A NEW LANDMARK IN LATIN-ENGLISH DICTIONARIES FOR THE MODERN STUDENT!

This totally revised and enlarged Latin-English dictionary is the first Latin dictionary ever to be compiled on the basis of modern lexicographical principles.

COMPREHENSIVE—More than 70,000 words and phrases.

DEFINITIVE—Based on the foremost Classical authorities and organized to achieve the utmost clarity, precision, and convenience.

MODERN—Obsolete definitions have been replaced by fresh translations that correspond to current English usage.

THE BANTAM NEW COLLEGE DICTIONARY SERIES

JOHN C. TRAUPMAN, Ph.D. in Classics, Princeton University, was chairman of the Department of Classics at St. Joseph's University (Philadelphia). He is the author of *The New College German & English Dictionary* (Bantam Books, 1981; Amsco School Publications, Inc. 1981), *Latin Is Fun: Lively Lessons for Beginners* (Amsco School Publications, Inc., Book I 1989, Book II 1994), and *Conversational Latin for Oral Proficiency* (Bolchazy-Carducci Publishers, Inc., 1996). He is an associate editor of *The Scribner-Bantam English Dictionary* (Scribner's, 1977; Bantam Books, 1979). He is a member of the Board of American Consultants to Lexus, Ltd., Glasgow, Scotland.

The Bantam New College

LATIN & ENGLISH DICTIONARY

Revised and Enlarged

JOHN C. TRAUPMAN, Ph.D.
St. Joseph's University, Philadelphia

BANTAM BOOKS
NEW YORK • TORONTO • LONDON • SYDNEY • AUCKLAND

THE BANTAM NEW COLLEGE
LATIN & ENGLISH DICTIONARY

A Bantam Book / April 1966

Bantam Revised and enlarged edition / March 1995

For information address: Bantam Books.

ISBN 0–553–57301–2

Published simultaneously in the United States and Canada

Bantam Books are published by Bantam Books, a division of Bantam Doubleday Dell Publishing Group, Inc. Its trademark, consisting of the words "Bantam Books" and the portrayal of a rooster, is Registered in U.S. Patent and Trademark Office and in other countries. Marca Registrade. Bantam Books, 1540 Broadway, New York, New York10036.

PRINTED IN THE UNITED STATES OF AMERICA

OPM 19 18 17 16 15 14 13 12 11

Contents

Preface to the Second Edition

This totally revised and expanded edition, with over 70,000 entries, includes not only additional authors, such as Martial, Juvenal, Suetonius, Tacitus, and Curtius, but also additional works by standard authors, such as the correspondence and philosophical essays of Cicero and the *Eclogues* and *Georgics* of Vergil. It also provides a much larger range of illustrative phrases, all of which are translated and arranged in alphabetical order. There are separate entries for prefixes and suffixes. As an additional new feature, this edition includes a Guide to Latin Grammar, which provides the following: the declension of nouns (including Greek nouns), pronouns, and adjectives; the irregular comparison of adjectives and adverbs; and the conjugation of verbs. There is also a list of Roman numerals.

The level of usage of Latin words and phrases is faithfully reflected in the level of usage of the English translations, so that, if the Latin word is colloquial, slang, or vulgar, the English translation corresponds. Variant spellings of Latin words are given within the entries. Additional features are provided in the Guide to the Dictionary.

The author wishes to thank Donald Reis, formerly of Bantam Books, under whose direction the first edition of this dictionary was undertaken. A debt of gratitude is due to the late Edwin B. Williams, former general editor of the New College Bantam Dictionary Series, for his guidance in the preparation of the first edition. Special thanks are due to James T. McDonough for proofreading the manuscript of the revised edition and for his many suggestions for improvement in both form and substance. The author gratefully acknowledges the kind support of Beverly Susswein, of Bantam Doubleday Dell, and Lawrence Weisburg, of Amsco School Publications.

A Guide to the Dictionary

The main entry, its inflected forms, spelling variants, and illustrative phrases are set in boldface. Part-of-speech labels are set in italics.

Centered periods within entry words indicate division points at which inflectional elements are to be added, without regard to syllabification, e.g.,

ord·ō -inis = ordō, ordinis

Compound words are generally given in their assimilated forms, e.g., **accurrō** rather than **adcurrō.** Cross-references are provided as guides for those using texts which employ the unassimilated forms, e.g.,

adc- = acc-

sēpiō *see* **saepio**

Spelling variants are indicated in bold type in parentheses after the part-of-speech abbreviation, e.g.,

affīnit·ās -ātis *f* **(adf-)** affinity, connection; relationship by marriage

However, nouns with both Greek and Latin endings are shown in full, e.g.,

troch·us *or* **troch·os -ī** *m* hoop

Tened·os *or* **Tened·us -ī** *f* Tenedos *(island off the coast of Troy)*

Adjectives of three endings, whether of the first and second or of the third declension, are shown with three endings; adjectives with a single ending are shown in the nominative, followed by the genitive ending, e.g.,

curv·us -a -um *adj* curved

simil·is -is -e *adj* similar

dīlig·ens -entis *adj* careful; diligent

When constructions are provided, cases are not shown with the most common prepositions **ab, ad, ex,** *or* **cum.** For all other prepositions, the case that the preposition governs is shown, e.g.,

stō stāre stetī statum *intr* to stand; *(w.* **ex)** to consist of; *(w. abl or* **in** *+ abl)* to depend on; *(w.* **per** *+ acc)* to be due to, thanks to

Synonymous meanings are separated by commas; distinct meanings are separated by semicolons. When a grammatical construction applies to several distinct meanings, thus extending beyond semicolons, the distinct meanings are numbered, e.g.,

perfugiō *intr (w.* **ad** *or* **in** *+ acc)* **1** to flee to for refuge; **2** to desert to; **3** to have recourse to

Discriminations between two or more meanings of an entry word are often shown by means of English words in parentheses, coming before or after the English meaning, e.g.,

argūt·us -a -um *adj* bright, smart *(person);* rustling *(leaves);* babbling *(brook);* chirping *(bird, cricket);* pungent *(smell);* expressive *(eyes, gestures)*

aspect·ō -āre -āvī -ātus *tr* **(ads-)** to look at, gaze at; *(of a place)* to face; to obey *(orders)*

However, words in parentheses, but not in italics, coming before or after a meaning are optional additions to the word in the target language, e.g.,

avuncul·us -ī *m* (maternal) uncle

abi·es -etis *f* fir (tree)

Level of usage of Latin words, indicated by the abbreviations *(coll)* for "colloquial," *(sl)* for "slang," and *(vulg)* for "vulgar," is reflected in the level of usage of the English translation of the Latin word, e.g.,

> **admutil·ō -āre** *tr* to clip close; *(coll)* to clip, cheat

> **ab·eō -īre -īvī** *or* **-iī itum** *vi* to go away, depart; **abi in malam rem!** *(sl)* go to hell!

> **cole·ī -ōrum** *mpl (vulg)* balls

Subject labels are given in italics and listed in alphabetical order, e.g.,

> **concurs·us -ūs** *m* a running together, concourse; *(astr)* conjunction; *(gram)* juxtaposition *(of letters); (leg)* joint-right; *(mil)* charge, clash

When an entry word is a proper noun, the proper noun is not repeated in English if the form is the same in Latin and in English; but when the proper noun has two possible endings, the form used in English is provided, e.g.,

> **Eurīpid·ēs -is** *m* Athenian tragic playwright *(480-406 B.C.)*

> **Eurōp·a -ae** *or* **Eurōp·ē -ēs** *f* Europa *(daughter of the Phoenician king Agenor)* **‖** (continent of) Europe

Substantives formed from adjectives are generally listed under the adjectives from which they are derived and are separated by vertical parallel bars, e.g.,

> **dialectic·us -a -um** *adj* logical **‖** *m* logician **‖** *f* logic **‖** *npl* dialectics

Proper nouns derived from adjectives or from common nouns are subsumed, in short entries, under the adjective and common noun respectively, e.g.,

> **daedal·us -a -um** *adj* skillful, artistic; intricately constructed **‖ Daedal·us -ī** *m* builder of the Labyrinth in Crete

> **Tarquini·us -a -um** *adj* Tarquinian **‖** *m* Tarquinius Priscus *(fifth king of Rome, c. 616-579 B.C.)* **‖** Tarquinius Superbus *(seventh and last king of Rome, c. 534-510 B.C.)*

> **cast·or -ōris** *m* beaver **‖ Castor** *son of Tyndareus, twin brother of Pollux*

Vertical parallel bars are used to separate different parts of speech of the entry word, for instance, pronominal adjectives from pronouns, e.g.,

> **alt·er -era -erum** *adj* one *(of two);* a second, the second; the next **‖** *pron* one *(of two),* the one, the other; a second one

Vertical parallel bars are used to separate past participles, when occurring as separate entries, from adjectives and substantives derived from them, e.g.,

> **impens·us -a -um** *pp of* **impendo ‖** *adj* high, costly, expensive; **‖** *f see* **impensa ‖** *n* high price

Vertical parallel bars are used to separate nouns in the singular from nouns in the plural when the plural of the nouns carries a special meaning, e.g.,

> **aed·es** *or* **aed·is -is** *f* room; apartment; shrine, temple **‖** *fpl* house, home

Vertical parallel bars are used to separate common nouns from proper nouns, e.g.,

> **urs·a -ae** *f* she-bear **‖ Ursa Major** *(astr)* Great Bear; **Ursa Minor** *(astr)* Little Bear

Vertical parallel bars are used to separate verb functions. Transitive *(tr),* reflexive *(refl),* passive (with intransitive sense) *(pass),* intransitive *(intr),* and impersonal *(v impers)* functions of verbs with their dependent constructions are clearly differentiated and are presented in the fixed order as listed above, e.g.,

> **ēmer·gō -gĕre -sī -sus** *vt* to raise *(from the water)* **‖** *refl or pass*

to rise ‖ *intr* to emerge; to rise *(in power)*

Illustrative phrases are provided at the end of entries in strict alphabetical order. However, when a Latin phrase illustrates a specific meaning, for instance, when the main entry is a prefix suffix, or preposition, the phrase is placed immediately after that meaning and introduced by a colon, e.g.,

-i·cō -āre *vbl suff* **1** used to form verbs from adjectives: **claudicāre** to be lame, to limp; **2** used to form verbs from other verbs: **fodicāre** to stab *(from* **fodĕre)**

For the sake of clarity, optional variants in illustrative phrases are placed in parentheses, e.g.,

vera et falsa *(or* **vera a falsis) dijudicare** to distinguish truth from falsehood

Vowel lengths are not shown on words within an entry except when clarity demands them, e.g.

succīdere [sub + caedere] to cut down (in order to distinguish it from **succĭdere [sub + cadere]** to collapse)

adversā viā up the road

nullā condicione by no means

de industriā on purpose

When a noun may be either masculine or feminine, the abbreviations are written together, but when a noun is generally, say, masculine but only rarely feminine or neuter, the rarer gender is shown in parentheses, e.g.,

serp·ens -entis *mf* serpent

pampin·us -ī *m (f)* vine shoot

sāl salis *m (n)* salt

Past participles are listed as separate entries when difference in form from the first person singular present indicative warrants such listing, provided they fall alphabetically more than one word before or after their verb, e.g.,

vīs·us -a -um *pp of* **video**

Similarly, the perfect form of a verb is listed as a separate entry in its alphabetical position, e.g.,

trīvī *perf of* **tero**

On the Latin-English side, the twofold purpose in marking the quantity of vowels is

1. to indicate accentuation of words
2. to provide the basis for scansion of Classical Latin verse

Thus, all vowels that are long by nature and occur in open syllables are marked, whereas vowels in closed syllables, whether long or short by nature, are not marked, since the syllable in either case is long. However, since a vowel followed by a mute and a liquid can be open or closed, its quantity is marked when it is long.

On the English-Latin side, Latin vowels are marked to distinguish:

1. words otherwise spelled alike: **lēvis** (smooth), **lĕvis** (light)
2. the ablative singular from the nominative singular of nouns of the first declension whenever the distinction is not clear from the context
3. the infinitive of verbs of the second conjugation from the infinitive of verbs of the third conjugation
4. the genitive singular and nominative and accusative plural from the nominative singular of the fourth declension whenever the distinction is not clear from the context

On the English-Latin side, a boldface dash represents the vocabulary entry, e.g.,

awake *adj* vigil, vigilans; **to be —** vigilare

PRONUNCIATION

Vowels

Classical Method

ă	*a* in ago: **compărō**
ā	*a* in father: **imāgō**
ĕ	*e* in pet: **propĕrō**
ē	*a* in late: **lēnis**
ĭ	*i* in hit: **ĭdem**
ī	*ee* in keen: **amīcus**
ŏ	*o* in often: **mŏdus**
ō	*o* in hope: **nōmen**
ŭ	*u* in put: **ŭt**
ū	*u* in rude: **ūtor**
y̆	*ü* in German Hütte: **my̆rta**
ȳ	*ü* in German über: **Tȳdeus**

Ecclesiastical Method

Generally the same as the Classical Method. However, in practice the different values of the vowels are frequently not rigidly adhered to.

Diphthongs

Classical Method

ae	*y* in by: **caecus**
au	*ow* in now: **nauta**
ei	*ey* in they: **hei**
eu	*eu* in feud: **Orpheus**
oe	*oi* in oil: **coepit**
ui	*uey* in gluey: **cui;** after **q**, *wee* in week: **qui**

Ecclesiastical Method

ae	*a* in late: **caecus**
au	as in Classical Method
ei	as in Classical Method
eu	*eu* in Italian neutro: **euge**
oe	*a* in late: **coepit**
ui	same as Classical Method

Consonants

Classical Method		Ecclesiastical Method	
b	English b	**b**	English b
c	always *c* in can: **cīvis, cantō, cedō**	**c**	before **e, i, ae,** or **oe** = *ch* in cherry: **celsus, civis, caelum, coepit,** but before other letters, *c* in can: **cantō, actus**
d	English d	**d**	English d
f	English f	**f**	English f
g	always *g* in go: **gallīna, genus, grātus, gula**	**g**	before **e** or **i** = *g* in gentle: **genus, regīna,** but before other letters except **g** and **n** (see under Consonant Groups) = *g* in go: **gallīna, grātus, gula, rogō**
h	English h	**h**	English h

j	*y* in yes: ***jam, jungō***	**j**	as in Classical Method
k	English k, but unaspirated	**k**	English k
l	English l	**l**	English l
m	English m, but in verse final **m** before an initial vowel or **h** in the following word was presumably not pronounced	**m**	English m
n	English n	**n**	English n
p	English p, but unaspirated	**p**	English p
q	English q	**q**	English q
r	trilled r as in the Romance languages	**r**	as in Classical Method
s	always *s* in sing: **mi*s*er, mor*s***	**s**	*s* in sing: ***s*alūs,** but when standing between two vowels or when final and preceded by a voiced consonant = *z* in dozen: **mi*s*er, mor*s***
t	English t, but unaspirated	**t**	as in Classical Method
u	*w* in wine, when unaccented, preceded by q, sometimes by s, and sometimes by g, and followed by a vowel: **q*u*i·a, s*u*ā·vis** (but **s*u*·ō·rum), dis·tin·g*u*ō** (but **ex·i·gŭ·*u*s)**	**u**	in Classical Method
v	*w* in wine: ***v*ī*v*ō**	**v**	English v
x	*x* (= **ks**) in six: **e*x*trā**	**x**	*x* (as **ks**) in six: **pa*x*;** but in words beginning with **ex** and followed by a vowel, **h,** or **s,** = *x* (as **gz**) in exhaust: **e*x*audī, e*x*hālō, e*x*solvō**
z	*dz* in adze: ***z*ōna**	**z**	as in Classical Method

Consonant Groups

	Classical Method		Ecclesiastical Method
bs	*ps* in apse: **o*bs*idō, ur*bs***	**bs**	**bs** in obsession: **o*bs*idō,** but in the final position = **bs** (= **bz**) in observe: **ur*bs***
bt	*pt* in captain: **o*bt*inēre**	**bt**	*bt* in obtain: **o*bt*inēre**
cc	*kk* in bookkeeper: **e*cc*e, o*cc*īdō, o*cc*āsum, o*cc*lūdō**	**cc**	before **e** or **i** = *tch* in catch: **e*cc*e, o*cc*īdō;** but before other letters = *kk* in bookkeeper; **o*cc*āsum, o*cc*lūdō**
ch	*ch* in chaotic: **pul*ch*er**	**ch**	as in Classical Method
gg	*gg* in leg guard: **a*gg*er**	**gg**	before **e** or **i** = *dj* in adjourn: **a*gg*er;** but before other letters = *gg* in leg guard: **a*gg*rĕgō**
gn	*ny* in canyon: **di*gn*us**	**gn**	as in Classical Method
gu	see consonant **u**	**gu**	as in Classical Method

ph	*p-h* in **top-heavy**: ***ph*ōca**	*ph*	**ph** in **phoenix**: ***ph*ōca**
qu	see consonant **u**	**qu**	as in Classical Method
sc	*sc* in **scope**: ***sc*iō, *sc*ūtum**	**sc**	before **e** or **i** = **sh** in **shin**: **a*sc*endō, sciō;** but before other letters = **sc** in scope: ***sc*andō, *sc*ūtum**
su	see consonant **u**	**su**	as in Classical Method
th	*t* in **take**: ***th*eātrum**	**th**	as in Classical Method
ti	*ti* in English patio: **nā*ti*ō**	**ti**	when preceded by **s, t,** or **x,** or when followed by a consonant = **ti** in English pa**ti**o: **hos*ti*a, admix*ti*ō, fort*i*ter;** but when unaccented, followed by a vowel, and preceded by any letter except **s, t,** or **x** = **tzy** in ri**tzy: nā*ti*ō, pre*ti*um**

Syllabification

1. Every Latin word has as many syllables as it has vowels or diphthongs: **ae•ger, fī•li•us, Bai•ae**
2. When a word is divided into syllables:
   a) a single consonant between two vowels goes with the following syllable (**h** is regarded as a consonant; **ch, ph, th, qu,** and sometimes **gu** and **su** are regarded as single consontants)*; **a•ger, ni•hil, a•qua, ci•hor•rē•um**
   b) the first consonant of a combination of two or more consonants goes with the preceding vowel: **tor•men•tum, mit•tō, mon•strum**
   c) a consonant group consisting of a mute (**b, c, d, g, p, t**) followed by **l** or **r** is generally left undivided and goes with the following vowel: **pā•trēs, a•cris, du•plex.** In Classical poetry this combination is often treated like any other pair of consonants: **pāt•rēs**, ac•ris, dup•lex
   d) prefixes form separate syllables even if the division is contrary to above rules: **ab•est, ob•lā•tus, abs•ti•nē•**ō, ab•stō
3. A syllable ending in a vowel or diphthong is called *open;* all others are called *closed*
4. The last syllable of a word is called the *ultima;* the next to last is called the *penult;* the one before the penult is called the *antepenult*

* The double consonant **x** goes with the preceding vowel: **dix•it**

Quantity of Vowels

1. A vowel is *long* (**lēvis**) or *short* (**lĕvis**) according to the length of time required for its pronunciation
2. A vowel is long:
   a) before **ns, nf,** (and perhaps **gn**): **ingēns, īnfāns, (māgnus)**
3. A vowel is short:
   a) before another vowel or **h: dĕa, trăhō**
   b) generally before **nd** and **nt: amăndus, amănt**
4. Diphthongs are long: **causa**

Quantity of Syllables

1. Syllables are distinguished as *long* or *short* according to the length of time required for their pronunciation
2. A syllable is long:
   a) if it contains a long vowel or a diphthong: **vē·nī scrī·bō, caus·ae** (such a syllable is said to be *long by nature)*
   b) if it contains a short vowel followed by **x, z,** or any two consonants except a mute (**b, d, g, p, t, c**) followed by **l** or **r: sax·um, gaz·a, mit·tō, cur·sor** (such a syllable is said to be *long by position,* but the vowel is pronounced *short)*
3. A syllable is short:
   a) if it contains a short vowel followed by a vowel or by a single consonant (**h** is regarded as a consonant; **ch, ph, th, qu,** and sometimes **gu** and **su** are regarded as single consonants): **me·us, ni·hil, ge·rit, a·qua**
   b) if it contains a short vowel followed by a mute (**b, d, g, p, t, c**) plus **l** or **r,** but it is sometimes long in verse: **flă·grans, ba·ră·thrum, ce·lĕ·brō** (such a syllable is said to be *common)*

NOTE: In this dictionary, on the Latin-English side, long vowels are marked except before **x, z,** or two or more consonants unless the two consonants are a mute plus a liquid (e.g., **pātris**). The short penult of the infinitive of verbs of the third conjugation is marked with a breve (e.g., **vincĕre**) to distinguish it from the long penult of the infinitive of verbs of the second conjugation (e.g., **vidēre**). In addition, the short syllable of words is marked to contrast it with the long syllable of otherwise homographs, e.g., **concīdĕre** (to kill) and **concĭdĕre** (to collapse); **ănus** (old woman) and **ānus** (anus, rectum).

Accent

1. Words of two syllables are accented on the first syllable: **om´nēs, tan´gō, ge´rit**
2. Words of more than two syllables are accented on the penult if it is long: **a·mī´cus, re·gun´tur,** and on the antepenult if the penult is short: **fa·mi´lĭ·a, ge´rĭ·tur**
3. These rules apply to words with enclitics appended (**-ce, -dum, -met, -ne, -que, -ve**): **vos´met, lau·dat´ne, de´ă·que** (nominative), **dē·a´que** (ablative)
4. In the second declension, the contracted genitive and the contracted vocative of nouns in **-ius** and the contracted genitive of those in **-ium** retain the accent of the nominative: **Vir·gĭ´lī, in·gĕ´nī**
5. Certain words which have lost a final **-e** retain the accent of the complete forms: **il·līc´** for **il·lī´ce, tan·tōn´** for **tan·tō´ne**
6. Certain compounds of **faciō,** in which a feeling for the individuality of the components was preserved, retain the accent of the simple verb: **be·ne·fă´cit**

Guide to Latin Grammar

Nouns

First Declension Singular		Second Declension Singular		
	rosa *f*	**sonus** *m*	**puer** *m*	**ager** *m*
	rose	sound	boy	field
Nom	ros**a**	son**us**	puer	ager
Gen	ros**ae**	son**ī**	puer**ī**	agr**ī**
Dat	ros**ae**	son**ō**	puer**ō**	agr**ō**
Acc	ros**am**	son**um**	puer**um**	agr**um**
Abl	ros**ā**	son**ō**	puer**ō**	agr**ō**

First Declension Plural		Second Declension Plural		
Nom	ros**ae**	son**ī**	puer**ī**	agr**ī**
Gen	ros**ārum**	son**ōrum**	puer**ōrum**	agr**ōrum**
Dat	ros**īs**	son**īs**	puer**īs**	agr**īs**
Acc	ros**ās**	son**ōs**	puer**ōs**	agr**ōs**
Abl	ros**īs**	son**īs**	puer**īs**	agr**īs**

Second Declension Singular

	vir *m*	dōnum *n*	**servos** *m*	**fīlius** *m*	**ingenium** *n*
	man	gift	servant	son	talent
Nom	vir	dōn**um**	serv**os**	fīli**us**	ingeni**um**
Gen	vir**ī**	dōn**ī**	serv**ī**	fīl·**iī** *or* **-ī**	ingen·**iī** *or* **-ī**
Dat	vir**ō**	dōn**ō**	serv**ō**	fīli**ō**	ingeni**ō**
Acc	vir**um**	dōn**um**	serv**om**	fīli**um**	ingeni**um**
Abl	vir**ō**	dōn**ō**	serv**ō**	fīli**ō**	ingeni**ō**

Second Declension Plural

Nom	vir**ī**	dōn**a**	serv**ī**	fīli**ī**	ingeni**a**
Gen	vir**ōrum**	dōn**ōrum**	serv**ōrum**	fīli**ōrum**	igeni**ōrum**
Dat	vir**īs**	dōn**īs**	serv**īs**	fīli**īs**	ingeni**īs**
Acc	vir**ōs**	dōn**a**	serv**ōs**	fīli**ōs**	ingeni**a**
Abl	vir**īs**	dōn**īs**	serv**īs**	fīli**īs**	ingeni**īs**

Notes **(a)** The vocative singular of **-us** nouns ends in **-e: amīce**. The vocative singular (and sometimes the genitive singular) of **-ius** nouns ends in **-ī: fīlī, Tiberī**. But the vocative of **deus** is **deus**.

(b) The earlier inflection of masculine nouns of the second declension, down to Caesar and Cicero, followed the pattern of **servos.**

Third Declension Masculine/Feminine Nouns Singular

	rex *m* king	**mīles** *m* soldier	**princeps** *m* chief	**māter** *f* mother
Nom	rex	mīles	princeps	māter
Gen	rēgis	mīlitis	principis	mātris
Dat	rēgī	mīlitī	principī	mātrī
Acc	rēgem	mīlitem	principem	mātrem
Abl	rēge	mīlite	principe	mātre

Third Declension Masculine/Feminine Nouns Plural

Nom	rēgēs	mīlitēs	principēs	mātrēs
Gen	rēgum	mīlitum	principum	mātrum
Dat	rēgibus	mīlitibus	principibus	mātribus
Acc	rēgēs	mīlitēs	principēs	mātrēs
Abl	rēgibus	mīlitibus	principibus	mātribus

Third Declension Masculine/Feminine Nouns Singular

	hostis *m* enemy	**custōs** *m* guard	**vigil** *m* fireman	**nox** *f* night
Nom	hostis	custōs	vigil	nox
Gen	hostis	custōdis	vigilis	noctis
Dat	hostī	custōdī	vigilī	noctī
Acc	host·em *or* -im	custōdem	vigilem	noctem
Abl	host·e *or* -ī	custōde	vigile	nocte

Third Declension Masculine/Feminine Nouns Plural

Nom	hostēs	custōdēs	vigilēs	noctēs
Gen	hostium	custōdum	vigilum	noctium
Dat	hostibus	custōdibus	vigilibus	noctibus
Acc	host·ēs *or* -īs	custōdēs	vigilēs	noctēs
Abl	hostibus	custōdibus	vigilibus	noctibus

Third Declension Neuter Nouns Singular

	nōmen *n* name	**caput** *n* head	**opus** *n* work	**iter** *n* road	**mare** *n* sea	**animal** *n* animal	**cor** *n* heart
Nom	nōmen	caput	opus	iter	mare	animal	cor
Gen	nōminis	capitis	operis	itineris	maris	animālis	cordis
Dat	nōminī	capitī	operī	itinerī	marī	animālī	cordī
Acc	nōmen	caput	opus	iter	mare	animal	cor
Abl	nōmine	capite	opere	itinere	marī	animālī	corde

Third Declension Neuter Nouns Plural

Nom	nōmina	capita	opera	itinera	maria	animālia	corda
Gen	nōminum	capitum	operum	itinerum	marium	animālium	—
Dat	nōminibus	capitibus	operibus	itineribus	maribus	animālibus	cordibus
Acc	nōmina	capita	opera	itinera	maria	animālia	corda
Abl	nōminibus	capitibus	operibus	itineribus	maribus	animālibus	cordibus

Notes (a) Masculine and feminine ĭ-stem nouns, such as **hostis,** regularly end in **-is** in the nominative singular, and always have **-ium** in the genitive plural. The accusative singular ends in **-em** *or* **-im**, and the ablative in **-e** *or* **-ī**, and the accusative plural in **-ēs** *or* **-īs.**

(b) A number of monosyllabic nouns with mute stems (like **cor**) lack the genitive plural.

	Fourth Declension Singular			**Fifth Declension Singular**	
	fructus *m*	**manus** *f*	**genū** *n*	**diēs** *m*	**rēs** *f*
	fruit	hand	knee	day	thing
Nom	fruct**us**	man**us**	gen**ū**	di**ēs**	r**ēs**
Gen	fruct**ūs**	man**ūs**	gen**ūs**	di**ēī**	r**ĕī**
Dat	fruct**uī**	man**uī**	gen**ū**	di**ēī**	r**ĕī**
Acc	fruct**um**	man**um**	gen**ū**	di**em**	r**em**
Abl	fruct**ū**	man**ū**	gen**ū**	di**ē**	r**ē**

	Fourth Declension Plural			**Fifth Declension Plural**	
Nom	fruct**ūs**	man**ūs**	gen**ua**	di**ēs**	r**ēs**
Gen	fruct**uum**	man**uum**	gen**uum**	di**ērum**	r**ērum**
Dat	fruct**ibus**	man**ibus**	gen**ibus**	di**ēbus**	r**ēbus**
Acc	fruct**ūs**	man**ūs**	gen**ua**	di**ēs**	r**ēs**
Abl	fruct**ibus**	man**ibus**	gen**ibus**	di**ēbus**	r**ēbus**

Note (a) Nouns of the fourth declension are mostly masculine nouns. The following nouns in **-us** are feminine: **acus** needle; **domus** house; **manus** hand; **porticus** colonnade; **tribus** tribe; **īdūs** *(pl)* Ides; also most names of trees, such as **quercus** oak.

(b) All fifth-declension nouns are feminine, except **diēs** *m* "day" and **merīdiēs** *m* "midday, noon." But **diēs** is sometimes feminine in the singular, especially in phrases indicating a fixed time, and regularly when used of time in general, e.g., **constitūtā diē** on the appointed day; **longa diēs** a long time.

Greek Nouns

First Declension

Greek nouns that end in **-ē** are feminine; those that end in **-ās** and **-ēs** are masculine. In the plural, when found, they are declined like regular Latin nouns of the first declension.. In the singular they are declined as follows:

	Aenēās *m*	Anchīsēs *m*	Pēnelopē *f*	Persēs *m*
	Aeneas	Anchises	Penelope	Persian
Nom	Aenē**ās**	Anchīs**ēs**	Pēnelop**ē**	Pers**ēs**
Gen	Aenē**ae**	Anchīs**ae**	Pēnelop**ēs**	Pers**ae**
Dat	Aenē**ae**	Anchīs**ae**	Pēnelop**ae**	Pers**ae**
Acc	Aenē·**am** *or* **-ān**	Anchīs·**ēn, -am**	Pēnelop**ēn**	Pers·**ēn** *or* **-am**
Abl	Aenē**ā**	Anchīs·**ē** *or* **-ā**	Pēnelop**ē**	Pers·**ē** *or* **-ā**
Voc	Aenē·**ā** *or* **-ă**	Anchīs·**ē** *or* **-ā** *or* **-ă**	Pēnelop**ē**	Pers·**ē** *or* **-ă**

Second Declension

Greek nouns of the second declension end in **-os** *or* **-ōs** and are masculine or feminine; those ending in **-on** are neuter. In the plural, when found, they are declined like regular Latin nouns. They are mostly proper names and are declined as follows in the singular:

	Lesbŏs *f*	**Athōs** *m*	**Īlion** *n*	**Panthūs** *m*
	Lesbos	Athos	Ilium	Panthus
Nom	Lesb·**ŏs** *or* **-us**	Ath·**ōs** *or* **-o**	Īli·**on** *or* **-um**	Panth**ūs**
Gen	Lesb**ī**	Ath·**ō** *or* **-ōnis**	Īli**ī**	Panth**ī**

DAT	Lesbō	Athō	Īliō	Panthō
ACC	Lesb·**on** *or* **-um**	Ath·**ōn** *or* **-ōnem**	Īli·**on** *or* **-um**	Panth**ūn**
ABL	Lesbō	Athō *or* **-ōne**	Īliō	Panthō
VOC	Lesbō	Athōs	Īli·**on** *or* **-um**	Panthū

THIRD DECLENSION SINGULAR

	hērōs *m* hero	**basis** *f* base	**nāïs** *f* naiad	**tigris** *mf* tiger	**lampas** *f* torch
NOM	hērōs	basis	nāïs	tigris	lampas
GEN	hērōïs	bas·**eōs** *or* **-idos**	nāïd·**os** *or* **-is**	tigr·**is** *or* **-idis**	lampados
DAT	hērōï	basī	nāïdī	tigrī	lampadī
ACC	hērōa	bas·**in** *or* **-ida** *or* **-im**	nāïda	tigr·**in** *or* **-idem**	lampada
ABL	hērōë	basī	nāïde	tigr·**ī** *or* **-ide**	lampade

THIRD DECLENSION PLURAL

NOM	hērōĕs	basēs	nāïdĕs	tigrēs	lampadĕs
GEN	hērō**um**	bas·**eōn** *or* **-ium**	nāïd**um**	tigr**ium**	lampad**um**
DAT	hērōï**bus**	basi**bus**	nāïdi**bus**	tigri**bus**	lampadi**bus**
ACC	hērōăs	bas**īs** *or* **-ēis**	nāïdăs	tigr·**īs** *or* **-idăs**	lampadăs
ABL	hērōï**bus**	basi**bus**	nāïdi**bus**	tigri**bus**	lampadi**bus**

THIRD DECLENSION PROPER NAMES

NOM	Dīdō	Capys	Paris	Orphēus
GEN	Dīdōnis *or* Dīdūs	Capyos	Paridis	Orph·eī *or* **-eōs**
DAT	Dīdōnī *or* Dīdō	Capyī	Paridī	Orph·eō *or* -eī
ACC	Dīdō *or* Dīdō**nem**	Capy**n**	Parid·**em** *or* **-im** *or* **-in**	Orphe·**um** *or* **-a**
ABL	Dīdōne *or* **-ō**	Capyë	Paridē *or* Parī	Orpheō
VOC	Dīdō	Capy	Pari	Orphēu

NOM	Periclēs	Simoīs	Atlās	Selīnūs
GEN	Pericl·**īs** *or* **-ī**	Simoënt·**is** *or* **-os**	Atlantis	Selīnuntis
DAT	Pericl·**ī** *or* **-ĭ**	Simoëntī	Atlantī	Selīnuntī
ACC	Pericl·**em** *or* **-ea** *or* **-ēn**	Simoënta	Atlanta	Selīnuntā
ABL	Pericle	Simoënte	Atlante	Selīnunte
VOC	Pericl·**ēs** *or* **-ē**	Simoīs	Atlā	Selīnūs

NOTES (a) The regular Latin forms may be used for most of the above.

(b) Most stems in **ĭd-** *(nom:* **-is)**, as **tigris,** often have also the forms of **i**-stems: *gen:* **-ĭdis** or **-ĭdos** *or* **-is;** *acc:* **-ĭdem** *or* **-ĭda** *or* **-im** *or* **-in;** *abl:* **-ĭde** *or* **-ī.** However, most feminine proper names have *acc* **-idem** *or* **-ida,** *abl:* **-ide, —** not **-im** *or* **-ī.**

(c) Stems in **ant-, ent-,** and a few in **unt-** follow the model of **Simoīs, -entis, Atlās, -antis** and **Selīnūs -untis.**

(d) Many Greek names, of the third declension in Latin, pass over into the first declension in the plural, as, **Hyperid·ae -ārum,** etc.

(e) Many names in **-ēs** belonging to the third declension have also genitive in **-ī,** e.g., **Pericl·ēs -is** *or* **-ī.**

(f) Greek names in **-ēus,** like **Orphēus,** have forms of the second and third declensions.

(g) Greek nouns of the third declension end in **-ĕs** in the nominative plural, as **Phrygĕs** Phrygians, and end in **-ăs** in the accusative plural, as **Phrygăs** Phrygians.

Pronouns

Personal Pronouns

	ego I	**tu** you	**is** he	**ea** she	**id** it
			SINGULAR		
	1st Pers	*2nd Pers*		*3rd Pers*	
NOM	ego	tū	is	ea	id
GEN	meī	tuī	ejus	ejus	ejus
DAT	mihi *or* mī	tibi	eī	eī	eī
ACC	mē	tē	eum	eam	id
ABL	mē	tē	eō	eā	eō
			PLURAL		
	1st Pers	*2nd Pers*		*3rd Pers*	
NOM	nōs	vōs	eī *or* iī	eae	ea
GEN	nostrum nostrī	vestrum vestrī	eōrum	eārum	eōrum
DAT	nōbīs	vōbīs	eīs	eīs	eīs
ACC	nōs	vōs	eōs	eās	ea
ABL	nōbīs	vōbīs	eīs	eīs	eīs

NOTES (a) The forms **nostrum** and **vestrum** are used partitively, e.g., **ūnusquisque nostrum** each one of us; otherwise, the forms **nostrī** and **vestrī** are used, e.g., **meminit vestrī** he remembered you.
(b) The form **mī** is sometimes used in poetry instead of **mihi.**

Reflexive Pronouns

		SINGULAR	
	1st Pers	*2nd Pers*	*3rd Pers*
NOM	——	——	——
GEN	meī	tuī	suī
DAT	mihi	tibi	sibi
ACC	mē	tē	sē *or* sēsē
ABL	mē	tē	sē *or* sēse

NOTES (a) The reflexive of the third persons serves for *all genders.* Thus, **suī** may mean "of himself", "of herself", or "of itself".
(b) All of the reflexive pronouns can serve as reciprocal pronouns, e.g., **inter se culpant** they blame each other (one another).

		PLURAL	
	1st Pers	*2nd Pers*	*3rd Pers*
NOM	——	——	——
GEN	nostrī	vestrī	suī
DAT	nōbīs	vōbīs	sibi
ACC	nōs	vōs	sē *or* sēsē
ABL	nōbīs	vōbīs	sē *or* sēsē

Demonstrative Pronouns

	hic this (one)	**haec** this (one)	**hoc** this (one)
		SINGULAR	
	masc	*fem*	*neut*
NOM	hic	haec	hoc
GEN	hujus	hujus	hujus
DAT	huic	huic	huic
ACC	hunc	hanc	hōc
ABL	hōc	hāc	hōc
		PLURAL	
	masc	*fem*	*neut*
NOM	hī	hae	haec
GEN	hōrum	hārum	hōrum
DAT	hīs	hīs	hīs
ACC	hōs	hās	haec
ABL	hīs	hīs	hīs

	ille that (one)	**illa** that (one)	**illud** that (one)
		SINGULAR	
	masc	*fem*	*neut*
NOM	ille	illa	illud
GEN	illīus	illīus	illīus
DAT	illī	illī	illī
ACC	illum	illam	illud
ABL	illō	illā	illō
		PLURAL	
	masc	*fem*	*neut*
NOM	illī	illae	illa
GEN	illōrum	illārum	illōrum
DAT	illīs	illīs	illīs
ACC	illōs	illās	illa
ABL	illīs	illīs	illīs

NOTES (a) **Iste, ista, istud** ("that") is declined like **ille.**
(b) **Ille** and **iste** appear in combination with the demonstrative particle **-c,** shortened from **-ce** (giving the sense "that there") in the following forms:

	masc	*fem*	*neut*
		SINGULAR	
NOM	illic	illaec	illuc *or* illoc
ACC	illunc	illanc	illuc *or* illoc
ABL	illōc	illāc	illōc
		PLURAL	
	masc	*fem*	*neut*
NOM	——	——	illaec
ACC	——	——	illaec

	SINGULAR		
	masc	*fem*	*neut*
NOM	istic	istaec	istuc *or* istoc
ACC	istunc	istanc	istuc *or* istoc
ABL	istōc	istāc	istōc

	PLURAL		
	masc	*fem*	*neut*
NOM	——	——	istaec
ACC	——	——	istaec

īdem the same **eadem** the same **idem** the same

	SINGULAR		
	masc	*fem*	*neut*
NOM	īdem	eadem	idem
GEN	ejusdem	ejusdem	ejusdem
DAT	eīdem	eīdem	eīdem
ACC	eundem	eandem	idem
ABL	eōdem	eādem	eōdem

	PLURAL		
	masc	*fem*	*neut*
NOM	eīdem *or* iīdem	eaedem	eadem
GEN	eōrundem	eārundem	eōrundem
DAT	eīsdem *or* īsdem	eīsdem *or* īsdem	eīsdem *or* īsdem
ACC	eōsdem	eāsdem	eadem
ABL	eīsdem *or* īsdem	eīsdem *or* īsdem	eīsdem *or* īsdem

Intensive Pronouns

ipse -self **ipsa** -self **ipsum** -self

	SINGULAR		
	masc	*fem*	*neut*
NOM	ipse	ipsa	ipsum
GEN	ipsīus	ipsīus	ipsīus
DAT	ipsī	ipsī	ipsī
ACC	ipsum	ipsam	ipsum
ABL	ipsō	ipsā	ipsō

	PLURAL		
	masc	*fem*	*neut*
NOM	ipsī	ipsae	ipsa
GEN	ipsōrum	ipsārum	ipsōrum
DAT	ipsīs	ipsīs	ipsīs
ACC	ipsōs	ipsās	ipsa
ABL	ipsīs	ipsīs	ipsīs

Relative Pronouns

	quī who, that	**quae** who, that	**quod** which, that
		SINGULAR	
	masc	*fem*	*neut*
NOM	quī	quae	quod
GEN	cujus	cujus	cujus
DAT	cui	cui	cui
ACC	quem	quam	quod
ABL	quō	quā	quō
		PLURAL	
	masc	*fem*	*neut*
NOM	quī	quae	quae
GEN	quōrum	quārum	quōrum
DAT	quibus	quibus	quibus
ACC	quōs	quās	quae
ABL	quibus	quibus	quibus

NOTE (a) The interrogative adjective **quī, quae, quod** (what? what kind of? which?), is declined throughout like the relative pronoun.

Interrogative Pronouns

	quis who?	**quid** what?
	masc & fem	*neut*
NOM	quis	quid
GEN	cujus	cujus
DAT	cui	cui
ACC	quem	quid
ABL	quō	quō

NOTES (a) The rare form of the plural follows the declension of the relative pronoun.

(b) **Quī** is sometimes used for **quis** in indirect questions.

(c) **Quis,** when modifying words denoting persons, is sometimes an adjective: **quis homō** = what man? whereas **quī homō** = what sort of man?

(d) The pronoun **quis** and the pronominal adjective **quī** may be strengthened by adding **-nam,** e. g., **quisnam** just who? exactly who?; **quidnam** just what?, exactly what?; **quīnam, quaenam, quodnam** of exactly what kind?

Indefinite Pronouns

	aliquis somone	**aliqua** someone	**aliquid** something
		SINGULAR	
	masc	*fem*	*neut*
NOM	aliquis (aliquī)	aliqua	aliquid (aliquod)
GEN	alicujus	alicujus	alicujus
DAT	alicui	alicui	alicui
ACC	aliquem	aliquam	aliquid (aliquod)
ABL	aliquō	aliquā	aliquō
		PLURAL	
	masc	*fem*	*neut*
NOM	aliquī	aliquae	aliqua
GEN	aliquōrum	aliquārum	aliquōrum
DAT	aliquibus	aliquibus	aliquibus
ACC	aliquōs	aliquās	aliqua
ABL	aliquibus	aliquibus	aliquibus

NOTES (a) The indefinite adjective **aliquī** "some" is declined in the same way as the indefinite pronoun **aliquis** "someone" except in the three cases indicated above in parentheses: nominative masculine singular, neuter nominative singular, and neuter accusative singular.

(b) **Quis** is used instead of **aliquis** after **nē, sī, nisi,** and **num,** e.g., **sī quis** "if anyone".

	quīdam, quaedam a certain person		**quiddam** a certain thing
		SINGULAR	
	masc	*fem*	*neut*
NOM	quīdam	quaedam	quiddam
GEN	cujusdam	cujusdam	cujusdam
DAT	cuidam	cuidam	cuidam
ACC	quendam	quandam	quiddam
ABL	quōdam	quādam	quōdam
		PLURAL	
	masc	*fem*	*neut*
NOM	quīdam	quaedam	quaedam
GEN	quōrundam	quārundam	quōrundam
DAT	quibusdam	quibusdam	quibusdam
ACC	quōsdam	quāsdam	quaedam
ABL	quibusdam	quibusdam	quibusdam

NOTES (a) The corresponding pronomimal adjective differs only in these forms: **quoddam** for **quiddam.**

(b) There are two indefinite relative pronouns: **quīcumque** and **quisquis** "whoever". **Quīcumque** declines only the first part; **quisquis** declines both but has only **quisquis, quidquid,** and **quōquō** in common use.

Adjectives

First and Second Declensions Singular

	bonus good			**tener** tender		
	masc	*fem*	*neu*	*masc*	*fem*	*neut*
Nom	bon**us**	bon**a**	bon**um**	tener	tener**a**	tener**um**
Gen	bon**ī**	bon**ae**	bon**ī**	tener**ī**	tener**ae**	tener**ī**
Dat	bon**ō**	bon**ae**	bon**ō**	tener**ō**	tener**ae**	tener**ō**
Acc	bon**um**	bon**am**	bon**um**	tener**um**	tener**am**	tener**um**
Abl	bon**ō**	bon**ā**	bon**ō**	tener**ō**	tener**ā**	tener**ō**

First and Second Declensions Plural

	masc	*fem*	*neu*	*masc*	*fem*	*neut*
Nom	bon**ī**	bon**ae**	bon**a**	tener**ī**	tener**ae**	tener**a**
Gen	bon**ōrum**	bon**ārum**	bon**ōrum**	tener**ōrum**	tener**ārum**	tener**ōrum**
Dat	bon**īs**	bon**īs**	bon**īs**	tener**īs**	tener**īs**	tener**īs**
Acc	bon**ōs**	bon**ās**	bon**a**	tener**ōs**	tener**ās**	tener**ā**
Abl	bon**īs**	bon**īs**	bon**īs**	tener**īs**	tener**īs**	tener**īs**

First and Second Declensions Singular

	sacer sacred		
	masc	*fem*	*neut*
Nom	sacer	sacr**a**	sacr**um**
Gen	sacr**ī**	sacr**ae**	sacr**ī**
Dat	sacr**ō**	sacr**ae**	sacr**ō**
Acc	sacr**um**	sacr**am**	sacr**um**
Abl	sacr**ō**	sacr**ā**	sacr**ō**

First and Second Declensions Plural

	masc	*fem*	*neut*
Nom	sacr**ī**	sacr**ae**	sacr**a**
Gen	sacr**ōrum**	sacr**ārum**	sacr**ōrum**
Dat	sacr**īs**	sacr**īs**	sacr**īs**
Acc	sacr**ōs**	sacr**ās**	sacr**a**
Abl	sacr**īs**	sacr**īs**	sacr**īs**

Nine Irregular Adjectives

alter the other .... *see below*
alius another .... *see below*
nullus none .... same as tōtus
neuter neither .... same as uter
sōlus alone .... same as tōtus
tōtus whole .... *see below*
ullus any .... same as tōtus
ūnus one .... same as tōtus
uter which (of two)? ..... *see below*

First and Second Declension Irregular Adjectives

They are declined in the singular as follows (the plural is regular):

	masc	*fem*	*neut*	*masc*	*fem*	*neut*
Nom	ali**us**	ali**a**	ali**ud**	alter	alter**a**	alter**um**
Gen	alter**īus** al**īus**	alter**īus** al**īus**	alter**īus** al**īus**	alter**īus**	alter**īus**	alter**īus**
Dat	ali**ī**	ali**ī**	ali**ī**	alter**ī**	alter**ī**	alter**ī**
Acc	ali**um**	ali**am**	ali**ud**	alter**um**	alter**am**	alter**um**
Abl	ali**ō**	ali**ā**	ali**ō**	alter**ō**	alter**ā**	alter**ō**

	masc	*fem*	*neut*	*masc*	*fem*	*neut*
Nom	uter	utr**a**	utr**um**	tōt**us**	tōt**a**	tōt**um**
Gen	utr**īus**	utr**īus**	utr**īus**	tōt**īus**	tōt**īus**	tōt**īus**
Dat	utr**ī**	utr**ī**	utr**ī**	tōt**ī**	tōt**ī**	tōt**ī**
Acc	utr**um**	utr**am**	utr**um**	tōt**um**	tōt**am**	tōt**um**
Abl	utr**ō**	utr**ā**	utr**ō**	tōt**ō**	tōt**ā**	tōt**ō**

Third Declension Adjectives of Three Endings: Singular

alacer lively

	masc	*fem*	*neut*
Nom	alacer	alacris	alacre
Gen	alacris	alacris	alacris
Dat	alacrī	alacrī	alacrī
Acc	alacrem	alacrem	alacre
Abl	alacrī	alacrī	alacrī

Third Declension Adjectives of Three Endings: Plural

	masc	*fem*	*neut*
Nom	alacrēs	alacrēs	alacria
Gen	alacrium	alacrium	alacrium
Dat	alacribus	alacribus	alacribus
Acc	alacr·ēs *or* -īs	alacr·ēs *or* -īs	alacria
Abl	alacribus	alacribus	alcribus

Third Declension Adjectives of Two Endings: Singular

	fortis brave		**fortior** braver	
	masc & fem	*neut*	*masc & fem*	*neut*
Nom	fortis	forte	fortior	fortius
Gen	fortis	fortis	fortiōris	fortiōris
Dat	fortī	fortī	fortiōrī	fortiōrī
Acc	fortem	forte	fortiōrem	fortius
Abl	fortī	fortī	fortiō·re *or* -rī	fortiō·re *or* -rī

Third Declension Adjectives of Two Endings: Plural

	masc & fem	*neut*	*masc & fem*	*neut*
Nom	fortēs	fortia	fortiōrēs	fortiōra
Gen	fortium	fortium	fortiōrum	fortiōrum
Dat	fortibus	fortibus	fortiōribus	fortiōribus
Acc	fort·ēs *or* -īs	fortia	fortiōr·ēs *or* -īs	fortiōra
Abl	fortibus	fortibus	fortiōribus	fortiōribus

Third Declension Adjectives of One Ending: Singular

	audax bold		**potens** powerful		**vetus** old	
	masc & fem	*neut*	*masc & fem*	*neut*	*masc & fem*	*neut*
Nom	audax	audax	potens	potens	vetus	vetus
Gen	audācis	audācis	potentis	potentis	veteris	veteris
Dat	audācī	audācī	potentī	potentī	veterī	veterī
Acc	audācem	audax	potentem	potens	veterem	vetus
Abl	audācī	audācī	potentī	potentī	vetere	vetere

Third Declension Adjectives of One Ending: Plural

	masc & fem	*neut*	*masc & fem*	*neut*	*masc & fem*	*neut*
Nom	audācēs	audācia	potentēs	potentia	veterēs	vetera
Gen	audācium	audācium	potentium	potentium	veterum	veterum
Dat	audācibus	audācibus	potentibus	potentibus	veteribus	veteribus
Acc	audāc·ēs -īs	audācia	potentia	potentia	veterēs	vetera
Abl	audācibus	audācibus	potentibus	potentibus	veteribus	veteribus

Comparison of Irregular Adjectives

Positive	*Comparative*	*Superlative*
bonus, *good*	melior, *better*	optimus, *best*
exter, *external*	exterior, *outer*	extrēmus, *outermost*
frūgī, *thrifty*	frūgālior, *thriftier*	frūgālissimus, *thriftiest*
magnus, *big*	major, *bigger*	maximus, *biggest*
malus, *bad*	pējor, *worse*	pessimus, *worst*
multus, *bad*	plūs, *more*	plūrimus, *most*
nēquam, *worthless*	nēquior, *worse*	nēquissimus, *worst*
posterus, *following*	posterior, *later*	postrēmus, postumus, *last*
superus, *upper*	superior, *higher*	suprēmus, summus, *highest*
———	dēterior, *worse*	dēterrimus, *worst*
———	inferior, *lower*	infimus, īmus, *lowest*
———	interior, *inner*	intimus, *innermost*
———	ocior, *swifter*	ocissimus, *swiftest*
———	potior, *preferable*	potissimus, *most important*
———	prior, *former*	prīmus, *first*
———	propior, *nearer*	proximus, *nearest*
falsus, *false*	———	falsissimus, *most false*
fīdus, *faithful*	———	fīdissimus, *most faithful*
novus, *new*	(recentior), *more recent*	novissimus, *latest, newest*
sacer, *sacred*	———	sacerrimus, *most sacred*
vetus, *old*	(vetustior), *older*	veterrimus, *oldest*

NOTES (a) For the declension of the comparative degree, see **fortior, fortius** above.

(b) Adjectives in **-er** form the superlative by adding **-rimus** to the nominative of the positive. The comparative is regular. Thus:

ācer, *sharp*	ācrior, *sharper*	ācerrimus, *sharpest*
celer, *swift*	celerior, *swifter*	celerrimus, *swiftest*
miser, *wretched*	miserior, *more w.*	miserrimus, *most w.*

(c) Five adjectives in **-ilis** form the superlative by adding **-limus** to the stem of the positive. The comparison is regular. Thus:

facilis, *easy*	facilior, *easier*	facillimus, *easiest*
difficilis, *difficult*	difficilior, *more d.*	difficillimus *most d.*
similis, *similar*	similior, *more s.*	simillimus, *most s.*
dissimilis, *unlike*	dissimilior, *more u.*	dissimillimus, *most u.*
humilis, *low*	humilior, *lower*	humillimus, *lowest*

Adverbs

Comparison of Irregular Adverbs

bene, *well*	melius, *better*	optimē, *best*
diū, *long*	diūtius, *longer*	diūtissimē, *longest*
magnopere, *greatly*	magis, *more*	maximē, *most*
male, *badly*	pejus, *worse*	pessimē, *worst*
multum, *much*	plūs, *more*	plūrimum, *most*
nēquiter, *worthlessly*	nēquius, *more w.*	nēquissimē, *most w.*
nūper, *recently*	———	nūperrimē, *most r.*
parum, *little*	minus, *less*	minimē, *least*
prope, *near*	propius, *more c.*	proximē, *most c.*
saepe, *often*	saepius, *oftener*	saepissimē, *most o.*
secus, *otherwise*	sētius, *otherwise*	———
———	potius, *rather*	potissimum, *especially*
———	prius, *previously*	prīmum, *first*

First Conjugation Verbs

Principal parts:	amō	I love
	amāre	to love
	amāvī	I loved, I have loved
	amātus	(having been) loved

Indicative Mood

Active Voice		*Passive Voice*	
Singular	*Plural*	*Singular*	*Plural*
PRESENT			
amō	**amāmus**	**amor**	**amāmur**
amās	**amātis**	**amā•ris** *or* **-re**	**amāminī**
amat	**amant**	**amātur**	**amantur**
IMPERFECT			
amābam	**amābāmus**	**amābar**	**amābāmur**
amābās	**amābātis**	**amābā•ris** *or* **-re**	**amābāminī**
amābat	**amābant**	**amābātur**	**amābantur**
FUTURE			
amābō	**amābimus**	**amābor**	**amābimur**
amābis	**amābitis**	**amābe•ris** *or* **-re**	**amābiminī**
amābit	**amābunt**	**amābitur**	**amābuntur**
PERFECT			
amāvī	**amāvimus**	**amātus sum**	**amātī sumus**
amāvistī	**amāvistis**	**amātus es**	**amātī estis**
amāvit	**amāvē•runt** *or* **-re**	**amātus est**	**amātī sunt**
PLUPERFECT			
amāveram	**amāverāmus**	**amātus eram**	**amātī erāmus**
amāverās	**amāverātis**	**amātus erās**	**amātī erātis**
amāverat	**amāverant**	**amātus erat**	**amātī erant**
FUTURE PERFECT			
amāverō	**amāverimus**	**amātus erō**	**amātī erimus**
amāveris	**amāveritis**	**amātus eris**	**amātī eritis**
amāverit	**amāverint**	**amātus erit**	**amātī erunt**

Subjunctive Mood

Active Voice		*Passive Voice*	
Singular	*Plural*	*Singular*	*Plural*
PRESENT			
amem	amēmus	amer	amēmur
amēs	amētis	amē•ris *or* -re	amēminī
amet	ament	amētur	amentur
IMPERFECT			
amārem	amārēmus	amārer	amārēmur
amārēs	amārētis	amārē•ris *or* -re	amārēminī
amāret	amārent	amārētur	amārentur
PERFECT			
amāverim	amāverimus	amātus sim	amātī sīmus
amāveris	amāveritis	amātus sīs	amātī sītis
amāverit	amāverint	amātus sit	amātī sint
PLUPERFECT			
amāvissem	amāvissēmus	amātus essem	amātī essēmus
amāvissēs	amāvissētis	amātus essēs	amātī essētis
amāvisset	amāvissent	amātus esset	amātī essent

Imperative Mood

Active Voice		*Passive Voice*	
Singular	*Plural*	*Singular*	*Plural*
PRESENT			
amā *(2nd pers)*	amāte *(2nd pers)*	amāre *(2nd pers)*	amāminī *(2nd pers)*
FUTURE			
amātō *(2nd pers)*	amātōte *(2nd pers)*	amātor *(2nd pers)*	———
amātō *(3rd pers)*	amantō *(3rd pers)*	amātor *(3rd pers)*	amantor *(3rd pers)*

Infinitive	**Participle**	**Infinitive**	**Participle**
PRESENT			
amāre	am•ans, -antis	amārī	———
PERFECT			
amāvisse	———	amātus esse	amātus
FUTURE			
amātūrus esse	amātūrus	amātum īrī	amandus *(gerundive)*

	Gerund	**Supine**
GEN	amandī	———
DAT	amandō	———
ACC	amandum	amātum
ABL	amandō	amātū

Second Conjugation Verbs

Principal parts:	**moneō**	I advise
	monēre	to advise
	monuī	I advised, have advised
	monitus	(having been) advised

Indicative Mood

Active Voice		*Passive Voice*	
Singular	*Plural*	*Singular*	*Plural*
Present			
moneō	monēmus	moneor	monēmur
monēs	monētis	monē•ris *or* -re	monēminī
monet	monent	monētur	monentur
Imperfect			
monēbam	monēbāmus	monēbar	monēbāmur
monēbās	monēbātis	monēbā•ris *or* -re	monēbāminī
monēbat	monēbant	monēbātur	monēbantur
Future			
monēbō	monēbimus	monēbor	monēbimur
monēbis	monēbitis	monēbe•ris *or* -re	monēbiminī
monēbit	monēbunt	monēbitur	monēbuntur
Perfect			
monuī	monuimus	monitus sum	monitī sumus
monuistī	monuistis	monitus es	monitī estis
monuit	monuē•runt *or* -re	monitus est	monitī sunt
Pluperfect			
monueram	monuerāmus	monitus eram	monitī erāmus
monuerās	monuerātis	monitus erās	monitī erātis
monuerat	monuerant	monitus erat	monitī erant
Future Perfect			
monuerō	monuerimus	monitus erō	monitī erimus
monueris	monueritis	monitus eris	monitī eritis
monuerit	monuerint	monitus erit	monitī erunt

Subjunctive Mood

Active Voice		*Passive Voice*	
Singular	*Plural*	*Singular*	*Plural*
PRESENT			
moneam	moneāmus	monear	moneāmur
moneās	moneātis	moneā·ris *or* -re	moneāminī
moneat	moneant	moneātur	moneantur
IMPERFECT			
monērem	monērēmus	monērer	monērēmur
monērēs	monērētis	monērē·ris *or* -re	monērēminī
monēret	monērent	monērētur	monērentur
PERFECT			
monuerim	monuerimus	monitus sim	monitī sīmus
monueris	monueritis	monitus sīs	monitī sītis
monuerit	monuerint	monitus sit	monitī sint
PLUPERFECT			
monuissem	monuissēmus	monitus essem	monitī essēmus
monuissēs	monuissētis	monitus essēs	monitī essētis
monuisset	monuissent	monitus esset	monitī essent

Imperative Mood

Active Voice		*Passive Voice*	
Singular	*Plural*	*Singular*	*Plural*
PRESENT			
monē *(2nd pers)*	monēte *(2nd pers)*	monēre *(2nd pers)*	monēminī *(2nd pers)*
FUTURE			
monētō *(2nd pers)*	monētōte *(2nd pers)*	monētor *(2nd pers)*	———
monētō *(3rd pers)*	monentō *(3rd pers)*	monētor *(3rd pers)*	monentor *(3rd pers)*

Infinitive	**Participle**	**Infinitive**	**Participle**
PRESENT			
monēre	mon·ens, -entis	monērī	———
PERFECT			
monuisse	———	monitus esse	monitus
FUTURE			
monitūrus esse	monitūrus	monitum īrī	monendus *(gerundive)*

	Gerund	**Supine**
GEN	monendī	———
DAT	monendō	———
ACC	monendum	monitum
ABL	monendō	monitū

Third Conjugation Verbs

Principal parts:	regō	I rule
	regĕre	to rule
	rexī	I ruled, have ruled
	rectus	(having been) ruled

Indicative Mood

Active Voice		*Passive Voice*	
Singular	*Plural*	*Singular*	*Plural*
Present			
regō	**regimus**	**regor**	**regimur**
regis	**regitis**	**rege•ris** *or* **-re**	**regiminī**
regit	**regunt**	**regitur**	**reguntur**
Imperfect			
regēbam	**regēbāmus**	**regēbar**	**regēbamur**
regēbās	**regēbātis**	**regēbā•ris** *or* **-re**	**regēbāminī**
regēbat	**regēbant**	**regēbātur**	**regēbantur**
Future			
regam	**regēmus**	**regar**	**regēmur**
regēs	**regētis**	**regēr•is** *or* **-re**	**regēminī**
reget	**regent**	**regētur**	**regentur**
Perfect			
rexī	**reximus**	**rectus sum**	**rectī sumus**
rexistī	**rexistis**	**rectus es**	**rectī estis**
rexit	**rexē•runt** *or* **-re**	**rectus est**	**rectī sunt**
Pluperfect			
rexeram	**rexerāmus**	**rectus eram**	**rectī erāmus**
rexerās	**rexerātis**	**rectus erās**	**rectī erātis**
rexerat	**rexerant**	**rectus erat**	**rectī erant**
Future Perfect			
rexerō	**rexerimus**	**rectus erō**	**rectī erimus**
rexeris	**rexeritis**	**rectus eris**	**rectī eritis**
rexerit	**rexerint**	**rectus erit**	**rectī erunt**

Subjunctive Mood

Active Voice		*Passive Voice*	
Singular	*Plural*	*Singular*	*Plural*
PRESENT			
regam	**regāmus**	**regar**	**regāmur**
regās	**regātis**	**regā·ris** *or* **-re**	**regāminī**
regat	**regant**	**regātur**	**regantur**
IMPERFECT			
regerem	**regerēmus**	**regerer**	**regerēmur**
regerēs	**regerētis**	**regerē·ris** *or* **-re**	**regerēminī**
regeret	**regerent**	**regerētur**	**regerentur**
PERFECT			
rexerim	**rexerimus**	**rectus sim**	**rectī sīmus**
rexeris	**rexeritis**	**rectus sīs**	**rectī sītis**
rexerit	**rexerint**	**rectus sit**	**rectī sint**
PLUPERFECT			
rexissem	**rexissēmus**	**rectus essem**	**rectī essēmus**
rexissēs	**rexissētis**	**rectus essēs**	**rectī essētis**
rexisset	**rexissent**	**rectus esset**	**rectī essent**

Imperative Mood

Active Voice		*Passive Voice*	
Singular	*Plural*	*Singular*	*Plural*
PRESENT			
rege *(2nd pers)*	**regite** *(2nd pers)*	**regĕre** *(2nd pers)*	**regiminī** *(2nd pers)*
FUTURE			
regitō *(2nd pers)*	**regitōte** *(2nd pers)*	**regitor** *(2nd pers)*	———
regitō *(3rd pers)*	**reguntō** *(3rd pers)*	**regitor** *(3rd pers)*	**reguntor** *(3rd pers)*

Infinitive	**Participle**	**Infinitive**	**Participle**
PRESENT			
regĕre	**reg·ens, -entis**	**regī**	—
PERFECT			
rexisse	—	**rectus esse**	**rectus**
FUTURE			
rectūrus esse	**rectūrus**	**rectum īrī**	**regendus** *(gerundive)*

	Gerund	**Supine**
GEN	**regendī**	———
DAT	**regendō**	———
ACC	**regendum**	**rectum**
ABL	**regendō**	**rectū**

Third Conjugation Verbs in *-io*

Principal parts:	**capiō**	I take
	capĕre	to take
	cēpī	I took, have taken
	captus	(having been) taken

Indicative Mood

Active Voice		*Passive Voice*	
Singular	*Plural*	*Singular*	*Plural*
Present			
capiō	**capimus**	**capior**	**capimur**
capis	**capitis**	**cape•ris** *or* **-re**	**capiminī**
capit	**capiunt**	**capitur**	**capiuntur**
Imperfect			
capiēbam	**capiēbāmus**	**capiēbar**	**capiēbāmur**
capiēbās	**capiēbātis**	**capiēbā•ris** *or* **-re**	**capiēbāminī**
capiēbat	**capiēbant**	**capiēbātur**	**capiēbāntur**
Future			
capiam	**capiēmus**	**capiar**	**capiēmur**
capiēs	**capiētis**	**capiē•ris** *or* **-re**	**capiēminī**
capiet	**capient**	**capiētur**	**capientur**
Perfect			
cēpī	**cēpimus**	**captus sum**	**captī sumus**
cēpistī	**cēpistis**	**captus es**	**captī estis**
cēpit	**cēpē•runt** *or* **-re**	**captus est**	**captī sunt**
Pluperfect			
cēperam	**cēperāmus**	**captus eram**	**captī erāmus**
cēperās	**cēperātis**	**captus erās**	**captī erātis**
cēperat	**cēperant**	**captus erat**	**captī erant**
Future Perfect			
cēperō	**cēperimus**	**captus erō**	**captī erimus**
cēperis	**cēperitis**	**captus eris**	**captī eritis**
cēperit	**cēperint**	**captus erit**	**captī erunt**

Subjunctive Mood

Active Voice		Passive Voice	
Singular	*Plural*	*Singular*	*Plural*
PRESENT			
capiam	**capiāmus**	**capiar**	**capiāmur**
capiās	**capiātis**	**capiā·ris** *or* **-re**	**capiāminī**
capiat	**capiant**	**capiātur**	**capiantur**
IMPERFECT			
caperem	**caperēmus**	**caperer**	**caperēmur**
caperēs	**caperētis**	**caperē·ris** *or* **-re**	**caperēminī**
caperet	**caperent**	**caperētur**	**caperentur**
PERFECT			
cēperim	**cēperimus**	**captus sim**	**captī sīmus**
cēperis	**cēperitis**	**captus sīs**	**captī sītis**
cēperit	**cēperint**	**captus sit**	**captī sint**
PLUPERFECT			
cēpissem	**cēpissēmus**	**captus essem**	**captī essēmus**
cēpissēs	**cēpissētis**	**captus essēs**	**captī essētis**
cēpisset	**cēpissent**	**captus esset**	**captī essent**

Imperative Mood

Active Voice		Passive Voice	
Singular	*Plural*	*Singular*	*Plural*
PRESENT			
cape *(2nd pers)*	**capite** *(2nd pers)*	**capĕre** *(2nd pers)*	**capiminī** *(2nd pers)*
FUTURE			
capitō *(2nd pers)*	**capitōte** *(2nd pers)*	**capitor** *(2nd pers)*	———
capitō *(3rd pers)*	**capiuntō** *(3rd pers)*	**capitor** *(3rd pers)*	**capiuntor** *(3rd pers)*

Infinitive	Participle	Infinitive	Participle
PRESENT			
capĕre	**cap·iens, -entis**	**capī**	———
PERFECT			
cēpisse	———	**captus esse**	**captus**
FUTURE			
captūrus esse	**captūrus**	**captum īrī**	**capiendus** *(gerundive)*

	Gerund	Supine
GEN	**capiendī**	———
DAT	**capiendō**	———
ACC	**capiendum**	**captum**
ABL	**capiendō**	**captū**

Fourth Conjugation Verbs

Principal parts:	**audiō**	I hear
	audīre	to hear
	audīvī	I heard, have heard
	audītus	(having been) heard

Indicative Mood

Active Voice		*Passive Voice*	
Singular	*Plural*	*Singular*	*Plural*
PRESENT			
audiō	**audīmus**	**audior**	**audīmur**
audīs	**audītis**	**audī·ris** *or* **-re**	**audīminī**
audit	**audiunt**	**audītur**	**audiuntur**
IMPERFECT			
audiēbam	**audiēbāmus**	**audiēbar**	**audiēbāmur**
audiēbās	**audiēbātis**	**audiēbā·ris** *or* **-re**	**audiēbāminī**
audiēbat	**audiēbant**	**audiēbātur**	**audiēbantur**
FUTURE			
audiam	**audiēmus**	**audiar**	**audiēmur**
audiēs	**audiētis**	**audiē·ris** *or* **-re**	**audiēminī**
audiet	**audient**	**audiētur**	**audientur**
PERFECT			
audīvī	**audīvimus**	**audītus sum**	**audītī sumus**
audīvistī	**audīvistis**	**audītus es**	**audītī estis**
audīvit	**audīvēr·unt** *or* **-re**	**audītus est**	**audītī sunt**
PLUPERFECT			
audīveram	**audīverāmus**	**audītus eram**	**audītī erāmus**
audīverās	**audīverātis**	**audītus erās**	**audītī erātis**
audīverat	**audīverant**	**audītus erat**	**audītī erant**
FUTURE PERFECT			
audīverō	**audīverimus**	**audītus erō**	**audītī erimus**
audīveris	**audīveritis**	**audītus eris**	**audītī eritis**
audīverit	**audīverint**	**audītus erit**	**audītī erunt**

Subjunctive Mood

Active Voice		*Passive Voice*	
Singular	*Plural*	*Singular*	*Plural*
PRESENT			
audiam	**audiāmus**	**audiar**	**audiāmur**
audiās	**audiātis**	**audiā·ris** *or* **-re**	**audiāminī**
audiat	**audiant**	**audiatur**	**audiantur**
IMPERFECT			
audīrem	**audīrēmus**	**audīrer**	**audīrēmur**
audīrēs	**audīrētis**	**audīrē·ris** *or* **-re**	**audīrēminī**
audīret	**audīrent**	**audīrētur**	**audīrentur**
PERFECT			
audīverim	**audīverimus**	**audītus sim**	**audītī sīmus**
audīveris	**audīveritis**	**audītus sīs**	**audītī sītis**
audīverit	**audīverint**	**audītus sit**	**audītī sint**
PLUPERFECT			
audīvissem	**audīvissēmus**	**audītus essem**	**audītī essēmus**
audīvissēs	**audīvissētis**	**audītus essēs**	**audītī essētis**
audīvisset	**audīvissent**	**audītus esset**	**audītī essent**

Imperative Mood

Active Voice		*Passive Voice*	
Singular	*Plural*	*Singular*	*Plural*
PRESENT			
audī *(2nd pers)*	**audīte** *(2nd pers)*	**audīre** *(2nd pers)*	**audīminī** *(2nd pers)*
FUTURE			
audītō *(2nd pers)*	**audītōte** *(2nd pers)*	**audītor** *(2nd pers)*	———
audītō *(3rd pers)*	**audiuntō** *(3rd pers)*	**audītor** *(3rd pers)*	**audiuntor** *(3rd pers)*

Infinitive	Participle	Infinitive	Participle
PRESENT			
audīre	**audi·ens, -entis**	**audīrī**	———
PERFECT			
audīvisse	———	**audītus esse**	**audītus**
FUTURE			
audītūrus esse	**audītūrus**	**audītum īrī**	**audiendus** *(gerundive)*

	Gerund	Supine
GEN	**audiendī**	———
DAT	**audiendō**	———
ACC	**audiendum**	**audītum**
ABL	**audiendō**	**audītū**

Conjugation of *sum*

Principal parts:	**sum**	I am
	esse	to be
	fuī	I was, have been
	futūrus	about to be

Indicative Mood

Singular	*Plural*
PRESENT	
sum	sumus
es	estis
est	sunt
IMPERFECT	
eram	**erāmus**
erās	**erātis**
erat	**erant**
FUTURE	
erō	**erimus**
eris	**eritis**
erit	**erunt**
PERFECT	
fuī	**fuimus**
fuistī	**fuistis**
fuit	**fuē-runt** *or* **-re**
PLUPERFECT	
fueram	**fuerāmus**
fuerās	**fuerātis**
fuerat	**fuerant**
FUTURE PERFECT	
fuerō	**fuerimus**
fueris	**fueritis**
fuerit	**fuerint**

Subjunctive Mood

Singular	*Plural*
PRESENT	
sim	sīmus
sīs	sītis
sit	sint
IMPERFECT	
essem	**essēmus**
essēs	**cssētis**
esset	**essent**
PERFECT	
fuerim	**fuerīmus**
fuerīs	**fuerītis**
fuerit	**fuerint**
PLUPERFECT	
fuissem	**fuissēmus**
fuissēs	**fuissētis**
fuisset	**fuissent**

Imperative Mood

Singular	*Plural*
PRESENT	
es *(2nd pers)*	**este** *(2nd pers)*
FUTURE	
estō *(2nd pers)*	**estōte** *(2nd pers,*
estō *(3rd pers)*	**suntō** *(3rd pers)*

Infinitive	**Participle**
PRESENT	
esse	———
PERFECT	
fuisse	———
FUTURE	
futūrus esse	**futūrus**

Conjugation of *volo, nolo, malo*

Principal parts:

volō	I wish	**velle**	to wish	**voluī**	I wished
nōlō	I do not wish	**nolle**	to be unwilling	**nōluī**	I did not wish
mālō	I prefer	**malle**	to prefer	**māluī**	I preferred, have preferred

Indicative Mood

PRESENT	volō vīs vult volumus vultis volunt	nōlō nōn vīs nōn vult nōlumus nōn vultis nōlunt	mālō māvīs māvult mālumus māvultis mālunt
IMPERFECT	volēbam	nōlēbam	mālēbam
FUTURE	volam	nōlam	mālam
PERFECT	voluī	nōluī	māluī
PLUPERFECT	volueram	nōlueram	mālueram
FUTURE PERFECT	voluerō	nōluerō	maluero

Subjunctive Mood

PRESENT	velim velīs velit velīmus velītis velint	nōlim nōlīs nōlit nōlīmus nōlītis nōlint	mālim mālīs mālit mālīmus mālitis mālint
IMPERFECT	vellem	nollem	mallem
PERFECT	voluerim	nōluerim	māluerim
PLUPERFECT	voluissem	nōluissem	māluissem

Imperative Mood

PRESENT	nōlī; nōlīte *(2nd pers)*
FUTURE	nōlītō; nōlītōte *(2md pers)* nōlītō; nōluntō *(3rd pers)*

Infinitive

PRESENT	velle	nolle	malle
PERFECT	voluisse	nōluisse	māluisse

Participle

PRESENT	vol•ens, -entis	nōl•ens, -entis	————

Conjugation of *eo*

Principal parts:		
	eō	I go
	īre	to go
	īvī *or* iī	I went
	itum (est)	people went

Indicative Mood

	Singular	*Plural*
Present	eō	īmus
	īs	ītis
	it	eunt
Imperfect	ībam	ībāmus
Future	ībō	ībimus
Perfect	īvī *or* iī	īvimus *or* iimus
Pluperfect	īveram *or* ieram	īverāmus *or* ierāmus
Future Perfect	īverō *or* ierō	īverimus *or* ierimus

Subjunctive Mood

Present	eam	eāmus
Imperfect	īrem	irēmus
Perfect	īverim *or* ierim	īverīmus *or* ierīmus
Pluperfect	īvissem *or* iissem	īvissēmus *or* iissēmus

Imperative Mood

Present	ī *(2nd pers)*	īte *(2nd pers)*
Future	**ītō** *(2nd pers)*	**ītōte** *(2nd pers)*
	ītō *(3rd pers)*	**euntō** *(3rd pers)*

	Infinitive	**Participle**
Present	īre	iens, euntis
Perfect	īvisse *or* isse	———
Future	itūrus esse	itūrus
		eundum *(gerundive)*

	Gerund	**Supine**
Gen	eundī	———
Dat	eundō	———
Acc	eundum	itum
Abl	eundō	itū

Conjugation of *fio*

Principal parts:	**fīō**	I am made, become
	fierī	to be made, become
	factus sum	I was made, became

Indicative Mood

	Singular	*Plural*
PRESENT	fīō	fīmus
	fīs	fītis
	fit	fīunt
IMPERFECT	fīēbam	fīēbāmus
FUTURE	fīam	fīēmus
PERFECT	factus sum	factī sumus
PLUPERFECT	factus eram	factī erāmus
FUTURE PERFECT	factus erō	factī erimus

Subjunctive Mood

PRESENT	fīam	fīāmus
IMPERFECT	fierem	fierēmus
PERFECT	factus sim	factī sīmus
PLUPERFECT	factus essem	factī essēmus

Imperative Mood

Singular	*Plural*
fī	fīte

	Infinitive	**Participle**
PRESENT	fierī	———
PERFECT	factus esse	factus
FUTURE	factum īrī	faciendus *(gerundive)*

Roman Numerals

	Cardinal	*Ordinal*	
1	ūnus, ūna, ūnum	prīmus	I
2	duo, duae, duo	secundus	II
3	trēs, tria	tertius	III
4	quattuor	quartus	IV
5	quinque	quintus	V
6	sex	sextus	VI
7	septem	septimus	VII
8	octō	octāvus	VIII
9	novem	nōnus	IX
10	decem	decimus	X
11	undecim	undecimus	XI
12	duodecim	duodecimus	XII
13	tredecim	tertius decimus	XIII
14	quattuordecim	quartus decimus	XIV
15	quindecim	quintus decimus	XV
16	sēdecim	sextus decimus	XVI
17	septendecim	septimus decimus	XVII
18	duodēvīgintī	duodēvīcēsimus	XVIII
19	ūndēvīgintī	ūndēvīcēsimus	XIX
20	vīgintī	vīcēsimus	XX
21	vīgintī ūnus	vīcēsimus prīmus	XXI
	ūnus et vīgintī		
22	vīgintī duo	vīcēsimus secundus	XXII
	duo et vīgintī		
30	trīgintā	trīcēsimus	XXX
40	quadrāgintā	quadrāgēsimus	XL
50	quinquāgintā	quinquāgēsimus	L
60	sexāgintā	sexāgēsimus	LX
70	septuāgintā	septuāgēsimus	LXX
80	octōgintā	octōgēsimus	LXXX
90	nōnāgintā	nōnāgēsimus	XC
100	centum	centēsimus	C
101	centum ūnus	centēsimus prīmus	CI
	centum et ūnus		
200	ducentī, -ae, -a	ducentēsimus	CC
300	trecentī, -ae, -a	trecentēsimus	CCC
400	quadringentī, -ae, -a	quadringentēsimus	CCCC
500	quingentī, -ae, -a	quingentēsimus	D
600	sescentī, -ae, -a	sescentēsimus	DC
700	septingentī, -ae, -a	septingentēsimus	DCC
800	octingentī, -ae, -a	octingentēsimus	DCCC
900	nongentī, -ae, -a	nongentēsimus	DCCCC
1,000	mille	millēsimus	M
2,000	duo mīlia	bis millēsimus	MM
10,000	decem mīlia	deciēs millēsimus	CCIↃↃ
100,000	centum mīlia	centiēs millēsimus	CCCIↃↃↃ

NOTES (a) **-ensimus** and **-iens** are often written in the numerals instead of **-ēsimus** and **-iēs.**
(b) The declension of **ūnus, ūna, ūnum** is indicated under "Nine Irregular Adjectives," p. 17.

Declension of duo and tres

	masc	*fem*	*neut*			
NOM	duo	duae	duo	trēs	trēs	tria
GEN	duōrum	duārum	duōrum	trium	trium	trium
DAT	duōbus	duābus	duōbus	tribus	tribus	tribus
ACC	duōs, duo	duās	duo	trēs (trīs)	trēs (trīs)	tria
ABL	duōbus	duōbus	duōbus	tribus	tribus	tribus

LATIN — ENGLISH

A

A. *abbr* **Aulus** *(Roman first name, praenomen); (leg)* **Absolvo** I acquit; *(pol)* **Antiquo** I vote "no" *(on the bill)*

-a *masc suf* indicating occupation or profession, *e.g.:* **agricola** one who tills a field, farmer; **scriba** one who writes, scribe

-ā *advl suf* forms adverbs which are also used as prepositions, *e.g.,* **suprā** above

ā *or* **āh** *interj* ah!

ā *or* **ab** *prep (w. abl)* **1** *(of agency)* by, at the hands of: **a Caesare in servitutem redactus** reduced to slavery by Caesar; **2** *(of time)* since, from, after: **a puero** since childhood; **a somno** after a sleep; **3** *(of space)* from, away from: **a castris perfuga** a deserter from the camp; **4** *(named)* after: **oppidum a Latini filiā appellatum** a town named after the daughter of Latinus; **5** on: **a dextro latere** on the right side; **6** in: **a tergo** in the rear; **ab una parte corporis** in one part of the body; **7** *(of cause, motive)* out of, from: **ab singulari amore** out of unparalleled love; **8** *(designating an office):* **ab epistulis** secretary; **a rationibus** accountant; **9** *(in respect to):* **dolere ab stomacho** to have a stomachache (to ache in respect to the stomach); **10** on the side of: **ab senatu stare** to side with the Senate (to stand on the side of the Senate)

ā- *or* **ab- abs-** *pref (before initial* **f** *becomes* **au-: auferre** to take away; *before* **p** *becomes* **as-: asportare** to take away, carry off) *with the sense of:* **1** from, away, away from: **abducere** to lead away; **2** off: **abscidere** to cut off; **3** at a distance: **abesse** to be at a distance, be absent; **4** completely, thoroughly: **abuti** to use up, exhaust by using; **5** the absence of what the noun implies: **amens** demented; **6** a more remote degree of relationship: **abnepos** great-great-grandson

abactus *pp of* **abigo**

abac·us -ī *m* cupboard; game board; abacus *(calculator);* panel; tray

abaliēn·ō -āre -āvī -ātus *tr* to alienate, estrange; to sell; to separate; **alicujus animum a se abalienare** to turn s.o. else's attention away from oneself

Abantiad·ēs -ae *m* descendant of Abas

Ab·ās -antis *m* king of Argos, father of Acrisius, and grandfather of Perseus

abav·us -ī *m* great-great-grandfather

Abdēr·a -ōrum *npl or* **Abdēr·a -ae** *f* town in S. Thrace, notorious for the alleged stupidity of its people

abdicāti·ō -ōnis *f* abdication, renunciation, resignation

abdĭc·ō -āre -āvī -ātus *tr* to abdicate, renounce, resign; to disinherit ‖ *refl* **se magistratu abdicare** to resign from office

ab·dīcō -dīcĕre -dixī -dictus *tr (in augury)* to disapprove of, forbid

abditē *adv* secretly, privately

abdit·us -a -um *adj* hidden, secret; secluded; abstruse; **abditus a conspectu** hidden from view

ab·dō -dĕre -didī -ditus *tr* to hide; to remove, withdraw; to banish; to plunge *(e.g., a sword)*

abdōm·en -inis *n* abdomen, belly; *(fig)* gluttony, greed

ab·dūcō -dūcĕre -duxī -ductus *tr* to lead away, take away; to withdraw *(troops);* to seduce; to alienate; *(w.* **ab**) to distinguish from; **animum abducere** to distract attention

ab·eō -īre -iī -itum *intr* to go away, depart; to disappear: **ab oculis** *(or* **e conspectu**) **abire** to disappear from sight; to pass away, die; *(of time)* to pass, elapse; to change, be changed; to retire; **abi in malam rem!** *(sl)* go to hell!

abequit·ō -āre -āvī *intr* to ride off

aberrāti·ō -ōnis *f* wandering; escape, relief

aberr·ō -āre -āvī -ātum *intr* to wander, go astray; to get lost; to make a mistake, go wrong; to do wrong; to digress; *(of a stream)* to overflow; *(w.* **ab**) **1** to disagree with; **2** to get one's mind off *(e.g., sadness);* **3** to deviate from; **4** to differ from

abesse *inf of* **absum**

abhinc *adv (w. acc or abl of time)* ago; **abhinc annos centum** a hundred years ago

abhorr·eō -ēre -uī *intr* to shrink back; *(w.* **ab**) **1** to be averse to; **2** to be inconsistent with; **3** to differ from; **4** to be free from

abiegn·us -a -um *adj* (**-gne·us** *or* **-gine·us** *or* **-gni·us**) fir

abi·es -etis *f* fir (tree); ship; spear; writing tablet

ab·igo -igĕre -ēgī -actus *tr* to drive away, get rid of; to banish, expel

abit·us -ūs *m* departure; outlet; end

abjectē *adv* negligently; unworthily

abject·us -a -um *adj* dejected, downhearted; undistinguished; unimportant; despicable; groveling

ab·jiciō -jicĕre -jēcī -jectus *tr* (**abic-**) to throw away, throw down; to push away; to understate; to belittle, slight; to give up; to humble, debase; to cow, reduce to despair; to sell cheaply, sacrifice; to express carelessly *or* perfunctorily; to discard; to cease to wear, take off; to expose *(a child to die);* to leave *(a corpse)* unburied; to turn down *(an offer);* to give up *(practices, intentions, attitudes);* **animam** *(or* **vitam) abjicere** to give up (this) life; **arma abjicere** to throw down one's arms ‖ *refl* to throw oneself down, fall down; **se ad pedes alicujus abjicere** to throw oneself down at s.o.'s feet; **se in herba abjicere** to fall down on the grass

abjūdic·ō -āre -āvī -ātus *tr* to take away *(by judicial decree);* to reject

abjun·gō -gĕre -xī -ctus *tr* to unyoke; to detach ‖ *refl (w.* **ab)** to detach oneself from, give up *(an activity);* **se ab hoc refractariolo dicendi genere abjungere** to depart from this quibbling style of speaking

abjūr·ō -āre -āvī -ātus *tr* to deny under oath

ablātīv·us -a -um *adj & m* ablative

ablāt·us -a -um *pp of* **aufero**

ablēgāti·ō -ōnis *f* sending off; banishment

ablēg·ō -āre -āvī -ātus *tr* to send away; to remove, banish; to dismiss, get rid of

abligū(r)r·iō -īre -īvī *or* **-iī** *tr* to eat up; *(coll)* to gobble up, waste, squander

abloc·ō -āre -āvī -ātus *tr* to lease, rent out

ab·lūdō -lūdĕre *intr* to be unlike; *(w.* **ab)** to differ from, fall short of

ab·luō -luĕre -luī -lūtus *tr* to wash away, cleanse, remove; *(poet)* to bathe, refresh

abneg·ō -āre -āvī -ātus *tr* to refuse, turn down

abnep·ōs -ōtis *m* great-great-grandson

abnept·is -is *f* great-great-granddaughter

abnoct·ō -āre *intr* to spend the night

abnorm·is -is -e *adj* irregular, unorthodox

ab·nuō -nuĕre -nuī *tr* to refuse *(to do s.th.);* to deny *(an assertion, allegation, one's guilt);* to repudiate responsibility for *(a crime);* to reject, refuse *(an offer);* to refuse to grant *(e.g., an interview);* to refuse to submit to *(authority);* to forbid, rule out *(e.g., hope);* to decline *(battle);* to refuse to perform *(a duty, task);* to disown *(children); (w. acc & inf)* to forbid *(the occurrence of an event);* **non abnuere** to admit, not to deny ‖ *intr* to say "no"; *(w.* **de** + *abl)* to say "no" to; **de societate haud abnuerunt barbari** the barbarians did not say "no" to (the idea of) an alliance

abnūt·ō -āre *intr* to keep saying "no" *(with a nod)*

abol·eō -ēre -ēvī -itus *tr* to abolish, efface; to destroy, obliterate; to banish from the mind, efface the memory of; to allow *(a practice)* to lapse, drop; to prohibit, ban; to put an end to *(an institution);* to rescind *(a law);* **abolere memoriam** *(w. gen)* to blot out the memory of *(s.th. unpleasant);* **abolere reum** *(leg)* to give up prosecuting a defendant

abol·escō -escĕre -ēvī *intr* to decay, vanish, die out; *(of things)* to be forgotten; *(of a memory)* to fade

aboliti·ō -ōnis *f* abolition, rescinding *(of a law, sentence);* amnesty

aboll·a -ae *f* cloak; *(fig)* wearer of a cloak

abōminand·us -a -um *adj* ill-omened; detestable, abominable

abōmin·or -ārī -ātus sum *tr* to loathe, detest; to seek to avert *(e.g., a bad omen, destruction)* by prayer

Aborīgin·ēs -um *mpl* aborigines, original inhabitants, natives

ab·orior -orīrī -ortus sum *intr* to miscarry; to fail; *(of stars, etc.)* to set

aborti·ō -ōnis *f* miscarriage, abortion

abortīv·us -a -um *adj* prematurely born ‖ *n* drug causing abortion

abort·us -ūs *m* miscarriage; **abortum facere** to have *or* to cause a miscarriage

ab·rādō -rādĕre -rāsī -rāsus *tr* to scrape off, shave; *(fig)* to squeeze out, rob

ab·ripiō -ripĕre -ripuī -reptus *tr* to take away by force, kidnap; to seize *(as booty);* to squander; *(of the wind)* to blow, drive *(off course);* to rescue *(from a bad situation);* **abripere mordicus** to bite off ‖ *refl* to hurry away, get away

ab·rōdō -rōdĕre -rōsī -rōsus *tr* to gnaw off

abrogāti·ō -ōnis *f* repeal

abrog·ō -āre -āvī -ātus *tr* to repeal, annul

abroton·um -ī *n* **(hab-)** southernwood *(aromatic medicinal plant)*

ab·rumpō -rumpĕre -rūpī -ruptus *tr* to break off; to tear, sever; to burst apart *(e.g., the clouds);* to rupture *(a body part);* to put an end to, cut short ‖ *refl (w. abl)* to dissociate oneself from

abruptē *adv* abruptly; rashly

abrupti·ō -ōnis *f* breaking off *(of relations);* divorce

abrupt·us -a -um *pp of* **abrumpo** ‖ *adj* abrupt, steep ‖ *n* precipice

abs *prep (w. abl, confined almost exclusively to the combination* **abs te)** by, from

abs- *pref see* **ā-, ab-, abs-**

abs·cēdō -cēdĕre -cessī -cessum *intr* **(aps-)** to go away, depart; to vanish; to retire *(from work);* to desist; *(w. dat)* to cease to support; *(of feelings, illness)* to pass; *(of heavenly bodies)* to move farther away; *(mil)* to retreat; **non abscedere a corpore** not to leave the body *(of a deceased person)*

abscessi·ō -ōnis *f* diminution, loss

abscess·us -ūs *m* departure; absence; remoteness

abs·cīdō -cīdĕre -cīdī -cīsus *tr* **(aps-)** to cut off, chop off; to cut short; to destroy *(hope);* to banish *(from the mind)*

ab·scindō -scindĕre -scĭdī -scissus *tr* to tear off, break off; to renounce; to divide

abscīs·us -a -um *pp of* **abscīdo** ‖ *adj* steep, precipitous; concise; abrupt
absconditē *adv* secretly; obscurely; profoundly
abscondit·us -a -um *adj* concealed, secret; abstruse, profound
abscon·dō -děre -dī *or* **-didī -ditus** *tr* to hide; to keep secret, conceal; to lose sight of, leave behind; to shroud (in darkness); *(w.* **in** + *acc)* to plunge *(weapon)* into ‖ *refl & pass* to hide
abs·ens -entis *pres p of* **absum** ‖ *adj* absent; in spite of being absent; non-existent; **praesens absens** whether present or absent
absenti·a -ae *f* **(aps-)** absence; non-appearance in court
absil·iō -īre -(i)ī *intr* to jump away
absimil·is -is -e *adj (w. dat)* unlike
absinth·ium -(i)ī *n* wormwood *(plant yielding bitter extract, used in flavoring wine)*
abs·is -idis *f* **(aps-)** vault, arch; orbit *(of a star)*
ab·sistō -sistěre -stitī *intr* to stand back, retire, withdraw, depart; to cease
absolūtē *adv* absolutely, perfectly
absolūti·ō -ōnis *f* exhaustiveness, completeness; perfection; acquittal; release *(from an obligation)*
absolūtōri·us -a -um *adj* of acquittal, granting acquittal
absolūt·us -a -um *adj* perfect, complete, unqualified
absol·vō -věre -vī -ūtus *tr* **(aps-)** to release, set free; to detach; to acquit; to get *(s.o.)* acquitted; *(of single juror)* to vote for the acquittal of; to complete, finish *(task, transaction);* to put the finishing touches to *(an operation);* to pay off, discharge *(an account, debt); (w. gen or abl of the charge)* to prove *(s.o.)* innocent of; **verbo** *(or* **paucis** *or* **breviter) absolvere** to sum up, put in a nutshell
abson·us -a -um *adj* **(aps-)** discordant, harsh *(sound);* unpleasant, jarring; *(w. dat or abl)* inconsistent with
absor·beō -bēre -buī *(or* **-psī)** **-ptus** *tr* **(aps-)** to swallow, devour; to absorb; to engross; to engulf
absque *prep* **(aps-)** *(w. abl)* without, apart from, but for: **absque me foret** had it not been for me; **absque unā hāc foret** but for this one thing
abstēmi·us -a -um *adj* abstemious, temperate, sober
abster·geō -gēre -sī -sus *or* **absterg·ō -ěre** *tr* **(aps-)** to wipe off, wipe dry; to expel, banish; **fletum abstergere** to wipe away tears
absterr·eō -ēre -uī -itus *tr* **(aps-)** to scare away; to deter
abstin·ens -entis *adj* temperate, fore-bearing; chaste; *(w. gen or abl)* showing restraint in respect to, not greedy for
abstinenter *adv* with restraint
abstinenti·a -ae *f* restraint, self-control; integrity; *(w. gen or abl)* **1** restraint in respect to; **2** abstinence from
abs·tineō -tinēre -tinuī -tentus *tr* **(aps-)** to withold, keep away, hold back; to restrain ‖ *refl (w. abl or* **ab)** to refrain from, keep oneself from ‖ *intr* to abstain, refrain; *(w. gen, abl or w.* **ab,** *w. inf, w.* **quin** *or* **quominus)** to refrain from
abst·ō -āre *intr* **(aps-)** to stand at a distance, stand aloof
abstra·hō -hěre -xī -ctus *tr* **(aps-)** to pull away, draw away, remove; to detach; to split; to deduct, subtract; to distract, divert; to exclude, except
abstrū·dō -děre -sī -sus *tr* **(aps-)** to push away; to conceal, suppress ‖ *pass* to be concealed *(by intervening object)*
abstrūs·us -a -um *pp of* **abstrudo (aps-)** ‖ *adj* hidden, concealed, secret; profound, abstruse; reserved *(person);* secluded
abstulī *perf of* **aufero**
absum abesse āfuī āfutūrus *intr* to be away, be absent, be distant; to be missing; to be unsuitable, be inappropriate; to be wanting; *(w. abl or* **ab)** to be removed from, keep aloof from, be disinclined to; *(w.* **ab) 1** to be different from; **2** to be inconsistent with; **3** to be free from; **4** to be unsuitable for, be unfit for; *(w. dat)* to be of no help to; **ab hoc consilio abesse** to have no part in this strategy; **a culpa abesse** to be free of guilt; **a periculis abesse** to avoid dangers; **legatos haud procul afuit quin violarent** they came close to outraging the ambassadors; **non multum aberat ab eo quin** he was not far from, he was almost on the point of; **tantum aberat a bello, ut** he was so averse to war, that
absūm·ō -ěre -psī -ptus *tr* to take away, diminish; to consume, use up, waste; to exhaust; to destroy; to spend *(time);* to cause the death of, carry off ‖ *pass (w.* **in** + *acc)* to disappear into
absurdē *adv* **(aps-)** out of tune; absurdly
absurd·us -a -um *adj* **(aps-)** out of tune; absurd, illogical, senseless, silly
Absyrt·us -ī *m* brother of Medea and son of Aeëtes, the king of Colchis, brother of Medea
abund·ans -antis *adj* abundant, overflowing; affluent; more than enough; *(of rivers)* in flood; *(w. gen or abl)* abounding in, rich in
abundanter *adv* abundantly; profusely
abundanti·a -ae *f* abundance; affluence; lavishness; profusion
abundē *adv* abundantly, amply

abūsi·ō -ōnis *f* incorrect use *(of words)*
abusque *prep (w. abl)* all the way from
ab·ūtor -ūtī -ūsus sum *intr (w. abl)* **1** to use up; **2** to misuse, abuse
Abӯd·os *or* **Abӯd·us -ī** *f* town on the Hellespont
ac *conj (usually before consonants)* and, and also, and moreover; *(connecting a more emphatic sentence element)* and in particular, and what is more; *(connecting a sentence element which strengthens or corrects the first element)* and in fact; *(in comparisons)* than, as
Acadēmi·a -ae *f* Academy *(where Plato taught);* Platonic philosophy; Cicero's villa near Puteoli
Acadēmic·us -a -um *adj* Academic **‖** *m* Academic philosopher **‖** *npl* Cicero's treatise on Academic philosophy
acalanth·is -idis *f* goldfinch *(bird)*
acanth·us *or* **acanth·os -ī** *m (bot)* acanthus *(plant on whose leaves the architectural ornament of capitals of Corinthian columns was patterned)*
Acarnāni·a -ae *f* district in N.W. Greece
Acast·us -ī *m* son of Pelias
ac·cēdō -cēdĕre -cessī -cessum *tr* **(adc-)** to come up to, approach **‖** *intr* to approach; *(w.* **ad***)* to come up to, approach; *(w. dat or* **ad***)* **1** to agree with, approve of; **2** to be like, resemble; *(w.* **ad** *or* **in** *+ acc)* to enter upon, undertake; **accedit ut** or **quod** there is the additional fact that
acceler·ō -āre -āvī -ātus *tr* to speed, quicken **‖** *intr* to hurry
accen·dō -dĕre -dī -sus *tr* to light *(a fire, lamp);* to set on fire; to arouse *(emotions);* to aggravate *(conditions);* to work up, incite *(people);* to raise *(prices);* to light up, brighten; **accensa lumina** lamplighting time, dusk
accens·eō -ēre -uī -us *tr* to regard; to assign *(as attendant)*
accens·us -a -um *pp of* **accendo ‖** *adj* on fire
accens·us -ī *m* attendant, orderly **‖** *mpl* rear-echelon troops
accent·us -ūs *m* accent, intonation
accepti·ō -ōnis *f* accepting, receiving
accept·ō -āre -āvī -ātus *tr* to accept, receive *(regularly);* to be given *(a name)*
accept·or -ōris *m* recipient; approver
acceptr·ix -īcis *f* recipient *(female)*
accept·us -a -um *pp of* **accipio ‖** *adj* welcome, pleasing, acceptable **‖** *n* receipt; credit side *(in account books);* **acceptum facere** *(or* **ferre***)* to treat *(a debt)* as paid off; **acceptum fieri** *(w. dat)* to be set down to the credit of; **acceptum referre** *(w. dat)* to set down to the credit side, have *(him, her, etc.)* to thank for
accersō *or* **arcess·ō -ĕre -īvī** *or* **-iī -ītus** *tr* to call, summon; to bring, procure
accessi·ō -ōnis *f* approach; addition, increase; additional payment, bonus; intensification; appendage, accessory; addition to one's resources; **accessionem facere** to make progress, gain ground; **accessio temporis** *(leg)* extra time *(added to possessorship)*
access·us -ūs *m* act of approaching, approach; attack; rising *(of heavenly bodies);* blowing *(of the wind);* going at, tackling *(a task);* right to approach, access; entry, way in, passage; **accessus et recessus aestuum** flow and ebb of the tide
Accher·uns -untis *mf* lower world
ac·cī·dō -cīdĕre -cīdī -cīsus *tr* to cut down; to impair, weaken; to decimate
ac·cĭdō -cĭdĕre -cĭdī *intr* to happen, occur, come to pass; *(w. dat of person affected)* to happen to, befall; *(w. adv)* to turn out; *(w. abl of cause)* to happen as the result of; *(w. dat)* to strike *(s.o. as), e.g.:* **hoc tibi insolentia praeter opinionem accidebat** this struck you as exceptional insolence; *(w.* **in** *+ acc)* **1** to fall upon; **2** to be applicable to; *(w. dat or* **ad***)* to fall at *(e.g., s.o.'s feet);* **aures** *(or* **auribus** *or* **ad aures***)* **accidere** *(w. gen)* to reach the ears of; **accidit ut** *(w. subj or* **quod** *w. indic)* it happens that; **si quid mihi acciderit** if anything should happen to me
accin·gō -gĕre -xī -ctus *tr* to gird; to gird up, tuck up *(one's clothing)* **‖** *refl & pass (w. abl)* to arm oneself with, equip oneself with; **accingi** *or* **se accingere** *(w. dat or* **ad** *or* **in** *+ acc)* to prepare oneself for, to enter upon, to undertake; **ferro accingi** to put on the sword
ac·ciō -cīre -cīvī -cītus *tr* to call, send for, invite; **mortem sibi accire** to commit suicide
ac·cipiō -cipĕre -cēpī -ceptus *tr* to take, receive, accept; to welcome, entertain; to hear, learn, understand; to interpret, explain; to undertake *(a task);* to assume *(a responsibility);* to take *(medicine, food);* to incur *(a wound, loss);* to accept *(a post, office);* to borrow *(money);* to approve of, agree to; to have room for, accommodate; to welcome, entertain; to accept as valid, admit; to learn, hear, be told of; to infer, conclude; *(geol)* to let in *(the sea);* **accipere dareque** to exchange; **actionem accipere** *(leg)* to be granted a hearing; **auribus accipere** to hear, learn by listening; **initium** *(or* **originem** *or* **ortum***)* **accipere** to begin; **finem accipere** to come to an end
accipi·ter -tris *m* hawk
accīs·us -a -um *pp of* **accīdō ‖** *adj* impaired, ruined; troubled, disordered
accīt·us -ūs *m* summons, call

Acc·ius -(i)ī *m* Roman tragic poet *(170–85? B.C.)*

acclāmāti·ō -ōnis *f* **(adc-)** shout *(of approval or disapproval)*

acclām·ō -āre -āvī -ātus *tr* to hail, acclaim ‖ *intr* to shout *(in approval); (w. dat)* to shout at

acclār·ō -āre -āvī *tr* **(adc-)** to clarify

acclīnāt·us -a -um *adj* prostrate; sloping; *(w. dat)* **1** leaning on; **2** inclined toward, disposed to

acclīn·ō -āre -āvī -ātus *tr* **(adc-)** *(w. dat or* **in** *+ acc)* to lean *or* rest *(s.th.)* against ‖ *refl (w.* **ad***) (fig)* to be inclined toward

acclīv·is -is -e *adj* **(adc-)** sloping upwards, uphill, steep

acclīvit·ās -ātis *f* **(adc-)** slope, ascent

accol·a -ae *m* **(adc-)** neighbor

ac·colō -colěre -coluī -cultus *tr* **(adc-)** to dwell near

accommodātē *adv* **(adc-)** suitably, fittingly; comfortably

accommodāti·ō -ōnis *f* **(adc-)** adjustment; compliance, accommodation

accommodāt·us -a -um *adj* **(adc-)** *(w. dat or* **ad***)* fit for, adapted to, suitable for

accommod·ō -āre -āvī -ātus *tr* **(adc-)** *(w. dat or* **ad***)* to adjust *or* adapt *or* apply *(s.th.)* to ‖ *refl (w.* **ad***)* to apply *or* devote oneself to

accommod·us -a -um *adj* **(adc-)** *(w. dat)* fit for, adapted to, suitable for

accrē·dō -děre -didī -ditum *intr* **(adc-)** *(w. dat)* to believe, put faith in, trust

accr·escō -escěre -ēvī -ētum *intr* **(adc-)** to grow larger, increase; to be added

accrēti·ō -ōnis *f* **(adc-)** increase

accubiti·ō -ōnis *f* **(adc-)** reclining *(at meals)*

accub·ō -āre *intr* to lie nearby; to recline at table; *(w. dat)* to lie near

accūd·ō -ěre *tr* **(adc-)** to coin

ac·cumbō -cumběre -cubuī -cubitum *intr* **(adc-)** to take one's place at table; *(w.* **cum***)* to lie down with

accumulātē *adv* **(adc-)** abundantly

accumulāt·or -ōris *m* **(adc-)** hoarder

accumul·ō -āre -āvī -ātus *tr* **(adc-)** to heap up, accumulate, amass; to load, overwhelm

accūrātē *adv* **(adc-)** carefully, accurately, exactly, meticulously

accūrāti·ō -ōnis *f* **(adc-)** carefulness, accuracy

accūrāt·us -a -um *adj* **(adc-)** careful, accurate, exact; studied

accūr·ō -āre -āvī -ātus *tr* **(adc-)** to take care of, attend to; *(w. subj,* **ut, ne***)* to see to it (that, that not)

ac·currō -curręre -currī *or* **-cucurrī -cursum** *intr* **(adc-)** to run up; *(w.* **ad** *or* **in** *+ acc)* to run to

accurs·us -ūs *m* **(adc-)** running, concourse; *(mil)* attack, charge

accūsābil·is -is -e *adj* reprehensible

accūsāti·ō -ōnis *f* accusation; *(leg)* (bill of) indictment

accūsātīv·us -a -um *adj & m* accusative

accūsāt·or -ōris *m* accuser, prosecutor; informant

accūsātōriē *adv* like an accuser, prosecutorial

accūsātōri·us -a -um *adj* accuser's, prosecutor's

accūsātr·ix -īcis *f* accuser *(female)*

accūsit·ō -āre -āvī -ātus *tr* to keep on accusing

accūs·ō -āre -āvī -ātus *tr* to accuse; to prosecute; to reproach, blame; *(w. gen of the charge or w.* **de** *+ abl)* to accuse of

ac·er -eris *n* maple tree; maple wood

a·cer -cris -cre *adj* sharp, pointed; alert, vigilant; shrewd; energetic, active; excited, eager, enthusiastic; strict, stern, hard; pinched, sharp *(features);* strong *(drink);* fierce, sharp *(bite);* bright, vivid *(color);* strong, pungent *(odor);* strong, bitter *(taste);* wild, savage *(animal);* fierce, relentless *(enemy);* violent *(storm);* biting *(cold);* strong, high *(wind);* swift *(river);* intense *(hunger, pain);* drastic *(remedy);* strong, powerful *(incentive);* serious, critical *(situation); (coll)* huge, terrific; **naribus acer** keen-scented

acer·a -ae *f* incense box

acerbē *adv* bitterly, harshly

acerbit·ās -ātis *f* bitterness, harshness, sharpness, sourness; distress, painful experience; ill-feeling, bitterness; satirical quality *(of writing)*

acerb·ō -āre -āvī -ātus *tr* to embitter; to exacerbate; render *(s.th.)* disagreeable

acerb·us -a -um *adj* bitter, harsh, sour *(flavor, taste);* unripe, green *(fruit);* cruel, hostile, pitiless *(enemy);* harsh *(speech, remark);* untimely, premature *(death);* bitter *(feelings; cold);* rough *(winter);* strict, severe *(person in authority); (in a weakened sense)* troublesome, disagreeable

acern·us -a -um *adj* maple

acerr·a -ae *f* incense box

acersecom·ēs -ae *m* young man

acervātim *adv* in heaps; briefly

acerv·ō -āre -āvī -ātus *tr* to heap *or* pile up

acerv·us -ī *m* heap, pile; multitude; *(in logic)* sorites

acescō acescěre acuī *intr* to turn sour

Acest·ēs -ae *m* king of Sicily

acētābul·um -ī *n* vinegar bottle

acēt·um -ī *n* sour wine, vinegar; *(fig)* sharp tongue

Achaemen·ēs -is *m* first king of Persia, great-grandfather of Cyrus

Achaemenid·ēs -ae *m* follower of Ulysses who was left behind in Sicily
Achaemeni·us -a -um *adj (poet)* Persian; Parthian
Achae·us -a -um *adj & m* Achaean; Greek
Achai·a *or* **Achāï·a -ae** *f* province in N. part of Peloponnesus on Gulf of Corinth; Greece
Achāï·cus -a -um *adj & m* Achaean; Greek
Achāt·ēs -ae *m* companion of Aeneas ‖ river in Sicily
Achelō·is -idis *f* daughter of Acheloüs; a Siren; a water nymph
Achelōi·us -a -um *adj* of the river Acheloüs; of Acheloüs *(the river god);* descended from Acheloüs
Achelō·üs -ī *m* river in N.W. Greece, flowing between Aetolia and Acarnania; god of this river
Acher·ōn -ontis *or* **Acher·uns -untis** *m (f)* Acheron *(river in Hades);* god of this river
Acher·uns -untis *mf* lower world
Acheruntic·us -a -um *adj* of the lower world
Acherūsi·us -a -um *adj* of the river Acheron
Achill·ās -ae *m* Egyptian who murdered Pompey
Achill·ēs -is *or* **-ī** *or* **-eī** *m* Greek warrior, son of Peleus and Thetis
Achillē·us -a -um *adj* of Achilles
Achillīd·ēs -ae *m* son *or* descendant of Achilles
Achīv·us -a -um *adj* Achaean, Greek
Acīdali·a -ae *f* Venus
acid·us -a -um *adj* sour, tart; *(of sound)* harsh, shrill; sharp, keen; pungent; unpleasant, disagreeable
aci·ēs -ēī *f* sharpness, sharp edge; keenness of vision; glance; eyesight, eye; pupil *(of the eye);* mental power; battleline, battle array; battlefield, battle; debate
acīnac·ēs -is *m* scimitar
acin·um -ī *n or* **acin·us -ī** *m* berry; grape; seed in berry
acipens·er -eris *or* **acipens·is -is** *m* sturgeon
āc·is -idis *m* son of Faunus, loved by Galatea, changed into a river
acl·ys -ydis *f* small javelin
aconīt·um -ī *n (bot)* wolfsbane; strong poison
ac·or -ōris *m* sour taste, sourness
acqui·escō -escĕre -ēvī -ētum *intr* **(adqu-)** to become quiet; to rest; to die; *(w. abl, dat, or* **in** *+ abl)* **1** to find rest in; **2** to acquiesce in, be content with; **3** find pleasure in, rejoice in
acquī·rō -rĕre -sīvī -sītus *tr* **(adqu-)** to acquire, obtain, gain, win
Acrae·us -a -um *adj (title of the gods)* dwelling on the heights, on high
Acrag·ās -antis *m* town on S.W. coast of Sicily *(poetic and Greek for Agrigentum)*
acrātophor·um -ī *n* vessel for holding unmixed wine
acrēdul·a -ae *f* bird *(species unknown)*
ācricul·us -a -um *adj* irritable, peevish
ācrimōni·a -ae *f* sharpness, pungency; irritation; energy
Acrisiōnē·us -a -um *adj* of Acrisius
Acrisiōniad·ēs -ae *m* descendant of Acrisius; Perseus
Acris·ius -(i)ī *m* king of Argos, father of Danaë, grandfather of Perseus
ācriter *adv* sharply, keenly; clearly, in a distinctive manner; closely, attentively; with vigor, with enthusiasm; severely; vehemently; bitterly, hard
ācroām·a -atis *n* entertainment
acroās·is -is *f* public lecture
Acroceraunī·a -ōrum *npl* promontory in Epirus on the Adriatic Sea
Acrocorinth·us -ī *f* citadel of Corinth
act·a -ae *f* seashore; seaside resort; beach party
act·a -ōrum *npl see* **actum**
Actae·ōn -onis *m* grandson of Cadmus, changed into a stag, and devoured by his own dogs
Actae·us -a -um *adj* Attic, Athenian; **Actaea virgo** Athena
Actiac·us -a -um *adj* of Actium; celebrating the victory of Actium
acti·ō -ōnis *f* doing, performance, action, activity; proceedings; act, deed; proposal, measure; delivery *(of orator or actor);* plot, action *(of play); (leg)* suit, right to bring a suit; **gratiarum actio** expression of gratitude; **naturales actiones** physiological functions
actit·ō -āre -āvī -ātus *tr* to do *(repeatedly);* to plead *(cases regularly);* to act *(often)* in *(plays)*
Acti·um -ī *n* promontory in Epirus *(where Octavian defeated Antony and Cleopatra in 31 B.C.)*
actīv·us -a -um *adj* practical *(philosophy); (gram)* active
act·or -ōris *m* doer, performer; agent, manager; actor, player; herdsman; *(leg) (with or without* **causae)** **1** defense counsel; **2** prosecutor; **actor summarum** cashier
Act·or -ŏris *m* companion of Aeneas
actuāriol·um -ī *n* small, fast boat
actuāri·us -a -um *adj* swift ‖ *m* stenographer ‖ *f* swift passenger ship *(having both sails and oars)*
act·um -ī *n* act, deed; transaction ‖ *npl* great deeds, exploits, achievements; official records *(of events; of business transacted by the Senate, emperors, etc.);* decrees *(of a magistrate, general, etc.);* **acta diurna** day-by-day record of events;

acta Herculis labors of Hercules; **acta mittere** to publish the news

actuōsē *adv* actively, energetically

actuōs·us -a -um *adj* active, energetic

actus *pp of* **ago** ‖ *adj* finished, past

act·us -ūs *m* act, performance; physical movement; driving *(of cattle or wagon);* right of way; cow path; wagon track; path, course *(of sun);* linear land measure *(120 ft.);* sequence *(of numbers);* drawing *(of breath);* transaction *(of business);* performance *(of a play);* act *(of a play);* delivery *(of a speech);* **deducere in actus** to dramatize; **in actu esse** to be active

actūtum *adv* instantly, immediately

acul·a *or* **aquol·a -ae** *f* small stream

aculeāt·us -a -um *adj* prickly; *(of insects)* having a sting; *(fig)* stinging, barbed

acule·us -ī *m* sting, proboscis *(of insects);* barb *(of arrow);* spike; sharp point; sarcasm; **aculeum emittere** *(fig)* to shoot one's wad, spend all one's money

acūm·en -inis *n* point, sharpness; sting *(of insects);* cunning; clever trick; **ingenii acumen** mental acumen

acuō acuĕre acuī acūtus *tr* to sharpen, make pointed; to whet; to tune *(musical instruments);* to stir emotionally; to stimulate; to quicken *(one's pace)*; to accent *(syllable)*

ac·us -ūs *f* needle, pin; hairpin; curling iron; **ab acia et acu** in great detail; **acu rem tangere** to hit the nail on the head

acūtē *adv* acutely, sharply, keenly

acūtul·us -a -um *adj* somewhat sharp, rather subtle

acūt·us -a -um *pp of* **acuo** ‖ *adj* sharp, pointed; shrill *(sound);* keen *(senses, mind);* shrewd, intelligent *(person);* piercing *(cold);* fiercely hot *(sun);* nimble *(movement);* pungent *(smell, taste);* subtle *(distinction)*

ad *prep (w.* **acc**) *(of space)* to, towards, at, near; *(often w.* **usque**) reaching to, as far as; for the purpose of, to; according to; in consequence of; with respect to; compared with; at the house of, with; in the company of; before *(judge, magistrate);* *(of time)* toward, about, until, at, on, by; *(with numbers)* about, almost; **ad diem** on the right day, promptly; **ad extremum** to the very end; **ad manum** on hand, available; **ad omnia** in all directions; **ad prima** to the highest degree; **ad summam** in short; **ad summum** at most; **ad tempus** on time, in time; **ad ultimum** utterly; **ad unum** one and all

ad- *pref* **1** at: **adclāmāre** *(or* **acclamare**) to shout at; **2** toward, aiming at: **adire** to go toward; **3** bringing things together: **adstringere** *(or* **astringere** to tie up; **4** towards a purpose: **adjurare** to swear to, swear by; **5** of increase or addition: **addere** to add; **6** of intensity: **adamare** to love deeply

adacti·ō -ōnis *f* administering *(an oath)*

adactus *pp of* **adigo**

adact·us -ūs *m* bringing together; snapping *(of jaws)*

adaequē *adv* equally

adaequ·ō -āre -āvī -ātus *tr* to make level; to equal, match, come up to the level of; *(fig)* to put on the same level; **adaequare solo** to level to the ground ‖ *intr* to be on the same level, be equal; *(of votes)* to be equally divided *(for acquittal and for condemnation); (w. dat)* to be level with; *(w. abl)* to be on a par with, be equal to *(in some respect)*

adamantē·us -a -um *adj* made of steel

adamantin·us -a -um *adj* hard as steel, adamantine; **saxa adamantina** diamonds

adam·ās -antis *m* adamant; steel; diamond

adambul·ō -āre *intr (w. dat or* **ad**) to walk beside

adam·ō -āre -āvī -ātus *tr* to love deeply; to fall in love with

adaper·iō -īre -uī -tus *tr* to uncover, throw open; to open up; to disclose to view, make visible; to open wide *(mouth, door);* to uncover *(head as sign of respect); (med)* to loosen *(bowels)*

adapertil·is -is -e *adj* that can be opened

adapert·us -a -um *adj* open *(door, flower)*

adapt·ō -āre -āvī -ātus *tr* to adapt, modify; *(w. dat)* to fit to

adaqu·ō -āre *tr* to water ‖ *intr* to fetch water

adauct·us -ūs *m* growth

adau·geō -gēre -xī -ctus *tr* to increase; to increase the number of; to exaggerate; *(w. abl)* to crown with

adaugesc·ō -ĕre *intr* to begin to grow

adbib·ō -ĕre -ī *tr* to begin to drink; to listen attentively to

adbīt·ō -ĕre *intr* to approach

adc- = acc-

addec·et -ēre *v impers* it is proper

addens·eō -ēre *or* **addens·ō -āre** *tr* to close *(ranks)*

ad·dīcō -dīcĕre -dixī -dictus *tr (w. dat)* **1** *(leg)* to assign *(property)* to; **2** to give custody of *(debtor)* to *(creditor);* **3** to sell *(by sale or auction)* to; **4** to award *(prizes, provinces)* to; **5** to ascribe to *(author);* **6** to condemn, doom to ‖ *refl & pass (w. dat)* to give one's support to ‖ *intr (in augury)* to be favorable

addict·us -a -um *adj (w. dat)* addicted to, a slave of; *(w. inf)* bound to *(do s.th.)* ‖ *mf* person enslaved for debt or theft

ad·discō -discĕre -didicī *tr* to learn in addition

additāment·um -ī *n* addition

ad·dō -dĕre -didī -ditus *tr* to add; to give

additionally; to add by way of exaggeration; to increase; to quicken *(one's pace);* to impart; to insert; to put *(into a container); (w. dat)* 1 to attach to, fit onto; 2 to serve *(a drink)* to; 3 to give to, confer on, inflict on; 4 to attribute to; 5 to intensify *(feelings);* **manus in vincla addere** to tie one's hands

addoc·eō -ēre -uī *tr* to teach in addition, teach new *(skills, etc.)*

addubit·ō -āre -āvī -ātus *tr* to call into doubt ‖ *intr* to begin to feel doubt; to hesitate

addū·cō -cĕre -xī -ctus *tr* to lead up, bring up; to bring with one, bring along; to import; to bring up *(reinforcements);* to lead *(the mind to);* to introduce *(arguments);* to draw together, wrinkle; to induce; to sail *(a ship to);* to bring *(water to a town);* to shut *(door);* to shorten *(rein);* to draw back *(bowstring);* to bend *(bow); (of time, conditions)* to bring on; *(leg)* to prosecute, bring to trial; **(in judicium) adducere** to take to court

adduct·us -a -um *adj* drawn tight, strained; narrow, tight *(place);* strict, serious *(character)*

ad·edō -edĕre -ēdī -ēsus *tr* to nibble at; to eat up; to waste; *(of fire)* to scorch; *(of water)* to erode

ad·empti·ō -ōnis *f* taking away

ad·eō -īre -iī *or* **-īvī -itus** *tr* to approach; to attack; to consult; to visit; to undertake, set about, undergo; to consult *(an oracle)* ‖ *intr* to go up, come up; *(w.* **ad)** 1 to go up to, approach; 2 to enter upon, undertake, set about; 3 to meet *(danger);* **ad rempublicam adire** to go into politics

adeō *adv* to such a degree, so; even, indeed, truly; very, extremely; *(following pronouns and numerals, to give emphasis)* precisely, exactly; quite, just, chiefly; *(at the beginning of sentence)* thus far, to such an extent; *(w.* **ut** *+ subj)* to the end that; *(w.* **ne** *+ subj)* to the end that...not; *(w.* **dum, donec,** *etc.)* to the point of time when; **adeo non** much less

ad·eps -ipis *mf* fat; corpulence

adepti·ō -ōnis *f* obtaining, acquisition

adeptus *pp of* **adipiscor**

adequit·ō -āre -āvī -ātum *intr* to ride up; *(w. dat or* **ad)** to ride up to, ride towards

adesse *inf of* **adedo** *& of* **adsum**

adēsur·iō -īre -īvī *intr* to be very hungry

adēsus *pp of* **adedo**

ad·haereō -haerēre -haesī -haesum *intr (w. dat, abl,* **ad** *or* **in** *+ acc)* 1 to cling to, stick to; 2 to keep close to, hang on to; 3 *(anat)* to be attached to; 4 *(of land)* to be contiguous with, be near; **lateri adhaerere** to stick to *(a person's)* side; **memoriae adhaerere** to stick in one's memory

adhae·rescō -rescĕre -sī -sum *intr* to stick; to falter; *(w. dat, abl,* **in** *+ abl, or* **ad)** 1 to stick to, cling to; 2 to be devoted to; 3 to correspond to, accord with; 4 *(of weapons)* to become lodged in; 5 to run aground on

adhaesi·ō -ōnis *f* clinging, adhesion

adhaes·us -ūs *m* clinging, adhesion

Adherb·al -is *m* son of Micipsa (king of Numidia), murdered by Jugurtha

adhib·eō -ēre -uī -itus *tr* to stretch out *(hands);* to apply *(remedies, fetters, treatment);* to administer *(medicine);* to call in *(as advisor, witness, expert);* to invite *(as a guest);* to cite *(an authority); (w. abl)* to supply *(s.o.)* with; **animum adhibere** *(w. dat)* to turn one's attention to; **fidem adhibere** *(w. dat)* to lend credence to ‖ *refl* to conduct oneself, behave

adhinn·iō -īre -iī *or* **-īvī -ītus** *tr* to whinny after; to lust after ‖ *intr (w. dat or* **ad** *or* **in** *+ acc)* 1 to whinny after; 2 to lust after, crave; 3 to chuckle in delight at

adhortāti·ō -ōnis *f* exhortation, encouragement

adhortāt·or -ōris *m* fan, supporter

adhort·or -ārī -ātus sum *tr* to cheer on, encourage

adhūc *adv* thus far, hitherto; till now; as yet, still; besides, in addition, moreover; to a greater degree, still further; *(w. numerals)* besides; **nihil adhuc** nothing as yet

ad·igō -igĕre -ēgī -actus *tr* to drive *(cattle);* to move up *(siege engine);* to assemble *(ships);* to hurl *(weapon);* to inflict *(wound);* to plunge *(weapon)* into; **aliquem jus jurandum adigere** to have s.o. swear allegiance; **provinciam in verba sua et Pompeii jus jurandum adigere** to have the province swear allegiance to himself and Pompey

ad·imō -imĕre -ēmī -emptus *tr (w. dat)* to take away from; **alicui vitam** *(or* **libertatem) adimere** to deprive s.o. of life *or* liberty

adipātus -a -um *adj* fatty, greasy; gross, bombastic ‖ *n* pastry *(made in fat)*

ad·ipiscor -ipiscī -eptus sum *tr* to get, obtain; to arrive at, reach; to inherit; to win *(victory);* **mortem adipisci** to commit suicide

aditiāl·is -is -e *adj* inaugural

aditi·ō -ōnis *f* a going to

adit·us -ūs *m* doorway, entrance, passage; extent to which a door is opened, opening; approach; arrival; access; entrance; right of entry, admittance; right to hold *(an office);* audience, interview; beginning, commencement; chance, opportunity; hostile approach, attack; chance of attacking, an "opening"; **primus aditus** first encounter *(with a person)*

adjac·eō -ēre -uī *tr* to adjoin ‖ *intr (w. dat or* **ad**) to lie near; to border
adjecti·ō -ōnis *f* addition; annexation
adjectīv·us -a -um *adj* adjectival ‖ *n* adjective
ad·jiciō -jicĕre -jēcī -jectus *tr* to add; to increase; *(w. dat or* **ad**) **1** to hurl *(weapon, insults)* at; **2** to add *(s.th.)* to; **c** to turn *(eyes, attention)* to; *(w.* **in** *+ acc)* to hurl *(weapon)* at
adjūdic·ō -āre -āvī -ātus *tr* to adjudge, award; to ascribe, assign
adjūment·um -ī *n* help, support
adjunct·a -ōrum *npl* attendant circumstances; **ad nomina adjuncta** epithets, nicknames
adjuncti·ō -ōnis *f* joining, union; addition; *(rhet)* repetition
adjun·gō -gĕre -xī -ctus *tr (w. dat)* **1** to yoke *or* harness *(animal)* to; **2** to add *(ingredients);* **3** to ascribe *(qualities)* to; **4** to bestow *(praise, honor)* on; *(w. dat or* **ad**) **1** to add, attach *(s.th.)* to; **2** to apply, direct *(mind, attention, etc.)* to; **uxorem adjungere** to get married ‖ *refl (w. dat)* to join
adjūr·ō -āre -āvī -ātus *tr* to swear to; to swear by ‖ *intr* to swear
adjūtābil·is -is -e *adj* helpful
adjūt·ō -āre -āvī -ātus *tr* to help ‖ *intr (w. dat)* to be of assistance to
adjūt·or -ōris *m* helper, assistant; aide, adjutant, deputy; supporting actor
adjūtōr·ium -(i)ī *n* help, support
adjūtr·ix -īcis *f* helper *(female)*
ad·juvō -juvāre -jūvī -jūtus *tr* to help; to encourage; to keep *(the fire)* going; *(med)* to relieve; *(w.* **ad** *or* **in** *+ acc)* to contribute to ‖ *v impers* it helps, it is an advantage, it is useful
adl- = all-
admātūr·ō -āre *tr* to bring to maturity, ripen; to speed up, expedite
ad·mētior -mētīrī -mensus sum *tr* to prop, support
Admēt·us -ī *m* king of Pherae in Thessaly, husband of Alcestis
admīgr·ō -āre *intr (w.* **ad**) to move to
adminicul·ō -āre -āvī -ātus *tr* to prop up
adminicul·um -ī *n* prop, support, stake, pole; rudder; aid; assistant
adminis·ter -trī *m* assistant; server, waiter
administr·a -ae *f* assistant, handmaid; waitress
adminstrāti·ō -ōnis *f* handling, administration, management, government; method of dealing with ‖ *fpl* administrative function *or* duties; administrative qualities
adminstrāt·or -ōris *m* administrator, director, manager
administr·ō -āre -āvī -ātus *tr* to administer, direct
admīrābil·is -is -e *adj* admirable, wonderful; strange, surprising; **admirabile est** it is remarkable
admīrābilit·ās -ātis *f* admiration, wonder; wonderfulness
admīrābiliter *adv* admirably; astonishingly
admīrāti·ō -ōnis *f* admiration, wonder; surprise
admīrāt·or -ōris *m* admirer
admīr·or -ārī -ātus sum *tr* to admire, wonder at; to be surprised at
admi·sceō -scēre -scuī -xtus *tr* to mix in, add; to involve, implicate; to join, mingle; *(w. dat,, w.* **ad** *or* **in** *+ acc or* **cum**) to add *(s.th.)* to, to mix *or* mix up *(s.th.)* with ‖ *refl* to get involved
admissār·ius -(i)ī *m* stallion; *(fig)* stud
admissi·ō -ōnis *f* audience, interview
admiss·um -ī *n* crime
ad·mittō -mittĕre -mīsī -missus *tr* to let in, admit; to allow; to let loose; to listen to; to put at a gallop; to let *(water, hair)* flow; to allow; to commit *(crime)*; **facinus in se admittere** to commit a crime; **ad animum admittere** to consider; **auribus** (*or* **ad aures**) **admittere** to listen to ‖ *intr (in augury)* to be propitious
admixti·ō -ōnis *f* admixture
admixtus *pp of* **admisceo**
admoderātē *adv* appropriately
admodum *adv* to the limit; very, quite, fully; *(w. numbers)* just about; *(w. negatives)* at all; *(in answers)* quite so, yes
admoen·iō -īre -īvī -ītus *tr* to besiege
admol·ior -īrī -ītus sum *tr* to pile up; **manūs admoliri** *(w. dat)* to lay violent hands on ‖ *intr (w.* **ut** *+ subj)* to struggle to
admon·eō -ēre -uī -itus *tr* to admonish, remind, suggest; to warn; *(w. acc or gen)* to recall
admoniti·ō -ōnis *f* admonition, reminder, suggestion
admonit·or -ōris *m* reminder
admonit·um -ī *n* advice, warning
admonit·us -ūs *m* advice; suggestion; warning; command *(given to an animal)*
admordeō admordēre — admorsus *tr* to bite at; *(fig)* to fleece
admōti·ō -ōnis *f* moving, movement
ad·moveō -movēre -mōvī -mōtus *tr* to move up, bring up, bring near; to lead on, conduct; to employ *(fear, flattery); (w. dat or* **ad**) **1** to move *or* bring *(s.th.)* to; **2** to apply *(s.th.)* to; **3** to direct *(attention, etc.)* to; **aurem admovere** to give heed; **calcar** *(or* **stimulum**) **admovere** *(w. dat)* to spur
admūg·iō -īre *intr (w. dat)* to bellow to
admurmurāti·ō -ōnis *f* murmuring

admurmur·ō -āre -āvī -ātum *intr* to murmur *(in approval or disapproval)*
admutil·ō -āre -āvī -ātus *tr* to clip close; *(coll)* to clip, cheat
adn- = ann-
ad·oleō -olēre -oluī -ultus *tr* to honor, worship, sacrifice to; to burn *(ritually);* to cremate; to light *(pyre);* to destroy by fire, burn; **adolere altaria donis** to pile the altar high with gifts; **flammis adolere penatis** *(fig)* to light the hearth; **honores adolere** *(dat)* to make burnt offerings to
adol·eō -ēre *intr* to smell
adolesc·ens -entis *m* young man **‖** *f* young lady
adol·escō -escĕre -ēvī adultum *intr* **(adul-)** to grow up; to become mature; to increase; *(of habits, etc.)* to become established
Adōn·is -is *or* **-idis** *m* son of Cinyras (king of Cyprus), loved by Venus, killed by a wild boar
adoper·iō -īre -uī -tus *tr* to cover up; to close
adopert·us -a -um *adj* covered; veiled; hiding; shut, closed; *(poet)* clothed
adopīn·or -ārī -ātus sum *tr* to suppose, conjecture further
adoptāti·ō -ōnis *f* adoption *(into a family)*
adopti·ō -ōnis *f* adoption *(into a family)*
adoptīv·us -a -um *adj* adoptive
adopt·ō -āre -āvī -ātus *tr* to adopt; to select; to graft *(plants)*
ad·or -ōris *n* spelt *(hardy European type of wheat)*
adōrāti·ō -ōnis *f* adoration, worship
adōre·a -ae *f* reward for valor; praise, glory
adōre·us -a -um *adj* of spelt, of wheat
ad·orior -orīrī -ortus sum *tr* to rise up against, attack; to attempt; to undertake
adorn·ō -āre -āvī -ātus *tr* to adorn; to equip, get ready
adōr·ō -āre -āvī -ātus *tr* to implore, entreat; to ask for; to adore, worship
adp- = app-
adq- = acq-
adr- = arr-
ad·rādō -rādĕre -rāsī -rāsus *tr* to shave close
Adrast·us -ī *m* king of Argos, father-in-law of Tydeus and Polynices
Adri- = Hadri-
adsc- = asc-
adsi- = assi-
adso- = asso-
adsp- = asp-
adst- = ast-
adsu- = assu-
ad·sum -esse -fuī -futūrus *intr* to be present; to appear; *(of conditions)* to exist; *(of time, events)* to be at hand; to be of assistance; *(of an assembly)* to convene; *(w. dat)* **1** to share in, participate in; **2** to assist, stand by; **3** *(leg)* to serve as attorney to; **4** *(of gods)* to look favorably on; **adesse animo** (*or* **animis**) to pay attention; to cheer up; **adesse illi corporis pulchritudo** he has a handsome physique
adt- = att-
adūlāti·ō -ōnis *f* flattery; fawning, cringing
adūlāt·or -ōris *m* flatterer
adūlātōri·us -a -um *adj* flattering
adulesc·ens -entis *m* **(adol-)** young man **‖** *f* young lady
adulescenti·a -ae *f* **(adol-)** youth, young people
adulescentul·a -ae *f* girl
adulescentul·us -ī *m* boy
adūl·ō -āre *tr* to fawn on *(like a dog)*
adūl·or -ārī -ātus sum *tr* to fawn on **‖** *intr* *(w. dat)* to kowtow to
adult·er -era -erum *adj* adulterous, unchaste; cross-bred *(plants);* debased *(coinage);* **adultera clavis** skeleton key **‖** *m* lover, adulterer **‖** *f* adulteress
adulterīn·us -a -um *adj* adulterous; counterfeit
adulter·ium -(i)ī *n* adultery; adulteration
adulter·ō -āre -āvī -ātus *tr* to defile, corrupt; to adulterate; to counterfeit; to falsify *(documents)* **‖** *intr* to commit adultery
adult·us -a -um *adj* grown, mature, adult
adumbrātim *adv* in outline
adumbrāti·ō -ōnis *f* sketch, outline
adumbrāt·us -a -um *adj* shadowy, sketchy; spurious
adumbr·ō -āre -āvī -ātus *tr* to shade; to obscure *(truth);* to sketch; to counterfeit
aduncit·ās -ātis *f* curvature
adunc·us -a -um *adj* curved, hooked
adurg·eō -ēre *tr* to be in hot pursuit of
ad·ūrō -ūrĕre -ussī -ustus *tr* to scorch, singe; to cause a burning sensation in, to burn; to nip, freeze; to desiccate; *(med)* to cauterize
adusque *prep* all the way to, right up to
adusti·ō -ōnis *f* burning; *(med)* burn; heatstroke
adust·us -a -um *pp of* **aduro ‖** *adj* scorched; **nivibus adustus** frostbitten; **sole adustus** sunburned
advectīci·us -a -um *adj* imported, foreign
advect·iō -ōnis *f* transportation
advect·ō -āre *tr* to import
advect·us -ūs *m* importation
adve·hō -hĕre -xī -ctus *tr* to convey; to ship; to import **‖** *pass* to ride; **equo advehi (ad** *or* **in** + *acc)* to ride to; **navi advehi (in** + *acc)* to sail to
advēl·ō -āre *tr* to veil; to wreathe
adven·a -ae *mf* stranger, foreigner
ad·veniō -venīre -vēnī -ventum *intr* to

arrive; *(of periods of time, events)* to draw near, approach, be imminent; *(w.* **ad** *or* **in** *+ acc, or acc of limit of motion)* to arrive at, come to, reach; *(w. dat) (of possession)* to come into the hands of; *(pres participle)* at *or* upon my (your, his, her, etc.) arrival; **advenientem ilico ad cenam adduxi** immediately upon his arrival I took him to dinner

adventīci·us -a -um *adj* foreign; imported; extraneous; unusual; migratory *(birds)*; **cena adventicia** reception; **ex adventicio** from an extraneous source

advent·ō -āre -āvī -ātum *intr* to keep coming closer; to turn up *(at a place)*; *(of tide)* to come in; *(of time, events)* to draw near

advent·or -ōris *m* visitor, guest; customer

advent·us -ūs *m* arrival, approach; visit; (official) visitation

adversāri·us -a -um *adj* **(-vors-)** *(w. dat)* turned towards, opposed to, opposite ‖ *mf* adversary ‖ *npl* journal, notebook, memoranda; assertion *(of opponent)*

adversātr·ix -īcis *f* **(-vors-)** opponent *(female)*

adversi·ō -ōnis *f* directing

advers·ō -āre -āvī -ātus *tr* **(-vors-)** to turn, direct; **animum adversare** to direct attention; *(w.* **ne)** to be careful not to

advers·or -ārī -ātus sum *intr* **(-vors-)** to put up opposition; to be unfavorable; *(w. dat)* **1** to oppose, resist; **2** to be incompatible with; **3** to be inconsistent with

adversum *or* **adversus** *adv* **(-vors-)** in the opposite direction ‖ *prep (w. acc)* facing, opposite, towards; in the direction of; in the opposite direction to, against; to the disadvantage of; *(after verbs expressing hostile intent)* to meet, face; compared with; contrary to; in the eyes of; in criticism of; in reply to, in response to; **adversus clivum** *(or* **collem)** uphill

advers·us -a -um *adj* **(-vors-)** opposite, in front; facing; unfavorable; hostile; *(astr)* diametrically opposite; **adversā viā** up the road; **adverso flumine** upstream; **frontibus adversis** head-on; **res adversae** misfortunes; **ventus adversus** head wind ‖ *n* trouble, adversity, misfortune; the opposite; **in adversum** forwards; *(of several things)* in the opposite direction; **in adversum subire** to go uphill; **per adversum** in the opposite direction

adver·tō -tĕre -tī -sus *tr* **(-vor-)** *(w. dat or* **in** *+ acc)* **1** to turn *or* direct *(s.th.)* toward; **2** to steer *(ship)* towards; **animos** *(or* **aures** *or* **oculos)** **advertere** to attract attention; **animum advertere** *(w. dat or* **ad)** to pay attention to, heed, observe ‖ *intr* to land; *(w.* **in** *+ acc)* to punish

advesper·ascit -ascĕre -āvit *v impers* evening approaches

advigil·ō -āre -āvī -ātum *intr* to be vigilant, keep watch; *(w. dat)* to keep watch over, bestow attention on; *(w.* **pro** *+ abl)* to watch out for

advocāt·a -ae *f* supporter *(female)*

advocāti·ō -ōnis *f* legal assistance; legal counsel; the bar; period of time allowed to procure legal assistance; delay, adjournment

advocāt·us -ī *m* helper, supporter; *(leg)* attorney

advoc·ō -āre -āvī -ātus *tr* to call; to convoke; to invoke; to invoke the help of; to invite *(to a meal)*; to consult; to cite; *(leg)* to adjourn

advol·ō -āre -āvī -ātum *intr (w. dat or* **ad)** **1** to fly toward; **2** to rush at; **3** *(mil)* to swoop down on

advol·vō -vĕre -vī -ūtus *tr (w. dat or* **ad)** to roll *(s.th.)* to *or* toward ‖ *refl* **se advolvere ad genua** *(or* **genibus)** *(w. gen)* to fall prostrate before

advor- = adver-

adyt·um -ī *n* sanctuary; *(fig)* tomb

Aeacidēi·us -a -um *adj* of the descendants of Aeacus; **Aeacideia regna** Aegina

Aeacid·ēs -ae *m* descendant of Aeacus

Aeac·us *or* **Aeac·os -ī** *m* king of Aegina, father of Peleus, Telamon, and Phocus, and judge of the dead

aed·ēs *or* **aed·is -is** *f* room, apartment; shrine, temple ‖ *fpl* house

aedicul·a -ae *f* chapel, shrine; small room, closet; small house ‖ *fpl* small house

aedificāti·ō -ōnis *f* constructing, building; structure, building

aedificātiuncul·a -ae *f* tiny building

aedificāt·or -ōris *m* builder, architect; **aedificator mundi** creator of the world

aedific·ium -(i)ī *n* building, edifice

aedific·ō -āre -āvī -ātus *tr* to build; **locum aedificare** to erect buildings on a site ‖ *intr* to erect a building

aedīlici·us -a -um *adj* aedile's ‖ *m* ex-aedile

aedīl·is -is *m* **(ēd-)** aedile *(Roman magistrate charged with the supervision of public buildings, markets, grain supply, games, and theatrical productions)*; magistrate in Italian and other towns; **aedilis cerealis** aedile in charge of the grain supply

aedīlit·ās -ātis *f* aedileship

aedis *see* **aedes**

aeditu·us *or* **aeditim·us** *or* **aeditum·us -ī** *m* sacristan

Aedu·ī -ōrum *mpl* **(Haed-)** Gallic tribe occupying the territory between the Saône and the Loire

Aeēt·ēs *or* **Aeēt·ās -ae** *m* Aeētes *(king of Colchis and father of Medea)*

Aeētae·us -a -um *adj* of Aeëtes
Aeēti·as -adis *f* daughter of Aeëtes *(i.e., Medea)*
Aegae·us -a -um *adj* **(Aegē·us, Ēgē·us)** Aegean ‖ *n* Aegean Sea
Aegāt·ēs -um *fpl* Aegatian Islands *(three islands off the W. coast of Sicily)*
ae·ger -gra -grum *adj* sick; *(w. abl of cause or* **ex)** sick from; diseased; weary, exhausted; depressed; depraved *(character, mind);* labored *(breathing, words);* corrupt *(institutions)* ‖ *mf* patient
Aeg·eūs -ēī *m* king of Athens and father of Theseus
Aegīd·ēs -ae *m* son of Aegeus, Theseus
Aegīn·a -ae *f* island off Attica ‖ mother of Aeacus
aeg·is -idis *f* shield of Minerva and of Jupiter; aegis, protection
Aegisth·us -ī *m* son of Thyestes and murderer of Agamemnon
aegrē *adv* painfully; with difficulty; reluctantly; hardly, scarcely; **aegre ferre** (*or* **pati**) to take (it) hard, resent
aegr·eō -ēre *intr* to be sick
aegresc·ō -ĕre *intr* to become sick; to get worse; to be distressed
aegrimōni·a -ae *f* distress, trouble
aegritūd·ō -inis *f* sickness; sorrow
aegr·or -ōris *m* illness
aegrōtāti·ō -ōnis *f* sickness, disease; sorrow
aegrōt·ō -āre -āvī -ātum *intr* to be sick; **animo aegrotare** to be mentally ill
aegrōt·us -a -um *adj* sick; love-sick
Aegypti·us -a -um *adj* of Egypt, Egyptian
Aegypt·us -ī *f* Egypt ‖ *m* mythical king of Egypt, whose 50 sons married the 50 daughters of his brother Danaüs
aelinon *interj* exclamation of sorrow, said to signify "alas for Linus"
Aemili·us -a -um *adj* name of a Roman clan *(nomen), esp.* Lucius Aemilius Paullus, who defeated Perseus at Pydna in 168 B.C.; **Via Aemilia** road from Ariminum to Placentia
aemul·a -ae *f* rival *(female);* rival city
aemulāti·ō -ōnis *f* emulation, rivalry
aemulāt·or -ōris *m* rival, imitator
aemulāt·us -ūs *m* emulation, rivalry
aemul·or -ārī -ātus sum *or* **aemul·ō -āre** *tr* to emulate, rival ‖ *intr (w. dat)* to be jealous of
aemul·us -a -um *adj (w. gen or dat)* **1** jealous of, striving after; **2** *(of things)* similar to, comparable to ‖ *m* rival
Aenead·ēs -ae *m* descendant of Aeneas; Trojan; Roman; Augustus
Aenē·ās -ae *m* son of Venus and Anchises, and hero of Vergil's epic
Aenē·is -idis *or* **-idos** *f* the *Aeneid*
aēne·um *or* **ahēneum** *or* **a(h)ē·um -ī** *n* bronze vessel, cauldron, pot
aēne·us *or* **ahēne·us** *or* **a(h)ēn·us -a -um** *adj* bronze; hard as bronze; bronze-colored
Aenīd·ēs -ae *m* son of Aeneas, Ascanius
aenigm·a -atis *n* enigma, riddle
aēnum *see* **aēneum**
aēnus *see* **aeneus**
Aeoli·a -ae *f* realm of Aeolus, king of winds; group of islands near Sicily
Aeoli·ī -ōrum *or* **Aeol·ēs -um** *mpl* Aeolians *(in N.W. Asia Minor)*
Aeol·is -idis *or* **idos** *f* Aeolia *(N.W. part of Asia Minor)*
Aeol·us -ī *m* god of winds
aequābil·is -is -e *adj* equal; alike; consistent, uniform; fair, impartial
aequābilit·ās -ātis *f* equality; uniformity; impartiality
aequābiliter *adv* equally; uniformly
aequaev·us -a -um *adj* of the same age, coeval
aequāl·is -is -e *adj* equal; of equal importance; even, level; of the same age; contemporary; symmetrical; affecting all equally, universal, general; *(of conditions, etc.)* comparable; uniform *(in consistency, shape, color, content, style);* homogeneous; *(of natural phenomena)* regular, continuous; *(of weather)* settled; equally balanced *(contest); (w. dat)* level with, on a level with, on a par with; *(w.* **ad)** equally disposed to ‖ *mf* comrade; contemporary
aequālit·ās -ātis *f* equality *(of age, status, merit)*; regularity; evenness; smoothness
aequāliter *adv* equally; evenly
aequanimit·ās -ātis *f* calmness, patience; kindness; impartiality
aequāti·ō -ōnis *f* equal distribution
aequē *adv* equally; justly, fairly; **aeque...ac** *or* **atque** *or* **et** just as if; **aeque...quam** as...as, in the same way as
Aequ·ī -ōrum *mpl* a people of central Italy
aequilībrit·ās -ātis *f* balance
aequilībr·ium -(i)ī *n* horizontal position; equilibrium
aequinoctiāl·is -is -e *adj* equinoctial
aequinoct·ium -(i)ī *n* equinox
aequiperābil·is -is -e *adj (w. dat or* **cum)** comparable to
aequiper·ō -āre -āvī -ātus *tr* **(-par-)** to compare; to equal, rival, come up to; *(w. dat, w.* **ad** *or* **cum)** to compare *(s.th.)* to ‖ *intr (w. dat)* to become equal to, be equal to
aequit·ās -ātis *f* evenness; conformity; symmetry; equity; calmness; **animi aequitas** equanimity
aequ·ō -āre -āvī -ātus *tr* to make level; to smooth (out); to equalize; to equal, match, rival; to reach as high *(or* as deep) as; to keep pace with; to balance

(scales); (w. dat) to liken to; **gradus aequare** to keep pace; **solo aequare** to raze to the ground; **sortes aequare** to shake up the lots fairly

aequ·or -oris *n* level surface; plain; sea

aequore·us -a -um *adj* of the sea, marine

aequ·us -a -um *adj* level, even, flat, smooth; on a level *(with)*, as tall *or* as high *(as)*; fair-minded, impartial, just, reasonable; evenly balanced; *(of laws, treaties)* giving equal rights, fair; *(of persons)* on an equal footing, equal *(in strength, etc.)*; *(of qualities)* matching, equal, alike; *(of love)* reciprocated; *(of verse)* regular, uniform; *(of movement)* steady, calm; *(of the mind)* calm, resigned; *(of things)* favorable, advantageous; *(w. dat)* **1** inclined towards; **2** sympathetic to, favorable to; **3** content with; **aequā mente** with calmness, patiently; **aequa pars** a half; **aequā parte** on a basis of equality; **aequi facere** to regard as immaterial, regard as a matter of indifference; **aequis manibus** *(of battles)* equally balanced; **aequo animo** with calmness, patiently; **aequo campo** *(mil)* on a level field *(offering advantage to neither side)*; **aequo fronte** *(mil)* in a straight line, in line; **aequo Marte** *(of battles)* evenly balanced; **aequo pede** on even terms, on an equal footing; **aequum est** it is right (that); **aequum solo ponere** to raze to the ground; **ex inferiore loco loquitur sive ex aequo sive ex superiore** whether he speaks before the judges on the bench or in the Senate, or from the rostra ‖ *n* level, plain; justice, fairness; **ex aequo** from the same level; *(fig)* equally

ā·ēr -ĕris *m* air; atmosphere; sky; weather; mist

aerāment·um -ī *n* bronze utensil

aerāri·us -a -um *adj* copper, bronze; of mines; financial, fiscal ‖ *m* coppersmith; low-class Roman citizen ‖ *f* mine; smelting furnace ‖ *n* treasury; funds contained in the treasury; *(specifically)* public treasury at Rome, kept in the temple of Saturn in the Forum; **aerarium militare** treasury for veterans' benefits; **aerarium sanctius** a special inner treasury; *(in Rome)* the part of the treasury containing a special war reserve

aerāt·us -a -um *adj* copper, bronze; rich

aere·us -a -um *adj* bronze; bronze-armored; bronze-beaked *(ships)*

āēre·us -a -um *adj see* **aërius**

aerif·er -era -erum *adj* carrying (bronze) cymbals

aerip·ēs -edis *adj* bronze-footed

Āëri·us -a -um *adj* aerial, lofty; airy; airborne; **aerium mel** dew

Āërop·ē -ēs *or* **Āërop·a -ae** *f* Aërope *(wife of Atreus, mother of Agamemnon and Menelaus)*

aerūginōs·us -a -um *adj* rusty

aerūg·ō -inis *f* copper rust, verdigris; corroding passion, envy, greed

aerumn·a -ae *f* trouble; distress; task

aerumnābil·is -is -e *adj* distressing

aerumnōs·us -a -um *adj* full of troubles, distressed; causing distress, calamitous

aes aeris *n* copper, bronze; bronze object; armor; statue; utensil; trumpet; money, cash; bronze coin, a copper; inscribed bronze tablet; payment; reward; **aes album** *(or* **candidum)** brass; **aes alienum** debt; **aes et libra** *(leg)* (symbolical) copper coin and scales *(used in transactions over property, emancipation of slaves, etc.)*; **aes militare** military pay; **in meo aere sum** I am free of debt

Aeschin·ēs -is *m* famous Athenian orator and opponent of Demosthenes ‖ Milesian orator contemporary of Cicero ‖ follower of Socrates

Aeschyl·us -ī *m* Athenian tragic poet *(525–456 B.C.)*

Aesculāp·ius -(i)ī *m* god of medicine

aesculēt·um -ī *n* **(esc-)** oak forest

aescule·us -a -um *adj* oak

aescul·us -ī *f* **(esc-)** Italian oak

Aeserni·a -ae *f* town in Samnium

Aesernīn·us -a -um *adj* of Aesernia

Aes·ōn -onis *m* father of Jason

Aesonid·ēs -ae *m* son of Aeson, Jason

Aesoni·us -a -um *adj* of Aeson, of Jason

Aesōp·us -ī *m* Aesop

aest·ās -ātis *f* summer; summer heat, summer weather

aestif·er -era -erum *adj* sultry; *(of a constellation)* that brings on the hot weather

aestimābil·is -is -e *adj* valuable

aestimāti·ō -ōnis *f* **(-tum-)** appraisal, assessment; esteem; value; **litis** *(or* **litium) aestimatio** *(leg)* assessment of damages *or* penalty

aestimāt·or -ōris *m* appraiser

aestim·ō -āre -āvī -ātus *tr* **(-tum-)** to appraise, rate, value, estimate; to esteem highly; to judge; to consider, think; *(w. gen or abl of value)* to consider worth; **litem (lites) aestimare** *(leg)* to assess the damages; **magni** *(or* **parvi) aestimare** to consider *(s.th. or s.o.)* worth much *(or* little)

aestīv·a -ōrum *npl* summer camp; campaign season, campaign; summer pastures

aestīvē *adv* scantily *(clad)*

aestīv·ō -āre -āvī -ātum *intr* to spend the summer

aestīv·us -a -um *adj* summer; **occasus aestivus** northwest; **oriens aestivus** northeast

aestuār·ium -(i)ī *n* estuary, lagoon; marsh; air shaft

aestu·ō -āre -āvī -ātum *intr* to boil, seethe; to burn, glow; to undulate, swell; to be tossed, heave; to waver; to be in heat, be all worked up

aestuōsē *adv* hotly, impetuously

aestuōs·us -a -um *adj* sultry; billowy; raging, seething; passionate; wavering

aest·us -ūs *m* agitation; glow, heat, sultriness; surge, billows; tide

aet·ās -ātis *f* lifetime, age; period of life; generation; passage of time; age group; era; **aetatem agere** to spend one's life; **aetatem exigere** to live out one's life; **id** *(or* **hoc)** **aetatis** at this time of life; **media** *(or* **constans,** *or* **firmata)** **aetas** middle age; **provecta aetas** old age

aetātul·a -ae *f* tender age

aeternit·ās -ātis *f* eternity; immortality; *(of things)* durability; courtesy title of the Emperor

aeternō *adv* forever

aetern·ō -āre *tr* to perpetuate, immortalize

aeternum *adv* forever; constantly

aetern·us -a -um *adj* eternal, everlasting, immortal; imperishable; durable; permanent, enduring a lifetime; *(of events)* remembered for ever; **in aeternum** forever

aeth·ēr -eris *m* upper air *(opp* **āēr);** sky, heaven; upper world *(opp* **Hades)**

aetheri·us -a -um *adj* ethereal, heavenly; of the upper world

Aethiopi·a -ae *f* Ethiopia

Aethi·ops -opis *m* Ethiopian; black man; *(poet)* Egyptian

aethr·a -ae *f* pure air, serene sky; air, sky, heavens

Aethr·a -ae *f* wife of Aegeus and mother of Theseus ‖ daughter of Oceanus and mother of Hyas ‖ wife of Hyperion

Aetn·a -ae *or* **Aetn·ē -ēs** *f* Mt. Etna

Aetnae·us -a -um *adj* of Etna; **fratres Aetnaei** the Cyclopes

Aetōli·a -ae *f* district in N.W. Greece

Aetōlic·us *or* **Aetōli·us -a -um** *adj* Aetolian

Aetōl·us -a -um *adj* of Aetolia, Aetolian; of Diomedes; of Meleager, like those of Meleager; of Tydeus ‖ *mpl* Aetolians

aevit·ās -ātis *f* age, lifetime

aev·um -ī *n or* **aev·us -ī** *m* age, lifetime, life; time, period; generation; eternity; **ad hoc aevi** hitherto; **aevo** *(or* **aevis)** for ages; **aevum agere** *(or* **agitare, degere, exigere)** to spend one's life; **ex ineunte aevo** from one's earliest years; **in** *(or* **per)** **(omne) aevum** forever; **primum aevum** early youth

Ā·fer -fra -frum *adj* African; **Afer turbo** S.W. Wind ‖ *m* African ‖ Publius Terentius Afer *(i.e., Terence, playwright, d. 159* B.C.*)* ‖ *mpl* Africans; inhabitants of the Roman province of N. Africa

affābil·is -is -e *adj* **(adf-)** affable; kind

affābilit·ās -ātis *f* **(adf-)** affability

affabrē *adv* **(adf-)** skillfully, ingeniously

affatim *or* **ad fatim** *adv* **(adf-)** sufficiently, enough

affāt·us -ūs *m* **(adf-)** address, discourse

affectāti·ō -ōnis *f* **(adf-)** disposition, state of mind; affectation, conceit

affectāt·or -ōris *m* **(adf-)** *(w. gen)* aspirant to

affectāt·us -a -um *adj* **(adf-)** affected

affecti·ō -ōnis *f* **(adf-)** frame of mind, mood; feeling; attitude, point of view; inclination, partiality; affection

affect·ō -āre -āvī -ātus *tr* **(adf-)** to grasp; to strive after, aim at; to try to win over; to affect; *(w. inf)* to aim to; **iter** *(or* **viam)** **affectare** to set out on a journey; **spem affectare** to cherish a hope

affect·us -a -um *adj* **(adf-)** furnished, provided; gifted; weakened, sick; affected, moved, touched

affect·us -ūs *m* **(adf-)** state, disposition, mood; feeling, emotion; affection

afferō afferre attulī allātus *tr* **(adf-)** to bring; to carry, convey; to report, announce; to introduce; to apply, employ, exert, exercise; to produce, cause, occasion; to impart; to allege; to assign; to contribute; to help; to offer for sale; **auxilium** *(or* **opem)** **afferre** to bring help; **causam afferre** *(w. gen or dat)* to be the cause of; **in judicium causam afferre** to prefer charges; **manus afferre** *(w. dat)* to lay violent hands on, attack

af·ficiō -ficĕre -fēcī -fectus *tr* **(adf-)** to treat, handle, manage; to influence, move; to attack, afflict; to impair; *(w. adv)* to treat *(in a certain way); (abl and verb may be rendered by the English verb corresponding to the Latin abl):* **cruce afficere** to crucify; **honoribus afficere** to honor; **supplicio afficere** to punish

af·fīgō -fīgĕre -fīxī -fīxus *tr* **(adf-)** *(w. dat or* **ad)** to fasten, attach, nail to; to apply *(as a remedy);* **animo affigere** to impress on the mind

af·fingō -fingĕre -finxī -fictus *tr* **(adf-)** to form, fashion besides; to make up, invent; *(w. dat)* **1** to attach, affix, add, join, contribute *(s.th.)* to; **2** to connect with, associate with; **3** to ascribe to, attribute to

affīn·is -is -e *adj* **(adf-)** adjoining, neighboring; related by marriage; *(w. dat or* **ad)** taking part in, privy to, associated with; subject to *(an affliction)* ‖ *mf* neighbor; in-law

affīnit·ās -ātis *f* **(adf-)** affinity, connection; relationship by marriage

affirmātē *adv* **(adf-)** with solemn assurance, positively

affirmāti·ō -ōnis *f* **(adf-)** affirmation, assertion, declaration; emphasis

affirm·ō -āre -āvī -ātus *tr* **(adf-)** to strengthen; to confirm, encourage; to assert

affix·us -a -um *pp of* **affigo (adf-)** ‖ *adj (w. dat)* **1** *(of guards, attendants)* assigned to; **2** attached to, devoted to; **3** intent on

afflāt·us -ūs *m* **(adf-)** blast, breeze; breath; inspiration

afflictāti·ō -ōnis *f* affliction

afflict·ō -āre -āvī -ātus *tr* **(adf-)** to strike repeatedly; *(of storms)* to toss about; to shatter, damage; to trouble, distress, torment; *(mil)* to harass ‖ *refl & pass* to be troubled

afflict·or -ōris *m* **(adf-)** subverter

afflict·us -a -um *adj* **(adf-)** damaged, shattered; downhearted; vile

afflī·gō -gĕre -xī -ctus *tr* **(adf-)** to knock down; to batter; to injure, damage; to distress, afflict; *(fig)* to crush

affl·ō -āre -āvī -ātus *tr* **(adf-)** to blast *(w. heat, lightning)*; *(w. dat)* **1** to breathe on, blow on; **2** to impart to ‖ *intr (of winds)* to blow; *(of smells)* to be wafted; to blow favorably ‖ *pass (of sounds or smells)* to carry toward

afflu·ens -entis *adj* **(adf-)** flowing; affluent; abounding, numerous

affluenter *adv* **(adf-)** lavishly, abundantly

affluenti·a -ae *f* **(adf-)** flow; abundance; extravagance

afflu·ō -ĕre -xī -xum *intr* **(adf-)** *(w. dat or* **ad)** **1** to flow to *or* towards, glide by; **2** to flock to; *(w. abl)* to abound in

af·for -fārī -fātus sum *tr* **(adf-)** to address, accost ‖ *pass* to be destined

affore = adfutur·us -a -um esse

afforem = adessem

afformīd·ō -āre *intr* **(adf-)** to be afraid

afful·geō -gēre -sī *intr* **(adf-)** to shine, beam; to dawn; to appear; *(w. dat)* to shine on

af·fundō -fundĕre -fūdī -fūsus *tr* **(adf-)** *(w. dat)* **1** to pour, sprinkle *(s.th.)* on; **2** to send *or* dispatch *(s.o.)* to ‖ *refl & pass (w. dat)* to prostrate oneself before

aflu·ō -ĕre -xī *intr* **(abf-)** to flow away; to be abundant; *(w. abl)* to abound in; *(w.* **ex)** to issue from, come from

Afrāni·us -a -um *adj* Roman clan name *(nomen), esp.* Lucius Afranius *(comic poet)* ‖ Lucius Afranius *(one of Pompey's generals)*

Āfric·a -ae *f* originally the district of Carthage, made a Roman province after the 3rd Punic War in 146 B.C.; continent of Africa; *(fig)* inhabitants of Africa

Āfricān·us -a -um *adj* African ‖ *m* Roman honorary name *(agnomen)* conferred upon the two Scipios

Āfric·us -a -um *adj* African ‖ *m* S.W. wind

Agamemn·ō(n) -onis *m* king of Mycenae, son of Atreus and Aërope, brother of Menelaus, murdered by his wife Clytemnestra

Agamemnonid·ēs -ae *m* son of Agamemnon *(i.e., Orestes)*

Agamemnoni·us -a -um *adj* of Agamemnon, descended from Aga-memnon

Aganipp·ē -ēs *f* fountain on Mt. Helicon sacred to the Muses

agās·ō -ōnis *m* stable boy; driver; lackey

Agathocl·ēs -is *m* king of Sicily, son of a potter, famous for his war with Carthage over the possession of Sicily *(361–287 B.C.)*

Agāv·ē -ēs *f* wife of Echion, king of Thebes, and mother of Pentheus

agedum *interj* come on!; well!

agell·us -ī *m* little field, plot

agēm·a -atis *n (mil)* honor guard

Agēn·or -oris *m* son of Belus, king of Phoenicia, father of Cadmus and Europa, and ancestor of Dido

Agēnorid·ēs -ae *m* descendant of Agenor; Cadmus; Perseus

a·ger -grī *m* (arable) land, (tilled) field *(opp:* **campus** = untilled, open land); ground; soil; farm, estate; territory, land, district; country *(opp:* **urbs)**; **ager publicus** state-owned land; **in agrum** in depth *(opp:* **in fronte** in frontage) ‖ *mpl* countryside

agg·er -eris *m* rubble; soil; rampart; breakwater; dike, dam; fortification; ramp; pile, heap, collection; ridge, mound, hill; funeral pyre; **agger ripae** bank *(of river)*; **agger (viae)** causeway

agger·ō -āre -āvī -ātus *tr* to pile up, fill up; to amass; to increase; *(fig)* to stimulate, intensify

ag·gerō -gerĕre -gessī -gestus *tr* **(adg-)** to bring forward; to pile up; *(w. dat)* to heap *(accusations, benefits)* on

aggest·us -ūs *m* **(adg-)** accumulation; terrace

agglomer·ō -āre -āvī -ātus *tr* **(adg-)** to gather together ‖ *refl & intr* to gather

agglūtin·ō -āre -āvī -ātus *tr* **(adg-)** to glue, paste; to solder ‖ *refl (w.* **ad)** to stick close to

aggravesc·ō -ĕre *intr* **(adg-)** to grow heavy; *(of diseases)* to get worse

aggrav·ō -āre -āvī -ātus *tr* **(adg-)** to weigh down; to make *(conditions)* worse, aggravate; to increase the force of *(a blow)*; *(fig)* to burden, oppress

ag·gredior -gredī -gressus sum *tr* **(adg-)** to approach; to address; to attack; *(w. inf)* to undertake to ‖ *intr (w.* **ad)** *(fig)* to tackle

aggreg·ō -āre -āvī -ātus *tr* **(adg-)** to assemble; *(w.* **in** *acc)* include (in); to implicate; *(leg) (w. dat)* to lump together with ‖ *refl & pass* to flock together; *(w. dat or* **ad)** to join

aggressi·ō -ōnis *f* **(adg-)** attack; *(rhet)* introduction

aggressus *pp of* **aggredior (adg-)**

agil·is -is -e *adj* agile, nimble, quick; busy, active

agilit·ās -ātis *f* agility, nimbleness, quickness; activity

agitābil·is -is -e *adj* mobile

agitāti·ō -ōnis *f* motion, movement, agitation; activity; waving *(of arms)*

agitāt·or -ōris *m* driver; charioteer

agit·ō -āre -āvī -ātus *tr* to set in motion; to drive on, impel; to hunt; to scour *(for game);* to brandish, wave *(weapon);* to pursue *(an objective);* to shake *(reins);* to drive *(vehicle);* to ride *(horse);* to tend *(flocks);* to urge, support, insist on; to practice *(justice, a trade)*; to exercise *(the body);* to engage in *(conversation);* to enjoy *(peace, fame);* to observe, celebrate; to obey, carry out; to spend, pass *(time);* to toss, disturb; to distress; to stimulate, arouse *(mind, emotions);* to deride, insult; to criticize; to discuss; to cherish *(hope);* **secum** *(or* **animo** *or* **mente)** to think about, consider, ponder; *(w. indirect question)* to debate *(in one's mind)* ‖ *intr* to live, spend one's life

Aglaur·ōs -ī *f* daughter of Cecrops

agm·en -inis *n* herd, flock, troop, crowd; body, mass; army column; procession; retinue, escort; course, flow *(of a stream);* movement *(of oars);* **agmen claudere** *(or* **cogere)** to bring up the rear; **agmen ducere** to form the van; **agmen primum** the van; **agmine** *(or* **uno agmine** *or* **agmine facto)** in marching formation; in a body

agn·a -ae *f* lamb *(female)*

ag·nascor -nascī -nātus sum *intr* to be born subsequently *(after the father has made his will);* **testamentum agnascendo rumpitur** a will is broken by the subsequent birth (of a son)

agnāti·ō -ōnis *f* blood relationship *(on the father's side)*

agnāt·us -ī *m* relative *(on the father's side)*

agnell·us -ī *m* little lamb

agnīn·a -ae *f* mutton, lamb

agniti·ō -ōnis *f* recognition, acknowledgement, admission; knowledge

ag·noscō -noscěre -nōvī -nitus *tr* to recognize, identify; to acknowledge; to own up to, admit to

agn·us -ī *m* lamb

-āg·ō -inis *fem suf* mostly formed from verbs in **-āre: imago** image; also from other sources: **cartilago** cartilage

agō agěre ēgī actus *tr* to drive, lead, conduct; to chase, hunt; to drive away, steal; to spend *(time);* to do; to manage, administer, carry on; to transact; to discuss; to play, act the part of; to plead *(a case);* to exercise, practice; to hold *(an office);* to celebrate *(triumph);* to work at, be busy on; to have in mind, plan; to push *(siege works)* forward; to emit *(smoke, flames);* to trace *(one's descent);* *(fig)* to dispel *(fear, hunger, etc.);* to spend, pass *(time, life); (of plants)* to put forth *(roots, sprouts);* to drive *(chariot);* to sail *(ship);* to construct *(anything linear: rampart, tunnel);* **agere furti** to accuse of theft; **agere reum** to indict a defendant; **aliud** *(or* **aliam rem) agere** not to attend to one's business; **animam agere** to breathe one's last; **gratias agere** to thank; **in crucem agere** to crucify; **iter** *(or* **cursum) agere** to make one's way; **nugas agere** to act foolishly; **praedam** *(or* **boves) agere** to rustle cattle; **primas partes agere** to play the lead role; **proelium agere** to do battle; **quid agis?** how do you do? **quo agis?** what's your point?; **satis agere** to have more than enough to do; **spumas agere** to foam *(at the mouth)* ‖ *refl* to go, come; to grow; to behave, comport oneself ‖ *pass* to be done, happen, occur, come to pass; to be involved, be at stake; **bene agitur** things turn out well; **quid agitur?** what's going on? ‖ *intr* to take action, act; to be busy; to bargain; to live, dwell; *(theat)* to act; **age!** come on! *(in assent)* O.K., very well; **bene (male) agere cum aliquo** to treat s.o. well (badly); **cum populo** *(or* **ad populum) agere** to address the people; **quo tu agis?** where are you off to?

ag·ōn -ōnis *m* contest

agrāri·us -a -um *adj* agrarian ‖ *mpl* land-reform party

agrest·is -is -e *adj* rustic, country; boorish; wild; savage

agricol·a -ae *m* farmer, peasant

Agricol·a -ae *m* Gnaeus Julius Agricola *(father-in-law of Tacitus)*

agricultūr·a -ae *f* agriculture

Agrigent·um -ī *n* city on S. coast of Sicily *(modern Agrigento)*

agripet·a -ae *m* colonist, settler

Agripp·a -ae *m* Marcus Vipsanius Agrippa *(son-in-law of Augustus, husband of Julia, and father of Agrippina)*

Agrippīn·a -ae *f* Vipsania Agrippina, daughter of Agrippa, wife of Tiberius and mother of Drusus *(d. 20* A.D.*)* ‖ Vipsania Agrippina Major, wife of Germanicus and mother of Caligula *(d. 33* A.D.*)* ‖ Julia Agrippina Minor, daughter of the previous Agrippina and

Germanicus, and mother of Nero *(murdered by Nero in 59 A.D.)*

āh *interj* ah!, ha!, oh!

aha *interj* aha!

ai *interj (denoting grief)* ah!

āin = aisne *(see* **aio)**

aiō *tr & intr (used mainly in pres and imperf indic)* I say; I say yes, I say so; I assert, tell relate; **ain (= aisne) tandem?** *(or* **ain tu?** *or* **ain tute** *or* **ain vero?)** *(coll) (expressing surprise)* do you really mean it?, you don't say!, really?

Āj·ax -ācis *m* son of Telamon, king of Salamis **‖** son of Oïleus, king of the Locri

-al -ālis *neut suf* forms neuter nouns: **animal** animal; **cubital** elbow cushion

āl·a -ae *f* wing; armpit; squadron *(of cavalry);* flank *(of battle line)*

alabas·ter -trī *m,* **alabastr·um -ī** *n* perfume box

ala·cer *or* **ala·cris -cris -cre** *adj* lively, brisk; quick; eager; active; cheerful

alacrit·ās -ātis *f* liveliness, briskness; quickness; eagerness; cheerfulness

alap·a -ae *f* slap

ālār·is -is -e *adj (mil)* consisting of auxiliary cavalry

ālāri·us -a -um *adj* consisting of auxiliary troops **‖** *mpl* auxiliaries, allies

ālāt·us -a -um *adj* winged

alaud·a -ae *f* lark

Alb·a -ae *f* town *(also called Alba Longa)* founded by Ascanius

Albān·ī -ōrum *mpl* inhabitants of Alba Longa

Albān·um -ī *n* Alban estate; Alban wine

albāt·us -a -um *adj* dressed in white

alb·eō -ēre -uī *intr* to be white

albesc·ō -ĕre *intr* to become white, whiten; to dawn; *(of hair)* to turn gray

albic·ō -āre -āvī -ātum *or* **albic·or -ārī -ātus sum** *intr* to be white, be whitish

albid·us -a -um *adj* white, whitish

Albi·ōn -ōnis *f* Britain

albitūd·ō -inis *f* whiteness

Albul·a -ae *f* earlier name of the Tiber River

albul·us -a -um *adj* whitish

alb·um -ī *n* white; white tablet, record, list, register

Albune·a -ae *f* fountain at Tibur; nymph of that fountain

alb·us -a -um *adj* flat white; bright, shining, clear *(sky, light, sun, etc.);* favorable; clad in white; light-skinned, fair; whitened, made white; favorable, auspicious; gray *(hair);* pale *(from fear, sickness);* **album opus** stucco work; **albus aterne sit nescire** not to know a person from Adam *(literally, not to know whether he is white or black)* **‖** *m* white man

Alcae·us -ī *m* Greek lyric poet from the Island of Lesbos *(fl. 610 B.C.)*

alcēd·ō -inis *f* kingfisher, halcyon

alcēdoni·a -ōrum *npl* halcyon days; *(fig)* deep calm, tranquillity

alc·ēs -is *f* elk

Alcest·is -is *f* loyal wife of Admetus

Alcibiad·ēs -ae *or* **-is** *or* **-ī** *m* Athenian politician, disciple of Socrates *(450?–404 B.C.)*

Alcīd·ēs -ae *m* descendant of Alceus, *esp.* Hercules

Alcimed·ē -ēs *f* wife of Aeson and mother of Jason

Alcino·ūs -ī *m* king of the Phaeacians, who entertained Ulysses

Alc(u)mēn·a -ae *or* **Alcmēn·ē -ēs** *f* wife of Amphitryon and mother of Hercules by Jupiter

alcy·ōn -onis *f* **(hal-)** halcyon *(bird believed to build its nest on the sea)*

Alcyon·ē -ēs *or* **Alcyon·a -ae** *f* **(Hal-)** daughter of Aeolus and wife of Cyex *(both of whom were changed into halcyons)* **‖** wife of Meleager **‖** one of the Pleiades

āle·a -ae *f* dice game; gambling; die; risk, gamble; **aleā ludere** to gamble; **jacta alea est** the die is cast

āleāri·us -a -um *adj* gambling

āleāt·or -ōris *m* gambler

āleātōri·us -a -um *adj* gambling

Ālect·ō -ūs *f* **(Āll-)** one of the three Furies

ālc·ō -ōnis *m* gambler

āl·es -itis *adj* winged **‖** *mf* winged creature, bird **‖** *m* poet; Cupid **‖** *f* augury, omen

alesc·ō -ĕre *intr* to grow up

Alexan·der -drī *m* Paris, son of Priam and Hecuba **‖** Alexander the Great, king of Macedon *(356–323 B.C.)*

Alexandrē·a -ae *f* **(-drī·a)** Greek city of N. Egypt, founded by Alexander the Great

Alexandrīn·us -a -um *adj* Alexandrine; characteristic of Alexandria

alg·a -ae *f* seaweed

alg·ens -entis *adj* cold; **algens toga** thin toga

al·geō -gēre -sī *intr* to be cold; to feel cold; to endure cold; *(fig)* to be left out in the cold

al·gescō -gescĕre -sī *intr* to catch a cold

algid·us -a -um *adj* cold

Algid·us -a -um *adj* of Mt. Algidus **‖** *m* mountain in Latium, S. of Tusculum

alg·or -ōris *m* cold; fit of shivering

alg·us -ūs *m* the cold

aliā *adv* by another way

aliās *adv* at another time, at other times; previously; subsequently; in other circumstances, otherwise; apart from this, in any case, besides; all the same, nevertheless; **alias...alias** at one time...at another, sometimes...sometimes

āliāt·um -ī *n* food flavored with garlic

alibī *adv* elsewhere; otherwise, in other respects; in another passage *(in a book, speech);* **alibi...alibi** in one place...in another, here...there; **alibi aliter** differently in different places; **alius alibi** one in one place, another in another

alic·a -ae *f* emmer *(type of wheat)*

alicāri·us -a -um *adj* of emmer ‖ *f* prostitute

alicubi *adv* somewhere; anywhere; occasionally

alicul·a -ae *f* light cape

alicunde *adv* from somewhere; from someone else

aliēnāti·ō -ōnis *f* transfer *(of property);* alienation; aversion; **alienatio mentis** insanity

aliēnigen·a -ae *m* foreigner, stranger *(born in another country)*

aliēn·ō -āre -āvī -ātus *tr* to transfer, sell; to give up *(children)* for adoption; to alienate, set at variance; to treat as an enemy; to remove, separate; to drive mad; **a sensu alienare** to deprive of feeling; **paene alienatā mente** almost driven mad ‖ *pass* to fall into s.o. else's hands; *(mil)* to fall into the enemy's hands; *(w.* **ab)** to recoil from

aliēn·us -a -um *adj* another's; foreign; contrary; hostile; strange; unsuitable; incongruous, inconsistent; inconvenient; **alienum est** it is out-of-place ‖ *m* stranger, foreigner ‖ *n* another's property; foreign soil ‖ *npl* another's affairs

ālif·er *or* **alig·er -era -erum** *adj* winged, wearing wings

alimentāri·us -a -um *adj* **(alum-)** relating to welfare

aliment·um -ī *n* **(alum-)** nourishment, food, provisions; fuel ‖ *npl* means of livelihood; alms

alimōni·a -ae *f or* **alimōn·ium -(i)ī** *n* nourishment, food; support; cost of living

aliō *adv* to another place, elsewhere; to another topic; to another policy; for another purpose; **alio...alio** in one direction...in another; **alius alio** one in one direction, another in another

aliōquī(n) *adv* otherwise, in other respects, for the rest; apart from these considerations; besides; in general; in any case

aliorsum *or* **aliōvorsum** *adv* **(-sus)** in another direction; in a different manner; in a different sense

ālip·ēs -edis *adj* wing-footed, swift-footed

alipt·ēs *or* **alipt·a -ae** *m* wrestling trainer, rubdown man

aliquā *adv* somehow; to some extent

aliquam *adv* to some degree; **aliquam multi** fairly many

aliquamdiū *adv* **(-quan-)** for some time; for a considerable distance

aliquandō *adv* sometime or other, once; at any time, ever; now and then; for once, now; finally, now at last; someday *(in the future)*

aliquantill·um -ī *n* a bit

aliquantisper *adv* for a while

aliquantō *adv* somewhat, to some extent, a little, rather

aliquantulum *adv* somewhat

aliquantul·us -a -um *adj* little ‖ *n* a small amount

aliquantum *adv* somewhat, a little, rather

aliquant·us -a -um *adj* considerable ‖ *n* a certain amount *(of);* a certain degree *(of);* a bit, a part

aliquātenus *adv* for some distance; to a certain extent; in some respects, partly; up to a point

ali·quī -qua -quod *adj* some; *(after a negative,* **si,** *etc.)* any at all

aliquid *adv* to some extent

ali·quid -cūjus *pron* something, anything; something important; **ad aliquid esse** *(of a term)* to be relative; **aliud aliquid** something else; **aliquid vini** some wine; **est aliquid** *(w. inf)* it is something to ‖ *adv* to some degree

ali·quis -cūjus *pron* someone, somebody, anyone; someone important

aliquō *adv* to some place, somewhere

aliquot *indecl adj* some, several

aliquotiens *adv* several times

aliquōvorsum *adv* in one direction or another

aliter *adv* otherwise, else; **aliter...aliter** in one way...in another; **aliter atque aliter** now in one way, now in another; **aliter esse** *or* **aliter se habere** to be different; **non** *(or* **haud) aliter quam** *(or* **ac) si** just as if

aliubī *adv* elsewhere; **aliubi...aliubi** here...there

āl·ium -(i)ī *n* **(all-)** garlic

aliunde *adv* from another place; **aliunde...aliunde** from one place...from another; **alius aliunde** one from one place, another from another

ali·us -a -ud *adj (gen singl is generally* **alterius;** *dat:* **alteri)** another, other, different; *(w.* **ac, atque, et, nisi, quam)** other than ‖ *pron* another; **alii...alii** some...others; **alius...alius** one...another, the one...the other; **alius atque alius** first one person, then another; **alius ex alio** one after another

al·lābor -lābī -lapsus sum *intr* **(adl-)** to glide, slide, slip; to flow

allabōr·ō -āre *intr* **(adl-)** to work hard

allacrim·ō -āre *intr* **(adl-)** to weep

allaps·us -ūs *m* **(adl-)** slithering

allātr·ō -āre -āvī -ātus *tr* **(adl-)** to bark

at; *(fig)* to revile; *(of sea)* to break against

allāt·us -a -um *pp of* **affero**

allaudābil·is -is -e *adj* praiseworthy

allaud·ō -āre *tr* **(adl-)** to praise highly

all·ēc -ēcis *n* **(hall-)** fish sauce

Allect·ō -ūs *f* **(ālec-)** Alecto *(one of the three Furies)*

allect·ō -āre *tr* **(adl-)** to allure, entice

allēgāti·ō -ōnis *f* **(adl-)** intercession; allegation

allēgāt·us -ūs *m* **(adl-)** prompting, instigation

allēg·ō -āre -āvī -ātus *tr* **(adl-)** to commission; to deputize; to put up; to dispatch; to allege; to instigate; *(w. dat)* to lay *(prayers)* before

al·lĕgō -legĕre -lēgī -lectus *tr* **(adl-)** to select; to appoint *(to an office)*

allēgori·a -ae *f* allegory

allevāment·um -ī *n* **(adl-)** alleviation

allevāti·ō -ōnis *f* lifting; alleviating, easing

allev·ō -āre -āvī -ātus *tr* **(adl-)** to lift up, raise; to alleviate; to comfort; to lighten

Alli·a -ae *f* tributary of the Tiber where the Gauls defeated the Romans in 390 B.C.

allice·faciō -facĕre -fēcī -factus *tr* to entire, allure

al·liciō -licĕre -lexī -lectus *tr* **(adl-)** to attract; to bring on *(sleep);* to attract the attention of; to win over

allī·dō -dĕre -sī -sus *tr* **(adl-)** *(w. dat or* **ad** *or* **in** *+ acc)* to dash *(s.th.)* against ‖ *pass* to be shipwrecked

Alliens·is -is -e *adj* of the Allia River; of the battle at the Allia River

allig·ō -āre -āvī -ātus *tr* **(adl-)** to bind; to bandage *(wounds);* to tie up; to grip firmly; to hold together; to freeze solid; to curdle *(milk);* to curb, restrict; to fetter; to hinder, detain; to involve, implicate; *(w.* **ad***)* to bind *(s.th.)* to; *(of laws)* to be binding on

al·linō -linĕre -lēvī -litus *tr* **(adl-)** to smudge; *(w. dat)* to smear *(s.th.)* on

all·ium -(i)ī *n* garlic

Allobrog·ēs -um *mpl* Gallic tribe in Gallia Narbonensis

allocūti·ō -ōnis *f* **(adl-)** address; pep talk

alloqu·ium -(i)ī *n* **(adl-)** address; conversation; reassuring words

allo·quor -quī -cūtus sum *tr* **(adl-)** to speak to, address; to invoke *(gods);* to console, comfort

allubesc·ō -ĕre *intr* to be lovely

alluc·eō -ēre -xī *intr (w. dat)* be a light for

allūdi·ō -āre *intr* **(adl-)** to play, frolic

allū·dō -dĕre -sī -sus *tr* **(adl-)** to play with ‖ *intr* to play, joke; *(of waves) (w. dat)* to lap; *(w. dat or* **ad***)* to allude playfully to

allu·ō -ĕre -ī *tr* **(adl-)** *(of rivers, the sea)* to flow past, lap, touch; *(of water)* to touch, wet *(a part of the body)*

alluvi·ēs -ēī *f* **(adl-)** pool *(left by flood waters);* silt

alluvi·ō -ōnis *f* **(adl-)** flood; alluvial land

alm·us -a -um *adj* nourishing; kind, gracious

aln·us -ī *f* alder tree; *(fig)* ship

al·ō -ĕre -uī -tus *or* **-itus** *tr* to nurse, breast-feed; to feed, nourish; to promote the growth of; to raise *(children, animals);* to support *(family, etc.); (of places, employment)* to provide a livelihood for; to foment *(discord);* to encourage; to promote the interests of; to increase; to strengthen

alo·ē -ēs *f (bot)* aloe *(whose bitter juice was used as a purgative);* bitterness

Alōeus *m* a son of Poseidon and Canace

alogi·a -ae *f* folly, nonsense

Alōïd·ae -ārum *mpl* the giants Otus and Ephialtes, sons of Poseidon and Iphimedeia, the wife of Aloeus

Alp·ēs -ium *fpl* Alps

alpha *indecl n* alpha *(first letter of the Greek alphabet)*

Alphē·us *or* **Alphī·us** *or* **Alphē·os -ī** *m* Alpheus *(chief river of the Peloponnesus)*

Alpic·us -a -um *adj* Alpine

Alpīn·us -a -um *adj* Alpine

alsī *perf of* **algeo** *and* **algesco**

als(i)·us -a -um *adj* chilly, cold

altār·ia -ium *npl* altar; burnt-offerings

altē *adv* high, on high, highly; from a great height; deeply, far, remotely; intensely, profoundly

alt·er -era -erum *adj* one *(of two);* a second, the second, the next ‖ *pron* one *(of two),* the one, the other; a second one, the second one, the next one; anyone else; another *(one's fellow man);* **alter...alter** the one...the other, the former...the latter; **unus et** *(or* **aut***)* **alter** one or two

alterās *adv* at another time

altercāti·ō -ōnis *f* altercation, dispute; *(phil)* debate

altercāt·or -ōris *m* disputant

alterc·ō -āre *or* **alterc·or -ārī -ātus sum** *intr* to argue, wrangle; to argue back and forth *(in court)*

alternīs *adv* by turns, alternately

altern·ō -āre -āvī -ātus *tr* to do by turns; to alternate, arrange in alternating order; to exchange ‖ *intr* to alternate

altern·us -a -um *adj* one after another, alternate; mutual; every other; **alternā vice** *(or* **alternis vicibus***)* alternately; in turn, successively; **in alternum** for one another, reciprocally; **ire per alternas vices** to go back and forth

alteru·ter -tra -trum *(fem also* **altera utra;** *neut also* **alterum utrum***)* *adj* one

(of two), either, one or the other ‖ *pron* one, either one, one or the other
Althae·a -ae *f* mother of Meleager
alticinct·us -a -um *adj* energetic
altil·is -is -e *adj* fattened, fat; *(fig)* rich ‖ *f* fattened fowl
altison·us -a -um *adj* sounding from on high; sublime
altiton·ans -antis *adj* thundering on high
altitūd·ō -inis *f* height; depth; *(fig)* profundity *(of mind);* loftiness *(of style)*; **ad** *or* **in altitudinem** vertically
altiusculē *adv* rather high
altiuscul·us -a -um *adj* rather high
altivol·ans -antis, altivol·us -a -um *adj* high-flying
alt·or -ōris *m* foster father
altrim secus *adv* on the other side
altrinsecus *adv* **(alter-)** on the other side
altr·ix -īcis *f* foster mother; wet nurse; *(of the earth)* nourisher; motherland
altrōvorsum *adv* **(-sus)** on the other hand
alt·us -a -um *adj* high; deep; profound *(wisdom);* deep, loud *(sound);* intense *(heat, cold);* thick *(fog);* high-born, ancient *(lineage)* ‖ *n* high seas, the deep; heaven; **ab alto** from on high, from heaven; **ex alto** far-fetched; **ex alto petere** *(or* **repetere)** to go far afield for
ālūcin·or -ārī -ātus sum *intr* **(hāl-, alluc-)** to ramble on; to rave
alumn·a -ae *f* foster daughter
alumn·us -ī *m* foster son
alūt·a -ae *f* soft leather; shoe; purse
alv(e)ār·ium -(i)ī *n* beehive
alveol·us -ī *m* bowl, basin; bathtub; river bed; game board
alve·us -ī *m* hollow; tub; bathtub; riverbed; hull of boat; game board; beehive
alv·us -ī *f (m)* belly, bowels, stomach; womb; rectum; boat; beehive; **alvum purgare** *(or* **solvere)** to move the bowels; **alvus fusa** *(or* **cita)** diarrhea
am- *pref see* **ambi-**
amābil·is -is -e *adj* lovable, lovely, attractive; delightful
amābilit·ās -ātis *f* attractiveness
amābiliter *adv* lovingly, delightfully
Amalthē·a -ae *f* nymph who fed infant Jupiter with goat's milk ‖ Cumaean sibyl
āmandāti·ō -ōnis *f* sending away
āmand·ō -āre -āvī -ātus *tr* **(amend-)** to send away
am·ans -antis *adj* loving, affectionate; **amans patriae** patriotic ‖ *mf* lover
amanter *adv* lovingly, affectionately
āmanuens·is -is *m* secretary
amārac·us -ī *mf* marjoram *(aromatic plants whose leaves are used as seasoning)*
amarant·us -ī *m* amaranth *(imaginary flower that never fades)*
amārē *adv* bitterly
amāriti·ēs -ēī *f* bitterness
amāritūd·ō -inis *f* bitterness; tang; sadness
amār·or -ōris *m* bitterness
amār·us -a -um *adj* bitter, pungent, tangy; shrill; brackish; **nux amara** almond
Amaryll·is -idis *f* conventional name for a shepherdess
amāsi·ō -ōnis *m* lover
amāsiuncul·a -ae *f* darling
amāsiuncul·us -ī *m* lover
amās·ius -(i)ī *m* lover
amāt·a -ae *f* loved one
Amāt·a -ae *f* mother of Lavinia
Amath·ūs -untis *f* town in Cyprus
Amathūsiac·us -a -um *adj* of Amathus
Amathūsi·us -a -um *adj* of Amathus ‖ *f* Venus
amāti·ō -ōnis *f* love affair
amāt·or -ōris *m* lover; friend; **amator patriae** patriot
amātorcul·us -ī *m* poor little lover
amātōriē *adv* lovingly
amātōri·us -a -um *adj* erotic, love ‖ *n* love charm
amātr·ix -īcis *f* mistress, girl friend
Amaz·ōn -onis *or* **Amazon·is -idis** *f* Amazon
Amazonic·us -a -um *adj* Amazonian
amb- *pref see* **ambi-**
ambact·us -ī *m* vassal
ambāg·ēs -is *f* winding, labyrinth; double-talk; digression; ambiguity, obscurity; **per ambages** enigmatically
amb·edō -esse -ēdī -ēsus *tr* to eat up; to waste, squander; *(of fire)* to char
ambestr·ix -īcis *f* gluttonous woman
ambi- *pref (before vowels usually* **amb-;** *before consonants* **ambi-, am-, an-)** around
ambig·ō -ĕre *tr* to go around, avoid; to call into question, debate ‖ *intr* to waver, hesitate, be undecided; to argue, debate, wrangle ‖ *v impers* **ambigitur** it is uncertain
ambiguē *adv* indecisively; ambiguously; in an untrustworthy manner
ambiguit·ās -ātis *f* ambiguity
ambigu·us -a -um *adj* wavering, changeable; uncertain; disputed; unreliable, untrustworthy; ambiguous, dark, obscure ‖ *n* doubt, uncertainty; paradox
amb·iō -īre -īvī *or* **-iī -itus** *tr* to go the round of; to go around, encircle; to throng; to go round, go past; to embrace; to include; *(pol)* to campaign for ‖ *intr* to move in an orbit; to rotate
ambiti·ō -ōnis *f* ambition *(in good and bad sense);* popularity; flattery; partiality, favoritism; pomp, ostentation; *(pol)* campaigning *(by lawful means)*
ambitiōsē *adv* ambitiously; ostentatiously; from a desire to please
ambitiōs·us -a -um *adj* winding; public-

ity-conscious; ambitious; ostentatious; eager for popularity

ambit·us -ūs *m* winding, revolution; circuit, circumference, border; orbit; ostentation; circumlocution; *(pol)* illegal campaign practices, bribery; **ambitus verborum** *(or* **orationis)** phrase; *(rhet)* rounded and balanced sentence, period

ambiv·ium -(i)ī *n* road junction

amb·ō -ae -ō *adj* both, two ‖ *pron* both, the two

Ambraci·a -ae *f* district of Epirus

Ambraciens·is -is -e *adj* of Ambracia

Ambraciōt·ēs -ae *m* an Ambracian

Ambraci·us -a -um *adj* of Ambracia

ambrosi·a -ae *f* food for the gods; imaginary healing plant

ambrosi·us -a -um *adj* **(-e·us)** ambrosial, divine

ambūbāi·a -ae *f* Syrian singer and courtesan ‖ *(bot)* wild endive

ambulācr·um -ī *n* walk, avenue

ambulāti·ō -ōnis *f (act; place)* walk

ambulātiuncul·a -ae *f* short walk; small promenade

ambulāt·or -ōris *m* stroller *(person);* peddler

ambulātōri·us -a -um *adj* movable

ambul·ō -āre -āvī -ātus *tr* to traverse, travel ‖ *intr* to walk, take a walk; to march; to travel; to strut; *(of things)* to extend, run; **bene ambula!** bon voyage!

amb·ūrō -ūrĕre -ussī -ustus *tr* to burn up; to scorch; to scald; to cremate; *(of cold)* to numb, nip

ambustulāt·us -a -um *adj* half-roasted

amell·us -ī *m (bot)* wild aster *(plant having daisylike flowers of various colors)*

ām·ens -entis *adj* insane; foolish

āmenti·a -ae *f* insanity; folly

āment·ō -āre -āvī -ātus *tr* **(amm-)** to fit *(a javelin)* with a strap

āment·um -ī *n* **(amm-)** strap

Ameri·a -ae *f* town in Umbria

Amerīn·us -a -um *adj* of Ameria; produced in Ameria ‖ *m* Amerian

am·es -itis *m* pole for fowler's net; fence rail

amethystināt·us -a -um *adj* dressed in violet-blue

amethystin·us -a -um *adj* violet-blue; set with amethysts ‖ *npl* violet-blue garments

amethyst·us -ī *f* amethyst

amīc·a -ae *f* girlfriend, lady friend; mistress

amīcē *adv* in a friendly way

ami·ciō -cīre -cuī *or* **-xī -tus** *tr* to wrap around; to cover, clothe, wrap

amīciter *adv* in a friendly way

amīciti·a -ae *f* friendship

amictori·um -ī *n* wrap

amict·us -ūs *m* wrap, cloak; clothing; fashion *(in dress)*

amīcul·a -ae *f* girl friend

amicul·um -ī *n* wrap, mantle ‖ *npl* clothing

amīcul·us -ī *m* pal, buddy

amīc·us -a -um *adj* friendly; supportive; favorable, congenial; helpful; dear, welcome; **amicus reipublicae** patriotic ‖ *m* friend; lover; partisan, supporter; disciple ‖ *f see* **amica**

āmigr·ō -āre *intr* to move (away)

Amilcar *see* **Hamilcar**

āmissi·ō -ōnis *f* loss

amit·a -ae *f* aunt *(father's sister)*

Amitern·um -ī *n* town in the Sabine district, birthplace of Sallust

ā·mittō -mittĕre -mīsī -missus *tr* to lose; to let slip, miss; to let go, release; to let fall, drop; **animam** *(or* **spiritum)** **amittere** to lose one's life; **fidem amittere** to break one's word; **spe amissā** having given up hope

amm- = adm-

amment·ō -āre *see* **amento**

amment·um -ī *n* **(āmen-)** strap

amnicol·a -ae *mf* riverside plant

amnicul·us -ī *m* brook

amn·is -is *m (f)* river; **secundo amni** downstream

am·ō -āre -āvī -ātus *tr* to love, like, be fond of; to fall in love with; **amabo (te)** *(coll)* please ‖ *intr* to be in love

amoenē *adv* charmingly, pleasantly

amoenit·ās -ātis *f* charm

amoen·us -a -um *adj* charming, pleasant

āmōl·ior -īrī *tr* to remove; to put aside, put away; to get rid of, put out of the way, dispose of *(a person);* to refute ‖ *refl* to remove oneself, clear out

amōm·um -ī *n (bot)* spice plant; spice obtained from this plant

am·or -ōris *m* love; affection; object of affection, love; liking, fondness, attachment; strong desire, yearning; love song; Cupid; **amor patriae** patriotism ‖ *mpl* love affair

āmōti·ō -ōnis *f* removal

ā·moveō -movēre -mōvī -mōtus *tr* to remove; to withdraw, put away; to lay aside *(suspicion, etc.);* to get rid of; to banish; to deprive of rights; to dispel *(fear);* to steal; **ex animo amovere** to put out of one's mind ‖ *refl* to retire, withdraw

Amphiarā·üs -ī *m* famous Greek seer, son of Oecle(u)s *(or* Apollo) and Hypermestra, one of the Seven against Thebes

Amphiarēïad·ēs -ae *m* descendant of Amphiaraus, his son Alcmaeon

amphiboli·a -ae *f* ambiguity

Amphilochi·a -ae *f* small district at the E. end of the Ambracian Gulf

Amphiloch·us -ī *m* son of Amphiaraus, and founder of Argos Amphilochium the chief town of Amphilocia
Amphī·ō(n) -onis *m* son of Zeus and Antiope, twin brother of Zethus, and husband of Niobe
Amphīoni·us -a -um *adj* of Amphion
Amphipol·is -is *f* town in Macedonia, near the mouth of the Strymon
amphitheātr·um -ī *n* amphitheater
Amphitrīt·ē -ēs *f* wife of Neptune; *(fig)* the sea
Amphitry·ō(n) *or* **Amphitru·ō -ōnis** *m* husband of Alcmena
Amphitryōniad·ēs -ae *m* Hercules
amphor·a -ae *f* amphora; liquid measure *(c. 7 gallons)*
ampl·a -ae *f* opportunity
amplē *adv* amply; grandly, splendidly
am·plector -plectī -plexus sum *tr* to embrace, hug; to cling to; to accept gladly, welcome; to comprise, extend over, cover, include; to encircle *(enemy forces);* to grasp, grip; to understand; *(of serpent)* to coil itself around; *(mil)* to occupy
amplex·ō -āre *or* **amplex·or -ārī -ātus sum** *tr* to embrace; to welcome; to cling to, grasp; to espouse, cherish
amplex·us -ūs *m* circuit; embrace, caress; coil *(of snake)*
amplificātiō -ōnis *f* extension, enlargement; *(rhet)* amplification
amplificāt·or -ōris *m* enhancer
amplificē *adv* splendidly
amplific·ō -āre -āvī -ātus *tr* to enlarge, extend, widen; to increase; to extol; *(rhet)* to enlarge upon, develop
ampli·ō -āre -āvī -ātus *tr* to widen, enlarge; to enhance; to postpone *(judgment);* adjourn *(court in order to gather more evidence);* to magnify, glorify; *(leg)* to postpone *(trial)*
ampliter *adv* splendidly; fully, very
amplitūd·ō -inis *f* width, size, bulk, extent; greatness, dignity, importance; high rank; *(rhet)* amplification, development
amplius *adv* any further, any more, any longer; besides; further, more, longer; **amplius hoc** what is more, in addition; **amplius uno die** one day longer; **nec amplius** no longer; **nemo amplius** no one else; **nihil amplius** nothing else; **quid amplius (quam)** what else (than) **II** *n* more, a larger amount; **amplius negoti** more trouble
ampliusculē *adv* rather more freely
ampl·us -a -um *adj* ample, large, wide, spacious; strong, great, powerful; grand, imposing; eminent, prominent, illustrious
Ampsanct·us -ī *m* valley and lake in Samnium with toxic exhalations, regarded as an entrance to the lower world
ampull·a -ae *f* bottle; bombast
ampullār·ius -(i)ī *m* bottle-maker
ampull·or -ārī -ātus sum *intr* to be bombastic
amputāti·ō -ōnis *f* pruning
amput·ō -āre -āvī -ātus *tr* to lop off, prune; to curtail, shorten; **amputata loqui** to speak disconnectedly
Amūl·ius -(i)ī *m* king of Alba Longa, brother of Numitor, and granduncle of Romulus and Remus
amurc·a -ae *f* dregs of oil
Amycl·ae -ārum *fpl* town in Laconia, the birthplace of Castor and Pollux
Amyclae·us -a -um *adj* of Amyclae
Amyclīd·ēs -ae *m* Hyacinthus *(worshiped at Amyclae)*
amygdal·a -ae *f* almond tree
amygdal·um -ī *n* almond
amyst·is -idis *f* drinking bottoms up
an *conj (introducing the second or further part of a multiple question, direct or indirect)* or, or whether; **haud scio an** I am inclined to think, probably
anabathr·a -ōrum *npl* bleachers
Anacre·ōn -ontis *m* lyric poet of Teos *(fl 540 B.C.)*
anadēm·a -atis *n* headband
anaglypt·a -ōrum *npl* work in bas-relief
anagnost·ēs -ae *m* reader, reciter
analect·a -ae *m* slave who cleaned up the crumbs
analectr·is -idis *f* shoulder pad *(to improve the figure)*
analogi·a -ae *f* ratio; *(gram)* analogy *(similarity in inflection and derivatives of words); (phil)* method of reasoning from similar cases
anancaec·um -ī *n* large cup that must be emptied "bottoms up"
anapaest·us -a -um *adj (pros)* anapestic **II** *m* anapest (◡ ◡ —) **II** *n* poem in anapestic meter; anapestic line *or* passage
Anāp·us -ī *m* river in Sicily
an·as -atis *f* duck
anaticul·a -ae *f* **(anet-)** *(sometimes as term of endearment)* duckling
anatīn·us -a -um *adj* **(anet-)** duck's
anatocism·us -ī *m* compound interest
Anaxagor·ās -ae *m* Greek philosopher, teacher of Pericles and Euripides *(500?–428 B.C.)*
Anaximan·der -drī *m* Greek philosopher of Miletus *(610–547 B.C.)*
Anaximen·ēs -is *m* Greek philosopher of Miletus *(fl 544 B.C.)*
an·ceps *or* **ancip·es -cipitis** *adj* two-headed, facing in two directions; exposed on both sides; two-edged; twin-peaked; amphibious; of doubtful allegiance, untrustworthy; unreliable, unpredictable; *(of a person)* undecided, wavering; *(of a battle)* fought on two

fronts; *(of enemies)* attacking on both sides; *(of dangers, evils)* arising from two sources, double, twofold; *(of roads)* leading in two directions; *(of battles)* undecided, hanging in the balance; *(of words)* ambiguous; *(of situations)* hazardous, critical ‖ *n* danger, peril

Anchīs·ēs -ae *m* son of Capys, lover of Venus, and, by her, father of Aeneas

Anchīsē·us -a -um *adj* of Anchises

Anchīsiad·ēs -ae *m* son of Anchises, Aeneas

ancīl·e -is *n* small figure-eight shield *(esp. one of twelve such kept by the Salii in the shrine of Mars and carried in religious processions)*

ancill·a -ae *f* slave girl

ancillār·is -is -e *adj* having the status of a slave girl

ancillul·a -ae *f* little slave girl

Ancōn·a -ae *f* seaport in N. Picenum

ancor·a -ae *f* **(anch-)** anchor

ancorāl·e -is *n* anchor cable

ancorāri·us -a -um *adj* of an anchor

Anc·us Marti·us -ī *m* the fourth king of Rome

Ancȳr·a -ae *f* Ankara, capital of Galatia

andabat·a -ae *m* blindfolded gladiator

And·ēs -ium *fpl* village near Mantua, birthplace of Vergil

Andri·us -a -um *adj* of the Greek island of Andros ‖ *mpl* people of Andros ‖ *f* woman from Andros

Androge·ōs -ō *or* **Androge·ōn -ōnos** *or* **Androge·us -ī** *m* Androgeüs *(son of Minos and Pasiphaë, whose death Minos avenged by attacking Athens)*

androgyn·us -ī *m or* **androgynē -ēs** *f* hermaphrodite

Andromach·a -ae *or* **Andromach·ē -ēs** *f* Hector's wife

Andromed·a -ae *or* **Andromed·ē -ēs** *f* daughter of Cepheus and Cassiope, rescued from a sea monster by Perseus

andr·ōn -ōnis *m* corridor

Andronīc·us -ī *m* Livius Andronicus *(fl 241 B.C., first epic and dramatic poet of Latin literature)*

Andr·os *or* **Andr·us -ī** *f* Aegean island

ānell·us -ī *m* little ring

anēt(h)·um -ī *n (bot)* dill *(aromatic herb whose seeds and leaves are used as seasoning)*

-āne·us -a -um *adjl suf* chiefly from nouns denoting a place: **circumforaneus** connected with (the business) of the forum

anfract·us -ūs *m* curve *(of road, seashore);* spiral, coil; *(astr)* orbit; *(rhet)* circumlocution

angell·us -ī *m* small angle

angin·a -ae *f* tonsillitis; throat infection

angiport·us -ūs *m or* **angiport·um -ī** *n* alley

ang·ō -ĕre *tr* to choke, strangle; to distress; to tease; to trouble

ang·or -ōris *m* strangling, suffocation; anguish

anguicom·us -a -um *adj* snake-haired

anguicul·us -ī *m* small snake

anguif·er -era -erum *adj* snaky, having snakes in place of hair, snake-haired; *(of places)* snake-infested

anguigen·a -ae *m* offspring of a dragon; Theban

anguill·a -ae *f* eel

anguine·us -a -um *adj* snaky; serpent-like

anguīn·us -a -um *adj* snaky

anguip·ēs -edis *adj* serpent-footed

angu·is -is *mf* snake, serpent ‖ **Anguis** *m* Dragon, Serpent, Hydra *(constellations)*

Anguiten·ens -entis *m* Ophiuchus *(constellation)*

angulār·is -is -e *adj* angular

angulāt·us -a -um *adj* **(angl-)** angular

angul·us -ī *m* angle, corner; nook, recess; **ad pares angulos** *(or* **rectis angulis)** at right angles

angustē *adv* within narrow limits; closely; hardly, scarcely; briefly, concisely

angusti·ae -ārum *fpl* narrow place; defile; narrow passage, strait; shortage, scarcity, want, deficiency; difficulty, tight spot; limitations; distress, straits; narrow-mindedness; poverty of vocabulary; **angustiae spiritūs** shortness of breath

angusticlāvi·us -a -um *adj* wearing a tunic with a narrow purple stripe *(a sign of equestrian rank)*

angust·ō -āre -āvī -ātus *tr* to narrow down; to reduce in size *or* amount; to choke

angust·us -a -um *adj* narrow, close; short, brief *(time);* scanty *(means);* tight *(reins);* difficult, critical; narrow-minded; base, mean ‖ *n* a confined space; narrowness; critical condition, danger; **in angustum adducere** *(or* **cogere, concludere, deducere)** to narrow down, compress, reduce

anhēlāti·ō -ōnis *f* panting

anhēlit·us -ūs *m* panting, difficulty in breathing, puffing; breath, breathing; vapor

anhēl·ō -āre -āvī -ātus *tr* to breathe out, to pant after ‖ *intr* to pant, puff; to exhale; *(of fire, sea)* to roar

anhēl·us -a -um *adj* panting

anicul·a -ae *f* little old lady

Aniē(n)s·is -is -e *or* **Aniēn·us -a -um** *adj* of the Anio *(Tiber tributary)*

anīl·is -is -e *adj* of an old woman; **aniles fabulae** old wives' tales

anīlit·ās -ātis *f* old age *(of women)*

anīliter *adv* like an old woman

anim·a -ae *f* air, wind, breeze; breath; breath of life, life; soul *(as principle of life, opposed to* **animus** *as principle of*

thought and feelings); spirit, ghost; **animam agere** to gasp for breath; **animam ducere** to draw a breath; **animam edere** *(or* **efflare** *or* **emittere** *or* **exspirare)** to breathe one's last; **animam trahere** to struggle to breathe
animadversi·ō -ōnis *f* attention, observation; mention; remark; criticism; punishment
animadvers·or -ōris *m* observer
animadver·tō -tĕre -tī -sus *tr* (**-vort-**) to pay attention to, attend to; to notice, observe, realize; to criticize; to punish
anim·al -ālis *n* animal; living creature
animāl·is -is -e *adj* consisting of air; animate, living ‖ *mfn* living creature, animal
anim·ans -antis *adj* living, animate ‖ *mfn* living thing; animal
animāti·ō -ōnis *f* living being
animāt·us -a -um *adj* courageous; inclined, disposed; *(w.* **erga** *or* **in** *+ acc)* disposed toward
anim·ō -āre -āvī -ātus *tr* to make alive, animate; to encourage
animōsē *adv* courageously; eagerly
animōs·us -a -um *adj* courageous; energetic; violent *(wind, fire)*; proud; spunky *(horse)*
animul·a -ae *f* little soul, little life
animul·us -ī *m* darling
anim·us -ī *m (cf* **anima)** intellect, understanding; mind; thought, reason; memory; knowledge; sense, consciousness; judgment, opinion; imagination; heart, feelings, passions; spirit, courage, morale; disposition, character; pride, haughtiness; will, purpose, desire, inclination; pleasure, delight; confident hope; **aequo animo** patiently, calmly; **animi causā** for amusement; **animo libenti** gladly; **bono animo esse** to take heart; **ex animo** from the bottom of the heart, sincerely; **ex animo effluere** to slip one's mind; **in animo habere** *(w. inf)* to have in mind to, intend to
Ani·ō -ōnis *m* tributary of the Tiber
Ani·us -ī *m* king and priest on Delos
ann- = adn-
Ann·a -ae *f* sister of Dido ‖ **Anna Perenna** goddess of the returning year
annāl·is -is -e *adj* lasting a year, annual; **lex annalis** law fixing the minimum age for holding public offices ‖ *mpl* annals, chronicle
annat·ō -āre -āvī -ātum *intr* (**adn-**) *(w. dat or* **ad)** to swim to
anne *conj (alternate form of* **an)** or, or whether
anne·ctō -ctere -xuī -xus *tr* (**adn-**) *(w. dat or* **ad)** to tie, connect, annex *(s.th.)* to; *(w. dat)* to apply *(s.th.)* to
annex·us -ūs *m* connection
annicul·us -a -um *adj* (**-ucul-**) one year old; lasting only one year
annī·tor -tī -sus *or* **-xus sum** *intr* (**adn-**) try one's hardest; to give support; *(w. dat or w.* **ad)** to lean on; *(w.* **ut** *or inf)* to strive to
anniversāri·us -a -um *adj* employed annually, renewed annually; occurring every year, growing every year; *(of games, festivals, sacrifices)* celebrated annually, annual
ann·ō -āre -āvī -ātum *intr* (**adn-**) *(w. dat, w.* **ad**, *w. acc of limit of motion)* to swim to *or* towards; *(w. dat)* to swim along with
annōn *conj* or not; **suntne di annon?** are there gods or not?
annōn·a -ae *f* year's crop; grain; price of grain; cost of living; high price
annōs·us -a -um *adj* aged, old
annotāti·ō -ōnis *f* (**adn-**) notation, remark
annōtin·us -a -um *adj* last year's
annot·ō -āre -āvī -ātus *tr* (**adn-**) to note *(in writing)*, put on record; to observe, notice; to register, designate
annumer·ō -āre -āvī -ātus *tr* (**adn-**) *(w. dat)* to count out *(money)* to; *(w. dat or* **in** *+ acc)* to add *(s.th.)* to, include *(s.o.)* among
annunti·ō -āre -āvī -ātus *tr* (**adn-**) to announce, make known, proclaim
an·nuō -nuĕre -nuī -nūtus *tr* (**adn-**) to designate by a nod; to indicate, declare; *(w. dat)* to promise, grant *(s.th.)* to ‖ *intr* to nod assent; *(w. dat)* to nod assent to, be favorable to, smile on
ann·us -ī *m* year; season; age, time of life; year of office; year's produce, crops; **ad annum** for the coming year, a year from now; **anno** last year; **anno exeunte** *(or* **anno pleno)** at the end of the year; **annum** *(or* **in annum)** for a year; **annus meus (tuus,** *etc.)* my (your, *etc.)* year of office; **annus solidus** a full year
annu·us -a -um *adj* lasting a year; annual, yearly ‖ *npl* yearly pay, pension
an·quīrō -quīrĕre -quīsīvī -quīsītus *tr* to search carefully; to examine, inquire into; *(w. gen or abl of the charge)* to accuse *(s.o.)* of ‖ *intr* to hold an inquest
ans·a -ae *f* handle; *(fig)* opportunity
ansāt·us -a -um *adj* having handles; **homo ansatus** man with arms akimbo
ans·er -eris *m* goose *(male)*, gander
Antae·us -ī *m* Libyan giant, son of Earth, killed by Hercules ‖ name of a Carthaginian general
ante *adv* before, previously, in the past; in front; forwards; **ante...quam** before; **anno ante** a year ago; **multis annis ante** many years before that
ante *prep (w. acc)* **1** before, in front of: **ante urbis portas** before the city gates;

2 before *(in time):* **ante diem** before the due date, too early; *(in dates):* **ante diem quartum Idus Martias** *(instead of* **quarto die ante Idus Martias)** *or abbr* **a.d. IV Id. Mart.** three days before the Ides of March; **ante tempus** before time, prematurely; **3** *(in preference, choice)* more than, above; **ante omnia** first of all; above all

ante- *pref (used in the senses of the adv)*

anteā *adv* before, previously, formerly; **jam antea** already in the past

anteact·us -a -um *adj (of time)* that has passed

anteambul·ō -ōnis *m* one who runs before *(to clear the way),* blocker

ante·capiō -capĕre -cēpī -ceptus *tr* to receive beforehand; to take possession of beforehand, preoccupy; to anticipate

ante·cēdō -cēdĕre -cessī -cessus *tr* precede; to outdo, surpass **||** *intr (w. dat)* **1** to have precedence over; **2** to excel, surpass

antecell·ō -ĕre *tr* to surpass **||** *intr (w. dat) (w. abl of respect or* **in** *+ abl)* to surpass *(s.o.)* in

antecessi·ō -ōnis *f* antecedent cause

antecess·or -ōris *m (mil)* scout **||** *mpl* advance guard

antecurs·or -ōris *m (mil)* scout **||** *mpl* vanguard

ante·eō -īre -īvī *or* **-iī** *tr* to precede; to surpass; to anticipate, prevent **||** *intr* to precede; to take the lead; *(w. dat)* **1** to go before; **2** to surpass

ante·ferō -ferre -tulī -lātus *tr* to prefer; to anticipate

antefix·um -ī *n* antefix *(image, statue, etc., affixed to roofs and gutters of temples or homes)*

ante·gredior -gredī -gressus sum *tr* to precede

antehab·eō -ēre -uī *tr* to prefer

antehāc *adv* before now, formerly

antelātus *pp of* **antefero**

antelogi·um -ī *n* preamble, introduction

antelūcān·us -a -um *adj* pre-dawn

antemerīdiān·us -a -um *adj* before noon

ante·mittō -mittĕre -mīsī -missus *tr* to send out ahead

Antemn·ae -ārum *fpl* ancient town in Latium

Antemnāt·ēs -ium *mpl* the people of Antemnae

antenn·a *or* **antemn·a -ae** *f* yardarm, sail yard, sail

Antēn·or -oris *m* Trojan founder of Patavium *(Padua)*

Antēnorid·ēs -ae *m* descendant of Antenor; native of Patavium *(Padua)*

anteoccupāti·ō -ōnis *f (rhet)* anticipation of an opponent's arguments

antepart·um -ī *n* **(-pert-)** thing *or* property acquired in the past

ante·pēs -pedis *m* forefoot

antepīlān·ī -ōrum *mpl* front ranks *(soldiers drawn up in the first two lines of a battle formation)*

antepoll·eō -ēre *tr* to surpass in strength **||** *intr (w. dat)* to be superior to *(s.o.)* in strength

ante·pōnō -pōnĕre -posuī -positus *tr* to place *or* station in front of; to place before *(in time);* to prefer, esteem more highly; *(w. dat)* to give *(a person)* preference over *(another)* to serve *(food);* to put *(a word, prefix, or letter)* before *(a word)*

antepot·ens -entis *adj* very wealthy

antequam *or* **ante...quam** *conj* before; sooner...than

Anter·ōs -ōtis *m* avenger of unrequited love *(son of Venus and Mars)*

ant·ēs -ium *mpl* rows *(of vines, soldiers, etc.)*

antesignān·us -ī *m* soldier fighting in front of the standards to defend them; leader, protagonist

ante·stō *or* **anti·stō -stāre -stitī** *intr* to excel; *(w. dat)* to be superior to

antest·or -ārī -ātus sum *tr* to call as witness

ante·veniō -venīre -vēnī -ventus *tr* to come before, arrive ahead of; to anticipate, thwart; to surpass **||** *intr* to arrive first; to become more distinguished; *(w. dat)* **1** to anticipate; **2** to get ahead of; **3** to be better than, surpass

antever·tō -tĕre -tī -sus *tr* **(-vort-)** to go *or* come before; to anticipate, to prefer **||** *intr* to act first; to go out first, set out first; *(w. dat)* to outweigh

antevol·ō -āre *intr* to dash out ahead

Antiānus -a -um *adj* of Antium

Antiās -ātis *adj* of Antium **||** *mpl* people of Antium

Antiātīnus -a -um *adj* of Antium

Anticat·ō -ōnis *m* title of the books which Caesar wrote in answer to Cicero's panegyric *Cato*

anticipāti·ō -ōnis *f* preconception

anticip·ō -āre -āvī -ātus *tr* to anticipate; to have a preconceived idea of; **viam anticipare** to take the lead *(in a race)*

antīc·us -a -um *adj* front, foremost

Anticyr·a -ae *f* name of several Greek towns famous for their hellbore *(used to cure insanity)*

antideā, antideō, antidhāc *adv* old forms for **anteā, anteō, antehāc**

antidot·um -ī *n or* **antidot·os** *or* **antidot·us -ī** *f* antidote

Antigon·ē -ēs *or* **Antigon·a -ae** *f* Antigone *(daughter of Oedipus* **||** *daughter of Laomedon)*

Antigon·us -ī *m* Greek name, *esp.* one of

the generals of Alexander the Great ‖ Antigonus Doson
Antiloch·us -ī *m* son of Nestor
Antiochī·a -ae *f* **(-chē·a)** Antioch, chief city of Syria
Antioch·us -ī *m* name of seven kings of Syria ‖ Academic philosopher, teacher of Cicero and Brutus
Antiop·a -ae *or* **Antiop·ē -ēs** *f* Antiopa *(mother, by Jupiter, of Amphion and Zethus)*
Antiphat·ēs -ae *m* king of the Laestrygonians ‖ son of Sarpedon, killed by Turnus
antiquāri·us -a -um *adj & m* antiquarian
antīquē *adv* in former times; in the good old style
antīquit·ās -ātis *f* antiquity; the ancients; the good old days
antīquitus *adv* in former times, of old; from ancient times; in the old style
antīqu·ō -āre -āvī -ātus *tr* to reject *(law, bill)*
antīqu·us -a -um *adj* **(-tic-)** old, ancient; old-fashioned, venerable; long-standing *(friendship);* located *or* lying in front ‖ *mpl* ancients, ancient authors ‖ *n* antiquity; old custom
antisophist·ēs -ae *m (rhet)* opponent in argument
antist·es -itis *m* high-priest *(of temple or deity);* authority *(of an art, philosophical school)* ‖ *f* high-priestess
Antisthen·ēs -is *or* **-ae** *m* pupil of Socrates and founder of Cynic philosophy *(455?–360 B.C.)*
antistit·a -ae *f* high-priestess
antithet·on -ī *n (rhet)* antithesis
Ant·ium -(i)ī *n* coastal town in Latium *(modern Anzio)*
antli·a -ae *f* pump; treadmill
Antōni·us -a -um *adj* Roman clan name *(nomen), esp.* Marcus Antonius *(orator, consul in 99 B.C.)* ‖ Marcus Antonius *(triumvir, consul in 44 B.C.)*
antr·um -ī *n* cave, cavern
Anūb·is -is *or* **-idis** *m* jackal-headed Egyptian god
ānulār·ius -(i)ī *m* ring maker
ānulāt·us -a -um *adj* wearing a ring
ānul·us -ī *m* ring, signet ring
ān·us -ī *m* anus, rectum; ring
ăn·us -ūs *f* old woman; hag
-ān·us -a -um *adjl suf* **1** from common nouns: **urbanus** of the cit; **2** from place names: **Romanus** from *or* of Rome, Roman; **3** from personal names: **Claudi-anus** of Claudius, Claudian
anxiē *adv* uneasily
anxiet·ās -ātis *f* anxiety, worry; meticulousness
anxif·er -era -erum *adj* disquieting
anxitūd·ō -inis *f* anxiety, worry
anxi·us -a -um *adj* worried, anxious, uneasy; meticulous
Anx·ur -uris *m & n* coastal town of Latium *(modern Terracina)*
Anyt·us -ī *m* one of Socrates' three accusers
Āonid·ēs -um *fpl* Muses *(named after the section of Boeotia, called Aonia, where Mt. Helicon is located)*
Āoni·us -a -um *adj* Boeotian; Theban; of the Muses; of Helicon; poetic ‖ *f* Boeotia
Aorn·os -ī *adj (masc only)* having no birds, birdless
apage *interj* go!; scram!
Apamē·a -ae *f* name of several towns in Asia Minor, *esp.* that in Syria and that in Phrygia
apēliōt·ēs -ae *m* east wind
Apell·ēs -is *m* Greek painter *(fl 4th cent. B.C.)*
Āpennīnicol·a -ae *m* **(App-)** inhabitant of the Apennines
Āpennīnigen·a -ae *adj (masc only)* born on the Apennines
Āpennīn·us -a -um *adj* **(App-)** Apennine ‖ *m* Apennine Mountains
a·per -prī *m* wild boar; meat of wild boar as food
aper·iō -īre -uī -tus *tr* to open, uncover, lay bare, disclose, reveal; to prove, demonstrate; to explain; to recount; to cut open, split; to usher in *(a new year);* to introduce *(a subject); (mil)* to spread out *(forces); (topog)* to bring into view; **locum aperire** *(w. dat)* to open the way to, afford an opportunity for ‖ *refl (of flowers)* to open; to come into view
apertē *adv* openly, frankly, candidly
apert·ō -āre *tr* to bare
apert·us -a -um *pp of* **aperio** ‖ *adj* bare, uncovered, exposed; without decks; clear *(style);* frank, candid; plain, evident; accessible, unobstructed ‖ *n* open space; **in aperto** in the open; **in aperto esse** to be clear, evident, well known, notorious
ap·ex -icis *m* point, tip; top, summit; conical flamen's hat; cap, crown; crowning glory; long mark over a vowel, macron
ap(h)eliōt·ēs -ae *m* the E. wind
aphract·us -ī *f or* **aphract·um -ī** *n* cargo ship without a deck
Aphrodīsi·a -ōrum *npl* festival in honor of Aphrodite
aphronit·um -ī *n* washing soda, sodium carbonate
apiār·ius -iī *m* beekeeper
apiastr·um -ī *n* a variety of balm
Apīc·ius -iī *m* gourmet of the lst cent. A.D.
apicul·a -ae *f* little bee
apin·ae -ārum *fpl* trifles, nonsense
ap·is -is *f (gen pl:* **-um & -ium)** bee
Āp·is -is *or* **-idis** *m* Egyptian sacred bull
ap·iscor -iscī -tus sum *tr* to pursue; to get,

reach, gain; to get, obtain; *(lit & fig)* to grasp; to get hold of; **litem apisci** to win a lawsuit

ap·ium -iī *n* celery; parsley

aplustr·e -is *or* **aplustr·um -ī** *n (naut)* curved ornamental stern

Apoclēt·ī -ōrum *mpl* select committee *(of Aetolian League)*

apodytēr·ium -(i)ī *n* dressing room *(of a bath)*

apolactiz·ō -āre *tr* to kick aside

Apollinār·is -is -e *adj* of Apollo; **ludi Apollinares** games in honor of Apollo, instituted after the victory at Cannae ‖ *n* place sacred to Apollo

Apoll·ō -inis *m* son of Jupiter and Latona, twin brother of Diana, god of the sun, divination, archery, healing, poetry, and music

Apollodōr·us -ī *m* rhetorician, teacher of Augustus

Apollōni·a -ae *f* name of several cities: on the S. coast of Illyricum; on the S. coast of the Black Sea; in Crete

apolog·us -ī *m* story, fable

Apon·us -ī *m* warm spring near Padua

apophorēt·a -ōrum *npl* presents for departing house guests

apoproēgmen·a -ōrum *npl* things that have been rejected

aposphrāgism·a -atis *n* device on signet ring, seal

apothēc·a -ae *f* warehouse, storeroom

apparātē *adv* **(adp-)** sumptuously

apparāti·ō -ōnis *f* **(adp-)** preparation

apparāt·us -a -um *adj* **(adp-)** getting *or* making ready, preparing; providing

apparāt·us -ūs *m* equipment, apparatus, gear; equipping, organization; armaments; stock, store; rhetorical devices; pomp, magnificence

appār·ens -entis *adj* **(adp-)** visible

appāreō -ēre -uī -itum *intr* **(adp-)** to appear, become visible, be visible; to be seen, show oneself, show up; to materialize, take shape; to appear, look *(e.g., unhappy);* to be perceptible *(to the senses);* to be clearly…, be seen to be; *(of facts)* to be clear, be evident, be obvious; *(w. dat)* **1** to wait on, serve; **2** to obey *(laws);* **nec caput nec pes apparet mihi** I can make neither head nor tail of it; **nusquam apparere** to have disappeared ‖ *v impers* it is evident, it is clear; **ut apparet** apparently

appāriti·ō -ōnis *f* **(adp-)** attendance, service; provision ‖ *fpl* household servants

appārit·or -ōris *m* servant; attendant of public official *(e.g., aide, lictor, secretary)*

appar·ō -āre -āvī -ātus *tr* **(adp-)** to prepare; to provide; to organize *(weddings, public games, war);* *(w. inf or* **ut)** to get ready to ‖ *refl (w.* **in** *+ acc)* to prepare oneself for, equip oneself for

appellāti·ō -ōnis *f* **(adp-)** addressing; *(w.* **ad)** appeal to *(in general; to higher authority);* naming, calling by name; designation, name, title; pronunciation; *(gram)* common noun

appellāt·or -ōris *m (leg)* one who appeals, appellant

appell·ō -āre -āvī -ātus *tr* **(adp-)** to speak to, address, accost; to appeal to, call on, beseech; to make overtures to, approach; to invoke *(god as witness);* to demand payment of; to call up *(to pay a debt or obligation);* to recognize (as), style officially; to name, call; to mention by name, use the name of, mention; to pronounce; to designate, term, call; to demand payment of; *(leg)* to sue; **imperatorem appellare** to hail as "Imperator" ‖ *intr* to appeal

ap·pellō -pellĕre -pulī -pulsus *tr* **(adp-)** *(w. dat or* **ad)** **1** to drive *(s.th.)* to; **2** to move *(military equipment, personnel)* to; **3** to steer *(ship)* to ‖ *pass (w.* **ad)** *(of a ship)* to put in at ‖ *intr (of a ship)* to land

appendicul·a -ae *f* small addition

append·ix -icis *f* addition; related topic; hanger-on

appen·dō -dĕre -dī -sus *tr* **(adp-)** to hang; to weigh; to pay out; *(fig)* to weigh, consider

Appenn- = **Āpenn-**

appet·ens -entis *adj* **(adp-)** greedy; *(w. gen)* eager for, craving

appetenter *adv* **(adp-)** greedily, avidly

appetenti·a -ae *f* **(adp-)** *(w. gen)* the craving for, desire for; **cibi appetentia** appetite (for food)

appetīti·ō -ōnis *f* **(adp-)** grasping; desire, appetite; *(w. gen)* **1** the craving for; **2** the reaching out for; **appetitio naturalis** *(or* **ex natura** *or* **animi)** instinctive desire, appetite *(for),* impulse *(towards)*

appetīt·us -ūs *m* **(adp-)** desire, appetite *(esp. natural or instinctive)*

appet·ō -ĕre -īvī *or* **-iī -ītus** *tr* **(adp-)** to try to reach; to lay hold of; to strive after, aim for; to seek the friendship of; to court; to make for, head for; to attack, assault; to have an appetite for *(food);* to tackle *(a job)* ‖ *intr (of events)* to approach, draw near

Appiān·us -a -um *adj* of Appia, a town in Phrygia ‖ of Appius Claudius the decemvir ‖ *m* Appian of Alexandria *(historian of the 2nd cent. A.D.)*

Appi·as -adis *f* a nymph of the Appian fountain, near the temple of Venus Genetrix ‖ title of Venus

Appiet·ās -ātis *f* the rank *or* status of an Appius

apping·ō -ĕre *tr* **(adp-)** to paint; to write *(s.th.)* in addition *(to a verbal picture)*

Appi·us -a -um *adj* Appian; **aqua Appia** Appian Aqueduct *(built by Appius Claudius Caecus);* **via Appia** Appian Way *(road between Rome and Capua, built by the same man)* ‖ *m* Roman first name, *esp.* of the Claudian clan: Appius Claudius Crassus *(consul and decemvir in 451 B.C.)* ‖ Appius Claudius Caecus *(censor in 312 B.C.)* ‖ Appius Claudius Caudex *(consul in 264 B.C.)* ‖ Appius Claudius Pulcher *(consul in 54 B.C., censor in 50 B.C.)* ‖ **Appi Forum** town in Latium on the Appian Way

applau·dō -dĕre -sī -sus *tr* **(adp-)** to strike, slap; **terrae applaudere** to dash to the ground ‖ *intr* to applaud

applicāti·ō -ōnis *f* **(adp-)** application

applicāt·us -a -um *adj* **(adp-)** *(w.* **ad)** inclined to; *(w. dat)* lying close to, attached to

applicit·us -a -um *adj* **(adp-)** *(w. dat)* adjacent to

applic·ō -āre -āvī *or* **-uī -ātus** *or* **-itus** *tr* **(adp-)** to bring into close contact; *(w. dat or* **ad)** **1** to apply, attach, add, join *(s.th.)* to; **2** to steer *(ship)* toward; **3** to apply *(mind, attention)* to; *(w.* **ad)** to place *(geographically)* near to ‖ *refl* to lean (against); to sit down (on); *(w.* **ad)** to devote oneself to, apply oneself to ‖ *intr (of ships)* to put in (*at*), land

applōdō *see* **applaudo**

applōr·ō -āre -āvī *intr* **(adpl-)** to lament

ap·pōnō -pōnĕre -posuī -positus *tr* **(adp-)** to serve *(food); (w. dat or* **ad)** to put or lay *(s.th.)* near, at, *or* beside; *(w. dat)* **1** to set *(food)* before; **2** to appoint, assign *(s.o.)* to; **3** to reckon *(s.th.)* as; **modum apponere** *(dat)* set a limit to

apporrect·us -a -um *adj* **(adp-)** stretched out near *or* beside

apport·ō -āre -āvī -ātus *tr* **(adp-)** to carry, bring (to); to bring along, bring with one; to import; to present *(a play);* to bring in its train, cause; *(w. dat)* to carry *(s.th.)* to

apposc·ō -ĕre *tr* to demand in addition

apposítē *adv* **(adp-)** appropriately

apposit·us -a -um *pp of* **appono** ‖ *adj (w.* **ad)** suited to; *(w. dat)* situated near, bordering on

appōt·us -a -um *adj* **(adp-)** drunk

apprec·or -ārī -ātus sum *tr* **(adp-)** to pray to, worship

apprehen·dō *or* **appren·dō -dĕre -dī -sus** *tr* **(adp-)** to seize, take hold of; to arrest; to take up *(topic); (mil)* to occupy

apprīmē *adv* **(adp-)** chiefly; very

ap·primō -primĕre -pressī -pressus *tr* **(adp-)** *(w. dat)* to press *(s.th.)* close to

approbāti·ō -ōnis *f* **(adp-)** approbation, approval; proof; decision

approbāt·or -ōris *m* **(adp-)** one who seconds *or* approves

approbē *adv* **(adp-)** very well

approb·ō -āre -āvī -ātus *tr* **(adp-)** to approve; to prove; to prove *(statement)* true

appromitt·ō -ĕre *tr* **(adp-)** to promise in addition

apprōn·ō -āre -āvī -ātus *refl* **(adp-)** to lean forward

approper·ō -āre -āvī -ātus *tr* **(adp-)** to hasten, speed up ‖ *intr* to hurry

appropinquāti·ō -ōnis *f* **(adp-)** approach

appropinqu·ō -āre -āvī *intr* **(adp-)** to approach; *(w. dat or* **ad)** to come near, approach

appugn·ō -āre -āvī -ātus *tr* **(adp-)** to fight, attack

appuls·us -ūs *m* **(adp-)** landing; approach; influence, impact

aprīcāti·ō -ōnis *f* sunbathing

aprīc·or -ārī -ātus sum *intr* to sunbathe

aprīc·us -a -um *adj* sunny ‖ *n* sunny spot; sunshine, light of day

Aprīl·is -is -e *adj* of April; **mensis Aprilis** April ‖ *m* April *(second month of the old calendar until 153 B.C.)*

aprugn·us -a -um *adj* of a wild boar

aps- = abs-

apsinth·ium -(i)ī *n* **(abs-)** *(bot)* wormwood *(yielding a bitter abstract used in flavoring wine)*

apsūmēd·ō -inis *f* a devouring

aptē *adv* closely; suitably

apt·ō -āre -āvī -ātus *tr* to fasten, fit, adjust; to make ready, equip

apt·us -a -um *adj* tied, bound, fastened; fitted together; suitable, adapted; neat, orderly, in good order, in good condition; handy, convenient; *(w. abl)* provided with; *(w.* **ex** *or adv)* following from, dependent on; *(w.* **ad** *or* **in** *acc)* **1** equipped for, ready for; **2** efficient at, good at; **3** convenient for; **4** useful for; **5** favorable for; **causae inter se aptae** connected causes

apud *prep (w. acc)* at, by, near, among; at the house of; in *(a building, town);* in the care of, in the hands of, in possession of; before, in the presence of; in the writings of; (with influence) over; **apud gentes** *(or* **homines)** in the whole world; **apud me (te)** in my (your) care; at my (your) house; **apud mensam** at table; **apud principia** on parade; **apud se esse** to be in one's right mind

Āpūli·a -ae *f* district in S.W. Italy

Āpulic·us -a -um *adj* Apulian

Āpul·us -a -um *adj* Apulian

aqu·a -ae *f* water; rain, rainfall; aqueduct; **aquā et igni interdicere** to outlaw *(lit-*

erally, to forbid from water and fire); **aquam praebere** *(w. dat)* to entertain *(guests)* ‖ *fpl* spa, baths
aquaeduct·us -ūs *m* aqueduct
aquāliculus -ī *m* potbelly
aquāl·is -is -e *adj* water- ‖ *m* washbasin
aquāri·us -a -um *adj* of water ‖ *m* water-conduit inspector ‖ *n* water supply
Aquār·ius -(i)ī *m (astr)* Aquarius *(constellation and sign of the zodiac)*
aquātic·us -a -um *adj* growing in water; watery, moist, humid ‖ *npl* well-watered places; marshes
aquātil·is -is -e *adj* living or growing in water, aquatic; watery
aquāti·ō -ōnis *f* fetching water; water hole
aquāt·or -ōris *m* water carrier
aquil·a -ae *f* eagle *(bird; Roman legionary standard); (fig)* legion; gable *(of house)*
Aquilēi·a -ae *f* town in Venetia at head of the Adriatic
aquil·ex -egis *m* water finder, dowser; water conduit inspector
aquilif·er -erī *m* standardbearer
aquilīn·us -a -um *adj* eagle's
aquil·ō -ōnis *m* north wind; North
aquilōni·us -a -um *adj* northerly
aquil·us -a -um *adj* swarthy
Aquīn·ās -ātis *adj* of Aquinum ‖ *m* citizen of Aquinum
Aquīn·um -ī *n* town of the Volsci, birthplace of Juvenal
Aquītāni·a -ae *f* province in S.W. Gaul
aquol·a *or* **acul·a -ae** *f* **(aquu-)** brook; small amount of water
aqu·or -ārī -ātus sum *intr* to fetch water
aquōs·us -a -um *adj* well-watered; rainy; humid; *(med)* dropsical
aquul·a -ae *f* brook
ār·a -ae *f* altar ‖ **Ara** *(astr)* Altar *(constellation)*
arabarch·ēs -ae *m* customs officer in Egypt
Arabi·a -ae *f* Arabia
Arabic·us *or* **Arabi·us** *or* **Arab·us -a -um** *adj* Arabian
Arab·s -is *m* Arab
Arachn·ē -ēs *f* Lydian girl whom Minerva changed into a spider
arāne·a -ae *f* spider; cobweb
arāneol·a -ae *f* small spider
arāneol·us -ī *m* small spider
arāneōs·us -a -um *adj* full of cobwebs; resembling cobwebs
arāne·us -a -um *adj* spider's ‖ *m* spider ‖ *n* spider web
Ar·ar -aris *(acc:* **Arrarim)** *m* Rhone tributary *(modern Saône)*
arāti·ō -ōnis *f* cultivation, tilling; agriculture; arable land
arātiuncul·a -ae *f* small plot; small farm
arāt·or -ōris *m* farmer ‖ *adj* plow-
arātr·um -ī *n* plow
Arāt·us -ī *m* Greek author, from Soli in Cilicia, of poem on astronomy *(fl 270 B.C.)*
Arax·ēs -is *m* river in Armenia ‖ river in S. Persia
arbi·ter -trī *m* eyewitness, spectator; judge; *(leg)* arbitrator *(with wider discretionary power than a* **judex**); ruler, director, controller
arbitr·a -ae *f* eyewitness
arbitrāriō *adv* uncertainly
arbitrāri·us -a -um *adj* discretionary; arbitrary
arbitrāt·us -ūs *m* decision; inclination, pleasure; **arbitratu** *(w. gen)* at the discretion of; *(leg)* according to the decision of *(an official arbitrator);* **arbitratu meo, tuo** *(coll)* to my (your) heart's content
arbitr·ium -(i)ī *n* (process of) arbitration *(before an arbitrator);* independent judgment; settlement *(of a matter);* mastery, power, control; wishes, desires; whim, caprice; **ad arbitrium nostrum** as much as we please; **mei arbitrii est** it is in my power; **sui arbitrii esse** to be one's own master; **suo arbitrio** on one's own initiative
arbitr·ō -āre -āvī -ātus *tr* to think, judge; *(w. a predicate)* to consider ‖ *pass (of a dispute)* to be settled
arbitr·or -ārī -ātus sum *tr & intr* to decide or judge *(as an arbitrator);* to consider, judge, think; to reckon, suppose, imagine; *(w. inf)* to think it proper
arb·or *or* **arb·ōs -oris** *f* tree; mast, oar, ship; gallows
arboret·um -ī *n* plantation of trees
arbore·us -a -um *adj* of a tree; tree-like
arbuscul·a -ae *f* small tree, sapling
Arbuscul·a -ae *f* actress in the time of Cicero
arbust·us -a -um *adj* wooded, planted with trees ‖ *n* orchard; vineyard planted with trees ‖ *npl* trees
arbute·us -a -um *adj* of arbutus
arbut·um -ī *n* wild strawberry *(fruit of arbutus)*
arbut·us -ī *f* arbutus, strawberry tree
arc·a -ae *f* chest, box, safe; coffin; prison cell
Arcădi·a -ae *f* district in central Peloponnesus, famed for its pastoral beauty
Arcădic·us *or* **Arcădi·us -a -um** *adj* Arcadian
arcānō *adv* in secret; in confidence
arcān·us -a -um adj secret, concealed; private; trustworthy *(friend)* ‖ *n* secret; sacred mystery
Arc·as -ados *m* inhabitant of Arcadia, Arcadian ‖ Arcas, son of Callisto by Jupiter, eponymous hero of Arcadia ‖ Mercury, who was born on Mt. Cyllene in Arcadia

arc·eō -ēre -uī *tr* to shut up, enclose; to keep out *(rain, cold);* to keep at a distance, keep off; to hinder, prevent; to control, govern; to prevent, stop; *(w. abl)* to protect from, rescue from

Arcesil·ās -ae *or* **Arcesilā·ūs -ī** *m* philosopher of the 3rd cent. B.C., founder of the Middle Academy

arcessīt·us -a -um *pp of* **arcesso (accers-)** ‖ *adj* foreign; far-fetched; self-inflicted *(death)*

arcessīt·us -ūs *m* call, summons

arcess·ō *or* **accers·ō -ĕre -īvī** *or* **-iī -ītus** *tr* to send for, summon; to raise *(money);* to drag in *(gratuitously);* to induce *(sleep, tears)*; to bring upon oneself *(troubles);* to derive; to import; *(leg)* to arraign

archetyp·us -a -um *adj* original, autograph ‖ *n* original

Archiloch·us -ī *m* Greek iambic and elegaic poet of Paros *(c. 714–676 B.C.)*

archimagīr·us -ī *m* chef

Archimēd·ēs -is *or* **-ī** *m* Greek scientist of Syracuse *(287?–212 B.C.)*

archipīrāt·a -ae *m* pirate captain

architect·ō -āre -āvī -ātus *tr* to design

architect·ōn -onis *m* architect

architect·or -ārī -ātus sum *tr* to design; to build; *(fig)* to devise

architectūr·a -ae *f* architecture

architect·us -ī *m* architect; designer, deviser

arch·ōn -ontis *m* archon *(a chief magistrate of Athens)*

Archȳt·as -ae *m* Pythagorean philosopher of the 4th cent. B.C.

arcisell·ium -(i)ī *n* chair *(with rounded back)*

arciten·ens -entis *adj* holding a bow; **dea arcitenens** Diana ‖ **Arcitenens** *m* Apollo; *(astr)* Sagittarius *(constellation and sign of the zodiac)*

Arctophyl·ax -ācis *m (astr)* Boötes *(constellation)*

arct·os -ī *m* North Pole; North; north wind; night ‖ **Arctos** *m* the Great and Little Bear *(double constellation)*

arctūr·us -ī *m* brightest star in Boötes

arcuāt·us -a -um *adj* bow-shaped; covered *(carriage)*

arcul·a -ae *f* small box

arculār·ius -iī *m* maker of small jewel boxes

arcu·ō -āre -āvī -ātus *tr* to curve

arc·us -ūs *m* bow; rainbow; curve; arch; triumphal arch; one of the five zones of the sky

ardali·ō -ōnis *m* busybody

arde·a -ae *f* heron ‖ **Ardea** town in Latium

Arde·ās -ātis *adj* of Ardea ‖ *mpl* the people of Ardea

Ardeātīn·us -a -um *adj* of Ardea

ard·ens -entis *adj* blazing, burning, hot, fiery; gleaming; intense *(emotions);* zealous, eager; high *(fever);* bright *(colors, stars)*

ardenter *adv* ardently, passionately; eagerly

ardeō ardēre arsī arsūrus *tr* to be in love with ‖ *intr* to be on fire, burn, blaze; to flash, glow; to smart, burn; *(of countries)* to be in turmoil; *(of corpses)* to be cremated; *(of seas)* to be rough

ardesc·ō -ĕre *intr* to catch fire; to gleam, glitter; *(of passions)* to become more intense

ard·or -ōris *m* heat, flame; flashing, brightness; heat *(of passions);* loved one, flame

Arduenn·a -ae *f* forest in the N. of Gaul *(modern Ardennes)*

ardu·us -a -um *adj* steep, high; uphill; erect; difficult; *(of hopes)* difficult to realize ‖ *n* height; difficulty; **in arduum** *(or* **per arduum)** upwards, uphill; high into the air

āre·a -ae *f* open space; forecourt *(of temple);* park, playground; building site; threshing floor; bald spot

āre·faciō -facĕre -fēcī -factus *tr* to dry up

Arelāte *indecl n* town in S. Gaul *(Arles)*

arēna *see* **harena**

ār·ens -entis *adj* dry, parched; parching *(thirst)*

ār·eō -ēre *intr* to be dry; to be thirsty

Arēopagīt·ēs -ae *m* member of the Areopagus

Arēopag·us -ī *m* criminal court in Athens; hill where this court met

Ar·ēs -is *m* Greek god of war *(counterpart of Mars)*

ār·escō -escĕre -uī *intr* to become dry; to wither; *(of streams)* to run dry

aretālog·us -ī *m* teller of tall tales

Arethūs·a -ae *f* nymph pursued by river god Alpheus in the Peloponnesus and changed into a fountain ‖ fountain at Syracuse

Arē·us -a -um *adj* of Ares; **Areus pagus** court of the Areopagus

Argē·ī -ōrum *mpl* figures of men made of straw and thrown annually into the Tiber

argentāri·us -a -um *adj* silver; silvery; financial; banker's ‖ *m* banker ‖ *f* banking; bank; silver mine

argentāt·us -a -um *adj* silver-plated; *(hum)* concerned with money

argenteol·us -a -um *adj* **(-tiol-)** silver

argente·us -a -um *adj* silver, silvery; *(hum)* of money ‖ *m* silver coin

argent·um -ī *n* silver; silver plate; money, cash; **argentum bigatum** silver coin stamped with a two-horse chariot; **argentum signatum** silver coin; **argentum vivum** mercury, quicksilver

Argē·us *or* **Argei·us** *or* **Argī·us -a -um** *adj* Argive; Greek
Arg·ī -ōrum *mpl or* **Argos** *n (only nom & acc)* Argos *(town in N.E. Peloponnesus)*
Argīlēt·um -ī *n (also* **Argī lētum)** district in Rome between the Quirinal and Capitoline HIlls
argill·a -ae *f* potter's clay
Arginūs(s)·ae -ārum *fpl* group of three islands off the coast of Asia Minor, the scene of an Athenian naval victory in 406 B.C.
argīt·is -idis *f* vine with white grapes
Argīv·us -a -um *adj* Argive; Greek
Arg·ō -ūs *(acc & abl:* **Argō)** *f* Jason's ship
Argolic·us -a -um *adj* Argive; Greek
Argol·is -idis *adj (fem only)* Argive ‖ Argive woman ‖ the Argolid *(district around Argos)*
Argonaut·a -ae *m* Argonaut
Argos *n (only nom & acc)* Argos *(see* **Argi)**
Argō·us -a -um *adj* of the Argo
argūmentāti·ō -ōnis *f* argumentation; proof
argūment·or -ārī -ātus sum *tr* to adduce as proof; to support by arguments; *(w.* **de** *+ abl)* to conclude from ‖ *intr* to adduce arguments, argue
argūment·um -ī *n* evidence, proof; argument; theme, plot; topic, subject; motif *(of artistic representation);* **ex argumento** from the facts of the case
arg·uō -uěre -uī -ūtus *tr* to prove; to reveal, betray; to accuse, charge, impeach *(person);* to find fault with *(thing);* to prove guilty, convict
Arg·us -ī *m* many-eyed monster set over Io and killed by Mercury
argūtāti·ō -ōnis *f* creaking
argūtē *adv* shrewdly
argūti·ae -ārum *fpl* subtlety; sophistry; wit
argūt·ō -āre -āvī *tr* to say childishly
argūt·or -ārī -ātus sum *intr* to chatter
argūtul·us -a -um *adj* somewhat subtle
argūt·us -a -um *adj* clearcut, bright, distinct; piercing; bright, smart, witty *(person);* clear-voiced, melodious; rustling *(leaves);* babbling *(brook);* chirping *(birds, crickets);* pungent *(smell);* expressive *(eyes, gestures)*
argyrasp·is -idis *adj* wearing a silver shield
-āri·a -ae *fem suf* forms nouns **1** denoting a place: **argentaria** a bank; **2** a female agent: **libraria** female secretary
Ariadn·a -ae *or* **Ariadn·ē -ēs** *f* Ariadna *(daughter of King Minos; she extricated Theseus from the Labyrinth)*
Arīci·a -ae *f* town in Latium on the Via Appia
āridul·us -a -um *adj* somewhat dry
ārid·us -a -um *adj* dry, parched; withered; meager; dry *(style)*
ari·ēs -etis *m* ram; battering ram; bulwark *(used as breakwater);* **ariete crebro** with constant ramming ‖ **Aries** Aries *(sign of Zodiac)*
ariet·ō -āre -āvī -ātus *tr* to batter, ram; **inter se arietari** to collide ‖ *intr* to collide; to trip; *(w.* **in** *+ acc)* to ram against
Ariobarzān·ēs -is *m* king of Cappadocia
Arī·ōn -onis *m* early Greek poet and musician, rescued from drowning by a dolphin
Ariovist·us -ī *m* king of Germanic tribe
-ār·is -is -e *adjl suf* collateral with **-ālis** but used when the stem contains an **l: consularis** consular
arist·a -ae *f* ear of grain
Aristae·us ī *m* son of Apollo and Cyrene *(said to have taught man beekeeping and to have been the first to plant olive trees)*
Aristarch·us -ī *m* Alexandrine critic and scholar *(fl 156 B.C.);* stern critic
Aristīd·ēs -ae *m* Athenian politician and general in thetime of Persian Wars, famous for his honesty ‖ author from Miletus
aristolochi·a -ae *f (bot)* birthwort *(plant believed to aid in childbirth)*
Aristophan·ēs -is *m* Greek comic playwright *(c. 450?–385? B.C.)*
Aristotel·ēs -is *or* **-ī** Aristotle *(384–322 B.C.)*
arithmētic·us -a -um *adj* of numbers ‖ *f or npl* arithmetic
āritūd·ō -inis *f* dryness
-ar·ium -(i)ī *n suf* denoting a place, *e.g.,* **armāmentārium** place for keeping arms, arsenal
-ār·ius -(i)ī *m suf* denoting "dealer in", *e.g.,* **librārius** bookseller
arm·a -ōrum *npl* armor, defensive arms *(opp* **tela** weapons to throw or thrust); war, warfare; camp life; armed men, troops; equipment, tools; utensils; nature's arms *(teeth, claws, etc.)*; **ad arma adire** *(or* **venire)** to resort to military force; **arma conferre cum** to clash with; **arma ferre contra** *or* **in** *(w. acc)* to fight against; **arma inferre** *(dat)* to make war on; **arma ponere** *(or* **deponere)** to lay down one's arms; **arma venatoria** hunting gear; **levia arma** light-armed troops
armāment·a -ōrum *npl* ship's gear; equipment
armāmentār·ium -(i)ī *n* arsenal
armāriol·um -ī *n* cabinet, chest, closet
armār·ium -(i)ī *n* cupboard, chest; bookcase
armātūr·a -ae *f* outfit, equipment; armor; light-armed troops

armāt·us -a -um *adj* armed; equipped ‖ *m* armed man, soldier

armāt·us -ūs *m* amor; **gravis armatus** heavy-armed troops

Armeni·a -ae *f* **(-min-)** country in N.E. Asia Minor

armeniāc·um -ī *n* apricot

armeniāc·us -ī *f* apricot tree

Armeni·us -a -um *adj* Armenian; **prunum Armenium** apricot ‖ *m* an Armenian

armentāl·is -is -e *adj* of the herd

armentār·ius -(i)ī *m* herdsman

arment·um -ī *n* herd

armif·er -era -erum *adj* arms-bearing, armed, warlike; **deus armifer** Mars; **dea armifera** Minerva

armig·er -era -erum *adj* armed; producing warriors; *(of a field sown with dragon's teeth)* producing armed men ‖ *m* armed man; bodyguard; armor-bearer ‖ *f* armor-bearer *(female);* **Jovis armigera** Jove's armor-bearer *(i.e., the eagle)*

armill·a -ae *f* armlet, bracelet

armillātus -a -um *adj* wearing a bracelet

Armilustr·um -ī *n* ceremony of purifying arms

armipot·ens -entis *adj* powerful in arms, valiant

armison·us -a -um *adj* reverberating with arms

arm·ō -āre -āvī -ātus *tr* to arm; to rouse to arms

arm·us -ī *m* shoulder, shoulder blade, upper arm; flank *(of animal)*

Arniens·is -is -e *adj* name of one of the tribes at Rome

ar·ō -āre -āvī -ātus *tr* to plow, till

Arpīnās -ātis *adj* of Arpinum

Arpīn·um -ī *n* town in Latium, birthplace of Marius and Cicero

arq- = arc-

arquāt·us -a -um *adj* jaundiced

arr- = adr-

arrab·ō -ōnis *m* earnest money, token payment, deposit; **arrabo amoris** token of love

arrect·us -a -um *pp of* **arrigo** ‖ *adj* upright; steep

arrēp·ō -ĕre -sī *intr* **(adr-)** *(w. dat or* **ad)** to creep towards, steal up on

Arrēt·ium -(i)ī *n* town in Etruria, known for its pottery

arrexī *perf of* **arrigo**

arrī·deō -dēre -sī -sus *tr* **(adr-)** to smile at ‖ *intr (w. dat)* **1** to smile at, smile on; **2** to laugh with; **3** to be favorable to; **4** to please

ar·rigō -rigĕre -rexī -rectus *tr* **(adr-)** to erect; to arouse, excite; to prick up *(ears);* **animum arrigere** to arouse courage; **in digitos arrectus** on tiptoe; **oculi arrecti** staring eyes

ar·ripiō -ripĕre -ripuī -reptus *tr* **(adr-)** to snatch, seize eagerly; to get hold of; to obtain, acquire; to head eagerly for *(destination);* to jump at *(a chance, excuse); (of disease)* to attack; to assail, attack suddenly; *(fig)* to grasp quickly; *(leg)* to arrest, arraign

arrīsī *perf of* **arrideo**

arrō·dō -dĕre -sī -sus *tr* **(adr-)** to gnaw at, nibble away part of

arrog·ans -antis *adj* **(adr-)** arrogant

arroganter *adv* **(adr-)** arrogantly

arroganti·a -ae *f* **(adr-)** arrogance; presumption

ar·rogō -āre -āvī -ātus *tr* **(adr-)** to question; to lay claim to, arrogate; to claim to possess; to assign, attribute

arrōsī *perf of* **arrodo**

arrōsus *pp of* **arrodo**

Arrun·s -tis *m* Etruscan proper name, tradionally given to the younger sons

ars artis f skill; craft, trade; craftsmanship; work of art; invention, device; trick, stratagem; *(mil)* tactic; profession, occupation; method, way, manner, means; artificial means, artificiality; science, theory; manual, textbook; **arte** cunningly; **bonae** *(or* **liberales) artes** liberal arts; **ex arte** systematically; **istae artes** evil practices, bad habits

Arsac·ēs -is *m* first king of the Parthians; title of his successors

arsī *perf of* **ardeo**

Artaban·us -ī *m* name of several Parthian kings

artē *or* **arctē** *adv* closely, tightly; *(to love)* deeply, dearly; *(to sleep)* soundly

Artem·is -idis *f* Greek counterpart of Diana

artēri·a -ae *f* windpipe; artery

arthrītic·us -a -um *adj* arthritic

articulātim *adv* piecemeal; *(to speak)* articulately, distinctly

articul·ō -āre *tr* to articulate

articul·us -ī *m* joint, knuckle; finger; toe; limb; point of time, juncture; *(gram)* single word *(of a sentence); (gram)* clause; *(gram)* (definite, indefinite) article; *(gram)* pronoun, pronominal adjective; **in articulo temporis** in the nick of time

artif·ex -icis *adj* **(-tuf-)** skilled, ingenious, professional; creative, productive; cunning; skillfully made, cunningly wrought; *(w. gen,* **ad** *or* **in** *+ acc)* skilled in, expert in; broken, trained *(horse)*

artif·ex -icis *m* craftsman, artist, master, professional; performer, actor, musician; author *(of book);* originator, contriver; *(w. gen or* **ad** *or* **in** *+ abl)* expert in

artificiōsē *adv* skillfully; systematically

artificiōs·us -a -um *adj* skillful, ingenious, accomplished; artificial

artific·ium -(i)ī *n* skill, talent; work of art;

trade, profession; cleverness, cunning; theory
arti·us -a -um *adj* sound in mind and body
art·ō -āre -āvī -ātus *tr* **(arct-)** to pack closely; to compress, contract; to limit; to tighten
artolagan·us -ī *m* cake
artopt·a -ae *m* bread pan; baker
artu·a -ōrum *npl* limbs
art·us -a -um *adj* close, tight; confined, restricted; narrow; dense; firm; scanty, small; needy; parsimonious, stingy; strict; sound *(sleep)* ‖ *n* narrow space; tight spot, difficulty; **in artum colligere** to summarize
art·us -ūs *m* joint; limb
ārul·a -ae *f* small altar
arund·ō -inis *f* reed; shaft, arrow; pipe, flute; pen; fishing rod; hobby-horse; *(in weaving)* comb
arvīn·a -ae *f* grease
arv·us -a -um *adj* arable, plowed ‖ *n* arable land, soil, land; plain; region; grain
arx arcis *f* citadel; fortress, stronghold; place of refuge; hilltop, peak; *(fig)* mainstay, protection; summit, pinnacle; **arcem facere e cloaca** *(prov)* to make mountains out of molehills; **arx caeli** height of heaven; **arx corporis** head; **Romae septem arces** seven hills of Rome
-ās *advl suf:* **alias** elsewhere
-ās -ātis *adjl suf* 1 originally used in ethnic adjectives from the names of Italian towns: **Arpinas** of *or* connected with Arpinum; 2 extended to other stems to form adjectives and substantives: **optimas** aristocratic; **optimates** artistocrats
ās assis *m* pound *(divisible into 12 ounces);* bronze coin, penny; jugerum *(c. 3/5 of an acre);* undivided estate; **heres ex asse** sole heir; **non assis facere** not to give a hoot about
Ascān·ius -(i)ī *m* son of Aeneas and Creusa and founder of Alba Longa
ascen·dō -dĕre -dī -sus *tr* **(ads-)** to climb; to mount *(horse);* to board *(ship)* ‖ *intr* to climb up, ascend; *(of voice, river)* to rise; *(w.* **ad** *or* **in** *+ acc)* to climb, climb up to; *(w.* **super** *or* **supra** *+ acc)* to rise above, surpass; **per gradūs ascendere** to climb the stairs
ascensi·ō -ōnis *f* climbing up, ascent
ascens·us -ūs *m* **(ads-)** ascent; means of ascending, approach; step, degree; flight of stairs; *(fig)* climb, rise
asci·a -ae *f* ax, hatchet; mason's trowel; **sub asciā** while still under construction
asc·iō -īre *tr* **(ads-)** to associate with oneself
asc·iscō -iscĕre -īvī -ītus *tr* **(ads-)** to adopt; to approve *(a bill);* to assume, arrogate; to receive, admit *(as ally, citizen, etc.);* to hire; *(w.* **in** *+ acc)* to admit *(to citizenship, the senate);* **inter patricios asciscere** to admit to the patrician order
ascīt·us -a -um *adj* acquired *(as opposed to innate)*
Asclēpiad·ēs -is *m* famous doctor of Prusa in Bithynia, who practised in Rome *(d. 40 B.C.)*
ascop·a -ae *f* small leather pouch
Ascr·a -ae *f* birthplace of Hesiod in Boeotia, near Mt. Helicon
Ascrae·us -a -um *adj* of Ascra; **Ascraeus poeta** *or* **senex** Hesiod
ascrī·bō -bĕre -psī -ptus *tr* **(ads-)** to add *(by writing);* to impute, ascribe; to enroll, register; to reckon, number, class
ascriptīci·us -a -um *adj* **(ads-)** enrolled, registered
ascripti·ō -ōnis *f* **(ads-)** addition *(in writing)*
ascriptīv·us -ī *m* **(ads-)** *(mil)* reserve
ascript·or -ōris *m* **(ads-)** supporter
Asculān·us -ī *m* inhabitant of Asculum
Asc(u)l·um -ī *n* chief town of Picenum in N. Italy
asell·a -ae *f* ass *(female)*
asell·us -ī *m* ass, donkey
Asi·a -ae *f* Asia; Asia Minor *(modern Turkey);* kingdom of Troy
Asiān·us -a -um *adj & m* Asian
Asiātic·us -a -um *adj* connected with Asia or the East *(esp. Asia Minor and the Roman province of Asia);* **mare Asiaticum** Carpathian Sea
asīl·us -ī *m* horsefly
asinārī·us -a -um *adj* connected with asses; **via asinaria** a road S.E. of Rome ‖ *m* ass-driver
asin·us -ī *m* ass; fool
Ās·is -idis *f* Asia; Asia Minor
Āsi·us -a -um *f* of Asia, of Asia Minor
Āsōp·us *or* **Āsōp·os -ī** *m* a river in Boeotia, personified as the father of Aegina
asōt·us -ī *m* playboy, rake
asparag·us -ī *m* asparagus
aspargō *see* **aspergo**
aspectābil·is -is -e *adj* visible
aspect·ō -āre -āvī -ātus *tr* **(ads-)** to look at, gaze at; to look with respect at; *(of a place)* to face; to obey *(orders)*
aspectus *pp of* **aspicio**
aspect·us -ūs *m* **(ads-)** look, sight, glance; sense of sight; eyes, expression in the eyes, look; range of vision, view; appearance, aspect; sight, vision; **primo aspectu** at first sight; **sub oculorum aspectum cadere** to come into view; **uno aspectu** at a glance
aspell·ō -ĕre *tr* to drive away
asp·er -era -erum (asprīs = asperīs) *adj* rough, uneven; harsh, severe, stormy *(climate);* grating, hoarse *(sound);* pungent, strong *(odor);* rough, hard; un-

kind, cruel, bitter, rude *(character);* austere, rigid *(person);* wild, fierce *(animal);* rough, annoying, adverse *(circumstances);* embossed *(cup, etc.);* craggy; rugged *(style)*

asperē *adv* roughly; harshly, sternly, severely

asper·gō -gĕre -sī -sus *tr* **(ads-) (-spar-)** to sprinkle, scatter; to taint; *(w. dat)* to sprinkle *(s.th.)* on

asperg·ō -inis *f* **(ads-) (-spar-)** sprinkling; spray

asperit·ās -ātis *f* uneveness, roughness; severity, fierceness; difficulty, trouble

aspernāti·ō -ōnis *f* disdain

aspernor -ārī -ātus sum *tr* to disdain, spurn, reject

asper·ō -āre -āvī -ātus *tr* to make rough *or* uneven, roughen; to exasperate; to make worse

aspersi·ō -ōnis *f* sprinkling

aspiciō aspicĕre aspexī aspectus *tr* **(ads-)** to catch sight of, spot; to look at; to inspect, look over; to look *(a person)* in the eye; to visit; to consider; to picture

aspīrāti·ō -ōnis *f* **(ads-)** breathing; exhalation; *(gram)* aspiration *(making an h sound)*

aspīr·ō -āre -āvī -ātum *intr* to breathe, blow; *(w. dat or* **ad** *or* **in** *+ acc)* to aspire to, desire to reach *or* obtain, come near to obtaining; *(w. dat)* to favor

asp·is -idis *f* asp *(poisonous snake of N. Africa)*

asportātiō -ōnis *f* removal

asport·ō -āre -āvī -ātus *tr* to carry away, remove; *(of vehicles)* to haul away

asprēt·a -ōrum *npl* rough terrain

Assarac·us -ī *m* king of Troy, son of Tros, and grandfather of Aeneas

assecl·a -ae *m* **(ads-)** hanger-on

assectāti·ō -ōnis *f* **(ads-)** (political) support

assectāt·or -ōris *m* **(ads-)** attendant, companion; disciple; devotee; *(pol)* supporter

assect·or -ārī -ātus sum *tr* **(ads-)** to follow closely; to escort; to be an adherent of, follow

assecul·a -ae *m* **(ads-)** hanger-on

assensi·ō -ōnis *f* **(ads-)** approval, applause; agreement, belief ‖ *fpl* expressions of approval

assens·or -ōris *m* **(ads-)** backer, supporter

assens·us -ūs *m* **(ads-)** assent, approval; agreement; belief

assentāti·ō -ōnis *f* **(ads-)** assent, agreement; flattery

assentātiuncul·a -ae *f* **(ads-)** bit of flattery

assentāt·or -ōris *m* **(ads-)** yes-man

assentātōriē *adv* **(ads-)** flatteringly

assentātr·ix -īcis *f* **(ads-)** flatterer *(female)*

assen·tiō -tīre -sī -sum *or* **assen·tior -tīrī -sus sum** *intr* **(ads-)** to agree; *(w. dat)* assent to, agree with, approve

assent·or -ārī -ātus sum *intr* **(ads-)** to agree always; *(w. dat)* **1** to agree always with; **2** to humor

asse·quor -quī -cūtus sum *tr* **(ads-)** to pursue, go after; to catch up to, reach; to gain, obtain, procure; to achieve, attain, win *(wisdom, citizenship, etc.);* to come up to, equal, match; to comprehend, understand

ass·er -eris *m* pole; joist, rafter; pole on which a litter was carried

asser·ō -ĕre -uī -tus *tr* **(ads-)** to set free, liberate *(slave);* to protect, defend; to claim, appropriate; **in servitutem asserere** to claim *(s.o.)* as one's slave

as·serō -serĕre -sēvī -sītus *tr (w. dat)* to plant *(s.th.)* close to

asserti·ō -ōnis *f* **(ads-)** declaration of civil status

assert·or -ōris *m* **(ads-)** defender, protector, champion; *(leg)* claimant *(who claims a person as his slave)*

asserv·iō -īre -īvī *or* **-iī** *intr* **(ads-)** *(w. dat)* to apply oneself to

asserv·ō -āre -āvī -ātus *tr* **(ads-)** to preserve; keep *(records);* to watch; to keep in custody; *(mil)* to guard

assessi·ō -ōnis *f* **(ads-)** company, (legal) support, standing by

assess·or -ōris *m* **(ads-)** adviser; *(leg)* counselor

assess·us -ūs *m* **(ads-)** legal assistance

assevēranter *adv* **(ads-)** emphatically

assevērāti·ō -ōnis *f* **(ads-)** assertion; emphasis; earnestness; *(rhet)* emphasizing particle *(e.g.,* **eheu)**

assevēr·ō -āre -āvī -ātus *tr* **(ads-)** to assert emphatically; *(of things)* to give clear evidence of; to be serious about ‖ *intr* to be serious

as·sideō -sidēre -sēdī -sessus *tr* **(ads-)** to sit near; *(mil)* to besiege ‖ *intr* to sit nearby; *(w. dat)* **1** to sit near, stand by, take care of, keep *(s.o.)* company; **2** to be busily engaged in; **3** *(of places)* to be situated close to; **4** to attend to, mind; **5** to resemble; **6** *(mil)* to encamp near; **7** *(mil)* to set up a blockade against

as·sīdō -sīdĕre -sēdī *intr* **(ads-)** to sit down; *(of birds)* to land, alight

assiduē *adv* **(ads-)** assiduously, continually

assiduit·ās -ātis *f* **(ads-)** constant presence; persistence, frequent recurrence

assiduō *adv* **(ads-)** continually

assidu·us -a -um *adj* **(ads-)** constantly present; persistent, incessant; tireless, busy; restless *(sea)* ‖ *m* taxpayer; rich man

assignāti·ō -ōnis *f* **(ads-)** allotment *(of land)*

assign·ō -āre -āvī -ātus *tr* **(ads-)** to mark out, allot, assign *(land); (w. dat)* **1** to confer *(honors)* on; **2** to ascribe to, impute to; **3** to attribute to; **4** to entrust to the care of

as·siliō -silīre -siluī -sultum *intr* **(ads-)** to jump; *(w. dat)* **1** to jump upon, leap at; **2** *(mil)* to make a sudden assault on; *(w.* **ad) 1** to jump to; **2** to have recourse to

assimil·is -is -e *adj* **(ads-)** *(w. gen or dat)* similar to, like

assimiliter *adv* **(ads-)** in like manner

assimulāti·ō -ōnis *f* **(ads-)** similarity; comparison; pretense

assimulāt·us -a -um *adj* **(ads-)** similar; counterfeit

assimul·ō -āre -āvī -ātus *tr* **(ads-) (-mil-)** to pretend; to resemble, imitate; *(w. dat)* to compare to

as·sistō -sistere -titī *intr* **(ads-)** to stop; to stand nearby; *(w.* **ad)** to stand at *or* near; *(w. dat)* to assist, defend; *(mil) (w.* **in** + *acc)* to take up a position against; *(leg)* to assist in court; *(leg) (w. dat)* to assist, defend

assitus *pp of* **assero**

assol·eō -ēre *intr* **(ads-)** to be usual

asson·ō -āre *intr* **(ads-)** *(w. dat)* to echo

assuctus *pp of* **assugo**

assūdesc·ō -ĕre *intr* **(ads-) (-asc-)** to break out into a sweat

assue·faciō -facĕre -fēcī -factus *tr* **(ads-)** to train; *(w. dat or* **ad** *or inf)* to accustom *(s.o.)* to

assu·escō -escĕre -ēvī -ētus *tr* **(ads-)** *(w. dat)* to accustom *(s.o.)* to, make *(s.o.)* familiar with ‖ *intr (w. dat,* **ad,** *or w. inf)* to become used to; *(w. dat)* to become intimate with

assuētūd·ō -inis *f* **(ads-)** habit, custom; intimacy

assuēt·us -a -um *pp of* **assuesco** ‖ *adj* accustomed, customary, usual; *(w. abl)* trained in; *(w. dat,* **ad** *or* **in** + *acc or inf)* accustomed to, used to; *(w. dat)* intimate with

assū·gō -gĕre -xī -ctus *tr* **(ads-)** to suck in

assul·a -ae *f* splinter, chip, shaving

assulātim *adv* into splinters

assult·ō -āre -āvī -ātus *tr* **(ads-)** to assault ‖ *intr (w. dat)* to jump at, jump to

assult·us -ūs *m* **(ads-)** assault

assūm·ō -ĕre -psī -ptus *tr* **(ads-)** to take in addition, add; to adopt; to usurp; to claim, assume; to employ, hire; to derive, borrow; to gain, acquire *(qualities);* to take *(food, drink, bait);* to take along *(as companion);* **sibi assumere** to lay claim to

assumpti·ō -ōnis *f* **(ads-)** assumption; adoption; acquisition; claim; *(in logic)* minor premise; *(rhet)* taking up *(of a point)*

assumptīv·us -a -um *adj* **(ads-)** resting on external evidence, extrinsic

assū·ō -ĕre *tr* **(ads-)** *(w. dat)* to sew *(e.g. patch)* on

assur·gō -gĕre -rexī -rectum *intr* **(ads-)** to stand up; to rise; to increase, swell; *(of hair)* to stand on end; *(w. dat)* to rise out of respect for

ass·us -a -um *adj* roasted; dry *(sunbathing without anointing)* ‖ *n* roast

assuxī *perf of* **assugo**

Assyri·a -ae *f* Assyria

Assyri·us -a -um *adj* Assyrian ‖ *mpl* Assyrians

ast *conj (old form of* **at)** but

Astart·ē -ēs *f* Syro-Phoenician goddess, counterpart of Venus

Asteri·a -ae *f* sister of Leto, who was metamorphosed into a quail at Delos

astern·ō -ĕre *tr* **(ads-)** to strew ‖ *pass* to prostrate oneself

astic·us -a -um *adj* city, urban

astipulāt·or -ōris *m* **(ads-)** legal assistant; supporter, adherent

astipul·or -ārī -ātus sum *intr* **(ads-)** *(w. dat)* to side with

astit·uō -uĕre -uī -ūtus *tr* to place near; *(w.* **ad)** to make *(s.o.)* stand near

ast·ō -āre -itī *intr* **(ads-)** to stand erect, stand up, stand nearby; *(w. dat)* to assist

Astrae·a -ae *f* goddess of justice

astrep·ō -ĕre -uī *tr* **(ads-)** to assail *(with shouts)* ‖ *intr* to shout in support

astrictē *adv* **(ads-)** concisely; strictly

astrict·us -a -um *pp of* **astringo** ‖ *adj* drawn together, tight; stingy; concise

astrif·er -era -erum *adj* starry

astri·ngō -ngĕre -nxī -ctus *tr* **(ads-)** to tighten, bind fast; to obligate; to restrain; to freeze; to pledge; *(fig)* to numb; *(fig)* to compress, abridge; to occupy *(attention);* to embarrass; to implicate *(in a crime);* **fidem astringere** to give one's word; **inter se astringere** to fasten together

astrologi·a -ae *f* astronomy; astrology

astrolog·us -ī *m* astronomer; astrologer

astr·um -ī *n* star; constellation ‖ *npl* stars; sky, heaven

astr·uō -ĕre -ī -ctus *tr* **(ads)** to build as an additional structure; **nobilitatem alicui astruere** to add nobility to s.o.

astū *indecl n* **(asty)** *the* city *(i.e., Athens)*

astup·eō -ēre -uī *intr (w. dat)* to be amazed at, be enthralled by

ast·us -ūs *m* cunning; trick

astūtē *adv* slyly

astūti·a -ae *f* cunning; astuteness; trick

astūt·us -a -um *adj* cunning, clever

Astyag·ēs -is *m* king of Media and grandfather of Cyrus

Astyan·ax -actis *m* son of Hector and Andromache

asȳl·um -ī *n* refuge, asylum

at *conj* but; *(in a transition)* but on the other hand; *(in anticipation of an opponent's objection)* but, it may be objected; *(in an ironical objection)* but really, but after all; *(after a negative clause, to introduce a qualification)* but at least; **at contra** but on the contrary; **at tamen** but at least

Atābul·us -ī *m* sirocco, S.E. wind

Atalant·a -ae *or* **Atlant·ē -ēs** *f* daughter of King Schoeneus, defeated by Hippomenes in a footrace ‖ daughter of Iasius and participant in the Calydonian boar hunt

atat *(or* **attat)** *interj (expressing surprise or fear)* aha!, oh!

atav·us -ī *m* great-great-great-grandfather; ancestor

ātell·a -ae *f* Campanian town

ātellān·a -ae *f* comic farce *(originated in Atella)*

ā·ter -tra -trum *adj* flat black *(different from* **niger** glossy black); dark; gloomy; malicious; poisonous; unlucky, ill-omened

Atham·ān -ānis *m* inhabitant of Athamia

Athamāni·a -ae *f* district in Epirus

Athamantē·us -a -um *adj* of Athamas *(referring to Phrixus or Palaemon)*

Atham·ās -antis *m* king of Thessaly, father of Helle and Phrixus by Nephele, and of Learchus and Melecertes by Ino

Athēn·ae -ārum *fpl* Athens

Athēniens·is -is -e *adj* Athenian

Athēnodōr·us -ī *m* Stoic philosopher, teacher of Augustus

athe·os -ī *m* atheist

āthlēt·a -ae *m* athlete; boxer; wrestler

āthlēticē *adv* athletically

āthlētic·us -a -um *adj* athletic ‖ *f* athletics

Ath·os *or* **Atho -ōnis** *m* mountain on the peninsula of Acte in Chalcidice

ātīn·a -ae *f* town in Latium ‖ town in Lucania

ātīn·ās -ātis *m* of Atina ‖ *mpl* the people of Atina

Atl·ā(n)s -antis *m* Atlas *(giant supporting the sky, son of Iapetus and Clymene)* ‖ Mt. Atlas *(on N.W. coast of Africa)*

Atlantē·us -a -um *adj* Atlantic

Atlantiad·ēs -ae *m* grandson of Atlas, Mercury ‖ great-grandson of Atlas, Hermaphroditus

Atlantic·us -a -um *adj* Atlantic

Atlant·is -idis *or* **-idos** *f* daughter *or* female descendant of Atlas

atom·os -ī *f* atom

atque *conj* and *(used before vowels and "h") see* **ac**

atquī *conj* but yet, and yet; however, rather, and yet

ātrāment·um -ī *n* ink; **atramentum sutorium** black shoe polish

ātrāt·us -a -um *adj* dressed in black *(for mourning)*

Atr·eūs -eī *m* son of Pelops, brother of Thyestes, father of Agamemnon and Menelaus

ātricol·or -ōris *adj* black

Atrīd·ēs -ae *m* descendant of Atreus

ātriens·is -is *m* butler

ātriol·um -ī *n* small hall, anteroom

ātrit·ās -ātis *f* blackness

ātrīt·us -a -um *adj* blackened

ātr·ium -(i)ī *n* atrium *(first main room of Roman house)*; hall *(of temple or public building)* ‖ *npl* house; palace

atrōcit·ās -ātis *f* hideousness; fierceness, brutality, cruelty; severity, rigor

artōciter *adv* horribly, fiercely, cruelly, grimly

Atrop·os -ī *f* one of the three Fates

atrōt·us -a -um *adj* invulnerable

atr·ox -ōcis *adj* atrocious, horrible; hideous; frightful; cruel, fierce; harsh, stern, unyielding, grim

attactus *pp of* **attingo**

attact·us -ūs *m* **(adt-)** touch, contact

attag·ēn -ēnis *m* woodcock *(game bird)*

attagēn·a -ae *f* woodcock *(game bird)*

Attalic·us -a -um *adj* of Attalus; Pergamean; rich, splendid; covered with gold brocade ‖ *npl* gold brocade

Attal·us -ī *m* king of Pergamum

attamen *conj* but still, but yet

attat *or* **attatae** *interj see* **atat**

attegi·a -ae *f* hut, cottage

attemperātē *adv* **(adt-)** on time, at the right time

attempt·ō -āre -āvī -ātus *tr* **(adt-)** to attempt; to test; to tempt, try to seduce; to call into question; to attack

atten·dō -dĕre -dī -tus *tr* **(adt-)** to notice, mark; to pay attention to, mind, consider; **animo attendere** to listen to; **animum attendere** to pay attention; **aures attendere** to listen closely ‖ *intr* to pay attention, listen

attentē *adv* **(adt-)** attentively

attenti·ō -ōnis *f* attention

attentō *see* **attemptō**

attent·us -a -um *pp of* **attendo** ‖ *adj* attentive; careful; frugal; industrious

attenuātē *adv* plainly, in a plain style

attenuāt·us -a -um *adj* weak, weakened; shortened, brief; over-refined, affected; plain, bald *(style)*

attenu·ō -āre -āvī -ātus *tr* **(adt-)** to weaken; to thin; to lessen, diminish; to impoverish ‖ *pass* to become thinner, shrink

at·terō -terĕre -trīvī -trītus *tr* **(adt-)** to rub (against), wear away, wear out; to reduce in dimensions, diminish; to impair *(faculties, qualities)*; to reduce *(military forces)*; to weaken, exhaust; to waste, fritter away; destroy

attest·or -ārī -ātus sum *tr* **(adt-)** to attest
attex·ō -ĕre -uī -tus *tr* **(adt-)** to add *(by weaving);* to add on
Atth·is -idis *f* Attica
Attic·a -ae *f* district of Greece, with Athens as its capital
Atticē *adv* in the Athenian style
Atticiss·ō -āre *tr & intr* to speak in the Athenian (Attic) manner
Attic·us -a -um *adj* Attic, Athenian **ǁ** *m* Titus Pomponius Atticus *(friend of Cicero, 109–32 B.C.)* **ǁ** *f* daughter of Atticus
attigō *see* **attingo**
at·tineō -tinēre -tinuī -tentus *tr* **(adt-)** to hold tight, hold on to, hold back; to reach for **ǁ** *intr (w.* **ad)** to pertain to, relate to, refer to, concern; **quod ad me attinet** as far as I am concerned
at·tingō -tingĕre -tigī -tactus *tr* **(adt-)** to touch, come in contact with; to reach, arrive at; to touch *(food),* taste; to touch, lie near, border; to touch upon, mention lightly; to touch, strike, attack; to touch, affect; to undertake, engage in; to take in hand, manage; to resemble; to concern, belong to
Att·is -idis *m* priest of Cybele
attoll·ō -ĕre *tr* **(adt-)** to lift up, raise; to erect; to stir up *(dust, sea);* to cause *(river)* to rise; to hold aloft, carry; to exalt; to uplift; **iras atollere** to rouse anger **ǁ** *refl & pass* to rise; to appear; to grow
atton·deō -dēre -dī -sus *tr* **(adt-)** to clip, shave, shear; to prune; to crop; *(fig)* to fleece, cheat, clip
attonit·us -a -um *adj* **(adt-)** thunderstruck, stunned, dazed, astonished; inspired; frantic, frenzied
atton·ō -āre -uī -itus *tr* **(adt-)** to strike with lightning; to drive crazy
attorqu·eō -ēre *tr* **(adt-)** to wind up *(before hurling)*
attra·hō -hĕre -xī -ctus *tr* **(adt-)** to attract; to drag in; to cause to happen, bring on; to draw toward oneself; to bend *(a bow);* to draw up *(the feet);* to contract, draw together
attrect·ō -āre -āvī -ātus *tr* **(adt-)** to touch, handle; to appropriate to oneself
attrepid·ō -āre *intr* **(adt-)** to hobble along
attrib·uō -uĕre -uī -ūtus *tr* **(adt-)** to allot, assign; to appoint *(to a post);* to put under the command of; to attribute; to bestow, give; to impose *(taxes)*
attribūti·ō -ōnis *f* **(adt-)** *(gram)* predicate; *(leg)* transference of a debt *(to another person, obligating him)*
attribūt·um -ī *n* **(adt-)** *(gram)* predicate
attrīt·us -a -um *pp of* **attero ǁ** *adj* worn away, wasted; thin; hardened
au *interj* ouch!
au·ceps -cupis *m* fowler, bird trapper; poulterer; spy, eavesdropper
auctār·ium -(i)ī *n* addition, overweight *(in a purchase)*
auctific·us -a -um *adj* increasing
aucti·ō -ōnis *f* increase; auction
auctiōnāri·us -a -um *adj* auction-
auctiōn·or -ārī -ātus sum *intr* to hold an auction
auctit·ō -āre *tr* to keep increasing
auct·ō -āre *tr* to increase; *(w. abl)* to bless with
auctor -ōris *m* originator, author; writer, historian; reporter, harbinger *(of news);* acknowledged expert, authority *(for statment or theory)*; proposer *(of a law);* supporter, backer; vendor, seller; progenitor *(of a clan, family, race);* founder *(of city);* model, example; adviser, counselor; teacher; guarantor, security; leader, statesman; source, thrower, dealer *(of missile, wound, death);* **auctor esse** *(w.* **ut, ne** + *subj)* to advocate, advise; to move that, propose that; **faenoris auctor** lender; **me auctore** on my initiative; **pecuniae auctor** person responsible for or owing a sum of money; **rerum omnium auctor parensque** the Creator *(literally, the author and parent of all things);* **sine auctore** anonymous
auctōrāment·um -ī *n* contract; pay
auctōrit·ās -ātis *f* origination, source, cause; view, opinion, judgment; advice, encouragement; power, authority, weight, influence, prestige; leadership; importance, significance, worth, consequence; example, model, precedent; authority *(for establishing a fact);* document, record; decree *(of senate);* right of ownership, title
auctōr·ō -āre -āvī -ātus or **auctōr·or ārī** *tr* to hire out, sell **ǁ** *refl & pass* to hire oneself out
auct·us -a -um *pp of* **augeo ǁ** *adj* blessed *(with children, good omens)*
auct·us -ūs *m* increase, growth; abundance, prosperity
aucup·ium -(i)ī *n* fowling; trap; eavesdropping; **aucupia verborum** quibbling
aucup·ō -āre -āvī -ātus *or* **aucup·or -ārī -ātus sum** *tr* to lie in wait for, watch for; to chase, strive after, catch **ǁ** *intr* to trap birds
audāci·a -ae *f* boldness, courage, daring; recklessness, effrontery, audacity; bold deed **ǁ** *fpl* adventures
audāc(i)ter *adv* boldly
aud·ax -ācis *adj* bold, daring; reckless
aud·ens -entis *adj* bold, daring
audenti·a -ae *f* boldness, daring
audeō audēre ausus sum *tr* to dare, risk; **vix ausim** *(old perf subj active)* **credere**

I could scarcely dare to believe ‖ *intr* to dare, be bold

audi·ens -entis *m* hearer, listener ‖ *mpl* audience

audienti·a -ae *f* hearing, attention; **audientiam facere** to command attention, command silence

aud·iō -īre -īvī *or* **-iī -ītus** *tr* to hear, listen to; to be taught by, learn from; to grant; to accept, agree with, yield to; to obey; to be called, be named; to be reported, be regarded

audīti·ō -ōnis *f* hearsay, rumor

audīt·ō -āre -āvī *tr* to hear

audīt·or -ōris *m* hearer; student

audītōr·ium -(i)ī *n* lecture hall; the audience

audīt·us -ūs *m* hearing, sense of hearing; hearsay

auferō auferre abstulī ablātus *tr* to take away, bear off; to remove, withdraw; to steal; to sweep away, kill, destroy; to gain, obtain; to learn, understand; to mislead; to lead into a digression; to abduct; to captivate; **pedes auferre** to go away ‖ *pass* **e conspectu auferri** to disappear from sight ‖ *refl* to go away

Aufid·us -ī *m* river in Apulia

au·fugiō -fugĕre -fūgī *tr* to shun, flee from ‖ *intr* to run away, escape

Aug·ē -ēs *f* mother of Telephus by Hercules

Augē·ās -ae *m* king of Elis, whose stables were cleaned by Hercules

au·geō -gēre -xī -ctus *tr* to increase, enlarge, augment, spread; to magnify; to exalt; to exaggerate; to emphasize; to enrich; to honor, advance, promote; to reinforce; to feed *(flame);* to raise *(voice);* to endow

augesc·ō -ĕre *intr* to begin to grow; to become larger, increase; to prosper; *(of river)* to rise

aug·ur -uris *mf* augur *(priest who foretold future by observing birds);* seer

augurācul·um -ī *n* place of augury *(later known as the* **arx**)

augurāl·is -is -e *adj* augural, augur's ‖ *n* area in a Roman camp where the general took the auguries

augurāti·ō -ōnis *f* prophesying

augurātō *adv* after taking the auguries

augurāt·us -ūs *m* office of augur

augurāt·us -a -um *adj* consecrated after taking the auspices

augur·ium -(i)ī *n* observation of omens, interpretation of omens, augury; sign, omen; prophecy; foreboding

auguri·us -a -um *adj* of augurs; **ius augurium** the right to take auguries

augur·ō -āre -āvī -ātus *or* **augur·or -ārī -ātus sum** *tr* to consult by augury; to consecrate by augury; to predict, prophesy; to conjecture, imagine ‖ *intr* to act as augur; to take auspices

August·a -ae *f* title of wife, mother, grandmother, daughter, or sister of the emperor

Augustāl·is -is -e *adj* of Augustus; **sodales Augustales** priests of deified Augustus ‖ *npl* games in honor of Augustus

Augustān·us -a -um *adj* Augustan

augustē *adv* reverently, solemnly

Augustiān·ī -ōrum *mpl* Nero's claque in the theater

Augustīn·us -a -um *adj* of Augustus

august·us -a -um *adj* august, sacred, venerable; majestic

August·us -a -um *adj* Augustan, imperial; **mensis Augustus** August ‖ *m* honorary cognomen of Octavius Caesar after 27 B.C. and of subsequent emperors

aul·a -ae *f* inner court, hall *(of house);* palace; royal court; people of the royal court, the court

aulae·um -ī *n* curtain ‖ *npl* curtain, tapestries

aulic·us -a -um *adj* courtly, princely ‖ *m* courtier

Aul·is -is *or* **-idis** *f* port in Boeotia from which Greeks sailed for Troy

auloed·us -ī *m* singer accompanied by reed pipe

aur·a -ae *f* breeze; breath of air, wind; air, atmosphere; heights, heaven; upper world; odor, exhalation; daylight, publicity; **ad auras ferre** to make known, publicize; **ad auras venire** to come to the upper world; **aura auri** the gleam of gold; **auram captare** to sniff the air; **aura popularis** popular favor; **auras fugere** to hide; **aura spei** breath of hope; **sub auras** to light, into the air; into the open air

aurāri·us -a -um *adj* gold, golden ‖ *f* gold mine

aurāt·us -a -um *adj* made of gold; gold-plated; golden; glittering; **aurata pellis** the Golden Fleece

Aureli·us -a -um *adj* Roman clan name *(nomen), esp.* Marcus Aurelius *(Roman Emperor* A.D. *161–180)* ‖ named after an Aurelius, *esp.* Via Aurelia *(running along the Etruscan coast to the Maritime Alps)*

aureol·us -a -um *adj* gold; splendid

aure·us -a -um *adj* gold, golden; gilded, gilt; beautiful, magnificent; brilliant ‖ *m* gold coin

auricom·us -a -um *adj* golden-haired; with golden foliage

auricul·a -ae *f* **(ōr-)** ear; *(leg)* **auriculam tangere** to agree to be a witness

aurif·er -era -erum *adj* producing *or* containing gold; *(of trees)* bearing golden apples

aurif·ex -icis *m* **(auru-)** goldsmith

aurīg·a -ae *mf* (ōr-) charioteer; *(fig)* pilot ‖ **Auriga** *m* Auriga *(constellation)*
aurīgāti·ō -ōnis *f* chariot-driving
aurigen·a -ae *m* offspring of gold *(i.e., Perseus)*
aurig·er -era -erum *adj* gold-bearing; gilded
aurīg·ō -āre -āvī -ātum *intr* to drive a chariot; to compete in a chariot race
aur·is -is *f* ear; **aurem admovere** to listen; **auribus servire** to flatter; **aures adhibere** to pay attention; **in aurem dextram** *(or* **in aurem utramvis) dormire** to sleep soundly, be unconcerned
auriscalp·ium -(i)ī *n (med)* earpick, probe
aurītul·us -ī *m (long-eared)* ass
aurīt·us -a -um *adj* long-eared; attentive; nosey; **testis auritus** witness by hearsay only ‖ *m* rabbit, hare
aurōr·a -ae *f* dawn, daybreak; the East ‖ **Aurora** goddess of dawn
aur·um -ī *n* gold; color of gold, golden luster; gold cup; gold necklace; gold jewelry; gold plate; golden fleece; gold money; Golden Age
Auranc·a -ae *f* town in Campania, birthplace of the poet Lucilius
Auranc·us -a -um *adj* of Arunca ‖ *mpl* people of Arunca
auscultāti·ō -ōnis *f* obedience
auscultāt·or -ōris *m* listener
auscult·ō -āre -āvī -ātus *tr* to listen to; to overhear ‖ *intr* (w. dat) to obey, listen to
ausim *see* **audeo**
Auson·ēs -um *mpl* Ausonians *(ancient inhabitants of central Italy)*
Ausoni·a -ae *f (poet)* Italy
Ausonid·ae -ārum *mpl (poet)* Italians
Ausoni·us -a -um *adj (poet)* Ausonian, Italian ‖ *mpl (poet)* Ausonians, Italians
ausp·ex -icis *mf* augur, soothsayer; *(fig)* guide, director, protector ‖ *mpl* witnesses *(at a marriage ceremony)*
auspicātō *adv* after taking the auspices; auspiciously
auspicāt·us -a -um *adj* consecrated *(by auguries);* auspicious, lucky
auspic·ium -(i)ī *n (often used in the plural)* auspices *(from behavior of birds or chickens);* right to take the auspices; sign, omen; command, leadership, authority; inauguration; **auspicia incerta** ambiguous auspices; **auspicium habere** to have the right to take auspices; **auspicium facere** *(of birds)* to give a sign; **pullarium in auspicium mittere** to send the keeper of chickens to take the auspices; **tuis auspiciis** under your command *(or* leadership)
auspic·ō -āre -āvī *intr* to take the auspices
auspic·or -ārī -ātus sum *tr* to inaugurate, make a ceremonial beginning of; to enter upon ‖ *intr* to take auspices; to make a start
aus·ter -trī *m* south wind; the South
austērē *adv* austerely, severely
austērit·ās -ātis *f* austerity
austēr·us -a -um *adj* austere, stern, harsh *(person);* pungent *(odor);* harsh *(taste);* drab, dark *(color);* serious *(talk);* gloomy, hard *(circumstances);* dry *(wine)*
austrāl·is -is -e *adj* southern; **cingulus** *(or* **regio** *or* **ora) australis** torrid zone
austrīn·us -a -um *adj* southerly, from the south; southern
aus·us -a -um *pp of* **audeo** ‖ *n* daring attempt, enterprise, venture; outrage
aut *conj* or; *(correcting what precedes)* or rather, or else; *(adding emphatic alternative)* or at least; **aut...aut** *(introducing two or more logically exclusive alternatives)* either...or; **unus aut alter** one or two
autem *conj (regularly follows an emphatic word)* but, on the other hand, however; *(in transitions)* now
autheps·a -ae *f* cooker *(utensil)*
autograph·us -a -um *adj* written with one's own hand, autograph
Autolyc·us -ī *m* father of Anticlea, maternal grandfather of Ulysses
automat·on *or* **automat·um -ī** *n* automaton
automat·us -a -um *adj* automatic, spontaneous, voluntary
Automed·ōn -ontis *m* charioteer of Achilles ‖ a charioteer
Autono·ē -ēs *f* daughter of Cadmus, wife of Aristaeus, and mother of Actaeon
autumnāl·is -is -e *adj* autumn-, fall-
autumn·us -a -um *adj & m* autumn
autum·ō -āre -āvī -ātus *tr* to assert, say
auxiliār·is -is -e *adj* auxiliary ‖ *mpl* auxiliary troops, auxiliaries
auxiliāri·us -a -um *adj* auxiliary
auxiliāt·or -ōris *m* helper
auxiliāt·us -ūs *m* help, aid
auxili·or -ārī -ātus sum *intr (w. dat)* **1** to give help to; **2** *(of things)* to be helpful to, be of use to; **3** *(med)* to relieve, heal, cure
auxil·ium -(i)ī *n* help; *(med)* relief, remedy; **auxilio esse** *(w. dat)* to be of assistance to ‖ *npl* auxiliary troops; reinforcements
avārē *adv* greedily
avāriter *adv* greedily
avāriti·a -ae *f* avarice, greed; gluttony
avār·us -a -um *adj* greedy, avaricious; *(w. gen)* eagerly desirous of, greedy for
avē! *see* **aveo**
āve·hō -hĕre -xi -ctus *tr* to haul away ‖ *pass* to ride away, sail away
ā·vellō -vellĕre -vellī *(or* **-vulsī** *or* **-volsī) -vulsus** *(or* **-volsus)** *tr* to pull *or* pluck

away; to tear off; to separate, remove ‖ *refl & pass (w.* **ab)** to tear oneself away from, withdraw from

avēn·a -ae *f* oats; reed, stalk, a straw; shepherd's pipe

Aventīn·us -a -um *adj* Aventine ‖ *m & n* Aventine Hill *(one of the Seven Hills of Rome)* ‖ son of Hercules

av·eō -ēre *tr* to desire, long for, crave; *(w. inf)* to long to ‖ *intr* to say good-bye; **ave!, avete!** hello!, farewell!, good-bye!; **avere jubeo** I send greetings

Avernāl·is -is -e *adj* of Lake Avernus

Avern·us -a -um *adj* birdless; of Lake Avernus ‖ *m* Lake Avernus *(near Cumae, reputed entrance to the underworld)*

āverr·ō -ēre -ī *tr* to sweep away

āverrunc·ō -āre *tr* to avert

āversābil·is -is -e *adj* abominable

āvers·or -ārī -ātus sum *tr* **(-vor-)** to repulse, reject, refuse; to shun, avoid; to send away ‖ *intr* to turn away *(in displeasure, shame, contempt)*

āvers·or -ōris *m* embezzler

āvers·us -a -um *pp of* **averto** ‖ *adj* turned back, reversed; rear, in the rear; *(of blows)* coming from the rear; distant, remote; out-of-the-way; disinclined, alienated, unfavorable, hostile; *(w. dat or* **ab)** averse to, hostile to, opposed to, estranged from ‖ *n* the back part, the back; **in aversum** backwards ‖ *npl* the back; hinterland

ā·vertō -vertēre -vertī -versus *tr* **(-vor-)** to turn away, avert; to embezzle, misappropriate; to divert, distract; to alienate ‖ *refl* to retire ‖ *intr* to withdraw, retire

avi·a -ae *f* grandmother; old wives' tale

āvi·a -ōrum *npl* wasteland

aviāri·us -a -um *adj* of birds, bird ‖ *n* aviary; haunt of wild birds

avidē *adv* eagerly, greedily

avidit·ās -ātis *f* eagerness, longing; avarice

avid·us -a -um *adj* eager, earnest; greedy; voracious, gluttonous; *(w. gen or dat or* **in** *acc)* eager for

av·is -is *f* bird; sign, omen; **avis alba** *(or* **rara)** rarity

avīt·us -a -um *adj* grandfather's; ancestral; old

āvi·us -a -um *adj* pathless; out-of-the-way, lonely; untrodden; wandering, straying; going astray

āvocāment·um -ī *n* diversion, recreation

āvocāti·ō -ōnis *f* distraction

āvoc·ō -āre -āvī -ātus *tr* to call away; to divert, remove, withdraw; to amuse; to distract *(attention);* to interrupt *(work)*

āvol·ō -āre -āvī -ātum *intr* to fly away; to dash off

āvulsus *pp of* **avello**

avuncul·us -ī *m* (maternal) uncle; **avunculus magnus** granduncle

av·us -ī *m* grandfather; forefather

-ax -ācis *suf* implying tendency, ability: **capax** ability to hold, **dicax** tendency to talk, **pertinax** tendency to hold on

Axen·us -ī *m* Black Sea

āxill·a -ae *f* armpit

ax·is -is *m* axle; wagon, chariot; the earth's axis; north pole; vault of heaven; region, climate, country; board, plank

B

babae *interj* great!, wonderful!

Babyl·ō -ōnis *m* Babylonian; rich man

Babyl·ōn -ōnis *f* city on the Euphrates River

Babylōni·a -ae *f* country between Tigris and Euphrates

Babylōnic·a -ōrum *npl* Babylonian tapestry

Babylōniēns·is -is -e *adj* Babylonian

Babylōni·us -a -um *adj* Babylonian ‖ *mpl* Babylonians

bāc·a -ae *f* berry; olive; fruit; pearl

bācāt·us -a -um *adj* adorned with pearls; **monile bacatum** pearl necklace

bacc·ar -aris *n* cyclamen *(plant with showy white, pink, or red flowers)*

Bacch·a -ae *f* Bacchante *(female member of the orgiastic cult of Bacchus)*

bacchābund·us -a -um *adj* raving

Bacchān·āl -ālis *n* site sacred to Bacchus ‖ *npl* Bacchanalian orgies

bacchant·ēs -(i)um *fpl* Bacchantes

bacchāti·ō -ōnis *f* orgy, revelry

Bacchē(i)·us, Bacchic·us, Bacchi·us -a -um *adj* Bacchic

bacch·or -ārī -ātus sum *intr* to celebrate the rites of Bacchus; to revel, rage, run wildly about; *(of a place)* to be the scene of Bacchanalian orgies; *(of a rumor)* to run wild

Bacch·us -ī *m* god of wine; *(fig)* vine, wine

baceol·us -a -um *adj (coll)* nutty

bācif·er -era -erum *adj* bearing berries; bearing olives

bacill·um -ī *n* small staff, wand; lictor's staff

Bactr·a -ōrum *npl* Bactra *(capital of Bactria, a province of Parthia)*

Bactriān·us -a -um *adj* Bactrian ‖ *mpl* Bactrians

Bactri·us -a -um *adj* Bactrian

bacul·um -ī *n or* **bacul·us -ī** *m* a cane; (lictor's) staff; scepter

badiz·ō -āre *intr* to go, walk

Baeticāt·us -a -um *adj* dressed in clothes of Baetican wool

Baetic·us -a -um *adj* of the Baetis river ‖ *mpl* the people of Baetica ‖ *f* Baetica *(Roman province in S. Spain)*

Baet·is -is *m* river in Spain *(modern Guadalquivir)*
Baeturi·a -ae *f* part of the province of Baetica
Bagō·ās -ae *m* eunuch *(used to guard women's quarters)*
Bagrad·a -ae *m* river in N. Africa
Bāi·ae -ārum *fpl* resort town at N. end of Bay of Naples ‖ villa at Baiae
Bāi·ānus -a -um *adj* of Baiae
bājul·ō -āre *tr* to carry, bear
bājul·us -ī *m* porter
bālaen·a *or* **ballaen·a -ae** *f* **(balēn-)** whale
balanāt·us -a -um *adj* anointed with balsam; embalmed
balan·us -ī *mf* acorn; date; balsam; type of shell-fish
balatr·ō -ōnis *m* jester, buffoon
bālāt·us -ūs *m* bleating
balb·us -a -um *adj* stammering, lisping ‖ **Balbus** *m* Roman family name, cognomen, *esp.* Lucius Cornelius Balbus, a supporter of Caesar, defended by Cicero in 56 B.C.
balbūt·iō *or* **balbutt·iō -īre** *tr & intr* to stammer, stutter; to babble
Baliāric·us -a -um *adj* Balearic
Baliār·is -is -e *adj* **(Bale-)** Balearic; **Baliares insulae** Balearic Islands *(Majorca and Minorca)*
baline·um -ī *n* bath
ballēna *see* **balaena**
Balli·ō -ōnis *m* actor playing the worthless fellow; worthless fellow
ballist·a -ae *f* **(bālis-)** artillery piece *(for hurling stones and other missiles)*
ballistār·ium -iī *n* artillery emplacement
balne·ae -ārum *fpl* **(balin-)** baths
balneāri·us -a -um *adj* **(balin-)** of a bath ‖ *npl* baths
balneāt·or -ōris *m* **(balin-)** bath superintendent
balneol·ae -ārum *fpl* baths
balneol·um -ī *n* small bath
balne·um -ī *n* **(balin-)** *(pl also:* **balne·ae -ārum)** bathroom; public baths; bathing, taking a bath
bāl·ō -āre -āvī -ātum *intr* to bleat
balsam·um -ī *n* balsam tree ‖ *npl* balsam *(used as perfume)*
balte·us -ī *m or* **balte·um -ī** *n* belt; shoulder-strap; woman's belt
bal·ux -ūcis *f* gold dust
Bandusi·a -ae *f* pleasant fountain on Horace's Sabine farm
Bantīn·us -a -um *adj* of the town of Bantia in Apulia
baptistēr·ium -iī *n* bath
barāthr·um -ī *n* abyss, chasm, pit; lower world
barb·a -ae *f* beard *(of man or animals);* **barbam demittere** to grow a beard; **barbam vellere** to tuck on the beard *(as a sign of insult)*
barbar·a -ae *f* foreign woman
barbarē *adv* in a foreign langue; savagely; *(of diction, etc.)* rudely
barbari·a -ae *or* **barbari·ēs -ēī** *f* foreign country; strange land; rudeness, lack of culture; barbarity, brutality
barbaric·us -a -um *adj* barbarian; barbaric; foreign, outlandish
barbariēs *see* **barbaria**
barbarism·us -ī *m* barbarism *(error in pronunciation or expression)*
barbar·us -a -um *adj* foreign; barbarous ‖ *mf* foreigner; barbarian ‖ *n* barbarism
barbātul·us -a -um *adj* wearing a short beard
barbāt·us -a -um *adj* bearded; adult; old-time ‖ *m* old-timer
barbig·er -era -erum *adj* bearded
barbit·os -ī *m (f)* lyre
barbul·a -ae *f* short beard
Barc·a -ae *m* name of Carthaginian family to which Hamilcar, Hannibal, and Hasdrubal belonged
Barcae·ī -ōrum *mpl* the people of Barce *(city of Cyrenaica)*
barcal·a -ae *m* simpleton
Barcīn·us -a -um *adj* of the Barca family, Barcan
bard·us -a -um *adj* stupid, dull
bār·is -idos *f* flat-bottomed boat
Bār·ium -(i)ī *n* coastal town in Apulia *(modern Bari)*
bār·ō -ōnis *m* dunce, blockhead
barrīt·us -ūs *m* trumpeting *(of elephants);* war cry
barr·us -ī *m* elephant
bascaud·a -ae *f* basin *(of British origin)*
bāsiāti·ō -ōnis *f* kissing; kiss
bāsiāt·or -ōris *m* one who kisses
basilic·a -ae *f* basilica, courthouse
basilicē *adv* royally
basilic·us -a -um *adj* royal; splendid
bāsi·ō -āre -āvī -ātus *tr* to kiss
bāsiol·um -ī *n* little kiss, peck
bas·is -is *f* base, support; pedestal; base *(of a triangle)*
bās·ium -(i)ī *n* kiss
Bassar·eūs -eī *m* Bacchus
Bassaric·us -a -um *adj* of Bacchus
Bassar·is -idos *f* Bacchante
Bastarn·ae -ārum *mpl* **(Bat-)** Germanic tribe close to the mouth of the Danube
Batāv·us -a -um *adj* of the Batavi, Batavian ‖ *mpl* people of Lower Germany
batioc·a -ae *f* drinking cup
Bat·ō -ōnis *m* Illyrian rebel leader
bā(t)tu·ō -āre *tr* to beat, pound; *(vulg)* to screw ‖ *intr* to fence
Batt·us -ī *m* legendary founder of Cyrene
Battiad·ēs -ae *m* inhabitant of Cyrene
Bauc·is -idis *f* wife of Philemon

Baul·ī -ōrum *mpl* town between Baiae and Misenum
baxe·a -ae *f* kind of sandal
beātē *adv* happily **||** *interj* great!; bravo!
beātit·ās -ātis *f* happiness
beātitūd·ō -inis *f* happiness
beātul·us -a -um *adj (of a deceased person)* of blessed memory
beāt·us -a -um *adj* happy; prosperous; fertile; abundant; wealthy, rich; sumptuous **||** *n* happiness
Bebryci·a -ae *f* territory of the Bébryces in Asia Minor
Bebryci·us -a -um *adj* of Bebrycia *or* of the Bebryces
Bedriac·um -ī *n* **(Betr-)** village between Mantua and Cremona
Belg·ae -ārum *mpl* inhabitants of N. Gaul
Belgic·us -a -um *adj* of the Belgae; **Gallia Belgica** N. part of the province of Gallia Comata, occupied by the Belgae
Belg·ium -iī *n* country of the Belgae
Bēlīd·ēs -ae *m* descendant of Belus
Bēlīd·ēs -um *fpl* Danaids *(descendants of Belus)*
bellāri·a -ōrum *npl* sweets, dessert
bellāt·or -ōris *adj (masc only)* warlike; **bellator equus** war horse **||** *m* warrior, fighter
bellātōri·us -a -um *adj* warlike
bellātr·ix -īcis *f* warrior *(female)*
bellē *adv* prettily, nicely, well; **belle esse** to have a nice time; **belle est** all is well *(of health)*; **se belle habere** to be in good health
Belleroph·ōn -ontis *or* **Bellerophont·ēs -ae** *m* slayer of Chimera and rider of Pegasus
Bellerophontē·us -a -um *adj* of Bellerophon
belliātul·us -a -um *adj* pretty little
belliāt·us -a -um *adj* pretty
bellicōs·us -a -um *adj* warlike
bellic·us -a -um *adj* war-, military; warlike, fierce **||** *n* bugle; bugle call
bellig·er -era -erum *adj* warring; war-
belliger·ō -āre -āvī -ātum *or* **belliger·or -ārī -ātus sum** *intr* to fight a war, be at war, fight
bellipot·ens -entis *adj* mighty *or* valiant in war**||** *m* Mars
bell·ō -āre -āvī -ātum *or* **bell·or -ārī -ātus sum** *intr* to wage war, be at war; to fight
Bellōn·a -ae *f* **(Duell-)** goddess of war
bellul·us -a -um *adj* pretty, cute
bell·um -ī *n* **(duell-)** war; warfare
bell·us -a -um *adj* pretty; fine, nice
bēlu·a -ae *f* beast, brute, monster
bēluāt·us -a -um *adj* embroidered with figures of beasts
bēluōs·us -a -um *adj* full of monsters
Bēl·us -ī *m* Baal **||** king of Tyre and father of Dido **||** king of Egypt, father of Danaüs and Aegyptus
Bēnāc·us -ī *m* lake near Verona *(modern Lago di Garda)*
bene *adv* well; thoroughly, very, quite; elegantly; **bene ambula!** bon voyage!; **bene audire** to be well spoken of; **bene dicite!** hush!; **bene emere** to buy at a bargain; **bene esse** *(w. dat)* to be well with, to be doing all right; **bene est** it's O.K.; **bene ferre** to put up with in good spirits; **bene sum** *or* **mihi bene est** I am content; **se bene habere** to be happy, be content; to do well; **bene sentire de** (+ *abl)* to have sound views about; **bene sperare** to be optimistic; **bene vendere** to sell at a good price **||** *interj (w. acc or dat) (in drinking to health)* here's to you!
benedicē *adv* with friendly words
benedī·cō -cĕre -xi -ctus *intr (w. dat)* to speak well of, praise; *(eccl)* to bless
bene·faciō -facĕre -fēcī -factus *tr* to do *(s.o.)* a service, confer a benefit on; **multa erga** (+ *acc)* **benefacere** to do many kindnesses to
beneficenti·a -ae *f* beneficence, kindness
beneficiāri·ī -ōrum *mpl* soldiers exempt from menial tasks
benefic·ium -(i)ī *n* **(benif-)** kindness, favor, benefit, service; help, support; promotion; right, privilege; **beneficio** *(w. gen)* thanks to; **beneficium accipere et reddere** to receive and return a favor
benefic·us -a -um *adj* generous, liberal, obliging
Benevent·um -ī *n* town in Samnium in S. Italy *(modern Benevento)*
benevolē *adv* **(beniv-)** kindly
benevol·ens -entis *adj* **(beniv-)** kindhearted, benevolent, obliging
benevolenti·a -ae *f* **(beniv-)** benevolence, kindness, goodwill; favor
benevol·us -a -um *adj* **(beniv-)** kind, benevolent **||** *m* well-wisher
benignē *adv* kindly, courteously; mildly; generously, liberally
benignit·ās -ātis *f* kindness, friendliness, courtesy; generosity
benign·us -a -um *adj* kind-hearted; mild; liberal; favorable; bounteous
be·ō -āre -āvī -ātus *tr* to make happy; to bless; to enrich; to refresh
Berecynt(h)i·us -a -um *adj* Berecyntian; epithet of Cybele
Berecynt·us -ī *m* mountain in Phrygia sacred to Cybele
Berenīc·ē -ēs *f* female name, *esp.* the daughter of the Jewish King Agrippa I; **crinis Berenices** "hair of Berenice" *(constellation, named after the wife of Ptolemy Euergetes)*
bēryll·us -ī *m* beryl *(precious stone)*

bēs be(s)sis *m* two thirds; **bes alter** one and two thirds; **faenus bessibus** interest at ⅔% per month *or* 8% per year
bēsāl·is -is -e *adj* comprising two-thirds
Bess·ī -ōrum *mpl* a people of Thrace
Bessic·us -a -um *adj* of the Bessi
besti·a -ae *f* beast, wild beast
bestiāri·us -a -um *adj* of wild beasts **ll** *m* wild-beast fighter
bestiol·a -ae *f* insect
bēt·a -ae *f* beet
bēta *indecl n* beta *(second letter of the Greek alphabet)*
bētāce·us -a -um *adj* of a beet
bētiz·ō -āre *intr* to be languid
bi- *pref* consisting of, having, measuring two of the things named, *e.g.:* **bimar·is -is -e** of *or* connected with two seas
bibliopōl·a -ae *m* bookseller
bibliothēc·a -ae *f* library
bibliothēcār·ius -iī *m* librarian
bib·ō -ĕre -ī *tr* to drink; to visit, live near *(river); (fig)* to take in, absorb **ll** *intr* to drink; to guzzle
bibul·us -a -um *adj* fond of drinking; absorbent; thirsty; *(of ears)* eager to hear
bi·ceps -cipitis *adj* two-headed; twin-peaked
biclīn·ium -(i)ī *n* table for two
bicol·or -ōris *adj* two-colored, of two colors
bicorn·is -is -e *adj* two-horned; two-pronged
bicorp·or -oris *adj* double-bodied
bid·ens -entis *adj* with two teeth; with two points; two-pronged **ll** *m* hoe, mattock; sacrificial animal; sheep
bident·al -ālis *n* place struck by lightning
Bidīn·us -a -um *adj* of Bidis *(town in Sicily)*
bīdu·um -ī *n* two-day period; two days
bienn·ium -(i)ī *n* two-year period; two years; **in** *(or* **per)** **biennium** for two years
bifāriam *adv* on both sides, twofold; in two parts; in two ways; in two directions
bifāri·us -a -um *adj* double, twofold
bif·er -era -erum *adj* bearing (fruit *or* flowers) twice (a year)
bifid·us -a -um *adj* split in two, forked, cloven
bifor·is -is -e *adj* having two doors; having two holes *or* openings; *(of sound)* double, coming from double pipes
biformāt·us -a -um *adj* double, having two forms
beform·is -is -e *adj* double, having two forms
bifr·ons -ontis *adj* two-faced
bifurc·us -a -um *adj* two-pronged **ll** *n* crotch
bīg·ae -ārum *fpl* two-horse chariot; team of horses
bīgāt·us -a -um *adj (of a coin)* stamped with the image of a two-horse chariot
bijug·is -is -e *or* **bijug·us -a -um** *adj* two-horse
Bilbil·is -is *f* town in Hispania Tarraconensis, birthplace of Martial
bilībr·is -is -e *adj* two-pound
bilingu·is -is -e *adj* two-tongued; bilingual; deceitful, two-faced
bīl·is -is *f* bile; wrath; **bilis atra** melancholy; insanity; **bilem movere** *(w. dat)* to get *(s.o.)* angry
-bil·is -is -e *adj/ suf* denoting ability, *e.g.:* **terribilis** able to frighten
bil·ix -īcis *adj* with a double thread
bilustr·is -is -e *adj* lasting for two lustra *(i.e., ten years)*
bimar·is -is -e *adj* situated between two seas
bimarīt·us -ī *m* bigamist
bimāt·er -ris *adj* having two mothers, twice-born *(Bacchus)*
bimembr·is -is -e *adj* half-man, half-beast **ll** *m* centaur
bime(n)str·is -is -e *adj* two-month-old; lasting two months
bīmul·us -a -um *adj* two-year-old
bīm·us -a -um *adj* two-year-old; lasting two years
bīn·ī -ae -a *adj* two by two, two each; two at a time; two *(per day, year, etc.);* a set of, a pair of; double, twofold; **inter bina castra** between the two camps
binoct·ium -(i)ī *n* period of two nights
binōmin·is -is -e *adj* having two names
Bi·ōn -ōnis *f* Greek philosopher, noted for his sharp sayings
Biōnē·us -a -um *adj* typical of Bion, satirical
bipalm·is -is -e *adj* two palms long *or* broad
bipartītō *adv see* **bipertito**
bipat·ens -entis *adj* opening in two directions
bipedāl·is -is -e *adj* two-foot (long, broad, *or* high)
bipennif·er -era -erum *adj* wielding a two-edged ax
bipenn·is -is -e *adj* two-edged **ll** *f* two-edged ax
bipertītō *adv* **(-part-)** in two parts; **bipertito esse** to be divided
bipertīt·us -a -um *adj* **(-part-)** divided into two parts, bipartite
bip·ēs -edis *adj* two-footed, biped
birēm·is -is -e *adj* two-oared; with two banks of oars **ll** *f* ship with two banks of oars
bis *adv* twice; doubly
Bīsalt·ae -ārum *mpl* a people of Macedonia
Bīsalt·is -is *f* Theophane, daughter of Bisaltes

Biston·es -um *mpl* fierce tribesmen in Thessaly
bisulc·us -a -um *adj* split; forked
Bīthȳni·a -ae *f* a district, later a Roman province, on the N.W. coast of Asia Minor
Bīthȳnic·us -a -um *or* **Bīthȳn·us -a -um** *adj* Bithynian
bīt·ō -ĕre *intr* to go
bitūm·en -inis *n* asphalt, pitch
bivi·us -a -um *adj* two-way ‖ *n* crossroads, intersection
blaes·us -a -um *adj* lisping; slurring
blandē *adv* flatteringly; coaxingly, seductively, charmingly
blandidic·us -a -um *adj* smooth-spoken, using flattering words
blandiloquentul·us -a -um *or* **blandiloqu·us -a -um** *adj* smooth, smooth-tongued
blandīment·um -ī *n* flattery, compliment; charm
blandi·or -īrī -ītus sum *intr* (*w. dat*) **1** to flatter; **2** to coax; **3** to allure; **4** to charm, please; **5** *(of dogs)* to fawn on; *(w.* **ut** + *subj)* to coax, persuade with blandishments to ‖ *refl (w. dat)* to delude oneself
blanditer *adv* flatteringly
blanditi·a -ae *or* **blanditi·ēs -ēī** *f* flattery, compliment; charm
bland·us -a -um *adj* smooth; flattering; fawning; alluring, charming, winsome, pleasant
blater·ō -āre -āvī -ātus *tr* to utter *(in a babbling way)* ‖ *intr* to babble
blatt·a -ae *f* cockroach; *(insect)* bookworm; clothes-moth
blenn·us -ī *m (coll)* idiot, blockhead
blite·us -a -um *adj* silly; tasteless ‖ *n* worthless stuff, trash
blit·um -ī *n* tasteless vegetable *(kind of spinach)*
boāri·us -a -um *adj* **(bov-)** cattle-
Boc(c)h·us -ī *m* king of Mauretania, who betrayed Jugurtha to the Romans ‖ king of Mauretania in the time of Julius Caesar
Boeb·ē -ēs *f* lake in Thessaly
Boeōti·a -ae *f* district N. of Attica
Boeōti·us -a -um *or* **Boeōt·us -a -um** *adj* Boeotian ‖ *mpl* Boeotians
Boi·ī -ōrum *mpl* Celtic people who migrated from Gaul into N. Italy
bōj·a -ae *f* collar worn by criminals
bōlēt·us -ī *m* mushroom
bol·us -ī *m* throw *(of the dice)*; cast *(of the net)*; *(fig)* haul, piece of good luck, gain; choice morsel
bombax *interj* strange!; indeed!
bomb·us -ī *m* booming; buzzing, humming
bombȳcin·us -a -um *adj* silk, silken
bomb·ȳx -ȳcis *m* silkworm; silk; silk garment
Bon·a De·a -ae *f* Roman goddess of chastity and fertility, worshipped by women
bonit·ās -ātis *f* goodness, integrity, good behavior; excellence, high quality *(of things)*
Bonn·a -ae *f* city in Lower Germany *(modern Bonn)*
Bonōni·a -ae *f* city of Cisalpine Gaul *(modern Bologna)*
Bonōniens·is -is -e *adj* of Bologna
bon·us -a -um *adj* good; *(morally)* good; cheerful *(face)*; sound, valid, well-founded *(arguments)*; pretty, shapely; *(w. dat)* good for; *(w.* **ad***)* good at; *(w. dat or* **ad***)* good, kind towards; **bona aetas** prime of life; **bonae artes** liberal arts, liberal education; **bonae rei esse** to be wealthy; **bonae res** good things, desirable things; wealth; **bonae vires** full strength; **bona forma** good appearance; **bone vir!** sir!; my good fellow!; **bono animo esse** *(or* **bonum animum habere***)* to be of good cheer, be in a good mood; to be well-disposed; **bono modo** in moderation; **bono periculo** with little risk; **bonum est** *(w. inf)* it is good to; **bonus a tempestatibus** free from storms, fine; **bonus stomachus** good humor; **cum bona pace** *(w. gen)* with the full consent of; **(cum) bonā veniā tuā** with your kind permission; **viri boni** decent citizens; *(pol)* conservatives ‖ *mpl* decent people; brave men; *(pol)* conservatives ‖ *n* good thing, good; **bono esse alicui** to be good for s.o., be profitable to s.o.; **cui bono?** for whose benefit? ‖ *npl* goods, property
bo·ō -āre *or* **-ĕre** *intr* to bawl; to bellow, roar
Boōt·ēs -ae *m* Boötes *(constellation)*
bore·ās -ae *m* north wind; the North ‖ **Boreās** god of the north wind
borē·us -a -um *adj* north, northern
Borysthen·ēs -is *m* Scythian river *(modern Dnieper)*
bōs bovis *m (gen pl:* **boum** *or* **bovum;** *dat & abl pl:* **bōbus** *or* **būbus***)* ox, bull ‖ *mpl* cattle ‖ *f* cow
Bosp(h)or·us *or* **Bosp(h)or·os -ī** *m* strait between Thrace and Asia Minor, connecting Propontis and Black Sea
botell·us -ī *m* small sausage
botul·us -ī *m* a black pudding
bovīl·e -is *n* ox stall, cow stable
Bovill·ae -ārum *fpl* town in Latium on the Appian Way, about 12 miles S. of Rome
bovill·us -a -um *adj* cattle-
brabeut·a -ae *m* umpire
brāc·ae -ārum *fpl* pants, trousers
brācāt·us -a -um *adj* wearing trousers; foreign, barbarian; effeminate
brā(c)chiāl·is -is -e *adj* of the arm

brā(c)chiol·um -ī *n* dainty arm
brā(c)ch·ium -(i)ī *n* arm, lower arm; claw; branch; tendril; arm of the sea; *(naut)* yardarm
brācil·is -is -e *adj (esp. of a tunic)* to be worn with trousers
bracte·a -ae *f* **(bratt-)** gold leaf; gold foil
bracteol·a -ae *f* **(bratt-)** very thin gold leaf
brassic·a -ae *f* cabbage
bratt- = bract-
Brenn·us -ī *m* Celtic chieftain who captured Rome about 390 B.C. ‖ Galatian chieftain who invaded Greece in 279 B.C.
brevī *adv* briefly, in a few words; shortly, in a short time; **brevi ante (post)** shortly before (afterwards)
breviār·ium -(i)ī *n* abridgment, summary
brevicul·us -a -um *adj* rather short
breviloqu·ens -entis *adj* concise, of few words
breviloquenti·a -ae *f* conciseness
brevi·ō -āre -āvī -ātus *tr* to shorten; to abbreviate; to pronounce *(a syllable)* short
brev·is -is -e *adj* short, little; low; stunted *(trees); (of depth)* shallow; brief; transient; short-lived; compressed, concise *(style);* small *(amounts, weights);* modest, simple; small, narrow, confined *(space);* **ad** *(or* **in) breve tempus** for (only) a short time ‖ *f (gram)* short syllable ‖ *n* a short space of time; **ad** *(or* **in) breve** for (only) a short time; **brevi** in a few words, briefly; in a short time, soon; for (only) a short time; after a lapse of a short space of time; **brevi ante** shortly before; **brevi post** shortly after; **in brevi** in a few words, briefly ‖ *npl* shallow water, shallows
brevit·ās -ātis *f* brevity; smallness; shortness; stunted size *(of trees);* short period of time; shortness of life; *(pros)* short quantity; *(rhet)* conciseness, terseness
breviter *adv* for (only) a short time; within a short space of time, quickly; in (only) a few words, briefly; to (only) a short distance; *(pros)* short
Brigant·es -um *mpl* a people of N. Britannia
Brīsē·is -idos *f (acc:* **Brīsēida)** slave and concubine of Achilles
Britann·ī -ōrum *mpl* Britons
Britanni·a -ae *f* **(Britt-)** Britain
Britannic·us -a -um *adj* British ‖ *m* name taken by Germanicus, son of Claudius and Messalina
Britann·us -a -um *adj* British
Brit(t)·ō -ōnis *m* Briton
Brixi·a -ae *f* town in Cisalpine Gaul *(modern Brescia)*
brocch·us -a -um *adj* buck-toothed
Brom·ius -(i)ī *m* Bacchus
Bront·ēs -ae *m* Brontes *(a Cyclops)*
brūm·a -ae *f* winter solstice, shortest day; (dead of) winter; winter's cold
brūmāl·is -is -e *adj* wintry
Brundis·ium -(i)ī *n* port in S.E. Italy on the Adriatic Sea *(modern Brindisi)*
Bruti·ī -ōrum *mpl* inhabitants of the toe of Italy
Brūt·us -ī *m* Roman family name, cognomen, *esp.* Lucius Junius Brutus *(drove out Tarquinius Superbus)* ‖ Marcus Junius Brutus *(one of the murderers of Julius Caesar)*
brūt·us -a -um *adj* heavy, unwieldy; dull, stupid
būbīl·e -is *n* cow stable
būb·ō -ōnis *mf* owl
būbul·a -ae *f* beef
bubulcit·or -ārī *intr* to tend cattle, be a herdsman; to ride herd
bubulc·us -ī *m* herdsman
būb(u)l·us -a -um *adj* ox-, bull's, cow's; **corius bubulus** oxhide, oxhide whip; **oculus bublus** bull's-eye
būcaed·a -ae *m (coll)* flogged slave
bucc·a -ae *f* cheek; loudmouth; trumpeter; parasite; mouthful; **dicere quidquid in buccam venerit** to say whatever came into his head
buccell·a -ae *f* small mouthful; morsel
bucc·ō -ōnis *f (coll)* fathead
buc(c)ul·a -ae *f* little cheek; visor
bucculent·us -a -um *adj* having fat cheeks; loud-mouthed
būcer(i)·us -a -um *adj* horned
būcin·a -ae *f (curved)* trumpet; war trumpet; shepherd's horn
būcināt·or -ōris *m* trumpeter
būcin·us -ī *m* trumpeter
būcolic·us -a -um *adj* pastoral, bucolic
būcul·a -ae *f* heifer
būf·ō -ōnis *m* toad
-bul·a -ae *fem suf* forms feminine nouns denoting instrument or agent, *e.g.:* **fibula** safety pin
bulb·us -ī *m* bulb; onion
būl·ē -ēs *f (Greek)* council, senate
būleut·a -ae *m* councilor
būleutēr·ium -(i)ī *n* meeting place of a Greek council
bull·a -ae *f* bubble; boss, stud, knob; amulet; locket *(hung around neck of children)*
bullāt·us -a -um *adj* inflated, bombastic; studded; wearing a bulla *(i.e., still a child)*
bull·iō -īre *intr* to bubble, boil
bullul·a -ae *f* little bubble
-bulum -ī *neut suf* denoting instrument or place, *e.g.:* **venabulum** hunting instrument, spear; **stabulum** place for cattle to stand, stable

būmast·us -a -um *adj* having large grapes
būr·a -ae *or* **būr·is -is** *f* curved handle of plow
Būsīr·is -idos *or* **-idis** *m* king of Egypt who sacrificed strangers and was killed by Hercules
bustirap·us -ī *m* grave robber
bustuāri·us -a -um *adj* of a tomb, of a pyre; **gladiator bustiarius** gladiator who fought at a tomb in honor of the dead
bust·um -ī *n* pyre; grave mound, tomb; *(pej) (applied to a person)* ruination
būte·ō -ōnis *m* buzzard
Būt(h)rōt·um (·on) -ī *n or* **Būt(h)rōt·os -ī** *f* town on the coast of Epirus
buxēt·um -ī *n* plantation of boxwood trees
buxif·er -era -erum *adj* producing boxwood trees
bux·um -ī *n (bot)* boxwood tree; *(object made of the hard wood of the boxwood tree):* (spinning) top, comb, writing tablet, flute
bux·us -ī *f* boxwood tree
Byrs·a -ae *f* **(Bur-)** citadel of Carthage
Byzant·ium -(i)ī *n* city on the Bosporus, later named Constantinople

C

C *abbr* **centum** (one hundred)
C. *abbr* **Gaius** *(Roman first name, praenomen)*
caballīn·us -a -um *adj* horse's; **fons caballinus** *(pej)* "nag's spring" *(i.e., Hippocrene)*
caball·us -ī *m* horse, nag; packhorse; riding horse; **Gorgoneus caballus** Pegasus *(sprung from the blood of the Gorgon Medusa)*
Cabīr·us -ī *m* deity worshiped on Lemnos and Samothrace *(e.g., Bacchus)*
cacātur·iō -īre -iī *intr (vulg)* to want to shit
cachinnāti·ō -ōnis *f* horselaugh
cachinn·ō -āre -āvī -ātum *intr* to laugh loud, roar *(with laughter)*
cachinn·us -ī *m* loud laugh; *(fig)* rippling *(of waves)*
cac·ō -āre -āvī -ātus *tr & intr (vulg)* to shit
cacoēth·es -is *n* malignant tumor; **cacoethes scribendi** an itch to write
cacozēli·a -ae *f* bad taste *(in style)*
cacozēl·os -on *adj (of style)* in bad taste
cacul·a -ae *m (sl)* soldier's slave
cacūm·en -inis *n* point, tip, top, peak; young shoot; **extremum cacumen** outer limit
cacūmin·ō -āre -āvī -ātus *tr* to make pointed
Cāc·us -ī *m* giant son of Vulcan, living on the Aventine Hill and slain by Hercules
cadāv·er -eris *n* corpse, carcass
cadāverōs·us -a -um *adj* cadaverous, ghastly
Cadmē·is -idos *adj (fem only)* of Cadmus ‖ *f* daughter of Cadmus
Cadmē·us -a -um *adj* Cadmean, Theban; **Tyros Cadmea** Tyre, home city of Cadmus ‖ *f* citadel of Thebes
Cadm·us -ī *m* son of Phoenician king Agenor, brother of Europa, and founder of the citadel of Thebes; **Cadmi terra** Phoenicia
cadō cadĕre cecidī cāsum *intr* to fall, sink, drop; to be slain, die, be sacrificed; to happen, occur, turn out, come to pass; to belong, refer, be suitable, apply; to flag, decline, decay; to vanish, fail, cease; to derive *(from a source)*; *(of parts of the body)* to fall out, be shed; *(of heavenly bodies)* to sink, set; *(of wind, sea, noise)* to die down; *(of words)* to fall from one's lips; *(of efforts)* to come to nothing; *(w.* **in** *+ acc)* **1** to come upon, arrive at by chance; **2** to fall upon *(the enemy)*; **3** to coincide with *(a time, period)*; **4** to fall due on *(a date)*; **5** to be consistent *or* compatible with, fit; **6** *(of words, clauses)* to end, terminate in *(e.g., a long syllable)*; **7** to fall into *(a category)*; *(w.* **ad** *or* **in** *+ acc)* to lapse into, degenerate into; **apte cadere ad** to be exactly adapted to; **causā cadere** *(leg)* to lose one's case, be convicted; *(fig)* to be in the wrong; **formulā cadere** to lose one's case on a technicality; **huc cadere** to fall so low; **numerose cadere** to sound rhythmical
cādūceāt·or -ōris *m* herald
cādūce·us -ī *m* herald's staff, caduceus
cādūcif·er -era -erum *adj* with herald's staff
cādūc·us -a -um *adj* falling; fallen; inclined to fall, tottery, unsteady; frail, perishable, transitory; *(of hopes, words)* futile; *(of persons)* destined to die, doomed; *(of fire)* likely to go out; *(of streams)* likely to dry up; *(of vines)* drooping; *(leg)* lapsed, without heir; *(mil)* fallen in battle
cadurc·um -ī *n* coverlet; *(fig)* marriage bed
cad·us -ī *m* (large) jar
Cadūsi·ī -ōrum *mpl* the people of Cadusia *(near the Caspian Sea)*
caecigen·us -a -um *adj* born blind
Caecili·us -a -um *adj* Roman clan name, nomen
caecit·ās -ātis *f* blindness; **caecitas animi** moral blindness; **caecitas mentis** mental blindness, lack of discernment
caec·ō -āre -āvī -ātus *tr* to blind; to obscure the judgment of; **astu caecare** *(fig)* to pull the wool over *(s.o.'s)* eyes

Caecub·um -ī *n* Caecuban wine *(from Caecubum in S. Latium)*
Caecul·us -ī *m* son of Vulcan and founder of Praeneste
caec·us -a -um *adj* blind; invisible; vague, random, aimless; uncertain, unknown; unsubstantiated; blinding; obscure, mysterious; dark, gloomy; concealed, disguised; unforeseeable *(dangers)*; **die caeco emere** to buy on credit *(i.e., to buy with no definite date of payment)*
caed·ēs -is *f* murder, slaughter, massacre; bloodshed, gore; the slain
caedō caedĕre cecīdī caesus *tr* to hack at; to chop; to strike, beat; to fell; to cut off, cut to pieces; to cut through, sever; to kill, murder; to crack, smash, break; to use up, consume; *(hum)* to devour; **sermones caedere** to exchange chitchat
caedu·us -a -um *adj* ready for felling
caelām·en -inis *n* engraving
caelāt·or -ōris *m* engraver
caelāt·um -ī *n* engraved work
caelātūr·a -ae *f* engraving
cael·ebs -ibis *adj* **(-eps)** unmarried, single *(whether bachelor or widower)*; *(of trees)* not supporting vines
cael·es -itis *adj* heavenly ‖ *mpl* gods
caelest·is -is -e *adj* heavenly, celestial; supernatural, divine ‖ *mf* deity; godlike person ‖ *npl* heavenly bodies
caelibāt·us -ūs *m* celibacy
caelicol·a -ae *mf* inhabitant of heaven *(god or goddess)*
caelif·er -era -erum *adj* supporting the sky
Caelimontān·us -a -um *adj* located on the Caelian Hill
caelipot·ens -entis *adj* powerful in heaven
caelit·ēs -um *mpl* gods in heaven
Caeli·us -a -um *adj* Roman clan name *(nomen)*
Caeli·us Mons *(gen:* **Caeliī Montis)** *m* Caelian Hill *(in Rome)*
cael·ō -āre -āvī -ātus *tr* to engrave in relief, emboss; to carve; to cast; to fashion, compose; to adorn
cael·um -ī *n* engraver's chisel
cael·um -ī *n* sky, heaven(s); air, climate, weather; universe, world; **caelum apertum** *(or* **patens)** the open air; **in caelo esse** to be in seventh heaven; **positio caeli** *(geog)* latitude
caement·um -ī *n* **(cēm-)** *(also used in pl)* crushed stone
Caen·eūs -eī *or* **-eos** *m* child of Elatus, born a girl, but changed into a boy
Caenīn·a -ae *f* ancient city of Latium *(defeated by Romulus)*
Caen·is -idis *f* child of Elatus, born a girl, but changed into a boy
caenōs·us -a -um *adj* filthy, muddy
caen·um -ī *n* **(cēn-)** filth, mud, slime; *(applied to persons) (sl)* scum
caep·a *or* **cēp·a -ae** *f or* **caep·e** *or* **cēp·e** *(nom, acc, and abl) n* onion
Caepi·ō -ōnis *m* Roman family name *(cognomen), esp.* in the *gens Servilia*
Caer·e -itis *or* **-ētis** *n* city in Etruria *(modern Cerveteri)*
Caer·es -itis *or* **-etis** *adj* of Caere ‖ *mpl* the people of Caere
Caerētān·us -a -um *adj* of Caere
caerimōni·a -ae *f* rite, ceremony; sanctity; awe, reverence ‖ *fpl* rites, ceremonies; practices
caerul·a -ōrum *npl* blue expanse *(of the sky)*; blue waters *(of the sea)*
caerul(e)·us -a -um *adj* blue; blue-eyed; dark-blue; greenish-blue; dark
Caes·ar -aris *m* Gaius Julius Caesar *(102?–44 B.C.)* ‖ honorary title of Octavian and succeeding emperors ‖ cognomen of various members of the imperial family
Caesarē·a -ae *f* name of several towns, *esp.* two in Palestine, one in Cappadocia, and one in Mauretania
Caesare·us -a -um *or* **Caesariān·us -a -um** *adj* connected with Julius Caesar; connected with Augustus; imperial
Caesariān·us -i *m* soldier *or* supporter of Julius Caesar; supporter *or* servant of the Roman emperor
caesariāt·us -a -um *adj* long-haired
caesari·ēs -ēī *f* long, flowing hair
caesim *adv* by chopping, by cutting; with a slashing blow; *(rhet)* in short clauses, in a clipped style
caesi·us -a -um *adj* bluish-gray; blue-eyed; gray-eyed; cat-eyed ‖ **Caesius** Roman clan name *(nomen)*
Caes·ō -ōnis *m* **(Kaes-)** Roman first name *(praenomen)*
caesp·es -itis *m* sod, turf; grass; altar of sod; rampart made of turf; mound of earth *(esp. as the covering of a grave)*
caest·us -ūs *m* **(cest-)** boxing glove
caes·us -a -um *pp of* **caedo** ‖ *npl*— **inter caesa et porrecta** *(fig)* at the eleventh hour *(literally, between the victim being slain and offered)*
caetr·a -ae *f* **(cēt-)** short Spanish shield
caetrāt·us -a -um *adj* armed with a shield ‖ *mpl* soldiers armed with a shield; Greek peltasts
Caīc·us -ī *m* **(Cay-)** river in Mysia
Caiēt·a -ae *f* nurse of Aeneas ‖ town on the coast of Latium
cai·ō -āre *tr* to beat, thrash
Caïus *see* **Gaius**
Cala·ber -bra -brum *adj* Calabrian
Calabri·a -ae *f* region of S.E. Italy
Cala·ïs -ïs *m (winged)* son of Boreas and Orithyia, and brother of Zetes
calamāri·us -a -um *adj* for holding pens

Calam·is -idis *m* Greek sculptor of the 5th cent. B.C.
calamis·ter -tri *m* curling iron
calamistrāt·us -a -um *adj* curled *(with a curling iron)*
calamistr·um -ī *n* curling iron
calamit·ās -ātis *f* calamity, disaster; *(mil)* defeat
calamitōsē *adv* disastrously
calamitōs·us -a -um *adj* disastrous; liable to disaster; blighted *(fields);* hit by disaster, ill-starred ‖ *m* victim of a disaster
calam·us -ī *m* reed;, stalk, shoot *(of a plant);* pen *(for writing on paper, as opposed to* **stilus** *of metal or bone for writing on wax);* arrow; fishing rod; lime rod *(smeared at top with lime to catch birds);* vine prop; *(mus)* reed pipe; *(collectively or pl)* Panpipes
calathisc·us -ī *m* small wicker basket
calath·us -ī *m* wicker basket; vessel for holding cheese *or* curdled milk; wine cup
Cālāti·a -ae *f* town in Campania
calāt·or -ōris *m* **(kal-)** servant; priest's attendant
calautic·a -ae *f* type of woman's head-dress
calc·ar -āris *n* spur; *(fig)* stimulus
calceāment·um -ī *n* footwear, shoe
calceār·ium -(i)ī *n* show allowance
calceāt·or -ōris *m* shoemaker
calceāt·us -ūs *m* footwear, shoes
calce·ō -āre -āvī -ātus *tr* to put shoes on; to shoe *(animals)*
calceolār·ius -(i)ī *m* shoemaker
calceol·us -ī *m* small shoe, half-boot; slipper
calce·us -ī *m* shoe; **calcei mullei** *(or* **patricii)** red shoes worn by senators who had held curule office; **calceos mutare** *(fig)* to become a senator *(from the shoes that senators wore);* **calceos poscere** to leave the table *(literally, to call for one's shoes)*
Calc(h)·ās -antis *m Calchas (Greek seer at Troy)*
calci- *see* **calce-**
calcitr·ō -āre -āvī -ātum *intr* to kick; to be recalcitrant, kick up one's heels
Calc(h)ēd·ōn -ōnis *f* Calchedon *(town on the Asiatic side of the Bosphorus, opposite Byzantium)*
calcitr·ō -āre -āvī -ātum *intr* to kick
calcitr·ō -ōnis *m* kicker; blusterer
calc·ō -āre -āvī -ī.tus *tr* to trample; to trample on; to tread *(grapes)*; to set foot on; to tread on accidentally, trip upon; *(fig)* to spurn; **viam calcare** to tread a path
calculāt·or -ōris *m* arithmetic teacher; accountant, bookkeeper
calcul·us -ī *m* pebble, stone; kidney stone; counter of an abacus; piece *(used in games);* **calculus albus** white pebble *(of acquittal);* **calculos** *(or* **calculum)** **ponere** *(or* **subducere)** to make a calculation *(esp. gains or losses);* **calculus ater** black pebble *(of condemnation);* vote, decision, sentence; **parem calculum ponere cum** to return an equivalent gift to
calda, caldārius, caldus *see* **calid-**
Calēdoni·a -ae *f* Caledonia, Scotland
cal(e)·faciō -facĕre -fēcī -factus *tr* to warm, heat; to rouse, excite
calefact·ō -āre -āvī -ātus *tr* to warm, heat
Calend- *see* **Kalend-**
Calēn·us -a -um *adj* of Cales ‖ *n* wine from Cales *(in Campania)*
cal·eō -ēre -uī *intr* to be warm, be hot; to feel warm; to glow; to be flushed *(with wine);* to be hot *(with lust);* to be busy, have one's hands full
Cal·ēs -ium *fpl* Campanian town famous for its wine
cal·escō -escĕre -uī *intr* to get warm, get hot; to become excited, get hot
caliandrum *see* **caliendrum**
calidē *adv* promptly, quickly
calid·us -a -um *adj* **(cald-)** warm, hot; eager, rash; hot-headed; hasty; intoxicating *(wine);* high *(fever)* ‖ *f* warm water ‖ *n* hot drink; heat
caliendr·um -ī *n* **(-lian-)** wig *(for women)*
calig·a -ae *f* army boot; *(fig)* military service
caligāt·us *or* **caligāri·us -a -um** *adj* wearing army boots ‖ *m (mil)* private
cālīginōs·us -a -um *adj* misty, foggy
cālīg·ō -inis *f* darkness; mist, fog; dark smoke; gloom; obscurity; mental blindness; dizziness
cālīg·ō -āre *tr* to veil in darkness, obscure; to make dizzy ‖ *intr* to be dark, be gloomy; to steam, reek; to be wrapped in mist *or* darkness; to be blind, grope
caligul·a -ae *f* small army boot ‖ **Caligula** *m* nickname given by soldiers to Emperor Gaius when he was a small boy
cal·ix -icis *m* cup; *(fig)* wine
Callaec·ī -ōrum *mpl* a people in the N.W. corner of Spain
callaïn·us -a -um *adj* turquoise
call·eō -ēre -uī *tr* to know by experience; to have skill in; *(w. inf)* to know how to, be able to ‖ *intr* to grow hard, be callused; *(fig)* to be thick-skinned, be callous; *(w. abl)* to be experienced in, be skilled in
callidē *adv* skillfuly; well; cunningly
callidit·ās -ātis *f* skill; shrewdness; cunning ‖ *fpl* clever tricks
callid·us -a -um *adj* expert, adroit, skillful; ingenious, clever; cunning, wily;

(w. gen, dat, or **in** + *abl)* experienced in; *(w. inf)* skilled at
Callimach·us -ī *m* Alexandrine poet and grammarian *(fl c. 270 B.C.)*
Calliop·ē -ēs *or* **Calliop(ē)·a -ae** *f* Calliope *(Muse of epic poetry)*
call·is -is *mf* rough footpath ‖ *mpl* mountain pasturage; cattle trails
Callistō *indecl f* daughter of Lycaon *(king of Arcadia),* changed into a she-bear and then into the constellation Ursa Major
callōs·us -a -um *adj* thick-skinned, callused; solid, hard
call·um -ī *n or* **call·us -ī** *m* hard skin; *(lit & fig)* callousness; **callum obducere** to produce insensitivity
cal·ō -āre -āvī -ātus *tr* **(kal-)** to announce; to convoke
cāl·ō -ōnis *m* soldier's slave; drudge
cal·or -ōris *m* warmth, heat; glow; passion, love; fire, zeal; fever
Calp·ē -ēs *f* Gibraltar
Calpurni·us -a -um *adj* name of a plebeian clan ‖ *f* Calpurnia *(wife of Julius Caesar)*
calt(h)·a -ae *f (bot)* marigold
caltul·a -ae *f (woman's)* yellow slip *(tied below the breasts)*
calumni·a -ae *f* **(kal-)** false accusation, malicious charge; frameup; conviction for malicious prosecution; false statement, misrepresentation; trickery; sham
calumniāt·or -ōris *m* malicious accuser; shyster
calumni·or -ārī -ātus sum *tr* to accuse fasely; to misinterpret, misrepresent; to blame unjustly; to find fault with ‖ *intr* to bring false accusation; to practice legal chicanery
calv·a -ae *f* bald head, scalp; skull
calvit·ium -(i)ī *n* baldness
calv·us -a -um *adj* bald
cal·x -cis *f* heel; (back of the) hoof; *(fig)* foot, kick; **calcibus caedere** to kick
cal·x -cis *f* lime, limestone; pebble *(used in games);* finish line, goal; **ad calcem pervenire** to reach the goal
Calyd·ōn -ōnis *or* **-ōnos** *f* town in Aetolia, site of the boar hunt led by Meleager
Calydōn·is -idos *adj (fem only)* Calydonian ‖ *f* Calydonian woman *(Dejanira)*
Calydōni·us -a -um *adj* Calydonian
Calyps·ō -ūs *f* nymph *(daughter of Atlas)* who entertained Ulysses on the island of Ogygia
camara *see* **camera**
camell·a -ae *f* drinking cup
camēl·us -ī *m* camel
Camēn·a -ae *f* Muse; poem; poetry
camer·a -ae *f* **(-mar-)** vault, arched roof, arch; flat boat with arched covering
Camerīn·um -ī *n* town in Umbria
Camill·a -ae *f* Volscian female warrior, ally of Turnus against Aeneas
Camill·us -ī *m* Marcus Furius Camillus, who liberated Rome from the Gauls in 390 B.C.
camīn·us -ī *m* fireplace; furnace, forge; vent of subterranean fires; **oleum addere camino** *(prov)* to pour oil on the fire
cammar·us -ī *m* lobster
Campānia -ae *f* district on E. coast of central Italy below Latium
Campān·us -a -um *adj* Campanian
campes·ter *or* **campes·tris -tris -tre** *adj* flat, level; overland *(march); (of city)* situated in a plain; *(of army)* fighting in a plain; *(of sports, elections)* held in the Campus Martius ‖ *n* loincloth ‖ *npl* flat lands
camp·us -ī *m* open field *(opp:* **ager** tilled field); flat space, plain; level surface; *(fig)* field of action, subject of debate; **Campus Martius** Field of Mars *(near the Tiber, used for sports, elections, military exercises)*
cam·ur *or* **cam·urus -ura -urum** *adj* crooked; concave
Canac·ē -ēs *f* daughter of Aeolus, who committed incest with her brother Macareus
canāl·is -is *mf* pipe, conduit; gutter, open drain; channel *(of a river; of the sea);* flow *(of language)*
cancell·ī -ōrum *mpl* railing, grating; barrier *(at sports, public events);* boundaries, limits; **intra cancellos** in a confined space
can·cer -crī *m* crab; the South; tropical heat; *(med)* cancer ‖ **Cancer** *(astr)* Cancer, the Crab *(sign of the zodiac)*
cande·faciō -facĕre -fēcī -factus *tr* to make white; to make white-hot
candēl·a -ae *f* candle, taper; waxed cord
candelābr·um -ī *n* candlestick, candelabrum; lampstand
cand·ens -entis *adj* white, shining, glistening; white-hot *(iron)*
cand·eō -ēre -uī *intr* to be shining white, glitter, shine; to be white-hot
cand·escō -escĕre *intr* to become white, begin to glisten; to get white-hot
candidātōri·us -a -um *adj* of a candidate, candidate's
candidāt·us -a -um *adj* clothed in white ‖ *m* candidate
candidē *adv* in dazzling white; clearly, simply, sincerely
candidul·us -a -um *adj* white, gleaming
candid·us -a -um *adj (cf* **albus** flat white) shiny white, white, bright, dazzling, gleaming, sparkling; lucky, favorable, happy; fair *(complexion);* candid, frank *(person);* bright, cheerful *(mood, circumstances);* clear, bright *(day); (of*

winds) bringing clear weather; white, silvery *(poplar, hair);* clear, unaffected *(style);* **candidus limes** Milky Way; **candida sententia** vote of acquittal

cand·or -ōris *m* brightness, radiance; fair complexion; candor, sincerity, kindness; clarity *(of style)*

cān·ens -entis *adj* gray, white

cān·eō -ēre -uī *intr* to be gray

cānesc·ō -ĕre *intr* to become gray; to grow old; *(of discourse)* to become dull, lose force

cān·ī -ōrum *mpl* gray hair(s)

Canicul·a -ae *f (astr)* Canicula, Sirius, Dog Star

canīn·us -a -um *adj* canine; snarling, spiteful; **canina littera** letter R

can·is -is *mf* dog; worst throw *(in dice)* ‖ **Canis** *m (astr)* Canis Major *or* Sirius

canistr·um -ī *n* wicker basket *(for bread, flowers, etc.)*

cāniti·ēs -ēī *f* grayness; *(fig)* gray hair; *(fig)* old age

cann·a -ae *f* reed; reed pipe, flute

cannab·is -ae *f or* **cannab·um -ī** *n* hemp, marijuana; hempen rope

Cann·ae -ārum *fpl* town in Apulia where Hannibal defeated the Romans in 216 B.C.

Cannens·is -is -e *adj* of Cannae

canō canĕre cecinī cantus *tr* to sing; to play *(musical instrument);* to speak in a singsong tone; to sing of; to prophesy, predict; *(mil)* to blow, sound; **signa** *(or* **classicum)** **canere** to sound the signal for battle ‖ *intr* to sing; to play *(on musical instrument); (of birds)* to sing; *(of roosters)* to crow; *(of frogs)* to croak; **receptui canere** to sound the retreat; **tibiā canere** to play the flute

Canōp·us -ī *m* town on W. mouth of the Nile

can·or -ōris *m* tune, sound, melody, song; tone *(of instruments)*

canōr·us -a -um *adj* melodious, musical; singsong, jingling ‖ *n* melody

Cantabr·ī -ōrum *mpl* tribe in N. Spain

Cantabri·a -ae *f* district in N. Spain

cantām·en -inis *n* incantation, spell

cantāt·or -ōris *m* singer

canthar·is -idis *f* beetle; Spanish fly

canthar·us -ī *m* wide-bellied drinking vessel with handles, tankard

cant(h)ērīn·us -a -um *adj* of a horse

cant(h)ēr·ius -(i)ī *m* gelding; eunuch

canth·us -ī *m* iron rim; wheel

cantic·um -ī *n* song; aria in Roman comedy

cantilēn·a -ae *f* old song, gossip; **cantilenam eandem canere** *(fig)* to harp on the same theme

canti·ō -ōnis *f* singing; incantation, spell, charm

cantit·ō -āre -āvī -ātus *tr* to keep on singing *or* playing

Cant·ium -(i)ī *n* district of Britain *(modern Kent)*

cantiuncul·a -ae *f* catchy tune

cant·ō -āre -āvī -ātus *tr* to sing; to play; to sing of, celebrate; to harp on, keep repeating; to drawl out; to predict; *(of birds)* to sing, crow, warble; *(of actor)* to play the part of ‖ *intr* to sing; to play; *(of instruments)* to sound; to drawl; *(of rooster)* to crow; **ad surdas aures cantare** *(fig)* to preach to deaf ears

cant·or -ōris *m* singer; poet; eulogist; actor, player; musician

cantr·ix -īcis *f* singer, player *(female)*

cant·us -ūs *m* song, tune, melody; incantation; magic spell; prediction; poetry

cān·us -a -um *adj* gray; white; gray-haired; old; age-old *(things);* whitened, foam-capped *(sea); (of trees, plants)* covered with silvery foliage

Canusīn·a -ae *f* garment made of Canusian wool

Canus·ium -(i)ī *n* town in Apulia *(modern Canosa)*

capācit·ās -ātis *f* capacity

Capan·eūs -ēī *m* one of the "Seven against Thebes", killed by lightning

cap·ax -ācis *adj* capacious, spacious, wide, roomy; *(of mind)* able to grasp, receptive; *(w. gen, dat or inf)* big enough for; *(w. gen)* **1** capable of, capable of holding; **2** susceptible of; **3** capable of understanding; **capax navium** navigable

capēd·ō -inis *f* cup, bowl *(used in sacrifices)*

capēduncul·a -ae *f* small cup *or* bowl *(used in sacrifices)*

capell·a -ae *f* she-goat, nanny goat ‖ **Capella** *(star in the constellation Auriga)*

Capēn·a -ae *f* Porta Capena *(gate in the Servian Wall marking the start of the Via Appia)*

ca·per -prī *m* he-goat, billy goat

caperr·ō -āre -āvī -ātus *tr & intr* to wrinkle

capess·ō -ĕre -īvī *or* **-iī -ītus** *tr* **(-iss-)** to try to reach, make for; to seize, get hold of, snatch at; to take up, engage in; **arma capessere** to take up arms, go to war; **cursum** *(or* **viam)** **capessere** to take the road (to); **flammam capessere** to catch fire; **poenas capessere** to exact punishment; **rem publicam capessere** to engage in politics ‖ *refl & intr* to go

Caphēr·eūs -eī *m* **(-phār-)** rocky promontory at the S.E. end of Euboea

capillāment·um -ī *n* wig, toupeé

capillār·e -is *n* hair oil

capillāt·us -a -um *adj* long-haired

capill·us -ī *m* hair *(of the head); (single)*

hair; *(of plants)* fibers; hair, fur *(of animals)*

capiō capĕre cēpī captus *(archaic fut:* **capsō)** *tr* to take hold of, grasp; to occupy; to take up *(arms);* assume *(office);* to put on *(clothes, armor);* to catch, capture; to catch *(fish);* to bag *(game);* to captivate, charm; to cheat, mislead, seduce, delude; to trap; to defeat, overcome; to keep under control; to be able to hold, have room for; to convince; to reach, arrive at, land at; to exact *(tribute, penalty);* to extort, accept as a bribe; to take, obtain, enjoy, reap *(profit, advantage);* to cherish, cultivate, adopt *(habits, etc.);* to form, come to, reach *(conclusions, plans, thoughts, resolutions, purposes);* to take, derive, draw, obtain *(examples, proofs, instances);* to receive, experience *(impressions, feelings); (of feeling)* to come over; to suffer, be subjected to *(injury);* to hold, contain, be large enough for; to comprehend, grasp; **animo capere** to grasp, get, understand; **consilium capere** to form a plan; **fidem capere** to be credible; **finem capere** to come to an end; **radicem capere** to take root; **quietem capere** to get some rest, go to sleep; **usu capere** to acquire, inherit **‖** *refl* **se non capere** not to contain oneself, not to control oneself

capi·ō -ōnis *f* taking; **usus capio** acquiring ownership by continuous possession

cap·is -idis *f* bowl *(with one handle, used in sacrifices)*

capistr·ō -āre -āvī -ātus *tr* to halter, muzzle

capistr·um -ī *n* halter, muzzle

capit·āl *or* **capit·āle -ālis** *n* capital offense; crime punishable by death

capitāl·is -is -e *adj* relating to the head *or* life; *(leg)* affecting a person's life *or* civil status; *(of crime)* punishable by death, punishable by loss of civil rights; dangerous, deadly, fatal; mortal *(enemy);* first-class, fine

capitāliter *adv* with bitter hostility

capit·ō -ōnis *m (coll)* bighead

Capitōlīn·us -a -um *adj* Capitoline **‖** *m* Capitoline Hill **‖** *mpl* persons in charge of the Capitoline games **‖** *n see* **Capitolium**

Capitōl·ium -(i)ī *n* the Capitol *(temple of Jupiter on the summit of Mons Tarpeius);* the Capitoline Hill *(including temple and citadel);* citadel *(of any city)*

capitulātim *adv* briefly, summarily

capitul·um -ī *n* small head; *(as term of endearment)* dear fellow; end, point *(of an instrument, pole, etc.)*

Cappadoci·a -ae *f* country in E. Asia Minor between Cilicia and Pontus

Cappadoc·us -a -um *adj* Cappadocian

Cappad·ox -ocis *m* inhabitant of Cappadocia; *(pej)* Asiatic

cappar·is -is *f* pickled flower bud of the caper plant *(prickly shrub)*

capr·a -ae *f* she-goat **‖ Capra** *(astr)* star in the constellation Auriga

capre·a -ae *f* wild she-goat; **Capr(e)ae Palus** Goat's Pool *(in Campus Martius, site of Circus Flaminius)*

Capre·ae -ārum *fpl* Isle of Capri

capreol·us -ī *m* chamois, roebuck; rafter

Capricorn·us -ī *m (astr)* Capricorn

caprific·us -ī *f* wild fig tree

caprigen·us -a -um *adj* of goats; **caprigenum pecus** herd of goats

caprimulg·us -ī *m* country bumpkin *(literally, goat milker)*

caprīn·us -a -um *adj* goat-; **de lanā caprinā rixari** *(fig)* to fight over nothing

caprip·ēs -edis *adj* goat-footed

caps·a -ae *f* container, holder, box, case *(esp. for scrolls)*

capsō *see* **capio**

capsul·a -ae *f* small box

capt·a -ae *f* captive *(female)*

captāti·ō -ōnis *f* hunt, quest; **captatio verborum** verbalism

captātor -ōris *m* seeker; legacy hunter; **aurae popularis captator** publicity hound

capti·ō -ōnis *f* trick, fraud; loss, disadvantage; verbal quibble

captiōsē *adv* slyly, trickily

captiōs·us -a -um *adj* tricky, captious; harmful, disadvantageous

captiuncul·a -ae *f* quibble, sophism

captīvit·ās -ātis *f* captivity; capture

captīv·us -a -um *adj* captured; captive; prisoner's; caught *(in hunting, fishing)* **‖** *mf* prisoner-of-war

capt·ō -āre -āvī -ātus *tr* to try to catch; to keep reaching for; to chase after; to strive after, long for, desire earnestly; to try to find; to try to trap, lure; to try to get the better of *(in an argument);* to adopt *(plan);* to try to cause *(laughter, response in others);* to watch for *(an opportunity);* to begin *(conversation);* **aure** *(or* **auribus)** **captare** to try to hear, listen in on, eavesdrop on; **cenam captare** to sponge a meal

captūr·a -ae *f* capture; quarry, kill; catch *(in fishing)*

capt·us -a -um *pp of* **capio ‖** *adj* captive; **oculis et auribus captus** blind and deaf; **mente captus** crazy

capt·us -ūs *m* grasping, taking; capacity, potentiality

Capu·a -ae *f* chief city of Campania

capūd·ō -inis *f* primitive sacrificial vessel

capulār·is -is -e *adj (sl)* ready for the grave

capul·us -ī *m* coffin; hilt, handle

cap·ut -itis *n* head; top, summit; point; principal point, main item; essential thing, matter of prime importance; end *(of anything, esp. when rounded or resembling a head, e.g., of a pole);* source *(of river);* root *(of plant);* top *(of tree);* head, leader; capital *(of country);* main point *(of discourse);* chapter, heading; substance, summary; beginning, first part *(of a speech, action; initial letter, beginnning of a word or sentence);* main course; *(com)* capital; *(leg)* life, civil status; **capitis accusare** to accuse of a capital crime; **capitis damnare** to condemn to death; **capitis res** matter of life and death; **caput demittere** to hang one's head; **diminutio capitis** loss of civil rights; **diminutio capitis maxima** condemnation to death *or* slavery; **diminutio capitis media** loss of citizenship; **diminutio capitis minima** change of status *(as by adoption, marriage)*

Cap·ys -yis *or* **-is** *m* son of Assaracus and father of Anchises **||** companion of Aeneas **||** eighth king of Alba Longa

carbase·us -a -um *adj* linen, canvas

carbas·us -a -um *adj* linen **||** *f* sail, canvas; awning; linen cloth **||** *npl* linen clothing

carb·ō -ōnis *m* charcoal

carbōnār·ius -(i)ī *m* charcoal burner *(person),* collier

carbuncul·us -ī *m* (live) coal, ember; garnet; *(med)* carbuncle, tumor

carc·er -eris *m* prison; prisoners; *(coll)* jailbird **||** *mpl* starting gate *(at racetrack);* **ad carceres a calce revocari** to start over from scratch *(literally, to be called back from the chalk line, i.e., finish line, to the starting gate)*

carcerāri·us -a -um *adj* prison-

carchēs·ium -(i)ī *n* drinking cup; masthead *(of ship)*

cardiac·us -a -um *adj* suffering from heartburn **||** *m* dyspeptic

card·ō -inis *m* **(kar-)** pivot and socket; hinge; turning point; axis, pole; boundary; region, district *(of a country);* the earth *(as pivot of the universe);* **cardo extremus** old age; **cardo rerum** critical juncture; **cardo summus** zenith *(of the sky)*

cardu·us -ī *m* thistle

cārē *adv* at a high price, dearly

cārect·um -ī *n* a bed of sedge *(reed grass, having solid rather than hollow stems)*

car·eō -ēre -uī *intr (w. abl or gen)* **1** to be without; **2** to miss; **3** to be free from *(trouble, pain, blame)*; **4** to keep away from, be absent from; **5** to abstain from; **6** to fail to achieve, be denied; **7** to go without

cār·ex -icis *f* sedge, reed grass *(having solid rather than hollow stems)*

Cāri·a -ae *f* district in S.W. Asia Minor

cari·ēs -ēī *f* decaying; decay, rot; shriveling up

carīn·a -ae *f* keel; ship **|| Carinae** *fpl* the Keels *(district in Rome between the Esquiline and Caelian Hills)*

cārīnār·ius -(i)ī *m* dyer of yellow

cariōs·us -a -um *adj* rotten, decayed; crumbly; wrinkled *(old age)*

cār·is -idis *f* shrimp

cārit·ās -ātis *f* dearness, costliness, high price, high cost of living; affection

carm·en -inis *n* song, tune; poem; poetry; lyric poetry; incantation; oracular utterance; ritual formula; legal formula; adage

Carment·a -ae *or* **Carment·is -is** *f* Roman goddess, mother of Evander

Carmentāl·is -is -e *adj* of Carmenta; **Porta Carmentalis** gate at Rome in the Servian Wall

Carment·is -is *or* **Carment·a -ae** *f* Roman goddess, the mother of Evander

carnār·ium -(i)ī *n* meat hook

carnār·ius -(i)ī *m* butcher, dealer in meat

Carnead·ēs -is *m* Greek Academic philosopher of the 2nd cent. B.C.

Carneadē·us -a -um *adj* characteristic of Carneades

carnif·ex -icis *m* **(carnu-)** executioner; murderer, butcher; scoundrel

carnificīn·a -ae *f* **(carnu-)** execution; torture

carnific·ō -āre -āvī -ātus *tr* to execute, butcher

car·ō -nis *or* **carn·is -is** *f* meat; **caro bubula** beef; **caro ferina** venison; **caro putida** carrion; *(fig)* rotten egg

Carpathi·us -a -um *adj* of the island of Carpathus *(between Crete and Rhodes);* **Carpathius senex (vates)** Proteus

carpatīn·a -ae *f* rough-leather shoe

carpent·um -ī *n* two-wheeled covered carriage *(used esp. by women)*

carp·ō -ere -sī -tus *tr* to pluck, pick; to carp at; to enjoy, make use of; to crop *(grass); (mil)* to harass; to cut to pieces; to card *(wool); (of wild animals)* to tear at; **auras vitales carpere** to breathe the breath of life; **diem carpere** to make the most of the present; **gyrum carpere** to go in a circle; **iter** *(or* **viam)** **carpere** to make one's way, travel; **pensum** *(or* **vellera)** **carpere** to spin

carptim *adv* piecemeal, separately; selectively; at different times; at various points; gradually

carpt·or -ōris *m* carver *(at table)*

carrūc·a -ae *f* four-wheeled carriage

carr·us -ī *m,* **carr·um -ī** *n* Gallic type of wagon

Carthae·us -a um *adj* of Carthaea *(town on the Greek island of Ceos)*
Carthāginiens·is -is -e *adj* **(Kar-)** Carthaginian
Carthāg·ō -inis *f* **(Kar-)** Carthage *(city in N. Africa, founded in 9th cent.* B.C.*)*
Carthēi·us -a -um *adj see* **Carthaeus**
caruncul·a -ae *f* scrap of meat
cār·us -a -um *adj* dear, expensive; dear, loving, affectionate
Cār·us -ī *m* Roman family name *(cognomen)*
cas·a -ae *f* cottage, cabin, hut
Casc·a -ae *m* Roman family name *(cognomen), esp.* Gaius and Publius Servilius Casca Longus *(two of Caesar's assassins)*
casc·us -a -um *adj* old-time, primitive
cāseol·us -ī *m* small piece of cheese
cāse·us -ī *m or* **cāse·um -ī** *n* cheese
casi·a -ae *f* wild cinnamon tree; fragrant shrub
Caspi·us -a -um *adj* Caspian; **mare Caspium** Caspian Sea; **sinus Caspius** Caspian Sea; **Caspiae pylae** *(or* **portae)** name of passes in the Caucasus mountains S. of the Caspian Sea
Cassandr·a -ae *f* prophetic daughter of Priam and Hecuba, believed by no one
cassid·a -ae *f* metal helmet
Cassiop·ē -ēs *or* **Cassiopē·a -ae** *f* wife of Cepheus and mother of Andromeda, afterwards changed into a constellation
cass·is -idis *f* metal helmet
cass·is -is *m (often pl)* hunting net, snare; spider web; **casses alicui tendere** to set a trap for s.o.
cassiter·um -ī *n* tin
Cass·ius -(i)ī *m* Gaius Cassius Longinus *(of one Caesar's murderers)*
cass·ō -āre *intr* to totter
cass·us -a -um *adj* empty, hollow; *(fig)* empty, groundless, pointless; *(w. abl)* deprived of, devoid of, without; **cassus lumine** without life; **in cassum** to no purpose, pointlessly
Castali·a -ae *f* spring at Delphi, associated with Apollo and Muses
Castal·is -idis *adj (fem only)* Castalian; **sorores Castalides** Muses ‖ *f* Muse
Castali·us -a -um *adj* of Castalia, of Apollo, of the Muses, of the Delphic oracle, Castalian
castane·a -ae *f* chestnut tree; chestnut
castē *adv* chastely, purely, spotlessly; virtuously; devoutly
castellān·us -a -um *adj* of a fort(ress) ‖ *mpl* occupants of a fort(ress)
castellātim *adv* one fort(ress) after another; **castellatim dissipati** (troops) stationed in various fortresses
castell·um -ī *n* fort, fortress; *(fig)* stronghold, refuge; small reservoir *or* center of distribution on an aqueduct
castēri·a -ae *f* rower's quarters
castīgābil·is -is -e *adj* punishable
castīgāti·ō -ōnis *f* correction, punishment; censure, reproof
castīgāt·or -ōris *m* castigator
castīgātōri·us -a -um *adj* reproving
castīgāt·us -a -um *adj* firm *(breast)*
castīg·ō -āre -āvī -ātus *tr* to correct, make right; to reprove, find fault with
castimōni·a -ae *f* purity, morality; chastity; ceremonial purification
castit·ās -ātis *f* chastity, purity
cast·or -oris *m* beaver ‖ **Castor** Castor, son of Tyndareus, twin brother of Pollux, brother of Helen and Clytemnestra, and patron of sailors; **aedes** *(or* **templum)** **Castoris** temple of Castor (and Pollux)
castore·um -ī *n* strong-smelling secretion of beavers, used in medicine
castr·a -ōrum *npl* camp; day's march; the service, army life; *(pol)* party; *(phil)* school; **bina castra** two camps; **castra facere** *(or* **munire** *or* **ponere)** to construct a camp; **castra habere** to be encamped; **castra movere** to break camp; **castra una** one camp
castrens·is -is -e *adj* camp-, military; characteristic of soldiers; **corona castrensis** crown conferred on first soldier to enter an enemy's camp
castr·ō -āre -āvī -ātus *tr* to castrate
castr·um -ī *n* fort, fortress ‖ *npl see* **castra**
cast·us -a -um *adj* chaste, pure, guiltless; *(of places)* free from crime; holy, religious, pious, sacred
casul·a -ae *f* little hut, little cottage
cās·us -ūs *m* falling; fall, downfall, overthrow, end; chance, event, occurrence; occasion, opportunity; emergency; misfortune, accident; plight; eventuality, possible situation, contingency; death; fate; *(gram)* case; **non consulto sed casu** not on purpose but accidentally
cataclysm·os -ī *m* deluge
catafract- *see* **cataphract-**
catagraph·us -a -um *adj* print *(dress)*
catamīt·us -ī *m* catamite ‖ **Catamītus** Ganymede
cataphag·ās -ae *m* glutton
cataphract·ēs -ae *m* coat of mail
cataphract·us -a -um *adj* clad in mail
cataplūs *m (nom only)* putting into port, ship's arrival
catapult·a -ae *f* catapult
catapultāri·us -a -um *adj* catapulted, shot *(from a catapult)*
cataract·a *or* **catarract·a -ae** *or* **catar(r)(h)act·ēs -ae** *f* rapids, cataract; sluice; portcullis
cataractri·a -ae *f (fictitious)* spice
catast·a -ae *f* platform on which slaves were displayed for sale

catē *adv* skillfully, wisely
catēj·a -ae *f* javelin
catell·a -ae *f* puppy *(female);* small chain *(worn by women)*
catell·us -ī *m* puppy; small chain
catēn·a -ae *f* chain; series; curb, restraint ‖ *fpl* chains, fetters
catēnāt·us -a -um *adj* chained
caterv·a -ae *f* crowd, throng, band, mob; troop *(of actors); (mil)* troop
catervārius -a -um *adj* in a crowd
catervātim *adv* in groups; in herds, in flocks; in crowds
cathedr·a -ae *f* armchair, cushioned seat; sedan chair; teacher's chair
Catilīn·a -ae *m* Lucius Sergius Catiline *(leader of conspiracy in 63 B.C.)*
catill·ō -āre -āvī -ātum *intr* to lick the plate
catill·us -ī *m or* **catill·um -ī** *n* plate
catīn·us -ī *m* plate, bowl, dish
Cat·ō -ōnis *m* Marcus Porcius Cato *(model of Roman aristocratic conservatism, 239–149 B.C.)* ‖ Marcus Porcius Cato Uticensis *(grandson of the former, arch-enemy of Julius Caesar, 95–45 B.C.)*
Catull·us -ī *m* Gaius Valerius Catullus *(lyric and elegaic poet of Verona, 86–54 B.C.)* ‖ a mime writer
catul·us -ī *m* puppy; whelp, cub ‖
Catulus Roman family name *(cognomen), esp.* Quintus Lutatius Catulus *(consul in 78 B.C.)*
cat·us -a -um *adj* clever; sly
Caucasi·us -a -um *adj* of the Caucasus; **portae Caucasiae** pass through the Caucusus Mountains
Caucas·us -ī *m* Caucasus Mountains
caud·a -ae *f* tail **(cōd-)** *(of an animal);* tail-end; *(vulg)* penis; **caudam jactare** *(w. dat)* to flatter; **caudam movere** to wag the tail; **caudam trahere** to be mocked
caude·us -a -um *adj* wooden
caud·ex -icis *m* **(cōd-)** trunk *(of tree);* block *(of wood to which one was tied for punishment);* book, tablet; ledger; *(coll)* blockhead
caudicāl·is -is -e *adj* wood-splitting
Caudīn·us -a -um *adj* of Caudium, Caudine; **Furculae Caudinae** Caudine Forks *(where Romans suffered a great defeat at the hands of Samnites)*
Caud·ium -(i)ī *n* town in Samnium
caul·ae -ārum *fpl* fence; sheepfold; *(anat)* pores
caulicul·us -ī *m* small stalk; small cabbage
caul·is -is *f* stalk, stem; cabbage
caup·ō -ōnis *m* innkeeper
caupōn·a -ae *f* inn, tavern; innkeeper *(female);* retail shop
caupōni·us -a -um *adj* of an inn *or* shop
caupōn·or -ārī -ātus sum *tr* to trade in, traffic in
caupōnul·a -ae *f* small inn; small shop
caus·a *or* **causs·a -ae** *f* cause, grounds, motive, reason; good reason, just cause; pretext, pretense; inducement, occasion; side, party, faction; condition, situation, position; responsibility, blame; *(leg)* case, trial, plea; *(med)* case, symptoms; *(rhet)* matter of discussion, subject matter; matter, business, concern; **causā** *(postpositive) (w. gen)* for the sake of, because of; **animi causā** for the sake of amusement; **causae amicitiae** ties of friendship; **causae necessitudinis** friendly relations; **causam agere** *(or* **dicere** *or* **orare)** to plead a case; **causam cognoscere** *(of a judge)* to examine a case; **in causā esse** to be responsible; **meā causā** for my sake; as far as I am concerned, for all I care; **non sine causā** with good reason; **ob hanc causam** because of this; **per causam** *(w. gen)* under the pretense of; **valetudinis causā** for reasons of (poor) health; **vestrā causā** in your interests
causāri·us -a -um *adj* sick; **missio causaria** *(mil)* medical discharge ‖ *m* soldier with medical discharge
causi·a -ae *or* **cause·a -ae** *f* wide-brimmed Macedonian hat
causidic·us -ī *m* lawyer; shyster
causific·or -ārī -ātus sum *intr* to make excuses
caus·or -ārī -ātus sum *tr* to give as an excuse, pretend
caussa *see* **causa**
causul·a -ae *f* poor reason; *(leg)* petty lawsuit
cautē *adv* cautiously, carefully; without risk
cautēl·a -ae *f* precaution, caution
caut·ēs -is *f* **(cōt-)** *(usu. pl)* rock, crag, cliff; *(fig)* hard-heartedness
cautim *adv* warily, cautiously
cauti·ō -ōnis *f* caution, wariness; guarantee, provision; *(leg)* bond, bail; **mea** *(or* **mihi)** **cautio est** I must see to it, I must take care
caut·or -ōris *m* wary person; *(leg)* bondsman
caut·us -a -um *pp of* **caveo** ‖ *adj* cautious, careful; safe, secure
cavaed·ium -(i)ī *n* inner court of a Roman house
cave·a -ae *f* cavity; enclosure for animals: cage, den, hole, stall, beehive; auditorium, theater; **prima cavea** section of auditorium for nobility; **ultima cavea** section for lower classes
caveō cavēre cāvī cautus *tr* to guard against, beware of; to keep clear of; to stipulate, decree, order; to guarantee; **cave canem!** beware of the dog! ‖ *intr* to be careful, look out, be on one's guard;

(w. abl or **ab)** to be on one's guard against; *(w.* **ab)** to get a guarantee from; *(w. dat)* **1** to guarantee, give a guarantee to; **2** to provide for, take care of; **cave tangere (= noli tangere)** do not touch!

cavern·a -ae *f* hollow; cavity *(in tooth);* cavern; hole; den, lair; hold *(of ship)* **II** *fpl* vault *(of sky)*

cavill·a -ae *f* jeering, scoffing

cavillāti·ō -ōnis *f* banter, scoffing; quibbling

cavillāt·or -ōris *m* scoffer; quibbler

cavill·or -ārī -ātus sum *tr* to scoff at, mock, criticize, satirize **II** *intr* to scoff, jeer; to quibble

cav·ō -āre -āvī -ātus *tr* to hollow out, excavate, dig a hole in; to pierce, run through

cav·us -a -um *adj* hollow, hollowed; concave, vaulted; deep-channeled *(river)* **II** *m & n* depression; cave, cavern; burrow, hole *(of an animal);* hole, cavity, hollow; aperture, perforation; **cavum aedium** inner court of a house

-ce demonstrative enclitic appended to pronouns and adverbs (like colloquial English *here, there,* with *this* or *that);* **hice** *(for* **hicce)** this *(here);* **hujusce** of this *(here);* (when followed by the enclytic **-ne,** the form becomes **-ci: hicine, sicine)**

Cē·a *or* **Cī·a -ae** *or* **Cē·os -ī** *f* Ceos *(Greek island in the Cyclades)*

Cecropi·a -ae *f* Athens

Cecropid·ēs -ae *m* descendant of King Cecrops; **Cecropidae** Athenians

Cecrop·is -idis *or* **idos** *f* female descendant of Cecrops; Aglauros; Procne; Philomela; Athenian woman

Cecropi·us -a -um *adj* of Cecrops; Athenian

Cecr·ops -opis *m* first king of Athens

cēd·ens -entis *adj* unresisting

cēdō cēděre cessī cessus *tr* to grant, concede, yield, give up **II** *intr* to go, move, walk, walk along; to go away, depart, withdraw; *(usu. w.* **vitā)** to pass away, die; *(of time)* to pass; *(of events)* turn out; *(w. dat)* **1** to befall, fall to the lot of; **2** to yield to, submit to, give in to; **3** to be inferior to; **4** to comply with, conform to, obey; *(w.* **in** + *acc)* **1** to result in; **2** to be changed into, become; *(w.* **pro** + *abl)* **1** to pass for; **2** to be the equivalent of; **3** to be the price of; **bonis** *(or* **possessionibus) alicui cedere** to give up *or* cede one's property to s.o.; **foro cedere** to go bankrupt

cedo *(pl:* **cette)** *(old impv)* give here, hand over, bring here; let's hear, tell, out with; look at; **cedo dum!** all right! **cedo ut inspiciam** let me have a look

cedr·us -ī *f* cedar; cedarwood; cedar-wood oil

Celaen·ō -ūs *f* daughter of Atlas and one of the Pleiades **II** one of the Harpies **II** greedy woman

cēlāt·um -ī *n* secret

cele·ber -bris -bre *adj* crowded, populous, frequented; well-attended; famous; well-known, common, usual; solemn, festive; numerous, repeated, frequent

celebrāti·ō -ōnis *f* large assembly; festival, celebration; widespread use **II** *fpl* throngs

celebrāt·us -a -um *adj* crowded, populous; much-frequented; celebrated, famous; solemn, festive; common, current

celebrit·ās -ātis *f* crowd; large assembly; publicity; frequency; fame

celebr·ō -āre -āvī -ātus *tr* to frequent; to crowd, fill; to inhabit; to celebrate, observe; to honor, worship; to escort, attend; to practice, exercise; to announce, publicize; **sermone celebrare** to discuss

cel·er -eris -ere *adj* fast; agile, quick; hurried; rash, hasty; passing quickly

celere *adv* quickly

Celer·ēs -um *mpl* mounted bodyguards of Roman kings

celerip·ēs -edis *adj* swift-footed **II** *m* race horse

celerit·ās -ātis *f* speed; quickness; excessive speed

celeriter *adv* quickly; soon, early

celer·ō -āre -āvī *tr* to quicken, speed up **II** *intr* to be quick, rush, hurry

celeum·a -atis *n* boatswain's call *(giving time to the rowers)*

Cele·us -ī *m* king of Eleusis and father of Triptolemus

cell·a -ae *f* storeroom; silo; small room; *(coll)* hole-in-the-wall, poor man's apartment; sanctuary *(of temple where statue stood);* cell *(of beehive);* cubicle *(in a bathing establishment or in a brothel);* porter's room

cellāri·us -a -um *adj* of a storeroom **II** *m* one in charge of the storeroom

cellul·a -ae *f* **(-ola)** small storeroom; small room; porter's lodge; slave's room

cēl·ō -āre -āvī -ātus *tr* to hide, conceal; to keep secret, keep quiet about; to conceal the identity of; *(w. acc of thing and acc of person from whom one conceals)* to keep *(s.o.)* in the dark about *(s.th.),* hide *(s.th.)* from *(s.o.)* **II** *refl & pass* to pass out of view; **celari de** *(w. abl)* to be kept in ignorance of

cel·ox -ōcis *adj* swift, quick **II** *f* light, fast boat

cels·us -a -um *adj* high, lofty, towering, prominent; erect; lofty *(thoughts);* high *(rank);* proud; *(of head)* held high; tall *(animals, person, trees, buildings)*

Celt·ae -ārum *mpl* Celts
Celtib·ēr -ērī *mpl* a Celtiberian ‖ *mpl* Celtiberians *(early people of central Spain)*
cēn·a -ae *f* dinner; dish, course
cēnācul·um -ī *n* dining room *(usually on the upper floor);* upper floor, attic; attic apartment
cēnātic·us -a -um *adj* dinner
cēnāti·ō -ōnis *f* dining room
cēnātōri·a -ōrum *npl* formal wear; dinner apparel
cēnāt·us -a -um *adj* having dined; stuffed from feasting
cēnit·ō -āre *intr* to dine often
cēn·ō -āre -āvī -ātus *tr* to dine on, eat ‖ *intr* to dine, eat dinner
cens·eō -ēre -uī -us *tr* to think, believe, suppose, imagine, expect; to esteem, appreciate, value; *(of senator)* to propose, move, vote; to recommend; to suggest, advise; *(of the Senate and other bodies and supreme magistrates)* to decide, resolve; *(of the censor)* to estimate, rate, assess, tax; to register *(possessions); (w. abl)* to measure by; **censeo** *(in replies)* I think so; **quid censes?** what is your opinion? *(formula used by the presiding magistrate to invite a senator to express his opinion)* ‖ *pass (w. abl)* to be valued for, have one's reputation based on; *(as deponent)* to reckon, count (as)
censi·ō -ōnis *f* tax assessment; punishment *(imposed by the censor)*
cens·or -ōris *m* censor *(one of two magistrates who took the census and exercised general control over morals);* severe judge of morals; critic
censōri·us -a -um *adj* of the censors; subject to censure; rigid, stern; **funus censorium** public funeral; **homo censorius** ex-censor; **lex censoria** contract *(drawn up by censors)* for leasing buildings
censūr·a -ae *f* office of censor, censorship; censure
cens·us -ūs *m* census; register of the census; income bracket; wealth, property; rich presents; **censum agere** *(or* **habere)** to hold a census; **censu prohibere** to exclude from citizenship
centaurē·um -ī *n* **(-i·um, -i·on)** centaury *(herb)*
Centaurē·us -a -um *adj* of Centaurs
Centaur·us -ī *m* Centaur *(half-man, half-horse); (astr)* Centaurus *(a constellation)*
centēn·ī -ae -a *adj* one hundred each; **deciens centena milia passuum** ten hundred thousand (one million) paces, one thousand miles
centēsim·us -a -um *adj* hundredth ‖ *f* hundredth part, one percent; *(com)* 1% monthly, 12% annually
centi·ceps -cipitis *adj* hundred-headed
centiēs *adv* **(-iens)** a hundred times; *(fig)* a good many times
centiman·us -a -um *adj* hundred-handed
cent·ō -ōnis *m* patchwork, quilt
centr·um -ī *n* center
centum *indecl adj* hundred
centumgemin·us -a -um *adj* hundredfold
centumpl·ex -icis *adj* hundredfold
centumpond·ium -(i)ī *n* hundred pounds, hundred-pound weight
centumvirāl·is -is -e *adj* of the centumvirs
centumvir·ī -ōrum *mpl* panel of one hundred *(jurors chosen annually to try civil suits under a quaestor, esp. concerning inheritances)*
centuncul·us -ī *m* piece of patchwork; blanket *(made of patchwork)*
centuri·a -ae *f (mil)* company, century *(nominally 100 soldiers); (pol)* century, voting division; unit of land *(100 heredia, 200 jugera, i.e., c. 133 acres)*
centuriātim *adv (mil, pol)* by companies *or* centuries
centuriāt·us -a -um *adj (mil, pol)* divided into companies *or* centuries; **comitia centuriata** centuriate assembly *(legislative body that met in the Campus Martius to elect high magistrates, decree war, etc.)*
centuriāt·us -ūs *m* rank of centurion; division into centuries
centuri·ō -ōnis *m* centurion *(commander of an infantry company)*
centuri·ō -āre -āvī -ātus *tr* to divide into centuries or companies
centuriōnāt·us -ūs *m* rank of centurion; revision of the list of centurions
centuss·is -is *m* a hundred *asses (coins, i.e., about $1)*
cēnul·a -ae *f* light dinner
cēnum *see* **caenum**
Ceōs *see* **Cea**
cēpa *or* **cepe** *see* **caepa**
Cephallāni·a -ae *f* Greek island in the Ionian Sea
Cephal·us -ī *m* husband of Procris, whom he accidentally killed
Cēphē·is -idos *f* daughter of Cepheus, Andromeda
Cephēi·us -a -um *adj* descended from Cepheus
Cēphēnes -um *mpl* a people of Ethiopia
Cēphēn·us -a -um *adj* of the Cephenes, Ethiopian
Cēph·eūs -ĕī *m* king of the Cephenes, father of Andromeda
Cēphīs·os -ī *m* Cephissus *(river in Attica; river in Phocis)*
cēr·a -ae *f* wax; writing tablet *(covered with wax);* wax seal; wax bust of an ancestor; cell *(of beehive)*
Ceramīc·us -ī *m* cemetery of Athens

cērār·ium -(i)ī *n* fee for affixing a seal
cerast·ēs -ae *m* horned serpent
ceras·um -ī *n* cherry
ceras·us -ī *f* cherry tree; cherry
cērāt·us -a -um *adj* waxed ‖ *n* wax-salve *(made of wax and oil)*
Cerber·us -ī *m* three-headed dog guarding entrance to lower world
cercopithēc·us -ī *m* long-tailed monkey
cercūr·us -ī *m* swift-sailing ship
cerd·ō -ōnis *m* (common) laborer
Cereāl·is -is -e *adj* of Ceres; of grain; **arma Cerealia** utensils for grinding and baking ‖ *npl* festival of Ceres *(April 10)*
cerebrōs·us -a -um *adj* hot-headed
cerebr·um -ī *n* brain; head, skull; hot temper; *(fig)* brains
Cer·ēs -eris *f* goddess of grain and fruits and mother of Proserpina; grain, wheat; bread; food
cēre·us -a -um *adj* of wax, waxen; wax-colored; soft, pliant ‖ *m* candle
cērinth·a -ae *f* wax flower
cērin·us -a -um *adj* wax-colored
Cermal·us -ī *m* **(Germ-)** part of the Palatine Hill in Rome
cernō cernĕre crēvī crētus *tr* to sift; to distinguish, make out, see; to understand, see; to decide, decree, determine; **hereditatem cernere** to accept an inheritance formally; **vitam cernere** to decide a question of life or death
cernu·us -a -um *adj* leaning forward; headfirst
cērōm·a -atis *n* wrestler's oil; *(fig)* wrestler
cērōmatic·us -a -um *adj* smeared with oil, oily, greasy
cerrīt·us -a -um *adj* possessed by Ceres, crazy, frenzied
certām·en -inis *n* contest, match; rivalry; *(mil)* battle, combat
certātim *adv* with a struggle, in rivalry
certāti·ō -ōnis *f* contest; rivalry, discussion, debate
certē *adv* surely, certainly; of course; *(in answers)* certainly; *(to restrict an assertion)* at least
certō *adv* for sure; in fact, really
cert·ō -āre -āvī -ātus *tr* to contest ‖ *pass* to be fought over ‖ *intr (w.* **de** *+ abl)* to fight over, struggle for; *(w.* **cum)** to fight with, struggle with, compete with; *(w. inf)* to strive to; *(leg)* to debate
cert·us -a -um *adj* certain; fixed; regular; specific, particular, definite; faithful, trusty; unerring; unwavering; **certiorem facere** to inform; **certum est mihi** *(w. inf)* I am determined ‖ *n* certainty; **certum habere** to regard as certain; **pro certo** for sure; **pro certo habere** to be assured
cērul·a -ae *f* piece of wax; **cerula miniata** red pencil *(of a critic)*
cēruss·a -ae *f* ceruse, white paint
cērussāt·us -a -um *adj* painted white
cerv·a -ae *f* doe
cervīc·al -ālis *n* pillow, cushion
cervīcul·a -ae *f* slender neck
cervīn·us -a -um *adj* of a stag
cerv·ix -īcis *f (often in plural with same meaning as singular)* neck; **in cervicibus nostris esse** *(fig)* to be on our necks; **a cervicibus nostris avertere** *(fig)* to get *(s.o.)* off our necks; **cervicibus sustinere** to shoulder *(responsibility)*
cerv·us -ī *m* stag, deer; *(mil)* palisade
cessāti·ō -ōnis *f* cessation; letup; delay; idleness, inactivity
cessāt·or -ōris *m* loafer
cessāt·us -a -um *adj* having been in abeyance; *(of land)* having been left fallow; spent in idleness
cessi·ō -ōnis *f (leg)* surrendering
cess·ō -āre -āvī -ātum *intr* to cease; to let up, slack off, become remiss; to be idle, do nothing; to lie fallow; to fail, not function; *(w. inf)* to hesitate to, be slow to; *(of things)* to stop, give out; *(of things)* to be at rest, be motionless; *(of things)* to be neglected, remain unused; *(w. abl or* **ab)** to be free of, be clear of, be wanting in; *(leg)* to fail to take action, default; *(leg)* to fail to appear in court
cessus *pp of* **cedo**
cest·os *or* **cest·us -ī** *m* brassière
cestrosphendon·ē -ēs *f* artillery piece for hurling stones
cētār·ium -(i)ī *n* fish pond
cētār·ius -(i)ī *m* fishmonger; fisherman
cētē *see* **cetus**
cētera *adv* otherwise, in all other respects, for the rest
cēterōquī(n) *adv* otherwise, in all other respects, for the rest
cēterum *adv* but, still; for the rest, otherwise; however that may be
cēter·us -a -um *adj* the other, the remaining, the rest of ‖ *pron masc pl & fem pl* the others, all the rest, everybody else ‖ *n* the rest; **de cetero** for the rest; otherwise; for the future; **in ceterum** in the future
Cethēg·us -ī *m* Gaius Cornelius Cethegus *(fellow conspirator of Catiline)*
cette *see* **cedo**
cēt·us *or* **cēt·os -ī** *(nom & acc npl:* **cētē)** *m* large sea animal: whale, shark, dolphin, seal; sea-monster
ceu *conj (in comparisons)* as, just as; *(in comparative conditions)* as if, just as if; **ceu cum** as when
cēv·eō -ēre *intr (cf.* **criso)** *(of a male) (sl)* to move the hips, shake it up

Cē·yx -ȳcis *m* king of Trachis, changed into a kingfisher *(bird)*
Chaerōnē·a -ae *f* town in Boeotia where Philip of Macedon defeated the Greeks in 338 B.C.
Chalcidic·us -a -um *adj* of Chalchis *(in Euboea);* of Cumae *(in Italy)*
Chaldae·us -a -um *adj* Chaldean ‖ *m* astrologer, fortuneteller
chalybēï·us -a -um *adj* steel-
Chalyb·es -um *mpl* people of Pontus in Asia Minor noted as steel-workers and iron-workers
chal·ybs -ybis *m* steel; iron
Chāon·es -um *mpl* tribe in Epirus
Chāoni·us -a -um *adj* Chaonian; of Epirus ‖ *f* Chaonia *(in Epirus)*
Cha·os -ī *n* chaos, the unformed world; **a Chao** from the beginning of the world
char·a -ae *f* wild cabbage (?)
Charit·ēs -um *fpl* the Graces
Char·ōn -onis *m* ferryman of the lower world
chart·a -ae *f* sheet of papyrus; thin sheet of metal ‖ *fpl (fig)* writings
chartul·a -ae *f* sheet of papyrus; note
Charybd·is -is *f* whirlpool between Italy and Sicily *(regarded as a female monster); (fig)* cruel person
Chatt·ī -ōrum *mpl* Germanic tribe
Chauc·ī -ōrum *mpl* Germanic tribe
Chēl·ae -ārum *fpl (astr)* the Claws *(of the constellation Scorpio); (astr)* Libra
chelydr·us -ī *m* poisonous water snake
chelys *(gen not in use; acc:* **chelyn)** *f* tortoise; lyre
cheragr·a -ae *f* arthritis in the hand
chīliarch·ēs -ae *or* **chīliarch·us -ī** *m* commander of 1,000 men; Persian chancellor *(highest office next to the king)*
Chimaer·a -ae *f* fire-breathing female monster, with lion's head, goat's body, and dragon's tail
Chimaerifer·a -ae *adj (fem only) (of Lycia)* that produced the Chimaera
Chi·os *or* **Chi·us -ī** *f* Chios *(Greek island off the coast of Ionia)*
chīrograph·um -ī *n* **(-graf-)** one's handwriting; manuscript; written promise; **falsum chirographum** forgery
Chīr·ō(n) -ōnis *m* Chiron *(Centaur, tutor of Hercules, Achilles, etc.); (astr)* Chiron *(constellation)*
chīronom·ōn -untos *adj* gesticulating
chīronom·os -ī *m* pantominist
chīrurgi·a -ae *f* surgery
chīrurgic·us -ī *m* surgeon
chīrurg·us -ī *m* surgeon
Chi·us -a -um *adj & mf* Chian ‖ *n* Chian wine ‖ *npl* Chian cloth
chlamydāt·us -a -um *adj* wearing a military cape
c(h)lam·ys -ydis *or* **-ydos** *f* military cape; gold-brocaded cape
Choeril·us -ī *m* incompetent panegyrist of Alexander the Great
chorāg·ium -(i)ī *n* stage properties
chorāg·us -ī *m* theatrical producer
choraul·ēs -ae *m* flute player *(who accompanied the choral dance)*
chord·a -ae *f* string *(of musical instrument);* cord, rope
chorē·a -ae *f* dance
chorē·us -ī *m* trochee (— ◡)
chorocitharist·ēs -ae *m* one who accompanied a chorus on the lyre
chor·us -ī *m* chorus; choir
Chrem·ēs -ētis *m* miserly old character in plays of Terence
Christiān·us -ī *m* Christian
Christ·us -ī *m* Christ
Chrȳsē·ïs -idis *or* **-idos** *f* Agamemnon's slave girl, daughter of Chryses
Chrȳs·ēs -ae *m* priest of Apollo
Chrȳsipp·us -ī *m* famous Stoic philosopher *(290–210 B.C.)*
chrȳsolith·os -ī *m* chrysolite, topaz
chrȳs·os -ī *m* gold
cibāri·us -a -um *adj* of food; common, coarse *(food for slaves)* ‖ *npl* rations, provisions, food allowance
cibāt·us -ūs *m* food; feed, fodder
cib·ō -āre -āvī -ātus *tr* to feed
cibōr·ium -(i)ī *n* chalice
cib·us -ī *m* food; feed; meal; nutriment; fuel; **cibum capere** to take food, eat food, eat a meal
cicād·a -ae *f* cicada; harvest fly
cicātrīcōs·us -a -um *adj* scarred, covered with scars
cicātr·ix -īcis *f* scar
cicc·us -ī *m* core of pomegranate; *(sl)* junk
cic·er -eris *m* chickpea; testicle
Cicer·ō -ōnis *m* Cicero *(Marcus Tullius Cicero, orator and politician, 106–43 B.C.)* ‖ Quintus Tullius Cicero *(his brother, 102–43 B.C.)* ‖ Marcus Tullius Cicero *(his son, consul in 30 B.C.)*
cichorē·um *or* **cichōri·um -ī** *n* endive
cicima(li)ndr·um -ī *n* comic name for an imaginary seasoning
Cicon·es -um *mpl* Thracian tribe
cicōni·a -ae *f* stork
cic·ur -uris *adj* tame
cicūt·a -ae *f* hemlock tree; hemlock poison; pipe, flute *(carved from hemlock wood)*
-cīd·a -ae *m suf* denoting one who cuts *or* kills *(e.g.,* **lapicida** stonecutter; **matricida** murderer of one's mother)
cidar·is -is *f* tiara *(of Persian king)*
cieō ciēre cīvī citus *tr* to set in motion, move; to stir up, rouse up, muster; to call for, send for; to summon for help; to invoke, appeal to; to bring about; to

cause, make; **lacrimas ciere** to shed tears; **stragem ciere** to wreak havoc

Cilici·a -ae *f* country and Roman province in S.E. Asia Minor

cilic·ium -(i)ī *n* rug *or* blanket of goat's hair

Cilici·us -a -um *adj* Cilician ‖ *n* garment made of goat's hair

Ciliss·a -ae *f* Cilician woman

Cil·ix -icis *adj & m* Cilician

-cill·um -ī *neut suf* forms diminutives: **corcillum** heart

-cill·us -ī *masc suf* forms diminutives from diminutives: **penicillus** (small) painter's brush

Cim·ber -brī *m* Cimbrian ‖ Roman family name *(cognomen)*

Cimbr·ī -ōrum *mpl* Germanic tribe that invaded Gaul and Italy at the end of the 2nd cent. B.C. and was defeated by Marius

Cimbric·us -a -um *adj* Cimbrian

cīm·ex -icis *m* bedbug

Cimmeri·ī -ōrum *mpl* people in the Crimea ‖ people living in perpetual darkness in caves at Cumae

cinaedic·us -a -um *adj* lewd

cinaed·us -ī *m* catamite; homosexual

cincinnāt·us -a -um *adj* curly-haired ‖ **Cicinnatus** *m* Lucius Quinctius Cincinnatus *(Roman war hero, appointed dictator in 458 B.C.)*

cincinn·us -ī *m* lock of curled hair; *(rhet)* artificial expression

cincticul·us -ī *m* small belt *or* sash

cinctūr·a -ae *f* belt, sash

cinctus *pp of* **cingo**

cinct·us -ūs *m* tucking up; belt, sash; **cinctus Gabinius** Gabinian style of wearing toga *(usually employed at religious festivals)*

cinctūt·us -a -um *adj* wearing a belt *or* sash; old-fashioned

cinefact·us -a -um *adj* reduced to ashes

cinerār·ius -(i)ī *m* hairdresser

cin·gō -gĕre -xī -ctus *tr* to surround, encircle; to enclose *(a space);* to wreathe *(head);* to tuck up *(garment)* ‖ *pass* to get dressed; to form a circle; **cingi in proelia** to gear up for battle; **ferrum cingi** to put on one's sword

cingul·a -ae *f* belt; sash; girth; sword belt; chastity belt

cingul·um -ī *n* belt; sword belt; sash; girdle; chastity belt

cingul·us -ī *m* zone *(of the earth)*

cinīfl·ō -ōnis *m* hairdresser

cin·is -eris *m (f)* ashes; ruin, death

-cin·ium -(i)ī *neut suf* denoting activity or profession *(e.g.,* **latrocinium** robbing, robbery)

Cinn·a -ae *m* Lucius Cornelius Cinna *(notorious consul 87–84 B.C.)*

cinnamōm·um *or* **cinnam·um -ī** *n* cinnamon ‖ *npl* cinnamon sticks

cinxī *perf of* **cingo**

Cinyr·ās -ae *m* father of Myrrha, and, by her, also father of Adonis

cip(p)·us -ī *m* stake, post, pillar; gravestone; *(mil)* palisade

Circa *see* **Circe**

circā *adv* around, round about; all around, in the vicinity ‖ *prep (w. acc)* around, surrounding, about, in the neighborhood of, near; through; attending, escorting; concerning, in respect to; *(of time)* around, about, towards; *(w. numbers)* about, nearly, almost

Circae·us -a -um *adj* of Circe

circāmoer·ium -(i)ī *n* area on both sides of a city wall

Circ·ē -ēs *or* **Circ·a -ae** *f* Circe *(famous witch, daughter of Sol and Perse)*

circens·is -is -e *adj* of the racetrack ‖ *mpl* races

circin·ō -āre -āvī -ātus *tr* to make round; to circle

circin·us -ī *m (geometer's)* compass

circiter *adv* about, nearly, approximately ‖ *prep (w. acc)* about, near

circlus *see* **circulus**

circueō *see* **circumeo**

circuitiō *see* **circumitio**

circuit·us -ūs *m* circuit; going around, revolution; detour; circumference; beating around the bush; *(rhet)* period

circulātim *adv* in groups

circulāt·or -ōris *m* peddler; itinerant performer

circulātr·ix -īcis *f* peddler *(female);* itinerant performer *(female)*

circul·or -ārī -ātus sum *intr* to gather a crowd around oneself

circ(u)l·us -ī *m* circle, circuit; ring, hoop; social circle; *(astr)* orbit

circum *adv* about, all around ‖ *prep (w. acc)* around, about; in the neighborhood of

circum- *suf* around, about: **circumstare** to stand around

circum·agō -agĕre -ēgī -actus *tr* to turn around; to turn *(e.g., a wheel);* to sway ‖ *refl & pass* to turn around; *(of feelings)* to change; to change *(in form);* to go out of one's way; *(of time)* to pass, roll around

circumar·ō -āre -āvī *tr* to plow around

circumcaesūr·a -ae *f* contour, outline

circumcī·dō -dĕre -dī -sus *tr* to cut around, trim; to cut short, cut down on; to abridge, shorten; to circumcise

circumcircā *adv* all around

circumcīs·us -a -um *pp of* **circumcido** ‖ *adj* steep, inaccessible; abridged

circumclū·dō -dĕre -sī -sus *tr* to shut in, enclose; *(mil)* to surround; *(fig)* circumvent

circumcol·ō -ĕre *tr* to live near
circumcurs·ō -āre -āvī *tr & intr* to run around
circum·dō -dăre -dedī -datus *tr* to surround, enclose, encircle; *(w. dat)* to place *or* put *(s.th.)* around
circumdū·cō -cĕre -xī -ctus *tr* lead around, draw around; *(w. double acc)* to lead *(s.o.)* around to; **aliquem omnia praesidia circumducere** to lead s.o. around to all the garrisons
circumducti·ō -ōnis *f* perimeter; *(w. gen)* cheating out of; *(rhet)* period
circum·eō -īre -īvī *or* **-iī -itus** *tr* to go around, go around to, visit, make the rounds of; to surround, encircle, encompass; to circumvent, deceive, cheat ‖ *intr* to go around, make a circuit
circumequit·ō -āre *tr* to ride around *(on horseback)*
circumerr·ō -āre -āvi *tr & intr* to wander around, prowl around
circum·ferō -ferre -tūlī -lātus *tr* to carry around, hand around; to publicize, spread around; to purify; **oculos circumferre** to glance about ‖ *pass* to revolve
circumfle·ctō -ctĕre -xī -xus *tr* to turn around, wheel about
circumfl·ō -āre *tr* to blow around; *(fig)* to buffet
circumflu·ō -ĕre -xī *tr* to flow around; to surround; to overflow ‖ *intr* to be overflowing, abound
circumflu·us -a -um *adj* flowing around; surrounded *(by water)*
circumforāne·us -a -um *adj* strolling about from market to market, itinerant; around the forum
circumfrem·ō -ĕre -uī *intr* to groan all around
circum·fundō -fundĕre -fūdī -fūsus *tr* to pour around; to surround, cover, envelop ‖ *refl & pass* to crowd around; *(w. dat)* to cling to
circumgem·ō -ĕre *tr* to growl around *(e.g., a sheepfold)*
circumgest·ō -āre *tr* to carry around
circum·gredior -gredī -gressus sum *tr* to surround *(esp. to attack)*
circu(m)iti·ō -ōnis *f* going around; patrolling; beating around the bush
circumitus *see* **circuitus**
circumjac·eō -ēre *intr (w. dat)* to lie near, border on, be adjacent to
circumject·us -ūs *m* an encompassing
circum·jiciō -jicĕre -jēcī -jectus *tr* to throw *or* place around; to surround; *(w. dat)* to throw *(s.th.)* around *(s.o. or s.th.)*; **fossam circumjicere** to dig a trench all around
circumject·us -a -um *adj* surrounding, encompassing, taking in
circumlāt·us -a -um *pp of* **circumfero**
circumlav·ō -āre *or* **-ĕre** *tr* to wash around, wash the sides of
circumlīg·ō -āre -āvī -ātus *tr* to bind; *(w. dat)* to tie *(s.th.)* to
circum·linō -linĕre -lēvī -litus *tr* to smear all over, to anoint; to cover; *(fig)* to clothe
circumlu·ō -ĕre *tr* to flow around
circumluvi·ō -ōnis *f* island *(formed by a river flowing in a new channel)*
circum·mittō -mittĕre -mīsī -missus *tr* to send around
circummūg·iō -īre *intr* to moo around
circummūn·iō -īre -īvī -ītus *tr* (**-moen-**) to fortify *(with wall, moat, etc.)*
circummūnīti·ō -ōnis *f* investment *(of town)*; circumvallation
circumpadān·us -a -um *adj* situated along the Po River
circumpend·eō -ēre *intr* to hang around
circumplaud·ō -ĕre *tr* to applaud from every direction
circumple·ctor -ctī -xus sum *tr* to embrace; to surround
circumplic·ō -āre -āvī -ātus *tr* to wind up; to coil around; *(w. dat)* to wind *(s.th.)* around
circum·pōnō -pōnĕre -posuī positus *tr* *(w. dat)* to place *or* set *(s.th.)* around
circumpōtāti·ō -ōnis *f* round of drinks
circumrēt·iō -īre *tr* to snare
circumrō·dō -dĕre -sī -sus *tr* to nibble all around; to hesitate to say; to slander
circumsaep·iō -īre -sī -tus *tr* (**-sēp-**) to fence in, enclose
circumscind·ō -ĕre *tr* to strip off
circumscrī·bō -bĕre -psī -ptus *tr* to draw a line around, mark the boundaries of; to limit, circumscribe; to set aside; to defeat the purpose of; to trap, defraud
circumscriptē *adv* concisely; *(rhet)* in periodic style
circumscripti·ō -ōnis *f* encircling; circle; limits, boundary; outline, definition; cheating; *(rhet)* periodic sentence
circumscript·or -ōris *m* cheat
circumscript·us -a -um *pp of* **circumscribo** ‖ *adj* restricted; concise; *(rhet)* periodic, rounded-off
circumsec·ō -āre -uī -tus *tr* to cut around; to circumcize
circum·sedeō -sedēre -sēdī -sessus *tr* to beset, besiege, blockade
circumsēpiō *see* **circumsaepio**
circumsessi·ō -ōnis *f* blockading
circum·sīdō -sīdĕre -sēdī -sessus *tr* to besiege, surround, invest
circumsil·iō -īre *tr & intr* to hop around
circum·sistō -sistĕre -stetī *tr* to stand around, surround
circumson·ō -āre -uī -ātus *tr* to make resound, cause to re-echo ‖ *intr* to resound everywhere; *(w. dat)* to resound to

circumson·us -a -um *adj* noisy
circumspectātr·ix -īcis *f* spy *(female)*
circumspecti·ō -ōnis *f* looking around; circumspection, caution
circumspect·ō -āre *tr* to watch for, search carefully for; to catch sight of ‖ *intr* to keep looking around, look around anxiously
circumspect·us -a -um *pp of* **circumspicio** ‖ *adj* well-considered, guarded *(words);* circumspect, cautious
circumspect·us -ūs *m* consideration; commanding view; contemplation
circum·spiciō -spicĕre -spexī -spectus *tr* to look around at, survey; to catch sight of; to consider, examine ‖ *refl* to think highly of oneself ‖ *intr* to be circumspect, be cautious, be on the watch
circumstant·ēs -ium *mpl* bystanders
circum·stō -stāre -stetī *tr* to surround, envelop; *(of terror, etc.)* to grip ‖ *intr* to stand around
circumstrep·ō -ĕre -uī -itus *tr* to shout at on all sides, surround with noise *or* shouts
circumsurg·ens -entis *adj (of mountains)* rising all around
circumtent·us -a -um *adj* tightly covered
circumter·ō -ĕre *tr* to rub shoulders with, crowd around
circumtext·us -a -um *adj* with embroidered border
circumton·ō -āre -uī *tr* to crash around, thunder around
circumtons·us -a -um *adj* clipped *or* trimmed all around
circumvā·dō -dĕre -sī *tr* to attack on every side; *(of terror)* to grip
circumvag·us -a -um *adj* flowing around, encircling
circumvall·ō -āre -āvī -ātus *tr* to blockade ‖ *refl* to form a blockade
circumvecti·ō -ōnis *f* carting around *(of merchandise);* circular course, revolution *(of sun)*
circumvect·ō -āre -āvī -ātus *tr* to carry around ‖ *pass* to travel around, sail around
circumve·hor -hī -ctus sum *tr* to ride around (to), sail around (to), travel around (to); to travel past
circumvēl·ō -āre *tr* to envelop, cover
circum·veniō -venīre -vēnī -ventus *tr* to enclose, surround; to go around to; to distress, beset; to circumvent, cheat; to prosecute *or* convict unjustly
circumver·tō -tĕre -tī -sus *tr* (-vor-) to turn *(s.th.)* around ‖ *pass* to turn around; **rota circumvertitur axem** the wheel revolves around its axle
circumvest·iō -īre *tr* to clothe
circumvinc·iō -īre *tr* to tie up
circumvīs·ō -ĕre *tr* to look around, glare around at
circumvolit·ō -āre -āvī *tr & intr* to fly around, dash about, rove around; to hover around
circumvol·ō -āre -āvī *tr* to fly around, dart around ‖ *intr* to hover about, hover over, flit about
circumvol·vō -vĕre -vī -ūtus *tr* to wind, roll around ‖ *refl & pass (w. dat or acc)* to revolve around, wind oneself around
circ·us -ī *m* circle; racetrack; *(astr)* orbit
Circ·us Falamini·us -ī *m* racetrack built by Gaius Flaminius Nepos in the Campus Martius in 220 B.C.
Circ·us Maxim·us -ī *m* oldest racetrack in Rome, between the Palatine and Aventine Hills
cirrāt·us -a -um *adj* curly-haired
Cirrh·a -ae *f* (Cyrr-) town near Delphi, sacred to Apollo
Cirrhae·us -a -um *adj* of Cirrha; of Apollo
cirr·us -ī *m* lock, curl; forelock
Cirt·a -ae *f* town in Numidia
Cirtens·ēs -ium *mpl* inhabitants of Cirta
cis *prep (w. acc)* on this side of *(on the Roman side of); (of time)* within
cis- *pref* used in the sense of the preposition
Cisalpīn·us -a -um *adj* Cisalpine *(on the Roman side of the Alps)*
cis·ium -(i)ī *n* gig *(light, two-wheeled carriage)*
Cisp·ius -(i)ī *m* (Cesp-) one of the summits of the Esquiline Hill
Cisrhenān·us -a -um *adj* dwelling on the W. side of the Rhine
Cissē·is -idis *f* daughter of Cisseus *(i.e., Hecuba)*
Ciss·eūs -eī *m* king of Thrace and father of Hecuba
cist·a -ae *f* box, chest *(esp. of wicker);* ballot box
cistell·a -ae *f* small box
cistellātr·ix -īcis *f* female slave in charge of the money box
cistellul·a -ae *f* small box
cistern·a -ae *f* cistern, reservoir
cistophor·us -ī *m* Asiatic coin *(with a representation of a bearer of the cista of Dionysus on it)*
cistul·a -ae *f* small box
citātim *adv* quickly, hurriedly
citāt·us -a -um *adj (of animals)* speeded up; *(of limbs)* moved quickly; *(of pace, actions)* quick, speedy; *(of bowels)* loose; **citato equo** at full gallop
citāt·us -ūs *m* impulse
citeri·or -or -us *adj* on this side, near *(to Rome);* earlier; *(nearer to the present)* later, more recent; more down-to-earth, nearer home; *(w. abl)* earlier than
citerius *adv* short of
Cithaer·ōn -ōnis *m* Greek mountain range dividing Attica from Boeotia

cithar·a -ae *f* lyre
citharist·a -ae *m* lyre player
citharistri·a -ae *f* lyre player *(female)*
cithariz·ō -āre *intr* to play the lyre
citharoed·us -ī *m* singer *(playing the lyre)*
citim·us -a -um *adj* (lying) nearest
citius *adv* sooner, rather; **dicto citius** no sooner said than done; **serius aut citius** sooner or later
cito *adv* quickly; soon
cit·ō -āre -āvī -ātus *tr* to excite, rouse; to call, summon; to call to witness, appeal to; to arouse, produce; to cite *(as an authority)*
citrā *adv* on this side, on the near side; **citra cadere** to fall short ‖ *prep (w. acc)* **1** on this side of, on the near side of: **citra mare** on this side of the sea, in Italy; **2** *(of time)* since, before: **citra Trojana tempora** before the Trojan period; **3** just short of, less than, except: **peccavi citra scelus** I committed a fault just short of a crime; **4** regardless of *(e.g., a person's wishes)*: **citra senatūs populique auctoritatem** regardless of *or* without regard for the authority of the senate and the people
citre·us -a -um *adj* of citrus wood
citrō *adv* to this side, this way; **ultro (et) citro** *(or* **citro ultroque)** to and fro, up and down; mutually
citr·um -ī *n* wood of the citron tree; table *(made of citron wood)*
citr·us -ī *f* citron tree
cit·us -a -um *pp of* **cieo** ‖ *adj* quick
cīvic·us -a -um *adj* civil; civilian; suitable for one as a civilian; **corona civica** civic crown *(given to war hero for saving s.o.'s life)*
cīvīl·is -is -e *adj* civil, civic; civilian; forensic, legal; political; unassuming; **jus civile** private *or* civil law; civil rights; **ratio civilis** political science; **res civilis** *(or* **civiles)** politics; **vir civilis** statesman
cīvīlit·ās -ātis *f* politics; courtesy
cīvīliter *adv* like a citizen; as an ordinary citizen should; politely
cīv·is -is *mf* citizen; fellow citizen; private citizen
cīvit·ās -ātis *f* state; community; city; citizenship
clād·ēs -is *f* disaster; loss; *(mil)* defeat, carnage; destruction; ruins; *(of person)* scourge, destroyer
clam *adv* secretly, privately; stealthily; **clam habere aliquem** to keep s.o. in the dark ‖ *prep (w. abl or acc)* without the knowledge of; **neque clam me est** nor is it unknown to me; **clam patre** without the father's knowledge
clāmāt·or -ōris *m* loudmouth
clāmitāti·ō -ōnis *f* bawling, racket
clāmit·ō -āre -āvī -ātus *tr & intr* to cry out, yell
clām·ō -āre -āvī -ātus *tr* to shout, yell; to proclaim; to call upon ‖ *intr* to shout
clām·or -ōris *m* shout; acclamation; applause; battle cry; noise; wailing
clāmōsē *adv* with a shout, loudly
clāmōs·us -a -um *adj* yelling, noisy; loud-barking *(dog)*
clanculum *adv* secretly; privately ‖ *prep (w. acc)* unknown to
clandestīnō *adv* secretly
clandestīn·us -a -um *adj* clandestine
clang·ō -ĕre *intr (of eagle)* to scream
clang·or -ōris *m* clang, noise; blast *(of trumpet)*; cry, scream *(of bird)*; baying *(of dog)*
clārē *adv* clearly; out loud; brightly; with distinction, honorably; **clare legere** to read aloud
clār·eō -ēre *intr* to be clear, be distinct, be bright; to be evident; to be famous
clār·esco -escĕre -uī *intr* to become clear, become distinct; to become bright; to become famous; *(of sound)* to get loud
clārigāti·ō -ōnis *f* reparation; fine
clārig·ō -āre -āvī -ātum *intr* to demand satisfaction, demand reparation
clārison·us -a -um *adj* clear-sounding
clārit·ās -ātis *f* loudness; clarity; brightness; distinction, renown
clāritūd·ō -inis *f* brightness; fame
Clari·us -a -um *adj* of the island of Claros, *esp.* as epithet of Apollo
clār·ō -āre -āvī -ātus *tr* to clarify, explain; to light up, illuminate; to make famous
Clar·os -ī *f* town in Asia Minor famous for a temple and oracle of Apollo
clār·us -a -um *adj* loud; clear, bright; plain, manifest; famous; notorious; **clara lux** broad daylight; **clarior luce** clearer than daylight; **vir clarissimus** gentleman of the Senate
classiāri·us -a -um *adj* naval ‖ *mpl* marines
classicul·a -ae *f* flotilla
classic·us -a -um *adj* first-class, belonging to the highest class of citizens; naval ‖ *m* trumpeter who summoned the *comitia centuriata* ‖ *mpl* marines, sailors ‖ *n* battle signal; bugle call; **classicum canere** to sound the bugle *(to begin battle; to announce a capital trial or an execution)*
class·is -is *f* fleet; *(social)* class; grade, class *(of pupils)*; band, group; **classi** with a fleet, at sea; in a naval battle
clāt(h)rāt·us -a -um *adj* barred
clāt(h)r·ī -ōrum *mpl* bars; railings
claud·eō -ēre *or* **claud·ō -ĕre** *intr* to be lame, to limp; to falter; to be imperfect
Claudiān·us -a -um *adj* connected with

members of the Claudian clan, *esp.* the Emperor Claudius
claudicāti·ō -ōnis *f* limping
claudic·ō -āre *intr* to be lame, to limp; to incline to one side; to be halting, be defective; to be deficient, fall short
Claud·ius -(i)ī *m* Appius Claudius Caecus *(censor in 312 B.C. and builder of the Appian Way and Appian aqueduct)* ‖ the Roman Emperor Claudius *(Tiberius Claudius Nero Germanicus, reigned 41–54 A.D.)*
clau·dō -dĕre -sī -sus *tr* to shut, close; to bring to a close, conclude; to shut up; to lock up, imprison; *(mil)* to blockade, hem in; to limit; to cut off, block; to keep secret, suppress *(feelings, thoughts);* **agmen claudere** to bring up the rear; **numeris** *(or* **pedibus) claudere** to put into verse; **transitum claudere** to block traffic
claud·us -a -um *adj* **(clōd-)** lame, limping; crippled, imperfect, defective; wavering; untrustworthy
claustell·um -ī *n* **(clos-)** keyhole
claustr·a -ōrum *npl* lock, bolt, bar; gate; dam, dike; barrier, barricade; cage, den; fortress; defenses
clausul·a -ae *f* close, conclusion *(of a letter, speech, argument; of a transaction);* clause *(in a law or document);* end *(of a word, of a line of verse); (rhet)* close of a periodic sentence with particular regard to its rhythm
claus·us -a -um *pp of* **claudo** ‖ *adj* closed, inaccessible *(place); (of a person)* impervious to feelings; shut, locked up; enclosed *(in a container)* ‖ *n* enclosure
Claus·us -ī *m* a Sabine chief, reputed ancestor of the *gens Claudia* ‖ *mpl* members of the *gens Claudia*
clāv·a -ae *f* cudgel, club
clāvār·ium -iī *n* soldier's allowance for shoe nails
clāvāt·or -ōris *m* club-bearer
clāvīcul·a -ae *f* tendril; key; pivot
clāvig·er -era -erum *adj* carrying a club; carrying keys ‖ *m* club bearer *(Hercules);* key bearer *(Janus)*
clāv·is -is *f* key; hook *(for rolling a hoop);* **clavīs adimere uxori** to take the keys away from a wife, get a divorce
clāv·us -ī *m* nail; rivet; rudder, helm; purple stripe *(worn on the tunic, broad for senators and their sons, narrow for equites);* **clavo** *(or* **clavo trabali) figere** to nail; *(fig)* to nail down, clinch; **clavum rectum tenere** to keep a steady course; **clavus anni** beginning of the year; **clavus trabalis** spike *(large nail)*
clēm·ens -entis *adj* gentle, mild, kind, compassionate; mild, calm *(weather)*
clēmenter *adv* gently, mildly, kindly, compassionately; at an easy pace; **colles clementer adsurgentes** gently rising hills
clēmenti·a -ae *f* mildness, clemency, compassion
Cleopatra -ae *f* daughter of Ptolemy Auletes and queen of Egypt *(d. 31 B.C.)*
clep·ō -ĕre -sī -tus *tr* to steal
clepsydr·a -ae *f* water clock; *(fig)* time *(allotted to speakers);* **clepsydram dare** *(w. dat)* to give *(s.o.)* the floor; **clepsydram petere** to ask to have the floor
clept·ēs -ae *m* thief
cli·ens -entis *m* client *(e.g., ex-slave protected by a former owner acting as patron);* follower, retainer; vassal ‖ *mpl* clients *(the citizens of an Italian or other city in their relationship to their Roman patronus)*
client·a -ae *f* client *(female)*
clientēl·a -ae *f* clientele; patronage, protection; clientship *(the relationship of a provincial city or a foreign people to their Roman patronus);* vassalage ‖ *fpl* allies, dependants
clientul·us -ī *m (as term of contempt)* just a poor client
clīnām·en -inis *n* swerve
clīnāt·us -a -um *adj* bent, inclined
clīnic·us -ī *m* clinical physician *(who tends patients at their bedside)*
Clī·ō -ūs *f* Muse of history
clipeāt·us -a -um *adj* armed with a *(round)* shield
clipe·um -ī *n or* **clipe·us -ī** *m* round bronze shield; medallion; disc *(of sun)*
clītell·ae -ārum *fpl* packsaddle
clītellāri·us -a -um *adj* carrying a packsaddle
clīvōs·us -a -um *adj* hilly; steep
clīv·us -ī *m* sloping ground, incline, hill; slope, pitch; *(fig)* uphill struggle; **adversus clivum** uphill; **primi clivi** foothills
Clīv·us Sac·er *(gen:* **Clīv·i Sac·ri)** *m* Sacred Incline *(part of the Via Sacra ascending the Capitoline Hill, also called* **Clivus Capitolinus)**
cloāc·a -ae *f* sewer, drain; **cloaca maxima** main sewer *(draining the area of the Roman Forum)*
Cloācīn·a -ae *f* Venus *(the "purifier")*
Clōdi·a -ae *f* sister of the notorious tribune Clodius
Clōdiān·us -a -um *adj* Clodian, of the Clodian faction
Clōd·ius -(i)ī *m* Publius Clodius Pulcher *(notorious tribune of the plebs, enemy of Cicero, killed in 52 B.C.)*
Cloeli·a -ae *f* Roman girl who was given as hostage to Porsenna and escaped by swimming the Tiber back to Rome
Clōthō *(gen not in use; acc:* **Clōthō)** *f* one of the three Fates

clu·eō -ēre *or* **clu·eor -ērī** *intr* to be spoken of as, be known for; **ut nomen cluet** as the word implies

clūn·is -is *mf* buttock ‖ *mpl & fpl* buttocks; hind quarters *(of an animal)*

clūr·a -ae *f* ape

clūrīn·us -a -um *adj* of apes

Clūs·ium -(i)ī *n* chief Etruscan town

Clūs·ius -(i)ī *m* Janus

Clymen·ē -ēs *f* mother of Phaëthon

clyst·ēr -ēris *m* an injection; *(fig)* syringe

Clyt(a)em(n)estr·a -ae *f* Clytemnestra *(wife of Agamemnon, sister of Helen, Castor, and Pollux, and mother of Electra, Iphigenia, and Orestes)*

Cn. *abbr* **Gnaeus** *(Roman first name, praenomen)*

Cnid·os *or* **Cnid·us -ī** *f* town in Caria, famous for the worship of Venus

coacervāti·ō -ōnis *f* accumulation

coacerv·ō -āre -āvī -ātus *tr* to gather into a heap; to accumulate; to make *(by heaping up)*

coac·escō -escĕre -uī *intr* to become sour

coacti·ō -ōnis *f* collection *(of money)*; abridgment

coact·ō -āre *tr* to force

coact·or -ōris *m* collector *(of money, taxes)*; **agminis coactores** rearguard elements

coact·us -a -um *pp of* **cogo** ‖ *adj* forced, unnatural, hypocritical ‖ *n* felt cloth ‖ *npl* felt cloak

coact·us -ūs *m* coercion, compulsion

coaedific·ō -āre -āvī -ātus *tr* to build *(a town)*; to build up *(an area)*, fill with buildings

coaequ·ō -āre -āvī -ātus *tr* to level off; to treat as equal, equate

coagmentāti·ō -ōnis *f* union; joint

coagment·ō -āre -āvī -ātus *tr* to join together; to construct; to fit *(words)* together

coagment·um -ī *n* joint

coāgul·um -ī *n* rennet *(curdled milk taken from the stomach of young mammals)*; curds

coal·escō -escĕre -uī -itum *intr* **(cōl-)** to grow together, coalesce; *(of wounds)* to close; to become unified; to grow firm, take root; to become established, thrive

coangust·ō -āre -āvī -ātus *tr* **(conang-)** to contract, compress; to limit, restrict

coarct- *see* **coart-**

coargu·ō -ĕre -ī *tr* to bring out into the open *(usu. s.th. undesirable)*; to prove conclusively, demonstrate; to refute, prove wrong *or* guilty; *(w. gen of the charge)* to prove *(s.o.)* guilty of

coartāti·ō -ōnis *f* crowding together; tightening

coart·ō -āre -āvī -ātus *tr* to narrow, make narrower; to crowd together, confine; to pack *(e.g., the Forum)*; to shorten; to abridge

coax·ō -āre *intr (of frogs)* to croak

Cōcal·us -ī *m* mythical king of Sicily who protected Daedalus

Coccēi·us -a -um *adj* Roman clan name *(nomen), esp.* Marcus Cocceius Nerva, emperor A.D. 96–98

coccināt·us -a -um *adj* dressed in scarlet

coccin(e)·us -a -um *adj* scarlet ‖ *npl* scarlet clothes; scarlet coverlets

cocc·um -ī *n* scarlet

coc(h)le·a -ae *f* snail

coc(h)leār·(e) -is *n* spoon

cocilendr·um -ī *n* an imaginary magical seasoning

cocl·es -itis *m* person blind in one eye ‖ **Cocles** Horatius Cocles *(commonly called Horatio and famous for defending the Pons Sublicius against Porsenna's army)*

coctil·is -is -e *adj* baked; brick-

coct·or -ōris *m* cook

coct·us -a -um *pp of* **coquo** ‖ *adj* cooked; roasted; baked *(bricks)*; ripe; *(fig)* mild ‖ *n* cooked food

Cōcyt·us -ī *m* river of the lower world

Cōdēt·a -ae *f* piece of ground in the Campus Martius

cōdex *see* **caudex**

cōdicill·ī -ōrum *mpl* **(-cell-)** fire logs; set of writing tablets; note; petition to the emperor; rescript from the emperor; supplement to a will, codicil

Codr·us -ī *m* last king of Athens

coēgi *perf of* **cogo**

coel- *see* **cael-**

Coel·ē -ēs *adj (fem only)* **Coele Syria** "Hollow Syria" *(the S. part of Syria, esp. the region between Lebanon and Antilebanon)*; **Coele Thessalia** the plain of Thessaly

co·emō -emĕre -ēmī -emptus *tr* to buy up

coëmpti·ō -ōnis *f* fictitious sale of an estate; marriage *(contracted by fictitious sale of contracting parties)*

coëmptiōnāl·is -is -e *adj* of a marriage by fictitious sale

coen- *see* **caen-**

co·eō -īre -iī -itus *tr* **societatem coire** to form an alliance ‖ *intr* to come together; to meet, assemble; to be united, combine; to mate, copulate; to have sexual intercourse; to congeal, curdle; to agree; to conspire; to clash *(in combat)*; *(of wounds)* to close

cœ̄p·ī -isse -tus *(v. defect) tr & intr* to begin

cœ̄pt·ō -āre -āvī -ātus *tr* to begin eagerly; *(w. inf)* to try to ‖ *intr* to make a beginning

cœ̄pt·um -ī *n (usu. pl)* undertaking, enterprise, attempt

coept·us -ūs *m* beginning; undertaking
coëpulōn·us -ī *m* dinner guest
coërc·eō -ēre -uī -itus *tr* to enclose, confine, hem in; to limit; to restrain, check, control
coërciti·ō -ōnis *f* physical restraint, coercion; inflicting of summary punishment by a magistrate; right to inflict summary punishment
coët·us -ūs *m* coming together, meeting; crowd, company; gang; combination
Coe·us -ī *m* Titan, father of Latona
cōgitātē *adv* deliberately, carefully
cōgitāti·ō -ōnis *f* thinking, deliberating; reflection; thought, plan, idea; reasoning power, imagination
cōgitāt·us -a -um *adj* well-considered, deliberate ‖ *npl* thoughts, ideas
cōgit·ō -āre -āvī -ātus *tr* to consider, ponder, reflect on; to imagine; *(w. inf)* to intend to ‖ *intr* to think
cognāti·ō -ōnis *f* relationship by birth; agreement, resemblance, affinity; relatives, family
cognāt·us -a -um *adj* related by birth; related, similar, akin ‖ *mf* relative
cogniti·ō -ōnis *f* learning, acquiring knowledge; knowledge; notion, idea; recognition; *(w. gen)* knowledge of, acquaintance with; *(leg)* inquiry, hearing, trial
cognit·or -ōris *m* attorney; defender, protector; witness
cognitūr·a -ae *f* the duty of an attorney
cognit·us *pp of* **cognosco** ‖ *adj* acknowledged, known; familiar
cognit·us -ūs *m* act of getting to know; **dignus cognitu** worth knowing; **jucundus cognitu** pleasant to know
cognōm·en -inis *n* surname, family name *(e.g.,* **Caesar;** *a second* **cognomen,** *called* **agnomen** *by later grammarians, was given as an honorary name to a person for some achievement, e.g.,* **Africanus);** additional title of a god *(e.g.,* **Jupiter Feretrus);** nickname; derived name *(esp. of places);* **a duce Tarpeiā mons est cognomen adeptus** the hill took its name from Tarpeia *(the enemy's)* guide
cognōment·um -ī *n* family name; name
cognōmināt·us -a -um *adj* synonymous
cognōmin·is -is -e *adj* like-named, with the same name
cognōmin·ō -āre -āvī -ātus *tr* to give *(s.o.)* a surname *or* nickname
cogn·oscō -oscĕre -ōvī -itus *tr* to become acquainted with, get to know, learn; to recognize, identify; to inquire into, investigate; *(mil)* to reconnoiter; **cognovisse** to know
cōgō cōgĕre coēgī coactus *tr* to gather together, collect; to assemble; to round up; to gather *(crops);* to collect, raise *(money, taxes);* to force, compel; to pressure; to exact, extort; to infer, conclude; to prove conclusively; to compress *(into a mass);* to abridge; to shorten, restrict in time; to form *(e.g., wrinkles by contraction);* to thicken, condense, curdle; **agmen cogere** to bring up the rear; **in ordinem cogere** to bring to order, bring back into line
cohaer·ens -entis *adj* adjoining, continuous; consistent; harmonious
cohaerenti·a -ae *f* organic structure
cohae·reō -rēre -sī -sum *intr* to stick *or* cling together, cohere; to be consistent, be in agreement; *(w.* **cum)** **1** to be closely connected with; **2** to be in harmony with; **3** to be consistent with; **inter se cohaerere** to be consistent
cohae·rescō -rescĕre -sī *intr* to stick together, cohere; to adhere
cohēr·ēs -ēdis *mf* joint-heir
cohib·eō -ēre -uī -itus *tr* to hold together, hold close; to confine; to clothe; to keep *(information, etc.)* secret, suppress; to check the growth of *(e.g., power);* to withold *(assent);* to hold back, repress *(emotions);* to check, stop *(an action, etc.); (w. acc & inf)* to prevent ‖ *refl* to remain, stay *(in a place);* to exercise self-restraint
cohonest·ō -āre *tr* to honor, pay respect to; to make respectable
cohorr·escō -escĕre -uī *intr* to shiver all over
cohor·s -tis *f* barnyard; retinue, escort; *(mil)* cohort *(comprising 3 maniples or 6 centuries and forming one-tenth of a legion, or 600 men)*
cohortāti·ō -ōnis *f* encouragement
cohorticul·a -ae *f* little cohort
cohort·or -ārī -ātus sum *tr* to encourage, cheer up, urge on
coïti·ō -ōnis *f* meeting; encounter; conspiracy; coalition
coït·us -ūs *m* meeting; junction, meeting place; sexual intercourse
col- *pref see* **con-**
-col·a -ae *masc suf* denotes a person who inhabits, tills, or worships: **amnicola** one who dwells by the river; **agricola** one who tills the field; **Junonicola** one who worships Juno
colaph·us -ī *m* punch
Colchic·us, Colch·us -a - um *adj* Colchian, of Colchis
Colch·is -idis *f* country on E. end of the Black Sea ‖ Colchian woman, Medea
cōle·ī -ōrum *mpl (vulg)* balls; **si coleos haberemus** if we had the balls *(i.e., if we dared assert ourselves)*
cōl·is -is *m* stalk; cabbage
collabasc·ō -ĕre *intr* **(conl-)** to waver, totter

collabefact·ō -āre *tr* **(conl-)** to shake hard
collabe·fīō -fierī -factus sum *intr* **(conl-)** to collapse, be ruined; to sink down
collā·bor -bī -psus sum *intr* **(conl-)** to fall down, collapse; to sink
collacrimāti·ō -ōnis *f* **(conl-)** weeping
collacrim·ō -āre -āvī -ātus *tr* **(conl-)** to cry bitterly over **‖** *intr* to cry together
collacte·a -ae *f* **(-ti·a)** foster sister
collār·e -is *n or* **collār·is -is** *m* collar
Collāti·a -ae *f* old town in Latium
Collātīn·us -ī *m* husband of Lucretia
collāti·ō -ōnis *f* **(conl-)** bringing together; contribution of money, collection, fund; comparison; *(gram)* comparison; **collatio prima** comparative; **collatio secunda** superlative
collāt·or -ōris *m* **(conl-)** contributor
collātus *pp of* **confero**
collaudāti·ō -ōnis *f* **(conl-)** warm praise
collaud·ō -āre -āvī -ātus *tr* **(conl-)** to praise highly
collax·ō -āre *tr* to loosen
collect·a -ae *f* contribution of money
collectāne·us -a -um *adj* collected from various sources
collectīci·us -a -um *adj* hastily gathered
collecti·ō -ōnis *f* **(conl-)** gathering; recapitulation; inference; *(phil)* syllogism
collectus *pp of* **colligo** (to collect)
collect·us -ūs *m* collection
collēg·a -ae *m* **(conl-)** colleague *(in office);* associate; fellow member
collēg·ium -(i)ī *n* **(conl-)** association in office; official body, board, college; guild, corporation; club, society
collībert·us -ī *m* **(conl-)** fellow ex-slave
collib·uit *or* **collub·uit -uisse -itum** *v impers* **(conl-)** it pleases
collī·dō -dĕre -sī -sus *tr* **(conl-)** to smash to pieces, crush; to strike together; to cause to clash, set at variance **‖** *pass* to be at variance, conflict; *(of teeth)* to chatter
colligāti·ō -ōnis *f* **(conl-)** binding together, connection
collig·ō -āre -āvī -ātus *tr* **(conl-)** to tie together, connect; to unite, combine; to unite *(by social, political ties);* to fasten, chain; to hinder, stop; **vasa colligare** to gather up one's gear **‖** *refl (w. dat)* to join up with
col·ligō -ligĕre -lēgī -lectus *tr* **(conl-)** to pick up; to gather together, collect; to attain, acquire *(esp. by natural processes);* to compile *(in a book);* to build (up) *(a reputation);* to hitch up, tuck up *(clothing);* to furl *(sails);* to gather in *(the reins);* to harvest *(fruit, crops);* to summarize, sum up; to contract, compress, concentrate; to acquire gradually, amass; to infer, conclude, gather; *(of numbers, totals)* to amount to; to enumerate; **animum** *(or* **mentem)** **colligere** to compose oneself; **ignes colligere** to catch fire; **vasa colligere** *(mil)* to gather up one's gear, break camp **‖** *refl & pass* to pull oneself together; to amount to; *(of winds, clouds, dust)* to gather; *(of anger)* to build up
collīne·ō -āre -āvī -ātus *tr* **(-ni·ō) (conl-)** to aim, direct **‖** *intr* to hit the mark
col·linō -linĕre -lēvī -litus *tr* **(conl-)** to smear; to defile
Collīn·us -a -um *adj* of the Quirinal Hill; **Collina Porta** Colline Gate *(near the Quirinal Hill)*
colliquefact·us -a -um *adj* **(conl-)** melted, dissolved
coll·is -is *m* hill
collocāti·ō -ōnis *f* **(conl-)** arrangement; giving in marriage
collocāt·us -a -um *adj* **(conl-)** *(geog)* located, lying
colloc·ō -āre -āvī -ātus *tr* **(conl-)** to place *(in a particular place);* to put in order, arrange; to station, deploy *(troops);* to give in marriage; to lodge, quarter; to occupy, employ; to spend, invest *(money);* to bestow; *(w.* **in** + *acc or abl)* to devote *(time, energy)* to; **in tuto** *(or* **in tutum)** **collocare** to make safe **‖** *pass* to occur, be found
collocuplēt·ō -āre -āvī -ātus *tr* **(conl-)** to enrich
collocūti·ō -ōnis *f* **(conl-)** conversation; debate, discussion; conference
colloqu·ium -(i)ī *n* **(conl-)** conversation; discussion, conference; interview
collo·quor -quī -cūtus sum *tr* **(conl-)** to talk to **‖** *intr* to talk (with), converse; *(w. acc & inf)* to say in conversation (that)
collubet *see* **collibet**
collūc·eō -ēre *intr* **(conl-)** to shine brightly, be entirely illuminated; *(fig)* to glitter
colluctāti·ō -ōnis *f* **(conl-)** struggling
colluct·or -ārī -ātus sum *intr* **(conl-)** *(w.* **cum)** to wrestle *(with)*
collū·dō -dĕre -sī -sum *intr* **(conl-)** to play together; to be in collusion; *(w. dat)* to play with
coll·um -ī *n or* **coll·us -ī** *m* neck; bottleneck
col·luō -luĕre -luī -lūtus *tr* **(conl-)** to wash out, rinse; to wash away
collūsi·ō -ōnis *f* **(conl-)** collusion
collūs·or -ōris *m* **(conl-)** playmate; fellow gambler
collustr·ō -āre -āvī -ātus *tr* **(conl-)** to light up; to survey, inspect; *(in painting)* to represent in bright colors
collutulent·ō -āre *tr* **(conl-)** to soil, defile
colluvi·ō -ōnis *or* **colluvi·ēs -ēī** *f* **(conl-)** sewage; dregs; impurities; impure mixture; turmoil; rabble

collyb·us -ī *m* **(collu-)** conversion of currency; rate of exchange
collȳr·a -ae *f* pasta, noodles, macaroni
collȳric·us -a -um *adj* **jus collyricum** noodle soup
colō colĕre coluī cultus *tr* to till, cultivate, work; to live in; to guard, protect; to honor, revere, worship; to adorn, dress; to practice, follow; to experience, live through, spend
colocāsi·a -ae *f* lotus, water lily
colōn·a -ae *f* peasant woman
colōni·a -āe *f* colony; *(coll)* town; settlers, colonists; **coloniam deducere** *(or* **mittere)** to send out settlers
colōnic·us -a -um *adj* colonial
colōn·us -ī *m* farmer; colonist, settler
Coloph·ōn -ōnis *m* city in Ionia, one of the "birthplaces" of Homer
col·or *or* **col·os -ōris** *m* color, tint; external condition; complexion; tone, style; luster; grace; colorful pretext
colōrāt·us -a -um *adj* colored, tinted; tanned; swarthy; trumped up
colōr·ō -āre -āvī -ātus *tr* to color; to tan; *(fig)* to give a certain tone to
colossē·us -a -um *adj* colossal
coloss·us *or* **coloss·os -ī** *m* colossus *(any large statue of a Roman emperor, made to rival the orginal Colossus)* ‖ **Colossus Rhodi** the Colossus of Rhodes
colostr·a -ae *f or* **colostr·ūm -ī** *n* **(-lust-)** first milk after childbirth, colostrum
colu·ber -brī *m* snake, adder
colubr·a -ae *f* snake, adder *(female)*
colubrif·er -era -erum *adj* snaky
colubrīn·us -a -um *adj* cunning
cōl·um -ī *n* strainer, colander
columb·a -ae *f* pigeon, dove *(female)*
columb·ar -āris *n* pigeonhole
columbār·ium -(i)ī *n* pigeonhole; niche in a sepulcher
columbīn·us -a -um *adj* of a dove *or* pigeon ‖ *m* little dove
columb·us -ī *m* pigeon, dove
columell·a -ae *f* small column
colum·en -inis *n* height, summit, peak; roof; ridgepole; head, leader; *(fig)* "crown", "jewel"; *(fig)* cornerstone *(of an argument); (fig)* very embodiment *(of a quality);* **summum columen** highest point *(of an orbit)*
column·a -ae *f* column, pillar; support; waterspout; *(vulg)* penis; **columnae Herculis** *(or* **Hesperiae)** the Pillars of Hercules; **columna Maenia** whipping post *(in the Forum for thieves and slaves and to which debtors were summoned for trial);* **Protei columnae** the Pillars of Proteus, the "borders of Eygpt" ‖ *fpl* portico; bookshop
columnār·ium -(i)ī *n* tax on house pillars
columnār·ius -(i)ī *m* debtor *(convicted at the* **Columna Maeniga)**
columnāt·us -a -um *adj* supported by pillars; **os columnatum** *(fig)* the head supported by one's arms
colurn·us -a -um *adj* of hazelwood
col·us -ī *or* **-ūs** *mf* distaff
colūte·a -ae *f* pod-like kind of fruit
cōlȳphi·a -ōrum *npl* choice cuts of meat, loin cuts
com- *pref see* **con-**
com·a -ae *f* hair *(of head);* mane; fleece; foliage; grass; *(poet)* rays
com·ans -antis *adj* hairy, long-haired; plumed *(helmet);* leafy; **comans stella** comet
cōmarch·us -ī *m* village chief
comāt·us -a -um *adj* long-haired; leafy; **Gallia Comata** Gaul other than the province existing after the conquest by Caesar
combib·ō -ĕre -ī *tr* **(conb-)** to drink up; to absorb; to swallow, engulf; to repress, conceal *(tears);* to absorb *(knowledge)*
combib·ō -ōnis *m* **(conb-)** drinking partner
comb·urō -ūrere -ussī -ustus *tr* **(conb-)** to burn up, consume; *(fig)* to ruin
com·edō -edĕre *(or* **-esse) -ēdī -ēsus** *(or* **estus)** *tr* to eat up, consume; to squander ‖ *refl* to pine away; *(fig)* feast one's eyes on
com·es -itis *mf* companion; fellow traveler; associate, partner; attendant; staff member; concomitant
comesse *see* **comedo**
comestus *pp of* **comedo**
comēsus *pp of* **comedo**
comēt·ēs -ae *m* comet
cōmicē *adv* like a comedy
cōmic·us -a -um *adj* of comedy, comic; **comicum aurum** stage money ‖ *m* actor, playwright *(of comedy)*
cōminus *see* **comminus**
cōm·is -is -e *adj* polite; *(w. dat or* **erga** *or* **in** *+ acc)* kind toward
cōmī(s)sābund·us -a -um *adj* riotous; drunken; boozing
cōmī(s)sāti·ō -ōnis *f* drinking party
cōmī(s)sāt·or -ōris *m* reveler
cōmī(s)s·or -ārī -ātus sum *intr* to carouse, make merry
cōmit·ās -ātis *f* politeness, kindness
comitāt·us -a -um *adj* **(by)** accompanied *(w. abl);* **comitatior** accompanied by a larger following, better attended
comitāt·us -ūs *m* escort, retinue; court *(of emperor, king);* company *(traveling together),* caravan
cōmiter *adv* politely; kindly
comitiāl·is -is -e *adj* of the assembly; **dies comitialis** day on which the comitia could transact business; **morbus comi-**

tialis epilepsy *(so called because its occurrence could cause an assembly to be adjourned)*
comitiāt·us -ūs *m (pol)* assembly
comit·ium -iī *n* comitium, assembly place, voting place ‖ *npl* popular assembly; elections; **comitia habere** to hold elections
comit·ō -āre -āvī -ātus *or* **comit·or -ārī -ātus sum** *tr* to accompany; to escort; to share *(a fate);* to attend *(a funeral); (of ancestral busts)* to be carried at *(a funeral)* ‖ *intr (w. dat)* to be present with, attend
comm·a -atis *n (gram)* phrase, part of a line
commacul·ō -āre -āvī -ātus *tr* to spot; to defile
commanip(u)lār·is -is *m* army buddy
commarīt·us -ī *m* fellow husband
commeāt·us -ūs *m* passage; traffic; convoy; *(mil)* furlough; *(mil)* lines of communication; *(mil)* supplies; **in commeatu esse** to be on furlough
commedit·or -ārī *tr* to practice hard; to imitate
com·mēiō -mēiĕre -mi(n)xī mi(n)ctus *tr (sl)* to wet, pee
commemin·ī -isse *(v. defect) tr & intr* to remember well
commemorābil·is -is -e *adj* memorable
commemorāti·ō -ōnis *f* **(conm-)** reminder; recollection, remembrance
commemor·ō -āre -āvī -ātus *tr* **(conm-)** to remember; to bring up, mention, relate
commendābil·is -is -e *adj* commendable
commendātīci·us -a -um *adj* of recommendation, of introduction
commendāti·ō -ōnis *f* recommendation; commendation, praise; approval, esteem; excellence
commendāt·or -ōris *m* backer
commendātr·ix -īcis *f* backer *(female)*
commendāt·us -a -um *adj* recommended; acceptable, suitable
commend·ō -āre -āvī -ātus *tr* to entrust; to recommend; to commit *(to writing, posterity);* to commend ‖ *refl (w. dat)* to devote oneself to
commentāriol·um -ī *n* notebook; essay
commentār·ium -(i)ī *n or* **commentār·ius -(i)ī** *m* **(conm-)** notebook, diary, journal; record, register; textbook; (collection of) notes; **a commentariis** official in charge of records
commentāti·ō -ōnis *f* careful study; treatise, commentary, textbook; *(rhet)* argument
commentīci·us -a -um *adj* thought-out; imaginary, fictitious
comment·or -ārī -ātus sum *tr* to think over, consider; to contrive, make up; to write, compose; to discuss; to practice, prepare *(a speech)*
comment·or -ōris *m* inventor, deviser
comment·us -a -um *pp of* **comminiscor** ‖ *adj* fictitious, invented, pretended ‖ *n* invention; fabrication; intention
comme·ō -āre -āvī -ātum *intr* to come and go; to back and forth; to travel repeatedly; *(of water)* to pass, flow; to travel around; to commute; to pass *(from one state to another)*
commerc·ium -(i)ī *n* trade, commerce; dealing, business; communication, correspondence; exchange *(of goods),* trafficking; goods, merchandise; sexual intercourse; *(leg)* right to engage in trade, commercial rights; *(w. gen)* right to buy and sell *(a commodity), e.g.:* **commercium agri** right to buy and sell land; **commercium linguae** common language *(shared by various tribes);* **jus commercii** trading rights
commerc·or -ārī -ātus sum *tr* **(conm-)** to purchase
commer·eō -ēre -uī -itus *or* **commer·eor -ērī -itus sum** *tr* **(conm-)** to deserve fully, merit; to be guilty of
com·mētior -mētīrī -mensus sum *tr* **(conm-)** to measure; *(w.* **cum)** to measure *(s.th.)* in terms of
commēt·ō -āre -āvī *intr* to go often, come and go
commigr·ō -āre -āvī -ātum *intr* to move, migrate
commīlit·ium -(i)ī *n* military comradeship
commīlit·ō -ōnis *m* army buddy
commināti·ō -ōnis *f* violent threat
com·mingō -mingĕre -minxī -mictus *tr (sl)* to pee on; to wet *(bed);* **commictum caenum** *(sl)* dirty skunk
com·miniscor -minisci -mentus sum *tr* to think up, contrive; to fabricate *(lie);* to state falsely, pretend, allege
commin·or -ārī -ātus sum *tr* to threaten, make a threat of
commin·uō -uĕre -uī -ūtus *tr* to lessen considerably; to smash, shatter; *(fig)* to crush, humiliate
comminus *adv* hand to hand; near at hand; **comminus conferre signa** to engage in hand-to-hand fighting
commi·sceō -scēre -scuī -xtus *tr* to mix together; to confuse; to unite, bring together; *(w.* **cum)** to discuss with
commiserāti·ō -ōnis *f (rhet)* appeal for compassion *or* pity
commiseresc·ō -ĕre *intr (w. gen)* to feel pity for ‖ *v impers* **me commiserescit ejus** I pity him
commiser·or -ārī -ātus sum *tr* to feel sympathy for ‖ *intr (rhet)* to try to evoke sympathy

commīsī *perf of* **committo**
commissi·ō -ōnis *f* commencement
commissūr·a -ae *f* connection; joint
commiss·us -a -um *pp of* **committo** ‖ *n* offense, crime; secret, trust; undertaking; thing confiscated
commītig·ō -āre *tr* **(conm-)** to soften up
com·mittō -mittĕre -mīsī -missus *tr* **(conm-)** to bring together; to join together, make continuous, connect, combine; to cause to compete, match *(for a fight, etc.)*; to begin, commence *(games)*; to undertake; to commit *(crime)*, do *(s.th. wrong)*; to incur *(penalty)*; to bring about, effect; to give up, forfeit, hand over; to engage in *(battle, war)*; *(w. dat)* **1** to take *(a person or matter)* before *(s.o.)* for a verdict, decision, *or* approval; **2** to entrust *(a person or thing)* to *(s.o.)*; **hostes pugnae** *(or* **proelio) committere** to engage the enemy; **memoriae committere** to commit to memory; **omnes inter se committere** to set all at variance with one another; **proelium** *(or* **pugnam) committere** to go into action, engage the enemy ‖ *refl (w.* **in** + *acc)* to venture into ‖ *intr* to commit an offense, break the law
commodē *adv* properly, appropriately; neatly; adequately, satisfactorily; at the right moment; conveniently, readily; helpfully, obligingly; tastefully; comfortably
commodit·ās -ātis *f* timeliness, right time; proportion, symmetry; convenience, comfort; pleasantness, kindness; *(rhet)* aptness of expression
commodō *adv* suitably, conveniently
commod·ō -āre -āvī -ātus *tr* to adjust, adapt; to bestow, supply, lend, give; **aurem** *(or* **aures) commodare** to lend an ear; **manum commodare** to lend a helping hand ‖ *refl* **mihi te commodare** to put yourself at my disposal ‖ *intr* to be obliging; *(w. dat)* to be accommodating to, help
commodulē *or* **commodulum** *adv* nicely, conveniently
commodum *adv* at a good time; in the nick of time; **commodum cum** just at the time when
commod·um -ī *n* convenience; opportunity; profit, advantage; privilege; loan; pay, reward; **commodo tuo** at your convenience; **ex commodo** *(or* **per commodum)** *(w. gen)* at the convenience of
commod·us -a -um *adj* convenient, suitable, fit; timely; opportune *(time)*; comfortable; advantageous; agreeable, obliging, pleasant *(person)*; good *(health)*; **quod commodum est** just as you please
Commod·us -ī *m* Roman Emperor *(son of Marcus Aurelius, reigned* A.D. *180–192)*
commōl·ior -īrī -ītus sum *tr* to set in motion, move with effort
commone·faciō -facĕre -fēcī -factus *tr* to call to mind; *(w. acc of person and gen of thing)* to remind *(s.o.)* of
common·eō -ēre -uī -itus *tr* to remind, warn; *(w. gen or* **de** + *abl)* to remind *(s.o.)* of
commoniti·ō -ōnis *f* reminder
commo(n)str·ō -āre -āvī -ātus *tr* to point out; to show where *(a person, thing, place)* is
commorāti·ō -ōnis *f* stay; delay *(rhet)* dwelling on a point
com·morior -morī -mortuus sum *intr (w. dat or* **cum)** to die with
commor·or -ārī -ātus sum *tr* to stop, detain ‖ *intr* to linger, stay, stop off; **in sententiā commorari** to stick to an opinion
commōti·ō -ōnis *f* motion; commotion; **animi commotio** excitement
commōtiuncul·a -ae *f* slight agitation
commōt·us -a -um *adj* excited, nervous; deranged *(mind)*; angry; impassioned; *(rhet)* lively *(style)*
com·moveō -movēre -mōvī -mōtus *tr* to stir up, shake; to disturb, upset; to excite, shake up; to arouse, provoke; to generate, produce; *(fig)* to touch, move; to influence; to impress; to cause, start *(a war, battle)*; to dislodge *(an enemy)*; to call in *(a debt)*
commūn·e -is *n* common property; community; **in commune 1** publicly; **2** for the good of all; **3** jointly; **4** in general terms
commūnicāti·ō -ōnis *f* sharing; *(rhet)* deliberating with the audience
commūnic·ō -āre -āvī -ātus *or* **commūnic·or -ārī -ātus sum** *tr* to share; to unite, link; to impart, communicate; to discuss together; to plan together
commūni·ō -ōnis *f* sharing; kinship, association
commūn·iō -īre -īvī *or* **-iī -ītus** *tr* **(-moen-)** to fortify; to build and fortify; *(fig)* to strengthen, fortify
commūn·is -is -e *adj* **(conm-)** common, joint; common, ordinary; public; universal, general; familiar; courteous; democratic; *(of arguments)* applicable to either side; **communis est conjectura** it is open to conjecture; **communis est aestimatio** it is a matter of opinion; **loca communia** public places; **loci communes** general topics; **sensus communis** civic *or* public spirit ‖ *n see* **commune** ‖ *npl* the common good; *(poet)* common lot
commūnit·ās -ātis *f* sharing, partnership, joint possession; social ties, fellowship, togetherness; affability

commūniter *adv* in common
commūnīti·ō -ōnis *f* road building; *(fig)* preparation, introduction
commurmur·ō -āre *or* **commurmur·or -ārī -ātus sum** *intr* to murmur, grumble
commūtābil·is -is -e *adj* changeable, subject to change; interchangeable
commūtāti·ō -ōnis *f* change, alteration; shift; exchange; reversal
commūtāt·us -ūs *m* change
commūt·ō -āre -āvī -ātus *tr* to change, alter; to interchange, exchange; to barter; to give in exchange; *(w. abl or* **cum***)* to exchange *(s.th.)* for; **verba commutare** to exchange words, talk
cōm·ō -ĕre -psī -ptus *tr* to set, do, braid *(the hair);* to adorn, deck out
cōmoedi·a -ae *f* comedy
cōmoedicē *adv* as in comedy
cōmoed·us -a -um *adj* of comic actors ‖ *m* comic actor
comōs·us -a -um *adj* with long hair; hairy; leafy
compaciscor *see* **compeciscor**
compacti·ō -ōnis *f* framework
compact·us -a -um *pp of* **compingo** ‖ *adj* compact, well-built ‖ *n* compact
compāg·ēs -is *f* construction; joint, seam; structure, framework; *(anat)* joint
compāg·ō -inis *f* **(conp-)** (act of) fastening; connection; framework, structure
comp·ar -aris *adj* **(conp-)** similar, alike; equal; *(w. dat)* matching, resembling ‖ *mf* buddy; playmate; perfect match; spouse
comparābil·is -is -e *adj* **(conp-)** comparable, similar
comparātē *adv* **(conp-)** comparatively
comparāti·ō -ōnis *f (from* **con-** + **parō***)* preparation; acquisition, procuring, obtaining, provision *(by purchasing or otherwise);* arrangement, settlment
comparāti·ō -ōnis *f (from* **compar-** + **ō***)* comparison; relative position *(of planets); (gram)* comparative degree; *(rhet)* argument based on the law of probability; **ex comparatione** *(w. gen)* in comparison with; **comparatio pro portione** proportion
comparātīv·us -a -um *adj* **(conp-)** comparative; *(gram)* that is in the comparative degree
compār·eō -ēre -uī *intr* **(conp-)** to be visible, be plain, be evident; to appear; to be at hand, be present
compar·ō -āre -āvī -ātus *tr (from* **con-** + **parō***)* to prepare, make preparations for; to purchase; to plan, devise; to put together, get together, provide; to match; to set up *(courts, a body of laws);* to procure, get, collect; to appoint; to establish, institute; to raise *(troops);* to compose *(writings);* **comparare inter se** *(esp. of consuls)* to arrange, settle
compar·ō -āre -āvī -ātus *tr (from* **compar-** + **ō***)* to unite; to match, pit; to align; to estimate; to compare *(with or to);* to point out by way of comparison
compas·cō -cĕre — -tus *tr & intr* **(conp-)** to feed together
compascu·us -a -um *adj* **(conp-)** of public grazing; **compascuus ager** public pasture land
compec·iscor -iscī -tus sum *intr* **(-pac-)** to make a compact, reach an agreement
compect·us -a -um *adj* in agreement ‖ *n* agreement, compact; **(de) compecto** by previous agreement
comped·iō -īre — -ītus *tr* **(conp-)** to shackle
compedīt·us -a -um *pp of* **compedio** ‖ *adj* shackled ‖ *m* shackled slave
compēgī *perf of* **compingo**
compellāti·ō -ōnis *f* **(conp-)** rebuke; *(rhet)* addressing, apostrophizing
compell·ō -āre -āvī -ātus *tr* **(conp-)** to address, speak to; to call upon, appeal to; to challenge; *(w. predicate adj)* to call *(s.o., e.g., disloyal, etc.);* to rebuke, call to account; *(leg)* to arraign
com·pellō -pellĕre -pulī -pulsus *tr* **(conp-)** to drive together, round up; to crowd together; to compel, drive; *(of wind, waves)* to drive, push, force; *(w.* **in** + *acc)* to drive *(s.o.)* into; *(w.inf or* **ut** + *subj)* to compel *(s.o.)* to *(do s.th.);* to coerce, constrain; to reduce by force *(to some state or condition);* to clench *(teeth);* to localize, concentrate *(fighting)*
compendiāri·us -a -um *adj* **(conp-)** short, abridged; **via compendiaria** shortcut
compend·ium -(i)ī *n* **(conp-)** careful weighing; saving *(of money);* profit; shortening, abridging; shortcut; **compendium facere** *(w. gen)* to save oneself the trouble of; **compendi fieri** to be brief; **compendio servire** to serve one's own private interests
compensāti·ō -ōnis *f* compensation
compens·ō -āre -āvī -ātus *tr* **(conp-)** to compensate for, make up for; to balance mentally
comper·cō -cĕre -sī *tr* **(conp-)** to save up, hoard up
comperendināti·ō -ōnis *f or* **comperendināt·us -ūs** *m* **(conp-)** *(leg)* two-day adjournment
comperendin·ō -āre -āvī -ātus *tr* **(conp-)** to adjourn *(court)* for two days; to put off *(defendant)* for two days
comper·iō -īre -ī -tus *or* **comper·ior -īrī -tus sum** *tr* **(conp-)** to find out, discover, learn; **compertum habeo** *or* **compertum mihi est** I know for certain

compern·is -is -e *adj* **(conp-)** having thighs close together

compert·us -a -um *adj* ascertained; well authenticated; *(w. gen)* convicted of; **compertum habeo** I have verified; **nihil comperti** no certainty; **pro comperto** *(to regard)* as certain; **res comperta** *(or* **compertae)** reliable information

comp·ēs -edis *f* **(conp-)** *(usu. pl)* shackles *(for the feet),* fetters; bond *(of love)*

compesc·ō -ĕre -uī *tr* **(conp-)** to confine, restrain; to imprison; to close, block *(entrances);* to check the movement of, steady; to stop, restrain *(activity of any kind);* to calm *(a storm);* to control *(a person);* to subdue, quell, crush *(an enemy, a mutiny);* to curb *(one's tongue, one's words);* to stifle *(feelings, fears, laughter);* to quench *(thirst);* to allay *(hunger);* **compesce dicere injuste!** stop speaking unfairly!; **compesce digito labellum!** put your finger to your lip! *(to indicate silence)*

competīt·or -ōris *m* **(conp-)** competitor; rival claimant *(to the throne);* rival bidder *(at an auction); (pol)* fellow candidate

competītr·ix -īcis *f* **(conp-)** competitor *(female)*

compet·ō -ĕre -īvī *or* **-iī -ītum** *intr* **(conp-)** to come together, meet; *(of events)* to coincide; to be adequate, be suitable; *(w.* **ad)** to be capable of ‖ *v impers* **si competit** if it is convenient; *(w.* **ut)** if it happens that

compīlāti·ō -ōnis *f* **(conp-)** burglary

compīl·ō -āre -āvī -ātus *tr* **(conp-)** to pillage; to plagiarize

com·pingō -pingĕre -pēgī -pactus *tr* **(conp-)** to put together, construct; to compose; to lock up, put *(in jail)*

Compitāl·ia -ium *npl* **(Conp-)** festival of the Lares at crossroads, celebrated twice annually at the crossroads with flowers

Compitālici·us -a -um *adj* **(Conp-)** of the crossroads

Compitāl·is -is -e *adj* **(Conp-, Compet-)** associated with the festival at the crossroads

compit·um -ī *n* **(conp-)** crossroads; *(fig)* crucial decision

complac·eō -ēre -uī *or* **-itum** *intr* **(conp-)** *(w. dat)* to suit just fine

complān·ō -āre -āvī -ātus *tr* **(conp-)** to level; to raze

comple·ctor -ctī -xus sum *tr* **(conp-)** to embrace, hug; to display affection for, display esteem for; to clasp *(the right hand); (of sleep)* to hold in its embrace; *(fig)* to embrace, take up *(a cause, a course of action);* to grip, grasp, cling to; to encircle, surround, enclose; to comprise; to take in, include within its limits *(an area); (of power, reputation, knowledge)* to extend over, embrace; to involve, associate, include *(in a relationship, class, activity);* to include, cover *(in a book or speech);* to state in a concise manner, sum up; to grasp, understand; **animo** *(or* **mente) complecti** to comprehend, take in; **memoriā complecti** to keep in mind

complēment·um -ī *n* **(conp-)** complement, completion

compl·eō -ēre -ēvī -ētus *tr* **(conp-)** to fill, fill up; to fill with sound, make resound; to supply, furnish; to complete; to impregnate; to bring *(a legion)* to full strength; *(mil)* to man

complēt·us -a -um *adj* **(conp-)** complete, perfect

complexi·ō -ōnis *f* **(conp-)** combination, collection, group; *(rhet)* summary

complex·us -ūs *m* **(conp-)** embrace; *(fig)* love, affection; close combat; mental grasp; grouping *(of words);* envelopment

complicāt·us -a -um *adj* **(conp-)** complicated

complic·ō -āre -āvī *(or* **-uī) -ātus** *(or* **-itus)** *tr* **(conp-)** to fold up

complō·dō -dĕre -sī -sus *tr* **(conp-)** to clap *(the hands)* together

complōrāti·ō -ōnis *f or* **complōrāt·us -ūs** *m* **(conp-)** wailing, lamentation

complōr·ō -āre -āvī -ātus *tr* **(conp-)** to mourn for

complūr·ēs -ēs -a *or* **-ia** *adj* **(conp-)** several, a fair number of

complūriens *adv* **(-iēs) (conp-)** sever[al] times, a good many times

compluscul·ī -ae -a *adj* **(conp-)** sever[al]

compluv·ium -(i)ī *n* **(conp-)** compluvi[um] *(quadrangular, inward-sloping cen[tral] part of the roof of a Roman hou[se] direct rain to a pool below, c[f.]* **impluvium)**

com·pōnō -pōnĕre -posuī -posi[tus] **(conp-)** to put together, join; to [...] *(things together);* to store up, h[...] lay aside, put away; to build; [...] pose, write; to arrange, settle, agr[...] to match; to match up *(pairs);* [...] pare; to treat as comparable; t[...] *(e.g., deeds with words);* to la[...] *dead);* to put in an urn; to b[...] range in order, lay out; to ar[...] tematically; to arrange prope[...] to deploy *(troops);* to arran[...] ganize *(a plan of action);* [...] fabricate *(a false report, st[...]* oncile; to concoct, contriv[...] *revolt);* to subdue *(rebe[...]* soothe, appease *(a person[...]* *(estranged friends);* to s[...] *problems, affairs);* **bellu[...]**

to end a war *(by coming to terms);* **in maestitiam compositus** putting on the appearance of sadness; **vultum componere** to put on a false front

comport·ō -āre -āvī -ātus *tr* **(conp-)** to bring together, bring in, collect, accumulate

comp·os -otis *adj* **(conp-)** *(w. gen or abl)* in possession of, master of, having control over; **compos animi** *(or* **mentis)** sane; **compos sui** self-controlled; **compos voti** having one's prayer answered

compositē *adv* **(conp-)** in an orderly manner; *(of actions)* deliberately; **composite dicere** to speak logically

compositi·ō -ōnis *f* **(conp-)** putting together, fitting together, connecting, arranging, composition; matching *(of gladiators, etc.);* reconciliation *(of friends);* orderly arrangement *(of words)*

compositō *adv* **(conp-)** by prearrangement

composit·or -ōris *m* **(conp-)** writer

compos(i)tūr·a -ae *f* **(conp-)** structure

composit·us -a -um *pp of* **compono** ‖ *adj* compound *(words, etc.);* composite, blended; orderly, tidy; calm *(sea);* composed, calm ‖ *n* compound medication; **de** *(or* **ex) composito** by agreement, as agreed ‖ *npl* law and order, settled situation

compotāti·ō -ōnis *f* **(conp-)** drinking party

compot·iō -īre -īvī -ītus *tr* **(conp-)** *(w. acc of person and abl of thing)* to make *(s.o.)* master of ‖ *pass (w. abl)* to attain

compōt·or -ōris *m,* **compōtr·ix -īcis** *f* **(conp-)** drinking partner

comprans·or -ōris *m* **(conp-)** dinner companion, fellow guest

comprecāti·ō -ōnis *f* **(conp-)** public supplication

comprec·or -ārī -ātus sum *tr* **(conp-)** to pray earnestly to, implore, invoke; *(w. acc of thing)* to pray for; *(w.* **ut** + *subj)* to pray that

omprehen·dō -dĕre -dī -sus *or* **compren·dō -dĕre -dī -sus** *tr* **(conp-)** to bind together, unite; to hold together *(e.g., w. ropes)*; to take hold of, grasp; to catch; to attack; to arrest; to capture; to occupy; to detect; to comprehend; to express; to describe, recount; **animo** *(or* **mente) omprehendere** to apprehend, appreciate; **ignem comprehendere** to catch fire; **nemoriā comprehendere** to remember; **umero comprehendere** to count, enuerate

nprehensibil·is -is -e *adj* **(conp-) dibilis)** comprehensible, intelligible

prehensi·ō *or* **comprensi·ō -ōnis** *f* **onp-)** seizing; arrest; comprehension, rception; combining; *(rhet)* period

prendō *see* **comprehendo**

compressi·ō -ōnis *f* **(conp-)** pressing closely; embrace; *(rhet)* compression

compress·or -ōris *m* rapist

compress·us -ūs *m* **(conp-)** compression; embrace; rape

com·primō -primĕre -pressī -pressus *tr* **(conp-)** to press together, compress; to close; to embrace; to check, curb; to keep back, suppress, withhold, conceal; to rape; to hold *(one's breath);* **compressis manibus sedere** to sit on folded hands, not lift a finger; **ordines comprimere** to close ranks

comprobāti·ō -ōnis *f* **(conp-)** full approval

comprobāt·or -ōris *m* **(conp-)** enthusiastic approver

comprob·ō -āre -āvī -ātus *tr* **(conp-)** to approve, sanction, acknowledge; to prove, establish, verify; to cofirm; to justify

comprōmiss·um -ī *n* **(conp-)** *(leg)* compromise *(agreement between the parties to abide by the arbitrator's decision)*

comprō·mittō -mittĕre -mīsī -missum *intr* **(conp-)** *(leg)* to compromise *(to agree to abide by the arbitrator's decision)*

comptiōnāl·is -is -e *adj (of worn-out goods)* suitable to be sold in batches

compt·us -a -um *pp of* **como** ‖ *adj (of hair)* set, neatly arranged; *(of person)* dressed up; *(of speech, writing)* polished

compt·us -ūs *m* hairdo

compulī *perf of* **compello**

compulsus *pp of* **compello**

compun·gō -gĕre -xī -ctus *tr* **(conp-)** to puncture, prick; to tatoo; to prod

comput·ō -āre -āvī -ātus *tr* **(conp-)** to compute, count

computresc·ō -ĕre *intr* **(conp-)** to rot

Cōm·um -ī *n* Como *(town N. of Po River, modern Como)*

con- *pref (also:* **co-, col-, com-, cor-) 1** together: **conjungere** to join together; **2** up, completely, fully: **consumere** to use up; **concredere** to trust completely; **3** with: **conspirare** to plot with *(s.o.);* **4** hard: **conjicere** to throw hard, fling

cōnām·en -inis *n* effort, struggle; support; *(often pl)* endeavor, attempt

cōnāt·um -ī *n* effort; venture

cōnāt·us -ūs *m* effort; endeavor; thrust *(with weapon)*

concac·ō -āre -āvī -ātus *tr (vulg)* to soil, shit

concaed·ēs -ium *fpl* log barricade

concale·faciō -facĕre -fēcī -factus *tr* to warm up, heat

concal·esc·ō -escĕre -uī *intr* to grow quite warm; to glow *(e.g., with love)*

concall·escō -escĕre -uī *intr* to grow hard; *(fig)* to become insensitive

concamerāt·us -a -um *adj* vaulted

Concān·us -ī *m* one of a Spanish tribe that drank horse's blood

concastīg·ō -āre -āvī -ātus *tr* to dress down; to chastise, punish

concav·ō -āre *tr* to curve, bend

concav·us -a -um *adj* concave, hollow; deep-sunken *(eyes);* deep *(valley)*

con·cēdō -cēdĕre -cessī -cessus *tr* to give up; to pardon, overlook; to grant ‖ *intr* to go away; to withdraw, retire; to pass away, die; *(w. dat)* **1** to yield to, succumb to; **2** to submit to, comply with; **3** to make allowances for, pardon; **4** to be inferior to; *(w.* **in** + *acc)* to pass over to, be merged into; **fato** *(or* **naturae** *or* **vitā) concedere** to die

concelebr·ō -āre -āvī -ātus *tr* to frequent; to fill; to pursue *(studies);* to enliven; to celebrate; to publish, proclaim

concēnāti·ō -ōnis *f* dinner party

concenti·ō -ōnis *f* singing together

concenturi·ō -āre *tr* to assemble by centuries *(groups of hundreds); (fig)* to marshal

concent·us -ūs *m* concert; harmony; shouting in unison; blending

concepti·ō -ōnis *f* conception; *(leg)* formula

concept·us -a -um *pp of* **concipio** ‖ *adj* **concepta verba** formula

concept·us -ūs *m* conception; embryo, fetus

concerp·ō -ĕre -sī -tus *tr* to tear up, tear to shreds; *(fig)* to cut up, revile

concertāti·ō -ōnis *f* wrangling

concertāt·or -ōris *m* rival

concertātōri·us -a -um *adj* controversial

concert·ō -āre -āvī -ātus *tr* to quarrel over; to rival ‖ *intr* to fight, quarrel

concessi·ō -ōnis *f* concession; admission *(of guilt with a plea for mercy)*

concess·ō -āre -āvī *intr (w. inf)* to cease to, stop *(doing s.th.)*

concess·us -ā -um *pp of* **concedo** ‖ *adj* allowable, lawful ‖ *n* concession

concess·us -ūs *m* permission; **concessu Caesaris** with Caesar's permission

conch·a -ae *f* clam, oyster, mussel, murex; clamshell, oyster shell; pearl; purple dye; trumpet *(of Triton);* vessel *(for ointments, etc.);* vulva

conch·is -is *f* bean

conchīt·a -ae *m* clam digger

conchul·a -ae *f* a small shellfish

conchȳliāt·us -a -um *adj* purple

conchȳl·ium -(i)ī *n* shellfish, clam, oyster; murex; purple dye, purple ‖ *npl* purple garments

concĭd·ō -ĕre -ī *intr* to collapse; to fall *(in battle); (fig)* to decline, fall, fail, decay, perish; *(of winds)* die down

concī·dō -dĕre -dī -sus *tr* to cut up, cut to pieces, kill; to beat severely; *(fig)* to demolish *(w. arguments); (rhet)* to chop up *(sentences)*

con·cieō -ciēre -cīvī -cītus *or* **con·ciō -cīre -cīvī -cītus** *tr* to assemble; to shake; *(fig)* to stir up

conciliābul·um -ī *n* public meeting place

conciliāti·ō -ōnis *f* union, bond; conciliating; inclination, bent

conciliāt·or -ōris *m* mediator; agent

conciliātrīcul·a -ae *f* madame *(of a brothel);* dear matchmaker

conciliātr·ix -īcis *f* match-maker; promoter *(of relationships)*

conciliāt·us -a -um *adj (w.* **ad)** endeared to, disposed toward

conciliāt·us -ūs *m* union, joining

concili·ō -āre -āvī -ātus *tr* to bring together, unite; to win over; to bring about *(by mediation);* to acquire, win

concil·ium -(i)ī *n* popular assembly *(esp. that of the plebs in Rome);* private meeting; council; union; association; a hearing in council; deliberation, debate; *(pol)* a league of states; **in uno concilio** together

concin·ens -entis *adj* harmonious

concinnē *adv* nicely, daintily

concinnit·ās -ātis *or* **concinnitūd·ō -inis** *f* elegance; excessive refinement

concinn·ō -āre -āvī -ātus *tr* to prepare for use, make ready; to repair; to touch up; to make up, concoct; to give rise to; to make, drive *(e.g., insane);* **lacrumentem concinnas tuam uxorem** you are making your wife cry

concinn·us -a -um *adj* symmetrical; elegant; courteous, nice; polished

concin·ō -ĕre -uī *tr* to sing of; to prophesy ‖ *intr* to sing *or* play together; *(fig)* to agree

conciō *see* **concieo**

conciō *see* **contio**

concipil·ō -āre -āvī *tr* to seize, carry off

con·cipiō -cipĕre -cēpī -ceptus *tr* to take in, absorb; to imagine, think; to understand, perceive; to conceive; to produce, form; *(of things)* to contain, hold; to contract *(disease);* to catch *(fire);* to entertain *(hope);* to frame *(in formal language);* to announce *(in formal language); (w. abl, adv,* **ab, ex)** to draw, derive from *(a source);* to utter solemnly; **verba concepta** solemn utterance

concīsē *adv* concisely

concīsi·ō -ōnis *f (rhet)* dividing a sentence into short phrases

concīs·us -a -um *pp of* **concīdo** ‖ *adj* cut up, cut short, terse; minute, very small

concitātē *adv* vigorously, vividly

concitāti·ō -ōnis *f* rapid movement; excitement; disturbance, riot

concitāt·or *or* **concit·or -ōris** *m* instigator, ring-leader; rabble-rouser

concitāt·us -a -um *adj* excited; rapid
concit·ō -āre -āvī -ātus *tr* to stir up, rouse, urge; to spur on *(horses, etc.)*; to agitate, stir up, disturb; to awaken; to summon, assemble; to galvanize into action; to infuriate; to bring about, cause, occasion
concitor *see* **concitator**
conclāmāti·ō -ōnis *f* loud shouting, yell; acclamation
conclāmit·ō -āre *intr* to keep on shouting, keep on yelling
conclām·ō -āre -āvī -ātus *tr* to shout, yell; to call to *(for help)*; to call repeatedly by name, bewail *(the dead)*; to exclaim; **jam conclamatum est** *(coll)* all's lost; **vasa conclamare** *(mil)* to give the signal to pack up; **ad arma conclamare** to sound the call to arms
conclāv·e -is *n* room; public toilet
conclū·dō -dĕre -sī -sus *tr* to shut up, enclose; to include, comprise; to round off, conclude *(speech, letter)*; to end rhythmically; to deduce, conclude
conclūsē *adv (rhet)* in a rhythmical cadence
conclūsi·ō -ōnis *f* conclusion; *(mil)* blockade; *(rhet)* summation
conclūsiuncul·a -ae *f* false conclusion
conclūs·us -a -um *pp of* **concludo** ‖ *adj* confined, restricted
concol·or -ōris *adj* of the same color
concomitāt·us -a -um *adj* escorted
conco·quō -quĕre -xī -ctus *tr* to cook thoroughly; to boil down; to digest; to stomach, put up with; to cook up, concoct *(ideas)*; to weigh seriously; to ripen ‖ *intr* to digest one's food
concordi·a -ae *f* harmony, concord
concorditer *adv* harmoniously
concord·ō -āre -āvī -ātum *intr* to be of one mind; to be in harmony, agree
concor·s -dis *adj* of the same mind, agreeing, harmonious
concoxī *perf of* **concoquo**
concrēbr·escō -escĕre -uī *intr* to grow strong
concrēd·ō -ĕre -idī -itus *tr* to entrust; to confide *(a secret)*
concrem·ō -āre -āvī -ātus *tr* to burn to ashes, burn down
concrep·ō -āre -uī *intr* to rattle, creak, grate, clash, sound, make noise; **digitis concrepare** to snap the fingers ‖ *tr* to cause to sound *or* to rattle
con·crescō -crescĕre -crēvī -crētum *intr* to grow together; to congeal; to curdle; to clot; to stiffen; to take shape, grow, increase
concrēti·ō -ōnis *f* condensing, congealing; matter, substance
concrēt·us -a -um *pp of* **concresco** ‖ *adj* grown together, compounded; solid, hard; frozen; matted; condensed, dense; curdled; inveterate, ingrained; dim *(light)* ‖ *n* hardness; solid matter
concrēvī *perf of* **concresco**
concrīmin·or -ārī -ātus sum *intr* to make bitter charges
concruci·ō -āre *tr* to torture
concubīn·a -ae *f* concubine
concubīnāt·us -ūs *m* free love
concubīn·us -ī *m* catamite, homosexual
concubit·us -ūs *m* reclining together; sexual intercourse
concubi·us -a -um *adj* **concubiā nocte** at bedtime ‖ *n* intercourse
conculc·ō -āre -āvī -ātus *tr* trample under foot, despise, treat with contempt
concumbō concumbĕre concubuī concubitum *intr* to sleep together; *(w.* **cum***)* to sleep with, have intercourse with
concup·iscō -iscĕre -īvī *or* **-iī -ītus** *tr* to long for; to strive for
concūr·ō -āre *tr* to take good care of
concur·rō -rĕre -rī -sum *intr* to run together, flock together; to unite; to strike one another, crash; to happen at the same time, coincide; *(mil)* to clash; *(w.* **ad***)* to have recourse to; *(of jaws)* to snap together; *(of facts, statements)* to agree
concursāti·ō -ōnis *f* running together, assembly; rushing about; *(mil)* skirmish
concursāt·or -ōris *m* skirmisher
concursi·ō -ōnis *f* concourse; *(gram)* collocation *(of vowels)*; *(rhet)* repetition for emphasis
concurs·ō -āre -āvī -ātus *tr* to run around to; **domos concursare** to run from house to house ‖ *intr* to rush around excitedly, dash up and down; *(mil)* to skirmish
concurs·us -ūs *m* a running together, concourse, assembly; combination; collision *(of atoms)*; *(astr)* conjunction; *(gram)* juxtaposition *(of letters)*; *(leg)* joint right; *(mil)* charge, clash
concussi·ō -ōnis *f* shaking; earthquake
concuss·us -ūs *m* shaking, shock
concu·tiō -tĕre -ssī -ssus *tr* to bang together; to convulse; to shake; to shatter; to harass, upset, shock; to stir up; to wave *(weapon, hand)*; to weaken, shake *(authority, confidence)*
condal·ium -(i)ī *n* (slave's) ring
condec·et -ēre *v impers* it befits
condecor·ō -āre -āvī -ātus *tr* to adorn; to grace
condemnāt·or -ōris *m* accuser; *(leg)* prosecutor
condemn·ō -āre -āvī -ātus *tr* to condemn, doom; to blame; *(leg)* to prosecute successfully, convict, sentence
condens·ō -āre -āvī -ātus *tr* to pack together
condens·us -a -um *adj* crowded, packed
condici·ō -ōnis *f* contract, arrangement;

stipulation, terms, condition; state, situation, circumstances; state of health; legal status; rank, place; marriage contract, marriage; prospective marriage partner, good match; nature, character; choice, option; **eā condicione ut** on the condition that; **in condicione manere** to stick to an agreement; **nullā condicione** by no means; **sub condicione** conditionally; **vitae condicio** living conditions

condī·cō -cĕre -xī -ctus *tr* to talk over, arrange together; **(ad) cenam condicere** *(w. dat)* to make a dinner engagement with

condignē *adv* very worthily

condign·us -a -um *adj (w. abl)* fully deserving of, fully worthy of

condīment·um -ī *n* seasoning, spice

cond·iō -īre -īvī *or* **-iī -ītus** *tr* to season; to pickle, preserve; to embalm; *(fig)* to give zest to

condiscipul·a -ae *f* schoolmate *(female)*

condiscipulāt·us -ūs *m* companionship at school

condiscipul·us -ī *m* schoolmate

condi·scō -scĕre -dicī *tr* to learn by heart

condīti·ō -ōnis *f* seasoning; method of preserving *(food)*

condit·or -ōris *m* founder, builder; originator *(of a practice; of a product)*; organizer; creator; *(as honorary title)* preserver; author, writer

condīt·or -ōris *m* seasoner

conditōr·ium -(i)ī *n* coffin; tomb

condīt·us -a -um *pp of* **condio** ‖ *adj* seasoned, spicy; elegant *(style)*

condit·us -a -um *pp of* **condo** ‖ *adj* concealed, secret; sunken *(eyes)*

condixī *perf of* **condico**

con·dō -dĕre -didī -ditus *tr* to build, found; to write, compose; to establish *(a practice, institution)*; to store up, hoard; to preserve; to keep safe; to plunge *(a weapon)*; to drown out *(a sound)*; to put *(in prison, chains)*

condoce·faciō -facĕre -fēcī -factus *tr* to train well

condoc·eō -ēre -uī -tus *tr* to teach thoroughly

condol·escō -escĕre -uī *intr* to begin to ache, get very sore; *(fig)* to feel grief

condōnāti·ō -ōnis *f* donation

condōn·ō -āre -āvī -ātus *tr* to give, present; to permit; to deliver over *(to enemy, for punishment)*; to adjudge; *(w. double acc)* to make *(s.o.)* a present of *(s.th.)*; *(w. acc of thing and dat of person)* to forgive, pardon *(s.o. an offense)*

condorm·iō -īre *intr* to sleep soundly

condorm·iscō -iscĕre -īvī *or* **-iī** *intr* to fall soundly asleep

condūcibil·is -is -e *adj* advantageous, profitable; *(w.* **ad** *or* **in** *+ acc)* just right for

condu·cō -cĕre -xī -ctus *tr* to bring together, collect, assemble; to connect, unite; to rent; to borrow; to induce, bribe; to employ, hire; to contract for, undertake a contract in connection with *(buildings, etc.)* ‖ *intr* to be of use; *(w. dat)* **1** to be useful to, be of use to; **2** to be profitable to; **3** to be fitting for; **4** to be conducive to; *(w.* **ad** *or* **in** *+ acc)* to be conducive to

conductīci·us -a -um *adj* mercenary; rented *(house)*

conducti·ō -ōnis *f* bringing together; recapitulation; the taking of a lease, renting

conduct·or -ōris *m* contractor; lessee, tenant

conduct·us -a -um *pp of* **conduco** ‖ *mpl* hired men; mercenaries ‖ *n* rented apartment, rented house; lease, contract

conduplicāti·ō -ōnis *f* doubling; *(hum)* embrace

conduplic·ō -āre -āvī -ātus *tr* to double; **corpora conduplicare** to embrace

condūr·ō -āre -āvī -ātus *tr* to harden

cond·us -ī *m* storeroom manager

cōne·ctō -ctĕre -xuī -xus *tr* **(conn-)** to tie; to connect, join, link; to state as a conclusion; **nodum conectere** to tie a knot; **per affinitatem conexus** *(w. dat)* related by marriage to

cōnexi·ō -ōnis *f* logical conclusion

cōnexuī *perf of* **conecto**

cōnex·us -a -um *pp of* **conecto** ‖ *adj* linked; related, associated; interdependent ‖ *n* logical connection, necessary consequence

cōnex·us -ūs *m* connection

confābul·or -ārī -ātus sum *tr* to discuss ‖ *intr* to have a talk

confarreāti·ō -ōnis *f* solemn marriage ceremony before the Pontifex Maximus and ten witnesses

confarre·ō -āre -āvī -ātus *tr* to marry with solemn rites; to contract *(marriage)*

confātāl·is -is -e *adj* bound by the same fate

confecti·ō -ōnis *f* preparation; completion; conclusion, end; compiling; mastication

confect·or -ōris *m* finisher, executor; destroyer

confer·ciō -cīre — -tus *tr* to stuff, cram, pack together; to stuff full

con·ferō -ferre -tulī -lātus *or* **collātus** *tr* to bring together; to contribute *(money, etc.)*; to condense, compress; to assemble *(ideas, plans, etc.)*; to discuss, talk over; to bear, convey, direct; to devote, apply; to confer, bestow, give, lend, grant; to ascribe, impute, assign; to postpone; *(w.* **in** *+ acc)* to change *(s.o. or s.th.)* into; to compare, contrast; **capita conferre** to put heads together, confer; **gradum conferre cum** to walk together with;

lites conferre to quarrel; **pedem cum pede conferre** to fight toe to toe; **sermones conferre cum** to engage in conversation with; **signa conferre** to begin fighting ‖ *refl (w.* **in** + *acc)* **1** to go to, head for; **2** to have recourse to; **3** to join *(a group, etc.)*

confertim *adv (mil)* shoulder to shoulder

confert·us -a -um *pp of* **confercio** ‖ *adj* crowded, packed, thick, dense; *(mil)* shoulder to shoulder

confervēfac·iō -ĕre *tr* to make glow, make melt

confer·vescō -vescĕre -buī *or* **-vuī** *intr* to begin to boil

confessi·ō -ōnis *f* confession, acknowledgment; admission of guilt; token, proof

confess·us -a -um *pp of* **confiteor** ‖ *adj* acknowledged, incontrovertible ‖ *m* confessed criminal ‖ *n* admission; **ex confesso** admittedly, beyond doubt; **in confessum venire** to be generally admitted

confestim *adv* immediately, suddenly

conficiens -entis *adj* productive, efficient; *(w. gen)* **1** productive of; **2** efficient in ‖ *npl (w. gen)* sources of

con·ficiō -ficĕre -fēcī -fectus *tr* to make, manufacture, process, refine; to do, perform, accomplish; to carry out, discharge; to celebrate *(a rite, festival);* to make ready, prepare; to complete, execute, fulfill; to bring about, cause; to bring together, collect; to secure, obtain; to use up, wear out, exhaust; to finish off, destroy, kill; to run through, waste *(money, inheritance);* to chew *(food);* to disgest *(food);* to spend, pass *(time);* to compose, write; to set down in writing, record; to demonstrate; to cover *(a distance); (of grief, worry)* to overwhelm

conficti·ō -ōnis *f* fabrication

confictus *pp of* **confingo**

confīd·ens -entis *adj* trustful; self-confident; presumptuous, smug

confīdenter *adv* confidently; smugly

confīdenti·a -ae *f* confidence; self-confidence, smugness

confīdentiloqu·us -a -um *adj* speaking confidently

confī·dō -dĕre -sus sum *intr* to have confidence, be confident; *(w. dat)* to confide in, rely on, trust, believe

confī·gō -gĕre -xī -xus *tr* to fasten, join together; to pierce, transfix; *(fig)* to paralyze

con·fingō -fingĕre -finxī -fictus *tr* to make up, fabricate

confīn·is -is -e *adj* having common boundaries, adjoining; *(fig)* akin

confīn·ium -(i)ī *n* common boundary, frontier; border; *(fig)* borderline ‖ *npl* limits, confines

confinxī *perf of* **confingo**

con·fīō -fierī *intr* to be accomplished; to occur, happen; *(w.* **ex**) to be made from

confirmāti·ō -ōnis *f* confirmation, encouragement; verification; *(rhet)* presentation of evidence

confirmāt·or -ōris *m* guarantor

confirmāt·us -a -um *adj* resolute, confident, courageous; established, well-attested

confirmit·ās -ātis *f* firmness; stubbornness

confirm·ō -āre -āvī -ātus *tr* to strengthen; to establish on a firm basis; to develop *(mind, character);* to reinforce; to sanction, ratify; to encourage; to corroborate; to assert positively; *(w. acc & inf)* to prove that; to prove the existence of; to give assurances of, affirm; *(mil)* to strengthen *(a position)* ‖ *refl* to recover, gain strength ‖ *pass* to become mature

confisc·ō -āre -āvī -ātus *tr* to deposit in a treasury; to confiscate *(for the public treasury)*

confīsi·ō -ōnis *f* confidence

con·fiteor -fitērī -fessus sum *tr* to confess, acknowledge, admit; to reveal ‖ *intr* to confess; *(poet)* to admit defeat

confixī *perf of* **configo**

confixus *pp of* **configo**

conflagrāti·ō -ōnis *f* conflagration; eruption *(of a volcano)*

conflagr·ō -āre -āvī -ātum *intr* to burn, be on fire; to be burnt down; *(fig)* to be utterly destroyed

conflicti·ō -ōnis *f* conflict

conflict·ō -āre -āvī -ātus *tr (usu. used in the passive)* to strike down; to ruin; to afflict, torment; to buffet

conflict·or -ārī -ātus sum *intr* to struggle, wrestle

conflict·us -ūs *m* clash, collision

conflī·gō -gĕre -xī -ctus *tr* to knock together, beat, clap ‖ *intr* to clash, fight, battle; *(w.* **cum**) to come into conflict with, clash with; *(w.* **adversus** + *acc or* **contra** + *acc)* to fight against; **inter se confligere** to collide with one another

confl·ō -āre -āvī -ātus *tr* to kindle, ignite; to inflame *(passions);* to melt down *(metals);* to raise *(army, money, etc.);* to concoct *(a lie);* to run up *(debt);* to bring about, cause, to hatch *(plot);* to organize *(riot)*

conflu·ens -entis *m (often pl)* confluence

conflu·ō -ĕre -xī *intr* to flow together; *(fig)* to flock together, come in crowds; *(of things)* to gather

con·fodiō -fodĕre -fōdī -fossus *tr* to dig up *(soil)*; to stab; *(fig)* to harm

confore = confuturum esse to be about to happen

conformāti·ō -ōnis *f* shape, form; fashion;

idea, notion; arrangement *(of words)*; expression *(in voice)*; *(rhet)* figure of speech

conform·ō -āre -āvī -ātus *tr* to shape, fashion, put together; to describe, delineate; to train, educate; to bring into harmony

confoss·us -a -um *pp of* **confodio** ‖ *adj* full of holes, punctured

confractus *pp of* **confringo**

confragōs·us -a -um *adj* rough, rugged ‖ *npl* rugged terrain

confrem·ō -ĕre -uī *intr* to grumble; to resound, ring

confric·ō -āre — -ātus *tr* to rub vigorously; to massage

con·fringō -fringĕre -frēgī -fractus *tr* to smash, crush; to ruin, undo ‖ *pass (of ships)* to be wrecked

con·fugiō -fugĕre -fūgī *intr* to flee, take refuge, run for help; *(w.* **ad)** **1** to have recourse to; **2** to appeal to

confug·ium -(i)ī *n* place of refuge, sanctuary, shelter

confulg·eō -ēre -sī *intr* to glitter, sparkle

con·fundō -fundĕre -fūdī -fūsus *tr* to pour together, blend, mingle; to mix up, jumble together, confuse, bewilder; to spread, diffuse

confūsē *adv* in confusion

confūsi·ō -ōnis *f* mixing, blending; confusion, mixup; **confusio oris** blush

confūs·us -a -um *pp of* **confundo** ‖ *adj* confused; troubled *(look)*

confūt·ō -āre -āvī -ātus *tr* to keep from boiling over; to repress, stop; to confute

confu·tuō -tuĕre -tuī -tūtus *tr (vulg)* to screw; **quidquid puellarum confutuere** to screw any and every girl

congel·ō -āre -āvī -ātus *tr* to cause to freeze up, harden; to curdle; *(fig)* to chill; **in lapidem congelare** to petrify ‖ *intr* to freeze, freeze up; to become hard; to become inactive

congemināti·ō -ōnis *f* doubling

congemin·ō -āre -āvī -ātus *tr* to double

congem·ō -ĕre -uī -itus *tr* to deplore deeply ‖ *intr* to gasp, sigh, groan

con·ger -grī *m* eel

congeri·ēs -ēī *f* heap, pile

con·gerō -gerĕre -gessī -gestus *tr* to bring together; to heap up, build up; to build, erect; to keep up, multiply; to repeat *(arguments)*; *(w.* **in** + *acc)* **1** to shower *(weapons)* on; **2** to heap *(curses, favors)* upon

congerr·ō -ōnis *m* playmate

congestīci·us -a -um *adj* piled up

congestus *pp of* **congero**

congest·us -ūs *m* heap, mass

congiāl·is -is -e *adj* holding a gallon

congiāri·us -a -um *adj* holding a gallon ‖ *n* gift of one gallon *(e.g., of olive oil apiece to the people)*; bonus *(to the army)*; gift of money *(to the people)*; gift, donation

cong·ius -(i)ī *m* liquid measure *(about 6 pints)*

conglaci·ō -āre -āvī *intr* to freeze up

conglisc·ō -ĕre *intr* to blaze up

conglobāti·ō -ōnis *f* massing together

conglob·ō -āre -āvī -ātus *tr* to make round, form into a ball; to mass together

comglomer·ō -āre -āvī -ātus *tr* to roll up; to group together, crowd together ‖ *refl (w.* **in** + *acc)* to crowd into

conglūtināti·ō -ōnis *f* gluing together; *(fig)* combining *(of words)*

conglūtin·ō -āre -āvī -ātus *tr* to glue, cement; *(fig)* to cement

congraec·ō -āre -āvī -ātus *tr* to squander like a Greek

congrātulāti·ō -ōnis *f* congratulations

congrātul·or -ārī -ātus sum *intr* to offer congratulations; *(of several persons)* to express their joy

con·gredior -gredī -gressus sum *tr* to meet, accost, address; to engage ‖ *intr* to come together, meet; *(w.* **cum)** **1** to meet with; **2** to associate with; **3** to fight against

congregābil·is -is -e *adj* gregarious

congregāti·ō -ōnis *f* flocking together, congregation, union, association

congreg·ō -āre -āvī -ātus *tr* to herd together; to assemble; to group together ‖ *pass* to flock together; **pares cum paribus facillime congregantur** *(prov)* birds of a feather flock together

congressi·ō -ōnis *f* meeting, conference

congressus *pp of* **congredior**

congress·us -ūs *m* meeting, association, society; union, combination; hostile encounter; fight; sexual intercourse

congru·ens -entis *adj* coinciding, corresponding; suitable; consistent; self-consistent, uniform

congruenter *adv* consistently; *(w. dat or* **ad)** in conformity with; **congruenter naturae vivere** to live in conformity with nature

congruenti·a -ae *f* consistency; similarity; good proportion

congru·ō -ĕre -ī *intr* to coincide; to correspond, agree, be consistent; *(w.* **ad** *or* **cum)** to correspond to, agree with, be consistent with; *(w. dat or* **in** + *acc)* to agree with

congru·us -a -um *adj* agreeing

cōniciō *or* **cōiciō** *see* **conjicio**

cōnif·er *or* **cōnig·er -era -erum** *adj* coniferous

cōnī·tor -tī -xus sum *or* **-sus sum** *intr* to make a great effort, struggle, exert oneself; *(w.* **in** + *acc)* to struggle toward, try to reach

cōn·īveō -īvēre -īvī *or* **-ixī** *intr* **(conn-)** to

close the eyes; to blink; *(of sun, moon)* to be eclipsed; to be drowsy; *(w.* **in** + *acc)* to connive at, overlook
conjecti·ō -ōnis *f* throwing, barrage *(of missiles);* conjecture; guesswork; interpretation *(of dreams, etc.);* prophecy; **conjectionem facere** to draw a conclusion
conject·ō -āre -āvī -ātus *tr* **(coject-)** to conjecture, infer
conject·or -ōris *m* interpreter of dreams, seer
conjectr·ix -īcis *f* interpreter of dreams, seeress
conjectūr·a -ae *f* **(coject-)** conjecture, guess; inference; interpretation
conjectūrāl·is -is -e *adj* conjectural
conject·us -ūs *m* throwing together; crowding together; connecting; heap, crowd, pile; throwing, hurling; turning, directing *(eyes);* casting *(a glance);* barrage *(of stones, missiles);* **ad** *(or* **intra)** **teli conjectum venire** to come within range of a weapon
con·jiciō -jicĕre -jēcī -jectus *tr* to hurl, cast; pile together; to conclude, infer; to conjecture; to interpret ‖ *refl* **se in fugam** *(or* **in pedes)** **conjicere** to take to one's heels
conjugāl·is -is -e *adj* conjugal
conjugāti·ō -ōnis *f (gram)* etymological relationship *(of words)*
conjugāt·or -ōris *m* uniter *(said of Hymen, god of marriage)*
conjugiāl·is -is -e *adj* marriage-
conjug·ium -(i)ī *n* union *(e.g., of body and soul);* marriage, wedlock; mating *(of animals); (fig)* spouse
conjug·ō -āre -āvī -ātus *tr* to join in marriage; to form *(a friendship);* **verba conjugata** *(gram)* cognates
conjunctē *adv* conjointly; at the same time; hypothetically; in intimacy
conjunctim *adv* jointly
conjuncti·ō -ōnis *f* combination, union; association, connection; friendship, intimacy; marriage; relationship *(by blood or marriage);* sympathy, affinity; *(gram)* conjunction
conjunct·us -a -um *adj (w. dat or abl)* bordering on, near; *(w. dat or abl or* **cum)** **1** connected with; **2** agreeing with, conforming with ‖ *n* connection
conjun·gō -gĕre -xī -ctus *tr* to join together; to unite in making *(war);* to join in marriage; to unite *(by bonds of friendship); (w. dat)* to add *(e.g., words)* to *(e.g., a letter)*
con·junx -jugis *m* **(-jux)** spouse, husband ‖ *mpl* married couple ‖ *f* spouse, wife; fiancée; bride; the female *(of animals)*
conjūrāti·ō -ōnis *f* plot, conspiracy; alliance
conjūrāt·us -a -um *adj* bound together by an oath, allied, associated; *(mil)* sworn in ‖ *mpl* conspirators
conjūr·ō -āre -āvī -ātum *intr* to take an oath together; to plot, conspire
conjux *see* **conjunx**
conl- = **coll-**
conm- = **comm-**
Con·ōn -ōnis *(acc:* **-ōna)** famous Athenian admiral *(fl c. 400 B.C.)* ‖ famous mathematician and astronomer of Samos *(Ē c. 230 B.C.)*
cōnōpī·um -ī *n* **(-pē·um)** mosquito net; bed with net, canopy bed
cōn·or -ārī -ātus sum *tr* to try
conquassāti·ō -ōnis *f* severe shaking, disturbance
conquass·ō -āre -āvī -ātus *tr* to shake hard; *(fig)* shatter, upset, disturb
conque·ror -rī -stus sum *tr* to complain bitterly about, deplore ‖ *intr* to complain bitterly
conquesti·ō -ōnis *f* complaining, complaint; *(rhet)* appeal for sympathy; *(w. gen, w.* **de** + *abl or* **adversus** + *acc)* complaint about
conquest·us -ūs *m* loud complaint
conqui·escō -escĕre -ēvī -ētum *intr* to rest, take a rest; to go to sleep; to find rest, find recreation; to keep quiet, remain inactive; to slacken; to lie dormant; to stop, pause
con·quiniscō -quiniscĕre -quexī *intr* to crouch down, squat
conquī·rō -rĕre -sīvī *or* **-siī -sītus** *tr* to search for, look for; to procure, bring together, collect; *(fig)* to go after *(e.g., pleasures)*
conquīsīti·ō -ōnis *f* search, procuring, collection; *(mil)* recruitment, draft
conquīsīt·or -ōris *m* **(-quist-)** recruiting officer
conquīsīt·us -a -um *pp of* **conquiro** ‖ *adj* select, choice
conr- = **corr-**
consaep·iō -īre -sī -tus *tr* **(-sēp-)** to fence in, enclose
consaept·um -ī *n* **(-sēp-)** enclosure
consalūtāti·ō -ōnis *f* exchange of greetings
consalūt·ō -āre -āvī -ātus *tr* to greet *(as a group),* greet cordially ‖ *intr* **inter se consalutare** to greet one another, exchange greetings
consān·escō -escĕre -uī *intr* to heal up; to recover
consanguine·us -a -um *adj* related by blood ‖ *m* brother ‖ *mpl* relatives ‖ *f* sister
consanguinit·ās -ātis *f* blood relationship; **consanguinitate propinquus** closely related
consauci·ō -āre -āvī -ātus *tr* to wound severely

consceleråt·us -a -um *adj* wicked, depraved, criminal; *(fig)* rotten to the core
consceler·ō -āre -āvī -ātus *tr* to stain with guilt, dishonor, disgrace
conscen·dō -dĕre -dī -sus *tr* to climb up, ascend; to climb *(tree);* to mount *(horse, chariot);* to board *(ship);* **aequor navibus conscendere** to go to sea ‖ *intr* to climb up; to climb aboard
conscensi·ō -ōnis *f* embarkation; **in naves conscensio** boarding the ships
conscienti·a -ae *f* joint knowledge; consciousness, knowledge; conscience; scruples; remorse
con·scindō -scindĕre -scidī -scissus *tr* to tear up, tear to pieces; *(fig)* to tear apart, abuse
consc·iō -īre -īvī *tr* to have on one's conscience
consc·iscō -iscĕre -īvī *or* **-iī -ītus** *tr* to decree, decide on; *(w.* **sibi)** to inflict on oneself; **sibi mortem consciscere** to decide on suicide
consci·us -a -um *adj* cognizant, conscious, aware; *(w. gen or dat)* having knowledge of, privy to ‖ *mf* partner; accomplice; confidant(e), confederate
conscre·or -ārī -ātus sum *intr* to clear the throat
conscrī·bō -bĕre -psī -ptus *tr* to enlist, enroll; to write up, compose; to prescribe
conscripti·ō -ōnis *f* record
conscript·us -a -um *pp of* **conscribo** ‖ *m* senator; **patres conscripti** gentlemen of the Senate ‖ *n (leg)* deposition
consec·ō -āre -uī -tus *tr* to cut up into small pieces, dismember
consecrāti·ō -ōnis *f* consecration; deification *(of emperors)*
consecr·ō -āre -āvī -ātus *tr* to consecrate; to dedicate to the gods below, doom to destruction, execrate; to immortalize; to hallow; to deify
consectāri·us -a -um *adj* conclusive
consectāti·ō -ōnis *f* eager pursuit
consectātr·ix -īcis *f* eager pursuer
consecti·ō -ōnis *f* cutting up
consect·or -ārī -ātus sum *tr* to follow eagerly, go after; to chase, hunt; to overtake; to imitate, follow
consecūti·ō -ōnis *f* effect, consequences; *(rhet)* order, sequence
consen·escō -escĕre -uī *intr* to grow old, grow old together; to become gray; to become obsolete; to waste away, fade, decline; to degenerate
consensi·ō -ōnis *f* agreement, unanimity; harmony; plot
consens·us -ūs *m* agreement, unanimity; harmony; plot; **consensu** with one accord; **in consensum vertere** to become a general custom
consentāne·us -a -um *adj (w. dat or* **cum)** **1** agreeing with; **2** according to, in accord with; **3** proper for; **consentaneum est** it is reasonable ‖ *npl* concurrent circumstances
consenti·ens -entis *adj* unanimous
consen·tiō -tīre -sī -sus *tr* to agree on; to consent to; **bellum consentire** to agree on war, vote for war ‖ *intr* to agree; *(w. inf)* to agree to, plot to; *(w.* **cum)** to fit in with, be consistent with
consēp- = consaep-
consequ·ens -entis *adj* reasonable; corresponding; logical; suitable ‖ *n* consequence, conclusion
consequenter *adv* consequently
consequenti·a -ae *f* consequence; natural sequence; **per consequentias** consequently
conse·quor -quī -cūtus sum *tr* to follow, follow up, pursue, go after; to catch up with, catch; to reach, attain to; to arrive at; *(fig)* to follow, copy, imitate; to obtain, get, acquire; to understand; *(of speech)* to do justice to; *(of time)* to come after, follow; to result from
con·serō -serĕre -sēvī -situs *tr* to sow, plant
conser·ō -ĕre -uī -tus *tr* entwine, tie, join, string together; **manum** *(or* **manūs) conserere** to fight hand-to-hand; **proelium** *(or* **pugnam) conserere** to begin to fight
consertē *adv* in close connection
conserv·a -ae *f* fellow slave *(female)*
conservāti·ō -ōnis *f* preservation
conservāt·or -ōris *m* preserver, defender
conservātr·ix -īcis *f* protectress
conservit·ium -(i)ī *n* fellowship in slavery
conserv·ō -āre -āvī -ātus *tr* to keep safe, preserve, maintain; to act in accordance with, observe; *(fig)* to keep intact
conserv·us -ī *m* fellow slave
consess·or -ōris *m* one who sits next to another *(at a feast, assembly, court of justice, public games)*
consess·us -ūs *m* a sitting together, an assembly, a court, an audience
consīderātē *adv* deliberately, with caution
consīderāti·ō -ōnis *f* consideration, examination
consīderāt·us -a -um *adj* cautious; well-considered, deliberate
consīder·ō -āre -āvī -ātus *tr* to inspect, examine; to consider, reflect on
consid·ium -(i)ī *n* court of justice
con·sīdō -sīdĕre -sēdī *or* **-sīdī -sessum** *intr* to sit down, be seated; to hold sessions, be in session; to settle, stay *(in residence);* to settle, sink; *(fig)* to sink; to subside, calm down; *(mil)* to encamp, take up a position

consign·ō -āre -āvī -ātus *tr* to seal, sign; to certify, vouch for; to record *(in a sealed document);* to put on record
consil·escō -escĕre -uī *intr* to fall silent; to become still, calm down
consiliāri·us -a -um *adj* counseling **‖** *m* counselor, consultant; cabinet member *(of an emperor)*
consiliāt·or -ōris *m* counselor
consiliō *adv* intentionally
consili·or -ārī -ātus sum *intr* to deliberate; to give advice
consil·ium -(i)ī *n* consultation, deliberation; advice; council; council of war; plan, stratagem; measure; decision; purpose, intention; policy; judgment, wisdom, discretion, sense; *(emperor's)* cabinet; **consilio** *(or* **consiliis) alicujus** on s.o.'s instructions; **consilium capere** *(or* **inire** *or* **suscipere)** to form a plan, come to a decision; **consilium mihi est** *(w. inf)* I intend to; **in consilio esse** to be available for consultation; **non est consilium mihi** *(w. inf)* I don't mean to; **privato consilio** for one's own purpose
consiluī *perf of* **consilesco**
consimil·is -is -e *adj* quite similar; *(w. gen or dat)* just like
consip·iō -ĕre *intr* to be sane
con·sistō -sistĕre -stitī *intr* to come to a stop, stop, pause, halt; *(w.* **cum)** to talk with; to take a stand; to stand still; to grow hard, become solid, set; *(of ships)* to come to anchorage, to ground; *(of travelers)* to halt on a journey; to be firm, be steadfast, endure; to be, exist; to come into existence; to continue in existence, remain; to occur, take place; *(mil)* to take up a position, be posted, make a stand; *(w. abl or* **in** + *abl)* **1** to consist of; **2** to depend on; **3** to be based on; **4** to base one's case on; *(w. abl, w.* **in** + *abl, w.* **de** *or* **ex** + *abl)* comprised of
consiti·ō -ōnis *f* sowing, planting
consit·or -ōris *m* sower, planter
consitūr·a -ae *f* sowing, planting
consōbrīn·a -ae *f* first cousin *(female)*
consōbrīn·us -ī *m* first cousin
consoc·er -erī *m* father-in-law
consociāti·ō -ōnis *f* association
consociāt·us -a -um *adj* shared
consoci·ō -āre -āvī -ātus *tr* to join in *(plans, activities);* to share **‖** *intr* to enter into a partnership
consōlābil·is -is -e *adj* consolable
consōlāti·ō -ōnis *f* consolation, comfort; encouragement; allaying
consōlāt·or -ōris *m* comforter
consōlātōri·us -a -um *adj* comforting; **litterae consolatoriae** letter of condolence
consōlor -ārī -ātus sum *tr* to console, comfort; to reassure, soothe, encourage; to relieve
consomni·ō -āre -āvī *tr* to dream about
conson·ō -āre -uī *intr* to sound together, ring, resound, reecho; *(w. dat or* **cum)** to harmonize with, agree with; **inter se consonare** to agree, be in accord
conson·us -a -um *adj* harmonious
consōp·iō -īre -īvī *or* **-ītus** *tr* to put to sleep
consor·s -tis *adj* having a common lot; common; shared in common **‖** *mf* partner **‖** *m* brother **‖** *f* sister
consorti·ō -ōnis *f* partnership; association; fellowship
consort·ium -(i)ī *n* community of goods; partnership; participation; *(w. gen)* partnership in
conspect·us -a -um *pp of* **conspicio ‖** *adj* visible; in full sight; conspicuous, striking
conspect·us -ūs *m* look, sight, view; (sense of) sight; mental view; appearance on the scene; **conspectu in medio** before all eyes
consper·gō -gĕre -sī -sus *tr* to sprinkle; to splatter
conspiciend·us -a -um *adj* worth seeing; distinguished
conspicill·um -ī *n* lookout (post)
con·spiciō -spicĕre -spexī -spectus *tr* to look at attentively, observe, fix the eyes upon; to catch sight of, spot; to look at with admiration; to face *(e.g., the Forum)* **‖** *pass* to be conspicuous, be noticed, be admired; to attract attention
conspic·or -ārī -ātus sum *tr* to catch sight of, spot, see; *(in a passive sense)* to be conspicuous
conspicu·us -a -um *adj* visible, in sight; conspicuous, striking, remarkable, distinguished
conspīrāti·ō -ōnis *f* agreement, unanimity, harmony; plot
conspīrāt·us -a -um *adj* conspiring, conspiratorial
conspīr·ō -āre -āvī -ātum *intr* to act in harmony; to agree; to conspire
conspons·or -ōris *m* co-guarantor
con·spuō -spuĕre -spuī -spūtus *tr* to spit on
conspurc·ō -āre -āvī -ātus *tr* to defile, mess up; to defile sexually
conspūt·ō -āre -āvī -ātus *tr* to spit on
constabil·iō -īre -īvī *or* **-iī -ītus** *tr* to stabilize, put on a firm basis
const·ans -antis *adj* constant, uniform, steady, fixed, stable, regular, invariable, persistent; consistent; *(fig)* faithful, trustworthy
constanter *adv* constantly, steadily, uniformly, invariably; consistently
constanti·a -ae *f* constancy, steadiness, firmness, perseverance; consistency,

harmony; steadfastness; self-possession

consternāti·ō -ōnis *f* consternation, dismay, alarm; disorder, disturbance; mutiny; wild rush, stampede

constern·ō -āre -āvī -ātus *tr* to shock; to startle; to stampede; to derange; *(w.* **ad** *or* **in** + *acc)* to drive *(by fear, etc.)* to *(some action)*

con·sternō -sterněre -strāvī -strātus *tr* to spread, cover; to pave; to thatch; **constrata navis** ship with deck

constīp·ō -āre -āvī -ātus *tr* to pack together

constit·uō -uěre -uī -ūtus *tr* to set up, erect; settle *(e.g., people in a place);* to establish; to settle on, fix *(date, price, penalty);* to arrange, organize; to designate, appoint, assign; to decide, arbitrate, decree, judge; *(mil)* to station, post, deploy; *(w. inf)* to decide to

constitūti·ō -ōnis *f* constitution, nature; disposition; regulation, ordinance; definition; *(rhet)* issue, point of discussion

constitūt·us -a -um *pp of* **constituo ǁ** *adj* ordered, arranged; **bene constitutum corpus** good constitution **ǁ** *n* agreement, arrangement

con·stō -stāre -stitī *intr* to stand together; to agree, correspond; to stand firm, be constant; to stand still, stand firm; to be in existence; *(com)* to tally, be correct; *(w. abl of price)* to cost; **ratio constat** the account tallies, is correct **ǁ** *v impers* it is a fact, it is known; **non mihi satis constat** I have not quite made up my mind; **satis constat** it is an established fact, all agree

constrāt·us -a -um *adj* paved **ǁ** *n* platform; deck *(of ship);* flooring

con·stringō -stringěre -strinxī -strictus *tr* to tie together, tie up; to chain; *(fig)* to restrain, inhibit, control; to bound, limit, confine; to limit in time; to knit *(the brow);* to tone up *(the body); (rhet)* to condense

constructi·ō -ōnis *f* building, construction; arrangement *(of words)*

constru·ō -ěre -xī -ctus *tr* to heap up; to construct; to arrange in a group; *(gram)* to construct

constuprāt·or -ōris *m* rapist

constupr·ō -āre -āvī -ātus *tr* to rape

consuā·deō -dēre -sī -sus *tr* to advocate **ǁ** *intr (w. dat)* to try to persuade

Consuāl·ia -ium *npl* feast of Consus *(ancient Italic god of fertility, celebrated on August 21 and December 15)*

consuās·or -ōris *m* adviser

consūcid·us -a -um *adj* very juicy

consūd·ō -āre -āvī *intr* to sweat profusely

consuē·faciō -facěre -fēcī -factus *tr* to accustom, inure

consu·escō -escěre -ēvī -ētus *tr* to accustom, inure **ǁ** *intr* to become accustomed; *(w. inf)* to become accustomed to, get used to; *(w.* **cum)** to cohabit with

consuēti·ō -ōnis *f* sexual intercourse

consuētūd·ō -inis *f* custom, habit; usage, idiom; social ties; sexual intercourse; **ad consuetudinem** *(w. gen)* according to the custom of; **(ex) consuetudine** from habit; **pro mea consuetudine** as is my habit; **ut fert consuetudo** as is usual

consuēt·us -a -um *pp of* **consuesco ǁ** *adj* customary

con·sul -sulis *m* consul *(one of the two highest magistrates of the Roman Republic);* **consul designatus** consul-elect; **consulem creare** *(or* **dicere,** *or* **facere)** to elect a consul; **consul ordinarius** regular consul *(who entered office in January 1);* **consul suffectus** substitute consul *(chosen in the course of the year to fill a vacancy)*

consulār·is -is -e *adj* consular; **aetas consularis** minimum legal age to be consul *(42 years);* **comitia consularia** consular elections; **vir consularis** a man of consular rank **ǁ** *m* ex-consul

consulāriter *adv* like a consul, in a manner worthy of a consul

consulāt·us -ūs *m* consulship; **consulatum gerere** to hold the consulship; **consulatum petere** to run for the consulship; **se consulatu abdicare** to resign from the consulship

consul·ō -ěre -uī -tus *tr* to consult; to consider; to advise *(s.th.),* offer as advice; **boni (optimi) consulere** to think well (very highly) of **ǁ** *intr* to deliberate, reflect; *(w. dat)* to look after; *(w.* **ad** *or* **in** + *acc)* to reflect on, take into consideration; *(w.* **in** + *acc)* to take measures against; *(w.* **de** + *abl)* to pass sentence on

consultāti·ō -ōnis *f* mature deliberation, consideration; consulting; inquiry; subject of consultation

consultē *adv* deliberately, with due deliberation, prudently

consultō *adv* on purpose

consult·ō -āre -āvī -ātus *tr* to reflect on, consider maturely; to ask *(s.o.)* for advice, consult **ǁ** *intr* to deliberate; *(w. dat)* to look after, take care of; **in medium** *(or* **in commune)** **consultare** to look after the common good

consult·or -ōris *m* counselor, consultant; advisee, client

consultr·ix -īcis *f* protectress

consult·us -a -um *pp of* **consulo ǁ** *adj* skilled, experienced **ǁ** *m* expert; **juris consultus** legal expert, attorney **ǁ** *n* deliberation, consideration; decree, decision; response *(from an oracle);* **bene consultum** a good measure; **male**

consultum an ill-advised measure; **senatūs consultum** decree of the Senate

consummāt·us -a -um *adj* consummate, perfect

consumm·ō -āre -āvī -ātus *tr* to sum up; *(of numbers)* to add up to; to finish, accomplish, perfect; to complete *(public works)*

consūm·ō -ĕre -psī -ptus *tr* to consume, use up, exhaust; to devour; to wear out; to waste

consumpti·ō -ōnis *f* consumption; wasting

consumpt·or -ōris *m* spend-thrift

con·suō -suĕre -suī -sūtus *tr* to sew up

consur·gō -gĕre -rexī -rectum *intr* to stand up; to rise in a body; *(w.* **ad** *or* **in** *+ acc)* to aspire to

consurrecti·ō -ōnis *f* rising up, standing up in a body

Cons·us -ī *m* ancient Italic deity of agriculture and fertility

consusurr·ō -āre -āvī *intr* to whisper to one another

contābē·faciō -facĕre -fēcī -factus *tr (fig)* to run *(s.o.)* down

contāb·escō -escĕre -uī *intr* to waste away

contabulāti·ō -ōnis *f* flooring; story

contabul·ō -āre -āvī -ātus *tr* to cover with boards; to construct with multiple stories; to bridge, span

contact·us -ūs *m* touch, contact; contagion; *(fig)* infection

contāg·ēs -is *f* touch, contact

contāgi·ō -ōnis *f* touching; touch, contact; contagion, infection

contāg·ium -(i)ī *n* touch, contact; contagion; moral contamination

contāmināt·us -a -um *adj* contaminated, polluted; vile

contāmin·ō -āre -āvī -ātus *tr* to contaminate, pollute; to adulterate; to defile, desecrate; to ruin, spoil

contechn·or -ārī -ātus sum *intr* to devise plots; to think up tricks

conte·gō -gĕre -xī -ctus *tr* to cover up; to hide; to protect; to put a roof on; to bury

contemer·ō -āre -āvī -ātus *tr* to defile

contem·nō -nĕre -psī -ptus *tr* to regard with contempt, look down on, despise; to treat with contempt; to pay no attention to, disregard; to have nothing to do with

contemplāti·ō -ōnis *f* viewing, surveying; contemplation, consideration

contemplāt·or -ōris *m* contemplator, observer

contemplāt·us -ūs *m* contemplation

contempl·ō -āre -āvī -ātus *or* **contempl·or -ārī -ātus sum** *tr* to observe, survey, gaze on, contemplate

contemptim *adv* contemptuously; fearlessly

contempti·ō -ōnis *f* scorn; contempt; disregarding, belittling

contempt·or -ōris *m* despiser

contemptr·ix -īcis *f* despiser *(female)*

contempt·us -a -um *pp of* **contemno** ‖ *adj* contemptible

contempt·us -ūs *m* contempt; **contemptui esse** to be an object of contempt

conten·dō -dĕre -dī -tus *tr* to stretch, draw tight; to tune *(instrument)*; to aim, shoot, hurl; to strain, exert; to assert, hold, allege; to compare, contrast; **cursum** *(or* **iter)** **contendere** to make one's way ‖ *intr* to exert oneself; to contend, compete, fight; to dispute, argue; to travel, march; to match, contrast; *(w.* **de** *+ abl)* to demand from; *(w. inf)* to be in a hurry to; *(w.* **in** *+ acc)* to rush to, head for; *(w.* **ad)** to strive for, aspire to; *(w.* **cum) 1** to contend with, argue with; **2** to fight with

contentē *adv (from* **contendo)** vehemently, vigorously

contentē *adv (from* **contineo)** in a restricted way, sparingly

contenti·ō -ōnis *f* stretching, tension; exertion, effort; competition; quarrel; contrast, comparison, antithesis; *(gram)* comparison of adjectives; *(rhet)* crescendo; **in contentionem venire** *or* **vocari** *(or* **in contentione poni)** to become the subject of a dispute

content·us -a -um *pp of* **contendo** ‖ *adj* tense, strained; energetic

content·us -a -um *pp of* **contineo** ‖ *adj* content, satisfied

contermin·us -a -um *adj* neighboring; *(w. dat)* adjacent to

con·terō -terĕre -trīvī -trītus *tr* to grind to powder, pulverize, crush; to wear out; *(fig)* to wear down; *(fig)* to trample on; to expunge, wipe out; to waste *(time, effort)*; to exhaust *(topic)*

conterr·eō -ēre -uī -itus *tr* to scare the life out of

contest·or -ārī -ātus sum *tr* to call to witness; *(fig)* to prove, attest; **litem contestari** to open a lawsuit by calling witnesses

contex·ō -ĕre -uī -tus *tr* to weave together; to make by joining, devise, build; to link, join *(words)*; to compose *(writings)*; to dream up

contextē *adv* in a coherent manner

context·us -a -um *pp of* **contexo** ‖ *adj* interwoven; coherent; continuous, uninterrupted

context·us -ūs *m* joining together; coherence; continuity, connection; structure; plan, course

contic·escō -escĕre *or* **contic·iscō -iscĕre -uī** *intr* to become quite still, fall completely silent; to keep silence; *(fig)* to abate, cease

conticin·ium -(i)ī *n* silence of the night
contignāti·ō -ōnis *f* floor, story
contign·ō -āre -āvī -ātus *tr* to lay a floor on
contigu·us -a -um *adj* contiguous, touching, adjoining, within reach; *(w. dat)* bordering on, near
contin·ens -entis *adj* continuous, unbroken; homogeneous; adjacent, close; next, immediately following; self-controlled, moderate; restrained; *(w. dat)* contiguous with ‖ *f* interior *(of a country);* mainland ‖ *n* main point *(of argument);* **ex continenti** (*or* **in continenti**) without delay
continenter *adv* in unbroken succession; without interruption; *(sitting)* close together; moderately
continenti·a -ae *f* repression; self-control
con·tineō -tinēre -tinuī -tentus *tr* to hold *or* keep together; to keep within bounds, confine; to contain, comprise, include; to control, repress
con·tingō -tingĕre -tigī -tactus *tr* to come into contact with; to touch, border on; to reach, attain; to infect; to contaminate; *(fig)* to touch, affect ‖ *intr* to happen, turn out, come to pass; *(w. dat)* to touch, border on ‖ *v impers* it happens, turns out; *(w. dat)* it befalls one
continuāti·ō -ōnis *f* unbroken series, succession; *(rhet)* period
continu·ō -āre -āvī -ātus *tr* to make continuous, join together, connect; to extend *(in time or space);* to continue, carry on, draw out, prolong; to pass, occupy *(time)* ‖ *pass (w. dat)* **1** to be contiguous with, adjacent to; **2** to follow closely upon ‖ *intr* to continue, last
continuō *adv* immediately; right from the first; without more ado; continuously; necessarily
continu·us -a -um *adj* continuous, unbroken; successive; **dies continuos quinque** (for) five days in a row
conti·ō -ōnis *f* meeting, rally; public meeting *(of the people or soldiers);* speech, pep talk; **contionem habere** to give a speech; to give a pep talk
contiōnābund·us -a -um *adj* haranguing, holding forth
contiōnāl·is -is -e *adj* like in assembly; demogogic
contiōnāri·us -a -um *adj* mob-like
contiōnāt·or -ōris *m* demogogue
contiōn·or -ārī -ātus sum *intr* to hold forth at a rally, to harangue; to come to a rally ‖ *tr (w. acc & inf)* to say at a rally (that)
contiuncul·a -ae *f* small rally
contoll·ō -ĕre *tr* **gradum contollere** to step up *(to a person)*
conton·at -āre *v impers* it is thundering loud
contor·qeō -quēre -sī -tus *tr* to twist, whirl; to throw hard; to twist *(words)* around
contortē *adv* intricately
contortiōn·ēs -um *fpl* intricacies *(of language)*
contort·or -ōris *m* perverter; **contortor legum** shyster
contortul·us -a -um *adj* terribly complicated
contortuplicāt·us -a -um *adj* all tangled up
contort·us -a -um *pp of* **contorqueo** ‖ *adj* involved, intricate
contrā *adv* in opposition, opposite, in front, face to face; in turn, in return; on the other hand; on the other side; reversely, in the opposite way, the other way; on the contrary, conversely; **contra atque** (*or* **ac**) contrary to, otherwise than; **contra dicere** to reply; to raise objections; **contra dicitur** the objection is raised; **contra ferire** to make a counterattack; **contra qua fas est** contrary to divine law; **contra quam senatus consuluisset** contrary to what the Senate would have decided; **quin contra** nay on the contrary
contrā *prep (w. acc)* **1** opposite, opposite to, facing, towards: **contra septentriones** facing north; **2** *(in a hostile sense)* against, with, in opposition to: **contra patriam exercitum ducere** to lead an army against one's country; **3** injurious to, unfavorable to: **quod contra se ipsum sit dicere** to say what is against one's own interests; **4** in defiance of: **contra senatum proficisci** to depart in defiance of the Senate; **5** in violation of: **contra jus gentium** in violation of international law; **6** contrary to, the reverse of **contra exspectationem omnium** contrary to universal expectation; **contra spem** contrary to hope, unexpectedly; **7** in comparison with: **nunc contra istum librum faveo orationi quam nuper dedi** now in comparison with that book I prefer the speech which I recently gave *(you)*
contracti·ō -ōnis *f* contraction; shortening *(of syllable);* **contractio animi** depression; **contractio nervorum** cramp
contractiuncul·a -ae *f* slight mental depression
contract·us -a -um *pp of* **contraho** ‖ *adj* contracted; narrow, limited *(place);* brief; pinching *(poverty);* limited in scope; parsimonious; terse *(style)*
contract·us -ūs *m* contraction
contrā·dīcō -dīcĕre -dixī -dictum *tr* to contradict ‖ *intr (w. dat)* **1** to contradict; **2** to speak against
contrādicti·ō -ōnis *f* objection, refutation
contra·hō -hĕre -xī -ctus *tr* to draw to-

gether; to contract; to collect, assemble; to shorten, narrow, abridge; to lessen; to wrinkle; to bring about, accomplish, cause, produce, incur; to conclude *(a bargain);* to transact *(business);* to settle *(an account);* to complete *(business arrangements)*

contrāposit·um -ī *n* antithesis

contrāriē *adv* in opposite directions; in a different way

contrāri·us -a -um *adj* opposite; contrary, conflicting; hostile, antagonistic; from the opposite direction; reciprocal, mutual; *(w. dat)* opposed to, contrary to ‖ *n* the opposite, the contrary, the reverse; antithesis; **contrario** on the contrary; **e(x) contrario** on the contrary; on the opposite side; **in contraria** *(or* **contrarium)** in the opposite direction; **in contaria versus** changed into its opposite

contrectābiliter *adv* **(-tract-)** appreciably, tangibly

contrectāti·ō -ōnis *f* **(-tract-)** handling, touching; fondling, caressing

contrect·ō -āre -āvī -ātus *tr* **(-tract-)** to touch, handle; *(sl)* to fondle; *(sl)* to have sexual intercouse with; to deal with *(a subject)*

contrem·iscō -iscĕre *tr* to shudder at ‖ *intr* to tremble all over; to waver

contrem·ō -ĕre -uī *intr* to tremble all over; to quake

contrib·uō -uĕre -uī -ūtus *tr* to bring together, enroll together; to associate, unite incorporate; to contribute, add

contrist·ō -āre -āvī -ātus *tr* to sadden; to cast gloom over, darken, cloud

contrīt·us -a -um *pp of* **contero** ‖ *adj* worn out, common, trite

contrōversi·a -ae *f* controversy, quarrel, dispute; debate; civil lawsuit, litigation; subject of litigation; contradiction; question

contrōversiōs·us -a -um *adj* controversial

contrōvers·us -a -um *adj* disputed, controversial; questionable, undecided

contrucīd·ō -āre -āvī -ātus *tr* to cut down, massacre; *(sl)* to make a mess of

contrū·dō -dĕre -sī -sus *tr* to push hard; to crowd together

contrunc·ō -āre -āvī -ātus *tr* to hack to pieces

contubernāl·is -is *m* army buddy; junior staff officer; *(coll)* husband *(of slave);* personal attendant; companion, colleague ‖ *f* wife *(of slave)*

contubern·ium -(i)ī *n* sharing the same tent; wartime friendship; army tent; serving as a junior staff officer; concubinage; marriage *(among slaves);* hovel *(of slave couple)*

contudī *perf of* **contundo**

contu·eor -ērī -itus sum *tr* to look intently at; to catch sight of; to be within sight of *(a place)*

contuit·us *or* **contūt·us -ūs** *m* sight, observation

contumāci·a -ae *f* insubordination, defiance; *(leg)* contempt

contumāciter *adv* defiantly

contum·ax -ācis *adj* insubordinate, defiant

contumēli·a -ae *f* mistreatment; outrage; abuse; insult, affront

contumēliōsē *adv* abusively; outrageously

contumēliōs·us -a -um *adj* insulting, outrageous, humiliating; abusive, rude

contumul·ō -āre -āvī -ātus *tr* to bury

con·tundō -tundĕre -tudī -tūsus *tr* to crush, grind, pound; to bruise; *(fig)* to crush, subdue; to baffle; to outdo *(performance)*

conturbāti·ō -ōnis *f* disorder; dismay, consternation

conturbāt·or -ōris *m* bankrupt

conturbāt·us -a -um *adj* confused, distracted, in confusion

conturb·ō -āre -āvī -ātus *tr* to confuse, throw into confusion; to disturb; to upset *(plans);* **rationes** *(or* **rationem) conturbare** to be bankrupt ‖ *intr* to go bankrupt

cont·us -ī *m* pole

contūsus *pp of* **contundo**

cōnūbiāl·is -is -e *adj* conjugal

cōnūb·ium -(i)ī *n* intermarriage; right to intermarry; marriage; sexual intercourse; **jus conubi** right to intermarry

cōn·us -ī *m* cone; apex *(of helmet)*

convad·or -ārī -ātus sum *tr* to subpoena

conval·escō -escĕre -uī *intr* to grow strong, thrive; to convalesce; *(fig)* to improve; *(leg)* become valid

convall·is -is *f* valley

convās·ō -āre -āvī -ātus *tr* to pack, pack up

convect·ō -āre -āvī -ātus *tr* to gather

convect·or -ōris *m* fellow passenger

conve·hō -hĕre -xī -ctus *tr* gather, bring in *(esp. the harvest);* to convey, ship *(to one place)*

con·vellō -vellĕre -vellī -vulsus *tr* **(-vols-)** to tear away, pull off, pluck, wrest; to tear to pieces, dismember; to break, shatter; *(fig)* to turn upside down, subvert, overthrow; **convellere signa** to break camp

conven·ae -ārum *mpl or fpl* strangers; refugees, vagabonds, the homeless

conveni·ens -entis *adj* agreeing, harmonious, consistent; appropriate; *(w. dat or* **cum)** consistent with, appropriate to; *(w.* **ad)** appropriate for, suitable for

convenienter *adv* consistently; suitably; *(w.* **cum** *or* **ad)** in conformity with

convenienti·a -ae *f* agreement, accord, harmony; conformity

con·veniō -venīre -vēnī -ventus *tr* to meet, go to meet; to interview; *(leg)* to sue; **Regulus convenit me in praetoris officio** Regulus met me at the installation of a praetor ‖ *intr* to come together, meet, gather; to make an agreement; to coincide; to converge; to unite, combine; to come to an agreement, agree; to fit; *(w.* **ad)** to fit *(as a shoe fits the foot); (w. dat or* **cum** *or* **ad** *or* **in** *+ acc)* to be applicable to, appropriate to; **bene convenire** to be on good terms; to fit well; **in matrmonium cum viro convenire** *(of a bride)* to get married; **viro in manum convenire** *(of a bride)* to come under the control of her husband ‖ *v impers* it is befitting; it is agreed; **bene convenit nobis** we get along well; **convenit inter se** *(w. dat)* there is harmony among

conventīci·us -a -um *adj* coming together, met by chance ‖ *n* fee paid for attending the assembly

conventicul·um -ī *n* small gathering; small meeting place

conventi·ō -ōnis *f* assembly; agreement, contract

convent·um -ī *n* contract, agreement

convent·us -ūs *m* gathering, assembly; congress; district court; company, corporation; agreement; **ex conventu** by agreement; of one accord; **conventum agere** to hold court

converber·ō -āre -āvī -ātus *tr* to beat soundly, bash

conver·rō -rĕre -rī -sus *tr* **(-vorr-)** to sweep out; to brush thoroughly; *(fig)* to scoop up *(e.g., an inheritance)*

conversāti·ō -ōnis *f* familiarity, close association *(with people);* **conversatio parit contemptum** *(prov)* familiarity breeds contempt

conversi·ō -ōnis *f* rotation; cycle; transposition, inversion; alteration; political change, upheaval; *(rhet)* repetition of word at end of clause; *(rhet)* balancing of phrases; *(rhet)* period

convers·ō -āre -āvī -ātus *tr* to turn around ‖ *refl* to revolve

conver·tō -tĕre -tī -sus *tr* **(-vor-)** to rotate; to turn back, reverse; *(fig)* to turn, direct *(attention, laughter);* to convert, transform; to translate; to turn upside down; to convulse, shake; to turn *(e.g., horse)* around; to shift, transfer; to transpose, invert *(an arrangement);* to turn aside, divert; to distract *(the mind);* to repulse *(attackers);* **ad se** *(or* **in se)** **convertere** to attract *(e.g., attention);* **in fugam convertere** to put to flight; **signa convertere** to face about; **terga convertere** to turn tail ‖ *refl* to turn around; *(mil)* to retreat ‖ *intr* to return; to change, turn; *(w.* **in** *+ acc)* to be changed into, turn into

convest·iō -īre *tr* to clothe, cover

convex·us -a -um *adj* rounded off; arched, convex; concave; sloping down ‖ *n* vault, arch, dome

convīciāt·or -ōris *m* heckler

convīci·or -ārī -ātus sum *intr* to jeer; *(w. dat)* to heckle, jeer at

convīc·ium -(i)ī *n* noise, chatter; wrangling; jeers, heckling, abuse; cry of protest; reprimand; **aliquem conviciis consectari** to heckle s.o.

convīcti·ō -ōnis *f* socializing, association, companionship; companions

convict·or -ōris *m* bosom pal

convict·us -ūs *m* socializing, association

con·vincō -vincĕre -vīcī -victus *tr* to refute, prove wrong; *(leg)* to convict; to prove, demonstrate clearly; **devotionem convincere** *(of a god)* to grant a request

convīs·ō -ĕre -ī -us *tr* to examine, search; to go to visit

convīv·a -ae *m (f)* guest; dinner guest

convīvāl·is -is -e *adj* convivial, festive

convīvāt·or -ōris *m* host; master of ceremonies

convīv·ium -(i)ī *n* banquet, dinner party; party; **convivium agitare** *(coll)* to throw a party ‖ *npl* dinner guests

convī·vō -vĕre -xī -ctum *intr* to live together; to live at the same time; *(w.* **cum)** to dine with

convīv·or -ārī -ātus sum *intr* to feast together, have a party

convocāti·ō -ōnis *f* calling together

convoc·ō -āre -āvī -ātus *tr* to convoke

convol·ō -āre -āvī -ātum *intr* to flock together

convol·vō -vĕre -vī -ūtus *tr* to roll together; to roll up *(scroll);* to fasten together, interweave; to wrap; **terga convolvere** *(of snakes)* to writhe ‖ *refl* to roll along; to go in a circle

convom·ō -ĕre -uī -itus *tr* to vomit all over

convortō *see* **converto**

convulner·ō -āre -āvī -ātus *tr* **(-vol-)** to wound seriously

convulsus *pp of* **convello**

coöper·iō *or* **cōperi·ō -īre -uī -tus** *tr* **(cōp-)** to cover; to overwhelm

coöptāti·ō -ōnis *f* **(cōp-)** coöptation *(election of a colleague by incumbents)*

coöpt·ō -āre -āvī -ātus *tr* **(cōp-)** to coöpt

coör·ior -īrī -tus sum *intr* to rise; to be born; to originate; to appear suddenly; *(of war)* to break out; *(mil)* to go on the attack

coört·us -ūs *m* rising, originating

Cō·os *or* **Co·us -ī** *f* small island in the Aegean, famous for its wine and fine linen

cōp·a -ae *f* barmaid
cophin·us -ī *m* basket
cōpi·a -ae *f* abundance, supply, store; plenty; multitude, large number; wealth, prosperity; opportunity, means; command of language, fluency; *(w. gen)* power over; *(w. dat)* access to; **copia dicendi** *(or* **verborum)** command of language, wide vocabulary, richness of expression; **pro copiā** as one's circumstances allow ‖ *fpl* troops, armed forces; provisions, supplies
cōpiol·ae -ārum *fpl* small contingent of troops
cōpiōsē *adv* abundantly; *(rhet)* fully, at length, eloquently
cōpiōs·us -a -um *adj* plentiful; well-supplied, rich; eloquent, fluent; *(w. abl)* abounding in, rich in
cop·is -idis *f* small, curved sword
cōpō *see* **caupo**
cōp·s -is *adj* rich, well-supplied; *(of the chest)* swelling *(with pride)*
copt·a -ae *f* crisp cake
cōpul·a -ae *f* cord, string, rope, leash; *(fig)* tie, bond
cōpulāti·ō -ōnis *f* coupling, joining, union; combining *(of words)*
cōpulāt·us -a -um *adj* closely connected; compound, complex; close, intimate *(relationship)*
cōpul·ō -āre -āvī -ātus *tr* to couple, join; *(fig)* to unite; *(w. dat or* **cum)** to couple with, join to, combine with ‖ *refl & pass* to unite *(for practical purposes)*
cōpul·or -ārī -ātus sum *tr* to join, clasp; **dextras copulari** to shake hands
coqu·a -ae *f* cook *(female)*
coquīn·ō -āre -āvī -ātum *intr* to be a cook
coquīn·us -a -um *adj* of cooked and baked food
co·quō -quĕre -xī -ctus *tr* to cook; to fry, roast, boil, bake; to brew; to bake *(bricks, bread);* to fire *(pottery);* to smelt *(ore);* to season *(lumber);* to burn, parch; to ripen; to digest *(food);* to disturb, worry; to concoct, dream up; to hatch *(plots)*
coqu·us *or* **coc·us -ī** *m* cook
cor cordis *n* heart; mind, judgment; dear friend; **aliquid cordi habere** to take s.th. to heart; **cordi esse** *(w. dat)* to please, be dear to, be agreeable to; **cor habere** to have common sense; **si vobis non fuit cordi** *(w. acc & inf)* if it was not to your liking that ‖ *npl* friends, souls
coracīn·us -ī *m* dark-colored species of fish
corall·ium -(i)ī *n* **(cūrali-)** coral
cōram *adv* in person, personally; publicly, openly; in someone's presence, face to face ‖ *prep (coming before or after abl)* before, in the presence of, face to face with
corb·is -is *m (f)* wicker basket
corbīt·a -ae *f* slow-sailing merchant ship
corbul·a -ae *f* small basket
corcōta *see* **crocota**
corcōtāri·us -a -um *adj* concerned with saffron-colored clothes
corcul·um -ī *n* little heart; sweetheart; poor fellow; the Wise *(name given to Publius Scipio Nasica)*
Corcȳr·a -ae *f* island off coast of Epirus, sometimes identified with Scheria, the island of Alcinoüs
cordātē *adv* wisely, prudently
cord·ax -ācis *m* trochaic meter; indecent dance
cordol·ium -(i)ī *n* heartache
Cordub·a -ae *f* Cordova *(in S. Spain)*
cordȳl·a -ae *f* baby tuna
Corfīn·ium -(i)ī *n* town in central Italy, center of the Social War
coriandr·um -ī *n (bot)* coriander *(aromatic herb, used as seasoning)*
Corinn·a -ae *f* Greek lyric poetess *(fl c. 500 B.C.)*
Corinthiac·us -a -um *or* **Corinthiens·is -is -e** *adj* Corinthian
Corinthi·us -a -um *adj* Corinthian; **aes Corinthium** alloy of gold, silver, and copper used in expensive jewelry ‖ *mpl* Corinthians ‖ *npl* costly Corinthian products
Corinth·us *or* **Corinth·os -ī** *f* Corinth
Coriolān·us -ī *m* Gnaeus Marcius Coriolanus *(notorious Roman general who led the Volsci against Rome)*
cor·ium -(i)ī *n or* **cor·ius -(i)ī** *m* skin, hide; leather; bark; peel, rind; *(sl)* one's hide; **corio suo ludere** *(sl)* to risk one's own hide; **corium alicujus petere** *(sl)* to be after s.o.'s hide
Cornēli·us -a -um *adj* Roman clan name *(nomen)* and tribal name; **lex Cornelia** a law proposed by any member of the Cornelian clan *(esp. Sulla)*
corneol·us -a -um *adj* made of horn; *(fig)* hard, tough
corne·us -a -um *adj* of horn; of cornel wood; of the cornel tree
cornic·en -inis *m* horn blower
cornīc·or -ārī -ātus sum *tr (sl)* to croak, say in a croaking voice ‖ *intr* to caw
cornīcul·a -ae *f* poor little crow
corniculār·ius -(i)ī *m* soldier decorated with horn-shaped medal for bravery; adjutant to a centurion
cornicul·um -ī *n* **(cornu-)** little horn; *(mil)* horn-shaped decoration
cornig·er -era -erum *adj* horned
cornip·ēs -edis *adj* hoofed
corn·ix -īcis *f* crow; *(pej)* old crow
corn·ū -ūs *or* **corn·um -ī** *n* horn *(of animals, insects);* drinking vessel *(made from a horn);* funnel *(made from a horn);*

horn, trumpet; lantern; funnel; oil cruet; hoof; bill *(of bird);* horn *(of moon);* tip *(of a bow);* branch *(of river);* arm *(of lake);* tongue *(of land);* crest socket *(of helmet);* roller end *(of scroll); (mil)* wing, flank; **cornua addere** *(w. dat)* to give courage to, add strength to; **cornua sumere** to gain strength; **cornu Copiae** cornucopia; **cornu Indicum** ivory

corn·um -ī *n* cornel cherry; spear

corn·us -ī *f* cornel cherry tree; dogwood tree; spear, shaft, javelin

coroll·a -ae *f* small garland

corollār·ium -(i)ī *n* garland; gilt wreath *(given as reward to actors);* gift, tip

corōn·a -ae *f* crown, garland; circle of bystanders; *(mil)* cordon of besiegers; *(mil)* ring of defense; **corona civica** decoration for a saving a life; **corona muralis** decoration for being the first to scale an enemy wall; **corona navalis** decoration for naval victory; **corona obsidialis** decoration for breaking a blockade; **sub corona vendere** to sell *(captives)* as slaves; **sub corona venire** *(of captives)* to be sold at auction ‖ **Corona** *(astr)* Ariadne's crown, Corona Borealis

corōnāri·us -a -um *adj* for a crown; **aurum coronarium** gold collected in the provinces for a victorious general's crown

Corōnē·a -ae *f* town in Boeotia

Corōn·eus -eī *m* king of Phocis, whose daughter was changed into a crow

Corōnīd·ēs -ae *m* Aesculapius, son of Coronis

corōn·is -idis *f* symbol for showing the end of a book, colophon

Corōn·is -idis *f* mother, by Apollo, of Aesculapius

corōn·ō -āre -āvī -ātus *tr* to crown, wreathe; to enclose, encircle, shut in

corporat·us -a - um *adj* incorporated; having a tangible body

corpore·us -a -um *adj* physical, of the body, bodily; corporeal, substantial; of flesh

corpulent·us -a -um *adj* corpulent

corp·us -oris *n* body; matter, substance; flesh; plumpness; trunk *(of tree);* corpse; person, individual; frame, structure, framework; community; corporation; society, union, guild; particle, grain; sum *(of money); (literary)* corpus; *(in geometry)* a solid; **corporis** *(w. noun)* body, bodily, physical; **corporis custos** bodyguard; **corpus reipublicae** the body politic; **toto corpore** with all one's strengh

corpuscul·um -ī *n* puny body; particle, atom; *(coll)* little fellow

corrā·dō -dĕre -sī -sus *tr* **(conr-)** to scrape together, rake up; *(coll)* to scrape *(money)* together

correcti·ō -ōnis *f* **(conr-)** correction, improvement, amendment; rhetorical restatement

correct·or -ōris *m* **(conr-)** corrector, reformer

correct·us -a -um *pp of* **corrigo** ‖ *adj* improved, correct

corrēp·ō -ĕre -sī -tum *intr* **(conr-)** to creep, slink; **in dumeta correpere** *(coll)* to beat around the bush, indulge in jargon

correptē *adv* **(conr-)** with a short vowel *or* syllable

correptius *adv* **(conr-)** more briefly; **correptius exire** to end in a short vowel

correptus *pp of* **corripio (conr-)** ‖ *adj* short *(syllable, vowel)*

correxī *perf of* **corrigo**

corrīd·eō -ēre *intr* **(conr-)** to laugh out loud

corrigi·a -ae *f* shoelace

cor·rigō -rigĕre -rexī -rectus *tr* **(conr-)** to straighten out; to smooth out; to correct, improve, reform; to make up for *(delay);* to make the best of

cor·ripiō -ripĕre -ripuī -reptus *tr* **(conr-)** to take hold of, snatch up; to seize *(a person);* to seize unlawfully; *(of a current)* to carry off; to steal, carry off; to enrapture, sweep off one's feet; to attack suddenly; to speed up, rush; to shorten, contract; to abridge *(a literary work);* to reproach; to cut short *(period of time); (gram)* to pronounce *(a word)* with a short syllable, pronounce *(a syllable)* short; **arma corripere** to go to war; **gradum corripere** to pick up the pace; **igne** *(or* **flammā) corripere** to ignite, set on fire; **in se corripere** to absorb ‖ *refl* to bestir oneself, jump up, hurry off

corrōbor·ō -āre -āvī -ātus *tr* **(conr-)** to strengthen, invigorate; *(fig)* to fortify, encourage; *(mil)* to reinforce ‖ *refl & pass* to become mature

cor·rōdō -rōdĕre -rōsī -rōsus *tr* **(conr-)** to gnaw, chew up

corrog·ō -āre -āvī -ātus *tr* **(conr-)** to go asking for, collect, drum up, solicit; to invite, summon

corrōsus *pp of* **corrodo**

corrūg·ō -āre -āvī -ātus *tr* **(conr-)** to wrinkle; **nares corrugare** *(w. dat)* to make s.o. turn up his nose

cor·rumpō -rumpĕre -rūpī -ruptus *tr* **(conr-)** to burst, to break to pieces, smash; to destroy completely, ruin, waste; to mar; to corrupt; to adulterate; to falsify, tamper with; to bribe; to seduce

corru·ō -ĕre -ī *tr* **(conr-)** to shatter, wreck, ruin ‖ *intr* to fall down, tumble, sink; *(fig)* to fall, fail, sink

corruptē *adv* **(conr-)** corruptly, perversely; in a lax manner

corruptēl·a -ae *f* **(conr-)** corruption, seduction; bribery; corrupting influence
corrupti·ō -ōnis *f* **(conr-)** corruption, ruining, breaking up; corrupt condition
corrupt·or -ōris *m or* **corruptr·ix -īcis** *f* **(conr-)** corrupter, seducer, briber
corrupt·us -a -um *pp of* **corrumpo (conr-)** ‖ *adj* corrupt, spoiled, bad, ruined
Corsic·a -ae *f* Corsica
cort·ex -icis *m (f)* bark, shell, hull, rind; cork; **nare sine cortice** to swim without a cork life preserver; *(fig)* to be on one's own
cortīn·a -ae *f* kettle, caldron; tripod; *(fig)* vault of heaven
corulus *see* **corylus**
cōrus *see* **caurus**
corusc·ō -āre -āvī *tr* to shake, wave, brandish ‖ *intr* to flit, flutter; to oscillate; to tremble; to flash, gleam
corusc·us -a -um *adj* oscillating, vibrating, tremulous; flashing, gleaming, glittering
corv·us -ī *m raven; (mil)* grapnel
Coryb·ās -antis *m* priest of Cybele
Corybant·ēs -um *mpl* the Corybantes *(priests of goddess Cybele)*
Corybanti·us -a -um *adj* of the Corbyantes
Cōryci·us -a -um *adj* of the Corycian mountain-caves on Mt. Parnasus
Cōrycid·es -um *fpl* **nymphae Corycides** the Muses
cōryc·us -ī *m* punching bag
corylēt·um -ī *n* cluster of hazel trees
coryl·us -ī *f* **(-rul-)** hazel tree
corymbif·er -era -erum *adj* wearing *or* carrying clusters of ivy berries ‖ *m* Bacchus
corymb·us -ī *m* cluster *(esp. of ivy berries)*
coryphae·us -ī *m* leader, head
cōrӯt·os *or* **cōrӯt·us -ī** *m* quiver
cōs- = cons-
cōs cōtis *f* whetstone
cosmēt·a -ae *f* slave girl in charge of the wardrobe
cosmic·os -ē -on *adj* worldly, fashionable
cosm·os -ī *m* the universe, cosmos ‖ a chief magistrate of Crete
cost·a -ae *f* rib; *(fig)* side, wall
cost·um -ī *n* perfume
cothurnāt·us -a -um *adj* wearing buskins; suitable to tragedy, tragic
cothurn·us -ī *m* high boot; hunting boot; buskin *(worn by tragic actors);* subject of tragedy; tragedy; lofty style of Greek tragedy
cōtīd- = cottid-
cottab·us -ī *m* game which consisted of flicking drops of wine on a bronze vessel
cottan·a -ōrum *npl* **(-on·a)** Syrian figs
cottīdiānō *adv* **(cōt-, quōt-)** daily
cottīdiān·us -a -um *adj* **(cōt-, quōt-)** daily; everyday, ordinary
cottīdiē *adv* **(cōt-, quōt-)** daily
coturn·ix -īcis *f* quail
Cot·ys -yis *m* name of several Thracian kings
Cotӯt·ō -ūs *f* Thracian goddess of orgiastic rites
Cotytti·a -ōrum *npl* festival of Cotytto
Coüs *see* **Coos**
Cō·us -a -um *adj* Coan, of Cos ‖ *n* Coan wine ‖ *npl* Coan garments
covinnār·ius -(i)ī *m* soldier who fought from a chariot
covinn·us -ī *m* war chariot *(of Britons and Belgae, with scythes attached to the axles);* coach *(for travel)*
cox·a -ae *f* hip; haunch *(of an animal)*
coxend·ix -īcis *f* hip; hipbone
crābr·ō -ōnis *m* hornet; **irritare crabrones** *(fig)* to stir up a hornet's nest
cramb·ē -ēs *f* cabbage; **crambe repetita** warmed-over cabbage; *(fig)* same old story, hackneyed writing
Crant·or -ōris *m* Greek Academic philosopher *(fl 300 B.C.)*
crāpul·a -ae *f* drunkenness; hangover; **crapulam obdormire** to sleep off a hangover
crāpulāri·us -a -um *adj* for getting rid of a hangover
crās *adv* tomorrow
crassē *adv* thickly; rudely, confusedly; dimly
crassitūd·ō -inis *f* thickness, density; dregs
crass·us -a -um *adj* thick, dense; stout, plump; *(fig)* dense, dull
Crass·us -ī *m* Lucius Licinius Crassus *(famous orator, d. 90 B.C.)* ‖ Marcus Licinius Crassus Dives *(triumvir) (112?–53 B.C.)*
crastin·us -a -um *adj* tomorrow's; **die crastini** *(old abl form)* tomorrow ‖ *n* tomorrow; **in crastinum differre** to put off till tomorrow
crāt·ēr -ēris *m or* **crātēr·a -ae** *f* mixing bowl; bowl; crater of a volcano ‖ **Crater** *m (astr)* Bowl *(a constellation)*
crāt·is -is *f* wickerwork; lattice work; harrow; ribs of shield; crisscross structure; cage; *(anat)* rib cage; *(mil)* faggots *(for filling trenches)*
creāti·ō -ōnis *f* election, appointment; procreation *(of children)*
creāt·or -ōris *m* creator; procreator, father; founder; one who appoints
creātr·ix -īcis *f* creatress; mother
crē·ber -bra -brum *adj* numerous, crowded; repeated; frequent; luxuriant, prolific *(growth)*
crēbr·escō -escĕre -uī *intr* to increase; to become frequent; to become widespread; to gain strength
crēbrit·ās -ātis *f* frequency; density
crēbrō *adv* repeatedly, frequently, again and again; thickly, densely

crēdibil·is -is -e *adj* credible, trustworthy; convincing, plausible; likely; **credibile est** *(w. acc & inf)* it is probable that
crēdibiliter *adv* credibly
crēdit·or -ōris *m* creditor, lender
crēd·ō -ĕre -idī -itus *tr* to lend, loan; to entrust; to believe, accept as true; to believe in; to think, suppose, imagine; *(w. predicate adj)* to believe to be, regard as ‖ *intr (w. dat)* to believe, put faith in, have trust *or* confidence in; **credas** one would imagine, you can imagine; **credo** *(in replies)* I think so; *(parenthetical)* I suppose ‖ *refl (w. dat)* to entrust oneself to ‖ *v impers* **satis creditum est** it is believed on good evidence
crēdulit·ās -ātis *f* credulity, trustfulness
crēdul·us -a -um *adj* credulous, trustful; gullible; *(w. dat or* **in** *+ acc)* trusting in
crem·ō -āre -āvī -ātus *tr* to burn; to burn alive; *(of fire)* to consume; to cremate; *(w. dat)* to offer as a burnt offering to
Cremōn·a -ae *f* town in N. Italy
Cremōnens·is -is -e *adj* of Cremona
crem·or -ōris *m* thick broth; gravy; thickened juice
cre·ō -āre -āvī -ātus *tr* to create; to produce; to elect *or* appoint *(to office);* to cause, occasion; to beget, bear
Cre·ōn -ontis *or* **Cre·ō -onis** *or* **-ōnis** *m* Creon *(brother of Jocasta and brother-in-law of Oedipus)* ‖ Creon *(king of Corinth who gave his daughter in marriage to Jason)*
crep·er -era -erum *adj* dark; *(fig)* obscure, uncertain, doubtful
crepid·a -ae *f* slipper, sandal
crepidāt·us -a -um *adj* wearing sandals *or* slippers
crepīd·ō -inis *f* base, pedestal; pier; dike; curb, sidewalk
crepidul·a -ae *f* small sandal *or* slipper
crepitācill·um -ī *n* small rattle
crepit·ō -āre -āvī -ātum *intr* to make noise, rattle, creak, chatter, rumble, rustle; *(of flames)* to crackle
crepit·us -ūs *m* noise, rattle, creak, chatter, rumble, rustle, crackle; *(vulg)* fart; **crepitum ventris emittere in convivio** *(vulg)* to let a fart at a dinner party; **crepitus digitorum** snap(ping) of the fingers
crep·ō -āre -uī *tr* to rattle; to talk noisily about, rattle on about ‖ *intr* to make noise, rattle, crackle, creak, chatter, rustle; *(of the stomach)* to rumble; *(of doors)* to creak; *(of flames)* to crackle; *(vulg)* to fart
crepundi·a -ōrum *npl* toy rattle; **in crepundiis** in earliest childhood
crepuscul·um -ī *n* twilight; dimness, obscurity ‖ *npl* darkness
Crē·s -ētis *m* a Cretan; Cretan dog
crescō crescĕre crēvī crētum *intr* to come into being, arise; to grow, grow up; to increase *(in size, amount, numbers, length, quantity, dimensions);* to swell; to expand; *(of rivers)* to rise; *(of period of time)* to advance, progress; to prosper, thrive; to become great; to swell with pride; **crescunt nobis animi** our spirits rise; **die crescente** as the day progressed
Crēsi·us -a -um *adj* Cretan
Cress·a -ae *adj (fem only)* Cretan; of chalk ‖ *f* Cretan woman; Ariadne
crēt·a -ae *f* whitish clay; clayey soil; chalk; finish line *(in a chariot race);* **creta figularis** *(or* **figlina)** potter's clay; **creta fullonia** fuller's earth; **creta sutoria** shoe polish
Crēt·a -ae *or* **Crēt·ē -ēs** *f* Crete; *(fig)* the Cretans
Crētae·us -a -um *adj* Cretan
Crētān·ī -ōrum *mpl* Cretans
crētāt·us -a -um *adj* whitened with chalk *(feet of slaves about to be auctioned off);* dressed in white *(as candidate)*
Crētens·is -is -e *adj & m* Cretan ‖ *n* Cretan wine
crēte·us -a -um *adj* of chalk, of clay, clayey
Crētic·us -a -um *adj* Cretan ‖ *m (pros)* Cretic (foot) (— ◡ —)
crēti·ō -ōnis *f (leg)* formal acceptance of an inheritance; *(leg)* terms laid down for making the declaration of acceptance
Crēt·is -idis *adj (fem only)* Cretan
crētōs·us -a -um *adj* clayey
crētul·a -ae *f* white clay
crēt·us -a -um *pp of* **cerno** *and of* **cresco** ‖ *adj (w. abl or* **ab** *or* **de)** sprung from
Creūs·a -ae *f* daughter of Priam and wife of Aeneas ‖ daughter of Creon (king of Corinth), and wife of Jason ‖ mother of Ion
crībr·um -ī *n* sieve; **imbrem in cribrum gerere** *(fig)* to swim against the tide *(literally, to carry rain water in a sieve)*
crīm·en -inis *n* indictment; reproach; guilt; crime; **esse in crimine** to be arraigned; **in crimen adduci** *(or* **poni** *or* **venire** *or* **vocari)** to be indicted; *(of actions)* to be called into question
crīmināl·is -is -e *adj (leg) (opp.* **civilis)** criminal
crīmināti·ō -ōnis *f* indictment; accusation; slander
crīmināt·or -ōris *m* accuser
crīmin·ō -āre *or* **crīmin·or -ārī -ātus sum** *tr* to indict, accuse; to slander; to complain of; to denounce
crīminōsē *adv* by way of accusation, accusingly; slanderously
crīminōs·us -a -um *adj* accusatory, reproachful; shameful

crīnāl·is -is -e *adj* for the hair; **acus crinalis** hairpin ‖ *n* hairpin
crīn·is -is *m (f)* hair *(of the head);* lock of hair; tail of a comet
crīnīt·us -a -um *adj* long-haired; **crinita draconibus ora** *(Medusa's)* snake-haired head; **crinitae angue sorores** snake-haired sisters; **stella crinita** *(or* **sidus crinitum**) comet
crīs·ō -āre -āvī -ātum *intr (sl) (of a woman)* to wiggle the buttocks, shake it up *(cf.* **ceveo**)
crisp·ans -antis *adj* curly; wrinkled
crisp·ō -āre -āvī -ātus *tr* to curl, wave *(hair);* to wave, brandish *(weapons)*
crispul·us -a -um *adj* having short curly hair
crisp·us -a -um *adj* curled, waved; curly-headed; wrinkled; tremulous, quivering
crist·a -ae *f* cockscomb; crest, plume; mons veneris
cristāt·us -a -um *adj* crested, plumed
critic·a -ōrum *npl* literary criticism
critic·us -ī *m* critic
croce·us -a -um *adj* of saffron; yellow, golden
crocin·um -ī *n* saffron oil *(used as perfume)*
crōc·iō *or* **groc·iō -īre** *intr* to croak
crocodīl·us -ī *m* (**-dill-**) crocodile
crocōt·a -ae *f* saffron-colored dress *(worn by women and transvestites)*
crocōtāri·us -a -um *adj* of saffron-colored clothes
crocōtul·a -ae *f* saffron-colored dress
croc·us -ī *m or* **croc·um -ī** *n* saffron; saffron color; saffron oil
Croes·us -ī *m* king of Lydia, famous for his wealth *(590?–546 B.C.)*
crotalistri·a -ae *f* castinet dancer
crotal·um -ī *n* castanet
Crotō(n) -ōnis *or* **Crotōn·a -ae** *f* Crotona *(town in S. Italy)*
cruciābilitāt·ēs -um *fpl* torments
cruciābiliter *adv* with torture
cruciāment·um -ī *n* torture
cruciāt·us -ūs *m* torture; mental torment; instrument of torture
cruci·ō -āre -āvī -ātus *tr* to put on the rack, torture; *(fig)* to torment ‖ *refl or pass* to suffer mental anguish
crūdēl·is -is -e *adj* cruel, hardhearted; *(w.* **in** + *acc)* cruel toward
crūdēlit·ās -ātis *f* cruelty
crūdēliter *adv* cruelly
crūd·escō -escĕre -uī *intr* to become fierce; *(of battle, disease)* to get rough
crūdit·ās -ātis *f* indigestion
crūd·us -a -um *adj* bloody, bleeding; uncooked *(food);* raw *(meat; wound);* unripe, green *(fruit);* untanned *(hide);* undigested *(food);* suffering from indigestion; hoarse; hardy, vigorous *(old age);* coarse, rude; fierce, wild, savage
cruent·ō -āre -āvī -ātus *tr* to bloody, stain with blood; *(fig)* to wound
cruent·us -a -um *adj* gory, blood-stained; bloodthirsty; blood-red
-cr·um -ī *neut suf* denoting place or instrument: **sepulcretum** cemetery; **involucrum** wrapper, envelope
crumēn·a -ae *f* (**-mīn-**) purse, pouch; *(fig)* money supply
crumill·a -ae *f* small purse
cru·or -ōris *m* blood, gore ‖ *mpl* bloodshed, murder
cruppellāri·ī -ōrum *mpl* warriors in full armor
crūrāl·is -is -e *adj* of the shin; **fasciae crurales** puttees
crūricrepid·a -ae *m (hum) (of one who has chains rattling around his legs)* "rattle-legs"
Crūrifrag·ius -(i)ī *m (comic slave name)* "Broken-shins"
crūs crūris *n* leg; shin; upper support of a bridge
cruscul·um -ī *n* little leg
crusm·a -atis *n* tune
crust·a -ae *f* crust, shell; peel, rind; inlaid work
crustul·um -ī *n* cookie
crust·um -ī *n* pastry
Crustumīnus -a -um *adj* of Crustumerium *or* Crustumium *(town in the Sabine district)*
crux crucis *f* cross; crucifixion; torment; tormentor; **ī in malam crucem!** *(coll)* go hang yourself!
crypt·a -ae *f* (**cru-**) underground passage, covered gallery; tunnel; crypt
cryptoportic·us -ūs *f* covered walk
crystallin·us -a -um *adj* (**crus-**) made of crystal ‖ *npl* crystal vases
crystall·us -ī *f or* **crystall·um -ī** *n* (**crus-**) crystal
cub·ans -antis *adj* lying down; low-lying
cubiculāri·us -a -um *adj* bedroom- ‖ *m* chamberlain
cubicul·um -ī *n* bedroom; emperor's box in the theater *or* circus; **a cubiculo** (imperial) chamberlain
cubīl·e -is *n* bed, couch; marriage bed; lair, nest, hole; kennel
cubit·al -ālis *n* elbow cushion
cubitāl·is -is -e *adj* of the elbow; one cubit long *(i.e., 17 to 21 inches)*
cubit·ō -āre -āvī -ātum *intr* to lie down, be in the habit of lying down; *(w.* **cum**) to go to bed with, have intercourse with
cubit·um -ī *n* elbow; forearm; cubit; **cubitum ponere** *(fig)* to sit down to dinner
cubitūr·a -ae *f* reclining, lying down

cubit·us -ūs *m* lying down; sexual intercourse

cub·ō -āre -uī *or* **-āvī -itum** *intr* to lie, lie down; to recline at table; to lie in bed; to take one's rest, sleep; to be confined to bed; *(of bones)* to rest; *(of roof)* to slope; *(of towns)* to lie on a slope; *(w.* **cum)** to have intercourse with

cub·us -ī *m* cube; lump

cucull·us -ī *m* cowl, hood

cucūl·us -ī *m* cuckoo; *(pej)* ninny

cucum·a -ae *f* large kettle *(for cooking)*

cucum·is -is *or* **-eris** *m* cucumber

cucurbit·a -ae *f* gourd; *(sl)* dolt, dummy; *(med)* cupping glass

cūd·ō -ĕre *tr* to strike, beat, pound; to thresh; to forge; to coin, stamp

cuicuimodī *or* **quoiquoimodī** *adj* of any kind

cūj·ās *or* **cūj·ātis -ātis** *interrog pron* from what country?; **Scipio eum percontatus est quis et cujas esset** Scipio asked who he was and from what country he came

cūjus *(gen of* **quī, quae, quod, quis, quid)** *pron (interrog)* whose, of whom ‖ *(interrog)* whose?

cūjusnam *(gen of* **quisnam, quidnam)** *pron (interrog)* just whose, exactly whose?

-cul·a -ae *fem suf* forms diminutives: **uxorcula** dear wife

culcit·a -ae *f* mattress, feather tick; cushion, pillow

culcitell·a *or* **culcitul·a -ae** *f* small cushion

cūleus *see* **culleus**

cul·ex *or* **cul·ix -icis** *mf* gnat

culīn·a -ae *f* kitchen; cuisine

culle·us -ī *m* **(cūle-)** leather bag *(for holding liquids);* leather sack *(in which criminals were sewn and drowned); (sl)* scrotum

culm·en -inis *n* peak; summit; stalk; *(fig)* pinnacle, height; **fabae culmen** bean stalk

culm·us -ī *m* stalk, stem; straw, thatch; hay

culp·a -ae *f* fault, blame; sense of guilt; imperfection, fault, defect; *(poet)* cause of blame; **in culpā esse** *(or* **versari)** to be at fault

culpit·ō -āre *tr* to blame

culp·ō -āre -āvī -ātus *tr* to blame, reproach; to find fault with, complain of

cult·a -ōrum *npl* standing crops; grain fields

cultē *adv* elegantly, sophisticatedly

cultell·us -ī *m* small knife

cul·ter -trī *m* knife; razor; plowshare

culti·ō -ōnis *f* cultivation, tilling

cult·or -ōris *m* tiller, cultivator, planter, farmer; inhabitant; supporter; worshiper

cultrār·ius -(i)ī *m* one who slew the victim

cultr·ix -īcis *f* cultivator *(female);* worshiper *(female);* inhabitant *(female)*

cultūr·a -ae *f* tilling, cultivating; agriculture; cultivation *(e.g., of the mind, important friendships)*

cult·us -a -um *pp of* **colo** ‖ *adj* tilled, cultivated; neat, prim; refined, civilized, cultured

cult·us -ūs *m* tilling, cultivation; care, tending *(of flocks);* training, education; culture, refinement, civilization; high style of living; luxury; style of dress, fancy clothes; fancy outfit; worship, reverence; cult; management *(of a household);* **cultus corporis** personal care, personal grooming; **cultus vitae** standard of living

culull·us -ī *m* drinking cup

-cul·um -ī *neut suf* 1 denoting places: **cubiculum** place for sleeping; 2 denoting instruments: **curriculum** small chariot

cūl·us -ī *m (sl)* ass, anus

-cul·us -ī *masc suf* 1 forming diminutives: **pisciculus** little fish; 2 nouns ending in **-o, -onis** and **-o -inis** take the form **-un-** before the suffix **-culus: sermunculus** small talk; **homunculus** little man, puny person

cum *prep (w. abl)* 1 *(accompaniment)* with, together with; 2 *(time)* at the same time with, at the time of, at, with; 3 *(circumstance, manner, etc.)* with, under, in, in the midst of, among, in connection with; **cum eo quod** *or* **cum eo ut** on the condition that; **cum pace** peacefully; **cum prima luce** at dawn; **cum primis** especially, particularly; **mecum** at my house; with me

cum, quum, *or* **quom** *conj* when, at the time when; whenever; while, as; since, now that, because; although; **cum maxime** just when; especially when, just while; just then; **cum primum** as soon as; **cum...tum** both...and, not only...but also, while...so too; **praesertim cum** *or* **cum praesertim** especially since; **quippe cum** since of course; **utpote cum** seeing that

Cūm·ae -ārum *fpl* town on the coast of Campania, residence of its famous Sibyl

Cūmae·us -a -um *adj* Cumaean

Cūmān·us -a -um *adj* Cumaean ‖ *n* Cicero's estate near Cumae

cūmātil·is -is -e *adj* sea-colored

cumb·a *or* **cymb·a -ae** *f* boat, skiff

cumer·a -ae *f* bin

cumīn·um -ī *n* cumin *(medicinal plant, said to produce paleness)*

cummi *indecl n or* **cumm·is -is** *f* **(gumm-)** gum

cumque, cunque, *or* **quomque** *adv* at any time

cumulātē *adv* fully, completely, abundantly
cumulāt·us -a -um *adj* heaped; abundant, vast, great; *(w. gen or abl)* abounding in
cumul·ō -āre -āvī -ātus *tr* to heap up, pile up; accumulate; to fill up, overload; to increase, augment; *(fig)* to crown
cumul·us -ī *m* heap, pile; increase; *(fig)* finishing touch, crown; *(fig)* peak, pinnacle; **summus cumulus** highest point
cūnābul·a -ōrum *npl* cradle
cūn·ae -ārum *fpl* cradle; *(poet)* nest
cunctābund·us -a -um *adj* hesitant
cunct·ans -antis *adj* hesitant, slow to act; clinging
cunctanter *adv* hesitantly, slowly
cunctāti·ō -ōnis *f* hesitation, reluctance, delay
conctāt·or -ōris *m* dawdler, slow-poke, procrastinator ‖ **Cunctātor** Quintus Fabius Maximus Cunctator *(cautious general who constantly avoided battles with Hannibal, d. 203 B.C.)*
cunct·or -ārī -ātus sum *intr* to hesitate, delay, linger; to be in doubt; **cunctatu brevi** after a moment's hesitation
cunct·us -a -um *adj* all together, the whole, all, entire
-cund·us -a -um *adjl suf* denoting a tendency: **iracundus** inclined toward anger, irascible
cuneātim *adv* in the form of a wedge, in tight formation
cuneāt·us -a -um *adj* wedge-shaped
cune·ō -āre -āvī -ātus *tr* to fasten with a wedge; *(fig)* to wedge in, squeeze in
cuneol·us -ī *m* small wedge; pin
cune·us -ī *m* wedge; wedge-form section of seats in the theater; *(mil)* troops formed in shape of wedge
cunīculōsus -a -um *adj* full of rabbits
cunīcul·us -ī *m* rabbit; burrow, hole; tunnel; water conduit, channel; *(mil)* mine
cunil·a -ae *f (bot)* savory *(aromatic plant used as seasoning)*
cunniling·us -a -um *adj (vulg)* cunt-sucking
cunnu·s -ī *m (vulg)* cunt
cunque *see* **cumque**
cūp·a -ae *f* vat
cuped- = cupped-
cupidē *adv* eagerly
Cupīdine·us -a -um *adj* Cupid's, charming, alluring
cupidit·ās -ātis *f* eagerness, longing, desire; passion, lust; ambition; greed; object of one's desire
cupīd·ō -inis *mf* eagerness, desire; carnal desire, lust; greed ‖ **Cupido** *m* Cupid, son of Venus
cupid·us -a -um *adj* eager; lecherous; ambitious; *(w. gen)* desirous of, longing for, fond of, enthusiastic about
cupi·ens -entis *adj* eager, enthusiastic; *(w. gen)* desirous of, longing for, fond of, enthusiastic about
cupienter *adv* eagerly
cup·iō -ĕre -īvī *or* **-iī -ītus** *tr* to wish, be eager for, long for, desire
cupīt·or -ōris *m* daydreamer
cuppēdenār·ius -(i)ī *m* pastry baker
cuppēdi·a -ōrum *npl or* **cūpēdi·a -ae** *f* sweets; delicacies; sweet tooth
cuppēdinār·ius -(i)ī *m* **(cūpēd-)** confectioner
cuppēd·ō -inis *f see* **cupido**
cupp·ēs -edis *adj* gluttonous
cupressēt·um -ī *n* cypress grove
cupresse·us -a -um *adj* cypress-
cupressif·er -era -erum *adj* cypress-bearing
cupress·us -ī *or* **-ūs** *f* cypress tree
cūr *or* **qūr** *or* **cuūr** *or* **quor** *adv* why
cūr·a -ae *f* care, concern, worry; carefulness, attention, pains; (a person's) attention; heartache; object of concern; sweetheart; task, reponsibility, post; administration, management, charge; trusteeship, care; guardian, keeper; study, reflection; literary effort, study, literary work; *(w. gen)* eagerness for, anxiety about, zeal for; *(med)* treatment; *(med)* cure; **in curā esse** *(w. dat)* to be a matter of concern to, be dear to; **in curā habere** to hold dear, care dearly about; **curā** purposely; **curae esse** *(w. dat)* to be of concern to; to be dear to; **curae habere** to hold dear
cūrābil·is -is -e *adj* troublesome; needing medical treatment
cūral·ium *or* **corall·ium -(i)ī** *n* coral
cūrāti·ō -ōnis *f* management, administration; office; *(med)* treatment
cūratius *adv* more carefully
cūrāt·or -ōris *m* superintendent, manager; *(leg)* guardian
cūrātūr·a -ae *f* care, attention; superintendence
cūrāt·us -a -um *adj* well cared-for; anxious, sollicitous, earnest
curculi·ō -ōnis *m* **(gurg-)** weevil; *(vulg)* penis
curculiuncul·us -ī *m* little weevil; *(fig)* trifle
Cur·ēs -ium *mpl* ancient Sabine town
Cūrēt·es -um *mpl* people of Crete who attended Jupiter at his birth
cūri·a -ae *f* Senate Building; meeting of the Senate; curia, ward *(one of the 30 wards into which Romulus had divided the people)*
cūriāl·is -is -e *adj* belonging to a ward ‖ *m* ward member
cūriātim *adv* by wards
cūriāt·us -a -um *adj* composed of wards; passed by the assembly of wards; **comitia**

curiata assembly of wards, curiate assembly
cūri·ō -ōnis *m* ward boss; **curio maximus** chief ward boss
cūriōsē *adv* carefully; curiously
cūriōsit·ās -ātis *f* curiosity, inquisitiveness
cūriōs·us -a -um careful, diligent; curious, inquisitive; careworn
cur·is *or* **quir·is -ītis** *f* spear
cūr·ō -āre -āvī -ātus *tr* to take care of, look after, attend to, trouble oneself about; to worry about; to take charge of, see to; to procure; to provide for the payment of, settle up; to attend to *(the body with food, washing, etc.); (med)* to treat; *(med)* to cure; **cura ut** see to it that; *(at end of letter)* **cura ut valeas** take care of yourself; **cutem curare** to look after one's appearance
curriculō *adv* at full speed, on the double
curricul·um -ī *n* race; lap; racetrack; racing chariot; *(fig)* career
currō currĕre cucurrī cursus *tr* to run over, skim over, traverse ‖ *intr* to run, dash; to sail; to move quickly, flow along; to fly; *(of night, day)* to pass
curr·us -ūs *m* chariot, car; war chariot; triumphal car; triumph; racing chariot; *(poet)* plow wheel; *(poet)* ship
cursim *adv* on the double, quickly
cursit·ō -āre -āvī *intr* to keep running around, run up and down; to vibrate
curs·ō -āre -āvī *intr* to run around, run up and down
curs·or -ōris *m* runner, racer; courier; errand boy
cursūr·a -ae *f* running; haste, speed
curs·us -ūs *m* running, speeding, speed; trip; course, direction; suitable time *or* weather for travel; rapid movement, flow; progress; **magno cursu** at top speed; **cursus honorum** political career
Curt·ius -a -um *adj* Roman clan name *(nomen), esp.* Quintus Curtius Rufus *(who wrote a history of Alexander the Great's campaigns)* ‖ **Lacus Curtius** area of the Roman Forum that was once a pond
curt·ō -āre -āvī -ātus *tr* to shorten; *(hum)* to circumcise
curt·us -a -um *adj* shortened; gelded, castrated; *(hum)* circumcised; broken; defective
curūl·is -is -e *adj* official, curule; **aedilis curulis** patrician aedile; **sella curulis** curule chair, official chair *(inlaid with ivory, used by consuls, praetors, and patrician aediles)*
curvām·en -inis *n* curve, bend
curvātūr·a -ae *f* curvature; **curvatura rotae** rim of a wheel
curv·ō -āre -āvī -ātus *tr* to curve, bend, arch; *(fig)* to affect, move, stir
curv·us -a -um *adj* curved, bent; crooked; concave, arched; hollow, winding *(stream, shore); (fig)* crooked ‖ *n* wrong, crookedness
-c·us -a -um *adjl suffix* formed from nouns: **bellicus** warlike
cusp·is -idis *f* point; bayonet; spearhead; spear, javelin; trident; scepter; sting *(of a scorpion)*
custōdēl·a -ae *f* charge, custody *(of a person or thing)*
custōdi·a -ae *f* protection, safekeeping, defense; preservation *(of a practice, etc.);* place for safekeeping; watch, care; sentry, guard; sentry post; custody, confinement, prison; prisoner, *(collectively)* prisoners; **custodiam agitare** to be on guard; **in liberā custodiā** under surveillance, under house arrest
custōd·iō -īre -īvī *or* **-iī -ītus** *tr* to guard, watch over, protect, defend; to hold in custody; to keep an eye on; to keep carefully, preserve; **memoriā custodire** to keep in mind
cust·ōs -ōdis *m* guard; guardian; watchman; protector; jailer; *(mil)* sentinel; **custos corporis** bodyguard ‖ *mpl* garrison ‖ *f* guardian; protectress; container
cutīcul·a -ae *f* skin
cut·is -is *f* skin; **cutem curare** to look after one's appearance; *(fig)* to look after one's own skin
Cyan·ē -ēs *f* spring in Syracause; nymph who was changed into that spring
cyathiss·ō -āre -āvī *intr* to ladle out wine
cyath·us -ī *m* ladle; liquid measure *(half pint)*
cybae·a -ae *f* merchant ship
Cybel·ē -ēs *f* (-bēbē) Phrygian goddess of fertility, worshipped in Rome as Ops *or* Magna Mater ‖ mountain of Phrygia
Cybelēi·us -a -um *adj* of Cybele
Cybel·us -ī *m* mountain in Phrygia
cyb·ium -(i)i *n* young tuna fish
cycladāt·us -a -um *adj* wearing a formal gown
Cyclad·ēs -um *fpl* Cyclades *(group of islands, roughly forming a circle, in the Aegean Sea)*
cycl·as -adis *f* woman's formal gown ‖ **Cyclas** one of the Cyclades Islands
cyclic·us -a -um *adj* cyclic; **poeta cyclicus** cyclic poet *(one of a group of poets treating epic sagas revolving around the Trojan War)*
Cyclopi·us -a -um *adj* Cyclopian
Cycl·ops -ōpis *m* one-eyed giant of Sicily, *esp.* Polyphemus
cycn·us -ī *m* (cyg-) swan; *(fig)* poet ‖ **Cycnus** king of the Ligurians, changed into a swan, and placed among the stars as a constellation ‖ son of Neptune
Cyd·ōn -ōnis *adj* Cydonian, of Cydonea

(a city on the N. coast of Crete) ‖ *m* inhabitant of Cydonea

Cydōnae·us -a -um *adj* (**-ē·us**) Cydonian; *(esp. as poetic epithet for arrows)* Cretan

Cydōne·a -ae *f* city on the N. coast of Crete

Cydōni·us -a -um *adj* Cretan ‖ *n* quince

cygnus *see* **cycnus**

cylindr·us -ī *m* cylinder; roller *(for rolling the ground);* cylindrical jewel

Cyllēn·ē -ēs *or* **-ae** *f* mountain in Arcadia where Mercury was said to have been born

Cyllēnē·us *or* **Cyllēni·us -a -um** *adj* of Mt. Cyllene ‖ *m* Mercury

cymb·a -ae *f* **(cum-)** boat, skiff

cymbal·um *or* **cymbal·on -ī** *n (usu. pl, esp. as used in the worship of Cybele)* cymbal; *(fig)* tedious speaker

cymb·ium -(i)ī *n* small cup

Cynicē *adv* like the Cynics

Cynic·us -a -um *adj* Cynic, relating to the Cynic philosophy ‖ *m* Cynic philosopher, *esp.* Diogenes, its founder *(412–323 B.C.)*

cynocephal·us -ī *m* dog-headed ape

Cynosūr·a -ae *f (astr)* Cynosure *(the constellation Ursa Minor)*

Cynthi·us -a -um *adj* of Mt. Cynthus; Cynthian ‖ *m* Apollo ‖ *f* Diana

Cynth·us -ī *m* low mountain on Delos, where Latona is said to have given birth to Apollo and Diana

cypariss·us -ī *f* cypress tree

cypress·us -ī *or* **-ūs** *f* cypress tree; box made of cypress

Cypri·us -a -um *adj* Cypriote; **aes Cyprium** copper ‖ *f* Venus

Cypr·us *or* **Cyp·ros -ī** *f* Cyprus *(island off S. coast of Asia Minor)*

Cypsel·us -ī *m* despot of Corinth *(reigned 655–625 B.C.)*

Cȳrēn·ē -ēs *f or* **Cyrēn·ae -ārum** *fpl* chief city of Greek settlement in N.E. Africa

Cȳrēnae·us *or* **Cȳrēnaic·us -a -um** *or* **Cȳrēnens·is -is -e** *adj* of Cyrene

Cȳrē·us -a -um *adj* of Cyprus

Cyrnē·us -a -um *adj* Corsican

Cyrn·os -ī *f* Greek name for Corsica

Cȳr·us -ī *m* father of Cambyses and founder of the Persian monarchy in 559 B.C. *(d. 529 B.C.)* ‖ Cyrus the Younger, son of Darius Nothus, whose famous march against his brother Artaxerxes is recorded by Xenophon *(d. 401 B.C.)*

Cyt·ae -ārum *fpl* town in Colchis, reputed birthplace of Medea

Cytae·is -idis *f* Medea

Cythēr·a -ōrum *npl* island off the S. coast of the Peloponnesus, famous for the worship of Venus

Cytherē·is -idis *f* Venus

Cythereī̈·us -a -um *adj* Cytherean; **heros Cythereïus** Aeneas ‖ *f* Venus

Cytherē·us -a -um *adj* Cytherean ‖ *f* Venus

cytis·us -ī *mf or* **cytis·um -ī** *n* clover

Cytōriāc·us -a -um *adj* of Cytorus, Cytorian; **pecten Cytoriacus** comb made of boxwood

Cytōr·us *or* **Cytōr·os -ī** *m* mountain in Paphlagonia, famous for its boxwood

Cȳzicēn·us -a -um *adj* of Cyzicus

Cyzic·um -ī *n or* **Cyzic·us** *or* **Cyzic·os -ī** *f* town on S. coast of Propontis

D

D *abbr* **quingenti** five hundred

D. *abbr* **Decimus** *(Roman first name, praenomen)*

Dāc·ī -ōrum *mpl* Dacians

Dāci·a -ae *f* Roman province on the lower Danube *(roughly modern Rumania)*

Dācic·us -a -um *adj* Dacian ‖ *m* gold coin struck under Domitian, conqueror of Dacia

dactylic·us -a -um *adj (pros)* dactylic

dactyliothēc·a -ae *f* ring case

dactyl·us -ī *m (pros)* dactyl (— ∪ ∪)

daedal·us -a -um *adj* skillful, artistic; intricately constructed ‖ **Daedal·us -ī** *m* builder of the Labyrinth in Crete and the first person to construct wings and fly

Damascēn·us -a -um *adj* of Damascus ‖ *npl* plums from Damascus

Damasc·us *or* **Damasc·os -ī** *f* city in Syria

damm·a *or* **dām·a -ae** *f* deer; venison

damnāti·ō -ōnis *f* condemnation; *(w. gen of the crime)* conviction on the charge of; **damnatio ambitūs** conviction on illegal campaign practices; **condemnatio pecuniae** a fine

damnātōri·us -a -um *adj (leg)* guilty *(verdict)*

damnāt·us -a -um *adj (leg)* found guilty; hateful, damn

damnific·us -a -um *adj* harmful

damnigerul·us -a -um *adj* injurious

damn·ō -āre -āvī -ātus *tr (leg)* to find guilty, convict; to sentence, condemn; to secure the condemnation of; to offer as a sacrifice, doom to the gods below; to pass judgment on *(a case); (w. dat of the aggrieved person)* to deliver by judicial sentence to, award *(s.o. s.th.); (w. abl)* to fine *(s.o.)* in the amount of; *(w. gen or abl)* to find fault with for; *(w. gen or abl of the charge)* to find *(s.o.)* guilty of; **aliquem voti damnare** to condemn s.o. to the amount he has vowed; **capite (***or* **capitis) damnare** to condemn to death; **de majestate damnare** to find guilty of treason; **exilio damnari** to be sentenced to ex-

ile; **voti damnare** to oblige *(s.o.)* to fulfill a vow
damnōsē *adv* ruinously
damnōs·us -a -um *adj* damaging, destructive; prodigal; **canes damnosi** crap *(worst throw of dice)*
damn·um -ī *n* loss, damage, harm; fine; defect; *(w. gen)* forfeiture of; *(mil)* losses; **damnum explere** *(or* **sarcire)** to make good a loss; **damnum facere** to incur a loss; to cause loss *(to another);* **naturae damnum** a natural defect
Dana·ē -ēs *f* daughter of Acrisius and mother, by Zeus, of Perseus
Danaïd·es -um *fpl* fifty daughters of Danaüs
Dana·üs -ī *m* Danaüs *(son of Belus and brother of Aegyptus and king of Argos)* ‖ *mpl* Greeks
danist·a -ae *m* moneylender, banker
danistic·us -a -um *adj* moneylending, banking
danō *see* **do**
Dānuv·ius -(i)ī *m* Upper Danube *(opp:* **Hister** = Lower Danube)
Daphn·ē -ēs *f* nymph pursued by Apollo and changed into a laurel tree
Daphn·is -idis *(acc:* **-im** *or* **-in)** *m* handsome young Sicilian shepherd, inventor of pastoral poetry
dapin·ō -āre *tr* to serve *(food)*
dap·s -is *f* ceremonial feast; feast; banquet; feed *(for animals)*
dapsil·is -is -e *adj* sumptuous, costly
Dardanid·ēs -ae *m* descendant of Dardanus; Trojan; Roman
Dardan·is -idis *or* **-idos** *adj (fem only)* Trojan
Dardan·us -a -um *adj* Dardanian, Trojan; Roman *(descendant of Aeneas)* ‖ *m* son of Jupiter and ancestor of the Trojan race ‖ *mpl* Illyrian tribe; a people of Asia Minor
Dārē·us *or* **Dārī·us -ī** *m* Darius *(521–485 B.C., Persian king whose generals were defeated by the Greeks at Marathon in 490 B.C.)* ‖ Darius Nothus *(424–405 B.C., son of Artaxerxes I)* ‖ Darius Codomanus *(last king of Persia, reigned 336–331 B.C.)*
datāri·us -a -um *adj* to be handed out, to be given away
datātim *adv* giving *or* tossing from hand to hand *(in games)*
dati·ō -ōnis *f* giving, allotting; transfer *(e.g., of property)*
datīv·us -a -um *adj & m (gram)* dative
dat·ō -āre -āvī -ātus *tr* to keep giving
dat·or -ōris *m* giver
dat·us -ūs *m* giving
Daul·is -idis *f* town in Phocis, famous for fable of Procne and Philomela
Daun·us -ī *m* mythical king of Apulia, the father of Turnus
dē *prep (w. abl)* **1** *(of space)* down from, from, away from, out of; **2** *(of origin)* from, of, descended from: **Priami de stirpe Diores** Diores of Priam's lineage; **3** *(of separation)* from among, out of: **noctem de die facere** to make night out of day; **4** *(in partitive sense)* of, out of: **dimidium de praedā dare** to give half of the booty; **5** *(of time)* immediately after; **diem de die** day after day; **6** *(of reference)* about, on, concerning, of, in respect to: **oratio de domo sua** a speech concerning his own home; **7** according to, in imitation of: **castae de more puellae** like a chaste girl *(literally, according to the manner of a chaste girl);* **8** *(of cause)* for, on account of, because of: **quā de causā** for that reason, wherefore; **9** *(of which s.th. is made)* **templum de marmore** a marble temple, a temple (made) of marble; **10** *(indicating persons over whom victory is gained)* over: **de Samnitibus triumphavit** he held a triumph for his victory over the Samnites; **11** *(indicating change)* from, out of: **de templo carcerem facere** to make a prison out of a temple; **de improviso** unexpectedly; **de industriā** on purpose; **de integro** afresh, all over again; **de nocte** *(or* **de vigiliā)** at night; **de novo** anew
dē- (**dĕ** before vowels and **h)** *pref* indicating: **1** motion down from or away: **dependere** to hang down; **2** removal, deprivation: **despolire** to despoil; **3** left behind: **derelinquere** to leave behind; **4** reversal of process: **deonerare** to unload; **5** completely, to the end: **depugnare** to fight it out, fight to the finish; **6** down, from the right path or state or norm: **deformis** ugly; **7** intensity: **deamare** to love passionately
de·a -ae *(dat & abl pl:* **deābus)** *f* goddess
dealb·ō -āre -āvī -ātus *tr* to whiten, whitewash
deambulāti·ō -ōnis *f* strolling, walking about, walk, stroll
deambul·ō -āre -āvī -ātum *intr* to go for a walk
deam·ō -āre -āvī -ātus *tr* to love passionately
dearm·ō -āre -āvī -ātus *tr* to disarm
deartu·ō -āre -āvī -ātus *tr* to tear limb from limb, dismember
deasci·ō -āre -āvī -ātus *tr* to smooth with an ax; *(fig)* to cheat, con
dēbacch·or -ārī -ātus sum *intr* to rant and rave
dēbellāt·or -ōris *m* conqueror
dēbell·ō -āre -āvī -ātus *tr* to fight it out

with, wear down, subdue ‖ *intr* to fight it out to the end; to bring a war to an end

dēb·eō -ēre -uī -itus *tr* to owe; to be responsible for; *(w. inf)* **1** to have to, be obliged to; **2** to be destined to; **debeo abire** I ought to leave ‖ *pass (w. dat)* to be due to

dēbil·is -is -e *adj* crippled, frail, feeble; ineffective

dēbilit·ās -ātis *f* lameness; debility, weakness, feebleness

dēbilitāti·ō -ōnis *f* disabling, enfeebling

dēbilit·ō -āre -āvī -ātus *tr* to disable; to debilitate, weaken; to unnerve; *(fig)* to paralyze

dēbiti·ō -ōnis *f* debt

dēbit·or -ōris *m* debtor; person under obligation

dēbit·um -ī *n* debt; obligation

dēblater·ō -āre -āvī -ātus *tr & intr* to blurt out

dēcant·ō -āre -āvī -ātus *tr* to repeat monotonously; to reel off ‖ *intr* to sing on to the end; to stop singing

dē·cēdō -cēdĕre -cessī -cessum *intr* to withdraw, depart, clear out; to retreat; to make way, make room, yield; to disappear; to die; to abate, subside, cease; to go wrong; *(w. dat)* to give in to; *(w.* **de** *+ abl)* to give up, abandon, relinquish

decem *indecl adj* ten

Decem·ber -bris -bre *adj* December, of December; **mensis December** (month of) December *(tenth month of the Roman calendar until 153 B.C.)* ‖ **Decem·ber -bris** *m* December

decemjug·is -is *m* ten-horse chariot

decemped·a -ae *f* ten-foot measuring rod, ten-foot rule

decempedāt·or -ōris *m* surveyor

decempl·ex -icis *adj* tenfold

decemprīm·ī *or* **decem prīm·ī -ōrum** *mpl* ten-man council *(governing Italic towns)*

decemscalm·us -a -um *adj* ten-oared

decem·vir -virī *m* decemvir *(member of a board of ten)*

decemvirāl·is -is -e *adj* decemviral; **leges decemvirales** laws passed by the decemviri

decemvirāt·us -ūs *m* decemvirate

decemvir·ī -ōrum *mpl* board of ten *(appointed in Rome at different times and for various purposes: maintaining Sibylline books, distribution of land; codifying the XII Tables; deciding whether a person was free or slave);* **decemviri sacris faciundis** commission for attending to religious matters

decenn·is -is -e *adj* ten-year, lasting ten years

dec·ens -entis *adj* decent, proper, becoming; handsome, pretty

decenter *adv* decently, properly

decenti·a -ae *f* decency, propriety

dē·cernō -cernĕre -crēvī -crētus *tr* to sift, separate; to decide, determine, settle; to resolve, decree, vote; to decide by combat; to fight, combat ‖ *intr* to contend, compete, struggle; to put forward a proposal; *(w.* **de** *or* **pro** *+ abl)* to fight over, fight for *(in court)*

dēcerp·ō -ĕre -sī -tus *tr* to pluck off, tear off, break off; to gather *(fruit, grapes);* to pick *(flowers);* to derive *(e.g., benefits, satisfaction);* **aliquid de gravitate decerpere** to detract somewhat from dignity

dēcertāti·ō -ōnis *f* decisive struggle

dēcert·ō -āre -āvī -ātum *intr* to fight it out, decide the issue

dēcessi·ō -ōnis *f* withdrawing; retirement, departure *(from a province);* decrease; disappearance

dēcess·or -ōris *m* retiring official; predecessor *(opp:* **successor)**

dēcess·us -ūs *m* withdrawal; retirement *(of an official from a province);* decease, death

dec·et -ēre -uit *(used only in inf and 3rd sing & pl) tr* to befit; to lend grace to; to adorn ‖ *v impers (w. inf)* it is proper for *(s.o.)* to; *(w. dat & inf)* it is proper *or* right for *(s.o.)* to

dēcĭ·dō -dĕre -dī *intr* to fall down; to die; to drop; to sink; *(of things)* to fail, go wrong; to end up, land; *(of plants)* to wilt

dēcī·dō -dĕre -dī -sus *tr* to cut off, cut away; to cut down; to cut short, terminate; to settle *(a matter);* **pennas decidere** *(w. dat) (fig)* to clip *(s.o.'s)* wings ‖ *intr (w.* **cum)** to come to terms with

deciens *adv* **(-iēs)** ten times; **deciens centena milia** *(or simply* **deciens)** a million; **bis deciens** two million

decimānus *see* **decumanus**

decimum *adv* for the tenth time

decim·us -a -um *adj* **(-cum-)** the tenth; **cum decimo** tenfold; **cum decimo effecit ager** the field produced a tenfold return

dē·cipiō -cipĕre -cēpī -ceptus *tr* to deceive, cheat; to dupe, mislead; to frustrate, disappoint; to escape the notice of; **aliquem laborum decipere** to make s.o. forget his troubles

dēcīsi·ō -ōnis *f* settlement

dēcīsum *pp of* **dēcīdō**

Dec·ius -(i)ī *m* Publius Decius Mus *(father and son, who gave their lives to save the Roman army)*

dēclāmāti·ō -ōnis *f* practice in public speaking; practice speech; theme *(in a practice speech)*

dēclāmāt·or -ōris *m* student of public speaking, declaimer

dēclāmātōri·us -a -um *adj* rhetorical

dēclāmit·ō -āre -āvī -ātus *tr* to plead *(cases)* ‖ *intr* to practice public speaking
dēclām·ō -āre -āvī -ātus *tr* to recite ‖ *intr* to practice public speaking, declaim
dēclārāti·ō -ōnis *f* declaration, disclosure, announcement; **declaratio amoris** an expression of affection
dēclār·ō -āre -āvī -ātus *tr* to make clear, make evident, disclose; to proclaim, announce officially; to show, prove, demonstrate; to mean, express, signify; to declare *(e.g., s.o. consul)*
dēclīnāti·ō -ōnis *f* deviation, swerve; inclination; avoidance; digression; *(gram)* declension
dēclīn·ō -āre -āvī -ātus *tr* to deflect; to parry, avoid; *(gram)* to decline, conjugate ‖ *intr* to deviate; to digress
dēclīvē -is *n* slope; **per declive** downwards
dēclīv·is -is -e *adj* sloping, steep, down-hill
dēclīvit·ās -ātis *f* sloping terrain
dēcoct·or -ōris *m* bankrupt
dēcoct·us -a -um *pp of* **decoquo** ‖ *adj* luscious; ripe; over-ripe; mellow *(style)* ‖ *f* cold drink
dēcoll·ō -āre -āvī -ātus *tr* to behead
dēcōl·ō -āre -āvī *intr* to drain away, come to naught, fail
dēcol·or -ōris *adj* off-color, faded; dark-skinned; degenerate, depraved
dēcolōr·ō -āre -āvī -ātus *tr* to discolor, stain, deface; to disgrace
dēco·quō -quĕre -xī -ctus *tr* to boil down, boil thoroughly; to bring to ruin; to digest *(food)* ‖ *intr* to go bankrupt
dec·or -ōris *m* beauty, grace, elegance, charm; ornament
decōrē *adv* beautifully, gracefully; suitably, properly
decor·ō -āre -āvī -ātus *tr* to beautify, adorn, embellish; to decorate, honor
decōr·us -a -um *adj* beautiful, graceful; glorious, noble; suitable, proper, decorous ‖ *n* grace; propriety
dēcoxī *perf of* **decoquo**
dēcrepit·us -a -um *adj* decrepit, broken down, worn out
dē·crescō -crescĕre -crēvī -crētum *intr* to grow less, become fewer, diminish, fade; *(of time)* to grow shorter; *(of water)* to subside, go down
dēcrēt·us -a -um *pp of* **decerno** ‖ *n* decree, decision; principle
decum·a -ae *f* **(-cim-)** one-tenth; tithe, land tax; largess to the people
decumān·us -a -um *adj* **(-cim-)** paying tithes; of the tenth legion, of the tenth cohort; subject to the 10% tax; **porta decumana** main gate of Roman camp on the side turned away from the enemy ‖ *m* tax collector ‖ *mpl* men of the tenth legion ‖ *f* tax collector's wife
decumāt·ēs -ium *adj* subject to tithes
dē·cumbō -cumbĕre -cubuī *intr* to lie down; to recline at table; to fall *(in battle)*
decuri·a -ae *f* decury *(unit in Roman government consisting of ten families)*; group of ten *(organized for work, recreation, etc.)*; panel *(from which jury members were selected)*; social club, society
decuriāti·ō -ōnis *f or* **decuriāt·us -ūs** *m* dividing into decuries
decuri·ō -āre -āvī -ātus *tr (fig)* to divide into groups; *(pol)* to divide into groups of ten
decuri·ō -ōnis *m* squad leader *(in the cavalry or navy in charge of ten men)*; councilman *(of a municipality or colony)*; chief chamberlain
dē·currō -currĕre -(cu)currī -cursus *tr* to run down, hurry down *(e.g., a path)*; to travel over *(a course)*, to cover *(a distance)*; to make straight for; to turn to *(s.o.)* for help; to pass through *(life)*; to run through *(mentally, in a speech)*, discuss, treat ‖ *intr* to run down; to run for exercise, jog; *(of liquids)* to run down, flow down; *(of terrain)* to slope down; *(of rivers, ships)* to run down to the sea; *(of ships, travelers)* to come to land; to travel downstream; *(mil)* to run through a drill, carry out maneuvers, parade ‖ *v impers* **eo decursum est ut** it got to the point where
dēcursi·ō -ōnis *f* raid; *(mil)* drill, maneuvers, dress parade
dēcurs·us -ūs *m* running down; downward course; *(mil)* maneuvers; *(mil)* dress parade; *(mil)* attack from higher ground; *(rhet)* the flow *(of a sentence, verse)*; **decursio honorum** completion of a political career
dēcurtāt·us -a -um *adj* cut down, cut off short, mutilated; clipped *(style)*
dec·us -oris *n* beauty, glory, honor, dignity; virtue, worth; source of glory ‖ *npl* achievements
dēcuss·ō -āre -āvī -ātus *tr* to divide crosswise *(in the form of an X)*
dēcu·tiō -tĕre -ssī -ssus *tr* to shake off, beat off, strike down; to chop off *(head)*; to break down *(wall with battering ram)*
dēdec·et -ēre -uit *v impers* it ill befits; *(w. inf)* it is a disgrace to
dēdecor·ō -āre -āvī -ātus *tr* to disgrace, dishonor, bring shame to; to make a sham of
dēdecōr·us -a -um *adj* disgraceful, dishonorable, unbecoming
dēdec·us -oris *n* disgrace, dishonor, shame; vice, crime, outrage; *(mil)* disgraceful defeat; **dedecori esse** *(w. dat)* to be a source of disgrace to; **dedecus admittere** to incur disgrace; **per dedecus** disgracefully

dēdicāti·ō -ōnis *f* dedication, consecration
dēdic·ō -āre -āvī -ātus *tr* to dedicate, consecrate, set aside; to declare *(property in a census return)*
dēdign·or -ārī -ātus sum *tr* to disdain, look down on; *(w. double acc)* to scorn *(s.o.)* as; **aliquem maritum dedignari** to regard s.o. as an unworthy husband
dē·discō -discĕre -didicī *tr* to unlearn, forget
dēditīc·ius -(i)ī *m* prisoner-of-war
dēditi·ō -ōnis *f* surrender
dēdit·us -a -um *pp of* **dedo** ‖ *adj (w. dat)* given to, devoted to; addicted to; *(w.* **in** *+ acc)* absorbed in ‖ *mpl* prisoners-of-war
dēd·ō -ĕre -idī -itus *tr* to give up, surrender; to devote; to apply; to abandon; **deditā operā** on purpose; **neci** *(or* **ad necem)** **dedere** to put to death
dēdoc·eō -ēre -uī -tus *tr* to cause to forget; *(w. inf)* to teach *(s.o.)* not to
dēdol·eō -ēre -uī *intr* to feel pain no more
dēdol·ō -āre -āvī -ātus *tr* to hew into shape
dēdū·cō -cĕre -xī -ctus *tr* to lead *or* draw down; to launch *(ship);* to accompany, escort; to lead out *(colonists to new colony);* to conduct *(bride to husband),* give *(bride)* away; to evict; to subtract, deduct; to summon *(as witness);* to divert; to mislead; to derive *(name);* to compose *(poetry);* to comb out *(hair);* to draw out *(thread in spinning);* to lure *(into a trap); (leg)* to arraign; *(pol)* to install *(in a position of authority);* **rem huc** *(or* **eo)** **deducere ut** to bring things to the point that
dēducti·ō -ōnis *f* draining *(of water);* settling of colonists; subtraction, deduction; inference; *(leg)* eviction; **rationis deductio** line of reasoning; **sine ulla reductione** in full
dēduct·or -ōris *m* escort
dēduct·us -a -um *pp of* **deduco** ‖ *adj* drawn down; bent inwards, concave; lowered, modest; subtle, well-wrought *(poem);* **nasus deductus** pug nose
deërr·ō -āre -āvī -ātum *intr* to go astray, wander away, get lost; to stray; to go wrong
dēfaec·ō -āre -āvī -ātus *tr* to remove the dregs of, strain; *(fig)* to clear up
dēfatīgāti·ō -ōnis *f* **(-fet-)** exhaustion
dēfatīg·ō -āre -āvī -ātus *tr* **(-fet-)** to exhaust
dēfatiscor *see* **defetiscor**
dēfecti·ō -ōnis *f* failure; defection, desertion; weakening, exhaustion; *(astr)* eclipse; *(gram)* ellipsis; **defectio animi** mental breakdown; **in defectione esse** to be in revolt
dēfect·or -ōris *m* defector, deserter
dēfect·us -a -um *pp of* **deficio** ‖ *adj* weak, worn out
dēfect·us -ūs *m* failing, failure; desertion, defection; *(astr)* eclipse
dēfen·dō -dĕre -dī -sus *tr* to defend, protect, guard; to repel, beat off, avert; to keep off *(the cold, heat);* to answer *(a charge);* to support, uphold *(argument);* to play the part of *(a character); (leg)* to defend; *(w. dat)* to ward off *(s.th. harmful)* from; **solstitium pecori defendere** to ward off the noonday heat from the flock, protect the flock from the noonday heat
dēfensi·ō -ōnis *f* defense
dēfensit·ō -āre -āvī -ātus *tr* to defend (often); **causas defensitare** to be a lawyer
dēfens·ō -āre -āvī -ātus *tr* to defend, protect
dēfens·or -ōris *m* defender, protector; champion *(leg)* defense lawyer; *(leg)* defendant; *(leg)* guardian
dēfensus *pp of* **defendo**
dē·ferō -ferre -tulī -lātus *tr* to bring *or* carry down; to bear off, carry away; to drive *(ship)* off course; to offer, confer, grant; to inform against, indict; to give an account of; to announce, report; to recommend; to register; **aliquem ad aerarium deferre** to recommend s.o. for a monetary reward; **ad consilium deferre** to take into consideration
dēfer·vescō -vescĕre -v(u)ī *or* **-buī** *intr* to stop boiling, cool off; *(fig)* to calm down
dēfess·us -a -um *adj* weary, tired
dēfetigō *see* **defatigo**
dē·fetiscor -fetiscī -fessus sum *intr* **(-fat-)** to get tired; *(w. inf)* to tire of
dē·ficiō -ficĕre -fēcī -fectus *tr* to fail, disappoint; to desert, abandon ‖ *intr* to fail, be a failure; *(of supplies, etc.)* to run short, run out; *(of strength, morale)* to fail, sink; *(of sun, moon)* to be eclipsed; *(of a family line, race)* to become extinct; *(of fire)* to die out; *(w. dat or* **ad)** to be insufficient for; *(com)* to be bankrupt; *(mil, pol)* to defect; *(pol)* to secede
dēfī·gō -gĕre -xī -xus *tr* to fix, fasten down; to drive down; to fix, concentrate *(eyes, attention);* to root to the spot, astound; to bewitch; **in terra defigere** to stick *or* plant *or* set *(s.th.)* up in the ground; to stick *(weapon into s.o.)*
dēfin·gō -gĕre -xī *tr* to form, mold; to disfigure
dēfīn·iō -īre -īvī *or* **-iī -ītus** *tr* to mark out the limits of *(a place);* to limit, restrict; to define; to fix, determine, appoint; to bring to a finish, put an end to; to assign, prescribe
dēfīnītē *adv* precisely

dēfīnīti·ō -ōnis *f* boundary; *(fig)* marking out, prescribing; definition
dēfīnītīv·us -a -um *adj* finite, limited; definite, precise
dēfinxī *perf of* **defingo**
dē·fīō -fierī *intr* to fail, be lacking, be in short supply
dēflagrāti·ō -ōnis *f* conflagration
dēflagr·ō -āre -āvī -ātus *tr* to burn down ‖ *intr* to burn down; to perish, be destroyed; *(of passions)* to cool off
dē·flectō -flectĕre -flexī -flexus *tr* to deflect, bend aside, turn away, divert; *(fig)* to modify, twist; to bend *(a bow);* to lead astray ‖ *intr* to digress, deviate
dēfl·eō -ēre -ēvī -etus *tr* to cry bitterly for; to lament; to mourn as lost ‖ *intr* to cry bitterly
dēflocc·ō -āre -āvī -ātus *tr* to rub the nap off *(cloth); (fig)* to fleece
dēfloccāt·us -a -um *adj (hum)* bald
dēflōr·escō -escĕre -uī *intr* to shed blossoms; *(fig)* to fade, droop
dēflu·ō -ĕre -xī -xum *intr* to flow *or* float down; to glide down; to slide, fall; to drain off, run dry; to vanish, pass away, cease; to go out of style; *(w.* **ab)** to be descended from
dē·fodiō -fodĕre -fōdī -fossus *tr* to dig down; to hollow out; to bury, hide, conceal
dēfore = dēfutūrum esse
dēformāti·ō -ōnis *f* configuration; disfigurement
dēform·is -is -e *adj* shapeless; misshapen, disfigured, ugly; degrading; degraded; humiliating; unbecoming
dēformit·ās -ātis *f* deformity, ugliness, hideousness; vileness; lack of good taste *(in writing)*
dēformiter *adv* without grace; shamefully
dēform·ō -āre -āvī -ātus *tr* to form from a pattern; to sketch, delineate; to deform, disfigure, mar
dēfossus *pp of* **defodio**
dēfraud·ō *or* **dēfrūd·ō -āre -āvī -ātus** *tr* to defraud, rob; to cheat; **animum** *(or* **se** *or* **genium suum) defraudare** to deny oneself some pleasure
dēfrēm·ō -ĕre -uī *intr* to quiet down
dēfrēnāt·us -a -um *adj* unbridled
dēfric·ō -āre -uī -tus *or* **-ātus** *tr* to rub down; to brush *(teeth);* to scour; *(fig)* to satirize
dē·fringō -fringĕre -frēgī -fractus *tr* to break off, break to pieces
dēfrūdō *see* **defraudo**
dēfrut·um -ī *n* new wine
dē·fugiō -fugĕre -fūgī *tr* to run away from, avoid, shirk; to evade *(e.g., authority, law)* ‖ *intr* to run off
dēfunct·us -a -um *pp of* **defungor** ‖ *adj* finished; dead
dē·fundō -fundĕre -fūdī -fūsus *tr* to pour out; to empty
dēfun·gor -gī -ctus sum *intr (w. abl)* **1** to perform, carry out; **2** to finish, be done with; **3** to have done with, get rid of; **defunctus honoribus** having ended a public career; **defunctus jam sum** I'm safe now; **defungi (vitā)** to die; **quasi defunctus regis imperio** as if carrying out the king's order; **suā morte defunctus est** he died a natural death
dēfūsus *pp of* **defundo**
dēfutūt·us -a -um *adj (vulg)* worn out from excessive sex
dēgen·er -eris *adj* degenerate; unworthy; ignoble
dēgener·ō -āre -āvī -ātus *tr* to disgrace, dishonor; to fall short of ‖ *intr* to degenerate; *(w.* **ad** *or* **in** *+ acc)* to sink to
dēger·ō -ĕre *tr* to carry off
dēg·ō -ĕre *tr* to spend, pass *(time);* to spend one's time in ‖ *intr* to spend one's time, live
dēgrandin·at -āre *v impers* it is hailing hard
dēgrav·ō -āre — -ātus *tr* to weigh down; *(fig)* to burden, distress, inconvenience, overpower
dē·gredior -gredī -gressus sum *intr* to march down, go down, walk down, descend; *(from a standard)* to depart; **ad pedes degredi** to dismount
dēgrunn·iō -īre *intr* to grunt loud
dēgust·ō -āre -āvī -ātus *tr* to taste; *(fig)* to taste, sample, try, experience; *(of weapon)* to graze
dehinc *adv* from here, from now on, after this; then, next; hereafter
dehisc·ō -ĕre *intr* to part, divide, gape, yawn; to develop a crack; *(w.* **in** *+ acc)* to split open and reveal
dehonestāment·um -ī *n* blemish, disfigurement, dishonor, disgrace
dehonest·ō -āre -āvī -ātus *tr* to dishonor, disgrace
dehort·or -ārī -ātus sum *tr* to dissuade, discourage; **multa me dehortantur a vobis** many things tell me to keep my distance from you
dein *see* **deinde**
deinceps *adv* one after another, in succession, in order; without interruption; *(of time)* from now on, from then on, after that, after this, next; *(of space)* beyond that; **et deinceps** and so on
deinde *or* **dein** *adv (of place)* from that place, from there; *(of time)* then, thereafter, thereupon, afterwards; *(in enumerating facts, presenting arguments)* secondly, in the next place
Dēïphob·us -ī *m* son of Priam and Hecuba, and husband of Helen after Paris' death

Dējanīr·a -ae *f* daughter of Oeneus and wife of Hercules
dējecti·ō -ōnis *f (leg)* eviction
dēject·us -a -um *pp of* **dejicio ll** *adj* low, depressed, sunken *(place);* downhearted, depressed, despondent
dējer·ō -āre -āvī -tum *tr & intr* **(-jūr-)** to swear solemnly
dē·jiciō -jicĕre -jēcī -jectus *tr* to throw down, fling down; to fell, kill *(sacrificial victim); (of winds)* to drive off course; to depose, fire *(from office);* to lower *(eyes);* to banish *(feelings); (leg)* to evict; *(mil)* to dislodge; *(w. abl or* **de** *+ abl)* to deprive *(s.o.)* of, prevent *(s.o.)* from obtaining, rob *(s.o.)* of; **a re publica oculos dejicere** to take one's eyes off the government; **de gradu** *(or* **de loco** *or* **de statu) dejicere** to throw off balance; **mente sua dejectus** driven out of one's mind; **sortem dejicere** to cast a lot *(into an urn)*
dējun·gō -gĕre -xī -ctus *tr* to unyoke; to sever
dējūrō *see* **dejero**
dējuv·ō -āre *tr* to refuse to help
dēlā·bor -bī -psus sum *intr* to slip down, fall down, sink; to glide down, float down; *(of water)* to flow down; *(fig)* to stoop, condescend; *(w.* **ad)** to be inclined toward, be partial to; *(w.* **in** *+ acc)* to sneak in among
dēlacer·ō -āre -āvī -ātus *tr* to tear to pieces
dēlāment·or -ārī -ātus sum *tr* to grieve deeply for
delass·ō -āre -āvī -ātus *tr* to tire out, weary
dēlāti·ō -ōnis *f* reporting; informing, denouncing; **nominis delatio** indicting a person
dēlāt·or -ōris *m* reporter; *(leg)* informer
dēlātus *pp of* **defero**
dēlēbil·is -is -e *adj* able to be obliterated
dēlectābil·is -is -e *adj* delightful; delicious
dēlectāment·um -ī *n* delight; amusement, pastime
dēlectāti·ō -ōnis *f* delight, pleasure, amusement; satisfaction
dēlect·ō -āre -āvī -ātus *tr* to delight; to amuse, charm; to attract, allure; **delectari** *(w. abl)* to delight in **ll** *v impers* **me ire delectat** I like to go, I enjoy going
dēlect·us -ūs *m* choosing, choice; *(mil)* recuitment; *(mil)* recruits
dēlēgāti·ō -ōnis *f (leg)* assignment to a third party of a creditor's interest in a debt
dēlēg·ō -āre -āvī -ātus *tr* to assign, appoint *(s.o. to a task);* to ascribe *(credit, blame);* to transfer *(ownership of property)*
dēlēnific·us -a -um *adj* soothing, ingratiating
dēlēnīment·um -ī *n* allurement, bait; solace, comfort
dēlēn·iō -īre -iī -ītus *tr* **(-līn-)** to soothe, calm down, console, appease; to allure, win over
dēlēnīt·or -ōris *m* charmer
dēl·eō -ēre -ēvī -ētus *tr* to destroy; to annihilate; to overthrow; to extinguish; to raze; to blot out, erase; to put an end to, abolish
dēlētr·ix -īcis *f* destroyer *(female)*
Dēliac·us -a -um *adj* Delian, of Delos
dēlīberābund·us -a -um *adj* deep in thought
dēlīberāti·ō -ōnis *f* considering, weighing; deliberation, consultation; **habet res deliberationem** the matter requires thought
dēlīberātīv·us -a -um *adj* deliberative; requiring deliberation
dēlīberāt·or -ōris *m* thoughtful person
dēlīberāt·us -a -um *adj* resolved upon, determined
dēlīber·ō -āre -āvī -ātus *tr* to weigh, think over; to resolve; to consult *(an oracle)* **ll** *intr* to deliberate; *(w.* **de** *+ abl)* to think over; *(w.* **cum)** to consult
dēlīb·ō -āre -āvī -ātus *tr* to sip, take a sip of; to taste, take a taste of, nibble at; to take away, subtract, remove; to touch on *(subject)*
dēlibr·ō -āre -āvī -ātus *tr* to strip the bark off
dēlibūt·us -a -um *adj* anointed; defiled, smeared, stained; steeped
dēlicātē *adv* delicately; luxuriously
dēlicāt·us -a -um *adj* delicate, dainty, tender; pampered; frivolous; fastidious, squeamish; self-indulgent; luxurious **ll** *mf* favorite
dēlici·ae -ārum *fpl* delight, pleasures; sweetheart, darling; pet, favorite; comforts, luxuries; ornaments; mannerisms, airs; **delicias facere** to enjoy oneself; to have fun *(at s.o. else's expense);* **delicias facere** *(w. dat) (sl)* to play around with *(a girl);* **esse in deliciis** *(w. dat)* to be the pet *or* favorite of; **habere in deliciis** to have as a pet *or* favorite
dēliciol·ae -ārum *fpl* darling
dēlic·ium -(i)ī *n* darling; pet
dēlic·ō -āre *tr* **(-qu·ō)** to make clear
dēlict·um -ī *n* fault, offense, wrong; defect *(in a thing)*
dēlicu·us -a -um *adj* **(-liqu-)**lacking, missing
dēlig·ō -āre -āvī -ātus *tr* **(-leg-)** to tie up, fasten; *(med)* to bandage
dē·ligō -ligĕre -lēgī -lectus *tr* to pick off; to pick out, choose, select; to gather *(mil)* to draft; *(mil)* to hold a draft in *(a place)*

dēlin·g(u)ō -g(u)ĕre -xī *tr* to lick off; to have a lick of
dēlīni- = deleni-
dēlin·ō -ĕre — -itus *tr* to smudge
dē·linquō -linquĕre -līquī -lictus *tr (w. neut pron)* to commit *(an offense);* **majora delinquere** to commit greater wrongs; **si quid deliquero** if I commit some offense ‖ *intr* to be missing; to be wanting, fall short; to do wrong, commit an offense
dē·liquescō -liquescĕre -licuī *intr* to melt, dissolve; to pine away
dēliqui·ō -ōnis *f* failure; *(w. gen)* failure to get; *(astr)* eclipse
dēliqu·ium -(i)ī *n* failure
dēliquō *see* **delico**
dēlīrāment·um -ī *n* nonsense, delusion, absurdity
dēlīrāti·ō -ōnis *f* silliness, folly, madness; infatuation; dotage
dēlīr·ō -āre *intr* to be off the beam, be crazy; to rave
dēlīr·us -a -um *adj* crazy, silly; senseless; in dotage
dēlit·escō -escĕre -uī *intr* **(-tisc-)** to conceal oneself, lie hidden, lurk
dēlītig·ō -āre *intr* to rant, have it out
Dēli·us -a -um *adj* Delian, of Delos, of Apollo ‖ *m* Apollo
Dēl·os -ī *f* sacred island in the Cyclades, where Apollo and Diana were born
Delph·ī -ōrum *mpl* town in Phocis, in Central Greece, famous for the shrine and oracle of Apollo ‖ people of Delphi
Delphic·us -a -um *adj* of Delphi; of Apollo ‖ *f* three-legged table
delphīn·us -ī *or* **delph·īn -īnis** *m* dolphin ‖ **Delphinus** *(astr)* Dolphin *(constellation)*
Delph·is -idis *f* Delphic priestess of Apollo
delta *indecl n* delta *(letter of the Greek alphabet)* ‖ **Delta** the Delta *(of the Nile River)*
Deltōt·on -ī *n (astr)* Triangle *(constellation)*
dēlūbr·um -ī *n* shrine, sanctuary
dēluct·ō -āre -āvī *or* **dēluct·or -ārī -ātus sum** *intr* to wrestle
dēlūdific·ō -āre -āvī -ātus *tr* to make fun of
dēlū·dō -dĕre -sī -sus *tr* to fool, con
dēlumb·is -is -e *adj* lame
dēlumb·ō -āre *tr* to lame in the loins; *(fig)* to weaken
dēmad·escō -escĕre *intr* to become drenched, become wet; to be moistened
dēmand·ō -āre -āvī -ātus *tr* to hand over, entrust
dēmān·ō -āre -āvī *intr* to run down
dēmarch·us -ī *m* demarch *(chief of a village in Attica); (fig)* tribune of the people
dēm·ens -entis *adj* demented, out of one's mind; senseless, reckless
dēmens·us -a -um *pp of* **dēmetior** ‖ *n* ration, allowance
dēmenter *adv* insanely
dēmenti·a -ae *f* insanity; folly
dēment·iō -īre *intr* to be insane
dēmer·eō -ēre -uī -itus *or* **dēmer·eor -ērī -itus sum** *tr* to earn, merit, deserve; to serve well, do a service to, win the favor of
dēmer·gō -gĕre -sī -sus *tr* to sink; to plunge, dip; to bury ‖ *pass (of heavenly bodies)* to set
dēmessus *pp of* **demeto**
dēmet·ior -īrī -mensus sum *tr* to measure out
dē·metō -metĕre -messuī -messus *tr* to mow, reap, harvest; to pick *(flowers, fruit);* to cut off
Dēmētr·ius -(i)ī *m* Demetrius Poliorcetes, son of Antigonus, and king of Macedonia ‖ Demetrius of Phaleron, famous orator and politician at Athens
dēmigrāti·ō -ōnis *f* emigration
dēmigr·ō -āre -āvī -ātum *intr* to migrate, emigrate, move, depart; *(fig)* to pass on, die
dēmin·uō -uĕre -uī -ūtus *tr* to make smaller, lessen, diminish; to deduct; *(w. abl)* to deprive of; *(w.* **de** *+ abl)* to deduct from; **capite deminuere** to deprive of civil rights
dēminūti·ō -ōnis *f* lessening, diminution, abridging; *(leg)* right of disposing of property; **capitis diminutio** loss of civil rights; **provinicae diminutio** shortening of term of office
dēmīr·or -ārī -ātus sum *tr* to be surprised at, be amazed at
dēmissē *adv* low; humbly, modestly; abjectly
dēmissīci·us -a -um *adj* allowed to hang down, flowing; *(of clothes)* ankle-length
dēmissi·ō -ōnis *f* letting down, sinking, lowering; **demissio animi** low morale
dēmiss·us -a -um *pp of* **demitto** ‖ *adj* low, low-lying *(place);* drooping *(lips, etc.);* bent *(head);* flowing, long *(hair); (of clothes)* hanging down, full-length; *(fig)* downhearted, dejected; *(fig)* poor, humble; *(w. abl)* descended from
dēmītig·ō -āre *tr* to calm down
dē·mittō -mittĕre -mīsī -missus *tr* to drop, let drop, let sink; to lower; to dip; to sink *(a well);* to bring downstream; to shed *(blood);* to land *(ship);* to let down *(hair);* to grow *(beard);* to move down *(troops from a higher place);* **animum** *(or* **mentem)** **demittere** to become discouraged; **demittere aures ad** to deign to listen to ‖ *refl* to descend, go down; to stoop, bend down; *(fig)* to plunge into;

(geog) to slope downwards ‖ *pass* to descend, go down

dēmiurg·us -ī *m* **(dami-)** magistrate in a Greek state

dēm·ō -ĕre -psī -ptus *tr* to take away, remove, withdraw; *(w. dat or abl or* **ab** *or* **de** + *abl)* to take away from, remove from, subtract from, withhold from; **vincla pedibus demere** to remove the fetters

Dēmocrit·us -ī *m* philosopher from Abdera in Thrace and founder of the atomic theory *(born c. 460 B.C.)*

dēmōl·ior -īrī -ītus sum *tr* to demolish, pull down

dēmōlīti·ō -ōnis *f* demolishing

dēmonstrāti·ō -ōnis *f* pointing out; explanation; description

dēmonstrātīv·us -a -um *adj* showy

dēmonstrāt·or -ōris *m* one who points out, indicator

dēmonstr·ō -āre -āvī -ātus *tr* to point out clearly; to state precisely, explain, describe; to mention, speak of; to demonstrate, prove, establish

Dēmoph(o)·ōn -ontis *m* son of Theseus and Phaedra

dēmor·ior -ī -tuus sum *tr* to be dying for ‖ *intr* to die; to die off; to become extinct

dēmor·or -ārī -ātus sum *tr* to delay, detain; to hinder, block ‖ *intr* to wait

Dēmosthen·ēs -is *or* **-ī** *m* greatest Greek orator *(384–322 B.C.)*

dē·moveō -movēre -mōvī -mōtus *tr* to remove, move away; to dispossess, expel; to oust

demptus *pp of* **demo**

dēmūgīt·us -a -um *adj* bellowing, lowing

dēmul·ceō -cēre -sī *tr* to stroke lovingly, pet

dēmum *adv* at last, finally; not till then; *(to give emphasis)* precisely, exactly, just; *(to give assurance)* in fact, certainly, to be sure, as a matter of fact; **decimo demum anno** not till the tenth year; **modo demum** only now, not until now; **nunc demum** now at last, not until now; **post demum** not until afterwards; **tum demum** then finally, not until then

dēmurmur·ō -āre *tr* to grumble through *(e.g., a performance)*

dēmūtāti·ō -ōnis *f* transformation

dēmūt·ō -āre -āvī -ātus *tr* to change; to make worse ‖ *intr* to fail; to change one's mind

dēnār·ius -iī *m* denarius *(about $1)*; money

dēnarr·ō -āre -āvī -ātus *tr* to recount in detail

dēnās·ō -āre *tr* to bite the nose off *(s.o.'s face)*

dēnat·ō -āre *intr* to swim downstream

dēneg·ō -āre -āvī -ātus *tr* to deny, refuse, turn down ‖ *intr* to say no

dēn·ī -ae -a *adj* in sets of ten, ten each, in tens; tenth

dēnicāl·is -is -e *adj* purifying from death; **feriae denicales** purification service *(after death in the household)*

dēnique *adv* finally, at last; in short, in a word; *(for emphasis)* just, precisely; *(ironical)* of course; **octavo denique mense** not till after the eighth month; **tum denique** then at last, only then, not till then

dēnōmin·ō -āre -āvī -ātus *tr (w.* **ab** *or* **ex)** to name after

dēnorm·ō -āre *tr* to make crooked *or* irregular; to disfigure, spoil

dēnot·ō -āre -āvī -ātus *tr* to mark down, specify; to take careful note of; to observe closely

dens dentis *m* tooth; ivory; point, prong; fluke; *(of an elephant)* tusk; **albis dentibus deridere aliquem** *(prov)* to laugh heartily at s.o.; **dens Indus** elephant's tusk

densē *adv* closely, thickly, in quick succession, repeatedly

denseō *see* **denso**

densit·ās -ātis *f* closeness; thickness

dens·ō -āre -āvī -ātus *or* **dens·eō -ēre** *tr* to thicken; to press close together; to close *(ranks)*; to condense

dens·us -a -um *adj* dense, close, thick, crowded; frequent, repeated; intense *(love, cold)*; concise *(style)*

dentāl·ia -ium *npl* plow beam

dentāt·us -a -um *adj* toothed; serrated; *(of paper)* polished smooth

dentifrangibul·us -a -um *adj (hum)* tooth-breaking ‖ *m* thug ‖ *n* fist

dentifric·ium -(i)ī *n* tooth powder

dentileg·us -ī *m (hum)* toothpicker *(one who picks up teeth after they have been knocked out)*

dentiscalp·ium -(i)i *n* toothpick

dent·iō -īre *intr* to teethe

dēnū·bō -bĕre -psī -ptum *intr (of a woman)* to marry beneath her rank; to go through a mock marriage

dēnūd·ō -āre -āvī -ātus *tr* to strip naked, strip bare; to expose, leave unprotected; *(fig)* to lay bare

dēnumer·ō -āre -āvī -ātus *tr* to pay *(money)* in full, pay down

dēnuntiāti·ō -ōnis *f* intimation; warning, threat; announcement, proclamation; **senatūs denuntiatio** senate ordinance; **testimoni denuntiatio** summons to testify

dēnunti·ō -āre -āvī -ātus *tr* to intimate; to give notice of; to announce officially; to give official warning to; to warn, threaten; *(mil)* to report to; **denuntiare testimonium** *(w. dat)* to give *(s.o.)* a summons to testify

dēnuō *adv* anew, once more, all over again; **denuo alius** yet another

deoner·ō -āre *tr* to unload

deopt·ō -āre *tr* to choose

deorsum *adv* **(-sus)** downwards, down; *(of position)* down below, underneath

deoscul·or -ārī -ātus sum *tr* to shower with kisses

dēpasciscor *see* **depeciscor**

dēpact·us -a -um *adj* fastened down

dēparc·us -a -um *adj* very stingy

dē·pascō -pascĕre -pāvī -pastus *or* **dē·pascor -pascī -pastus sum** *tr* to eat up; to feed on; to graze on; to feed the cattle on *(grass, etc.);* to consume, to destroy, waste; *(fig)* to prune off *(excesses in style)*

dēpec·iscor -iscī -tus sum *tr* **(-pac-)** to agree on, come to terms on; to bargain for

dēpe·ctō -ctĕre — -xus *tr* to comb out; *(fig)* to flog

dēpecūlāt·or -ōris *m* embezzler, crook

dēpecūl·or -ārī -ātus sum *tr* to embezzle; to steal

dē·pellō -pellĕre -pulī -pulsus *tr* to drive off, drive away; to drive out; to avert; *(mil)* to dislodge; *(w.* **quin** *or w.* **ab** *or* **de** *+ abl)* to deter from, dissuade from, wean from **ll** *intr* to deviate

dēpend·eō -ēre -ī *intr* to hang down; *(w. abl)* to be derived from; *(w.* **ab** *or* **de** *+ abl)* to depend on; *(w.* **ex)** to hang down from

dēpen·dō -dĕre -dī -sus *tr* to pay up; to pay *(penalty)*

dēper·dō -dĕre -didī -ditus *tr* to lose completely; to ruin, destroy

dēper·eō -īre -iī *tr* to be hopelessly in love with **ll** *intr* to go to ruin, perish; to be lost, be finished

dēpexus *pp of* **depecto**

dēpilāt·us -a -um *adj* plucked; *(fig)* swindled, gypped

dē·pingō -pingĕre -pinxī -pictus *tr* to paint, portray; to embroider; *(fig)* to portray, describe, represent

dēplan·gō -gĕre -xī *tr* to beat one's breast in mourning over; to grieve over, cry one's heart out over

dēplex·us -a -um *adj* grasping

dēplōrābund·us -a -um *adj* complaining bitterly; sobbing

dēplōr·ō -āre -āvī -ātus *tr* to cry over, mourn; to despair of **ll** *intr* to cry bitterly, take it hard

dēplu·it -ĕre -it *v impers* it is raining hard, is pouring down

dē·pōnō -pōnĕre -posuī (posīvī) -pos(i)tus *tr* to put down, put aside; to get rid of; to bet; to deposit; *(w.* **apud** *+ acc)* to entrust to, commit to the care of; **bellum deponere** to give up war; **imperium deponere** to relinquish power

dēpopulāti·ō -ōnis *f* ravaging, pillaging

dēpopulāt·or -ōris *m* marauder

dēpopul·ō -āre -āvī -ātus *or* **dēpopul·or -ārī -ātus sum** *tr* to ravage, pillage, lay waste; *(of diseases)* to ravage; *(fig)* to wreck, destroy

dēport·ō -āre -āvī -ātus *tr* to carry down; to carry away; to bring home, win *(victory);* to transport; to banish

dē·poscō -poscĕre -poposcī *tr* to demand; to require, call for; to request earnestly; to challenge

dēposit·us -a -um *pp of* **depono ll** *adj* despaired of **ll** *n* deposit *(as down-payment; for safekeeping);* **depositi agere** to sue for breach of trust; **depositi damnare** to convict of breach of trust

dēprāvātē *adv* perversely

dēprāvāti·ō -ōnis *f* distorting; *(fig)* distortion; perversity, perversion

dēprāv·ō -āre -āvī -ātus *tr* to make crooked, distort; to pervert, corrupt, seduce; to misrepresent

dēprecābund·us -a -um *adj* imploring

dēprecāti·ō -ōnis *f* supplication, averting by prayer; invocation, earnest entreaty; *(w. gen)* intercession against *(danger, etc.)*

dēprecāt·or -ōris *m* intercessor; *(w. gen)* champion of

dēprec·or -ārī -ātus sum *tr* to pray against, avert by prayer; to pray for, beg for; to intercede on behalf of; to plead in excuse **ll** *intr* to pray; to make an entreaty

dēprehen·dō -dĕre -dī -sus *or* **dēpren·dō -dĕre -dī -sus** *tr* to get hold of; to arrest; to catch, intercept; to surprise, catch in the act; to detect, discover; to perceive, understand; to embarrass

dēprehensi·ō -ōnis *f* detection

dēpress·us -a -um *pp of* **deprimo ll** *adj* low *(voice);* low-lying *(land)*

dē·primō -primĕre -pressī -pressus *tr* to depress, weigh down; to plant deep; to dig *(e.g., trench);* to sink *(ship)* **ll** *pass* to sink

dēproeli·or -ārī *intr* to fight it out, battle fiercely

dēprōm·ō -ĕre -psī -ptus *tr* to take down; to bring out, produce; **pecuniam ex arca depromere** to get the money out of the safe

dēproper·ō -āre *tr* to make in a hurry **ll** *intr* to hurry

deps·ō -ĕre -uī -tus *tr* to knead; *(vulg)* to feel up

dēpud·et -ēre -uit *v impers* **eum depudet** he is ashamed

dēpūg·is -is *adj* **(-pȳg-)** *(masc & fem only)* with thin buttocks

dēpugn·ō -āre -āvī -ātum *intr* to fight hard; to fight it out **ll** *v impers (pass)* **depugnatum est** they fought hard

dēpulsī *perf of* **depello**
dēpulsi·ō -ōnis *f* averting; *(rhet)* defense
dēpuls·ō -āre *tr* to push aside; **de via depulsare** to push out of the way
dēpuls·or -ōris *m* averter
dēpulsus *pp of* **depello**
dēpung·ō -ĕre *tr* to mark off *(in an account by punching holes)*
dēpurg·ō -āre -āvī -ātus *tr* to clean (out) thoroughly
dēput·ō -āre -āvī -ātus *tr* to prune; to reckon, consider
dēpȳgis *see* **depugis**
dēque *adv* down, downwards
dērād·ō -ĕre -rāsī -rāsus *tr* to shave off; to scrape off
dērect·us -a -um *pp of* **derigo;** *see* **directus**
dērelicti·ō -ōnis *f* neglect
dēre·linquō -linquĕre -līquī -lictus *tr* to leave behind, abandon
dērepente *adv* suddenly
dērēp·ō -ĕre -sī *intr* to creep down
dēreptus *pp of* **deripio**
dērī·deō -dēre -sī -sus *tr* to deride ‖ *intr* to laugh it off *(i.e., get off scot-free)*
dērīdicul·us -a -um *adj* quite ridiculous, absurd ‖ *n* derision; absurdity; **deridiculo esse** to be the butt of ridicule
dērig·escō -escĕre -uī *intr* to grow stiff, grow rigid; to curdle
dērigō *see* **dirigo**
dē·ripiō -ripĕre -ripuī -reptus *tr* to tear off; to remove; to seize; to tear down, pull down
dērīs·or -ōris *m* scoffer
dērīs·us -ūs *m* derision
dērīvāti·ō -ōnis *f* diverting *(of streams);* divergence of sense; derivation *(of words)*
dērīv·ō -āre -āvī -ātus *tr* to draw off, divert; to derive
dērō·dō -dĕre — -sus *tr* to nibble away at
dērŏg·ō -āre -āvī -ātus *tr* to propose to repeal *(a law)* in part; to restrict, modify; to take away
dērōs·us -a -um *adj* gnawed away, nibbled
dēruncin·ō -āre -āvī -ātus *tr* to plane off; *(fig)* to rip off
dēru·ō -ĕre -ī *tr* to throw down, demolish; *(w.* **de** *+ abl)* to detract from
dērupt·us -a -um *adj* rough, steep ‖ *npl* crevasses, crags
dēsaev·iō -īre -(i)ī -ītum *intr* to rage furiously, vent one's rage; to run wild
dēsalt·ō -āre -āvī -ātus *tr* to dance; **canticum desaltare** to dance a number
descen·dō -dĕre -dī -sum *intr* to climb down, descend, come down; to dismount; to fall, sink; to sink in, penetrate; *(fig)* to go down, sink down, penetrate; *(fig)* to lower oneself, stoop, yield; *(mil)* to march down
descensi·ō -ōnis *f* descent; sailing down; **descensio Tiberina** sailing down the Tiber
descens·us -ūs *m* climbing down, descent; slope
desc·iscō -iscĕre -īvī *or* **-iī -ītum** *intr* to revolt, defect; *(fig)* to depart, deviate; *(w.* **ab)** to deviate from, break allegiance with, revolt from; **a me descii** I abandoned my own principles; **in monstrum desciscere** to degenerate into a monster
descrī·bō -bĕre -psī -ptus *tr* to write out, transcribe, copy; to describe, portray, design, sketch
descriptē *see* **discripte**
descripti·ō -ōnis *f* diagram, plan; transcript; description; **descriptio criminis** indictment
descriptus *pp of* **describo**
dēsec·ō -āre -uī -tus *tr* (**-sic-**) to cut off
dēser·ō -ĕre -uī -tus *tr* to desert, abandon, forsake; *(leg)* forfeit
dēsert·or -ōris *m* deserter
dēsert·us -a -um *pp of* **desero** ‖ *adj* deserted; uninhabited ‖ *npl* wilderness, desert
dēserv·iō -īre *intr (w. dat)* to be a slave to, serve devotedly
dēs·es -idis *adj* sitting down, sitting at ease; lazy, idle; apathetic, listless
dēsicc·ō -āre *tr* to dry up; to drain
dē·sideō -sidēre -sēdī *intr* to sit idle, remain inactive
dēsīderābil·is -is -e *adj* desirable
dēsīderāti·ō -ōnis *f* missing, feeling the absence, yearing; **desideratio voluptatum** yearning for pleasures
dēsīder·ium -(i)ī *n* longing, missing, feeling of loss; want, need, desire; request, petition; **ex desiderio laborare** to be homesick; **me desiderium tenet** *(w. gen)* I miss, am homesick for
dēsīder·ō -āre -āvī -ātus *tr* to miss, long for; to call for, require; *(mil)* to lose *(men)* in combat ‖ *pass* to be lost, be missing, be a casualty
dēsidi·a -ae *f* idleness, inactivity; laziness; apathy
dēsidiābul·um -ī *n (coll)* place to lounge, hangout
dēsidiōsē *adv* idly
dēsidiōs·us -a -um *adj* idle, lazy; causing idleness *or* laziness; spent in idleness
dē·sīdō -sīdĕre -sēdī *or* **-sīdī** *intr* to sink; to subside; to settle down; **in imo desidere** to settle at the bottom
dēsignāti·ō -ōnis *f* specification; layout; appointment; election
dēsignātor *see* **dissignator**
dēsign·ō -āre -āvī -ātus *tr* to mark out, point out, designate; to outline; to define, trace; *(of words)* to denote, indicate; to earmark; to appoint, elect; **consul designatus** consul-elect

dē·siliō -silīre -siluī *or* **-silīvī** *or* **-siliī -sultum** *intr* to jump down; to dismount
dē·sinō -sinĕre -sīvī *or* **-s(i)ī -situs** *tr* to give up, abandon, finish with; *(w. inf)* to stop *(doing s.th.)*; **furere desinere** to stop raging ‖ *intr* to stop, come to a stop, end; to stop speaking; *(w. gen)* to cease from; *(w.* **in** *+ acc)* to end in; **similiter desinere** to have similar endings
dēsipi·ens -entis *adj* foolish, silly
dēsipienti·a -ae *f* foolishness
dēsip·iō -ĕre *intr* to be silly, fool around
dē·sistō -sistĕre -stitī *intr* to stop, desist; to get stuck, stick; *(w. abl or w.* **ab** *or* **de** *+ abl)* to desist from, abandon, give up *(an action begun)*; **desistere a defensione** to give up the defense
dēsitus *pp of* **desino**
dēsōl·ō -āre -āvī -ātus *tr* to leave desolate, leave empty; to leave alone, forsake, abandon; **desolatus** *(w. abl)* deprived of
despect·ō -āre *tr* to look down on, overlook, command a view of; *(fig)* to look down on, despise
despect·us -a -um *pp of* **despicio** ‖ *adj* contemptible
despect·us -ūs *m* commanding view, view; contempt, scorn
despēranter *adv* hopelessly
despērāti·ō -ōnis *f* desperation, despair
despērāt·us -a -um *adj* desperate, hopeless; despaired of
despēr·ō -āre -āvī -ātus *tr* to despair of ‖ *intr* to despair, give up hope; *(w.* **de** *+ abl)* to despair of
despicāti·ō -ōnis *f* contempt ‖ *fpl* feelings of contempt
despicāt·us -a -um *adj* despicable; **aliquem despicatum habere** to hold s.o. in contempt
despicāt·us -ūs *m* contempt
despici·ens -entis *adj* contemptuous; *(w. gen)* contemptuous of
despicienti·a -ae *f* contempt
de·spiciō -spicĕre -spexī -spectus *tr* to despise, look down on ‖ *intr* to look down; *(w.* **in** *+ acc)* to look down on, have a view of
despic·or -ārī -ātus sum *tr* to despise, disdain
despoliāt·or -ōris *m* robber
dēspoli·ō -āre -āvī -ātus *tr* to strip, rob, plunder
despon·deō -dēre -dī -sus *tr* to pledge, promise solemnly; to promise in marriage; **animum** *(or* **animos)** **despondere** to lose heart, despair
dēspons·ō -āre *tr* to betroth
despūm·ō -āre -āvī -ātus *tr* to skim (off); to work off *(i.e., digest)* ‖ *intr* to stop foaming
despu·ō -ĕre *tr* to spit out, spit down; to avert by spitting; *(fig)* to reject ‖ *intr* to spit on the ground *(to avert evil, etc.)*
desquām·ō -āre -āvī -ātus *tr* to scale *(fish)*; *(fig)* to peel off
destill·ō -āre -āvī -ātus *tr* to drip, distill ‖ *intr* to drip, trickle down
destimul·ō -āre *tr* to goad on
destināti·ō -ōnis *f* designation; nomination; purpose, intention; **locus destinationis** destination
destināt·us -a -um *adj* obstinate; fixed, determined; **animus morti destinatus** a mind set on death; **destinatum est mihi** *(w. inf)* I have made up my mind to ‖ *n* design, intention; mark *(aimed at)*; **ex destinato** according to plan
destin·ō -āre -āvī -ātus *tr* to lash down, secure; to fix, determine, resolve; to earmark; to appoint, designate; to arrange the purchase of; to aim at ‖ *intr* to make up one's mind ‖ *v impers* **destinatum mihi est** I have made up my mind
destit·uō -uĕre -uī -ūtus *tr* to set apart; to set down, place; to forsake; to leave high and dry, betray, desert; *(w.* **ab***)* to rob of, leave destitute of
destitūti·ō -ōnis *f* forsaking, abandonment; disappointment
destrict·us -a -um *adj* severe, rigid
de·stringō -stringĕre -strinxī -strictus *tr* to strip; to unsheathe; to give *(s.o.)* a rubdown; to brush gently against, skim; *(of weapon)* to graze; *(fig)* to criticize, satirize
destructi·ō -ōnis *f* pulling down *(e.g., of walls)*; destruction, demolition; refutation
destru·ō -ĕre -xī -ctus *tr* to pull down, demolish; *(fig)* to ruin
dēsubitō *or* **dē subitō** *adv* suddenly
dēsūdasc·ō -ĕre *intr* to begin to sweat all over
dēsūd·ō -āre -āvī -ātum *intr* to sweat; *(w. dat) (fig)* to sweat over
dēsuē·fiō -fierī -factus sum *intr (w.* **ab***)* to become unused to, get away from
dēsu·escō -escĕre -ēvī -ētum *intr (w. inf)* to become unaccustomed to, get away from
dēsuētūd·ō -inis *f* disuse, lack of use
dēsuēt·us -a -um *pp of* **desuesco** ‖ *adj* unused, out of use, obsolete; out of practice; *(w. dat)* unused to, unfamiliar with
dēsult·or -ōris *m* circus rider *(who leaps from one horse to another)*; **amoris desultor** fickle lover, "butterfly"
dēsultōri·us -a -um *adj* of a circus rider; **equus desultorius** show horse
dēsultūr·a -ae *f* jumping down
dē·sum -esse -fuī -futurus *intr* to fall short, fail; to fail in one's duty; to be absent, be missing; *(w. dat)* **1** to be absent from, be missing from; **2** to fail to

support; **sibi deësse** to sell oneself short; **tempori deësse** *(or* **occasioni temporis)** **deësse** to pass up the opportunity

dēsūm·ō -ĕre -psī -ptus *tr* to pick out, choose; to undertake; **sibi hostem desumere** to take on an enemy

dēsuper *adv* from above

dēsur·gō -gĕre -rexī -rectum *intr* to rise; **cenā desurgere** to get up from the table; *(euphem)* to go to the toilet

dēte·gō -gĕre -xī -ctus *tr* to detect, uncover, expose, lay bare; to reveal, disclose, betray

dēten·dō -dĕre — -sus *tr* to loosen; to strike *(a tent)*

dētentus *pp of* **detineo**

dēter·geō -gēre -sī -sus *or* **dēter·gō -gĕre** to wipe off, wipe away; *(fig)* to wipe clean

dēteri·or -or -us *adj* inferior, worse, poorer; lower in value; weaker

dēterius *adv* worse

dētermināti·ō -ōnis *f* boundary; conclusion, end

dētermin·ō -āre -āvī -ātus *tr* to bound, limit; *(rhet)* to conclude *(sentence, period)*

dē·terō -terĕre -trīvī -trītus *tr* to rub away, wear away; to wear out; to lessen, weaken, detract from; **calces alicujus deterere** to tread on s.o.'s heels

dēterr·eō -ēre -uī -itus *tr* to deter, frighten away, discourage; *(w. abl or* **ab** *or* **de** *+ abl, or w.* **ne, quin,** *or* **quominus)** to deter *(s.o.)* from, discourage *(s.o.)* from

dētersus *pp of* **detergeo**

dētestābil·is -is -e *adj* detestable

dētestāti·ō -ōnis *f* detestation; curse; *(leg)* formal renunciation

dētest·or -ārī -ātus sum *tr* to curse; to invoke *(the gods)* to avert; to plead against; to detest; *(w.* **in** *+ acc)* to call *(e.g., vengeance)* upon; **invidiam detestari** to avert jealousy, avoid unpopularity

dētex·ō -ĕre -uī -tus *tr* to weave, finish weaving; *(fig)* to finish (off)

dē·tineō -tinēre -tinuī -tentus *tr* to hold back, keep back; to hold up, detain; to occupy, keep busy; *(w.* **ab** *or* **de** *+ abl)* to keep back from; *(w. abl or* **in** *+ abl)* to occupy *(day, mind)* with, keep *(s.o.)* busy with

dēton·deō -dēre -dī -sus *tr* to cut off, shear off; *(fig)* to strip off

dēton·ō -āre -uī *intr* to stop thundering; *(of Jupiter)* to thunder down

dētonsus *pp of* **detondeo**

dētor·queō -quēre -sī -tus *tr* to twist *or* bend aside; to twist out of shape; to turn aside; to turn, direct; to avert *(eyes);* to divert, pervert; to distort, misrepresent *(words)*

dētracti·ō -ōnis *f* (**-trect-**) taking away, wresting; removal; *(rhet)* ellipsis

dētractō *see* **detrecto**

dētract·or -ōris *m* detractor

dētra·hō -hĕre -xī -ctus *tr* to drag down, drag away, pull down, pull away; to remove, withdraw; to deprive, rob, strip; to induce to come down *(e.g., an enemy from a strong position);* to disparage, detract, slander; *(w. dat or* **de** *+ abl)* to rob *(s.o.)* of

dētrectāti·ō -ōnis *f* drawing back, avoidance; **militiae detrectatio** draft dodging

dētrectāt·or -ōris *m* detractor; shirker

dētrect·ō -āre -āvī -ātus *tr* (**-trac-**) to draw back from, shirk, decline, reject; to disparage; to demean; **militiam detrectare** to dodge the draft

dētrīmentōs·us -a -um *adj* detrimental

dētrīment·um -ī *n* detriment, loss, harm; **detrimentum accipere** *(or* **capere)** to incur a loss; **detrimentum inferre** *(or* **afferre)** to cause harm *or* loss

dētrītus *pp of* **detero**

dētrīvī *perf of* **detero**

dētrū·dō -dĕre -sī -sus *tr* to push down, push away, push off; to postpone; *(mil)* to dislodge; *(leg)* to evict; **aliquem de sua sententia detrudere** to force s.o. to change his mind

dētrunc·ō -āre -āvī -ātus *tr* to cut off, lop off; to mutilate; to behead

dētulī *perf of* **deferro**

dēturb·ō -āre *tr* to beat down, tear down, strike down; to eject, expel, dispossess; *(mil)* to dislodge; **aliquem de sanitate deturbare** to drive a person mad

dēturp·ō -āre *tr* to disfigure

Deucali·ōn -ōnis *m* son of Prometheus who, together with his wife Pyrrha, survived the Deluge

deūn·x -cis *m* eleven-twelfths; **heres ex deūnce** heir to eleven-twelfths

de·ūrō -ūrĕre -ussī -ustus *tr* to burn up, destroy; *(of frost)* to nip

de·us -ī *(nom pl:* **deī** *or* **dī(ī);** *gen pl:* **deōrum** *or* **deum;** *dat and abl pl:* **deīs, dīs** *or* **diīs;** *vocative sg:* **deus)** *m* god, deity ‖ *mpl (of people in high places)* the powers that be; **di boni!** good heavens!; **di hominesque** all the world; **di meliora!** Heaven forbid!; **dis volentibus** with the help of the gods; **di te ament!** bless your little heart!

deustus *pp of* **deuro**

dē·ūtor -ūtī *intr (w. abl)* to mistreat

dēvast·ō -āre -āvī -ātus *tr* to devastate

dēve·hō -hĕre -xī -ctus *tr* to carry down, carry away, carry off, ship off ‖ *pass* to ride down; to sail down

dēvellō dēvellĕre dēvellī *or* **dēvōlsī dēvulsus** *or* **dēvolsus** *tr* to pluck

dēvēl·ō -āre *tr* to unveil

dēvener·or -ārī -ātus sum *tr* to worship; to avert by prayer

dē·veniō -venīre -vēnī -ventum *intr* to come down, arrive; *(w. acc of extent of motion or w.* **ad** *or* **in** *+ acc)* to arrive at, reach; *(w.* **ad**) to happen to, befall

dēverber·ō -āre -āvī -ātus *tr* to thrash soundly

dēverb·ium -(i)ī *n* spoken parts of a play, unaccompanied by music

dēvers·or -ārī -ātus sum *intr* to stay as a guest; *(w.* **apud** *+ acc)* to stay at the house of

dēvers·or -ōris *m* **(-vor-)** guest

dēversōriol·um -ī *n* small inn

dēversōri·us -a -um *adj* **(-vor-)** of an inn, fit to stay at; **taberna deversoria** inn ‖ *n* inn

dēverticul·um -ī *n* **(-vort-)** side road; detour; digression; refuge; inn, tavern; *(coll)* dive; *(fig)* loophole

dēver·tō -tĕre -tī -sum *or* **dēver·tor -tī -sus sum** *intr* **(-vort-)** to turn aside, turn away; to stay as guest, spend the night; *(w.* **ad** *or* **apud** *+ acc)* to stay with, stay at the house of; *(w.* **ad**) to have recourse to

dēvex·us -a -um *adj* inclining, sloping, steep; *(w.* **ad**) prone to, inclined to

dēvin·ciō -cīre -xī -ctus *tr* to tie up, clamp; *(fig)* to obligate, unite closely ‖ *refl* **se vino devincire** *(coll)* to get tight on wine

dē·vincō -vincĕre -vīcī -victus *tr* to beat decisively, trounce

dēvinctus *pp of* **devincio** ‖ *adj (w. dat)* strongly attached to

dēvītāti·ō -ōnis *f* avoidance

dēvīt·ō -āre -āvī -ātus *tr* to avoid

dēvi·us -a -um *adj* out of the way; off the beaten track; living apart, solitary, sequestered; inconsistent ‖ *npl* wilderness

dēvoc·ō -āre -āvī -ātus *tr* to call down; to call off; to recall; to call away; to allure; **deos ad auxilium devocare** to invoke the gods for help

dēvol·ō -āre -āvī -ātum *intr* to fly down; to fly away; to hasten down, hasten away

dēvol·vō -vĕre -vī -ūtus *tr* to roll down; *(w.* **de**) to roll down from ‖ *pass* to roll down, go tumbling down; *(w.* **ad**) to fall back on

dēvor·ō -āre -āvī -ātus *tr* to devour, gulp down; to consume, waste; *(of sea)* to engulf, swallow up; to swallow, mumble *(words);* to repress *(tears);* to bear with patience

dēvor- = dever-

dēvorti·a -ōrum *npl* side roads, detour

dēvōti·ō -ōnis *f* self-sacrifice; cursing; outlawing; incantation, spell; **capitis** *(or* **vitae) devotio** sacrifice of one's life

dēvōt·ō -āre -āvī -ātus *tr* to bewitch, jinx

dēvōt·us -a -um *pp of* **devoveo** ‖ *adj* devoted, faithful; accursed; *(w. dat)* **1** devoted to; **2** addicted to

dē·voveō -vovēre -vōvī -vōtus *tr* to devote, vow, sacrifice, dedicate; to mark out, doom, destine; to curse; to bewitch

dēvulsus *pp of* **devello**

dext·ans -antis *m* five-sixths

dextell·a -ae *f* little right hand; right-hand man

dex·ter -tera -terum *or* **-tra -trum** *adj* right, on the right side; handy, dexterous; lucky, propitious, favorable; opportune, right ‖ *f* right hand, right side, the right; **a dextrā laevāque** to the right and left, right and left, everywhere; **dextrā** with the right hand; *(fig)* with valor; **dextrā** *(w. gen or acc)* to the right of; **dextrae jungere dextram** to shake hands; **dextram dare** *(or* **tendere)** to give a pledge of friendship

dexterē *or* **dextrē** *adv* dexterously, skillfully; **dextre fortunā uti** *(fig)* to play the cards right

dexterit·ās -ātis *f* dexterity; readiness to help

dextrorsum *or* **dextrorsus** *or* **dextrōversum** *adv* **(-vor-)** to the right, towards the right side

dī *see* **deus**

Dī·a -ae *f* ancient name of the island of Naxos ‖ mother of Mercury

diabathrār·ius -(i)ī *m* shoemaker

diadēm·a -ātis *n* diadem

diadēmāt·us -a -um *adj* wearing a diadem, wearing a crown

diaet·a -ae *f* room; cabin *(of ship);* annex *(to the main building); (med)* regimen *(proper exercise, etc.)*

dialecticē *adv* logically

dialectic·us -a -um *adj* dialectical, logical ‖ *m* dialectician, logician ‖ *f* logic, dialectics ‖ *npl* dialectics

dialect·os -ī *f* dialect

Diāl·is -is -e *adj* of Jupiter; of Jupiter's high priest; **apex Dialis** high priest's miter; **flamen Dialis** high priest of Jupiter

dialog·us -ī *m* dialogue, conversation; literary composition in the form of a dialogue

Diān·a *or* **Diān·a -ae** *f* Diana *(Roman goddess, identified with Artemis); (fig)* Diana's temple; *(fig)* moon; **iracunda Diana** lunacy

Diāni·us -a -um *adj* Diana's ‖ *n* enclosure sacred to Diana

diāri·a -ōrum *npl* daily ration

dibaph·us -ī *f* crimson robe; official robe *(of a magistrate or augur)*

dic·a -ae *f (leg)* lawsuit, case, judicial proceedings; **dicam scribere** *(w. dat)* to sue s.o.; **dicas sortiri** to select a jury

dicācit·ās -ātis *f* sarcasm

dicācul·us -a -um *adj* sarcastic
dicāti·ō -ōnis *f* declaration of intent of becoming a citizen
dic·ax -ācis *adj* witty, sharp; sarcastic
dichorē·us -ī *m (pros)* double trochee (— ∪ — ∪)
dici·ō -ōnis *f* jurisdiction; sway, authority, control, rule, dominion, sovereignty; **in** *(or* **sub) dicione esse** *(w. gen)* to be under the control of, be subject to, be under the jurisdiction of; **in dicionem redigere** *(w. gen) or* **dicioni subjicere** *(w. gen)* to bring *(s.o.)* under the control of
dicis causā *or* **grātiā** *adv* for show, for the sake of appearances
dic·ō -āre -āvī -ātus *tr* to dedicate, consecrate; to deify; to inaugurate; to set apart, devote; *(w. dat)* to devote *(e.g., time, energy, self)* to
dīcō dīcĕre dixī dictus *tr* to say; to tell, relate; to indicate, mention, specify, point out; to nominate, appoint; to fix, set *(day, date);* to speak, deliver, recite; to pronounce, utter, articulate; to call, name; to assert, state; to describe; to predict; *(w. double acc)* to appoint *(s.o.)* as; **causam dicere** to plead *or* defend a case; **diem dicere** *(w. dat)* to set a date for; **facete dictum!** well put!; **sententiam dicere** to express an opinion; **testimonium dicere** to give evidence
dicrot·a -ae *f* bireme
dicrot·um -ī *n* bireme
Dictae·us -a -um *adj* of Mt. Dicte, Dictaean, Cretan
dictamn·us *or* **dictamn·os -ī** *f (bot)* dittany *(aromatic plant, believed to have magical powers)*
dictāt·a -ōrum *npl* lessons, rules; dictation
dictāt·or -ōris *m* dictator *(emergency magistrate in Rome, legally appointed for a maximum six-month term);* chief magistrate *(of Italic town)*
dictātōri·us -a -um *adj* of a dictator
dictātr·ix -īcis *f* mistress of ceremonies
dictātūr·a -ae *f* dictatorship
Dict·ē -ēs *f* mountain in Crete, the alleged birthplace of Jupiter
dicti·ō -ōnis *f* saying, speaking, uttering; diction, style; conversation; oracular response, prediction; **dictio causae** pleading of a case; **dictio testimoni** right to give testimony; **juris dictio** administration of justice; jurisdiction
dictit·ō -āre -āvī -ātus *tr* to keep saying, to state emphatically; **causas dictitare** to practice law
dict·ō -āre -āvī -ātus *tr* to reiterate, say repeatedly; to dictate; to compose; to suggest, remind
dict·us -a -um *pp of* **dico ‖** *n* saying, word, statement; witticism; maxim, proverb; prediction; order, instruction; promise, assurance; derisive remark; **dicta dicere** to make (witty *or* cutting) remarks; **dictis manere** to stick to one's promises
Dictynn·a -ae *f* Cretan goddess Britomartis, identified with Diana
-dicus -a -um *adjl suf;* **-dic·us -ī** *masc suf* denotes one who speaks: **veridicus** saying the truth; **causidicus** one who pleads cases, lawyer
dī·dō *or* **dis·dō -dĕre -didī -ditus** *tr* to publicize, disseminate; to distribute, hand out
Dīd·ō -ūs *or* **-ōnis** *(acc:* **Dīdō** *or* **Dīdōn)** *f* daughter of Tyrian king Belus, and foundress and queen of Carthage
dīdū·cō -cĕre -xī -ctus *tr* to draw apart, open; to part, sever, separate, split; to undo, untie; to divide, distribute; to scatter, disperse; to untie *(knot);* to break up *(friendships);* to deploy *(forces);* to digest *(food);* to open wide *(mouth); (in mathematics)* to divide; **animus diductus** *(w. abl)* the mind torn between *(alternatives)*
dīducti·ō -ōnis *f* separation into parts, distribution
diēcul·a -ae *f* little while
diērect·us -a -um *adj (coll)* finished, done for; **abi** *(or* **i) dierectus!** *(sl)* go straight to blazes!
di·ēs -ēī *m (but occasionally feminine when referring to a fixed day or time in general)* day; time, period, space of time, interval; daylight; light of day; anniversary; daybreak; season; **diem dicere** *(w. dat)* to impeach, bring an accusation against; **diem ex die** from day to day, day after day; **diem noctemque** day and night; **dies meus** my birthday; **in diem** for the moment; for a future day; **in dies** (more and more) every day; **multo denique die** not till late in the day; **postridie ejus diei** the day after that; **post tertium ejus diei** two days after that
Diespi·ter -tris *m* Jupiter
diffām·ō -āre -āvī -ātus *tr* to spread the news of; to defame, slander
differenti·a -ae *f* difference, diversity; distinguishing characteristic; specific difference, species
differit·ās -ātis *f* difference
differō differre distulī dīlātus *tr* to carry in different directions; to scatter, disperse; to publicize; to postone; to put *(a person)* off; to humor; to get rid of; to bewilder; to disquiet **‖** *intr* to differ, be different; *(w.* **ab)** to differ from **‖** *v impers* there is a difference; **multum differt** there is a great difference
differt·us -a -um *adj* stuffed; crowded, overcrowded

difficil·is -is -e *adj* difficult, hard; surly; hard to manage, hard to please
difficiliter *adv* (**-culter**) with difficulty, barely
difficult·ās -ātis *f* difficulty, hardship, trouble, distress; surliness; poverty, financial embarrassment
difficulter *adv* with difficulty, barely
diffid·ens -entis *adj* diffident, lacking in confidence; anxious, nervous
diffidenter *adv* without confidence, distrustfully
diffidenti·a -ae *f* diffidence, mistrust, distrust
diffī·dō -dĕre -sus sum *intr (w. dat)* to distrust; to despair of; *(w. acc & inf)* to have no confidence that; *(w. inf)* to expect not to
dif·findō -findĕre -fidī -fissus *tr* to split, divide; **diem diffindere** *(fig)* to put off the day of the trial
diffing·ō -ĕre *tr* to form differently, remodel; to alter
diffissus *pp of* **diffindo**
diffit·eor -ērī *tr* to disavow, disown
diffl·ō -āre -āvī -ātus *intr* to blow away; to disperse
difflu·ō -ĕre -xī -ctum *intr* to flow in different directions, flow away; to dissolve, melt away, disappear; *(w. abl)* to wallow in *(e.g., luxury)*
dif·fringō -fringĕre -frēgī -fractus *tr* to shatter, break apart, smash
dif·fugiō -fugĕre -fūgī *intr* to flee in different directions; to disperse; to disappear
diffug·ium -(i)ī *n* dispersion
diffundit·ō -āre *tr* to pour out, scatter; to waste
dif·fundō -fundĕre -fūdī -fūsus *tr* to pour out; to scatter, diffuse, spread, extend; to bottle *(wine);* to give vent to; to cheer up, gladden
diffūsē *adv* diffusely; fully
diffūsil·is -is -e *adj* diffusive
diffūs·us -a -um *pp of* **diffundo ‖** *adj* extending over a wide area; extensive *(writings);* diffuse, expansive *(speech)*
diffutūt·us -a -um *adj (vulg)* exhausted by too much sex
dī·gerō -gerĕre -gessī -gestus *tr* to distribute in all directions; to spread about, disperse, divide; to arrange; to interpret
dīgesti·ō -ōnis *f* arrangement; *(rhet)* enumeration
dīgestus *pp of* **digero**
digitul·us -ī *m* little finger
digit·us -ī *m* finger; inch *(one sixteenth of a Roman foot);* toe; **digitis concrepare** to snap the fingers; **digito uno attingere** to touch lightly, touch tenderly; **digitum intendere ad** to point the finger at; **digitum tollere** to make a bid; **digitus index** index finger; **digitus medius** *or* **summus** middle finger; **digitus minimus** little finger; **digitus pollex** thumb; **digitus quartus** ring finger; **in digitos arrectus** on tiptoe; **primus** *(or* **prior)** **digitus** fingertip
dīgladi·or -ārī -ātus sum *intr* to fight in a gladiatorial contest
dignāti·ō -ōnis *f* esteem, respect; dignity, honor; rank, status
dignē *adv* worthily
dignit·ās -ātis *f* worth, worthiness; dignity; authority, rank, reputation, distinction, majesty; self-respect; dignitary; political office
dign·ō -āre -āvī -ātus *or* **dign·or -ārī -ātus sum** *tr (w. abl)* to think worthy of; *(w. inf)* to think fit to; *(w. double acc)* to think *(s.o.)* worthy of being *(e.g., a son)*
dignosc·ō *or* **dīnosc·ō -ĕre** *tr* to distinguish; *(w. abl)* to distinguish *(s.o.)* from; **dominum ac servum dignoscere** to know the difference between master and slave
dign·us -a -um *adj* worthy, deserving; fit, adequate, suitable, deserved, proper; *(w. abl)* worthy of
dīgre·dior -dī -ssus sum *intr* to move apart, separate; to deviate; to digress
dīgressi·ō -ōnis *f* parting, separation; deviation; digression
dīgressus *pp of* **digredior**
dīgress·us -ūs *m* departure; digression
dījūdicāti·ō -ōnis *f* decision
dījūdic·ō -āre -āvī -ātus *tr* to decide, settle; **vera et falsa** *(or* **vera a falsis) dijudicare)** to distinguish between truth and falsehood
dījun- = disjun-
dī·lābor -lābī -lapsus sum *intr* to fall apart, break up; *(of ice)* to melt; to disperse; to decay; *(of time)* to slip by; *(of water)* to flow in different directions
dīlacer·ō -āre -āvī -ātus *tr* to tear to pieces
dīlāmin·ō -āre *tr* to split in two; to crack *(nuts)*
dīlani·ō -āre -āvī -ātus *tr* to tear to pieces
dīlapid·ō -āre -āvī -ātus *tr* to demolish *(a structure of stone); (coll)* to squander
dīlapsus *pp of* **dilabor**
dīlarg·ior -īrī -ītus sum *tr* to hand out generously, lavish
dīlāti·ō -ōnis *f* postponement, delay; *(leg)* adjournment
dīlāt·ō -āre -āvī -ātus *tr* to dilate, stretch, broaden, extend, enlarge; *(fig)* to amplify, spread, extend; to drawl out
dīlāt·or -ōris *m* procrastinator, slowpoke
dīlātus *pp of* **differo**
dīlaud·ō -āre *tr* to praise enthusiastically
dīlect·us -a -um *pp of* **diligo ‖** *adj* beloved, dear
dīlect·us -ūs *m* selection; *(mil)* selective

service, draft; draftees; recruitment; **dilectum habere** to conduct a draft; **legiones ex novo dilectu conficere** to bring the legions to full strength with new draftees

dīlid·ō -ĕre *tr* to smash to pieces

dīlig·ens -entis *adj* careful, accurate; exacting, strict; thrifty; industrious; *(w. gen)* **1** observant of; **2** devoted to, fond of; *(w.* **ad** *or* **in** + *acc)* **1** careful in, careful to; **2** conscientious about

dīligenter *adv* carefully, diligently; thoroughly, well

dīligenti·a -ae *f* care, diligence, industry, attentiveness; economy, frugality; *(w. gen)* regard for

dī·ligō -ligĕre -lexī -lectus *tr* to love, esteem; to like; to value, appreciate

dīlōrīc·ō -āre -āvī -ātus *tr* to tear open

dīlūc·eō -ēre *intr* to be clear, be evident; *(w. dat)* to be obvious to

dī·lūcescō -lūcescĕre -luxī *intr* to get light, dawn

dīlūcidē *adv* clearly, distinctly

dīlūcid·us -a -um *adj* clear, distinct, plain, evident

dīlūcul·um -ī *n* daybreak, dawn

dīlūd·ium -(i)ī *n* intermission

dīl·uō -uĕre -uī -ūtus *tr* to wash away; to break up, separate; to dilute; to get rid of *(worries, annoyances);* to atone for; to explain

dīluvi·ēs -ēī *f* flood, deluge

dīluvi·ō -āre *tr* to flood, inundate

dīluv·ium -(i)ī *n* flood, deluge

dimach·ae -ārum *mpl* soldiers who fight either on foot or on horseback

dīmān·ō -āre *intr* to flow in different directions; *(fig)* to spread around

dīmensi·ō -ōnis *f* measurement, dimensions

dī·mētior -mētīrī -mensus sum *tr* to measure out; to count off

dīmēt·or -ārī -ātus sum *tr* to measure *or* mark off

dīmicāti·ō -ōnis *f* fight, combat, struggle; contest, rivalry

dīmic·ō -āre -āvī -ātus *intr* to contend, fight, struggle; **de capite** *(or* **de vitā)** **dimicare** to fight for one's life

dīmidi·a -ae *f* half

dīmidiāt·us -a -um *adj* half, in half

dīmidi·us -a -um *adj* half; broken (in two); **dimidius patrum, dimidius plebis** half patrician, half plebeian; **parte dimidiā auctus** twice as large **‖** *n* half; **dimidio longior** twice as long; **dimidium militum quam** half as many soldiers as

dīmi·nuō -nuĕre -nuī -nūtus *tr* to shatter

dīmissi·ō -ōnis *f* dismissal; sending out; *(mil)* discharge

dī·mittō -mittĕre -mīsī -missus *tr* to send away, let go; to dismiss *(an assembly);* to spread; to set free, release; to let off; to scatter, distribute; to let go of, let loose; to let go, let slip, forgo *(a chance, an opportunity);* to divorce *(a wife); (fin)* to settle *(a debt); (fin)* to pay off *(a creditor); (mil)* to discharge *(a soldier),* disband *(an army)*

dimminuō *see* **dīminu·ō**

dī·moveō -movēre -mōvī -mōtus *tr* to move apart, part, separate; to disperse, scatter; to dismiss; to lure away

Dindymēn·ē -ēs *f* Cybele *(named after Dindymus, a mountain in Phrygia sacred to Cybele)*

Dindym·us *or* **Dindym·os -ī** *m* Mt. Dindymus

dīnoscō *see* **dignosco**

dīnumerāti·ō -ōnis *f* enumeration, counting up

dīnumer·ō -āre -āvī -ātus *tr* to enumerate, count up; to count out, pay

diōbolār·is -is -e *adj* costing two obols *(about 2¢)*

Diodot·us -ī *m* Stoic philosopher and tutor of Cicero *(d. 59 B.C.)*

dioecēs·is -is *or* **-eōs** *f* district; governor's jurisdiction

dioecēt·ēs -ae *m* treasurer; secretary of revenue

Diogen·ēs -is *m* Ionic philosopher *(5th cent. B.C.)* **‖** Cynic philosopher from Sinope, in Pontus *(412?–323 B.C.)*

Diomēd·ēs -is *m* son of Tydeus and king of Argos, and hero at Troy

Diō(n) -ōnis *m* Dion *(brother-in-law of the elder Dionysius, the tyrant of Syracuse, and a pupil and friend of Plato's)*

Diōn·ē -ēs *or* **Diōn·a -ae** *f* mother of Venus

Dionȳsi·a -ōrum *npl* festival of Dionysus

Dionȳs·ius -(i)ī *m* tyrant of Syracuse *(430–367 B.C.)* **‖** Dionysius the Younger *(397–330? B.C.)*

Dionȳs·us *or* **Dionȳs·os -ī** *m* Greek god of wine and fertility, equated with Bacchus

diōt·a -ae *f* two-handled wine jar

Dīphil·us -ī *m* Greek comic writer of Sinope, used by Plautus

diplōm·a -atis *n* travel pass *(to travel free on the Imperial post);* certificate

dips·as -adis *f* poisonous snake whose bite provokes thirst

Dipyl·on -ī *n* N.W. gate at Athens

dipyr·us -a -um *adj* twice burned

Dīr·a -ae *f* Fury *(goddess of revenge)*

dīr·ae -ārum *fpl* bad omens; curses

Dircae·us -a -um *adj* Dircean, Boeotian; **cycnus Dircaeus** Boeotian swan *(Pindar, lyric poet from Boeotia)*

Dirc·ē -ēs *f* famous spring in Boeotia

dīrectē *adv* **(der-)** in a straight line

dīrectō *adv* **(dēr-)** in a straight line; directly, without intervening procedures

dīrect·us *or* **dērect·us -a -um** *pp of* **dirigo**

‖ *adj* straight, direct; level; upright, vertical, perpendicular; *(fig)* direct, straightforward, simple; **in directum** *(or* **per directum)** in a straight line; **in directo** on a straight stretch *(of road)*
diremptus *pp of* **dirimo**
dirempt·us -ūs *m* **separation**
dīrepti·ō -ōnis *f* plundering, pillaging ‖ *fpl* acts of pillage; a scramble for a share
dīrept·or -ōris *m* plunderer
dīreptus *pp of* **diripio**
dirib·eō -ēre -uī -itus *tr* to sort *(votes taken out of the ballot box)*
diribiti·ō -ōnis *f* sorting *(of votes)*
diribit·or -ōris *m* sorter (of ballots)
diribitōr·ium -iī *n* sorting room
dīrigō dīrigĕre dīrexī dīrectus *tr* **(dē-)** to direct; to put in order, arrange, line up, straighten out; to level *(a surface);* to construct *(roads, tunnels, along a given line); (mil)* to deploy
dir·imō -imĕre -ēmī -emptus *tr* to take apart; to part, separate, divide; to break off, disturb, interrupt; to separate, dissolve; to put off, delay; to break off, end, bring to an end; to nullify, bring to naught
dī·ripiō -ripĕre -ripuī -reptus *tr* to tear apart, tear to pieces; to lay waste, pillage; to loot, rob; to steal; to snatch away; to whip out *(sword);* to run after, compete for the company of *(person)*
dīrit·ās -ātis *f* frightfulness; dire event
dī·rumpō -rumpĕre -rūpī -ruptus *tr* to break to pieces, smash, shatter; to break off *(friendship);* to sever *(ties)* ‖ *pass* to burst *(w. laughter, envy, etc.)*
dīru·ō -ĕre -ī -tus *tr* to pull apart, demolish, destroy, overthrow; to scatter; to bankrupt; *(mil)* to break up *(enemy formation)*
dīr·us -a -um *adj* dire, awful, fearful; ominous, ill-omened; dreadful; cruel, relentless, fierce; **temporibus diris** in the reign of terror; **venena dira** deadly poisons
dīs dītis *adj* rich; fertile; generous; expensive; *(w. abl)* abounding in ‖ **Dis** *m* Pluto *(king of the lower world)*
dis- *pref* (unchanged before initial **c p t s; dī-** before **b d g l m n r,** consonantal **u** and sometimes **i; dif-** before **f; dir-** *(by rotacism)* before vowels and **h** *(with rare exceptions);* it commonly signifies **1** separation or dispersion or both: **diffugere** to flee away; **discedere** to draw apart; **2** the reversal of a previous process: **disjungere** to disunite, separate; **3** a negative sense: **displicere** to displease, not please
dis·cēdo -cēdĕre -cessī -cessum *intr* to go away, depart; to separate, be severed; to disperse, be dissipated, disappear; to split open, come apart; *(of wife)* to separate *(from husband);* to deviate, swerve; to pass away, cease; *(mil)* to march off, break camp; *(mil)* to come off *(victorious, etc.); (w. abl)* **1** to forsake *(e.g., friends);* **2** to deviate from, swerve from; *(w.* **ex** *or* **de** *+ abl)* to depart from; *(w.* **ad)** to depart for; *(w.* **in** *+ acc)* to vote for; **discedere in Catonis sententiam** to vote for Cato's proposal; **ut discedatur ab** apart from
disc·ens -entis *m* learner, apprentice, trainee
disceptāti·ō -ōnis *f* dispute, difference of opinion; discussion, debate
disceptāt·or -ōris *m,* **disceptātr·ix -īcis** *f* arbitrator
discept·ō -āre -āvī -ātus *tr* to debate, dispute, discuss, treat; to decide, settle ‖ *intr* to act as judge, arbitrate; to argue; to be at stake
dis·cernō -cernĕre -crēvī -crētus *tr* to separate, mark off, divide; to keep apart; to distinguish between; to discern, make out
discerp·ō -ĕre -sī -tus *tr* to mangle, mutilate; *(fig)* to tear apart *(with words, arguments)*
discessi·ō -ōnis *f* separation, division; divorce; *(in the Senate)* division, formal vote; **discessio sine ulla varietate** unanimous vote
discess·us -ūs *m* separation, parting; departure; banishment; marching off
discid·ium -(i)ī *n* parting; discord, disagreement; divorce
discīd·ō -ĕre -ī *tr* to cut up
discinct·us -a -um *pp of* **discingo** ‖ *adj* without a belt; dissolute, loose; effeminate, voluptuous
di·scindō -scindĕre -scĭdī -scissus *tr* to tear apart, tear open, rend; **amicitias discindere** to break off the ties of friendship
discin·gō -gĕre -xī -ctus *tr* to take off; to loosen; to disarm
disciplīn·a -ae *f* instruction, training, teaching, education; learning, knowledge, science; discipline, branch of study; custom, habit; system; **militaris disciplina** basic training; **reipublicae disciplina** statesmanship
discipul·a -ae *f* pupil *(female)*
discipul·us -ī *m* pupil; disciple, follower
discissus *pp of* **discindo**
disclū·dō -dĕre -sī -sus *tr* to keep apart, shut off; to seal up, seal off; to assign
discō discĕre didĭcī *tr* to learn; to get to know, become acquainted with; to be told *(e.g., the truth); (w. inf)* to learn how to
discobol·us -ī *m* discus-thrower
discol·or -ōris *adj* of a different color; of different colors; *(w. dat)* different from

discondūc·ō -ĕre *intr* to be unprofitable, be prejudicial

disconven·iō -īre *intr* to disagree; to be inconsistent ‖ *v impers* there is disagreement

discordābil·is -is -e *adj* discordant, disagreeing

discordi·a -ae *f* discord, dissension, disagreement; mutiny

discordiōs·us -a -um *adj* prone to discord, mutinous

discord·ō -āre *intr* to quarrel, disagree; *(w. dat or* **ab)** **1** to be be out of harmony with; **2** to be opposed to

discor·s -dis *adj* discordant; at variance; contradictory, inconsistent; warring *(winds, etc.); (w. abl)* inconsistent with, different from

discrepanti·a -ae *f* discrepancy, dissimilarity, difference

discrepāti·ō -ōnis *f* disagreement, dispute

discrepit·ō -āre *intr* to be completely different

discrep·ō -āre -āvī *or* **-uī** *intr* to be different in sound, sound different; to be out of tune; to disagree; to be different, vary; to be inconsistent; to be disputed; *(w. dat or abl or* **ab** *or* **cum)** **1** to disagree with; **2** to be different from; **3** to be inconsistent with ‖ *v impers* there is a difference of opinion, it is a matter of dispute, it is undecided

discrī·bō -bĕre -psī -ptus *tr* to distribute, divide; to classify; to assign, apportion; *(w.* **in** *+ acc)* to distribute among, divide among

discrīm·en -inis *n* dividing line; interval, intervening space, division, distance, separation; discrimination, difference, distinction; critical moment, turning point; crisis, jeopardy, peril, danger, risk; decision, determination; decisive battle; difference in pitch; **res in discrimine est** the situation is at a critical stage; **parvum discrimen leti** narrow escape from death

discrīmin·ō -āre -āvī -ātus *tr* to divide, separate; to apportion

discriptē *adv* in an orderly way, lucidly, distinctly

discripti·ō -ōnis *f* distribution, classification

discript·us -a -um *pp of* **discribo** ‖ *adj* well-arranged, sorted, classified

discruci·ō -āre -āvī -ātus *tr* to torture; to distress, torment

discumbō discumbĕre discubuī discubitum *intr (of several)* to take their places at the table; *(of several)* to go to bed

discup·iō -ĕre *tr (coll)* to want badly; *(w. inf) (coll)* to be dying to

dis·currō -currĕre -cucurri *or* **-currī -cursum** *intr* to run in different directions, scamper about, run up and down, dash around

discurs·us -ūs *m* running up and down, running about; *(mil)* pincer movement

disc·us -ī *m* discus

discu·tiō -tĕre -ssī -ssus *tr* to knock apart; to smash to pieces, shatter; to shake off; to break up, disperse *(an assembly, gathering);* to dispel *(danger, sleep);* to frustrate, bring to naught; to suppress, destroy

disertē *adv* eloquently, clearly

disertim *adv* clearly, distinctly

disert·us -a -um *adj* fluent, eloquent; clear, articulate

disject·ō -āre -āvī -ātus *tr* to toss about

disject·us -a -um *pp of* **disjicio** ‖ *adj* scattered; dilapidated

disject·us -ūs *m* scattering

dis·jiciō -jicĕre -jēcī -jectus *tr* to drive apart, scatter; to tear to pieces; to ruin; to frustrate, wreck; *(mil)* to break up *(enemy formation)*

di(s)junctē *adv* in separate words, separately

di(s)juncti·ō -ōnis *f* separation, alienation; divination; variation; dilemma; *(rhet)* asyndeton *(succession of phrases or clauses without conjunction)*

di(s)junct·us -a -um *adj* separate, distinct; distant, remote; disjointed, disconnected, incoherent; logically opposed ‖ *npl* opposites

di(s)jun·gō -gĕre -xī -ctus *tr* to unyoke; to sever, divide, part, remove; to separate; to alienate

dispālesc·ō -ĕre *intr* to be spread abroad, get around

dispāl·or -ārī -ātus sum *intr* to wander around; to straggle, stray off

dis·pandō -pandĕre — -pansus *tr* **(-pen-)** to stretch out, extend; to expand

dis·pār -paris *adj* different, unlike; unequal; ill-matched

disparāt·us -a -um *adj* separate, distinct; negatively opposite *(e.g.,* **sapere et non sapere** to be wise and not to be wise)

disparil·is -is -e *adj* dissimilar

dispariliter *adv* differently

dispar·ō -āre -āvī -ātus *tr* to separate; to make different ‖ *intr* to be different

dispartiō, dispartior *see* **dispertio**

dispectus *pp of* **dispicio**

dis·pellō -pellĕre -pulī -pulsus *tr* to dispel, drive away; to disperse

dispend·ium -(i)ī *n* expense, cost; loss *(as result of a transaction)*

dispendō *see* **dispando**

dis·pennō -pennĕre — -pessus *tr* to stretch out, extend; to expand

dispensāti·ō -ōnis *f* weighing out, doling out; management, superintendence, administration; office of treasurer

dispensāt·or -ōris *m* household manager, chief butler; cashier; treasurer

dispens·ō -āre -āvī -ātus *tr* to weigh out, pay out; to distribute, manage *(household stores);* to regulate, manage

dispercut·iō -ĕre *tr* to knock out; **cerebrum dispercutere** *(w. dat)* to knock *(s.o.'s)* brains out

disper·dō -dĕre -didī -ditus *tr* to spoil, ruin; to squander

disper·eō -īre -iī *intr* to go to ruin; to go to waste; to be undone, perish; **disperii!** *(coll)* I'm finished!; **dispeream si** *(coll)* I'll be darned if

disper·gō -gĕre -sī -sus *tr* **(-sparg-)** to scatter about, disperse; to splatter; to distribute, scatter *(e.g., men)* without organization; to spread, extend *(war, rumor, etc.)*

dispersē *adv* here and there; occasionally

dispersus *pp of* **dispergo**

dispers·us -ūs *m* dispersal

dispert·iō -īre -īvī *or* **-iī -ītus** *or* **dispert·ior -īrī -ītus sum** *tr* to distribute, divide; to assign *(e.g., gates, areas)* as posts to be guarded

dispertīti·ō -ōnis *f* distribution, sharing

dispessus *pp of* **dispando**

di·spiciō -spicĕre -spexī -spectus *tr* to see clearly, make out, distinguish, detect; to consider carefully, perceive, discover; to reflect on **||** *intr* to see clearly

displic·eō -ēre -uī -itum *intr* to be unpleasant, be displeasing; *(w. dat)* to displease; **sibi displicere** to be dissatisfied with oneself; to be in a bad mood

dis·plōdō -plōdĕre — -plōsus *tr & intr* to burst apart

dis·pōnō -pōnĕre -posuī -positus *tr* to place here and there; to distribute; to arrange, set in order; to station, post, assign; to adjust; to dispose; **diem disponere** to arrange the day's schedule

dispositē *adv* orderly, methodically

dispositi·ō -ōnis *f* orderly arrangement, development *(of a theme)*

dispositūr·a -ae *f* order, arrangement

disposit·us -a -um *pp of* **dispono || adj** well-arranged; methodical, orderly

disposit·us -ūs *m* order, arrangement

dispud·et -ēre -uit *v impers (w. inf)* it's a great shame to

dispulsus *pp of* **dispello**

dispun·gō -gĕre -xī -ctus *tr* to check, balance, audit *(accounts)*

disputāti·ō -ōnis *f* argument, discussion, debate

disputāt·or -ōris *m* disputant

disput·ō -āre -āvī -ātus *tr* to dispute, discuss; *(com)* to estimate; to examine, treat, explain **||** *intr* to argue, argue one's case

disquīr·ō -ĕre *tr* to examine closely

disquīsīti·ō -ōnis *f* inquiry, investigation

disrumpō *see* **dirumpo**

dissaep·iō -īre -sī -tus *tr* to separate, wall off, fence off

dissaept·um -ī *n* partition, barrier

dissāvi·or *or* **dissuāvi·or -ārī** *tr* to kiss passionately

dissec·ō -āre -uī -tus *tr* to cut up, dissect

dissēmin·ō -āre -āvī -ātus *tr* to disseminate

dissensi·ō -ōnis *f* difference of opinion, disagreement; dissension; conflict, incompatibility

dissens·us -ūs *m* dissension, discord

dissentāne·us -a -um *adj* disagreeing, dissenting; conflicting; contrary

dissen·tiō -tīre -sī -sum *intr* to dissent, disagree; to differ, be in conflict, be inconsistent; *(w. dat or* **ab** *or* **cum)** to differ with; *(w.* **ab)** to differ from, be opposed to

disserēn·at -āre -āvit *v impers* it is clearing up

dis·serō -serĕre -sēvī -situs *tr* to scatter; to sow here and there; to stick in the ground at intervals

disser·ō -ĕre -uī -tus *tr* to discuss; to examine; to arrange **||** *intr (w.* **de** *+ abl)* to discuss

disserp·ō -ĕre *intr* to creep around; to spread gradually

disserti·ō -ōnis *f* severance, a disconnecting

dissert·ō -āre -āvī -ātus *tr* to discuss

dissertus *pp of* **dissero** *(to discuss)*

dis·sideō -sidēre -sēdī *intr* to be distant, be remote; to live far apart; to disagree; to differ, be unlike; *(of garment)* to be on crooked; *(w.* **ab** *or* **cum)** to disagree with

dissignāti·ō -ōnis *f* arrangement

dissignāt·or -ōris *m* **(dēsig-)** master of ceremonies; usher *(at theater);* undertaker, mortician

dissign·ō -āre -āvī -ātus *tr* to regulate; to arrange; to contrive

dissil·iō -īre -uī *intr* to fly apart, burst, split, break up; to be dissolved

dissimil·is -is -e *adj* dissimilar, different; *(w. gen or dat or w.* **atque** *or* **ac)** different from

dissimiliter *adv* differently

dissimilitūd·ō -inis *f* difference

dissimulābiliter *adv* furtively

dissimulanter *adv* secretly, slyly

dissimulanti·a -ae *f* faking, hiding

dissimulāti·ō -ōnis *f* dissimulation; Socratic irony; pretended ignorance

dissimulāt·or -ōris *m* dissembler, faker

dissimul·ō -āre -āvī -ātus *tr* to conceal, disguise; to keep secret; to pretend not to see, ignore

dissipābil·is -is -e *adj* **(dissu-)** that may be dissipated

dissipāti·ō -ōnis *f* **(dissu-)** dispersal, dissipation; distribution
dissip·ō *or* **dissup·ō -āre -āvī -ātus** *tr* to scatter, disperse; to demolish, overthrow; to squander, dissipate; to circulate, spread; to drive away *(worries); (mil)* to break up *(enemy formation)*
dissitus *pp of* **dissero** *(to scatter)*
dissociābil·is -is -e *adj* incompatible; irreconcilable
dissociāti·ō -ōnis *f* separation
dissoci·ō -āre -āvī -ātus *tr* to dissociate, separate; to ostracize; to set at variance; to divide into factions; to detach
dissolūbil·is -is -e *adj* dissoluble, separable
dissolūtē *adv* disconnectedly, loosely; carelessly
dissolūti·ō -ōnis *f* dissolution, breakup; abolition; destruction; refutation; looseness, dissoluteness; *(rhet)* asyndeton
dissolūt·us -a -um *adj* disconnected, loose; careless, negligent, remiss; loose, dissolute **‖** *n (rhet)* asyndeton
dissol·vō -vĕre -vī -ūtus *tr* to dissolve, melt; to dismantle; to disband; to make to disappear; to free, release; to loosen, undo; to solve *(problem);* to break up; to pay *(debt);* to refute; to weaken, wear out; to put an end to, do away with; to refute *(argument);* **animam dissolvere** to die; **legem dissolvere** to rescind a law; **poenam dissolvere** to pay the penalty
disson·us -a -um *adj* dissonant, discordant, jarring, confused *(sounds); (w. abl)* differing from, different from
dissor·s -tis *adj* having a different fate; *(w.* **ab)** unshared by
dissuā·deō -dēre -sī -sus *tr* to advise against; to dissuade **‖** *intr* to argue against an idea
dissuāsi·ō -ōnis *f* dissuasion; *(w. gen)* opposition to, objection to
dissuās·or -ōris *m* opponent
dissuāvior *see* **dissavior**
dissult·ō -āre *intr* to fly apart, burst
dissu·ō -ĕre -uī -tus *tr* to take the stitches out of, undo
dissupō *see* **dissipo**
distaed·et -ēre *v impers (w. gen)* it makes *(one)* tired of; **me distaedet loqui** I'm sick and tired of talking
distanti·a -ae *f* distance, remoteness; difference, diversity
disten·dō *or* **disten·nō -dĕre -dī -tus** *tr* to stretch apart, stretch out; to distend; to cause to swell *or* bulge; to fill to capacity; to distract; to perplex **‖** *pass* to swell; to bulge
distent·us -a -um *pp of* **distendo ‖** *adj* distended **‖** *pp of* **distineo ‖** *adj* busy, occupied, distracted
distermin·ō -āre -āvī -ātus *tr* to serve as a boundary between, separate by a boundary, divide, limit
distich·on -ī *n (pros)* couplet
distinctē *adv* distinctly, clearly
distincti·ō -ōnis *f* distinction, differentiation, discrimination; distinctive quality *(of a thing);* difference; punctuation mark; division, paragraphing
distinct·us -a -um *pp of* **distinguo ‖** *adj* distinct, separate; studded, adorned; varied, diversified; lucid *(speaker);* eminent
distinct·us -ūs *m* distinction, difference
dis·tineō -tinēre -tinuī -tentus *tr* to keep apart, separate; to detain, hold back, hinder; to employ, engage; to divert; to put off, delay; to keep divided; to stand in the way of; to distract
distin·guō -guĕre -xī -ctus *tr* to mark off; to distinguish; to specify; to set off *(w. colors, gold, etc.);* to punctuate
dist·ō -āre *intr* to stand apart, be separate, be distant; to differ; *(w. dat or* **ab)** to differ from; *(w. abl)* to be separated by *(a period of time)* **‖** *v impers* there is a difference, it makes a difference
distor·queō -quēre -sī -tus *tr* to twist, distort; to curl *(lips);* to roll *(eyes);* **cogitationem distorquere** to rack one's brains
distorti·ō -ōnis *f* twisting; contortion
distort·us -a -um *pp of* **distorqueo ‖** *adj* distorted, misshapen, deformed; perverse
distracti·ō -ōnis *f* pulling apart; dividing; discord, dissension
distract·us -a -um *adj* severed; rarefied; distracted, perplexed
distra·hō -hĕre -xī -ctus *tr* to pull *or* drag apart, separate forcibly; to tear away, drag away, remove; to distract; to sever; to alienate; to prevent, frustrate; to end, settle *(e.g., disputes);* to sell retail; to sell *(land)* in lots
distrib·uō -uĕre -uī -ūtus *tr* to distribute
distribūtē *adv* methodically
distribūti·ō -ōnis *f* distribution, apportionment, division
district·us -a -um *adj* drawn in opposite directions; distracted; busy, engaged
di·stringō -stringĕre -strinxī -strictus *tr* to draw apart; to distract, draw attention to
distrunc·ō -āre -āvī -ātus *tr* to cut in two, hack apart
distulī *perf of* **differo**
disturbāti·ō -ōnis *f* demolition
disturb·ō -āre *tr* to throw into confusion; to demolish; to break up *(a marriage);* to frustrate
dītesc·ō -ĕre *intr* to get rich
dīthyrambic·us -a -um *adj (pros)* dithyrambic

dithyramb·us -ī *m* dithyramb *(song in honor of Bacchus)*

dīti·ae -ārum *fpl* riches

dīt·ō -āre -āvī -ātus *tr* to enrich, make rich ‖ *pass* to get rich

diū *adv* by day, in the daytime; long, for a long time; in a long time; **diu noctuque** by day and by night; **jam diu** this long; **satis diu** long enough

diurn·us -a -um *adj* of the day, by day, day-, daytime; daily, of each day; day's, of one day; **merum diurnum** daytime drinking ‖ *n* account book ‖ *npl* record, journal, diary

dī·us *or* **dīv·us -a -um** *adj* godlike, divine; divinely inspired; having the brightness of day

diūtīnē *adv* for a long time

diūtīn·us -a -um *adj* long, lasting, long-lasting

diūtissimē *adv* for a very long time; longest; **jam diutissime** long long ago

diūtius *adv* longer, still longer; **paulum diutius** a little too long

diūturnit·ās -ātis *f* length of time, long duration; durability

diūturn·us -a -um *adj* long, long-lasting; chronic

dīv·a -ae *f* goddess

dīvāric·ō -āre -āvī -ātus *tr* to stretch out, spread ‖ *pass* to stand *or* sit with legs apart

dī·vellō -vellĕre -vellī -vulsus *or* **-volsus** *tr* to tear apart; to tear away; to untie; to wrest, remove, separate; to estrange

dīvend·ō -ĕre -idī -itus *tr* to sell retail

dīverber·ō -āre -āvī -ātus *tr* to split; to batter; to zip through, fly through

diverb·ium -(i)ī *n (theat)* dialogue

dīversē *adv* **(-vor-)** in different directions, differently

dīversit·ās -ātis *f* distance; diversity; difference; difference of opinion; difference of method; direct opposite; inconsistency; *(w. gen or* **inter** + *acc)* difference between

dīvers·us -a -um *adj* **(-vor-)** in different directions; *(of roads)* running *or* leading in different directions; moving from opposite directions, converging; facing *or* turned in two *(or more)* directions; *(w.* **ab**) leading away from; situated at a distance from each other, apart, separate; distant, remote; opposite; of the opposing side *(in war)*, hostile; unsettled, irresolute; dissimilar, distinct; inconsistent; different *(from one another in quality, quantity, purpose, degree, effect, etc.); (w. dat or gen or* **ab** *or* **quam)** different from, the reverse of ‖ *mpl* individuals ‖ *n* opposite direction, different quarter, opposite side, opposite view; **ex diverso** from a different direction; on opposite sides; from *or* on the opposing side; in contrast, on the other hand; on the contrary; from a different point of view, in turn; in reverse, vice versa; **in diversum** in a different direction; for a different reason; to a different effect; vice versa; **per diversum** crosswise ‖ *npl* different parts; **in diversa** in different directions; **per diversa** for different reasons

dīver·tō -tĕre -tī -sum *intr* **(-vor-)** to go different ways; to turn off; to stop off, stay

dīv·es -itis *adj* rich; costly; precious, sumptuous; plentiful; *(w. gen or abl)* rich in, abounding in

dīvex·ō -āre -āvī -ātus *tr* to ravage; to harass

dīvidi·a -ae *f* worry, trouble; nuisance; dissension, antagonism

dī·vidō -vidĕre -vīsī -vīsus *tr* to divide; to distribute, share; to break up, destroy; to arrange, apportion; to separate, distinguish; to segregate, keep apart; to accompany *(songs with music);* **dimidium dividere** to go halves *(w. s.o.);* **sententiam dividere** to break down a proposal *(so as to vote on each part separately)*

dīvidu·us -a -um *adj* divisible; divided, separated; forked

dīvīnāti·ō -ōnis *f* clairvoyance; forecasting, predicting, divination; *(leg)* selection of the most suitable prosecutor

dīvīnē *adv* through divine power; prophetically; divinely, gorgeously

dīvīnit·ās -ātis *f* divinity, godhead; prophetic power, clairvoyance; excellence

dīvīnitus *adv* from heaven, from god; providentially; prophetically; divinely, in a godlike manner; excellently

dīvīn·ō -āre -āvī -ātus *tr* to divine, predict; to guess

dīvīn·us -a -um *adj* divine, heavenly; divinely inspired, prophetic; godlike; gorgeous, excellent; **divinum jus** natural law; **divinum jus et humanum** natural and positive law; **divinum scelus** sacrilege; **rem divinam facere** to worship; to sacrifice; **res divina** rite; **res divinae** religious affairs, religion; celestial matters ‖ *m* prophet ‖ *npl* divine matters; religious duties; **divina humanaque** things divine and human, the whole world; **divina humanaque agere** to perform religious and secular duties

dīvīsi·ō -ōnis *f* division, distribution

dīvīs·or -ōris *m* distributor; agent hired by a candidate to give out bribes

dīvīs·us -a -um *pp of* **divido** ‖ *adj* separate, distinct

dīvīs·us -ūs *m* division, distribution; **facilis divisui** easily divided

dīviti·ae -ārum *fpl* riches; richness *(of soil);* costly things
dīvolg- = divulg-
dīvor- = diver-
dīvort·ium -(i)ī *n* divorce; fork *(of road or river);* **divortium facere cum** to divorce *(a woman)*
dīvulgāt·us -a -um *adj* common, widespread
dīvulg·ō -āre -āvī -ātus *tr* to divulge, spread among the people; to publish *(book);* to publicize, advertise
dīvulsus *pp of* **divello**
dīv·us *or* **dī·us -a -um** *adj* divine, deified ‖ *m* god, deity; title applied to dead emperors ‖ *n* sky; the open; **sub divo** out in the open; **sub divum rapere** to bring out into the open
dō dare dědī datus (danit = dat; danunt = dant; dane = dasne; duim, duis, duit = dem, dēs det; *(in Plautus:* **dan = dasne; datin = datisne; dabin = dabisne; duas = des)** *tr* to give; to offer, dedicate; to pay out *(money);* to confer; to permit, grant; to give up, hand over; to communicate, tell; to ascribe, impute, assign; to cause, make; to furnish, afford, present; to admit; to administer *(medicine);* to utter, give expression to, announce; **amplexus dare** to embrace; **comoediam dare** to present a comedy; **concilium** *(or* **contionem) dare** to allow a private person to address the assembly; **conspectum dare** to make visible; **damnum dare** to cause damage; **fabulam dare** to present a play; **jus** *(or* **jura) dare** to give laws, give a constitution, administer justice; **leto** *(or* **morti) dare** to send *(s.o.)* to *(his)* death; **legem dare** to enact a law; **litteras dare** to mail a letter; **locum dare** *(w. dat)* to make way for; **manūs dare** to surrender; **nomen dare** to enlist; **operam dare** *(w. dat)* to pay attention to, devote attention to, look out for; **palam dare** to make clear; **poenam** *(or* **poenas** *or* **supplicium) dare** to pay the penalty; **satis dare** *(w. dat)* to give satisfaction to, satisfy; **Senatum dare** to allow a private person to address the Senate; **spatium dare** to make room; **terga dare** to take to one's heels; **velum dare** to set sail; **veniam dare** to grant pardon; **venum dare** to put up for sale ‖ *refl* to present oneself; to plunge, rush; **se dare militem** *(or* **militiae)** to enlist in the service
doc·eō -ēre -uī -tus *tr* to teach, instruct; to give instructions to; to tell, inform *(s.o. of a fact); (w. double acc)* to teach *(s.o. s.th.);* **fabulam docere** to produce a play, put on a play
dochm·ius -iī *m (pros)* dochmiac foot *(consisting of iamb and cretic)* (◡ ——◡ —)
docil·is -is -e *adj* easily taught, teachable; ready to listen
docilit·ās -ātis *f* aptitude for learning
doctē *adv* skillfully; cleverly
doct·or -ōris *m* teacher
doctrīn·a -ae *f* teaching, instruction, education, training; lesson; erudition, learning; science
doct·us -a -um *pp of* **doceo** ‖ *adj* learned, skilled, experienced, trained; clever, shrewd; *(w. abl or ad or* **in** *+ abl)* skilled in, clever at
document·um -ī *or* **docum·en -inis** *n* **(doci-)** example, model, pattern; object lesson, warning; proof, evidence
Dōdōn·a -ae *f* town in Epirus, famous for the oracular oak tree sacred to Jupiter
Dōdōnae·us -a -um *adj* of Dodona
Dōdōn·is -idis *adj (fem only)* of Dodona
dodr·ans -antis *m* three-fourths; **heres ex dodrante** heir to three-fourths of an estate
dōdrantāri·us -a -um *adj* **tabulae dondrantariae** account books connected with the Valerian Law of 86 B.C., which reduced debts by three-fourths
dogm·a -atis *n* doctrine, tenet
Dolabell·a -ae *m* Roman family name *(cognomen)* in the *gens Cornelia, esp.* Publius Cornelius Dolabella, Cicero's son-in-law *(d. 43 B.C.)*
dolābr·a -ae *f* pickax, mattock
dol·ens -entis *adj* painful, smarting; distressing; grieving
dolenter *adv* painfully; with sorrow
dol·eō -ēre -uī -itus *tr* to give pain to, hurt ‖ *intr* to feel pain; to hurt, be sore, ache, smart; to grieve, be sorry, be hurt; take offense; *(w. dat)* to give pain to, afflict; **caput mihi dolet** I have a headache
dōliār·is -is -e *adj (coll)* fat, tubby
dōliol·um -ī *n* small barrel
dōl·ium -iī *n* large earthenware barrel
dol·ō -āre -āvī -ātus *tr* to chop; to beat up, drub; *(fig)* to hack out *(e.g., a poem)*
dol·ō -ōnis *m* pike *(having a wooden shaft and a short iron point);* topsail
Dol·ōn -ōnis *m* Dolon *(Trojan spy)*
Dolop·es -um *mpl* tribe of Thessaly
dol·or -ōris *m* pain, ache; grief, distress; indignation, resentment, chagrin; pathos; object of grief; **capitis dolor** headache; **dentium dolor** toothache; **esse dolori** *(w. dat)* to be a cause of grief *or* resentment to
dolōsē *adv* shrewdly, slyly
dolōs·us -a -um *adj* wily, cunning
dol·us -ī *m* trick; deceit, cunning; **dolus malus** *(leg)* malice aforethought, fraud
domābil·is -is -e *adj* able to be tamed
domesticātim *adv* at home, by use of one's domestics
domestic·us -a -um *adj* of the house *or*

home; domestic, household; familiar, private, personal; native, of one's own country; **bellum domesticum** civil war ‖ *mpl* members of the household, one's staff
domī *see* **domus**
domicēn·ium -(i)ī *n* a meal at home
domicil·ium -(i)ī *n* residence, home
domin·a -ae *or* **domn·a -ae** *f* lady of the house; mistress, owner; lady; sweetheart; wife; *(as a title of courtesy)* Ma'am
domin·ans -antis *adj* ruling, dominant; **nomen dominans** word in its literal sense, normal word ‖ *m* ruler
domināti·ō -ōnis *f* mastery; tyranny, despotism; dominion, kingdom ‖ *fpl* control; supremacy; rulers
dominăt·or -ōris *m* arbitrary ruler, lord
dominātr·ix -īcis *f* ruler, mistress
dominăt·us -ūs *m* absolute rule, sovereignty; ownership; mastery
dominic·us -a -um *adj* master's; mistress's; owner's; belonging to the emperor ‖ **Dominic·a -ae** *f (eccl)* the Lord's day, Sunday
domin·ium -(i)ī *n* rule, dominion; ownership; banquet, feast
domin·or -ārī -ātus sum *intr* to be master, be lord, have dominion; to domineer; *(w.* **in** *+ acc or abl)* to lord it over, dominate
domin·us -ī *m* owner, proprietor; master, ruler, lord; tyrant; commander; lover; manager *(of a troupe)*; *(as a courtesy title)* Sir; *(as imperial title)* His Imperial Highness; **convivii dominus** host ‖ **Dominus** *(eccl)* the Lord
domiport·a -ae *f* house-carrier *(snail)*
Domitiān·us -ī *m* Domitian *(Titus Flavius Domitianus, son of Vespasian and Roman emperor, 81–96 A.D.)*
domit·ō -āre -āvī *tr* to train, break in
domit·or -ōris *m* tamer; conqueror
domitr·ix -īcis *f* tamer *(female)*
domit·us -ūs *m* taming
domīt·us -a -um *adj* house-bound, kept at home
dom·ō -āre -uī -itus *tr* to tame, break in; to domesticate; to master, subdue, vanquish, conquer
dom·us -ūs *or* **-ī** *(dat:* **domō** *or* **domuī**; *abl* **domō** *or* **domū**; *loc:* **domī,** *rarely* **domō** *or* **domuī**; *gen pl:* **domōrum** *or* **domuum)** *f* house, home; mansion, palace; family, household; school *(of philosophers)*; building *(of any sort)*; seat *(an an activity)*; **domi** at home; by one's own resources; **domi militiaeque** at home and in the field; in peace and in war; **domi tuae** at your home; **domo** from home; from the house; from one's own resources; **domum** *(to one's)* home; *(coll)* into one's pocket
dōnābil·is -is -e *adj* worthy of a gift
dōnār·ium -(i)ī *n* gift repository of a temple; sanctuary; altar; votive offering
dōnāti·ō -ōnis *f* donation
dōnātīv·um -ī *n (mil)* bonus
dōnec *(also* **dōnicum)** *conj* while; as long as; until
dōn·ō -āre -āvī -ātus *tr* to present, grant; to condone, excuse; to forgive, let off; to give up, sacrifice; **aliquem civitate donare** to present s.o. with citizenship; **civitatem alicui donare** to bestow citizenship on s.o.
dōn·um -ī *n* gift, present; votive offering, sacrifice; **ultima dona** funeral rites, obsequies
dorc·as -adis *f* gazelle
Dōr·ēs *or* **Dōr·īs -um** *mpl* Dorians *(one of the four Hellenic tribes, inhabiting the Peloponnese in the classical period; also, the inhabitants of Doris in N. Greece)*
Dōricē *adv* in the Dorian dialect
Dōric·us -a -um *adj* Doric ‖ *mpl* the Dorians
Dōr·is -idis *or* **-idos** *adj (fem only)* Dorian, Doric ‖ *f* district in N. Greece ‖ the S.W. tip of Caria with its offshore islands ‖ a sea-goddess, wife of Nereus and mother of fifty sea nymphs
Dōri·us -a -um *adj* Dorian
dorm·iō -īre -īvī *or* **-iī -ītum** *intr* to sleep; to fall asleep; to be idle, be unconcerned
dormītāt·or -ōris *m* night-prowler
dormīt·ō -āre -āvī *intr* to be sleepy, be drowsy; to nod, fall asleep
dormīt·or -ōris *m* sleeper
dormītōri·us -a -um *adj* for sleeping; **cubiculum dormitorium** bedroom
dors·um -ī *n* back; ridge; reef
doryphor·os *or* **doryphor·us -ī** *m* spearman
dōs dōtis *f* dowry; endowment
Dossenn·us -ī *m* hunchback, clown *(well-known character in early Italic comedy)*
dōtāl·is -is -e *adj* of a dowry, given as a dowry, dotal
dotāt·us -a -um *adj* endowed; **dotatissimus** richly endowed
dōt·ō -āre -āvī -ātus *tr* to endow
drachm·a *or* **drachum·a -ae** *f* drachma *(Greek coin approximately the value of a denarius, c. $1)*
drachumiss·ō -āre *intr* to work for a drachma a day
drac·ō -ōnis *m* dragon; huge serpent ‖ **Draco** Draco *(Athenian lawgiver, notorious for his severity, c. 621 B.C.)*; *(astr)* Dragon *(constellation)*
dracōnigen·us -a -um *adj* sprung from a dragon; **urbs draconigena** Thebes
drāpet·a -ae *m* runaway slave
drauc·us -ī *m* athlete
drom·as -adis *m* dromedary, camel
drom·os -ī *m* parade ground

drop·ax -acis *m* hair-remover

Druid·ēs -um *or* **Druid·ae -ārum** *mpl* Druids *(priests and sages of the Gauls and Britons)*

Drūsill·a -ae *f* Livia Drusilla *(second wife of Augustus and mother of Tiberius, 58 B.C.–A.D. 29)* ‖ sister of Caligula ‖ daughter of Caligula, murdered in infancy

Drūs·us -ī *m* Livius Drusus *(tribune of the people with Gaius Gracchus in 122 B.C.)* ‖ Marcus Livius Drusus *(former's son, famous orator and tribune of the people in 91 B.C.)* ‖ Nero Claudius Drusus *(son of Livia, brother of Tiberius, 38 B.C.–A.D. 9)*

dry·as -adis *f* dryad *(wood nymph)*

Dryop·ē -ēs *f* mother of Amphissus

Dryop·es -um *mpl* a people of Epirus

dubiē *adv* doubtfully; **haud dubie** undoubtedly, indubitably

dubitābil·is -is -e *adj* doubtful

dubitanter *adv* doubtingly, hesitantly

dubitāti·ō -ōnis *f* doubt, uncertainty; wavering, hesitancy; hesitation, delay; *(rhet)* pretended embarrassment *(to win over sympathy)*

dubit·ō -āre -āvī -ātus *tr* to doubt; to consider, ponder, wonder ‖ *intr* to be doubtful, be in doubt, be uncertain, be perplexed; to deliberate; to waver, hesitate, delay

dubi·us -a -um *adj* wavering, doubtful, dubious, uncertain; precarious, critical; adverse, difficult; dim *(light)*; overcast *(sky)*; indecisive *(battle)*; **haud pro dubio habere** to regard as beyond doubt; **in dubium venire** to come into question; **in dubium vocare** to call into question; **procul dubio** undoubtedly

ducāt·us -ūs *m* military leadership, command

ducēnāri·us -a -um *adj* receiving an annual salary of 200,000 sesterces *(c. $50,000)*

ducēn·ī -ae -a *adj* two hundred each

ducentēsim·a -ae *f* half-percent tax

ducent·ī -ae -a *adj* two hundred

ducentiens *adv* (**-iēs**) two hundred times

dūcō dūcĕre duxī ductus *tr* to lead, guide, direct, conduct; to command; to march; to draw, pull; to draw out, prolong; to stall *(s.o.)*; to pull at *(oars)*; to mislead, take in, fool; to draw, attract; to draw *(lots)*; to draw in, breathe in; to sip, drink; to trace; to construct, form, fashion, shape; to run, build *(a wall from one point to another)*; to drive *(vehicles)*; to assume, get *(a name)*; *(of a man)* to marry; to calculate, compute; to regard, consider, hold, account; to derive, trace *(lineage)*; to spin *(wool)*; *(of a road)* to lead, take *(s.o.)*; **ducere triumphum** to hold a triumph; **id parvi ducere** to consider it of little importance; **initium** *(or* **rationem)** **ducere** to take acccount *(of)*, pay attention *(to)*; **principium ducere** *(w.* **ab)** to start from, originate from, trace to, e.g.: **belli initium a fame ducere** to trace the beginning of the war to hunger; **uxorem ducere** *(of the groom)* to get married, take a wife

ductil·is -is -e *adj (of a river)* that is led along a course

ductim *adv* in a continuous stream

ductit·ō -āre -āvī -ātus *tr* to take home, marry *(a woman)*; to lead on, trick

duct·ō -āre -āvī -ātus *tr* to lead; to draw; to accompany, escort

duct·or -ōris *m* leader, commander, general; guide; pilot

duct·us -ūs *m* drawing, conducting; line, row; leadership, command; **aquae ductus** aqueduct; **oris ductus** facial expression

dūdum *adv* a short time ago; just now; once, formerly; **cum dudum** just as; **haud dudum** not long ago, just now; **jam dudum** for some time; **jam dudum eum exspecto** I have been waiting for him a long time; **quam dudum** how long; **ut dudum** just as

Duill·ius *or* **Duīl·ius -(i)ī** *m* Duilius *(Roman consul who won Rome's first naval victory, off Sicily, in 260 B.C.)*

duim, duis duit *see* **do**

dulcēd·ō -inis *f* sweetness; pleasantness, charm, delightfulness

dulc·escō -escĕre *intr* to become sweet

dulciāri·us -a -um *adj* **pistor dulciarius** confectioner, pastry baker

dulcicul·us -a -um *adj* rather sweet

dulcif·er -era -erum *adj* full of sweetness, sweet

dulc·is -is -e *adj* sweet; pleasant, delightful; dear, affectionate, kind

dulciter *adv* sweetly; pleasantly

dulcitūd·ō -inis *f* sweetness

dūlicē *adv* like a slave

Dūlich·ium -iī *n or* **Dūlichi·a -ae** *f* Dulichium *(island in the Ionian Sea)*

Dūlich·ius -(i)ī *m* Ulysses

dum *adv* up to now, yet, as yet; now; **age dum!** *(pl:* **agite dum!)** come now!; all right!; **nemo dum** no one (as) yet; **non dum** not yet

dum *conj* while; as long as; until; provided that, if only; **dum modo** *or* **dummodo** provided that, if only; **exspectabam dum rediret** I was waiting for him to return

dūmēt·um -ī *n* thicket, underbrush

dummodo *conj* provided that

dūmōs·us -a -um *adj* overgrown with bushes, bushy

dumtaxat *adv (with numbers)* up to, at most, not exceeding; *(with small numbers)* only, just; not less than, at least;

(limiting a statement) at any rate, at least, strictly speaking; up to a point ‖ *conj* provided that, as long as; **non dumtaxat...sed** not just...but also

dūm·us -ī *m* bush, bramble

du·o -ae -o *(dat & abl pl:* **duōbus, duābus, duōbus)** *adj* two

duodeciens *adv* **(-ciēs)** twelve times

duodecim *indecl adj* twelve

duodecim·us -a -um *adj* **(-cum-)** twelfth

duodēn·ī -ae -a *adj* twelve each, twelve, apiece; a dozen; **duodenis assibus** at 12%

duodēquadrāgēsim·us -a -um *adj* thirty-eighth

duodēquadrāgintā *indecl adj* forty-eight

duodēquinquāgēsim·us -a -um *adj* forty-eighth

duodētrīciens *adv* **(-ciēs)** twenty-eight times

duodētrīgintā *indecl adj* twenty-eight

duodēvīcēn·ī -ae -a *adj* eighteen each

duodēvīgintī *indecl adj* eighteen

duoetvīcēsimān·ī -ōrum *mpl* soldiers of the twenty-second legion

duoetvīcēsim·us -a -um *adj* **(-cens-)** twenty-second

duovirī *see* **duumviri**

dupl·a -ae *f* a double amount of money; double the price

dupl·ex -icis *adj* twofold, double; divided into two; in double rows; double, twice as big; twice as long; complex, compound; two-faced, double-dealing, false

duplicār·ius -iī *m* soldier receiving double pay

dupliciter *adv* doubly; in two ways; into two categories

duplic·ō -āre -āvī -ātus *tr* to double up, bend over; to double *(in size, length, quantity)*

dupl·us -a -um *adj* double, twice as much, twice as large ‖ *f see* **dupla** ‖ *n* double the price; **in duplum** twice the amount; **in duplum ire** to pay twice as much

dupond·ius -(i)ī *m or* **dupond·ium -(i)ī** *n* two-ass coin *(worth c. 2¢)*

dūrābil·is -is -e *adj* durable, lasting

dūracin·us -a -um *adj* having a hard berry

dūrām·en -inis *n* hardness

dūrate·us -a -um *adj* wooden

dūrē *or* **dūriter** *adv* hard, sternly, rigorously, roughly; stiffly, awkwardly

dūr·escō -escĕre -uī *intr* to grow hard, harden; to become solid

dūrit·ās -ātis *f* hardness, toughness; harshness

dūriter *see* **dure**

dūriti·a -ae *or* **dūriti·ēs -ēī** *f* hardness; austerity; strictness, harshness, rigor; oppressiveness; insensibility, callousness

dūriuscul·us -a -um *adj* somewhat hard, rather harsh

dūr·ō -āre -āvī -ātus *tr* to harden, solidify; *(fig)* to harden, inure, toughen up; to make insensible; to dull, blunt ‖ *intr* to be tough, be inured; to become hard; *(of liquids)* to become solid; to endure, last, hold out; to continue unchanged, remain; *(of food)* to keep; *(of hills)* to continue unbroken, extend

dūr·us -a -um *adj* hard; lasting; rough *(to the senses);* tough, hardy; rough, rude, uncouth; shameless, brazen; harsh, cruel; callous, insensitive; severe, oppressive; parsimonious

duum·vir *or* **duo·vir** *or* **II·vir -virī** *m* duumvir *(member of a board of two) (see* **duumvirī)**

duumvirāt·us -ūs *m* duumvirate, office of duumvir

duumvir·ī -ōrum *or* **duovir·ī** *or* **II·virī -ōrum** *mpl* two-man board; **duumviri ad aedem faciendam** two-man board for the construction of a temple; **duumviri juri dicundo** two-man board of colonial magistrates; pair of judges; **duumviri navales** two-man board to equip the navy; **duumviri perduellionis** criminal court *(to try cases of treason);* **duumviri sacrorum** two-man board in charge of the Sibylline books

dux ducis *m (f)* general; guide; leader, head, ringleader; driver *(of chariot);* captain *(of ship),* commander *(of naval force);* **dux gregis** shepherd

Dymant·is -idos *f* daughter of Dymas, Hecuba

Dym·ās -antis *m* father of Hecuba

dynam·is -is *f* store, plenty

dynast·ēs -ae *m* ruler, (Eastern) prince

Dyrr(h)ach·ium -(i)ī *n* Adriatic port in Illyria, serving as landing place for those sailing from Italy to Greece *(modern Durazzo)*

dysenteri·a -ae *f* dysentery

dyspepsi·a -ae *f* indigestion

E

ē *prep see* **ex**

ē- *pref see* **ex-**

-ē *advl suf* forms adverbs from **o**-stem adjectives: **clare** clearly; but in prosody, **benĕ, malĕ**

eā *adv* there; that way

ea ejus *pron* she

eādem *adv* the same way, by the same route; at the same time; likewise, by the same token

eāpropter *adv* therefore

eapse = ipsa *(old feminine emphatic form of* **ipse)**
eātenus *adv* to such a degree, so far
ebenus *see* **hebenus**
ebes *see* **hebes**
ēbib·ō -ĕre -ī -itus *tr* to drink up, drain; *(of things)* to absorb, swallow up; to spend on drinks
ebiscum *see* **hibiscum**
ēbīt·ō -ĕre *intr* to go out
ēbland·ior -īrī -ītus sum *tr* to coax out, obtain by flattery
Eborāc·um -ī *n* **(Ebur-)** town in Britain *(modern York)*
eborāt·us -a -um *adj* **(ebur-)** adorned with ivory
ēbriet·ās -ātis *f* drunkenness
ēbriol·us -a -um *adj* tipsy
ēbriōsit·ās -ātis *f* habitual drunkenness, heavy drinking
ēbriōs·us -a -um *adj* addicted to drinking; *(of grapes)* addictive
ēbri·us -a -um *adj* drunk; drunken *(acts, words),* of a drunk; *(fig)* intoxicated *(e.g., w. love, power)*
ēbull·iō -īre -iī *or* **īvī** *tr* to babble about; **animam ebullire** *(coll)* to give up the ghost ‖ *intr* to bubble up
ebul·um -ī *n or* **ebul·us -ī** *f (bot)* dwarf elder *(small tree having clusters of white flowers and red or blackish berry-like fruit)*
eb·ur -oris *n* ivory; ivory object *(e.g., statue, flute, scabbard);* elephant's tusk; elephant; curule chair *(of a magistrate, ornamented with ivory)*
eburāt·us -a -um *adj* inlaid with ivory
eburneol·us -a -um *adj* made of ivory
eburne·us *or* **eburn·us -a -um** *adj* ivory; white as ivory; **dentes eburnei** tusks; **ensis eburneus** sword with ivory hilt
ec- *pref (prefixed to interrogatives with intensive or indefinite force, e.g.,* **ecquis** is there anyone who?)
ēcastor *interj (used mainly by women)* by Castor!
ecca, eccam, eccās *see* **ecce**
ecce *interj* see!, look!, look here! here!; *(followed by accusative in early literature; also followed by nominative from time of Cicero on)* **ecce me** here I am!; **ecce nos** here we are!; *(colloquially combined with the pronouns* **is, ille, iste: ecca** *(i.e.,* **ecce + ea)** *(fem sing)* here she is!; *(neut pl)* here they are!; **eccam** *(i.e.,* **ecce + eam)** here she is!; **eccilla** *or* **eccistam** there she is!; **eccillum** *or* **eccum** here he is!; **eccos** here they are!; *(calling attention to something non-visual)* mark this!; *(in vivid narrative, introducing a surprising event)* lo and behold!
eccerē *interj* there!
eccheum·a -atis *n* pouring out
eccill- *see* **ecce**
eccist- *see* **ecce**
ecclēsi·a -ae *f* Greek assembly of the people; *(eccl)* church, congregation
eccōs *interj see* **ecce**
eccum *interj see* **ecce**
ecdic·us -ī *m* public prosecutor; public defender
ecf- = eff-
echidn·a -ae *f* viper ‖ **Echidna** Hydra; **Echidna Lernaea** Lernaean Hydra ‖ monstrous mother of Cerberus, half woman and half serpent
Echidnē·us -a -um *adj* of Echidna; **canis Echidneus** Cerberus
Echīnad·es -um *fpl* cluster of small islands off Acarnania
echīn·us -ī *m* sea urchin; dishpan
Echī·ōn -onis *m* hero who sprang from the dragon's teeth sown by Cadmus, married Agave, and became father of Pentheus ‖ an argonaut
Echīonid·ēs -ae *m* Pentheus, son of Echion
Echīoni·us -a -um *adj* Cadmean, Theban
ēch·ō -ūs *(acc:* **-ō** *or* **-ōn)** *f* nymph who was changed by Hera into an echo
eclog·a -ae *f* literary selection; eclogue
eclogāri·ī -ōrum *mpl* excerpted literary passages
ecquando *adv* ever, at any time; *(in indirect questions)* whether ever
ecquī *conj (in indirect questions)* whether
ecqu·ī -ae *(or* **-a) -od** *interrog adj* any at all, really any
ec·quid -cūjus *pron* anything at all; *(in questions)* whether, if at all
ec·quis -cūjus *pron* any at all, anyone at all; *(in indirect questions)* whether anyone
ecquō *adv* anywhere
ecule·us -ī *m* foal, colt; small equestrian statue; torture rack; hobbyhorse
edācit·ās -ātis *f* gluttony
ed·ax -ācis *adj* gluttonous; *(fig)* devouring, destructive
ēdent·ō -āre -āvī -ātus *tr (sl)* to knock the teeth out of
ēdentul·us -a -us *adj* toothless, old
edepol *interj* by Pollux!, gad!
eder·a *or* **heder·a -ae** *f* ivy
ēdī·cō -cĕre -xī -ctus *tr* to proclaim; to decree; to appoint
ēdicti·ō -ōnis *f* edict, decree
ēdict·ō -āre -āvī -ātus *tr* to proclaim, publish
ēdict·um -ī *n* edict, proclamation; edict of a praetor listing rules he would follow in his capacity as judge
ē·discō -discĕre -didicī *tr* to learn by heart, learn thoroughly
ēdisser·ō -ĕre -uī -tus *tr* to explain in detail, analyze fully

ēdissert·ō -āre -āvī -ātus *tr* to explain fully, explain in detail
ēditīci·us -a -um *adj* set forth, proposed; **judices editicii** panel of jurors *(subject to challenge by defendant)*
ēditi·ō -ōnis *f* statement, account; publication; edition *(of book); (leg)* declaration *(of the form of judicial procedure to be followed)*
ēdit·us -a -um *adj* high; raised, rising; *(fig)* exalted; **locus editus** height, hill **‖** *n* height; ordinance; **ex edito** from a height; **in edito** on a hill; *(fig)* on a pedestal
ēd·ō -ĕre -idī -itus *tr* to give out, put forth, bring forth, emit; to give birth to, bear; to publish; to tell, announce, disclose; to show, display, produce, perform; to bring about, cause; to bring forward *(witnesses); (leg)* to give the defendant notice of; **animam edere** to give up the ghost
edō edĕre *(or* **esse) ēdī ēsus** *tr* to eat; *(fig)* to devour, consume, destroy; **pugnos edere** *(sl)* to eat fists, eat a knuckle sandwich
ēdoc·eō -ēre -uī -tus *tr* to teach thoroughly; to instruct clearly; to inform; to show clearly; *(w. double acc)* to teach *(s.o. s.th.)* well
ēdol·ō -āre -āvī -ātus *tr* to hew out: *(fig)* to hew into shape
ēdom·ō -āre -uī -itus *tr* to conquer thoroughly; to overcome *(vices, difficulties)*
Ēdōn·ī -ōrum *or* **Ēdōn·es -um** *mpl* Thracian tribe noted for its heavy drinking
Ēdōn·is -idis *adj (fem only)* Edonian **‖** *f* Bacchante
Ēdōn·us -a -um *adj* Edonian
ēdorm·iō -īre -īvī *or* **-iī ītus** *tr* to sleep off; to sleep through *(e.g., a lecture);* **crapulam edormire** to sleep off a hangover **‖** *intr* to sleep soundly
ēdormisc·ō -ĕre *tr* to sleep off
ēducāti·ō -ōnis *f* raising *(of children, animals)*
ēducāt·or -ōris *m* fosterer; foster father
ēducātr·ix -īcis *f* foster mother; nurse
ēduc·ō -āre -āvī -ātus *tr* to bring up, raise *(children, animals);* to produce *(fruit, grain)*
ēdū·cō -cĕre -xī -ctus *tr* to draw out, to take away; to build high; to drain off *(liquids);* to draw *(sword);* to spend *(time);* to lead out *(army);* to raise *(children, animals);* **in jus educere** to take to court
edūl·ia -ium *npl* eatables
edūl·is -is -e *adj* edible, eatable
ēdūr·ō -āre *intr* to last, endure
ēdūr·us -a -um *adj* hard, tough; *(fig)* tough
Ēēti·ōn -ōnis *m* father of Andromache and king of Thebe in Cilicia
effarciō *see* **effercio**
effāt·us -a -um *pp of* **effor ‖** *adj* solemnly pronounced **‖** *n* pronouncement; axiom, proposition
effectē *adv* consummately
effecti·ō -ōnis *f* accomplishment, performance; efficient cause
effectīv·us -a -um *adj* effective; practical
effect·or -ōris *m,* **effectr·ix -īcis** *f* producer, author
effect·us -a -um *pp of* **efficio ‖** *adj* finished, complete **‖** *n* effect
effect·us -ūs *m* effecting; completion; effect, result; **ad effectum adducere** to bring to completion; **cum effectu** in fact, actually; **effectu** in effect, to all intents and purposes; **sine effectu** without a decisive result
effēminātē *adv* effeminately
effēmināt·us -a -um *adj* **(ecf-)** effeminate
effēmin·ō -āre -āvī -ātus *tr* **(ecf-)** to make a woman of; to represent as a woman, regard as female; to emasculate **‖** *pass* to become unmanly
efferāt·us -a -um *adj* wild, savage
effer·ciō *or* **effarciō -cīre -sī -tus** *tr* **(ecfer-, ecfar-)** to stuff; to fill in *(e.g., a ditch)*
efferit·ās -ātis *f* wildness, barbarism
effer·ō -āre -āvī -ātus *tr* **(ecf-)** to make wild, brutalize; to exasperate
efferō efferre extulī ēlātus *tr* **(ecf-)** to carry out, bring out, bring forth; to utter, express, to publish, spread *(news);* to carry out for burial, bury; to produce, bear; to name, designate; to lift up, raise; to promote, advance; to bring out, expose; to praise, extol; to sweep off one's feet; *(w.* **ex)** copy out *(of some text);* **in lucem efferre** *(of fields)* to produce *(crops);* **gressum** *(or* **pedem) efferre** to go forth **‖** *refl* to arise; to be haughty, be conceited **‖** *pass (fig)* to be carried away
effert·us -a -um *pp of* **effercio ‖** *adj* chock-full, crammed, bulging
efferv·eō -ēre *or* **efferv·ō -ĕre** *intr* to boil over; *(of bees, etc.)* to come pouring out; *(of volcano)* to erupt
efferv·escō -escĕre -ī *intr* to boil, boil over; to burst forth; to get all worked up; to seethe; to rage; *(of words) (fig)* to become heated
effer·us -a -um *adj* very wild, savage
effēt·us -a -um *adj* worn out, spent; vain, delusive; *(w. gen)* incapable of
efficācit·ās -ātis *f* efficiency
efficāciter *adv* efficiently, effectively
effic·ax -ācis *adj* efficient, effective, efficacious
effici·ens -entis *adj* efficient, effective; **res efficientes** *(phil)* efficient causes
efficienter *adv* efficiently

efficienti·a -ae *f* efficiency, efficacy, influence

ef·ficiō -ficĕre -fēcī -fectus *tr* **(ecf-)** to bring about, bring to pass, effect, cause, produce; to make, form; to construct; to finish, complete, accomplish; to show, prove; *(w.* **ut)** to bring it about that; to carry out *(an order); (of component parts)* to constitute; to cover *(a distance in travel); (of numbers)* to amount to, add up to; *(of a field)* to produce, yield; to compose *(a speech, an essay); (w. double acc)* to elect *(s.o., e.g., consul)* ‖ *pass* to follow; **ita efficitur ut** thus it follows that

effictus *pp of* **effingo**

effigi·ēs -ēī *or* **effigi·a -ae** *f* effigy, likeness, semblance; opposite number; copy, imitation; image; statue, figure, portrait; ghost, phantom

ef·fingō -fingĕre -finxī -fictus *tr* **(ecf-)** to mold, form, fashion; to imitate; to wipe out, wipe clean; to represent, portray; to imagine

effiō *pass of* **efficio**

efflāgitāti·ō -ōnis *f* urgent demand

efflāgitāt·us -ūs *m* insistence

efflāgit·ō -āre *tr* to demand, insist on; to pester *(s.o. with requests)*

efflictim *adv* **(ecf-)** passionately

efflict·ō -āre *tr* **(ecf-)** to strike dead

efflī·gō -gĕre -xī -ctus *tr* **(ecf-)** to strike dead, exterminate

effl·ō -āre -āvī -ātus *tr* **(ecf-)** to breathe out; **animam efflare** to expire

efflōr·escō -escĕre -uī *intr* **(ecf-)** to bloom; *(fig)* to flourish

efflu·ō -ĕre -xī *intr* **(ecf-)** to flow out, flow forth, run out; to slip away, drop out, disappear; *(of rumor)* to get out, circulate; *(of secret)* to leak out; **ex animo** *(or* **memoriā) effluere** to slip one's mind

effluv·ium -(i)ī *n* outlet

effo·diō -dĕre -dī -ssus *tr* **(ecf-, exf-)** to dig up; to gouge out *(eyes);* to hollow out; to root out; to make *(by digging);* to erase; **humum** *(or* **terram) effodere** to dig a hole in the ground

(ef·for) -fārī -fātus sum *tr* **(ecf-)** to say out loud, tell; *(in augury)* to mark off, consecrate *(an area)* ‖ *intr* to speak out

effossus *pp of* **effodio**

effrēnātē *adv* **(ecf-)** without restraint, out of control

effrēnāti·ō -ōnis *f* impetuosity

effrēnāt·us -a -um *adj* **(ecf-)** unbridled; *(fig)* unbridled, unrestrained

effrēn·us -a -um *adj* unbridled; *(fig)* uncontrolled

ef·fringō -fringĕre -frēgī -fractus *tr* **(ecf-)** to break open, smash, break off; to break down *(door)*

ef·fugiō -fugĕre -fūgī *tr* **(ecf-, exf-)** to escape; to keep away from *(a person or place);* to avoid; to escape the grasp of, slip out of *(the hands);* to escape the notice of ‖ *intr* to escape, slip away; *(w. abl or w.* **ab** *or* **ex)** to escape from

effug·ium -(i)ī *n* escape, flight; means of escape; avoidance

efful·geō -gēre -sī *or* **effulg·ō -ĕre** *intr* to shine forth, gleam, flash, glitter; *(fig)* to shine forth

effult·us -a -um *adj* propped up

ef·fundō -fundĕre -fūdī -fūsus *tr* **(ecf-)** to pour out, pour away; to emit; to utter *(sounds);* to allow *(rain water)* to run off; to shed *(tears);* to hurl, shower *(weapons); (w.* **in** + *acc)* to shower *(praises)* on; *(of the stomach)* to throw up; to give up, let go, abandon, resign; to knock down, overturn *(walls, buildings);* to produce in abundance; to lavish, waste *(money, energy); (of tree)* to spread out *(branches);* to empty out *(bags, etc.);* to give vent to, pour out ‖ *refl & pass* to come pouring out; *(of rain)* to pour down; *(of a river) (w.* **ab)** to begin to flow from, have its source at; **super ripam effundi** to overflow its banks

effūsē *adv* far and wide; at random, in disorder; lavishly; immoderately

effūsi·ō -ōnis *f* **(ecf-)** outpouring, rushing out; shedding; effusion; profusion, lavishness, extravagance ‖ *fpl* excesses

effūs·us -a -um *pp of* **effundo** ‖ *adj* spread out, extensive; *(of troops)* thinly spread out *(over a large area);* straggly, disorderly; relaxed, loose; disheveled; lavish; unrestrained; immoderate; *(w.* **in** + *acc)* very prone to *(some weakness),* passionately devoted to *(some cause);* **effusissimis habenis** at full speed

effūt·iō -īre -īvī *or* **-iī -ītus** *tr & intr* to blab, babble

effut·uō -uĕre -uī -ūtus *tr* **(ecf-)** *(vulg)* to wear out through excessive sex

ēgelid·us -a -um *adj* tepid; cool

eg·ens -entis *adj* needy, poor; *(w. gen)* in need of, needing

egēn·us -a -um *adj* needy, destitute; *(w. gen)* in need of, needing

eg·eō -ēre -uī *intr* to be needy, suffer want; *(w. gen)* **1** to be in need of; **2** to lack, be without; **3** to want, desire, miss

Ēgeri·a -ae *f* nymph whom King Numa visited at night for advice

ē·gerō -gerĕre -gessī -gestus *tr* to carry out, take away, remove; to discharge, vomit, emit

egest·ās -ātis *f* need, want, poverty; *(w. gen)* lack of

ēgesti·ō -ōnis *f* squandering

ēgestus *pp of* **egero**

ego *pron* I

egomet *pron* I personally, I and nobody else
ē·gredior -gredī -gressus sum *tr* to go beyond, pass; to quit; *(fig)* to surpass ‖ *intr* to go out, come out; to march out; to set sail; to disembark, land; to go up, climb; *(fig)* to digress
ēgregiē *adv* exceptionally, singularly, uncommonly, splendidly
ēgregi·us -a -um *adj* exceptional, uncommon; distinguished, illustrious; **vir egregius** *(title given under the Empire to officials of equestrian rank)* the honorable...
ēgressus *pp of* **egredior**
ēgress·us -ūs *m* way out, exit; departure; disembarking, landing; mouth *(of river);* digression ‖ *mpl* comings and goings
ēgurgit·ō -āre *tr* to pour out, lavish
ehem *interj (expressing pleasant surprise)* ha!, aha!
ēheu *interj (expressing pain)* oh!
eho *interj (often expressing rebuke)* look here!, see here!; **eho dum!** look here now!
ei *interj* **hei** *(expressing fear or dismay)* ah!
ēia *or* **hēia** *interj (expressing joy or surpise)* ah!; ah ha!; good!; *(expressing haste)* quick!, come on!; **eia age** come on!, up then!
ējacul·or -ārī -ātus sum *tr* to squirt ‖ *refl (of water, etc.)* to squirt
ējectāment·a -ōrum *npl* refuse; jetsam
ējecti·ō -ōnis *f* ejection; banishment, exile
ēject·ō -āre -āvī -ātus *tr* to spout forth; to keep throwing up *(e.g., blood)*
ēject·us -ūs *m* emission
ējer·ō -āre -āvī -ātus *tr* (**ējūr-**) to refuse under oath, abjure, forswear; to deny under oath; to resign, abdicate; to disown, abandon
ē·jiciō -jicĕre -jēcī -jectus *tr* to throw out, drive out, put out, eject, expel; to banish; to utter; to run aground; to reject, disapprove; to boo *(s.o.)* off the stage ‖ *refl (of passions)* to come to the fore, break out ‖ *pass* to be stranded
ējulāti·ō -ōnis *f* lamenting
ējulāt·us -a - um *adj* wailing
ējul·ō -āre *intr* (**hēj-**) to wail, lament
ējūrō *see* **ejero**
ējusdemmodī *see* **modus**
-ēl·a, -ell·a -ae *fem suf* forms diminutives chiefly from verbs: **querela** complaint *(from* **queri** to complain)
ēlā·bor -bī -psus sum *intr* to glide off; to slip away, escape; to pass away, disappear; *(w. abl or* **super** *+ acc)* to glance off
ēlabōrāt·us -a -um *adj* studied, overdone; elaborate, finished
ēlabōr·ō -āre -āvī -ātus *tr* to work out, elaborate; to produce ‖ *intr* to make a great effort, take great pains; *(w. inf)* to strive to
ēlāmentābil·is -is -e *adj* pathetic
ēlangu·escō -escĕre -ī *intr* to slow down, slacken, let up
ēlapsus *pp of* **elabor**
ēlātē *adv* proudly
ēlāti·ō -ōnis *f* elation, ecstasy
ēlātr·ō -āre *tr* to bark out
ēlāt·us -a -um *pp of* **effero** ‖ *adj* high, elevated; exalted; haughty, proud
ē·lavō -lavāre -lāvī -lautus *or* **-lōtus** *tr* to wash out; *(coll)* to clean out, rob ‖ *intr* to be cleaned out, be wrecked; **elavare bonis** *(coll)* to be broke
Ele·a -ae *f* town in Lucania in S. Italy, modern Velia, birthplace of Eleatic philosophy
Eleāt·ēs -ae *m* inhabitant of Elea *(i.e., Zeno)*
Eleātic·ī -ōrum *mpl* Eleatics, Eleatic philosophers *(Parmenides and Zeno)*
ēlecebr·a -ae *f* (**exl-**) snare; seductress
ēlectē *adv* tastefully
ēlectil·is -is -e *adj* choice, dainty
ēlecti·ō -ōnis *f* choice, selection
ēlect·ō -āre *tr* to select, choose; to wheedle out, coax out *(a secret)*
Ēlectr·a -ae *f* daughter of Agamemnon and Clytemnestra ‖ Pleiad, daughter of Atlas and mother of Dardanus
ēlectr·um -ī *n* amber; gold-silver alloy ‖ *npl* amber beads
ēlect·us -a -um *pp of* **eligo** ‖ *adj* select, choice; *(mil)* elite
ēlect·us -ūs *m* choice
ēleg·ans -antis *adj* elegant; choosy; fine, choice, select
ēleganter *adv* elegantly, tastefully
ēleganti·a -ae *f* elegance, refinement, taste, propriety
elegē·um -ī *n* (**gīum**) elegaic poem
eleg·ī -ōrum *mpl* elegaic verses
elegī·a -ae *f* (**-gē·a**) elegy
Elel·eūs -eī *m (epithet of)* Bacchus
elementāri·us -a -um *adj* engaged in learning the rudiments; **senex elementarius** old schoolteacher
element·um -ī *n* first principle, element; atom, particle; letter of the alphabet ‖ *npl* rudiments, elements; beginnings; ABC's
elench·us -ī *m (pear-shaped)* pearl ‖ *mpl* criticisms
elephantomach·a -ae *m* fighter mounted on an elephant
elephant·us -ī *or* **eleph·ās -antis** *m* elephant; *(fig)* ivory
Ēlē·us -a -um *adj* of Elis *(in the Peloponnese)*
Eleus·īn -īnis *f* Eleusis *(town in Attica, sacred to Demeter, the Roman Ceres)*

Eleusīn·us -a -um *adj* Eleusinian; **Eleusina Mater** Demeter *or* the Roman Ceres
eleutheri·a -ae *f* freedom
ēlev·ō -āre -āvī -ātus *tr* to lift up, raise; to alleviate; to lessen; to make light of
Ēli·as -adis *adj (fem only)* Elian, Olympic
ēlic·iō -ĕre -uī -itus *tr* to elicit, draw out; to lure out, entice; to conjure up
ēlicitus *pp of* **elicio**
Ēlic·ius -(i)ī *m (epithet of)* Jupiter
ēlī·dō -dĕre -sī -sus *tr* to knock out, strike out, tear out, force out; to shatter, smash to pieces, crush; to force out, stamp out
ē·ligō -ligĕre -lēgī -lectus *tr* **(-leg-)** to pluck out; to pick out, choose
ēlīmin·ō -āre *tr* to carry outside; to spread abroad
ēlīm·ō -āre -āvī -ātus *tr* to file; to finish off, perfect
ēlingu·is -is -e *adj* speechless; *(fig)* inarticulate
ēlingu·ō -āre *tr* to tear out *(s.o.'s)* tongue
Ēl·is -idis *f* **(Āl-)** town and district on the W. coast of the Peloponnesus in which Olympia is located
-ēl·is -is -e *adj/ suf* formed from nouns and adjectives: **crudelis** cruel
Eliss·a *or* **Elīs·a -ae** *f* Dido
ēlīsus *pp of* **elido**
ēl·ix -icis *m* drainage ditch
ēlix·us -a -um *adj* boiled; *(sl)* soused
-ell·a -ae *fem suf* forms diminutives: **cistella** a little box
ellam = ecce + illam there she is!
elleborōs·us -a -um *adj* crazy
ellebor·us -ī *m or* **ellebor·um -ī** *n* **(hell-)** hellebore *(plant used to cure mental illness)*
ellips·is -is *f* ellipsis
ellum = ecce + illum there he is!
-ell·us -ī *masc suf* forms diminutives: **agellus** small plot
ēloc·ō -āre -āvī -ātus *tr* to lease out, rent out
ēlocūti·ō -ōnis *f* style of speaking, delivery
ēlog·ium -(i)ī *n* saying, maxim; inscription, epitaph; codicil *(in a will)*; criminal record
ēloqu·ens -entis *adj* eloquent
ēloquenter *adv (used in comp & supl degree)* eloquently
ēloquenti·a -ae *f* eloquence
ēloqu·ium -(i)ī *n* eloquence
ēlo·quor -quī -cūtus sum *tr* to speak out, declare; to divulge, tell **‖** *intr* to speak, give a speech
ēlōtus *pp of* **elavo**
ēlū·ceō -cēre -xī *intr* to shine forth; to glitter
ēluct·or -ārī -ātus sum *tr* to struggle out of, struggle through *(e.g., deep snow)*; to surmount *(difficulties)* **‖** *intr* to force a way out
ēlūcubr·ō -āre -āvī -ātus *or* **ēlūcubr·or -ārī -ātus sum** *tr* to compose by lamplight
ēlū·dō -dĕre -sī -sus *tr* to elude, parry, avoid; to escape, shun; to delude, deceive; to make fun of; to get the better of, outmaneuver **‖** *intr* to end the game; to behave outrageously with impunity, have free play *(for outrageous conduct)*
ēlū·geō -gēre -xī *tr* to mourn for **‖** *intr* to cease to mourn
ēlumb·is -is -e *adj* **(-bus -a -um)** having a dislocated hip; bland *(style)*
ē·luō -luĕre -luī -lūtus *tr* to wash off, wash clean; to wash away; to rinse out; *(fig)* to wash away, get rid of **‖** *intr (coll)* to loose one's property, be cleaned out
ēlūsus *pp of* **eludo**
ēlūt·us -a -um *pp of* **eluo ‖** *adj* watery, insipid; weak
ēluvi·ēs -ēī *f* inundation, overflow; sewage; ravine
ēluvi·ō -ōnis *f* deluge
Elvīn·a -ae *f* **(Hel-)** epithet of Ceres
Ēlysi·us -a -um *adj* Elysian
Ēlys·ium -iī *n* realm of the blessed in the lower world
em *interj* **(hem)** *(in offering some object or fact to s.o., often followed by a dat)* here (there) you are!
emācit·ās -ātis *f* fondness for shopping, mania for buying
ēmad·escō -escĕre -uī *intr* to become soaked
ēmancipāti·ō -ōnis *f* **(-cup-)** emancipation; transfer of property
ēmancipāt·us -a -um *adj* transferred; sold
ēmancip·ō -āre -āvī -ātus *tr* **(-cup-)** to transfer; to declare *(a son)* free and independent, emancipate; to surrender, abandon
ēmān·ō -āre -āvī -ātum *intr* to flow down; to trickle out, leak out; to become known **‖** *v impers* **emanabat** *(w. acc & inf)* word got out that
Ēmathi·a -ae *f* Macedonia; Thessaly, Pharsalus
Ēmath·is -idis *adj (fem only)* Macedonian **‖** *fpl* the Pierides
Ēmathi·us -a -um *adj* Macedonian, Thessalian, Pharsalian
ēmātūr·escō -escĕre -uī *intr* to begin to ripen; to soften; *(fig)* to mellow
em·ax -ācis *adj* fond of shopping; *(fig) (of a prayer)* bargaining with the gods, haggling
emblēm·a -atis *n* mosaic; inlay
embol·ium -(i)ī *n* interlude; insertion *(in literary work)*
ēmendābil·is -is -e *adj* capable of correction
ēmendātē *adv* faultlessly

ēmendāti·ō -ōnis *f* emendation
ēmendāt·or -ōris *m*, **ēmendātr·ix -īcis** *f* corrector, reformer
ēmendāt·us -a -um *adj* faultless
ēmendīc·ō -āre -āvī -ātus *tr* to get by begging
ēmend·ō -āre -āvī -ātus *tr* to emend, correct; to reform, improve, revise; to atone for
ēmensus *pp of* **emetior**
ēment·ior -īrī -ītus sum *tr* to falsify, fabricate, feign ‖ *intr* to tell a lie
ēmerc·or -ārī -ātus sum *tr* to buy up; to obtain through bribery
ēmer·eō -ēre -uī -itus *or* **ēmer·eor -ērī -itus sum** *tr* to earn; to lay under obligation, do *(s.o.)* a favor; *(mil)* to serve out *(term of service)* ‖ *intr* to serve out one's time in the army
ēmer·gō -gĕre -sī *tr* to raise *(from the water)* ‖ *refl & pass* to raise oneself up, rise ‖ *intr* to emerge; to rise *(in power);* to extricate oneself; *(w.* **ex)** to get clear of
ēmerit·us -a -um *pp of* **emereo** ‖ *adj (mil)* discharged; *(fig)* ready to be let out to pasture ‖ *m* veteran
ēmersus *pp of* **emergo**
emetic·a -ae *f* an emetic
ē·mētior -mētīrī -mensus sum *tr* to measure out; to traverse, travel over; to live through; to impart
ēmet·ō -ĕre *tr* to mow down
ēmi- = hemi-
ēmic·ō -āre -uī -ātum *intr* to dart out, dash out; *(of liquids)* to spurt out; *(of flame)* to shoot out; *(fig)* to stand out, be conspicuous
ēmigr·ō -āre -āvī -ātum *intr* to move out, depart; **e vita emigrare** to pass on
ēmināti·ō -ōnis *f* threatening, blustering
ēmin·ens -entis *adj* projecting, prominent, high; eminent
ēminenti·a -ae *f* projection, prominence; *(in painting)* highlights, foreground
ēmin·eō -ēre -uī *intr* to stand out, project; to be conspicious; *(in paintings)* to be highlighted, stand out against a background
ēmin·or -ārī *tr* to threaten
ēminus *adv* at long range, at a distance; from afar
ēmīr·or -ārī -ātus sum *tr* to be greatly surpised at, stand aghast at
ēmissār·ium -(i)ī *n* drain, outlet
ēmissār·ius -(i)ī *m* scout, spy
ēmissīci·us -a -um *adj* spying; **oculi emissicii** prying eyes
ēmissi·ō -ōnis *f* discharge, hurling, shooting; releasing, letting off
ēmissus *pp of* **emitto**
ēmiss·us -ūs *m* emission, sending forth; hurling, shooting
ē·mittō -mittĕre -mīsī -missus *tr* to send out; to hurl, shoot; to let go, let slip, let loose, drop, release, let out; to publish; to allow to escape; to emancipate, set at liberty; to utter; to pass up *(opportunity);* **animam emittere** to give up the ghost ‖ *refl & pass (w.* **ex)** to break out of
emō emĕre ēmī emptus *tr* to buy; *(w. gen or abl of price)* to buy *(s.th.)* at; to pay for; to gain, obtain; to bribe; **bene emere** to buy at a bargain; **in diem emere** to buy on credit; **male emere** to pay dearly for
ēmoder·or -ārī *tr* to moderate
ēmodul·or -ārī *tr* to sing the praises of, celebrate in song
ēmōl·ior -īrī -ītus sum *tr* to accomplish with great effort
ēmoll·iō -īre -īvī *or* **-iī -ītus** *tr* to soften; to make mild; to enervate
ēmol·ō -ĕre — *tr* to grind up
ēmolument·um -ī *n* profit; advantage
ēmon·eō -ēre *tr* to admonish earnestly
ēmor·ior -ī -tuus sum *intr* to die; to die off; *(of a fire)* to die down; *(of river)* to peter out; *(fig)* to die out
ēmortuāl·is -is -e *adj* of death
ēmortuus *pp of* **emorior**
ē·moveō -movēre -mōvī -mōtus *tr* **(exm-)** to move out, remove, expel; to dislodge; to shake *(e.g., foundations of a wall)*
Empedocl·ēs -is *or* **-ī** *m* philosopher of Sicily who is said to have jumped into crater of Mt. Etna *(fl 444 B.C.)*
emphas·is (-is) *f* emphasis, stress
empīric·us -ī *m* empiricist *(physician who relies on experience rather than on scientific theory)*
empor·ium -(i)ī *n* market town; trade mart, market
empti·ō -ōnis *f* buying, purchase; thing purchased, purchase
emptit·ō -āre -āvī -ātus *tr* to be in the habit of buying, buy *(regularly)*
empt·or -ōris *m* buyer, customer
empt·um -ī *n* a purchase
emptus *pp of* **emo**
ēmūg·iō -īre *tr* to bellow out
ēmul·geō -gēre — -sus *tr* to drain off *(milk);* to drain *(a swamp)*
ēmunct·us -a -um *adj* refined; snobbish; **naris emunctae esse** to have discriminating tastes
ēmun·gō -gĕre -xī -ctus *tr* to blow the nose of; to swindle; *(w. abl)* to cheat *(s.o.)* of ‖ *refl & pass* to blow one's nose
ēmūn·iō -īre -īvī *or* **-iī -ītus** *tr* to build up; to fortify; to make a road through *(woods)*
ēn *interj (in questions)* really?; *(in commands)* come on!; *(to call attention)* hey!
ēnarrābil·is -is -e *adj* describable, intelligible

ēnarrāti·ō -ōnis *f* description; analysis
ēnarr·ō -āre -āvī -ātus *tr* to explain in detail; to describe; to interpret
ēnascor ēnascī ēnātus sum *intr* to grow out, sprout, arise; to be born
ēnat·ō -āre -āvī -ātum *intr* to swim away, escape by swimming; *(fig)* to get away with it
ēnātus *pp of* **enascor**
ēnāvig·ō -āre -āvī -ātus *tr* to sail across, traverse ‖ *intr* to sail away; *(fig)* to escape
encaust·us -a -um *adj* burnt in, painted in encaustic *(i.e., with molten wax as paint)*
Encelad·us *or* **Encelad·os -ī** *m* one of the giants whom Jupiter buried under Mount Etna
endrom·is -idis *f* athlete's bathrobe
Endymi·ōn -ōnis *m* handsome young man with whom Luna fell in love and who was doomed to everlasting sleep on Mt. Patmos; any handsome young man
ēnec·ō *(or* **ēnicō)** **-āre -uī** *(or* **-āvī)** **-tus** *(or* **-ātus)** *tr* to kill, kill off; to exhaust, wear out; *(coll)* to kill, pester to death
ēnervāt·us -a -um *adj* without sinews, without muscles; without energy
ēnerv·is -is -e *or* **enerv·us -a -um** *adj* weak, feeble
ēnerv·ō -āre -āvī -ātus *tr* to weaken, enervate, render impotent
ēnicō *see* **eneco**
enim *conj* namely, for instance; yes, indeed, certainly; in fact, to be sure; *(in replies)* of course, no doubt; for, because
enimvērō *adv* yes indeed, to be sure, certainly; *(ironically)* of course
Enīp·eūs -eī *m* tributary of the River Peneus in Thessaly
ēnīsus *pp of* **enitor**
ēnit·eō -ēre -uī *intr* to shine out, sparkle; to be conspicuous
ēnit·escō -escěre *intr* to begin to shine, begin to brighten; to become conspicuous
ēnī·tor -tī -sus *or* **-xus sum** *tr* to work one's way up, climb; to give birth to ‖ *intr* to exert oneself, make an effort; *(w. inf)* to struggle to, strive to
ēnixē *adv* strenuously, earnestly
ēnix·us -a -um *pp of* **enitor** ‖ *adj* strenuous, earnest
Enni·us -(i)ī *m* father of Latin literature, writer of tragedy, comedy, epic, and satire *(239–169* B.C.*)*
Ennosigae·us -ī *m (epithet of Neptune)* Earthshaker
ēn·ō -āre -āvī -ātum *intr* to swim out, swim away, escape by swimming
ēnōdātē *adv* without knots; clearly
ēnōdāti·ō -ōnis *f* solution, explanation
ēnōd·is -is -e *adj* without knots; clear
ēnōd·ō -āre -āvī -ātus *tr* to explain, clarify
ēnorm·is -is -e *adj* enormous; shapeless, irregular; ill-fitting *(clothes);* extravagant *(style)*
ēnormit·ās -ātis *f* enormity; irregular shape
ēnōt·escō -escěre -uī *intr* to become known
ēnot·ō -āre -āvī -ātus *tr* to take notes of, note down
ensicul·us -ī *m* little sword
ensif·er *or* **ensig·er -era -erum** *adj* with a sword, wearing a sword
ens·is -is *m* sword
-ens·is -is -e *adjl suf* forms adjectives mainly from words denoting places: **Atheniensis** Athenian, from Athens
enterocēl·ē -ēs *f* hernia of the intestines
enterocēlic·us -a -um *adj* suffering from an intestinal hernia
entheāt·us -a -um *adj* filled with divine frenzy
enthe·us -a -um *adj* inspired; inspiring, that fills with divine frenzy
enthȳmēm·a -atis *n* thought, reflection; *(phil)* condensed syllogism
ēnū·bō -běre -psī *intr (of a woman)* to marry outside her rank
ēnucleātē *adv* precisely
ēnucleāt·us -a -um *adj* precise, to the point; straightforward, simple *(style);* fine-drawn *(agruments)*
ēnucle·ō -āre -āvī -ātus *tr (fig)* to examine carefully; to weigh *(one's decision)*
ēnumerāti·ō -ōnis *f* enumeration
ēnumer·ō -āre -āvī -ātus *tr* to count up; to count out, pay out; to recount, detail, enumerate
ēnuntiāti·ō -ōnis *f* announcement; *(in logic)* assertion; proposition *(gram)* pronunciation *(of a word or syllable)*
ēnunti·ō -āre -āvī -ātus *tr* to disclose, reveal, betray; to say, assert, express; to proclaim publicly; *(gram)* to pronounce *(a word or syllable)*
ēnupti·ō -ōnis *f* right of a woman to marry outside her clan
ēnutr·iō -īre -īvi *or* **-iī -ītus** *tr* to nourish, raise, bring up
Enȳ·ō (-us) *f* Greek goddess of war
eō īre īvī *or* **iī itum** *intr* to go; to walk, sail, ride; *(of time)* to pass; *(of events)* to go on, happen, turn out; *(of things)* to give way; *(mil)* to march; *(w. abl)* to stem from; **in sententiam ire** *(pol)* to vote for a bill
eō *adv* there, to that place; to that end, to that purpose; so far, to such an extent, to such a pitch; on that account, for that reason, with that in view; **eo ero brevior** I will be all the briefer; **eo magis** all the more; **eo maxime quod** especially because; **eo quo** to the place to which; **quo...eo** the...the...; **quo plus potestis, eo moderatius imperio uti debetis** the

more power you have, the more moderately you ought to use that power; **eo quod** because; **eo...ut** to such an extent...that

eōdem *adv* to the same place, purpose, *or* person

Ēōs *(nom only) f* Dawn *(the Latin Aurora, daughter of Hyperion and Theia or Euryphaëssa)*

Ēō·us -ī *m* morning star ‖ inhabitant of the East ‖ one of the horses of the sun ‖ dawn

Ēō·us -a -um *adj* of the dawn; Eastern, oriental ‖ *m* morning star; dawn; an oriental

Epamīnond·ās -ae *m* famous Theban general who defeated the Spartans in two great battles *(c. 371 B.C.)*

epaphaeres·is -is *f* a second close :lip *(of the hair)*

Epaph·us -ī *m* son of Jupiter and Io

ēpast·us -a -um *adj* eaten up

Epē·us *or* **Epī·us -ī** *m* builder of the Trojan horse

ephēb·us -ī *m (Greek)* young man

ephēmer·is -idis *or* **-idos** *f* diary; journal

Ephes·us *or* **Ephes·os -ī** *f* city on the coast of Asia Minor with famous temple of Diana

ephippiāt·us -a -um *adj* riding a saddled horse

ephipp·ium -iī *n* saddle

ephor·us -ī *m* ephor *(Spartan magistrate)*

Ephyr·a -ae *or* **Ephyr·ē -ēs** *f* ancient name of Corinth

Epicharm·us -ī *m* Sicilian Greek writer of early comedy *(530?–440 B.C.)*

epichys·is -is *f* wine ladle

epicōp·us -a -um *adj* **phaselus epicopus** rowboat

epicroc·us -a -um *adj* thin yellow *(garment)* ‖ *n* thin yellow garment

Epicūr·us -ī *m* Greek philosopher, born on Samos *(342–270 B.C.)*

epic·us -a -um *adj* epic ‖ **Epic·i -orum** *mpl* Epic poets

epidictic·us -a -um *adj* showy

epidīpn·is -idis *f* dessert

epigramm·a -atis *or* **-atos** *n* inscription, epitaph; short poem, epigram

epilog·us -ī *m* epilogue, peroration

epimēni·a -ōrum *npl* month's rations

Epimēth·eūs -eī *m* son of Iapetus and brother of Prometheus

epinīc·ion -iī *n* victory song

epiraed·ium -iī *n* horse-drawn carriage

Ēpīrōt·ēs -ae *m* native of Epirus

Ēpīr·us *or* **Ēpīr·os -ī** *f* district of N.W. Greece

epistol·ium -iī *n* note

epistul·a -ae *f* **(-tol-)** letter

epistulār·is -is -e *adj* **(-tol-)** concerned with letters; **chartae epistulares** writing paper

epitaph·ium -(i)ī *n* eulogy

epithalam·ium -(i)ī *n* wedding song

epithēc·a -ae *f* addition, increase

epitom·a -ae *or* **epitom·ē -ēs** *f* epitome, abridgment

epitȳr·um -ī *n* olive salad

epoch·ē -ēs *f* suspension of judgment

ep·ops -opis *m* hoopoe *(an Old World bird having a fanlike crest and a slender downward-curving bill)*

epos *(nom & acc only) n* epic

ēpōt·us -a -um *adj* **(exp-)** drunk dry, drained to the dregs

epul·ae -ārum *fpl* courses, dishes; sumptuous meal; **epulae regum** dinner fit for a king

epulār·is -is -e *adj* at dinner, of a dinner; **sermo epularis** talk at dinner, table talk

epulāti·ō -ōnis *f* banqueting

epul·ō -ōnis *m* dinner guest; **Tresviri** *(or* **Septemviri) Epulones** college of priests who superintended the state dinner to the gods

epul·or -ārī -ātus sum *tr* to feast on ‖ *intr* to attend a dinner; *(w. abl)* to feast on

epul·um -ī *n* banquet, feast

equ·a -ae *f* mare

equ·es -itis *m* rider; trooper, cavalryman; cavalry ‖ *mpl* cavalry

Equ·es -itis *m* knight; capitalist *(member of Roman middle class);* equestrian order, bourgeoisie

eques·ter *or* **equest·ris -tris -tre** *adj* equestrian; cavalry; middle-class

equidem *adv* truly, indeed, in any event; of course, to be sure; *(w. first person)* for my part, as far as I am concerned

equīn·us -a -um *adj* horse's

equīri·a -ōrum *npl* **(equirr-)** horse race

equitāt·us -ūs *m* cavalry

equit·ō -āre -āvī -ātum *intr* to ride, ride a horse

equule·us -ī *m* foal, colt; small equestrian statue; torture rack

equ·us -ī (equos *and* **equom** *in pre-Augustan period,* **ecus** *and* **ecum** *from Aug. period to end of 1st cent. A.D.,* **equus** *and* **equum** *after that) m* horse; **equis virisque** *(or* **equis viris)** *(fig)* with might and main; **equo merere** to serve in the cavalry; **equo vehi** to ride a horse; **equus bipes** sea horse; **in equo** mounted ‖ *mpl* chariot

er·a *or* **her·a -ae** *f* lady of the house

ērādīc·ō -āre -āvī -ātus *tr* **(exr-)** to uproot; to destroy utterly

ērā·dō -dĕre -sī -sus *tr* to scratch out, erase, obliterate

eran·us -ī *m* mutual insurance society *(in Greece)*

Erāt·ō *(nom and voc only) f* Muse of erotic poetry; Muse

Eratosthen·ēs -is *m* Alexandrine geographer, poet, and philosopher *(276–196 B.C.)*
erc- *see* **herc-**
Ereb·us -ī *m* god of darkness, son of Chaos and brother of Night; lower world
Erechth·eūs -eī *m* king of Athens, son of Hephaestus ‖ grandson of former and son of Pandion
Erechthē·us -a -um *adj* of Erechtheus; *(poet)* Athenian
Erechthīd·ae -ārum *mpl* descendants of Erechtheus; *(poet)* Athenians
ērect·us -a -um *pp of* **erigo** ‖ *adj* erect, upright; noble, elevated, lofty; haughty; attentive, alert, tense; resolute, courageous
ērēp·ō -ēre -sī *tr* to crawl through *(a field);* to crawl up *(a mountain)* ‖ *intr* to crawl out
ērepti·ō -ōnis *f* robbery
ērept·or -ōris *m* robber
ēreptus *pp of* **eripio**
Eretri·a -ae *f* city on the island of Euboea, birthplace of the philosopher Menedemus
Eretriac·ī -ōrum *mpl* philosophers of the school of Menedemus
ergā *(prep) (w. acc)* to, towards; against; next to
ergastul·um -ī *n* prison *(on a large estate where unruly slaves were kept);* chain gang
ergō *adv* therefore, consequently; *(resumptive)* well then, I say, as I was saying; *(w. imperatives)* then, now
ergō *prep (w. preceding gen)* for the sake of, in consequence of; **illius ergo** for his sake
Erichthon·ius -iī *m* king of Athens ‖ son of Dardanus, father of Tros, and king of Troy
ēric·ius -(i)ī *m* hedgehog; *(mil)* beam with iron spikes
Ēridan·us -ī *m* Po river *(so called by the Greeks); (astr)* constellation
erifug·a -ae *m* runaway slave
ē·rigō -rigĕre -rexī -rectus *tr* to set up straight, straighten out *(e.g., tree);* to set up, erect; to cheer up, encourage; to arouse, excite; *(mil)* to deploy troops on a slope ‖ *refl & pass* to raise oneself, get up
Ērigon·ē -ēs *f (astr)* Virgo *(constellation)*
erīl·is -is -e *or* **herīl·is -is -e** *adj* master's, mistress's
Erīn·ys -yos *f* Fury; *(fig)* frenzy
Eriphȳl·a -ae *or* **Eriphȳl·ē -ēs** *f* wife of the seer Amphiaraus; a treacherous wife
ē·ripiō -ripĕre -ripuī -reptus *tr* to snatch away, pull out, tear out; to deliver, rescue; to rob; *(w. dat or w.* **ab** *or* **ex***)* to take away from, rescue from ‖ *refl* to escape
-ern·us -a -um *adjl suf* forms adjectives denoting times: **hestiernus** yesterday's
ērogāti·ō -ōnis *f* expenditure, outlay, payment
ērogit·ō -āre *tr* to try hard to find out
ērog·ō -āre -āvī -ātus *tr* to allocate, expend; to bequeath; *(w.* **in** *+ acc)* **1** to allocate to, spend on; **2** to bequeath to
Er·ōs -ōtis *m* Love, Cupid, Eros
errābund·us -a -um *adj* wandering, straggling
errātic·us -a -um *adj* erratic, wandering; **stella erratica** planet
errāti·ō -ōnis *f* wandering
errāt·um -ī *n* error, mistake
errāt·us -ūs *m* roving, wandering about
err·ō -āre -āvī -ātum *intr* to wander, roam; to lose one's way, stray; to waver; to err, make a mistake, be mistaken; *(w.* **in** *+ abl)* to be mistaken about
err·ō -ōnis *m* vagrant, vagabond
err·or -ōris *m* wandering; wavering, uncertainty; error; cause of error, deception; maze, winding, intricacy
ērubescendus -a -um *adj* enough to make one blush, shameful
ērub·escō -escĕre -uī *tr* to blush at; to be ashamed of; to respect ‖ *intr* to grow red, redden; to blush
ērūc·a -ae *f (bot)* cole *(type of cabbage)*
ēruct·ō -āre -āvī -ātus *tr* to belch, vomit
ērud·iō -īre -iī *or* **-īvī -ītus** *tr* to educate, teach, instruct; *(w. double acc)* to teach *(s.o. s.th.)*
ērudītē *adv* learnedly
ērudīti·ō -ōnis *f* instructing, instruction; erudition, learning
ērudītul·us -a -um *adj* somewhat experienced, somewhat skilled
ērudīt·us -a -um *adj* educated, learned, accomplished
ēruī *perf of* **eruo**
ē·rumpō -rumpĕre -rūpī -ruptus *tr* to cause to break out; to give vent to; **iram in hostes erumpere** to vent one's wrath on the enemy ‖ *intr* to burst out, break out
ēru·ō -ĕre -ī -tus *tr* to uproot, dig out; to tear out *(eyes);* to undermine, demolish, destroy; to draw out, elicit; to churn up *(sea);* to plow up
ērupti·ō -ōnis *f* eruption; *(mil)* sortie, sally
ēruptus *pp of* **erumpo**
er·us *or* **her·us -ī** *m* master of the house, head of the family; lord, owner
ērutus *pp of* **eruo**
erv·um -ī *n (bot)* vetch *(cultivated for its edible seeds)*
Erycīn·us -a -um *adj* of Mt. Eryx *(in N.W. Sicily);* of Venus; Sicilian ‖ *f* Venus
Erymanth·is -idos *f* Callisto *(changed first into a bear and then into a constellation)*
Erymanth·us -ī *m* mountain range in Arcadia, where Hercules killed a boar

Erythē·a -ae *f* small island in the Bay of Gades, home of the giant Geryon
erythīn·us -ī *m* red mullet *(fish)*
Er·yx -ycis *or* **Eryc·us -ī** *m* Eryx *(mountain on N.W. coast of Sicily, famous for its temple to Venus)* ‖ son of Venus and Butes, half-brother of Aeneas
esc·a -ae *f* dish; food; bait
escāri·us -a -um *adj* of food; of bait ‖ *npl* dishes, courses
escen·dō -dĕre -dī -sus *tr & intr* to climb, climb up; to sail up
escensi·ō -ōnis *f* climbing up; hostile raid *(from the coast)*
escens·us -ūs *m* ascent
-esc·ō -ĕre *vbl suf* formed from nouns and adjectives, with inchoative force: **senescere** to begin to be old, get old
esculent·us -a -um *adj* edible ‖ *npl* edibles, foodstuffs
esculētum *see* **aesculetum**
esculus *see* **aesculus**
-ēsim·us *or* **-ensim·us -a -um** *suf* used to form ordinal numbers from 20 to 1000
ēsit·ō -āre -āvī -ātus *tr* (essi-) to be used to eating
Esquili·ae -ārum *fpl* Esquiline Hill
Esquilīn·us -a -um *adj* Esquiline ‖ *f* Esquiline gate
esse *inf of* **sum** to be; *inf of* **ēdō** to eat
essedār·ius -(i)ī *m* soldier *or* gladiator fighting from a chariot
essed·um -ī *m* Gallic war chariot; light traveling carriage
essenti·a -ae *f* essence
essitō *see* **esito**
-ess·ō -ĕre -īvī *or* **-iī -ītus** *vbl suf* with conative force: **capessere** to try to catch, snatch at, catch at eagerly, strive for
estr·ix -īcis *f* glutton *(female)*
ēsuriāl·is -is -e *adj* (ess-) of hunger
ēsur·iō -īre — -ītus *tr* (ess-) to be hungry for ‖ *intr* to be hungry
essuri·ō -ōnis *m* a hungry man
ēsurīti·ō -ōnis *f* hunger
ēsus *pp of* **edo**
ēs·us -ūs *m* eating
et *adv* besides, also; even, I mean
et *conj* and; *(for emphasis)* and even, yes and; *(antithetical)* however, but; **et...et** both...and, not only...but also
etenim *conj* for, and as a matter of fact
etēsi·ae -ārum *mpl (fpl)* periodic winds *(on the Aegean Sea)*
ēthic·ē -ēs *f* ethics
ēthologi·a -ae *f* portrayal of character
ētholog·us -ī *m* impersonator
etiam *adv & conj* also, and also, besides, likewise; *(of time)* yet, as yet, still, even now; *(in affirmation)* yes, yes indeed, certainly, by all means; *(emphatic)* even, rather; *(w. emphatic imperatives)* but just; **etiam atque etiam** again and again
etiamnunc *or* **etiamnum** *adv* even now, even at the present time, still
etiamsī *conj* even if, although
etiamtum *or* **etiamtunc** *adv* even then, till then, still
Etrūri·a -ae *f* district N. of Rome
Etrusc·us -a -um *adj* Etruscan, of Etruria
etsī *conj* even if, although
-ēt·um -ī *neut suf* formed mainly from names of plants to denote the place where they grow: **rosetum** rose bed
etymologi·a -ae *f* etymology
eu *interj (sometimes ironic)* fine!, great!
Euān *or* **Euhān** *m* cult title of Bacchus, cult cry
eu·ans *or* **euh·ans -antis** *adj* crying Eu(h)an *(Bacchic cry)*
euax *interj* hurray!
Euboe·a -ae *f* Greek island off E. coast of Attica and Boeotia
Euēn·us -ī *m* a king of Aetolia, father of Marpessa ‖ river in Aetolia
euge *or* **eugepae** *interj* terrific!
euhans *see* **euans**
Euhēmer·us -ī *m* Greek writer who attempted to prove that all ancient myths were basically historical events *(fl 316 B.C.)*
Euh·ius -iī *m* Bacchus
Euhoe *or* **Euoe** *interj* ecstatic cry of revelers at festival of Bacchus
Euius *see* **Euhius**
Eumenid·ēs -um *fpl* Eumenides *or* Erinyes *or* Furies *(goddesses of vengeance)*
eunūch·us -ī *m* eunuch
Euoe *see* **Euhoe**
Euphorb·us -ī *m* brave Trojan warrior whose soul Pythagoras asserted had transmigrated to himself
Euphrāt·ēs -is *or* **-ae** *or* **-ī** *m* Euphrates River
Eupol·is -idis *or* **-is** *m* Athenian comic playwright *(446?–411 B.C.)*
Eurīpid·ēs -is *m* Athenian tragic playwright *(485–405 B.C.)*
eurīp·us -ī *m* channel; trench running between the arena and the seats in the Circus Maximus ‖ **Euripus** strait between Boeotia and Euboea
Eurōp·a -ae *or* **Eurōp·ē -ēs** *f* Europe ‖ Europa, daughter of Agenor and mother of Sarpedon, Rhadamantus, and Minos by Jupiter, who, in the shape of a bull, carried her off to Crete
Eurōt·ās -ae *m* chief river of Laconia in S. Greece, on which Sparta stood
Eur·us -ī *m* S.E. wind; east wind; wind
Eurydic·ē -ēs *f* wife of Orpheus
Eurysth·eūs -eī *m* king of Argos who imposed the Twleve Labors on Hercules
Euryt·is -idos *f* daughter of Eurytus, king of Oechalia *(i.e., Iole)*
-e·us -a -um *adjl suf* formed from nouns,

usually to denote material: **ligneus** (made) of wood, wooden
euschēmē *adv* gracefully
Euterp·ē -ēs *f* Muse *(later associated with the reed pipe)*
Euxīn·us Pont·us -ī *m* Black Sea
ēvā·dō -dĕre -sī -sus *tr* to pass, pass by; to pass through, escape ‖ *intr* to go out; to turn out to be, become, prove to be; to get away; to climb
ēvag·or -ārī -ātus sum *tr* to stray beyond, transgress ‖ *intr (fig)* to spread; *(mil)* to maneuver
ēval·escō -escĕre -uī *intr* to grow strong; to increase; *(of a word or expression)* to gain currency; *(w. inf)* to be able to; *(w.* **in** *+ acc)* to develop into
ēvalid·us -a -um *adj* very strong
Evan·der *or* **Evan·drus -drī** *m* Evander *(Arcadian who founded Pallanteum at the foot of the Palatine Hill)*
ēvān·escō -escĕre -uī *intr* to vanish, pass away, die away; to be forgotten; *(of liquids)* to evaporate
ēvānid·us -a -um *adj* vanishing
ēvast·ō -āre -āvī -ātus *tr* to devastate, wreck completely
ēvāsus *pp of* **evado**
ēve·hō -hĕre -xī -ctus *tr* to carry out; to spread abroad; to lift up, raise ‖ *pass* to ride, sail, drift
ē·vellō -vellĕre -vellī *or* **-vulsī -vulsus** *tr* to pluck out; to eradicate; to extract *(teeth)*
ē·veniō -venīre -vēnī -ventum *intr* to come out, come forth; to come to pass, happen; to turn out, result, end ‖ *v impers* it happens
ēvent·um -ī *n* event, occurrence; result, effect, consequence; fortune; experience
ēvent·us -ūs *m* event, accident, fortune, lot, fate; good fortune, success; issue, consequence, result
Evēn·us -ī *m* river in Aetolia
ēverber·ō -āre -āvī -ātus *tr* to hit hard; to beat up
ēverricul·um -ī *n* broom; dragnet
ēver·rō -rĕre -rī -sus *tr* to sweep out; *(fig)* to clean out, strip
ēversi·ō -ōnis *f* overthrow, subversion, destruction
ēvers·or -ōris *m* destroyer
ēversus *pp of* **everro** *and of* **everto**
ēver·tō -tĕre -tī -sus *tr* **(-vor-)** to overturn, turn upside down; to overthrow; to turn out, expel; to subvert, destroy, ruin
ēvestīgāt·us -a -um *adj* tracked down
ēvictus *pp of* **evinco**
ēvid·ens -entis *adj* evident, visible, plain, clear, obvious
ēvidenter *adv* plainly, obviously
ēvidenti·a -ae *f* obviousness; evidence; *(rhet)* vividness
ēvigil·ō -āre -āvī -ātus *tr* to watch through *(the night);* to work through the night writing *(e.g., books)* ‖ *intr* to be wide-awake; *(fig)* to be on one's toes
ēvīl·escō -escĕre -uī *intr* to depreciate, become worthless
ēvin·ciō -cīre -xī -ctus *tr* to tie up; to crown, wreathe
ē·vincō -vincĕre -vīcī -victus *tr* to conquer completely, trounce; to prevail over
ēvinctus *pp of* **evincio**
ēvirāt·us -a -um *adj* effeminate
ēvir·ō -āre -āvī -ātus *tr* to castrate, emasculate
ēviscer·ō -āre -āvī -ātus *tr* to disembowel, gut, eviscerate; to mangle
ēvītābil·is -is -e *adj* avoidable
ēvītāti·ō -ōnis *f* avoidance
ēvīt·ō -āre -āvī -ātus *tr* to avoid, escape
ēvocāt·ī -ōrum *mpl* veterans called up again, reenlisted veterans
ēvocāt·or -ōris *m* recruiter
ēvoc·ō -āre -āvī -ātus *tr* to call out, summon; to challenge; to evoke, excite, stir; *(mil)* to call up *(for service)*
ēvolgō *see* **evulgo**
ēvol·ō -āre -āvī -ātum *intr* to fly out, fly away; to rush out; *(fig)* to soar
ēvolūti·ō -ōnis *f* unrolling a scroll; *(fig)* reading
ēvolsi·ō -ōnis *f* extraction
ēvol·vō -vĕre -vī -ūtus *tr* to roll out, unroll, unfold; to spread; to read, study; to disclose; to free, extricate; to repel; to evolve, develop
ēvom·ō -ĕre -uī -itus *tr* to vomit, spew out, disgorge
ēvulg·ō -āre -āvī -ātus *tr* **(-vol-)** to divulge, make public
ēvulsi·ō -ōnis *f* extraction
ēvulsus *pp of* **evello**
ex *or* **ē** *prep (w. abl)* **1** *(of space)* out of, from: **ex concilio ire** to come out of the assembly; **2** *(of space)* down from: **se ex altissimo praecipitare** to jump down from a great height; **3** *(of space)* up from: **e lecto surgere** to get up from his bed; **4** *(of time)* from, from...onward, following, since: **ex eo** *(or* **ex illo** *or* **ex quo)** from that time on, ever since then; **5** *(of time)* right after: **ex imbre** right after the rain; **6** *(of material of which s.th. consists)* of: **statua ex auro** a statue of gold; **7** *(of parentage, racial origin)* by, from: **tres filios ex ea generavit** he had three children by her; **8** *(of cause or origin)* from, through, by, on account of, by reason of: **ex aere alieno commotus** upset because of his debts; **9** *(derivation of a word)* from, after: **appellata est ex viro virtus** "manliness" is derived from "man"; **10** *(in partitive sense)* of, out of, from among: **paucos ex suis deperdidit**

he lost few of his own men; **11** *(indicating extent):* **copiae ex parte deletae, ex parte captae** troops partly destroyed, partly captured; **12** *(indicating repetition)* after: **bella ex bellis serere** to sow the seeds of war after war; **dies ex die** day after day; **13** *(indicating recovery)* **ex vulnere refectus** recovered from a wound; **14** *(indicating point from which action is performed)* from: **ex equo pugnare** to fight from a horse *(i.e., on horseback);* **ex itinere pugnare** to fight en route; **15** *(indicating conformity)* after, according to, in conformity with: **ex consuetudine cotidianā** according to their daily habit; **17** *(w. verbs of learning)* from: **ex litteris tuis intellexi** I understood from your letter

ex- or **ē-** *pref* (**ex-** normally before vowels, **c, q, p, s, t; s** is sometimes absorbed, e.g., **expectare; ex** is dropped in **escendere, epotare; e-** before **g, b, d, r, l, m, n, i, u;** with **f, ff-** is commonly formed, also **ecf-**) **1** out: **exire** to go out; **2** away: **ēfugere** to run away; **3** well, thoroughly: **ēdiscere** to learn thoroughly, learn by heart; **4** hard, up: **ēverberare** to beat hard, beat up; **5** *(negative, deprivation)* -less, un-: **exsanguis** unbloody; **exos** boneless; **6** up: **exaggerare** to pile up

exacerb·ō -āre -āvī -ātus *tr* to exasperate, enrage; to exacerbate, make worse

exacti·ō -ōnis *f* driving out, expulsion; demanding; exaction, collection; supervision *(of public works)*

exact·or -ōris *m* expeller; collector; supervisor

exact·us -a -um *pp of* **exigo ‖** *adj* exact, precise

exac·uō -uĕre -uī -ūtus *tr* to sharpen; to stimulate, spur, inflame

exadversum *or* **exadversus** *adv* (**-vor-**) on the opposite side **‖** *prep (w. dat or acc)* across from, right opposite

exaedificāti·ō -ōnis *f* construction

exaedific·ō -āre -āvī -ātus *tr* to finish building, build, construct; *(fig)* to complete

exaequāti·ō -ōnis *f* leveling; uniformity

exaequ·ō -āre -āvī -ātus *tr* to level, make level; *(fig)* to equal, regard as equal **‖** *pass (w. dat)* to be put on the same level with

exaestu·ō -āre -āvī -ātum *intr* to seethe, boil; to ferment

exaggerāti·ō -ōnis *f* exaltation; *(rhet)* intensification *(by repetition or piling up);* **animi exaggeratio** broadening of the mind

exagger·ō -āre -āvī -ātus *tr* to pile up; to enlarge; to enhance

exagitāt·or -ōris *m* critic

exagit·ō -āre -āvī -ātus *tr* to stir up, keep on the move; to scare away; to criticize, satirize; to irritate; to arouse *(feelings)*

exagōg·a -ae *or* **exagoge -ēs** *f* exportation

exalb·escō -escĕre -uī *intr* to turn pale

exām·en -inis *n* swarm; crowd; tongue of a scale; weighing, consideration

examussim *adv* exactly

exāmin·ō -āre -āvī -ātus *tr* to weigh, balance; to examine **‖** *intr* to swarm

exancl·ō -āre -āvī -ātus *tr* to draw off, drain; to go through *(e.g., a war)*

exanimāl·is -is -e *adj* dead, lifeless; deadly

exanimāti·ō -ōnis *f* breathlessness; terror, panic

exanim·is -is -e *or* **exanim·us -a -um** *adj* breathless, terrified; lifeless; fainting

exanim·ō -āre -āvī -ātus *tr* to knock the breath out of; to wind, tire, weaken; to deprive of life, kill; to scare out of one's wits; to dishearten; to agitate

exanimus *see* **exanimis**

exar·descō -descĕre -sī -sum *intr* to catch fire; *(lit & fig)* to flare up

exār·escō -escĕre -uī *intr* to become quite dry, dry up

exarm·ō -āre -āvī -ātus *tr* to disarm

exar·ō -āre -āvī -ātus *tr* to plow up; to raise, produce; to write *(on wax with a stylus),* write down, note; to furrow, wrinkle; **frontem rugis exarare** to knit one's brows

exasper·ō -āre -āvī -ātus *tr* to make rough, roughen; to exasperate; to make worse

exauctōr·ō -āre -āvī -ātus *tr (mil)* to discharge; *(mil)* to give a dishonorable discharge to

exaud·iō -īre -īvī *or* **-iī -ītus** *tr* to hear clearly; to discern; to perceive, understand; to listen to; to grant

exaug·eō -ēre *tr* to increase greatly

exaugurāti·ō -ōnis *f* deconsecration

exaugur·ō -āre -āvī -ātus *tr* to deconsecrate

exauspic·ō -āre -āvī *intr (w.* **ex**) *(hum)* to come out of *(e.g., chains)* with good auspices

exb- = **eb-**

exballist·ō -āre *tr* to finish off, batter down the defenses of

exbibō *see* **ebibo**

exc- = **exsc-**

excaec·ō -āre -āvī -ātus *tr* to blind; to block up *(a river, pipe);* to dim, darken

excalceāt·us -a -um *adj* unshod; *(of an actor)* not wearing the buskin, acting in comedy **‖** *mpl* comic actors

excalce·ō -āre *tr* **excalceare pedes** take off the shoes

excandescenti·a -ae *f* mounting anger, outburst of anger

excand·escō -escĕre -uī *intr* to grow white

hot; to burst into a rage, flare up, reach a pitch *(of emotion)*

excant·ō -āre -āvī -ātus *tr* to charm away

excarnific·ō -āre -āvī -ātus *tr* (**-nu-**) to tear to pieces, torture to death; to torment *(mentally)*

excav·ō -āre -āvī -ātus *tr* to hollow out

ex·cēdō -cēdĕre -cessī -cessus *tr* to exceed, pass, surpass ‖ *intr* to go out, go away, withdraw, depart, disappear; to die; **e medio** *(or* **e vita) excedere** to depart this life

excell·ens -entis *adj* excellent, superior

excellenter *adv* excellently

excellenti·a -ae *f* excellence, superiority; **per excellentiam** par excellence

excell·ō -ĕre -uī *intr* to excel; *(w. dat or* **super** *+ acc)* to be superior to, surpass; *(w. abl or* **in** *+ abl)* to be superior in, excel in

excelsē *adv* high, loftily

excelsit·ās -ātis *f* loftiness

excels·us -a -um *adj* high, lofty; tall; eminent ‖ *n* height, high ground; high social status; **in excelso aetatem** *(or* **vitam) agere** to be in the limelight

excepti·ō -ōnis *f* exception, restriction, limitation; *(leg)* objection raised by a defendant against an accuser's statement; *(leg)* a limiting clause

except·ō -āre -āvī -ātus *tr* to catch; to pick up

exceptus *pp of* **excipio**

ex·cernō -cernĕre -crēvī -crētus *tr* to sift out, separate

excerp·ō -ĕre -sī -tus *tr* to pick out, extract, to choose; to gather; to leave out, omit

excerpt·um -ī *n* excerpt

excess·us -ūs *m* departure; death; digression

excetr·a -ae *f* water-snake; spiteful woman

excidi·ō -ōnis *f* destruction

excid·ium -iī *n* destruction, overthrow; cause of destruction

excĭd·ō -ĕre -ī *intr* to fall out; *(of an utterance)* to slip out; to pass away, perish; to degenerate; to disappear; to be forgotten; *(w.* **in** *+ acc)* to degenerate into; *(w. abl or* **ex)** **1** to be deprived of, lose; **2** to forget, miss; *(w. dat or* **de** *+ abl)* **1** to fall from; **2** to escape from *(lips);* **e memoriā excidere** to slip one's mind

excī·dō -dĕre -dī -sus *tr* to cut out, cut off, cut down; to raze, demolish; *(fig)* to banish, eliminate

excieō *see* **excio**

exc·iō -īre -īvī *or* **-iī -ītus** *or* **-ĭtus** *or* **exci·eō -ēre** *tr* to call *(s.o.)* out, summon; to awaken; to disturb; to frighten; to stir up, excite; to produce, occasion

ex·cipiō -cipĕre -cēpī -ceptus *tr* to take out, remove; to rescue; to exempt; to take, receive, catch, capture; to follow, succeed to; to intercept; to be exposed to; to incur; to welcome; to take up eagerly; to listen to, overhear; to except, make an exception of; to reach *(a place);* to mention in particular; to take on, withstand

excīsi·ō -ōnis *f* destruction

excīsus *pp of* **excīdo**

excitāt·us -a -um *adj* excited, lively, vigorous; loud

excit·ō -āre -āvī -ātus *tr* to wake up, rouse; to raise, stir up; to erect, construct, produce; to cause, occasion; *(fig)* to arouse, awaken, inspire, stimulate, enliven, encourage; to startle

excītus *or* **excĭtus** *pp of* **excio**

excīvī *pp of* **excio**

exclāmāti·ō -ōnis *f* exclamation

exclām·ō -āre -āvī -ātus *tr & intr* to exclaim, shout, yell

exclū·dō -dĕre -sī -sus *tr* to exclude, shut out, shut off; to remove, separate; to hatch; *(coll)* to knock out *(an eye);* to prevent

exclūsi·ō -ōnis *f* exclusion

exclūsus *pp of* **excludo**

excoctus *pp of* **excoquo**

excōgitāti·ō -ōnis *f* thinking up, inventing, contriving

excōgitāt·us -a -um *adj* carefully thought up; choice

excōgit·ō -āre -āvī -ātus *tr* to think up, devise, contrive

ex·colō -colĕre -coluī -cultus *tr* to tend, cultivate, work carefully; to refine, ennoble, perfect, improve; to adorn; to worship

ex·coquō -coquĕre -coxī -coctus *tr* to cook out, boil away; to dry up; to bake thoroughly; to temper *(steel)*

excor·s -dis *adj* senseless, silly

excrēment·um -ī *n* excretion *(spittle, urine, etc.);* excrement

excreō *see* **ex(s)creo**

ex·crescō -crescĕre -crēvī -crētum *intr* to grow out; to grow up, rise up

excruciābil·is -is -e *adj* deserving torture

excruci·ō -āre -āvī -ātus *tr* to torture, torment

excubi·ae -ārum *fpl* standing guard; sentry; watchfire

excubit·or -ōris *m* sentry

excub·ō -ĕre -uī -itum *intr* to sleep out of doors; to be attentive, be on the alert; *(mil)* to stand guard

excū·dō -dĕre -dī -sus *tr* to beat out, strike out; to hammer out; to forge; to hatch *(eggs); (fig)* to hammer into shape, write up

exculc·ō -āre -āvī -ātus *tr* to kick out; to tread down on; to stomp

excultus *pp of* **excolo**

excūrāt·us -a -um *adj* carefully attended to

ex·currō -currĕre -cucurrī *or* **-currī -cursum** *intr* to run out, dash out; *(mil)* to sally forth, make an incursion; to project, extend; *(fig)* to fan out, expand

excursi·ō -ōnis *f* sally, sortie; excursion, short trip *(away from a place);* journey, expedition; digression; outset, opening *(of a speech)*

excurs·or -ōris *m* skirmisher; emissary; courier

excurs·us -ūs *m* sally, sortie, raid, charge; expedition, short trip *(away from a place);* journey; digression; *(geog)* projection

excūsābil·is -is -e *adj* excusable

excūsātē *adv* excusably, without blame

excūsāti·ō -ōnis *f* excuse

excūsāt·us -a -um *adj* free from blame, exempt

excūs·ō -āre -āvī -ātus *tr* to free from blame, excuse; to except; to make excuses for, apologize for; to allege in excuse, plead as an excuse

excussus *pp of* **excutio**

excūsus *pp of* **excudo**

excu·tiō -tĕre -ssī -ssus *tr* to shake out, shake off, shake loose; to knock out *(e.g., teeth); (of a horse)* to throw; to shake out *(a garment);* to jilt, give the cold shoulder to; to toss, throw, shoot; to search; to examine, investigate; to discover; *(fig)* to shake off

exd- = ed-

exdorsu·ō -āre *tr* to fillet

exec- *see* **exsec-**

ex·edō -esse *or* **-edĕre -ēdī -ēsus** *tr* to eat up, consume; to destroy; to prey on; to make hollow; to wear away, corrode; to emaciate

exedr·a -ae *f (semi-circular recess in a wall for sitting, often used for lectures)* sitting room; lecture hall

exedr·ium -(i)ī *n* small sitting room

exempl·ar *or* **exempl·āre -āris** *n* copy; transcript; likeness; pattern, model, ideal

exemplār·is -is -e *adj* following a model **||** *m* copy; transcript

exempl·um -ī *n* sample, example, typical instance; precedent; pattern, make, character; model, pattern *(of conduct);* object lesson; warning; copy; transcript; portrait

exemptus *pp of* **eximo**

exenter·ō -āre -āvī -ātus *tr* **(-int-)** to disembowel, gut; *(fig)* to empty *(purse)*

ex·eō -īre -īvī *or* **-iī -itus** *tr* to pass beyond, cross; to ward off, avoid; *(fig)* to exceed **||** *intr* to go out, go forth; to go away, withdraw, depart, retire; to march out; to disembark; to pour out, gush out, flow out; to escape, be freed; to pass away, perish; *(of time)* to run out; to get out, become public; to burgeon forth; *(of hills)* to rise

exeq- = exseq-

exerc·eō -ēre -uī -itus *tr* to exercise, train; to keep *(s.o.)* busy, keep *(s.o.)* going; to supervise; to cultivate, work *(the soil);* to occupy *(the mind);* to practice *(medicine, patience, skills, etc.);* to carry into effect; to annoy, bother; to worry; to last through *(e.g., winter);* to levy, collect *(taxes);* to use *(instruments, materials);* to wield *(power, authority);* to run *(a business);* to carry on *(investigation); (mil)* to drill, train; **aleam exercere** to gamble; **causidicos exercere** to keep the lawyers busy; **faenus exercere** to lend money at interest; **imperium exercere** to wield power; **justitiam exercere** to administer justice; **legem exercere** to enforce a law; **quaestionem de sicariis exercere** to conduct prosecutions for murder; **vectigalia exercere** to levy taxes, collect taxes **||** *refl* to exercise, do exercises

exercitāti·ō -ōnis *f* exercise, practice, experience, training; cultivation; *(w. gen)* practice in

exercitāt·us -a -um *adj* experienced, trained, disciplined; troubled

exercit·ium -(i)ī *n* exercise, training, practice; written exercise; proficiency

exercit·ō -āre -āvī -ātus *tr* to keep in training, train, exercise; to habituate; to trouble

exercit·or -ōris *m* trainer

exercit·us -a -um *pp of* **exerceo ||** *adj* disciplined; experienced; trying, tough; troubled, harassed

exercit·us -ūs *m* army; infantry; army of followers; swarm, flock, multitude; *(pol)* assembly of the people

exerō *see* **exsero**

exēs·or -ōris *m* corrosive factor, underminer

exēsus *pp of* **exedo**

exf- *see* **eff-**

exhalāti·ō -ōnis *f* exhalation, vapor

exhāl·ō -āre -āvī -ātus *tr* to exhale, give off; **animam** *(or* **vitam) exhalare** to breathe one's last **||** *intr* to exhale; to steam

exhau·riō -rīre -sī -stus *tr* to draw out, empty; to drain, exhaust; to deplete; to take away, remove; to drain dry; to bring to an end; to undergo, endure; to carry out *(task);* to discuss fully

exhērēd·ō -āre -āvī -ātus *tr* to disinherit

exhēr·ēs -ēdis *adj* disinherited

exhib·eō -ēre -uī -itus *tr* to hold out; to present, produce; to display, exhibit; to cause, occasion; to render, make

exhilar·ō -āre -āvī -ātus *tr* to cheer up

exhorr·escō -escěre -uī *tr* to shudder at ‖ *intr* to be terrified
exhortāti·ō -ōnis *f* encouragement ‖ *fpl* words of encouragement
exhort·or -ārī -ātus sum *tr* to encourage, exhort
ex·igō -igěre -ēgī -actus *tr* to drive out, push out, thrust out, expel; to demand, exact, collect; to require; to pass, spend, complete *(life, time);* to finish, conclude; to ascertain; to weigh, consider, estimate; to examine; to test; to dispose of
exiguē *adv* slightly, sparingly, barely; briefly
exiguit·ās -ātis *f* shortness, smallness; meagerness, scantiness, scarcity
exigu·us -a -um *adj* slight, short, small, meager, scanty, poor, paltry, inadequate; a little, a bit of ‖ *n* a bit, a small amount
exiliō *see* **exsilio**
exīl·is -is -e *adj* thin, small, meager, feeble, poor; dreary; depleted *(ranks);* worthless; insincere; *(rhet)* dry, flat, jejune *(style)*
exīlit·ās -ātis *f* thinness; meagerness; dreariness
exīliter *adv* concisely; drearily; parsimoniously; jejunely
exilium *see* **exsilium**
exim *see* **exinde**
eximiē *adv* exceptionally
eximi·us -a -um *adj* excepted; exempt; choice, select; special, exceptional
ex·imō -iměre -ēmī -emptus *tr* to take out, take away, remove; to exempt; to free, release, let off; to make an exception of; to waste, lose *(time);* to banish *(worries)*
exin *see* **exinde**
exinān·iō -īre -īvī *or* **-iī -ītus** *tr* to empty; to drain, dry up; to weaken; to strip; *(fig)* to clean out, fleece
exinde *or* **exim** *or* **exin** *adv* from that place, from that point; *(in enumerating)* after that, next, then, furthermore; *(of time)* from that point, after that, then; accordingly
existimāti·ō -ōnis *f* **(-tum-)** opinion, view, judgment, favorable opinion; appraisal; decision, verdict; reputation, good name; *(com)* credit; **vulgi existimatio** public opinion; **existimatio tibi est** it is for you to judge
existimāt·or -ōris *m* critic, judge
existim·ō -āre -āvī -ātus *tr* **(-tum-)** to form an opinon of, judge, consider, regard; to think, suppose; **in hostium numero existimare** to regard as an enemy
existō *see* **exsisto**
exitiābil·is -is -e *adj* deadly, fatal
exitiāl·is -is -e *adj* deadly, fatal
exiti·ō -ōnis *f* going out, exit
exitiōs·us -a -um *adj* deadly, destructive
exit·ium -(i)ī *n* destruction, ruin; cause of destruction; death
exit·us -ūs *m* going out, exit, departure; way out, outlet; end, close, conclusion; **ad exitum adducere** to bring to a close
exl- = el-
exlecebra *see* **elecebra**
ex·lex -lēgis *adj* without law, exempt from the law; lawless
exm- = em-
exo- = exso-
exobsecr·ō -āre -āvī -ātus *tr* **(exops-)** to beg earnestly, entreat
exocul·ō -āre -āvī -ātus *tr* to knock the eyes out of
exod·ium -(i)ī *n* finale; farce *(presented after the main feature)*
exol·escō -escěre -ēvī -ētum *intr* **(exs-)** to decay, fade; to become obsolete; to grow up, become an adult
exolēt·us -a -um *adj* full-grown ‖ *m (fig)* male prostitute
exoner·ō -āre -āvī -ātus *tr* to unload; to empty; *(fig)* to relieve, free
exoptābil·is -is -e *adj* highly desirable, long-awaited
exoptāt·us -a -um *adj* longed-for, welcome, desired
exopt·ō -āre -āvī -ātus *tr* to long for, wish earnestly for, desire greatly
exōrābil·is -is -e *adj* accessible, sympathetic
exōrābul·a -ōrum *npl* enticements, bait, entreaties
exōrāt·or -ōris *m* successful petitioner
exor·dior -dīrī -sus sum *tr & intr* to begin, start, commence
exord·ium -(i)ī *n* beginning, start, commencement; origin; introduction
exor·ior -īrī -tus sum *intr* to come out, come forth, rise, appear; to begin, arise, be caused, be produced
exornāti·ō -ōnis *f* embellishment
exornāt·or -ōris *m* embellisher
exorn·ō -āre -āvī -ātus *tr* to fit out, furnish, equip, provide, supply; to adorn, embellish, decorate, set off
exōr·ō -āre -āvī -ātus *tr* to prevail upon, win over; to gain *or* obtain by entreaty; to appease
exors·us -a -um *pp of* **exordior** ‖ *npl* beginning, commencement; introduction, preamble
exors·us -ūs *m* beginning, commencement; introduction
exortus *pp of* **exorior**
exort·us -ūs *m* rising; the East
ex·os -ossis *or* **exoss·is -is -e** *adj* boneless
exoscul·or -ārī -ātus sum *tr* to kiss lovingly, kiss tenderly
exoss·ō -āre -āvī -ātus *tr* to bone, take the bones out of

exostr·a -ae *f* movable stage; **in exostra** in public
exōs·us -a -um *adj* hating, detesting
exōtic·us -a -um *adj* foreign, exotic; **Graeca exoctica** Magna Graecia *(S. Italy)*
exp- = exsp-
expall·escō -escĕre -uī *tr* to turn pale at, dread **II** *intr* to turn pale
expalliāt·us -a -um *adj* robbed of one's cloak
expalp·ō -āre -āvī -ātus *tr* to coax out
ex·pan·dō -dĕre -dī -sus *or* **-passus** *tr* to spread out, unfold, expand
expassus *pp of* **expando**
expatr·ō -āre -āvī -ātus *tr* to squander
expav·escō -escĕre -ī *tr* to panic at **II** *intr* to panic
expect- = exspect-
expecūliāt·us -a -um *adj* stripped of one's savings
exped·iō -īre -īvī *or* **-iī -ītus** *tr* to untie, unwrap; to unfetter; to extricate *(a person from a confined position);* to disentangle; to get ready; to clear for action; to clear *(roads of obstacles);* to solve, clear up *(problems);* to settle *(a debt);* to get *(s.o.)* out of *(troubles);* to put in order, arrange, settle, adjust, set right; to explain, clear up; to disclose; to recount, relate; to supply, provide; to accomplish, achieve **II** *refl* to prepare oneself, get ready **II** *intr* to be useful, be profitable; to set out *(on a military expedition);* to turn out *(in a certain manner);* *(w. dat)* to be useful to **II** *v impers (w. inf)* it is useful to, is advantageous to
expedītē *adv* freely, nimbly; quickly, expeditiously; unambiguously
expedīti·ō -ōnis *f* (military *or* naval) expedition, campaign; special mission; *(rhet)* proof by elimination
expedīt·us -a -um *adj* unencumbered, unhampered, unobstructed; ready, prompt; ready at hand, convenient; agile; *(of roads)* easy to travel, fast; quick *(mind);* *(mil)* light-armed; **in expedito** in readiness, at hand; without hindrance
ex·pellō -pellĕre -pulī -pulsus *tr* to drive out, expel; to disown
expen·dō -dĕre -dī -sus *tr* to weigh out; to pay out, pay down, lay out, expend; to rate, estimate; to ponder, consider; to pay *(penalty)*
expens·us -a -um *adj* paid out, spent **II** *n* payment, expenditure
expergē·faciō -facĕre -fēcī -factus *tr* to awaken, wake up; to arouse
exper·giscor -giscī -rectus sum *intr* to wake up; to be alert
experg·ō -ĕre -ī -itus *tr* to wake up
experi·ens -entis *adj* enterprising, active; *(w. gen)* ready to undergo
experienti·a -ae *f* test, trial, experiment; experience, practice; effort
experīment·um -ī *n* test, experiment, proof; experience; person serving as a test, test-case
exper·ior -īrī -tus sum *tr* to test, try, prove; to experience, endure, find out; to try to do, attempt; to measure strength with **II** *intr* to go to court
experrectus *pp of* **expergiscor**
exper·s -tis *adj (w. gen)* **1** having no share in, having no part in; **2** devoid of, free from, without
expert·us -a -um *pp of* **experior II** *adj* tried, tested, proved; *(w. gen)* experienced in
expetess·ō -ĕre *tr* to desire, long for
expet·ō -ĕre -īvī *or* **-iī -ītus** *tr* to ask for, demand; to exact *(penalty);* to ask about; to aim at, head for; to desire, long for **II** *intr (w.* **in** *+ acc)* to befall; to fall upon, assail
expiāti·ō -ōnis *f* expiation, atonement; satisfaction; purification
expictus *pp of* **expingo**
expīlāti·ō -ōnis *f* pillaging, ransacking, looting
expīlāt·or -ōris *m* plunderer, looter, robber
expīl·ō -āre -āvī -ātus *tr* to plunder, rob, ransack; to plagiarize
ex·pingō -pingĕre -pinxī -pictus *tr* to paint; to depict
expi·ō -āre -āvī -ātus *tr* to purify; to atone for, expiate; to avenge; to appease; to avert *(a curse, bad omen)*
expīrō *see* **exspiro**
expisc·or -ārī -ātus sum *tr* to go fishing for *(information)*
explānātē *adv* plainly, clearly
explānāti·ō -ōnis *f* explanation; clear pronunciation
explānāt·or -ōris *m* interpreter
explānāt·us -a -um *adj* plain
explān·ō -āre -āvī -ātus *tr* to explain, make clear; to flatten out; to pronounce distinctly
explaudō *see* **explodo**
explēment·um -ī *n* filling, stuffing
expl·eō -ēre -ēvī -ētus *tr* to fill up; to complete; to satisfy *(desires);* to make good *(losses);* to fulfill, perform, accomplish, discharge
explēti·ō -ōnis *f* satisfying, fulfillment
explēt·us -a -um *adj* full, complete, perfect
explicātē *adv* clearly, plainly
explicāti·ō -ōnis *f* unfolding, uncoiling; analysis; interpretation
explicāt·or -ōris *m,* **explicātr·ix -īcis** *f* explainer, interpreter
explicāt·us -a -um *adj* plain, clear-cut, straightforward

explicāt·us -ūs *m* unfolding; explanation, interpretation
explicit·us -a -um *adj* disentangled; simple, easy
explic·ō -āre -āvī *(or* **-uī) -ātus** *(or* **-itus)** *tr* to unfold, unroll; to spread out; to loosen, undo; to set free; to arrange, adjust, settle; to exhibit; to explain; to display
ex·plōdō -plōdĕre -plōsī -plōsus *tr* **(-plaud-)** to drive off the stage *(by clapping);* to boo; to disapprove of, discredit
explōrātē *adv* after careful examination; for sure, for certain
explōrāti·ō -ōnis *f* exploration, examination
explōrāt·or -ōris *m* scout, spy
explōrāt·us -a -um *adj* sure, certain; safe, secure; *(w. abl)* clear of; **exploratum** *(or* **pro explorato) habere** to know for sure
explōr·ō -āre -āvī -ātus *tr* to explore, investigate; to probe, search; to test, try, try out; *(w. acc & inf)* to ascertain that; *(w.* **ut, ne)** to insure (that; that not); *(mil)* to reconnoiter
explōsi·ō -ōnis *f* driving off the stage, booing
expol·iō -īre -īvī *or* **-iī -ītus** *tr* to polish; to finish off *(a building e.g., with plaster); (fig)* to embellish, adorn, refine
expolīti·ō -ōnis *f* polishing, finishing off, embellishing
expolīt·us -a -um *adj* polished, lustrous; refined
ex·pōnō -pōnĕre -posuī -positus *or* **-postus** *tr* to put out, bring out (into the open); to expose *(children to die);* to leave in an exposed position; to display, put on show; to make available; to reveal; to publish; to exhibit; to relate; to explain; to offer, tender; to set on shore, land; to send *(s.o.)* sprawling; *(w. dat or* **ad** *or* **adversus** *+ acc)* to expose to
expor·rigō *or* **expor·gō -rigĕre -rexī -rectus** *tr* to stretch out, spread (out); **exporge frontem!** *(coll)* quit frowning! ‖ *refl (geog)* to extend, reach
exportāti·ō -ōnis *f* exportation
export·ō -āre -āvī -ātus *tr* to carry out; to export
ex·poscō -poscĕre -poposcī *tr* to demand, beg, insist upon; to demand the surrender of; *(w. double acc)* to ask *(s.o.)* for *(s.th.)*
expositīci·us -a -um *adj* foundling
expositi·ō -ōnis *f* exposing; *(rhet)* statement, description, explanation
exposit·us -a -um *pp of* **expono** ‖ *adj* frank; affable; plain, trite
expostulāti·ō -ōnis *f* insistent demand; complaint
expostul·ō -āre -āvī -ātus *tr* to demand, insist on; to complain of; *(w.* **cum** *of person)* to complain about *(s.th)* to *(s.o.)* ‖ *intr (w.* **cum)** to lodge a complaint with
expostus *pp of* **expono**
expōtus *see* **epōtus**
express·us -a -um *adj* distinct, clear, express; *(w.* **ad)** closely modeled on
ex·primō -primĕre -pressī -pressus *tr* to press out, squeeze out; to extort; to press upwards, raise; to model, form, portray; to stamp *(a design on a surface);* to represent; to imitate, copy; *(w.* **ad)** to model on *(a pattern);* to describe; to express; to translate; to pronounce, articulate; **exprimere in melius** to improve on
exprobrāti·ō -ōnis *f (w. gen)* reproach arising from
exprobr·ō -āre -āvī -ātus *tr* to reproach, find fault with; *(w. dat)* to cast *(s.th.)* up to, put the blame for *(s.th.)* on ‖ *intr (w. dat)* to complain to
exprōm·ō -ĕre -psī -ptus *tr* to bring out, fetch out *(from storage);* to give vent to; to disclose, display, exhibit; to utter, express, state; to bring into play, put to use
expugnābil·is -is -e *adj* vulnerable to attack
expugnāci·or -or -us *adj* more potent
expugnāti·ō -ōnis *f* assault; *(w. gen)* assault on; ruin
expugnāt·or -ōris *m* attacker; **expugnator pudicitiae** rapist
expugn·ō -āre -āvī -ātus *tr* to assault, storm; to break into, plunder *(a home);* to defeat; *(fig)* to overcome, sweep aside *(conditions, purposes); (fig)* to achieve, accomplish; *(fig)* to extort, wrest, gain; to persuade, overcome the resistance of
expulsi·ō -ōnis *f* expulsion
expuls·ō -āre -āvī -ātus *tr* to drive out, expel
expuls·or -ōris *m* expeller
expulsus *pp of* **expello**
expultr·ix -īcis *f* expeller *(female)*
expun·gō -gĕre -xī -ctus *tr* to expunge; *(fin)* to cancel *(a debt),* check off the list as paid; *(vulg)* to prick thoroughly
expurgāti·ō -ōnis *f* **(-pūrig-)** justification, excuse; cleansing
expurg·ō -āre -āvī -ātus *tr* **(-pūrig-)** to cleanse, purify; to cure; to vindicate; to excuse, justify
expūtesc·ō -ĕre *intr* to rot away
exput·ō -āre -āvī -ātus *tr* to prune, lop off; to consider; to figure out
exquīrō exquīrĕre exquīsīvī exquīsītus *tr* **(-quaer-)** to look into, ask about; to look for; to search, examine; to find out; **pretium exquirire** to work out a price

exquīsītē *adv* carefully, accurately; exquisitely
exquīsīt·us -a -um *pp of* **exquiro** ‖ *adj* carefully considered; meticulous; choice, exquisite
exr- = **er-**
exrādīcitus *adv* (**ērād-**) utterly
exsaev·iō -īre *intr* to lose its fury
e(x)sangu·is -is -e *adj* bloodless; pale; feeble; causing paleness
ex(s)ar·ciō -cīre -sī -tus *tr* (**ex(s)er-**) to patch up, mend
ex(s)ati·ō -āre -āvī -ātus *tr* to satisfy fully
exsaturābil·is -is -e *adj* appeasable
exsatur·ō -āre -āvī -ātus *tr* to satisfy completely, glut
exsce- = **esce-**
ex(s)cindō ex(s)cindĕre ex(s)cidī ex(s)cissus *tr* to annihilate, demolish; to exterminate *(a people)*
ex(s)cre·ō -āre -āvī -ātus *tr* to cough up, spit out
exscrī·bō -bĕre -psī -ptus *tr* to write down; to write out in full; to copy; *(fig)* to take after, resemble
ex(s)culp·ō -ĕre -sī -tus *tr* to carve out; to scratch out, erase; *(fig)* to extort
ex(s)ec·ō *or* **ex(s)ic·ō -āre -uī -tus** *tr* to cut out, cut away, cut off; to castrate; to deduct
ex(s)ecrābil·is -is -e *adj* accursed; bitter, merciless, deadly; amounting to execration
ex(s)ecrāti·ō -ōnis *f* curse, execration; solemn oath
ex(s)ecrāt·us -a -um *adj* accursed, detestable
ex(s)ecr·or -ārī -ātus sum *tr* to curse ‖ *intr* to take a solemn oath
ex(s)ecti·ō -ōnis *f* cutting out
ex(s)ecūti·ō -ōnis *f* execution, performance; administration *(of a province);* development *(of a subject)*
ex(s)ecūtus *pp of* **ex(s)equor**
ex(s)equi·ae -ārum *fpl* funeral procession; funeral service; **ex(s)equias ire** to attend a funeral
ex(s)equiāl·is -is -e *adj* funeral; **carmina exsequialia** dirges
ex(s)e·quor -quī -cūtus sum *tr* to follow out; to accompany to the grave; to perform, execute, carry out; to follow up, investigate; to pursue, go after; to avenge, punish; to say, tell, relate; to describe; to enumerate, go through; *(rhet)* to develop *(a topic);* **verbis exsequi** to enumerate
ex(s)er·ō -ĕre -uī -tus *tr* to untie, disconnect; to stretch out *(one's arms);* to stick out *(one's tongue);* to bare, uncover
ex(s)ert·ō -āre -āvī -ātus *tr* to keep on stretching *or* sticking out
ex(s)ertus *pp of* **ex(s)ero** ‖ *adj* uncovered, bare; protruding
ex(s)ībil·ō -āre -āvī -ātus *tr* to hiss off the stage
ex(s)iccāt·us -a -um *adj* dry, uninteresting
ex(s)icc·ō -āre -āvī -ātus *tr* to dry up; to drain dry
ex(s)icō *see* **ex(s)eco**
exsign·ō -āre -āvī -ātus *tr* to mark down exactly, write down in detail
ex(s)il·iō -īre -uī *intr* to jump out; to be startled; **ex(s)ilire gaudio** to jump for joy
ex(s)il·ium -(i)ī *n* exile; place of exile
ex·(s)istō -(s)istĕre -(s)titī -(s)titum *intr* to come out, come forth; to appear, emerge; to exist, be; to arise, proceed; to turn into; to be visible ‖ *v impers* it follows as a consequence
ex(s)ol·vō -vĕre -vī -ūtus *tr* to loosen, untie; to release, set free; to discharge, pay; to keep, fufill; to satisfy *(hunger);* to break open, wound; to solve; to explain; to throw off, get rid of; to repay, requite; to give out *(awards, punishment)*
ex(s)omn·is -is -e *adj* sleepless
ex(s)or·beō -bēre -psī *tr* to absorb; to suck up, drain; to gulp down; to exhaust; *(fig)* to gobble up *(wealth, etc.)*
ex(s)or·s -tis *adj* without lots; chosen specially; *(w. gen)* having no share in, free from
ex(s)pati·or -ārī -ātus sum *intr* to go off course; to flow away from its course; to digress; to expatiate
ex(s)pectābil·is -is -e *adj* expected, anticipated
ex(s)pectāti·ō -ōnis *f* expectation, anticipation, suspense; **exspectationem facere** to cause suspense
ex(s)pectāt·us -a -um *adj* expected, awaited, desired
exspect·ō -āre -āvī -ātus *tr* to await, wait for, look out for; to hope for, anticipate, long for ‖ *intr* to wait with anticipation
exsper·gō -gĕre — -sus *tr* to sprinkle, scatter
ex(s)pēs *adj (only in nom sing)* hopeless, without hope
ex(s)pīrāti·ō -ōnis *f* breathing out, exhalation
ex(s)pīr·ō -āre *tr* to breathe out, exhale, emit ‖ *intr* to be exhaled; to expire, breathe one's last; *(fig)* to come to an end, cease
ex(s)plend·escō -escĕre -uī *intr* to glitter, shine; to become conspicuous
ex(s)poli·ō -āre -āvī -ātus *tr* to strip; to pillage
ex(s)p·uō -uĕre -uī -ūtus *tr* to spit out; *(fig)* to banish *(e.g., cares)*
ex(s)tern·ō -āre -āvī -ātus *tr* to startle, scare; to terrify; to stampede

ex(s)till·ō -āre -āvī *intr* to drip, trickle out; to melt
ex(s)timulāt·or -ōris *m* instigator
ex(s)timul·ō -āre -āvī -ātus *tr* to goad; *(fig)* to stir up
ex(s)tincti·ō -ōnis *f* extinction
ex(s)tinct·or -ōris *m* extinguisher; suppressor; destroyer
ex(s)tin·guō -guĕre -xī -ctus *tr* to extinguish, put out; to destroy, kill; to abolish, annul ‖ *pass* to die, die out; to be forgotten
ex(s)tirp·ō -āre -āvī -ātus *tr* to pull up by the roots, extirpate, root out, eradicate
ex(s)t·ō -āre ex(s)titī *intr* to stand out, protrude, project; to stand out, be prominent, be conspicuous; to be visible; to appear; to exist, be extant
ex(s)tructi·ō -ōnis *f* erection, construction
exstruct·um -ī *n* platform
ex(s)tru·ō -ĕre -xī -ctus *tr* to pile up; to build, erect, construct
ex(s)uct·us -a -um *pp of* **ex(s)ugo** ‖ *adj* dried up
ex(s)ūd·ō -āre -āvī -ātus *tr* to sweat over; to exude ‖ *intr* to ooze out
ex(s)ū·gō -gĕre -xī -ctus *tr* to suck out; *(fig)* to draw out *(moisture)*
ex(s)·ul -ulis *mf* exile, refugee
ex(s)ul·ō -āre -āvī *intr* to be an exile, be a refugee
ex(s)ultāti·ō -ōnis *f* exultation, jumping for joy
ex(s)ultim *adv* friskily
ex(s)ult·ō -āre -āvī *intr* to jump up; to frisk about; *(of horses)* to rear, prance; *(of heart)* to throb; to exult, rejoice, jump for joy; to revel, run riot; to boast; *(of speech)* to jump around
ex(s)uperābil·is -is -e *adj* conquerable
ex(s)uperanti·a -ae *f* superiority
ex(s)uper·ō -āre -āvī -ātus *tr* to surmount; to tower above; to exceed; to be too strong for, overpower; to outdo; to outlive ‖ *intr* to rise; to be superior, excel, to be conspicuous; to gain the upper hand; *(of flames)* to shoot up
ex(s)urd·ō -āre -āvī -ātus *tr* to deafen; to dull *(the senses)*
ex(s)ur·gō -gĕre -rexī *intr* to get up, rise, stand up; to swell; *(fig)* to recover strength; **foras ex(s)urgere** to get up and go out
exsuscit·ō -āre -āvī -ātus *tr* to rouse from sleep; to fan *(fire)*; to excite, stir up
ext·a -ōrum *npl* vital organs
extāb·escō -escĕre -uī *intr* to waste away; to pine away; to disappear
extār·is -is -e *adj* used for cooking the sacrificial victim; sacrificial
extemp(u)lō *adv* immediately, right away; on the spur of the moment
exten·dō -dĕre -dī -tus *or* **-sus** *tr* to stretch out, spread out, extend; to enlarge, increase; to widen; to prolong, continue; to pass, spend; to exert, strain; **labellum extendere** to pout *(literally, to extend the lip)*; **vires omnes imperii extendere** to do everything in one's power ‖ *refl* to exert oneself ‖ *pass* to stretch out, extend; to be stretched out at full length
extent·ō -āre -āvī -ātus *tr* to exert, strain
extent·us -a -um *pp of* **extendo** ‖ *adj* extensive, wide; level; **per funem extentum ire** to walk a tightrope
extenuāti·ō -ōnis *f* belittlement
extenuāt·us -a -um *adj* thinned, reduced; trifling; weak, faint
extenu·ō -āre -āvī -ātus *tr* to thin out; to lessen; to detract from
exter *or* **exter·us -a -um** *adj* exterior, outward; foreign, strange; **mare exterum** the ocean *(as opposed to the Mediterranean Sea)* ‖ *m* foreigner
exterebr·ō -āre -āvī -ātus *tr* to bore out; to extort
exter·geō -gēre -sī -sus *or* **exter·gō -gĕre** *tr* to wipe out, wipe away; to wipe clean; *(fig)* to clean out
exteri·or -or -us *adj* exterior, outer
exterius *adv* on the outside
extermin·ō -āre -āvī -ātus *tr* to drive out, banish; to put aside, put away; to dismiss *(from the mind)*
extern·us -a -um *adj* external, outward; foreign, strange ‖ *m* foreigner, stranger, foreign enemy ‖ *npl* foreign goods
ex·terō -terĕre -trīvī -trītus *tr* to rub out, wear away; *(fig)* to crush
exterr·eō -ēre -uī -itus *tr* to terrify; *(w. abl)* to frighten out of
extersī *perf of* **extergeo**
extersus *pp of* **extergeo**
exters·us -ūs *m* the wiping
exterus *see* **exter**
extex·ō -ĕre -uī -tus *tr* to unweave; *(fig)* to cheat
extim·escō -escĕre -uī *tr* to become terribly afraid of, dread ‖ *intr* to become afraid
extim·us -a -um *adj* outermost, farthest, most remote
extisp·ex -icis *m* soothsayer *(who makes predictions by inspecting the entrails of animals)*
extispic·ium -(i)ī *n* the examination of entrails as a means of divination
extoll·ō -ĕre *tr* to lift up; to erect; to postpone; to extol, praise; to raise, exalt; to keep raised, hold up; to beautify; **animos extollere** to raise the morale ‖ *refl & pass (of heavenly bodies)* to rise
extor·queō -quēre -sī -tus *tr* to wrench, wrest; to dislocate; to extort
extorr·is -is -e *adj* driven out of one's country, banished, exiled

extorsī *perf of* **extorqueo**
extort·or -ōris *m* extortionist
extort·us -a -um *pp of* **extorqueo** ‖ *adj* deformed
extrā *adv* outside, on the outside; from the outside; **extra quam** except in the case that; **extra quam si** unless ‖ *prep (w. acc)* **1** outside, outside of: **extra nostrum ordinem** outside our class; **extra ordinem** outside the usual order, extraordinarily, exceptionally; **extra sortem** by direct appointment *(literally, outside the casting of lots);* **2** beyond (the limits of): **extra meum fundum** beyond (the limits of) my farm; **extra teli jactum** beyond the range of the weapon, out of range; **3** beyond the scope of, not subject to: **extra leges** beyond the scope of the laws, not subject to the laws; **4** free from, without: **extra modum** immoderately, abnormally *(literally, without measure);* **extra numerum** not in meter; off-key; **extra numerum es mihi** *(fig)* you don't count in my eyes; **5** apart from, except: **omnes extra me** everyone except me; **6** aside from: **extra jocum** all joking aside
extra·hō -hĕre -xī -ctus *tr* to pull out, drag out; to draw *(water)* out; to pull up *(to higher ground);* to prolong; to waste *(time);* to extricate, rescue; to remove; to tow *(a ship)* out
extrāne·us -a -um *adj* extraneous, external, irrelevant; foreign ‖ *mf* stranger; foreigner
extraordinārī·us -a -um *adj* extraordinary
extrāri·us -a -um *adj* outward, external; unrelated *(by family ties)*
extrēm·a -ōrum *npl* extremities, last measures, last resort; end *(e.g., of life, of strip of land); (mil)* rear elements
extrēmit·ās -ātis *f* extremity, end
extrēmō *adv* finally, at last
extrēmum *adv* finally, at last; for the last time
extrēm·us -a -um *adj* extreme, outermost, on the end; latest, last, hindmost; the last part of, end of; the tip of, the edge of; *(of degree)* utmost, extreme; lowest; **extrema aetas** advanced old age; **extrema cauda** tip of the tail; **extremā lineā amare** to love at a distance; **extrema manus** final touches; **extremis digitis attingere** to touch lightly; to hold tenderly; to touch lighly on; **extremo tempore** finally; **extremus ignis** flickering flame; **in extremo libro secundo** at the end of the second book ‖ *n* end; limit; edge; tip; bottom; extremity; conclusion; **ad extremum** at last; at the end; utterly; **in extremo** in mortal danger, in a crisis
extrīc·ō -āre -āvī -ātus *or* **extrīc·or -ārī -ātus sum** *tr* to extricate; to clear up; to obtain with difficulty
extrinsecus *adv* from the outside, from abroad; outside, on the outside
extrītus *pp of* **extero**
extrīvī *perf of* **extero**
extrū·dō -dĕre -sī -sus *tr* to push out; to eject, expel, drive out; to keep out *(e.g., the sea with dikes)*
ex·tumeō -ēre -uī *intr* to swell up
ex·tundō -tundĕre -tudī -tūsus *tr* to beat out, hammer out; to fashion; to devise; to extort, get *(a promise, concession)* out of
exturb·ō -āre -āvī -ātus *tr* to drive out, chase out, drive away; to divorce; to knock out; to disturb, upset; **matrimonio exturbare** to divorce *(a woman)*
exūber·ō -āre -āvī -ātum *intr* to grow luxuriantly; to abound
exul *see* **exsul**
exulō *see* **exsulo**
exulcer·ō -āre -āvī -ātus *tr* to make sore; to aggravate; to exasperate; to wound the feelings of
exulul·ō -āre -āvī -ātus *tr* to invoke with cries ‖ *intr* to howl, ululate
exunctus *pp of* **exungo**
exund·ō -āre -āvī *intr* to gush up, well up; to overflow; **in litora exundare** to wash ashore
exun·g(u)ō -g(u)ĕre -xī -ctus *tr* to rub down with oil
ex·uō -uĕre -uī -ūtus *tr* to take off, pull off; to shake off; to undress; to strip; to deprive *(of possessions);* to release; to cast aside, cast off; to bare
exurg·eō -ēre *tr* to squeeze out
ex·ūrō -ūrĕre -ussī -ustus *tr* to burn out; to burn up; to burn down; to dry up; to consume, destroy; to purge away; *(fig)* to inflame; **vivum** *(or* **vivam) exurere** to burn alive
exusti·ō -ōnis *f* conflagration
exust·us -a -um *pp of* **exuro**
exūtus *pp of* **exuo** ‖ *adj* bare; **unum pedem exutus** with one foot bare
exuvi·ae -ārum *fpl* spoils; souvenir; hide, skin; slough *(of snake);* clothing; symbols of the gods *(e.g., lightning bolt, scepter, etc., carried in procession)*
exuv·ium -(i)ī *n* spoils

F

fab·a -ae *f* bean
fabāl·is -is -e *adj* bean-; **stipulae fabales** bean stalks
fabell·a -ae *f* short story; fable; play
fa·ber -bra -brum *adj* skilled ‖ *m* crafts-

man; smith; carpenter; builder; **faber aerarius** coppersmith; **faber ferrarius** blacksmith; **faber marmoris** marble worker; **faber navalis** ship builder; **faber sandapilarum** bier maker; **faber tignarius** carpenter

Fab·ius -(i)ī *m* Quintus Fabius Maximus Cunctator *(see* **cunctātor)**

fabrē *adv* skillfully

fabrēfact·us -a -um *adj* constructed by craftsmen

fabric·a -ae *f* craft, trade, industry; workshop; workmanship; process of building, construction, production; **fabricam fingere** *(w.* **ad)** *(coll)* to pull a trick on

fabricāti·ō -ōnis *f* construction; structure

fabricāt·or -ōris *m* builder, producer, creator, architect

fabric·or -ārī -ātus sum *or* **fabric·ō -āre -āvī -ātus** *tr* to make, build, construct, produce; to forge; to prepare, form; to coin *(words)*

fabrīl·is -is -e *adj* craftsman's, carpenter's, smith's, builder's, sculptor's; skilled ‖ *npl* tools

fābul·a -ae *f* story, tale; talk, conversation; conversation piece; small talk; gossip; affair, matter; myth, legend; drama, play; dramatic poem; **fabula est** *(w. acc & inf)* legend has it that, the story goes that; **fabulae!** *(coll)* baloney!; **fabulam dare** *(or* **docere)** to present a play; **lupus in fabula!** *(coll)* speak of the devil!; **quae haec est fabula?** *(coll)* what's that you are saying?

fābulār·is -is -e *adj* legendary; **historia fabularis** mythology

fābulāt·or -ōris *m* story-teller; writer of fables

fābul·or -ārī -ātus sum *tr* to say, invent ‖ *intr* to talk, chat, gossip

fābulōs·us -a -um *adj* legendary; incredible; fictitious, mythical ‖ *n* myth, legend

fabul·us -ī *m* bean

facess·ō -ĕre -īvī *or* **-iī -ītus** *tr* to do eagerly, perform, accomplish; to bring on, cause, create; **negotium alicui facessere** to cause s.o. trouble; *(leg)* to bring a case against s.o.; **rem facessere** *(leg)* to sue ‖ *intr* to go away, depart, take off; *(lit & fig)* to retire; **cubitum facessere** to go to sleep

facētē *adv* facetiously, humorously, wittily, amusingly, brilliantly

facēti·ae -ārum *fpl* clever thing, clever talk, witticism, humor

facēt·us -a -um *adj* witty, humorous; fine, elegant; brilliant

faci·ēs -ēī *f* face; look, facial expression; appearance; make, form, shape, outline; nature, character; pretense, pretext; **a facie** in the face, in front; **in facie** *(w. gen)* in the presence of; **in faciem** *(w. gen)* so as to give the appearance of; into the presence of; **primā facie** at first sight

facilĕ *adv* easily, without trouble; unquestionably, far, by far; generally; quite, fully; promptly, readily, willingly; pleasantly, well; **non facile** hardly

facil·is -is -e *adj* easy; nimble; convenient, suitable; ready, quick; easygoing, good-natured; favorable; prosperous; gentle *(breeze);* easily borne, slight *(loss);* tame, obedient *(animals);* **ex** *(or* **e) facili** easily; **facile est** *(w. inf)* it is easy to; **facile est de** (+ *abl)* it does not matter about; **facilis victu** well-to-do, well-off; **facilius est ut** it is more likely that; **in facili esse** to be easy

facilit·ās -ātis *f* facility, ease, easiness; readiness; fluency; aptitude; good nature; courteousness; levity

faciliter *adv (pedantic for* **facile)**

facinorōs·us -a -um *adj & m* **(-ner-)** criminal; wicked

facin·us -oris *n* deed, act; event; crime, outrage; criminal

faciō facĕre fēcī factus (faxim = fēcerim; faxō = fēcerō) *tr* to make; to do, perform; to fashion, frame, create; to build, erect; to produce, compose; to produce *(young);* to bring about, cause, occasion; to acquire, get, gain; to incur, suffer; to render, grant, give, confer; to assert, say, represent, depict; to choose, appoint; to follow, practice; to regard, prize, value; **aliquem certiorem facere de** (+ *abl)* to inform s.o. about; **copiam facere** *(w. dat)* to afford *(s.o.)* the opportunity; **dies facere** to spend days; **fac ita esse** suppose it were so, granted that it is so; **fidem facere** to give one's word; **gratiam facere** to grant pardon, excuse; **gratum (pergratum) facere** *(w. dat)* to do s.o. a (great) favor; **pecuniam** *(or* **stipendium) facere** to make money, earn money; **pretium facere** to name the price; **promissum facere** to fulfill a promise; **sacra facere** to sacrifice, offer sacrifice; **verba facere** to speak; **viam facere** *(w. dat)* to make way for ‖ *intr* to do, act; to take part, take sides; *(w. dat or* **ad)** to be satisfactory for, be fit for, do for; *(of medicines)* to work; *(w.* **ad)** to be effective in dealing with; **suā causā** *(or* **suā re) facere** to act in one's own interests; *(euph. for relieving oneself)* to do one's duty

facteon = faciendum

facti·ō -ōnis *f* doing; making; party, faction; partisanship; band, group; troupe *(of actors);* social set, association; **quae haec factio est?** *(coll)* what's this all about?

factiōs·us -a -um *adj* busy; well-connected; belonging to a faction; factious, subversive, revolutionary
factit·ō -āre -āvī -ātus *tr* to keep doing, keep making; to practice *(e.g., trade); (w. double acc)* to declare *(s.o.)* to be *(e.g., heir)*
fact·or -ōris *m* maker; perpetrator *(of crime);* **factores et datores** pitchers and catchers *(in ballgame)*
fact·us -a -um *pp of* **facio** ‖ *n* deed, act; accomplishment, exploit; misdeed; **dictum factum** no sooner said than done
facul·a -ae *f* little torch
facult·ās -ātis *f* opportunity; feasibility; ability, capacity, skill; material resources; *(of things)* power, potency; supply *(of money, ships, men);* convenience; *(w. gen)* **1** power over; **2** skill in; **facultas ingenii** expertise ‖ *fpl* talents; resources
fācundē *adv* eloquently
fācundi·a -ae *f* eloquence
facundit·ās -ātis *f* eloquence
fācund·us -a -um *adj* eloquent
faece·us -a -um *adj* foul
faecul·a -ae *f* **(fēc-)** wine lees *(when dried, used as medicine or spice)*
faenebr·is -is -e *adj* **(fēn-)** of interest; lent at interest
faenerāti·ō -ōnis *f* **(fēn-)** lending at interest, investment
faenerātō *adv* with *or* at interest
faenerāt·or -ōris *m* **(fēn-)** money lender, investor
faener·or -ārī -ātus sum *or* **faener·ō -āre -āvī -ātus** *tr* **(fēn-)** to lend at interest; to invest *(money)*; to finance; to ruin *(e.g., a province)* through high interest rates ‖ *intr* to yield interest, bring profit
faene·us -a -um *adj* made of hay
faenicul·um -ī *n* fennel *(used as seasoning or medicine)*
faenīl·ia -ium *npl* **(fēn-)** hayloft
faenisec·a -ae *m* **(fēn-)** reaper, farmer
faen·um -ī *n* **(fēn-)** hay; **faenum habet in cornu** *(sl)* he's crazy *(literally, he has hay on his horns)*
faen·us -oris *n* **(fēn-)** interest; debt *(as result of heavy interest); capital; (fig)* profit, gain, advantage; **faenore** at interest; **in faenore** on loan
faenuscul·um -ī *n* **(fēn-)** a little interest
fae·x -cis *or* **fex fēcis** *f* wine lees, dregs; sediment; slag; impure mixture; *(fig)* scum
fāgine·us *or* **fāgin·us** *or* **fāge·us -a -um** *adj* beech
fāg·us -ī *f* beech tree
fal·a *or* **phal·a -ae** *f* movable wooden siege tower; scaffold
falāric·a -ae *f* **(phal-)** incendiary missile
falcār·ius -(i)ī *m* sickle maker
falcāt·us -a -um *adj* fitted with scythes; sickle-shaped, curved
falcif·er -era -erum *adj* scythe-bearing
falc·ō -ōnis *m* pigeon-toed person
Faleri·ī -ōrum *mpl* city of Etruria
Falern·us -a -um *adj* Falernian; **ager Falernus** district in N. Campania, famous for its wine ‖ *n* Falernian wine
Falisc·us -a -um *mpl* Faliscan ‖ *mpl* a people of S. E. Etruria
fallāci·a -ae *f* deception, deceit, trick
fallācit·ās -ātis *f* deceptiveness
fallāciter *adv* deceptively; falsely
fall·ax -ācis *adj* deceptive, deceitful; spurious, false
fall·ens -entis *adj* deceptive
fallō fallĕre fefellī falsus *tr* to cause to fall, trip; to lead into error, mislead; to deceive, trick, dupe, cheat; to fail to live up to, disappoint; to while away *(time);* to escape the clutches of; to escape the notice of, slip by; to disguise; **faciem alicujus fallere** to impersonate s.o.; **fidem fallere** to break one's word; **oculos fallere** to be invisible; **opinionem fallere** *(w. gen)* to fail to live up to the expectations of ‖ *pass* **nisi** *(or* **ni) fallor** unless I'm mistaken ‖ *intr* to go unnoticed ‖ *v impers* **me fallit** I am wrong
falsār·ius -(i)ī *m* forger
falsē *adv* falsely
falsidic·us -a -um *adj* speaking falsely, lying
falsific·us -a -um *adj* acting dishonestly
falsijūri·us -a -um *adj* swearing falsely
falsiloqu·us -a -um *adj* lying
falsimōni·a -ae *f* trick, deception
falsipar·ens -entis *adj* bastard
falsō *adv* mistakenly, wrongly, erroneously; falsely, deceitfully
fals·us -a -um *adj* false, untrue; mistaken, wrong, erroneous; lying, deceitful; vain, groundless, empty; spurious, sham, fictitious ‖ *n* error; lying; lie, falsehood; perjury
fal·x -cis *f* sickle; pruning hook, pruning knife; *(mil)* hook for pulling down walls
fām·a -ae *f* talk, rumor, report, news; saying, tradition; *(w. gen)* reputation *(for)*; fame, renown, name; infamy, notoriety; public opinion
famēlic·us -a -um *adj* famished
fam·ēs -is *f* hunger; starvation; famine; fasting; *(fig)* craving; *(rhet)* bald style, poverty of expression
fāmigerāti·ō -ōnis *f* rumor
fāmigerāt·or -ōris *m* gossip, rumormonger
famili·a -ae *or* **-ās** *f* household slaves, domestics; gang of slaves; retinue of servants; household; house, family; family estate; sect, school; **familia gladiatorum** stable of gladiators; **familiam**

ducere to head a sect; **pater familias** head of the family

familiār·is -is -e *adj* domestic, family-, household-; familiar, intimate; private, personal *(as opposed to public); (in augury)* one's own *(part of the sacrificial animal);* **res familiaris** one's private property, estate, patrimony ‖ *m* servant, slave; acquaintance; close friend

familiārit·ās -ātis *f* close friendship, intimacy; familiarity; *(of things)* close relationship

familiāriter *adv* in the manner of a close friend; thoroughly; as if at home, in a familiar manner; familiarly

fāmōs·us -a -um *adj* much talked of; famous, renowned; infamous; slanderous, libelous; **carmen famosum** lampoon

famul·a -ae *f* maid, slave-girl

famulār·is -is -e *adj* of slaves, servile

famulāt·us -ūs *m* slavery, servitude

famul·or -ārī -ātus sum *intr* to be a slave; *(w. dat)* to serve

famul·us -a -um *adj* servile ‖ *m* servant, attendant; slave ‖ *f see* **famula**

fānātic·us -a -um *adj* belonging to a temple; fanatic, enthusiastic, inspired; frantic ‖ *mf* temple attendant

fand·us -a -um *adj* that may be spoken

fān·um -ī *n* shrine, sanctuary; temple

fār farris *n* spelt *(type of wheat);* coarse meal, grits; sacrificial meal; bread; dog biscuit ‖ *npl* grain

far·ciō -cīre -sī -tus *tr* to stuff; to fatten *(birds for table); (w.* **in + acc**) to cram into ‖ *refl* to gorge oneself

farfar·us *or* **farfer·us -ī** *m* coltsfoot *(plant w. heart-shaped leaves)*

farīn·a -ae *f* flour; powder; *(fig)* character, quality

-fāriam *advl suf* forms multiplicative adverbs denoting -sided: **multifariam** many-sided

farrāg·ō -inis *f* mash *(for cattle); (fig)* medley, hodgepodge

farrāt·us -a -um *adj* filled with grain, made with grain

fart·is -is *f* stuffing, filling; mincemeat; **fartim facere ex hostibus** to make mincemeat of the enemy

fart·or -ōris *m* fattener of poultry

far·tus -us -a -um *pp of* **farcio** ‖ *adj* well-fed; crammed, gorged

fās *indecl n* divine law; sacred duty, divine will, fate; right; natural law; **fas est** it is right, it is lawful; it is permissible; **fas tibi est** you have the right; **omne fas est fidere** there is every reason to trust

fasci·a -ae *f* bandage; bra(ssière); diaper; headband, fillet; wisp of cloud

fasciātim *adv* in bundles

fascicul·us -ī *m* small bundle

fascin·ō -āre -āvī -ātus *tr* to cast an evil eye on, bewitch, jinx; to envy

fascin·um -ī *n or* **fascin·us -ī** *m* evil eye; jinx; witchcraft; charm, amulet; *(vulg)* penis

fasciol·a -ae *f* ribbon; headband

fasc·is -is *m* bundle, pack, parcel; fagot; load, burden; baggage ‖ *mpl* fasces *(bundle of rods and ax, carried before high magistrates by lictors as symbols of authority);* high office, supreme power, consulship

fassus *pp of* **fateor**

fast·ī -ōrum *mpl* calendar, almanac; annals; register of higher magistrates ‖ **Fasti** poem by Ovid

fastīd·iō -īre -īvī *or* **-iī -ītus** *tr* to despise, snub, turn up the nose at ‖ *intr* to feel disgust, feel squeamish; to be snobbish, be haughty

fastīdiōsē *adv* fastidiously, squeamishly; disdainfully, snobbishly

fastīdiōs·us -a -um *adj* fastidious, squeamish; disdainful, snobbish; refined, delicate; nauseating

fastīd·ium -(i)ī *n* fastidiousness, distaste, squeamishness, disgust, loathing; snobbishness, haughtiness; **(in) fastidio esse** to be repugnant; **in fastidium ire** to become repugnant

fastīgātē *adv* sloped, at an angle

fastīgāt·us -a -um *adj* rising to a point; sloping down

fastīg·ium -(i)ī *n* gable; pediment; roof; ceiling; slope; height, elevation; top, edge; depth, depression; completion; rank, dignity; main point, heading; highlight *(of a story, etc.)*

fastīg·ō -āre -āvī -ātus *tr* to make pointed; to taper; to cause to slope, incline ‖ *refl & pass* to taper; to narrow

fastōs·us -a -um *adj* disdainful

fast·us -a -um *adj (of day)* lawful *(for transaction of business);* **dies fastus** court day ‖ *mpl see* **fasti**

fast·us -ūs *m* contempt; arrogance

fātāl·is -is -e *adj* fateful, destined, preordained; fatal, deadly; **deae fatales** the Fates

fātāliter *adv* by fate, by destiny

fateor fatērī fassus sum *tr* to admit, acknowledge, confess; to profess, declare; **fatendi modus** *(gram)* the indicative mood ‖ *intr* to admit guilt, confess; to say yes; *(w. inf)* to agree to

fātican·us -a -um *adj* (**-cin-**) prophetic

fātidic·us -a -um *adj* prophetic

fātif·er -era -erum *adj* fatal, deadly

fatīgāti·ō -ōnis *f* fatigue

fatīg·ō -āre -āvī -ātus *tr* to fatigue, weary, tire out; to wear down; to worry, torment, bother; to pray to constantly

fātiloqu·a -ae *f* prophetess

fatisc·ō -ĕre *or* **fatisc·or -ī** *intr* to split, crack, give way; *(fig)* to become exhausted, wear out
fatuē *adv* foolishly
fatuit·ās -ātis *f* silliness
fāt·um -ī *n* divine utterance, oracle; fate, destiny, doom; calamity; ruin; death; *(fig)* cause of death, cause of ruin; **ad fata novissima** to the last; **fato functus** dead; **fato obire** to meet death; **fatum est** it is fated; **fatum proferre** to put off fate, prolong life **‖** *npl* what fate has in store, the future
fātus *pp of* **for**
fatu·us -a -um *adj* silly, foolish; clumsy; tasteless *(food)* **‖** *m* fool
fauc·ēs -ium *(poet: abl singl:* **fauce)** *fpl* throat; gullet; neck; strait, channel; pass, gorge; mouth *(of river);* entrance *(to harbor, home, building, cave, lower world);* jaws, maw *(of wild animals);* crater *(of volcano);* neck *(of vase, jar);* **fauces premere** *(w. gen)* to throttle s.o.
Faun·us -ī *m* king of Latium, father of Latinus and worshiped as the Italian Pan **‖** *mpl* Fauns, woodland spirits
faustē *adv* favorably, auspiciously
faustit·ās -ātis *f* fertility; good fortune, happiness
Faustul·us -ī *m* shepherd who rescued and raised Romulus and Remus
faust·us -a -um *adj* auspicious, favorable; lucky **‖ Faustus** personal name *(agnomen)* of the son of the dictator Sulla
faut·or *or* **favit·or -ōris** *m,* **fautr·ix -īcis** *f* patron, supporter, fan
fave·a -ae *f* favorite girl, pet slave girl
faveō favēre fāvī fautum *intr (w. dat)* to be favorable to, favor, support, side with; *(w. inf)* to be eager to; **favere linguis** *(or* **ore)** to observe a reverential silence
favill·a -ae *f* ashes, embers; *(fig)* spark, beginnings
favitor *see* **fautor**
Favōn·ius -(i)ī *m* West Wind *(also called Zephyrus)*
fav·or -ōris *m* favor, support; applause; appreciation *(shown by applause)*
favōrābil·is -is -e *adj* popular
favōrābiliter *adv* in order to win popularity
fav·us -ī *m* honeycomb **‖** *mpl* honey
fax facis *f* torch; wedding torch, wedding; funeral torch, funeral; meteor, shooting star, comet; firebrand; fire, flame; guiding light; instigator; flame of love; stimulus, incitement; cause of ruin *or* destruction; **dicendi faces** fiery eloquence; **dolorum faces** pangs of grief
faxim, faxō *see* **facio**
febrīcul·a -ae *f* slight fever
febrīculōs·us -a -um *adj* fever-ridden; prone to fevers
febr·is -is *f* fever
Febru·a -ōrum *npl* Roman festival of purification and expiation, celebrated on February 15
Februāri·us -a -um *adj & m* February *(twelfth month of the Roman calendar until the reform of 153* B.C.*)*
febru·um -ī *n* purification
fēcundit·ās -ātis *f* fertility, fruitfulness; *(rhet)* overstatement
fēcund·ō -āre -āvī -ātus *tr* to fertilize
fēcund·us -a -um *adj* fertile, fruitful; abundant, rich; fertilizing; *(w. gen or abl)* rich in, abounding in
fel fellis *n* gallbladder; gall, bile; bitterness, animosity; poison
fēl·ēs *or* **fēl·is -is** *f* cat
fēlīcit·ās -ātis *f* fertility; luck, piece of luck; felicity, happiness
fēlīciter *adv* fruitfully, abundantly; luckily; happily; sucessfully; favorably
fēlis *see* **feles**
fēl·ix -īcis *adj* fruit-bearing; fruitful, fertile; favorable, auspicious; lucky; happy; successful; well-aimed
fellāt·or -ōris *m* one who practices oral sex
fell·ō -āre -āvī -ātus *tr* to practice oral sex with **‖** *intr* to practice oral sex
fēmell·a -ae *f* girl, young lady
fēmin·a -ae *f* female; woman
femināl·ia -ium *npl* stockings *(to cover the thighs)*
fēmine·us -a -um *adj* woman's; effeminate, unmanly
fēminīn·us -a -um *adj* female; *(gram)* feminine
fem·ur -oris *or* **-inis** *n* thigh
fēn- = faen-
fenestr·a -ae *f* window; hole *(for earrings); (fig)* opening, opportunity; *(mil)* breach *(in a wall)*
-f·er -era -erum *adjl suf* denotes bearing, carrying, or bringing: **conifer** bearing cones
fer·a -ae *f* wild beast, wild animal
ferāciter *adv* fruitfully
ferācius *adv* more fruitfully
Fērāl·ia -ium *npl* **(Fĕr-)** festival of the dead, celebrated on February 17th or 21st
fērāl·is -is -e *adj* associated with death *or* the dead; funeral-; deadly, fatal, gloomy, dismal; **papilio feralis** funerary butterly *(symbolizing the soul)*
fer·ax -ācis *adj* fertile, fruitful; *(w. gen)* productive of
fercul·um -ī *n* food tray; dish; course; litter *(for carrying spoils in a victory parade or cult images in a religious procession)*
fercul·us -ī *m* litter bearer
ferē *or* **fermē** *adv* approximately, nearly, almost, about, just about; generally, as a

rule, usually; *(w. negatives)* practically; **haud fere** *(or* **non fere)** hardly ever; **nemo fere** practically no one

ferentār·ius -(i)ī *m* light-armed soldier; eager helper

Feretr·ius -(i)ī *m* epithet of Jupiter on the Capitoline Hill

feretr·um -ī *n* litter, bier

fēri·ae -ārum *fpl* holidays, vacation; *(fig)* leisure

fēriāt·us -a -um *adj* vacationing, taking it easy; dressed for the holiday; unemployed; **dies feriatus** holiday

fericulum = ferculum

ferīn·us -a -um *adj* of wild animals; brutish; **caro ferina** venison; **vita ferina** life in the wild ‖ *f* venison

fer·iō -īre *tr* to strike, hit, shoot, knock; to kill; to slaughter, sacrifice *(an animal);* to coin; *(fig)* to strike, reach, affect; *(fig)* to cheat, trick; **cornu ferire** to butt; **foedus ferire** to conclude a treaty; *(fig)* to strike a bargain; **securi ferire** to behead; **verba ferire** to coin words

ferit·ās -ātis *f* wildness, fierceness

fermē *see* **ferē**

ferment·um -ī *n* ferment; yeast

ferō ferre tulī *or* **tetulī lātus** *tr* to bear, carry; to bear, produce; to bear, endure; to lead, drive, conduct, direct; to bring, offer; to receive, acquire, obtain, win; to carry off, plunder, ravage; to manifest, display; to make known, report, say, tell; to call; to propose, bring forward; to allow, permit; to cause, create; to set in motion; to call, name; *(of circumstances, etc.)* to suggest; *(in accounting)* to enter; to carry *(e.g., a ward in an election);* **aditum ferre** to approach; **aegre ferre** to be annoyed at; to take it hard; **caelo supinas manus ferre** to raise the hands heavenward in prayer; **crimina ferre in** *(w. acc)* to bring charges against; **cursum** *(or* **iter)** **ferre** to go, proceed, pursue a course; **hunc inventorem artium ferunt** they call him the inventor of the arts; **in oculis ferre** *(fig)* to have before one's eyes, have on one's mind; **judicem ferre** to propose as judge; **judicem ferre** *(w. dat)* to propose a judge to *(i.e., to go to court with);* **laudibus ferre** to extol; **legem ferre** to propose a bill; **moleste ferre** to be annoyed at; **ore ferre** to show *(by one's looks);* **osculum ferre** *(w. dat)* to give *(s.o.)* a kiss; **pedem** *(or* **pedes)** **ferre** to come, go, move, get going; **prae se ferre** to display, manifest; **repulsam ferre** to experience defeat *(at polls);* **responsum ferre** to get an answer; **sententiam ferre** to pass judgment; to cast a vote; **signa ferre** *(mil)* to begin marching; **suffragium ferre** to cast a vote, cast a ballot; **ventrem ferre** to be pregnant ‖ *refl* to go, proceed; to rush, flee; *(of rivers)* to flow; **se ferre obviam** *(w. dat)* to rush to meet ‖ *pass (of things)* to be carried along; to extend; *(of sounds)* to carry ‖ *intr* to say *(e.g.,* **ut ferunt** as people say, as they say); to allow, permit *(e.g.,* **si occasio tulerit** if the occasion permit); to lead *(e.g.,* **iter ad oppidum ferebat** the road led to the town)

ferōci·a -ae *f* fierceness, ferocity; fighting spirit; pride, presumption

ferōc·iō -īre *intr* to rampage

ferōcit·ās -ātis *f* fierceness, ferocity; aggressiveness; presumption

ferōciter *adv* ferociously, aggressively; defiantly, arrogantly

Fērōni·a -ae *f* early Italic goddess of groves and springs, and patroness of ex-slaves

fer·ox -ōcis *adj* fierce, ferocious; warlike; defiant; arrogant

ferrāment·um -ī *n* tool, implement

ferrāri·us -a -um *adj* iron, of iron; **faber ferrarius** blacksmith; **officina** *(or* **taberna)** **ferraria** blacksmith shop ‖ *fpl* iron mines; iron works

ferrātil·is -is -e *adj* fit to be chained

ferrāt·us -a -um *adj* iron-plated; iron-tipped; in chains; in armor; **calx ferrata** spur ‖ *mpl* soldiers in armor

ferre·us -a -um *adj* iron, of iron; cruel, hardhearted; firm, unyielding; armored; inexorable, inflexible *(fate, laws);* **ferreus somnus** death

ferricrepin·us -a -um *adj (coll)* clanking with chains

ferriter·ium -(i)ī *n (coll)* brig *(jail)*

ferriter·us -ī *m (coll)* glutton for punishment

ferritrīb·ax -ācis *adj (coll)* chainsore *(from dragging chains)*

ferrūgine·us -a -um *adj* rust-colored, dark, dusky

ferrūg·ō -inis *f* rust, verdigris; dark-red; dark color; gloom

ferr·um -ī *n* iron; tool, implement; iron object: sword, dart, arrowhead, ax, plowshare, crowbar, spade, scissors, stylus, curling iron, *(surgical)* knife; gladiatorial fight; **ferro atque igni** with fire and sword; **ferro decernere** to decide by force of arms; **ferrum sumere** to resort to arms

ferrūm·en -inis *n* adhesive, cement

fertil·is -is -e *adj* fertile, fruitful, productive; fertilizing; life-giving; profitable, lucrative; *(w. gen, dat, or abl)* productive of

fertilit·ās -ātis *f* fertility

ferul·a -ae *f* reed, stalk; rod, whip

fer·us -a -um *adj* wild; uncultivated, untamed; savage, uncivilized; rude, cruel, fierce; wild, bleak *(place)* ‖ *m* wild beast;

wild horse; lion; stag ‖ *f* wild beast, wild animal
ferve·faciō -facĕre -fēcī -factus *tr* to heat, boil
ferv·ens -entis *adj* seething, burning, hot; red-hot *(iron); (of mind)* in turmoil; *(fig)* hot, heated, violent, impetuous, ardent; **fervens ira oculis** anger sparkling in the eyes
ferventer *adv (fig)* heatedly, impetuously
ferv·eō -ēre *or* **ferv·ō -ĕre -ī** *intr* to boil, seethe, steam; to foam; to swarm; to be busy, bustle about; *(fig)* to burn, glow, rage, rave; **fervet opus** the work goes on at a feverish pace
fervesc·ō -ĕre *intr* to become boiling hot, grow hot, begin to boil
fervid·us -a -um *adj* boiling, seething, hot; fermenting *(grapes);* hot, highly spiced; *(fig)* hot, fiery, violent, impetuous, hot-blooded
fervō *see* **ferveo**
ferv·or -ōris *m* heat; boiling; fermenting; fever; raging *(of the sea); (fig)* heat, vehemence, ardor, passion
Fescenni·a -ae *f* town in Etruria
Fescennīn·us -a -um *adj* Fescennine ‖ *mpl* Fescennine verses *(coarse, boisterous form of dramatic dialogue)*
fess·us -a -um *adj* tired out, worn out; weakened *(by wounds, disease, etc.); (fig)* demoralized, depressed; *(w. abl)* weary of, sick of
festīnanter *adv* quickly
festīnāti·ō -ōnis *f* hurry, haste
festīnātō *adv* hurriedly
festīn·ō -āre -āvī -ātus *tr* to perform, *(or* make *or* do) without delay; to move *(s.th.)* quickly; to accelerate; **jussa festinare** to carry out orders promptly ‖ *intr* to rush, hurry; to bustle; to be in a hurry; *(w. inf)* to be anxious to, lose no time in
festīn·us -a -um *adj* hasty, speedy
festīvē *adv* gaily; *(coll)* humorously; *(coll)* delightfully, neatly, nicely
festīvit·ās -ātis *f* festivity, gaiety, fun; *(rhet)* humor, liveliness *(of speaker, speech)*
festūc·a -ae *f* **(fis-)** stalk; rod *(with which slaves were tapped when freed)*
fest·us -a -um *adj* festive, joyous, in holiday mood; **dies festus** holiday ‖ *n (often plural in singular sense)* holiday, festival; **festum agere** to observe a holiday
fētiāl·is -is -e *adj* negotiating, diplomatic; fetial, of the fetial priests ‖ *m* fetial *(member of a college of priests who performed the ritual in connection with declaring war and making peace)*
fētid·us -a -um *adj* **(foet-)** fetid, stinking
fētūr·a -ae *f* breeding, bearing; offspring, young
fēt·us -a -um *adj* pregnant, breeding; fruitful, teeming, productive
fēt·us -ūs *m* childbirth; laying *(of eggs); (of plants)* producing, bearing; offspring, young; fruit, produce; *(fig)* product *(of mind or imagination)*
fī *interj (at a bad smell)* phew!
fi·ber -brī *m* beaver
fibr·a -ae *f* fiber, filament; lobe *(of liver, lungs)* ‖ *fpl* entrails
fībul·a -ae *f* clasp, safety pin, brooch; barrette; clamp; bolt, peg; chastity clamp *(worn through the prepuce to prevent sexual intercourse)*
ficēdul·a -ae *f* **(-cēd-)** beccafico, fig-pecker *(small bird)*
fictē *adv* falsely, fictitiously
fictil·is -is -e *adj* clay-, earthen ‖ *n* jar; clay statue ‖ *npl* earthenware
ficti·ō -ōnis *f* forming, formation; disguising; supposition; fiction
fict·or -ōris *m* shaper, sculptor, molder; attendant of priest who kneaded the sacrificial cake
fictr·ix -īcis *f* maker, molder *(female)*
fictūr·a -ae *f* shaping, fashioning
fict·us -a -um *pp of* **fingo** ‖ *adj* false, fictitious; insincere *(person, character, emotions);* false *(witness);* **vox ficta** falsehood ‖ *n* falsehood; pretense; fiction
fīcul·a -ae *f* little fig
fīculn(e)·us -ā -um *adj* of a fig tree
fīc·us -ī *or* **-ūs** *f* fig; fig tree; **prima ficus** early autumn ‖ *fpl* hemorrhoids
fideicommiss·um -ī *n* trust fund
fidēli·a -ae *f* earthen pot, bucket; **duo parietes de eādem fideliā dealbare** *(prov)* to kill two birds with one stone *(literally, to whitewash two walls with one bucket)*
fidēl·is -is -e *adj* faithful, loyal; trustworthy, true, sure; safe *(ship, port, advice, etc.); (w. dat or* **ad**) faithful to ‖ *m* confidant
fidēlit·ās -ātis *f* fidelity, loyalty
fidēliter *adv* faithfully, loyally; securely, certainly
Fīdēn·ae -ārum *fpl* ancient town near Rome *(once the rival of Rome)*
fīd·ens -entis *adj* self-confident; bold; *(w. gen)* confident in
fīdenter *adv* confidently; boldly
fīdenti·a -ae *f* self-confidence; assurance; boldness
fid·ēs -eī *f* trust, faith, reliance, confidence; credence, belief; trustworthiness, conscientiousness, honesty; promise, assurance; word, word of honor; protection, guarantee; safe conduct; confirmation, proof; *(com)* credit; **bonae fidei** in good faith; **bonā fide** *(or* **ex bonā fide)** in good faith; really, genuinely; **de fide**

malā in bad faith; **Di vostram fidem!** for heaven's sake!; **fide decedere** to cease to be loyal; **fidei causā** as proof of *(one's)* trustworthiness; **fidem dare** to give one's word; **fidem alicujus decipere** to deceive s.o. through (misplaced) trust, betray s.o.'s trust; **fidem facere** *(w. dat)* 1 to convince; 2 to place trust in; **fidem fallere** to break one's word; **fidem firmare** to make good one's word, back up one's promise; **fidem habere** to be credible, be believed, have credibility; **fidem habere** *(w. dat)* to have confidence in, give credence to; **fidem obsecrare** to beg for support *or* protection; **fidem obligare** to pledge one's word, make a solemn promise, guarantee one's loyalty; **fidem obstringere** *(w. dat)* to pledge one's word to; **fidem praestare** *(or* **servare** *or* **tenere** *or* **retinere)** to keep one's word; **fides publica** promise of immunity; safe conduct; **in fide manere** to remain loyal; **meā (tuā) fide** on my *(your)* word; **optimā fide** with the utmost honesty; **pro fidem deum!** for heaven's sake!; **res fidesque** capital and credit

fid·ēs -is *f* string *(of musical instrument)* ‖ *fpl* stringed instrument, lyre; *(fig)* lyric poetry; **fidibus canere** to play the lyre; **fidibus discere** to learn to play the lyre; **fidibus scire** to know how to play the lyre

fidī *perf of* **findo**

fidic·en -inis *m* lyre player; *(fig)* lyric poet

fidicin·a -ae *f* lyre player *(female)*

fidicul·a -ae *f* small lyre ‖ *fpl* torture rack

Fid·ius -(i)ī *m* epithet of Jupiter; **medius fidius!** honest to goodness!, so help me God!

fidō fidĕre fisus sum *intr (w. dat or abl)* to trust, put confidence in

fidūci·a -ae *f* trust, confidence, reliance; self-confidence; trustworthiness; guarantee; *(w. gen)* confident hope of; *(leg)* deposit, pledge, security; **fiduciā** *(w. gen)* with reliance on

fidūciāri·us -a -um *adj* held in trust, fiduciary; of a trustee

fid·us -a -um *adj* trusty, dependable; certain, sure, safe

figlīn·us -a -um *adj* **(figul-)** potter's

figment·um -ī *n* figment; unreality

fi·gō -gĕre -xī -xus *or* **-ctus** *tr* to fix, fasten, affix, attach, nail; to drive in; to pierce; to erect, set up; to build; to put up, hang up, post; **cruci** *(or* **in cruce)** **figere** *(or simply* **figere)** to crucify; **dicta animo figere** to let the words sink in; **lumine figere** *(poet)* to stare at

figulār·is -is -e *adj* potter's

figul·us -ī *m* potter; bricklayer

figūr·a -ae *f* figure, shape, form; phantom, host; nature, kind; figure of speech

figūrāti·ō -ōnis *f* forming; form, shape; description, sketch

figūrāt·us -a -um *adj* figurative

figūr·ō -āre -āvī -ātus *tr* to shape, form, mold, fashion; to train; *(w.* **in** *+ acc)* to transform into; *(rhet)* to embellish *(a speech)* with rhetorical figures

filātim *adv* thread by thread

fili·a -ae *f (dat & abl pl:* **filiābus)** daughter

filicāt·us -a -um *adj* engraved with fern patterns

filiol·a -ae *f* little daughter, dear daughter

filiol·us -ī *m* little son, dear son

fil·ius -(i)ī *m* son; **terrae filius** a nobody

fil·ix -icis *f* fern

fil·um -ī *n* thread; fillet; string, cord; wick; figure, shape *(of a woman);* build *(of a person);* texture, quality, style *(of speech); (fig)* character; **filo pendere** to hang by a thread, be in a precarious situation

fimbri·ae -ārum *fpl* fringe, border

fim·us -ī *m* dung, manure; mire

findō findĕre fidī fissus *tr* to split ‖ *refl & pass* to fork, split

fingō fingĕre finxī fictus *tr* to shape, form; to mold, model *(in clay, wax);* to arrange *(esp. the hair),* trim; to imagine, suppose, think; to contrive, invent; to pretend, feign; to train, influence *(s.o.)* to be; to compose *(poetry);* to disguise *(looks);* to trump up *(charges); (w. double acc)* to represent as, depict as; **ars fingendi** sculpture; **linguā fingere** to lick ‖ *refl* to pretend to be; *(w.* **ad)** 1 to adapt oneself to; 2 to be subservient to

fīni·ens -entis *m* horizon

fīn·iō -īre -īvī *or* **-iī -ītus** *tr* to limit; *(fig)* to set bounds to, limit, restrain; to mark out, fix, determine; to put an end to, finish, complete ‖ *pass & intr* to come to an end

fīn·is -is *m (f)* boundary, border, limit; end; purpose, aim; extreme limit, summit, highest degree; starting point; goal; death; **eādem fini** within the same period; **fine** *(w. gen)* up to, as far as; **finem facere** *(w. gen or dat)* to put an end to; **in fine** in conclusion; **quā fine** *(or* **quā fini)** up to the point where; up to what point?; **quem ad finem** how long, to what extent ‖ *mpl* boundaries, country, territory, land

fīnītē *adv* to a limited degree; specifically

finitim·us -a -um *adj* **(-tum-)** neighboring, bordering; *(w. dat)* 1 bordering on; 2 *(fig)* bordering on, akin to ‖ *mpl* neighbors

fīnīt·or -ōris *m* surveyor

fīnīt·us -a -um *pp of* **finio** ‖ *adj* limited; *(rhet)* rhythmical

fīō fierī factus sum *intr* to come into being, arise; to be made; to be done; to become, get; to happen, occur; *(of events, festivals, etc.)* to take place, be held; *(of physical phenomena)* to arise, develop; *(w. gen of price)* to be valued at; *(in arithmetic)* to equal; **fiat** so be it; **fieri non potest quin** it is inevitable that; **fieri potest ut** it is possible that; **ita fit ut** *(or* **quo fit ut)** thus it happens that; **plurimi fieri** to valued highly; **quid fiet?** *(w. dat)* what's going to happen to?; **quoad fiat** as far as is possible **II** *v impers* a sacrifice is being offered

firmām·en -inis *n* prop, support

firmāment·um -ī *n* prop, support; mainstay; main point

firmāt·or -ōris *m* promoter

firmē *adv* firmly, steadily

firmit·ās -ātis *f* firmness, stability; strength

firmiter *adv* firmly, tight, ; securely, safely; resolutely

firmitūd·ō -inis *f* firmness, strength, durability; vigor; stability; **memoriae firmitudo** unfaltering memory

firm·ō -āre -āvī -ātus *tr* to strengthen, support, reinforce; to encourage; to assure; to fortify; to put *(laws, institutions)* on a firm footing, establish; to guarantee; to assert, affirm; to substantiate, vouch for *(a statement or its veracity);* **aliquem in se** *(or* **sibi) firmare** to make sure of the loyalty of; **animum firmare** to get up one's courage; **fidem firmare** to make good one's word, back up one's promise; **gradum firmare** to walk resolutely; **oculos** *(or* **vultum) firmare** to look determined **II** *refl* to brace oneself

firm·us -a -um *adj* firm, strong; stable; hardy, sound *(health);* solid, substantial *(food);* steadfast, trusty; lasting

fiscāl·is -is -e *adj* fiscal, of the imperial treasury

fiscell·a -ae *f* small basket

fiscin·a -ae *f* wicker basket, wickerwork; **cum porcis cum fiscina** *(fig)* lock, stock, and barrel *(literally, with pigs and with wicker basket)*

fisc·us -ī *m* basket; money box; imperial treasury *(distinct from state treasury:* **aerarium);** state revenues

fissil·is -is -e *adj* easily split; split

fissi·ō -ōnis *f* dividing, splitting

fiss·us -a -um *pp of* **findo II** *adj* cloven, divided **II** *n* split

fistūca *see* **festuca**

fistul·a -ae *f* pipe, tube; water pipe; hollow reed; flute; *(med)* fistula

fistulāt·or -ōris *m* who who plays a shepherd's pipe

fistulāt·us -a -um *adj* provided with pipes

fīsus *pp of* **fido**

fix·us -a -um *pp of* **figo II** *adj* fixed, immovable; irrevocable; *(w. abl)* fitted with

flābellifer·a -ae *f* female slave who waved a fan

flābellul·um -ī *n* small fan

flābell·um -ī *n* fan

flābil·is -is -e *adj* of air

flābr·a -ōrum *npl* gusts of wind; breezes, winds

flacc·eō -ēre *intr* to be flabby; to lose heart; *(of a speech)* to get dull

flacc·escō -escĕre -uī *intr* to become flabby; to wither, droop

flaccid·us -a -um *adj* flaccid, flabby; weak, feeble

flacc·us -a -um *adj* flabby; flap-eared

flagell·ō -āre -āvī -ātus *tr* to whip

flagell·um -ī *n* whip; scourge; riding crop; young shoot, sucker; tentacle *(of polyp);* pang *(of conscience)*

flāgitāti·ō -ōnis *f* demand

flāgitāt·or -ōris *m* persistent demander

flāgitiōsē *adv* shamefully, disgracefully

flāgitiōs·us -a -um *adj* shameful, disgraceful, scandalous

flāgit·ium -(i)ī *n* shame, disgrace, scandal; good-for-nothing

flāgit·ō -āre -āvī -ātus *tr* to demand; *(w. double acc, or w.* **ab)** to demand *(s.th.)* of *(s.o.)*

flagr·ans -antis *adj* blazing, flaming, hot; shining, glowing, glittering; ardent, hot, vehement, eager

flagranter *adv* vehemently, ardently

flagranti·a -ae *f* blaze, glow; passionate love; **flagiti flagrantia** utter disgrace

flagritrib·a -ae *m (coll) (said of a slave)* victim of constant whipping, whipping boy

flagr·ō -āre -āvī *tr* to burn with love for **II** *intr* **(fragl·ō)** to blaze, be on fire; *(w. abl)* **1** to glow with, flare up in; **2** to be the victim of *(e.g., envy)*

flagr·um -ī n whip; whipping

flām·en -inis *m* flamen *(priest of a specific deity);* **flamen Dialis** priest of Jupiter

flām·en -inis *n* gust, gale; breeze

flāminic·a -ae *f* wife of a flamen; priestess

Flāminīn·us -ī *m* Titus Quintus Flamininus *(consul of 198 B.C, and conqueror of Philip V of Macedon at Cynoscephalae in 197 B.C.)*

flāmin·ium -(i)ī *n* office of flamen, priesthood

Flāmini·us -a -um *adj* Flaminian; **via Flaminia** road leading N. from Rome to Ariminum **II** *m* Gaius Flaminius *(conqueror of Insubrian Gauls in 223 B.C., and builder of the Circus Flaminius and Flaminian road)*

flamm·a -ae *f* flame, fire, blaze; star; torch; burning fever; glow, passion; sweetheart; danger; flare-up *(of violence);* **flammam**

adjicere *(or* **suggerere)** *(w. dat)* to fan the flames of; **flammam concipere** to catch fire; **in flamma** in flames, ablaze

flammār·ius -(i)ī *m* maker of bridal veils

flammeol·um -ī *n (flame-colored)* bridal veil

flammesc·ō -ĕre *intr* to become inflamed, become fiery

flamme·us -a -um *adj* flaming, fiery; flashing *(eyes);* flame-colored ‖ *n (flame-colored)* bridal veil

flammif·er -era -erum *adj* fiery

flamm·ō -āre -āvī -ātus *tr* to set on fire; *(fig)* to get *(s.o.)* all excited ‖ *pass* to glow, flame

flammul·a -ae *f* little flame

flāt·us -ūs *m* blowing, breathing, breath; breeze, wind; snorting; arrogance; **flatum emittere** *(sl)* to break wind

flāv·ens -entis *adj* yellow, golden

flāv·eō -ēre *intr* to be yellow, be blond(e)

flāvesc·ō -ĕre *intr* to become yellow, become golden-yellow

Flāvi·us -a -um *adj* Flavian; **gens Flavia** Flavian clan *(to which the emperors Vespasian, Titus, and Domitian belonged)*

flāv·us -a -um *adj* yellow; blond; reddish-yellow, golden ‖ *m* gold coin

flēbil·is -is -e *adj* pitiful, pathetic, deplorable; tearful

flēbiliter *adv* tearfully, mournfully

fle·ctō -ctĕre -xī -xus *tr* to bend, curve; to turn, wheel about, turn around; to wind, twist; to curl *(hair);* to direct, avert, turn away *(eyes, mind, etc.);* to double, sail around *(a cape);* to inflect *(voice);* to change *(mind);* to persuade, move, appease; to handle *(reins, tiller);* to guide, steer; **animum** *(or* **mentem)** **flectere** to give way, bend; **viam** *(or* **iter) flectere** *(w.* **ad)** to make one's way toward, head toward; **vultum flectere** to change one's expression ‖ *refl & pass (geog)* to wind, curve ‖ *intr* to turn; to go

flēmin·a -um *npl* swollen ankles

fl·eō -ēre -ēvī -ētus *tr* to cry for, mourn (for) ‖ *intr* to cry

flēt·us -ūs *m* crying ‖ *mpl* tears

flexanim·us -a -um *adj* moving, touching, persuasive

flexī *perf of* **flecto**

flexibil·is -is -e *adj* flexible; shifty

flexil·is -is -e *adj* flexible, pliant

flexiloqu·us -a -um *adj* ambiguous

flexi·ō -ōnis *f* bending, turning; winding *(path);* inflection *(of voice)*

flexip·ēs -edis *adj* creeping *(ivy)*

flexuōs·us -a -um *adj* winding

flexūr·a -ae *f* bending, winding

flex·us -a -um *pp of* **flecto** ‖ *adj* curved, twisting; involved, obscure *(language);* modulated *(voice); (of a syllable)* having a circumflex

flex·us -ūs *m* bending, curving, turning, winding; bend, curve; shift, change, transition; curling *(of hair);* inflection *(of voice)*

flict·us -ūs *m* clashing, banging together, collision

flō flāre flāvī flātus *tr* to blow; to breathe, exhale; to coin *(money);* to play *(flute, songs)* ‖ *intr* to blow; to breathe

flocc·us -ī *m* tuft of wool; down; **flocci facere** *(or* **pendere)** to think little of, not give a hoot about

Flōr·a -ae *f* goddess of flowers *(honored on April 28-May 3)*

Flōrāl·ia -ium *npl* festival of Flora *(on April 28)*

Flōrālici·us -a -um *adj* of the Floralia

Flōrāl·is -is -e *adj* connected with Flora *or* her festival

flōr·ens -entis *adj* blooming; prosperous; flourishing; illustrious; strong, powerful; vivid *(speaker); (w. abl)* in the prime of, at the height of

flōr·eō -ēre -uī *intr* to blossom, bloom; *(of wine)* to foam, froth, ferment; *(of arts)* to flourish; to be prosperous, be eminent; *(w. abl)* **1** to abound in; **2** to swarm with, be filled with; **aetate florere** to be in one's prime

flōr·escō -escĕre -uī *intr* to begin to bloom; to increase in renown

flōre·us -a -um *adj* flowery; made of flowers

flōridul·us -a -um *adj* flowery; pretty; in the bloom of youth

flōrid·us -a -um *adj* flowery; covered with flowers; fresh, pretty; florid *(style)*

flōrif·er -era -erum *adj* flowery

flōrileg·us -a -um *adj (of bees)* going from flower to flower

flōs flōris *m* flower; bud, blossom; best *(of anything);* prime *(of life);* youthful beauty; innocence, chastity; crown, glory; aroma *(of wine);* best period, heyday, zenith; *(rhet)* literary ornament

floscul·us -ī *m* little flower; flower, pride, glory; *(rhet)* literary ornament

fluctifrag·us -a -um *adj* surging, wave-breaking *(shore)*

fluctig·er -era -erum *adj* wave-borne

fluctuāti·ō -ōnis *f* wavering, vacillation

fluctu·ō -āre -āvī -ātus *or* **fluctu·or -ārī -ātus sum** *intr* to fluctuate, undulate, wave; to be restless; to waver, vacillate

fluctuōs·us -a -um *adj* rough *(sea)*

fluct·us -ūs *m* wave; flowing, undulating; turbulence, commotion; disorder, unrest; **fluctus in simpulo** *(prov)* tempest in a teacup

flu·ens -entis *adj* loose, flowing; *(mor-*

ally) loose; smooth, fluent *(speech, composition)*
fluent·a -ōrum *npl* flow, stream, river
fluenter *adv* like a wave
fluid·us -a -um *or* **flūvid·us -a -um** *adj* flowing, fluid; soft; relaxing
fluit·ō -āre *intr* to float, swim; to sail; to toss about; to hang loose, flap; to be uncertain, waver; to stagger; *(of fluids)* to flow
flūm·en -inis *n* flowing, stream; river; *(fig)* flood *(e.g., of tears, words);* **flumine adverso** upstream; **secundo flumine** downstream
flūmine·us -a -um *adj* river-
flu·ō -ĕre -xī -xum *intr* to flow; to run down, drip; to overflow; to fall gradually, sink, drop, slip; to droop; to pass away, vanish, perish; *(of time)* to slip by; *(of plans)* to proceed, develop; to melt; to be fluent; to be monotonous; *(w.* **ab** *or* **ex) 1** to spring from, arise from, proceed from; **2** *(of words)* to be derived from; *(of crowds)* to stream, flock; *(of branches)* to spread; *(of clothes, hair)* to hang loosely, flow; *(phil)* to be in a state of transition *or* flux
fluviāl·is -is -e *adj* river-, of a river
flūvidus *see* **fluidus**
fluviātil·is -is -e *adj* river-, found in rivers; **equus fluviatilis** hippopotamus; **fluviatiles naves** river boats
fluv·ius -(i)ī *m* river; running water; stream
fluxī *perf of* **fluo**
flux·us -a -um *adj* flowing, loose; careless; loose, dissolute; frail, weak; transient, perishable
fōcāl·e -is *n* scarf
fōcil·ō -āre -āvī -ātus *tr* to warm, revive; *(fig)* to foster, cherish
fōcul·um -ī *n* stove
focul·us -ī *m* brazier; *(fig)* fire
foc·us -ī *m* hearth, fireplace; brazier; funeral pile; altar; *(fig)* home, family
fodic·ō -āre -āvī -ātus *tr* to poke, nudge
fodiō fodĕre fōdī fossus *tr* to dig, dig out; *(fig)* to prod
foecund- = fecund-
foedē *adv* foully, cruelly, shamefully
foederāt·us -a -um *adj* federated, allied
foedifrag·us -a -um *adj* treaty-breaking, treacherous
foedit·ās -ātis *f* foulness, hideousness
foed·ō -āre -āvī -ātus *tr* to make filthy, foul up; to make hideous, disfigure; to mutilate, mangle; to ravage savagely *(land);* to darken, dim *(light);* to pollute, defile; to disgrace
foed·us -eris *n* treaty, charter; league; compact, agreement; law; **aequo foedere** on equal terms, mutually; **foedere certo** by fixed law; **foedere pacto** by fixed agreement; **foedus icere** to conclude a treaty; **foedus rumpere** to break a treaty
foed·us -a -um *adj* foul, filthy, disgusting; horrible, shocking
foen- = faen-
foet·eō -ēre *intr* **(faet-, fēt-)** to stink
foetid·us -a -um *adj* **(faet-, fēt-)** fetid, stinking
foet·or -ōris *m* **(faet-, fēt-)** stink, stench
foetu- = fētu-
foliāt·us -a -um *adj* leafy **‖** *n* perfume *(made from aromatic leaves)*
fol·ium -(i)ī *n* leaf; petal; **folium recitare Sibyllae** *(coll)* to tell the gospel truth *(literally, to read aloud the leaf of the Sibyl)*
follicul·us -ī *m* small bag, sack; shell, skin; eggshell; large inflated ball
foll·is -is *m* bag, sack; punching bag; inflated ball; bellows; moneybag; puffed-out cheeks
follīt·us -a -um *adj* enclosed in a sack
fōment·um -ī *n* compress, dressing; *(fig)* remedy, solace, alleviation
fōm·es -itis *m* tinder
fon·s -tis *m* spring, fountain; spring water, water; stream; headwaters, source *(of river); (fig)* source, origin
fontān·us -a -um *adj* spring-
fonticul·us -ī *m* little spring, little fountain
for fārī fātus sum *tr & intr* to say, speak
forābil·is -is -e *adj* vulnerable; *(w. abl)* vulnerable to
forām·en -inis *n* hole, opening; socket; pore; stop *(in musical pipe)*
forās *adv (w. verbs implying motion)* out, outside, out of doors; *(w. verbs of selling, lending)* into the hands of outsiders; *(w. verbs of publishing)* into the light of day; **vocatus ad cenam foras** invited out to dinner; **foras cenare** to eat out
forc·eps -ipis *f* tongs; tweezers; pliers; clippers; claw *(of a crab)*
ford·a -ae *f* pregnant cow
fore = futur·us -a -um esse to be about to be
forem = essem
forens·is -is -e *adj* of the Forum, in the Forum; public *(as opp. to domestic);* forensic, of the lawcourts *(because the lawcourts were located in the Forum)* **‖** *npl* street clothes
forf·ex -icis *f* scissors; tongs, forceps
forficul·ae -ārum *fpl* scissors
foric·a -ae *f* public toilet
for·is -is *f* door; entrance, opening **‖** *fpl* double doors; **in foribus** in the doorway
forīs *adv* outside, out of doors; outside the Senate, among the people; among strangers, in public life; abroad, in foreign countries; from outside, from abroad; **a foris** from outside; **foris cenare** to eat out; **foris esse** to be bankrupt

form·a -ae *f* form, shape, figure; beauty, good looks; image; mold, stamp; shoemaker's last; vision, apparition, phantom; species, form, nature, sort, kind; outline, design, sketch, plan; map

formāl·is -is -e *adj* formal

formāment·um -ī *n* shape

formāt·or -ōris *m* shaper, creator

formātūr·a -ae *f* fashioning, shaping

Formi·ae -ārum *fpl* town on S. coast of Latium

formīc·a -ae *f* ant

formīcīn·us -a -um *adj* ant-like

formīdābil·is -is -e *adj* terrifying, formidable

formīd·ō -āre -āvī -ātus *tr* to dread ‖ *intr* to be afraid

formīd·ō -inis *f* fear, terror; *(religious)* dread, awe; bogy; threats

formīdolōsē *adv* **(-dul-)** dreadfully, terribly

formīdolōs·us -a -um *adj* **(-dul-)** formidable, alarming; fearful, frightened

form·ō -āre -āvī -ātus *tr* to form, shape, mold, build; *(w.* **in** + *acc)* to transform into, make into; to make, produce, invent; to imagine; to shape, direct; to instruct; to depict, represent; *(gram)* to inflect

formōsē *adv* beautifully, gracefully

formōsit·ās -ātis *f* beauty, good looks

formōs·us -a -um *adj* shapely, beautiful, handsome, good-looking

formul·a -ae *f* nice shape, beauty; list, register; legal position; formula; contract, agreement; rule, regulation; pattern, type; charter *(of a government); (leg)* regular form of judicial procedure; *(leg)* provisions *(of a law); (phil)* principle; **formula quaestionis** the rule of evidence; **formulam accipere** to be sued; **formulam edere** *(or* **intendere** *or* **scribere)** to bring an action, bring suit

fornācāl·is -is -e *adj* of an oven

fornācul·a -ae *f* small oven

forn·ax -ācis *f* oven, furnace; kiln; forge

fornicāti·ō -ōnis *f* arch, vaulting

fornicāt·us -a -um *adj* arched

forn·ix -icis *m* arch, vault; arcade; brothel

fornus *see* **furnus**

for·ō -āre -āvī -ātus *tr* to bore, pierce

fors *adv* perhaps, chances are

for·s -tis *f* chance, luck, accident; **forte** by chance, accidentally, by accident; perhaps; **vidistine forte eum?** did you happen to see him?

forsan *or* **forsit** *or* **forsitan** *adv* perhaps

fortasse *or* **fortassis** *adv* perhaps

forte *see* **fors**

forticul·us -a -um *adj* quite bold, rather brave

fort·is -is -e *adj* brave, courageous; strong, mighty, powerful; resolute, steadfast, firm; loud, noisy *(sounds); (of cities)* rich in resources *or* manpower; decent, honorable *(conduct);* drastic *(remedies);* vigorous *(speakers);* strong, potent *(medicine, wine)*

fortiter *adv* bravely, boldly; strongly, vigorously, firmly; justifiably

fortitūd·ō -inis *f* fortitude, bravery, courage; strength; resolution

fortuītō *adv* fortuitously, by chance, accidentally; haphazardly

fortuīt·us -a -um *adj* fortuitous, accidental; random, haphazard

fortūn·a -ae *f* chance, luck, fate, fortune; good luck, prosperity; bad luck, misfortune; lot; opportunity; circumstances; state, rank, position; property, goods, fortune; **fortunae mandare** to leave to chance; **fortunam alicujus sequi** to follow s.o.'s leadership; **fortunam suam sequi** to follow one's star; **fortunam temptare** *(or* **periclitari)** to tempt fate; **in fortuna positus esse** *(or* **fortunae subjectus esse)** to be left to chance, be dependent on luck; **per fortunas!** *(in earnest entreaties)* for heaven's sake! ‖ *fpl* riches, fortune

fortūnātē *adv* happily; prosperously; successfully

fortūnāt·us -a -um *adj* fortunate, lucky, prosperous; happy; rich

fortūn·ō -āre -āvī -ātus *tr* to make happy, make prosperous; to bless

forul·ī -ōrum *mpl* bookshelves

for·um -ī *n* forum, civic center; shopping center, marketplace; market town; trade, commerce; public life, public affairs; jurisdiction; popular assembly; the bar, the courts; game board; **ad forum deducere** to escort *(a young man)* to the Forum to assume the toga of manhood; **cedere foro** to go bankrupt; **extra suum forum** beyond his jurisdiction; **Forum Boarium** cattle market; **Forum Olitorium** produce market; **Forum Piscatorium** fish market; **Forum Romanum** Roman Forum; **in foro** outside one's home, in public; **forum agere** to hold court; **forum attingere** to enter public life; **in foro versari** to be engaged in business

For·um Appiī *(gen:* **Fori Appiī)** *n* town in Latium on the Via Appia

for·us -ī *m* gangway; tier of seats; tier of a beehive

foss·a -ae *f* ditch, trench; moat; canal; **fossam deprimere** to dig a ditch

fossi·ō -ōnis *f* digging

foss·or -ōris *m* digger; *(fig)* lout

fossūr·a -ae *f* digging

fossus *pp of* **fodio**

fōtus *pp of* **foveo**

fove·a -ae *f* small pit; *(lit & fig)* pitfall

foveō fovēre fōvī fōtus *tr* to warm, keep warm; to refresh, soothe; to bathe; to massage; to freshen *(breath);* to nurse *(wounds);* to fondle, caress; to cherish *(hope);* to foster, nurture; to take the side of; to support, encourage; to pamper

fract·us -a -um *pp of* **frango** ‖ *adj* interrupted, irregular; weak, feeble

frāg·a -ōrum *npl* strawberries

fragil·is -is -e *adj* fragile, brittle; crackling; frail, flimsy; unstable; impermanent, uncertain

fragilit·ās -ātis *f* fragility; frailty

fraglō *see* **flagro**

fragment·um -ī *n* fragment, remnant

frag·or -ōris *m* crash, noise, uproar, din; applause; clap of thunder

fragōs·us -a -um *adj* broken, uneven, rough; crashing, roaring

frāgr·ō *or* **frāgl·ō -āre -āvī** *intr* to smell sweet, be fragrant; to reek

frame·a -ae *f* German spear

frangō frangĕre frēgī fractus *tr* to break to pieces, smash to pieces, shatter; to grind, crush *(grain);* to curl *(hair);* to make *(waters)* choppy; to violate, break *(treaty, law, promise); (fig)* to break down, overcome, crush, dishearten, humble; to repress *(feelings);* to weaken, soften; to inflict a crushing blow on *(a nation); (esp. of old age)* to exhaust, wear out; to break the force of; to move, touch; **diem mero frangere** to break up the day with wine; **iter frangere** to force a way; **navem frangere** to wreck a ship ‖ *pass* to suffer shipwreck; to relent

frātell·us -ī *m* little brother

frā·ter -tris *m* brother; cousin; *(euphem)* (homosexual) sex partner; **frater germanus** full brother; **frater patruelis** first cousin *(on father's side)*

frātercul·us -i *m* little brother

frāternē *adv* like a brother

frāternit·ās -ātis *f* brotherhood

frātern·us -a -um *adj* fraternal; brotherly; brother's

frātricīd·a -ae *m* murderer of a brother, fratricide

fraudāti·ō -ōnis *f* swindling

fraudāt·or -ōris *m* swindler, cheat

fraud·ō -āre -āvī -ātus *tr* to swindle, cheat, defraud; to embezzle; *(w. abl)* to cheat *(s.o.)* out of

fraudulenti·a -ae *f* dishonesty

fraudulent·us -a -um *adj* fraudulent, dishonest; deceitful, treacherous

frau·s -dis *f* fraud, deception, trickery; error, delusion; offense, crime; harm, damage; *(person)* fraud, cheat; **sine fraude** without harm to oneself, unscathed; without risk of punishment, with impunity; **fraudem legi facere** to violate the law

fraxine·us -a -um *adj* made of ash wood

fraxin·us -ī *f* ash tree; spear *(made of ash wood)*

fraxinus -a -um *adj* of ash wood

frēgī *perf of* **frango**

fremibund·us -a -um *adj* (-meb-) roaring

fremid·us -a -um *adj* growling

fremit·us -ūs *m* roar, growl, rumble, hum; din, noise; grumbling, muttering; loud buzz of approval

frem·ō -ĕre -uī -itus *tr* to grumble at, complain loudly about; to demand angrily, clamor for; to declare noisily ‖ *intr* to roar, growl, snort, howl; to grumble; to resound

frem·or -ōris *m* roaring, grumbling; murmuring

frend·ō -ĕre -uī *intr* to gnash the teeth; **dentibus frendere** to gnash the teeth

frēnī *see* **frenum**

frēn·ō -āre -āvī -ātus *tr* to bridle, curb; *(fig)* to curb

frēn·um -ī *n or* **frēn·a -ōrum** *npl or* **frēn·ī -ōrum** *mpl* reins; bridle, bit; *(fig)* curb, control, restraint; *(poet)* riding *(on horseback);* **frena** *(or* **frenos** *or* **frenum) accipere** *(or* **pati)** to take the bit, learn obedience; **frena** *(or* **frenos) dare** *(or* **effundere** *or* **immittere** *or* **laxare** *or* **remittere)** to loosen the reins; **frena (ab)rumpere** to snap the reins, bolt; **frena** *(or* **frenos) tenere** *(or* **moderari)** *(w. gen)* to hold the reins of, be in control of; **in frenis** *(or* **sub freno)** under control

frequ·ens -entis *adj* crowded, packed, filled; in crowds, numerous; frequent, repeated, usual, common; full, plenary *(Senate session); (of persons)* constant, regular; *(may be rendered adverbially)* often, frequently, *e.g.:* **frequens et audivi et adfui** I was often at your side and heard you speak; *(w. abl)* **1** crowded with; **2** densely covered with; **frequens emporium** well-stocked market; **frequens est** *(w. inf)* it is a common practice to

frequentāti·ō -ōnis *f* piling up, concentration

frequenter *adv* in crowds, in large numbers; frequently, in quick succession; commonly, widely; **frequenter habitari** *(or* **coli)** to be densely populated

frequenti·a -ae *f* crowd; crowded assembly, large attendance; dense mass; populousness; populous district; crowdedness; abundance; multitude; population; frequency; conscientious performance *(of duties)*

frequent·ō -āre -āvī -ātus *tr* to crowd, people, populate; *(w. abl)* to pack with, stock with, crowd with; to assemble in a crowd; to crowd around *(a person);* to attend *(e.g., games)* in large numbers; to sue frequently; to say over and over again; to do often, repeat; to use frequently; to frequent, resort to; to visit often; to celebrate, observe *(festival, ceremony);* to attend *(a meeting, school, lecture);* to appear on *(the stage);* to inhabit *(a place)* ‖ *pass* to become common

fretens·is -is -e *adj* **mare fretense** Strait of Messina

fret·um -ī *n* strait, channel; sea, the deep; waters; *(fig)* seething flood

frēt·us -a -um *adj (w. dat or abl)* relying on, confident of, depending on; *(w. acc & inf)* confident that

fret·us -ūs *m* strait

fric·ō -āre -uī -tus *or* **-ātus** *tr* to rub; to chafe; to rub down, massage

frictus *pp of* **frigo**

frīgefact·ō -āre *tr* to cool

frīg·eō -ēre *intr* to be cold, be chilly; to freeze; *(fig)* to be numbed, be lifeless, be dull; *(fig)* to get a cool reception, get the cold shoulder; *(of words)* to fall flat; *(of an old man)* to lack vigor; to have nothing to do, be idle

frīgesc·ō -ĕre frixī *intr* to become cold, become chilled; to become lifeless; *(of a speech)* to fall flat

frīgid·a -ae *f* cold water

frīgidāri·us -a -um *adj* cooling

frīgidē *adv* feebly; coolly

frīgidul·us -a -um *adj* rather cold; rather faint

frīgid·us -a -um *adj* cold, cool; numbed, dull, lifeless; indifferent, unimpassioned; flat, insipid, trivial ‖ *f* cold water

frīg·ō frīgĕre frixī frictus *tr* to roast, fry

frīg·us -oris *n* cold, coldness, chill, coolness; frost; cold of winter, winter; coldness of death, death; chill, fever; shudder, chill; cold region; cold reception; coolness, indifference; slowness, inactivity ‖ *npl* cold spell

frigutt·iō -īre *intr* to stutter

fringill·a -ae *f* a songbird

fri·ō -āre -āvī -ātus *tr & refl & pass* to crumble

fritill·us -ī *m* dice box

frīvol·us -a -um *adj* frivolous, trifling, worthless, sorry, pitiful ‖ *npl* trifles

frixī *perf of* **frigesco** *and* **frigo** *and* **frigeo**

frondāt·or -ōris *m* pruner

frond·eō -ēre *intr* to have leaves; *(of places)* to be green with trees

frondesc·ō -ĕre *intr* to get leaves

fronde·us -a -um *adj* leafy

frondif·er -era -erum *adj* leafy

frondōs·us -a -um *adj* full of leaves, leafy

fron·s -dis *f* foliage; leafy bough, green bough; chaplet, garland

fron·s -tis *f* forehead, brow; front end, front; face, look; façade; vanguard; exterior, appearance; outer end of a scroll; sense of shame; **a fronte** in front; **frons firma** *(fig)* a bold front; **frons prima** front line; **frontem contrahere** *(or* **adducere** *or* **constringere** *or* **obducere)** to frown; **frontem ferire** to tap oneself on the forehead *(in annoyance)*; **frontem remittere** *(or* **exporrigere)** to smooth the brow, cheer up, relax; **frontis tenerae videri** to seem to blush *(literally, to seem to be of sensitive brow);* **in fronte** *(in measuring land)* in breadth, in frontage; **salvā fronte** without shame; **tenuis frons** low forehead

frontāl·ia -ium *npl* frontlet *(ornament for forehead of horse)*

front·ō -ōnis *m* person with bulging forehead

fructuāri·us -a -um *adj* productive; subject to land tax

fructuōs·us -a -um *adj* fruitful, productive

fructus *pp of* **fruor**

fruct·us -ūs *m* fruit, produce; proceeds, profit, income, return, revenue; enjoyment, satisfaction; benefit, reward, results, consequence

frūgāl·is -is -e *adj* thrifty, frugal

frūgālit·ās -ātis *f* frugality, economy; temperance; honesty; worth

frūgāliter *adv* frugally, economically; temperately

frūgēs *see* **frux**

frūgī *indecl adj* frugal; temperate; honest; worthy; useful; proper; **frugi esse** to do the right thing

frūgif·er -era -erum *adj* fruitful, productive, fertile; profitable

frūgifer·ens -entis *adj* fruitful

frūgileg·us -a -um *adj (of ants)* food-gathering

frūgipar·us -a -um *adj* fruitful

fruitus *pp of* **fruor**

frūmentāri·us -a -um *adj* of grain, grain-; grain-producing; of provisions; **res frumentaria** *(mil)* supplies, quartermaster ‖ *m* grain dealer; *(mil)* forager

frūmentāti·ō -ōnis *f (mil)* foraging

frūmentāt·or -ōris *m* grain merchant; *(mil)* forager

frūment·or -ārī -ātus sum *intr (mil)* to forage

frūment·um -ī *n* grain; wheat ‖ *npl* grain fields; crops

frūn·iscor -iscī -ītus sum *tr* to enjoy

fruor fruī fructus sum *or* **fruitus sum** *tr* to enjoy; ‖ *intr (w. abl)* **1** to enjoy, delight in; **2** to enjoy the company of; **3** *(law)* to have the use and enjoyment of

frustillātim *adv* in bits

frustrā *adv* in vain, uselessly, for nothing; without reason, groundlessly; **frustra**

discedere to go away disappointed; **frustra esse** to be mistaken; **frustra habere** to have *(s.o.)* confused
frustrām·en -inis *n* deception, error
frustrāti·ō -ōnis *f* deception; frustration
frustrāt·us -ūs *m* deception; **frustratui habere** *(coll)* to take for a sucker
frustr·ōr -ārī -ātus sum *or* **frustr·ō -āre** *tr* to deceive, trick; to disappoint; to frustrate
frustulent·us -a -um *adj* full of crumbs
frust·um -ī *n* crumb, bit, scrap; **frustum pueri** *(coll)* whippersnapper
frutect·um *or* **fruticēt·um -ī** *n* thicket, shrubbery **II** *npl* bushes
frut·ex -icis *m* shrub, bush; stem, trunk; *(coll)* blockhead
fruticētum *see* **frutectum**
frutic·ō -āre -āvī *or* **frutic·or -ārī** *intr* to sprout; to become bushy; *(fig) (of hair)* to become bushy
fruticōs·us -a -um *adj* bushy, overgrown with bushes
frux frūgis *f or* **frūg·ēs -um** *fpl* produce; crops; grain; vegetables; bread, meal; barley meal *(for sacrifice);* fruits, benefit; *(singl)* morality, honesty; **ad frugem bonam se recipere** to turn over a new leaf; **bonae frugi esse** to be honest, be thrifty; **expers frugis** worthless; **frugem facere** to do the decent thing
fūcāt·us -a -um *adj* artificial *(color);* dyed, colored, painted; phony
fūc·ō -āre -āvī -ātus *tr* to dye, tint; to apply makeup to; to disguise, falsify
fūcōs·us -a -um *adj* painted, colored; artificial, spurious
fūc·us -ī *m* (red) paint; rouge; drone; beeglue; disguise; pretense, deceit
fūdī *perf of* **fundo**
fue *or* **fu** *interj* phui!
fug·a -ae *f* flight, escape; avoidance; exile; speed, swift passage; disappearance; *(w. gen)* avoidance of, escape from; **fugae sese mandare** *(or* **fugam capere** *or* **fugam capessere** *or* **fugam facere** *or* **se in fugam conferre** *or* **se in fugam conjicere** *or* **sese in fugam dare)** to flee; **in fugam conferre** *(or* **in fugam conjicere** *or* **in fugam dare** *or* **in fugam impellere)** to put to flight; **fugam petere** to look for a means of escape
fugācius *adv* more cautiously, with one eye on flight
fug·ax -ācis *adj* apt to flee, fleeing; shy, timid; swift; transitory; *(w. gen)* shy of, shunning, avoiding, steering clear of, averse to
fugi·ens -entis *adj* fleeing, retreating; *(w. gen)* avoiding, averse to
fugiō fugĕre fūgī fugitus *tr* to escape, escape from, get away from; to run away from, shun, avoid; to succeed in avoiding; to vanish from; to be repelled by; to leave *(esp. one's country);* to be averse to, dislike; to escape the notice of, be unknown to; **fuge** *(w. inf)* do not...!; **fugere conspectum** *(w. gen)* to keep out of sight of; **fūgit me ratio** I made a mistake; **fūgit me scribere** it slipped my mind to write **II** *intr* to flee, escape, run away; to go into exile; to vanish; to pass away, perish; to begin to decay; *(w.* **ab)** to keep away from, shrink from; *(of things)* to slip out of one's grasp *or* control
fugit·ans -antis *adj* fleeing; *(w. gen)* averse to
fugit·ō -āre *tr* to run away from, shun **II** *intr* to run away
fugitīv·us -a -um *adj & m* runaway, fugitive
fug·ō -āre -āvī -ātus *tr* to put to flight, rout, drive away, chase away; to exile, banish; to avert
fulcīm·en -inis *n* support, prop
ful·ciō -cīre -sī -tus *tr* to prop up, support; to sustain, strengthen; **pedibus fulcire** to tread
fulcr·um -ī *n* bedpost; couch leg; *(fig)* bed, couch
ful·geō -gēre -sī *or* **fulg·ō -ĕre** *intr* to gleam, flash, blaze, shine, glare; to be conspicuous, be illustrious
fulgid·us -a -um *adj* flashing, shining
fulgō *see* **fulgeo**
fulg·or -ōris *m* flash; flash of lightning, lightning; brightness; splendor, glory; *(astr)* meteor; *(astr)* bright star
fulg·ur -uris *m* flash of lightning; place struck by lighning
fulgurāl·is -is -e *adj* of lightning; *(books)* on lightning
fulgurāt·or -ōris *m* interpreter of lightning
fulgurīt·us -a -um *adj* struck by lightning
fulgur·ō -āre -āvī -ātum *intr* to lighten, send lightning **II** *v impers* it is lightning
fulic·a -ae *or* **ful·ix -icis** *f* waterfowl *(perhaps the coot)*
fūlīg·ō -inis *f* soot *(used as a cosmetic, in paint, in medications, in ink)*
fulix *see* **fulica**
full·ō -ōnis *m* fuller *(person who shrank, beat, pressed, cleaned, and whitened cloth with chalk)*
fullōni·a -ae *f* fuller's craft, fulling
fullōnic·a -ae *f* fuller's craft, fulling; fuller's shop
fullōni·us -a -um *adj* fuller's
fulm·en -inis *n* thunderbolt, lightning bolt; *(fig)* bolt out of the blue
fulment·a -ae *f* heel
fulmine·us -a -um *adj* of lightning, lightning-; shine, sparkling, flashing
fulmin·ō -āre -āvī -ātum *intr* to lighten; *(fig)* to flash

fulsī *perf of* **fulcio** *and* **fulgeo**
fultūr·a -ae *f* support, prop
fultus *pp of* **fulcio**
fulv·us -a -um *adj* yellow, yellowish brown, reddish yellow, tawny; strawberry-blond
fūme·us -a -um *adj* smoky, murky
fūmid·us -a -um *adj* smoky, full of smoke; smoking; steaming
fūmif·er -era -erum *adj* smoking
fūmific·ō -āre -āvī *intr* to smoke; to burn incense
fūmific·us -a -um *adj* smoking, steaming
fūm·ō -āre -āvī *intr* to smoke, fume; to steam; to reek
fūmōs·us -a -um *adj* smoky; grimy from smoke; smoked *(food)*
fūm·us -ī *m* smoke; fume; steam, vapor ‖ *mpl* clouds of smoke
fūnāl·e -is *n* taper of wax-soaked rope; chandelier, candelabrum
fūnambul·us -ī *m* tightrope walker
functi·ō -ōnis *f* performance
funct·us -a -um *pp of* **fungor** ‖ *adj* dead ‖ *mpl* the dead
fund·a -ae *f* sling; pebble *(used in a sling)*; dragnet
fundām·en -inis *n* foundation; **fundamina ponere** to lay the foundations
fundāment·um -ī *n* foundation; *(fig)* basis, ground, beginning; **a fundamentis** utterly; **fundamenta agere** *(or* **jacĕre** *or* **locare)** to lay the foundation(s)
fundāt·or -ōris *m* founder
fundāt·us -a -um *adj* well-founded, established
Fund·ī -ōrum *mpl* town in Latium
fundit·ō -āre -āvī -ātus *tr* to sling, hurl with a sling; *(fig)* to sling *(e.g., words)* around
fundit·or -ōris *m* slinger
funditus *adv* from the bottom, utterly, entirely
fund·ō -āre -āvī -ātus *tr* to found; to put on a firm basis, establish; to secure, make fast ‖ *pass (w. abl)* to be based on
fundō fundĕre fūdī fūsus *tr* to pour, pour out; to smelt *(metals)*; to cast *(in metal)*; to pour in streams, shower, hurl; to pour out, empty; to spread, extend, diffuse; to bring forth, bear, yield in abundance; to throw to the ground, bring down; to give up, lose, waste; to pour out *(words)*; *(mil)* to pour in *(troops)*; *(mil)* to rout
fund·us -ī *m* bottom; farm, estate; *(leg)* sanctioner, authority
fūnebr·is -is -e *adj* funeral-, funerary; deadly, murderous
fūnerāt·us -a -um *adj* done in, killed; **prope funeratus** almost sent to *(one's)* grave
fūnere·us -a -um *adj* funerary, mourning; deadly, fatal
fūner·ō -āre -āvī -ātus *tr* to bury; to bring *(s.o.)* to his grave, kill
fūnest·ō -āre -āvī -ātus *tr* to defile with murder, desecrate
fūnest·us -a -um *adj* funereal, mourning; lamentable; polluted *(through contact with a corpse)*; deadly, fatal, calamitous; sad, dismal, mournful
fungīn·us -a -um *adj* of a mushroom
fun·gor -gī -ctus sum *tr* to perform, execute; **diem** *(or* **vitam)** **fungi** to die ‖ *intr (w. abl)* **1** to perform, execute, discharge, do; **2** to busy oneself with, be engaged in; **3** to finish complete; *(w.* **pro** *+ abl)* to act as; **fato** *(or* **morte** *or* **vitā** *or* **officio)** **fungi** to die
fung·us -ī *m* mushroom, fungus; candle snuffer; *(fig)* clown
fūnicul·us -ī *m* cord
fūn·is -is *m* rope, cable, cord; rigging; **funem reducere** *(fig)* to change one's mind; **per extentum funem ire** *(lit & fig)* to walk a tightrope; **sequi potius quam ducere funem tortum** to follow the lead rather than to lead
fūn·us -eris *n* funeral, funeral rites, burial; corpse; death; murder; havoc, ruin, destruction; **sub funus** on the brink of the grave ‖ *npl* shades of the dead
fūr fūris *mf* thief; *(fig)* rogue
fūrācissimē *adv* just like a thief
fūr·ax -ācis *adj* thievish
furc·a -ae *f* fork; fork-shaped prop *(for supporting vines, bleachers, etc.)*; pillory *(used to punish slaves)*; *(topog)* defile, pass
furcifer·a -ae *f* rascal *(female)*
furcif·er -erī *m* rogue, rascal
furcill·a -ae *f* pitchfork; **furcillā extrudi** *(coll)* to be given the bum's rush
furcill·ō -āre -āvī -ātus *tr* to support, prop up
furcul·a -ae *f* fork-shaped prop ‖ *fpl* narrow pass, defile; **Furculae Caudinae** Caudine Forks *(mountain pass in Samnium where Roman army was trapped in 321 B.C. and made to pass under the yoke)*
furenter *adv* furiously
furf·ur -uris *m* chaff; bran
furi·a -ae *f* frenzy, madness, rage; remorse; madman ‖ **Furia** Fury *(one of the three goddesses of vengeance: Megaera, Tisiphone, and Alecto)*
furiāl·is -is -e *adj* frenzied, frantic, furious; infuriated; of the Furies
furiāliter *adv* frantically
furibund·us -a -um *adj* frenzied, frantic, mad; inspired
fūrīn·us -a -um *adj* of thieves
furi·ō -āre -āvī -ātus *tr* to drive mad, infuriate
furiōsē *adv* in a rage, in a frenzy

furiōs·us -a -um *adj* frenzied, frantic, mad, furious; maddening
furn·us -ī *m* **(for-)** oven; bakery
fur·ō -ĕre *intr* to be out of one's mind; to rush furiously around; to rage, rave
fūr·or -ārī -ātus sum *tr* to steal, pilfer; to pillage; to plagiarize; to obtain by fraud ‖ *refl* to steal away
fur·ŏr -ōris *m* madness, rage, fury, passion; furor, excitement; prophetic frenzy, inspiration; passionate love
furtific·us -a -um *adj* thievish
furtim *adv* secretly; imperceptibly
furtīvē *adv* secretly, stealthily
furtīv·us -a -um *adj* stolen; secret, hidden, furtive
furt·um -ī *n* theft, robbery; trick; secret action, intrigue; secret love ‖ *npl* intrigues; secret love affair; stolen goods
fūruncul·us -ī *m* petty thief
furv·us -a -um *adj* black, dark, gloomy, eerie; **dies furvus** unlucky day
fuscin·a -ae *f* trident
fusc·ō -āre -āvī -ātus *tr* to darken, blacken
fusc·us -a -um *adj* dark; dim, ill-lit *(room);* hoarse *(voice);* dark-skinned, swarthy; low, muffled *(sound)*
fūsē *adv* widely, extensively; in great detail; loosely, roughly
fūsil·is -is -e *adj* molten, liquid-
fūsi·ō -ōnis *f* outpouring, effusion
fust·is -is *m* club; stick; beating to death *(as military punishment)*
fustitudin·us -a -um *adj (hum)* whip-happy
fustuār·ium -(i)ī *n* beating to death *(as military punishment)*
fūs·us -a -um *pp of* **fundo** ‖ *adj* spread out; broad, wide; diffuse *(style)*
fūs·us -ī *m* spindle
futtile *adv* uselessly, in vain
futtil·is -is -e *adj* **(fūtil-)** brittle; futile, worthless; trifling
futtilit·ās -ātis *f* **(fūtil-)** futility, uselessness
fut·uō -uĕre -uī -ūtus *tr (vulg)* to have intercourse with, screw *(a woman)*
futūr·us -a -um *adj* coming, future; impending, imminent; **tempus futurum** *(gram)* future tense ‖ *n* the future; **in futurum** for the future ‖ *npl* future events, the future
futūti·ō -ōnis *f (vulg)* sex, screwing
futūt·or -ōris *m (vulg)* sex partner
futūtr·ix -īcis *adj (fem only) (vulg)* lecherous ‖ *f* sex partner *(female)*

G

gabat·a -ae *f* plate, dish
Gabi·ī -ōrum *mpl* ancient town just outside Rome
Gabīni·us -a -um *adj* of the Gabinian clan
Gabīn·us -a -um *adj* of Gabii ‖ *mpl* the people of Gabii
Gād·ēs -um *fpl or* **Gād·is -is** *f* Cadiz *(in S. Spain)*
Gādītān·us -a -um *adj* of Gades ‖ *mpl* the people of Gades ‖ *fpl* dancing girls from Gades ‖ *n* dance by Gades dancing girls
gaes·um -ī n **(gēs-)** Gallic spear
Gaetūl·us -a -um *adj* Gaetulian, African ‖ *mpl* a people in N.W. Africa along the Sahara Desert
Gāï·a -ae *f* Gaia *(archaic feminine form of Gaius, surviving in ritual and legal language as a name for any woman)*
Gā·ïus -iī Gaius *(Roman praenomen; the names of Gaius and Gaia were formally given to the bridegroom and bride respectively at the wedding ceremony)*
Galat·ae -ārum *mpl* Galatians *(a people of central Asia Minor)*
Galatē·a -ae *f* sea nymph loved by Acis and Polyphemus
Galati·a -ae *f* Galatia *(Roman province in Asia Minor)*
Galb·a -ae *m* Roman emperor *(A.D. 68–69)*
galbane·us -a -um *adj* of galbanum
galban·um -ī *n* galbanum *(resinous sap of a Syrian plant)*
galbe·us -ī *m* armband *(worn as ornament or for medical purposes)*
galbināt·us -a -um *adj* dressed in chartreuse
galbin·us -a -um *adj* chartreuse; yellowish; *(fig)* effeminate ‖ *npl* chartreuse clothes
gale·a -ae *f* helmet *(usu. of leather)*
galeāt·us -a -um *adj* helmeted
gale·ō -āre *tr* to equip with a helmet
galēricul·um -ī *n* leather cap
galērīt·us -a -um *adj* wearing a leather cap
galēr·um -ī *n or* **galēr·us -ī** *m* leather cap; ceremonial cap *(worn by pontifices, flamines, etc.);* wig
gall·a -ae *f* gallnut *(nutlike growth on a plant)* ‖ *f* Gallic woman
Gall·ī -ōrum *mpl* Gauls *(inhabitants of modern France, Belgium, and N. Italy)*
Galli·a -ae *f* Gaul
Gallicān·us -a -um *adj* Gallic
gallicin·ium -(i)ī *n* cockcrow, daybreak
Gallic·us -a -um *adj* Gallic; belonging to the priests of Cybele; **canis Gallicus** a breed of hunting dog ‖ *f* Gallic shoe
gallīn·a -ae *f* chicken, hen; *(as term of endearment)* chick
gallīnāce·us -a -um *adj* of domestic fowl; **gallus gallinaceus** rooster; **lac gallinaceum** *(hum)* hen's milk *(i.e., an impossible thing)*
gallīnār·ius -(i)ī *m* poultry farmer; one who looks after the poultry used in augury
Gallograec·ī -ōrum *mpl* Galatians *(Celts*

who migrated from Gaul to Asia Minor in 3rd cent. B.C.)

Gall·us -a -um *adj* Gallic ‖ *m* a Gaul; priest of Cyblele; Galatian

gall·us -ī *m* rooster

gāne·a -ae *f or* **gāne·um -ī** *n* low-class restaurant, dive; gluttonous eating

gāne·ō -ōnis *m* glutton

gāneum *see* **ganea**

Gangarid·ae -ārum *mpl* an Indian people near the Ganges

Gang·ēs -is *m* Ganges River

Gangētic·us -a -um *adj* Indian

gann·iō -īre *intr* to snarl

gannīt·us -ūs *m* snarling

Ganymēd·ēs -is *m* Ganymede *(handsome boy carried off to Olympus by an eagle to become the cupbearer of the gods and catamite of Zeus)*

Ganymēdē·us -a -um *adj* of Ganymede

Garamant·ēs -um *mpl* tribe in N. Africa

Garamant·is -idos *adj (fem only) (poet)* African

Gargān·us -ī mountain in S.E. Italy

Gargar·a -ōrum *npl* a peak in the Ida mountain range; town in that region

garr·iō -īre -īvī *tr* to chatter, prattle; **nugas garrire** to talk nonsense ‖ *intr* to chatter, chat; *(of frogs)* to croak

garrulit·ās -ātis *f* talkativeness; chattering

garrul·us -a -um *adj* garrulous, talkative; blabbing; *(of birds)* chattering; *(time)* for chattering

gar·um -ī *n* fish sauce

gaud·ens -entis *adj* cheerful

gaudeō gaudēre gavīsus sum *tr* to rejoice at; **gaudium gaudere** to feel joy ‖ *intr* to rejoice; *(w. abl)* to be glad about, feel pleased at, delight in; **in se gaudere** *(or* **in sinu)** **gaudere** to be secretly glad

gaud·ium -(i)ī *n* joy, gladness, delight; cause of joy, source of delight; **gaudium nuntiare** to announce good news; **mala mentis gaudia** gloating

gaul·us -ī *m* bucket

gausap·a -ae *f or* **gausap·e -is** *or* **gausap·um -ī** *n* coarse woolen cloth; felt; shaggy beard

gāvīsus *pp of* **gaudeo**

gaz·a -ae *f* royal treasure; treasure, riches

gelasīn·us -ī *m* dimple

gelidē *adv* coldly; indifferently

gelid·us -a -um *adj* cold, icy, frosty; ice-cold, stiff, numbed ‖ *f* ice-cold water

gel·ō -āre -āvī -ātus *tr & intr* to freeze

Gelōn·ī -ōrum *mpl* Scythian tribe

gel·u -ūs *n or* **gel·um -ī** *n* cold; frost; ice; chill, coldness *(of death, old age, fear)*

gemebund·us -a -um *adj* groaning

gemellipar·a -ae *f* mother of twins

gemell·us -a -um *adj & m* twin

gemināti·ō -ōnis *f* doubling; repetition

gemin·ō -āre -āvī -ātus *tr* to double; to join, unite; to pair; to do repeatedly ‖ *intr* to become double

gemin·us -a -um *adj* twin; paired, double, twofold, two, both; similar ‖ *m* twin

gemit·us -ūs *m* sigh, groan

gemm·a -ae *f* bud; gem, jewel; jeweled goblet; signet ring, signet; eye *(of a peacock's tail);* literary gem; pebble *(for marking days);* a piece in a game-board

gemm·ans -antis *adj* adorned with gems; decorated

gemmāt·us -a -um *adj* set with gems, jeweled

gemme·us -a -um *adj* set with jewels, jeweled; brilliant, glittering, sparkling

gemmi·fer -fera -ferum *adj* containing gems; gem-producing

gemm·ō -āre -āvī -ātum *intr* to sprout, bud; to sparkle

gem·ō -ĕre -uī -itus *tr* to sigh over, lament ‖ *intr* to sigh, groan, moan; to creak

Gemōni·ae -ārum *fpl* steps on the Aventine slope from which the corpses of criminals were thrown into the Tiber River

gen·a -ae *f* cheek; eyelid ‖ *fpl* cheeks; region about the eyes, eyes

geneālog·us -ī *m* genealogist

gen·er -erī *m* son-in-law; daughter's fiancé; brother-in-law

generāl·is -is -e *adj* general, universal

generāliter *adv* in general, generally

generasc·ō -ĕre *intr* to be generated

generātim *adv* by species, by classes; in general, generally

generāt·or -ōris *m* producer, father

gener·ō -āre -āvī -ātus *tr* to beget, procreate, father; *(of places, of the body)* produce; to engender, arouse *(emotions)*

generōsē *adv* with dignity, nobly

generōsit·ās -ātis *f* good breeding, nobility of stock

generōs·us -a -um *adj* of good stock, high-born, noble; noble-minded; high-spirited

genes·is -is *f* birth; horoscope

genesta *see* **genista**

genetīv·us -a -um *adj* inborn, innate; *(gram)* genitive ‖ *m (gram)* genitive case

genetr·ix -īcis *f* (**-nit-**) mother, ancestress

geniāl·is -is -e *adj* nuptial, bridal; genial; joyous, merry, festive

geniāliter *ad* merrily

geniculāt·us -a -um *adj* knotted, having knots, jointed

genist·a -ae *f* (**-nest-**) broom plant

genitābil·is -is -e *adj* productive

genitāl·is -is -e *adj* generative, productive; of birth; **dies genitalis** birthday ‖ *n* genital organ

genitāliter *adv* fruitfully

genit- = genet-

genit·or -ōris *m* father; creator; source, cause
genitrix *see* **genetrix**
genitūr·a -ae *f* horoscope
genitus *pp of* **gigno**
gen·ius -iī *m* guardian spirit *(of person, place, or thing); (hum)* personfication of all natural appetites, natural inclination; talent
gen·ō -ĕre *see* **gigno**
gen·s -tis *f (Roman)* clan *(sharing the same nomen and, theoretically, the same ancestor);* stock; tribe; nation, people; country; class, set, race; species, breed; descendant, offspring; *(poet)* herd, flock, hive ‖ *fpl* the peoples of the world; rest of the world *(apart from the Romans),* foreign nations; **longe gentium abire** to be far, far away; **minime gentium** by no means; **ubi gentium** where in the world
gentic·us -a -um *adj* tribal; national
gentīlici·us -a -um *adj* of a Roman clan, of the extended family
gentīl·is -is -e *adj* family, hereditary; tribal; national ‖ *m* clansman, kinsman
gentīlit·ās -ātis *f* clan relationship
gen·ū -ūs *n* knee; **genibus minor** kneeling; **genibus nixus** on one's knees; **genuum junctura** knee joint
genuāl·ia -ium *npl* garters
genuī *perf of* **gigno**
genuīn·us -a -um *adj* innate, natural
genuīn·us -a -um *adj* of the cheek; jaw, of the jaw ‖ *mpl* back teeth
-gen·us -a -um *adjl suf* forms adjectives meaning "born of": **caeligenus** heavenborn
gen·us -eris *n* race, descent, lineage, breed, stock, family; noble birth; tribe; nation, people; descendant, offspring, posterity; kind, sort, species, class; rank, order, division; fashion, style, way; matter, respect; genus; sex; *(gram)* gender; **aliquid id genus** *(acc of respect instead of gen of quality)* something of that sort; **genus humanum** *(or* **genus hominum)** the human race, mankind; **in omni genere** in every respect; **sui generis** in a class of its *(her, his, their)* own, unique
geōgraphi·a -ae *f* geography
geōmetr·ēs -ae *m* geometer, mathematician
geōmetri·a -ae *f* geometry
geōmetric·us -a -um *adj* geometrical ‖ *f* geometry ‖ *npl* geometry
georgic·us -a -um *adj* agricultural ‖ *npl* Georgics *(poems on farming by Vergil)*
ger·ens -entis *adj (w. gen)* managing *(e.g., a business)*
germānē *adv* sincerely
Germān·ī -ōrum *mpl* Germans
Germāni·a -ae *f* Germany
Germānic·us -a -um *adj* Germanic ‖ *m* cognomen of Tiberius's nephew and adoptive son *(15 B.C.–A.D. 19)*
germānit·ās -ātis *f* brotherhood, sisterhood *(relationship between brothers and sisters of the same parents; relationship between colonies of the same mother-city)*
germān·us -a -um *adj* having the same parents; brotherly, sisterly; genuine, real, true ‖ *m* full brother ‖ *f see* **germana**
germ·en -inis *n* sprout, shoot; bud; embryo
germin·ō -āre -āvī -ātus *tr* to put forth, grow *(hair, wings, etc.)* ‖ *intr* to sprout
gerō gerĕre gessī gestus *tr* to bear, carry *(in one's hands); (of things)* to have in it, contain; to bear *(fruit);* to bear, carry *(in the womb);* to wear *(clothing);* to have; to hold *(consulship, etc.);* to spend, pass *(time);* to bring; to display, exhibit; to entertain *(feelings);* to assume; to carry on, manage; to govern, regulate, administer; to carry out, transact, do, accomplish; **bellum gerere** to fight a war, carry on a war; **dum ea geruntur** while that was going on; **gerere morem** *(w. dat)* to gratify; **personam gerere** *(w. gen)* to play the part of; **rem gerere** to run a business, conduct an affair ‖ *refl* to behave; *(w.* **pro** *+ abl)* to claim to be for; se **medium gerere** to remain neutral
ger·ō -ōnis *m* porter
gerr·ae -ārum *interj* nonsense!
gerulifigul·us -ī *m* accomplice; *(w. gen)* accomplice in
gerul·us -ī *m* porter
Gēry·ōn -onis *or* **Gēryon·ēs -ae** *m* Geryon *(three-headed monster of Spain that was slain by Hercules)*
gessī *perf of* **gero**
gestām·en -inis *n* load; article(s) worn; load, pack, burden; vehicle, litter ‖ *npl* ornaments; accouterments; arms
gestāti·ō -ōnis *f* ride *(on horseback, in litter, in vehicle);* drive *(place),* walk *(place)*
gestāt·or -ōris *m* bearer, carrier
gesti·ō -ōnis *f* performance
gest·iō -īre -īvī *or* **-iī** *intr* to be delighted, be thrilled; to be eager; *(w. inf)* to be itching to, long to
gestit·ō -āre -āvī *tr* to be in the habit of carrying *or* wearing
gest·ō -āre -āvī -ātus *tr* to bear, wear, carry; to take for a ride *(in a litter, in a vehicle, on horseback);* to spread, blab, tell; to cherish, harbor *(thoughts)* ‖ *pass* to ride, drive, sail *(esp. for pleasure)*
gest·or -ōris *m* tattler
gestuōs·us -a -um *adj* gesturing; suggestive
gest·us -a -um *pp of* **gero** ‖ *adj* **res gestae** deeds, accomplishments ‖ *n* business; deed

gest·us -ūs *m* gesture; gesticulation; posture, bearing, attitude
Get·ae -ārum *mpl* Thracian tribe on the Lower Danube
Geticē *adv* in Getic, in the Getic language
Getic·us -a -um *adj* of the Getae; Thracian
gibb·us -ī *m or* **gibb·a -ae** *f* hump
Gigant·ēs -um *mpl* Giants *(race of gigantic size that tried to storm heaven and were placed under various volcanoes)*
gignō gignĕre genuī genitus *or* **gen·ō -ĕre** *tr* to beget, bear, produce; to cause, occasion; to give rise to, bring about; to create, begin ‖ *pass* to be born; *(of faculties, parts of the body)* to be produced; *(w. abl)* to be born of, spring from; *(phil)* to come into being
gilv·us -a -um *adj* pale-yellow; **equus gilvus** palomino
gingīv·a -ae *f* gum *(of mouth)*
-gintā *indecl suf* forms numerals from 30 to 90
glabell·us -a -um *adj* bald, smooth
gla·ber -bra -brum *adj* bald, smooth ‖ *m* young slave, favorite slave
glaciāl·is -is -e *adj* icy, frozen
glaci·ēs -ēī *f* ice
glaci·ō -āre -āvī -ātus *tr* to turn into ice, freeze ‖ *intr* to congeal, harden
gladiāt·or -ōris *m* gladiator; ruffian; assassin ‖ *mpl* gladiatorial combat, gladiatorial show; **gladiatores dare** *(or* **edere)** to stage a gladiatorial show
gladiātōri·us -a -um *adj* gladiatorial; **munus gladiatorium** gladiatorial show ‖ *n* gladiator's pay
gladiātūr·a -ae *f* gladiatorial profession
glad·ius -(i)ī *m* sword; murder, death; **gladium educere** *(or* **stringere)** to draw the sword; **gladium recondere** to sheathe the sword; **jus** *(or* **potestas) gladii** right to try and punish a capital crime *(granted by emperor to provincial governors)*
glaeb·a -ae *f* **(glēb-)** lump of earth, clod; soil, land; lump, piece
glaebul·a -ae *f* **(glēb-)** small lump; bit of land, small farm
glaesum *see* **glesum**
glandif·er -era -erum *adj* acorn-bearing
gland·ium -(i)ī *n* candy
glan·s -dis *f* acorn, beechnut, chestnut; pellet *(for a sling)*; *(anat)* head of the penis
glāre·a -ae *f* gravel
glāreōs·us -a -um *adj* full of gravel, gravelly
glaucōm·a -atis *(acc fem singl:* **glaucumam)** *n* cataract; **glaucumam ob oculos objicere** *(w. dat)* to throw dust into *(s.o.'s)* eyes
glau·cus -a -um *adj* gray-green, grayish; bright, sparkling ‖ **Glauc·us -ī** *m* leader of the Lycians in the Trojan War ‖ fisherman of Euboea who was changed into a sea deity ‖ son of Sisyphus
glēb- = glaeb-
glēs·um *or* **glaes·um -ī** *n* amber
glī·s -ris *m* dormouse *(small, furry-tailed Old World rodent resembling a small squirrel in appearance and habits)*
glisc·ō -ĕre *intr* to grow, swell up, spread, blaze up; to grow, increase
globōs·us -a -um *adj* spherical, round
glob·us -ī *m* ball, sphere, globe; crowd, throng, gathering; clique
glomerām·en -inis *n* ball, globe
glomer·ō -āre -āvī -ātus *tr* to form into a ball; to gather up, roll up; to collect, gather together, assemble ‖ *refl & pass* to gather, assemble
glom·us -eris *n* ball of yarn
glōri·a -ae *f* glory, fame; pride; feeling of pride; source of pride, pride and joy; false pride, vanity, boasting; glorious deed; thirst for glory, ambition
glōriāti·ō -ōnis *f* boasting, pride
glōriol·a -ae *f* bit of glory
glōri·or -ārī -ātus sum *tr (only w. neuter pron as object)* to boast about; **haec gloriari** to boast about this, be proud of this; **idem gloriari** to make the same boast, be proud of the same thing ‖ *intr* to be proud; to boast; *(w. abl or w.* **de** *or* **in** + *abl)* to take pride in, boast about; *(w.* **adversus** + *acc)* to boast *or* brag to *(s.o.)*
glōriōsē *adv* gloriously, proudly; boastfully, pompously
glōriōs·us -a -um *adj* glorious, illustrious; eager for glory, ambitious; boastful; proud
glossēm·a -atis *n* word to be glossed
glūb·ō -ĕre *tr* to peel, skin
glūt·en -inis *n* glue
glūtināt·or -ōris *m* bookbinder
glūtin·ō -āre -āvī -ātus *tr* to glue together; *(med)* to close *(wounds)*
glutt·iō -īre -īvī *or* **-iī -ītus** *tr* **(glūt-)** to gulp down
glutt·ō -ōnis *m* glutton
Gnae·us *or* **Gnē·us -ī** *m* Roman first name *(praenomen, abbreviated Cn.)*
gnār·us -a -um *adj* skilled, expert; known, familiar; *(w. gen)* having knowledge of, familiar with, expert in, experienced in
gnāta *see* **nata**
gnātus *see* **natus**
gnōbilis *see* **nobilis**
gnoscō *see* **nosco**
Gnōsi·a -ae *or* **Gnōsi·as -adis** *or* **Gnōs·is -idis** *f* Ariadne *(daughter of King Minos of Cnossos)*
Gnō(s)s·us -ī *f* Cnossos *(ancient capital of Crete and residence of King Minos)*
gnōtus *see* **notus**
gōb·ius -(i)ī *m* **(cōb-)** goby *(small fish)*

Gorgi·as -ae *m* famous orator and sophist from Sicily *(480–c.390 B.C.)*
Gorg·ō -ōnis *f* Gorgon *(one of three daughters of Phorcys and Ceto: Stheno, Medusa, and Euryale)*
Gorgone·us -a -um *adj* Gorgonian; **Gorgoneus equus** Pegasus; **Gorgoneus lacus** the spring Hippocrene *(on Mt. Helicon)*
grabāt·us -ī *m* cot; army cot
Gracch·us -ī *m* Roman family name *(cognomen);* Tiberius Sempronius Gracchus *(social reformer, and tribune in 133 B.C.)* ‖ Gaius Sempronius Gracchus *(younger brother of Tiberius and tribune in 123 B.C.)*
gracil·is -is -e *adj* slim, slender; thin, skinny; poor; slight, insignificant; plain, simple *(style)*
gracilit·ās -ātis *f* slenderness; thinness, leanness, meagerness
grācul·us -ī *m* **(gracc-)** jackdaw *(glossy, black European bird resembling the crow)*
gradātim *adv* step by step, gradually, little by little
gradāti·ō -ōnis *f* flight of steps; tiers of seats *(in theater); (rhet)* series of propositions of ascending emphasis
gradior gradī gressus sum *intr* to go, walk, step
Grādīv·us *or* **Gradīv·os -ī** *m* epithet of Mars
grad·us -ūs *m* step, pace, walk, gait; step, degree, grade, stage; approach, advance, progress; status, rank; station, position; step, rung, stair; footing, stance; **concito gradu** on the double; **de gradu dejicere** *(fig)* to throw off balance; **gradum celerare** *(or* **corripere)** to pick up the pace; **gradum conferre** *(mil)* to come to close quarters; **gradūs ferre** *(mil)* to charge; **pleno gradu** on the double; **per gradūs** by degrees; **per gradūs ascendere** to climb the stairs; **suspenso gradu** on tiptoe
Graecē *adv* Greek, in Greek; **Graece discere (legere, loqui, scire)** to learn (read, speak, know) Greek
Graeci·a -ae *f* Greece; **Magna Graecia** Greek cities along the coast of S. Italy
graeciss·ō -āre *intr* to ape the Greeks; to speak Greek
graec·or -ārī *intr* to go Greek, act like a Greek
Graecul·us -a -um *adj (pej)* Greek through and through, hundred-percent Greek ‖ *mf (pej)* Greekling, dirty little Greek
Graec·us -a -um *adj & mf* Greek ‖ *n* Greek, Greek language
Grājugen·a -ae *m* Greek *(by birth)*
Grāj·us -a -um *adj* Greek ‖ *mpl* Greeks
grall·ae -ārum *fpl* stilts
grallāt·or -ōris *m* stilt walker
grām·en -inis *n* grass; meadow, pasture; plant, herb
grāmine·us -a -um *adj* grassy, of grass
grammatic·us -a -um *adj* grammatical, of grammar ‖ *m* teacher of literature and language; philologist ‖ *f & npl* grammar; philology
grammatist·a -ae *f* elementary school teacher
grānāri·a -ōrum *npl* granary
grandaev·us -a -um *adj* old, aged
grandesc·ō -ĕre *intr* to grow, grow big
grandicul·us -a -um *adj* rather large; pretty tall
grandif·er -era -erum *adj* productive, producing large crops
grandiloqu·us -ī *m* big talker
grandin·at -āre *v impers* it is hailing
grand·iō -īre *tr* to enlarge, increase
grand·is -is -e *adj* full-grown, grown up, tall; large, great; aged; important; powerful, strong; lengthy *(book, speech);* intense *(emotions);* proud, noble *(words, sentiments);* grand, lofty *(style);* dignified *(person);* loud, strong *(voice);* heavy *(debt);* dignified *(speaker);* **aevo** *(or* **aetate) grandis** advanced in years, elderly
grandit·ās -ātis *f* grandeur
grand·ō -inis *f (m)* hail
grānif·er -era -erum *adj (of an ant)* grain-carrying
grān·um -ī *n* small particle, grain; seed; kernel; stone *(in fruit);* **granum piperis** peppercorn
graphiār·ium -(i)i *n* case for holding a stylus, "pencil box"
graphicē *adv* in the manner of a painter; vividly, graphically; *(coll)* perfectly, properly, thoroughly
graphic·us -a -um *adj* artistic; *(coll)* exquisite, first-class
graph·ium -(i)ī *n* stylus
grassāt·or -ōris *m* tramp; bully, hoodlum; mugger, prowler
grassātūra -ae *f* holliganism
grass·or -ārī -ātus sum *intr* to advance, press on; to prowl; to run riot, rage; *(w.* **adversus** *or* **in** *+ acc)* to attack, waylay, mug
grātē *adv* willingly, with pleasure; gratefully
grātēs *(gen not in use) fpl* thanks, gratitude; **grates agere** *(w. dat)* to thank; **grates habere** *(w. dat)* to feel grateful toward
grāti·a -ae *f* grace, charm, pleasantness, loveliness; influence, prestige; popularity; love, friendship; service; favor, kindness; thanks, gratitude; cause, reason, motive; **cum gratiā** *(w. gen)* to the satisfaction of; with the approval of; **eā gratiā**

ut for the reason that; **exempli gratiā** for example; **gratiā** *(w. gen) (postpositive)* for the sake of, on account of; **gratiam facere** *(w. dat of person and gen of thing)* pardon *(s.o.)* for *(a fault)*; **gratias agere** *(w. dat)* to thank; **gratias habere** *(w. dat)* to be grateful to; **in gratiam** *(w. gen)* in order to win the favor of, in order to please; **in gratiam habere** to regard *(s.th.)* as a favor; **meā gratiā** for my sake; **quā gratiā?** why?

Grāti·ae -ārum *fpl* Graces *(Aglaia, Euphrosyne, and Thalia)*

grātificāti·ō -ōnis *f* kindness, favor

grātific·or -ārī -ātus sum *tr* to give up, surrender, sacrifice **||** *intr (w. dat)* **1** to do *(s.o.)* a favor; **2** to gratify, please *(s.o.)*; **3** to humor *(s.o.)*

grātiōs·us -a -um *adj* popular, influential; obliging

grātīs *adv* gratis, free, for nothing

grāt·or -ārī -ātus sum *intr* to rejoice; to express gratitude; *(w. dat)* to congratulate; **invicem inter se gratari** to congratulate one another

grātuītō *adv* gratuitously, gratis, for nothing; for no particular reason

grātuīt·us -a -um *adj* done for mere thanks, gratuitous, free, spontaneous; voluntary; unprovoked

grātulābund·us -a -um *adj* congratulating

grātulāti·ō -ōnis *f* congratulation; rejoicing, joy; public thanksgiving

grātulāt·or -ōris *m* well-wisher

grātul·or -ārī -ātus sum *intr* to be glad, rejoice; *(w. dat)* **1** to congratulate; **2** to render thanks to

grāt·us -a -um *adj* pleasing, pleasant, agreeable, welcome; thankful, grateful; deserving thanks, earning gratitude; popular **||** *n* favor; **gratum facere** *(w. dat)* to do *(s.o.)* a favor

gravanter *adv* reluctantly

grāvātē *adv* with difficulty; unwillingly, grudgingly

gravātim *adv* with difficulty; unwillingly

gravēdinōs·us -a -um *adj* prone to catch colds, susceptible to colds

gravēd·ō -inis *f* cold, head cold

graveol·ens -entis *adj* stinking

gravesc·ō -ĕre *intr* to grow heavy; *(fig)* to get worse

graviditās -ātis *f* pregnancy

gravid·ō -āre -āvī -ātus *tr* to impregnate

gravid·us -a -um *adj* loaded, filled, full; pregnant; *(w. abl)* teeming with

grav·is -is -e *adj* heavy, weighty; burdensome; grave, serious; troublesome, oppressive, painful, harsh, hard, severe, unpleasant; indigestible *(food)*; important, influential; venerable, dignified; grave, serious; pregnant; hostile; relentless; obnoxious *(person)*; exorbitant *(prices)*; low, deep *(voice)*; flat *(note)*; harsh, bitter, offensive *(smell, taste)*; impressive *(speech)*; stormy *(weather)*; labored *(breathing)*; oppressive *(heat)*; unhealthy *(climate, place, season)*; dangerous *(animal, person)*; *(mil)* heavy-armed

gravit·ās -ātis *f* weight; severity, harshness; seriousness; importance; dignity, influence, authority; pregnancy; violence, vehemence; offensiveness *(of smell)*; unhealthfulness *(of climate, place, season)*

graviter *adv* heavily, ponderously; hard, violently, vehemently; severely, harshly; unpleasantly; sadly, sorrowfully; with dignity, with propriety, with authority; *(to feel)* deeply; *(to smell)* offensive; *(to speak)* impressively; **graviter ferre** to take *(s.th.)* hard

grav·ō -āre -āvī -ātus *tr* to weigh down, load (down); to be burdensome to, be oppressive to; to aggravate; to increase

grav·or -ārī -ātus sum *tr* to feel annoyed at, object to; to refuse, decline; to bear with reluctance, regard as a burden **||** *intr* to feel annoyed

gregāl·is -is -e *adj* of the herd *or* flock; common; **miles gregalis** a private; **sagulum gregale** a private's uniform **||** *mpl* comrades, companions

gregāri·us -a -um *adj* of the flock *or* herd; common, ordinary; **miles gregarius** a private **||** *m (mil)* a private

gregātim *adv* in flocks, in herds, in crowds

grem·ium -(i)ī *n* lap, bosom; womb

gressus *pp of* **gradior**

gress·us -ūs *m* step; course, way

gre·x -gis *m* flock, herd; swarm; company, group, crowd, troop, set, clique, gang; theatrical cast, troupe

gruis *see* **grus**

grunn·iō -īre -īvī *or* **-iī -ītum** *intr* **(grund-)** to grunt

grunnīt·us -ūs *m* grunt, grunting

gru·ō -ĕre *intr (of a crane)* to honk

grū·s *or* **gru·is -is** *mf* crane

gryps grȳpis *m* griffin *(fabled monster having the head and wings of an eagle and the body of a lion)*

gubernāc(u)l·um -ī *n* rudder, tiller, helm **||** *npl (fig)* helm

gubernāti·ō -ōnis *f* navigation

gubernāt·or -ōris *m* navigator, pilot, helmsman; ruler, governor, director

gubernātr·ix -īcis *f* directress

gubern·ō -āre -āvī -ātus *tr* to navigate, pilot; to direct, govern

gul·a -ae *f* gullet, throat; palate, appetite; gluttony

gulōs·us -a -um *adj* appetizing, dainty; fond of fine foods

gurg·es -itis *m* abyss, gulf, whirlpool; waters, flood, depths, sea; spendthrift

gurguli·ō -ōnis *m* gullet; windpipe

gurgust·ium -(i)ī *n* dark hovel; *(fig)* hole in the wall

gustātōr·ium -(i)ī *n* appetizer

gustāt·us -ūs *m* sense of taste; flavor, taste

gust·ō -āre -āvī -ātus *tr* to taste; *(fig)* to enjoy; to overhear ‖ *intr* to have a snack

gust·us -ūs *m* tasting; flavor, taste; appetizer; small portion, taste

gutt·a -ae *f* drop; spot, speck

guttātim *adv* drop by drop

guttāt·us -a -um *adj* spotted

guttul·a -ae *f* tiny drop

gutt·ur -uris *n (m)* gullet, throat, neck ‖ *npl* throat, neck

gūt·us -ī *m* **(gutt-)** cruet, flask

Gy·ās -ae *m* hundred-armed giant

Gȳg·ēs -is *or* **-ae** *m* king of Lydia *(reigned 716–678 B.C.)*

gymnasiarch·us -ī *m* manager of a gymnasium

gymnas·ium -(i)ī *n* gymnasium

gymnastic·us -a -um *adj* gymnastic

gymnic·us -a -um *adj* gymnastic

gymnosophist·ae -ārum *mpl* Hindu Stoics

gynaecē·um -ī *or* **gynaec·īum -(i)ī** *n* women's apartment in a Greek house

gypsāt·us -a -um *adj* covered with gypsum, white with gypsum

gyps·ō -āre -āvī -ātus *tr* to whiten with gypsum *(the feet of slaves put up for auction);* to plaster up

gyps·um -ī *n* gypsum; plaster of Paris

gȳr·us -ī *m* circle, cycle, ring; *(astr)* orbit, course; **in gypros ire** to go in circles; **in gyrum** in a circle; all around

H

ha *interj* expression of joy, satisfaction, *or* laughter

habēn·a -ae *f* strap ‖ *fpl* reins; *(fig)* reins of government; **habenae rerum** reins of state; **habenas adducere** *(or* **dare** *or* **effundere** *or* **immittere)** *(w. dat)* to give free rein to; **habenas premere** to tighten the reins; **immissis habenis** at full speed

hab·eō -ēre -uī -itus *tr* to have; to hold; to possess; to own; to keep, retain, detain; to have at one's disposal, have available; to have on one's side, have in one's favor; to control, have under one's control; to involve, entail; to have knowledge of *(facts, information);* to afford, give *(e.g., pleasure);* to have on, wear *(clothes);* to treat, handle, use; *(of a vessel)* to hold, contain; to be made up of, consist of; *(of feelings)* to beset, come over, grip; to hold, conduct *(meeting, inquiry, census);* to deliver, give *(speech),* give *(a talk);* to keep, observe *(a law, edict, practice); (of owner, inhabitant)* to occupy, inhabit; to pronounce, utter *(words);* to spend, live *(life, youth);* to hold, manage, govern, wield; to hold, think, consider, believe; to occupy, engage, busy; to occasion, produce, render; to know, be informed of, be acquainted with; to take, accept, endure, bear; **animo habere** *(w. inf)* to have in mind to, intend to; **certum habere** to regard as certain; **comitia habere** to hold an assembly; to hold elections; **contionem habere** to hold a meeting *or* rally; **gratiam habere** to be grateful; **in animo habere** to have on one's mind, have in mind; **justum habere** *(w. inf)* to have a duty to; **locum priorem habere** to have the lead *(in a race);* **melius habere** *(w. inf)* to think it better to; **necesse habere** *(w. inf)* to have an obligation to; **parum habere** *(w. inf)* to think it a minor matter to; **parum habere violasse** to think nothing of having violated; **pro certo habere** to regard it as certain; **pro explorato habere** to regard it as an established fact; **rus me nunc habet** I am now in the country; **secum habere** to have with one *or* in one's possession, have in one's company; **secum** *(or* **sibi)** **habere** to keep *(s.th.)* to oneself, keep secret ‖ *refl (w. adv)* to be, feel *(well, etc.);* **bene vos habetis** you are doing fine; **me male habeo** I'm doing lousy; **quo pacto te habes?** how are you doing?; **sic res se habet** that's the situation, that's the way things are; **singulos ut sese haberet rogitans** asking each and every one how he was doing ‖ *intr (w. adv or abl)* to be, live, dwell *(in a place);* **habet!** *(said of gladiator receiving fatal wound)* he's had it!; **hic ego habeo** I live here ‖ *v impers* **bene habet** (that's) fine!, O.K. then!; **sic habet** that's how it is

habil·is -is -e *adj* handy; easy to handle; suitable, convenient; active; *(of vehicles)* easy to control

habilit·ās -ātis *f* aptitude

habitābil·is -is -e *adj* fit to live in

habitāti·ō -ōnis *f* residence; (cost of) rent

habitāt·or -ōris *m* inhabitant; occupant, tenant *(of house, apartment)*

habit·ō -āre -āvī *tr* to live in, inhabit ‖ *intr* to dwell, live

habitūd·ō -inis *f* condition, appearance; bearing

habitur·iō -īre *tr* to like to have

habit·us -a -um *pp of* **habeo** ‖ *adj* in good

physical condition; **corpulentior et habitior videri** to look stouter and in better physical condition

habit·us -ūs *m* condition *(of the body);* physical make-up, build, looks, form, shape; circumstances; style, style of dress; character, quality; disposition, state of feeling; posture

hāc *adv* this way, in this way

hactenus *adv* to this place, thus far; until now, hitherto, so far; to this extent, so much; *(in writing)* to this point; **haec hactenus** enough of this

Hadri·a -ae *f* **(Adr-)** Adriatic Sea

Hadriac·us -a -um *adj* Adriatic

Hadriān·us -a -um *adj* **(Adr-)** Adriatic ‖ *m* Hadrian *(Roman emperor, A.D. 117–138)*

Hadriātic·us -a -um *adj* Adriatic

haec hōrum *(neut pl of* **hoc)** *adj & pron* these

haec hūjus *(older form:* **haece;** *gen:* **hujusce)** *(fem of* **hic)** *adj* this; the present, the actual; the latter; *(occasionally)* the former; **haec…haec** one…another ‖ *pron* this one, she; the latter; *(occasionally)* the former; **haec…haec** one…another one; **haecine (haec** *w. interrog enclitic* **-ne)** is this…?

haece *see* **haec**

haecine *see* **haec**

Haed·ī -ōrum *mpl (astr)* the Kids *(pair of stars in the constellation Auriga)*

haedili·a -ae *f* little goat

haedill·us -ī *m (term of endearment)* little goat

haedīn·us -a -um *adj* kid's, goat's

haedul·us -ī *m* little kid, little goat

haed·us -ī *m* young goat, kid

Haemōni·a -ae *f* Thessaly

Haem·us *or* **Haem·os -ī** *m* mountain range in N. Thrace

hae·reō -rēre -sī -sum *intr* to cling, stick; to hang around, linger, stay, remain fixed, remain in place; to be rooted to the spot; to come to a standstill, stop; to be embarrassed, be at a loss, hesitate, be in doubt; *(w. dat or abl or w.* **in** *+ abl)* **1** to cling to, stick to, be attached to; **2** to loiter in, hang around in, waste time in *(a place)* *or* at *(an activity);* **3** to adhere to, stick by *(an opinion, purpose);* **4** to gaze upon; **5** to keep close to; **in terga** *(or* **tergis** *or* **in tergis) hostium haerere** to keep on the enemy's tail

haeresc·ō -ĕre *intr* to stick together

haeres·is -is *f* philosophical school

haesitābund·us -a -um *adj* hesitating, faltering

haesitanti·a -ae *f* hesitancy

haesitāti·ō -ōnis *f* hesitation, indecision

haesitāt·or -ōris *m* hesitator

haesit·ō -āre -āvī -ātum *intr* to get stuck; to hesitate; to stammer; to be undecided, be at a loss

hahae, hahahahae *interj* expression of joy, satisfaction, *or* laughter

halagor·a -ae *f* salt market

hāl·ans -antis *adj* fragrant

hāl·ēc *or* **(h)all·ēc -ēcis** *n* **(·ex)** fish sauce; fish soup

haliaeët·os -ī *m* osprey *(large hawk that preys on fish, also called fish hawk)*

hālit·us -ūs *m* breath; steam, vapor

hal(l)ūcin·ō -āre *or* **hālūcin·or -ārī -ātus sum** *tr* to say in a distracted state ‖ *intr* to have hallucinations; to ramble

hāl·ō -āre *tr* to exhale ‖ *intr* to be fragrant

halopant·a -ae *m* scoundrel

halōs·is -is *(acc:* **-in)** *f* capture

halt·ēr -ēris *m* weight held in the hand by an athlete

hālūcinor *see* **hal(l)ucino**

ham·a *or* **am·a -ae** *f* bucket

Hamādry·as -adis *(dat pl:* **Hamādryasin)** *f* wood nymph

hāmātil·is -is -e *adj* with hooks

hāmāt·us -a -um *adj* hooked

Hamilc·ar -aris *m* Carthaginian general in the First Punic War, surnamed Barca, and father of Hannibal *(d. 228 B.C.)*

hāmiōt·a -ae *f* fisher(man)

Hamm·ō(n) *or* **Amm·ōn -ōnis** *m* Ammon *(Egyptian god, represented as a ram, who had a famous oracle in Libya and was identified with Jupiter Ammon);* **ultimus Ammon Afrorum** deepest Africa

hāmul·us -ī *m* small hook

hām·us -ī *m* hook, fishhook; barb

Hannib·al -alis *m* son of Hamilcar Barca and famous general in the Second Punic War *(240–182 B.C.)*

har·a -ae *f* pen, coop, stye

(h)arēn·a -ae *f* sand; seashore, beach; arena ‖ *fpl* desert

(h)arēnāri·a -ae *f* sandpit

(h)arēnōs·us -a -um *adj* sandy

hariol·a -ae *f* fortuneteller *(female)*

hariol·or -ārī -ātus sum *intr* to foretell the future; to talk gibberish

hariol·us -ī *m* fortuneteller

harmoni·a -ae *f* harmony ‖ **Harmonia** wife of Cadmus, founder and first king of Thebes

harpag·ō -āre -āvī -ātus *tr (coll)* to hook *(to steal)*

harpag·ō -ōnis *m* hook; harpoon; grappling hook; greedy person

Harpalyc·ē -ēs *f* Thracian princess, raised as a warrior

harpast·um -ī *n* handball

harp·ē -ēs *f* sickle; scimitar

Harpȳj·a -ae *f* harpy *(creature with head of a woman and body of a bird)*

(h)arundif·er -era -erum *adj* reed-bearing

(h)arundine·us -a -um *adj* of reeds
(h)arund·ō -inis *f* reed, cane, fishing rod; pen; shepherd's pipe; shaft, arrow; fowler's rod; weaver's comb; **(h)arundo Indica** bamboo
(h)arusp·ex -icis *m* soothsayer *(interpreter of internal organs, prodigies, and lightning)*
(h)aruspic·a -ae *f* soothsayer *(female)*
(h)aruspicīn·us -a -um *adj* of divination ‖ *f* the art of divination
(h)aruspic·ium -(i)ī *n* divination
(H)asdrub·al -alis *m* brother of Hannibal *(d. 207 B.C.)* ‖ son-in-law of Hamilcar Barca *(d. 221 B.C.)*
hast·a -ae *f* spear *(weapon; spear stuck into ground at public auction; symbol of the centumviral court, which dealt with cases of property and inheritance);* **sub hastā vendere** to sell at auction
hastāt·us -a -um *adj* armed with a spear ‖ *mpl* soldiers in the first line of a Roman battle formation
hastīl·e -is *n* shaft; spear; rod
(h)au *interj* oh!, ow!, ouch!
haud *or* **haut** *or* **hau** *adv* hardly; not, not at all, by no means
hau(d)quāquam *adv* by no means whatsoever, not at all
hau·riō -rīre -sī -stus *tr* to draw, draw up, draw out; to drain, drink up; to spill, shed *(blood); (of water)* to swallow up, engulf; *(of flames)* to devour; to consume, use up *(resources);* to scoop up; to hollow out; to derive; *(fig)* to have one's fill of; *(fig)* drink in
haustr·um -ī *n* scoop *(on a water-wheel)*
haustus *pp of* **haurio**
haust·us -ūs *m* drawing *(of water);* drinking, swallowing; drink, draft; handful; stream *(of blood)*
haut *see* **haud**
haveō *see* **aveo**
hebdom·as -ados *f* week; a group of seven; fever occurring at seven-day intervals
Hēb·ē -ēs *f* goddess of youth, daughter of Juno, and cupbearer of the gods
(h)eben·us -ī *m* ebony
heb·eō -ēre *intr* to be blunt, be dull; *(of light)* to grow dim; *(of anger)* to die down; *(fig)* to be sluggish, be inactive
heb·es -etis *adj* blunt, dull; faint, dim; dull, obtuse, stupid
hebesc·ō -ĕre *intr* to grow blunt, grow dull; to become faint *or* dim; to lose vigor
hebet·ō -āre -āvī -ātus *tr* to blunt, dull, dim
Hebr·us -ī *m* principal river in Thrace
Hecat·ē -ēs *f* goddess of magic and witchcraft, identified with Diana
hecatomb·ē -ēs *f* hecatomb *(public sacrifice of 100 oxen to the gods)*
Hect·or -oris *m* son of Priam and Hecuba, husband of Andromache
Hecub·a -ae *or* **Hecub·ē -ēs** *f* **(-cab-)** wife of Priam *(was metamorphosed into a dog)*
(h)eder·a -ae *f* ivy
(h)ederig·er -era -erum *adj* wearing ivy
(h)ederōs·us -a -um *adj* overgrown with ivy
hēdycr·um -ī *n* perfume
hei, hēia *see* **ei, ēia**
Helen·a -ae *or* **Helen·ē -ēs** *f* Helen of Troy *(wife of Menelaus, sister of Clytemnestra, Castor, and Pollux)*
Helen·us -ī *m* prophetic son of Priam and Hecuba
Hēliad·es -um *fpl* daughters of Helios and sisters of Phaëthon, who were changed into poplar trees and whose tears were changed into amber
helic·a -ae *f* spiral
Helicā·ōn -onis *m* the son of Antenor and founder of Patavium
Helicāoni·us -a -um *adj* of Helicaon *(i.e., of Patavium)*
Helic·ē -ēs *f (astr)* Big Bear *(constellation Ursa Major); (poet)* N. regions
Helic·ōn -ōnis *m* mountain in Boeotia sacred to Muses and Apollo
Helicōniad·es *or* **Helicōnid·es -um** *fpl* Muses
Helicōni·us -a -um *adj* of Helicon
hēliocamīn·us -ī *m* sun-room
Hell·as -adis *or* **-ados** *f* (mainland of) Greece
Hell·ē -ēs *f* daughter of Athamas and Nephele who, while riding the golden-fleeced ram, fell into the Hellespont *(= Helle's Sea)* and drowned
hellebor- = ellebor-
Hellespont·us -ī *m* Hellespont *(modern Dardanelles)*
hellu·ō -ōnis *m* glutton; squanderer
hellu·or -ārī -ātus sum *intr* to be a glutton
(h)el·ops *or* **ell·ops -opis** *m* highly-prized fish *(perhaps the sturgeon)*
helvell·a -ae *f* delicious herb
Helvēti·us -a -um *adj* Helvetian ‖ *mpl* Helvetians *(a people of ancient Switzerland)*
helv·us -a -um *adj* pale-yellow
hem *interj (expression of surprise)* well!
hēmerodrom·us -ī *m* courier
hēmicill·us -ī *m (pej)* mule
hēmicycl·ium -(i)ī *n* semicircle of seats
hēmīn·a -ae *f* half a sextarius *(half a pint)*
hendecasyllab·ī -ōrum *mpl (pros)* hendecasyllabics *(verses with eleven syllables)*
hēpatiāri·us -a -um *adj* of the liver
heptēr·is -is *f* galley *(perhaps)* with seven banks of oars
hera *see* **era**

Hēr·a -ae *f* Greek goddess, identified with Juno
Hēraclē·a -ae *f* name of numerous towns *(esp. a part of Lucania on the Siris River and, in Sicily, a town between Lilybaeum and Agrigentum)* **‖** epic poem on the subject of Hercules
Hēraclīt·us -ī *m* early Greek philosopher of Ephesus who believed fire to be the primary element *(Ē 513 B.C.)*
Hērae·a -ōrum *npl* festival in honor of the Greek goddess Hera
herb·a -ae *f* blade; stalk; herb; plant; grass, lawn; **adhuc tua messis in herba est** *(prov)* don't count your chickens before they are hatched *(literally, your harvest is still on the stalk);* **herba mala** weed
herbesc·ō -ĕre *intr* to sprout
herbe·us -a -um *adj* grass-green
herbid·us -a -um *adj* grassy; full of weeds
herbif·er -era -erum *adj* grassy, grass-producing; made of herbs; bearing magical herbs
herbigrad·us -a -um *adj (of a snail)* that crawls on the grass
herbōs·us -a -um *adj* grassy; made with herbs; resembling vegetation
herbul·a -ae *f* small plant
(h)ercisc·ō -ĕre *intr* to divide an inheritance
hercle *or* **hercule** *or* **ercle** *interj (used for emphasis or to express strong feeling, normally used by the male sex only)* by Hercules!
(h)erct·um -ī *n* inheritance
Herculānens·is -is -e *adj* of Herculaneum **‖** *m* district of Herculaneum **‖** *mpl* inhabitants of Herculaneum
Herculāne·um -ī *n* town on the Bay of Naples, destroyed by the volcano of Mt. Vesuvius in A.D. 79
Hercul·ēs -is *or* **-ī** *or* **-eī** *m* son of Jupiter and Alcmena, husband of Deianira
Herculēs *or* **Herc(u)le** *interj* by Hercules! *(see* **hercle)**
Herculē·us -a -um *adj* of Hercules
Hercyni·us -a -um *adj* Hercynian, of Hercynia *(a region of the forest-covered mountains extending from the Rhine to the Carpathians)*
here *see* **heri**
hērēdipet·a -ae *m* legacy hunter
hērēditāri·us -a -um *adj* of an inheritance; inherited, hereditary
hērēdit·ās -ātis *f* inheritance; hereditary succession; **hereditas sine sacris** an inheritance without encumbrances
hērēd·ium -(i)ī *n* inherited estate
hēr·ēs -ēdis *m* heir *(to an estate, throne);* **heres ex dodrante** heir to three-quarters of an estate; *(w. ordinal numbers, indicating order of succession):* **heres Pelopis tertius** Pelop's heir third in order of succession *(i.e., Agamemnon)* **‖** *f* heiress
herī *or* **heri** *or* **here** *adv* yesterday
herif-, herīl- = **erif-, eril-**
Hermaphrodīt·us -ī *m* son of Hermes and Aphrodite who combined with the nymph Salmacis to become one bisexual person
Hermathēn·a -ae *f* a herm *(i.e., a quadrangular pillar)* with a bust of Athena
Herm·ēs -ae *m* Greek god identified with Mercury; herm *(quadrangular pillar with the bust of Hermes, or later, of other gods)*
Hermion·ē -ēs *or* **Hermion·a -ae** *f* Hermione *(daughter of Helen and Menelaus and wife of Orestes)*
Herm·us -ī *m* gold-rich river in the Greek district of Aeolis
Hērodot·us -ī *m* father of Greek history, born at Halicarnassus on coast of Asia Minor *(484–425 B.C.)*
hērōïc·us -a -um *adj* heroic, epic
hērōïn·a -ae *f* demigoddess, heroine
hērō·is -idis *f* demigoddess, heroine
hēr·ōs -ōös *m* hero *(mythological figure; a man with heroic qualities)*
hērō·us -a -um *adj* heroic, epic **‖** *m* dactylic hexameter; a dactyl
Hersili·a -ae *f* wife of Romulus
herus *see* **erus**
Hēsiod·us -ī *m* Hesiod *(early Greek poet from Boeotia, 8th cent. B.C.)*
Hēsion·ē -ēs *or* **Hēsion·a -ae** *f* Hesione *(daughter of Laomedon, king of Troy, whom Hercules rescued from a sea monster)*
Hesperi·a -ae *f* the land of the evening star *(i.e., Italy and Spain)*
Hesperid·es -um *fpl* daughters of Hesperus who guarded the golden apples beyond Mount Atlas
Hesper·us *or* **Hesper·os -ī** *m* evening star
hestern·us -a -um *adj* yesterday's
hetairi·a -ae *f* secret society
hetairic·ē -ēs *f* Macedonian mounted guard
heû! *interj (expression of pain or dismay)* oh!, ah!
heûs! *interj (to draw attention)* say there!, hey!
hexame·ter -tra -trum *adj (pros)* hexameter, having six metrical feet *(applied esp. to dactylic hexamter)* **‖** *mpl* verse in this meter
hexaphor·um -ī *n* litter carried by six men
hexēr·is -is *f* ship *(perhaps)* with 6 banks of oars
hiāt·us -ūs *m* opening; open mouth; mouthing, bluster; basin *(of a fountain); (w. gen)* greedy desire for; chasm; *(pros)* hiatus
Hibēr·ēs -um *mpl* Spaniards **‖** tribe south of the Caucasus
Hībēri·a -ae *f* Iberian peninsula *(Greek name for Spain)*

Hibēric·us -a -um *adj* Spanish
hībern·a -ōrum *npl (mil)* winter quarters; winter-quartering
hībernācul·a -ōrum *npl* winter bivouac; winter residence
Hiberni·a -ae *f* Ireland
hībern·ō -āre -āvī -ātum *or* **hībern·or -ārī -ātus sum** *intr* to spend the winter; to stay in winter quarters; *(fig)* to hibernate
hībern·us -a -um *adj* winter-, in winter, wintry; designed for winter use
Hibēr·us -ī *m* river in Spain *(modern Ebro)*
hibisc·um -ī *n (bot)* hibiscus *(plant w. large, showy flowers)*
hibrid·a -ae *mf* **(hyb-)** hybrid, mongrel, half-breed
hīc *(or* **hic) hūjus** *(older form:* **hīce hūjusce)** *adj* this; the present, the actual; the latter; *(occasionally)* the former; **hic**...**hic** one...another ‖ *pron* this one, he; this man; myself, yours truly *(i.e., the speaker or writer);* the latter; *(occasionally)* the former; *(in court)* the defendant, my defendant; **hic**...**hic** one...another; **hicine (hic +** *interrog enclitic* **-ne)** is this...?
hīc *adv* here, in this place; at this point; in this affair, in this particular
hīce *see* **hic**
hīcine *see* **hic**
hiemāl·is -is -e *adj* winter, wintry; stormy
hiem·ō -āre -āvī -ātum *intr* to spend the winter; to be wintry, be cold, be stormy
hiem·s *or* **hiem·ps -is** *f* winter; cold; storm
Hiemps·ala -alis *m* name of several N. African kings, *esp.* a grandson of Massinissa and cousin of Jugurtha, by whom he was killed
Hier·ō(n) -ōnis *m* Hieron *(ruler of Syracuse and patron of philosophers and poets, d. 466 B.C.)* ‖ Hieron *(ruler of Syracuse and friend of the Romans in First Punic War, 306?–215 B.C.)*
Hierosolym·a -ae *f or* **Hierosolym·a -ōrum** *npl* Jerusalem
hiet·ō -āre *intr* to keep yawning
hilarē *adv* cheerfully, merrily
hilar·is -is -e *adj* cheerful, merry
hilarit·ās -ātis *f* cheerfulness
hilaritūd·ō -inis *f* cheerfulness
hilar·ō -āre -āvī -ātus *tr* to cheer up
hilarul·us -a -um *adj* cheerful little
hilar·us -a -um *adj* cheerful, merry
hill·ae -ārum *fpl* smoked sausage
(H)īlōt·ae -ārum *mpl* Helots *(serfs of the Spartans)*
hīl·um -ī *n (usu. after a neg.)* the least bit
hinc *adv* from here, from this place; on this side, here; for this reason; from this source; after this, from now on, henceforth; *(partitive)* of this, of these; **hinc illinc** from one side to the other
hinn·iō -īre -iī *intr* to whinny, neigh
hinnīt·us -ūs *m* neighing
hinnule·us -ī *m* fawn, young deer
hi·ō -āre -āvī *tr* to mouth, sing with mouth wide open ‖ *intr* to open, be open; to gape; to yawn; to make eyes *(in surprise or greedy anticipation); (rhet)* to be disjointed
hippagōg·os -ī *f* ship for transporting horses
Hipparch·us -ī *m* son of Pisistratus, tyrant of Athens, slain in 514 B.C.
Hippi·ās -ae *m* son of Pisistratus (tyrant of Athens), and tyrant of Athens himself *(527–510 B.C.)*
hippocentaur·us -ī *m* centaur
Hippocrat·ēs -is *m* founder of scientific medicine *(c. 460–380 B.C.)*
Hippocrēn·ē -ēs *f* spring on Mt. Helicon, sacred to the Muses and produced when the hoof of Pegasus hit the ground there
Hippodam·ē -ēs *or* **Hippodamē·a** *or* **Hippodamī·a -ae** *f* Hippodamia *(daughter of Oenamaüs, king of Elis, and wife of Pelops)* ‖ Hippodamia *(daughter of Adrastus and wife of Pirithoüs)*
hippodrom·os -ī *m* racetrack
Hippolyt·ē -ēs *or* **Hippolyt·a -ae** *f* Hippolyte *(Amazonian wife of Thesesus)* ‖ wife of Acastus, king of Magnesia
Hippolyt·us -ī *m* **(Ipp-)** son of Theseus and Hippolyte
hippoman·es -is *n* discharge of a mare in heat; membrane of the head of a newborn foal
Hippomen·ēs -is *m* young man who competed with Atalanta in a race and won her as his bride
Hippōn·ax -actis *m* Greek satirist *(Ē 540 B.C.)*
hippotoxot·ae -ārum *mpl* mounted archers
hippūr·us -ī *m* goldfish
hīr·a -ae *f* empty gut
hircīn·us -a -um *adj* **(-quīn-)** goat-, of a goat
hircōs·us -a -um *adj* smelling like a goat
hirc·us -ī *m* **(-qu·us)** goat
hirne·a *or* **hirni·a -ae** *f* jug
hirsūt·us -a -um *adj* hairy, hirsute, shaggy; bristly; prickly; rude
Hirt·ius -(i)ī *m* Aulus Hirtius *(consul in 43 B.C. and author of the eighth book of Caesar's Memoirs on the Gallic War)*
hirt·us -a -um *adj* hairy, shaggy; uncouth
hirūd·ō -inis *f* leech, bloodsucker
hirundinīn·us -a -um *adj* swallow's
hirund·ō -inis *f* swallow *(bird)*
hisc·ō -ĕre *tr* to murmur, utter ‖ *intr* to (begin to) open, gape, yawn; to open the mouth; to split open
Hispān·ī -ōrum *mpl* Spaniards
Hispāni·a -ae *f* Spain
Hispāniens·is -is -e *adj* Spanish

hispid·us -a -um *adj* hairy, shaggy; rough, rugged *(terrain)*
(H)is·ter -trī *m* Lower Danube *(also applied to the whole river)*
histori·a -ae *f* history; account, story; theme *(of a story)*
historic·us -a -um *adj* historical ‖ *m* historian
histric·us -a -um *adj* theatrical
histri·ō -ōnis *m* actor
histriōnāl·is -is -e *adj* theatrical; histrionic
histriōni·a -ae f dramatics, art of acting
hiulcē *adv* with frequent hiatus
hiulc·ō -āre *tr* to split open
hiulc·us -a-um *adj* split, split open; open, gaping; with hiatus
hōc hūjus *(old form:* **hōce;** *gen:* **hūjusce)** *(neut of* **hic)** *adj* this; the present, the actual; the latter; *(occasionally)* the former ‖ *pron* this one, it; the latter; *(occasionally)* the former; *(w. gen)* this amount of, this degree of, so much; **hoc erat quod** this was the reason why; **hoc est** that is, I mean, namely; **hocine (hoc** + *interrog enclitic* **-ne)** is this...?; **hoc facilius** all the more easily
hōce *see* **hoc**
hōcine *see* **hoc**
hodiē *adv* today; nowadays; still, to the present; at once, immediately; **hodie mane** this morning; **numquam hodie** *(coll)* never at all
hodiern·us -a -um *adj* today's; **hodiernus dies** this day, today
holit·or -ōris *m* grocer
holitōri·us -a -um *adj* vegetable
hol·us -eris *n* vegetable; *(collectively)* vegetables; **holus atrum** cabbage-like plant growing on the seashore
holuscul·um -ī *n (pej)* vegetables
Homērē·us -a -um *or* **Homērī·us -a -um** *adj* Homeric
Homēric·us -a -um *adj* Homeric
Homēr·us -ī *m* Homer
homicīd·a -ae *m* murderer
homicīd·ium -(i)ī *n* homicide, murder, manslaughter
hom·ō -inis *mf* human being, man, person, mortal; mankind, human race; fellow; fellow creature; member of a military force; **mi homo!** my good man! ‖ *mpl* people; **inter homines esse** to be alive; to see the world
homull·us -ī *or* **homunci·ō -ōnis** *or* **homuncul·us -ī** *m* poor guy
honest·a -ae *f* lady
honestāment·um -ī *n* ornament
honest·ās -ātis *f* good reputation, respectability; sense of honor, respect; beauty, grace; integrity; decency ‖ *fpl* respectable persons, decent people
honestē *adv* honorably, respectably, decently; honestly, fairly; **honeste genitus** *(or* **natus)** high-born
honest·ō -āre -āvī -ātus *tr* to honor, dignify; to grace, adorn; to put a good face on
honest·us -a -um *adj* honored, respected; honorable, decent, respectable; handsome; well-born, of high rank ‖ *n* a virtue, a good
hon·or *or* **hon·ōs -ōris** *m* honor, esteem; position, office, post; mark of honor, reward, prize, acknowledgment; recompense, fee; offering, sacrifice, rites *(to the gods or the dead);* grace, beauty, charm; glory, fame, reputation; **honor mortis** *(or* **sepulturae)** funeral rites; **honoris causā** out of respect, with all respect; **in honore esse** to meet general approval; **praefari honorem** to begin with an apology; **pugnae honor** military glory; **tempus honoris** term of office
honōrābil·is -is -e *adj* honorable, respectable
honōrār·ium -(i)ī *n* honorarium
honōrāri·us -a -um *adj* complimentary, honorary; **summa (pecunia) honoraria** sum of money contributed by a magistrate to the treasury on entering office
honōrātē *adv* with honor, honorably
honōrāt·us -a -um *adj* honored, respected; in high office; honorable, respectable; **honoratum habere** to hold in honor
honōrificē *adv* honorably, respectfully
honōrific·us -a -um *adj* conferring honor, complimentary
honōr·ō -āre -āvī -ātus *tr* to honor, respect; to embellish, decorate
honōr·us -a -um *adj* conferring honor, complimentary; deserving honor
honōs *see* **honor**
hoplomach·us -ī *m* heavy-armed gladiator
hōr·a -ae *f* hour; time; season; **ad horam** on time, punctually; **horas quaerere** to ask what time it is; **in diem et horam** continually; **in horam vivere** to live from hand to mouth; **quota hora est?** what time is it? ‖ *fpl* hours; time; clock; **horas inspicere** to look at the clock; **horas quaerere ab aliquo** to ask s.o. the time; **omnibus horis** at all hours, at all times; **omnium horarum** suited to all occasions; **quotas horas nuntiare** to say what time it is, tell the time
Hor·a -ae *f* wife of Quirinus *(i.e., of deified Romulus),* called Hersilia before her death
Hōr·ae -ārum *fpl* Hours *(daughters of Jupiter and Themis, who kept watch at the gates of heaven)*
hōrae·us -a -um *adj* pickled; seasoned; in season
Horāt·ius -(i)ī *m* Horace *(Quintus Horatius Flaccus, poet, 65–8 B.C.)* ‖ Horatio

(Horatius Cocles, defender of the bridge across the Tiber in the war with Porsenna)

horde·um -ī *n* **(ord-)** barley

hōri·a -ae *f* fishing boat

hōriol·a -ae *f* small fishing boat

horiz·ōn -ontos *m* horizon

hornō *adv* this year, during this year

hornōtin·us -a -um *adj* this year's

horn·us -a -um *adj* this year's

hōrolog·ium -iī *n* clock, water clock, sundial

hōroscop·us *or* **hōroscop·os -ī** *m* horoscope; eastern horizon

horrend·us -a -um *adj* horrendous, horrible; awesome

horr·ens -entis *adj* dreadful, awful

horr·eō -ēre -uī *tr* to dread; to shudder at, shrink from; to be amazed at; to regard *(gods, etc.)* with awe ‖ *intr* to stand on end, stand up straight; to get gooseflesh; to shiver, tremble; to bristle; to look frightful, look unkempt; to have a gloomy character

horr·escō -escĕre -uī *tr* to dread, become terrified at ‖ *intr* to stand on end; *(of the sea)* to become rough; to begin to shake *or* shiver; to start, be startled

horre·um -ī *n* barn, shed; silo, granary; wine cellar; storehouse *(of bees)*, beehive

horribil·is -is -e *adj* horrible, terrifying; amazing; rough, uncouth

horridē *adv* roughly, rudely; harshly

horridul·us -a -um *adj* rather shaggy; somewhat shabby; *(rhet)* somewhat unsophisticated *(style)*

horrid·us -a -um *adj* shaggy, prickly; bristly *(pig)*; choppy *(sea)*; disheveled *(appearance)*; rugged, wild *(terrain)*; rude, uncouth *(manner)*; horrible; shivering *(from cold)*

horrif·er -era -erum *adj* causing shudders; freezing, chilling; terrifying

horrificē *adv* awfully, in a frightening way

horrific·ō -āre -āvī *tr* to make rough, ruffle; to terrify, frighten

horrific·us -a -um *adj* frightful, terrifying

horrison·us -a -um *adj* frightening *(sound)*, frightening to hear

horr·or -ōris *m* bristling; shivering, shuddering; horror, dread; awe, reverence; chill; thrill

horsum *adv* this way

hortām·en -inis *n* injunction; encouragement; incentive

hortāment·um -ī *n* encouragement

hortāti·ō -ōnis *f* exhortation, encouragement

hortāt·or -ōris *m* backer, supporter, rooter; instigator

hortāt·us -ūs *m* encouragement, cheering, cheer

Hortens·ius -(i)ī *m* Quintus Hortensius *(lawyer and friendly competitor of Cicero, 114–50 B.C.)*

hort·or -ārī -ātus sum *tr* to encourage, cheer, incite, instigate; to give a pep talk to *(soldiers)*

hortul·us -ī *m* little garden

hort·us -ī *m* garden; garden used by Epicurus as a place of teaching; *(fig)* philosophical system ‖ *mpl* park

hosp·es -itis *m* host, entertainer; guest, visitor; friend; stranger, foreigner

hospit·a -ae *f* hostess; guest, visitor; friend; stranger, foreigner

hospitāl·is -is -e *adj* host's; guest's; hospitable ‖ *npl* guest room

hospitālit·ās -ātis *f* hospitality

hospitāliter *adv* hospitably, as a guest

hospit·ium -(i)ī *n* hospitality; ties of hospitality, friendship; welcome; guest room; lodging; inn

hospit·or -ārī -ātus sum *intr* to be put up *(as a guest)*

hosti·a -ae *f* victim, sacrificial animal; **hostia major** full-grown victim

hostiāt·us -a -um *adj* bringing sacrificial victims

hostic·us -a -um *adj* hostile, of the enemy; foreign ‖ *n* enemy territory

hostific·us -a -um *adj* hostile, bitter

hostīl·is -is -e *adj* enemy-, hostile

hostīliter *adv* like an enemy, in a hostile manner

Hostīl·ius -(i)ī *m* Tullus Hostilius *(third king of Rome)*

hostīment·um -ī *n* compensation

host·iō -īre *tr* to get even with ‖ *intr* to get even

host·is -is *mf* (public) enemy; stranger

hūc *adv* here, to this place; to this point, so far; to such a pitch; for this purpose; **huc atque illuc** here and there, in different directions; **hucine? (huc +** *interrog enclitic)* so far?

hui! *interj* wow!

hūjus(ce)modī *adj (indecl)* of this sort, this kind of

hūmānē *adv* like a human being; politely, gently, with compassion

hūmānit·ās -ātis *f* human nature; humanity; kindness, compassion, human feeling; courtesy; culture, refinement, civilization

hūmāniter *adv* like a human being; reasonably; gently, with compassion

hūmānitus *adv* humanly; humanely, kindly, compassionately

hūmān·us -a -um *adj* of a human being, human; humane, kind, compassionate; courteous; cultured, refined, civilized

humāti·ō -ōnis *f* burial

hūme- = **ume-**
hūmid- = **umid-**
humil·is -is -e *adj* low, low-lying, low-growing; short *(in stature);* humble; lowly, poor, obscure; insignificant; petty, unimportant; small-minded, cheap; humiliated, humbled
humilit·ās -ātis *f* lowness, lack of stature; lowliness, insignificance; small-mindedness; humiliation; humility, subservience
humiliter *adv* low, deeply; abjectly
hum·ō -āre -āvī -ātus *tr* to bury
hum·us -ī *f* ground, earth, soil; land, region, country; **humi** on *(or* in) the ground
hyacinthin·us -a -um *adj* of the hyacinth; crimson
hyacinth·us *or* **hyacinth·os -ī** *m* hyacinth ‖ **Hyacinth·us** *or* **Hyacinth·os -ī** *m* Hyacinth *(Spartan youth who was accidentally killed by Apollo and from whose blood hyacinths sprang)*
Hyad·es -um *fpl* Hyades *(group of 7 stars in the head of the constellation Taurus whose rising indicated rain)*
hyaen·a -ae *f* hyena
hyal·us -ī *m* glass
Hyantē·us -a -um *adj* Boeotian
Hy·ās -antis *m* son of Atlas; **sidus Hyantis** the Hyades
Hybl·a -ae *or* **Hybl·ē -ēs** *f* Sicilian town on the slopes of Mt. Aetna, famous for its honey
Hyblae·us -a -um *adj* of Hybla; **Hyblaeus liquor** honey
hybrid·a -ae *mf* hybrid, mongrel, half-breed
Hydasp·ēs -is *m* tributary of the Indus River
Hȳdr·a -ae *f* Hydra *(seven-headed water snake killed by Hercules)* ‖ monster guarding the gate to the lower world *(mother of Cerberus)* ‖ *(astr)* Hydra *or* Anguis *(constellation)*
hydraulic·us -a -um *adj* hydraulic
hydraul·us -ī *m* water organ
hydri·a -ae *f* water jug, urn
Hydrocho·us -ī *m (astr)* Aquarius
hydrōpic·us -a -um *adj* dropsical
hydr·ops -ōpis *m* dropsy
hydr·us *or* **hydr·os -ī** *m* water snake; snake; dragon
Hygī·a -ae *f* goddess of health
Hȳlae·us -ī *m* centaur who wounded Milanion, the lover of Atalanta
Hyl·ās -ae *m* favorite of Hercules who was carried off by the nymphs
Hyll·us -ī *m* son of Hercules and husband of Iole
Hym·ēn -enis *or* **Hymenae·us** *or* **Hymenae·os -ī** *m* Hymen *(god of marriage);* wedding ceremony; wedding; wedding song
Hymett·us *or* **Hymett·os -ī** *m* mountain in E. Attica, famous for its honey and marble
Hypan·is -is *m* river in Sarmatia *(modern Yuzhnyy Bug)*
hyperpat·on -ī *n (rhet)* transposition of words *or* clauses
hyperbol·ē -ēs *f* hyperbole
Hyperbore·ī -ōrum *mpl* people in the land of the midnight sun
Hyperī·ōn -onis *or* **-onos** *m* son of Titan and Earth, father of the Sun
Hypermestr·a -ae *or* **Hypermestr·ē -ēs** *f* only one of the 50 daughters of Danaüs who did not kill her husband on her wedding night
hypocaust·um *or* **hypocaust·on -ī** *n* subfloor heating chamber
hypodidascal·us -ī *m* assitant teacher
hypomnēm·a -atis *n* note, reminder
hypothec·a -ae *f (fin)* collateral
Hypsipyl·ē -ēs *f* queen of Lemnos at the time of the Argonauts
Hyrcāni·a -ae *f* country on S.E. side of the Caspian Sea
Hyrcān·us -a -um *adj* of Hyrcania; **mare Hyrcanum** Caspian Sea
hysteric·us -a -um *adj* having a gynecological ailment

I

ia- = **ja-**
-i·a -ae *fem suf* forms abstract nouns from adjectives: **audacia** boldness *(from* **audax** bold)
Iacch·us -ī *m* Bacchus; wine
iambē·us -a -um *adj (pros)* iambic
iambic·us -a -um *adj (pros)* iambic
iamb·us -ī *m (pros)* iamb (◡ —); iambic trimeter *(consists of three double feet, i.e., of six iambic feet);* iambic poem; iambic poetry
ianthin·us -a -um *adj* violet-colored ‖ *npl* violet clothes
Īapet·us -ī *m* a Titan, father of Prometheus, Epimetheus, and Atlas
Iāpyd·es -um *mpl* (**-pud-**) an Illyrian tribe
Iāp·yx -ygis *adj* Iapygian ‖ *m* son of Daedalus who ruled in S. Italy ‖ wind that blew from Apulia to Greece
Īas·ius -(i)ī *m* son of Jupiter and Electra and brother of Dardanus
Iās·ō(n) -onis *m* Jason *(son of Aeson and leader of the Argonauts)*
iasp·is -idis *f* spear
Ībēr- = **Hiber-**
ibi *or* **ibī** *adv* there, in that place; then, on that occasion; therein
ibidem *or* **ibīdem** *adv* in the same place, just there; in the place already mentioned, therein, thereon; at that very

moment, there and then; at the same time; in the same matter

īb·is -is *or* **-idis** *f* ibis *(bird sacred to the Egyptians)*

Īcariōt·is -idis *adj* of Penelope ‖ *f* Penelope *(daughter of Icarius)*

Īcari·us -a -um *adj* of Icarus, Icarian; of the Icarian Sea; **Canis Icarius** *(astr)* Dog Star ‖ *m* father of Penelope ‖ *n* Icarian Sea

Īcar·us -ī *m* son of Daedalus, who, on his flight from Crete with his father, fell into the sea

ichneum·ōn -onis *m* ichneumon *(Egyptian rat that eats crocodile eggs)*

īcī *perf of* **ico**

-īci·us -a -um *adjl suf* **1** used to form adjectives from nouns denoting officers, relationships, etc.: **tribunicius** tribunician; **patricius** patrician; **2** denoting the time of birth, of a birthday: **nātālicius** of the time of birth, belonging to a birthday; **3** used to form adjectives from past participles: **expositicius** exposed, foundling; **4** used to form adjectives from nouns denoting materials: **latericius** brick-, of brick *(from* **later** brick)

-icō *vbl suf* **1** used to form verbs from adjectives: **claudicare** to be lame, to limp *(from* **claudus** lame, limping); **2** used to form verbs from other verbs: **fodicare** to stab *(from* **fodere** to stab, dig)

īc·ō -ĕre -ī -tus *tr* to hit, strike, shoot; to sting, bite; **foedus icere** to conclude a treaty

īc·ōn -onis *f* image

īconic·us -a -um *adj* giving an exact image

icteric·us -a -um *adj* jaundiced

ict·is -idis *f* weasel

ictus *pp of* **ico**

ict·us -ūs *m* stroke, blow, hit; cut; sting, bite; wound; range; *(musical or metrical)* beat; *(fig)* shock, blow; **sub ictum** within range

id *adv* for that reason, therefore

id ejus *(neut of* **is)** *adj* this, that, the aforesaid ‖ *pron* it; a thing, the thing; **ad id** for that purpose; **aliquid id genus** s.th. of that sort, s.th. like that; **cum eo ut** on condition that, with the stipulation that; **eo plus** the more; **ex eo** from that time on; as a result of that, consequently; **id consili** some sort of plan, some plan; **id temporis** at that time; of that age; **in id** to that end; **in eo esse** to depend on it; **in eo esse ut** to be so far gone that, to get to the point where

Īd·a -ae *or* **Īd·ē -ēs** *f* mountain range near Troy ‖ mountain in Crete where Jupiter was brought up

Īdae·us -a -um *adj* Idaean, of Mt. Ida *(in Crete or near Troy)*

Īdal·ium -(i)ī *n* city in Cyprus dear to Venus

idcircō *adv* on that account, for that reason, therefore

īdem eadem ĭdem *adj* the same, the very same, exactly this; *(often equivalent to a mere connective)* also, likewise ‖ *pron* the same one

identidem *adv* again and again, continually; now and then, at intervals

ideō *adv* therefore

idiōt·a -ae *m* layman, amateur; private individual

īdōl·on -ī *n* apparition, ghost

idōneē *adv* suitably

idōne·us -a -um *adj* suitable, fit, proper; *(w. dat or w.* **ad** *or* **in** *+ acc)* fit for, capable of, suited for, convenient for, sufficient for

Īd·ūs -uum *fpl* Ides *(15th day of March, May, July, and October, and 13th day of the other months; interest, debts, and tuition were often paid on the Ides)*

ie- = je-

-iens *or* **-iēs** *advl suf* forming numerals and adjectives to denote a number of times: **centiens** a hundred times; **totiens** so many times

iens euntis *pres p of* **eo**

-iens·is -is -e *adjl suf* used to form ethnic adjectives from place names: **Carthaginiensis** Carthaginian

igitur *adv* then, therefore, accordingly; *(resumptive after parenthetical matter)* as I was saying; *(in summing up)* so then, in short

ignār·us -a -um *adj* ignorant, unaware, inexperienced; unsuspecting; senseless; unknown, strange, unfamiliar; *(w. gen)* unaware of, unfamiliar with, ignorant of

ignāvē *adv* listlessly, lazily

ignāvi·a -ae *f* listlessness, laziness; cowardice

ignāviter *adv* listlessly, lazily

ignāv·us -a -um *adj* listless, lazy, idle, inactive; relaxing; cowardly; unproductive, useless

ignesc·ō -ĕre *intr* **(-nis-)** to catch fire, become inflamed, burn; *(fig)* to flare up

igne·us -a -um *adj* of fire, on fire, fiery; red-hot; fiery, ardent *(person)*

ignicul·us -ī *m* small fire, little flame; sparkle; *(lit & fig)* spark

ignif·er -era -erum *adj* fiery

ignigen·a -ae *m* son of fire *(epithet of Bacchus)*

ignip·ēs -edis *adj* fiery-footed

ignipot·ens -entis *adj* lord of fire *(epithet of Vulcan)*

ign·is -is *m* fire; watch fire, fire signal; torch; lightning, bolt of lightning; funeral pyre; star; brightness, glow, splendor; *(fig)* fire, rage, fury, love, passion; flame, sweetheart; agent of destruction, fanatic ‖ *mpl* love poems

ignōbil·is -is -e *adj* unknown, obscure, insignificant, undistinguished; low-born, ignoble

ignōbilit·ās -ātis *f* obscurity; humble birth

ignōmini·a -ae *f* ignominy, dishonor, disgrace; *(mil)* dishonorable discharge; **ignominiā afficere** to dishonor, disgrace; **ignominia senātūs** public censure imposed by the Senate

ignōminiōs·us -a -um *adj* disgraced; ignominious, disgraceful, shameful ‖ *m (person)* disgrace

ignōrābil·is -is -e *adj* unknown

ignōranti·a -ae *f* ignorance

ignōrāti·ō -ōnis *f* ignorance

ignōr·ō -āre -āvī -ātus *tr* to not know, be ignorant of, be unfamiliar with; to be unaware of, know nothing about; to fail to recognize; to mistake, misunderstand; to ignore, disregard, take no notice of

ignosc·ens -entis *adj* forgiving, indulgent

ig·noscō -noscĕre -nōvī -nōtum *intr (w. dat)* to pardon, forgive, excuse; *(w. dat of person and acc of the offense)* to pardon, forgive, excuse *(s.o. a fault)*

ignōt·us -a -um *adj* unknown, unfamiliar, strange; inglorious; unnoticed; low-born, ignoble; vulgar; ignorant

īl·ex -icis *f* holm oak *(European evergreen oak with foliage resembling that of a holly)*

Īli·a -ae *f* Rhea Silvia *(daughter of Numitor and mother of Romulus and Remus)*

īl·ia -ium *npl* flank, side *(of the body extending from the hips down to the groin)* guts, intestines; belly, groin, private parts

Īliac·us -a -um *adj* Trojan

Īli·as -adis *f Iliad;* Trojan woman

īlicet *adv (ancient form for adjourning an assembly)* you may go; *(expressing dismay)* it's all over!, finished!; at once, immediately

īlicō *adv* on the spot, right then and there, immediately

īlign(e)·us -a -um *adj* of holm oak

Īl·ios -iī *f* Ilium, Troy

Īlīthyi·a -ae *f* goddess who aided women in childbirth

Īl·ium -iī *n or* **Īl·ion -iī** *n or* **Īl·ios -iī** *f* Ilium, Troy

Īli·us -a -um *adj* of Ilium, Trojan

illā *adv* that way

ill·a -īus *adj fem* that; that famous ‖ *pron* that one, she

illabefact·us -a -um *adj* (**inl-**) unbroken, uninterrupted; unimpaired

illā·bor -bī -psus sum *intr* (**inl-**) to flow; to sink, fall; to fall in, cave in; to slip; *(w. dat or w.* **ad** *or* **in** + *acc)* to flow into, enter into, penetrate

illabōr·ō -āre *intr* (**inl-**) *(w. dat)* to work at, work on

illāc *adv* that way

illacessīt·us -a -um *adj* (**inl-**) unprovoked

illacrimābil·is -is -e *adj* (**inl-**) unlamented, unwept; inexorable

illacrim·ō -āre -āvī *or* **illacrim·or -ārī -ātus sum** *intr* (**inl-**) *(w. dat)* to cry over

ill·aec *(acc:* **-anc;** *abl:* **-āc)** *adj fem* that ‖ *pron* she

illaes·us -a -um *adj* (**inl-**) unharmed

illaetābil·is -is -e *adj* (**inl-**) sad, melancholy

illapsus (**inl-**) *pp of* **illabor**

illaque·ō -āre -āvī -ātus *tr* (**inl-**) to trap, entangle

illātus (**inl-**) *pp of* **infero**

illaudāt·us -a -um *adj* (**inl-**) unworthy of praise, unpraised

ill·e -īus *adj masc* that; that famous; the former; **ille aut ille** this or that, such and such ‖ *pron* that one; he; the former one

illecebr·a -ae *f* (**inl-**) attraction, allurement

illecebrōs·us -a -um *adj* (**inl-**) alluring, seductive

illectus (**inl-**) *pp of* **illicio**

illect·us -a -um *adj* (**inl-**) unread

illect·us -ūs *m* (**inl-**) allurement

illepidē *adv* (**inl-**) inelegantly, rudely

illepid·us -a -um *adj* (**inl-**) inelegant, lacking refinement

illēvī *perf of* **illino**

ill·ex -icis *mf* (**inl-**) lure, decoy

ill·ex -ēgis *adj* (**inl-**) lawless

illexī *perf of* **illicio**

illībāt·us -a -um *adj* (**inl-**) undiminished, unimpaired, intact

illīberāl·is -is -e *adj* (**inl-**) stingy

illīberālit·ās -ātis *f* (**inl-**) stinginess

illīberāliter *adv* (**inl-**) stingily

ill·ic *(acc:* **-unc;** *abl:* **-ōc)** *adj masc* that ‖ *pron* he

illic *adv* there, in that place; in that matter, therein

il·liciō -licĕre -lexī -lectus *tr* (**inl-**) to allure, attract; to seduce, mislead

illicitāt·or -ōris *m* (**inl-**) hired bidder *(one who bids at an auction to make others bid higher)*

illicit·us -a -um *adj* (**inl-**) unlawful

illī·dō -dĕre -sī -sus *tr* (**inl-**) to smash to pieces, crush; *(w. dat or w.* **ad** *or* **in** + *acc)* to smash *(s.th.)* against

illig·ō -āre -āvī -ātus *tr* (**inl-**) to attach, connect; to tie, bind; to oblige, obligate; to impede; to involve, tie up

illim *adv* from there

illīm·is -is -e *adj* unmuddied, clear

illinc *adv* from there; on that side

il·linō -linĕre -lēvī -litus *tr* (**inl-**) to cover;

to smear; *(w. dat)* to smear *or* spread *(s.th.)* on, cake *(s.th.)* on
illiquefact·us -a -um *adj* **(inl-)** melted
illīsī *perf of* **illido**
illīsus *pp of* **illido**
illi(t)terāt·us -a -um *adj* **(inl-)** uneducated, illiterate
illitus *pp of* **illino**
illō(c) *adv* there, at that place; at that point
illōt·us *or* **illaut·us -a -um** *adj* **(inl-)** unwashed, dirty
illūc *adv* to that place, in that direction; to that person, to him, to her; to that matter; to that point
ill·ūc *(acc; -***ūc;** *abl* **-ōc)** *adj neut* that **||** *pron* it
illūc·eō -ēre *intr* **(inl-)** *(w. dat)* to shine on
illū·cescō -cescĕre -xī *intr* **(inl-)** to grow light, dawn; to begin to shine
ill·ud -īus *adj neut* that; the former **||** *pron* it
illū·dō -dĕre -sī -sus *tr* **(inl-)** to make fun of, ridicule; to waste, fritter away *(time, life)* **||** *intr (w. dat) (coll)* to play around with *(sexually)*
illūminātē *adv* **(inl-)** clearly
illūmin·ō -āre -āvī -ātus *tr* **(inl-)** to illuminate, light up, make bright; to illustrate
illūsī *perf of* **illudo**
illūsi·ō -ōnis *f* **(inl-)** irony
illustr·is -is -e *adj* **(inl-)** bright, clear, brilliant; plain, distinct, evident; distinguished, famous, illustrious, noble
illustr·ō -āre -āvī -ātus *tr* **(inl-)** to light up, illuminate; to make clear, clear up, explain; to make famous; to embellish
illūsus *pp of* **illudo**
illuvi·ēs -ēī *f* **(inl-)** filth, dirtiness; mud; inundation; *(of a person) (pej)* scum
illuxī *perf of* **illucesco**
Illyric·us -a -um *adj* Illyrian **||** *n* Illyria
Illyri·us -a -um *adj & m* Illyrian **||** *f* Illyria *(on the E. coast of the Adriatic Sea)*
Īl·us -ī *m* son of Tros, father of Laomedon, and founder of Ilium **||** Ascanius
-im *advl suf*
imāgināri·us -a -um *adj* imaginary
imāginātiōn·ēs -um *fpl* imaginings
imāgin·or -ārī -ātus sum *tr* to imagine
imāg·ō -inis *f* image, likeness, picture, bust; bust of ancestor; ghost, vision; echo; appearance, semblance, shadow; mental picture, concept, thought, idea; figure of speech, simile, metaphor
imbēcillit·ās -ātis *f* **(inb-)** weakness, feebleness; helplessness
imbēcill·us -a -um *adj* **(inb-)** weak, feeble; helpless; *(of medicine)* ineffective
imbell·is -is -e *adj* **(inb-)** anti-war; unwarlike; peaceful, quiet; ineffective *(weapon); (pej)* unfit for war, soft
im·ber -bris *m* rain, rainstorm; *(lit & fig)* shower; rain cloud; rainwater; water *(in general);* snowstorm; hail-storm; flood of tears
imberb·is -is -e *or* **imberb·us -a -um** *adj* **(inb-)** beardless
imbib·ō -ĕre -ī *tr* **(inb-)** to imbibe, drink in; **(animo) imbibere** to absorb, form *(e.g., an opinion)*
imbīt·ō -ĕre *tr* **(inb-)** to enter
imbr·ex -icis *f* tile
imbric·us -a -um *adj* rainy
imbrif·er -era -erum *adj* rainy
im·buō -buĕre -buī -būtus *tr* to wet, soak; to dip; to moisten; to stain, taint, infect; to imbue, fill, steep; to instruct; *(w.* **ad)** to introduce to
imitābil·is -is -e *adj* imitable, capable of being imitated
imitām·en -inis *n* imitation, copy; image, likeness
imitāment·um -ī *n* imitation **||** *npl* pretense
imitāti·ō -ōnis *f* imitation; mimicking, copying; copy, counterfeit
imitāt·or -ōris *m,* **imitātr·ix -īcis** *f* imitator
imitāt·us -a -um *adj* fictitious, copied
imit·or -ārī -ātus sum *tr* to imitate, copy; to portray; to ape
immad·escō -escĕre -uī *intr* **(inm-)** to become wet
immāne *adv* **(inm-)** savagely
immān·is -is -e *adj* **(inm-)** huge, enormous, monstrous; inhuman, savage
immānit·ās -ātis *f* **(inm-)** vastness, enormity; savageness, cruelty
immansuēt·us -a -um *adj* **(inm-)** untamed, savage, wild
immātūrit·ās -ātis *f* **(inm-)** immaturity; prematureness; overanxiousness
immātūr·us -a -um *adj* **(inm-)** immature; unripe; premature
immedicābil·is -is -e *adj* **(inm-)** incurable
immem·or -oris *adj* **(inm-)** forgetful, forgetting; negligent, heedless; **immemor patriae** forgetting (one's) country
immemorābil·is -is -e *adj* **(inm-)** not worth mentioning; untold
immemorāt·a -ōrum *npl* **(inm-)** novelties, things hitherto untold
immensit·ās -ātis *f* **(inm-)** immensity **||** *fpl* immense stretches
immens·us -a -um *adj* **(inm-)** immense, unending, immeasurable, huge **||** *n* infinity, infinite space
immer·ens -entis *adj* **(inm-)** undeserving, innocent
immer·gō -gĕre -sī -sus *tr* **(inm-)** to immerse, dip, plunge; to overwhelm, drown; *(w.* **in** *+ acc)* to dip *(s.th.)* into **||** *refl (w.* **in** *+ acc)* **1** to plunge into; **2** to insinuate oneself into
immeritō *adv* **(inm-)** undeservedly, innocently

immerit·us -a -um *adj* **(inm-)** undeserving, innocent; undeserved; **immerito meo** through no fault of mine
immersābil·is -is -e *adj* **(inm-)** unsinkable
immersī *perf of* **immergo**
immersus *pp of* **immergo**
immētāt·us -a -um *adj* **(inm-)** unmeasured, undivided
immigr·ō -āre -āvī -ātum *intr* **(inm-)** to immigrate; *(w.* **in** *+ acc)* **1** to move into; **2** to invade
immin·eō -ēre *intr* **(inm-)** to project, stick out; to be near, be imminent; to threaten, menace; *(w. dat)* **1** to look out over, overlook *(a view)*; **2** to hover over, loom over, threaten; *(w. dat or* **in** *+ acc)* to be intent on, be eager for
immin·uō -uere -uī -ūtus *tr* **(inm-)** to lessen, curtail; to weaken, impair; to infringe upon, encroach upon, violate, subvert, destroy
imminūti·ō -ōnis *f* **(inm-)** lessening; mutilation; *(rhet)* understatement
im·misceō -miscēre -miscuī -mixtus *tr* **(inm-)** to mix in, intermix, blend; *(fig)* to mix up, confuse; **manūs manibus immiscere** *(of boxers)* to mix it up ‖ *refl & pass (w. dat)* **1** to join, join in with, mingle with, get lost in *(e.g., a crowd)*; **2** to blend with, disappear in *(e.g., the night, a cloud)*
immiserābil·is -is -e *adj* **(inm-)** unpitied
immisericorditer *adv* **(inm-)** unmercifully
immisericor·s -dis *adj* **(inm-)** merciless
immīsī *perf of* **immitto**
immissi·ō -ōnis *f* **(inm-)** letting *(e.g., saplings)* grow
immissus *pp of* **immitto**
immīt·is -is -e *adj* **(inm-)** unripe, sour, green *(fruit)*; sour *(wine)*; harsh; rude; cruel, ruthless, pitiless
im·mittō -mittere -mīsī -missus *tr* **(inm-)** to send *(to or into)*; to steer *(a ship)*; to guide *(a horse)*; to insert; to let in, let go in, admit; to let go of, let drop; to let fly, throw; to let *(death, ills)* loose *(on)*; to direct the flow of *(water, air, etc., into or against)*; **habenas immittere** to slacken the reins ‖ *refl & pass* to go *(into)*; to leap *(into)*; *(geog)* to extend *(to, into)*
immixtus (inm-) *pp of* **immisceo**
immō *adv (in contradiction or correction of preceding words)* nay, on the contrary, or rather, more precisely; *(in confirmation of preceding words)* quite so, yes indeed; **immo vero** yes and in fact
immōbil·is -is -e *adj* **(inm-)** motionless, unshaken; immovable; fixed, unalterable; clumsy, unwieldy
immoderātē *adv* **(inm-)** immoderately
immoderāti·ō -ōnis *f* **(inm-)** lack of moderation, excess
immoderāt·us -a -um *adj* **(inm-)** unmeasured, limitless; immoderate, uncontrolled, excessive
immodestē *adv* **(inm-)** immoderately, shamelessly
immodesti·a -ae *f* **(inm-)** lack of self-control; excesses; insubordination
immodest·us -a -um *adj* **(inm-)** immoderate, uncontrolled
immodicē *adv* **(inm-)** excessively
immodic·us -a -um *adj* **(inm-)** huge, enormous; immoderate, excessive; *(w. gen or abl)* given to, excessive in
immodulāt·us -a -um *adj* **(inm-)** unrhythmical
immolāti·ō -ōnis *f* **(inm-)** sacrifice
immolāt·or -ōris *m* **(inm-)** sacrificer
immōlīt·us -a -um *adj* **(inm-)** constructed, erected ‖ *npl* buildings
immol·ō *or* **inmol·ō -āre -āvī -ātus** *tr* **(inm-)** to sprinkle the feet of *(the victim)* with coarse flour in preparation for sacrifice; to immolate, sacrifice
immor·deō -dēre — -sus *tr* to bite into; *(fig)* stimulate
immor·ior -ī -tuus sum *intr* **(inm-)** *(w. dat)* to die in, die upon; *(fig)* to get sick over
immor·or -ārī -ātus sum *intr* **(inm-)** *(w. dat)* to dwell upon
immors·us -a -um *adj* bitten into; excited, stimulated
immortāl·is -is -e *adj* **(inm-)** immortal
immortālit·ās -ātis *f* **(inm-)** immortality
immortāliter *adv (coll)* **(inm-)** infinitely, eternally
immortuus (inm-) *pp of* **immorior**
immōt·us -a -um *adj* **(inm-)** unmoved, immovable; unshaken, undisturbed, steadfast
immūg·iō -īre -īvī *or* **-iī -ītum** *intr* **(inm-)** to bellow; to roar
immulg·eō -ēre *tr* **(inm-)** to milk
immunditi·a -ae *f* **(inm-)** dirtiness, filth
immund·us -a -um *adj* **(inm-)** dirty, filthy
immūn·iō -īre -īvī *or* **-iī** *tr* **(inm-)** to reinforce, fortify
immūn·is -is -e *adj* **(inm-)** without duty *or* office; tax-exempt; free, exempt; pure, innocent; *(w. abl or* **ab)** free from, exempt from; *(w. gen)* **1** free of, free from; **2** devoid of, without; **3** having no share in
immūnit·ās -ātis *f* **(inm-)** immunity, exemption; exemption from tribute
immūnīt·us -a -um *adj* **(inm-)** unfortified; unpaved *(road)*
immurmur·ō -āre *intr* **(inm-)** to grumble; *(w. dat) (of the wind)* to whisper among
immūtābil·is -is -e *adj* **(inm-)** immutable, unchangeable; changed
immūtābilit·ās -ātis *f* **(inm-)** immutability

immūtāti·ō -ōnis *f* **(inm-)** exchange, substitution; *(rhet)* metonymy
immūtāt·us -a -um *adj* **(inm-)** unchanged
immūt·ō -āre -āvī -ātus *tr* **(inm-)** to change, alter; to substitute
inm- = imm-
impācāt·us -a -um *adj* **(inp-)** unsubdued
impactus *pp of* **impingo**
impall·escō -escĕre -uī *intr* **(inp-)** *(w. abl)* to turn pale at
imp·ār -aris *adj* **(inp-)** uneven, odd *(numbers);* uneven *(in size or length);* unlike *(in color or appearance);* unequal; unfair; ill-matched; crooked; *(w. dat)* **1** not a match for, inferior to; **2** unable to cope with
imparāt·us -a -um *adj* **(inp-)** unprepared
impariter *adv* **(inp-)** unequally
impast·us -a -um *adj* **(inp-)** unfed, hungry
impati·ens -entis *adj* **(inp-)** impatient; *(w. gen)* **1** impatient with; **2** unable to endure, unable to take *(e.g., the heat);* **impatiens irae** unable to restrain one's anger
impatienter *adv* **(inp-)** impatiently; intolerably
impatienti·a -ae *f* **(inp-)** *(w. gen)* inability *or* unwillingness to endure
impavidē *adv* **(inp-)** fearlessly
impavid·us -a -um *adj* **(inp-)** fearless, undismayed
impedīment·um -ī *n* **(inp-)** impediment, hindrance; difficulty **‖** *npl* baggage; mule train
imped·iō -īre -īvī *or* **-iī -ītus** *tr* **(inp-)** to entangle; to hamper, hinder; to entwine, encircle; to clasp, embrace; to block *(road);* to hinder, prevent; to embarrass; *(w.* **ne, quin,** *or* **quominus)** to prevent *(s.o.)* from
impedīti·ō -ōnis *f* **(inp-)** hindrance **‖** *npl* cases of obstruction
impedīt·us -a -um *adj* **(inp-)** hampered; obstructed, blocked; difficult, intricate; impassable; busy, occupied
impēgī (inp-) *perf of* **impingo**
im·pellō -pellĕre -(pe)pulī -pulsus *tr* **(inp-)** to strike against, strike; to reach *(the ears);* to push, drive, drive forward, impel, propel; to urge, persuade; to stimulate, induce; to force, compel; to put to rout; to swell *(sails)*
impend·eō -ēre *intr* **(inp-)** to be near, be at hand, be imminent, threaten; *(w. dat)* to hang over; *(w. dat or* **in** *+ acc)* to hover over, loom over
impendiōs·us -a -um *adj* **(inp-)** extravagant, free-spending
impend·ium -(i)ī *n* **(inp-)** expense, cost, outlay; interest *(paid out);* loss
impen·dō -dĕre -dī -sus *tr* **(inp-)** to weigh out, pay out; to expend, devote, apply, employ; *(w.* **in** *+ acc)* **1** to spend *(money)* on; **2** to expend *(effort)* on; **3** to pay *(attention)* to
impenetrābil·is -is -e *adj* **(inp-)** impenetrable
impens·a -ae *f* **(inp-)** expense, cost, outlay; waste; contribution; **impensam facere** to incur an expense; **meis impensis** at my expense
impensē *adv* **(inp-)** at a high cost, expensively; with great effort
impens·us -a -um *pp of* **impendo ‖** *adj* high, costly, expensive; strong, vehement; earnest **‖** *n* high price
imper·ans -antis *m* **(inp-)** master, ruler
imperāt·or -ōris *m* **(inp-)** commander, general; commander in chief; emperor; director; master, ruler
imperātōri·us -a -um *adj* **(inp-)** of a general, general's; imperial
imperātr·ix -īcis *f* **(inp-)** controller, mistress
imperāt·um -ī *n* **(inp-)** command, order
impercept·us -a -um *adj* **(inp-)** unperceived, unknown
imperc·ō -ĕre *intr (w. dat)* **(inp-)** to spare, take it easy on
impercuss·us -a -um *adj* **(inp-)** noiseless
imperdit·us -a -um *adj* **(inp-)** not killed, unscathed
imperfect·us -a -um *adj* **(inp-)** unfinished; imperfect; undigested *(food)*
imperfoss·us -a -um *adj* **(inp-)** unpierced, not stabbed
imperiōs·us -a -um *adj* **(inp-)** masterful, commanding; imperial; magisterial; tyrannical, overbearing, domineering, imperious
imperītē *adv* **(inp-)** unskillfully, clumsily; in an ignorant manner
imperīti·a -ae *f* **(inp-)** inexperience, awkwardness, ignorance
imperit·ō -āre -āvī -ātus *tr & intr* **(inp-)** to command, rule, govern
imperīt·us -a -um *adj* **(inp-)** inexperienced, unfamiliar, ignorant, unskilled; *(w. gen)* inexperienced in, unacquainted with, ignorant of
imper·ium -(i)ī *n* **(inp-)** supreme administrative power *(exercised by the kings, subsequently by certain magistrates and provincial governors, and later by Roman emperors);* absolute authority *(in any sphere);* dominion, sway, government; empire; command, order; right to command; authority; exercise of authority; military commission, military command; mastery; sovereignty; realm, dominion; public office, magistracy; term of office
imperjūrāt·us -a -um *adj* **(inp-)** sacrosanct
impermiss·us -a -um *adj* **(inp-)** forbidden
imper·ō -āre -āvī -ātus *tr* **(inp-)** to requi-

sition, give orders for, order, demand; *(w. acc of thing and dat of source demanded from)* to demand *(e.g., hostages)* from ‖ *intr* to be in command, rule, be master; *(w. dat)* to give orders to, order, command, govern, master, exercise control over; *(gram)* to express a command

imperterrit·us -a -um *adj* **(inp-)** undaunted, fearless

impert·iō -īre *tr* **(inp-)** *(w. dat)* to impart, communicate, bestow, assign, direct *(s.th.)* to, share *(s.th.)* with; *(w. acc of person and abl of thing)* to present *(s.o.)* with

imperturbāt·us -a -um *adj* **(inp-)** unperturbed, unruffled

impervi·us -a -um *adj* **(inp-)** impassable; *(w. dat)* impervious to

impete *(abl singl) m* with an assault, with a charge

impetibil·is -is -e *adj* **(inp-)** intolerable

impet·ō -ĕre *tr* **(inp-)** to make for; to attack

impetrābil·is -is -e *adj* **(inp-)** obtainable; successful

impetrāti·ō -ōnis *f* **(inp-)** obtaining one's request

impetr·iō -īre *tr* **(inp-)** to try to obtain through favorable omens

impetr·ō -āre -āvī -ātus *tr* **(inp-)** to obtain, procure *(by asking)*; to achieve, accomplish, bring to pass

impet·us -ūs *m* **(inp-)** attack, assault; rush; impetus; impetuosity, vehemence, vigor; violence, fury, force; wide expanse *(of sea, sky)*; *(w. gen)* sudden burst of; *(w. inf or* **ad***)* impulse to *(do s.th.)*; **animi impetus** impulse, urge; **omni impetu** with all one's might

impex·us -a -um *adj* **(inp-)** uncombed, unkempt, tangled

impiē *adv* **(inp-)** wickedly

impiet·ās -ātis *f* **(inp-)** impiety, irreverence, lack of respect; disloyalty

impi·ger -gra -grum *adj* **(inp-)** diligent, active, energetic

impigrē *adv* **(inp-)** energetically, actively

impigrit·ās -ātis *f* **(inp-)** energy, activity

im·pingō -pingĕre -pēgī -pactus *tr* **(inp-)** *(w. dat or* **in** *+ acc)* **1** to fasten to; **2** to pin against, force against, dash against; **3** to press *or* force *(s.th.)* on; **4** to fling at

impi·ō -āre -āvī -ātus *tr* **(inp-)** to desecrate; to make disrepectful

impi·us -a -um *adj* **(inp-)** impious, godless, irreverent, disrespectful; disobedient; disloyal; wicked, unscrupulous; **Tartara impia** Tartarus, the abode of the impious

implācāt·us -a -um *adj* **(inp-)** implacable, inexorable, insatiable

implacid·us -a -um *adj* **(inp-)** restless; rough, wild

impl·eō -ēre -ēvī -ētus *tr* **(inp-)** to fill up; to satisfy; to fatten; to make pregnant; to enrich; to cover with writing, fill up *(a book)*; to discharge, execute, implement; to complete, end; to occupy, take up *(time)*; to make up, amount to; to fulfill, satisfy *(wishes, hopes, prophecies, appetites)*

implex·us -a -um *adj* **(inp-)** entwined; involved

implicāti·ō -ōnis *f* **(inp-)** interweaving; network; **implicatio rei familiaris** financial embarrassment

implicāt·us -a -um *adj* **(inp-)** involved, intricate

implicisc·or -ī *intr* **(inp-)** to become confused

implicitē *adv* **(inp-)** intricately

implicitus *pp of* **implico** ‖ *adj* confused; **implicitus morbo** disabled by sickness

implic·ō -āre -āvī -ātus *or* **-āre -uī -itus** *tr* **(inp-)** to entwine, wrap; to intertwine; to involve; to envelop; to embrace, clasp, grasp; to connect, join, unite; to implicate; to kindle *(a fire)* ‖ *refl* **se dextrae implicare** to clasp *(s.o.'s)* right hand ‖ *pass* to be intimately associated; to be embroiled

implōrāti·ō -ōnis *f* **(inp-)** imploring

implōr·ō -āre -āvī -ātus *tr* **(inpl-)** to implore, appeal to; *(w. double acc)* to beg *(s.o.)* for; *(w.* **ab***)* to ask for *(s.th.)* from

impl·uit -uĕre -uit *or* **-ūvit -ūtum** *intr* **(inp-)** *(w. dat)* to rain on

implūm·is -is -e *adj* **(inp-)** featherless, unfledged; without wings

impluviāt·us -a -um *adj* **(inpl-)** square, shaped liked an impluvium

impluv·ium -(i)ī *n* **(inp-)** impluvium, rain basin *(square basin built into the floor of the atrium to hold rain water; (rarely =* **compluvium:** *square opening in the roof of the atrium of a Roman house to get rid of smoke and let in light and air)*

impolītē *adv* **(inp-)** simply, without fancy words

impolīt·us -a -um *adj* **(inp-)** unpolished, rough; lacking culture; *(of materials)* in the crude state

impollūt·us -a -um *adj* **(inp-)** unsullied

im·pōnō -pōnĕre -posuī -positus *or* **-postus** *tr* **(inp-)** to impose; *(w. dat or* **in** *+ acc)* to place on, lay on, set on; *(w. dat or* **super** *+ acc)* to build *(house, bridge, city)* on; *(w. dat or* **ad***)* to station *(soldiers)* in *or* at; *(w. dat or* **ad** *or* **in** *+ acc)* to apply *(remedies)* to; *(w. dat)* **1** to place *(s.o.)* in command *or* control of, put *(s.o.)* in charge of; **2** to put *(garments)* on *(s.o.)*; **3** to impose *(taxes, terms, laws, responsibilites, limits, etc.)* on; **4** to inflict *(wounds, blows, punishment)* on; *(w. dat, w.* **in** *+ acc,* **in** *+ abl, or* **supra** *+*

acc) to place, put, set, lay *(s.th. or s.o.)* on ‖ *intr (w. dat)* **1** to impose upon; **2** to trick, cheat

import·ō -āre -āvī -ātus *tr* **(inp-)** to bring in, import; to introduce; to bring about, cause; *(w. dat)* to inflict *(damage, trouble)* on

importūnit·ās -ātis *f* **(inp-)** importunity, rudeness, insolence; unfitness

importūn·us -a -um *adj* **(inp-)** inconvenient; unsuitable, out of place; troublesome, annoying; lacking consideration for others, rude, ruthless; stormy *(weather);* grim *(looks);* ill-omened

importuōs·us -a -um *adj* **(inp-)** without a harbor

imp·os -otis *adj* **(inp-)** out of control; *(w. gen)* not having control of; **impos animi** *(or* **mentis** *or* **sui)** out of one's mind

impositus (inp-) *pp of* **impono** ‖ *adj* situated, located

impossibil·is -is -e *adj* **(inp-)** impossible

impostus *pp of* **impono**

imposuī *perf of* **impono**

impot·ens -entis *adj* **(inp-)** impotent, powerless; lacking self-control, uncontrollable, wild, violent; *(w. gen)* having no control over; **impotens sui** *(or* **animi)** out of one's mind

impotenter *adv* **(inp-)** impotently, weakly; without self-control, lawlessly, intemperately

impotenti·a -ae *f* **(inp-)** weakness, helplessness; lack of self-control, violence, fury, lawlessness

impraesentiārum *adv* **(inp-)** for the present, under present circumstances

imprans·us -a -um *adj* **(inp-)** without breakfast *or* lunch, fasting

imprecāti·ō -ōnis *f* **(inp-)** the calling down of curses, imprecation

imprec·or -ārī -ātus sum *tr* **(inp-)** to call down *(a curse);* to invoke

impressī *perf of* **imprimo**

impressi·ō -ōnis *f* **(inp-)** pressure; attack, charge; rhythmical beat; emphasis; impression *(on the mind)*

impressus *pp of* **imprimo**

imprīmīs *or* **in prīmīs** *adv* **(inp-)** in the first place; chiefly, especially

im·primō -primĕre -pressī -pressus *tr* **(inp-)** to press down; to impress, imprint, stamp *(a seal, marks, patterns)*; to thrust, drive in *(esp. weapons);* to plant *(the feet, kisses); (fig)* to impress; **animum quasi ceram imprimere** to impress the mind like wax

improbāti·ō -ōnis *f* **(inp-)** disapproval; *(leg)* discrediting *(of a witness)*

improbē *adv* **(inp-)** badly, wickedly, wrongfully; recklessly; persistently

improbit·ās -ātis *f* **(inp-)** wickedness, depravity; roguishness

improb·ō -āre -āvī -ātus *tr* **(inp-)** to disapprove of, condemn, blame, reject

improbul·us -a -um *adj* **(inp-)** somewhat impudent, naughty

improb·us -a -um *adj* below standard, inferior; bad, shameless; rebellious, unruly; restless, indomitable, self-willed; cruel, merciless; persistent; disloyal, ill-disposed; *(of language)* offensively rude

imprōcēr·us -a -um *adj* **(inp-)** undersized

imprōdict·us -a -um *adj* **(inp-)** not postponed

imprompt·us -a -um *adj* **(inp-)** slow

improperāt·us -a -um *adj* **(inp-)** unhurried

impropri·us -a -um *adj* **(inp-)** *(gram)* improper, incorrect

improsp·er -era -erum *adj* **(inp-)** unfortunate

improsperē *adv* **(inp-)** unfortunately

imprōvidē *adv* **(inp-)** without foresight, thoughtlessly

imprōvid·us -a -um *adj* **(inp-)** not foreseeing, not anticipating; *(w. gen)* indifferent to

imprōvis·us -a -um *adj* **(inp-)** unexpected; **de improviso** *(or* **ex improviso** *or* **improviso)** unexpectedly ‖ *npl* emergencies

imprūd·ens -entis *adj* **(inp-)** not foreseeing, unsuspecting; off one's guard; inconsiderate; foolish, imprudent; *(w. gen)* **1** unaware of, ignorant of; **2** heedless of; **3** not experienced in

imprūdenter *adv* **(inp-)** without foresight, thoughtlessly, unintenionally; foolishly, imprudently

imprūdenti·a -ae *f* **(inp-)** thoughtlessness; ignorance, imprudence

impūb·ēs -eris *or* **impūb·is -is -e** *adj* **(inp-)** youthful, young, underage; beardless *(cheeks);* innocent, chaste, celibate, virgin; **anni impubes** childhood years

impud·ens -entis *adj* **(inp-)** shameless

impudenter *adv* **(inp-)** shamelessly, impudently; immodestly

impudenti·a -ae *f* **(inp-)** shamelessness, impudence; immodesty

impudīciti·a -ae *f* immodesty, lewdness, shamelessness

impudīc·us -a -um *adj* **(inp-)** immodest, lewd, shameless

impugnāti·ō -ōnis *f* **(inp-)** assault, attack

impugn·ō -āre -āvī -ātus *tr* **(inp-)** to assault, attack; *(fig)* to impugn; *(w. acc & inf)* to assert in opposition *(that)*

impulsi·ō -ōnis *f* **(inp-)** pressure; impulse

impuls·or -ōris *m* **(inp-)** instigator

impulsus *pp of* **impello**

impuls·us -ūs *m* **(inp-)** blow, impact, shock; impulse; instigation, incitement

impūne *adv* **(inp-)** with impunity, unpunished, scot-free; safely, unscathed

impūnit·ās -ātis *f* **(inp-)** impunity
impūnītē *adv* **(inp-)** with impunity
impūnīt·us -a -um *adj* **(inp-)** unpunished; unrestrained; safe
impurāt·us -a -um *adj* **(inp-)** filthy
impūrē *adv* **(inp-)** impurely
impūrit·ās -ātis *f* **(inp-)** impurity
impūriti·ae -ārum *fpl* **(inp-)** filth
impūr·us -a -um *adj* **(inp-)** impure; unclean, filthy
imputāt·us -a -um *adj* **(inp-)** unpruned, untrimmed
imput·ō -āre -āvī -ātus *tr* **(inp-)** to charge to someone's account, enter in an account; *(w. dat)* **1** to charge to; **2** to ascribe to; **3** to give credit for *(s.th.)* to; **4** to put the blame for *(s.th.)* on
īmul·us -a -um *adj* cute little
īm·us -a -um *adj* deepest, lowest; last; the bottom of, the foot of, the tip of **‖** *n* bottom, depth; **ab imo** utterly; **ab immo ad summum** from top to bottom; **ex imo** utterly, completely **‖** *npl* lower world
in *prep (w. abl)* **1** in, on, upon; **2** among; **3** at; **4** before; **5** under; **6** *(of time)* during, within, in, at, in the course of, on the point of; **7** in case of; **8** in relation to; **9** subject to; **10** affected by; **11** engaged in, involved in **‖** *(w. acc)* **1** into; **2** up to, as far as *(a point of space or time)*; **3** *(indicating person towards whom feelings are directed)* towards, to, for; **4** until; **5** about, respecting; **6** *(w. verbs of opposition or hostility)* against; **7** for, with a view to; **8** according to, after; *(w. verbs of sending, traveling)* to *(a country, city)*; **9** *(w. verbs of spending)* on; **10** *(w. verbs of distributing)* among
in- *pref* **(n** *is assimilated to following* **l, m,** *and* **r;** *becomes* **m** *before* **b** *and* **p;** *disappears before* **gn) 1** *combines, usu. with verbs, in the local or figurative senses of the preposition, e.g.,* **inaedificare** to build in *(a place); also with intensive force, e.g.,* **increpare** to make a loud noise; **2** *inchoative:* **insudare** to begin to sweat, break out in a sweat; **3** *negative or privative pref, e.g.:* **incognitus** unknown
inaccess·us -a -um *adj* inaccessible
inac·escō -escĕre -uī *intr* to turn sour
Īnachid·ēs -ae *m* descendant of Inachus *(esp.* Perseus and Epaphus)
Īnach·us *or* **Īnach·os -ī** *m* first king of Argos and father of Io
inacuī *perf of* **inacesco**
inadsc- = inasc-
inadt- = inatt-
inadust·us -a -um *adj* unburned
inaedific·ō -āre -āvī -ātus *tr* to build on, build as an addition, erect, construct; to wall up, barricade; *(w.* **in** + *abl)* to build *(s.th.)* on top of
inaequābil·is -is -e *adj* uneven
inaequābiliter *adv* unevenly, unequally
inaequāl·is -is -e *adj* uneven, unequal; unlike; changeable, inconstant
inaequālit·ās -ātis *f* unevenness
inaequāliter *adv* unevenly
inaequāt·us -a -um *adj* unequal
inaequ·ō -āre -āvī -ātus *tr* to level off
inaestimābil·is -is -e *adj* inestimable; invaluable; valueless
inaestu·ō -āre *intr* to seethe; to flare up
inaffectāt·us -a -um *adj* unaffected, natural
inamābil·is -is -e *adj* hateful, revolting
inamāresc·ō -ĕre *intr* to become bitter
inambitiōs·us -a -um *adj* unambitious
inambulāti·ō -ōnis *f* walking about, strutting about
inambul·ō -āre -āvī *intr* to walk up and down; to stroll about
inamoen·us -a -um *adj* unpleasant
ināni·ae -ārum *fpl* emptiness
inānilogist·a -ae *m* chatterbox
inānīment·um -ī *n* empty space
inanim·us -a -um *adj* inanimate
inān·is -is -e *adj* empty, void; deserted, abandoned, unoccupied; hollow; worthless, idle; lifeless, unsubstantial; penniless; unprofitable; groundless **‖** *n* empty space, vacuum; emptiness; worthlessness
inānit·ās -ātis *f* empty space, emptiness; uselessness, worthlessness
ināniter *adv* uselessly, vainly
inarāt·us -a -um *adj* untilled, unplowed
inar·descō -descĕre -sī *intr* to catch fire, burn, glow
ināresc·ō -ĕre *intr* to become dry, dry up
inarsī *perf of* **inardesco**
inascens·us -a -um *adj* not climbed
inassuēt·us -a -um *adj* unaccustomed
inattenuāt·us -a -um *adj* undiminished; unappeased
inaud·ax -ācis *adj* timid
inaud·iō - īre -īvī *or* **-iī -ītus** *tr* **(indau-)** to hear, learn, get wind of
inaudīt·us -a -um *adj* unheard-of, unprecedented; unusual; without a court hearing
inaugurātō *adv* after taking the auspices
inaugur·ō -āre -āvī -ātus *tr* to inaugurate, consecrate, install **‖** *intr* to take the auspices
inaurāt·us -a -um *adj* gilded, gilt
inaur·es -ium *fpl* earrings
inaur·ō -āre -āvī -ātus *tr* to goldplate, gild; to line the pockets of *(s.o.)* with gold
inauspicātō *adv* without consulting the auspices
inauspicāt·us -a -um *adj* undertaken without auspices; unlucky
inaus·us -a -um *adj* unattempted
inb- = imb-

incaedu·us -a -um *adj* uncut, unfelled
incal·escō -escĕre -uī *intr* to get warm, get hot; to get excited
incalfac·iō -ĕre *tr* to warm, heat
incallidē *adv* unskillfully
incallid·us -a -um *adj* unskillful; stupid, simple, clumsy
incand·escō -ĕscere -uī *intr* to become white; to get white-hot
incantāt·us -a -um *adj* enchanted
incān·us -a -um *adj* grown gray
incassum *adv* in vain
incastīgāt·us -a -um *adj* unscolded, unpunished
incautē *adv* incautiously, recklessly
incaut·us -a -um *adj* incautious, inconsiderate, thoughtless, reckless; unforeseen, unexpected; unguarded
in·cēdō -cēdĕre -cessī -cessum *intr* to go, walk, move; to step, stride, strut; to proceed; to come along, happen, occur, appear, arrive; to advance, go on; *(of troops)* to march, advance
incelebrāt·us -a -um *adj* unheralded
incēnāt·us -a -um *adj* supperless
incendiārius -(i)ī *m* agitator; arsonist
incend·ium -(i)ī *n* fire; heat
incen·dō -dĕre -dī -sus *tr* to light, set on fire, burn; to light up, make bright; *(fig)* to inflame, fire up, excite, enrage
incēn·is -is -e *adj* dinnerless
incensi·ō -ōnis *f* burning
incensus *pp of* **incendo**
incens·us -a -um *adj* not registered *(w. the censor)*
incepti·ō -ōnis *f* inception, beginning; undertaking
incept·ō -āre -āvī -ātus *tr* to begin; to undertake
incept·or -ōris *m* beginner, originator
incept·us -a -um *pp of* **incipio** ‖ *n* beginning; undertaking, attempt, enterprise; subject, theme
in·cernō -cernĕre -crēvī -crētus *tr* to sift
incēr·ō -āre -āvī -ātus *tr* to wax, cover with wax, coat with wax
incertē *adv* uncertainly
incertō *adv* uncertainly
incert·ō -āre -āvī -ātus *tr* to render doubtful, make uncertain
incert·us -a -um *adj* uncertain; vague, obscure; doubtful; unsure, hesitant ‖ *n* uncertainty, insecurity; contingency; **in incertum** for an indefinite time
incessī *perf of* **incedo**
incess·ō -ĕre -ī *or* **-īvī** *or* **-uī** *tr* to fall upon, assault; to reproach, accuse, attack
incess·us -ūs *m* walk, gait, pace; trampling; invasion, attack; advance; procession
incestē *adv* impurely, sinfully; indecently
in·cīdō -cidĕre -cidī -cāsum *intr* to happen, occur; *(w.* **ad** *or* **in** *+ acc)* to fall into, fall upon; *(w.* **in** *+ acc)* **1** to come upon unexpectedly, fall in with; **2** to attack; *(w. dat or* **in** *+ acc)* **1** to occur to *(mentally)*; **2** to fall on *(a certain day)*; **3** to befall, happen to; **4** to agree with
incī·dō -dĕre -dī -sus *tr* to carve, engrave, inscribe; to cut, sever; *(fig)* to cut into, cut short, put an end to, break off, interrupt
incīl·e -is *n* ditch, trench
incin·gō -gĕre -xī -ctus *tr* to drape; to wreathe; to invest, surround
incin·ō -ĕre *tr* to sing; to play
incipessō *see* **incipisso**
in·cipiō -cipĕre -cēpī -ceptus *tr & intr* to begin, start
incipiss·ō -ĕre *tr* to begin
incīsē *or* **incīsim** *adv* in short phrases
incīsi·ō -ōnis *f* incision; *(rhet)* short phrase
incīsus *pp of* **incīdo**
incitāment·um -ī *n* incentive
incitāti·ō -ōnis *f* inciting, rousing; speed
incitāt·us -a -um *adj* rapid, speedy; **equo incitato** at full gallop
incit·ō -āre -āvī -ātus *tr* to incite, urge on, spur on, drive on; to stimulate; to inspire; to stir up, arouse; to increase; **currentem incitare** *(fig)* to spur a willing horse ‖ *refl* to rush
incit·us -a -um *adj* rapid, swift; immovable; **ad incita** *(or* **ad incitas)** **adigere** to bring to a standstill
inclāmit·ō -āre -āvī -ātus *tr* to cry out against, revile, abuse
inclām·ō -āre -āvī -ātus *tr* to call out to; to invoke; to shout at, scold, revile ‖ *intr* to yell
inclār·escō -escĕre -uī *intr* to become famous
inclēm·ens -entis *adj* harsh, unmerciful; violent *(movement)*
inclēmenter *adv* harshly; rudely
inclēmenti·a -ae *f* harshness, cruelty
inclīnāti·ō -ōnis *f* leaning; inclination, tendency, bias; change; *(gram)* inflection
inclīnāt·us -a -um *adj* inclined, prone; sinking; low, deep; *(gram)* inflected
inclīn·ō -āre -āvī -ātus *tr* to bend, turn; to turn back, drive back, repulse; to shift *(e.g., blame)*; to change; *(gram)* to inflect *(nouns or verbs)* ‖ *refl & pass* to lean, bend, turn; to change *(esp. for the worse)* ‖ *pass (mil)* to fall back ‖ *intr* to bend, turn, lean, dip, sink; to change, deteriorate; to change for the better
inclit·us -a -um *adj* famous
inclū·dō -dĕre -sī -sus *tr* to shut in, confine, lock up; to include; to insert; to block, shut off, obstruct; to restrain, control; to close, end *(e.g., a day)*
inclūsi·ō -ōnis *f* locking up, confinement
inclut·us -a -um *adj* famous

incoct·us -a -um *pp of* **incoquo ‖** *adj* uncooked, raw; undigested
incōgitābil·is -is -e *adj* thoughtless, inconsiderate
incōgit·ans -antis *adj* unthinking, thoughtless
incōgitanti·a -ae *f* thoughtlessness
incōgitāt·us -a -um *adj* thoughtless, inconsiderate
incōgit·ō -āre -āvī -ātus *tr* to think up
incognit·us -a -um *adj* not investigated; unknown, unrecognized, unidentified, incognito; unparalleled
incohāt·us *or* **inchoāt·us -a -um** *adj* only begun, unfinished, imperfect; temporary *(structure)*
incoh·ō -āre -āvī -ātus *tr* to begin
incol·a -ae *mf* inhabitant; resident alien
incol·ō -ĕre -uī *tr* to live in, inhabit, occupy **‖** *intr* to live, reside
incolum·is -is -e *adj* unharmed, safe and sound, unscathed, alive; *(w. abl)* safe from
incolumit·ās -ātis *f* safety
incomitāt·us -a -um *adj* unaccompanied
incommendāt·us -a -um *adj* unprotected
incommodē *adv* at the wrong time; inconveniently; annoyingly; improperly; unfortunately
incommodestic·us -a -um *adj (coll)* ill-timed, inconvenient
incommodit·ās -ātis *f* inconvenience; unsuitableness; disadvantage
incommod·ō -āre -āvī -ātum *intr (w. dat)* to inconvenience, be inconvenient for, be annoying to
incommod·us -a -um *adj* inconvenient; troublesome, tiresome, annoying; disadvantageous, unfavorable; unpleasant, disagreeable **‖** *n* inconvenience, discomfort; disadvantage; misfortune, trouble; *(med)* ailment; *(mil)* setback, disaster
incommūtābil·is -is -e *adj* unchangeable
incomparābil·is -is -e *adj* unequaled, incomparable
incompert·us -a -um *adj* unknown, undetermined; forgotten
incompositē *adv* in disorder
incomposit·us -a -um *adj* disordered, poorly arranged, poorly written; clumsy, awkward *(movements);* disorganized *(troops)*
incomprehensibil·is -is -e *adj* incomprehensible
incompt·us -a -um *adj* unkempt, messy; untidy; simple, unstudied; unpolished *(writing, speech)*
inconcess·us -a -um *adj* forbidden, unlawful
inconcili·ō -āre -āvī -ātus *tr* to deceive, trick; to rob, fleece
inconcinn·us -a -um *adj* clumsy, awkward; absurd
inconcuss·us -a -um *adj* unshaken
inconditē *adv* confusedly
incondit·us -a -um *adj* unorganized, disorderly, confused; irregular; rough, undeveloped *(style);* raw *(jokes)*
inconsīderātē *adv* thoughtlessly
inconsīderāt·us -a um *adj* thoughtless
inconsōlābil·is -is -e *adj* inconsolable; *(fig)* incurable
inconst·ans -antis *adj* inconsistent, fickle, shifty
inconstanter *adv* inconsistently
inconstanti·a -ae *f* inconsistency, fickleness
inconsultē *adv* indiscreetly
inconsult·us -a -um *adj* indiscreet, ill-advised; not consulted
inconsult·us -ūs *m* lack of consultation; **inconsultu meo** without consulting me
inconsumpt·us -a -um *adj* unconsumed
incontāmināt·us -a -um *adj* untainted
incontent·us -a -um *adj* loose, untuned *(string)*
incontin·ens -entis *adj* intemperate
incontinenter *adv* without self-control, intemperately
incontinenti·a -ae *f* lack of self-control
inconveni·ens -entis *adj* unsuitable, dissimilar
inco·quō -quĕre -xī -ctus *tr* to boil *(in or with);* to dye
incorrect·us -a -um *adj* uncorrected
incorruptē *adv* honestly, fairly
incorrupt·us -a -um *adj* intact, unspoiled, untainted; uncorrupted; not open to bribes, incorruptible; chaste; genuine, authentic
incoxī *perf of* **incoquo**
incrēb(r)·escō -escĕre -uī *intr* to grow; to rise; to increase; to spread
incrēdibil·is -is -e *adj* incredible
incrēdibiliter *adv* incredibly
incrēdul·us -a -um *adj* incredulous
incrēment·um -ī *n* growth, increase; increment, addition; addition to the family, offspring
increpit·ō -āre -āvī -ātus *tr* to scold, rebuke
increp·ō -āre -uī *or* **-āvī -itus** *or* **-atus** *tr* to cause to make noise, cause to ring; to rattle; *(of Jupiter)* to thunder at; to scold, rebuke; to protest against; *(of sounds)* to strike *(the ears); (w. acc & inf)* to say reproachfully that, to remark indignantly that **‖** *intr* to make noise; to snap, rustle, rattle, clash; to speak angrily; *(of a bow)* to twang; *(of flying object)* to whiz, whir; **suspicio tumultūs increpat** the suspicion of a riot sounds the alarm
incr·escō -escĕre -ēvī *intr* to grow, increase; *(w. dat or abl)* to grow in *or* upon
incrētus *pp of* **incerno**
incrēvī *perf of* **incerno** *and* **incresco**

incruentāt·us -a -um *adj* unbloodied
incruent·us -a -um *adj* bloodless, without bloodshed
incrust·ō -āre -āvī -ātus *tr* to coat, cover with a coat, encrust
incub·ō -āre -uī -itum *intr (w. dat)* **1** to lie in *or* upon; **2** to lean on; **3** to brood over; **4** to watch jealously over
incū·dō -dĕre -dī -sus *or* **-ssus** *tr* to indent by hammering; to emboss
inculc·ō -āre -āvī -ātus *tr* to impress, inculcate; *(w. dat)* to force *(s.th.)* upon
inculpāt·us -a -um *adj* blameless
incultē *adv* uncouthly, roughly
incult·us -a -um *adj* untilled, uncultivated; neglected, slovenly; rough, uneducated, uncivilized ‖ *npl* desert, wilderness, the wilds
incult·us -ūs *m* neglect; dirt, squalor
in·cumbō -cumbĕre -cubuī -cubitum *intr (w. dat or* **in** *+ acc)* **1** to lean on *or* against; **2** to lie down on *(bed, couch);* **3** to bend to *(the oars);* **4** to light on, fall on; **5** *(fig)* to press upon, burden, oppress, weigh down; **6** to apply oneself to, take pains with; **7** to pay attention to; *(w.* **ad** *or* **in** *+ acc)* to be inclined towards, lean towards
incūnābul·a -ōrum *npl* baby clothes; *(fig)* cradle, infancy; birthplace; origin, source
incūrāt·us -a -um *adj* neglected; uncured
incūri·a -ae *f* carelessness, negligence
incūriōsē *adv* carelessly
incūriōs·us -a -um *adj* careless, unconcerned, indifferent; neglected
in·currō -currĕre -currī *or* **-cucurrī -cursus** *tr* to attack ‖ *intr (w. dat or* **in** *+ acc)* **1** to run into, rush at, charge, attack; **2** to invade; **3** to extend to; **4** to meet, run into; **4** to fall on, coincide with
incursi·ō -ōnis *f* incursion, invasion, raid; attack; collision
incurs·ō -āre -āvī -ātus *tr* to attack; to invade ‖ *intr (w. dat or* **in** *+ acc)* **1** to attack; **2** to run into, bump against; **3** to strike, meet *(e.g., the eyes);* **4** to affect, touch, move
incurs·us -ūs *m* attack; invasion, inroad, raid; collision, impact
incurv·ō -āre -āvī -ātus *tr* to bend, curve
incurv·us -a -um *adj* bent, crooked
inc·ūs -ūdis *f* anvil
incūsāti·ō -ōnis *f* accusation
incūs·ō -āre -āvī -ātus *tr* to blame, find fault with, accuse
incussī *perf of* **incutio**
incussus *pp of* **incutio**
incuss·us -ūs *m* shock
incustōdīt·us -a -um *adj* unguarded; unconcealed; imprudent
incūs·us -a -um *pp of* **incudo** ‖ *adj* forged; embossed; **lapis incusus** indented millstone
incu·tiō -tĕre -ssī -ssus *tr* to throw; to produce; *(w. dat or* **in** *+ acc)* to strike *(s.th.)* on *or* against; *(w. dat)* **1** to strike into, instill in; **2** to throw at, to fling upon; **metum incutere** *(w. dat)* to strike fear into; **scipione in caput alicujus incutere** to beat s.o. over the head with a stick
indāgāti·ō -ōnis *f* investigation, search
indāgāt·or -ōris *m*, **indāgātr·ix -īcis** *f* investigator
indāg·ō -āre -āvī -ātus *tr* to track down, hunt; to investigate, explore
indāg·ō -inis *f* dragnet; **indagine agere** to ferret out
indaudiō *see* **inaudio**
inde *adv* from there; from that source, therefrom; from that time on, after that, thereafter; then; from that cause
indēbit·us -a -um *adj* that is not owed, not due
indec·ens -entis *adj* unbecoming, improper, indecent
indecenter *adv* improperly, indecently
indec·eō -ēre *tr* to be improper for ‖ *intr* (*w. dat*) to be inappropriate to
indēclīnāt·us -a -um *adj* unchanged, constant
indec·or -oris *or* **indecor·is -is -e** *adj* disgraceful, dishonorable, cowardly
indecōrē *adv* indecently, improperly
indecor·ō -āre -āvī -ātus *tr* to disgrace
indecōr·us -a -um *adj* unsightly
indēfens·us -a -um *adj* undefended
indēfess·us -a -um *adj* tireless; not tired
indēflēt·us -a -um *adj* unwept
indēject·us -a -um *adj* undemolished
indēlēbil·is -is -e *adj* indestructible, indelible
indēlībāt·us -a -um *adj* undiminished
indemnāt·us -a -um *adj* unconvicted
indēplōrāt·us -a -um *adj* unwept
indēprens·us -a -um *adj* undetected
indeptus *pp of* **indipiscor**
indēsert·us -a -um *adj* unforsaken
indēspect·us -a -um *adj* unfathomable
indēstrict·us -a -um *adj* unscathed
indētons·us -a -um *adj* unshorn
indēvītāt·us -a -um *adj* unavoidable, unerring *(e.g., arrow)*
ind·ex -icis *m* index, sign, mark; indication, proof; title *(of book);* informer, spy; index finger
Indi·a -ae *f* India
indicāti·ō -ōnis *f* setting the price; statement, declaration
indīc·ens -entis *adj* not speaking; **me indicente** without a word from me
indic·ium -(i)ī *n* information, disclosure, evidence; indication, proof; permission to give evidence; reward for giving evidence; **indicio esse** to give evidence; to be an indication *or* proof; **indicium**

afferre *(or* **deferre)** to adduce evidence; **indicium facere** to give away a secret; to give an indication *or* warning

indic·ō -āre -āvī -ātus *tr* to point out; to reveal, disclose; to betray, inform against; to put a price on ‖ *intr* to give evidence

in·dīcō -dīcĕre -dixī -dictus *tr* to proclaim, announce, publish; to summon, convoke; to impose *(a fine);* **bellum indicere** to declare war; **diem indicere** to set a date

indict·us -a -um *adj* unsaid; **causā indictā** without a hearing

Indic·us -a -um *adj* Indian ‖ *m* Indian ‖ *n* indigo

indidem *adv* from the same place; from the same source, from the same thing

indiffer·ens -entis *adj* (morally) indifferent; unconcerned, indifferent

indigen·a -ae *adj masc & fem* native

indig·ens -entis *adj* indigent; *(w. gen)* in need of

indigenti·a -ae *f* indigence, need; craving

indig·eō -ēre -uī *intr (w. gen or abl)* **1** to need, be in need of; **2** to require; *(w. gen)* to crave, desire

indig·es -etis *adj* indigenous, native ‖ *m* native god; national hero

indīgest·us -a -um *adj* unarranged, disorderly, confused, in confusion

indignābund·us -a -um *adj* highly indignant

indign·ans -antis *adj* indignant; *(w. gen)* resentful of

indignāti·ō -ōnis *f* indignation, displeasure; provocation, occasion for indignation ‖ *fpl* expressions of indignation

indignē *adv* unworthily; undeservedly; shamefully, outrageously; **indigne ferre** *(or* **pati)** to be indignant at

indignit·ās -ātis *f* unworthiness; indignation; indignity, shameful treatment; enormity, shamelessness

indign·or -ārī -ātus sum *tr* to be indignant at, displeased at, angry at, offended by

indign·us -a -um *adj* unworthy, undeserving; undeserved; shameful, scandalous; *(w. abl)* **1** unworthy of; **2** not deserving; **3** not worth; *(w. gen)* unworthy of, undeserving of; **indignum!** shame!

indig·us -a -um *adj* needy, indigent; *(w. gen or abl)* in need of

indīlig·ens -entis *adj* careless

indīligenter *adv* carelessly

indīligenti·a -ae *f* carelessness

ind·ipiscor -ipiscī -eptus sum *or* **indipisc·ō -ĕre** *tr* to obtain, get; to win, acquire ‖ *intr (w.* **de** *+ abl)* to gain one's point about

indīrept·us -a -um *adj* unplundered

indiscrēt·us -a -um *adj* closely connected, inseparable; used indiscriminately; indistinguishable; **indiscretum est** it makes no difference

indisert·us -a -um *adj* without eloquence

indisposit·us -a -um *adj* confused, disordered

indissolūbil·is -is -e *adj* imperishable, indestructible

indistinct·us -a -um *adj* indistinct; applied without distinction

inditus *pp of* **indo**

indīvidu·us -a -um *adj* indivisible; inseparable; equal, impartial ‖ *n* atom, indivisible particle

in·dō -dĕre -didī -ditus *tr* to put, place; to introduce; to impart, give; *(w.* **in** *+ acc)* to put *or* place *(s. th.)* into *or* on, insert into

indocil·is -is -e *adj* slow to learn; impossible to teach; untrained, ignorant

indoctē *adv* unskillfully

indoct·us -a -um *adj* untaught, untrained; ignorant, uninformed

indolenti·a -ae *f* freedom from pain; insensibility to pain

indol·ēs -is *f* inborn quality, natural quality; nature, character; natural ability, talent; *(w. gen)* natural capacity for, natural tendency toward

indol·escō -escĕre -uī *intr* to feel sorry; to feel resentment

indomābil·is -is -e *adj* untamable

indomit·us -a -um *adj* untamed, wild; indomitable; unrestrained; unmanageable

indorm·iō -īre -īvī *or* **-iī -ītum** *intr* to fall asleep; to grow careless; *(w. dat or abl or* **in** *+ abl)* **1** to fall asleep at *or* on; **2** to fall asleep over; **3** to become careless about

indōtāt·us -a -um *adj* without dowry; poor; without funeral rites; **ars indotata** *(rhet)* unadorned style

indubitābil·is -is -e *adj* indubitable

indubitāt·us -a -um *adj* undoubted

indubit·ō -āre *intr (w. dat)* to begin to distrust, begin to doubt

indubi·us -a -um *adj* undoubted, certain

indūci·ae *or* **indūti·ae -ārum** *fpl* armistice, truce

indū·cō -cĕre -xī -ctus *tr* to lead in, bring in; to introduce; to induce; to seduce; to overlay, drape, wrap, cover; to put on, clothe; to strike out, erase; to repeal, cancel; to present, exhibit; to mislead, delude; *(w.* **in** *+ acc)* **1** to lead to, lead into, lead against; **2** to bring into, introduce into; **3** to enter into *(account books); (w. dat or* **super** *+ acc)* to put *(item of apparel, esp. shoes)* on, spread *(s.th.)* over, wrap *(s.th.)* around, draw *(s.th.)* over; **animum** *(or* **in animum)** **inducere** to make up one's mind, convince oneself, be convinced, conclude, suppose, imagine

inducti·ō -ōnis *f* bringing in, introduction, admission; resolution, determination; intention; induction, generalization; **animi inductio** inclination; **erroris inductio** deception

induct·or -ōris *m (hum) (referring to a whip)* persuader

induct·us -a -um *pp of* **induco** ‖ *adj* alien, adventitious

induct·us -ūs *m* inducement

indūcul·a -ae *f* slip, petticoat

indulg·ens -entis *adj* indulgent, lenient; *(w. dat or* **in** *+ acc)* lenient toward, kind toward

indulgenter *adv* indulgently, leniently, kindly

indulgenti·a -ae *f* indulgence, leniency, kindness

indul·geō -gēre -sī -sus *tr (w. dat)* to grant, concede *(s.th.)* to; **veniam indulgere** *(w. dat)* to make allowances for ‖ *refl* **sibi indulgere** to be self-indulgent, take liberties ‖ *intr (w. dat)* **1** to be lenient toward, be kind to, be tender to; **2** to yield to, give way to; **3** to indulge in, be addicted to; **4** to make allowance for; **5** *(of deities, fate, etc.)* to look favorably on, show kindness to; **6** to take pleasure in; **7** to devote oneself to *(an activity)*

ind·uō -uĕre -uī -ūtus *tr* to put on *(e.g., a tunic);* to cover, wrap, clothe, array; to envelop; to engage in; to assume, put on; to assume the part of; to involve; *(w. dat)* to put *(e.g., a tunic)* on *(s.o.)*

indup- = imp-

indūr·escō -escĕre -uī *intr* to become hard, harden

indūr·ō -āre -āvī -ātus *tr* to harden

indūruī *perf of* **induresco**

Ind·us -a -um *adj* Indian ‖ *m* Indian; Ethiopian; mahout

industri·a -ae *f* industry, diligence; **de** *(or* **ex)** **industria** diligently; **industriā** *(or* **de** *or* **ex industria)** *(or* **ob industriam)** on purpose, deliberately

industriē *adv* industriously, diligently

industri·us -a -um *adj* industrious, diligent, painstaking

indūti·ae *or* **indūci·ae -ārum** *fpl* armistice, truce

indūt·us -ūs *m* wearing; clothing

induvi·ae -ārum *fpl* clothes

inebri·ō -āre -āvī -ātus *tr* to make drunk; *(fig)* to fill *(e.g., the ear with gossip)*

inedi·a -ae *f* fasting; starvation

inēdit·us -a -um *adj* not made known, unknown, unpublished

inēleg·ans -antis *adj* inelegant, undistinguished

inēleganter *adv* without style, poorly; without clear thought

inēluctābil·is -is -e *adj* inescapable

inēmor·ior -ī *intr (w. dat)* to die *(of starvation)* in the sight of *(a feast)*

inempt·us -a -um *adj* unpurchased; without ransom

inēnarrābil·is -is -e *adj* indescribable

inēnarrābiliter *adv* indescribably

inēnōdābil·is -is -e *adj* inexplicable

in·eō -īre -īvī -iī -itus *tr* to enter; to enter upon, undertake, form; to begin, engage in; **ab ineunte pueritiā** from earliest boyhood; **consilium inire** to form a plan; **in consilium inire ut** *(or* **qua** *or* **quemadmodum)** to plan how to *(do s.th.);* **ineunte vere** at the beginning of spring; **inire numerum** *(w. gen)* to go into an enumeration of, enumerate; **inire rationem** *(w. gen)* to form an estimate of; **inire rationem ut** *(or* **qua** *or* **quemadmodum)** to consider, find out, *or* figure out how to *(do s.th.);* **viam inire** to begin a trip; to find a way, devise a means

ineptē *adv* foolishly, absurdly, inappropriately, pointlessly

inepti·a -ae *f* foolishness ‖ *fpl* nonsense; trifles

inept·iō -īre *intr* to be absurd, make a fool of oneself

inept·us -a -um *adj* foolish, silly; inept, awkward, absurd; unsuitable, out of place; tactless, tasteless

inerm·is -is -e *or* **inerm·us -a -um** *adj* unarmed, defenseless; undefended; toothless *(gums);* harmless; peaceful

inerr·ans -antis *adj* not wandering, fixed

inerr·ō -āre -āvī *intr* to wander about

iner·s -tis *adj* unskilled, incompetent; inactive, sluggish; weak, soft, helpless; stagnant, motionless; ineffective; dull, insipid; numbing *(cold);* expressionless *(eyes);* uneventful, leisurely *(time)*

inerti·a -ae *f* lack of skill, ignorance, rudeness; inactivity; laziness

inērudīt·us -a -um *adj* uneducated; crude, inconsiderate

inesc·ō -āre -āvī -ātus *tr* to bait; *(fig)* to bait, trap; to gorge

inēvect·us -a -um *adj* mounted

inēvītābil·is -is -e *adj* inevitable, inescapable

inexcīt·us -a -um *adj* unexcited, calm

inexcūsābil·is -is -e *adj* without excuse; admitting no excuse

inexercitāt·us -a -um *adj* untrained

inexhaust·us -a -um *adj* unexhausted, not wasted; inexhaustible

inexōrābil·is -is -e *adj* inexorable, relentless; unswerving, strict

inexperrect·us -a -um *adj* unawakened

inexpert·us -a -um *adj* untried, untested; novel; *(w. abl or* **adversus** *or* **in** *+ acc)* inexperienced in, unaccustomed to

inexpiābil·is -is -e *adj* inexpiable, not to

be atoned for; irreconcilable, implacable
inexplēbil·is -is -e *adj* insatiable
inexplēt·us -a -um *adj* unsatisfied, unfilled
inexplicābil·is -is -e *adj* inextricable; inexplicable, baffling; impassable *(road);* involved, unending *(war);* incurable *(disease)*
inexplōrātō *adv* without reconnoitering
inexplorāt·us -a -um *adj* unexplored; unfamiliar; not investigated
inexpugnābil·is -is -e *adj* impregnable, unassailable; invincible
inexspectāt·us -a -um *adj* unexpected, unforeseen
inextinct·us -a -um *adj* unextinguished; insatiable
inexsuperābil·is -is -e *adj* insuperable, insurmountable
inextrīcābil·is -is -e *adj* inextricable
infabrē *adv* unskillfully
infabricāt·us -a -um *adj* unshaped, untrimmed, unwrought
infacētē *adv* boorishly
infacēti·ae -ārum *fpl* crudities
infacēt·us -a -um *adj* not witty, not funny, dull, stupid
infācund·us -a -um *adj* ineloquent
infāmi·a -ae *f* bad reputation; disrepute, disgrace; scandal; *(w. gen)* stigma of; *(pol)* public disgrace *(involving loss of some civil rights)*
infām·is -is -e *adj* infamous, notorious, disreputable, disgraceful; disgraced; *(w.* **in** *+ acc or abl)* suspected of misconduct with; **infamis digitus** middle finger *(used in obscene gestures)*
infām·ō -āre -āvī -ātus *tr* to defame, dishonor, disgrace; to smear *(esp. groundlessly)* ‖ *pass (w.* **in** *+ acc)* to be suspected of misconduct with
infand·us -a -um *adj* unspeakable, shocking
inf·ans -antis *adj* speechless, unable to speak; baby-, infant-, young; childish, silly; *(fig)* tongue-tied ‖ *mf* infant
infanti·a -ae *f* infancy; childishness; inability to speak; lack of eloquence; young children
infar- = infer-
infatu·ō -āre -āvī -ātus *tr* to make a fool of
infaust·us -a -um *adj* ill-omened, unpropitious; unfortunate
infect·or -ōris *m* dyer
infect·us -a -um *pp of* **inficio** ‖ *adj* not made, not done, undone, unfinished; unwrought *(metals);* unachieved; infeasible; **foedere infecto** without concluding a treaty; **re infectā** without achieving the objective
infēcundit·ās -ātis *f* unfruitfulness
infēcund·us -a -um *adj* unfruitful
infēlicit·ās -ātis *f* bad luck, misfortune
infēlīciter *adv* unhappily; unluckily, unsuccessfully
infēlīc·ō -āre *tr* to make unhappy
infēl·ix -īcis *adj* unfruitful; unhappy; unfortunate, unlucky; causing misfortune, ruinous; ill-omened; pessimistic
infensē *adv* with hostility, aggressively
infens·ō -āre -āvī -ātus *tr* to antagonize; to make dangerous ‖ *intr* to be hostile
infens·us -a -um *adj* hostile, antagonistic; dangerous; *(w. dat or* **in** *+ acc)* **1** hostile to; **2** dangerous to
infer- = infar-
infer·ciō -cīre -sī -ctus *tr* (**-far-**) to stuff, cram
infer·a -ōrum *npl* lower world
infer·ī -ōrum *mpl* the dead; the world below
inferi·ae -ārum *fpl* rites and offerings to the dead
inferi·or -or -us *adj* lower, farther down; *(fig)* inferior; subsequent; later, more recent *(period); (w. abl or* **in** *+ abl)* inferior, worse in *(some respect)*
inferius *adv* lower, at a lower level; too low; at a later stage
infernē *adv* below, beneath
infern·us -a -um *adj* lower; infernal, of the lower world
inferō inferre intulī illātus *tr* to bring in, carry in; to import; to introduce; to bring forward, adduce, produce; *(w. dat)* to cause *(injury, death, delay)* to; to bury, inter; *(w.* **in** *+ acc)* to reduce to; *(w. dat)* to pay *(money)* to *(e.g., the treasury);* **arma** *(or* **bellum)** **inferre** *(w. dat)* to make war on; **gradum** *(or* **pedem** *or* **signa)** **inferre** to advance *(usually to attack);* **conversa signa inferre** *(w. dat)* to turn around and attack; **faces** *(or* **ignem)** **inferre** *(w. dat)* to set fire to; **honores inferre** to offer a sacrifice; **manūs inferre** *(w. dat)* to lay hands on; **nomen in tabulas inferre** to enter one's name in the records ‖ *refl & pass* to enter; to rush in *or* on; to go, march, charge, plunge; **se in periculum inferre** to expose oneself to danger ‖ *intr* to infer, conclude
infer·us -a -um *adj* lower; southern
inferv·eō -ēre *intr* to come to a boil
infervesc·ō -ĕre *intr* to simmer, come to a boil, start to boil
infestē *adv* hostilely, violently
infest·ō -āre -āvī -ātus *tr* to annoy, harass, bother; to attack; to damage; *(of diseases, pests)* to infest
infest·us -a -um *adj* hostile, antagonistic; aggressive, warlike; troubled *(times, conditions); (of weapons)* poised to strike; *(of armies)* taking the offensive; *(of things)* harmful, troublesome; *(of*

places) threatened, exposed to danger, insecure; *(w. abl)* 1 dangerous *or* unsafe because of; 2 infested with

inficēt- = infacēt-

in·ficiō -ficĕre -fēcī -fectus *tr* to dip, dye, tint; to infect; to stain; to corrupt, spoil; to imbue, instruct; *(fig)* to poison, infect

infidēl·is -is -e *adj* unfaithful, untrue, disloyal

infidēlit·ās -ātis *f* infidelity, disloyalty

infidēliter *adv* disloyally

infidī *perf of* **infindo**

infid·us -a -um *adj* untrustworthy, treacherous

in·figō -figĕre -fixī -fixus *tr* to drive in, nail, thrust; to imprint, fix, impress; *(w. dat)* **1** to drive into, thrust into; **2** to impale on; **3** to imprint on *or* in; **4** to fasten to, attach to

infimātis *see* **infumatis**

infim·us -a -um *(superl of* **inferus)** *adj* **(-fum-)** lowest, last; worst; humblest; **ab infimo colle** at the foot of the hill; **infimum mare** the bottom of the sea ‖ *n* bottom

in·findō -findĕre -fidī -fissus *tr (w. dat)* to cut *(e.g., furrows)* into

infinit·ās -ātis *f* endlessness, infinity; *(phil)* the Infinite

infinītē *adv* without bounds, without end, infinitely; without exception

infinīti·ō -ōnis *f* boundlessness, infinity

infinīt·us -a -um *adj* unlimited, boundless; without end, endless, infinite; countless; indefinite

infirmāti·ō -ōnis *f* invalidation; refutation

infirmē *adv* weakly, faintly, feebly

infirmit·ās -ātis *f* weakness, feebleness; infirmity; inconstancy

infirm·ō -āre -āvī -ātus *tr* to weaken, enfeeble; to refute, disprove; to annul

infirm·us -a -um *adj* weak, faint, feeble; infirm, sick; trivial; inconstant

infissus *pp of* **infindo**

infit *v defect* he, she, it begins

infiti·ae -ārum *fpl* denial; **infitias ire** *(w. acc)* to deny, refuse to acknowledge as true; to disown, repudiate

infitiāl·is -is -e *adj* negative

infitiāti·ō -ōnis *f* denial

infitiāt·or -ōris *m* repudiator

infiti·ōr -ārī -ātus sum *tr* to deny, repudiate, disown; to contradict

infixī *perf of* **infigo**

infixus *pp of* **infigo**

inflammāti·ō -ōnis *f* setting on fire; *(med)* inflammation; **animi inflammatio** inspiration; **inflammationem inferre** *(w. dat)* to set on fire

inflamm·ō -āre -āvī -ātus *tr* to set on fire, kindle, light up; *(med)* to inflame; *(fig)* to excite

inflāti·ō -ōnis *f* swelling up; flatulence; **habet inflationem faba** beans cause gas

inflātius *adv* rather pompously

inflāt·us -a -um *adj* blown up, inflated; swollen; haughty; turgid *(style)*

inflāt·us -ūs *m* puff, blast; inspiration

infle·ctō -ctĕre -xī -xus *tr* to bend, curve, bow; to tilt, slant; to turn aside; to change *(course);* to influence; to inflect, modulate *(voice)* ‖ *refl & pass* to curve; to change course; to turn around; *(of a person)* to change

inflēt·us -a -um *adj* unwept

inflexī *perf of* **inflecto**

inflexibil·is -is -e *adj* inflexible

inflexi·ō -ōnis *f* bending; modification, adaptation

inflexus *pp of* **inflecto**

inflex·us -ūs *m* curve, bend, winding

inflī·gō -gĕre -xī -ctus *tr (w. dat)* **1** to strike *(s.th.)* against, smash *(s.th.)* against; **2** to inflict *(wound)* on; **3** to bring *(e.g., disgrace)* to

infl·ō -āre -āvī -ātus *tr (of wind)* to blow on; to blow *(horn),* play *(flute); (of a deity)* to inspire; to inflate, fill with conceit; to puff up *(cheeks);* to fill *(sails);* to distend, bloat; to amplify *(sound);* to inflate *(price)*

influ·ō -ĕre -xī *intr (w.* **in** *+ acc)* **1** to flow into; **2** *(fig)* to spill over into, stream into, pour into; **3** *(of words, ideas)* to sink into, penetrate

in·fodiō -fodĕre -fōdī -fossus *tr* to dig; to bury

informāti·ō -ōnis *f* formation *(of an idea);* sketch; idea

inform·is -is -e *adj* unformed, shapeless; ugly, hideous

inform·ō -āre -āvī -ātus *tr* to form, shape; to sketch *(in words),* give an idea of; to instruct, educate

infor·ō -āre -āvī -ātus *tr* to bring into court

infortūnāt·us -a -um *adj* unfortunate

infortūn·ium -(i)ī *n* misfortune; *(euphem. for punishment)* trouble

infossus *pp of* **infodio**

infrā *adv* below, underneath; down south; down the coast; downstream; lower down *(on the page or in the work);* below the surface; later ‖ *prep (w. acc)* **1** below, beneath, under; **2** inferior *(in quality, rank, etc.)* to; **3** smaller than; **4** lower *(in number)* than; **5** beneath the dignity of, degrading to; **6** submissive to; **7** south of; **infra et supra Ephesum** south and north of Ephesus; **8** after, later than; **9** falling short of *(a target)*

infracti·ō -ōnis *f* breaking; **animi infractio** discouragement

infract·us -a -um *pp of* **infringo** ‖ *adj* broken; disjointed *(words);* weakened;

humble, subdued *(tone);* **infractos animos gerere** to feel down and out
infragil·is -is -e *adj* unbreakable, indestructible; vigorous *(voice)*
infrēgī *perf of* **infringo**
infrem·ō -ĕre -uī *intr* to growl, bellow, roar; to rage
infrēnāt·us -a -um *adj* unbridled
infrend·eō -ēre *or* **infrend·ō -ĕre** *intr* to grit the teeth; **dentibus infrendere** to grit the teeth
infrēn·is -is -e *or* **infrēn·us -a -um** *adj* unbridled
infrēn·ō -āre -āvī -ātus *tr* to bridle; to harness; *(fig)* to curb
infrēnus *see* **infrenis**
infrequ·ens -entis *adj* uncrowded, not numerous; poorly attended; thinly populated; unusual, infrequent *(words);* inconstant; irregular; *(mil)* undermanned, below strength; *(mil)* absent without leave
infrequenti·a -ae *f* small number, scantiness; poor attendance; emptiness; depopulated condition *(of a place)*
in·fringō -fringĕre -frēgī -fractus *tr* to break; to break in; to bend; to break up *(sentences);* to impair, affect adversely; to subdue; to weaken, break down; to cause to relent; to foil *(an action);* to render null and void
infr·ons -ondis *adj* leafless
infructuōs·us -a -um *adj* unfruitful; pointless
infūcāt·us -a -um *adj* painted over
infūdī *perf of* **infundo**
infūl·a -ae *f* bandage; fillet *(worn by priests, by sacrificial victims; displayed as a sign of submission);* festoon *(hung on doorposts at a wedding)*
infumāt·is -is *m* **(infim-)** one of the lowest *(in rank)*
infumus *see* **infimus**
in·fundō -fundĕre -fūdī -fūsus *tr* to pour in, pour on, pour out; *(w. dat or* **in** *+ acc)* **1** to pour into, pour upon; **2** to administer to; **3** to shower *(gifts)* upon; **4** to rain *(missiles)* upon; **5** to stretch out *(the body)* upon; **6** to instil *(ideas, feelings)* in **‖** *refl & pass (w. dat)* to spread out on, relax on
infusc·ō -āre -āvī -ātus *tr* to darken, obscure; to stain, corrupt, sully
infūs·us -a -um *pp of* **infundo ‖** *adj* diffused; permeating; fallen *(snow);* crowded; **conjugis infusus gremio** relaxing on the lap of his spouse; **infusis humero capillis** with his hair streaming over his shoulders
ingemin·ō -āre -āvī -ātus *tr* to redouble; to repeat; **ingeminare voces** to call repeatedly; **ignes ingeminare** to flash repeatedly **‖** *intr* to increase in intensity, get worse
ingem·iscō -iscĕre -uī *intr* **(-esc-)** to groan, heave a sigh; *(w. dat or* **in** *+ abl)* to groan over, sigh over
ingem·ō -ĕre -uī *tr* to groan over, sigh over **‖** *intr* to groan, moan; *(w. dat)* to sigh over
ingener·ō -āre -āvī -ātus *tr* to engender, generate, produce; *(fig)* to implant
ingeniāt·us -a -um *adj* naturally endowed, talented
ingeniōsē *adv* ingeniously
ingeniōs·us -a -um *adj* ingenious, clever, talented; *(w. dat or* **ad)** naturally suited to
ingenit·us -a -um *adj* inborn, natural
ingen·ium -(i)ī *n* innate quality; nature, temperament, character; bent, inclination; mood; natural ability, talent, intellect; bright person; gifted writer; skill, ingenuity; clever device
ing·ens -entis *adj* huge, vast; great, mighty, powerful; a great amount of, a great number of; very important, momentous; proud, haughty, heroic *(character); (w. abl)* outstanding in; **ingens pecunia** a lot of money
ingenuē *adv* liberally; frankly
ingenuī *perf of* **ingigno**
ingenuit·ās -ātis *f* noble birth; noble character; frankness
ingenu·us -a -um *adj* native, indigenous; natural; free-born; like a freeman, noble; ingenuous, frank
in·gerō -gerĕre -gessī -gestus *tr* to carry in, throw in, heap; to ingest *(food, drink, esp. in large amounts);* to hurl, shoot *(missiles);* to pour out *(angry words);* to heap *(abuse);* to rain *(blows); (w. dat)* to force *(unwelcome things)* on *(s.o.);* to say repeatedly
in·gignō -gignĕre -genuī -genitus *tr* to cause *(plants)* to grow; *(fig)* to implant *(qualities, etc.)*
inglōri·us -a -um *adj* inglorious, without glory, inconspicuous
ingluvi·ēs -eī *f* crop, maw; gluttony
ingrātē *adv* unpleasantly; unwillingly; ungratefully
ingrātific·us -a -um *adj* ungrateful
ingrātiīs *or* **ingrātīs** *f abl pl* unwillingly, against one's will; against another's will; *(w. gen or poss adj)* against the wishes of
ingrāt·us -a -um *adj* unpleasant, unwelcome; ungrateful; receiving no thanks, unappreciated; thankless
ingravesc·ō -ĕre *intr* to get heavier; to become pregnant; *(of troubles)* to grow worse; to become more serious; to become weary; to become dearer *(in price); (of prices)* to become inflated; to become more important
ingre·dior -dī -ssus sum *tr* to enter; to undertake; to begin; to walk in, follow

(footsteps) ‖ *intr* to go in, enter; to go, walk, walk along; to begin, commence; to begin to speak; *(mil)* to go to the attack; *(w.* **in** + *acc)* **1** to go into, enter; **2** to enter upon, begin, take up, undertake; *(w. dat)* to walk on; **in rem publicam ingredi** to enter politics

ingressi·ō -ōnis *f* entering; walking; gait, pace; beginning

ingress·us -ūs *m* entry; walking; gait; beginning; *(mil)* inroad

ingru·ō -ĕre -ī *intr* to come, come on, rush on; *(of war)* to break out; *(of rain)* to pour down; *(w. dat or* **in** + *acc)* to fall upon, attack

ingu·en -inis *n* groin; swelling, tumor ‖ *npl* private parts

ingurgit·ō -āre -āvī -ātus *tr* to pour in; to gorge, stuff ‖ *refl* to stuff oneself; *(w.* **in** + *acc)* **1** to steep oneself in; **2** to devote oneself to

ingustāt·us -a -um *adj* untasted

inhabil·is -is -e *adj* clumsy, unhandy, unwieldy; *(w. dat or* **ad**) unfit for

inhabitābil·is -is -e *adj* uninhabitable

inhabit·ō -āre -āvī -ātus *tr* to inhabit ‖ *intr* (*w. dat or* **in** + *abl)* to live in

inhae·reō -rēre -sī -sum *intr* to stick, cling, adhere; to be inherent; *(w. dat, w.* **ad** *or* **in** + *acc)* **1** to cling to; **2** to be closely connected with; **3** to gaze upon

inhae·rescō -rescĕre -sī *intr* to begin to stick, become attached; to become stuck; to become fixed *(in the mind)*

inhal·ō -āre -āvī -ātus *tr (w. dat)* to breathe *(e.g., bad breath)* on *(s.o.)*

inhib·eō -ēre -uī -itus *tr* to hold back, curb, check, control; to use, employ, apply; to inflict *(punishment)*; **retro navem** *(or* **navem remis**) **inhibere** to back up the ship ‖ *intr* to row backwards, backwater; **remis inhibere** to backwater

inhibiti·ō -ōnis *f* backing up

inhi·ō -āre -āvī -ātus *tr* to gape at; to pore over; to cast longing eyes at ‖ *intr* to stand open-mouthed, be amazed; *(w. dat)* to be eager for

inhonestē *adv* dishonorably, disgracefully; dishonestly

inhonest·ō -āre -āvī -ātus *tr* to dishonor, disgrace

inhonest·us -a -um *adj* dishonorable, disgraceful, shameful; indecent; ugly, degrading

inhonōr·us -a -um *adj* defaced

inhorr·eō -ēre -uī *intr* to stand on end, bristle

inhorr·escō -escĕre -uī *intr* to stand on end, bristle; to vibrate; to shiver, tremble, shudder

inhospitāl·is -is -e *adj* inhospitable, unfriendly

inhospitālit·ās -ātis *f* inhospitality

inhospit·us -a -um *adj* inhospitable

inhūmānē *adv* inhumanly; rudely; heartlessly

inhūmānit·ās -ātis *f* inhumanity; churlishness; stinginess; heartlessness

inhūmāniter *adv* impolitely; heartlessly

inhūmān·us -a -um *adj* uncivilized; ill-bred, discourteous; heartless, brutal

inhumāt·us -a -um *adj* unburied

inibi *or* **inibī** *adv* there, in that place; near at hand

inimīc·a -ae *f (personal)* enemy *(female)*

inimīcē *adv* with hostility, in an unfriendly way

inimīciti·a -ae *f* unfriendliness, enmity ‖ *fpl* feuds

inimīc·ō -āre -āvī -ātus *tr* to make into enemies, set at odds

inimīc·us -a -um *adj* unfriendly, hostile; harmful ‖ *m (personal)* enemy; **inimicissimus suus** his bitterest *(personal)* enemy ‖ *f (personal)* enemy *(female)*

inīque *adv* unequally, unevenly; unfairly

inīquit·ās -ātis *f* unevenness; inequality; disadvantage; unfairness

inīqu·us -a -um *adj* uneven, unequal; not level, sloping; unfair; adverse, harmful; dangerous, unfavorable; prejudiced; excessive; impatient, discontented; **iniquo animo** impatiently, unwillingly ‖ *m* enemy, foe

initi·ō -āre -āvī -ātus *tr* to initiate, begin; to initiate *(into mysteries)*

init·ium -(i)ī *n* entrance; beginning ‖ *npl* elements; first principles; sacred rites, sacred mysteries

initus *pp of* **ineo**

init·us -ūs *m* entrance; beginning

in·jiciō -jicĕre -jēcī -jectus *tr* to throw, inject; to hurl, discharge *(missiles)*; to impose, apply; to inspire, infuse; to cause, occasion; to furnish *(a cause)*; to bring up, mention *(a name)*; *(w. dat)* to put *(e.g., a cloak)* on *(s.o.)*; **manicas alicui injicere** to put handcuffs on s.o.; **manum injicere** *(w. dat)* **1** to lay hands on; **2** take possession of ‖ *refl (w. dat or* **in** + *acc)* **1** to throw oneself into, rush into, expose oneself to; **2** to fling oneself down on; **3** *(of the mind)* to turn itself to, concentrate on, reflect on

injūcundit·ās -ātis *f* unpleasantness

injūcundius *adv* rather unpleasantly

injūcund·us -a -um *adj* unpleasant

injūdicāt·us -a -um *adj* undecided

injun·gō -gĕre -xī -ctus *tr* to join, attach, fasten; *(w. dat)* **1** to join to, attach to, fasten to; **2** to inflict on; **3** to impose *(e.g., taxes)* on

injūrāt·us -a -um *adj* not under oath

injūri·a -ae *f* injustice, wrong, outrage; insult, affront; harshness, severity; revenge; injury, damage, harm; ill-gotten goods; **injuriā** unjustly, undeservedly, innocently; **per injuriam** unjustly; outrageously

injūriōsē *adv* unjustly, wrongfully

injūriōs·us -a -um *adj* unjust, wrongful; insulting; harmful

injūri·us -a -um *adj* unjust, wrong

injūr·us -a -um *adj* unjust

injussū *(abl only) m* without orders; **injussu meo** without my orders

injuss·us -a -um *adj* unasked, unbidden, voluntary

injustē *adv* unjustly

injustiti·a -ae *f* injustice

injust·us -a -um *adj* unjust

inl- = ill-

inm- = imm-

innābil·is -is -e *adj* unswimmable

in·nascor -nascī -nātus sum *intr (w. dat)* **1** to be born in; **2** *(of plant life)* grow in *or* on; *(w.* **in** + *abl)* **1** to originate in; **2** *(of plant life)* to grow in; **3** *(of minerals)* to occur in, be native to

innat·ō -āre -āvī *tr* to swim **‖** *intr (w. dat)* to swim around in, float on; *(w.* **in** + *acc)* to swim into

innāt·us -a -um *pp of* **innascor ‖** *adj* innate, inborn, natural

innāvigābil·is -is -e *adj* unnavigable

in·nectō -nectěre -nexuī -nexus *tr* to entwine; to tie, fasten together; to join, attach, connect; *(fig)* to devise, invent, plan

innī·tor -tī -xus sum *or* **-sus sum** *intr (w. abl)* to lean on, rest on, be supported by

inn·ō -āre *tr* to swim; to sail, sail over **‖** *intr (w. abl)* **1** to swim in, float on; **2** to sail on; **3** *(of the sea)* to wash against *(a shore)*

innoc·ens -entis *adj* harmless; innocent; upright; unselfish; *(w. gen)* innocent of

innocenter *adv* innocently, blamelessly; harmlessly

innocenti·a -ae *f* innocence; integrity; unselfishness

innocuē *adv* harmlessly; innocently

innocu·us -a -um *adj* harmless, innocuous; innocent; unharmed

innōt·escō -escěre -uī *intr* to become known; to become notorious

innov·ō -āre -āvī -ātus *tr* to renew, restore **‖** *refl (w.* **ad** + *acc)* to return to

innoxi·us -a -um *adj* harmless; safe; innocent; unhurt; *(w. gen)* innocent of

innub·a -ae *adj (fem only)* unmarried

innūbil·us -a -um *adj* cloudless

innū·bō -běre -psī *intr (of a girl) (w. dat)* to marry into *(a family)*

innumerābil·is -is -e *adj* innumerable

innumerābilit·ās -atis *f* countless number

innumerābiliter *adv* in countless ways; countless times

innumerāl·is -is -e *adj* innumerable

innumer·us -a -um *adj* countless

in·nuō -nuěre -nuī -nūtum *intr* to give a nod; *(w. dat)* to nod to

innupt·a -ae *adj (fem only)* unmarried **‖** *f* unmarried girl, maiden

innutr·iō -īre -īvī *or* **-iī -ītus** *tr (w. abl)* to bring up in

Īn·ō -ūs *f* daughter of Cadmus and Harmonia, wife of Athamas and mother of Learchus and Melicertes

inoblīt·us -a -um *adj* unforgetful

inobrut·us -a -um *adj* not overwhelmed

inobservābil·is -is -e *adj* unnoticed

inobservanti·a -ae *f* inattention

inobservāt·us -a -um *adj* unobserved

inoccidu·us -a -um *adj* never setting

inodōr·us -a -um *adj* odorless

inoffens·us -a -um *adj* unobstructed, uninterrupted, unhindered; unimpaired; smooth *(path)*

inofficiōs·us -a -um *adj* irresponsible; unobliging; **testamentum inofficiosum** a will passing over the relatives

inol·ens -entis *adj* odorless

inol·escō -escěre -ēvī *tr* to implant **‖** *intr* to become inveterate; *(w. dat)* to grow in, develop in

inōmināt·us -a -um *adj* ill-starred, inauspicious

inopi·a -ae *f* lack, want, need, poverty; scarcity; helplessness; *(rhet)* barrenness *(of style); (rhet)* lack of subject matter

inopīn·ans -antis *adj* unsuspecting, taken by surprise, off one's guard

inopīnanter *adv* unexpectedly

inopīnātō *adv* unexpectedly, by surprise

inopīnāt·us -a -um *adj* unexpected, unsuspected, surprising **‖** *n* surprise; **ex inopinato** by surprise, unexpectedly

inōpīn·us -a -um *adj* unexpected

inopiōs·us -a -um *adj (hum) (w. gen)* in need of

in·ops -opis *adj* without means *or* resources; poor, needy, destitute; helpless, weak, forlorn; *(rhet)* bald *(style);* poor *(expression);* deficient in vocabulary; pitiful, contemptible; *(w. gen)* destitute of, stripped of, without; *(w. abl)* lacking in, deficient in, poor in

inōrāt·us -a -um *adj* not presented; **re inoratā** without presenting one's case

inordināt·us -a -um *adj* disordered

inornāt·us -a -um *adj* unadorned; unheralded; *(rhet)* plain *(style)*

inp- = imp-

inquam *v defect (the following forms are found: pres:* **inquam, inquis, inquit, inquimus, inquiunt;** *imperfect:* **inquiebat;** *fut:* **inquies, inquiet;** *perfect:* **inquii, inquisti;** *persent subj:* **inquiat;** *impv:* **inque** *or* **inquito)** to say; *(after one or more words of direction quotation, e.g.,*

Desilite, inquit, milites et..."Jump down, fellow soldiers", he says, " and..."); *(in emphatic repetition, e.g.,* **tuas, tuas inquam suspiciones**...your suspicions, yes I say yours...); **inquit** it is said, one says, they say
inqui·ēs -ētis *adj* restless
inquiēt·ō -āre -āvī -ātus *tr* to disquiet, disturb
inquiēt·us -a -um *adj* restless, unsettled
inquilīn·us -ī *m* tenant, lodger
inquinātē *adv* filthily
inquināt·us -a -um *adj* filthy, foul
inquin·ō -āre -āvī -ātus *tr* to mess up, defile, contaminate
inquī·rō -rĕre -sīvī *or* **-siī -sītus** *tr* to search for, inquire into, examine, pry into ‖ *intr* to hold an investigation; to hold a preliminary hearing
inquīsīti·ō -ōnis *f* search, inquiry, investigation; preliminary hearing; *(w. gen)* search for, inquiry into, investigation of
inquīsīt·or -ōris *m* inspector, examiner; spy; *(leg)* investigator
inquīsīt·us -a -um *pp of* **inquiro** ‖ *adj* not investigated, unexamined
inquisīvī *perf of* **inquiro**
inquit *see* **inquam**
inquiunt *see* **inquam**
inr- = irr-
insalūbr·is -is -e *adj* unhealthy, unhealthful
insalūtāt·us -a -um *adj* ungreeted
insānābil·is -is -e *adj* incurable
insānē *adv* insanely, madly
insāni·a -ae *f* insanity, madness, frequency; rapture; mania; excess; **ad insaniam** to the point of madness
insān·iō -īre -īvī *or* **-iī -ītum** *intr* to be insane; to be absurd; to be wild, rave; *(w.* **in** *+ acc)* to be crazy about
insānit·ās -ātis *f* insanity
insānum *adv (coll)* exceedingly, very
insān·us -a -um *adj* insane, crazy; absurd, foolish; excessive, extravagant; monstrous, outrageous; inspired; maddening
insatiābil·is -is -e *adj* insatiable; voracious; that cannot cloy
insatiābiliter *adv* insatiably
insatiet·ās -ātis *f* insatiable desire
insaturābil·is -is -e *adj* insatiable
insaturābiliter *adv* insatiably
inscen·dō -dĕre -dī -sus *tr* to climb up; to get up on *(horse, chariot)* ‖ *intr* to climb up; **in arborem inscendere** to climb a tree; **in currum inscendere** to climb into a chariot; **in navem inscendere** to board a ship
inscensi·ō -ōnis *f* mounting; **in navem inscensio** embarkation
inscensus *pp of* **inscendo**
insci·ens -entis *adj* unaware; silly, ignorant, stupid
inscienter *adv* ignorantly; inadvertently
inscītē *adv* ignorantly, unskillfully
inscīti·a -ae *f* ignorance; inexperience; lack of skill; neglect
inscīt·us -a -um *adj* ignorant; stupid
insci·us -a -um *adj* unaware; ignorant, silly, stupid
inscri·bō -bĕre -psī -ptus *tr* to inscribe; to ascribe; to title *(a book); (w. dat)* **1** to assign, attribute to; **2** to apply to; **3** to address *(a letter)* to; *(w. dat or* **in** *+ abl)* to write *(s.th.)* on *or* in; **aedes venales** *(or* **mercede)** **inscribere** to advertise a house for sale
inscripti·ō -ōnis *f* inscribing; branding *(of slaves);* inscription; title *(of book)*
inscript·us -a -um *pp of* **inscribo** ‖ *adj* unwritten; *(of a book)* entitled ‖ *n* inscription; brand (mark); title *(of a book)*
insculp·ō -ĕre -sī -tus *tr* to cut, carve, engrave; *(w. dat or abl or* **in** *+ abl)* to cut, carve, *or* engrave on; **in animo** *(or* **in mente)** **insculpere** to imprint on the mind
insēdī *perf of* **insideo** *and* **insido**
insectāti·ō -ōnis *f* hot pursuit
insectāt·or -ōris *m* persecutor
insect·or -ārī -ātus sum *or* **insect·ō -āre** *tr* to pursue, chase, attack; to heckle, harrass
insect·us -a -um *adj* indented, notched; **animalia insecta** insects ‖ *n* insect
insecūtus *pp of* **insequor**
insēdābiliter *adv* unquenchably
insen·escō -escĕre -uī *intr (w. dat)* to grow old amidst, grow old over; *(of the moon)* to wane
insensil·is -is -e *adj* imperceptible
insepult·us -a -um *adj* unburied
insequ·ens -entis *adj* next, following, succeeding
inse·quor -quī -cūtus sum *tr* to follow (immediately behind); to succeed, follow up; to attack, go for; to persecute; to catch up with; to reproach; to strive after ‖ *intr* to follow, come next; to pursue the point; *(w. inf)* to proceed to
in·serō -serĕre -sēvī -situs *tr* to sow, plant; to graft on *(a cutting);* to graft a cutting on *(a tree); (lit & fig)* to implant; **singulos hortos cujusque generis surculis serere** to plant each garden with one kind of cutting
inser·ō -ĕre -uī -tus *tr* to insert; to introduce; to include *(in a book, speech);* to involve; to join, enroll, associate; to mingle, blend; **manūs inserere** *(w. dat)* to lay hands on, seize; **oculos inserere** *(w.* **in** *+ abl)* to look into *(e.g., s.o.'s heart)*
insert·ō -āre -āvī -ātus *tr* to insert
inserv·iō -īre -īvī *or* **-iī -ītus** *tr* to serve, obey ‖ *intr* to be a slave, be a subject; *(w. dat)* **1** to serve, be subservient to; **2** to be

subject to; **3** to be devoted to; **4** to pay attention to

insessus *pp of* **insideo** *and* **insido**

insēvī *perf of* **insero** (to plant)

insībil·ō -āre -āvī -ātum *intr (of the wind)* to whistle

in·sideō -sidēre -sēdī -sessus *tr* to hold, occupy **‖** *intr* to sit down; to settle down; to be deep-seated; *(w. abl or* **in** + *abl)* **1** to sit on; **2** to settle down on *or* in; **3** *(fig)* to be fixed in, be stamped in

insidi·ae -ārum *fpl* ambush; plot, trap; **insidias dare** *(or* **collocare** *or* **parare** *or* **struere)** *(w. dat)* to lay a trap for

insidiāt·or -ōris *m* soldier in ambush; *(fig)* plotter, subversive

insidi·or -ārī -ātus sum *intr (w. dat)* **1** to lie in wait for; **2** to plot against; **3** to watch for, be on the lookout for *(e.g., opportunity)*

insidiōsē *adv* insidiously, by underhand means

in·sīdō -sīděre -sēdī -sessus *tr* to occupy, keep possession of, possess **‖** *intr* to sink in, penetrate; *(of diseases)* to become deep-seated; *(w. dat)* to settle in *or* on; *(w.* **in** + *abl)* to become fixed in, become imbedded in

insign·e -is *n (s.th. worn or carried as an indication of rank or status)* insignia, mark; coat of arms; signal; honor, distinction; brilliant passage, gem; *(mil)* decoration, medal **‖** *npl* insignia, regalia, uniform; outer trappings

insign·iō -īre -īvī *or* **-iī -ītus** *tr* to make conspicuous, distinguish, mark

insign·is -is -e *adj* conspicuous, distinguished; prominent, eminent, extraordinary, singular

insignītē *adv* notably, extraordinarily

insigniter *adv* remarkably

insignīt·us -a -um *adj* marked, conspicuous, clear, glaring; distinguished, striking, notable

insil·ia -ium *npl* treadle *(of a loom)*

insil·iō -īre -uī *or* **-īvī** *tr* to jump up on, mount **‖** *intr (w. dat)* to jump on; *(w.* **in** + *acc)* **1** to jump into *or* on(to); **2** to mount; **3** to climb aboard

insimulāti·ō -ōnis *f* allegation *(of a crime);* charge, accusation

insimul·ō -āre -āvī -ātus *tr* to allege; to charge, accuse

insincēr·us -a -um *adj* adulterated; not genuine, insincere

insinuāti·ō -ōnis *f (rhet)* winning sympathy *(in a speech)*

insinu·ō -āre -āvī -ātus *tr* to bring in secretly, sneak in **‖** *refl (w.* **inter** + *acc)* to wriggle in between, work one's way between *or* among; **se insinuare in familiaritatem** *(w. gen)* to ingratiate oneself with

insipi·ens -entis *adj* foolish

insipienter *adv* foolishly

insipienti·a -ae *f* foolishness

in·sistō -sistěre -stitī *tr* to stand on, trample on; to set about, keep at *(a task, etc.);* to follow, chase after; **iter** *(or* **viam)** **insistere** to pursue a course **‖** *intr* to stand, stop, come to a stop; to pause; *(w. dat)* **1** to tread on the heels of, pursue closely; **2** to press on with; **3** to dwell upon; *(w. dat or* **in** + *abl)* to persist in; *(w.* **ad** *or* **in** + *acc)* **1** to keep at, keep after, keep the pressure on; **2** pursue vigorously

insiti·ō -ōnis *f* grafting; grafting time

insitīv·us -a -um *adj* grafted; *(fig)* spurious

insit·or -ōris *m* grafter *(of trees)*

insit·us -a -um *pp of* **insero ‖** *adj* inborn, innate; incorporated

insociābil·is -is -e *adj* incompatible

insōlābiliter *adv* unconsolably

insol·ens -entis *adj* unaccustomed, unusual; immoderate, excessive; extravagant; insolent; *(w. gen or* **in** + *abl)* **1** unaccustomed to; **2** inexperienced in; **in aliena re insolens** free with someone else's money

insolenter *adv* unusually; excessively; insolently

insolenti·a -ae *f* unusualness, novelty, strangeness, inexperience; affectation; insolence, arrogance

insolesc·ō -ěre *intr* to become proud, become insolent; to become elated

insolid·us -a -um *adj* soft

insolit·us -a -um *adj* unaccustomed; inexperienced; unusual, strange, uncommon **‖** *n* the unusual

insomni·a -ae *f* insomnia

insomn·is -is -e *adj* sleepless

insomn·ium -(i)ī *n* sleeplessness; dream; vision in a dream *or* trance

inson·ō -āre -uī *intr* to make noise; to sound, resound, roar; **calamis insonare** to play the reed pipe; **flagello insonare** to crack the whip; **pennis insonare** to flap the wings

ins·ons -ontis *adj* innocent; harmless

insōpīt·us -a -um *adj* sleepless

insop·or -ōris *adj* sleepless

inspeciōs·us -a -um *adj* homely

inspecti·ō -ōnis *f* inspection

inspect·ō -āre -āvī -ātus *tr* to look at, view, observe, examine **‖** *intr* to look on; **inspectante Roscio** with Roscius looking on, under the eyes of Roscius

inspectus *pp of* **inspicio**

inspēr·ans -antis *adj* not hoping, not expecting

inspērāt·us -a -um *adj* unhoped for, unexpected, unforeseen; unwelcome; **(ex) insperato** unexpectedly

insper·gō -gĕre -sī -sus *tr* to sprinkle on
in·spiciō -spicĕre -spexī -spectus *tr* to inspect, look into, examine; to look at, watch; to consider; to comprehend, grasp; to investigate; to look at, consult *(books);* to look into *(the mirror)* ‖ *intr (w.* **in** + *acc)* to look into
inspīc·ō -āre -āvī -ātus *tr* to make pointed
inspīr·ō -āre -āvī -ātus *tr* to inspire, infuse, enkindle ‖ *intr (w. dat)* to blow on, breathe on
inspoliāt·us -a -um *adj* undespoiled
insp·uō -uĕre -uī -ūtus *tr* to spit on ‖ *intr (w. dat)* to spit on
inspūt·ō -āre -āvī -ātus *tr* to spit on
instābil·is -is -e *adj* unstable, unsteady; not remaining still; *(fig)* changeable
inst·ans -antis *adj* present; immediate, threatening, urgent
instanter *adv* vehemently, insistently
instanti·a -ae *f* presence; earnestness, insistence; concentration
instar *indecl n* image, likeness, appearance, resemblance; *(w. gen)* like, equal to, as large as, worth, as good as; **ad instar** *(w. gen)* according to the standard of
instaurāti·ō -ōnis *f* renewal, repetition
instaurātīv·us -a -um *adj* begun anew, repeated
instaur·ō -āre -āvī -ātus *tr* to set up; to renew, repeat, start all over again *(esp. games and celebrations because of alleged bad omens in the initial event);* to repay, requite
in·sternō -sternĕre -strāvī -strātus *tr* to cover; to lay *(a floor, deck)*
instīgāt·or -ōris *m*, **instīgātr·ix -īcis** *f* instigator, ringleader
instīg·ō -āre -āvī -ātus *tr* to instigate, goad on, stimulate, incite
instill·ō -āre -āvī -ātus *tr (w. dat)* to pour *(s.th.)* on, instill *(s.th.)* in
instimulāt·or -ōris *m* instigator
instimul·ō -āre -āvī -ātus *tr* to stimulate, urge on, goad on
instinct·or -ōris *m* instigator
instinct·us -a -um *adj* aroused, fired up; infuriated; inspired
instipul·or -ārī -ātus sum *intr* to bargain
instit·a -ae *f* border, flounce; band, ribbon; *(fig)* lady
institī *perf of* **insisto** *and* **insto**
institi·ō -ōnis *f* standing still
instit·or -ōris *m* salesman, huckster
instit·uō -uĕre -uī -ūtus *tr* to set, fix, plant; to set up, erect, establish; to arrange; to build, make, construct; to prepare; to provide, furnish; to institute, organize, set up; to appoint, designate; to undertake, begin; to control, direct, govern; to teach, train, instruct, educate; *(w. inf)* to decide to
institūti·ō -ōnis *f* arrangement; custom; instruction, education; **morum institutio** established custom ‖ *fpl* principles of education
institūt·um -ī *n* plan, program; practice, custom, usage; precedent; principle; decree, regulation, stipulation, terms; purpose, intention; **ex instituto** according to custom, by convention ‖ *npl* teachings, precepts, principles of education
in·stō -stāre -stitī *tr* to follow, pursue; to work hard at; to menace, threaten ‖ *intr* to be at hand, approach, be impending; to insist; *(w. dat or* **in** + *abl)* to stand on *or* in; *(w. dat)* **1** to be close to; **2** to be on the heels of, pursue closely; **3** to harass
instrātus *pp of* **insterno**
instrāvī *perf of* **insterno**
instrēnu·us -a -um *adj* lethargic
instrēp·ō -āre -uī -itum *intr* to creak, rattle
instructi·ō -ōnis *f* construction; array, formation; instruction
instructius *adv* with better preparation
instruct·or -ōris *m* supervisor; preparer
instruct·us -a -um *pp of* **instruo** ‖ *adj* equipped, furnished; prepared, arranged; instructed, versed
instruct·us -ūs *m* equipment; *(rhet)* stock-in-trade *(of an orator)*
instrūment·um -ī *n* instrument, tool, utensil; equipment; dress, outfit; repertory, stock-in-trade; means, supply, provisions; *(leg)* document, deed, instrument
instru·ō -ĕre -xī -ctus *tr* to build up, construct; to furnish, prepare, provide, fit out; to instruct; *(mil)* to deploy
insuās·um -ī *n* dark-orange color
insuāv·is -is -e *adj* unpleasant, disagreeable
insūd·ō -āre -āvī *intr* to sweat, break a sweat; *(w. dat)* to drip sweat on
insuēfact·us -a -um *adj* accustomed
insu·escō -escĕre -ēvī -ētus *tr* to accustom, familiarize ‖ *intr (w. dat, w.* **ad** *or w. inf)* to get used to
insuēt·us -a -um *adj* unusual; *(w. gen or dat, w.* **ad** *or w. inf)* unused to
insuēvī *perf of* **insuesco**
insul·a -ae *f* island; apartment building
insulān·us -ī *m* islander
insulār·ius -(i)ī *m* superintendent *(of an apartment building)*
insulsē *adv* in poor taste; insipidly, absurdly
insulsit·ās -ātis *f* lack of taste; silliness, absurdity
insuls·us -a -um *adj* unsalted, without taste; coarse, tasteless, insipid; silly, absurd; bungling ‖ *fpl* silly creatures *(i.e., women)*
insult·ō -āre -āvī -ātus *tr* to insult, scoff at, taunt; *(of votaries)* to dance about in

‖ *intr* to jump, gambol, prance; to gloat; *(w. abl)* 1 to jump in, cavort in, gambol on, jump upon; 2 to gloat over; *(w. dat or* **in** + *acc)* 1 to scoff at; 2 to gloat over

insultūr·a -ae *f* jumping on *or* in

in·sum -esse -fuī *intr* to be there, exist; *(w. dat or* **in** + *acc)* 1 to be in, be on; 2 to be implied in, be contained in, belong to

insūm·ō -ĕre -psī -ptus *tr* to spend, devote, waste; *(w. dat or* **in** + *acc)* to devote to, apply to; *(w. abl or* **in** + *abl)* to expend on; **operam insumere** *(w. dat)* to devote effort to, waste effort on

in·suō -suĕre -suī -sūtus *tr* to sew up; *(w. dat)* 1 to sew up in; 2 to embroider *(s.th.)* on

insuper *adv* above, overhead, on top; from above; moreover, besides, in addition ‖ *prep (w. acc)* above, over, over and above; *(w. abl)* in addition to, besides

insuperābil·is -is -e *adj* insurmountable; unconquerable

insur·gō -gĕre -rexī -rectum *intr* to rise, stand up, stand high, tower; to rise, increase, grow, grow intense; to rise to power; *(of language)* to soar; *(w. dat)* 1 to rise up against; 2 to strain at *(e.g., oars)*

insusurr·ō -āre -āvī -ātus *tr (w. dat)* to whisper *(s.th.)* to; **insusurrare in aurem** *(w. gen)* to whisper in *(s.o.'s)* ear; **sibi cantilenam insusurrare** to hum a tune to oneself ‖ *intr* to whisper; *(of wind)* to blow gently

intāb·escō -escĕre -uī *intr* to melt away gradually, dissolve gradually; *(fig)* to waste away, pine away

intactil·is -is -e *adj* intangible

intact·us -a -um *adj* untouched; uninjured, intact; unpolluted; untried; unmarried, virgin, chaste

intact·us -ūs *m* intangibility

intāmināt·us -a -um *adj* unsullied

intect·us -a -um *pp of* **intego** ‖ *adj* uncovered; naked; open, frank

integell·us -a -um *adj* fairly pure *or* chaste; in fair condition

inte·ger -gra -grum *adj* whole, complete, intact; unhurt, unwounded; healthy, sound; new; fresh; pure, chaste; untouched, unaffected; unbiased; unattempted; unconquered; unbroken *(horse);* not worn, unused; inexperienced; virtuous, honest, blameless; healthy, sane; *(mil)* having suffered no losses; **ab** *(or* **de** *or* **ex) integro** anew, all over again; **in integrum restituere** to restore to a former condition; to pardon; **integrum alicui esse** *(w. inf)* to be in someone's power to

inte·gō -gĕre -xī -ctus *tr* to cover up; to protect

integrasc·ō -ĕre *intr* to start all over again

integrāti·ō -ōnis *f* renewal, new beginning

integrē *adv* wholly, entirely; honestly; correctly

integrit·ās -ātis *f* soundness; integrity; innocence; purity, chastity

integr·ō -āre -āvī -ātus *tr* to make whole; to heal, repair; to renew, begin again; to refresh, reinvigorate

integument·um -ī *n* covering; lid; wrapping; protection

intellectus *pp of* **intellego**

intellect·us -ūs *m* intellect; perception; comprehension, understanding

intelleg·ens -entis *adj* intelligent; *(w. gen)* appreciative of; *(w.* **in** + *abl)* versed in

intellegenter *adv* intelligently

intellegenti·a -ae *f* intelligence; understanding, knowledge; perception, judgment, discrimination, taste; skill; concept, notion; *(w. gen)* knowledge of, understanding of; *(w.* **in** + *abl)* judgment in

intelle·gō -gĕre -xī -ctus *tr* to understand, perceive, comprehend; to realize, recognize; to have an accurate knowledge of, be an expert in ‖ *intr (in answers)* I understand, I get it

intemerāt·us -a -um *adj* undefiled, pure, chaste; pure, undiluted

intemper·ans -antis *adj* intemperate, without restraint; lewd

intemperanter *adv* intemperately

intemperanti·a -ae *f* intemperance, lack of self-control; extravagance; *(w. gen)* unrestrained use of

intemperāri·ae -ārum *fpl* wild outbursts; wildness

intemperātē *adv* intemperately

intemperāt·us -a -um *adj* excessive

intemperi·ēs -ēī *f* wildness, excess; outrageous conduct, excesses; **intemperies aquarum** heavy rain; **intemperies caeli** stormy weather

intempestīvē *adv* at a bad time, at the wrong time

intempestīv·us -a -um *adj* untimely; unseasonable *(weather);* poorly timed

intempest·us -a -um *adj* unseasonable; dark, dismal; unhealthy; **nox intempesta** dead of night

intemptāt·us -a -um *adj* **(-tent-)** unattempted, untried

inten·dō -dĕre -dī -tus *or* **-sus** *tr* to stretch, stretch out, extend, spread out; to stretch, bend *(e.g., a bow);* to aim, shoot *(weapon);* to spread *(sails); (of winds)* to fill *(sails);* to cover *(e.g., with festoons);* to increase, magnify, intensify; to intend; to urge, incite; to aim at, intend; to assert, maintain; to raise *(voice);* to stretch *(truth);* to direct, turn, focus *(mind, attention);* to pitch *(tent);* **cursum** *(or* **iter) intendere** to direct one's course

‖ *intr (w.* **in** + *acc)* **1** to direct one's effort to, apply oneself to; **2** to turn to
intentātus *see* **intemptatus**
intentē *adv* intently, attentively
intenti·ō -ōnis *f* stretching, straining; tension, tautness; attention; effort, exertion; aim, intention; accusation; *(leg)* statement of the charge
intent·ō -āre -āvī -ātus *tr* to stretch out; to aim, direct; to threaten; to brandish threateningly; **manūs intentare** to shake hands; **oculos intentare** to fix one's gaze *(on)*
intent·us -a -um *pp of* **intendo** ‖ *adj* tense, taut; intent, attentive; eager; tense, nervous; strict *(discipline);* vigorous *(speech)*
intent·us -ūs *m* stretching out, extending *(of the palms)*
intep·eō -ēre -uī *intr* to be lukewarm
intep·escō -escĕre -uī *intr* to get warm, be warmed
inter *prep (w. acc)* **1** between, among, amidst; **2** during, within, in the course of; **inter cenam** during dinner; **inter haec** during these events, in the meantime; **inter talia opera** during such frenetic activites; **3** *(in classifying)* among, in, with; **inter se** each other, one another, mutually
inter- *pref* with one of the senses of the preposition
interaestu·ō -āre *intr* to retch
interāment·a -ōrum *npl* framework of a ship
Interamn·a -ae *f* town in Latium on the Liris River ‖ town in Umbria, birthplace of Tacitus
interāresc·ō -ĕre *intr* to dry up
interātim *adv* meanwhile
interbib·ō -ĕre *tr* to drink up
interbīt·ō -ĕre *intr* to come to nothing
intercalār·is -is -e *adj* intercalary, added *(to the calendar)*
intercal·ō -āre -āvī -ātus *tr* to intercalate, add *(to the calendar)*
intercapēd·ō -inis *f* interruption, break, pause
inter·cēdō -cēdĕre -cessī -cessum *intr* to come *or* go in between; *(of time)* to intervene, pass, occur; to act as an intermediary; to intercede; *(of tribunes)* to exercise the veto; *(w. dat)* **1** to veto, protest against; **2** to interfere with, obstruct, hinder
intercepti·ō -ōnis *f* interception
intercept·or -ōris *m* embezzler
interceptus *pp of* **intercipio**
intercessi·ō -ōnis *f* intercession, mediation; *(tribune's)* veto
inter·cĭdō -cidĕre -cĭdī *intr* to fall short, miss the mark; to happen in the meantime; to drop out, be lost
inter·cīdō -cīdĕre -cīdī -cīsus *tr* to cut through, sever; to cut off, cut short; to cut the seals of, tamper with *(documents)*
intercin·ō -ĕre *tr* to interrupt with song *or* music
inter·cipiō -cipĕre -cēpī -ceptus *tr* to intercept; to trap *(animals);* to draw *(water illegally from the aqueduct);* to steal, usurp *(rights, honors);* to interrupt, cut off, cut short *(a conversation)*; to appropriate; to misappropriate; to receive by mistake *(e.g., poison); (mil)* to cut off *(the enemy); (mil)* to capture; *(mil)* to be struck by *(e.g., spear intended for another)*
intercīsē *adv* piecemeal
intercīsus *pp of* **intercido**
interclū·dō -dĕre -sī -sus *tr* to shut off, shut out, cut off; to stop, block up; to hinder, prevent; to blockade, shut in; to cut off, intercept; to separate, divide
interclūsi·ō -ōnis *f* stopping; parenthetical matter; **animae interclusio** shortwindedness
interclūsus *pp of* **intercludo**
intercolumn·ium -(i)ī *n* space between columns, intercolumniation
inter·currō -currĕre -cucurrī -cursum *intr* to intervene, mediate; to mingle; to rush in
intercurs·ō -āre -āvī -ātum *intr* to crisscross; **inter se intercursare** to crisscross each other
intercurs·us -ūs *m* intervention
interc·us -utis *adj* between the skin and flesh; **aqua intercus** dropsy
inter·dīcō -dīcĕre -dixī -dictus *tr* to forbid, prohibit ‖ *intr* to issue a prohibition, issue an injunction; **aquā et igni interdicere** *(w. dat)* to outlaw *(s.o.),* banish *(s.o.) (literally, to prohibit s.o. from receiving water and fire)*
interdicti·ō -ōnis *f* prohibiting; **aquae et igni interdictio** banishment
interdict·um -ī *n* prohibition; contraband; injunction *(by praetor or promagistrate)*
interdictus *pp of* **interdico**
interdiū *or* **interdiūs** *adv* by day, in the daytime
interdixī *perf of* **interdico**
inter·dō -dăre -dedī -datus *tr* (**·duō**) to place between, place at intervals, interpose; **ciccum** *(or* **floccum** *or* **nihil)** **interduim** *(sl)* I don't give a hoot
interduct·us -ūs *m* punctuation
interdum *adv* sometimes, now and then, occasionally; meanwhile
interdu·ō *see* **interdo**
intereā *adv* meanwhile, in the interim; anyhow, nevertheless
interemptus *pp of* **interimo**
inter·eō -īre -iī -itum *intr* to die; to be

done for, be finished, perish, be lost; to become extinct

interequit·ō -āre -āvī -ātus *tr* to ride between *(e.g., the ranks or columns)* ‖ *intr* to ride *(on horseback)* in between

interfāti·ō -ōnis *f* interruption

interfecti·ō -ōnis *f* killing

interfect·or -ōris *m*, **interfectr·ix -īcis** *f* killer, murderer

inter·ficiō -ficĕre -fēcī -fectus *tr* to kill; to destroy

inter·fīō -fierī *intr* to be destroyed

inter·fluō -fluĕre -flūxī *tr* to flow between ‖ *intr* to flow in between

inter·fodiō -fodĕre -fōdī -fossus *tr* to pierce, penetrate

interf·or -ārī -ātus sum *tr & intr* to interrupt

interfug·iō -ĕre *intr* to slip in between

interfulg·eō -ēre *intr (w. abl)* to shine amid *or* among

interfūs·us -a -um *adj* spread here and there; *(w. acc)* flowing between

interibi *adv* in the meantime

interim *adv* meanwhile; for the moment; sometimes; however, anyhow

inter·imō -imĕre -ēmī -emptus *tr* to do away with, abolish; to kill

interi·or -or -us *adj* inner, interior; internal; inner side of; more remote *(places, peoples, esp. far from the seacoast);* secret, private; deeper, more profound; more intimate, more personal, more confidential

interiti·ō -ōnis *f* ruin, destruction; *(violent or untimely)* death

interit·us -ūs *m* ruin; *(violent or untimely)* death; dissolution *(of institutions, society, material things);* extinction

interius *adv* on the inside; inwardly; in the middle; too short; *(to listen)* closely; more deeply

interjac·eō -ēre *intr (w. dat)* to lie between

interjaciō *see* **interjicio**

interjecti·ō -ōnis *f (gram)* interjection; *(rhet)* parenthetical remark *or* phrase

interject·us -a -um *pp of* **interjicio** ‖ *adj (w. dat or* **inter** *+ acc)* set *or* lying between

interject·us -ūs *m* interposition; interval

inter·jiciō -jicĕre -jēcī -jectus *tr* to interpose; *(w. dat or* **inter** *+ acc)* **1** to throw *or* set *(s.th.)* between; **2** to intermingle *(s.th.)* with, intermix *(s.th.)* with

interjun·gō -gĕre -xī -ctus *tr* to join together; to clasp

inter·lābor -lābī -lapsus sum *intr* to glide in between, flow in between

inter·legō -legĕre -lēgī -lectus *tr* to pick *or* pluck here and there

inter·linō -linĕre -lēvī -litus *tr* to smear; to daub in the gaps *(of a structure);* to tamper with *(a document to falsify it)*

interlo·quor -quī -cūtus sum *intr* to interrupt

interlū·ceō -ēre -xī *intr* to shine through; to be lightning now and then; to be transparent; to be plainly visible

interlūni·a -ōrum *npl* new moon

interlu·ō -ĕre *tr* to flow between; to wash

intermenstru·us -a -um *adj* of the new moon ‖ *n* new moon

interminät·us -a -um *adj* endless

intermin·or -ārī -ātus sum *tr (w. dat)* to threaten *(s.o.)* with *(s.th.)* ‖ *intr* to threaten

inter·misceō -miscēre -miscuī -mixtus *tr* to intermingle

intermissi·ō -ōnis *f* intermission, pause, interruption; interval of time; *(leg)* adjournment

inter·mittō -mittĕre -mīsī -missus *tr* to interrupt, break off, suspend; to omit, neglect; to leave gaps in, leave unoccupied, leave undefended; to allow *(time)* to pass ‖ *intr* to pause, stop

intermixtus *pp of* **intermisceo**

inter·morior -morī -mortuus sum *intr* to die suddenly; to faint

intermortu·us -a -um *adj* dead; unconscious; *(fig)* half-dead

intermundi·a -ōrum *npl* outer space

intermūrāl·is -is -e *adj* intermural, between two walls

internāt·us -a -um *adj (w. dat)* growing among *or* between

internecīn·us -a -um *adj* internecine, exterminating, of extermination

interneci·ō -ōnis *f* massacre

internecīv·us -a -um *adj* exterminating; **bellum internecivum** war of extermination

internec·ō -āre -āvī -ātus *tr* to exterminate

internect·ō -ĕre *tr* to intertwine

internit·eō -ēre *intr* to shine out

internōd·ium -(i)ī *n (anat)* space between two joints

inter·noscō -noscĕre -nōvī -nōtus *tr* to distinguish, pick out; *(w.* **ab***)* to distinguish *(one thing)* from *(another)*

internunti·ō -āre *intr* to exchange messages

internunt·ius -(i)ī *m*, **internunti·a -ae** *f* messenger, courier; mediator, go-between

intern·us -a -um *adj* internal; civil, domestic

in·terō -terĕre -trīvī -trītus *tr* to rub in; to crumble up

interpellāti·ō -ōnis *f* interruption

interpellāt·or -ōris *m* interrupter; petitioner

interpell·ō -āre -āvī -ātus *tr* to interrupt, break in on; to disturb, obstruct; to raise an objection; to accost with a request

interpol·is -is -e *adj* patched up, touched up, made like new

interpol·ō -āre -āvī -ātus *tr* to refurbish, touch up; to make like new

inter·pōnō -pōnere -posuī -positus *tr* to insert, interpose, intersperse; to add as an ingredient; to include *(in a speeech or book);* to introduce, bring into play; to introduce as witness *or* participant; to admit *(a person);* to let *(time)* pass; to alter, falsify *(writings);* to allege, use as a pretext; *(w.* **inter** *+ acc)* to place between; **auctoritatem interponere** to assert one's authority, exert one's influence; **fidem interponere** to give one's one's word; **fidem suam in eam rem interponere** to give his word in that matter; **operam** *(or* **studium) interponere** to apply effort ‖ *refl* to interfere; to intervene in order to veto; *(w. dat or* **in** *+ acc)* to interfere with, meddle with, get mixed up with ‖ *pass (of time)* to elapse in the meantime, intervene; to lie between; *(of writing)* to contain insertions

interpositi·ō -ōnis *f* insertion; introduction; inclusion; parenthetical statement

interpositus *pp of* **interpono**

interposit·us -ūs *m* interposition

interpr·es -etis *mf* mediator, negotiator; middleman, broker; interpreter; expounder; translator

interpretāti·ō -ōnis *f* interpretation, explanation; meaning; translation

interpret·or -ārī -ātus sum *tr* to interpret, construe; to infer, conclude; to decide; to translate

inter·primō -primere -pressī -pressus *tr* to squeeze; **fauces interprimere** to choke

interpuncti·ō -ōnis *f* punctuation

interpunct·um -ī *n* pause *(between words and sentences);* punctuation mark

interpunct·us -a -um *adj* well-divided; *(w. abl)* interspersed with

interpun·gō -gere -xī -ctus *tr* to divide *(words)* with punctuation, punctuate; to intersperse

interqui·escō -escere -ēvī *intr* to rest awhile; to pause awhile

interregn·um -ī *n* interregnum *(time between the death of one king and election of another or similar interval between consuls)*

inter·rex -rēgis *m* interrex, regent

interrit·us -a -um *adj* undaunted

interrogāti·ō -ōnis *f* question; interrogation, cross-examination; argument developed by question and answer

interrogāt·um -ī *n* question; **ad interrogatum respondere** to answer the question

interrog·ō -āre -āvī -ātus *tr* to ask, question; to interrogate, cross-examine; to sue; to seek information from; **casus interrogandi** *(gram)* genitive case; **sententiam interrogare** to ask *(a senator's)* opinion; **lege** *(or* **legibus) interrogare** *(leg)* to arraign, indict ‖ *intr* to ask a question, ask questions; to argue, reason

interrumpō interrumpere interrūpī interruptus *tr* to break apart, break in half; to break up, smash; to divide, scatter; to interrupt, break off

interruptē *adv* with interruptions

interruptus *pp of* **interrumpo**

intersaep·iō -īre -sī -tus *tr* to fence off, enclose; to stop up, close, cut off

inter·scindō -scindere -scidī -scissus *tr* to tear apart, tear down; to cut off, separate

interscrī·bō -bere -psī -ptus *tr* to write *(s.th.)* in between

interser·ō -ere -uī *tr* to interpose; to allege as an excuse

interspīrāti·ō -ōnis *f (rhet)* breathing pause, correct breathing *(in delivering a speech)*

interstinct·us -a -um *adj* blotchy

interstin·guō -guere -xī -ctus *tr* to spot, blotch; to extinguish

interstring·ō -ere *tr* to strangle

inter·sum -esse -fuī *intr* to be present, assist, take part; to differ; to be of interest; *(w. dat)* 1 to be present at, attend; 2 take part in; *(w.* **in** *+ acc)* to be present at ‖ *v impers* there is a difference; it makes a difference; it is of importance; it is of interest; *(w.* **inter** *+ acc or* **in** *+ abl)* there is a difference between; *(w. gen or with fem of poss pronouns* **meā, tuā, nostrā,** *etc.)* it makes a difference to, it is of importance to, it concerns (me, you, us, etc.); *(w. gen of value, e.g.,* **magni, permagni, tanti,** *or w. adv* **multum, plurimum, maxime)** it makes a (great, very great, such a great) difference, it is of (great, very great, such great) concern; **ne minimum quidem interest** there is not the slightest difference; **nihil omnino interest** there is no difference whatever

intertext·us -a -um *adj* interwoven

intertra·hō -here -xī -ctus *tr (w. dat)* to take *(s.th.)* away from

intertrīment·um -ī *n* wear and tear; loss, wastage

interturbāti·ō -ōnis *f* confusion, turmoil

interturb·ō -āre -āvī *tr* to confuse

intervall·um -ī *n* interval, space, distance; gap, opening; interval of time, spell; pause; break, intermission; contrast, difference *(in degree, quality, etc.);* **ex intervallo** at *or* from a distance; after a while; at intervals; **ex intervallis** at intervals; **longo intervallo** after a long while, much later;

per intervallum *(or* intervalla) at intervals

inter·vellō -vellĕre -vulsī -vulsus *tr* to pluck here and there

inter·veniō -venīre -vēnī -ventus *tr* to interfere with ‖ *intr* to happen along, come on the scene; to intervene, intrude; to happen, crop up; *(w. dat)* to interfere with, interrupt, put a stop to, come in the way of, oppose, prevent

intervent·or -ōris *m* intruder, untimely visitor

intervent·us -ūs *m* intervention; intrusion; mediation

interver·tō -tĕre -tī -sus *tr* **(-vort-)** to divert, embezzle

intervīs·ō -ĕre -ī -us *tr* to drop in on; to visit from time to time

intervolit·ō -āre -āvī *intr* to flit about

intervom·ō -ĕre -uī -itus *tr (w.* **inter** *+ acc)* to throw up amongst

intervulsus *pp of* **intervello**

intestābil·is -is -e *adj* infamous, notorious; detestable, shameful

intestātō *adv* intestate

intestāt·us -a -um *adj* intestate; unconvicted by witnesses

intestīn·us -a -um *adj* internal ‖ *n* alimentary canal; intestine; **intestinum tenue** small intestine

intexī *perf of* **intego**

intex·ō -ĕre -uī -tus *tr* to interweave, interlace; to weave; to embroider; to surround, envelop

intib·um -ī *n* **(inty-)** endive

intimē *adv* intimately, cordially

intim·us -a -um *adj* **(-tum-)** innermost; deepest, most abstruse, most profound; most secret, most intimate ‖ *m* close friend

intin·gō -gĕre -xī -ctus *tr* to dip, soak; to color *(w. cosmetics)*

intolerābil·is -is -e *adj* intolerable; irresistible

intolerand·us -a -um *adj* intolerable

intoler·ans -antis *adj* intolerable; *(w. gen)* unable to stand, unable to put up with

intoleranter *adv* intolerably, immoderately, excessively

intoleranti·a -ae *f* impatience

inton·ō -āre -uī -itus *tr* to thunder forth ‖ *intr* to thunder

intons·us -a -um *adj* unshorn, untrimmed; long-haired; rude

intor·queō -quēre -sī -tus *tr* to twist, turn, roll; *(w.* **circum** *+ acc)* to wrap *(s.th.)* around; *(w. dat or* **in** *+ acc)* to hurl *(e.g., spear)* at

intort·us -a -um *adj* twisted; tangled; *(fig)* crooked

intrā *adv* on the inside, inside, within; inward

intrā *prep (w. acc)* **1** inside, within; **intra parietes** within the walls, at home, privately; **intra se** to oneself, privately; by oneself, alone; in one's own country, at home; **2** inside *(a period of time)*, within, during, in the course of, in less than; **intra hos dies** within these (last few) days; **3** within the limits of, without passing beyond, on this side of, short of *(a certain point)*; **modice hoc facere aut etiam intra modum** to do this with moderation and even keep on the safe side of moderation; **intra teli jactum progredi** to come within range; **intra (et) extra** inside and out, on both sides

intrābil·is -is -e *adj* approachable

intractābil·is -is -e *adj* intractable, unmanageable; formidable

intractāt·us -a -um *adj* untamed; unbroken *(horse)*; unattempted

intrem·iscō -iscĕre -uī *intr* to begin to tremble

intrem·ō -ĕre -uī *intr* to shake, tremble, shiver

intrepidē *adv* calmly, intrepidly

intrepid·us -a -um *adj* calm, intrepid, not nervous; untroubled

intrīc·ō -āre -āvī -ātus *tr* to entangle, involve

intrinsecus *adv (opp:* **extrinsecus)** on the inside; to the inside, inwards

intrīt·us -a -um *adj* not worn away; *(fig)* not worn out

intrō *adv* inwards, inside, in

intr·ō -āre -āvī -ātus *tr & intr* to enter; to penetrate

intrōdū·cō -cĕre -xī -ctus *tr* to bring in, lead in; to introduce; to raise *(a subject, point)*

intrōducti·ō -ōnis *f* introduction

intrō·eō -īre -īvī *or* **-iī -itum** *tr & intr* to enter

intrō·ferō -ferre -tulī -lātus *tr* to carry in; *(w.* **in** *+ acc)* to carry into; **pedem introferre** *(w.* **in** *+ acc)* to set foot in

intrō·gredior -gredī -gressus sum *intr* to step inside

introit·us -ūs *m* entrance; hostile entry; invasion; beginning, prelude

intrōlātus *pp of* **introfero**

intrō·mittō -mittĕre -mīsī -missus *tr* to let in, admit; to send in; to introduce

introrsum *adv* **(-sus)** inwards, towards the inside; *(fig)* inwardly

intrō·rumpō -rumpĕre -rūpī -ruptus *tr* to break in, enter by force

intrōspect·ō -āre *tr* to look in on

intrō·spiciō -spicĕre -spexī -spectus *tr* to look into; to look at, regard; *(fig)* to look into, examine ‖ *intr (w.* **in** *+ acc) (lit & fig)* to look into, inspect

intub·um -ī *n* endive

intu·eor -ērī -itus sum *or* **intu·or -ī** *tr* to look at, gaze at; to consider, take into consideration; to look up to, have regard for; to keep an eye on; to examine visually, inspect **terram intueri** to look down at the ground

intum·escō -escĕre -uī *intr* to swell up, rise; *(of voice)* to grow louder; *(of river)* to rise, become swollen; to become angry; to get a big head, swell with pride

intumulāt·us -a -um *adj* unburied

intuor *see* **intueor**

inturbid·us -a -um *adj* undisturbed, quiet

intus *adv* inside, within; at home, in; to the inside; from within

intūt·us -a -um *adj* unsafe; unprotected, unguarded, defenseless

inul·a -ae *f* elecampane *(tall, coarse plant with yellow flowers)*

inult·us -a -um *adj* unavenged; unpunished

inumbr·ō -āre -āvī -ātus *tr* to shade; to cover

inundāti·ō -ōnis *f* inundation, flood

inund·ō -āre -āvī -ātus *tr* to inundate, flood ‖ *intr* to overflow; **sanguine inundare** to run red with blood

inun·g(u)ō -g(u)ĕre -xī -ctus *tr* to anoint

inurbānē *adv* impolitely, rudely

inurbān·us -a -um *adj* impolite; unsophisticated, rude, rustic

inur·geō -gēre -sī *intr* to butt

in·ūrō -ūrĕre -ussī -ustus *tr* to burn in, brand, imprint; *(w. dat)* **1** to brand upon, imprint upon, affix to; **2** to inflict upon

inūsitātē *adv* unusually, strangely

inusitāt·us -a -um *adj* unusual, strange, uncommon, extraordinary

inustus *pp of* **inuro**

inūtil·is -is -e *adj* useless; unprofitable; impractical; injurious, harmful

inūtilit·ās -ātis *f* uselessness; harmfulness

inūtiliter *adv* uselessly; harmfully

invā·dō -dĕre -sī -sus *tr* to come *or* go into, enter; to enter upon, undertake, attempt; to invade, attack, rush upon; *(fig)* to seize, take possession of ‖ *intr* to come *or* go in; to invade; *(w.* **in** *+ acc)* **1** to invade; to assail; **2** to seize; **3** to get possession of; **4** to rush to embrace

inval·escō -escĕre -uī *intr* to grow stronger; *(fig)* to increase in power; to grow in frequency; to predominate

invalid·us -a -um *adj* weak; feeble; dim *(light, fire)*; inadequate; ineffectual

invāsī *perf of* **invado**

invāsus *pp of* **invado**

invecti·ō -ōnis *f* importation, importing; arrival by boat

inve·hō -hĕre -xī -ctus *tr* to carry in, bring in, ship in *(by cart, horse, boat, etc.)*; *(w. dat)* to bring *(e.g., evils)* upon ‖ *refl (w. acc or* **in** *+ acc)* to rush against, attack ‖ *pass* to ride, drive, sail; *(w. acc or* **in** *+ acc)* **1** to ride into, sail into; **2** to attack; **3** to inveigh against, attack *(w. words)*; **invehi equo** to ride a horse; **invehi nave** to sail

invendibil·is -is -e *adj* unsaleable

in·veniō -venīre -vēnī -ventus *tr* to come upon, find, come across, discover; to find out; to invent, devise; to learn, ascertain; to get, reach, earn

inventi·ō -ōnis *f* inventiveness; inventing, invention

invent·or -ōris *m*, **inventr·ix -īcis** *f* inventor, author, discoverer

invent·us -a -um *pp of* **invenio** ‖ *n* invention, discovery

invenust·us -a -um *adj* having no sex appeal; homely, unattractive; unlucky in love

inverēcund·us -a -um *adj* disrespectful, immodest, shameless

inverg·ō -ĕre *tr (w. dat or* **in** *+ acc)* to pour upon

inversi·ō -ōnis *f* inversion *(of words)*; irony; allegory

invers·us -a -um *pp of* **inverto** ‖ *adj* turned upside down; turned inside out; **manus inversa** back of the hand

inver·tō -tĕre -tī -sus *tr* to invert, turn upside down, upset, reverse, turn inside out; to transpose, reverse; to pervert, abuse, misrepresent; to use ironically

invesperasc·it -ĕre *v impers* evening is approaching, twilight is falling

investīgāti·ō -ōnis *f* investigation; search

investīgāt·or -ōris *m* investigator

investīg·ō -āre -āvī -ātus *tr* to track, trace, search after; to investigate, search into, search after

inveter·ascō -ascĕre -āvī *intr* to begin to grow old, get old; to become fixed, become established; to become rooted, grow inveterate; to become obsolete

inveterāti·ō -ōnis *f* chronic illness

inveterāt·us -a -um *adj* inveterate, long-standing

invexī *perf of* **inveho**

invicem *or* **in vicem** *adv* in turn, taking turns, one after another, alternately; mutually, each other; **defatigatis invicem integri succedunt** fresh troops take turns in relieving the exhausted troops

invict·us -a -um *adj* unconquered; invincible

invid·ens -entis *adj* envious, jealous

invidenti·a -ae *f* envy, jealousy

invideō -vidēre -vīdī -vīsus *tr* to envy, be jealous of ‖ *intr (w. dat)* to envy, begrudge; *(w. dat of person and abl of cause or* **in** *+ abl)* to begrude *(s.o. s.th.)*, to envy *(s.o.)* because of *(s.th.)*

invidi·a -ae *f* envy, jealousy; unpopularity; **invidiae esse** *(w. dat)* to be the cause

of envy to; **invidiam habere** to be unpopular
invidiōsē *adv* spitefully; so as to bring unpopularity on an opponent
invidiōs·us -a -um *adj* envious; spiteful; envied; enviable, causing envy
invid·us -a -um *adj* envious, jealous; *(w. dat)* hostile to, unfavorable to
invigil·ō -āre -āvī -ātum *intr* to be alert, be on one's toes; *(w. dat)* to be on the lookout for, keep an eye on, pay attention to, watch over; *(w.* **pro** *+ abl)* to watch over
inviolābil·is -is -e *adj* inviolable; invulnerable, indestructible
inviolātē *adv* inviolately
inviolāt·us -a -um *adj* inviolate, unhurt; inviolable
invīsitāt·us -a -um *adj* unusual, strange; not seen before, unknown
invīs·ō -ĕre -ī -us *tr* to visit, go to see; to look into, inspect; to look after; to catch sight of
invīs·us -a -um *pp of* **invideo** ‖ *adj* unseen; hated, detested; hostile
invītāment·um -ī *n* attraction, allurement, inducement
invītāti·ō -ōnis *f* invitation; challenge
invītāt·us -ūs *m* invitation
invītē *adv* unwillingly, against one's wishes
invīt·ō -āre -āvī -ātus *tr* to invite; to entertain; to summon, challenge; to ask, request; to allure, attract; to encourage, court
invīt·us -a -um *adj* reluctant, unwilling, against one's will; **invītā Minervā** against one's better judgment, against the grain
invi·us -a -um *adj* without roads, trackless, impassable ‖ *npl* rough terrain
invocāti·ō -ōnis *f* invocation
invocāt·us -a -um *adj* unbidden
invoc·ō -āre -āvī -ātus *tr* to invoke, call upon; to call out *(name of one's girlfriend in rolling dice)*; to pray for; to address *(with an honorific title)*
involāt·us -ūs *m* flight
involgō *see* **invulgo**
involit·ō -āre -āvī *intr (w. dat)* (of long hair) to trail over
invol·ō -āre -āvī -ātus *tr* to swoop down on, pounce on ‖ *intr* to swoop down; *(w.* **in** *+ acc)* to swoop down on
involūcr·um -ī *n* wrapper; cover; envelope; *(fig)* cover-up, front
involūt·us -a -um *adj* complicated
invol·vō -vĕre -vī -ūtus *tr* to wrap up; to involve, envelop; to cover completely, overwhelm; *(w. dat or* **in** *+ acc)* to pile *(s.th.)* on ‖ *refl (w. dat) (fig)* to get all wrapped up in
involvol·us -ī *m* caterpillar *(which rolls up the leaves it infests)*
invulg·ō -āre -āvī -ātus *tr* (**-vol-**) to reveal, publicize ‖ *intr* to give public evidence
iō *interj* ho!
Ī·ō -ūs *or* **-ōnis** *f (acc & abl:* **Īō***)* Io *(daughter of Argive King Inachus, changed into a heifer and driven by Juno over the world)*
Iocast·a -ae *or* **Iocast·ē -ēs** *f* Jocasta *(wife of Laius, and mother as well as wife of Oedipus)*
Iölā·us -ī *m* son of Iphicles and companion of Hercules
Iöl·ē -ēs *f* daughter of Eurytus, who fell in love with Hercules
Iōn·es -um *mpl* Ionians *(Greek inhabitants of the W. coast of Asia Minor)*
Iōnic·us -a -um *adj* Ionic ‖ *m* Ionic dancer ‖ *npl* Ionic dance
Īoni·us -a -um *adj* Ionian ‖ *f* Ionia *(coastal district of Asia Minor)* ‖ *n* Ionian Sea *(off W. coast of Greece)*
iōta *indecl n* iota *(ninth letter of the Greek alphabet)*
Īphianass·a -ae *f* Iphigenia
Īphigenī·a -ae *f* daughter of Agamemnon and Clytemnestra, who was to have been sacrificed at Aulis but was saved by Artemis
Īphit·us -ī *m* Argonaut, son of Eurytus and Antiope
ips·a -īus *or* **-ĭus** *adj* self, very, just, mere, precisely; in person; by herself, alone; of her own accord ‖ *pron* she herself; lady of the house
ips·e *or* **ips·us -īus** *or* **-ĭus** *adj* self, very, just, mere, precisely; in person; by himself, alone; of his own accord ‖ *pron* he himself; master; host
ipsim·a -ae *f (coll)* boss
ipsim·us -ī *m (coll)* boss
ips·um -īus *or* **-ĭus** *adj* self, very, just, mere, precisely; by itself, alone; of itself, spontaneously; **nunc ipsum** just then ‖ *pron* it itself, that itself; **ipsum quod**...the very fact that
ipsus *see* **ipse**
īr·a -ae *f* wrath, resentment
īrācundē *adv* angrily; passionately
īrācundi·a -ae *f* quick temper; anger, wrath, passion, violence; resentment
īrācund·us -a -um *adj* hot-tempered, irritable; angry; resentful
īrasc·or -ārī *intr* to get angry, fly into a rage; *(w. dat)* to get angry with
īrātē *adv* angrily
īrāt·us -a -um *adj* irate, angry, enraged; *(w. dat)* angry at
Īr·is -idis *f* goddess of the rainbow and messenger of the gods
īrōnī·a -ae *f* irony
irrās·us -a -um *adj* unshaven
irratiōnāl·is -is -e *adj* (**inr-**) irrational

irrau·cescō -cescĕre -sī *intr* (**inr-**) to become hoarse
irredivīv·us -a -um *adj* irreparable
irred·ux -ucis *adj* one-way *(road)*
irreligāt·us -a -um *adj* (**inr-**) not tied
irreligiōsē *adv* (**inr-**) impiously, blasphemously
irreligiōs·us -a -um *adj* (**inr-**) irreligious, impious
irremeābil·is -is -e *adj* (**inr-**) from which there is no return, one-way
irreparābil·is -is -e *adj* (**inr-**) irretrievable; irreparable *(damage)*
irrepert·us -a -um *adj* (**inr-**) undiscovered, not found
irrēp·ō -ĕre -sī -tum *intr* (**inr-**) to creep in; *(fig)* to sneak in; *(w.* **ad** *or* **in** *+ acc)* to creep toward *or* into; *(fig)* to sneak up on
irreprehens·us -a -um *adj* (**inr-**) blameless
irrequiēt·us -a -um *adj* (**inr-**) restless
irresect·us -a -um *adj* (**inr-**) untrimmed
irresolūt·us -a -um *adj* (**inr-**) not loosened, still tied, unrelaxed
irrēt·iō -īre -īvī *or* **-iī -ītus** *tr* (**inr-**) to net, trap in a net
irretort·us -a -um *adj* (**inr-**) not turned back; **oculo irretorto** without one backward glance
irrever·ens -entis *adj* (**inr-**) irreverent, disrespectful
irreverenter *adv* (**inr-**) irreverently, disrespectfully
irreverenti·a -ae *f* (**inr-**) irreverence, disrespect
irrevocābil·is -is -e *adj* (**inr-**) irrevocable; implacable, relentless
irrevocāt·us -a -um *adj* (**inr-**) not called back, not asked back
irrī·deō -dēre -sī -sus *tr* (**inr-**) to ridicule, laugh at ‖ *intr* to laugh, joke; *(w. dat)* to laugh at
irrīdiculē *adv* (**inr-**) with no sense of humor
irrīdicul·um -ī *n* (**inr-**) laughing stock
irrigāti·ō -ōnis *f* (**inr-**) irrigation
irrig·ō -āre -āvī -ātus *tr* (**inr-**) to irrigate, water; to inundate; *(fig)* to diffuse; *(fig)* to flood, steep, soak
irrigu·us -a -um *adj* (**inr-**) wet, soaked, well-watered; refreshing
irrīsī (**inr-**) *perf of* **irrideo**
irrīsi·ō -ōnis *f* (**inr-**) ridicule, mockery
irrīs·or -ōris *m* (**inr-**) reviler, mocker
irrīsus (**inr-**) *pp of* **irrideo**
irrīs·us -ūs *m* (**inr-**) mockery, derision; laughing stock, object of derision
irrītābil·is -is -e *adj* (**inr-**) easily excited; easily enraged, irritable; sensitive
irrītām·en -inis *n* (**inr-**) incentive; provocation
irrītāment·um -ī *n* (**inr-**) incentive; provocation
irrītāti·ō -ōnis *f* (**inr-**) incitement; irritation, provocation; stimulant
irrīt·ō -āre -āvī -ātus *tr* (**inr-**) to provoke, annoy; to incite; to excite, stimulate; to bring on *(a calamity, etc.)*
irrit·us -a -um *adj* (**inr-**) not valid, null and void; futile, pointless, useless; unsuccessful *(person)*
irrogāti·ō -ōnis *f* (**inr-**) imposition *(e.g., of a fine)*
irrog·ō -āre -āvī -ātus *tr* (**inr-**) to impose, inflict; to object to *(proposals)*
irrōr·ō -āre -āvī -ātus *tr* (**inr-**) to moisten with dew; to sprinkle, water; **aquam capiti irrorare** to sprinkle water on (s.o.'s) head
irruct·ō -āre *intr* (**inr-**) to belch
ir·rumpō -rumpĕre -rūpī -ruptus *tr* (**inr-**) to rush into, break down ‖ *intr* to rush in; *(w. dat or* **in** *+ acc)* **1** to rush into, rush through; **2** *(fig)* to intrude upon
irru·ō -ĕre -ī *intr* (**inr-**) to rush in, force one's way in; *(w. dat or* **in** *+ acc)* **1** to rush into; **2** to rush on; **3** to invade, attack; **irruere in odium** *(w. gen)* to incur the anger of
irrūpī (**inr-**) *perf of* **irrumpo**
irrupti·ō -ōnis *f* (**inr-**) bursting in; forcible entry; *(mil)* incursion; assault
irrupt·us -a -um (**inr-**) *pp of* **irrumpo** ‖ *adj* unbroken
Īr·us -ī *m* beggar in the palace of Ulysses in Ithaca
is ejus *adj* this, that, the said, the aforesaid ‖ *pron* he; **is qui** he who, the person who, the one who
Īs·is -is *or* **-idis** *f* Egyptian goddess
Ismari·us -a -um *adj* of Mt. Ismarus in Thrace; Thracian
Īsocrat·ēs -is *m* orator and teacher of rhetoric at Athens *(436–338 B.C.)*
ista *see* **iste**
istāc *adv* that way
istactenus *adv* thus far
istaec *see* **istic**
ist·e -a -ud *adj* that of yours; this, that, the very, that particular; such, of such a kind; that terrible, that despicable ‖ *pron* that one; *(in court)* your client
Isthm·us *or* **Isthm·os -ī** *m (f)* Isthmus of Corinth
ist·ic -aec -oc *or* **-uc** *adj* that, that of yours ‖ *pron* the one, that one
istīc *adv* there, in that place; herein; on this occasion
istinc *adv* from there; from your side; from what you have
istīusmodī *or* **istīmodī** *or* **istīus modī** *or* **istī modī** *adj* that kind of; **istiusmodi scelus** that kind of crime
istō *adv* where you are; therefore; in that matter
istōc *adv* there, to where you are

istorsum *adv* in that direction, that way

istūc *adv* there, to that place, to where you are, that way; **istuc veniam** I'll come to that matter

istūcine *see* **istic**

istud *see* **iste**

ita *adv* thus, so, in this manner, in that way; *(of natural consequence)* thus, accordingly, therefore, under these circumstances; *(in affirmation)* yes, true, exactly; *(in questions)* really?, truly?; **ita...ut** *(in comparisons)* just as...so; *(introducing contrast)* whereas...at the same time; *(as adversative)* although...nevertheless; *(introducing result clauses)* so *or* in such a way that; *(as correlatives)* both...and, both...as well as; *(in restriction)* on the condition that, insofar as, on the assumption that; *(of degree)* to such a degree...that, so much...that, so...that; **non ita** not very, not especially; **quid ita?** how so?, what do you mean?

Ītali·a -ae *f* Italy

Ītalic·us -a -um *adj* Italic

Ītal·is -idis *adj* Italian **||** *fpl* Italian women

Ītali·us -a -um *adj* Italian **||** *f see* **Italia**

Ītal·us -a -um *adj* Italian

itaque *adv* and so, and thus, accordingly, therefore, consequently

item *adv* likewise, besides, moreover

it·er -ineris *n* journey, trip; walk; march; day's march; day's journey; route; right of way; duct, passage; method, course, way, road; **ex** *(or* **in)** **itinere** en route, on the way; **iter facere** to take a trip; to travel; to make way;*(mil)* to march; **iter flectere** to change course; **iter patefacere** to clear a way; **iter terrestre** overland route; **itinere** en route; **maximis itineribus** by marching at top speed

iterāti·ō -ōnis *f* repetition

iter·ō -āre -āvī -ātus *tr* to repeat, renew; to plow again

iterum *adv* again, a second time; **iterum atque iterum** repeatedly, again and again

Ithac·a -ae *or* **Ithac·ē -ēs** *f* Ithaca (*island off W. coast of Greece in the Ionian Sea and home of Odysseus*)

itidem *adv* in the same way

iti·ō -ōnis *f* going

it·ō -āre -āvī *intr* to go

it·us -ūs *m* going; departure

It·ys -yos *m* son of Tereus and Procne, who was killed by Procne and served up as food to Tereus

iu- = ju-

Ixī·ōn -onis *or* **-onos** *m* Ixion *(king of the Lapiths, who was tied to a wheel by Jupiter for trying to seduce Juno and sent flying into Tartarus)*

Ixīonid·ēs -ae *m* son of Ixion *(esp.* Pirithous)

Ixīoni·us -a -um *adj* of Ixion

J

jac·eō -ēre -uī -itum *intr* to lie, lie down; to recline *(at table);* to lie ill, be sick; to rest; to lie dead, to have fallen *(in battle); (of structures, cities)* to lie in ruins; to linger, stay *(in a place); (of places)* to lie, be stituated; *(of places)* to be low-lying, lie low; *(of fields)* to lie idle; *(of prices)* to be low; *(of persons)* to feel low, be despondent; *(of the eyes, face)* to be downcast; *(of hair)* to hang loose; *(of the sea)* to be calm; *(of duties, responsibilities)* to be neglected; to lie prostrate, be powerless; *(of arguments)* to fail, be refuted; to be low in s.o.'s opinion; **amici jacentem animum incitare** to cheer up a friend's despondent mood; **animi militum jacent** the morale of the soldiers is low; **Brundisi jacere** to linger in Brundisi; **in orbem jacere** *(of a group of islands)* to lie in a circle, form a circle; **jacere cum** to have sexual intercourse with; **mihi ad pedes jacere** to lie prostrate at my feet

jaciō jacĕre jēcī jactus *tr* to throw, cast, fling; to toss *(head, limbs);* to hurl *(charges, insults);* to lay *(foundations);* to build, establish, set, found, construct; to emit, produce *(heat, light, sparks);* to sow, scatter *(seed);* to throw down; to throw away; to mention, utter, declare, intimate; **contumeliam in aliquem jacere** to hurl the charge of defiance at s.o., charge s.o. with defiance; **fundamenta jacere** to lay the foundations; **voces jaciuntur** words are uttered **||** *refl* to leap; to rush, burst

jact·ans -antis *adj* boastful, showing off; proud

jactanter *adv* boastfully; ostentatiously; arrogantly

jactanti·a -ae *f* bragging; ostentation

jactāti·ō -ōnis *f* tossing to and fro; swaying; shaking; writhing; bragging, showing off; **jactatio animi** agitation; **jactatio corporis** gesticulation; **jactatio maritima** seasickness

jactāt·us -ūs *m* tossing, waving

jactit·ō -āre *tr* to display, show off

jact·ō -āre -āvī -ātus *tr* to throw, hurl; to toss about, shake; to wave, brandish; to throw away, throw out; to throw overboard; to throw aside, reject; to disturb, disquiet, stir up; to make restless, cause to toss; to consider, discuss; to throw out, mention; to brag about, show off **||** *refl* to boast, show off, throw one's weight around **||** *pass* to toss, rock

jactūr·a -ae *f* throwing away, throwing overboard; loss, sacrifice

jactus *pp of* **jacio**
jact·us -ūs *m* toss, throw, cast
jaculābil·is -is -e *adj* missile
jaculāti·ō -ōnis *f* hurling
jaculāt·or -ōris *m* thrower, hurler; light-armed soldier; spearman; hunter
jaculātr·ix -īcis *f* huntress
jacul·or -ārī -ātus sum *tr* to throw; to shoot at; *(fig)* to aim at, strive after
jacul·us -a -um *adj* throwing, casting ‖ *n* dart, javelin; casting net
jājūn- = jejun-
Jālysi·us -a -um *adj* of Jalysos, a town on the island of Rhodes
Jālys·us -ī *m* son of the god Helios, and eponym of the town Jalysos ‖ famous portrait of Jalysus by Protogenes
jam *adv (in the present)* now, already; *(in the past)* already, by then, by that time; *(in the future)* very soon, right away; *(in transition)* now, next, moreover; *(for emphasis)* actually, precisely, quite; *(in conclusion)* then surely; **jam ante(a)** even before that; **jam dudum** long ago, long since; **jam inde** immediately; **jam inde ab** all the while from, continuously from; **jam jam** *(for emphasis or emotive effect)* at last, now finally **jam…jam** at one time…at another; first…then; **jamjamque** at any time now, now all but…; **jam nunc** even now; **jam pridem** long since; **jam primum** to begin with, first of all; **jam tum** even then, even at that time; **quid jam?** *(coll)* what (is the matter) now?
Jānicul·um -ī *n* Roman hill on right bank of the Tiber
Jānigen·a *adj (masc & fem only)* born of Janus
jānit·or -ōris *m* doorman, porter
jānitr·ix -īcis *f* portress
janthin·us -a -um *adj* violet ‖ *n* the color violet ‖ *npl* violet clothes
jānu·a -ae *f* door; doorway, entrance; *(fig)* entrance, approach, gateway; **janua leti** gateway of death, gateway to the lower world
Jānuāri·us -a -um *adj* of Janus; **mensis Januarius** January *(first month, after 153 B.C., of the Roman year)* ‖ *m* January
jān·us -ī *m* covered passage, arcade; **janus imus, janus medius, janus summus** bottom archway, middle archway, top archway *(three archways on the east side of the Forum, where money changers and merchants conducted their business)* ‖ **Jānus** Janus *(old Italic deity, represented as having two faces)* ‖ temple of Janus *(at the bottom of the Argiletum in the Forum)* ‖ **Janus Geminus** *(or* **Janus Quirinus** *or* **Janus Quirini)** shrine of Janus in the Forum consisting of an archway, with doors at the ends that were closed in times of peace
Jāpyd·es -um *mpl* the people of Japydia
Jāpydi·a -ae *f* country in the N. part of Illyria
Jāpygi·a -ae *f* Greek name for part of S.E. Italy, including some or all of Calabria and Apulia
Jāp·yx -ygis *or* **-ygos** *adj* Japygian ‖ *m* son of Daedalus, who gave his name to Japygia ‖ river in Apulia ‖ the N.W.N. wind, which favors the crossing from Italy to Greece
Jarb·a(s) -ae *m* Jarbas *(king of the Gaetulians in N. Africa, whom Dido rejected as a suitor)*
Jarbīt·a -ae *m* Mauretanian, Moor
Jardan·is -idis *f* daughter of Jardanus, king of Lydia *(i.e., Omphale)*
Jās·ō(n) -onis *m* Jason *(son of Aeson, leader of the Argonauts, and husband of Medea)*
Jāsoni·us -a -um *adj* Jason's
Jasp·is -idis *or* **-idos** *f* jasper
Jās·us -ī *f town on the coast of Caria*
jātralipt·ēs -ae *m* masseur
Jāz·yx -ygis *m* member of a people dwelling near the Danube
jec·ur -oris *or* **-ineris** *or* **-inoris** *n* liver; *(as the seat of emotions)* anger, lust
jecuscul·um -ī *n* little liver
jējūnē *adv (fig)* dryly
jējūniōs·us -a -um *adj* **(jājūn-)** *(hum)* abounding in hunger, hungry
jējūnit·ās -ātis *f* **(jājūn-)** fasting; dryness *(of style)*
jējūn·ium -(i)ī *n* fasting, fast; hunger, leanness
jējūn·us -a -um *adj* **(jājūn-)** fasting; hungry; thin; insignificant, paltry; poor *(land);* jejune *(style)*
jentācul·um -ī *n* **(jājen-)** breakfast
jent·ō -āre -āvī *intr* to eat breakfast
Jocast·a -ae *f* wife of Laïus and mother and wife of Oedipus
jocāti·ō -ōnis *f* jesting, humor
jocineris *gen of* **jecur**
joc·or -ārī -ātus sum *or* **joc·ō -āre** *tr* to say in jest ‖ *intr* to joke, crack a joke, be joking
jocōsē *adv* humorously, as a joke, jokingly
jocōs·us -a -um *adj* humorous, funny; fond of jokes
joculār·is -is -e *adj* humorous, funny
joculāri·us -a -um *adj* ludicrous
joculāt·or -ōris *m* joker
jocul·or -ārī -ātus sum *intr* to joke
jocul·us -ī *m* joke; **joculo** as a joke, in fun
joc·us -ī *m (pl:* **joc·ī -ōrum** *mpl,* **joc·a -ōrum** *npl)* joke; laughing stock; child's play; **joco remoto** all joking aside; **per jocum** as a joke
jub·a -ae *f* mane; crest

jub·ar -aris *n* radiance, brightness; sunshine
jubāt·us -a -um *adj* crested
ju·beō -bēre -ssī -ssus *tr* to order; to prescribe *(a task);* to designate, appoint; *(med)* prescribe; *(pol)* to order, decree, ratify; **jube fratrem tuum salvere** *(in letters)* best regards to your brother; say good- bye to your brother
jūcundē *adv* pleasantly, delightfully
jūcundit·ās -ātis *f* pleasantness, delight, enjoyment ‖ *fpl* favors
jūcund·us -a -um *adj* pleasant, delightful, agreeable
Jūdae·us -a -um *adj* Jewish ‖ *mf* Jew ‖ *f* Judea, Palestine
Jūdaïc·us -a -um *adj* Jewish; of Judea; *(mil)* stationed in Judea
jūd·ex -icis *m* judge; juror; arbitrator; umpire; critic, scholar; **judex morum** censor; **me judice** in my judgment
jūdicāti·ō -ōnis *f* judicial investigation; *(fig)* judgment, opinion
jūdicāt·us -a -um *adj* decided, determined ‖ *m* condemned person ‖ *n* judicial decision, judgment; precedent; fine; **judicatum facere** to carry out a decision; **judicatum solvere** to pay a fine
jūdicāt·us -ūs *m* judgeship
jūdiciāl·is -is -e *adj* judicial, forensic
jūdiciāri·us -a -um *adj* judiciary
jūdic·ium -(i)ī *n* trial, court; sentence; jurisdiction; opinion, decision; faculty of judging, judgment, good judgment, taste, tact, discretion; criterion; **ad judicium ire** to go to court; **in judicio esse** to be under investigation; **in judicium deducere** *(or* **vocare)** to take to court; **in judicium venire** to come before the court; **judicium agere** to conduct a trial; **judicium dare** *(or* **reddere)** *(of a praetor)* to grant an action; **judicium facere (in** + *acc)* to pass judgment against; **judicium tenere** *(or* **vincire)** to win a case; **judicium privatum** civil suit; **judicium publicum** criminal trial; **meo judicio** in my judgment; **suo judicio** intentionally; **suprema judicia** last will and testament
jūdic·ō -āre -āvī -ātus *tr* to judge; to examine; to sentence, condemn; to form an opinion of; to conclude; to declare, proclaim; *(w. dat of person and acc of the offense)* to convict *(s.o.)* of; *(w. gen)* to find *(s.o.)* guilty of; *(w. dat of person and gen of the offense)* to convict *(s.o.)* of
jugāl·is -is -e *adj* yoked together; nuptial
jugāti·ō -ōnis *f* tying up
jūger·um -ī *n* jugerum *(land measure, about ⅔ of an acre)*
jūg·is -is -e *adj* continuous, perennial, inexhaustible
jūgl·ans -andis *f* walnut tree; walnut
jugōs·us -a -um *adj* hilly
Jugul·ae -ārum *fpl (astr)* Orion's Belt *(3 stars in the constellation Orion)*
jugul·ō -āre -āvī -ātus *tr* cut the throat of, kill, murder; to destroy; to silence
jugul·um -ī *n,* **jugul·us -ī** *m* throat
jug·um -ī *n* yoke, collar; pair, team; crossbar *(of loom);* thwart *(of boat);* common bond, union; wedlock; pair, couple; mountain ridge; *(mil)* yoke *(consisting of a spear laid crosswise on two upright spears, under which the conquered had to pass)* ‖ *npl* heights
Jugurth·a -ae *m* king of Numidia *(160–104 B.C.)*
Jūli·a -ae *f* aunt of Julius Caesar and wife of Marius ‖ daughter of Julius Caesar and wife of Pompey *(d. 54 B.C.)* ‖ daughter of Augustus by Scribonia *(39 B.C.–A.D. 14)*
Jūli·us -a -um *adj* Julian; of July; **mensis Julius** July ‖ *m* Roman first name *(praenomen);* July
Jūl·us -ī *m* son of Aeneas *(also called Ascanius)*
jūment·um -ī *n* beast of burden, horse, mule
junce·us -a -um *adj* of reeds; slim, slender
juncōs·us -a -um *adj* overgrown with reeds
junctim *adv* side by side; in succession
juncti·ō -ōnis *f* joining, combination, union
junctūr·a -ae *f* joining, uniting, joint, juncture; connection, relationship; combination
junct·us -a -um *pp of* **jungo** ‖ *adj* connected, associated, united, attached
junc·us -ī *m* reed
jun·gō -gĕre -xī -ctus *tr* to join, join together, unite, connect; to yoke, harness; to couple, pair, mate; to bridge *(a river);* to bring together, associate, ally; to add; to compose *(poems);* to combine *(words)*
jūni·or -ōris *adj (mas & fem only)* younger ‖ *mpl* younger men *(esp. of military age, between 17 and 46 years)*
jūniper·us -ī *f* juniper
Jūni·us -a -um *adj* June, of June; **mensis Junius** June ‖ *m* Roman first name *(praenomen);* June
jūn·ix -īcis *f* heifer
Jūn·ō -ōnis *f* daughter of Saturn and wife and sister of Jupiter *(commonly identified with Hera);* woman's tutelary deity *(corresponding to a male's* **genius);** **Juno Lucina** goddess of childbirth *(applied to Juno and Diana);* **Juno inferna** name of Proserpina *(queen of the lower world);* **Junonis avis** peacock; **Junonis stella** planet Venus
Juppiter *(or* **Jūpiter** *or* **Diespiter) Jovis** *m* son of Saturn, brother and husband of

Juno, and chief god of the Romans *(commonly identified with Zeus)*

jurāt·or -ōris *m* judge; assistant censor

jūrāt·us -a -um *adj* being under oath; having given one's word

jūre *adv* rightfully; with good reason, deservedly; correctly

jūreconsult·us -ī *m* **(jūris-)** legal expert

jūreperītus *see* **jurisperitus**

jurg·ium -(i)ī *n* quarrel **‖** *npl* reproaches, abuse

jurg·ō -āre -āvī -ātus *tr* to scold **‖** *intr* to quarrel

jūridiciāl·is -is -e *adj* juridical

jūrisconsult·us -ī *m* **(jūre-)** legal expert, lawyer

jūrisdicti·ō -ōnis *f* administration of justice; jurisdiction

jūrisperīt·us -ī *m* **(jūre-)** legal expert, lawyer

jūr·ō -āre -āvī -ātus *tr* to swear; to swear by, attest, call to witness; to swear to, attest; to promise under oath, vow **‖** *intr* to swear, take an oath; *(w.* **in** *+ acc)* **1** to swear allegiance to; **2** to swear to observe *(the laws, etc.);* **3** to conspire against; **in haec verba jurare** to swear according to the prescribed form; **in verba alicujus jurare** to swear allegiance to s.o.; **jurare calumniam** to swear that the accusation is not false

jūs jūris *n* juice, broth, gravy

jūs jūris *n* law, the laws *(as established by society and custom rather than statute law);* legal system, right, justice; law court; legal right, authority, permission; prerogative; jurisdiction; **in jus ire** to go to court; **jura dare** to prescribe laws, administer justice; **jure** by right, rightfully; **jus dicere** to sit as judge, hold court; **jus gentium** law available to aliens as well as to citizens; international law; **jus praetorium** principles of law contained in a praetor's edict; **jus publicum** constitutional law; **mei juris** subject to my control; **pro jure suo** without exceeding one's rights, at will, freely; in one's own right; **sui juris** *(or* **suo jure)** legally one's own master; **summum jus** strict letter of the law

jūsjūrandum *or* **jūs jūrandum** *(gen:* **jūr·isjūrand·ī** *or* **jūr·is jūrand·ī)** *n* oath; **aliquem jurejurando adigere** to bind s.o. with an oath, have s.o. take an oath

jussū *(abl only) m* by order; **meo jussu** by my order

juss·us -a -um *pp of* **jubeo ‖** *n* order, command, bidding

justē *adv* justly, rightly

justific·us -a -um *adj* just-dealing

justiti·a -ae *f* justice, fairness

justit·ium -(i)ī *n* suspension of legal business, legal holiday; period of mourning; *(fig)* standstill

just·us -a -um *adj* just, fair; justified, well-founded; formal; in due order, according to protocol, regular **‖** *n* justice; due measure; **plus quam justo** more than due measure, too much **‖** *npl* rights, one's due; regular tasks, formalities; ceremonies, due ceremony; funeral rites, obsequies

Jūturn·a -ae *f* nymph, sister of Turnus, the king of the Rutuli

jūtus *pp of* **juvo**

juvenāl·is -is -e *adj* youthful; juvenile **‖ Juvenalis** *m* Juvenal *(Decimus Junius Juvenalis, Roman satirist in the time of Domitian and Trajan, c.* A.D.*62–142)*

juvenc·us -a -um *adj* young **‖** *m* bullock; young man **‖** *f* heifer; girl

juven·escō -escěre *intr* to grow up; to become young again

juvenīl·is -is -e *adj* youthful; juvenile; cheerful

juvenīliter *adv* youthfully, boyishly

juven·is -is -e *adj* young **‖** *m* young man *(between the ages of 20 and 45);* warrior **‖** *f* young lady

juven·or -ārī -ātus sum *intr* to act like a kid

juvent·a -ae *f* youth

juvent·ās -ātis *f or* **juvent·ūs -ūtis** *f* youth, prime of life, manhood; *(collectively)* young people, the young, youth

juv·ō juvāre jūvī jūtus *tr* to help; *(of terrain)* to give *(one)* an advantage; to back up *(an opinion);* to benefit, do good to; to please, delight **‖** *v impers (w. inf)* it helps to; **juvat me** it delights me, I am glad, I am relieved

juxtā *adv* nearby, in close proximity; alike, in like manner, equally; *(w.* **ac, atque, et, quam,** *or* **cum)** as well as, just the same as **‖** *prep (w. acc)* **1** close to, near to, next to; **2** next to, immediately after; **3** near, bordering on; **4** next door to

juxtim *adv* near; equally

K

K. *abbr* **Kaeso** *(Roman first name, praenomen)*

Kalend·ae -ārum *fpl* **(Cal-)** Kalends *(first day of the Roman month);* **tristes Kalendae** gloomy Kalends *(because interest was due on the Kalends)*

Kalendār·ium -(i)ī *n* account book, ledger

Karthāginiens·is -is -e *adj* **(Carth-)** Carthaginian

Karthāg·ō -inis *f* **(Carth-)** Carthage

L

L *abbr* the number 50

L. *abbr* **Lucius** *(Roman first name, praenomen)*

labasc·ō -ĕre *intr* to break up, dissolve; to waver; to give in, yield

lābēcul·a -ae *f* blemish, stain

labe·faciō -facĕre -fēcī -factus *tr* to cause to totter; to shake, weaken; *(fig)* to cause to waver, shake; *(fig)* to undermine *(authority, power)*

labefactāti·ō -ōnis *f* loosening

labefact·ō -āre -āvī -ātus *tr* to shake, loosen, make unsteady; to undermine the authority of; to undermine *(loyalty, etc.)*

lăbell·um -ī *n* lip

lābell·um -ī *n* small basin

labeōs·us -a -um *adj* thick-lipped

lāb·ēs -is *f* fall, falling down; stroke, blow; disaster; cause of disaster; blot, stain; blemish, defect; disgrace, discredit; *(geol)* subsidence, landslide; **labem dare** to collapse

labi·a -ae *f* (thick) lip

Labīcān·us -a -um *adj* of the town of Labici; **via Labicana** a road entering Rome from the S.E.‖ *n* territory of the Labici

Labīc·ī -ōrum *mpl* small town about 15 miles S.E. of Rome ‖ *mpl* people of Labici

Labiēn·us -a -um *adj* Roman clan name *(nomen), esp.* Titus Labienus *(Caesar's officer who defected to Pompey, d. 45 B.C.)*

labiōs·us -a -um *adj* thick-lipped

lab·ium -(i)ī *n* lip; **labiis aliquem ductare** *(prov)* to lead s.o. by the nose

lab·ō -āre -āvī *intr* to totter, wobble; to waver, hesitate, be undecided; to fall to pieces, go to ruin

lābor lābī lapsus sum *intr* to glide, slide, slip; to fall, sink; to slip away, disappear, escape; *(of time)* to slip by, pass; *(of liquids, rivers)* to flow; *(of the sun)* to sink down; *(of day)* to decline; *(of style)* to run smoothly; *(of words)* to slip out; *(of a building)* to collapse; *(fig)* to fade; *(fig)* to fall into error, go wrong; **memoriā labi** to have a lapse of memory; **mente labi** to go out of one's mind

lab·or *or* **lab·os -ōris** *m* effort, exertion; work, labor; trouble, distress, suffering; cause of distress; wear and tear; product of work, production; drudgery; **lunae** *(or* **solis)** **labores** eclipse of the moon *(or* sun)

labōrif·er -era -erum *adj* struggling, hard-working

labōriōs·us -a -um *adj* laborious; full of troubles, troublesome; energetic, industrious, hard-working

labōr·ō -āre -āvī -ātus *tr* to work at; to make by toil; to produce *(grain, etc.); (w. internal acc)* to be worried about, be concerned about, *e.g.:* **hoc homines timent, hoc laborant** people fear this, they are worried about this; **nihil laboro de iis** I am not concerned about them; **nihil laboro, nisi ut salvus sis** my only concern is that you are O.K. *(literally, I am concerned as to nothing except that you be well)* ‖ *intr* to work, perform physical work; to suffer, be troubled; to exert oneself; *(w. abl of cause or* **ab** *or* **ex)** **1** to suffer *(physical pain)* from, *e.g.:* **(a) stomacho** *(or* **ex stomacho)** **laborare** to have stomach trouble; **e dolore laborare** to suffer pain; **e renibus laborare** to have kidney problems; **laborantes utero puellae** pregnant girls, girls in labor *(i.e., in giving birth);* **2** to be distressed at, be anxious about, be worried about, be in trouble because of: **laborat de aestimatione sua** he is anxious *or* worried about his reputation; **ex aere alieno laborare** to be heavily in debt, be in trouble because of debt; **e dolore laborare** to be afflicted with grief; **ex inscientia laborare** to suffer from ignorance; **cujus manu sit percussus, non laboro** I do not concern myself over by whose hand he was struck; *(w.* **in** *+ abl)* **1** to be in trouble over, be in danger because of, *e.g.:* **in re familiari valde laborare** to be in deep trouble over personal finances, be in deep financial trouble; **2** to take pains with, exert oneself on behalf of, *e.g.:* **multo plus est in reliqua causa laborandum** much greater pains must be taken with the rest of the case *or* lawsuit; *(w.* **in** *+ acc)* to strive for, work for, *e.g.:* **in divitias luxuriamque laborare** to strive for wealth and luxury; *(w. inf or* **ut** *+ subj)* to strive to, try to, take pains to, make an effort to, *e.g.:* **laborabat ut reliquas civitates adjungeret** he tried to annex the rest of the communities; *(w.* **de** *+ abl)* to be anxious about, be worried about; **luna laborat** *(astr)* the moon is in eclipse; **silvae laborantes** the groaning forests; **suis laborantibus succurrere** to help his own people in difficulty

labōs *see* **labor**

lăbr·um -ī *n* lip; edge

lābr·um -ī *n* basin, tub, bathtub

labrusc·a -ae *f* wild vine

labrusc·um -ī *n* wild grape

labyrinthē·us -a -um *adj* labyrinthine

labyrinth·us -ī *m* labyrinth, maze *(esp. that built by Daedalus on Crete)*

lac lactis *n* milk; milky sap of plants
Lacaen·a -ae *f* Spartan woman
Lacedaem·ō(n) -onis *f* Sparta
Lacedaemōni·us -a -um *adj* Spartan
lac·er -era -erum *adj* mangled, lacerated; *(of things)* badly damaged
lacerāti·ō -ōnis *f* laceration, tearing, mangling
lacern·a -ae *f* mantle, cloak
lacernāt·us -a -um *adj* cloaked
lacer·ō -āre -āvī -ātus *tr* to lacerate, tear, mangle; to batter, damage; to rack *(w. pain);* to slander, abuse; to waste *(time);* to wreck *(a ship); (fig)* to murder *(a song, speech)*
lacert·us -a -um *adj* muscular ‖ *m* lizard; upper arm; muscle ‖ *mpl* muscles, brawn ‖ *f* lizard *(female)*
lacess·ō -ĕre -īvī *or* **-iī -ītus** *tr* to provoke, exasperate; to challenge; to move, arouse
Laches·is -is *f* one of the three Fates
lacini·a -ae *f* flap *(of a garment)*
Lacīn·ium -(i)ī *n* promontory in Bruttium with a temple to Juno
Lac·ō(n) -ōnis *m* Spartan; Spartan dog
Lacōni·a -ae *f* district of the Peloponnesus of which Sparta was the chief city
Lacōnic·us -a -um *adj* Spartan ‖ *n* sweat bath, sauna
lacrim·a -ae *f* (-rum-) tear(drop); *(bot)* gumdrop *(from plant)* ‖ *fpl* tears; dirge
lacrimābil·is -is -e *adj* worthy of tears, deplorable
lacrimābund·us -a -um *adj* tearful, about to break into tears
lacrim·ō -āre -āvī -ātus *tr* **(-rum-)** to cry for, shed tears over ‖ *intr* to cry, shed tears
lacrimōs·us -a -um *adj* crying, tearful; causing tears, bringing tears to the eyes
lacrimul·a -ae *f* teardrop, little tear; *(fig)* crocodile tear
lacrum- = lacrim-
lact·ans -antis *adj* milk-giving
lactāri·us -a -um *adj* milky
lact·ens -entis *adj* unweaned, still breast-feeding; milky, juicy, tender; full of milk ‖ *m* suckling
lacteol·us -a -um *adj* milk-white
lact·ēs -ium *fpl* small intestines; *(as a dish)* chitterlings; **laxae lactes** empty stomach
lactesc·ō -ĕre *intr* to turn to milk
lacte·us -a -um *adj* milky, full of milk; milk-colored, milk-white
lact·ō -āre -āvī -ātus *tr* to cajole, induce
lactūc·a -ae *f* lettuce
lacūna -ae *f* ditch, hole, pit; pond, pool; *(fig)* hole, gap
lacūn·ar -āris *n* paneled ceiling
lacūn·ō -āre -āvī -ātus *tr* to panel
lacūnōs·us -a -um *adj* sunken; pitted
lac·us -ūs *m* vat; tank, pool, reservoir, cistern; lake
lae·dō -dĕre -sī -sus *tr* to knock, strike; to hurt; to rub open; to wound; to break *(promise, pledge);* to harm *(reputation, interests);* to offend, outrage, violate; *(w.* **ad)** to smash *(s.th.)* against; *(poet)* to mar
laen·a -ae *f* lined coat
Lāërt·ēs -ae *m* father of Odysseus
Lāërtiad·ēs -ae *m* son of Laërtes, Odysseus
laesī *perf of* **laedo**
laesi·ō -ōnis *f* attack, provocation
Laestrȳg·ōn -onis *or* **-onos** *m* Laestrygonian *(one of the mythical races of cannibals in Italy, founders of Formiae)*
Laestrȳgoni·us -a -um *adj* Lyaestrygonian, of Formiae
laes·us -a -um *pp of* **laedo** ‖ *adj* harmed; **res laesae** adversity
laetābil·is -is -e *adj* cheerful, glad
laet·ans -antis *adj* joyful, glad
laetāti·ō -ōnis *f* rejoicing, joy
laetē *adv* joyfully, gladly
laetific·ans -antis *adj* joyous
laetific·ō -āre -āvī -ātus *tr* to gladden, cheer up ‖ *pass* to rejoice
laetific·us -a -um *adj* joyful, cheerful
laetiti·a -ae *f* joyfulness, gladness, exuberance
laet·or -ārī -ātus sum *intr* to rejoice, be glad
laet·us -a -um *adj* glad, cheerful, rejoicing; happy; fortunate, auspicious; fertile, rich *(soil);* smiling *(grain);* sleek, fat *(cattle);* bright, cheerful *(appearance);* cheering, welcome *(news)*
laevē *adv* awkwardly
laev·us -a -um *adj* left, on the left side; awkward, stupid; ill-omened; lucky, propitious ‖ *f* left hand, left side ‖ *n* the left ‖ *npl* the area on the left
lagan·um -ī *n,* **lagan·us -ī** *m* pancake
lagēna *see* **lagoena**
lagē·os -ī *f* a Greek variety of vine
Lāgē·us -a -um *adj* of Lagus *(i.e., of the Ptolemies),* Egyptian
lagoen·a *or* **lagōn·a** *or* **lagēn·a** *or* **lagūn·a -ae** *f* bottle
lagō·is -idis *f* grouse
lagūna *see* **lagoena**
laguncul·a -ae *f* flask
Lāg·us -ī *m* Ptolemy I, King of Egypt
Lāïad·ēs -āe *m* son of Laius *(Oedipus)*
Lāï·us -ī *m* Laius *(father of Oedipus)*
lall·ō -āre *intr* to sing a lullaby
lām·a -ae *f* swamp, bog
lamber·ō -āre *tr* to tear to pieces
lamb·ō -ĕre -ī *tr* to lick, lap; *(of a river)* to lap, flow by; *(of ivy)* to cling to
lāment·a -ōrum *npl* lamentation
lāmentābil·is -is -e *adj* pitiable; doleful; mournful, sorrowful

lāmentāri·us -a -um *adj* sorrowful, pitiful
lāmentāti·ō -ōnis *f* lamentation
lāment·or -ārī -ātus sum *tr* to lament ‖ *intr* to lament, wail, cry
lami·a -ae *f* witch, sorceress
lāmin·a *or* **lammin·a** *or* **lamn·a -ae** *f* plate, thin sheet *(of metal or wood);* blade; *(coll)* cash; peel, shell
lamp·as -adis *or* **-ados** *f* torch; brightness; light *(of the sun, moon, stars); (w. numerals)* day; meteor; lamp
Lam·us -ī *m* king of the Laestrygonians ‖ son of Hercules and Omphale
lān·a -ae *f* wool; working in wool, spinning; **lana aurea** golden fleece; **lanam trahere** to card wool; **lanas ducere** to spin wool; **rixari de lanā caprinā** *(prov)* to fight over nothing *(literally, to fight over goat wool)*
lānār·ius -(i)ī *m* wool worker
lānāt·us -a -um *adj* woolly ‖ *fpl* sheep
lance·a -ae *f* lance, spear
lancin·ō -āre -āvī -ātus *tr* to squander
lāne·us -a -um *adj* woolen; soft
langue·faciō -facĕre -fēcī -factus *tr* to make tired
langu·ens -entis *adj* languid, drooping, listless
langu·eō -ēre *intr* to be tired, be weary; to be weak, be feeble *(from disease);* to be sick; *(fig)* to be languid, listless; to be without energy; *(of water)* to be sluggish; *(of plants)* to droop, wilt
langu·escō -escĕre -uī *intr* to become weak, grow faint; to become listless; to decline, decrease; to relax
languidē *adv* weakly; slugglishly
languidul·us -a -um *adj* languid; wilted, drooping *(plants)*
languid·us -a -um *adj* weak, faint; weary; languid, sluggish; listless; lazy; drooping, wilting *(plants)*
langu·or -ōris *m* weakness, faintness, languor; listlessness, sluggishness; apathy; idleness
laniāt·us -ūs *m* mangling ‖ *mpl* mental anguish
laniēn·a -ae *f* butcher shop
lānific·ium -(i)ī *n* weaving
lānific·us -a -um *adj* spinning, weaving, of spinning, of weaving
lānig·er -era -erum *adj* fleecy ‖ *m* sheep *(ram)* ‖ *f* sheep *(ewe)*
lani·ō -āre -āvī -ātus *tr* to tear to pieces, mangle
lanist·a -ae *m* gladiator trainer, fencing master; *(pej)* ringleader
lānit·ium -(i)ī *n* wool
lan·ius -(i)ī *m* butcher; *(pej)* executioner, butcher
lantern·a -ae *f* **(lāt-)** lantern
lanternār·ius -(i)ī *m* guide
lānūg·ō -inis *f* down *(of plants, on cheeks)*
Lānuv·ium -(i)ī *n* town in Latium on the Appian Way
lan·x -cis *f* dish, platter; pan *(of a pair of scales);* **aequā lance** impartially
Lāöco·ōn -ontis *m* son of Priam and priest of Apollo, who, with his two sons, was killed by sea serpents
Lāömedontē·us *or* **Lāömedonti·us -a -um** *adj* Trojan
Lāömedontiad·ēs -ae *m* son of Laomedon, Priam ‖ *mpl* Trojans
lapath·um -ī *n or* **lapath·us -ī** *f* sorrel *(plant)*
lapicīd·a -ae *m* stonecutter, quarry worker
lapicīdīn·ae -ārum *fpl* stone quarry
lapidāri·us -a -um *adj* stone; **latomiae lapidariae** stone quarries ‖ *m* stonecutter
lapidāti·ō -ōnis *f* throwing stones, stoning
lapidāt·or -ōris *m* stone thrower
lapide·us -a -um *adj* of stones, stone, stony; **lapideus imber** shower of meteoric stones; **lapideus sum** *(fig)* I am petrified
lapid·ō -āre -āvī -ātus *tr* to throw stones at, stone ‖ *v impers* it is raining stones
lapidōs·us -a -um *adj* full of stones, stony; hard as stone; gritty *(bread)*
lapill·us -ī *m* small stone, pebble; precious stone, gem; piece, counter *(in a game);* voting pebble
lap·is -idis *m* stone; milestone; platform; boundary stone, landmark; tombstone; precious stone, gem, pearl; stone statue; marble table; **lapides loqui** to speak harsh words
Lapith·ae -ārum *mpl* mountain tribe in Thessaly that fought the centaurs
lapp·a -ae *f* bur *(prickly head or seed vessel of certain plants)*
lapsi·ō -ōnis *f* sliding, slipping; *(fig)* tendency
laps·us -ūs *m* falling, fall, sliding, slipping, gliding, flow, flight; blunder, slip; fall from favor; lapse *(of time);* course *(of the stars);* **lapsus rotarum** rolling wheels
laqueār·ia -ium *npl* paneled ceiling
laqueāt·us -a -um *adj* paneled, having a paneled ceiling
laque·us -ī *m* noose; snare; *(fig)* snare, trap ‖ *mpl* subtleties
Lār Laris *(gen plur:* **Larum** *or* **Larium)** *m* tutelary deity, household god; hearth, home ‖ *mpl* hearth, home, house, household, family
lard·um -ī *n* bacon
Lārenti·a -ae *f (also* **Acca Lārentia)** wife of Faustulus who reared Romulus and Remus
largē *adv* liberally, generously; in large numbers, in large quantities; to a great extend *or* degree

largific·us -a -um *adj* bountiful
largiflu·us -a -um *adj* gushing
largiloqu·us -a -um *adj* talkative
larg·ior -īrī -ītus sum *tr* to give generously, bestow freely; to lavish; to confer; to grant, concede; to condone, overlook; *(w. dat)* to overlook in favor of: **rogo ut amori nostro plusculum, quam concedat veritas, largiare** I beg you to overlook a little more than truth would allow, in favor of our affection (for each other) ‖ *intr* to give bribes, engage in bribery; *(of time, conditions)* to allow
largit·ās -ātis *f* generosity, bounty
largiti·ō -ōnis *f* generosity; bribery
largīt·or -ōris *m* generous donor; spendthrift; briber
larg·us -a -um *adj* abundant, plentiful, large, much; generous; bountiful, profuse
lārid·um -ī *n* bacon
Lāriss·a -ae *f* (-rīs-) town in Thessaly on the Peneus River, famous for its beauty
Lārissae·us -a -um *adj* (-rīs-) of Larissa
Lār·ius -(i)ī *m* Lake Como
lar·ix -icis *f* larch tree
Lar·s -tis *m* first name *(praenomen)* of Etruscan origin, *usu.* given to the eldest son
larv·a -ae *f* mask; ghost; demon
larvāt·us -a -um *adj* bewitched
lasan·um -ī *n or* **lasan·us -ī** *m* chamber pot
lāsarpīcif·er -era -erum *adj* producing asafetida *(used as an anti-spasmodic)*
lascīvi·a -ae *f* frisking, playfulness; lewdness, sexual freedom; fun
lascīvibund·us -a -um *adj* frisky
lascīv·iō -īre -iī -ītum *intr* to frolic, be frisky; to run riot, run wild; to be in heat
lascīv·us -a -um *adj* playful, frisky; brash, impudent; licentious, horny; luxuriant *(growth)*
lāserpīc·ium -(i)ī *n* silphium *(plant yielding asafetida, used as an anti-spasmodic)*
lassitūd·ō -inis *f* tiredness, lassitude
lass·ō -āre -āvī -ātus *tr* to tire out, exhaust
lassul·us -a -um *adj* somewhat tired
lass·us -a -um *adj* tired, exhausted
lātē *adv* widely, extensively; profusely; **late longeque** far and wide; **late patere** to cover a wide field, have wide application
latebr·a -ae *f* hiding place, hideaway, hideout; *(fig)* loophole
latebricol·a -ae *mf* person who hangs around dives and brothels
latebrōsē *adv* secretly
latebrōs·us -a -um *adj* full of holes; hidden, secret; porous
lat·ens -entis *adj* hidden, secret
latenter *adv* in secret
lat·eō -ēre -uī *intr* to hide, lie hidden; to lurk; to be out of sight, be invisible; to lie below the surface; to keep out of sight, sulk; to live a retired life, remain in obscurity, remain unknown; to escape notice; to be in safety; to avoid a summons, lie low; to be obscure; to take shelter
lat·er -eris *m* brick, tile; brickwork; **laterem lavare** *(prov)* to waste effort *(literally, to wash sun-dried bricks of clay);* **lateres ducere** to make bricks
laterām·en -inis *n* earthenware
latercul·us -ī *m* small brick; tile; biscuit
laterici·us -a -um *adj* brick, of brick ‖ *n* brickwork
lātern·a -ae *f* **(lant-)** lantern
latesc·ō -ěre *intr* to hide
lat·ex -icis *m* liquid, fluid; water; spring; wine; oil
latibul·um -ī *n* hiding place, hideout, lair, den; *(fig)* refuge
lāticlāvi·us -a -um *adj* having a broad crimson stripe *(distinctive mark of senators, military tribunes of the equestrian order, and of sons of distinguished families)* ‖ *m* senator; nobleman
lātifund·ium -(i)ī *n* large estate, ranch
Latīnē *adv* Latin, in Latin; in proper Latin; in plain Latin; **Latine docere** to teach Latin; **Latine loqui** to speak Latin; to speak correct Latin; *(coll)* to talk turkey; **Latine reddere** to translate Latin; **Latine scire** to understand Latin
Latīnit·ās -ātis *f* pure Latin, Latinity; Latin rights and privileges
Latīn·us -a -um *adj* Latin; possessing Latin rights and privileges ‖ *m* Latinus *(king of Latium, who gave his daugher Lavinia in marriage to Aeneas)* ‖ *mpl* the Latins, people of Latium ‖ *f* Latin (language) ‖ *n* Latin (language); **in Latinum convertere** to translate into Latin
lāti·ō -ōnis *f* bringing, rendering; formal proposal *(of a law);* **suffragii latio** the franchise
latitāti·ō -ōnis *f* lying in concealment
latit·ō -āre -āvī *intr* to keep hiding oneself; to be concealed, hide, lurk; to lie low *(in order to avoid a summons)*
lātitūd·ō -inis *f* breadth, width; latitude; size, extent; wide area; richness of expression; **latitudo verborum** drawl; **in latitudine** *(or* **per latitudinem)** horizontally; **in latitudinem** in width
lātius *adv* of late
Lati·us -a -um *adj* of Latium, Latin, Roman ‖ *n* Latium *(district in W. central Italy, in which Rome is situated);* **jus Latii** *(or* **jus Latium)** Latin political rights and privileges
Lātō·is -idis *f* daughter of Latona, Diana
lātom- = lautom-
Lātōn·a -ae *f* mother of Apollo and Diana *(equated with the Greek goddess Leto)*

Lātōnigen·a -ae *mf* child of Latona, Apollo, Diana
Lātōni·us -a -um *adj* of Latona ‖ *f* Diana
lāt·or -ōris *m* bringer, bearer; proposer *(of a law)*
Lātō·us -ī *m* son of Latona, Apollo
lātrāt·or -ōris *m* barker; dog
lātrāt·us -ūs *m* barking
lātrīn·a -ae *f* washroom, toilet
lātr·ō -āre -āvī -ātus *tr* to bark at, snarl at ‖ *intr* to bark; *(fig)* to rant
latr·ō -ōnis *m* mercenary; robber, bandit, brigand; *(of animal or hunter)* predator; *(in chess)* pawn
latrōcin·ium -(i)ī *n* military service *(as a mercenary)*; brigandage, banditry, vandalism, piracy; robbery, highway robbery; villany, outrage; band of robbers
latrōcin·or -ārī -ātus sum *intr* to serve as a mercenary; to be a bandit, be a pirate
latruncul·us -ī *m* small-time bandit; piece *(on a battle-game board)*
lātumi·ae -ārum *fpl* stone quarry; prison
lātus *pp of* **fero**
lāt·us -a -um *adj* wide, broad; extensive; widespread; drawling *(pronunciation)*; **in latum** in width; **latus clavus** broad vertical crimson stripe on the tunic of men of the senatorial class
lat·us -eris *n* side, flank; body, person; lungs; lateral surface; coast; *(mil)* flank; **a latere** *(mil)* on the flank; **a latere** *(w. gen)* **1** at the side of, in the company of; **2** from among the friends of; **aperto latere** *(mil)* on the exposed flank; **in latus cubare** to lie on one's side; **latere tecto** scot-free; **latus dare** to expose oneself; **latus tegere** *(w. gen)* to walk by the side of, to escort
latuscul·um -ī *n* small side
laudābil·is -is -e *adj* laudable
laudābiliter *adv* laudably
laudāti·ō -ōnis *f* commendation; eulogy, panegyric, funeral oration; *(in court)* testimony by a character witness
laudāt·or -ōris *m* praiser; eulogist, panegyrist; *(leg)* character witness
laudāt·us -a -um *adj* praiseworthy, commendable, excellent
laud·ō -āre -āvī -ātus *tr* to praise, commend; to name, quote, cite; to pronounce the funeral oration over, eulogize
laure·a -ae *f* laurel tree; laurel branch; laurel crown, bay wreath; triumph
laureāt·us -a -um *adj* laureate, laureled, crowned with laurel; **litterae laureatae** communiqué announcing victory
Laurent·ēs -um *mpl* Laurentians *(people of Lanuvium)*
Laurentin·us *or* **Laurenti·us -a -um** *adj* Laurentian
laureol·a -ae *f* little laurel crown; triumph
laure·us -a -um *adj* laurel, of laurel ‖ *f see* **laurea**
lauricom·us -a -um *adj* laurel-covered *(mountain)*
laurif·er -era -erum *or* **laurig·er -era -erum** *adj* producing laurels; crowned with laurels
laur·us -ī *or* **-ūs** *f* laurel tree, bay; laurel branch; triumph
lau·s -dis *f* praise, commendation; fame, glory; reputation; approval; praiseworthy deed; merit, worth; **laus est** *(w. inf or* **ut** *w. subj)* it is praiseworthy to ‖ *fpl* eulogy; praises; **laudibus ferre** *(or* **efferre** *or* **tollere)** **in** *(or* **ad)** **caelum** to praise to the skies
Laus·us -ī *m* son of Numitor and brother of Rhea Silvia ‖ son of Mezentius, killed by Aeneas
lautē *adv* sumptuously, splendidly
lauti·a -ōrum *npl* state banquet *(given to foreign ambassadors and state guests)*
lautiti·a -ae *f* luxury, high living
lautumi·ae *or* **lātomi·ae** *or* **lātumi·ae -ārum** *fpl* stone quarry *(esp. used as a prison)*
laut·us -a -um *adj* expensive, elegant, fine; well-heeled; refined, fashionable
lavābr·um -ī *n* bath
lavāti·ō -ōnis *f* washing, bathing, bath; bathing kit
Lāvīni·us -a -um *adj* Lavinian, of Lavinium ‖ *n* town in Latium founded by Aeneas ‖ *f* wife of Aeneas
lav·ō lavāre *(or* **lavĕre)** **lāvī lautum** *(or* **lavātum** *or* **lōtum)** *tr* to wash, bathe; to wet, drench; to wash away ‖ *refl & pass & intr* to wash, wash oneself, bathe
laxāment·um -ī *n* relaxation, respite, letup, mitigation
laxāt·us -a -um *adj* loose, extended *(e.g., ranks)*
laxē *adv* loosely, widely; freely
laxit·ās -ātis *f* roominess; extent, width; freedom of movement
lax·ō -āre -āvī -ātus *tr* to extend, widen, expand; to spread out, scatter; to open up *(passage, hole)*; to undo; to loose *(bonds, bolts, doors)*; to untie; to relax *(body, mind)*; to slacken; to mitigate; *(fig)* to release, relieve; to unstring *(bow)* ‖ *refl* to increase in size, spread out ‖ *pass* to relax ‖ *intr (of prices)* to go down
lax·us -a -um *adj* roomy, wide; loose, slack; prolonged, extended *(time)*; far off, distant *(date)*; low *(price)*; loose-hanging *(clothes)*; wide-open *(door)*; gaping *(joints, holes)*; *(fig)* relaxed, easygoing
le·a -ae *f* lioness
leaen·a -ae *f* lioness
Lēan·der -drī *m* youth of Abydos who

swam across the Hellespont every night to his girlfriend

Learch·us -ī *m* son of Athamas and Ino, killed by his mad father

leb·ēs -ētis *m* cauldron

lectīc·a -ae *f* litter

lectīcār·ius -(i)ī *m* litter bearer

lectīcul·a -ae *f* small litter; small bier

lecti·ō -ōnis *f* selection; reading, reading aloud; perusal; **lectio senatūs** revision of the Senate roll *(by censors)*

lectisterniāt·or -ōris *m* slave who arranged the seating at table

lectistern·ium -(i)ī *n* ritual feast *(at which images of the gods were placed on couches at the table)*

lectit·ō -āre -āvī -ātus *tr* to read and reread; to like to read

lectiuncul·a -ae *f* light reading

lect·or -ōris *m* reader *(esp. a slave who read aloud to his master)*

lectul·us -ī *m* cot; small bed, small couch, settee; humble bier

lect·us -ī *m* bed; couch; dining couch; bier; **lectus genialis** marriage bed *(placed in the atrium)*

lect·us -a -um *pp of* **lego** ‖ *adj* select, choice, special, elite

Lēd·a -ae *f* mother of Helen, Clytemnestra, Castor, and Pollux

lēgāti·ō -ōnis *f* embassy, mission, legation; members of an embassy; work *or* report of work of a mission; nominal staff appointment; command of a legion; **legatio libera** junket

lēgāt·um -ī *n* bequest, legacy

lēgāt·us -ī *m* deputy, representative; ambassador, envoy; adjutant *(of a consul, proconsul, or praetor)*; **legatus Augusti** governor of an imperial province; commander *(of a legion)*

lēgī *perf of* **lĕgo** (to read)

lēgif·er -era -erum *adj* lawgiving

legi·ō -ōnis *f* legion *(divided into 10 cohorts and numbering between 4,200 and 6,000 men)*; army, active service

legiōnāri·us -a -um *adj* legionary ‖ *m* legionary soldier

lēgirup·a -ae *or* **lēgirupi·ō -ōnis** *m* lawbreaker

lēgitimē *adv* legitimately, lawfully; properly

lēgitim·us -a -um *adj* legitimate; lawful; regular, right, just, proper; genuine; professional *(boxers, gladiators)* ‖ *npl* legal formalities

legiuncul·a -ae *f* under-manned legion

lēg·ō -āre -āvī -ātus *tr* to commission; to send on a public mission, despatch; to delegate, deputize; to bequeath, will; *(fig)* to entrust

lĕgō lĕgĕre lēgī lectus *tr* to read, peruse; to recite, read aloud; to gather, collect, pick; to pick out, choose; to pick one's way through, cross; to sail by, coast along; to pick up, steal; to pick up *(news, rumor)*; **fila legere** to wind up the thread of life; **senatum legere** to read off the Senate roll

lēgulē·ius -(i)ī *m* pettifogger

legūm·en -inis *n* leguminous plant; vegetable; pulse; bean

lemb·us -ī *m* cutter, yacht *(built for speed)*, speedboat

lemm·a -ătis *n* theme, subject matter; epigram

Lemnicol·a -ae *m* inhabitant of Lemnos *(i.e., Vulcan)*

lemniscāt·us -a -um *adj* heavily decorated with combat ribbons

lemnisc·us -ī *m* ribbon which hung down from a victor's wreath

Lemni·us -a -um *adj* Lemnian ‖ *m* Lemnian *(i.e., Vulcan)* ‖ *mpl* the people of Lemnos

Lemn·os *or* **Lemn·us -ī** *f* large island in the N. Aegean Sea

Lemur·ēs -um *mpl* ghosts

Lemūri·a -ōrum *npl* night festival to drive ghosts from the house

lēn·a -ae *f* madame *(of brothel)*

Lēnae·us -a -um *adj* Bacchic; **latices Lenaei** wine ‖ *m* Bacchus

lēnē *adv* gently

lēnīm·en -inis *n* consolation

lēnīment·um -ī *n* alleviation

lēn·iō -īre -īvī *or* **-iī -ītus** *tr* to soothe, alleviate, calm ‖ *intr* to calm down

lēn·is -is -e *adj* mild, gentle, soft, smooth, calm; gentle *(slope)*; weak, mild *(medicine)*; quiet *(sleep)*; mellow *(wine)*; tolerable, moderate *(conditions)*; kind *(person)*

lēnit·ās -ātis *f* mildness, gentleness, softness, smoothness; tenderness, clemency

lēniter *adv* mildly, gently, softly, smoothly; quietly, calmly; halfheartedly; *(of style)* smoothly

lēnitūd·ō -inis *f* mildness, gentleness, softness, smoothness

lēn·ō -ōnis *m* pimp, brothel keeper

lēnōcin·ium -(i)ī *n* pimping, pandering; allurement; alluring makeup; sexy clothes; flattery

lēnōcin·or -ārī -ātus sum *intr* to be a pimp; *(w. dat)* **1** to play up to, pander to; **2** to stimulate, promote

lēnōni·us -a -um *adj* pimp's

len·s -tis *f* lentil

lentē *adv* slowly; indifferently, halfheartedly; calmly, leisurely, deliberately

lentesc·ō -ĕre *intr* to get sticky; *(fig)* to soften, weaken

lentiscif·er -era -erum *adj (of a region)* producing mastic trees

lentisc·us -ī *f* mastic tree *(small evergreen*

tree that yields an aromatic resin called mastic); toothpick *(made of mastic wood)*

lentitūd·ō -inis *f* slowness; insensibility, apathy, dullness

lent·ō -āre -āvī -ātus *tr* to bend *(under strain)*

lentul·us -a -um *adj* somewhat slow

lent·us -a -um *adj* sticky, clinging; pliant, limber; slow, sluggish; lingering; irresponsive, reluctant, indifferent, backward; slow-moving; tedious; drawling; at rest, at leisure, lazy; calm, unconcerned

lēnul·us -ī *m* little pimp

lēnuncul·us -ī *m* small boat, skiff

le·ō -ōnis *m* lion ‖ **Leo** *(astr)* Leo *(constellation and sign of the zodiac)*

Leōnid·ās -ae *m* king of Sparta *(who fell at Thermopylae after a gallant stand in 480 B.C.)*

leōnīn·us -a -um *adj* lion's, of a lion

Leontīn·ī -ōrum *mpl* town in E. Sicily

lep·as -adis *f* limpet *(shellfish)*

lepidē *adv* charmingly, pleasantly, neatly; *(as affirmativbe answer)* yes; *(of approval)* great!

lepid·us -a -um *adj* charming, delightful, neat; witty, amusing *(writings, remarks)*

lep·ōs *or* **lep·or -ōris** *m* pleasantness, charm, attractiveness

lep·us -oris *m* hare ‖ **Lepus** *(astr)* Lepus, the Hare *(constellation)*

lepuscul·us -ī *m* little hare

Lern·a -ae *f* marsh near Argos, where Hercules slew the Hydra

Lernae·us -a -um *adj* Lernaean

Lesbi·us -a -um *adj* of Lesbos, Lesbian ‖ *f* fictitious name given by Catullus to his mistress Clodia ‖ *n* Lesbian wine

Lesb·os *or* **Lesb·us -ī** *f* large island in the N. Aegean, birthplace of Alcaeus and Sappho

less·us *(gen does not occur; acc:* **lessum)** *m* loud wailing

lētāl·is -is -e *adj* lethal, fatal, mortal

Lēthae·us -a -um *adj* of Lethe; infernal; causing drowsiness

lēthargic·us -ī *m* lazy fellow

lētharg·us -ī *m* lethargy

Lēth·ē -ēs *f* Lethe *(river of forgetfulness in lower world)*

lētif·er -era -erum *adj* deadly, fatal; **locus letifer** mortal spot

lēt·ō -āre -āvī -ātus *tr* to kill

lēt·um -ī *n* death; ruin, destruction; **leto dare** to put to death

Leuc·as -adis *f* "White Island", island off W. Greece

leucasp·is -idis *adj* armed with a white shield

Leucipp·us -ī *m* philosopher, teacher of Democritus, and one of the founders of Atomism *(5th cent. B.C.)*

Leuctr·a -ōrum *npl* small town in Boeotia where Epaminondas defeated the Spartans in 371 B.C.

levām·en -inis *n* alleviation, comfort, consolation

levāment·um -ī *n* alleviation, comfort, consolation

levāti·ō -ōnis *f* lightening, easing; relief, comfort; lessening, mitigation

levicul·us -a -um *adj* somewhat vain

levidens·is -is -e *adj* poor, inferior

levifid·us -a -um *adj* untrustworthy

lĕv·is -is -e *adj* light, not heavy; light-armed; lightly dressed; easily digested; thin, poor *(soil);* nimble; flitting; slight, small; unimportant, trivial; unfounded *(rumor);* easy, simple; mild; gentle, easy-going; capricious, unreliable, fickle; lacking authority; lacking power; unsubstantial, thin; **in levi habere** to make light of

lēv·is -is -e *adj* smooth; slippery; hairless, beardless; delicate, tender; effeminate; smooth *(style)*

levisomn·us -a -um *adj* light-sleeping

lĕvit·ās -ātis *f* lightness; mobility, nimbleness; levity, frivolity; *(fig)* shallowness

lēvit·ās -ātis *f* smoothness; *(fig)* fluency

leviter *adv* lightly; slightly, a little, somewhat; easily, without difficulty; nimbly

lev·ō -āre -āvī -ātus *tr* to lift up, raise; to lighten, relieve, ease; to console, comfort; to lift off, remove; to lessen, weaken; to release, free; to take away; to avert; to restore, refresh

lēv·ō -āre -āvī -ātus *tr* to make smooth, polish; to soothe

lēv·or -ōris *m* smoothness

lex lēgis *f* motion, bill; law, statute; rule, regulation; principle, precept; condition, stipulation; **ad legem** neatly; **eā lege ut** with the stipulation that, on condition that; **lege** *(or* **legibus)** legally; **lege agere** to go to court, take legal action; **legem abrogare** to repeal a law; **legem derogare** to amend a bill *or* law; **legem ferre** to propose a bill; **legem jubere** *(of the assembly)* to sanction a law; **legem perferre** to get a bill *or* law passed **leges** constitution; **leges pacis** terms of peace; **sine legibus** without restraint, without control

lībām·en -inis *n* libation; firstfruits

lībāment·um -ī *n* libation; firstfruits

lībāti·ō -ōnis *f* libation

lībell·a -ae *f* small silver coin, one tenth of a denarius *(c. 10¢);* small sum; *(carpenter's)* level; **ad libellam** to a tee, exactly; **heres ex libella** sole heir

libell·us -ī *m* booklet, pamphlet; notebook; journal, diary; program; handbill, advertisement; petition; answer to a petition; letter; written accusation, indictment; libel; satirical verse

lib·ens -entis *adj* **(lub-)** willing, ready, glad; merry, cheerful; **libenti animo** willingly

libenter *adv* **(lub-)** willingly, gladly, with pleasure

lī·ber -brī *m* book, work, treatise; catalog, list, register; letter, rescript; bark *(of a tree)*

līb·er -era -erum *adj* free; open, unoccupied; unrestricted; unprejudiced; outspoken, frank; uncontrolled, unrestricted; *(of states or municipalities)* independent, autonomous; exempt; free of charge; *(w. abl or* **ab)** free from, exempt from; *(w. gen)* free of ‖ *mpl see* **liberi**

Līb·er -erī *m* Italian fertility god, later identified with Bacchus; wine

Līber·a -ae *f* Proserpine ‖ Ariadne *(the wife of Bacchus)*

Līberāl·ia -ium *npl* festival of Liber *(held on March 17, at which young men received the toga virilis)*

līberāl·is -is -e *adj* relating to freedom, relating to civil status, of free citizens; worthy of a freeman, honorable, gentleman's; courteous; liberal, generous; handsome

līberālit·ās -ātis *f* courtesy, politeness; liberality, generosity; grant, gift

līberāliter *adv* like a freeman, nobly; liberally *(e.g., educated);* courteously; liberally, generously

līberāti·ō -ōnis *f* liberation, freeing; release *(from debt); (leg)* acquittal

līberāt·or -ōris *m* liberator

līberē *adv* freely; frankly; ungrudgingly; like a freeman, liberally

līber·ī -ōrum *or* **-um** *mpl* children; sons; **jus trium liberorum** a privileged status granted by the *Lex Papia Poppaea* of A.D. 9 to fathers of three or more children *(occasionally extended to others)*

līber·ō -āre -āvī -ātus *tr* to free, set free, release; to acquit; to cancel, get rid of *(e.g., debts);* to pay for, cover *(an expense);* to exempt; to manumit; to cross *(threshold);* to draw *(a sword);* to clear *(positions of hostile forces); (w. abl or w.* **ab** *or* **ex)** to free from, release from, acquit of; **fidem liberare** to keep one's promise; **nomina liberare** to cancel debts; **promissa liberare** to fulfill promises ‖ *refl* to pay up a debt

lībert·a -ae *f* freedwoman, ex-slave

lībert·ās -ātis *f* liberty, freedom; status of a freeman; political freedom; freedom of speech, freedom of thought; frankness

lībertīn·us -a -um *adj* of the status of a freedman ‖ *m* freedman, ex-slave ‖ *f* freedwoman, ex-slave

lībert·us -ī *m* freedman, ex-slave

lib·et -ēre -uit *or* **libitum est** *v impers* **(lub-)** *(w. dat)* it pleases, it is pleasant for, is agreeable to, is nice for *(s.o.); (w. inf)* it is nice, pleasant to *(do s.th.);* **mihi libet** I feel like, want; **qui libet** any you like to mention; **si lubet** if you please; **ut lubet** as you please

libīdin·or -ārī -ātus sum *intr* to gratify lust

libīdinōsē *adv* willfully; arbitrarily

libīdinōs·us -a -um *adj* **(lub-)** willful; arbitrary; lustful, lecherous

libīd·ō -inis *f* **(lub-)** desire, longing, inclination, pleasure; will, willfulness, arbitrariness, caprice, fancy; lust, sexual desire; rut, heat; **ad** *(or* **per) libidinem** *(w. gen)* at the pleasure of; **ex libidine** arbitrarily; **libidinem habere in** *(w. abl)* to be fond of, take pleasure in

libīt·a -ōrum *npl* will, pleasure

Libitīn·a -ae *f* burial goddess; implements for burial; grave; death

līb·ō -āre -āvī -ātus *tr* to taste, sip; to pour as a libation, offer, consecrate; to touch lightly, barely touch, graze; to spill, waste; to extract, collect, compile

lībr·a -ae *f* balance, scales; plummet, level; pound *(of 12 ounces)*

lībrāment·um -ī *n* weight; balance, ballast; level surface, horizontal plane; gravity

lībrāri·a -ae *f* forelady *(who weighed out wool for slaves to spin)*

librāriol·us -ī *m* copyist, scribe

librāri·us -a -um *adj* book-, of books; **taberna libraria** bookstore ‖ *m* copyist, scribe, secretary; bookseller ‖ *n* bookcase

lībrāri·us -a -um *adj* weighing a pound

lībrāt·or -ōris *m* surveyor

lībrāt·us -a -um *adj* horizontal, level; poised; well-aimed

lībrīl·is -is -e *adj* one-pound

lībrit·or -ōris *m* artilleryman

lībr·ō -āre -āvī -ātus *tr* to balance; to poise, level, hurl, launch; to sway

līb·um -ī *n or* **līb·us -ī** *m* cake *(usu. used in sacrficial offerings);* **libum natale** birthday cake

Liburni·a -ae *f* district of Illyria between Istria and Dalmatia

Liburn·us -a -um *adj* Liburnian ‖ *mf* Liburnian ‖ *f* Liburnian galley

Liby·a -ae *or* **Liby·ē -ēs** *f* Libya *(general term for all of N. Africa)*

Libyc·us -a -um *adj* Libyan, N. African

Lib·ys -yos *adj* of N. Africa, N. African ‖ *m* N. African

Libyss·us -a -um *adj* N. African

Libystīn·us *or* **Liby·us -a -um** *adj* Libyan; N. African

Libyst·is -idis *adj (fem only)* N. African

lic·ens -entis *adj* free, unrestrained; licentious; forward, pushy, bold

licenter *adv* freely, without restraint; licentiously; boldly
licenti·a -ae *f* license, freedom; unruly behavior, lawlessness; outspokenness; licentiousness; free imagination; *(w. gen of gerund)* freedom to *(do s.th.)*; **ludendi licentia** (unrestricted) freedom to play
lic·eō -ēre -uī *intr* to be for sale; *(w. abl or gen of price)* to cost, fetch
lic·eor -ērī -itus sum *tr* to bid on, bid for, make an offer for ‖ *intr* to bid
lic·et -ēre -uit *or* **-itum est** *v impers* it is permitted, it is lawful; *(w. dat & inf)* it is all right for *(s.o.)* to; **licet** *(to express assent)* yes, O.K.; **mihi licet** I may, I can *(often w. neut. pron as subject)*: **si tibi hoc licitum est** if you are allowed to do this; *(w. the force of a conjunction, w. subj)* although, granting that
Lich·ās -ae *m* companion of Hercules
līch·ēn -ēnos *m* lichen *(resin used to cure skin diseases)*; ringworm *(a skin disease)*
licitāti·ō -ōnis *f* bidding *(at auction)*; haggling
licitāt·or -ōris *m* bidder
licit·or -ārī -ātus sum *tr* to bid for
licit·us -a -um *adj* permissible, lawful, legitimate ‖ *n* lawful action
lict·or -ōris *m* lictor *(attendant and bodyguard of a magistrate)*
li·ēn -ēnis *m* spleen
liēnōs·us -a -um *adj* splenetic
ligām·en -inis *n* string, tie; bandage
ligāment·um -ī *n* bandage
lignār·ius -(i)ī *m* carpenter
lignāti·ō -ōnis *f* gathering of lumber
lignāt·or -ōris *m* woodcutter, lumberjack
ligneol·us -a -um *adj* wooden
ligne·us -a -um *adj* wooden; woody; tough, wiry *(person)*
lign·or -ārī -ātus sum *intr* to gather wood
lign·um -ī *n* wood; *(also pl)* firewood *(as opp. to* **materia** = lumber for building); stump; log, plank; writing tablet; tree; stone *(of olive, fruit)*; *(various objects made of wood)*: spear-shaft, money box, writing tablet, wooden mask, boat; **in silvam ligna ferre** *(prov)* to carry coals to Newcastle *(literally, to carry logs into the woods)*; **mobile lignum** puppet
lig·ō -āre -āvī -ātus *tr* to tie, tie up, bandage; to close *(a deal)*; to draw tight, knot; to cement *(an alliance)*; to unite in harmony; *(w. dat or* **ad**) to tie to
lig·ō -ōnis *m* mattock, hoe; farming
ligul·a *or* **lingul·a -ae** *f* shoe strap; flap; *(geog)* tongue of land
Lig·ur *or* **Lig·us -uris** *mf* Ligurian
Liguri·a -ae *f* Liguria *(district along the N.W. coast of Italy)*
ligūr(r)·iō -īre -īvī *or* **-iī -ītus** *tr* to lick; to pick at, eat daintily; *(fig)* to be dying for; *(fig)* to sponge on
ligū(r)rīti·ō -ōnis *f* constant hankering for food
Ligus *see* **Ligur**
Ligusc·us *or* **Ligustic·us** *or* **Ligustīn·us -a -um** *adj* Ligurian
ligustr·um -ī *n (bot)* privet *(widely used for hedges)*
līl·ium -(i)ī *n (bot)* lily; *(mil)* trench lined with sharp stakes
līm·a -ae *f* file; *(fig)* revision, polishing; **limae labor** *(fig)* the work of polishing
līmātius *adv* in a more polished style
līmātul·us -a -um *adj* refined, sensitive *(judgment)*
līm·ax -ācis *mf* snail
limbulāri·us -a -um *adj* hem-; **textores limbularii** tassel makers, hemmers
limb·us -ī *m* fringe, hem, tassel
līm·en -inis *n* lintel, threshold; doorway, entrance; outset, beginning; starting gate *(at racetrack)*; house, home
līm·es -itis *m* country trail; path; road along a boundary; boundary, frontier; *(fig)* limit; boundary marker; channel *(of river)*; course *(of life)*; track, trail *(of a shooting star)*; line of color, streak
līm·ō -āre -āvī -ātus *tr* to file; *(fig)* to polish, refine; to file down, take away from, lessen; to get down to *(the truth)*
līmōs·us -a -um *adj* muddy; growing in mud
limpid·us -a -um *adj* limpid, clear
līmul·us -a -um *adj* squinting
līm·us -a -um *adj* squinting; sidelong
līm·us -ī *m* mud; dirt, grime
līm·us -ī *m* ceremonial apron *(trimmed with purple and worn by priests at sacrifice)*
līne·a -ae *f* line; string, thread; fishing line; plumb line; outline; boundary line, limit; **ad lineam** *(or* **rectā lineā**) in a straight line; vertically; horizontally; **extremā lineā amare** to love at a distance; **lineas transire** to go out of bounds
līneāment·um -ī *n* line; characteristic, feature; outline ‖ *npl* lineaments, lines *(of the face)*
līne·ō -āre -āvī -ātus *tr* to make straight, make perpendicular
līne·us -a -um *adj* flaxen, linen
lin·gō -gĕre -xī -ctus *tr* to lick; to lap up
lingu·a -ae *f* tongue; speech, language, dialect; eloquence; utterance; style *(of s.o.'s speech)*; *(of animals)* note, song, bark; *(geog)* tongue of land; **favete linguis!** observe a sacred silence!; **linguam comprimere** *(or* **tenere**) to hold one's tongue; **linguā promptus** insolent, cheeky; **utraque lingua** both languages *(Greek and Latin)*
lingul·a -ae *f* shoe strap; flap; *(geog)* tongue of land

linguläc·a -ae *mf* gossip, chatterbox
līnig·er -era -erum *adj* wearing linen
linō linĕre lēvī *or* **līvī litus** *tr* to smear; to erase; to cover, coat; *(fig)* to mess up
linquō linquĕre līquī *tr* to leave, forsake; to depart from; to leave alone; to leave in a pinch ‖ *pass* to faint; **animo linqui** to faint ‖ *v impers* **relinquitur** *(w.* **ut)** it remains to *(do s.th.)*
linteātus -a -um *adj* canvas-
linte·ō -ōnis *f* linen-weaver
linteol·um -ī *n* small linen cloth
lin·ter -tris *f* skiff; vat, tank
linte·us -a -um *adj* linen ‖ *n* linen; linen cloth; canvas, sail; kerchief
lintricul·us -ī *m* small boat
līn·um -ī *n* flax; linen; thread; rope, line; fishing line; net; linen dress
Lin·us *or* **Lin·os -ī** *m* son of Apollo and instructor of Orpheus and Hercules
Lipar·a -ae *or* **Lipar·ē -ēs** *f* Lipara *(island off the N. coast of Sicily)* ‖ *fpl* the Aeolian Islands
Liparae·us -a -um *or* **Liparens·is -is -e** *adj* of Lipara
lipp·iō -īre -īvī *or* **-iī -ītum** *intr* to have sore eyes; *(of eyes)* to burn
lippitūd·ō -inis *f* running eyes, inflammation of the eyes
lipp·us -a -um *adj* with sore eyes; burning *(eyes); (fig)* half-blind
lique·faciō -facĕre -fēcī -factus *(pass:* **lique·fīō -fierī -factus sum)** *tr* to melt, dissolve; to decompose; to waste, weaken
liqu·ens -entis *adj* clear, limpid; flowing, gliding
liqueō liquēre liquī *or* **licuī** *intr* to be liquid; to be clear ‖ *v impers* it is clear, is apparent, is evident; **liquet mihi** *(w. inf)* I am free to; **non liquet** *(leg)* it is not clear *(legal formula used by a hung jury)*
liquescō liquescĕre licuī *intr* to melt; to decompose; to grow soft, grow effeminate; to become clear; *(fig)* to melt away
liquidē *adv* clearly
liquidiuscul·us -a -um *adj* gentler
liquidō *adv* clearly, plainly, certainly
liquid·us -a -um *adj* liquid, fluid, flowing; clear, transparent; evident; pure *(pleasure);* clear *(voice);* calm *(mind)* ‖ *n* liquid, water; clearness, certainty
liqu·ō -āre -āvī -ātus *tr* to melt, dissolve; to strain, filter
līqu·or -ī *intr* to flow; to melt; *(fig)* to waste away; **in lacrimas liqui** to dissolve into tears
liqu·or -ōris *m* fluidity; liquid, fluid; sea
Līr·is -is *m* river between Latium and Campania
līs lītis *f (old form:* **stlīs stlītis)** matter of dispute; quarrel, dispute; wrangling; *(leg)* lawsuit, litigation; *(leg)* charge, accusation; **lis capitis** criminal charge; **litem aestimare** *(or* **taxare)** to assess damages; **litem intendere** *(or* **litem inferre)** *(w. dat)* to bring a suit against, sue *(s.o.)*
litāti·ō -ōnis *f* successful sacrifice *(i.e., obtaining of favorable omens from a sacrifice)*
litātō *adv* with favorable omens
lītera *see* **littera**
Līternum -ī *n* town on the coast of Campania
litic·en -inis *m* trumpeter
lītigāt·or -ōris *m (leg)* litigant
lītigiōs·us -a -um *adj* litigious; quarrelsome; disputed
lītig·ium -(i)ī *n* quarrel, dispute
lītig·ō -āre -āvī -tum *intr* to squabble; *(leg)* to go to court
lit·ō -āre -āvī -ātus *tr* to propitiate; to offer by way of atonement; to atone for; **litandum est** atonement must be made ‖ *intr* to obtain favorable omens from a sacrifice; *(of a sacrifice)* to give favorable omens; *(w. dat)* to appease, propitiate
lītorāl·is -is -e *adj* shore-, of the shore
lītore·us -a -um *adj* at *or* along the seashore
litter·a *or* **līter·a -ae** *f* letter *(of the alphabet);* handwriting; **ad litteram** verbatim; **littera salutaris** *(leg) (i.e.,* **A = absolvo)** vote of acquittal; **littera tristis** *(leg) (i.e.,* **C = condemno)** vote of guilty ‖ *fpl* epistle, letter, dispatch; edict, ordinance; literature, books, literary works; book learning, liberal education, scholarship; branch of learning; records, account; inscription; **in litteras digerere** to arrange in alphabetical order; **litteras discere** to learn to read and write; **litteras scire** to know how to read and write, be literate
litterāri·us -a -um *adj* of reading and writing; **ludus litterarius** elementary school
litterātē *adv* legibly, in a clear handwriting; literally; learnedly
litterāt·or -ōris *m* elementary-school teacher, schoolmaster
litterātūr·a -ae *f* writing; alphabet; grammar; writings, literature
litterāt·us -a -um *adj* learned, scholarly; liberally educated; devoted to literature; *(of time)* devoted to studies; marked *or* inscribed with letters ‖ *m* man of culture; teacher of literature; scholar
litterul·a -ae *f* small letter ‖ *fpl* short letter, note; slight literary endeavors; ABC's
litūr·a -ae *f* erasure; erased passage; correction; smudge, smear
litus *pp of* **lino**
līt·us -oris *n* seashore, beach, coast;

riverbank; **litus arare** *(prov)* to waste effort *(literally, to plow the shore)*

litu·us -ī *m* cavalry trumpet, clarion; *(fig)* signal; augur's wand *(a crooked staff carried by an augur);* **lituus meae profectionis** signal for my departure

līv·ens -entis *adj* livid; black-and-blue

līv·eō -ēre *intr* to be black-and-blue, be livid; to be envious; *(w. dat)* to be jealous of

līvesc·ō -ĕre *intr* to turn black-and-blue

Līvi·a -ae *f* second wife of Augustus and mother of Tiberius and Drusus (58 B.C.–A.D. 29)

līvidul·us -a -um *adj* inclined to be jealous, somewhat envious

līvid·us -a -um *adj* leaden *(in color);* blue; black-and-blue; jealous, envious, spiteful

Līv·ius -(i)ī *m* Livy *(Titus Livius Patavinus, historian, 58 B.C.–A.D. 17)* **II** Livius Andronicus *(a Greek who was the first to write Latin poetry, both tragedies and comedies; his first drama was staged in 240 B.C.; he also translated the Odyssey into Saturnian verse)*

līv·or -ōris *m* leaden color; bluish color; black-and-blue mark; jealousy, envy, spite

lix·a -ae *m* peddler *(around a camp),* camp follower

locār·ius -(i)ī *m* ticket broker, gouger *(one who buys up theater seats an an investment)*

locāti·ō -ōnis *f* arrangement, placement; renting out, contract, lease

locāt·or -ōris *m* lessor

locāt·um -ī *n* lease, contract

locell·us -ī *m* small box

locit·ō -āre *tr* to lease out

loc·ō -āre -āvī -ātus *tr* to place, put, set, lay; to establish, constitute, set; to lay *(foundations);* to station *(troops);* to rent out, lease; to contract for; to invest *(effort);* to lend at interest; to farm out *(taxes);* **locare in matrimonium** *(or* **nuptiis** *or* **nuptum)** *(w. dat)* to give in marriage *(to s.o.)*

locul·us -ī *m* little place, spot; pocket

locupl·ēs -ētis *adj* rich; *(w. abl)* rich in, well supplied with; reliable, responsible; **locuples oratione** *(or* **in dicendo) esse** to be a polished speaker

locuplēt·ō -āre -āvī -ātus *tr* to make rich, enrich; to embellish *(a building)*

loc·us -ī *(pl:* **loc·ī -ōrum** *mpl* passages, verses; **loc·a -ōrum** *npl* physical places) *m* place; site; spot; locality, district; seat; town, village; period (of time); opportunity, room, occasion; situation, position; category; rank, degree, birth; office, post; passage *(in a book);* topic, subject, point, division; *(mil)* post, station; *(in astrology)* house; **adhuc locorum** until now; **ad id locorum** until then; **ex aequo loco dicere** to speak in the Senate; to hold a conversation; **ex** *(or* **de) loco superiore dicere** to speak from the Rostra; **ex loco inferiore dicere** to speak before a judge, speak in court; **inde loci** since then; **in eo loci** in such a condition; **in locum** *(w. gen)* in place of, as a substitute for, instead of; **interea loci** meanwhile; **loca** *(vulg)* female genitals; **loci communes** general topics; public places, parks; **loco** *(w. gen)* in stead of, in place of; **loco** *(or* **in loco)** at the right time; on the spot; **loco cedere** to give way, yield; **loco movere** to dislodge; to dislocate *(a limb);* **locum dare** to make way; **locum habere** to be valid, be applicable, hold good; **locum facere** to clear the way; **locum mutare** to change one's residence, move; **locus publicus** public building, public square; **mentem (meam, tuam, ejus) loco movere** *(or* **pellere)** to drive (me, you, him) out of (my, your, his) mind; **nullo loco** under no circumstances; **postea loci** afterwards; **post id locorum** afterwards; **stare loco** to stand still; **ubicumque loci** whenever

lōcust·a -ae *f* locust

Lōcust·a -ae *f* **(Lūc-)** woman notorious as poisoner in the time of Claudius and Nero

locūti·ō -ōnis *f* speech; way of speaking; expression; word; pronunciation

locūtus *pp of* **loquor**

lōd·ix -īcis *f* blanket

logic·us -a -um *adj* logical **II** *npl* logic

log·os *or* **log·us -ī** *m* word; witticism **II** *mpl* mere words, empty talk

lōlīgō *see* **lolligo**

lol·ium -(i)ī *n* darnel *(type of grass)*

lollīg·ō -inis *f* **(lōl-)** squid

lollīguncul·a -ae *f* small squid

lōment·um -ī *n* a face cream *(for cleansing skin)*

Londīn·ium -(i)ī *n* London

longaev·us -a -um *adj* aged

longē *adv* far, far off, a long way off; away, distant; out of reach; long, for a long period; *(to speak)* at greater length; *(w. comparatives)* far, by far, much; **longe lateque** far and wide

longinquit·ās -ātis *f* length, extent; remoteness, distance; length, duration

longinqu·us -a -um *adj* long, extensive; far off, distant, remote; from afar, foreign; long, prolonged, continued, tedious; **e(x) longinquo** from far away; **in longinquo** far away

longitūd·ō -inis *f* length; **in longitudinem** **1** lengthwise, in length; **2** to an immoderate length, too far; **3** for the distant future; **longitudine** *(or* **per longitudinem)** lengthwise

longiuscul·us -a -um *adj* pretty long

longur·ius -(i)ī *m* long pole

long·us -a -um *adj* long; spacious; protracted; tedious; **longa navis** battleship; **longum est** *(w. inf)* it would take too long to **II** *n* length; **in** *(or* **per) longum** for a long while; **ne longum faciam** to make a long story short

loquācit·ās -ātis *f* talkativeness

loquāciter *adv* long-windedly; at length, in detail

loquācul·us -a -um *adj* rather talkative

loqu·ax -ācis *adj* loquacious, talkative

loquēl·a -ae *f* **(-quell-)** speech; word, expression

loqu·ens -entis *adj* articulate

loquit·or -ārī -ātus sum *intr* to chatter away

loquor loquī locūtus sum *tr* to say; to talk of, speak about; to tell, tell of, mention; *(fig)* to declare, show, indicate **II** *intr* to speak; to rustle, murmur; **Latine loqui** to speak Latin; *(coll)* to talk turkey; **male loqui** to speak abusively

lōrār·ius -(i)ī *m* slave driver

lōrāt·us -a -um *adj* tied with thongs

lōre·us -a -um *adj* made of strips of leather; **vostra faciam latera lorea** *(coll)* I'll cut your hide to ribbons

lōrīc·a -ae *f* breastplate; parapet; **libros mutare loricis** to exchange books for arms

lōrīcāt·us -a -um *adj* wearing a breastplate, mail-clad

lōrip·ēs -edis *adj* bowlegged

lōr·um -ī *n* strip of leathter, thong, strap; dog's leash; whip, scourge; leather badge **II** *npl* reins

Lōt·is -idis *f* a nymph who changed into a lotus tree to escape the advances of Priapus

Lōtophag·ī -ōrum *mpl* Lotus-eaters

lōt·os *or* **lōt·us -ī** *f* lotus *(fabulous plant bringing forgetfulness to those who eat its fruit);* flute *(of lotus wood)*

lōtus *see* **lautus**

Lu·a -ae *f* cult partner of Saturn *(to whom captured arms were dedicated)*

lub- = lib-

lubenti·a -ae *f* pleasure

lūbric·ō -āre -āvī -ātus *tr* to oil, grease, make smooth

lūbric·us -a -um *adj* slippery; smooth; slimy; *(of streams)* gently flowing, gliding; deceitful, tricky; precarious, ticklish *(situations, undertakings)* **II** *n* precarious situation, critical period; unstable condition; **in lubrico poni** to be placed in a dangerous situation; **in lubrico versari** to be in a precarious situation

Lūc·a bōs *(gen:* **Lūc·ae bovis)** *f* elephant

Lūcāni·a -ae *f* district in S.W. Italy

Lūcān·us -a -um *adj* Lucanian **II** *m* Lucanian **II** Lucan *(Marcus Annaeus Lucanus, epic poet, condemned to death by Nero, A.D. 39–65)*

lūc·ar -āris *n* funds allocated for public games *(derived from a forest tax)*

lucell·um -ī *n* slight profit

lū·ceō -cēre -xī *intr* to shine, be light, glow, glitter, be clear; *(fig)* to be clear, be apparent, be conspicuous **II** *v impers* it is light, day is dawning

Lūcer·ēs -um *mpl* **(Lŭc-)** one of the three original Roman tribes

lucern·a -ae *f* oil lamp; *(fig)* midnight oil; **ad lucernam** after dark; **ante lucernas** before nightfall; **vinum et lucernae** wine and lamps *(i.e., evening festivities)*

lūcescō lūcescere luxī *intr* **(-cisc-)** to begin to shine **II** *v impers* it is getting light

Lūci·a -ae *f* female name

lūcidē *adv* clearly, distinctly

lūcid·us -a -um *adj* shining, bright, clear; lucid

lūcif·er -era -erum *adj* shiny

Lūcif·er -erī *m (astr)* morning star **II** *(astr)* planet Venus **II** son of Aurora and Cephalus

lūcifug·us -a -um *adj* light-shunning; avoiding the public eye, sulking

Lūcil·ius -(i)ī *m* Gaius Lucilius *(first Roman satiric poet, c. 180–102 B.C.)*

Lūcīn·a -ae *f* goddess of childbirth; childbirth

lūciscō *see* **lucesco**

Lūc·ius -(i)ī *m* Roman first name *(praenomen; abbr: L.)*

Lucmo *see* **Lucumo**

Lucrēti·a -ae *f* wife of Collatinus, who, having been raped by Sextus Tarquinius, committed suicide in 509 B.C.

Lucrēt·ius -(i)ī *m* Spurius Lucretius *(father of Lucretia and consul in 509 B.C.)* **II** Lucretius *(Titus Lucretius Carus, philosophical poet, 94?–55? B.C.)*

lucrificābil·is -is -e *or* **lucrific·us -a -um** *adj* profitable

lucrifug·a -ae *m* person not interested in profit, spendthrift

Lucrīn·us -a -um *adj* Lucrine; **Lacus Lucrinus** Lucrine Lake *(near Baiae, famous for its oysters)*

lucripet·a -ae *m* profiteer

lucr·or -ārī -ātus sum *tr* to gain, win *(as profit)* **II** *intr (w.* **ex)** to profit from

lucrōs·us -a -um *adj* profitable

lucr·um -ī *n* profit, gain; wealth; greed, love of gain; **lucri facere** to gain for oneself; to make profit; **lucri fieri** to be gained; **lucro esse** *(w. dat)* to be advantageous to *(s.o.);* **ponere in lucro** *(or* **in lucris)** to regard as gain; **vivere de lucro** to be lucky to be alive

luctām·en -inis *n* wrestling; struggle, effort

luct·ans -antis *adj* reluctant

luctāti·ō -ōnis *f* wrestling; struggle, effort

luctāt·or -ōris *m* wrestler

luctific·us -a -um *adj* causing sorrow, calamitous

luctison·us -a -um *adj* sad-sounding

luct·or -ārī -ātus sum *or* **luct·ō -āre** *intr* to wrestle; *(w.* **cum)** to struggle with, grapple with; *(w. inf)* to struggle to

luctuōsē *adv* so as to cause sadness

luctuōsius *adv* more pitifully

luctuōs·us -a -um *adj* causing sorrow, sorrowful; sad, feeling sad

luct·us -ūs *m* sorrow, mourning, grief, distress; signs of sorrow, mourning clothes; source of grief

lūcubrāti·ō -ōnis *f* working by lamp light; evening gossip

lūcubr·ō -āre -āvī -ātus *tr* to compose at night ‖ *intr* to burn the midnight oil

lūculentē *adv* splendidly, well; *(to beat)* soundly; *(to sell)* at an excellent price

lūculenter *adv* brilliantly, smartly

lūculent·us -a -um *adj* bright, brilliant; excellent, fine; good-looking

Lūcull·us -ī *m* Lucius Licinius Lucullus *(Roman general and politician, 117–56 B.C.)*

Luc(u)m·ō -ōnis *m* Etruscan personal name

lūc·us -ī *m* sacred grove; woods

lūdi·a -ae *f* actress; gladiator *(female)*

lūdibr·ium -(i)ī *n* toy, plaything; derision; object of derision, butt of ridicule; frivolous behavior; sham, pretense; *(fig)* sucker; **ludibrio esse** *(w. dat)* to be made a fool of by *(s.o.)*, be taken in by *(s.o.)*; **ludibrio habere** to take *(s.o.)* for a sucker ‖ *npl* outrages, insults

lūdibund·us -a -um *adj* playful, playing around, having fun; without effort, without danger; carefree

lūdi·cer -cra -crum *adj* for sport, in sport; *(theat)* of the stage, dramatic, acting; **ludicra ars et scaena tota** dramatic art and the stage in general; **ludicra exercitatio** sports; **ludicra res** drama; **ludicras partes sustinere** *(theat)* to play a dramatic role, act on the stage; **ludicrum praemium** sports award; ‖ *n* sport, game; toy; show, public game; stage play

lūdificābil·is -is -e *adj* used in mockery

lūdificāti·ō -ōnis *f* ridiculing, mocking; fooling, tricking

lūdificāt·or -ōris *m* mocker

lūdificāt·us -ūs *m* mockery

lūdific·ō -āre -āvī -ātus *or* **lūdific·or -ārī -ātus sum** *tr* to make a fool of, take for a sucker; to fool, trick

lūdi·ō -ōnis *m or* **lūd·ius -(i)ī** *m* actor

lū·dō -dĕre -sī -sus *tr* to play; to spend *(time)* in play; to lose *(money)* in gambling; to amuse oneself with, do for amusement, practice as a pastime; to imitate, mimic, do a takeoff on, ridicule; to tease, tantalize; to deceive, delude; **operam ludere** to waste one's efforts; ‖ *intr* to play; to have fun; to jest, joke; to frolic; *(sl)* to play around, make love; **aleā ludere** to play dice; **pilā ludere** to play ball

lūd·us -ī *m* play, game, sport, pastime, diversion; mere child's play; joke, fun; *(sl)* playing around, fooling around, lovemaking; school; public show, public game; **amoto ludo** all joking aside; **in ludum ire** to go to school; **ludum alicui dare** *(w. dat)* to allow s.o. to enjoy himself; **ludum frequentare** to attend school; **ludus gladiatorius** gladiatorial school; **ludus (litterarius, litterarum)** (elementary) school; **per ludum** as a joke, for fun ‖ *mpl* public games, public exhibition; games, tricks; **ludos facere** *(or* **ludos reddere)** *(w. dat)* **1** to play tricks on; **2** to put on a show for; **3** to make fun of; **ludos sibi facere** to amuse oneself; **ludi circenses** festival of public games, contests, *or* theatrical shows held at the racetrack; **ludi magister** school teacher; **ludi magni** special votive games; **ludi plebeii** games given annually by the plebeian aediles on Nov. 4-17; **ludi Romani** games given annually by the curule aediles on Sept. 4-19; **ludi scaenici** public events held in the theater, plays

luell·a -ae *f* expiation, atonement

lu·ēs -is *f* infection, contagion, plague, pestilence; calamity

Lugdūnens·is -is -e *adj* of Lyons

Lugdūn·um -ī *n* Lyons *(town in E. Gaul)*

lū·geō -gēre -xī -ctus *tr* to mourn, lament, deplore ‖ *intr* to mourn, be in mourning; to be in mourning clothes

lūgubr·ia -ium *npl* mourning clothes

lūgubr·is -is -e *adj* mourning; doleful; disastrous

lumbifrag·ium -(i)ī *n* physical wreck

lumbrīc·us -ī *m* earthworm; *(as a term of reproach)* worm

lumb·us -ī *m* loin ‖ *mpl* loins; genitals

lūm·en -inis *n* light; lamp, torch; brightness, sheen, gleam; daylight; light of the eye, eye; light of life, life; window, window light; luminary, celebrity; glory, pride; *(leg) (usu. pl)* the amount of light falling on a building to which the owner is entitled; *(rhet)* strong point *(of an argument)*; *(rhet)* brilliant phrase *or* expression; **ad lumina prima** until lamp-lighting time, until dusk; **lumen adferre** *(w. dat)* to shed light on *(a subject)*; **lumen vitale** light enjoyed by living creatures,

life; **lumina amittere** to go blind; **luminibus captus** blind; **sub lumina prima** around dusk, just before dusk
lūminōs·us -a -um *adj* luminous, dazzling; *(fig)* bright, conspicuous
lūn·a -ae *f* moon; month; night; crescent *(worn as an ornament by senators on their shoes);* **ad lunam** by moonlight; **luna laborans** moon in eclipse, eclipse of the moon; **luna minor** waning moon
Lūn·a -ae *f* town in N. Etruria near modern Carrara
lūnār·is -is -e *adj* lunar, of the moon
lūnāt·us -a -um *adj* crescent-shaped
lūn·ō -āre -āvī -ātus *tr* to make crescent-shaped, curve
lūnul·a -ae *f* little crescent *(ornament worn by women)*
lu·ō -ĕre -ī *tr* to wash; to cleanse, purge; to set free, let go; to pay *(debt, penalty);* to pay as a fine; to suffer, undergo; to atone for, expiate; to satisfy, appease; to avert by expiation *or* punishment; **poenas luere** to suffer a punishment *(by way of expiation)*
lup·a -ae *f* she-wolf; flirt, prostitute
lupān·ar -āris *n* brothel
lupāt·us -a -um *adj* jagged *(like wolf's teeth)* ‖ *npl* jagged bit *(for spunky horses)*
Luperc·al -ālis *n* shrine on the Palatine Hill sacred to Pan
Lupercāl·ia -ium *npl* Lupercalia *(festival of Lycaean Pan, celebrated in February)*
Luperc·us -ī *m* Pan
lupill·us -ī *m (bot)* small lupine
lupīn·us -a -um *adj* wolf's, lupine ‖ *m & n (bot)* lupine *(plant having clusters of flowers of various colors*
lup·us -ī *m* wolf; *(fish)* pike; jagged bit *(for horse);* grapnel
lurc(h)·ō -ōnis *m* glutton
lūrid·us -a -um *adj* pale-yellow, wan, ghastly, lurid; causing paleness
lūr·or -ōris *m* sallowness, sickly yellow color
-lus -la -lum *suf* forming diminutives, e.g., **lapillus** pebble, **agellus** little field, plot, **homunculus** little man
luscini·a -ae *f* nightingale
lusciniol·a -ae *f* little nightingale
luscin·ius -(i)ī *m* nightingale
lusciōs·us *or* **luscitiōs·us -a -um** *adj* partly blind
lusc·us -a -um *adj* one-eyed
lūsī *perf of* **ludo**
lūsi·ō -ōnis *f* play, game
Lūsitān·ī -ōrum *mpl* Lusitanian
Lūsitāni·a -ae *f* Lusitania *(modern Portugal and W. part of Spain)*
lūsit·ō -āre *intr* to like to play
lūs·or -ōris *m* player; gambler; humorous writer; joker
lustrāl·is -is -e *adj* lustral, propitiatory; quinquennial
lustrāti·ō -ōnis *f* purification, lustration; wandering, traveling
lustr·ō -āre -āvī -ātus *tr* to purify; to travel over, traverse; to check, examine; to go around, encircle; to light up, make bright, illuminate; to scan *(with the eyes);* to consider, review; to survey; *(mil)* to review *(troops)*
lustr·or -ārī -ātus sum *intr* to frequent brothels
lustr·um -ī *n* haunt, den, lair; wilderness; brothel; sensuality; purificatory sacrifice, lustration; lustrum, period of five years; period of years; **ingens lustrum** a century
lūsus *pp of* **ludo**
lūs·us -ūs *m* play, game, sport, amusement; playing around *(amorously)*
lūteol·us -a -um *adj* yellowish
lute·us -a -um *adj* of mud, of clay; muddy; dirty, grimy; (morally) dirty, filthy
lūte·us -a -um *adj* golden-yellow, yellow, orange
lutit·ō -āre *tr* to splatter with mud; *(fig)* to throw mud at
lut·ō -āre -āvī -ātus *tr* to cover with mud, daub; *(fig)* to smear
lutulent·us -a -um *adj* muddy; dirty; *(fig)* filthy; turbid *(style)*
lut·um *or* **lut·us -ī** *n* mud, mire; clay; **in luto esse** *(or* **haerere)** *(fig)* to be in a pickle; **pro luto esse** to be dirt-cheap
lūt·um -ī *n* yellow pigment, yellow
lux lūcis *f* light; light of day, life; daylight; public view, publicity; the public, the world; light of hope, encouragement; glory; elucidation; **luce** *(or* **luci)** by daylight, in the daytime; **lux aestiva** summer; **lux brumalis** winter; **(cum) primā luce** at daybreak
lux·ō -āre -āvī -ātus *tr* to dislocate *(a limb)*
lux·or -ārī -ātus sum *intr* to live riotously, have a ball
luxuri·a -ae *or* **luxuri·ēs -eī** *f* luxuriance; luxury, extravagance, excess, sumptuousness
luxuri·ō -āre -āvī -ātum *or* **luxur·ior -ārī -ātus sum** *intr* to grow luxuriantly; to luxuriate; *(of the body)* to swell up; *(of animals)* to be frisky; to lead a wild life
luxuriōsē *adv* luxuriously, voluptuously
luxuriōs·us -a -um *adj* luxuriant; exuberant; extravagant; voluptuous; highly fertile *(land)*
lux·us -ūs *m* luxury, extravagance, excess; splendor, pomp, magnificence
Lyae·us -a -um *adj* Bacchic ‖ *m* Bacchus; wine
Lycae·us -a -um *adj* Lycaean *(esp. applied to Pan);* **Mons Lycaeus** Mount

Lycaeus *(mountain in Arcadia where Jupiter and Pan were worshiped)*
Lycā·ōn -onis *m* king of Arcadia, whose daughter Callisto was changed into a she-bear and transferred to the sky as the Great Bear
Lycāon·is -idis *f* daughter of Lycaon *(i.e., Callisto)*
Lycāoni·us -a -um *adj* descended from Lycaon of Arcadia; **axis Lycaonia** North Pole *(where Callisto as the Great Bear is located)*
lychnūch·us -ī *m* lamp stand; **lychnuchus pensilis** chandelier
lychn·us -ī *m* lamp, chandelier
Lyci·a -ae *f* country in S. Asia Minor
Lycī·um -ī *n* **(Lycē-)** the Lyceum *(gymnasium near Athens where Aristotle taught)* ‖ Lyceum *(name given by Cicero to the gymnasium in his Tusculan villa)*
Lyci·us -a -um *adj* of Lycia, Lycian ‖ *mpl* Lycians
Lycomēd·ēs -is *m* king of the Greek island of Scyros, father of Deidamia
Lycophr·ōn -onis *or* **-onos** *m* Alexandrine poet, noted for his obscure style *(born c. 320 B.C.)*
Lycōr·is -idis *or* **-idos** *f* name under which the poet Gallus wrote about his mistress Cytheris
Lycorm·ās -ae *m* old name for the Aetolian river Evenus
Lycti·us -a -um *adj* Cretan, of Lyctos *(a town in Crete)*
Lycurgē·us -a -um *adj* Lycurgan *(resembling the orator Lycurgus, noted for his relentlessness as prosecutor)*
Lycurgīd·ēs -ae *m* son of the Arcadian king Lycurgus *(i.e., Ancaeus, killed by the Calydonian boar)*
Lycurg·us -ī *m* traditional founder of the Spartan constitution ‖ Athenian orator, contemporary with Demosthenes *(born c. 396 B.C.)* ‖ son of Dryas and king of the Edones, who persecuted Bacchus and his worshipers
Lyc·us -ī *m* king of Thebes and husband of Dirce ‖ name of numerous rivers in Asia Minor, *esp.* a tributary of the Menander
Lȳdi·a -ae *f* country in W. Asia Minor
Lȳdi·us -a -um *adj* Lydian
Lȳd·us -a -um *adj* Lydian ‖ *mf* Lydian; Etruscan
lygd·os -ī *f* marble from Paros
lymph·a -ae *f* water nymph; *(poet)* water
lymphātic·us -a -um *adj* frenzied
lymphāt·us -a -um *adj* frenzied, frantic
lymph·ō -āre *tr* to drive crazy ‖ *pass* to be in a state of frenzy
Lyncest·is -idis *adj (fem only)* of the Lycestae, a people of W. Macedonia
Lync·eus -eī *m* Argognaut, famed for his sharp eyesight ‖ son of Aegyptus and husband of Hypermestra
Lyncē·us -a -um *adj* of Lynceus the Argonaut; keen-sighted, Lynceus-like
Lyncīd·ēs -ae *m* descendant of Lynceus, husband of Hypermestra *(esp. his great-grandson Perseus)*
lyn·x -cis *or* **-cos** *mf* lynx
lyr·a -ae *f* lyre; *(fig)* lyric poetry ‖ **Lyra** *(astr)* Lyra *(constellation)*
Lyrcē·us -a -um *adj* of Mt. Lyrceum on the borders of Arcadia and Argolis
lyric·us -a -um *adj* of the lyre; lyric ‖ *m* lyric poet ‖ *npl* lyric poetry
Lyrnēs·is -idis *or* **-idos** *f* Briseis *(Achilles' slave girl from Lyrnesos, a town in Phrygia)*
Lȳsan·der -drī *m* Spartan general and statesman *(d. 395 B.C.)*
Lȳsi·ās -ae *m* Athenian orator *(c. 459–c. 380 B.C.)*
Lȳsimach·us -ī *m* bodyguard of Alexander the Great, who later became King of Thrace

M

M *abbr* **mille** one thousand
M. *abbr* **Marcus** *(Roman first name, praenomen)*
M'. *abrr* **Manius** *(Roman first name, praenomen)*
Macarē·is -idos *f* daughter of Macareus *(i.e., Isse)*
Macar·eus -eī *or* **-eos** *m* son of Aeolus *(who lived in incest with his sister Canace)*
macc·us -ī *m* clown *(in Atellan farces)*
Maced·ō -onis *m* Macedonian
Macedoni·a -ae *f* Macedonia
Macedonic·us -a -um *adj* Macedonian
Macedoniens·is -is -e *adj* Macedonian
Macedoni·us -a -um *adj* Macedonian
macellār·ius -(i)ī *m* grocer
macell·um -ī *n* grocery store; *(fig)* groceries
mac·eō -ēre *intr* to be lean, be skinny
ma·cer -cra -crum *adj* lean; skinny; poor *(soil)*; scraggly *(plants)*
Ma·cer -cri *m* Gaius Licinius Macer *(Roman historian and orator, d. 66 B.C.)* ‖ Gaius Licinius Macer Calvus *(son of the former, and orator and poet, 82–46 B.C.)* ‖ Marcus Aemilius Macer *(poet and friend of Vergil and Ovid)*
māceri·a -ae *f* brick *or* stone wall; garden wall
mācer·ō -āre -āvī -ātus *tr* to soak; to soften, tenderize; to weaken, wear down; to worry, annoy, torment ‖ *refl & pass* to fret, worry

macesc·ō -ĕre *intr* to grow thin; *(of fruit)* to shrivel
machaer·a -ae *f* **(macch-)** (single-edged) sword
machaerophor·us -ī *m* soldier armed with a single-edged sword
Machā·ōn -onos *m* famous physician of the Greek army in the Trojan War and son of Aesculapius
Machāoni·us -a -um *adj* of Machaon; *(fig)* medical
māchin·a -ae *f* large mechanism, machine; crane, derrick; pulley, windlass, winch; revolving stage; siege engine; platform on which slaves were exhibited for sale (= **catasta**); cage, pen; *(fig)* scheme, stratagem
māchināment·um -ī *n* contrivance, device; *(mil)* siege engine;
māchinār·ius -(i)ī *m* crane operator
māchināti·ō -ōnis *f* mechanism; machine; trick; art of making machines; *(mil)* field piece
māchināt·or -ōris *m* engineer, machinist; *(fig)* contriver
māchin·or -ārī -ātus sum *tr* to engineer, design, contrive; to scheme
māchinōs·us -a -um *adj* containing a mechanism
maci·ēs -ēī *f* leanness, thinnness; barrenness; poverty *(of soil; of style)*
macilent·us -a -um *adj* skinny
macresc·ō -ĕre *intr* to grow thin
macritūd·ō -inis *f* leanness
macrocoll·um -ī *n* large-size sheet of papyrus
mactābil·is -is -e *adj* deadly
mactāt·us -ūs *m* sacrifice
mactē *interj* well done!; good luck!; bravo!; *(w. gen, acc, or abl)* hurrah for; **macte virtute esto!** bless you for your excellence!; well done!
mact·ō -āre -āvī -ātus *tr* to glorify, honor; to slay *(sacrificially)*, sacrifice; to kill, slaughter, put to death; to destroy, overthrow, ruin; to trouble; *(w. abl)* to afflict *or* punish with
mact·us -a -um *adj* glorified; struck, smitten
macul·a -ae *f* spot, stain; mesh *(of net)*; *(fig)* blemish, defect
maculōs·us -a -um *adj* spotted; stained
made·faciō -facĕre -fēcī -factus *(pass:* **made·fīō -fierī -factus sum)** *tr* to wet, moisten, drench, soak
mad·ens -entis *adj* wet, moist; flowing *(hair)*; melting *(snow)*; reeking *(w. blood)*
mad·eō -ēre -uī *intr* to be wet, be moist, be soaked, be drenched; to drip; to flow; *(coll)* to be soused; to be full, overflow
mad·escō -escĕre -uī *intr* to become wet, become moist; *(coll)* to get loaded
madidē *adv* drunkenly
madid·us -a -um *adj* wet, moist, drenched; dyed, steeped; *(coll)* drunk, loaded
mad·or -ōris *m* moisture
maduls·a -ae *m* *(coll)* souse, drunkard
Maean·der *or* **Maean·dros** *or* **Maean·drus -drī** *m* river in Asia Minor, famous for its winding course; winding; winding border; devious course
Maecēn·ās -ātis *m* Gaius Cilnius Maecenas *(adviser to Augustus and friend of Vergil and Horace, d. 8 B.C.)*
maen·a -ae *f* sprat *(fish)*
Maenal·is -idis *adj* of Mt. Maenalus, Arcadian; **Maenalis ursa** Callisto *(who was changed into the Great Bear)*
Maenal·us *or* **Maenal·os -ī** *m or* **Maenal·a -ōrum** *npl* Mt. Maenalus *(in Arcadia, sacred to Pan)*
Maen·as -adis *f* Bacchante; frenzied woman
Maeni·us -a -um *adj (name of a Roman clan)* Maenian; **Maenia Columna** pillar in the Forum at which the **triumviri capitales** held court and at which thieves, slaves, and debtors were tried and flogged
Maeon·es -um *mpl* Maeonians *(ancient name of the Lydians)*
Maeoni·a -ae *f* E. part of Lydia; *(from the alleged ancestry of its people)* Etruria
Maeonid·ēs -ae *m* native of Maeonia; Homer; Etruscan
Maeon·is -idis *adj (fem only)* Lydian ‖ *f* Maeonian woman *(esp. Arachne or Omphale)*
Maeoni·us -a -um *adj* Lydian; Homeric; Etruscan ‖ *f see* **Maeonia**
Maeōt·ae -ārum *mpl* a Scythian people on Lake Maeotis *(Sea of Azov)*
Maeōt·is -idis *adj* Maeotic; Scythian; **Maeotis lacus** Sea of Azov
Maeōti·us -a -um *adj* Maeotian, of the Maeotae *(a Scythian people)*
maer·eō -ēre *tr* to mourn for, grieve for ‖ *intr* to mourn, grieve
maer·or -ōris *m* mourning, grief
maestē *adv* mournfully, sadly
maestiter *adv* mournfully, sadly
maestiti·a -ae *f* sadness, sorrow, grief; gloom; dullness *(of style)*
maestitūd·ō -inis *f* sadness
maest·us -a -um *adj* mourning, sad, gloomy
Maev·ius -(i)ī *m* poetaster often ridiculed by Vergil and Horace
māgāl·ia -ium *npl* huts
mage *see* **magis**
mag·ē -ēs *f* magic
magic·us -a -um *adj* magic; **artes magicae** magic
magis *or* **mage** *adv* more, to a greater extent, in a higher degree, rather; **eo magis** (all) the more; **magis...atque**

rather...than; **magis aut minus** more or less; **magis est ut, quod** it is more the case that; **magis magisque** more and more; **magis...quam** rather...than; **non magis...quam** not so much...as

magis·ter -trī *m* chief, master, director; teacher; adviser, guardian; ringleader, author; *(in apposition with noun in the gen)* expert; **navis magister** captain, pilot; **magister morum** censor; **magister sacrorum** chief priest

magister·ium -(i)ī *n* directorship, presidency, superintendence; control, governance; instruction; **magisterium morum** censorship

magistr·a -ae *f* directress, mistress; instructress, teacher

magistrāt·us -ūs *m* magistracy; magistrate, official; military command

magmentār·ium -(i)ī *n* receptacle for a part of the sacrificial animal

magnanimit·ās -ātis *f* magnanimity; high ideals; bravery

magnanim·us -a -um *adj* magnanimous, noble, big-hearted; brave

magnāri·us -a -um *adj* wholesale; **magnarius negotiator** wholesale dealer

Magn·ēs -ētis *adj* of Magnesia, Magnesian

magn·ēs -ētis *adj* magnetic; **magnes lapis** magnet

Magnēsi·a -ae *f* district in E. Thessaly on the Aegean Sea **||** city in Caria near the Menander River **||** city in Lydia near Mt. Sipylus

magnēsi·us -a -um *adj* magnetic; **saxum magnesium** lodestone

magnidic·us -a -um *adj* talking big

magnificē *adv* magnificently, splendidly; pompously

magnificenti·a -ae *f* magnificence, grandeur, splendor; pompousness

magnific·ō -āre -āvī -ātus *tr* to make much of

magnific·us -a -um *adj* magnificent, splendid; sumptuous; proud

magniloquenti·a -ae *f* pompous language, braggadocio; *(rhet)* lofty style

magniloqu·us -a -um *adj* **(-loc-)** sublime; bragging

magnitūd·ō -inis *f* magnitude; size; large quantity, large number; vastness, extent; greatness; importance; power, might; high station, dignity, high rank; dignity of character; length *(of time);* intensity *(of storm, etc.);* strength, loudness *(of voice)*

magnopere *or* **magnō opere** *adv* greatly, very much; particularly; strongly, earnestly, heartily

magn·us -a -um *(comp:* **major;** *superl:* **maximus)** *adj* big, large; important; great; distinguished; impressive; complete, utter, full, pure; high, powerful *(in rank);* long *(time);* high *(price);* loud *(voice);* heavy *(rain);* advanced *(age);* noble *(character);* **magna itinera** forced marches; **Magna Mater** Cybele; **magno casu occidere** to happen by pure chance; **mare magnum** the ocean; **vir magno jam natu** a man advanced in years **||** *n* great thing; great value; boast, proud claim; **magni (pretii) aestimare** *(or* **magni habere)** to value highly, have a high regard for; **magno emere (vendere)** to buy (sell) at a high price; **magnum spirare** to be proud

Māg·ō -ōnis *m* brother of Hannibal

mag·us -a -um *adj* magic; **artes magae** magic **||** *m* magician; learned man *(among the Persians)*

Māi·us -a -um *adj & m* May **||** *f* daughter of Atlas and Pleione and mother of Mercury by Jupiter

mājāl·is -is *m* castrated hog; *(as term of abuse)* swine

mājest·ās -ātis *f* majesty, dignity, grandeur; sovereign power, sovereignty; authority; *(as a crime of diminishing the majesty of the Roman people)* high treason; **majestas laesa** *(or* **imminuta)** high treason

māj·or -or -us *(comp of* **magnus)** *adj* bigger, larger; greater; more important; **annos natu major quadraginta** forty years older; **in majus ferre** to exaggerate; **majoris (pretii)** at a higher price; **major natu** older **||** *mpl see* **majores ||** *npl* worse things, worse sufferings

mājōr·ēs -um *mpl* ancestors, forefathers

mājuscul·us -a -um *adj* somewhat greater; a little older

māl·a -ae *f* cheekbone, upper jaw **||** *fpl* cheeks; *(fig)* jaws *(e.g., of death)*

malaci·a -ae *f* calm at sea, dead calm

malaciss·ō -āre -āvī -ātus *tr* to soften (up)

malac·us -a -um *adj* soft; luxurious

male *adv (comp:* **pējus;** *superl:* **pessimē)** badly, wrongly; wickedly, cruelly, maliciously; unfortunately, unsuccessfully; awkwardly; excessively, extremely, very much; *(w. adjectives having a bad sense)* terribly, awfully; **male accipere** to treat roughly; **male audire** to be ill spoken of; **male dicere** *(w. dat)* to say nasty things to; **male existimare de** *(w. abl)* to have a bad opinion of; **male emere** to buy at a high price; **male facere** *(w. dat)* to treat badly, treat cruelly; **male factum!** *(coll)* too bad!; **male ferre** to take (it) hard; **male fidus** unsafe; **male gratus** ungrateful; **male habere** to harass; **male metuere** to be terribly afraid of; **male perdere** to ruin utterly; **male sanus** insane; **male vendere** to sell at a loss; **male vivere** to be a failure in life

maledic·ax -ācis *adj* abusive, foul-mouthed
maledicē *adv* abusively, slanderously
maledīc·ens -entis *adj* abusive, foul-mouthed
male·dīcō -dīcěre -dixī -dictum *intr (w. dat)* 1 to speak ill of, abuse, slander; 2 to say nasty things to
maledicti·ō -ōnis *f* abusive language, abuse
maledictit·ō -āre -āvī *intr (w. dat)* to keep saying nasty things to
maledict·um -ī *n* insult, taunt
maledic·us -a -um *adj* abusive, foul-mouthed; slanderous
male·faciō -facěre -fēcī -factum *intr* to do wrong; *(w. dat)* to injure, do wrong to
malefact·or -ōris *m* malefactor
mal(e)fact·um -ī *n* wrong, injury
maleficē *adv* mischievously
maleficenti·a -ae *f* harm, wrong, mischief
malefic·ium -(i)ī *n* evil deed, crime, offense; harm, injury, wrong, mischief; **maleficium admittere** *(or* **committere)** to commit a crime
malefic·us -a -um *adj* wicked, vicious, criminal ‖ *m* mischief-maker
malesuād·us -a -um *adj* seductive
malevol·ens -entis *adj* malevolent, spiteful, malicious ‖ *mf* spiteful person
malevolenti·a -ae *f* malevolence, spitefulness, ill will
malevol·us -a -um *adj* malevolent, spiteful, nasty
Māliac·us -a -um *adj* Malian, of Malis; **sinus Maliacus** Malian Gulf *(in S. Thessaly, modern Gulf of Zeitouni)*
Māliens·is -is -e *adj* of Malis *(a district of S. Thessaly)*
malignē *adv* spitefully; jealously; grudgingly; scantily, poorly
malignit·ās -ātis *f* spite, malice, jealously; stinginess
malign·us -a -um *adj* spiteful, malicious, jealous; stingy; *(fig)* unproductive *(soil)*; scanty *(light)*
maliti·a -ae *f* malice, ill-will, bad behavior ‖ *fpl* devilish tricks
malitiōsē *adv* wickedly; craftily
malitiōs·us -a -um *adj* malicious, crafty, wicked, devilish
malleol·us -ī *m* small hammer, small mallet; fiery arrow
malle·us -ī *m* hammer, mallet; **malleus ferreus** pole-ax *(for slaughtering sacrificial animals)*
mālō *or* **māvolō malle māluī** *tr* to prefer; **pecuniam quam sapientiam malle** to prefer money to wisdom; *(w. inf)* to prefer to *(do s.th.)*; *(w. acc & inf, w.* **ut**) to prefer that ‖ *intr (w. dat)* to incline toward, be more favorably disposed to
mālobathr·um -ī *n* malobathrum oil *(used as perfume)*
mal·um -ī *n* evil, ill; harm; punishment; disaster; hardship, trouble
māl·um -ī *n* apple; **aureum malum** quince; **felix malum** lemon; **malum Persicum** peach; **malum Punicum** *(or* **malum granatum)** pomegranate; **malum silvestre** crab apple
mal·us -a -um *adj* bad; ill, evil; ugly; unpatriotic; adverse, unfavorable; unsucessful; harmful; inappropriate, misplaced; insulting, abusive *(words)*; humble *(birth)*; **i in malam rem!** *(sl)* go to hell!; **mala aetas** old age; **res mala** trouble ‖ *n see* **malum**
māl·us -ī *m* mast *(of ship)*; pole
māl·us -ī *f* apple tree
malv·a -ae *f* mallow *(used as food or mild laxative)*
Mam. *abbr* **Māmercus** *(Roman first name, praenomen)*
Mām·ers -ertis *m* Mars
Māmertīn·ī -ōrum *mpl* inhabitants of Messana who precipitated the First Punic war
mamill·a -ae *f* breast, teat
mamm·a -ae *f* breast *(of a woman)*; dug *(of an animal)*; *(baby talk)* mummy, mamma
mammeāt·us -a -um *adj* large-breasted
mammōs·us -a -um *adj* large-breasted, chesty
mānābil·is -is -e *adj* penetrating *(cold)*
manc·eps -ipis *m* purchaser; contractor
mancip·ium -(i)ī *n* (**-cup-**) formal purchase; possession, right of ownership; slave; **mancipio accipere** to take possession of; **mancipio dare** to turn over possession of; **res mancipi** possessions *(basic to running a farm e.g., land, slaves, livestock, farm implements)*; **res nec mancipi** possessions *(other than those needed to run a farm)*
mancip·ō -āre -āvī -ātus *tr* (**-cup-**) to sell, transfer
manc·us -a -um *adj* crippled, maimed; *(fig)* defective, weak
mandāt·um -ī *n* command, order, commission ‖ *npl* instructions
mandāt·us -ūs *m* command, order
mand·ō -āre -āvī -ātus *tr* to hand over; to commit, entrust; to command, order, enjoin; to commission; to delegate *(authority)*; to send a message about, report; to prescribe, specify; **humo aliquem mandare** to bury s.o.; **memoriae** *(or* **animo) mandare** to commit to memory, record ‖ *refl* **se fugae mandare** to run away
man·dō -děre -dī -sus *tr* to chew; to champ; to eat, devour; **humum mandere** to bite the dust
mandr·a -ae *f* stable, stall; column of pack animals *or* cattle; checkerboard
mandūc·us -ī *m* mask representing a glutton

māne *indecl n* morning ‖ *adv* in the morning; on the following morning; **bene mane** early in the morning; **cras mane** tomorrow morning; **heri mane** yesterday morning; **hodie mane** this morning; **postridie ejus diei mane** the following morning

man·eō -ēre -sī -sus *tr* to wait for, await ‖ *intr* to stay, remain; to stop off, pass the night; to last, endure, continue, persist; to be left over; **in condicione manere** to stick to an agreement; **in sententiā manere** to stick to an opinion

mān·ēs -ium *mpl* spirits of the dead; lower world; mortal remains

mang·ō -ōnis *m* slave dealer; pushy salesman

manic·ae -ārum *fpl* handcuffs; grappling hook; long sleeves; gloves

manicāt·us -a -um *adj* long-sleeved

manicul·a -ae *f* little hand

manifestē *adv* plainly, distinctly

manifestō *adv* red-handed; plainly, manifestly, evidently

manifest·ō -āre -āvī -ātus *tr* to reveal; to make known; to clarify

manifest·us -a -um *adj* manifest, plain, clear, distinct; exposed, brought to light, detected, caught; *(w. gen)* caught in, convicted of; *(w. inf)* known to

manipl = manipul-

manipulār·is -is -e *adj (mil)* of a maniple *or* company; **miles manipularis** private

manipulātim *adv (mil)* by companies

manip(u)l·us -ī *m* handful *(esp. of hay); (coll)* gang; *(mil)* maniple, company *(three of which constituted a cohort)*

Manl·ius -(i)ī *m* Marcus Manlius Capitolinus *(consul in 392 B.C., who, in 389 B.C. saved the Capitoline from the invading Gauls)* ‖ Titus Manlius Torquatus *(consul in 340 B.C., famous for his military discipline)*

mannul·us -ī *m* little pony

mann·us -ī *m* pony

mān·ō -āre -āvī -ātus *tr* to pour out; to shed *(tears)* ‖ *intr* to drip, trickle; *(w. abl)* to drip with; to leak; to flow, pour; to stream; *(of rumors)* to spread, circulate; *(of secrets)* to leak out; *(fig)* to be derived, emanate

mansi·ō -ōnis *f* staying; stopover

mansit·ō -āre -āvī *intr* to stay on

mansuē·faciō -facĕre -fēcī -factus *(pass:* **mansuē·fīō -fierī -factus sum)** *tr* to tame; to civilize

mansu·ēs -is *or* **-ētis** *adj* tame, mild

mansu·escō -escĕre -ēvī -ētus *tr* to tame ‖ *intr* to become tame; *(fig)* to become gentle; to relent; to grow less harsh

mansuētē *adv* gently, mildly

mansuētūd·ō -inis *f* mildness, gentleness

mansuēt·us -a -um *adj* tame; mild, gentle

mansus *pp of* **mando** *and* **maneo**

mantēl·e -is *n* hand towel; napkin; tablecloth

mantēl·ium -(i)ī *n* hand towel; napkin

mantell·um -ī *n* **(-tēl-)** mantle

mantic·a -ae *f* knapsack

Mantinē·a -ae *f* town in Arcadia, where the Spartans were defeated by the Thebans in 362 B.C.

mantiscin·or -ārī -ātus sum *intr* to predict, prophesy

mant·ō -āre *tr* to wait for ‖ *intr* to stay, remain, wait

Mant·ō -ūs *f* prophetic daughter of Tiresias

Mantu·a -ae *f* town in N. Italy, birthplace of Vergil

manuāl·e -is *n* wooden case for a book

manuāl·is -is -e *adj* that can be held in hand, hand-sized *(e.g., rocks)*

manubi·ae -ārum *fpl* money derived from the sale of booty; *(coll)* proceeds from robbery, loot

manubiāl·is -is -e *adj* obtained from the sale of booty

manubiāri·us -a -um *adj (coll)* bringing in the loot

manūbr·ium -(i)ī *n* handle; hilt

manufestāri·us -a -um *adj* **(mani-)** plain, obvious

manule·a -ae *f* long sleeve

manuleār·ius -(i)ī *m* sleeve maker

manuleāt·us -a -um *adj* long-sleeved

manūmissi·ō -ōnis *f* manumission, freeing *(of a slave)*

manū·mittō -mittĕre -mīsī -missus *tr* to manumit, set free *(a slave)*

manupret·ium -(i)ī *n* workman's pay, wages; *(fig)* pay, reward

man·us -ūs *f* hand; band, gang, company; force, violence, close combat; finishing touch; handwriting; work; workmanship; trunk *(of elephant);* twigs *(of a tree); (leg)* power of a husband over his wife and children; *(med)* surgery; **ad manum** close at hand, within easy reach; **ad manum habere** to have at hand, have in readiness; **ad manum venire** to come within reach; **ad manus pervenire** to resort to fighting; **aequā manu** *(or* **aequis manibus)** on even terms; **a manu servus** secretary; **de manu** personally; **e manu** at a distance, from a distance; **in manibus esse** *(gen)* to be in the power of; be under the jurisdiction of; **inter manus** under one's hand, in one's arms; **inter manus habere** to have in hand, be busied with; **manibus pedibusque** *(fig)* with might and main; **manu** by hand, artificially; in deed; by force; *(mil)* by force of arms; **manu (e)mittere** to set *(a slave)* free; **manu factus** man-made; **manum committere** *(or* **conserere** *or* **conferre)** to begin to fight; **manum dare**

to lend a hand; **manum injicere** *(w. dat)* to lay hands on, arrest; **manūs dare** *(or* **manūs dedere)** to surrender; **manus extrema** *(or* **summa** *or* **ultima)** finishing touches; **manus (ferrea)** grappling iron; **manu tenere** to know for sure; **media manus** a go-between; **per manūs** by hand; by force; from hand to hand, from mouth to mouth, from father to son; **plenā manu** generously; **prae manibus** *(or* **prae manu)** at hand, in readiness; **sub manu** *(or* **sub manum)** at hand, near; immediately, promptly; **suspensā manu** reluctantly

mapāl·ia -ium *npl* African huts; *(fig)* a mess

mapp·a -ae *f* napkin; flag *(used in starting races at the racetrack)*

Marath·ōn -ōnis *f* site in E. Attica of the victory of Miltiades over the Persians *(490 B.C.)*

Marathōni·us -a -um *adj* of Marathon

Marcell·us -ī *m* Roman family name *(cognomen)* in the gens Claudia; Marcus Claudius Marcellus *(nephew of Augustus, 43–23 B.C.)*

marc·eō -ēre *intr* to wither, droop, shrivel; to be weak, be feeble; be decrepit, be run-down; to slack off

marcesc·ō -ĕre *intr* to begin to wither, begin to droop; to become weak, become run-down; to become lazy

marcid·us -a -um *adj* withered, droopy; groggy

Marc·ius -(i)ī *m* Ancus Marcius *(fourth king of Rome)*

marcul·us -ī *m* small hammer

mar·e -is *n* sea; saltwater; **mare caelo miscere** to raise a huge storm; *(fig)* to have all hell break loose; **mare inferum** Tyrrhenian Sea; **mare magnum** the ocean; **mare nostrum** Mediterranean Sea; **mare superum** Adriatic Sea; **trans mare** overseas, abroad

Mareōt·a -ae *f* town and lake near Alexandria in Egypt

Mareōtic·us -a -um *adj* Mareotic; Egyptian

margarīt·a -ae *f or* **margarīt·um -ī** *n* pearl

margin·ō -āre -āvī -ātus *tr* to furnish with a border; to curb *(a street)*

marg·ō -inis *f* margin, edge, border; frontier; bank *(of a stream)*

Mariān·ī -ōrum *mpl* partisans of Marius

Marīc·a -ae *f* nymph of Minturnae, mother of Latinus

marīn·us -a -um *adj* sea-, marine; seagoing

marisc·a -ae *f* a fig; **tumidae mariscae** the piles

marīt·a -ae *f* wife

marītāl·is -is -e *adj* marital, nuptial; matronly, of a married woman

maritim·us -a -um *adj* (**-tum-**) sea-, of the sea; seafaring, maritime; *(fig)* changeable *(like the sea)*; **ora maritima** seacoast ‖ *npl* seacoast

marīt·ō -āre -āvī -ātus *tr* to provide with a husband *or* wife, marry; to train *(a vine to a tree)* ‖ *pass* to get married

marīt·us -a -um *adj* matrimonial, nuptial ‖ *m* husband ‖ *f* wife

Mar·ius -(i)ī *m* Gaius Marius *(conqueror of Jugurtha and of the Cimbri and Teutons, and seven times consul, 157–86 B.C.)*

marm·or -oris *n* marble; marble statue, marble monument; marble vessel; milestone; smooth surface of the sea ‖ *npl* marble pavement

marmore·us -a -um *adj* marble, made of marble; marble-like

Mar·ō -ōnis *m* cognomen of Vergil

marr·a -ae *f* hoe, weeding hook

Mar·s -tis *m* god of war and father of Romulus and Remus; battle, war; engagement; *(astr)* Mars; **aequo Marte** on an equal footing, in an even battle; **stella** *(or* **sidus) Martis** *(astr)* the planet Mars; **suo Marte** by his own exertions, independently

Mars·ī -ōrum *mpl* Marsians *(a people of S. central Italy, regarded as tough warriors)*

marsupp·ium -(i)ī *n* purse, pouch

Marsy·ās *or* **Marsy·a -ae** *m* satyr who challenged Apollo with the flute and was flayed alive upon his defeat ‖ statue of Marsyas in the Roman Forum

Martiāl·ēs -ium *mpl* college of priests of Mars; troops of the **legio Martia** *(Martian legion)*

Martiāl·is -is *m* Martial *(Marcus Valerius Martialis, famous for his epigrams, c. A.D. 40–120)*

Marticol·a -ae *m* worshiper of Mars

Marti·us -a -um *adj* Martian, of Mars; sacred to Mars; descended from Mars; of March; **mensis Martius** March *(third month of the year after the year 153 B.C., originally the first month)* ‖ *m* March

mās maris *adj* male, masculine; manly, brave ‖ *m* male

masculīn·us -a -um *adj* male, masculine

mascul·us -a -um *adj* male, masculine; manly, vigorous ‖ *m* male

mass·a -ae *f* mass, lump; *(coll)* chunk of money; bulk, size; heavy weight *(used in exercising)*

Massaget·ae -ārum *mpl* a nomadic tribe of Scythia

Massic·us -a -um *adj* Massic ‖ *m* Mt. Massicus *(between Latium and Campania, famous for its wine)* ‖ *n* Massic wine

Massili·a -ae *f* Greek Colony on S. coast of Gaul *(modern Marseilles)*

Massyl·ī -ōrum *mpl* tribe of E. Numidia
mastīgi·a *or* **mastīgi·ās -ae** *m* rascal *(whip-needer)*
mastrūc·a -ae *f* skeepskin; *(pej)* ninny
mastrūcāt·us -a -um *adj* dressed in a sheepskin coat
masturbāt·or -ōris *m* masturbator
masturb·or -ārī -ātus sum *intr* to masturbate
matar·a -ae *or* **matar·is -is** *f* Celtic javelin
matell·a -ae *f* chamber pot
matelli·ō -ōnis *m* small pot
mā·ter -tris *f* mother; matron; foster mother; *(in addressing an old woman)* ma'am; *(of animals)* dam; cause, origin, source; motherland, native land; native city; **Magna mater** Cybele; **mater familias** lady of the house
matercul·a -ae *f* little mother, poor mother
māt·erfamiliās -risfamiliās *f* lady of the house, mistress of the household
māteri·a -ae *or* **māteri·ēs -ēī** *f* matter, stuff, material; lumber *(for building);* fuel; subject, subject matter, theme, topic; cause, source; occasion, opportunity; capacity, natural ability; disposition
māteriār·ius -(i)ī *m* lumber merchant
māteriāt·us -a -um *adj* built with lumber; **male materiatus** built with poor lumber
māteriēs *see* **materia**
māteri·or -ārī -ātus sum *intr* to gather wood
mātern·us -a -um *adj* maternal, mother's, of a mother
māterter·a -ae *f* aunt, mother's sister; **matertera magna** grandaunt, grandmother's sister
mathēmatic·a -ae *or* **mathēmatic·ē -ēs** *f* mathematics; astrology
mathēmatic·us -a -um *adj* mathematical, of arithmetic, of geometry **||** *m* mathematician; astrologer
Matīn·us -ī *m* mountain in Apulia near Horace's birthplace
mātricīd·a -ae *m* murderer of one's mother
mātricīd·ium -(i)ī *n* murder of one's mother, matricide
mātrimōn·ium -(i)ī *n* matrimony, marriage; **in matrimonium accipere** to marry *(a man);* **in matrimonium dare** *(or* **collocare)** to give in marriage; **in matrimonium ducere** to marry *(a woman)*
mātrim·us -a -um *adj* having a mother still living
mātrōn·a -ae *f* married woman, matron, wife; lady
Mātrōnāl·ia -ium *npl* festival celebrated by married women on March 1 in honor of Mars
mātrōnāl·is -is -e *adj* matronly, wifely, womanly
matt·a -ae *f* straw mat
matul·a -ae *f* pot; chamber pot; *(pej)* blockhead
mātūrātē *adv* promptly
mātūrē *adv* at the right time; in good time, in time; at an early date; at an early age; quickly; prematurely
mātūr·escō -escĕre -uī *intr* to get ripe, ripen, mature
mātūrit·ās -ātis *f* ripeness, maturity; harvest season; the proper time; *(fig)* maturity, height, perfection
mātūr·ō -āre -āvī -ātus *tr* to ripen, bring to maturity; to speed up, hasten; *(w. inf)* to be too quick in doing **||** *intr* to hurry; **maturato opus est** there is no time to lose
mātūr·us -a -um *adj* ripe, mature, full-grown; opportune, at the right time; *(of winter, etc.)* early, coming early; advanced in years; marriageable; mellow
Mātūt·a -ae *f* goddess of the dawn
mātūtīn·us -a -um *adj* morning, early; **dies matutinus** early part of the day; **tempora matutina** morning hours
Mauritāni·a -ae *f* country of N.W. Africa
Maur·us -a -um *adj* Moorish; African
Maurūsi·us -a -um *adj* Moorish, Mauretanian
Māvor·s -tis *m* Mars; warfare; *(astr)* Mars
Māvorti·us -a -um *adj* Martian, of Mars; warlike, martial **||** *m* Meleager *(son of Mars)*
maxill·a -ae *f* jaw
maximē *adv* **(-xum-)** very, most, especially, particularly; just, precisely, exactly; *(in sequences)* in the first place, first of all; *(in affirmations)* by all means, certainly, yes; **immo maxime** certainly not; **nuper maxime** just recently; **quam maxime** as much as possible; **tum cum maxime** at the precise moment when; **tum maxime** just then; **ut maxime…ita maxime** the more…so much the more
maximit·ās -ātis *f* magnitude
maxim·us -a -um *(superl of* **magnus)** *adj* **(-xum-)** biggest, largest; tallest; greatest *(in amount, number, value, power, or reputation); (with or without* **natu)** oldest; highest, utmost; most important, leading, chief; **maximā voce** at the top of one's lungs
mazonom·um -ī *n* serving dish
meāmet = meā, *abl fem sing of* **meus,** *strengthened by* **-met**
meāpte = meā, *abl fem sing of* **meus,** *strengthened by* **-pte**
meāt·us -ūs *m* motion, movement; course, channel
mecastor *interj* by Castor! *(used by women)*
mēcum = cum me
mēd = mē *(archaic form of acc and abl)*

medd·ix -icis *m* (**mēd-**) magistrate *(among the Oscans)*; **meddix tuticus** chief magistrate
Mēdē·a -ae *f* daughter of Aeëtes, the king of Colchis, and wife of Jason
Mēdē·is -idos *adj* magical
med·ens -entis *m* doctor
med·eor -ērī *tr* to heal ‖ *intr (w. dat)* to heal, cure; *(w.* **adversus** *or* **contra** *+ acc)* to be good for *(e.g., a cold, headache)*
Mēd·ī -ōrum *mpl* Medes; Parthians; Persians
Mēdi·a -ae *f* country of the Medes S. of the Caspian Sea
mediān·us -a -um *adj* central ‖ *n* central part, middle
mediast(r)īn·us -ī *m* servant *(without any specific skill)*
mēdic·a -ae *f* alfalfa
medicābil·is -is -e *adj* curable
medicām·en -inis *n* medicine, medication; drug, antidote; remedy; tincture; cosmetic; *(fig)* remedy
medicāment·um -ī *n* medicine, medication; potion; *(fig)* relief, antidote; *(rhet)* embellishment
medicāt·us -a -um *adj* healing, having healing powers; imbued with magical substances
medicāt·us -ūs *m* magic charm
medicīn·a -ae *f* medicine *(medication; science of medicine)*; remedy; doctor's office; *(w. gen) (fig)* cure for, remedy for; **medicinam exercere** *(or* **facere**) to practice medicine
medicīn·us -a -um *adj* of medicine
medic·ō -āre -āvī -ātus *tr* to medicate, cure; to dye; to poison
medic·or -ārī -ātus sum *tr* to cure ‖ *intr (w. dat)* to heal, cure
medic·us -a -um *adj* medical; healing ‖ *m* doctor, surgeon ‖ *f* physician *(female)*, midwife
Mēdic·us -a -um *adj* Median, of the Medes
medīdi·ēs -ēī *f (early form of* **meridies**) noon; south
mediē *adv* moderately
mediet·ās -ātis *f* mean; middle
medimn·um -ī *n or* **medimn·us -ī** *m* bushel *(containing six modii or "pecks")*
mediocr·is -is -e *adj* of medium size, medium, average, ordinary; undistinguished; mediocre; narrow, small; intermediate
mediocrit·ās -ātis *f* moderate size *or* amount; middle course, mean; moderation; mediocrity ‖ *fpl* moderate passions
mediocriter *adv* moderately, fairly; not particularly, not very, not much; calmly; with moderation; *(w. neg.)* in no slight degree, considerably, extraordinarily
Mediolānens·is -is -e *adj* of Milan
Mediolān·um -ī *n* Milan
medioxum·us -a -um *adj (coll)* in the middle, intermediate
meditāment·um -ī *n* practice, drill, exercise *(in school, in the army)*
meditātē *adv* intentionally
meditāti·ō -ōnis *f* reflection, contemplation; practice; rehearsal; *(w. gen)* reflection on
meditāt·us -a -um *adj* premeditated
mediterrāne·us -a -um *adj* inland ‖ *n* interior *(of a country)*
medit·or -ārī -ātus sum *tr* to think over, reflect on; to practice, rehearse; to have in mind, intend; to plan, design ‖ *refl* to practice, train ‖ *intr* to prepare one's speech, rehearse; *(w.* **de** *+ abl)* to reflect on, think about;
meditull·ium -(i)ī *n* the interior *(of a country)*; middle, center
medi·us -a -um *adj* middle, central, the middle of, in the middle; intermediate; moderate; intervening *(time)*; middling, ordinary, common; undecided, neutral, ambiguous; **dies medius** *(or* **lux media, sol medius**) midday; the south; **in mediā viā** in the middle of the road; **media pars** half; **medium mare** the high seas ‖ *n* the middle part, center; the general public; intervening space; intermediate stage; **de** *(or* **ē**) **medio** from the scene; **in medio** in mid-course; within reach; **in medio positus** made available to all; **in medio ponere** to disclose; **in medium** on behalf of the general public; for the common good; **in medium proferre** to make public; **in medium** *(or* **in medio**) **relinquere** to leave undecided; **medio temporis** in the meanwhile
medius fidius *interj* so help me God!; honest to God!
med·ix -icis *see* **meddix**
medull·a -ae *f* marrow; *(fig)* middle ‖ *fpl (fig)* heart; **imis medullis** in the innermost heart, deep within one's heart
medullitus *adv* with all one's heart
medullul·a -ae *f* **anseris medullula** goose down
Mēd·us -a -um Mede, of the Medes ‖ *m* son of Aegeus and Medea, the eponymous hero of the Medes
Medūs·a -ae *f* one of the three Gorgons, whose look turned people to stone
Medūsae·us -a -um *adj* Medusan; **equus Medusaeus** Pegasus
Megaer·a -ae *f* one of the three Furies
Megalens·ia *or* **Megalēs·ia -ium** *npl* festival of Cybele, celebrated on the 4th of April
Megalens·is -is -e *adj* of the Magna Mater *or* Cybele; **ludi Megalenses** games in honor of Cybele

Megar·a -ae *f* wife of Hercules, whom he killed in a fit of madness
Megar·a -ae *f or* **Megar·a -ōrum** *npl* town near Athens on the Saronic Gulf ‖ Greek town in Sicily
Megarē·us *or* **Megaric·us -a -um** *adj* of Megara, Megarean
megistān·es -um *mpl* grandees
meherc(u)le *or* **mehercules** *interj* by Hercules!
mēj·ō -ĕre mixī *or* **minxī mictum** *or* **minctum** *intr (coll)* to pee
mel mellis *n* honey; **meum mel** *(as term of endearment)* my honey ‖ *npl* drops of honey
melancholic·us -a -um *adj* melancholy
melandry·um -ī *n* piece of salted tuna
Melanipp·a -ae *f or* **Melanipp·ē -ēs** *f* Melanippe *(daughter of Aeolus or Desmon, the mother of two children by Neptune)*
Melanth·ius -(i)ī *m* goatherd of Ulysses
melcul·um -ī *n (term of endearment)* little honey
Melea·ger *or* **Melea·gros -grī** *m* Meleager *(son of King Oeneus of Calydon and participant in the famous Calydonian boar hunt)*
Meleagrid·es -um *fpl* sisters of Meleager who were changed into birds
mēl·ēs -is *f* badger
Melicert·a -ae *or* **Melicert·ēs -ae** *m* Melicertes *(son of Ino and Athamas, who was changed into a sea- god, called Palaemon by the Greeks and Portunus by the Romans)*
melic·us -a -um *adj* musical, melodious; lyric
melilōt·os -ī *m* clover-like plant
melimēl·a -ōrum *npl* honey apples
mēlīn·a -ae *f* (**mell-**) leather pouch
Mēlīn·um -ī *n* pigment; Melian white *(from Melos)*
meli·or -or -us *(comp of* **bonus**) *adj* better; kinder, more gracious; **melius est** *(w. inf, w. acc & inf)* it is (would be) preferable to, that
melisphyll·um -ī *n* balm *(herb of which bees are fond)*
Melit·a -ae *or* **Melit·ē -ēs** *f* Malta; a sea nymph
Melitens·is -is -e *adj* Maltese
melius *(comp of* **bene**) *adv* better
meliusculē *adv* pretty well
meliuscul·us -a -um *adj* a little better
mell·a -ae *f* mead *(mixture of honey and water)*
mellicul·us -a -um *adj* sweet as honey
melli·fer -fera -ferum *adj* producing honey
mellific·ō -āre *intr* to make honey
mellill·a -ae *f (term of endearment)* little honey
mellīn·a -ae *f* sweetness, delight
mellīn·a -ae *f* (**mēlī-**) leather pouch *(made from the skin of a badger)*
mellīt·us -a -um *adj* honeyed; sweet as honey
mel·os -eos *n or* **mel·um -ī** *n or* **mel·os -ī** *m* song, tune
Melpomen·ē -ēs *f* Muse of tragic poetry
membrān·a -ae *f* membrane, skin; slough *(of a snake)*; parchment; film
membrānul·a -ae *f* small piece of parchment
membrātim *adv* limb by limb; singly, piecemeal; in short sentences
membr·um -ī *n* member, organ, limb, genital; part, division *(of a thing)*; apartment, room; member *(of a group)*; *(gram)* clause; *(rhet)* small section of a speech or literary work
mēmet *pron (emphatic form of* **mē**) me
memin·ī -isse *(imperative:* **memento; mementote**) *tr* to remember ‖ *tr (w. gen)* to remember, be mindful of
Memn·ōn -ōnis *m* son of Tithonus and Aurora, king of the Ethiopians, killed by Achilles ‖ statue in Egypt *(actually of Amenhotep III)*
Memnonid·es -um *fpl* birds that rose from the pyre of Memnon
Memnoni·us -a -um *adj* Memnonian; Oriental; Moorish; black
mem·or -oris *adj* mindful, remembering having a good memory; careful, thoughtful; observant; *(w. gen)* mindful of, remembering
memorābil·is -is -e *adj* memorable, remarkable
memorand·us -a -um *adj* worth mentioning, notable
memorāt·us -ūs *m* mention
memori·a -ae *f* memory; remembrance; period of recollection, time, lifetime; a memory, past event, history; historical account; **in memoriā habere** to bear in mind; **in memoriā redire** *(or* **regredi**) to recollect; **in memoriam** *(w. gen)* in memory of; **in memoriā inducere** *(or* **redigere**) to call to mind; **memoriā** *(w. gen)* in the time of; **memoriā tenere** to keep in mind; to remember; **memoriae causā** as a reminder; **memoriae mandare** *(or* **tradere**) to commit to memory; **memoriae prodere** to hand down to posterity; **paulo supra hanc memoriam** not long ago; **post hominum memoriam** within the memory of man; **superiore memoriā** in earlier times
memoriāl·is -is -e *adj* for memoranda
memoriol·a -ae *f* weak memory
memoriter *adv* from memory, by heart; accurately, correctly
memor·ō -āre -āvī -ātus *tr* to mention, bring up; to name, call ‖ *intr (w.* **de** + *abl)* to speak of

Memph·is -is *or* **-idos** *f* capital city of Pharaonic Egypt
Memphītic·us -a -um *adj* Egyptian
Menan·der *or* **Menan·dros -drī** *m* Greek playwright of Attic New Comedy *(342–291 B.C.)*
Menandrē·us -a -um *adj* of Menander
mend·a -ae *f* fault, blemish; slip of the pen
mendāciloqui·or -or -us *adj* more false
mendāc·ium -(i)ī *n* lie
mendāciuncul·um -ī *n* white lie, fib
mend·ax -ācis *adj* mendacious, lying, false ‖ *m* liar
mendīcābul·um -ī *n* beggar
mendīcit·ās -ātis *f* begging
mendīc·ō -āre -āvī -ātus *or* **mendīc·or -ārī -ātus sum** *tr* to beg, beg for ‖ *intr* to beg, be a beggar
mendīcul·us -a -um *adj* beggarly
mendīc·us -a -um *adj* needy, poverty-stricken; paltry *(meal)* ‖ *m* beggar
mendōsē *adv* faultily, carelessly
mendōs·us -a -um *adj* full of physical defects; full of faults, faulty, incorrect, erroneous; blundering
mend·um -ī *n* defect, fault; blunder
Menelā·us -ī *m* son of Atreus, brother of Agamemnon, and husband of Helen
Menēn·ius -(i)ī *m* Menenius Agrippa *(told the plebs the fable of the belly and the limbs, 494 B.C.)*
Menoec·eūs -eī *or* **-eos** *m* son of Theban king Creon, who hurled himself off the city walls to save the city
Menoetiad·ēs -ae *m* son of Menoetius *(i.e., Patroclus)*
Menoet·ius -(i)ī *m* one of the Argonauts and father of Patroclus
men·s -tis *f* mind, intellect; frame of mind, attitude; will, inclination; understanding, reason; thought, opinion, intention, plan; courage, boldness; passion, impulse; **addere mentem** to give courage; **captus mente** crazy; **demittere mentem** to lose heart; **in mentem venire** to come to mind; **mentis suae esse** to be in one's right mind
mens·a -ae *f* table; meal, course, dinner; guests at table; counter; bank; sacrificial table, altar; **mens secunda** dessert
mensār·ius -(i)ī *m* banker; treasury official; **triumviri mensarii** board of three treasury officials
mensi·ō -ōnis *f* measure, measuring; *(pros)* quantity *(of a syllable)*
mens·is -is *(gen pl:* **mensium** *or* **mensum)** *m* month; **primo mense** at the beginning of the month
mens·or -ōris *m* surveyor
menstruāl·is -is -e *adj* for a month
menstru·us -a -um *adj* monthly; lasting for a month ‖ *n* rations for a month; month's term of office; monthly payment
mensul·a -ae *f* small table
mensūr·a -ae *f* measuring, measurement; standard of measure; amount, size, proportion, capacity, extent, limit, degree; **mensura duorum digitorum** a pinch *(e.g., of salt)*
mensus *pp of* **metior**
ment·a *or* **menth·a -ae** *f* mint
menti·ens -entis *m (phil)* sophism, fallacy
menti·ō -ōnis *f* mention; **mentionem facere** *(w. gen or* **de** *+ abl)* to make mention of; **mentiones serere** *(w.* **ad***)* to throw hints to
ment·ior -īrī -ītus sum *tr* to invent, fabricate; to feign, imitate, fake ‖ *intr* to lie; to act deceitfully
Ment·ōr -ŏris *m* friend of Ulysses ‖ Greek silversmith of 4th cent. B.C.; *(fig)* a work by Mentor
ment·um -ī *n* chin
me·ō -āre -āvī -ātum *intr* to go, pass
mēopte *pron (emphatic form of* **mē***)* me, me myself
mephīt·is -is *f* sulfurous fumes
merāc(u)l·us -a -um *adj* pretty pure
merāc·us -a -um *adj* undiluted, pure
mercābil·is -is -e *adj* buyable
merc·ans -antis *m* merchant
mercāt·or -ōris *m* merchant, dealer
mercātōri·us -a -um *adj* mercantile, trading, business; **navis mercatoria** merchant ship
mercātūr·a -ae *f* commerce, trade, trading; purchase ‖ *fpl* goods, wares
mercāt·us -ūs *m* market, marketplace; fair; trade, traffic
mercēdul·a -ae *f* poor pay; low rent
mercennāri·us *or* **mercēnāri·us -a -um** *adj* hired, paid, mercenary ‖ *m* common laborer
merc·ēs -ēdis *f* pay, wages; bribe; reward, recompense; cost; price; payment *(esp. for effort, pain, misfortune)*; injury, detriment; stipulation, condition; retribution, punishment; rent, income, interest; **unā mercede duas res assequi** *(prov)* to kill two birds with one stone *(literally, to buy two things for the price of one)*
mercimōn·ium -(i)ī *n* merchandise, goods, wares
merc·or -ārī -ātus sum *tr* to purchase ‖ *intr* to trade, buy and sell
Mercuriāl·is -is -e *adj* of Mercury ‖ *mpl* corporation of merchants in Rome
Mercur·ius -(i)ī *m* Mercury *(son of Jupiter and Maia, messenger of the gods, patron of commerce, diplomacy, gambling, etc.)*; *(astr)* Mercury; **sidus** *(or* **stella)** **Mercurii** the planet Mercury
merd·a -ae *f* droppings, excrement
merend·a -ae *f* lunch, snack

mer·eō -ēre -uī -itus *or* **mer·eor -ērī -itus sum** *tr* to deserve, merit, be entitled to; to win, gain *(glory, fame, reproach);* to earn *(money);* **merere pecuniam ut** to accept money on condition that; **stipendia** *(or* **stipendium) merere** *(mil)* to serve ‖ *intr* to serve; to serve in the army; *(w.* **de** + *abl)* to serve, render service to, do a favor for; **bene de re publica merere** *(or* **mereri)** to serve one's country well; **de te merui** I have done you a favor, I have treated you well; **equo merere** to serve in the cavalry

meretrīciē *adv* like a prostitute

meretrīci·us -a -um *adj* prostitute's

meretrīcul·a -ae *f* cute little wench; *(pej)* the little wench

meretr·ix -īcis *f* prostitute, hooker

merg·ae -ārum *fpl* pitchfork; device for reaping

merg·es -itis *f* sheaf of wheat

mer·gō -gĕre -sī -sus *tr* to dip, plunge, sink; to flood, inundate, engulf, swallow up; to swamp, overwhelm; to bury; to drown ‖ *refl* to dive ‖ *pass* to sink; *(of heavenly bodies)* to go down; to drown; to go bankrupt

merg·us -ī *m* seagull

merīdiān·us -a -um *adj* midday, noon; southern, southerly

merīdiāti·ō -ōnis *f* siesta

merīdi·ēs -ēī *m* midday, noon; south; **spectare ad meridiem** to face south

merīdi·ō -āre -āvī *or* **merīdi·or -ārī -ātus sum** *intr* to take a siesta

Mērion·ēs -ae *m* charioteer of Idomeneus of Crete in Trojan War

meritō *adv* deservedly, rightly

merit·ō -āre -āvī -ātus *tr* to earn regularly

meritōri·us -a -um *adj* rented, hired ‖ *npl* rented lodgings

merit·us -a -um *adj* deserved, just, right, proper, deserving; guilty ‖ *n* service, favor, kindness; merit, worth; blame, fault, offense

merobib·us -a -um *adj* drinking unmixed wine

Merop·ē -ēs *f* one of the Pleiades, daughter of Atlas and Pleione

Merop·s -is *m* king of Ethiopia, husband of Clymene, and reputed father of Phaëthon

mer·ops -opis *m* bee-eater *(bird)*

mers·ō -āre -āvī -ātus *tr* to keep dipping *or* plunging; to drown; *(fig)* to engulf ‖ *pass (w. dat)* to plunge into

mersus *pp of* **mergo**

merul·a -ae *f* blackbird

mer·us -a -um *adj* pure, unmixed, undiluted; *(fig)* nothing but, mere ‖ *n* (undiluted) wine

mer·x -cis *f* merchandise, wares; **mala merx** *(fig)* bad lot

Messallīn·a -ae *f* Valeria Messallina *(wife of Claudius and mother of Britannicus)* ‖ Statilia Messalina *(wife of Nero)*

Messān·a -ae *f* town in N.E. Sicily

Messāpi·us -a -um *adj* of Messapia, of Calabria ‖ *f* town and district of Messapia in S.E. Italy

mess·is -is *f (acc:* **messem** *or* **messim)** harvest; harvest time; **adhuc tua messis in herbā est** *(prov)* don't count your chickens before they are hatched *(literally, your harvest is still on the stalk, i.e., in early stages of growth)*

mess·or -ōris *m* reaper, mower

messōri·us -a -um *adj* reaper's

messuī *perf of* **meto**

messus *pp of* **meto**

mēt·a -ae *f* marker for measuring a lap at a racetrack; haystack; *(fig)* goal, end; *(fig)* turning point

metall·um -ī *n* metal ‖ *npl* mine

metamorphōs·is -is *f* transformation

metaphor·a -ae *f* metaphor

mētāt·or -ōris *m* planner; **metator urbis** city planner

Metaur·us -ī *m* river in Umbria

Metell·us -ī *m* Roman family name *(cognomen);* Quintus Caecilius Metellus Numidicus *(commander of the Roman forces against Jugurtha, 109–107 B.C.)*

Mēthymn·a -ae *f* town on the Island of Lesbos

metīculōsus *see* **metuculosus**

mētior mētīrī mensus sum *tr* to measure; to traverse, travel; to judge, estimate; *(w. dat)* to measure *(s.th.)* out to, distribute *(s. th.)* among; *(w. abl)* to judge *(s.o.)* by the standard of

metō metĕre messuī messus *tr* to reap, mow, gather, harvest; *(fig)* to mow down *(e.g., with the sword)*

mēt·or -ārī -ātus sum *tr* to measure off; to lay out *(e.g., a camp)*

metrēt·a -ae *f* liquid measure *(about nine gallons)*

metūculōs·us -a -um *adj* **(metīc-)** fearful; scary; awful

metu·ens -entis *adj* afraid, anxious

met·uō -uĕre -uī -ūtus *tr* to fear, be afraid of ‖ *intr* to be afraid, be apprehensive

met·us -ūs *m* fear, anxiety; **in metu esse** to be in a state of alarm; to be an object of concern

me·us -a -um *adj* my ‖ *pron* mine; **meā interest** it is of importance to me; **meum est** *(w. inf)* it is my duty to; **meus est** *(coll)* I've got him, he's mine

Mezent·ius -(i)ī *m* Etruscan ruler of Caere, slain by Aeneas

mī = mihi

mīc·a -ae *f* crumb, morsel

Micips·a -ae *m* son of Masinissa and king of Numidia *(148–118 B.C.)* ‖ *mpl (fig)* Numidians, N. Africans
mic·ō -āre -uī *intr* to vibrate, quiver; to twinkle, sparkle, flash
mictur·iō -īre *intr* to have to urinate
Mid·ās -ae *m* king of Phrygia, at whose touch everything turned to gold *(8th cent. B.C.)*
migrāti·ō -ōnis *f* moving, changing residence; migration; *(fig)* metaphorical use
migrō -āre -āvī -ātus *tr* to move, transport; *(fig)* to violate *(a law)* ‖ *intr* to move, change residence; migrate; *(fig)* to change, turn
mīl·es -itis *m* soldier; infantryman; private; *(fig)* army
Mīlēsi·us -a -um *adj* Milesian, of Miletus
Mīlēt·us -ī *f* town on W. coast of Asia Minor ‖ *m* founder of the town of Miletus
mīl·ia -ium *npl* thousands; *see* **mille**
mīliār·ium -(i)ī *n* milestone
mīlitār·is -is -e *adj* military
mīlitāriter *adv* in a military manner, like a soldier
mīlitāri·us -a -um *adj* soldierly, military
mīliti·a -ae *f* army; war; the military; military discipline; **militiae** in war, on the battlefield, in the army; **militiae domique** abroad and at home, on the war front and on the home front
mīlit·ō -āre -āvī -ātum *intr* to be a soldier, do military service
mil·ium -(i)ī *n* millet *(a food grain)*
mille *(indecl) adj* thousand; **mille homines** a thousand people ‖ **mīlia** *npl (declinable noun) (gen:* **mīlium)** thousands; *(w. gen):* **duo milia hominum** two thousand people; **duo milia passuum** two miles *(literally, two thousands of paces)*
millēsim·us *or* **millensim·us -a -um** *adj* thousandth
milliār·ium -(i)ī *n* milestone
milliens *or* **milliēs** *adv* a thousand times; innumerable times
Mil·ō -ōnis *m* Titus Annius Papinianus Milo *(defended by Cicero on a charge of having murdered Clodius in 52 B.C.)*
Miltiad·ēs -is *m* Athenian general victorious at Marathon *(490 B.C.)*
mīlvīn·us *or* **miluīn·us -a -um** *adj* rapacious *(as a kite)*
mīlv·us *or* **milv·os** *or* **mīlu·us -ī** *m* kite *(bird of prey);* flying gurnard *(fish); (astr)* mistakenly taken by Ovid as a constellation
mīm·a -ae *f* actress *(of mimes)*
Mimallon·is -idis *f* a Bacchante
Mim·ās -antis *m* one of the Giants
mīmicē *adv* like a mime actor
mīmic·us -a -um *adj* suitable for the mime, farcical
Mimnerm·us -ī *m* Greek elegaic poet of Colophon on the W. coast of Asia Minor *(fl 630 B.C.)*
mīmul·a -ae *f* miserable little actress
mīm·us -ī *m* mime, farce; actor *(of a mime); (fig)* farce
min·a -ae *f* Greek unit of weight, equal to 100 drachmas, or 100 Roman denarii; Greek coin *(about 100 denarii, i.e., about $100)*
mināci·ae -ārum *fpl* threats
mināciter *adv* threateningly
min·ae -ārum *fpl* threats; projecting points of a wall
minanter *adv* threateningly
mināti·ō -ōnis *f* threatening
min·ax -ācis *adj* threatening, menacing; projecting, jutting out
min·eō -ēre *intr* to project, jut out
Minerv·a -ae *f* goddess of wisdom and of the arts and sciences, identified with Athena; *(fig)* skill, genius; spinning and weaving; **invitā Minervā** against one's better judgment
mingō mingĕre minxī *or* **mixī minctum** *or* **mictum** *intr* (coll) to pee
miniān·us -a -um *adj* vermilion
miniātul·us -a -um *adj* reddish
minimē *or* **minumē** *adv* least of all, least, very little; by no means, certainly not, not in the least; *(w. numerals)* at least; **minime gentium** *(coll)* by no means
minim·us *or* **minum·us -a -um** *(superl of* **parvus)** *adj* smallest, least, very small; slightest, very insignificant; youngest; shortest *(time);* **minimus natu** youngest ‖ *n* the least, minimum; lowest price; **minimo emere** to buy at a very low price; **minimo provocare** to provoke on the flimsiest pretext
mini·ō -āre -āvī -ātus *tr* to color red, paint red
minis·ter -trī *m* servant, attendant, helper; waiter; agent, subordinate, tool
minister·ium -(i)ī *n* activity of a servant *or* attendant, service, attendance; task, duty; office, ministry; occupation, work; agency, instrumentality ‖ *npl* servants
ministr·a -ae *f* servant, attendant, helper; waitress; handmaid
ministrāt·or -ōris *m or* **ministrātr·ix -īcis** *f* assistant, helper
ministr·ō -āre -āvī -ātus *tr* to serve, wait on; to tend; to execute, carry out *(orders); (w. dat)* to hand out *(s.th.)* to; *(w. abl)* to supply *(s.o. or s.th.)* with
minitābund·us -a -um *adj* threatening, menacing
minit·ō -āre *or* **minit·or -ārī -ātus sum** *tr* to make threats of *(e.g., war); (w. acc of thing and dat of person)* to threaten to bring *(e.g., evil, harm)* upon, hold *(s.th.)* threateningly over *(s.o.)* ‖ *intr* to jut out,

project; to be menacing, make threats; *(w. dat)* to threaten

min·or -or -us *(comp of* **parvus)** *adj* smaller, less; shorter *(time);* inferior, less important; *(w. abl)* **1** *(of time)* too short for; **2** inferior to; **3** unworthy of; *(w. inf)* unfit to, incapable of; **dimidio minor quam** half as small as; **minor capitis** deprived of civil rights; **minores facere filios quam** to think less of the sons than of; **minor natu** younger ‖ *mpl* descendants, posterity ‖ *n* less; **minoris emere** to buy at a lower price; **minus praedae** less booty

Mīn·ōs -ōis *or* **-ōnis** *m* son of Zeus and Europa, king of Crete, husband of Pasiphaë, and, after his death, judge in the lower world

Mīnōtaur·us -ī *m* monstrous offspring of Pasiphaë, half man and half bull, kept in the Labyrinth

minum- = minim-

min·uō -uĕre -uī -ūtus *tr* to diminish, lessen, reduce; to weaken, lower; to modify *(plans);* to settle *(controversies);* to limit *(authority);* to offend against, try to cheapen *(e.g., the majesty of the Roman people)* ‖ *intr* to diminish, abate, ebb; **minuente aestu** at ebbtide

minus *adv* less; not; by no means, not at all

minuscul·us -a -um *adj* smallish

minūt·al -ālis *n* hash, hamburger

minūtātim *adv* piecemeal; bit by bit

minūtē *adv* in a small-minded way

minūtul·us -a -um *adj* tiny

minūt·us -a -um *adj* small, minute; petty, narrow-minded

Miny·ae -ārum *mpl* descendants of Minyas, *esp.* the Argonauts

Miny·ās -ae *m* king of Thessaly

mīrābil·is -is -e *adj* remarkable, extraordinary, amazing, wonderful

mīrābiliter *adv* amazingly

mīrābund·us -a -um *adj* astonished, wondering

mīrācul·um -ī *n* wonder, marvel; surprise, amazement; *(pej)* freak; **septem miracula** the seven wonders *(of the ancient world)*

mīrand·us -a -um *adj* fantastic

mīrāti·ō -ōnis *f* astonishment, wonder

mīrāt·or -ōris *m,* **mīrātr·ix -īcis** *f* admirer

mīrē *adv* surprisingly, strangely; uncommonly; wonderfully; **mire quam** it is strange how, strangely

mīrificē *adv* wonderfully

mīrific·us -a -um *adj* causing wonder, wonderful; fascinating

mīrimodīs *adv* in a strange way

mirmill·ō -ōnis *m* gladiator *(who fought with Gallic arms)*

mīr·or -ārī -ātus sum *tr* to be amazed at, be surprised at; to look at with wonder, admire

mīr·us -a -um *adj* amazing, surprising, astonishing; wonderful; **mirum est** *(w. acc & inf)* it is surprising that; **est mirum quam** *(or* **mirum quantum)** it is amazing how, it is amazing to what extent

miscellāne·a -ōrum *npl* **(miscill-)** hash, hodgepodge

misceō miscēre miscuī mixtus *tr* to mix, blend, mingle; to combine, associate, share; to give and take; to mix up, confuse, turn upside down; to mix, prepare, brew; to fill *(with confused noise, etc.);* to unite sexually; **arma** *(or* **manūs** *or* **proelium** *or* **proelia)** **miscere** to join battle

misell·us -a -um *adj* poor little

Mīsēn·um -ī *n* promontory and town near the Bay of Naples

mis·er -era -erum *adj* poor, pitiful; wretched, miserable, unhappy; sorry, worthless

miserābil·is -is -e *adj* miserable, pitiable; piteous

miserābiliter *adv* pitiably; piteously

miserand·us -a -um *adj* pitiful; deplorable

miserāti·ō -ōnis *f* pity, compassion, sympathy; appeal for sympathy

miserē *adv* wretchedly, miserably, unhappily; pitifully; desperately

miser·eō -ēre -uī -itum *or* **miser·eor -ērī -itus sum** *intr (w. gen)* to pity, feel sorry for, sympathize with ‖ *v impers (w. acc of person who feels pity and gen of object of pity), e.g.,* **miseret** *(or* **miseretur)** **me aliorum** I feel sorry for the others

miseresc·ō -ĕre *intr* to feel pity, feel sympathetic; *(w. gen)* to pity, feel sorry for ‖ *v impers (w. acc of person who feels pity and gen of object of pity), e.g.,* **me miserescit viri** I feel sorry for the man, I pity the man

miseri·a -ae *f* pitiful condition, misery, distress, trouble

misericordi·a -ae *f* pity, sympathy, compassion; mercy

misericor·s -dis *adj* sympathetic, merciful

miseriter *adv* sadly

miser·or -ārī -ātus sum *tr* to deplore; to pity ‖ *intr* to feel pity

missicul·ō -āre -āvī -ātus *tr* to keep sending

missil·is -is -e *adj* missile, flying ‖ *npl* missiles

missi·ō -ōnis *f* release, liberation; sending off, dispatching; military discharge; dismissal from office; **missio cum ignominiā** dishonorable discharge; **sine missione** without letup, to the death

missit·ō -āre -āvī -ātus *tr* to keep sending

missus *pp of* **mitto**
miss·us -ūs *m* letting go, throwing, hurling; sending
mītesc·ō -ĕre *intr* to grow mild; to grow mellow, become ripe; *(fig)* to get soft; *(fig)* to become gentle, become tame; *(of feelings)* to become less intense, abate, cool off
Mithr·ās -ae *m* Mithra(s) *(sun-god of the Persians)*
Mithridāt·ēs -is *m* Mithridates the Great *(king of Pontus from 120 to 63 B.C.)*
Mithridātē·us *or* **Mithridātic·us -a -um** *adj* Mithridatic
mītigāti·ō -ōnis *f* mitigation
mītig·ō -āre -āvī -ātus *tr* to mellow, ripen; to soften; to calm down, appease; to make more tolerable, alleviate; to tone down *(a statement);* to soothe, mollify *(feelings);* to civilize
mīt·is -is -e *adj* mellow, ripe, soft; calm, placid; mild, gentle
mitr·a -ae *f* miter, turban
mittō mittĕre mīsī missus *tr* to send; to let fly, throw, hurl, launch; to emit, shed; to let out, utter; to let go of, drop; to free, release; to discharge, dismiss; to pass over in silence; to send for, invite; to pass up, forego; to dedicate *(a book);* to yield, produce; to export; to forget, dismiss *(from the mind);* **sanguinem mittere** to bleed; **sanguinem provinciae mittere** *(fig)* to bleed a province dry; **sub leges orbem mittere** to subject the world to laws; **voces mittere** to utter words
mītul·us -ī *m* limpet *(kind of mussel)*
mixtim *adv* promiscuously
mixtūr·a -ae *f* mixing, blending
mixtus *pp of* **misceo**
Mnēmosyn·ē -ēs *f* mother of the Muses
mnēmosyn·on -ī *n* souvenir
mōbil·is -is -e *adj* mobile, movable, portable; nimble, active; shifty, changing; impressionable, excitable
mōbilit·ās -ātis *f* mobility; agility, quickness; shiftiness, fickleness
mōbiliter *adv* quickly, rapidly
mōbilit·ō -āre -āvī -ātus *tr* to impart motion to, endow with motion
moderābil·is -is -e *adj* moderate
moderām·en -inis *n* control
moderanter *adv* under control
moderātē *adv* with moderation
moderātim *adv* gradually
moderāti·ō -ōnis *f* controlling, control, regulation; curbing, checking; guidance; moderation, self-control
moderāt·or -ōris *m or* **moderātr·ix -īcis** *f* controller, director, guide
moderāt·us -a -um *adj* controlled, well-regulated, orderly, restrained
moder·ō -āre -āvī -ātus *or* **moder·or -ārī -ātus sum** *tr* to control, direct, guide ‖ *intr (w. dat)* **1** to moderate, restrain; **2** to allay, mitigate
modestē *adv* with moderation, discreetly; modestly
modesti·a -ae *f* moderation, restraint; discretion; modesty, sense of shame, sense of honor, dignity; propriety; mildness *(of weather)*
modest·us -a -um *adj* moderate, restrained; modest, discreet; orderly, obedient
modiāl·is -is -e *adj* containing a *modius or* peck
modicē *adv* moderately, with restraint; in an orderly manner; only slightly
modic·us -a -um *adj* moderate; small; modest, unassuming; ordinary; puny, trifling
modificāt·us -a -um *adj* regulated *(in length),* measured
mod·ius -(i)ī *m modius,* peck *(one-sixth of a medimnus or bushel);* **pleno modio** in full measure
modo *adv* only, merely, simply; *(of time)* just now, just recently, lately; presently, in a moment; **modo...deinde** *(or* **tum, postea, interdum)** first...then, at one time...next time; **modo...modo** now...now, sometimes...sometimes, at one moment...at another; **non modo...sed etiam** *(or* **verum etiam)** not only...but also ‖ *conj* if only, provided that
modulātē *adv* according to measure, in time; melodiously
modulāt·or -ōris *m* director, musician
modul·or -ārī -ātus sum *tr* to regulate the time of, measure rhythmically; to modulate; to sing; to play
modul·us -ī *m* small measure; small stature; unit of measurement
mod·us -ī *m* measured amount, quantity; standard of measurement, unit of measurement, measure; time, rhythm; size, extent, length; due *or* proper measure, limit, boundary; rule, regulation; way, manner, style, mode; kind, form, type; *(gram)* voice *(of a verb); (mus)* measure, beat, note, tone; *(poet)* verse, poetry, meter; *(rhet)* rhythmic pattern; **ad modum** *(or* **in modum)** in time, rythmically; **ad modum** *(w. gen) or* **in modum** *(w. gen)* in the manner of, like; **cujusdam modi** of a certain kind, a certain kind of; **cujusdam modi pugna** a certain kind of fight; **cum modo** with restraint, moderately; **ejus modi homo** that kind of person; **ex Tusco modo** in the Etruscan manner *or* style; **hujus modi homo** this kind of person; **modo** moderately; **modum adhibere** *(or* **constituere** *or* **facere** *or* **imponere** *or* **ponere** *or* **statuere)** to impose a limit, set bounds;

nullo modo in no way, not at all; **omni modo** in every case; **praeter** *(or* **supra)** **modum** excessively; **pro modo** *(w. gen)* in proportion to; **quem ad modum** how; **quemnam ad modum** just how; **quid modi?** what limit?; **quonam modo** just how; **sine modo** without restraint ‖ *mpl* tune, melody, song; poetry, poems

moech·a -ae *f* adulteress

moechiss·ō -āre *tr* to commit adultery with

moech·or -ārī -ātus sum *intr* to have an affair, commit adultery

moech·us -ī *m* adulterer

moen·ia -ium *npl* town walls, ramparts, fortifications; fortified town; castle, stronghold; defenses

moeniō *see* **munio**

moerus *see* **murus**

Moes·ī -ōrum *mpl* people of the Lower Danube basin

Moesi·a -ae *f* Moesia *(Roman province S. of the Danube and extending to the Black Sea)*

mol·a -ae *f* millstone; mill; flour ‖ *fpl* mill

molār·is -is *m* millstone; molar *(tooth)*

mōl·ēs -is *f* mass, bulk, pile; massive structure; dam, mole, pier; mass *(of people, etc.)*; burden, effort, trouble; calamity; might, greatness

molestē *adv* with annoyance; with difficulty, with trouble; **moleste ferre** to be annoyed at, be disgruntled at, barely stand *or* tolerate

molesti·a -ae *f* annoyance, trouble; worry; affectation *(of style)*

molest·us -a -um *adj* annoying, troublesome, distressing; labored, affected *(style)*

mōlīm·en -inis *n* great exertion, great effort; attempt, undertaking

mōlīment·um -ī *n* great exertion, great effort

mōl·ior -īrī -ītus sum *tr* to do with great effort, strain at, exert oneself over; to wield, heave, hurl *(missiles)*; to wield *(a weapon, an instrument)*; to get *(a ship)* under way; to get *(a vehicle)* moving; to rouse *(bodies of men)* to action; to work hard at; to build, erect *(usu. huge constructions)*; to displace, shift from its position; to undertake, attempt; to perform; to cause, occasion ‖ *intr* to exert oneself, struggle, take great pains; to make one's way *(w. effort)*, proceed

mōlīti·ō -ōnis *f* building, erection; (the action of) shifting *or* moving; **rerum molitio** the creation

mōlīt·or -ōris *m* builder; contriver, schemer

mōlītr·ix -īcis *f* contriver *(female)*

molitus *pp of* **molo** ‖ *adj* ground, milled

molītus *pp of* **molior**

mollesc·ō -ĕre *intr* to become soft; to become gentle; to become effeminate

mollicul·us -a -um *adj* tender, dainty

moll·iō -īre -īvī *or* **-iī -ītus** *tr* to make soft, soften; *(fig)* to soften, mitigate; to demoralize

mollip·ēs -edis *adj* tender-footed

moll·is -is -e *adj* soft; springy; flexible; flabby; mild, calm; easy; gentle *(slope)*; sensitive, impressionable; tender, touching; weak, effeminate; amatory *(verses)*; changeable, untrustworthy

molliter *adv* softly; gently, smoothly; effeminately; voluptuously; patiently, with fortitude

molliti·a -ae *or* **molliti·ēs -ēī** *f* softness; flexibility; tenderness; sensitivity; weakness, irresolution; effeminacy, voluptuousness

mollitūd·ō -inis *f* softness; flexibility; susceptibiltiy

mol·ō -ĕre -uī -itus *tr* to grind

Moloss·us -a -um *adj* Molossian ‖ *m* Molossian hound ‖ *mpl* Molossians *(a people of Epirus)*

mōl·y -yos *n* magic herb

mōm·en -inis *n* movement, motion; momentum

mōment·um -ī *n* movement, motion; alteration; turn, critical time; moment; impulse; momentum; influence; importance; motive

Mon·a -ae *f* Isle of Anglesey

monēdul·a -ae *f* jackdaw *(bird)*

mon·eō -ēre -uī -itus *tr* to call to mind, remind, advise, point out; to warn; to foretell; to teach; to inform

monēr·is -is *f* galley

Monēt·a -ae *f* Juno Moneta *(in whose temple on the Capitoline Hill money was coined)*; mint; coin, money; stamp, die *(for money)*

monētāl·is -is -e *adj* of the mint ‖ *m* superintendent of the mint

monīl·e -is *n* necklace

monim- = monum-

monit·a -ōrum *npl* warnings; prophecies; precepts

moniti·ō -ōnis *f* reminder; warning

monit·or -ōris *m* reminder; counselor; teacher; prompter

monit·us -ūs *m* reminder; warning ‖ *mpl* promptings, warnings

monogramm·us -a -um *adj* sketchy, shadowy; unsubstantial, hollow

monopod·ium -(i)ī *n* table with a single central leg

monotrop·us -a -um *adj* single, alone

mon·s -tis *m* mountain; hill; mountain range; mass, heap; **montīs auri polliceri** *(prov)* to make wild promises *(literally, to promise mountains of gold)*; **summus mons** mountaintop ‖ *mpl* hill country, the hills

monstrāti·ō -ōnis *f* pointing out
monstrāt·or -ōris *m* displayer, demonstrator
monstr·ō -āre -āvī -ātus *tr* to show, point out; to make known; to demonstrate, teach; to indicate, suggest; to appoint, designate ‖ *intr* to show the way
monstr·um -ī *n* sign, portent, wonder; warning; monster, monstrosity; atrocity; monstrous event
monstruōsē *adv* unnaturally
monstruōs·us -a -um *adj* unnatural, monstrous, strange
montān·us -a -um *adj* mountain-, of a mountain; mountainous ‖ *mpl* hill-dwellers *(esp. of the seven hills of Rome)* ‖ *npl* mountainous regions
monticol·a -ae *m* mountaineer
montivag·us -a -um *adj* wandering over the mountains
montōs·us *or* **montuōs·us -a -um** *adj* mountainous
monument·um -ī *n* reminder; monument, memorial; literary work, book; history; record *(written or oral);* token of identification ‖ *npl* recorded tradition; **annalium monumenta** annals; **litterarum monumenta** literary record, document
Mopsopi·us -a -um *adj* Athenian ‖ *f* Athens; *(ancient name for)* Attica
mor·a -ae *f* delay; pause; spell, period of time; stop-off; *(mil)* division *(of the Spartan army of from 300 to 700 men);* **haud morā** without hesitation; **in morā esse** to be a hindrance; **in morā habere** to allow to be a hindrance; **mora est** it will take too long; **moram afferre** to present difficulties, waste time; **moram facere** to obstruct; to cause delay
mōr·a -ae *f* fool
mōrāl·is -is -e *adj* moral
morāt·or -ōris *m* obstructionist; loiterer; *(in court)* lawyer who spoke only to gain time
mōrāt·us -a -um *adj* -mannered, -natured; in character; *(of a thing)* natured; **bene moratus** well-mannered, civilized; **male moratus** ill-mannered, rude; **mirabiliter moratus** he is a strange creature
morbid·us -a -um *adj* sickly; causing sickness, unwholesome
morbōs·us -a -um *adj* sickly; sex-crazy, horny; **morbosus in** *(w. acc)* mad about
morb·us -ī *m* sickness, disease, ailment; fault, vice; distress; **in morbum cadere** *(or* **in morbum incidere)** to fall sick
mordācius *adv* more bitingly; *(fig)* more radically
mord·ax -ācis *adj* biting, snapping; *(fig)* sharp, stinging, caustic; snarling; pungent, tart
mordeō mordēre momordī morsus *tr* to bite; to eat, devour; to grip; *(of cold)* to nip; *(of words)* to cut, hurt; *(of a river)* to bite its way through
mordic·ēs -um *mpl* bites; incisor teeth
mordicus *adv* by biting, with the teeth; *(fig)* tightly, doggedly
mōrē *adv* foolishly
morēt·um -ī *n* salad
moribund·us -a -um *adj* dying, at the point of death; mortal; deadly
mōriger·ō -āre *or* **mōriger·or -ārī -ātus sum** *intr (w. dat)* **1** to humor, pamper; **2** to yield to; **3** to comply with
mor·ior -ī -tuus sum *intr* to die; *(fig)* to decay, pass away, die out; *(of fires)* to die out; *(of flowers)* to wither, die off; **moriar nisi** *(coll)* hope to die if…not
morm·ȳr -ȳris *f* Pontic fish
mor·or -ārī -ātus sum *tr* to delay, detain; to entertain, hold the attention of; to hinder, prevent; **nihil morari** *(w. acc)* **1** to disregard, care nothing for, not value; **2** to have nothing against, have nothing to say against ‖ *intr* to delay, linger, loiter; to stay, remain; to wait; **quid moror?** *(or* **quid multis morer?)** why should I drag out the point?, to make a long story short
mōrōsē *adv* morosely, crabbily
mōrōsit·ās -ātis *f* moroseness, crabbiness
mōrōs·us -a -um *adj* morose, crabby; fastidious, particular; *(fig)* stubborn *(disease)*
Morph·eūs -eos *(acc:* **-ea)** *m* god of dreams
mors mortis *f* death; destruction; corpse; bloodshed; **morte communi** of natural causes; **mortem obire** *(or* **oppetere)** to meet death; **mortem** *(or* **morti) occumbere** to die; **mortem sibi consciscere** to commit suicide *(literally, to decide on death for oneself);* **mortis honos** burial; **mortis poena** death penalty
mors·a -ōrum *npl* bits, little pieces
morsiuncul·a -ae *f* peck, kiss
morsus *pp of* **mordeo**
mors·us -ūs *m* bite; pungency; grip; corrosion; gnawing pain; sting; vicious attack
mortāl·is -is -e *adj* mortal, subject to death; human; transient; man-made ‖ *m* mortal, human being
mortālit·ās -ātis *f* mortality; mortals, mankind
morticīn·us -a -um *adj & m* carrion
mortif·er *or* **mortif·erus -era -erum** *adj* lethal, deadly, fatal
mortiferē *adv* mortally
mortuāl·ia -ium *npl* dirges
mortu·us -a -um *adj* dead, deceased; withered, decayed; scared to death; over and done with; half-hearted, feeble ‖ *m* dead person ‖ *mpl* the dead
mōrul·us -a -um *adj* dark, blackberry-colored

mōr·um -ī *n* black mulberry
mōr·us -ī *f* black mulberry tree
mōr·us -a -um *adj* foolish ‖ *mf* fool
mōs mōris *m* custom, usage, practice; caprice, mood; nature; manner; fashion, style; rule, regulation, law; **de more** *(or* **ex more)** according to custom; **more** in the customary manner; **more** *(or* **in morem** *or* **de more)** *(w. gen)* in the manner of, like; **morem gerere** *(w. dat)* to humor *(s.o.),* to indulge *(s.o. or one's feelings);* **mos majorum** tradition; **nullo more** *(or* **sine more)** without restraint, wildly; lawlessly; **supra morem** more than is usual ‖ *mpl* morals; character; behavior; customs; laws; **ex meis moribus** according to my wishes
Mōs·ēs *or* **Moys·ēs -is** *m* Moses
mōti·ō -ōnis *f* motion, movement
mōtiuncul·a -ae *f* slight attack of fever
mōt·ō -āre -āvī -ātus *tr* to keep moving
mōtus *pp of* **moveo**
mōt·us -ūs *m* motion, movement; gesture; dancing; change *(e.g., of fortune);* impulse, inspiration; passion; revolt, riot; tactical move; *(rhet)* figure of speech; **in motu** active; **in motu esse** to be in a state of flux; **motus animi** emotion; **motus mentis** thought process; **motus pedum** activity; **motus terrae** earthquake
mov·ens -entis *adj* active; restless, shifting; **res moventes** movable property *(e.g., clothes, furniture)* ‖ *npl* motives
moveō movēre mōvī mōtus *tr* to move; to stir, shake, disturb; to cause, occasion, promote; to begin; to undertake; to trouble, torment; to touch, influence, affect; to throw into political turmoil; to eject, expel *(from office, post);* to degrade; to remove, take away; to dislodge *(the enemy);* to shake; cause to waver; to plow; to strum, play *(a musical instrument);* to dissuade; to exert, exercise; to turn over in the mind, ponder; **aliquem loco movere** to dislodge s.o.; **bellum movere** to bring on a war, begin a war; **senatu movere** to remove from the Senate roll; **signa movere** to begin a march; **ventrem movere** to move the bowels; **vocem movere carmine** to raise the voice in song ‖ *refl* to move; to dance; *(of heavenly bodies)* to rise; *(of riots)* to break out; **se ex loco movere** to budge from the spot ‖ *pass & intr* to move; to shake, quake, throb ‖ *intr* to move off, depart; *(of buds)* to sprout, come out
mox *adv* soon, presently; hereafter; next, then; later on
Moys·ēs -is *m* Moses
mūcid·us -a -um *adj* sniveling, snotty; moldy, musty
Mūc·ius -(i)ī *m* Roman clan name *(nomen);* Gaius Mucius Cordus Scaevola *(tried to kill Porsenna and, when caught, deliberately burned his right hand)*
mucr·ō -ōnis *m* sharp point, sharp edge; tip; sword; edge, boundary; keenness
mūc·us -ī *m* **(mucc-)** mucus, snot
mūgient·ēs -ium *mpl* oxen
mūg·il *or* **mūg·ilis -ilis** *m* gray mullet *(a sea fish)*
mūgīn·or -ārī -ātus sum *intr* to dilly-dally
mūg·iō -īre -īvī *or* **-iī -ītum** *intr* to moo, bellow, low; to roar, rumble; *(of a bugle)* to blast, sound
mūgīt·us -ūs *m* mooing, bellowing; roaring, rumbling
mūl·a -ae *f* mule
mul·ceō -cēre -sī -sus *or* **mul(c)tus** *tr* to stroke, pet; to stir gently; to soothe, alleviate; to appease; to gladden, delight
Mulcib·er -erī *or* **-eris** *m* Vulcan; *(fig)* fire
mulc·ō -āre -āvī -ātus *tr* to beat up, cudgel; to mistreat, injure; to worst *(in battle)*
mulctr·a -ae *f* milk pail
mulctrār·ium -(i)ī *or* **mulctr·um -ī** *n* milk pail
mul·geō -gēre -sī -sus *or* **-ctus** *tr* to milk
muliebr·is -is -e *adj* woman's, womanly, feminine; womanish, effeminate; *(of deities)* presiding over the lives of women; *(gram)* feminine; **pars muliebris** *(or* **partes muliebres)** female sexual organs ‖ *npl* female sexual organs; **viri muliebria patiuntur** men play the role of women *(i.e., let themselves be used as catamites)*
muliebriter *adv* like a woman; effeminately
muli·er -eris *f* woman; wife
mulierāri·us -a -um *adj* woman's ‖ *m* womanizer, wolf
muliercul·a -ae *f* little *(or* weak *or* foolish) woman; sissy
mulierōsit·ās -ātis *f* weakness for women
mulierōs·us -a -um *adj* woman-crazy
mūlīn·us -a -um *adj* mulish
mūli·ō -ōnis *m* mule driver
mūliōni·us -a -um *adj* mule driver's
mullul·us -ī *m* little mullet *(fish)*
mull·us -ī *m* red mullet *(fish)*
mulsī *perf of* **mulceo** *and* **mulgeo**
muls·us -a -um *pp of* **mulceo** *and of* **mulgeo** ‖ *adj* honeyed, sweet as honey ‖ *f (term of endearment)* honey ‖ *n* mead *(wine mixed with honey)*
mult·a -ae *f* fine; penalty; loss of money; **multam certare** to contest a fine; **multam committere** to incur a fine; **multam dicere** *(w. dat of person and acc of the fine)* to fine *(s. o. a certain amount);* **multam subire** to incur a fine, be fined
multa *adv* much, very; earnestly
mult·a -ōrum *npl* many things; much; **ne multa** in short

multangul·us -a -um *adj* having many angles, many-angled
multātīci·us -a -um *adj* of a fine; **multaticia pecunia** fine
multāti·ō -ōnis *f* fine, penalty
multēsim·us -a -um *adj* trifling, negligible
mult·ī -ōrum *mpl* many men, many; multitude, mass, common people
multibib·us -a -um *adj* fond of drinking, heavy-drinking
multicav·us -a -um *adj* porous
multīci·a -ōrum *npl* diaphanous garments
multifāriam *adv* in many places
multifid·us -a -um *adj* divided into many parts; splintered *(wood); (of a river)* having many tributaries
multiform·is -is -e *adj* multiform, manifold
multifor·us -a -um *adj* many-holed; *(flute)* having many stops
multigen·er -eris *or* **multigen·us -a -um** *adj* of many kinds, various
multijug·is -is -e *or* **multijug·us -a -um** *adj* many yoked together; many tied together; *(fig)* various
multiloqu·ax -ācis *adj* talkative
multiloqu·ium -(i)ī *n* talkativeness
multiloqu·us -a -um *adj* talkative
multimodīs *adv* in many ways
multiplex -icis *adj* with many folds; winding, serpentine; manifold; many; *(in comparisons)* many times as great, far greater; varied, complicated; versatile, changeable, many-sided; sly, cunning **||** *n* manifold return
multiplicābil·is -is -e *adj* manifold, many
multipliciter *adv* in various ways
multiplic·ō -āre -āvī -ātus *tr* to multiply, increase, enlarge; to have *(or* use *or* practice) on many occasions
multipot·ens -entis *adj* mighty, powerful
multitūd·ō -inis *f* great number, multitude, crowd, throng; rabble, common people; population
multivol·us -a -um *adj* passionate
multō *adv (w. comparatives)* much, far, by far, a great deal; **multo aliter ac** far otherwise than, much different from; **multo ante** long before; **multo post** long after; **non multo secus fieri** to turn out just about the same
mult·ō -āre -āvī -ātus *tr* to punish; to fine
mult·us -a -um *(comp:* **plures;** *superl:* **plurimus)** *adj* many a, much, great; abundant, considerable, extensive; tedious, long-winded; full, numerous, thick, loud, heavy; constant; **ad multum diem** till late in the day; **multā nocte** late at night; **multo die** late in the day; *(with plural nouns)* many **||** *mpl see* **multi** **||** *n* much; **multi** of great value, highly; **multi facere** to think highly of, make much of; **multum est** it is of great importance; **multum temporis** a great deal of time, much time **||** *npl see* **multa**
multum *adv* much, a lot, greatly, very; often, frequently; *(w. comparatives)* much, far; **multum valere** to have considerable influence
mūl·us -ī *m* mule
Mulvi·us -a -um *adj* Mulvian; **Mulvius pons** Mulvian bridge *(across the Tiber, above Rome on the Via Flaminia)*
Mumm·ius -(i)ī *m* Lucius Mummius Achaicus *(conqueror of Corinth, 146 B.C.)*
mundān·us -a -um *adj* of the world **||** *m* world citizen
mundē *or* **munditer** *adv* neatly, cleanly
munditi·a -ae *or* **munditi·ēs -ēī** *f* neatness, cleanliness; elegance; politeness; refinement of language
mundul·us -a -um *adj* trim, neat
mund·us -a -um *adj* neat, clean, nice; fine, smart, sharp, elegant; choice *(words)* **||** *m* neat person; world, earth, universe; heavens; mankind; beauty aids; **in mundo** ready, in store; **mundus caeli** firmament
mūnerār·ius -(i)ī *m* producer of gladiatorial shows
mūnerigerul·us -ī *m* bearer of presents
mūner·ō -āre -āvī -ātus *or* **mūner·or -ārī -ātus sum** *tr* to reward, honor, present; *(w. acc of thing and dat of person)* to present *(s.th.)* to
mūni·a -ōrum *npl* official duties *or* functions
mūnic·eps -ipis *mf* citizen of a municipality; fellow citizen, fellow countryman
mūnicipāl·is -is -e *adj* municipal; *(pej)* provincial
mūnicipātim *adv* by municipalities
mūnicip·ium -(i)ī *n* municipality, town *(whose people were Roman citizens, but otherwise autonomous)*
mūnificē *adv* generously
mūnificenti·a -ae *f* generosity
mūnific·ō -āre -āvī -ātus *tr* to treat generously
mūnific·us -a -um *adj* generous; splendid
mūnīm·en -inis *n* defense
mūnīment·um -ī *n* defense, protection, fortification, rampart; *(fig)* shelter, defense, safeguard
mūn·iō -īre -īvī *or* **-iī -ītus** *tr* **(moen-)** to defend with a wall, wall in; to fortify, strengthen, defend, protect, secure; to build *(road);* to provide with a road; *(fig)* to guard, shelter, protect, support
mūn·is -is -e *adj* obliging, ready to be of service
mūnīti·ō -ōnis *f* building, fortifying, defending; fortification, rampart, trenches,

lines; **munitio fluminum** bridging of rivers; **munitio viae** road construction
mūnīt·ō -āre *tr* to open up *(a road)*
mūnīt·or -ōris *m* builder *(of fortifications)*
mūnīt·us -a -um *pp of* **munio** ‖ *adj* well-fortified, well-protected; *(fig)* safe, protected
mūn·us -eris *n* **(moen-)**service, function, duty; gift; favor, kindness; tax, duty; public entertainment, gladiatorial show; tribute *(to the dead)*, rite, sacrifice; public office; **in munere** *(or* **munere** *or* **pro munere)** as a gift
mūnuscul·um -ī *n* small gift
mūraen·a -ae *f* moray *(eel-like fish)*
mūrāl·is -is -e *adj* wall-, of a wall; wall-destroying; wall-defending
mūr·ex -icis *m* murex, mollusk *(yielding purple dye)*; purple dye, purple; jagged rock; spiked trap *(as defense against cavalry attack)*
muri·a -ae *or* **muri·ēs -ēī** *f* brine *(used for pickling)*
muriātic·um -ī *n* pickled fish
mūricid·us -ī *m* **(murr-)** mouse killer; *(fig)* coward
murmill·ō -ōnis *m* gladiator *(with Gallic arms, who fought against an opponent who used a net)*
murm·ur -uris *n* murmur, murmuring; buzz, hum; roar, crash; growling, grumbling; rumbling; hubbub
murmurill·um -ī *n* low murmur
murmur·ō -āre -āvī -ātus *tr* to murmur against ‖ *intr* to mutter, grumble; to rumble, roar
murr·a *or* **murrh·a** *or* **myrrh·a -ae** *f* myrrh tree; myrrh
murr·a -ae *f* fluorspar *(mineral from which expensive vases were made)*
murre·us -a -um *adj* **(myrrh-)** myrrh-colored, reddish-brown
murre·us -a -um *adj* made of fluor-spar
murt- = myrt-
mūr·us -ī *m* wall; city wall(s); dike; rim *(of dish or pot)*; *(fig)* defender, champion
mūs mūris *m* mouse; rat
Mūs·a -ae *f* Muse *(patron goddess of poetry, song, dance, literature, etc.)*; poem, song; talent; poetic inspiration
Mūsae·us *or* **Mūsē·us -a -um** *adj* of the Muses, musical, poetic ‖ *n* institute of philosophy and research at Alexandria
Mūsae·us -ī *m* pre-Homeric bard in the time of Orpheus
musc·a -ae *f* fly; *(fig)* nosey person
muscār·ium -(i)ī *n* fly swatter
muscipul·a -ae *f or* **muscipul·um -ī** *n* mousetrap
muscōs·us -a -um *adj* mossy
muscul·us -ī *m* little mouse; muscle; *(mil)* mantelet
musc·us -ī *m* moss
mūsic·a -ae *or* **mūsic·ē -ēs** *f or* **mūsic·a -ōrum** *npl* music; art of music *(including poetry)*
mūsicē *adv* pleasantly, elegantly
mūsic·us -a -um *adj* relating to the Muses; musical; melodious, tuneful; poetic; *(of a person)* expert in music ‖ *mf* musician
mussit·ō -āre -āvī -ātus *tr* to bear in silence ‖ *intr* to be silent; to mutter, grumble
muss·ō -āre -āvī -ātus *tr* to bear in silence; to brood over ‖ *intr* to mutter, murmur; to hesitate; *(of bees)* to hum
mustāce·us -ī *m or* **mustāce·um -ī** *n* wedding cake *(baked with must and set on laurel leaves)*
mustēl·a -ae *f* **(-tell-)** weasel
mustēlīn·us -a -um *adj* **(-tell-)** of a weasel
muste·us -a -um *adj* fresh; *(of a book)* in the early stages
must·um -ī *n* fresh grape juice, must; vintage
mūtābil·is -is -e *adj* changeable; fickle
mūtābilit·ās -ātis *f* mutability; fickleness
mūtāti·ō -ōnis *f* mutation, change; exchange, interchange; translation; **mutatio animi** change of heart
mutil·ō -āre -āvī -ātus *tr* to chop off, lop off, crop; to mutilate; to reduce; to rob
mutil·us -a -um *adj* mutilated; maimed; having chopped-off horns
Mutin·a -ae *f* town of N. Central Italy, S. of the Po *(modern Modena)*, where Decimus Brutus was besieged by Antony *(44–43 B.C.)*
Mutinens·is -is -e *adj* of Mutina
mūtiō *see* **muttio**
mutītiō *see* **muttitio**
mūt·ō -āre -āvī -ātus *tr* to change, shift; to alter; to exchange, interchange, barter, sell; to modify, transform; to vary; to change for the better; to change for the worse; *(w.* **in** *+ acc)* to change *(s.th. or s.o.)* into; *(w. abl or w.* **cum** *or* **pro** *+ abl)* to exchange *or* substitute *(s.th. or s.o.)* for; **mutare fidem** to change allegiance, change sides; **mutare latus** to roll over *(in bed)*; *(of fish)* to flip over ‖ *pass* to change; *(w.* **in** *+ acc)* to change into; *(w. abl)* to change in respect to: **silvae foliis mutantur** the forests change their leaves ‖ *intr* to change; **mutare in melius** *(or* **peius)** to change for the better *(or* for the worse) ‖ *v impers* **non mutat** it makes no difference
mūt·ō *see* **mutto**
mutt·iō -īre -īvī -ītus *tr* **(mūt-)** to mutter
muttīti·ō *or* **mūtīti·ō -ōnis** *f* **(mūt-)** muttering
mutt·ō *or* **mūt·ō -ōnis** *m (vulg)* penis
mūtuē *adv* mutually; in turn
mūtuit·or -ārī *tr* to wish to borrow

mutūniāt·us -a -um *adj (vulg)* having a large penis
mūtuō *adv* mutually, in return
mūtu·or -ārī -ātus sum *tr* to borrow; to obtain, get; to derive
mūt·us -a -um *adj* mute; dumb speechless; silent, still, noiseless; **muta persona** non-speaking actor ‖ *npl* dumb animals
mūtu·us -a -um *adj* mutual, reciprocal, interchangeable; borrowed, lent ‖ *n* loan; reciprocity; **aliquid mutuum accipere** *(or* **sumere)** to borrow s.th.; **aliquid mutuum dare** *(w.* **cum)** to lend s.th. to *(s.o.);* **mutuas pecunias sumere ab** to borrow money from; **mutuum argentum rogare ab** to ask *(s.o.)* for a loan of cash; **mutuum facere cum aliquo** to reciprocate s.o.'s feelings ‖ *npl (w. advl sense)* mutually, reciprocally; **in mutua** towards each other; **per mutua** with one another
Mycēn·ae -ārum *fpl or* **Mycēn·ē -ēs** *f* Mycenae *(city of King Agamemnon in Argolis)*
Mycēn·is -idis *f* Mycenaean girl *(i.e., Iphigenia)*
Mygdon·es -um *mpl* a people of Thrace, some of whom later migrated to Phrygia
Mygdoni·us -a -um *adj* Phrygian
myopar·ōn -ōnis *m* galley
myrīc·a -ae *or* **myrīc·ē -ēs** *f* tamarisk
Myrmidon·es *or* **Myrmidon·ēs -um** *mpl* Myrmidons *(people of Thessaly whom Achilles led in battle)*
Myr·ōn -ōnis *m* famous Greek sculptor *(5th cent.* B.C.*)*
myropōl·a -ae *m* perfumer
myropōl·ium -(i)ī *n* perfume shop
myrrh- = murr-
myrtēt·um -ī *n* **(mur-)** myrtle grove
myrte·us -a -um *adj* **(mur-)** myrtle; crowned with myrtle
Myrtō·um Mar·e *(gen:* **Myrtō·ī Mar·is)** *n* Myrtoan Sea *(between the Peloponnesus and the Cyclades)*
myrt·um -ī *n* myrtle berry
myrt·us -ūs *or* **-ī** *f* myrtle tree
Mȳsi·us -a -um *adj* Mysian ‖ *f* Mysia *(country in N.W. Asia Minor)*
myst·a *or* **myst·ēs -ae** *m* priest of the mysteries of Ceres; an initiate
mystagōg·us -ī *n* initiator; tourist guide
mystēr·ium -(i)ī *n* **(mist-)** secret religion, secret service, secret rite; divine mystery; secret; **mysteria facere** to hold service; **mysteria Romana** festival of Bona Dea
mystic·us -a -um mystic
Mytilēn·ae -ārum *fpl or* **Mytilēn·ē -ēs** *f* Mytilene *(chief of the island of Lesbos)*
Mytilēnae·us -a -um *or* **Mytilēnens·is -is -e** *adj* of Mytilene

N

N. *abbr* **Numerius** *(Roman first name, praenomen);* **Nonae** the Nones; **Nummus** coin
Nabatae·us -a -um *adj* Nabataean; Eastern ‖ *mpl* Nabataeans *(a people of N. Arabia)*
nabl·ia -ium *npl* Phoenician harp
nactus *pp of* **nanciscor**
Naeviān·us -a -um *adj* of Naevius
Naev·ius -(i)ī *m* Gnaeus Naevius *(early Roman dramatic and epic poet, c. 270–200* B.C.*)*
Nāï·as -adis *or* **Nā·is -idis** *or* **-idos** *f* Naiad, water nymph,
nam *conj* for; for in that case; *(affirmative)* yes, to be sure; *(transitional)* now, but now, on the other hand
namque *conj* for in fact, for no doubt, for surely
nan·ciscor -ciscī -ctus sum *or* **nactus sum** *tr* to get, obtain; to come across, find; to arrive at; to experience, meet with; to contract *(a disease)*
nān·us -ī *m* dwarf, midget
Napae·ae -ārum *fpl* dell nymphs
nāp·us -ī *m* turnip
Narb·ō -ōnis *m* Narbonne *(city in S. Gaul, from which the province of Narbonese took its name)*
Narbōnens·is -is -e *adj* Narbonese
narciss·us -ī *m (bot)* narcissus ‖ **Narcissus** son of Cephisus and the nymph Liriope, who was changed into a narcissus ‖ powerful freedman of Claudius
nard·um -ī *n or* **nard·us -ī** *f* nard, spikenard *(fragrant ointment)*
nār·is -is *f* nose; **homo acutae naris** *(or* **emunctae naris)** a man of keen perception; **homo naris obesae** dimwit *(literally, thick-nosed man)* ‖ *fpl* nostrils, nose; **nares corrugare** to cause *(s.o.)* to turn up his nose; **naribus ducere** to smell; **naribus uti** *(w.* **ad)** to turn up the nose at
Narni·a -ae *f* town in Umbria
Narniens·is -is -e *adj* of Narnia
narrābil·is -is -e *adj* to be told
narrāti·ō -ōnis *f* narrative
narrātiuncul·a -ae *f* anecdote
narrāt·or -ōris *m* narrator
narrāt·um -ī *n* account, narrative
narrāt·us -ūs *m* narrative, tale
narr·ō -āre -āvī -ātus *tr* to tell, relate, narrate, recount; to describe, tell about ‖ *intr* to speak, tell; **bene narrare** *(w.* **de** + *abl)* to tell good news about *(s.o.);* **male narrare** *(w.* **de** + *abl)* to tell bad news about *(s.o.);* **tibi narro** *(coll)* I'm telling you, I assure you; **quam tu mihi nunc**

navem narras? *(coll)* now, what's this ship you're talking about?

narthēc·ium -(i)ī *n* medicine chest

narus *see* **gnarus**

Nāryci·us -a -um *adj* of Narycum *(birthplace of Ajax, son of Oileus)*

nascor nascī nātus sum *intr* **(gn-)** to be born; to begin, orginate, spring forth, proceed; to be produced; *(of plants)* to grow; *(of rocks, minerals)* to be found, occur; *(astr)* to rise

Nāsīc·a -ae *m* Roman honorary name *(agnomen)* Publius Cornelius Scipio Nasica *(consul in 191 B.C.)*

Nās·ō -ōnis *m* Ovid *(Publius Ovidius Naso, Roman poet, 43 B.C.–A.D. 17)*

nass·a -ae *f* wicker trap *(for catching fish); (fig)* trap

nassitern·a -ae *f* large water jug

nasturc·ium -(i)ī *n (bot)* watercress

nās·us -ī *m or* **nās·um -ī** *n* nose; sense of smell; sagacity; scorn; satirical wit; spout, nozzle

nāsūtē *adv* sarcastically

nāsūt·us -a -um *adj* big-nosed; sarcastic, satirical

nāt·a *or* **gnāt·a -ae** *f* daughter

nātālici·us -a -um *adj* birthday; natal, congenital; **dies natalicius** birthday ‖ *f* birthday party

nātāl·is -is -e *adj* of birth, natal, congenital; **dies natalis** birthday ‖ *m* birthday; foundation day *(of city, temple, etc.)* ‖ *mpl* birth, origin, parentage; **natalibus suis restituere** *(or* **reddere)** to confer the status of a free-born citizen on *(one born into slavery)*

nat·ans -antis *adj* swimming; swimming in the sea, marine ‖ *mf* fish

natāti·ō -ōnis *f* swimming, swim

natāt·or -ōris *m* swimmer

nat·ēs -ium *fpl see* **natis**

nāti·ō -ōnis *f* tribe, nation, people; race, stock; *(pej)* breed

nat·is -is *f* buttock, rump ‖ *fpl* buttocks, rear end

nātīv·us -a -um *adj* born; inborn, innate, original; native, local; produced by nature, natural; primitive *(words)*

nat·ō -āre -āvī -ātus *tr* to swim (across) ‖ *intr* to swim, float; to flow; to overflow; *(of eyes)* to be glassy; *(of birds)* to fly, glide; to waver, fluctuate; to hover; to move to and fro

natr·ix -icis *f* water snake

nātūr·a -ae *f* nature, natural constitution; character, temperament; ability; distinctive feature *or* characteristic; naturalness *(in art);* order of the world, course of things; element, substance; sex organs; **in naturā** *(or* **in rerum naturā)** **esse** to be the natural choices, to be the alternatives; **naturā** *(or* **per naturam)** naturally; **natura fluminis** the natural course of the river; **natura rerum** (physical) nature; **suā naturā** of its own accord

nātūrāl·is -is -e *adj* natural; by birth, one's own *(father, son, etc.);* produced by nature; according to nature

nātūrāliter *adv* naturally, by nature

nāt·us *or* **gnāt·us -a -um** *pp of* **nascor** ‖ *adj* born; *(w. dat or* **ad** *or* **in** *+ acc)* born for, made for, naturally suited to, fit for; *(w.* **annos)** at the age of..., ...years old, *e.g.,* **annos viginti natus** at the age of twenty, twenty years old; **non amplius novem annos natus** no more than nine years old; **pro re nata** *(or* **e re nata)** under the existing circumstances, as matters stand; **res nata** the situation, the way things are ‖ *m* son ‖ *mpl* children ‖ *f* daughter

nauarch·us -ī *m* ship's captain, skipper

nauclēric·us -a -um captain's ‖ *m* ship owner, captain

nauclēr·us -ī *m* ship's captain

naucul·or -ārī -ātus sum *intr* to go boating, go sailing

nauc·um -ī *n* trifle; *(mostly in gen of value with a negative)* **non nauci esse** to be good for nothing; **non nauci habere** to regard as worthless

naufrag·ium -(i)ī *n* shipwreck; wreck, ruin, destruction; wreckage; *(fig)* shattered remains; **naufragium facere** to be shipwrecked; *(of things)* to be lost ‖ *npl* remnants, shattered remains; **naufragia Caesaris amicorum** the remnants of Caesar's friends

naufrag·ō -āre -āvī *intr* to suffer shipwreck

naufrag·us -a -um *adj* shipwrecked, of the shipwrecked; causing shipwreck, dangerous to shipping; *(fig)* ruined ‖ *m* shipwrecked person

naul·um -ī *n* fare

naumachi·a -ae *f* simulated naval engagement *(staged as an exercise or for amusement)*

naumachiār·ius -(i)ī *m* person taking part in a mock sea fight

Naupact·us -ī *f* town on the N. shore of the Gulf of Corinth

Naupliad·ēs -ae *m* son of Nauplius, Palamedes

Naupl·ius -(i)ī *m* king of Euboea who wrecked the Greek fleet to avenge the death of his son Palamedes

nause·a -ae *f* seasickness; vomiting, nausea; **nausea fluens** vomiting

nause·ō -āre -āvī *tr* to make *(s.o.)* throw up; *(fig)* to belch forth, throw up, utter ‖ *intr* to be seasick; to vomit; to feel squeamish, feel disgust; to cause disgust

nauseol·a -ae *f* slight squeamishness

Nausica·ā -ae *f* daughter of Alcinoüs, king of the Phaeacians
naut·a *or* **nāvit·a -ae** *m* sailor, seaman, mariner; captain
naute·a -ae *f* nausea; bilge water
nautic·us -a -um *adj* nautical, sailor's **||** *mpl* sailors, seamen
nāvāl·is -is -e *adj* naval, of ships, of a ship; **castra navalia** camp for the protection of ships; **forma navalis** shape of a ship **||** *n* tackle, rigging **||** *npl* dock, dockyard, shipyard; rigging
nāvē *adv* industriously
nāvicul·a -ae *f* small ship
nāviculāri·us -a -um *adj* of a small ship **||** *m* skipper; ship owner **||** *f* shipping business
nāvifrag·us -a -um *adj* dangerous, treacherous, causing shipwreck
nāvigābil·is -is -e *adj* navigable
nāvigāti·ō -ōnis *f* sailing, navigation, voyage
nāvig·er -era -erum *adj* navigable
nāvig·ium -(i)ī *n* ship; boat
nāvig·ō -āre -āvī -ātus *tr* to sail across, navigate **||** *intr* to sail, put to sea; *(fig)* to swim
nāv·is -is *f* ship; *(astr)* Argo *(constellation);* **navem appellere** *(or* **navem terrae applicare)** to land a ship; **navem deducere** to launch a ship; **navem solvere** to set sail; **navem subducere** to beach a ship; **navi** *(or* **navibus)** by ship, by sea; **navis aperta** ship without a deck; **navis longa** battleship; **navis mercatoria** merchant vessel; **navis oneraria** transport, cargo ship; **navis praetoria** flagship; **navis tecta** ship with a deck
nāvit·a *see* **nauta**
nāvit·ās -ātis *f* energy, zeal
nāviter *adv* energetically, zealously, actively, busily; utterly, completely
nāv·ō -āre *tr* to do *or* perform energetically, conduct *or* carry out with vigor; **operam navare** to act energetically; **operam navare** *(w. dat)* to render assistance to
nāv·us -a -um *adj* **(gn-)** energetic, busy
Nax·os -ī *f* largest island of the Cyclades in the Aegean Sea
nē *interj (nearly always with a personal or demonstrative pronoun)* indeed, certainly, surely; **ne ego homo infelix fui** I was indeed an unhappy man **||** *adv* not; **ne...quidem** *(to negate emphatically the words placed between)* not even; **ne timete!** do not fear! **||** *conj* that not, lest; so as to prevent *(s.th. from happening);* much less, let alone; **ne dicam** not to mention; **ne mentiar** to tell the truth; **ne multa** *(or* **ne multi)s** to make a long story short **||** *conj (after verbs and nouns denoting fear)* that
-ne *enclitic (introducing a question and added to the first important word of a clause; it does not imply anything about the expected answer); (introducing an alternative in a question)* Or...?; *(in indirect questions)* whether; *(introducing a double or multiple indirect question)* whether
nebul·a -ae *f* mist, fog, vapor; cloud; smoke; darkness, obscurity
nebul·ō -ōnis *m* loafer, good-for-nothing
nebulōs·us -a -um *adj* foggy
nec *or* **neque** *adv* not **||** *conj* nor, and not; **nec...et** not only...but also; **nec...nec** *(or* **neque...neque)** neither...nor; **nec non** *(introducing an emphatic affirmative)* and certainly, and besides
necdum *or* **nequedum** *conj* and not yet, nor yet
necessāriē *or* **necessāriō** *adv* necessarily, of necessity
necessāri·us -a -um *adj* necessary, indispensable, needful, requisite; inevitable; pressing, urgent; connected by blood or friendship, related, closely connected **||** *mf* relative, kinsman; friend **||** *npl* necessities
necesse *indecl adj* necessary; unavoidable, inevitable; requisite; **necesse esse** to be necessary; **necesse habere** to regard as necessary, regard as inevitable
necessit·ās -ātis *f* necessity, inevitability; compulsion, urgency; requirement; privation, want; relationship, connection, friendship
necessitūd·ō -inis *f* necessity, need, want, distress; relationship, bond, connection, friendship **||** *fpl* ties of friendship; relatives, friends, personal connections
necessum *indecl adj* necessary, requisite; inevitable
necne *conj* or not
nec·ō -āre -āvī -ātus *tr* to kill, murder
necopīn·ans -antis *adj* unaware
necopīnātō *adv* unexpectedly, by surprise
necopīnāt·us -a -um *adj* unexpected; **ex necopinato** unexpectedly
necopīn·us -a -um *adj* unexpected; unsuspecting; careless, off-guard
nect·ar -aris *n* nectar *(drink of the gods);* nectar *(term for honey, milk, wine, poetry, sweetness)*
nectare·us -a -um *adj* of nectar, sweet *(or* delicious) as nectar
nectō nectĕre nexuī *or* **nexī nexus** *tr* to tie, connect, fasten together, join; to weave; to clasp; to imprison; to fetter; to devise, contrive; *(fig)* to attach
nēcubi *conj* lest anywhere, so that nowhere
nēcunde *conj* lest from anywhere
nēdum *conj (after an expressed or implied negative)* much less, still less; *(after an affirmative)* not to say, much more

nefand·us -a -um *adj* unspeakable, heinous

nefāriē *adv* wickedly, foully

nefāri·us -a -um *adj* nefarious, heinous, criminal ‖ *n* crime, foul deed

nefās *indecl n* crime, wrong, wickedness; act contrary to divine law, sin; criminal, monster; **fas atque nefas** right and wrong; **nefas est** *(w. inf)* it is a crime to; **per omne fas ac nefas** by hook or by crook ‖ *interj* shocking!, dreadful!

nefast·us -a -um *adj* forbidden, unlawful; impious, irreligious; criminal; **dies nefastus** day unfit for business, legal holiday ‖ *n* outrage

negāti·ō -ōnis *f* denial

negit·ō -āre -āvī *tr* to keep denying; to turn down, refuse repeatedly

neglecti·ō -ōnis *f* **(nec-)** neglect

neglectus (nec-) *pp of* **neglego** ‖ *adj* neglected, despised, slighted

neglect·us -ūs *m* **(nec-)** neglect

negleg·ens -entis *adj* **(nec-)** negligent, careless, indifferent

neglegenter *adv* **(nec-)** carelessly

neglegenti·a -ae *f* **(nec-)** negligence, carelessness, neglect; **epistularum neglegentia** failure to write

negle·gō -gĕre -xī -ctus *tr* **(nec-)** to be unconcerned about; to neglect, disregard, overlook; to do without; to slight; to make light of; *(w. inf)* to fail to

neg·ō -āre -āvī -ātus *tr* to deny; *(w. acc + inf)* to say that...not ‖ *refl* to refuse one's services ‖ *intr* to say no; to refuse; *(w. dat)* to say no to, turn down *(regarding marriage or sexual favors, dinner invitation, etc.)*

negōtiāl·is -is -e *adj* business-

negōti·ans -antis *m* business man

negōtiāti·ō -ōnis *f* business, trade; business deal; business establishment

negōtiāt·or -ōris *m* businessman; banker; salesman, dealer

negōtiol·um -ī *n* minor matter

negōti·or -ārī -ātus sum *intr* to conduct business; to do banking; to trade; **homo negotians** businessman

negōtiōs·us -a -um *adj* business; busy; **dies negotiosus** workday

negōt·ium -(i)ī *n* business; occupation, employment; matter, thing, affair; situation; difficulty; trouble; banking, moneylending; trade, commerce; **dare negotium alicui ut** to give s.o. the job of; **in magno negotio habere** *(w. inf)* to make a point of; **negotium gerere** to conduct business; **negotium suum** private affairs; **non negotium est quin** there is nothing to do but; **quid negoti est?** what's the matter?; **quid negoti tibi est?** what business is it of yours?; **suum negotium agere** to mind one's own business ‖ *npl* commercial activities, business transactions; lawsuits

Nēl·eūs -eī *or* **-eos** *m* king of Pylos and father of Nestor

Nēlīd·ēs -ae *m* descendant of Neleus

Neme·a -ae *or* **Neme·ē -ēs** *f* Nemea *(town in Argolis, where Hercules slew a lion and founded the Nemean games)*

Neme·a -ōrum *npl* Nemean games *(held every two years at Nemea)*

Nemeae·us -a -um *adj* Nemean

Nemes·is -eōs *f* goddess of vengeance

nēm·ō -inis *mf* no one, nobody; a person of no consequence, a nobody; **nemo alius** no one else; **nemo dum** no one yet; **nemo non** every; **nemo quisquam** nobody at all; **nemo unus** no single person, no one by himself; **non nemo** someone, many a one, a few

nemorāl·is -is -e *adj* sylvan

nemorens·is -is -e *adj* of a grove; of Diana's grove

nemoricultr·ix -īcis *f* denizen *(female)* of the forest

nemorivag·us -a -um *adj* roaming the woods

nemorōs·us -a -um *adj* wooded; covered with foliage

nempe *adv (in confirmation or in sarcasm)* of course, naturally; *(in questions)* do you mean?

nem·us -oris *n* cluster of trees; grove; sacred grove

nēni·a -ae *f* **(naen-)** funeral song; doleful song; incantation; ditty

neō nēre nēvī nētus *tr* to spin; to weave

Neoptolem·us -ī *m* the son of Achilles *(also called Pyrrhus)*

nep·a -ae *f* scorpion; crab

Nephelē·is -idos *f* Helle *(daughter of Nephele and Athamas)*

nep·ōs -ōtis *m* grandson; nephew; descendant; spendthrift, playboy; **seri nepotes** distant descendants ‖ **Nepos** Cornelius Nepos *(Roman biographer and friend of Cicero, c. 100–25 B.C.)*

nepōtul·us -ī *m* little grandson

nept·is -is *f* granddaughter; descendant *(female)*

Neptūni·us -a -um *adj* of Neptune

Neptūn·us -ī *n* Neptune *(god of the sea and brother of Jupiter)*

nēquam *(comp:* **nēquior;** *superl:* **nēquissimus)** *indecl adj* worthless, bad, good for nothing; naughty; **nequam facere** to be naughty

nēquāquam *adv* by no means, not at all

neque *see* **nec**

nequedum *see* **necdum**

nequ·eō -īre -īvī *or* **-iī -ītum** *intr (w. inf)* to be unable to, be incapable of; *(w.* **quin)** to be unable to keep oneself from; **nequit** *(w.* **quin)** it is impossible to

nēqui·or -or -us *(comp of* **nequam)** *adj* worse, more worthless

nēquīquam *or* **nēquicquam** *adv* pointlessly, for nothing, to no purpose; without good reason; with impunity

nēquissim·us -a -um *(superl of* **nequam)** *adj* worst, most worthless

nēquiter *adv* wickedly; wrongly, with poor results; worthlessly; *(in playful use)* naughtily

nēquiti·a -ae *or* **nēquiti·ēs -ēī** *f* worthlessness, vileness, wickedness; naughtiness

Nērē·is -idis *f* Nereid, sea nymph *(one of the fifty daughters of Nereus)*

Nēr·eūs -eī *or* **-eos** *m* son of Oceanus and Tethys, and husband of Doris, and father of the Nereids; sea

Nērīnē -ēs *f* daughter of Nereus

Nēriti·us -a -um *adj* of Neritus; **dux Neritius** Ulysses; **Neritia ratis** ship of Ulysses

Nērit·os *or* **Nērit·us -ī** *f* island near Ithaca

Ner·ō -ōnis *m* Nero Claudius Caesar *(A.D. 38–68; reigned A.D. 54–68)*

Nerōniān·us -a -um *adj* Nero's, Neronian

Nerv·a -ae *m* Marcus Cocceius Nerva *(A.D. 30–98; reigned A.D. 96–98)*

nervōsē *adv* strongly, vigorously

nervōs·us -a -um *adj* sinewy, brawny, muscular

nerv·us *or* **nerv·os -ī** *m* sinew, tendon, muscle; string, wire; bowstring; thong; strap; leather covering of a shield; *(vulg)* penis; prison ‖ *mpl* power, vigor, strength, nerve, force, energy; **nervi belli pecunia** money, the sinews of war; **nervi conjurationis** the force *(i.e., the leaders)* behind the conspiracy

nesc·iō -īre -īvī *or* **-iī -ītus** *tr* not to know, be ignorant of, be unacquainted with; *(w. inf)* not to know how to, be unable to; **nescio modo** somehow or other; **nescio quando** sometime or other; **nescio quid** something or other; **nescio quis** someone or other

nesci·us -a -um *adj* unaware, ignorant; unknown; *(w. gen or* **de** *+ abl)* ignorant of, unaware of; *(w. inf)* not knowing how to, unable to, incapable of; *(w. acc & inf)* unaware that, not knowing that

Ness·us -ī *m* centaur who was slain by Hercules with a poisoned arrow for trying to molest his wife

Nest·or -oris *m* son of Neleus, king of Pylos, and wise counselor of the Greeks at Troy

Nestorid·ēs -ae *m* son of Nestor *(i.e., Antilochus)*

neu *see* **neve**

neu·ter -tra -trum *adj* neither *(of two);* neuter; of neither sex ‖ *pron* neither one *(of two)*

neutiquam *or* **ne utiquam** *adv* on no account, in no way

neutrāl·is -is -e *adj (gram)* neuter

neutrō *adv* to neither side, in neither direction

neutrubi *adv* in neither the one place nor the other

nēve *or* **neu** *conj* or not, and not; **neve…neve** *(or* **neu…neu)** neither…nor

nex necis *f* death; violent death, murder, slaughter; **necem (sibi) consciscere** to decide to commit suicide *(literally, to decide on death for oneself);* **neci** *(or* **ad necem) dare** *(or* **mittere)** to put to death

nexil·is -is -e *adj* plaited, intertwined

nex·um -ī *n* slavery for debt; voluntary servitude for debt

nex·us -a -um *pp of* **necto** ‖ *m* bondman *(person who has pledged his person as security for a debt)*

nex·us -ūs *m* bond; tie *(of kinship, etc.);* legal obligation; grip *(in wrestling);* embrace; combination ‖ *mpl* coils *(of snake);* knotty problem

nī *adv* not; **quid ni?** why not? ‖ *conj (in prohibition or negative purpose)* that not; *(in negative condition)* if not, unless

nīcētēr·ium -(i)ī *n* prize

nict·ō -āre -āvī -ātum *or* **nict·or -ārī -ātus sum** *intr* to blink; to wink; *(w. dat)* to wink at

nīdāment·um -ī *n* material for a nest

nīd·or -ōris *m* steam, vapor, smell

nīdul·us -ī *m* small nest

nīd·us -ī *m* nest; nestlings, brood; pigeonhole *(fig)* home ‖ *mpl* nestlings, brood

ni·ger -gra -grum *adj* black; dark; swarthy; dismal; unlucky, ill-omened; bad *(character);* malicious

nigr·ans -antis *adj* black, dusky

nigr·escō -escĕre -uī *intr* to grow black, grow dark

nigr·ō -āre -āvī -ātus *tr* to blacken ‖ *intr* to be black

nigr·or -ōris *m* blackness, darkness

nihil *or* **nīl** *indecl n* nothing; *(w. partitive gen)* no, not a bit of *(e.g.,* **nihil cibi** no food); **nihil agere** to do nothing, sit still; **nihil aliud** nothing else; **nihil boni** no good, not a bit of good; **nil est** *(in replies)* it is pointless, it's no good; **nihil dum** nothing so far; **nihil est mihi cum** I have nothing to do with; **nihil est** it doesn't matter; **nihil est quod** *(or* **cur** *or* **quamobrem)** there is no reason why; **nihil est ubi** *(or* **quo)** there is no place where *(or* to which); **nihil quicquam** nothing whatever; **non nihil** a considerable amount, quite a lot; to a considerable extent

nihilōminus *adv* nevertheless, just the same; no less

nihil·um *or* **nīl·um -ī** *n* nothing; **ad nihilum**

venire to come to nothing; **de nihilo** for nothing, for no reason; **nihili facere** *(or* **pendere)** to consider as worthless; **nihil** *(w. comparatives or words expressing difference, e.g.:* **nihil carius** nothing dearer); **nihilo minus** nonetheless, nevertheless; **pro nihilo putare** *(or* **ducere** *or* **habere)** to regard as worthless, disregard

nīl *see* **nihil**

Nīliac·us -a -um *adj* Nile, of the Nile; Egyptian

nīlum *see* **nihilum**

Nīl·us -ī *m* Nile; god of the Nile; a type of conduit

nimbāt·us -a -um *adj* light, frivolous

nimbif·er -era -erum *adj* stormy

nimbōs·us -a -um stormy, rainy

nimb·us -ī *m* rain cloud, storm cloud; cloud; rainstorm, heavy shower; shower, spray; *(fig)* storm; *(fig)* dense crowd

nimiō *adv* far, much; **nimio plus** far more, much more

nīmīrum *adv* no doubt, certainly sure; *(ironically)* of course

nimis *adv* very, very much, too much; **non nimis** not particularly

nimium *adv* too, too much; very much; **nimium quam** *(or* **nimium quantum)** very much indeed, ever so much, very; **nimium quam es barbarus** you are as uncouth as can be; **non nimium** not particularly, not very much

nimi·us -a -um *adj* very much; very great; too great, extraordinary, excessive; extravagant, intemperate; over-eager; overconfident; *(w. gen or abl of respect)* intemperate in, going overboard about; *(w. dat)* too much for, too strong for; **nimio opere** to excess ‖ *n* excess

ning(u)it ningĕre ninguit *or* **ninxit** *v impers* it is snowing

ningu·ēs -ium *fpl* snow flakes; snow; snowdrifts

Nin·os *or* **Nin·us -ī** *m* king of Assyria, legendary founder of Nineveh; Nineveh

Niob·a -ae *or* **Niob·ē -ēs** *f* Niobe *(daughter of Tantalus and wife of Amphion; she was turned into a weeping mountain)*

Nīr·eūs -eī *or* **-eos** *m* second-handsomest Greek at Troy *(after Achilles)*

Nīsē·is -idis *f* daughter of Nisus, Scylla

nisi *conj* unless, if not; except; **nisi si** unless, if not; **nisi quia** *(or* **quod)** except that

nīsus *pp of* **nitor**

nīs·us *or* **nix·us -ūs** *m* pressure, effort; labor pains; soaring, flight; posture; **nisu immotus eodem** immobile in the same posture

Nīs·us -ī *m* king of Megara and father of Scylla ‖ friend of Euryalus *(in the Aeneid)*

nītēdul·a -ae *f* dormouse *(squirrel-like rodent)*

nit·ens -entis *adj* shining, bright, sparkling; brilliant; beautiful, glamorous; sleek *(cattle);* prosperous, thriving; illustrious, outstanding

nit·eō -ēre -uī *intr* to shine, gleam, glisten; to be glamorous; to glow with health; *(of animals)* to be sleek; *(of style)* to be brilliant; *(of fields, plants)* to be luxuriant

nit·escō -escĕre -uī *intr* to become shiny, become bright; to begin to glow *(with health or beauty);* to grow sleek; *(of plants)* to begin to thrive

nitidē *adv* brightly

nitidiusculē *adv* somewhat more sprucely

nitidiuscul·us -a -um *adj* a little more shiny

nitid·us -a -um *adj* shining, bright; glowing, radiant, handsome *(with health or beauty);* spruce, well-groomed; glossy, lustrous *(hair);* sleek *(animals);* luxuriant, lush *(plants, fields);* cultivated, refined; elegant *(style)*

nit·or -ōris *m* brightness, sheen; luster; glamour, beauty, healthy glow; elegance *(of style);* dignity *(of character)*

nītor nītī nixus sum *(usually in the literal sense) or* **nīsus sum** *(usually in the figurative sense) intr* to make an effort, struggle, strain, strive; to be in labor; to push forward, advance, climb, fly; to contend, insist; *(w. abl or* **in** *+ acc)* to lean on, support oneself on; *(w. abl or* **in** *+ abl)* to depend on, rely on, trust to; *(w.* **ad)** to aspire to; *(w. inf)* to try to, endeavor to, struggle to

nitr·um -ī *n* soda, potash; cleanser

nivāl·is -is -e *adj* snowy; covered with snow; cold, wintry; *(fig)* cold, chilly

nive·us -a -um *adj* snowy, covered with snow; snow-white; cooled with snow

nivōs·us -a -um *adj* snowy

nix nivis *f* snow ‖ *fpl (fig)* gray hair

nix·or -ārī -ātus sum *intr* to struggle hard; *(w. abl)* to lean on, rest on

nixus *pp of* **nitor**

nix·us -ūs *see* **nisus**

nō nāre nāvī *intr* to swim, float; to sail; to fly; *(of eyes)* to be glazed

nōbil·is -is -e *adj* known, familiar; noted; notable, remarkable, noteworthy; famous; notorious; noble; thoroughbred; fine, excellent; *(w. abl of cause)* famous for, noted for; **nobile est** *(w. acc & inf)* it is well-known that ‖ *m* notable, nobleman, aristocrat

nōbilit·ās -ātis *f* fame, renown; noble birth; nobility; the nobility, the nobles; excellence

nōbiliter *adv* with distinction

nōbilit·ō -āre -āvī -ātus *tr* to make generally

known, call attention to; to make famous; to make notorious
noc·ens -entis *adj* harmful; *(w. abl)* guilty of ‖ *m* guilty person, criminal
noc·eō -ēre -uī -itum *intr (w. dat)* to harm, injure; **haud ignarus nocendi** well aware of the mischief
nocīv·us -a -um *adj* harmful, injurious
noctif·er -erī *m* evening star *(night-bringer)*
noctilūc·a -ae *f* moon *(she who shines by night)*
noctivag·us -a -um *adj (esp. of heavenly bodies)* wandering at night
noctū *adv* by night, at night
noctu·a -ae *f* owl *(night bird)*
noctuābund·us -a -um *adj* traveling by night
noctuīn·us -a -um *adj* of owls
nocturn·us -a -um *adj* nocturnal, of night, at night, by night, night-
noctuvigil·us -a -um *adj* awake at night
nocu·us -a -um *adj* harmful
nōd·ō -āre -āvī -ātus *tr* to tie in a knot, knot
nōdōs·us -a -um *adj* knotty
nōd·us -ī *m* knot; knot *(in wood)*; node *(in stem of grass or plant)*; bond, tie; obligation; knotty point, problem, difficulty; coil *(of serpent)*; check, restraint; **igneus nodus** fireball
Nōl·a -ae *f* town of Campania E. of Naples *(where Augustus died)*
nōlō nolle nōluī *tr (w. inf)* to be unwilling to, wish not to, refuse to ‖ *intr* to be unwilling; *(2nd person imperative w. inf to form negative command)* do not...: **noli** *(pl:* **nolite) tangere** do not touch!
Nom·as -adis *or* **-ados** *mf* nomad; Numidian
nōm·en -inis *n* name; clan *(or* middle) name *(e.g., Julius, as distinct from the praenomen, or first name, e.g., Gaius, and the cognomen, or family name, e.g., Caesar)*; good name, reputation; title; stock, race; bond, claim, debt; debtor; pretext, pretense, excuse; authority; sake, behalf; reason, cause; responsibility; heading, category; entry *(of a loan, etc., in a ledger)*; *(gram)* noun; **aetatis nomine** on the pretext of age; on account of age; **eo nomine** on that account; **nomen alicujus accipere** *(or* **recipere)** *(of a presiding judge)* to consent to hear the case against s.o.; **nomen dare** *(or* **edere** *or* **profiteri)** to enlist *(in the army; as a colonist)*; **nomen deferre** *(w. gen)* to bring an accusation against, accuse *(s.o.)*; **nomen dissolvere** *(or* **nomen expedire** *or* **nomen solvere)** *(com)* to liquidate an account, pay off a debt; **nomen Latinum** those with Latin rights; **nomen Romanum** the Roman people; **nomina facere** *(com)* to enter a business transaction in a ledger; **nomina magna** big shots, celebrities; **nomina sua exigere** to collect one's debt; **nomine** *(w. gen)* by the authority of, in the name of; on the pretext of; in the guise of; **non re sed nomine** not in reality but in name only; **oppidum nomine Nola** a town named Nola; **per nomen** *(w. gen)* on the pretext of; in the guise of; **sub nomine** *(w. gen)* by the authority of, in the name of; **suo nomine** on one's own responsibility, independently; **uno nomine** in a word
nōmenclāt·or -ōris *m* name-caller *(slave who accompanied his master and discreetly identified those whom they met, esp. during a political campaign)*
Nōment·um -ī *n* town in Latium on the Sabine border
nōminātim *adv* by name, expressly
nōminātī·ō -ōnis *f* nomination for office; name, term
nōminātīv·us -a -um *adj & m (gram)* nominative
nōminit·ō -āre -āvī -ātus *tr* to name, call, term
nōmin·ō -āre -āvī -ātus *tr* to name, call by name; to mention by name; to make famous; to nominate for office; to denounce, arraign
nomism·a -atis *n* coin; coinage; voucher, token
nōn *adv* not; no; by no means
Non. *abbr* **Nonae**
Nōn·ae -ārum *fpl* Nones *(the ninth day before the Ides, and so the fifth day in all months, except March, May, July, and October, in which the Nones occurred on the seventh)*
nōnāgensim·us -a -um *adj* **(-gēs-)** ninetieth
nōnāgiens *adv* **(-giēs)** ninety times
nōnāgintā *indecl adj* ninety
nōnān·us -a -um *adj* of the ninth legion ‖ *m* soldier of the ninth legion
nōnāri·a -ae *f* prostitute
nōndum *adv* not yet
nōngent·ī -ae -a *adj* nine hundred
nōnne *adv (interrog particle in questions expecting a positive answer)* is it not?; *(in indirect questions)* whether not; **nonne vides?** you see, don't you?, don't you see?; **quaeritur nonne ire statim velis** the question is whether you do not wish to go at once
nōnnull·us -a -um *adj* some, a certain amount of; many a ‖ *pl* some, not a few
nōnnumquam *adv* **(-nunq-)** sometimes
nōnnusquam *adv* in some places
nōn·us -a -um *adj* ninth ‖ *f* ninth hour
nōn·us decim·us -a -um *adj* nineteenth
Nōric·us -a -um *adj* of Noricum ‖ *n*

Noricum *(Roman province between the Danube and the Alps)*

norm·a -ae *f (carpenter's)* square; *(fig)* standard, norm of behavior

nōs *pron* we; us

noscit·ō -āre -āvī -ātus *tr* to examine closely, observe; to know, recognize

noscō noscĕre nōvī nōtus *tr* **(gn-)** to get to know, become acquainted with, learn; to recognize; to examine, inquire into; to approve of; **novisse** to have become acquainted with, *(and therefore)* to know

nōsmet *pron (emphatic form of* **nōs**) we ourselves; us ourselves

nos·ter -tra -trum *adj* our, our own ‖ *pron* ours; **noster** our friend; **nostri** our men, our soldiers, our side, our friends

nostrās -ātis *adj* born *or* produced in our country, native, of our country, indigenous

not·a -ae *f* note; mark; sign; letter, character; punctuation mark; brand *(of wine);* marginal note, critical mark; tattoo marks, brand; distinctive mark, distinctive quality; stamp *(on coin);* stigma; nickname; black mark *(against one's name);* reproach, disgrace; nod, sign, beck; sign of the zodiac; **in notam alicujus** so as to humiliate s.o.; **per notas scribere** to write in code ‖ *fpl* letters of the alphabet; shorthand notes; memoranda

notābil·is -is -e *adj* notable, noteworthy, memorable; conspicuous

notābiliter *adv* notably, remarkably; perceptibly

notār·ius -(i)ī *m* stenographer; secretary

notāti·ō -ōnis *f* notation, mark; black mark *(of censor);* choice; observation; etymology

notāt·us -a -um *adj* noted, distinguished

nōt·escō -escĕre -uī *intr* to become known

noth·us -a -um *adj* bastard, illegitimate; mongrel, crossbreed; spurious; *(of the moon's light)* reflected

nōti·ō -ōnis *f* acquaintance; *(fig)* notion, idea; *(leg)* investigation

nōtiti·a -ae *or* **nōtiti·ēs -ēī** *f* acquaintance, knowledge; awareness; fame; notion, conception; familiarity *(w. things);* **notitia ei cum Perseo est** he is familiar with Perseus; **notitiam feminae habere** to have sex with a woman

nōt·ō -āre -āvī -ātus *tr* to mark; to mark out; to note, observe; to write down; to record; to take down in shorthand; to mark critically; to brand; to indicate, denote; to reproach; to indicate by a sign; *(of things)* to be a sign of; to mention *(in a speech or writing)*

nōt·or -ōris *m* guarantor

nōt·us -a -um *pp of* **nosco** ‖ *adj* known, well-known; notorious; familiar, customary; **notum est** *(w. acc + inf)* it is common knowledge that; **notum facere** *(w. acc & inf)* to make it known that; **notum habere** *(w. acc & inf)* to be informed that ‖ *m* an acquaintance; one who knows

novācul·a -ae *f* razor

novāl·is -is *f or* **novāl·e -is** *n* field plowed for the first time, reclaimed land; cultivated field; fallow land; crops

novātr·ix -īcis *f* innovator *(female)*

novē *adv* newly, in an unusual manner

novell·us -a -um *adj* new, fresh, young; newly acquired

novem *indecl adj* nine

Novem·ber *or* **Novem·bris -bris -bre** *adj* November; **mensis November** *(9th month of the Roman calendar until 153 B.C.)* ‖ **Novem·ber -bris** *m* November

novemdecim *indecl adj* **(noven-)** nineteen

novendiāl·is -is -e *adj* **(novem-)** nine-day; occurring on the ninth day; **cineres novendiales** *(fig)* ashes not yet cold ‖ *n* nine-day festival *(to mark the appearance of an omen);* funeral feast *(held nine days after death)*

novēn·ī -ae -a *adj* in groups of nine, nine each, nine

novensil·ēs -ium *mpl* new gods *(introduced from abroad)*

noverc·a -ae *f* stepmother

novercāl·is -is -e *adj* stepmother's, of a stepmother; like a stepmother

novīci·us -a -um *adj* new, brand new; recently imported *(slaves);* recently discovered *(things); (pej)* new-fangled

noviens *or* **noviēs** *adv* nine times

novissimē *adv* of late, very recently

novissim·us -a -um *adj* latest, last, final; most recent; most extreme, utmost; **novissimum agmen** *(mil)* the rear; **novissima verba** parting words ‖ *mpl (mil)* rear guard ‖ *npl* the worst

novit·ās -ātis *f* newness, novelty; innovation; rareness, strangeness, unusualness; unexpectedness; recently acquired rank *(condition of being a* **novus homo**); **novitas rerum** revolution

nov·ō -āre -āvī -ātus *tr* to make new, renew, renovate; to repair; to refresh; to change; to coin *(words);* **res renovare** to bring about a revolution

nov·us -a -um *adj* new; young; fresh; novel; unexpected; strange, unusual, unheard-of; recent, modern; unused; inexperienced; renewed, revived, as good as new; newly recuited *(soldiers);* inexperienced; subversive *(plans, activities);* fallow *(field);* newly arrived *(in a place);* **novae tabernae** new shops *(on N. side of the Forum);* **novus homo** self-made man *(first man of a family to reach a curule office);* **res nova** a new development; **res novae** revolution

nox noctis *f* night; night activity; sleep; death; darkness, blindness; mental darkness, ignorance; gloom; **ad multam noctem** till late at night; **nocte** *(or* **de nocte)** at night, by night; **noctem et diem** night and day; **sub noctem** at nightfall ‖ *fpl* **noctes et dies** night and day, continually

nox·a -ae *f* harm, injury; offense; fault, guilt, responsibility; **in noxā esse** to be guilty of wrongdoing; **noxae** *(or* **ad** *or* **in** + *acc)* **dedere** to hand *(s.o.)* over for punishment; **noxā** *(or* **noxis) solutus** *(of a slave in a formula of sale)* guilty of no prior injurious conduct

noxi·us -a -um *adj* harmful, noxious; guilty; *(w. gen)* guilty of ‖ *f* harm, damage, injury; blame, guilt; fault; offense; **in noxiā esse** to be at fault

nūbēcul·a -ae *f* little cloud; gloomy expression

nūb·ēs -is *f or* **nūb·is -is** *m* cloud; gloom; veil

nūbif·er -era -erum *adj* cloudy; cloud-capped; cloud-bringing *(wind)*

nūbigen·a -ae *adj (masc only) (of the Centaurs, whom Ixion fathered on a cloud-image of Hera; of Phrixus, son of the cloud-goddess Nephele)* born of clouds

nūbil·is -is -e *adj* marriageable

nūbil·us -a -um *adj* cloudy; cloud-bringing *(wind);* troubled; gloomy, melancholy

nūbō nūbere nupsī -nuptum *intr* (of a woman) to marry; *(w. dat)* to marry *(a man);* to be married to *(a man)* ‖ *refl* to get married

Nūceri·a -ae *f* town in Campania

Nūcerīn·us -a - um *adj* of Nuceria

nucifrangibul·um -ī *n (coll)* nut-cracker *(i.e., teeth)*

nucle·us -ī *m* nut; kernel, stone *(of fruit)*

nudius *adv* it is now the…day since, *e.g.,* **nudius tertius** it is now the third day since *(by Roman reckoning, the day before yesterday);* **nudius dies dedi ad te epistolam** it is now the third day since I mailed you a letter; ago, *e.g.,* **nudius tertius decimus** thirteen days ago *(twelve days ago by our reckoning, since the Romans counted both the first and last day)*

nūd·ō -āre -āvī -ātus *tr* to strip, bare; to lay bare, uncover; to explain; to strip *(a person of office or rank);* to empty *(a building)* of all its occupants; *(mil)* to leave undefended; *(w. abl)* to divest of; **terga nudare** to expose their backs *(to attack)*

nūd·us -a -um *adj* nude, naked; lightly clothed; bare, empty; defenseless; poor, needy; mere, simple, sole, only; *(w. gen or abl or w.* **ab)** bare of, without, stripped of, deprived of

nūg·ae -ārum *fpl* nonsense, baloney; trivia; trash, junk; good-for-nothing, a nobody; **nugae** *(or* **nugas)!** nonsense!; baloney!; **nugae sunt** it's no use; **nugas agere** to waste one's effort

nūgāt·or -ōris *m* joker; fibber; babbler; braggart

nūgātōri·us -a -um *adj* worthless, useless, nonsensical; frivolous

nūg·ax -ācis *adj* nonsensical; frivolous

nūgigerul·us -ī *m* dealer in women's apparel

nūg·or -ārī -ātus sum *intr* to talk nonsense; *(w. dat)* to tell tall stories to

null·us -a -um *adj* no; *(coll)* not, not at all; non-existent; of no account ‖ *pron* none

num *adv (of time, used only w.* **etiam)** now, *e.g.,* **etiam num** now, even, now, still ‖ *adv (interrog particle expecting negative answer)* surely not, really, actually, *e.g.,* **num ista est nostra culpa?** is that really our fault?; that isn't our fault, is it? ‖ *conj (in indirect questions)* whether

Num. *abbr* **Numerius** *(Roman first name, praenomen)*

Num·a -ae *m* Numa Pompilius *(second king of Rome)*

numell·a -ae *f* shackle, restrainer

nūm·en -inis *n* nod; will, consent; divine will; divine power; divine majesty; divinity, deity, godhead

numerābil·is -is -e *adj* easily counted, few in number

numerāt·um -ī *n* cold cash

numerāt·us -a -um *adj* counted out, paid down; in cold cash

numerō *adv* at the right time, just now; too soon

numer·ō -āre -āvī -ātus *tr* to number, count; to pay out, pay down *(money);* to consider; to enumerate, mention; to relate, recount; to reckon as one's own, possess, own; *(w.* **in** + *abl or* **inter** + *acc)* to count among, include in *(a category);* *(w.* **in** + *acc)* to allocate to; *(w. pred. adj)* to treat as, class as; **Senatum numerare** to count the Senate *(to see whether a quorum is present)*

numerōsē *adv* rhythmically

numerōs·us -a -um *adj* numerous; rhythmical

numer·us -ī *m* number; mere cipher; class, category; rank, position; estimation, regard; portion *(of work),* part, function; *(often w.* **suus)** the proper number, the full number, full complement; *(gram)* number; *(mil)* division, troop; *(mus, rhet)* rhythm, meter, verse; *(mus)* tune; *(pros)* quantity, measure; **ad numerum** *(or* **in numerum)** *(mus, pros, rhet)* rhythmically, in time; **aliquo (nullo) numero esse** to be of some (no) account; **extra numerum** *(mus)* off beat, out of time; **in numero esse** to be included in a group; **in numero habere** *(w. gen)* to be regarded as, be ranked among; **nullo numero esse** to be of no account; **numero** at the right time, just now; too soon, too early; **numero huc advenis ad prandium** you are arriving here too early for lunch; **suum numerum navium habere** to have one's full complement of ships; **super** *(or* **supra) numerum** not attached to the regular staff ‖ *mpl* mathematics; astronomy; notes of the scale; melody; **ad numeros** *(mus, pros)* rhythmically, in time; **in numeris esse** to be on active duty; **omnibus numeris perfectus** perfect in every detail

Numid·a -ae *m* Numidian

Numidi·a -ae *f* Numidia *(country of N. Africa; Roman province, extending W. and S. of Carthage)*

Numidic·us -a -um *adj* Numidian

Numit·or -ōris *m* king of Alba, brother of Amulius, father of Ilia *(or* Rhea Silvia), and grandfather of Romulus and Remus

nummāri·us -a -um *adj* financial; *(pej)* mercenary, venal

nummāt·us -a -um *adj* rich; **bene nummatus** well-to-do, well-off

nummulār·ius -(i)ī *m* money changer

nummul·ī -ōrum *mpl* petty cash

numm·us -ī *m* coin; cash, money; sesterce *(small silver coin, worth about a dime);* small sum, trifle; **in nummis habere** to have in cash

numquam *adv* **(nun-)** never; **non numquam** sometimes

numquid *adv (to introduce direct question):* **numquid meministi?** do you remember?; *(to introduce an indirect question)* whether

nunc *adv* now; nowadays, today; now, in view of this, but as matters now stand; **nunc ipsum** at this very moment; **nunc...nunc** at one time...at another, once...once

nuncupāti·ō -ōnis *f* name, title; public pronouncing *(of vows);* nomination *(to some position)*

nuncup·ō -āre -āvī -ātus *tr* to name, call; to take *(a vow)* publicly; to appoint *(as heir);* to utter the name of, invoke; to address *(a person)*

nundin·ae -ārum *fpl* market day *(occurring regularly at intervals of eight days, i.e., every ninth day by Roman reckoning);* marketplace; market town; mart

nundināl·is -is -e *adj* market-

nundināti·ō -ōnis *f* marketing, trading

nundin·or -ārī -ātus sum *tr* to traffic in; to buy ‖ *intr* to hold a market, attend a market; to trade; to gather in crowds

nundin·um -ī *n* market time; **inter nundinum** the time between two market periods; **trinum nundinum** a sequence of three market periods *(i.e., 24 days)*

nunq- = numq-

nunti·a -ae *f* messenger *(female)*

nuntiāti·ō -ōnis *f* announcement *(by an augur)*

nunti·ō -āre -āvī -ātus *tr* to bring word of; to announce, declare; to report *(omens);* to give warning of *(some future event);* **gaudium nuntiare** to bring good news; **salutem nuntiare** to send greetings

nunti·us -a -um *adj* bringing news, announcing ‖ *m* messenger, courier; message, news; order, injunction; **nuntium remittere** *(w. dat)* to send a letter of divorce to, to divorce *(a wife)* ‖ *n* message, communication

nūper *adv* recently, lately; in modern times

nūper·us -a -um *adj* recent

nupt·a -ae *f* bride, wife

nupti·ae -ārum *fpl* marriage, wedding

nuptiāl·is -is -e *adj* nuptial, wedding

nur·us -ūs *f* daughter-in-law; young lady, young married woman

nusquam *adv* nowhere; on no occasion; for nothing, to nothing; **nusquam alibi** nowhere else; **nusquam esse** not to exist; **nusquam gentium** nowhere in the world; **plebs nusquam alio nata, quam ad serviendum** the plebs, born for nothing else than to serve

nūt·ō -āre -āvī -ātus *intr* to keep nodding; to sway to and fro, totter; to waver

nūtrīcāt·us -ūs *m* breast-feeding

nūtrīc·ius -(i)ī *m (child's)* guardian

nūtrīc·ō -āre -āvī -ātus *or* **nūtrīc·or -ārī -ātus sum** *tr* to breast-feed, nurse; to nourish, promote the growth of *(plants, animals);* to rear, bring up, support; to take care of, attend to; to cherish, cultivate

nūtrīcul·a -ae *f* nanny; wet-nurse; *(of persons or things)* fosterer

nūtrīm·en -inis *n* nourishment

nūtrīment·um -ī *n* nourishment ‖ *npl* upbringing *(of a child)*

nūtr·iō -īre -īvī *or* **-iī -ītus** *or* **nūtrior nūtrīrī nūtrītus sum** *tr* to breast-feed, suckle; to support with food, nourish; to feed *(animals, plants, fire);* to build up *(resources);* to take care of, attend to *(the skin, hair);* to bring up *(a child);* to raise *(animals, crops);* to give rise to, foster, promote *(a condition, feeling);* to treat *(a wound, sick person);* to look after *(material things);* to deal gently with *(faults, people at fault)*

nūtrīt·or -ōris *m* one who feeds

nūtr·ix -īcis *f* nurse ‖ *fpl* breasts

nūt·us -ūs *m* nod; hint, intimation; nod of assent; will, pleasure; command; gravitation, gravitational pull; **nutus et renutus** nod of assent and nod of dissent

nux nucis *f* nut; nut tree; almond tree; **nuces relinquere** *(fig)* to put away childish things; **nux abellana** *(or* **avellana)** hazelnut; **nux castanea** chestnut; **nux Graeca** (sweet) almond; **nux juglans** walnut; **nux pinea** pine cone

Nyctē·is -idis *f* Antiope *(daughter of Nycteus, wife of Lycus (king of Thebes) and mother of Amphion and Zethus)*

Nyct·eūs -eī *or* **-eos** *m* father of Antiope

nymph·a -ae *or* **nymph·ē -ēs** *f* bride; nymph; *(fig)* water

Nȳs·a -ae *f* legendary mountain on which Bacchus was alleged to have been born *(usually located in India)*

Nȳsae·us *or* **Nȳsi·us -a -um** *adj* of Nysa, Nysaean

Nȳs·eūs -eī *or* **-eos** *m* Bacchus

Nȳsigen·a -ae *m* native of Nysa

O

ō *interj* oh!

Ōari·on -ōnis *m* Orion

Ōax·ēs *or* **Ōax·is -is** *m* river in Crete *(or perhaps on the E. frontier of the Empire)*

ob *prep (w. acc)* **1** before, in front of: **ob oculos** *(or* **ob os)** before one's eyes, right in front of s.o., under s.o.'s very nose; **2** on account of, because of, for: **quam ob rem** for which reason, accordingly, wherefore; **quas ob causas** for what reasons, why; **3** for the sake of, in the interest of: **ob rem publicam** for the sake of the country; **4** as a reward *or* punishment for, in return for: **ob mendacium tuum** in punishment for your lie; **5** *(in connection with bribes)* in payment for: **ob tua edicta pecuniae dabantur** you were given money *(i.e., bribes)* in payment for your edicts; **6** in connection with: **ob rem** to the purpose, usefully, profitably; **ob suam partem** on one's own account

ob- *pref (also* **oc-, of-, og-, op-**; the **b** is lost in **omitto** and **operio)** conveying the sense of: **1** movement towards a meeting: **obeo** to go to meet; **2** covering a surface: **oblimo** to cover with mud; **obduco** to cover the surface of; **3** protecting: **obduco** to draw *or* place as a protection *or* obstacle; **4** of overwhelming: **opprimo** to oppress; **5** counterbalancing: **oppono** to set off against by way of balance; **6** confrontation: **obsto** *(w. dat)* to stand in the way, obstruct; **7** surprise or the unexpected: **obvenio** *(w. dat)* to fall to the lot of; **8** pleasant effect: **oblecto** to delight, entertain; **9** hostility: **obtrecto** to mistreat, disparage; **10** assault: **occido** to kill

obaerāt·us -a -um *adj* deeply in debt ‖ *m* debtor

obambul·ō -āre -āvī -ātus *tr* to prowl all over, prowl about *(e.g., the city)* ‖ *intr* to walk about; to wander; to prowl about; *(w. dat)* to prowl about near; *(w.* **ante** + *acc)* to wander around in front of

obarm·ō -āre -āvī -ātus *tr* to arm

obar·ō -āre -āvī -ātus *tr* to plow up, plow over

obb·a -ae *f* decanter, beaker

obbrūt·escō -escĕre -uī *intr* to grow dull

obc- = occ-

ob·dō -dĕre -didī -ditus *tr* to set before; to fasten *(a bolt);* to close, lock *(a door);* to expose

obdorm·iō -īre -īvī *or* **-iī -ītum** *intr* to fall asleep

obdorm·iscō -iscĕre *intr* to fall fast asleep

ob·dūcō -dūcĕre -duxī -ductus *tr (w.* **ad)** to lead *(troops)* toward *or* against; to extend in front as a barrier *or* protection; to fasten *(bolt);* to obstruct, block; to screen, protect; to cover the surface of; to draw over as a covering; to veil, envelop; to swallow; to put on *(clothes);* to bring forward as an opposing candidate; to pass *(time);* to dig *(ditch); (w. dat of thing protected)* to draw *or* place *(s.th.)* over; *(w. dat or* **ad)** to pit *(s.o. or s.th.)* against; **tenebras obducere** *(w. dat)* to cast darkness over

obducti·ō -ōnis *f* veiling, covering

obduct·ō -āre *tr* to introduce as a rival

obduct·us -a -um *pp of* **obduco** ‖ *adj* cloudy; gloomy; **obductus cicatrix** a closed scar

obdūr·escō -escĕre -uī *intr* to grow hard, harden; to become insensitive; **Gorgonis vultu obdurescere** to become petrified *(literally, to grow hard at the sight of the Gorgon)*

obdūr·ō -āre -āvī -ātum *intr* to stick it out

ob·eō -īre -īvī *or* **-iī -itus** *tr* to go to meet; to travel, travel to, travel across; to wander through, traverse, encircle; to visit; to run over, review, enumerate *(in a speech);* to undertake, engage in; **diem edicti** *(or* **diem** *or* **diem suum** *or* **diem extremum** *or* **mortem)** **obire** to meet one's death ‖ *intr* to go; to pass away, die; to fade, disappear; *(of heavenly bodies)* to set

obequit·ō -āre -āvī -ātum *intr* to ride up *(on horseback); (w. dat)* to ride up to

oberr·ō -āre -āvī -ātum *intr* to ramble about, wander around; *(w. abl)* **1** to wander among; **2** to make a mistake on *or* at

obēs·us -a -um *adj* obese; swollen; crude, coarse
ōb·ex -icis *mf* bar, bolt; barrier
obf- = off-
obg- = ogg-
obhae·rescō -rescĕre -sī *intr* to get stuck
obīr·ascor -ascī -ātus sum *intr (w. dat)* to get angry with
obiter *adv* on the way, as one goes along; *(fig)* in passing, incidentally
obitus *pp of* **obeo**
obit·us -ūs *m* approach, visit; death, passing; ruin, downfall; *(astr)* setting
objac·eō -ēre -uī *intr (w. dat)* to lie before, lie at
objectāti·ō -ōnis *f* reproach
object·ō -āre -āvī -ātus *tr* to oppose; to expose, endanger; to throw in the way; to cause *(delay)*; *(w. dat)* **1** to impute to, throw up *(faults)* to; **2** to bring a charge of *(e.g., madness)* against, fling *(charges, abuse)* at; *(w. dat & acc & inf)* to throw a hint to *(s.o.)* that
object·us -a -um *pp of* **objicio** ‖ *adj* lying in the way, lying in front; *(w. dat)* **1** opposite; **2** exposed to ‖ *npl* charges
object·us -ūs *m* interposition; obstacles, hindrance; protection; *(w. gen)* protection afforded by
ob·jiciō -jicĕre -jēcī -jectus *tr* to hold up as an example; to bring up, cite *(before an opponent as a ground for disapproval or condemnation)*, throw up in one's face; to set up as a defense, use as a barrier *or* defense; to bar, shut *(the gates to prevent entry by an enemy)*; to throw in, use, deploy *(troops)*; *(w. dat)* **1** to throw *or* set *(e.g., food, fodder)* before; **2** to expose *(people)* to *(the wild beasts)*; **3** *(coll)* to toss *or* hand out *(money)* to; **4** to put *(a bandage)* on *(a part of the body)*; **5** to turn *(a ship)* so as to face *(e.g., a hostile shore)*; to set up as a defense against; **6** to hold out *(false hopes, incentives, temptations)* to; **7** to throw up *(faults, weaknesses, etc.)* to, lay *(faults)* to one's charge; **hi exercitui Caesaris luxuriem objiciebant** they were charging Caesar's army with extravagance; **8** to subject *(s.o.)* to *(danger, misfortune)*; **9** to bring up, throw in *(troops)* against; **exceptionem objicere** to raise an objection; **interdum metus animo objicitur** at times fear crosses my mind; **portas objicere** to bar the gates; **religionem objicere** to raise the matter of religious scruples *(as a hindrance to some action)*; **signum objicere** to raise an omen as an objection *(to some action)* ‖ *refl (w. dat)* to expose oneself to; **turba oculis meis modo se objecit** a crowd just came into view ‖ *pass (w. dat)* to happen to, befall, occur to; *(geog) (w. dat)* to be located near *or* opposite (to)
objurgāti·ō -ōnis *f* scolding, rebuke
objurgāt·or -ōris *m* critic
objurgātōri·us -a -um *adj* reproachful
objurgit·ō -āre -āvī -ātus *tr* to keep on scolding
objurg·ō -āre -āvī -ātus *tr* to scold, rebuke, reprimand; to correct; to deter
oblangu·escō -escĕre -ī *intr* to taper off
oblātrātr·ix -īcis *f* nagging woman
oblātus *pp of* **offero**
oblectām·en -inis *n* delight
oblectāment·um -ī *n* delight, amusement, pastime
oblectāti·ō -ōnis *f* delight, amusement; attraction; *(w. gen)* diversion from
oblect·ō -āre -āvī -ātus *tr* to delight, amuse, entertain, attract; to spend *(time)* pleasantly ‖ *refl* to amuse oneself, enjoy oneself
oblēvī *perf of* **oblino**
ob·līdō -līdĕre -līsī -līsus *tr* to rush; to squeeze *(the throat)*, strangle
obligāti·ō -ōnis *f* binding, pledging; obligation
obligāt·us -a -um *adj* obliged, under obligation; *(w. dat)* owed by right to, due to
oblig·ō -āre -āvī -ātus *tr* to tie up, bandage; to bind, obligate, put under obligation, make liable; to hamper; to earmark; to embarrass; to mortgage *(property)*; *(w dat)* to pledge to, devote to; **fidem obligare** to pledge one's word, make a solemn promise; to guarantee one's loyalty ‖ *refl* to bind oneself, pledge oneself ‖ *pass* to be liable; *(w. abl)* **1** to be guilty of; **2** to be obliged to, compelled to
oblīm·ō -āre -āvī -ātus *tr* to cover with mud; to dissipate, squander
ob·linō -linĕre -lēvī *or* **līvī -itus** *tr* to smear, daub, coat; to seal up *(jar)*; *(fig)* to sully, sully the reputation of; *(fig)* to overload
oblīquē *adv* sideways; zigzag; *(fig)* indirectly
oblīqu·ō -āre -āvī -ātus *tr* to turn aside, twist, shift, slant; to avert *(eyes)*
oblīqu·us -a -um *adj* slanting, crosswise, sideways; zigzag; from the side; indirect *(language)*; sly; envious; downhill *(road)*; **obliquus oculus** disapproving look; envious look ‖ *n* side; **ab** *(or* **ex***)* **obliquo** from the side, at an angle, obliquely; **in obliquum** at an angle, sideways; **per obliquum** diagonally across
oblīsī *perf of* **oblido**
oblīsus *pp of* **oblido**
oblit·escō -escĕre -uī *intr* to hide, disappear
oblitter·ō -āre -āvī -ātus *tr* (**-līt-**) to erase; to cancel; *(fig)* to blot out; **nomina oblitterare** to cancel debts

oblituī *perf of* **oblitesco**
oblītus *pp of* **oblino**
oblītus *pp of* **obliviscor**
oblīvi·ō -ōnis *f* oblivion; forgetting; forgetfulness
oblīviōs·us -a -um *adj* forgetful, oblivious; *(wine)* causing forgetfulness
oblī·viscor -viscī -tus sum *tr* to forget ‖ *intr* to forget; *(w. gen)* to forget, neglect, disregard, be indifferent to
oblīv·ium -(i)ī *n* forgetfulness, oblivion
oblocūt·or -ōris *m* one who contradicts
oblong·us -a -um *adj* oblong
ob·loquor -loquī -locūtus sum *intr (w. dat)* 1 to interrupt; 2 to rail at; 3 to accompany *(musically)*
obluct·or -ārī -ātus sum *tr (w. dat)* to struggle with, fight against
oblūdi·ō -āre *intr* to make a fool of oneself
oblūd·ō -ĕre *tr* to play jokes on
obmōl·ior -īrī -ītus sum *tr* to make a barricade of; to block up *(a gap)*
obmurmur·ō -āre -āvī -ātum *intr (w. dat)* to roar in answer to
obmūt·escō -escĕre -uī *intr* to become silent, hush up; to cease
obnāt·us -a -um *adj (w. dat)* growing on *(e.g., a river bank)*
ob·nītor -nītī -nixus sum *intr* to strain, struggle, put on the pressure; *(w. dat)* 1 to press against, lean against; 2 to resist, oppose
obnixē *adv* with all one's might; obstinately
obnix·us -a -um *pp of* **obnitor** ‖ *adj* steadfast, firm, obstinate
obnoxiē *adv* guiltily; submissively
obnoxiōsius *adv* more slavishly
obnoxiōs·us -a -um *adj* submissive
obnoxi·us -a -um *adj* submissive, servile, obedient; weak, timid; *(w. dat)* 1 subservient to; 2 at the mercy of; 3 exposed to *(harm, danger, storms, etc.)*; 4 indebted to, under obligation to; 5 legally liable to, answerable to; **obnoxium est** *(w. inf)* it is dangerous to
ob·nūbō -nūbĕre -nupsī -nuptus *tr* to veil, cover *(the head)*
obnuntiāti·ō -ōnis *f* announcement *(of omens)*
obnunti·ō -āre -āvī -ātum *intr* to make an announcement; to make an announcement that the omens are adverse; to announce bad news
oboedi·ens -entis *adj* obedient; *(w. dat or* **ad**) obedient to; **dicto oboediens** obedient to the command
oboedienter *adv* obediently
oboedienti·a -ae *f* (-**bēd-**) obedience
oboed·iō -īre -īvī *or* **-iī -ītum** *intr (w. dat)* 1 to obey, listen to; 2 *(of things)* to respond to
obol·eō -ēre -uī *tr* to smell of ‖ *intr* to smell, stink
obor·ior -īrī -tus sum *intr* to rise. rise up, appear; *(fig) (of thoughts, sudden events)* occur, spring up
obp- = opp-
obrēp·ō -ĕre -sī -tus *tr* (**opr-**) to creep up on, sneak up on ‖ *intr* to creep up; *(w. dat)* 1 to creep up on, sneak up on, take by surprise; 2 to trick, cheat; *(w.* **in** + *acc)* to steal over; **obrepere ad honores** to worm one's way into high positions
obrept·ō -āre -āvī -ātum *intr* (**opr-**) to sneak up
obrēt·iō -īre -īvī *or* **-iī -ītus** *tr* to entangle
obrig·escō -escĕre -uī *intr* to stiffen; to freeze
obrōd·ō -ĕre *tr* to gnaw at
obrog·ō -āre -āvī -ātum *intr (w. dat)* to supersede
obru·ō -ĕre -ī -tus *tr* to cover up, cover, hide, bury; to overwhelm, overthrow; to sink, cover with water, swamp; to overflow; to overpower, surpass, obscure, eclipse ‖ *intr* to fall to ruin
obruss·a -ae *f* test, proof
obsaep·iō -īre -sī -tus *tr* (**-sēp-**) to fence in; to block *(road)*; *(fig)* to block
obsatur·ō -āre -āvī -ātus *tr* to cloy ‖ *pass (w. gen)* to have enough of
obscaen- = obscen-
obscaev·ō -āre -āvī -ātum *intr (w. dat)* to augur well for; to augur ill for
obscēnē *adv* (**-scaen-**) obscenely
obscēnit·ās -ātis *f* (**-scaen-**) obscenity
obscēn·us -a -um *adj* (**-scaen-**) obscene, indecent; dirty, filthy; ominous ‖ *m* sexual pervert; foul-mouthed person ‖ *npl* sexual *or* excretory parts *or* functions, private parts
obscūrāti·ō -ōnis *f* obscuring, darkening; disappearance
obscūrē *adv* indistinctly, dimly; in an underhand manner; cryptically; imperceptibly; **obscure ferre** to conceal, keep secret
obscūrit·ās -ātis *f* obscurity
obscūr·ō -āre -āvī -ātus *tr* (**ops-**) to obscure, darken; to cover, hide; to suppress; to veil *(words)*; *(of love)* to blind
obscūr·us -a -um *adj* (**ops-**) obscure; dark, shady; dim, indistinct, dimly seen, shadowy; barely visible; not openly expressed, unpublicized; obscure, unintelligible; secret; reserved; vague, uncertain; gloomy ‖ *n* the dark, darkness; obscurity; **in obsucro est** it is not clear, it is doubtful
obsecrāti·ō -ōnis *f* (**ops-**) entreaty; public supplication of the gods
obsecr·ō -āre -āvī -ātus *tr* (**ops-**) to entreat, appeal to, implore; **fidem obse-**

crare to beg for protection *or* support; **te obsecro** I beseech you, please
obsecund·ō -āre -āvī -ātum *intr* (**ops-**) (*w. dat*) to comply with, humor
obsecūtus *pp of* **obsequor**
obsēp- = **obsaep-**
obsequ·ens -entis *adj* (**ops-**) compliant, obedient; indulgent, gracious *(gods); (w. dat)* obedient to
obsequenter *adv* (**ops-**) compliantly
obsequenti·a -ae *f* (**ops-**) compliance, deference
obsequiōs·us -a -um *adj* (**ops-**) compliant, deferential
obsequ·ium -(i)ī *n* (**ops-**) compliance, indulgence; obedience, allegiance
ob·sequor -sequī -secūtus sum *intr* (**ops-**) (*w. dat*) **1** to comply with, yield to, give in to; **2** to gratify, humor
obser·ō -āre -āvī -ātus *tr* (**ops-**) to bolt, lock up
ob·serō -serĕre -sēvī -situs *tr* (**ops-**) to sow *or* plant thickly; to fill, cover
observābil·is -is -e *adj* perceptible; capable of being guarded against
observ·ans -antis *adj* attentive; *(w. gen)* **1** respectful of; **2** attentive to; **3** careful about
observanti·a -ae *f* regard, respect; *(w. gen or* **in** *+ acc)* regard for, respect for
observāti·ō -ōnis *f* (**ops-**) observation; caution, care; observance, usage, practice; remark, observation; safeguarding, protection
observāt·or -ōris *m* observer
observit·ō -āre -āvī -ātus *tr* to watch carefully, note carefully
observ·ō -āre -āvī -ātus *tr* to watch; to watch out for *(dangers, opportunities);* to watch for *(to ensnare);* to take careful note of; to guard; to observe, keep, obey, comply with; to pay attention to, pay respect to; to regard as important *or* authoritative; to keep to *(a date); (w. predicate)* to regard as, accept as; to adopt *(a course of action); (w.* **ut**) to follow *(such a course of action)* that
obs·es -idis *mf* (**opses**) hostage; guarantee, pledge; bail
obsessi·ō -ōnis *f* blockade
obsess·or -ōris *m* (**ops-**) frequenter, regular visitor; blockader
ob·sideō -sidēre -sēdī -sessus *tr* (**ops-**) to sit near *or* at, remain by *or* near; to frequent; to block, choke; to occupy, fill; to look out for, watch closely; to keep guard over; *(mil)* to besiege, blockade
obsidiāl·is -is -e *adj (mil)* for breaking a blockade
obsidi·ō -ōnis *f (mil)* blockade, siege
obsid·ium -(i)ī *n* (**ops-**) *(mil)* blockade, siege; status of hostage
ob·sīdō -sīdĕre -sēdī -sessus *tr* to take possession of, occupy *(so as to bar passage); (mil)* to besiege, blockade
obsignāt·or -ōris *m* sealer; witness; **obsignator testamenti** witness to a will
obsign·ō -āre -āvī -ātus *tr* (**ops-**) to seal, to sign and seal; *(fig)* to stamp
ob·sistō -sistĕre -stitī -stitum *intr* (**ops-**) (*w. dat*) **1** to stand in the way of, block; **2** to resist, oppose; **3** to disapprove of, forbid
obsitus (**ops-**) *pp of* **obsero** (to sow) ‖ *adj (w. abl)* overgrown with, covered with
obsole·faciō -facĕre -fēcī -factus *tr (pass:* **obsole·fīō -fierī -factus sum** *intr* to degrade, lower the dignity of
obsol·escō -escĕre -ēvī -ētum *intr* to go out of style, become obsolete; to fade away; to suffer degradation; *(of reputation)* to become tarnished; *(of persons)* to sink into obscurity
obsolētē *adv* shabbily
obsolēt·us -a -um *adj* out of date, obsolete; worn out; shabby, threadbare; soiled, dirty; low, poor; *(of language)* hackneyed, trite
obsōnāt·or -ōris *m* (**ops-**) shopper *(for groceries)*
obsōnāt·us -ūs *m* (**ops-**) shopping *(for groceries)*
obsōn·ium -(i)ī *n* (**ops-**) shopping; groceries ‖ *npl* groceries; pension
obsōn·ō -āre -āvī -ātus *or* **obsōn·or -ārī -ātus sum** *tr* (**ops-**) to shop for *(groceries);* **famem obsonare** to work up an appetite ‖ *intr* to go shopping; to provide food; *(w.* **de** *+ abl)* to provide a feast for
obsŏn·ō -āre -āvī -ātum *intr* (w. dat) to drown out
obsorb·eō -ēre -uī *tr* (**ops-**) to gulp down
obstanti·a -ae *f* obstacle
obstetr·ix -īcis *f* (**ops-**) midwife
obstinātē *adv* resolutely, with determination; obstinately, stubbornly
obstināti·ō -ōnis *f* determination; obstinacy, stubbornness
obstināt·us -a -um *adj* determined, fixed; obstinate, stubborn
obstin·ō -āre -āvī -ātus *tr* (**ops-**) to set one's mind on, persist in ‖ *intr (w.* **ad**) to persist in
obstipescō *see* **obstupesco**
obstīp·us -a -um *adj* bent, bent forwards, bowed; **capite obstipo stare** to stand with bowed head
obstit·us -a -um *adj* struck by lightning
ob·stō -stāre -stitī -stātum *intr* (**ops-**) to stand in the way, raise opposition; *(w. dat)* **1** to stand in the way of, block the path of; **2** to block the view of, stand in front of; **3** to oppose, object to, resist, obstruct; **4** to constitute a boundary to;

(w. **ne** *or* **quin** *or* **quominus** *or* **cur non)** to prevent *(s.o.)* from

obstrep·ō -ĕre -uī -itus *tr* (ops-) to fill with noise, drown out ‖ *intr* to make a racket, make noise; *(w. dat)* 1 to shout at, drown out, interrupt with shouts; 2 *(of the sea)* to resound against

obstrin·gō -gĕre -xī obstrictus *tr* (ops-) to tie a rope tightly around *(a neck); (w.* **ob** *+ acc)* to tie onto; to tie up, shut in, confine; *(fig)* to involve, put under obligation *(by an agreement, oath);* to pledge, promise *(s.th.);* **fidem obstringere** *(w. dat)* to pledge one's word to; **in verba alicujus obstringere** to have *(s.o.)* swear loyalty to s.o. ‖ *refl & pass (w. abl)* 1 to get involved in; 2 to be guilty of

obstructi·ō -ōnis *f* obstruction

obstructus *pp of* **obstruo**

obstrū·do -dĕre -sī -sus *tr* (obt-) to gulp down; *(w. dat)* to force *(s.th.)* upon, thrust *(s.th.)* upon

obstru·ō -ĕre -xī -ctus *tr* (ops-) to pile up, block up, stop up; *(w. dat)* to block *or* close *(e.g., a road)* against

obstrūsus *pp of* **obstrudo**

obstupe·faciō -facĕre -fēcī -factus *tr* to stun, astonish, strike dumb, daze; *(of drinks)* to stupefy; to paralyze *(emotions, etc.)*

obstup·escō -escĕre -uī *intr* (-stip-) to be astounded, be stunned, be paralyzed; to be struck with awe *or* wonder; *(of the body)* to become numb

obstupid·us -a -um *adj* (ops-) struck dumb, stunned, dazed, astounded

ob·sum -esse -fui *or* **offuī -futūrus** *intr (w. dat)* 1 to be opposed to, be against; 2 to be prejudicial to; 3 to be harmful to; **nihil obest dicere** there is no harm in saying

ob·suō -suĕre -suī -sūtus *tr* to sew on; to sew up

obsurd·escō -escĕre -uī *intr* to become deaf; *(fig)* to turn a deaf ear

ob·tegō -tegĕre -texī -tectus *tr* (opt-) to cover up *(w. clothing);* to protect; to conceal, screen; to keep secret

obtemperāti·ō -ōnis *f (w. dat)* obedience to, submissiveness to

obtemper·ō -āre -āvī -ātum *intr* (opt-) *(w. dat)* to comply with, be submissive to, obey

obten·dō -dĕre -dī -tus *tr* (opt-) to spread, stretch out; to offer as an excuse; to envelop; to conceal; to allege ‖ *pass (w. dat)* to lie opposite; **obtentā nocte** under cover of darkness

obtent·us -ūs *m* (opt-) screen, cover; pretext, pretense

ob·terō -terĕre -trīvī -trītus *tr* to trample on, trample down, crush; *(fig)* to trample on, degrade, destroy, crush

obtestāti·ō -ōnis *f* calling to witness; solemn invocation; solemn appeal

obtest·or -ārī -ātus sum *tr* (opt-) to call as witness; to make an appeal to, implore, entreat

obtex·ō -ĕre -uī -tus *tr* to cover, veil

obtic·eō -ēre -uī *intr* (opt-) to be silent

obtic·escō -escĕre -uī *intr* (opt-) to fall silent; to be dumbstruck

ob·tineō -tinēre -tinuī -tentus *tr* (opt-) to hold on to, keep up, persist in; to possess; to maintain, preserve, uphold; to remain in charge of; to retain military control of; to achieve *(a goal),* gain *(one's point);* to secure *(rights);* to win *(one's case);* to secure *(one's rights);* to cover, extend over; to constitute; to comprise; *(of conditions)* to prevail over; to hold *(a rank, position; an opinion);* **auctoritatem obtinere** *(w. gen)* to have the authority of; **locum obtinere** *(w. gen)* to fulfill the function of; **rem obtinere** to be successful, be victorious; **vim obtinere** *(w. gen)* to have the force of ‖ *intr* to carry the day, get one's way, succeed; *(of an opinion, report)* to be generally accepted

ob·tingō -tingĕre -tigī *intr* (opt-) to happen, occur; *(w. dat)* to happen to, befall

obtorp·escō -escĕre -uī *intr* (opt-) to become numb, become stiff; to become insensible

obtor·queō -quēre -sī -tus *tr* (opt-) to twist; to restrain with a noose

obtrectāti·ō -ōnis *f* (opt-) detraction, disparagement

obtrectāt·or -ōris *m* (opt-) detractor

obtrect·ō -āre -āvī -ātus *tr* (opt-) to treat spitefully, mistreat, disparage; to carp at ‖ *intr (w. dat)* to detract from, disparage

obtrītus *pp of* **obtero**

obtrīvī *perf of* **obtero**

obtrūdō *see* **obstrudo**

obtrunc·ō -āre -āvī -ātus *tr* (opt-) to cut off, cut down; *(in battle)* to cut down, kill

ob·tueor -tuērī -tuitus sum *or* **optu·or -ī** *tr* (opt-) to gaze at, gaze upon; to see clearly

ob·tundō -tundĕre -tudī -tūsus *or* **-unsus** *tr* (opt-) to beat, beat on, thump on; to blunt; *(fig)* to pound away at, stun; to deafen; to annoy

obturb·ō -āre -āvī -ātus *tr* (opt-) to throw into disorder; *(fig)* to disturb, confuse, distract

obtur·gescō -gescĕre -tursī *intr* to begin to swell

obtūr·ō -āre -āvī -ātus *tr* (opt-) to block up, plug up; **aures obturare** to refuse to listen; **os alicujus obturare** to shut s.o. up

obtūs·us *or* **obtuns·us -a -um** *pp of*

obtundo ‖ *adj* dull; blunt; husky, coarse *(voice); (of utterances)* obtuse; *(of actions)* blunt, lacking in refinement
obtūt·us -ūs *m* **(opt-)** stare, gaze
obumbr·ō -āre -āvī -ātus *tr* to overshadow, shade; to darken, obscure; to cover, screen
obunc·us -a -um *adj* hooked
obust·us -a -um *adj (of a stake)* having an end burned to a point; nipped *(by cold)*
obvāg·iō -īre *intr* to bawl
obvall·ō -āre -āvī -ātus *tr* to fortify *(with a rampart)*
ob·veniō -venīre -vēnī -ventum *intr* to come up, happen, come one's way; *(w. dat)* **1** to fall to *(s.o.'s)* lot; **2** to come to *(s.o.'s)* notice
obvers·or -ārī -ātus sum *intr* to make an appearance, show oneself; *(fig)* to appear *(before one's eyes, mind)*
obvers·us -a -um *adj (w.* **ad)** **1** turned toward, facing; **2** inclined to; *(w. dat)* engaged in ‖ *m* opponent
ob·vertō -vertĕre -vertī -versus *tr* **(-vor-)** *(w. dat or* **ad)** to turn *(s.th.)* towards *or* in the direction of; *(w.* **in** *+ acc)* to turn *(e.g., soldiers)* to face *(e.g., the enemy)* ‖ *pass (w.* **ad)** to turn toward
obviam *or* **ob viam** *adv (w. dat)* **1** to meet, in order to meet, in the way of; **2** *(fig)* opposed to; **effundi obviam** *(w. dat)* to pour *or* rush out to meet; **obviam esse** *(w. dat)* **1** to meet; **2** to oppose, resist; **3** to be at hand, be handy; **obviam ire** *(or* **obviam procedere)** *(w. dat)* **1** to go to meet; **2** to face up to *(dangers);* **obviam obsistere** *(w. dat)* to stand in the way of; **obviam prodire** *(or* **proficisci** *or* **progredi)** *(w. dat)* to go to meet; **obviam venire** *(w. dat)* to come *or* go to meet
obvigilāt·um -ī *n* vigilance
obvi·us -a -um *adj* in the way; exposed, open; accessible *(person);* ready, at hand; *(w. dat)* **1** to meet, so as to meet; **2** opposed to; **3** exposed to, open to; **obvius esse** *(w. dat)* to meet, encounter
obvol·vō -vĕre -vī -ūtus *tr* to wrap up, cover up
occaec·ō -āre -āvī -ātus *tr* **(obc-)** to blind; to darken, obscure; to hide; *(of fear)* to numb
occall·escō -escĕre -uī *intr* **(obc-)** to become thick-skinned, become callused; *(fig)* to become callous, become insensitive
occan·ō -ĕre -uī *intr (mil)* to sound the charge
occāsi·ō -ōnis *f* opportunity, good time, right moment, chance; pretext; *(mil)* surprise, raid; **ex occasione** at the right time; **occasionem amittere** to lose the opportunity; **occasionem arripere** to seize the opportunity; **per occasionem** *(or* **occasiones)** at the right time
occāsiuncul·a -ae *f* nice little opportunity
occās·us -ūs *m* setting; sunset; the West; *(fig)* downfall, ruin, death
occāti·ō -ōnis *f* harrowing, breaking up of the soil
occāt·or -ōris *m* harrower
oc·cēdō -cēdĕre -cessī -cessum *intr* to go up; **obviam occedere** *(w. dat)* to go to meet
occent·ō *or* **occant·ō -āre -āvī -ātus** *tr* **(obc-)** to serenade; to satirize in verse
occept·ō -āre -āvī -ātus *tr* to begin
occid·ens -entis *m* the setting sun; the West
occīdi·ō -ōnis *f* massacre, annihilation; **occidione occidere** to massacre
oc·cīdō -cīdĕre -cīdī -cīsus *tr* to kill; to murder; to knock down; to bring about the ruin of; *(fig)* to be the death of; to pester to death
oc·cĭdō -cidĕre -cĭdī -cāsum *intr* to fall, fall down; *(of the sun)* to set; to fall, be slain; *(of hope, etc.)* to fade; *(of species)* to become extinct, die out; *(fig)* to be ruined, be done for; **occidi!** I'm finished! **vita occidens** the twilight of life
occidu·us -a -um *adj* setting; western; *(fig)* sinking, fading, dying
occill·ō -āre -āvī -ātus *tr* to smash
oc·cinō -cinĕre -cecinī *or* **-cinuī** *or* **occan·ō -ĕre -uī** *intr* to sing inauspiciously, sound ominous
oc·cipiō -cipĕre -cēpī -ceptus *tr & intr* **(-cup-)** to begin
occipit·ium -(i)ī *or* **occip·ut -itis** *n* back of the head
occīsi·ō -ōnis *f* murder, killing
occīs·or -ōris *m* murderer, killer
occīsus *pp of* **occīdō**
occlāmit·ō -āre -āvī -ātus *tr* to shout at ‖ *intr* to shout, yell
occlū·dō -dĕre -sī -sus *tr* **(obc-)** to close up, shut up, lock up; to close access to *(buildings);* to restrain
occ·ō -āre -āvī -ātus *tr* to harrow, break up *(the soil)*
occub·ō -āre *intr* to lie; to rest; **crudelibus umbris occubare** to lie dead in the cruel lower world
occulc·ō -āre -āvī -ātus *tr* to trample down
occul·ō -ĕre -uī -tus *tr* to cover; to cover up, hide
occultāti·ō -ōnis *f* concealment, hiding
occultāt·or -ōris *m* one who conceals
occultē *adv* secretly, in secret
occult·ō -āre -āvī -ātus *tr* to hide, conceal; to suppress, keep *(facts, information)* secret ‖ *refl & pass* to hide
occult·us -a -um *pp of* **occulo** ‖ *adj* hidden, secret; clandestine; recondite *(expressions);* invisible *(forces of nature);*

reserved *(person)* ‖ *n* concealment; secret; **ex occulto** from a concealed position; **in occulto** in hiding; **per occultum** without being observed, secretly

oc·cumbō occumbĕre occubuī occubitus *tr* to meet *(death)* ‖ *intr* to fall dying; *(w. dat or abl)* to meet *(death)*; **occumbere per** *(w. acc)* to die at the hands of

occupāti·ō -ōnis *f* occupation, employment, business; business engagement, task, job; occupying *(of a town)*; preoccupation, concentration, close attention

occupāt·us -a -um *adj* occupied, busy, engaged

occup·ō -āre -āvī -ātus *tr* to occupy; to seize; to grasp, grab; to win, gain; to attack, strike down; to outstrip, overtake; to fill up, occupy *(a space)*; to assume *(title, position)*; to invest; to loan, lend; to head for, reach; to forestall; to take by surprise; to take the lead over *(competitor)*; *(w. inf)* to be the first to

oc·currō -currĕre -currī *or* **-cucurrī -cursum** *intr* **(obc-)** to run up; *(w. dat)* **1** to run up to, run to meet, hurry to meet; **2** to rush against, attack; **3** to resist, oppose, counteract; **4** to meet, answer, reply to, object to; **5** to relieve, remedy; **6** to occur to, suggest itself to, present itself to; **7** run into, run up against, get involved in

occursāti·ō -ōnis *f* hustle and bustle; excited welcome; officiousness

occurs·ō -āre -āvī -ātus *tr* **(obc-)** to run to meet ‖ *intr (w dat)* **1** to run to meet, come to meet, meet; **2** to attack, charge, oppose; **3** *(of thoughts)* to occur to

occurs·us -ūs *m* meeting; *(w. gen)* running into *(s.o. or s.th.)*

Ōceanīt·is -idis *or* **-idos** *f* ocean nymph, daughter of Oceanus

ōcean·us -ī *m* ocean ‖ **Ōceanus** Oceanus *(son of Uranus and Ge and father of the river gods and ocean nymphs)*

ocell·us -ī *m* eye; gem; darling

ōcim·um -ī *n* basil *(seasoning)*

ocin·um -ī *n* fodder *(possibly clover)*

ōci·or -or -us *adj* swifter, quicker

ōcius *adv (superl:* **ōcissimē**) more swiftly, more quickly; sooner; more easily; immediately, on the spot; *(w. abl)* rather than; **ocius serius** sooner or later; **quam ocissime** as quickly as possible

ocre·a -ae *f* greave, shin guard

ocreāt·us -a -um *adj* wearing shin guards

octaphoros *see* **octophoros**

octāv·a -ae *f* one-eighth; eighth hour of the day *(i.e., 2:00 p.m.)*

Octāvi·a -ae *f* sister of Augustus, wife of Gaius Marcellus, and later of Marc Antony *(64–11 B.C.)* ‖ daughter of Claudius and wife of Nero *(murdered in A.D. 62)*

Octāv·ius -(i)ī *m* Gaius Octavius *(Augustus, who, upon adoption by Julius Caesar, became Gaius Julius Caesar Octavianus, 63 B.C.–A.D. 14)*

octāvum *adv* for the eighth time

octāv·us -a -um *adj* eighth; **octava pars** one-eighth ‖ *f see* **octāva** ‖ *n* **cum octavo efficere** to produce an eightfold yield

octāv·us decim·us -a -um *adj* eighteenth

octiens *or* **octiēs** *adv* eight times

octingentēsim·us -a -um *adj* eight hundreth

octingent·ī -ae -a *adj* eight hundred

octip·ēs -edis *adj* eight-footed

octiplicāt·us -a -um *adj* eightfold

octō *indecl adj* eighteen

Octō·ber -bris -bre *adj* October, of October; **mensis October** October *(8th month of the Roman calendar until 153 B.C.)* ‖ **Octo·ber -ris** *m* October

octōdecim *indecl adj* eighteen

octōgēnāri·us -a -um *adj & m* octogenarian

octōgēn·ī -ae -a *adj* eighty each

octōgē(n)sim·us -a -um *adj* eightieth

octōgiē(n)s *adv* eighty times

octōjug·is -is -e *adj* eight-horse

octōn·ī -ae -a *adj* eight at a time, eight each

octōphor·os -os -on *adj* **(octa-)** carried by eight men ‖ *n* litter carried by eight men

octupl·us -a -um *adj* eightfold ‖ *n* eightfold fine

octuss·is -is *m* sum of eight "asses" *(small coins, i.e., 8¢)*

oculāt·us -a -um *adj* having eyes; exposed to view, conspicuous; **oculatus testis** eyewitness

ocule·us -a -um *adj* many-eyed

oculissim·us -a -um *adj (hum)* dearest

oculitus *adv (to love s.o.)* like one's own eyes, dearly

ocul·us -ī *m* eye; eye, bud *(in plants)*; sight, vision; mind's eye; **aequis oculis** contentedly; **altero oculo captus** blind in one eye; **ante oculos** in full view; *(fig)* obvious; **ante oculos ponere** to imagine; **ex oculis abire** to go out of sight, disappear; **in oculis** in view, in public, in the limelight; **in oculis ferre** *(or* **gestare)** to hold dear, value; **oculos adjicere** *(w.* **ad)** to eye; to covet; **oculos dejicere ab** to take one's eyes off; *(fig)* to lose sight of; **oculos pascere** *(w. abl)* to feast one's eyes on; **sub oculis** *(w. gen)* in the presence of, under the very nose of

ōdī odisse ōsus *tr* to have taken a dislike to, dislike, hate, be disgusted with

odiōsē *adv* hatefully; unpleasantly

odiōsic·us -a -um *adj (hum)* odious, unpleasant, annoying

odiōs·us -a -um *adj* odious, unpleasant, annoying
od·ium -(i)ī *n* dislike, aversion, hatred; object of hatred, nuisance; dissatisfaction, disgust; offensive conduct, insolence; **odio esse** *(w. dat)* to be hateful to, be disliked by, be hated by ‖ *npl* feelings of hatred
od·or *or* **od·ōs -ōris** *m* odor, smell, scent; stench; pleasant smell, fragrance; perfume; inkling, suggestion, hint ‖ *mpl* perfume
odōrāti·ō -ōnis *f* smell, smelling
odōrāt·us -a -um *adj* fragrant, scented
odōrāt·us -ūs *m* smell, smelling; sense of smell
odōrif·er -era -erum *adj* fragrant
odōr·ō -āre -āvī -ātus *tr* to make fragrant
odōr·or -ārī -ātus sum *tr* to sniff at, scent; to aspire to, aim at; to be sniffing after, search for, investigate; to get a smattering of
odōr·us -a -um *adj* smelly; fragrant; keen-scented
odōs *see* **odor**
Odrys·ae -ārum *mpl* a people of the Thracian interior
Odrysi·us -a -um *adj & m* Thracian
Odyssē·a *or* **Odyssī·a -ae** *f* the Odyssey
Oea·ger *or* **Oea·grus -grī** *m* Oeager *(king of Thrace and father of Orpheus)*
Oeagri·us -a -um *adj* Thracian
Oea·gus -grī *m* king of Thrace and father of Orpheus
Oebalid·ēs -ae *m* male descendant of Oebalus *(see* **Oebalus)** ‖ *mpl* Castor and Pollux
Oebali·us -a -um *adj* Spartan; Tarentine; Sabine ‖ *f* Tarentum *(Spartan colony in S. Italy)*
Oebal·us -ī *m* king of Sparta, father of Tyndareus, and grandfather of Helen, Clytemnestra, Castor and Pollux
Oedip·ūs -odis *or* **-ī** *m* Oedipus
Oen·eūs -eī *or* **-eos** *m* king of Calydon, husband of Althaea, and father of Meleager and Dejanira
Oenīd·ēs -ae *m* descendant of Oeneus; Meleager; Diomedes
Oenoma·ūs -ī *m* king of Pisa in the Peloponnesus and father of Hippodamia
oenophor·um -ī *n* wine-bottle basket
Oenopi·a -ae *f* ancient name of Aegina
oenopōl·ium -(i)ī *n* wine shop
Oenōtri·us -a -um *adj* Oenotrian, Italic ‖ *f* ancient name of S.E. Italy; Italy
oestr·us -ī *m* horsefly, gadfly; fancy, inspiration
oesyp·um -ī *n* (-sop-) lanolin
Oet·a -ae *or* **Oet·ē -ēs** *f* Mt. Oeta *(in S. Thessaly, on which Hercules died)*
Oetae·us -a -um *adj* Oetean ‖ *m* Hercules
ofell·a -ae *f* small chunk of meat
off·a -ae *f* lump; dumpling; lump, swelling
offectus *pp of* **officio**
offen·dō -děre -dī -sus *tr* to bump, bump against, stub, strike, hit; to hit upon, come upon, meet with, bump into, stumble upon, find; to offend, shock; to annoy, disgust; to hurt *(feelings);* to injure *(reputation);* **nihil offendere** to suffer no damage, receive no injury ‖ *intr* to blunder, make a mistake; to give offense, be offensive; to fail, take a loss, be defeated, come to grief; to run aground; *(w. dat or* **in** *+ abl)* to hit against, bump against; *(w. dat)* to give offense to; *(w.* **in** *+ acc)* to take offense at; **terrae offendere** to run aground
offens·a -ae *f* offense, affront; displeasure, resentment, hatred; crime; **offensā** *(w. gen)* out of hatred for
offensi·ō -ōnis *f* stubbing; tripping, stumbling; obstacle; setback, mishap; detriment; affront, outrage ‖ *fpl* offensive acts; feelings of displeasure
offensiuncul·a -ae *f* slight mishap
offens·ō -āre -āvī -ātus *tr & intr* to bump
offens·us -a -um *pp of* **offendo** ‖ *adj* offensive, odious; *(w. dat)* offended at, displeased with
offens·us -ūs *m* bump; shock; offense
offerō offerre obtulī oblātus *tr* to offer, bring forward, present, show; to cause; to confer, bestow; to inflict; to deliver, hand over ‖ *refl (w. adj)* to show oneself to be; *(w. dat)* **1** to meet, encounter; **2** to expose oneself to *(e.g., danger);* **3** to give oneself up to *(an authority);* **4** to offer one's services to, volunteer for ‖ *refl & pass (esp. of an apparition)* to appear; *(of an idea)* to suggest itself
offerūment·a -ae *f (said humorously of a blow or welt)* present
officīn·a *or* **opificīn·a -ae** *f* shop, workshop, factory; office; artist's studio; training school
of·ficiō -ficěre -fēcī -fectum *intr (w. dat)* to get in the way of, interfere with, oppose; to obstruct, hinder; to be detrimental to
officiōsē *adv* obligingly, courteously
officiōs·us -a -um *adj* ready to serve, obliging; dutiful; officious
offic·ium -(i)ī *n* service, favor, kindness, courtesy; obligation, duty; function, part; social obligation, social call, social visit; ceremony; ceremonial observance, attendance; official duty; employment, business, job; sense of duty, conscience; allegiance; **officio togae virilis interesse** to attend the ceremony of the assuming of the manly toga
of·fīgō -fīgěre -fixī -fixus *tr* to fasten down, nail down, drive in
offirmāt·us -a -um *adj* determined

offirm·ō -āre -āvī -ātus *refl & intr* to steel oneself, be determined
offlect·ō -ĕre *tr* to turn *(s.th.)* around
offrēnāt·us -a -um *adj* curbed
offrēn·ō -āre -āvī -ātus *tr (fig)* to curb
offūci·a -ae *f* cosmetic; *(fig)* trick, deception
offul·geō -gēre -sī *intr (w. dat)* to shine on
of·fundō -fundĕre -fūdī -fūsus *tr* to pour out; to cover; to fill; to eclipse ‖ *pass (w. dat)* to pour out over, spread over
oggann·iō -īre -īvī *or* **-iī -ītus** *tr or intr* to growl
ogger·ō -ĕre *tr* to bring, offer
Ōgyg·ēs -is *or* **Ōgyg·us -ī** *m* mythical king of Thebes, in whose reign the Deluge allegedly occurred
Ōgygi·us -a -um *adj* Theban; **Ōgygius deus** Theban god *(i.e., Bacchus)*
oh *interj* oh!
ōhē *or* **ohē** *interj* whoa!
Oīl·eūs -eī *or* **-eos** *m* king of Locris in N. Greece and father of Ajax the archer
ole·a -ae *f* olive; olive tree
oleāgin·us -a -um *adj* olive, of an olive tree
oleāri·us -a -um *adj* oil, of oil ‖ *m* oil merchant
oleas·ter -trī *m* oleaster, wild olive tree
Ōleni·us -a -um *adj* of Olenus *(town in Achaia and Aetolia)*; Achaian, Aetolian
ol·ens -entis *adj* smelling; fragrant; smelly, stinking; musty
ol·eō -ēre -uī *tr* to smell of, smell like; *(fig)* to betray ‖ *intr* to smell; *(w. abl)* to smell of
ole·um -ī *n* olive oil, oil; *(fig)* palestra; **oleum addere camino** *(prov)* to pour oil on the fire; **oleum et operam perdere** to waste time and effort
ol·faciō -facĕre -fēcī -factus *tr* to smell
olfact·ō -āre -āvī -ātus *tr* to sniff at
olid·us -a -um *adj* smelly
ōlim *adv* once, once upon a time; at the time; for a good while; someday *(in the future)*, hereafter; now and then, at times; ever, at any time
olit- = holit-
olīv·a -ae *f* olive; olive tree; olive wreath; olive branch; olive staff
olīvēt·um -ī *n* olive grove
olīvi·fer -fera -ferum *adj* producing olives, olive-growing
olīv·um -ī *n* olive oil; ointment; *(fig)* palestra
oll·a -ae *f* pot, jar
olle *or* **ollus = ille**
ol·or -ōris *m* swan
olōrīn·us -a -um *adj* swan-
olus *see* **holus**
Olympi·a -ae *f* Olympia *(region in Elis, in the Peloponnesus, where the Olympic games were held)*
Olympi·a -ōrum *npl* Olympic games
Olympiac·us -a -um *adj* Olympic
Olympi·as -adis *or* **-ados** *f* Olympiad *(period of 4 years between Olympic games, starting in 776 B.C., according to which the Greeks reckoned time)* ‖ wife of Philip V of Macedon and mother of Alexander the Great
Olympic·us -a -um *adj* Olympic, of the games held at Olympia
Olympionīc·ēs -ae *m* Olympic victor
Olympi·us -a -um *adj* Olympian *(cult title of Zeus)*; *(of games)* Olympic, held at Olympia; *(of temple)* dedicated to Olympian Zeus
Olymp·us -ī *m* Mt. Olympus *(on the boundary of Macedonia and Thessaly, regarded as the home of the gods)*
omās·um -ī *n* tripe
ōm·en -inis *n* omen *(good or bad)*; foreboding; **omen accipere** to believe an event to be an omen; **prima omina** first marriage; **(procul) omen abesto!** *(or* **quod omen di avertant!)** God forbid!
ōment·um -ī *n* fatty membrane covering the bowels; the bowels
ōmināt·or -ōris *m* diviner
ōmin·or -ārī -ātus sum *tr* to foretell, predict, forebode
ōminōs·us -a -um *adj* ominous
omīsī *perf of* **omitto**
omiss·us -a -um *pp of* **omitto** ‖ *adj* remiss, negligent, heedless
omittō omittĕre omīsī omissus *tr* to let go; to let go of, let fall, drop; to give up, abandon; to omit, pass over; to overlook, disregard; to release from custody; to allow to escape; to discard
omnigen·us -a -um *adj (also indecl)* every kind of
omnimodīs *or* **omnimodō** *adv* by all means, wholly
omnīnō *adv* altogether, entirely, wholly; *(w. numerals)* in all; *(in generalizations)* in general; *(in concessions)*, no doubt, to be sure, yes, by all means; **haud omnino** *(or* **non omnino)** not quite, not entirely; absolutely not, not at all; not expressly; **omnino nemo** absolutely no one
omnipar·ens -entis *adj* all-producing *(earth)*
omnipot·ens -entis *adj* omnipotent
omn·is -is -e *adj* all, every; every kind of; the whole ‖ *mpl* all, everybody ‖ *n* the universe ‖ *npl* all things, everything; all nature; all the world
omnitu·ens -entis *adj* all-seeing
omnivag·us -a -um *adj* roving everywhere
omnivol·us -a -um *adj* all-craving
Omphal·ē -ēs *f* Lydian queen who bought Hercules as a slave for a year
ona·ger *or* **ona·grus -grī** *m* wild ass
onāg·os -ī *m* ass-driver

Onchesmīt·ēs -ae *m* wind blowing from Onchesmus *(harbor in Epirus)*

onerāri·us -a -um *adj* carrying freight; **jumenta oneraria** beasts of burden; **oneraria** *(or* **navis oneraria)** freighter, transport

oner·ō -āre -āvī -ātus *tr* to load, load down, burden; *(fig)* to overload, oppress; *(fig)* to pile on, aggravate

onerōs·us -a -um *adj* onerous, burdensome, oppressive; heavy

on·us -eris *n* burden; load; freight, cargo; trouble; tax burden; fetus, embryo; **oneri esse** *(w. dat)* to be a burden to

onust·us -a -um *adj* loaded down, burdened; filled, full

on·yx -ychis *mf* onyx; onyx box

opācit·ās -ātis *f* shade, darkness

opāc·ō -āre -āvī -ātus *tr* to shade, make shady

opāc·us -a -um *adj* shady; dark, obscure **II** *npl* **opaca locorum** shady places; **opaca viarum** dark streets

opell·a -ae *f* light work; small effort

oper·a -ae *f* effort, pains, exertion; work; care, attention; service, assistance; leisure, spare time; laborer, workman, artisan; a day's work *(by one person);* **operae esse** *(or* **operae pretium esse)** to be worthwhile; **operam dare** to take pains, exert oneself, be busied, pay attention, give attention, apply oneself; **operam funeri dare** to attend a funeral; **operam magistro dare** *(or* **reddere)** to attend a teacher's lectures, study under a teacher; **operam ludere** *(or* **perdere)** to waste one's time and effort; **operam sermoni dare** to listen to a conversation; **operam tonsori dare** to go see a barber, get a haircut; **operā meā (tuā,** *etc.)* through my (your, *etc.)* agency, thanks to me (you, *etc.)*

operāri·us -a -um *adj* working; working for hire **II** *m* workman **II** *f* working woman

opercul·um -i *n* lid, cover

operīment·um -ī *n* lid, cover

oper·iō -īre -uī -tus *tr* to cover, cover up; to shut; to hide; to clothe; to bury; to bury with a shower of missiles

oper·or -ārī -ātus sum *intr* to work hard, take pains; *(w. dat)* **1** to work hard at, be busied with, be engaged in; **2** to perform *(religious services);* **3** to attend; **4** to worship

operōsē *adv* with great effort, at great pains

operōs·us -a -um *adj* active, busy, painstaking; troublesome, difficult, elaborate; efficacious, powerful *(drugs)*

opertus *pp of* **operio II** *adj* closed; hidden; secret **II** *n* secret; secret place; **in operto** inside, in secret **II** *npl* depth; veiled oracles

operuī *perf of* **operio**

opēs *see* **ops**

ophīt·ēs -ae *m* serpentine *(type of marble)*

Ophiūsi·us -a -um *adj* Cyprian **II** *f* old name of Cyprus

ophthalmi·ās -ae *m* a type of fish

ophthalmic·us -ī *m* eye-doctor

Opic·us -a -um *adj* Oscan; boorish; ignorant *(esp. of Latin),* uncultured

opif·er -era -erum *adj* helpful

opif·ex -icis *m* maker, creator; craftsman, mechanic

opificīn·a -ae *f* workshop

opific·ium -(i)ī *n* work

ōpili·ō -ōnis *m* shepherd

opīmē *adv* splendidly; richly

opīmit·ās -ātis *f* prosperity

opīm·us -a -um *adj* fat, plump; fertile, fruitful; rich, enriched; abundant, plentiful; sumptuous, splendid; lucrative; noble; **spolia opima** armor stripped from one general by another on the field of battle

opīnābil·is -is -e *adj* conjectural, imaginary

opīnāti·ō -ōnis *f* mere opinion, conjecture, supposition, hunch

opīnāt·us -a -um *adj* supposed, imagined

opīnāt·us -ūs *m* supposition

ōpīni·ō -ōnis *f* opinion; conjecture, guess, supposition; expectation; general impression; estimation; rumor; reputation, bad reputation; **amplius opinione** beyond expectation, beyond all hopes; **celerius opinione** sooner than expected; **hac opinione ut** under the impression that; **in opinione esse** *(w. acc & inf)* to be of the opinion that; **praebere opinionem timoris** to convey the impression of fear; **praeter opinionem** contrary to expectation, sooner than expected; **ut opinio mea est** as I suppose

opīn·ō -āre *or* **opīn·or -ārī -ātus sum** *tr* to suppose, imagine, conjecture **II** *intr (parenthetical)* to suppose, imagine

opiparē *adv* splendidly, sumptuously

opipar·us -a -um *adj* splendid, sumptuous, ritzy

opisthograph·us -a -um *adj* written on the back; **in opisthographo** on the reverse side of a document

opitul·or -ārī -ātus sum *intr (w. dat)* to bring help to, assist

oport·et -ēre -uit *v impers* it is right, it is proper; **me abire oportet** I ought to go, I should go

op·pangō -pangĕre -ēgī -pactus *tr* to affix, imprint

oppect·ō -ĕre *tr* to comb off; *(coll)* to pluck, pick at, eat

oppēdō -ĕre *intr* (vulg) *(w. dat)* **1** to fart at; **2** *(fig)* to deride, mock

opper·ior -īrī -tus sum *tr* to wait for; *(w.*

num) to wait and see whether ‖ *intr* to wait

oppet·ō -ĕre -īvī *or* **-iī -ītus** *tr* to meet, encounter *(prematurely)* ‖ *intr* to meet death; die

oppidān·us -a -um *adj* of a town, in a town; *(pej)* provincial ‖ *mpl* townspeople

oppidō *adv* absolutely, quite; *(as affirmative answer)* exactly, extremely; **oppido quam breve intervallum** an extremely short distance

oppidul·um -ī *n* small town

oppid·um -ī *n* town

oppigner·ō -āre -āvī -ātus *tr* to pledge

oppīl·ō -āre -āvī -ātus *tr* to shut up, shut off

oppl·eō -ēre -ēvī -ētus *tr* to fill up, fill completely

op·pōnō -pōnĕre -posuī -positus *tr* to put, place, station; to oppose; to expose, lay bare, open; to wager; to mortgage; to bring forward, adduce, allege; to reply, object; to compare; **currum opponere** to block a rival's chariot

opportūnē *adv* at the right time

opportūnit·ās -ātis *f* opportunity, chance *(to do s.th.)*; right time, opportuneness; advantage; suitability, fitness, convenience

opportūn·us -a -um *adj* opportune, suitable, convenient; advantageous, useful; exposed; **tempore opportunissimo** in the nick of time

oppositi·ō -ōnis *f* opposition

opposit·us -a -um *pp of* **oppono** ‖ *adj* opposite; *(w. dat)* opposite, across from

oppressi·ō -ōnis *f* force, violence, violent seizure; suppression, overthrow

oppressiuncul·a -ae *f* slight pressure

oppressus *pp of* **opprimo**

oppress·us -ūs *m* pressure

op·primō -primĕre -pressī -pressus *tr* **(obp-)** to press down, weigh down; to pressure, put pressure on; to shut; to overwhelm; to put down, quell; to sink *(ship)*; to subvert, overthrow, crush, overpower; to conceal, suppress; to catch

opprobrāment·um -ī *n* disgrace, scandal

opprobr·ium -(i)ī *n* **(obp-)** disgrace, scandal, reproach; cause of disgrace; taunt, abuse, abusive word

opprobr·ō -āre -āvī -ātus *tr* **(obp-)** to throw up *(s.th.)* to *(s.o. as a reproach)*

oppugnāti·ō -ōnis *f* **(opr-)** assault; *(fig)* attack, accusation

oppugnāt·or -ōris *m* **(obp-)** assailant

oppugn·ō -āre -āvī -ātus *tr* to assault, attack, storm; *(fig)* attack, assail

ops opis *f* power, might; help, aid; influence, weight; **non opis est nostrae** it is not in our power; **ope meā** with my help; **opem ferre** *(w. dat)* to bring help to, help ‖ *fpl* wealth, resources, means; military *or* political resources; **(ex) summis opibus** with all one's might ‖ **Ops** *(goddess of abundance (sister and wife of Saturn and mother of Jupiter)*

ops- = obs-

optābil·is -is -e *adj* desirable

optāti·ō -ōnis *f* wishing, wish

optātō *adv* according to one's wish

optāt·us -a -um *adj* longed-for, desired, welcome ‖ *n* wish, desire

optigō *see* **obtego**

optim·ās -ātis *m* **(-tum-)** aristocrat ‖ *mpl* aristocracy, aristocratic party

optimē *(superl of* **bene)** *adv* **(-tum-)** very well; thoroughly; best; most opportunely, just in time

optim·us -a -um *(superl of* **bonus)** *adj* **(-tum-)** very good, best; excellent; most beneficial, most advantageous; *(of a legal title)* most valid, having the soundest basis; **in optimam partem** most favorably; **optimā fide** with the utmost honesty; **optimum est** *(w. inf)* it is best to; **optimum factu est** *(w. inf)* the best thing to do is to; **ut optimus maximusque** *(leg) (of property)* in its optimum condition *(i.e., free from all encumbrances)*

opti·ō -ōnis *f* option, choice ‖ *m* helper, assistant; *(mil)* adjutant

optīv·us -a -um *adj* chosen

opt·ō -āre -āvī -ātus *tr* to choose, select; to pray for; to wish for, desire

optum- = optim-

opul·ens -entis *adj* opulent, rich

opulentē *or* **opulenter** *adv* richly

opulenti·a -ae *f* opulence, wealth; resources; power

opulentit·ās -ātis *f* opulence; power

opulent·ō -āre -āvī -ātus *tr* to make rich, enrich

opulent·us -a -um *adj* opulent, rich; sumptuous; powerful

op·us -eris *n* work; product of work: structure, building; literary work, composition, book; work of art, workmanship; deed, achievement; literary genre; occupation, employment; what a person is expected to do, function, business; *(w. gen) (poet)* a thing the size of; *(mil)* offensive works, siege works; *(mil)* defensive works, fortifications; **dulce opus peragere** to perform one's pleasant business *(i.e., sexual intercourse)*; **in opere** at work; **magno opere** greatly, to a great extent; **majore (summo) opere** to a greater (the greatest) extent; **opere** *(w. gen)* through the agency of; **quanto opere** how much, how greatly; **tanto opere** so much, so greatly; **operis alicujus esse** to be s.o.'s doing; **opus est** *(w. dat of person in need and abl of person or thing needed)* to need, *e.g.*,

opus est mihi duce I need a leader; **sui operis esse** to be part of one's business
opuscul·um -ī *n* little work, minor work
-or -ōris *m suf* forms nouns denoting **1** abstracts, *e.g.:* **candor** whiteness; **amor** love; **2** doer of the action of the verb, *e.g.,* **amator** lover
ōr·a -ae *f* boundary, border, edge; coastline, coast; region, district; cable, hawser; *(fig)* people of the coast, people of the region; division of the world; **ora maritima** seacoast ‖ *fpl* region, land; **orae extremae** the most distant lands, farthest shores; **orae luminis** *(or* **orae superae)** the upper world
ōrāc(u)l·um -ī *n* oracle; prophesy
ōrāri·us -a -um *adj* coasting; **navis oraria** coasting vessel, coaster
ōrāt·a -ōrum *npl* prayer, requests
ōrāti·ō -ōnis *f* faculty of speech; speech, language; style of speech, manner of speaking, style, expression; oration, speech; theme, subject; prose; eloquence; dialect; imperial rescript; **orationem habere** to give a speech; **oratio soluta** *(or* **oratio prorsa)** prose; **orationis pars** part of speech
ōrātiuncul·a -ae *f* short speech, insignificant speech
ōrāt·or -ōris *m* orator, speaker; suppliant; spokesman
ōrātōriē *adv* oratorically
ōrātōri·us -a -um *adj* orator's, oratorical
ōrātr·ix -īcis *f* suppliant *(female)*
ōrāt·us -ūs *m* request
orb·a -ae *f* orphan
orbāt·or -ōris *m* murderer *(of s.o.'s children or parents)*
Orbil·ius -(i)ī *m* Lucius Orbilius Pupillus *(Horace's teacher in Venusia)*
orb·is -is *m* circle; disk, ring; orbit *(of heavenly bodies);* quoit; hoop; wheel; spinning wheel; potter's wheel; round shield; eye socket, eye; globe, earth, world, universe; region, territory, country; circuit, round; rotation; cycle, period; zodiac; *(rhet)* balance; **magnus orbis** a year; **orbis caeli** vault of heaven; **Orbis Lacteus** Milky Way; **orbis luminis** eye; **orbis noster** our section of the world; **orbis oculi** eyeball; **orbis terrae** *(or* **terrarum)** earth, world, universe
orbit·a -ae *f* rut; *(astr)* orbit; *(fig)* routine
orbit·ās -ātis *f* childlessness, widowhood, orphanhood
orbitōs·us -a -um *adj* full of ruts
orb·ō -āre -āvī -ātus *tr* to bereave of parents, father, mother, children, husband, *or* wife; to strip, rob, deprive; to make destitute
orb·us -a -um *adj* bereaved, bereft; destitute; orphaned, fatherless; childless; widowed; *(w. gen or abl or* **ab)** bereft of, without ‖ *mf* orphan
orc·a -ae *f* vat
Orcad·es -um *fpl* islands N. of Scotland *(modern Orkneys)*
orch·as -adis *f* a kind of olive
orchestr·a -ae *f* senatorial seats *(in the theater);* orchestra *(area in front of the Greek stage where the chorus sang and danced)*
Orc·us -ī *m* lower world; Pluto *(king of the lower world);* death
orde- = horde-
ordināri·us -a -um *adj* ordinary, usual, regular; normally elected *(consul)*
ordinātim *adv* in order, in good order; in sucession; regularly
ordināti·ō -ōnis *f* orderly arrangement; orderly government
ordināt·us -a -um *adj* regular; appointed
ordin·ō -āre -āvī -ātus *tr* to set in order, arrange, regulate; to govern, rule; to record chronologically
ordior ordīrī orsus sum *tr* to begin, undertake; to describe ‖ *intr* to begin; to begin to speak
ord·ō -inis *m* line, row; series; row of seats *(in theater);* order, methodical arrangement; order, class; social standing, rank, position; *(mil)* line, file *(of soldiers),* company, century, command of a company *or* century; **amplissimus ordo** senatorial order; **ex ordine** in succession, without a break; **extra ordinem** extraordinarily, especially, uncommonly; **in ordine** *(mil)* in regular order, in battle array; **in ordinem cogere** *(or* **redigere)** to put *(s.o.)* in his place, tell *(s.o.)* off; **ordine** *(or* **in ordine** *or* **per ordinem)** in order, in sequence; in a straight line; in detail; with regularity, regularly ‖ *mpl* officers of a company; promotions
Orē·as -adis *or* **-ados** *f* Oread *(mountain nymph)*
Orest·ae -ārum *mpl* tribe on the borders of Macedonia and Epirus
Orest·ēs -is *or* **-ae** *m* son of Agamemnon and Clytemnestra
orex·is -is *f* craving, appetite
organic·us -ī *m* organist
organ·um -ī *n* instrument, implement; musical instrument; water organ; organ pipe; **organum hydraulicum** water organ
orgi·a -ōrum *npl* Bacchic revels; orgies
orichalc·um -ī *n* copper ore; brass
ōricill·a -ae *f* little ear; lobe
ori·ens -entis *m* rising sun, morning sun; morning; day; land of the rising sun, Orient, the East
orīg·ō -inis *f* origin, source, beginning, start; birth, lineage, descent; race, stock, family; founder, progenitor; derivation *(of a word)*

Ōrī·ōn -ōnis *or* **-ōnos** *m* giant hunter, killed by Diana and turned into a constellation; *(astr)* Orion

orior orīrī ortus sum *intr* to rise; to get up; to become visible, appear; to be born, originate, be descended; to proceed, begin, start; *(of a spring, river)* to rise; *(of living creatures)* to come into existence, be born; *(of plants)* to come up, sprout; *(of events)* to arise, crop up; **homo a se ortus** a self-made man

Ōrīthȳi·a -ae *f* daughter of Erechtheus, king of Athens

oriund·us -a -um *adj* descended; *(w. abl)* originating from, originally from *(a place)*

ornāment·um -ī *n* equipment, trappings, apparatus; ornament, decoration; trinket, jewel; *(fig)* distinction; pride and joy; *(rhet)* rhetorical device

ornātē *adv* ornately, elegantly

ornātr·ix -īcis *f* hairdresser *(female)*

ornāt·us -ūs *m* equipment; apparel, outfit; furniture; decoration, ornament; preparation; *(rhet)* rhetorical embellishment

orn·ō -āre -āvī -ātus *tr* to equip, fit out, furnish; to outfit, dress; to set off, decorate, adorn; to show *(s.o.)* respect; *(w. abl)* 1 to honor with; 2 *(of things)* to give distinction to, enhance

orn·us -ī *f (bot)* mountain ash

ōr·ō -āre -āvī -ātus *tr* to beg, entreat, implore, plead with; to ask for; *(w. double acc)* to ask *(s.o.)* for; *(leg)* to plead *(a case)* ‖ *intr* to plead, beg, pray; *(w.* **cum***)* to plead with, argue with

Orōd·ēs -is *m* name of several eastern kings, *esp.* Orodes II of Parthia, whose general defeated Crassus at Carrhae *(53 B.C.)*

Oront·ēs -is *or* **-ae** *m* chief river of Syria ‖ companion of Aeneas

Orontē·us -a -um *adj* from the River Orontes, Syrian

Orph·eūs -eī *or* **-eos** *m* famous musician and poet, husband of Eurydice

Orphē·us *or* **Orphic·us -a -um** *adj* Orphic

ors·us -a -um *pp of* **ordior** ‖ *npl* beginnings; utterance, words; attempt

ors·us -ūs *m* beginning; attempt, undertaking

orthographi·a -ae *f* spelling

ortus *pp of* **orior**

ort·us -ūs *m* rising; sunrise, daybreak; the East; birth *(of living creatures)*; origin; source; **solis ortus** sunrise; the East; beginning, dawning *(of a period)*

Ortygi·a -ae *or* **Ortygi·ē -ēs** *f* Ortygia *(old name of Delos)* ‖ Ortygia *(island in the port of Syracuse)* ‖ Ortygia *(old name of Ephesus)*

Ortygi·us -a -um *adj* of Ortygia, Delian; Syracusan

or·yx -ygis *m* gazelle

oryz·a -ae *f* rice

os ossis *n* bone; marrow, innermost parts; kernel *(of a nut)*; stone *(of fruit)* ‖ *npl* bones; skeleton; **ossa legere** to collect the bones *(from a pyre)*

ōs ōris *n* mouth; beak; voice, speech; expression; lip, face, countenance, look; sight, presence *(of a person)*; impudence; mask; opening, orifice, front; **favete ore!** observe a respectful silence!; **habere aliquid in ore** to be talking about s.th. continually; **in ora hominum venire** to become a household name; **in ore omnium esse** to be on the lips of all; **in os aliquem laudare** to praise s.o. to his face; **os amnis** mouth of a river; **os durum** hardened look *or* expression; **os laedere** *(w. dat)* to insult s.o. to his/her face; **os oblinere** *(w. dat)* to hoodwink *(s.o.)*; **os ostendere** to show one's face; **os timidum** expression of fear; **os venae** opening in a blood vessel; **per ora ferri** to go from mouth to mouth; **per** *(or* **praeter)** **ora nostra** before our eyes; **summo ore** just with the lips; **tria Dianae ora** the three forms of Diana; **uno ore** unanimously

osc·en -inis *mf* bird of augury *(e.g, crow, raven, owl)*

oscill·um -ī *n* small mask

oscit·ans -antis *adj* yawning; *(fig)* indifferent, bored

oscit·ō -āre -āvī -ātus *or* **oscit·or -ārī -ātus sum** *intr* to gape; to yawn

osculāti·ō -ōnis *f* kissing

oscul·or -ārī -ātus sum *tr* to kiss; *(fig)* to make a fuss over

oscul·um -ī *n* kiss; mouth, lips *(usually, puckered for a kiss)*; **breve osculum** peck

Osc·us -a -um *adj* Oscan ‖ *mpl* Oscans *(ancient people of Campania and Samnium)*

Osīr·is -is *or* **-idis** *m* Egyptian god, husband of Isis

ōs·or -ōris *m* hater

Oss·a -ae *f* mountain in N.E. Thessaly

osse·us -a -um *adj* bony

osten·dō -dĕre -dī -tus *or* **-sus** *tr* to hold out for inspection; to show, exhibit, display, expose; to stretch out, stretch forth; to bring to one's attention; to expose; to reveal, disclose; to declare, make known; to represent in art; **os ostendere** to show one's face ‖ *refl* to show oneself, appear; **se optime ostendere** to appear very friendly

ostentāti·ō -ōnis *f* display; ostentation, showing off; mere show, pretense

ostentāt·or -ōris *m* show-off

ostent·ō -āre -āvī -ātus *tr* to show, exhibit; to show off, display, parade, boast of; to declare, point out, set forth

ostent·um -ī *n* portent, prodigy
ostent·us -ūs *m* display, show; **ostentui** for appearances
Osti·a -ae *f or* **Osti·a -ōrum** *npl* Ostia *(port town at mouth of Tiber)*
ostiār·ium -(i)ī *n* tax on doors
ostiār·ius -(i)ī *m* doorman
ostiātim *adv* from door to door
ost·ium -(i)ī *n* door; entranceway; entrance, mouth
ostre·a -ae *f or* **ostre·um -ī** *n* oyster
ostreāt·us -a -um *adj* covered with oyster shells; *(fig)* black-and-blue
ostreōs·us -a -um *adj* abounding in oysters
ostri·fer -fera -ferum *adj* producing oysters, oyster-bearing
ostrīn·us -a -um *adj* purple
ostr·um -ī *n* purple dye; purple; purple garment, purple coverlet
ōsus *pp of* **odi**
-ōs·us -a -um *adjl suf (formed chiefly from nouns)* abounding in, rich in, full of: **ostreosus** abounding in oysters
Oth·ō -ōnis *m* Marcus Salvius Otho *(Roman emperor in A.D. 69)* ‖ Lucius Roscius Otho *(author of the law of 67 B.C. reserving 14 rows in theaters for the equestrian order)*
Othr·ys -yos *m* mountain range in S. Thessaly
ōtiol·um -ī *n* bit of leisure
ōti·or -ārī -ātus sum *intr* to take it easy
ōtiōsē *adv* at leisure; leisurely, without haste; calmly, fearlessly
ōtiōs·us -a -um *adj* at leisure, relaxing, having nothing to do; free from official obligations; quiet, calm; undisturbed; unconcerned, indifferent, neutral; passionless; having no practical use, useless; superfluous, unnecessary; leading a peaceful existence; *(of land)* unoccupied, vacant ‖ *m* private person *(not holding public office)*; civilian, non-combatant
ōt·ium -(i)ī *n* leisure, free time, relaxation; freedom from public affairs, retirement; peace, quiet; peaceful relations *(with another country)*; ease, idleness, inactivity; calm weather; respite, lull; **(in) otio** *(or* **per otium)** at leisure, undisturbed
ovāti·ō -ōnis *f* ovation, minor triumph *(in which the victor went on foot rather than driving a chariot)*
ovāt·us -a -um *adj* triumphal, of an ovation
Ovid·ius -(i)ī *m* Ovid *(Publius Ovidius Naso, Latin poet, born at Sulmo, 43 B.C.–A.D. 17)*
ovīl·e -is *n* sheepfold; voting enclosures in the Campus Martius
ovīlis -is -e *adj* sheep-, of sheep
ovill·us -a -um *adj* sheep-, of sheep ‖ *f* mutton, lamb
ov·is -is *f* sheep; wool; simpleton
ov·ō -āre -āvī -ātum *intr* to rejoice; to hold a celebration; to celebrate a minor triumph
ōv·um -ī *n* egg ‖ *npl* wooden balls used to mark the laps at the racetrack
oxycomin·a -ōrum *npl* pickled olives
oxygar·um -ī *n* fish sauce containing vinegar

P

P. *abbr* **Publius** *(Roman first name, praenomen)*
pābulāti·ō -ōnis *f* foraging
pābulāt·or -ōris *m* forager
pābul·or -ārī -ātus sum *intr* to forage; to feed, graze; *(coll)* to make a living
pābul·um -ī *n* feed, fodder; pasturage, grass; *(fig)* nourishment, fuel
pācāl·is -is -e *adj* of peace
pācāt·us -a -um *adj* peaceful, quiet, calm; *(of people)* living in peace; of peacetime; **pacatae ramus olivae** the olive branch, symbolic of peace; **vici male pacati** villages not completely pacified ‖ *n* peaceful countryside
Pachȳn·um -ī *n or* **Pachȳn·os -ī** *f* S.E. point of Sicily
pācif·er -era -erum *adj* peace-bringing, peaceful; *(of olive and laurel)* symbolizing peace
pācificāti·ō -ōnis *f* pacification
pācificāt·or -ōris *m* peacemaker
pācificātōri·us -a -um *adj* peace-making
pācific·ō -āre -āvī -ātus *tr* to pacify, appease ‖ *intr* to make peace, conclude peace
pācific·us -a -um *adj* peace-making; peaceable
pac·iscor -iscī -tus sum *tr* to bargain for, agree upon; to stipulate; to barter; to become engaged to ‖ *intr* to come to an agreement, strike a bargain, make a contract; *(w. inf)* to agree to, pledge oneself to
pāc·ō -āre -āvī -ātus *tr* to pacify, soothe; to reclaim *(land)*
pact·a -ae *f* fiancée; bride
pacti·ō -ōnis *f* pact, contract, agreement; treaty, terms; condition, stipulation; collusion; *(leg)* settlement *(in a dispute)*; **pactio nuptialis** marriage contract
Pactōl·us *or* **Pactōl·os -ī** *m* river in Lydia famous for its gold
pact·or -ōris *m* contractor, party *(in a contract)*; negotiator
pact·us -a -um *pp of* **paciscor** *and* **pango** ‖ *n* pact, contract, agreement; way, man-

ner; **aliquo pacto** somehow; **hoc pacto** in this way; **in pacto manere** to stick to an agreement; **quo pacto** how, in what way

Pācuv·ius -(i)ī *m* Marcus Pacuvius *(c. 220–133 B.C., Roman tragic poet, native of Brundisium and nephew of Ennius)*

Pad·us -ī *m* Po River *(in N. Italy)*

Padūs·a -ae *f* one of the mouths of the Po River

pae·ān -ānis *m* hymn to Apollo; paean, hymn of praise, victory song ‖ **Paean** epithet of Apollo as god of healing

paedagōg·ium -iī *n* **(pēd-)** training school for pages

paedagōg·us -ī *m* **(pēd-)** slave in charge of school children; *(fig)* guide, leader

paedīc·ō -ōnis *m* **(pēd-)** homosexual, pederast

paedīc·ō -āre -āvī -ātus *tr* **(pēd-)** to have homosexual relations with *(boys)*

paed·or -ōris *m* **(ped-)** filth

pael·ex -icis *f* **(pēl-, pell-)** concubine, mistress

paelicāt·us -ūs *m* **(pēl-)** concubinage

Paelign·ī -ōrum *mpl* **(Pēl-)** a people of central Italy

paene *adv* nearly, almost

paeninsul·a -ae *f* peninsula

paenitend·us -a -um *adj* regrettable

paenitenti·a -ae *f* **(poen-)** repentance, regret

paenit·eō -ēre -uī paenitūrus *tr* **(poen-)** to cause to regret; to displease ‖ *intr (w. gen)* to regret ‖ *v impers (w. acc of person), e.g.,* **me paenitet** I am sorry; *(w. acc of person and gen of thing), e.g.,* **me paenitet consili** I regret the plan, I am dissatisfied with the plan; *(w. acc of person and inf or* **quod**), *e.g.,* **eos paenitet animum tuum offendisse** *(or* **eos paenitet quod animum tuum offenderint**) they regret having offended your feelings

paenul·a -ae *f* travel coat; raincoat

paenulāt·us -a -um *adj* wearing a traveling coat *or* raincoat

pae·ōn -ōnis *m (pros)* metrical foot containing one long and three short syllables *(first paeonic: — ∪ ∪ ∪; second paeonic: ∪ — ∪ ∪; third paeonic: ∪ ∪ — ∪; fourth paeonic: ∪ ∪ ∪ —)*

Paeon·es -um *mpl* a people inhabiting Paeonia

Paeoni·a -ae *f* Paeonia *(the country N. of Macedonia)*

paeōni·us -a -um *adj* healing, medicinal; **herba paeonia** peony

Paestān·us -a -um *adj* of Paestum

Paest·um -ī *n* town in Lucania in S. Italy, famous for its roses

paetul·us -a -um *adj* slightly squint-eyed

paet·us -a -um *adj* squinting, squint-eyed; leering ‖ **Paetus** *m* Roman family name *(cognomen)*

pāgān·us -a -um *adj* of a village, rustic; ignorant ‖ *m* villager, peasant; *(pej)* yokel

Pagas·a -ae *f or* **Pagas·ae -ārum** *fpl* town on the E. coast of Thessaly from which the Argo set sail

Pagasae·us -a -um *adj* Pagasean ‖ *m* Jason

pāgātim *adv* by villages, village by village, in every village

pāgell·a -ae *f* small page *or* sheet

pāgin·a -ae *f* page; *(poet)* piece of writing; **in imā paginā** at the bottom of the page

pāginul·a -ae *f* small page *or* sheet

pāg·us -ī *m* village; canton, province; country people, villagers

pāl·a -ae *f* spade

palaestr·a -ae *f* palestra, wrestling school, gymnasium; school of rhetoric; rhetorical training; school; wrestling; exercise; brothel

palaestricē *adv* as at the palestra

palaestric·us -a -um *adj* of the palestra, gymnastic ‖ *f* gymnastics

palaestrīt·a -ae *m* wrestling coach; director of a palestra

palam *adv* openly, publicly, plainly; **palam esse** to be public, be well known; **palam facere** to make public, disclose ‖ *prep (w. abl)* before, in the presence of, face to face with

Palātīn·us -a -um *adj* Palatine; imperial

Palāt·ium -(i)ī *n* Palatine Hill; palace; a temple on the Palatine

palāt·um -ī *n or* **palāt·us -ī** *m (anat)* palate; *(fig)* taste; *(fig)* literary taste

pale·a -ae *f* chaff

paleār·ia -ium *npl* dewlap *(fold of skin that hangs from the neck of a bovine animal)*

Pal·ēs -is *f* Italic goddess of shepherds and flocks

Palīc·ī -ōrum *mpl* twins sons of Jupiter and the nymph Thalia

Palīl·is -is -e *adj* of Pales ‖ *npl* feast of Pales *(celebrated April 21)*

palimpsest·um -ī *n* palimpsest *(parchment from which writing has been erased and new writing put on)*

Palinūr·us -ī *m* pilot of Aeneas who fell overboard and drowned ‖ promontory named after Palinurus

paliūr·us *or* **paliūr·os -ī** *mf (bot)* Christ's thorn

pall·a -ae *f* ladies' long outdoor dress *(counterpart of the male's toga);* male outer garment *(restricted to non-Romans);* tragic actor's costume

pallac·a -ae *f* concubine

Pallacīn·a -ae *f* section of Rome near the Circus Flaminius

Palladi·us -a -um *adj* of Pallas, associated with Pallas Athene *(Minerva)* ‖ *n* statue of Pallas; Palladium *(Trojan statue of Pallas allegedly stolen by Odysseus and said subsequently to have been brought to Rome, since the safety of the city depended on it)*

Pallantē·um -ī *n* city in Arcadia, the home of Pallas ‖ city founded by Evander in Italy where Rome later stood

Pallantē·us -a -um *adj* of Pallas *(great-grandfather of Evander)*

Pall·ās -antis *m* great-grandfather of Evander ‖ son of Evander ‖ son of Pandion and brother of Aegeus ‖ father of Minerva

Pall·as -adis *or* **-ados** *f* Athene; olive oil, oil; olive tree; Palladium *(Trojan statue of Pallas)*

pall·ens -entis *adj* pale; chartreuse, yellowish; sick-looking; dim *(light)*

pall·eō -ēre -uī *intr* to be pale, look pale; to have a pale *(greenish or yellowish)* color; to fade; to be dim; *(w. dat)* to grow pale over, worry about

pall·escō -escĕre -uī *tr* to turn pale at ‖ *intr* to turn pale; to turn yellow; to fade, grow dim

palliāt·us -a -um *adj* wearing a Greek cloak; **fabula palliata** Latin play with Greek setting and characters

pallidul·us -a -um *adj* somewhat pale

pallid·us -a -um *adj* pallid, pale; gray-green, yellow-green, chartreuse

palliolātim *adv* in a mantle

palliolāt·us -a -um *adj* wearing a pallium

palliol·um -ī *n* short cloak; hood

pall·ium -(i)ī *n* pallium *(rectangular material worn mainly by men, esp. Greek men, as an outer garment);* bed cover, couch cover

pall·or -ōris *m* pallor, pale complexion; **pallorem ducere** to turn pale

pallul·a -ae *f* small outer garment *(see* **palla)**

palm·a -ae *f* palm of the hand, hand; palm tree, date; palm branch; palm wreath; palm of victory, first prize; victory; victor *(carrying a palm);* oar, oar blade

palmār·is -is -e *adj* excellent, deserving of the palm *or* prize ‖ *n* masterpiece

palmāri·us -a -um *adj* prize-winning, excellent ‖ *n* masterpiece

palmāt·us -a -um *adj* embroidered with palm-branch design; **tunica palmata** embroidered tunic *(with palm-branch design, worn by a general)*

palm·es -itis *m* vine shoot, vine branch, vine; branch, twig *(of any tree)*

palmēt·um -ī *n* palm grove

palmi·fer -fera -ferum *adj* producing palms, palm-bearing

palmōs·us -a -um *adj* full of palm trees

palmul·a -ae *f* oar blade; date *(fruit of the palm tree)*

pāl·or -ārī -ātus sum *intr* to roam about, wander aimlessly

palpāti·ō -ōnis *f* stroking ‖ *fpl* flatteries

palpāt·or -ōris *m* flatterer

palpebr·a -ae *f* eyelid

palpit·ō -āre -āvī *intr* to throb, palpitate, quiver

palp·ō -āre -āvī -ātus *or* **palp·or -ārī -ātus sum** *tr* to stroke, pat; to wheedle, coax; to flatter ‖ *intr (w. dat)* **1** to coax; **2** to flatter

palp·us -ī *m* palm of the hand; coaxing, flattery

palūdāment·um -ī *n* general's cloak

palūdāt·us -a -um *adj* wearing a general's cloak

palūdōs·us -a -um *adj* swampy

palumb·ēs -is *mf* pigeon, dove

pāl·ŭs -ī *m* stake, post; wooden sword *(used in practice)*

pal·ūs -ūdis *f* swamp, marsh; sedge

palus·ter *(or* **-tris) -tris -tre** *adj* swampy, marshy; growing in a swamp; used, *or* located in a swamp ‖ *npl* swamp, marshland

pampine·us -a -um *adj* of vine tendrils, made of vine leaves; **odor pampineus** bouquet of wines

pampin·us -ī *m (f)* vine shoot, tendril; vine leaf; tendril *(of any kind)*

Pā·n -nos *m* Pan *(Greek god of flocks, shepherds, and woods, often identified with Faunus)*

panacē·a -ae *f or* **panac·ēs -is** *mf or* **panac·ēs -is** *n* panacea, cure-all

Panaetōlic·us -a -um *adj* Pan-Aetolian

pānār·ium -(i)ī *n* breadbox; breadbasket; food basket; picnic basket

Panchāī·a -ae *f* region in Arabia famous for its frankincense

panchrest·os -os -on *adj* good for everything, universally useful; **panchreston medicamentum** *(hum)* bribery *(the cure-all medication)*

pancraticē *adv (coll)* fine, splendidly; **pancratice valere** to get along splendidly

pancrat·ium *or* **pancrat·ion -iī** *n* contest which included the skills of boxing and wrestling

Pandar·us -ī *m* famous Lycian archer in the Trojan army ‖ companion of Aeneas, killed by Turnus

pandicul·or -ārī -ātus sum *intr (of a person while yawning)* to stretch

Pandī·ōn -onis *or* **-onos** *m* king of Athens and father of Procne and Philomela

Pandīoni·us -a -um *adj* of Pandion

pan·dō -dĕre -dī -sus *or* **passus** *tr* to spread out, extend, expand, unfold; to open, lay open, throw open; to open up *(a road);* to

make *(a place)* accessible, open *(a building);* to reveal, make known, publish; *(mil)* to deploy
pand·us -a -um *adj* curved
pangō pangĕre panxī *or* **pepegī** *or* **pēgī pactus** *tr* to fasten, fix, drive in; to fix, set *(boundaries);* to settle *(a matter);* to agree upon, determine; to write, compose, celebrate, record; to promise in marriage; to provide; **indutias pangere cum** to conclude an armistice with
pānice·us -a -um *adj* made of bread; **milites panicei** *(coll)* Breadville brigade *(humorous coinage applied to bakers)*
pānicul·a -ae *f* tuft
pānic·um -ī *n* Italian millet *(cereal grass, raised for its seed or small grains to be used as food)*
pān·is -is *m* bread; loaf of bread; **panem coquere** to bake bread; **panis cibarius** coarse bread; **panis secundus** stale bread
Pānisc·us -ī *m* little Pan
pannicul·us -ī *m* rag
pannōs·us -a -um *adj* tattered, threadbare; dressed in rags
Pannoni·us -a -um *adj* Pannonian ‖ *f* Pannonia *(country of Lower Danube in the area of modern Austria)*
pannūce·us *or* **pannūci·us -a -um** *adj* ragged; shriveled, wrinkled
pann·us -ī *m* patch; rag
Panop·ē -ēs *or* **Panopē·a -ae** *f* a sea nymph
pans·a -ae *adj (masc & fem only)* flat-footed ‖ **Pansa** *m* Roman family name *(cognomen), esp.* Gaius Vibius Pansa *(cos. 43 B.C.)*
pansus *pp of* **pando**
panthēr·a -ae *f* panther
Panthoid·ēs -ae *m* son of Panthus, *(i.e., Euphorbus, a Trojan warrior)*
Panth·us -ī *m* priest of Apollo at Troy and father of Euphorbus
pantic·ēs -um *mpl* guts; sausages
papae *interj (in delight)* great!, wonderful!; *(in pain)* ouch!; *(in astonishment)* wow!
pāp·as -ae *or* **-atis** *m* papa *(baby-talk for pedagogue)*
papāv·er -eris *n (m)* poppy; poppyseed
papāvere·us -a -um *adj* of poppies
Paphi·ē -ēs *f* Paphian goddess, Venus; *(poet)* heterosexual love
Paphi·us -a -um *adj* of Paphos
Paph·os -ī *f* town in S.W. Cyprus sacred to Venus ‖ *mf* child of Pygmalion
pāpili·ō -ōnis *m* butterfly; moth
papill·a -ae *f* nipple, teat; breast
papp·ō -āre *tr* to eat *(soft food)*
papp·us -ī *m* hairy seed *(of certain plants)*
papul·a -ae *f* pimple
papȳrif·er -era -erum *adj* papyrus-producing
papȳr·us -ī *f or* **papȳr·um -ī** *n* papyrus
pār paris *adj* equal, like, on a par, equally matched, well-matched; suitable, adequate; of equal size; *(w. dat or* **cum)** equal to, comparable to, similar to, as large as; *(w. limiting abl, w.* **ad** *or* **in** + *acc)* equal, similar, alike in; **par est** it is right, it is proper; **par proelium** even *or* indecisive battle; **ut par est** *(used parenthetically)* as is only right ‖ *m* companion; equal, mate, spouse; **pares cum paribus facillime congregantur** *(prov)* birds of a feather flock together ‖ *n* pair, couple, the like; **par pari** tit for tat
parābil·is -is -e *adj* available
parasīt·a -ae *f* parasite *(female)*
parasītas·ter -trī *m* poor parasite
parasītāti·ō -ōnis *f* sponging
parasītic·us -a -um *adj* parasitical
parasīt·or -ārī -ātus sum *intr* to be a parasite, sponge, freeload
parasīt·us -ī *m* parasite, sponger, freeloader
parātē *adv* with perparation; carefully; readily, promptly
parāti·ō -ōnis *f* preparing, procuring, acquisition
paratragoed·ō -āre *intr* to talk in the tragic style, be melodramatic, ham it up
parāt·us -a -um *adj* prepared, ready; ready at hand, available; furnished, equipped; learned, well-versed, skilled; *(w. dat or* **ad) 1** ready for; **2** equipped to; *(w. inf)* prepared to, ready to; *(w. abl or* **in** + *abl)* versed in, experienced in
parāt·us -ūs *m* preparation; equipment, outfit; clothing, apparel; *(food at dinner table)* spread
Parc·a -ae *f* goddess of Fate, Fate
parcē *adv* sparingly, thriftily; moderately, with restraint; stingily; rarely
parcēprōm·us -ī *m* stingy person
parcō parcĕre pepercī parsūrus *tr* to spare, use sparingly ‖ *intr* to be sparing, economize; *(w. dat)* **1** to spare, use carefully; **2** to show mercy to, take it easy on; **3** to show consideration for; **4** to abstain from, refrain from; *(w. inf)* to cease to
parc·us -a -um *adj* thrifty, economical, frugal; stingy; moderate, conservative; slight, little, scanty, paltry *(thing given)*
pard·us -ī *m* leopard
pār·ens -entis *adj* obedient, submissive ‖ *mpl* subjects
par·ens -entis *m* parent, father; ancestor, grandparent; founder; inventor; **parens patriae** father of one's country ‖ *mpl* ancestors ‖ *f* parent, mother; mother country; mother city
parentāl·is -is -e *adj* parental; **dies parentalis** memorial day ‖ *npl* festival in honor of dead ancestors and relatives
parent·ō -āre -āvī -ātum *intr* to hold a memorial service in honor of dead par-

ents *or* relatives; *(w. dat)* **1** to offer sacrifice to *(the dead);* **2** to avenge *(dead person with the death of another person);* **3** to appease, satisfy

pār·eō -ēre -uī -itum *intr* to appear, be visible, be evident, be at hand; *(w. dat)* **1** to obey, be obedient to; **2** to comply with; **3** to be subject to, be subservient to; **4** to yield to, gratify, satisfy *(pleasures, etc.);* **5** to fulfill *(promises)*

pari·ēs -etis *m* wall *(inner or outer wall of house or other building);* **intra parietes** in private, at home, under one's own roof

parietin·ae -ārum *fpl* tumble-down walls; *(lit & fig)* ruins

Parīl·ia -ium *npl* **(Palīl-)** festival of Pales *(April 21)*

Parīl·is -is -e *adj* **(Palīl-)** connected with Pales *or* her festival

paril·is -is -e *adj* equal, like; **aetas parilis** same age, like age

pariō parĕre peperī partus *tr* to bear, bring forth, give birth to; *(of animals)* to produce, spawn, lay *(eggs); (of countries, of the earth)* to produce, be a source of; *(of things)* to give rise to; *(fig)* to create, devise, cause, accomplish; to acquire

Par·is -idis *m* son of Priam and Hecuba ‖ pantomime actor in the reign of Nero ‖ pantomime actor in the reign of Domitian

pariter *adv* equally, in like manner, as well, alike; at the same time, at one and the same time, together; side by side; evenly, uniformly; in equal quantity *or* degree; at once; **pariter ac** *(or* **atque** *or* **ut)** as well as; **pariter ac si** just as if; **pariter cum** together with, at the same time as

parit·ō -āre *tr (w. inf)* to get ready to

Par·ium *or* **Par·ion -iī** *n* town of the Troad near the entrance to the Propontis *(modern Kemer)*

Pari·us -a -um *adj* Parian, of Paros

parm·a -ae *f* small round shield

parmāt·us -a -um *adj* armed with a small, round shield, light-armed

parmul·a -ae *f* small round shield

Parnās·is -idis *or* **Parnāsi·us -a -um** *adj* of Parnassus, Parnassian

Parnās·us *or* **Parnās·os -ī** *m* mountain forming the backdrop to Apollo's shrine at Delphi

par·ō -āre -āvī -ātus *tr* to prepare, make ready, provide, furnish; to get, procure, acquire, gather, purchase ‖ *refl* to get ready ‖ *intr* to get ready, make preparations, make arrangements; *(w. dat or* **ad)** to get ready for

paroch·a -ae *f* room and board *(which provincials had to provide for traveling Roman officials)*

paroch·us -ī *m* official host *(provided accommodations for traveling Roman dignitaries)*

parops·is -idis *f* dish for serving dessert

Par·os *or* **Par·us -ī** *f* Greek island of the Cyclades, famous for its white marble

parr·a -ae *f* owl

Parrhas·is -idis *or* **-idos** *f* Arcadian woman; Callisto *(as Ursa Major)*

Parrhasi·us -a -um *adj* Arcadian; **Parrhasia virgo** Callisto *(as Ursa Major)* ‖ *f* district in Arcadia

parricīd·a -ae *mf* parricide *(murderer of one's parent or close relative);* assassin of a high magistrate; murderer; traitor, outlaw

parricīd·ium -(i)ī *n* parricide *(murder of a parent or close relative);* murder; assassination; high treason

par·s -tis *f* part, portion, share, section; fraction; side, direction, region; part, function, duty; part of body, member *(esp. genital organs);* **ab omni parte** in every respect; **a parte** partly; **exiguā parte** in a slight degree; **ex alterā parte** on the other hand; **ex parte** partly; **ex eā parte** *(or* **in eam partem) quatenus** to the extent that; **in eam partem** in that direction; in that sense; **in parte** *(of* **in partem)** partly, in part; in such a manner; **in parte alicujus rei esse** to form part of s.th., be included in s.th.; **in pejorem partem rapere** to put a worse construction on; **in utramque partem** in both directions; **magnā ex parte** to a great degree; **major pars populi** the majority; **maximam partem** for the most part; **minor pars populi** a minority; **pars dimidia (tertia, quarta,** *etc.)* one half (one-third, one-fourth, *etc.);* **pars...pars, pars...alii** some...others; **pars orationis** *(gram)* part of speech; **parte** in part, partly; **pro meā parte** to the best of my ability; **pro ratā parte** in a fixed proportion; **pro parte** in part, partially; **pro parte semissā** half and half; **pro suā parte** *(or* **pro virili parte)** to the best of one's ability ‖ *fpl* part, role; task, function; character; political party; pieces, fragments; scraps *(esp. of food);* **omnibus partibus** in all respects; **partes obscenae** privates, private parts; **per partes** *(or* **partibus)** (so much) at a time, in stages; **tres partes** three-fourths; **tuae partes sunt** the task *(or* decision) devolves on you

parsimōni·a -ae *f* parsimony, thrift

Parthā·ōn -onis *m* king of Calydon, the son of Agenor and Epicaste and father of Oeneus

Parthāoni·us -a -um *adj* of Parthaon; Calydonian

parthenic·ē -ēs *f (bot)* chamomile *(plant*

with white flowers, used medicinally and as tea)

Parthenopae·us -ī *m* one of the Seven against Thebes, the son of Meleager and Atalanta

Parthenop·ē -ēs *f* ancient name of Naples *(named after the Siren Parthenope who was supposedly buried there)*

Parthi·a -ae *f* Parthia *(country located S.E. of the Caspian Sea)*

Parthic·us -a -um *adj* Parthian; honorary title of several Roman Emperors

Parth·us -a -um *adj & m* Parthian

partic·eps -ipis *adj (w. gen)* sharing in, taking part in **II** *m* partner, confederate; *(w. gen)* partner in

particip·ō -āre -āvī -ātus *tr* to make *(s.o.)* a partner; to share *(s.th.)*

particul·a -ae *f* bit, particle, grain

partim *adv* partly, in part, to some extent; for the most part; *(w. gen or* **ex**) some of; **partim…partim** some…others, partly…partly

parti·ō -ōnis *f* bringing forth, producing

part·iō -īre -īvī -ītus *or* **part·ior -īrī -ītus sum** *tr* to share; to distribute, apportion, divide

partītē *adv* with proper divisions

partīti·ō -ōnis *f* division, distribution, sharing; classification; *(rhet)* division of a speech

partitūd·ō -inis *f* bearing *(of young)*

partur·iō -īre -īvī *tr* to teem with; to be ready to produce; to bring forth, yield; *(fig)* to brood over **II** *intr* to be in labor

part·us -a -um *pp of* **pario II** *adj* acquired **II** *n* acquisition; gain; store

part·us -ūs *m* giving birth; birth; young, offspring; embryo; *(fig)* beginnings

parum *adv & indecl n* a little, too little, insufficiently; **parum est** it is not enough; **parum habere** to regard as unsatisfactory; **satis eloquentiae sapientiae parum** enough eloquence but too little wisdom

parumper *adv* for a little while, just for a moment

parvit·ās -ātis *f* smallness

parvul·us -a -um *adj* (**-vol-**) tiny; slight, petty; young **II** *n* childhood, infancy; **ab parvulis** from childhood, from infancy

parv·us -a -um *(comp:* **minor;** *superl:* **minimus)** *adj* small, little, puny; short; young; brief, short *(time);* slight; insignificant, unimportant; low, cheap *(price)* **II** *n* a little, trifle; childhood, infancy; **a parvis** *(or* **a parvo)** from childhood, from infancy; **parvi esse** to be of little importance; **parvi facere** *(or* **aestimare** *or* **habere** *or* **ducere)** to think little of, care little for; **parvi pretii** of little worth; **parvi refert** it makes little difference, it matters little; **parvo** at a low price; **parvo animo esse** to be small-minded

pasceol·us -ī *m* moneybag

pascō pascĕre pāvī pastus *tr* to feed; to be food for; to pasture, keep, raise *(animals); (of land)* to provide food for; to cultivate, cherish; to feed *(fire; flames of passion);* to pile up *(debts);* to grow *(beard);* to lay waste, ravage *(fields);* to use *(land)* as pasturage; to feast *(the eyes, the mind)* **II** *refl & pass* to support oneself; *(w. abl)* to get rich on, grow fat on **II** *pass (of animals)* to graze; to feed; *(w. abl)* **1** to feast on, thrive on; **2** to gloat over **II** *intr* to feed, graze

pascu·us -a -um *adj* grazing, pasture **II** *n* pasture

Pāsipha·ē -ēs *or* **Pāsipha·a -ae** *f* Pasiphaë *(daughter of Helios, sister of Circe, wife of Minos, and mother of Phaedra, Ariadne, and the Minotaur)*

pass·er -eris *m* sparrow; flounder; **passer marinus** ostrich *(because imported from overseas)*

passercul·us -ī *m* little sparrow

passim *adj* here and there; all over the place; at random, without order, indiscriminately

passit·ō -āre *intr (of a starling)* to sing

passīv·us -a -um *adj (gram)* passive

passus *pp of* **pando** *and of* **patior II** *adj* spread out, extended, open; disheveled; *(of grapes and other fruits spread out in the sun)* dried, dry **II** *f* raisin **II** *n* raisin wine

pass·us -ūs *m* step, pace; footstep, track; **mille passūs** thousand paces, a mile; **tria milia passuum** three miles

pastill·us -ī *m* lozenge

pasti·ō -ōnis *f* pasture, grazing

past·or -ōris *m* shepherd

pastōrāl·is -is -e *adj* pastoral

pastōrici·us -a -um *or* **pastōri·us -a -um** *adj* shepherd's, pastoral

pastus *pp of* **pasco**

past·us -ūs *m* the feeding of animals; pasture; fodder, feed

patagiār·ius -(i)ī *m* fringe maker

patagiāt·us -a -um *adj (tunic)* with fringes

Patar·a -ae *f or* **Patar·a -ōrum** *npl* town in Lycia with an oracle of Apollo

Patar·eūs -eī *or* **-eos** *m* Apollo

Patavīn·us -a -um *adj* of Patavium

Patav·ium -(i)ī *n* city in N. Italy, birthplace of Livy *(modern Padua)*

pate·faciō -facĕre -fēcī -factus *(pass:* **pate·fīō -fierī)** *tr* to uncover, reveal; to open *(gates, windows, buildings, containers, etc.);* to throw open; to open up, make accessible; to bring to light; to disclose; *(mil)* to deploy; *(mil) (w. dat)* to expose to *(attack)*

patefacti·ō -ōnis *f* disclosure

patell·a -ae *f* pan, dish, plate
pat·ens -entis *adj* open, accessible; extensive; exposed; evident
patentius *adv* more openly; more clearly
pat·eō -ēre -uī *intr* to stand open, be open; to be accessible; to be exposed; to open, stretch out, extend; to be clear, be plain, be well-known; to be attainable, be free; *(of the mind)* to be open, be receptive; *(of wounds)* to gape; **late patere** to have wide application, cover a wide field
pa·ter -tris *m* father; **pater cenae** host; **pater familias** head of the family; **quartus pater** great-great-grandfather ‖ *mpl* forefathers; patricians; senators; **patres conscripti** gentlemen of the Senate
pater·a -ae *f* flat dish, saucer *(used esp. in making libations)*
paterfamiliās patrisfamiliās *m* head of the family
patern·us -a -um *adj* father's, paternal, fatherly; ancestral; of a native country, native
pat·escō -escĕre -uī *intr* to be opened, be open; to stretch out, extend; to be disclosed, be divulged, become evident; *(mil)* to be deployed
pathic·us -a -um *adj* lustful
patibil·is -is -e *adj* tolerable; sensitive
patibulāt·us -a -um *adj* fastened to a yoke *or* gibbet, pilloried
patibul·um -ī *n* pillory *(fork-shaped yoke to which criminals were fastened)*; fork-shaped gibbet
pati·ens -entis *adj* hardy, tough; hard; stubborn, unyielding; patient, tolerant; *(w. gen or* **ad**) able to endure, inured to, able to take; **amnis patiens navium** navigable river
patienter *adv* patiently
patienti·a -ae *f* patience, endurance; resignation; submissiveness; sexual submission
patin·a -ae *f* dish, pan
patinārī·us -a -um *adj* of pans; in a pan; **strues patinaria** pile of dishes
patior patī passus sum *tr* to experience, undergo, suffer; to put up with, allow; to submit to *(sexually)*; **aegre pati** to resent, be displeased with
patrāt·or -ōris *m* perpetrator
patrāt·us -ī *adj (masc only)* **pater patratus** plenipotentiary senator *(sent on a foreign mission)*
patri·a -ae *f* native land, native city, home
patricē *adv* like a patrician
patriciāt·us -ūs *m* status of patrician
patrici·us -a -um *adj & m* patrician
patrimōn·ium -(i)ī *n* patrimony, inheritance
patrim·us -a -um *adj* having a father still living
patriss·ō -āre *intr* to take after one's father
patrīt·us -a -um *adj* father's, inherited from one's father
patri·us -a -um *adj* father's, of a father, fatherly; ancestral; traditional, hereditary; native ‖ *f see* **patria**
patrō -āre *tr* to bring about, effect, achieve, perform; to finish, conclude; **bellum patrare** to bring a war to an end; **jus jurandum patrare** to take an oath *(confirming a treaty)*; **pacem patrare** to conclude a peace; **promissa patrare** to fulfill promises ‖ *intr* to reach a sexual climax
patrōcin·ium -(i)ī *n* patronage, protection; legal defense, legal representation
patrōncin·or -ārī -ātus sum *intr* to be a patron, afford protection; *(w. dat)* to serve *(s.o.)* as patron, protect, defend
Patrŏcl·us -ī *m* son of Menoetius and friend of Achilles
patrōn·a -ae *f* legal protectress, patroness; defender; safeguard
patrōn·us -ī *m* legal protector, patron; advocate *(in court)*; defender
patruēl·is -is -e *adj* on the father's side, cousin's; **frater patruelis** cousin; **soror patruelis** cousin *(female)* ‖ *m* cousin
patru·us -a -um *adj* of a *(paternal)* uncle ‖ *m* father's brother, paternal uncle; **patruus magnus** great-uncle, granduncle
patul·us -a -um *adj* open, standing open; spreading, spread out, broad
pauciloqu·ium -(i)ī *n* reticence
paucit·ās -ātis *f* paucity, scarcity, small number
paucul·ī -ae -a *adj* just a few, very few ‖ *npl* few words
pauc·i -ae -a *adj* few ‖ *pron masc pl* few, a few; the select, elite; **inter paucos** *(or* **in paucas** *or* **in pauca** *or* **in paucis**) *(in connection with an adj)* among a few, especially, unusually, uncommonly ‖ *pron neut pl* a few things, a few words; **paucis** in a few words, briefly
paul(l)ātim *adv* little by little, gradually, by degrees; a few at a time
paul(l)isper *adv* for a little while
paul(l)ō *adv (as abl. of degree of difference in comparisons)* a little, somewhat; **paulo ante** a little earlier; **paulo post** a little later
paul(l)ulō *adv* somewhat, a little; cheaply, at a low price
paul(l)ulum *adv* somewhat, a little
paul(l)ul·us -a -um *adj* very little ‖ *n* very little, a bit; **paullulum pecuniae** a bit of money, very little money
paul(l)um *adv* a little, to some extent
paul(l)·us -a -um *adj* small, little ‖ *n* a bit, trifle; **post paulum** after a bit

Paul(l)·us -ī *m* Lucius Aemilius Paulus Macedonicus *(conqueror of Macedonia at Pydna in 168 B.C.)*
paup·er -eris *adj* poor *(financially);* scanty, meager; *(w. gen)* poor in ‖ *mf* pauper
paupercul·us -a -um *adj* poor little
pauperi·ēs -ēī *f* poverty
pauper·ō -āre -āvī -ātus *tr* to impoverish; *(w. abl)* to rob *(s.o.)* of
paupert·ās -ātis *f* poverty
paus(s)·a -ae *f* pause, intermission, stop, end; **pausam dare** *(or* **facere)** to make a pause, take a break; **pausam facere** *(w. dat)* put an end to
pauxillātim *adv* little by little
pauxillisper *adv* bit by bit
pauxillulum *adv* a little, a bit ‖ *n (w. gen)* a bit of
pauxillul·us -a -um *adj* tiny
pauxill·us -a -um *adj* very little, tiny ‖ *n* small amount
pavefact·us -a -um *adj* frightened
paveō pavēre pāvī *tr* to be scared of, be terrified at ‖ *intr* to be terrified, tremble with fear
pavesc·ō -ĕre *tr* to get scared of ‖ *intr* to begin to be alarmed
pāvī *perf of* **pasco** *and of* **paveo**
pavidē *adv* in panic
pavid·us -a -um panicky, alarmed, trembling with fear, startled; with beating heart, nervous; causing alarm
pavīment·ō -āre *tr* to pave
pavīment·um -ī *n* pavement; floor
pav·iō -īre -īvī *or* **-iī -ītus** *tr* to strike, beat
pavit·ō -āre *tr* to be panicky over ‖ *intr* to quake with fear, be scared to death; to shiver *(w. fever)*
pāv·ō -ōnis *or* **pāv·us -ī** *m* peacock
pav·or -ōris *m* panic, terror, dread; dismay; quaking, shivering; **pavorem injicere** *(w. dat)* to strike terror into
pax pācis *f* peace; peace treaty; reconciliation; compact, agreement; harmony, tranquility; favor, pardon *(from the gods);* **cum bona pace** with full consent; **pace tuā** with your leave, with your permission
pax *interj* quiet, enough!
pecc·ans -antis *m* offender, sinner
peccāt·um -ī *n* fault, mistake, slip; moral offense, sin
pecc·ō -āre -āvī -ātum *intr* to make a mistake, blunder; to make a slip in speaking; to be wrong; to sin
pecorōs·us -a -um *adj* rich in cattle
pect·en -inis *m* comb; plectrum; rake; pubic bone; pubic region; scallop *(as seafood)*
pectō pectĕre pex(u)ī pexus *or* **pexitus** *tr* to comb; to card *(wool); (hum)* to thrash
pect·us -oris *n* breast, chest; heart, feeling; soul, conscience; mind, understanding; person, character; **toto pectore** heart and soul
pecū *(gen not in use; pl:* **pecua)** *n* flock, herd ‖ *npl* farm animals; cattle; pastures
pecuāri·us -a -um *adj* **(pequ-)** of sheep, of cattle; **res pecuaria** livestock ‖ *m* cattleman, cattle breeder, rancher ‖ *f* livestock ‖ *npl* herds of cattle, herds of sheep
pecūlāt·or -ōris *m* embezzler
pecūlāt·us -ūs *m* **(peq-)** embezzlement
pecūliār·is -is -e one's own, as one's own private property; special; exceptional, singular
pecūliāriter *adv* specially
pecūliāt·us -a -um *adj* well off
pecūli·ō -āre -āvī -ātus *tr* to provide with personal property
pecūl·ium -(i)ī *n* personal property *or* savings *(of a slave or a son under his father's control)*
pecūni·a -ae *f* money; property, possessions
pecūniāri·us -a -um *adj* pecuniary, financial, money
pecūniōs·us -a -um *adj* rich, well-off; profitable
pec·us -oris *n* cattle, herd, flock; sheep; head of cattle; livestock; **pecus equinum** stud; *(pej)* cattle
pec·us -udis *f* head of cattle; beast; sheep; domestic animal; land animal *(as opposed to birds and fish); (pej)* brute, beast, swine
pedāl·is -is -e *adj* one-foot-long
pedār·ius -(i)ī *m* senator of lower standing *(who lets others step all over him)*
pedāt·us -ūs *m* one of the three formal stages in issuing an ultimatum
ped·es -itis *m* infantryman, footsoldier; pedestrian; **equites peditesque** all Roman citizens
pedes·ter *or* **pedes·tris -tris -tre** *adj* infantry; pedestrian; on land, by land; written in prose; prosaic, plain
pedetem(p)tim *adv* by feeling one's way, step by step, slowly, cautiously
pedic·a -ae *f* foot chain, fetter; trap, snare
pedīculōs·us -a -um *adj* lousy
pēd·is -is *mf* louse
pedisequ·a -ae *f* attendant, handmaid
pedisequ·us -ī *m* attendant
peditastell·us -ī *m* poor infantryman
peditāt·us -ūs *m* infantry
pēdit·um -ī *n (vulg)* fart
Pedi·us -a -um *adj* name of a Roman clan *(nomen) (esp. Quintus Pedius, Caesar's nephew);* **lex Pedia** law providing a trial for Caesar's murderers
pēdō pēdĕre pepēdī pēditum *intr (vulg)* to fart
Ped·ō -ōnis *m* Roman family name *(cog-*

nomen), esp. Albinovanus Pedo, a poet and friend of Ovid

ped·um -ī *n* shepherd's crook

Pēgase·us *or* **Pēgasēï·us -a -um** *adj* of Pegasus, Pegasean

Pēgas·is -idis *or* **-idos** *adj (fem only)* of Pegasus *(with reference to Hippocrene)* ‖ *f* fountain nymph ‖ *fpl* Muses

Pēgas·us *or* **Pegas·os -ī** *m* winged horse that sprang from the blood of Medusa

pegm·a -atis *n* bookcase; scaffold

pējerātiuncul·a -ae *f* petty oath

pējerāt·us -a -um *adj* (**-jūr-**) offended by false oaths; **jus pejeratum** false oath

pējer·ō -āre -āvī -ātus *tr* (**-jūr-**) to swear falsely by ‖ *intr* to swear a false oath; *(coll)* to lie

pējerōs·us -a -um *adj* (**-jūr-**) perjured

pēj·or -or -us *(comp of* **malus**) *adj* worse

pējus *(comp of* **male**) *adv* worse

pelagi·us -a -um *adj* of the sea

pelag·us -ī *n* sea, open sea

pēlam·is -idis *or* **pēlam·ys -ydis** *f* young tuna fish

Pelasg·ī -ōrum *mpl* aborigines of Greece; *(poet)* certain early inhabitants of Italy; *(poet)* Greeks *(opp:* Trojans); *(poet)* Argives *(opp:* Thebans)

Pēl·eūs -eī *or* **-eos** *m* king of Thessaly, son of Aeacus, husband of Thetis, and father of Achilles

Pēli·as -adis *adj (fem only)* of Mt. Pelion, from Mt. Pelion

Peli·ās -ae *m* king of Iolcos in Thessaly and uncle of Jason

Pēlīd·ēs -ae *m* descendant of Peleus; Achilles; Neoptolemus

Pēl·ion -(i)ī *n* mountain in E. Thessaly

Pēli·us *or* **Pēliac·us -a -um** *adj* of Mt. Pelion

Pell·a -ae *or* **Pell·ē -ēs** *f* Pella *(city in Macedonia, birthplace of Alexander the Great)*

pellāci·a -ae *f* charm, allurement

Pellae·us -a -um *adj* of *or* from Pella; **Pellaeus juvenis** Alexander

pell·ax -ācis *adj* seductive, alluring

pellecti·ō -ōnis *f* perusal

pel·liciō -licĕre -lexī *or* **licuī -lectus** *tr* to captivate, allure, entice, coax

pellicul·a -ae *f* small *or* thin hide, skin

pelli·ō -ōnis *m* furrier

pell·is -is *f* skin, hide; leather; felt; tent; shield cover; **detrahere pellem** to expose one's true character *(literally, to take off one's hide);* **ossa ac pellis** mere skin and bones

pellīt·us -a -um *adj* clothed in skins; wearing a leather coat

pellō pellĕre pepulī pulsus *tr* to push, beat, strike, knock; to beat *(drum, chest);* to knock at *(door);* thrust; to drive, impel; to rouse, stimulate; to drive away, eject, expel; to banish; to repel, drive back, rout; to strum *(lyre, etc.);* to affect, impress, strike; to stomp *(the earth)*

pelluc- = perluc-

Pelopēï·as -ados *or* **Pelopē·us -a -um** *adj* Pelopian, of Pelops; Mycenaean; Phrygian

Pelopē·is -idos *f* descendant of Pelops *(female)*

Pelopid·ae -ārum *mpl* descendants of Pelops

Peloponnens·is -is -e *adj* (**-nnēs-**) Peloponnesian

Peloponnēsiac·us *or* **Peloponnēsi·us -a -um** *adj* Peloponnesian

Peloponnēs·us *or* **Peloponnēs·os -ī** *f* Peloponnesus *(modern Morea)*

Pel·ops -opis *m* son of Tantalus, father of Atreüs and Thyestes, and grandfather of Agamemnon and Menelaüs

pelōr·is -idos *m* large mussel

Pelōr·us *or* **Pelōr·os -ī** *m* N.E. promontory of Sicily

pelt·a -ae *f* small leather shield

peltast·a -ae *m* soldier armed with a small leather shield

peltāt·us -a -um *adj* armed with a small leather shield

Pēlūs·ium -(i)ī *n* city on the E. mouth of the Nile

pelv·is -is *f* basin, shallow bowl

penāri·us -a -um *adj* for storing food; **cella penaria** pantry

Penāt·ēs -ium *mpl* Penates, household gods; Penates of the State; hearth; house; home *(also applied to a nest, a hive, a temple)*

penātig·er -era -erum *adj* carrying the houshold gods

pendeō pendēre pependī *intr* to hang (down), be suspended; to hang loose; to be flabby; to be weak; to be in suspense, be uncertain, hesitate; to hang around, loiter; to hang in the air, hover, float; to overhang; *(of plants)* to droop; *(w. abl or* **ab, de,** *or* **ex** + *abl)* **1** to hang down from, hang by; **2** to depend on, be dependent upon; **3** to be based on, hinge on; **4** to result from; **5** to hang onto; *(w.* **in** + *abl)* to be poised on, hover in, hover over; **animi pendere** to be in suspense, be perplexed; **pendere ab ore** *(w. gen)* to hang on *(s.o.'s)* words, listen with rapt attention to; **pendere ex vultu** *(w. gen)* to gaze intently at *(s.o.'s)* face

pendō pendĕre pependī pensus *tr* to weigh, weigh out; to pay, pay out; to ponder, consider, value, esteem; **flocci pendere** to think little of; **magni (parvi) pendere** to think much (little) of; **poenas pendere** to pay the penalty; **supplicia pendere** to suffer punishment

pendul·us -a -um *adj* hanging, hanging down; doubtful, uncertain

Pēnē·is -idos *or* **Pēnēj·us -a -um** *adj* of the Peneus River *(in Thessaly)*

Pēnelop·a -ae *or* **Pēnelop·ē -ēs** *f* Penelope *(daughter of Icarius and Periboea and wife of Ulysses)*

penes *prep (w. acc of person only)* in the possession of, in the power of, belonging to, resting with; at the house of, with; **penes se esse** to be in one's senses, be in one's right mind

penetrābil·is -is -e *adj* penetrating, piercing; penetrable

penetr·āl·e -is *n see* **penetralis**

penetrāl·is -is -e *adj* penetrating, piercing; inner, internal, interior ‖ *n* inner part, inmost recess *(of a building);* inner shrine *(of a temple);* shrine of the Penates; house, home ‖ *npl* the interior, center; inner chambers; sanctuary; *(geog)* the interior, hinterlands

penetr·ō -āre -āvī -ātus *tr* to penetrate, enter; to cross *(river);* **pedem penetrare intra** *(w. acc)* to set foot inside ‖ *refl* to go; **foras se penetrare** to go outside ‖ *intr* to penetrate, enter; *(w.* **ad***)* to go as far as, go all the way to, reach, gain entrance to; *(w.* **in** *+ acc)* to enter, penetrate

Pēnē·us *or* **Pēnī·os -ī** *m* the Peneüs River *(largest river in Thessaly)* ‖ river god, the father of Cyrene and Daphne

pēnicill·us -ī *m or* **pēnicill·um -ī** *n* paint brush; sponge

pēnicul·us -ī *m* brush; sponge

pēn·is -is *m* tail; penis; lechery

penitē *adv* deep down inside

penitus *adv* internally, inside, deep within, deeply; from within; thoroughly, through and through; heartily

penit·us -a -um *adj* inner, inward

penn·a -ae *f* feather; wing; flight

pennāt·us -a -um *adj* feathered

pennig·er -era -erum *adj* winged, feathered

pennipot·ens -entis *adj* able to fly

pennul·a -ae *f* little wing

pensil·is -is -e *adj* hanging; supported on arches; suspended in mid-air

pensi·ō -ōnis *f* payment *(esp. by installments),* installment; rent money; compensation

pensit·ō -āre -āvī -ātus *tr* to pay; to weigh, ponder, consider ‖ *intr* to be taxable

pens·ō -āre -āvī -ātus *tr* to weigh out; to weigh, ponder, consider, examine; to compare, contrast; to pay; to atone for; to repay, compensate, requite

pens·um -ī *n* work quota; duty, task; consideration, scruple; **nihil pensi habere** *(or* **ducere***)* to have no scruples; **pensi esse** *(w. dat)* to be of value to, be of importance to; **pensi habere** *(or* **ducere***)* to value, consider of importance

pensus *pp of* **pendo**

pentēr·is -is *f* galley, quinquereme

Penthesilē·a -ae *f* Amazon warrior queen, killed by Achilles at Troy

Penth·eūs -eī *or* **-eos** *m* king of Thebes, son of Echion and Agave, grandson of Cadmus

pen·um -ī *n or* **pen·us -ūs** *f (m) or* **pen·us -oris** *n* food, provisions *(in the pantry)*

pēnūri·a -ae *f* want, need, dearth

pen·us -ūs *f (m) see* **penum**

pependī *perf of* **pendeo** *and of* **pendo**

pepercī *perf of* **parco**

peperī *perf of* **pario**

pepl·um -ī *n or* **pepl·us -ī** *m* robe for the statue of Athena

pepulī *perf of* **pello**

per *prep (w. acc) (of space)* through; all over *(an area, space),* throughout; along *(a linear direction); (of time)* through, during, for, in the course of, over a period of; *(of agency)* through, by, by means of, at the hands of; *(of means or manner)* through, by, under pretense of; *(w. refl pron)* for one's *or* its own sake, on its own account, by: **multiplicare VI** per IIII fit XXIIII multiplying 6 by 4 gives 24; **per causam** on the grounds *(that);* **per manūs tradere** to pass from hand to hand; **per me** as far as I am concerned; **per me stat** it is due to me *(that),* it is my fault *(that);* **per omnia** in all respects, throughout; **per speciem** on the pretext *(of);* **per omnes deos jurare** to swear by all the gods; **per se** in itself, by itself *(or* himself, herself, *etc.);* **per tempus** at the right time; **per Tiberim** along the Tiber

per- *pref* conveying the idea of: **1** through: **perfringere** to break through; **2** intensive force: **perfacile** very easy; **3** throughly, to the end: **perficere** to complete; **perlegere** to read through to the end; **perdomare** to tame thoroughly; **4** of going in the wrong direction: **pervertere** to turn the wrong way; **perfidia** treachery *(a trust, gone in the wrong direction)*

-per *advl suf* denoting the duration or the number of times, *e.g.:* **paulisper** for a little while

pēr·a -ae *f* pouch *(bag slung over the shoulder for carrying the day's provisions)*

perabsurd·us -a -um *adj* completely absurd

peraccommodāt·us -a -um *adj* very convenient

perā·cer -cris -cre *adj* very sharp

peracerb·us -a -um *adj* very harsh, very sour

peracesc·ō -ĕre *intr* to turn completely sour

peracti·ō -ōnis *f* conclusion; last act *(of a play)*
peractus *pp of* **perago**
peracūtē *adv* very acutely
peracūt·us -a -um *adj* very sharp; very clear *(voice, intellect)*
peradulesc·ens -entis *adj* very young
peradulescentul·us -ī *m* very young man
peraequē *adv* quite equally, uniformly; in all cases, invariably; **omnes peraeque** all alike
peragit·ō -āre -āvī -ātus *tr* to harass
per·agō -agĕre -ēgī -actus *tr* to carry through to the end, complete, accomplish; to pierce; to travel through; to harass, disturb, trouble; to describe, relate, go over; to work, till, cultivate *(the soil);* to fulfill *(hopes, promises);* to live out *(a period of time);* to come to the end of *(of period of time);* to treat *(a subject)* thoroughly; to use up *(resources);* to deliver *(a speech); (leg)* to prosecute to a conviction; **partes peragere** to play the part
peragrāti·ō -ōnis *f* traveling
peragr·ō -āre -āvī -ātus *tr* to travel through, travel, traverse ‖ *intr (fig)* to spread, penetrate
peram·ans -antis *adj (w. gen)* very fond of
peramanter *adv* very lovingly
perambul·ō -āre -āvī -ātus *tr* to walk through; to walk about in; to travel about in, tour
peramīcē *adv* in a very friendly way
peram·ō -āre -āvī -ātus *tr* to show a great liking for
peramoen·us -a -um *adj* very pleasant, very charming
perampl·us -a -um *adj* very large; very spacious
perangustē *adv* very narrowly
perangust·us -a -um *adj* very narrow
perantīqu·us -a -um *adj* very ancient, very old
perapposit·us -a -um *adj* very suitable, very appropriate
perardu·us -a -um *adj* very difficult
perargūt·us -a -um *adj* very clear; very sharp, very witty
perarmāt·us -a -um *adj* heavily armed
perar·ō -āre -āvī -ātus *tr* to plow through; to furrow; to write on *(a wax tablet);* to inscribe
pērātim *adv* bag by bag
perattentē *adv* very attentively
peraudiend·us -a -um *adj* that must be heard to the end
perbacch·or -ārī -ātus sum *tr* to carouse through *(e.g., the night)*
perbeāt·us -a -um *adj* very happy
perbellē *adv* very prettily
perbene *adv* very well
perbenevol·us -a -um *adj* very friendly, very well-disposed
perbenignē *adv* very kindly
perbib·ō -ĕre -ī *tr* to drink up, drink in, imbibe
perbīt·ō -ĕre *intr* to perish, die
perbland·us -a -um *adj* very attractive, very charming
perbon·us -a -um *adj* very good, excellent
perbrev·is -is -e *adj* very short, very brief; **perbrevi** *(or* **perbrevi tempore)** in a very short time
perbreviter *adv* very briefly
perc·a -ae *f* perch *(fish)*
percalefact·us -a -um *adj* warmed through and through
percal·escō -escĕre -uī *intr* to become quite hot
percall·escō -escĕre -uī *tr* to become thoroughly versed in ‖ *intr* to become very hardened
percār·us -a -um *adj* very dear; very costly
percaut·us -a -um *adj* very cautious
percelebr·ō -āre -āvī -ātus *tr* to make widely known ‖ *pass* to be quite famous
percel·er -eris -ere *adj* very rapid
perceleriter *adv* very rapidly
per·cellō -cellĕre -culī -culsus *tr* to knock down, beat down, overthrow; to scare to death; to ruin; to send scurrying; *(lit & mil)* to hit hard
percens·eō -ēre -uī *tr* to count up; to review, survey; to travel all through *(a country)*
percepti·ō -ōnis *f* comprehension; reaping, harvesting ‖ *fpl* concepts
percept·us -a -um *pp of* **percipio** ‖ *n* rule, principle
percī·dō -dĕre -dī -sus *tr* to smash to pieces
perci·eō -ēre *or* **perc·iō -īre -īvī** *or* **-iī -ītus** *tr* to stir up, set in motion; to excite
per·cipiō -cipĕre -cēpī -ceptus *tr* to get a good hold of; to catch; to occupy, seize; to gather in, harvest, reap; *(of the senses)* to take in, perceive, feel; *(of feelings)* to get hold of, get the better of, come over *(s.o.)*; to learn, know, comprehend, perceive
percit·us -a -um *pp of* **percieo** *and of* **percio** ‖ *adj* aroused, provoked; impetuous, excitable
percoctus *pp of* **percoquo**
percol·ō -āre -āvī -ātus *tr* to strain, filter
percolō -colĕre -coluī -cultus *tr* to reverence, revere, worship; to beautify; to crown, complete
percōm·is -is -e *adj* very courteous
percommodē *adv* very conveniently; very well; very suitably
percommod·us -a -um *adj* very convenient, very comfortable; very suitable
percontāti·ō -ōnis *f* thorough investigation

percontāt·or -ōris *m* inquisitive fellow; interrogator
percont·or -ārī -ātus sum *tr* to question, investigate, interrogate; *(w. double acc)* to ask *(s.o. s.th.)*
percontum·ax -ācis *adj* very defiant
per·coquō -quĕre -xī -ctus *tr* to cook thoroughly; to heat thoroughly; to ripen; to scorch, blacken
percrēb(r)·escō -escĕre -uī *tr* to become widespread; to get to be widely believed
percrep·ō -āre -uī *intr* to resound, ring
percruci·or -ārī -ātus sum *intr* to be tormented
perculsus *pp of* **percello**
percult·us -a -um *pp of* **percolō** ‖ *adj* decked out; *(coll)* all dolled up
percupid·us -a -um *adj (w. gen)* very fond of
percup·iō -ĕre -iī -ītus *tr* to desire greatly; *(w. inf)* to be very eager to, be dying to
percūriōs·us -a -um *adj* very curious
percūr·ō -āre -āvī -ātus *tr* to treat successfully, heal
percurrō percurrĕre per(cu)currī percursus *tr* to run through, run along, run over, pass over, speed over; *(fig)* to scan briefly, look over; *(in a speech)* to treat in succession, go over, run over; *(of feelings)* to run through, penetrate, pierce ‖ *intr* to run fast, hurry along; *(w.* **ad)** to dash to; *(w.* **per** + *acc)* **1** to run through *or* across, travel through; **2** *(fig)* to run through, mention quickly, treat in succession
percursāti·ō -ōnis *f* traveling; a tour
percursi·ō -ōnis *f* quick survey
percurs·ō -āre -āvī -ātum *tr & intr* to roam about
percussi·ō -ōnis *f* hitting, striking; snapping *(of fingers)*; *(mus)* beat, time
percuss·or -ōris *m* assassin
percussus *pp of* **percutio**
percuss·us -ūs *m* impact; striking
percu·tiō -tĕre -ssī -ssus *tr* to beat *or* hit hard; to strike *(w. lightning, sword, etc.)*; *(of snakes)* to bite; to knock at *(door)*; to strum *(lyre, etc.)*; to smash; to pierce, stab, run through; to shoot; to kill; to shock, make a deep impression on; to astound; to dig *(ditch)*; to coin *(money)*; to trick, cheat; **fusti percutere** to beat to death; **securi percutere** to behead
perdecōr·us -a -um *adj* very pretty
perdēlīr·us -a -um *adj* very silly, quite irrational; quite crazy
perdeps·ō -ĕre -uī *tr* to knead thoroughly; *(sl)* to feel up *(sexually)*
Perdiccās -ae *m* founder of the Macedonian monarchy ‖ Perdiccas II, King of Macedonia from 454 to 413 B.C. ‖ Perdiccas III *(d. 359 B.C.)* ‖ distinguished general of Alexander the Great *(d. 321 B.C.)*
perdifficil·is -is -e *adj* very difficult
perdifficiliter *adv* with great difficulty
perdign·us -a -um *adj (w. abl)* quite worthy of
perdīlig·ens -entis *adj* very diligent, very conscientious
perdīligenter *adv* very diligently, very conscientiously
per·discō -discĕre -didicī *tr* to learn thoroughly, learn by heart
perdisertē *adv* very eloquently
perditē *adv* recklessly, desperately
perdit·or -ōris *m* destroyer
perdit·us -a -um *adj* ruined, done-for; degenerate; infamous; reckless, incorrigible, hopeless; lost
perdit·us -ūs *m* ruination
perdiū *adv* for a very long time
perdiūturn·us -a -um *adj* protracted, long-lasting
perdīv·es -itis *adj* very rich
perd·ix -īcis *mf* partridge ‖ **Perdix** Perdix, nephew of Daedalus, who was changed into a partridge
per·dō -dĕre -didī -ditus *tr* to wreck, ruin, destroy; to waste, squander; to lose; **perdere operam** to waste one's efforts
perdoc·eō -ēre -uī -tus *tr* to teach thoroughly
perdoctē *adv* very skillfully
perdoct·us -a -um *pp of* **perdoceo** ‖ *adj* very learned, very skillful
perdol·eō -ēre -uī -itum *intr* to be annoyed; to be a cause of annoyance
perdolesc·ō -ĕre *intr* to become hurt, become annoyed
perdom·ō -āre -uī -itus *tr* to tame completely, subdue, subjugate
perdormisc·ō -ĕre *intr* to sleep on, keep on sleeping
perdū·cō -ĕre -xī -ctus *tr* to lead, guide *(to a destination)*; to bring *(to court)*; *(of roads)* to lead *(to)*; *(of a pimp)* to take *(s.o.)* to *(s.o. else's bed)*; to cover, spread; to prolong, drag out; to induce; to seduce; *(w.* **ad)** **1** to lead, guide, escort to; **2** to build, run *(wall, ditch, road, etc.)* to; **3** to prolong, drag out, continue *(s.th.)* to *or* until; **4** to win over to, convince of
perduct·ō -āre -āvī -ātus *tr* to lead, guide
perduct·or -ōris *m* guide; pimp
perdūdum *adv* long long ago
perduelli·ō -ōnis *f* treason
perduell·is -is *m* enemy
perdūr·ō -āre -āvī -ātum *intr* to last, hold out
per·edō -edĕre -ēdī -ēsus *tr* to eat up, devour; *(of things)* to eat away
perēgī *perf of* **perago**
peregrē *adv* abroad, away from home; from abroad; **peregre abire** *(or* **peregre exire)** to go abroad
peregrīn·a -ae *f* foreign woman

peregrīnābund·us -a -um *adj* traveling around, touring
peregrīnāti·ō -ōnis *f* living abroad; foreign travel, touring; *(of animals)* roaming, ranging
peregrīnāt·or -ōris *m* traveler *(abroad)*, tourist
peregrīnit·ās -ātis *f* foreign manners, outlandish ways; alien status
peregrīn·or -ārī -ātus sum *intr* to live abroad; to travel abroad; *(fig)* to be a stranger
peregrīn·us -a -um *adj* foreign; strange; alien, exotic; outlandish; *(fig)* strange; *(fig)* inexperienced; **amores peregrini** love affairs with foreign women; **praetor peregrinus** praetor who tried cases involving disputes between foreigners and Roman citizens; **terror peregrinus** fear of a foreign enemy **‖** *mf* foreigner, alien
perēleg·ans -antis *adj* very elegant
perēleganter *adv* very elegantly
perēloqu·ens -entis *adv* very eloquent
peremn·is -is -e *adj* **auspicia peremnia** auspices taken before crossing a river
peremptus *pp of* **perimo**
perendiē *adv* the day after tomorrow
perendin·us -a -um *adj* **dies perendinus** the day after tomorrow
perenn·is -is -e *adj* perennial, continual, everlasting
perenniserv·os -ī *m* slave for life
perennit·ās -ātis *f* continuance, perpetuity
perenn·ō -āre *intr* to last
pērenticīd·a -ae *m (hum)* purse snatcher
per·eō -īre -iī -itum *intr* to pass away, pass on, die; to go to waste, perish, be destroyed; to be lost, be ruined, be undone; to be desperately in love, pine away; *(of snow)* to melt away; *(of iron)* to rust away; **perii!** *(coll)* I'm finished!, I'm washed up!
perequit·ō -āre -āvī -ātus *tr* to ride through *(on horseback)* **‖** *intr* to ride around *(on horseback)*
pererr·ō -āre -āvī -ātus *tr* to roam around, wander through; to survey, look *(s.o.)* over **‖** *intr* to roam all around
perērudīt·us -a -um *adj* very learned, erudite
perēsus *pp of* **peredo**
perexcels·us -a -um *adj* very high up
perexiguē *adv* very sparingly
perexigu·us -a -um *adj* tiny; insignificant; very short *(day)*
perexpedīt·us -a -um *adj* readily available
perfacētē *adv* very wittily
perfacēt·us -a -um *adj* very witty
perfacile *adv* very easily
perfacil·is -is -e *adj* very easy
perfamiliār·is -is -e *adj* very close, intimate **‖** *mf* very close friend
perfectē *adv* completely; perfectly
perfecti·ō -ōnis *f* completion; perfection
perfect·or -ōris *m* perfecter; **dicendi perfector** stylist
perfect·us -a -um *pp of* **perficio ‖** *adj* complete, finished; perfect; *(gram)* perfect; **praeteritum perfectum** perfect tense
per·ferō -ferre -tulī -lātus *tr* to carry through; to endure to the end, bear with patience, put up with; to drive home *(a weapon);* to deliver *(message),* bring news of; to cause *(news)* to reach; to keep up *(an attitude, activity)* to the end; *(of things)* to be capable of accommodating; *(pol)* to get *(a law)* passed
per·ficiō -ficere -fēcī -fectus *tr* to complete, finish, bring to an end; to accomplish, carry out, execute; to perfect; to cause; *(w.* **ut, ne**) to bring it about (that, that not)
perfic·us -a -um *adj* that completes *or* perfects
perfidē *adv* dishonestly
perfidēl·is -is -e *adj* completely trustworthy
perfidi·a -ae *f* treachery, perfidy
perfidiōsē *adv* treacherously
perfidiōs·us -a -um *adj* treacherous, false
perfid·us -a -um *adj* treacherous, false; untrustworthy, dishonest, sneaky **‖** *m* a sneak
perfī·gō -gere -xī -xus *tr* to pierce
perflābil·is -is -e *adj* airy; invisible
perflāgitiōs·us -a -um *adj* utterly disgraceful
perflāt·us -ūs *m* draft
perfl·ō -āre -āvī -ātus *tr* to blow across, blow through; to blow throughout *(a period)* **‖** *intr* to blow hard, blow continuously
perfluctu·ō -āre -āvī -ātus *tr* to surge through
perflu·ō -ere -xī -xus *intr* to flow along; to leak all over; *(w.* **per**) to flow through
per·fodiō -fodere -fōdī -fossus *tr* to dig through; to pierce, stab
perfor·ō -āre -āvī -ātus *tr* to bore through, pierce; to make by boring
perfortiter *adv* very bravely
perfoss·or -ōris *m* borer; **parietum perfossor** burglar *(literally, one who bores through walls)*
perfossus *pp of* **perfodio**
perfractus *pp of* **perfringo**
perfrem·ō -ere *intr* to snort loud
perfrequ·ens -entis *adj* very crowded, overcrowded
perfric·ō -āre -uī -tus *or* **-ātus** *tr* to rub hard, rub all over; **os perfricare** to rub away blushes, put on a bold front
perfrīgefac·iō -ere *tr (fig)* to send a chill over, make shudder

perfrīgescō perfrīgescĕre perfrixī perfrictum *intr* to become chilled; to catch a bad cold
perfrīgid·us -a -um *adj* ice-cold
per·fringō -fringĕre -frēgī -fractus *tr* to break through; to break into; to break to pieces, smash; to break down *(a door); (fig)* to break up *(conspiracy); (fig)* to break *(the law); (med)* to fracture
per·fruor -fruī -fructus sum *intr (w. abl)* **1** to enjoy fully; **2** to perform gladly
perfug·a -ae *m* military deserter; political turncoat; refugee
per·fugiō -fugĕre -fūgī *intr* (w. **ad** *or* **in** + *acc)* **1** to flee to for refuge; **2** to desert to; **3** to have recourse to
perfug·ium -(i)ī *n* place of refuge, shelter, sanctuary; way of escape; *(fig)* an escape; excuse, defense; means of protection *or* safety
perfuncti·ō -ōnis *f* performance, performing, discharge
perfunctus *pp of* **perfungor**
per·fundō -fundĕre -fūdī -fūsus *tr* to drench, bathe; to flood; to sprinkle; to dye; *(of river)* to flow through; *(of sun)* to drench *(w. light, color); (fig)* to fill, steep, inspire ‖ *refl & pass* to bathe, take a bath
perfun·gor -gī -ctus sum *tr* to enjoy ‖ *intr (w. abl)* **1** to perform, discharge, fulfill; **2** to endure, undergo; **3** to get rid of; **4** to be finished with, be done with; **5** to enjoy
perfur·ō -ĕre *intr* to rage wildly, rage on and on
perfūsus *pp of* **perfundo**
Pergam·a -ōrum *npl or* **Pergam·um -ī** *n* Pergamum *(citadel of Troy),* Troy
Pergame·us -a -um *adj* Trojan ‖ *f* Pergamea *(name given by Aeneas to his city on Crete)* ‖ *mpl* Trojans
Pergam·os -ī *f or* **Pergam·um -ī** *n or* **Pergam·on -ī** *n* Pergamum *(city of Mysia famous for its library and temple of Aesculapius)*
pergaud·eō -ēre *intr* to be very glad
pergn·oscō -oscĕre -ōvī *tr* to be well-acquainted with
per·gō -gĕre -rexī -rectus *tr* to go on interruptedly with, continue; *(w. inf)* to continue to; **iter pergere** to go on one's way ‖ *intr* to go straight on, continue, proceed; *(w.* **ad)** **1** to make one's way toward; **2** to pass on to, proceed to *(esp. a topic);* **perge modo!** go on now!, now get going!
pergraec·or -ārī *intr (coll)* to go completely Greek, have a ball
pergrand·is -is -e *adj* very large, huge; **pergrandis natu** very old
pergraphic·us -a -um *adj* perfectly drawn
pergrāt·us -a -um *adj* very pleasant ‖ *n* distinct pleasure; **pergratum mihi feceris si** you would be doing me a very great favor if
pergrav·is -is -e *adj* very heavy; very important; very impressive
pergraviter *adv* very seriously
pergul·a -ae *f* open porch *(used for business, as a school, as a brothel)*
perhib·eō -ēre -uī -itus *tr* to present; to assert, regard, maintain; to call, name; to adduce, cite; **testimonium perhibere** to bear witness
perhīlum *adv* very little
perhonōrificē *adv* with all due respect, very respectfully
perhonōrific·us -a -um *adj* very complimentary; very respectful
perhorr·escō -escĕre -uī *tr* to begin to shudder at; to develop a terror of ‖ *intr* to begin to tremble violently
perhūmāniter *adv* very kindly
perhūmān·us -a -um *adj* very kind
Pericl·ēs -is *m* famous Athenian statesman *(495–429 B.C.)*
perīclitāti·ō -ōnis *f* test, experiment
perīclit·or -ārī -ātus sum *tr* to test, put to the test, try; to jeopardize; to risk ‖ *intr* to be in danger, be in jeopardy; to run a risk; *(w. abl)* to be in danger of losing *(life, reputation, etc.);* **capite periclitari** to risk one's life
perīculōsē *adv* dangerously
perīculōs·us -a -um *adj* dangerous, risky, perilous
perīc(u)l·um -ī *n* danger, peril, risk; trial, attempt; experiment, test; literary venture; *(leg)* case, trial, lawsuit, legal record, sentence; **periculum facere** to run the risk; try it out; *(w. gen)* to test, put to the test *(e.g., s.o.'s loyalty);* **periculum facere ex aliis** to learn from the mistakes of others; **periculum intendere** *(w. dat)* to expose *(s.o.)* to danger, endanger *(s.o.);* **volo periculum facere an** I want to see whether
peridōne·us -a -um *adj* very suitable; *(w. dat or* **ad)** well-adapted to, well-suited to
Perillē·us -a - um *adj* of Perillus
Perill·us -ī *m* Athenian sculptor who made for the tyrant Phalaris a bronze bull in which to roast people alive
perillustr·is -is -e *adj* very clear; very illustrious, very distinguished
perimbēcill·us -a -um *adj* very weak, very feeble
per·imō -imĕre -ēmī -emptus *tr* to take away completely; to destroy; to kill
perimpedīt·us -a -um *adj* rough *(terrain);* full of obstacles
perincommodē *adv* very inconveniently
perincommod·us -a -um *adj* very inconvenient
perinde *adv* in the same manner, equally,

just as, quite as; *(w.* **ac, atque, ut, prout,** *or* **quam)** just as; *(w.* **ac si, quasi, tamquam,** *or* **quamsi)** just as if; **non perinde** not particularly, not as much as one would expect
perindulg·ens -entis *adj* very tender; *(w.* **ad)** very tender toward
perinfirm·us -a -um *adj* very weak
peringeniōs·us -a -um *adj* very gifted
perinīqu·us -a -um *adj* very unfair; very upset, very annoyed; very impatient; very reluctant; **periniquo animo pati** *(or* **ferre)** to be quite upset at, be very reluctant about
perinsign·is -is -e *adj* very remarkable
perinvīt·us -a -um *adj* very unwilling
period·us -ī *f (rhet)* period *(a group of at least two words organically related in grammar and sense, and spoken without pause)*
peripatētic·us -a -um *adj* Peripatetic, Aristotelian ‖ *mpl* Peripatetics, Aristotelians
peripetasmat·a -um *npl* curtains, drapes
Periph·ās -antis *m* king of Attica, changed into an eagle by Zeus
periphras·is -is *f (acc:* **-in)** circumlocution
perīrāt·us -a -um *adj* very angry; *(w. dat)* very angry with
periscel·is -idis *f* anklet
peristrōm·a -atis *n* carpet; bedspread
peristȳl·ium -(i)ī *or* **peristȳl·um** *or* **peristȳl·on -ī** *n* peristyle *(inner court surrounded by a colonnade)*
perītē *adv* skillfully, expertly
perīti·a -ae *f* experience, practical knowledge, skill; *(w. gen)* experience in, familiarity with, knowledge of
perīt·us -a -um *adj (w. gen or abl, w.* **in** + *abl or* **ad)** experienced in, skillful in, expert in *or* at, familiar with; *(w. inf)* skilled in, expert at, *e.g.,* **peritus cantare** skilled in singing; **juris peritus** expert in the law, legal adviser, lawyer
perjūcundē *adv* very pleasantly
perjūcund·us -a -um *adj* very pleasant
perjūr·ium -(i)ī *n* perjury; false oath; false promise
perjūrō -āre *tr* **(-jer-)** to swear falsely by ‖ *intr* to swear a false oath, commit perjury; *(coll)* to lie
perjūr·us -a -um *adj* **(-jer-)** perjured, oath-breaking; *(coll)* lying
per·lābor -lābī -lapsus sum *intr* to glide along, skim across *or* over; *(w.* **per** + *acc)* **1** to slip through; **2** to slip along, glide along; *(w.* **ad)** to come, move, glide, *or* slip toward; *(w.* **in** + *acc)* to glide into, slip into
perlaet·us -a -um *adj* very glad, most joyful
perlapsus *pp of* **perlabor**
perlātē *adv* very extensively
perlat·eō -ēre -uī *intr* to be completely hidden
perlātus *pp of* **perfero**
perlecti·ō -ōnis *f* thorough perusal
per·legō -legĕre -lēgī -lectus *tr* to scan, survey thoroughly, to read through; to recount *(in a speech)*
perlepidē *adv* very nicely
perlev·is -is -e *adj* very light; very slight
perleviter *adv* very lightly; very slightly
perlib·ens -entis *adj* **(-lub-)** very willing
perlibenter *adv* **(-lub-)** very gladly, very willingly
perlīberāl·is -is -e *adj* very well-bred
perlīberāliter *adv* very generously
perlib·et -ēre *v impers* **(lub-) perlibet me** *(w. inf)* I should very much like to
perliciō *see* **pellicio**
perlit·ō -āre -āvī -ātus *tr* to sacrifice *(in order to get a favorable omen);* ‖ *intr* **bove perlitare** to sacrifice an ox *(to obtain a favorable omen)*
perlongē *adv* a long way off
perlonginqu·us -a -um *adj* very long; very tedious
perlong·us -a -um *adj* very long
perlub- = perlib-
per·lūceō -lūcēre *intr* **(pell-)** to shine clearly, be bright; to be clearly visible; to be transparent; to be clear, be intelligible
perlūcidul·us -a -um *adj* transparent
perlūcid·us -a -um *adj* **(pell-)** very bright; transparent
perluctuōs·us -a -um *adj* very sad
per·luō -luĕre -luī -lūtus *tr* to wash thoroughly; to wash off; to bathe
perlustr·ō -āre -āvī -ātus *tr* to traverse; to scan, survey, review
permade·faciō -facĕre -fēcī -factus *tr* to soak through and through, drench
permad·escō -escĕre -uī *intr* to become drenched
permagn·us -a -um *adj* very big; very great; very important ‖ *n* great thing; **permagno** at a very high price, very dearly; **permagnum aestimare** *(w. inf)* to think it quite something to
permānanter *adv* pervasively
permānasc·ō -ĕre *intr (of a report)* to leak out
perman·eō -ēre -sī -sum *intr* to last, continue, hold out, remain, persist; *(of the voice)* to remain steady; **permanere esse** to continue to be
permān·ō -āre -āvī -ātus *tr* to seep through, penetrate ‖ *intr* to penetrate; *(w.* **ad** *or* **in** + *acc)* **1** to seep through to; **2** to seep into, penetrate; **3** *(fig)* to reach, extend to, penetrate
permansi·ō -ōnis *f* persistence, continuance

permarīn·us -a -um *adj* seagoing
permātūr·escō -escěre -uī *intr* to become fully ripe
permediocr·is -is -e *adj* completely normal, very moderate
permeditāt·us -a -um *adj* well-rehearsed, well-trained
permējō -mējěre -mi(n)xī -i(n)ctus *tr (sl)* to soak with urine, urinate all over
permensus *pp of* **permetior**
perme·ō -āre -āvī -ātus *tr* to go through, cross over, cross ‖ *intr (w.* **in** *+ acc)* to penetrate; *(w.* **per** *+ acc)* to penetrate, permeate
Permess·us -ī *m* river in Boeotia sacred to Apollo and the Muses
per·mētior -mētīrī -mensus sum *tr* to measure exactly; to travel over, traverse; to pass right through *(a period of time);* **permetiri oculis** to take stock of, eye appraisingly
per·mingō -mingěre -minxī -mi(n)ctus *tr (sl)* to soak with urine, urinate all over
permīr·us -a -um *adj* very surprising, truly amazing
per·misceō -miscēre -miscuī mixtus *tr* to mix together, blend thoroughly, intermingle; to unite *(by marriage); (fig)* to involve, embroil; *(fig)* to mix up, confuse, treat as identical; to throw into confusion ‖ *pass (w.* **cum**) to combine with; *(w. abl or* **ex**) to consist of, be made up of
permissi·ō -ōnis *f* permission; unconditional surrender; *(as rhetorical device)* concession
permiss·us -a -um *pp of* **permitto** ‖ *n* permission
permiss·us -ūs *m* permission, leave
permitiāl·is -is -e *adj* destructive
permiti·ēs -ēī *f* wasting away; ruin; *(of persons)* source of ruin, ruination
per·mittō -mittěre -mīsī -missus *tr* to let through, let go through; to hurl; to give up, surrender; to concede, relinquish; to let loose, let go; to let, permit, allow, grant; *(w. dat)* to surrender *(s.th.)* to, entrust *(s.th.)* to, grant *(s.th.)* to; *(w.* **in** *+ acc)* to send flying at, hurl at
permixtē *or* **permixtim** *adv* confusedly; indiscriminately
permixti·ō -ōnis *f* mixture; confusion, bedlam
permixt·us -a -um *pp of* **permisceo** ‖ *adj* confused; promiscuous; composite
permodest·us -a -um *adj* very modest, very moderate
permolestē *adv* with much trouble; **permoleste ferre** to be quite annoyed at
permolest·us -a -um *adj* very troublesome, very annoying
permol·ō -ěre *tr* to grind up; **alienas uxores permolere** *(sl)* to have sex with other men's wives
permōti·ō -ōnis *f* excitement; **animi permotio** *(or* **mentis permotio)** deep emotion
per·moveō -movēre -mōvī -mōtus *tr* to stir up, churn up *(the sea);* to move deeply, make a deep impression on; to excite, agitate, upset; to influence, induce
permul·ceō -cēre -sī -sus *tr* to stroke, pet; to soothe, calm down, relax; to smoothe *(one's hair);* to charm, delight; to appease
permultō *adv* by far, much, far
permultum *adv* very much; **permultum ante** very often before; **permultum interest** it makes a world of difference
permult·us -a -um *adj* very much; *(w. pl nouns)* very many ‖ *n* a lot, much
permūn·iō -īre -īvī *or* **-iī -ītus** *tr* to fortify thoroughly; to finish fortifying
permūtāti·ō -ōnis *f* interchange; exchange; bartering; substitution, switch; reversal *(of an arrangment);* turning upside down, revolution; alternation, transformation
permūt·ō -āre -āvī -ātus *tr* to change *or* alter completely, transform; to interchange; to remit by bill of exchange; to reverse *(an order, arrangmement);* to turn topsy-turvy *(w. abl or* **cum** *or* **pro** *+ abl)* **1** to exchange for, replace with; **2** to receive in exchange for; **3** to acquire at the price of; **4** to substitute for
pern·a -ae *f* ham
pernecessāri·us -a -um *adj* very necessary; very closely related ‖ *m* close friend; close relative
pernecesse *indecl neut adj* very necessary, indispensable
perneg·ō -āre -āvī -ātus *tr* to deny flatly; to turn down flat
per·neō -nēre -nēvī -nētus *tr (of the Fates)* to spin out
perniciābil·is -is -e *adj* ruinous
pernici·ēs -ēī *f* ruin, destruction, disaster; pest, curse
perniciōsē *adv* perniciously, ruinously
perniciōs·us -a -um *adj* pernicious, ruinous
pernīcit·ās -ātis *f* agility, nimbleness, swiftness
pernīciter *adv* nimbly, swiftly
perni·ger -gra -grum *adj* jet black; very dark *(eyes)*
pernimium *adv* much too much
pern·ix -īcis *adj* agile, nimble, swift
pernōbil·is -is -e *adj* very famous
pernoct·ō -āre -āvī -ātum *intr* to spend the night
per·noscō -noscěre -nōvī -nōtus *tr* to examine thoroughly; to become fully acquainted with, get accurate knowledge of
pernōt·escō -escěre -uī *intr* to become generally known

per·nox -noctis *adj* all-night; **luna pernox** full moon
pernumer·ō -āre -āvī -ātus *tr* to count up
pēr·ō -ōnis *m* clodhopper *(worn by peasants and soldiers)*
perobscūr·us -a -um *adj* very obscure; very vague
perō·dī -disse -sus *tr* to detest, loathe
perodiōs·us -a -um *adj* very annoying
perofficiōsē *adv* with attention, with great devotion; very politely
pērōnāt·us -a -um *adj* wearing clodhoppers
peropportūnē *adv* very conveniently, most opportunely
peropportūn·us -a -um *adj* most opportune, very convenient, well-timed
peroptātō *adv* very much in accordance with one's wishes
peroptāt·us -a -um *adj* greatly desired, longed-for
peropus *indecl n* great need; **peropus est** *(w. acc & inf)* it is essential that
perōrāti·ō -ōnis *f* peroration, summation
perornāt·us -a -um *adj* very flowery
perorn·ō -āre -āvī -ātus *tr* to enhance the prestige of
perōr·ō -āre -āvī -ātus *tr* to bring *(a case, discussion)* to a close ‖ *intr* to bring a speech to a close; *(leg)* to wind up a case, give the summation
perōs·us -a -um *adj* hating, detesting; hated, hateful
perpāc·ō -āre -āvī -ātus *tr* to silence completely; to pacify thoroughly
perparcē *adv* most stingily
perparvul·us -a -um *adj* tiny
perparv·us -a -um *adj* very small
perpast·us -a -um *adj* well-fed
perpauc·ī -ae -a *adj* very few ‖ *npl* very few words
perpaucul·ī -ae -a *adj* very few
perpaulum *adv* somewhat, slightly
perpaul·um -ī *n* small bit
perpaup·er -eris *adj* very poor
perpauxill·um -ī *n* little bit
perpave·faciō -facĕre -fēcī -factus *tr* to frighten the daylights out of
per·pellō -pellĕre -pulī -pulsus *tr* to push hard; to urge strongly, force; to drive all the way
perpendicul·um -ī *n or* **perpendicul·us -ī** *n* plumb line; **ad perpendiculum** perpendicularly
perpen·dō -dĕre -dī -sus *tr* to weigh carefully, consider; to value, judge
perperam *adv* incorrectly, wrongly; by mistake
Perpern·a *or* **Perpenn·a -ae** *m* Roman family name *(cognomen)*, *esp.* Marcus Perperna Vento, partisan and later murderer of Sertorius
perp·es -etis *adj* continuous, uninterrupted
perpessi·ō -ōnis *f* endurance
per·petior -petī -pessus sum *tr* to endure, put up with, stand; to allow, permit
perpetr·ō -āre -āvī -ātus *tr* to accomplish, go through with, carry out, perform; to perpetrate, commit; to fulfill *(a promise)*; *(w.* **ut***)* to bring it about that
perpetuē *adv* constantly
perpetuit·ās -ātis *f* perpetuity
perpetuō *adv* constantly; forever
perpetu·ō -āre -āvī -ātus *tr* to perpetuate
perpetu·us -a -um *adj* perpetual, continuous; general, universal; whole; **quaestiones perpetuae** standing courts; permanent committees ‖ *n* **in perpetuum** continuously; forever
perplac·eō -ēre *intr (w. dat)* to please immensely
perplexābil·is -is -e *adj* perplexing, puzzling
perplexābiliter *adv* perplexingly
perplexē *or* **perplexim** *adv* confusedly, unintelligibly
perplex·or -ārī *intr* to cause confusion
perplex·us -a -um *adj* intricate, complicated; ambiguous; muddled, mistaken; baffling *(words)*
perplicāt·us -a -um *adj* entangled
perplu·ō -ĕre *intr (of roof, etc.)* to let the rain in; *(of rain)* to come in
perpol·iō -īre -īvī *or* **-iī -ītus** *tr* to bring to a high polish; *(fig)* to polish up, perfect
perpolīt·us -a -um *adj* polished, refined
perpopul·or -ārī -ātus sum *tr* to ravage, devastate
perpōtāti·ō -ōnis *f* heavy drinking; drinking party
perpōt·ō -āre -āvī -ātus *tr* to drink up ‖ *intr* to drink heavily, carouse
per·primō -primĕre -pressī -pressus *tr* to press hard, squeeze hard
perpropinqu·us -a -um *adj* very near ‖ *m* very close relative
perprūrisc·ō -ĕre *intr* to begin to itch all over
perpugn·ax -ācis *adj* very belligerent
perpul·c(h)er -c(h)ra -c(h)rum *adj* very beautiful, very handsome
perpulsus *pp of* **perpello**
perpurg·ō -āre -āvī -ātus *tr* to cleanse thoroughly, clean up; *(fig)* to clear up
perpusill·us -a -um *adj* puny
perput·ō -āre -āvī -ātus *tr* to prune back hard; to explain in detail
perquam *adv* very, extremely
per·quīrō -quīrĕre -quīsīvī *or* **-quīsiī -quīsītus** *tr* to search carefully for; to examine carefully
perquīsītius *adv* more accurately, more critically
perquīsīt·or -ōris *m* enthusiast
perrārō *adv* very rarely
perrār·us -a -um *adj* very rare

perrecondit·us -a -um *adj* recondite
perrectus *pp of* **pergo**
perrēp·ō -ĕre -sī *tr* to creep through; to crawl along *(the ground)*
perrept·ō -āre -āvī *tr* to creep through, sneak through ‖ *intr* to creep around
perrexī *perf of* **pergo**
Perrhaeb·us -a -um *adj* of Perrhaebia *(a mountainous region of N. Thessaly)* ‖ *m* inhabitant of Perrhaebia
perrīdiculē *adv* most absurdly
perrīdicul·us -a -um *adj* utterly absurd
perrogāti·ō -ōnis *f* passage *(of a law)*
perrog·ō -āre *tr* to ask for in turn; to question in turn; to poll *(opinions); (pol)* **sententias perrogare** to have roll call *(in the Senate)*
per·rumpō -rumpĕre -rūpī -ruptus *tr* to break through, force one's way through; to break in two, shatter, smash; to offend against, violate ‖ *intr* to break through, make a breakthrough
Pers·a *or* **Pers·ēs -ae** *m* Persian
Pers·a -ae *f* a daughter of Oceanus, wife of the sun, and mother of Circe, Perses *(father of Hecate),* Aeëtes, and Pasiphaë
persaepe *adv* very often
persalsē *adv* very wittily
persals·us -a -um *adj* very witty
persalūtāti·ō -ōnis *f* round of greetings, greeting all in turn
persalūt·ō -āre -āvī -ātus *tr* to salute one after another
persanctē *adv* very solemnly
persapi·ens -entis *adj* very wise
persapienter *adv* very wisely
perscienter *adv* very skillfully
per·scindō -scindĕre -scĭdī -scissus *tr* to tear to pieces; to split
perscīt·us -a -um *adj* very clever, very smart
per·scrībō -scrībĕre -scripsī -scriptus *tr* to write out; to describe fully, give in detail; to finish writing; to record, register; to enter *(into an account book);* to write out in full *(as opposed to abbreviating);* **pecuniam perscribere** to write a check for *(a certain sum of money)*
perscripti·ō -ōnis *f* entry, official record; check, payment by check
perscript·or -ōris *m* bookkeeper, accountant
perscriptus *pp of* **perscribo**
perscrūt·or -ārī -ātus sum *tr* to search *or* examine thoroughly, scrutinize
persec·ō -āre -uī -tus *tr* to dissect; to cut through; to lance *(a boil)*
persect·or -ārī -ātus sum *tr* to follow eagerly, investigate
persecūti·ō -ōnis *f* pursuit; *(leg)* right to sue; *(leg)* prosecution, suing
persecūtus *pp of* **persequor**
per·sedeō -sedēre -sēdī -sessum *intr* to remain seated
persegn·is -is -e *adj* very slow-moving
Persē·is -idis *or* **-idos** *adj (fem only)* of Persa; of Perseus ‖ *f* daughter of Persa *(Hecate, Circe)* ‖ Persa
persen·tiō -tīre -sī -sus *tr* to perceive clearly, to feel deeply
persentisc·ō -ĕre *tr* to become fully conscious of; to begin to feel deeply
Persephon·ē -ēs *f* daughter of Demeter and Zeus and queen of the lower world *(named Proserpina by the Romans)*
persequ·ens -entis *adj* pursuing; *(w. gen)* given to the pursuit *or* practice of
perse·quor -quī -cūtus sum *tr* to follow persistently, follow up; to be in hot pursuit of, be on the heels of; to chase after, catch up to; to follow verbatim; to imitate, copy; to take vengeance on; to follow out, execute; to describe, explain; *(leg)* to prosecute
Pers·ēs *or* **Pers·a -ae** *or* **Pers·eus -eī** *or* **-eos** *m* Perseus *(last king of Macedonia, conquered by Aemilius Paulus at Pydna in 169 B.C.)*
Pers·eus -eī *or* **-eos** *m* son of Jupiter and Danaë, and slayer of Medusa ‖ *see* **Perses**
Persē·us *or* **Persē̆i·us -a -um** *adj* of Perseus *(son of Jupiter and Danaë)*
persevēr·ans -antis *adj* persevering, persistent, relentless
persevēranter *adv* persistently
persevēranti·a -ae *f* perseverance
persevēr·ō -āre -āvī -ātus *tr* to persist in ‖ *intr* to persevere
persevēr·us -a -um *adj* very strict
Persi·a -ae *or* **Pers·is -idis** *or* **-idos** *f* Persia
Persic·us -a -um *adj* Persian; *(fig)* luxurious, soft; of Perseus *(king of Macedonia);* **malum Persicum** peach ‖ *mpl* Persians ‖ *f* peach tree ‖ *n* peach ‖ *npl* Persian history
per·sīdō -sīdĕre -sēdī *intr* to sink down; *(w.* **ad** *or* **in** *+ acc)* to penetrate
persign·ō -āre -āvī -ātus *tr* to record in detail *(articles in an inventory)*
persimil·is -is -e *adj* very similar; *(w. gen or dat)* very similar to
persimpl·ex -icis *adj* very simple
Pers·is -idis *or* **-idos** *adj (fem only)* Persian ‖ *f* Persia; Persian woman
Pers·ius -(i)ī *m* Persius *(Aulus Persius Flaccus, satirist in the reign of Nero, A.D. 34–62)*
persoll·a -ae *f* little mask; *(pej)* you ugly little thing!
persōl·us -a -um *adj* all alone
per·solvō -solvĕre solvī -solūtus *tr* to solve; to explain; to pay up, pay in full; to pay *(a penalty);* to fulfill *(a vow);* to carry out *(a duty);* to render *(thanks);* to offer *(sacrifice); (w. gen)* pay the pen-

alty for *(a crime); (w. dat)* to pay *(the penalty)* at the hands of; to solve *(a problem, riddle);* **ab omnibus ei poenae persolutae sunt** punishment was inflicted on him by all; **debitum naturae persolvere** to pay one's debt to nature *(i.e., to die);* **honorem dis persolvere** to offer sacrifices to the gods; **grates dis persolvere** to render thanksgiving to the gods; **gratiam dis persolvere** to render thanks to the gods; **justa persolvere** to pay honors to the dead; **poenas dis hominibusque persolvere** to suffer punishment at the hands of gods and men; **vectigalia persolvere** to pay taxes; **vota persolvere** to fulfill vows

persōn·a -ae *f* mask; part, character; pretense; personality; person; *(gram)* person; *(leg)* the person involved in a case; **ab** *(or* **ex** *or* **in) suā personā** *(acting, speaking)* in one's own name, on one's own behalf; **in personā** *(w. gen)* in the case of, in the instance of; **mea persona** my personality *or* character; **personae fictio** personification; **persona muta** a character with no speaking part

persōnāl·is -is -e *adj* personal

persōnāliter *adv* personally

persōnāt·us -a -um *adj* wearing a mask, masked; *(fig)* under false pretenses, putting on a front; **pater personatus** the father in the play; **personata fabula** a play in which actors wear masks; **personatus histrio** an actor wearing a mask

persōn·ō -āre -uī -ātus *tr* to make *(a place)* resound; to shout out; to sing loudly, belt out *(a song);* **aurem personare** to make the ear ring ‖ *intr* to resound, reecho; *(of a musician w. abl. of instrument)* to play loudly on *(e.g., the lyre); (of a singer)* to sing loudly; **citharā personare** to produce loud music on the lyre

perspargō *see* **perspergo**

perspectē *adv* intelligently

perspect·ō -āre -āvī -ātus *tr* to examine carefully; to watch steadily ‖ *intr* to look all around, have a look around

perspect·us -a -um *pp of* **perspicio** ‖ *adj* well-known, clear, evident; **res penitus perspectae** matters clearly understood

perspecul·or -ārī -ātus sum *tr* to explore thoroughly; *(mil)* to reconnoiter

persper·gō -gĕre -sī -sus *tr* **(-spar-)** to sprinkle; to strew *(w. flowers)*

perspexī *perf of* **perspicio**

perspic·ax -ācis *adj* sharp-sighted; keen, penetrating, perspicacious

perspicienti·a -ae *f* clear perception

per·spiciō -spicĕre -spexī -spectus *tr* to see through; to look through; to look closely at, look over, examine, inspect, observe; to discern, ascertain; to prove

perspicuē *adv* clearly

perspicuit·ās -ātis *f* clarity

perspicu·us -a -um *adj* clear; transparent; clearly visible, conspicuous; plain, evident; lucid *(expression)*

perspīr·ō -āre *intr* to blow steadily

perspissō *adv* very slowly

persternō -sternĕre -strāvī -strātus *tr* to pave *(a road)* along its full length

perstimul·ō -āre -āvī -ātus *tr* to stimulate; to continue to stir up

per·stō stāre -stitī -stātum *intr* to stand firm, hold one's ground; to remain standing; to remain unchanged, last; to be firm, persevere, hold out; *(of soldiers)* to continue under arms; *(of things)* to remain stationary; *(w. inf)* to continue obstinately to *(do s.th.)*

perstrātus *pp* of **persterno**

perstrep·ō -ĕre -uī *intr* to make a loud noise, make a lot of noise

perstringō perstringĕre perstrinxī perstrictum *tr* to tie, tie up; to make unfavorable mention of; *(of sounds)* to grate on; to blunt, deaden *(the senses);* to dazzle *(the eyes);* to deafen *(the ears); (of a weapon)* to graze; to glance over; to touch lightly on; to wound *(s.o.'s)* feelings, offend; **Crassus meis litteris perstrictus est** Crassus was offended by *(or* took offense at) my letter; **horror ingens spectantes perstrinxit** a deep shudder came over the onlookers

perstudiōsē *adv* enthusiastically

perstudiōs·us -a -um *adj (w. gen)* very fond of, enthusiastic about

persuā·deō -dēre -sī -sum *intr (w. dat)* to persuade, convince; **sibi persuasum habere** to have oneself convinced

persuāsi·ō -ōnis *f* convincing; conviction, belief

persuāstr·ix -īcis *f* seductress

persuāsum *pp of* **persuadeo**

persuās·us -ūs *m* persuasion

persubtīl·is -is -e *adj* of very fine texture; very subtle, very ingenious

persult·ō -āre -āvī -ātus *tr* to prance about; to scour *(woods)* ‖ *intr* to gambol, prance, run around

per·taedet -taedēre -taesum est *v impers (w. acc of person = subject in English and gen of thing = object in English)* to be weary of, be sick and tired of, be bored with, *e.g.,* **me hujus negotii pertaedet** I am sick and tired of this business

perte·gō -gĕre -xī -ctus *tr* to cover up, cover completely; to roof over

pertempt·ō -āre -āvī -ātus *tr* **(-tent-)** to test thoroughly; to sound *(s.o.)* out; to consider well; *(fig)* to fill, pervade; **gaudia pertemptant pectus** joy fills *(their)* hearts

perten·dō -děre -dī -sus *or* **-tus** *tr* to press on with, continue, carry out ‖ *intr* to press on, continue, persevere, keep going
pertenu·is -is -e *adj* very thin, very slight, very small, very fine
perterebr·ō -āre -āvī -ātus *tr* to bore through
perter·geō -ēre -sī -sus *tr* to wipe off; *(of air)* to brush lightly against
perterre·faciō -facěre -fēcī -factus *tr* to scare the life out of
perterr·eō -ēre -uī -itus *tr* to frighten, terrify; *(w.* **ab)** to frighten *(s.o.)* away from
perterricrep·us -a -um *adj* terrible-sounding, rattling frightfully
pertex·ō -ěre -uī -tus *tr* to bring to an end, go through with, accomplish; to complete the composition of *(a speech, writing)*
pertic·a -ae *f* pole; rod, staff; ten-foot measuring pole; *(fig)* measure
pertimefact·us -a -um *adj* thoroughly frightened
pertim·escō -escěre -uī *tr* to be alarmed at, become afraid of ‖ *intr* to become very frightened *or* alarmed
pertināci·a -ae *f* stubbornness; perseverance, determination
pertināciter *adv* stubbornly, tenaciously; through thick and thin
pertin·ax -ācis *adj* very tenacious; persevering, steadfast; stubborn
pertin·eō -ēre -uī *intr* to reach, extend; *(w.* **per** + *acc)* **1** to pervade; **2** reach; *(w.* **ad)** **1** to extend to, reach; **2** to pertain to, relate to, concern; **3** to apply to, be applicable to, suit, be suitable to; **4** to be conducive to; **5** to belong to; **quod pertinet** *(w.* **ad)** as regards
perting·ō -ěre *tr* to get as far as, reach ‖ *intr* to extend; **collis in inmensum pertingens** a hill extending a very long distance
pertoler·ō -āre -āvī -ātus *tr* to put up with, endure to the end
pertorqu·eō -ēre *tr* to twist, distort
pertractātē *adv* in a trite manner
pertractāti·ō -ōnis *f* handling, treatment
pertract·ō -āre -āvī -ātus *tr* to handle; *(fig)* to treat systematically; to examine in detail
per·trahō -trahěre -traxī -tractus *tr* to drag along; to drag by force *(to s.th. unpleasant)*; to lure, lead on *(an enemy)*; to tow
pertrect- = **pertract-**
pertrist·is -is -e *adj* very sad; very stern
pertulī *perf of* **perfero**
pertumultuōsē *adv* very excitedly, hysterically
per·tundō -tunděre -tudī -tūsus *tr* to punch a hole through, perforate
perturbātē *adv* in confusion
perturbāti·ō -ōnis *f* confusion, disorder; riot; distress, agitation; strong emotion
perturbātr·ix -īcis *f* disturbing element
perturbāt·us -a -um *adj* disturbed, troubled; excited, alarmed; embarrassed
perturb·ō -āre -āvī -ātus *tr* to throw into confusion, confuse; to disturb; to embarrass; to upset; to alarm
perturp·is -is -e *adj* downright shameful
pertūs·us -a -um *pp of* **pertundo** ‖ *adj* perforated; tattered *(clothes)*
pērul·a -ae *f* small satchel
perun·g(u)ō -g(u)ěre -xī -ctus *tr* to anoint thoroughly
perurbān·us -a -um *adj* very polite; very sophisticated ‖ *m* snob
per·ūrō -ūrěre -ussī -ustus *tr* to burn up; to consume; to inflame, rub sore; to scorch; *(of cold)* to nip, bite; *(fig)* to fire, inflame
Perusi·a -ae *f* town in Etruria *(modern Perugia)*
Perusīn·us -a -um *adj* of Perusia ‖ *mpl* inhabitants of Perusia ‖ *n* an estate in Perusia
perussī *perf of* **peruro**
perustus *pp of* **peruro**
perūtil·is -is -e *adj* very useful
per·vādō -vāděre -vāsī -vāsus *tr* to pass through, go through; to pervade ‖ *intr* to spread; to penetrate; *(w.* **ad** *or* **in** + *acc)* **1** to go as far as, spread to; **2** to reach, arrive at; **3** to penetrate; *(w.* **per** + *acc)* to spread through *or* over
pervagāt·us -a -um *adj* widespread, prevalent, well-known; general, common; of widespread application
pervag·or -ārī -ātus sum *tr* to spread through *or* over, pervade ‖ *intr* to wander all over, range about; *(w.* **ad)** **1** to spread to, extend to; **2** to be known as far as
pervag·us -a -um *adj* wandering about
perval·eō -ēre *intr (of a magnet)* to retain (its) power
pervariē *adv* in various versions
pervast·ō -āre -āvī -ātus *tr* to devastate
pervāsus *pp of* **pervado**
perve·hō -hěre -xī -ctus *tr* to bring, carry, convey; to bring *(e.g, supplies)* through ‖ *pass* to ride, drive, sail; **in portum pervehi** to sail into port, reach port
pervell·ō -ěre -ī *tr* to pull hard; to pinch hard; to excite, arouse; to cause to twinge; *(fig)* to disparage; **aurem alicui pervellere** to pull s.o.'s ear *(as a reminder)*
per·veniō -venīre -vēnī -ventus *tr* to come to, reach ‖ *intr* to come up; to arrive; *(w.* **ad** *or* **in** + *acc)* **1** to arrive at, reach; **2** *(fig)* to attain to
pervēn·or -ārī *tr* to search through, scour *(e.g., all the city)*

perversē *adv* **(-vors-)** wrongly, perversely
perversāriō *adv* **(-vors-)** in a wrong-headed way, wrongly
perversit·ās -ātis *f* perversity, unreasonableness; distortion
pervers·us -a -um *adj* **(-vors-)** turned the wrong way, awry, crooked; cross-eyed; *(fig)* crooked, wrong, perverse; *(fig)* spiteful, malicious
per·vertō -vertĕre -vertī -versus *tr* **(-vort-)** to overturn, upset, knock down; to invert the order of; to cause to face in the opposite direction; to bend out of shape, distort; to misrepresent, falsify *(statements);* to divert to an improper use, misuse, abuse; to undo, destroy; to pervert, spoil
pervesperī *adv* late in the evening
pervestīgāti·ō -ōnis *f* thorough search, examining, investigation
pervestīg·ō -āre -āvī -ātus *tr* to track down; to examine in detail; *(fig)* to trace, detect
pervet·us -eris *adj* very old, ancient
pervetust·us -a -um *adj* very ancient
pervexī *perf of* **perveho**
perviam *adv* **perviam facere** to make accessible
pervicāci·a -ae *f* persistence; *(pej)* stubbornness; **pervicacia in hostem** obstinate resistance to the enemy
pervicācius *adv* more stubbornly
pervic·ax -ācis *adj* persistent, determined; *(pej)* headstrong, stubborn
pervīcī *perf of* **pervinco**
pervictus *pp of* **pervinco**
per·videō -vidēre -vīdī -vīsus *tr* to look over, survey; to see through; to examine, investigate; to realize, perceive fully
pervig·eō -ēre -uī *intr* to continue to thrive
pervig·il -ilis *adj* wide-awake, ever watchful
pervigilāti·ō -ōnis *f* religious vigil
pervigil·ium -(i)ī *n* all-night vigil
pervigil·ō -āre -āvī -ātus *tr* to spend *or* pass *(nights, days)* without sleep ‖ *intr* to stay awake all night, keep an all-night vigil
pervīl·is -is -e *adj* very cheap
per·vincō -vincĕre -vīcī -victus *tr* to defeat completely, completely get the better of; to outdo; to outbid; to convince; to prove ‖ *intr* to win, succeed; to carry a point; *(w.* **ut)** to succeed in, bring it about that; **non pervicit ut referrent consules** he did not succeed in having the consuls make a formal proposal
pervīsus *pp of* **pervideo**
pervi·us -a -um *adj* crossable, passable; open at both ends; perforated; acessible; open to entreaty ‖ *n* passage
per·vīvō -vīvĕre -vixī *intr* to live on, go on living
pervolgō *see* **pervulgo**
pervolit·ō -āre -āvī -ātus *tr & intr* to fly about, flit about
pervol·ō -āre -āvī -ātus *tr* to fly through, fly about, flit about; to dart through, pass quickly over ‖ *intr* to fly about, flit about; *(w.* **in** + *acc)* to fly through to, arrive at, reach
per·volō -velle *tr* to wish very much; **te quam primum pervelim videre** I'd like very much to see you as soon as possible
pervolūt·ō -āre -āvī -ātus *tr* to turn over often, read through *(a book scroll)*
per·volvō -volvĕre -volvī -volūtus *tr* to roll *(s.o.)* over; to keep reading, read through *(a scroll)* ‖ *refl* to roll around ‖ *pass* to be busy
pervor- = perver-
pervulgāt·us -a -um *adj* **(-vol-)** widely known, very common
pervulg·ō -āre -āvī -ātus *tr* **(-vol-)** to make known, make public, publicize; to frequent ‖ *refl* to prostitute oneself
pēs pedis *m* foot *(of body, of table, of couch; in verse);* rope at lower part of a sail, sheet; **ad pedes descendere** to dismount *(in order to fight on foot);* **ad pedes pugna** an infantry fight; **aequis pedibus labi** to sail on an even keel; **ante pedes** in plain view; **in pedes** feet first; **pede dextro** *(or* **felice** *or* **secundo)** auspiciously *(the right foot being associated with good omens);* **pedem conferre** to come to close quarters; **pedem ferre** to come; to go; **pedem ponere** *(w.* **in** + *abl)* to set foot in; **pedem referre** to step back, retreat; **pedes tollere** to lift the legs *(for sexual intercourse);* **pedibus** on foot; **pedibus claudere** to set to verse, put in meter; **pedibus ire in sententiam** *(w. gen)* to vote in favor of the proposal of; **pedibus itur in sententiam** the proposal is put to a vote; **pedibus merere** *(or* **pedibus mereri)** to serve in the infantry; **pedibus vincere** to win a footrace; **plano pede** on level ground; **pugna ad pedes** infantry battle; **se in pedes conjicere** *(or* **se in pedes conferre** *or* **se in pedes dare** *or* **se pedibus dare)** to take to one's heels; **servus a pedibus** footman; **sub pedibus** under one's sway
pessimē *(superl of* **male)** *adv* **(-sum-)** worst; most wickedly; most unfortunately; by a stroke of bad luck
pessim·us -a -um *(superl of* **malus)** *adj* **(-sum-)** worst; most villainous; most distressing
Pessin·ūs -untis *m* Galatian town on the borders of Phrygia, famous for its cult of Cybele
pessul·us -ī *m* bolt *(of a door)*
pessum *adv* down, to the ground, to the bottom; **pessum dare** *(or* **pessumdare**

as one word) to send to the bottom, sink, drown, ruin, destroy; **pessum ire** to go down, sink, go to pot

pestif·er -era -erum *adj* pestilential; destructive, pernicious, disastrous ‖ *m* troublemaker

pestiferē *adv* disastrously

pestil·ens -entis *adj* pestilential, unhealthful; *(fig)* disastrous

pestilenti·a -ae *f* pestilence, plague; unhealthful atmosphere *or* climate

pestilit·ās -ātis *f* pestilence, plague

pest·is -is *f* contagious disease; plague; death, destruction; instrument of death *or* destruction; *(of persons)* troublemaker, anarchist, subversive

petal·ium -(i)ī *n* thin sheet of metal

petasāt·us -a -um *adj* wearing a hat; *(fig)* ready to travel

petas·ō -ōnis *m* ham

petasuncul·us -ī *m* little ham

petas·us -ī *m* broad-rimmed hat

petaur·um -ī *n* springboard

Petēli·a -ae *f* town in Bruttium, besieged by Hannibal

petess·ō -ĕre *tr* **(-tiss-)** to be eager for, pursue; **pugnam petessere** to be spoiling for a fight

petīti·ō -ōnis *f* attack, blow, thrust, aim; petition, request, application; *(leg)* claim, suit, suing, right to sue; *(pol)* candidacy, political campaign; **petitioni se dare** to become a candidate

petīt·or -ōris *m* applicant; *(leg)* plaintiff; *(pol)* political candidate

petītr·ix -īcis *f (leg)* plaintiff *(female)*

petītur·iō -īre *intr (pol)* to be eager for office

petīt·us -a -um *pp of* **peto** ‖ *adj* **longe petitus** far-fetched ‖ *n* request

pet·ō -ĕre -īvī *or* **-iī -ītus** *tr* to make for, head for; to attack; to strive after; to aim at; to demand, require, exact; to ask for; to claim, lay claim to, sue for; to beg, entreat; to look for, go in search of, search for; to run after, chase *(girls);* to go and fetch; to obtain; to draw *(a sigh);* to run for *(office);* to refer to, relate to; *(w. dat or* **ad** *or* **in** *+ acc)* to demand *(s.o. or s.th.) (for a specific purpose), e.g.,* **custodem in vincla petere** to demand that the watchdog be chained; **astra petere** to mount to the stars; **terram petere** to fall to the earth

petorrit·um -ī *n* **(-tōri-)** open four-wheeled carriage *(of Celtic origin)*

petr·a -ae *f* rock, crag

Petr·a -ae *f* Petra *(name of several towns, esp. the chief town of Arabia Petraea)*

Petrei·us -ī *m* Roman clan name *(nomen), esp.* Marcus Petreius *(legate of Gaius Antonius against Catiline and later of Pompey in the Civil War)*

Petrīn·um -ī *n* place near Sinuessa on the border between Latium and Campania ‖ estate in this area

petr·ō -ōnis *m* yokel

Petrōn·ius -(i)ī *m* Petronius Arbiter *(author and master of cermonies at the court of Nero)*

petul·ans -antis *adj* petulant, brash, smart-alecky; *(of sexual behavior)* horny

petulanter *adv* brashly, rudely

petulanti·a -ae *f* petulance, brashness; *(of speech)* rudeness; *(of sexual behavior)* horniness

petulc·us -a -um *adj* butting, apt to butt

Peuceti·a -ae *f* Peucetia *(S. section of Apulia)*

Peuceti·us -a -um *adj* of Peucetia

pexī *perf of* **pecto**

pex·us -a -um *pp of* **pecto** ‖ *adj* neatly combed; new, still having the nap on

Phaeāc·es -um *mpl* Phaeacians *(people living on a utopian island, according to the Odyssesy)*

Phaeāci·us -a -um *adj* Phaeacian ‖ *f* Phaeacia *(sometimes identified with Corcyra and ruled by King Alcinoüs)*

Phaeāc·us -a -um *adj* Phaeacian

Phae·ax -ācis *or* **-ācos** *m* Phaeacian ‖ *m* Phaeacian; well-fed man

Phaedr·a -ae *f* daughter of Minos and wife of Theseus

Phaedr·us -ī *m* one of the Socratic circle, who gave his name to a dialogue of Plato ‖ Epicurean philosopher of Athens, who taught Cicero ‖ writer of fables, freedman of Augustus

Phaesti·as -adis *or* **-ados** *adj (fem only)* a woman of Phestum

Phaesti·us -a -um *adj* of Phestum

Phaest·um -ī *n* town in S. Crete

Phaët(h)·ōn -ontis *or* **-ontos** *m* son of Helios, who was killed by Zeus while driving his father's chariot

Phaëthonte·us -a -um *adj* of Phaëthon

Phaët(h)ontiad·es -um *fpl* sisters of Phaëthon, who were turned into trees

Phaëthont·is -idis *or* **-dos** *adj (fem only)* of Phaëthon ‖ *fpl* sisters of Phaëthon

Phaëthūs·a -ae *f* the eldest sister of Phaëthon

pha·ger -grī *m* fish *(sea-bream?)*

phalang·a -ae *f* wooden roller *(for moving ships and siege engines)*

phalangīt·ae -ārum *mpl* soldiers belonging to a Macedonian phalanx

phal·anx -angis *f* phalanx *(compact body of heavy-armed men in battle formation first developed by the Macedonians)*

phalāric·a -ae *f* **(fal-)** firebrand, fiery missile *(shot by a catapult or thrown by hand)*

Phalar·is -idis *m* a tyrant of Agrigentum on S. coast of Sicily, notorious for the bronze bull in which he roasted his victims *(c. 570–554 B.C.)*

phaler·ae -ārum *fpl* military medals; medallions *(worn by horses on the forehead and chest)*

phalerāt·us -a -um *adj* wearing medals, decorated; ornamental

Phalēr·eus -eī *or* **-eos** *m* Demetrius of Phalerum *(Athenian statesman)*

Phalēric·us -a -um *adj* of Phaleron

Phalēr·um -ī *n* Athenian harbor

phantasm·a -atis *n* phantom, ghost

Pha·ōn -ōnis *f* legendary Lesbian, reputed lover of Sappho

pharetr·a -ae *f* quiver

pharetrāt·us -a -um *adj* carrrying a quiver

Phari·us -a -um *adj* of Pharos, Pharian; *(poet)* Egyptian

pharmaceutri·a -ae *f* witch, sorceress

pharmacopōl·a -ae *m* druggist; *(pej)* quack

Pharnac·ēs -is *m* Pharnaces I *(king of Pontus and grandfather of Mithridates, died c. 169 B.C.)* ‖ Pharnaces II *(son of Mithridates the Great, easily defeated by Caesar at Zela in 47 B.C.)*

Phar·os *or* **Phar·us -ī** *f (m)* Pharos *(island lying off Alexandria);* lighthouse *(built on the E. tip of Pharos by Ptolemy II Philadelphus);* a lighthouse *(in general); (poet)* Egypt

Pharsālic·us -a -um *adj* of Pharsalus

Pharsāli·us -a -um *adj* Pharsalian ‖ *f* Pharsalia *(district of Thessaly)*

Pharsāl·os *or* **Pharsāl·us -ī** *f* town in Thessaly near which Caesar defeated Pompey *(48 B.C.)*

phasēl·us *or* **phasēl·os -ī** *mf* kidney bean; light passenger ship

Phāsiac·us -a -um *adj* of the River Phasis in Colchis; Colchian

phāsiān·a -ae *f* pheasant *(female)*

phāsiān·us -ī *m* pheasant

Phāsi·as -ados *adj (fem only)* Colchian ‖ *f* Medea

Phās·is -idis *or* **-idos** *m* river in Colchis

phasm·a -atis *n* specter, ghost

Phēgēi·us -a -um *adj* of Phegeus, king of Psophis in Arcadia, the father of Alphesiboea

Phēm·ius -(i)ī *m* minstrel of Ithaca

Phene·us *or* **Phene·os -ī** *m or* **Phene·on -ī** *n* a town and stream with subterranean channels in Arcadia

Pher·ae -ārum *fpl* city in Thessaly, home of Admetus

Pherae·us -a -um *adj* of Pherae

Phereclē·us -a -um *adj* of Phereclus *(the builder of Paris' ship)*

phial·a -ae *f* saucer

Phīdiac·us -a -um *adj* of Phidias

Phīdi·ās -ae *m* Greek sculptor and friend of Pericles *(fl 440 B.C.)*

Philaen·ī -ōrum *mpl* two Carthaginian brothers who agreed to be buried alive to establish the frontier between Carthage and Cyrene

Philamm·ōn -ōnis *m* legendary musician, son of Apollo

philēm·a -atis *n* kiss

Philēm·ō(n) -onis *m* Philemon *(pious rustic who was changed into an oak tree while his wife Baucis was changed into a linden tree)*

Philippens·is -is -e *adj* of Philippi ‖ *mpl* the people of Philippi

Philippē·us -a -um *adj* of Philip II of Macedon *(esp. as epithet of gold coins minted by Philip)*

Philipp·ī -ōrum *mpl* city in Macedonia where Octavian and Antony defeated Brutus and Cassius *(42 B.C.)*

Philippic·ae -ārum *fpl* Philippics *(series of vitriolic speeches directed at Antony by Cicero)*

Philippopol·is -eōs *f* city in Thessaly

Philipp·us -ī *m* name of several kings of Macedon *(esp. Philip II, father of Alexander, c. 382–336 B.C.)*

Philist·us -ī *m* historian, from Syracuse *(d. 356 B.C.)*

philiti·a *or* **phiditi·a -ōrum** *npl* public meals at Sparta

Phillyrid·ēs -is *m* son of Philyra *(i.e., Chiron)*

Phil·ō(n) -ōnis *m* Philo *(Academic philosopher and teacher of Cicero)*

Philoctēt·ēs -ae *m* Greek warrior who was abandoned by the Greek army on the island of Lemnos

philologi·a -ae *f* love of study; study of literature

philolog·us -a -um *adj* learned, scholarly ‖ *m* scholar

Philomēl·a -ae *f* daughter of Pandion; she and her sister Procne were changed into nightingales

philosoph·a -ae *f* philosopher *(female)*

philosophē *adv* philosophically

philosophi·a -ae *f* philosophy

philosoph·or -ārī -ātus sum *intr* to pursue philosophy; to philosophize, moralize

philosoph·us -a -um *adj* philosophical ‖ *m* philosopher

philtr·um -ī *n* love potion

philyr·a -ae *f* inner bark of the lime tree *(from which bands for chaplets were made)*

Philyr·a -ae *f* nymph, the mother of Chiron by Saturn

Philyrēi·us -a -um *adj* of Philyra; of Chiron; **heros Philyraeius** Chiron

phīm·us -ī *m* dice box

Phīnēi·us -a -um *adj* of Phineus

Phīn·ēus -ēī *or* **-eos** *m* king of Thrace, plagued by the Harpies
Phīnid·ēs -ae *m* descendant of Phineus
Phlegeth·ōn -ontis *m* river of fire in the lower world
Phlegethont·is -idis *adj (fem only)* of Phlegethon
Phlegrae·us -a -um *adj* of Phlegra *(where the Giants were said to have been struck by lightning in battle with the gods)*
Phlegy·ae -ārum *mpl* a people of Thessaly
Phlegy·ās -ae *m* king of the Lapiths, son of Ares, and father of Ixion
Phlī·ūs -untis *f* city of N.E. Peloponnesus
phōc·a -ae *or* **phōc·ē -ēs** *f* seal
Phōcae·a -ae *f* Ionian city on the coast of Asia Minor
Phōcaeens·is -is -e *adj* of Phocaea ‖ *mpl* the people of Phocaea
Phōcae·us -a -um *adj* of Phocaea ‖ *mpl* the people of Phocaea
Phōcaïc·us *or* **Phōci·us -a -um** *adj* Phocian
Phōc·is -idis *or* **-idos** *f* region of central Greece containing the oracle of Delphi
Phoeb·as -ados *f* prophetess, priestess of Apollo
Phoeb·ē -ēs *f* Phoebe *(moon goddess, the sister of Phoebus, identified with Diana);* night
Phoebēi·us -a -um *adj* of Phoebus *(as sun-god and as god of prophecy, music, and healing);* of Aesculapius; **ales Phoebeius** the raven; **anguis Phoebeius** the snake of Aesculapius
Phoebē·us -a -um *adj* of Phoebus
Phoebigen·a -ae *m* son of Phoebus *(i.e., Aesculapius)*
Phoeb·us -ī *m* Apollo as sun-god; sun
Phoenic·a -ae *or* **Phoenīc·ē -ēs** *f* Phoenicia
Phoenīc·es -um *mpl* Phoenicians
phoenīcopter·us -ī *m* flamingo
Phoeniss·a -ae *f* Phoenician woman *(esp. Dido)*
phoen·ix -īcis *or* **-īcos** *m* phoenix *(a bird said to live 500 years and from whose ashes a young phoenix would be born)*
Phoen·ix -īcis *or* **-īcos** *m* Phoenician ‖ son of Amyntor and companion of Achilles ‖ son of Agenor and brother of Cadmus
Phol·us -ī *m* name of a Centaur
phōnasc·us -ī *m* voice teacher
Phorc·is -idos *f* daughter of Phorcus; Medusa ‖ *fpl* the Graeae
Phorc·us -ī *m* son of Neptune and father of Medusa and the other Gorgons and the Graeae
Phorcȳn·is -idis *or* **-idos** *f* Medusa
Phormi·ō -ōnis *m* Athenian admiral *(died c. 428 B.C.)* ‖ Peripatetic philosopher who lectured Hannibal on military science
Phraāt·ēs -ae *m* king of Parthia
phrenēs·is -is *f* frenzy, delirium
phrenētic·us -a -um *adj* frenetic, frantic, delirious
Phrix·us *or* **Phrix·os -ī** *m* son of Athamas and Nephele and brother of Helle
phronēs·is -is *f* wisdom
Phryg·es -um *mpl* Phrygians
Phrygi·a -ae *f* a country comprising part of the central and W. Asia; *(poet)* Troy
phrygi·ō -ōnis *m* **(fryg-)** embroiderer
Phrygi·us -a -um *adj & mf* Phrygian; Trojan
Phrȳn·ē -ēs *f* Athenian courtesan who offered to rebuild Thebes when it was destroyed by Alexander the Great
Phry·x -gis *or* **-gos** *adj* Phrygian *(often w. reference to Troy or the Trojans)*
Phthī·a -ae *f* home of Achilles in Thessaly
Phthī·as -adis *f* woman from Phthia
Phthīōt·a *or* **Phthiot·ēs -ae** *m* native of Phthia
P(h)thīōtic·us -a -um *adj* of Phthia
phthis·is -is *f* tuberculosis
Phthī·us -a -um *adj* of Phthia
phȳ *interj* bah!
phylac·a -ae *f* prison
Phylac·ē -ēs *f* city of Thessaly, where Protesilaus was king
Phylacē·is -idos *adj (fem only)* of Phylace, *or* of Phylacus, the founder of Phylace
Phylacēi·us -a -um *adj* of Phylace *or* Phylacus; **conjunx Phylaceia** Laodamia *(wife of Protesilaus)*
Phylacid·ēs -ae *m* descendant of Phylacus, son of Diomede *(esp. Protesilaus)*
phylarch·us -ī *m* tribal chief
Phyllēi·us -a -um *adj* of the city of Phyllus in Thessaly; **Phylleius juvenis** Caeneus
Phyll·is -idis *or* **-idos** *f* daughter of King Sithon of Thrace, who was changed into an almond tree ‖ stock female name in poetry
physic·a -ae *or* **physic·ē -ēs** *f* natural science
physicē *adv* scientifically
physic·us -a -um *adj* natural, physical, belonging to natural philosophy *or* physics ‖ *m* natural philosopher, physicist ‖ *npl* natural science
physiognōm·ōn -onis *m* physiognomist
physiologi·a -ae *f* natural science
piābil·is -is -e *adj* expiable
piāculār·is -is -e *adj* expiatory; demanding expiatory rites ‖ *npl* expiatory sacrifices
piācul·um -ī *n* propitiatory sacrifice, victim; atonement, expiation; remedy; crime, sacrilege; punishment
piām·en -inis *n* atonement
pīc·a -ae *f* magpie, jay
picāri·a -ae *f* place where pitch is made
pice·a -ae *f* pine tree, spruce
Pīc·ens -entis *adj* Picene, of Picenum

Pīcentīn·us -a -um *adj* of Picenum; of Picentia *(town in S. Campania)*
Pīcēn·um -ī *n* distinct on the Adriatic coast of central Italy
Pīcēn·us -a -um *adj & m* Picene ‖ *n see* **Picenus**
pice·us -a -um *adj* made of pitch; pitch-black
pic·ō -āre -āvī -ātus *tr* to tar, coat with pitch
pict·or -ōris *m* painter ‖ **Pictor** Quintus Fabius Pictor *(earliest Roman historian, who wrote a history of Rome in Greek, fl 225 B.C.)*
pictūr·a -ae *f* painting; (art of) painting; embroidery
pictūrāt·us -a -um *adj* painted; embroidered
pict·us -a -um *pp of* **pingo** ‖ *adj* painted; embroidered *(in color);* **tabula picta** a painting
pīc·us -ī *m* woodpecker ‖ **Picus** son of Saturn and grandfather of Latinus; Picus was changed by Circe into a woodpecker
piē *adv* dutifully; affectionately
Pīeri·a -ae *f* district of S. E. Macedonia
Pīer·is -idos *f* daughter of Pieros; Muse ‖ *fpl* the nine Muses
Pīeri·us -a -um *adj* Pierian; poetic; musical ‖ *f see* **Pieria** ‖ *fpl* Muses
Pīer·os *or* **Pīer·us -ī** *m* Pieros *(King of Emathia, or Macedonia, who named his nine daughters after the Muses; they were defeated in a contest with the Muses and were changed into birds)*
piet·ās -ātis *f* sense of responsibility, sense of duty; devotion, piety; *(of gods)* due regard *(for human beings);* kindness, tenderness; loyalty to the gods and country; *(w dat or* **adversus** *or* **erga** *or* **in** + *acc)* respect for, devotion to, loyalty to
pi·ger -gra -grum *adj* apathetic, slow, lazy; reluctant, unwilling; numbing *(cold);* slow-moving, tedious *(war, etc.);* backward, slow, dull
pig·et -ēre -uit *or* **-itum est** *v impers* it irks, pains, annoys; *(w. gen of cause of feeling), e.g.:* **piget stultitiae meae** I am irked by my own foolishness; *(w. inf), e.g.:* **illa me composuisse piget** I regret having written those verses
pigmentār·ius -(i)ī *m* paint dealer
pigment·um -ī *n* pigment, paint, color; coloring *(of style)*
pignerāt·or -ōris *m* mortgagee
pigner·ō -āre -āvī -ātus *tr* to mortgage; to pawn; *(fig)* to pledge
pigner·or -ārī -ātus sum *tr* to take as a pledge, accept in good faith; to lay claim to; to assure
pign·us -eris *or* **-oris** *n* pledge, security, guarantee; hostage; mortgage; income from mortgages; wager, stake; *(fig)* pledge, assurance ‖ *npl* children
pigrē *adv* slowly, sluggishly
pigriti·a -ae *or* **pigriti·ēs -ēī** *f* sluggishness, laziness
pigr·ō -āre -āvī *or* **pigr·ōr -ārī** *intr* to be slow, be sluggish, be lazy
pīl·a -ae *f (vessel for pounding)* mortar; pillar; pier; funerary monument *(w. cavity for mortal remains)*
pĭl·a -ae *f* ball; ball game; globe; ballot *(used by jury);* **mea pila est** the ball is mine, I've won; **pilā ludere** to play ball
pīlān·us -ī *m* soldier in the third rank in battle
pīlāt·us -a -um *adj* armed with javelin
Pīlāt·us -ī *m* Pontius Pilate *(prefect of Judea, A.D. 26–36)*
pīlent·um -ī *n* ladies' carriage
pilleāt·us -a -um *adj* **(pīl-)** wearing a felt skullcap *(as a symbol of freed status)*
pilleol·us -ī *m* (small) skullcap
pille·um -ī *n or* **pille·us -ī** *m or* **pīle·um -ī** *n* felt cap *or* hat *(worn by Romans at festivals, esp. at the Saturnalia, and given to a slave when freed as a symbol of his freedom);* freedom
pilōs·us -a -um *adj* hairy
pīl·um -ī *n* javelin
Pīlumn·us -ī *m* primitive Italic deity
pīl·us -ī *m* maniple *or* company of the triarii; company of veteran reserves; **primi pili centurio** chief centurion of a legion; **primus pilus** chief centurion *(of the triarii and therefore of the legion)*
pil·us -ī *n* hair; **non pili facere** to not care a whit for
Pimpl·a -ae *f* spring in Pieria sacred to the Muses
Pimplē·a -ae *or* **Pi(m)plē·is -idis** *or* **idos** *f* Muse
Pi(m)plē(i)·us -a -um *adj* of Pimpla ‖ *f* the spring at Pimpla
pīn·a -ae *f* a bivalve shellfish
Pīnāri·us -a -um *adj* name of a patrician clan at Rome, concerned with the cult of Hercules
Pindaric·us -a -um *adj* Pindaric
Pindar·us -ī *m* Pindar *(Greek lyric poet from Thebes in Boetoia, 519–438 B.C.)*
Pind·us -ī *m* mountain range separating Thessaly from Macedonia, connected with the Muses
pīnēt·um -ī *n* pine forest
pīne·us -a -um *adj* pine-, of pine
pingō pingĕre pinxī pictus *tr* to draw, paint; to embroider; to depict, represent, portray; to stain, color; to decorate; *(rhet)* to embellish
pingu·e -is *n* fat
pinguesc·ō -ĕre *intr* to get fat; to become fertile
pingu·is -is -e *adj* fat; fatty, greasy; *(of*

lamps) full of oil; *(of torches)* full of pitch; juicy; full-bodied *(wine);* rich, full *(sound);* rich, fertile *(land);* fat, sleek *(cattle);* thick *(in dimension);* strong *(words); (of altars)* caked with fat and blood; dense; stupid, dull; clumsy *(writing);* quiet, comfortable *(life, home, retreat);* **crura luto pinguia** legs caked with mud

pīnif·er *or* **pīnig·er -era -erum** *adj* pine-producing, pine-covered

pinn·a -ae *f* feather; wing; flight; fin; feathered arrow; pinnacle, battlement

pinnāt·us -a -um *adj* feathered, winged

pinnig·er -era -erum *adj* winged; feathered; having fins

pinnip·ēs -edis *adj* wing-footed

pinnipot·ens -entis *adj* able to fly

pinnirap·us -ī *m* crest-snatcher *(gladiator who tried to get the crest of his opponent's helmet)*

pinnul·a -ae *f* little wing

pīnotēr·ēs -ae *m* hermit crab

pinsit·ō -āre *tr* to pound (continually)

pī(n)s·ō -ĕre -ī *(or* **-uī)** **-us** *(or* **-itus)** *tr* to pound

pīn·us -ūs *or* **-ī** *f* pine tree, fir tree; pine forest; ship; torch; wreath of pine

pi·ō -āre -āvī -ātus *tr* to appease by sacrifice, propitiate; to honor with religious rites, worship; to purify with religious rites; to atone for, expiate; to avert

pip·er -eris *n* pepper

pipinn·a -ae f childish term for the penis

pīpil·ō -āre *intr* to chirp

pīpi·ō -āre *intr* to chirp

pīpul·um -ī *n or* **pīpul·us -ī** *m* shrieking, yelling

Pīrae·eūs *or* **Pīrae·us -ī** *m or* **Pīrae·a -ōrum** *npl* Piraeus *(principal harbor of Athens)*

Pīrae·us -a -um *adj* of Piraeus ‖ *mpl* inhabitants of Piraeus

pīrāt·a -ae *m* pirate

pīrātic·us -a -um *adj* pirate ‖ *f* piracy; **piraticam facere** to practice piracy

Pīrēn·ē -ēs *or* **Pīrēn·a -ae** *f* Pirene (*spring on the citadel of Corinth near which Bellerophon caught Pegasus*)

Pīrēn·is -idos *adj (fem only)* of the spring of Pirene

Pīritho·ūs -ī *m* son of Ixion and king of the Lapiths

pir·um -ī *n* pear

pir·us -ī *f* pear tree

Pīs·a -ae *f or* **Pīs·ae -ārum** *fpl* Pisa *(capital of Pisatis in Elis on the Alpheus River)*

Pīs·ae -ārum *fpl* Pisa *(ancient city of N. Etruria, alleged to have been founded by the people of Greek Pisa)*

Pīsae·us -a -um *adj* of Pisa ‖ *f* Hippodamia

Pīsān·us -a -um *adj* of Pisa *(in Etruria)*

Pisaur·um -ī *n* city in Umbria on the Adriatic coast *(modern Pisaro)*

piscāri·us -a -um *adj* fish; of fishing; **forum piscarium** fish market

piscāt·or -ōris *m* fisherman; fishmonger

piscātōri·us -a -um *adj* fishing; fish

piscāt·us -ūs *m* fishing; fish; *(fig)* good haul

piscicul·us -ī *m (lit & fig)* little fish

piscīn·a -ae *f* fish pond; swimming pool

piscīnār·ius -(i)ī *m* person fond of swimming pools *or* of fish ponds

pisc·is -is *m* fish ‖ **Pisces** *mpl (astr)* Pisces *(constellation)*

pisc·or -ārī -ātus sum *intr* to fish

piscōs·us -a -um *adj* full of fish

pisculent·us -a -um *adj* well-stocked with fish

Pisid·a -ae *m* Pisidian *(inhabitant of Pisidia, referred to in contempt for the alleged addiction of the Pisidians to augury)*

Pisidi·a -ae *f* region in S. Asia Minor

Pīsistratid·ae -ārum *mpl* sons of Pisistratus *(Hippias & Hipparchus)*

Pīsistrat·us -ī *m* enlightened tyrant of Athens *(560–527 B.C.)*

pīsō *see* **pinso**

Pīs·ō -ōnis *m* Roman family name *(cognomen)* of the Calpurnian clan ‖ Gnaeus Calpurnius Piso *(consul 7 B.C., accused of the murder of Germanicus in A.D. 19)* ‖ Gaius Calpurnius Piso *(alleged leader of the conspiracy against Nero in A.D. 65)*

pistill·um -ī *n or* **pistill·us -ī** *m* pestle

pist·or -ōris *m* miller; baker

Pistōriens·is -is -e *adj* of Pistorium *(town in Etruria)*

pistōri·us -a -um *adj* baker's; **opus pistorium** pastry

pistrill·a -ae *f* small mill; small bakery

pistrīn·a -ae *f* flour mill; bakery

pistrīnens·is -is -e *adj* of *or* belonging to a bakery

pistrīn·um -ī *n* flour mill; bakery; drudgery

pistr·is -is *or* **pistr·ix -īcis** *f* sea monster; whale, shark; swift ship; *(astr)* the Whale *(constellation)*

pīstus *pp of* **pi(n)so**

pīs·um -ī *n* pea

Pitan·ē -ēs *f* Aeolian settlement on the coast of Asia Minor near Pergamum

pithēc·ium -(i)ī *n* little monkey

Pitthē·is -idos *f* daughter of Pittheus *(i.e., Aethra)*

Pitth·eūs -eī *or* **-eos** *m* king of Troezen and father of Aethra, the mother of Theseus

Pitthē·us *or* **Pitthēi·us -a -um** *adj* of Pittheus

pītuīt·a -ae *f* phlegm; rheum; head cold

pītuītōs·us -a -um *adj* full of phlegm, phlegmatic

pity·ōn -ōnos *m* woods of pine trees

pi·us -a -um *adj* conscientious, dutiful; god-fearing, godly, holy; fatherly, motherly, brotherly, sisterly; affectionate; patriotic; good; sacred, holy *(objects connected with religion)*

pix pīcis *f* a sphinx

pix picis *f* pitch ‖ *fpl* chunks of pitch

plācābil·is -is -e *adj* easily appeased; pacifying, appeasing

plācābilit·ās -ātis *f* readiness to forgive, conciliatory disposition

plācām·en -inis *n* means of appeasing, peace-offering

plācāment·um -ī *n* means of appeasing, peace-offering

plācātē *adv* calmly, quietly

plācāti·ō -ōnis *f* pacifying, propitiating

plācāt·us -a -um *adj* calm, quiet; appeased, reconciled

plac·ens -entis *adj* pleasing

placent·a -ae *f* flat cake, pancake

placenti·a -ae *f* agreeableness

Placenti·a -ae *f* town on the river Po *(modern Piacenza)*

plac·eō -ēre -uī -itum *intr (w. dat)* to please, satisfy, give pleasure to, be acceptable to; **sibi placere** to be pleased with oneself ‖ *v impers* it seems right, seems proper; it is settled, is agreed; it is resolved, is decided; **eis placitum est ut considerarent** they decided to consider; **senatui placuit** the senate decided

placidē *adv* calmly, gently, quietly

placid·us -a -um *adj* calm; gentle; quiet, peaceful; tame *(animal)*

placit·ō -āre *intr* to be very pleasing

placit·us -a -um *adj* pleasing, acceptable; agreed upon ‖ *n* principle, belief, tenet; **ultra placitum laudare** to praise excessively

plāc·ō -āre -āvī -ātus *tr* to calm, quiet; to appease; to reconcile

plāg·a -ae *f* blow; wound, gash, welt; *(fig)* blow

plăg·a -ae *f* region, tract, zone; hunting net; mesh of a net; curtain; *(fig)* trap

plagiār·ius -(i)ī *m* plunderer; kidnapper; plagiarist

plāgig·er -era -erum *adj* covered with welts

plāgigerul·us -a -um *adj* covered with welts

plāgipatid·ēs -ae *m* whipping boy

plāgōs·us -a -um *adj* quick to use the rod

plagul·a -ae *f* curtain

plagūsi·a -ae *f* a kind of shellfish

planctus *pp of* **plango**

planct·us -ūs *m* beating

planc·us -a -um *adj* flatfooted

plānē *adv* clearly, distinctly; legibly; completely, quite; certainly, to be sure

plan·gō -gĕre -xī -ctus *tr* to strike, beat; to beat *(head, breast as sign of grief)*; to lament, bewail; *(fig)* to wring the hands ‖ *pass* to beat one's breast; *(of bird)* to flap its wings ‖ *intr* to wail

plang·or -ōris *m* striking, beating; beating of the breast, wailing

plāniloqu·us -a -um *adj* outspoken

plānip·ēs -edis *m* barefooted actor *(in the role of a slave)*

plānit·ās -ātis *f* distinctness

plāniti·ēs -ēī *or* **plāniti·a -ae** *f* flat surface, level ground, plain

plant·a -ae *f* sprout, shoot, young plant, seedling; *(anat)* sole

plantār·ia -ium *npl* cuttings, slips

plantār·ium -(i)ī *n* seedling bed *(for starting seedlings)*

plān·us -a -um *adj* flat, level, even; plain, clear ‖ *n* level ground; plain; **de plano** easily; **e plano** out of court

plan·us -ī *m* tramp; con-man

plasm·a -atis *n* phoney accent

Platae·ae -ārum *fpl* Plataea *(town in Boeotia where the Greeks defeated the Persians in 479 B.C.)*

Plataeens·is -is -e *adj* of Plataea ‖ *mpl* Plataeans

platale·a -ae *f* spoonbill *(waterfowl)*

platan·ōn -ōnis *m* grove of plane trees

platan·us -ī *or* **-ūs** *f* plane tree

plate·a *or* **platē·a -ae** *f* street

Plat·ō(n) -ōnis *m* Plato *(Greek philosopher, 429–348 B.C.)*

Platōnic·us -a -um *adj* Platonic ‖ *mpl* Platonists

plau·dō -dĕre -sī -sus *tr* **(plōd-)** to slap, clap, beat ‖ *intr* to clap, beat, flap; *(w. dat)* to applaud, approve of; **alis plaudere** to flap the wings; **manibus plaudere** to clap the hands

plausibil·is -is -e *adj* deserving of applause

plaus·or *or* **plōs·or -oris** *m* applauder

plaustr·um -ī *n* **(plos-)** wagon, cart; **plaustrum percellere** *(fig)* to upset the applecart ‖ **Plaustrum** *(astr)* the Great Bear *(constellation)*

plausus *pp of* **plaudo**

plaus·us -ūs *m* clapping, flapping; applause

Plautīn·us -a -um *adj* of Plautus

Plauti·us -a -um *adj* of Plautus

Plaut·us -ī *m* Plautus *(Titus Maccius Plautus, Roman writer of comedies, born in Umbria, c. 254–184 B.C.)*

plēbēcul·a -ae *f* rabble

plēbēi·us *or* **plēbēj·us -a -um** *adj* plebeian, of the common people; common, low, vulgar ‖ *m* plebeian

plēbicol·a -ae *m* democrat; demagogue

plēbis(s)cīt·um -ī *n* decree of the assembly of the plebeians

plebs *or* **pleps plēbis** *or* **plēb·ēs -ēī** *f* the

plebeians, common people; the masses, proletariat
plectil·is -is -e *adj* plaited, braided
plectō plectĕre plexī plexus *tr* to plait, braid
plect·ō -ĕre *tr* to beat; to punish
plectr·um -ī *n* plectrum; *(fig)* lyre
Plēi·as -adis *or* **-ados** Pleiad ‖ *fpl* Pleiades *(seven daughters of Atlas and Pleione, who were placed among the stars)*
Plēïon·ē -ēs *f* daughter of Oceanus and Tethys, wife of Atlas, and mother of the Pleiades
Plēmyr·ium -(i)ī *n* headland at the S. end of the Bay of Syracuse
plēnē *adv* fully, completely
plēn·us -a -um *adj* full; stout, plump; pregnant; filled, satisfied; full, packed; strong, loud *(voice);* full-length, unabridged, uncontracted; plentiful; advanced *(years);* complete
ple·ō -ēre *tr* to fill
plērumque *adv* generally, mostly, for the most part; often, frequently
plēr·usque -aque -umque *adj* a very great part of, the greater part of, most; a good many; **plerique omnes** nearly all ‖ *mpl* most people, the majority ‖ *n* the greatest part
Pleur·ōn -ōnis *f* a city in Aetolia
-pl·ex -icis *adj suf usu.* formed from numerals, equivalent to the English "-fold", *e.g.:* **centumplex** hundredfold
plex·us -a -um *pp of* **plecto** ‖ *adj* plaited
plicātr·ix -īcis *f* woman who folds clothes, folder
plic·ō -āre -āvī *or* **-uī -ātus** *or* **-itus** *tr* to fold, wind, coil up
Plīn·ius -(i)ī *m* Pliny the Elder *(Gaius Plinius Secundus, author of a work on natural history, d. A.D. 79)* ‖ Pliny the Younger *(Gaius Plinius Caecilius Secundus (his nephew), author of Letters and Panegyric to Trajan, A.D. 61–114)*
plīpi·ō -āre *intr (of a hawk)* to caw
plōdō *see* **plaudo**
plōrābil·is -is -e *adj* dismal
plōrātill·us -a -um *adj* tearful
plōrāt·or -ōris *m* mourner
plōrāt·us -ūs *m* wailing, crying
plōr·ō -āre -āvī -ātus *tr* to cry over ‖ *intr* to cry aloud, wail
plostell·um -ī *n* small cart
plostr·um -ī *n* wagon
ploxen·um -ī *n* **(-xin-)** wagon body
pluit pluĕre pluit *v impers (tr)* it is raining *(stones, blood, etc.)* ‖ *v impers (intr)* it is raining; *(w. abl)* it is raining *(stones, etc.)*
plūm·a -ae *f* down, soft feather; *(collectively)* down, feathers
plūmātil·e -is *n* dress embroidered with feathers
plūmāt·us -a -um *adj* covered with feathers
plumbe·us -a -um *adj* lead-, of lead, leaden; oppressive *(weather);* dull *(blade);* cheap *(wine);* stupid
plumb·um -ī *n* lead; pellet *(for a sling);* pipe; ruler *(for drawing lines);* **plumbum album** *(or* **candidum)** tin
plūme·us -a -um *adj* downy; filled with down; like feathers
plūmip·ēs -edis *adj* with feathered feet
plūm·ō -āre -āvī -ātum *tr* to cause to be covered with feathers
plūmōs·us -a -um *adj* feathered, covered with feathers
plūrāl·is -is -e *adj (gram)* plural
plūrāliter *adv (gram)* in the plural
plūr·ēs -ēs -a *adj* more; several; too many; **pluribus (verbis)** at great length, in greater detail ‖ *mpl* most people, the majority; the dead, "the majority" ‖ *npl* more things
plūrifāriam *adv* extensively, in many places
plūrimum *adv* **(-rum-)** very much, especially, commonly, generally, mostly; **plurimum valere** to be most powerful, have the greatest influence
plūrim·us -a -um *(superl of* **multus)** *adj* **(-rum-)** many a; most; very much; very many; very great, very intense; very powerful, very violent; **plurimam salutem dare** to send warmest greetings ‖ *mpl* most people, a very great number of people ‖ *n* a great deal; **plurimi facere** to think very highly of, think a great deal of; **plurimi vendere** to sell at the highest price; **quam plurimo vendere** to sell at the highest possible price; **quam plurimum** as much as possible
plūs *adv* more; **multo plus** much more; **plus minus** more or less; **paulo plus** a little more
plūs plūris *(comp of* **multus)** *adj* more ‖ *n* more, too much; **plus animi** more courage; **plus nimio** much too much; **plus plusque** more and more; **pluris esse** *(gen of value)* to be of more value, be worth more, be higher, be dearer ‖ *npl* more things; **quid plura?** why say more?, in short
pluscul·us -a -um *adj* a little more, somewhat more ‖ *n* a little more
plute·us -ī *m or* **plute·um -ī** *n* barrier, screen; low wall; parapet; headboard *or* footboard of bed *or* couch; *(fig)* couch; *(fig)* dining couch; bier; lectern; bookcase; *(mil)* movable mantlet *or* shed used to protect soldiers in siege works
Plūt·ō(n) -ōnis *m* Pluto *(king of the lower world, husband of Proserpina, and brother of Jupiter and Neptune)*
Plūtōni·us -a -um *adj* of Pluto

pluvi·a -ae *f* rain
pluviāl·is -is -e *adj* rain-, of rain, rainy
pluvi·us -a -um *adj* rain-, of rain, rainy; **pluvia aqua** rain water; **pluvius arcus** rainbow **‖** *f* rain
pōcill·um -ī *n* small drinking cup
pōc(u)l·um -ī *n* drinking cup; drink, draft; **poculum (ducere** *or* **exhaurire)** to drain a cup
poda·ger -gra -grum *adj* suffering from sore feet
podagr·a -ae *f* arthritis
podagrōs·us -a -um *adj* arthritic
Podalīri·us -ī *m* legendary physician, son of Aesculapius
pōd·ex -icis *m (sl)* ass, behind
pod·ium -(i)ī *n* balcony; box seat *(for the emperor)*
Poeantiad·ēs -is *m* son of Poeas, Philoctetes
Poeanti·us -a -um *adj* of Poeas **‖** *m* Philoctetes
Poe·ās *or* **Poe·ans -antis** *m* father of Philoctetes
poēm·a -atis *n (dat & abl pl:* **poematibus** *or* **poematis)** poem; poetry
poēmat·ium -(i)ī *n* short poem
poen·a -ae *f* punishment; penalty, fine; compensation, recompense, retribution, satisfaction; hardship, loss, pain; *(in games)* penalty; **poenam** *(or* **poenas)** **dare** *(or* **dependere, pendere, persolvere, reddere, solvere, suscipere, sufferre)** to pay the penalty; **poenam** *(or* **poenas) capere** *(or* **exigere, persequi, petere, repetere, reposcere)** to exact a penalty, demand satisfaction; **poena mortis** death penalty
Poenici·us -a -um *adj* Punic, Carthaginian
Poenīn·ī -ōrum *mpl* the Pennine Alps *(from Mont Blanc to Monte Rosa)*
poeniō *see* **punio**
Poenul·us -ī *m* little Phoenician *(i.e., Zeno the Stoic)*
Poen·us -a -um *adj* Phoenician; Carthaginian **‖** *m* Carthaginian *(esp. Hannibal)*
poēs·is -is *f* art of poetry; poetry, poems
poēt·a -ae *m* poet; playwright; *(fig)* person of great skill, artist
poētic·a -ae *or* **poētic·ē -ēs** *f* art of poetry; poetics
poeticē *adv* poetically
poētic·us -a -um *adj* poetic
poētri·a -ae *f* poetess
poētr·is -idis *or* **-idos** *f* poetess
pol *interj* by Pollux!; Gads!; **certo pol** most assuredly
Polem·ōn -ōnis *m* Platonic philosopher, disciple of Xenocrates and teacher of Zeno
Polemōnē·us -a -um *adj* professing the philosophy of Polemon
polent·a -ae *f* pearl barley
polentāri·us -a -um *adj* caused by eating barley
pol·iō -īre -īvī *or* **-iī -ītus** *tr* to polish; to smooth; *(fig)* to polish
polītē *adv* in a polished manner, with taste, smoothly, elegantly
polītic·us -a -um *adj* political
polīt·us -a -um *adj (lit & fig)* polished, smooth
poll·en -inis *n or* **poll·is -inis** *mf* flour
poll·ens -entis *adj* strong, powerful
pollenti·a -ae *f* might, power
poll·eō -ēre *intr* to be strong, be powerful; to be capable, be able; to have influence; *(of medicines)* to be efficacious; **in re publica plurimum pollere** to have tremendous influence in politics
poll·ex -icis *m* thumb; big toe; **pollicem premere** to press the thumb *(against the index finger to indicate approval);* **pollicem vertere** to turn the thumb down *(to indicate disapproval)*
pollic·eor -ērī -itus sum *tr* to promise
pollicitāti·ō -ōnis *f* promise
pollicit·or -ārī -ātus sum *tr* to keep promising
pollicit·us -a -um *pp of* **polliceor ‖** *n* promise
pollināri·us -a -um *adj* flour
polli(n)ct·or -ōris *m* mortician
pollin·gō -gĕre -xī -ctus *tr* to prepare *(a corpse),* lay out
Polli·ō -ōnis *m* Gaius Asinius Pollio *(orator, poet, historian, and patron of literature, 76* B.C.*–*A.D. *4)*
poll·is -inis *mf* flour
pol·lūceō -lūcēre -luxī -luctus *tr* to offer up *(as a sacrifice);* to serve *(food, a meal)*
pollūcibiliter *adv* sumptuously
polluctūr·a -ae *f* sumptuous dinner
pol·luō -luĕre -luī -lūtus *tr* to pollute; to violate; to dirty, soil
Poll·ux *or* **Poll·ūcēs -ūcis** *m* Pollux *(son of Tyndareus and Leda, twin brother of Castor, and patron of boxers)*
pol·us -ī *m* pole *(either end of the axis on which the heavenly spheres were believed to revolve);* star; sky; heaven; **polus australis** South Pole; **polus superior** North Pole
Polyb·ius -iī *m* Greek historian and friend of Scipio Aemilianus *(c. 203–120* B.C.*)*
Polyclīt·us -ī *m* **(-clēt-)** Polycletus *(Greek sculptor of Argos, fl c. 452–412* B.C.*)*
Polycrat·ēs -is *m* ruler of Samos in the 6th cent. B.C., patron of the arts and close friend of Anacreon
Polydam·ās -antos *m* **(Pōl-)** Trojan warrior, son of Panthus and friend of Hector
Polydōrē·us -a -um *adj* of Polydorus
Polydōr·us -ī *m* youngest son of Priam and Hecuba

Polyhymni·a -ae *f* one of the Muses; Muse of lyric poetry
Polym(n)est·ōr -oris *m* king of Thracian Chersonese, husband of Ilione (the daughter of Priam), and murderer of Polydorus
Polynīc·ēs -is *m* son of Oedipus and Jocasta, and brother of Eteocles, Antigone, and Ismene, and leader of the Seven against Thebes
Polyphēm·us -ī *m* son of Neptune and one of the Cyclopes
pōlyp·us -ī *m* polyp *(sea animal; tumor)*
Polyxen·a -ae *or* **Polyxen·ē -ēs** *f* Polyxena *(daughter of Priam and Hecuba whom Pyrrhus, son of Achilles, sacrificed at his father's tomb)*
Polyxeni·us -a -um *adj* of Polyxena
pōmāri·us -a -um *adj* fruit, of fruit trees ‖ *m* fruit vendor ‖ *n* orchard
pōmēr·ium -(i)ī *n* **(-moer-)** space kept free of buildings inside and outside a city wall
pōmif·er -era -erum *adj* fruit-bearing
Pōmōn·a -ae *f* Roman goddess of fruit
pōmōs·us -a -um *adj* loaded with fruit
pomp·a -ae *f* solemn procession; parade; retinue; pomp, ostentation
Pompēī·a *or* **Pompēj·a -ae** *f* Julius Caesar's second wife, the daughter of Quintus Pompeius Rufus *(consul in 88 B.C.)* ‖ a daughter of Pompey, who married Faustus Cornelius Sulla
Pompēiān·us *or* **Pompējān·us -a -um** *adj* Pompeian ‖ *mpl* inhabitants of Pompeii ‖ soldiers *or* followers of Pompey
Pompēī·us *or* **Pompēj·us -ī** *m* Gnaeus Pompeius Strabo *(father of the the triumvir)* ‖ Pompey the Great *(Gnaeus Pompeius Magnus, Roman general and politician, 106–48 B.C.)* ‖ Sextus Pompeius Magnus *(his younger son, killed in 35 B.C.)*
Pompēj·i -ōrum *mpl* city about 10 miles S. of Naples, destroyed by Vesuvius in A.D. 79
Pompil·ius -(i)ī *m* Numa Pompilius *(second king of Rome and traditional founder of Roman state religion)*
pompil·us -ī *m* pilot-fish
Pompōniān·us -a -um *adj* of a member of the Pomponian clan
Pompōn·ius -(i)ī *m* Lucius Pomponius *(of Bononia, a writer of Atellan farces (c. 109–32 B.C.)* ‖ Titus Pomponius Atticus *(the friend and correspondent of Cicero (109–32 B.C.)* ‖ Publius Pomponius Secundus *(writer of dramatic verse)*
Pomptīn·us -a -um *adj* Pomptine; **Pomptinae paludes** Pomptine Marshes *(in Latium)*
pōm·um -ī *n* fruit; fruit tree
pōm·us -ī *f* fruit tree
ponder·ō -āre -āvī -ātus *tr (lit & fig)* to weigh
ponderōs·us -a -um *adj* weighty, massive; *(fig)* dignified
pondō *indecl n* pound, pounds; *(in advl sense)* in weight; *(where specific number of pounds is given, the numeral is usually expressed in the neuter:* **argenti pondo bina selibras in militem praestare** to offer two and a half pounds of silver per soldier); **auri quinque pondo** five pounds of gold; **duo pondo saxum** a two-pound rock; **quot pondo ted esse censes nudum?** how many pounds do you think you weigh nude?
pond·us -eris *n* weight; mass; burden; importance; stability of character ‖ *npl* balance, equilibrium
pōne *adv* behind, after, back ‖ *prep (w. acc)* behind
pōnō pōnĕre posuī pos(i)tus *tr* to put, set, place; to put down, put aside; to pitch *(camp);* to station, post *(troops);* to lay *(foundation, keel);* to build, found *(town, colony, building);* to plant *(tree); (of trees)* to shed leaves; to serve *(food);* to stage *(a play);* to lay down *(arms);* to take off *(clothes, ornaments);* to cut *(beard, hair, fingernails);* to arrange, smooth *(the hair);* to take *(steps);* to deposit *(money);* to bet *(money);* to lend *(money)* at interest; to set aside, store; to lay out, spend *(time, effort, etc.);* to file *(legal claim);* to lay down *(rule, law);* to stage *(a play);* to yield up *(life, breath);* to get rid of, drop; to esteem, value; to classify; to appoint *(to specific position);* to calm *(sea);* to lay *(egg);* to fix *(penalty, price);* to offer *(award);* to depict *(in art);* to assume, suppose; to quote, cite; to state *(in writing or speech);* to pose, ask *(question);* to spend *(time, money, energy);* to give as security; to give *(a name);* to lay out for burial; *(w.* **in** *+ abl)* to base *or* stake *(upon);* **finem ponere** *(w. dat)* to put an end to; **genu ponere** to kneel down; **in loco** *(or* **loco** *or* **in numero) ponere** to place in a class *or* category; **in medio ponere** to make accessible to all; **modum ponere** *(w. dat)* to limit, set bounds to ‖ *intr (of snow)* to fall; *(of wind)* to drop, stop; to be neutral
pon·s -tis *m* bridge; gangway; drawbridge; deck
Ponti·ae -ārum *fpl* island in the Tuscan Sea S. of Circeii
ponticul·us -ī *m* small bridge
Pontic·us -a -um *adj* Pontic, of Pontus *(region around the Black Sea);* **mare Ponticum** Black Sea; **nux Pontica** hazelnut; **radix Pontica** rhubarb
pontif·ex -icis *m* **(-tuf-)** pontiff, pontifex,

priest *(one of a board of 15);* **pontifex maximus** chief pontiff
pontificāl·is -is -e *adj* pontifical
pontificāt·us -ūs *m* pontificate
pontific·us -a -um *adj* pontifical
pont·ō -ōnis *m* ferry
pont·us -ī *m* sea; sea water
Pont·us -ī *m* Euxine *or* Black Sea; region around the Black Sea **ll** Pontus *(kingdom of Mithridates, between Bithynia and Armenia, after 63 B.C. a Roman province)*
pop·a -ae *m* priest's assistant *(who slew the victim)*
popan·um -ī *n* sacrificial cake
popell·us -ī *m* rabble, mob
popīn·a -ae *f* low-class restaurant, dive; food sold at a low-class restaurant
popīn·ō -ōnis *m* diner at a low-class restaurant
popl·es -itis *m* hollow of the knee; knee; **duplicato poplite** on bended knee; **contento poplite** with a stiff knee
Poplicola *see* **Publicola**
poposcī *perf of* **posco**
poppysm·a -atis *n* smacking of the lips *(to indicate satisfaction)*
populābil·is -is -e *adj* destructible
populābund·us -a -um *adj* ravaging
populār·is -is -e *adj* of the people, people's; approved by the people, popular; favoring the people, democratic; demagogic; of the same country, native; common, coarse **ll** *mf* fellow countryman; party member; fellow member, associate; *(w. gen)* partner *or* associate in **ll** *mpl* people's party, democrats **ll** *npl* general-admission seats
populārit·ās -ātis *f* courting popular favor; fellow citizenship
populāriter *adv* like the people; like a demagogue, to win popular favor; **populariter loqui** to use slang
populāti·ō -ōnis *f* ravaging
populāt·or -ōris *m,* **populātr·ix -īcis** *f* ravager, destroyer
populāt·us -ūs *m* devastation
pōpule·us -a -um *adj* of poplars, poplar-
pōpulif·er -era -erum *adj* poplar-bearing
pōpuln(e)us -a -um *adj* of poplar
popul·ō -āre -āvī -ātus *or* **popul·or -rī -ātus sum** *tr* to ravage, devastate, lay waste; *(fig)* to pillage, ruin, spoil
pŏpul·us -ī *m* the people *(as political community);* nation; public, crowd; citizens *(as opposed to soldiers),* civilians; region, district
pōpul·us -ī *f* poplar tree
por- *pref* giving the sense of "forth", *e.g.:* **portendo** to stretch forth
porc·a -ae *f* sow
porcell·a -ae *f* little sow, suckling pig
porcell·us -ī *m* little hog, suckling pig
Porci·a -ae *f* daughter of Cato Uticensis, married first to Marcus Bibulus, consul in 59 B.C., and afterwards to Marcus Brutus, the assassin of Julius Caesar
porcīnār·ius -(i)ī *m* pork seller
porcīn·us -a -um *adj* hog's, pig's **ll** *f* pork
Porc·ius -(i)ī *m* Cato *(Marcus Porcius Cato the Censor 235–149 B.C.)* **ll** Cato Uticensis *(Marcus Porcius Cato Uticensis (95–46 B.C.)*
porcul·a *or* **porculēn·a -ae** *f* little sow
porcul·us -ī *m* little pig
porc·us -ī *m* pig, hog
porgō *see* **porrigo**
porphyrētic·us -a -um *adj* made of porphyry *(a purple-streaked marble)*
porphyri·ō -ōnis *f* type of waterfowl
Porphyri·ōn -ōnis *m* one of the Giants who fought against the gods
porphyrīt·ēs -ae *adj* of porphyry **ll** *m* porphyry
Porphyr·ius -(i)i *m* Porphyry *(Neo-Platonic philosopher, born A.D. 233, who edited the works of Plotinus)*
porrecti·ō -ōnis *f* extending, stretching out
porrect·us -a -um *pp of* **porrigo** *and* **porricio ll** *adj* stretched out, extended, extensive, long; protracted; laid out, dead; *(fig)* wide-spread **ll** *npl* offerings
por·riciō -ricĕre -rexī -rectus *tr* to offer up; **inter caesa et porrecta** *(prov)* at the last moment, at the eleventh hour *(literally, between the slaughtering and the offering)*
por·rigō -rigĕre -rexī -rectus *tr* to reach out, stretch out, extend; to stretch out *(in sleep or death);* to offer, present, hand; to lengthen *(a syllable)* **ll** *refl & pass* to extend
porrīg·ō -inis *f* dandruff
Porrim·a -ae *f* cult name of the birth-goddess Antevorta
porrō *adv* forwards; farther on, on; far off, at a distance; long ago; in the future, hereafter; again, in turn; next, furthermore, moreover, on the other hand
porr·um -ī *n or* **porr·us -ī** *m* leek; chive
Porsenn·a *or* **Porsēn·a** *or* **Porsinn·a -ae** *m* Lars Porsen(n)a *(king of Clusium in Etruria who sided with Tarquin in a war against Rome)*
port·a -ae *f* city-gate; gate; entrance; outlet; camp-gate *(of which there were always four:* **praetoria, principalis, decumanus, quaestoria)**
portāti·ō -ōnis *f* carrying
porten·dō -dĕre -dī -tus *tr* to indicate, foretell, portend, predict
portentific·us -a -um *adj* abnormal
portentōs·us -a -um *adj* abnormal, unnatural; monstrous

portent·um -ī *n* portent, omen, sign; monstrosity, monster; fantasy, far-fetched fiction; *(as term of contempt)* monster

portentus *pp of* **portendo**

porthm·eūs -eī *or* **-eōs** *m* ferryman *(i.e., Charon)*

porticul·a -ae *f* small portico

portic·us -ūs *f* portico, colonnade; *(mil)* gallery *(formed by placing vineae end to end);* Stoicism

porti·ō -ōnis *f* portion, share; ratio, proportion; installment, payment; **pro portione** proportionately, relatively

portiscul·us -ī *m* gavel *(used to keeping time for rowers)*

portit·or -ōris *m* customs officer; ferryman, boatman

port·ō -āre -āvī -ātus *tr* to carry; to bring

portōr·ium -(i)ī *n* port-duty, customs duty; tax *(on peddlers)*

portul·a -ae *f* small gate

Portūn·us -ī *m* tutelary deity of harbors

portuōs·us -a -um *adj* having good harbors

port·us -ūs *m* port, harbor; haven, refuge; mouth of a river

posc·a -ae *f* sour drink

poscō poscĕre poposcī *tr (weaker than* **flāgitō**) to ask, request, beg, demand; to ask for in marriage; *(at auction)* to bid for; *(of things)* to require, demand, need, call for, make necessary; *(w.* **ab**) to ask for *(s.th.)* from, demand *(s.th.)* of; *(w. double acc)* to demand *(s.th.)* of *(s.o.)*, ask *(s.o.)* for *(s.th.)*

posculent·us -a -um *adj* drinkable

pōsi·a -ae *f* **(paus-)** unripe olive

Posīd·ēs -ae *m* favorite freedman of the Emperor Claudius

Posīdōn·ius -(i)ī *m* Stoic philosopher at Rhodes, teacher of Cicero *(135–51 B.C.)*

positi·ō -ōnis *f* putting, placing, setting; position, posture; situation

posit·or -ōris *m* builder

positūr·a -ae *f* posture; formation

posit·us -a -um *pp of* **pono ‖** *adj* situated, located; stretched out, lying down

posit·us -ūs *m* position, site; arrangement; *(gram)* position *(of a syllable)*

possessi·ō -ōnis *f* possession; getting possession, occupation; estate

possessiuncul·a -ae *f* small estate

possess·or -ōris *m* possessor, occupant; *(leg)* defendant

possibil·is -is -e *adj* possible

pos·sideō -sidēre -sēdī -sessus *tr* to possess, occupy; to have, own; to dwell in, live in; *(fig)* to take hold of; *(poet)* to take up *(space)* with one's bulk

pos·sīdō -sīdĕre *tr* to take possession of, occupy, seize

possum posse potuī *intr* to be able; **multum (plus, plurimum) posse** to have much (more, very great) influence; **non possum quin exclamem** I can't help shouting out; **quantum** *(or* **ut) fieri potest** as far as is possible

post *also* **poste** *adv (of place)* behind, back, backwards; *(of time)* later, afterwards; *(of order)* next; **aliquanto post** somewhat later; **multis post annis** many years later **‖** *prep (w. acc) (of place)* behind; *(of time)* after, since

post- *pref used in the senses of the adverb*

posteā *adv* afterwards, after this, after that, hereafter, thereafter

posteāquam *conj (also as two words)* after; ever since, from the time that

posteri·or -or -us *adj* later, next, following; latter, posterior; inferior; hind *(e.g., legs)*

posterit·ās -ātis *f* the future, afterages, posterity, later generations; offspring *(of animals);* **in posteritatem** in the future

posterius *adv* later, at a later date

poster·us -a -um *adj* following, ensuing, next, subsequent, future **‖** *mpl* future generations, posterity, descendants **‖** *n* future time; next day; consequence; **in posterum** until the next day; for the future

post·ferō -ferre *tr* to treat as less important, esteem less; to sacrifice

postgenit·us -a -um *adj* born later **‖** *mpl* later generations

posthab·eō -ēre -uī -itus *tr* to consider of secondary importance; to slight, neglect; *(w. dat)* to think *(s.th.)* less important than

posthāc *adv* hereafter, in the future

posthinc *or* **post hinc** *adv* from here, next

posthōc *or* **post hōc** *adv* after this, afterwards

postibi *adv* afterwards, then

postīcul·um -ī *n* small building in the rear, outhouse

postīc·us -a -um *adj* rear-, back- **‖** *n* back door

postid *adv* then, afterwards

postideā *adv* afterwards, after that

postilēn·a -ae *f* rump; buttocks

postili·ō -ōnis *f* sacrifice demanded by the gods to make up for a previous omission in sacrifice

postillā(c) *adv* afterwards

post·is -is *m* doorpost; door **‖** *mpl* double doors

postlīmin·ium -(i)ī *n* right to return home and resume one's former rank and privileges after exile or capture; recovery, restoration

pos(t)merīdiān·us -a -um *adj* afternoon

postmerīdiē *adv* in the afternoon

postmodo *or* **postmodum** *adv* after a bit, a little later, afterwards

postpart·or -ōris *m* successor, heir

post·pōnō -pōněre -posuī -positus *tr* to consider of secondary importance; to postpone; *(w. dat)* to consider *(s.th.)* of less importance than, set *(s.th.)* aside in favor of; **omnibus rebus postpositis** laying aside everything

postprincip·ium -(i)ī *n (also written as two words)* sequel; **postprincipia** *(mil)* second line of battle

postput·ō -āre -āvī -ātus *tr (also written as two words)* to consider of secondary importance; *(w.* **prae** *+ abl)* to consider *(s.th.)* less important than

postquam *conj* after, when

postrēmō *adv* at last; finally

postrēmum *adv* for the last time, last of all

postrēm·us -a -um *(superl of* **posterus)** *adj* last; latest, most recent; last in line, rear; least important; lowest, worst ‖ *n* the end; **ad postremum** in the end, finally; in the last place

postrīdiē *adv* on the day after, on the following day; **postridie mane** the next morning ‖ *prep (w. gen), e.g.,* **postridie ejus diei** on the day after that; *(w. acc), e.g.,* **postridie ludos** on the day after the games

postrīduō *adv* on the day after

postscaen·ium -(i)ī *n* backstage

post·scrībō -scrīběre -scripsī -scriptus *tr (w. dat)* to add *(e.g., a name)* to; **Tiberi nomen suo postscribere** to add the name of Tiberius to his own

postulāt·a -ōrum *npl* demands, claims, requests

postulāti·ō -ōnis *f* demand, request, desire; complaint; *(leg)* application for permission to present a claim

postulāt·or -ōris *m* one who makes demands; plaintiff

postulāt·um -ī *n* demand; request

postulāt·us -ūs *m* petition, request

postul·ō -āre -āvī -ātus *tr* to demand, claim; to look for as due, expect; *(of things)* to require; *(leg)* to arraign, prosecute; *(leg)* to apply for *(a writ from the praetor to prosecute)*

Postumi·us -a -um *adj* Roman clan name *(nomen), esp.* Aulus Postumius Tubertus *(father-in-law of Cincinnatus)* ‖ Gaius Postumius *(a soothsayer consulted by Sulla)*

postum·us -a -um *adj* last, latest-born; born after the father's death

Postum·us -ī *m* Roman first name *(praenomen),* subsequently in use as a family name *(cognomen)*

postus *pp of* **pono**

Postvert·a -ae *f* goddess presiding over breech births

posuī *perf of* **pono**

pōtāti·ō -ōnis *f* drinking; drinking party

pōtāt·or -ōris *m* drinker

pot·ens -entis *adj* capable; mighty, powerful, strong; efficacious, potent; influential; *(w. gen)* **1** capable of, equal to, fit for; **2** having power over; **3** presiding over; **4** having obtained *(one's wish);* **5** having carried out *(an order)*

potentāt·us -ūs *m* political power, rule, dominion

potenter *adv* powerfully, mightily, effectually, vigorously; according to one's ability

potenti·a -ae *f* force, power; political power *(esp. unconstitutional power in contrast to* **potestas)**

potēr·ium -iī *n* goblet

potest·ās -ātis *f* power, ability, capacity; efficacy, force; public authority, rule, power, sway, dominion, sovereignty, empire; magisterial power, magistracy, office; possibility, opportunity *(to choose, decide),* discretion, power of choice; permission; person in office, magistrate, ruler; property, quality

Pothīn·us -i *m* minister of Ptolemy XIII of Egypt, who ordered the assassination of Pompey the Great

potin *or* **potin'** = **potisne** can you?

pot·iō -īre -īvī -ītus *tr (w. acc and gen)* to put *(s.o.)* under the power of

pōti·ō -ōnis *f* drinking; drink, draught; magic potion

pōtiōnāt·us -a -um *adj (w. abl)* having been given a drink of

pot·ior -īrī -ītus sum *tr* to acquire, get possession of ‖ *intr (w. abl)* to acquire, get possession of, become master of, get hold of

poti·or -or -us *(comp of* **potis)** *adj* more powerful; more precious; better, preferable, superior; more important; *(w. gen)* having greater control over

potis *or* **pote** *indecl adj* able, capable; possible

potissimum *adv* chiefly, especially

potissim·us -a -um *adj* chief, principal, most important

pōtit·ō -āre -āvī -ātus *tr* to drink (habitually)

pōtiuncul·a -ae *f* a little drink

potius *adv* rather, more, by preference; **potius quam** more than, rather than

Potni·as -ados *adj (fem only)* of Potniae *(a Boeotian village)*

pōt·ō -āre -āvī -ātus *or* **-us** *tr* to drink; to absorb ‖ *intr* to drink

pōt·or -ōris *m* drinker; a drunk

pōtr·ix -īcis *f* drinker *(female)*

pōtulent·us -a -um *adj* drinkable; tipsy ‖ *npl* drinks

pōt·us -a -um *pp of* **poto** ‖ *adj* drunk

pōt·us -ūs *m* drinking; a drink

prae *adv* before, in front; in preference ‖ *prep (w. abl)* **1** *(in its literal sense, usu.*

w. refl pron, in certain phrases) before, in front of: **prae se** in front of oneself, publicly, openly, plainly; **prae se ferre** to display, manifest, profess; **prae manu** at hand; **2** compared with, in comparison with: **Gallis prae magnitudine corporum suorum brevitas nostra contemptui est** in comparison with the size of their own bodies the Gauls hold our shortness of stature in contempt; **3** by reason of, in consequence of, because of, for: **prae laetitiā lacrimare** to weep for joy; **nec loqui prae maerore potuit** he could not speak because of his grief; **4** in consequence of, out of: **prae pudore** out of shame

prae- *pref* indicating **1** position in front, ahead: **praecedere** to go in front, go ahead; **2** position in the end: **praeurere** to burn at the extremity; **praeacuere** to sharpen to a point; **3** temporal precedence: **praedicere** to tell in advance; **4** with adjectives, pre-eminence in the quality concerned: **praeacutus** very sharp; **5** rank: **praeesse** to be in charge; **praetor** one in charge; **6** protection: **praesidium** defense, protection

praeac·uō -uĕre -uī -ūtus *tr* to sharpen to the point

praeacūt·us -a -um *adj* very sharp; pointed

praealt·us -a -um *adj* very high; very deep

praeb·eō -ēre -uī -itus *tr* to hold out, offer, present; to supply, give; to exhibit, represent, show; to give up, yield, surrender; to cause, occasion; to permit, allow; **praebere aurem** *(or* **aures)** *(w. dat)* to listen to; **praebere exemplum** to set an example; **praebere suspicionem** to cause suspicion ‖ *refl* to show oneself, behave; to offer oneself as

praebib·ō -ĕre -ī -itus *tr (w. dat)* to drink *(e.g., a toast)* to

praebit·or -ōris *m* supplier

praecalid·us -a -um *adj* very hot

praecalv·us -a -um *adj* very bald

praecant·ō -āre -āvī -ātus *tr* **(-cen-)** to cast a spell over ‖ *intr (w. dat)* to recite a spell over

praecantr·ix -īcis *f* witch, enchantress

praecān·us -a -um *adj* prematurely gray

prae·caveō -cavēre -cāvī -cautus *tr* to take precautions against, guard against, try to avoid ‖ *intr* to take precautions, be on one's guard; *(w. dat)* to look out for, look after; *(w. abl)* to guard against, be on one's quard against

prae·cēdō -cēdĕre -cessī -cessus *tr* to precede, go out before, lead; to surpass ‖ *intr* to excel; *(w. dat)* to excel, be superior to

praecell·ens -entis *adj* excellent, outstanding, preeminent

praecell·ō -ĕre *tr* to surpass, outdo ‖ *intr* to distinguish oneself, excel; to take precedence; *(w. dat)* **1** to rule over; **2** to surpass

praecels·us -a -um *adj* towering

praecenti·ō -ōnis *f* musical prelude

praecentō *see* **praecanto**

praecentus *pp of* **praecino**

praecēpī *perf of* **praecipio**

praec·eps -ipitis *adj* headfirst; downhill, steep, precipitous; sinking *(sun);* swift, rushing, violent; hasty, rash, inconsiderate; dangerous ‖ *n* edge of a cliff, cliff; *(fig)* brink; danger; **in praeceps** *(or* **per praeceps)** headlong, straight downward; **in praecipiti** on the edge; *(fig)* on the brink of disaster

praeceps *adv* headfirst

praecepti·ō -ōnis *f* preconception; precept, rule; instruction; *(leg)* receiving *(of an inheritance)* in advance *(of the general partition of an estate)*

praecept·or -ōris *m,* **praceptr·ix -īcis** *f* teacher, tutor

praecept·um -ī *n* instruction, bit of advice; rule; maxim; order, direction

praecerp·ō -ĕre -sī -tus *tr* to pick beforetime; *(w. dat) (fig)* to snatch away from

praecī·dō -dĕre -dī -sus *tr* to lop off, cut off; to cut short; to cut, cut through; to damage, mutilate; to break off, end suddenly *(a speech, etc.);* to end, destroy *(hopes, etc.);* to refuse, decline

praecin·gō -gĕre -xi -ctus *tr* to gird; to surround, ring; to dress ‖ *pass* to be surrounded, be ringed; **altius praecinctus** with tunic tucked up higher; *(fig)* more energetic(ally); **ense cingi** to wear a sword; **male cinctus** improperly dressed; **recte cinctus** properly dressed

prae·cinō -cinĕre -cinuī -centus *tr* to predict; *(w. dat)* to predict *(s.th.)* to ‖ *intr* to make predictions; *(w. dat)* to sing *or* play before *or* at *(e.g., sacrifice, dinner, etc.)*

prae·cipiō -cipĕre -cēpī -ceptus *tr* to take in advance, occupy in advance; to receive in advance; to grasp beforehand, anticipate; to teach, instruct, direct, advise, order, bid, warn; to prescribe; **aliquantulum viae** *(or* **temporis)** **praecipere** *(or* **iter praecipere)** to get a headstart; **animo** *(or* **cogitatione)** **praecipere** to imagine beforehand, reckon on, anticipate, expect; **artem nandi praecipere** to give swimming instructions; **gaudium praecipere** to rejoice in advance; **oculis praecipere** to see beforehand, get a preview of; **opinione praecipere** to suspect; **pecuniam mutuam praecipere** to get an advance loan

praecipitanter *adv* at top speed

praecipit·ō -āre -āvī -ātus *tr* to throw down headfirst; to hasten, hurry, precipitate ‖ *refl* to throw oneself down, throw oneself headfirst, jump down, dive; to sink ‖ *intr* to rush headfirst, rush at top speed, rush thoughtlessly; to fall, sink; to be ruined

praecipuē *adv* especially, chiefly

praecipu·us -a -um *adj* special, peculiar, particular; chief, principal; distinguished, excellent, extraordinary ‖ *n* excellence, superiority ‖ *npl* outstanding *or* important elements; **praecipua rerum** highlights

praecīsē *adv* briefly, concisely; absolutely

praecīs·us -a -um *pp of* **praecido** ‖ *adj* abrupt, precipitous; rugged, rough; brief, shortened *(speech);* clipped *(words)*

praeclārē *adv* very clearly; excellently; *(to express agreement)* very good, excellent

praeclār·us -a -um *adj* very clear; very nice; splendid, noble, distinguished, excellent; famous; notorious

praeclū·dō -dĕre -sī -sus *tr* to shut, shut off, obstruct, bar the way of; to hinder, impede, stop; to preclude *(an action, event);* **portas consuli praecludere** to shut the gates in the consul's face; **vocem praecludere alicui** to shut s.o. up, hush s.o. up

praec·ō -ōnis *m* crier, herald; auctioneer; *(fig)* eulogist

praecōgit·ō -āre -āvī -ātus *tr* to premeditate

praecognit·us -a -um *adj* known beforehand, foreseen

prae·colō -colĕre -coluī -cultus *tr* to cultivate prematurely; *(fig)* to embrace prematurely

praecomposit·us -a -um *adj* arranged beforehand; studied, self-conscious

praecōni·us -a -um *adj* of a public crier; of an auctioneer ‖ *n* crier's office; proclamation, announcement; praising, praise

praeconsum·ō -ĕre -psī -ptus *tr* to spend *or* use up beforehand

praecontrect·ō -āre *tr* to consider in advance

praecoqu·is -is -e *adj* premature; precocious

praecordi·a -ōrum *npl* midriff; lower chest; chest; diaphragm; insides, stomach; breast, heart *(as seat of emotions)*

praecor·rumpō -rumpĕre -rūpī -ruptus *tr* to bribe in advance

prae·cox -cocis *adj* premature; early, precocious

praecupid·us -a -um *adj (w. gen)* very fond of

praecurrent·ia -ium *npl* antecedents

prae·currō -currĕre -(cu)currī cursus *tr* to precede, anticipate; to outdo, surpass ‖ *intr* to run out ahead, take the lead; *(w.* **ante** *+ acc)* to run out ahead of; *(w. dat)* to outdo

praecursi·ō -ōnis *f* previous occurrence; *(mil)* skirmish; *(rhet)* warmup *(of the audience)*

praecurs·or -ōris *m* forerunner; spy; *(mil)* scout; *(mil)* advance guard

praecursōri·us -a -um *adj* sent in advance

prae·cutiō -cutĕre *tr* to wave, brandish in front

praed·a -ae *f* booty, spoils, plunder; prey; *(of fish)* catch; *(in hunting)* the game; prize, profit; **praedae esse** *(w. dat)* to fall prey to; **vocamus in partem praedamque Jovem** we invite Jupiter to share the game

praedābund·us -a -um *adj* pillaging, plundering, marauding

praedamn·ō -āre -āvī -ātus *tr* to condemn beforehand; **spem praedamnare** to give up hope too soon

praedāti·ō -ōnis *f* plundering

praedātor -ōris *m* marauder, looter, vandal; hunter; greedy man

praedātōri·us -a -um *adj* marauding, looting; graspy, greedy

praedāt·us -ūs *m* robbery

praedēlass·ō -āre *tr* to tire out, weaken beforehand

praediāt·or -ōris *m* real-estate dealer

praediātōri·us -a -um *adj* concerned with real-estate; **jus praediatorium** *(leg)* mortgage law

praedicābil·is -is -e *adj* praiseworthy, laudable

praedicāti·ō -ōnis *f* announcement, publication; praise, commendation

praedicāt·or -ōris *m* eulogist

praedĭc·ō -āre -āvī -ātus *tr* to announce; to report; to assert; to praise, recommend

prae·dīcō -dīcĕre -dixī -dictus *tr* to mention beforehand *or* earlier; to prearrange; to predict; to order beforehand, command beforehand

praedicti·ō -ōnis *f* prediction

praedict·um -ī *n* prediction, prophecy; command, order; **velut ex praedicto** as if by prearrangement

praediol·um -ī *n* small estate, small farm

praedisc·ō -ĕre *tr* to learn beforehand, find out in advance

praedisposit·us -a -um *adj* previously arranged

praedit·us -a -um *adj* gifted; *(w. abl)* endowed with, provided with, furnished with

praed·ium -iī *n* estate, farm; collateral *(consisting of land);* **praedium urbanum** *(whether in town or in the country)* building site

praedīv·es -itis *adj* very rich

praedīvīn·ō -āre -āvī -ātus *tr* to know in advance, have a presentiment of
praed·ō -ōnis *m* robber; pirate
praedoct·us -a -um *adj* instructed beforehand
praed·or -ārī -ātus sum *tr* to raid, plunder, loot, rob; *(fig)* to rob, ravish; **amores alicujus praedari** to steal s.o.'s sweetheart away ‖ *intr* to plunder, loot, make a raid; *(w.* **ex)** to prey on, profit by, take advantage of, *e.g.,* **ex alterius inscientiā praedari** to prey on *or* take advantage of another's ignorance
prae·dūcō -dūcĕre -duxī -ductus *tr* to run *or* construct *(trench, wall)* out in front *(as a defense)*
praedulc·is -is -e *adj* very sweet; *(fig)* very satisfying *(honor, reward)*
praedūr·us -a -um *adj* very tough *(skin);* tough, brawny
praeēmin·eō *or* **praemin·eō -ēre** *tr* to surpass, excel ‖ *intr* to project, stick out
prae·eō -īre -īvī *or* **-iī** *tr* to lead, precede; to read out, dictate, lead *(prayers)* ‖ *intr* to go out ahead, take the lead; *(w. dat)* to walk in front of
praefāti·ō -ōnis *f* preface, introduction; formula
praefātus *pp of* **praefor**
praefectūr·a -ae *f* supervision, superintendence; office of prefect, superintendency; government of a district; prefecture *(Italian city governed by a Roman prefect);* territory of a prefecture, district
praefect·us -ī *m* prefect, supervisor, superintendent; command; governor; *(w. gen or dat)* supervisor of, commander of, prefect *or* governor of
prae·ferō -ferre -tulī -lātus *tr* to hold out, carry in front; *(w. dat or* **quam)** to prefer *(one thing)* to *(another);* to anticipate; to display, reveal, betray; to offer, present; to offer as a model ‖ *refl & pass (w. dat)* to surpass ‖ *pass* to ride past, ride by, march past; to outflank
paefer·ox -ōcis *adj* very defiant
praeferrāt·us -a -um *adj* iron-tipped; *(coll)* chained *(slave)*
praefervid·us -a -um *adj (lit & fig)* boiling
praefestīn·ō -āre -āvī -ātus *tr* to hurry past; *(w. inf)* to be in a big hurry to
praefic·a -ae *f* hired mourner *(female)*
prae·ficiō -ficĕre -fēcī -fectus *tr* to put *(s.o.)* in charge; *(w. double acc)* to appoint *(s.o.)* as; *(w. dat)* to put *(s.o.)* in charge of, set *(s.o.)* over, appoint *(s.o.)* to command
praefīd·ens -entis *adj* too trustful; overconfident; *(w. dat)* too trustful of; **homines sibi praefidentes** overconfident people
praefī·gō -gĕre -xī -xus *tr* to fix, fasten, set up in front, fasten on the end; *(w. abl)* to tip with; *(w.* **in** + *abl)* to impale on; **capistris praefigere** to muzzle
praefīn·iō -īre -īvī *or* **-iī ītus** *tr* to determine in advance; to prescribe, appoint; to limit
praefīnītō *adv* in the prescribed manner
praefiscinē *or* **praefiscinī** *or* **praefascinē** *adv* so as to avoid bad luck; meaning no offense
praefixī *perf of* **praefigo**
praefix·us -a -um *pp of* **praefigo** ‖ *adj* **cuspidibus praefixus** pointed; **ferro praefixus** iron-tipped
praeflōr·ō -āre -āvī -ātus *tr* to deflower beforehand; *(fig)* to tarnish
praeflu·ō -ĕre *tr & intr* to flow by
praefōc·ō -āre -āvī -ātus *tr* to suffocate; to block *(windpipe, road)* ‖ *pass* to choke
prae·fodiō -fodĕre -fōdī -fossus *tr* to bury beforehand; to dig in front of; **portas praefodere** to dig trenches in front of the gates
prae·for -fārī -fātus sum *tr* to say beforehand, utter in advance, preface; to address in prayer beforehand; to fortell; to invoke ‖ *intr* to pray beforehand; *(w. dat)* to pray before
praefractē *adv* obstinately
praefract·us -a -um *pp of* **praefringo** ‖ *adj* determined; abrupt
praefrīgid·us -a -um *adj* very cold
prae·fringō -fringĕre -frēgī -fractus *tr* to break off at the tip; to break to pieces, smash
praeful·ciō -cīre -sī -tus *tr* to prop up, support in front; *(w. dat)* to use *(s.o.)* as a prop *or* support for
praeful·geō -gēre -sī *intr* to shine forth, glitter, sparkle
praegelid·us -a -um *adj* very cold
praegest·iō -īre *intr* to be very eager
praegn·ans -antis *or* **praegn·ās -ātis** *adj* pregnant; *(w. abl)* full of, swollen with
praegracil·is -is -e *adj* lanky
praegrand·is -is -e *adj* huge; very great; very powerful
praegrav·is -is -e *adj* very heavy; weighed down; very troublesome
praegrav·ō -āre -āvī -ātus *tr* to weigh down; to outweigh; *(fig)* to burden
prae·gredior -gredī -gressus sum *tr* to go in advance of, go ahead of; to go by, go past; *(fig)* to outstrip ‖ *intr* to walk out in front; *(w. dat)* to precede, lead
praegressi·ō -ōnis *f* procession; *(fig)* precedence
praegress·us -ūs *m* prior occurrence
praegustāt·or -ōris *m* taster, sampler
praegust·ō -āre -āvī -ātus *tr* to taste beforehand, sample, get a sample of

praehib·eō -ēre -uī -itus *tr* to offer, furnish, supply; to utter, speak; **operam praehibere** to offer help

praejac·eō -ēre *tr* to lie before, be located in front of ‖ *intr (w. dat)* to lie before

praejūdicāt·us -a -um *adj* decided beforehand; prejudiced; **opinio praejudicata** prejudice ‖ *n* prejudged matter; prejudice; **id pro praejudicato ferre** to take it as a foregone conclusion

praejūdic·ium -(i)ī *n* preliminary hearing; prejudice; presumption; precedent, example

praejūdic·ō -āre -āvī -ātus *tr* to decide beforehand, prejudge ‖ *intr (w. dat of disadvantage)* to be prejudicial to

prae·juvō -juvāre -jūvī *tr* to help in advance

prae·lābor -lābī -lapsus sum *tr & intr* to glide along, glide, by, float by

praelamb·ō -ĕre *tr* to lick beforehand

praelarg·us -a -um *adj* very ample

praelātus *pp of* **praefero**

praelaut·us -a -um *adj* plush

praelecti·ō -ōnis *f* lecture

prae·legō -legĕre -lēgī -lectus *tr* to lecture on; to sail past

praelig·ō -āre -āvī -ātus *tr* to tie up; *(w. dat)* to tie *(s.th.)* to

praelong·us -a -um *adj* very long; very tall

prae·loquor -loquī -locūtus sum *tr* to make *(a speech)* before s.o. else; to say by way of preface; *(leg)* to present *(a case)* first; ‖ *intr* to speak first

prae·lūceō -lūcēre -lūxī *tr (fig)* to enkindle *(hope)* ‖ *intr (w. dat)* **1** to throw light on; **2** to outshine, outdo, surpass; **3** to light the way for

praelūsi·ō -ōnis *f* prelude

praelustr·is -is -e *adj* magnificent

praemandāt·a -ōrum *npl (leg)* warrant for arrest

praemand·ō -āre -āvī -ātus *tr* to recommend beforehand; to order in advance

praemātūrē *adv* too soon, prematurely

praemātūr·us -a -um *adj* premature

praemedicāt·us -a -um *adj* protected by drugs *or* charms

praemeditāti·ō -ōnis *f* premeditation, prior consideration

praemedit·or -ārī -ātus sum *tr* to think over beforehand; to practice; to practice on *(e.g., a lyre);* **mala praemeditata** premeditated crimes

praemerc·or -ārī -ātus sum *tr* to buy in advance

praemetu·ens -entis *adj* apprehensive, anxious

praemetuenter *adv* anxiously; cautiously

praemetu·ō -ĕre *tr* to fear beforehand ‖ *intr (w. dat)* to be apprehensive about

praemin·eō -ēre *tr* to surpass, exceed ‖ *intr* to stand out prominently

prae·mittō -mittĕre -mīsī -missus *tr* to send out ahead, send in advance ‖ *intr* to send word

praem·ium -(i)ī *n* prize, reward, recompense; exploit *(worthy of reward);* gift, bribe

praemolesti·a -ae *f* apprehension, presentiment of trouble

praemōl·ior -īrī *tr* to prepare beforehand, work at in advance

praemon·eō -ēre -uī -itus *tr* to forewarn; to warn of; to foreshadow, presage, predict

praemonit·us -ūs *m* premonition, forewarning

praemonstrāt·or -ōris *m* guide

praemonstr·ō -āre -āvī -ātus *tr* to point out the way to, guide, direct; to predict

praemor·deō -dēre -dī *or* **-sī -sus** *tr* to bite the tip off *(s.th.); (fig)* to crib, pilfer

praemor·ior -ī -tuus sum *intr* to die too soon, die prematurely

praemūn·iō -īre -īvī -ītus *tr* to fortify in front; to protect, secure ‖ *intr (fig) (of a lawyer)* to prepare one's defenses

praemūnīti·ō -ōnis *f (rhet)* preparation, conditioning *(of the minds of the hearers)*

praenarr·ō -āre -āvī -ātus *tr* to relate beforehand

praenat·ō -āre -āvī *tr & intr* to float past, flow by

praenāvig·ō -āre -āvī -ātum *tr & intr* to sail by

Praenest·e -is *n (f)* ancient town in Latium *(c. 20 miles S.E. of Rome, modern Palestrina)*

Praenestīn·us -a -um *adj & m* Praenestine

praenit·eō -ēre -uī *intr (w. dat)* **1** to outshine; **2** to appear more attractive to

praenōm·en -inis *n* first name

prae·noscō -noscĕre -nōvī *tr* to find out beforehand, foreknow

praenōti·ō -ōnis *f* innate idea, preconception

praenūbil·us -a -um *adj* heavily clouded; dark, gloomy

praenunti·a -ae *f* harbinger, omen

praenunti·ō -āre -āvī -ātus *tr* foretell

praenunti·us -a-um *adj* foreboding ‖ *m* forecaster, harbinger, omen

praeoccupāti·ō -ōnis *f* seizing beforehand, advance occupation

praeoccup·ō -āre -āvī -ātus *tr* to occupy before another; to preoccupy; to anticipate, prevent

praeol·et -ēre *or* **praeolit -ĕre** *v impers* a smell is emitted, there is a strong smell; **praeolit mihi quo tu velis** I scent your wishes before you express them

praeopt·ō -āre -āvī -ātus *tr* to prefer

praepand·ō -ĕre *tr* to spread, extend; *(fig)* to reveal

praeparāti·ō -ōnis *f* preparation

praeparāt·us -a -um *adj* prepared, supplied, furnished, ready ‖ *n* stores; **ex ante preparato** from the stores; *(fig)* by previous arrangement

praepar·ō -āre -āvī -ātus *tr* to get ready, prepare, prepare for; to gather together; to furnish beforehand; to plan in advance

praepedīment·um -ī *n* impediment

praeped·iō -īre -īvī *or* **-(i)ī -ītus** *tr* to shackle, chain; to hinder, obstruct, hamper; to embarrass

praepend·eō -ēre *intr* to hang down in front

praep·es -etis *adj (of birds of omen)* flying straight ahead, of good omen; winged, swift of flight ‖ *mf* bird of good omen; bird, large bird

praepilāt·us -a -um *adj* tipped with a ball; **missile praepilatum** blunted missile

praepingu·is -is -e *adj* very fertile

praepoll·eō -ēre -uī *intr* to be very powerful; to be superior; *(w. dat)* to surpass in power

praeponder·ō -āre -āvī -ātus *tr* to outweigh; to regard as superior ‖ *intr* to weigh more

prae·pōnō -pōnĕre -posuī -positus *tr (w. dat)* **1** to place, set, put *(s.th.)* in front of *or* before *(s.o.)*; **2** to serve *(s.o. food)*; **3** to entrust *(s.o.)* with; **4** to put *(s.o.)* in charge of *or* in command of; **5** to prefer *(s.o. or s.th.)* to, give priority to

praeport·ō -āre -āvī -ātus *tr* to carry before oneself

praepositi·ō -ōnis *f* preference; prefixing; *(gram)* preposition

praeposit·um -ī *n* preferable thing *(i.e., s.th. short of absolute good)*

praeposit·us -a -um *pp of* **praepono** ‖ *adj* preferred, preferable ‖ *m* prefect, commander ‖ *n* that which is desirable, a desirable good

praeposterē *adv* out of the proper order

praeposter·us -a -um *adj* inverted, in the wrong order; badly timed; topsy-turvy; preposterous

praeposuī *pref of* **praepono**

praepot·ens -entis *adj* very powerful; *(w. gen)* in full control of

praeproperanter *or* **praeproperē** *adv* very quickly, too fast

praeproper·us -a -um *adj* very quick; overhasty, sudden

praepūt·ium -(i)ī *n* foreskin

praequam *conj* in comparison to; **nihil hoc est, praequam alios sumptūs facit** this is nothing in comparison to the other expenses that he runs up

praequest·us -a -um *adj* complaining beforehand; **multa praequestus** having first voiced many complaints

praeradi·ō -āre *tr* to outshine

praerapid·us -a -um *adj* very swift

praereptus *pp of* **praeripio**

praerig·escō -escĕre -uī *intr* to become very stiff

prae·ripiō -ripĕre -ripuī -reptus *tr* to snatch away, carry off; to anticipate, forestall; to count on too soon, presume upon; *(w. dat)* to snatch from

prae·rōdō -rōdĕre -rōsī -rōsus *tr* to bite the end of, nibble at; **digitos praerodere** to bite the fingernails

praerogātīv·us -a -um *adj* asked before others; *(pol)* voting first, privileged; **omen praerogativum** omen to vote first ‖ *f (pol)* first tribe *or* century to vote; *(pol)* vote of the first tribe *or* century to vote; *(pol)* previous election; sure sign, omen

praerōsī *perf of* **praerodo**

praerōsus *pp of* **praerodo**

prae·rumpō -rumpĕre -rūpī -ruptus *tr* to break off, tear away *(s.th.)* in front

praerupt·us -a -um *adj* broken off, broken up; rough *(terrain)*; steep; hasty, impetuous; *(of an utterance)* cut short ‖ *n* precipice, steep place; *(fig)* dangerous undertaking

praes *adv* at hand

prae·s -dis *m* bondsman, surety; collateral

praesaep- = praesep-

praesāgāti·ō -ōnis *f* power of knowing the future, presentiment

praesāg·iō -īre -īvī *or* **-iī** *or* **praesāg·ior -īrī** *tr* to have forebodings of, feel beforehand; to forebode, portend

praesāgīti·ō -ōnis *f* presentiment, strange feeling; prophetic power

praesāg·ium -(i)ī *n* presentiment prophetic instinct; portent; prediction

praesāg·ō -āre -āvī *tr* to have a presentiment of

praesāg·us -a -um *adj* prophetic

praesc·iō -īre -īvī -ītus *tr* to know beforehand

praesc·iscō -iscĕre -(i)ī *tr* to find out *or* learn beforehand

praesci·us -a -um *adj* prescient, having foreknowledge; **praescius venturi** foreseeing the future

prae·scrībō -scrībĕre -scripsī -scriptus *tr* to prefix in writing; to describe beforehand; to determine in advance, prescribe, ordain; to dictate; to outline, map out; to put forward as an excuse

praescripti·ō -ōnis *f* heading, title; preface; pretext; rule, law; limit, restriction

praescript·um -ī *n* regulation, rule; boundary line; route

praesec·ō -āre -uī -tus *tr* to cut off; to cut away; to pare *(nails)*

praesegmin·a -um *npl* clippings
praes·ens -entis *adj* present, in person, face to face; at hand; existing, contemporary; prompt, immediate, instant; impending; efficacious, powerful, effective; influential; resolute; *(of a god)* read to help, propitious; *(of payment)* in cash; **in praesens tempus** for the present; **in rem prasentem venire** to come to the very spot; **(in) re praesenti** on the spot; **praesens pecunia** cold cash; **praesenti die** on the day in question; **sermo praesens** a face-to-face talk ‖ *n* present time; **ad** *(or* **in)** **praesens** for the present; **in praesenti** on the spot; in the present case; on the present occasion
praesensī *perf of* **praesentio**
praesensi·ō -ōnis *f* presentiment; preconception
praesensus *pp of* **praesentio**
praesentāne·us -a -um *adj (of a poison)* having an immediate effect
praesentāri·us -a -um *adj* paid in cash on the spot
praesenti·a -ae *f* presence; efficacy, effect; **animi praesentia** presence of mind; resolution; **in praesentiā** at present, in the present state of affairs; **in praesentiā esse** to be present, be available; **in praesentiam** for the present
praesen·tiō -tīre -sī -sensus *tr* to feel beforehand, to realize in advance, have strange feelings about
praesēp·e -is *n or* **praesēp·ēs -is** *f* **(-saep-)** stall, stable; crib, manger; *(coll)* brothel; *(coll)* lodgings, room
praesēp·iō -īre -sī -tus *tr* **(-saep-)** to fence in, barricade
praesertim *adv* especially, particularly; **praesertim cum** especially because
praeserv·iō -īre *intr (w. dat)* to serve *(s.o.)* as a slave
praes·es -idis *m* guard, guardian, protector, defender; president, superintendent; captain, pilot; governor *(of a province)* ‖ *f* guardian, protectress
praesid·ens -entis *m* president, ruler
prae·sideō -sidēre -sēdī *tr* to guard, protect, defend; to command, be in command of ‖ *intr* to be in charge, be in command; *(w. dat)* **1** to watch over, guard, protect; **2** to preside over, direct, manage; **3** to command
praesidiāri·us -a -um *adj* on garrison duty
praesid·ium -(i)ī *n* protection, defense; assistance; *(mil)* guard, garrison; *(mil)* garrison post, defensive position; *(naut)* convoy; **praesidium agitare** to stand guard
praesignific·ō -āre -āvī -ātus *tr* to indicate in advance, foretoken
praesign·is -is -e *adj* outstanding
praeson·ō -āre -uī *tr & intr* to sound beforehand
praesparg·ō -ĕre *tr* to strew, scatter
praestābil·is -is -e *adj* excellent, outstanding; of outstanding importance
praest·ans -antis *adj* outstanding
praestanti·a -ae *f* excellence, preëminence, superiority
praestantissimē *adv* exceptionally well
praestern·ō -ĕre *tr* to strew in front
praest·es -itis *m* guardian, protecting deity
praestīgi·ae -ārum *fpl* sleight of hand; juggling; tricks; illusion
praestīgiāt·or -ōris *m,* **praestīgiātr·ix -īcis** *f* juggler; magician; imposter
praestin·ō -āre -āvī -ātus *tr* to buy, shop for, bargain for
praesti·tuō -tuĕre -tuī -tūtus *tr* to fix *or* set up beforehand; to prescribe
praestitus *pp of* **praesto**
praestō *adv* at hand, ready, present, here; **praesto esse** *(w. dat)* **1** to be on hand for, attend, serve, be helpful to, aid; **2** to be in the way of, resist, oppose
prae·stō -stāre -stitī -stitus *(fut participle:* **praestātūrus)** *tr* to be superior to, outdo; to show, exhibit, give evidence of, display; to answer for, be responsible for, take upon oneself; to perform, discharge, fulfill; to keep, maintain, retain; to present, offer, supply; **fidem praestare** to keep one's word; **impetūs populi praestare** to be responsible for popular outbreaks; **nihil praestare** to be answerable for nothing; **officia praestare** to perform duties; **socios salvos praestare** to keep the allies safe; **terga hosti praestare** to show one's back to the enemy, retreat; **virtutem praestare** to display courage ‖ *refl* to show oneself, behave ‖ *intr* to stand out, be outstanding, be preëminent ‖ *v impers* it is preferable, it is better
praestōl·or -ārī -ātus sum *or* **praestōl·ō -āre** *tr* to wait for, expect ‖ *intr (w. dat)* to wait for, await
prae·stringō -stringĕre -strinxī -strictus *tr* to draw together, constrict, squeeze; to graze; *(fig)* to touch lightly on; to blunt *(an edge);* to blind, dazzle *(the eyes);* to dazzle, baffle; to throw into the shade
praestru·ō -ĕre -xī -ctus *tr* to build up, to block up, stop up; to build up *(e.g., confidence)* beforehand
praes·ul -ulis *or* **praesultāt·or -ōris** *m* dancer *(at the head of a religious procession)*
praesult·ō -āre -āvī -ātum *intr (w. dat)* to dance in front of, jump around in front of
prae·sum -esse -fuī -futūrus *intr* to preside; **in provinciā praeesse** to govern a

province; *(w. dat)* 1 to preside over, be in charge of, be in command of; 2 to be preëminent in

prae·sūmō -sūmĕre -sumpsī -sumptus *tr* to take in advance; to anticipate, presume, take for granted

praesumpti·ō -ōnis *f* anticipation; presumption; *(rhet)* anticipation *(of an opponent's objections)*

praesūt·us -a -um *adj* sewed up; covered

praete·gō -gĕre -xī -ctus *tr* to protect; to shelter

praetempt·ō -āre -āvī -ātus *tr* to try out in advance, test in advance; to grope for

praeten·dō -dĕre -dī -tus *tr* to hold *or* stretch in front of oneself; to present; to offer an an excuse, give as pretext, allege, pretend; *(w. dat)* to hold *(e.g., a toga)* in front of *(e.g., the eyes)* ‖ *pass* *(of places) (w. dat)* to lie to the front of *or* opposite

praetent·ō -āre *tr* to allege

praetep·escō -escĕre -uī *intr (of love)* to glow, grow warm

praeter *conj* besides, other than ‖ *prep (w. acc)* 1 *(of place)* past, by, along, before, in front of: **praeter castra copias suas ducere** to lead his troops past *or* in front of the camp; 2 beyond in degree, surpassing: **praeter spem** beyond hope, unexpectedly; 3 despite, contrary to: **praeter speciem** despite appearances; **praeter consuetudinem** contrary to normal usage, contrary to custom; 4 in addition to, as well as, besides: **praeter haec** besides this, moreover; **praeter id quod** in addition to the fact that; 5 except, but, other than: **nunc quidem praeter nos nemo est** now there's really no one but us; 6 exclusive of, except for: **praetores quotannis praeter paucos locupletati sunt** the praetors with few exceptions were getting rich every year

praeter *adv* by, past

praeter- *pref* by, past

praeterag·ō -ĕre *tr (w. double acc)* to drive *(e.g., a horse)* past *(a place)*

praeterbīt·ō -ĕre *tr & intr* to go by *or* past

praeter·dūcō -dūcĕre -duxī -ductus *tr* to lead by, conduct past

praetereā *adv (also written as two words)* besides, moreover; hereafter, thereafter

praeter·eō -īre -īvī *or* **-iī -itus** *tr* to go past, pass by; to skip, pass over in silence; to escape the notice of; to go beyond; to surpass ‖ *intr* to go by

praeterequit·ans -antis *adj* riding by *(on horseback)*

praeter·ferō -ferre -tulī -lātus *tr (w. double acc)* to carry *or* take *(s.o.)* past *(s.th.)* ‖ *pass* to move by *(a place)*

praeterflu·ō -ĕre *tr & intr* to flow by

praeter·gredior -gredī -gressus sum *tr* to march by, go past; to surpass ‖ *intr* to march by, go past

praeterhāc *adv* in addition

praeterit·us -a -um *pp of* **praetereo** ‖ *adj* past, bygone, former; *(gram)* **(tempus) praeteritum** past tense

praeter·lābor -lābī -lapsus sum *tr & intr* to glide by, slip past

praeterlātus *pp of* **praeterfero**

praeterme·ō -āre *tr & intr* to go past

praetermissi·ō -ōnis *f* leaving out, omission; passing over, neglecting; *(w. gen)* omission of

praeter·mittō -mittĕre -mīsī -missus *tr* to let pass, let go by; to leave undone; to pass over, omit, disregard, overlook, neglect

praeternāvig·ō -āre *tr* to sail past

prae·terō -terĕre -trīvī *tr* to wear down in front

praeterquam *or* **praeter quam** *conj* except that; **praeterquam qui** apart from a person who; **praeterquam quod** apart from the fact that; *(w. illipsis)* **num quo crimine is esset accusatus praeterquam veneni?** had he ever been charged with any crime except that of poisoning?; **praeterquam bis** except on two occasions

praetertulī *perf of* **praeterfero**

praetervecti·ō -ōnis *f* passing by; sailing past; riding by

praeter·vehor -vehī -vectus sum *tr & intr* to pass by *or* past; to ride by; to sail by; to march *or* go by

praetervol·ō -āre *tr & intr* to fly by; *(of opportunity)* to slip by; to escape

praetex·ō -ĕre -uī -tus *tr* to border, edge, fringe; to adorn in front; *(fig)* to cloak, conceal, disguise; to use as a pretext, allege, pretend

praetext·a -ae *f* crimson-bordered toga *(worn by higher magistrates and by freeborn boys and possibly girls)*; tragedy; **praetextas docere** to put on tragedies

praetextāt·us -a -um *adj* wearing the toga praetexta *(crimson-bordered toga)*; underage, juvenile; **mores praetextati** loose morals

praetext·um -ī *n* adornment, glory; pretext, cloak

praetext·us -a -um *pp of* **praetexo** ‖ *adj* bordered; wearing the crimson-bordered toga; **fabula praetexta** Roman tragic drama ‖ *f see* **praetexta** ‖ *n* pretext, pretense, excuse

praetext·us -ūs *m* show, appearance; pretext

praetim·eō -ēre *intr* to be apprehensive

praetinct·us -a -um *adj* previously dipped

praet·or -ōris *m* praetor *(judicial magistrate, accompanied by six lictors)*; *(during early days of the Republic)* chief magistrate, chief executive; *(in Italian municipalities)* chief magistrate; **praetor peregrinus** praetor who had jurisdiction over cases involving a Roman and a foreigner; **praetor urbanus** *(or* **urbis)** praetor with jurisdiction over cases involving Roman citizens; **pro praetore** magistrate with extended governorship, or other persons ranked as such

praetōriān·us -a -um *adj* praetorian, belonging to the emperor's bodyguard; **miles praetorianus** a praetorian guard ‖ *mpl* praetorian guard

praetōrici·us -a -um *adj* received from the praetor *(at public games)*

praetōri·us -a -um *adj* of the commander in chief, of the commander *or* general; praetor's; propraetor's; **cohors praetoria** general's bodyguard; **comitia praetoria** praetorial elections; **navis praetoria** flagship; **porta praetoria** camp gate nearest the general's tent; **turba praetoria** crowd around the praetor ‖ *n* general's quarters, headquarters; official residence of the governor in a province; council of war; emperor's bodyguard; palace, mansion

praetor·queō -quēre -sī -tus *tr* to twist beforehand; to strangle first

praetract·ō -āre *tr* to consider in advance

praetrepid·ō -āre *intr* to tremble in anticipation

praetrepid·us -a -um *adj* very nervous, trembling

praetrīvī *perf of* **praetero**

praetrunc·ō -āre -āvī -ātus *tr* to cut off; to lop off the tip of

praetulī *perf of* **praefero**

Praetūtiān·us -a -um *adj* of the Praetutii *(a people of Picenum)*

praetūr·a -ae *f* praetorship; propraetorship

praeumbr·ans -antis *adj* casting a shadow; *(fig)* overshadowing

praeust·us -a -um *adj* burnt at the tip, hardened by fire at the point; frostbitten

praeut *conj* as compared with, when compared with

praeval·ens -entis *adj* exceptionally powerful, exceptionally strong

praeval·eō -ēre -uī *intr* to be stronger, have more power; to have greater influence; to have the upper hand

praevalid·us -a -um *adj* unusually strong, unusually powerful, imposing; too strong

praevāricāti·ō -ōnis *f (leg)* collusion

praevāricāt·or -ōris *m (leg)* prosecutor in collusion with the defense

praevaric·or -ārī -ātus sum *intr (leg) (of an attorney)* to act in collusion with his opposite to secure a particular outcome to a trial

praevār·us -a -um *adj* very crooked; very knock-kneed

prae·vehor -vehī -vectus sum *tr (of a river)* to flow by ‖ *intr* to ride in front, ride by; to sail by

prae·veniō -venīre -vēnī -ventus *tr* to come before, precede, get the jump on, anticipate; to prevent ‖ *intr* to come before, precede

praeverb·ium -(i)ī *n (gram)* prefix

praeverr·ō -ĕre *tr* to sweep *(the ground)* before

praever·tō -tĕre -tī -sus *or* **prae·vertor -vertī -versus sum** *tr* **(-vort-)** to go before, precede, outrun, outstrip; to turn to first, attend to first; to prefer; to come before, anticipate; to prevent; to reoccupy; *(w. dat or* **prae** *+ abl)* to prefer *(s.o. or s.th.)* to ‖ *intr (w. dat or* **ad)** to go first to, turn to first, attend to first

prae·videō -vidēre -vīdī -vīsus *tr* to foresee

praeviti·ō -āre -āvī -ātus *tr* to taint *or* pollute beforehand

praevi·us -a -um *adj* going before, leading the way

praevol·ō -āre -āvī *intr* to fly out in front

pragmatic·us -a -um *adj* experienced, worldly-wise ‖ *m* legal adviser

pran·deō -dēre -dī -sus *tr* to eat for breakfast, eat for lunch ‖ *intr* to have breakfast, have lunch

prand·ium -(i)ī *n* breakfast; lunch

pransit·ō -āre *intr* to usually eat breakfast *or* lunch

prans·or -ōris *m* guest at lunch

pransōri·us -a -um *adj* suitable for lunch

prans·us -a -um *pp of* **prandeo** ‖ *adj* having had breakfast *or* lunch, after eating; well-fed; **pransus potus** having been wined and dined

prasināt·us -a -um *adj* wearing a green outfit

prasiniān·us -ī *m* fan of the green faction *(at the racetrack)*

prasin·us -a -um *adj* green; **factio prasina** the Greens *(one of the stables of horses at the racetrack)*

prātens·is -is -e *adj* meadow-, growing in a meadow

prātul·um -ī *n* small meadow

prāt·um -ī *n* meadow; *(fig)* broad expanse of the sea ‖ *npl* meadow grass

prāvē *adv* crookedly; improperly, wrongly, badly, poorly; **prave facti versūs** poorly written verses

prāvit·ās -ātis *f* crookedness, distortion; impropriety, irregularity; perverseness, depravity

prāv·us -a -um *adj* crooked, distorted, deformed; irregular, improper, wrong, bad; perverse, vicious

Praxitel·ēs -ī *or* **-ūs** *or* **-ae** *m* Athenian sculptor *(4th cent. B.C.)*

Praxitelī·us -a -um *adj* of Praxiteles

precāriō *adv* upon request
precāri·us -a -um *adj* obtained by prayer; dependent on another's will, uncertain, precarious
precāti·ō -ōnis *f* prayer; **precationes facere** to say prayers
precāt·or -ōris *m* intercessor, suppliant
precēs = *pl of* **prex**
preci·ae -ārum *fpl* grapevine
prec·or -ārī -ātus sum *tr* to entreat, supplicate, pray to; to pray for; to wish for; *(w. double acc)* to pray to *(s.o.)* for; *(w. acc of thing and abl of person)* to request *(s.th.)* from; *(w.* **pro** + *abl)* to entreat *(e.g., the gods)* on behalf of; *(w.* **ut, ne)** to pray that, pray that not; **longum Augusto diem precari** to wish Augustus long life ‖ *intr* to pray; *(w.* **ad)** to pray to, *e.g.,* **di ad quos precantur** the gods to whom they pray; **male precari** to curse, utter curses
prehen·dō *or* **pren·dō -dĕre -dī -sus** *tr* to take hold of, grasp, seize; to detain; to arrest; to catch, surprise; to reach, arrive at; to grasp, understand; *(w.* **in** + *abl)* to catch a person in the act of; *(mil)* to occupy
prēl·um -ī *n* wine press, oil press; clothes press
premō premĕre pressī pressus *tr* to press, squeeze; to lie down on *(the ground); (of things)* to be on top of, rest on; to bury *(in the ground);* to trample on; to get on top of, have sex with *(a woman);* to hug *(the shore);* to suppress, hide; to cover, crown; to press hard, bear down on; to weigh down, burden; to put emphasis on *(a point of argument);* to chase, attack; to weigh down, load; to press together, close; to choke, throttle; to block *(an entranceway);* to keep shut up, prevent from escaping; to curb, stop *(movement, an action, a process);* to depress, lower; to submerge, sink; to drown out *(a noise); (of sleep, death)* to overcome, overpower; *(of darkness)* to cover, hide; to mark, impress; to prune; to pressure, urge, importune; to degrade, humble, disparage; to abridge, condense, compress *(words, thoughts);* to press *(wine, oil);* to subjugate; *(geog)* to hem in, surround; **forum premere** to frequent the forum, walk about in the forum; **oculos premere** to close the eyes *(of a dead person);* **pollicem premere** to give the good luck sign *(by pressing the thumb against the index finger);* **vestigia premere** *(w. gen)* **1** to follow hard upon the tracks of; **2** *(fig)* to follow in *(s.o.'s)* tracks; **vocem premere** to fall silent ‖ *refl & pass* to lower oneself *(in dignity),* stoop ‖ *refl* to huddle together
prensāti·ō -ōnis *f (pol)* campaign
prens·ō *or* **prehens·ō -āre -āvī -ātus** *tr* to take hold of, clutch at, grab; to buttonhole ‖ *intr (pol)* to campaign
prensus *pp of* **prendo**
pressē *adv* distinctly, with articulation; concisely; accurately, simply
pressī *perf of* **premo**
pressi·ō -ōnis *f* pressure *(exerted by the fulcrum of a lever);* fulcrum
press·ō -āre -āvī -ātus *tr* to press, exert pressure on; to weigh down
pressūr·a -ae *f* pressure
press·us -a -um *pp of* **premo** ‖ *adj* closed, shut tight; compact, dense; low *(sound),* subdued *(voice);* tight *(embrace);* deliberate *(pace);* concise *(style);* **basia pressa** one kiss after another; **copia lactis pressi** a supply of cheese
press·us -ūs *m* pressure; expression *(of the face)*
pretiōsē *adv* at great cost, expensively
pretiōs·us -a -um *adj* precious, valuable; expensive; extravagant
pret·ium -(i)ī *n* price; value, worth; reward, return, recompense; bribe; pay, wages; ransom; **ad pretium redigere** to put a price on; **in pretio esse** to be prized; to be held in high esteem; **in pretio habere** to prize, hold in high esteem; **pretio meo (tuo)** at my (your) expense; **pretium curae esse** to be worth the trouble; **pretium facere** to set a price; **pretium habere** to have value, be worth something; **pretium operae esse** to be worth the effort, be worthwhile
prex precis *f (usu. pl)* prayer; request; intercession; curse, imprecation
Priamē·is -idos *f* daughter of Priam, Cassandra
Priamēi·us -a -um *adj* of Priam
Prīāmid·ēs -ae *m* son of Priam
Priam·us -ī *m* Priam *(son of Laomedon, husband of Hecuba, father of Hector, Paris, Cassandra, etc., king of Troy)*
Priāp·us -ī *m* son of Dionysus and Aphrodite, god of gardens and vineyards, and protector of flocks
prīdem *adv* formerly, previously; once *(in the past);* long ago; **haud ita pridem** not so long ago, not long before; **jam pridem** long ago; **quam pridem?** for how long?; how long ago?
prīdiān·us -a -um *adj* of the day before
prīdiē *adv* the day before
Priēn·ē -ēs *f* coastal town in Ionia, opposite Miletus
prīm·a -ōrum *npl* first part, beginning; first principles *or* elements; **cum primis** among the first, especially; chiefly; first of all; **in primis** above all, chiefly, particularly, especially
prīm·ae -ārum *fpl* lead, first rank, highest

place, highest importance; **primas dare** *(w. dat)* to attach supreme importance to

prīmaev·us -a -um *adj* youthful

prīmān·ī -ōrum *mpl* soldiers of the first legion

prīmāri·us -a -um *adj* first in rank; first-rate

prīmē *adv* to the highest degree

prīmigeni·us -a -um *adj* first-born

prīmipīlār·is -is *m* ranking centurion of a legion

prīmipīl·us -ī *m* ranking centurion of a legion

prīmiti·ae -ārum *fpl* first fruits; *(fig)* beginnings; **a primitiis** from the beginning, thoroughly

prīmitus *adv* originally, at first; for the first time

prīmō *adv* first, in the first place; at first, at the beginning

prīmord·ium -(i)ī *n* origin, beginning; commencement; beginning of a new reign

prīmōr·is -is -e *adj* first, leading; the front of, the beginning of; tip of; first, earliest; front *(teeth, battle line);* principal; basic; leading *(men);* **digituli primores** fingertips; **in labris primoribus** on the tip of one's tongue ‖ *mpl* leaders, chiefs; *(mil)* front ranks

prīmulum *adv* for the first time; at first, first of all

prīmul·us -a -um *adj* very first

prīmum *adv* first, in the first place, before all else; at first; for the first time; **cum primum** *(or* **ubi primum** *or* **ut primum)** as soon as; **primum dum** in the first place; **quam primum** as soon as possible

prīmumdum *adv* in the first place

prīm·us -a -um *adj* first; foremost; principal; distinguished; nearest; basic, fundamental; first-class; that is in the earliest stages; the front of; front *(teeth);* the tip of, end of; **prīmā fronte** *(or* **facie)** outwardly, at first glance; **primas partes agere** to play the lead role; **primi pedes** forefeet; **primis digitis** with *or* at the fingertips; **primo anno** at the beginning of the year *or* season; **primo quoque tempore** at the very earliest opportunity; **primus in provinciam introiit** he was the first to enter the province; **primus quisque** the very first, the first possible; each in turn ‖ *mpl* leading citizens ‖ *fpl see* **primae** ‖ *n* beginning; front; **a primo** from the first; **in primō** in the beginning; *(mil)* at the head of the column ‖ *npl see* **prima**

princ·eps -ipis *adj* first; earliest; original; leading, in front; foremost, chief ‖ *m* leader, chief; emperor; *(mil)* maniple, company; *(mil)* captain, company commander, centurion; *(mil)* rank of centurion; **princeps primus** a centurion ranking second among the six centurions of a legion ‖ *mpl (mil)* soldiers of the second line *(between the* **hastati** *and the* **triarii)**, second line

principāl·is -is -e *adj* first, foremost; original, primitive; chief, principal; of the emperor; **via principalis** *(mil)* main street *(of a camp);* **porta principalis** *(mil)* main gate *(of a camp)*

principāt·us -ūs *m* first place; post of commander in chief; principate; rule, sovereignty; origin, beginning; **principatum tenere** to occupy first place, be in the lead

principi·a -ōrum *npl* first principles; foundations; *(mil)* front line, front-line troops; *(mil)* headquarters

principiāl·is -is -e *adj* initial

principiō *adv* in the beginning, at first

princip·ium -(i)ī *n* beginning, start; starting point; origin; beginner, originator; basis; premise; *(pol)* first to vote; *(pol)* right to vote first; **a principio** in the beginning, at first; **de principio** right from the start; **principium capere** *(or* **sumere** *or* **exordiri)** to begin; **principium ducere ab** to originate with ‖ *npl* foundations; *(mil)* headquarters; *(mil)* the second line in order of battle; *(phil)* rudimentary particles of matter, elements

pri·or -or -us *comp; no positive exists) adj* previous, preceding, prior, former; more fundamental, basic; better, superior, preferable; *(of kings, rulers)* the elder; **in priorem partem** in a forward direction; **priores partes agere** to play a more important role ‖ *mpl* forefathers, ancestors, ancients ‖ *fpl (only acc)* lead, preference ‖ *npl* earlier events

priscē *adv* in the old-fashioned style

prisc·us -a -um *adj* old, ancient; old-time, old-fashioned; former, previous

Prisc·us -ī *m* Roman family name *(cognomen), esp.* Lucius Tarquinius Priscus *(the fifth king of Rome)* ‖ Quintus Servilius Priscus Fidenas *(conqueror of the Veientes and Fidenates in 435 B.C.)* ‖ Helvidius Priscus *(prominent Stoic under Nero and Vespasian)*

pristin·us -a -um *adj* former, earlier; pristine, primitive, original; preceding, previous, yesterday's ‖ *n* **in pristinum restituere** to restore to its former condition

pristis *see* **pistrix**

prius *adv* earlier, before, previously, sooner, first; sooner, rather

priusquam *conj (also written as two words)* before

prīvātim *adv* privately, in private; as a private citizen; at home

prīvāti·ō -ōnis *f* removal, negation

prīvāt·us -a -um *adj* private; personal, individual, peculiar; isolated; ordinary *(language)* ‖ *m* private citizen; civilian; subject *(of a ruler)* ‖ *n* privacy, retirement; private property, private land; **ex privato** out of one's own pocket; **in privato** in private; **in privatum** for private use

Prīvern·ās -ātis *adj* of Privernum ‖ *mpl* the people of Privernum

Prīvern·um -ī *n* Latin town founded by the Volscians

prīvigna -ae *f* stepdaughter

prīvign·us -ī *m* stepson ‖ *mpl* stepchildren

prīvilēg·ium -(i)ī *n* privilege, special right; *(pol)* special bill directed against *or* in favor of an individual

prīv·ō -are *tr (w. abl)* **1** to deprive of, rob of; **2** to release from, relieve of, free from

prīv·us -a -um *adj* every, each, single; own, private; *(w. gen)* deprived of

prō *adv (w.* **quam** *or* **ut)** just as, according as ‖ *prep (w. abl)* before, in front of; in the presence of; for, on behalf of, in favor of, in the service of, on the side of; instead of, for, in lieu of; just as, the same as, for; in proportion to; according to; in comparison with; by virtue of; in name of; **esse pro** (+ *abl)* to be as good as, be the equivalent of; **esse** *(or* **stare pro** + *abl)* to be on the side of *(s.o.)*; **pro certo habere** to regard *(s.th.)* as certain; **pro eo** just the same; **pro eo atque** *(or* **ac)** just as, the same as; **pro eo quod** in view of the fact that; **pro eo quantum** in proportion to, according as; **pro eo ut** instead of the case being that; **pro herede** in his capactiy as heir; **pro occiso relictus** left for dead; **pro rostro orationem habere** to speak from the rostrum; **pro se quisque** each one for himself, individually; **pro sententiā dicere** to state as his opinion; **pro testimonio dicere** to state by way of evidence; **pro vallo carros objiciunt** they put their wagons in the way to serve as a barricade; **utrum pro ancilla me habes an filia?** do you regard me as a maid or a daughter? ‖ *interj* oh!; **pro di immortales!** oh, heavens above!

pro- *pref* **1** forward movement: **progredi** to go forward; **2** downward movement: **proclivis** downhill; **3** action in front: **protegere** to cover in front; **4** bringing into the open: **prodere** to bring out, publish; **5** priority in time: **providere** to see beforehand; **6** advantage: **prodesse** *(w. dat)* to be advantageous to, be good for

proāgor·us -ī *m* mayor *(in some Greek provincial towns)*

proauct·or -ōris *mf* early ancestor

proavi·a -ae *f* great-grandmother

proavīt·us -a -um *adj* great-grandfather's, ancestral

proav·us -ī *m* great-grandfather; ancestor, forefather

probābil·is -is -e *adj* worthy of approval, commendable, acceptable; pleasing, agreeable; probable, plausible, likely

probābilit·ās -ātis *f* probability

probābiliter *adv* probably

probāti·ō -ōnis *f* approval, approbation; criterion, test; proof

probāt·or -ōris *m* approver, supporter, backer

probāt·us -a -um *adj* approved, acceptable; tried, tested, good; esteemed

probē *adv* correctly, well, satisfactorily; thoroughly, very, very much; **haud probe** not really, no; **pereo probe** *(coll)* I'm absolutely a goner

probit·ās -ātis *f* probity, uprightness, honesty, goodness; sexual purity; good behavior

problēmat·a -ōrum *npl (rhet)* difficult questions for debate, problems

prob·ō -āre -āvī -ātus *tr* to approve, commend, esteem; to make good, represent as good, make acceptable; to pronounce judgment on; to pronounce approval of; to make credible, prove, show, demonstrate; to test, try, inspect; **probare pro** *(w. abl)* to pass *(s.o.)* off as ‖ *pass* **probari pro** *(w. abl)* to pass for, be taken for

probosc·is -idis *f* snout; trunk *(of an elephant)*

probriperlecebr·ae -ārum *fpl* temptations

probrōs·us -a -um *adj* scandalous, shameful, abusive

probr·um -ī *n* abuse, invective, reproach; shameful act; lewdness, indecency; shame, disgrace; charge of disgraceful conduct

prob·us -a -um *adj* good, honest, upright, virtuous, decent; *(coll)* real, proper, downright

Prob·us -ī *m* Roman family name *(cognomen), esp.* Marcus Valerius Probus *(grammarian of the 1st cent.* A.D.*)*

Proc·a *or* **Proc·ās -ae** *m* Proca *(king of Alba Longa and father of Numitor and Amulius)*

procācit·ās -ātis *f* brashness

procāciter *adv* brashly

proc·ax -ācis *adj* brash

prō·cēdō -cēdĕre -cessī -cessum *intr* to proceed, go forward, advance; to make progress; to come out *(in public)*, show oneself, appear; to come forth, arise; *(of time)* to pass, elapse; to turn out, result, succeed; to continue

procell·a -ae *f* violent wind, squall, hurricane, storm; *(fig)* violence, commotion, storm; *(mil)* charge

prōcell·ō -ĕre *tr* to throw down ‖ *refl* **se procellere in mensam** to flop down at the table

procellōs·us -a -um *adj* gusty

prōcērē *adv* far

procer·ēs -um *mpl* leading men *(of a society, etc.)*; leaders *(of a profession, art)*

prōcērit·ās -ātis *f* height, tallness; length ‖ *fpl* the different heights

prōcērius *adv* farther, to a greater extent, more

prōcēr·us -a -um *adj* tall *(person, tree)*; long *(neck, beak)*; lofty *(idea)*; *(pros)* long; **palmae procerae** open palms

prōcessī *perf of* **procedo**

prōcessi·ō -ōnis *f* advance

prōcess·us -a -um *pp of* **procedo** ‖ *adj* advanced *(age)*

prōcess·us -ūs *m* advance, progress

Prochyt·a -ae *or* **Prochyt·ē -ēs** *f* small island off the Campanian coast

proc·ī -ōrum *mpl* class of leading citizens under the Servian constitution

prō·cidō -cidĕre -cidī *intr* to fall forwards, fall over, fall down, fall prostrate

prōcinctū *(abl only) m* **in procinctu** ready for combat, on red alert

prōclāmāt·or -ōris *m* loudmouth

prōclām·ō -āre -āvī -ātus *tr* to yell out; to exclaim; *(w. acc & inf)* to cry out that ‖ *intr* to yell; to practice public speaking

Procl·ēs -is *m* one of the first pair of kings to reign at Sparta, together with Eurysthenes

prōclīn·ō -āre -āvī -ātus *tr* to bend, bend forward; **res proclinata** critical situation, crisis

prōclīv·e -is *n* slope, descent; **in proclivi esse** to be easy

prōclīvī *adv* downhill; effortlessly

prōclīv·is -is -e *or* **prōclīv·us -a -um** *adj* sloping down; sloping forward; downhill; easy; *(w.* **ad***)* inclined to, disposed to, ready for; *(of years, seasons)* declining; *(fig)* going downhill, insecure; *(w.* **ad***)* inclined to

prōclīvit·ās -ātis *f* proclivity, tendency, predispostion

prōclīviter *adv* readily; easily, effortlessly

prōclīv·us *see* **proclivis**

Procn·ē -ēs *f* **(Prog-)** Procne *(daughter of Pandion, sister of Philomela, wife of Tereus, and mother and murderess of Itys; she was changed into a swallow)*; swallow

proc·ō -āre *or* **proc·or -ārī** *tr* to require, demand

prōcons·ul -ulis *m* vice-consul, proconsul; governor of a province; military commander

prōconsulār·is -is -e *adj* proconsular

prōconsulāt·us -ūs *m* proconsulship, proconsulate

prōcrastināti·ō -ōnis *f* procrastination

prōcrastin·ō -āre -āvī -ātus *tr* to put off till the next day, postpone ‖ *intr* to procrastinate

prōcreāti·ō -ōnis *f* procreation

prōcreāt·or -ōris *m* procreator; creator

prōcreātr·ix -īcis *f* mother

prōcre·ō -āre -āvī -ātus *tr* to procreate, beget; to produce

prōcresc·ō -ĕre *intr* to spring forth, be produced; to continue to grow, grow up

Procr·is -is *or* **-idis** *f* wife of Cephalus, who mistook her for a wild beast and shot her with bow and arrow

Procrust·ēs -ae *m* notorious robber in Attica who stretched his victims to the length of his bed or mutilated them if they were too tall

prōcub·ō -āre -uī *intr* to lie stretched out

prōcū·dō -dĕre *tr (lit & fig)* to hammer out, forge

procul *adv* at a distance, in the distance; far away, a great way off; from a distance, from far; **haud procul afuit quin legatos violarent** they came close to outraging the ambassadors; **non procul ab** not far from

prōculc·ō -āre -āvī -ātus *tr* to trample upon, trample down

Proculēi·us -ī *m* Roman clan name *(nomen), esp.* Gaius Proculeius *(friend of Augustus and literary patron)*

prōcumbō prōcumbĕre prōcubuī prōcubitum *intr* to fall down, sink down; to lean forward, bend over, be broken down; to lie down; *(fig)* to go to ruin; *(topog)* to extend, spread

prōcūrāti·ō -ōnis *f* attention; *(w. gen)* **1** concern for, care for; **2** responsibility for, charge over; **3** management of, administration of; **4** procuratorship of; **5** expiation of

prōcūrāt·or -ōris *m* procurator, manager, administrator; agent, deputy; governor of a (minor) province

prōcūrātr·ix -īcis *f* superintendent *(female)*

prōcūr·ō -āre -āvī -ātus *tr* to look after, attend to; to administer *(as procurator)*; to have charge of; to avert by sacrifice; to expiate ‖ *intr* to serve as procurator

prō·currō -currĕre -(cu)currī -cursum *intr* to run out ahead, dash forward; to jut out, project

prōcursāti·ō -ōnis *f* sally, charge

prōcursātōr·ēs -um *mpl* skirmishers

prōcurs·ō -āre *intr* to keep charging out; to continue to skirmish

prōcurs·us -ūs *m* sally, charge

prōcurv·us -a -um *adj* curving forwards; curving, winding *(shore)*

proc·us -ī *m* suitor; gigolo ‖ *mpl* class of leading citizens in the Servian constitution; **impudentes proci** shameless candidates

Procy·ōn -ōnis *m (astr)* Lesser Dog Star *(the constellation Canis Minor)*

prōdactus *pp of* **prodigo**

prōdeambul·ō -āre *intr* to go out for a walk

prōd·eō -īre -iī -itum *intr* to go out, come out, go forth, come forth; *(of plants)* to come out; to appear in public; to come forward *(in the assembly or court);* to appear *(on stage);* to go ahead, advance; **in proelium prodire** to go into battle; **obviam prodire** *(w. dat)* to out to meet *(s.o.); (e.g., of a cliff)* to jut out, project

prō·dīcō -dīcĕre -dixī -dictus *tr* to set *(a date)* beforehand *(for some activity);* **praetor reo atque accusatoribus diem prodixit** *(leg)* the praetor announced the date of the trial to the defendant as well as the plaintiffs

Prodic·us -ī *m* sophist of Ceos, contemporary with Socrates

prōdigē *adv* lavishly

prōdigenti·a -ae *f* extravagance; **prodigentia opum** wasting of resources

prōdigiāl·is -is -e *adj* marked with prodigies

prōdigiāliter *adv* to a fantastic degree

prōdigiōs·us -a -um prodigious; freakish

prōdig·ium -(i)ī *n* prodigy, portent; unnatural crime, monstrous crime; monster, freak

prōd·igō -igĕre -ēgī *tr* to squander, waste

prōdig·us -a -um *adj* wasteful; lavish, openhanded; *(w. gen)* free with; **animae prodigus** free with *or* careless with one's life; **herbae prodigus locus** spot with luxurious growth of grass

prōditi·ō -ōnis *f* betrayal, treason; **proditionem agere** *(w. dat)* to commit treason against, betray

prōdit·or -ōris *m* betrayer, traitor

prō·dō -dĕre -didī -ditus *tr* to bring out, bring forth, produce; to reveal, disclose; *(of a writer, esp. w.* **memoriā** *or* **memoriae** *or* **ad memoriam**) to record, relate, report, hand down, transmit; to proclaim; to appoint; to give up, surrender; to forsake, betray; to prolong; *(w. dat)* **1** to betray to; **2** to reveal to

prōdoc·eō -ēre *tr* to teach publicly

prodrom·us -ī *m* forerunner; northerly winds *(that precede the Etesian winds)*

prō·dūcō -dūcĕre -duxī ductus *tr* to bring out, bring forth; to produce; to promote, advance; to bring to light; to bring into the world; to raise, bring up; to educate; to drag out, protract; to lengthen *(a syllable);* to lead on, induce; to put off, adjourn; to put *(a slave)* up for sale; to produce, perform *(on the stage); (leg)* to bring to court

prōduct·a -ōrum *npl* preferable things, preferences

prōductē *adv* long; **producte litteram dicere** to pronounce the letter *or* vowel long

prōducti·ō -ōnis *f* lengthening

prōduct·ō -āre *tr* to drag out

prōduct·us -a -um *pp of* **produco** ‖ *adj* lengthened, prolonged, long

proēgmen·on -ī *n* preference

proeliār·is -is -e *adj* battle-, of battle

proeliāt·or -ōris *m* combatant

proeli·or -ārī -ātus sum *intr* to battle

proel·ium -(i)ī *n* battle, combat, fight ‖ *npl* fighting men, warriors

Proetid·es -um *fpl* daughters of Proetus, who were driven mad by Hera and imagined that they were cows

Proët·us -ī *m* Proëtus, king of Argos *or* Tiryns, twin-brother of Acrisius

profān·ō -āre -āvī -ātus *tr* to profane

profān·us -a -um *adj* unconsecrated, ordinary; impious; ill-omened

profātus *pp of* **profor**

prōfēcī *perf of* **proficio**

profecti·ō -ōnis *f* setting out, departure; source *(of money)*

profectō *adv* really, actually

profectus *pp of* **proficiscor**

prōfectus *pp of* **proficio**

prōfect·us -ūs *m* progress, advance; success; profit

prō·ferō -ferre -tulī -lātus *tr* to bring forward, advance, bring out; to extend, enlarge; to put off, postpone; to produce, discover, invent; to make known, publish; to express; to mention, cite, quote; **in medium** *(or* **in lucem**) **proferre** to publish, disclose; **pedem proferre** to advance; **res proferre** *(leg)* to declare a recess; **signa proferre** *(mil)* to march forward

professi·ō -ōnis *f* public acknowledgment, profession, declaration; registration *(at which property, etc., was declared);* profession, business

profess·or -ōris *m* professor, teacher

professōri·us -a -um *adj* professorial; professional, expert

professus *pp of* **profiteor**

profest·us -a -um *adj* non-holiday, ordinary; **dies profestus** workday

prō·ficiō -ficĕre -fēcī -fectum *intr* to make progress, make headway, advance; to have success; to be useful, do good, help, be conducive; **nihil proficere** to do no good

pro·ficiscor -ficiscī -fectus sum *intr* to set out, start, go, depart; to originate, proceed, arise

pro·fiteor -fitērī -fessus sum *tr* to declare

publicly, acknowledge, confess, profess; to offer freely, promise, volunteer; to follow as a profession, practice *(e.g., law);* to make a declaration of, register *(property, etc., before a public official);* **indicium profiteri** to volunteer evidence, testify freely; **nomen profiteri** to put one's name in as a candidate; **se adjutorem profiteri** *(w.* **ad)** to volunteer to help *(s.o.)* ‖ *intr* to make a confession, make an admission; to be a professor, be a teacher

prōflīgāt·or -ōris *m* big spender

prōflīgāt·us -a -um *adj* profligate

prōflīg·ō -āre -āvī -ātus *tr* to knock to the ground, knock down; to defeat; to bring to an end, do away with, finish off; to ruin, crush; to degrade, debase

prōfl·ō -āre -āvī -ātus *tr* to breathe out

prōflu·ens -entis *adj* flowing along; fluent *(speech)* ‖ *f* running water

prōfluenter *adv* easily, effortlessly

prōfluenti·a -ae *f* fluency

prōflu·ō -ĕre -xī *intr* to flow out; to flow along; *(fig)* to proceed; **gravedo profluit** the head cold results in a runny nose

prōfluv·ium -(i)ī *n* flow

pro·for -fārī -fātus sum *tr* to say, declare ‖ *intr* to speak out

prōfūdī *perf of* **profundo**

pro·fugiō -fugĕre -fūgī -fugitūrus *tr* to run away from, escape from ‖ *intr* to run away, escape; *(w.* **ad)** to take refuge with, take refuge at the house of

profug·us -a -um *adj* fugitive; banished, exiled; nomadic ‖ *m* refugee

pro·fundō -fundĕre -fūdī -fūsus *tr* to pour, pour out; to shed *(blood, tears)* freely; to utter; to give vent to; to spend freely, squander; **animam** *(or* **spiritum) profundere** to breathe one's last; **vitam pro patriā profundere** to give one's life for one's country ‖ *refl & pass* to come pouring out; to sprout

profund·us -a -um *adj* deep; boundless, vast; dense *(forest, cloud);* high; infernal; *(fig)* bottomless, boundless ‖ *n* depth; the deep, deep sea; abyss

profūsē *adv* in disorder, haphazardly, helter-skelter; extravagantly

profūsi·ō -ōnis *f* profusion

profūs·us -a -um *pp of* **profundo** ‖ *adj* extravagant, lavish, profuse; excessive, expensive

prōgen·er -erī *m* grandaughter's husband

prōgener·ō -āre -āvī -ātus *tr* to beget, give birth to; to produce

prōgeni·ēs -ēī *f* offspring, progeny; line, family; lineage, descent

prōgenit·or -ōris *m* progenitor

prō·gignō -gignĕre -genuī -genitus *tr* to beget, produce

prōgnāriter *adv* precisely, exactly

prognāt·us -a -um *adj (w. abl or* **ab** *or* **ex)** born of, descended from ‖ *m* child; grandson

Prognē *see* **Procne**

prognostic·on *or* **prognostic·um -ī** *n* sign of the future, prognostic

prō·gredior -gredī -gressus sum *intr* to go forward, march forward; to advance; to go on, make headway, make progress; to go forth, go out

prōgressi·ō -ōnis *f* progress, advancement; increase, growth; *(rhet)* climax

prōgressus *pp of* **progredior**

prōgress·us -ūs *m* progress, advance; march *(of time or events)*

prōh *interj* oh!; **proh di immortales!** oh, heavens above!

prohib·eō -ēre -uī -itus *tr* to hold back, check, hinder, prevent, avert, keep off; to prohibit; to preclude; to keep away; to defend, protect; *(w.* **ne, quominus,** *or in negative contexts* **quin)** to keep *(s.o.)* from *(doing s.th.)*

prohibiti·ō -ōnis *f* prohibition

proïnde *or* **proïn** *(or* **proin** *as monosyllable) adv* so then, consequently, accordingly; equally; likewise; **proinde atque** *(or* **ac** *or* **ut** *or* **quam)** just as, exactly as; **proinde atque si** *(or* **ac si** *or* **quasi)** just as if

prōjēcī *perf of* **projicio**

prōjectīci·us -a -um *adj* exposed, abandoned *(child)*

prōjecti·ō -ōnis *f* stretching out; **projectio bracchii** stretching out of the arm

prōject·us -a -um *pp of* **projicio** ‖ *adj* jutting out; prostrate, stretched out; abject, contemptible; downcast; *(w.* **ad)** prone to

prōject·us -ūs *m* projection, extension

prō·jiciō -jicĕre -jēcī -jectus *tr* to throw down; to throw away, abandon, forsake; to fling from oneself as unwanted, discard; to hold out, extend; to banish, exile; to neglect, desert; to blurt out; to give up, sacrifice; to put off, delay; to throw overboard; *(w.* **in** + *acc or* **ad)** to abandon to *(a fate),* expose to; **projicere in exilium** to drive out, banish ‖ *refl* to throw oneself, plunge; to rush; *(w.* **in** + *acc)* to give way to *(a feeling, tears, habit);* **se projicere ad pedes** *(w. gen)* to throw oneself at the feet of; **se projicere ex nave** to jump overboard; **se projicere in Forum** to rush into the Forum; **se projicere in muliebres fletus** to give way to unmanly weeping ‖ *pass (geog)* to extend; *(of a promontory)* to jut out ‖ *intr* to jut out

prō·lābor -lābī -lapsus sum *intr* to glide forward, slip *or* move forward; to fall forwards, fall on one's face; to slip out; *(of words)* to slip out, escape; to be led on, led astray *(by fear, greed, etc.); (fig)* to fail, go to ruin, collapse; **prolabi per equi caput** to go flying over the head of the horse

prōlapsi·ō -ōnis *f* slipping

prōlapsus *pp of* **prolabor**

prōlāti·ō -ōnis *f* extension *(of territory);* adducing, mentioning *(of precedents);* delay, postponement

prōlāt·ō -āre *tr* to extend; to put off, delay

prōlātus *pp of* **profero**

prōlect·ō -āre -āvī -ātus *tr* to lure

prōl·ēs -is *f* offspring, progeny, children; descendants; race, stock; child; young man

prōlētār·ius -(i)ī *m* proletarian ‖ *mpl* proletariat

prōli·ciō -cĕre *tr* to entice, bring out, lead on; to incite

prōlixē *adv* freely, wildly, readily, cheerfully

prōlix·us -a -um *adj* long, freely growing, wild *(beard, hair, etc.);* favorable *(circumstances)*

prōlocūtus *pp of* **proloquor**

prōlog·us -ī *m* prologue *(of a play);* actor who gives the prologue

prōloquor -quī -cūtus sum *tr & intr* to speak out

prōlub·ium -(i)ī *n* desire, inclination, yen

prōlū·dō -dĕre -sī -sum *tr* to be a prelude to ‖ *intr* to practice; *(of boxers)* to spar, shadowbox

prō·luō -luĕre -luī -lūtus *tr* to wash out, flush, wash off; *(of water)* to wash away; to wet, drench; to wash clean, wash out

prōlūsi·ō -ōnis *f* practice fight, dry run; sparring

prōlūtus *pp of* **proluo**

prōluvi·ēs -ēī *f* flood; discharge, excrement

prōmercāl·is -is -e *adj* sold in the open market

prōmer·eō -ēre -uī -itus *or* **prōmer·eor -ērī -itus sum** *tr* to deserve, merit, earn ‖ *intr* to be deserving; *(w.* **de** *+ abl)* to deserve the gratitude of; **bene de multis promerere** *(or* **promereri)** to deserve the full gratitude of many people

prōmerit·um -ī *n* favor; reward, due; merit; guilt; **bene (male) promeritum** a good (bad) turn

Promēth·eūs -eī *or* **-eos** *m* son of Iapetus and Clymene, brother of Epimetheus, and discoverer of use of fire, which he taught to men

Promēthē·us -a -um *adj* Promethean, of Prometheus

Promēthīd·ēs -ae *m* son of Prometheus, Deucalion *(who, with his wife Pyrrha, survived the Deluge)*

prōmin·ens -entis *adj* prominent, projecting ‖ *n* headland

prōmin·eō -ēre -uī *intr* to jut out, stick out, stick up; *(of persons)* to lean out, bend forward; *(w.* **in** *+ acc)* to reach down to, reach out for

prōmiscam *or* **promiscē** *or* **prōmiscuē** *adv* in common; without distinction; all at the same time *or* in the same place

prōmisc(u)·us -a -um *adj* promiscuous, haphazard, indiscriminate; in common, open to all; common

prōmissi·ō -ōnis *f* promise

prōmiss·or -ōris *m* one who promises *or* guarantees

prōmiss·us -a -um *adj* allowed to grow, long ‖ *n* promise; prediction

prō·mittō -mittĕre -mīsī -missus *tr* to send forth; to let *(e.g., hair)* grow; to promise, guarantee; to predict as certain; to give hope of; **ad cenam** *(or* **ad aliquem) promittere** to accept an invitation to dinner *(or* to s.o.'s home); **damni infecti promittere** to guarantee compensation for damage done; **promittere (in matrimoniam)** to promise *(one's daughter)* in marriage ‖ *refl (w.* **ad)** to have expectations of attaining; **sibi promittere** to promise oneself, look forward to, count on

prōm·ō -ĕre -(p)sī -ptus *tr* to bring out, draw out; to produce *(arguments);* to bring to light, reveal; to bring out, express *(ideas, emotions)*

prōmon·eō -ēre *tr* to warn openly

prōmontōr·ium -(i)ī *n* promontory

prōmōt·a -ōrum *npl* second choice

prō·moveō -movēre -mōvī -mōtus *tr* to move *(s.th.)* forward, cause to advance; to enlarge, extend; to effect, accomplish; to encourage, egg on; to promote *(to higher office);* to bring to light, reveal; to postpone; **gradum** *(or* **pedem) promovere** to step forward; **nihil promovere** to accomplish nothing, do no good, make no progress ‖ *intr* to make headway

promptārius *see* **promptuarius**

promptē *adv* readily; willingly; fluently

prompt·ō -āre *tr* to give out, distribute; to be treasurer of

promptuāri·us -a -um *adj* of a storehouse, storage-; **cella promptuaria** *(coll)* jail, cooler ‖ *n* storeroom, cupboard

prompt·us -a -um *pp of* **promo** ‖ *adj* at hand, readily available; easy; glib *(tongue);* brought to light, evident; bold, enterprising; *(w. dat or* **ad** *or* **in** *+ acc)* **1** readily inclined to; **2** ready *or* prepared for; *(w.* **in** *+ abl)* quick at; *(w.* **adversus** *+ acc)* ready for, prepared against; *(w. inf)* ready to, quick to; **promptum est** *(w. inf)* it is an easy matter to

prompt·us -ūs *m* **in promptu 1** within easy reach, at one's disposal *or* command; **2** in full view, in a prominent position; **3** within one's powers *or* capabilities; **4** at one's command; **in promptu esse** to be obvious; **in promptu gerere** *(or* **habere** *or* **ponere)** to display

prōmulgāti·ō -ōnis *f (pol)* promulgation, official publication *(of a proposed law)*

prōmulg·ō -āre -āvī -ātus *tr* to promulgate, to publish, publicize

prōmuls·is -idis *f* hors d'oeuvres

prōmuntur·ium *or* **prōmontor·ium -(i)ī** *n* promontory

prōm·us -ī *m* butler

prōmūtu·us -a -um *adj (fin)* on credit, advanced as a loan

prōnē *adv* downwards; slantwise

pronep·ōs -ōtis *m* great-grandson

pronept·is -is *f* great-grandaughter

pronoe·a -ae *f* divine providence

prōnōm·en -inis *n (gram)* pronoun; *(gram)* demonstrative pronoun

prōnub·a -ae *f* matron of honor *(who conducted the bride to the husband's home); (of Juno, Bellona, Tisiphone)* patroness of marriage

prōnuntiāti·ō -ōnis *f* proclamation, declaration; verdict; pronunciation *(of words);* proposition *(in logic); (rhet)* delivery

prōnuntiāt·or -ōris *m* narrator

prōnuntiāt·um -ī *n* proposition *(in logic)*

prōnunti·ō -āre -āvī -ātus *tr* to proclaim, announce; to express *(opinion, judgment);* to pronounce *(words);* to hold out, promise *(rewards)* publicly; to recite, deliver; to narrate, relate; **sententiam pronuntiare** *(pol)* to announce a motion *(for discussion in the Senate),* to put a motion to a vote **II** *intr (theat) (of an actor)* speak one's lines

prōnūper *adv* quite recently

prōnur·us -ūs *f* grandson's wife

prōn·us -a -um *adj* leaning, inclined, bending, stooping, bent over, bent forwards; swift, rushing, dashing, moving swiftly along; sloping, steep *(hill, road);* sinking, setting *(sun, etc.);* downhill; easy; *(w. dat or* **ad** *or* **in** *+ acc)* inclined toward, disposed toward, prone to; *(w. dat)* inclined to favor *(e.g., a winner)* **II** *n* downward tendency, gravity **II** *npl* slopes

pro(h)oemi·or -ārī *intr* to make an introduction *or* preface

pro(h)oem·ium *or* **pro(h)ēm·ium -(i)ī** *n* introduction, preface; prelude; *(fig)* prelude *(e.g., to a fight)*

propāgāti·ō -ōnis *f* propagation, reproduction; prolongation; transmission *(to posterity);* **nominis propagatio** perpetuation of the name

propāgāt·or -ōris *m* one who extends *(s.th.)* in time; **propagator provinciae** grantor of an extended provincial command

propāg·ō -āre -āvī -ātus *tr* to produce *(plants)* from slips; to produce *(offspring);* to propagate *(race, religion);* to extend *(territory);* to prolong *(a period, life);* to cause *(a family name, tradition)* to endure, hand down *(to posterity)*

propāg·ō -inis *f* slip *(from which a plant is propagated);* offspring, progeny; race, line; descendants

prōpalam *adv* openly, publicly

prōpatul·us -a -um *adj* open **II** *n* open space; **in propatulo habere** to display

prope *(comp:* **propius;** *superl:* **proxime)** *adv* near, nearby; *(of time)* near, at hand; *(of degree)* nearly, almost, practically, just about; *(w.* **ab** *+ abl)* close by, near to; **prope est cum** the time has come when **II** *prep (w. acc)* near, near to; **prope diem** very soon, any day now

propediem *adv* very soon, any day now

prō·pellō -pellěre -pulī -pulsus *tr* to propel, drive forward; to push over, overturn, upset; to drive away, drive out; to banish, expel

propemodo *or* **propemodum** *adv* nearly, practically, almost

prōpen·deō -dēre -dī -sum *intr* to hang down; *(w.* **in** *+ acc)* to be inclined to, be favorably disposed to

prōpensē *adv* readily, willingly

prōpensi·ō -ōnis *f* propensity

prōpens·us -a -um *pp of* **propendeo II** *adj* weighty; approaching; inclined; ready, willing; *(w. dat, w.* **ad** *or* **in** *+ acc)* favorably disposed to, partial to; **propenso animo** with ready mind, willingly; **propensus in alteram partem** inclined toward the other point of view

properanter *adv* hastily, quickly

properanti·a -ae *f* haste

properāti·ō -ōnis *f* haste

properātō *adv* hastily, speedily

properāt·us -a -um *adj* hurried, hasty, speedy **II** *n* speed; **properato opus est** speed is required

properē *adv* hastily, in haste, quickly; without hesitation

properip·ēs -edis *adj* quick-moving, quick-footed

proper·ō -āre -āvī -ātus *tr* to speed up; to prepare hastily, do in haste **II** *intr* to be quick; to go *or* move quickly

Propert·ius -(i)ī *m* Sextus Aurelius Propertius *(Latin elegiac poet, native of Umbria, c. 50–15 B.C.)*

proper·us -a -um *adj* quick, speedy

prōpex·us -a -um *adj* combed forward

prophēt·a -ae *m* prophet

propīn *n (only nom and acc in use)* apéritif

prōpīnāti·ō -ōnis *f* toast

prōpīn·ō -āre -āvī -ātus *tr* to drink *(e.g., a*

cup of wine) as a toast; to drink a toast to *(s.o.)*; *(w. dat)* **1** to drink *(e.g., a cup of wine as a toast)* to; **2** to pass on *(a cup)* to

propinqu·a -ae *f* relative *(female)*

propinquē *adv* near at hand

propinquit·ās -ātis *f* proximity, nearness, vicinity; relationship, affinity; friendship

propinqu·ō -āre -āvī -ātus *tr* to bring on; to hasten **‖** *intr* to approach; *(w. dat)* to draw near to, approach

propinqu·us -a -um *adj* near, neighboring; *(of time)* near, at hand; closely related; *(w. dat)* akin to; **in spe propinquā missionis** in the hope of an early discharge; **nulla propinqua spes** no hope for the near future; **spes propinqui reditūs** hope for an early return **‖** *mf* relative **‖** *n* neighborhood; **in propinquo** in the vicinity; *(of time, events)* near at hand, in the offing

propi·or -or -us *adj* nearer, closer; *(of time)* earlier; later, more recent; more closely related, more like, more nearly resembling; more imminent; more intimate, closer *(tie)*; of more importance, of more concern; *(of battle)* fought at close range; shorter *(route)*; *(w. dat)* **1** nearer to, closer to; **2** closer to *(in resemblance)*, more like; **3** to be favorably disposed to; *(w. acc or w.* **ab** *+ abl)* closer to **‖** *npl* closer side *(e.g., of a river)*; more recent events

propiti·ō -āre -āvī -ātus *tr* to propitiate

propiti·us -a -um *adj (w. dat)* **1** propitious towards; **2** favorably disposed towards

propnigē·um *or* **propnigē·on -ī** *n* sweat room *(of a bath)*

Prōpoetid·es -um *fpl* Cyprian girls who denied the divinity of Venus, becoming the first prostitutes, subsequently turned to stone

propōl·a -ae *f* retailer

prōpollu·ō -ĕre *tr* to further pollute

prō·pōnō -pōnĕre -posuī -positus *tr* to put *or* place forward, expose to view, display; to propose, suggest; to imagine; to offer, propose; to say, report, relate, publish; to threaten; to denounce; to design, determine, intend

Propontiac·us -a -um *adj* of the Propontis

Propont·is -idis *or* **-idos** *f* Propontis, Sea of Marmora

prōporrō *adv* furthermore; wholly

prōporti·ō -ōnis *f* proportion, symmetry; *(gram)* analogy

prōport·ō -āre *tr* to cite

prōpositi·ō -ōnis *f* proposition; intention, purpose; theme; basic assumption *(in logic)*

prōposit·us -a -um *pp of* **propono ‖** *adj* exposed, open; accessible; impending, at hand **‖** *n* intention, purpose; main point, theme; first premise *(in logic)*; **mihi propositum** it is my intention, it is my plan; **propositum habere** to have as one's object

prōpraet·or -ōris *m* propraetor *(ex-praetor as governor of a province)*

propriē *adv* in the strict sense; properly; strictly for oneself, personally; peculiarly, especially

propriet·ās -ātis *f* property, peculiarity, quality

proprītim *adv* specifically, properly

propri·us -a -um *adj* own, very own; special, peculiar, individual, particular, personal; lasting

propter *adv* near, near at hand

propter *prep (w. acc)* near, close, next to; on account of, because of, for the sake of; through, by means of; **propter quod** wherefore

propterea *or* **propter eā** *adv* for that reason, therefore, on that account; **propterea quod** for the very reason that

prōpudiōs·us -a -um *adj* shameful

prōpud·ium -(i)ī *n* shameful act; *(said of a person)* disgrace

prōpugnācul·um -ī *n* rampart, battlement; defense; *(fig)* safeguard

prōpugnāti·ō -ōnis *f* defense, vindication; protection

prōpugnāt·or -ōris *m* defender, champion

prōpugn·ō -āre -āvī -ātus *tr* to defend **‖** *intr* to come out and fight; to fight a defensive action, repel an assault; *(fig)* to put up a defense

prōpulsāti·ō -ōnis *f* repulse

prōpuls·ō -āre -āvī -ātus *tr* to drive off, repel; *(fig)* to ward off, repel

prōpulsus *pp of* **propello**

Propylae·a -ōrum *npl* Propylaea *(monumental gateway, esp. the entrance to the Athenian Acropolis)*

prōquaest·or -ōris *m* proquaestor *(magistrate who, after his quaestorship in Rome, was associated as a financial officer with a proconsul in the administration of a province)*

prōquam *or* **prō quam** *conj* just as, according as

prōr·a -ae *f* prow; *(fig)* ship; **mihi prora et puppis est** my intention from first to last is *(literally, it is prow and stern to me)*

prōrēp·ō -ĕre -sī -ptum *intr* to creep ahead, crawl out

prōrēt·a -ae *m* lookout man at the prow

prōreus *m (nom only)* look-out man at the prow

prō·ripiō -ripĕre -ripuī -reptus *tr* to drag forth, drag out; to rush **‖** *refl* to rush, dash

prōrogāti·ō -ōnis *f* extension *(of a term of office)*; putting off

prōrog·ō -āre -āvī -ātus *tr* to extend, prolong; to put off, postpone

prors·a *or* **prōs·a -ae** *f* prose

prorsum *or* **prōsum** *adv* forwards, straight ahead; *(as an intensive)* altogether, absolutely; *(w. negatives)* absolutely, at all, *e.g.*, **prorsum nihil** absolutely nothing, nothing at all

prorsus *or* **prōsus** *adv* forward; straight *(to the destination); (intensifying a word, phrase, etc., which it may either precede or follow)* altogether, absolutely; *(w. a negative)* absolutely, at all; *(emphasizing the second and stronger of two related terms)* more than that, even; *(connecting a clause or sentence with what precedes)* in fact, all in all; *(in summing up)* in short, in a word; *(w. demonstrative pron or adv, emphasizing correspondence)* exactly, just

prō·rumpō -rumpĕre -rūpī -ruptus *tr* to make *(s.th.)* burst forth; to give vent to; to emit ‖ *pass* to rush forth, rush out ‖ *intr* to rush forth; *(of vapors, etc.)* to burst forth; *(of news)* to come out; *(mil)* to make an attack

prōru·ō -ĕre -ī -tus *tr* to overthrow, demolish ‖ *intr* to rush forth; to tumble

prōrupt·us -a -um *pp of* **prorumpo** ‖ *adj* unrestrained

prōs·a -ae *f* prose

prōsāpi·a -ae *f* stock, race, line

proscaen·ium -(i)ī *n* **(-scēn-)** stage

pro·scindō -scindĕre -scidī -scissus *tr* to plow up, break up; *(fig)* to criticize harshly, cut to pieces

proscrī·bō -bĕre -psī -ptus *tr* to publish in writing; to proclaim, announce; to advertise *(for sale, etc.);* to confiscate *(property);* to punish with confiscation; to proscribe, outlaw *(people)*

proscripti·ō -ōnis *f* advertisement; proscription, political purge; notice of confiscation; notice of outlawry

proscriptur·iō -īre *intr* to be eager to hold a proscription *or* purge

proscript·us -a -um *pp of* **proscribo** ‖ *m* outlaw

prōsec·ō -āre -uī -tus *tr* to cut off *(esp. parts of a sacrificial victim)*

prōsecūtus *pp of* **prosequor**

prōsed·a -ae *f* prostitute

prōsēmin·ō -āre -āvī -ātus *tr* to sow, scatter about, plant; to propagate, raise

prōsen·tiō -tīre -sī *tr* to sense *or* realize beforehand, get wind of

prō·sequor -sequī -secūtus sum *tr* to escort, attend; to pursue *(enemy);* to chase, follow; to follow up *(actions, words);* to go on with, continue *(a topic);* to describe in detail; to follow, imitate; to honor, reward *(with)*; to send *(s.o.)* on his *or* her way with gifts; *(of events)* to occur after, succeed

prōser·ō -ĕre *tr* to stick out *(e.g., the tongue)*

Prōserpīn·a -ae *f* daughter of Ceres and wife of Pluto

prōserp·ō -ĕre *intr* to creep *or* crawl forwards, creep along

proseuch·a -ae *f* synagogue

prōsil·iō -īre -uī *or* **-īvī** *or* **-iī** *intr* to jump forward, jump up; to jump to one's feet; *(of blood)* to spurt; *(of sparks)* to shoot out, fly; to dash

prōsoc·er -erī *m* wife's grandfather; husband's grandfather

prosōdi·a -ae *f* the tone *or* accent of a syllable, prosody

prosōpopoei·a -ae *f* impersonation

prospect·ō -āre -āvī -ātus *tr* to view, look out at, gaze upon; *(of places)* to look towards, command a view of, face; to look for, hope for; *(w. indir. ques.)* to look to see *(what, whether)*

prospectus *pp of* **prospicio**

prospect·us -ūs *m* distant view; view; faculty of sight; a sight *(thing seen)*

prospecul·or -ārī -ātus sum *tr* to look out for, watch for ‖ *intr* to look around, reconnoiter

prosper *see* **prosperus**

prosperē *adv* favorably, luckily, as desired, successfully

prosperit·ās -ātis *f* success, good fortune, prosperity; **prosperitas valetudinis** good health

prosper·ō -āre *tr* to cause to succeed, make happy

prosp·erus *or* **prosp·er -era -erum** *adj* successful, fortunate, lucky, favorable, prosperous

prospicienti·a -ae *f* foresight, precaution

pro·spiciō -spicĕre -spexī -spectus *tr* to see in the distance; to spot; to command a view of; to watch for; to look out for, provide for; to foresee ‖ *intr* to look forward; to look into the distance, have a view; to be on the lookout, exercise foresight; *(w.* **in** *+ acc)* to command a view of, overlook; **ex superioribus in urbem prospicere** to have a view of the city from a vantage point; **parum prospiciunt oculi** the eyes are nearsighted

pro·sternō -sternĕre -strāvī -strātus *tr* to throw to the ground, knock down; *(of sickness)* to strike down; to wreck, ruin, overthrow, subvert; to demean ‖ *refl* to debase oneself; **se prosternere ad pedes** *(w. gen)* to throw oneself at the feet of, fall down before

prostibil·is -is *f* prostitute

prostibul·um -ī *n* prostitute

prostit·uō -uĕre -uī -ūtus *tr* to expose for sale; to prostitute
prostitūt·a -ae *f* prostitute
pro·stō -stāre -stitī -stitum *intr* to project, stick out; *(of wares)* to be set up for sale; to prostitute oneself, be a prostitute
prostrātus *pp of* **prosterno**
prōstrāvī *perf of* **prosterno**
prōsubig·ō -ĕre *tr* to dig up in front
prō·sum -desse -fuī -futūrus *intr* to be useful, do good, be profitable; *(w. dat)* to be good for, do *(s.o.)* good; **multum prodesse** to do a lot of good
prōsum *adv see* **prorsum**
Prōtagor·ās -ae *m* Greek sophist, contemporary of Socrates, born at Abdera *(c. 485–415 B.C.)*
prōte·gō -gĕre -xī -ctus *tr* to cover in front, cover up; to cover with a roof; to shelter, protect; *(fig)* to cover, defend, protect
prōtēl·ō -āre -āvī -ātus *tr* to chase away
prōtēl·um -ī *n* team of oxen in tandem; row, series
prōten·dō -dĕre -dī -tus *tr* to stretch forth, stretch out, extend
prōtent·us -a -um *pp of* **protendo** ‖ *adj* extended
prōtenus *see* **protinus**
prō·terō -terĕre -trīvī -trītus *tr* to wear down; to rub out; to trample down, trample under foot; *(fig)* to trample upon, rub out, crush
prōterr·eō -ēre -uī -itum *tr* to scare away
protervē *adv* brashly, brazenly
protervit·ās -ātis *f* brashness
proterv·us -a -um *adj* brash, brazen
Prōtesilāē·us -a -um *adj* of Protesilaus
Prōtesilā·us -ī *m* first Greek casualty in the Trojan War, husband of Laodamia
Prōt·eūs -eī *or* **-eos** *m* a god of the sea with power to assume various forms
prothȳmē *adv* willingly, readily
prothȳmi·a -ae *f* willingness, readiness
prōtinam *adv* immediately
prōtinus *or* **prōtenus** *adv* straight on, forward, farther on; continuously, right on, without pause; on the spot
prōtoll·ō -ĕre *tr* to stretch out *(hand);* to put off, postpone
prōtopraxi·a -ae *f (fin)* priority *(among creditors receiving payment)*
prō·trahō -trahĕre -traxī -tractus *tr* to drag forward, drag out; to produce; to reveal, bring to light
prōtrītus *pp of* **protero**
prōtrīvī *perf of* **protero**
prōtrū·dō -dĕre -sī -sus *tr* to push forwards, push out; to postpone
prōturb·ō -āre -āvī -ātus *tr* to drive ahead, drive on in confusion; to drive away, repel; to knock down
proüt *(or* **prout,** *scanned as one syllable) conj* as, just as; in sor far as, in as much as; *(introducing alternatives)* **prout...ita** according to whether...or
prōvect·us -a -um *adj* advanced; **aetate provectus** advanced in years; **nox provecta erat** the night had been far advanced
prōve·hō -hĕre -xī -ctus *tr* to carry forwards; to transport, convey; to lead, lead on; to promote, advance, raise ‖ *pass* to ride, drive, move, *or* sail ahead
prō·veniō -venīre -vēnī -ventum *intr* to go on, proceed; to succeed; to come out, appear; *(of plants, seeds)* to come out, come up, grow; to come about, happen
prōvent·us -ūs *m* result, outcome; success; yield, produce; harvest
prōverb·ium -iī *n* proverb
prōvexī *perf of* **proveho**
prōvid·ens -entis *adj* prudent
prōvidenter *adv* prudently, with foresight
prōvidenti·a -ae *f* foresight, foreknowledge; precaution; **providentia deorum** divine providence
prō·videō -vidēre -vīdī -vīsus *tr* to see in the distance; to see coming; to foresee; to provide for; to provide against, guard against, avert, avoid; to look after, look out for, care for; to prepare, make ready; *(w.* **ut***)* to see to it that ‖ *intr* to exercise forethought, take precautions; *(w. dat or* **de** *+ abl)* to look after, care for ‖ *v impers* **provisum est** care was taken
prōvid·us -a -um *adj* foreseeing; prudent, cautious; provident; *(w. gen)* providing for
prōvinci·a -ae *f* province; sphere of administration *or* jurisdiction; office, duty, charge; public office, commission, command, administration; sphere of action
prōvinciāl·is -is -e *adj* provincial, of a province; in a province; **bellum provinciale** war in a province; **molestia provincialis** annoyance of administering a province ‖ *m* provincial
prōvinciātim *adv* province by province
prōvīsi·ō -ōnis *f* foresight; precaution; *(w. gen)* precaution against
prōvīsō *adv* with forethought
prōvīs·ō -ĕre *tr* to go out to see; to be on the lookout for
prōvīs·or -ōris *m* lookout *(person);* provider
prōvīsū *m (abl only)* by looking forward; *(w. objective gen)* **1** by foreseeing *(e.g., danger);* **2** by providing, providing for
prōvīsus *pp of* **provideo**
prō·vīvō -vīvĕre -vixī *intr* to live on, go on living
prōvocāti·ō -ōnis *f* challenge; *(leg)* appeal
prōvocāt·or -ōris *m* challenger; a type of gladiator
prōvoc·ō -āre -āvī -ātus *tr* to challenge *(a*

person, a statement); to provoke; to exasperate; to stir, stimulate; **bellum provocare** to provoke a war; **beneficio provocatus** touched *or* stirred by an act of kindness; **in aleam provocare** to challenge to a game of dice; **provocare maledictis** to provoke *or* exasperate with nasty remarks ‖ *intr (leg)* to appeal; *(leg) (w.* **ab)** to appeal from the decision of *(a magistrate); (leg) (w.* **ad)** to appeal to *(a higher authority)*

prōvol·ō -āre -āvī *intr* to fly out, rush out, dash out

prōvol·vō -věre -vī -ūtus *tr* to roll forward, roll along; to roll over, overturn; to humble; to ruin ‖ *refl* to prostrate oneself, fall down, grovel

prōvom·ō -ěre *tr* to vomit, throw up

prōvorsus *adv* straight ahead

prōvulg·ō -āre -āvī -ātus *tr* to make publicly known

prox *interj (comic representation of a fart):* **dum enitor, prox! jam paene inquinavi pallium** as I struggle to my feet, bang! I darn near soiled by clothes

proxenēt·a -ae *m* business agent

proximē *adv* **(-umē)** *(superl of* **prope)** *(of place)* nearest, next; *(of time)* most recently, just recently; *(w. acc)* **1** close to, next to, at the side of; **2** very much like, resembling; *(w. dat) (of place)* next to; **proxime atque** almost as much as, nearly the same as; **proxime Pompeium sedebam** I was sitting next to Pompey; **quam proxime** *(w. dat or acc)* as close as possible to

proximit·ās -ātis *f* proximity, vicinity; resemblance, similarity; close relationship

proximō *adv* very *(or* just) recently

proxim·us -a -um *adj* **(-xum-)** nearest, next; adjoining; living nearby; readiest at hand; *(of time)* immediately preceding, previous, most recent, following, latest, last; just mentioned; closely related; *(of affections)* closely devoted; *(of cause)* immediate, proximate; *(of an argument)* relevant; very like *(in character, resemblance);* nearest *(in degree);* next *(in rank, worth),* second-best; next in order; most direct *(route);* **proximum est ut** (+ *subj)* it is most likely that; the next point is that; the next thing is to ‖ *m* close relative, next of kin; heir next in succession; friend, intimate ‖ *n* neighborhood; the house next door; the recent past; **de proximo** aptly, very closely; **ex proximo** from the readiest source; close by; **in proximo** within easy reach; close at hand; **in proximum** for the following day

prūd·ens -entis *adj* foreseeing; conscious, aware; skilled, skillful, experienced; prudent, discreet, sensible, intelligent; *(w. gen or abl or w.* **in** + *abl)* **1** aware of, conscious of; **2** familiar with; **3** skilled in, experienced in, versed in ‖ *m* expert; *(leg)* jurist

prūdenter *adv* prudently, cautiously; skillfully

prūdenti·a -ae *f* foreseeing; prudence, discretion, good sense; **prudentia juris publici** *(leg)* knowledge of *or* experience in public law

pruīn·a -ae *f* frost; winter; **pruinae** a covering of frozen snow

pruīnōs·us -a -um *adj* frosty

prūn·a -ae *f* live coal

prūnice·us -a -um *adj* made of plum-tree wood

prūniti·us -a -um *adj* of plum-tree wood

prūn·um -ī *n* plum

prūn·us -ī *f* plum tree

prūrīg·ō -inis *f* itch, tickle; yen

prūr·iō -īre *intr* to itch, tickle; to have an itch; to be sexually aroused; *(w.* **in** + *acc)* to be itching for

Prūsi·ās *or* **Prūsi·a -ae** *m* Prusias *(name of several kings of Bithynia, esp. Prusias Cholus, d. about 182 B.C., with whom Hannibal took refuge after his defeat)*

prytanē·um *or* **prytanī·um -ī** *n* town hall *(in some Greek cities where the Prytanes, or magistrates, held meetings and dined)*

prytan·is -is *m* magistrate in some Greek states

psall·ō -ěre -ī *intr* to play the cithara

psaltēr·ium -(i)ī *n* cithara *(form of harp)*

psalt·ēs -ae *m* cithara-player, citharist

psaltri·a -ae *f* citharist *(female)*

Psamath·ē -ēs *f* a sea nymph, wife of Aeacus and mother of Phocus ‖ daughter of the Argive King Crotopus

psec·as -adis *f* female slave who perfumed her lady's hair; typical name of maidservants

psell·us -a -um *adj* faltering in speech

psēphism·a -atis *n (pol)* plebiscite of the Greek assembly

Pseudocat·ō -ōnis *m* a make-believe Cato

Pseudol·us -ī *m* "Little Liar" *(title of a play by Plautus)*

pseudomen·os *or* **pseudomen·us -ī** *m (phil)* fallacious syllogism

Pseudophilipp·us -ī *m* "False Philip" *(i.e., Andriscus, who claimed to be the son of Perseus of Macedon and was defeated by the Romans in 148 B.C.)*

pseudothyr·um -ī *n* hidden door

psīlocitharist·a -ae *m* one who plays the lyre without singing in accompaniment

psithi·us -a -um *adj* the name of a type of vine ‖ *fpl* grapes

psittac·us -ī *m* parrot

Psōph·is -idos *f* town in Arcadia to the S. of Mt. Erymanthus

Psȳch·ē -ēs *f* girlfriend of Cupid, made immortal by Jupiter
psychomantī·um *or* **psychomantē·um -ī** *n* place of séance
-pte *enclitic (added to pronouns, usu. w. poss adj and esp. in abl)* self, own; **sonitu suopte titinant aures** the ears are ringing (with their own sound)
ptisanār·ium -(i)ī *n* gruel
Ptolomae·um -ī *n* name of a gymnasium **ll** tomb of the Ptolemies
Ptolemae·us -ī *m* Ptolemy *(name of a series of thirteen Egyptian kings descended from Latus, one of Alexander the Great's generals)*
pūb·ens -entis *adj* full of sap, succulent, vigorous
pūber *see* **pubes**
pūbert·ās -ātis *f* puberty; manhood; sign of maturity, beard; physical signs of puberty
pūb·ēs *or* **pūb·er -eris** *adj* grown up, adult; downy, covered with down **ll** *mpl* grown-ups, men
pūb·ēs -is *f* pubic hair; private parts; puberty; adult population, manpower; throng
pūb·escō -escĕre *intr* to reach the age of puberty, arrive at maturity; *(of plants)* to grow up, ripen; *(of meadows, fields)* to be clothed, covered *(e.g., with flowers)*
pūblic·a -ae *f* prostitute
pūblicān·us -a -um *adj* of public revenues **ll** *m* revenue agent, publican, tax collector **ll** *f* public prostitute
pūblicāti·ō -ōnis *f* confiscation; disclosure
pūblicē *adv* publicly; officially, on behalf of the state, for the state; at public expense; generally, universally; **publice dicere** to speak officially
pūblicitus *adv* at public expense, at the expense of the state; publicly
Pūblici·us -a -um *adj* Publician *(Roman clan name, nomen)*; **Clivus Publicius** Publician Slope *(road leading up to the Aventine Hill)*
pūblic·ō -āre -āvī -ātus *tr* to confiscate; to throw open to the general public; to prostitute
Pūblicol·a -ae *m* **(Popl-)** Publius Valerius Publicola *(regarded as one of the first consuls, fl 509 B.C.)*
pūblic·us -a -um *adj* public, of the people, common; of the state, state, national; ordinary, vulgar; general; **causa publica** affair of national importance; *(leg)* federal case *(i.e., criminal case)*; **id bono publico facere** to do it for the public good; **publica acta** the public record, the official gazette; **res publica** state, government, politics, public life, country; **rem publicam inire** to enter politics **ll** *m* public official **ll** *n* public, publicity; public property; national treasury; federal revenue; **de publico** at public expense; **in publico** in public, publicly; **in publicum prodire** to go out in public; **in publicum redigere** to hand over to the national treasury **ll** *f* prostitute
pudend·us -a -um *adj* shameful, scandalous; **pars pudenda** genitals **ll** *npl* genitals
pud·ens -entis *adj* modest, bashful
pudenter *adv* modestly, bashfully
pud·eō -ēre -uī *or* **puditum est** *tr* to make ashamed, put to shame **ll** *intr* to be ashamed **ll** *v impers (w. acc of person and gen or abl of cause of feeling), e.g.,* **me tui pudet** I am ashamed of you
pudibund·us -a -um *adj* modest, bashful
pudīcē *adv* chastely, modestly, decently; in a subdued style
pudīciti·a -ae *f* chastity, purity
pudīc·us -a -um *adj* chaste, pure
pud·or -ōris *m* shame, sense of shame, decency, modesty; sense of honor, propriety; cause for shame, disgrace; blush
puell·a -ae *f* girl; girlfriend, sweetheart; young wife
puellār·is -is -e *adj* young girl's, girlish, youthful
puellāriter *adv* girlishly
puellul·a -ae *f* little girl; little sweetheart
puell·us -ī *m* little boy, lad; catamite
pu·er *also* **pu·erus -erī** *m* boy, lad; servant, slave; page; bachelor; **a pueris** *(or* **a puero)** from childhood on; **ex pueris excedere** to outgrow childhood
puerasc·ō -ĕre *intr* to approach boyhood
puercul·us -ī *m* little son
puerīl·is -is -e *adj* boyish, childish, youthful, puerile
puerīliter *adv* like a child, childishly
puer(i)ti·a -ae *f* childhood; boyhood
puerper·a -ae *f* woman in labor; woman who has given birth
puerper·ium -(i)ī *n* childbirth, delivery, giving birth
puerper·us -a -um *adj* easing labor pains, helping childbirth
puertia *see* **pueritia**
puerul·us -ī *m* little boy; little slave
pūg·a *or* **pȳg·a -ae** *f* rear, buttocks
pug·il -ilis *m* boxer
pugilāti·ō -ōnis *f* boxing
pugilātōri·us -a -um *adj* boxing-; **follis pugilatorius** punching bag
pugilāt·us -ūs *m* boxing match
pugilicē *adv* like a boxer
pugillār·is -is -e *adj* hand-size **ll** *mpl & npl* set of tablets; notebook
pūgi·ō -ōnis *m* dagger
pūgiuncul·us -ī *m* small dagger
pugn·a -ae *f* fistfight, brawl; fight, combat, battle

pugnācit·ās -ātis *f* pugnacity, aggressiveness
pugnāciter *adv* aggressively
pugnācul·um -ī *n* fortress
pugnant·ēs -ium *mpl* fighters, warriors
pugnant·ia -ium *npl* contradictions, inconsistencies
pugnāt·or -ōris *m* fighter, combatant
pugnātōri·us -a -um *adj* used in fighting; **arma pugnatoria** combat weapons
pugn·ax -ācis *adj* pugnacious, scrappy, aggressive; quarrelsome; dogged
pugne·us -a -um *adj* of the fist; **hospitio pugneo accipere** *(hum)* to welcome s.o. with a reception of fists; **merga pugnea** *(hum)* punch reaper
pugn·ō -āre -āvī -ātus *tr* to fight; **clara pugna ad Perusiam pugnata est** a brilliant battle was fought at Perusia; **proelia, bella pugnare** to fight battles, wars ‖ *intr* to fight; to contend, dispute; *(w. dat or* **cum)** **1** to fight, fight against, struggle with, oppose; **2** to contradict
pugn·us -ī *m* fist
pulchell·us -a -um *adj* cute little
pul·c(h)er -c(h)ra -c(h)rum *adj* beautiful, fair, handsome
Pul·cher -chri *m* Roman family name *(cognomen)* in the Claudian clan, *esp.* Publius Clodius Pulcher *(tribune of 58 B.C.)*
pulchrē *adv* beautifully, attractively; thoroughly, perfectly; *(in gloating or irony)* nicely; *(as exclamation)* fine!; **pulchre mihi est** I am fine
pulchritūd·ō -inis *f* **(pulcr-)** beauty; excellence, attractiveness
pūlē·ium -(i)ī *n (bot)* pennyroyal, mint; *(fig)* fragrance, pleasantness
pūl·ex *or* **pūl·ix -icis** *m* flea
pullār·ius -(i)ī *m* keeper of the sacred chickens
pullāt·us -a -um *adj* wearing black, in black, in mourning
pullul·ō -āre -āvī -ātus *intr* to sprout; *(of animals)* to produce young
pull·us -a -um *adj* dark-gray, dark, blackish; mourning-; **toga pulla** mourning toga ‖ *n* dark-gray garment
pull·us -ī *m* young *(of animals),* foal, offspring, chick; favorite boy, catamite; sprout, shoot ‖ *mpl* chickens *(used in divination)*
pulmentār·ium -(i)ī *n* relish, appetizer
pulment·um -ī *n* relish; appetizer; food
pulm·ō -ōnis *m* lung
pulmōne·us -a -um *adj* of the lungs, pulmonary
pulp·a -ae *f* lean meat; *(pej)* flesh *(man's carnal nature)*
pulpāment·um -ī *n* meat; game
pulpit·um -ī *n* platform; stage
pulp·ō -āre *intr* to make the sound of a vulture
puls pultis *f* pulse, porridge, mush
pulsāti·ō -ōnis *f* knock
puls·ō -āre -āvī -ātus *tr* to batter, keep hitting; to knock at; to strum *(lyre);* to beat on, strike against; *(fig)* to jolt ‖ *intr* to throb
pulsus *pp of* **pello**
puls·us -ūs *m* push, pushing; beat, beating, striking, stamping; blow, stroke; trampling; *(fig)* impression, influence
pultāti·ō -ōnis *f* knocking *(at door)*
Pultiphagōnid·ēs -ae *m (humorous patronymic)* son of Porridge-eater
pultiphag·us -ī *m* porridge eater
pult·ō -āre *tr* to knock at
pulvere·us -a -um *adj* dust-, of dust; dusty; fine as dust; raising dust
pulverulent·us -a -um *adj* dusty; raising dust; covered with dust
pulvill·us -ī *m* small cushion
pulvīn·ar -āris *n* cushioned couch; sacred couch for the images of the gods; seat of honor
pulvīnār·ium -(i)ī *n* cushioned seat of a god; *(naut)* dry dock
pulvīn·us -ī *m* pillow, cushion; seat of honor
pulv·is -eris *m (f)* dust, powder; scene of action, arena, field; effort, work
pulviscul·us -ī *m* fine dust; fine powder
pūm·ex -icis *m (f)* pumice *(esp. used to polish books and also used as a depilatory);* lava
pūmice·us -a -um *adj* pumice-; lava-
pūmic·ō -āre -āvī -ātus *tr* to polish with pumice
pūmili·ō -ōnis *m* midget, dwarf; pygmy
pūmil·ius -(i)ī *m* dwarf, pygmy
pūmil·us -a -um *adj* of short stature, dwarf
punctim *adv* with the point, with the pointed end
punct·um -ī *n* prick, puncture; point; spot, dot; moment; *(gram)* clause, phrase; *(math)* point; *(pol)* vote, ballot *(dot made on wax tablet to indicate vote);* **puncto temporis eodem** at the same instant; **punctum temporis** moment, point in time, instant
pungō pungĕre pupugī *or* **pepugī punctus** *tr* to prick, puncture, dent; to sting, bite; to cause *(a wound);* to stab; *(fig)* to sting, annoy, disturb
Pūnicān·us -a -um *adj* Punic, Carthaginian, in the Carthaginian style
Pūnicē *adv* **(Poen-)** Punic, in the Punic language
pūnice·us -a -um *adj* **(poen-)** reddish, scarlet, crimson ‖ **Puniceus (Poen-)** Punic, Carthaginian
Pūnic·us -a -um *adj* **(Poen-)** Punic, Carthaginian; red, crimson, reddish, pink; **Punicum malum** *(or* **pomum)** pomegranate ‖ *n* pomegranate

pūn·iō -īre -īvī *or* **-iī -ītus** *or* **pūn·ior -īrī -ītus -sum** *tr (older form:* **poen-**) to punish; to avenge ‖ *intr* to inflict punishment

pūnīti·ō -ōnis *f* punishment

pūnit·or -ōris *m* avenger

pūp·a -ae *f* doll, puppet; girl, kid

pūpill·a -ae *f* orphan girl, ward; minor; *(anat)* pupil

pūpillār·is -is -e *adj* of an orphan, belonging to an orphan

pūpill·us -ī *m* orphan boy, ward

Pūpini·us -a -um *adj* **ager Pupinius** a barren district between Rome and Tusculum

Pūpi·us -a -um *adj* Roman clan name *(nomen), esp.* Publius Pupius *(a tragedian)*

pupp·is -is *(acc sing usu.* **puppim**) *f* stern; ship; *(coll)* back; **a puppi** astern

pūpul·a -ae *f* little girl, kid; *(anat)* pupil, eye

pūpul·us -ī *m* little boy, kid

pūp·us -ī *m* boy, child, kid

pūrē *adv* clearly, brightly; plainly, simply; chastely, purely

purgām·en -inis *n* dirt, filth; means of expiation, purification

purgāment·a -ōrum *npl* offscourings, dirt, filth, garbage; *(term of abuse)* trash, garbage

purgāti·ō -ōnis *f* cleansing, cleaning, cleanup; justification

purgāt·us -a -um *adj* cleansed, clean, pure

purg·ō -āre -āvī -ātus *tr* to cleanse, clean; to clear, clear away, remove; to clear of a charge; to excuse, justify; to refute; to purify ritually; to purge *(the body)* ‖ *refl & pass (of water, the sky)* to become clear

pūrific·ō -āre -āvī -ātus *tr* to purify

pūriter *adv* purely, cleanly; **vitam puriter agere** to lead a clean life

purpur·a -ae *f* purple dye *(ranging in shade from blood-red to deep violet);* purple, deep-red, royal purple, crimson; royal-purple cloth; royal-purple robe; royalty; consular diginity; imperial dignity

purpurāri·us -a -um *adj* (royal) purple; relating to the purple dyeing *or* to the selling of purple cloth

purpurasc·ō -ĕre *intr* to turn purple

purpurāt·us -a -um *adj* wearing royal purple ‖ *m* courtier

purpure·us -a -um *adj* purple, crimson, royal purple *(and various shades as applied to roses, poppies, grapes, lips, flesh, blood, wine, dawn, sun at sunrise, hair)*

purpurissāt·us -a -um *adj* rouged

purpuriss·um -ī *n* rouge; red dye

pūr·us -a -um *adj* pure, clear, clean; cleared, cleansed; cleansing, purifying; chaste; plain, naked, unadorned, natural; plain *(toga),* without crimson border; faultless *(style); (leg)* unconditional, absolute; *(leg)* subject to no religious claims ‖ *n* clear sky

pūs pūris *n* pus; *(fig)* venom, malice

pusill·us -a -um *adj* petty, puny ‖ *n* bit, trifle

pūsi·ō -ōnis *m* little boy

pūsul·a *or* **pussul·a** *or* **pustul·a -ae** *f* pimple; blister

pusulāt·us *or* **pustulāt·us -a -um** *adj* refined, purified *(silver)*

putām·en -inis *n* shell *(of nuts, eggs, turtles);* peel *(of fruit)*

putāti·ō -ōnis *f* pruning

putāt·or -ōris *m* pruner

pute·al -ālis *n* low wall *(around a well or sacred spot),* stone enclosure; **puteal Libonis** stone enclosure in Roman Forum near which much business was transacted

puteāl·is -is -e *adj* of a well

pūtē·faciō -facĕre -fēcī -factus *tr* to cause to rot; to cause to crumble

pūt·eō -ēre -uī *intr* to stink; to be rotten

Puteolān·us -a -um *adj* of Puteoli

Puteol·ī -ōrum *mpl* Puteoli *(commercial city on the coast of the Bay of Naples, modern Pozzuoli)*

pu·ter *or* **pu·tris -tris -tre** *adj* putrid, rotting; crumbling; flabby

pūt·escō -escĕre -uī *intr* to become rotten

pute·us -ī *m* well; pit; dungeon

pūtidē *adv* disgustingly; affectedly

pūtidiuscul·us -a -um *adj* rather tedious

pūtid·us -a -um *adj* stinking, rotten; worn-out *(brain);* rotten *(person);* offensive *(words, actions);* unnatural, disgusting *(style)*

putill·us -a -um *adj* tiny

put·ō -āre -āvī -ātus *tr* to trim, prune; to think, ponder, consider, judge; to suppose, imagine; to reckon, estimate, value; to believe in, recognize *(gods);* to clear up, settle *(accounts);* **magni putare** to think highly of; **pro certo putare** to regard as certain ‖ *intr* to think, imagine, suppose

pūt·or -ōris *m* stench; rottenness

putre·faciō -facĕre -fēcī -factus *tr* to rot; to cause to crumble, soften

putresc·ō -ĕre *intr* to become rotten, get moldy

putrid·us -a -um *adj* rotten; flabby

putris *see* **puter**

put·us -a -um *adj (ancient word for* **purus** *and usu. used in combination with* **purus**) pure, bright, perfectly pure; splendid; unmixed; unmitigated; **certum pondus argenti puri puti** a certain weight of perfectly pure silver ‖ *m* boy

pyct·a *or* **pyct·ēs -ae** *m* boxer

Pydn·a -ae *f* Pydna *(city in Macedonia near which Aemilius Paulus defeated Perseus, king of Macedonia, 169 B.C.)*
pyel·us -ī *m* bathtub
pȳg·a -ae *f* rear, buttocks
pȳgarg·us -ī *m* kind of antelope
Pygmae·ī -ōrum *mpl* Pygmies *(a dwarfish race, esp. in Africa, said to have been constantly at war with cranes, by whom they were always defeated)*
Pygmae·us -a -um *adj* of the Pygmies; avis **Pygmaeus** a crane
Pygmali·ōn -ōnis *or* **-ōnos** *m* son of Belus and brother of Dido ‖ king of Cyprus who fell in love with a statue
Pylad·ēs -ae *or* **-is** *m* son of Strophius and friend of Orestes
Pyladē·us -a -um *adj* worthy of Pylades
Pyl·ae -ārum *fpl* Thermopylae
Pylaemen·ēs -is *m* king of the Paphlagonians and ally of Priam
Pylaïc·us -a -um of Thermopylae
Pyli·us -a -um *adj* of Pylos ‖ *m* Nestor
Pyl·os -ī *f* Pylos *(home of Nestor in S.E. Peloponnesus)*
pyr·a -ae *f* pyre
pȳram·is -idis *or* **-idos** *f* pyramid; cone
Pȳram·us -ī *m* neighbor and boyfriend of Thisbe
Pȳrēnae·us -a -um *adj* of the Pyrenees
Pȳrēn·ē -ēs *f (geog)* the Pyrenees
Pyrēn·eūs -eī *m* king of Thrace who tried to rape the Muses
pyrethr·um -ī *n* Spanish camomile *(medicinal plant)*
Pygens·is -is -e *adj* of (the town of) Pyrgi
Pyrg·ī -ōrum *mpl* town on the coast of Etruria
Pyriphlegeth·on -ontos *m* one of the rivers of the lower world *(= Phlegethon)*
pyrōp·us -ī *m* bronze
Pyrrh·a -ae *f* daughter of Epimetheus, wife of Deucalion, and survivor of the Deluge
Pyrrhi·as -adis *adj (fem only)* of (the town of) Pyrrha in Lesbos
Pyrrh·ō(n) -ōnis *m* Pyrrho *(philosopher of Elis, contemporary of Aristotle and founder of the school of Skepticism, c. 360–270 B.C.)*
Pyrrhōnē·us -a -um *adj* of the school founded by Pyrrho
Pyrrh·us -ī *m* son of Achilles and founder of Epirus *(also called Neoptolemus)* ‖ king of Epirus who invaded Italy against the Romans in 280 B.C. *(319–272 B.C.)*
Pȳthagor·ās -ae *m* Greek philosopher and mathematician *(6th cent. B.C.)* ‖ a servant of Nero
Pȳthagorē·us *or* **Pȳthagoric·us -a -um** *adj* Pythagorean
Pȳthi·as -adis *f* typical name for a slave girl in comedy
Pȳthic·us -a -um *adj* Pythian, Delphic
Pȳthi·us -a -um *adj* Pythian, Delphic ‖ *m* Apollo ‖ *f* Pythia *(priestess of Apollo at Delphi)* ‖ *npl* Pythian games *(held in honor of Apollo every four years at Delphi)*
Pȳth·ō -ūs *f* ancient name of Delphi *or* its oracle
Pȳth·ōn -ōnis *or* **-ōnos** *m* dragon slain by Apollo near Delphi
pȳtism·a -atis *n* mouthful of wine *(spat out after tasting)*
pȳtiss·ō -āre *tr* to spit out *(wine after tasting it)*
pyx·is -idis *or* **-idos** *f* powder box, cosmetic box

Q

Q. *abbr* **Quīntus** *(first name, praenomen)*
quā *adv (interrog)* by which road? which way? in which direction? by which route? where? by what means? how? ‖ *(rel)* where; to the extent that; in so far as; in as much as; in the manner in which, as ‖ *(indef)* by any route; by any chance, in any way; **qua...qua** partly...partly, both...and
quācumque *adv* **(-cunq-)** wherever, by whatever way, in whatever way; by whatever means, howsoever
quādamtenus *adv* to a certain point, only so far and no farther
quadr·a -ae *f* square table, dining table; square crust; square bit, cube *(of cheese, etc.)*; slice *(of bread, cake)*
quadrāgēn·ī -ae -a *adj* forty each
quadrāgēsim·us -a -um *adj* **(-gensi-)** fortieth ‖ *f* one-fortieth; 2½% tax
quadrāgiēs *adv* **(-giens)** forty times
quadrāgintā *indecl adj* forty
quadr·ans -antis *m* one-fourth, a quarter; penny *(smallest coin, worth one sixth of Roman* **as**); quarter of a pound; quarter pint *(quarter of a* **sextarius**); **quadrante lavatum ire** to take a bath for a penny *(usual price of a bath)*
quadrant·al -ālis *n* five-gallon jar
quadrantāri·us -a -um *adj* quarter; **mulier quadrantaria** two-bit wench *(woman who sells herself for a pittance)*; **tabulae quadrantariae** record of debts reduced to a fourth
quadrāt·us -a -um *adj* square; stocky *(build)*; 90-degree *(angle)*; compact *(style)*; cube, cubic ‖ *n* square; square object; cube
quadri- *pref* consisting of, having four of the things named
quadrīdu·um -ī *n* four-day period; **in quadriduo** within four days; **quadriduo**

for a period of four days; within the next four days; **quadriduo ante (post)** four days before (after)

quadrienn·ium -(i)ī *n* four-year period, four years

quadrifāriam *adv* in four directions; in four ways; in four places; in fours

quadrifid·us -a -um *adj* split into four parts

quadrīg·a -āe *f or* **quadrīg·ae -ārum** *fpl* four-horse team *(running four abreast);* four-horse chariot

quadrīgāri·us -a -um *adj* connected with chariot racing

quadrīgār·ius -(i)ī *m* chariot racer

quadrīgāt·us -a -um *adj (of a coin)* stamped with the image of a four-horse chariot

quadrīgul·ae -ārum *fpl (figurine of a)* four-horse chariot

quadrijūg·is -is -e *or* **quadrijug·us -a -um** *adj* drawn by a four-horse team *(yoked abreast); (of horses)* yoked four abreast ‖ *mpl* four-horse team

quadrilībr·is -is -e *adj* four-pound

quadrīmul·us -a -um *adj* only four years old

quadrīm·us -a -um *adj* four-year-old

quadringēnāri·us -a -um *adj* consisting of four hundred men each

quadringēn·ī -ae -a *adj* four hundred each

quadringentēsim·us -a -um *adj* four-hundredth

quadringentiē(n)s *adv* four hundred times

quadripertītō *adv* in four parts, in four divisions

quadripertīt·us -a -um *adj* four-fold

quadrirēm·is -is -e *adj* having four banks of oars *(or possibly with four rowers to every bench)* ‖ *f* quadrireme

quadriv·ium -(i)ī *n* crossroads

quadr·ō -āre -āvī -ātus *tr* to make square; to complete; *(rhet)* to round out, give rhythmic finish to *(a speech)* ‖ *intr* to make a square; to be exact; *(of accounts)* to agree, come out right, tally; *(w. dat or* **in** *+ acc)* to suit, fit

quadr·um -ī *n* square; **in quadrum redigere sententiam** *(rhet)* to balance a sentence *(by changing word order)*

quadruped·ans -antis *adj* galloping ‖ *mpl* horses

quadruped·us -a -um *adj* galloping

quadrup·ēs -edis *adj* four-footed; on all fours ‖ *mf* quadruped

quadruplāt·or -ōris *m* informer *(who received ¼ of the forfeiture);* corrupt judge

quadrupl·ex -icis *adj* quadruple, fourfold

quadruplic·ō -āre -āvī -ātus *tr* to quadruple

quadrupl·or -ārī -ātus sum *intr* to be an informer, be a whistleblower

quadrupl·us -a -um *adj* quadruple, fourfold ‖ *n* four times the amount

quaerit·ō -āre -āvī -ātus *tr* to keep looking for; to keep asking

quae·rō -rĕre -sīvī *or* **-siī -sītus** *tr* to look for, search for; to try to get; to get, obtain; to try to gain, earn, acquire; to miss, lack; to require, demand, call for; to ask, interrogate; to examine, investigate; to plan, devise, aim at; *(w. inf)* to try to, wish to; *(w.* **ab** *or* **de** *or* **ex** *+ abl)* to ask *(s.th.)* of *or* from *(s.o.)* ‖ *intr* to hold an examination; *(w.* **de** *+ abl)* to ask about; **quid quaeris?** *(introducing a short, clinching remark)* what more can I say?; **si quaeris** *(or* **si quaerimus**) to tell the truth

quaesīti·ō -ōnis *f (leg)* questioning under torture

quaesīt·or -ōris *m (leg)* judge *(praetor or other official who presided over a criminal trial)*

quaesīt·us -a -um *pp of* **quaero** ‖ *adj* select, special; far-fetched; artificial, affected ‖ *npl* gains, earnings, acquisitions, store

quaes·ō -ĕre *tr* to try to obtain; to beg, ask for, request ‖ *intr* to carry out a search; **quaeso** *(usually parenthetical)* please; *(w. direct questions)* please tell me; *(in exclamations)* just look!; take note!

quaesticul·us -ī *m* slight profit

quaesti·ō -ōnis *f* inquiry, investigation, questioning, examination; *(leg)* judicial investigation, criminal trial, court of inquiry, court; *(leg)* questioning under torture, third degree; *(leg)* question, subject of investigation, case; *(leg)* court record; *(w.* **de** *+ abl of the nature of the charge)* court investigating a charge of *(e.g., forgery);* **in quaestione versari** to be under investigation; **quaestio extraordinaria** investigation by a special board; **quaestio inter sicarios** murder trial, court investigating a murder; **quaestio perpetua** standing court; **quaestioni praesse** to preside over a case; **servos in quaestionem dare** *(or* **ferre**) to hand over slaves for questioning under torture

quaestiuncul·a -ae *f* minor *or* trivial question; small problem, puzzle

quaest·or -ōris *m* quaestor *(serving, at various periods as: financial officer; treasury official; public prosecutor of criminal offenses; aide to a provincial governor; army paymaster; personal aide to the emperor);* **pro quaestore** acting quaestor, vice-quaestor

quaestōri·us -a -um *adj* quaestor's, of a quaestor; employed in a quaestor's office; qualified for the rank of quaestor; having quaestorian rank *(i.e., having held* *the office of quaestor);* **ager quaestoria** conquered land sold on behalf of the state treasury; **porta quaestoria** the gate nearest the quaestor's tent *(perhaps* **porta decumana)** ‖ *m* ex-quaestor ‖ *n* quaestor's tent in a camp; quaestor's residence in a province

quaestuōs·us -a -um *adj* profitable, productive; acquiring wealth; eager to make a profit, acquisitive; good at moneymaking; enriched, wealthy

quaestūr·a -ae *f* quaestorship; *(fig)* public funds

quaest·us -ūs *m* gain, profit; acquisition; way of gaining a livelihood, job, occupation, business, trade; income; *(fig)* benefit, advantage; **ad quaestum** for profit, to make a profit; **in quaestu esse** to be profitable; **in quaestu habere** to derive profit from; **pecuniam in quaestu relinquere** to deposit money at interest; **quaestui rem publicam habere** to use public office for personal profit; **quaestum facere** to make money, make a living; **quaestūs facere** to make gains

quālibet *adv* **(-lub-)** anywhere, everywhere; in any way, as you please

quāl·is -is -e *adj* what sort of, what kind of; of such a kind, such as, as; *(w. quotations and citations)* as, as for example; **in hoc bello, quale** in this war, the likes of which; **qualis erat!** what a man he was!

quāl·iscumque -iscumque -ecumque (-cunque) *adj* of whatever kind; of any kind whatsoever, any at all; **homines, qualescumque sunt** people, no matter what kind they are; **qualiscumque** *(or* **qualecumque)** **est** such as it is, for what it is worth

quāl·islibet -islibet -elibet *adj* of whatever kind, of whatever sort

quāl·isnam -isnam -enam *adj* just what kind of

quālit·ās -ātis *f* quality, nature; property, characteristic; high quality; *(gram)* mood *(of a verb)*

quāliter *adv* as, just as

quāl·us -ī *m or* **quāl·um -ī** *n* wicker basket, straw basket

quam *adv (in questions and exclamations)* how, how much; *(in comparisons)* as, than; *(with superlatives)* as…as possible, *e.g.,* **quam celerrime** as fast as possible; **quam plurimo vendere** to sell at the highest price possible; **quam primum** as soon as possible; *(indicating numerical proportion)* **dimidium (duplex,** *etc.)* **quam** half as much as (twice as much as, *etc.); (as the correlative of* **tam)** the…the: **quam magis id reputo, tam magis uror** the more I think it over, the madder I get; *(after verbs of preferring)* than: **praestat nemini imperare quam alicui servire** it is preferable to rule over no one than to be a slave to someone

quamdiū *or* **quam diū** *interrog & rel adv* how long ‖ *conj* as long as

quamlibet *adv* **(-lub-)** as much as you please

quamobrem *or* **quam ob rem** *adv* for what reason, why; for which reason, wherefore, why

quamquam *conj* although

quamvīs *adv (with adj or adv)* however, no matter how; ever so; **illa quamvis ridicula essent** no matter how funny they were ‖ *conj* although

quānam *adv* by what route *or* way

quandō *adv (in questions)* when, at what time; *(indefinite, after* **si, ne, num)** ever, at any time ‖ *conj* when, because, since

quandōcumque *adv* **(-cunque)** at some time or other, some day ‖ *conj* whenever; as often as, no matter when

quandōque *adv* at some time, at one time or other, some day ‖ *conj* whenever; as often as; since

quandōquidem *conj* in as much as, whereas, seeing that

quantill·us -a -um *interrog adj* how much?, how little?

quantit·ās -ātis *f* quantity; size

quantō *adv* by how much, how much; **quanto…tanto** the…the: **quanto longior nox est, tanto brevior dies it** the longer night is, the shorter the day becomes

quantopere *or* **quantō opere** *adv* by how much, how much; with how great effort, how carefully

quantulum *adv* how little; **quantulum interest utrum** how little difference it makes whether

quantul·us -a -um *adj* how great, how much, how little, how small, how insignificant

quantuluscumque quantulacumque quantulumcumque *adj* however small, however unimportant

quantum *adv* as much as, so much as, as great an extent; how much, how far, to what extent; *(w. comparatives)* the more, the greater; **quantum in me fuit** as much as I could, to the best of my ability; **quantum maximā voce potuit** at the top of his voice; **quantum potest** as much *(or* fast, quickly, soon, long, *etc.)* as possible

quantumcumque *adv* as much as; however much, however little; to whatever degree, as far as

quantumlibet *adv (also written as two words)* however much

quantusquantus quantaquanta quantumquantum *adj (also written as two* *words)* however big, however great, of whatever degree ‖ *n* however much, whatever

quantumvīs *adv (also written as two words)* however; **quantumvis rusticus** however unsophisticated, although unsophisticated

quant·us -a -um *adj (interrogative or exclamatory)* how great, how much, of what size, of what importance, of what worth ‖ *n* **in quantum** to whatever extent, as far as; **quanti** *(gen of price)* how much, how high, how dearly, at what price; **quanto** *(abl of price)* at what price, for how much; **quantum frumenti** how much grain ‖ *pl* how many

quant·uscumque -acumque -umcumque *adj* however great; of whatever size; however small; however trifling; however important *(or* unimportant); **quanticumque** at whatever price, at whatever cost

quant·uslibet -alibet -umlibet *adj* however great; ever so great

quant·usvīs -avīs -umvīs *adj* of whatever size, amount, degree, *etc.,* you wish; however big, however great, no matter how great

quāpropter *adv* wherefore, why

quāquā *adv* by whatever route, in whatever way

quāquam *adv* in any way; anywhere

quārē *or* **quā rē** *adv* by what means, how; in what way, from what cause, why; whereby; wherefore; **nec quid nec quare** without why or wherefore

quart·a -ae *f* a fourth, one quarter

Quart·a -ae *f* female first name *(praenomen)*

quartadecumān·ī -ōrum *mpl* **(-decim-)** *mpl* soldiers of the 14th legion

quartān·us -a -um *adj* occurring every fourth day ‖ *f* quartan fever ‖ *mpl* soldiers of the 4th legion

quartār·ius -(i)ī *m* quarter pint

quartō *adv* for the fourth time

quartum *adv* for the fourth time; in the fourth place, fourthly

quart·us -a -um *adj* fourth

quart·us decim·us -a -um *adj* fourteenth

quasi *adv* as it were, so to speak; about, nearly, almost; allegedly ‖ *conj* on the charge that; as would be the case if; *(expressing the supposed reason for an action)* on the grounds that; *(introducing a hypothetical situation after verbs of asserting or supposing)* saying that, believing that, to the effect that: **sparsit rumorem, quasi…bellum gerere non possit** he spread a rumor to the effect that he could not fight a war

quasill·um -ī *n or* **quasill·us -ī** *m* small basket

quassāti·ō -ōnis *f* (violent) shaking

quass·ō -are *tr* to keep shaking, keep tossing, keep waving; to batter, shatter, smash to pieces; *(fig)* to shake, weaken ‖ *intr (of the head)* to keep on shaking

quass·us -a -um *pp of* **quatio** ‖ *adj* shattered, broken; quavering *(voice);* chopped *(wood)*

quate·faciō -facĕre -fēcī -factus *tr* to shake; *(fig)* to weaken

quātenus *adv* how far, to what point; as far as, till when, how long; to what extent; **est quatenus** there is an extent to which ‖ *conj* as far as; insofar as, in as much as, seeing that, since, as

quater *adv* four times

quater decie(n)s *adv* fourteen times

quatern·ī -ae -a *adj* four together, four in a group, four each

quatiō quatĕre — quassus *tr* to shake, cause to tremble, cause to vibrate; to brandish, wave about; to beat, strike, drive; to batter, crush; *(fig)* to touch, move, affect; *(fig)* to plague, harass

quattuor *indecl adj* four

quattuordecim *indecl adj* fourteen

quattuor·vir -virī *m* member of a board of four *(one of the four chief magistrates of a municipium; member of a committee of four at Rome)*

quattuorvirāt·us -ūs *m* membership on the board of four

quāvīs *adv* anyway you like, in any possible way

quax·ō -āre *intr (of frogs)* to croak

-que *enclitic conj* and; **-que…-que** *(mostly poetical)* both…and; **terrā marīque** on land and on sea

-que *suf used in the formation of certain adverbs and conjunctions, e.g.:* **itaque** and so, therefore; *esp. to give indefinite force to relative pronouns and adverbs, e.g.,* **quandoque** at some time or other, someday

quemadmodum *or* **quem ad modum** *adv* in what way, how ‖ *conj* just as, as

qu·eō -īre -īvī *or* **-iī -ītum** *intr* to be able; *(w. inf)* to be able to

quercēt·um -ī *n* oak forest

querce·us -a -um *adj* oak-, of oak

querc·us -ūs *f* oak tree; oak-leaf crown *(awarded to a soldier who saved a citizen in battle);* acorns

querēl·a -ae *f* **(-ell-)** complaint; grievance, protest; difference of opinion

queribund·us -a -um *adj* full of complaints; whining *(voice)*

querimōni·a -ae *f* complaint, grievance; elegy

querit·or -ārī *intr* to keep complaining

quern·us -a -um *adj* oak-, of oak

queror querī questus sum *tr* to complain of, complain about; to lament ‖ *intr* to complain; *(of birds)* to sing, warble, sing sadly, coo mournfully

Querquētulān·us -a -um *adj (as name of various places and deities associated with oaks)* oak-, covered with oak trees; **mons Querquetulanus** Oak Hill *(an old name for the Caelian Hill in Rome*; **Porta Querquetulana** Oak Gate *(probably between the Caelian and the Esquiline Hills)*

querquēt·um -ī *n* oak forest

querul·us -a -um *adj* complaining, full of complaints, querulous; plaintive; warbling, cooing

questi·ō -ōnis *f* complaining

questus *pp of* queror

quest·us -ūs *m* complaint; plaintive note *(of the nightingale)*

quī quae *or* **qua quod** *adj (interrog)* which, what, what kind of; *(indef)* any ‖ *pron (rel)* who, that; *(indef, after* **si, nisi, num, ne)** anyone

quī *adv* how; why; at what price; whereby; in some way, somehow

quia *conj* because

quianam *adv (interrog)* why in fact?

quicquam cūjusquam *pron* anything

quicque cūjusque *pron* each (one)

quīcum *(old abl of* **quī** *and* **cum)** *pron* with whom, with which

quīcumque quaecumque quodcumque *(also* **-cunque, -quomque)** *pron & adj (rel & indef)* whoever, whosoever, everyone who, whatever, whatsoever, everything ever

quid *adv* how?; why? **quid agis?** how do you do?; **quid plura?** why say more?

quid cūjus *pron (interrog)* what?; *(w. gen)* what kind of?: **quid mulieris uxorem habes?** what sort of woman do you have as your wife?; *(indef, after* **si, nisi, num, ne)** anything

quīdam quaedam quiddam *pron* a certain one, a certain person, a certain thing

quīdam quaedam quoddam *adj* a certain; *(to soften an expression)* a kind of, what one might call

quidem *adv (emphasizing the word before it)* indeed, in fact; *(qualifying or limiting)* at least, at any rate; *(concessive)* it is true; of course; all right; *(exemplifying)* for example; **ne...quidem** *(emphasizing the intervening word)* not even, *e.g.*, **ne tu quidem** not even you

quidnam cūjusnam *pron (interrog)* just what?

quidnam *adv* why in the world

quidnī *adv* why not?

quidpiam cūjuspiam *pron* anything, something

quidpiam *adv* in some respect

quidquid *or* **quicquid** *(gen and dat not in use; abl:* **quōquō)** *pron* whatever, whatsoever, everything which; **per quidquid deorum** by all the gods

quidquid *adv* to whatever extent, the further

quīdum *adv* how so?

qui·ēs -ētis *f* quiet, rest, peace; calm, lull; neutrality; sleep; dream; sleep of death, death

qui·escō -escĕre -ēvī -ētum *intr* (contracted forms: **quiesse = quievisse; quierunt = quieverunt; quierem = quieveram)** to rest, keep quiet, be inactive; to fall asleep; to sleep, be asleep; to lie still, be still, be undisturbed; to say no more, be quiet; *(of the dead)* to find rest; to pause, make a pause; *(of a person)* to be calm, remain calm, be unruffled; *(of physical forces, of conditions)* to die down, subside, be still; *(of things)* to cease to operate; to be neutral, keep neutral, take no action; to refrain from violence, make no disturbance, remain peaceful; *(of troops)* to make no move; *(w. inf)* to cease to, stop; to take no steps to, omit to; *(w.* **ab** + *abl)* to be free from

quiētē *adv* quietly, calmly

quiēt·us -a -um *adj* at rest, resting, free from exertion, inactive; quiet; peaceful, undisturbed; netural; calm; still, silent; idle ‖ *npl* period of peace

quīlibet quaelibet quidlibet (-lubet) *pron* anyone, any you wish, no matter who, anything, anything you wish, no matter what, everything

quīlibet quaelibet quodlibet (-lubet) *adj* any, any at all, any you wish

quīn *adv (interrog)* why not; *(corroborative)* in fact, as a matter of fact ‖ *conj* so that not, without; **facere non possum, quin ad te mīttam librum** I can't help sending you the book; **nullo modo introire possem, quin viderent me** I just couldn't walk in without their seeing me; *(after verbs of preventing, opposing)* from: **milites aegre sunt retenti quin oppidum oppugnarent** the soldiers could barely be kept from assaulting the town; *(after verbs of hestitation, doubt, suspicion):* **non dubito quin** I do not doubt that; *(esp. representing a nominative of a relative pronoun with a negative)* that...not: **nemo aspicere potest quin dicat** no one can look on without saying; **nemo est quin velit** there is no one who does not prefer

quīnam quaenam quodnam *adj* which, what, just which, just what

quīnavīcēnāri·us -a -um *adj* of twenty-five; **lex annorum quinavicenaria** the law prohibiting those under twenty-five years of age from making contracts

Quincti·us -a -um *adj* Roman clan name *(nomen), esp.* Lucius Quinctius Cincinnatus *(called on his farm to become dictator in 458 B.C.)* ‖ Titus Quinctius Flamininus *(consul in 198 B.C., who "liberated" Greece from Macedonia)* ‖ Publius Quinctius *(represented by Cicero in his first case, in 81 B.C.)*

quinc·unx -uncis *m* five-twelfths; 5% *(interest);* the figure five *(as arranged on dice or cards)*

quindeciē(n)s *adv* fifteen times

quindecim *indecl adj* fifteen

quindecimprīm·ī -ōrum *mpl* executive board of fifteen *(magistrates of a municipality)*

quindecimvirāl·is -is -e *adj* of the board of fifteen

quindecimvir·ī -ōrum *mpl* board of fifteen; **quindecimviri Sibylini** board of fifteen in charge of the Sibylline Books

quingēnāri·us -a -um *adj* of five hundred each, consisting of five hundred *(men, pounds, etc.)*

quingēn·ī -ae -a *adj* five hundred each

quingentēsim·us -a -um *adj* five-hundredth

quingent·ī -ae -a *adj* five hundred

quingentiē(n)s *adv* five hundred times

quīn·ī -ae -a *adj* five each; **quini deni** fifteen each; **quini viceni** twenty-five each

quinquāgēn·ī -ae -a *adj* fifty each

quinquāgēsim·us -a -um *adj* fiftieth ‖ *f* 2% tax

quinquāgintā *indecl adj* fifty

Quinquātr·ūs -uum *fpl or* **Quinquātr·ia -ium** *npl* festival in honor of Minerva *(celebrated from March 19 to 23 esp. by the trades and professions under her patronage);* **quinquatrūs minores** *(or* **minusculae)** festival of Minerva held on June 13

quinque *indecl adj* five

quinquennāl·is -is -e *adj* quinquennial, occurring every five years; five-year, lasting five years

quinquenn·is -is -e *adj* five-year-old, of five years

quinquenn·ium -(i)ī *n* five-year period, five years

quinqueped·al -ālis *n* five-foot ruler

quinquepertīt·us -a -um *adj* five-fold, divided into five parts

quinqueprīm·ī -ōrum *mpl* five-man board of magistrates

quinquerēm·is -is -e *adj* having five banks of oars ‖ *f* quinquereme

quinque·vir -virī *m* member of a five-man board *(created at various times for various purposes)*

quinquevirāt·us -ūs *m* membership on a board of five

quinquiē(n)s *adv* five times

quinquipl·ex -icis *adj* fivefold; **cera quinquiplex** tablet consisting of five sheets

quinquiplic·ō -āre -āvī -ātus *tr* to multiply by five

Quint·a -ae *f* woman's name *(praenomen)*

quintadecimān·ī -ōrum *mpl* **(-decum-)** soldiers of the 15th legion

quintān·us -a -um *adj* of the fifth ‖ *mpl* members of the fifth legion ‖ *f* camp street running between the 5th and 6th maniple *(used as a market street of the camp)*

Quintiliān·us -ī *m* Quintilian *(Marcus Fabius Quintilanus, orator and professor of rhetoric, A.D. c. 35–95)*

Quintīl·is *or* **Quinctīl·is -is -e** *adj & m* July *(fifth month of the old Roman calendar until 153 B.C.; renamed* **Julius** *after the Julian reform of the calendar)*

Quint·ius *or* **Quinct·ius -(i)ī** *m* Roman clan name *(nomen)*

quintō *or* **quintum** *adv* for the fifth time

quint·us -a -um *adj* fifth ‖ **Quintus** *m* Roman first name *(praenomen)*

quint·us decim·us -a -um *adj* fifteenth

quippe *adv* of course, naturally, obviously, by all means ‖ *conj* since, for; **quippe qui** since he *(is, was, will be one who),* inasmuch as he; **multa Caesar questus est quippe qui vidisset** Caesar complained a lot since he had seen

quippiam = quidpiam

quippinī *adv* why not?; of course, to be sure

Quirīnāl·is -is -e *adj* of Quirinus *(i.e., Romulus);* **collis Quirinalis** Quirinal Hill *(one of the seven hills of Rome)* ‖ *npl* festival in honor of Romulus *(celebrated on February 17)*

Quirīn·us -a -um *adj* of Quirinus ‖ *m* Quirinus *(epithet of Romulus after his deification, of Janus, of Augustus, and of Antony)*

Quir·īs -ītis *m* Roman citizen; inhabitant of Cures *(Sabine town) (after the union of the Sabines and Romans, the Romans called themselves* **Quirites** *in their peace-time capacity. They were styled on all solemn occasions* **Populus Romanus Quirites(que)**; *in later times it was distorted into* **Populus Romanus Quirites)**

quirītāti·ō -ōnis *f* shrieking, shriek

quirītāt·us -ūs *m* shriek, scream

Quirītēs -ium *mpl (pl form of* **Quirīs)** *(see* **Quiris)** Roman citizens; **jus Quiritium** legal rights enjoyed by Roman citizens

quirīt·ō -āre *tr & intr* to shriek, scream

quis cūjus *pron (interrog)* who, which one; *(indef)* anyone

quīs = quibus

quisnam quaenam *(see* **quidnam)** *pron (interrog)* who, just who

quispiam cūjuspiam *pron* someone
quispiam quaepiam quodpiam *adj* any
quisquam cūjusquam *pron* anyone
quisque cūjusque *pron* each, each one, everybody, everyone; **doctissimus quisque** everyone of great learning, all the most learned; **optimus quisque** all the best ones
quisque quaeque quodque *or* **quidque** *or* **quicque** *adj* each
quisquili·ae -ārum *fpl or* **quisquili·a -ōrum** *npl* refuse, scraps, trash, junk
quisquis *(gen and dat not in use; abl:* **quōquō)** *pron* whoever, whosoever; everyone who; everyone, each
quīvīs quaevīs quidvīs *pron* anyone at all, anyone you please; **quivis unus** any one person
quō *adv (interrog)* where?, to what place?; what for?, to what purpose?; *(after* **si, nisi,** *or* **ne)** to any place, anywhere; **quo...eo** the...the; **quo magis...eo magis** the more...the more ‖ *conj* where, to which place; whereby, wherefore; *(replacing* **ut** *when the clause contains a comparative)* in order that, so that
quoad *adv* how far; to what extent; by what time, how soon; how long; **est modus quoad** there is a limit up to which ‖ *conj* as long as; as far as; until, until such time as
quōcircā *adv* for which reason, wherefore, therefore, that's the reason
quōcumque (-cunque, -quomque) *adv* to whatever place, wherever
quod *conj* because; as for the fact that; the fact that; insofar as; as far as; **quod si** *(or* **quodsi)** but if
quōdammodō *or* **quōdam modo** *adv* in a way
quoi = cui
quoiquoimodī *see* **cuicuimodi**
quoivīsmodī *see* **cuivismodi**
quōjus = cujus
quōlibet *adv* anywhere you please, anywhere at all
quom *see* **cum**
quōminus *conj* that not; *(after verbs of hindering)* from, *e.g.,* **deterrere aliquem quominus aliquid habeat** to keep s.o. from having s.th.
quōmodo *adv (interrog)* how, in what way; *(rel)* just as, as
quōmodocumque *adv* in whatever way, however
quōmodonam *interrog adv* where?, whereto?; to what purpose?, to what end?
quōnam *interrog* where on earth?, just where(to)? **quonam usque** just how much longer? to what possible degree? to what conceivable end?
quondam *adv* once, at one time, formerly; at times, once in a while; someday, one day *(in the future)*
quōniam *conj* because, seeing that, now that
quōpiam *adv* at any place, anywhere
quōquam *adv* to any place; in any direction, anywhere
quoque *adv (always succeeds the word it emphasizes)* too
quōquō *adv* to whatever place, wherever
quōquōmodo *adv* in whatever way, however
quōquōversum *adv* **(-vorsum, -sus)** in every direction, every way
quorsum *interrog & rel adv* **(-sus)** in what direction, whereto; to what end, why
quot *indecl adj (interrog)* how many; *(correlative)* as many; **quot Kalendis** every first of the month; **quot mensibus** every month
quotannīs *adv* every year
quotcumque *indecl adj* however many
quotēn·ī -ae -a *adj* how many each
quotīdiān·us -a -um *adj* **(cōt-, cott-)** daily
quotīdiē *adv* **(cōt-, cott-)** daily
quotiē(n)s *adv (interrog)* how many times; *(correlative)* as often as, whenever
quotīe(n)scumque *or* **quotiē(n)scunque** *adv* however many, no matter how many
quotquot *indecl adj* however many; **quotquot annis** every year; **quotquot mensibus** every month
quotum·us -a -um *adj* which in number, which in order
quot·us -a -um *adj* which, what; what a small, what a trifling; **quota hora est?** what time is it?; **quota pars** *(or* **portio)** what part, what portion; **quotus quisque** how few?; **quotus quisque philosophorum invenitur** how few of the philosophers are found *or* how rarely is one of the philosophers found?
quot·uscumque -acumque -umcumque *adj* just what, just which
quōusque *adv* how far, how long, till when; to what degree
quōvīs *adv* to any place whatsoever, anywhere; **quovis gentium** anywhere in the world
qūr *or* **quūr** *see* **cur**

R

rabidē *adv* rabidly, madly; furiously
rabid·us -a -um *adj* rabid, mad; furious, raving, uncontrolled
rabi·ēs *(gen not in use) f* madness; *(fig)* rage, anger, fury, wild passion; ferocity *(of animals);* rabies
rabiōsē *adv* furiously, madly
rabiōsul·us -a -um *adj* half-mad

rabiōs·us -a -um *adj* rabid *(animal);* mad; frenzied, furious
rabō -ōnis *m (shortened form of* **arrabo)** token payment, earnest money
rabul·a -ae *m* ranting lawyer
racēmif·er -era -erum *adj* clustered; covered with grape clusters
racēm·us -ī *m* cluster, bunch *(esp. of grapes); (fig)* wine
radi·ans -antis *adj* shining, beaming, radiant
radiāt·us -a -um *adj* spoked; having rays, radiant
rādīcitus *adv* by the roots, root and all; *(fig)* completely, utterly
rādīcul·a -ae *f* small root; radish
radi·ō -āre *or* **radi·or -ārī** *intr* to radiate, shine
radiōs·us -a -um *adj* radiant
rad·ius -(i)ī *m* stake, stick; spoke; ray, beam; shuttle; radius; measuring rod; elongated variety of olive
rād·ix -īcis *f* root; radish; foot *(of hill or mountain);* base, foundation; basis, origin
rā·dō -dĕre -sī -sus *tr* to scrape, scratch; to shave; to scratch out, erase; to graze, touch in passing; to strip off; *(of wind)* to lash
raed·a -ae *f* **(rēd-)** four-wheeled carriage, coach
raedār·ius -(i)ī *m* coach driver
Raeti·us -a -um *adj* **(Rhaet-)** Rhaetian ‖ *f* Rhaetia *(Alpine country between Germany and Italy)*
Raetic·us -a -um *adj* **(Rhaet-)** Rhaetian
Raet·us -a -um *adj & m* **(Rhaet-)** Rhaetian
rall·us -a -um *adj* thin, threadbare
rāmāl·ia -ium *npl* brushwood, undergrowth
rāment·a -ae *f or* **rāment·um -ī** *n* chip, shaving
rāmes *see* **ramex**
rāme·us -a -um *adj* of branches, of boughs
rām·ex -icis *m or* **ram·es -itis** *m* rupture; blood vessel of the lung ‖ *mpl* lungs
Ramn·ēs *or* **Ramnens·ēs -ium** *mpl* one of the three original Roman tribes; *(fig)* blue bloods
rāmōs·us -a -um *adj* having many branches, branching; branch-like
rāmul·us -ī *m* twig
rām·us -ī *m* branch, bough; branch *(of an antler);* genealogical branch
rān·a -ae *f* frog; **rana quaxat** the frog croaks
ranc·ens -entis *adj* putrid, stinking
rancidul·us -a -um *adj* stinky, rank; rather disgusting
rancid·us -a -um *adj* rancid, rank, stinking; disgusting
ranc·ō -āre *intr (of a tiger)* roar
rānuncul·us -ī *m* little frog, tadpole
rapācid·a -ae *m (hum patronymic)* son of a thief
rapācit·ās -ātis *f* rapacity, greediness
rap·ax -ācis *adj* rapacious, grasping, greedy for plunder; insatiable
raphan·us -ī *m* radish
rapidē *adv* rapidly; *(to burn)* fiercely
rapidit·ās -ātis *f* rapidity, velocity, swiftness, rush
rapid·us -a -um *adj* tearing away, seizing; fierce, consuming, white-hot *(fire);* rapid, swift, rushing, impetuous
rapīn·a -ae *f* rapine, pillage; prey
rap·iō -ĕre -uī -tus *tr* to seize and carry off; to snatch, tear, pluck; to drag off; to hurry, drive, cause to rush; to carry off by force, ravish; to ravage, lay waste; to lead on hurriedly; **flammam rapere** to catch fire; **in jus rapere** to haul off to court ‖ *refl* to hurry, dash, take off
raptim *adv* hurriedly; suddenly
rapti·ō -ōnis *f* abduction, ravishing
rapt·ō -āre *tr* to seize and carry off; to abduct, kidnap; to drag away; to drag along; to plunder; **in jus raptare** to haul off to court
rapt·or -ōris *m* plunderer, robber; abductor
rapt·us -a -um *pp of* **rapio** ‖ *n* plunder, loot
rapt·us -ūs *m* snatching away; looting, robbery; abduction, kidnapping
rāpul·um -ī *n* little turnip
rāp·um -ī *n* turnip
rārē *adv* rarely; sparsely; loosely
rārē·faciō -facĕre -fēcī -factus *tr* to rarefy, thin out
rārē·fīō -fierī -factus sum *intr* to become less solid, rarefy
rāresc·ō -ĕre *intr* to grow thin, lose density, become rarefied; to grow wider, widen out, open up; to become fewer; to disappear, die away
rārit·ās -ātis *f* looseness of texture; thinness; small number; sparseness; infrequency; rarity
rārō *adv* rarely, seldom
rār·us -a -um *adj* wide apart, of loose texture, thin; scattered, far apart; scarce, sparse; few; uncommon, rare; unusual; *(mil)* in open rank
rāsī *perf of* **rado**
rāsil·is -is -e *adj* shaved smooth, scraped, polished
rāsit·ō -āre -āvī -ātus *tr* to shave (regularly)
rastell·us -ī *m* rake *(usu. of wood)*
rastr·um -ī *(pl:* **rastr·ī -ōrum** *mpl) n* rake; mattock
rāsus *pp of* **rado**
rati·ō -ōnis *f* calculation, computation, reckoning, account; register; matter, affair, business, transaction; consideration,

respect; grounds; guiding principle; scheme, system, method; procedure; theory, doctrine; science; relation, connection, reference; fashion, way, style; reasoning, reason, judgment, understanding; reasonableness; order, law, rule; view, opinion; *(w. gen)* a reason for; **(libertus) a rationibus** bookkeeper, accountant; **fugit te ratio** *(coll)* you're off your rocker; **non erat ratio amittere ejusmodi occasionem** there was no reason to pass up that kind of opportunity; **pares rationes facere cum** to square accounts with; **popularis ratio** popular cause; **pro ratione** proportionately; according to the rule, properly; **propter rationem** *(w. gen)* out of regard for; **ratio aeraria** rate of exchange; **ratio atque usus** theory and practice; **ratio constat** the account tallies; **ratione** with good reason; according to the rules, properly; **rationem conferre** *(or* **deferre** *or* **referre)** *(w. gen)* to render *or* give an account of, account for; **rationem (de)ducere** to make a calculation, reckon; **rationem habere cum** to have to do with; **rationem inire** to calculate, make a calculation; to embark on a scheme; **ratio vitae** pattern of life, life style

ratiōcināti·ō -ōnis *f* exercise of the reasoning powers, reasoning; theory, theorizing; deduction, inference

ratiōcinātīv·us -a -um *adj* concerned with reasoning, syllogistic

ratiōcināt·or -ōris *m* accountant

ratiōcin·or -ārī -ātus sum *tr & intr* to calculate, reckon; to reason, argue, conclude, infer

ratiōnāl·is -is -e *adj* rational; theoretical; dialectical

ratiōnār·ium -(i)ī *n* financial survey

rat·is -is *f* raft; *(poet)* ship, craft ‖ *fpl* pontoons

ratiuncul·a -ae *f* small account; trifling reason; petty argumentation

rat·us -a -um *pp of* **reor** ‖ *adj* reckoned, calculated; fixed, established, settled, certain, sure; approved; **pro rata parte** *(or* **pro ratā)** in proportion, proportionately; **ratum facere** *(or* **efficere)** to confirm, ratify, approve; **ratum habere** *(or* **ducere)** to consider valid, regard as certain *or* sure

raucison·us -a -um *adj* hoarse-sounding

rauc·us -a -um *adj* raucous, hoarse; screaming, strident; scraping; deep, deep-voiced

raud·us *n* **(rōd-, rūd-)** copper coin; lump

rauduscul·um -ī *n* **(rōd-, rūd-)** bit of money

Ravenn·a -ae *f* Ravenna *(port and naval base)*

rāv·iō -īre *intr* to be hoarse

rāv·is -is *f* hoarseness

rāv·us -a -um *adj* grayish

re- *pref (also* **red-)** *denoting* **1** movement back, in reverse: **revocare** to call back; **2** reversal of an action, un-: **retegere** to uncover; **3** restoration: **revalescere** to recover again; **4** response: **respondere** to respond; **rescribere** to answer *(in writing);* **5** opposition: **rebellare** to rebel; **6** separation: **removere** to remove; **7** repeated action: **replere** to refill; **reïterare** repeat again and again

re·a -ae *f* defendant; guilty woman

Rēa *see* **Rhea**

rēapse *adv* **(-abs-)** in fact, actually, really

Reāt·e -is *n* Sabine town

Reātīn·us -a -um *adj* of Reate

rebellāti·ō -ōnis *f* rebellion

rebellātr·ix -īcis *adj (fem only)* rebellious; **rebellatrix Germania** rebellious Germany

rebelli·ō -ōnis *f* rebellion

rebell·is -is -e *adj* rebellious ‖ *mpl* rebels

rebell·ium -(i)ī *n* rebellion

rebell·ō -āre -āvī -ātum *intr* to rebel

rebīt·ō -ĕre *intr* to go back

rebo·ō -āre *tr* to make reecho ‖ *intr* to reecho, bellow back

recalcitr·ō -āre *intr* to kick back

recal·eō -ēre *intr* to get warm again; *(of a river)* to run warm *(e.g., w. blood)*

recal·escō -escĕre -uī *intr* to grow warm again

recal·faciō -facĕre -fēcī *tr* to warm up again

recalv·us -a -um *adj* bald in front, with receding hairline

recand·escō -escĕre -uī *intr* to grow white; *(w. dat)* to grow hot, glow in response to

recanō *see* **recino**

recant·ō -āre -āvī -ātus *tr* to recant; to charm back, charm away ‖ *intr* to reecho

reccidō *see* **recido**

re·cēdō -cēdĕre -cessī -cessum *intr* to go back; to go away, withdraw, recede; to give ground, fall back; to depart; to vanish; to stand back, be distant

recell·ō -ĕre *intr* to recoil

recens *adv* just, recently, lately

rec·ens -entis *adj* recent, fresh, young; newly arrived, just arrived; modern; fresh; rested; **recentissimus** latest ‖ *npl* recent events

recens·eō -ēre -uī -sus *tr* to count, enumerate, number, survey; to recount, go over again, retell; *(mil)* to review; *(pol) (of a censor)* to revise the roll of, review, enroll

recensi·ō -ōnis *f* revision

recensus *pp of* **recenseo**

recens·us -ūs *m* review; census; valuation *(of property)*

recēpī *perf of* **recipio**
receptācul·um -ī *n* receptacle, container; reservoir; place of refuge, shelter; hiding place
recepti·ō -ōnis *f* reception
recept·ō -āre *tr* to take back; to welcome frequently into the home, entertain; to tug at ‖ *refl* to beat a hasty retreat
recept·or -ōris *m or* **receptr·ix -īcis** *f* shelterer; concealer
recept·us -a -um *pp of* **recipio** ‖ *n* obligation
recept·us -ūs *m* taking back, recantation; way of escape; refuge; return; *(mil)* retreat; **(signum) receptui canere** to sound the retreat
recessī *perf of* **recedo**
recessim *adv* backwards
recess·us -ūs *m* retreat, withdrawal; departure; secluded spot, retreat; inner room, central chamber; recess; background
recharmid·ō -āre *ref* to stop being a Charmides *(character in Roman comedy)*
recidīv·us -a -um *adj* recurring, returning; rebuilt
recī·dō -dĕre -dī -sus *tr* to cut back, cut off, cut away, cut down; to abridge, cut short
re·cĭdō -cidĕre -cĭdī -cāsum *or* **reccĭd·ō -ĕre** *intr* to fall back; to jump back, recoil; to suffer a relapse; *(fig)* to fall back, sink, relapse; to turn out, result; *(w.* **ad** *or* **in** *+ acc)* to pass to, be handed over to
recin·gō -gĕre -xī -ctus *tr* to loosen, undo, take off
recin·ō -ĕre *tr* to repeat, reecho ‖ *intr* to sound a warning
reciper- = recuper-
re·cipiō -cipĕre -cēpī -ceptus *tr* to keep back, keep in reserve; to withdraw, bring back, carry back; to retake, recover, regain; to take in, accept, receive, welcome; to gain, collect, take in, make *(money);* to take up, assume, undertake; to guarantee, pledge; *(mil)* to retake, recapture, seize, take, occupy; **ad se** *(or* **in se)** **recipere** to take upon oneself, take the responsibility for, promise, guarantee ‖ *refl* to get hold of oneself again, regain composure, recover, come to again; to retreat, escape; **se recipere** *(w.* **ad** *or* **in** *+ acc)* to retreat to, escape to, find refuge in
reciproc·ō -āre -āvī -ātus *tr* to move back and forth; to turn back; to back up *(e.g., a ship),* reverse the direction of; to reverse, convert *(a proposition)* ‖ *intr (of the tide)* to ebb and flow, rise and fall
reciproc·us -a -um *adj* ebbing and flowing, going backwards and forwards
recīsus *pp of* **recido**
recitāti·ō -ōnis *f* reading aloud, recitation
recitāt·or -ōris *m* reader, reciter
recit·ō -āre -āvī -ātus *tr* to read out, read aloud, recite; to name in writing, appoint, constitute; **senatum recitare** to have roll call in the Senate
reclāmāti·ō -ōnis *f* cry of disapproval; shout of protest
reclāmit·ō -āre *intr* to voice disapproval; *(w. dat)* to protest against
reclām·ō -āre -āvī -ātus *tr* to protest ‖ *intr* to raise a protest, shout objections; to reverberate; *(w. dat)* to express disapproval to, contradict
reclīn·is -is -e *adj* reclining, leaning back
reclīn·ō -āre -āvī -ātus *tr* to bend back, lean back, rest; *(w.* **ab***)* to distract *(s.o.)* from ‖ *refl* to lean
reclū·dō -dĕre -sī -sus *tr* to open; to lay open, disclose; to draw *(sword);* to break up *(the soil)*
recoctus *pp of* **recoquo**
recōgit·ō -āre -āvī -ātum *tr* to consider, think over ‖ *intr* (w. **de** + *abl)* to think again about, reconsider
recogniti·ō -ōnis *f* formal inspection
reco·gnoscō -gnoscĕre -gnōvī -gnitus *tr* to call to mind again, review; to recognize; to look over, examine, inspect, investigate; to certify, authorize
recol·ligō -ligĕre -lēgī -lectus *tr* to gather again, gather up, collect; **te recollige!** get hold of yourself! take heart! ‖ *refl* to pull oneself together
re·colō -colĕre -coluī -cultus *tr* to till again; to honor again; to call to mind, think over, consider; to cultivate once more; to practice again, resume
recomment·or -ārī -ātus sum *tr* to remember, recall
recomminisc·or -ī *tr* to call to mind again, recall
recomposit·us -a -um *adj* rearranged
reconciliāti·ō -ōnis *f* winning back again, reestablishment, restoration; reconciliation
reconciliāt·or -ōris *m* reconciler; **pacis reconciliator** restorer of peace
reconcili·ō -āre -āvī -ātus *tr* to bring back, regain, recover; to restore, reestablish; to win over again, conciliate; to bring together again, reconcile
reconcinn·ō -āre *tr* to set right again, repair
recondit·us -a -um *adj* hidden, concealed; recondite, abstruse, profound; reserved *(person)*
recon·dō -dĕre -didī -ditus *tr* to put back again; to put away, hoard; to hide, conceal; to plunge *(sword);* to close *(eyes)* again; to store up *(in the mind)*
reconfl·ō -āre *tr* to rekindle

reco·quō -quĕre -xī -ctus *tr* to cook, boil, *or* bake again; to recast, remold

recordāti·ō -ōnis *f* recollection, remembrance

record·or -ārī -ātus sum *tr & intr* to recall, recollect, remember

recoxī *perf of* **recoquo**

recre·ō -āre -āvī -ātus *tr* to recreate, restore, renew; *(fig)* to revive, refresh

recrep·ō -āre *intr* to reecho

re·crescō -crescĕre -crēvī *intr* to grow again; to be renewed

recrūd·escō -escĕre -uī *intr (of a wound)* to open up again; *(of a revolt)* to break out again

rectā *adv* by a direct route, straight

rectē *adv* in a straight line; rightly, correctly; suitably, properly, well; quite; *(in answers)* well, right, quite well, fine

recti·ō -ōnis *f* direction, controlling

rect·or -ōris *m* guide, controller; rider, driver *(of an animal);* leader; master; pilot; tutor; *(mil)* commander; *(naut)* helmsman, pilot; *(pol)* ruler, governor

rect·us -a -um *pp of* **rego ‖** *adj* in a straight line, straight, direct; correct, right, proper, appropriate; just, upright, conscientious, virtuous; standing erect; *(impartial)* judge; straight-forward *(expression);* sheer *(cliff);* **aere recto cantare** to play a reed pipe; **casus rectus** *(gram)* nominative case; **funis rectus** tightrope; **rectis oculis** with eyes not lowered, without flinching **‖** *n* right; uprightness, rectitude, virtue; **in rectum** in a straight line; in a vertical position *or* direction, vertically; straight forward

recub·ō -āre *intr* to lie on one's back, lie down, rest

rēcul·a -ae *f* little thing

recultus *pp of* **recolo**

re·cumbō -cumbĕre -cubuī *intr* to lie down (again); to recline *(esp. at table);* to sink down *(e.g., in a swamp);* to fall; *(of fog)* to settle down

recuperāti·ō -ōnis *f* recovery

recuperāt·or -ōris *m* (-cip-) recoverer; *(leg)* arbiter *(member of a bench of from 3 to 5 men who expedited cases needing speedy decisions)*

recuperātōri·us -a -um *adj* (**-cip-**) of the special court for summary civil suits

recuper·ō -āre -āvī -ātus *tr* (**-cip-**) to regain, recover, get back; to win over again

recūr·ō -āre -āvī -ātus *tr* to restore, refresh, restore to health

recur·rō -rĕre -rī -sum *intr* to run back, hurry back; to return *(to the starting point of a cycle);* to recur, come back *(to the mind); (of a process)* to run in the oppposite direction; to revert *(to a former condition); (w.* **ad**) to have recourse to

recurs·ō -āre *intr* to keep running back; to keep recurring

recurs·us -ūs *m* return; retreat

recurv·ō -āre -āvī -ātus *tr* to curve, bend back

recurv·us -a -um *adj* curving, curved, bent, crooked

recūsāti·ō -ōnis *f* refusal; *(leg)* objection, protest; *(leg)* counterplea

recūs·ō -āre -āvī -ātus *tr* to raise objections to, reject, refuse; *(w. inf)* to be reluctant to, refuse to **‖** *intr* to raise an objection; to make a rebuttal

recuss·us -a -um *adj* reverberating

recu·tiō -tĕre -ssī -ssus *tr* to strike *(so as to cause to resound)*

recutīt·us -a -um *adj* raw *(skin, from being rubbed);* circumcised

red- *see* **re-**

redactus *pp of* **redigo**

redambul·ō -āre *intr* to walk back

redam·ō -āre *tr* to love in return

redardesc·ō -ĕre *intr* to blaze up again

redargu·ō -ĕre -ī *tr* to disprove, refute, contradict; to disprove the existence of

redauspic·ō -āre *intr* to take the auspices again

red·dō -dĕre -didī -ditus *tr* to give back, return, restore, replace; to repay; to repeat *(words);* to recite, rehearse *(words);* to produce *(a sound);* to ascribe, attribute; to translate; to utter in response; to render, make; to give as due, pay, grant, deliver; to reflect, reproduce, imitate; **animam a pulmonibus reddere** to exhale *(literally, to give back a breath from the lungs);* **causam reddere** to give a reason *or* explanation; **conubia reddere** to grant intermarriage rights; **judicium reddere** to administer justice; to grant a trial; **jura reddere** to administer justice; **litteras reddere** to deliver a letter; **morbo naturae debitum reddere** to die of disease; **poenas reddere** to suffer punishment; **qui te nomine reddet** who will bear your name; **rationem reddere** to render an account *(financial or other);* **reddere hosti cladem** to pay back the enemy for the massacre; **talia ei reddere** to answer him in words such as this; **veniam reddere** *(w. dat)* to forgive; **verbum pro verbo reddere** to translate word for word; **vitam reddere** to die **‖** *refl* to return

redempti·ō -ōnis *f* ransoming; bribing; revenue collection

redempt·ō -āre *tr* to ransom (repeatedly)

redempt·or -ōris *m* contractor; revenue agent

redemptūr·a -ae *f* undertaking of public contracts

redemptus *pp of* **redimo**

red·eō -īre -iī -itum *intr* to go back, come back, return; *(of a speaker)* to return *(to the theme)*; *(w.* **ad)** **1** to return to, revert to; **2** to fall back on, have recourse to; **3** to be reduced to; **4** *(of power, inheritances, etc.)* to revert to, devolve upon; **ad se redire** to come to again, regain consciousness; to control oneself

redhāl·ō -āre *tr* to exhale

redhib·eō -ēre -uī -itus *tr (of a vendor)* to take back *(a defective purchase)*; *(of a purchaser)* to return *(a defective purchase)*

red·igō -igĕre -ēgī -actus *tr* to drive back, lead back, bring back; to call in, collect, raise, make *(money)*; to gather in *(crops)*; to repel *(the enemy)*; to reduce *(in quantity, number, or to a condition)*; to force, compel, subdue; *(w. double acc)* to render, make; *(w.* **in** *or* **sub** *+ acc)* to bring under the power of; **ad vanum et irritum redigere** to make meaningless; to make null and void; **in memoriam redigere** to remember, recall; **in ordinem redigere** to bring into line; **in provinciam redigere** to reduce to the status of a province; **in potestatem redigere** *(w. gen)* to bring under the control of; **in publicum** *(or* **in aerarium) redigere** to turn over *(money)* to the public treasury

redimīcul·um -ī *n* band, chaplet, fillet; chain, fetter

redim·iō -īre -iī -ītus *tr* to crown, wreathe; to surround, encircle

red·imō -imĕre -ēmī -emptus *tr* to buy back; to ransom, redeem; to buy off, ward off, avert; to pay for, compensate for, atone for; *(com)* to get by contract, collect under contract

redintegrāti·ō -ōnis *f* renewal; repetition

redintegr·ō -āre *tr* to make whole again, restore, revive, refresh; *(mil)* to bring to full strength

redipisc·or -ī *tr* to get back

rediti·ō -ōnis *f* return

redit·us -ūs *m* return; *(fig)* restoration; *(astr)* orbit, revolution; *(fin)* revenue, proceeds, return; **(in) reditu esse** to yield a return

redivia *see* **reduvia**

redivīv·us -a -um *adj* second-hand

redol·eō -ēre -uī *tr* to smell of, smell like ‖ *intr* to smell, be redolent

redōn·ō -āre -āvī -ātus *tr* to restore, give back again; to give up, abandon

redorm·iō -īre *intr* to go back to sleep (again)

redū·cō -cĕre -xī -ctus *tr* to lead back, bring back; to draw back; to revive *(a practice)*; to escort *(an official, as mark of honor, to his home)*; to remarry *(after a separation)*; to restore to normal, restore to a previous condition; to withdraw *(troops)*; *(leg)* to make retrospective; **gradum reducere** to draw back; **in gratiam reducere** to restore to favor; **in memoriam reducere** to recall; **rem huc reducere ut** to make it possible that

reducti·ō -ōnis *f* restoration

reduct·or -ōris *m* restorer

reduct·us -a -um *pp of* **reduco** ‖ *adj* remote, secluded, aloof

redunc·us -a -um *adj* bent backwards, curved backwards

redundanti·a -ae *f* excess; redundancy

redund·ō -āre -āvī -ātum *tr* to cause to overflow; **aqua redundata** the overflow ‖ *intr* to overflow; to be too numerous, be too large; *(of writers)* to be excessive; to be soaked *(e.g., w. blood)*; *(w. abl)* to abound in; *(w.* **ex** *or* **de** *+ abl)* to stream from, overflow with

reduvi·a *or* **redivi·a -ae** *f* hangnail

red·ux -ucis *adj* **(redd-)** guiding back, rescuing; that brings back home *(esp. a soldier on a foreign mission)*; brought back, restored

reduxī *perf of* **reduco**

refecti·ō -ōnis *f* restoration, repairing; regaining one's strength; convalescence

refectus *pp of* **reficio**

refell·ō -ĕre -ī *tr* to refute, disprove

refer·ciō -cīre -sī -tus *tr* **(refarc-)** to stuff, cram, choke, crowd

refer·iō -īre *tr* to strike back

referō referre rettulī relātus *tr* to bring back, carry back; to give back, return, restore; to pay back, repay; to (re)echo *(a sound)*; to renew, revive, repeat; to direct, focus, turn *(mind, attention)*; to present again, represent; to say in turn, reply; to announce, report, relate, tell; to note down, enter, register, record; to consider, regard; to refer, attribute, ascribe; to bring up, spit out, vomit; **gradum referre** to go back, retreat; **gratiam referre** to do a return favor; **gratias referre** to return thanks, show gratitude; **pedem referre** to go back, retreat; **pedes fertque refertque** he walks up and down; **rationes referre ad aerarium** to make an accounting to the treasury; **vestigia referre** to retrace footsteps ‖ *refl* to go back, return ‖ *intr (pol)* to make a motion, make a proposal; **ad senatum referre** *(w.* **de** *+ abl)* to bring before the Senate the matter of, make a proposal to the Senate about ‖ *v impers* it is of importance, it is of consequence; **meā (tuā, nostrā) refert** it is of importance *or* of advantage to me (you, us); **non refert utrum** it makes no difference whether; **parvi refert** *(w. inf)* it is of little importance, of little advantage to; **quid refert?** what's the difference?

refert·us -a -um *pp of* **refercio** ‖ *adj* packed, crammed; crowded
referv·eō -ēre *intr* to boil over, bubble over
refervesc·ō -ĕre *intr* to begin to boil *or* bubble
refībul·ō -āre *tr* to unpin
re·ficiō -ficĕre -fēcī -fectus *tr* to rebuild, repair, restore; to revive *(hope, etc.)*; to refresh, invigorate; to get *(e.g., money)* back again; to reappoint
refī·gō -gĕre -xī -xus *tr* to unfasten, undo; to take down *(posters, etc.)*; to annul *(laws)*
refing·ō -ĕre *tr* to refashion
refixus *pp of* **refigo**
reflāgit·ō -āre *tr* to demand again, ask back
reflāt·us -ūs *m* headwind
re·flectō -flectĕre -flexī -flexus *tr* to bend back *or* backwards, turn around, turn away; *(fig)* to turn back, bring back, change
refl·ō -āre -āvī -ātus *tr* to breathe out again ‖ *intr* to blow in the wrong direction
reflu·ō -ĕre *intr* to flow back, run back; to overflow
reflu·us -a -um *adj* ebbing, receding
refocill·ō -āre -āvī -ātus *tr* to rewarm; to revive
reformāt·or -ōris *m* reformer
reformīdāti·ō -ōnis *f* dread
reformīd·ō -āre -āvī -ātus *tr* to dread, stand in awe of; to shrink from, shun
reform·ō -āre -āvī -ātus *tr* to reshape, remold, transform
re·foveō -fovēre -fōvī -fōtus *tr* to warm again; to restore, revive, refresh
refractāriol·us -a -um *adj* a bit refractory, somewhat stubborn
refractus *pp of* **refringo**
refrāg·or -ārī -ātus sum *or* **refrāg·ō -āre** *intr (w. dat)* to oppose, resist, thwart
refrēn·ō -āre -āvī -ātus *tr* to curb, restrain, keep down, control
refric·ō -āre -uī -ātus *tr* to rub open, scratch open; to irritate, reopen *(a wound)*; *(fig)* to exasperate; *(fig)* to renew ‖ *intr* to break out again
refrīger·ō -āre -āvī -ātus *tr* to cool, cool off, chill; to refresh; to weary, exhaust ‖ *pass* to grow cool; to grow weary
re·frīgescō -frīgescĕre -frixī *intr* to grow cool, become cool; *(fig)* to lose force, flag, abate, fail, grow dull, grow stale; *(fig)* to fall flat
re·fringō fringĕre -frēgī -fractus *tr* to break open, break down; to tear off *(clothes)*; *(fig)* to break, check, destroy, put an end to
re·fugiō -fugĕre -fūgī *tr* to run away from; to avoid ‖ *intr* to run away, escape; to disappear
refug·ium -(i)ī *n* place of refuge; recourse
refug·us -a -um *adj* receding, vanishing ‖ *m* fugitive, refugee
reful·geō -gēre -sī *intr* to gleam, reflect *(light)*, glitter
re·fundō -fundĕre -fūdī -fūsus *tr* to pour back, pour out ‖ *pass* to flow back; to overflow
refūtāti·ō -ōnis *f* refutation
refūtāt·us -ūs *m* refutation
refūt·ō -āre -āvī -ātus *tr* to repress, suppress; to refute, disprove
rēgāliol·us -ī *m* wren
rēgāl·is -is -e *adj* regal, kingly; royal
rēgāliter *adv* royally; despotically
regel·ō -āre -āvī -ātus *tr* to thaw
re·gerō -gerĕre -gessī -gestus *tr* to carry back, throw back; *(fig)* to throw back *(remarks)*
rēgi·a -ae *f* palace; court *(royal or imperial establishment)*; capital; *(in camp)* king's tent; regia *(originally the house of King Numa in the Roman Forum and later the residence of the Pontifex Maximus)*
rēgiē *adv* royally; despotically
Rēgiens·is -is -e *or* **Rēgīn·us -a -um** *adj* **(Rhēg-)** of Rhegium ‖ *mpl* inhabitants of Rhegium *(in Bruttium in S. Italy)*
rēgific·us -a -um *adj* fit for a king
Rēgill·um -ī *n or* **Rēgill·ī -ōrum** *mpl* Sabine town from which the Fabian clan is said to have come
Rēgill·us -ī *m* family name *(cognomen)* in the Aemilian clan ‖ name of a small lake south of Gabii *(now dried up)* where the Romans defeated the Latins in 496 B.C.
regim·en -inis *n* steering *(of a ship)*; steering oar; control *(of a horse)*; direction, control *(of public and private affairs)*
rēgīn·a -ae *f* queen
Rēgīn·us -a -um (Rhēg-) of Rhegium *(in Bruttium)* ‖ *mpl* inhabitants of Rhegium
regi·ō -ōnis *f* straight line, line, direction; boundary, boundary line; region, area, quarter, neighborhood; ward *(of Rome)*; district, province *(of a country)*; department, sphere; geographical position; **ab recta regione** in a straight line; **de recta regione deflectere** to veer off the straight path; **e regione** in a straight line, directly; *(w. gen or dat)* in the opposite direction to, exactly opposite; **rectā regione** by a direct route
regiōnātim *adv* by districts
rēgi·us -a -um *adj* king's, royal, regal; like a king, worthy of a king, magnificent ‖ *mpl* king's troops ‖ *f see* **regia**
reglūtin·ō -āre *tr* to unglue
regnāt·or -ōris *m* ruler, sovereign
regnātr·ix -īcis *adj (fem only)* reigning, imperial
regn·ō -āre -āvī -ātum *intr* to reign; to be

supreme, hold sway; to dominate; to rule the roost, play (the part of a) king; *(w. gen)* to be king of; *(w.* **in** + *acc)* to rule over

regn·um -ī *n* monarchy, royal power, kingship; absolute power, despotism; supremacy, control, direction, sovereignty; kingdom, realm; domain, estate

regō regĕre rexī rectus *tr* to keep in a straight line; to keep on a proper course; to guide, conduct; to guide *(morally);* to manage, direct; *(mil)* to command; *(pol)* to rule, govern; **imperium regere** to exercise dominion, rule supreme; **regere finīs** *(leg)* to mark out the limits

re·gredior -gredī -gressus sum *intr* to step *or* go back; to come back, return; *(mil)* to march back, retreat

regressi·ō -ōnis *f (mil)* withdrawl; *(rhet)* repetition

regress·us -ūs *m* return; retreat

rēgul·a -ae *f* ruler *(for drawing straight lines or measuring);* rod, bar; rule, standard, model, principle *(in conduct, language)*

rēgul·us -ī *m* petty king; prince **‖ Regulus** Marcus Atilius Regulus *(Roman general who refused to let himself be ransomed in the First Punic War)* **‖** Marcus Aquilius Regulus *(an informer under Nero, later a successful advocate)*

regust·ō -āre -āvī -ātus *tr* to taste again; *(fig)* to delve again into *(e.g., literature)*

reject·a -ōrum *npl (phil)* things which, while not absolutely bad, should be avoided

rejectāne·us -a -um *adj* to be rejected

rejecti·ō -ōnis *f* rejection; *(leg)* challenging; **rejectio judicum** challenging potential jury members

rejectus *pp of* **rejicio**

re·jiciō -jicĕre -jēcī -jectus *tr* to throw back; to throw over one's shoulders; to beat back, repel; to reject; to refer, direct, assign; to postpone; *(leg) (of judges)* to challenge, overrule; **rem rejicere** *(w.* **ad**) to refer the matter *(to s.o. for decision);* **potestas rejiciendi** *(leg)* right to challenge

relā·bor -bī -psus sum *intr* to slide *or* glide back; to sink down *(upon a couch); (of rivers)* to flow back; to sail back; *(fig)* to return

relangu·escō -escĕre -ī *intr* to faint; to be relaxed, relax; to weaken

relāti·ō -ōnis *f* report *(made by a magistrate to the Senate or the Emperor);* repetition; **relatio criminis** *(leg)* responding to a charge

relāt·or -ōris *m (pol)* proposer of a motion in the Senate

relātus *pp of* **refero**

relāt·us -ūs *m* official report; narration; recital

relaxāti·ō -ōnis *f* relaxation; easing off, mitigation

relax·ō -āre -āvī -ātus *tr* to stretch out, widen, open; to loosen, open; to release, set free; to relax; to cheer up; to mitigate

relectus *pp of* **relego**

relēgāti·ō -ōnis *f* banishment; sending into retirement

relēg·ō -āre -āvī -ātus *tr* to send away, remove; to send into retirement, retire; to banish; to relegate; to shift *(blame, responsibility);* to give back

re·lĕgō -legĕre -lēgī -lectus *tr* to collect again, gather up; to travel over, sail over again; to go over, review *(in thought, in a speech);* to reread

relentesc·ō -ĕre *intr* to slack off, cool off

relev·ō -āre -āvī -ātus *tr* to lighten; to lift up *or* raise again; *(fig)* to relieve, ease the pain of; to lessen in force; to soothe

relicti·ō -ōnis *f* abandonment

relictus *pp of* **relinquo ‖** *adj* abandoned, forsaken

relicuus *see* **reliquus**

relīd·ō -ĕre *tr* to dash back *(in the direction from which s.th. came)*

religāti·ō -ōnis *f* tying back *or* up

religi·ō -ōnis *f* religion; religious scruple, sense of right, conscience; misgivings; reverence, awe; *(pej)* superstition; sanctity, holiness; sect, cult; mode of worship; object of veneration, sacred object, sacred place; divine service, worship, ceremonies; religious practice, ritual; religious taboo; manifestation of divine sanction; *(w. gen)* scruple about, scrupulous regard for

religiōsē *adv* religiously, reverently, piously; scrupulously, conscientiously, carefully, exactly

religiōs·us -a -um *adj* religious, reverent, pious, devout; scrupulous, conscientious, exact, precise, accurate; superstitious; sacred, holy, consecrated; subject to religious claims, under religious liability

relig·ō -āre -āvī -ātus *tr* to tie back, tie up; to moor *(ship);* to untie, unfasten; to bind *(with a wreath, ribbon)*

re·linō -linĕre -lēvī *tr* to unseal

re·linquō -linquĕre -līquī -lictus *tr* to leave behind, not take along; to bequeath; to let remain; to leave alive; to forsake, abandon, leave in the lurch; to relinquish, resign; to leave unmentioned; **in medio** *(or* **in medium) relinquere** to leave *(a question)* open; **locum integrum relinquere** to leave the place untouched

reliqu·ī -ōrum *mpl* the rest, the others; the survivors; posterity

reliqui·ae -ārum *fpl* remains, remnants

reliqu·us -a -um *adj (also* **-cuus)** remaining, left over, left; subsequent, future *(time);* outstanding *(debt)* **‖** *mpl see*

reliqui ‖ *n* remainder, rest, residue; **in reliquum** in the future, for the future; **nihil reliqui facere** to leave nothing undone, leave no stone unturned; **reliquum est** *(w. inf or* **ut)** it only remains to; **reliquum aliquid facere** *(or* **aliquid reliqui facere)** to leave s.th. behind, neglect s.th.

rellig- = **relig-**

relliqu- = **reliq-**

relū·ceō -cēre -xī *intr* to reflect light, gleam, shine out, blaze

relū·cescō -cescĕre -xī *intr* to grow bright again, clear

reluct·or -ārī -ātus sum *intr* to fight back, put up a struggle, resist; to be reluctant

remacresc·ō -ĕre *intr* to shrink and become thin

remaledīc·ō -ĕre *intr* to return abuse

remand·ō -ĕre *tr* to chew again

reman·eō -ēre -sī -sum *intr* to stay behind; to remain, continue *(in a certain state)*

remān·ō -āre *intr* to flow back

remansi·ō -ōnis *f* staying behind

remed·ium -(i)ī *n* remedy, cure

remensus *pp of* **remetior**

reme·ō -āre -āvī -ātus *tr* to retrace, relive ‖ *intr* to go back, come back, return

re·mētior -mētīrī -mensus sum *tr* to remeasure; to retrace, go back over

rēm·ex -igis *m* rower, crew member

Rēm·ī -ōrum *mpl* a people of Gaul *(near modern Rheims)*

rēmigāti·ō -ōnis *f* rowing

rēmig·ium -(i)ī *n* rowing; oars; oarsmen, rowers; **remigium alarum** flapping of wings

rēmig·ō -āre -āvī *intr* to row

remigr·ō -āre -āvī -ātum *intr* to move back

reminisc·or -ī *tr* to call to mind, remember ‖ *intr* to remember; *(w. gen)* to be mindful of, be conscious of, remember

re·misceō -miscēre — -mixtus *tr* to mix up, intermingle; **veris falsa remiscere** to mix in lies with the truth

remissē *adv* mildly, gently

remissi·ō -ōnis *f* release; easing, letting down, lowering; relaxing *(of muscles)*; relaxation, recreation; mildness, gentleness; submissiveness; abating, diminishing; remission *(of debts)*

remiss·us -a -um *adj* relaxed, loose, slack; mild, gentle; remiss; easy-going, indulgent; gay, merry, light; low, cheap *(price)*; **remissiore uti genere dicendi** to speak in a lighter vein

re·mittō -mittĕre -mīsī -missus *tr* to send back; to release; to slacken, loosen; to emit, produce, let out, give off; to return, restore; to reecho *(a voice)*; to give up, reject, resign, concede; to relax, relieve *(the mind)*; to pardon; to remit, *(penalty, debt, obligation)*; *(w. inf)* to stop *(doing s.th.)*; **frontem** *(or* **os** *or* **vultum)** **remittere** to relax the tense expression; **loqui remittere** to stop speaking; **nihil remittere** to spare no effort; **repudium remittere** to send a notice of divorce ‖ *intr (of wind, rain)* to let up, slack off

remixtus *pp of* **remisceo**

remōl·ior -īrī -ītus sum *tr* to push *or* move back *or* away, heave back

remollesc·ō -ĕre *intr* to soften again; to weaken

remoll·iō -īre -īvī -ītus *tr* to soften

remor·a -ae *f* hindrance, delay

remorāmin·a -um *npl* hindrances, delays

remor·deō -dēre -dī -sus *tr* to bite back; to attack in return; to worry, nag

remor·or -ārī -ātus sum *tr* to hinder, delay, hold back ‖ *intr* to loiter, linger, delay, stay behind

remōtē *adv* at a distance, far away

remōti·ō -ōnis *f* withdrawal; removal, elimination *(of a condition)*; **remotio criminis** the shifting of a charge

remōt·us -a -um *adj* removed, out of the way, far off, remote, distant; *(fig)* remote, apart, separate; dead; *(w.* **ab)** **1** removed from, separate from, apart from; **2** clear of, free from

re·moveō -movēre -mōvī -mōtus *tr* to move back, withdraw; to put away, remove; to shroud, veil; to substract; *(fig)* to put out of sight, set aside, abolish

remūg·iō -īre *intr* to bellow back; *(fig)* to reecho, resound

remul·ceō -cēre -sī -sus *tr* to stroke, smooth back; **caudam remulcere** to put the tail between the legs *(in fear)*

remulc·um -ī *n* towline, towrope

Remul·us -ī *m* a king of Alba Longa

remūnerāti·ō -ōnis *f* remuneration, recompense, reward

remūner·or -ārī -ātus sum *or* **remūner·ō -āre** *tr* to repay, remunerate

Remūri·a -ōrum *npl* **(Le-)** festival held in May to appease the spirits of the dead

remurmur·ō -āre *tr & intr* to murmur in reply

rēm·us -ī *m* oar; **ad remos dare** to assign *(s.o.)* as rower; **remi corporis** *(fig)* hands and feet *(of a swimmer)*; **remis** by rowing; **remis incumbere** to lean to the oars

Rem·us -ī *m* twin brother of Romulus

renarr·ō -āre *tr* retell

re·nascor -nascī -nātus sum *intr* to be born again; to rise again, spring up again, be restored; to reappear; to recur

renāvig·ō -āre *intr* to sail back

ren·eō -ēre *tr* to unravel, undo

rēn·ēs -(i)um *mpl* kidneys

renīd·ens -entis *adj* beaming, glad

renīd·eō -ēre *intr* to reflect (light), glitter,

shine; to smile, grin all over; to beam with joy

renīdesc·ō -ĕre *intr* to grow bright, gleam, begin to glitter

renī·tor -tī *intr* to fight back, put up a struggle, resist

ren·ō -āre -āvī *intr* to swim back, float back

rēn·ō -ōnis *m* **(rhē-)** reindeer skin *(used for clothing)*

renōd·ō -āre -āvī -ātus *tr* to tie back in a knot; to untie

renovām·en -inis *n* renewal, new form

renovāti·ō -ōnis *f* renovation, renewal; revision; *(fin)* compound interest

renov·ō -āre -āvī -ātus *tr* to make new again; to renovate, repair, restore; to plow up *(a fallow field);* to reopen *(a wound);* to revive *(an old custom, etc.);* to start *(a battle)* all over again; to refresh *(the memory);* to repeat, keep repeating, reaffirm; **faenus renovare in singulos annos** *(fin)* to compound the interest on a yearly basis

renumer·ō -āre -āvī -ātus *tr* to count over again, recount; to pay back, repay

renuntiāti·ō -ōnis *f* formal *or* official report, announcement

renunti·ō -āre -āvī -ātus *tr* to report; to announce; to retract *(a promise, statement);* to renounce *(an alliance, a friendship);* to reject; to call off *(a previous engagement); (w. double acc)* to announce *or* declare *(s.o.)* elected as; *(w. acc & inf)* to bring back word that; **legationem renuntiare** *(of an ambassador)* to give an account of an embassy; **repudium renuntiare** to break off an engagement; **sibi renuntiare** to say to oneself, remind oneself **‖** *intr* to take back a message; *(w. dat)* to withdraw from, renounce, give up

renunt·ius -(i)ī *m* reporter

renu·ō -ĕre -ī *tr* to nod refusal to, turn down, decline, say no to, reject **‖** *intr* to shake the head in refusal; *(w. dat)* to say no to, deny *(a charge)*

renūt·ō -āre -āvī *intr* to refuse emphatically

reor rērī ratus sum *tr* to think, deem; *(w. acc & inf)* to think that; *(w. acc & adj as objective complement)* to regard *(s.th.)* as **‖** *intr* to think, suppose

repāgul·a -ōrum *npl* bolts, bars; *(fig)* restraints, regulations, rules, limits

repand·us -a -um *adj* curved backwards, concave; *(shoes)* with turned-up toes

reparābil·is -is -e *adj* capable of being repaired, reparable, retrievable

reparc·ō -ĕre repersī *intr (w. dat)* to be sparing with, take it easy on

repar·ō -āre -āvī -ātus *tr* to get again, acquire again; to recover, retrieve, make good; to restore, renew; to repair; to recruit *(a new army);* **vina merce reparare** to get wine in exchange for wares, barter for wine

repastināti·ō -ōnis *f* the act of turning *(the ground)* over again for planting

repastin·ō -āre -āvī -ātus *tr* to turn *(the ground)* over again for planting

re·pectō -pectĕre -pexī -pexus *tr* to comb back; to comb again

repellō repellĕre reppulī repulsus *tr* to drive back, push back, repel; to reject; to remove; to refute

repen·dō -dĕre -pendī -pensus *tr* to repay, pay back; to ransom; *(fig)* to repay in kind, requite, recompense, reward; to compensate for; to balance, balance out; **magna rependere** to pay back in full

rep·ens -entis *adj* sudden, unexpected; completely new

repensus *pp of* **rependo**

repente *adv* suddenly, all of a sudden; unexpectedly

repentīnō *adv* suddenly; unexpectedly, without warning

repentīn·us -a -um *adj* sudden, unexpected; hasty, impetuous

reperc·ō -ĕre *intr (w. dat)* **1** to be sparing with; **2** to refrain from

repercussī *perf of* **repercutio**

repercuss·us -a -um *pp of* **repercutio ‖** *adj* rebounding; reflected, reflecting; echoed, echoing

repercuss·us -ūs *m* reverberation, echo, repercussion; reflection

reper·cutiō -cutĕre -cussī -cussus *tr* to make *(s.th.)* rebound, make reverberate, make reflect

reperiō reperīre repperī repertus *tr* to find, discover; to find again; to get, procure, win; to find out, ascertain, realize; to invent, devise

repertīci·us -a -um *adj* newly discovered

repert·or -ōris *m* discoverer, inventor, author

repert·us -a -um *pp of* **reperio ‖** *npl* discoveries, inventions

repetīti·ō -ōnis *f* repetition; *(w.* **in** *+ acc)* going back to; *(rhet)* anaphora

repetīt·or -ōris *m* claimant

repet·ō -ĕre -īvī *or* **-iī -ītus** *tr* to head back to, try to reach again, return to; to aim at again; to fetch back; to attack again; to persecute again; to demand anew; to demand back, claim, demand in compensation, retake; to trace back, retrace; to trace in thought, think over, recall, recollect; to repeat, undertake again, resume, renew; **animo** *(or* **memoriā)** **repetere** to recall; **lex de pecuniis** *(or* **rebus)** **repetundis** law on extortion *(literally, law concerning recovering money or property);* **memoriam repetere** to recall the memory; **pecuniam repetere** to sue for the recovery of money; **poenam** *(or* **poenas) repetere** to demand satisfaction; **res repetere** to sue for the recovery of property; **reus pecuniarum repetundarum** guilty of extortion ‖ *intr (w.* **ad)** to head back to

repetund·ae -ārum *fpl* money extorted; extortion; **repetundarum argui** to be charged with extortion; **repetundarum teneri** to be held on an extortion charge

repexus *pp of* **repecto**

repl·eō -ēre -ēvī -ētus *tr* **(reppl-)** to refill, replenish; to fill to the brim; to make up for, replace, compensate for; *(mil)* to recruit, bring *(an army)* to full strength

replēt·us -a -um *pp of* **repleo** ‖ *adj* filled, full; *(of the body)* well-filled out; *(w. abl or gen)* **1** full of; **2** fully endowed with

replicāti·ō -ōnis *f* folding back, rolling back, rolling up; reflex action

replic·ō -āre -āvī -ātus *tr* to fold back, turn back; to unfold

rēp·ō -ĕre -sī *intr* to crawl, creep

re·pōnō -pōnĕre -posuī -positus *or* **-postus** *tr* to put back, set back, lay *(e.g., the head)* back; to replace; to restore; to substitute; to lay out, stretch out *(the body);* to lay aside, store, keep, preserve; to renew, repeat; to place, class; to repay, requite; **in sceptra reponere** to reinstate in power; **membra reponere** *(w. ab or* **in** *+ abl)* to stretch out on *(e.g., a bed);* **se in cubitum reponere** to rest on one's elbow; **spem reponere** *(w.* **in** *+ abl)* to put one's hopes in *or* on, count on

report·ō -āre -āvī -ātus *tr* to bring back; to report; **victoriam reportare** to win a victory

reposc·ō -ĕre *tr* to demand back; to ask for, claim, require, demand

repositōr·ium -(i)ī *n* large serving dish

repos(i)t·us -a -um *pp of* **repono** ‖ *adj* out-of-the-way, remote

repost·or -ōris *m* restorer

repostus *pp of* **repono**

repōti·a -ōrum *npl* second round of drinks, seconds

repperī *perf of* **reperio**

reppulī *perf of* **repello**

repraesentāti·ō -ōnis *f* vivid presentation; *(fin)* cash payment

repraesent·ō -āre -āvī -ātus *tr* to present again, show, exhibit, display, depict; to do immediately, accomplish instantly; to rush, speed up *(e.g., plans);* to anticipate; to pay in cash; to apply *(medicines)* immediately

reprehen·do *or* **repren·dō -dĕre -ī -sus** *tr* to hold back; to restrain, check; to blame, find fault with, criticize; to refute; *(leg)* to prosecute, convict, condemn

repre(he)nsi·ō -ōnis *f* checking, check; finding fault, blame, criticism, rebuke; *(rhet)* refutation; *(rhet)* self-correction

reprehens·ō -āre *tr* to hold back (continually)

reprehens·or -ōris *m* critic

reprendō *see* **reprehendo**

reprensō *see* **reprehenso**

repress·or -ōris *m* one who represses

re·primō -primĕre -pressī -pressus *tr* to hold back, keep back; to restrain, limit, confine, curb, repress, suppress ‖ *refl* to control oneself; *(w.* **ab)** to refrain from

reprōmissi·ō -ōnis *f* counter-promise, promise in return

reprō·mittō -mittĕre -mīsī -missus *tr* to promise in return ‖ *intr (leg) (w. dat)* to make a counter-promise to *(s.o.)*

rept·ō -āre -āvī -ātum *intr* to crawl around

repudiāti·ō -ōnis *f* repudiation; refusal, rejection; refusal to approve a policy

repudi·ō -āre -āvī -ātus *tr* to repudiate, scorn; to refuse, reject; to jilt; to divorce

repudiōs·us -a -um *adj* objectionable, offensive

repud·ium -(i)ī *n* repudiation, separation, divorce; **repudium renuntiare** *(or* **remittere)** *(w. dat)* to send a letter of divorce to

repuerasc·ō -ĕre *intr* to become a child again; to behave childishly

repugn·ans -antis *adj* contradictory, inconsistent ‖ *npl* contradictions, inconsistencies

repugnanter *adv* reluctantly

repugnanti·a -ae *f* contradiction, inconsistency; conflicting demands; incompatibility

repugn·ō -āre -āvī -ātum *intr* to fight back; *(w. dat)* **1** to oppose, offer opposition to, fight against, be against; **2** to disagree with, be inconsistent with, be incompatible with; *(w.* **contra** *+ acc)* to fight against

repuls·a -ae *f* defeat at the polls; rebuff, cold shoulder; **repulsa consulatūs** defeat in running for the consulship; **repulsam ferre** to suffer a defeat, lose an election

repuls·ans -antis *adj* throbbing; reechoing

repuls·us -a -um *pp of* **repello** ‖ *adj* rejected, spurned

repuls·us -ūs *m* reverberation, echo

repung·ō -ĕre *tr* to goad again

repurg·ō -āre -āvī -ātus *tr* to clean again; to purge away, remove

reputāti·ō -ōnis *f* rethinking, reconsideration, review; subject of thought, reflection

reput·ō -āre -āvī -ātus *tr* to think over, reflect upon, reconsider; to count back, calculate

requi·ēs -ētis *f* rest, relief; relaxation;

break, pause, intermission; recreation, amusement, hobby; *(w. gen)* rest from
requi·escō -escĕre -ēvī -ētus *tr* to put to rest, quiet down, calm down ‖ *intr* to rest, take a rest; to come to rest, stop, end; to relax; to find peace, be consoled, find relief; to rest, lie quietly, sleep; *(of the dead)* to rest, sleep
requiēt·us -a -um *adj* rested up
requīrit·ō -āre *tr* to keep asking for; to be on a constant lookout for
re·quīrō -quīrĕre -quīsīvī *or* **-quīsiī -quīsītus** *tr* to look for, search for, hunt for; to miss; to ask; to ask for, demand, require; *(w.* **ab** *or* **de** + *abl)* to ask *or* demand *(s.th.)* from *or* of
requīsītum -ī *n* a need
rēs reī *or* **rēī** *f* thing; matter, affair; object; cirumstance; event, occurrence; deed; condition, case; reality, truth, fact; property, possessions, wealth; estate, effects; benefit, advantage, interest, profit; business affair, transaction; cause, reason, motive, ground; historical event; theme, topic, subject matter; *(leg)* case, suit; *(mil)* operation, campaign, battle; *(pol)* state, government, politics; **ab re** contrary to interests, disadvantageous, useless; **ad rem pertinere** to be relevant to the matter at hand; **ex re** according to circumstances, according to the situation; **ex re istius** for his good; **ex re publica** for the common good, in the public interest; **ex tua re** to your advantage; **in re** *(or* **re ipsā** *or* **reāpse** *or* **re verā)** in fact, in reality; **in re praesenti** on the spot; **in rem** for the good, useful, advantageous; **in rem praesentem** on the spot; **nil ad rem est** *(frequently with ellipsis of* **est)** it is not to the point, it is irrelevant; **ob eam rem** for that reason; **ob rem** to the purpose; **pro re** according to circumstances; **quae res?** what's that? what are you talking about?; **re** in fact, in practice, in reality, actually, really; **rem agere** *(leg)* to conduct a case; **rem gerere** *(mil)* to conduct a military operation; **rem solvere** to settle a matter; **res capitalis** *(or* **res capitis)** *(leg)* a case involving the death penalty *or* loss of civil rights; **res familiaris** private property; **res frumentaria** grain situation; grain supply; foraging; **res judiciaria** administration of justice, department of justice; **res mihi tecum** I have some business with you; **res pecuaria et rustica** livestock; **res rustica** agriculture; **res publica** state, government, politics, public life, commonwealth, country; **res sit mihi cum his** let me handle them; **res soli** real property, real estate *(as contrasted with* **res mobilis)**; **res uxoria** marriage; dowry; **res Veneris** sexual intercourse, love making ‖ *fpl* physical phenomena; property; affairs, public affairs; **rerum** *(w. superl adj)* the best in the world: **rerum facta est pulcherrima Roma** Rome became the most beautiful city in the world; **rerum potiri** to get control of the government; **rerum scriptor** historian, annalist; **res gestae** exploits, accomplishments, military achievements; **res novae** revolution; **res Persicae** Persian history, Parthian history; **res prolatae** business adjourned *(for the holiday)*; **res publicas inire** to enter politics; **res secundae** prosperity; **summa rerum** world; universe; **tibi res tuas habe** *(formula for divorce)* take your things and go!
resacr·ō *or* **resecr·ō -āre** *tr* to ask again for; to free from a curse
resaevi·ō -īre *intr* to go wild again
resalūtāti·ō -ōnis *f* a greeting in return
resalūt·ō -āre -āvī -ātus *tr* to greet in return
resān·escō -escĕre -uī *intr* to heal again
resar·ciō -cīre -sī -tus *or* **-sus** *tr* to patch up, repair; to make good *(a loss)*
re·scindō -scindĕre -scĭdī -scissus *tr* to tear off; to cut down; to tear open; to rescind, repeal; *(fig)* to expose
re·sciscō -sciscĕre -scīvī *or* **-sciī -scītus** *tr* to find out, learn, ascertain
re·scrībō -scrībĕre -scripsī -scriptus *tr* to write back in reply; to rewrite, revise; to enlist, enroll; to pay back, repay ‖ *intr* to write a reply
rescript·um -ī *n* imperial rescript
resec·ō -āre -uī -tus *tr* **(-sic-)** to cut back, cut short; to reap; *(fig)* to trim, curtail; **ad vivum resecare** to cut to the quick
resecr·ō *see* **resacro**
resectus *pp of* **reseco**
resecūtus *pp of* **resequor**
resēmin·ō -āre *tr* reproduce
re·sequor -sequī -secūtus sum *tr* to reply to, answer
reser·ō -āre -āvī -ātus *tr* to unlock, unbar, open; to disclose; to begin *(a year)*
reserv·ō -āre -āvī -ātus *tr* to reserve, hold back; to spare; to hold on to; to store
res·es -idis *adj* remaining, left; lazy, idle, inactive; slow, sluggish; calm
re·sideō -sidēre -sēdī *intr* to sit down, settle back; to sink down, settle, subside; to calm down
re·sīdō -sīdĕre -sēdī *or* **-sīdī** *intr* to sit down; *(of a person lying down)* to sit up; *(of birds)* to perch; *(after rising or climbing)* to fall back, sink back; *(of things)* to come to rest, lodge; *(of colonists)* to settle; *(of water)* to go down, subside; *(of swellings)* to go down, shrink; *(of natural features)* to dip (down); *(of wind, flame, rain)* to die down; *(of a person)* to

quiet down; *(of activity, condition)* to diminish in intensity, abate; *(mil)* to encamp

residu·us -a -um *adj* remaining, left; in arrears, outstanding *(money)* ‖ *n* the remainder, the rest

resign·ō -āre -āvī -ātus *tr* to unseal, open; to disclose; to give up, resign; to annul, cancel; to destroy *(confidence)*

resil·iō -īre -uī *or* **-iī** *intr* to spring back, jump back; to recoil; to contract

resīm·us -a -um *adj* turned-up, snub

rēsīn·a -ae *f* resin *(secreted by various trees, used to preserve and season wine, used as a depilatory, etc.)*

rēsināt·us -a -um *adj* rubbed with resin, resined

resip·iō -ĕre *tr* to taste of, taste like, have the flavor of

resip·iscō -iscĕre -īvī *or* **-iī** *or* **-uī** *intr* to come to one's senses

resist·ens -entis *adj* firm, tough

re·sistō -sistĕre -stitī *intr* to stand still, stop, pause; to stay, stay behind, remain; to resist, put up resistance; to rise again; *(w. dat)* **1** to be opposed to, resist; **2** to reply to

resolūt·us -a -um *adj* loose, limp; effeminate

re·solvō -solvĕre -solvī -solūtus *tr* to untie, unfasten, undo; to open; to dissolve, melt, thaw; to relax *(the body)*; to stretch out *(the limbs)*; to unravel; to cancel; to dispel; to unnerve, enervate; to release, set free

resonābil·is -is -e *adj* resounding, answering *(echo)*

reson·ans -antis *adj* echoing

reson·ō -āre -āvī *tr* to repeat, reecho, resound with, make ring ‖ *intr* to resound, ring, reecho; *(w.* **ad***)* to resound in answer to

reson·us -a -um *adj* resounding, re- echoing

resorb·eō -ēre *tr* to suck in, swallow again

respargō *see* **respergo**

respect·ō -āre *tr* to look back on; to keep an eye on, care for; to have regard for, respect; to gaze at, look at ‖ *intr* to look back; to look around

respectus *pp of* **respicio**

respect·us -ūs *m* backward glance, looking back; looking around; refuge; respect, regard, consideration; **respec-tum habere** *(w. dat or* **ad***)* to have respect for

resper·gō -gĕre -sī -sus *tr* **(-spar-)** to sprinkle, splash, spray; to defile

respersi·ō -ōnis *f* sprinkling, splashing

respersus *pp of* **respergo**

re·spiciō -spicĕre -spexī -spectus *tr* to look back at, see behind oneself; to look around for; to look back upon *(the past, etc.)*; to look at, gaze at; to regard, contemplate, consider; to notice; to look after, take care of, see to; to respect ‖ *intr* to look back; to look around; *(w.* **ad***)* to look at, gaze at

respīrām·en -inis *n* respiration, breathing; exhalation; letup, rest, pause *(to catch one's breath)*, breathing space

respīrāti·ō ōnis *f* respiration, breathing; breathing pause; *(fig)* exhalation, emission of vapor

respīrāt·us -ūs *m* respiration

respīr·ō -āre -āvī -ātus *tr* to breathe, breathe out, exhale ‖ *intr* to breathe, take a breath, breathe again; to recover *(from fright, etc.)*; *(of combat, passions, etc.)* to slack off, die down, subside; **a continuis cladibus respirare** to catch one's breath again after continuous fighting; **ab metu respirare** to recover from a shock

resplend·eō -ēre *intr* to glitter

respon·deō -dēre -dī -sus *tr* to answer; to say in reply; to say in refutation; **ficta respondere** to make up answers; **hoc quod rogo responde** answer my question; **multa respondere** to give a lengthy reply; **par pari respondere** to give tit for tat; **verbum verbo respondere** to answer word for word ‖ *intr* to answer, reply; *(of officials, seers, priests)* to give an official *or* formal reply; to echo; to satisfy the claims *(of a creditor)*; *(leg)* to answer a summons to appear in court; *(of lawyers)* to give an opinion, give legal advice; *(of priests)* to give a response *(from a god)*; *(w. dat)* **1** to answer, reply to; **2** to match, balance, correspond to, be equal to; **3** to resemble; **4** to measure up to; **amori amore respondere** to return love for love; **nominibus respondere** to pay off debts

responsi·ō -ōnis *f* response, answer, reply; refutation; *(rhet)* **sibi ipsi responsio** a reply to one's own arguments

responsit·ō -āre -āvī *intr* to give professional legal advice

respons·ō -āre *intr* to answer, reply; to reecho; *(w. dat)* **1** to answer to, agree with; **2** to resist, defy; **3** to talk back to *(in disobedience)*

respons·or -ōris *m* respondent

respons·us -a -um *pp of* **respondeo** ‖ *n* answer, response; oracular response; *(leg)* professional advice; **responsum auferre** *(or* **ferre***)* *(w.* **ab***)* to receive an answer from; **responsum referre** to deliver an answer

rēspūblica reīpūblicae *f* state, government, politics, public life, commonwealth, country; **rempublicam inire** to enter politics; *(see also* **res publica***)*

respu·ō -ĕre -ī *tr* to spit out; to cast out, eject, expel; to refuse, to reject

restagn·ō -āre *intr* to form pools; to run over, overflow; to be inundated
restaur·ō -āre -āvī -ātus *tr* to restore, rebuild; to renew, take up again
resticul·a -ae *f* thin rope, cord
restincti·ō -ōnis *f* quenching
restin·guō -guĕre -xī -ctus *tr* to quench, extinguish, put out; to snuff out; to exterminate, destroy
resti·ō -ōnis *f* rope dealer; *(hum)* roper *(person who is whipped with ropes)*
restipulāti·ō -ōnis *f* counterclaim
restipul·or -ārī -ātus sum *tr* to stipulate in return ‖ *intr* to make a counterclaim
rest·is -is *f (acc:* **restem** *or* **restim)** rope
restit·ō -āre *intr* to stay behind, lag, behind; to keep offering resistance
restitr·ix -īcis *f* stay-at-home *(female)*
resti·tuō -tuĕre -tuī -tūtus *tr* to set up again; to restore, rebuild, reconstruct; to renew, reestablish, revive; to bring back, restore, reinstate; to give back, return, replace; to restore, repair, remedy; to reenact *(a law);* to reverse; to revoke, undo, cancel, make void; to make good, compensate for, repair
restitūti·ō -ōnis *f* restoration; reinstatement, pardon; recall *(from exile)*
restitūt·or -ōris *m* restorer, rebuilder
restitūtus *pp of* **restituo**
re·stō -stāre -stitī *intr* to stand firm, stand one's ground, resist; to stay behind, stay in reserve; to be left over ‖ *v impers (w. inf or* **ut)** it remains to *(do s.th.)*
restrictē *adv* sparingly; exactly, precisely
restrict·us -a -um *pp of* **restringo** ‖ *adj* tied back, tight; stingy; moderate, strict, stern
re·stringō -stringĕre -strinxī -strictus *tr* to tie *(the hands, arms)* behind one; to draw tight, tie; to tighten; to draw back the cover from *(s.th. concealed); (of dogs)* to show *(the teeth) (fig)* restrain; *(fig)* to restrict the activity of
resūd·ō -āre *intr* to sweat, ooze
result·ō -āre *intr* to rebound; to resound, reverberate
resūm·ō -ĕre -psī -ptus *tr* to resume; to recover *(strength)*
resu·ō -ĕre -uī -ūtus *tr* to undo the stitching of
resupīn·ō -āre -āvī -ātus *tr* to throw *(s.o.)* on his back, throw over, throw down; *(coll)* to knock for a loop; to break down *(door)*
resupīn·us -a -um *adj* lying on the back; bent back, thrown back; leaning backward; proud *(gait)*
resur·gō -gĕre -rexī -rectum *intr* to rise again; to appear again
resuscit·ō -āre *tr* to resuscitate
retardāti·ō -ōnis *f* retardation
retard·ō -āre -āvī -ātus *tr* to retard, slow down, hold back, delay; to keep back, check, hinder ‖ *intr* to lag behind
retax·ō -āre *tr* to rebuke
rēt·e -is *n* net; *(fig)* trap
rete·gō -gĕre -xī -ctus *tr* to uncover; to unclothe, expose; to open; to reveal, make visible; to disclose *(secrets)*
retempt·ō -āre -āvī -ātus *tr* to attempt again, try again; to test again
reten·dō -dĕre -dī -tus *or* **-sus** *tr* to release from tension, unbend, relax
retenti·ō -ōnis *f* holding back; slowing down; withholding *(assent)*
retent·ō -āre *tr* to hold back, hold tight; to attempt again; to retain the loyalty of; to keep *(feelings)* in check
retentus *pp of* **retendo** *and* **retineo**
retexī *perf of* **retego**
retex·ō -ĕre -uī -tus *tr* to unravel; to cancel, reverse, annul, undo; to weave anew; to renew, repeat; to correct, revise; to retract *(words)*
rēti·a -ae *f* net
rētiār·ius -(i)ī *m* net-man *(gladiator who tried to entangle his opponent in a net)*
reticenti·a -ae *f* reticence; *(rhet)* abrupt pause; **poena reticentiae** punishment for suppression of truth
retic·eō -ēre -uī *tr* to be silent about, suppress, keep secret ‖ *intr* to be silent, keep silent; *(w. dat)* to make no answer to
rēticulāt·us -a -um *adj* covered with a net; net-shaped, reticulate
rēticul·um -ī *n* small net; hair net; meshwork bag *(for protecting bottles);* racket *(for playing ball)*
retinācul·a -ōrum *npl* cable, rope
retin·ens -entis *adj (w. gen)* clinging to, sticking to
retinenti·a -ae *f* retention
re·tineō -tinēre -tinuī -tentus *tr* to hold back, keep back; to restrain; to keep, retain; to hold in reserve; to preserve, maintain, uphold; to hold, engross *(attention);* to detain, delay
retinn·iō -īre *intr* to ring again, ring out, tinkle in response
reton·ō -āre *intr* to resound
retor·queō -quēre -sī -tus *tr* to twist *or* bend back; to hurl back *(weapons);* **mentem retorquere** to change the mind; **oculos retorquere** *(w.* **ad)** to look back wistfully at
retorrid·us -a -um *adj* parched, dried out, withered; wily, shrewd
retortus *pp of* **retorqueo**
retractāti·ō -ōnis *f* holding back, hesitation; **sine retractatione** without hesitation
retractāt·us -a -um *adj* revised
retract·ō *or* **retrect·ō -āre** *tr* to rehandle, take in hand again, undertake once more,

take up once more; to reexamine, review; to revise ‖ *intr* to refuse, decline; to be reluctant

retract·us -a -um *adj* remote, distant

retra·hō -hĕre -xī -ctus *tr* to draw back, withdraw, pull back; to bring to light again, make known again; *(fig)* to drag away, remove

retrectō *see* **retracto**

retrib·uō -uĕre -uī -ūtus *tr* to hand back; to repay

retrō *adv* backwards, back; to the rear; behind, on the rear; in the past, formerly, back, past; in return; on the contrary, on the other hand; in reverse order *(of words);* counting back to an earlier date, retrospectively; *(w. reference to reasoning)* back to first principles

retro·agō -agĕre -ēgī -actus *tr* to drive backward; to reverse the order of, invert; to repeat backwards

retrō·cēdō -dĕre -cessī -cessum *intr* to move backward; to withdraw, retire

retrorsum *adv* **(-sus)** back, backwards, in reverse; in reverse order

retrū·dō -dĕre — -sus *tr* to push back; to hide, conceal

retundō retundĕre retudī *(or* **rettudī)** **retunsus** *(or* **retūsus)** *tr* to pound back; to dull, blunt; *(fig)* to deaden, weaken, repress, restrain

retuns·us *or* **retūs·us -a -um** *pp of* **retundo** ‖ *adj* blunt, dull; *(fig)* dull

re·us -ī *m (either of the two parties involved in litigation)* defendant, the accused, plaintiff; convict, criminal, culprit; *(w. gen)* person charged with; **in reos recipere** *(or* **referre)** to list among the accused; **reum agere** to try a defendant; **reum facere** to indict, bring a defendant to trial; **reum postulare** to prosecute, force to face a trial

reval·escō -escĕre -uī *intr* to regain one's strength, recover; to become valid again

re·vehō -vehĕre -vexī -vectus *tr* to carry back, bring back ‖ *pass* to ride back, drive back; to sail back; *(fig)* to go back *(e.g., to an earlier period)*

re·vellō -vellĕre -vellī -vulsus *tr* to pull out, pull back, tear off, tear out; to tear up *(the ground),* dig up; *(fig)* to unmask *(deception)*

revēl·ō -āre -āvī -ātus *tr* to unveil, uncover

re·veniō -venīre -vēnī -ventum *intr* to come again, come back, return

rēvērā *adv* in fact, actually

reverber·ō -āre -āvī -ātus *tr* to beat back

reverend·us -a -um *adj* venerable, awe-inspiring; deserving respect

rever·ens -entis *adj* reverent, respectful

reverenter *adv* respectfully

reverenti·a -ae *f* reverence, respect

rever·eor -ērī -itus sum *tr* to revere, respect, stand in awe of

reversi·ō -ōnis *f* **(-vor-)** turning back *(before reaching one's destination);* recurrence

revert·ō -ĕre -ī *or* **re·vertor -vertī -versus sum** *intr* **(-vor-)** to turn back, turn around, come back, return; *(in speaking)* to return, revert

revictus *pp of* **revinco**

revid·eō -ēre *tr* to go back to see

revin·ciō -cīre -xī -ctus *tr* to tie back, tie behind, tie up

re·vincō -vincĕre -vīcī -victus *tr* to conquer in turn; to refute, convict of falsehood; *(w. acc or gen of the charge)* to convict *(s.o.)* of

revinctus *pp of* **revincio**

revir·escō -escĕre -uī *intr* to become green again; to grow young again; to grow again, grow strong again, revive

revīs·ō -ĕre *tr* to revisit; to look back to see ‖ *intr* to come *or* go back; *(w.* **ad)** **1** to look at again, look back at; **2** to return to, revisit

re·vīviscō -vīviscĕre -vixī *intr* **(-escō)** to come back to life, be restored to life, revive; *(fig)* to recover, gain strength

revocābil·is -is -e *adj* capable of being recalled; **non revocabilis** irrevocable

revocām·en -inis *n* recall

revocāti·ō -ōnis *f* calling back, recall; calling away; retraction

revoc·ō -āre -āvī -ātus *tr* to call back, recall; to call off, withdraw *(troops);* to call back *(a performer)* for an encore; to bring back to life, revive; *(leg)* to arraign again; to regain *(strength, etc.);* to resume *(career, studies);* to revoke, retract; to check, control; to cancel; *(w.* **ad)** to refer, apply, subject, submit *(s.o. or s.th.)* to

revol·ō -āre -āvī *intr* to fly back

revolsus *see* **revulsus**

revolūbil·is -is -e *adj* able to be rolled back; **non revolubilis** irrevocable *(fate)*

revol·vō -vĕre -vī -ūtus *tr* to roll back, unroll, unwind; to retravel; to unroll, read over, read again *(a scroll);* to reexperience; to go over, think over ‖ *pass* to revolve; to come around again, recur, return

revom·ō -ĕre -uī *tr* to throw up again, disgorge

revor- = **rever-**

revorr·ō -ĕre *tr* to sweep back

revulsus *pp of* **revello**

rex rēgis *m* king; patron; queen bee

Rhadamanth·us *or* **Rhadamanth·os -ī** *m* son of Jupiter, brother of Minos, and one of the three judges in the lower world

Rhaet·ī -ōrum *mpl* people of Rhaetia

Rhaeti·a -ae *f* Alpine country between Germany and Italy

Rhamn·ūs -untos *f* Attic deme famous for its statue of Nemesis

Rhamnūsi·us -a -um *adj* of the deme of Rhamnus; **Rhamnusia virgo** the goddess worshiped at Rhamnus *(i.e., Nemesis)*

rhapsōdi·a -ae *f* Homeric lay, selection from Homer; **rhapsodia secunda** second book *(of Homer)*

Rhe·a -ae *f* Cybele

Rhe·a Silvi·a -ae *f* daughter of Numitor and mother of Romulus and Remus by Mars, the god of war

rhēd- = raed-

Rhēg·ium -(i)ī *n (also* **Rēg-**) town on the toe of Italy

Rhēnān·us -a -um *adj* of *or* on the Rhine

rhēn·ō -ōnis *f* reindeer skin *(used as clothing)*

Rhēn·us -ī *m* the Rhine

Rhēs·us -ī *m* Thracian king who fought as an ally of Troy

rhēt·or -oris *m* rhetorician, teacher of rhetoric; orator

rhētoric·a -ae *or* **rhētoric·ē -ēs** *f* rhetoric, public speaking

rhētoric·a -ōrum *npl* treatise on rhetoric

rhētoricē *adv* rhetorically, in an oratorical manner

rhētoric·us -a -um *adj* rhetorician's, rhetorical; **doctores rhetorici** professors of rhetoric; **libri rhetorici** textbooks on rhetoric

rhīnocer·ōs -ōtis *or* **-ōtos** *m* rhinoceros; vessel made of a rhinoceros's tusk; **pueri nasum rhinocerotis habent** the children turn up their noses

rhō *indecl n* rho *(seventeenth letter of the Greek alphabet)*

Rhodan·us -ī *m* the Rhone River

Rhodiens·is -is -e *or* **Rhodi·us -a -um** *adj* Rhodian, of Rhodes ‖ *mpl* Rhodians

Rhodop·ē -ēs *f* mountain range in Thrace

Rhodopēj·us -a -um *adj* Thracian

Rhod·os *or* **Rhod·us -ī** *f* Rhodes *(island off the S.W. coast of Asia Minor)*

Rhoetē·us -a -um *adj* Trojan; of the promontory of Rhoeteum; **Rhoeteus ductor** Aeneas; **Rhoeteum profundum** sea near the promontory of Rhoeteum ‖ *n* promontory on the Dardanelles near Troy

rhomb·us -ī *m* magic wheel; turbot *(fish)*

rhomphae·a -ae *f* long javelin

rhythmic·us -a -um *adj* rhythmical ‖ *m* teacher of prose rhythm

rhythm·os *or* **rhythm·us -ī** *m* rhythm; symmetry

rhyt·ion -iī *n* conical cup *or* urn

rīc·a -ae *f* veil *(worn by Roman women at sacrifice)*

rīcin·ium -(i)ī *n* short mantle with a cowl

rict·um -ī *n* snout; wide-open mouth

rict·us -ūs *m* snout; wide-open mouth; **risu rictum diducere** to break into a broad grin ‖ *mpl* jaws, gaping jaws

rīdeō rīdēre rīsī rīsus *tr* to laugh at, ridicule; to smile upon ‖ *intr* to laugh; to smile, grin; *(w. dat or* **ad**) to smile at, laugh at

rīdibund·us -a -um *adj* laughing

rīdiculāri·us -a -um *adj* funny, laughable ‖ *npl* jokes

rīdiculē *adv* jokingly, humorously; ridiculously

rīdiculōs·us -a -um *adj* funny, amusing; ridiculous

rīdicul·us -a -um *adj* funny, amusing, laughable; ridiculous, silly ‖ *m* joker, clown ‖ *n* joke

riēn·ēs -ium *mpl* kidneys

rig·ens -entis *adj* rigid, stiff

rig·eō -ēre -uī *intr* to be stiff, be rigid; to be numb; to stand on end, stand erect; to stand stiff; to be unmoved by entreatics

rig·escō -escēre -uī *intr* to grow stiff, become numbed; to stiffen, harden; to stand on end

rigid·a -ae *f (vulg)* penis in erect state

rigidē *adv* rigorously, severely

rigid·us -a -um *adj* rigid, stiff, hard, inflexible; stern, severe; rough, rude; erect *(penis)*

rig·ō -āre *tr* to wet, moisten, water; to conduct, convey *(water)*

rig·or -ōris *m* stiffness; numbness, cold; hardness; sternness

rigu·us -a -um *adj* constantly flowing, irrigating; well-watered, irrigated; ‖ *npl* irrigated areas, flood plain; irrigation ditches

rīm·a -ae *f* crack; chap *(in the skin);* **rimas agere** to cause cracks to develop; **rimas ducere** to develop cracks

rīm·or -ārī -ātus sum *tr* to lay open, tear open; to pry into, search, examine; to search for *(facts);* to rummage about for; to ransack; **naribus rimari** to sniff at; **oculis rimari** to scrutinize

rīmōs·us -a -um *adj* full of cracks; leaky

ringor ringī rictus sum *intr* to open the mouth wide; to show the teeth; to snarl; *(fig)* to be snappy

rīp·a -ae *f* river bank; **aequoris ripa** seashore

Ripae·us -a -um *adj (also* **Rhip-**) of the Rhipean mountains; **mons R(h)ipaeus** legendary mountain range in the extreme north

rīpul·a -ae *f* riverbank

risc·us -ī *m* chest, trunk

rīsion·ēs -um *fpl* laughs

rīs·or -ōris *m* scoffer; teaser

rīs·us -ūs *m* laugh, laughter, smile; laughingstock; **risum contirere** to keep from laughing; **risum movere** *(w. dat)* to make *(s.o.)* laugh; **risūs captare** to try to make people laugh, try to get a laugh

rīte *adv* according to religious usage; duly, justly, rightly, fitly; in the usual way, customarily

rīt·us -ūs *m* rite, ceremony; custom, habit, way, manner, style; **ritū** *(w. gen)* in the manner of, like; **pecudum ritū** like cattle

rīvāl·is -is *m* one who uses the same stream, neighbor; one who uses the same mistress, rival

rīvālit·ās -ātis *f* rivalry

rīvul·us *or* **rīvol·us -ī** *m* brook

rīv·us -ī *m* brook, stream; artificial watercourse, channel; flow *(of water in the aqueducts)*

rix·a -ae *f* brawl, fight; squabble

rix·or -ārī -ātus sum *intr* to brawl, come to blows, fight; to squabble

rōbīginōs·us -a -um *adj* **(rub-)** rusty; envious

rōbīg·ō -inis *f* rust; blight, mildew; film *(on teeth),* tartar

rōbore·us -a -um *adj* **(-bur-)** oak-

rōbor·ō -āre -āvī -ātus *tr* to strengthen

rōb·ur *or* **rob·us -oris** *n* hardwood; oak; prison *(at Rome, also called Tullianum);* objects made of hardwood: lance, club, bench; physical strength, power, toughness; power *(of mind);* best part, flower, choice, cream, élite; stronghold

rōb·us -a -um *adj* red

rōbust·us -a -um *adj* hardwood; oak; robust, strong, tough *(body);* firm, solid *(character)*

rō·dō -děre -sī -sus *tr* to gnaw, gnaw at; to rust, corrode; to say nasty things about, slander, run down

rogāl·is -is -e *adj* of a funeral pyre

rogāti·ō -ōnis *f* proposal, bill *(in the Roman assembly);* request, invitation; *(rhet)* question; **rogationem ferre** to introduce a bill; **rogationem perferre** to pass a bill; **rogationem suadere** to back, push, *or* speak in favor of a bill; **rogationi intercedere** to veto a bill

rogātiuncul·a -ae *f* inconsequential bill; minor question

rogāt·or -ōris *m* proposer *(of a bill to the Roman assembly);* poll clerk *(who collects and counts votes);* beggar

rogāt·us -ūs *m* request

rogitāti·ō -ōnis *f (pol)* bill

rogit·ō -āre -āvī -ātus *tr* to keep asking (for)

rog·ō -āre -āvī -ātus *tr* to ask, ask for, beg, request; to question; to invite; to nominate for election; to bring forward for approval, introduce, propose *(bill); (w. double acc)* to ask *(s.o. for s.th.);* **legem rogare** to introduce a bill; **milites sacramento rogare** to swear in soldiers; **senatorem sententiam rogare** to ask a senator for his opinion, ask a senator how he votes; **sententias rogare** to call the roll *(in the Senate);* **populum rogare** to ask the people about a bill, to propose *or* introduce a bill; **primus sententiam rogari** to have the honor of being the first *(senator)* to be asked his view, be the first to vote

rog·us -ī *m or* **rog·um -ī** *n* funeral pyre; *(fig)* grave, destruction

Rōm·a -ae *f* Rome; Roma *(goddess of Rome)*

Rōmān·us -a -um *adj* Roman ‖ *mpl* Romans

Rōmule·us -a -um *adj* of Romulus; Roman

Rōmulid·ae -ārum *mpl* descendants of Romulus, Romans

Rōmul·us -a -um *adj* of Romulus; Roman ‖ *m* Romulus *(son of Rhea Silvia and Mars, twin brother of Remus, and founder as well as first king of Rome)*

rōrāri·ī -ōrum *mpl* skirmishers *(light-armed Roman troops who usually initiate an attack and then withdraw)*

rōrid·us -a -um *adj* dewy

rōrif·er -era -erum *adj* dewy, dew-bringing

rōr·ō -āre -āvī -ātus *tr* to drip, trickle, pour drop by drop; to moisten ‖ *intr* to drop dew, scatter dew

rōs rōris *m* dew; moisture; spray; water; teardrop; **ros Arabus** perfume; **ros marinus** *(or* **maris)** rosemary *(see* **rosmarinum);** **rores pluvii** drizzle; **rores sanguinei** drops of blood

ros·a -ae *f* rose; rosebush; rose bed; wreath of roses

rosāce·us -a -um *adj (crown)* of roses; **oleum rosaceum** rose oil

rosār·ium -(i)ī *n* rose garden

roscid·us -a -um *adj* wet with dew; consisting of dew; dewy *(conditions; as epithet of the moon, stars, associated with dew);* moistened, sprayed

Rosc·ius -(i)ī *m* Lucius Roscius Otho *(Cicero's friend, whose law in 67 B.C. reserved 14 rows of seats in the theater for members of the equestrian order)* ‖ Quintus Roscius *(famous Roman actor and friend of Cicero, d. 62 B.C.)* ‖ Sextus Roscius *(of Ameria, defended by Cicero in a patricide trial in 80 B.C.)*

Rōse·a -ae *f* low-lying district between Reate and the Veline Lake

rosēt·um -ī *n* rose bed, rose garden

rose·us -a -um *adj* made of roses; rose-colored *(covering a wide range of reds);* rosy, pink *(dawn, sunset, cheeks, skin)*

Rōse·us -a -um *adj* of Rosea

rosmarīn·um -ī *n* rosemary *(shrub used in medicines, in perfumes, and as a seasoning)*

rostell·um -ī *n* little beak; pointed nose *(of a rodent)*

rostrāt·us -a -um *adj* beaked; *(ship)* having a pointed bow; **columna rostrata** column adorned with the beaks of conquered vessels to commemorate a naval victory; **corona rostrata** navy medal *(awarded to the first man to board an enemy ship)*

rostr·um -ī *n* bill, beak; snout, muzzle; curved bow *(of ship)* ‖ *npl* rostrum *(in the Roman Forum, so called because it was adorned with the beaks of ships taken from the battle of Antium, 338 B.C.)*; **pro rostris orationem habere** to give a speech from the rostrum

rōsus *pp of* **rodo**

rot·a -ae *f* wheel; potter's wheel; torture wheel; mill wheel; magic wheel; child's hoop; disk *(of a heavenly body)*; chariot, car *(of sun, moon, time)*; **aquarum rota** water wheel

rot·ō -āre -āvī -ātus *tr* to turn, whirl about ‖ *pass* to roll around; to revolve

rotul·a -ae *f* little wheel

rotundē *adv* smoothly, elegantly

rotundit·ās -ātis *f* roundness

rotund·ō -āre -āvī -ātus *tr* to make round; *(fig)* round off *(numbers)*

rotund·us -a -um *adj* rolling, revolving; round, circular, spherical; rounded, perfect; well-turned, smooth, polished *(style)*

rube·faciō -facĕre -fēcī -factus *tr* to make red, redden

rebell·us -a -um *adj* reddish

rub·ens -entis *adj* red; blushing

rub·eō -ēre *intr* to be red, be ruddy; to be bloody; to blush

ru·ber -bra -brum *adj* red *(including shades of orange)*; ruddy; **Saxa Rubra** village on the Via Flaminia N. of Rome; **Mare Rubrum** Red Sea

rub·escō -escĕre -uī *intr* to get red, redden; to blush

rubēt·a -ae *f* toad

rūbet·a -ōrum *npl* bramble bushes, thicket of brambles

rube·us -a -um *adj* bramble, of brambles

Rubic·ō(n) -ōnis *m* Rubicon *(small stream marking the boundary between Italy and Cisalpine Gaul)*

rubicundul·us -a -um *adj* reddish

rubicund·us -a -um *adj* red, reddish; ruddy, flushed *(complexion)*

rubid·us -a -um *adj* red; ruddy

rūbīg- = robig-

rub·or -ōris *m* redness; blush; bashfulness, sense of shame; shame, disgrace

rubrīc·a -ae *f* red clay; red ochre; red chalk; chapter heading *(of book of law, painted red)*

rub·us -ī *m* bramble bush; blackberry bush; blackberry

ructātr·ix -īcis *adj (fem only) (of foods)* that causes belching

ruct·ō -āre -āvī -ātus *or* **ruct·or -ārī -ātus sum** *tr & intr* to belch

ruct·us -ūs *m* belch, belching

rud·ens -entis *m* rope ‖ *mpl* rigging

Rudi·ae -ārum *fpl* town in Calabria in S. Italy *(birthplace of Ennius)*

rudiār·ius -(i)ī *m* retired gladiator

rudīment·um -ī *n* first attempt, beginning; early training; **rudimentum adulescentiae ponere** to pass the beginning of his youth; **rudimentum militare** basic training ‖ *npl* first lessons; fruits of one's early training

Rudīn·us -ā -um *adj* of Rudiae

rud·is -is *f* stick; rod; practice sword; wooden sword *(presented to a retiring gladiator)*

rud·is -is -e *adj* in the natural state; raw, undeveloped, rough, wild, unformed; inexperienced, unskilled, ignorant; uncultured, uncivilized; unsophisticated; *(of land)* not yet cultivated, virgin; *(of wool)* uncombed; *(of artefacts)* crude, roughly fashioned; *(of movement)* awkward, clumsy; *(of fruit)* unripe; *(of animals)* unbroken; *(of recruits)* raw; *(of literary works)* crude, unpolished, rough; *(w. gen or abl, w.* **ad** *+ acc or* **in** *+ abl)* inexperienced in, ignorant of, awkward at

rud·ō -ĕre -īvī -ītum *intr* (**rūd-**) to roar, bellow; *(of a donkey)* to bray; *(of inanimate things)* to creak loudly

rud·or -ōris *m* roar, bellow

rūd·us -eris *n* crushed stone; rubble; piece of brass

rūful·us -a -um *adj* reddish

Rūful·ī -ōrum *mpl* military tribunes appointed by a general *(as opposed to military tribunes elected by the people)*

rūf·us -a -um *adj* red; red-haired ‖ **Rufus** *m* frequent Roman family name

rūg·a -ae *f* wrinkle; crease, small fold; shallow groove

rūg·iō -īre *intr* to bellow, roar

rūg·ō -āre *intr* to become wrinkled, become creased

rūgōs·us -a -um *adj* wrinkled, shriveled; corrugated

ruīn·a -ae *f* tumbling down, fall; collapse; debris, ruins; crash; catastrophe, disaster, destruction; defeat; wrecker, destroyer; *(fig)* downfall, ruin; *(fig)* source of ruin *or* destruction; **ruinam dare** *(or* **trahere**) to fall with a crash

ruīnōs·us -a -um *adj* liable to ruin, going to ruin, tumbling; ruined, dilapidated

Rull·us -ī *m* Roman family name *(cognomen) (esp.* Publius Servilius Rullus, whose agrarian bill was defeated by Cicero in 63 B.C.)

rum·ex -icis *mf* sorrel *(grown as a vegetable, used in salads)*
rūmific·ō -āre *tr* to report
rūmifer·ō -āre *tr* to carry reports of
Rūmīn·a -ae *f* Roman goddess who was worshiped near the fig tree under which the she-wolf had suckled Romulus and Remus
Rūmīnāl·is -is -e *adj* **ficus Ruminalis** fig tree of Romulus and Remus
rūminātī·ō -ōnis *f* chewing of the cud; *(fig)* rumination, thinking over
rūmīn·ō -āre -āvī -ātus *tr* to chew again ‖ *intr* to chew the cud
rūm·or -ōris *m* rumor, hearsay; shouting, cheering, noise; popular opinion, current opinion; reputation, fame; notoriety; calumny; **adverso rumore esse** to be in bad repute, be unpopular
rumpi·a -ae *f* long Thracian javelin
rumpō rumpĕre rūpī ruptus *tr* to break, break down, break open; to burst, burst through; to tear, split; to cause to snap; to tear, rend *(hair, clothes);* to cause *(s.th.)* to break; to force, make *(e.g., a path)* by force; to break in on, interrupt, cut short; to break, violate *(a law, treaty);* to break out in, utter *(complaints, etc.);* **amores rumpere** to break off a love affair; **nuptias rumpere** to annul a marriage; **silentium** *(or* **silentia) rumpere** to break silence ‖ *refl & pass* to burst forth, erupt
rūmuscul·ī -ōrum *mpl* gossip
rūn·a -ae *f* dart
runc·ō -āre -āvī -ātus *tr* to weed, weed out
ru·ō -ĕre -ī -tus *tr* to throw down, hurl to the ground; to level *(e.g,, sand dunes);* to destroy, overthrow, lay waste; to sweep headlong; to upturn, churn up ‖ *intr* to dash, rush, hurry; *(of vehicles)* to go fast; *(of buildings)* to fall down, collapse; *(of fortunes)* to go to ruin; *(of rain)* to come pouring down; *(of the sun)* to set rapidly; *(w.* **in** *+ acc)* **1** to charge, swoop down on; **2** to proceed with haste *or* impatience to *(an action);* **curru in bella ruere** to go into battle on the double
rūp·ēs -is *f* cliff
rupt·or -ōris *m* breaker, violator
ruptus *pp of* **rumpo**
rūricol·a -ae *mf* rustic, peasant ‖ *m* ox
rūrigĕn·a -ae *m* one born in the country, farmer
rūr·ō -āre *intr* to live in the country
rursus *or* **rursum** *or* **rūsum** *adv* back, backwards; on the contrary, on the other hand; in turn; again, a second time; *(in the direction from which one has come)* back again; once more; **rursus rursusque** again and again; **rursum prorsum** *(or* **rursus (ac) prorsus)** back and forth, backward and forward
rūs rūris *n* the country, countryside, lands, fields; farm, estate; **rure redire** to return from the country; **ruri** in the country; **ruri** *(or* **rure) vitam agere** to live in the country; **rus ire** to go into the country ‖ *npl* countryside
rusc·um -ī *n or* **rusc·us -ī** *m* broom *(of twigs)*
russāt·us -a -um *adj* red, ruddy; clothed in red
russ·us -a -um *adj* red, russet; red-haired
rustic·a -ae *f* country girl
rusticān·us -a -um *adj* rustic, country, rural
rusticātī·ō -ōnis *f* country life
rusticē *adv* like a farmer; plainly, simply; boorishly
rusticit·ās -ātis *f* simple country ways, rusticity; boorishness, coarseness
rustic·or -ārī -ātus sum *intr* to live in the country
rusticul·us -a -um *adj* of the country, in the country, rural; plain, simple, unspoiled, unsophisticated; coarse, boorish ‖ *m* farmer ‖ *f* country girl
rūstic·us -a -um *adj* of the country, rural, rustic, country-; plain, simple, provincial, rough, gross, awkward, prudish ‖ *m* rustic; *(pej)* hick ‖ *f* country girl
rūsum *see* **rursus**
rūt·a -ae *f* rue *(bitter herb);* bitterness, unpleasantness
rūt·a -ōrum *npl* minerals; **ruta caesa** *(or* **ruta et caesa)** *(leg)* everything mined *or* cut down on an estate, timber and minerals
rutābul·um -ī *n* spatula; poker *(instrument with flattened end)*
rūtāt·us -a -um *adj* flavored with rue *(a bitter herb);* bitter
rutil·ō -āre -āvī -ātus *tr* to make red, color red, dye red ‖ *intr* to glow red
rutil·us -a -um *adj* red, reddish yellow; strawberry-blond
rutr·um -ī *n* shovel
rūtul·a -ae *f* a bit of rue *(bitter herb)*
Rutul·ī -ōrum *mpl* ancient people of Latium whose capital was Ardea
rutus *pp of* **ruo**

S

Sab·a -ae *f* town in Arabia Felix, famous for its incense
Sabae·us -a -um *adj* Sabaean, of the Sabaeans *(people of S.W. Arabia)* ‖ *f* Sabaea *(country of the Sabaeans, modern Yemen)*
Sabāz·ius -(i)ī *m* Bacchus ‖ *npl* festival in honor of Bacchus
sabbat·a -ōrum *npl* Sabbath

sabbatāri·a -ae *f* Sabbath-keeper *(i.e., Jewish woman)*
Sabell·us -a -um *adj* Sabellian, Sabine ‖ *m* Sabine *(i.e., Horace)*
Sabīn·us -a -um *adj* Sabine; **herba Sabina** *(bot)* savin *(a juniper, used to produce a drug)*; **oleum Sabinum** oil derived from savin ‖ *m* Roman family name *(cognomen) (e.g.,* Flavius Sabinus, the father of the Emperor Vespasian) ‖ *mpl* an ancient people of central Italy ‖ *f* Sabine woman ‖ *n* Sabine wine; Horace's Sabine farm
sabul·um -ī *n or* **sabul·ō -ōnis** *m* gravel, coarse sand
saburr·a -ae *f* gravel; ballast
saburr·ō -āre -āvī -ātus *tr* to ballast; *(coll)* to gorge with food
Sac·ae -ārum *mpl* (**Sag-**) Scythian tribe
sacciper·ium -(i)ī *n* purse
sacc·ō -āre -āvī -ātus *tr* to filter, strain
saccō -ōnis *m (pej) (of a rich person)* moneybags
saccul·us -ī *m* little bag; pouch
sacc·us -ī *m* sack, bag; pouch; bag for straining liquids, strainer
sacell·um -ī *n* chapel, shrine
sa·cer -cra -crum *adj* sacred, holy, consecrated; devoted to a deity for destruction, accursed; detestable; criminal, infamous ‖ *n see* **sacrum**
sacerd·ōs -ōtis *m* priest ‖ *f* priestess
sacerdōtāl·is -is -e *adj* priestly
sacerdōt·ium -(i)ī *n* priesthood
sacrāment·um -ī *n* guarantee, deposit *(sum of money which each of the parties to a lawsuit deposits and which is forfeited by the loser)*; civil lawsuit; dispute; oath; voluntary oath of recruits; military oath; **eum obligare militiae sacramento** to swear him into the army; **justis sacramentis contendere** to argue on equal terms; **omnes sacramento adigere** *(or* **rogare**) *(mil)* to swear them all in; **sacramentum dicere** *(mil)* to sign up; **sacramentum dicere** *(w. dat)* to swear allegiance to
Sacrān·us -a -um *adj* of the Sacrani *(a people from Reate in Italy)*
sacrār·ium -(i)ī *n* shrine, chapel; sacristy
sacrāt·us -a -um *adj* hallowed, consecrated, holy, sacred
sacrif·er -era -erum *adj* carrying sacred objects
sacrificāl·is -is -e *adj* sacrificial
sacrificāti·ō -ōnis *f* sacrificing
sacrific·ium -(i)ī *n* sacrifice; **sacrificium facere** *(or* **perpetrare**) *(w. dat)* to offer a sacrifice to
sacrific·ō -āre -āvī -ātus *tr & intr* to sacrifice
sacrificul·us -ī *m* sacrificing priest
sacrific·us -a -um *adj* sacrificial
sacrileg·ium -(i)ī *n* sacrilege; temple robbing
sacrilĕg·us -a -um *adj* sacrilegious; profane, impious, wicked ‖ *m* temple robber; wicked person ‖ *f* impious woman
sacr·ō -āre -āvī -ātus *tr* to consecrate; to dedicate; to set apart, devote, give; to doom, curse; to hallow, declare inviolable; to hold sacred, worship; to immortalize
sacrōsanct·us -a -um *adj* sacred, inviolable, sacrosanct
sacr·um -ī *n* holy object, sacred vessel; holy place, temple, sanctuary; religious rite, act of worship, religious service; festival; sacrifice; victim ‖ *npl* worship, religion; secret, mystery; inviolability; **sacra facere** to sacrifice; **sine sacris hereditatis** *(fig)* godsend, windfall
saeclum *see* **saeculum**
saec(u)lār·is -is -e *adj* (**sēc-**) centennial
saec(u)l·um -ī *n* (**sēc-**) generation, lifetime; century; spirit of the age, fashion
saepe *adv* often
saepenumerō *or* **saepe numerō** *adv* oftentimes, on many occasions
saep·ēs -is *f* (**sēp-**) hedge, fence, enclosure
saepiculā *adv* often
saepīment·um -ī *n* (**sēp-**) hedge, fence, enclosure
saep·iō -īre -sī -tus *tr* (**sēp-**) to fence in, hedge in, enclose; to surround, encircle; to guard, fortify, protect, strengthen
saepissim·us -a -um *adj* very frequent
saepsī *perf of* **saepio**
saept·um -ī *n* (**sēp-**) fence, wall, enclosure; stake; sheepfold; voting booth ‖ *npl* enclosure; voting booths, polls
saeptus *pp of* **saepio**
saet·a -ae *f* (**sēt-**) bristle, stiff hair
saetig·er -era -erum *adj* (**sēt-**) bristly ‖ *m* wild boar
saetōs·us -a -um *adj* (**sēt-**) shaggy, bristly
saevē *adv* savagely, fiercely
saevidic·us -a -um *adj* spoken in anger
saev·iō -īre -iī -ītum *intr* to be fierce, be savage, be furious; *(of persons)* to be brutal, be violent
saeviter *adv* savagely, cruelly
saeviti·a -ae *f* rage, fierceness; brutality, savageness *(of persons)*
saevitūd·ō -inis *f* savageness
saev·us -a -um *adj* raging, fierce, cruel; brutal, savage, barbarous
sāg·a -ae *f* witch; wise woman
sagācit·ās -ātis *f* sagacity, shrewdness; keenness
sagāciter *adv* keenly, with keen scent *or* sight; with insight
Sagan·a -ae *f* name of a witch
Sagar·is -is *m* river flowing from Phyrgia into the Black Sea ‖ fictitous name of a Trojan

Sagarīt·is -idis *f* nymph, daughter of the river Sagaris, loved by Attis

sagāt·us -a -um *adj* wearing a military cloak

sag·ax -ācis *adj* keen-scented; sharp, preceptive *(mind)*

sagīn·a -ae *f* stuffing, fattening up; food, rations; rich food; fattened animal; fatness *(from overeating)*

sagīn·ō -āre -āvī -ātus *tr* to fatten

sāg·iō -īre *tr* to perceive quickly

sagitt·a -ae *f* arrow ‖ **Sagitta** *(astr)* Sagitta *(constellation);* an arrow in the constellation Sagittarius

sagittāri·us -a -um *adj* of *or* for an arrow ‖ *m* archer ‖ **Sagittārius** *m (astr)* Sagittarius *(constellation)*

sagittāt·us -a -um *adj* barbed

sagittif·er -era -erum *adj* carrying an arrow

Sagittipot·ens -entis *m (astr)* Sagittarius *(constellation)*

sagm·en -inis *n* tuft of sacred herbs *(plucked in the Capitol by the consul or praetor and worn by the Fetiales as a sign of inviolability)*

sagulāt·us -a -um *adj* wearing a military coat ‖ *m* soldier

sagul·um -ī *n* short military coat *(esp. that of general officers)*

sag·um -ī *n* coarse mantle; military uniform; **ad sagum ire** *(or* **sagum sumere)** to get into uniform; **in sagis esse** to be in uniform, to go to war

Saguntīn·us -a -um *adj & m* Saguntine

Sagunt·um -ī *n or* **Sagunt·us** *or* **Sagunt·os -ī** *f* Saguntum *(city on E. coast of Spain (modern Sagunto), which Hannibal attacked thus bringing on the First Punic War)*

sāl salis *m (n)* salt; salt water, sea; seasoning; flavor; good taste, elegance; pungency *(of words);* wit, humor, sarcasm ‖ *mpl* wisecracks

Salaci·a -ae *f* a sea goddess

salac·ō -ōnis *m* show-off, braggart

salamandr·a -ae *f* salamander

Salamīni·us -a -um *adj* of Salamis ‖ *mpl* people of Salamis

Salam·is -īnos *or* **-īnis** *(acc:* **Salamīna;** *(abl:* **Salamīne)** *f* island in the Saronic Gulf near Athens, opposite Eleusis ‖ city in Cyprus

Sal(a)pi·a -ae *f* port in N. Apulia

salapūt·ium -(i)ī *n* midget

Salāri·a -ae *f* Via Salaria *(from Porta Collina to the Sabine district)*

salāri·us -a -um *adj* salt, of salt; **annona salaria** revenue from salt works; **Via Salaria** Salt Road *(from the Porta Collina to the Sabine district)* ‖ *m* saltfish dealer ‖ *n* salary, allowance *(originally the allowance given to soldiers for salt); (fig)* meal

sal·ax -ācis *adj* lustful; salacious, provocative

salebr·a -ae *f* jolting; rut; roughness *(of speech)*

salebrōs·us -a -um *adj* rough, uneven

Sālentīn·ī -ōrum *mpl* **(Sall-)** a people who occupied the S.E. extremity of Italy

Salern·um -ī *n* town on the Campanian coast S.E. of Naples *(modern Salerno)*

Saliār·is -is -e *adj* Salian, of the Salii; sumptuous

Saliāt·us -ūs *m* Salian priesthood

salict·um -ī *n* willow grove

salient·ēs -ium *fpl* springs, fountains

salign·us -a -um *adj* willow

Sali·ī -ōrum *mpl* college of twelve priests dedicated to Mars who went in solemn procession through Rome on the Kalends of March

salill·um -ī *n* small salt shaker

salīn·ae -ārum *fpl* salt pits, salt works; **salinae Romanae** salt works at Ostia *(a state monopoly)*

salīn·um -ī *n* salt shaker

sal·iō -īre -uī *or* **-iī -tum** *tr (of an animal)* to mount ‖ *intr* to jump, leap, hop

Salisubsal(i)·ī -ōrum *mpl* dancing priests of Mars

saliunc·a -ae *f* wild nard *(aromatic plant)*

Sal·ius -(i)ī *m* priest of Mars *(see* **Salii)**

salīv·a -ae *f* saliva; taste, flavor

sal·ix -icis *f* willow tree

Sallentīnī *see* **Salentini**

Sallustiān·us -a -um *adj* of Sallust; **horti Sallustiani** park in the N. part of Rome owned by Sallust ‖ *m* imitator of Sallust's style ‖ *n* a Sallustian expression

Sallust·ius -(i)ī *m* Sallust *(Gaius Sallustius Crispus, Roman historian, 86–34 B.C.)* ‖ Gaius Sallustius Crispus *(his great-nephew and adopted son, an advisor to Agustus and Tiberius, d. A.D. 20)*

Salmac·is -idis *f* fountain at Halicarnassus on the W. coast of Asia Minor, which made all who drank from it soft and effeminate

Salmōn·eūs -eī *m* son of Aeolus who imitated lightning and was thrown by Jupiter into Tartarus

Salmōn·is -idis *or* **-idos** *f* Tyro *(daughter of Salmoneus)*

Sal·ō -ōnis *f* tributary of the River Ebro *(modern Jalon)*

Salōn·ae -ārum *fpl* city on the Illyrian coast *(near modern Split)*

salp·a -ae *f* saupe *(type of fish)*

salsāment·um -ī *n (usu. pl)* salted food *(esp. fish)*

salsē *adv* facetiously, humorously

salsipot·ens -entis *adj* ruling the sea

salsūr·a -ae *f* (process of) pickling

sals·us -a -um *adj* salted; briny, salty;

facetious, humorous, witty ‖ *npl* salty food; witty remarks, satirical writings

saltāti·ō -ōnis *f* dancing, dance

saltāt·or -ōris *m* dancer

saltātōri·us -a -um *adj* dance-, for dancing

saltātr·ix -īcis *f* dancing girl

saltāt·us -ūs *m* dance

saltem *adv* at least, in any event, anyhow; **non** *(or* **neque)** **saltem** not even

salt·ō -āre -āvī -ātus *tr & intr* to dance

saltuōs·us -a -um *adj* wooded, covered with forest

salt·us -ūs *m* defile, pass; wooded pasture; opening in the woods, glade; forest; jungle; ravine; *(vulg)* female pudenda

salt·us -ūs *m* jump, leap; *(fig)* step, stage; **saltum dare** to leap

salū·ber *or* **salū·bris -bris -bre** *adj* healthful, healthy, wholesome; *(w. dat or* **ad)** good for, beneficial to

salūbrit·ās -ātis *f* healthiness, wholesomeness; health, soundness

salūbriter *adv* healthfully; healthily; beneficially; **emere salubriter** to buy cheaply

saluī *pref of* **saliō**

sal·um -ī *n* billow; sea in motion; high seas; **aerumnoso navigare salo** *(poet)* to sail a sea of troubles; **tirones salo nauseāque confecti** recruits, hit hard by seasickness

sal·ūs -ūtis *f* health; welfare; prosperity; safety; greeting, best regards; **salutem dicere** *(abbr:* **s.d.)** to send greetings; *(at end of letter)* to say goodbye; **salutem magnam dicere** *(w. dat)* to send warm greetings to, bid fond farewell to, say goodbye to; **salutem plurimam dicere** *(abbr:* **s.p.d)** to send warmest greetings; *(at end of letter)* to give best regards

salūtār·is -is -e *adj* salutary, healthful, wholesome; beneficial, advantageous, useful; *(w.* **ad)** good for, beneficial for; *(w. dat)* beneficial to; **ars salutaris** art of healing; **salutaris littera** vote of acquittal *(letter* **A** *for* **Absolvo)**

salūtāriter *adv* beneficially

salūtāti·ō -ōnis *f* greeting, salutation; formal morning reception at the house of an important person; callers; **ubi salutatio defluxit** when morning callers have dispersed

salūtāt·or -ōris *m,* **salūtātr·ix -īcis** *f* morning caller

salūtif·er -era -erum *adj* health-giving

salūtigerul·us -a -um *adj* bringing greetings

salūt·ō -āre -āvī -ātus *tr* to greet, wish well; to send greetings to; to pay respects to, pay a morning call on; to pay reverence to *(gods);* to welcome; *(w. double acc)* to hail as

salvē *adv* well; in good health; **saltine** *(or* **satisne) salve?** *(supply* **agis** *or* **agit** *or* **agitur)** *(coll)* everything O.K.?

salv·eō -ēre *intr* to be well, be in good health; to be getting along well; **salve, salvete** *(or* **salveto)!** hello!, good morning!, good day!; goodbye!; **salvebis a meo Cicerone** my son Cicero wishes to be remembered to you; **te salvere jubeo** I bid you good day; **vale, salve** goodbye

salv·us -a -um *adj* well, sound, safe, unharmed; living, alive; *(w. noun or pronoun in an abl absolute)* without violation of, without breaking, *e.g.,* **salvā lege** without breaking the law; **salvos sum** *(coll)* I'm O.K.

Samae·ī -ōrum *mpl* inhabitants of Cephallenia

sambūc·a -ae *f* triangular stringed instrument, small harp

sambūcistri·a -ae *f* harpist *(female)*

Sam·ē -ēs *or (less frequently)* **Sam·os -ī** *f* ancient name of the island of Cephallenia

Samiol·us -a -um *adj* of Samian ware

Sami·us -a -um *adj* of Samos, Samian; **Juno Samia** Juno worshiped at Samos; **testa Samia** Samian potsherd *(noted for its thinness);* **vir Samius** Pythagoras ‖ *mpl* Samians ‖ *npl* delicate Samian pottery

Samn·īs -ītis *adj* Samnite ‖ *m* gladiator armed with Samnite weapons ‖ *mpl* the Samnites

Samn·ium -(i)ī *n* country of central Italy, whose inhabitants were the offshoot of the Sabines

Sam·os *or* **Sam·us -ī** *(acc:* **-um** *or* **-on)** *f* an island off the W. coast of Asia Minor, famous as the birthplace of Pythagoras ‖ *see* **Same**

Samothrāc·a -ae *f* Samothrace *(island off the Thracian coast)*

Samothrāc·es -um *mpl* Samothracians

Samothrāci·us -a -um *adj* Samothracian ‖ *f* Samothrace *(island in N. Aegean Sea)*

sam(p)s·a -ae *f* crushed olive

sānābil·is -is -e *adj* curable

sānāti·ō -ōnis *f* healing, curing

san·ciō -cīre -xi -ctus *tr* to fulfill *(a threat, prophecy);* to ratify *(laws, agreements, treaties);* to enact *(a law);* to sanction *(a policy, practice);* to confirm the possession of *(property);* to condemn; *(w. abl of the penalty)* to make *(an offense, a person)* punishable by law with; **Solon capite sanxit qui in seditione non alterius utrius partis fuisset** Solon condemned to death anyone who did not side with one party or the other in a revolution

sanctē *adv* solemnly, reverently, religiously, conscientiously, purely

sanctimōni·a -ae *f* sanctity, sacredness; chastity

sancti·ō -ōnis *f* consecration; sanctioning; penalty clause *(that part of the law that provided for penalties against those breaking that law),* sanction

sanctit·ās -ātis *f* sanctity, sacredness, inviolability; integrity; purity

sanctitūd·ō -inis *f* sanctity

sanct·or -ōris *m* enactor *(of laws)*

sanct·us -a -um *adj* consecrated, hallowed, sacred, inviolable, holy; venerable, august, divine; chaste

Sanc·us -ī *m* epithet of Semo *(a god of Sabine origin)*

sandaliāri·us -a -um *adj* sandal-maker's; **Apollo Sandaliarius** Apollo of Shoemakers' Street

sandaligerul·ae -ārum *fpl* maids who brought slippers to their mistress

sandal·ium -iī *n* sandal *(one in which the toes were covered; cf.* **solea**)

sandapil·a -ae *f* cheap coffin

sand·yx -ȳcis *f* vermilion, scarlet

sānē *adv* sanely, reasonably, sensibly; certainly, doubtless, truly, very; *(ironically)* of course, naturally; *(w. negatives)* really, at all; *(in concessions)* to be sure, however; *(in answers)* yes, of course; *(w. imperatives)* then; **haud** *(or* **non**) **sane** not very; **nihil sane** absolutely nothing; **sane quam** extremely

sanesc·ō -ĕre *intr* to get well; to heal

Sangari·us -a -um *adj* living near the Sangaris River *(in Phrygia)* ‖ *m* Sangaris River

sanguin·ans -antis *adj* bleeding; bloodthirsty

sanguināri·us -a -um *adj* bloodthirsty

sanguine·us -a -um *adj* bloody, bloodstained; blood-red

sanguinolent·us -a -um *adj* bloody, bloodstained; blood-red; vindictive

sangu·is -inis *m* blood; descent, parentage, family; descendant; murder, bloodshed; *(fig)* lifeblood, source of vitality, life, strength; forcefulness, life, vigor *(of a speech);* **sanguinem dare** to bleed; **sanguinem effundere** *(or* **profundere**) to bleed heavily; **sanguinem haurire** to shed *(s.o.'s)* blood; **sanguinis missio** *(med)* bloodletting; **sanguinem mittere** *(of a physician)* to let blood, bleed

sani·ēs -ēī *f* blood *(from a wound);* gore; foam, froth; venom

sānit·ās -ātis *f* health; sanity; common sense, discretion; solidity, healthy foundation *(for victory, etc.);* soundness, propriety *(of style)*

sann·a -ae *f* mocking grimace, sneer, face

sanni·ō -ōnis *m* clown

sān·ō -āre -āvī -ātus *tr* to cure, heal; to correct, repair; to allay, quiet, relieve

Sanquāl·is -is -e *adj* of Sancus *(Sabine deity);* **Sanqualis avis** osprey

Santon·ī -ōrum *mpl* Gallic tribe N. of the Geronne

Santonic·us -a -um *adj* of the Santoni; **herba** *(or* **virga**) **Santona** wormwood *(bitter aromatic herb used as a tonic)*

Santr·a -ae *m* a grammarian of the time of Varro

sān·us -a -um *adj* sound, hale, healthy; sane, rational, sensible; sober; *(w.* **ab**) free from *(faults, etc.)*

sanxī *perf of* **sancio**

sap·a -ae *f* (distilled) new wine

sāperd·a -ae *m* a fish *(from the Black Sea)*

sapi·ens -entis *adj* wise, sensible, judicious, discreet ‖ *m* sensible person; sage, philosopher; man of discriminating taste, connoisseur; title given to jurisconsults

sapienter *adv* wisely, sensibly

sapienti·a -ae *f* wisdom; common sense; philosophy; knowledge *(of principles, methods),* science

sap·iō -ĕre -īvī *or* **-iī** *tr* to have the flavor of, taste of; to smell like; to understand ‖ *intr* to have the sense of taste; to have sense, be sensible, be discreet, be wise

sāp·ō -ōnis *m* hair dye

sap·or -ōris *m* taste, flavor; delicacy; refinement, sense of taste

Saphh·ō -ūs *f* Greek lyric poetess of Lesbos *(born c. 612 B.C.)*

sarcin·a -ae *f* package, bundle, pack; burden *(of a womb);* sorrow, trouble ‖ *fpl* luggage, gear; movable goods, chattels, belongings

sarcināri·us -a -um *adj* luggage-, of luggage; **jumenta sarcinaria** pack animals

sarcināt·or -ōris *m* patcher, botcher

sarcināt·us -a -um *adj* loaded down

sarcinul·ae -ārum *fpl* small bundles, little trousseau

sar·ciō -cīre -sī -tus *tr* to patch, fix, repair

sarcophag·us -ī *m* stone coffin

sarcul·um -ī *n* garden hoe

Sardanapal(l)·us -ī *m* last king of Assyria *(c. 9th cent.)* whose decadence was legendary

Sard·ēs *or* **Sard·īs -ium** *fpl* Sardis *(capital of Lydia)*

Sardiān·us -a -um *adj* Sardian ‖ *mpl* inhabitants of Sardis

Sardini·a -ae *f* Sardinia

Sardiniens·is -is -e *adj* Sardinian

Sardis *see* **Sardes**

sardon·yx -ychis *or* **-ychos** *m (f)* sardonyx *(precious stone)*

Sardō·us *or* **Sard·us -a -um** *adj & m* Sardinian

sarg·us -ī *m* sar *(fish)*

sar·iō -īre -uī *intr* (**sarr-**) to hoe

sarīs(s)·a -ae *f* long Macedonian lance

sarīs(s)ophor·os -ī *m* Macedonian lancer

Sarmat·ae -ārum *mpl* Sarmatians *(barbarous people of S.E. Russia)*
Sarmati·a -ae *f* Sarmatia
Sarmaticē *adv* Sarmatian, in the Sarmatian language
Sarmatic·us -a -um *adj* Sarmatian
sarment·um -ī *n* brushwood ‖ *npl* twigs, fagots
Sarn·us -ī *n* river in Campania near Paestum *(modern Sarno)*
Sarpēd·ōn -onis *or* **-onos** *m* King of Lycia who was killed by Patroclus at Troy
Sarr·a -ae *f* old name for Tyre
sarrāc·um -ī *n* (serr-) wagon
Sarrān·us -a -um *adj* Tyrian, Phoenician; dyed (Tyrian) purple
sarriō *see* **sario**
sarsī *perf of* **sarcio**
sartāg·ō -inis *f* frying pan; hodgepodge
sart·us *or* **sarct·us -a -um** *pp of* **sarcio** ‖ *adj (occurring only with* **tectus)** in good repair; **aedem Castoris sartam tectam tradere** to hand over the temple of Castor in good repair ‖ *npl* repairs; **sarta tecta exigere** to complete the repairs
sat *indecl adj* enough, sufficient, adequate ‖ *n* enough; **sat agere** *(w. gen)* to have enough of, have one's hands full with
sat *adv* sufficiently, quite; **sat scio** I am quite sure
sat·a -ōrum *npl* crops
sat·agō -agĕre -ēgī *intr* to have trouble enough, have one's hands full
satell·es -itis *mf* bodyguard, attendant, follower; *(pej)* lackey; partisan; *(w. gen)* accomplice in *(crime)*
sati·ās -ātis *f* sufficiency; overabundance, satiety, satisfied desire
Saticul·us -ī *m* inhabitant of Saticula *(Samnite town)*
satiet·ās -ātis *f* sufficiency, adequacy; satiety, weariness, disgust
satin' *or* **satine** *adv* quite, really
sati·ō -āre -āvī -ātus *tr* to satisfy, appease; to avenge; to fill, glut; to saturate; to cloy
sati·ō -ōnis *f* sowing, planting ‖ *fpl* sown fields
satis *or* **sat** *indecl adj* enough, sufficient, adequate ‖ *n* enough; *(leg)* satisfaction, security, guarantee; **satis accipere** to receive a guarantee; **satis dare** *(w. dat)* to give a guarantee to; **satis facere** *(w. dat)* to satisfy; to pay *(a creditor);* to make amends to *(by word or deed),* apologize to; **satis facere** *(w. dat of person and acc & inf)* to satisfy *(s.o.)* with proof that, demonstrate sufficiently to *(s.o.)* that; **satis superque dictum est** more than enough has been said
satis *adv* enough, sufficiently, adequately; **satis bene** pretty well
satisdati·ō -ōnis *f* putting up bail, giving a guarantee
satis·dō -dare -dedī -datum *intr* (also written as two words) see **satis**
satis·faciō -facĕre -fēcī -factus *tr (also written as two words) see* **satis**
satisfacti·ō -ōnis *f* amends, satisfaction; apology, excuse
satius *(comp of* **satis)** *adj (neut only)* **satius est** *(w. inf)* it is better *or* preferable to
sat·or -ōris *m* sower, planter; father; promoter, author
satrapē·a *or* **satrapī·a -ae** *f* satrapy *(office or province of a satrap)*
satrap·ēs *or* **satrap·a -ae** *m* satrap *(provincial governor in the Persian empire)*
sat·ur -ura -urum *adj* full, well-fed, stuffed; plump; fertile; deep *(color)*
satur·a -ae *f* (satir-) dish of mixed ingredients; mixture, hodgepodge; medley, variety show; literary medley of prose and poetry; satire, satirical poem; **in** *(or* **per) saturam** at random; collectively, en block; **per saturam ferre** to propose as a rider to a bill
satureī·a -ōrum *npl* savory *(seasoning)*
saturit·ās -ātis *f* satiety; plenty, overabundance
Sāturnāli·a -ium *npl* festival in honor of Saturn, beginning on the 17th of December and lasting several days; **io Saturnalia!** cry of merrymakers at this festival; **non semper Saturnalia erunt** *(fig)* it won't be Christmas forever
Sāturni·a -ae *f* Juno *(daughter of Saturn)*
Sāturnīn·us -ī *m* Lucius Appuleius Saturninus *(demagogic tribune in 103 and 100 B.C.)*
Sāturni·us -a -um *adj* Saturnian; **Saturnius numerus** Saturnian meter *(archaic Latin meter based on stress accent)* ‖ *m* Jupiter; Pluto
Sāturn·us -ī *m* Saturn *(Italic god of agriculture, equated with the Greek god Cronos, ruler of the Golden Age, and father of Jupiter, Neptune, Juno, and Pluto)*
satur·ō -āre -āvī -ātus *tr* to fill, satisfy, glut, cloy, saturate; to satisfy, content
sat·us -a -um *pp of* sero (to plant) ‖ *npl see* **sata**
sat·us -ūs *m* sowing, planting; begetting; race, stock; seed *(of knowledge)*
satyrisc·us -ī *m* little satyr
satyr·us -ī *m* satyr; satyr play *(in which chorus consisted of satyrs)*
sauciāti·ō -ōnis *f* wounding
sauci·ō -āre -āvī -ātus *tr* to wound
sauci·us -a -um *adj* wounded; *(fig)* smitten, offended, hurt; melted *(snow)* ‖ *mpl* the wounded
sauroctοn·os -ī *m (as title of a statue)* lizard killer
Sauromat·ae -ārum *fpl* Sarmatians *(barbaric tribe of S. Russia)*

sāviāti·ō -ōnis *f* (suav-) kissing
sāviol·um -ī *n* (suav-) little kiss, peck
sāvi·or -ārī -ātus sum *tr* (suav-) to kiss
sāv·ium -(i)ī *n* (suav-) puckered lips; kiss
saxātil·is -is -e *adj* rock-, living among rocks ‖ *m* saxatile *(fish)*
saxēt·um -ī *n* rocky place; stone quarry
saxe·us -a -um *adj* rocky, stony; **umbra saxea** shade of the rocks
saxific·us -a -um *adj* petrifying, changing objects into stone
saxifrag·us -a -um *adj* rock-breaking
saxōs·us -a -um *adj* rocky, stony
saxul·um -ī *n* small rock *or* crag
sax·um -ī *n* boulder, rock; Tarpeian Cliff *(W. side of the Capitoline Hill)*
scabellum *see* **scabillum**
sca·ber -bra -brum *adj* itchy; rough, scurfy
scābī *perf of* **scabo**
scabi·ēs -ēī *f* itch; eczema; *(fig)* itch
scabill·um -ī *n* (-bell-) stool, footstool; castanet tied to the ankle
scabiōs·us -a -um *adj* itchy, mangy; moldy
scabō scabĕre scābī *tr* to scratch
Scae·a port·a -ae *f* Scaean gate *(W. gate of Troy)*
scaen·a -ae *f* (scēn-) stage; backdrop, scenery; scene; *(fig)* public view, publicity; melodramatic behavior; pretense; pretext; canopy *(of forest acting like a backdrop)*; **tibi scenae serviendum est** you must keep yourself in the limelight
scaenicē *adv* (scēn-) like on the stage
scaenic·us -a -um *adj* (scēn-) of the stage, theatrical, scenic; **ludi scaenici** plays
scaev·a -ae *f* favorable omen
Scaevol·a -ae *m* Gaius Mucius Cordus Scaevola *(Roman hero who infiltrated Porsenna's camp to kill Porsenna, and on being discovered, burned off his own right hand)* ‖ Quintus Mucius Scaevola *(consul in 95 B.C. and pontifex maximus)*
scaev·us -a -um *adj* left, on the left; perverse ‖ *f* sign *or* omen appearing on the left *(hence, unfavorable)*
scāl·ae -ārum *fpl* ladder; flight of stairs, stairs
scalm·us -ī *m* oarlock; oar; boat
scalpell·um -ī *n* scalpel
scalptōr·ium -(i)ī *n* back-scratcher
scalptūr·a -ae *f* engraving
scalp·ō -ĕre -sī -tus *tr* to carve; to scratch; to tickle, titillate
scalpr·um -ī *n* chisel; knife; penknife
scalpsī *perf of* **scalpo**
scalpurr·iō -īre *intr* to scratch
Scaman·der -drī *m* river at Troy *(also called Xantus)*
scamb·us -a -um *adj* bowlegged
scammōne·a -ae *f (bot)* scammony *(plant with trumpet-like flowers similar to the morning-glory, used as a laxative)*
scamn·um -ī *n* bench; stool; throne
scan·dō -dĕre -dī *tr* to climb, scale; to climb aboard; to mount ‖ *intr* to climb; *(of buildings)* to rise, tower
scandul·a -ae *f* shingle *(of a roof)*
Scantīni·us -a -um *adj* Roman clan name *(nomen)*; **lex Scantinia** law against unnatural vice
scaph·a -ae *f* light boat, skiff
scaph·ium -iī *n* (scaf-) boat-shaped drinking cup; chamber pot
scapul·ae -ārum *fpl* shoulder blades; shoulders; back
scāp·us -ī *m* shaft *(of a column)*; stalk *(of a plant)*
scarīf·ō -āre *tr* to scratch open
scar·us -ī *m* scar *(fish)*
scatebr·a -ae *f* bubbling spring
scat·eō -ēre -uī *or* **scat·ō -ĕre** *intr* to bubble up, gush out; to teem
scatur(r)īgi·ō -inis *f* spring
scaturr·iō -īre *intr* to bubble, gush; to bubble over with enthusiasm
scaur·us -a -um *adj* clubfooted
scaz·ōn -ontis *m* scazon *(iambic trimeter with a spondee in the last foot)*
scelerātē *adv* criminally, wickedly
scelerāt·us -a -um *adj* profaned, desecrated; outlawed; criminal, wicked, infamous; **campus sceleratus** open field near the Colline gate where unchaste Vestals were buried alive; **vicus sceleratus** street on Esquiline Hill where Tullia, daughter of Servius Tullius, drove over her father's corpse ‖ *m* criminal; rascal
sceler·ō -āre -āvī -ātus *tr* to defile
scelerōs·us -a -um *adj* steeped in wickedness
scelestē *adv* wickedly, criminally
scelest·us -a -um *adj* wicked, villainous, criminal
scel·us -eris *n* wicked deed, crime, wickedness; calamity; criminal
scēn- = scaen-
sceptrif·er -era -erum *adj* sceptered
sceptr·um -ī *n* scepter ‖ *npl* kingship, dominion, authority; kingdom; **sceptra Asiae tenere** to hold sway in Asia
sceptūch·us -ī *m* scepter-bearer *(high officer of state in the East)*
sched·a *or* **scid·a -ae** *f* sheet, page
sc(h)ēm·a -ae *f,* **sc(h)ēm·a -atis** *or* **-atos** *n* figure, form; style; figure of speech
schid·a -ae *f* (scid-) sheet *(of papyrus)*; one of the strips forming a sheet of papyrus
Schoenē·is -idos *f* daughter of Schoeneus, Atalanta
Schoenēi·us -a -um *adj* of Schoeneus ‖ *f* Atalanta
Schoen·eus -eī *m* king of Boeotia and father of Atalanta

schoenobat·ēs -ae *m* tightrope-walker
schoen·us -ī *m* cheap perfume
schol·a -ae *f* school; lecture hall; lecture; learned debate; sect, followers
scholastic·us -a -um *adj* school, scholastic ‖ *m* rhetoric teacher, rhetorician; grammarian
scida *see* **scheda**
scidī *perf of* **scindo**
sci·ens -entis *adj* aware of a fact, cognizant; having full knowledge, with one's eyes wide open; *(w. gen)* cognizant of, familiar with, expert in; *(w. inf)* knowing how to
scienter *adv* wisely, expertly
scienti·a -ae *f* knowledge, skill, expertise; science; *(w.* **de** *or* **in** *+ abl)* expertise in, skill in
sciī *perf of* **scio**
scīlicet *adv* of course, evidently, certainly; *(ironically)* naturally, of course; *(as an explanatory particle)* namely, that is to say
scill·a -ae *f* **(squi-)** squill *(seaside plant of the lily family)*
scīn = scisne, *i.e.,* **scis + ne** do you know?
scindō scindere scidī scissus *tr* to cut, split, tear apart, tear open; to divide, separate; to interrupt
scintill·a -ae *f* spark; speck
scintill·ō -āre *intr* to sparkle, flash
scintillul·a -ae *f* little spark
sciō scīre scīvī *or* **sciī scītus** *tr* to know; to realize, understand; to have skill in; *(w. inf)* to know how to
Scīpiad·ās -ae *m* one of the Scipio family, a Scipio
scīpi·ō -ōnis *m* ceremonial staff *or* baton *(generally made of ivory and carried by persons of rank, such as a seer or a general at his triumph)* ‖ **Scīpiō** family name *(cognomen)* in the famous gens Cornelia ‖ Publius Cornelius Scipio Africanus Major *(victor in the Second Punic War, 236–184 B.C.)* ‖ Publius Cornelius Scipio Aemilianus Africanus Minor *(victor in Third Punic War, c. 185–132 B.C.)*
Scīr·ōn -ōnis *or* **-ōnos** *m* robber who waylaid travelers on the road near Megara *(killed by Theseus)*
s(c)irpe·us -a -um *adj* wicker-, of wicker ‖ *f* wickerwork
s(c)irpicul·a -ae *f* wicker basket
s(c)irpicul·us -ī *m* wicker basket
s(c)irp·us -ī *m* bulrush
sciscitāt·or -ōris *m* interrogator
sciscit·ō -āre *or* **sciscit·or -ārī -ātus sum** *tr* to ask, question, interrogate; to consult; *(w. acc of thing asked and* **ex** *or* **ab** *of person asked)* to ask *(s.th.)* of *(s.o.)*, check on *(s.th.)* with *(s.o.)* ‖ *intr* (w. **de** + *abl)* to ask about
sciscō sciscere scīvī scītus *tr (pol)* to approve, adopt, enact, decree; to learn, ascertain
sciss·or -ōris *m* carver *(person cutting meat at the table)*
scissūr·a -ae *f* crack, cleft
sciss·us -a -um *pp of* **scindo** ‖ *adj* split, rent; furrowed *(cheeks)*; shrill *(voice)*
scītāment·a -ōrum *npl* delicacies, choice tidbits
scītē *adv* expertly
scīt·or -ārī -ātus sum *tr* to ask; to consult *(oracle)*; *(w. acc of thing and* **ab** *or* **ex)** to ask *(s.th.)* of *(s.o.)* ‖ *intr* (w. **de** + *abl)* to ask *or* inquire about
scītul·us -a -um *adj* neat, pretty
scīt·um -ī *n* statute, decree
scīt·us -a -um *adj* experienced, skillful; suitable, proper; judicious, sensible, witty; smart, sharp *(appearance)*; *(w. gen)* skilled in, expert at
scīt·us -ūs *m* decree, enactment
sciūr·us -ī *m* squirrel
scīvī *perf of* **scio** *and of* **scisco**
-sc·ō -ere *vbl suf normally used only in the present system with inchoative force, e.g.,* **lūcescō** to begin to shine
scob·is -is *f* sawdust, scrapings, filings
scom·ber -brī *m* mackerel
scōp·ae -ārum *fpl* broom
Scop·ās -ae *m* Greek sculptor from the island of Paros *(4th cent. B.C.)*
scopulōs·us -a -um *adj* rocky, craggy
scopul·us -ī *m* rock, cliff, crag; promontory; archery target
scorpi·ō -ōnis *or* **scorp·ius** *or* **scorp·ios -(i)ī** *m* scorpion; *(mil)* catapult ‖ **Scorpio** *(astr)* Scorpion *(constellation)*
scortāt·or -ōris *m* a john *(prostitute's customer)*
scorte·us -a -um *adj* leather
scort·ōr -ārī *intr* to associate with prostitutes
scort·um -ī *n* prostitute; sex fiend *(of either sex)*
screāt·us -ūs *m* clearing of the throat
scre·ō -āre *intr* to clear the throat, hawk, hem
scrīb·a -ae *m* clerk, secretary
scrib(i)līt·a -ae *f* cheese cake
scrībō scrībere scripsī scriptus *tr* to write, draw; to write down; to write out, compose; to draw up, draft *(a law, treaty, decree)*; to create *(characters, episodes in a play)*; to lay down in writing, prescribe; to register *(a person)*; to draft *(colonists to a place)*; to name *(in a will)*; to enlist *(soldiers)*; *(w. double acc)* to appoint *(s.o.)* as ‖ *intr* to write
scrīn·ium -(i)ī *n* case for scrolls; letter case; portfolio
scripsī *perf of* **scribo**

scripti·ō -ōnis *f* writing; composition; spelling; wording, text
scriptit·ō -āre -āvī -ātus *tr & intr* to keep writing, write regularly
script·or -ōris *m* writer; scribe, secretary; author; **rerum scriptor** historian
scriptul·a -ōrum *npl* lines on a game board
scriptūr·a -ae *f* writing; composing; written work, composition; tax paid on public pastures; testamentary provision
script·us -a -um *pp of* **scribo** ‖ *n* composition, treatise, work, book; actual text *(of a law, document);* literal meaning, letter *(as opposed to spirit);* **duodecim scripta** a type of game board; **orationem de scripto dicere** to read off a speech; **voluntas legis, non tantum scriptum** the spirit of the law, not only the letter *(of the law)*
scrīpul·um -ī *n* **(script-)** small weight, smallest measure of weight, scruple *(one twenty-fourth of an uncia, or ounce)*
scrob·is -is *mf* ditch, trench; grave
scrōf·a -ae *f* breeding sow
scrōfipasc·us -ī *m* pig breeder
scrūpe·us -a -um *adj* full of sharp rocks, made of jagged rocks, jagged
scrūpōs·us -a -um *adj* full of sharp rocks, jagged, rough
scrūpulōsē *adv* scrupulously, precisely, carefully
scrūpulōs·us -a -um *adj* full of sharp projections of rock, jagged; scrupulous, meticulous, precise
scrūpul·us -ī *m* uneasy feeling, scruple, worry, headache; thorny problem
scrūp·us -ī *m* rough *or* sharp stone; uneasiness
scrūt·a -ōrum *npl* trash, junk
scrūtāt·or -ōris *m* examiner
scrūt·or -ārī -ātus sum *tr* to scrutinize, examine
sculp·ō -ĕre -sī -tus *tr* to carve, chisel, engrave
sculpōne·ae -ārum *fpl* clogs, wooden shoes
sculpsī *perf of* **sculpo**
sculptil·is -is -e *adj* carved, engraved
sculpt·or -ōris *m* sculptor
sculptūr·a -ae *f* carving; sculpture
sculptus *pp of* **sculpo**
scurr·a -ae *m* jester, comedian; city slicker
scurrīl·is -is -e *adj* scurrilous, offensive
scurrīlit·ās -ātis *f* offensive humor, scurrility
scurrīliter *adv* with offensive humor, like a buffoon
scurr·or -ārī *intr* to clown around
scūtāl·e -is *n* thong of a sling
scūtār·ius -(i)ī *m* shield-maker
scūtāt·us -a -um *adj* carrying a shield ‖ *mpl* troops armed with shields
scutell·a -ae *f* saucer, shallow bowl
scutic·a -ae *f* whip
scūtigerul·us -a -um *m* shield-bearer
scutr·a -ae *f* pan, flat dish
scutul·a -ae *f* wooden roller
scutulāt·us -a -um *adj* diamond-shaped ‖ *npl* checkered clothing
scūtul·um -ī *n* small shield
scūt·um -ī *n* oblong shield; *(fig)* shield, defense, protection
Scyll·a -ae *f* female monster on Italian side of Straits of Messina, that snatched and devoured sailors from passing ships ‖ daughter of Nisus who betrayed her father by cutting off his purple lock of hair
Scyllae·us -a -um *adj* Scyllan
scymn·us -ī *m* cub, whelp
scyph·us -ī *m* goblet, cup
Scȳr·os *or* **Scȳr·us -ī** *f* island off Euboea
Scyth·a *or* **Scyth·ēs -ae** *m* Scythian *(member of nomadic tribe N. of the Black Sea)*
Scythi·a -ae *f* country N. of the Black Sea
Scythic·us -a -um *adj* Scythian
Scyth·is -idis *f* Scythian woman
s. d. *abbr* **salutem dicere**
sē *or* **sēsē** *(gen:* **suī;** *dat:* **sibi;** *acc & abl:* **sē** *or* **sēsē** *pron (refl)* himself, herself, itself, themselves; one another; **ad se** *(or* **apud se)** at home; **apud se** in one's senses; **inter se** each other, one another, mutually; **in se** associated with each other, one another, together; **per se** by himself *(herself, etc.),* alone
sē- *pref (also* **sēd-, sŏ-)** *added to verbs, etc.:* **1** *in the sense of "apart", "aside", e.g.:* **seducere** to take aside; **seditio** a going apart, mutiny; **2** *sometimes privative, e.g.:* **socors** lacking in vitality, inactive
sēb·um -ī *n* tallow, grease, suet
sē·cēdō -cēdĕre -cessī -cessum *intr* to withdraw; to depart; to rebel, go on a sit-down strike, secede; **in otium secedere** to retire
sē·cernō -cernĕre -crēvī -crētus *tr* to separate; to dissociate; to distinguish; to reject, set aside
sēcessi·ō -ōnis *f* withdrawal; secession
sēcess·us -ūs *m* retirement, retreat; isolated spot; country retreat
sēclū·dō -dĕre -sī -sus *tr* to shut off, shut up; to shut out; to seclude, bar; to hide
sec·ō -āre -uī -tus *tr* to cut, cut off; to reap; to carve *(meat);* to split up *(in classification);* to cut through, traverse *(e.g., the sea);* to cut short; to settle, decide; to follow, chase; to castrate; *(med)* to cut out, excise, cut off, amputate; **viam secare** to open up a path
sēcrēti·ō -ōnis *f* dividing, separating *(into constituent parts)*
sēcrētō *or* **sēcrētē** *adv* separately, individually, apart; secretly; in private; away from one's companions
sēcrēt·us -a -um *pp of* **secerno** ‖ *adj* sepa-

rate; isolated, solitary; secret; *(w. gen or abl)* deprived of, in need of ‖ *n* secret, mystery; mystic rite, mystic emblem; secret nature *(of a business);* abstruseness *(of a subject);* private conversation *or* interview, audience; isolated spot; **a secreto** (*or* **in secreto** *or* **in secretum**) in private; **secreto in occulto cum aliquo agere** to discuss *(s.th.)* with s.o. in a private conversation; **secretum dare (petere)** to grant (ask for) an audience

sect·a -ae *f* path; way, method, course; school of thought; political party; code of behavior; **secta (vitae)** way of life, occupation

sectāri·us -a -um *adj* followed (by the flock)

sectāt·or -ōris *m* follower, adherent

sectil·is -is -e *adj* cut, divided

secti·ō -ōnis *f* cutting; auctioning off of confiscated property; a buying up of confiscated property in lots; right to confiscated property; things so to be sold, lots

sect·or -ōris *m* speculator in confiscated estates *(one who buys up confiscated property with the intention of reselling);* **sector zonarius** purse-snatcher

sect·or -ārī -ātus sum *tr* to keep following, follow eagerly, run after; to hunt *(game);* to go about searching for; to imitate; to run after *(girls);* to avenge; to follow *(an example, practice);* to go regularly to, frequent; to aim continually at *(an objective)*

sectūr·a -ae *f* incision; stone quarry

sectus *pp of* **seco**

sēcubit·us -ūs *m* sleeping alone

sēcub·ō -āre -uī *intr* to sleep by oneself; to live alone

secuī *perf of* **seco**

sēcul- = saecul-

secund·a -ōrum *npl* success

secund·ae -ārum *fpl (theat)* secondary role in a play; *(fig)* second fiddle

secundān·ī -ōrum *mpl* soldiers of the second legion

secundāri·us -a -um *adj* secondary; second-rate, inferior

secundō *adv* secondly

secund·ō -āre -āvī -ātus *tr* to favor, further; to make *(conditions)* favorable for travel; **secundans ventus** favorable wind, tail wind

secundum *adv* after, behind ‖ *prep (w. acc)* **1** *(of space)* beside, by, along, alongside: **ire secundum me** to walk beside me; **legiones secundum flumen duxit** he led the troops along the river; **2** *(of time)* immediately after: **secundum ludos** immediately after the games; **3** *(in rank or quality)* next to, after: **secundum deos homines hominibus utiles esse possunt** next to the gods, people can be helpful to people; **4** *(of agreement)* according to, in compliance with: **secundum naturam vivere** to live in accordance with nature; **5** *(leg)* in favor of, to the advantage of; **abscentibus secundum praesentes facillime dabat** when a party (to the suit) was absent, he would very readily decide in favor of the party present

secund·us -a -um *adj* following; next, second *(in time; in rank);* backing, favorable, supporting; secondary, subordinate, inferior, second-string; alternate *(heir); (w. dat or* **ab**) second only to; **anno secundo** the next year; **a mensis fine secunda dies** the second-last day of the month; **in secundam aquam** with the current; **res secundae** success, prosperity; **secundae partes** supporting role; **secunda mensa** dessert; **secundo flumine** downstream, with the current; **secundo lumine** on the following day; **secundo mari** with the tide; **secundo populo** with the backing of the people; **secundus panis** stale bread; **secundus ventus** tailwind, fair wind ‖ **Secundus** *m* Roman first name *(praenomen)* ‖ *fpl see* **secundae** ‖ *npl see* **secunda**

sēcūrē *adv* securely, safely

secūricul·a -ae *f* hatchet

secūrif·er -era -erum *adj* carrying an ax, ax-carrying

secūrig·er -era -erum *adj* carrying an ax, ax-wielding

secūr·is -is *f (acc: usu.* **securim**) ax, hatchet; *(fig)* blow, mortal blow; *(fig) (from the ax in the fasces, usu. pl)* power of life and death, supreme authority, sovereignty; **graviorem rei publicae infligere securim** to inflict a more serious blow on the State

sēcūrit·ās -ātis *f* freedom from care, unconcern, composure; freedom from danger, security, safety; false sense of security; carelessness

sēcūr·us -a -um *adj* carefree; secure, safe; cheerful; careless; offhand

secus *indecl n* sex; **secus muliebre** females; **secus virile** males

secus *adv* otherwise, differently; **haud** (*or* **haut** *or* **non**) **secus ac** (*or* **non secus quam**) not otherwise than, just as, exactly as; **haud** (*or* **haut** *or* **non**) **secus si** exactly as if, just as though; **si secus accidet** if it turns out otherwise *(than expected),* if it turns out badly

secūt·or -ōris *m* chaser *(gladiator who fought against the net-man)*

secūtus *pp of* **sequor**

sed *or* **set** *conj* but; but also

sēdātē *adv* sedately, calmly

sēdāti·ō -ōnis *f* calming

sēdāt·us -a -um *adj* calm, composed
sēdecim *indecl adj* sixteen
sēdēcul·a -ae *f* little seat, low stool
sedentāri·us -a -um *adj* sedentary
sedeō sedēre sēdī sessum *intr* to sit, remain seated; *(of magistrates, esp. judge)* to sit, preside, hold court, be a judge; *(of an army)* to remain encamped; to keep the field; to settle down to a blockade; to be idle, be inactive; *(of clothes)* to fit; *(of places)* to be low-lying; to sink, settle; to be firm, be fixed, be established; to stick fast, be stuck; to be determined
sēd·ēs -is *f* seat, chair, throne; residence, home; last home, burial place; base, foundation, bottom
sēdī *perf of* **sedeo**
sedīl·e -is *n* seat, chair **II** *npl* seats in the theater; rowers' benches
sēditi·ō -ōnis *f* sedition, insurrection, mutiny; dissension, quarrel, disagreement; warring *(of elements)*
sēditiōsē *adv* seditously, in mutiny
sēditiōs·us -a -um *adj* seditious, mutinous; quarrelsome; troubled
sēd·ō -āre -āvī -ātus *tr* to calm, settle, still
sēdū·cō -cĕre -xī -ctus *tr* to lead aside, draw aside, lead off, withdraw; to carry off; to lead astray; to put aside; to divide, split
sēducti·ō -ōnis *f* taking aside
sēduct·us -a -um *pp of* **seduco II** *adj* distant, remote
sēdulit·ās -ātis *f* application, earnestness; officiousness
sēdulō *adv* diligently; intentionally
sēdul·us -a -um *adj* diligent, busy; officious
sēduxī *perf of* **seduco**
seg·es -etis *f* grainfield; crop; arable land
Segest·a -ae *f* town in N.W. Sicily
Segestān·us -a -um *adj* of Segesta **II** *mpl* people of Segesta **II** *n* territory of Segesta
segmentāt·us -a -um *adj* trimmed with a flounce *(decorative border)*
segment·um -ī *n* section, segment; trimming, flounce; zone *(of the earth)*
segnip·ēs -edis *adj* slow-footed
segn·is -is -e *adj* slow; inactive; sluggish, lazy
segniter *adv* slowly; lazily
segniti·a -ae *or* **segniti·ēs -ēī** *f* slowness; inactivity; laziness
sēgreg·ō -āre -āvī -ātus *tr* to segregate, separate; to dissociate; **ad sese segregandos a ceteris** for the purpose of dissociating themselves from the rest; **sermonem segregare** to break off a conversation; **suspicionem a se segregare** to ward off suspicion from oneself
Sējāniān·us -a -um *adj* of Sejanus **II** *mpl* partisans of Sejanus
Sējān·us -ī *m* Roman family name *(cognomen) (esp. Lucius Aelius Sejanus, the notorious praetorian prefect under the Emperor Tiberius)*
sējugāt·us -a -um *adj* separated, detached
sējug·is -is *m* six-horse chariot
sējug·ō -āre -āvī -ātus *tr (w.* **ab**) to separate from, detach from
sējunctim *adv* separately
sējuncti·ō -ōnis *f* separation, division
sējun·gō -gĕre -xī -ctus *tr* to separate, part, sever; *(fig)* to sever, part, disconnect; to distinguish
sēlecti·ō -ōnis *f* choice, selection
sēlectus *pp of* **seligo**
sēlēgī *perf of* **seligo**
Seleucī·a -ae *f* name of several towns in Asia
Seleuc·us -ī *m* name of a line of six kings of Syria, whose ancestor, Seleucus Nicator, was a general under Alexander the Great and founded the Syrian monarchy *(c. 358–280 B.C.)*
sēlībr·a -ae *f* half pound
sē·ligō -ligĕre -lēgī -lectus *tr* to select
Selīn·ūs -untis *f* town on the S.W. coast of Sicily **II** town on the coast of Cilicia
sell·a -ae *f* chair, stool *(normally without back or armrests);* portable chair, sedan chair; **sella curulis** magistrate's chair
sellāriol·us -a -um *adj (place)* for sitting *or* lounging
sellār·ius -(i)ī *m* lecher
sellistern·ium -(i)ī *n* sacred banquet in honor of goddesses
sellul·a -ae *f* stool; sedan chair
sellulāri·us -a -um *adj* sedentary; **artifex sellularius** craftsman who sits at his job **II** *mpl* sedentary craftsmen
sēmanimis *see* **semianimis**
semel *adv* once, one time; but once, once and for all; the first time; ever, at some time, at any time; **semel aut iterum** once or twice
Semel·ē -ēs *or* **Semel·a -ae** *f* Semele (*daughter of Cadmus and mother of Bacchus by Jupiter*)
Semelē̆i·us -a -um *adj* of Semele
sēm·en -inis *n* seed; seedling, young plant, shoot: offspring; race, stock; *(in physics)* particle; *(fig)* instigator, root: **semen omnium malorum** root of all evils
sēmenstris *see* **semestris**
sēmentif·er -era -erum *adj* seed-bearing, fruitful
sēment·is -is *f* sowing, planting; young crops; **ut sementem feceris, ita metes** *(prov)* as you sow, so shall you reap
sēmentīv·us -a -um *adj* at seed time, of the sowing season
sēmerm·is -is -e *adj* half-armed
sēmestr·is -is -e *adj* **(-mens-)** for six months, half-yearly, semi-annual
sēmēs·us -a -um *adj* half-eaten

sēmet = *emphatic form of* **se**
sēmi- *pref before nouns and adjectives with the sense of* "half-" *(sometimes* **sēm-** *before vowels, e.g.:* **semesus** half-eaten; **sem(i)animus** half-alive; *also reduced to* **sē-** *e.g.:* **selibra** half pound
sēmiadapert·us -a -um *adj* half-open
sēmianim·is -is -e *or* **sēm(i)anim·us -a -um** *adj* half-dead
sēmiapert·us -a -um *adj* half-open
sēmib·ōs -ōvis *adj (masc only)* half-ox; **semibos vir** the Minotaur
sēmica·per -prī *m (masc only)* half-goat *(i.e., Pan or Faunus)*
sēmicrem(āt)·us -a -um *adj* half-burned
sēmicubitāl·is -is -e *adj* half-cubit long *or* wide
sēmide·us -a -um *adj* semidivine ‖ *m* demigod
sēmidoctus -a -um *adj* half-educated
sēm(i)erm·is -is -e *or* **sēm(i)erm·us -a -um** *adj* half-armed
sēm(i)ēs·us -a -um *adj* half-eaten
sēmifact·us -a -um *adj* half-finished
sēmifer·us -a -um *adj* half-beast; half-savage ‖ *m* centaur
sēmifult·us -a -um *adj* half-propped
sēmigermān·us -a -um *adj* half-German
semigraec·us -a -um *adj* half-Greek
sēmigrav·is -is -e *adj* half-drunk
sēmigr·ō -āre -āvī -ātum *intr* (w. **ab**) to go away from, move away from
sēmihi·ans -antis *adj* half-open
sēmihom·ō -inis *adj (masc only)* half-man, half-beast; subhuman
sēmihōr·a -ae *f* half hour
sēmi·lacer -lacera -lacerum *adj* half-mangled
sēmilaut·us -a -um *adj* half-washed
sēmilīb·er -era -erum *adj* half-free
sēmilix·a -ae *f (pej) (of a commander)* sad sack, little more than a camp follower
sēmi·marīnus -marīna -marīnum *adj* half-submerged
sēmim·ās -aris *adj* half-male, gelded, castrated ‖ *m* hermaphrodite
sēmimortu·us -a -um *adj* half-dead
sēminār·ium -(i)ī *n* nursery garden; *(fig)* breeding ground
sēmināt·or -ōris *m* originator
sēmin·(ex) -ecis *adj* half-killed, half-dead
sēmin·ium -(i)ī *n* breeding; stock
sēmin·ō -āre *tr* to sow; to beget, procreate; to produce
sēminūd·us -a -um *adj* half-naked
sēmipāgān·us -ī *m* little clown
sēmiplēn·us -a -um *adj (forces)* at half-strength; *(ships)* half-manned
sēmiputāt·us -a -um *adj* half-pruned
Semīram·is -idis *f* famous queen of Assyria, builder of Babylon and consort and successor of King Ninus
Semīrami·us -a -um *adj* of Semiramis; Babylonian
sēmirās·us -a -um *adj* half-shaven
sēmireduct·us -a -um *adj* bent back halfway
sēmi·refectus -refecta -refectum *adj* half-repaired
sēm·is -issis *m* half; half an **as** *(small coin);* ½% per month *or* 6% per annum; **non semissis homo** worthless fellow
sēmisen·ex -is *m* elderly gent
sēmisepult·us -a -um *adj* half-buried
sēmisomn·is -is -e *or* **sēmisomn·us -a -um** *adj* half-asleep
sēmisupīn·us -a -um *adj* half-prone
sēmit·a -ae *f* path, lane, track
sēmitāl·is -is -e *adj* of byways, backroad
sēmitāri·us -a -um *adj* back-alley
sēm(i)ustilāt·us -a -um *adj* (**-tul-**) half-burned
sēmi·vir -virī *adj* half-man, half-beast; unmanned; unmanly ‖ *m* half-man; eunuch
sēmivīv·us -a -um *adj* half-alive, half-dead
sēmod·ius -iī *m* half a peck
sēmōt·us -a -um *adj* remote, distant; private, intimate ‖ *npl* faraway places
sē·moveō -movēre -mōvī -mōtus *tr* to separate, remove, exclude
semper *adv* always, ever
sempitern·us -a -um *adj* everlasting
Semprōnius *see* **Gracchus**
sēmunci·a -ae *f* half ounce *(one twenty-fourth of a Roman pound);* trifle
sēmunciāri·us -a -um *adj* half-ounce; **faenus semunciarium** interest at the rate of one twenty-fourth of the capital *(i.e., about 5% per annum)*
sēmust·us -a -um *adj* half-burned
senācul·um -ī *n* open-air meeting place of the Senate in the Forum
sēnāriol·us -ī *m (pros)* trifling trimeter
sēnāri·us -a -um *adj (pros)* six-foot *(verse)* ‖ *m (pros)* iambic trimeter
senāt·or -ōris *m* senator
senātōri·us -a -um *adj* senatorial; in the Senate; of a senator
senāt·us -ūs *m* Senate; Senate session; **senatūs consultum** *(also* **senatus-consultum)** decree of the Senate; **senatum dare** *(or* **praebere)** to grant an audience with the Senate; to give *(s.o.)* the floor
Senec·a -ae *m* Lucius Annaeus Seneca *(Stoic philosopher and instructor of Nero, 4 B.C.–A.D. 65)*
senect·us -a -um *adj* aged, old ‖ *f* old age, senility
senect·ūs -ūtis *f* old age; old person
sen·eō -ēre *intr* to be old
sen·escō -escĕre -uī *intr* to get old; to decline, become feeble, lose strength; to wane, draw to a close

sen·ex -is *adj* aged, old ‖ *m* old man
sēn·ī -ae -a *adj* six each, in groups of six, six at a time; *(used in multiplication):* **aspice bis senos cycnos!** see those twelve swans!; **seni deni** sixteen each
senīl·is -is -e *adj* of old people, of an old man; aged; senile
sēni·ō -ōnis *m* a six *(on dice)*
seni·or -or (-us) *(comp of* **senex)** *adj* older, elder; more mature *(years)* ‖ *m* elderly person, an elder *(over 45 years of age)*
sen·ium -iī *n* feebleness of age, decline, senility; decay; grief, trouble; gloom; crabbiness; old man
sens·a -ōrum *npl* thoughts, sentiments, ideas
sensī *perf of* **sentio**
sensicul·us -ī *m* petty aphorism
sensif·er -era -erum *adj* producing a sensation
sensil·is -is -e *adj* capable of sensation, sentient
sensim *adv* gropingly; tentatively; carefully; gradually, gently
sens·us -a -um *pp of* **sentio** ‖ *npl see* **sensa**
sens·us -ūs *m* capacity for feeling, sensation; sense *(of hearing, etc.);* self-awareness, consciousness; awareness *(of conditions, situations);* feeling, emotion, sentiment; attitude, frame of mind; idea, thought; understanding, judgment, viewpoint; meaning, sense *(of a word);* intent, plan of action; self-contained expression, sentence; **communes sensūs** commonplaces, trite topics; **cum sensu** with taste; **sensus communis** civic pride, concern for the common good
sententi·a -ae *f* opinion, view, judgment; purpose, intention; *(in the Senate)* motion, proposal; meaning, sense; plan of action; sentence; maxim; *(leg)* verdict, sentence; **de sententiā** *(w. gen)* in accordance with the wishes of; **ex animi (mei) sententiā** *(in an oath)* to the best of (my) knowledge; **ex meā sententiā** in my opinion; to my liking; **in sententiam alicujus pedibus ire** to vote in favor of s.o.'s proposal *(literally, to go on foot to s.o.'s proposal);* **sententiam dicere** *(in the Senate)* to express a view; **sententia est** *(w. inf)* I intend to; **sententiam pronuntiare** *(or* **dicere)** to pronounce *or* give the verdict
sententiol·a -ae *f* phrase; maxim
sententiōsē *adv* sententiously, in moralizing style
sententiōs·us -a -um *adj* full of meaning, pregnant, sententious
senticēt·um -ī *n* thorny bush
sentīn·a -ae *f* bilge water; cesspool; bilge; *(fig)* dregs, scum, rabble
sen·tiō -tīre -sī -sus *tr* to perceive with the senses, feel, hear, see, smell; to realize; to observe, notice; to experience; to think, judge ‖ *intr (leg)* to vote, decide
sent·is -is *m* thorny bush, briar
sentisc·ō -ĕre *tr* to begin to realize; to begin to observe, perceive
sent·us -a -um *adj* rough, rugged; untidy *(person)*
s(e)orsum *or* **s(e)orsus** *adv* apart, separately; *(w. abl or* **ab)** apart from
sēparābil·is -is -e *adj* separable
sēparātim *adv* apart, separately
sēparāti·ō -ōnis *f* severing, separation
sēparātius *adv* less closely, more widely
sēparāt·us -a -um *adj* separate, distinct, different
sēpar·ō -āre -āvī -ātus *tr* to separate, divide, part; to distinguish
sepelībil·is -is -e *adj* that may be buried
sepeliō sepelīre sepelīvī *or* **sepeliī sepultus** *tr* to bury; *(fig)* to overwhelm, ruin, destroy, suppress
sēpēs *see* **saepes**
sēpi·a -ae *f* **(saep-)** cuttlefish
sēpīment·um *see* **saepimentum**
sēpio *see* **saepio**
sēpiol·a -ae *f* little cuttle fish
sē·pōnō -pōnĕre -posuī -positus *tr* to set aside, drop, discard; to banish; to disregard, forget; to separate, pick out, select; to reserve; to remove, take away, exclude; to distinguish
sēposit·us -a -um *adj* remote, distant; select; distinct; private
seps sēpos *mf* snake
sēpse = *emphatic* **sē**
septem *indecl adj* seven
Septem·ber -bris -bre *adj* September, of September; **mensis September** September *(seventh month of the old Roman calendar until 153 B.C.)* ‖ **Semptem·ber -bris** *m* September
septemdecim *indecl adj* **(-ten-)** seventeen
septemflu·us -a -um *adj* seven-mouthed *(Nile)*
septemgemin·us -a -um *adj* sevenfold
septempedāl·is -is -e *adj* seven-foot, seven-foot-high
septempl·ex -icis *adj* sevenfold
septemrēm·is -is -e *adj* having rowers arranged in sevens
septem·vir -virī *m* septemvir *(member of a board of seven, established in 44 B.C. to distribute land to veterans)* ‖ *mpl* board of seven officials; **septemviri epulonum** college of priests responsible for sacred feasts
septemvirāl·is -is -e *adv* of the septemvirs, septemviral ‖ *mpl* septemvirs
septemvirāt·us -ūs *m* office of the septemvirs
septemvirī *see* **septemvir**
septentri·ō -ōnis *m* the North; **ad** *or* **in septentrionem** to the north, northward

septentriōnāl·is -is -e *adj* **(septem-)** northern; **Oceanus septentrionalis** the North Sea ‖ *npl* northern regions, the North
septentriōn·ēs -um *mpl* **(septem-)** *(seven stars near the North Pole belonging to the Great Bear)* Great Bear; *(the seven stars of the Little Bear)* Little Bear; northern regions, the North; north wind
septēnār·ius -(i)ī *m (pros)* heptameter *(verse of seven feet)*
septendecim *indecl adj* **(septem-)** seventeen
septēn·ī -ae -a *adj* seven each, in groups of seven; **septeni deni** seventeen each, seventeen in a group
septentr- = septemtr-
septiens *or* **septiēs** *adv* seven times
septimān·us -a -um *adj* of *or* on the seventh ‖ *mpl* soldiers of the seventh legion
septimum *adv* for the seventh time
septim·us -a -um *adj* **(-tum-)** seventh
septim·us decim·us -a -um *adj* seventeenth
septingentēsim·us -a -um *adj* seven hundreth
septingent·ī -ae -a *adj* seven hundred
septuāgēsim·us -a -um *adj* seventieth
septuāgintā *indecl adj* seventy
septuenn·is -is -e *adj* seven-year-old
septum *see* **saeptum**
septun·x -cis *m* seven ounces; seven-twelfths
septus *pp of* **sepio** *(see* **saepio)**
sepulc(h)rāl·is -is -e *adj* of a tomb, sepulchral, funeral
sepulc(h)rēt·um -ī *n* grave, tomb
sepulc(h)r·um -ī *n* grave, tomb
sepultūr·a -ae *f* burial
sepultus *pp of* **sepelio**
Sēquan·us -a -um *adj* of the Sequani ‖ *mf* the Seine River ‖ *mpl* the Sequani *(a tribe of E. Gaul)*
sequ·ax -ācis *adj* following, pursuing; penetrating *(fumes);* eager
sequ·ens -entis *adj* next, following
seques·ter -tra -trum *(or* **-ter -tris -tre)** *adj* intermediate; negotiating; **pace sequestrā** under the protection of a truce ‖ *m* trustee *(with whom money or property is deposited);* agent, go-between ‖ *n* **sequestro dare** *(or* **ponere)** to put in trust
sequius *or* **secius** *(comp of* **secus)** *adv* less; worse, more unfavorably; differently, otherwise; **nec eo secius** nonetheless; **nihilo** *(or* **nilo) sequius** nevertheless
sequor sequī secūtus sum *tr* to follow; to escort, accompany, go with; to chase, pursue; to come after *(in time);* to go after, aim at; to head for ‖ *intr* to go after, follow, come next; *(of words)* to come naturally
Ser. *abbr* **Servius** *(Roman first name, praenomen)*
ser·a -ae *f* bolt, bar *(of door)*
Serāp·is -is *or* **-idis** *m* **(Sar-)** Egyptian god of healing
serēnit·ās -ātis *f* fair weather; serenity; favorableness
serēn·ō -āre -āvī -ātus *tr* to make fair, clear up, brighten
serēn·us -a -um *adj* clear, bright, fair; cloudless; cheerful, serene ‖ *n* clear sky, fair weather
Sēr·es -um *mpl* Chinese
seresc·ō -ĕre *intr* to dry off
Sergi·us -(i)ī *m* Roman clan name *(nomen) esp.* Lucius Sergius Catilina *(praetor in 68 B.C. and leader of the conspiracy put down by Cicero in 63 B.C.)*
sēri·a -ae *f* large jar
sēri·a -ōrum *npl* serious matters, serious business
Sēric·us -a -um *adj* Chinese ‖ *npl* silks
seri·ēs -ēī *f* series, row, succession; train, sequence, order, connection; lineage
sēriō *adv* seriously, in all sincerity
sērius *adv* later; too late; **serius ocius** sooner or later
sēri·us -a -um *adj* serious, earnest ‖ *n* serious matter; seriousness, earnestness ‖ *npl see* **seria**
serm·ō -ōnis *m* conversation, talk; discussion, discourse; common talk, rumor, gossip; language; diction; prose, everyday language
sermōncin·or -ārī -ātus sum *intr* to talk, converse
sermuncul·us -ī *m* small talk
ser·ō -ĕre -uī -tus *tr* to join, connect; to entwine, wreathe; to compose, combine, contrive
serō serĕre sēvī satus *tr* to sow, plant; *(fig)* to sow the seed of
sērō *adv (comp:* **sērius;** *superl:* **sērissimē)** late; too late
serp·ens -entis *mf (large)* snake, serpent, dragon ‖ **Serpens** *m (astr)* Draco *(constellation);* Serpens *(constellation, in the hand of Ophiuchus)*
serpentigen·a -ae *m* dragon offspring
serpentip·ēs -ĕdis *adj* dragon-footed
serperastr·um -ī *n* splint *(for straightening the crooked legs of children); (mil)* officer who keeps his soldiers in check
serpillum *see* **serpyllum**
serp·ō -ĕre -sī *intr* to creep, crawl; to wind; to move along slowly, spread slowly
serpyll·um -ī *n* **(-pill-, -pull-)** wild thyme *(used for seasoning)*
serr·a -ae *f* saw
serrāc·um -ī *n* **(sarr-)** large wagon
serrāt·us -a -um *adj* serrated, toothed *(like a saw);* notched

serrul·a -ae *f* small saw
sert·a -ae *f* wreath
sert·a -ōrum *npl* wreathes; festoons
Sertōriān·ī -ōrum *mpl* partisans of Sertorius
Sertōr·ius -(i)ī *m* general of Marius, assassinated in Spain by Perperna *(c. 122–72 B.C.)*
sert·us -a -um *pp of* **sero** (to join) **‖** *f see* **serta ‖** *npl see* **serta**
seruī *perf of* **sero** (to join)
ser·um -ī *n* whey *(milk serum, the watery liquid separating from curds)*
sēr·us -a -um *adj* late; too late; occurring at a late hour; advanced, far gone; **anni seri** ripe years; **ulmus sera** slow-growing elm **‖** *n* late hour; **in serum rem trahere** to drag out the matter until late
serv·a -ae *f* slave *(female)*
servābil·is -is -e *adj* retrievable
serv·ans -antis *adj* keeping; *(w. gen)* observant of
servāt·or -ōris *m,* **servātr·ix -īcis** *f* savior, preserver, deliverer
servīl·is -is -e *adj* slave, servile
servīliter *adv* slavishly
serv·iō -īre -īvī *or* **-iī -ītum** *intr* to be a servant *or* slave; to be obedient; *(of buildings, land)* to be mortgaged; *(w. dat)* **1** to be a slave to, be subservient to; **2** to serve; **3** to comply with, conform to; **4** to humor; **5** to be devoted to; **6** to work at; **7** to serve, be of use to
servit·ium -(i)ī *n* slavery; slaves
servitūd·ō -inis *f* servitude, slavery
servit·ūs -ūtis *f* slavery; slaves; property liability, easement
Serv·ius Tull·ius -(i)ī *m* sixth king of Rome *(credited with building the Servian Wall of tufa around Rome)*
serv·ō -āre -āvī -ātus *tr* to watch over, preserve, protect; to store, preserve; to keep, retain; to serve; to keep to, continue to dwell in
servol·a -ae *f* **(-ula)** young slave girl
servolicol·a -ae *f* slave of a slave *(female)*
servol·us -ī *m* **(-ulus)** young slave
serv·us *or* **serv·os -a -um** *adj* slave, servant **‖** *mf* slave, servant
sescēnār·is -is -e *adj* **(sexc-)** a year and a half old
sescēnāri·us -a -um *adj* six-hundred-man *(cohort)*
sescēn·ī -ae -a *adj* six hundred each, in groups of six hundred
sescentiens *or* **sescentiēs** *adv* **(sexc-)** six hundred times
sēsē *see* **se**
sesqui *adv* **(-que)** more by a half, one and a half times
sesqui- *pref indicating that a quantity is multiplied by one and a half, e.g.,* **sesquihora** an hour and a half; *with ordinal numbers, it gives a number consisting of a unit and the fraction indicated by the numeral, e.g.,* **sesquitertius** one and a third times as big; **sesquioctavus** one and an eighth times as big
sesquialt·er -era -erum *adj* **(sesque-)** one and a half times
sesquihōr·a -ae *f* an hour and a half
sesquilībr·a -ae *f* one and a half pounds
sesquimod·ius -(i)ī *m* a peck and a half
sesquioctāv·us -a -um *adj* **(sesque-)** one and one-eighth times as big
sequiop·us -eris *n* **(sesque-)** one and a half days' work
sequipedāl·is -is -e *adj* one and a half feet long *(or high, wide, thick, square, etc.)*
sesqui·pēs -pedis *m* distance *or* length of one and a half feet
sesquiplāg·a -ae *f* a stroke and a half
sesquipl·ex -icis *adj* one and a half times as much
sesquipl·us -a -um *adj* one and a half times as big **‖** *n* one and a half times as much
sesquiterti·us -a -um *adj* **(sesque-)** one and a third times as big
sessibul·um -ī *n* seat, chair
sessil·is -is -e *adj (of the back of a centaur)* for sitting on; *(of plants)* low-growing
sessi·ō -ōnis *f* sitting; session; loafing
sessit·ō -āre -āvī -ātum *intr* to sit a lot, keep sitting, rest
sessiuncul·a -ae *f* small group *(sitting down together for a discussion)*
sess·or -ōris *m* spectator; resident
sessōr·ium -iī *n* sitting room
sestertil·um -ī *n (coll)* a mere 100,000 sesterces
sestert·ium -(i)ī *n (or declined as gen pl)* 100,000 sesterces
sestert·ius -iī *(gen pl:* **sestertium)** *(abbr:* **HS)** *m* sesterce *(small silver coin, equal to about one-fourth of a denarius, i.e., about 25¢, and used as the ordinary Roman unit in accounting; sums below 2000 sesterces are expressed by a cardinal number, e.g.,* **ducenti sesterii;** *sums from 2000 upwards are expressed by* **milia sestertium** *(or* **sestertia,** *with the distributives, or group-numbers (***bina, quinquagena,** *etc.); sums of 1,000,000 and upwards are expressed by the numeral adverb in* **-iens (-ies)** *with* **sestertium** *(taken as a gen pl or declined as a neuter singular noun:* **deciens** *(i.e.,* **deciens centena milia) sestertium** *= one million sesterces)*
Sest·os *or* **Sest·us -ī** *f* city on the Hellespont
sēt- = saet-
Sēti·a -ae *f* town in Latium famous for its wine *(modern Sezza)*
Sētīn·us -a -um *adj* Setine **‖** *n* Setine wine, wine from Setia

sētius *comp adv* **(sēc-)** later, more slowly; to a lesser degree, less readily; otherwise; **nihilo setius** just the same, nonetheless; **quo setius** *(w. subj)* so as to delay *or* prevent *(s.th. from happening):* **impedimento est Caepio quo setius lex feratur** Caepio is an impediment to having the law passed

seu *conj* or if; or; **seu...seu** whether...or

sevērē *adv* severely, sternly; seriously, in earnest; solemnly; **severe dicere** to speak plainly

sevērit·ās -ātis *f* severity, sternness; self-discipline; seriousness

sevēritūd·ō -inis *f* severity, sternness; seriousness *(of expression)*

sevēr·us -a -um *adj* severe, strict, austere; serious, grave; ruthless, grim; plain, unadorned *(style of writing, architecture)*

sēvī *perf of* **sero** (to plant)

sēvoc·ō -āre -āvī -ātus *tr* to call aside, call away; to remove, withdraw; to separate; to appropriate *(from the common fund)*

sēv·um -ī *n* tallow, grease, suet

Sex. *abbr* **Sextus** *(Roman first name, praenomen)*

sex *indecl adj* six

sexāgēnāri·us -a -um *adj* sixty-year-old

sexāgēn·ī -ae -a *adj* sixty each; sixty at a time; sixty

sexāgē(n)sim·us -a -um *adj* sixtieth

sexāgiens *or* **sexāgiēs** *adv* sixty times

sexāgintā *indecl adj* sixty

sexangul·us -a -um *adj* hexagonal

sexcēn- = sescen-

sexcēnāri·us -a -um *adj* six-hundred-man *(cohort)*

sexenn·is -is -e *adj* six-year-old; **sexenni die** in a six-year period

sexenn·ium -(i)ī *n* six-year period, six years

sexiens *or* **sexiēs** *adv* six times

sexprīm·ī *or* **sex prīm·ī -ōrum** *mpl* six-member council *(in provincial towns)*

sextadecimān·ī -ōrum *mpl* soldiers of the sixteenth legion

sext·ans -antis *m* one-sixth; small coin *(one-sixth of an* **as**); one-sixth of a pint

sextār·ius -(i)ī *m* pint

Sextīl·is -is -e *adj* of Sextilis *(the sixth month of the old Roman year, which began in March; Sextilis was afterwards called August in honor of Augustus)*

sextul·a -ae *f* sixth of an ounce

sextum *adv* for the sixth time

sext·us -a -um *adj* sixth

sext·us decim·us -a -um *adj* sixteenth

sex·us -ūs *m* sex; *(gram)* gender

sī *conj* if; **o si** *(expressing a wish)* if only!; **si forte** if by any chance, in the hope that; **si maxime** however much; **si minus** if not; **si modo** provided that; **si vero** *(expressing scepticism)* if really

sibī *see* **se**

sībil·a -ōrum *npl* hisses, hissing

sībil·ō -āre -āvī -ātus *tr* to hiss at; to whistle at ‖ *intr* to hiss; to whistle

sībil·us -a -um *adj* hissing; whistling ‖ *m & n* hissing; whistling; rustling

Sibyll·a -ae *f* **(Sibu-)** sibyl *(esp. the sibyl at Cumae)*

Sibyllīn·us -a -um *adj* Sibylline

sīc *adv* thus, so, in this way; thus, as follows; in these circumstances; in such a way, to such a degree; *(in assent)* yes

Sicān·ī -ōrum *mpl* ancient people of Italy who migrated to Sicily

Sicāni·a -ae *f* Sicily

Sicān·is -idis *adj* Sicilian

Sicāni·us -a -um *adj* Sicilian ‖ *f* Sicily

Sicān·us -a -um *adj* Sicilian ‖ *mpl see* **Sicani**

sīcār·ius -(i)ī *m* murderer, assassin; **inter sicarios accusare (defendere)** to prosecute (defend) on a murder charge

siccē *adv* firmly; *(rhet)* plainly

siccit·ās -ātis *f* dryness; drought; firmness, solidity; plainness *(of style)*

sicc·ō -āre *tr* to dry, dry up; to drain; **cruores siccare** to stanch the blood

siccocul·us -a -um *adj* dry-eyed

sicc·us -a -um *adj* dry; thirsty; sober; firm, solid *(body);* solid *(argument);* dry, insipid *(style)*

Sicili·a -ae *f* Sicily

sicilicissit·ō -āre *intr* to act like a Sicilian

sīcīlicul·a -ae *f* sickle

Siciliens·is -is -e *adj* Sicilian

sīcine *adv* is this how...?

sīcubi *adv* if anywhere, wheresoever

sīcul·a -ae *f* little dagger; *(vulg)* penis

Sicul·ī -ōrum *mpl* ancient Italic people who migrated to Sicily; Sicilians

sīcunde *conj* if from some place

sīcut *or* **sīcutī** *conj* as, just as; *(in elliptical clauses)* just as, like; *(introducing a comparison)* as it were, so to speak; *(introducing an example)* as for instance; *(of condition)* as, in the same condition as; as if, just as if; **sicut...ita** although...yet

sīcutī *adv (archaic form of* **sicut)**

Sicy·ōn -ōnis *mf* town in the N. Peloponnesus

Sicyōni·us -a -um *adj* Sicyon ‖ *mpl* inhabitants of Sicyon

sīdere·us -a -um *adj* starry; star-spangled; heavenly, divine

sīdō sīdĕre sīdī *intr* to sit down; to settle; *(of birds)* to land; to sink; to settle down, subside; *(of ships)* to be grounded

Sīd·ōn -ōnis *f* city of Phoenicia

Sīdōn·is -idis *adj* Phoenician ‖ *f* Dido; Europa; Anna

Sīdōni·us -a -um *adj* Sidonian, Phoenician; Theban ‖ *mpl* Sidonians

sīd·us -eris *n* constellation; star, heavenly

body; sky, heaven; light, glory, beauty, pride; season; climate, weather; *(in astrology)* star, destiny

Sigambr·ī -ōrum *mpl* German tribe

Sīgē·um *or* **Sīgē·on -ī** *n* promontory near Troy

Sīgē(i)·us -a -um *adj* Sigean; Trojan

sigillār·ia -ium *or* **-iōrum** *npl* small objects of pottery stamped in relief with figures *or* ornamentation ‖ art market in Rome ‖ festival forming the final day of the Saturnalia

sigillāt·us -a -um *adj* adorned with little figures *or* patterns in relief

sigill·um -ī *n* statuette, figurine; stamped *or* embossed figure, a relief; figure woven in tapestry

sigm·a -atis *n* semicircular couch *(for reclining at table)*

signāt·or -ōris *m* sealer, signer; witness

signāt·us -a -um *adj* marked with a stamp, coined

signif·er -era -erum *adj* bearing the constellations, starry ‖ *m* standard-bearer; chief, leader

signific·ans -antis *adj* clear, distinct, expressive; significant, meaningful

significanter *adv* clearly, graphically; meaningfully, significantly

significāti·ō -ōnis *f* signal, indication, sign, mark; meaning, sense, signification; emphasis; expression of approval, applause

signific·ō -āre -āvī -ātus *tr* to show, indicate, express, point out; to intimate; to notify, publish; to portend; to mean, signify ‖ *intr* to make signs, indicate

Signīn·us -a -um *adj* of *or* from Signia *(town in Latium, modern Segni, famous for its astringent variety of wine)*; **opus Signinum** waterproof plaster

signipot·ens -entis *adj* ruling over the constellations

sign·ō -āre -āvī -ātus *tr* to mark, stamp, impress, imprint; to seal, seal up; to coin; to signify, indicate, express; to adorn; to distinguish, note

sign·um -ī *n* sign; indication, proof; military standard, banner; password; cohort, maniple; omen; symptom; shop sign; statue; a figure *(in a relief, picture, or embroidery)*; device on a seal, seal; heavenly sign, constellation; **ab signis discedere** to break ranks, disband; **signa conferre** to engage in close combat; to concentrate troops; **signa constituere** to halt; **signa conversa ferre** to wheel around and attack; **signa ferre** to break camp; **signa movere in hostem** to advance against the enemy; **signa proferre** to march forward; **signa servare** to keep the order of battle; **signa sequi** to march in rank; **signa subsequi** to keep the order of battle; **signa transferre** to desert, join the other side; **signis collatis** in regular battle formation

sīlān·us -ī *m* waterspout *(originally designed as a head of Silenus*

Silar·us -ī *m* **(Siler-)** Sele River *(forming the boundary between Lucania and Campania and flowing by the town of Paestum)*

sil·ens -entis *adj* silent, calm, quiet ‖ *mpl* the dead

silent·ium -(i)ī *n* silence; inactivity; **silentium facere** to obtain silence; to keep silent; **silentium significare** to call for silence

Sīlēn·us -ī *m* teacher and companion of Bacchus, usually drunk; a Silenus *(wood-spirit)*

sil·eō -ēre -uī *tr* to leave unmentioned, say nothing about ‖ *intr* to be silent, be still; to keep silent; to be hushed; to rest, cease

sil·er -eris *n* willow

silesc·ō -ĕre *intr* to become silent, fall silent, become hushed

sil·ex -icis *mf* flint stone, lava stone *(used in road paving and other construction)*; cliff, crag; *(fig)* hardheartedness

silicern·ium -(i)ī *n* funeral meal; *(coll)* old fossil

silīg·ō -inis *f* winter wheat; wheat flour

siliqu·a -ae *f* pod, husk ‖ *fpl* pulse *(the edible seeds of certain leguminous plants, as lentils, peas)*

sillyb·us -ī *m* label *(giving the title of the scroll)*

sīl·ō -ōnis *m* snub nose

silua *see* **silva**

siluī *perf of* **sileo**

silūr·us -ī *m* European catfish

sīl·us -a -um *adj* snub-nosed

silv·a *or* **silū·a -ae** *f* woods, forest; shrubbery, bush, foliage, crop, growth; mass, quantity; material, supply

Silvān·us -ī *m* god of woods ‖ *mpl* woodland gods

silvesc·ō -ĕre *intr (of a vine)* to run wild

silvestr·is -is -e *adj* wooded, overgrown with woods; woodland, living in the woods; wild, growing wild; rural, pastoral ‖ *npl* woodlands

silvicol·a -ae *mf* denizen of the forest

silvicultr·ix -īcis *adj (fem only)* living in the woods

silvifrag·us -a -um *adj (of the wind)* forest-smashing

silvōs·us -a -um *adj* wooded, woody

sīmi·a -ae *f* ape

simil·is -is -e *adj* similar; *(w. gen, mostly of persons, or dat, mostly of things)* similar to, resembling, like; **homines inter se similes** people resembling one another; **veri similis** probable, realistic ‖ *n* comparison, parallel

similiter *adv* similarly; **similiter atque** *(or* **ac)** just as; **similiter ut si** just as if
similitūd·ō -inis *f* likeness, resemblance; imitation; analogy; comparison, simile; monotony; *(w. gen or dat)* similarity to; **est homini cum deo similitudo** there is a resemblance between man and a god
sīmiol·us -ī *m* little monkey
simītū *adv* at the same time; *(w.* **cum** *+ abl)* together with
sīm·ius -iī *m* monkey, ape
Simo·īs -entis *m* stream at Troy
Simōnid·ēs -is *m* lyric poet of the Greek island of Ceos *(fl 500 B.C.)* ‖ iambic poet of the Greek island of Amorgos *(7th cent. B.C.)*
simpl·ex -icis *adj* single, simple; unmixed; plain, natural; frank; naive; in single file
simplicit·ās -ātis *f* simplicity; candor, frankness
simpliciter *adv* simply, plainly; frankly, candidly
simpul·um -ī *n* small ladle
simpu(v)·ium -(i)ī *n* libation bowl
simul *adv* together, at the same time; likewise; *(w. abl or* **cum)** together with; **simul atque** *(or* **ac** *or* **et)** as soon as; **simul...simul** both...and ‖ *conj* as soon as
simulācr·um -ī *n* image, likeness, representation; form, shape, phantom, ghost; conception; sign, emblem; mere shadow; portraiture, characterization
simulām·en -inis *n* imitation, copy
simul·ans -antis *adj* imitating; *(w. gen)* imitative of, able to imitate
simulātē *adv* insincerely, deceitfully
simulāti·ō -ōnis *f* faking, bluffing, bluff, pretense; **simulatione** *(w. gen)* under the pretense of
simulāt·or -ōris *m* imitator; pretender, phoney
simul·ō -āre -āvī -ātus *tr* **(simil-)** to imitate, copy; to represent; to put on the appearance of, simulate
simult·ās -ātis *f* enmity, rivalry, feud; jealousy; grudge
sīmul·us -a -um *adj* rather snub-nosed
sīm·us -a -um *adj* snub-nosed
sīn *conj* if however, if on the other hand, but if
sināp·i *or* **sināp·e -is** *n*, **sināp·is -is** *f* (white) mustard
sincērē *adv* sincerely, honestly
sincērit·ās -ātis *f (physical)* soundness; purity; sincerity, integrity
sincēr·us -a -um *adj* sound, whole, clean; untainted; sincere, real, genuine
sincip·ut -itis *or* **sincipitāment·um -ī** *n* half a head *(as food);* cheek, jowl *(of a hog);* brain
sind·ōn -ōnis *f* fine cotton *or* linen fabric, muslin
sine *prep (w. abl)* without
singillātim *or* **singulātim** *adv* singly
singlāriter *see* **singulariter**
singulār·is -is -e *adj* single, alone, one at a time; specific, peculiar, special; individual; unique ‖ *mpl* crack troops
sing(u)lāriter *adv* singly; particularly
singulāri·us -a -um *adj* single, separate; unique
singulātim *adv* singly, individually
singul·ī -ae -a *adj* single, one at a time, individual; one each, one apiece; **in singulos dies** on each successive day; every day, daily *(w. comp or words denoting increase or decrease):* **crescit in dies singulos hostium numerus** the number of the enemy increases daily; **in singulos homines** per man ‖ *mpl* individuals
singultim *adv* sobbingly, with sobs
singult·iō -īre *intr* to hiccup; to throb
singult·ō -āre -āvī -ātus *tr* to gasp out; to utter with sobs ‖ *intr* to gasp, sob
singult·us -ūs *m* sob, gasp; squirt *(of water, etc.);* death rattle
singul·ī -ae -a *adj* one by one, single; each one, one apiece
sinis·ter -tra -trum *adj* left, on the left; *(because in Roman augury the augur faced south, having the East on the left)* favorable, auspicious, lucky; *(because in Greek augury the augur faced north, having the East on his right)* unfavorable, inauspicious, unlucky; wrong, perverse, improper ‖ *mpl* soldiers on the left flank ‖ *f* left, left hand; left side; **a sinistrā** on the left ‖ *n* left side
sinisterit·ās -ātis *f* awkwardness
sinistrē *adv* badly, wrongly
sinistr(ō)rsum *or* **sinistrō(r)sus** *adv* to the left
sinō sinĕre sīvī *or* **siī situs** *tr* to allow; **sine modo** only let, if only
Sin·ōn -ōnis *m* Greek soldier who talked the Trojans into dragging the wooden horse into Troy
Sinōp·a -ae *or* **Sinōp·ē -ēs** *f* Sinope *(Greek colony on the S. coast of the Euxine or Black Sea)*
Sinuess·a -ae *f* **(Sino-)** city near the border between Latium and Campania
sīn·um -ī *n* large drinking cup
sinu·ō -āre -āvī -ātus *tr* to wind, curve; to fill out *(sails)*
sinuōs·us -a -um *adj* winding, sinuous, serpentine
sīn·us -ī *m* large drinking cup
sin·us -ūs *m* indentation, curve, fold, hollow; fold of the toga about the breast, pocket, purse; breast, bosom, lap; bay, gulf, lagoon; winding coast; valley, hollow; heart *(e.g., of a city),* interior; intimacy; **in sinu meo est** he/she is dear to me

sīpar·ium -(i)ī *n (theat)* curtain; **post siparium** behind the scenes
sīp(h)·ō -ōnis *m* siphon; fire engine
sīphuncul·us -ī *m* small pipe
Sipyl·us *or* **Sipyl·os -ī** *m* mountain in Lydia on which Niobe was changed into a rock
sīquandō *or* **si quandō** *conj* if ever
sīquidem *conj* if in fact
siremps *or* **sirempse = si rem ipsam** *adj* the same; **sirempse legem ussit esse Jupiter** Jupiter ordered the law to be the same
Sīr·ēn -ēnis *f* Siren *(sea nymph that had the power of charming sailors to their death with her song)*
Sīri·us -a -um *adj* of Sirius, of the Dog Star **ǁ** *m* Sirius, Dog Star *(in the constellation Canis Major)*
sirp·e -is *n (bot)* silphium *(from which gum was extracted)*
sīr·us -ī *m* underground silo
sīs = sī vīs please, if you please
sistō sistěre stitī *or* **stetī status** *tr* to cause to stand, make stand, put, place, set; to set up *(monument);* to establish; to stop, check, arrest; to put an end to; to produce in court; **pedem** *(or* **gradum) sistere** to halt, stop; **vadimonium sistere** to answer bail, show up in court **ǁ** *refl* to present oneself, appear, come **ǁ** *pass* **sisti non potest** the crisis cannot be met, the case is hopeless **ǁ** *intr* to stand, rest; to stop, stay; to stand firm, last, endure; to show up in court; *(w. dat or* **contra** *+ acc)* to stand firm against
sistrāt·us -a -um *adj* with a tambourine
sistr·um -ī *n* tambourine, rattle
Sīsyphid·ēs -ae *m* descendant of Sisyphus, Ulysses
Sisyphi·us -a -um *adj* of Sisyphus; **sanguine cretus Sisyphio** born of the stock of Sisyphys *(i.e., Ulysses)*
Sīsyph·us *or* **Sīsyph·os -ī** *m* Sisyphus *(son of Aeolus, king of Corinth, whose punishment in Hades was to roll a rock repeatedly up a hill)*
sitell·a -ae *f* lottery urn
Sīth·ōn -onis *adj* Thracian
Sīthon·is -idis *or* **-idos** *or* **Sīthoni·us -a -um** *adj* Thracian **ǁ** *mpl* Thracians
sitīculōs·us -a -um *adj* thirsty
siti·ens -entis *adj* thirsting, thirsty; arid, parched; parching; *(w. gen)* thirsting for, eager for
sitienter *adv* thirstily, eagerly
sit·iō -īre *tr* to thirst for **ǁ** *intr* to be thirsty
sit·is -is *f* thirst; *(w. gen)* thirst for
sitīt·or -ōris *m* thirsty person; **sititor aquae** thirster for water
sittybus *see* **sillybus**
situl·a -ae *f* bucket; basin, urn
sit·us -a -um *pp of* **sino ǁ** *adj* situated, located, lying; founded; *(w.* **in** *+ abl)* resting on, dependent on
sit·us -ūs *m* position, situation, site; structure; neglect; mustiness; dust, dirt; idleness, inactivity, lack of use
sīve *or* **seu** *conj* or if; or; **sive...sive** whether...or
sīvī *perf of* **sino**
smaragd·us *or* **smaragd·os -ī** *f (m)* emerald
smar·is -idis *f* a small sea fish
smīl·ax -acis *adj (bot)* smilax *(an evergreen climbing plant)*
Sminth·eūs -eī *m* epithet of Apollo
Smyrn·a -ae *f* town on W. coast of Asia Minor
sobol- = subol-
sōbriē *adv* soberly, moderately; sensibly
sōbriet·ās -ātis *f* sobriety
sobrīn·a -ae *f* cousin *(female, on the mother's side)*
sobrīn·us -ī *m* cousin *(on the mother's side)*
sōbri·us -a -um *adj* sober; temperate; sensible, reasonable
soccul·us -ī *m* small slipper
socc·us -ī *m* slipper; low shoe *(worn by actors in comedy); (fig)* comedy
soc·er *or* **soc·erus -erī** *m* father-in-law
soci·a -ae *f* associate, companion, ally, partner *(female)*
sociābil·is -is -e *adj* compatible, intimate
sociāl·is -is -e *adj* allied, confederate; nuptial, conjugal; sociable
sociāliter *adv* sociably
socienn·us -ī *m* buddy; partner
societ·ās -ātis *f* companionship, fellowship; association, society; partnership; alliance, confederacy
soci·ō -āre -āvī -ātus *tr* to unite, associate; to share
sociofraud·us -ī *m* double-crosser, heel
soci·us -a -um *adj* joint, allied, confederate; held in common, common **ǁ** *m* associate, companion, ally, partner **ǁ** *f see* **socia**
socordi·a -ae *f* silliness, stupidity; apathy, laziness
socordius *adv* too apathetically
soc·ors -ordis *adj* silly, stupid; apathetic, lazy, inactive
Sōcrat·es -is *m* Athenian philosopher *(469–399 B.C.)*
Sōcratic·ī -ōrum *mpl* Socratics
socr·us -ūs *f* mother-in-law
sodālici·us -a -um *adj* of companionship **ǁ** *n* companionship, intimacy; society, secret society
sodāl·is -is *m* companion, fellow, buddy, crony; member *(of a society, priestly college, etc.);* accomplice; **sodālis Augustalis** member of a fraternity associated with the cult of Augustus

sodālit·ās -ātis *f* companionship, fellowship; society, club, association; secret society
sodālit- = sodalic-
sōdēs = si audes if you will, please
sōl sōlis *m* sun; sunlight, sunshine; day
sōlāciol·um -ī *n* a bit of comfort
sōlāc·ium -(i)ī *n* **(sōlāt-)** comfort, relief
sōlām·en -inis *n* comfort
sōlār·is -is -e *adj* sun-; **lumen solare** sunlight, sunshine
sōlār·ium -(i)ī *n* sundial; clock; sunny spot, balcony
sōlāt- = solac-
sōlāt·or -ōris *m* comforter
solduri·ī -ōrum *mpl* retainers *(of a chieftain)*
soldus *see* **solidus**
sole·a -ae *f* sole; sandal *(with toes exposed; cf.* **sandalium)**; fetter; sole *(flatfish)*
soleār·ius -(i)ī *m* sandal-maker
soleāt·us -a -um *adj* wearing sandals
soleō solēre solitus sum *intr (w. inf)* to be in the habit of, be used to; usually: *e.g.,* **solet cenare sero** he usually eats late; *(w.* **cum** *+ abl)* to have sex with
solidē *adv* solidly; thoroughly, downright; firmly
solidit·ās -ātis *f* solidity
solid·ō -āre -āvī -ātus *tr* to make firm; to make dense; to strengthen
sol(i)d·us -a -um *adj* solid, firm, dense; whole, entire; genuine; trustworthy; resolute **II** *n* entire sum, total; a solid; mass, substance; solid earth
sōliferre·um -ī *n* all-iron spear
sōlistim·us -a -um *adj* **(-umus)** perfect; **tripudium solistimum** perfectly auspicious omen
sōlitāri·us -a -um *adj* solitary, lonely
sōlitūd·ō -inis *f* loneliness; deprivation; solitude; wilderness; *(w. gen)* state of being forsaken by **II** *fpl* desert, wilderness
solit·us -a -um *adj* usual, customary, characteristic **II** *n* the usual, the customary; **formosior solito** more handsome than usual; **magis** *(or* **plus)** **solito** more than usual
sol·ium -(i)ī *n* seat, chair; throne; dominion, sway; bathtub; stone coffin
sōlivag·us -a -um *adj* roaming alone; single, solitary
sollemn·is -is -e *adj* annual, periodic; solemn, religious; usual **II** *n* usage, practice; solemn rite, solemnity, ceremony; feat; sacrifice; festival, games *(in honor of Roman holy days)*
sollemniter *adv* solemnly, religiously
soll·ers -ertis *adj* **(sōl-)** skilled, skillful, expert, clever
sollerti·a -ae *f* **(sōl-)** skill, shrewdness; clever plan; *(w. gen)* skill in
sollicitāti·ō -ōnis *f* vexation; anxiety; incitement, instigation
sollicitē *adv* anxiously, with solicitude; diligently
sollicit·ō -āre -āvī -ātus *tr* to shake, disturb; to disquiet, annoy, molest; to worry, make anxious; to provoke, tempt; to stir up, incite to revolt
sollicitūd·ō -inis *f* anxiety, uneasiness; worry; solicitude; *(w. gen)* anxiety over
sollicit·us -a -um *adj* stirred up, stormy *(sea);* tossed *(by the waves);* troubled, disturbed, restless; solicitous, anxious, worried; incited to revolt
sollif- = solif-
sollist- = solist-
soloecism·us -ī *m* mistake in grammar, solecism
Sol·ō(n) -ōnis *m* Solon *(famous Athenian legislator c. 640–560* B.C.*)*
sōl·or -ārī -ātus sum *tr* to console; to relieve, mitigate *(fear, etc.)*
sōlstiāl·is -is -e *adj* of the summer solstice; midsummer's; solar
sōlstit·ium -(i)ī *n* summer solstice, midsummer, summer heat
sol·um -ī *n* bottom, ground, floor; soil, land, country; sole *(of foot, shoe)*
sōlum *adv* only, merely, barely; **non solum...sed etiam** not only...but also
sōl·us -a -um *adj* only, single, sole, alone; lonely, solitary
solūtē *adv* loosely, freely, without hindrance; negligently; without vigor
solūti·ō -ōnis *f* loosening; payment
solūt·us -a -um *adj* loose, untied, unbandaged; negligent; free; fluent; unrhythmical; uncontrolled; exempt, free; unbiased; unbridled
sol·vō -vĕre -vī *or* **-uī -ūtus** *tr* to loosen, untie *(a cord);* to release; to dissolve, break up; to detach, disengage; to unlock, open; to melt; to relax *(the body);* to smooth, soothe; to impair, weaken, destroy; to acquit; to accomplish, fulfill; to pay, pay off; to solve, explain; to break *(a siege);* to break down *(a barrier);* to undergo *(punishment);* to get rid of *(feelings);* to loosen *(the bowels);* to remove *(surgical dressings);* to unharness, unyoke *(animals);* to disperse into the atmosphere, dissipate; to enervate, sap the strength of *(a person);* **crines solvere** to let down the hair *(in mourning);* **navem** *(or* **ratem)** **solvere** to cast off, set sail; **ora solvere** to open the mouth *(to speak)* **II** *intr* to weigh anchor, set sail
Solym·a -ōrum *npl* Jerusalem
Solym·us -a -um *adj* of Jerusalem **II** *mpl* mountain tribe, supposed to have given its name to Jerusalem
somniculōsē *adv* sleepily, drowsily

somniculōs·us -a -um *adj* sleepy, drowsy
somnif·er -era -erum *adj* soporific, sleep-inducing; deadly *(poison)*
somni·ō -āre -āvī -ātus *tr* to dream of; to day-dream about, imagine; **somnium somniare** to have a dream ‖ *intr* to dream; to daydream
somn·ium -(i)ī *n* dream, vision; day-dreaming
somn·us -ī *m* sleep; night; sleep of death; indolence
sonābil·is -is -e *adj* noisy
sonip·ēs -ĕdis *adj* loud-hoofed ‖ *m* steed
sonit·us -ūs *m* sound, noise, clang
sonivi·us -a -um *adj* noisy
son·ō -āre -uī -itus *tr* to utter, say sound, express; to denote, mean; to sound like ‖ *intr* to sound; to ring, resound, make a noise; to be spoken of as
son·or -ōris *m* sound, noise, clang
sonōr·us -a -um *adj* sonorous, loud, noisy, clanging
sons sontis *adj* guilty, criminal; *(w. abl of the crime)* guilty of ‖ *m* guilty one, criminal
sontic·us -a -um *adj* serious, critical
sonuī *perf of* **sono**
son·us -a -um *adj/ suf denotes "sounding", e.g.:* **raucisonus** hoarse-sounding
son·us -ī *m* sound, noise; tone
sophi·a -ae *f* wisdom
sophist·ēs *or* **sophist·a -ae** *m* sophist
Sophocl·ēs -is *or* **-ī** Greek writer of tragedies *(c. 495–406 B.C.)*
Sophoclē·us -a -um *adj* Sophoclean
soph·us -a -um *adj* wise ‖ *m* wise man, sage
sōp·iō -īre -īvī *or* **-iī -ītus** *tr* to put to sleep; to stun, knock unconscious; *(fig)* to calm, settle, lull
sop·or -ōris *m* deep sleep; stupor; apathy; sleeping potion
sopōrāt·us -a -um *adj* stupefied; unconscious; buried in sleep; allayed *(grief);* soporific
sopōrif·er -era -erum *adj* sleep-inducing
sopōr·us -a -um *adj* drowsy
Sōract·e -is *n* mountain in Etruria about 25 miles N.E. of Rome
sōrac·um -ī *n* box, carton
sorb·eō -ēre -uī -itus *tr* to suck in, gulp down; to absorb; *(fig)* to swallow
sorbil(l)·ō -āre -āvī -ātus *tr* to sip
sorbilō *adv* drop by drop, bit by bit
sorbiti·ō -ōnis *f* broth
sorb·um -ī *n* **(sorv-)** Juneberry
sorb·us -ī *f* **(sorv-)** Juneberry tree
sord·eō -ēre *intr* to be dirty, be shabby; to appear worthless
sord·ēs -is *f* dirt, filth; shabbiness, squalor; greed, stinginess; moral turpitude; meanness *(of behavior);* low rank, low condition; rabble, scum; **sordes verborum** vulgarity ‖ *fpl* rags, dark clothes *(often worn as a sign of mourning)*
sord·escō -escĕre -uī *intr* to become dirty, become soiled
sordidāt·us -a -um *adj* in shabby clothes *(esp. as sign of mourning)*
sordidē *adv* vilely; greedily
sordidul·us -a -um *adj* rather soiled, rather shabby; *(fig)* low
sordid·us -a -um *adj* dirty, filthy; shabby; soiled, stained; dressed in mourning clothes; low *(rank);* vulgar
sorditūd·ō -inis *f* dirt, filth
sōr·ex -icis *m* shrewmouse
sōricīn·us -a -um *adj* squealing like mice
sōrīt·ēs -ae *m* sorites *(logical conclusion drawn from cumulative arguments)*
sor·or -ōris *f* sister; cousin; companion, playmate; **sorores doctae** Muses; **sorores tres** three Fates; **sorores tristes** gloomy Fates
sororicīd·a -ae *m* murderer of a sister
sorōri·us -a -um *adj* sister's, of a sister; sisterly; **stuprum sororium** incest with a sister
sors sortis *f* lot; casting of lots, decision by lot; prophecy; fate, destiny, lot in life; portion, share; sort, kind
sorsum *see* **seorsum**
sortileg·us -a -um *adj* prophetic ‖ *m* soothsayer, fortuneteller
sort·iō -īre -īvī *or* **-iī -ītus** *or* **sort·ior -īrī -ītus sum** *tr* to cast lots for; to allot, assign by lot, appoint by lot; to obtain by lot; to choose, select; to share, divide; to receive, get by chance ‖ *intr* to cast *or* draw lots
sortīti·ō -ōnis *f* drawing lots, determining by lots
sortītō *adv* by lot; by fate
sortīt·us -ūs *m* lottery
Sosi·ī -ōrum *mpl* the Sosii *(two brothers famous as booksellers in Rome at the time of Horace)*
sosp·es -itis *adj* safe and sound; auspicious, lucky
sospit·a -ae *f* preserver *(epithet of Juno)*
sospitāl·is -is -e *adj* beneficial
sospit·ō -āre *tr* to preserve, protect
Sōt·ēr -ēris *m* savior, protector
Sōtēri·a -ōrum *npl* party for a person recovering from an illness
Sp. *abbr* **Spurius** *(Roman first name, praenomen)*
spād·ix -īcis *m* chestnut-brown horse
spad·ō -ōnis *m* eunuch
spar·gō -gĕre -sī -sus *tr* to scatter, sprinkle, strew; to disperse; to disseminate; to spot, dapple
sparsi·ō -ōnis *f* sprinkling
spars·us -a -um *pp of* **spargo** ‖ *adj* freckled, spotty
Spart·a -ae *or* **Spart·ē -ēs** *f* Sparta *(capital of Laconia)*

Spartac·us -ī *m* Thracian gladiator who led a revolt of gladiators against Rome in 73–71 B.C.

Spartān·us -a -um *adj* Spartan

Spartiāt·ēs -ae *m* Spartan

Spartiātic·us *or* **Spartic·us -a -um** *adj* Spartan

spart·um *or* **spart·on -ī** *n* Spanish broom *(fibrous plant used in making ropes, nets, etc.)*

sparul·us -ī *m* bream *(fish)*

spar·us *m or* **spar·um -ī** *n* hunting spear

spath·a -ae *f* broad two-edged sword

spati·or -ārī -ātus sum *intr* to stroll, take a walk; to walk solemnly; to spread out

spatiōsē *adv* extensively; long

spatiōs·us -a -um *adj* extensive; spacious; wide; *(of time)* long, lengthy; *(of vowel)* long; *(w. advl force)* with its *(his, etc.)* great size

spat·ium -(i)ī *n* space, room, extent; open space, public square; distance *(between two points);* walk, promenade *(place);* lap *(of a race);* racetrack; interval, period; time, opportunity; *(pros)* measure, quantity

speci·ēs -ēī *f* sight, view; outward appearance; outline, shape; fine appearance, beauty; deceptive appearance, show, semblance, pretense, pretext; resemblance; display, splendor; apparition; image, statue; idea, notion; reputation; species, sort; *(leg)* specific legal situation *or* case; **ad** *(or* **in)** **speciem** for show; **in speciem** *(or* **per speciem)** as a pretext, for the sake of appearances; **primā specie** at first sight; **specie** outwardly, to all appearances; **specie** *(w. gen)* **1** in the guise of; **2** on the pretext of

specill·um -ī *n* probe *(surgical instrument)*

specim·en -inis *n* mark, sign, proof; example; model, ideal

speciō specĕre spexī spectus *tr* to look at

speciōsē *adv* splendidly

speciōs·us -a -um *adj* handsome, good-looking, beautiful; plausible; specious

spectābil·is -is -e *adj* visible; remarkable

spectāc(u)l·um -ī *n* sight, spectacle; public performance, show; stage play; theater

spectām·en -inis *n* sign, proof

spectāti·ō -ōnis *f* observation, view; examining, testing

spectāt·or -ōris *m* observer; spectator; critic, judge ‖ *mpl* audience

spectātr·ix -īcis *f* onlooker, observer; spectator *(female)*

spectāt·us -a -um *adj* tried, tested, proved; esteemed, distinguished

specti·ō -ōnis *f* observing the auspices; right to take the auspices

spect·ō -āre -āvī -ātus *tr* to observe, watch; to face in the direction of; to consider; to bear in mind; to aim at, tend towards; to examine, test

spectr·um -ī *n* specter, apparition

specul·a -ae *f* lookout, watchtower; summit; **in speculis** on the lookout

speculābund·us -a -um *adj* on the lookout

speculār·is -is -e *adj* transparent ‖ *n* windowpane *(of mica)*, window

speculāt·or -ōris *m* spy; explorer

speculātōri·us -a -um *adj* for spying, for reconnaissance ‖ *f* reconnaissance ship

speculātr·ix -īcis *f* spy *(female)*

specul·or -ārī -ātus sum *tr* to reconnoiter, observe, watch for

specul·um -ī *n* mirror *(made of polished metal)*

spec·us -ūs *m (n)* cave, cavern; *(any artificial excavation)* hole, pit, tunnel, ditch; cavity *(of a wound, etc.)*

spēlae·um -ī *n* **(-lē-)** den, cave

spēlunc·a -ae *f* cave

spērābil·is -is -e *adj* to be hoped for

spērāt·us -a -um *adj* hoped for, desired ‖ *f* fiancée

Sperchē·is -idos *adj (fem only)* of the Spercheus River

Sperchē·us -ī *m* **(-chi-)** Spercheus *(large river in Thessaly)*

spernō spernĕre sprēvī sprētus *tr* to spurn, scorn, reject; to speak disdainfully of; to separate, dissociate

spēr·ō -āre -āvī -ātus *tr* to hope for, expect, look forward to; to trust, trust in; to anticipate, await in fear; *(w. acc & inf; also w. nom & inf in imitation of the Greek; also w.* **ut** *+ subj)* I hope that; **id quod non spero** I hope that is not the case, I hope not ‖ *intr* to hope; **bene sperare** to be optimistic; **non spero** I hope not

spēs speī *f* hope; expectation; anticipation, apprehension *(of evil);* person *or* thing on which hopes are based, *e.g.:* **Gaius Marius spes subsidium patriae** Gaius Marius, the hope and safeguard of our country; *(applied to one's offspring)* one's hopes for the future, *e.g.:* **mea carissima filiola et spes reliqua nostra** my dearest little daughter and our only remaining hope; **in spe** in prospect; **in spe** *(w. gen)* with the prospect of; **in spem** *(w. gen)* so as to give the promise of; **praeter spem** beyond all expectation

sp(h)aer·a -ae *f* sphere, globe; ball; one of the imaginary spheres in which the heavenly bodies were supposed to travel around the earth; working model of the universe

sphaeristēr·ium -iī *n* ball field, ball court

Sphin·x -gis *or* **-gos** *f* sphinx *(esp. the Sphinx of Boeotia whose riddle Oedipus was able to solve)*; the Sphinx of Egypt at Giza

spīc·a -ae *f* point; ear *(of grain);* tuft, top, head *(of plants)*
spīce·us -a -um *adj* made of ears of grain
spīcul·um -ī *n* point; sting; dart, arrow
spīc·um -ī *n* ear *(of grain)*
spīn·a -ae *f* thorn; thornbush; prickle *(of animals);* spike *(of asparagus);* backbone, spine; *(fig)* thorny question
spīnēt·um -ī *n* thorn hedge, thorny thicket
spīne·us -a -um *adj* made of thorns
spīnif·er *or* **spīnig·er -era -erum** *adj* prickly, thorny
spīnōs·us -a -um *adj* thorny, prickly; *(fig)* thorny, difficult; obscure *(style)*
spint·ēr -ēris *m* bracelet
Spinth·ēr -ēris *m* Roman family name *(cognomen)*
spintri·a -ae *m* male prostitute *(given to particularly perverted acts)*
spinturnīc·ium -iī *n* bird of ill omen
spīn·us -ī *or* **-ūs** *f* thornbush
spīr·a -ae *f* coil *(of serpent);* chin strap
spīrābil·is -is -e *adj* good to breathe, life-giving *(air)*
spīrācul·um -ī *n* pore; vent
spīrāment·um -ī *n* vent; air hole; windpipe; breathing space, pause; **animae spiramenta** lungs
spīrit·us -ūs *m* breathing, breath; breeze, wind; air, air current; wind of the bowels; breath of life, life; inspiration; spirit, soul; character, courage; enthusiasm, vigor; pride, arrogance; morale; *(gram)* aspiration; **extremus** *(or* **ultimus)** **spiritus** one's last breath; **spiritum ducere** to take a breath
spīr·ō -āre -āvī -ātus *tr* to breathe, blow; to exhale; to give off the odor of, smell of; to aspire to, aim at **‖** *intr* to breathe; to be alive; to breathe after exertion, recover one's breath; *(of the wind)* to blow, blow auspiciously, be favorable; *(of things)* to give off an odor; *(of a quality)* to emanate; to have poetic inspiration
spissāment·um -ī *n* stopper, plug
spissāt·us -a -um *adj* condensed, concentrated
spissē *adv* thickly, closely, tightly; with effort, slowly
spissesc·ō -ĕre *intr* to condense, become thick, become more compact
spissigrad·us -a -um *adj* slow-paced
spiss·ō -āre -āvī -ātus *tr* to condense, concentrate; to pack tightly; to intensify *(efforts)*
spiss·us -a -um *adj* thick; tight; dense; solid, compact; slow, sluggish; late; closely-woven, thick; packed, crowded; *(of blows, kisses)* coming thick and fast
splēn splēnis *m* spleen
splend·eō -ēre *intr* to be clear and bright; to shine, gleam; to become glossy; to be illustrious, be glorious; to be resplendent
splendesc·ō -ĕre *intr* to become bright, begin to shine; *(w. abl)* to take on luster from
splendidē *adv* splendidly, brilliantly
splendid·us -a -um *adj* clear and bright, gleaming, glistening, sparkling; spotless, noble *(character);* splendid; sumptuous; showy; illustrious
splend·or -ōris *m* splendor; brightness, brilliance; clearness
splēniāt·us -a -um *adj* wearing a patch
splēn·ium -iī *n* patch
spoliāti·ō -ōnis *f* stripping, plundering; unjust deprivation *(of honor, dignity);* ousting *(from office)*
spoliāt·or -ōris *m,* **spoliātr·ix -īcis** *f* despoiler, robber
spoliāt·us -a -um *adj* stripped, robbed
spoli·ō -āre -āvī -ātus *tr* to strip; to pillage, plunder, rob; to take away *(possessions)*
spol·ium -iī *n* hide, skin; spoils, booty, loot **‖** *npl* arms, equipment, etc., stripped from an enemy; **spolia opima** the spoils taken by a Roman general from the enemy leader he had killed in single combat; **spolia secunda** lesser spoils
spond·a -ae *f* bedframe, sofa frame; bed, sofa
spondā(u)l·ium -(i)ī *n* ritual hymn accompanied by a flute
spondeō spondēre spopondī sponsus *tr* to promise solemnly, pledge, vow; to promise in marriage; to vouch for, back up **‖** *intr (leg)* to give a guarantee, put up bail; *(w.* **pro** + *abl)* to vouch for
spondē·us -ī *m (pros)* spondee *(foot consisting of two long syllables)*
spondyl·us -ī *m* a kind of shellfish, mussel
spongi·a -ae *f* **(-ge-)** sponge; sponge eraser; quilted corslet
spons·a -ae *f* fiancée
sponsāl·ia -ium *npl* engagement; engagement party
sponsi·ō -ōnis *f* solemn promise; guarantee; bet; *(leg)* agreement between two parties that the loser pay a certain sum to the winner
spons·or -ōris *m* guarantor, surety; **Ammonius sponsor promissorum Cleopatrae** Ammon, who backs up the promises of Cleopatra
spons·us -a -um *pp of* **spondeo** **‖** *m* fiancé, bridegroom **‖** *f see* **sponsa** **‖** *n* agreement, engagement
spons·us -ūs *m* contract
sponte *(abl only) f (of persons, mostly with poss adj)* of one's own accord, voluntarily, deliberately, purposely; by oneself, unaided; *(of things)* of itself, spontaneously; on its own account, for its own

sake; **meā (suā,** *etc.)* **sponte** of my own *(his own, her own, etc.)* accord; **sponte aetatis** as a consequence of one's years; **sponte naturae (suae)** of its own nature, naturally, spontaneously; **suā sponte** considered in itself, inherently, essentially

spopondī *perf of* **spondeo**

sport·a -ae *f* plaited basket

sportell·a -ae *f* little basket

sportul·a -ae *f* little basket *(in which gifts of food were given by the patron to his clients);* dole, present *(of food or money);* gift

sprēt·or -ōris *m* despiser, scorner

sprētus *pp of* **sperno**

sprēvī *perf of* **sperno**

spūm·a -ae *f* foam, froth; hair dye; **spumas agere ore** to froth at the mouth

spūmāt·us -a -um *adj* covered with foam

spūmesc·ō -ĕre *intr* to grow foamy

spūme·us -a -um *adj* foaming

spūmif·er *or* **spūmig·er -era -erum** *adj* foaming

spūm·ō -āre -āvī -ātum *intr* to foam, froth; *(of places, things)* to be covered with foam; **equi terga spumantia** the back of the horse soaked with sweat

spūmōs·us -a -um *adj* full of foam, foaming; bombastic

spuō spuĕre spuī spūtus *tr* to spit, spit out ‖ *intr* to spit

spurcāt·us -a -um *adj* foul, filthy

spurcē *adv* filthily; offensively; in filthy language

spurcidic·us -a -um *adj* foul-mouthed, smutty, obscene

spurcific·us -a -um *adj* smutty

spurciti·a -ae *or* **spurciti·ēs -ēī** *f* filth, smut

spurc·ō -āre -āvī -ātus *tr* to make filthy, foul up; to defile

spurc·us -a -um *adj (morally)* filthy

spūtātilic·us -a -um *adj* deserving to be spit on, contemptible, disgusting

spūtāt·or -ōris *m* spitter

spūt·ō -āre -āvī -ātus *tr* to spit, spit out; to avert *(by spitting)*

spūt·um -ī *n* spit, sputum

squāl·eō -ēre -uī *intr* to be rough, be scaly; to be coated, be clotted, be stiff; to be covered with filth, be caked with mud; *(of clouds, shade)* to be dark, be murky; *(of places)* to be covered with weeds, be overgrown; *(of land)* to lie waste *(from neglect, barrenness); (of persons)* to wear mourning clothes

squālidē *adv* harshly, roughly

squālid·us -a -um *adj* rough, scaly; stiff, caked with dirt; squalid; in mourning; coarse *(speech);* barren, waste *(land)*

squāl·or -ōris *m* squalor, dirtiness; desolation; uncouthness *(of style);* squalid clothes *(as a sign of mourning)*

squal·us -ī *m* a type of sea fish

squām·a -ae *f* scale; scale armor; scale-like yellow band on the abdomen of a bee

squāme·us -a -um *adj* scaly

squāmif·er *or* **squāmig·er -era -erum** *adj* scaly ‖ *mpl* fish

squāmōs·us -a -um *adj* covered with scales, scaly

squill·a -ae *f* **(scill-)** shrimp, crayfish

st *interj* shhh!, ssst!

stabilīment·um -ī *n* support, prop; *(fig)* mainstay

stabil·iō -īre -īvī -ītus *tr* to stabilize; to establish firmly

stabil·is -is -e *adj* stable, firm, steady; steadfast, unwavering, immutable

stabilit·ās -ātis *f* stability, firmness, steadiness, durability

stabiliter *adv* firmly; steadfastly

stabul·ō -āre -āvī -ātus *tr* to stable *or* house *(animals)* ‖ *intr* to have a stall

stabul·um -ī *n* stable, stall; lair; hut; brothel; *(coll)* flea bag, cheap lodgings

stact·a -ae *or* **stact·ē -ēs** *f* myrrh oil

stad·ium -iī *n* furlong; running track, stadium; stade *(= 625 feet)*

Stagīr·a -ōrum *npl* town in Macedonia, birthplace of Aristotle

Stagīrīt·ēs -ae *m* Aristotle

stāgn·ō -āre -āvī -ātus *tr* to overflow, inundate ‖ *intr* to form a pool; to be inundated

stāgn·um -ī *n (expanse of water, natural or artificial)* pool, lake, lagoon, swamp, straits; alloy of silver and lead ‖ *npl* the depths

stalagm·ium -(i)ī *n* eardrop, earring *(w. pendant)*

stām·en -inis *n* vertical threads of a loom, warp; thread; string *(of an instrument);* fillet *(worn by priests)*

stāmine·us -a -um *adj* consisting of threads; wrapped in threads

Stat·a -ae *f* a goddess who gave protection against fire

statāri·us -a -um *adj* standing, stationary; *(of plays, actors, speakers)* free from violent action, calm, quiet ‖ *mpl* actors in a refined type of comedy ‖ *f* refined comedy

statēr·a -ae *f* scales; **statera aurificis** goldsmith's scales

staticul·us -ī *m* pose

statim *adv* at once, on the spot

stati·ō -ōnis *f* standing still, stationary position; station, post; position; residence; anchorage; **in statione** at one's post, on guard ‖ *fpl* sentries

Stāt·ius -(i)ī *m* Publius Papinius Statius *(poet of the Silver Age of Latin literature, c. A.D. 40–96)*

statīv·us -a -um *adj* stationary ‖ *npl* biv-

ouac; halts; **cum die stativorum** with a rest-day *(on the march)*
stat·or -ōris *m* attendant *(of provincial governor, later of the emperor)* ‖ **Stator** *m* cult title of Jupiter
statu·a -ae *f* statue
statūm·en -inis *n* rib *(of a hull)*
stat·uō -uĕre -uī -ūtus *tr* to cause to stand; to bring to a stop; to fix in the ground, plant; to erect, build; to set up *(a statue)*, set up a statue of; to found *(a city)*; to establish *(a practice, precedent, principle, state of affairs)*; to decide, settle *(matters)*; to decree; to strengthen, support; to appoint *(a time, place)*; *(w. double acc)* to appoint *(s.o.)* as; to determine, fix, set *(a price, payment; penalty, punishment)*; to draw up, arrange *(a battle line)*; *(w.* **utrum***)* to make up one's mind whether, decide whether; *(w. inf)* to decide to, resolve to; *(w.* **ut** *+ subj)* to decide that; *(w. pred. noun or adj)* to judge, deem; **statuere finem** *(w. dat)* set a limit to
statūr·a -ae *f* stature, height; **brevis (longae) staturae homo** a person of short (tall) stature
stat·us -a -um *pp of* **sisto** ‖ *adj* fixed, set *(times, places, seasons)*; regular, average, normal
stat·us -ūs *m* position; posture; social standing, rank, prestige; state of affairs, situation, condition; *(gram)* mood of the verb; *(leg)* legal position *(in regard to rights, obligations)*; *(mil)* position; *(rhet)* point at issue; **status rei publicae** type of government, form of constitution
statūt·us -a -um *adj* upstanding
steg·a -ae *f (naut)* deck
stell·a -ae *f* star; constellation; **stella comans** *(or* **crinita***)* comet; **stella diurna** Lucifer; **stella errans** planet; **stella de caelo lapsa** shooting star; **stella marina** starfish; **stellae quinque** the five *(recognized)* planets *(i.e., Mars, Mercury, Venus, Jupiter, Saturn)*
stell·ans -antis *adj* starry; star-shaped, starlike
stellāt·us -a -um *adj* set with stars, starry; made into a star; **stellatus Argo** *(fig)* Argo with bright eyes
stellif·er *or* **stellig·er -era -erum** *adj* starbearing, starry
stel(l)i·ō -ōnis *m* newt, lizard *(with spotted back)*
stemm·a -atis *n* genealogical tree, family tree, lineage ‖ *npl* antiquity, history
stercore·us -a -um *adj (vulg)* full of shit
stercor·ō -āre -āvī -ātus *tr* to fertilize, manure
sterculīnum *see* **sterquilinium**
sterc·us -oris *n* manure, dung
steril·is -is -e *adj* sterile, barren; causing barrenness, blighting; empty, bare; unprofitable; unrequited; wild *(tree)*
sterilit·ās -ātis *f* sterility
stern·ax -ācis *adj* bucking *(horse)*
sternō sternĕre strāvī strātus *tr* to strew, spread; to cover *(couch, horse)* with a cloth; to pave *(a road, floor)*; to strike down, lay low, slay; to raze; to overwhelm, defeat utterly; to flatten, smooth; to calm, calm down; **triclinium sternere** to set the table; ‖ *pass* to stretch out *(on the ground)*
sternūment·um -ī *n* sneeze
sternu·ō -ĕre -ī *tr* to give *(an omen)* by sneezing ‖ *intr* to sneeze
Sterop·ē -ēs *f* one of the Pleiades
Sterop·ēs -ae *m* a Cyclops working in Vulcan's blacksmith shop
sterquilīn·ium -(i)ī *or* **sterquilīn·um -ī** *or* **sterculīn·um -ī** *n* manure pile
stert·ō -ĕre *intr* to snore
Stēsichor·us -ī *m* Greek lyric poet of Himera in Sicily *(c. 640–555 B.C.)*
stetī *perf of* **sto**
Sthenel·us -ī *m* king of Mycenae, son of Perseus, and father of Eurystheus ‖ king of the Ligurians and father of Cycnus, who was changed into a swan
stibad·ium -iī *n* semicircular seat
stigm·a -atis *n* mark, brand; stigma *(of disgrace)*
stigmati·ās -ae *m* branded runaway slave
stigmōs·us -a -um *adj* branded
still·a -ae *f* drop; mere drop
stillicid·ium -(i)ī *n* drip, dripping
still·ō -āre -āvī -ātus *tr & intr* to drip
stil·us -ī *m* stylus *(pointed instrument for writing)*; composition; style
stimulāti·ō -ōnis *f* stimulation, incitement
stimulātr·ix -īcis *f* a tease *(female)*
stimule·us -a -um *adj* of goads
stimul·ō -āre -āvī -ātus *tr* to goad, torment; to spur on, incite, excite
stimul·us -ī *m* goad, prick; *(fig)* stimulus, incentive, spur; *(mil)* pointed stake concealed below the ground
stingu·ō -ĕre *tr* to extinguish
stīpāti·ō -ōnis *f* crowd, throng
stīpāt·or -ōris *m* attendant, bodyguard ‖ *mpl* retinue
stīpendiāri·us -a -um *adj* liable to taxes, tributary ‖ *mpl* tributary peoples; mercenary troops
stīpend·ium -(i)ī *n* tax, tribute, tariff; *(mil)* pay; military service; year's service; campaign; **emereri stipendia** to have served out one's term; **emeritis stipendiis** at the end of one's military service, at discharge; **merere** *(or* **mereri***)* **stipendia** to serve in the army
stīp·es -itis *m* log; trunk; branch, tree; *(pej)* blockhead
stīp·ō -āre -āvī -ātus *tr* to pack, cram,

crowd; to crowd around, accompany in a groups
stips stipis *f* donation, gift; alms
stipul·a -ae *f* stalk, blade; stubble; *(mus)* reed pipe
stipulāti·ō -ōnis *f* agreement, bargain; *(leg)* formal promise
stipulātiuncul·a -ae *f* insignificant promise
stipulāt·us -a -um *adj* promised
stipul·or -ārī -ātus sum *tr (of a buyer)* to demand a guarantee from *(the seller that the purchase is fair by asking the formal question "spondesne? dabisne?", i.e., "do you promise? will you give?")* ‖ *intr (leg)* to make a solemn promise *(by answering "spondeo, dabo", i.e., "I promise, I shall give")*
stīri·a -ae *f* icicle
stirpitus *adv* by the roots
stirp·s *or* **stirp·ēs** *or* **stirp·is -is** *f (m)* stock, stem, stalk; root; plant, shrub; race, lineage; offspring, descendant; character, nature; source, origin, beginning, foundation
stīv·a -ae *f* plow handle
stlattāri·us -a -um *adj* imported
stō stāre stetī statum *intr* to stand; *(of buildings, cities)* to stand still, remain standing; to last, endure; to stand firm; to stand upright; *(of hair)* to stand on end; *(of eyes)* to remain fixed; *(of battle)* to continue; *(of a ship)* to be moored, ride at anchor; to be motionless; to be stuck; *(w.* **ex***)* to consist of; to take sides; *(w. abl or* **in** *+ abl)* to depend on, rest with; *(w.* **per** *+ acc of person)* to depend on, be due to, be the fault of, thanks to; **per me stetit quin** *(or* **ne** *or* **quominus***)* **proelio dimicaretur** it was due to me that there was no battle; thanks to me, there was no battle; **per me stetit ut** it was due to me that ‖ *v impers (w. inf)* it is a fixed resolve; **mihi stat** *(w. inf)* it is my fixed resolve to, I have made up my mind to
Stōic·a -ae *f* Stoic philosophy
Stōicē *adv* stoically, like a Stoic
Stōic·us -a -um *adj & m* Stoic
stol·a -ae *f* dress *(female outer garment, counterpart of the male toga);* ceremonial gown *(worn by musicians)*
stolāt·us -a -um *adj* wearing a **stola;** *(fig)* ladylike
stolidē *adv* stupidly, brutishly
stolid·us -a -um *adj* dull, stupid, slow, insensitive; *(of things)* inert
stomach·or -ārī -ātus sum *tr* to be indignant at ‖ *intr* to be angry, fume
stomachōsē *adv* irritably
stomachōsius *adv* rather angrily
stomachōs·us -a -um *adj* irritable
stomach·us -ī *m* stomach; esophagus, gullet; taste; appetite; irritation, annoyance; **stomachum movere** *(or* **facere***)* to cause annoyance; **stomachus bonus** good appetite; good humor, patience
store·a *or* **stori·a -ae** *f* straw mat
strab·ō -ōnis *m* squinter ‖ **Strabo** *see* **Pompeius**
strāg·ēs -is *f* devastation; heap; pile of debris; havoc; massacre
strāgul·us -a -um *adj* covering, serving as a covering ‖ *n* rug, carpet; bedspread; horse blanket
strām·en -inis *n* straw
strāment·um -ī *n* straw; covering; saddlecloth; **stramentum agreste** straw bed
strāmine·us -a -um *adj* straw-, made of straw
strangul·ō -āre -āvī -ātus *tr* to strangle; to suffocate; to constrict; to stifle
strangūri·a -ae *f* strangury *(difficulty with urinating)*
stratēgēm·a -atis *n* stratagem; ruse
stratēg·us -ī *m* commander, general
stratiōtic·us -a -um *adj* soldierly
strāt·um -ī *n* quilt, blanket; bed, couch; horse blanket, saddlecloth; pavement; **strata viarum** paved streets
strātūr·a -ae *f* paving *(of roads)*
strāt·us -a -um *pp of* **sterno** ‖ *n see* **stratum**
strāvī *perf of* **sterno**
strēn(u)·a -ae *f* good-luck omen; lucky gift sent at the New Year
strēnuē *adv* briskly, quickly, actively, strenuously
strēnuit·ās -ātis *f* briskness, vigor, liveliness
strēnu·us -a -um *adj* brisk, vigorous, active; fast *(ship);* restless
strepit·ō -āre *intr* to be noisy; to clatter; to rustle
strepit·us -ūs *m* noise, din, racket; crash, bang, clank; rumble; rustle; creak, squeak
strep·ō -ĕre -uī -itus *tr* to shout ‖ *intr* to make a noise *(of any kind);* to rattle, clatter, clang; to rumble; to rustle; to creak, squeak; to roar; to hum; to murmur; *(of muscial instruments)* to sound, blare; *(of places)* to ring, resound, be filled
stri·a -ae *f* groove, channel, furrow
striāt·us -a -um *adj* grooved, fluted, furrowed ‖ *f* scallop *(sea animal)*
strictim *adv* superficially, cursorily
strictūr·a -ae *f* mass of hardened iron
strict·us -a -um *pp of* **stringo** ‖ *adj* close, tight, narrow
strīd·eō -ēre -ī *or* **strīd·ō -ĕre -ī** *intr* to make a high-pitched noise; to hiss, whistle; to whizz; to shriek, scream; to grate; to buzz; *(of a wound)* to gurgle; *(of wings)* to whirr
strīd·or -ōris *m* shrill sound, hiss; whiz-

zing; shriek, scream; whine; harsh noise, grating; whirring *(of wings)*

strīdul·us -a -um *adj* shrill, strident; hissing, whistling; creaking

strigil·is -is *f* scraper, strigil *(used by athletes to scrape off the mud)*

strig·ō -āre *intr* to stop; to give out

strigōs·us -a -um *adj* lean, shriveled; bald *(style)*

stringō stringĕre strinxī strictus *tr* to strip, clip; to draw *(a sword);* to draw tight, tie tight; to string *(a bow);* to pick *(fruit);* to strip off *(leaves);* to press together, compress; to graze, scratch; to border on; to touch lightly on *(a subject); (of a river)* to erode

string·or -ōris *m* **(strīg-)** twinge, shock

strix strigis *f* owl, screech owl

stroph·a -ae *f* **(strof-)** trick, feat of skill

Strophad·es -um *fpl* island home of the Harpies

strophiār·ius -(i)ī *m* bra-maker

stroph·ium -iī *n* brassiere, bra; head band

Stroph·ius -(i)ī *m* king of Phocis and father of Pylades

structil·is -is -e *adj* for building; **caementum structile** concrete

struct·or -ōris *m* builder, mason, carpenter; carver *(at table)*

structūr·a -ae *f* construction; structure

structus *pp of* **struo**

stru·ēs -is *f* pile, heap; row of sacrificial cakes

stru·ix -īcis *f* heap, pile

strūm·a -ae *f* tumor, swollen gland

strūmōs·us -a -um *adj (med)* scrofulous

stru·ō -ĕre -xī -ctus *tr* to build, erect; to deploy *(troops);* to arrange, regulate; to occasion; to compose; to construct *(words);* to plot, design, aim at; to load with

strūt(h)ē·us -a -um *adj* **malum strutheum** *n (a small variety of)* quince

strūthocamēl·us -ī *m* ostrich

struxī *perf of* **struo**

Strȳm·ōn -onis *or* **-onos** *m* river on the Macedonian-Thracian border

Strȳmon·is -idis *f* Thracian woman

Strȳmoni·us -a -um *adj* of the Strymon, Thracian

stud·eō -ēre -uī *tr* to desire, be eager for; to make *(s.th.)* one's concern **||** *intr (w. dat)* **1** to be eager for, be keen on, be enthusiastic about; **2** take pains with, busy oneself with, apply oneself to; **3** to pursue; **4** to study; **5** to be a partisan of

studiōsē *adv* eagerly, enthusiastically, diligently

studiōs·us -a -um *adj* eager, keen, enthusiastic; studious; *(w. gen)* partial to *(a person or cause); (w. gen or dat)* eager for, keen on, enthusiastic about, devoted to, fond of, desirous of; **litterarum studiosus** studious

stud·ium -(i)ī *n* eagerness, keenness, enthusiasm; devotion *(to a person);* support, goodwill *(esp. in a political sense),* party spirit; study; *(w. gen)* eagerness for, enthusiasm for; *(w.* **ad** *or* **in** *+ acc)* enthusiasm for **||** *npl* studies; **studia contraria** opposite parties

stultē *adv* foolishly

stultiloquenti·a -ae *f or* **stultiloqu·ium -(i)ī** *n* silly talk

stultiloqu·us -a -um *adj* talking foolishly

stultiti·a -ae *f* foolishness, silliness

stultivid·us -a -um *adj (foolishly)* seeing things that are not there

stult·us -a -um *adj* foolish, silly

stūp·a -ae *f* tow, coarse flax, hemp

stupe·faciō -facĕre -fēcī -factus *(pass:* **stupe·fīō -fierī -factus sum)** *tr* to stupefy, stun, shock

stup·eō -ēre -uī *tr* to be amazed at, marvel at **||** *intr* to be knocked senseless, be stunned, be astounded, be amazed; to be stopped in one's tracks

stup·escō -escĕre -uī *intr* to become amazed, become bewildered

stūpe·us -a -um *adj* of tow, hempen

stupidit·ās -ātis *f* stupidity

stupid·us -a -um *adj* amazed, astounded; stupid

stup·or -ōris *m* numbness; stupor; bewilderment, confusion; dullness, stupidity

stupp·a -ae *f* hemp, coarse flax

stuppe·us -a -um *adj* hempen

stupr·ō -āre -āvī -ātus *tr* to ravish, rape, to defile; **struprum inferre** *(w. dat)* to have sex with; to violate

stupr·um -ī *n* immorality; illicit sex; fornication *(as distinct from adultery);* rape

stupuī *perf of* **stupeo**

sturn·us -ī *m* starling

Stygi·us -a -um *adj* Stygian; hellish; deadly; dismal, melancholy

Stymphāli(c)·us -a -um *adj* Stymphalian

Stymphāl·um -ī *n or* **Stymphāl·us** *or* **Stymphal·os -ī** *m* district in Arcadia famous for its vicious birds of prey which were killed by Hercules as one his Twelve Labors

Sty·x -gis *or* **-gos** *f* chief river in the lower world; river in Arcadia

suādēl·a -ae *f* persuasion

suā·deō -dēre -sī -sus *tr* to recommend, suggest, propose; to urge, impel, induce **||** *intr (w. dat)* to advise, urge, suggest to, propose to; **sibi suadere** *(w. acc & inf)* to satisfy *or* convince oneself that

suāsi·ō -ōnis *f* recommendation; support, backing *(a proposal);* persuasive eloquence

suās·or -ōris *m* adviser; advocate, supporter

suāsōri·a -ae *f* rhetorical exercise *(giving of advice based on historical situations)*
suāsōri·us -a -um *adj* concerned with advice
suās·um -ī *n* dirty gray color
suāsus *pp of* **suadeo**
suās·us -ūs *m* advice
suāveol·ens -entis *adj* sweet-smelling, fragrant
suāviātiō *see* **saviatio**
suāvidic·us -a -um *adj* smooth *(verses);* smooth-talking
suāviloqu·ens -entis *adj* smooth-talking, charming
suāviloquenti·a -ae *f* charming way of talking, smooth talk
suāviolum *see* **saviolum**
suāvior *see* **savior**
suāv·is -is -e *adj* charming, pleasant, agreeable, attractive, nice
suāvit·ās -ātis *f* charm, pleasantness, attractiveness
suāviter *adv* charmingly, pleasantly, attractively, sweetly
suāvitūd·ō -inis *f (term of endearment)* honey, sweetie
suāvium *see* **savium**
sub *(prep) (w. abl)* **1** under, beneath, underneath: **sub sole ardente** under the blazing sun; **sub divo** under the sky, in the open; **2** under the surface of *(the earth, water):* **sub terrā** below the ground; **3** down in *(a depression, valley):* **urbs sub vallibus sita est** the city is located down in the valley; **4** close behind: **sub ipso ecce volat Diores** look, Diores comes flying close behind him; **5** close (up) to: **ager noster sub urbe** our land close to town; **6** close by: **sub dextrā (sinistrā)** on the right (left); **sub manu** close at hand; **7** at the foot of, close to, near, right under *(mountain, wall):* **sub radicibus montium** at the foothills of the mountains; **sub muro stare** to stand close to the wall; **8** immediately before, at the approach of: **sub vespere** at the approach of evening; **9** in the reign of, during the term of office of, under: **sub Tiberio Caesare** in the reign of Tiberius Caesar; **10** at the hands of: **majore sub hoste** at the hands of a greater enemy; **11** under the name *or* title of: **qui Caesareo juvenes sub nomine crescunt** these young men are growing up under Caesar's name; **12** on the pretext of: **sub excusatione valitudinis** on the pretext of poor health ‖ *(w. acc)* **1** to a position below, under, beneath: **ejus exercitum sub jugum miserat** he had sent his army under the yoke; **sub lectum repere** to crawl under the bed; **2** to a point at the foot of: **succedunt sub montem in quo** they advance to the foot of the mountain on which; **3** up *(walls, mountains):* **subire sub montem** to go up the mountain; **4** just before *(a point of time, event),* on the eve of: **sub idem tempus** at almost the same time; **sub ipsum spectaculum gladiatorium** on the eve of the gladiatorial show; **sub occasum solis** just before sunset; **5** directly after: **sub eas litteras statim recitatae sunt tuae** your letter was read aloud right after that letter; **6** in response to: **sub hanc vocem fremitus multitudinis fuit** at this statement a roar went up in the crowd; **7** into a state of subjection: **Ninus totam Asiam sub se redegit** Ninus subjected all of Asia to his control
sub- *pref* **1** *(before adjectives and verbs, giving the sense of reduced intensity):* **subamārus** somewhat bitter; **subridere** to smile; **2** *(compounded with verbs it gives the senses of the preposition):* **2a** *(position underneath):* **subscribere** to write underneath *or* below; **2b** *(movement up from below):* **subire** to go up, climb; **2c** *(movement down):* **succīdere** to cut down; **2d** *(movement close to):* **subsequi** to follow close behind; **2e** *(substitution):* **sublegere** to substitute; **2f** *(secret activity and removal):* **subnotare** to observe secretly; **subducere** to remove, steal; **3** *(before nouns, indicating lower rank):* **subcenturio** assistant centurion
subabsurdē *adv* a bit absurdly
subabsurd·us -a -um *adj* a bit absurd
subaccūs·ō -āre *tr* to blame, find some fault with
subacti·ō -ōnis *f* working *(of the soil);* development *(of the mind)*
subactus *pp of* **subigo**
subaerāt·us -a -um *adj (of gold)* having an inner layer of bronze
subagrest·is -is -e *adj* rather uncouth
subālār·is -is -e *adj* carried under the arms
subalb·us -a -um *adj* whitish, off-white
subamār·us -a -um *adj* somewhat bitter
subaquil·us -a -um *adj* somewhat dark *(complexion)*
subarroganter *adv* **(subadro-)** rather arrogantly
subauscult·ō -āre *tr* to eavesdrop on ‖ *intr* to eavesdrop
subbasilicān·us -ī *m* loafer *(hanging around the basilicas)*
subbib·ō -ĕre -ī *tr* to drink a little
subbland·ior -īrī *intr (w. dat)* to flirt with
subc- = succ-
subdifficil·is -is -e *adj* rather difficult, a bit difficult
subdiffīd·ō -ĕre *intr* to be a little distrustful
subditīci·us -a -um *adj* phoney
subditīv·us -a -um *adj* substituted, spurious

subditus *pp of* **subdo**
subdiū *adv* by day
sub·dō -dĕre -didī -ditus *tr* to put under; to subdue; to substitute; to forge, make up; to spread *(a rumor); (w. dat)* **1** to put *or* apply *(s.th.)* to, add *(s.th.)* to; **2** to subject *(s.o.)* to ‖ *refl* **se aquis subdere** to plunge into the water
subdoc·eō -ēre *tr* to instruct *(as an assistant instructor)*
subdolē *adv* rather cunningly
subdol·us -a -um *adj* underhand, sly, cunning
subdom·ō -āre *tr* to tame somewhat
subdubit·ō -āre *intr* to be rather undecided
sub·dūcō -dūcĕre -duxī -ductus *tr* to draw up from below; to pull up, raise; to remove, take away, steal; to haul up, beach *(a ship);* to withdraw *(troops);* to balance *(accounts)*
subducti·ō -ōnis *f* drydocking, beaching; calculation, computation
sub·edō -edĕre *or* **-esse -ēdī -ēsus** *tr* to eat away below *or* eat away at the bottom of; **scopulum unda subedit** water wears away the bottom of the cliff
sub·eō -īre -īvī *or* **-iī -itus** *tr* to enter *(a place; the mind);* to approach, attack; to undergo *(danger, punishment, etc.);* to help, support; to climb; to slip under; to dodge *(a blow)* ‖ *intr* to come *or* go up, climb; to follow; to advance, press forward; *(w.* **ad** *or* **in** + *acc)* **1** to come up against, attack; **2** to climb *(a mountain);* **3** to approach, enter
sūb·er -eris *n* cork tree, cork
subf- = **suf-**
subg- = **sugg-**
subhorrid·us -a -um *adj* rather coarse, rather uncouth
subigitāti·ō -ōnis *f (sl) (sexually)* fondling, feeling up
subigitātr·ix -īcis *f (sl)* a tease
subigit·ō -āre -āvī -ātus *tr (sl)* to arouse sexually by fondling, feel up
sub·igō -igĕre -ēgī -actus *tr* to turn up, till, plow *(the soil);* to knead *(dough);* to grind, reduce to a powder: **farina in pollinem subacta** flour reduced to a fine powder; to work *(wool into a smooth thread);* to rub down, massage *(the body, also in the erotic sense);* to tame, break in *(an animal);* to train, discipline *(the mind);* to conquer, subdue *(a country);* to row, propel *(a boat);* to make smooth *(by rubbing, polishing);* to lubricate; to whet, sharpen: **subigunt in cote securis** they sharpen their axes on a whetstone; to suppress, quell *(hostilities);* to subdue the spirit of, break the spirits of *(people); (w. inf or* **ut** + *subj)* to force, constrain *(s.o.)* to; *(w.* **ad***)* to drive to: **subegit nos ad necessitudinem dedendi res** he drove us to the necessity of giving up our property
subimpud·ens -entis *adj* rather shameless
subinān·is -is -e *adj* rather empty, rather pointless
subinde *adv* immediately afterwards; promptly; from then on; from time to time, now and then
subinsuls·us -a -um *adj* rather insipid
subinvid·eō -ēre *intr (w. dat)* to envy *(s.o.)* a little
subinvīs·us -a -um *adj* rather disliked, somewhat unpopular
subinvīt·ō -āre *tr* to invite unenthusiastically
subīr·ascor -ascī -ātus sum *intr* to be annoyed; *(w. dat)* to be peeved at
subitāri·us -a -um *adj* requiring prompt action; *(of troops)* hastily called up *(to meet an emergency); (of buildings)* hastily erected; **res subitaria** emergency
subitō *adv* suddenly, unexpectedly, at once; **subito dicere** to speak ex-tempore
subit·us -a -um *adj* coming on suddenly, sudden, unexpected; rash *(person);* emergency *(troops)* ‖ *n* emergency; **de subito** *(or* **per subitum***)* suddenly
subjac·eō -ēre -uī *intr* to lie nearby; *(w. dat)* to lie under, lie close to; **monti subjacere** to lie at the foot of the mountain
subjecti·ō -ōnis *f* subjection; substitution; forgery
subjectissimē *adv* most humbly
subject·ō -āre -āvī -ātus *tr* to toss up *(from below);* **stimulos subjectare** *(w. dat)* to prod s.o. on
subject·or -ōris *m* forger
subject·us -a -um *pp of* **subjicio** ‖ *adj (w. dat)* **1** located near, bordering (on); **2** subject to; **subjecta materia** subject matter ‖ *m* subject, subordinate, underling
sub·jiciō -jicĕre -jēcī -jectus *tr* to throw up, fling up; to bring up; to bring up close, expose; to suggest; to add, append; to suborn; to substitute; to forge; *(w. dat or* **sub** + *acc)* **1** to put, place *(s.th.)* under; **2** to subject *(s.o.)* to; **3** to classify *(s.th.)* under; **4** to submit *(s.th.)* to *(one's judgment)*
subjun·gō -gĕre -xī -ctus *tr (w. dat)* **1** to yoke *or* harness to; **2** to join to, connect with, add to; **3** to make subject to
sub·labor -lābī -lapsus sum *intr* to sink, fall down, collapse; to glide imperceptibly; to fall back, fail
sublātē *adv* loftily, in lofty tones
sublāti·ō -ōnis *f* elevation, raising
sublāt·us -a -um *pp of* **suffero** *and of* **tollo** ‖ *adj* elated
sublect·ō -āre *tr* to coax, cajole

sub·legō -legĕre -lēgī -lectus *tr* to gather up, pick up; to steal; to kidnap; to substitute; to overhear, pick up
sublest·us -a -um *adj* weak; trifling
sublevāti·ō -ōnis *f* alleviation
sublev·ō -āre -āvī -ātus *tr* to lift up, raise, support; to assist; to encourage; to promote, further *(an activity);* to lighten, alleviate; to make up for *(a fault)* ‖ *refl* to get up
sublic·a -ae *f* stake, pile *(esp. for a bridge)*
sublici·us -a -um *adj* resting on piles; **pons sublicius** wooden bridge *(across the Tiber, built by Ancus Marcius, third king of Rome)*
subligācul·um -ī *n* loincloth, shorts
sublig·ar -āris *n* loincloth, shorts
sublig·ō -āre -āvī -ātus *tr (w. dat)* to tie *or* fasten *(e.g., a sword)* to *or* below
sublīmē *adv* aloft, on high
sublīmen *adv* upwards, on high
sublīm·is -is -e *adj* high, raised up, lifted high; *(of ideas)* lofty, grand, exalted; borne aloft, through the sky; aspiring; having lofty ideals; exalted in rank, eminent, distinguished; lofty, majestic *(style)* ‖ *npl* the heights
sublīmit·ās -ātis *f* loftiness, sublimity
sublīm·us -a -um *adj* high, lofty
sublingul·ō -ōnis *m (hum)* dish-licker, dishwasher
sub·linō -linĕre -lēvī -litus *tr* to smear over, coat *(a surface);* to smear the underside of; **os sublinere** *(w. dat)* to pull a practical joke on
sublūc·eō -ēre *intr* to shine faintly; *(w. dat)* to shine through
sub·luō -luĕre -luī -lūtus *tr* to wash underneath; to flow at the foot of *(a mountain);* to wash *(the underside of the body);* **quid solium subluto podice perdis?** why do you ruin the bathtub with washing your behind?
sublustr·is -is -e *adj* dimly lighted; throwing some light, glimmering, flickering
subm- = summ-
sub·nascor -nascī -nātus sum *intr (w. dat)* to grow up underneath
sub·nectō -nectĕre -nexuī -nexus *tr* to fasten, tie *(s.th.)* underneath; to confine; *(w. dat)* to fasten *or* tie *(s.th.)* below *(s.th. else)*
subneg·ō -āre -āvī -ātus *tr* to half-refuse
subni·ger -gra -grum *adj* blackish
subnīsus -a -um *adj* **(-nix-)** propped up; *(w. dat)* **1** propped up on, resting on, leaning on; **2** relying on, confiding in; **3** elated by
subnot·ō -āre -āvī -ātus *tr* to note down, record, register; to observe secretly
subnub·a -ae *f* rival *(female)*
subnūbil·us -a -um *adj* somewhat cloudy, overcast
sub·ō -āre *intr* to be in heat
subobscēn·us -a -um *adj* somewhat obscene, shady, off-color
subobscūr·us -a -um *adj* somewhat obscure
subodiōs·us -a -um *adj* rather tiresome, rather annoying
suboffend·ō -ĕre *intr* to give some offense
subol·et -ēre *v impers* there is a faint smell; **mihi subolet** I have an inkling, I have a sneaking suspicion
subol·ēs -is *f* offspring; children; the young *(of animals)*; race, stock
subolesc·ō -ĕre *intr* to grow up
subor·ior -īrī -tus sum *intr* to rise up in succession, arise, proceed
suborn·ō -are *tr* to equip, supply, provide; to employ as a secret agent, induce secretly, suborn; to dress up *(in a costume, disguise);* to prepare, instruct *(for some underhand purpose)*
subp- = supp-
subr- = surr-
sub·scrībō -scrībĕre -scripsī -scriptus *tr* to write underneath; to sign; to write down, record, register ‖ *intr (leg)* to sign an accusation, act as prosecutor; *(w. dat)* **1** to add in writing to; **2** to agree to; *(leg) (w.* **in** *+ acc)* to sign an accusation against, indict
subscripti·ō -ōnis *f* inscription underneath; signature; s.th. written under a heading; recording *(of an offense by the censor);* record, register; *(leg)* specification *(of crimes)* in an indictment, a count, charge
subscript·or -ōris *m (leg)* signer, co-signer *(of an accusation)*
subscriptus *pp of* **subscribo**
subsc·ūs -ūdis *f* **(sups-)** tenon of a dovetail
subsecīvus *see* **subsicivus**
subsec·ō -āre -uī -tus *tr* to clip, trim, cut off; to pare, clip *(nails)*
subsecūtus *pp of* **subsequor**
subsell·ium -(i)ī *n* seat, bench; stool; seat *or* bench on a lower level; seat in the Senate; *(leg)* seat in the court *(usu. where the judge, prosecution or the defense and their witnesses sat); (fig)* the bench, tribunal, court; seat in the theater; **versatus in utrisque subsellis** experienced as lawyer and judge ‖ *npl* the courts; bleachers *(where the poor people sat); (fig)* occupants of the bleachers
subsen·tiō -tīre -sī -sus *tr* to have some inkling of
sub·sequor -sequī -secūtus sum *tr* to follow close after; to pursue; to back up, support; to imitate; to adhere to, conform to; to come after, succeed *(in time or order)* ‖ *intr* to ensue
subserv·iō -īre *intr (w. dat)* **1** to be subject to; **2** to accommodate oneself to, humor; **3** to support, aid

subsicīv·us *or* **subsecīv·us -a -um** *adj* **(sup-)** *(of land)* left over *(after an allotment);* extra, spare *(time);* extra, overtime *(work)*

subsidiāri·us -a -um *adj* in reserve; *(mil)* reserve ‖ *mpl (mil)* reserves

subsid·ium -(i)ī *n* aid, support; mainstay; place of refuge; protection; *(mil)* reserves; military support, relief; **ad** *(or* **in) subsidium** for support; **subsidio esse** *(w. dat)* to be of help to ‖ *npl (mil)* reserves, reinforcements

sub·sīdō -sīdĕre -sēdī *tr* to lie in wait for ‖ *intr* to sit down, crouch down, settle down; to sink, subside, settle; to settle down, establish residence

subsignān·us -a -um *adj (mil)* special reserve *(troops)*

subsign·ō -āre -āvī -ātus *tr* to endorse, subscribe to *(an opinion);* to register, enter, record; to guarantee

subsil·iō -īre -uī *intr* **(suss-) (sups-)** to jump up

sub·sistō -sistĕre -stitī *tr* to hold out against ‖ *intr* to stand up; to make a stand, take a firm stand; to come to a standstill, stop; to stay behind; *(w. dat)* **1** to take a stand against, oppose, fight; **2** to meet *(an expense)*

subsort·ior -īrī -ītus sum *tr* to choose as a substitute by lot ‖ *intr* to choose a substitute by lot; *(in a passive sense)* to be chosen as a substitute

subsortīti·ō -ōnis *f* substitution by lot

substanti·a -ae *f* substance, essence; means, wealth, property

sub·sternō -sternĕre -strāvī -strātus *tr* to spread underneath; to cover; *(w. dat)* to put at the disposal of, make subservient to; **rem publicam libidini suae substernere** to misuse high office to serve one's lust

substit·uō -uĕre -uī -ūtus *tr* to submit, present; to substitute; *(w. dat or* **in locum** *w. gen)* to substitute for *or* in place of; **animo** *(or* **oculis) substituere** to imagine

subst·ō -āre *intr* to stand firm, hold out; *(w. dat)* to stand up to

substrātus *pp of* **substerno**

substrāvī *perf of* **substerno**

substrict·us -a -um *adj* tight, narrow, small

sub·stringō -stringĕre -strinxī -strictus *tr* to tie up, draw up; to restrain, control; *(w. dat)* to press *(s.th.)* close to

substructi·ō -ōnis *f* substructure, foundation

substru·ō -ĕre -xī -ctus *tr* to lay *(a foundation);* **vias glareā substruere** to lay a foundation of gravel on the roads

subsult·ō -āre *intr* to jump up and down

sub·sum -esse *intr* **(sup-)** to be near, be at hand; *(w. gen) (of feelings, qualities, underlying cause or meaning)* to form the foundation for, be at the bottom of; *(w. dat)* **1** to be below *or* underneath, be under; **2** to be at the foot of; **3** to be (located) at the edge of *(the sea);* **4** to be concealed in; **5** to be (worn) under *(e.g., a tunic);* **6** to be attached to *(a document);* **7** to be subject to, be subservient to

subsūt·us -a -um *adj* trimmed at the bottom

subtē(g)m·en -inis *n* weft, woof *(horizontal threads woven in between the warp threads in a loom);* yarn

subter *adv* **(sup-)** below, underneath ‖ *prep (w. abl)* beneath, below, underneath, under ‖ *(w. acc)* underneath, beneath; up to, close to, close beneath

subter·dūcō -dūcĕre -duxī -ductus *tr* **(sup-)** to remove secretly ‖ *refl* to steal away, sneak away

subter·fugiō -fugĕre -fūgī *tr* **(sup-)** to evade, avoid ‖ *intr* to run off secretly

subter·lābor -lābī *tr* to glide *or* flow under ‖ *intr* to slip away

sub·terō -terĕre -trīvī -trītus *tr* **(sup-)** to wear away underneath

subterrāne·us -a -um *adj* subterranean, underground

subtex·ō -ĕre -uī -tus *tr* to sew on; to veil, cover; *(fig)* to work up, compose; *(w. dat)* **1** to sew onto; **2** to throw *(a covering)* over; **3** to work *(s.th.)* into *(a story or plot)*

subtīl·is -is -e *adj* **(sup-)** finely woven; delicate; subtle; discriminating, refined; precise, matter-of-fact

subtīlit·ās -ātis *f* **(sup-)** fineness, minuteness; slenderness; exactness, precision; simplicity *(of style)*

subtīliter *adv* **(sup-)** finely, delicately; accurately; plainly, simply

subtim·eō -ēre *intr* to be a bit afraid

sub·trahō -trahĕre -traxī -tractus *tr* **(sup-)** to drag up from beneath, drag out, draw off; to withdraw, remove; to withhold; to misappropriate, steal; to undermine; to avert *(eyes); (w. dat)* to drag *(s.th.)* away from; *(w. abl)* to rescue *(s.o.)* from the threat of, snatch *(s.o.)* from *(impending danger, ruin);* **oculis subtrahere** to remove from sight ‖ *refl (w.* **ab)** to withdraw from, dissociate oneself from *(an activity, responsibility)*

subtrist·is -is -e *adj* rather sad

subtrītus *pp of* **subtero**

subtrīvī *perf of* **subtero**

subturpicul·us -a -um *adj* somewhat disgraceful

subturp·is -is -e *adj* rather disgraceful, somewhat scandalous

subtus *adv* below, underneath

subtūs·us -a -um *adj* somewhat bruised
subūcul·a -ae *f* undertunic *(worn by both sexes)*
subulc·us -ī *m* swineherd
Subūr·a -ae *f* noisy business and nightlife district in Rome, N.E. of the Forum between the Esquiline and Quirinal Hills
Subūrān·us -a -um *adj* of the Subura
suburbānit·ās -ātis *f* proximity to Rome
suburbān·us -a -um *adj* suburban, near Rome **II** *m* suburbanite **II** *n* suburban Rome
suburb·ium -(i)ī *n* suburb
suburg·eō -ēre *tr (w.* **ad)** to keep *or* turn *(a ship)* close to
subvecti·ō -ōnis *f* transportation
subvect·ō -āre -āvī -ātus *tr* to bring up regularly, transport regularly
subvect·us -ūs *m* bringing up, transportation
sub·vehō -vehĕre -vexī -vectus *tr* to carry *or* bring up, transport
sub·veniō -venīre -vēnī -ventum *intr (w. dat)* to come up to aid, reinforce
subvent·ō -āre *intr (w. dat)* to rush to the aid of
subver·eor -ērī *intr* to be a bit apprehensive
subvers·ō -āre *tr* **(-vors-)** to ruin completely
subvers·or -ōris *m* one who overthrows *(a law)*
subver·tō -tĕre -tī -sus *tr* **(-vort-)** to turn upside down, upset, overthrow, subvert
subvex·us -a -um *adj* sloping upward
subvol·ō -āre *intr* to fly up
subvolturi·us -a -um *adj* vulture-like
subvolv·ō -ĕre *tr* to roll up(hill)
subvor- = subver-
succav·us -a -um *adj* hollow underneath
succēdāne·us -a -um *adj* **(succī-)** killed as a substitute
suc·cēdo -cēdĕre -cessī -cessus *tr* to climb; to march on *or* against, advance as far as **II** *intr* to come up, climb; to come next, follow in succession; to turn out well, turn out successfully; *(w.* **ad, in,** *or* **sub** *+ acc)* to climb, climb up; *(w. dat)* **1** to succeed, follow; **2** become a successor to; **3** to succeed in *(an undertaking);* **4** to yield to, submit to; **5** to relieve *(e.g., tired troops);* **6** to enter, go below to *(e.g., a shelter, a grave); (w.* **ad** *or* **in** *+ acc) (fig)* to attain *(e.g., high honors),* enter upon *(an inheritance);* **bene succedere** to turn out well
succen·dō -dĕre -dī -sus *tr* to set on fire, set fire to; to light *(a fire); (fig)* to inflame, enkindle
succens·eō -ēre -uī *intr* **(susc-)** *(w. dat)* to be enraged at
succensus *pp of* **succendo**
succenturiāt·us -a -um *adj* **(subc-)** in reserve
succenturi·ō -āre -āvī -ātus *tr* **(subc-)** to receive *(s.o.)* as a substitute into a *centuria*
succenturi·ō -ōnis *m* **(subc-)** assistant centurion, substitute for a centurion
successi·ō -ōnis *f* succession
success·or -ōris *m* successor
success·us -ūs *m* approach, advance uphill; outcome; success
succīdāneus *see* **succedaneus**
suc(c)īdi·a -ae *f* leg *or* side of meat; *(fig)* extra income
suc·cīdō -cīdĕre -cīdī -cīsus *tr* **(subc-)** to cut down, cut off, mow down
suc·cĭdō -cidĕre -cĭdī *intr* **(subc-)** to sink, give way; to collapse, fail
succid·us -a -um *adj* **(sūci-)** juicy; *(coll)* plump *(girl)*
succidu·us -a -um *adj* sinking, falling, collapsing, giving way
succint·us -a -um *adj (of a person)* with clothes tucked up; *(of a statement)* concise; *(of a book)* compact; *(fig)* in a state of readiness; *(fig) (w. abl)* equipped with *(a means of defense, military strength);* **cultro succinctus** carrying a knife in his belt
succin·gō -gĕre -xī -ctus *tr* to tuck up; to put on *(a sword);* to equip, arm; to surround closely **II** *refl & pass (w. abl)* to gather up one's clothes with
succingul·um -ī *n* belt
succin·ō -ĕre *tr* to recite in a droning voice **II** *intr* to chime in *(in conversation); (w. dat)* to accompany *(in singing or playing)*
succīsus *pp of* **succīdo**
succlāmāti·ō -ōnis *f* shouting in reply
succlām·ō -āre -āvī -ātus *tr* **(subc-)** to shout out after; to interrupt with shouts, heckle; *(w. dat)* to shout out *(words)* at
subcoll·ō -āre -āvī -ātus *tr* to carry on one's shoulders
succontumēliōsē *adv* **(subc-)** rather insolently
suc·crescō -crescĕre -crēvī *intr* **(subc-)** to grow up; to be replenished; *(w. dat)* to attain to
succrisp·us -a -um *adj* **(subc-)** rather curly
succulent·us -a -um *adj* **(subc-)** succulent
suc·cumbō -cumbĕre -cubuī -cubitum *intr* **(subc-)** to fall back, sink back; to succumb, yield, submit
suc·currō -currĕre -currī -cursum *intr (w. dat)* **1** to run up to; **2** to run to help; **3** to occur to, enter the mind of; **4** *(topog)* to extend to the foot of **II** *v impers* the thought occurs
succ·us *or* **sūc·us -ī** *m* sap, juice; taste, flavor; *(fig)* vitality
succuss·us -ūs *m* shaking, jolt

succust·ōs -ōdis *m* **(subc-)** assistant guard
suc·cutiō -cutĕre -cussī -cussus *tr* to toss up; to jolt *(a rider, vehicle)*
sūcidus *see* **succidus**
sūcin·us -a -um *adj & n* amber
suctus *pp of* **sugo**
sucul·a -ae *f* winch, windlass
Sūcul·ae -ārum *fpl (astr)* Hyades
sūculent·us -a -um *adj* juicy, succulent
sūc·us -ī *m* juice; *(of the soil)* moisture; *(fig)* sap, vitality
sūdār·ium -(i)ī *n* handkerchief; towel
sūdātōri·us -a -um *adj* sweat-, for sweating **‖** *n* sweat room, sauna
sūdātr·ix -īcis *adj* causing sweat
sud·is -is *f* stake, pile; pike *(weapon);* sharp projection, spike
sūd·ō -āre -āvī -ātus *tr* to sweat, exude; to soak with sweat; *(fig)* to sweat at, sweat over **‖** *intr* to sweat; to drip
sūd·or -ōris *m* sweat; moisture; *(fig)* hard work
sūducul·um -ī *n (hum)* sweat-maker *(i.e., a whipping post)*
sūd·us -a -um *adj* dry; clear, cloudless **‖** *n* clear weather, bright sky
Suēbi·a -ae *f* district E. of the Elbe
Suēb·ī -ōrum *mpl* **(Suēv-)** generic name of a group of German tribes
suescō suescĕre suēvī suētus *tr* to accustom, familiarize **‖** *intr (w. dat or inf)* to become accustomed to
Suētōn·ius -(i)ī *m* Roman clan name *(nomen) (esp. that of Gaius Suetonius Tranquillus, biographer, born c.* A.D. *69)*
suēt·us -a -um *pp of* **suesco ‖** *adj* usual, familiar
Suēvī *see* **Suebi**
suf·ēs *or* **sūf·es -etis** *m* chief magistrate at Carthage
suffarcināt·us -a -um *adj* **(subf-)** stuffed, padded
suffarcin·ō -āre -āvī -ātus *tr* **(subf-)** to stuff, cram
suffect·us -a -um *pp of* **sufficio ‖** *adj* substitute; **consul suffectus** substitute consul *(appointed to complete an unexpired term of another consul)*
sufferō sufferre sustulī sublātus *tr* **(subf-)** to suffer, bear, endure; to place at s.o.'s disposal, offer
suf·ficiō -ficĕre -fēcī -fectus *tr* to lay the foundation for; to dip, tinge, dye; to appoint to a vacancy; to yield, supply, afford **‖** *intr* to be sufficient; *(w. dat)* to suffice for
suf·figō -figĕre -fixī -fixus *tr* to nail up, fasten
suffīm·en -inis *n* incense
suffīment·um -ī *n* incense
suff·iō -īre -īvī *or* **-(i)ī -ītus** *tr* to fumigate; to perfume
suffixus *pp of* **suffigo**
sufflām·en -inis *n* brake *(on a vehicle)*
sufflāmin·ō -āre -āvī -ātus *tr* to apply the brakes to
sufflāt·us -a -um *adj* puffed up, bloated; *(fig)* bombastic; *(fig)* fuming *(w. anger)*
suffl·ō -āre -āvī -ātus *tr* to blow up, inflate **‖** *intr* to blow, puff
suffōc·ō -āre -āvī -ātus *tr* to choke, suffocate
suf·fodiō -fodĕre -fōdī -fossus *tr* **(subf-)** to stab, pierce; to dig under *(walls)*
suffrāgāti·ō -ōnis *f* **(subf-)** voting *(in s.o.'s favor),* support
suffrāgāt·or -ōris *m* **(subf-)** voter; supporter *(at the polls),* partisan
suffrāgātōri·us -a -um *adj* **(subf-)** partisan
suffrāg·ium -(i)ī *n* **(subf-)** ballot, vote; right to vote, franchise; decision, judgment; applause, approbation; **suffragium ferre** to cast a ballot; **suffragium ferre** *(w.* **de** *or* **in** *+ abl)* to vote on
suffrāg·or -ārī -ātus sum *intr* to cast a favorable vote; *(w. dat)* to vote in favor of, support, vote for; **fortunā suffragante** with luck on our side
suffring·ō -ĕre *tr* **(subf-)** to break
suffug·ium -(i)ī *n* shelter, cover
sufful·ciō -cīre -sī -tus *tr* to prop up, underpin, support
suf·fundō -fundĕre -fūdī -fūsus *tr* **(subf-)** to pour in, fill; to suffuse, spread; to tinge, color; to infuse; **virgineum ore ruborem suffundere** *(w. dat)* to make *(s.o.)* blush like a girl
suffūr·or -ārī *tr* to filch, snitch
suffusc·us -a -um *adj* **(subf-)** darkish
suffūsus *pp of* **suffundo**
Sugambr·ī -ōrum *mpl* a German tribe living to the E. of the Lower Rhine, above the Ubii
sug·gerō -gerĕre -gessī -gestus *tr* **(subg-)** to supply, add; to suggest
suggest·um -ī *n* platform; stage
suggestus *pp of* **suggero**
suggest·us -ūs *m* platform; stage
suggrand·is -is -e *adj* **(subg-)** rather huge
sug·gredior -gredī -gressus sum *tr & intr* **(subg-)** to approach
sūgillāti·ō -ōnis *f* **(suggill-, subgill-)** bruise; affront
sūgill·ō -āre -āvī -ātus *tr* to beat black-and-blue; to affront, insult
sūgō sūgĕre suxī suctus *tr* to suck
suī *see* **se**
suī *perf of* **suo**
suill·us -a -um *adj* of swine; **caro suilla** pork; **grex suillus** herd of swine **‖** *f* pork
sulc·ō -āre -āvī -ātus *tr* to furrow; to plow; to score, make a line in
sulc·us -ī *m* furrow; ditch, trench *(for plants);* track *(of a wheel or meteor);* wrinkle; plowing; wake *(of a ship)*

sulf·ur -uris *n* sulfur
Sull·a -ae *m* **(Syll-)** Sulla *(Cornelius Sulla Felix, Roman general, dictator, and political reformer, 138–78 B.C.)*
Sullān·ī -ōrum *mpl* **(Syll-)** partisans of Sulla
sullātur·iō -īre *intr* to wish to be a Sulla
Sulm·ō -ōnis *m* town c. 90 miles E. of Rome, and birthplace of Ovid
Sulmōnens·is -is -e *adj* of Sulmo
sulp(h)·ur *or* **sulf·ur -uris** *n* sulfur
sulp(h)urāt·us -a -um *adj* saturated with sulfur
sulp(h)ure·us -a -um *adj* sulfurous
sultis = si vultis if you please
sum esse fuī futūrus *intr* to be; to exist; *(w. gen of possession)* to belong to, pertain to, be characteristic of, be the duty of; *(w. gen or abl of quality)* to be of, be possessed of, have; *(w. gen or abl of value)* to be valued at, cost; *(w. dat)* to belong to; *(w.* **ab)** to belong to; *(w.* **ad)** to be designed for; *(w.* **ex)** to consist of; **est** *(w. inf)* it is possible to, it is permissible to; **est** *(w.* **ut)** it is possible that; **sunt qui** there are those who, there are people who, they are of the type that
sumbolus *see* **symbolus**
sūm·en -inis *n* breast; teat, udder; breeding sow
summ- = subm-
summ·a -ae *f* main thing; chief point, gist, summary; sum, amount; contents, substance; sum of money; sum-total *(of hopes, etc.)*; the whole issue, the whole case; *(phil)* totality of matter, the universe; **ad summam** in short; generally, on the whole; as the crowning touch, to complete it all; **in summā** in all; **in summam** taken as a whole; **ad** *(or* **in) summam prodesse** *(or* **proficere)** to be of general good; **summa honoraria** honorarium, voluntary payment to a lawyer; **summa rerum** the world; supreme power; general welfare; **summa summarum** the whole universe
summān·ō -āre *intr* **(subm-)** to drip a bit
Summān·us -ī *m* Roman god of night lightning
summ·ās -ātis *adj* aristocratic, first-class
summātim *adv* on the surface; generally, summarily
summē *adv* very, extremely, intensely
summer·gō -gĕre -sī -sus *tr* **(subm-)** to sink, submerge, drown
summers·us -a -um *adj* **(subm-)** sunken; living underwater; *(sunk)* below the horizon
summer·us -a -um *adj* **(subm-)** nearly straight, nearly pure
sumministr·ō -āre -āvī -ātus *tr* **(subm-)** to furnish
summissē *or* **summissim** *adv* **(subm-)** in a low voice, softly; modestly, humbly
summissi·ō -ōnis *f* lowering, dropping
summiss·us -a -um *adj* lowered, stooping; lowered, soft *(voice)*; humble, unassuming; submissive; too submissive, abject; *(of hair)* worn long, let down
sum·mittō -mittĕre -mīsī -missus *tr* **(subm-)** to let down, lower, sink, drop; to let *(hair)* grow long; to lower, reduce, moderate, relax, lessen; to humble; to rear, produce, put forth; to send secretly; to send as a reinforcement; to send as a substitute; **animum summittere** *(w. dat)* to yield to ‖ *refl* to bend down, stoop over; to condescend; *(w. dat)* to give in to
summolestē *adv* **(subm-)** with some annoyance
summolest·us -a -um *adj* **(subm-)** rather annoying
summon·eō -ēre -uī -itus *tr* to give *(s.o.)* a gentle reminder, remind privately; **patres salutavit nominatim nullo summonente** he greeted senators by name, with no one prompting him
summopere *or* **summō opere** *adv* with the greatest diligence, with utmost effort
summōt·us -a -um *adj* secluded, distant
sum·moveō -movēre -mōvī -mōtus *tr* **(subm-)** to move up, advance; to clear *(e.g., the court)*; to remove; to expel, banish; to deny admission to, keep off; to clear from the path of a magistrate; to dispense with *(a procedure)*; to ward off *(heat, cold)*; *(fig)* to drive away, forget about *(e.g., worries)*; *(mil)* dislodge
summul·a -ae *f* small sum of money
summum *adv (w. numbers)* at most; at latest; **uno aut summum altero proelio** in one or at most two battles
summ·us -a -um *adj* highest, uppermost; the top of, the surface of; last, latest, the end of; greatest, best, top, consummate; finest, first-rate; at the height of *(a season)*; perfect *(peace, tranquility)*; closest, best *(friend)*; most distinguished; middle *(finger)*; *(of affairs, concerns)* most important, of highest importance; *(of a diner)* farthest to the left on the couch *(from the viewpoint of those dining)*; *(of a couch)* to the left of the middle couch; **omnia summa facere** to do one's utmost; **res summa** *(or* **res summae)** critical situation; **res summa** *(or* **respublica summa)** the welfare of the state, the general welfare; **summa cena** main course; **summa manus** finishing touches; **summa mensa** main course; **summa rudis** head instructor in a gladiatorial school *(literally, top practice-sword)*; **summo jure** with the full force of the law ‖ *m* head of the table; ‖ *f see* **summa** ‖ *n* top,

surface; highest place, head of the table; **ab summo aut ab imo** at the top or the bottom of the page ‖ *npl* extremities *(of the body or its parts);* general purport *(of a writing)*

sūmō sūmĕre sumpsī sumptus *tr* to take up; to put on, dress oneself in, wear; to exact, inflict *(penalty);* to take up, begin, enter upon; to eat, consume; to assume, suppose, take for granted; to cite, adduce, mention; to assume, appropriate *(a title, name);* to embrace *(a practice, way of life);* to borrow *(words, ideas from other people);* to select; to purchase, buy; to adopt *(a child);* **aliquid mutuum sumere** to borrow s.th.; **arma sumere** to take up arms; **in se sumere** to take upon oneself, assume; **mortem** *(or* **exitium)** *(usu. w.* **sponte)** **sumere** to commit suicide; **supplicium sumere** to exact punishment

sumpti·ō -ōnis *f* assumption, premiss

sumptuāri·us -a -um *adj* expense-, relating to expenses; *(of laws)* sumptuary, against extravagance

sumptuōsē *adv* sumptuously, expensively

sumptuōs·us -a -um *adj* costly, expensive; lavish, wasteful

sumptus *pp of* **sumo**

sumpt·us -ūs *m* cost, expense; **sumptui esse** *(w. dat)* to be expensive for; **sumptum suum exercere** to earn one's keep; **sumptu tuo** at your expense

Sūn·ium *or* **Sun·ion -iī** *n* S.E. promontory of Attica

suō suĕre suī sūtus *tr* to sew, stitch, tack together

suōmet = *emphatic form of* **suo**

suopte = *emphatic form of* **suo**

suovetaurīl·ia -ium *npl* **(suovi-)** sacrifice of a pig, sheep, and bull

supell·ex *or* **suppell·ex -ectilis** *f* furniture, household utensils; tableware; outfit, equipment

sup·er -era -erum *adj see* **superus**

super *adv* on the top, on the surface, above; besides, moreover; in addition to what has been said; **satis superque** enough and to spare; **super esse** to be left over ‖ *prep (w. acc)* over, above; upon, on top of; *(w. numbers)* over, more than; besides, over and above; **alius super alium** one on top of another, one after another; **super cenam** *(or* **mensam)** over dinner, at table *(i.e., during the meal);* **super omnia** *(or* **cuncta)** above all, more than anything ‖ *(w. abl)* above, over, upon, on; concerning, about, in the matter of; besides, in addition to; at *(e.g., midnight)*

super·a -ōrum *npl* upper world, sky; heaven; heavenly bodies

superā *adv* above

superābil·is -is -e *adj* surmountable, climbable; conquerable

superad·dō -dĕre -didī -ditus *tr* to add besides, add to boot

super·ans -antis *adj* predominant; outstanding, remarkable

superāt·or -ōris *m* conqueror

superbē *adv* arrogantly, haughtily, snobbishly

superbi·a -ae *f* arrogance, haughtiness, snobbishness; pride

superbiloquenti·a -ae *f* haughty tone, arrogant speech

superb·iō -īre *intr* to be haughty; to be proud; to be superb, be magnificent; *(w. abl)* to take pride in

superb·us -a -um *adj* arrogant, haughty, snobbish; proud; overbearing, tyrannical; fastidious, disdainful; superb, magnificent; *(of an honor)* that is a source of pride; *(w. abl)* proud of; **ales superba** the phoenix

supercil·ium -(i)ī *n* eyebrow; frown, will *(of Jupiter);* stern looks; summit, brow *(of a hill);* arrogance, superciliousness; artificial eyebrow

superēmin·eō -ēre *tr* to tower over, top

superfici·ēs -ēī *f* top, surface; *(leg)* fixtures, improvements, buildings *(i.e., anything upon the property but not the land itself)*

superfix·us -a -um *adj* stuck *or* impaled on top of; **rumpiis superfixa capita** heads stuck on top of long spears

super·fīō -fierī *intr* to be over and above; to be left over

superfix·us -a -um *adj* superabundant, running over; *(w. abl)* abounding in

superflu·ō -ĕre -xī *intr* to overflow; to be superfluous

superfuī *perf of* **supersum**

super·fundō -fundĕre -fūdī -fūsus *tr (w. abl)* to shower *(s.th.)* with; *(w. dat)* to pour *(s.th.)* upon ‖ *refl & pass* to spread, spread out, extend

super·gredior -gredī -gressus sum *tr* to walk *or* step over; to surpass

super·ī -ōrum *mpl* the gods above; men on earth; mortals; upper world

superimmin·eō -ēre *intr (w. dat)* to stand over *(s.o. in a threatening manner)*

superimpend·ens -entis *adj* overhanging, towering overhead

super·impōnō -impōnĕre -imposuī -positus *tr* to place on top, place overhead

superimposit·us -a -um *adj* superimposed

superincid·ens -entis *adj* falling from above

superincub·ans -antis *adj* lying above *or* on top

superin·cumbō -cumbĕre -cubuī *intr* to lean over; *(w. dat)* to lay oneself down on

superindu·ō -ĕre -ī *tr* to put on over one's other clothes
superin·jiciō -jicĕre -jēcī -jectus *tr* to throw on top
superin·sternō -sternĕre -strāvī -strātus *tr (w. abl)* to cover *(w. s.th.)*
superi·or -or -us *(comp of* **superus)** *adj* higher, upper; the upper part of; past, previous, preceding; older, elder, more advanced; superior, stronger; victorious, conquering; greater; **de loco superiore dicere** to speak from the tribunal, handle a case in court; to speak from the rostra; **ex loco superiore pugnare** to fight from a vantage point
superius *adv (e.g., mentioned)* above
super·jaciō -jacĕre -jēcī -jectus *or* **-jactus** *tr* to throw on top; to overshoot *(a target)*; **fidem superjacere** to exceed the bounds of credibility; **natare superjecto aequore** to swim in the flood waters
superjūmentār·ius -(i)ī *m* one charged with looking after the beasts of burden
superlāt·us -a -um *adj* exaggerated
superne *adv* above, from above; on top; **de superne** from above
supern·us -a -um *adj* upper; situated high up; supernal, celestial
super·ō -āre -āvī -ātus *tr* to go over, pass over, rise above; to pass, go past, go beyond; to sail past, double; to outdo, surpass; to surmount *(difficulties)*; to live past, live beyond; to overcome, vanquish; to arrive before *or* ahead of; **vitā superare** to survive, outlive ‖ *intr* to mount, ascend; to be superior, have the advantage; to be left over, survive; to be superfluous; to be abundant; to remain to be done; *(w. dat)* to pass over, pass above
superobru·ō -ĕre *tr (also written as two words)* to cover completely, smother
superoccup·ō -āre *tr* to pounce on
superpend·ens -entis *adj* towering overhead
super·pōnō -pōnĕre -posuī -positus *tr (w. dat)* to put *(s.th.)* upon; *(w.* **in** *+ acc)* to put *(s.o.)* in charge of
superquam quod *conj* in addition to the fact that
superscand·ō -ĕre *tr* to step over, climb over
superscrībō -scrībĕre -scripsī -scriptus *tr* to write over *or* on top of
super·sedeō -sedēre -sēdī -sessum *tr* **(-sid-)** to sit on top of ‖ *intr* to sit on top; *(w. abl)* to refrain from, give up, steer clear of; *(w. inf)* to stop *(doing s.th.)*
superstagn·ō -āre -āvī *intr (of a river)* to overflow and form swamps
superst·es -itis *adj* standing by as a witness; surviving; posthumous; *(w. gen or dat)* outliving, surviving *(s.o.)*; **superstes esse** to live on; **superstes esse** *(w. gen or dat)* to outlive *(s.o.)*
superstiti·ō -ōnis *f* superstition; blind adherence to rules
superstitiōsē *adv* superstitiously
superstitiōs·us -a -um *adj* superstitious; ecstatic; blindly adhering to rules
superstit·ō -āre *intr* to be left
superst·ō -āre -stetī *tr* to stand over ‖ *intr (w. dat)* to stand on, stand over
superstrāt·us -a -um *adj* spread over *(as a covering)*
superstru·ō -ĕre -xī -ctus *tr* to build on top
super·sum -esse -fuī -futūrus *intr* to be left over, still exist, survive; to abound; to overflow; to be excessive; to be superfluous; to be adequate, suffice; *(w. dat)* to outlive, survive *(s.o.)*
superte·gō -gĕre -xī -ctus *tr* to cover over
superurg·ens -entis *adj* putting on pressure, adding pressure
super·us *or* **super -a -um** *adj* upper; of this world, of this life; northern; **ad auras superas redire** to come back to life; **mare superum** Adriatic Sea ‖ *mpl see* **superi** ‖ *npl see* **supera**
supervac(u)āne·us -a -um *adj* superfluous
supervacu·us -a -um *adj* superfluous
supervād·ō -ĕre *tr* to go over, climb over
super·vehor -vehī -vectus sum *tr* to sail, ride, *or* drive by *or* past
super·venio -venīre -vēnī -ventus *tr* to come upon, come on top of; to overtake; to come over, close over, cover; to surprise ‖ *intr* to arrive suddenly; *(w. dat)* to come upon by surprise
supervent·us -ūs *m* sudden arrival, unexpected arrival
super·vīvō -vīvĕre -vixī *intr (w. dat)* to outlive
supervolit·ō -āre -āvī *tr* to hover over
supervol·ō -āre -āvī *tr* to fly over ‖ *intr* to fly across
supīn·ō -āre -āvī -ātus *tr* to turn over *(by plowing)*
supīn·us -a -um *adj* face-up; lying on one's back; turned upwards; sloping, sloping upwards; *(of streams)* flowing upwards *(to their source)*; on one's back; lazy, careless, indifferent
supp- = subp-
suppactus *pp of* **suppingo (subp-)**
suppaenitet -ēre *v impers* **(subp-)** *(w. acc of person and gen of thing regretted), e.g.,* **illum furoris suppaenitet** he somewhat regrets the outburst
suppalp·or -ārī *intr* **(subp-)** *(w. dat)* to coax *(s.o.)* a little
supp·ār -aris *adj* nearly equal
supparasīt·or -ārī *intr (w. dat)* to flatter *(s.o.)* a little like a parasite

suppar·um -ī *n or* **suppar·us -ī** *m* linen dress; small sail
suppeditāti·ō -ōnis *f* **(subp-)** good supply
suppedit·ō -āre -āvī -ātus *tr* **(subp-)** to supply, furnish ‖ *intr* to stand by; to be on hand, be in stock, be available; *(w. dat)* to be at hand for; *(w.* **ad** *or* **in** *+ acc)* to be adequate for
suppēd·ō -ĕre *intr (vulg)* to fart quietly
suppernāt·us -a -um *adj* hamstrung
suppeti·ae -ārum *fpl* assistance
suppeti·or -ārī -ātus sum *intr* **(subp-)** *(w. dat)* to help, assist
suppet·ō -ĕre -īvī *or* **-iī -ītum** *intr* to be at hand, be in stock, be available; *(w. dat)* **1** to be at hand for, be available to; **2** to be equal to, suffice for; **3** to correspond to
suppīl·ō -āre -āvī -ātus *tr* **(subp-)** to filch, snitch
sup·pingō -pingĕre -pēgī -pactus *tr* **(subp-)** to fasten underneath
supplant·ō -āre -āvī -ātus *tr* **(subp-)** to trip up, cause to stumble
supplēment·um -ī *n* **(subp-)** *(mil)* reinforcement(s)
suppl·eō -ēre -ēvī -ētus *tr* **(subp-)** to fill up; to make good *(losses, damage, etc.)*; *(mil)* to bring to full strength
suppl·ex -icis *adj* kneeling, on one's knees, in entreaty; humble, submissive ‖ *mf* suppliant
supplicāti·ō -ōnis *f* public thanksgiving, day of prayer; thanksgiving for victory; day of humiliation
suppliciter *adv* suppliantly, humbly
supplic·ium -(i)ī *n* **(subp-)** kneeling down, bowing down, humble entreaty; public prayer, supplication; *(because criminals were beheaded kneeling)* execution, death penalty; punishment, torture; suffering, pain; **supplicium dare** to atone; **supplicium dare** *(or* **pendere,** *or* **expendere,** *or* **luere)** to pay the penalty, suffer punishment; **supplicium sumere** *(or* **exigere)** to exact punishment; to accept reparation; *(w.* **ab, ex, ex** *+ abl)* to exact punishment from, put *(s.o.)* to death
supplic·ō -āre -āvī -ātum *intr* **(subpl)** *(w. dat)* to go on one's knees to, entreat, beg
supplo·dō -dĕre -sī -sus *tr* **(subp-)** to stamp *(the foot)*
supplōsi·ō -ōnis *f* **(subp-)** stamping *(one's foot)*
sup·pōnō -pōnĕre -posuī -positus *tr* **(subp-)** *(w. dat)* **1** to put, place, set *(s.th.)* under; **2** to put *(s.th.)* next to, add *(s.th.)* to; **3** to substitute *(s.th.)* for; **potentiam in gratiae locum supponere** to substitute power for influence
support·ō -āre -āvī -ātus *tr* **(subp-)** to bring up, transport
suppositīci·us -a -um *adj* **(subp-)** spurious
suppositi·ō -ōnis *f* substitution
suppositus *pp of* **suppono**
suppostr·ix -īcis *f* unfair substituter *(female)*
suppressi·ō -ōnis *f* holding back *(of money)*, embezzlement
suppress·us -a -um *adj* soft *(voice)*; soft-spoken *(person)*
sup·primō -primĕre -pressī -pressus *tr* **(subp-)** to press down *or* under; to sink; to repress, stop; to suppress, keep secret; to stifle *(an utterance)*; to detain in one's private custody; to retain *(another's money)* in one's possession; to suppress *(feelings)*
supprōm·us -ī *m* assistant butler
suppud·et -ēre *v impers* **(subp-)** to cause *(s.o.)* a slight feeling of shame; *(w. acc of person and gen of cause), e.g.:* **eorum me suppudet** I am a bit ashamed of them
suppūr·ō -āre -āvī -ātum *intr* to fester
supp·us -a -um *adj* lying on one's back, supine; upside down
supput·ō -āre -āvī -ātus *tr* to trim off the lower branches of; to count, compute
suprā *adv* on top, above; up above; earlier; beyond, more; **supra quam** more than ‖ *prep (usu. w. acc; also w. abl) (sometimes following its object or separated from it by intervening words)* on, on top of; over, above; beyond; *(of time)* before, earlier than; north of; to the far side of; *(of amount)* over, beyond; in charge of; *(w. reference to position at the dining table, from the standpoint of those eating)* on the left of; **Atticus supra me, infra Verrius accubebat** Atticus sat to the left of me, Verrius to the right of me; **gallinaceus supra viri umerum deinde in capite astitit** the rooster stood on the man's shoulder and then on his head; **supra caput** *(in a threatening way)* (hanging) over one's head; **supra terram** above ground
suprālāti·ō -ōnis *f* exaggeration
suprālāt·us -a -um *adj* exaggerated
suprascand·ō -ĕre *tr* to climb over
suprāscript·us -a -um *adj* written above *(as a correction)*
suprēmum *adv* for the last time; as a final tribute
suprēm·us -a -um *(superl of* **superus)** *adj* last, latest, final; highest; greatest, supreme, extreme; critical, desperate *(time)*; closing, dying, final; **suprema manus** finishing touches; **suprema multa** maximum fine; **supremum judicium** last will and testament; **supremum supplicium** death penalty; **supremus mons** mountain top ‖ *n* last moment ‖ *npl* moment of death; funeral rites
supt- = subt-
Sur- = Syr-

sūr·a -ae *f (anat)* calf
surcul·us -ī *m* shoot, sprout, twig; slip, graft
surdas·ter -tra -trum *adj* somewhat deaf
surdit·ās -ātis *f* deafness
surd·us -a -um *adj* deaf; silent, noiseless; unheeding; dull, faint
Sūrēn·a -ae *m* grand vizier *(in Parthia)*
surgō surgĕre surrexī surrectum *intr* to get up; to stand up; to rise; to spring up and grow tall
surr- = subr-
surrancid·us -a -um *adj* **(subr-)** somewhat rancid *or* spoiled
surrauc·us -a -um *adj* **(subr-)** somewhat hoarse
surrectus *pp of* **surgo** *and* **surrigo**
surrēmig·ō -āre *intr* to row along
Surrentīn·us -a -um *adj* of Surrentum *(modern Sorrento)*
sur·rēpō -rēpĕre -repsī -reptum *tr* **(subr-)** to creep under, crawl under ‖ *intr* to creep up; *(w. dat)* to creep up on
surreptīci·us -a -um *adj* **(subr-)** surreptitious; stolen
surreptus *pp of* **surrepo** *and of* **surripio**
sur·rīdeo -rīdēre -rīsī *intr* **(subr-)** to smile
surrīdiculē *adv* **(subr-)** rather humorously
sur·rigō -rigĕre -rexī -rectus *tr* **(subr-)** to raise, lift up, erect
surring·or -ī *intr* **(subr-)** to grimace, make a face; to be somewhat annoyed
sur·ripiō -ripĕre -ripuī -reptus *tr* **(subr-)** to snatch secretly, pilfer; *(w. dat)* to pilfer *(s.th.)* from
surrīsī *perf of* **surrīdēre**
surrog·ō -āre -āvī -ātus *tr* **(subr-)** to propose as a substitute
surrostrān·ī -ōrum *mpl* **(subr-)** loafers around the Rostra *(in the Forum)*
surrub·eō -ēre *intr* **(subr-)** to blush slightly
surrūf·us -a -um *adj* **(subr-)** reddish
sur·ruō -ruĕre -ruī -rutus *tr* **(subr-)** to dig under; to loosen at the base; to tear down, demolish; *(fig)* to undermine, subvert
surrustic·us -a -um *adj* **(subr-)** rather unsophisticated
surrutil·us -a -um *adj* **(subr-)** reddish
surrutus *pp of* **surruo**
sursum *adv* **(sursus, sūsum, sūsus)** upwards, high up; **sursum desorsum** up and down
sūs suis *m* pig, hog; boar ‖ *f* sow
Sūs·a -ōrum *npl* capital of Persia
suscenseō *see* **succenseo**
suscept·um -ī *n* enterprise, undertaking
suscepti·ō -ōnis *f* undertaking
sus·cipiō -cipĕre -cēpī -ceptus *tr* to catch *(s.th. before it falls);* to support; to pick up, resume *(conversation);* to bear *(children);* to accept, receive *(under one's protection);* to take up, undertake; to acknowledge, recognize *(a child)* as one's own
suscit·ō -āre -āvī -ātus *tr* to stir up, shake up; to build, erect; to cause *(s.th.)* to rise; to wake *(s.o.)* up; to encourage; to stir up *(rebellion, love, etc.);* to rouse *(from inactivity);* to have *(s.o.)* stand up in court *(as witness)*
suspect·ō -āre -āvī -ātus *tr* to gaze up at; to suspect
suspect·us -a -um *pp of* **suspicio** ‖ *adj* suspect, suspected, mistrusted
suspect·us -ūs *m* view from below; respect, esteem
suspend·ium -(i)ī *n* hanging; hanging oneself
suspen·dō -dĕre -dī -sus *tr* to hang up, hang; to prop up, support; to keep in suspense; to check *(temporarily);* to interrupt ‖ *pass (w.* **ex)** to depend on
suspens·us -a -um *adj* hanging, balanced; raised, poised; in suspense, uncertain, hesitant; marked by uncertainty; vague *(language); (w.* **ex)** dependent upon; **in suspenso** in suspense, on tenterhooks; undecided
suspic·ax -ācis *adj* suspicious; mistrustful
suspiciō suspicĕre suspexī suspectus *tr* to look up at; to look up to, admire; to mistrust, suspect ‖ *intr* to look up; *(w.* **in** *+ acc)* to look up at *or* into
suspici·ō -ōnis *f* suspicion, mistrust; inkling; faint indication, trace, suggestion; *(w. gen)* suspicion *(of); (w. acc & inf or* **quasi)** suspicion that; **in suspicionem cadere** to fall under suspicion; **in suspicionem venire** to come under suspicion; **Tarentinorum defectio jam diu in suspicione Romanis fuerat** the revolt of the Tarentines long been suspected by the Romans
suspīciōsē *adv* suspiciously
suspīciōs·us -a -um *adj* mistrustful, suspicious; suspicious-looking; *(w.* **in** *+ acc)* suspicious of
suspic·ō -āre *or* **suspic·or -ārī -ātus sum** *tr* to mistrust, suspect; to suppose, surmise, believe
suspīrāt·us -ūs *m* deep breath, sigh; labored breathing
suspīr·ium -(i)ī *n* deep breath, sigh; **suspirium ducere** *(or* **repetere** *or* **trahere)** to take a deep breath, sigh
suspīr·ō -āre -āvī -ātus *tr* to sigh for ‖ *intr* to sigh, heave a sigh
susque dēque *adv* up and down; **de Octavio susque deque est** it's all one *(i.e., of no consequence)* as far as Octavian is concerned
suss- = subs-
sustentāti·ō -ōnis *f* delay
sustent·ō -āre -āvī -ātus *tr* to build up; to hold upright; to support; to sustain *(w.*

food); to maintain; to provide *(s.o. w. food, money, etc.),* support, maintain; to uphold *(the law);* to endure, hold up against; to hold back, keep in check; to delay, put off

sus·tineō -tinēre -tinuī *tr* to hold up, support; to hold back, hold in check; to uphold *(the law);* to sustain, support *(w. food, etc.);* to bear, endure *(trouble);* to hold up, delay, put off

sustoll·ō -ĕre *tr* to lift up, raise; to kidnap

sustulī *perf of* **tollo**

sūsum *see* **sursum**

susurrāt·or -ōris *m* mutterer, whisperer

susurr·ō -āre *tr & intr* to mutter, murmur, whisper

susurr·us -a -um *adj* whispering

susurr·us -ī *m* low, gentle noise; murmur, whisper, buzz, hum

sūt·a -ōrum *npl* coat of mail

sūtēl·ae -ārum *fpl* patches; tricks

sūtil·is -is -e *adj* sewn together; **cumba sutilis** boat made of skins; **rosae sutiles** a wreath of roses

sūt·or -ōris *m* shoemaker

sūtōri·us -a -um *adj* shoemaker's **II** *m (hum)* Shoemaker Emeritus

sūtrīn·us -a -um *adj* shoemaker's **II** *f* shoemaker's shop

Sūtr·ium -(i)ī *n* town in Etruria

sūtūr·a -ae *f* stitch; seam

sūt·us -a -um *pp of* **suo II** *npl* joints

su·us -a -um *or* **su·os -a -om** *adj* his own, her own, its own, their own, one's own; due, proper, peculiar **II** *pron masc pl* one's own people, one's own family, one's own friends **II** *pron neut pl* one's own property

Sybar·is -is *f* town in S. Italy noted for its luxurious living **II** *m* Sybaris *(boy's name, suggestive of decadence)*

Sybarīt·a -ae *m* Sybarite

Sybarītic·us -a -um *adj* Sybarite; *(fig)* erotic

Sȳchae·us -ī *m* husband of Dido

sȳcophant·a -ae *m* swindler; slanderer; cunning parasite

sȳcophanti·a -ae *f* deceptive trickery

sȳcophantiōsē *adv* deceitfully

sȳcophant·or -ārī -ātus sum *intr* to cheat; *(w. dat)* to pull a fast one on

Syēn·e -ēs *f* town in Egypt *(modern Aswan)*

Sylla *see* **Sulla**

syllab·a -ae *f* syllable

syllabātim *adv* syllable by syllable

Symaethē·us -a -um *adj* of the River Symaethus

Symaeth·is -idis *f* daughter of the river-god Symaethus

Symaeth·us -ī *m* River Symaethus in Sicily near Catana

symbol·a -ae *or* **symbol·ē -ēs** *f* contribution *(of money to a feast); (coll)* blows

symbol·us -ī *m* **(sumb-)** symbol, mark, token

symphōni·a -ae *f* harmony; symphony, band *(of singers or musicians)*

symphōniac·us -a -um *adj* concert-, musical; **pueri symphoniaci** choristers **II** *mpl* musicians

Symplēgad·es -um *fpl* two islands in the Black Sea which floated about and dashed against each other until they were fixed in place a split second after the Argo sailed by them

symplegm·a -atis *n* tangled group *(of persons embracing or wrestling)*

syngraph·a -ae *f* promissory note

syngraph·us -ī *m* written contract; pass *(for safe-conduct)*

synhedr·us -ī *m* senator *(in Macedonia)*

syn(h)od·ūs -ontos *m* bream *(fish)*

Synnad·a -ōrum *npl or* **Synn·as -adis** *f* town in Phrygia, famous for its colored marble

synthesin·a -ae *f* dinner shirt

synthes·is -is *f* a set of matching articles; dinner service; (matching) dinner clothes

Syph·ax -ācis *m* **(Syf-)** king of Numidia at the time of the Second Punic War, siding with Carthage *(d. 203 B.C.)*

Syrācosi·us -a -um *adj* Syracusan

Syrācūs·ae -ārum *fpl* Syracuse *(chief city of Sicily)*

Syrācūsān·us *or* **Syrācūsi·us -a -um** *adj* Syracusan

Syri·a -ae *f* **(Sur-)** Syria *(usu. including Phoenicia and Palestine)*

Syriac·us -a -um *adj* Syrian; from Syria; produced in Syria

Syriātic·us -a -um *adj* Syrian

Sȳr·inx -ingos *f* nymph who was pursued by Pan and changed into a reed

Syri·us -a -um *adj & m* Syrian; of Syros in the Cyclades

syrm·a -atis *n* robe with a train *(worn esp. by actors in tragedies);* tragedy

Syrophoen·ix -icis *m* Syrophoenician *(Phoenica was regarded as part of Syria)*

syrt·is -is *f* sand bank, sand dune **II Syrtis** *f* Gulf of Sidra in N. Africa **II** Gulf of Gabes **II** *fpl* name of an area of sand dunes on the coast between Carthage and Cyrene

Syr·us -a -um *adj* **(Sur-)** Syrian **II** *mf* Syrian; proper name of a slave

T

T. *abbr* **Titus** *(Roman first name, praenomen)*

tabān·us -ī *m* horse fly

tabell·a -ae *f* small board, panel; plaque; writing tablet; page *(of a bound note-*

book); ballot; picture, painting; votive tablet; game board; placard, notice; door panel ‖ *fpl* notebook

tabellāri·us -a -um *adj (leg)* regulating voting by secret ballot ‖ *m* mail carrier, courier

tāb·eō -ēre *intr* to waste away; to melt; to decay; to drip; **tabentes genae** sunken cheeks

tabern·a -ae *f* hut; booth, stall, shop; inn; **taberna diversoria** *(or* **meritoria)** inn

tabernācul·um -ī *n* tent; **tabernaculum capere** *(of an augur)* to set up a tent in which to take the auspices

tabernār·ius -(i)ī *m* shopkeeper

tāb·ēs -is *f* melting; wasting, decay; dwindling, shrinking; decaying matter, rot; disease; moral corruption; means of corruption

tāb·escō -escĕre -uī *intr* to begin to decay; to begin to melt; to rot

tābidul·us -a -um *adj* rotting; wasting

tābid·us -a -um *adj* wasting, decaying; melting; corrupting; infectious

tābific·us -a -um *adj* wasting; melting; *(fig)* gnawing

tabul·a -ae *f* plank, board; writing tablet; painting *(on a panel of wood);* game board; votive tablet; door panel; placard, advertisement; auction notice; will; record; counting board ‖ *fpl* account books, records, register, lists; **tabulae novae** clean slate *(i.e., cancellation of debts)*

tabulār·ium -(i)ī *n* archives; archives building

tabulār·ius -(i)ī *m* accountant, bookkeeper

tabulāti·ō -ōnis *f* flooring; floor, story

tabulāt·us -a -um *adj* boarded ‖ *n* floor, story; layer; deck *(of a ship);* row *(of trees)*

tāb·um -ī *n* rot, putrid matter; infectious disease, plague

tac·eō -ēre -uī -itus *tr* to be silent about, pass over in silence ‖ *intr* to be silent, be still

tacitē *adv* silently; secretly, privately; without publicity; tacitly, without express statement; imperceptibly, quietly

taciturnit·ās -ātis *f* taciturnity; silence; failure to communicate

taciturn·us -a -um *adj* taciturn, silent; noiseless, hushed, quiet

tacit·us -a -um *adj* silent; mute; unmentioned; secret; *(leg)* tacit; **per tacitum** in silence

Tacit·us -ī *m* Gaius(?) Cornelius Tacitus *(Roman historian, c. A.D. 55–115)*

tactil·is -is -e *adj* tangible

tacti·ō -ōnis *f* touch, touching; feeling, sense of touch

tactus *pp of* **tango**

tact·us -ūs *m* touch; handling; *(fig)* contact, influence

taed·a -ae *f* pine wood; pitch; pine board; pine tree; torch; wedding torch; *(fig)* wedding

tae·det -dēre -sum est *v impers* it irks; *(w. acc of person and gen of the cause), e.g.,* **me taedet sermonis tui** I am sick of your talk, your talk irks me

taedi·fer -fera -ferum *adj* carrying a torch, torch-bearing

taed·ium -(i)ī *n* tediousness; weariness, boredom; feeling of disgust; object of disgust; nuisance

Taenarid·ēs -ae *m* man from Taenarus, Spartan *(esp. Hyacinthus)*

Taenar·is -idis *adj (fem only)* Spartan ‖ *f* Spartan woman

Taenari·us *or* **Taenare·us -a -um** *adj* of Taenarus, Taenarian; *(poet)* Spartan, Laconian

Taenar·um *or* **Taenar·on -ī** *n, or* **Taenar·os** *or* **Taenar·us -ī** *mf* Taenarus *(promontory at the S. tip of the Peloponnesus, near which a cavern was thought to lead to the lower world);* Hades

taeni·a -ae *f* band, ribbon; string

taesum est *see* **taedet**

tae·ter -tra -trum *adj* **(tet-)** offensive, revolting, loathsome; hideous; *(of actions)* monstrous, horrible

taetrē *adv* foully, hideously

taetricus *see* **tetricus**

tag·ax -ācis *adj* light-fingered *(thief)*

Tag·ēs -is *m* Etruscan god, originator of divination and grandson of Jupiter

tālār·is -is -e *adj* ankle-length ‖ *npl* ankle-length clothes; sandals; winged sandals; *(fig)* means of getting away

tālāri·us -a -um *adj* of dice; **ludus talarius** game of dice

talāsiō *interj* **(-lass-)** wedding cry

tāle·a -ae *f* rod, bar, stake

talent·um -ī *n* talent *(Greek weight, varying from state to state, but equal to about 50 lbs.; also a unit of currency, consisting of 60 minae, or about 600 denarii, or about $600);* **talentum magnum** Attic talent *(so called to distinguish it from talents from other cities of lower value)*

tāli·ō -ōnis *f (leg)* punishment in kind, exaction of compensation in kind

tāl·is -is -e *adj* such, of that kind; so great, so excellent; **talis…qualis** such…as

tāliter *adv* in such a way

tālitr·um -ī *n* fillip *(flick with the tip of the middle finger and the thumb)*

talp·a -ae *mf* mole *(animal)*

Talthyb·ius -(i)ī *m* herald of Agamemnon

tāl·us -ī *m* ankle; anklebone; foot; knucklebone *(used in playing dice);* **talis ludere** to play dice; **talos jacere** to roll the dice

tam *adv* to such an extent, to such a degree, so, so much; **tam...quam** the...the; **tam magis...quam magis** the more...the more

tamar·ix -īcis *f* tamarisk *(ornamental shrub or short tree)*

tamdiū *or* **tam diū** *adv* so long, how long; **tamdiu quam** *(or* **tamdiu dum)** as long as

tamen *adv* yet, nevertheless, still, just the same

tamendem *adv* all the same

tamenetsī *conj* even though ‖ *adv* all the same, nevertheless

Tames·is -is *m or* **Tames·a -ae** *f* Thames River

tametsī *conj* even if, although

tamquam *conj* **(tan-)** as, just as, as much as; just as if; **tamquam si** just as if

Tanagr·a -ae *f* town in Boeotia

Tana·is -is *m* river of Sarmatia *(modern River Don)*

Tanaqu·il -ilis *f* wife of the elder Tarquin

tandem *adv* at last, in the end, finally; *(expressing urgency or impatience)* now, tell me, please, just; **quousque tandem** just how long?

tangō tangĕre tetigī tactus *tr* to touch; to handle, meddle with; to taste; to come to, reach; to border on; to hit, beat; to wash; to anoint; to gall; to move to pity; to dupe; to touch upon, mention; to touch, be related to; to undertake; **de caelo** *(or* **fulmine)** **tangere** to strike with lightning

tanquam *see* **tamquam**

Tantale·us -a -um *adj* of Tantalus

Tantalid·ēs -ae *m* descendant of Tantalus *(e.g., Atreus, Aegisthus, Agamemnon, Menelaus)*

Tantal·is -idos *f* female descendant of Tantalus *(e.g., Niobe, Hermione)*

Tantal·us -ī *m* son of Jupiter and father of Pelops and Niobe; he was punished in Hades with constant hunger and thirst

tantill·us -a -um *adj* so small, so little ‖ *n* a bit; **tantillo minus** a little less

tantisper *adv* just so long *(and no longer);* just for the moment

tantopere *or* **tantō opere** *adv* so much, so greatly, to such a degree, so earnestly, so hard

tantulum *adv* so little, in the least

tantul·us -a -um *adj* so little, so small ‖ *n* so little, such a trifle; **tantulo vendere** to sell for such a trifling amount

tantum *adv (see also the neut of* **tantus)** so much, so greatly, to such a degree, so far, so long, so; only, just, but just; hardly, scarcely; **non tantum** all but, almost; **non tantum omnes opitulari voluerunt** almost all wished to be of assistance; **non tantum...sed etiam** not only...but also; **tantum modo** only

tantummodo *adv* only

tantundem *adv* just as much, just as far, to the same extent

tant·us -a -um *adj* of such size, so big, so great; so much; so little; so important ‖ *pron neut* so much; so little; so small an amount, so small a number; to such an extent *or* degree; **alterum tantum** twice the amount; **in tantum** to such an extent; **tanti** of such value, worth so much, at so high a price; of little account, of such small importance; **tanto** *(as abl of price)* at such a price, for so much; *(w. comparatives)* by so much, so much the; **tanto melior!** so much the better!; **tanto nequior!** so much the worse!; **tanto ante (post)** so much earlier (later); **tantum est** that is all; **tantum abesse ut...ut** to be so far (from being the case) that; **tantum afuit ut periculosum rei publicae putaret exercitum ut** (+ *subj)* so far was he from thinking that the army was a threat to the country that...; **ter (quater) tantum** three (four) times as much

tant·usdem -adem -undem *adj* just as big, just as large, just as great ‖ *n* the same quantity, just as much; *(w. advl force)* to the same degree, just as much; **tantidem** at the same price; **tantundem est** it comes to the same thing

tapēt·a -ae *m or* **tapēt·um -ī** *n* carpet; tapestry; coverlet

tapēt·ia -ium *npl* tapestry

taratantara *n* sound produced by the trumpet; **at tuba taratantara dixit** but the trumpet went "taratantara"

tardē *adv* slowly; with difficulty; late; **cum tardissime** at the latest

tardesc·ō -ĕre *intr* to become slow; to falter

tardip·ēs -edis *adj* limping

tardit·ās -ātis *f* tardiness; slowness; procrastination; dullness, stupidity

tarditūd·ō -inis *f* tardiness; slowness

tardiuscul·us -a -um *adj* rather slow, slowish, dragging

tard·ō -āre -āvī -ātus *tr* to slow down, delay, hinder; to check *(emotions);* to dull *(the senses)* ‖ *intr* to go slow, take it easy; to hold back

tard·us -a -um *adj* tardy, slow; lingering; mentally slow, mentally retarded; deliberate; crippling; *(of events)* long drawn out, making slow progress

Tarentīn·us -a -um *adj* Tarentine ‖ *mpl* Tarentines

Tarent·um -ī *n* Tarentum *(town on S. coast of Italy, modern Taranto)* ‖ a section on the west side of the Campus Martius

tarm·es -itis *m* woodworm, borer

Tarpēi·us -a -um *adj* Tarpeian; **mons**

Tarpeius *(or* **Tarpeia rupes** *(or* **Tarpeium saxum)** Tarpeian cliff *(on the Capitoline Hill from which criminals were thrown)* ‖ *f* Roman girl who treacherously opened the citadel to the Sabine attackers

tarpezīt·a -ae *m* **(trap-)** banker, money-changer

Tarquiniān·us -a -um *adj* of the Tarquins

Tarquiniens·is -is -e *adj* of the town of Tarquinii ‖ *mpl* inhabitants of Tarquinii

Tarquini·ī -ōrum *mpl* Tarquinii *(important Etruscan city on the W. coast of Italy, about seventy miles N. of Rome, modern Tarquinia)*

Tarquini·us -a -um *adj* Tarquinian ‖ *m* Tarquinius Priscus *(fifth king of Rome, c. 616–579 B.C.)* ‖ Tarquinius Superbus *(seventh and last king of Rome, c. 534–510 B.C.)*

Tarracīn·a -ae *f or* **Terracīn·ae -ārum** *fpl* Terracina *(town in Latium)*

Tartar·a -ōrum *npl or* **Tartar·us** *or* **Tartar·os -ī** *m* Tartarus *(lower level of Hades reserved for notorious criminals)*

Tartare·us -a -um *adj* of Tartarus, infernal

tat *or* **tatae** *interj* expression of surprise

tat·a -ae *m (coll)* daddy; grandpa

Tat·ius -(i)ī *m* Titus Tatius *(king of the Sabines who later ruled jointly with Romulus until the latter had him killed)*

tau *indecl n* the Greek letter tau

taure·us -a -um *adj* bull's, of a bull; **terga taurea** bulls' hides; drums ‖ *f* rawhide, whip

Taur·ī -ōrum *mpl* inhabitants of Chersonesus Tauricus *(modern Crimea)*

Tauric·us -a -um *adj* Tauric ‖ *mpl* the Tauri

taurif·er -era -erum *adj (of regions)* bull-producing

tauriform·is -is -e *adj* bull-shaped

taurīn·us -a -um *adj* bull's; made of bull's hide; bull-like ‖ **Taurīn·us -a -um** of the Taurini *(a Ligurian tribe)* ‖ *mpl* the Taurini

Tauri·us -a -um *adj* Roman clan name *(nomen);* **ludi Taurii** games held in the Circus Flaminius in honor of the gods of the lower world

taur·us -ī *m* bull; bronze bull made as an instrument of torture ‖ **Taurus** *(astr)* Taurus *(constellation)* ‖ **Taurus** the Taurus mountain range in S.E. Asia Minor

taxāti·ō -ōnis *f* evaluation, assessment; *(leg)* maximum sum

taxill·us -ī *m* small die *(for playing dice)*

tax·ō -āre -āvī -ātus *tr* to appraise, assess the value of; to reproach

tax·us -ī *f* yew tree

Tāyget·ē -ēs *f (astr)* one of the seven Pleiads forming the constellation of the Pleiades

Tāyget·us -ī *m* mountain range in Laconia, separating it from Messenia to the W.

tē *pron, acc & abl of* **tu**

-te = *suf for* **tu** *and* **te**

Teān·um -ī *n* town in Campania *(modern Teano)* ‖ town in Apulia *(modern Civitate)*

techn·a *or* **techin·a -ae** *f* trick

technyph·ion -iī *n* a little workroom

Tecmess·a -ae *f* mistress of Ajax son of Telamon

tectē *adv* cautiously, guardedly

tect·or -ōris *m* plasterer

tectōriol·um -ī *n* bit of plasterwork

tectōri·us -a -um *adj* plaster-, of plaster; **opus tectorium** plasterwork, stucco ‖ *n* plaster, stucco; fresco painting; beauty preparation

tect·um -ī *n* roof; ceiling; canopy; cover, shelter; house

tect·us -a -um *pp of* **tego** ‖ *adj* concealed; secret; guarded *(words);* reserved, secretive *(person)* ‖ *n see* **tectum**

tēcum = cum te

tēd- = taed-

Tege·a -ae *f* town in S.E. Arcadia

Tegeae·us -a -um *adj* Tegean, Arcadian ‖ *m* Pan ‖ *f* Arcadian maiden *(esp. Atalanta and Callisto)*

Tegeāt·ēs -ae *m* inhabitant of Tegea

teg·es -etis *f* piece of matting *(used for lying on or as a covering)*

tegetīcul·a -ae *f* small piece of matting

tegill·um -ī *n* hood, cowl

tegim·en *or* **teg(u)m·en -inis** *n (applied to clothing, armor, skin of an animal or of fruit)* cover, covering; vault *(of heaven)*

tegiment·um *or* **teg(u)ment·um -ī** *n (applied to clothing, armor, skins, shells)* cover, covering

tegō tegĕre texī tectus *tr* to cover; to protect, shelter; to hide; to bury; **tegere latus** *(w. gen)* to escort *(s.o.)*

tēgul·a -ae *f* tile ‖ *fpl* roof tiles, tiled roof; siding for walls

tegumen *see* **tegimen**

tegumentum *see* **tegimentum**

tēl·a -ae *f* web; warp *(horizontal threads of a loom);* yarn beam; loom; *(fig)* design, plan

Telam·ōn -ōnis *m* son of Aeacus, brother of Peleus, king of Salamis, and father of Ajax and Teucer

Telamōniad·ēs -ae *m* son of Telamon *(esp. Ajax)*

Telamōn·ius -(i)ī *m* Ajax *(son of Telamon)*

Tēlegon·us -ī *m* son of Ulysses and Circe

Telemach·us -ī *m* son of Ulysses and Penelope

Tēleph·us -ī *m* king of Mysia, wounded by

the spear of Achilles and later cured by its rust

tēlin·um -ī *n* perfume made of fenugreek

tell·ūs -ūris *f* the earth; ground, earth; land, country; dry land

tēl·um -ī *n* missile, weapon; spear, javelin, dart; sword, dagger; ax; shaft *(of light);* **cum telis** *(or* **telo)** armed

temerāri·us -a -um *adj* casual, accidental; rash, thoughtless

temere *adv* by chance, without cause; at random; rashly, thoughtlessly; **non temere** not lightly; not easily; hardly ever; **nullus dies temere intercessit quo non scriberet** hardly a day ever went by without his writing

temerit·ās -ātis *f* chance, accident; rashness, thoughtlessness ‖ *fpl* foolhardy acts

temer·ō -āre -āvī -ātus *tr* to darken, blacken; to violate, disgrace, defile

Temes·ē -ēs *f or* **Temes·a -ae** *f* town in Bruttium noted for its copper mines

tēmēt·um -ī *n* intoxicating liquor

temn·ō -ĕre *tr* to slight

tēm·ō -ōnis *m* pole, tongue *(of a carriage or plow);* wagon

Tempē *indecl npl* scenic valley between Mt. Olympus and Mt. Ossa in Thessaly

temperāment·um -ī *n* blend; moderation; temperate heat; restraint, balance

temper·ans -antis *adj* self-controlled

temperanter *adv* moderately

temperanti·a -ae *f* self-control, moderation

temperātē *adv* moderately

temperāti·ō -ōnis *f* blending; composition; proportion, symmetry; temperament; organization, constitution; control, controlling power

temperāt·or -ōris *m* controller; temperor of metal

temperāt·us -a -um *adj* tempered; self-controlled; moderate

temperī *or* **temporī** *adv* in time, on time; in due time, at the right time

temperi·ēs -ēī *f* blending; climate; mild climate, moderate temperature

temper·ō -āre -āvī -ātus *tr* to compound, combine, blend, temper; to regulate, modify *(in regard to temperature);* to adjust; to tune; to govern, control, rule; to control *(by steering)* ‖ *intr* to be moderate, exercise restraint; *(w. dat)* to exercise control over; *(w. abl or* **ab** *+ abl, w.* **quin, quominus, ne,** *w. inf)* to refrain from

tempest·ās -ātis *f* time, period, season, occasion; stormy weather, storm; misfortune, disaster; hail *(of weapons)*

tempestīvē *adv* at the right time

tempestīvit·ās -ātis *f* right time, timeliness

tempestīvō *adv* at the right time

tempestīv·us -a -um *adj* timely, seasonable, fit; ripe, mature; in good time, early

templ·um -ī *n* space marked off in the sky *or* on the earth for the observation of omens; open space, quarter; site for a temple; temple, shrine, sanctuary

temporāl·is -is -e *adj* temporary; temporal

temporāri·us -a -um *adj* temporary; changeable *(character)*

tempore *or* **temporī** *adv* in time, on time; in due time, at the right time

temptābund·us -a -um *adj* making constant attempts, trying

temptām·en -inis *n* attempt, effort; *(w. gen)* test of

temptāment·um -ī *n* attempt, effort; temptation, trial

temptāti·ō -ōnis *f* trial; attack *(of sickness, of an enemy); (w. gen)* attack on

temptāt·or -ōris *m* assailant, attacker

tempt·ō -āre -āvī -ātus *tr* **(tent-)** to test, feel, probe; to attempt; to attack; to try to influence, tamper with, tempt, try to induce; to urge, incite, sound out; to worry, distress

temptus *pp of* **temno**

temp·us -oris *n* time; period, season; occasion, opportunity; right time, good time, proper period; times, condition, state, position; need, emergency; *(anat)* temple; *(pros)* measure, quantity, cadence; **ad tempus** *(or* **temporis causā)** to suit the occasion; **ante tempus** before time, too soon; **ex tempore** on the spur of the moment; **idem temporis** at the same time; **id temporis** at that time; **in ipso tempore** in the nick of time; **in tempore** at the right moment; just in time; as occasion offers; **in tempus** temporarily, for a time; **per tempus** just in time; **primum tempus** spring; **pro tempore** as time permits; according to circumstances; to suit the occasion; **tempore** at an opportune time; **tempori cedere** to yield to circumstances; **tempus in ultimum** to the last extremity; **tunc tempus** for the time, at the time

tēmulent·us -a -um *adj* intoxicated

tenācit·ās -ātis *f* tenacity; miserliness

tenāciter *adv* tightly, firmly

ten·ax -ācis *adj* holding tight, gripping, clinging; sticky; firm; obstinate; stingy; *(w. gen)* clinging to

tendicul·ae -ārum *fpl* little snare, little noose, little trap

tendō tendĕre tetendī tentus *or* **tensus** *tr* to stretch, stretch out, hold out, spread; to strain; to head for; to aim, shoot *(an arrow);* to bend *(a bow);* to tune *(an instrument);* to pitch *(a tent)* ‖ *intr* to pitch tents, be encamped; to travel, sail, move, march; to endeavor; to contend, fight; to exert oneself; *(w. inf)* to try to; *(w.* **ad)** **1** to tend toward, be inclined toward; **2** to move toward, travel to, aim for; *(w.* **contra** *+ acc)* to fight against

tenebr·ae -ārum *fpl* darkness; night; blindness; dark place, haunts; unconsciousness; death; lower world; obscurity, low station; ignorance; gloomy state of affairs

tenebricōs·us -a -um *adj* dark, gloomy; hidden, concealed *(lust)*

tenebric·us -a -um *adj* dark, gloomy

tenebrōs·us -a -um *adj* dark, gloomy

Tened·os *or* **Tened·us -ī** *f* Tenedos *(island off the coast of Troy)*

tenellul·us -a -um *adj* tender little, dainty little

tenell·us -a -um *adj* dainty

ten·eō -ēre -uī -tus *tr* to hold, hold tight; to keep; to grasp, comprehend; to comprise; to possess, occupy, be master of; to hold back, restrain, repress; to charm, amuse; to have control of, get the better of; to keep, detain; to hold to, stick to, insist on *(an opinion); (w. inf)* to know how to; **cursum** *(or* **iter** *or* **viam) tenere** to continue on a course; ‖ *refl* to remain *(in a place),* stay put ‖ *intr* to hold out, last, keep on; to continue, persist; to continue on a course; *(w.* **quin, quominus, ne** *or inf)* to refrain from; *(w.* **ut, ne)** to make good one's point (that, that not)

ten·er -era -erum *adj* tender, soft, delicate; young, youthful; impressionable; weak; effeminate; voluptuous

tenerasc·ō *or* **teneresc·ō -ĕre** *intr* to grow weak; to become flabby

tenerē *adv* softly

tenerit·ās -ātis *f* weakness

teneritūd·ō -inis *f* tender age

tēnesm·os -ī *m* straining at stool

ten·or -ōris *m* uninterrupted course; continuity; **uno tenore** uninterruptedly

Tēn·os -ī *f* island of the Cyclades

tens·a -ae *f* car carrying images of the gods in procession

tens·us -a -um *pp of* **tendo** ‖ *adj* stretched, drawn tight; stretched out

tentīg·ō -inis *f* lust

tentō *see* **tempto**

tentōr·ium -iī *n* tent

tent·us -a -um *pp of* **tendo** *and* **teneo** ‖ *adj* stretched, drawn tight

Tentyr·a -ōrum *npl* town in Upper Egypt

tenuī *perf of* **teneo**

tenuicul·us -a -um *adj* poor, paltry

tenu·is -is -e *adj* thin; fine; delicate; precise; shallow *(groove, etc.);* slight, puny, poor, insignificant; plain, simple; small, narrow

tenuit·ās -ātis *f* thinness, fineness; leanness; simplicity; precision; poverty; simpleness *(of style)*

tenuiter *adv* thinly; slightly; poorly, indifferently; exactly, minutely; superficially

tenu·ō -āre -āvī -ātus *tr* to make thin; to contract; to dissolve; to lessen; to weaken; to rarefy; to make *(the voice)* shrill; to emaciate *(the body)*

ten·us -oris *n* trap, snare

tenus *prep (w. abl, always placed after the noun)* as far as, up to, down to; **nomine** *(or* **verbo) tenus** as far as the name goes, nominally

Te·os *or* **Te·us -ī** *f* town on the coast of Asia Minor, the birthplace of Anacreon

tepe·facio -facĕre -fēcī -factus *tr* to warm up

tepefact·ō -āre *tr* to be in the habit of warming

tep·eō -ēre -uī *intr* to get warm; to grow lukewarm; to glow with love; to be cool, be indifferent

tep·escō -escĕre -uī *intr* to grow warm; to grow lukewarm, grow indifferent

tepid·us -a -um *adj* warm, lukewarm, tepid

tep·or -ōris *m* warmth; coolness, lack of heat *(in a bath);* lack of fire *(in a speech)*

tepuī *perf of* **tepeo** *and* **tepesco**

ter *adv* three times

-ter *advl suf* of third-declension adjectives: **audacter** boldly; stems in **-nt-** drop **-t-**: **prudenter** prudently; also of second-declension adjectives: **humaniter** kindly

-ter -teri *or* **-trī** *m* **-tera -terum** *or* **-tra -trum** *adjl suf* ofen used to forming pairs: **magister** master, **minister** servant; **noster** our, **vester** your

terdeciens *or* **terdeciēs** *adv* thirteen times

terebinth·us -ī *f* terebinth, turpentine tree

terebr·a -ae *f* drill

terebr·ō -āre -āvī -ātus *tr* to bore, drill a hole in, pierce

terēd·ō -inis *f* grubworm

Tēreid·ēs -ae *m* Itys *(son of Tereus)*

Terentiān·us -a -um *adj* of the Terentian clan; *esp.* written, portrayed, *etc.,* by the poet Terence

Terent·ius -(i)ī *m* Terence *(Marcus Terentius Afer, Roman comic poet, c. 190–159* B.C.*)*

ter·es -etis *adj* smooth, well-rounded; polished, shapely; round, cylindrical; *(fig)* fine, elegant

Tēr·eus -eī *or* **-eos** *m* evil king of Thrace, husband of Procne, and father of Itys

tergemin·us -a -um *adj* triplet, triple

ter·geō -gēre -sī -sus *or* **terg·ō -ĕre** *tr* to wipe off, wipe dry; to scour; to clean, cleanse

tergīn·um -ī *n* rawhide; scourge

tergiversāti·ō -ōnis *f* refusal; evasion, subterfuge
tergivers·or -ārī -ātus sum *intr* to turn one's back; to be shifty
tergō *see* **tergeo**
terg·um -ī *n or* **terg·us -oris** *n* back; ridge; hide; leather; leather objects: bag, shield, drum; *(mil)* rear; **a tergo** in the rear, from behind; **in tergum** backward
terment·um -ī *n* sore caused by friction
term·es -itis *m* branch, bough
Terminal·ia -ium *or* **-iōrum** *npl* festival in honor of Terminus *(god of boundaries, celebrated on February 23)*
termināti·ō -ōnis *f* the marking of the boundaries of a territory *(esp. w. boundary stones or posts);* boundary; tract of land along a boundary; end, goal *(of an activity);* decision, determining; *(rhet)* arrangement, ending *(of a sentence)*
termin·ō -āre -āvī -ātus *tr* to mark off with boundaries, bound, limit; to fix, determine, define; to terminate, conclude; to settle *(an issue); (rhet)* to round out *(a sentence)*
termin·us -ī *m* boundary, limit, bound ‖ **Terminus** god of boundaries
tern·ī -ae -a *adj* three apiece, three each, three at a time; three in a row
terō terĕre trīvī trītus *tr* to rub; to wear down; to wear out *(by constant handling);* to make *(words, expressions)* trite *(by repetition),* run into the ground; to travel *(a road)* repeatedly; to trample, crush; to spend, waste *(time);* to smooth, polish; to sharpen; to thresh *(grain);* to grind *(grain);* **otium terere** to waste time in idleness
Terpsichor·ē -ēs *f* Muse of dancing, of lyric poetry; *(fig)* poetry
terr·a -ae *f* the earth; land; earth, ground, soil; country, region, territory; **in terrā** *(or* **terris)** in the world, in existence; *(as contrasted with heaven)* on earth; *(astr)* the planet earth; **terrā ortus** sprung from the earth, indigenous; **terrae filius** a nobody; **terrae** *(or* **terrarum) motus** earthquake
terrāneol·a -ae *f* crested lark
terrēn·us -a -um *adj* earthly, terrestrial; earthen ‖ *n* land, ground
terr·eō -ēre -uī -itus *tr* to frighten, scare, terrify; to deter
terrestr·is -is -e *adj* of the earth, on the earth; land, earth; terrestrial; **proelium terrestre** land battle
terre·us -a -um *adj* earth-born
terribil·is -is -e *adj* terrible, frightful
terricul·a -ae *f* bogy; scary thing
terrific·ō -āre *tr* to terrify
terrific·us -a -um *adj* terrifying, awe-inspiring, alarming
terrigen·a -ae *m* earth-born creature
terriloqu·us -a -um *adj* ominous, alarming
terripav·ium -(i)ī *n* **(-pud·ium, -puv·ium)** *(etymologizing forms of* **tripudium)** *see* **tripudium**
territ·ō -āre -āvī *tr* to keep frightening; to try to scare, intimidate
territōr·ium -(i)ī *n* land around a town, territory, suburbs
terr·or -ōris *m* terror, alarm, dread
terruī *perf of* **terreo**
ter(r)unc·ius -(i)ī *m* copper coin *(weighing three* **unciae** *= three- twelfths of an* **as** *or one-fortieth of a* **denarius,** *i.e., less than 1¢);* **heres ex teruncio** heir to one fourth an estate
ters·us -a -um *pp of* **tergeo** ‖ *adj* clean, neat; terse; polished *(writing)*
tertiadecimān·ī -ōrum *mpl* soldiers of the thirteenth legion
tertiān·us -a -um *adj* recurring every three days, *(in our system: every other day),* tertian *(fever)* ‖ *mpl* soldiers of the third legion
tertiō *adv* in the third place, thirdly; the third time
tertium *adv* for the third time
terti·us -a -um *adj* third
terti·us decim·us -a -um *adj* thirteenth
teruncius *see* **terrunicus**
tervenēfic·us -ī *m (term of abuse)* three-time killer, absolute villain
tesqu·a -ōrum *npl* wilderness, wilds
tessell·a -ae *f* cubed mosaic stone
tesselāt·us -a -um *adj* tesselated
tesser·a -ae *f* cube; die; watchword, countersign; tally, token; ticket
tesserār·ius -(i)ī *m (mil)* officer of the day
tesserul·a -ae *f* small cube; ticket
test·a -ae *f* brick, tile; jug, crock; potsherd; shellfish; shell *(of a crustacean, snail, etc.);* fragment, splinter *(esp. of a broken tooth or bone)*
testāmentāri·us -a -um *adj* pertaining to a will, testamentary ‖ *m* forger
testāment·um -ī *n* testament, will
testāti·ō -ōnis *f* testifying to a fact; *(leg)* deposition
testāt·or -ōris *m* testator *(one who makes a will)*
testāt·us -a -um *adj* well-attested; witnessed
testicul·us -ī *m* testicle
testificāti·ō -ōnis *f* testifying; proof, evidence
testific·or -ārī -ātus sum *tr* to give as evidence, give proof of; to testify to; to vouch for; to invoke *(e.g., a god)* as one's witness; *(fig)* to give proof of
testimōn·ium -(i)ī *n* testimony
test·is -is *mf* witness ‖ *m* testicle
test·or -ārī -ātus sum *tr* to give as evidence; to show, prove, vouch for; to call

to witness, appeal to ‖ *intr* to be a witness, testify; to make a will

test·ū -ūs *n see* **testum**

testūdine·us -a -um *adj* of a tortoise; made of tortoise shell

testūd·ō -inis *f* tortoise; tortoise shell; lyre, lute; arch, vault; *(mil)* protective shed *(for besiegers)*

testul·a -ae *f* potsherd

test·um -ī *n* earthenware lid; pot with a lid

tēte = *emphatic form of* **te**

tetendī *perf of* **tendo**

Tēth·ys -yos *f* wife of Oceanus and mother of the sea nymphs; ocean, sea

tetigī *perf of* **tango**

tetradrachm·um -ī *n* **(-trach-)** Greek silver coin *(worth four drachmas or four denarii or $4)*

tetra·ō -ōnis *m* game bird *(black grouse?)*

tetrarch·ēs -ae *m* tetrarch *(ruler of ¼ of a country)*; petty prince

tetrarchi·a -ae *f* tetrarchy

tetrastich·on -ī *n* four-line poem

tetric·us -a -um *adj* stern, gloomy, crabby; harsh, rough

tetrissit·ō -āre *intr* to quack

Teu·cer *or* **Teu·crus -crī** *m* son of Telamon and half-brother of Ajax ‖ son of Scamander of Crete, father-in-law of Dardanus, and later king of Troy

Teucri·a -ae *f* Troy, land of the Teucrians

Teucr·us -a -um *adj* Teucrian, Trojan ‖ *mpl* Trojans

Teuthrantē·us -a -um *adj* Mysian

Teuthranti·us -a -um *adj* of Teuthras; **turba Teuthrantia** fifty daughters of Thespius

Teuthr·ās -antis *m* ancient king of Mysia, father of Thespius

Teuton·ēs -um *or* **Teuton·ī -ōrum** *mpl* Teutons

Teutonic·us -a -um *adj* Teutonic

tex·ō -ĕre -uī -tus *tr* to weave; to plait; to build; to compose

textil·is -is -e *adj* woven; brocaded ‖ *n* fabric

text·or -ōris *m* weaver

textrīn·um -ī *n* weaving; weaving room

textr·ix -īcis *f* weaver *(female)*

textūr·a -ae *f* texture; web; fabric

text·us -a -um *pp of* **texo** ‖ *n* woven cloth, fabric; web

text·us -ūs *m* texture

texuī *perf of* **texo**

Thā·is -idis *or* **-idos** *f* notorious Athenian prostitute

thalam·us -ī *m* woman's room; bedroom; marriage bed; marriage

thalassic·us *or* **thalassin·us -a -um** *adj* sea-green, aquamarine

Thal·ēs -ae *m* Thales *(early Ionian philosopher of Miletus, regarded as one of the Seven Sages, Ē 575 B.C.)*

Thalī·a *or* **Thalē·a -ae** *f* Muse of comedy and light verse ‖ one of the Graces ‖ a Nereid, sea nymph

thall·us -ī *m* green bough; green stem

Thaps·os -ī *f* city of N. Africa where Caesar defeated the Pompeians *(46 B.C.)*

Thasi·us -a -um *adj* of Thasos; **Thasius lapis** Thasian marble

Thas·os -ī *f* island in the Aegean Sea, off the coast of Thrace

Thaumantē·us -a -um *adj* descended from Thaumas *(a Titan)*

Thaumanti·as -adis *or* **Thaumant·is -idis** *f* Iris *(daughter of the Titan Thaumas)*

theātrāl·is -is -e *adj* theatrical

theātr·um -ī *n* theater

Thēb·ae -ārum *fpl* Thebes *(capital of Boeotia, founded by Cadmus)* ‖ Thebes *(city of Upper Egypt)* ‖ place in Mysia, home of Eetion

Thēba·is -idis *or* **-idos** *adj (fem only)* of Boeotian Thebes; of Thebes in Mysia; of Egyptian Thebes; **Thebais nupta** Theban bride *(i.e., Andromache)* ‖ *f* Theban woman; district around Egyptian Thebes, the Thebaid

Thēbān·us -a -um *adj & mf* Theban *(of Boeotia, Egypt, or Mysia)*

thēc·a -ae *f* case, box

them·a -atis *n* position of the planets *or* stars at one's birth, horoscope; *(rhet)* theme, topic proposed for debate in a school of rhetoric

Them·is -is *f* goddess of justice and of prophecy

Themistocl·ēs -is *m* Themistocles *(Athenian admiral and statesman, c. 528–459 B.C.)*

Themistoclē·us -a -um *adj* Themistoclean

thensaurius *or* **thensaurus** *see* **thesaurus**

Theocrit·us -ī *m* founder of Greek pastoral poetry, born at Syracuse *(3rd cent. B.C.)*

theolog·us -ī *m* theologian

theologūmen·a -ōn *npl* essays on the gods

therm·ae -ārum *fpl* hot baths, public baths *(which included rooms for social activities, lecture halls, theater, restaurants, workout rooms)*

Thermōd·on -ontis *m* river in Pontus, around which the Amazons were said to have lived

Thermōdontiac·us -a -um *adj* of the River Thermodon *(often applied to Amazons, esp. Hippolyta and Penthesilea, or to things connected with them)*

thermopōl·ium -(i)ī *n* hot-drink shop

thermopot·ō -āre *tr* to supply with warm drinks

Thermopyl·ae -ārum fpl **(-pul-)** Thermopylae *(famous pass in Thessaly, defended by Leonidas and his 400 Spartans in 480 B.C.)*

thermul·ae -ārum *fpl* small hot bath
Thersīt·ēs -ae *m* Greek soldier at Troy notorious for his ugliness
thēsaur·us -ī *m* **(thens-)** storehouse; store, treasure, hoard
Thēs·eūs -eī *or* **-eos** *m* king of Athens, son of Aegeus and husband *(or* lover) first of Ariadne and later of Phaedra
Thēsē·us -a -um *adj* of Theseus
Thēsīd·ae -ārum *mpl* Athenians
Thēsīd·ēs -ae *m* Hippolytus *(son of Theseus)* ‖ *mpl* Athenians
thes·is -is *f (rhet)* general question *(opp:* a particular case)
Thespiad·es -um *fpl* descendants of Thespius *(fifty sons of Thespius's fifty daughters)*
Thespi·ae -ārum *fpl* town in Boeotia near Mt. Helicon
Thesp·is -is *m* traditional founder of Greek tragedy *(his first presentation was in 535 B.C.)*
Thespi·us -a -um *adj* Thespian ‖ *m* a king of Mysia who had fifty daughters; *see* **Thespiades** ‖ *fpl* town in Boeotia near Mt. Helicon
Thessali·a -ae *f* Thessaly *(most northerly district of Greece)*
Thessalic·us -a -um *adj* Thessalian
Thessal·is -idis *or* **-idos** *adj (fem only)* Thessalian ‖ *f* Thessalian woman *(esp. a witch)*
Thessal·us -a -um *adj* Thessalian ‖ *mpl* people of Thessaly
Thestorid·ēs -ae *m* Calchas *(famous Greek seer in the Trojan War)*
thēta *indecl n* the Greek letter theta *(written on tablets by jurors voting for the death sentence)*
Thet·is -idis *or* **-idos** *f* sea nymph, daughter of Nereus and Doris, wife of Peleus, and mother of Achilles
thias·us -ī *m* Bacchic dance; troupe of Bacchic dancers
Thisb·ē -ēs *f* girl in Bablyon, loved by Pyramus ‖ small town in Boeotia
Thoantē·us -a -um *adj* of Thoas
Tho·ās -antis *m* king of the Taurians, slain by Orestes ‖ king of Lemnos and father of Hypsipyle
thol·us -ī *m* rotunda
thōr·ax -ācis *m* breastplate
Thrāc·a -ae *or* **Thrāc·ē -ēs** *f* Thrace *(country N. of the Aegean)*
Thrāci·us -a -um *adj* Thracian ‖ *f* Thrace
Thraex *see* **Threx**
Thr·ax -ācis *m* Thracian
Thre(i)ss·a -ae *f* Thracian woman
Thr·ex -ēcis *or* **Thr·aex -aecis** *m* Thracian gladiator *(i.e., armed like a Thracian with saber and small shield)*
thron·us -ī *m* throne
Thūcȳdid·ēs -is *or* **-ī** *m* Thucydides *(Greek historian of the Peloponnesian War, c. 456–400 B.C.)*
Thūl·ē *or* **T(h)ȳl·ē -ēs** *f* island located in the far north, perhaps Iceland or part of Scandinavia
thunn·us -ī *m* tuna fish
thūr- = **tur-**
Thūri·ī -ōrum *mpl* Thurii *(Greek city on the Tarentine Gulf in S. Italy)*
Thūrīn·us -a -um *adj & m* Thurian
thū·s -ris *n* incense, frankincense
Thybris *see* **Tiberis**
Thyēn·ē -ēs *f* nymph who nursed Bacchus
Thyest·ēs -ae *or* **-is** *m* son of Pelops, brother of Atreus, and father of Aegisthus
thymbr·a -ae *f (bot)* savory *(used as a spice in cooking)*
thym·um -ī *n (bot)* thyme *(common garden herb used as seasoning)*
Thyni·a -ae *f* Bithynia *(country of Asia Minor on the S. coast of the Black Sea)*
Thȳniac·us -a -um *adj* Bithynian
Thȳn·us -a -um *adj & m* Bithynian
thynn·us -ī *m* tuna fish
Thyōn·eūs -eī *m* Bacchus
thyrs·us -ī *m* Bacchic wand twined with vine leaves and ivy, and crowned with a pine cone
Ti. *abbr* **Tiberius** *(Roman first name, praenomen)*
tiār·a -ae *f or* **tiār·ās -ae** *m* tiara
Tiberīn·is -idis *or* **-idos** *adj (fem only)* of the Tiber
Tiberīn·us -a -um *adj* of the Tiber River ‖ *m* eponymous hero of the Tiber River
Tiber·is *or* **Tibr·is** *or* **Thybr·is -is** *m* Tiber River
Tiber·ius -(i)ī *m* Tiberius *(Roman first name, praenomen); esp.* Tiberius Claudius Nero Caesar *(successor of Augustus, 42 B.C.–A.D. 37, ruling from A.D. 14–37)* ‖ Tiberius Sempronius Gracchus *(socialist reformer, killed in 133 B.C.)*
tībi·a -ae *f* shinbone, tibia; flute
tībiāl·e -is *n* stocking
tībīc·en -inis *m* flutist; prop; pillar
tībīcin·a -ae *f* flutist *(female)*
Tibull·us -ī *m* Albius Tibullus *(Roman elegiac poet, c. 54–19 B.C.)*
Tīb·ur -uris *n* town of Latium on the Anio *(modern Tivoli)*
Tīburn·us -a -um *adj* of Tibur ‖ *m* legendary founder of Tibur
Tībur·s -tis *adj* of Tibur ‖ *mpl* inhabitants of Tibur ‖ *n* estate at Tibur
Tīburtīn·us -a -um *adj* of Tibur; travertine *(stone)* ‖ *n* estate at Tibur
Tīburt·us -ī *m* legendary founder of Tibur *(see* **Tiburnus)**
Tīcīn·us -ī *m* tributary of the Po
Tigellīn·us -ī *m* notorious favorite of Nero
tigill·um -ī *n* beam; log
tignāri·us -a -um *adj* carpenter's; **faber**

tignarius carpenter; **officina tignaria** carpenter's shop

tign·um -ī *n* beam, plank; lumber

tigr·is -is *mf* tiger

tigr·is -is *or* **-idis** *f* tigress

Tigr·is -is *or* **-idis** *m* Tigris River

tili·a -ae *f* lime tree

Tīmae·us -ī *m* Greek historian of Sicily *(c. 346–250 B.C.)* ‖ Pythagorean philosopher of Locri in S. Italy *(after whom Plato names one of his dialogues, 5th cent. B.C.)*

Timāv·us -ī *m* river which flows into the gulf of Trieste

Tīmāgen·ēs -is *m* brilliant rhetorician in the time of Augustus

timefact·us -a -um *adj* frightened

tim·eō -ēre -uī *tr* to fear, be afraid of ‖ *intr* to be afraid; *(w. dat or* **de** *or* **pro** *+ abl)* to fear for; *(w.* **ab** *+ abl of source of fear)* to fear harm from

timidē *adv* timidly, fearfully

timidit·ās -ātis *f* timidity, fearfulness, cowardice

timid·us -a -um *adj* timid, fearful, cowardly; *(w. gen)* afraid of

tim·or -ōris *m* fear; alarm, dread

tinctil·is -is -e *adj* obtained by dipping

tinctus *pp of* **tingo**

tine·a -ae *f* moth *(destructive of clothes, books),* bookworm

tin·g(u)ō -g(u)ĕre -xī -ctus *tr* to dip, soak; to dye, color; to tinge; to imbue

tinnīment·um -ī *n* ringing

tinn·iō -īre -īvī *or* **-iī -ītus** *tr & intr* to ring

tinnīt·us -ūs *m* ring, ringing; tinkling, jingling

tinnul·us -a -um *adj* ringing, tinkling; shrill

tintin(n)ābul·um -ī *n* bell; doorbell; cowbell

tintinnācul·us -a -um *adj* jingling ‖ *mpl* chain gang

tintin(n)·ō -āre *or* **tintin(n)·iō -īre** *intr* to ring

tīn·us -ī *f* laurustinus *(evergreen shrub having white or pinkish flowers)*

-tin·us -a -um *adjl suf forms adjectives from adverbs denoting time, e.g.:* **crastinus** tommorrow's; **pristinus** antique, ancient

-ti·ō -ōnis *fem suf forms verbal nouns to denote the action of the verb, e.g.:* **actio** act, action; *appears as* **-sio** *from verbs which form the supine in* **-sum,** *e.g.:* **cursio** running

Tīph·ys -yos *m* pilot of the Argo

tippūl·a -ae *f* water spider

Tīresi·ās -ae *m* famous blind seer at Thebes at the time of Oedipus

Tīridāt·ēs -ae *m* name of three kings of Parthia

tīr·ō -ōnis *m* novice, beginner; young man who has just come of age; *(mil)* recruit ‖ **Tiro** Marcus Tullius Tiro *(Cicero's secretary)*

tīrōcin·ium -(i)ī *n* apprenticeship; beginning, first try; *(mil)* first campaign; *(mil)* military inexperience; *(mil)* body of raw recruits

tīruncul·us -ī *m* beginner, recruit

Tīryn·s -thos *f* town in the Argolid where Hercules was raised

Tīrynthi·us -a -um *adj* Tirynthian ‖ *m* Hercules ‖ *mpl* the people of Tiryns ‖ *f* Alcmena

Tīsamen·us -ī *m* son of Orestes and king of Argos

tisan·a -ae *f* pearl barley

tisanār·ium -(i)ī *n* gruel; **tisanarium oryzae** rice gruel

Tīsiphon·ē -ēs *f* one of the three Furies who haunted murderers

Tīsiphonē·us -a -um *adj* belonging to Tisiphone; *(fig)* deserving of punishment by the Furies, guilty

Tīt·ān -ānos *or* **Tītān·us -ī** *m* Titan; sun; Prometheus ‖ *mpl* Titans *(giant sons of Uranus and Ge who rebelled against Uranus and put Cronus on the throne)*

Tītāni·us -a -um *adj* of the Titans, Titanic *(esp. of the sun, moon, or Prometheus)* ‖ *m* sun-god ‖ *f* Latona *(mother of Apollo and Diana)* ‖ Diana ‖ Pyrrha *(as descendant of Prometheus)* ‖ Circe *(as daughter of Sol or Helios)*

Tīthōni·us -a -um *adj* Tithonian ‖ *f* Aurora *(wife of Tithonus)*

Tīthōn·us -ī *m* son of Laomedon and husband of Aurora from whom he received the gift of immortality without eternal youth

Titiens·is -is -e *adj* of the Tities tribe

Tit·iēs -ium *mpl* one of the three original Roman tribes

tītillāti·ō -ōnis *f* tickling, titillation;

tītill·ō -āre *tr* tickle, titillate

Titi·us -a -um *adj* Roman clan name *(nomen)*

tittibilīc·ium -(i)ī *n* trifle

titubanter *adv* falteringly

titubanti·a -ae *f* stumbling *(in speech)*

titubāti·ō -ōnis *f (lit & fig)* stumbling

titub·ō -āre -āvī -ātum *intr* to stagger, reel, totter; to falter, waver; to stumble, slip up *(in speech)*

titul·us -ī *m* inscription; label; title, heading *(of a book, chapter);* chapter *(of a book);* personal title; identification tag; notice, advertisement; pretext, ostensible motive; claim to fame; title of honor; renown; *(w. gen)* 1 honor *or* distinction arising from; 2 reputation for

Tit·us -ī *m* Roman first name *(praenomen); esp.* Titus Tatius *(a Sabine king who is said to have ruled with Romulus until the*

latter had him killed) ‖ the Emperor Titus *(Titus Flavius Vespasianus, son of Vespasian; ruled* A.D. *79–81)*

Tity·os *or* **Tity·us -ī** *m* Tityus *(giant slain by Apollo for attempting to rape Latona and thrown into Tartarus)*

Tītyr·us *or* **Tity·os -ī** *m* shepherd in Vergil's pastorals, sometimes identified with Vergil himself

Tlēpolem·us -ī *m* son of Hercules

Tmar·os -ī *m* mountain in Epirus

Tmōlīt·ēs -is *adj (masc only)* of Mt. Tmolus ‖ *m* wine from Mt. Tmolus

Tmōli·us -a -um *adj* of Mt. Tmolus

Tmōl·us -ī *m* **(Tim-)** Tmolus *(mountain in Lydia famous for its wines)*

toculli·ō -ōnis *m* loan shark

todill·us -ī *m* type of small bird

tōfīn·us -a -um *adj* made of tufa

tōf·us -ī *m* **(toph-)** tufa *(sandstone, used extensively in Republican Rome as building stone)*

tog·a -ae *f* toga *(outer garment of a Roman citizen);* **toga atra** dark toga *(unwhitened toga worn as sign of mourning);* **toga candida** white toga *(fulled with chalk and worn by candidates for office);* **toga picta** brocaded toga *(worn by triumphant generals);* **toga praetexta** crimson-bordered toga *(worn by magistrates and freeborn children);* **toga pulla** dark-gray toga *(worn by mourners);* **toga pura** *(or* **virilis** *or* **libera)** toga of manhood *(worn by young men from about the age of sixteen)*

togāt·a -ae *f* Latin comedy *(on Roman themes and in Roman dress)*

togātār·ius -(i)ī *m* actor in a *fabula togata*

togātul·us -ī *m (pej)* miserable Roman *(of clients paying duty calls)*

togāt·us -a -um *adj* wearing a toga, true Roman; having a civilian occupation *or* status, civilian; peacetime-; **fabula togata** *(theat)* Latin comedy *(written on a native theme and presented in Roman dress);* **Gallia Togata** Cisalpine Gaul *(between the Alps and the Po River)* ‖ *m* Roman citizen; civilian; humble client ‖ *f* prostitute; *see* **togata**

togul·a -ae *f (pej)* little toga

tolerābil·is -is -e *adj* tolerable; patient

tolerābiliter *adv* without stress

toler·ans -antis *adj* tolerant; *(w. gen)* tolerant of, enduring

toleranter *adv* patiently

toleranti·a -ae *f* toleration, endurance

tolerāti·ō -ōnis *f* toleration, endurance

tolerāt·us -a -um *adj* tolerable, endurable

toler·ō -āre -āvī -ātus *tr* to tolerate, endure; to support, maintain, sustain

tollēn·ō -ōnis *m* crane, lift, derrick

tollō tollĕre sustulī sublātus *tr* to lift, raise; to raise *(the voice);* to draw *(lots);* to have *(a child);* to acknowledge *(a child);* to raise, educate; to weigh *(anchor); (of a ship)* to take on board; *(of a ship)* to have the capacity of; *(of a vehicle)* to pick up, take as a passenger; to win, carry off *(a prize);* to reap *(a profit);* to remove; to do away with, destroy; to cancel, abolish, abrogate; to lift, steal; to uplift, cheer up, excite; to erect, build up; to waste *(time);* **amicum tollere** to cheer up a friend; **animos tollere** to boost morale; **deos tollere** to deny the existence of the gods; **de medio tollere** to kill; **diem tollere** to take a day off *(from work);* **in crucem** *(or* **in furcam)** **tollere** to crucify ‖ *refl (of plants)* to grow high; **in caelum se tollere** to ascend *or* climb into the sky ‖ *pass* to climb up, rise

Tolōs·a -ae *f* city in Narbonese Gaul *(modern Toulouse)*

Tolōsān·us -a -um *adj* **(Toloss-)** of Tolosa ‖ *mpl* people of Tolosa

Tolōs·as -ātis *adj* produced in Tolosa ‖ *mpl* people of Tolosa

tolūtim *adv* at a trot, jogging

tomāc(u)l·um -ī *n* sausage

tōment·um -ī *n* pillow stuffing

Tom·ī -ōrum *mpl or* **Tom·is -is** *f* Tomi *(town on the Black Sea in modern Romania, where Ovid spent his years in exile)*

Tomīt·ae -ārum *mpl* people of Tomi

Tomītān·us -a -um *adj* of Tomi

tom·us -ī *m* a length of papyrus, sheet

Ton·ans -antis *m* Thunderer *(epithet of several gods, esp. Jupiter)*

tondeō tondēre totondī tonsus *tr* to clip, shear, shave; to prune; to reap, mow; to crop, browse on; *(fig)* to fleece, rob; **usque ad cutem tondere** *(fig)* to swindle, fleece *(literally, the clip right down to the skin)*

tonitrāl·is -is -e *adj* thunderous

tonitr·us -ūs *m or* **tonitr·um -ī** *n* thunder ‖ *mpl or npl* claps of thunder

ton·ō -āre -uī -itūrus *tr* to thunder forth *(words)* ‖ *intr* to thunder

tons·a -ae *f* oar

tonsil·is -is -e *adj* clipped

tonsill·a -ae *f* **(tōs-)** tonsil

tonsit·ō -āre *tr* to shear regularly

tons·or -ōris *m* **(tōs-)** shearer; barber

tonsōri·us -a -um *adj* shaving; barber's

tonstrīcul·a -ae *f* little hairdresser, little barber *(female)*

to(n)strīn·a -ae *f* barber shop

tonstrīn·um -ī *n* trade of a barber, barbering

tonstr·ix -īcis *f* hairdresser, barber *(female)*

tonsūr·a -ae *f* clipping, shearing; **capillorum tonsura** haircut

tons·us -a -um *pp of* **tondeo** ‖ *f see* **tonsa**

tons·us -ūs *m* haircut; hairdo

tonuī *perf of* **tono**
tōph·us -ī *m* (**tōf-**) tufa *(sandstone used as building material esp. in the Republican period)*
topiāri·us -a -um *adj* garden, landscape ‖ *m* gardener, landscaper ‖ *f* landscaping
topic·a -ōrum *npl* "commonplaces" *(title of work by Aristotle on which Cicero based his work on this topic)*
topic·ē -ēs *f (rhet)* resourcefulness in finding topics for speeches
-t·or -ōris *masc suf, formed from verbs to denote the doer of the action of the verb, e.g.:* **amator** lover; *becomes* **-sor** *from verbs which form the past participle in* **-sus**, *e.g.:* **tonsor** shearer, barber
tor·al -ālis *n* valance; coverlet
torcul·ar -āris *or* **torcul·um -ī** *n* wine press, oil press
toreum·a -atis *n* embossed work, relief
-tōr·ium -(i)ī *neut suf often denoting places, e.g.,* **praetorium** headquarters of the praetor *or* commander
torment·um -ī *n* windlass; catapult, artillery piece; shot; torture rack; *(lit & fig)* torture ‖ *npl* artillery
tormin·a -um *npl* colic, bowel trouble
torminōs·us -a -um *adj* suffering from colic, colicky
torn·ō -āre -āvī -ātus *tr* to turn on a lathe
torn·us -ī *m* lathe
torōs·us -a -um *adj* brawny, muscular
torpēd·ō -inis *f* numbness, lethargy, listlessness; stingray *(fish)*
torp·eō -ēre -uī *intr* to numb; to be stiff; to be stupefied; to be groggy
torp·escō -escĕre -uī *intr* to grow numb; to grow listless
torpid·us -a -um *adj* numbed, paralyzed; groggy
torp·or -ōris *m* torpor, numbness; grogginess
torpuī *perf of* **torpeo** *and* **torpesco**
torquāt·us -a -um *adj* wearing a collar *or* necklace ‖ **Torquatus** *m* Titus Manlius Torquatus *(legendary Roman hero who wore a necklace taken from a gigantic Gaul he had slain)*
tor·queō -quēre -sī -tus *tr* to twist, turn, wind; to bend out of shape; to hurl; to wind up *(catapult);* to turn *(so as to face in the opposite direction);* to roll *(eyes);* to crane *(neck);* to divert the course of; to spin; to curl *(hair);* to wreathe *(the head); (fig)* to torment; **aliquem torquere** *(w.* **in** *or* **adversus, contra** + *acc)* to torture s.o. to give evidence against *(s.o.)*
torqu·ēs *or* **torqu·is -is** *m(f)* necklace; collar *(of twisted metal, as military decoration)*
torr·ens -entis *adj* burning, seething; rushing, roaring *(stream);* fiery *(speech)* ‖ *m* torrent; current
torr·eō -ēre -uī tostus *tr* to roast, bake; to burn, scorch; to parch
torr·escō -escĕre -uī *intr* to become burned; to become parched
torrid·us -a -um *adj* baked, parched; dried up; frostbitten
torr·is -is *or* **torr·us -ī** *m* firebrand
torruī *perf of* **torreo**
torsī *perf of* **torqueo**
tortē *adv* crookedly
tortil·is -is -e *adj* twisted, winding, spiral, coiled
tort·ō -āre *tr* to twist, coil ‖ *pass* to writhe
tort·or -ōris *m* torturer
tortuōs·us -a -um *adj* tortuous, winding; *(fig)* complicated
tort·us -a -um *adj* bent, crooked, curved; coiled, twisted; curly *(hair);* winding *(road, labyrinth)*
tort·us -ūs *m* twist, coil; **tortūs dare** *(of a serpent)* to form loops
torul·us -ī *m* headband; tuft *(of hair)*
tor·us -ī *m* knot; bulge; muscle, brawn; bed, couch; mattress; cushion; mound; boss; flowery expression; **torus genialis** conjugal bed
torvit·ās -ātis *f* grimness
torv·us -a -um *adj* grim
tostus *pp of* **torreo**
tot *indecl adj* so many, as many; **tot...quot** as many ... as
totiens *or* **totiēs** *adv* so often, so many times
totondī *perf of* **tondeo**
tōt·us -a -um *adj* the whole, all, entire; **totus in illis** totally absorbed in those matters ‖ *n* the whole matter, all; **ex toto** totally; **in toto** on the whole, in general; **in totum** totally
toxic·um -ī *n* poison *(originally, a poison in which arrowheads were dipped)*
trabāl·is -is -e *adj* of *or* for beams; **clavus trabalis** spike; **telum trabale** beam-like shaft
trabe·a -ae *f* ceremonial robe *(with purple stripes and worn by magistrates, augurs, and as dress uniform of the equites)*
trabeāt·us -a -um *adj* wearing a *trabea*
trab·s -is *f* beam, plank; timber; tree; object made of beams: roof, shaft, table, battering ram
Trāch·īn -īnis *or* **Trāch·ȳn -ȳnos** *f* Trachis *(town in Thessaly on Mount Oeta, where Hercules had himself cremated)*
Trāchīni·us -a -um *adj* of Trachin (Trachis) ‖ *m* Ceyx *(king of Trachin)* ‖ *fpl* "Women of Trachis" *(title of a play by Sophocles)*
tractābil·is -is -e *adj* manageable; *(of weather)* fit for navigation

tractāti·ō -ōnis *f* handling, management; discussion, treatment *(of a subject)*
tractātr·ix -īcis *f* masseuse
tractāt·us -ūs *m* touching, handling; management
tractim *adv* little by little, slowly; in a drawn-out manner
tract·ō -āre -āvī -ātus *tr* to drag around, haul, pull; to touch, handle; to deal with, treat; to manage, control; to wield; to conduct, carry on, transact; to practice; to discuss; *(of an actor)* to play the role of; to examine, consider; **male tractare** to mistreat ‖ *refl* to behave, conduct oneself ‖ *intr* to carry on a discussion
tract·us -a -um *pp of* **traho** ‖ *adj* fluent; lengthy, continuous *(discourse)*
tract·us -ūs *m* dragging; dragging out, extension *(e.g., of a war);* track, trail; tract, expanse, extent, distance; region, district
tradidī *perf of* **trado**
trāditi·ō -ōnis *f* handing over, surrender; transmission; item of traditional belief, custom, tradition
trādit·or -ōris *m* betrayer, traitor
trā·dō -dĕre -didī -ditus *tr* to hand over, surrender, deliver; to betray; to hand down, bequeath, transmit, pass on; to relate, recount; to teach ‖ *refl (w. dat)* **1** to surrender to; **2** to devote oneself to
trā·dūcō -dūcĕre -duxī -ductus *tr* to bring across *or* over, transfer; to convert, bring over; *(w.* **ad** *or* **in** *+ acc)* to cause *(s.o.)* to change *(from one attitude, habit, etc.)* to *(another);* to exhibit, display; to disgrace; to pass, spend; *(gram)* to derive; **traducere equum** *(of a member of the equestrian order who passed the censor's inspection)* to lead one's horse in the parade
trāducti·ō -ōnis *f* transference; passage *(of time);* metonymy; use of homonyms *or* homophones
trāduct·or -ōris *m* conveyor
trāductus *pp of* **traduco**
trād·ux -ucis *mf* vine branch *(trained across the space between trees in a vineyard)*
trāduxī *perf of* **traduco**
tragicē *adv* as in tragedy
tragicocōmoedi·a -ae *f* melodrama
tragic·us -a -um *adj* of tragedy, tragic; in the tragic style, grand, solemn; of a tragic nature, tragic ‖ *m* writer of tragedies
tragoedi·a -ae *f* tragedy
tragoed·us -ī *m* tragic actor
trāgul·a -ae *f* javelin
trag·us *or* **trag·os -ī** *m* body odor of the armpits; a fish *(of unknown type)*
trah·ax -ācis *adj* greedy
trahe·a -ae *f* sledge, drag *(used as a threshing device)*
tra·hō -hĕre -xī -ctus *tr* to draw, drag, trail; *(in a temporal sense)* to bring in its wake; to draw out, pull out, extract; to drag out, protract; to lead, to come leading *(an animal); (of a river)* to carry along; to carry off *(as plunder);* to rob *(persons);* to take along *(on a trip);* to contract, wrinkle *(the brow);* to pull toward one; *(of physical forces)* to attract; to attract, lure, fascinate *(persons);* to draw *(water);* to draw *(conclusions);* to take on, assume; to acquire, get; to spin, manufacture; to win over *(to the other side);* to refer, ascribe; to distract; to keep on considering, ponder; **animam** *(or* **spiritum)** **trahere** to draw in breath; **pedem trahere** *(of a lame person)* to drag one foot
Trājān·us -ī *m* Trajan *(Marcus Ulpius Trajanus, Roman emperor,* A.D. *98–117)*
trājecti·ō -ōnis *f* crossing, passage; transposition *(of words);* shift of meaning; exaggeration
trājectus *pp of* **trajicio**
trāject·us -ūs *m* crossing over, passage
trā·jiciō -jicĕre -jēcī -jectus *tr* to throw *(a weapon)* across; *(of a weapon)* to pierce, pass through; to place *(a bridge, a bar)* across; to pass through, break through; to move, shift *(s.th. from one place to another); (w. double acc)* to bring *(e.g., troops)* across *(e.g., a river, mountain); (w.* **trans** *+ acc)* to lead across; *(w.* **in** *+ acc)* to lead over into; to shift *(words from one part of the sentence to another)* ‖ *intr* to cross over
trālāt- = translat-
Trall·ēs -ium *fpl* Tralles *(town in Lydia on the Menander River, variously set in Caria and Lydia)*
Tralliān·us -a -um *adj* of Tralles
trāloqu·or -ī *tr* to talk over, enumerate, recount
trālūceō *see* **transluceo**
trām·a -ae *f* woof, warp *(in some form of weaving)*
trām·es -itis *m* path, track, trail
trāmi- = transmi-
trānatō = transnato
trān·ō *or* **transn·ō -āre -āvī -ātus** *tr* to swim across; to pass through, permeate ‖ *intr* to swim across; to pass through
tranquillē *adv* quietly, calmly
tranquillit·ās -ātis *f* tranquillity, stillness, calmness
tranquill·ō -āre -āvī -ātus *tr* to calm, quiet, compose
tranquill·us -a -um *adj* tranquil, calm, quiet ‖ *n* calm, quiet, tranquillity; calm sea
Tranquill·us -ī *m* Gaius Suetonius Tranquillus *(biographer of the Emperors, born c.* A.D. *69)*

trans *prep (w. acc)* across, over, beyond
trans- *pref (used with verbs or verbal derivatives in the sense of the preposition)*
transab·eō -īre -īvī *or* **-iī** *tr* to pierce, pass right through *(and go some distance beyond)*
transacti·ō -ōnis *f* business transaction, business deal
transact·or -ōris *m* manager, negotiator
transactus *pp of* **transigo**
transad·igō -igĕre -ēgī -āctus *tr* to pierce; to run *(s.o.)* through; *(w. double acc)* to run *(e.g., a sword)* through *(s.o.)*
Transalpīn·us -a -um *adj* Transalpine
transbīt·ō -ĕre *intr* to come *or* go across
transcen·dō -dĕre -dī -sus *tr* to climb *or* step over, surmount; to overstep, transgress ‖ *intr* to climb *or* step across
trans·cīdō -cīdĕre -cīdī -cīsus *tr* to flog thoroughly
trans·scrībō -scrībĕre -scripsī -scriptus *tr* to transcribe, copy off; *(leg)* to transfer, convey
trans·currō -currĕre -(cu)currī -cursum *tr & intr* to hurry, run *or* dash over; to run through; to run past; *(in writing)* to pass over quickly; to skim *(in reading)*
transcurs·us -ūs *m* running through, passage; cursory mention, cursory treatment *(of a subject)*
transd- = trad-
transenn·a -ae *f* **(trās-)** lattice work; lattice window; fowler's net
trans·eō -īre -īvī *or* **-iī -itus** *tr* to cross; to desert; to pass *(in a race);* to pass over, make no mention of; to treat cursorily; to overstep; to surpass ‖ *intr* to go over, go across, pass over; to pass by, go by; to shift *(to another opinion, topic, etc.); (of time)* to pass by; to pass away; *(w.* **ad** *+ acc)* **1** to cross over to *(a place);* **2** to desert to; *(w.* **in** *+ acc)* to change into; *(w.* **per** *+ acc)* to penetrate, permeate
trans·ferō -ferre -tulī -lātus *(or* **trālātus)** *tr* **(trāf-)** to carry *or* bring across; to transfer *(by writing);* to copy; to shift; to transform; to postpone; to translate; to use figuratively
trans·fīgō -figĕre -fixī -fixus *tr* to pierce; to run *(s.o.)* through
transfigūr·ō -āre -āvī -ātus *tr* to transform
transfixus *pp of* **transfigo**
trans·fodiō -fodĕre -fōdī -fossus *tr* to stab, pierce, run through
transform·is -is -e *adj* transformed
transform·ō -āre -āvī -ātus *tr* to transform
transfossus *pp of* **transfodio**
transfret·ō -āre -āvī -ātum *intr* to cross the sea
transfug·a -ae *m* deserter, turncoat
trans·fugiō -fugĕre -fūgī *intr* to go over to the enemy, desert
transfug·ium -(i)ī *n* desertion
trans·fundō -fundĕre -fūdī -fūsus *tr* to transfuse; to pour; *(w.* **in** *+ acc)* to pour *(a liquid)* into; *(w.* **ad** *+ acc) (fig)* to shift *(affection, allegiance)* to
transfūsi·ō -ōnis *f* pouring from one vessel into another; *(fig)* intermarriage
transfūsus *pp of* **transfundo**
trans·gredior -gredī -gressus sum *tr* to cross, pass over; to exceed ‖ *intr* to go across; to cross over *(to another party)*
transgressi·ō -ōnis *f* crossing; transition; transposition *(of words)*
transgressus *pp of* **transgredior**
transgress·us -ūs *m* crossing
transiciō *see* **transjicio**
transiect- = transject-
trans·igō -igĕre -ēgī -actus *tr* to pierce, run through; to finish; to settle, transact; to accomplish, perform, conclude; to pass, spend ‖ *intr* to come to an agreement, reach an understanding
transil·iō *or* **transsil·iō -īre -uī** *tr* to jump over, jump across; to overstep; to skip, omit ‖ *intr* to jump across
transit·ans -antis *adj* passing through
transiti·ō -ōnis *f* crossing, passage; switching *(to another party);* contagion, infection; passageway
transitōri·us -a -um *adj* affording a passage *(from one place to another)*
transitus *pp of* **transeo**
transit·us -ūs *m* crossing, passage; passing; traffic; crossing over, desertion; change, period of change, transition; transference of possession *(of); fading (of colors);* **in transitu** in passing; **per transitum** by way of transition
translātīci·us -a -um *adj* **(trāl-)** transmitted, traditional, customary; usual, common
translāti·ō -ōnis *f* **(trāl-)** transfer, shift; transporting; translation; metaphor, figure
translātīv·us -a -um *adj* **(trāl-)** transferable
translāt·or -ōris *m* middleman *(in a transfer)*
translātus *pp of* **transferro**
transleg·ō -ĕre *tr (w. dat)* to read out to *(s.o.)*
transloqu·or -ī *tr* **(trāl-)** to recount from the beginning
transluc·eō -ēre *intr* **(trāl-)** to shine through; to be reflected
transmarīn·us -a -um *adj* from beyond the seas, foreign, overseas
transme·ō -āre *tr & intr* **(trām-)** to cross, pass through
transmigr·ō -āre -āvī -ātum *intr* **(trām-)** to move, change residence; to migrate, emigrate

transmin·eō -ēre *intr* to stick out on the other side
transmissi·ō -ōnis *f* crossing, passage
transmissus *pp of* **transmitto**
transmiss·us -ūs *m* passing over, crossing, passage
trans·mittō -mittěre -mīsī -missus *tr* **(trām-)** to send across; to transmit; to let pass; to hand over, entrust; to pass over, leave unmentioned; to endure; *(w.* **in** + *acc)* to send *(s.o.)* across to *or* into; *(w.* **per** + *acc)* to let *(s.o.)* pass through ‖ *intr* to cross over, cross, pass *(from one place to another)*
transmontān·ī -ōrum *mpl* people living across the mountains
trans·moveō -movēre -mōvī -mōtus *tr* to move, transfer
transmūt·ō -āre -āvī -ātus *tr* to change, shift
transnat·ō -āre -āvī -ātus *tr* **(trān-)** to swim (across) ‖ *intr* to swim across
transnō *see* **trano**
transnōmin·ō -āre -āvī -ātus *tr (w. double acc)* to rename as
Transpadān·us -a -um *adj* beyond *or* N. of the Po River
transpect·us -ūs *m* view, prospect
trans(s)pic·iō -ěre *tr* to look through
trans·pōnō -pōněre -posuī -positus *tr* to transfer, move across
transport·ō -āre -āvī -ātus *tr* to transport
transpositus *pp of* **transpono**
transrhenān·us -a -um *adj* beyond the Rhine, E. of the Rhine
transs- = trans-
transtiberīn·us -a -um *adj* across the Tiber
transtin·eō -ēre *intr* to provide a link *(from one side to the other)*
transtr·um -ī *n* crossbeam; rower's seat, thwart
transult·ō -āre *intr* to jump across
transūt·us -a -um *adj* pierced through *(w. a pointed object)*
transvecti·ō -ōnis *f* **(trāv-)** transportation; riding past *(in review)*
trans·vehō -vehěre -vexī -vectus *tr* **(trāv-)** to transport; to carry past *(in a parade)* ‖ *pass* to ride by *(in a parade)*; *(of time)* to elapse
transverber·ō -āre *tr* to pierce through and through, transfix
transversāri·us -a -um *adj* lying crosswise ‖ *n* crosspiece
transversē *adv* crosswise; across one's course
transvers·us *or* **transvors·us -a -um** *adj* **(trāv-)** lying across, lying crosswise; inopportune; astray; in the wrong direction ‖ *n* wrong direction; **de transverso** unexpectedly; **ex transverso** unexpectedly; sideways
transvolit·ō -āre *tr* to flit through, fly through
transvol·ō -āre -āvī -ātus *tr & intr* **(trāv-)** to fly over, fly across, fly by
transvorsus *see* **transversus**
trapēt·um -ī *n or* **trapēt·us -ī** *m* oil press
trapezīt·a -ae *m* banker, money-changer
trapezophor·um -ī *n* ornate table
Trapez·os -untis *or* **-untos** *f* city in Pontus on the Black Sea
Trasumēn·us -ī *m* **(-menn-)** Lake Trasimene *(lake in Etruria, modern Trasimeno, where Hannibal defeated the Romans in 217 B.C.)*
trāv- = transv-
traxī *perf of* **traho**
Trebi·a -ae *f* river which flows into the Po near Placentia *(modern Trebbia River, near which Hannibal defeated the Romans in 218 B.C.)*
Trebulān·us -a -um *adj* of Trebula *(town in central Campania)*; **ager Trebulanus** district of Trebula
trecēn·ī -ae -a *adj* three hundred each; three hundred each time ‖ *mpl* lots of three hundred *(men)*
trecentēsim·us -a -um *adj* three-hundredth
trecentiē(n)s *adv* three hundred times
trechedipn·um -ī *n* light garment worn to dinner
tredecim *indecl adj* thirteen
tremebund·us -a -um *adj* trembling, shivering
treme·faciō -facěre -fēcī -factus *tr* to shake, cause to shake
tremend·us -a -um *adj* awe-inspiring, terrible
trem·escō -escěre -uī *tr* to tremble at ‖ *intr* to tremble
trem·ō -ěre -uī *tr* to tremble at ‖ *intr* to tremble, shiver, quake
trem·or -ōris *m* trembling, shivering; dread; cause of fright, terror
tremuī *perf of* **tremo** *and* **tremesco**
tremul·us -a -um *adj* trembling, quivering, tremulous, shivering
trepidanter *adv* tremblingly, nervously
trepidāti·ō -ōnis *f* nervousness, alarm; trembling
trepidē *adv* nervously, in alarm
trepid·ō -āre -āvī -ātus *tr* to start at, be startled by ‖ *intr* to be nervous, be jumpy, be alarmed; *(of a flame)* to flicker; *(of streams)* to rush along
trepid·us -a -um *adj* nervous, jumpy; restless; bubbling; perilous, critical, alarming; **in re trepida** in a ticklish situation
trēs trēs tria *adj* three; *(denoting a small number)* a couple of
tress·is -is *m* sum of three *"pennies"*; mere trifle
tresvirī *(gen:* **triumvirōrum)** *mpl* triumvirs

Trēver·ī *or* **Trēvir·ī -ōrum** *mpl* people E. of Gaul
tri- *pref* consisting of three of the things named, *e.g.*, **tricornis** having three horns
triangul·us -a -um *adj* triangular ‖ *n* triangle
triāri·ī -ōrum *mpl* soldiers of the third rank in a battle line, reserves
trib·as -adis *f* female sexual pervert
Triboc·ī -ōrum *mpl* tribe which settled on the Rhine in the region of modern Alsace
tribuāri·us -a -um *adj* tribal
tribuī *perf of* **tribuo**
tribūl·is -is *m* fellow tribesman
trībul·um -ī *n* threshing sledge *(wooden platform with iron teeth underneath)*
tribul·us -ī *m* caltrop *(thistle)*
tribūn·al -ālis *n* platform; tribunal, judgment seat; *(in camp)* general's platform; cenotaph; **pro tribunali** *(or* **in** *or* **e tribunali)** officially
tribūnāt·us -ūs *m* tribuneship
tribūnici·us -a -um *adj* tribunician, tribune's ‖ *m* ex-tribune
tribūn·us -ī *m* tribune; **tribunus aerarius** paymaster; **tribunus militaris** *(or* **militum)** military tribune *(six in each legion, serving under the legatus, and elected by the people or at times appointed by the commander)*; **tribunus plebis** tribune of the people *(initially two, eventually ten in number, serving in the interests of the plebeians)*
trib·uō -uĕre -uī -ūtus *tr* to divide; to distribute, bestow, confer, assign; to give, present; to concede, grant, allow; to ascribe, impute; to devote, spend
trib·us -ūs *f* tribe *(orginally three in number and eventually increased to thirty-five)*
tribūtāri·us -a -um *adj* tributary, subject to tribute; **tributariae tabellae** letters of credit
tribūtim *adv* by tribes, tribe by tribe
tribūti·ō -ōnis *f* distribution
tribūt·um -ī *n or* **tribūt·us -ī** *m* tribute, tax; contribution
tribūt·us -a -um *pp of* **tribuo** ‖ *adj* arranged by tribes
trīc·ae -ārum *fpl* tricks; nonsense
trīcēn·ī -ae -a *adj* thirty each; thirty at a time, in groups of thirty
tric·eps -ipitis *adj* three-headed
trīcēsim·us -a -um *adj* **(-cens-)** thirtieth
trichil·a *or* **tricli·a** *or* **tricle·a -ae** *f* bower, arbor; summer house
trīciens *or* **trīciēs** *adv* thirty times
triclea *see* **trichila**
triclia *see* **trichila**
trīclīn·ium -(i)ī *n* dining couch *(running around three sides of a table)*; dining room
trīc·ō -ōnis *m* schemer
trīc·or -ārī *intr* to cause trouble; to pull tricks
tricorp·or -oris *adj* triple-bodied
tricusp·is -idis *adj* three-pronged
trid·ens -entis *adj* three-pronged ‖ *m* trident
Tridentif·er *or* **Tridentig·er -erī** *m* Trident Bearer *(epithet of Neptune)*
tridu·um -ī *n* three-day period, three days
trienn·ia -ium *npl* triennial festival *(celebrated every three years)*
trienn·ium -(i)ī *n* three-year period, three years
tri·ens -entis *m* one third; coin *(one third of a "penny")*; third of a pint
trientābul·um -ī *n* land given by the State to those from whom the State had borrowed, equivalent to one third of the sum which the state owed
trienti·us -a -um *adj* sold for a third
triērarch·us -ī *m* captain of a trireme
triēr·is -is -e *adj* having oars *or* rowers arranged in threes ‖ *f* trireme
trietēric·us -a -um *adj* triennial, recurring every three years ‖ *npl* festival of Bacchus
trietēr·is -idis *or* **-idos** *f* three-year period; triennial festival in honor of Bacchus
trifāriam *adv* in three places, on three sides; under three headings
trifauc·is -is -e *adj* triple-throated
trifid·us -a -um *adj* three-forked; split into three parts
trifīl·is -is -e *adj* having three threads *or* strands of hair
Trifolīn·us -a -um *adj* belonging to the district of Trifolium near Naples
trifol·ium -(i)ī *n* clover
triform·is -is -e *adj* triple-form *(of the goddess having the three aspects of Luna, Diana, and Hecate; of three-headed Geryon; of the Chimera as composed of a lion, snake, and goat)*
tri·fūr -fūris *m* archthief
trifurcif·er -erī *m* archvillain, hardened criminal
trigemin·us -a -um *adj* **(terg-)** threefold, triple ‖ *mpl* triplets
trīgintā *indecl adj* thirty
trig·ō(n) -ōnis *or* **-ōnos** game of catch *(played with three players standing to form a triangle)*; ball *(used in this game)*
trigōnāl·is -is -e *adj* **pila trigonalis** ball used in the game of catch
trilībr·is -is -e *adj* three-pound
trilingu·is -is -e *adj* three-tongued
tril·ix -īcis *adj* three-ply, triple-stranded
trime(n)str·is -is -e *adj* of three months
trimetr·us -ī *m (pros)* trimeter *(metric line consisting of three double feet, e.g.,*

iambic trimeter, or a line consisting of six iambic feet)
trimod·ius -iī *m* measure of three pecks
trīmul·us -a -um *adj* three-year-old
trīm·us -a -um *adj* three-year-old
-trīn·a -ae *f suf* denoting the place where an activity is conducted: **tonstrīna** barbershop *(from* **tondere** to cut, shear, clip)
Trīnacr·is -idis *adj* Sicilian
Trīnacri·us -a -um *adj* Sicilian ‖ *m* Empedocles ‖ *f* Sicily
trīn·ī -ae -a *adj* threefold, triple; three each, three at a time; *(w. nouns occurring only in pl)* three: **trinae litterae** three letters, three epistles
Trinobant·ēs -ium *mpl* a British tribe near Essex
trinoctiāl·is -is -e *adj* occurring on three successive nights
trinōd·is -is -e *adj* triple-knotted
trinumm·us -ī *m* popular name for a newly introduced coin of high value ‖ **Trinummus** title of a play by Plautus
triōbol·um -ī *n* three-obol coin, half-dramcha *or* half-denarius piece *(c. 50¢)*
triōn·ēs -um *mpl* team of three oxen used in plowing ‖ **Triōnēs** Great and Little Bear *(constellations)*
Triop·ās -ae *adj (masc & fem only)* of Erysichthon
Triopē·is -idos *f* Mestra *(daughter of Erysichthon and granddaughter of Triopas, king of Thessaly)*
Triopē·ius -(i)ī *m* Erysichthon *(son of Triopas, king of Thessaly)*
triparc·us -a -um *adj* extremely stingy, triply stingy
tripartītō *adv* in three parts, into three parts
tripartīt·us -a -um *adj* **(-pert-)** divided into three parts, threefold
tripector·us -a -um *adj* triple-bodied, triple-chested
tripedāl·is -is -e *adj* three-foot
tripertītus *see* **tripartitus**
trip·ēs -edis *adj* three-legged, three-footed
tripl·ex -icis *adj* threefold, triple ‖ *n* three times as much, triple portion
tripl·us -a -um *adj* triple, threefold
Triptolem·us -ī *m* son of Celeus the king of Eleusis, favorite of Ceres, inventor of agriculture and one of the judges in the lower world
tripudi·ō -āre -āvī -ātum *intr* to perform a ritual dance *(tripudium)*
tripud·ium -(i)ī *n* war dance *(ritual dance in triple time, originally performed by priests in honor of Mars);* favorable omen *(when the sacred chickens ate hungrily, letting some grains fall to the ground in the process)*
trip·ūs -odis *or* **-odos** *m* tripod *(three-footed caldron);* oracle, Delphic oracle
triquetr·us -a -um *adj* triangular; Sicilian
trirēm·is -is -e *adj* having three banks of oars ‖ *f* trireme
trīs *see* **tres**
triscel·um -ī *n* triangle
triscurri·a -ōrum *npl* fantastic nonsense
tristicul·us -a -um *adj* somewhat sad
tristific·us -a -um *adj* saddening
tristimōni·a -ae *f or* **tristimōn·ium -(i)ī** *n* sadness
trist·is -is -e *adj* sad, sorrowful; bringing sorrow, saddening; gloomy, sullen; stern, harsh; disagreeable, offensive *(odor);* bitter, sour *(taste);* unpleasant *(sound)*
tristiter *adv (to cry)* bitterly; distressingly
tristiti·a -ae *or* **tristiti·ēs -ēī** *f* sadness, gloom, gloominess, depression; severity, sternness
trisulc·us -a -um *adj* three-forked
tritavi·a -ae *f* great-great-great-great-grandmother
tritav·us -ī *m* great-great-great-great-grandfather
trīticei·a -ae *f* facetious name of a fish invented to make a pun with *hordeia*
trītice·us -a -um *adj* wheat-
trītic·um -ī *n* wheat
Trīt·ōn -ōnis *m* son of Neptune who blows through a shell to calm the seas ‖ river flowing through Lake Tritonis in N. Africa where Minerva was said to be born
Trītōniac·us -a -um *adj* Tritonian, associated with Minerva
Trītōn·is -idis *or* **-idos** *f* Minerva
Trītōni·us -a -um *adj* Tritonian ‖ *f* Tritonia *(i.e., Minerva)*
trīt·or -ōris *m* grinder
trītūr·a -ae *f* threshing; kneading
trīt·us -a -um *pp of* **tero** ‖ *adj* worn, well-worn; beaten *(path);* experienced, expert; common, trite
trīt·us -ūs *m* rubbing, friction
triumphāl·is -is -e *adj* triumphal; having had a triumph ‖ *npl* triumphal insignia *(without the actual triumph)*
triump(h)e *interj* a cheer shouted in the parade of triumphing generals *or* in the procession of the Arval Brothers
triumph·ō -āre -āvī -ātus *tr* to triumph over, vanquish ‖ *intr (w.* **de** *or* **ex** *+ abl)* to celebrate a triumph *(over a people)*
triumph·us -ī *m* triumph, victory parade; victory; **triumphum agere** *(w.* **de** *or* **ex** *+ abl)* to celebrate a triumph over *(a conquered people)*
triumv·ir -irī *m* triumvir, commissioner; mayor *(of a provincial town)* ‖ *mpl* triumvirs; **triumviri capitales** superintendents of prisons and executions

triumvirāl·is -is -e *adj* triumviral, of the triumvirs

triumvirāt·us -ūs *m* triumvirate *(appointed at various times to serve various purposes)*

trivenēfic·a -ae *f* nasty old witch

trīvī *perf of* **tero**

Trivi·a -ae *f* epithet of Diana

triviāl·is -is -e *adj* appropriate for the street corners, common, vulgar

triv·ium -(i)ī *n* crossroads, intersection; public street; the "gutter"

trivi·us -a -um *adj* of *or* at the crossroads; worshiped at the crossroads **II** *f see* **Trivia**

-tr·ix -īcis *fem suf corresponding to the masc suf* **-tor** *and denoting female agents, e.g.,* **tonstrix** hairdresser, barber

Trō·as *or* **Trō·jas -adis** *or* **-ados** *adj (fem only)* Trojan **II** *f* Troad, district of Troy; Trojan woman

trochae·us -ī *m (pros)* trochee *(metrical foot)* (— ◡), tribrach *(metrical foot)* (◡ ◡ ◡)

trochle·a *or* **trochli-ae** *f* block and tackle

troch·us *or* **troch·os -ī** *m* hoop

Troez·ēn -ēnis *or* **-ēnos** *f* town in the Argolid on the E. shore of the Pelo–ponnesus

Troezēni·us -a -um *adj* of Troezen

Trōi·a *or* **Trōj·a -ae** *f* Troy

Trōic·us -a -um *adj* Trojan

Trōil·us -ī *m* son of Priam, killed by Achilles

Trōi·us *or* **Trōj·us -a -um** *adj* Trojan **II** *f see* **Troia**

Trōjān·us -a -um *adj & m* Trojan

Trōjugen·a *adj (masc & fem only)* Trojan-born, born at Troy, of Trojan descent, Trojan **II** *m* Trojan

Tromentīn·us -a -um *adj* name of one of the rustic tribes of early Rome

tropae·um -ī *n* trophy, war memorial *(originally armor taken from the enemy and hung on a stake, but later a permanent war monument, set up to mark the defeat of an enemy)*

Trophōn·ius -(i)ī *m* Boeotian oracular god with a shrine at Lebadea

Trōs Trōis *m* Tros *(son of Erichthonius and grandson of Dardanus and king of Phrygia after whom Troy was named)* **II** a Trojan

trucīdāti·ō -ōnis *f* slaughter, massacre, butchery

trucid·ō -āre *tr* to slaughter, massacre, cut down

trucil·ō -āre *intr (of a thrush)* to chirp

truculentē *or* **truculenter** *adv* grimly, fiercely

truculenti·a -ae *f* ferocity, savagery; harshness; **truculentia caeli** harsh weather

truculent·us -a -um *adj* grim, fierce

trud·is -is *f* pointed pole, pike

trū·dō -dĕre -sī -sus *tr* to push, shove; to thrust; to force, drive; to put forth *(buds)*

trull·a -ae *f* dipper, ladle, scoop; brazier; wash basin

-tr·um -ī *neut suf denoting instrument, e.g.:* **aratrum** plow

trunc·ō -āre -āvī -ātus *tr* to lop off, maim; to amputate

trunc·us -a -um *adj* lopped; stripped *(of branches and leaves),* trimmed; maimed, mutilated; imperfect, undeveloped **II** *m* tree trunk; trunk, body *(of a human being);* chunk of meat; blockhead

trūsī *perf of* **trudo**

trūs·ō -āre *intr (w. dat)* to keep ramming *(s.o.) (i.e., have sexual intercourse with a girl)*

trūsus *pp of* **trudo**

trutin·a -ae *f* pair of scales; criterion

trutin·or -ārī -ātus sum *tr* to weigh, balance

tru·x -cis *adj* savage, grim, fierce

trybl·ium -(i)ī *n* a kind of bowl

trȳgōn·us ī *m* stingray

tū *pron* you *(singl)*

tuātim *adv* in your manner, as is typical of you

tub·a -ae *f* trumpet *(with a stright tube, as opposed to the* **cornu***) used in war, at religious ceremonies, at the start of public shows, at weddings, funerals, etc.)*

tūb·er -eris *n* lump, hump, swelling; **tuber terrae** *(bot)* truffle *(underground fungus used as food)*

tub·er -eris *f* exotic type of fruit tree **II** *m* exotic kind of fruit

Tūbert·us -ī *m* Roman family name *(cognomen), esp.* Aulus Postumius Tubertus *(dictator in 431 B.C. and conqueror of the Aequi at Algidus)*

tubic·en -inis *m* trumpeter

tubilustr·ium -(i)ī *n* festival of trumpets *(celebrated on March 23 and May 23 and including a ritual cleaning of the trumpets)*

tuburcin·or -ārī -ātus sum *tr (coll)* to gobble up

tub·us -ī *m* tube, pipe

tuccēt·um *or* **tūcēt·um -ī** *n* sausage

Tucci·us -a -um *adj* Roman clan name *(nomen), esp.* Tuccia *(a Vestal Virgin who vindicated her chastity by carrying water in a sieve)*

tudit·ō -āre *tr* to keep hitting

-tūd·ō -inis *fem suf forms abstract nouns, chiefly from adjectives, e.g.:* **fortitudo** bravery, *from* **fortis** brave

tueor *or* **tuor tuērī tuitus sum** *or* **tūtus sum** *tr* to look at, gaze at, watch, observe; to took after, take care of; to guard, defend, protect; to keep in good order, maintain; to keep up *(practice);* to preserve the memory of

tugur·ium -(i)ī *n* hut, hovel

tuiti·ō -ōnis *f* protection, support; upkeep, maintenance; **tuitio sui** self-defense

tulī *perf of* **ferro**

Tulli·a -ae *f* Roman female name

Tulliān·um -ī *n* state dungeon at the foot of the Capitoline Hill, said to have been added by Servius Tullius to the *Carcer Mamertinus*

Tulliol·a -ae *f* little Tullia

Tull·ius -(i)ī *m* Roman clan name *(nomen), esp.* Marcus Tullius Cicero *(Roman orator and politician, 106-43 B.C.)* ‖ Servius Tullius *(6th king of Rome)*

Tull·us -ī *m* early first name *(praenomen), esp.* Tullus Hostilius, the third king of Rome

tum *adv* then, at that time; at that moment; in those days; next; moreover, besides; **cum...tum** both...and especially, not only...but also, if...then surely; **tum cum** at the point when, at the time when, just then when; **tum...tum** first...then, at one time...at another, now...now, both...and, partly...partly

tume·faciō -facĕre -fēcī -factus *tr* to cause to swell; *(fig)* to puff up *(with pride)*

tum·eō -ēre -uī *intr* to be swollen, swell up; to be inflated; *(of language or speaker)* to be bombastic; *(of a person)* to be excited, be in a dither, be in a rage; to be proud

tum·escō -escĕre -uī *intr* to begin to swell (up); *(of wars)* to brew; to grow excited; to become enraged; to become inflated

tumid·us -a -um *adj* swollen, swelling; bloated; rising high; proud, puffed up; arrogant; incensed, enraged, exasperated; bombastic

tum·or -ōris *m* tumor, swelling; protuberance, bulging; elevation *(of the ground);* commotion, excitement; anger, rage; vanity, pride

tumuī *perf of* **tumeo** *and* **tumesco**

tumul·ō -āre -āvī -ātus *tr* to bury

tumulōs·us -a -um *adj* hilly, rolling

tumultuāri·us -a -um *adj* confused, disorderly; makeshift; *(mil)* emergency-, drafted hurriedly to meet an emergency; **exercitus tumultuarius** emergency army; **pugna tumultuaria** irregular battle *(i.e., not fought in regular battle formation)*

tumultuāti·ō -ōnis *f* commotion

tumultu·ō -āre *or* **tumultu·or -ārī -ātus sum** *intr* to make a disturbance; to be in an uproar; *(mil)* to fight in a disorganized way

tumultuōsē *adv* disorderly, in confusion; in panic

tumultuōs·us -a -um *adj* boisterous, turbulent; panicky; **somnia tumultuosa** nightmares

tumult·us -ūs *m* commotion, uproar; insurrection, rebellion, civil war; confusion *(of the mind);* outbreak *(of crime); (mil)* sudden attack

tumul·us -ī *m* mound; rising; ground swell; burial mound; **tumulus inanis** cenotaph

tūn = tūne (tū + ne) do you?

tunc *adv (of time past)* then, at that time; *(of future time)* then, in that event; *(of succession in time)* thereupon; *(in conclusion)* consequently, in that case; **tunc cum** then when, just when; only when; **tunc demum** not until then; **tunc maxime** just then; **tunc primum** then for the first time; **tunc quando** whenever; **tunc quoque** then too; **tunc vero** then to be sure, exactly then

tundō tundĕre tutudī tunsus *or* **tūsus** *tr* to beat, pound, hammer, thump; to buffet; to thresh; *(fig)* to harp on

tunic·a -ae *f* tunic *(ordinary half-sleeved knee-length garment worn by both sexes);* military tunic *(made of mail or hides as armor);* skin, peel, husk, coating; *(anat, bot)* tunic; **tunica molesta** tunic with inflammable material, in which criminals were burned alive; **tunica recta** *(woven on a warp-weighted loom)* bridal tunic; **tunica palmata** tunic embroidered with palm-leaf design, worn by triumphing generals and by magistrates presiding over games

tunicāt·us -a -um *adj* wearing a tunic; in shirt sleeves; coated; covered with (hard) skin, tunicate

tunic(u)l·a -ae *f* short tunic; thin skin; thin coating

tunsus *pp of* **tundo**

tuor *see* **tueor**

turb·a -ae *f* turmoil, disorder, uproar, commotion; brawl; crowd, mob, gang; multitude; common crowd, masses; a large number; *(coll)* rumpus, to-do

turbāment·a -ōrum *npl* means of disturbance

turbātē *adv* in confusion

turbāti·ō -ōnis *f* confusion, disorder

turbāt·or -ōris *m* ringleader, rabble-rouser, demagogue

turbāt·us -a -um *adj* confused, disorderly; disturbed, annoyed

turbell·ae -ārum *fpl* stir, row; **turbellas facere** to cause quite a row

turben *see* **turbo** *m*

turbidē *adv* confusedly, in disorder

turbid·us -a -um *adj* confused, wild, boisterous; muddy, turbid; troubled, perplexed; vehement; disheveled *(hair)*; stormy *(weather, sky)*

turbine·us -a -um *adj* cone-shaped; gyrating like a spinning-top

turb·ō -inis *m or* **turb·en -inis** *n* whirl, twirl; eddy; spinning, revolution; coil; spinning top; reel; spindle; wheel; tornado, whirlwind; wheel of fortune; *(fig)* whirlwind, storm

turb·ō -āre -āvī -ātus *tr* to throw into confusion, disturb, agitate; to break, disorganize *(ranks in battle)*, cause to break ranks; to confuse; to alarm; to muddy; to stir *(a liquid in order to thicken it)*; to stir up *(ingredients; emotions)*; to jumble up *(sounds)*; to wipe out *(tracks, clues)*; to tamper with *(documents)*; to squander *(a fortune)* ‖ *intr* to behave in a disorderly manner, go wild; to be in a state of commotion; to riot, revolt

turbulentē *or* **turbulenter** *adv* boisterously, tumultuously, confusedly

turbulent·us -a -um *adj* turbulent, wild, stormy; disturbed, confused; seditious, trouble-making

turd·a -ae *f or* **turd·us -ī** *m* thrush

tūre·us -a -um *adj* of frankincense

tur·geō -gēre -sī *intr* to be swollen, be puffed up; to be bombastic

turgesc·ō -ĕre *intr* to begin to swell (up); to begin to blow up *(in anger)*

turgidul·us -a -um *adj* poor swollen *(eyes)*

turgid·us -a -um *adj* swollen, puffed up; inflated; turgid, bombastic

tūribul·um -ī *n* censer

tūricrem·us -a -um *adj* incense-burning

tūrif·er -era -erum *adj* producing incense

tūrileg·us -a -um *adj* incense-gathering

turm·a -ae *f* troop, squadron *(of cavalry, originally consisting of 30 men)*; crowd, group

turmāl·is -is -e *adj* of a squadron; equestrian ‖ *mpl* troopers

turmātim *adv* by troops, by squadrons, squadron by squadron

Turn·us -ī *m* king of the Rutuli, killed by Aeneas

turpicul·us -a -um *adj* ugly little; somewhat indecent

turpificāt·us -a -um *adj* corrupted, degenerate

turpilucricupid·us -a -um *adj (coll)* eager to make a fast buck

turp·is -is -e *adj* ugly, deformed; foul, filthy, nasty; disgraceful, shameless; dirty, obscene, indecent

turpiter *adv* repulsively; disgracefully, scandalously, shamelessly

turpitūd·ō -inis *f* ugliness, deformity; foulness; disgrace; moral turpitude

turp·ō -āre -āvī -ātus *tr* to disfigure; to soil, defile, pollute; to disgrace

turrif·er -era -erum *adj see* **turriger**

turrig·er -era -erum *adj* turreted; *(of Cybele)* wearing a turreted crown *(representing earth with its cities)*

turr·is -is *f* turret, tower; howdah *(on an elephant)*; *(fig)* castle, mansion

turrīt·us -a -um *adj* turreted; fortified with turrets; crowned with turrets, adorned with a turret crown

turt·ur -uris *m* turtledove

tūs tūris *m* incense, frankincense

Tusculānens·is -is -e *adj* Tusculan

Tusculān·us -a -um *adj* Tusculan ‖ *n* Tusculan estate *(esp. Cicero's)*

tuscul·um -ī *n* a little incense

Tuscul·us -a -um *adj* Tusculan ‖ *n* Tusculum *(town in Latium near Alba Longa, about 12 miles S. of Rome)*

Tusc·us -a -um *adj* Etruscan

tussicul·a -ae *f* slight cough

tuss·iō -īre *intr* to cough, have a cough

tuss·is -is *(acc:* **tussim;** *abl singl:* **tussi)** *f* cough

tūsus *pp of* **tundo**

tūtām·en -inis *or* **tūtāment·um -ī** *n* means of protection; protector

tūtě = tū + te *emphatic form of* **tū**

tūtē *adv* safely

tūtēl·a -ae *f* care, charge, protection, defense; guardianship; charge, thing protected; support, maintenance *(of persons)*; upkeep *(of buildings)*; guardian, keeper; **in suam tutelam (per)venire** *(or* **tutelam accipere** *or* **suae tutelae fieri)** *(of a minor)* to become capable of managing one's own affairs

tūtemet = tū + te + met *emphatic form of* **tū**

tūtō *adv* safely, securely, without risk of harm; **tuto esse** to exist safely

tūt·ō -āre *or* **tūt·or -ārī -ātus sum** *tr* to guard, protect, defend; to keep safe, watch, preserve; to ward off, avert; *(w.* **ab** *+ abl or w.* **ad** *or* **adversus** *+ acc)* to protect *(s.o.)* from, guard *(s.o.)* against

tūt·or -ōris *m* protector; *(leg)* guardian *(of minors, of women of any age, etc.)*

tutudī *perf of* **tundo**

tūt·us -a -um *pp of* **tueor** ‖ *adj* safe, secure; cautious, prudent ‖ *n* safe place, shelter, security; **ex tuto** from a safe place, in safety

tu·us -a -um *(also* **tu·os -a -om)** *adj* your; your dear *(friend, etc.)*, dear to you; typical of you; devoted to you; *(of circumstances)* favorable to you ‖ *pron* yours; **de tuo** at your expense; **in tuo** on your land; **quid tua?** what business is it of yours?; **tua** your girlfriend, your sweetheart; **tuā interest** *(or* **tuā refert** it is of importance to you; **tui** your friends, your people, your family, your soldiers; **tuum est** *(w. inf)* it is your duty to, it's up to you to; **tuum est quod** it is thanks to you that

tuxtax *adv (a word meant to imitate the sound of blows)* whack, wham; **tuxtax meo tergo erit** *(coll)* it's going to be wham, whack all over my back

Tȳd·eūs -eī *or* **-eos** *m* Tydeus *(son of Oeneus, one of the Seven against Thebes, and father of Diomedes)*

Tȳdīd·ēs -ae *m* Diomedes *(son of Tydeus)*

tympaniz·ō -āre *intr* to play the drum

tympanotrīb·a -ae *m* timbrel player, drummer

tympan·um *or* **typan·um -ī** *n* drum, revolving cylinder; solid circular wheel *(used on carts and wagons);* dentated wheel *(used as a waterwheel); (mus)* drum, timbrel *(esp. used in the worship of Cybele or Bacchus)*

Tyndar·eūs -eī *or* **Tyndar·us -ī** *m* king of Sparta, husband of Leda, father of Castor and Clytemnestra, and reputed father of Pollux and Helen

Tyndarid·ēs -ae *m* descendant of Tyndareus *(esp. Castor and Pollux)*

Tyndar·is -idis *f* descendant of Tyndareus *(esp. Helen and Clytemnestra)*

Typhō·eūs -eī *or* **-eos** *or* **Tȳph·ōn -ōnis** *m* giant who was struck by Jupiter with lightning and buried under Mt. Etna

Tȳphōe·us -a -um *adj* of the monster Typhoeus

Tȳph·ōn -ōnis *m see* **Typhoeus**

typ·us -ī *m* figure, image, bas-relief *(on the wall)*

tyrannicē *adv* tyrannically

tyrannicīd·a -ae *m* assassin of a tyrant

tyrannic·us -a -um *adj* tyrannical

tyrann·is -idis *or* **-idos** *f* tyranny, despotism

tyrannocton·us -ī *m* tyrannicide, assassin of a tyrant

tyrann·us -ī *m* monarch, sovereign; *(in a Greek city-state)* unconstituional (absolute) ruler

Tyrianthin·a -ōrum *npl* clothes of a violet color

Tyri·us -a -um *adj* Tyrian, Phoenician; Carthaginian; Theban; crimson *(because of the famous dye produced at Tyre)* ‖ *mpl* Tyrians; Carthaginians

Tȳr·ō -ūs *or* **-ōnis** *f* daughter of Salmoneus and mother of Pelias and Neleus by Poseidon

Tyr·os *or* **Tyr·us -ī** *f* Tyre *(commercial city of Phoenicia, famous for its crimson dye, or "Tyrian purple"; its dye works were active until destroyed by the Crusaders)*

tȳrotarīch·os -ī *m* dish of salted fish and cheese *(as an example of a plain diet)*

Tyrrhēni·a -ae *f* Etruria

Tyrr(h)ēnic·us -a -um *adj* Etrurian, Etruscan

Tyrr(h)ēn·us -a -um *adj* Etrurian, Etruscan; **mare Tyrrhenum** Tyrrhenian Sea *(lying between the W. coast of Italy, Sardinia, and Sicily);* **Tyrrhenae volucres** the Sirens ‖ *mpl* Etruscans *(Pelasgian people who migrated to Italy, perhaps from Lydia in Asia Minor)*

Tyrtae·us -ī *m* Spartan poet *(7th cent. B.C.)*

Tyrus *see* **Tyros**

U

ūb·er -eris *adj* rich, fertile; fruitful, productive; plentiful; plenty of; valuable; copious *(tears); (of things)* rich in content; imaginative *(writer, style); (fig)* productive ‖ *n* (woman's) breast, nipple; udder; bosom *(of the earth);* fertility; fertile soil, fruitful field

ūberius *adv* more fully, in greater abundance; more fruitfully; with greater exuberance

ūbert·ās -ātis *f* richness; fertility; productiveness; abundance; richness of content

ūbertim *adv* copiously; **urbertim flere** to cry bitterly

ubī *or* **ubĭ** *adv (interrog)* where; **ubi gentium** *(or* **terrarum**) *(coll)* where in the world ‖ *conj* where, in which; whereby; with whom, by whom; when, whenever

ubīcumque *conj* wherever, wheresoever ‖ *adv* anywhere, everywhere

Ubi·ī -ōrum *mpl* German tribe on the Lower Rhine

ubīnam *adv* just where?, wherever?; **ubinam gentium** where in the world

ubiquāque *adv* everywhere

ubīque *adv* everywhere, anywhere

ubiubī *conj* wherever

ubivīs *adv* anywhere, everywhere, wherever you please; **ubivis gentium** *(coll)* anywhere in the world

ūd·ō -ōnis *m* felt slipper

ūd·us -a -um *adj* wet, moist; humid

Ūf·ens -entis *m* river in Latium

-ūg·ō -inis *fem suf formed from names of materials to denote a superficial film, e.g.:* **ferrugo** (iron) rust; *formed from nouns, e.g.:* **versperugo** the Evening Star

-ul·a -ae *fem suf forms diminutives, e.g.:* **arcula** small box *or* chest

-ulent·us -a -um *adj suf forms adjectives meaning "abounding in", "full of", e.g.:* **vīnulentus** full of wine, intoxicated

ulcer·ō -āre -āvī -ātus *tr* to cause to fester; *(fig)* to wound
ulcerōs·us -a -um *adj* ulcerous
ulciscor ulciscī ultus sum *tr* to avenge oneself on, take revenge on, punish; to avenge, requite
ulc·us -eris *n* ulcer, sore
ūlīg·ō -inis *f* moisture, dampness
Ulix·ēs -is *or* **-eī** *or* **-ī** *m* Ulysses *(king of Ithaca, son of Laertes, husband of Penelope, and father of Telemachus and Telegonus)*
ull·us -a -um *adj* any
ulme·us -a -um *adj* elm, made of elm; *(hum)* elm-whipped
ulmitrib·a -ae *m (coll)* slaphappy *(from being flogged with elm whips)*
ulm·us -ī *f* elm tree **||** *fpl* elm whips
uln·a -ae *f* elbow; arm; *(as measure of length, span of the outstretched arms, c. 45 inches)* ell
ulpic·um -ī *n* type of garlic
ulteri·or -or -us *adj* farther, on the farther side, more remote; further, additional, more; longer; in a higher degree; worse; **Gallia Ulterior** Transalpine Gaul; **Hispania Ulterior** the western of the two provinces of the Iberian peninsula **||** *mpl* more remote people, those beyond **||** *npl* things beyond
ulterius *adv* to a more distant place, farther away; to a further extent, further, more than that; **ulterius quam** further than
ulterius *prep (w. acc)* beyond
ultimō *adv* finally, last of all
ultimum *adv* finally; for the last time
ultim·us -a -um *adj* **(-tum-)** farthest, most distant, extreme; earliest; latest, final, last; greatest; lowest; meanest **||** *n* last thing, end; **ad ultimum** to the end; to the extreme; in the highest degree; to the last degree, utterly; *(in an enumeration)* finally; **in ultimo** finally **||** *npl* extremes; the worst
ulti·ō -ōnis *f* vengeance, revenge
ult·or -ōris *m* avenger, punisher
ultrā *adv* beyond, farther, besides **||** *prep* **1** *(w. acc) (in a physical sense)* on the farther side of, beyond, past: **nihil est ultra altitudinem montium quo pertimendum est** there is nothing beyond *(i.e., except)* the heights of the mountains that needs to be feared; **2** *(in the temporal sense)* to a point later than, at a later time than, after, past; to a time further back than, earlier than: **ultra mediam noctem** till past midnight; **3** *(of number, measure, degree)* over, beyond, more than, over and above: **non ultra tres versus** not more than three verses; **4** *(in negative sentences, indicating the limit of an activity)* **nihil ultra nervos atque cutem morti concederat atrae** he had conceded to dark death nothing but sinews and skin *(i.e., his body)*
ultr·ix -īcis *adj (fem only)* avenging *(esp. of the Furies and other agents of retribution)* **||** *f* avenger
ultrō *adv* to the farther side, beyond; on the other side; on both sides, in both directions; at the opposite end of the scale, conversely; besides, moreover, too; into the bargain, to boot; of one's own accord, without being asked; without being spoken to; unprovoked; **bella inferre ultro** to go to war (although) unprovoked; **ultro et citro** back and forth; **ultro tributa** expenditure incurred by the government for public works
ultus *pp of* **ulciscor**
ulul·a -ae *f* owl
ululāt·us -ūs *m* howling *(esp. of dogs and wolves);* ulutation, wailing *(esp. of mourners);* war cry
ulul·ō -āre -āvī -ātus *tr* to howl out, howl at **||** *intr* to howl; to ululate, wail; *(of places)* to resound
ulv·a -ae *f (bot)* sedge, rush
-ul·um -ī *neut suf forming diminutive neuter nouns:* **speculum** mirror
-ul·us *m and* **-ul·a** *f suf* **1** *forming diminutives:* **calculus** little stone; **2** *adjectives denoting repeated action:* **credulus** regularly believing, credulous; **3** *adjectives denoting diminished intensity:* **ūmidulus** dampish; **4** *nouns denoting instruments:* **furculus** pitchfork; **5** *nouns denoting endearment:* **uxorcula** dear wife
umbell·a -ae *f* umbrella, parasol
Um·ber -bra -brum *adj* Umbrian, of Umbria **||** *m* Umbrian
umbilīc·us -ī *m* navel, bellybutton; midriff; middle, center; projecting end of dowels *or* cylinders on which scrolls were rolled; cockle, sea snail; **ad umbilicum** *(or* **ad umbilicos)** to the end of the scroll *or* book
umb·ō -ōnis *m* boss *(of a shield);* shield; elbow
umbr·a -ae *f* shade; shadow; phantom, ghost; mere shadow *(of one's former self);* semblance; darkness, gloom; shelter, cover; privacy, retirement; umber *(fish);* **rhetorica umbra** rhetorician's school **||** *fpl* darkness of night; lower world
umbrāc(u)l·um -ī *n* shade; bower, arbor; school; umbrella, parasol
umbrāticol·a -ae *mf* lounger *(in the shade)*
umbrātic·us -a -um *adj* too fond of the shade, lazy, inactive; secluded; private; **umbraticus doctor** private tutor; pedant

umbrātil·is -is -e *adj* carried out in the shade, private, retired; academic
Umbri·a -ae *f* Umbria *(district in central Italy)*
umbrif·er -era -erum *adj* shady
umbr·ō -āre -āvī -ātus *tr* to shade, cast a shadow on; to overshadow
umbrōs·us -a -um *adj* shady
ūmect·ō -āre -āvī -ātus *tr* **(hūm-)** to wet, moisten
ūmect·us -a -um *adj* **(hūm-)** moist, damp
ūm·eō -ēre *intr* to be moist, be damp, be wet
umer·us -ī *m* **(hum-)** shoulder
ūmesc·ō -ĕre *intr* to become moist, become wet
ūmidul·us -a -um *adj* dampish
ūmid·us -a -um *adj* **(hūm-)** moist, damp, wet; green *(lumber)* ‖ *n* wet place
ūmif·er -era -erum *adj* laden with moisture
ūm·or -ōris *m* **(hūm-)** moisture; liquid, fluid
umquam *or* **unquam** *adv* ever, at any time
ūnā *adv* together; **unā cum** together with; **unā venire** to come along
ūnanim·ans -antis *adj* of one mind, of one accord
ūnanimit·ās -ātis *f* unanimity
ūnanim·us -a -um *adj* **(ūnian-)** unanimous; of one mind, of one heart
unci·a -ae *f* one-twelfth; ounce *(one-twelfth of a pound or* **libra**); *(of interest rate)* 1% a year; *(in length)* inch *(25 mm, one twelfth of a foot or* **pes**)
unciāri·us -a -um *adj* containing one-twelfth; one-ounce; one-inch
unciātim *adv* ounce by ounce, little by little
uncīnāt·us -a -um *adj* hooked, barbed
uncīn·us -ī *m* hook
unciol·a -ae *f* a mere twelfth
unc·ō -āre *intr (of a bear)* to grunt
uncti·ō -ōnis *f* rubdown with oil; *(fig)* wrestling
unctit·ō -āre *tr* to keep rubbing with oil, keep oiling
unctiuscul·us -a -um *adj* somewhat too oily; unctuous
unct·or -ōris *m* anointer, rubdown man, masseur
unct·um -ī *n* sumptuous dinner
unctūr·a -ae *f* anointing
unct·us -a -um *pp of* **ung(u)o** ‖ *adj* greasy; resinous; sumptuous
uncul·us -a -um *adj* any at all
unc·us -a -um *adj* hooked, barbed; crooked ‖ *m* hook, clamp; grappling iron
und·a -ae *f* water; stream, river; wave; sea, seawater; current *(of air)*; *(fig)* stream, tide, agitated mass
unde *adv* from where, whence; from whom; **unde unde** *(or* **undeunde**) by hook or by crook
ūndeciens *or* **ūndeciēs** *adv* eleven times
ūndecim *indecl adj* eleven
ūndecim·us -a -um *adj* **(-decum-)** eleventh
undecumque *adv* **(-cun-)** from whatever place, from whatever source
ūndēn·ī -ae -a *adj* eleven in a group, eleven each, eleven
ūndēnōnāgintā *indecl adj* eighty-nine
ūndēoctōgintā *indecl adj* seventy-nine
ūndēquadrāgēsim·us -a -um *adj* thirty-ninth
ūndēquadrāgintā *indecl adj* thirty-nine
ūndēquinquāgēsim·us -a -um *adj* forty-ninth
ūndēquinquāgintā *indecl adj* forty-nine
ūndēsexāgintā *indecl adj* fifty-nine
undētrīcēsim·us -a -um *adj* twenty-ninth
ūndētrīgintā *indecl adj* twenty-nine
ūndēvīcēsimān·ī -ōrum *mpl* soldiers of the nineteenth legion
ūndēvicēsim·us -a -um *adj* nineteenth
ūndēvīgintī *indecl adj* nineteen
undique *adv* from all directions, on all sides, everywhere; in all respects, completely
undison·us -a -um *adj* of roaring waves; **undisoni dei** gods of the roaring waves
und·ō -āre -āvī -ātum *intr* to move in waves, undulate; to billow; to overflow
undōs·us -a -um *adj* full of waves, billowy; wave-washed *(shore)*
ūnetvīcē(n)sim·us -a -um *adj* twenty-first
ūnetvīcēsimān·ī -ōrum *mpl* soldiers of the twenty-first legion
ungō *or* **unguō ung(u)ĕre unxī unctus** *tr* to oil, grease, anoint
ungu·en -inis *n* fat, grease; ointment
unguentāri·us -(i)ī *m* perfumer
unguentāt·us -a -um *adj* anointed; perfumed, wearing perfume
unguent·um -ī *n* ointment; perfume
unguicul·us -i *m* fingernail; toenail; **a teneris unguiculis** from earliest childhood
ungu·is -is *m* fingernail; toenail; claw, talon; hoof; **ad unguem** to a tee, complete, perfect; **de tenero ungui** from earliest childhood
ungul·a -ae *f* hoof; claw, talon; *(fig)* horse
unguō *see* **ungo**
ūnicē *adv* singularly; particularly; **unice unus** one and only
ūnicol·or -ōris *adj* of one and the same color, monochrome
ūnicorn·is -is -e *adj* one-horned
ūnic·us -a -um *adj* one and only, sole; singular, unique; uncommon
ūniform·is -is -e *adj* uniform, having only one shape

ūnigen·a -ae *adj (masc & fem only)* only-begotten, only; of the same parentage
ūniman·us -a -um *adj* one-handed
ūni·ō -ōnis *f* single large pearl
ūnisubsell·ium -(i)ī *n* seat for one
ūniter *adv* jointly
ūniversāl·is -is -e *adj* universal
ūniversē *adv* generally, in general
ūniversit·ās -ātis *f* aggregate, whole; whole world, universe
ūnivers·us -a -um *adj* **(-vors-)** all, all together; all taken collectively; whole, entire **‖** *n* the whole; whole world, universe; **in universum** on the whole, in general
ūnocul·us -ī *m* one-eyed person
ūnomammi·a -ae *adj (fem)* single-breasted *(Amazon)*
unquam *or* **umquam** *adv* ever, at any time
ūnumquicquid *pron* every little thing
ūn·us -a -um *adj* one, single, only, sole; one and the same; *(indefinite)* one, some; **unus et alter** one or two; **unus quisque** each one, every single one **‖** *pron* someone, a mere individual; **ad unum** to a man
unxī *perf of* **ung(u)o**
ūpili·ō -ōnis *m* shepherd
upup·a -ae *f* hoopoe *(bird with fan-like crest and downward-curving bill);* hoe, mattock
-ūr·a -ae *fem suf forms nouns form nouns ending in* **-tor** *to denote office:* **praetura** praetorship *(from* **paetor);** *forms nouns mainly from verbal derivatives in* **-tus: natura** nature *(from* **natus)**
Ūrani·a -ae *or* **Ūrani·ē -ēs** *f* Muse of astronomy
urbānē *adv* politely, courteously; with sophistication; wittily
urbānit·ās -ātis *f* living in the city, city life; refinement; politeness; sophistication; wit; raillery
urbān·us -a -um *adj* of the city, city; courteous; sophisticated; witty; brash, forward **‖** *m* city dweller; *(pej)* city slicker
urbicap·us -ī *m* conqueror of cities
urbic·us -a -um *adj* city-, of the city
urbi·us -a -um *adj* **urbius clivus** slope on the Esquiline Hill
ur·bs *or* **ur·ps -bis** *f* city; the city of Rome
urceol·us -ī *m* little pitcher, little pot
urce·us -ī *m* pitcher, water pot
urc·ō -āre *intr (of a lynx)* to snarl
ūrēd·ō -inis *f* blight *(on plants)*
urgeō urgēre ursī *tr* to prod on, urge forward; to pressure, put pressure on *(s.o.);* to crowd, hem in; to follow up, keep at, stick by **‖** *intr* to be urgent; to be insistent
ūrīn·a -ae *f* urine
ūrināt·or -ōris *m* diver
ūrīn·ō -āre *or* **ūrin·or -ārī** *intr* to dive
-ur·iō -īre -īvī *or* **-iī** *suf forming desideratives* **(cenaturire** to wish to eat)
Ūrī·ōn -ōnis *m* Orion
Ūr·ios -iī *m* cult title of Zeus, as the sender of favorable winds
urn·a -ae *f* pot, jar; water pot; voting urn; urn of fate; cinerary urn; money jar; liquid measure *(= one half of an amphora)*
urnul·a -ae *f* small urn
ūrō ūrěre ussī ustus *tr* to burn; to burn up, reduce to ashes, consume; to scorch, parch, dry up; to sting, pain; to nip, frostbite; to rub sore; to corrode; to annoy, gall, burn up, make angry; to inflame *(w. love)*
urps *see* **urbs**
urs·a -ae *f* she-bear **‖ Ursa Major** *(astr)* Great Bear *(constellation);* **Ursa Minor** *(astr)* Little Bear *(constellation)*
ursī *perf of* **urgeo**
ursīn·us -a -um *adj* bear-, bear's
urs·us -ī *m* bear
urtīc·a -ae *f (bot)* stinging nettle *(causing a burning rash upon contact)*; desire, itch
ūrūc·a *or* **ūrīc·a -ae** *f* caterpillar
ūr·us -ī *m* wild ox
Ūsīpet·ēs -um *mpl* German tribe on the Rhine
ūsitātē *adv* in the usual way, as usual
ūsitāt·us -a -um *adj* usual, customary, familiar; **usitatum est** *(w. inf)* it is customary to
uspiam *adv* anywhere, somewhere, in some place or other
usquam *adv* anywhere *(in any place or to any place)*
usque *adv* all the way, right on; all the time, continuously; even, as much as; *(without addition of an adv or prep)* to the fullest extent, completely; **usque ab** *(w. abl)* all the way from; ever since; **usque ad** *(w. acc)* all the way to; all the way back in time to; **usque adeo** *(or* **usque eo) ut** to such an extent that; **usque quaque** every moment, continually; on all occasions, in everything **‖** *prep (w. acc)* up to, as far as, right until
usquequāque *or* **usque quāque** *adv* everywhere, as far as one can go in either direction; *(fig)* in every conceivable situation; in every possible respect, wholly
ussī *perf of* **uro**
usti·ō -ōnis *f* burning
ust·or -ōris *m* cremator
ustul·ō -āre -āvī -ātus *tr* to scorch, singe
ustus *pp of* **uro**
ūsū·capiō -capěre -cēpī -captus *tr (leg)* to acquire ownership of *(by long use)*

ūsūcapi·ō -ōnis *f (leg)* acquisition of ownership *(through long use)*

ūsūr·a -ae *f* use, enjoyment; interest *(on capital)*

ūsūrāri·us -a -um *adj* for use and enjoyment; paying interest, interest-bearing

ūsurpāti·ō -ōnis *f* use; *(w. gen)* making use of, use of

ūsurp·ō -āre -āvī -ātus *tr* to use, make *(constant)* use of, employ; to exercise *(a right);* to put into practice *(a custom, operation);* to take possession of, acquire; to usurp; to name, call, speak of; to assume *(a title, honor, esp. arbitrarily);* to take up *(an inheritance);* to perceive *(with the senses),* observe, experience; **memoriam usurpare** *(w. gen)* to invoke the memory of

ūsus *pp of* **utor**

ūs·us -ūs *m* use, enjoyment; practice, employment; experience, skill; usage, custom; familiarity; usefulness, advantage, benefit; occasion, need, necessity; **ex usu esse** *(or* **usui esse)** *(w. dat)* to be useful to, be a good thing for; **in usu** in one's everyday experience; **in usu esse** to be in use; to be customary; **in usu (meo, tuo,** *etc.)* **est** it is to (my, your, *etc.)* advantage; **in usu habere** *(or* **continere)** to keep in use; **quis usus est?** *(w. gen)* what useful purpose is served by?; **scientia et usus** theory and practice; **si usus veniat** if the need should arise, if the opportunity should present itself; **usus adest** a good opportunity comes along; **usus est** *(w. abl)* there is a need of; **usus et fructus** use and enjoyment; **usu venit** it happens, it occurs; **usus venit** *(w. dat)* the need arises for

ūsusfructus *(gen:* **ūsūsfructūs)** *m* use and enjoyment, usufruct

ut *(or* **utī,** *an older form, increasingly rare after Cicero, but affected by archaizing authors) adv (in direct and indirect questions; in exclamations)* how; **ut miser est qui!** how pitiful is the man who! ‖ *conj (comparative)* as; *(adversative)* although; *(temporal)* when, while; *(purpose)* in order that; *(result, after* **adeo, eo, sic, talis, tam, tantus)** (to such a degree, so, such, so great) that; *(concessive)* granted that; *(introducing examples)* as, as for example; *(after verbs of fearing)* lest, that not; *(introducing an explanation or reason)* as, as being, inasmuch as; *(introducing indirect commands)* that; **ut maxime** at most; **ut perinde** *(or* **proinde)** according to the degree to which; **ut qui** (= **quippe qui)** as is natural for one who; **ut puta** *(indicating an example)* as say, as for example

utcumque *or* **utcunque** *or* **utquomque** *adv* however; whenever; one way or another

ūt·ens -entis *adj* having money to spend

ūtensil·is -is -e *adj* useful ‖ *npl* utensils, materials, provisions, similar things

ū·ter -tris *m (n)* bag, skin, bottle; inflated bag to keep swimmers afloat

u·ter -tra -trum *adj* which *(of the two)* ‖ *pron* which one *(of the two);* one or the other

utercumque utracumque utrumcumque *adj* whichever *(of the two)* ‖ *pron* whichever one *(of the two)*

uterlibet utralibet utrumlibet *adj* whichever *(of the two)* you please ‖ *pron* whichever one *(of the two)* you please, either one *(of the two)*

uterque utraque utrumque *adj* each *(of the two),* both; **sermones utriusque linguae** conversations in both languages *(i.e., Greek and Latin)* ‖ *pron* each one *(of the two),* both; **uterque insaniunt** both are insane

uter·us -ī *m or* **uter·um -ī** *n* belly, abdomen; womb; potbelly *(of a man);* **uterum gerere** to be pregnant

utervīs utravīs utrumvīs *adj* whichever *(of the two)* you please, either ‖ *pron* whichever one *(of the two)* you please, either one

utī *see* **ut**

ūtibil·is -is -e *adj* useful, practical

Utic·a -ae *f* city in Africa, N.W. of Carthage, where the younger Cato committed suicide in 46 B.C.

Uticens·is -is -e *adj* of Utica ‖ *m* posthumous title of Cato

ūtil·is -is -e *adj* useful, profitable, practical; *(w. dat or* **ad** + *acc)* fit for, useful for, practical in

ūtilit·ās -ātis *f* usefulness, advantage

ūtiliter *adv* usefully, profitably

utinam *conj (introducing a wish)* if only, would that

utīque *adv* anyhow, at least, at any rate; in particular, especially; without condition, absolutely; *(after negatives)* on any account; *(in obeying instructions)* without fail; **cur utique** exactly why

ūtor ūtī ūsus sum *intr (w. abl)* **1** to use, make use of: **coqui his condimentis utuntur** cooks use these seasonings; **2** to enjoy: **valetudine prosperā uti** to enjoy good health; **3** to practice, experience: **portis patefactis eo die pace primum usi sunt** as the gates were thrown open they experienced peace for the first time on that day; **4** to enjoy the friendship *or* companionship of: **multos jam annos te usi sumus** for many years now we have enjoyed your friendship; **5** *(w. adv or abl of manner)* to treat: **om-**

nibus sociis clementiā uti to treat all our allies with kindness; **familiariter utebar Caesare** I was on familiar terms with Caesar; **6** to hold *(office, military command):* **honore uti** to hold office; **tribuni milites et imperio et insignibus consularibus usi sunt** the military tribunes held military commands and wore the consular insignia; **7** to handle, manage, control: **bene armis, optime equis usus est** he managed arms well and horses very well; **8** to consume *(food or drink):* **qui vetere vino utuntur** who drink old wine; **9** to wear *(clothes):* **solutis vestibus utuntur Gratiae** the Graces wear loose dresses; **10** to live *or* spend one's time *(in a place):* **eo mari uti consuerunt** they were used to living on (the coast of) that sea; **11** to play *(a musical instrument):* **qui fidibus aut tibiis uti volunt** those who want to play the lyre or the flute

utpote *adv (reinforcing explanatory phrases or clauses)* as one might expect, as is natural, naturally, inasmuch as; **utpote cum** as you might expect since; **utpote qui** inasmuch as *(he is one)* who, inasmuch as he, because he

utrār·ius -(i)ī *m* water carrier, water boy

utric(u)lār·ius -(i)ī *m* bagpipe player

utrimque *or* **utrinque** *adv* from *or* on both sides, on either side; **utrimque constitit fides** on both sides their word of honor held good

utrō *adv* to which of the two sides, in which direction

utrobīque *adv* on both sides, on either hand

utrōlibet *adv* to either side

utrōque *adv* to both sides, in both directions

utrōqueversum *adv* **(-vors-)** in both directions

utrubi *adv* at *or* on which of the two sides

utrubīque *adv* on both sides, on either hand

utrum *conj* whether

utut *adv* in whatever way, however

ūv·a -ae *f* grape; grapes; bunch of grapes; vine; swarm of bees; *(anat)* uvula; **uva passa** raisin *(literally, grape spread out to dry)*

ūvesc·ō -ĕre *intr* to become moist; *(fig)* to get drunk

ūvidul·us -a -um *adj* a little moist, dampish

ūvid·us -a -um *adj* wet, moist, damp; humid; drunk

ux·or -ōris *f* wife; mate *(of animals)*

uxorcul·a -ae *f* dear (little) wife

uxorcul·ō -āre -āvī *intr* to play the role of a wife

uxōri·us -a -um *adj* of a wife, wifely; very fond of a wife; henpecked

V

V, v is used in this dictionary to represent consonantal *u*

vac·ans -antis *adj* vacant, unoccupied; at leisure; unemployed; unattached, single; *(w. abl)* lacking, without; **puella vacans** a single girl ‖ *npl* unoccupied estates

vacāti·ō -ōnis *f* freedom, exemption *(from duty, service, etc.);* exemption from military service; payment for being exempted from military service; vacation, holiday, day off

vacc·a -ae *f* cow

vaccīn·ium -(i)ī *n (bot)* hyacinth

vaccul·a -ae *f* heifer

vacē·fīō -fierī *intr* to become empty, be emptied, be vacated

vacerr·a -ae *f* fence post

vacerrōs·us -a -um *adj (pej)* cracked, crazy

vacillāti·ō -ōnis *f* tottering

vacill·ō -āre -āvī -ātum *intr* **(vacc-)** to stagger, reel; to vacillate, waver; to be untrustworthy

vacīvē *adv* at leisure

vacīvit·ās -ātis *f* want, lack

vacīv·us -a -um *adj* **(voc-)** *(of a place)* unoccupied, vacant; *(w. gen)* free of, devoid of, free from

vac·ō -āre -āvī -ātum *intr* **(voc-)** to be empty, be vacant; to be unoccupied; to be ownerless; to be without, not to contain; to be free, be carefree; to be at leisure, have free time; *(of things)* to lie idle; to be *(romantically)* unattached; *(w. abl or* **ab)** **1** to be free from; **2** to be devoid of; **3** to abstain from; **4** to be exempt from *(duty, responsibility); (w. dat or w.* **ad** *or* **in** *+ acc)* to be free for, have time for, have spare time for; *(w. inf)* to have leisure to, have time to; **populo vacare** to remain aloof from the people; **res publica et milite et pecuniā vacat** the country is relieved from furnishing an army and money; **semper philosophiae vaco** I always have time for philosophy ‖ *v impers (w. dat)* there is time for, there is room for; *(w. inf)* there is time to *or* for

vacuāt·us -a -um *adj* empty

vacuē·faciō -facĕre -fēcī -factus *tr* to empty, clear, free

vacuit·ās -ātis *f* freedom, exemption; emptiness; empty space; vacancy *(in an office); (w. gen or w.* **ab)** freedom from *(s.th. undesirable)*

Vacūn·a -ae *f* Sabine goddess, later identified with Victory

Vacūnāl·is -is -e *adj* of the goddess Vacuna

vacu·ō -āre -āvī -ātus *tr* to empty, clear, free; to strip *(a place of defenders, inhabitants)*

vacu·us -a -um *adj* empty, clear, free; vacant; worthless, useless; single, umarried; widowed; at leisure; carefree; *(w. gen or abl or w.* **ab)** free from, devoid of, without; *(w. dat)* free for

vadimōn·ium -(i)ī *n (leg)* promise *(to appear in court)*, bail *(given as a guarantee of one's appearance in court)*; **vadimonium deserere** to default, jump bail; **vadimonium differre** to postpone appearance in court, grant a continuance; **vadimonium facere** to put up bail; **vadimonium sistere** to appear in court

vadis *see* **vas**

vādō vādĕre vāsī *intr* to go, make one's way, advance

vad·or -ārī -ātus sum *tr (of a plaintiff)* to demand that *(s.o.)* put up bail; to sue

vadōs·us -a -um *adj* shallow

vad·um -ī *n or* **vad·us -ī** *m* shallow place, shallow, ford; shallow part of the sea, shoal; bottom *(of the sea)*, depths; sea, waters

vae *interj* woe!; *(w. acc or dat)* woe to

va·fer -fra -frum *adj* sly, cunning; subtle; ingenious

vafrē *adv* slyly, cunningly

vagē *adv* far and wide

vāgīn·a -ae *f* sheath, scabbard; hull *(of ear of grain)*

vāg·iō -īre -īvī *or* **-iī** *intr (esp. of an infant)* to cry, bawl; *(of hares)* to squeal

vāgīt·us -ūs *m* cry

vāg·or -ōris *m* cry *(of a baby)*

vag·or -ārī -ātus sum *or* **vag·ō -āre** *intr* to wander, range, roam

vag·us -a -um *adj* wandering, roaming; shifting, inconstant; rambling *(speech)*; roundabout *(explanation)*; haphazard, erratic; fickle; *(of lovers)* changing from one partner to another; **stella vaga** planet

vāh *interj (expressing dismay, pain, annoyance, contempt, or surpise)* ah!, oh!

vaha *interj (expressing pleasant surprise)* aha!

valdē *adv* greatly, intensely; *(w. adj or adv)* very; *(as affirmative reply)* yes, certainly, to be sure

valē *interj* goodbye!

val·ens -entis *adj* strong, powerful; healthy, well; coarse *(fabrics)*; strong *(medicine)*; vigorous *(plants)*; potent, effective *(remedies; arguments)*

valenter *adv* strongly; energetically

valentul·us -a -um *adj* sturdy, robust

val·eō -ēre -uī valitūrus *intr* to be strong; to be vigorous; to be powerful; to be effective; to prevail, succeed; to be influential; to be valid; to be strong enough, be adequate, be capable, be able; to be of value, be of worth; to mean, signify; **te valere jubeo** I bid you farewell, goodbye to you; **vale** *(pl:* **valete)** goodbye; **vale dicere** to say goodbye, take leave

Valeriān·us -a -um *adj* belonging to Valerius

Valeri·us -a -um *adj* Roman clan name *(nomen), esp.* Publius Valerius Publicola, recorded as one of the first two consuls in 509 B.C.

valesc·ō -ĕre *intr* to grow strong, thrive; to grow powerful

valētūdinār·ium -(i)ī *n* hospital

valētūd·ō -inis *f* state of health; good health; ill health, illness; **bona** *(or* **commoda** *or* **firma** *or* **prospera** *or* **secunda)** **valetudo** good health; **adversa** *(or* **infirma** *or* **mala)** poor health; **valetudinis causā** for reasons of (poor) health

Valgi·us -a -um *adj* Roman clan name *(nomen), esp.* Gaius Valgius Rufus *(an Augustan poet and grammarian)*

valg·us -a -um *adj* knock-kneed

validē *adv* strongly, vehemently; *(in replies)* of course, certainly, definitely

valid·us -a -um *adj* strong, powerful, able; healthy; robust; fortified; influential; efficacious

vallār·is -is -e *adj* of a rampart; **corona vallaris** crown awarded to the first soldier to scale the enemy's rampart

vall·ēs *or* **vall·is -is** *f* valley

vall·ō -āre -āvī -ātus *tr* to fortify with a rampart, wall in; to protect, defend

vall·um -ī *n* palisade of stakes on top of an embankment; rampart

vall·us -ī *m* stake, pale; rampart with palisades, stockade; tooth *(of a comb)*

valv·ae -ārum *fpl* folding doors, double doors

vānesc·ō -ĕre *intr* to vanish, fade

vānidic·us -a -um *adj* lying; boasting ‖ *m* liar; boaster

vāniloquenti·a -ae *f* empty talk, mere talk

vāniloquidōr·us -ī *m* liar, windbag

vāniloqu·us -a -um *adj* talking nonsense; lying; bragging

vānit·ās -ātis *f* falsity, unreality, deception, untruth; bragging; lying; vanity; worthlessness; frivolity

vānitūd·ō -inis *f* falsehood

vann·us -ī *f* winnowing fan

vān·us -a -um *adj* empty, vacant; groundless; pointless; hollow, unreal; lying, false; boastful; conceited, vain ‖ *n* emptiness; uselessness; deceptive appearance

vapidē *adv* poorly, badly

vapid·us -a -um *adj* flat, vapid, spoiled, bad; morally corrupt

vap·or -ōris *m* vapor, steam; warmth *(of the sun)*
vapōrār·ium -(i)ī *n* steam room
vapōr·ō -āre -āvī -ātus *tr* to steam up; to warm, heat ‖ *intr* to steam
vapp·a -ae *f* sour wine; *(pej)* brat, good-for-nothing
vāpulār·is -is -e *adj* in for a flogging
vapul·ō -āre *intr* to get a beating; *(of savings, etc.)* to take a beating
vārē *adv* in a straddling manner
varianti·a -ae *f* diversity, variety
Vāriān·us -a -um *adj* of Varus *(i.e., Publius Quintilius Varus, whose legions were cut to pieces in Germany)*
variāti·ō -ōnis *f* diversification; variation; divergence
vāric·ō -āre -āvī -ātus *intr* to spread the legs, stand with legs spread apart
varicōs·us -a -um *adj* vericose
vāric·us -a -um *adj* with legs wide apart
variē *adv* variously; in different degrees; differently; severally, respectively; in a varied style; with changing colors
variet·ās -ātis *f* variety, difference, diversity; vicissitudes; inconstancy
vari·ō -āre -āvī -ātus *tr* to vary, diversify, change, make different; to give variety to; to variegate ‖ *intr* to change color; to vary, differ, change; to be diversified; to differ in opinion; to waver; **bellum variante fortunā** a war with varying success, a war with ups and downs ‖ *v impers* **si variaret** if there were a difference of opinion
vari·us -a -um *adj* variegated, of different colors; varied; composed of different elements, motley; many-sided *(personality);* conflicting *(opinions, reports);* changing, fluctuating *(conditions, fortunes);* versatile; inconstant, unsteady; untrustworthy, fickle *(character)*
Var·ius -(i)ī *m* Lucius Varius Rufus *(epic and tragic poet and friend of Virgil and Horace, died c. 12 B.C.)*
var·ix -icis *mf* varicose vein
Varr·ō -ōnis *m* Roman family name, *(cognomen), esp.* Gaius Terentius Varro *(consul in 216 B.C. and joint commander at Cannae)* ‖ Marcus Terentius Varro *(antiquarian, philologist, and librarian, 116–27 B.C.)* ‖ Publius Terentius Varro Atacinus *(born 82 B.C., poet, translator of Apolllonius Rhodius' "Argonautica")*
vār·us -a -um *adj* knock-kneed; bent, crooked; opposed, contrary
vas vadis *m (leg)* bondsman *(person who provides surety or bail)*
vās vāsis *or* **vās·um -ī** *(pl:* **vās·a -ōrum)** *n* vessel, dish; utensil, implement ‖ *npl* equipment, gear; **vasa colligere** *(mil)* to pack up one's gear; **vasa conclamare** *(mil)* to give the signal to pack the gear; **vasa coquitatoria** pots and pans
vāsār·ium -(i)ī *n* allowance for furnishings *(given to a provincial governor)*
vasculār·ius -(i)ī *m* metal worker; seller of housewear items
vascul·um -ī *n* small vessel
vastāti·ō -ōnis *f* devastation
vastāt·or -ōris *m* devastator
vastē *adv* vastly, widely; coarsely, harshly; violently
vastific·us -a -um *adj* devastating
vastit·ās -ātis *f* wasteland, desert; state of desolation, emptiness; devastation, destruction; vastness, immensity; great open spaces
vastiti·ēs -ēī *f* ruin, destruction
vast·ō -āre -āvī -ātus *tr* to leave desolate; to lay waste; to cut *(troops)* to pieces
vast·us -a -um *adj* desolate; devastated; vast, enormous; uncouth; clumsy; unrefined *(pronunciation)*
vāt·ēs *or* **vat·is -is** *m* seer, prophet; bard, poet ‖ *f* prophetess; poetess
Vāticān·us -a -um *adj* Vatican; **mons** *(or* **collis)** **Vaticanus** hill in Rome on the right bank of the Tiber
vāticināti·ō -ōnis *f* prophesying, soothsaying, prophecy
vāticināt·or -ōris *m* prophet, seer
vāticin·ium -(i)ī *n* prophecy
vāticin·or -ārī -ātus sum *tr* to foretell, prophcsy; to keep harping on ‖ *intr* to prophesy; to rant and rave, talk wildly
vāticin·us -a -um *adj* prophetic
vatill·um -ī *n* brazier
vātis *see* **vates**
vati·us -a -um *adj* knock-kneed
-ve *conj (enclitic)* or; **-ve…-ve** either…or
vēcordi·a -ae *f* **(vae-)** senselessness; madness
vēc·ors -ordis *adj* **(vae-)** senseless; insane
vectāti·ō -ōnis *f* riding *(on horseback or in a carriage)*
vectīg·al -ālis *n* tax; revenue; duty; tariff; private income; produce providing personal income; payment given to a magistrate *or* provincial governor; private income *or* revenue; **vectigal aedilicium** payment exacted by an aedile to finance games
vectīgāl·is -is -e *adj (of persons, cities, etc.)* subject to taxation, taxed, taxable; *(of land, etc.)* yielding taxes; **pecunia vectigalis** money raised by taxes
vecti·ō -ōnis *f* conveyance, transporting
vect·is -is *m* crowbar, lever; bar, bolt *(on a door or gate)*
Vect·is -is *f* Isle of Wight
vect·ō -āre -āvī -ātus *tr* to carry, transport *(by an habitual agent or means of*

conveyance) ‖ *pass* to ride, drive, travel; **equo vectari** to ride a horse; **nave vectari** to sail

vect·or -ōris *m* bearer, carrier; rider; passenger

vectōri·us -a -um *adj* of transportation; **navigia vectoria** cargo ships

vectūr·a -ae *f* transportation, conveyance; freight costs; fare

vectus *pp of* **veho**

Vēdiov·is *or* **Vējov·is -is** *m* Anti-Jove *(Etruscan divinity of the lower world, identified with the Jupiter of the lower world)* ‖ Little Jove *(identified with the infant Jupiter)*

veget·ō -āre *tr* to invigorate

veget·us -a -um *adj* vigorous; lively *(rhythm, time, mind, thoughts)* vivacious, energetic; invigorating; vivid *(colors)*; **intervallum temporis vegetissimum agricolis** a space of time extremely busy for the farmers

vēgrand·is -is -e *adj* not huge, puny

vehem·ens -entis *adj* (vēm-) vehement; intense *(heat, cold)*; strong, powerful *(force)*; strong *(taste, flavor)*; potent *(drink, medicine)*; severe *(pain)*; serious *(illness)*; drastic *(actions)*; forceful, strongly expressive, tremendous *(writing, speech)*; imperious, overmastering; forceful *(arguments)*; violent *(men, animals, natural phenomena)*; vigorous, active *(person)*; ardent, great *(love)*

vehementer *adv* (vēm-) vehemently, impetuously; with great force, violently; firmly, strongly; energetically; in an impassioned manner; *(w. reference to feelings)* strongly, overpoweringly; *(modifying adjectives)* immensely, tremendously

vehic(u)l·um -ī *n* vehicle, wagon, cart; means of transportation; **praefectus vehiculorum** director of the imperial post

veh·is -is *m (f)* wagonload

vehō vehěre vexī vectus *tr* to carry, convey, transport ‖ *pass* to travel, ride, sail, be borne along

Vei·ens -entis *or* **Veientān·us -a -um** *adj* of Veii

Vei·ī *or* **Vē·ī -ōrum** *mpl* old Etrurian city about 12 miles from Rome, captured by Camillus *(396 B.C.)*

Vējov·is -is *or* **Vēdjovis -is** *m* ancient deity worshiped on the Capitol at Rome, considered to be the lower-world counterpart of Jupiter

vel *adv* even, actually; perhaps; for instance; **vel...vel** either...or

Vēlābrens·is -is -e *adj* of the Velabrum

Vēlābr·um -ī *n* low ground between the Capitoline and Palatine where a market was located

vēlām·en -inis *n* drape, covering, veil; clothing, robe; olive branch wrapped in woll *(symbol carried by a suppliant)*

vēlāment·um -ī *n* covering, wrapping; a wrap; olive branch wrapped in wool *(symbol carried by a suppliant)*; *(fig)* screen, cover-up

vēlār·ium -(i)ī *n* awning *(over the open-air theater)*

vēlāt·ī -ōrum *mpl (mil)* reserves

vēl·es -itis *m* light-armed soldier, skirmisher

Veli·a -ae *f* the Velia *(ridge connecting the Palatine and Oppian hills at Rome)* ‖ town and port in Lucania

Veliens·is -is -e *adj* of the Velia in Rome ‖ of Velia *(Lucanian town)*

vēlif·er -era -erum *adj* sail-, sailing; **carina velifera** sailboat, sailing ship

vēlificāti·ō -ōnis *f* sailing

vēlific·ō -āre -āvī -ātus *or* **vēlific·or -ārī -ātus sum** *tr* to sail through ‖ *intr* to sail; *(w. dat)* 1 to be under full sail toward, set one's course for; 2 to be hell-bent on *(e.g., high office)*

Velīn·us -a -um *adj* of Velia *(Lucanian town and port)*; of the River Velinus; **lacus Valinus** Valine Lake *(fed by the Veline river)*; **tribus Velina** one of the 35 Roman tribes, belonging to that region

Velīn·us -ī *m* river and lake in the Sabine territory

vēlitār·is -is -e *adj* of light-armed troops

vēlitāti·ō -ōnis *f* skirmishing

Velitern·us -a -um *adj* of Velitrae

vēlitēs = *pl of* **veles**

vēlit·or -ārī -ātus sum *or* **vēlit·ō -āre** *intr* to make an irregular attack, skirmish; *(fig)* to indulge in a verbal skirmish

Velitr·ae -ārum *fpl* Volscian town in Latium on the S. side of the Alban Hills

vēlivol·us -a -um *adj* speeding along under sail; sail-covered *(sea)*

Vēli·us -a -um *adj* Roman clan name, *(nomen), esp.* Velius Longus *(a grammarian of the age of Trajan)*

velle *inf of* **volo**

vellic·ō -are *tr* to pluck, pinch, nip; to carp at, rail at

vellō vellěre vellī *or* **vulsī** *or* **volsī vulsus** *or* **volsus** *tr* to pluck, pull, tear at, tear away, tear out; to tear up, tear down, destroy

vell·us -eris *n* fleece, skin, pelt; wool ‖ *npl* fleecy clouds

vēl·ō -āre -āvī -ātus *tr* to veil, wrap, envelop; to cover, clothe; to encircle, crown; to cover up, hide; to adorn *(temples, etc., ritually)*; **velatus** sail-clad, fitted with sails

vēlōcit·ās -ātis *f* velocity, speed

vēlōciter *adv* speedily, swiftly

vēl·ox -ōcis *adj* speedy, swift

vēl·um -ī *n* sail; veil; curtain, awning, covering; **plenis velis** full speed ahead; **remis velisque** *(fig)* with might and main; **(ventis) vela dare** to set sail; **vela facere** to spread one's sails

velut *or* **velutī** *adv* as, just as, even as; as for example; *(to introduce a simile)* as, as it were; *(in elliptical clauses)* like; **velut** *(or* **velut si)** just as if, just as though, as if, as though

vēmens *see* **vehemens**

vēn·a -ae *f* blood vessel *(whether vein or artery); (contrasted with* **arteria)** vein; artery *(believed to conduct air or food and drink to the body);* duct *(in the body);* penis; vein, streak *(in wood, stone, minerals);* vein *(of ore);* channel, trench; watercourse; store of talent *or* ability; natural disposition; strength; **vena aquae** streamlet ‖ *fpl (fig)* heart, core

vēnābul·um -ī *n* hunting spear

Venā·fer -fra -frum *or* **Venāfrān·us -a -um** *adj* of Venafrum

Venāfr·um -ī *n* Samnite town in S. central Italy

vēnālici·us -a -um *adj* for sale ‖ *m* slave dealer ‖ *npl* merchandise, imports and exports

vēnāl·is -is -e *adj* for sale; open to bribe ‖ *mf* slave offered for sale

vēnātic·us -a -um *adj* hunting

vēnāti·ō -ōnis *f* hunt, hunting; wild-beast show; game

vēnāt·or -ōris *m* hunter

vēnātōri·us -a -um *adj* hunter's

vēnātr·ix -īcis *f* huntress

vēnātūr·a -ae *f* hunting

vēnāt·us -ūs *m* hunting

vendibil·is -is -e *adj* marketable; on sale; attractive, popular, acceptable

venditāti·ō -ōnis *f* advertising; showing off

venditāt·or -ōris *m* hawker, self-advertiser

venditi·ō -ōnis *f* sale

vendit·ō -āre -āvī -ātus *tr* to try to sell; to advertise; to give as a bribe ‖ *refl (w. dat)* to ingratiate oneself with

vendit·or -ōris *m* vendor, seller; recipient of a bribe

vend·ō -ere -idī -itus *tr* to put up for sale; to sell, vend; to sell *(s.o.)* out, betray; to advertise; to praise, recommend

venēfic·a -ae *f* poisoner; sorceress, witch; *(term of abuse)* hag, witch

venēfic·ium -(i)ī *n* poisoning; poison; magical herb; magic, supernatural influence; dye; *(fig)* pernicious moral influence, malicious speech

venēfic·us -a -um *adj* poisoning, poisonous; magic ‖ *m* poisoner; sorcerer, magician

venēnāt·us -a -um *adj* poisonous, venomous; filled with poison; magic; bewitched, enchanted; *(fig)* venomous, bitter

venēnif·er -era -erum *adj* poisonous, venomous

venēn·ō -āre -āvī -ātus *tr (lit & fig)* to poison

venēn·um -ī *n* poison; drug, potion; magic charm; sorcery; ruin; dye; virulence *(of speech)*

vēn·eō -īre -iī -itūrus *intr* to go up for sale, be sold

venerābil·is -is -e *adj* venerable, revered

venerābund·us -a -um *adj* reverend; reverential, worshiping

venerand·us -a -um *adj* venerable, august

venerāti·ō -ōnis *f* veneration, reverence, deep respect

venerāt·or -ōris *m* respecter, adorer; admirer

Venere·us *or* **Veneri·us -a -um** *adj* of Venus; of sexual love, erotic; **res Veneriae** sexual intercourse ‖ *m* Venus throw *(best throw of the dice, when each of the four dice turns up a different number)* ‖ *mpl* attendants in Venus' temple

vener·or -ārī -ātus sum *or* **vener·ō -āre** *tr* to venerate, revere, worship, pray to; to implore, beg; to pray for

Venet·ī -ōrum *mpl* a people in N.E. Italy in the region of modern Venice ‖ a tribe in Gallia Lugdunensis

Veneti·a -ae *f* district of the Veneti in W. Gaul

Venetic·us -a -um *adj* of the Veneti *(of Gallia Lugdunensis)*

Venet·us -a -um *adj* Venetian; bluish ‖ *m* Venetian; a Blue *(i.e., a member of one of the racing factions in Rome)*

veni·a -ae *f* kindness, favor, goodwill; permission; pardon, forgiveness; **veniam dare** *(w. dat)* **1** to grant forgiveness to; **2** to do a favor to; **3** to grant permission to; **veniam petere** to ask permission; **veniā vestrā** with your leave

Venīli·a -ae *f* Italian nymph *(wife of Faunus or of Janus)*

veniō venīre vēnī ventum *intr* to come; to be coming, be on the way; to appear in court; to come to dinner; *(of plants)* to come up; *(w.* **in** *+ acc)* **1** to come into; **2** to enter into *(an agreement, friendship, etc.);* **3** to fall into *(e.g., trouble, disgrace, etc.);* **in buccam venire** to be on the tip of the tongue; **in mentem venire** to come to mind

vēn·or -ārī -ātus sum *tr & intr* to hunt

vent·er -ris *m* stomach, belly; womb; embryo, unborn child; belly, protuberance;

appetite, gluttony
ventil·ō -āre -āvī -ātus *tr* to fan, wave; to display, show off
venti·ō -ōnis *f* coming
ventit·ō -āre -āvī -ātum *intr* to keep coming, come regularly
ventōs·us -a -um *adj* windy, full of wind; of the wind; wind-like, swift as the wind; conceited; fickle
ventricul·us -ī *m* belly; ventricle *(of the heart)*
ventriōs·us -a -um *adj* pot-bellied
ventul·us -ī *m* breeze
vent·us -ī *m* wind; intestinal wind; *(fig)* storm; **ventum emittere** to break wind
vēnūcul·a -ae *f* grape *(of the type well suited for preserving)*
vēn·um *(gen not in use; dat:* **vēnō)** *n* sale, that which is for sale; for sale; **venum** *(or* **veno) dare** to put up for sale, sell; to sell as a slave; **venum** *(or* **veno) dari** to be sold; **venum** *(or* **veno) ire** to go up for sale, be sold
vēnum·dō -dare -dedī -datus *tr* **(-und-)** to put up for sale, sell
ven·us -eris *f* beauty, charm; sexual intercourse, sex; mating; beloved, love ‖ **Venus** Venus *(goddess of love and beauty; planet);* Venus-throw *(see* **Venereus)**
Venusi·a -ae *f* town in Apulia *(birthplace of Horace, modern Venosa)*
Venusīn·us -a -um *adj* of Venusia
venust·ās -ātis *f* beauty, charm, attraction
venustē *adv* prettily, charmingly
venustul·us -a -um *adj* cute, pretty
venust·us -a -um *adj* charming, attractive; interesting *(writing, writer)*
vēpallid·us -a -um *adj* very pale
veprēcul·a -ae *f* little brier bush
vepr·ēs -is *m (f)* brier, bramble bush
vēr vēris *n* spring, springtime; youth
vērātr·um -ī *n (bot)* hellebore *(used as a drug to treat insanity)*
vēr·ax -ācis *adj* truthful
verbēn·a -ae *f (bot)* verbena *(plant with clusters of flowers of various colors)* ‖ *fpl* sacred branches worn by heralds and priests
verb·er -eris *n* scourge, rod, whip; flogging, scourging; thong *(of a sling and similar weapon)* ‖ *npl* strokes, flogging
verberābilissum·us -a -um *adj* altogether deserving of a flogging
verberābund·us -a -um *adj* flogging all the way
verberāti·ō -ōnis *f* flogging
verberetill·us -a -um *adj* deserving of a flogging
verbere·us -a -um *adj* deserving of a flogging
verber·ō -āre -āvī -ātus *tr* to flog, scourge, whip; to batter, beat
verber·ō -ōnis *m* rascal *(deserving of flogging)*
verbivēlitāti·ō -ōnis *f* verbal skirmish
verbōsē *adv* verbosely
verbōs·us -a -um *adj* verbose
verb·um -ī *n* word; verb; saying, expression; proverb; mere talk, mere words; formula; **ad verbum** word for word, verbatim; **verba dare** *(w. dat)* to cheat *(s.o.);* **verba facere** to speak, make a speech; **verbi causā** *(or* **verbi gratiā)** for instance; **verbo** orally; in a word, briefly; nominally, in name only; in theory; **verbo de verbo** *(or* **verbum pro verbo** *or* **verbum verbo)** word for word
Vercell·ae -ārum *fpl* town in N.W. Gaul *(modern Vercelli)*
Vercingetor·ix -igis *m* famous leader of the Arverni in the Gallic War
vercul·um -ī *n (term of endearment)* sweet springtime
vērē *adv* really, truly
verēcundē *adv* bashfully, modestly
verēcundi·a -ae *f* bashfulness, shyness, modesty; respect, awe, reverence; sense of shame; feeling of disgrace, disgrace, shame
verēcund·or -ārī *intr* to be bashful, be shy, feel ashamed
verēcund·us -a -um *adj* bashful, shy, modest, reserved
verēd·us -ī *m* fast hunting horse
verend·us -a -um *adj* awesome ‖ *npl* sexual organs
ver·eor -ērī -itus sum *tr* to revere, have respect for; to fear ‖ *intr* to feel uneasy, be anxious, be afraid; *(w. gen)* to stand in awe of, be afraid of; *(w. dat)* to be afraid for; *(w.* **de** *+ abl)* to be apprehensive about; *(w.* **ut)** to be afraid that not; *(w.* **ne)** to be afraid that
veretr·um -ī *n* male sexual organ
Vergili·ae -ārum *fpl (astr)* Pleiades *(constellation)*
Vergil·ius *or* **Virgil·ius -(i)ī** *m* Roman clan name *(nomen), esp.* Vergil *(Publius Vergilius Maro, epic poet of the Augustan Age, 70–19 B.C.)*
Vergīni·us -a -um *adj* Roman clan name *(nomen), esp.* Lucius Verginius *(said to have killed his daughter to save her from the lust of Appius Claudius and thus to have brought about the overthrow of the decemvirs in 449 B.C.)* ‖ *f* his daughter
verg·ō -ĕre *tr* to cause to move in a downward direction, incline; to tilt down ‖ *intr* to turn, incline; to slope back *or* away; to decline; to lie, be situated; *(w.* **ad) 1** to verge toward; **2** to face (toward); **3** to incline toward, tend toward

(usu. a worse condition); 3 *(w.* **in** + *acc)* to sink into, lapse into *(lethargy, old age)*

vēridic·us -a -um *adj* truthful, speaking the truth; truly spoken

vēriloqu·ium -(i)ī *n* argument based on the true meaning of a word

vērīsimil·is -is -e *adj* probable, likely; realistic

vērīsimilitūd·ō -inis *f* probability, likelihood

vērit·ās -ātis *f* truth, truthfulness; real life, reality; honesty, integrity; correctness *(in eytmology and grammar);* **ex veritate** in accordance with the truth

vēriverb·ium -(i)ī *n* truthfulness

vermiculāt·us -a -um *adj* inlaid with wavy lines, vermiculated

vermicul·us -ī *m* grubworm, maggot; **in vermiculo** in the larval state

vermin·a -um *npl* stomach cramps

verm·is -is *m* worm

vern·a -ae *mf* home-born slave *(born in the master's house);* native

vernācul·us -a -um *adj* of home-born slaves; home-grown, native, domestic; of the neighborhood; indigenous; proletarian; *(of troops)* levied locally; *(w. gen)* native to *(a place)* ‖ *mf* home-born slave

vernīl·is -is -e *adj* servile; obsequious

vernīlit·ās -ātis *f* slavishness; rude behavior, impudence

vernīliter *adv* slavishly

vern·ō -āre *intr* to show signs of spring; to burgeon, break into bloom; to be young

vernul·a -ae *mf* young slave *(born in the master's house);* native

vern·us -a -um *adj* spring, of spring; **tempus vernum** springtime

vērō *adv* in truth, in fact; certainly, to be sure; even; however

Vērōn·a -ae *f* city in N. Italy, birthplace of Catullus

Vērōn(i)ens·is -is -e *adj* Veronese

verp·a -ae *f* penis *(as protruded from the foreskin)*

verp·us -a -um *adj* circumsized; having the foreskin drawn back

verr·ēs -is *m* pig, boar ‖ **Verres** Gaius Cornelius Verres *(notorious governor of Sicily in 73–70 B.C.)*

verrīn·us -a -um *adj* of a boar, of a pig, pork

ver·rō -rěre -rī -sus *tr* **(vor-)** to pull, drag, drag away, carry off; to sweep, scour, brush; *(of the wind)* to whip across, sweep *(the land)*

verrūc·a -ae *f* wart *(on the body);* small failing, minor blemish

verrūcōs·us -a -um *adj* full of warts; *(fig)* full of blemishes

verrunc·ō -āre *intr* to turn out well

versābil·is -is -e *adj* shifting, movable

versābund·us -a -um *adj* revolving

versātil·is -is -e *adj* capable of turning, revolving, movable; versatile

versicapill·us -a -um *adj* having hair that has turned gray, graying

versicol·or -ōris *adj* changing colors, of various colors

versicul·us -ī *m* short line, single line *(of verse or prose),* versicle ‖ *mpl* poor little verses

versificāti·ō -ōnis *f* versification

versificāt·or -ōris *m* versifier

versific·ō -āre *tr* to put into verse ‖ *intr* to write verse

versipell·is -is *m* one can change appearance at will; werewolf

vers·ō -āre -āvī -ātus *tr* **(vor-)** to keep turning, spin, whirl; to twist, bend, wind *(material in order to change its shape);* to turn *(the eyes)* this way and that *(in uncertainty);* to keep shifting *(the limbs in restlessness);* to keep turning, maneuver *(a vehicle, a horse);* to swing *(a weapon)* in all directions; to stir *(the contents of a vessel, esp. the lots in an urn);* to keep turning over *(the ground, as in plowing); (fig)* to influence, sway *(a person in one direction or another); (pej)* to manipulate *(a person); (fig)* to turn over in the mind, ponder, consider; *(w.* **in** + *acc)* to focus *(the mind)* on; *(rhet)* to vary the expression *(of an idea)* ‖ *refl* to keep going around, keep on revolving; to spin around *(so as to face in the opposite direction)*

vers·or -ārī -ātus sum *intr* **(vor-)** to come and go frequently; to live, stay; to be, be in operation, obtain; *(w. adverbs)* to behave *(in a certain way);* to revolve; to spin around *(so as to face in the opposite direction);* to toss, writhe; *(w.* **in** + *abl)* 1 to be involved in, be engaged in, be busy with; 2 to stay in, live in, pass one's time in *(a place, among persons, or in surroundings);* 3 *(of things)* to be concerned with, have to do with; 4 to be subject to; 5 *(of an idea, mental image)* to be constantly present in *(the mind);* 6 *(of a speaker)* to dwell on; **in ore vulgi versari** to be constantly on people's lips

versōri·a -ae *f (naut)* rope used to set sail at an angle in order to tack

versum *adv* **(vor-)** *(usu. after another adv of direction)* back; **rusum vorsum** backward; **sursum versum** up and down

versūr·a -ae *f* **(vor-)** rotation; loan *(of money to pay another debt);* **versuram facere** *(w.* **ab)** to get a loan from *(s.o. to pay another);* **versurā solvere** to pay off *(another debt)* with borrowed money

versus *pp of* **verro** *and* **verto**

vers·us -ūs *m* (**vor-**) turning; furrow; line, row; turn, step *(in a dance); (poet)* line, verse

versus *or* **versum** *adv* (**vor-**) *(w.* **ad)** towards, in the direction of; *(w.* **in** + *acc)* into, in towards; **si in urbem versus venturi erunt** if they intend to come into the city; **sursum versus** upwards

versūtē *adv* (**vor-**) cunningly

versūti·ae -ārum *fpl* cunning, tricks

versūtiloqu·us -a -um *adj* smooth-talking, sly

versūt·us -a -um *adj* (**vors-**) clever, shrewd, ingenious; sly, cunning, deceitful

vert·ex -icis *m* (**vor-**) whirlpool, eddy, strong current; whirlwind, tornado; crown *or* top of the head; head; top, summit *(of mountain);* pole *(of the heavens);* **ex vertice** from above

verticōs·us -a -um *adj* swirling, full of whirlpools

vertīg·ō -inis *f* turning, whirling; dizziness

vert·ō -ĕre -ī versus *tr* (**vor-**) to turn, turn around, spin; to reverse; to invert, tilt; to change, alter, transform; to turn over, plow; to overturn, knock down; to destroy; to subvert, ruin; to ascribe, impute; to translate; *(w.* **ab)** to deflect from ‖ *refl (w.* **in** + *acc)* to change into ‖ *pass (w.* **in** + *acc)* to turn into; *(w.* **in** + *abl)* **1** to be in *(a place or condition);* **2** to be engaged in, be involved in ‖ *intr* to turn; to change; to turn out; *(w.* **in** + *abl)* to center on, depend upon

vertrag·us -ī *m* Gallic greyhound

Vertumn·us -ī *m* (**Vor-**) god of the changing seasons

ver·ū -ūs *n* spit *(for roasting);* javelin, dart

veruīn·a -ae *f* spit; small javelin

vērum *adv* truly; yes; *(in responses)* true but, yes but; but in fact; but yet, but even; yet, still; **non solum** *(or* **modo** *or* **tantum)...verum** *(usu. followed by* **et, etiam** *or* **quoque)** not only...but also

vērumtamen *adv* nevertheless

vēr·us -a -um *adj* true, actual, genuine, real; fair, reasonable ‖ *n* truth, reality; honor, duty, right; **veri similis** probable; realistic; **veri similitudo** probability

verūt·um -ī *n* dart, javelin

verūt·us -a -um *adj* armed with a javelin *or* dart

verv·ex -ēcis *m* wether, castrated hog; *(term of abuse)* muttonhead

vēsāni·a -ae *f* (**vae-**) insanity, madness

vēsāni·ens -entis *adj* raging

vēsān·us -a -um *adj* (**vae-**) insane; furious, savage, raging

vesc·or -ī *intr (w. abl)* to feed on, eat, to feast on, enjoy

vesc·us -a -um *adj* nibbled off; little, feeble; corroding, consuming

Veser·is -is *m* stream in Campania where Publius Decius Mus and Titus Manius Torquatus defeated the Latins in 340 B.C.

vēsīc·a -ae *f* bladder; bombast; objects made of bladder: purse, cap, football, lantern

vēsīcul·a -ae *f* little bladder; little bag

vesp·a -ae *f* wasp

Vespāsiān·us -ī *m* Vespasian *(Titus Flavius Vespasianus Sabinus, Roman Emperor,* A.D. *70–79)*

Vespāsi·us -a -um *adj* Roman clan name *(nomen), esp.* Vespasia Polla *(mother of the Emperor Vespasian)*

vesp·er -erī *or* **-eris** *m* evening; supper; the West; **ad vesperum** toward evening; **primo vespere** early in the evening; **sub vespere** towards evening; **tam vesperi** so late in the evening; **vespere** *or* **vesperi** in the evening

vesper·a -ae *f* evening

vesper·ascō -ascĕre -āvī *intr* to grow towards evening; **vesperascente die** as the day was getting late ‖ *v impers* evening is coming

vespertili·ō -ōnis *m* bat

vespertīn·us -a -um *adj* evening-, in the evening; western

vesperūg·ō -inis *f* evening star

vespill·ō -ōnis *m* mortician

Vest·a -ae *f* Roman goddess of the hearth

Vestāl·is -is -e *adj* Vestal, of Vesta; **virgo Vestalis** Vestal virgin

ves·ter -tra -trum *adj* (**vos-**) your *(pl);* ‖ *pron* yours; **vestri** your friends, your relatives, your soldiers, your school, your party; **vestrum est** *(w. inf)* it is up to you to; **voster** your master

vestibul·um -ī *n* entrance, forecourt; beginning

vestīg·ium -(i)ī *n* footstep, step; footprint, track; trace, vestige; moment, instant

vestīg·ō -āre *tr* to track, trace; to check, find out

vestīment·um -ī *n* clothing; garment; blanket

Vestīn·us -a -um *adj* of the Vestini ‖ *mpl* the Vestini *(Oscan-speaking tribe of the central Apennines)*

vest·iō -īre -īvī *or* **-iī -ītus** *tr* to dress, clothe; to adorn, array, attire; *(fig)* to dress, clothe

vestiplic·a -ae *f* laundress, folder *(employed in ironing and folding clothes)*

vest·is -is *f* garment, dress; clothing; coverlet; tapestry; blanket; slough, skin *(of a snake);* **vestem mutare** to change one's clothes; to put on mourning clothes; **vestis longa** full dress including the full-length stola

vestispic·a -ae *f* female servant in charge of clothes

vestīt·us -ūs *m* clothing, clothes, dress, apparel; ornament *(of speech);* **mutare vestitum** to put on mourning clothes; **redire ad suum vestitum** to end the mourning period

Vesuvi·us -a -um *adj* of Mt. Vesuvius; **mons Vesuvius** Mt. Vesuvius

veter·a -um *npl* tradition, antiquity

veterāmentāri·us -a -um *adj* dealing in second-hand clothes

veterān·us -a -um *adj & m* veteran

veter·ascō -ascĕre -āvī *intr* to grow old

veterāt·or -ōris *m* old hand, expert; sly old fox

veterātōriē *adv* cunningly, slyly

veterātōri·us -a -um *adj* cunning

veter·ēs -um *mpl* the ancients; ancient authors

veterīn·us -a -um *adj* of burden ‖ *fpl & npl* beasts of burden

veternōs·us -a -um *adj* lethargic; sleepy, drowsy

vetern·us -ī *m* lethargy; old age; drowsiness; listlessness *(of old age)*

vetit·um -ī *n* prohibition

vet·ō -āre -uī -itus *tr* (**vot-**) to forbid, prohibit, oppose; to veto; *(w. inf, w.* **ne, quominus**) to prevent from; *(w. inf, w. acc & inf, w.* **ne**, *w.* **quin**) to forbid *(s.o. to do s.th.)*

vetul·us -a -um *adj* poor old

vet·us -eris *adj* old, aged; long-standing ‖ *mpl see* **veteres** ‖ *npl see* **vetera**

vetust·ās -ātis *f* age; ancient times, antiquity; long duration, great age

vetust·us -a -um *adj* old, ancient; old-time, old-fashioned, good old *(days, etc.);* antiquated

vexām·en -inis *n* shaking, quaking

vexāti·ō -ōnis *f* shaking, jolting, tossing; distress

vexāt·or -ōris *m* jostler; harasser; troublemaker

vexī *perf of* **veho**

vexillār·ius -(i)ī *m* standard-bearer ‖ *mpl* special reserves

vexillāti·ō -ōnis *f (mil)* detachment

vexill·um -ī *n* standard, flag, banner *(esp. the red flag hoisted above the general's tent as the signal for battle);* replica of the military banner, awarded for distinguished service; detachment of troops; **vexillum praeponere** to hoist the red flag *(as the signal for battle)*

vex·ō -āre *tr* to shake, toss; to vex, annoy; to harass *(troops)*

vi·a -ae *f* way, road, street, highway; march, journey; method; right way, right method; **inter vias** on the road; **in via** *(frontage)* on the road; **viam munire** to build a road; *(fig)* to pave the way; isle *(in the theater);* **via recta** a direct route; **via vitae** pathway of life

viāl·is -is -e *adj* of the highway

viāri·us -a -um *adj* for highway maintenance

viāticāt·us -a -um *adj* provided with traveling money

viātic·us -a -um *adj* for the trip, for traveling, travel ‖ *n* travel allowance, provisions for the journey; *(mil)* soldier's saving fund

viāt·or -ōris *m* traveler; passenger; *(leg)* bailiff

vīb·ex -īcis *f* welt *(from a blow)*

vibr·ō -āre *tr* to brandish, wave around; to hurl ‖ *intr* to vibrate, quiver; *(of the tongue)* to flick

vīburn·um -ī *n (bot)* viburnum *(ornamental shrub, the bark of which was used in medicine)*

vīcān·us -a -um *adj* village- ‖ *mpl* villagers

Vic·a Pot·a *(gen:* **Vic·ae Pot·ae**) *f* a goddess of victory

vicāri·us -a -um *adj* substitute ‖ *m* substitute, deputy, proxy; under-slave *(kept by another slave)*

vīcātim *adv* from street to street; from village to village; in hamlets

vice *prep (w. gen)* on account of; like, after the manner of

vicem *adv* in turn ‖ *prep (w. gen)* instead of, in place of; on account of; like, after the manner of

vīcēnāri·us -a -um *adj* of the number twenty

vīcēn·ī -ae -a *adj* twenty each, twenty apiece, twenty at a time, twenty in a group

vīcēsimān·ī -ōrum *mpl* soldiers of the twentieth legion

vīcēsimāri·us -a -um *adj* derived from the 5% tax

vīcēsim·us -a -um *adj* (**vīcens-**) twentieth ‖ *f* 5% tax

vīcess·is -is *m* coins worth 20 "asses" *(i.e., c. 20¢)*

vici·a -ae *f* vetch *(grown for its edible seeds and used as fodder for animals)*

vīciē(n)s *adv* twenty times

vīcināl·is -is -e *adj* neighboring, nearby

vīcīni·a -ae *f* neighborhood; nearness, proximity

vīcīnit·ās -ātis *f* neighborhood, proximity; the neighborhood *(i. e., the neighbors)*

vīcīn·us -a -um *adj* neighboring, nearby, near; imminent ‖ *mf* neighbor ‖ *n* neighborhood; **ex vicino** of a similar nature; **in vicino** in close proximity

vicis *(gen; the nom singl and gen pl do not*

occur; acc singl: **vicem;** *abl singl:* **vice)** *f* change, interchange, alternation; succession; exchange; interaction; return, recompense, retaliation; fortune, misfortune, condition, fate; plight, lot; changes of fate; duty, office, position; function, capacity, office; **ad vicem** (*w. gen*) after the manner of; **in vicem** *(or* **in vices** *or* **per vices)** in turn, alternately; **in vicem** *(or* **invicem)** *(w. gen)* instead of, in place of; **vice** in return; **vice** *(w. gen) or* **vicem** *(w. gen)* in place of, as a substitute for; **vice versā** *(or* **vicibus versis)** vice-versa, conversely; **vicibus** in return

vicissim *or* **vicissātim** *adv* in turn, again

vicissitūd·ō -inis *f* change, interchange; regular succession, alternation; reversal, vicissitude; reciprocation

victim·a -ae *f* **(-tum-)** victim; sacrifice

victimār·ius -(i)ī *m* **(-tum-)** assistant at sacrifices

victit·ō -āre -āvī -ātum *intr* to live, subsist; *(w. abl)* to live on, subsist on

vict·or -ōris *m* victor; *(in apposition)* **victor exercitus** victorious army

victōri·a -ae *f* victory

victōriāt·us -ī *m* victory coin *(of silver, stamped with the image of victory)*

Victōriol·a -ae *f* figurine of Victory

victr·ix -īcis *adj (fem & neut only)* victorious, triumphant

victus *pp of* **vinco**

vict·us -ūs *or* **-ī** *m* living, means of livelihood; way of life; food, sustenance

vīcul·us -ī *m* hamlet

vīc·us -ī *m* village, hamlet; ward, quarter *(in a city);* street, block

vidēlicet *adv* clearly, evidently; *(in irony)* of course, naturally; *(in explanations)* namely

viden = vidēsne? do you see?, do you get it?

videō vidēre vīdī vīsus *tr* to see, look at; to know; to consider; to understand, realize; *(w.* **ut)** to see to it that, take care that ‖ *pass* to seem, appear ‖ *v impers pass* it seems right, it seems good; **dis visum est** the gods decided *(literally, it seemed (right) to the gods*

vidu·a -ae *f* widow; spinster

viduit·ās -ātis *f* bereavement; want, lack; widowhood

vīdul·us -ī *m* leather travel bag, suitcase, knapsack

vidu·ō -āre -āvī -ātus *tr* to deprive, bereave; *(w. gen or abl)* to deprive of; **viduata** left a widow

vidu·us -a -um *adj* bereft, destitute; unmarried; *(w. abl or* **ab)** bereft of, destitute of, without ‖ *f see* **vidua**

Vienn·a -ae *f* chief city of the Allobroges in Gallia Narbonensis *(modern Vienne)*

viēt·or -ōris *m* cooper

viēt·us -a -um *adj* shriveled

vig·eō -ēre -uī *intr* to thrive, be vigorous, flourish

vig·escō -escěre -uī *intr* to become vigorous, gain strength, become lively

vīgēsim·us -a -um *adj* twentieth

vig·il -ilis *adj* awake, wakeful; alert, one one's toes ‖ *m* watchman, guard, sentinel; fireman, policeman

vigil·ans -antis *adj* watchful, alert; disquieting *(worries)*

vigilanter *adv* vigilantly, alertly

vigilanti·a -ae *f* wakefulness; vigilance, alertness

vigil·ax -ācis *adj* alert; disquieting, sleep-disturbing *(worries)*

vigili·a -ae *f* wakefulness, sleeplessness, insomnia; vigil; vigilance, alertness; watch *(one of the four divisions of the night for keeping watch); (mil)* standing guard; *(mil)* guards, sentinels; **vigilias agere** *(or* **agitare** *or* **servare)** to keep watch

vigil·ō -āre -āvī -ātus *tr* to spend *(the night)* awake; to make, do, perform, write *(s.th.)* while awake at night ‖ *intr* to stay awake; to be watchful; to be alert; *(w. dat)* to be attentive to

vīgintī *indecl adj* twenty

vīgintī·vir -virī *m* member of a board of twenty *(appointed by Caesar in 59 B.C. to distribute parcels of land in Campania)* ‖ member of a board of twenty in municipal administration

vīgintīvirāt·us -ūs *m* membership on the board of twenty

vig·or -ōris *m* vigor, liveliness

vīlic·a -ae *f* **(vill-)** foreman's wife, manager's wife

vīlic·ō -āre -āvī -ātum *intr* **(vill-)** to be a foreman, be a manager *(of an estate)*

vīlic·us -ī *m* **(vill-)** foreman, manager *(of an estate)*

vīl·is -is -e *adj* cheap, inexpensive; common, worthless, contemptible

vīlit·ās -ātis *f* lowness of price, cheapness, low price; worthlessness

vīliter *adv* cheaply, at a low price

vill·a -ae *f* country home; farmhouse; **villa rustica** farmhouse, homestead; **villa urbana** *(also in the country, with no farm attached)* country villa

villic- = vilic-

villōs·us -a -um *adj* hairy, shaggy, bushy

villul·a -ae *f* small farmhouse; small villa

vill·um -ī *n* drop of wine

vill·us -ī *m* hair; fleece; nap *(of cloth)*

vīm·en -inis *n* osier; basket

vīment·um -ī *n* osier

Vīmināl·is -is -e *adj* Viminal; **Viminalis collis** Viminal Hill *(one of the seven hills of Rome)*

vīmine·us -a -um *adj* made of osiers
vīn *or* **vīn'** = **visne?** do you wish?, ya' wanna?
vīnāce·us -a -um *adj* grape, of grape ‖ *n* grape seed
Vīnāl·ia -ium *npl* wine festival; **Vinalia priora** earlier wine festival *(celebrated on April 23, when libations of wine from the previous year were poured to Jupiter);* **Vinalia rustica** country wine festival *(celebrated on August 19 and 20 in honor of Jupiter in thanksgiving for the successful harvest)*
vīnāri·us -a -um *adj* wine- ‖ *m* wine dealer; vintner ‖ *npl* wine flasks
vincibil·is -is -e *adj* easily won
vin·ciō -cīre -xī -ctus *tr* to bind, tie; to wrap; to encircle, surround; to restrain; *(med)* to bandage; *(med)* to ligature; *(rhet)* to link together, arrange rhythmically
vincō vincĕre vīcī victus *tr* to conquer; to get the better of, beat, defeat; to outdo; to convince, refute, persuade; to prove, demonstrate; to outlast, outlive ‖ *intr* to win, be victorious; to prevail; to succeed
vinct·us -a -um *pp of* **vincio** ‖ *adj* fettered, in bonds
vincul·um *or* **vincl·um -ī** *n* chain; fetter, cord, band; sandal strap; thong, rope; mooring cable; tether ‖ *npl* bonds, fetter; imprisonment; prison; **vincula publica** chains worn by a state prisoner; **aliquem in vincula conjicere** to put s.o. into chains
Vindelic·us -a -um *adj* of the Vindelici ‖ *mpl* people living between the Raetian Alps and the Danube
vindēmi·a -ae *f* vintage
vindēmiāt·or -ōris *m* grape picker
vindēmiol·a -ae *f* small vintage; minor sources of income
Vindēmit·or -ōris *m (astr)* a star in Virgo
vind·ex -icis *adj* avenging ‖ *m (leg)* claimant; defender, protector, champion; liberator; avenger, punisher
Vind·ex -icis *m* Roman family name *(cognomen), esp.* Gaius Julius Vindex *(leader of a rebellion in Gaul against Nero in* A.D. *69)*
vindicāti·ō -ōnis *f* avenging, punishment; *(leg)* claim
vindici·ae -ārum *fpl* legal claim; things *or* persons claimed; championship, protection; **vindicias dare** *(or* **dicere** *or* **decernere)** to hand over the things *or* persons claimed
vindic·ō -āre -āvī -ātus *tr* to lay legal claim to; to protect, defend; to appropriate; to demand; to demand unfairly; to claim as one's own; to avenge, punish; **in libertatem vindicare** to set free, liberate *(literally, to claim for freedom)*
vindict·a -ae *f* rod used in the ceremony of setting slaves free; defense, protection; vengeance, revenge, satisfaction
vīne·a *or* **vīni·a -ae** *f* vineyard; vine; *(mil)* shed *(used to defend besiegers against enemy missiles)*
vīnēt·um -ī *n* vineyard
vīnipoll·ens -entis *adj* powerful through wine
vīnit·or -ōris *m* vine dresser
vinnul·us -a -um *adj* charming
vīnolenti·a -ae *f* **(vīnul-)** wine drinking, intoxication
vīnolent·us -a -um *adj* **(vīnul-)** drunk
vīnōs·us -a -um *adj* addicted to wine; tasting *or* smelling of wine
vīn·um -ī *n* wine
viol·a -ae *f* violet *(flower; color; dye)*
violābil·is -is -e *adj* vulnerable
violār·ium -(i)ī *n* bed of violets
violār·ius -(i)ī *m* dyer of violet
violāti·ō -ōnis *f* violation, profanation
violāt·or -ōris *m* violator, profaner
viol·ens -entis *adj* violent, raging
violenter *adv* violently, vehemently
violenti·a -ae *f* violence
violent·us -a -um *adj* violent
viol·ō -āre -āvī -ātus *tr* to violate; to outrage, harm by violence
vīper·a -ae *f* viper; *(poisonous)* snake
vīpere·us -a -um *adj* viper's; snake's
vīperīn·us -a -um *adj* viper's, snake's
Vipsāni·us -a -um *adj* Roman clan name *(nomen);* **porticus Vipsania** Vipsanian portico *(forming part of the Pantheon built by Agrippa in the Campus Martius)* ‖ Agrippa *(Marcus Vipsanius Agrippa, Augustus' friend and sucessful admiral)* ‖ *f* Vipsania *(esp. Vipsania Agrippina, daughter of Agrippa and the first wife of Emperor Tiberius)*
vir virī *m* man; he-man, hero; husband; lover; manhood, virility; *(mil)* infantryman
virāg·ō -inis *f* female warrior; heroine
Virb·ius -(i)ī *m* local deity, the reincarnation of Hipppolytus, worshipped with Diana at Aricia ‖ son of Hippolytus
virect·um -ī stretch of green
vir·eō -ēre -uī *intr* to be green; to be fresh, be vigorous, flourish
virēs = *pl of* **vis**
vir·escō -escĕre -uī *intr* to turn green
virg·a -ae *f* twig, sprout; graft; rod, switch *(for flogging);* wand; walking stick, cane; colored stripe in a garment; branch of a family tree
virgāt·or -ōris *m* flogger
virgāt·us -a -um *adj* made of twigs *or* osiers; striped
virgēt·um -ī *n* osier thicket
virge·us -a -um *adj* of twigs, of kindling wood

virgi(n)dēmi·a -ae *f (hum)* harvest of birch rods *(i.e., a sound flogging)*
virgināl·is -is -e *adj* maiden's, girl's, girlish ‖ *n* female organ
virginārī·us -a -um *adj* girl's
virgine·us *or* **virgini·us -a -um** *adj* virgin, of *or* for a virgin; proper to a virgin; of virgins
virginit·ās -ātis *f* girlhood; virginity
virg·ō -inis *f (marriageable)* girl, maiden; virgin ‖ **Virgo** Virgo *(constellation; aqueduct constructed by Marcus Vipsanius Agrippa)*
virgul·a -ae *f* little twig; wand; **virgula divina** divining rod
virgult·um -ī *n* thicket; shrub ‖ *npl* brushwood; firewood; slips *(of trees)*
virgult·us -a -um *adj* covered with brushwood
virguncul·a -ae *f* lass, young girl
Viriāt(h)·us -ī *m* Lusitanian who led a guerilla war against Rome *(147–140 B.C.)*
virid·ans -antis *adj* green
virid(i)ār·ium -(i)ī *n* garden
virid·is -is -e *adj* green; fresh, young ‖ *npl* greenery
viridit·ās -ātis *f* greenness; freshness
virid·ō -āre *tr* to make green ‖ *intr* to turn green
Vir(i)domar·us -ī *m* Insubrian leader killed in battle by Marcus Claudius Marcellus, 222 B.C., who thereby won the *spolia opima*
virīl·is -is -e *adj* male, masculine; adult; manly; *(gram)* masculine; **pars virilis** male sexual organ; **pro virili parte** *(or* **portione)** to the best of one's ability ‖ *npl* manly *or* heroic deeds; male sexual organs
virīlit·ās -ātis *f* manhood, virility
virīliter *adv* manfully, like a man
virīpot·ens -entis *adj* almighty
virītim *adv* man by man; per man; individually
vīrōs·us -a -um *adj* slimy; strong-smelling, fetid, stinking
virt·ūs -ūtis *f* manliness, manhood, virility; strength; valor, gallantry; excellence, worth; special property; moral excellence, goodness, virtue; good quality, high quality *(of persons, animals, things)*; potency, effectiveness *(of drugs, medications)*; **virtute** *(w. gen)* through the good services of, thanks to ‖ *fpl* achievements; gallant deeds
vīr·us -ī *n* venom; slime; stench, pungency; saltiness
vīs *(gen not in use; dat & abl:* **vi;** *acc:* **vim;** *pl:* **vīr·ēs -ium)** *f* power, strength, force; influence; energy; hostile force, violence, attack; amount, quantity; meaning, force *(of words)*; binding force *(of a law)*; value, amount; **magna vis** *(w. gen)* a large number of, a large amount of; **omnis vis** *(w. gen)* the whole range of, the sum total of; **per vim** forcibly; **suā vi** in itself, intrinsically; **summā vi** with utmost energy; **vi** by force; **vim adferre** *(w. dat)* **1** to do violence to; **2** to rape; **3** to kill; **vim adferre sibi** *(or* **vitae suae)** to take one's own life; **vim facere** to make an assault; **vim habere** *(w. gen)* to be equivalent *(in amount)* to ‖ **vires** *fpl* strength; resources; potency, power *(of herbs, drugs)*; *(mil)* military strength, fighting power; control, influence; financial resources, assets; powers of intellect, capability; meaning *(of words)*; value, amount; **pro viribus** with all one's might
viscāt·us -a -um *adj* smeared with birdlime
viscer·a -um *npl* fleshy parts of the body *(as distinct from skin and bones)*; viscera, internal organs; womb; heart, vitals, bowels; *(fig)* innermost part, bowels, heart; center *(esp. of the earth)*; *(fig)* bosom friend, favorite; *(fig)* person's flesh and blood *(family, offspring)*
viscerāti·ō -ōnis *f* public distribution of meat
visc·ō -āre -āvī -ātus *tr* to catch in birdlime
visc·um -ī *n or* **visc·us -ī** *m* mistletoe; birdlime
visc·us -eris *n (anat)* organ; entrails ‖ *npl see* **viscera**
vīsend·us -a -um *adj* worth going to see, worth visiting
vīsī *perf of* **viso**
vīsi·ō -ōnis *f* appearance, apparition; notion, idea
vīsit·ō -āre -āvī -ātus *tr* to keep seeing; to visit, go to visit
vīs·ō -ĕre -ī *tr* to look at with attention, view; to come *or* go to look at; to find out; to go and see, visit; to look in on *(the sick)* ‖ *intr* to go and look; *(w.* **ad)** to go to visit, call on *(esp. an invalid)*
vispillō *see* **vespillo**
viss·iō -īre *intr (sl)* to fart softly
vīs·um -ī *n* sight, appearance
Visurg·is -is *m* river in N. Germany *(modern Weser)*
vīsus *pp of* **video**
vīs·us -ūs *m* (faculty of) sight; thing seen, sight, vision
vīt·a -ae *f* life; way of life; means of living, livelihood; manner of life; course of life, career; biography
vītābil·is -is -e *adj* undesirable, deserving to be shunned
vītābund·us -a -um *adj* taking evasive action

vītāl·is -is -e *adj* of life, vital; life-giving; likely to live, staying alive; able to survive; living, alive ‖ *npl (anat)* vital parts
vītāliter *adv* vitally
vītāti·ō -ōnis *f* avoidance
Vitell·ius -(i)ī *m* Vitellius *(Aulus Vitellius, Roman Emperor, from January 2 to December 22,* A.D. *69)*
vitell·us -ī *m* little calf; yolk *(of egg)*
vīte·us -a -um *adj* of the vine
vīticul·a -ae *f* little vine
vītif·er -era -erum *adj* producing vines, vine-producing
vītigen·us -a -um *adj* produced from the vine
viti·ō -āre -āvī -ātus *tr* to spoil, corrupt, violate, mar; to falsify
vitiōsē *adv* faultily, badly, corruptly; **vitiose se habere** to be defective
vitiōsit·ās -ātis *f* corrupt *or* bad condition
vitīos·us -a -um *adj* faulty, defective; (morally) corrupt, bad, depraved
vīt·is -is *f* vine; vine branch; centurion's staff; centurionship
vītisāt·or -ōris *m* vine planter
vit·ium -(i)ī *n* fault, flaw; defect, disorder; sin, offense, vice; flaw in the auspices; injurious quality, disadvantage; augural impediment, unfavorable augury; **in vitio esse** to be in a defective state, be defective; *(leg)* legal defect, technicality; **meo vitio pereo** I am ruined through my own fault; **vitio** *(w. gen)* through the fault of; **vitio dare** *(or* **vertere)** to regard as a fault; **vitium capere** *(or* **facere)** to develop a defect; **vitium dicere** *(w. dat)* to insult s.o.
vīt·ō -āre -āvī -ātus *tr* to avoid, evade
vīt·or -ōris *m* basket-maker
vitre·us -a -um *adj* glass, of glass; glassy ‖ *npl* glassware
vītric·us -ī *m* stepfather
vitr·um -ī *n* glass; blue dye
vitt·a -ae *f* headband, fillet
vittāt·us -a -um *adj* wearing a fillet
vitul·a -ae *f* heifer
vitulīn·us -a -um *adj & f* veal
vītul·or -ārī *intr* to shout for joy
vitul·us -ī *m* calf, young bull; foal; seal
vituperābil·is -is -e *adj* blameworthy
vituperāti·ō -ōnis *f* blaming, censuring; blame; scandalous conduct, blameworthiness
vituperāt·or -ōris *m* censurer
vituper·ō -āre -āvī -ātus *tr* to criticize, find fault with; to declare *(an omen)* invalid
vīvācit·ās -ātis *f* will to live; life-force; vitality
vīvār·ium -(i)ī *n* game preserve, zoo; fish pond
vīvāt·us -a -um *adj* animated, lively
vīv·ax -ācis *adj* long-lived; long-lasting, enduring; quick to learn
vīvē *adv* in a lively manner
vīverād·ix -īcis *f* rooted cutting *(i.e., having roots)*
vīvescō *or* **vīviscō vīviscĕre** *intr* to become alive, come to life; to grow lively, get full of life
vīvid·us -a -um *adj* teeming with life, full of life; true to life, vivid, realistic; quick, lively *(mind);* vivid *(expression)*
vīvirād·ix -īcis *f see* **viveradix**
vīviscō *see* **vivesco**
vīvō vīvĕre vixī victum *intr* to be alive, live; to be still alive, survive; to reside; *(w. abl or* **de** *+ abl)* to live on, subsist on
vīv·us -a -um *adj* alive, living; lively; fresh; natural *(rock);* speaking *(voice);* **argentum vivum** quicksilver; **calx viva** lime ‖ *n (com)* capital; **ad vivum resecare** to cut to the quick
vix *adv* scarcely; hardly, with difficulty, barely
vixdum *adv* hardly then, scarcely yet
vocābul·um -ī *n* word, term; name, designation; noun; common noun
vōcāl·is -is -e *adj* having a voice, gifted with speech, speaking; gifted with song, singing; tuneful ‖ *f (gram)* vowel
vocām·en -inis *f* name, designation
vocāti·ō -ōnis *f* invitation *(to dinner); (leg)* summons
vocāt·or -ōris *m* inviter, host
vocāt·us -ūs *m* summons, call
vōciferāti·ō -ōnis *f* loud cry, yell
vōcifer·ō -āre *or* **vōcifer·or -ārī -ātus sum** *tr & intr* to shout, yell
vocit·ō -āre -āvī -ātus *tr* to call habitually, usually call, name; to shout out again and again
voc·ō -āre -āvī -ātus *tr* to call, name; to summon; to call upon, invoke *(the gods);* to invite *(to dinner); (w. double acc)* to call *(s.o. s.th.);* to call for, require; *(w.* **de** *+ abl)* to name *(s.o., s.th.)* after; *(mil)* to challenge; **ad se vocare** to summon; **aliquem ex jure manum consertum vocare** *(leg)* to call out of court to settle the issue by physical combat; **in arma vocare** to call to arms; **in dubium vocare** to call into question; **in jus vocare** to summon to court; **in odium vocare** to bring into disfavor; **in periculum vocare** to lead into danger
vōcul·a -ae *f* weak voice; soft note, soft tone; whisper, gossip
volaem·um -ī *n* **(volē-)** type of large pear
Volāterr·ae -ārum *fpl* old Etruscan hill town *(modern Volterra)*
Volāterrān·us -a -um *adj* of Volaterrae
volātic·us -a -um *adj* flying, winged; transitory, passing; inconstant

volātil·is -is -e *adj* able to fly; rapid; transitory

volāt·us -ūs *m* flight

Volcānāl·ia -ium *npl* **(Vulc-)** festival of Vulcan *(August 23)*

Volcāni·us -a -um *adj* **(Vulc-)** of Vulcan; **acies Vulcania** Vulcan's battleline *(i.e., fire spreading in a line);* **arma Vulcania** arms made by Vulcan *(for Achilles)*

Volcān·us -ī *m* **(Vul-)** Vulcan *(god of fire, son of Jupiter)*

vol·ens -entis *adj* willing; permitting; ready; favorable **‖** *m* well-wisher

Voles·us -ī *m* Roman family name *(nomen), esp.* the father of Publius Valerius Publicola

volg- = vulg-

volit·ans -antis *m* winged insect

volit·ō -āre -āvī -ātum *intr* to flit about, fly about, flutter; to move quickly; to hover, soar

vol·ō -āre -āvī -ātum *intr* to fly

volō velle voluī *tr* to wish, want; to propose, determine; to hold, maintain; to mean; to prefer **‖** *intr* to be willing

Vologēs·us -ī *m* name of several Arsacid kings of Parthia

volōn·ēs -um *mpl* volunteers *(slaves who enlisted after the battle of Cannae, 216 B.C.)*

volpēs *see* **vulpes**

Volsc·us -a -um *adj* Vulscan **‖** *mpl* Volscians *(ancient people in S. Latium, subjugated by the Romans in 5th & 4th cent. B.C.)*

volsell·a -ae *f* tweezers

Volsini·ī -ōrum *mpl* Etruscan city

volsus *pp of* **vello**

volt = *older form of* **vult** he *(or* she *or* it) wishes

voltis = *older form of* **vultis** you wish

Voltumn·a -ae *f* Etruscan goddess in whose temple the twelve Etruscan states met

Volt·ur -uris *m* **(Vul-)** mountain of Apulia near the border of Samnium

Volturn·um -ī *n* town at the mouth of the Volturnus river **‖** old name of Capua

Volturn·us -ī *m* river flowing from the Apennines to the coast of Campania **‖** name for a S.E. wind

voltus *see* **vultus**

volūbil·is -is -e *adj* turning, spinning, revolving, swirling; voluble, rapid, fluent; changeable

volūbilit·ās -ātis *f* whirling motion; roundness; volubility; fluency; mutability

volūbiliter *adv* rapidly; fluently

volu·cer -cris -cre *adj* flying, winged; rapid, speedy

volu·cer -cris *m* bird

volucr·is -is *f* bird; fly; **volucris Junonis** the bird of Juno *(i.e., a peacock)*

voluī *perf of* **volo**

volūm·en -inis *n* roll, book; chapter; whirl, eddy; coil; fold

Volumni·us -a -um *adj* Roman clan name *(nomen)*

voluntāri·us -a -um *adj* voluntary **‖** *mpl* volunteers

volunt·ās -ātis *f* will, wish, desire, purpose, aim, intention; inclination; goodwill, sympathy; willingness, approval; choice, option; last will and testament; attitude *(good or bad);* meaning *(of words);* **ad voluntatem** *(w. gen)* according to the wishes of; **de** *(or* **ex)** **voluntate** *(w. gen)* at the desire of; **voluntate** *(w. gen)* with the consent of

volup *adv* to one's satisfaction, with pleasure; **volup esse** to be a source of pleasure; **volup facere** *(w. dat)* to cause *(s.o.)* pleasure

voluptābil·is -is -e *adj* agreeable, pleasant

voluptāri·us -a -um *adj* pleasant, agreeable; voluptuous **‖** *m* voluptuary

volupt·ās -ātis *f* pleasure, enjoyment, delight **‖** *fpl* sensual pleasures; games, sports, public performances

voluptuōs·us -a -um *adj* pleasant, agreeable; giving pleasure

Volusi·us -a -um *adj* Roman clan name *(nomen), esp.* name of a Roman epic poet, mocked by Catullus

volūtābr·um -ī *n* wallow *(for swine)*

volūtābund·us -a -um *adj* wallowing about

volūtāti·ō -ōnis *f* rolling about, tossing about; wallowing; restlessness

volūt·ō -āre -āvī -ātus *tr* to roll about, turn over; to engross; to think over **‖** *pass* to wallow, luxuriate

volūtus *pp of* **volvo**

volva *see* **vulva**

vol·vō -vĕre -vī -ūtus *tr* to roll, turn about, wind; *(of a river)* to roll *(e.g., rocks)* along; to breathe; to unroll, read *(books, scrolls);* to pour out, utter fluently; to consider, weigh; *(of time)* to bring on, bring around; to form *(a circle);* to undergo *(troubles)* **‖** *pass* to roll, tumble; to revolve **‖** *intr* to revolve; to roll on, elapse

vōm·er *or* **vōm·is -eris** *m* plowshare; *(vulg)* penis

vomic·a -ae *f* sore, boil, abscess, ulcer; annoyance

vōmis *see* **vomer**

vomit·ō -āre *intr* to vomit *(frequently)*

vomiti·ō -ōnis *f* vomiting

vomit·us -ūs *m* vomiting; vomit

vom·ō -ĕre -uī -itus *tr & intr* to vomit, throw up

vorāg·ō -inis *f* deep hole, abyss, chasm, depth

vor·ax -ācis *adj* swallowing, devouring; greedy, ravenous
vor·ō -āre -āvī -ātus *tr* to swallow, devour; *(fig)* to devour *(by reading)*
vors- = vers-
vort- = vert-
vōs *pron* you *(pl); (refl)* yourselves
vōsmet *pron (emphatic form of* **vōs)** you yourselves
voster *see* **vester**
vōtīv·us -a -um *adj* votive, promised in a vow
votō *see* **veto**
vōt·um -ī *n* solemn vow *(made to a deity);* votive offering *(made for a prayer answered);* prayer, wish; thing wished for, wish; **compos voti** *(or* **voto) esse** to have had one's prayer answered; **in voto est** *(w. inf)* it is *(my)* wish to; **in voto est** *(w.* **ut** + *subj or w. acc & inf)* it is *(my)* wish that; **voti reus** obligated to fulfill a vow; **voto major** surpassing one's fondest hopes; **votum est** *(w. inf)* it is *(my)* hope to; **votum est** *(w.* **ut** + *subj or w. acc & inf)* it is *(my)* hope that
voveō vovēre vōvī vōtus *tr* to vow, promise solemnly, pledge, devote *(to a deity);* to wish, wish for
vox vōcis *f* voice; sound, tone, cry, call; word *(written or spoken);* utterance, saying, expression; proverb; language; accent
Vulcānus *see* **Volcanus**
vulgār·is -is -e *adj* **(vol-)** common, general, usual, everyday; low-class; unimportant, routine *(business);* well-known, often repeated *(story)*
vulgāriter *adv* **(vol-)** in the usual way; commonly
vulgāt·or -ōris *m* **(vol-)** divulger
vulgāt·us -a -um *adj* **(vol-)** common, general; well-known; notorious
vulgivag·us -a -um *adj* roving; promiscuous
vulg·ō -āre -āvī -ātus *tr* **(vol-)** to spread, publish, broadcast; to divulge; to prostitute; to level, make common
vulgō *adv* **(vol-)** generally, publicly, everywhere
vulg·us -ī *n* **(vol-)** masses, public, people; crowd; herd, flock; rabble, populace; **in vulgus** *(or* **in vulgum)** to the general public, publicly
vulnerāti·ō -ōnis *f* **(vol-)** wounding, wound
vulner·ō -āre -āvī -ātus *tr* **(vol-)** to wound; to damage
vulnific·us -a -um *adj* inflicting wounds
vuln·us -eris *n* **(vol-)** wound; blow, stroke; blow, disaster
vulpēcul·a -ae *f* **(vol-)** little fox, sly little fox
vulp·ēs -is *f* **(vol-)** fox; craftiness, cunning
vuls·us *or* **vols·us -a -um** *pp of* **vello** ‖ *adj* plucked, beardless, effeminate
vulticul·us -ī *m* **(vol-)** mere look
vult·um *see* **vultus**
vultuōs·us -a -um *adj* **(vol-)** full of airs, affected, stuck-up
vult·ur -uris *m* **(vol-)** vulture ‖ **Vultur** *m* mountain in Apulia
vulturīn·us -a -um *adj* **(vol-)** vulture-like, of a vulture
vultur·ius -(i)ī *m* **(vol-)** vulture
Vulturn·us -ī *m* **(Vol-)** principal river of Campania *(modern Volturno)*
vult·us -ūs *m* **(vol-)** face; looks, expression, features; look, appearance
vulv·a -ae *f* **(vol-)** wrapper, cover; womb; female genitalia, vulva; sow's womb *(as a delicacy)*

X

X = decem ten
Xanthipp·e -ēs *f* wife of Socrates
Xanthipp·us -ī *m* father of Pericles ‖ Spartan commander of the Carthaginians in the First Punic War
Xanth·us -ī *m* river at Troy, identified with the Scamander River ‖ river and town of the same name in Lycia ‖ name applied by Vergil to a river in Epirus
xen·ium -iī *n* gift, present *(given by a guest to a host or by a host to a guest)*
Xenocrat·ēs -is *m* Greek philosopher, a disciple of Plato
Xenophan·ēs -is *m* early Greek philosopher *(c. 565–470 B.C.)*
Xenoph·ōn -ontis *m* Greek historian and pupil of Socrates *(c. 430–354 B.C.)*
xērampelin·ae -ārum *fpl* reddish-purple clothes
Xerx·ēs -is *m* Persian king, defeated at Salamis *(c. 519–465 B.C.)*
xiphi·ās -ae *m* swordfish
xyst·us -ī *m or* **xyst·um -ī** *n* open colonnade *or* portico, walk

Y

Y, y letter adopted from Greek into the Roman alphabet for the transliteration of words containing an upsilon *(for which* u *was used earlier),* and pronounced approximate as German ü. It appears to have been in use by the time of Cicero; but its use was restricted to foreign words

Z

Zacynth·us *or* **Zacynth·os -ī** *f* island off W. Greece ‖ name for Saguntum, supposed to have been colonized by people from Zacynthus
Zaleuc·us -ī *m* traditional lawgiver of the Locrians
Zam·a -ae *f* town in Numidia where Scipio defeated Hannibal and brought the Second Punic War to an end *(202 B.C.)*
zāmi·a -ae *f* harm, damage, loss
Zanclae·us -a -um *adj* of Zancle
Zancl·ē -ēs *f* old name of Messana in N. Sicily
Zanclēi·us -a -um *adj* of Zancle
zēlotypi·a -ae jealousy
zēlotyp·us -a -um *f* jealous
Zēn·ō(n) -ōnis *m* Zeno the Stoic *(founder of Stoic philosophy and native of Citium in Cyprus, 335–263 B.C.)* ‖ Zeno *(Epicurean philosopher, the teacher of Cicero and Atticus, born c. 150 B.C.)*
Zephyr·us *or* **Zephyr·os -ī** *m* zephr; west wind; wind
Zēt·ēs -ae *m* one of the two sons of Boreas *(Aquilo)*
Zēth·us *or* **Zēt·os -ī** *m* son of Jupiter and Antiope and brother of Amphion
Zeux·is -idis *m* Greek painter of Heraclea in Lucania *(fl c. 400 B.C.)*
zinzi·ō -āre *intr (of a blackbird)* to sing
zmaragd·us -ī *mf* emerald
zōdiac·us -a -um *adj* of the zodiac; **zodiacus circulus** *(or* **orbis)** the zodiac ‖ *m* zodiac
Zōil·us -ī *m* a native of Amphipolis, proverbially stern critic of Homer, Plato, and others
zōn·a -ae *f* belt, sash; money belt; zone
zōnāri·us -a -um *adj* of a belt ‖ *m* belt maker
zōnul·a -ae *f* little belt
zōthēc·a -ae *f* niche; bay, recess
zōthēcul·a -ae *f* little alcove

A

a *indef article (when modifying a substantive, is unexpressed in Latin);* **— little carelessly** parum attente; **— little later** paulo post; **ten denarii — pound** decem denarii per libras; **twice — year** bis in anno
aback *adv* **taken —** attonit•us -a -um
abandon *tr* (de)relinquĕre
abandonment *s* derelicti•o -onis *f*
abashed *adj* erubesc•ens -entis
abate *tr (to lower)* imminuĕre; *(to slacken)* laxare; *(price)* remittĕre ‖ *intr (to lessen)* imminuĕre; *(to decline)* decedĕre; *(of passion)* defervescĕre
abbey *s* abbati•a ae *f*
abbot *s* abb•as -atis *m*
abbreviate *tr* breviare
abbreviation *s* not•a -ae *f*
ABC's *spl* primae litter•ae -arum *fpl;* **to know one's —** litteras scire
abdicate *tr* abdicare ‖ *intr* se abdicare
abdication *s* abdicati•o -onis *f*
abdomen *s* abdom•en -inis *n*
abduct *tr* abducĕre; *(a girl)* rapĕre
abduction *s* rapt•us -ūs *m*
aberration *s (departure from right)* err•or -oris *m; (deviation from straight line)* declinati•o -onis *f*
abet *tr* adjuvare; **to — a crime** minister in maleficio esse
abeyance *s* **to be in —** jacēre
abhor *tr* abhorrēre ab *(w. abl)*
abhorrence *s* detestati•o -onis *f*
abhorrent *adj* **(to)** alien•us -a -um *(abl or* ab + *abl)*
abide *tr* tolerare ‖ *intr* manēre; **— by** stare in *(w. abl)*
abiding *adj* mansur•us -a -um
ability *s (power)* potest•as -atis *f; (mental capacity)* ingen•ium -(i)i *n;* **to the best of one's —** pro sua parte
abject *adj* abject•us -a -um
abjectly *adv* abjecte, humiliter
ablative *s* ablativ•us -i *m*
able *adj (having the power)* pot•ens -entis; *(having mental ability)* ingenios•us -a -um; **not — to fight** non pugnae potens; **not to be — to** nequire *(w. inf);* **to be — to** posse *(w. inf)*
able-bodied *adj* valid•us -a -um
ablution *s* abluti•o -onis *f*
ably *adv* ingeniose
abnormal *adj* enorm•is -is -e
aboard *adv* in nave: **to go — a ship** navem conscendĕre
abode *s* domicil•ium -(i)i *n*
abolish *tr* tollĕre, abolēre
abolition *s* aboliti•o -onis *f*
abominable *adj* detestabil•is -is -e
abominably *adv* execrabiliter, odiose
abominate *tr* abominari, detestari
abomination *s* detestati•o -onis *f; (terrible crime)* flagit•ium -(i)i *n*
aborigines *spl* aborigin•es -um *mfpl*
abortion *s* abort•us -ūs *m;* **to perform an —** partum abigĕre
abortive *adj* abortiv•us -a -um; *(unsuccessful)* irrit•us -a -um
abound *intr* abundare, superesse; **to — in** abundare *(w. abl)*
abounding *adj* **— in** abund•ans -antis *(w. dat or abl)*
about *adv (almost)* fere, ferme; *(approximately)* circa, circiter; **in — ten days** decem circiter diebus
about *prep (of place)* circa, circum *(w. acc); (of number)* circa, ad *(w. acc); (of time)* circa, sub *(w. acc); (concerning)* de *(w. abl)*
above *adv* supra, insuper; **from —** desuper, superne
above *prep* supra, super *(w. acc);* **— all** ante omnia; **— all others** praeter omnes ceteros; **to be —** *(e.g., bribery)* indignari *(w. acc)*
abrasion *s* attrit•us -ūs *m*
abreast *adv* pariter; **to walk — of s.o.** latus alicui tegĕre
abridge *tr* breviare, contrahĕre; **to — a book** in compendium redigĕre
abridgment *s* epitom•e -es *f*
abroad *adv (in a foreign land)* peregre; *(of motion, out of doors)* foras; *(of rest, out of doors)* foris; **from —** extrinsec•us -a -um ; *(w. verbs)* peregre; **to be** *or* **go abroad** peregrinari; **to get —** *(of news)* divulgari
abrogate *tr* abrogare, rescindĕre
abrupt *adj (sudden)* subit•us -a -um; *(rugged)* praerupt•us -a -um
abruptly *adv* subito, repente
abruptness *s* rapidit•as -atis *f*
abscess *s* vomic•a -ae *f*
absence *s* absenti•a -ae *f;* **in my —** me absente
absent *adj* abs•ens -entis; **— without leave** *(mil)* infrequ•ens -entis
absent *tr* **to — oneself** se removēre; *(not show up)* non comparēre
absentee *s* abs•ens -entis *mf*
absolute *adj* absolut•us -a -um, summ•us -a -um; *(unlimited)* infinit•us -a -um; **— power** dominat•us -ūs *m,* tyrann•is -idis *f;* **— ruler** domin•us -i *m,* tyrann•us -i *m*
absolutely *adv (unconditionally)* praecise; *(completely)* utique, prorsus; **— nothing** nihil prorsus; **to rule — over** dominari *(w. dat)*
absolution *s* absoluti•o -onis *f*
absolve *tr* veniam dare *(w. dat);* **to — from** absolvĕre ab *(w. abl)*

absorb *tr* absorbēre, (com)bibĕre; *(fig)* tenēre
absorbent *adj* bibul•us -a -um
abstain *intr* **(from)** se abstinēre *(w. abl)*
abstemious *adj* abstemi•us -a -um
abstinence *s* abstinenti•a -ae *f; (from food)* inedi•a -ae *f*
abstract *tr* **(from)** abstrahĕre (ab + *abl); (an idea)* separare
abstract *s* compend•ium -(i)i *n;* **in the —** in abstracto
abstract *adj (idea)* mente percept•us -a -um; *(quantity)* abstract•us -a -um
abstraction *s* separati•o -onis *f; (idea)* noti•o -onis *f*
abstruse *adj* abstrus•us -a -um
absurd *adj* absurd•us -a -um
absurdity *s* inepti•a -ae *f*
abundance *s* abundanti•a -ae *f,* copi•a -ae *f*
abundant *adj* abund•ans -antis, larg•us -a -um; **to be —** abundare
abundantly *adv* abundanter, copiose
abuse *s (wrong use)* abus•us -ūs *m; (insult)* injuri•a -ae *f,* convic•ium -(i)i *n;* **to heap — on** contumeliosissime maledicĕre *(w. dat)*
abuse *tr (to misuse)* abuti *(w. abl); (sexually)* stuprare; *(w. words)* maledicĕre *(w. dat)*
abusive *adj* **(toward)** contumelios•us -a -um (in + *acc); (person)* maledic•us -a -um; **to be — to** abuti *(w. abl)*
abusively *adv* contumeliose
abyss *s* profund•um -i *n; (fig)* barathr•um -i *n*
academic *adj* academic•us -a -um
academy *s* academi•a -ae *f*
accede *intr* **to — to** assentire *(w. dat)*
accelerate *tr & intr* accelerare
acceleration *s* accelerati•o -onis *f*
accent *s* accent•us -ūs *m,* vo•x -cis *f; (peculiar tone of a people)* son•us -i *m;* **a Greek —** son•us -i *m* linguae Graecae; **to place an acute (grave, circumflex) — on a word** acutam (gravem, circumflexam) vocem in verbo ponĕre
accent *tr (in speaking)* acuĕre; *(in writing)* fastigare
accent mark *s* fastig•ium -(i)i *n*
accentuation *s (in speaking)* accent•us -ūs *m; (in writing, expr. by gerundive):* **careful in the — of syllables** in syllabis acuendis diligens
accept *tr* accipĕre, recipĕre; *(to approve of)* probare
acceptable *adj* **(to)** accept•us -a -um, probabil•is -is -e *(w. dat);* **to be — to** placēre *(w. dat)*
acceptably *adv* apte
acceptance *s* accepti•o -onis *f; (approval)* probati•o -onis *f*
access *s* adit•us -ūs *m,* access•us -ūs *m;* **— to books** copi•a -ae *f* librorum; **to gain — to** penetrare ad *(w. acc);* **to have — to** admitti *(w. dat)*
accessible *adj (of places)* pat•ens -entis; *(of persons)* facil•is -is -e; **to be — to** patēre *(w. dat)*
accession *s (addition)* accessi•o -onis *f;* **— to the throne** regni princip•ium -(i)i *n*
accessory *adj* adjunct•us -a -um; *(to a crime)* consci•us -a -um
accessory *s* affin•is -is *mf;* **— to this crime** affinis *mf* huic facinori
accident *s* cas•us -ūs *m;* **by —** casu
accidental *adj* fortuit•us -a -um; *(nonessential)* adventici•us -a -um
accidentally *adv* casu, forte
acclamation *s (shouts of applause)* clam•or -oris *m,* acclamati•o -onis *f; (oral vote)* conclamati•o -onis *f*
accommodate *tr (adapt)* **(to)** accommodare *(w. dat); (w. lodgings)* hospitium parare *(w. dat); (of an auditorium, etc.)* capĕre
accommodation *s* accommodati•o -onis *f; (convenience)* commodit•as -atis *f;* **—s** deversor•ium -(i)i *n*
accompaniment *s* concinenti•a -ae *f;* **to sing to the — of the flute** ad tibiam concinĕre
accompany *tr* comitari; *(mus)* concinĕre *(w. dat)*
accomplice *s* **(in)** partic•eps -itis *m (w. gen or* in + *abl)*
accomplish *tr* efficĕre, perficĕre
accomplished *adj (skilled)* erudit•us -a -um; *(of a speaker)* disert•us -a -um
accomplishment *s (completion)* peracti•o -onis *f;* **—s** re•s -rum *fpl* gestae
accord *s* consens•us -ūs *m;* **of one's own —** sua sponte, ultro; **to be in — with** convenire *(w. dat);* **with one —** unanimiter
accordance *s* **in — with** secundum *(w. acc),* pro *(w. abl),* ex *(w. abl)*
accordingly *adv* proinde, itaque
according to *prep* secundum *(w. acc)*
accost *tr* appellare, compellare; *(sexually)* lenare
account *s (financial)* rati•o-onis *f; (statement)* memori•a -ae *f; (story)* narrati•o -onis *f; (esteem)* reputati•o -onis *f;* **of little —** parvi pretii; **of no —** nullius pretii; **on — of** ob, propter *(w. acc);* **on that —** propterea; **to be entered into an —** rationibus inferri; **to call to —** rationem poscere; **to give an —** rationem reddere; **to take — of** rationem habēre *(w. gen)*
account *tr (to consider)* ducĕre; *(to esteem)* aestimare; **to — for** rationem reddere *(w. gen);* **to — for his absence** rationem adferre cur absit
accountable *adj* **(for)** re•us -a -um *(w. gen)*

accountant *s* ratiocinat•or -oris *m*
accredited *adj* aestimat•us -a -um
accretion *s* accessi•o -onis *f*
accrue *intr* accrescĕre; **to — to** accedĕre *(w. dat),* redundare in *(w. acc)*
accumulate *tr* accumulare ‖ *intr* crescĕre, augēri
accumulation *s* congest•us -ūs *m; (pile)* cumul•us -i *m*
accuracy *s (pains bestowed)* cur•a -ae *f; (exactness)* subtilit•as -atis *f*
accurate *adj* exact•us -a -um; *(of a definition, observation)* subtil•is -is -e
accurately *adv* exacte; subtiliter
accursed *adj* exsecrat•us -a -um
accusation *s* accusati•o -onis *f; (charge)* crim•en -inis *n;* **to bring an — against** accusare
accusative *s* accusativ•us -i *m*
accusatory *adj* accusatori•us -a -um
accuse *tr* **(of)** accusare *(w. gen or* de + *abl);* **to — falsely** calumniari
accused *s* re•us -i *m,* re•a -ae *f*
accuser *s* accusat•or -oris *m,* accusatr•ix -icis *f*
accusingly *adv* accusatorie
accustom *tr* **(to)** assuefacere *(w. abl, dat or* ad + *acc, or inf);* **to — oneself** *or* **become —ed to** assuescĕre *(w. dat),* ad, in *(w. acc);* **to be —ed to** solēre *(w. inf)*
ache *s* dol•or -oris *m*
ache *intr* dolēre; **my head —s** caput mihi dolet
achieve *tr* conficere; *(to win)* consequi
achievement *s* res, rei *f* gesta
acid *s* acid•um -i *n*
acid *adj* acid•us -a -um
acknowledge *tr* agnoscĕre; *(a child)* tollĕre
acknowledgement *s* confessi•o -onis *f; (money receipt)* apoch•a -ae *f*
acme *s* fastig•ium -(i)i *n*
acorn *s* glan•s -dis *f*
acoustics *spl* acustic•a -orum *npl*
acquaint *tr* **(with)** certiorem facĕre (de + *abl);* **to — oneself with** cognoscĕre
acquaintance *s* familiarit•as -atis *f; (person)* familiar•is -is *mf*
acquainted *adj* not•us -a -um; **— with** gnar•us -a -um *(w. gen);* **to become — with** cognoscĕre
acquiesce *intr* **(in)** acquiescĕre (in + *abl),* stare *(w. abl or* in + *abl)*
acquiescence *s* assens•us -ūs *m*
acquire *tr* adipisci, nancisci
acquisition *s* quaest•us -ūs *m; (thing acquired)* quaesit•um -i *n*
acquisitive *adj* quaestuos•us -a -um
acquit *tr* **(of)** absolvere (de + *abl);* **to — oneself** se gerĕre
acquittal *s* absoluti•o -onis *f*
acre *s* juger•um -i *n (actually .625 of an acre)*
acrid *adj* a•cer -cris -cre
acrimonious *adj* acerb•us -a -um
acrimony *s* acerbit•as -atis *f*
acrobat *s* funambul•us -i *m*
across *adv* in transversum
across *prep* trans *(w. acc)*
act *s (deed, action)* fact•um -i *n; (decree)* decret•um -i *n; (theat)* act•us -ūs *m;* **caught in the —** manifestari•us -a -um; **in the very —** in flagranti; **public —s** act•a -orum *npl*
act *tr (role)* agĕre ‖ *intr* agĕre; **to — as a friend** amicum agĕre; **to — as a servant** servile officium tueri
acting *s* acti•o -onis *f*
action *s* acti•o -onis *f,* act•us -ūs *m; (deed)* fact•um -i *n; (leg)* acti•o -onis *f; (mil)* pugn•a -ae *f; (of speaker)* gest•us -ūs *m;* **to bring an — against** actionem intendere in *(w. acc)*
actionable *adj (leg)* obnoxi•us -a -um
active *adj (life)* actuos•us -a -um; *(mind)* veget•us -a -um; *(busy)* impi•ger -gra -grum; *(gram)* activ•us -a -um; **verb in the — voice** verbum agendi modi
actively *adv* impigre; *(energetically)* gnaviter
activity *s* agitati•o -onis *f; (energy)* industri•a -ae *f,* gnavit•as -atis *f*
actor *s* histri•o -onis *m,* act•or -oris *m; (in comedy)* comoed•us -i *m; (in tragedy)* tragoed•us -i *m*
actress *s* mim•a -ae *f [Note: females did not normally act in regular Roman dramas]*
actual *adj* ver•us -a -um
actuality *s* verit•as -atis *f*
actually *adv* re verā
acumen *s* acum•en -inis *n*
acute *adj (angle, pain)* acut•us -a -um; *(vision, intellect)* a•cer -cris -cre
acutely *adv* acute, acriter
acuteness *s (of senses, intellect)* aci•es -ei *f*
adage *s* proverb•ium -(i)i *n*
adamant *adj* obstinat•us -a -um
adamant *s* adam•as -antis *n*
adapt *tr* accommodare, aptare
adaptation *s* accommodati•o -onis *f*
adapted *adj* apt•us -a -um
add *tr* **(to)** addĕre, adjicĕre *(w. dat or* ad + *acc); (in speaking)* superdicĕre; *(in writing)* subscribĕre; **to — up** computare; **to be —ed to** accedĕre *(w. dat or* ad + *acc)*
adder *s* colub•er -ri *m; (female)* colubr•a -ae *f*
addict *tr* **to be —ed to** se tradere *(w. dat)*
addicted *adj* **— to** dedit•us -a -um *(w. dat)*
addition *s* accessi•o -onis *f,* adjecti•o -onis *f;* **in —** praeterea, insuper; **in — to** praeter *(w. acc),* super *(w. acc)*
additional *adj* additici•us -a -um
address *s* alloqu•ium -(i)i *n; (on letter)* inscripti•o -onis *f; (speech)* conti•o -onis

f, orati•o -onis *f; (adroitness)* dexterit•as -atis *f*
address *tr (to speak to)* alloqui, compellare; *(a letter)* inscriběre
adduce *tr (witness, evidence)* producěre; *(arguments)* afferre
adept *adj* **(in)** perit•us -a -um (+ *gen or abl or* in + *abl)*
adequacy *s* sufficienti•a -ae *f*
adequate *adj* suffici•ens -entis; **to be —** sufficěre
adequately *adv* satis, apte
adhere *intr* **(to)** haerēre, cohaerēre *(w. dat, abl, or* in + *acc);* **to — to** *(fig)* stare in *(w. abl)*
adherence *s* adhaes•us -ūs *m*
adherent *s* assectat•or -oris *m*
adhesion *s* adhaesi•o -onis *f*
adhesive *adj* ten•ax -acis
adieu *interj* vale, valete; **to bid —** valēre jubēre
adjacent *adj* confin•is -is -e; **to be — to** adjacēre *(w. acc, dat,* ad + *acc)*
adjective *s* adjectiv•um -i *n*
adjectively *adv* pro apposito; **the word is used —** vocabulum pro apposito ponitur
adjoin *tr* adjacēre *(w. dat)*
adjoining *adj* conjunct•us -a -um
adjourn *tr* differre; *(leg)* ampliare ‖ *intr* diferri
adjournment *s* dilati•o -onis *f*; *(leg)* amplificati•o -onis *f*
adjudge *tr* adjudicare
adjudicate *tr* addicěre
adjunct *s* adjunct•um -i *n*
adjure *tr* obtestari
adjust *tr* **(to)** aptare, accommodare (*w. dat or* ad + *acc); (to put in order)* componěre ‖ *intr* **(to)** se accommodare (+ *dat or* ad + *acc)*
adjustment *s* accommodati•o -onis *f; (of a robe)* structur•a -ae *f*
adjutant *s* opti•o -onis *m*
administer *tr (to manage)* administrare; *(medicines)* adhibēre; *(oath)* adigěre; **to — justice** jus dicěre
administration *s* administrati•o -onis *f;* **— of justice** jurisdicti•o -onis *f;* **— of public affairs** procurati•o -onis *f* reipublicae
administrative *adj* ad administrationem pertin•ens -entis
administrator *s* administrat•or -oris *m,* procurat•or -oris *m*
admirable *adj* admirabil•is -is -e
admiral *s* classis praefect•us -i *m*
admiration *s* admirati•o -onis *f*
admire *tr* admirari
admirer *s* admirat•or -oris *m; (lover)* am•ans -antis *mf*
admiringly *adv use participle:* admir•ans -antis
admissible *adj* accipiend•us -a -um
admission *s* confessi•o -onis *f; (being let in)* adit•us -ūs *m,* access•us -ūs *m;* **by his own —** confessione sua
admit *tr (to allow to enter)* admittěre; *(e.g., into the senate)* asciscěre; *(to grant as valid)* dare; *(to acknowledge)* agnoscěre; **it is —ed** constat; **to — flatly** profiteri palam
admittedly *adv* sane
admonish *tr* admonēre
admonition *s (act)* admoniti•o -onis *f; (words used)* monit•um -i *n*
adolescence *s* adulescenti•a -ae *f*
adolescent *adj* adulesc•ens -entis
adolescent *s* adulescentul•us -i *m*
adopt *tr (a child)* adoptare; *(an adult)* arrogare; *(customs, laws)* asciscěre; *(a plan)* capěre, inire
adoption *s* adopti•o -onis *f; (of an adult)* arrogati•o -onis *f; (of a custom)* assumpti•o -onis *f*
adoptive *adj* adoptiv•us -a -um
adorable *adj* adorand•us -a -um
adoration *s* adorati•o -onis *f*
adore *tr* adorare; *(fig)* demirari
adorn *tr* decorare, ornare
adornment *s (act)* exornati•o -onis *f; (object)* ornament•um -i *n*
Adriatic *adj* Adriatic•us -a -um
adrift *adv* **to be —** fluctuare; **to set —** aperto mari committěre
adroit *adj* callid•us -a -um; *(dexterous)* dex•ter -tra -trum
adroitness *s* calliditas -atis *f;* dexterit•as -atis *f*
adulation *s* adulati•o -onis *f*
adult *adj* adult•us -a -um; **— population** pub•es -is *f*
adult *s* adult•us -i *m;* **—s** pub•es -is *f*
adulterate *tr* adulterare
adulteration *s* adulterati•o -onis *f*
adulterer *s* adult•er -eri *m*
adulteress *s* adulter•a -ae *f*
adulterous *adj* adulterin•us -a -um
adultery *s* adulter•ium -(i)i *n;* **to commit —** adulterare
advance *tr (to more forward)* promovēre; *(money)* in antecessum solvěre; *(a cause)* fovēre; *(to promote)* provehěre; *(an opinion)* praeferre ‖ *intr (to go forward)* proceděre; *(of steady movement on foot)* inceděre; *(in riding or sailing)* provehi; *(to progress)* proficěre; *(mil)* gradum *(or* pedem) inferre; **as the day —ed** die procedente
advance *s* progress•us -ūs *m;* **in —** ante; **to pay in —** pecuniam nondum debitam solvěre
advanced *adj* provect•us -a -um; **at an —ed age** provectā aetate; **—ed in years** grand•is -is -e natu *(or* aevo)
advance guard *s* primum agm•en -inis *n*
advance man *s* praecurs•or -oris *m*

advancement *s* promoti•o -onis *f*
advantage *s (benefit)* commod•um -i *n; (a real good)* bon•um -i *n; (profit)* emolument•um -i *n; (usefulness)* utilit•as -atis *f;* **to be of —** prodesse; **to have an — over** praestare *(w. dat);* **to take — of** uti *(w. abl); (pej)* sibi quaestui habēre; **to take — of an opportunity** occasionem nancisci
advantageous *adj* util•is -is -e, fructuos•us -a -um
advantageously *adv* utiliter
advent *s* advent•us -ūs *m*
adventure *s* cas•us -ūs *m*
adventurer *s* periclitat•or -oris *m*
adventurous *adj* aud•ax -acis
adverb *s* adverb•ium -(i)i *n*
adverbial *adj* adverbial•is -is -e
adverbially *adv* adverbialiter
adversary *s* adversar•ius -(i)i *m,* adversatr•ix -icis *f*
adversative *adj* adversativ•us -a -um
adverse *adj (mostly winds)* advers•us -a -um; *(times)* asp•er -era -erum; **— circumstances** re•s -rum *fpl* asperae
adversely *adv* male, infeliciter
adversity *s* re•s -rum *fpl* adversae; *(fig)* re•s -rum *fpl* asperae
advertise *tr* proscriběre
advertisement *s (poster)* proscripti•o -onis *f*
advice *s* consil•ium -(i)i *n;* **to ask s.o. for —** aliquem consulěre, aliquem consilium rogare; **to give —** suadēre *(w. dat)*
advisable *adj* **it is — to** expedit *(w. inf)*
advise *tr* suadēre *(w. dat)*
advisedly *adv* consulto
adviser *s* consult•or -oris *m*
advocate *s (leg)* advocat•us -i *m; (fig)* patron•us -i *m*
advocate *tr* suadēre
aedile *s* aedil•is -is *m*
aedileship *s* aedilit•as -atis *f*
aegis *s* aeg•is -idis *f; (fig)* tutel•a -ae *f*
aerial *adj* aëri•us -a -um
affability *s* affabilit•as -atis *f*
affable *adj* affabil•is -is -e
affably *adv* affabiliter
affair *s* negot•ium -i(i) *n,* res, rei *f; (love)* am•or -oris *m*
affect *tr (to influence)* afficěre; *(to move)* movēre; *(to pretend)* simulare
affectation *s* affectati•o -onis *f*
affected *adj* simulat•us -a -um; *(style)* putid•us -a -um
affection *s* am•or -oris *m,* affecti•o -onis *f*
affectionate *adj* am•ans -antis
affectionately *adv* amanter
affidavit *s* per tabulas testimon•ium -(i)i *n*
affiliated *adj* **to be — with a college** in collegio cooptari
affinity *s* affinit•as -atis *f;* **to have no — with** longe remot•us -a -um ab *(w. abl)*
affirm *tr* affirmare
affirmation *s* affirmati•o -onis *f*
affirmative *adj* affirm•ans -antis; **I reply in the —** aio; **to give an — answer** fateri ita se rem habere
affix *tr* affigěre
afflict *tr* affligěre; **to be —ed with** conflictari *(w. abl)*
affliction *s (cause of distress)* mal•um -i *n; (state of distress)* miseri•a -ae *f*
affluence *s* diviti•ae -arum *fpl*
affluent *adj* div•es -itis
afford *tr (opportunity, etc.)* praebēre; **I cannot —** res mihi non suppetit ad *(w. acc)*
affray *s* rix•a -ae *f*
affront *tr* contumeliā affligěre
affront *s* contumeli•a -ae *f*
afield *adv* in agro; *(astray)* vag•us -a -um, err•ans -antis
afloat *adj* nat•ans -antis; **to get a ship —** navem deducěre
afoot *adv* pedibus; **to be —** *(fig)* geri; **what is —?** quid geritur?
aforementioned *adj* supra dict•us -a -um
afraid *adj* timid•us -a -um; **to be — (of)** timēre; **to make —** terrēre
afresh *adv* de integro, de novo
Africa *s* Afric•a -ae *f*
African *adj* African•us -a -um
African *s* Af•er -ri *m*
after *prep* post *(w. acc),* ab, ex *(w. abl); (in rank or degree)* secundum *(w. acc);* **(and) — all** (et) re verā; **— an interval** interposito deinde spatio; **— that** subinde; **a little —** paulo post; **named — his father** a patre nominat•us -a -um: **right —** sub *(w. acc);* **the day —** postridie (quam)
after *conj* postquam
afternoon *s* postmeridian•um -i *n;* **in the —** post meridiem, postmeridie
afternoon *adj* postmeridian•us -a -um
afterthought *s* posterior cogitati•o -onis *f*
afterwards *adv* postea
again *adv* iterum, rursus; *(hereafter)* posthac; *(in turn)* invicem; *(further)* porro; **— and —** identidem; **once —** denuo; **over —** denuo
against *prep* contra *(w. acc); (in a hostile manner)* adversus *(w. acc),* in *(w. acc);* **— the current** adverso flumine; **to lean — a tree** se ad arborem applicare; **to be —** adversari
age *s (time of life)* aet•as -atis *f; (era)* saecul•um -i *n,* aet•as -atis *f;* **don't ask me my —** noli me percontari meum aevum; **of the same —** aequaev•us -a -um; **old —** senect•us -utis *f;* **to be of —** sui juris esse; **twelve years of —** duodecim annos nat•us -a -um; **under —** inpub•is -is -e
age *tr* aetate conficěre ‖ *intr* maturescěre; *(to grow old)* senescěre

aged *adj* aetate provect•us -a -um; **a man — forty** vi•r -i *m* annos quadraginta natus
agency *s* acti•o -onis *f; (means)* oper•a -ae *f; (office)* procurati•o -onis *f;* **through the — of** per *(w. acc)*
agent *s (doer)* act•or -oris *m*; *(com)* procurat•or -oris *m,* negotiorum curat•or -oris *m;* **man is a free —** homo sui juris est
agglomeration *s* congeri•es -ei *f*
aggrandize *tr* amplificare
aggrandizement *s* amplicati•o -onis *f*
aggravate *tr (to make worse)* aggravare; *(a wound)* ulcerare; *(to annoy)* vexare; **to become —d** ingravescĕre
aggravating *adj* molest•us -a -um
aggravation *s (annoyance)* vexati•o -onis *f*
aggregate *adj* tot•us -a -um; **in the —** in toto
aggression *s* incursi•o -onis *f;* **to commit — against** incursionem hostiliter facere in *(w. acc)*
aggressive *adj* hostil•is -is -e
aggressor *s* qui bellum ultro infert
aggrieve *tr* dolore afficĕre
aggrieved *adj* qui injuriam accepit
aghast *adj* stupefact•us -a -um; **to stand —** obstupescĕre
agile *adj* agil•is -is -e; *(mind)* veget•us -a -um
agility *s* agilit•as -atis *f*
agitate *tr (to move rapidly to and fro)* agitare; *(to excite)* agitare; *(to disturb)* perturbare
agitated *adj (sea)* tumultuos•us -a -um; *(fig)* turbulent•us -a -um
agitation *s (violent movement)* agitati•o -onis *f; (mental or political disturbance)* commoti•o -onis *f*
agitator *s* vulgi turbat•or -oris *m*
ago *adv* abhinc; **a short time —** haud ita pridem; **long —** jamdudum, multo ante; **some time —** pridem; **three years —** abhinc tres annos
agonize *intr* (ex)cruciari
agonizing *adj* cruci•abil•is -is -e
agony *s* acerbissimus dol•or -oris *m;* **to be in —** dolore angi
agrarian *adj* agrari•us -a -um
agree *intr* consentire; *(to make a bargain)* pascisci; *(of facts)* constare, convenire; **it had been —ed** convenerat; **it is generally —ed** fere convenit; **to — with s.o. about** assentire alicui de *(w. abl)*
agreeable *adj (pleasing)* grat•us -a -um; *(of persons)* commod•us -a -um; *(acceptable)* accept•us -a -um
agreeably *adv* grate, accommodate
agreement *s* consens•us -ūs *m; (pact)* pacti•o -onis *f,* pact•um -i *n; (proportion)* symmetri•a -ae *f;* **according to the —** ex pacto: **there is general —** fere convenit
agricultural *adj* rustic•us -a -um; **the Latins were an — people** Latini agriculturae studebant
agriculture *s* agricultur•a -ae *f*
ah *interj* ah!; *(of grief, indignation)* vah!; *(of admiration)* eja!; **— me** eheu!
ahead *adv use verb with prefix* prae- *or* pro-; **— of time** ante tempus; **to get — of s.o.** aliquem praevenire; **go —, tell mihi!** agedum, dic mihi!; **to walk — of s.o.** aliquem praecedĕre
aid *s* auxil•ium -(i)i *n*
aid *tr* adjuvare
aide-de-camp *s* opti•o -onis *m*
ail *tr* dolēre *(w. dat)*
ailment *s* mal•um -i *n*
aim *s (mark)* scop•us -i *m; (fig)* fin•is -is *m,* proposit•um -i *n*
aim *tr* (in)tendĕre ‖ *intr* **to — at** *(a target)* destinare; *(to try to hit)* petĕre; *(to try to attain)* affectare; *(virtue, renown)* spectare
aimless *adj* van•us -a -um
aimlessly *adv* sine ratione
air *s* a•ër -eris *(acc:* aëra) *m; (upper air)* aeth•er -eris *m; (air in motion)* aur•a -ae *f; (attitude)* habit•us -ūs *m;* **— shaft** aestuar•ium -(i)i *n;* **in the open —** sub divo; **to let in fresh —** auras admittĕre; **to put on —s** se jactare; **up in the —** *(fig)* in medio relict•us -a -um
air *tr* ventilare; *(to disclose)* patefacĕre
airhead *s (coll)* cucurbit•a -ae *f*
airily *adv* hilare
airing *s* ventilati•o -onis *f; (of an idea)* praedicati•o -onis *f*
airy *adj* perflabil•is -is -e
aisle *s* al•a -ae *f*
ajar *adj* semiapert•us -a -um
akimbo *adv* **to stand with arms —** ansat•us -a -um stare
akin *adj* (**to**) finitim•us -a -um *(w. dat)*
alabaster *s* alabas•ter -tri *m*
alacrity *s* alacrit•as -atis *f*
alarm *s (loud notice of danger)* clam•or -oris *m; (sudden fright)* pav•or -oris *m;* **to sound the —** signum monitorium dare; *(mil)* classicum canĕre
alarm *tr* perturbare; **to become —ed** expavescĕre
alas *interj* eheu!
albumen *s* album•en -inis *n*
alchemist *s* alchemist•a -ae *m*
alchemy *s* alchimi•a -ae *f*
alcohol *s* spirit•us -ūs *m* vini
alcoholic *adj* alcoholic•us -a -um
alcoholic *s* bibos•us -i *m*
alcove *s* zothec•a -ae *f*
ale *s* cerevisi•a -ae *f*
alert *adj* intent•us -a -um; **— mind** erecta men•s -tis *f*
alert *s* monitorium sign•um -i *n;* **on the —** intent•us -a -um; **to sound the —** signum monitorium dare

alert *tr (to warn)* praemonēre; *(to rouse)* excitare
alertness *s* alacrit•as -atis *f*
alias *s* nom•en -inis *n* mentitum
alibi *s (excuse)* speci•es -ei *f;* **to have an —** dicĕre se alibi fuisse; *(fig)* se excusare
alien *adj* peregrin•us -a -um
alien *s* alienigen•a -ae *mf*
alienate *tr* alienare
alienation *s* alienati•o -onis *f*
alight *intr* descendĕre; *(from a horse)* desilire; *(of birds)* **(on)** insidĕre *(w. dat)*
alight *adj* illustr•is -is -e
alike *adj* simil•is -is -e
alike *adv* pariter
alimony *s* alimon•ium -(i)i *n*
alive *adj* viv•us -a -um; *(fig)* ala•cer -cris -cre
all *adj* omn•is -is -e; *(denoting a unity of parts in a body)* univers•us -a -um; **— the most learned** doctissimus quisque
all *pron* omn•es -ium *mpl & fpl,* omn•ia -ium *npl;* **in —** in summā; **not at —** haudquaquam; **nothing at —** nihil omnino; **one's —** propr•ium -(i)i *n*
all *adv* **— over** undique; **— along** usque ab initio; **— but** tantum non; **— the better** tanto melius; **— the more** eo magis; **— too late** immo jam sero
allay *tr* sedare; **to be —ed** temperari
allegation *s* affirmati•o -onis *f*
allege *tr* arguĕre; **—ing that** tamquam *(w. subj)*
allegiance *s* fid•es -ei *f;* **to swear —** sacramentum dicĕre
allegorical *adj* allegoric•us -a -um
allegorize *intr* allegorice scribĕre, allegorizare
allegory *s* allegori•a -ae *f*
allergic *adj* **(to)** obnoxi•us -a -um *(+ dat)*
allergy *s* allergi•a -ae *f*
alleviate *tr* levare
alleviation *s* levati•o -onis *f*
alley *s* angiport•us -ūs *m*
alliance *s (by marriage)* affinit•as -atis *f; (of states)* foed•us -eris *n*
allied *adj (pol)* foederat•us -a -um, soci•us -a -um; *(related)* finitim•us -a -um
alligator *s* crocodil•us -i *m*
alliteration *s* alliterati•o -onis *f*
allocate *tr (funds)* attribuĕre; *(to assign)* distribuĕre
allocation *s (of funds)* attributi•o -onis *f; (money)* attribut•um -i *n*
allot *tr* assignare
allotment *s* assignati•o -onis *f;* **an — of land** ag•er -ri *m* assignatus
allow *tr* concedĕre *(w. dat),* sinĕre; **it is —ed** licet; **it is — by Caesar** licet per Caesarem; **to — for** indulgēre *(w. dat);* **to — of** admittĕre
allowable *adj* licit•us -a -um; **it is —** fas est
allowance *s (permission)* permissi•o -onis *f; (concession)* veni•a -ae *f; (portion)* porti•o -onis *f; (money)* stipend•ium -(i)i *n; (food)* diari•a -orum *npl*
alloy *s* mixtur•a -ae *f; (of metals)* temperati•o -onis *f*
alloy *tr* miscēre et temperare
all-seeing *adj* omnitu•ens -entis
all-time *adj* post hominum memoriam
allude *intr* **to — to** attingĕre
allure *tr* allicĕre
allurement *s* blandiment•um -i *n*
alluring *adj* bland•us -a -um
allusion *s* significati•o -onis *f*
allusive *adj* obliqu•us -a -um
allusively *adv* oblique
alluvial *adj* alluvi•us -a -um; **— soil** alluvi•o -onis *f*
alluvium *s* alluvi•o -onis *f*
ally *s* soc•ius -(i)i *m,* soci•a -ae *f*
ally *tr* sociare
almanac *s* fast•i -orum *mpl*
almighty *adj* omnipot•ens -entis
almond *s* amygdal•a -ae *f*
almond tree *s* amygdal•us -i *f*
almost *adv* paene, fere
alms *spl* stip•s -is *f*
aloft *adv (motion & rest)* sublime
alone *adj* sol•us -a -um; *(only)* un•us -a -um; **all —** persol•us -a -um; **to leave —** deserĕre; **to let —** mittĕre
alone *adv* solum
along *adv* porro, protinus; **all —** jamdudum; **— with** unā cum *(w. abl);* **to bring —** afferre; **to get — with** consentire cum *(w. abl)*
along *prep* per *(w. acc),* praeter *(w. acc)* secundum *(w. acc)*
aloof *adv* procul; **to keep — from the senate** curiā abstinēre; **to stand —** abstare
aloud *adv* clare
alphabet *s* element•a -orum *npl*
alphabetical *adj* litterarum ordine
alphabetically *adv* **to arrange —** in litteram digĕre
Alpine *adj* Alpin•us -a -um
Alps *spl* Alp•es -ium *fpl*
already *adv* jam
also *adv* etiam, et, necnon
altar *s* ar•a -ae *f*
alter *tr* mutare, commutare
alterable *adj* mutabil•is -is -e
alteration *s* mutati•o -onis *f*
altercation *s* altercati•o -onis *f*
alternate *adj* altern•us -a -um
alternate *tr & intr* alternare
alternately *adv* invicem, per vices
alternation *s* vicissitud•o -inis *f*
alternative *adj* alt•er -era -erum, alternat•us -a -um
alternative *s* alternata condici•o -onis *f,* opti•o -onis *f*
although *conj* quamquam

altitude *s* altitud•o -inis *f*
altogether *adv* omnino
altruism *s* beneficenti•a -ae *f*
always *adv* semper
amalgamate *tr* miscēre
amalgamation *s* mixti•o -onis *f*
amass *tr* cumulare
amateur *s* idiot•a -ae *m*
amatory *adj* amatori•us -a -um
amaze *tr* obstupefacĕre
amazed *adj* **(at)** stupefact•us -a -um (cum + *abl)*
amazement *s* stup•or -oris *m*
amazing *adj* mir•us -a -um
amazingly *adv* mirabiliter
Amazon *s* Amaz•on -onis *f*
Amazonian *adj* Amazoni•us -a -um
ambassador *s* legat•us -i *m*
amber *s* electr•um -i *n*
ambidextrous *adj* aequiman•us -a -um
ambiguity *s* ambiguit•as -atis *f*
ambiguous *adj* ambigu•us -a -um
ambition *s* ambiti•o -onis *f*
ambitious *adj* laudis *(or* gloriae) studios•us -a -um; *(worker)* assidu•us -a -um; *(self-seeking)* ambitios•us -a -um
amble *intr* ambulare
ambrosia *s* ambrosi•a -ae *f*
ambush *s* insidi•ae -arum *fpl*
ambush *tr* insidiari *(w. dat)*
ameliorate *tr* corrigĕre, meliorem *or* melius facĕre ‖ *intr* melior *or* melius fieri
amenable *adj* tractabil•is -is -e
amend *tr* emendare ‖ *intr* proficĕre
amendment *s* emendati•o -onis *f*
amends *spl* satisfacti•o -onis *f;* **to make —** satisfacĕre
amenity *s* amoenit•as -atis *f; (comfort)* commod•um -i *n*
America *s* Americ•a -ae *f;* **Central —** America Media; **North —** America Septentrionalis; **South —** America Australis
American *adj* American•us -a -um
American *s* American•us -i *m,* American•a -ae *f*
amethyst *s* amethyst•us -i *f*
amiable *adj* amabil•is -is -e
amiably *adv* suaviter
amicable *adj* amic•us -a -um
amicably *adv* amice
amid *prep* inter *(w. acc)*
amiss *adv* perperam; **to take —** aegre ferre
amity *s* amiciti•a -ae *f*
ammonia *s* ammoniac•a -ae *f*
ammonium *s* ammon•ium -(i)i *n*
ammunition *s* missilium copi•a -ae *f*
amnesty *s* veni•a -ae *f*
among *prep* inter *(w. acc),* apud *(w. acc);* **from —** ex *(w. abl)*
amorous *adj* amatori•us -a -um; *(sexual)* libidinos•us -a -um
amorphous *adj* inform•is -is -e
amount *s* summ•a -ae *f*
amount *intr* **to — to** efficĕre ad *(w. acc),* esse ad *(w. acc);* **it —s to the same thing** tantundem est; **to — to something** bonum exitum umquam factur•us -a -um esse; **what does it — to?** quid istuc valet?
amphitheater *s* amphitheatr•um -i *n*
ample *adj* ampl•us -a -um
amplification *s* amplificati•o -onis *f*
amplify *tr* amplificare
amply *adv* ample
amputate *tr* amputare
amputation *s* amputati•o -onis *f*
amuck *adv* **to run —** delirare
amulet *s* amulet•um -i *n*
amuse *tr* oblectare; **to — oneself** se oblectare
amusement *s* oblectati•o -onis *f; (that which amuses)* oblectament•um -i *n*
amusing *adj* festiv•us -a -um
an *indef article, unexpressed in Latin*
anachronism *s* temporum inversi•o -onis *f*
analogous *adj* analog•us -a -um
analogy *s* analogi•a -ae *f*
analysis *s* analys•is -is -eos *f;* **to make an — of a compound substance** compositum in principia redigĕre
analytical *adj* analytic•us -a -um
analytically *adv* per analysin
analyze *tr* in principia redigĕre; *(words)* subtiliter enodare
anapest *s* anapaestus pe•s -dis *m*
anapestic *adj* anapaestic•us -a -um
anarchist *s* civ•is -is *m* seditiosus
anarchy *s* effrenata licenti•a -ae *f;* **to cause —** turbare omnia et permiscēre; **to have —** nullum omnino imperium habēre
anathema *s* anathem•a -atis *n*
anatomical *adj* anatomic•us -a -um
anatomy *s* anatomi•a -ae *f*
ancestor *s* proav•us -i *m;* **—s** major•es -um *mpl*
ancestry *s* gen•us -eris *n*
anchor *s* ancor•a -ae *f;* **to lie at —** in ancoris stare; **to weigh —** ancoram tollĕre
anchor *tr* ad ancoras deligare ‖ *intr* in ancoris stare
anchorage *s* stati•o -onis *f*
ancient *adj* antiqu•us -a -um, vetust•us -a -um; **in — times** antiquitus; **the —s** veter•es -um *mpl; (authors)* antiqu•i -orum *mpl*
and *conj* et, ac, atque, -que; **— so forth** et perinde; **— then** deincepsque
anecdote *s* fabell•a -ae *f*
anemic *adj* exsangu•is -is -e
anew *adv* denuo
angel *s* angel•us -i *m*
angelic *adj* angelic•us -a -um
anger *s* ir•a -ae *f*
anger *tr* irritare
angle *s* angul•us -i *m*

angler *s* piscat•or -oris *m*
angrily *adv* irate
angry *adj* irat•us -a -um; **to be — (with)** irasci *(w. dat);* **to make —** irritare
anguish *s* ang•or -oris *m*
angular *adj* angular•is -is -e
animal *s* anim•al -alis *n; (wild beast)* besti•a -ae *f,* fer•a -ae *f; (domestic)* pec•us -oris *n*
animate *adj* animal•is -is -e
animate *tr* animare; *(fig)* excitare
animated *adj* veget•us -a -um
animation *s (bestowal of life)* animati•o -onis *f; (liveliness)* vig•or -oris *m*
animosity *s* acerbit•as -atis *f*
ankle *s* tal•us -i *m*
ankle-length *adj* talar•is -is -e
anklet *s* periscel•is -idis *f*
annalist *s* annalium script•or -oris *m*
annals *spl* annal•es -ium *mpl*
annex *s* diaet•a -ae *f*
annex *tr (nations)* adjicĕre, adjungĕre
annexation *s* adjecti•o -onis *f*
annihilate *tr* delēre, ex(s)tinguĕre
annihilation *s* exstincti•o -onis *f*
anniversary *adj* anniversari•us -a -um
anniversary *s* festus di•es -ei *m* anniversarius
annotate *tr* annotare
annotation *s* annotati•o -onis *f*
announce *tr* nuntiare, indicĕre; *(to report)* renuntiare; *(officially)* denuntiare; *(laws, etc.)* proscribĕre
announcement *s* denuntiati•o -onis *f; (report)* renuntiati•o -onis *f*
announcer *s* nunt•ius -(i)i *m*
annoy *tr* vexare, male habēre; **to be —ed at** stomachari ob *(w. acc)*
annoyance *s* molesti•a -ae *f*
annoying *adj* molest•us -a -um
annual *adj* annu•us -a -um
annually *adv* quotannis
annuity *s* annua pecuni•a -ae *f*
annul *tr (contract, law)* infirmare; *(a law)* abrogare; **to — a marriage** dirimĕre nuptias
annulment *s* infirmati•o -onis *f;* abrogati•o -onis *f*
anoint *tr* ung(u)ĕre
anointing *s* uncti•o -onis *f*
anomalous *adj* enorm•is -is -e; *(gram)* anomal•us -a -um
anomaly *s* enormit•as -atis *f; (gram)* anomali•a -ae *f*
anonymous *adj* sine nomine
anonymously *adv* sine nomine
another *adj* ali•us -a -ud; **—'s** alien•us -a -um; **at — time** alias; **in — place** alibi; **one after —** alius ex alio; **one —** inter se; **one…—** ali•us -a -ud…ali•us -a -ud; **to — place** alio
answer *tr* respondēre *(w. dat); (by letter)* rescribĕre *(w. dat); (to correspond to)* congruĕre cum *(w. abl)* ‖ *intr* **to — for** rationem reddere *(w. gen);* **to — to the name of** vocari
answer *s* respons•um -i *n; (solution)* explicati•o -onis *f*
answerable *adj* re•us -a -um; **to be — for** praestare *(acc)*
ant *s* formic•a -ae *f*
antagonism *s* adversit•as -atis *f*
antagonist *s* adversar•ius -(i)i *m,* adversatr•ix -icis *f*
antarctic *adj* antarctic•us -a -um
antecedent *adj* anteced•ens -entis
antecedent *s* anteced•ens -entis *n; (gram)* nom•en -inis *n* antecedens
antechamber *s* atriol•um -i *n*
antedate *tr* diem vero antiquiorem ascribĕre *(w. dat); (to precede in time)* aetate antecedĕre *(w. dat or acc)*
antelope *s* antilop•e -es *f*
antenna *s* antenn•a -ae *f*
antepenult *s* syllab•a -ae *f* antepaenultima
anterior *adj* anter•ior -ior -ius
anteroom *s* atriol•um -i *n*
anthem *s* hymn•us -i *m* elatior; **national —** patrium carm•en -inis *n*
anthology *s* anthologi•a -ae *f*
anticipate *tr* anticipare; *(to expect)* spectare; *(mentally)* praesumĕre
anticipation *s* anticipati•o -onis *f,* praesumpti•o -onis *f*
anticlimax *s* clim•ax -acis *f* inversa
antics *spl* mot•us -uum *mpl* ridiculi
antidote *s* antidot•ium -(i)i *n*
antipathy *s* antipathi•a -ae *f*
antiquarian *adj* antiquari•us -a -um
antiquarian *s* antiquar•ius -(i)i *m*
antiquated *adj* antiquat•us -a -um
antique *adj* prisc•us -a -um ; **— statues** sign•a -orum *npl* operis antiqui
antique *s* antiqui artificis op•us -eris *n*
antiquity *s* antiquit•as -atis *f*
anti-Semitic *adj* Judaeis avers•us -a -um
anti-Semitism *s* Judaeorum od•ium -(i) *n*
antithesis *s* contrar•ium -(i)i *n*
antler *s* corn•u -us *n*
antonym *s* verb•um -i *n* contrarium
anus *s* an•us -i *m*
anvil *s* inc•us -dis *f*
anxiety *s* anxiet•as -atis *f*
anxious *adj* anxi•us -a -um; *(eager)* **(for)** studios•us -a -um *(w. gen)*
anxiously *adv* anxie; *(eagerly)* avide
any *adj* ull•us -a -um; *(after* si, ne, nisi, num) quis, quid; **at — time** aliquando
any *adv* **— longer** diutius; **— more** amplius
anybody *pron* aliquis; *(after* si, nisi, ne, num) quis; *(interrog)* ecquis, numquis; *(after negative)* quisquam; **— you wish** quisvis, quislibet
anyhow *adv* quoquomodo; *(in any event)* utique
anyone *see* **anybody**

anything *pron* aliquid, quicquam; *(after* si, nisi, ne, num) quid; *(interrog)* ecquid, numquid; *(after negative)* quisquam; — **you wish** quidlibet; **hardly** — nihil fere
anyway *adv* quoquomodo; *(at least, in any event)* utique
anywhere *adv (in any place)* alicubi; *(frequently after* si) uspiam; *(usu. w. negative)* usquam; *(anywhere you please)* ubivis; *(to any place, usu. w.* si, ne, num) quo
aorta *s* grandis ven•a -ae *f* cordis
apart *adv* seorsum, separatim; — **from** praeter *(w. acc);* **to be** — distare; **to fall** — dilabi; **to set** — seponĕre; **to stand** — distare
apartment *s* cenacul•um -i *n*
apartment building *s* insul•a -ae *f*
apathetic *adj* lent•us -a -um
apathy *s* apathi•a -ae *f*
ape *s* sim•ius -(i)i *m,* simi•a -ae *f*
ape *tr* imitari
aperture *s* foram•en -inis *n*
apex *s* cacum•en -inis *n*
aphorism *s* sententi•a -ae *f*
aphrodisiac *s* sature•um -i *n*
apiary *s* alvear•ium -(i)i *n*
apiece *adv no exact Latin equivalent, but its sense is expressed by distributive numerals, e.g.:* **they went out with two garments** — cum binis vestimentis exierunt; **he stationed one legion — at Brindisium and Tarentum** legiones singulas posuit Brindisi, Tarenti
aplomb *s* confidenti•a -ae *f*
apocalypse *s* apocalyps•is -is *f*
apocryphal *adj* apocryph•us -a -um
apogee *s* apogae•um -i *n*
apologetic *adj* se excus•ans -antis
apologize *intr* satis facĕre; **to — for s.o.** aliquem excusare
apology *s* excusati•o -onis *f;* **to make an — for** excusare
apoplectic *adj* apoplectic•us -a -um
apoplexy *s* apoplexi•a -ae *f*
apostasy *s* apostasi•a -ae *f*
apostate *s* apostat•a -ae *m*
apostle *s* apostol•us -i *m*
apostolic *adj* apostolic•us -a -um
apostrophe *s* apostroph•e -es *f;* *(gram)* apostroph•us -i *f*
apothecary *s (drugstore)* tabern•a -ae *f* medicina; *(druggist)* medicamentar•ius -(i)i *m*
apotheosis *s* apotheosis -is *f*
appall *tr* exterrēre
apparatus *s* apparat•us -ūs *m*
apparel *s* vestit•us -ūs *m*
apparel *tr* vestire
apparent *adj* manifest•us -a -um; *(seeming)* fict•us -a -um
apparently *adv* specie, per speciem
apparition *s* speci•es -ei *f*
appeal *intr (leg) (to a magistrate)* appellare *(acc); (to the people)* provocare **(ad +** *acc);* **to — to** *(to be attractive to)* allicĕre; *(to the gods)* obtestari
appeal *s (leg)* appellati•o -onis *f; (to the people)* provocati•o -onis *f; (entreaty)* obtestati•o -onis *f; (attractiveness)* suavit•as -atis *f*
appealing *adj* suav•is -is -e; *(imploring)* suppl•ex -icis
appear *intr (to be visible)* apparēre; *(to show up)* comparēre; *(to arise suddenly)* oriri; *(to seem)* vidēri; *(in public, on the stage)* prodire; **to begin to** — patescĕre
appearance *s (becoming visible)* aspect•us -ūs *m; (outward show)* speci•es -ei *f; (likelihood)* similitud•o -inis *f; (vision)* vis•um -i *n;* **for the sake of —s** ad speciem; **to all —s** ut videtur; **to keep up —s** speciem gerĕre; **to make one's — in public** in publicum prodire; **to make one's appearance on the stage** in proscaenium prodire
appease *tr* placare
appeasement *s* placati•o -onis *f*
appellation *s* appellati•o -onis *f*
append *tr* subscribĕre
appendage *s* append•ix -icis *f*
appendix *s* append•ix -icis *f; (anat)* append•ix -icis *f* coli
appetite *s* appetit•us -ūs *m; (for food)* cibi appetenti•a -ae *f;* **lack of** — inedi•a -ae *f;* **to control the —s** appetitūs regĕre
appetizer *s* gustati•o -onis *f*
applaud *tr* applaudĕre *(w. acc or dat); (to praise)* approbare **||** *intr* plaudĕre
applause *s* plaus•us -ūs *m;* **to look for** — plausūs captare
apple *s* mal•um -i *n;* **— of my eye** meus ocell•us -i *m*
apple peel *s* malicor•ium -(i)i *n*
apple tree *s* mal•us -i *f*
appliance *s* instrument•um -i *n*
applicable *adj* **(to)** commod•us -a -um *(w. dat)*
applicant *s* petit•or -oris *m*
application *s (act of requesting)* petiti•o -onis *f; (act of applying)* adhibiti•o -onis *f; (industry)* sedulit•as -atis *f; (med)* foment•um -i *n*
apply *tr (to put on or to)* **(to)** adhibēre *(w. dat or* ad + *acc); (to wounds)* inponĕre *(w. dat or* in + *acc);* **to — oneself to** se conferre ad *(w. acc);* **to — the mind to** animum adhibēre ad *(w. acc)* **||** *intr* **to — to** pertinēre ad *(w. acc),* cadĕre in *(w. acc);* **to — for** petĕre
appoint *tr* designare, creare, dicĕre
appointment *s* creati•o -onis *f; (agreement to meet)* constitut•um -i *n; (order)* mandat•um -i *n;* **I have an — with you** constitutum tecum habeo; **to keep an** — ad constitutum venire

apportion *tr* dividĕre
apportionment *s* divisi•o -onis *f*
apposition *s* appositi•o -onis *f;* **a noun in — with** vocabulum appositum *(w. dat)*
appraisal *s* aestimati•o -onis *f; (com, fin)* taxati•o -onis *f*
appraise *tr* aestimare; *(com, fin)* taxare
appraiser *s* aestimat•or -oris *m; (com, fin)* taxat•or -oris *m*
appreciable *adj* aestimabil•is -is -e, haud exigu•us -a -um
appreciate *tr (to esteem)* magni aestimare; *(to discern)* cognosĕre
appreciation *s* aestimati•o -onis *f; (gratitude)* grati•a -ae *f;* **to show — to s.o. for** gratiam alicui referre ob *(+ acc)*
apprehend *tr (to arrest; to grasp)* apprehendĕre
apprehension *s (arrest; understanding)* apprehensi•o -onis *f; (fear)* tim•or -oris *m,* sollicitud•o -inis *f*
apprehensive *adj* sollicit•us -a -um
apprentice *s* tir•o -onis *m*
apprenticeship *s* tirocin•ium -(i)i *n*
apprize *tr* **(of)** certiorem facere (de + *abl)*
approach *tr* appropinquare *(w. dat); (to approximate)* accedĕre *(w. dat or* ad + *acc)* **II** *intr* appropinquare, accedĕre; *(of an event)* appetĕre
approach *s* access•us -ūs *m; (of time)* appropinquati•o -onis *f; (by sea)* appuls•us -ūs *m*
approachable *adj (person)* facil•is -is -e; *(place)* pat•ens -entis
approbation *s* approbati•o -onis *f*
appropriate *adj* conveni•ens -entis, apt•us -a -um, idone•us -a -um; **it is — to** convenit *(w. inf or acc & inf)*
appropriate *tr (to claim)* vindicare; *(to claim presumptuously)* arrogare; *(money)* **(to)** dicĕre *(w. dat)*
appropriately *adv* apte, congruenter
appropriateness *s* convenienti•a -ae *f,* congruenti•a -ae *f*
appropriation *s* vindicati•o -onis *f; (of money)* **(for)** destinati•o -onis *f* (in + *acc)*
approval *s* approbati•o -onis *f*
approve *tr* approbare; *(a law)* sciscĕre **II** *intr* **to — of** probare
approved *adj* probat•us -a - um
approximate *adj* proxim•us -a -um
approximate *tr* accedĕre ad *(w. acc)*
approximately *adv* prope, propemodum; *(w. numbers)* ad *(w. acc)*
approximation *s* **the nearest —** quod proximum est
apricot *s* armeniac•um -i *n*
apricot tree *s* armeniac•a -ae *f*
April *s* April•is -is *m or* mens•is -is *m* Aprilis; **on the first of —** Kalendis Aprilibus
apron *s* sublig•ar -aris *n*
apt *adj* apt•us -a -um; **to be — to** *(w. inf)* solēre *(w. inf)*
aptitude *s* **(for)** ingen•ium -(i)i *n* (ad + *acc)*
aptly *adv* apte
aptness *s (fitness)* convenienti•a -ae *f; (talent)* ingen•ium -(i)i *n; (tendency)* proclivit•as -atis *f*
aquatic *adj* aquatic•us -a -um
aqueduct *s* aquaeduct•us -ūs *m*
aquiline *adj (nose)* adunc•us -a -um
arable *adj* arabil•is -is -e; **— land** arv•um -i *n*
arbiter *s* arbit•er -ri *m*
arbitrarily *adv* ad arbitrium
arbitrary *s* libidinos•us -a -um; *(imperious)* imperios•us -a -um
arbitrate *tr & intr* disceptare
arbitration *s* arbitr•ium -(i)i *n*
arbitrator *s* arbi•ter -tri *m*
arbor *s* umbracul•um -i *n*
arc *s* arc•us -ūs *m*
arcade *s* portic•us -ūs *f*
arch *s* arc•us -ūs *m,* forn•ix -icis *f*
arch *tr* arcuare, fornicare
arch *adj (chief)* summ•us -a -um; **— enemy** summus adversar•ius -(i)i *m*
archaeological *adj* archaeologic•us -a -um
archaeologist *s* vi•r -ri *m* monumentorum antiquitatis peritissimus
archaeology *s* archaeologi•a -ae *f*
archaic *adj* prisc•us -a -um
archaism *s* locuti•o -onis *f* obsoleta
archbishop *s* archiepiscop•us -i *m*
archer *s* sagittar•ius -(i)i *m; (astr)* Arciten•ens -entis *m*
archery *s* ar•s -tis *f* sagittandi
archetype *s* archetyp•um -i *n*
archipelago *s* mar•e -is *n* insulis crebrum
architect *s* architect•us -i *m*
architectural *adj* architectonic•us -a -um
architecture *s* architectur•a -ae *f*
archives *spl* tabul•ae -arum *fpl; (place)* tabular•ium -(i)i *n*
arctic *adj* arctic•us -a -um
ardent *adj* ard•ens -entis
ardently *adv* ardenter
ardor *s* ard•or -oris *m*
arduous *adj* ardu•us -a -um
area *s (open space; in geometry)* are•a -ae *f; (region)* regi•o -onis *f*
arena *s* (h)aren•a -ae *f*
Argonaut *s* argonaut•a -ae *m*
argue *tr (to reason)* arguĕre; *(to discuss)* disceptare de *(w. abl);* **to — a case** causam agĕre **II** *intr* disputare; *(to wrangle)* altercari
argument *s (discussion)* disputati•o -onis *f; (heated)* altercati•o -onis *f; (reason in support of a position)* argument•um -i *n;* **the force of his —** vis *f* argumenti ejus; **to get into an —** in litem ambiguam descendĕre; **to put up an —** recusare

argumentation *s* argumentati·o -onis *f,* rati·o -onis *f*
argumentative *adj* litigios·us -a -um
aria *s* cantic·um -i *n*
arid *adj* arid·us -a -um; *(fig)* jejun·us -a -um
aridity *s* aridit·as -atis *f*
aright *adv* recte
arise *intr* surgĕre; *(of a group)* consurgĕre; *(of a storm, etc.)* oriri, cooriri; *(suddenly)* exoriri; *(to come into existence)* exsistĕre; *(to orginate)* (from) nasci (ex + *abl)*
aristocracy *s (class)* optimat·es -ium *mpl; (government)* optimatium dominat·us -ūs *m*
aristocrat *s* optim·as -atis *m*
aristocratic *adj* patrici·us -a -um
arithmetic *s* arithmetic·a -ae *f*
ark *s* arc·a -ae *f*
arm *tr* armare
arm *s* bracch·ium -(i)i *n; (upper arm)* lacert·us -i *m; (of the sea)* sin·us -ūs *m; (of a chair)* anc·on -onis *m;* **at —'s length** eminus *(adv);* **to carry in one's —s** in manibus gestare; **to carry under one's —s** sub ala portare; **with —s akimbo** ansat·us -a -um; **with folded —s** compressis manibus; **with open —s** sinu complexuque ‖ *spl* arm·a -orum *npl;* **by force of —** vi et armis; **to be under —** in armis esse; **to lay down —** ab armis discedĕre; **to take up —** arma sumĕre
armada *s* class·is -is *f* magna
armament *s* apparat·us -ūs *m* belli
armchair *s* anconibus fabrefacta sell·a -ae *f*
armed *adj* armat·us -a -um
armistice *s* induti·ae -arum *fpl;* **to break off an —** indutias tollĕre
armlet *s* bracchiol·um -i *n; (bracelet)* armill·a -ae *f*
armor *s* arm·a -orum *npl*
armorbearer *s* armig·er -eri *m*
armory *s* armamentar·ium -(i)i *n*
armpit *s* al·a -ae *f*
army *s* exercit·us -ūs *m; (in battle)* aci·es -ei *f; (on the march)* agm·en -inis *n;* **to join the —** ad militiam ire
aroma *s* arom·a -atis *n; (of wine)* flo·s -ris *m*
aromatic *adj* aromatic·us -a -um
around *adv* circum, circa; **all —** undique
around *prep* circum *(w. acc); (approximately)* circa, ad *(w. acc)*
arouse *tr* suscitare; *(to wake up)* e somno excitare; *(fig)* excitare; **to — suspicion** suspicionem movēre
arraign *tr* accusare
arraignment *s* accusati·o -onis *f*
arrange *tr (to set in order)* ordinare; *(the hair)* componĕre, comĕre; *(a plan, meeting)* constituĕre; *(matters, a cloak to hang properly)* collocare; *(to agree)* pacisci; *(to put each thing separately in its place)* digerĕre; **—ed in a circle** in orbe disposit·us -a -um
arrangement *s* ord·o -inis *m; (of the year, of elections)* ordinati·o -onis *f; (of matters, of a garment)* collocati·o -onis *f; (of a speech, of books)* context·us -ūs *m;* **the — was that** convenit ut
array *s* vestit·us -ūs *m; (mil)* aci·es -ei *f*
array *tr* vestire; *(mil)* instituĕre
arrears *s* reliqu·a -orum *npl,* residuae pecuni·ae -arum *fpl;* **to be in —** relinqui
arrest *s* prehensi·o -onis *f*
arrest *tr* (ap)prehendĕre; *(movement)* tardare; **to — the attention of all** omnes in se convertĕre
arrival *s* advent·us -ūs *m; (by sea)* appuls·us -ūs *m*
arrive *intr* advenire; *(by ship or on horseback)* advehi; *(of a ship)* appelli; **to — at** pervenire ad *(w. acc);* **to — before the messengers** nuntios praevenire; **to — in** *(a place, country)* pervenire in *(w. acc)*
arrogance *s* arroganti·a -ae *f*
arrogant *adj* arrog·ans -antis
arrogantly *adv* arroganter
arrow *s* sagitt·a -ae *f*
arrowhead *s* spicul·um -i *n*
arsenal *s* armamentar·ium -(i)i *n; (naval)* naval·ia -ium *npl*
arsenic *s* arsenic·um -i *n*
arson *s* incend·ium -(i)i *n* malo dolo
arsonist *s* incendiar·ius -(i)i *m*
art *s* ar·s -tis *f; (practice of some craft)* artific·ium -(i)i *n;* **fine —s** art·es -ium *fpl* elegantes; **to study —** arti studēre
artery *s* arteri·a -ae *f*
artful *adj* callid·us -a -um
artfully *adv* callide
art gallery *s* pinacothec·a -ae *f*
article *s (object)* res rei *f; (ware)* mer·x -cis *f; (term)* condici·o -onis *f; (clause in a law)* cap·ut -itis *n; (gram)* articul·us -i *m;* **— of faith** decret·um -i *n* fidei
articulate *tr* articulatim dicĕre
articulate *adj* dilucid·us -a -um
articulately *adv* articulate
articulation *s (distinct utterance)* explanati·o -onis *f; (anat)* commissur·a -ae *f*
artifice *s* artific·ium -(i)i *n*
artificial *adj (produced by human hands)* artificios·us -a -um; *(not genuine)* factici·us -a -um
artificially *adv* arte; *(by human hands)* manu
artillery *s* torment·a -orum *npl*
artisan *s* opif·ex -icis *m; (usu. in hard material)* fa·ber -bri *m*
artist *s (of any of the fine arts)* artif·ex -icis *m; (painter)* pict·or -oris *m*
artistic *adj* artif·ex -icis

artistically *adv* artificiose
as *conj & adv* ut; *(while)* ut, dum, cum; *(as article of comparison, denoting equality)* atque, ac; *(for example)* velut, ut, sicut; *(because)* cum; **—...—** *(degree)* tam...quam, aeque...atque; **— far —** quoad; **— good —** aeque bonus atque; **— great —** tantus...quantus; **— if** quasi; **— is** ut est; **— it were** tamquam; **— long —** tamdiu, tantisper dum, quam diu; **— many —** totidem; **— much** tantum; **— often —** toties...quoties; **— soon —** cum primum: **— though** quasi; **— well as** ac, atque; **— yet** adhuc; **just — if** perinde ac si; **not — yet** nondum
ascend *tr & intr* ascendĕre
ascendency *s (superior influence)* potenti•a -ae *f;* **to gain the —** superior fieri
ascension *s* ascensi•o -onis *f*
ascent *s* ascensi•o -onis *f,* ascens•us -ūs *m;* **during the — to the summit** dum in summum ascenditur
ascertain *tr* comperire
ascetic *adj* ascetic•us -a -um
ascetic *s* ascet•a -ae *m*
asceticism *s* duriti•a -ae *f*
ascribe *tr* ascribĕre
ash *s* cin•is -is -eris *m; (tree)* fraxin•us -i *f;* **—es** cin•is -is -eris *m; (esp. ashes of the dead)* ciner•es -um *mpl*
ashamed *adj* pudibund•us -a -um; **I am —ed of** pudet me *(w. gen);* **I am — to tell** pudet me referre; **there is nothing to be —ed of** non est quod pudeatur
ashen *adj* pallid•us -a -um
ashore *adv (motion)* in terram; *(rest)* in litore; **to go —** in terram egredi
Asia *s* Asi•a -ae *f*
Asian *adj* Asian•us -a -um
Asiatic *adj* Asiatic•us -a -um
aside *adv* seorsum; **to call —** evocare; **to set** *or* **put —** seponĕre; **to take —** seducĕre; **to turn —** deflectĕre
aside from *prep* praeter *(w. acc)*
asinine *adj* asinin•us -a -um
ask *tr* rogare; *(to beg, petition for, esp. of a request made to a superior)* petĕre; *(to demand)* poscĕre, postulare; **to ask s.o. for s.th.** aliquem aliquid rogare; **to — that (that not)** rogare *(w.* ut *or* ne + *subj);* **I — you this question** hoc te rogo; **to — further questions** quaerĕre ultra; **to — many questions** multa quaerĕre *or* rogare; **to — one question after another** aliud ex alio quaerĕre; **to — questions** interrogare; **to — why** requirĕre quamobrem ‖ *intr* **to — about** percontari; **to — for** petĕre
askance *adv* **to look — (at)** limis oculis aspicĕre
asleep *adj* dormi•ens -entis; **half —** semisomn•us -a -um; **to be (sound) —** (arte) dormire; **to fall —** obdormiscĕre
asp *s* asp•is -idis *f*
asparagus *s* asparag•us -i *m*
aspect *s* aspect•us -ūs *m*
aspen *s* popul•us -i *f* tremula
asperity *s* acerbit•as -atis *f*
aspersion *s* opprobr•ium -(i)i *n;* **to cast — on** calumniari
asphalt *s* bitum•en -inis *n*
asphyxiation *s* asphyxi•a -ae *f*
aspirant *s* **(to)** appetit•or -oris *m (w. gen)*
aspiration *s* affectati•o -onis *f;* **to have lofty —s** magna spectare
aspire *intr* **to — to** appetĕre, affectare
aspiring *adj* **(after)** appet•ens -entis *(w. gen)*
ass *s* asin•us -i *m,* asin•a -ae *f; (fool)* asin•us -i *m; (anat)* clun•es -ium *mpl*
assail *tr* appetĕre; *(mil)* oppugnare
assailable *adj* expugnabil•is -is -e
assailant *s* oppugnat•or -oris *m*
assassin *s* percuss•or -oris *m*
assassinate *tr* per insidias interficĕre
assassination *s* caed•es -is *f* per insidias
assault *s* oppugnati•o -onis *f;* **aggravated —** *(leg)* vis *f;* **— and battery** vis *f* inlata; **sexual —** stuprati•o -onis *f;* **to take by —** expugnare
assault *tr (a person)* manus inferre *(w. dat); (sexually)* stuprum inferre *(w. dat); (in speech)* invehi in *(w. acc); (mil)* oppugnare
assay *tr (metals)* spectare
assay *s (of metals)* obruss•a -ae *f*
assemblage *s* congregati•o -onis *f*
assemble *tr* cogĕre; *(to call together)* convocare ‖ *intr* convenire
assembly *s* coet•us -ūs *m; (mil, pol)* conti•o -onis *f; (electoral)* comiti•a -orum *npl;* **in the —** pro contione; **to hold an —** comitia *(or* contionem) habēre
assent *s* assens•us -ūs *m*
assent *intr* **(to)** assentiri *(w. dat);* **to — to a request** petenti annuĕre
assert *tr* affirmare, confirmare; *(to maintain, claim)* asserĕre
assertion *s* affirmati•o -onis *f; (claim)* asserti•o -onis *f*
assess *tr* taxare; *(for tax purposes)* censēre
assessment *s* taxati•o -onis *f; (for tax purposes)* cens•us -ūs *m*
assessor *s* cens•or -oris *m*
assets *spl* bon•a -orum *npl*
assiduous *adj* assidu•us -a -um
assiduously *adv* assidue
assign *tr* attribuĕre; *(land, duties)* assignare; *(time)* praestituĕre; *(task)* delegare; *(to allege)* afferre; *(in writing)* praescribĕre
assignment *s* attributi•o -onis *f; (of land, duties)* assignati•o -onis *f; (in school)* pens•um -i *n*
assimilate *tr* assimulare; *(food)* digerĕre; *(knowledge)* concipĕre

assimilation *s* digesti•o -onis *f*
assist *tr* adesse *(w. dat),* adjuvare
assistance *s* auxil•ium -(i)i *n;* **to be of — to** auxilio esse *(w. dat)*
assistant *s* adjut•or -oris *m,* adjutr•ix -icis *f*
associate *s* soc•ius -(i)i *m*
associate *adj* soci•us -a -um
associate *tr* consociare, adjungĕre ‖ *intr* **to — with** familiariter uti *(w. dat)*
association *s* societ•as -atis *f;* **— with s.o** consociati•o -onis *f (w. gen)*
assort *tr* digerĕre
assortment *s (arrangement)* digesti•o -onis *f;* **a large — of jewelry** gemm•ae -arum *fpl* plurimae et cujuve generis
assuage *tr* allevare
assume *tr* assumĕre; *(a task)* suscipĕre; *(improperly)* arrogare; *(to take for granted in argument)* ponĕre; *(a role)* induĕre
assumption *s* assumpti•o -onis *f; (improper)* arroganti•a -ae *f; (hypothesis)* sumpti•o -onis *f*
assurance *s* fiduci•a -ae *f; (confidence)* confidenti•a -ae *f; (guarantee)* fid•es -ei *f*
assure *tr (to promise)* confirmare, affirmare; **to be** *or* **feel —ed** confidĕre
assured *adj (e.g, victory)* explorat•us -a -um
assuredly *adv* profecto
asterisk *s* asterisc•us -i *m*
asthma *s* asthm•a -atis *n;* **to have —** suspirio laborare
asthmatic *adj* asthmatic•us -a -um
astonish *tr* stupefacĕre
astonished *adj* attonit•us -a -um; **to be — at** obstupescĕre *(w. dat)*
astonishing *adj* mir•us -a -um
astonishingly *adv* admirabiliter
astonishment *s* admirati•o -onis *f; (speechlessness)* stup•or -oris *m*
astound *tr* (ob)stupefacĕre; **to be —d** stupēre
astray *adv* vag•us -a -um; **to go —** errare; **to lead s.o. —** aliquem transversum agĕre
astride *adv* equitantium modo posit•us -a -um
astrologer *s* astrolog•us -i *m,* mathematic•us -i *m*
astrology *s* astrologi•a -ae *f*
astronomer *s* astrolog•us -i *m*
astronomical *adj* astronomic•us -a -um
astronomy *s* astronomi•a -ae *f*
astute *adj* astut•us -a -um
asunder *adv* seorsum; *use verb with prefix* dis- *or* se-; **to tear —** discerpĕre
asylum *s* asyl•um -i *n*
at *prep (of place)* ad *(w. acc); (strictly, near)* apud *(w. acc); (usu. with names of towns, harbors, villas)* in *(w. abl), or locative case; (at the house of)* apud *(w. acc); (of time) use abl case;* **— all** omnino, prorsum; **— first** primo, initio; **— home** domi; **— least** duxtaxat, utique; **— once** momento, continuo; **— present** in praesentiā; **— the right time** in tempore
atheism *s* deos esse negare *(used as a neuter noun)*
atheist *s* athe•os -i *m*
Athenian *adj* Athenae•us -a -um
Athenian *s* Atheniens•is -is *m*
Athens *s* Athen•ae -arum *fpl*
athlete *s* athlet•a -ae *mf*
athletic *adj* athletic•us -a -um
athletics *spl* ar•s -tis *f* athletica
atlas *s* orbis terrarum descripti•o -onis *f*
atmosphere *s* cael•um -i *n*
atmospheric *adj* caeli *(gen)*
atom *s* atom•us -i *f*
atomic *adj* atomic•us -a -um; **— bomb** pyrobol•um -i *n* atomicum; **— energy** vis *f* atomica; **— theory** atomorum doctrin•a -ae *f*
atone *intr* **to — for** (ex)piare
atonement *s* expiati•o -onis *f*
atrocious *adj* atro•x -ocis
atrocity *s (atrociousness)* atrocit•as -atis *f; (deed)* atrox facin•us -eris *n*
atrophy *s* atrophi•a -ae *f*
atrophy *intr* tabescĕre
attach *tr (to fasten to)* annectĕre, adjungĕre; *(e.g., meaning)* subjicĕre; **to — importance to s.th.** aliquid magni aestimare; **to — oneself to s.o.** se alicui adjungĕre; **to be —ed to** adhaerēre *(w. dat)*
attachment *s (contact)* junctur•a -ae *f; (devotion)* stud•ium -(i)i *n;* **my — to the Roman people** studium meum in populum Romanum
attack *s* impet•us -ūs *m; (usu. on a town)* oppugnati•o -onis *f; (by cavalry)* incurs•us -ūs *m; (of a disease)* tentati•o -onis *f; (verbal)* petiti•o -onis *f*
attack *tr* aggredi; *(esp. w. physical force)* adoriri, vim inferre *(w. dat); (towns)* oppugnare; *(of a disease)* tentare, invadĕre; *(verbally)* petĕre; **—ed by a sudden illness** corrept•us -a -um subitā valetudine
attacker *s* aggress•or -oris *m; (mil)* oppugnat•or -oris *m*
attain *tr* adipisci, consequi; **to — to** pervenire ad *(w. acc)*
attainable *adj (by request)* impetrabil•is -is -e; **to be —** patēre
attempt *s* conat•us -ūs *m*
attempt *tr* conari, temptare, moliri
attend *tr (to accompany)* comitari; *(to escort)* prosequi; *(school, wedding, senate session)* frequentare; *(to be present at, e.g., a meeting)* adesse *(w. dat); (of a doctor)* assidēre *(w. dat);* **to — to** procurare, animadvertĕre
attendance *s (in great numbers)* frequenti•a -ae *f; (of a doctor)* assiduit•as -atis *f*

attendant *adj* adjunct•us -a -um; **— circumstances** adjunct•a -orum *npl*
attendant *s (to officials)* apparit•or -oris *m; (servant)* minist•er -ri *m,* ministr•a -ae *f; (of a temple)* aeditu•us -i *m*
attention *s* attentus anim•us -i *m,* animi attenti•o -onis *f;* **to attract —** animos hominum ad se convertere; **to call — to** indicare; **to call for —** animadverti jubēre; **to hold our —** animos nostros tenēre; **to pay — to** operam dare *(w. dat)*
attentive *adj* attent•us -a -um
attentively *adv* attente
attenuate *tr* attenuare, extenuare
attentuation *s* extenuati•o -onis *f*
attest *tr* testificare
attestation *s* testificati•o -onis *f*
attic *s* cenacul•um -i *n*
Attic *adj* Attic•us -a -um
Attica *s* Attic•a -ae *f*
attire *tr* vestire
attire *s* vestit•us -ūs *m*
attitude *s* habit•us -ūs *m; (of the body)* stat•us -ūs *m*
attorney *s* cognit•or -oris *m*
attorney general *s* advocat•us -i *m* fisci
attract *tr (lit & fig)* trahĕre; **to — a buyer** emptorem adducĕre; **to — the attention of all** oculos omnium in se convertĕre
attraction *s* vis *f* attractionis; *(fig)* illecebr•a -ae *f*
attractive *adj* illecebros•us -a -um
attractively *adv* blande
attractiveness *s* lep•os -oris *m*
attributable *adj* ascribend•us -a -um
attribute *s* propr•ium -(i)i *n,* qualit•as -atis *f*
attribute *tr* (at)tribuĕre; *(to attribute wrongly)* affingĕre
attrition *s* attrit•us -ūs *m*
attune *tr* modulari
auburn *adj* fulv•us -a -um
auction *s* aucti•o -onis *f; (by the state)* hast•a -ae *f;* **to hold an —** auctionem habēre
auction *tr* **to —off** auctione vendĕre; *(by the state)* sub hasta vendĕre
auctioneer *s* praec•o -onis *m*
audacious *adj* aud•ax -acis
audaciously *adv* audacter
audacity *s* audaci•a -ae *f*
audible *adj* clar•us -a -um
audibly *adv* clarā voce
audience *s* auditor•es -um *mpl,* spectator•es -um *mpl; (bystanders)* coron•a -ae *f;* **to ask for a private —** secretum petĕre
audit *s* rationum inspecti•o -onis *f*
audit *tr* inspicĕre
auditory *adj* auditori•us -a -um
Augean *adj* Augiae *(gen)*
auger *s* terebr•a -ae *f*
augment *tr* augēre, ampliare ‖ *intr* augēri
augmentation *s* increment•um -i *n*
augur *s* aug•ur -uris *m;* **—'s staff** litu•us -i *m*
augur *intr* augurari
augury *s* augur•ium -(i)i *n*
August *s* August•us -i *m or* mens•is -is *m* Augustus; **on the first of —** Kalendis Augustis
Augustan *adj* Augustal•is -is -e
aunt *s (pateral)* amit•a -ae *f; (maternal)* materter•a -ae *f*
auricle *s* auricul•a -ae *f*
auspices *spl* auspic•ium -(i)i *n;* **to take the —** auspicari; **under the —s of** sub clientela *(w. gen);* **without taking the —s** inauspicato
auspicious *adj* fel•ix -icis
auspiciously *adv* feliciter
austere *adj* auster•us -a -um
austerely *adv* austere
austerity *s* austerit•as -atis *f*
authentic *adj* genuin•us -a -um
authenticate *tr* recognoscĕre
authenticity *s* auctorit•as -atis *f*
author *s (originator)* auct•or -oris *mf; (writer)* script•or -oris *m; (inventor)* condit•or -oris *m*
authoritative *adj* grav•is -is -e; *(reliable)* cert•us -a -um; *(imperious)* imperios•us -a -um
authority *s* auctorit•as -atis *f; (leave)* licenti•a -ae *f; (power of a magistrate)* imper•ium -(i)i *n; (expert)* auct•or -oris *m;* **on good —** gravi auctore; **the authorities** magistrat•us -uum *mpl*
authorization *s* auctorit•as -atis *f*
authorize *tr* **to — s.o. to** auct•or -oris *m* esse alicui *(w. gerundive)*
authorship *s (origin)* auct•or -oris *m*
autobiography *s* lib•er -ri *m* de vita sua
autocracy *s* dominati•o -onis *f*
autocrat *s* domin•us -i *m*
autocratic *adj* tyrannic•us -a -um
autograph *s* chirograph•um -i *n*
autograph *tr* manu suā scribĕre
automatic *adj* automatari•us -a -um
automaton *s* automat•on -i *n*
autumn *s* autumn•us -i *m*
autumn(al) *adj* autumnal•is -is -e
auxiliaries *spl* auxili•a -orum *npl*
auxiliary *adj* auxiliar•is -is -e
avail *tr* prodesse *(w. dat);* **to — oneself of** uti *(w. abl);* **what do laws —?** quid leges faciunt? ‖ *intr* valēre
avail *s* **but to no —** sed frustra; **to be of no —** usui non esse
available *adj* in promptu
avalanche *s* nivis ruin•a -ae *f*
avarice *s* avariti•a -ae *f*
avaricious *adj* avar•us -a -um
avariciously *adv* avare
avenge *tr* ulcisci, vindicare
avenger *s* ult•or -oris *m,* vind•ex -icis *mf*
avenging *adj* ultr•ix -icis
avenue *s* vi•a -ae *f*

average *s* med•ium -(i)i *n;* **on the —** peraeque
average *adj* peraeque duct•us -a -um
average *tr (to calculate)* peraeque ducĕre; *(to amount to)* peraequare
aversion *s* fastid•ium -(i)i *n;* **to have an — for** fastidire
avert *tr* avertĕre
aviary *s* aviar•ium -(i)i *n*
avid *adj* avid•us -a -um
avidly *adv* avide
avocation *s* stud•ium -(i)i *n*
avoid *tr* evitare; *(a blow)* declinare
avoidable *adj* evitabil•is -is -e
avoidance *s* vitati•o -onis *f*
avow *tr* fateri
avowal *s* confessi•o -onis *f*
avowedly *adv* ex professo
await *tr* exspectare, manēre
awake *adj* vigil•ans -antis, desomn•is -is -e; **to be —** vigilare
awaken *tr* somno excitare ‖ *intr* expergisci
award *s* praem•ium -(i)i *n*
award *tr* tribuĕre; *(leg)* addicĕre
aware *adj* gnar•us -a -um; **to be — of** scire
awareness *s* conscienti•a -ae *f*
away *adv use verbs with prefix* ab-; **— with you!** abi hinc!; **far —** procul; **to be —** abesse; **to fly —** avolare; **to go —** abire
awe *s* reverenti•a -ae *f;* **to stand in — of** verēri
aweful *adj* terribil•is -is -e
awefully *adv* terribiliter
awesome *adj* verend•us -a -um
awhile *adv* paulisper, aliquamdiu
awkward *adj* inept•us -a -um; *(unwieldly)* inhabil•is -is -e
awkwardly *adv* inepte
awkwardness *s* inepti•a -ae *f*
awl *s* subul•a -ae *f*
awning *s* velar•ium -(i)i *n*
awry *adv* oblique; **to go —** perquam evenire
ax *s* secur•is -is *f*
axiom *s* proloqu•ium -(i)i *n*
axis *s* ax•is -is *m*
axle *s* ax•is -is *m*
azure *adj* caerule•us -a -um

B

baa *s* balat•us -ūs *m*
baa *intr* balare
babble *s* garrulit•as -atis *f*
babble *intr* blatire; **to — on about** effutire
babbler *s* blater•o -onis *m*
babbling *adj* garrul•us -a -um
babe *s* inf•ans -antis *mf*
baboon *s* cynocephal•us -i *m*
baby *s* inf•ans -antis *mf*
baby *tr* indulgēre *(w. dat)*
babyish *adj* infantil•is -is -e
bacchanal *s* bacch•ans -antis *m,* bacch•a -ae *f*
Bacchanalia *spl* bacchanal•ia -ium *npl*
bacchanalian *adj* bacchanal•is -is -e
Bacchic *adj* bacchic•us -a -um
Bacchus *s* Bacch•us -i *m*
bachelor *s* caeleb•s -is *m; (degree)* bacchelaure•us -i *m*
bachelorhood *s* caelibat•us -ūs *m*
back *s* terg•um -i *n,* dors•um -i *n;* **at one's —** a tergo; **— of the classroom** posterior par•s -tis *f* scholae; **lying on one's —** resupin•us -a -um; **to climb on his —** super dorsum ejus ascendĕre; **to turn one's — on** contemnĕre
back *adv* retro, retrorsum; *or use verbs with prefix* re- *or* retro-
back *tr* favēre *(w. dat)* ‖ *intr* **to — away from** refugĕre; **to — down** recedĕre; **to — out** se recipĕre; **to — up** retrogradi; *(of water)* refluĕre
backbite *tr* **— a friend** amicum absentem rodĕre
backbiting *s* mors•us -ūs *m*
backbiter *s* maledic•us -i *m*
backboard *s* plute•us -i *m*
backbone *s* spin•a -ae *f*
back door *s* postic•um -i *n*
backer *s* faut•or -oris *m; (pol)* suffragat•or -oris *m*
background *s (in paintings)* abscedent•ia -ium *npl; (causes)* ort•ūs -ūs *m; (of a person)* prior aet•as -atis *f*
backside *s (anat)* clun•es -ium *mpl*
backstairs *spl* posticae scal•ae -arum *fpl*
backward *adv* retro, retrorsum
backward *adj (reversed)* supin•us -a -um; *(slow)* tard•us -a -um; **to be —** cunctari
backwardness *s* tardit•as -atis *f*
bacon *s* lard•us -i *m;* **to bring home the —** habēre panem
bad *adj* mal•us -a -um; *(usu. morally bad)* improb•us -a -um; *(health, weather)* advers•us -a -um; *(harmful)* noxi•us -a -um; *(road)* iniqu•us -a -um; *(rotten)* putid•us -a -um; **— news** acerbum nunt•ium -(i)i *n;* **it is — to** *(w. inf)* alienum est *(w. inf);* **to go —** corrumpi; **wine is — for you** alienum tibi vinum est
badge *s* insign•e -is *n*
badger *s* mel•es -is *f*
badger *tr* vexare
badly *adv* male; improbe; **to want —** valde cupĕre
badness *s* maliti•a -ae *f; (moral)* improbit•as -atis *f*
baffle *tr* eludĕre
bag *s* sacc•us -i *m; (dim.)* saccul•us -i *m*
baggage *s* sarcin•ae -arum *fpl; (mil)* impediment•a -orum *npl*
bail *s* vadimon•ium -(i)i *n;* **to be out on —** vadari; **to put up — for** spondēre pro *(w. abl)*

bail *tr* **to — s.o. out** *(leg)* aliquem vadari; *(fig)* aliquem e periculo servare; **to — out the boat** sentinam e navicula egerĕre; **to — out water** sentinam egerĕre
bailiff *s (in a courtroom)* viat•or -oris *m; (manager of an estate)* villic•us -i *m*
bailiwick *s* jurisdicti•o -onis *f*
bait *s* esc•a -ae *f; (fig)* incitament•um -i *n;* **to put the — on the hook** escam hamo imponĕre
bait *tr* inescare; *(to tease)* lacessĕre
bake *tr* coquĕre
baker *s* pist•or -oris *m,* pistr•ix -icis *f*
bakery *s* pistrin•a -ae *f*
balance *s (pair of scales)* trutin•a -ae *f; (equilibrium)* aequilibr•ium -(i)i *n; (in bookkeeping)* reliqu•a -orum *npl; (fig)* compensati•o -onis *f*
balance *tr* librare; **to — accounts** rationes dispungĕre; **to — joy with grief** laetitiam cum doloribus compensare ‖ *intr* constare; **the account —s** ratio constat
balance sheet *s* rati•o -onis *f* accepti et expensi
balancing *s* **— of accounts** dispuncti•o -onis *f*
balcony *s* maenian•um -i *n*
bald *adj* calv•us -a -um; *(style)* arid•us -a -um; **to be —** calvēre
baldness *s* calvit•ium -(i)i *n; (of style)* aridit•as -atis *f*
bale *s* fasc•is -is *m*
bale *tr (hay)* in fasces colligĕre
baleful *adj* pernicios•us -a -um
balk *s (of wood)* tign•um -i *n*
balk *tr* frustrari
ball *s* globul•us -i *m; (for playing)* pil•a -ae *f;* **—s** *(anat) (sl) (lit & fig)* cole•i -orum *mpl;* **to play —** pilā ludĕre
ballad *s* carm•en -inis *n*
ballast *s* saburr•a -ae *f*
ballast *tr* saburrare
ballet *s* pantomim•us -i *m*
ballet dancer *s* pantomim•us -i *m,* pantomim•a -ae *f*
ballot *s* suffrag•ium -(i)i *n;* **to cast a —** suffragium ferre
ballot box *s* cist•a -ae *f*
balm *s* balsam•um -i *n*
bamboo *s* arund•o -inis *f* Indica
ban *s* interdict•um -i *n*
ban *tr* interdicĕre
banana *s* arien•a -ae *f*
band *s (group)* man•us -ūs *f; (gang)* caterv•a -ae *f; (for the head)* inful•a -ae *f; (of musicians)* symphoni•a -ae *f*
band *intr* **to — together** conjungi; *(pej)* conjurare
bandage *s* fasci•a -ae *f*
bandage *tr (a wound)* astringĕre; *(an arm, etc.)* deligare
bandit *s* latr•o -onis *m*
banditry *s* latrocin•ium -(i)i *n*
bandy *tr* **to — words with s.o.** sermonem serĕre *(w. dat)*
bane *s (fig)* pest•is -is *f*
baneful *adj* pestifer•us -a -um
bang *s* sonit•us -ūs *m*
bang *tr* verberare; **to — together** concrepare ‖ *intr* sonitum facĕre; **to — on the door** fores pulsare
bangle *s* circul•us -i *m*
banish *tr (from the confines of a state)* exterminare; *(usual formula in time of Cicero)* aquā et igni interdicĕre; *(temporarily)* relegare; *(to some island)* deportare; *(cares, etc.)* pellĕre
banishment *s (act)* relegati•o -onis *f,* interdicti•o -onis *f* aquā et igni; *(state)* exil•ium -(i)i *n*
banister *s* epimed•ion -(i)i *n*
bank *intr* **to — on** niti *(w. abl)*
bank *s (of river)* rip•a -ae *f; (of earth)* agg•er -eris *m; (com)* argentari•a -ae *f*
banker *s* argentar•ius -(i)i *m*
banking *s* argentaria negotiati•o -onis *f;* **to be engaged in —** argentariam facĕre
bankrupt *s (person)* decoct•or -oris *m;* **to be —** decoquĕre; **to go —** foro cedĕre, conturbare
bankruptcy *s* decocti•o -onis *f*
banner *s* vexill•um -i *n*
banquet *s* conviv•ium -(i)i *n; (religious)* epul•ae -arum *fpl;* **to go to** *or* **attend a —** convivium inire
banter *s* cavillati•o -onis *f*
banter *intr* cavillari
bantering *s* cavillati•o -onis *f*
baptism *s* baptism•a -atis *n*
baptize *tr* baptizare
bar *s* vect•is -is *f; (of door)* ser•a -ae *f; (of gate)* ob•ex -icis *m; (ingot)* lat•er -eris *m; (legal profession)* for•um -i *n;* **—s** *(of a cage)* clathr•i -orum *mpl;* **of the —** forens•is -is -e; **to practice at the —** causas agĕre
bar *tr (the door)* obserare; *(to keep away)* prohibēre; **to — s.o. from campaigning** submovēre aliquem petitione; **to — s.o.'s way** obstare alicui
barb *s* ham•us -i *m; (sting)* acule•us -i *m*
barbarian *adj* barbar•us -a -um
barbarian *s* barbar•us -i *m,* barbar•a -ae *f*
barbaric *adj* barbaric•us -a -um
barbarism *s* barbari•a -ae *f; (in speech)* barbarism•us -i *m*
barbarity *s* ferocit•as -atis *f*
barbarous *adj* barbar•us -a -um
barbed *adj* hamat•us -a -um
barber *s* tons•or -oris *m,* tonstr•ix -icis *f*
barbershop *s* tonstrin•a -ae *f*
bard *s* vat•es -is *m*
bare *adj* nud•us -a -um; *(style)* press•us -a -um
bare *tr* nudare
barefaced *adj (shameless)* impud•ens

-entis; *(unconcealed)* evidentissim•us -a -um
barefoot *adj & adv* nudis pedibus
bareheaded *adj* nudo capite
barely *adv* vix, aegre
bargain *s* pact•um -i *n;* **a good —** empti•o -onis *f* secunda; **to buy at a —** bene emĕre; **to strike a —** pacisci
bargain *intr* pascisci; **to — for** depacisci
barge *s* lint•er -ris *f*
barge *intr* **to — in** *(coll)* intervenire
bark *s (of tree)* cort•ex -icis *m; (of dog)* latrat•us -ūs *m; (ship)* rat•is -is *f*
bark *intr* latrare; **to — at** allatrare
barking *s* latrat•us -ūs *m*
barley *s* horde•um -i *n*
barley *adj* hordeac•us -a -um; **— flour** hordeaca farin•a -ae *f*
barmaid *s* cauponae ministr•a -ae *f*
barn *s* horre•um -i *n*
barnyard *s* cohor•s -tis *f*
barometer *s* barometr•um -i *n*
barometric *adj* barometric•us -a -um
baron *s* bar•o -onis *m*
baroness *s* baroniss•a -ae *f*
barracks *spl* castr•a -orum *npl* stativa
barrel *s* cup•a -ae *f*
barrel hoop *s* circul•us -i *m* de cupa
barren *adj* steril•is -is -e
barrenness *s* sterilit•as -atis *f*
barricade *s* claustr•a -orum *npl,* agg•er -eris *m; (of logs)* concaed•es -ium *fpl*
barricade *tr* obsaepire
barrier *s* sept•um -i *n; (fig)* claustr•a -orum *npl*
barrister *s* causidic•us -i *m*
barter *s* permutati•o -onis *f* mercium
barter *tr* mutare *(w. acc of thing given and abl of thing received);* **to — booty for wine** praedam vino mutare ‖ *intr* **(with)** merces mutare (cum + *abl)*
base *adj* humil•is -is -e; *(morally)* turp•is -is -e; *(coinage)* adulterin•us -a -um
base *s (groundwork; of a column)* bas•is -is *f; (mil)* castr•a -orum *npl*
base *tr* fundare; **to — the country on laws** civitatem legibus fundare
baseless *adj* van•us -a -um
basement *s* cell•a -ae *f*
baseness *s* turpitud•o -inis *f*
bash *tr (coll)* percutĕre; **to — in** perfringĕre; **to — in a man's head** alicui caput perfringĕre
bashful *adj* verecund•us -a -um
bashfully *adv* verecunde
bashfulness *s* verecundi•a -ae *f*
basic *adj* prim•us -a -um
basilica *s* basilic•a -ae *f*
basin *s* pelv•is -is *f; (reservoir)* labr•um -i *n*
basis *s* bas•is -is *f*
bask *intr* **to — in the sun** apricari
basket *s* corb•is -is *f; (money basket)* fisc•us -i *m; (for flowers, fruit)* calath•us -i *m; (small food basket)* sportell•a -ae *f*
bas-relief *s* anaglypt•a -orum *npl; (on plates, vessels)* toreum•a -atis *n*
bass *s (fish)* perc•a -ae *f* fluvialis; *(mus)* son•us -i *m* gravissimus; **to sing —** voce imā cantare
bassinet *s* cun•ae -arum *fpl*
bastard *adj* spuri•us -a -um
bastard *s* noth•us -i *m*
baste *tr* lardo perfundĕre; *(in sewing)* suturam *(w. gen)* solute suĕre
bastion *s* propugnacul•um -i *n*
bat *s (bird)* vespertili•o -onis *m; (club)* clav•a -ae *f*
batch *s* mass•a -ae *f; (pile)* cumul•us -i *m*
bath *s* balne•um -i *n; (public)* balne•a -orum *npl; (bath and community center)* therm•ae -arum *fpl;* **to take a cold (hot) —** frigidā (calidā) aquā lavari
bathe *tr* lavare; *(face, sore limb)* fovēre ‖ *intr* lavari
bather *s* qui lavat; *(swimmer)* natat•or -oris *m;* **—s** lavant•es -ium *mpl*
bathing *s* lavati•o -onis *f; (swimming)* natati•o -onis *f*
bathroom *s* balneol•um -i *n; (toilet)* latrin•a -ae *f*
bathtub *s* sol•ium -(i)i *n*
baton *s* virg•a -ae *f*
battalion *s* cohor•s -tis *f*
batter *s* farin•a -ae *f* lacte ovisque mixta
batter *tr* verberare; *(to shake by battering)* percutĕre; **to — down** ariete dejicĕre
battering ram *s* ari•es -etis *m*
battle *s (general & mil)* pugn•a -ae *f; (mil)* proel•ium -(i)i *n*
battle *tr* certare ‖ *intr* proeliari
battle-ax *s* bipenn•is -is *f*
battle-cry *s* clam•or -oris *m* militum; *(of barbarians)* barit•us -ūs *m*
battlefield *s* loc•us -i *m* pugnae, aci•es -ei *f*
battle formation *s* aci•es -ei *f*
battlement *s* pinn•a -ae *f*
baubles *spl* tric•ae -arum *fpl*
bawd *s* len•a -ae *f*
bawdy *adj* obscen•us -a -um
bawl *intr* clamitare; *(to cry)* flēre; *(of babies)* vagire
bawling *s* vociferati•o -onis *f; (crying)* flet•us -ūs *m; (by a baby)* vagit•us -ūs *m*
bay *s (of the sea)* sin•us -ūs *m; (tree)* laur•us -i *f;* **at —** obsess•us -a -um; **to keep at —** arcēre
bay *adj (light-colored)* helv•us -a -um; *(horse)* spad•ix -icis; *(of bay tree)* laure•us -a -um
bay *intr* ululare
bayonet *s* pugi•o -onis *m*
bayonet *tr* pugione fodĕre
bazaar *s* for•um -i *n* rerum venalium
be *intr* esse; *(of a situation)* se habēre, versari; **— gone!** apage!; **that is the situation** sic res se habent; **to — absent**

abesse; **to — against** adversari; **to — among** interesse *(w. dat);* **to — for** favēre *(w. dat),* stare cum *(w. abl);* **to — present** adesse, interesse
beach *s* act•a -ae *f,* lit•us -oris *n*
beach *tr (a ship)* subducĕre
beacon *s* ign•is -is *m* in specula; *(lighthouse)* phar•us -i *f*
bead *s* bac•a -ae *f*
beagle *s* parvus can•is -is *m* venaticus
beak *s* rostr•um -i *n*
beaked *adj* rostrat•us -a -um
beaker *s (cup)* pocul•um -i *n; (decanter)* obb•a -ae *f*
beam *s (of wood)* trab•s -is *f; (of light)* jub•ar -aris *n; (ray)* rad•ius -(i)i *m*
beaming *adj* nit•ens -entis
bean *s* fab•a -ae *f; (kidney bean)* phasel•us -i *mf*
bear *tr (to carry)* portare, ferre; *(to endure)* ferre, pati; *(to produce)* ferre; *(to beget)* parĕre; **to — away** auferre; **to — in mind** recordari; **to — out** *(to confirm)* arguĕre; **to — witness** testari **||** *intr* **to — down on** *(to approach)* appropinquare *(w. dat); (to press)* inniti in *(w. acc); (to oppress)* opprimĕre; **to — with** indulgēre *(w. dat)*
bear *s* urs•us -i *m,* urs•a -ae *f*
bearable *adj* tolerabil•is -is -e
beard *s* barb•a -ae *f; (of grain)* arist•a -ae *f;* **to cut his first —** barbatorium facĕre; **to grow a —** barbam summittĕre
bearded *adj* barbat•us -a -um
beardless *adj* inberb•is -is -e
bearer *s (porter)* bajul•us -i *m; (of litter)* lecticar•ius -(i)i *m; (of letter)* tabellar•ius -(i)i *m; (of news)* nunt•ius -(i)i *m*
bearing *s (posture)* gest•us -ūs *m; (direction)* regi•o -onis *f;* **to get one's —s** regionem reperire; **to have a — on** pertinēre ad *(w. acc)*
beast *s* besti•a -ae *f,* belu•a -ae *f; (brutish person)* belu•a -ae *f*
beastly *adj* beluin•us -a -um
beast of burden *s* jument•um -i *n*
beat *tr (to punish)* verberare; *(to knock on)* pulsare; *(to conquer)* vincĕre; *(the breast, drum)* plangĕre; **to — back** repellĕre; **to — down** demoliri; **to — in** perfringĕre; **to — the daylights out of** pulchre percopolare **||** *intr* palpitare; **to — upon** *(of rain)* impluĕre in *(w. acc); (of waves)* illidĕre; **to — around the bush** circuitu uti, schemas loqui
beat *s (blow)* plag•a -ae *f,* ict•us -ūs *m; (of the heart)* palpitati•o -onis *f; (mus)* ict•us -ūs *m; (patrol area)* circuiti•o -onis *f*
beaten *adj (defeated)* vict•us -a -um; *(worn)* trit•us -a -um
beating *s* verberati•o -onis *f; (defeat)* repuls•a -ae *f; (of the heart)* palpitati•o -onis *f;* **to get a —** vapulare
beautiful *adj* pul•cher -chra -chrum; *(shapely)* formos•us -a -um
beautifully *adv* pulchre
beautify *tr* ornare
beauty *s* pulchritud•o -inis *f*
beaver *s* fi•ber -bri *m*
beaver skin *s* pell•is -is *f* fibrina
because *conj* quod, quia, quoniam
because of *prep* ob, propter *(w. acc)*
beck *s* nut•us -ūs *m;* **at the — and call** ad arbitrium
beckon *tr* nutu vocare
become *tr* decēre **||** *intr* fieri; **to — friends with me once again** in gratiam mecum redire
becoming *adj* dec•ens -entis
becomingly *adv* decenter
bed *s* lect•us -i *m; (in the garden)* areol•a -ae *f; (of a river)* alve•us -i *m;* **to go to —** cubitum ire; **to make the —** lectum sternĕre
bedaub *tr* oblinĕre
bedbug *s* sciniph•is -is *m*
bedding *s* stragul•um -i *n*
bedeck *tr* ornare
bedevil *tr (to enchant)* fascinare
bedfellow *s* soc•ius -(i)i *m* lecti
bedlam *s* tumult•us -ūs *m*
bedpost *s* fulcr•um -i *n*
bedraggled *adj* sordid•us -a -um
bedridden *adj* valetudinari•us -a -um; **to be —** lecto tenēri
bedroom *s* cubicul•um -i *n*
bedstead *s* spond•a -ae *f*
bedtime *s* hor•a -ae *f* somni
bee *s* ap•is -is *f*
beech tree *s* fag•us -i *f*
beef *s* bubul•a *f*
beefsteak *s* frust•um -i *n* bubulum
beehive *s* alve•us -i *m*
beekeeper *s* apiar•ius -(i)i *m*
beeline *s* **to make a — for** directā viā contendĕre ad *(w. acc)*
beer *s* cerevisi•a -ae *f*
beet *s* bet•a -ae *f*
beetle *s* scarabae•us -i *m*
befall *tr* contingĕre *(w. dat)* **||** *intr* accidĕre, contingĕre
befit *tr* decēre
befitting *adj* dec•ens -entis; **it is —** decet
before *prep (in front of)* ante *(w. acc),* pro *(w. abl); (in time)* ante *(w. acc); (in the presence of)* coram *(w. abl); (leg)* apud *(w. acc);* **— all things** imprimis; **— long** jamdudum; **— now** antehac
before *conj* antequam, priusquam
beforehand *adv* antea
befoul *tr* inquinare
befriend *tr* in amicitiam recipĕre
beg *tr* petĕre, orare **||** *intr* mendicare; **to — for** deprecari; *(alms)* mendicare; **to — s.o. to** aliquem deprecari ut *(w. subj);* **to — from door to door** ostiatim mendicare

beget *tr* gignĕre
beggar *s* mendic•us -i *m*
begging *s* mendicit•as -atis *f;* **to go —** mendicare
begin *tr & intr* incipĕre; *(without finishing)* inchoare; *(to initiate)* instituĕre; **to — with** primum (omnium)
beginner *s* tir•o -onis *m*
beginning *s (the act of starting)* incepti•o -onis *f; (the start itself)* init•ium -(i)i *n; (origin)* orig•o -inis *f;* **at the — of winter** ineunte *or* primā hieme; **in the —** inter initia; **—s** principi•a -orum *npl*
begrudge *tr* **to — my enemy his victory** amici victoriae invidēre
beguile *tr* fraudare
behalf *s* **on — of** pro *(w. abl)*
behave *intr* se gerĕre; **to — toward** uti *(w. abl);* **well-behaved** bene morat•us -a -um
behavior *s* mor•es -um *mpl;* **your — towards me was unfriendly** inimice te in me gessisti
behead *tr* decollare
beheading *s* decollati•o -onis *f*
behest *s* juss•um -i *n*
behind *adv* pone, a tergo; **to be left —** relinqui
behind *prep* post *(w. acc); (esp. w. verbs of motion)* pone *(w. acc); (in support)* pro *(w. abl);* **from —** a tergo; **to talk about a friend — his back** absentem amicum rodĕre
behind *s (coll)* clun•es -ium *mpl*
behold *tr* conspicĕre
behold *interj* ecce!, en!
behoove *tr* **it behooves you to** *(w. inf)* oportet te *(w. inf)*
beige *adj* rav•us -a -um
being *s* en•s -tis *n;* **human —** hom•o -inis *m*
bejewelled *adj* gemmat•us -a -um
belabor *tr (to thrash)* verberare; *(to harp on)* cantare
belch *s* ruct•us -ūs *m*
belch *tr* **to — forth** eructare ‖ *intr* ructare
beleaguer *tr* obsidēre
belfry *s* turr•is -is *f* campanis instructa
belie *tr (to prove false)* refellĕre; *(to disappoint)* frustrari; *(to disguise)* dissimulare
belief *s* fid•es -ei *f; (conviction) (in)* opini•o -onis *f (w. gen or* de + *abl)*
believe *tr (thing)* credĕre; *(person)* credĕre *(w. dat); (to suppose)* existimare; **to make —** simulare
believer *s* cred•ens -entis *mf*
bell *s (large)* campan•a -ae *f; (small)* tintinnabul•um -i *n*
belle *s* bella puell•a -ae *f*
belles-lettres *spl* litter•ae -arum *fpl* exquisitiores
belligerent *adj (at war)* belliger•ans -antis; *(scrappy)* pugn•ax -acis
bellow *intr* mugire
bellow *s* mugit•us -ūs *m*
bellows *spl* foll•is -is *m*
bell pepper *s* pip•er -eris *n* rotundum
bell tower *s* turr•is -is *f* campanis instructa
belly *s* ven•ter -tris *m; (womb)* uter•us -i *m*
bellyache *s* tormin•a -um *npl;* **to have a —** dolēre a torminibus
belong *intr* **to — to** esse *(w. dat); (to be related)* pertinēre ad *(w. acc); (to be a member of)* in numero *(w. gen)* esse
belongings *spl* bon•a -orum *npl*
below *adj* infer•us -a -um
below *adv* infra
below *prep* infra *(w. acc)*
belt *s* cingul•um -i *n; (of women's clothes)* zon•a -ae *f; (sword belt)* balte•us -i *m; (area)* zon•a -ae *f;* **to tighten one's —** sumptui parcĕre
bemoan *tr* deplorare
bench *s* scamn•um -i *n; (esp. for senators and judges)* subsell•ium -(i)i *n; (for rowers)* transtr•um -i *n*
bend *tr* flectĕre, curvare; *(to cause to lean)* inclināre; *(the bow)* intendĕre, flectĕre; *(to persuade)* inflectĕre; **to — back** reflectĕre; **to — down** deflectĕre ‖ *intr (e.g., of iron)* se inflectĕre; *(to give in)* cedĕre; **to — down** *or* **over** *(to stoop)* se inclinare, se demittĕre
bend *s* curvam•en -inis *n;* **— in the road** flex•us -ūs *m* viae
bending *s* inclinati•o -onis *f*
beneath *adv* subter
beneath *prep* sub *(w. acc or abl);* **he thinks these matters are — him** arbitratur has res infra se positas
benediction *s* benedicti•o -onis *f*
benefaction *s* benefic•ium -(i)i *n*
benefactor *s* largit•or -oris *m,* patron•us -i *m*
benefactress *s* patron•a -ae *f*
beneficence *s* beneficenti•a -ae *f*
beneficent *adj* benefi•cus -a -um
beneficial *adj* util•is -is -e, commod•us -a -um; **to be —** prodesse
benefit *s (deed)* benefic•ium -(i)i *n; (advantage)* commod•um -i *n;* **to have the — of** frui *(w. abl);* **to whose — is it?** cui bono est?
benefit *tr* prodesse *(w. dat),* juvare ‖ *intr* proficĕre; *(financially)* lucrari; **to — from** utilitatem capĕre ex *(w. abl)*
benevolence *s* benevolenti•a -ae *f*
benevolent *adj* benevol•us -a -um
benevolently *adv* benevole
benign *adj* benign•us -a -um
benignly *adv* benigne
bent *adj* flex•us -a -um, curv•us -a -um; **— backwards** recurv•us -a -um; **— forwards** pron•us -a -um; **— inwards** camur•us -a -um; **— on** *(fig)* attent•us -a -um ad *(w. acc)*
bent *s* curvatur•a -ae *f; (inclination)* inclinati•o -onis *f*

benumb *tr* torpore afficĕre
bequeath *tr* legare
bequest *s* legat•um -i *n*
bereave *tr* orbare
bereavement *s* orbit•as -atis *f*
bereft *adj* **— of** orbat•us -a -um *(w. abl or gen)*
berry *s* bac•a -ae *f*
berth *s (cabin)* diaet•a -ae *f; (space for ship at anchor)* stati•o -onis *f;* **to give wide — to** devitare
beseech *tr* obsecrare
beset *tr* urgēre; *(mil)* obsidēre
beside *prep* ad *(w. acc),* juxta *(w. acc);* **— the point** nihil ad rem; **to be — oneself** delirare; **to sit — s.o.** assidēre alicui; **to walk — s.o.** alicui latus tegĕre
besides *adv* praeterea, ultro
besides *prep* praeter *(w. acc)*
besiege *tr* obsidēre; *(fig)* circumsedēre
besmirch *tr* inquinare
best *adj* optim•us -a -um; *(most advantageous)* commodissim•us -a -um; **it is — to** optimum est *(w. inf),* maxime prodest *(w. inf)*
best *s* flo•s -ris *f;* **to do one's —** pro virili parte agĕre; **to have the — of it** praevalēre; **to make the — of it** aequo animo ferre; **to the — of one's ability** pro viribus
best *tr* exsuperare
bestial *adj* bestial•is -is -e
bestir *tr (to move)* ciēre; **to — oneself** *(to wake up)* expergisci
best man *s* pronub•us -i *m*
bestow *tr* **(on)** tribuĕre, deferre *(w. dat)*
bestowal *s* largiti•o -onis *f*
bestower *s* largit•or -oris *m*
bet *s* sponsi•o -onis *f;* **to lose a —** sponsionis condemnari; **to win a —** sponsione vincĕre
bet *tr* ponĕre; **to — that**...sponsionem facĕre *(w. acc & inf)*
betide *intr* evenire
betoken *tr* portendĕre
betray *tr* prodĕre; *(feelings)* arguĕre
betrayer *s* prodit•or -oris *m*
betroth *tr* despondēre
betrothal *s* sponsal•ia -ium *npl*
betrothed *adj* spons•us -a -um
better *adj* mel•ior -ior -ius; *(preferable)* praestant•ior -ior -ius; **— half** *(fig)* alter•a -ae *f;* **for the —** in melius; **it is — to** *(w. inf)* commodius est *(w. inf);* **to be —** *(in health)* melius esse; **to get —** convalescĕre; **to get the — of** praevalēre *(w. abl)*
better *adv* melius, potius
better *tr* meliorem *(or* melius) facĕre, corrigĕre; **to — oneself** proficĕre
betterment *s* correcti•o -onis *f*
betters *spl* melior•es -um *mpl*
between *prep* inter *(w. acc)*
bevel *tr* obliquare
beverage *s* pot•us -ūs *m*
bevy *s* gre•x -gis *m*
bewail *tr* deplorare
beware *intr* cavēre; **to — of** cavēre
bewilder *tr* confundĕre
bewildered *adj* confus•us -a -um
bewilderment *s* confusi•o -onis *f*
bewitch *tr* fascinare; *(to charm)* demulcēre
beyond *adv* ultra
beyond *prep* ultra *(w. acc),* extra *(w. acc); (motion)* trans *(w. acc);* **to go — the limits** egredi extra terminos
bias *s (prejudice)* inclinati•o -onis *f; (line)* line•a -ae *f* obliqua
bias *tr* inclinare
Bible *s* Bibli•a-orum *npl*
Biblical *adj* Biblic•us -a -um
bibliography *s* bibliographi•a -ae *f*
bicker *intr* altercari
bickering *s* altercati•o -onis *f*
bid *tr (to order)* jubēre; *(to invite)* invitare; *(at auction)* licitari; **to — farewell** valedicĕre
bid *s* licitati•o -onis *f;* **to make a —** licitationem facĕre
bidder *s* licitat•or -oris *m*
bidding *s (command)* juss•um -i *n; (at auction)* licitati•o -onis *f;* **at his —** jussu ejus; **to do s.o.'s —** jussum alicujus exsequi
bide *tr* **to — one's time** tempus idoneum opperiri
biennial *adj* biennial•is -is -e
bier *s* feretr•um -i *n; (euphem)* vitalis lect•us -i *m*
big *adj* magn•us -a -um, ing•ens -entis; **— with child** gravida; **— with young** praegn•ans -antis
bigamist *s* bimarit•us -i *m*
bigamy *s* bigami•a -ae *f*
big mouth *s* **to be a —** *(coll)* durae buccae esse
bigot *s* qui suae opinioni nimium fidit
bigoted *adj* obstinate suae opinioni de partibus *(or* de religione *or* de genere) dedit•us -a -um
bigotry *s* nimia suae de partibus *(or* de religione *or* de genere) opinioni fiduci•a -ae *f*
bile *s* bil•is -is *f*
bilge water *s* sentin•a -ae *f*
bilious *adj* bilios•us -a -um
bilk *tr* fraudare
bill *s (of bird)* rostr•um -i *n; (proposed law)* rogati•o -onis *f; (com)* rati•o -onis *f* debiti; **— of indictment** subscripti•o -onis *f;* **to introduce a —** legem ferre; **to pass a —** legem perferre; **to turn down a —** legem *or* rogationem antiquare
bill collector *s* flagitat•or -oris *m*
billet *s* hospit•ium -(i)i *n*
billion *s* billi•o -onis *f*

billow *s* fluct•us -ūs *m*
billowy *adj* fluctuos•us -a -um
bin *s (in wine cellar)* locul•us -i *m; (for grain)* lac•us -ūs *m*
bind *tr* ligare; *(wounds)* stringĕre; *(to obligate)* obligare; *(books)* conglutinare; **to — fast** devincĕre; **to — together** colligare; **to — up** alligare; *(med)* astringĕre
binding *adj* obligatori•us -a -um; *(law)* rat•us -a -um
binding *s* religati•o -onis *f*
binoculars *spl* binocular•es -um *mpl*
biographer *s* vitae script•or -oris *m*
biography *s* vit•a -ae *f*
biology *s* biologi•a -ae *f*
biologist *s* biologic•us -i *m*
biped *s* bip•es -edis *m*
birch *adj* betulin•us -a -um
birch tree *s* betul•a -ae *f*
bird *s* av•is -is *f;* **—s of a feather flock together** pares cum paribus facillime congregantur
birdcage *s* cave•a -ae *f*
birdcall *s* fistul•a -ae *f* aucupatoria
birdlime *s* visc•um -i *n*
bird's nest *s* nid•us -i *m*
birth *s* part•us -ūs *m; (lineage)* gen•us -eris *n*
birthday *s* di•es -ei *m* natalis
birthday cake *s* lib•um -i *n*
birthday party *s* natalici•a -ae *f*
birthplace *s* patri•a -ae *f*
birthright *s* ju•s -ris *n* e genere ortum
biscuit *s* crustul•um -i *n*
bisect *tr* in duas partes aequales secare
bishop *s* episcop•us -i *m*
bison *s* bis•on -ontis *m*
bit *s (for horse)* fren•um -i *n; (small amount)* aliquantul•um -i *n; (of food)* off•a -ae *f;* **a — of peace** aliquid quietis; **— by —** minutatim; **to cut (chop) to —s** minutatim secare (concidēre)
bitch *s* can•is -is *f*
bite *s* mors•us -ūs *m; (by an insect)* ict•us -ūs *m*
bite *tr* mordēre; *(of pepper, frost)* urĕre; *(of an insect)* icĕre
biting *adj (apt to bite)* mord•ax -acis; *(cutting)* asp•er -era -erum
bitter *adj (lit & fig)* amar•us -a -um; *(hatred)* asp•er -era -erum *(painful, sharp)* acerb•us -a -um; **— taste in the mouth** amarum o•s -ris *n*
bitterly *adv (denoting wounded feeling)* amare; *(implying anger or harshness)* aspere; *(implying hostility)* infense
bitterness *s* amarit•as -atis *f; (fig)* acerbit•as -atis *f; (wounded feeling)* amaritud•o -inis *f*
bitters *spl* absinth•ium -(i)i *n*
bivouac *s* excubi•ae -arum *fpl*
bivouac *intr* excubare
blab *tr* blaterare; **to — out** effutire ‖ *intr* deblaterare
black *adj (shiny black)* ni•ger -gra -grum; *(dull black)* a•ter -tra -trum; *(looks)* tru•x -cis
black *s (color)* nigr•um -i *n; (person)* Aethi•ops -opis *m;* **dressed in —** pullat•us -a -um
black-and-blue *adj* livid•us -a -um; **— mark** liv•or -oris *m*
blackberry *s* mor•um -i *n*
blackbird *s* merul•a -ae *f*
blacken *tr* nigrare
black eye *s* ocul•us -i *m* sugillatus
blacklist *s* proscripti•o -onis *f*
blacklist *tr* proscribĕre
black magic *s* magicae art•es -ium *fpl*
blackness *s* nigriti•a -ae *f*
blacksmith *s* ferrarius fa•ber -bri *m*
bladder *s* vesic•a -ae *f*
blade *s (edge)* lamin•a -ae *f; (of grass)* herb•a -ae *f; (of oar)* palm•a -ae *f*
blamable *adj* culpabil•is -is -e
blame *tr* improperare *(w. dat),* culpare; **you are to —** in culpā es
blame *s* culp•a -ae *f*
blameless *adj* inte•ger -gra -grum
blame-worthy *adj* vituperabil•is -is -e
blanch *tr* candefacĕre ‖ *intr* exalbescĕre, pallescĕre
bland *adj (food)* len•is -is -e
blandishment *s* blanditi•a -ae *f*
blank *adj* inan•is -is -e; *(expression)* stolid•us -a -um
blanket *s* lod•ix -icis *f; (dim.)* lodicul•a -ae *f*
blare *s* strepit•us -ūs *m*
blare *intr* strepare
blaspheme *tr* blasphemare
blasphemous *adj* blasphem•us -a -um
blasphemy *s* blasphemi•a -ae *f*
blast *s (of wind)* flam•en -inis *n; (of musical instrument)* flat•us -ūs *m;* **— of wind** flat•us -ūs *m*
blast *tr* discutĕre
blaze *s (glare)* fulg•or -oris *m; (fire)* incend•ium -(i)i *n;* **go to —s** *(coll)* i in malam crucem!
blaze *tr* **to — a trail** semitam notare ‖ *intr* ardēre; **fires were —ing** ignes flagrabant; **to — up** exardescĕre
bleach *tr* dealbare
bleachers *spl* anabathr•a -ōrum *npl*
bleak *adj* immit•is -is -e; *(outlook, hope)* incommod•us -a -um
bleary-eyed *adj* lipp•us -a -um; **to be —** lippire
bleat *intr* balare
bleating *s* balat•us -ūs *m*
bleed *intr* sanguinem fundĕre
bleeding *adj* crud•us -a -um
bleeding *s* sanguinis profusi•o -onis *f; (bloodletting)* sanguinis missi•o -onis *f*

blemish *s (flaw)* vit•ium -(i)i *n; (on the body)* mend•um -i *n; (moral)* macul•a -ae *f*
blemish *tr* maculare
blend *tr* commiscēre; **to — in** immiscēre ‖ *intr* **to — in with** se immiscēre *(w. dat)*
blend *s* mixtur•a -ae *f; (proportionate)* temperi•es -ei *f*
bless *tr* beare; *(consecrate)* consecrare; *(w. success)* secundare; *(eccl)* benedicĕre; **— your little heart!** di te ament!
blessed *adj* beat•us -a -um; *(of dead emperors)* div•us -a -um
blessing *s (thing)* bon•um -i *n; (eccl)* benedicti•o -onis *f*
blight *s* robig•o -inis *f; (fig)* tab•es -is *f*
blight *tr* robigine afficĕre; *(fig)* nocēre *(w. dat)*
blind *adj (lit & fig)* caec•us -a -um
blind *tr (lit & fig)* occaecare
blindfold *tr* oculos obligare *(w. dat)*
blindfolded *adj* oculis obligatis
blindly *adv* temere
blindness *s* caecit•as -atis *f*
blinds *spl (on window)* transenn•a -ae *f*
blink *intr* connivēre
bliss *s* beatitud•o -inis *f*
blissful *adj* beat•us -a -um
blissfully *adv* beate
blister *s* pustul•a -ae *f*
blister *intr* pustulare
bloated *adj* sufflat•us -a -um
block *s (of wood)* stip•es -itis *f; (of marble, stone)* mass•a -ae *f; (in a city)* vic•us -i *m; (obstruction)* impediment•um -i *n;* **— by —** vicatim
block *tr (e.g., the road)* obstruĕre; *(to choke up)* opplēre; **to — s.o.'s way** obstare alicui; **to — up** *(e.g. a window)* obstruĕre
blockade *s* obsidi•o -onis *f;* **to lift a —** obsidionem solvĕre; **to undergo a —** in obsidione teneri
blockade *tr* obsidēre
block and tackle *spl* trochle•a -ae *f*
blockhead *s* caud•ex -icis *m*
blood *s* sangu•is -inis *m; (outside the body)* cru•or -oris *m; (lineage)* gen•us -eris *n;* **to let —** sanguinem mittĕre; **there was bad — between him and Caesar** huic simultas cum Caesari intercedebat; **to stain with —** cruentare
bloodless *adj* exsangu•is -is -e; *(without bloodshed)* incruent•us -a -um
blood pressure *s* pressur•a -ae *f* sanguinis
blood-red *adj* sanguine•us -a -um
blood relative *s* consanguine•us -i *m*
bloodshed *s* caed•es -is *f*
bloodshot *adj* **— eyes** cruore suffusi ocul•i -orum *mpl*
bloodstained *adj* cruent•us -a -um
bloodsucker *s* sanguisug•a -ae *f*
bloodthirsty *adj* sanguinari•us -a -um
blood vessel *s* ven•a -ae *f*
bloody *adj* sanguine•us -a -um
bloom *s* flo•s -ris *m;* **to be in —** florid•us -a -um esse
bloom *intr* florēre; **to begin to —** florescĕre
blooming *adj* flor•ens -entis
blossom *s* flo•s -ris *m;* **to shed its —s** deflorēre
blossom *intr* florēre
blot *s* macul•a -ae *f*
blot *tr* maculare; **to — out** delēre; *(to erase)* oblit(t)erare
blotch *s (stain)* macul•a -ae *f; (on the skin)* var•us -i *m*
blotchy *adj* maculos•us -a -um
blow *s (stroke)* plag•a -ae *f; (blow which wounds)* ict•us -ūs *m; (w. the fist)* colaph•us -i *m; (fig)* plag•a -ae *f*
blow *tr* flare; *(a horn)* inflare; **to — out** *(candle)* ex(s)tinguĕre; **to — the nose** se emungĕre; **to — up** pulvere nitrato destruĕre ‖ *intr* flare; **to — over** *(of a storm)* cadĕre; **to — up** *(to get angry)* irasci
blowing *s* sufflati•o -onis *f*
blowup *s* scandal•um -i *n; (anger)* ir•a -ae *f*
blubber *s* ad•eps -ipis *m* balaenarum
blubber *intr (coll)* plorare
blue *adj* caerule•us -a -um; *(dark blue)* cyane•us -a -um; *(pale blue)* subcaerule•us -a -um; *(melancholy)* melancholic•us -a -um
blue *s* caeruleus col•or -oris *m; (concrete)* caerule•um -i *n;* **—s** melancholi•a -ae *f;* **to have the —s** melancholic•us -a -um esse
blue-grey *adj (eyes)* caesi•us -a -um
blueprint *s* form•a -ae *f*
bluff *s* rup•es -is *f; (false threat)* simulata audaci•a -ae *f*
bluff *tr* decipĕre ‖ *intr* simulatā audaciā uti
blunder *s* err•or -oris *m; (in writing)* mend•um -i *n*
blunder *intr* errare
blunderer *s* hom•o -inis *m* ineptus
blunt *adj (dull)* heb•es -itis; *(person)* inurban•us -a -um; *(speech)* impolit•us -a -um
blunt *tr* hebetare
bluntly *adv* liberius
bluntness *s* hebetud•o -inis *f; (fig)* rusticit•as -atis *f*
blur *s* macul•a -ae *f*
blur *tr* obscurare
blurred *adj* **the eyes are —** oculi caligant; **to have — vision** quasi per caliginem vidēre
blurt *tr* **to — out** effutire
blush *s* rub•or -oris *m*
blush *intr* erubescĕre
bluster *intr (to swagger)* declamare, se jactare; *(of the wind)* saevire

bluster *s (boasting)* jactati•o -onis *f; (din)* strepit•us -ūs *m*
blustery *adj* ventos•us -a -um
boar *s* a•per -pri *m*
board *s (of wood)* tabul•a -ae *f; (food)* vict•us -ūs *m; (council)* colleg•ium -(i)i *n; (judicial)* quaesti•o -onis *f; (for games)* alve•us -i *m*
board *tr* **to — a ship** navem conscendĕre; **to — up** contabulare ‖ *intr (to be a boarder)* victitare; **to — with** devertĕre apud *(w. acc)*
boarder *s* deversit•or -oris *m*
boarding house *s* deversor•ium -(i)i *n*
boardwalk *s* ambulacr•um -i *n* in litore
boast *intr* gloriari, se jactare
boast *s* jactanti•a -ae *f*
boastful *adj* glorios•us -a -um
boasting *s* gloriati•o -onis *f*
boat *s* navig•ium -(i)i *n*
boatman *s* naut•a -ae *m*
bode *tr* portendĕre
bodiless *adj* incorporal•is -is -e
bodily *adj* corporis *(gen)*
body *s* corp•us -oris *n; (corpse)* cadav•er -eris *n; (person)* hom•o -inis *m; (of troops)* man•us -ūs *f; (of cavalry)* turm•a -ae *f; (frame)* compag•es -ium *fpl;* **to come in a —** agmine facto occurrĕre
bodyguard *s* satellit•es -um *mpl; (of the emperor)* cohor•s -tis *f* praetoria
bog *s* pal•us -udis *f*
bog *tr* **to — down** mergĕre; **to get —ed down** in luto haesitare; *(fig)* haesitare
bogus *adj (counterfeit)* adulterin•us -a -um; *(sham)* simulat•us -a -um; *(fictitious)* commentici•us -a -um
boil *tr (to cause to boil)* fervefacĕre; *(to cook)* coquĕre; **to — down** *(food)* decoquĕre; *(facts)* coartare ‖ *intr* fervēre; *(fig)* bullire; **to — over** effervescĕre; **to — with indignation** indignatione bullire
boil *s (med)* furuncul•us -i *m*
boiler *s* ahen•um -i *n*
boisterous *adj (noisy)* turbid•us -a -um; *(stormy)* procellos•us -a -um
bold *adj* aud•ax -acis
bold-faced *adj* impud•ens -entis
boldly *adv* audacter
boldness *s* audaci•a -ae *f*
bolster *s* cervic•al -alis *n*
bolster *tr* fulcire
bolt *s (of a door)* pessul•us -i *m,* ser•a -ae *f; (of lightning)* ful•men -inis *n; (pin)* clav•us -i *m; (screw)* cochle•a -ae *f*
bolt *tr* obserare; **—ed doors** oppessulatae for•es -ium *fpl;* **to — down** *(food)* devorare ‖ *intr (of a horse)* se proripĕre; *(pol)* a factione deficĕre
bomb *s* missil•e -is *n* dirumpens
bomb *tr* missilibus dirumpentibus concutĕre
bombard *tr* tormentis verberare; *(fig)* lacessĕre
bombardment *s* tormentis verberati•o -onis *f*
bombast *s* ampull•ae -arum *fpl*
bombastic *adj* tumid•us -a -um; **to be —** ampullari
bond *s* vincul•um -i *n; (legal document)* syngraph•a -ae *f; (of love)* copul•a -ae *f*
bondage *s* servit•us -utis *f; (captivity)* captivit•as -atis *f*
bondsman *s (slave)* famul•us -i *m; (leg)* spons•or -oris *m*
bone *s* os, ossis *n; (of fish)* spin•a -ae *f*
bone *adj (of bone)* osse•us -a -um
bone *tr (to remove bones from)* exossare
boneless *adj* ex•os -ossis
bonfire *s* ign•es -ium *mpl* festi
bonnet *s* redimicul•um -i *n*
bonus *s* praem•ium -(i)i *n*
bony *adj* osse•us -a -um
boogieman *s* larv•a -ae *m*
book *s* li•ber -bri *m;* **by the —** *(fig)* pro modo; **to write a —** librum componĕre
bookbinder *s* glutinat•or -oris *m*
bookcase *s* forul•i -orum *mpl*
bookish *adj* libris dedit•us -a -um
bookkeeper *s* tabular•ius -(i)i *m,* dispensat•or -oris *m*
bookshelf *s* plute•us -i *m*
bookstore *s* librari•a -ae *f*
bookworm *s* tine•a -ae *f; (fig)* librorum hellu•o -onis *m*
boom *s (of ship)* longur•ius -(i)i *m; (of harbor)* repagul•um -i *n; (sound)* sonit•us -ūs *m; (of waves)* frag•or -oris *m*
boon *s* benefic•ium -(i)i *n*
boor *s* rustic•us -i *m*
boorish *adj* rustic•us -a -um
boorishness *s* rusticit•as -atis *f*
boost *tr* efferre
boot *s* calce•us -i *m; (soldier's)* calig•a -ae *f; (peasant's)* per•o -onis *m; (tragic)* cothurn•us -i *m*
boot *tr (coll)* calce petĕre ‖ *intr* prodesse; **to —** insuper
booth *s* tabern•a -ae *f*
border *s (edge)* marg•o -inis *mf; (seam)* fimbri•a -ae *f; (boundary)* fin•is -is *m; (frontier)* lim•es -tis *m;* **to mark the —** finem discernĕre
border *tr* attingĕre ‖ *intr* **to — on** attingĕre
bordering *adj* finitim•us -a -um
bore *tr* terebrare; *(a person)* obtundĕre; **to — a hole in** excavare; **to — a hole through s.th.** aliquid perforare; **to — out** exterebrare
bore *s (tool)* terebr•a -ae *f; (fig)* molest•us -i *m*
borer *s* terebr•a -ae *f*
born *adj* nat•us -a -um; **to be —** nasci; *(fig)* oriri
borough *s* municip•ium -(i)i *n*

borrow *tr* mutuari; *(fig)* imitari
borrowed *adj* mutu•us -a -um
bosom *s* sin•us -ūs *m; (of female)* mammill•ae -arum *fpl*
bosom friend *s* intimus familiar•is -is *m*
boss *s (owner)* domin•us -i *m; (coll)* ipsim•us -i *m; (ornamental fixture)* bull•a -ae *f; (on a shield)* umb•o -onis *m*
boss *tr* dominari in *(w. acc)*
botanical *adj* herbari•us -a -um
botanist *s* herbar•ius -(i)i *m*
botany *s* ar•s -tis *f* herbaria
botch *tr* male gerĕre
both *adj* amb•o -ae -o; *(of pairs)* gemin•us -a -um; *(each of two)* ut•erque, -raque, -rumque; **— parents** uterque par•ens -entis *m;* **in — directions** utroque; **on — sides** utrimque
both *pron* amb•o -ae -o; *(w. singular verb)* ut•erque, -raque, -rumque
both *conj* **—…and** et…et
bother *tr* vexare ‖ *intr* **to — about** operam dare *(w. dat)*
bother *s* negot•ium -(i)i *n*
bothersome *adj* molest•us -a -um
bottle *s* ampull•a -ae *f; (large)* lagoen•a -ae *f*
bottle *tr* in ampullas infundĕre
bottom *s* fund•us -i *m; (of a ship)* carin•a -ae *f; (of a mountain)* rad•ix -icis *m;* **the — of** im•us -a -um; **the — of the sea** imum mar•e -is *n*
bottom *adj* im•us -a -um
bottomless *adj* profund•us -a -um
bough *s* ram•us -i *m*
boulder *s* sax•um -i *n*
bounce *tr* repercutĕre; *(coll)* ejicĕre ‖ *intr* resilire
bounce *s (leap)* salt•us -ūs *m; (energy)* vig•or -oris *m*
bound *adj* alligat•us -a -um; **it is — to happen** necesse est accidat; **to be — for** tendĕre ad *or* in *(w. acc)*
bound *s (leap)* salt•us -ūs *m;* **to set —s** modum facĕre
bound *tr* terminare, continēre; **they are —ed on one side by the Rhine** unā ex parte flumine Rheno continentur ‖ *intr (to leap)* salire
boundary *s* fin•is -is *m; (esp. fortified)* lim•es -itis *m*
boundless *adj* infinit•us -a -um
bountiful *adj* larg•us -a -um
bounty *s* largit•as -atis *f*
bouquet *s* corollar•ium -(i)i *n; (of wine)* flo•s -ris *m*
bout *s* certam•en -inis *n*
bow *s* arc•us -ūs *m; (in a ribbon)* plex•us -ūs *m*
bow *s (of ship)* pror•a -ae *f; (bending)* capitis summissi•o -onis *f;* **to take a —** caput summittĕre
bow *tr* flectĕre; *(one's head)* demittĕre ‖ *intr* se demittĕre; **to — to** *(to accede to)* obtemperare *(w. dat)*
bowels *spl* alv•us -i *f*
bower *s* umbracul•um -i *n*
bowl *s* crater•a -ae *f; (for libations)* pater•a -ae *f*
bowlegged *adj* valg•us -a -um
bowman *s* sagittar•ius -(i)i *m*
bowstring *s* nerv•us -i *m*
box *s (chest)* arc•a -ae *f; (for books)* caps•a -ae *f; (for clothes, etc.)* cist•a -ae *f; (for perfume, medicine)* pyx•is -idis *f*
box *tr (to enclose in a box)* includĕre; *(an opponent)* pugillare cum *(w. abl);* **to — s.o. on the ear** alicui alapam adhibēre ‖ *intr* pugillare
boxer *s* pug•il -ilis *m*
boxing *s* pugillat•us -ūs *m*
boxing glove *s* caest•us -ūs *m*
boxing match *s* pugillat•us -ūs *m*
boy *s* pu•er -eri *m; (dim.)* puerul•us -i *m*
boyhood *s* pueriti•a -ae *f;* **from —** a puero
boyish *adj* pueril•is -is -e
bra *s* stroph•ium -(i)i *n*
brace *s (strap)* fasci•a -ae *f; (pair)* pa•r -ris *n; (prop)* fulment•um -i *n*
brace *tr (to bind)* ligare; *(to strengthen)* firmare; *(to prop)* fulcire; **to — oneself for** se comparare ad *(w. acc)*
bracelet *s* armill•a -ae *f*
bracket *s* mutul•us -i *m;* **—s** *(in writing)* unc•i -orum *mpl*
brag *intr* se jactare
braggart *s* jactat•or -oris *m*
bragging *s* jactanti•a -ae *f*
braid *s* limb•us -i *m; (of hair)* spir•a -ae *f*
braid *tr* plectĕre
brain *s* cerebr•um -i *n;* **—s** *(talent)* ingen•ium -(i)i *n;* **to have (no) —s** cor (non) habēre
brain *tr (sl)* caput elidĕre *(w. dat)*
brainless *adj* soc•ors -ordis
brainstorm *s* inflat•us -ūs *m* spiritūs
brain trust *s* consil•ium -(i)i *n* sapientium
brake *s (on wagon)* sufflam•en -inis *n; (thicket)* dumet•um -i *n;* **to apply the —s** rotam sufflaminare
bramble *s* dum•us -i *m; (thorny bush)* sent•is -is *m*
branch *s (of tree)* ram•us -i *m; (of pedigree)* stemm•a -atis *n; (of knowledge)* disciplin•a -ae *f*
branch *intr* **to — out** ramos porrigĕre; *(fig)* scindi, diffundi
branch office *s* officin•a -ae *f* auxiliaria
brand *s (mark)* stigm•a -atis *n; (com)* not•a -ae *f; (type)* gen•us -eris *n; (of fire)* fa•x -cis *f*
branding iron *s* caut•er -eris *m*
brandish *tr* vibrare
brandy *s* vini spirit•us -ūs *m*
brash *adj* temerari•us -a -um
brass *s* orichalc•um -i *n*

brassiere *s* stroph•ium -(i)i *n*
brat *s* procax pusi•o -onis *m*
brave *adj* fort•is -is -e
brave *tr* sustinēre
bravely *adv* fortiter
bravery *s* fortitud•o -inis *f*
bravo *interj* macte!
brawl *s* rix•a -ae *f*
brawl *intr* rixari
brawler *s* rixat•or -oris *m*
brawling *adj* jurg•ans -antis
brawn *s* lacert•us -i *m*
brawny *adj* lacertos•us -a -um
bray *intr* rudĕre
braying *s* rudit•us -ūs *m*
brazen *adj* aëne•us -a -um; *(fig)* impud•ens -entis
brazier *s* focul•us -i *m*
breach *s* ruin•a -ae *f; (of treaty)* dissid•ium -(i)i *n;* **— in the wall** ruin•a -ae *f* muri; **to commit a — of promise** fidem frangĕre; **to make a small — in the wall** aliquantulum muri discutĕre
bread *s* pan•is -is *m; (fig)* vict•us -ūs *m;* **loaf of —** panis *m;* **to earn one's —** sibi victum quaerĕre
bread basket *s* panar•ium -(i)i *n*
breadcrumb *s* mic•a -ae *f* panis
breadth *s* latitud•o -inis *f;* **in —** in latitudinem
break *tr (arm, dish, treaty, one's word)* frangĕre; *(the law)* violare; *(leg, ankle)* suffringĕre; *(silence)* rumpĕre; *(camp)* movēre; *(in several places)* diffringĕre; **to — a fall** casum mitigare; **to — apart** diffringĕre; **to — a treaty** foedus frangĕre; **to — down** *(to demolish)* demoliri; **to — down into** *(categories)* deducĕre in *(w. acc);* **to — formation** ordinem solvĕre; **to — in** *(a horse)* domare; **to — in pieces** confringĕre; **to — off** *(e.g., a branch)* praefringĕre; *(friendship or action)* dirumpĕre; *(a meeting, conversation)* interrumpĕre; **to — one's word** fidem frangĕre; **to — open** effringĕre; **to — up** dissolvĕre ‖ *intr* frangi, rumpi; *(of day)* illuscescĕre; *(of strength)* deficĕre; **to — forth** erumpĕre; **to —into** *(e.g., a house)* irrumpĕre *(w. acc or* intra + *acc); (e.g., a city)* invadĕre *(w. acc or* in + *acc);* **to — loose from** se eripĕre ex *(w. abl);* **to — off** *(to stop short)* repente desinĕre; **to — out** erumpĕre; *(of trouble)* exardescĕre; *(of war)* exoriri; *(of fire)* grassari; **to — up** dissolvi, dilabi; *(of a meeting)* dimitti; **to — with** dissidēre ab *(w. abl)*
break *s (of a limb)* ruptur•a -ae *f;* (interruption) intercaped•o -inis *f; (for rest)* intervall•um -i *n,* vacati•o -onis *f; (escape)* effug•ium -(i)i *n;* **— of day** prima lu•x -cis *f*
breakage *s* fractur•a -ae *f*
breakdown *s (of health)* debilit•as -atis *f; (mechanical)* defect•us -ūs *m; (division)* deducti•o -onis *f*
breaker *s* fluct•us -ūs *m* a saxo fractus
breakfast *s* jentacul•um -i *n;* **for —** in jentaculum; **to eat —** jentare
breakfast *intr* jentare
breakneck *adj* praec•eps -ipitis
breakup *s* dissoluti•o -onis *f*
breakwater *s* mol•es -is *f* lapidum in mari structa
breast *s* pect•us -oris *n; (of a woman)* mamm•a -ae *f; (when filled with milk)* ub•er -eris *n; (fig)* praecord•ia -ium *npl;* **to make a clean — of it** confiteri omnia
breastbone *s* stern•um -i *n*
breast-feed *tr* uberibus alĕre
breastplate *s* loric•a -ae *f*
breath *s* spirit•us -ūs *m,* anim•a -ae *f;* **— of air** aur•a -ae *f;* **deep —** anhelit•us -ūs *m;* **out of —** anhel•us -a -um; **to catch one's —** obstipescĕre; **to draw a —** spiritum trahĕre; **to hold one's —** animam continēre; **to take a —** animam *or* spiritum ducĕre; **to take one's — away** exanimare; **to waste one's —** operam perdĕre
breathe *tr* ducĕre, spirare; *(to whisper)* susurrare; **to — fire** flammas exspirare; **to — one's last** animam exspirare ‖ *intr* spirare, respirare; **to — upon** inspirare *(w. dat)*
breather *s (breathing space)* spat•ium -(i)i *n*
breathing *s* respirati•o -onis *f*
breathless *adj* exanim•is -is -e
breeches *spl* brac•ae -arum *fpl*
breed *s* gen•us -eris *n*
breed *tr* parĕre, gignĕre; *(to cause)* producĕre; *(to raise)* educare, alĕre; **familiarity —s contempt** conversatio parit contemptum
breeder *s (man)* generat•or -oris *m; (animal)* matr•ix icis *f; (fig)* nutr•ix -icis *f*
breeding *s* fetur•a -ae *f;* **good —** humanit•as -atis *f*
breeze *s* aur•a -ae *f*
breezy *adj* ventos•us -a -um
brethren *spl* fratr•es -um *mpl*
brevity *s* brevit•as -atis *f*
brew *s* cerevisiae ferment•um -i *n*
brew *tr* concoquĕre ‖ *intr* excitari
brewer *s* cerevisiae coct•or -oris *m*
brewery *s* officin•a -ae *f* ad cerevisiam concoquendam
bribe *s* pret•ium -(i)i *n,* praem•ium -(i)i *n,* pecuni•a -ae *f*
bribe *tr* (pecuniā) corrumpĕre
briber *s* corrupt•or -oris *m*
bribery *s* corrupti•o -onis *f; (pol)* ambit•us -ūs *m*
brick *s* lat•er -eris *m*

brick *adj* laterici•us -a -um
bricklayer *s* laterum struct•or -oris *m*
bridal *adj* nuptial•is -is -e; **— bed** genialis tor•us -i *m;* **— suite** thalam•us -i *m;* **— veil** flamme•um -i *n*
bride *s* nupt•a -ae *f*
bridegroom *s* marit•us -i *m*
bridesmaid *s* pronub•a -ae *f*
bridge *s* pon•s -tis *m*
bridge *tr* pontem imponěre *(w. dat)*
brief *adj* brev•is -is -e
brief *tr* edocēre
brief *s (leg)* commentar•ius -(i)i *m*
briefing *s* mandat•a -orum *npl*
briefly *adv* breviter, paucis (verbis)
brigade *s (infantry)* legi•o -onis *f; (cavalry)* turm•a -ae *f*
brigadier *s* tribun•us -i *m* militum
brigand *s* latr•o -onis *m*
brigandage *s* latrocin•ium -(i)i *n*
bright *adj* clar•us -a -um; *(stars, gems)* lucid•us -a -um; *(beaming)* nitid•us -a -um; *(smart)* a•cer -cris -cre; *(eyes)* veget•us -a -um
brighten *tr* illuminare ‖ *intr* lucescěre, clarescěre; **his face —ed up** vultus ejus in hilaritatem solutus est
brightly *adv* clare, lucide
brightness *s* nit•or -oris *m,* cand•or -oris *m; (of sky)* serenit•as -atis *f*
brilliance *s* splend•or -oris *m; (ability)* lu•x -cis *f;* **— of style** nit•or -oris *m* orationis
brilliant *adj* splendid•us -a -um; *(esp. fig: achievement, speech, battle, etc.)* luculent•us -a -um
brilliantly *adv* splendide, luculente
brim *s (rim)* or•a -ae *f; (border)* marg•o -inis *mf;* **to fill to the —** ad summam oram implēre
brimful *adj* ad summum plen•us -a -um
brimstone *s* sulf•ur -uris *n*
brine *s* salsament•um -i *n; (the sea)* sal•um -i *n*
bring *tr* (to) afferre (ad + *acc); (by carriage, etc.)* advehěre; *(letters, report, news)* perferre; **to — about** efficěre, perficěre; **to — along** afferre; **to — (s.o.) around** circumagěre (aliquem); **to — back** referre, reducěre; *(to recall)* revocare; *(by force, authority)* redigěre; **to — before a court of law** producěre in judicium; **to —** *(a matter)* **before the senate** ad senatum referre de *(w. abl);* **to — credit to** fidem ferre *(w. dat);* **to — down** deferre; *(e.g., a tower)* dejicěre; **to — forth** proděre, deproměre; *(to yield)* ferre; **to — forward** proferre; **to — in** inferre; *(on a vehicle)* invehěre; *(money, profit)* efficěre; **to — it about that** efficěre ut; **to — on** afferre; *(illness, fever)* adducěre; *(fig)* objicěre; **to — oneself to** animum inducěre ut *(w. subj);* **to — out** *(to reveal)* proferre; *(to elicit)* elicěre; *(the wine)* (ex)proměre; *(a book)* proděre; **to — over** perducěre; *(fig)* perducěre, conciliare; **to — to** adducěre; **to — together** conferre; *(to assemble)* cogěre, contrahěre; *(esp. forces)* comparare; *(estranged persons)* conciliare; **to — to pass** efficěre; **to — under one's control** subigěre; **to — up** subducěre; *(children)* educare; *(to vomit)* evoměre; *(a topic)* mentionem facěre de *(w. abl)*
brink *s* marg•o -inis *mf;* **on the — of death** morti vicin•us -a -um; **to be on the — of disaster** in summo discrimine versari
brisk *adj (lively)* ala•cer -cris -cre; *(wind)* vehement•ior -ior -ius; *(weather)* frigid•us -a -um; **to be —** vigēre
briskly *adv* alacriter
briskness *s* alacrit•as -atis *f,* vig•or -oris *m*
bristle *s* saet•a -ae *f*
bristle *intr* horrēre
bristly *adj* sactos•us -a -um
Britain *s* Britanni•a -ae *f*
British *adj* Britannic•us -a -um
brittle *adj* fragil•is -is -e
broach *tr* in medium proferre
broad *adj* lat•us -a -um; *(grin)* solut•us -a -um; *(general)* commun•is -is -e; **in — daylight** *(fig)* propalam; **to sleep till — daylight** ad multum diem dormire
broadcast *tr* divulgare
broaden *tr (to widen)* dilatare; *(to enlarge)* ampliare ‖ *intr* in latitudinem crescěre, latescěre
broadsword *s* glad•ius -(i)i *m*
brocade *s* seric•um -i *n* aureo *(or* argento) filo intertextum
broccoli *s* brassic•a -ae *f* oleracea Botyrtis
brochure *s* libell•us -i *m*
broil *s* rix•a -ae *f*
broil *tr* torrēre ‖ *intr* torrēri
broken *adj* fract•us -a -um; *(by age, hard times)* confect•us -a -um; *(faltering)* infract•us -a -um; **— in** domit•us -a -um
broken-hearted *adj* deject•us -a -um
broker *s* arillat•or -oris *m*
bronze *s* ae•s -ris *n*
bronze *adj* aëne•us -a -um
brooch *s* fibul•a -ae *f*
brood *s* prol•es -is *f; (of birds, etc. hatched together)* fetur•a -ae *f*
brood *intr* **to — over** *(lit & fig)* incubare *(w. dat),* parturire
brook *s* rivul•us -i *m*
brook *tr* tolerare, pati
broom *s* scop•ae -arum *fpl*
broth *s* ju•s -ris *n*
brothel *s* lupan•ar -aris *n*
brother *s* fra•ter -tris *m*
brotherhood *s* fraternit•as -atis *f; (organization)* sodalit•as -atis *f*
brother-in-law *s* lev•ir -iri *m*
brotherly *adj* fratern•us -a -um

brow *s* fron•s -tis *f; (of a hill)* dors•um -i *n;* **to knit the —** frontem contrahĕre
browbeat *tr* minis et terrore commovēre
brown *adj (w. a dash of yellow)* fulv•us -a -um; *(chestnut color)* spad•ix -icis; *(of skin)* adust•us -a -um
browse *intr* depasci
bruise *tr* contundĕre; *(to make black-and-blue)* sugillare
bruise *s* contusi•o -onis *f; (black-and-blue)* suggillati•o -onis *f*
bruise mark *s* liv•or -oris *m*
brunette *s* puell•a -ae *f* subfusca
brunt *s* tota vis *f*
brush *s (scrub brush)* penicul•us -i *m; (painter's)* penicill•us -i *m; (skirmish)* aggressi•o -onis *f; (bushes)* vigult•a -orum *npl*
brush *tr (lightly)* verrĕre; *(teeth)* purgare; *(shoes)* detergēre; **to — aside** spernĕre; **to — away** or **out** detergēre ‖ *intr* **to — past s.o.** aliquem praetereundo leviter terĕre
brutal *adj* imman•is -is -e
brutality *s* immanit•as -atis *f*
brutally *adv* immaniter
brute *adj* brut•us -a -um
brute *s* belu•a -ae *f*
brutish *adj* imman•is -is -e
bubble *s* bull•a -ae *f*
bubble *intr* bullire, bullare; *(of a spring)* scatēre
bubbling *s* bullit•us -ūs *m; (of a spring)* scatebr•a -ae *f*
bubbly *adj (person)* argutiis scat•ens -entis
buccaneer *s* pirat•a -ae *m*
buck *s* cerv•us -i *m; (he-goat)* hirc•us -i *m*
bucket *s* situl•a -ae *f;* **to kick the —** *(coll)* animam ebullire
buckle *s* fibul•a -ae *f*
buckle *tr* fibulā nectĕre ‖ *intr (to bend)* flecti; *(to collapse)* collabi; **to — down** se applicare; **to — up** se fibulā nectĕre
buckler *s* parm•a -ae *f*
bucolic *adj* bucolic•us -a -um
bud *s* gemm•a -ae *f; (of a flower)* cal•yx -ycis *m;* **to nip s.th. in the —** aliquid maturum occupare
bud *intr* gemmare
buddy *s* conger•o -onis *m*
budge *tr* ciēre, movēre ‖ *intr* se movēre, loco cedĕre
budget *s* pecuniae rati•o -onis *f*
buffalo *s* ur•us -i *m*
buffet *s (sideboard)* abac•us -i *m; (slap)* alap•a -ae *f*
buffet *tr* jactare
buffoon *s* scurr•a -ae *f;* **to play the —** scurrari
bug *s* cim•ex -icis *mf*
buggy *s (two-wheeled)* carpent•um -i *n; (four-wheeled)* pertorrit•um -i *n*
bugle *s* bucin•a -ae *f,* corn•u -us *n*
bugle call *s* classic•um -i *n*
bugler *s* bucinat•or -oris *m*
build *tr (house, ship)* aedificare; *(house, walls)* (ex)struĕre; *(bridge)* fabricare; *(wall, rampart)* ducĕre; *(road)* munire; *(hopes)* ponĕre; **to — up** exstruĕre
builder *s* aedificat•or -oris *m,* struct•or -oris *m*
building *s (act)* aedificati•o -onis *f,* exstructi•o -onis *f; (structure)* aedific•ium -(i)i *n*
building site *s* are•a -ae *f*
bulb *s* bulb•us -i *m*
bulge *intr (swell)* tumēre; *(to stand out)* prominēre
bulge *s* tub•er -eris *n*
bulk *s* amplitud•o -inis *f; (mass)* mol•es -is *f; (greater part)* major par•s -tis *f*
bulkiness *s* magnitud•o -inis *f*
bulky *adj (huge)* ing•ens -entis; *(difficulty to handle)* inhabil•is -is -e
bull *s* taur•us -i *m*
bulldog *s* can•is -is *m* Moloss•us
bulldozer *s* machin•a -ae *f* aggerandi
bullet *s* glan•s -dis *f* plumbea
bulletin *s* libell•us -i *m; (news)* nunt•ius -(i)i *m*
bulletin board *s* tabul•a -ae *f* publica
bullfrog *s* ran•a -ae *f* ocellata
bullion *s (gold)* aur•um -i *n* infectum; *(silver)* argent•um -i *n* infectum
bullock *s* juvenc•us -i *m*
bull's eye *s* scop•us -i *m* medius; **hit the —** scopum medium ferire
bully *s* scordal•us -i *m*
bully *tr* procaciter lacessĕre
bulwark *s (wall)* moen•ia -ium *npl; (any means of defense)* propugnacul•um -i *n; (fig)* ar•x -cis *f*
bump *s (swelling)* tub•er -eris *n; (thump)* plag•a -ae *f,* sonit•us -ūs *m*
bump *tr* pulsare, pellĕre ‖ *intr* **to — against** offendĕre
bumpy *adj* tuberos•us -a -um; *(road, ground)* iniqu•us -a -um
bun *s (roll)* lib•um -i *n,* collyr•is -idis *f*
bunch *s* fascicul•us -i *m; (of grapes)* racem•us -i *m; (group)* glob•us -i *m*
bunch *intr* **to — together** glomerari
bundle *s* fasc•is -is *m; (of straw)* manipul•us -i *m*
bundle *tr* **to — up** *(with clothes)* coöperire
bungle *tr (a job)* inscite gerĕre, inscite agĕre ‖ *intr* errare
bungler *s* imperit•us -i *m*
buoy *tr* **to — up** sublevare
buoyancy *s* levit•as -atis *f; (fig)* hilarit•as -atis *f*
buoyant *adj* lev•is -is -e; *(fig)* hilar•is -is -e
burden *s* on•us -eris *n*
burden *tr* onerare
burdensome *adj* oneros•us -a -um
bureau *s* minister•ium -(i)i *n; (chest)*

armar•ium -(i)i *n; (for clothes)* vestiar•ium -(i)i *n*
burglar *s* effractar•ius -(i)i *m*
burglary *s* (domūs) effractur•a -ae *f*
burial *s (act)* sepultur•a -ae *f; (ceremony)* fun•us -eris *n*
burial place *s* sepulchr•um -i *n*
burlesque *s* ridicula imitati•o -onis *f*
burly *adj* corpulent•us -a -um
burn *tr* urěre, cremare; **to — down** deurěre; **to — out** exurěre; **to — up** comburěre ‖ *intr* flagrare, ardēre; **to — down** deflagrare; **to — out** exstingui; **to — up** conflagrare
burn *s* adusti•o -onis *f; (injury)* ambust•um -i *n*
burning *adj* ard•ens -entis
burn-out *s* defecti•o -onis *f* virium
burrow *s* cunicul•us -i *m*
burrow *intr* defoděre
bursar *s* dispensat•or -oris *m*
burst *s (spurt)* impet•us -ūs *m; (noise)* frag•or -oris *m;* **— of anger** iracundiae impet•us -ūs *m;* **— of applause** clamor•es -um *mpl*
burst *tr* rumpěre; *(with noise)* disploděre; **to — asunder** dirumpěre; **to — open** effrangěre ‖ *intr* rumpi; **to — forth** prorumpěre; **to — in** irrumpěre; **to — out** erumpěre; **to — out laughing** risum effunděre
bury *tr* sepelire; *(to hide)* abděre; **to — the sword in his side** lateri abděre ensem
bush *s* frut•ex -icis *m; (thorny bush)* dum•us -i *m;* **to beat around the —** circuitione uti
bushel *s* medimn•us -i *m*
bushy *adj (full of bushes)* dumos•us -a -um; *(full of branches)* ramos•us -a -um; *(tail)* villos•us -a -um
busily *adv* impigre, sedulo
business *s* negot•ium -(i)i *n; (trade, calling)* ar•s -tis *f; (matter)* res, rei *f; (establishment)* officin•a -ae *f;* **I always made it my — to be present** ego id semper egi ut adessem; **to mind one's own —** negotium suum agěre; **what — do you have here?** quid negotii tibi hic est?; **what — is it of his?** quid illius interest?
business agent *s* negotiorum curat•or -oris *m*
businessman *s* negotiat•or -oris *m*
buskin *s* cothurn•us -i *m*
bust *s* imag•o -inis *f; (bosom)* pectus -oris *n; (woman's)* mammill•ae -arum *fpl*
bustle *s (hurry)* festinati•o -onis *f; (running to and fro)* discurs•us -ūs *m*
bustle *intr* festinare; **to — about** discurrěre
busy *adj* occupat•us -a -um; *(time)* operos•us -a -um; *(w. business matters)* negotios•us -a -um
busy *tr* **to — oneself** versari
busybody *s* ardali•o -onis *m*
but *prep* praeter *(w. acc)*
but *adv* modo, tantum
but *conj* sed; *(stronger)* at; **— if** quodsi; sin; **— if not** sin aliter
butcher *s* lan•ius -(i)i *m; (fig)* carnif•ex -icis *m*
butcher *tr (animals)* caeděre; *(people)* contrucidare
butcher shop *s* lanien•a -ae *f*
butchery *s* trucidati•o -onis *f*
butler *s* prom•us -i *m*
butt *s (mark)* met•a -ae *f; (backside)* clun•es -ium *mpl;* **— of ridicule** ludibr•ium -(i)i *n*
butt *tr* arietare ‖ *intr* **to — in** interpellare
butter *s* butyr•um -i *n*
butter *tr (bread)* (panem) butyro inducěre; **to — s.o. up** blandiri *(w. dat)*
buttercup *s* ranuncul•us -i *m* tuberosus
butterfly *s* papili•o -onis *m*
buttermilk *s* lactis ser•um -i *n*
buttock *s* clun•is -is *mf*
button *s* globul•us -i *m* vestiarius
button *tr* globulo nectěre
buttress *s* anter•is -idis *f*
buttress *tr* suffulcire
buxom *adj* ampl•us -a -um
buy *tr* **(from)** eměre, mercari de (w *abl*); **to — back** *or* **off** rediměre; **to — up** coëměre
buyer *s* empt•or -oris *m*
buying *s* empti•o -onis *f*
buzz *s* bomb•us -i *m*
buzz *intr* bombilare
buzzard *s* bute•o -onis *m*
by *prep (agency)* a, ab *(w. abl); (of place) (near)* apud *(w. acc); (along)* secundum *(w. acc); (past)* praeter *(w. acc); (in oaths)* per *(w. acc);* **— and —** mox; **— means of** per *(w. acc);* **— oneself** per se; *(alone)* sol•us -a -um
bygone *adj* praeterit•us -a -um; *(olden)* prisc•us -a -um
bylaw *s* praescript•um -i *n*
bypass *s* circuit•us -ūs *m*
bypass *tr* ambire
bystander *s* spectat•or -oris *m*
byway *s* deverticul•um -i *n*
byword *s* proverb•ium -(i)i n

C

cab *s (for hire)* cis•ium -(i)i *n* meritorium
cabbage *s* brassic•a -ae *f; (head of cabbage)* caul•is -is *m*
cabin *s (cottage)* cas•a -ae *f; (on a ship)* daiet•a -ae *f*
cabin boy *s* pu•er -eri *m* nauticus
cabinet *s* armar•ium -(i)i *n; (pol)* consil•ium -(i)i *n* principis
cabinet member *s* consiliat•or -oris *m*
cable *s* rud•ens -entis *m; (for anchor)* ancoral•e -is *n*

cackle *intr (of hens)* gracillare; *(of geese)* gingrire
cackle *s* gingrit•us -ūs *m*
cacophony *s* dissonae voc•es -ium *fpl*
cactus *s* cact•us -i *f*
cadaver *s* cadav•er -eris *n*
cadaverous *adj* cadaveros•us -a -um
cadence *s* numer•us -i *m*
cadet *s* discipul•us -i *m* militaris
cage *s* cave•a -ae *f; (for large animals)* sept•um -i *n*
cage *tr* in cavea *or* septo includĕre
caged *adj* caveat•us -a -um
cahoots *spl* **be in — with** colludĕre cum *(w. abl)*
cajole *tr* lactare
cake *s* placent•a -ae *f; (birthday cake)* lib•um -ī *n*
calamitous *adj* calamitos•us -a -um
calamity *s* calamit•as -atis *f;* **to suffer —** calamitatem perferre
calculate *tr* computare; *(fig)* existimare
calculated *adj* subduct•us -a -um
calculation *s* computati•o -onis *f; (fig)* ratiocinati•o -onis *f*
calculator *s* computat•or -oris *m*
caldron *s* cortin•a -ae *f; (of copper)* ahen•um -i *n*
calendar *s* fast•i -orum *mpl*
calends *spl* Kalend•ae -arum *fpl*
calf *s* vitul•us -i *m,* vitul•a -ae *f; (anat)* sur•a -ae *f*
caliber *s (fig)* ingen•ium -(i)i *n*
call *s* vocati•o -onis *f; (shout)* clam•or -oris *m; (visit)* salutati•o -onis *f; (summons)* accit•us -ūs *m;* **social —** offic•ium -(i)i *n;* **to make** *or* **pay a social —** officium peragĕre
call *tr (to summon)* ad se vocare; *(to name)* appellare, vocare; **to — aside** sevocare; **to — away** avocare; **to — back** revocare; **to — down** devocare; **to — forth** evocare; *(to cause)* provocare; *(fig)* elicĕre; **to — in** *(money)* cogĕre; *(for advice)* advocare; *(a doctor)* arcessĕre; **to — off** *(to cancel)* revocare, tollĕre; *(to read)* citare; **to — out** *(to call forth)* evocare; *(to shout)* exclamare; **to — to account** *(to upraid)* compellĕre; **to — together** convocare; **to — to mind** recordari; **to — to witness** testari; **to — up** *(mil)* evocare ‖ *intr* **to — for** *(to demand)* poscĕre; *(to require)* requirĕre; **to — on** *(to invoke)* invocare; *(for help)* implorare; *(to visit)* visĕre
caller *s* salutat•or -oris *m*
calling *s (profession)* ar•s -tis *f; (station)* stat•us -ūs *m*
callous *adj* callos•us -a -um; *(fig)* exper•s -tis sensūs; **to become —** occallescĕre; *(fig)* obdurescĕre
callus *s* call•us -i *m*
calm *adj (unruffled)* tranquill•us -a -um; *(sleep, sea, speech, old age)* placid•us -a -um; *(mentally)* aequ•us -a -um
calm *tr* sedare, tranquillare
calming *s* sedati•o -onis *f*
calmly *adv* tranquille, placide; *(of a person)* aequo animo
calmness *s (lit & fig)* tranquillit•as -atis *f;* **with —** aequo animo
calumny *s (abuse)* maledict•um -i *n; (slander)* calumni•a -ae *f*
camel *s* camel•us -i *m*
cameo *s* imag•o -inis *f* ectypa
camouflage *s* dissimulati•o -onis *f*
camouflage *tr* dissimulare
camp *s* castr•a -orum *npl;* **summer —** aestiv•a -orum; *npl* **winter —** hibern•a -orum *npl*
camp *adj* castrens•is -is -e
camp *intr* castra ponĕre
campaign *s (mil)* expediti•o -onis *f,* stipend•ium -(i)i *n; (pol)* **(for)** petiti•o -onis *f (w. gen)*
campaign *intr (mil)* stipendium merēre; *(pol)* ambire
campaigning *s (pol)* ambiti•o -onis *f*
camp follower *s* cal•o -onis *m*
camphor *s* camphor•a -ae *f*
can *s* pyx•is -idis *f* stannea
can *intr* posse; *(to have the power)* pollēre; **I — not** nequeo, non possum
canal *s* foss•a -ae *f* navigabilis
canary *s* fringill•a -ae *f* Canaria
cancel *tr* tollĕre; *(to cross out)* cancellare, delēre
cancellation *s* deleti•o -onis *f; (fig)* aboliti•o -onis *f*
cancer *s* can•cer -cri *m,* carcinom•a -atis *n*
cancerous *adj* concros•us -a -um
candid *adj* apert•us -a -um
candidate *s (for)* candidat•us -i *m (w. gen);* **to announce oneself as —** profiteri
candidly *adv* aperte, libere
candied *adj* succharo condit•us -a -um
candle *s* candel•a -ae *f*
candlestick *s* candelabr•um -i *n*
candor *s* cand•or -oris *m*
candy *s* sacchar•um -i *n* crystallinum
cane *s (walking stick)* bacul•us -i *m; (reed)* harund•o -inis *f*
cane *tr* baculo verberare
canine *adj* canin•us -a -um
canister *s* pyx•is -idis *f*
canker *s* rubig•o -inis *f*
cannibal *s* anthropophag•us -i *m*
cannon *s* torment•um -i *n*
cannonball *s* glob•us -i *m* missilis
canoe *s* scaph•a -ae *f*
canon *s* can•on -onis *m*
canonical *adj* canonic•us -a -um
canopy *s* canope•um -i *n*
cantata *s* carm•en -inis *n* ad musicam accommodatum

canteen *s (flask)* lagunculˑa -ae *f; (mil)* cauponˑa -ae *f* castrensis
canter *s* lenis quadrupedans gradˑus -ūs *m*
canter *intr* leniter currĕre
canticle *s* canticˑum -i *n*
canto *s* liˑber -bri *m*
canton *s* pagˑus -i *m*
canvas *s* linteˑum -i *n* crassum; *(for painting)* textilˑe -is *n*
cap *s* pilleˑus -i *m; (worn by certain priests)* galerˑus -i *m*
capability *s* facultˑas -atis *f*
capable *adj (skilled)* sollerˑs -tis, peritˑus -a -um; **(of)** capˑax -acis *(w. gen);* **— of enduring** *(cold, hunger, etc.)* patiˑens -entis *(w. gen);* **— of holding 500 spectators** capˑax -acis quingentorum spectatorum
capably *adv* scite
capacious *adj* capˑax -acis
capacity *s (extent of space)* capacitˑas -atis *f; (extent of mental power)* mensurˑa -ae *f; (ability)* ingenˑium -(i)i *n*
cape *s* promontorˑium -(i)i *n; (garment)* humeralˑe -is *n*
caper *s (leap)* exsultatiˑo -onis *f; (prank)* ludibrˑium -(i)i *n; (bold criminal act)* scelˑus -eris *n;* **to pull a —** scelus patrare
capital *adj (chief)* praecipuˑus -a -um; *(offense, punishment)* capitalˑis -is -e; *(letters)* uncialˑis -is -e
capital *s (chief city)* capˑut -itis *n; (archit)* capitulˑum -i *n; (com)* capˑut -itis *n,* sorˑs -tis *f*
capitalist *s* feneratˑor -oris *m*
capitol *s* capitolˑium -(i)i *n*
capitulate *intr* se dedĕre
capitulation *s* deditiˑo -onis *f*
capon *s* capˑo -onis *m*
caprice *s* libidˑo -inis *f*
capricious *adj* inconstˑans -antis
capriciously *adv* inconstanter
Capricorn *s* Capricornˑus -i *m*
capsize *tr* evertĕre **‖** *intr* everti
capsule *s* capsulˑa -ae *f; (bot)* vasculˑum -i *n*
captain *s (in infantry)* centuriˑo -onis *m; (in cavalry)* praefectˑus -i *m; (in navy)* navarchˑus -i *m; (of merchant ship)* navis magisˑter -tri *m*
caption *s* capitulˑum -i *n; (leg)* praescriptiˑo -onis *f*
captious *adj (tricky)* captiosˑus -a -um; *(carping)* morosˑus -a -um
captivate *tr* capĕre
captive *adj* captivˑus -a -um
captive *s* captivˑus -i *m,* captivˑa -ae *f*
captor *s* captˑor -oris *m; (of a city)* expugnatˑor -oris *m*
capture *s* comprehensiˑo -onis *f; (of a city)* expugnatiˑo -onis *f; (of animals)* capturˑa -ae *f*
capture *tr* capĕre, excipĕre; *(city)* expugnare; *(by surprise)* opprimĕre

car *s (chariot)* currˑus -ūs *m; (carriage)* raedˑa -ae *f; (modern)* automobilˑe -is *n*
caravan *s* commeatˑus -ūs *m*
carbon *s* carbonˑium -(i)i *n*
carbuncle *s* carbunculˑus -i *m*
carcass *s* cadavˑer -eris *n*
card *s* chartˑa -ae *f*
cardboard *s* chartˑa -ae *f* crassior
cardinal *adj* principalˑis -is -e; *(color)* ruˑber -bra -brum; *(numbers)* cardinalˑis -is -e
cardinal *s (eccl)* cardinalˑis -is *m*
care *s (anxiety, oversight, attention)* curˑa -ae *f; (diligence)* diligentiˑa -ae *f; (charge)* tutelˑa -ae *f; (watching over)* custodiˑa -ae *f;* **— was taken by the senate to** *(w.inf)* opera a senatu data est ut; **to take — of** curare
care *intr* curare; **to — for** *(to look after)* curare; *(to be fond of, with negatives)* morari; **I don't — for wine** ego vinum nihil moror
career *s* curriculˑum -i *n; (pol)* cursˑus -ūs *m* honorum
carefree *adj* securˑus -a -um
careful *adj (attentive)* diligˑens -entis; *(cautious)* cautˑus -a -um; *(of work)* accuratˑus -a -um
carefully *adv* diligenter; caute
careless *adj* neglegˑens -entis
carelessly *adv* neglegenter
carelessness *s* incuriˑa -ae *f; (stronger)* neglegentiˑa -ae *f*
caress *s* amplexˑus -ūs *m*
caress *tr* fovēre
cargo *s* onˑus -eris *n;* **to put a ship's — aboard** navem onerare
caricature *s* gryllˑus -i *m*
caricature *tr* in pejus fingĕre
carnage *s* stragˑes -is *f*
carnal *adj* carnalˑis -is -e
carnival *s* feriˑae -arum *fpl* ante quadragesimam
carnivorous *adj* carnivorˑus -a -um
carol *s* cantˑus -ūs *m*
carouse *intr* comissari
carp *s* cyprinˑus -i *m*
carp *intr* **to — at** carpĕre
carpenter *s* faˑber -bri *m* tignarius
carpentry *s* materiaturˑa -ae *f* fabrilis
carpet *s* tapetˑe -is *n*
carriage *s* vehiculˑum -i *n,* raedˑa -ae *f; (esp. women's)* carpentˑum -i *n*
carrier *s* bajulˑus -i *m*
carrion *s* carˑo -nis *f* morticina
carrot *s* carotˑa -ae *f*
carry *tr* ferre; *(of heavier things)* portare; *(by vehicle)* vehĕre; *(a law)* perferre; **to — away** auferre; evehĕre; **to — in** importare; invehĕre; **to — off** auferre; *(by force)* rapĕre; **to — on** *(to conduct)* exercēre: *(war)* gerĕre; **to — out** efferre; evehĕre; *(to perform)* exsequi; **to —**

through perferre; **to — weight** auctoritatem habēre ‖ *intr (of sound)* audiri; **to — on** pergĕre; *(to behave)* se gerĕre
cart *s* plaustr•um -i *n; (dim.)* plostell•um -i *n; (two-wheeled, drawn by oxen)* carr•us -i *m;* **putting the — before the horse** praeposteris consiliis
cart *tr* plaustro vehĕre; **to — off** plaustro evehĕre
carve *tr* sculpĕre; *(to engrave)* caelare; *(at table)* secare
carver *s (engraver)* caelat•or -oris *m; (at table)* sciss•or -oris *m*
carving *s* caelatur•a -ae *f*
carving knife *s* cultell•us -i *m*
cascade *s* praeceps aquae laps•us -ūs *m*
case *s (leg)* caus•a -ae *f; (matter, circumstances, condition)* res, rei *f; (instance)* exempl•um -i *n; (container)* involucr•um -i *n; (patient)* aeg•er -ri *m,* aegr•a -ae *f; (gram)* cas•us -ūs *m;* **if that's the —** si res sic habet; **in any —** utcumque; **in no —** nequaquam; **in the — of Priam** in Priamo; **since that's the —** quae cum ita sint
casement *s* biforis fenestr•a -ae *f*
cash *s* numm•i -orum *mpl;* numerat•um -i *n;* **in hard —** in nummis: **to pay —** praesenti pecuniā solvĕre
cash box *s* arc•a -ae *f*
cashier *s* dispensat•or -oris *m*
cash payment *s* repraesentati•o -onis *f*
cask *s* cad•us -i *m*
casket *s* capul•us -i *m*
cast *s (throw)* jact•us -ūs *m; (mold)* typ•us -i *m;* **— of characters** distributi•o -onis *f* partium in singulos actores
cast *tr* jacĕre; *(metal)* fundĕre; *(a vote)* ferre; **to — aside** abjicĕre; **to — down** dejicĕre; **to — in** injicĕre; **to — off** *(skin)* exuĕre; *(fig)* ponĕre; **to — out** ejicĕre, expellĕre; **to — upon** superinjicĕre; *(fig)* aspergĕre ‖ *intr* **to — off** navem solvĕre
castanet *s* crotal•um -i *n*
castaway *s* perdit•us -i *m*
caste *s* ord•o -inis *m*
castigate *intr* castigare
castle *s* castell•um -i *n*
castor oil *n* cicinum ole•um -i *n*
castrate *tr* castrare
castration *s* castrati•o -onis *f*
casual *adj* fortuit•us -a -um; *(person)* negleg•ens -entis
casually *adv* fortuito, casu
casualty *s* cas•us -ūs *m*
cat *s* fel•es -is *f*
cataclysm *s* cataclysm•os -i *m*
catacombs *spl* catacumb•ae -arum *fpl*
catalogue *s* catalog•us -i *m*
cataract *s* cataract•a -ae *f; (of the eyes)* glaucom•a -atis *n*
catastrophe *s* calamit•as -atis *f*
catcall *s* irrisi•o -onis *f*
catch *s (of fish)* praed•a -ae *f; (fastening)* fibul•a -ae *f;* **to think s.o. a great —** aliquem magni facĕre; **what's the — ?** quid est captatio?
catch *tr* capĕre; *(unawares)* excipĕre; *(to surprise)* deprehendĕre; *(falling object)* excipĕre, suscipĕre; *(in a net)* illaquēre; *(fish)* captare; *(birds)* excipĕre; **to — a cold** gravedine affligi; **to — fire** ignem *or* flammam concipĕre; **to — hell** convicium habēre; **to — his eye** experimentum oculorum ejus capĕre; **to — red-handed** deprehendĕre; **to — sight of** conspicĕre ‖ *intr* **to — at** arripĕre; **to — on** comprehendĕre; **to — up to** consequi
catching *adj (contagious)* contagios•us -a -um; *(fig)* grat•us -a -um
categorical *adj* categoric•us -a -um
categorically *adv* categorice
category *s* categori•a -ae *f*
cater *intr* cibum suppeditare; **to — to** indulgēre *(w. dat)*
caterer *s* obsonat•or -oris *m*
caterpillar *s* eruc•a -ae *f*
cathedral *s* ecclesi•a -ae *f* cathedralis
catholic *adj* catholic•us -a -um
cattle *s* pec•us -oris *n*
cauliflower *s* brassic•a -ae *f* oleracea botryitis
causal *adj* causal•is -is -e
cause *s* caus•a -ae *f; (motive)* rati•o -onis *f*
cause *tr* facĕre, efficĕre; *(to stir up)* movēre; **to — a quarrel** litem facĕre; **to — him to leave** facĕre ut abeat
causeless *adj* sine causa
causeway *s* agg•er -eris *m*
caustic *adj* caustic•us -a -um; *(fig)* mord•ax -acis
cauterize *tr* adurĕre
caution *s* cauti•o -onis *f;* **to use great —** diligenter circumspicĕre; **with —** pedetemptim
caution *tr* (ad)monēre
cautious *adj* caut•us -a -um
cautiously *adv* caute
cavalcade *s* pomp•a -ae *f*
cavalier *s* equ•es -itis *m*
cavalry *s* equitat•us -ūs *m*
cave *s* spec•us -ūs *m*
cavern *s* cavern•a -ae *f*
cavernous *adj* cavernos•us -a -um
caviar *s* ov•a -orum *npl* acipenseris
cavity *s* cav•um -i *n; (anat)* lacun•a -ae *f*
caw *intr* crocire, crocitare
cease *intr* desinĕre; *(temporarily)* intermittĕre
ceaseless *adj* perpetu•us -a -um
ceaselessly *adv* perpetuo
cedar *s* cedr•us -ūs *f*
cedar *adj* cedre•us -a -um
cede *tr* cedĕre *(w. abl)*

ceiling *s* camer•a -ae *f; (panelled)* lacun•ar -aris *n*
celebrate *tr* celebrare; *(in song)* canĕre
celebrated *adj* cele•ber -bris -bre
celebration *s* celebrati•o -onis *f; (of rites)* sollemn•e -is *n*
celebrity *s* celebrit•as -atis *f; (person)* vi•r -ri *m* illustris
celery *s* heleoselin•um -i *n*
celestial *adj* caelest•is -is -e
celibacy *s* caelibat•us -ūs *m*
celibate *adj* caeleb•s -is
cell *s* cell•a -ae *f*
cellar *s* hypoge•um -i *n*
cement *s* ferrum•en -inis *n*
cement *tr* ferruminare; *(to glue)* conglutinare ‖ *intr* coalescĕre
cemetery *s* sepulcret•um -i *n*
cenotaph *s* cenotaph•ium -(i)i *n*
censer *s* turibul•um -i *n*
censor *s* cens•or -oris *m*
censorship *s* censur•a -ae *f; (of literature)* literarum censur•a -ae *f*
censure *s* vituperati•o -onis *f*
censure *tr* animadvertĕre; *(officially)* notare
census *s* civium enumerati•o -onis *f; (in the Roman sense)* cens•us -ūs *m;* **to conduct a —** recensum populi agĕre
cent *s* centesim•a -ae *f;* **I don't owe anyone a red —** assem aerarium nemini debeo
centaur *s* centaur•us -i *m*
centenary *adj* centenari•us -a -um
centenary *s* centesimus ann•us -i *m*
center *s* med•ium -(i)i *n; (math)* centr•um -i *n;* **in the — of the town** in medio oppido
center *tr* in centrum ponĕre ‖ *intr* **to — on** niti *(w. abl)*
central *adj* medi•us -a -um
centralize *tr (authority)* ad unum deferre
centurion *s* centuri•o -onis *m*
century *s* saecul•um -i *n; (mil, pol)* centuri•a -ae *f*
ceramic *adj* fictil•is -is -e
ceramics *s* ar•s -tis *f* figlina; *(objects)* fictil•ia -ium *npl*
cereal *s* cereal•e-is *n*
cerebellum *s* cerebell•um -i *n*
cerebrum *s* cerebr•um -i *n*
ceremonial *adj* sollemn•is -is -e
ceremonial *s* sollemn•e -is *n; (religious)* rit•us -ūs *m*
ceremonious *adj* solemn•is -is -e; *(person)* officios•us -a -um
ceremoniously *adv* rite
ceremony *s* caerimoni•a -ae *f; (pomp)* apparat•us -ūs *m;* **religious ceremonies** religion•es -um *fpl*
certain *adj (sure)* cert•us -a -um; *(indefinite)* quidam quaedam quoddam; **for —** pro certo; **it is certain that** constat *(w. acc & inf)*
certainly *adv* profecto
certainty *s* cert•um -i *n; (belief)* fid•es -ei *f*
certificate *s* testimon•ium -(i)i *n*
certify *tr* confirmare
cessation *s* cessati•o -onis *f; (temporary)* intermissi•o -onis *f;* **— of hostilities** induti•ae -arum *fpl*
chafe *tr* urĕre; *(w. the hand)* fricare; *(to excoriate)* atterĕre; *(to vex)* irritare ‖ *intr* stomachari
chaff *s* pale•a -ae *f; (fig)* quisquili•ae -arum *fpl*
chagrin *s* stomach•us -i *m*
chagrined *adj* **to be —** stomachari
chain *s* caten•a -ae *f; (necklace)* torqu•es -is *mf; (fig)* seri•es -ei *f;* **dog on a —** can•is -is *m* catenis vinctus
chain *tr* catenas injicĕre *(w. dat)*
chaingang *s* compedit•i -orum *mpl*
chair *s* sell•a -ae *f; (w. rounded back)* arcisell•ium -(i)i *n; (of a teacher)* cathedr•a -ae *f; (of a magistrate)* sella *f* curulis
chair *tr (a meeting)* praesidēre *(w. dat),* praeesse *(w. dat)*
chairperson *s* praes•es -idis *mf*
chalice *s* cal•ix -icis *m*
chalk *s* cret•a -ae *f*
chalk *tr* cretā notare; *(cover with chalk)* cretā illinĕre; **to — up** notare
chalky *adj (chalk-like)* cretace•us -a -um; *(full of chalk)* cretos•us -a -um
challenge *s* provocati•o -onis *f; (leg)* rejecti•o -onis *f*
challege *tr* provocare; *(a claim)* vindicare; *(validity)* recusare; *(leg)* rejicĕre
challenger *s* provocat•or -oris *m*
challenging *adj* provoc•ans -antis
chamber *s (room)* conclav•e -is *n; (bedroom)* cubicul•um -i *n; (pol)* curi•a -ae *f*
chambermaid *s* ancill•a -ae *f* cubicularia
chamber pot *s* lasan•um -i *n*
champ *tr & intr* mandĕre; **to — on the bit** frena dente premĕre
champagne *s* vin•um -i *n* effervescens
champion *s* propugnat•or -oris *m*
championship *s* titul•us -i *m* victoriae
chance *s (accident)* cas•us -ūs *m; (opportunity)* potest•as -atis *f; (prospect)* sp•es -ei *f; (fig)* ale•a -ae *f;* **by —** casu, forte; **by some — or other** nescio quo casu; **game of —** ale•a -ae *f;* **to give s.o. a — to** potestatem alicui facĕre *(w. inf);* **to stand a —** potestatem habēre; **to take a —** periculum adire
chance *tr* periclitari ‖ *intr* accidĕre; *often expressed by the adverb* forte: **I —ed to see the aedile** aedilem forte conspexi; **to — on** occurrĕre *(w. dat)*
chance *adj* fortuit•us -a -um
chancel *s* cancell•us -i *m*
chancellor *s* cancellar•ius -(i)i *m*

chandelier *s* candelabr•um -i *n*
change *s* mutati•o -onis *f; (complete)* commutati•o -onis *f,* permutati•o -onis *f; (variety)* variet•as -atis *f; (of fortune)* vicissitud•o -inis *f; (coins)* numm•i -orum *mpl* minores; **— of clothes** mutati•o -onis *f* vestis; **— of heart** animi mutati•o -onis *f;* **for a —** varietatis causā
change *tr* mutare; *(completely)* commutare; **to — into** convertĕre in *(w. acc)* ‖ *intr* mutari, variare; *(of the moon)* renovari; **to — for the better (worse)** in meliorem (pejorem) partem mutari; **to — into** verti in *(w. acc)*
changeable *adj* mutabil•is -is -e; *(fickle)* inconst•ans -antis
changeless *adj* immutabil•is -is -e
changeling *s* supposit•us -i *m*
channel *s* canal•is -is *m; (of rivers)* alve•us -i *m; (arm of the sea)* fret•um -i *n; (groove)* stri•a -ae *f*
channel *tr* sulcare, excavare; *(to guide)* ducĕre
chant *s* cant•us -ūs *m*
chant *tr* cantare
chaos *s* cha•os -i *n; (confusion)* perturbati•o -onis *f*
chaotic *adj* confus•us -a -um
chap *s* fissur•a -ae *f; (person)* hom•o -inis *m; (boy)* pu•er -eri *m*
chap *tr* diffindĕre; **—ed lips** fissur•ae -arum *fpl* labrorum ‖ *intr* scindi
chapel *s* sacell•um -i *n*
chapter *s* cap•ut -itis *n*
char *tr* amburĕre
character *s* mor•es -um *mpl; (inborn)* indol•es -is *f,* ingen•ium -(i)i *n; (repute)* existimati•o -onis *f; (type)* gen•us -eris *n; (letter)* litter•a -ae *f; (theat)* person•a -ae *f;* **to assume the — of a plaintiff** petitoris personam capĕre
characteristic *s* propr•ium -(i)i *n*
characteristic *adj* propri•us -a -um; **it is — of a father to protect his family** patris est familiam suam tegĕre
characteristically *adv* proprie
characterize *tr* describĕre, pingĕre
charade *s* mim•us -i *m;* **—s** aenigm•a -atis *n* syllabicum
charcoal *s* carb•o -onis *m*
charge *s* accusati•o -onis *f; (leg)* crim•en -inis *n; (mil)* impet•us -ūs *m; (into enemy territory)* incurs•us -ūs *m; (command)* mandat•um -i *n; (trust)* cur•a -ae *f,* custodi•a -ae *f; (office)* mun•us -eris *n; (cost)* impens•a -ae *f;* **free of —** gratis; **to be in —** praeesse *(w. dat);* **to bring —s against** litem intendĕre *(w. dat);* **to put in — of** praeficĕre *(w. dat);* **to take — of** curare
charge *tr (to attack)* incurrĕre *(w. dat or acc); (to enjoin upon)* mandare *(w. dat of person and* ut *w. subj);* **to — a certain price for goods** pretium statuĕre merci; **to — an expense to the citizens** sumptum civibus inferre; **to — a fixed price** pretium certum constituĕre; **to — s.o. with** *(a crime)* arguĕre aliquem *(w. gen or abl of the charge)* ‖ *intr (to make a charge)* irruĕre
charger *s* bellat•or -oris *m*
chariot *s* curr•us -ūs *m; (for racing)* curricul•um -i *n; (for war)* essed•um -i *n*
charioteer *s* aurig•a -ae *m; (combatant in a chariot)* essedar•ius -(i)i *m*
charitable *adj* benign•us -a -um; *(lenient in judgment)* mit•is -is -e
charitably *adv* benigne
charity *s* liberalit•as -atis *f; (Christian love)* carit•as -atis *f*
charlatan *s* ostentat•or -oris *m; (quack doctor)* pharmacopol•a -ae *m*
charm *s (attractiveness)* venust•as -atis *f,* lep•os -oris *m; (spell)* carm•en -inis *n; (amulet)* amulet•um -i *n*
charm *tr (to bewitch)* incantare; *(to delight)* capĕre; **to lead a —ed life** vitam divinitus munitam gerĕre
charmer *s* fascinat•or -oris *m; (fig)* delici•ae -arum *fpl*
charming *adj* lepid•us -a -um; *(beautiful)* venust•us -a -um
chart *s* tabul•a -ae *f; (nautical)* nautica tabul•a -ae *f*
chart *tr* designare
charter *tr (to hire)* conducĕre; *(to grant a charter to)* diploma donare *(w. dat)*
charter *s (instrument conferring privileges)* diplom•a -atis *n*
chase *s (hunt)* venati•o -onis *f; (pursuit)* insectati•o -onis *f*
chase *tr (to hunt)* venari; *(to engrave)* caelare; *(romantically)* petĕre; **to — away** abigĕre ‖ *intr* **to — after** petĕre
chasing *s* caelatur•a -ae *f*
chasm *s* hiat•us -ūs *m*
chaste *adj* cast•us -a -um
chastely *adv* caste
chasten *tr (to chastise)* castigare; *(to moderate)* moderare
chastise *tr* castigare
chastisement *s* castigati•o -onis *f*
chastiser *s* castigat•or -oris *m*
chastity *s* castit•as -atis *f*
chat *s* familiaris serm•o -onis *m;* **to have a —** fabulari
chat *intr* fabulari
chattel *s* res, rei *f* mancipi; **—s** bon•a -orum *npl*
chatter *s* clang•or -oris *m; (idle talk)* garrulit•as -atis *f; (of teeth)* crepit•us -ūs *m*
chatter *intr* balbutire; *(of birds)* canĕre; **my teeth —** dentibus crepito
cheap *adj* vil•is -is -e; **to be — as dirt** pro luto esse; **to sell —er** minoris vendĕre

cheaply *adv* bene, vili (pretio); **to live —** parvo sumptu vivěre
cheapen *tr* pretium minuěre *(w. gen)*
cheapness *s* vilit•as -atis *f*
cheat *tr* decipěre; **to — s.o. out of his money** aliquem pecuniā fraudare
cheat *s* plan•us -i *m*
cheater *s* fraudat•or -oris *m*
check *tr (to restrain, e.g., an onset, flow of blood, eager horses)* inhibēre; *(to slow down)* retardare; *(accounts)* dispungěre; *(to verify)* comprobare; **to — off** notare
check *s (bill)* rati•o -onis *f; (restraint)* coërciti•o -onis *f; (reprimand)* reprehensi•o -onis *f; (disadvantage)* detriment•um -i *n;* **to hold in —** suppriměre; **to write a — for** argentum perscriběre *(w. dat)*
checkered *adj* vari•us -a -um
cheek *s* gen•a -ae *f; (when puffed out by eating, blowing)* bucc•a -ae *f*
cheekbone *s* maxill•a -ae *f*
cheer *s* clam•or -oris *m;* **to be of good —** bono animo esse
cheer *tr* hortari; **to — up** exhilare; **— up!** bono animo es!
cheerful *adj* hilar•is -is -e
cheerfully *adv* hilariter
cheerfulness *s* hilarit•as -atis *f*
cheerless *adj* illaetabil•is -is -e
cheese *s* case•us -i *m*
chef *s* coqu•us -i *m* peritus
chemical *adj* chemic•us -a -um
chemical *s* chemic•um -i *n*
chemist *s* chemiae perit•us -i *m*
chemistry *s* chemi•a -ae *f*
cherish *tr* fovēre; *(fig)* colěre
cherry *s* ceras•um -i *n*
cherry-red *adj* cerasin•us -a -um
cherry tree *s* ceras•us -i *f*
chess *s* latruncul•i -orum *mpl*
chest *s (anat)* pect•us -oris *n; (box)* arc•a -ae *f,* armar•ium -(i)i *n; (for clothes)* vestiar•ium -(i)i *n*
chestnut *s* castane•a -ae *f*
chestnut tree *s* castane•a -ae *f*
chew *tr* manducare; **to — the cud** ruminare; **to — out** *(coll)* objurgare
chicanery *s* praevaricati•o -onis *f*
chick *s* pull•us -i *m; (term of endearment)* pull•a -ae *f*
chicken *s* pull•us -i *m* gallinaceus, gallin•a -ae *f*
chicken-hearted *adj* ignav•us -a -um
chicory *s* cichore•um -i *n*
chide *tr* increpitare
chief *adj* princ•eps -ipis; *(first in rank)* primari•us -a -um; **— justice** summus jud•ex -icis *m*
chief *s* princ•eps -ipis *m; (ringleader)* cap•ut -itis *n*
chiefly *adv* praecipue, inprimis
chieftain *s* du•x -cis *m*
child *s* inf•ans -antis *mf,* fil•ius -(i)i *m;* **children** liber•i -orum *mpl;* **to bear a —** parturire; **with —** gravida
childbearing *s* part•us -ūs *m*
childbirth *s* part•us -ūs *m*
childhood *s* infanti•a -ae *f,* pueriti•a -ae *f;* **from —** a puero *or* a pueris
childish *adj* pueril•is -is -e
childishly *adv* pueriliter
childless *adj* orb•us -a -um
childlike *adj* pueril•is -is -e
chill *s* frig•us -oris *n; (of the body)* horr•or -oris *m*
chill *tr* refrigerare
chilly *adj* frigidul•us -a -um; *(susceptible to cold)* alsios•us -a -um
chime *s* son•us -i *m*
chime *intr* conciněre; **to — in** succiněre; *(to interrupt)* interpellare
chimera *s* chimaer•a -ae *f*
chimney *s* camin•us -i *m*
chin *s* ment•um -i *n;* **to drop the —** labrum demittěre
China *s* Ser•es -um *mpl*
china *s* murrhin•a -orum *npl*
Chinese *adj* Seric•us -a -um
chink *s* rim•a -ae *f; (sound)* tinnit•us -ūs *m*
chink *intr* tinnire
chip *s* assul•a -ae *f; (of pottery)* fragment•um -i *n*
chip *tr (wood)* ascio dedolare; *(to break off a piece of)* praeciděre; **to — in** *(money)* conferre
chipper *adj* ala•cer -cris -cre
chirp *s (of birds)* pipat•us -ūs *m; (of crickets)* strid•or -oris *m*
chirp *intr (of birds)* pipilare; *(of crickets)* striděre
chisel *s* scalpr•um -i *n*
chisel *tr* scalpro caeděre; *(to cheat)* emungěre; *(to borrow)* mutuare
chivalrous *adj* magnanim•us -a -um
chivalry *s (knighthood)* equestris dignit•as -atis *f; (spirit)* magnanimit•as -atis *f*
chococlate *s* chocolat•um -i *n*
choice *s* electi•o -onis *f; (power of choosing)* opti•o -onis *f; (diversity)* variet•as -atis *f*
choice *adj* elect•us -a -um
choir *s* chor•us -i *m*
choke *tr* strangulare ‖ *intr* strangulari
choking *s* strangulati•o -onis *f*
choose *tr* eligěre; **to — to** *(to prefer to)* malle *(w. inf)*
chop *s* ofell•a -ae *f;* **pork —** ofella *f* porcina
chop *tr (wood)* dolabrā caeděre; **to — off** praeciděre; **to — up** minutatim conciděre
choral *adj* symphoniac•us -a -um
chord *s* nerv•us -i *m*
chorus *s* chor•us -i *m*
chorus girl *s* ambubai•a -ae *f*
Christ *s* Christ•us -i *m*
christen *tr* baptizare

Christendom *s* cuncti Christian•i -orum *mpl*
Christian *adj* Christian•us -a -um
Christian *s* Christian•us -i *m*
Christianity *s* Christianism•us -i *m*
Christmas *s* fest•um -i *n* nativitatis Christi; **it won't be — forever** *(fig)* non semper Saturnalia erunt; **Merry — !** festum natalem Christi!; **to celebrate — all year long** *(fig)* semper Saturnalia agĕre
Christmas carol *s* cantic•um -i *n* de Christi natali
Christmas day *s* Christi di•es -ei *m* natalis
Christmas eve *s* di•es -ei *m* proximus ante festum nativitatis Christi
chronic *adj* long•us -a - um
chronicle *s* annal•es -ium *mpl*
chronological *adj* **in — order** conservatis notisque temporibus
chronology *s* temporum ord•o -inis *m*
chubby *adj* crass•us -a -um
chuckle *intr* pressā voce cachinnare
chum *s* convict•or -oris *m*
church *s* ecclesi•a -ae *f*
churl *s* rustic•us -i *m*
churlish *adj* importun•us -a -um
churlishly *adv* importune
cider *s* hydromel•um -i *n*
cinder *s* favill•a -ae *f*
cinnamon *s* cinnamom•um -i *n*
cipher *s* *(code)* not•a -ae *f; (a nobody)* numer•us -i *m; (zero)* nihil *n;* **to write in —** per notas scribĕre
circle *s* circul•us -i *m; (anything round)* orb•is -is *m;* **family —** coron•a -ae *f* domi; **to form a —** *(to stand in a circle)* in orbem consistĕre; **to ride in a —** in orbem equitare
circle *tr* circumdare, cingĕre ‖ *intr* circulum ducĕre
circuit *s* circuit•us -ūs *m;* **to make a —** circumire, circumagi
circuitous *adj* flexuos•us -a -um; **by a — route** circuitu; **to take a — route** circumagi
circular *adj* rotund•us -a -um
circulate *tr (to spread)* in vulgum spargĕre ‖ *intr (of money)* in usum venire; *(to flow)* circumfluĕre; *(of news)* percrebescĕre
circulation *s* circulati•o -onis *f*
circumcise *tr* circumcidĕre
circumcised *adj* recutit•us -a -um
circumcision *s* circumcisi•o -onis *f*
circumference *s* ambit•us -ūs *m; (geom)* peripheri•a -ae *f*
circumflex *s* circumflex•us -ūs *m*
circumlocution *s* circumlocuti•o -onis *f;* **by —** per ambitum verborum
circumscribe *tr* circumscribĕre
circumspect *adj* circumspect•us -a -um
circumspection *s* circumspecti•o -onis *f*
circumstance *s* res, rei *f; (circumstances collectively)* temp•us -oris *n;* **according to —s** pro re, pro tempore; **in humble —s** tenui re; **to yield to —** tempori cedĕre
circumstantial *adj (incidental)* adventici•us -a -um; **to rest on — evidence** conjecturā contineri
circumvent *tr* circumscribĕre
circumvention *s* circumscripti•o -onis *f*
circus *s* circ•us -i *m; (performance)* circens•es -ium *mpl*
cistern *s* cistern•a -ae *f*
citadel *s* ar•x -cis *f*
citation *s (summons)* vocati•o -onis *f; (quotation)* loc•us -i *m* allatus; *(act of quoting)* prolati•o -onis *f*
cite *tr (leg)* evocare, citare; *(to quote)* proferre; *(in writing)* ponĕre
citizen *s* civ•is -is *mf; (of a municipality)* munic•eps -ipis *mf*
citizenship *s* civit•as -atis *f*
city *adj* urban•us -a -um
city *s* urb•s -is *f*
city council *s* decurion•es -um *mpl*
civic *adj* civil•is -is-e
civil *adj* civil•is -is -e; *(polite)* urban•us -a -um; **— rights** civile ju•s -ris *n*
civilian *s* togat•us -i *m*
civilian *adj* togat•us -a -um, privat•us -a -um
civility *s* comit•as -atis *f*
civilization *s* cult•us -ūs *m*
civilize *tr* excolĕre
clad *adj* indut•us -a -um
claim *s (demand)* postulati•o -onis *f; (leg)* vindici•ae -arum *fpl; (land)* a•ger -gri *m* assignatus; *(assertion)* affirmati•o -onis *f;* **to lay — to** vindicare
claim *tr (to demand)* postulare; *(esp. leg)* vindicare; *(to assert)* affirmare; **to — the thing as ours** rem nostram vindicare
claimant *s* petit•or -oris *m*
clam *s* my•ax -acis *m*
clamber *intr* scandĕre; **to — down** descendĕre; **to — up** *(e.g., a mountain)* scandĕre
clammy *adj* umid•us -a -um
clamor *s* clam•or -oris *m*
clamor *intr* vociferari; **to — for** flagitare
clamp *s* confibul•a -ae *f*
clamp *tr* constringĕre
clan *s* gen•s -tis *f*
clandestine *adj* clandestin•us -a -um
clandestinely *adv* clam, furtim
clang *s* clang•or -oris *m*
clang *intr* clangĕre
clank *s* crepit•us -ūs *m*
clank *intr* crepare
clap *s (of hands)* plaus•us -ūs *m; (of thunder)* frag•or -oris *m;* **a loud — of thunder** gravis fragor *m*
clap *tr* **to — the hands** manūs complodĕre; **to — a man in prison** aliquem in vincula conjicĕre ‖ *intr* plaudĕre

claptrap *s* apparat•us -ūs *m*
clarification *s* explicati•o -onis *f*
clarify *tr* deliquare
clarion *s* litu•us -i *m*
clarity *s* clarit•as -atis *f*
clash *s* concurs•us -ūs *m; (sound)* crepit•us -ūs *m; (fig)* dissonanti•a -ae *f; (of colors)* repugnanti•a -ae *f*
clash *intr* concurrěre; *(to make a noise by striking)* concrepare; *(fig)* collidi
clasp *s* fibul•a -ae *f; (embrace)* amplex•us -ūs *m*
clasp *tr (to embrace)* amplecti; *(to grasp)* comprehenděre
class *s (pol)* class•is -is *f,* ord•o -inis *m; (of pupils)* class•is -is *f; (kind)* gen•us -eris *n*
class *tr (e.g., according to wealth)* describěre; **to — as** in numero *(w. gen)* habēre
classical *adj* classic•us -a -um
classics *spl* scriptor•es -um *mpl* classici
classification *s* descripti•o -onis *f*
classify *tr* describěre
clatter *s* strepit•us -ūs *m*
clatter *intr* strepare, crepitare
clause *s (gram)* articul•us -i *m,* membr•um -i *n; (leg)* cap•ut -itis *n*
claw *s* ungu•is -is *m; (of birds)* ungul•a -ae *f; (of a crab)* bracch•ium -(i)i *n*
claw *tr* lacerare
clay *s* lut•um -i *n; (white potter's clay)* argill•a -ae *f;* **made of —** fictil•is -is -e
clayey *adj* argillace•us -a -um
clean *adj* mund•us -a -um; *(lit & fig)* pur•us -a -um
clean *tr* mundare, purgare; **to — s.o. out** *(of money)* aliquem excatarissare
cleanliness *s* munditi•a -ae *f*
cleanly *adv* omnino, penitus
cleanse *tr* purgare; *(by washing)* abluěre; *(by rubbing)* detergēre
clear *adj* clar•us -a -um; *(unclouded)* seren•us -a -um; *(liquids)* limpid•us -a -um; *(transparent)* pellucid•us -a -um; *(voice)* liquid•us -a -um; *(style)* lucid•us -a -um; *(explanation)* illustr•is -is -e; *(manifest)* conspicu•us -a -um; *(conscience)* rect•us -a -um; *(mind)* sag•ax -acis; **— of** exper•s -tis *(w. gen);* **it is —** manifestum est; *(leg)* liquet; **to keep — of** evitare
clear *tr* purgare; *(to make open)* expedire; *(to acquit)* absolvěre; *(land)* exstirpare; *(the table)* mundare; *(profit)* lucrari; **to — away** detergēre, amovēre; *(by force)* amoliri; **to — out** emundare; **to — up** enodare **||** *intr (of weather)* disserenascěre; **— out!** apage!
clearance *s* purgati•o -onis *f; (space)* intervall•um -i *n*
clearly *adv* clare; *(obviously)* aperte
clearness *s* clarit•as -atis *f; (of sky)* serenit•as -atis *f; (of style)* perspicuit•as -atis *f*
clear-sighted *adj* **to be —** clare decerněre
cleavage *s* discid•ium -(i)i *n*
cleave *tr* finděre **||** *intr* **to — to** adhaerēre *(w. dat)*
cleaver *s* dolabr•a -ae *f*
cleft *s* rim•a -ae *f,* fissur•a -ae *f*
clemency *s* clementi•a -ae *f*
clement *adj* clem•ens -entis
clench *tr* comprimĕre; **to — the fist** manum comprimĕre
clergy *s* cler•us -i *m*
cleric *s* cleric•us -i *m*
clerk *s* scrib•a -ae *m*
clever *adj* callid•us -a -um
cleverly *adv* callide
cleverness *s* callidit•as -atis *f*
click *s* crepit•us -ūs *m*
click *intr* crepitare
client *s* cli•ens -entis *mf*
cliff *s* rup•es -is *f*
climate *s* cael•um -i *n*
climax *s* gradati•o -onis *f*
climb *tr* ascenděre; *(to the top)* conscenděre; **to — (up) a tree** in arborem inscenděre, arborem conscenděre **||** *intr* ascenděre
climb *s* ascens•us -ūs *m*
clinch vt confirmare
cling *intr (to)* adhaerēre *(w. abl or dat or* ab + *abl);* **to — together** cohaerēre
clink *s* tinnit•us -ūs *m*
clink *intr* tinnire
clip *s* fibul•a -ae *f*
clip *tr (to cut)* tondēre; *(words, tail)* mutilare
clipping *s* tonsur•a -ae *f;* **—s** resegmin•a -um *npl*
cloak *s* pall•ium -(i)i *n; (cape with hood for travel)* paenul•a -ae *f; (mil)* sag•um -i *n; (general's)* paludament•um -i *n;* **wearing a —** palliat•us -a -um
cloak *tr* dissimulare, tegěre
clock *s* horolog•ium -(i)i *n*
clod *s* glaeb•a -ae *f; (pej)* caud•ex -icis *m*
clog *s* sole•a -ae *f* lignea
clog *tr (to hinder, fetter)* impedire; *(to block up)* obstruěre
cloister *s* portic•us -ūs *f; (eccl)* monaster•ium -(i)i *n*
close *adj (near)* propinqu•us -a -um; *(dense)* dens•us -a -um; *(tight)* art•us -a -um; *(imtimate)* intim•us -a -um; *(shut)* occlus•us -a -um; *(atmosphere)* crass•us -a -um; **at — quarters** comminus *(adv);* **— attention** anim•us -i *m* attentissimus; **to be on the —est possible terms with s.o.** aliquo familiarissime uti; **to be — at hand** adesse, instare; **to keep — to** adhaerēre *(w. dat)*
close *tr* clauděre; *(eyes, lips)* preměre; *(to end)* finire; **in —ing** denique; **to — down**

claudĕre; **to — a bargain** pascisci; **to — up** praeclūdĕre ‖ *intr* coire, claudi; **to — in on the enemy** undique fauces hostium premĕre
close *s* fin•is -is *m;* **at the — of the year** exeunte anno; **to bring to a —** finire; **to draw to a —** terminari
close *adv* prope, juxta; **— to** *(near)* prope *(w. acc),* juxta *(w. acc); (almost)* paene
closely *adv* prope; *(attentively)* attente
closet *s* armar•ium -(i)i *n; (for clothes)* vestiar•ium -(i)i *n*
closing *adj* ultim•us -a -um
closing *s* conclusi•o -onis *f*
clot *s* concretus cru•or -oris *m*
clot *intr* concrescĕre
cloth *s* pann•us -i *m; (linen)* linte•um -i *n*
clothe *tr* vestire, indūĕre
clothes *spl* vestiment•a -orum *npl*
clothier *s* vestiar•ius -(i)i *m*
clothing *s* vestit•us -ūs *m;* **an article of —** vestiment•um -i *n*
cloud *s* nub•es -is *f; (dark storm cloud)* nimb•us -i *m;* **small —** nebecul•a -ae *f*
cloud *tr* nubibus velare; *(fig)* obscurare ‖ *intr* **to — up** nubescĕre
cloudburst *s* maximus im•ber -bris *m;* **I arrived in Capua in a —** maximo imbri Capuam veni
cloud-capped *adj* nubif•er -era -erum
cloudless *adj* seren•us -a -um
cloudy *adj* nubil•us -a -um; **somewhat —** subnubil•us -a -um; **to get —** nubilare
clout *s* ict•us -ūs *m;* **to have —** *(coll)* plurimum posse
clove *s (of garlic)* nucle•us -i *m*
cloven *adj* bisulc•us -a -um; **— hoofs** ungul•ae -arum *fpl* spissae
clover *s* trifol•ium -(i)i *n*
clown *s* scurr•a -ae *m*
clown *intr* **to — around** scurrari
clownish *adj* scurril•is -is -e
cloy *tr* satiare
cloying *adj* putid•us -a -um
club *s (cudgel)* clav•a -ae *f; (society)* sodalit•as -atis *f,* colleg•ium -(i)i *n*
club *tr* clavā dolare
cluck *intr* glocidare, singultire
cluck *s* singult•us -ūs *m*
clue *s* indic•ium -(i)i *n*
clump *s* mass•a -ae *f;* **— of trees** arbust•um -i *n*
clumsily *adv* inscite, rustice
clumsiness *s* insciti•a -ae *f,* rusticit•as -atis *f*
clumsy *adj* inscit•us -a -um, rustic•us -a -um; *(of things)* inhabil•is -is -e
cluster *s (of fruit, flowers, berries)* corymb•us -i *m; (of people)* coron•a -ae *f*
cluster *intr* congregari; **to — around** stipare
clutch *s* ungul•a -ae *f;* **from one's —es** e manibus; **in one's —es** in sua potestate
clutch *tr* arrigĕre
clutter *s* congeri•es -ei *f*
clutter *tr* **to — up** conturbare
coach *s (four-wheeled)* raed•a -ae *f; (two-wheeled, closed in, with arched top, for women)* carpent•um -i *n; (trainer)* exercit•or -oris *m; (of gladiators)* lanist•a -ae *m*
coach *tr* exercēre
coagulate *intr* coïre
coagulation *s* coagulati•o -onis *f*
coal *s* carb•o -onis *m*; lapis gagas (*gen*: lapidis gagatis)
coalesce *intr* coalescĕre
coalition *s* conjuncti•o -onis *f*
coal mine *s* fodin•a -ae *f* carbonaria
coarse *adj (materials)* crass•us -a -um; *(unfinished)* rud•is -is -e; *(manners)* incult•us -a -um
coarseness *s* crassitud•o -inis *f; (of manners)* rusticit•as -atis *f*
coast *s* or•a -ae *f;* **the — is clear** nihil obstat
coast *intr* **to — along the shore** oram praetervehi
coastal *adj* maritim•us -a -um
coastline *s* or•a -ae *f* maritima
coat *s* paenul•a -ae *f; (of animals)* pell•is -is *f; (of paint, plaster)* inducti•o -onis *f*
coat *tr* illinĕre, obducĕre; **—ed tongue** lingu•a -ae *f* fungosa
coating *s* inducti•o -onis *f*
coat of arms *s* insign•ia -ium *npl*
coat of mail *s* loric•a -ae *f*
coax *tr* blandiri
coaxing *s* blandiment•a -orum *npl*
coaxing *adj* bland•us -a -um
coaxingly *adv* blande
cobbler *s* sut•or -oris *m*
cobweb *s* arane•um -i *n*
cock *s* gall•us -i *m*
cock-a-doodle-do *interj* cocococo
cockeyed *adj* **— person** strab•o -onis *m*
cock fight *s* rix•a -ae *f* gallorum
cockroach *s* blatt•a -ae *f*
cocky *adj* jact•ans -antis
cocoa *s* fab•a -ae *f* Cacao
cocoanut *s* nu•x -cis *f* palmae Indicae
cocoon *s* globul•us -i *m*
coddle *tr* indulgēre *(w. dat)*
code *s (laws)* leg•es -um *fpl; (rules)* praecept•a -orum *npl; (system of symbols)* not•ae -arum *fpl;* **in —** per notas; **Justinian —** cod•ex -icis *m* Justinianeus
co-ed *s (coll)* condiscipul•a -ae *f*
codicil *s* codicill•i -orum *mpl*
codify *tr* digerĕre
coerce *tr* coercēre, cogĕre
coercion *s* coerciti•o -onis *f*
coeval *adj (with)* aequal•is -is -e *(w. dat)*
coexist *intr* simul existĕre
coffee *s* coffe•um -i *n;* **cup of —** pocill•um -i *n* caffei
coffeepot *s* oll•a -ae *f* caffei

coffer *s* arc•a -ae *f*
coffin *s* capul•us -i *m*
cog *s* den•s -tis *m*
cogent *adj* grav•is -is -e
cognate *adj* cognat•us -a -um
cognition *s* cogniti•o -onis *f*
cognizance *s* cogniti•o -onis *f;* **to take — of** cognitionem tractare de *(w. abl)*
cognizant *adj* **(of)** consci•us -a -um *(w. gen)*
cohabit *intr* consuescĕre
cohabitation *s* consuetud•o -inis *f*
coheir *s* coher•es -edis *mf*
cohere *intr* cohaerēre
coherence *s* context•us -ūs *m*
coherent *adj* cohaer•ens -entis
coherently *adv* constanter
cohesion *s* cohaerenti•a -ae *f*
cohesive *adj* ten•ax -acis
cohort *s* cohor•s -tis *f*
coil *s* spir•a -ae *f*
coil *tr* glomerare ‖ *intr* glomerari
coin *s* numm•us -i *m*
coin *tr (to mint)* cudĕre; *(to stamp)* signare; *(words)* fingĕre
coinage *s* monet•a -ae *f*
coincide *intr* **(with)** congruĕre (cum + *abl)*
coincidence *s* concursati•o -onis *f*
coincidental *adj* fortuit•us -a -um
coined *adj* monetal•is -is -e
cold *adj* frigid•us -a -um, gelid•us -a -um; **to be —** frigēre; **to become —** frigescĕre
cold *s* frig•us -oris *n; (med)* graved•o -inis *f;* **to catch a —** gravedinem contrahĕre; **to have a —** gravedine dolēre
coldly *adv (fig)* frigide
coldness *s* frig•us -oris *n*
colic *s* tormin•a -um *npl*
colicky *adj* colic•us -a -um
collapse *s* ruin•a -ae *f*
collapse *intr* collabi
collar *s* collar•e -is *n*
collar *tr* collo comprehendĕre
collar bone *s* jugul•um -i *n*
collate *tr* conferre
collateral *adj (lines of descent)* transvers•us -a -um; *(effect)* adjunct•us -a -um
collateral *s (com)* sponsi•o -onis *f*
colleague *s* colleg•a -ae *m*
collect *tr* conferre, colligĕre; *(to assemble)* convocare; *(money)* exigĕre; **to — oneself** mentem *or* animum colligĕre; **to — paintings and statues** tabulas signaque comparare ‖ *intr (of water)* colligi
collected *adj* **to be —** praesentis animi esse
collection *s (act)* collecti•o -onis *f; (pile or group collected)* congeri•es -ei *f; (literary)* corp•us -oris *n*
collective *adj* commun•is -is -e
collectively *adv* communiter, unā
college *s* colleg•ium -(i)i *n*
collegiate *adj* collegial•is -is -e
collide *intr* confligĕre
collision *s* conflicti•o -onis *f;* **a — of ships with one another** concurs•us -ūs *m* navium inter se
colloquial *adj* cotidian•us -a -um; **— language** serm•o -onis *m* cotidianus
collusion *s* collusi•o -onis *f;* **to be in — with** colludĕre cum *(w. abl)*
colon *s (anat)* col•um -i *n; (gram)* col•on -i *n*
colonel *s* tribun•us -i *m* militum
colonial *adj* colonic•us -a -um
colonist *s* colon•us -i *m*
colonize *tr* coloniam deducĕre in *(w. acc)*
colonnade *s* portic•us -ūs *f*
colony *s* coloni•a -ae *f*
color *s* col•or -oris *m;* **—s** vexill•um -i *n;* **with flying —s** magnā cum gloriā
color *tr* colorare; *(to dye)* tingĕre
colossal *adj* imman•is -is -e
colossus *s* coloss•us -i *m*
colt *s* equul•us -i *m*
column *s* column•a -ae *f; (line)* agm•en -inis *n*
comb *tr* pectĕre
comb *s* pect•en -inis *m*
combat *s* pugn•a -ae *f;* **— with wild beasts** venati•o -onis *f*
combat *tr* pugnare cum *(w. abl)*
combatant *s* pugnat•or -oris *m*
combative *adj* pugn•ax -acis
combination *s (act)* conjuncti•o -onis *f; (result)* junctur•a -ae *f; (of various ingredients)* compositi•o -onis *f;* **— of syllables** coït•us -ūs *m* syllabarum
combine *tr* conjungĕre, miscēre; *(in due proportion)* temperare ‖ *intr* coïre; *(of persons)* conspirare
combustible *adj* igni obnoxi•us -a -um
combustion *s* combusti•o -onis *f;* **during —** dum comburitur
come *intr* venire; *(to arrive)* pervenire; *(to happen)* fieri; *(of sleep)* accedĕre; **— here!** istoc accede!; **to — about** evenire, fieri; **to — across** occurrĕre *(w. dat);* **to — after** (sub)sequi; **to — again** revenire; **to — along** procedĕre; *(to accompany)* comitari; **to — apart** solvi; **to — at** *(in a hostile manner)* petĕre; **to — away** abscedĕre; **to — back** revenire; **to — before** praevenire; **to — between** intervenire; **to — by** praeterire; *(to get)* acquirĕre; **to — down** *(to descend)* descendĕre; *(e.g., to the sea)* devenire; **to — down from antiquity** ex antiquitate tradi; **to — down with an illness** morbo corripi; **to — first** antevenire; **to — forth** exire; *(fig)* exoriri; **to — forward** prodire; **to — in** introire; **to — into play** accedĕre; **to — near** appropinquare, accedĕre; **to — off** *(e.g., stem comes off the apple)* recedĕre ab *(w. abl);* **to — off victorious** victor discedĕre; **to — off without a loss** sine detrimento discedĕre; **to — on** pergĕre; *(to progress)* proficĕre;

to — on top of *(s.th. else)* supervenire *(w. dat);* **to — out (of)** exire (ex + *abl); (to be published)* edi, emitti; *(of teeth)* cadĕre; *(of evidence)* emergĕre; *(to end)* evenire; **to — over** supervenire; *(to a different part)* transgredi; *(of feelings, conditions)* obire, occupare; **to — round** *(fig)* transgredi; **to — to** advenire ad *or* in *(w. acc); (to cost)* vēnire *(w. gen of price); (after fainting)* resipiscĕre; **to — to a head** concoqui; **to — to one's senses** ad se redire; **to — to pass** evenire, fieri; **to — to the assistance of** subvenire*(w. dat);* **to — together** convenire; **to — up** subvenire; *(to occur)* provenire; **to — up to** *(to approach)* accedĕre ad *(w. acc);* **to — upon** *(to find)* invenire; (*to attack, as diseases)* ingruĕre *(w. dat)*; **whatever —s into s.o.'s head** quae cuique libuissent

comedian *s* scurr•a -ae *m; (theat)* comoed•us -i *m*

comedy *s* comoedi•a -ae *f*

comely *adj* venust•us -a -um

comet *s* comet•es -ae *m*

comfort *s* solat•ium -(i)i *n;* **—s** commod•a -orum *npl*

comfort *tr* consolari

comfortable *adj* commod•us -a -um; **make yourselves —** rogo ut vobis suaviter sit

comfortably *adv* commode

comforter *s* consolat•or -oris *m*

comforting *adj* consol•ans -antis

comic *adj* comic•us -a -um

comic *s* scurr•a -ae *m*

comical *adj* ridicul•us -a -um

coming *adj* ventur•us -a -um

coming *s* advent•us -ūs *m*

comma *s* comm•a -atis *n*

command *s (order)* juss•um -i *n; (mil)* imper•ium -(i)i *n; (jurisdiction)* provinci•a -ae *f;* **— of language** copi•a -ae *f* verborum; **to be in — of** praesse *(w. dat);* **to give a — to** imperare *(w. dat);* **to hold supreme military —** summam imperii tenēre; **to put s.o. in — of** aliquem praeficĕre *(w. dat)*

commander *s* du•x -cis *m,* praefect•us -i *m*

commander-in-chief *s* imperat•or -oris *m*

commandment *s* mandat•um -i *n*

commemerate *tr* celebrare

commemoration *s* celebrati•o -onis *f*

commence *tr & intr* incipĕre

commencement *s* init•ium -(i)i *n*

commend *tr* approbare; *(to recommend; to commit)* commendare

commendable *adj* probabil•is -is -e

commendation *s* commendati•o -onis *f,* lau•s -dis *f*

comment *intr* commentari; **to — on** annotare, commentari

comment *s* sententi•a -ae *f; (note)* annotati•o -onis *f*

commentary *s* commentar•ium -(i)i *n;* **—s** commentari•i -orum *mpl*

commentator *s* interpr•es -etis *m*

commerce *s* commerc•ium -(i)i; **to engage in —** negotiari

commercial *adj* mercatori•us -a -um

commiserate *intr* **to — with** misereri *(w. gen)*

commiseration *s* misericordi•a -ae *f*

commission *s* mandat•um -i *n; (group)* consil•ium -(i)i *n;* **out of —** ex usu; **to do business on —** ex mandato negotiari

commission *tr* delegare, mandare

commissioner *s* curat•or -oris *m;* **highway —** viarum curator *m;* **police —** praefect•us -i *m* vigilum; **water —** aquarum curator *m*

commit *tr (crime)* admittĕre; *(to entrust)* committĕre; **to — to memory** ediscĕre; **to — an error** errare; **to — a sin** peccare; **to — to prison** in carcerem conjicĕre; **to — to writing** litteris mandare

commitment *s* pign•us -oris *n*

committee *s* consil•ium -(i)i *n*

commodity *s* mer•x -cis *f*

common *adj (shared)* commun•is -is -e, public•us -a -um; *(ordinary)* cotidian•us -a -um, vulgar•is -is -e; *(well-known)* vulgat•us -a -um; *(gram)* commun•is -is -e; **— people** vulg•us -i *n;* **to have — sense** cor habēre

commoner *s* plebe•us -i *m;* **—s** pleb•s -is *f*

commonly *adv* vulgo, fere

commonplace *adj* vulgar•is -is -e

commonwealth *s* res, rei *f* publica

commotion *s* tumult•us -ūs *m*

commune *intr* confabulari

communicate *tr* communicare; *(information)* impertire ‖ *intr* **to — with** communicare *(w. dat)*

communicative *adj* affabil•is -is -e

communion *s* communi•o -onis *f*

community *s* civit•as -atis *f*

commutation *s* mutati•o -onis *f; (reduction)* remissi•o -onis *f*

commute *tr* commutare; **his death sentence was —ed to exile** capitis damnato exilium ei permissum est ‖ *intr (travel)* ultro citroque commeare

commuter *s* commeat•or -oris *m*

compact *adj* spiss•us -a -um

compact *s* pact•um -i *n; (esp. public)* foed•us -eris *n;* **to abide by the —** in pacto manēre; **to make a —** *(of two parties)* foedus inter se facĕre

compact *tr* densare

compactly *adv* spisse, confertim

companion *s* com•es -itis *m; (mil)* contubernal•is -is *m*

companionship *s* sodalit•as -atis *f;* **to enjoy s.o.'s —** aliquo familiariter uti

company *s (com)* societ•as -atis *f; (guests)*

conviv•ium -(i)i *n; (mil)* centuri•o -onis *f; (theat)* gre•x -gis *m*
comparable *adj* comparabil•is -is -e
comparative *adj* aliorum ratione habitā; *(gram)* comparativ•us -a -um
comparative *s (gram)* comparativ•um -i *n*, grad•us -ūs *m* comparativus
comparatively *adv* comparative
compare *tr* comparare, conferre; **—ed with** adversus *(w. acc)*
comparison *s* comparati•o -onis *f;* **in — with** adversus *(w. acc)*
compartment *s* locul•us -i *m*
compass *s (instrument)* circin•us -i *m; (magnetic)* ac•us -ūs *f* magnetica; *(limits)* fin•es -ium *mpl*
compass *tr* circumdare
compassion *s* misericordi•a -ae *f*
compassionate *adj* misericor•s -dis
compassionately *adv* misericorditer
compatibility *s* congruenti•a -ae *f*
compatible *adj* congru•us -a -um
compatriot *s* civ•is -is *m*
compeer *s* aequal•is -is *mf*
compel *tr* compellĕre, cogĕre
compendium *s* summar•ium -(i)i *n*
compensate *tr* compensare ‖ *intr* **to — for** repensare, rependĕre
compensation *s (act)* compensati•o -onis *f; (pay)* merc•es -edis *f; (for damages)* poen•a -ae *f*
compete *intr* certare
competence *s* facult•as -atis *f; (legal capacity)* ju•s -ris *n*
competent *adj* perit•us -a -um; *(leg)* locupl•es -etis
competently *adv* satis idoneë
competition *s* certam•en -inis *n*
competitor *s* petit•or -oris *m*
compilation *s (act)* collecti•o -onis *f; (result)* collectane•a -orum *npl*
compile *tr* componĕre
compiler *s* composit•or -oris *m*
complacency *s* am•or -oris *m* sui
complacent *adj* qui sibi placet
complain *tr (about)* queri (super + *abl)*
complaint *s* querel•a -ae *f; (leg)* crim•en -inis *n; (med)* vit•ium -(i)i *n;* **to raise —s** querelas facĕre
complement *s* complement•um -i *n; (mil)* numer•us -i *m;* **to give the legions their full — of men** complēre legiones
complete *adj (entire)* plen•us -a -um; *(untouched)* integ•er -ra -rum; *(finished)* perfect•us -a -um; *(set)* just•us -a -um
complete *tr (years)* complēre; *(public works)* consummare; *(to accomplish)* perficĕre, peragĕre
completely *adv* plane, prorsus
completion *s* completi•o -onis *f; (accomplishment)* perfecti•o -onis *f*, confecti•o -onis *f*
complex *adj* multipl•ex -icis
complexion *s* col•or -oris *m*
complexity *s* multiplex natur•a -ae *f*
compliance *s* obtemperati•o -onis *f;* **in — with an agreement** ex pacto et convento
compliant *adj* obsequ•ens -entis
complicate *tr* impedire
complicated *adj* implicat•us -a -um
complication *s* implicati•o -onis *f*
complicity *s* conscienti•a -ae *f*
compliment *s* blandiment•um -i *n;* **as a —** honoris gratiā; **to pay s.o. a —** gratulari *(w. dat)*
compliment *tr* gratulari *(w. dat)*
complimentary *adj* honorific•us -a -um
comply *intr* **to — with** obsequi *(w. dat)*
component *s* element•um -i *n*
compose *tr* componĕre; *(verses)* condĕre; *(to calm)* sedare; **to — oneself** tranquillari
composed *adj* tranquill•us -a -um
composer *s* script•or -oris *m; (mus)* musicorum modorum script•or -oris *m*
composite *adj* composit•us -a -um
composition *s (act)* compositi•o -onis *f; (in literature)* scripti•o -onis *f; (work composed)* script•um -i *n*
composure *s* tranquillit•as -atis *f;* **to bear with —** aequo animo ferre; **to lose one's —** perturbari
compound *adj* composit•us -a -um
compound *s* compositi•o -onis *f; (noun)* compositum verb•um -i *n*
compound *tr* componĕre, duplicare
compound interest *s* anatocism•us -i *m*
comprehend *tr* continēre; *(to understand)* comprehendĕre
comprehensible *adj* perspicu•us -a -um
comprehension *s (act of grasping)* comprehensi•o -onis *f; (power of understanding)* intellect•us -ūs *m*
comprehensive *adj* ampl•us -a -um
compress *tr* comprimĕre; *(to abridge)* coartare
compress *s (med)* foment•um -i *n*
compression *s* compressi•o -onis *f*
comprise *tr* continēre; **to be —ed of** constare ex *(w. abl)*
compromise *s (bilateral)* compromiss•um -i *n; (unilateral)* accommodati•o -onis *f*
compromise *tr* compromittĕre; *(to imperil)* in periculum ac discrimen vocare ‖ *intr* pacisci
compulsion *s* necessit•as -atis *f;* **by —** per vim
compulsory *adj* necessari•us -a -um
compunction *s* compuncti•o -onis *f;* **I feel — me paenitet**
computation *s* computati•o -onis *f*
compute *tr* computare
computer *s* computat•or -oris *m*
comrade *s* sodal•is -is *m; (mil)* contubernal•is -is *m*
comradeship *s* societ•as -atis *f*

con *tr (coll)* defraudare; **to — s.o out of his money** aliquem pecuniā defraudare
concave *adj* concav•us -a -um
conceal *tr* celare, occultare, abdĕre
concealed *adj* celat•us -a -um
concealment *s (act)* occultati•o -onis *f; (place)* latebr•ae -arum *fpl;* **to be in —** latebras agĕre
concede *tr* concedĕre
conceit *s* superbi•a -ae *f*
conceited *adj* superbiā tum•ens -entis
conceivable *adj* quod fingi potest
conceive *tr* concipĕre ‖ *intr* **to — of** fingĕre
concentrate *tr* in unum locum contrahĕre ‖ *intr* **to — on** animum intendĕre in *(w. acc)*
concentration *s* in unum locum contracti•o -onis *f; (fig)* animi intenti•o -onis *f*
concept *s* sententi•a -ae *f*
conception *s (in womb)* concept•us -ūs *m; (idea)* informati•o -onis *f*
concern *s (affair)* res, rei *f,* negot•ium -(i)i *n; (worry)* cur•a -ae *f; (importance)* moment•um -i *n;* **it is of — to me** mihi curae est
concern *tr* pertinēre ad *(w. acc); (to worry)* sollicitare; **as far as I'm —ed** per me; **it —s me** meā refert
concerned *adj* sollicit•us -a -um
concerning *prep* de *(w. abl)*
concert *s (mus)* concent•us -ūs *m,* symphoni•a -ae *f;* **in —** ex composito
concert *tr* **— a plan** consilium inire
concession *s* concessi•o -onis *f; (thing)* concess•um -i *n; (com)* conducti•o -onis *f;* **to make a —** concedĕre
conch *s* conch•a -ae *f*
conciliate *tr* conciliare
conciliation *s* conciliati•o -onis *f*
conciliatory *adj* pacific•us -a -um
concise *adj* press•us -a -um
concisely *adv* presse
conciseness *s* brevit•as -atis *f*
conclave *s* conclav•e -is *n*
conclude *tr (to end)* terminare; *(to infer)* colligĕre; **I must — my speech** mihi perorandum est; **to — a treaty** foedus icĕre
conclusion *s (end)* fin•is -is *m,* conclusi•o -onis *f; (of speech)* perorati•o -onis *f; (inference)* conclusi•o -onis *f;* **in —** ad ultimum; **they came to the — that** eis placuit ut; **to draw the —** colligĕre
conclusive *adj* firm•us -a -um
concoct *tr* concoquĕre; *(to contrive)* fingĕre, conflare
concoction *s* pot•us -ūs *m; (fig)* machinati•o -onis *f*
concomitant *adj* adjunct•us -a -um
concord *s* concordi•a -ae *f*
concordat *s* pact•um -i *n*
concourse *s* concurs•us -ūs *m*
concrete *adj* concret•us -a -um; **in the —, not in the abstract** re, non cogitatione
concrete *s* concret•um -i *n*
concubinage *s* concubinat•us -ūs *m*
concubine *s* concubin•a -ae *f*
concupiscence *s* libid•o -inis *f*
concur *intr* consentire
concurrence *s* consensi•o -onis *f*
concussion *s (med)* quassatur•a -ae *f*
condemn *tr* damnare; **to — to death** capitis damnare
condemnation *s* damnati•o -onis *f*
condensation *s* densati•o -onis *f*
condense *tr* (cond)densare ‖ *intr* densari
condescend *intr* se summittĕre
condescending *adj* fastidios•us -a -um
condescendingly *adv* fastidiose
condescension *s* comit•as -atis *f*
condition *s (state)* stat•us -ūs *m,* condici•o -onis *f; (stipulation)* condici•o -onis *f,* le•x -gis *f;* **in excellent —** habitissim•us -a -um; **in bad (good) —** male (bene) habit•us -a -um; **on — that** eā lege ut; **physical —** corporis habit•us -ūs *m*
condition *tr* informare
conditional *adj* condicional•is -is -e
conditionally *adv* condicionaliter
condole *intr* **to — with** dolēre cum *(w. abl)*
condolence *s* consolati•o -onis *f;* **I gave him my —** doloris ejus particeps factus sum; **letter of —** litter•ae -arum *fpl* consolatoriae
condone *tr* condonare
conducive *adj* util•is -is -e ad *(w. acc)*
conduct *s (behavior)* mor•es -um *mpl; (management)* administrati•o -onis *f*
conduct *tr (to lead)* adducĕre; *(to manage)* administrare
conductor *s* duct•or -oris *m*
conduit *s* canal•is -is *m*
cone *s* con•us -i *m*
confection *s* cupped•o -inis *f*
confectioner *s* cuppedinar•ius -(i)i *m*
confectionery *s* cuppedi•a -orum *npl*
confederacy *s (treaty)* foed•us -eris *n; (allied states)* civitat•es -um *fpl* foederatae
confederate *adj* foederat•us -a -um
confederate *s* soc•ius -(i)i *m*
confederation *s* civitat•es -um *fpl* foederatae
confer *tr* deferre, tribuĕre ‖ *intr* colloqui, conferre
conference *s* colloqu•ium -(i)i *n*
confess *tr* confiteri, fateri
confessedly *adv* ex confesso
confession *s* confessi•o -onis *f*
confidant *s* consci•us -(i)i *m,* consci•a -ae *f*
confide *tr* committĕre ‖ *intr* **to — in** confidĕre *(w. dat)*
confidence *s* fid•es -ei *f; (assurance)* fiduci•a -ae *f; (esp. self-confidence)* confidenti•a -ae *f;* **to have — in** fidem

habēre *(w. dat);* **to inspire — in** fidem facĕre *(w. dat)*
confident *adj* fid•ens -entis
confidential *adj (worthy of confidence)* fid•us -a -um; *(secret)* secret•us -a -um
confidently *adv* fidenter
configuration *s* figur•a -ae *f*
confine *tr* includĕre; *(to restrain)* cohibēre; *(to limit)* circumscribĕre
confined *adj* art•us -a -um, angust•us -a -um; **to be — to bed** lecto teneri
confines *spl* confin•ium -(i)i *n; (boundary)* fin•es -ium *mpl;* **on the — of** finitim•us -a -um *(w. dat);* **within the — of** in confinio *(w. gen)*
confirm *tr* confirmare; *(to prove)* comprobare; *(to ratify)* sancire
confirmation *s* confirmati•o -onis *f*
confirmed *adj* (con)firmat•us -a -um; *(habitual)* inveterat•us -a -um; *(proved)* comprobat•us -a -um
confiscate *tr* publicare
confiscation *s* publicati•o -onis *f*
conflagration *s* incend•ium -(i)i *n*
conflict *s* pugn•a -ae *f;* **to be in —** *(fig)* inter se repugnare
conflict *intr* inter se repugnare
conflicting *adj* repugn•ans -antis
confluence *s* conflu•ens -entis *m*
conform *intr (to)* obtemperare *(w. dat),* se accommodare ad *(w. acc)*
conformation *s* conformati•o -onis *f*
conformity *s* convenienti•a -ae *f;* **in — with** secundum *(w. acc)*
confound *tr (to confuse)* confundĕre; *(to disconcert)* exanimare
confounded *adj* nefand•us -a -um
confront *tr* obviam ire *(w. dat),* se opponĕre *(w. dat)*
confrontation *s* obstanti•a -ae *f*
confuse *tr* confundĕre, turbare
confused *adj* confus•us -a -um, turbat•us -a -um
confusedly *adv* confuse
confusion *s* confusi•o -onis *f*
confutation *s* refutati•o -onis *f*
confute *tr* confutare
congeal *tr* congelare ‖ *intr* concrescĕre, se congelare
congenial *adj* consentane•us -a -um
congenital *adj* nativ•us -a -um
congested *adj* refert•us -a -um
congestion *s (traffic)* frequenti•a -ae *f,* concurs•us -ūs *m;* **nasal —** stillati•o -onis *f*
congratulate *tr* gratulari *(w. dat)*
congratulations *spl* gratulati•o -onis *f;* **— !** macte virtute esto *(pl:* estote)!
congratulatory *adj* gratulabund•us -a -um
congregate *tr* congregare ‖ *intr* congregari
congregation *s* coët•us -ūs *m*
conical *adj* conic•us -a -um
conifer *s* arb•or -oris *f* conifera
conjectural *adj* conjectural•is -is -e
conjecturally *adv* ex conjectura
conjecture *s* conjectur•a -ae *f*
conjecture *tr* conjectare
conjugal *adj* conjugal•is -is -e
conjugate *tr* declinare
conjugation *s* declinati•o -onis *f*
conjunction *s* concurs•us -ūs *m; (gram)* conjuncti•o -onis *f*
conjure *tr (to beseech solemnly)* obtestari; **to — up** *(ghosts)* elicĕre; *(fig)* excogitare, effingĕre
conjurer *s* mag•us -i *m*
con-man *s* plan•us -i *m*
connect *tr* connectĕre; *(in a series)* serĕre
connected *adj* conjunct•us -a -um; *(by marriage)* affin•is -is -e; *(of buildings)* **(to)** adfict•us -a -um *(w. dat);* **to be closely — with** inhaerēre *(w. dat);* **to be — with s.o. by blood and race** aliquem sanguine ac genere contingĕre
connection *s* conjuncti•o -onis *f,* nex•us -ūs *m; (kin)* necessitud•o -inis *f; (by marriage)* affinit•as -atis *f*
connivance *s* indulgenti•a -ae *f*
connive *intr* connivēre
connoisser *s* doctus existimat•or -oris *m*
connotation *s* significati•o -onis *f* latens
connubial *adj* connubial•is -is -e
conquer *tr* vincĕre
conqueror *s* vict•or -oris *m,* victr•ix -icis *f*
conquest *s* victor•ia -ae *f*
consanguinity *s* consanguinit•as -atis *f*
conscience *s* conscienti•a -ae *f;* **guilty —** mala conscientia *f;* **to have no —** nullam religionem habēre
conscientious *adj* pi•us -a -um, religios•us -a -um
conscientiously *adv* diligenter
conscious *adj* consci•us -a -um
consciously *adv* scienter
consciousness *s (awareness)* conscienti•a -ae *f;* **to lose —** animum relinquĕre; **to regain —** resipiscĕre
conscript *s* tir•o -onis *m*
conscript *tr* conscribĕre
conscription *s* delect•us -ūs *m*
consecrate *tr* consecrare
consecration *s* consecrati•o -onis *f*
consecutive *adj* continu•us -a -um
consecutively *adv* continenter
consent *intr* consentire
consent *s* consens•us -ūs *m;* **to give one's —** permittĕre; **with the — of the people** secundo populo; **without my —** me invito
consequence *s* consecuti•o -onis *f,* event•us -ūs *m;* **a man of —** hom•o -inis *m* auctoritate praeditus; **as a —** ex eo; **it is of great —** magni interest; **it is of no —** nihil refert; **thing of no —** parva res, rei *f*
consequent *adj* consequ•ens -entis

consequential *adj* consentane•us -a -um
consequently *adv* igitur, itaque
conservation *s* conservati•o -onis *f*
conservative *adj* a rebus novandis abhorr•ens -entis; *(pol)* reipublicae statūs conservandi studios•us -a -um; **— party** optimat•es -um *mpl*
conserve *tr* conservare
consider *tr* considerare; *(to deem)* aestimare, ducĕre; *(to respect)* respicĕre
considerable *adj* aliquantul•us -a -um; *(of persons)* illustr•is -is -e; *(of size)* ampl•us -a -um
considerably *adv* aliquantum; *(w. comp)* multo, aliquanto
considerate *adj* human•us -a -um
consideration *s* considerati•o -onis *f; (regard)* respect•us -ūs *m; (ground, motive)* rati•o -onis *f; (payment)* pret•ium -(i)i *n;* **out of — for** ob *(w. acc);* **to have — for the wounded;** sauciorum rationem habēre; **to show — for s.th.** alicujus rei respectum habēre
considering *prep* pro *(w. abl)*
consign *tr* mandare
consignment *s* **goods given** (*or* **sent) on —** merc•es -ium *fpl* ex perscriptione traditae (*or* missae)
consist *intr* **to — of** constare ex *(w. abl),* consistĕre ex *(w. abl)*
consistency *s* constanti•a -ae *f; (viscosity)* crassitud•o -inis *f*
consistent *adj* const•ans -antis
consistently *adv* constanter
consolable *adj* consolabil•is -is -e
consolation *s* consolati•o -onis *f; (thing)* solac•ium -(i)i *n*
console *tr* consolari
consolidate *tr* solidare, stabilire
consonant *adj* conson•us -a -um
consonant *s* conson•ans -antis *f*
consort *s* conju•x -gis *mf*
consort *intr* **to — with** familiariter uti *(w. abl),* se associare cum *(w. abl)*
conspicuous *adj* conspicu•us -a -um
conspicuously *adv* insigniter
conspiracy *s* conjurati•o -onis *f*
conspirator *s* conjurat•us -i *m*
conspire *intr* conjurare
constable *s* viat•or -oris *m*
constancy *s* constanti•a -ae *f*
constant *adj (fixed)* const•ans -antis; *(loyal)* fid•us -a -um; *(incessant)* perpetu•us -a -um
constantly *adv* assidue, perpetuo
constellation *s* sid•us -eris *n*
consternation *s* consternati•o -onis *f;* **to be in —** trepidare; **to throw into —** perterrēre
constipated *adj* **he is —** venter ejus est astrictus
constipation *s* alv•us -i *f* astricta
constituent *s (part)* element•um -i *n;* **—s** *(pol)* suffragator•es -um *mpl*
constitute *tr* constituĕre
constitution *s (physical)* habit•us -ūs *m; (pol)* reipublicae leg•es -um *fpl*
constitutional *adj* legitim•us -a -um
constitutionally *adv* legitime
constrain *tr* cogĕre
constraint *s* vis *f;* **by —** per vim
construct *tr* construĕre; *(esp. things of mechanical kind)* fabricare
construction *s* constructi•o -onis *f,* fabricati•o -onis *f; (of a road)* muniti•o -onis *f; (interpretation)* interpretati•o -onis *f;(gram)* constructi•o -onis *f*
construe *tr* interpretari; *(gram)* construĕre
consul *s* cons•ul -ulis *m;* **— elect** consul *m* designatus
consular *adj* consular•is -is -e; **a man of — rank** consular•is -is *m*
consulship *s* consulat•us -ūs *m;* **during my —** me consule; **in the — of Caesar and Bibulus** Caesare et Bibulo consulibus; **to hold the —** consulatum gerĕre; **to run for the —** consulatum petĕre
consult *tr* consultare ‖ *intr* deliberare
consultation *s* consultati•o -onis *f*
consume *tr* consumĕre
consumer *s* empt•or -oris *m*
consuming *adj* ed•ax -acis
consummate *adj* summ•us -a -um
consummate *tr* consummare
consummation *s* consummati•o -onis *f; (end)* exit•us -ūs *m*
consumption *s* consumpti•o -onis *f; (disease)* tab•es -is *f*
consumptive *adj* **to be —** tabe laborare
contact *s* contact•us -ūs *m; (connection)* necessitud•o -inis *f;* **to come in — with** contingĕre
contagion *s* contag•ium -(i)i *n; (esp. fig)* contagi•o -onis *f*
contagious *adj* contagios•us -a -um
contain *tr* continēre; *(to hold, as a vessel)* capĕre
container *s* receptacul•um -i *n,* va•s -sis *n*
contaminate *tr* contaminare
contamination *s* contaminati•o -onis *f*
contemplate *tr* contemplari; *(some action)* considerare
contemplation *s* contemplati•o -onis *f; (of an action)* considerati•o -onis *f*
contemplative *adj* contemplativ•us -a -um
contemporaneous *adj* aequal•is -is -e
contemporaneously *adv* simul
contemporary *s* aequaev•us -i *m*
contempt *s* contempt•us -ūs *m*
contemptible *adj* contempt•us -a -um
contemptibly *adv* abjecte
contemptuous *adj* fastidios•us -a -um
contend *tr (to aver)* affirmare ‖ *intr* contendĕre; *(to dispute)* verbis certare; **to — against** adversari

contending *adj* avers•us -a -um
content *adj* **(with)** content•us -a -um *(w. abl)*
content *tr* satisfacĕre *(w. dat)*
contented *adj* content•us -a -um
contentedly *adv* aequo animo
contention *s* contenti•o -onis *f*
contentious *adj* pugn•ax -acis; *(litigious)* litigios•us -a -um
contentment *s* aequus anim•us -i *m*
contents *spl* quod inest, quae insunt; *(of a book)* argument•um -i *n; (see* **table of contents)**
contest *s* certam•en -inis *n*
contest *tr (to dispute)* resistĕre *(w. dat); (leg)* lege agĕre de *(w. abl)*
contestant *s* petit•or -oris *m*
context *s* context•us -ūs *m*
contiguous *adj* contigu•us -a -um
continence *s* continenti•a -ae *f*
continent *adj* contin•ens -entis
continent *s* par•s -tis *f* terrae
contingent *s* man•us -ūs *f*
continual *adj* continu•us -a -um; *(lasting)* perpetu•us -a -um
continually *adv* assidue, continenter
continuance *s* continuati•o -onis *f; (leg)* prolati•o -onis *f*
continuation *s* continuati•o -onis *f*
continue *tr* continuare; *(leg)* proferre ‖ *intr* pergĕre; *(to last)* persistĕre
continuity *s* continuit•as -atis *f*
continuous *adj* continu•us -a -um, perpetu•us -a -um
continuously *adv* continenter
contortion *s* contorti•o -onis *f*
contour *s* lineament•um -i *n*
contraband *s* interdict•a -orum *npl*
contraception *s* conceptionis inhibiti•o -onis *f*
contraceptive *adj* conceptionis inhibit•ens -entis
contraceptive *s* atoc•ium -(i)i *n*
contract *tr* contrahĕre ‖ *intr* contrahi; **to — for** pacisci, locare; *(of the party undertaking the work)* conducĕre; **to — for the making of a statue** statuam faciendam locare
contract *s* pact•um -i *n; (on the part of the hirer)* locati•o -onis *f; (on the part of the one hired)* redempti•o -onis *f*
contraction *s* contracti•o -onis *f; (of a word)* compend•ium -(i)i *n*
contractor *s* conduct•or -oris *m*
contradict *tr* contradicĕre; **to — oneself** secum pugnare, pugnantia loqui
contradiction *s* contradicti•o -onis *f; (inconsistency)* repugnanti•a -ae *f*
contradictory *adj* contradictori•us -a -um, repugn•ans -antis
contraption *s* machin•a -ae *f*
contrary *adj (opposite)* contrari•us -a -um; *(fig)* repugn•ans -antis; **— to** contra *(w. acc)*
contrary *s* contrar•ium -(i)i *n;* **on the —** contra
contrast *s* comparati•o -onis *f*, oppositi•o -onis *f*
contrast *tr* comparare, opponĕre ‖ *intr* discrepare
contribute *tr* contribuĕre, conferre ‖ *intr* **to — towards** conferre ad *or* in *(w. acc)*
contribution *s* contributi•o -onis *f; (money)* stip•s -is *f; (gift)* don•um -i *n*
contributor *s* collat•or -oris *m*, donat•or -oris *m*
contributory *adj* contribu•ens -entis
contrite *adj* paenit•ens -entis
contrition *s* paenitenti•a -ae *f; (eccl)* contriti•o -onis *f*
contrivance *s (act)* machinati•o -onis *f; (thing)* machin•a -ae *f*
contrive *tr* excogitare, machinari
control *s (restraint)* continenti•a -ae *f; (power)* moderati•o -onis *f*, potest•as -atis *f*
control *tr* continēre; *(to govern)* imperare *(w. dat)*
controller *s* moderat•or -oris *m*
controversial *adj* controvers•us -a -um
controversy *s* controversi•a -ae *f*
contusion *s* contusi•o -onis *f*
conundrum *s* aenigm•a -atis *n*
convalesce *intr* convalescĕre
convalescent *adj* convalesc•ens -entis
convene *tr* convocare ‖ *intr* coïre
convenience *s* commodit•as -atis *f; (thing)* commod•um -i *n;* **at your —** commodo tuo, ex commodo
convenient *adj* commod•us -a -um; *(time, occasion)* opportun•us -a -um
conveniently *adv* commode, opportune
convention *s* convent•us -ūs *m; (custom)* consuetud•o -inis *f*
conventional *adj* vulgat•us -a -um
converge *intr* vergĕre, coïre
conversant *adj* perit•us -a -um; **to be — with** versari in *(w. abl)*
conversation *s* colloqu•ium -(i)i *n*
conversational *adj* in colloquio usitat•us -a -um
converse *intr* colloqui
converse *s* convers•us -ūs *m*
conversely *adv* e converso
conversion *s* conversi•o -onis *f*
convert *tr* convertĕre
convert *s* neophyt•us -i *m*
convertible *adj* commutabil•is -is -e
convex *adj* convex•us -a -um
convey *tr* convehĕre, advehĕre; *(to impart)* significare; *(leg)* abalienare
conveyance *s (act)* advecti•o -onis *f; (vehicle)* vehicul•um -i *n; (leg)* abalienati•o -onis *f*
convict *s* qui ad poenam damnatus est
convict *tr* **(of)** convincĕre *(w. gen of the offense);* **—ed of a lie** mendacii manifest•us -a -um

conviction *s (leg)* damnati•o -onis *f; (belief)* persuasi•o -onis *f;* **it is my firm —** mihi persuasissimum est
convince *tr* persuadēre *(w. dat)*
convinced *adj* **I am firmly — that** plenus persuasionis sum *(w. acc & inf)*
convincing *adj* ad persuadendum apt•us -a -um; **there is — proof that** magno argumento est *(w. acc & inf)*
convivial *adj* hilar•is -is -e
conviviality *s* hilarit•as -atis *f*
convocation *s* convocati•o -onis *f*
convoke *tr* convocare
convoy *s (naut)* praesidiaria class•is -is *f*
convulse *tr* convellĕre
convulsions *spl* spasm•us -i *m;* **to have —** spasmo vexari
convulsive *adj* spastic•us -a -um
coo *intr* canĕre
cooing *s* cant•us -ūs *m*
cook *s* coqu•us -i *m,* coqu•a -ae *f*
cook *tr* coquĕre; **to — up** *(fig)* excogitare ‖ *intr* coquĕre
cooked *adj* elix•us -a -um
cookie *s* crustul•um -i *n*
cool *adj* frigidul•us -a -um; *(fearless)* impavid•us -a -um; *(indifferent)* frigid•us -a -um
cool *s* **to keep one's —** mentem compescere
cool *tr* refrigerare ‖ *intr* refrigerari; *(fig)* defervescĕre; **to — off** intepescĕre
cooling *adj* frigoric•us -a -um
coolness *s* frig•us -oris *n; (indifference)* lentitud•o -inis *f; (calmness)* aequus anim•us -i *m*
coop *s (for chickens)* cave•a -ae *f*
coop *tr* **to — up** includĕre
cooperate *intr* unā agĕre
cooperation *s* adjument•um -i *n*
cope *intr* **to — with** certare cum *(w. abl);* **to be able to — with** par *(w. dat)* esse; **to be unable to — with** impar *(w. dat)* esse
copious *adj* copios•us -a -um
copiously *adv* copiose
copper *s* cupr•um -i *n,* ae•s -ris *n*
copper *adj* cuprin•us -a -um
coppersmith *s* aerar•ius -(i)i *m*
copulate *intr* coïre
copulation *s* coït•us -ūs *m*
copulative *s (gram)* copulativ•us -a -um
copy *s* exempl•ar -aris *n*
copy *tr (to imitate)* imitari; *(in writing)* (from) exscribĕre (ex + *abl)*
coquette *s* lup•a -ae *f*
coquettish *adj* lasciv•us -a -um
coral *adj* coralin•us -a -um
coral *s* coral•ium -(i)i *n*
cord *s* funicul•us -i *m*
cordial *adj* benign•us -a -um; *(sincere)* sincer•us -a -um; **to give s.o. a — welcome** aliquem benigne excipĕre
cordiality *s* comit•as -atis *f*
cordially *adv* benigne, ex animo
cordon *s* coron•a -ae *f*
cordon *tr* **to — off** saepire
corduroy *s* textil•e -is *n* crassum et striatum
core *s (of fruit)* volv•a -ae *f; (fig)* nucle•us -i *m*
Corinth *s* Corinth•us -i *f*
Corinthian *adj* Corinthiac•us -a -um
cork *s* cort•ex -icis *m; (stopper)* obturament•um -i *n*
corn *s* ze•a -ae *f; (on toe)* call•us -i *m*
corned beef *s* bubul•a -ae *f* muriatica
corner *s* angul•us -i *m; (of street)* compit•um -i *n; (tight spot)* angusti•ae -arum *fpl*
corner *tr* impedire; *(com)* coëmĕre ad quaestum
cornice *s* coron•a -ae *f*
cornucopia *s* corn•u -ūs *n* copiae
corollary *s* corollar•ium -(i)i *n*
coronation *s* coronati•o -onis *f*
coronet *s* diadem•a -atis *n*
corporal *adj* corporal•is -is -e, corporis *(gen);* **— punishment** veber•a -orum *npl*
corporal *s* decuri•o -onis *m*
corporate *adj* corporat•us -a -um
corporation *s* colleg•ium -(i)i *n*
corporeal *adj* corporeal•is -is -e
corps *s* legi•o -onis *f*
corpse *s* cadav•er -eris *n*
corpulent *adj* corpulent•us -a -um
corpuscle *s* corpuscul•um -i *n*
correct *adj* correct•us -a -um
correct *tr* corrigĕre; *(to remove faults)* emendare; *(to chastise)* castigare
correction *s* correcti•o -onis *f;* emendati•o -onis *f;* castigati•o -onis *f*
corrective *adj* ad corrigendum apt•us -a -um
corrective *s* remed•ium -(i)i *n*
correctly *adv* probe, integre
correlation *s* mutua rati•o -onis *f*
correspond *intr* congruĕre; *(to each other)* inter se congruĕre; *(by letter)* epistularum commercium habēre
correspondence *s* congruenti•a -ae *f; (exchange of letters)* epistularum commerc•ium -(i)i *n*
correspondent *s* epistularum script•or -oris *m*
corridor *s* andr•on -onis *m*
corroborate *tr* confirmare
corrode *tr* erodĕre
corrosion *s* rosi•o -onis *f*
corrosive *adj* corrosiv•us -a -um; *(fig)* mord•ax -acis
corrupt *tr* corrumpĕre
corrupt *adj* corrupt•us -a -um, putrid•us -a -um; *(accessible to bribery)* venal•is -is -e; *(text)* depravat•us -a -um
corrupter *s* corrupt•or -oris *m,* corruptr•ix -icis *f*
corruption *s* corrupti•o -onis *f*
corsage *s* fascicul•us -i *m* florum

corselet *s (mil)* loric•a -ae *f*
cortege *s* comitat•us -ūs *m*
cosily *adv* commode
cosmetic *s* offucin•a -ae *f,* medicam•en -inis *n; (rouge-like)* fuc•us -i *m*
cost *s (price)* pret•ium -(i)i *n; (expense)* impens•a -ae *f;* **— of living** anon•a -ae *f*
cost *intr* constare *(usu. w. abl of definite price);* **how much does it —?** quanti constat?; **it —s nothing** gratis constat; **the victory — the lives of many** victoria morte multorum constitit; **to — 200 denarii** ducentis denariis constare
costliness *s* carit•as -atis *f*
costly *adj* pretios•us -a -um; *(extravagant)* sumptuos•us -a -um
costume *s* habit•us -ūs *m*
cosy *adj* commod•us -a -um
cot *s* grabat•us -i *m*
cottage *s* cas•a -ae *f*
cotton *s* gossyp•ium -(i)i *n*
cotton *adj* gossypin•us -a -um
couch *s* cubil•e -is *n; (esp. for dining)* lect•us -i *m*
cough *s* tuss•is -is *(acc:* tussim) *f;* **to have a bad —** male tussire
cough *tr* **to — up** extussire **||** *intr* tussire
council *s* concil•ium -(i)i *n*
councilor *s* consiliar•ius -(i)i *m*
counsel *tr* consulĕre
counselor *s* consiliat•or -oris *m*
count *s* com•es -itis *m*
count *s* computati•o -onis *f; (total)* summ•a -ae *f; (of indictment)* cap•ut -itis *n*
count *tr* numerare, computare; *(to regard)* habēre, ducĕre; **to — out** *or* **up** enumerare; **to — out to** annumerare *(w. dat)* **||** *intr* aestimari, habēri; **to — upon** confidĕre *(w. dat);* **you can — on it that** erit tibi perspectum *(w. acc & inf)*
countenance *s* vult•us -ūs *m*
countenance *tr* indulgēre *(w. dat)*
counter *s (of shop, kitchen)* abac•us -i *m; (in games)* calcul•us -i *m*
counteract *intr* obsistĕre *(w. dat); (a sickness)* medēri *(w. dat)*
counterattack *s* impet•us -ūs *m* contra hostium impetum
counterattack *intr* impetum contra hostium impetum facĕre
counterfeit *tr (to pretend)* simulare; *(money)* adulterare
counterfeit *s* monet•a -ae *f* adulterina
counterfeit *adj* simulat•us -a -um; *(money)* adulterin•us -a -um
counterfeiter *s* falsar•ius -(i)i *m*
countermand *tr* irritum facĕre
counterpart *s (person)* pa•r -ris *n; (thing)* res, rei *f* gemella
countersign *tr* contrascribĕre
countless *adj* innumerabil•is -is -e
country *s* terr•a -ae *f; (territory)* fin•es -ium *mpl; (not city)* ru•s -ris *n; (native)* patri•a -ae *f;* **of what —** cuj•as -atis; **of what — are you?** cujates estis?
country *adj* rustic•us -a -um
country estate *s* suburban•um -i *n*
country-fresh *adj* agrest•is -is -e
country house *s* vill•a -ae *f* urbana
countryman *s* civ•is -is *m*
countryside *s* agr•i -orum *mpl*
couple *s* pa•r -ris *n; (married couple)* marit•i -orum *mpl;* **a couple of** aliquantul•i -ae -a
couple *tr* copulare **||** *intr (of animals)* coïre
courage *s* virt•us -utis *f,* anim•us -i *m;* **to lose —** animum demittĕre; **to take —** bono animo esse
courageous *adj* fort•is -is -e
courageously *adv* fortiter
courier *s* curs•or -oris *m,* nunt•ius -(i)i *m; (letter carrier)* tabellar•ius -(i)i *m*
course *s (movement, of ship, of river, of stars, etc.)* curs•us -ūs *m; (of life)* rati•o -onis *f; (of water)* duct•us -ūs *m; (route)* it•er -ineris *n; (at table)* fercul•um -i *n; (order)* seri•es -ei *f; (for racing)* circ•us -i *m,* stad•ium -(i)i *n;* **in due —** mox; **in the — of** inter *(w. acc);* **of —** de more, nempe, profecto; *(sarcastically)* scilicet; **to be driven off —** cursu excuti; **to change —** iter flectĕre
court *s (leg)* for•um -i *n,* judic•ium -(i)i *n; (open area)* are•a -ae *f; (inner court of a house)* cavaed•um -(i)i *n; (palace)* aul•a -ae *f; (retinue)* comitat•us -ūs *m;* **to take to —** in judicium vocare
court *tr* colĕre, ambire; *(a woman)* petĕre; *(danger)* se offerre *(w. dat)*
court costs *spl* litis impens•ae -arum *fpl*
courteous *adj* com•is -is-e
courteously *adv* comiter
courtesan *s* meretr•ix -cis *f*
courtesy *s* comit•as -atis *f;* **— of** beneficio *(w. gen)*
courtesy call *s* offic•ium -(i)i *n*
courthouse *s* basilic•a -ae *f*
courtier *s* aulic•us -i *m*
courtly *adj* aulic•us -a -um
court-martial *s* judic•ium -(i)i *n* castrense
courtship *s* procati•o -onis *f*
courtyard *s* are•a -ae *f*
cousin *s (on mother's side; used also for cousin in general)* consobrin•us -i *m,* consobrin•a -ae *f; (on father's side)* patruel•is -is *mf*
cove *s* sin•us -ūs *m*
covenant *s* pact•um -i *n*
covenant *s* pacisci̇
cover *s (for concealment and shelter)* tegment•um -i *n; (lid)* opercul•um -i *n; (mil)* praesid•ium -(i)i *n; (pretense)* speci•es -ei *f;* **under — of the artillery** tormentis munit•us -a -um; **under — of darkness** nocte adjuvante
cover *tr* tegĕre, operire; *(to hide)* celare; **to**

— up obtegĕre; *(against the cold)* bene operire
coverlet *s* stragul•um -i *n; (for bed or couch)* toral•e -is *n*
covet *tr* concupiscĕre
covetous *adj* appet•ens -entis
covey *s* gre•x -gis *m*
cow *tr* domare
coward *s* hom•o -inis *m* ignavus
cowardice *s* ignavi•a -ae *f*
cowardly *adj* ignav•us -a -um
cower *intr* subsidĕre
coy *adj* verecund•us -a -um
coyly *adv* verecunde
coyness *s* verecundi•a -ae *f*
cozily *adv* commode
cozy *adj* commod•us -a -um
crab *s* can•cer -cri *m*
crabby *adj* moros•us -a -um
crack *s* rim•a -ae *f; (noise)* crepit•us -ūs *m;* **at the — of dawn** primā luce
crack *tr* findĕre; *(nuts, etc.)* perfringĕre; *(a code)* enodare; **to — jokes** joca dicĕre ‖ *intr* rimas agĕre; *(to sound)* crepitare; *(of the voice)* irraucescĕre; **to — down on** castigare
cracked *adj* rimos•us -a -um; *(crazy)* delir•us -a -um
cracker *s* crustul•um -i *n*
crackle *intr* crepitare
crackling *s* crepit•us -ūs *m*
cradle *s* cunabul•a -orum *npl*
cradle *tr* fovēre
craft *s (trade)* artific•ium -(i)i *n; (skill)* ar•s -tis *f; (cunning)* dol•us -i *m; (naut)* navig•ium -(i)i *n*
craftily *adv* callide
craftsman *s* artif•ex -icis *m*
craftsmanship *s* artific•ium -(i)i *n*
crafty *adj* callid•us -a -um
cram *tr* farcire; **to — together** constipare ‖ *intr (for an examination)* cuncta confertim menti inculcare
cramp *s* spasm•us -i *m*
cramp *tr* comprimĕre; **to be —ed for space** in angusto sedēre
crane *s (bird)* gru•s -is *mf; (machine)* tollen•o -onis *f*
crank *s (machine)* unc•us -i *m; (person)* moros•us -i *m*
crank *tr* volvĕre
crash *s* frag•or -oris *m*
crash *intr* fragorem dare; **to come —ing down** corruĕre
crass *adj* crass•us -a -um
crate *s* cist•a -ae *f*
crater *s* crat•er -eris *m*
crave *tr* concupiscĕre
craven *adj* ignav•us atque abject•us -a -um
craving *s* desider•ium -(i)i *n*
crawfish *s* astac•us -i *m*
crawl *intr* repĕre
crawl *s (of babies)* reptati•o -onis *f*
crayon *s* cret•a -ae *f*
craze *s* fur•or -oris *m*
craziness *s* dementi•a -ae *f*
crazy *adj (person)* dem•ens -entis; *(idea)* insuls•us -a -um; **— about birds** moros•us -a -um in aves; **to drive s.o. —** mentem *(w. gen)* alienare
creak *s* strid•or -oris *m*
creak *intr* stridēre
creaking *s* strid•or -oris *m*
creaking *adj* stridul•us -a -um
cream *s* crem•or -oris *m* lactis; *(fig)* flo•s -ris *m*
crease *s* plic•a -ae *f*
crease *tr* duplicare ‖ *intr* plicari
create *tr* creare; *(in the mind)* fingĕre
creation *s (act)* creati•o -onis *f; (world)* summ•a -ae *f* rerum, mund•us -i *m; (fig)* op•us -eris *n*
creative *adj* creatr•ix -icis; *(able)* ingenios•us -a -um
creator *s* creat•or -oris *m; (originator)* auct•or -oris *m,* opif•ex -icis *m*
creature *s (living)* anim•al -alis *n; (tool)* minis•ter -tri *m*
credence *s* fid•es -ei *f;* **to gain —** fidem habēre; **to give — to** credĕre *(w. dat)*
credentials *spl* testimoni•a -orum *npl*
credibility *s* fid•es -ei *f*
credible *adj* credibil•is -is -e; *(of persons)* locupl•es -etis
credit *s (faith)* fid•es -ei *f; (authority)* auctorit•as -atis *f; (reputation)* existimati•o -onis *f; (com)* fid•es -ei *f; (recognition)* lau•s -dis *f;* **to buy on —** in diem emĕre; **to have —** fide stare
credit *tr* credĕre *(w. dat); (com)* acceptum referre *(w. dat);* **to — my teacher with my success** successum meum magistro ascribo
creditable *adj* honest•us -a -um
credit card *s* tabell•a -ae *f* tributaria
creditor *s* credit•or -oris *m*
credulity *s* credulit•as -atis *f*
credulous *adj* credul•us -a -um
creed *s* fid•es -ei *f*
creek *s* riv•us -i *m*
creep *intr* repĕre; **it makes my skin —** facit ut horream
crescent *s* lun•a -ae *f* crescens
crescent-shaped *adj* lunat•us -a -um
crest *s* crist•a -ae *f*
crested *adj* cristat•us -a -um
crew *s* gre•x -gis *m; (naut)* naut•ae -arum *mpl; (rowers)* remig•es -um *mpl*
crib *s (manger)* praesep•e -is *n; (for a baby)* lectul•us -i *m*
cricket *s* gryll•us -i *m*
crier *s* praec•o -onis *m*
crime *s* scel•us -eris *n*
criminal *adj* scelest•us -a -um
criminal *s* scelest•us -i *m*
criminally *adv* nefarie

crimp *tr* crispare
crimson *adj* coccine•us -a -um
crimson *s* cocc•um -i *n*
cringe *intr* abhorrēre; *(to behave servilely)* se demittěre, adulari
cripple *s* claud•us -i *m*
cripple *tr* debilitare; *(fig)* frangěre
crippled *adj (in the hands)* manc•us -a -um; *(lame)* claud•us -a -um
crisis *s* discrim•en -inis *n*
criterion *s* norm•a -ae *f*
critic *s* reprehens•or -oris *m; (literary)* cens•or -oris *m*
critical *adj (relating to criticism; crucial)* critic•us -a -um; *(blaming)* censori•us -a -um
criticism *s* reprehensi•o -onis *f; (literary)* judic•ium -(i)i *n,* ar•s -tis *f* critica
criticize *tr* reprehenděre; *(literature)* judicare
croak *intr* coaxare; *(of ravens)* crocitare; *(to complain)* queritari; *(to die) (coll)* animam ebullire
croaking *s (of frogs)* clam•or -oris *m; (of ravens)* crocitati•o -onis *f; (complaining)* querimoni•a -ae *f*
crock *s* oll•a -ae *f*
crocodile *s* crocodil•us -i *m*
crook *s (shepherd's)* ped•um -i *n; (thief)* fu•r -ris *m*
crook *tr* curvare
crooked *adj* curvat•us -a -um; *(fig)* dolos•us -a -um
crop *s (of grain)* seg•es -itis *f; (of a bird)* ingluvi•es -ei *f*
crop *tr* tondēre; *(to harvest)* metěre; *(to browse)* carpěre
cross *s (structure)* cru•x -cis *f; (figure)* decuss•is -is *m; (fig)* cruciat•us -ūs *m*
cross *adj (across)* transvers•us -a -um; *(contrary)* contrari•us -a -um; *(peevish)* acerb•us -a -um; *(hybrid)* mixt•us -a -um
cross *tr* transire; *(a river)* trajicěre; *(a mountain)* transcenděre; *(to thwart)* frustrari, adversari; *(hybrids)* miscēre; **to — the legs** poplites alternis genibus imponěre; **to — out** expungěre
crossbar *s* tign•um -i *n* transversum; *(line)* line•a -ae *f* transversa
crossbow *s* arcuballist•a -ae *f*
crossbreed *s* hibrid•a -ae *mf*
crossbreed *tr* miscēre
crosscut *s* secti•o -onis *f* in transversum
cross-examination *f* interrogati•o -onis *f*
cross-examine *tr* interrogare
cross-eyed *adj* strab•us -a -um; **he is —** strabo est
crossing *s* transit•us -ūs *m; (of a river)* traject•us -ūs *m; (of roads)* biv•ium -(i)i *n; (of three roads)* triv•ium -(i)i *n; (of four roads)* quadriv•ium -(i)i *n*
crossroads *spl* quadriv•ium -(i)i *n; (esp. in the country)* compit•a -orum *npl*
crosswise *adv* decussatim
crotch *s (anat)* bifurc•um -i *n*
crouch *intr* subsidēre; **in a —** subsid•ens -entis
crow *s (bird)* corn•ix -icis *f; (of rooster)* gallicin•ium -(i)i *n*
crow *intr (of roosters)* cucurire; *(to boast)* gloriari
crowbar *s* vect•is -is *m*
crowd *s* frequenti•a -ae *f; (mob)* turb•a -ae *f; (of people flocking together)* concurs•us -ūs *m; (common people)* vulg•us -i *n*
crowd *tr* frequentare ‖ *intr* **to — around** stipare, circumfundi *(w. dat);* **to — together** congregari
crowded *adj* frequ•ens -entis; **— together** confert•us -a -um
crowing *s* cant•us -ūs *m*
crown *s (of king)* insign•e -is *n* regium; *(wreath)* coron•a -ae *f; (power)* regn•um -i *n; (top)* vert•ex -icis *m; (fig)* ap•ex -icis *m*
crown *tr* insigne regium capiti *(w. gen)* imponěre; **to — the temples with flowers** tempora floribus cingěre
crucifix *s* imag•o -inis *f* Christi crucifixi
crucifixion *s* crucis supplic•ium -(i)i *n*
crucify *tr* crucifigěre
crude *adj* rud•is -is -e, incult•us -a -um
crudely *adv* inculte
cruel *adj* crudel•is -is -e
cruelly *adv* crudeliter
cruelty *s* crudelit•as -atis *f*
cruet *s* gutt•us -i *m*
cruise *intr* circumvectari, navigare
cruise *s* navigati•o -onis *f*
crumb *s* mic•a -ae *f*
crumble *tr* friare ‖ *intr* friari; *(to fall down)* corruěre
crumbling *adj* friabil•is -is -e
crumple *tr* corrugare
crumpled *adj* corrugat•us -a -um
crunch *tr* dentibus frangěre
crush *tr* contunděre; *(fig)* oppriměre
crush *s* contusi•o -onis *f; (crowd)* frequenti•a -ae *f* densissima
crust *s* crust•um -i *n*
crusty *adj* crustos•us -a -um; *(fig)* cerebros•us -a -um
crutch *s* bacul•um -i *n*
cry *s (shout)* clam•or -oris *m; (of a baby)* vagit•us -ūs *m*
cry *tr* clamare; **to — out** exclamare ‖ *intr (to shout)* clamare; *(to shout repeatedly)* clamitare; *(to weep)* lacrimare, flēre; *(of infants)* vagire
crying *s* flet•us -ūs *m; (of a baby)* vagit•us -ūs *m*
crypt *s* crypt•a -ae *f*
cryptic *adj* occult•us -a -um
crystal *adj* cyrstallin•us -a -um
crystal *s* crystall•um -i *n*
crystal-clear *adj* pellucid•us -a -um

cub *s* catul•us -i *m*
cube *s* cub•us -i *m*
cubic *adj* cubic•us -a -um
cubit *s* cubit•um -i *n*
cuckoo *s* cucul•us -i *m*
cucumber *s* cucum•is -eris *m*
cud *s* rum•en -inis *n;* **to chew the —** ruminare
cudgel *s* fust•is -is *m*
cue *s (hint)* nut•us -ūs *m,* indic•ium -(i)i *n; (theat)* verb•um -i *n* monitorium
cuff *s (of sleeve)* extrema manic•a -ae *f; (blow)* colaph•us -i *m*
cull *tr* decerpĕre
culminate *intr* ad summum venire
culmination *s* fastig•ium -(i)i *n*
culpable *adj* culpand•us -a -um
culprit *s* re•us -i *m,* re•a -ae *f*
cultivate *tr (land, mind, friendship)* colĕre
cultivation *s* cultur•a -ae *f*
cultivator *s* cult•or -oris *m*
culture *s* cultur•a -ae *f*
culvert *s* cloac•a -ae *f*
cumbersome *adj* inhabil•is -is -e
cunning *adj (clever)* callid•us -a -um; *(sly)* astut•us -a -um
cup *s* pocul•um -i *n*
cupbearer *s* pocillat•or -oris *m*
cupboard *s* armar•ium -(i)i *n*
Cupid *s* Cupid•o -inis *m*
cupidity *s* cupidit•as -atis *f*
cupola *s* thol•us -i *m*
cur *s (coll)* can•is -is *m* nothus; *(fig)* scelest•us -i *m*
curable *adj* sanabil•is -is -e
curative *adj* medicabil•is -is -e
curator *s* curat•or -oris *m*
curb *s (& fig)* fren•um -i *n; (of the road)* crepid•o -inis *f*
curb *tr* frenare; *(fig)* refrenare
curbstone *s* crepid•o -inis *m*
curdle *tr* coagulare ‖ *intr* coïre
cure *s (remedy)* remd•ium -(i)i *n; (process)* sanati•o -onis *f*
cure *tr* sanare; *(to pickle)* salire
curiosity *s* curiosit•as -atis *f; (thing)* miracul•um -i *n*
curious *adj* curios•us -a -um; *(strange)* mirabil•is -is -e
curiously *adv* curiose
curl *s (natural)* cirr•us -i *m; (artificial)* cincinn•us -i *m*
curl *tr* crispare ‖ *intr* crispari; *(of smoke)* volvi
curler, curling iron *s* calamistr•um -i *n*
curly *adj* crisp•us -a -um
currency *s* monet•a -ae *f; (use)* us•us -ūs *m;* **to gain —** percrebrescĕre
current *adj (opinion)* vulgar•is -is -e; *(in general use)* usitat•us -a -um
current *s* vis *f* fluminis *n; (of air)* afflat•us -ūs *m;* **against the —** adverso flumine; **with the —** secundo flumine
curse *s* maledict•um -i *n; (fig)* pest•is -is *f*
curse *tr* maledicĕre *(w. dat)* ‖ *intr* maledicĕre
cursed *adj* exsecrabil•is -is -e
cursing *s* convic•ium -(i)i *n*
cursorily *adv* strictim
cursory *adj* lev•is -is -e, brev•is -is -e
curt *adj* abrupt•us -a -um
curtail *tr (to cut off a part of)* praecidĕre; *(to diminish)* minuĕre
curtain *s* aulae•um -i *n*
curvature *s* curvatur•a -ae *f*
curve *s (of road, river)* flex•us -ūs *m*
curve *tr* incurvare, flectĕre ‖ *intr* incurvari
curved *adj* curv•us -a -um; *(as a sickle)* falcat•us -a -um
cushion *s* pulvin•us -i *m; (for sitting on)* sedular•ium -(i)i *n; (fig)* levam•en -inis *n*
custard *s* artolagan•us -i *m*
custodian *s* cust•os -odis *m,* curat•or -oris *m*
custody *s* tutel•a -ae *f,* custodi•a -ae *f;* **to keep in —** custodire; **to take into —** in vincula conjicĕre
custom *s* mo•s -ris *m,* consuetud•o -inis *f;* **according to the — of the Roman people** more populi Romani
customary *adj* consuet•us -a -um; *(regularly occurring)* sollemn•is -is -e
customer *s* cli•ens -entis *m; (buyer)* empt•or -oris *m*
customs *spl (tax)* portor•ium -(i)i *n*
customs officer *s* portit•or -oris *m*
cut *tr* secare; *(to fell)* caedĕre; *(to mow)* succidĕre; **to — apart** dissecare; **to — away** recidĕre, abscindĕre; **to — down** caedĕre; *(to kill)* occidĕre; **to — in pieces** concidĕre; **to — off** praecidĕre; *(to intercept)* intercludĕre; **to — open** incidĕre; **to — out** exsecare; *(out of a rock, etc.)* excidĕre; **to — short** intercidĕre; *(to abridge)* praecidĕre; *(to interrupt)* interpellare; **to — short the school day** ludum artare; **to — to pieces** concidĕre; **to — up** minutatim concidĕre; *(the enemy)* trucidare
cuticle *s* cuticul•a -ae *f*
cutlass *s* ens•is -is *m*
cutlery *s* cultr•i -orum *mpl*
cutlet *s* frust•um -i *n*
cutthroat *s* sicar•ius -(i)i *m*
cutting *adj (sharp)* acut•us -a -um; *(fig)* acerb•us -a -um
cutting *s (act)* secti•o -onis *f; (thing)* segm•en -inis *n; (for planting)* taleol•a -ae *f*
cuttlefish *s* sepi•a -ae *f*
cycle *s* orb•is -is *m; (of events)* ord•o -inis *m*
cylinder *s* cylindr•us -i *m*
cylindrical *adj* cylindrat•us -a -um
cymbal *s* cymbal•um -i *n*
cynic *adj* cynic•us -a -um

cynic *s* cynic•us -i *m*
cynical *adj* acerb•us -a -um
cynicism *s* acerbit•as -atis *f*
cypress *s* cypress•us -i *f*

D

dab *s* massul•a -ae *f*
dab *tr* **to — on** illiněre
dabble *intr* **to — in** leviter attingěre
dad, daddy *s* tat•a -ae *m*
dactyl *s* dactyl•us -i *m*
dactylic *adj* dactylic•us -a -um
daffodil *s* asphodel•us -i *m*
daffy *adj (coll)* delir•us -a -um
dagger *s* pugi•o -onis *m*
daily *adj* co(t)tidian•us -a -um
daily *adv* co(t)tidie
dainties *spl* cuppedi•a -orum *npl*
dainty *adj* delicat•us -a -um
dairy *s* cell•a -ae *f* lactaria
dairy farm *s* fund•us -i *m* lactarius
daisy *s* bell•is -idis *f*
dale *s* vall•is -is *f*
dally *intr (to linger)* morari; *(to trifle)* nugari; *(amorously)* blandiri
dam *s* mol•es -is *f; (of animals)* mat•er -ris *f*
dam *tr* **to — up** (operibus) obstruěre
damage *s (loss)* damn•um -i *n; (injury)* nox•a -ae *f*
damage *tr* laeděre; *(a person)* fraudi esse *(w. dat);* **to — s.o.'s reputation** aestimationem alicujus violare
dame *s* domin•a -ae *f; (girl)* puell•a -ae *f*
damn *tr* damnare, exsecrari
damnable *adj* damnabil•is -is -e
damnably *adv* damnabiliter
damnation *s* damnati•o -onis *f*
damp *adj* (h)umid•us -a -um
dampen *tr* humectare; *(fig)* restringěre
dampness *s* ulig•o -inis *f*
damsel *s* puell•a -ae *f*
dance *s* saltat•us -ūs *m*
dance *tr* **to — a number** canticum desaltare ‖ *intr* saltare
dancing *s* saltati•o -onis *f*
dandelion *s* taraxac•um -i *n*
dandruff *s* porrig•o -inis *f*
dandy *adj* bell•us -a -um
dandy *s* hom•o -inis *m* bellus
danger *s* pericul•um -i *n;* **to be in — of** periclitari *(w. abl);* **to be in grave —** in praecipite esse
dangerous *adj* periculos•us -a -um
dangerously *adv* periculose; *(seriously)* graviter
dangle *tr* suspenděre ‖ *intr* penděre
dank *adj* (h)umid•us et frigid•us -a -um
dappled *adj* maculos•us -a -um; *(horse)* guttat•us -a -um
dare *tr* provocare ‖ *intr* audēre
daring *adj* aud•ax -acis
daring *s* audaci•a -ae *f*
dark *adj* obscur•us -a -um; *(in color)* fusc•us -a -um; *(gloomy)* a•ter -tra -trum; *(stern)* atr•ox -ocis; **—est night** spississima no•x -ctis *f;* **— eyes** nigri ocul•i -orum *mpl;* **to grow —** nigrescěre
dark *s* tenebr•ae -arum *fpl;* **after —** de nocte; **in the —** *(i.e., secretly)* clam et occulte; **to be in the —** *(i.e., ignorant)* caligare; **to keep in the —** celare
darken *tr* obscurare; *(colors)* fuscare
darling *adj* suavissim•us -a -um
darling *s* delici•ae -arum *fpl*
darn *tr* resarcire
darn *interj* hercule!
dart *s* spicul•um -i *n*
dart *intr (to move quickly)* provolare; *(of snake's tongue)* vibrare; **to — out** emicare
dash *tr (to splash)* aspergěre; *(hopes)* frustrari; **to — against** alliděre ad *(w. acc);* **to — off** *(letter)* scriptitare; **to — to pieces** discutěre; **to — to the ground** affligěre ‖ *intr* ruěre
dash *s* impet•us -ūs *m; (animation)* alacrit•as -atis *f; (small amount)* mensur•a -ae *f* duorum digitorum
dashing *adj* ala•cer -cris -cre; *(showy)* nitid•us -a -um
data *spl* fact•a -orum *npl*
date *s* di•es -ei *m,* temp•us -oris *n; (fruit)* palmul•a -ae *f;* **out of —** obsolet•us -a -um; **to —** adhuc; **up to —** rec•ens -entis
date *tr* diem ascriběre *(w. dat)* ‖ *intr* **to — from** originem trahěre ab *(w. abl)*
date palm *s* palm•a -ae *f*
dative *s* dativ•us -i *m*
daub *tr* obliněre
daughter *s* fili•a -ae *f*
daughter-in-law *s* nur•us -i *f*
daunt *tr* perterrēre
dauntless *adj* impavid•us -a -um
dauntlessly *adv* impavide
dawdle *intr* cessare
dawn *s* auror•a -ae *f;* **at —** primā luce
dawn *intr* dilucescěre; **to — on** *(fig)* occurrěre *(w. dat)*
day *s* di•es -ei *m;* **by —** interdiu; **— by —** in dies; **— and night** diem noctemque; **every —** co(t)tidie; **from — to —** in dies; **next —** postridie; **one —** *(in the past)* quodam die; **some —** olim; **the — after** postridie; **the — after that** postridie ejus diei; **the — after tomorrow** perendie; **the — before** pridie
day *adj* diurn•us -a -um
daybreak *s* **at —** primā luce; **before —** antelucio
daydream *s* somn•ium -(i)i *n*
daydream *intr* vigilans somniare
daylight *s* lu•x -cis *f*

daystar *s* Lucif•er -eri *m*
daytime *s* temp•us -oris *n* diurnum; **in the —** interdiu
daze *s* stup•or -oris *m*
daze *tr* obstupefacĕre
dazzle *tr* praestringĕre
dazzling *adj* fulgid•us -a -um
deacon *s* diacon•us -i *m*
dead *adj* mortu•us -a -um
dead *s* **— of night** media no•x -ctis *f;* **dead of winter** brum•a -ae *f;* **the —** man•es -ium, mortu•i -orum *mpl*
dead *adv* omnino, prorsus
deaden *tr* obtundĕre
dead end *s* fundul•a -ae *f; (fig)* cessati•o -onis *f*
deadly *adj* mortif•er -era -erum; *(hatred)* capital•is -is -e
deaf *adj* surd•us -a -um; **to be — to** non audire; **to go —** obsurdescĕre; **to turn a — ear** obsurdescĕre
deafen *tr* exsurdare
deaf-mute *adj* surd•us idemque mut•us -a -um
deafness *s* surdit•as -atis *f*
deal *s (quantity)* copi•a -ae *f,* vis *f; (com)* negot•ium -(i)i *n;* **a good — longer** multo diutius; **a good — of** aliquantum *(w. gen)*
deal *tr* partiri; **to — him a blow in the stomach** pugnos in ventrem ingerĕre **||** *intr (com)* negotiari; **easy to — with** tractabil•is -is -e; **to — with** *(a thing)* agĕre *(w. abl); (a person)* uti *(w. abl)*
dealer *s* negotiat•or -oris *m; (in a small shop)* coci•o -onis *m*
dealing *s* negotiati•o -onis *f;* **to have —s with** commercium habēre cum *(w. abl)*
dean *s* decan•us -i *m*
dear *adj (highly valued; high-priced)* car•us -a -um; **my — friend!** mi amice!
dear *interj* **O —!** *(in dismay)* hei!; *(in embarrassment)* au au!
dearly *adv (intensely)* valde; *(at high cost)* magni
dearness *s* carit•as -atis *f*
dearth *s* inopi•a -ae *f*
death *s* mor•s -tis *f; (in violent form)* ne•x -cis *f;* **to meet one's —** mortem obire; **to put to —** ad mortem dare
deathbed *s* tor•us -i *m* extremus
deathless *adj* immortal•is -is -e
deathlike *adj* mortuos•us -a -um
deathly *adj* pallid•us -a -um
debase *tr* depravare; *(coinage)* adulterare; **to — oneself** se demittĕre
debasement *s* adulterati•o -onis *f*
debatable *adj* controversios•us -a -um, ambigu•us -a -um
debate *s* disceptati•o -onis *f*
debate *tr* disceptare de *(w. abl)* **||** *intr* disserĕre
debater *s* disputat•or -oris *m*
debauchery *s* licenti•a -ae *f*
debilitate *tr* debilitare
debit *s* expens•um -i *n*
debit *tr* in expensum referre
debt *s* ae•s -ris *n* alienum; *(fig)* debit•um -i *n;* **to pay off a —** aes alienum persolvĕre; **to run up a —** aes alienum conflare
debtor *s* debit•or -oris *m*
decade *s* dec•as -adis *f*
decadence *s* occas•us -ūs *m*
decadent *adj* degen•er -era -erum
decalogue *s* decalog•us -i *m*
decamp *intr* castra movēre
decant *tr* diffundĕre
decanter *s* lagoen•a -ae *f*
decapitate *tr* detruncare
decay *s* tab•es -is *f; (fig)* defecti•o -onis *f*
decay *intr* putrescĕre, tabescĕre
decease *s* decess•us -i *m*
deceased *adj* defunct•us -a -um
deceit *s* frau•s -dis *f,* dol•us -i *m*
deceitful *adj* fall•ax -acis
deceitfully *adv* fallaciter
deceive *tr* decipĕre, fallĕre
December *s* Decem•ber -bris *m or* mens•is -is *m* December; **on the first of —** Kalendis Decembribus
decency *s* decor•um -i *n*
decent *adj* dec•ens -entis
decently *adv* decenter
deception *s* fallaci•a -ae *f*
deceptive *adj* fall•ax -acis
decide *tr & intr* decernĕre; **the Senate decided** senatui placuit; **to — to** *(w. inf)* constituĕre *(w. inf)*
decided *adj* cert•us -a -um
deciduous *adj* caduc•us -a -um
decimate *tr* decimare; *(fig)* depopulari
decipher *tr* enodare
decision *s* sententi•a -ae *f; (of deliberative body)* decret•um -i *n; (of Senate)* auctorit•as -atis *f; (leg)* judic•ium -(i)i *n*
decisive *adj* cert•us -a -um; **— battle** decretoria pugn•a -ae *f*
deck *s* pon•s -tis *m;* **ship with a —** nav•is -is *f* constrata
deck *tr* ornare; *(tables)* sternĕre; **—ed out in** subornat•us -a -um *(w. abl)*
declaim *intr* declamare
declamation *s* declamati•o -onis *f*
declamatory *adj* declamatori•us -a -um
declaration *s* declarati•o -onis *f; (of war)* denuniati•o -onis *f*
declarative *adj* declarativ•us -a -um
declare *tr* declarare; *(to say out plainly)* edicĕre; *(war)* indicĕre **||** *intr* **to — for** favēre *(w. dat)*
declension *s* declinati•o -onis *f*
declinable *adj* declinabil•is -is -e
decline *s (slope)* decliv•e -is *n; (of strength, etc.)* deminuti•o -onis *f;* **to cause a — in prices** pretia levare
decline *tr (to refuse)* recusare; *(gram)*

declinare, flectĕre; **to — battle** pugnam detrectare ‖ *intr* inclinare; *(to decay, fail)* deficĕre, decrescĕre; *(of prices)* laxare
decode *tr* enodare
decompose *tr* resolvĕre ‖ *intr* putrescĕre, dissolvi
decomposition *s* dissoluti•o -onis *f*
decorate *tr* ornare
decoration *s (act)* ornati•o -onis *f; (ornament)* ornament•um -i *n; (distinction)* dec•us -oris *n*
decorator *s* exornat•or -oris *m*
decorous *adj* decor•us -a -um
decorously *adv* decore
decorum *s* decor•um -i *n*
decoy *s* ill•ex -icis *mf*
decoy *tr* allicĕre
decrease *s* imminuti•o -onis *f*
decrease *tr* imminuĕre ‖ *intr* decrescĕre; *(of prices)* retro abire
decreasingly *adv* in minus
decree *s* decret•um -i *n; (of the Senate)* consult•um -i *n; (of the assembly)* scit•um -i *n*
decree *tr* decernĕre; **the people —ed** populus jussit
decrepit *adj* decrepit•us -a -um
decry *tr* vituperare
dedicate *tr* dedicare; *(a book)* dicare; **to — oneself to** se dedĕre *(w. dat)*
dedication *s* dedicati•o -onis *f; (of a book)* nuncupati•o -onis *f*
deduce *tr* deducĕre; *(to infer)* colligĕre
deduct *tr* deducĕre; **to — from the capital what has been paid in interest** de capite deducĕre quod usuris pernumeratum est
deduction *s* deducti•o -onis *f; (inference)* conclusi•o -onis *f*
deed *s* fact•um -i *n; (pej)* facin•us -oris *n; (leg)* syngraph•a -ae *f;* **good —** benefic•ium -(i)i *n*
deem *tr* ducĕre, habēre
deep *adj* alt•us -a -um; *(very deep)* profund•us -a -um; *(of sounds)* grav•is -is -e; *(of color)* satur; *(sleep)* art•us -a -um; *(recondite)* recondit•us -a -um; **— silence fell** ingens silentium factum est; **in — thought** cogitabund•us -a -um
deep *s* alt•um -i *n*
deepen *tr* defodĕre; *(e.g., affection)* augēre ‖ *intr* alt•ior -ior -ius fieri
deeply *adv* alte; *(inwardly)* penitus; *(fig)* graviter, valde; **to be — grieved** graviter dolēre; **to be — in love** graviter amare
deep-sunk *adj (eyes)* concav•us -a -um
deer *s* cerv•us -i *m,* cerv•a -ae *f*
deface *tr* deformare
defaced *adj* deform•is -is -e
defacement *s* deformit•as -atis *f*
defamation *s* obtrectati•o -onis *f*
defamatory *adj* probros•us -a -um
defame *tr* diffamare, infamare
default *s* delict•um -i *n*
defeat *s* repuls•a -ae *f; (mil)* clad•es -is *f*
defeat *tr* vincĕre, superare; *(to baffle)* frustrari; **to — a bill** rogationem antiquare
defect *s* vit•ium -(i)i *n*
defect *intr (to desert)* deficĕre
defection *s* defecti•o -onis *f; (to the enemy)* transfug•ium -(i)i *n*
defective *adj* vitios•us -a -um; *(gram)* defectiv•us -a -um
defend *tr* defendĕre; *(leg)* patrocinari *(w. dat)*
defendant *s* re•us -i *m,* re•a -ae *f*
defender *s* defens•or -oris *m; (leg)* patron•us -i *m*
defense *s (act)* defensi•o -onis *f;* praesid•ium -(i)i *n; (leg)* patrocin•ium -(i)i *n; (speech)* defensi•o -onis *f*
defenseless *adj* infens•us -a -um; *(unarmed)* inerm•is -is -e
defensible *adj* defensibil•is -is -e
defensive *adj* **— and offensive alliance** societ•as -atis *f* ad bellum defendendum atque inferendum facta; **—and offensive weapons** tela ad tegendum et adnocendum; **to put s.o. on the —** aliquem ad sua defendenda cogĕre
defer *tr* differre ‖ *intr* **to — to** obsequi *(w. dat)*
deference *s* observanti•a -ae *f;* **out of —** reverenter
deferential *adj* **(to)** observ•ans -antis *(w. gen)*
defiance *s* contempti•o -onis *f;* **in — of the law** invitis legibus
defiant *adj* insol•ens -entis
deficiency *s* defect•us -ūs *m; (of supplies, water, money)* penuri•a -ae *f*
deficient *adj* **(in)** in•ops -opis *(w. gen);* **to be —** deesse
deficit *s* lacun•a -ae *f;* **there is a —** deficit; **to make up the —** lacunam explēre
defile *s* fauc•es -ium *fpl*
defile *tr* inquinare; *(usu. fig)* contaminare
defilement *s* contaminati•o -onis *f*
define *tr* definire
definite *adj* definit•us -a -um
definitely *adv* definite, certe
definition *s* definiti•o -onis *f*
definitive *adj* definitiv•us -a -um
definitively *adv* definite
deflect *tr* deflectĕre
deflection *s* deflecti•o -onis *f*
deflower *tr* devirginare
deform *tr* deformare
deformed *adj* deform•is -is -e
deformity *s* deformit•as -atis *f*
defraud *tr* fraudare
defray *tr* suppeditare; **to — the costs** sumptūs suppeditare
deft *adj* agil•is -is -e, habil•is -is -e
deftly *adv* scite

defunct *adj* defunct•us -a -um
defy *tr* contemnĕre
degeneracy *s* mor•es -um *mpl* deteriores
degenerate *adj* degen•er -eris
degradation *s* ignomini•a -ae *f*
degrade *tr (to lower rank)* in ordinem redigĕre; *(fig)* dehonestare
degrading *adj* indign•us -a -um
degree *s* grad•us -ūs *m;* **to such a — that** adeo ut
deification *s* consecrati•o -onis *f*
deify *tr* inter deos referre
deign *tr* dignari
deism *s* deism•us -i *m*
deity *s* num•en -inis *n*
dejected *adj* demiss•us -a -um
dejection *s* animi abjecti•o -onis *f*
delay *s* mor•a -ae *f*
delay *tr* demorari ‖ *intr* morari
delectable *adj* delectabil•is -is -e
delegate *s* legat•us -i *m*
delegate *tr (to depute)* delegare; *(to entrust)* demandare
delegation *s (act)* mandat•us -ūs *m; (group)* legati•o -onis *f*
delete *tr* delēre
deleterious *adj* noxi•us -a -um
deliberate *adj* deliberat•us -a -um
deliberate *intr* deliberare, consulĕre
deliberately *adv* de industria
deliberation *s* deliberati•o -onis *f*
delicacy *s* subtilit•as -atis *f; (food)* cuppedi•a -ae *f,* matte•a -ae *f*
delicate *adj (of fine texture)* subtil•is -is -e; *(e.g., girl)* delicat•us -a -um; *(taste, work of art)* eleg•ans -antis; *(health)* infirm•us -a -um; *(matter)* lubric•us -a -um
delicious *adj* sapid•us -a -um
delight *s* delectati•o -onis *f; (cause of delight)* delici•ae -arum *fpl*
delight *tr* delectare ‖ *intr* **to — in** delectari *(w. abl)*
delighted *adj* **(with)** delectat•us -a -um *(w. abl)*
delightful *adj* suav•is -is -e
delightfully *adv* suaviter
delineate *tr* delineare, describĕre
delineation *s* descripti•o -onis *f*
delinquency *s* delict•um -i *n*
delinquent *adj* noxi•us -a -um
delinquent *s* nox•ius -(i)i *m,* noxi•a -ae *f*
delirious *adj* delir•us -a -um
delirium *s* delir•ium -(i)i *n*
deliver *tr (to hand over)* tradĕre; *(to free)* liberare; *(to surrender)* prodĕre; *(a speech)* habēre, dicĕre; *(sentence)* dicĕre; *(message)* referre; *(blow)* intendĕre; *(child)* obstetricari; *(a letter)* reddĕre
deliverance *s* liberati•o -onis *f*
deliverer *s* liberat•or -oris *m*
delivery *s (freedom)* liberati•o -onis *f; (of goods)* traditi•o -onis *f; (of a speech)* dicti•o -onis *f; (childbirth)* part•us -ūs *m*
delude *tr* deludĕre
deluge *s* diluv•ium -(i)i *n*
deluge *tr* obruĕre, inundare
delusion *s* delusi•o -onis *f*
demagogue *s* publicol•a -ae *m*
demand *s* postulati•o -onis *f*
demand *tr* postulare, flagitare
demarcation *s* confin•ium -(i)i *n*
demean *tr* **to — oneself** se demittĕre
demeanor *s* gest•us -ūs *m*
demerit *s* vit•ium -(i)i *n; (mark)* vitii not•a -ae *f*
demigod *s* her•os -oïs *m*
demise *s* decess•us -ūs *m*
democracy *s* civit•as -atis *f* popularis
democrat *s* civ•is -is *m* popularis
democratic *adj* popular•is -is -e; **— party** part•es -ium *fpl* populares
democratically *adv* populi voluntate
demolish *tr* demoliri
demolition *s* demoliti•o -onis *f*
demon *s* daem•on -onis *m*
demonstrable *adj* demonstrabil•is -is -e
demonstrably *adv* manifeste
demonstrate *tr (to show)* monstrare; *(to prove)* demonstrare
demonstration *s (proof)* demonstrati•o -onis *f; (display)* ostent•us -ūs *m*
demonstrative *adj* demonstrativ•us -a -um
demoralization *s* depravati•o -onis *f*
demoralize *tr (to corrupt)* depravare; *(to discourage)* percellĕre
demote *tr* loco movēre
demotion *s* a gradu moti•o -onis *f*
demure *adj* modest•us -a -um
demurely *adv* modeste
den *s* latibul•um -i *n*; *(in a home)* tablin•um -i *n*
deniable *adj* infitiand•us -a -um
denial *s* negati•o -onis *f; (refusal)* repudiati•o -onis *f;* **to give s.o. a flat —** praecise alicui negare
denomination *s (name)* denominati•o -onis *f; (sect)* sect•a -ae *f*
denominator *s* numer•us -i *m* dividens
denotation *s* denotati•o -onis *f*
denote *tr* declarare
denounce *tr (to inform against)* deferre; *(to condemn)* reprehendĕre
dense *adj* dens•us -a -um; *(crowded)* spiss•us -a -um; *(stupid)* crass•us -a -um
densely *adv* dense, crebro
density *s* densit•as -atis *f*
dent *s* not•a -ae *f*
dent *tr* imprimĕre, cavare
dented *adj* collis•us -a -um
dentist *s* dentium medic•us -i *m*
dentistry *s* dentium medicin•a -ae *f*
denude *tr* nudare
denunciation *s (by informer)* delati•o -onis *f; (condemnation)* reprehensi•o -onis *f*
deny *tr* negare

depart *intr* abire; *(to die)* obire; **to — for his province** abire in provinciam
departed *adj* defunct•us -a -um
department *s (of administration)* provinci•a -ae *f*, administrati•o -onis *f; (branch)* gen•us -eris *n*
departure *s* abit•us -ūs *m; (death)* obit•us -ūs *m*
depend *tr* **to — on** dependĕre de *(w. abl)*, niti *(w. abl)*; **it —s on you** in te positum est; **it — a lot on whether** plurimum refert num
dependable *adj* fid•us -a -um
dependant *s* cli•ens -entis *mf*
dependence *s* fiduci•a -ae *f*
dependency *s* provinci•a -ae *f*
dependent *adj* obnoxi•us -a -um
depict *tr (to paint)* pingĕre; *(in words)* describĕre, depingĕre
deplete *tr* deminuĕre
depletion *s* deminuti•o -onis *f*
deplorable *adj* miserabil•is -is -e
deplore *tr* deplorare
deploy *tr (mil)* expedire
deponent *adj (gram)* depon•ens -entis
depopulate *tr* vacuefacĕre
deportment *s* gest•us -ūs *m*
depose *tr* summovēre; *(leg)* testificari
deposit *s* deposit•um -i *n; (earnest money)* arrhab•o -onis *m; (of fluids)* sedim•en -inis *n;* **to put down 10 denarii as a —** decem denarios arrhaboni dare
deposit *tr (for safekeeping)* **(with)** deponĕre (apud + *acc)*
deposition *s (leg)* testimon•ium -(i)i *n*
depositor *s* deposit•or -oris *m*
depot *s (com)* empor•ium -(i)i *n; (mil)* armamentar•ium -(i)i *n*
depraved *adj* prav•us -a -um
depravity *s* pravit•as -atis *f*
deprecate *tr* deprecari
deprecation *s* deprecati•o -onis *f*
depreciate *tr* detrectare
depreciation *s* detrectati•o -onis *f; (of price)* vilit•as -atis *f*
depredation *s* spoliati•o -onis *f*
depress *tr* deprimĕre; *(fig)* infringĕre
depressed *adj (low-lying)* depress•us -a -um; *(despondent)* demiss•us -a -um; *(flat)* plan•us -a -um; *(hollow)* cav•us -a -um
depressing *adj* trist•is -is -e
depression *s* depressi•o -onis *f; (emotional)* anim•us -i *m* fractus
deprivation *s (act)* privati•o -onis *f; (state)* inopi•a -ae *f*
deprive *tr* privare
depth *s* altitud•o -inis *f;* **a hundred feet in —** *(as opposed to frontage)* centum pedes in agrum; **the —s** profund•um -i *n*
deputation *s* legati•o -onis *f*
deputy *s* legat•us -i *m*
derange *tr* conturbare
deranged *adj* mente capt•us -a -um
derangement *s (of mind)* mentis alientati•o -onis *f*
dereliction *s* derelicti•o -onis *f*
deride *tr* irridēre
derision *s* irrisi•o -onis *f*
derisive *adj* irrid•ens -entis
derivation *s* derivati•o -onis *f*
derivative *adj* derivativ•us -a -um
derive *tr* (de)ducĕre; *(words)* derivare ‖ *intr* procedĕre
derogatory *adj* indign•us -a -um
descend *intr* descendĕre; **to — on** *(to attack)* irrumpĕre in *(w. acc)*
descendant *s* progeni•es -ei *f;* **the —s** poster•i -orum *mpl*
descent *s* descens•us -ūs *m; (slope)* cliv•us -i *m; (lineage)* gen•us -eris *n*
describe *tr* describĕre
description *s* descripti•o -onis *f*
desecrate *tr* profanare
desecration *f* violati•o -onis *f*
desert *s* desert•a -orum *npl*
desert *tr* deserĕre, relinquĕre ‖ *intr* deserĕre; *(esp. mil)* transfugĕre
deserter *s* desert•or -oris *m; (mil)* transfug•a -ae *m*
desertion *s* deserti•o -onis *f; (esp. mil)* transfug•ium -(i)i *n*
deserts *spl* merit•a -orum *npl;* **he got his —** habet quod sibi debebatur
deserve *tr* merēre, merēri
deservedly *adv* merito, jure
deserving *adj* **(of)** dign•us -a -um *(w. abl)*
design *s (of a building, etc.)* descripti•o -onis *f; (drawing)* adumbrati•o -onis *f; (plan)* form•a -ae *f*
design *tr* designare; *(to draw in lines)* delineare; *(to sketch)* adumbrare; *(fig)* machinari
designate *tr* designare
designation *s (appointment)* designati•o -onis *f; (name)* nom•en -inis *n*
designer *s (of s.th. new)* invent•or -oris *m; (one who designs as an architect)* designat•or -oris *m; (of a stratagem)* fabricat•or -oris *m*
designing *adj* callid•us -a -um
desirable *adj* desiderabil•is -is -e
desire *s* cupidit•as -atis *f; (longing)* desider•ium -(i)i *n; (sexual)* libid•o -inis *f*
desire *tr* cupĕre, optare; *(to long for what is lacking)* desiderare
desirous *adj* **(of)** cupid•us -a -um *(w. gen)*
desist *intr* **(from)** desistĕre *(w. abl or* de *w. abl)*
desk *s* mens•a -ae *f* scriptoria
desolate *adj* desolat•us -a -um; *(of persons)* afflict•us -a -um
desolate *tr* desolare
desolation *s* solitud•o -inis *f*
despair *s* desperati•o -onis *f*
desperado *s* sicar•ius -(i)i *m*

desperate *adj (hopeless)* desperat•us -a -um; *(dangerous)* periculos•us -a -um; **in their — situation** in extremis rebus suis; **to take — measures** ad extrema descenděre
desperately *adv* vehementer; **to be — in love** perdite amare
desperation *s* desperati•o -onis *f*
despicable *adj* despicabil•is -is -e
despise *tr* despicěre, sperněre
despite *prep* contra *(w. acc)*
despoil *tr* spoliare
despondency *s* animi abjecti•o -onis *f*, tristiti•a -ae *f*
despondent *adj* abject•us -a -um; **to be —** animo demisso esse
despondently *adv* animo demisso
despot *s* tyrann•us -i *m*
despotic *adj* tyrannic•us -a -um
despotically *adv* tyrannice
despotism *s* dominati•o -onis *f*
dessert *s* secunda mens•a -ae *f*
destination *s* loc•us -i *m* destinationis
destine *tr* destinare
destiny *s* fat•um -i *n*, sor•s -tis *f*
destitute *adj* **(of)** inop•s -is *(w. gen or abl)*, eg•ens -entis *(w. gen)*
destitution *s* inopi•a -ae *f*
destroy *tr* destruěre, delēre; **to be —ed** interire
destroyer *s* delet•or -oris *m*, deletr•ix -icis *f*
destruction *s* exit•ium -(i)i *n*
destructive *adj* exitial•is -is -e
desultory *adj* inconst•ans -antis
detach *tr* sejungěre; *(by breaking)* abscinděre; *(by pulling)* avellěre
detached *adj* sejunct•us -a -um
detachment *s (act)* sejuncti•o -onis *f*; *(mil)* man•us -ūs *f*; *(aloofness)* secess•us -ūs *m*
detail *s* **—s** singul•a -orum *npl*; **in —** singulatim; **to go into —** per singula ire
detail *tr* exsequi, enarrare
detain *tr* tenēre, retinēre
detect *tr* detegěre, deprehenděre
detection *s* deprehensi•o -onis *f*
detective *s* inquisit•or -oris *m*
detention *s* retenti•o -onis *f*
deter *tr* deterrēre
detergent *s* smagm•a -atis *n*
deteriorate *tr* deteri•orem -orem -us facěre ‖ *intr* deteri•or -or -us fieri
determination *s (resolution)* constanti•a -ae *f*; *(decision)* consil•ium -(i)i *n*
determine *tr (to fix)* determinare; *(to decide)* constituěre
determined *adj (resolute)* firm•us -a -um; *(fixed)* cert•us -a -um
detest *tr* detestari
detestable *adj* detestabil•is -is -e
detestation *s* detestati•o -onis *f*
dethrone *tr* regno depellěre
detonate *intr* crepare
detonation *s* frag•or -oris *m*
detour *s* flex•us -ūs *m*; **to take a —** flectěre viam
detract *tr* detrahěre ‖ *intr* **to — from** obtrectare
detraction *s* obtrectati•o -onis *f*
detractor *s* obtrectat•or -oris *m*
detriment *s* detriment•um -i *n*
detrimental *adj* damnos•us -a -um; **to be — to** detrimento esse *(w. dat)*
devastate *tr* vastare
devastating *adj* damnos•us -a -um
devastation *s (act)* vastati•o -onis *f*; *(state)* vastit•as -atis *f*
develop *tr (to evolve)* evolvěre; *(to unfold)* explicare; *(to improve)* excolěre; *(a person)* alěre ‖ *intr* crescěre; *(to advance)* progredi; **to — into** evaděre in *(w. acc)*
development *s (unfolding)* explicati•o -onis *f*; *(advance)* progress•us -ūs *m*; **— of events** event•us -ūs *m*; **to attain full —** adolescěre
deviate *intr* **(from)** se declinare (de + *abl)*; *(to act in violation of)* **(from)** disceděre (ab + *abl)*; **not to — from the course** cursum tenēre
deviation *s* declinati•o -onis *f*
device *s* artific•ium -(i)i *n*, machin•a -ae *f*; *(plan)* consil•ium -(i)i *n*; *(emblem)* sign•um -i *n*
devil *s* diabol•us -i *m*; **go to the —!** abi in malam crucem!; **those —s!** istae larvae!
devilish *adj* diabolic•us -a -um; *(fig)* nefand•us -a -um
devious *adj* devi•us -a -um; *(person)* astut•us -a -um
devise *tr* excogitare
devoid *adj* exper•s -tis *(w. gen or abl)*; **to be — of** carēre *(w. abl)*
devolve *intr* **to — upon** ceděre in *(w. acc)*; *(by inheritance)* pervenire ad *(w. acc)*
devote *tr* devovēre, consecrare; **to — oneself to** se deděre *(w. dat)*
devoted *adj* **(to)** dedit•us -a -um *(w. dat)*, studios•us -a -um *(w. dat)*
devotee *s* cult•or -oris *m*
devotion *s* devoti•o -onis *f*; **—s** prec•es -um *fpl*
devour *tr* vorare; *(fig)* haurire
devout *adj* pi•us -a -um
devoutly *adv* pie
dew *s* ro•s -ris *m*
dewdrop *s* gutt•a roscida *f*
dewy *adj* roscid•us -a -um
dexterity *s* calliditas -atis *f*
dexterous *adj* callid•us -a -um
dexterously *adv* callide
diabolical *adj* diabolic•us -a -um
diadem *s* diadem•a -atis *n*
diagnose *tr* discerněre
diagnosis *s* diagnos•is -is *f*
diagonal *adj* diagonal•is -is -e
diagonally *adv* in transversum
diagram *s* form•a -ae *f*

dial *s (of clock)* hor•ae -arum *fpl*
dialect *s* dialect•us -i *f*
dialectic *adj* dialectic•us -a -um
dialectics *s* dialectic•a -ae *f*
dialogue *s* serm•o -onis *m; (written discussion)* dialog•us -i *m*
diameter *s* diametr•os -i *f*
diamond *s* adam•as -antis *m*
diaper *s* fasci•ae -arum *fpl*
diaphragm *s* sept•um -i *n* transversum
diarrhea *s* alvi defusi•o -onis *f*
diary *s* diar•ium -(i)i *n*
diatribe *s* convic•ium -(i)i *n*
dice *spl* ale•ae -arum *fpl; (the game)* ale•a -ae *f;* **to roll the —** aleas jactare; **to play —** aleā luděre
dictate *tr* dictare; *(to prescribe)* praescriběre
dictate *s* praescript•um -i *n*
dictation *s* dictati•o -onis *f;* **to take —** dictata exscriběre
dictator *s* dictat•or -oris *m*
dictatorial *adj* dictatori•us -a -um
dictatorship *s* dictatur•a -ae *f*
diction *s* dicti•o -onis *f*
dictionary *s* glossiar•ium -(i)i *n*
didactic *adj* didascalic•us -a -um
die *s* ale•a -ae *f;* **the — is cast** alea jacta est
die *intr* mori; **to — laughing** risu emori; **to — off** demori; **to — out** emori
diet *s (food)* victūs rati•o -onis *f; (dietary regime)* diaet•a -ae *f*
diet *intr* victūs rationem inire
dietary *adj* diatetic•us -a -um
differ *intr* differre; *(in opinion)* dissentire; *(to disagree)* discrepare
difference *s* differenti•a -ae *f; (wide difference)* distanti•a -ae *f; (disagreement)* discrepanti•a -ae *f;* **— of opinion** dissensi•o -onis *f;* **it makes no —** nihil interest; **there is no — between god and god** nihil inter deum et deum interest; **there isn't the slighest — between them** ne minimum quidem inter eos interest; **what — does it make whether...?** quid refert utrum...?
differentiate *tr* discerněre
differently *adv* aliter; *(variously)* varie, diverse
differing *adj* disson•us -a -um
difficult *adj* difficil•is -is -e; *(blocked up, e.g., a road)* impedit•us -a -um; **it is a — thing to** magnum est *(w. inf)*
difficulty *s* difficult•as -atis *f;* **with —** aegre
diffidence *s (distrust)* diffidenti•a -ae *f; (modesty)* verecundi•a -ae *f*
diffident *adj* diffid•ens -entis; *(modest)* verecund•us -a -um
diffuse *adj* diffus•us -a -um; *(verbally)* verbos•us -a -um
diffuse *tr* diffunděre
diffusely *adv* effuse
diffusion *s* diffusi•o -onis *f*
dig *tr* foděre; **to — a hole in the ground** terram excavare; **to — a hole in the wall (wood)** parietem (lignum) perfoděre; **to — up** *(e.g., the garden, the earth)* confoděre
digest *s* summar•ium -(i)i *n*
digest *tr* concoquěre
digestion *s* concocti•o -onis *f*
digestive *adj* peptic•us -a -um
digging *s* fossi•o -onis *f*
digit *s* numer•us -i *m*
dignified *adj* grav•is -is -e
dignify *tr* honestare
dignitary *s* vir -i *m* amplissimus
dignity *s* dignit•as -atis *f*
digress *intr* digredi
digression *s* digressi•o -onis *f*
dike *s* agg•er -eris *m*
dilapidated *adj* ruinos•us -a -um
dilate *tr* dilatare ‖ *intr* dilatari
dilatory *adj* cunctabund•us -a -um
dilemma *s (difficulty)* angusti•ae -arum *fpl; (logical)* dilemm•ā -atis *n;* **to be in a —** haerēre in salebra
diligence *s* diligenti•a -ae *f*
diligent *adj* dilig•ens -entis
diligently *adv* diligenter
dilute *tr* diluěre
dilution *s* mixtur•a -ae *f*
dim *adj* heb•es -etis, obscur•us -a -um; **to be —** hebēre; **to become —** hebescěre
dim *tr* hebetare ‖ *intr* hebescěre
dimension *s* mensur•a -ae *f;* **to take the —s of** mensuram *(w. gen)* agěre
diminish *tr* minuěre; *(weight, value, authority)* levare ‖ *intr* minui
diminutive *adj* exigu•us -a -um; *(gram)* deminutiv•us -a -um
diminutive *s* deminutiv•um -i *n*
dimness *s* hebetud•o -inis *f*
dimple *s* gelasin•us -i *m*
din *s* strepit•us -ūs *m;* **to make a —** strepare
dine *intr* cenare; **to — out** foris cenare
diner *s* conviv•a -ae *mf*
dingy *adj* squalid•us -a -um
dining couch *s* tor•us -i *m*
dining room *s* cenati•o -onis *f,* triclin•ium -(i)i *n*
dinner *s* cen•a -ae *f;* **to eat —** cenare, cenam suměre; **what did you have for —** quid in cenā habuisti?
dinner clothes *spl* cenatori•a -orum *npl*
dinner guest *s* conviv•a -ae *mf*
dinner party *s* conviv•ium -(i)i *n*
dint *s* **by — of** per *(w. acc)*
dip *tr* immergěre; *(to wet by dipping)* ting(u)ěre ‖ *intr* mergi; **to — into** *(fig)* attingěre
dip *s (decrease)* deminuti•o -onis *f; (slope)* declivit•as -atis *f;* **to take a —** natare
diphthong *s* diphthong•us -i *f*
diploma *s* diplom•a -atis *n*

diplomatic *adj (fig)* sag•ax -acis
dipper *s* trull•a -ae *f;* **Big Dipper** Urs•a -ae *f* Major; **Little Dipper** Urs•a -ae *f* Minor
dire *adj* dir•us -a -um
direct *adj* (di)rect•us -a -um
direct *vt* dirigĕre; *(to manage)* administrare; *(to order)* jubēre; *(a weapon)* intendĕre; *(a letter)* inscribĕre; **to — attention to** animum attendĕre ad *(w. acc)*
direction *s (act)* directi•o -onis *f; (quarter)* par•s -tis *f; (management)* administrati•o -onis *f; (instruction)* mandat•um -i *n; (order)* praecept•um -i *n;* **in all —s** in omnes partes; **in a sourtherly —** in meridiem versus; **in both —** utroque; **in every —** quoquoversus; **in the — of Gaul** in Galliam versus; **in the — of Rome** Romam versus
directive *s* mandat•um -i *n*
directly *adv* directe, rectā; *(immediately)* statim; **to go —** ire rectā
director *s* rect•or -oris *m*
directory *s (office of director)* magister•ium -(i)i *n; (list, catalog)* ind•ex -icis *m*
dirge *s* neni•a -ae *f*
dirt *s* sord•es -is *f (usu. pl); (mud)* lut•um -i *n*
dirt-cheap *adj* pro luto
dirtiness *s* spurciti•a -ae *f*
dirty *adj* sordid•us -a -um, spurc•us -a -um; *(fig)* obscen•us -a -um; **— old man** salax sen•ex -is *m;* **— talk** serm•o -onis *m* obscenus
dirty *tr* spurcare, foedare
disability *s* imbecillit•as -atis *f*
disable *tr (to weaken)* debilitare; *(to cripple)* mutilare; *(a ship)* afflictare
disabled *adj* invalid•us -a -um; *(maimed)* manc•us -a -um; **totally —** omnibus membris capt•us -a -um
disabuse *tr* errorem eripĕre *(w. dat)*
disadvantage *s* incommod•um -i *n*
disadvantaged *adj* incommodat•us -a -um
disadvantageous *adj* incommod•us -a -um, iniqu•us -a -um
disagree *intr* **(with)** dissentire (ab + *abl);* **the food —d with me** cibus stomachum offendit
disagreeable *adj* injucund•us -a -um; *(smell)* graveol•ens -entis; *(person)* importun•us -a -um
disagreement *s* dissensi•o -onis *f*
disallow *tr* vetare
disappear *intr* evanescĕre; **to — from sight** e conspectu fugĕre
disappearance *s* exit•us -ūs *m*
disapppoint *tr* fallĕre, frustrari
disappointment *s (act)* frustrati•o -onis *f; (result)* incommod•um -i *n*
disapproval *s* improbati•o -onis *f*
disapprove *tr* improbare ‖ *intr* **to — of** improbare
disarm *tr* exarmare
disarrange *tr* turbare
disarray *s* perturbati•o -onis *f*
disaster *s* calamit•as -atis *f; (mil)* clad•es -is *f*
disastrous *adj* calamitos•us -a -um
disastrously *adv* calamitose
disavow *tr* diffiteri, infiteri
disavowal *s* infitiati•o -onis *f*
disband *tr* dimittĕre ‖ *intr* dimitti
disbelief *s* incredulit•as -atis *f*
disbeliever *s* incredul•us -i *m*
disburse *tr* expendĕre, erogare
disbursement *s* erogati•o -onis *f,* impens•a -ae *f*
disc *s* orb•is -is *m*
discard *tr* abjicĕre
discern *tr (to distinguish)* discernĕre; *(to see clearly)* perspicĕre
discernible *adj* dignoscend•us -a -um
discerning *adj* perspic•ax -acis
discernment *s (faculty)* discrim•en -inis *n; (act)* perspicienti•a -ae *f*
discharge *s (release)* liberati•o -onis *f; (mil)* missi•o -onis *f; (of missiles)* conject•us -ūs *m,* emissi•o -onis *f; (of duty)* perfuncti•o -onis *f; (bodily)* defluxi•o -onis *f;* **dishonorable —** missio *f* cum ignominiā
discharge *tr (to perform)* perfungi *(w. abl); (mil)* dimittĕre; *(debt)* exsolvĕre; *(defendant)* absolvĕre; *(missiles)* immittĕre, conjicĕre
disciple *s* discipul•us -i *m*
discipline *s* disciplin•a -ae *f; (punishment)* castigati•o -onis *f*
discipline *tr* disciplinā instituĕre; *(to punish)* castigare
disclaim *tr* infitiari
disclaimer *s* infitiati•o -onis *f*
disclose *tr (to reveal)* patefacĕre, detegĕre; *(to tell)* promĕre; *(to divulge)* enuntiare
disclosure *s* patefacti•o -onis *f*
discolor *tr* decolorare ‖ *intr* decolorari; *(to fade)* pallescĕre
discomfit *tr* profligare
discomfort *s* incommod•um -i *n*
discomfort *tr* incommodare
disconcerting *adj* molest•us -a -um
disconnect *tr* disjungĕre
disconsolate *adj* maest•us -a -um
discontent *s* offensi•o -onis *f*
discontent *tr* offendĕre
discontented *adj* parum content•us -a -um
discontentedly *adv* animo iniquo
discontinue *tr* intermittĕre ‖ *intr* desinĕre
discord *s* discordi•a -ae *f; (mus)* dissonanti•a -ae *f*
discordant *adj* discor•s -dis; *(mus)* disson•us -a -um

discount *tr* deducĕre; *(to disregard)* praetermittĕre
discount *s (com)* decessi•o -onis *f*
discourage *tr* animum (animos) *(w. gen)* infringĕre; *(to dissuade)* dehortari; **to be —d** animo (animis) deficĕre, animum (animos) demittĕre
discouragement *s* animi infracti•o -onis *f*
discouraging *adj* advers•us -a -um
discourse *s* serm•o -onis *m; (written)* libell•us -i *m*
discourse *intr* **(on)** disserĕre de *(w. abl)*
discourteous *adj* inurban•us -a -um
discourteously *adv* inurbane
discourtesy *s* inurbanit•as -atis *f*
discover *tr* invenire; *(to explore)* explorare
discoverable *adj* indagabil•is -is -e
discoverer *s* invent•or -oris *m*
discovery *s* inventi•o -onis *f; (thing discovered)* invent•um -i *n*
discredit *s* dedec•us -oris *n;* macul•a -ae *f;* **to be a — to one's family** familiae suae dedecori esse; **to bring — upon oneself** maculam suscipĕre *(w. abl of cause)*
discredit *tr (to disbelieve)* non credĕre *(w. dat); (to disgrace)* labem inferre *(w. dat)*
discreet *adj* caut•us -a -um, prud•ens -entis
discrepancy *s* discrepanti•a -ae *f*
discretion *s (tact)* judic•ium -(i)i *n; (entire control)* arbitr•ium -(i)i *n;* **at one's —** ad arbitrium suum
discretionary *adj* lib•er -era -erum; **to give s.o. — power** liberum arbitrium alicui permittĕre
discriminate *tr* distinguĕre
discriminating *adj* discern•ens -entis
discrimination *s (act of distinguishing)* distincti•o -onis *f; (discernment)* discrim•en -inis *n; (prejudice)* opini•o -onis *f* praejudicata
discuss *tr* disputare
discussion *s* disputati•o -onis *f;* **there was a long — about** diu disputatum est de *(w. abl)*
disdain *tr* fastidire
disdain *s* fastid•ium -(i)i *n;* **to treat with —** dedignari
disdainful *adj* fastidios•us -a -um
disdainfully *adv* fastidiose
disease *s* morb•us -i *m*
diseased *adj* aegrot•us -a -um
disembark *tr* e nave exponĕre ‖ *intr* e nave exire
disenchant *tr* errorem demĕre *(w. dat)*
disengage *tr* expedire, eximĕre
disentangle *tr* explicare
disfavor *s* invidi•a -ae *f,* offens•a -ae *f;* **to be in great — with s.o.** magnā in offensā esse apud aliquem; **to fall into — with s.o.** suscipere invidiam apud aliquem
disfigure *tr* deformare
disfranchise *tr* civitatem adimĕre *(w. dat)*
disgorge *tr* evomĕre
disgrace *s* dedec•us -oris *n,* ignomini•a -ae *f; (thing)* flagit•ium -(i)i *n; (public disgrace)* ignomin•ia -ae *f;* **to become a source of —** to dedecori esse *(w. dat)*
disgrace *tr* dedecorare
disgraceful *adj* dedecor•us -a -um
disgracefully *adv* turpiter
disguise *s* vestit•us -ūs *m* alienus; *(fig)* person•a -ae *f;* **in —** mutatā veste
disguise *tr* dissimulare
disgust *s* taed•ium -(i)i *n*
disgust *tr* stomachum movēre *(w. dat);* **I am —ed with** me taedet *(w. gen),* me piget *(w. gen)*
disgusting *adj* foed•us -a -um
disgustingly *adv* foede
dish *s (flat)* patin•a -e *f; (large)* lan•x -cis *f; (course)* fercul•um -i *n;* **to wash the —es** vasa coquinatoria eluĕre
dishearten *tr* animum (animos) *(w. gen)* infringĕre; **to be —ed** animum (animos) demittĕre
disheveled *adj (hair)* pass•us -a -um
dishonest *adj* fraudulent•us -a -um; *(lying)* mend•ax -acis
dishonestly *adv* dolo malo
dishonesty *s* frau•s -dis *f*
dishonor *s* dedec•us -oris *n*
dishonor *tr* dedecorare
dishonorable *adj* inhonest•us -a -um
dishonorably *adv* inhoneste
dishpan *s* labr•um -i *n* (ad vasa coquinatoria eluenda)
disillusion *tr* errorem adimĕre *(w. dat)*
disinclination *s* declinati•o -onis *f*
disinfect *tr* contagia depellĕre de *(w. abl)*
disinfectant *s* remed•ium -(i)i *n* ad contagia depellenda aptum
disinherit *tr* exheredare
disintegrate *intr* dilabi
disinter *tr* effodĕre
disinterested *adj* inte•ger -gra -grum
disinterestedly *adv* integre
disjoin *tr* disjungĕre
disjointed *adj* incomposit•us -a -um
disjointedly *adv* incomposite
disk *s* orb•is -is *m*
dislike *s* od•ium -(i)i *n*
dislike *tr* aversari
dislocate *tr* luxare
dislocation *s* luxatur•a -ae *f*
dislodge *tr* depellĕre
disloyal *adj* perfid•us -a -um
disloyally *adv* perfide
disloyalty *s* perfidi•a -ae *f*
dismal *adj* maest•us -a -um
dismally *adv* maeste
dismantle *tr* diruĕre
dismay *s* consternati•o -onis *f*
dismay *tr* percellĕre
dismember *tr* membratim dividĕre

dismemberment *s* mutilati•o -onis *f*
dismiss *tr* dimittĕre; *(fear)* mittĕre
dismissal *s* dimissi•o -onis *f*
dismount *intr* ex equo desilire
disobedience *s* inobedienti•a -ae *f*
disobedient *adj* parum obedi•ens -entis
disobey *tr* non obedire *(w. dat)*
disorder *s* confusi•o -onis *f; (of mind)* perturbati•o -onis *f; (med)* mal•um -i *n; (pol)* tumult•us -ūs *m*
disordered *adj* turbat•us -a -um; *(of mind or body)* aegrot•us -a -um
disorderly *adj* inordinat•us -a -um; *(of troops)* effus•us -a -um; *(unruly)* turbulent•us -a -um
disorganization *s* dissoluti•o -onis *f*
disorganize *tr* conturbare
disorganized *adj* dissolut•us -a -um
disown *tr (statement)* infitiari; *(heir)* abdicare; *(thing)* repudiare
disparage *tr* obtrectare
disparagement *s* obtrectati•o -onis *f*
disparaging *adj* obtrect•ans -antis
disparate *adj* dispa•r -ris
disparity *s* discrepanti•a -ae *f*
dispassionate *adj* frigid•us -a -um
dispassionately *adv* frigide
dispatch *tr* mittĕre; *(to finish)* perficĕre; *(to kill)* interficĕre
dispel *tr* dispellĕre, depellĕre
dispensary *s* medicamentaria tabern•a -ae *f*
dispensation *s* distributi•o -onis *f; (exemption)* immunit•as -atis *f*
dispense *tr* distribuĕre; *(to release)* solvĕre ‖ *intr* **to — with** remittĕre
dispenser *s* dispensat•or -oris *m*
disperse *tr* dispergĕre, dissipare ‖ *intr* diffugĕre; *(gradually)* dilabi
dispersion *s* dispersi•o -onis *f*
dispirited *adj* animo fract•us -a -um
displace *tr* summovēre; **—ed person** profug•us -i *m*, profug•a -ae *f*
displacement *s* amoti•o -onis *f*
display *s (exhibit)* ostent•us -ūs *m; (ostentation)* ostentati•o -onis *f*
display *tr* ostendĕre; *(to show off)* ostentare
displease *tr* displicēre *(w. dat)*
displeased *adj* offens•us -a -um; **to be — at** aegre ferre
displeasing *adj* ingrat•us -a -um
displeasure *s* offens•a -ae *f*
disposable *adj* in promptu
disposal *s* dispositi•o -onis *f;* **at your —** penes te
dispose *tr* disponĕre, ordinare; *(to incline)* inclinare ‖ *intr* **to — of** *(to settle)* componĕre; *(to sell)* abalienare; *(to get rid of)* tollĕre
disposed *adj* inclinat•us -a -um; *(pej)* pron•us -a -um
disposition *s (arrangement)* dispositi•o -onis *f; (character)* indol•es -is *f*
dispossess *tr (of)* pellĕre *(w. abl)*
disproportion *s* inconcinnit•as -atis *f*
disproportionate *adj* inaequal•is -is -e
disproportionately *adv* inaequaliter
disprove *tr* refellĕre, redarguĕre
disputable *adj* disputabil•is -is -e
dispute *s (debate)* disputati•o -onis *f; (argument)* altercati•o -onis *f;* **beyond —** indisputabil•is -is -e; **that is a matter of —** id disputari potest
dispute *tr & intr* disputare
disputed *adj* controvers•us -a -um
disqualification *s* impediment•um -i *n*
disqualify *tr* excipĕre; **to — s.o. from** aliquem excipĕre ex *(w. abl) or* ne *or* quominus
disquiet *tr* inquietare
disquieted *adj* inquiet•us -a -um
disquisition *s* disputati•o -onis *f*
disregard *s* **(for)** incuri•a -ae *f (w. gen)*, neglegenti•a -ae *f (w. gen)*
disregard *tr* neglegĕre, omittĕre
disreputable *adj* infam•is -is -e
disrepute *s* infami•a -ae *f*
disrespect *s* neglegenti•a -ae *f*
disrespectul *adj (toward)* negleg•ens -entis (in + *acc)*
disrespectfully *adv* parum honorifice
disrupt *tr* disturbare
disruption *s* discid•ium -(i)i *n*
dissatisfaction *s* displicenti•a -ae *f*
dissatisfied *adj* parum content•us -a -um
dissatisfy *tr* male satisfacĕre *(w. dat)*
dissect *tr* insecare
dissection *s* incisi•o -onis *f*
dissemble *tr & intr* dissimulare
disseminate *tr* disseminare
dissension *s* dissensi•o -onis *f*
dissent *s* dissensi•o -onis *f*
dissent *intr* dissentire
dissertation *s* dissertati•o -onis *f*
dissimilar *adj* dissimil•is -is -e
dissimiliarity *s* dissimilitud•o -inis *f*
dissipate *tr* dissipare ‖ *intr* dissipari
dissipation *s* dissipati•o -onis *f*
dissolute *adj* dissolut•us -a -um
dissolution *s* dissoluti•o -onis *f*
dissolve *tr* dissolvĕre; *(to melt)* liquefacĕre; *(meeting)* dimittĕre ‖ *intr* liquescĕre; *(to break up)* dissolvi
dissonance *s* dissonanti•a -ae *f*
dissonant *adj* disson•us -a -um
dissuade *tr* dissuadēre *(w. dat)*
dissuasion *s* dissuasi•o -onis *f*
distaff *s* col•us -i *m*
distance *s* distanti•a -ae *f*, spat•ium -(i)i *n; (long way)* longinquit•as -atis *f;* **at a —** procul, longe
distant *adj* dist•ans -antis; *(remote)* longinqu•us -a -um; *(fig)* parum familiar•is -is -e; **to be —** abesse, distare
distaste *s* **(for)** fastid•ium -(i)i *n (w. gen)*
distasteful *adj (of food)* tet•er -ra -rum; *(fig)* odios•us -a -um

distemper *s* morb•us -i *m*
distend *tr* distendĕre; *(sails)* tendĕre
distil *tr & intr* stillare, destillare
distinct *adj (different)* divers•us -a -um; *(clear)* distinct•us -a -um
distinction *s (act of distinguishing)* distincti•o -onis *f; (the thing distinguished)* discrim•en -inis *n; (mark, badge)* insign•e -is *n; (honor)* hon•or -oris *m; (status)* amplitud•o -inis *f; (decoration)* praem•ium -(i)i *n*; **a man of —** vir -i *m* illustris; **without —** promiscue
distinctive *adj* propri•us -a -um
distinguish *tr* distinguĕre, discernĕre; **to — oneself** enitēre
distinguishable *adj* spectand•us -a -um
distinguished *adj* insign•is -is -e
distort *tr* distorquēre; *(words)* detorquēre; *(to misinterpret)* male interpretari
distortion *s* distorti•o -onis *f; (fig)* depravati•o -onis *f*
distract *tr* distrahĕre, vocare
distracted *adj* distract•us -a -um; *(distraught)* vecor•s -dis
distraction *s (cause)* avocament•um -i *n; (state)* distracti•o -onis *f* animi; *(w. verbs of loving, etc.)* **to —** efflictim
distraught *adj* vecor•s -dis
distress *s* miseri•a -ae *f*, dol•or -oris *m; (straits)* angusti•ae -arum *fpl*
distress *tr* angĕre, afflictare
distressed *adj* sollicit•us -a -um
distressing *adj* importun•us -a -um
distribute *tr* distribuĕre
distributer *s* distribut•or -oris *m*
distribution *s* distributi•o -onis *f*
district *s* regi•o -onis *f*
distrust *s* diffidenti•a -ae *f*
distrust *tr* diffidĕre *(w. dat)*
distrustful *adj* **(of)** diffid•ens -entis *(w. dat)*
distrustfully *adv* diffidenter
disturb *tr* perturbare; *(to render anxious)* sollicitare; *(to upset)* commovēre; *(s.o.'s sleep)* inquietare
disturbance *s* perturbati•o -onis *f; (pol)* tumult•us -ūs *m*
disturber *s* **— of the peace** turbat•or -oris *m* otii
disuse *s* desuetud•o -inis *f*
ditch *s* foss•a -ae *f*
ditty *s* cantilen•a -ae *f*
divan *s* lectul•us -i *m*
dive *s* salt•us -ūs *m; (coll)* popin•a -ae *f*
dive *intr* mergi; *(of a submarine)* urinari
diver *s* urinat•or -oris *m*
diverge *intr* deflectĕre, declinare; *(of view)* discrepare
diverse *adj* divers•us -a -um
diversification *s* variati•o -onis *f*
diversify *tr* variare
diversion *s (recreation)* oblectament•um -i *n; (of a river)* derivati•o -onis *f; (pastime)* avocati•o -onis *f*
diversity *s* diversit•as -atis *f*
divert *tr (rivers)* avertĕre, divertĕre; *(attention)* avocare; **to — s.o.'s anger and turn it on oneself** iram alicujus in se derivare
divest *tr* exuĕre, nudare; **to — oneself of** exuĕre, ponĕre
divide *tr* dividĕre; *(to distribute)* partiri; **to — the year into 12 months** annum in duodecim menses describĕre ‖ *intr* se scindĕre; **to — by ten** *(math)* decem partes dicĕre
divination *s* divinati•o -onis *f*
divine *adj* divin•us -a -um
divine *tr* divinare; *(to guess)* conjicĕre
divinely *adv* divinitus
diviner *s* aug•ur -uris *m*, harusp•ex -icis *m*
divinity *s* divinit•as -atis *f; (god)* num•en -inis *n*
divisible *adj* dividu•us -a -um
division *s* divisi•o -onis *f; (part)* par•s -tis *f; (mil)* legi•o -onis *f;* **— of opinion** dissensi•o -onis *f*
divorce *s* divort•ium -(i)i *n*
divorce *tr* divortium facĕre cum *(w. abl)*
divulge *tr* vulgare, divulgare
dizziness *s* vertig•o -inis *f*
dizzy *adj* vertiginos•us -a -um
do *tr* agĕre, facĕre; *(to carry out, succeed in doing)* efficĕre; **to — a hitch in the army** stipendia facĕre; **to — a kindness** beneficium facĕre; **to — s.o. in** aliquem pessum dare; **what have I to — with you?** quid mihi et tibi est? ‖ *intr* agĕre; *(for emphatic auxiliary, use* vero: **I — wish to go** cupio vero ire); *(when* **I —!** *is used to answer a question, repeat the verb in the question:* **— you believe? I —.** credisne? credo.); **how — you —?** quid agis?; **it will — you good** proderit tibi; **it won't — to** non satis est *(w. inf)*; **that'll —!** satis est!; **to — away with** tollĕre, perdĕre; **to — well** *(to make out well)* recte facĕre; *(to have good health)* bene valēre; **to — without** carēre *(w. abl)*; **to have enough to —** satagĕre; **what's doing?** quid agitur?
docile *adj* docil•is -is -e, tractabil•is -is -e
dock *s* naval•e -is *n; (leg)* cancell•i -orum *mpl*
docket *s* memnisc•us -i *m*
dockyard *s* naval•ia -ium *npl*
doctor *s* medic•us -i *m; (teacher)* doct•or -oris *m*
doctorate *s* doctoris grad•us -ūs *m*
doctrine *s* doctrin•a -ae *f*, dogm•a -atis *n*
document *s* instrument•um -i *n*
dodge *s* dol•us -i *m*
dodge *tr* eludĕre; *(to shift aside and so avoid)* declinare; **to — the draft** sacramentum detrectare
doe *s* cerv•a -ae *f*

dog *s* can•is -is *mf;* **to go to the —s** *(coll)* pessum ire
dogged *adj* pervic•ax -acis
doggedness *s* pervicaci•a -ae *f*
doggerel *s* inepti versicul•i -orum *mpl*
dog house, dog kennel *s* canis cubil•e -is *n*
dogma *s* dogm•a -atis *n*
dogmatic *adj* dogmatic•us -a -um; *(pej)* arrog•ans -antis
dogmatism *s* arroganti•a -ae *f*
dog star *s* canicul•a -ae *f*
doing *s* facin•us -eris *n*
dole *s* sportul•a -ae *f*
dole *tr* **to — out** parce dare
doleful *adj* lugubr•is -is -e
dolefully *adv* maeste
doll *s* pup•a -ae *f*
dollar *s* thaler•us -i *m*
dolphin *s* delphin•us -i *m*
dolt *s* caud•ex -icis *m*
domain *s (kingdom)* regn•um -i *n;* **public —** ag•er -ri *m* publicus
dome *s* thol•us -i *m*
domestic *adj* domestic•us -a -um
domestic *s* famul•us -i *m,* famul•a -ae *f*
domesticate *tr* domare
domicile *s* domicil•ium -(i)i *n*
dominant *adj* praeval•ens -entis; **to be —** auctoritate pollēre; **to become —** potent•ior -ior -ius fieri
dominate *intr* **(over)** dominari (in *acc)*
domination *s* domin•ium -(i)i *n*
domineer *intr* dominari
domineering *adj* imperios•us -a -um
dominion *s* imper•ium -(i)i *n*
don *tr* induĕre
donation *s* donati•o -onis *f*
done *adj* **have — with fear!** omitte timorem!; **no sooner said than —** dictum factum; **well done!** macte virtute!
donkey *s* asell•us -i *m*
donor *s* donat•or -oris *m,* donatr•ix -icis *f*
doom *s* fat•um -i *n*
doom *tr* damnare
door *s* janu•a -ae *f,* ost•ium -(i)i *n;* for•es -ium *fpl; (folding doors)* valv•ae -arum *fpl;* **out of doors** *(position)* foris; *(direction)* foras
doorkeeper *s* ostiar•ius -(i)i *m*
doorpost *s* post•is -is *m*
doorstep *s* lim•en -inis *n*
doorway *s* ost•ium -(i)i *n*
Doric *adj* Doric•us -a -um
dormant *adj* res•es -idis; *(hidden)* lat•ens -entis; **to lie —** jacēre
dormitory *s* dormitor•ium -(i)i *n*
dorsal *adj* dorsal•is -is -e
dose *s* mensur•a -ae *f*
dot *s* punct•um -i *n*
dot *tr* punctum imponĕre *(w. dat)*
dotage *s* sen•ium -(i)i *n*
dotard *s* sen•ex -is *m* delirus
dote *tr* **to — on** deamare
doting *adj* deam•ans -antis
double *adj* dupl•ex -icis; *(of pairs)* gemin•us -a -um; *(as much again)* dupl•us -a -um; *(meaning)* ambigu•us -a -um
double *s* dupl•um -i *n;* **on the —** curriculo, concitu gradu
double *tr* duplicare; *(a cape)* praetervehi ‖ *intr* duplicari
double-dealing *s* frau•s -dis *f*
double-dealing *adj* versut•us -a -um
double-edged *adj* bipenn•is -is -e
double-talk *s* simulati•o -onis *f* et fallaci•a -ae *f*
doubly *adv* dupliciter
doubt *s* dub•ium -(i)i *n; (distrust)* suspici•o -onis *f;* **there is no — that** non dubium est quin *(w. subj)*
doubt *tr* dubitare *(w. acc of neuter pronoun only; otherwise use* de + *abl);* **I do not — that** non dubito quin *(w. subj)*
doubtful *adj (of persons)* dubi•us -a -um; *(of things)* incert•us -a - um, anc•eps -ipitis
doubtfully *adv* dubie; *(hesitatingly)* dubitanter
doubtless *adv* haud dubie, sine dubio
dough *s* fari•na -ae *f* ex aqua subacta
doughty *adj* fort•is -is -e
douse *tr (to put out)* exstinguĕre; *(to drench)* madefacĕre
dove *s* columb•a -ae *f*
dowdy *adj* inconcinn•us -a -um
down *s* plum•a -ae *f; (of hair)* lanug•o -inis *f; (of plants)* papp•us -i *m*
down *adv* deorsum; *(often expressed by the prefix* de-: **to flow —** defluĕre); **to pay money —** repraesentare pecuniam; **to run —** decurrĕre; **— from** de *(w. abl);* **— to** usque ad *(w. acc)*
down *prep* de *(w. abl)*
down *adj* decliv•is -is -e; *(depressed)* demiss•us -a -um; *(financially)* ad inopiam redact•us -a -um; **to feel — and out** infractos animos gerĕre **to hit a man when he is —** jacentem ferire
downcast *adj (in low spirits)* demiss•us -a -um; **with — eyes** dejectis in terram oculis
downfall *s* occas•us -ūs *m*
downhearted *adj* animo fract•us -a -um
downhill *adj* decliv•is -is -e, pron•us -a -um; **it was all —** proclivia omnia erant; **the last part of the road is —** ultima via est prona
downhill *adv* per declive; **as his business went —** inclinatis rebus suis
downpour *s* im•ber -bris *m* maximus
downright *adv* prorsus, plane
downright *adj* direct•us -a -um; *(unmixed)* mer•us -a -um
downstream *adv* secundo flumine
downward *adj* decliv•us -a -um, pron•us -a -um

downwards *adv* deorsum
downy *adj* plume•us -a -um; *(of hair)* lanuginos•us -a -um
dowry *s* do•s -tis *f*
doze *intr* dormitare
dozen *adj & pron* duodecim *(indecl)*
drab *adj* cinere•us -a -um
draft *s (drink)* haust•us -ūs *m; (mil)* dilect•us -ūs *m; (breeze)* aur•a -ae *f; (first copy)* exempl•ar -aris *n; (money)* syngraph•a -ae *f; (of net)* jact•us -ūs *m; (of ship)* immersi•o -onis *f*
draft *tr (mil)* conscriběre
drag *s (fig)* impediment•um -i *n;* **to be a — on s. o.** aliquem retardare
drag *tr* trahěre; *(w. suddenness or violence)* rapěre; **to — away** abstrahěre; **to — down** detrahěre; **to — out** protrahěre **‖** *intr* trahi; **to — on** protrahi
dragnet *s* tragul•a -ae *f*
dragon *s* drac•o -onis *m*
drain *s* cloac•a -ae *f*
drain *tr (marshland)* siccare; *(a cup, the treasury, strength)* exhaurire
drainage *s* exsiccati•o-onis *f*
drainage ditch *s* incil•e -is *n*
drake *s* an•as -atis *m*
drama *s (single play)* fabul•a -ae *f; (genre)* dram•a -atis *n*
dramatic *adj* scenic•us -a -um; *(fig)* animum mov•ens -entis
dramatics *s* histrioni•a -ae *f*
dramatist *s* poet•a -ae *m* scaenicus
dramatize *tr* ad scaenam componěre
drape *s* aulae•um -i *n*
drape *tr (to wrap)* amicire; *(to cover)* velare
drapery *s* aulae•a -orum *npl*
drastic *adj* severissim•us -a -um
draw *tr (to pull)* trahěre; *(a picture)* delineare; *(inference)* colligěre; *(bow)* adducěre; *(sword)* educěre; *(water)* haurire; *(breath)* ducěre; *(geometrical figures)* describěre; **to — aside** seducěre; **to — apart** diducěre; **to — away** avertěre; **to — back** retrahěre; **to — blood** cruorem ducěre; **to — off** detrahěre, abducěre; *(wine)* deproměre; **to — out** extrahěre; *(fig)* elicěre; **to — the conclusion** colligěre; **to — together** contrahěre; **to — up** subducěre; *(to write)* componěre; *(mil)* instituěre **‖** *intr* **to — back** pedem referre; *(fig)* receděre; **to — near** appropinquare; **to — up to** *(of ships)* appetěre
drawback *s* impediment•um -i *n*
drawbridge *s* pon•s -tis *m* versatilis
drawer *s* locul•us -i *m*
drawing *s* pictur•a -ae *f* linearis
drawl *s* lentior pronuntiati•o -onis *f*
drawl *intr* voces lentius pronuntiando trahěre
dread *s* formid•o -inis *f*
dread *adj* dir•us -a -um
dreadful *adj* terribil•is -is -e
dreadfully *adv* horrendum in modum
dream *s* somn•ium -(i)i *n;* **in a —** in somno
dream *tr & intr* somniare; **to — about** somniare de *(w. abl)*
dreamer *s (fig)* nugat•or -oris *m*
dreamy *adj* somniculos•us -a -um
drearily *adv* triste
dreariness *s* solitud•o -inis *f*
dreary *adj (place)* vast•us -a -um; *(person)* trist•is -is -e
dredge *tr* machinā alveum *(w. gen)* perfoděre
dregs *spl* fae•x -cis *f; (fig)* sentin•a -ae *f*
drench *tr* madefacěre
dress *s* cult•us -ūs *m*
dress *tr* vestire, induěre; *(to deck out)* exornare; *(wounds)* curare; *(the hair)* coměre; **—ed in a (fancy) coat** subornat•us -a -um aliculā; **—ed in white** amict•us -a -um veste alba; **to — down** *(to chew out)* pilare; **to get —ed** amiciri; *(in fancy clothes)* se exornare **‖** *intr* se induěre
dresser *s* vestiar•ium -(i)i *n*
dressing *s* ornati•o -onis *f; (sauce)* ju•s -ris *n; (stuffing)* fart•um -i *n; (med)* foment•um -i *n*
dressing room *s (at a bath)* apodyter•ium -(i)i *n*
dribble *intr* stillare
drift *s (intent)* proposit•um -i *n*
drift *intr* fluitare
drifter *s* larifug•a -ae *m*
drill *s (tool)* terebr•a -ae *f; (mil)* exercitati•o -onis *f*
drill *tr (to bore)* terebrare; *(mil)* exercēre; *(students)* instituěre
drink *tr* biběre, potare; **to — in** *(fig)* haurire; **to — up** epotare **‖** *intr* biběre; **to — to** propinare *(w. dat)*
drink *s* pot•us -ūs *m,* poti•o -onis *f*
drinker *s* pot•or -oris *m; (habitual)* potat•or -oris *m*
drinking *s* poti•o -onis *f*
drinking *adj* bibos•us -a -um
drinking cup *s* scyph•us -i *m*
drinking straw *s* siph•o -onis *m*
drinkable *adj* potabil•is -is -e
drip *s* stillicid•ium -(i)i *n*
drip *intr* destillare
drive *tr* agěre, pellěre; *(to force)* compellěre; *(to steer)* gubernare; *(a vehicle)* agitare; *(to convey)* vehěre; **to — away** abigěre; *(fig)* depellěre; *(in confusion)* deturbare; **to — back** repellěre; **to — home** *(fig)* animo infigěre; **to — in** *(sheep, etc.)* cogěre; *(nails)* infigěre; **to — off** abigěre; **to — on** impellěre; **to — out** expellěre; **to — out of one's mind** infuriare; **to — up** subigěre **‖** *intr (in a*

carriage) vehi; **to — off** *(in a carriage)* avehi; **to — on** *or* **past** praetervehi
drive *s (in carriage)* vectur•a -ae *f; (energy)* vis *f,* impigrit•as -atis *f*
drivel *s* saliv•a -ae *f; (fig)* inepti•ae -arum *fpl*
drivel *intr (fig)* delirare
driver *s* agitat•or -oris *m; (of a chariot)* aurig•a -ae *m*
drizzle *s* levis pluvi•a -ae *f*
drizzle *intr* leniter pluĕre
dromedary *s* drom•as -adis *m*
drone *s (bee)* fuc•us -i *m; (buzz)* bomb•us -i *m; (person)* cessat•or -oris *m*
drone *intr* murmurrare
droop *tr* demittĕre ‖ *intr* languēre
drooping *adj* languid•us -a -um
drop *s* gutt•a -ae *f; (a drop as falling)* still•a -ae *f; (fall)* cas•us -ūs *m,* laps•us -ūs *m; (decrease)* deminuti•o -onis *f; (a little bit)* paulul•um -i *n;* **— by —** stillatim
drop *tr (purposely)* demittĕre, dejicĕre; *(to let slip)* omittĕre; *(to lay low)* sternĕre; *(a hint)* emittĕre; *(anchor)* jacĕre; *(work)* desistĕre ab *(w. abl)* ‖ *intr (to lessen)* cadĕre, concidĕre; *(to trickle)* (de)stillare; *(to fall)* decidĕre; *(esp. from the sky)* delabi, decidĕre; **to — behind** cessare; **to — down** decidĕre; **to — in on** visĕre; **to — off to sleep** obdormire; **to — out of** excidĕre de *(w. abl)*
drop-out *s* destit•or -oris *m* de schola
droppings *spl* merd•ae -arum *fpl*
drought *s* siccit•as -atis *f*
drove *s* gre•x -gis *m*
drown *tr* demergĕre; *(fig)* opprimĕre; **to — out** obscurare ‖ *intr* submergi
drowsily *adv* somniculose
drowsy *adj* somniculos•us -a -um
drub *tr* pulsare, verberare
drudge *s (slave)* mediastin•us -i *m*
drudgery *s* oper•a -ae *f* servilis
drug *s* medicament•um -i *n*
druggist *s* medicamentar•ius -(i)i *m*
drugstore *s* apothec•a -ae *f*
Druids *spl* Druid•ae -arum *mpl*
drum *s* tympan•um -i *n*
drum *tr* **to — up** exquirĕre ‖ *intr* tympanum pulsare; **to — on the table** mensam digitis pulsare
drummer *s* tympanist•a -ae *m*
drunk *adj* ebri•us -a -um; *(habitually)* ebrios•us -a -um
drunk, drunkard *s* ebrios•us -i *m,* ebrios•a -ae *f*
drunken *adj* ebri•us -a -um
drunkenness *s* ebriet•as -atis *f*
dry *adj* arid•us -a -um, sicc•us -a -um; *(thirsty)* sicc•us -a -um; *(wine)* auster•us -a -um; *(boring)* jejun•us -a -um
dry *tr* siccare; **to — out** exsiccare; **to — up** arefacĕre ‖ *intr* arescĕre
dryad *s* dry•as -adis *f*
drydock *s* siccum naval•e -is *n*
dry land *s* arid•um -i *n*
dryness *s* siccit•as -atis *f*
dry run *s* simulacr•um -i *n*
dual *adj* dual•is -is -e
dub *tr* appellare
dubious *adj* dubi•us -a -um; *(shady)* anc•eps -ipitis
duck *s* an•as -atis *f*
duck *tr (in the water)* deprimĕre; *(an issue)* evitare ‖ *intr* se inclinare
duckling *s* anaticul•a -ae *f*
duct *s* tub•us -i *m*
due *adj (owed)* debit•us -a -um; *(merited)* merit•us -a -um, just•us -a -um; **— honors** meriti honor•es -um *mpl;* **— to** propter *(w. acc),* causā *(w. gen);* **to be — to** fieri ab *(w. abl);* **to fall — on the fifth day** in quintum diem cadĕre
due *s* debit•um -i *n;* **—s** stipendi•a -orum *npl;* **to give everyone his —** suum cuique tribuĕre
due *adv* rectā; **— east** rectā ad orientem
duel *s* singulare certam•en -inis *n*
duel *intr* viritim pugnare
duet *s* bicin•ium -(i)i *n*
duffel bag *s* sarcinul•a -ae *f*
duke *s* du•x -cis *m*
dull *adj* heb•es -itis; *(mind)* tard•us -a -um
dull *tr* hebetare
dullness *s* tardit•as -atis *f*
duly *adv* rite, recte
dumb *adj* mut•us -a -um; *(fig)* stupid•us -a -um
dumbfounded *adj* obstupefact•us -a -um; *(speechless)* elingu•is -is -e
dummy *s* effigi•es -ei *f; (stupid person)* bar•o -onis *m*
dumpling *s* farinae subactae globul•us -i *m*
dumpy *adj* brev•is -is -e et obes•us -a -um
dunce *s* bar•o -onis *m*
dung *s* sterc•us -oris *n; (of birds)* merd•ae -arum *fpl*
dungeon *s* rob•ur -oris *n*
dupe *s* credul•us -i *m*
dupe *tr* decipĕre
duplicate *adj* dupl•ex -icis
duplicate *s* exempl•ar -aris *n*
duplicate *tr* duplicare
duplicity *s* duplicit•as -atis *f*
durability *s* firmit•as -atis *f*
durable *adj* durabil•is -is -e
duration *s (period of time itself)* spat•ium -(i)i *n; (lastingness)* diurnit•as -atis *f;* **of long —** diuturn•us -a -um; **of short —** brev•is -is -e
during *prep* inter *(w. acc),* per *(w. acc)*
dusk *s* crepuscul•um -i *n*
dusky *adj* fusc•us -a -um
dust *s* pulv•is -is -eris *m*
dust *tr* detergēre
dusty *adj* pulverulent•us -a -um

dutiful *adj* pi•us -a -um, officios•us -a -um
duty *s (social or moral)* offic•ium -(i)i *n; (task)* mun•us -eris *n; (tax)* portor•ium -(i)i *n;* **to be on —** *(mil)* stationem agĕre; **when I do my —** *(coll)* cum mea facio
dwarf *s* pumili•o -onis *m*
dwarfish *adj* pumil•us -a -um
dwell *intr* habitare; **to — upon** commorari in *(w. abl)*
dweller *s* incol•a -ae *mf*
dwelling place *s* sed•es -is *f*
dwindle *intr* imminui, decrescĕre
dye *s* tinctur•a -ae *f*
dye *tr* ting(u)ĕre, inficĕre
dying *adj* moribund•us -a -um
dynamic *adj (fig)* vehem•ens -entis
dynamics *spl* dynamic•a -ae *f*
dynasty *s* dom•us -ūs *f* regnatrix; **under the Flavian —** potiente rerum Flaviā domu
dysentery *s* dysenteri•a -ae *f*
dyspepsia *s* dyspepsi•a -ae *f*

E

each *adj & pron* quisque, quidque; *(of two)* uterque, utraque utrumque; *(individually)* singul•i -ae -a; **— and every** unusquisque, unaquaeque, unumquodque; **— day** cot(t)idie; **— other** inter se, invicem; **he stationed one legion — in Brundisium, Tarentum, and Sepontum** legiones singulas posuit Brindisi, Tarenti, Seponti
eager *adj* **(for)** cupid•us -a -um *(w. gen),* avid•us -a -um *(w. gen)*
eagerly *adv* cupide, avide
eagerness *s* avidit•as -atis *f*
eagle *s* aquil•a -ae *f*
ear *s* aur•is -is *f; (outer ear)* auricul•a -ae *f; (of corn)* spic•a -ae *f;* **to give — to** aurem praebēre *(w. dat)*
earache *s* auris dol•or -oris *m;* **to have an —** ab aure laborare
earl *s* com•es -itis *m*
early *adj (in the morning)* matutin•us -a -um; *(coming naturally early)* matur•us -a -um; *(before its time)* praematur•us -a -um, praec•ox -ocis; *(of early date)* antiqu•us -a -um; *(beginning)* prim•us -a -um; **from — youth** a prima adolescentia; **in — spring** primo vere; **in — times** antiquitus
early *adv (in the morning)* mane; *(too soon)* praemature; *(in good time)* mature; **— enough** satis temperi; **— in the morning** bene mane; **his father died —** pater ejus decessit mature
earmark *tr* destinare
earn *tr* merēre, merēri; **to — a living** quaestum facĕre
earnest *adj (eager)* intent•us -a -um; *(serious)* seri•us -a -um; **— money** arrab•o -onis *m*
earnest *s* **in —** ex bona fide, serio
earnestly *adv* intente, valde
earnestness *s* gravit•as -atis *f*
earnings *spl* quaest•us -ūs *m*
earrings *spl* inaur•es -ium *fpl; (of several pearls)* crotali•a -orum *npl*
earth *s* terr•a -ae *f; (globe)* orb•is -is *m* terrarum; **of —, made of —** terren•us -a -um, terre•us -a -um
earthen *adj* terren•us -a -um; *(pottery)* fictil•is -is -e
earthenware *s* fictil•ia -ium *npl*
earthly *adj (made of earth)* terren•us -a -um; *(opposed to heavenly)* terrestr•is -is -e; **for what — reason** quare tandem
earthquake *s* terrae mot•us -ūs *m*
earthwork *s* op•us -eris *n* terrenum
earthy *adj (humor)* terren•us -a -um
ease *s (leisure)* ot•ium -(i)i *n; (easiness)* facilit•as -atis *f;* **at one's —** otios•us -a -um; **to live in —** in otio vivĕre; **to set s.o.'s mind at —** alicujus animum tranquillum reddere; **to speak with —** solute loqui
ease *tr* levare; *(to assuage)* mitigare; **to — oneself** alvum exonerare
easily *adv* facile
east *adj* oriental•is -is -e
east *s* ori•ens -entis *m;* **from — to west** ab oriente ad occidentem; **on the —** ab oriente; **to sail —** ad *or* in orientem navigare
Easter *s* pasch•a -ae *f*
Easter *adj* paschal•is -is -e
easterly *adj* oriental•is -is -e
eastern *adj* oriental•is -is -e
Eastertime *s* temp•us -oris *n* paschale
eastward *adv* ad orientem
east wind *s* Eur•us -i *m*
easy *adj* facil•is -is -e; *(graceful)* lepid•us -a -um; *(without obstacles, e.g., a road)* expedit•us -a -um; *(life)* otios•us -a -um; **— to understand** intellectu facil•is -is -e
easygoing *adj* secur•us -a -um
eat *tr* esse; *(to live on)* vesci *(w. abl);* **to — away** corrodĕre; **to — breakfast** jentare; **to — dinner** cenare; **to — lunch** prandēre; **to — up** comesse ‖ *intr* esse, cenare; **to — and drink** cibum et potionem adsumĕre; **to — out** foris cenare
eatable *adj* esculent•us -a -um
eating *s* es•us -ūs *m*
eaves *spl* suggrund•ae -arum *fpl*
eavesdrop *intr* subauscultare; **— on** subauscultare
eavesdropper *s* auc•eps -ipis *m*
ebb *s* recess•us -ūs *m;* **— and flow** aestūs recessus *m* et access•us -ūs *m;* **to be at a low —** *(fig)* jacēre

ebb *intr* recedĕre; *(fig)* decrescĕre
ebony *s* eben•um -i *n*
eccentric *adj* abnorm•is -is -e
ecclesiastic *adj* ecclesiastic•us -a -um
echo *s* ech•o -us *f*, imag•o -inis *f*
echo *tr* repercutĕre; *(to repeat what s.o. has said)* subsequi; **to — a sound** sonum referre ‖ *vi* resonare
echoing *adj* reson•us -a -um
eclectic *adj* eclectic•us -a -um
eclipse *s* defecti•o -onis *f*
eclipse *tr* obscurare
eclogue *s* eclog•a -ae *f*
economic *adj* economic•us -a -um, ad opes publicas pertin•ens -entis
economical *adj* frugi *(indecl)*, parc•us -a -um
economically *adv* parce
economics *s* publicarum opum scienti•a -ae *f*
economist *s* qui rei publicae opes exponit
economize *intr* (on) parcĕre *(w. dat)*; *(of the state)* publicos sumptūs minuĕre
economy *s* frugalit•as -atis *f*; **public —** publicarum opum administrati•o -onis *f*
ecstasy *s (trance)* ecstas•is -is *f*; *(rapture)* elati•o -onis *f* voluptaria; **to be in —** laetitiā gestire
eddy *s* vort•ex -icis *m*
eddy *intr* in se volutari
edge *s (very often expressed by* extrem•us -a -um *modifying the substantive)*; *(margin)* marg•o -inis *mf*; *(of knife, etc.)* aci•es -ei *f*; *(of forest)* or•a -ae *f*; **on —** anxi•us -a -um; **on the —** in praecipiti
edge *tr (garment)* praetexĕre; *(to sharpen)* acuĕre ‖ *intr* **to — away** sensim abscedĕre; **to — closer** sensim appropinquare
edgewise *adv* **to get in a word —** vocem in sermonem insinuare
edging *s* limb•us -i *m*
edible *adj* edul•is -is -e
edict *s* edict•um -i *n*
edification *s* humanit•as -atis *f*
edifice *s* aedific•ium -(i)i *n*
edify *tr* ad humanitatem excolĕre
edit *tr* edĕre; *(to correct)* emendare
edition *s* editi•o -onis *f*
editor *s* edit•or -oris *m*
educate *tr* erudire, instituere
educated *adj* erudit•us -a -um
education *s* eruditi•o -onis *f*
educational *adj* scholastic•us -a -um
educator *s* praecept•or -oris *m*
eel *s* anguill•a -ae *f*
eerie *adj* prodigios•us -a -um
efface *tr* delēre
effect *s* effect•um -i *n*; *(show)* jactati•o -onis *f*; **cause and —** caus•a -ae *f* et consecuti•o -onis *f*; **—s** bon•a -orum *npl*; **for mere —** ad jactationem; **in —** reapse; **to go into —** valēre; **to have an —** valēre; *(med)* pollēre; **to have a beneficial — on** prodesse *(w. dat)*; **to have a harmful** *or* **negative — on** obesse *(w. dat)*; **to put into —** efficacem reddĕre; **to take —** operari; **to the same —** in eandem sententiam; **to this —** hujusmodi; **without —** frustra
effect *tr* conficĕre
effective *adj* profici•ens -entis, effic•ax -acis
effectively *adv* efficienter; **to speak —** plurimum in dicendo valēre
effectual *adj* effic•ax -acis
effeminancy *s* molliti•es -ei *f*
effeminate *adj* effeminat•us -a -um
effeminately *adv* effeminate
effete *adj* effet•us -a -um
efficacious *adj* effic•ax -acis
efficaciously *adv* efficaciter
efficacy *s* virt•us -utis *f*
efficiency *s* efficienti•a -ae *f*
efficient *adj* effici•ens -entis
efficiently *adv* efficienter
effigy *s* effigi•es -ei *f*
effort *s* nis•us -ūs *m*; **to be worth the —** pretium operae esse; **to make an —** eniti; **with great —** enixe
effortless *adj* facil•is -is -e
effortlessly *adv* sine labore
effrontery *s* os oris *n*; **you have the — to** *(w. inf)* os tibi inest ut *(w. subj)*
effusion *s* effusi•o -onis *f*
effusive *adj* effus•us -a -um
effusively *adv* effuse
egg *s* ov•um -i *n*; **fried —s** ova *npl* fricta; **hard-boiled —** ovum *n* durum excoctum; **scrambled —** ova *npl* permixta; **soft-boiled —** apal•um -i *n*; **to lay an —** ovum parĕre
egg *tr* **to — on** concitare
egghead *s* hom•o -inis *m* ingeniosus
egg-shaped *adj* oval•is -is -e
eggshell *s* putam•en -inis *n*
egg white *s* ovi alb•um -i *n*
egotism *s* am•or -oris *m* sui
egotist *s* sui amat•or -oris *m*
egotistical *adj* sibi soli consul•ens -entis
egress *s* egress•us -ūs *m*
egress *intr* egredi
eight *adj* octo *(indecl)*; **— times** octies
eighteen *adj* duodeviginti *(indecl)*
eighteenth *adj* duodevicesim•us -a -um
eighth *adj* octav•us -a -um
eighth *s* octava par•s -tis *f*
eightieth *adj* octogesim•us -a -um
eighty *adj* octoginta *(indecl)*
either *adj & pron* u•ter -tra -trum
either *conj* **—…or** vel…vel; *(where the alternatives are mutually exclusive)* aut…aut
eject *tr* ejicĕre
ejection *s* ejecti•o -onis *f*
eke *tr* **to — out a livelihood** victum aegre parare

elaborate *adj* elaborat•us -a -um
elaborate *tr* elaborare ‖ *intr* **(on)** singullatim loqui (de + *abl)*
elaboration *s* lim•a -ae *f*
elapse *intr* praeterire
elastic *adj* elastic•us -a -um
elasticity *s* elasticit•as -atis *f*
elated *adj* **to be —** efferri
elation *s* anim•us -i *m* elatus
elbow *s* cubit•um -i *n;* **resting on one's —** in cubitum erect•us -a -um; **to lean one one's —** cubito inniti; **to rub —s with** conversari cum *(w. abl)*
elbow *tr* cubitis pulsare; **to — one's way through the crowd** cubitis turbam depulsare de via
elder *adj* maj•or -or -us natu
elderberry *s (bush)* sambuc•us -i *f; (berry)* sambuc•um -i *n;* **— wine** vin•um -i *n* sambuceum
elderly *adj* aetate provect•ior -ior -ius
eldest *adj* maxim•us -a -um natu
elect *adj* designat•us -a -um; *(elite)* lect•us -a -um
elect *tr* creare, eligĕre
election *s (act of choosing)* electi•o -onis *f;* **—s** *(pol)* comiti•a -orum *npl;* **to hold —s** comitia habēre
election day *s* di•es -ei *m* comitialis
electioneering *s* ambiti•o -onis *f*
elective *adj (pol)* suffragiis creat•us -a -um; *(of choice)* elegend•us -a -um
elective *s* disciplin•a -ae *f* electa
electric(al) *adj* electric•us -a -um
electric chair *s* sell•a -ae *f* electrica
electricity *s* vis *f* electrica
electrify *tr* electricā vi afficĕre; *(to thrill)* vehementer excitare
electrocute *tr* vi electricā interficĕre
elegance *s* eleganti•a -ae *f*
elegant *adj* eleg•ans -antis
elegantly *adv* eleganter
elegiac *adj* elegiac•us -a -um; **— verse** eleg•i -orum *mpl*
elegy *s* elegi•a -ae *f*
element *s* element•um -i *n;* **—s** principi•a -orum *npl* rerum; *(fig)* rudiment•a -orum *npl;* **to be out of one's —** peregrinus et hospes esse
elemental *adj* primordi•us -a -um
elementary *adj* simpl•ex -icis; **— instruction** element•a -orum *npl*
elementary school *s* lud•us -i *m* litterarius
elementary school teacher *s* litterar•ius -(i)i *m,* litterari•a -ae *f*
elephant *s* elephant•us -i *m*
elevate *tr* levare, (at)tollĕre; *(fig)* efferre
elevated *adj* edit•us -a -um
elevation *s* elati•o -onis *f; (height)* altitud•o -inis *f; (hill)* loc•us -i *m* editus
eleven *adj* undecim *(indecl)*
eleventh *adj* undecim•us -a -um
elf *s* num•en -inis *n* pumilum
elicit *tr* elicĕre
eligible *adj (pol)* qui per leges deligi potest; *(bachelor)* optabil•is -is -e
eliminate *tr* amovēre, tollĕre
elimination *s use a verbal paraphrase*
elision *s* elisi•o -onis *f*
elite *adj* elect•us -a -um
elite *s* flo•s -ris *m*
elk *s* alc•es -is *f*
ellipsis *s* ellips•is -is *f*
elliptical *adj* elliptic•us -a -um
elm *s* ulm•us -i *f*
elocution *s* pronuntiati•o -onis *f*
elongate *tr* producĕre
elongated *adj* praelong•us -a -um
elope *intr* insciis atque invitis parentibus cum amatore *(or* amatrice) domo fugĕre
elopement *s* clandestina fug•a -ae *f* et nupti•ae -arum *fpl*
eloquence *s* eloquenti•a -ae *f; (natural)* facundi•a -ae *f*
eloquent *adj* disert•us -a -um
eloquently *adv* diserte
else *adj* **anyone —** quivis alius; **anything —?** aliquid amplius?; **no one —** nem•o -inis *m* alius; **nothing —** nihil aliud; **who — ?** quis alius?
else *adv (besides)* praeterea; *(otherwise)* aliter; **or —** alioquin; **somewhere —** *(position)* alibi; *(direction)* alio
elsewhere *adv (position)* alibi; *(direction)* alio
elucidate *tr* illustrare, explicare
elucidation *s* explicati•o -onis *f*
elude *tr* eludĕre
elusive *adj (difficult to grasp)* fug•ax -acis; *(difficult to describe)* recondit•us -a -um
Elysian *adj* Elysi•us -a -um; **— Fields** Camp•i -orum *mpl* Elysii
emaciate *tr* macerare
emaciated *adj* ma•cer -cra -crum; **to become —** emacrescĕre
emaciation *s* maci•es -ei *f*
emanate *intr* emanare
emanation *s* exspirati•o -onis *f*
emancipate *tr (a son)* emancipare; *(a slave)* manumittĕre
emancipation *s (of a son)* emancipati•o -onis *f; (of a slave)* manumissi•o -onis *f*
emasculate *tr* emasculare
emasculated *adj (lit & fig)* effeminat•us -a -um
embalm *tr* condire
embalmment *s* **different modes of —** corporum condiendorum mod•i -orum *mpl* diversi
embankment *s* agg•er -eris *m*
embargo *s* **to lay an — on ships** naves ab exitu prohibēre; **to lift the — on ships** naves dimittĕre
embark *tr* imponĕre ‖ *intr* (in navem) conscendĕre; **to — upon** *(fig)* ingredi
embarkation *s* conscensi•o -onis *f; (usu.*

expressed by the verb: **after the — of the army** exercitu in naves imposito)
embarrass *tr* perturbare; **to be —ed** erubescĕre; **to be —ed by a deformity** deformitatem iniquissime ferre
embarrassing *adj* erubescund•us -a -um
embarrassment *s* conturbati•o -onis *f; (financial)* angusti•ae -arum *fpl*
embassy *s* legati•o -onis *f*
embellish *tr* exornare; **to — facts rather than report them accurately** res gestas magis exornare quam fideliter narrare
embellishment *s (act)* exornati•o -onis *f; (result)* ornament•um -i *n*
ember *s* favill•a -ae *f*
embezzle *tr* peculari
embezzlement *s* peculat•us -ūs *m*
embezzler *s* peculat•or -oris *m*
embitter *tr* exacerbare
embittered *adj* exacerbat•us -a -um
emblazon *tr* insignire
emblem *s* indic•ium -(i)i *n; (badge)* insign•e -is *n*
emblematic *adj* symbolic•us -a -um
embodiment *s* effigi•es -ei *f*
embody *tr* includĕre, informare
emboss *tr* caelare
embrace *s* amplex•us -ūs *m*
embrace *tr* amplecti
embroider *tr* acu pingĕre
embroidery *s (art)* ar•s -tis *f* acu pingendi; *(product)* pictur•a -ae *f* in textili (facta); picta vest•is -is *f*
embroil *tr* implicare
embroilment *s* implicati•o -onis *f*
embryo *s* part•us -ūs *m* inchoatus
emend *tr* emendare
emendation *s* emendati•o -onis *f*
emerald *s* smaragd•us -i *f*
emerge *intr* emergĕre; *(to arise)* existĕre
emergency *s* discrim•en -inis *n*
emigrant *s* emigr•ans -antis *mf*
emigrate *intr* **(to)** emigrare (in + *acc)*
emigration *s* emigrati•o -onis *f*
eminence *s* praestanti•a -ae *f; (rise in the ground)* loc•us -i *m* editus
eminent *adj* emin•ens -entis, egregi•us -a -um, ornatissim•us -a -um
eminently *adv* insigniter
emissary *s* legat•us -i *m*
emission *s* emissi•o -onis *f*
emit *tr* emittĕre
emotion *s* animi mot•us -ūs *m;* **strong —** permoti•o -onis *f*
emotional *adj* affectūs animi mov•ens -entis
emperor *s* imperat•or -oris *m; (title chosen by Augustus)* princ•eps -ipis *m*
emphasis *s* vis *f,* impressi•o -onis *f*
emphasize *tr (a word)* premĕre; *(idea)* exprimĕre
emphatic *adj* grav•is -is -e
emphatically *adv* graviter
empire *s* imper•ium -(i)i *n*
empirical *adj* empiric•us -a -um
empirically *adv* ex experimentis
empiricism *s* empiric•e -es *f*
employ *tr (to use)* uti *(w. abl); (to hire)* adhibēre; **to — precaution** uti observatione
employer *s* conduct•or -oris *m*
employment *s (act)* us•us -ūs *m; (occupation)* quaest•us -ūs *m; (hiring)* conducti•o -onis *f*
empower *tr* potestatem *(w. dat)* facĕre
empress *s* imperatr•ix -icis *f*
emptiness *s* inanit•as -atis *f; (fig)* vanit•as -atis *f*
empty *adj* vacu•us -a -um, inan•is -is -e; *(street)* desert•us -a -um; *(fig)* van•us -a -um; *(stomach)* jejun•us -a -um
empty *tr (contents)* vacue facĕre; *(bottle, stomach)* exhaurire; *(to strip bare)* exinanire **‖** *intr (of river)* se effundĕre
empty-handed *adj* inan•is -is -e; *(without a gift)* immun•is -is -e
empty-headed *adj* frivol•us -a -um
emulate *tr (to rival)* aemulari; *(to imitate)* imitari
emulation *s* aemulati•o -onis *f*
emulous *adj* **(of)** aemul•us -a -um *(w. gen)*
enable *tr* facultatem *(w. dat)* facĕre
enact *tr* sancire; *(of the plebs)* sciscĕre; *(of the Roman people)* jubēre; *(of a absolute ruler)* imponĕre
enactment *s* sancti•o -onis *f*
enamel *s* smalt•um -i *n*
enamel *adj* smaltin•us -a -um
enamored *adj* **to be — of** deamare
encamp *intr* castra ponĕre
encampment *s* castr•a -orum *npl*
encase *tr* includĕre
encaustic *adj* encaustic•us -a -um
enchant *tr* fascinare; *(fig)* capĕre
enchanted *adj* incantat•us -a -um, capt•us -a -um
enchanting *adj (fig)* venust•us -a -um
enchantment *s* incantament•um -i *n; (fig)* illecebr•ae -arum *fpl*
enchantress *s* mag•a -ae *f*
encircle *tr* circumdare
enclose *tr* includĕre; *(with a fence)* saepire; **to — a document in a letter** libellum litteris subjicĕre
enclosure *s* saept•um -i *n*
encompass *tr* complecti
encore *s* revocati•o -onis *f;* **he received an —** revocatus est
encounter *s (meeting)* congress•us -ūs *m; (fight)* pugn•a -ae *f*
encounter *tr (unexpectedly)* occurrĕre *(w. dat),* offendĕre; *(the enemy)* obviam ire *(w. dat);* **to — death** mortem oppetĕre
encourage *tr* cohortari; *(of one cast down)* animum *or* animos *(w. gen)* confirmare

encouragement *s* hortat•us -ūs *m;* confirmati•o -onis *f*
encroach *intr* invadĕre; **to — upon** occupare; *(rights)* imminuĕre; **to — upon a neighbor's land** terminos agri proferre
encroachment *s* usurpati•o -onis *f; (on rights)* imminuti•o -onis *f*
encumber *tr* impedire
encumbrance *s* impediment•um -i *n*
encyclical *s* litter•ae -arum *fpl* publicae pontificales
encyclopedia *s* encyclopaedi•a -ae *f*
end *s* fin•is -is *m,* termin•us -i *m; (termination of life)* exit•um -i *n; (aim)* proposit•um -i *n; (of a speech)* perorati•o -onis *f;* **at the — of the letter** in extremis litteris; **at the — of the year** exeunte anno; **in the —** denique; **to come to an —** finem capĕre; **to put an — to** finem imponĕre *(w. dat);* **to the — of spring** ad ultimum ver; **toward the — of his life** tempore extremo; **to what — ?** quo?, quorsum?
end *tr* finire, terminare ‖ *intr* desinĕre, finem capĕre; *(of time)* exire
endanger *tr* in periculum vocare
endear *tr* carum reddĕre
endearing *adj* car•us -a -um
endearment *s* blanditi•ae -arum *fpl*
endeavor *s* conat•us -ūs *m*
endeavor *intr* conari, niti
ending *s* fin•is -is *m,* exit•us -ūs *m*
endless *adj* infinit•us -a -um
endlessly *adv* sine fine
endorse *tr* comprobare; *(a check)* chirographum a tergo *(w. gen)* inscribĕre
endow *tr* donare
endowed *adj* **(with)** praedit•us -a -um *(w. abl)*
endowment *s (of body or mind)* do•s tis *f; (financial)* dotati•o -onis *f*
endurable *adj* tolerabil•is -is -e
endurance *s* patienti•a -ae *f; (duration)* durati•o -onis *f*
endure *tr* tolerare ‖ *intr* durare
enduring *adj* toler•ans -antis; *(lasting)* durabil•is -is -e
enemy *s (public)* host•is -is *m; (private)* inimic•us -i *m,* inimic•a -ae *f*
enemy *adj* hostic•us -a -um, infest•us -a -um; inimic•us -a -um
energetic *adj* impi•ger -gra -grum
energy *s* vis *f*
enervate *tr* enervare
enforce *tr* **to — the law** legem exercēre
enfranchise *tr* civitate donare; *(a slave)* manumittĕre
enfranchisment *s* civitatis donati•o -onis *f; (of a slave)* manumissi•o -onis *f*
engage *tr (to employ)* adhibēre; *(attention)* occupare; *(to involve)* implicare; *(enemy)* proelium facĕre cum *(w. abl),* dimicare cum *(w. abl)* ‖ *intr* **to — in** suscipĕre, ingredi; **to — in battle** proeliari
engaged *adj (to marry)* spons•us -a -um; **to be — in** versari in *(w. abl)*
engagement *s (to marry)* pacti•o -onis *f* nuptialis; *(business)* occupati•o -onis *f; (mil)* proel•ium -(i)i *n;* **to break off the —** sponsum repudiare
engaging *adj* suav•is -is -e
engender *tr* gignĕre
engine *s* machin•a -ae *f*
engineer *s* machinat•or -oris *m; (mil)* fa•ber -bri *m*
engineering *s* machinalis scienti•a -ae *f*
English *adj* Anglic•us -a -um
English *s* **to know —** Anglice scire; **to speak —** Anglice loqui; **to teach —** Anglice docēre
engrave *tr* caelare
engraver *s* caelat•or -oris *m*
engraving *s* caelatur•a -ae *f*
engross *tr* **(in)** animum occupare in *(w. abl);* **to be —ed in** tot•us -a -um esse in *(w. abl)*
engulf *tr* devorare, mergĕre
enhance *tr* amplificare
enhancement *s* amplificati•o -onis *f*
enigma *s* aenigm•a -atis *n*
enigmatic *adj* ambigu•us -a -um
enigmatically *adv* per aenigmata
enjoin *tr* jubēre
enjoy *tr* frui *(w. abl); (to have the benefit of, e.g., good health, friendship)* uti *(w. abl)*
enjoyment *s* fruct•us -ūs *m; (the sense of pleasure itself)* delectati•o -onis *f*
enlarge *tr* amplificare
enlargement *s* amplificati•o -onis *f*
enlighten *tr (physically)* illustrare; *(mentally)* illuminare; *(to instruct)* erudire
enlightened *adj* erudit•us -a -um
enlightenment *s* humanit•as -atis *f*
enlist *tr (support)* conciliare; *(mil)* conscribĕre; *(to swear in)* sacramento adigĕre ‖ *intr* sacramentum dicĕre
enlistment *s* conscripti•o -onis *f*
enliven *tr* excitare
enmity *s* simult•as -atis *f;* **to be at — with** in simultate esse cum *(w. abl);* **to feel — toward** simultatem habēre cum *(w. abl)*
ennoble *tr* honestare, nobilitare
ennui *s* taed•ium -(i)i *n*
enormity *s* immanit•as -atis *f*
enormous *adj* imman•is -is -e
enormously *adv* praeter modum
enough *adj* satis *(indecl);* **— trouble** satis laboris; **time —** satis temporis
enough *adv* satis; **more than —** satis superque
enrage *tr* infuriare
enrapture *tr* rapĕre; **to be —d** gaudio efferri
enrich *tr* locupletare, ditare

enroll *tr* adscribĕre; **to — s.o. in the patrician order** aliquem inter patricios asciscĕre
enshrine *tr* consecrare
ensign *s (banner)* sign•um -i *n; (officer)* signif•er -eri *m*
enslave *tr* in servitutem redigĕre
enslavement *s* servit•us -utis *f*
ensnare *tr* illaquēre; *(fig)* illicĕre
ensue *intr* insequi
ensuing *adj* insequ•ens -entis
entail *tr* adferre
entangle *tr* implicare
entanglement *s* implicati•o -onis *f*
enter *tr* intrare, ingredi, inire; *(office)* inire; *(to pierce)* penetrare in *(w. acc)*; **to — in a memorandum** in libellum referre; **to — in an account book** in rationem inducĕre; **to — politics** rem publicam inire **ll** *intr* intrare, ingredi, inire; **to — into an alliance with s.o.** societatem cum aliquo facĕre; **to — upon** *(to undertake)* suscipĕre; *(a magistracy)* inire
enterprise *s (undertaking)* incept•um -i *n; (project)* op•us -eris *n; (venture)* aus•um -i *n; (pej)* facin•us -oris *n; (enterprising disposition)* alacer ac promptus anim•us -i *m*
enterprising *adj* ala•cer -cris -cre et prompt•us -a -um
entertain *tr (a guest)* excipĕre; *(idea)* admittĕre; *(to amuse)* oblectare
entertainer *s* ludi•o -onis *m; (host)* hosp•es -itis *m*
entertaining *adj* festiv•us -a -um
entertainment *s (amusement)* oblectati•o -onis *f; (cultural, esp. at a dinner party)* acroam•a -atis *n; (by the host)* hospit•ium -(i)i *n*; **public —s** spectacul•a -orum *npl*
enthrall *tr* captare
enthusiasm *s* stud•ium -(i)i *n*
enthusiastic *adj* studios•us -a -um
enthusiastically *adv* studiose
entice *tr* allicĕre
enticement *s* illecebr•a -ae *f*
enticing *adj* illecebros•us -a -um
entire *adj* tot•us -a -um, univers•us -a -um
entirely *adv* omnino
entirety *s expressed by* univers•us -a -um: **to look at the matter in its —** rem universam contemplari
entitle *tr (a book, essay)* inscribĕre; *(to name)* appellare; *(to give title to)* potestatem dare *(w. dat)*; **to be —d to do anything** jus aliquid faciendi habēre; dignus esse qui aliquid faciat
entity *s* en•s -tis *n*
entomb *tr* sepulchro condĕre
entomologist *s* entomologic•us -i *m*
entomology *s* entomologi•a -ae *f*
entourage *s* comitat•us -ūs *m*
entrails *spl* ext•a -orum *npl*
entrance *s* adit•us -ūs *m*, introit•us -ūs *m; (act)* ingressi•o -onis *f*; **at the — to the theater** in aditu theatri
entrance *tr* rapĕre
entrance hall *s* vestibul•um -i *n*
entrance way *s* ost•ium -(i)i *n*
entrap *tr* illaquēre
entreat *tr* obsecrare
entreaty *s* obsecrati•o -onis *f*
entree *s* cen•a -ae *f* altera
entrench *tr (lit & fig)* vallare; **to — oneself** subsidĕre
entrenchment *s* muniment•um -i *n*
entrepreneur *s* negotiat•or -oris *m*
entrust *tr* committĕre
entry *s (act)* ingressi•o -onis *f*, introït•us -ūs *m; (of house)* ost•ium -(i)i *n; (in accounts)* nom•en -inis *n*
entwine *tr* implicare, implectĕre
enumerate *tr* enumerare
enumeration *s* enumerati•o -onis *f*
enunciate *tr (words)* exprimĕre; *(to predicate)* enuntiare
enunciation *s (of sounds)* explanati•o -onis *f; (setting forth)* enuntiati•o -onis *f*
envelop *tr* involvĕre
envelope *s* involucr•um -i *n*
enviable *adj* invidios•us -a -um
envious *adj* invid•us -a -um
environment *s* circumject•a -orum *npl*
environs *spl* vicinit•as -atis *f*
envision *tr* fingĕre
envoy *s* legat•us -i *m*
envy *s* invidi•a -ae *f*
envy *tr* invidēre *(w. dat)*
enzyme *s* enzym•a -ae *f*
eons *spl* plurima saecul•a -orum *npl*
ephemeral *adj (brief)* brev•is -is -e; *(perishable)* caduc•us -a -um
epic *adj* epic•us -a -um
epic *s* epos *n (only in nom & acc)*, poem•a -atis *n* epicum
epicure *s* hellu•o -onis *m*
Epicurean *adj (of Epicurus)* Epicure•us -a -um; *(fig)* voluptari•us -a -um
Epicurean *s* Epicure•us -i *m; (hedonist)* voluptar•ius -(i)i *m*
epidemic *adj* epidem•us -a -um
epidemic *s* pestilenti•a -ae *f*
epidermis *s* epiderm•is -is *f*
epiglottis *s* epiglott•is -idis *f*
epigram *s* epigramm•a -atis *n*
epilepsy *s* comitalis morb•us -i *m*
epilogue *s* epilog•us -i *m*
epiphany *s* epiphani•a -ae *f*
episcopal *adj* episcopal•is -is -e
episode *s* embol•ium -(i)i *n*
epistle *s* epistol•a -ae *f*
epitaph *s* titul•us -i *m* (sepulcri)
epithet *s* epithet•on -i *n*
epoch *s* saecul•um -i *n*
equal *adj* aequ•us -a-um; *(matching)* pa•r -ris; **to be — to the task** muneri par esse

equal *s* pa•r -ris *mf & n;* **to be on an — with the gods** in aequo diis stare
equal *tr* aequare
equality *s* aequalit•as -atis *f;* **to be on — with** in aequo *(w. dat)* stare
equalization *s (act)* exaequati•o -onis *f; (state)* aequalit•as -atis *f*
equally *adv* aeque
equanimity *s* aequus anim•us -i *m*
equation *s* aequati•o -onis *f*
equator *s* aequat•or -oris *m*
equatorial *adj* aequinoctial•is -is -e
equestrian *adj* equestr•is -is -e
equestrian *s* equ•es -itis *m*
equidistant *adj* **to be —** aequo intervallo inter se distare
equilibrium *s* aequilibr•ium -(i)i *n*
equinox *s* aequinoct•ium -(i)i *n*
equip *tr* ornare; *(with arms)* armare
equipment *s* instrument•um -i *n,* apparat•us -ūs *m*
equitable *adj* aequ•us -a -um
equitably *adv* aeque
equity *s* aequ•um -i *n*
equivalence *s* aequalit•as -atis *f*
equivalent *adj* pa•r -ris, aequ•us -a -um; **one gold coin is — to ten silver ones** pro argenteis decem aureus unus valet
equivalent *s* quod idem valet
equivocal *adj* ambigu•us -a -um
equivocate *intr* tergiversari
era *s* temp•us -oris *n*
eradicate *tr* eradicare, exstirpare
eradication *s* exstirpati•o -onis *f*
erase *tr* eradĕre, delēre
erasure *s* litur•a -ae *f*
ere *conj* priusquam
ere *prep* ante *(w. acc);* **— long** mox; **— now** ante hoc tempus
erect *adj* erect•us -a -um
erect *tr (to raise)* errigĕre; *(to build)* exstruĕre; *(statue)* ponĕre, statuĕre
erection *s (building)* exstructi•o -onis *f; (setting up)* erecti•o -onis *f*
erotic *adj* erotic•us -a -um
err *intr* errare, peccare
errand *s* mandat•um -i *n*
erratic *adj* inconst•ans -antis
erroneous *adj* fals•us -a -um; **to be —** in erratis esse
erroneously *adv* perperam
error *s* err•or -oris *m; (in writing)* mend•um -i *n*
erudite *adj* erudit•us -a -um
erudition *s* eruditi•o -onis *f*
erupt *intr* erumpĕre
eruption *s* erupti•o -onis *f*
escalade *tr (to increase)* augēre; *(to intensify)* intendĕre ‖ *intr* (in)crescĕre, ingravescĕre
escapade *s* facin•us -oris *n* temerarium
escape *s* effug•ium -(i)i *n*
escape *tr* fugĕre; *(in a quiet way)* subterfugĕre; **to — the notice of** fallĕre ‖ *intr* effugĕre
escort *s* comitat•us -ūs *m; (protection)* praesid•ium -(i)i *n*
escort *tr* prosequi
especially *adv* praecipue, maxime
essay *s* experiment•um -i *n; (treatise)* libell•us -i *m*
essay *tr* conari
essence *s* essenti•a -ae *f*
essential *adj* necessari•us -a -um
essentially *adv* necessario
establish *tr* constituĕre; *(to settle firmly)* stabilare; *(to prove)* probare
establishment *s (act)* constituti•o -onis *f; (com)* negot•ium -(i)i *n*
estate *s (landed property)* fund•us -i *m,* a•ger -gri *m; (state)* stat•us -ūs *m*
esteem *s* aestimati•o -onis *f;* **to hold in high (highest) —** magni (maximi) facĕre
esteem *tr* aestimare; **to — highly (more, very highly)** magni (pluris, maximi) facĕre
estimable *adj* aestimand•us -a -um
estimate *s (valuation)* aestimati•o -onis *f; (judgment)* judic•ium -(i)i *n;* **to form an —** judicium facĕre; **to give an —** modum impensarum explicare
estimation *s* aestimati•o -onis *f*
estimator *s* aestimat•or -oris *m*
estrange *tr* alienare
estrangement *s* alienati•o -onis *f*
estuary *s* aestuar•ium -(i)i *n*
eternal *adj* aetern•us -a -um
eternally *adv* in aeternum
eternity *s* aeternit•as -atis *f*
ether *s* aeth•er -eris *m*
ethereal *adj* aethere•us -a -um
ethical *adj* moral•is -is -e
ethics *spl* ethic•e -es *f; (of an individual)* mor•es -ium *mpl*
etymology *s* etymologi•a -ae *f*
eulogize *tr* laudare
eulogy *s* laudati•o -onis *f*
eunuch *s* eunuch•us -i *m; (pej)* spad•o -onis *m*
euphemism *s* euphemism•us -i *m*
euphemistic *adj* **— expression** vo•x -cis *f* per euphemismum usurpata
euphony *s* vocalit•as -atis *f*
Europe *s* Europ•a -ae *f*
European *adj* Europae•us -a -um
evacuate *tr* vacuefacĕre; *(people)* deducĕre; *(bowels)* exonerare
evacuation *s (mil)* deducti•o -onis *f;* **— of the bowels** alvi purgati•o -onis *f*
evade *tr* eludĕre
evaluate *tr* aestimare
evaluation *s* aestimati•o -onis *f*
evangelical *adj* evangelic•us -a -um
evangelist *s* evangelist•a -ae *m*
evangelize *tr* evangelizare
evaporate *tr* exhalare ‖ *intr* exhalari

evaporation *s* exhalati•o -onis *f*
evasion *s (avoidance)* fug•a -ae *f; (dodging)* tergiversati•o -onis *f; (round-about speech)* ambag•es -um *fpl;* **to practice —** tergiversari
evasive *adj* ambigu•us -a -um
evasively *adv* ambigue
eve *s* vesp•er -eri *m; (of a feastday)* vigili•ae -arum *fpl;* **on the — of** sub *(w. acc)*
even *adj* aequal•is -is -e; *(level)* plan•us -a -um; *(of numbers)* pa•r -ris; **to get — with** ulcisci
even *adv* etiam; *(esp. to emphasize single words)* vel; **— if, — though** etsi, etiamsi; **— so** nihilominus; **not —** ne...quidem
evening *s* vesp•er -eri *m;* **all —** totā vesperā; **in the —** vespere, vesperi; **— falls** vesperascit; **good —!** salve!, *(pl:* salvete!); **toward —** sub vesperum; **in the early —** primo vespere; **yesterday —** heri vesperi; **very late in the —** pervespere
evening *adj* vespertin•us -a -um
evening star *s* Hesper•us -i *m*
evenness *s* aequalit•as -atis *f*
event *s* res, rei *f; (adverse)* cas•us -ūs *m; (outcome)* event•us -ūs *m;* **in all —s** saltem; **in any —** utique; **in the — of** si
eventful *adj* memorabil•is -is -e
eventual *adj* ultim•us -a -um
eventually *adv* aliquando
ever *adv (always)* semper; *(at any time)* umquam; *(after* si, nisi, num, ne) quando; **— since** ex quo (tempore); **for —** in aeternum; **greater than —** major quam umquam; **more than —** magis quam umquam
evergreen *adj* semperviv•us -a -um
everlasting *adj* sempitern•us -a -um
evermore *adv* **for —** in aeternum
every *adj* omn•is -is -e, quisque, quaeque, quodque; **— day** co(t)tidie, in dies; **— now and then** interdum; **— other day** alternis diebus
everybody *pron (each one)* quisque; *(all)* omn•es -ium *mpl; (stronger)* nem•o -inis *m* non; **— for himself** pro se quisque
everyday *adj* co(t)tidian•us -a -um; *(ordinary)* usitat•us -a -um
everyone *pron see* **everybody**
everything *pron* omn•ia -ium *npl*
everywhere *adv* ubique
evict *tr* expellěre, detruděre
eviction *s* expulsi•o -onis *f*
evidence *s* testimon•ium -(i)i *n; (information given)* indic•ium -(i)i *n;* **to give —** testari; **to give — against s.o.** testimonium dare in aliquem; **to turn state's —** indicium profiteri; **on what — will you convict me?** quo me teste convinces?
evidence *tr* testari
evident *adj* manifest•us -a -um; **it is —** apparet, manifestum est, constat
evidently *adv* manifeste
evil *adj* mal•us -a -um
evil *s* mal•um -i *n*
evildoer *s* malefact•or -oris *m*
evil-minded *adj* malevol•us -a -um
evince *tr* praestare
evoke *tr* evocare, excitare
evolution *s* progress•us -ūs *m*
evolve *tr* evolvěre per gradus ‖ *intr* evolvi per gradus
exact *adj* exact•us -a -um; *(persons)* dilig•ens -entis; **at the — time** ipso tempore
exact *tr* exigěre
exaction *s* exacti•o -onis *f*
exactly *adv* accurate; **— as** sic ut
exactness *s* accurati•o -onis *f*
exaggerate *tr* in majus extollěre; *(numbers)* augēre; **to — the facts** egredi veritatem, exceděre actae rei modum
exaggeration *s* superjecti•o -onis *f* veri; **falsehoods and —s** falsa et majora vero; **he is given to —** omnia in majus extollěre solet
exalt *tr* amplificare, efferre
exaltation *s* elati•o -onis *f*
examination *s* investigati•o -onis *f; (leg)* examinati•o -onis *f; (in school)* probati•o -onis *f;* **to fail an —** probatione caděre; **to pass an —** probatione feliciter evaděre
examine *tr* investigare, scrutari; *(witnesses)* interrogare; *(students)* probare
examiner *s* investigat•or -oris *m;* probat•or -oris *m*
example *s (illustration)* exempl•um -i *n; (lesson)* document•um -i *n;* **for —** exempli gratiā; **to set an —** exemplum praebēre
exasperate *tr* exasperare
exasperation *s* ir•a -ae *f*
excavate *tr* excavare
excavation *s* excavati•o -onis *f*
exceed *tr* exceděre, superare
exceedingly *adv* magnopere, valde
excel *tr* superare ‖ *intr* excellěre
excellence *s* excellenti•a -ae *f*
Excellency *s* illustrissim•us -i *m*
excellent *adj* praest•ans -antis
excellently *adv* egregie, optime
except *tr* excipěre
except *prep* praeter *(w. acc);* **— that** nisi quod
exception *s* excepti•o -onis *f;* **with the — of** praeter *(w. acc);* **with this —** hoc excepto; **without a single —** ne uno quidem excepto; **without —** ad un•um -am -um
exceptional *adj* praest•ans -antis
exceptionally *adv* praeter modum
excess *s* nim•ium -(i)i *n;* **to be in —** superesse; **to —** nimis; **to go to — in anything** nimium esse in aliqua re
excess *adj* nimi•us -a -um

excessive *adj* immodic•us -a -um
excessively *adv* immodice, nimis
exchange *s (of goods)* permutati•o -onis *f; (of money)* collyb•us -i *m*
exchange *tr* **(for)** permutare *(w. abl)*
excise *tr* excidĕre
excision *s* exsecti•o -onis *f*
excitable *adj* mobil•is -is -e; *(irritable)* irritabil•is -is -e
excite *tr* excitare; *(to inflame)* incendĕre
excitement *s* commoti•o -onis *f; (that which excites)* incitament•um -i *n;* **to feel —** excitari
exclaim *tr* exclamare; *(as a group)* conclamare; *(in reply)* succlamare
exclamation *s* exclamati•o -onis *f*
exclude *tr* excludĕre
exclusion *s* exclusi•o -onis *f*
exclusive *adj* propri•us -a -um; **— of** praeter *(w. acc)*
exclusively *adv* solum
excommunicate *tr* excommunicare
excommunication *s* excommunicati•o -onis *f*
excrement *s* excrement•um -i *n*
excrete *tr* excernĕre
excretion *s (act)* excreti•o -onis *f; (result)* excrement•um -i *n*
excruciating *adj* cruci•ans -antis, acerbissim•us -a -um
exculpate *tr* (ex)purgare
excursion *s* it•er -ineris *n* voluptatis causā susceptum
excusable *adj* excusabil•is -is -e
excuse *s* excusati•o -onis *f; (pretext)* praetext•um -i *n*
excuse *tr* ignoscĕre *(w. dat);* **to — oneself** se excusare
execute *tr (a criminal)* supplicio capitis afficĕre; *(to perform)* exsequi, efficĕre
execution *s* exsecuti•o -onis *f; (capital punishment)* supplic•ium -(i)i *n* capitis
executioner *s* carnif•ex -icis *m*
executive *adj* ad administrationem pertin•ens -entis
executive *s* administrat•or -oris *m*
executor *s* curat•or -oris *m* testamenti
exemplary *adj* eximi•us -a -um
exemplification *s* exempl•um -i *n*
exemplify *tr* exemplum *(w. gen)* exponĕre
exempt *tr* eximĕre
exempt *adj (from)* vacu•us -a -um (ab + *abl); (from tribute)* immun•is -is -e, lib•er -era -erum
exemption *s* immunit•as -atis *f; (from military service)* vacati•o -onis *f* militiae
exercise *s* exercitati•o -onis *f; (athletic)* palaestr•a -ae *f; (mil)* exercit•ium -(i)i *n; (literary)* them•a -atis *n*
exercise *tr* exercēre ‖ *intr* se exercēre
exert *tr* adhibēre; **to — oneself** viribus eniti
exertion *s* contenti•o -onis *f*
exhalation *s* exhalati•o -onis *f*
exhale *tr* exhalare ‖ *intr* exspirare
exhaust *tr* exhaurire; *(to tire)* defatigare, conficĕre
exhausted *adj* fatigat•us -a -um; **to be** *or* **become —** a viribus deficĕre
exhaustion *s* defecti•o -onis *f* virium
exhibit *tr* exhibēre; *(games)* edĕre
exhibition *s* exhibiti•o -onis *f; (display)* ostentati•o -onis *f; (public performance)* lud•i -orum *mpl; (gladiatorial show)* mun•us -eris *n*
exhilarate *tr* exhilare
exhilarating *adj* animum exhilar•ans -antis; **the morning air is —** exhilarant animos aurae matutinae
exhilaration *s* hilarit•as -atis *f*
exhort *tr* hortari
exhortation *s* hortam•en -inis *f; (act)* hortati•o -onis *f*
exhume *tr* exhumare
exigency *s* necessit•as -atis *f*
exile *s (temporary)* ex(s)il•ium -(i)i *n; (for life)* deportati•o -onis *f; (person)* exs•ul -ulis *mf*
exile *tr* exterminare; *(for a time)* relegare; *(for life)* deportare
exist *intr* esse, ex(s)istĕre; *(to be extant)* exstare; *(of human beings)* vivĕre
existence *s* existenti•a -ae *f; (of human beings)* vit•a -ae *f*
exit *s* exit•us -ūs *m*
exonerate *tr* absolvĕre
exorbitant *adj* immodic•us -a -um; **to make — demands** immodice postulare
exotic *adj* exotic•us -a -um
expand *tr* expandĕre, extendĕre ‖ *intr* expandi, se extendĕre
expanse *s* spat•ium -(i)i *n*
expansion *s* expansi•o -onis *f*
expatriate *tr* exterminare
expatriate *s* exs•ul -ulis *mf*
expect *tr* exspectare; **not —ing** necopin•ans -antis; **sooner than —ed** opinione celerius
expectancy *s* spe•s -i *f*
expectation *s* exspectati•o -onis *f;* **contrary to —** praeter opinionem
expectorate *tr & intr* exspuĕre
expediency *s* utilit•as -atis *f*
expedient *adj* util•is -is -e; **it is — that** expedit *(w. acc & inf)*
expedient *s* mod•us -i *m*
expedite *tr* expedire, maturare
expedition *s (mil)* expediti•o -onis *f; (speed)* celerit•as -atis *f;* **to lead troops on an —** copias educĕre in expeditionem
expeditious *adj* cel•er -eris -ere
expeditiously *adv* celeriter; **as — as possible** quam celerrime
expel *tr* expellĕre
expend *tr* impendĕre
expenditure *s* impens•a -ae *f*

expense *s* impens•a -ae *f*, sumpt•us -ūs *m;* **at great —** magno sumptu
expensive *adj* car•us -a -um, pretios•us -a -um, sumptuos•us -a -um
expensively *adv* sumptuose
experience *s* us•us -ūs *m*, experienti•a -ae *f;* **military —** usus *m* in re militari; **political —** usus *m* in republica; **a man of long —** vi•r -ri *m* longā experientiā
experience *tr* experiri, cognoscĕre; **to — in daily life** in usu habēre
experienced *adj* **(in)** perit•us -a -um *(w. gen)*
experiment *s* experiment•um -i *n*
experimental *adj* usu comparat•us -a -um
expert *adj* **(in)** perit•us -a -um *(w. gen)*
expertly *adv* scienter, callide
expertness *s* calliditas -atis *f*
expiate *tr* expiare, luĕre
expiation *s* expiati•o -onis *f*
expiration *s* exit•us -ūs *m;* **at the — of the fifth year** quinto anno exeunte
expire *intr* exspirare; *(of time)* exire
explain *tr* explanare, explicare
explanation *s* explanati•o -onis *f*
expletive *s* explement•um -i *n*
explicit *adj* explicat•us -a -um
explicitly *adv* aperte, plane
explode *tr* displodĕre; *(fig)* explodĕre ‖ *intr* displodi
exploit *s* facin•us -oris *n;* **—s** re•s -rum *fpl* gestae
exploit *tr* uti *(w. abl); (pej)* abuti *(w. abl)*
exploration *s* indagati•o -onis *f*
explore *tr* explorare, indagare
explorer *s* explorat•or -oris *m*
explosion *s* frag•or -oris *m*
exponent *s* interpr•es -itis *m*
export *tr* exportare, evehĕre
exporter *s* exportat•or -oris *m*
exports *spl* merc•es -ium *fpl* quae exportantur
expose *tr* exponĕre; *(to bare)* nudare; *(to uncover)* detegĕre; *(to danger)* objicĕre; **to be —ed to** patēre *(w. dat)*
exposition *s* expositi•o -onis *f*
exposure *s (to cold)* expositi•o -onis *f; (of guilt)* deprehensi•o -onis *f*
expound *tr* exponĕre, interpretari
express *adj* express•us -a -um
express *tr* exprimĕre; **to — oneself** loqui, dicĕre
expression *s* verb•um -i *n; (of the face)* vult•us -ūs *m;* **joy beyond —** gaudia majora quam quae verbis exprimi possint
expressive *adj* signific•ans -antis; *(fig)* loqu•ax -acis; **— of** ind•ex -icis *(w. gen)*
expressly *adv* plane
expulsion *s* exacti•o -onis *f*
expunge *tr* oblitterare
expurgate *tr* expurgare
exquisite *adj* exquisit•us -a -um
exquisitely *adv* exquisite
extant *adj* superst•es -itis; **to be —** exstare
extempore *adv* ex tempore
extemporaneous *adj* extemporal•is -is -e
extemporaneously *adv* ex tempore
extemporize *intr* subita dicĕre
extend *tr* extendĕre; **to — the empire** ampliare imperium; **to — the governor's term** prorogare imperium ‖ *intr* extendi; **to — to** tendĕre ad *(w. acc)*
extension *s* extenti•o -onis *f; (lengthening)* producti•o -onis *f; (e.g., of the fingers)* porrigi•o -onis *f; (of size)* prolati•o -onis *f*
extensive *adj* lat•us -a -um
extensively *adv* late
extent *s* spat•ium -(i)i *n; (of a country)* fin•es -ium *mpl;* **to a great —** magnā ex parte; **to some —** aliquā ex parte; **to this —** hactenus
extenuating *adj* **— circumstances** eae res quibus culpa minuitur
exterior *adj* exter•ior -ior -ius
exterior *s* speci•es -ei *f*
exterminate *tr* ad internecionem delēre
extermination *s* interneci•o -onis *f*
external *adj* extern•us -a -um
externally *adv* extrinsecus
extinct *adj* exstinct•us -a -um; **to become —** obsolescĕre
extinction *s* exstincti•o -onis *f*
extinguish *tr* exstinguĕre
extol *tr* laudibus efferre
extort *tr* extorquēre
extortion *s* pecuni•ae -arum *fpl* repetundae
extortionist *s* extort•or -oris *m*
extra *adj* addit•us -a -um
extra *adv* insuper, praeterea
extract *s (chemical)* expressi•o -onis *f; (literary)* excerpt•um -i *n; (synopsis)* compend•ium -(i)i *n*
extract *tr* extrahĕre; *(to squeeze out)* exprimĕre; *(teeth)* evellĕre; *(from a literary source)* excerpĕre
extraction *s (act)* evulsi•o -onis *f; (descent)* stirp•s -is *f;* **of German —** oriund•us -a -um a Germanis
extraneous *adj* alien•us -a -um
extraordinarily *adv* praeter modum
extraordinary *adj* extraordinari•us -a -um, insolit•us -a -um; *(outstanding)* eximi•us -a -um
extravagance *s* sumpt•us -ūs *m*
extravagant *adj (exceeding bounds)* immodic•us -a -um; *(in expenditure)* sumptuos•us -a -um; *(spending)* prodig•us -a -um
extravagantly *adv* immodice; *(expensively)* sumptuose; *(lavishly)* profuse, prodige
extreme *adj* extrem•us -a -um
extreme *s* extrem•um -i *n;* **from one — to another** ab imo ad summum; **in the —**

ad extremum; **to go to —s** descendĕre ad extrema
extremely *adv* summe, perquam
extremist *s* assectat•or -oris *m* rerum novarum
extremity *s* extremit•as -atis *f,* extrem•um -i *n;* **extremities of the body** eminentes part•es -ium *fpl* corporis; **we have been reduced to extremities** ad extrema perventum est
extricate *tr* expedire, extrahĕre
extrinsic *adj* extrane•us -a -um
extrude *tr* extrudĕre ‖ *intr* extrudi
exuberance *s (of growth)* luxuri•es -ei *f; (of spirit)* redundanti•a -ae *f*
exuberant *adj* luxurios•us -a -um; *(unrestrained)* effus•us -a -um; **to be —** *(of style)* redundare
exude *tr* exudare ‖ *intr* emanare
exult *intr* exsultare, gestire
exultant *adj* laetabund•us -a -um
exultantly *adv* laete
exultation *s* exsultati•o -onis *f*
eye *s* ocul•us -i *m; (of needle)* foram•en -inis *n; (of plant)* gemm•a -ae *f;* **blind in one —** lusc•us -a -um; **keep your —s open!** cave circumspicias!; **to be in the public —** scaenae servire; **to keep an — on** cavēre, in oculis habēre; **to shut one's —s to** conivēre
eye *tr* aspicĕre
eyeball *s* oculi orb•is -is *m*
eyebrow *s* supercil•ium -(i)i *n*
eyeglasses *spl* perspicill•a -orum *npl*
eyelash *s* palpebrarum pil•us -i *m*
eyelid *s* palpebr•a -ae *f*
eyesight *s* aci•es -ei *f;* **to lose one's —** oculos perdĕre
eyesore *s (fig)* res, rei *f* taetra
eyewitness *s* oculatus test•is -is *m*

F

fable *s* fabul•a -ae *f*
fabled *adj* fabulos•us -a -um
fabric *s* textil•e -is *n,* text•um -i *n; (framework)* fabric•a -ae *f*
fabricate *tr* fabricare; *(fig)* fingĕre
fabrication *s* fabricati•o -onis *f; (fig)* mendac•ium -(i)i *n*
fabulous *adj* mirabil•is -is -e
fabulously *adv* perquam
face *s* faci•es -ei *f,* o•s -ris *n; (forward part of anything)* fron•s -tis *f;* **— to —** coram; **— to — with** coram *(w. abl);* **on the — of it** primā facie; **to lose —** honestatem amittĕre; **to make a —** os ducĕre; **to one's —** coram
face *tr (to look towards)* aspicĕre; *(to withstand, e.g., danger)* obviam ire *(w. dat); (to confront)* se opponĕre *(w. dat)* ‖ *intr* spectare; **to — about** *(mil)* signa convertĕre; **to — north (south,** *etc.)* ad *or* in septentrionem (meridiem, *etc.)* spectare
face powder *s* fuc•us -i *m*
facet *s* gemmae superfici•es -ei *f; (fig)* aspect•us -ūs *m*
facetious *adj* facet•us -a -um
facetiously *adv* facete
facilitate *tr* facilius reddĕre
facility *s (skill)* facult•as -atis *f; (ease)* facilit•as -atis *f;* **—s** commod•a -orum *npl*
facing *s (archit)* tector•ium -(i)i *n*
facing *adj* adversus *(w. acc)*
facsimile *s* imag•o -inis *f*
fact *s* fact•um -i *n,* res, rei *f;* **as a matter of —** enimvero; **in —** vero, quidem; **the — that** quod
faction *s* facti•o -onis *f; (party)* part•es -ium *fpl*
factory *s* officin•a -ae *f*
faculty *s* facult•as -atis *f; (educ)* ord•o -inis *m*
fade *intr (of colors)* pallēre; *(of strength, etc.)* marcescĕre
fag, fagot *s (sl)* cinaed•us -i *m*
fail *tr (to disappoint)* deficĕre; *(to desert)* deserĕre, destituĕre; **time, voice, lungs — me** me dies, vox, latera deficiunt; **to — a test** probatione cadĕre; **words — me** quid dicam non invenio ‖ *intr* deficĕre; *(educ)* cadĕre; *(com)* decoquĕre
fail *s* **without —** certo, omnino
failing *s (deficiency)* defect•us -ūs *m, (fault)* vit•ium -(i)i *n; (ceasing)* remissi•o -onis *f*
failure *s (of strength, breath, supplies)* defecti•o -onis *f; (lack of success)* offensi•o -onis *f; (com)* ruin•a -ae *f* fortunarum; *(person)* hom•o -inis *m* perditus; *(fault)* vit•ium -(i)i *n*
faint *adj (weary)* fess•us -a -um; *(drooping)* languid•us -a -um; *(sight, etc.)* heb•es -itis; *(sound)* surd•us -a -um; *(colors)* pallid•us -a -um; *(courage)* timid•us -a -um
faint *intr* collabi, animo linqui
faint-hearted *adj* ignav•us -a -um
faintness *s (of impression)* levit•as -atis *f; (of body)* langu•or -oris *m*
fair *adj (handsome)* pul•cher -chra -chrum; *(complexion)* candid•us -a -um; *(hair)* flav•us -a -um; *(weather)* seren•us -a -um; *(wind)* secund•us -a -um; *(impartial)* aequ•us -a -um; *(ability)* mediocr•is -is -e; **— and square** sine fuco ac fallaciis
fair *s* nundin•ae -arum *fpl*
fairly *adv* aeque; *(somewhat)* aliquantulum; *(moderately)* mediocriter
fairness *s (justice)* aequit•as -atis *f; (of complexion)* cand•or -oris *m*
fairy *s (water fairy)* nymph•a -ae *f; (wood fairy)* dry•as -adis *f*

faith *s* fid•es -ei *f; in good* — ex bona fide; **to have — in** credĕre *(w. dat)*
faithful *adj* fid•us -a -um, fidel•is -is -e
faithfully *adv* fideliter
faithfulness *s* fidelit•as -atis *f*
faithless *adj* infidel•is -is -e
faithlessly *adv* perfide
falcon *s* falc•o -onis *m*
fall *s (drop)* cas•us -ūs *m; (by slipping)* laps•us -ūs *m; (autumn)* autumn•us -i *m; (e.g., of a tower)* ruin•a -ae *f; (of a town)* excid•ium -(i)i *n; (decrease)* deminuti•o -onis *f; (moral)* laps•us -ūs *m;* **the —s** desiliens aqu•a -ae *f*
fall *intr* cadĕre; *(several together)* concidĕre; *(to die)* occidĕre; *(to abate)* decrescĕre; *(violently)* corruĕre; *(to occur)* accidĕre, incidĕre; *(by lot)* contingĕre; **to — apart** dilabi; **to — at the feet of** procubare ad pedes *(w. gen);* **to — asleep** in somnum decidĕre; **to — away** desciscĕre; **to — back** recidĕre; *(to retreat)* pedem referre; **to — back on** recurrĕre ad *(w. acc);* **to — down on** *(e.g., the bed)* decidĕre in *(w. acc);* **to — due** cadĕre; **to — for** *(a person)* amore perdi in *(w. acc); (a trick)* falli *(w. abl);* **to — forwards** procidĕre, prolabi; **to — in love with** amare, coepisse amare; **to — into** incidĕre in *(w. acc);* **to — in with** *(to meet)* incidĕre in *(w. acc); (to agree)* congruĕre cum *(w. abl);* **to — into a trap** in plagas incidĕre; **to — into the hands of** in manus *(w. gen)* incidĕre, in potestatem *(w. gen)* devenire; **to — off** *(e.g., a wagon)* decidĕre de *or* ex *(w. abl); (fig)* in deterius mutari; **to — on** *(a certain day)* incidĕre in *(w. acc);* **to fall on the ground** in terram incidĕre; **to — on one's sword** in gladium incumbĕre; **to — on top of** incidĕre super *(w. acc);* **to — out** *(mil)* ordine egredi; **to — out of** excidĕre de *(w. abl);* **to — out with** *(in disagreement)* dissentire ab *(w. abl);* **to — short of** non contingĕre; **to — over** *(to topple over)* cadĕre; *(to stumble over)* pedem offendĕre ad *(w. acc);* **to — short** deficĕre; **to — short of the goal** metam non contingĕre; **to — sick** in morbum incidĕre; **to — to** *(of inheritances, etc.)* obvenire *(w. dat);* **to — to the ground** in terram decidĕre; **to — under** *(to be listed under)* cadĕre sub *(w. acc);* **to — under s.o.'s sway** in ditionem alicujus venire, in potestatem alicujus cadĕre; **to — upon** incidĕre ad *(w. acc); (to assail)* incidĕre in *(w. acc);* **to let —** demittĕre
fallacious *adj* fall•ax -acis
fallacy *s* capti•o -onis *f*
fallible *adj* errori obnoxi•us -a -um
fallow *adj (land)* noval•is -is -e; **to lie —** cessare
false *adj* fals•us -a -um; *(counterfeit)* adulterin•us -a -um
falsehood *s* comment•um -i *n*
falsely *adv* falso
falsify *tr (documents)* corrumpĕre; *(to tamper with)* vitiare
falsity *s* fals•um -i *n*
falter *intr (to stammer)* haesitare; *(to totter)* titubare
falteringly *adv* titubanter
fame *s* fam•a -ae *f,* clarit•as -atis *f*
famed *adj* clar•us -a -um
familiar *adj* **(with)** familiar•is -is -e *(w. dat); (well known)* not•us -a -um; **to be on — terms with** familiariter uti *(w. abl)*
familiarity *s* familiarit•as -atis *f;* **to be on terms of — with** familiariter uti *(w. abl)*
familiarize *tr* **(with)** assuefacĕre *(w. dat)*
family *s* famili•a -ae *f;* **— on the father's (mother's) side** paternum (maternum) gen•us -eris *n;* **to come from a good —** honesto loco nat•us -a -um esse
family *adj* familiar•is -is -e; **— inheritance** heredit•as -atis *f* gentilica; **— name** gentile nom•en -inis *n;* **— secrets** arcan•a -orum *npl* domūs; **— tree** gen•us -eris *n*
famine *s* fam•es -is *f*
famished *adj* famelic•us -a -um
famous *adj* clar•us -a -um
famously *adv* insigniter
fan *s* flabell•um -i *n; (admirer)* faut•or -oris *m; (winnowing)* vann•us -i *m*
fan *tr* ventilare; *(fire)* accendĕre; *(fig)* excitare
fanatic *adj* fanatic•us -a -um
fanaticism *s* fur•or -oris *m* religiosus
fancied *adj* fict•us -a -um
fanciful *adj* commentici•us -a -um
fancy *s* imaginati•o -onis *f; (caprice)* libid•o -inis *f; (liking)* prolub•ium -(i)i *n*
fancy *tr* imaginari
fang *s* den-s -tis *m*
fantastic *adj (unreal)* van•us -a -um; *(wonderful)* mir•us -a -um
far *adj* longinqu•us -a -um; **on the — side of the Po** ultra Padum
far *adv* procul; *(of degree)* longe; **as — as** quantum, quatenus; *(up to)* tenus *(always after the governed word) (w. abl or gen);* **as — as the neck** cervicibus tenus; **by —** longe, multo; **by — the wealthiest state** longe opulentissima civit•as -atis *f;* **— away** procul; **— and near** longe lateque; **— be it from me to say** equidem dicĕre nolim; **— from it!** minime!; **— off** procul; **— otherwise** longe aliter; **how —** quoad, quousque; **so —** hactenus; **thus —** hactenus; **to be — away (from)** longe abesse (ab + *abl);* **to be very — from the truth** longissime abesse a vero

farce *s (lit & fig)* mim•us -i *m*
farcical *adj* mimic•us -a -um
farcically *adv* mimice
fare *s (food)* vict•us -ūs *m; (money)* vectur•a -ae *f; (for sea travel)* nav•ium -(i)i *n; (passenger)* vect•or -oris *m*
fare *intr* agĕre, se habēre
farewell *interj* vale! *(pl:* valete!)
far-fetched *adj* conquisit•us -a -um
far-flung *adj* late pat•ens -entis
farm *s* fund•us -i *m*
farm *tr (to till)* arare, colĕre; *(taxes)* redimĕre; **to — out** locare
farmer *s* agricol•a -ae *m*
farm house *s* vill•a -ae *f* (rustica)
farming *s* agricultur•a -ae *f*
farm worker *s* colon•us -i *m*
farsighted *adj* provid•us -a -um
farther *adj* ulter•ior -ior -ius
farther *adv* longius, ulterius; **no — than** non ultra quam; **to advance —** procedĕre ulterius
farthermost *adj* ultim•us -a -um
farthest *adj* ultim•us -a -um
fasces *spl* fasc•es -ium *fpl*
fascinate *tr* capĕre
fascinating *adj* mirific•us -a -um
fascination *s* blanditi•a -ae *f*
fashion *s* mod•us -i *m,* mo•s -ris *m;* **to be in —** more fieri; **to go out of —** obsolescĕre
fashion *tr* fabricare; *(to form a figure of)* effingĕre
fashionable *adj* eleg•ans -antis; **it is —** moris est
fashionably *adv* ad morem
fast *adj (swift)* cel•er -eris -ere; *(firm)* firm•us -a -um; *(tight)* astrict•us -a -um; *(shut)* occlus•us -a -um; *(color)* stabil•is -is -e; *(talk)* expedit•us -a -um
fast *adv (swiftly)* celeriter; *(firmly)* firmiter; **to be — asleep** arte dormire
fast *s* jejun•ium -(i)i *n;* **to break the —** jejunium solvĕre; **to keep the —** jejunium servare
fast *intr* jejunare, cibo abstinēre
fasten *tr* affigĕre, astringĕre; *(to tie)* ligare; **to — down** defigĕre; **to — to** *(w. nails, rivets)* affigĕre *(w. dat or* ad + *acc); (by tying)* annectĕre, illigare *(w. dat or* ad + *acc);* **to — together** *(w. nails, etc.)* configĕre; *(by tying)* connectĕre, colligare ‖ *intr* **to — upon** arripĕre
fastener *s (clip)* fibul•a -ae *f*
fastening *s* vincul•um -i *n*
fastidious *adj* fastidios•us -a -um
fastidiously *adv* fastidiose
fasting *s* jejun•ium -(i)i *n*
fasting *adj* abstin•ax -acis
fat *adj* pingu•is -is -e; **to get —** pinguescĕre
fat *s* ad•eps -ipis *mf*
fatal *adj* fatal•is -is -e, letal•is -is -e
fatality *s* cas•us -ūs *m* fatalis
fatally *adv* fataliter
fate *s* fat•um -i *n,* sor•s -tis *f*
fated *adj* fatal•is -is -e
fateful *adj* fatal•is -is -e
Fates *spl* Parc•ae -arum *fpl*
father *s* pa•ter -tris *m;* **— of the family** paterfamilias *(gen:* patrisfamilias) *m;* **on the —'s side** patri•us -a -um
fatherhood *s* paternit•as -atis *f*
father-in-law *s* soc•er -eri *m*
fatherless *adj* orb•us -a -um
fatherly *adj* patern•us -a -um
fathom *s* uln•a -ae *f*
fathom *tr* penitus cognosĕre
fathomless *adj* profund•us -a -um
fatigue *s* (de)fatigati•o -onis *f*
fatigue *tr* (de)fatigare
fatigued *adj* (de)fatigat•us -a -um
fatten *tr* saginare ‖ *intr* **to — up** pinguescĕre
fatty *adj* pingu•is -is -e; **all — substances** omnia quae adipis naturam habent
fatuous *adj* fatu•us -a -um
fault *s* culp•a -ae *f,* delict•um -i *n;* **I am at —** in culpā sum, penes me culpa est; **to be at —** *(leg)* in noxā esse; **to find — with** vituperare
faultless *adj* inte•ger -gra -grum; *(without blemish)* emendat•us -a -um
faultlessly *adv* emendate
faulty *adj* vitios•us -a -um; *(having errors)* mendos•us -a -um
faun *s* faun•us -i *m*
favor *s* fav•or -oris *m; (good will of a party or nation)* grati•a -ae *f; (good turn)* benefic•ium -(i)i *n; (a favor done)* grati•a -ae *f;* **to ask s.o. a —** gratiam ab aliquo petĕre; **to be in — of** favēre *(w. dat);* **to be in — with s.o.** cum aliquo in gratiā esse; **to do s.o a —** gratum alicui facĕre; **to do s.o. a bigger —** gratius alicui facĕre; **to return s.o. a —** gratiam alicui referre; **to restore s.o. to —** aliquem in gratiam restituĕre
favor *tr* favēre *(w. dat),* secundare; **to — severer measures** asperiora suadēre
favorable *adj* prosper•us -a -um; *(wind, circumstances, auspices, gods)* secund•us -a -um; *(suitable)* idone•us -a -um
favorably *adv* benigne; **to be — disposed toward s.o.** bono animo esse in aliquem; **to hear —** benigne audire
favored *adj* grat•us -a -um
favorite *adj* dilect•us -a -um
favorite *s* delici•ae -arum *fpl*
favoritism *s* iniquit•as -atis *f*
fawn *s* hinnule•us -i *m*
fawn *intr* **to — on** adulari
fawning *adj* bland•us -a -um
fear *s* met•us -ūs *m; (timidity, as a variety of* metus) tim•or -oris *m;* **to be in —** in metu esse; **to be inspired with —** metum capĕre
fear *tr & intr* metuĕre, timēre

fearful *adj* **(of)** timid•us -a -um *(w. gen or* ad + *acc); (terrible)* terribil•is -is -e, dir•us -a -um
fearless *adj* impavidu•s -a -um
fearlessly *adv* impavide, intrepide
feasibility *s* possibilit•as -atis *f*
feasible *adj* possibil•is -is -e
feast *s* epul•ae -arum *fpl; (religious)* di•es -ei *m* festus
feast *tr* pascĕre; **to — one's eyes on** oculos pascĕre *(w. abl)* ‖ *intr* epulari
feat *s* facin•us -oris *n*; **— of arms** facinus *n* militare; **—s** re•s -rum *fpl* gestae
feather *s* penn•a -ae *f; (downy)* plum•a -ae *f*
feather *tr* **to — one's nest** opes accumulare
feathered *adj* pennat•us -a -um
feathery *adj* plumos•us -a -um
feature *s* lineament•um -i *n; (fig)* propri-et•as -atis *f*
February *s* Februar•ius -(i)i *m or* mens•is -is *m* Februarius; **on the first of —** Kalendis Februariis
federal *adj* foederat•us -a -um
federalize *tr* confoederare
federation *s* consociati•o -onis *f*
fee *s* merc•es -edis *f; (for tuition)* Minerv•al -alis *n; (for membership)* honorar•ium -(i)i *n*
feeble *adj* infirm•us -a -um; *(senses, impression made)* heb•es -etis
feebly *adv* infirme
feed *tr* pascĕre; *(to nourish)* alĕre; *(of streams, etc.)* servire *(w. dat)* ‖ *intr* **(on)** pasci *(w. abl)*
feed *s* pabul•um -i *n*
feeding *s* pasti•o -onis *f*
feel *tr (hunger, pain, heat, cold, etc.)* sentire; *(with hands)* tentare; **to — compassion for** misereri *(w. gen);* **to — grief** dolēre; **to — one's way** viam tentare; *(fig)* caute et cogitate rem tractare; **to — pain** dolore affici; **to — pity for** misereri *(w. gen);* **to — the pulse** *(med)* pulsum venarum attingĕre, venas tentare ‖ *intr* **to — good** se bene habēre; **to — happy** gaudēre; **to — sad** maest•us -a -um esse
feel *s* tact•us -ūs *m*
feeler *s* experiment•um -i *n;* **to send out a — to** tentare
feeling *s (touch, sensation)* tact•us -ūs *m; (sensibility)* sens•us -ūs *m; (emotion)* affect•us -ūs *m; (taste)* judic•ium -(i)i *n; (compassion)* misericordi•a -ae *f;* **to hurt s.o.'s —s** aliquem offendĕre
feign *tr* fingĕre, dissimulare
feint *s* simulati•o -onis *f*
felicitous *adj* fel•ix -icis
felicity *s* felicit•as -atis *f*
feline *adj* felin•us -a -um
fell *adj* dir•us -a -um
fell *tr (trees)* caedĕre; *(person)* sternĕre
fellow *s (companion)* soc•ius -(i)i *m; (coll)* hom•o -inis *m;* **my good —, what have you there?** mi homo, quid istuc est?; **young —** adulescentul•us -i *m*
fellow citizen *s* civ•is -is *mf*
fellow countryman *s* civ•is -is *m*
fellow creature *s* hom•o -inis *m*
fellow man *s* alt•er -erius *m*
fellow member *s* sodal•is -is *mf*
fellow passenger *s* convect•or -oris *m*
fellow soldier *s* commilit•o -onis *m*
fellow student *s* condiscipul•us -i *m*, condiscipul•a -ae *f*
fellowship *s* sodalit•as -atis *f; (award)* stipend•ium -(i)i *n* in sumptūs studiosorum
fellow townsman *s* munic•eps -ipis *m*
felon *s* scelest•us -i *m*
felonious *adj* scelest•us -a -um
felony *s* scel•us -eris *n*
felt *adj* coact•us -a -um
felt *s* coact•a -orum *npl*
female *adj* muliebr•is -is -e
female *s* muli•er -eris *f*
feminine *adj* muliebr•is -is -e, femin•eus -a -um; *(gram)* feminin•us -a -um
fence *s* saep•es -is *f*
fence *tr* saepire; **to — off** saepire ‖ *intr* batuĕre
fencing *s* gladii ar•s -tis *f*
fend *tr* **to — off** arcēre ‖ *intr* **to — for oneself** sibi consulĕre
ferment *s* ferment•um -i *n; (fig)* aest•us -ūs *m*
ferment *tr* fermentare; *(fig)* excitare ‖ *intr* fermentari; *(fig)* fervēre
fermentation *s* fermentati•o -onis *f*
fern *s* fil•ix -icis *f*
ferocious *adj* truculent•us -a -um
ferociously *adv* truculente
ferocity *s* saeviti•a -ae *f*
ferret *tr* **to — out** eruĕre
ferry *s* traject•us -ūs *m*
ferry *tr* trajicĕre
ferryboat *s* cymb•a -ae *f*
ferryman *s* portit•or -oris *m*
fertile *adj* fertil•is -is -e
fertility *s* fertilit•as -atis *f*
fertilize *tr* laetificare
fertilizer *s* laetam•en -inis *n*
fervent *adj* ard•ens -entis
fervently *adv* ardenter
fervid *adj* fervid•us -a -um
fervidly *adv* fervide
fervor *s* ferv•or -oris *m*
fester *intr* suppurare
festival *s* fest•um -i *n*
festive *adj* festiv•us -a -um
festivity *s (celebration)* solemn•ia -ium *npl; (gaiety)* festivit•as -atis *f*
festoon *s* sert•um -i *n*
fetch *tr (to summon)* arcessĕre; *(to go to get)* petĕre

fetid *adj* foetid•us -a -um
fetter *s* comp•es -edis *m*
fetter *tr* compedes imjicĕre *(w. dat); (fig)* impedire
feud *s* simult•as -atis *f*
fever *s* febr•is -is *f;* **high —** ardens febris *f;* **slight —** febricul•a -ae *f;* **to have** *(or* **to run) a —** febricitare
feverish *adj* febriculos•us -a -um
few *adj* pauc•i -ae -a; **a —** aliquot *(indecl);* **in a — words** paucis
fiasco *s* calamit•as -atis *f*
fiber *s* fibr•a -ae *f*
fibrous *adj* fibrat•us -a -um
fickle *adj* mobil•is -is -e
fickleness *s* mobilit•as -atis *f*
fiction *s* ficti•o -onis *f*
fictitious *adj* fict•us -a -um
fictitiously *adv* ficte
fiddle *s* fid•es -ium *fpl*
fiddle *intr* fidibus canĕre
fiddler *s* fidic•en -inis *m*
fidelity *s* fidelit•as -atis *f*
fidget *intr* trepidare
fidgety *adj* inquiet•us -a -um
field *s* a•ger -gri *m; (plowed)* arv•um -i *n; (undeveloped)* camp•us -i *m; (sports)* are•a -ae *f; (mil)* aci•es -ei *f; (of studies)* disciplin•a -ae *f*
fieldpiece *s* torment•um -i *n*
fiend *s* diabol•us -i *m*
fiendish *adj* diabolic•us -a -um
fierce *adj* atr•ox -ocis; *(intensive)* fer•ox ocis
fiercely *adv* atrociter; ferociter
fierceness *s* atrocit•as -atis *f;* ferocit•as -atis *f*
fiery *adj* igne•us -a -um; *(fig)* ard•ens -entis
fife *s* tibi•a -ae *f*
fifteen *adj* quindecim *(indecl);* **— times** quindecies
fifteenth *adj* quint•us decim•us -a -um
fifth *adj* quint•us -a -um; **for the — time** quinto
fifth *s* quinta par•s -tis *f*
fiftieth *adj* quinquagesim•us -a -um
fifty *adj* quinquaginta *(indecl)*
fig *s* fic•us -i *f*
fight *s* pugn•a -ae *f; (battle)* proel•ium -(i)i *n; (brawl)* rix•a -ae *f; (boxing)* pugilati•o -onis *f*
fight *tr* pugnare cum *(w. abl)* ‖ *intr* pugnare; *(to brawl)* rixari; *(to box)* pugilari; *(w. sword)* digladiari; **to — it out** depugnare; **to — hand to hand** cominus pugnare
figment *s* **— of the imagination** figment•um -i *n*
figurative *adj* translat•us -a -um
figuratively *adv* per translationem
figure *s* figur•a -ae *f; (any form)* form•a -ae *f; (in a painting)* imag•o -inis *f;* **to cut a —** *(to play a part)* partes agĕre
figure *tr (to think)* putare; **to — out** excogitare ‖ *intr* **to — on** niti *(w. abl)*
figured *adj (adorned w. figures)* sigillat•us -a -um
figure of speech *s* figur•a -ae *f* orationis
filament *s* fil•um -i *n*
filbert *s* nu•x -cis *f* avellana
file *s (for iron)* lim•a -ae *f; (for woodwork)* scobin•a -ae *f; (for papers)* scap•us -i *m; (cabinet)* scrin•ium -(i)i *n; (row)* ord•o -inis *m;* **in single —** singul•i -ae -a per ordinem
filial *adj* pi•us -a -um
filigree *s* diatret•a -orum *npl*
filings *spl* scob•is -is *f*
fill *s* **to have one's —** se replēre
fill *tr* implēre; *(office)* fungi *(w. abl);* **to — up** complēre, explēre ‖ *intr* **to — up on** se implēre *(w. abl)*
fillip *s* talitr•um -i *n*
filly *s* equul•a -ae *f*
film *s* membranul•a -ae *f*
filmy *adj* membranace•us -a -um; *(fig)* caliginos•us -a -um
filter *s* col•um -i *n*
filter *tr* percolare ‖ *intr* percolari
filtering *s* percolati•o -onis *f*
filth *s* sord•es -ium *fpl*
filthiness *s* squal•or -oris *m; (fig)* obscenit•as -atis *f*
filthy *adj* sordid•us -a -um; *(fig)* obscen•us -a -um
filtration *s* percolati•o -onis *f*
fin *s* pinn•a -ae *f*
final *adj* ultim•us -a -um
finally *adv* denique, postremo
finance *s (private)* res, rei *f* familiaris; *(public)* rati•o -onis *f* aeraria
finance *tr* faenerare
financial *adj* pecuniari•us -a -um
find *tr* invenire, reperire; *(to hit upon)* offendĕre; **to — out** cognoscĕre
finder *s* repert•or -oris *m*
findings *spl* compert•a -orum *npl*
fine *adj (thin)* tenu•is -is -e; *(opp. of coarse)* subtil•is -is -e; *(superior)* perbon•us -a -um; *(nice)* bell•us -a -um; *(weather)* seren•us -a -um; **— arts** art•es -ium *fpl* elegantiores *(or* ingenuae); **to feel —** se bene habēre
fine *s* mul(c)t•a -ae *f*
fine *tr* mul(c)tare
finery *s* munditi•ae -arum *fpl*
finesse *s* arguti•ae -arum *fpl*
finger *s* digit•us -i *m; (of glove)* digital•e -is *n;* **index —** index digitus *m;* **little —** minimus digitus *m;* **middle —** medius digitus *m; (as an obscene gesture)* digitus *m* inpudicus *or* infamis; **ring —** minimo proximus digitus *m;* **to point the — at** digitum intendĕre ad *(w. acc);* **to snap the —s** digitis concrepare

finger *tr* tractare; *(to inform on)* deferre; *(mus)* pulsare
fingernail *s* ungu•is -is *m*
fingertip *s* summus digit•us -i *m*
finicky *adj* fastidios•us -a -um; **— appetite** fastid•ium -(i)i *n*
finish *s* fin•is -is *m; (in art)* perfecti•o -onis *f; (polish)* politur•a -ae *f*
finish *tr* conficĕre; *(to put an end to)* terminare; **to — off** conficĕre; *(to use up)* consumĕre; *(to destroy)* perdĕre; *(to kill)* occidĕre; **to — speaking** sermonem finire ‖ *intr* desinĕre; **to add the —ing touch to** ultimam manum adferre *(w. dat)*
finite *adj* finit•us -a -um
fire *s* ign•is -is *m; (conflagration)* incend•ium -(i)i *n; (of artillery)* conject•us -ūs *m; (fig)* ard•or -oris *m;* **by — and sword** ferro ignique; **on —** flagr•ans -antis; **to be on —** ardēre; **to catch —** ignem concipĕre; **to set on —** incendĕre
fire *tr* accendĕre; *(missile)* conjicĕre
fire alarm *s* sign•um -i *n* monitorium incendii
firebrand *s* fa•x -cis *f*
fire chief *s* praefect•us -i *m* vigilum
fire engine *s* siph•o -onis *m*
fireman *s* vig•il -is *m*
fireplace *s* foc•us -i *m*
fireproof *adj* ignibus impervi•us -a -um
fireside *s* foc•us -i *m*
firewood *s* lign•um -i *n*
firm *adj* firm•us -a -um; *(foundation)* stabil•is •is -e; **to stand —** perstare
firm *s (com)* societ•as -atis *f*
firmament *s* cael•um -i *n*
firmly *adv* firme, firmiter; *(w. firm hold)* tenaciter
firmness *s* firmit•as -atis *f*
first *adj* prim•us -a -um; *(of two)* pri•or -or -us; **among the —** in primis
first *adv* primum; **at —** primo; **— of all** imprimis
first aid *s* prima curati•o -onis *f*
firstborn *adj* primogenit•us -a -um
first fruits *spl* primiti•ae -arum *fpl*
fiscal *adj* aerari•us -a -um; *(belonging to the emperor's finances)* fiscal•is -is -e
fish *s* pisc•is -is *m;* **little —** *(lit & fig)* piscicul•us -i *m*
fish *tr* piscari; **to — for** *(fig)* expiscari
fisherman *s* piscat•or -oris *m*
fishhook *s* ham•us -i *m*
fishing *s* piscat•us -ūs *m*
fishing line *s* lin•um -i *n*
fishing rod *s* arund•o -inis *f*
fish market *s* for•um -i *n* piscarium
fish pond *s* piscin•a -ae *f*
fishy *adj* pisculent•us -a -um; *(fig)* suspicios•us -a -um
fissure *s* fissur•a -ae *f*
fist *s* pugn•us -i *m;* **to make a —** pugnum facĕre
fistfight *s* **to have a —** pugnis certare
fit *s (of anger, etc.)* impet•us -ūs *m;* **a good —** vestiment•um -i *n* bene factum; **by — and starts** carptim; **fainting —** defecti•o -onis *f;* **—s** morb•us -i *m* comitialis; **to have the —s** *(fig)* delirare; *(in anger)* furĕre
fit *adj* **(for)** apt•us -a -um, idone•us -a -um *(w. dat); (healthy)* san•us -a -um
fit *tr* accommodare; *(to apply)* applicare; **to — out** instruĕre, ornare ‖ *intr* convenire; **to — in with** congruĕre cum *(w. abl);* **to — together** inter se cohaerēre
fitful *adj (sleep)* inquiet•us -a -um
fitly *adv* apte
fitness *s* convenienti•a -ae *f; (of persons)* habilit•as -atis *f*
fitting *adj* dec•ens -entis; **it is —** convenit, decet
five *adj* quinque *(indecl); (distributives)* quin•i -ae -a, *modifying nouns which have no singular, e.g.,* **five camps** quina castr•a -orum *npl;* **— times** quinquies; **— years** quinquenn•ium -(i)i *n*
fix *s* **a quick —** praesens remed•ium -(i)i *n;* **to be in a —** *(coll)* in angustiis versari
fix *tr (to repair)* reficĕre, corrigĕre; *(to patch)* resarcire; *(to arrange)* disponĕre; *(to adjust)* accommodare; *(meals)* parare; *(to fasten)* figĕre; *(the eyes)* intendĕre; *(time)* dicĕre; *(to avenge)* ulcisci ‖ *intr* **to — upon** inhaerēre *(w. dat)*
fixed *adj (day, boundaries)* cert•us -a -um; **— resolve** men•s -tis *f* solida; **— stars** stell•ae -arum *fpl* inerrantes; **— upon** *(intent upon)* intent•us -a -um *(w. dat)*
fixture *s* affix•um -i *n*
fizz *intr* sibilare
flabbiness *s* molliti•a -ae *f*
flabby *adj* flacc•us -a -um
flaccid *adj* flaccid•us -a -um
flag *s* vexill•um -i *n*
flag *tr* signo indicare ‖ *intr* languescĕre; *(to lose interest)* refrigescĕre
flagrant *adj* nefari•us -a -um
flagship *s* nav•is -is *f* praetoria
flail *s* pertic•a -ae *f*
flail *tr* fustibus cudĕre
flake *s* squam•a -ae *f;* **snow —s** plumeae niv•es -ium *fpl*
flaky *adj (sl)* delir•us -a -um
flame *s* flamm•a -ae *f*
flame *intr* flammare; **to — up** scintillare; *(fig)* exardescĕre
flank *s (of animal)* il•ia -ium *npl; (mil)* lat•us -eris *n;* **on the —** a latere
flank *tr* tegĕre latus *(w. gen)*
flap *s (of dress)* lacini•a -ae *f*
flap *tr* plaudĕre *(w. abl)* ‖ *intr (to hang loosely)* fluitare

flare *s* fulg•or -oris *m; (torch)* fa•x -cis *f*
flare *intr (to blaze)* coruscare; **to — up** *(of diseases)* urgēre; *(of anger, passions)* exardescĕre
flash *s* fulg•or -oris *m;* **— of lightning** ict•us -ūs *m* fulminis
flash *intr* fulgēre, coruscare
flashy *adj* fucat•us -a -um
flask *s* laguncul•a -ae *f*
flat *adj (level)* plan•us -a -um; *(not mountainous)* campes•ter -tris -tre; *(on one's back)* supin•us -a -um; *(on one's face)* pron•us -a -um; *(insipid)* vapid•us -a -um; **to fall —** *(e.g., of a play, speech)* frigēre
flatfooted *adj* plaut•us -a -um
flatly *adv* palam
flatness *s* planiti•es -ei *f*
flatten *tr* complanare; *(to prostrate)* prosternĕre
flatter *tr* blandiri
flatterer *s* adulat•or -oris *m*
flattering *adj* bland•us -a -um
flatulence *s* inflati•o -onis *f*
flaunt *tr* jactare
flaunting *adj* glorios•us -a -um
flaunting *s* jactati•o -onis *f*
flavor *s* sap•or -oris *m; (substance)* condiment•um -i *n*
flavor *tr* condire
flaw *s (defect)* vit•ium -(i)i *n; (chink)* rimul•a -ae *f*
flawless *adj* sine vitio
flax *s* lin•um -i *n*
flaxen *adj* line•us -a -um
flay *tr* deglubare
flea *s* pul•ex -icis *m*
flea market *s* for•um -i *n* rerum venalium
fleck *s* macul•a -ae *f*
fledgling *s* pull•us -i *m*
flee *tr* effugĕre ‖ *intr* fugĕre; **to — to** confugĕre ad *or* in *(w. acc)*
fleece *s* vell•us -eris *n*
fleece *tr (fig)* spoliare
fleecy *adj* lanig•er -era -erum
fleet *s* class•is -is *f*
fleet *adj* cel•er -eris -ere
fleet-footed *adj* celerip•es -edis
fleeting *adj* fug•ax -acis
flesh *s* car•o -nis *f;* **in the —** viv•us -a -um
flesh wound *s* car•o -nis *f* vulnerata
fleshy *adj* corpore•us -a -um; *(fat)* corpulent•us -a -um
flexibility *s* flexibilit•as -atis *f; (fig)* molliti•es -ei *f*
flexible *adj (lit & fig)* flexibil•is -is -e
flick *s* crepit•us -ūs *m; (of the finger)* talitr•um -i *n*
flick *tr* **to — away** excutĕre
flicker *intr (of a flame)* trepidare
flickering *adj* tremul•us -a -um; **— lamps** occidentes lucern•ae -arum *fpl*
flier *s* libell•us -i *m*
flight *s (flying)* volat•us -ūs *m; (escape)* effug•ium -(i)i *n; (covey)* gre•x -gis *m;* **— of steps** gradati•o -onis *f;* **to put to —** fugare; **to take to —** terga vertĕre
flighty *adj* lev•is -is -e
flimsy *adj* praetenu•is -is -e; *(trivial)* frivol•us -a -um
flinch *intr* tergiversari; *(to start)* absilire
fling *s* jact•us -ūs *m*
fling *tr* conjicĕre; **to — away** abjicĕre; **to — down** dejicĕre; **to — open** rejicĕre, patefacĕre
flint *s* sil•ex -icis *mf*
flinty *adj* silice•us -a -um
flippancy *s* protervit•as -atis *f*
flippant *adj* prompt•us -a -um atque lev•is -is -e
flippantly *adv* temere ac leviter
flirt *s* lup•us -i *m,* lup•a -ae *f*
flirt *intr* **to — with** *(a person)* subblandiri *(w. dat); (an idea)* ludĕre cum *(w. abl)*
flirtation *s* leves amor•es -um *mpl*
flit *intr* volitare
float *s (raft)* rat•es -is *f; (on fishing line)* cort•ex -icis *m*
float *tr (to launch)* deducĕre ‖ *intr* fluitare; *(in the air)* volitare
flock *s* gre•x -gis *m;* **in —s** gregatim
flock *intr* **to — around** circumfluĕre *(w. acc);* **to — to** affluĕre ad *(w. acc);* **to — together** congregari
floe *s* fragment•um -i *n* glaciei
flog *tr* verberare
flogging *s* verberati•o -onis *f;* **to get a —** vapulare
flood *s (deluge)* diluv•ium -(i)i *n; (of tears, words)* flum•en -inis *n;* **the Flood** inundanti•a -ae *f* terrarum
flood *tr (lit & fig)* inundare ‖ *intr* inundare
floodgates *spl* cataract•ae -arum *fpl;* **to open the — of** *(fig)* effundĕre habenas *(w. gen)*
floodtide *s* access•us -ūs *m*
floor *s (ground)* sol•um -i *n; (paved)* paviment•um -i *n; (story)* tabulat•um -i *n;* **to lay the —** pavimentum facĕre; *(on an upper story)* contabulare; **to throw on the —** in pavimentum projicĕre
floor *tr (to knock down)* sternĕre
flooring *s* contabulati•o -onis *f*
floral *adj* flore•us -a -um
flotilla *s* classicul•a -ae *f*
flounce *s* instit•a -ae *f*
flounder *s (fish)* pass•er -eris *m*
flounder *intr* volutari; *(in speech)* haesitare
flour *s* farin•a -ae *f; (finest)* poll•en -inis *m*
flourish *s (mus)* taratantara *n (indecl)*
flourish *tr* vibrare; *(to sound)* canĕre ‖ *intr* florēre; *(mus)* praeludĕre
flour mill *s* pistrin•a -ae *f*
flout *tr (to scorn)* spernĕre; *(to mock)* deridēre
flow *s* fluxi•o -onis *f; (of the tide)* access•us -ūs *m; (of words)* flum•en -inis *n*

flow *intr* fluĕre; **to — into** influĕre in *(w. acc)*; **to — past** praeterfluĕre
flower *s (lit & fig)* flo•s -ris *m*
flower *intr* florescĕre
flower bed *s* are•a -ae *f*
flowery *adj* florid•us -a -um
fluctuate *intr* jactari, se jactare
fluctuation *s* mutati•o -onis *f*
flue *s* cunicul•us -i *m* fornacis
fluency *s* volubilit•as -atis *f*
fluent *adj* volubil•is -is -e
fluently *adv* volubiliter
fluid *adj* fluid•us -a -um
fluid *s* um•or -oris *m*
fluke *s (of anchor)* den•s -tis *m; (luck)* fortuit•um -i *n*
flurry *s* commoti•o -onis *f;* **— of activity** festinati•o -onis *f*
flush *s (blush)* rub•or -oris *m; (onrush)* impet•us -ūs *m*
flush *tr (to purge)* proluĕre; **to — out** *(game)* excitare ‖ *intr* erubescĕre
fluster *tr* turbare, inquietare
flute *s* tibi•a -ae *f; (archit)* stri•a -ae *f*
fluting *s (archit)* striatur•a -ae *f*
flutist *s* tibic•en -inis *m*
flutter *s (of wings)* plaus•us -ūs *m; (bustle)* festinati•o -onis *f; (vibration)* trem•or -oris *m; (of the heart)* palpitati•o -onis *f*
flutter *intr (of a heart)* palpitare; *(of a bird)* volitare; *(w. alarm)* trepidare
flux *s* flux•us -ūs *m;* **to be in a state of —** fluĕre
fly *s* musc•a -ae *f*
fly *intr* volare; *(to flee)* fugĕre; **to — apart** dissilire; **to — away** *or* **off** avolare; **to — in the face of** lacessĕre; **to — open** dissilire, patēre; **to — out** evolare, provolare; **to — under** subtervolare; **to — up** subvolare
flying *adj* volatil•is -is -e
flying *s* volat•us -ūs *m*
foal *s* pull•us -i *m; (of horse)* equul•us -i *m; (of asses)* asell•us -i *m*
foal *tr & intr* parĕre
foam *s* spum•a -ae *f*
foam *intr* spumare; *(of sea)* aestuare
foaming *adj* spum•ans -antis
foamy *adj* spume•us -a -um
focus *tr* **to — attention** *(or* **mind)** **on** animum attendĕre ad *(w. acc)*
fodder *s* pabul•um -i *n*
foe *s (public)* host•is -is *m; (private)* inimic•us -i *m,* inimic•a -ae *f*
fog *s* nebul•a -ae *f*
foggy *adj* nebulos•us -a -um
foible *s* vit•ium -(i)i *n*
foil *s (for fencing)* rud•is -is *f; (leaf of metal)* lamin•a -ae *f; (very thin)* bracte•a -ae *f; (fig)* umbr•a -ae *f*
foil *tr* eludĕre, frustrari
fold *s* sin•us -ūs *m; (wrinkle)* rug•a -ae *f; (for sheep; the Church)* ovil•e -is *n*
fold *tr* plicare; **to — up** complicare
foliage *s* fron•s -dis *f*
folio *s* li•ber -bri *m* maximae formae
folk *s* homin•es -um *mpl;* **common —** vulg•us -i *n,* pleb•s -is *f*
folk music *s* music•a -ae *f* vulgaris
folk song *s* carm•en -inis *n* vulgare
follow *tr* sequi; *(closely)* instare *(w. dat),* assequi; *(immediately after)* subsequi; *(instructions)* parēre *(w. dat); (to understand)* intellegĕre; **to — the calling of a merchant, banker, soothsayer** mercaturam, argentarium, haruspicinam facĕre; **to — up** *(to the end)* persequi ‖ *intr* insequi; **it —s that** sequitur ut; **to — up on** persequi; **to — upon** supervenire *(w. dat)*
follower *s* sectat•or -oris *m; (hanger-on)* assec(u)l•a -ae *mf*
following *s (attendants)* comitat•us -ūs *m; (pol)* facti•o -onis *f*
following *adj* sequ•ens -entis, proxim•us -a -um, poster•us -a -um
folly *s* stultiti•a -ae *f*
foment *tr* fovēre
fond *adj* **(of)** am•ans -antis *(w. gen),* studios•us -a -um *(w. gen);* **to be — of** amare
fondle *tr* mulcēre, fovēre
fondly *adv* amanter
fondness *s* **(for)** *(persons, country)* carit•as -atis *f* (erga *w. acc);* **(for)** *(things)* stud•ium -(i)i *n (w. gen)*
food *s* cib•us -i *m*
fool *s* stult•us -i *m,* fatu•us -i *m;* **to make a — of** ludificare; **to make a — of oneself** fatuari, ineptire
fool *tr* fallĕre
foolhardily *adv* temere
foolhardy *adj* temerari•us -a -um
foolish *adj* stult•us -a -um
foolishly *adv* stulte
foot *s (of men, animals, tables, chairs)* pe•s -dis *m; (of mountain)* rad•ix -icis *m; (of pillar)* bas•is -is *f;* **on —** pedibus; **to set — in** pedem ponĕre in *(w. abl);* **to tread under —** calcare
foot *tr* **to — a bill** impensam sumĕre
football *s* pil•a -ae *f* pedalis
foothold *s* grad•us -ūs *m* stabilis
footing *s* grad•us -ūs *m;* **on an equal —** ex aequo; **to be on an equal — with** in aequo stare *(w. dat);* **to get one's —** locum capĕre; **to lose one's —** de gradu labi
footpath *s* semit•a -ae *f*
footprint *s* vestig•ium -(i)i *n*
footrace *s* curs•us -ūs *m*
foot soldier *s* ped•es -itis *m*
footstool *s* scabell•um -i *n*
footwear *s* calceament•um -i *n*
fop *s* hom•o -inis *m* delicatus
foppish *adj* delicat•us -a -um

for *prep (extent of time or space) render by acc; (price) render by gen or abl; (on behalf of; in place of; instead of; in proportion to, consideration of)* pro *(w. abl); (purpose)* ad *(w. acc); (cause)* causā *(w. gen)(always after the governed word),* ob *(w. acc); (after negatives)* prae *(w. abl); (toward)* erga *(w. acc); (out of, for, e.g., joy, fear)* prae *(w. abl); (to denote the appointment of a definite time)* in *(w. acc);* **as for** quod attinet ad *(w. acc);* **— all that** nec eo setius; **— nothing** gratis, gratuito; *(in vain)* frustra; **for the last three months** in ternos novissimos menses; **— the rest of the year** in reliquum anni tempus; **— these reasons** his de causis; **good — nothing** ad nullam rem util•is -is -e; **to be —** *(to be in favor of)* studēre *(w. dat),* favēre *(w. dat);* **to live — the day** in diem vivěre; **what —?** quare?
for *conj (generally first in a clause)* nam, siquidem, *(never first)* enim
forage *s* pabul•um -i *n*
forage *intr* pabulari
foray *s* incursi•o -onis *f*
forbear *intr* desistěre
forbearance *s* patienti•a -ae *f*
forbid *tr* vetare, prohibēre
forbidding *adj* odios•us -a -um
force *s* vis *(acc:* vim; *abl:* vi; *pl:* vires) *f;* **—s** *(mil)* vir•es -ium *fpl,* copi•ae -arum *fpl;* **in —** valid•us -a -um
force *tr* cogěre, impellěre; *(a door)* rumpěre; **to — down** detruděre; **to — out** extruděre, extorquēre; **to — s.o. to surrender** redigěre aliquem in dicionem
forced *adj (unnatural)* quaesit•us -a -um; **— march** magnum *or* maximum it•er -ineris *n*
forceps *spl* forc•eps -ipis *mf*
forcible *adj* per vim fact•us -a -um
forcibly *adv* per vim, vi
ford *s* vad•um -i *n*
ford *tr* vado transire
fore *adj* pr•ior -ior -ius
forearm *s* bracch•ium -(i)i *n*
forearm *tr* praemunire; **to be —ed** praecavēre
forebears *spl* major•es -um *mpl*
forebode *tr* portenděre
foreboding *s* portent•um -i *n; (feeling)* praesensi•o -onis *f*
foreboding *adj* presag•us -a -um
forecast *s* praedicti•o -onis *f,* conjectur•a -ae *f*
forecast *tr* praedicěre
forecastle *s* pror•a -ae *f*
foredoom *tr* praedestinare
forefather *s* atav•us -i *m;* **—s** major•es -um *mpl*
forefinger *s* index digit•us -i *m*
forego *tr* dimittěre
foregone conclusion *s* praejudicat•um -ī *n;* **to take it as —** id pro praejudicato ferre
foregoing *adj* pr•ior -ior -ius
forehead *s* fron•s -tis *f*
foreign *adj (of another country)* extern•us -a -um; *(opposite of home-produced)* adventici•us -a -um; *(that has come from abroad)* peregrin•us -a -um; *(not pertaining to)* alien•us -a -um; **to live (travel) in a — country** peregrinari
foreigner *s* peregrin•us -i *m,* peregrin•a -ae *f*
foreknowledge *s* providenti•a -ae *f*
foreman *s* procurat•or -oris *m; (on an estate)* villic•us -i *m*
foremost *adj* prim•us -a -um; *(of chief importance)* princ•eps -ipis
forenoon *s* antemeridianum temp•us -oris *n;* **in the —** ante meridiem
forensic *adj* forens•is -is -e
foreground *s* prior par•s -tis *f*
forerunner *s* praenunt•ius -(i)i *m,* praecurs•or -oris *m*
foresee *tr* providēre
foreseeing *adj* provid•us -a -um
foresight *s* providenti•a -ae *f; (precaution)* provisi•o -onis *f*
forest *adj* silvestr•is -is -e
forest *s* silv•a -ae *f*
forestall *tr* praeoccupare
foretell *tr* praedicěre
forethought *s* providenti•a -ae *f*
forewarn *tr* praemonēre
forever *adv* in perpetuum
forewarning *s* praemonit•us -ūs *m*
forfeit *s* mult•a -ae *f*
forfeit *tr* multari *(w. abl)*
forfeiture *s* amissi•o -onis *f*
forge *s* forn•ax -acis *f* ferraria
forge *tr* excuděre; *(a document) (strictly: to substitute)* subjicěre, supponěre; **to — a signature on** *(a document)* signo adulterino obsignare
forged *adj* fals•us -a -um
forger *s (of wills)* subject•or -oris *m; (of any document)* falsar•ius -(i)i *m*
forgery *s* fals•um -i *n*
forget *tr* oblivisci *(w. gen)*
forgetful *adj* oblivios•us -a -um
forgetfulness *s* oblivi•o -onis *f*
forgive *tr* ignoscěre *(w. dat)*
forgiveness *s* veni•a -ae *f*
forgiving *adj* ignosc•ens -entis
fork *s* furc•a -ae *f; (small fork)* furcul•a -ae *f; (in the road)* biv•ium -(i)i *n*
forked *adj* bifurc•us -a -um
forlorn *adj* destitut•us -a -um
form *s* form•a -ae *f; (document)* formul•a -ae *f; (gram)* figur•a -ae *f;* **in due —** rite
form *tr* formare; *(to produce)* efficěre; *(a plan, partnership, alliance)* inire; **to — a long line** agmen longum facěre; **to — an opinion** judicium facěre; **to — such**

bitter enmities tam graves simultates excipĕre ‖ *intr* nasci, fieri

formal *adj* just•us -a -um; *(stiff)* composit•us -a -um

formality *s* rit•us -ūs *m;* **formalities** just•a -orum *npl;* **with due —** rite

formation *s* conformati•o -onis *f;* **in —** instruct•us -a -um

former *adj* pr•ior-ior -ius; *(immediately preceding)* super•ior -ior -ius; *(original, olden)* pristin•us -a -um; **the —...the latter** ille...hic

formerly *adv* antehac, antea

formidable *adj* formidabil•is -is -e

formless *adj* inform•is -is -e

formula *s* formul•a -ae *f; (leg)* acti•o -onis *f*

forsake *tr* deserĕre

forswear *tr* adjurare

fort *s* castell•um -i *n*

forth *adv (often expressed in Latin by a prefix, e.g.,* **to go —** exire); **and so —** et cetera; **from that day —** inde, ex eo (die)

forthcoming *adj* futur•us -a -um; **to be —** praesto esse

forthright *adj* apert•us -a -um

forthwith *adv* protinus, extemplo

fortieth *adj* quadragesim•us -a -um

fortification *s* muniment•um -i *n*

fortify *tr* munire

fortitude *s* fortitud•o -inis *f*

fortress *s* castell•um -i *n*

fortuitous *adj* fortuit•us -a -um

fortuitously *adv* fortuito

fortunate *adj* fortunat•us -a -um

fortunately *adv* feliciter

fortune *s* fortun•a -ae *f; (estate)* op•es -ium *fpl,* res, rei *f;* **bad —** fortuna *f* adversa; **good —** fortuna *f* prospera; **to make a —** rem facĕre; **to squander one's —** rem dissipare; **to tell —s** hariolari

fortuneteller *s* hariol•us *m,* hariol•a -ae *f; (pej)* sortileg•us -i *m*

fortunetelling *s* hariolati•o -onis *f*

forty *adj* quadraginta *(indecl)*

forum *s* for•um -i *n*

forward *adv* prorsus, prorsum; *(often expressed by the prefix* pro-, *e.g.,* **to move —** promovēre)

forward *adj (cocky)* proterv•us -a -um; **— motion** progress•us -ūs *m*

foster *tr* alĕre, fovēre

foster brother *s* collacte•us -i *m*

foster child *s* alumn•us -i *m,* alumn•a -ae *f*

foster father *s* alt•or -oris *m*

foster mother *s* altr•ix -icis *f*

foster sister *s* collacte•a -ae *f*

foul *adj (dirty)* foed•us -a -um; *(language)* obscen•us -a -um; *(weather)* turbid•us -a -um; *(deed)* foed•us -a -um; *(smell)* te•ter -tra -trum; **— play** dol•us -i *m* malus; **to run — of** inruĕre in *(w. acc)*

foul *tr* inquinare; *(morally)* contaminare; **to — up** *(coll)* conturbare

foully *adv* foede

foul-mouthed *adj* maledic•us -a -um

found *tr* fundare, condĕre

foundation *s* fundament•um -i *n;* **to lay the — for** *(lit & fig)* fundamenta jacĕre *(w. gen)*

founder *s* condit•or -oris *m*

founder *intr (lit & fig)* pessum ire

foundling *s* expositic•ius -(i)i *m;* expositici•a -ae *f*

fountain *s* fon•s -tis *m*

fountainhead *s* cap•ut -itis *n* fontis

four *adj* quattuor *(indecl);* **— each** quatern•i -ae -a; **— times** quater; **— years** quadrenn•ium -(i)i *n;* **on all —** rep•ens -entis

fourfold *adj* quadrupl•us -a -um

four-footed *adj* quadrup•es -edis

fourscore *adj* octoginta *(indecl)*

fourteen *adj* quattuordecim *(indecl)*

fourteenth *adj* quart•us decim•us -a -um

fourth *adj* quart•us -a -um; **for the — time** quartum

fourth *s* quarta par•s -tis *f;* **three —s** tres part•es -ium *fpl*

fourthly *adv* quarto

fowl *s* av•is -is *f; (domestic)* gallin•a -ae *f*

fox *s* vulp•es -is *f;* **an old —** *(coll)* veterat•or -oris *m*

foyer *s* vestibul•um -i *n*

fracas *s (brawl)* rix•a -ae *f; (quarrel)* iurg•ium -(i)i *n*

fraction *s* par•s -tis *f* exigua; *(math)* fracti•o -onis *f*

fracture *s* fractur•a -ae *f*

fracture *tr* frangĕre

fragile *adj* fragil•is -is -e

fragility *s* fragilit•as -atis *f*

fragment *s* fragment•um -i *n*

fragrance *s* suavis od•or -oris *m*

fragrant *adj* suaveol•ens -entis

frail *adj* infirm•us -a -um

frailty *s* infirmit•as -atis *f*

frame *s (of a picture)* form•a -ae *f; (of the body* figur•a -ae *f; (of buildings, etc.)* compag•es -is *f; (of bed)* spond•a -ae *f;* **— of mind** habit•us -ūs *m* animi

frame *tr* fabricari; *(to contrive)* moliri; *(a picture)* in forma includĕre; *(a person)* falso insimulare; *(to draw up a form of words)* concipĕre

framework *s* compag•es -is *f; (of wood)* contignati•o -onis *f*

France *s* Galli•a -ae *f*

franchise *s* ju•s -ris *n* suffragii

frank *adj* lib•er -era -erum

frankincense *s* tu•s -ris *n*

frankly *adv* libere

frankness *s* libert•as -atis *f*

frantic *adj* fur•ens -entis

frantically *adv* furenter

fraternal *adj* fratern•us -a -um
fraternally *adv* fraterne
fraternity *s* sodalit•as -atis *f*
fraternize *intr* conversari
fratricide *s (doer)* fratricid•a -ae *m; (deed)* fratris parricid•ium -(i)i *n*
fraud *s* frau•s -dis *f; (leg)* dol•us -i *m* malus
fraudulent *adj* fraudulent•us -a -um
fraudulently *adv* fraudulenter
fraught *adj (with)* plen•us -a -um *(w. abl)*
fray *s* rix•a -ae *f; (contest)* certam•en -inis *n*
freak *s* monstr•um -i *n; (whim)* libid•o -inis *f;* **— of nature** lus•us -ūs *m* naturae
freakish *adj* monstruos•us -a -um
freckle *s* lentig•o -inis *f*
freckled *adj* lentiginos•us -a -um
free *adj* lib•er -era -erum; *(disengaged) (from)* vacu•us -a -um *(w. abl); (generous)* liberal•is -is -e; *(from duty, taxes)* immun•is -is -e; *(unencumbered)* expedit•us -a -um; **for —** gratis; **to be — from** vacare *(w. abl)*
free *tr* liberare; *(slave)* manumittĕre; *(son)* emancipare
freebooter *s* praed•o -onis *m*
freeborn *adj* ingenu•us -a -um
freely *adv* libere; *(of one's own accord)* sponte, ultro; *(frankly)* aperte; *(generously)* large
freedman *s* libert•us -i *m*
freedom *s* libert•as -atis *f*
freedwoman *s* libert•a -ae *f*
free will *s* volunt•as -atis *f;* **of one own —** suā sponte
freeze *tr & intr* gelare; **to — up** congelare
freezing *adj* gelid•us -a -um
freight *s (cargo)* on•us -eris *n; (cost)* vectur•a -ae *f*
freighter *s* nav•is -is *f* oneraria
French *adj* Gallic•us -a -um; **in —** Gallice; **to speak —** Gallice loqui
frenzied *adj* fur•ens -entis
frenzy *s* fur•or -oris *m*
frequency *s* frequenti•a -ae *f*
frequent *adj* frequ•ens -entis
frequent *tr* frequentare
frequenter *s* frequentat•or -oris *m*
frequently *adv* frequenter
fresco *s* op•us -eris *n* tectorium
fresh *adj (food, etc.)* rec•ens -entis; *(cool)* frigidul•us -a -um; *(not tired)* inte•ger -gra -grum; *(forward)* proterv•us -a -um; *(green)* virid•is -is -e; *(water)* dulc•is -is -e
freshen *tr* recreare, renovare ‖ *intr (of wind)* increbrescĕre; **to — up** se recreare
freshly *adv* recenter
freshman *s* tir•o -onis *m*
freshness *s* viridit•as -atis *f*
fret *intr* angi, stomachari
fretful *adj* stomachos•us -a -um
fretting *s* sollicitud•o -inis *f*
friction *s* fricti•o -onis *f*
fried *adj* frict•us -a -um; **— eggs** ov•a -orum *npl* in oleo fricta
friend *s* amic•us -i *m,* amic•a -ae *f,* familiar•is -is *mf; (of a thing)* amat•or -oris *m*
friendless *adj* amicorum in•ops -opis
friendliness *s* humanit•as -atis *f*
friendly *adj* amic•us -a -um; **in a — manner** amice
friendship *s* amiciti•a -ae *f*
frieze *s* zoöphor•us -i *m*
fright *s* terr•or -oris *m*
frighten *tr* terrēre; **to — away** absterrēre
frightening *adj* terrific•us -a -um
frightful *adj* terribil•is -is -e
frightfully *adv* foede
frigid *adj* frigid•us -a -um
frigidity *s* frigidit•as -atis *f*
frigidly *adv* frigide
frill *s (plaited border)* instit•a -ae *f;* **—s** *(fig)* tric•ae -arum *fpl*
fringe *s (trim)* fimbri•ae -arum *fpl; (border)* marg•o -inis *m*
fringe *adj (outer)* ultimus -a -um; *(secondary)* secundari•us -a -um
frisk *tr* scrutari ‖ *intr* lascivire
fritter *s* lagan•um -i *n*
fritter *tr* **to — away** terĕre
frivolity *s* levit•as -atis *f*
frivolous *adj* frivol•us -a -um
frivolously *adv* nugatorie
frizzle *tr* crispare
frizzled *adj* calamistrat•us -a -um
fro *adv* **to and —** huc illuc
frock *s* stol•a -ae *f*
frog *s* ran•a -ae *f*
frolic *intr* lascivire
from *prep* a(b) *(w. abl); (denoting strictly descent from above, but used in other senses; subtraction; source)* de *(w. abl); (from within, out of)* e(x) *(w. abl); (cause)* ob *(w. acc);* **— above** desuper; **— day to day** diem de die; **— within** intrinsecus; **— without** extrinsecus
front *s* fron•s -tis *f; (on the march)* primum agm•en -inis *n; (appearance)* speci•es -ei *f;* **in —** a fronte, adversus; **in — of** *(in the presence of)* coram *(w. abl); (position)* pro *(w. abl);* **the — of the house** frons *f* aedium
front *adj* pr•ior -ior -ius; *(teeth, feet)* prim•us -a -um; **— door** antic•um -i *n*
frontage *s* fron•s -tis *f;* **a hundred feet of —** centum pedes in fronte
frontal *adj* advers•us -a -um; **— attack** impet•us -ūs *m* ex adverso
frontier *s* lim•es -itis *m*
frontline *s (mil)* principi•a -orum *npl*
frost *s* pruin•a -ae *f*
frostbitten *adj* torrid•us -a -um
frosty *adj* gelid•us -a -um

froth *s* spum•a -ae *f*
froth *intr* spumare
frothy *adj* spume•us -a -um
frown *s* contracti•o -onis *f* frontis
frown *intr* frontem contrahĕre
frozen *adj* frigore concret•us -a -um
frugal *adj* frugi *(indecl)*
frugality *s* frugalit•as -atis *f*
frugally *adv* frugaliter
fruit *s* fruct•us -ūs *m; (esp. orchard fruit)* pom•um -i *n; (of tree)* mal•a -orum *npl;* **—s of the earth** frug•es -ium *fpl*
fruitful *adj* fecund•us -a -um; *(actually yielding fruit)* frugif•er -era -erum
fruitfully *adv* fecunde
fruitfulness *s* fecundit•as -atis *f*
fruitless *adj* steril•is -is -e; *(fig)* irrit•us -a -um
fruitlessly *adv* frustra
fruit tree *s* pom•us -i *f*
frustrate *tr (to break off, e.g., an undertaking)* dirimĕre, ad irritum redigĕre; *(to baffle)* frustrari
frustrating *adj* incommod•us -a -um
frustration *s* frustrati•o -onis *f*
fry *s (dish of things fried)* frix•a -ae *f*
fry *tr* frigĕre
frying pan *s* sartag•o -inis *f*
fuel *s* aliment•um -i *n;* **to add — to the flames** *(fig)* oleum addĕre camino
fugitive *s (from country or home)* profug•a -ae *mf; (pej)* fugitiv•us -i *m,* fugitiv•a -ae *f*
fugitive *adj* fugitiv•us -a -um
fulcrum *s (of lever)* pressi•o -onis *f*
fulfill *tr (a duty)* explēre, praestare; *(prophecy)* implēre; **to — a promise** promissum exsolvĕre
fulfilled *adj (prayer, hope)* rat•us -a -um
fulfillment *s (carrying out)* executi•o -onis *f; (of a prophecy, etc.)* perfecti•o -onis *f*
full *adj (of)* plen•us -a -um *(w. gen or abl); (filled up)* explet•us -a -um; *(entire)* solid•us -a -um; *(satisfied)* sat•ur -ura -urum; *(dress)* fus•us -a -um
full-blown *adj (flowers)* apert•us -a -um; *(mature)* adult•us -a -um
full-grown *adj* adult•us -a -um
fully *adv (completely)* plene; *(quite)* penitus, prorsus
full moon *s* plenilun•ium -(i)i *n*
fumble *tr (the ball)* demittĕre ‖ *intr* haesitare; **to — for** explorare
fume *s* halit•us -ūs *m*
fume *intr* exaestuare
fumigate *tr* fumigare, suffire
fumigation *s* suffit•us -ūs *m*
fun *s* joc•us -i *m;* **pure —** mera hilar•ia -ium *npl;* **to have —** se oblectare; **to make — of** eludĕre
function *s* mun•us -eris *n,* offic•ium -(i)i *n*
function *intr* fungi, munus implēre
functionary *s* magistrat•us -ūs *m*
fund *s* pecuni•a -ae *f* collecta; *(store of anything)* copi•a -ae *f;* **—s** pecunia *f,* op•es -um *fpl*
fundamental *adj* prim•us -a -um
fundamentally *adv* funditus, penitus
funeral *s* fun•us -eris *n; (funeral procession and obsequies)* exsequi•ae -arum *fpl;* **to attend a —** (con)venire in funus
funeral *adj* funere•us -a -um; **to perform the — rites** parentare
funereal *adj* funebr•is -is -e
fungus *s* fung•us -i *m*
funnel *s* infundibul•um -i *n*
funny *adj* ridicul•us -a -um
fur *s* vill•i -orum *mpl*
furious *adj* furios•us -a -um
furiously *adv* furiose
furl *tr* complicare; *(sail)* legĕre
furlough *s* commeat•us -ūs *m;* **on —** in commeatu; **to grant a —** commeatum dare; **to obtain a —** commeatum sumĕre
furnace *s* forn•ax -acis *f*
furnish *tr* suppeditare; *(to fit out)* ornare, instruĕre
furnished *adj* instruct•us -a -um
furniture *s* suppel•ex -ectilis *f*
furrow *s* sulc•us -i *m*
furry *adj* villos•us -a -um
further *adj* ulter•ior ior -ius
further *adv* ultra, longius
further *tr (to serve)* servire *(w. dat); (to promote)* promovēre; *(to aid)* adjuvare; **to — our own interests** nostris commodis servire
furtherance *s* progress•us -ūs *m*
furthermore *adv* porro, praeterea
furthest *adj* ultim•us -a -um
furthest *adv* longissime
furtive *adj* furtiv•us -a -um
furtively *adv* furtim, furtive
fury *s* fur•or -oris *m*
fuse *tr* fundĕre ‖ *intr* coalescĕre
fusion *s* fusur•a -ae *f*
fuss *s* perturbati•o -onis *f;* **to make a great — over nothing** laborare in angusto, tumultuari
fuss *intr* satagĕre, tumultuari
fussy *adj* fastidios•us -a -um
futile *adj* futil•is -is -e
futility *s* futilit•as -atis *f*
future *adj* futur•us -a -um; **for all — time** in posterum
future *s* futur•a -orum *npl,* posterum temp•us -oris *n;* **in the —** posthac, in posterum
futurity *s* posterit•as -atis *f*

G

gab *s* garrulit•as -atis *f*
gab *intr* garrire

gable *s* fastig•ium -(i)i *n*
gadfly *s* taban•us -i *m*
gag *s* joc•us -i *m*
gag *tr* os obstruěre *(w. dat)*
gaiety *s* hilarit•as -atis *f*
gaily *adv* hilare
gain *s* lucr•um -i *n*
gain *tr* consequi, acquirěre; *(victory)* consequi, adipisci; *(by asking)* impetrare; *(office, military command)* capěre; **to — access to a person** penetrare ad aliquem; **to — ground** *(fig)* increbrescěre; **to — possession of** potiri *(w. abl)*
gainful *adj* lucros•us -a -um
gainsay *tr* contradicěre *(w. dat)*
gait *s* incess•us -ūs *m*
gala *adj* festiv•us -a -um
gala *s* festivit•as -atis *f*
galaxy *s* orb•is -is *m* lacteus
gale *s* procell•a -ae *f*
gall *s* bil•is -is *f*
gall *tr* urěre
gallant *adj* fort•is -is -e; *(polite)* officios•us -a -um
gallant *s* amat•or -oris *m*
gallantly *adv* fortiter
gallantry *s* fortitud•o -inis *f*
gall bladder *s* fe•l -llis *n*
galleon *s* nav•is -is *f* oneraria
gallery *s* portic•us -ūs *f; (open)* peristyl•ium -(i)i *n; (for paintings)* pinacothec•a -ae *f*
galley *s* nav•is -is *f* longa; *(two banks of oars)* birem•is -is *f; (three banks of oars)* trirem•is -is *f; (kitchen)* culin•a -ae *f*
Gallic *adj* Gallic•us -a -um
galling *adj* mord•ax -acis
gallon *s* cong•ius -(i)i *n*
gallop *s* citissimus curs•us -ūs *m;* **at a —** citato equo
gallop *intr (of a horse)* quadrupedare; *(of the rider)* citato equo contenděre
gallows *s* patibul•um -i *n*
gallstone *s* calcul•us -i *m*
galore *adv* satis superque
galvanize *tr* incitare
gamble *tr* **to — away** in aleā perděre ‖ *intr* aleā luděre
gambler *s* aleat•or -oris *m*
gambling *s* ale•a -ae *f*
gambol *s* salt•us -ūs *m*
gambol *intr* lascivire
game *s* lud•us -i *m; (w. dice)* ale•a -ae *f; (venison)* praed•a -ae *f;* **to make — of** ludificari
gamecock *s* gall•us -i *m* rixosus
gander *s* ans•er -eris *m*
gang *s* gre•x -gis *m,* man•us -ūs *f*
gang *intr* **to — together** conjurare; **to — up on** conspirare in *(w. acc)*
gangrene *s* gangren•a -a *f*
gangster *s* grassat•or -oris *m*
gangway *s* for•us -i *m*
gap *s* hiat•us -ūs *m*
gape *intr* hiare; **to — at** attonito animo inhiare *(w. dat)*
gaping *adj* hi•ans -antis; *(fig)* stupid•us -a -um
garb *s* vestit•us -ūs *m*
garbage *s* quisquili•ae -arum *fpl*
garble *tr* corrumpěre
garden *s* hort•us -i *m*
gardener *s* hortulan•us -i *m; (ornamental)* topiar•ius -(i)i *m*
gardening *s* hortorum cult•us -ūs *m; (ornamental)* topiaria ar•s -tis *f*
gargle *intr* gargarizare
gargling *s* gargarizati•o -onis *f*
garland *s* coron•a -ae *f*
garlic *s* al•ium -(i)i *n*
garment *s* vestiment•um -i *n*
garner *tr* colligěre
garnish *tr* ornare
garret *s* cenacul•um -i *n*
garrison *s* praesid•ium -(i)i *n*
garrison *tr (a post w. troops)* praesidium collocare in *(w. abl)*
garrulity *s* garrulit•as -atis *f*
garrulous *adj* garrul•us -a -um
garter *s* periscel•is -idis *f*
gas *s (anat)* inflati•o -onis *f; (gasoline)* ole•um -i *n* bituminosum
gash *s* patens plag•a -ae *f*
gash *tr* caesim ferire
gasp *s* anhelit•us -ūs *m*
gasp *intr* anhelare; **to — for breath** singultare animam
gas station *s* stati•o -onis *f* olei bituminosi
gastric *adj* stomachi *(gen)*
gastronomy *s* gul•a -ae *f*
gate *s* port•a -ae *f*
gateway *s* adit•us -ūs *m*
gather *tr (to assemble)* colligěre; *(fruit, nuts, flowers)* legěre; *(to infer)* colligěre, conjicěre; *(to suspect)* suspicari; **to — up** colligěre ‖ *intr* convenire
gathering *s* convent•us -ūs *m; (collecting)* collecti•o -onis *f*
gaudily *adv* laute
gaudiness *s* lautiti•a -ae *f*
gaudy *adj* laut•us -a -um
gauge *s* modul•us -i *m*
gauge *tr* metiri
gaunt *adj* ma•cer -cra -crum
gauntlet *s* digital•ia -ium *npl;* **to throw down the —** provocare
gauze *s* co•a -orum *npl*
gawky *adj* inept•us -a -um
gay *adj* hilar•is -is -e; *(homosexual)* cinaed•us -a -um
gay *s* cinaed•us -i *m*
gaze *s* conspect•us -ūs *m; (fixed look)* obtut•us -ūs *m*
gaze *intr* tueri; **to — at** intueri
gazelle *s* dorc•as -adis *f*
gazette *s* act•a -orum *npl* diurna
gazetteer *s* itinerar•ium -(i)i *n*

gear *s* apparat•us -ūs *m*
gelatin *s* glutin•um -i *n*
gelding *s* canter•ius -(i)i *m*
gem *s* gemm•a -ae *f*
gender *s* gen•us -eris *n*
genealogy *s* propagin•es -um *fpl*
general *adj (as opposed to specific)* general•is -is -e; *(wide-spread)* vulgar•is -is -e; *(shared by all)* commun•is -is -e, public•us -a -um; **in —** ad summum, in universum
general *s* du•x -cis *m,* imperat•or -oris *m*
generalize *intr* in summam loqui
generally *adv (opp: specifically:* membratim) generatim; *(for the most part)* plerumque, fere
generalship *s* duct•us -ūs *m*
generate *tr* generare
generation *s (act of producing)* generati•o -onis *f; (age)* aet•as -atis *f*
generic *adj* general•is -is -e
generosity *s* liberalit•as -atis *f*
generous *adj* liberal•is -is -e
generously *adv* liberaliter
genesis *s* orig•o -inis *f*
genial *adj* com•is -is -e
geniality *s* comit•as -atis *f*
genially *adv* comiter
genitals *spl* genital•ia -ium *npl*
genitive *s* genitiv•us -i *m*
genius *s* vi•r -ri *m* ingeniosus
genteel *adj* urban•us -a -um
gentile *adj* gentil•is -is -e
gentile *s* gentil•is -is *mf*
gentility *s* nobilit•as -atis *f*
gentle *adj* mit•is -is -e; *(gradual)* moll•is -is -e; *(wind, etc.)* len•is -is -e; *(tame)* mansuet•us -a -um
gentleman *s* vi•r -ri *m* honestus
gentleness *s* clementi•a -ae *f; (gradualness)* lenit•as -atis *f; (tameness)* mansuetud•o -inis *f*
gently *adv* leniter, clementer; *(gradually)* sensim
gentry *s* optimat•es -um *mpl*
genuine *adj* sincer•us -a -um
genuinely *adv* sincere
genus *s* gen•us -eris *n*
geographer *s* geograph•us -i *m*
geographical *adj* geographic•us -a -um
geography *s* geographi•a -ae *f*
geological *adj* geologic•us -a -um
geologist *s* geolog•us -i *m*
geology *s* geologi•a -ae *f*
geometric(al) *adj* geometric•us -a -um
geometry *s* geometri•a -ae *f*
germ *s* germ•en -inis *n*
German *adj* Germanus -a -um
germane *adj* affin•is -is -e
Germany *s* Germani•a -ae *f*
germinate *intr* germinare
germination *s* germinat•us -ūs *m*
gerund *s* gerund•ium -(i)i *n*
gesticulate *intr* gesticulari
gesture *s* gest•us -ūs *m*
gesture *intr* gestu indicare
get *tr (to acquire)* nancisci; *(to receive)* accipĕre; *(by entreaty)* impetrare; *(to fetch)* afferre; *(to understand)* comprehendĕre; *(a cold)* incidĕre in *(w. acc);* **to — back** recuperare; **to — down** depromĕre; **to — hold of** prehendĕre; **to — in** *(crops)* condĕre; **to get** *(a defendant)* **off** expedire, servare; **to — out** *(a spot)* oblitterare; *(to extort)* extorquēre; **to — ready** parare; **to — rid of** tollĕre; *(a person)* amoliri; **to — the better of** superare; **to — together** cogĕre **||** *intr (to become)* fieri; **to — abroad** palam fieri; **to — along well** bene se habēre; **to — away** aufugĕre, evadĕre; **to — at** ulcisci; **to — back** reverti; **to — down** descendĕre; **to — dressed** amiciri; **to — even with** malum vicissim dare *(w. dat);* **to — in** pervenire; **to — off** aufugĕre; **to — on** procedĕre; *(a horse)* conscendĕre; **to — on well** bene se habēre; *(to succeed)* bene succedĕre; **to — out** exire; (e curru) descendĕre; **to — out of being led away** evadĕre ne seducatur; **to — over** *(a wall)* transcendĕre; *(difficulty)* superare; *(a sickness)* convalescĕre ex *(w. abl);* **to — ready** sese parare; **to — through** *(to complete)* conficĕre; **to — together** congregari, convenire; **to — under the table** mensam subire; **to — up** surgĕre; *(as a group)* consurgĕre; *(from sleep)* expergisci; *(out of respect to s.o.)* assurgĕre
ghastly *adj (deadly pale)* lurid•us -a -um; *(shocking)* foed•us -a -um
ghost *s* umbr•a -ae *f; (haunting spirit)* larv•a -ae *f;* **to give up the —** animam ebullire
ghostly *adj* spiritual•is -is -e
giant *s* gig•as -antis *m*
gibberish *s* nug•ae -arum *fpl*
gibbet *s* patibul•um -i *n*
gibe *s* irrisi•o -onis *f*
gibe *tr & intr* irridēre
giblets *spl* gingeri•a -orum *npl*
giddiness *s* vertig•o -inis *f*
giddy *adj* vertiginos•us -a -um; *(light-minded)* lev•is -is -e
gift *s* don•um -i *n,* mun•us -eris *n; (e.g., of beauty)* do•s -tis *f*
gifted *adj* ingenios•us -a -um; *(endowed)* praedit•us -a -um
gig *s (carriage)* cis•ium -(i)i *n*
gigantic *adj* praegrand•is -is -e
giggle *intr* summissim cachinnare
gild *tr* inaurare
gilded *adj* inaurat•us -a -um
gilding *s (art)* auratur•a -ae *f; (gilded work)* aur•um -i *n* inductum
gill *s* branchi•a -ae *f*

gilt *adj* inaurat•us -a -um
gin *s* junipero infectus spirit•us -ūs *m*
ginger *s* zinziberi *n (indecl)*
gingerly *adv* pedetemptim
giraffe *s* camelopardal•is -is *f*
gird *tr* cingĕre; **to — oneself** cingi
girder *s* tign•um -i *n*
girdle *s* cingul•um -i *n*
girdle *tr* cingĕre
girl *s* puell•a -ae *f; (unmarried girl)* virg•o -inis *f*
girlhood *s* puellaris aet•as -atis *f*
girlish *adj* puellar•is -is -e
girth *s (measure around)* ambit•us -ūs *m; (of a horse)* cingul•a -ae *f*
gist *s* summ•a -ae *f*
give *tr* dare; *(as a gift)* donare; *(to deliver)* tradĕre; **— it to "em"!** adhibete!; **not — a hoot about s.o.** aliquem dupundii non facĕre; **to — in marriage** in matrimonium dare; **to — away** donare; *(to betray)* prodĕre; **to — back** reddĕre; **to — forth** emittĕre; **to — oneself up to** se addicĕre *(w. dat)*; **to — off** emittĕre; **to — out** edĕre; **to — s.o. a dirty look** respicĕre aliquem minus familiari vultu; **to — s.o. the slip** alicui subterfugĕre; **to — up** *(hope, power)* deponĕre; *(to abandon)* dimittĕre; **to — up the ghost** animam ebullire; **to — way** *(to yield)* cedĕre; *(to comply)* obsequi; *(mil)* pedem referre ‖ *intr* **to — in** cedĕre
giver *s* dat•or -oris *m*
giving *s* dati•o -onis *f*
glacial *adj* glacial•is -is -e
glacier *s* mol•es -is *f* conglaciata
glad *adj* laet•us -a -um; **to be —** gaudēre
gladden *tr* laetificare
glade *s* nem•us -oris *n*
gladiator *s* gladiat•or -oris *m*
gladiatorial *adj* gladiatori•us -a -um; **— show** mun•us -eris *n*
gladiola *s* gladiol•us -i *m*
gladly *adv* libenter
gladness *s* gaud•ium -(i)i *n*
glamor *s* nit•or -oris *m*
glamorous *adj* nitid•us -a -um; **to be —** nitēre
glance *s* aspect•us -ūs *m;* **at a —** primō aspectu; **to cast a — at** strictim aspicĕre
glance *intr* **to — at** strictim aspicĕre; *(in reading)* strictim legĕre; **to — off** stringĕre
gland *s* glandul•a -ae *f*
glare *s* fulg•or -oris *m*
glare *intr* fulgēre; **to — at** torvis oculis tueri
glaring *adj* fulg•ens -entis; *(striking)* manifest•us -a -um
glass *s* vitr•um -i *n; (for drinking)* cal•ix -icis *m* vitreus
glass *adj* vitre•us -a -um
glassmaker *s* vitrar•ius -(i)i *m*
glassware *s* vitre•a -orum *npl*
glaze *tr* vitrum illinĕre *(w. dat)*
gleam *s* fulg•or -oris *m; (fig)* aur•a -ae *f;* **slight — of hope** levis aur•a -ae *f* spei
gleam *intr* coruscare
gleaming *adj* corusc•us -a -um
glean *tr* colligĕre
gleaning *s* spicileg•ium -(i)i *n*
glee *s* laetiti•a -ae *f*
gleeful *adj* laet•us -a -um
gleefully *adv* laete
glen *s* vall•is -is *f*
glib *adj* volubil•is -is -e
glibly *adv* volubiliter
glide *intr* labi
glimmer *s* lu•x -cis *f* dubia; **— of hope** specul•a -ae *f*
glimmer *intr* sublucēre
glimpse *s* aspect•us -ūs *m* brevis; **to have a — of** dispicĕre
glisten *tr* nitēre
glistening *adj* nitid•us -a -um
glitter *s* fulg•or -oris *m*
glitter *intr* fulgēre
gloat *intr* oculos pascĕre; **to — over** oculos pascĕre *(w. abl)*, insultare (in + *acc)*
globe *s* glob•us -i *m; (earth)* orb•is -is *m* terrarum
globular *adj* globos•us -a -um
globule *s* globul•us -i *m*
gloom *s* tenebr•ae -arum *fpl; (fig)* tristiti•a -ae *f*
gloomily *adv* maeste
gloomy *adj* tenebros•us -a -um; *(fig)* maest•us -a -um
glorification *s* glorificati•o -onis *f*
glorify *tr* glorificare
glorious *adj* glorios•us -a -um
gloriously *adv* gloriose
glory *s* glori•a -ae *f*
glory *intr* **(in)** gloriari (in + *abl)*
gloss *s (on a word)* interpretati•o -onis *f; (sheen)* nit•or -oris *m*
gloss *tr* annotare; **to — over** colorare
glossary *s* glossar•ium -(i)i *n*
glossy *adj* nitid•us -a -um
glove *s* chirothec•a -ae *f*
glow *s* ard•or -oris *m*
glow *intr* ardēre
glowing *adj* ard•ens -entis; *(w. heat)* cand•ens -entis; **to speak in — terms about** ornatissime loqui de *(w. abl)*
glowingly *adv* ferventer
glue *s* glut•en -inis *n*
glue *tr* glutinare; **to — together** conglutinare
glum *adj* maest•us -a -um
glut *tr* satiare
glutton *s* hellu•o -onis *m*
gluttonous *adj* gulos•us -a -um
gnarled *adj* nodos•us -a -um
gnash *tr* **to — the teeth** dentibus frendĕre

gnat *s* cul•ex -icis *m*
gnaw *tr & intr* roděre
gnawing *adj* mord•ax -acis
go *s (try)* conat•us -ūs *m;* **to have a — at** tentare; **to make a — of it** rem bene gerěre; **on the —** nav•us -a -um
go *intr* ire; **to — about** *(work)* aggredi; **to — abroad** peregre exire; **to — after** petěre; **to — against** obstare, adversari *(w. dat);* **to — along with** assentire *(w. dat);* **to — around** circumire; **to — aside** disceděre; **to — astray** errare; **to — back** reverti; **to — back on one's word** fidem fallěre; **to — before** praeire *(w. dat);* **to — between** intervenire; **to — beyond** egredi; *(fig)* exceděre; **to — by** *(to pass)* praeterire; *(the rules)* servare; *(promises)* stare *(w. abl);* **to — down** descenděre; *(of sun)* occiděre; *(of ship)* mergi; *(of price)* laxari; *(of swelling)* se summittěre; **to — for** petěre; *(to fetch a person)* adducěre; *(a thing)* adferre; *(the bait)* appetěre; **to — forth** exire; **to — in** introire; **to — into** inire; **to — off** abire; *(as gun)* disploděre; **to — on** *(to continue)* pergěre; *(to happen)* fieri, agi; **to — out** exire; *(of fire)* exstingui; **to — out ahead** anteceděre; **to — out of doors** prodire; **to — over** *(to cross)* transire; *(a subject)* percurrěre; *(to examine)* perscrutari; *(to repeat)* repetěre; **to — straight** rectum iter vitae insistěre; **to — through** *(to travel through)* obire; *(to suffer)* perferre; **to — through with** pertenděre; **to — to** adire, acceděre; **to — to and fro** commeare; **to — towards** petěre; **to — under** submergi; **to — up** subire *(w. acc); (of prices)* ingravescěre; **to — with** comitari
goad *s* stimul•us -i *m*
goad *tr* instigare; *(fig)* stimulare; *(to exasperate)* exasperare
goal *s* fin•is -is *m; (at the racetrack)* cal•x -cis *f*
goat *s* ca•per -pri *m,* capr•a -ae *f*
gobble *tr* devorare
gobbler *s* hellu•o -onis *m*
go-between *s* internunt•ius -(i)i *m,* internunti•a -ae *f*
goblet *s* pocul•um -i *n*
goblin *s* larv•a -ae *f*
god *s* de•us -i *m;* **God** De•us -i *m;* **— forbid!** Deus averruncet!; **— willing** Deo volente; **thank —** Deo gratias!; **ye —s** di superi!
god-awful *adj* taeterrim•us -a -um
goddess *s* de•a -ae *f*
godhead *s* deit•as -atis *f*
godless *adj* impi•us -a -um
godlike *adj* divin•us -a -um
godliness *s* piet•as -atis *f*
gold *adj* aure•us -a -um
gold *s* aur•um -i *n*
golden *adj* aure•us -a -um
goldfinch *s* cardel•is -is *f*
goldfish *s* hippur•us -i *m*
gold leaf *s* auri bracte•a -ae *f*
gold mine *s* aurifodin•a -ae *f*
goldsmith *s* aurif•ex -icis *m*
good *adj* bon•us -a -um; *(morally)* prob•us -a -um; *(useful)* util•is -is -e; *(beneficial)* salutar•is -is -e; *(kindhearted)* benevol•us -a -um; *(fit)* idone•us -a -um; **— for you!** macte virtute esto! *(pl:* estote!); **I am having a — time** mihi pulchre est; **it is — to** *(w. inf)* commodum est *(w. inf);* **it is not — to** *(w. inf)* non convenit *(w. inf);* **to be — for** prodesse *(w. dat);* **to do s.o. —** alicui prodesse; **to have a — time** *(to celebrate)* genio indulgēre; **to make —** compensare; **to seem —** videri
good *n* bon•um -i *n; (profit)* lucr•um -i *n;* **for —** in perpetuum; **—s** bon•a -orum *npl; (for sale)* merc•es -cium *fpl*
good *interj* bene!; **very —** bene sane!
goodbye *interj* vale! *(pl:* valete!); **to say —** vale jubēre
good-for-nothing *s* **to be a —** nihil hominis esse
good-for-nothing *adj* nequam *(indecl)*
goodly *adj (amount)* ampl•us -a -um; **a — number of** nonnull•i -ae -a
good-natured *adj* facil•is -is -e
goodness *s* bonit•as -atis *f; (moral)* probit•as -atis *f; (generosity)* benignit•as -atis *f*
goose *s* anser -eris *m*
gooseberry *s* acin•us -i *m* grossulae
gore *s* cru•or -oris *m*
gore *tr* cornibus confoděre
gorge *s* angusti•ae -arum *fpl*
gorge *tr* **to — oneself** se ingurgitare
gorgeous *adj* magnific•us -a -um
gorgeously *adv* laute
Gorgon *s* Gorg•o -onis *f*
gory *adj* cruent•us -a -um
gospel *s* evangel•ium -(i)i *n*
gossamer *s* arane•a -ae *f*
gossip *s (talk)* gerr•ae -arum *fpl; (person)* garrul•us -i *m,* gerrul•a -ae *f*
gossip *intr* garrire
gouge *tr* **to — out s.o.'s eye** oculum alicui eruěre
gourd *s* cucurbit•a -ae *f*
gourmand *s* hellu•o -onis *m*
gout *s* arthrit•is -idis *f; (in the feet)* podagr•a -ae *f; (in the hands)* chiragr•a -ae *f*
govern *tr* imperare *(w. dat),* gubernare
governess *s* magistr•a -ae *f*
government *s* res, rei *f* publica
governor *s (of a province)* praes•es -idis *m; (of an imperial province)* legat•us -i *m; (of a Roman province)* procons•ul -ulis *m; (of a smaller province)* procurat•or -oris *m*
governorship *s* praefectur•a -ae *f*

gown *s (of Roman citizen)* tog•a -ae *f; (of women)* stol•a -ae *f*
grab *tr* rapĕre; **to — hold of** invadĕre; **to — with both hands** injicĕre utramque manum *(w. dat)*
grace *s* grati•a -ae *f; (pardon)* veni•a -ae *f;* to say — *(before meals)* consecrationem recitare; *(after meals)* gratias agĕre
grace *tr (to adorn)* decorare; *(to add honor and distinction)* honestare
graceful *adj* decor•us -a -um
gracefully *adv* decore
gracefulness *s* venust•as -atis *f*
graceless *adj* illepid•us -a -um
Graces *spl* Grati•ae -arum *fpl*
gracious *adj* benign•us -a -um
graciously *adv* benigne
gradation *s* grad•us -ūs *m; (rhet)* gradati•o -onis *f*
grade *s* grad•us -ūs *m; (test)* not•a -ae *f*
gradient *s* proclivit•as -atis *f*
gradual *adj* per gradus
gradually *adv* gradatim, sensim
graduate *tr* ad gradum admittĕre ‖ *intr* gradum suscipĕre
graduate *s* qui gradum academicum adeptus est
graft *s* surcul•us -i *m; (pol)* ambit•us -ūs *m*
graft *tr* inserĕre
grain *s (single)* gran•um -i *n;* frument•um -i *n; (in wood)* fibr•a -ae *f;* **against the —** transversis fibris; *(fig)* invitā Minerā; **with a — of salt** cum grano salis
grammar *s* grammatic•a -ae *f*
grammarian *s* grammatic•us -i *m*
grammatical *adj* grammatic•us -a -um
granary *s* horre•um -i *n*
grand *adj* grand•is -is -e; **— old style of oratory** grandis orati•o -onis *f*
grandchild *s* nep•os -otis *m,* nept•is -is *f*
granddaughter *s* nept•is -is *f*
grandeur *s* majest•as -atis *f*
grandfather *s* av•us -i *m*
grandiloquent *adj* grandiloqu•us -a -um
grandmother *s* avi•a -ae *f*
grandson *s* nep•os -otis *m*
grant *tr (to bestow)* concedĕre; *(usu. s.th. that is due)* tribuĕre; *(to acknowledge)* fatēri; *(in geometry)* dare; **—ed, he himeself is nothing** esto, ipse nihil est; **— that** sit quidem ut; **to take for —ed** sumĕre
grant *s* concessi•o -onis *f;* **to make anyone a — of anything** aliquid alicui concedĕre
granular *adj* granos•us -a -um
grape *s* uv•a -ae *f,* acin•us -i *m*
grape picker *s* vindemit•or -oris *m*
grapevine *s* vit•is -is *f*
graphic *adj* express•us -a -um
graphically *adv* expresse, graphice
grapnel *s* unc•us -i *m*
grapple *intr* luctari
grappling iron *s* man•us -ūs *f* ferrea
grasp *s (act of grasping; comprehension)* comprehensi•o -onis *f;* **he escaped my — manus meas effugit; to wrest from one's —** de manibus extorquēre; **within one's —** inter manūs
grasp *tr* prehendĕre; *(mentally)* comprehendĕre ‖ *intr* **to — at** *(lit & fig)* captare
grasping *adj* avar•us -a -um
grass *s* gram•en -inis *n,* herb•a -ae *f*
grasshopper *s* grill•us -i *m*
grassy *adj* graminos•us -a -um
grate *s* clathr•i -orum *mpl; (hearth)* camin•us -i *m*
grate *tr* conterĕre ‖ *intr* stridēre; **to — upon s.o.** alicujus animum offendĕre
grateful *adj* grat•us -a -um
gratefully *adv* grate
gratification *s* gratificati•o -onis *f; (pleasure, delight)* volupt•as -atis *f,* delectati•o -onis *f;* **— of natural desires** expleti•o -onis *f* naturae
gratify *tr* gratificari *(w. dat)*
gratifying *adj* grat•us -a -um
grating *s* cancell•i -orum *mpl; (sound)* strid•or -oris *m*
gratis *adv* gratis
gratitude *s* grati•a -ae *f;* **to feel —** gratiam habēre; **to show —** gratiam referre
gratuitous *adj* gratuit•us -a -um
gratuitously *adv* gratuito
gratuity *s* stip•s -is *f*
grave *adj* grav•is -is -e; *(stern)* sever•us -a -um
grave *s* sepulcr•um -i *n*
gravedigger *s* tumulorum foss•or -oris *m*
gravel *s* glare•a -ae *f*
gravelly *adj* glareos•us -a -um
gravely *adv* graviter
gravestone *s* monument•um -i *n*
graveyard *s* sepulcret•um -i *n*
gravitate *intr* vergĕre
gravitation *s* ponderati•o -onis *f*
gravity *s (importance; gravitational pull)* gravit•as -atis *f; (personal)* severit•as -atis *f*
gravy *s* ju•s -ris *n*
gray *adj* can•us -a -um; **to become —** canescĕre
gray-eyed *adj* caesi•us -a -um
gray-headed *adj* can•us -a -um
grayish *adj* canesc•ens -entis
grayness *s* caniti•es -ei *f*
graze *tr (cattle)* pascĕre; *(to touch lightly)* perstingĕre ‖ *intr* pasci
grease *s* ad•eps -ipis *m*
greasy *adj* unct•us -a -um
great *adj* magn•us -a -um; *(thirst)* ing•ens -entis; **as — as** tant•us...quant•us -a -um; **— amount of money** ingens pecuni•a -ae *f;* **— big** grand•is -is -e; **it**

was really —! bene fuit merhercule; **how —** quant·us -a -um; **so —** tant·us -a -um; **very —** permagn·us -a -um, maxim·us -a -um
great-granddaughter *s* pronept·is -is *f*
great-grandfather *s* prova·us -i *m*
great-grandmother *s* proavi·a -ae *f*
great-grandson *s* pronep·os -otis *m*
greatness *s* magnitud·o -inis *f*
great-uncle *s* avuncul·us -i *m* major
greaves *spl* ocre·ae -arum *fpl*
Grecian *adj* Graec·us -a -um
greed *s* avariti·a -ae *f*
greedily *adv* avide
greediness *s* avariti·a -ae *f*
greedy *adj* avid·us -a -um
Greek *adj* Graec·us -a -um
Greek *s* Graec·us -i *m;* **to know (read, speak) —** Graece scire (legĕre, loqui)
green *adj* virid·is -is -e; *(dark-green)* prasin·us -a -um; *(fresh)* rec·ens -entis; *(unripe, e.g., apples)* crud·us -a -um; **to become —** virescĕre
green *s* col·or -oris *m* viridis; *(lawn)* loc·us -i *m* herbidus; **—s** holer·a -um *npl*
greenhouse *s* viridar·ium -(i)i *n* hibernum
greenish *adj* subvirid·is -is -e
greenness *s* viridit·as -atis *f; (fig)* crudit·as -atis *f*
greet *tr* salutare, salutem dicĕre *(w. dat)*
greeting *s* salutati·o -onis *f;* **to return a —** resalutare
gregarious *adj* gregal·is -is -e; *(person)* social·is -is -e
grenade *s* pyrobol·us -i *m*
grey *see* **gray**
greyhound *s* vertag·us -i *m,* vertag·a -ae *f*
gridiron *s* craticul·a -ae *f*
grief *s* maer·or -oris *m;* **good —!** mehercules!; **to come to —** perire
grievance *s* querell·a -ae *f*
grieve *tr* dolore afficĕre ‖ *intr* maerēre, dolēre
grievous *adj* grav·is -is -e
grievously *adv* graviter
griffin *s* gry·ps -pis *m*
grill *tr* assare; *(w. questions)* interrogare
grill *s* craticul·a -ae *f*
grim *adj* torv·us -a -um; *(e.g., winter)* deform·is -is -e
grimace *s* rict·us -ūs *m*
grimly *adv* torve
grin *s* subris·us -ūs *m* distortus
grin *intr* distorto vultu subridēre
grind *tr (grain)* molĕre; *(in mortar)* contundĕre; *(on whetstone)* exacuĕre; **to — out a song** canticum extorquēre; **to — the teeth** dentibus frendĕre
grindstone *s* co·s -tis *f*
grip *s* comprehensi·o -onis *f*
grip *tr* comprehendĕre
grisly *adj* horrend·us -a -um
grist *s* farin·a -ae *f*
gristle *s* cartilag·o -inis *f*
gristly *adj* cartilaginos·us -a -um
grit *s* haren·a -ae *f*
gritty *adj* harenos·us -a -um
grizzly *adj* can·us -a -um
groan *s* gemit·us -ūs *m*
groan *intr* gemĕre
grocer *s* olitar·ius -(i)i *m*
groceries *spl* obsoni·a -orum *npl*
grocery store *s* tabern·a -ae *f* cibaria
groggy *adj* titub·ans -antis
groin *s* ingu·en -inis *n*
groom *s* novus marit·us -i *m*
groom *tr* curare
groove *s* stri·a -ae *f*
groove *tr* striare
grope *intr* praetentare
gropingly *adv* pedetentim
gross *adj (corpulent)* crass·us -a -um; *(indelicate)* indecor·us -a -um; *(coarse)* rud·is -is -e; *(inordinate)* nimi·us -a -um; *(ignorance, folly)* ing·ens -entis
grossly *adv* nimium
grotesque *adj* distort·us -a -um
grotto *s* antr·um -i *n*
ground *s* sol·um -i *n,* terr·a -ae *f; (level ground)* sol·um -i *n; (reason)* rati·o -onis *f; (place)* loc·us -i *m;* **on the —** humi; **to be burnt to the —** ad solum exuri; **to fall to the —** ad terram decidĕre; **to gain —** proficĕre; **to level with the —** solo adaequare; **to lose —** recedĕre; *(mil)* pedem referre
ground *tr* fundare; *(to teach)* imbuĕre; *(a ship)* subducĕre; ‖ *intr (naut)* haerēre
ground floor *s* sol·um -i *n*
groundless *adj* van·us -a -um; *(false)* fals·us -a -um
groundwork *s* fundament·um -i *n*
group *s (band)* man·us -ūs *f; (class)* gen·us -eris *n; (crowd)* glob·us -i *m*
group *tr* disponĕre ‖ *intr* **to — around** circulari, stipari
grouping *s* dispositi·o -onis *f*
grouse *s (bird)* tetra·o -onis *m*
grove *s* nem·us -oris *n; (sacred grove)* luc·us -i *m*
grovel *intr* repĕre, se prosternĕre
grow *tr* colĕre, serĕre ‖ *intr* crescĕre; *(to become)* fieri; *(of vegetables)* nasci; *(to shoot up)* se promittĕre; **to let the hair, beard — long** capillam, barbam promittĕre; **to — back** renasci; **to — out** excrescĕre; **to — out of** *(e.g., a wall)* innasci *(w. dat or* in + *abl) (fig)* oriri ex *(w. abl);* **to — over** *(e.g., of a skin over a wound)* induci *(w. dat);* **to — up** adolescĕre; *(to arrive at puberty)* pubescĕre
grower *s* cult·or -oris *m*
growl *s* fremit·us -ūs *m*
growl *intr* fremĕre; **to — at** ogganire
grown-up *adj* adult·us -a -um

growth *s* increment•um -i *n;* **full —** maturit•as -atis *f*
grub *s* vermicul•us -i *m; (food)* vict•us -ūs *m*
grub *intr* effodĕre
grudge *s* invidi•a -ae *f;* **to hold a — against** succensēre *(w. dat)*
grudgingly *adv* invit•us -a -um *(adj in agreement with the subject)*
gruelling *adj* (de)fatig•ans -antis
gruesome *adj* tae•ter -tra -trum
gruff *adj* asp•er -era -erum
gruffly *adv* aspere
gruffness *s* asperit•as -atis *f*
grumble *intr* murmurare; **to — about** queri de *(w. abl)*
grumpy *adj* stomachos•us -a -um
grunt *s* grunnit•us -ūs *m*
grunt *intr* grunnire
guarantee *s* fid•es -ei *f; (money)* sponsi•o -onis *f; (person who guarantees)* va•s -dis *m; (in legal contracts)* satisdati•o -onis *f;* **to give, recieve a —** fidem dare, accipĕre
guarantee *tr* fidem dare *(w. dat),* spondēre
guaranteed *adj* spons•us -a -um
guarantor *s* spons•or -oris *m*
guard *s* custodi•a -ae *f; (mil)* praesid•ium -(i)i *n; (person)* cust•os -odis *mf;* **to be on one's — against** praecavēre; **to mount —** custodiam agĕre
guard *tr* custodire ‖ *intr* **to — against** cavēre
guarded *adj* caut•us -a -um
guardedly *adv* caute
guardian *s* cust•os -odis *mf; (of minor or orphan)* tut•or -oris *m*
guardianship *s* custodi•a -ae *f; (of minor or woman)* tutel•a -ae *f*
guardhouse *s* carc•er -eris *m* militaris
guess *s* conjecti•o -onis *f*
guess *tr & intr* conjicĕre, divinare
guest *s* hosp•es -itis *mf; (at dinner)* conviv•a -ae *mf*
guidance *s* duct•us -ūs *m; (advice)* consil•ium -(i)i *n;* **under the — of the deity** deo ducente
guide *s* duct•or -oris *m*
guide *tr (as a local guide)* ducĕre; *(to manage, control)* regĕre
guidebook *s* itinerar•ium -(i)i *n*
guild *s* colleg•ium -(i)i *n*
guile *s* dol•us -i *m*
guileful *adj* dolos•us -a -um
guileless *adj* simpl•ex -icis
guilt *s* culp•a -ae *f*
guilty *adj* son•s -tis; **— of** noc•ens *(w. gen or abl);* **to punish the —** sontes punire
guinea hen *s* meleagr•is -idis *f*
guise *s* speci•es -ei *f; (features, dress)* habit•us -ūs *m;* **under the — of** sub specie *(w. gen)*
guitar *s* cithar•a -ae *f* Hispanica
gulf *s* sin•us -ūs *m*
gull *s* merg•us -i *m*
gullet *s* gul•a -ae *f*
gullibility *s* credulit•as -atis *f*
gullible *adj* credul•us -a -um
gulp *s* singult•us -ūs *m*
gulp *tr* **to — down** obsorbēre ‖ *intr* singultare
gum *s* gummi *n (indecl); (anat)* gingiv•a -ae *f*
gumption *s* alacrit•as -atis *f*
gun *s* sclopet•um -i *n;* **to jump the —** signum praevertĕre; **to stick to one's —s** in sententiā stare
gurgle *intr* singultare; *(of a stream)* murmurare
gurgling *s* singult•us -ūs *m; (of a stream)* murmurati•o -onis *f*
gush *s* effusi•o -onis *f,* erupti•o -onis *f; (of water)* scatebr•a -ae *f;* **w. a — of tears** profusis lacrimis
gush *intr* scaturire; **to — out** prorumpĕre; *(of blood from a wound)* emicare
gust *s* flam•en -inis *n*
gusto *s* stud•ium -(i)i *n*
gusty *adj* procellos•us -a -um
gut *s* intestin•um -i *n*
gut *tr* extenterare; *(a building)* amburĕre
gutted *adj (by fire)* ambust•us -a -um
gutter *s* canal•is -is *m,* riv•us -i *m;* **to clean out the —** rivos deducĕre
guttural *adj* guttural•is -is -e
guy *s* **poor —** homuncul•us -i *m;* **that —** iste
guzzle *tr & intr* potare
guzzler *s* pot•or -oris *m*
gymnasium *s* gymnas•ium -(i)i *n*
gymnastic *adj* gymnastic•us -a -um
gymnastics *spl* palaestric•a -ae *f*
gynecology *s* gynaecologi•a -ae *f*
gypsum *s* gyps•um -i *n*
gyrate *intr* in gyrum verti

H

haberdasher *s* linte•o -onis *m*
haberdashery *s* tabern•a -ae *f* vestiaria
habit *s* consuetud•o -inis *f; (dress)* habit•us -ūs *m;* **to be in the — of** consuescĕre *(w. inf);* **to break the —** abscedĕre ab usu; **to get into the — of** se assuefacĕre *(w. inf)*
habitation *s* habitati•o -onis *f*
habitual *adj* usitat•us -a -um
habitually *adv* de more, ex more
habituate *tr* assuefacĕre
hack *s (cut)* plag•a -ae *f; (coach) (coll)* raed•a -ae *f* meritoria
hack *tr* caedĕre; **to — to pieces** concidĕre
hackneyed *adj* trit•us -a -um
haddock *s* gad•us -i *m*

hag *s* an•us -ūs *f*
haggard *adj* ma•cer -cra -crum
haggle *intr* licitari
haggler *s* licitat•or -oris *m*
hail *s* grand•o -inis *f (m)*
hail *intr* **it is —ing** grandinat
hail *tr* appellare
hail *interj* salve! *(pl:* salvēte!)
hailstone *s* grandinis gran•um -i *n*
hair *s (of head or beard)* capill•us -i *m*, *(or* capill•i -orum *mpl); (in locks or dressed)* crin•is -is *m; (hair as an orament, of men or women)* com•a -ae *f; (single)* pil•us -i *m; (of a animals)* saet•a -ae *f;* **he was within a — 's breadth of** nil propius est factum quam ut; **to split —s** cavillari
haircut *s* tons•us -ūs *m*
hairdresser *s* tonstri•x -icis *f*
hairless *adj (of head)* calv•us -a -um; *(of body)* gla•ber -bra -brum
hairnet *s* reticul•um -i *n*
hair oil *s* capillar•e -is *n*
hairpin *s* crinal•e -is *n*
hairy *adj* pilos•us -a -um; *(chest)* saetos•us -a -um, hirsut•us -a -um
hale *adj* **— and hardy** san•us et robust•us -a -um
half *s* dimidia par•s -tis *f*
half *adv* dimidio; *(partly)* partim; **— and —** pro parte semissā
half *adj* dimidiat•us -a -um, dimidi•us -a -um; **— the drinks** dimidiae potion•es -um *fpl*
half alive *adj* semiviv•us -a -um
half asleep *adj* semisomn•us -a -um
halfbreed *s* hybrid•a -ae *mf*
half brother *s (on mother's side)* fra•ter -tris *m* uterin•us; *(on father's side)* fra•ter -tris *m* consanguineus
half-burnt *adj* semiust•us -a -um
half-cooked *adj* semicoct•us -a -um
half-dead *adj* semianim•us -a -um
half-eaten *adj* semes•us -a -um
half-finished *adj* semiperfect•us -a -um
half-full *adj* semiplen•us -a -um
half-hour *s* semihor•a -ae *f*
half-moon *s* lun•a -ae *f* dimidiata; *(shape)* lunul•a -ae *f*
half-open *adj* semiapert•us -a -um
half pint *s (sl)* homuncul•us -i *m*
half pound *s* selibr•a -ae *f*
half sister *s (on mother's side)* sor•or -oris *f* uterina; *(on father's side)* sor•or -oris *f* consanguinea
halfway *adj* medi•us -a -um
half-year *adj* semestr•is -is -e
hall *s* atr•ium -(i)i *n*
hallo *interj* heus!
hallucinate *intr* alucinari
hallucination *s* alucinati•o -onis *f*
hallway *s* andr•on -onis *m; (at front of house)* vestibul•um -i *n*
halo *s* coron•a -ae *f*
halt *s* paus•a -ae *f*, mor•a -ae *f;* **to come to a —** consistĕre
halt *tr* sistĕre ‖ *intr* consistĕre; *(to limp)* claudicare
halter *s* capistr•um -i *n*
halting *adj* claud•us -a -um; *(fig)* haesitabund•us -a -um
halve *tr* ex aequo dividĕre
ham *s* pern•a -ae *f; (back of the knee)* popl•es -itis *m*
hamlet *s* vic•us -i *m*
hammer *s* malle•us -i *m*
hammer *tr* malleo tundĕre
hamper *s* corb•is -is *m*
hamstring *s* poplitis nerv•us -i *m*
hamstring *tr* poplitem succidĕre *(w. dat); (fig)* impedire
hand *s* man•us -ūs *f; (handwriting)* chirograph•um -i *n; (of dial)* gnom•on -onis *m; (worker)* operar•ius -(i)i *m;* **at —** praesto, ad manum; **by —** manu; **from — to —** de manu in manum; **— in —** junctis manibus; **— off!** noli(te) tangĕre; **—s up!** tolli(te) manus!; **left —** laev•a -ae *f*, sinistr•a -ae *f;* **old —** veterat•or -oris *m;* **on the one —, on the other** unā ex parte...alterā ex parte; *or use* hic...ille; **on the other —** contra; **right —** dext(e)r•a -ae *f;* **these things are not in our —s** haec non sunt in nostra manu; **to be near at —** subesse; **to have a — in s.th.** interesse alicui rei; **to have clean —s** manūs pecuniae abstinentes habēre; **to have in —** in manibus habēre; **to have one's —s full** satis agĕre; **to lay —s on** manum injicĕre *(w. dat);* **to live from — to mouth** in horam vivĕre; **to pass a thing from — to —** aliquid de manu in manum tradĕre; **to shake —s** dextram dextrae jungĕre; **to take in —** suscipĕre
hand *tr* tradĕre, porrigĕre; **to be —ed over to** *(by a judge)* adjudicari *(w. dat);* **to — around** circumferre; **to — down** tradĕre; **to — in** reddĕre; **to — over** tradĕre; *(to betray)* prodĕre
handbill *s* libell•us -i *m*
handbook *s* enchirid•ion -(i)i *n*
handcuffs *spl* manic•ae -arum *fpl*
handful *s* manipul•us -i *m*
handicraft *s* artific•ium -(i)i *n*
handiwork *s* opific•ium -(i)i *n*
handkerchief *s* sudar•ium -(i)i *n*
handle *s* manubr•ium -(i)i *n; (of a cup)* ansul•a -ae *f*
handle *tr* tractare
handling *s* tractati•o -onis *f*
handsome *adj* pul•cher -chra -chrum
handsomely *adv* pulchre; *(liberally)* liberaliter
handsomeness *s* pulchritud•o -inis *f*
handwriting *s* chirograph•um -i *n*

handy *adj (of things)* habil•is -is -e; *(of persons)* soller•s -tis; *(at hand)* praesto
hang *tr* suspenděre; *(by a line)* appenděre; *(the head)* demittěre ‖ *intr* pendēre; **—ing down** demiss•us -a -um; **to — down** dependēre; **to — on to** haerēre *(w. dat)*; **to — over** imminēre *(w. dat)*
hanger-on *s* assecl•a -ae *m*
hanging *adj* pensil•is -is -e
hanging *s (execution)* suspend•ium -(i)i *n*; **—s** aulae•a -orum *npl*
hangman *s* carnif•ex -icis *m*
hangout *s* latebr•ae -arum *fpl*
hangover *s* crapul•a -ae *f*; **to sleep off a —** crapulam obdormire
hanker *intr* **— for** desiderare
haphazard *adj* fortuit•us -a -um
happen *intr* acciděre, fieri, contingěre; **I happened to see** forte vidi; **it happens that** contingit ut; **to — upon** inciděre in *(w. acc)*
happily *adv* feliciter, beate
happiness *s* felicit•as -atis *f*
happy *adj* beat•us -a -um
harangue *s* conti•o -onis *f*; **to give a —** contionem habēre
harangue *tr & intr* contionari
harass *tr* vexare
harassment *s* vexati•o -onis *f*
harbinger *s* praenunt•ius -(i)i *m*, praenunti•a -ae *f*
harbor *s* port•us -ūs *m*
harbor *tr* excipěre; **to — hopes, thoughts** portare spes, cogitationes
hard *adj* dur•us -a -um; *(difficult)* difficil•is -is -e; *(severe)* a•cer -cris -cre; **to become —** durescěre
hard *adv* valde, sedulo, summā vi
harden *tr* durare; *(fig)* indurare ‖ *intr* durescěre; *(fig)* obdurescěre
hardhearted *adj* dur•us -a -um
hardiness *s* rob•ur -oris *n*
hardly *adv* vix, aegre; **— any** null•us -a -um fere
hardness *s* duriti•a -ae *f*; *(fig)* acerbit•as -atis *f*
hardship *s* lab•or -oris *m*
hardware *s* ferrament•a -orum *npl*
hardware store *s* tabern•a -ae *f* ferraria
hardy *adj* robust•us -a -um
hare *s* lep•us -oris *m*
harem *s* gynaece•um -i *n*
hark *interj* heus!
harken *intr* audire; **to — to** auscultare *(w. dat)*
harlot *s* meretr•ix -icis *f*
harm *s* injuri•a -ae *f*; **to come to —** detrimentum accipěre
harm *intr* nocēre *(w. dat)*, laeděre
harmful *adj* noxi•us -a -um
harmless *adj* innocu•us -a -um
harmonious *adj* canor•us -a -um; *(fig)* concor•s -dis
harmoniously *adv* consonanter; *(fig)* concorditer
harmonize *tr* componěre ‖ *intr* conciněre; *(fig)* consentire
harmony *s* harmoni•a -ae *f*; *(fig)* concordi•a -ae *f*
harness *s* equi ornament•a -orum *npl*
harp *s* lyr•a -ae *f*
harpist *s* psalt•es -ae *m*
harpoon *s* jacul•um -i *n* hamatum
harpoon *tr* jaculo hamato transfigěre
Harpy *s* Harpyi•a -ae *f*
harrow *s* irp•ex -icis *m*
harrow *tr* occare
harsh *adj* asp•er -era -erum; *(sound)* rauc•us -a -um; *(fig)* dur•us -a -um, inclem•ens -entis, sever•us -a -um
harshly *adv* aspere, severe
harshness *s* asperit•as -atis *f*
harvest *s* mess•is -is *f*
harvest *tr* metěre
hash *s* minut•al -alis *n*
hash *tr* comminuěre
haste *s* festinati•o -onis *f*; **in —** propere; **to make —** properare
hasten *tr & intr* properare
hastily *adv* propere, raptim; *(without reflection)* temere
hastiness *s* celerit•as -atis *f*; *(without reflection)* temerit•as -atis *f*
hasty *adj* temerari•us -a -um
hat *s* petas•us -i *m*
hatch *s (naut)* foram•en -inis *n*
hatch *tr (fig)* coquěre; *(of chickens)* ex ovis excluděre
hatchet *s* asci•a -ae *f*
hate *s* od•ium -(i)i *n*
hate *tr* odisse
hateful *adj* odios•us -a -um, invis•us -a -um; **to be —** to odio esse *(w. dat)*
hatefully *adv* odiose
hatred *s* od•ium -(i)i *n*
haughtily *adv* superbe
haughtiness *s* superbi•a -ae *f*
haughty *adj* superb•us -a -um
haul *s (catch)* captur•a -ae *f*; *(transport)* vectur•a -ae *f*
haul *tr* trahěre; **to — up** subducěre
haunch *s* clun•is -is *f*
haunt *s* loc•us -i *m* frequentatus; *(of animals)* lateb•rae -arum *fpl*
haunt *tr* frequentare; *(to disturb)* inquietare
haunted *adj* ab larvis frequentat•us -a -um
have *tr* habēre; *(to be obliged)* debēre; **I — confidence** fiducia est mihi
haven *s* port•us -ūs *m*
have-not *s* paup•er -eris *mf*
havoc *s* strag•es -is *f*; **to wreak —** stragem dare
hawk *s* accipi•ter -tris *mf*
hawk *tr* venditare; **to — up phlegm** pituitam exsecrare per tussim
hawker *s* circulat•or -oris *m*

hawk-eyed *adj* lynce•us -a -um
hawser *s* retinacul•um -i *n*
hay *s* faen•um -i *n*
hayloft *s* faenil•ia -ium *npl*
haystack *s* faeni met•a -ae *f*
hazard *s* pericul•um -i *n*
hazardous *adj* periculos•us -a -um
haze *s* nebul•a -ae *f*
hazelnut *s* nu•x -cis *f* avellana
hazy *adj* nebulos•us -a -um; *(fig)* obscur•us -a -um
he *pron* hic, is; *(male)* ma•s -ris *m*
head *s* cap•ut -itis *n; (mental faculty)* ingen•ium -(i)i *n; (fig)* princ•eps -ipis *m;* **back of the —** occipit•um -i *n;* **from — to foot** ab imis unguibus usque ad verticem summum; **— first** praec•eps -itis; **— over heels in love** tot•us -a -um in amore; **it all came to a head** in discrimen summa rerum adducta est; **to come into s.o's —** alicui in mentem venire; **to come to a —** *(of a boil)* caput facĕre; **to put —s together** capita conferre; **use your — !** cogita *(pl:* cogitate)! **wine goes to my —** vinum in cerebrum mihi abit
head *adj* prim•us -a -um
head *tr* praesse *(w. dat),* ducĕre ‖ *intr* **to — for** tendĕre ad *(w. acc)*
headache *s* capitis dol•or -oris *m*
heading *s* titul•us -i *m*
headland *s* promuntor•ium -(i)i *n*
headless *adj* trunc•us -a -um
leadlong *adv* praec•eps -itis
headquarters *spl* praetor•ium -(i)i *n*
head start *s* **to get a —** iter praecipĕre; *(fig)* aliquantum temporis praecipĕre
headstrong *adj* contum•ax -acis
headway *s* **to make —** proficĕre
headwind *s* vent•us -i *m* adversus
heady *adj (of wine)* fervid•us -a -um
heal *tr* mederi *(w. dat),* sanare ‖ *intr* sanescĕre; *(of wounds)* coalescĕre
healer *s* medic•us -i *m*
healing *adj* salutar•is -is -e
healing *s* sanati•o -onis *f*
health *s (good or bad)* valetud•o -inis *f;* **bad (delicate, good, ill) —** adversa (infirma, secunda, incommoda) valetud•o -inis *f;* **to be in good —** bene valēre; **to drink to the — of** propinare *(w. dat);* **to enjoy excellent —** optima valitudine uti
healthful *adj* salubr•is -is -e
healthily *adv* salubriter
healthy *adj* san•us -a -um; *(places)* salubr•is -is -e
heap *s* cumul•us -i *m,* acerv•us -i *m*
heap *tr* acervare; **to — up** accumulare, exstruĕre; **to —** *(blows, favors, abuse)* **upon** congerĕre (plagas, beneficia, maledicta) *(w. dat or* in + *acc)*
hear *tr* audire; *(to learn)* cognoscĕre, accipĕre
hearing *s (act)* auditi•o -onis *f; (sense)* audit•us -ūs *m; (leg)* cogniti•o -onis *f;* **hard of —** surdas•ter -tra -trum
hearken *intr* auscultare; **to — to** auscultare *(dat)*
hearsay *s* auditi•o -onis *f*
heart *s* cor cordis *n; (fig)* anim•us -i *m;* **from the —** animo; **my — was in my mouth** anima mihi in naso erat; **to learn by —** ediscĕre; **to love with all one's —** toto pectore amare
heartache *s (fig)* cur•a -ae *f*
heartbreak *s* ang•or -oris *m*
heartburn *s* praecordium dol•or -oris *m*
heartbroken *adj* ae•ger -gra -grum animi
heart-felt *adj* haud simulat•us -a -um
hearth *s* foc•us -i *m*
heartily *adv* cum summo studio
heartiness *s* alacrit•as -atis *f*
heartless *adj* inhuman•us -a -um
heartlessly *adv* inhumane
hearty *adj* sincer•us -a -um; *(meal)* laut•us -a -um
heat *s* cal•or -oris *m,* ard•or -oris *m; (fig)* ferv•or -oris *m;* **— of the day** aest•us -ūs *m*
heat *tr* calfacĕre ‖ *intr* calescĕre
heathen *adj* pagan•us -a -um
heathen *s* pagan•us -i *m*
heating *s* calefacti•o -onis *f*
heave *tr* attollĕre; **to — a sigh** gemitum ducĕre ‖ *intr (to swell)* fluctuare; *(of the chest)* anhelare
heaven *s* cael•um -i *n;* **— forbid!** dii meliora! **good —s !** pro divum fidem!; **thank —** dis gratia; **to move — and earth** caelum ac terras miscēre
heavenly *adj* caelest•is -is -e
heavily *adv* graviter; *(slowly)* tarde
heaviness *s* gravit•as -atis *f*
heavy *s* grav•is -is -e; *(sad)* maest•us -a -um; *(rain)* magn•us -a -um
Hebraic *adj* Hebraic•us -a -um
Hebrew *adj* Hebrae•us -a -um
Hebrew *s* Hebrae•us -i *m; (language)* lingu•a -ae *f* Hebraea; **to know (read, speak) —** Hebraice scire (legĕre, loqui)
hecatomb *s* hecatomb•e -es *f*
heckle *tr* interpellĕre
heckler *s* conviciat•or -oris *m*
hectic *adj* febriculos•us -a -um
hedge *s* saep•es -is *f*
hedge *tr* **to — in** saepire; **to — off** intersaepire ‖ *intr* tergiversari
hedgehog *s* eric•ius -(i)i *m*
heed *s* cur•a -ae *f;* **to take —** curare
heed *tr* curare, observare; *(to obey)* parēre *(w. dat)*
heedless *adj* incaut•us -a -um; **— of** immem•or -oris *(w. gen)*
heedlessness *s* neglegenti•a -ae *f*
heel *s* cal•x -cis *mf;* **to take to one's —** se in pedes conjicĕre

hefty *adj* robust•us -a -um; *(thing)* ing•ens -entis
heifer *s* juvenc•a -ae *f*
height *s* altitud•o -inis *f; (of person)* procerit•as -atis *f; (top)* culm•en -inis *n; (fig)* fastig•ium -(i)i *n*
heighten *tr* amplificare, augēre
heinous *adj* atr•ox -ocis
heir *s* her•es -edis *m;* **sole** *or* **universal —** her•es -edis *m* ex asse
heir apparent *s* her•es -edis *m* legitimus
heiress *s* her•es -edis *f*
heirloom *s* res, rei *f* hereditaria
hell *s* infer•i -orum *mpl;* **to catch —** convicium habēre
Hellenic *adj* Hellenic•us -a -um
Hellenism *s* Hellenism•us -i *m*
hellish *adj* infern•us -a -um
hello *interj* salve (*pl:* salvete)
helm *s* gubernacul•um -i *n*
helmet *s (of leather)* gale•a -ae *f; (of metal)* cass•is -idis *f*
helmsman *s* gubernat•or -oris *m*
help *s* auxil•ium -(i)i *n*
help *tr* adjuvare, opem ferre *(w. dat)*
helper *s* adjut•or -oris *m,* adjutr•ix -icis *f*
helpful *adj* util•is -is -e
helpless *adj* inop•s -is
helplessness *s* inopi•a -ae *f*
hem *interj* hem!, ahem!
hem *s* lacini•a -ae *f*
hem *tr* circumsuěre; **to — in** circumsidēre; *(by entrenchments)* circumvallare
hemisphere *s* hemisphaer•ium -(i)i *n*
hemlock *s* cicut•a -ae *f*
hemorrhage *s* sanguinis profluv•ium -(i)i *n*
hemorrhoids *spl* haemorrhoid•a -ae *f*
hemp *s* cannab•is -is *f*
hempen *adj* cannabin•us -a -um
hen *s* gallin•a -ae *f*
hence *adv* hinc; *(consequently)* igitur
henceforth *adv* posthac, dehinc
henchman *s* adjut•or -oris *m*
henpecked *adj* uxori•us -a -um
her *pron* eam, illam, hanc
her *adj* ejus, illius, hujus; **— own** su•us -a -um
herald *s* fetial•is -is *m; (crier)* praec•o -onis *m*
herald *tr* (prae)nuntiare
herb *s* herb•a -ae *f*
herd *s* gre•x -gis *m; (pej)* vulg•us -i *n*
herd *tr* **to — together** congregare ‖ *intr* **to — together** congregari
herdsman *s* armentar•ius -(i)i *m*
here *adv* hic; **— and now** depraesentiarium; **— and there** passim
hereafter *adv* posthac
hereby *adv* ex hoc, hinc
hereditary *adj* hereditari•us -a -um
heredity *s* gen•us -eris *n;* **by —** jure hereditario, per successiones
herein *adv* in hoc, in hac re, hic
heresy *s* haeres•is -is *f*
heretical *adj* haeretic•us -a -um
hereupon *adv* hic
herewith *adv* unā cum hac re
heritage *s* heredit•as -atis *f*
hermaphrodite *s* androgyn•us -i *m*
hermit *s* eremit•a -ae *m*
hermitage *s* eremitae cell•a -ae *f*
hernia *s* herni•a -ae *f*
hero *s* vi•r -ri *m; (demigod)* her•os -oïs *m*
heroic *adj (age)* heroïc•us -a -um; fortissim•us -a -um
heroically *adv* fortissime
heroine *s* virag•o -inis *f; (myth)* heroïn•a -ae *f*
heroism *s* virt•us -utis *f*
heron *s* arde•a -ae *f*
herring *s* hareng•a -ae *f*
hers *pron* ejus, illius
herself *pron (refl)* se; *(intensive)* ipsa; **by —** per se; **to —** sibi; **with —** secum
hesitant *adj* dubi•us -a -um
hesitantly *adv* cunctanter
hesitate *intr* dubitare
hesitation *s* dubitati•o -onis *f; (in speaking)* haesitati•o -onis *f*
heterogeneous *adj* divers•us -a -um
hew *tr* dolare, caeděre
hey *interj* ohe!; **— you!** heus tū!
hiatus *s* hiat•us -ūs *m*
hiccup *s* singult•us -ūs *m*
hiccup *intr* singultire
hidden *adj* occult•us -a -um; **to lie —** latēre
hide *s* cor•ium -(i)i *n; (pelt)* pell•is -is *f*
hide *tr* abděre, celare ‖ *intr* latēre
hide and seek *s* **to play —** per lusum latitare
hideous *adj* foed•us -a -um
hideously *adv* foede
hideousness *s* foedit•as -atis *f*
hiding *s* occultati•o -onis *f; (whipping)* verberati•o -onis *f*
hiding place *s* latebr•a -ae *f*
hierarchy *s* hierarchi•a -ae *f*
high *adj* alt•us -a -um; *(rank)* ampl•us -a -um; *(price)* magn•us -a -um; *(wind)* vehem•ens -entis; *(fever)* ard•ens -entis; *(note)* acut•us -a -um; *(expensive)* car•us -a -um; *(ground)* edit•us -a -um; *(virtue, good, etc.)* summ•us -a -um; **at a — price** magni (pretii) *or* magno pretio; **— opinion** magna opini•o -onis *f;* **— sea** alt•um -i *n;* **— tide** maximus aest•us -ūs *m*
high *adv* alte; **to aim —** magnas res appetěre; **from on —** desuper; **on —** sursum versum
highborn *adj* generos•us -a -um
high-flown *adj* inflat•us -a -um
highhanded *adj* insol•ens -entis
highhandedly *adv* insolenter
highlander *s* montan•us -i *m*
highlands *spl* regi•o -onis *f* montuosa
highlights *spl* praecipu•a -orum *npl* rerum

highly *adv (value)* magni; *(intensity)* vehementer, valde
high-minded *adj (noble)* magnanim•us -a -um; *(arrogant)* imperios•us -a -um
high priest *s* pontif•ex -icis *m,* sacerd•os -otis *m* maximus
high treason *s* majest•as -atis *f* (laesa); **convicted of —** de majestate damnat•us -a -um
highway *s* vi•a -ae *f*
hijacker *s* latr•o -onis *m*
hike *s* ambulati•o -onis *f*
hilarious *adj* hilar•is -is -e
hilariously *adv* hilare
hilarity *s* hilarit•as -atis *f*
hill *s* coll•is -is *m*
hillock *s* tumul•us -i *m*
hillside *s* cliv•us -i *m*
hilly *adj* clivos•us -a -um
hilt *s* capul•us -i *m*
him *pron* eum, illum, hunc; **of —** ejus, illius hujus
himself *pron (refl)* se; *(intensive)* ipse; **to —** sibi; **with —** secum
hind *s* cerv•a -ae *f*
hind *adj* poster•ior -ior -ius; **— end** *(coll)* sed•es -is *f*
hinder *tr* impedire, prohibēre; *(to block)* obstare *(w. dat)*
hindmost *adj* postrem•us -a -um
hindrance *s* impediment•um -i *n*
hinge *s* card•o -inis *m*
hinge *intr* **to — on** *(fig)* niti *(w. abl)*
hint *s* significati•o -onis *f;* **to throw clear —s** nec dubias significationes jacĕre
hint *tr* suggerĕre
hip *s* cox•a -ae *f*
hippodrome *s* hippodrom•os -i *m*
hippopotamus *s* hippopotam•us -i *m*
hire *s* conducti•o -onis *f*
hire *tr* conducĕre; **to — oneself out** auctorari; **to — out** locare
hired *adj* conduct•us -a -um, mercenari•us -a -um
hireling *s* mercenar•ius -(i)i *m*
his *adj* ejus, illius, hujus; **— own** su•us -a -um, propri•us -a -um
hiss *s* sibil•us -i *m*
hiss *tr & intr* sibilare
historian *s* historic•us -i *m*
historical *adj* historic•us -a -um
history *s* histori•a -ae *f;* **ancient —** antiqua historia *f;* **modern —** recentioris aetatis historia *f;* **to write a — of the Roman people** res gestas populi Romani perscribĕre
histrionic *adj* histrional•is -is -e
hit *s* plag•a -ae *f,* ict•us -ūs *m; (success)* success•us -ūs *m*
hit *tr* icĕre, ferire; *(of an illness)* affligĕre, occupare; **to — it off with** convenire cum *(w. abl);* **you've — the nail on the head** acu rem tetigisti ‖ *intr* **to — upon** offendĕre
hitch *s* nod•us -i *m;* **there is a —** haeret res (in salebrā)
hitch *tr* conjungĕre
hither *adv* huc
hither *adj* citer•ior -ior -ius
hitherto *adv (of time)* adhuc; *(of place)* huc usque
hive *s* alve•us -i *m*
hoard *s* acerv•us -i *m*
hoard *tr* coacervare, recondĕre
hoarder *s* accumulat•or -oris *m*
hoarse *adj* rauc•us -a -um; **to get —** irraucescĕre
hoarsely *adv* raucā voce
hoary *adj* can•us -a -um
hoax *s* frau•s -dis *f*
hobble *intr* claudicare
hobby *s* avocament•um -i *n*
hobnob *intr* conversari
hock *s* popl•es -itis *m*
hoe *s* sarcul•um -i *n*
hoe *tr* sarculare
hog *s* porc•us -i *m*
hogwash *s* quisquili•ae -arum *fpl*
hoist *tr* sublevare
hold *s (of ship)* cavern•a -ae *f;* **to get** *or* **take — of** prehendĕre; *(with both hands)* comprehendĕre
hold *tr* tenēre; *(to contain)* capĕre; *(to think)* habēre; *(elections, meeting, discussions)* habēre; *(office, consulship, etc.)* gerĕre; **able to —** *(e.g., of a theater)* cap•ax -acis *(w. gen);* **to — back** retinēre; *(laughter, tears)* tenēre; **to — court** *(leg)* quaerĕre; **to — forth** *(e.g., hands)* porrigĕre; *(to offer)* praebēre; **to — in** inhibēre, cohibēre; **to — in honor** in honore habēre; **to — off** arcēre; **to — one's breath** animam comprimĕre; **to — one's tongue** tacēre; **to — out** *(e.g., hands)* protendĕre; **to —** *(e.g., a compress)* **to** *(e.g., one's cheek)* admovēre (fomentum) ad (malam); **to — up** attollĕre; **to — up one's head** mentum tollĕre ‖ *intr* **to — back** cunctari; **to — forth** *(to speak)* contionari; **to — on to** tenēre; **to — out** *(to last)* durare, permanēre
holder *s* possess•or -oris *m; (instrument)* receptacul•um -i *n*
holding *s* possessi•o -onis *f*
hole *s* foram•en -inis *n; (of mice, etc.)* cav•um -i *n;* **to dig a — in the ground** locum in terra excavare; **to dig a — in the wall** parietem perfodĕre
hole-in-the-wall *s (cheap lodgings)* stabul•um -i *n*
holiday *s* di•es -ei *m* festus; **—s** feri•ae -arum *fpl;* **public —** di•es -ei *m* sollemnis
holiness *s* sanctit•as -atis *f*
hollow *adj* cav•us -a -um; *(fig)* inan•is -is -e

hollow *s* cav•um -i *n; (depression)* lacun•a -ae *f;* **— of the hand** cava man•us -ūs *f*
hollow *tr* **to — out** excavare
holly *s* il•ex -icis *n* aquifolium
holocaust *s* holocaust•um -i *n*
holy *adj* sanct•us -a -um
homage *s* cult•us -ūs *m;* **to pay —** **to** colĕre
home *s* aed•es -ium *fpl,* dom•us -ūs *f;* **at —** domi; **from —** domo
home *adv (motion)* domum; *(place where)* domi
home *adj* domestic•us -a -um
homeless *adj* tecto car•ens -entis
homeliness *s* rusticit•as -atis *f*
homely *adj* rustic•us -a -um
homemade *adj* domestic•us -a -um
homemaker *s* materfamilias *(gen:* matrisfamilias) *f*
homesick *adj* appet•ens -entis tecti sui; **to be —** ex desiderio tecti sui laborare
homesickness *s* tecti sui desider•ium -(i)i *n*
homestead *s* fund•us -i *m*
homeward *adv* domum
homicidal *adj* cruent•us -a -um
homicide *s (person)* homicid•a -ae *m; (deed)* homicid•ium -(i)i *n*
homily *s* tractat•us -ūs *m* moralis
homogeneous *adj* pari naturā praedit•us -a -um
homosexual *adj* cinaed•us -a -um; **— partner** *(euphem)* fra•ter -tris *m*
homosexual *s* cinaed•us -i *m*
hone *tr* acuĕre
honest *adj* prob•us -a -um; *(truthful)* ver•ax -acis; **— to God, — to goodness** mediusfidius
honesty *s* probit•as -atis *f*
honey *s* mel mellis *n; (term of endearment)* melill•a -ae *f*
honeycomb *s* fav•us -i *m*
honeysuckle *s* clymen•us -i *m*
honor *s* hon•or -oris *m; (mark of distinction)* dignit•as -atis *f;* **on your —** per fidem; **sense of —** pud•or -oris *m;* **word of —** fid•es -ei *f*
honor *tr* honorare; *(to respect)* colĕre
honorable *adj* honest•us -a -um
honorably *adv* honeste
honorary *adj* honorari•us -a -um
hood *s* cucull•us -i *m*
hoof *s* ungul•a -ae *f*
hook *s* unc•us -i *m; (esp. for fishing)* ham•us -i *m;* **by — or by crook** quocumque modo
hook *tr (to catch w. a hook)* inuncare; *(fig)* capĕre
hooked *adj* hamat•us -a -um; *(crooked)* adunc•us -a -um
hoop *s* circul•us -i *m; (toy)* troch•us -i *m; (shout)* clam•or -oris *m*
hoot *s* cant•us -ūs *m;* **not give a — about** pili facĕre *(w. acc)*

hoot *tr* explodĕre ‖ *intr* obstrepĕre; *(of owls)* canĕre
hop *s* salt•us -ūs *m*
hop *intr* salire, subsaltare
hope *s* spe•s -i *f*
hope *intr* sperare; **to — for** exspectare
hopeful *adj* bonae spei
hopefully *adv* magnā cum spe
hopefuls *spl (persons)* spe•s -rum *fpl*
hopeless *adj* desperat•us -a -um
hopelessly *adv* desperanter
hopelessness *s* desperati•o -onis *f*
horde *s* turb•a -ae *f; (wandering)* vaga multitud•o -inis *f*
horizon *s* fini•ens -entis *m*
horizontal *adj* librat•us -a -um
horizontally *adv* per libram
horn *s* corn•u -us *n*
horned *adj* cornig•er -era -erum
hornet *s* crab•o -onis *m*
horny *adj* sal•ax -acis
horoscope *s* horoscop•us -i *m;* **to have the same —** uno astro esse
horrible *adj* horribil•is -is -e
horribly *adv* horribili modo
horrid *adj* horrid•us -a -um
horrify *tr* horrificare
horror *s* horr•or -oris *m; (strong aversion)* od•ium -(i)i *n*
hors d'oevres *spl* promuls•is -idis *f*
horse *s* equ•us -i *m,* equ•a -ae *f*
horseback *s* **on —** in equo; **to fight on —** ex equo pugnare; **to ride on —** in equo vehi
horsehair *s* pil•us -i *m* equinus
horsefly *s* taban•us -i *m*
horseman *s* equ•es -itis *m*
horse race *s* curricul•um -i *n* equorum
horseradish *s* armoraci•a -ae *f*
horseshoe *s* sole•a -ae *f* (equi)
horsewhip *s* scutic•a -ae *f*
horsewhip *tr* scuticā verberare
horticultural *adj* ad hortorum cultum pertin•ens -entis
horticulture *s* hortorum cult•us -ūs *m*
hose *s (tube)* tubul•us -i *m; (stocking)* tibial•e -is *n*
hosiery *s* feminal•ia -ium *npl*
hospitable *adj* hospital•is -is -e
hospitably *adv* hospitaliter
hospital *s* valetudinar•ium -(i)i *n*
hospitality *s* hospitalit•as -atis *f*
host *s (entertainer)* hosp•es -itis *m; (army)* copi•ae -arum *fpl; (immense number)* multitud•o -inis *f; (wafer)* hosti•a -ae *f*
hostage *s* obs•es -idis *mf*
hostess *s* hospit•a -ae *f; (at an inn)* caupon•a -ae *f*
hostile *adj* infens•us -a -um; *(forces, soil)* hostil•is -is -e; **in a — manner** hostiliter, infense
hot *adj* calid•us -a -um; *(boiling)* ferv•ens

-entis; *(seething)* aestuos•us -a -um; *(of spices)* a•cer -cris -cre; *(fig)* ard•ens -entis; **to be —** calēre; **to become —** calescĕre; **to be in — water** *(coll)* in angustiis versari
hotel *s* hospit•ium -(i)i *n*
hot-headed *adj* cerebros•us -a -um
hot-tempered *adj* stomachos•us -a -um
hound *s* catul•us -i *m*
hound *tr* instare *(w. dat)*
hour *s* hor•a -ae *f;* **at all —s** omnibus horis; **from — to —** in horas
hourly *adv* in horas
house *s* dom•us -ūs *m,* aed•es -ium *fpl; (family)* dom•us -ūs *m,* gen•s -tis *f;* **at the — of** apud *(w. acc)*
house *tr* domo excipĕre; *(things)* condĕre
housebreaker *s* effractar•ius -(i)i *m*
household *adj* familiar•is -is -e
household *s* famili•a -ae *f*
householder *s* paterfamilias *(gen:* patrisfamilias) *m*
household gods *spl* Lar•es et Penat•es -um *mpl*
housekeeper *s* prom•us -i *m*
housekeeping *s* rei familiaris cur•a -ae *f*
housemaid *s* ancill•a -ae *f*
housewife *s* materfamilias *(gen:* matrisfamilias) *f*
hovel *s* tugur•ium -(i)i *n*
hover *intr* pendēre; **to — over** impendēre *(w. dat)*
how *adv* quomodo, quo pacto; *(to what degree)* quam; **— far is Rome from Veii?** quantum distat Roma a Veiis?; **— long ago** quam pridem, quam dudum; **— many** quot; **— much** quantum; **— often** quotiens; **— soon** quam dudum
however *adv (nevertheless)* tamen, autem; *(in whatever way)* quoquomodo; *(to whatever degree)* quamvis *(esp. w. adj or adv; followed by subj);* **— great** quant•uscumque -acumque -umcumque; **— many** quotquot; **— often** quotiescumque
howl *s* ululat•us -ūs *m*
howl *intr (lit & fig)* ululare
hub *s* ax•is -is *m*
hubbub *s* tumult•us -ūs *m; (noise of brawling)* convic•ium -(i)i *n*
huckster *s* instit•or -oris *m*
huddle *intr* coacervari; **—ed together** confert•i -ae -a
huddle *s* coron•a -ae *f*
hue *s* col•or -oris *m;* **to raise a — and a cry** conclamare; *(to complain)* conqueri
huff *s* offensi•o -onis *f;* **to be in a —** stomachari
huff *intr* stomachari
hug *s* complex•us -ūs *m*
hug *tr* complecti, amplecti
huge *adj* ing•ens -entis; *(of monstrous size)* imman•is -is -e; **— sum of money** ingens pecuni•a -ae *f*
hugeness *s* immanit•as -atis *f*
hulk *s (hull of unseaworthy ship)* alve•us -i *m* desertus; *(heavy ship)* nav•is -is *f* oneraria
hulking, hulky *adj* grav•is -is -e
hull *s* alve•us -i *m*
hum *s* murm•ur -uris *m; (of bees)* bomb•us -i *m*
hum *intr* murmurare; *(of bees)* bombilare
human *adj* human•us -a -um; **— feelings** humanit•as -atis *f*
human being *s* hom•o -inis *m*
humane *adj* human•us -a -um
humanely *adv* humane
humanity *s* humanit•as -atis *f; (people)* homin•es -um *mpl*
humanize *tr* excolĕre
humble *adj (modest)* summiss•us -a -um; *(obscure)* humil•is -is -e
humble *tr* deprimĕre; **to — oneself before s.o.** se summittĕre alicui
humbly *adv* summisse
humdrum *adj (dull)* molest•us -a -um; *(banal)* trit•us -a -um
humid *adj* humid•us -a -um
humidity *s* hum•or -oris *m*
humiliate *tr* deprimĕre
humiliating *adj* humil•is -is -e
humiliation *s* humilati•o -onis *f*
humility *s* humilit•as -atis *f*
humor *s* festivit•as -atis *f; (mood)* anim•us -i *m;* **he is in bad —** tristis est; **he is in good —** festivus est; **sense of —** festivit•as -atis *f*
humor *tr* indulgēre *(w. dat)*
humorous *adj* facet•us -a -um
humorously *adv* festive
hump *s* gibb•er -eris *m*
humpbacked *adj* gibb•er -era -erum
hunch *s* opini•o -onis *f;* **to have a —** opinari
hundred *adj* centum *(indecl);* **— times** centie(n)s
hundredfold *adj* centupl•ex -icis
hundredfold *s* centupl•um -i *n*
hundredth *adj* centesim•us -a -um
hunger *s* fam•es -is *f; (voluntary)* inedi•a -ae *f*
hunger *intr* esurire; **to — for** cupĕre
hungrily *adv* avide, voraciter
hungry *adj* esuri•ens -entis; **to be —** esurire
hunt *s* venati•o -onis *f*
hunt *tr* venari ‖ *intr* **to — for** quaerĕre
hunter *s* venat•or -oris *m; (horse)* equ•us -i *m* venaticus
hunting *s* venat•us -ūs *m;* **to go —** venari
hunting *adj* venatic•us -a -um; **— gear** venationis apparat•us -ūs *m* **— spear** venabul•um -i *n*
huntress *s* venatr•ix -icis *f*
hurdle *s* crat•es -is *f; (obstacle)* ob•ex -icis *mf*

hurl *tr* conjicěre
hurray *interj* evax!
hurricane *s* procell•a -ae *f*
hurried *adj* praeproper•us -a -um; *(too hasty)* praec•eps -ipitis
hurriedly *adv* raptim; *(carelessly)* negligenter
hurry *tr* rapěre; **to — away** abripěre **||** *intr* properare, festinare; *(to rush hurriedly)* ruěre; **to — along** se agěre
hurry *s* festinati•o -onis *f;* **in a —** festinanter; **to be in a —** festinare
hurt *s* injuri•a -ae *f*
hurt *adj* sauci•us -a -um; *(emotionally)* sauci•us -a -um, offens•us -a -um
hurt *tr* nocēre *(w. dat),* laeděre; *(fig)* offenděre **||** *intr* dolēre
husband *s* marit•us -i *m*
husbandry *s* agricultur•a -ae *f*
hush *s* silent•ium -(i)i *n*
hush *tr* compriměre; *(a secret)* celare **||** *intr* tacēre
hush *interj* st!
husk *s* follicul•us -i *m; (of beans, etc.)* siliqu•a -ae *f; (of grain)* glum•a -ae *f*
husky *adj* robust•us -a -um; *(of voice)* rauc•us -a -um
hustle *tr* truděre **||** *intr* inter se truděre
hustler *s* hom•o -inis *m* strenuus
hut *s* tugur•ium -(i)i *n*
hyacinth *s* hyacinth•us -i *m*
hybrid *s* hybrid•a -ae *f*
Hydra *s* Hydr•a -ae *f*
hydraulic *adj* hydraulic•us -a -um
hydrophobia *s* hydrophobi•a -ae *f*
hyena *s* hyaen•a -ae *f*
hymn *s* hymn•us -i *m*
hyperbole *s* hyperbol•e -es *f*
hypercritical *adj* nimis sever•us -a -um
hyphen *s* hyphen *(indecl) n*
hypochondriac *s* melancholic•us -i *m*
hypocrisy *s* simulati•o -onis *f*
hypocrite *s* simulat•or -oris *m*
hypocritical *adj* simulat•us -a -um
hypothesis *s* hypothes•is -is *m*
hypothetical *adj* hypothetic•us -a -um
hysteria *s* delirati•o -onis *f*
hysterical *adj* delir•us -a -um

I

I *pron* ego; **— myself** egomet
iamb *s (pros)* iamb•us -i *m*
iambic *adj (pros)* iambe•us -a -um
ice *s* glaci•es -ei *f*
iceberg *s* glaciei niviumque concreta stru•es -is *f*
ice water *s* nivata aqu•a -ae *f*
icicle *s* stiri•a -ae *f*
icy *adj* glacial•is -is -e
idea *s (notion)* noti•o -onis *f; (thought)* sententi•a -ae *f;* **it's a good — to** expedit *(w. inf)*
ideal *adj* perfect•us -a -um
ideal *s* exempl•ar -aris *n*
idealist *s* hom•o -inis *m* summae virtutis
idealistic *adj* omnibus virtutibus ornat•us -i *m*
identical *adj* idem eadem idem
identify *tr* agnoscěre
idiocy *s* fatuit•as -atis *f*
idiosyncrasy *s* propr•ium -(i)i *n*
idiot *s* fatu•us -i *m*
idiotic *adj* fatu•us -a -um
idle *adj* vacu•us -a -um; *(pointless)* van•us -a -um; *(lazy)* ignav•us -a -um; **to be —** cessare
idle *tr* **to — away** terěre **||** *intr* cessare, vacare
idleness *s* cessati•o -onis *f*
idler *s* cessat•or -oris *m*
idle talk *s* nug•ae -arum *fpl*
idly *adv* segniter
idol *s* simulacr•um -i *n; (eccl)* idol•um -i *n; (fig)* delici•ae -arum *fpl*
idolater *s* idololatr•es -ae *m*
idolatrous *adj* idololatric•us -a -um
idolatry *s* idololatri•a -ae *f*
idolize *tr* venerari
idyl *s* idyll•ium -(i)i *n*
if *conj* si; **as —** quasi, tamquam; **and —, but —** quodsi; **even —** etiamsi; **— not** ni, nisi; **— only** si modo
iffy *adj (coll)* dubi•us -a -um
igneous *adj* igne•us -a -um
ignite *tr* accenděre **||** *intr* flammam concipěre, exardescěre
ignoble *adj* ignobil•is -is -e; *(base)* turp•is -is -e
ignobly *adv* turpiter
ignominious *adj* ignominios•us -a -um
ignominiously *adv* ignominiose
ignominy *s* ignomini•a -ae *f*
ignoramus *s* nesap•ius -(i)i *m,* nesapi•a -ae *f*
ignorance *s* ignoranti•a -ae *f*
ignorant *adj* ignar•us -a -um; *(unlearned)* indoct•us -a -um; **to be — of** ignorare
ignorantly *adv* inscienter
ignore *tr* praeterire; *(to omit)* neglegěre
Iliad *s* Ili•as -adis *f*
ill *adj* aegrot•us -a -um; *(evil)* mal•us -a -um; **to be —** aegrotare; **to fall —** in morbum inciděre
ill *adv* male
ill *s* mal•um -i *n*
ill-advised *adj* inconsult•us -a -um
ill-boding *adj* infaust•us -a -um
ill-bred *adj* inhuman•us -a -um
ill-disposed *adj* **(toward)** malevol•us -a -um *(w. dat)*
illegal *adj* illicit•us -a -um
illegitimate *adj* haud legitim•us -a -um; *(of birth)* noth•us -a -um

illegitimately *adv* contra legem
ill-fated *adj* infel•ix -icis
ill-gotten *adj* male part•us -a -um
ill health *s* valetud•o -inis *f*; adversa
illiberal *adj* illiberal•is -is -e
illicit *adj* illicit•us -a -um
illicitly *adv* illicite
illiteracy *s* ignorati•o -onis *f* legendi scribendique
illiterate *adj* illiterat•us -a -um
illness *s* morb•us -i *m*
illogical *adj* absurd•us -a -um
illogically *adv* absurde
ill-omened *adj* infel•ix -icis
ill-starred *adj* infel•ix -icis
ill-tempered *adj* iracund•us -a -um
illuminate *tr* illuminare
illumination *s* illuminati•o -onis *f*
illusion *s* err•or -oris *m*
illusive *adj* van•us -a -um
illusory *adj* fall•ax -acis
illustrate *tr (to shed light on)* illustrare; *(to exemplify)* exempla *(w. gen)* adducĕre; *(to draw)* delineare; *(to picture)* in tabulis depingĕre
illustration *s (example)* exempl•um -i *n; (picture)* tabul•a -ae *f*
illustrious *adj* illustr•is -is -e
ill will *s* malevolenti•a -ae *f*
image *s* sign•um -i *n; (esp. a portrait or bust)* imag•o -inis *f; (esp. a figure of a god)* simulacr•um -i *n*
imagery *s* imagin•es -um *fpl*
imaginary *adj* commentici•us -a -um
imagination *s* cogitati•o -onis *f*
imaginative *adj* ingenios•us -a -um
imagine *tr* fingĕre
imbecile *s* fatu•us -i *m*
imbedded *adj* **(in)** infix•us -a -um (in + *abl)*
imbibe *tr* imbibĕre
imbue *tr* imbuĕre
imitate *tr* imitari
imitation *s (act)* imitati•o -onis *f; (thing)* imag•o -inis *f*
imitator *s* imitat•or -oris *m,* imitatr•ix -icis *f*
immaculate *adj* immaculat•us -a -um
immaterial *adj* incorporal•is -is -e; *(unimportant)* nullius momenti
immeasurable *adj* immens•us -a -um
immeasurably *adv* longe longeque
immediate *adj* proxim•us -a -um
immediately *adv* statim, confestim; **— after** sub *(w. acc)*
immemorial *adj* antiquissim•us -a -um; **from time —** ex omni memoria aetatum
immense *adj* immens•us -a -um
immensely *adv* vehementer
immensity *s* immensit•as -atis *f*
immerse *tr* (im)mergĕre
immersion *s* immersi•o -onis *f*
imminent *adj* immin•ens -entis; **to be —** instare
immobile *adj* immobil•is -is -e
immobility *s* immobilit•as -atis *f*
immoderate *adj* immodic•us -a -um
immoderately *adv* immodice
immodesty *s* immodesti•a -ae *f*
immolate *tr* immolare
immolation *s* immolati•o -onis *f*
immoral *adj* prav•us -a -um
immorality *s* perditi mor•es -um *mpl*
immortal *adj* immortal•is -is -e
immortality *s* immortalit•as -atis *f*
immortalize *tr* immortalitati tradĕre
immovable *adj (lit & fig)* immobil•is -is -e
immunity *s* immunit•as -atis *f*; **promise of —** fid•es -ei *f* publica
immutability *s* immutabilit•as -atis *f*
immutable *adj* immutabil•is -is -e
imp *s* pu•er -eri *m* protervus
impact *s* impuls•us -ūs *m*
impair *tr* imminuĕre
impale *tr* palo infigĕre; **— oneself on a pointed stake** se acuto vallo induĕre
impart *tr* impertire, communicare
impartial *adj* aequ•us -a -um
impartiality *s* aequit•as -atis *f*
impartially *adv* aequabiliter; **to judge —** aequo (animo) judicare
impassable *adj* impervi•us -a -um
impassioned *adj* vehem•ens -entis; **with — gestures** ardenti motu gestuque
impassive *adj* sensu car•ens -entis
impatience *s* impatienti•a -ae *f*
impatient *adj* iniquo animo; **to be — with** iniquo animo ferre
impatiently *adv* iniquo animo
impeach *tr* nomen *(w. gen)* deferre
impeachment *s* delati•o -onis *f* nominis
impede *tr* impedire
impediment *s* impediment•um -i *n; (in speech)* haesitati•o -onis *f*
impel *tr* impellĕre
impending *adj* immin•ens -entis
impenetrable *adj* impenetrabil•is -is -e; *(fig)* occult•us -a -um
impenitence *s* impaenitenti•a -ae *f*
imperative *adj* inst•ans -antis; *(gram)* imperativ•us -a -um
imperceptible *adj* tenuissim•us -a -um
imperceptibly *adv* sensim
imperfect *adj* imperfect•us -a -um
imperfection *s* vit•ium -(i)i *n*
imperfectly *adv* imperfecte
imperial *adj (of an emperor)* principal•is -is -e; *(becoming an emperor)* august•us -a - um
imperil *tr* in discrimen adducĕre
imperious *adj* imperios•us -a -um
imperiously *adv* imperiose
imperishable *adj* incorrupt•us -a -um
impermeable *adj* impervi•us -a -um
impersonal *adj (detached)* incurios•us -a -um; *(gram)* impersonal•is -is -e
impersonally *adv* impersonaliter

impersonate *tr* sustinēre partes *(w. gen)*
impertinence *s* protervit•as -atis *f*
impertinent *adj* proterv•us -a -um; *(not to the point)* nihil ad rem
impertinently *adv* proterve
impervious *adj* impervi•us -a -um
impetuosity *s* impet•us -ūs *m*
impetuous *adj* violent•us -a -um
impetus *s* impet•us -ūs *m*
impiety *s* impiet•as -atis *f*
impinge *intr* **— on** incidĕre *(w. dat)*
impious *adj* impi•us -a -um; *(stronger)* nefari•us -a -um
impiously *adv* impie; *(stronger)* nefarie
impish *adj* proterv•us -a -um
implacable *adj* implacabil•is -is -e
implacably *adv* implacabiliter
implant *tr* inserĕre, ingenerare
implement *s* instrument•um -i *n; (iron tool)* ferrament•um -i *n*
implement *tr* exsequi
implicate *tr* implicare
implication *s* indic•ium -(i)i *n;* **by —** tacite
implicit *adj* tacit•us -a -um; *(absolute)* summ•us -a -um
implicitly *adv* tacite
implied *adj* tacit•us -a -um; **to be — in** inesse in *(w. abl)*
implore *tr* implorare
imply *tr* significare
impolite *adj* inurban•us -a -um
impolitely *adv* inurbane
impoliteness *s* inurbanit•as -atis *f*
impolitic *adj* inconsult•us -a -um
import *tr* importare, invehĕre
import *s (meaning)* significati•o -onis *f;* **—s** importatici•a -orum *npl*
importance *s* moment•um -i *n;* **of —** grav•is -is -e; **to be a person of great —** plurimum pollēre; **to be of great —** magni esse
important *adj* magn•us -a -um; *(weighty)* grav•is -is -e; **an — and wealthy city** gravis atque opulenta civit•as -atis *f;* **to be —** magni (momenti *or* negotii) esse; **to be very —** maximi (momenti *or* negotii) esse
importunate *adj* importun•us -a -um
importune *tr* flagitare, sollicitare
impose *tr* imponĕre; *(to enjoin)* injungĕre **‖** *intr* **to — upon** abuti *(w. abl)*
imposition *s (excessive burden)* importunit•as -atis *f; (act) use* imponĕre
impossibility *s* impossibilit•as -atis *f*
impossible *adj* impossibil•is -is -e; **it is —** non fieri potest
imposter *s* fraudat•or -oris *m*
imposture *s* frau•s -dis *f*
impotence *s* infirmit•as -atis *f; (sexual)* sterilit•as -atis *f*
impotent *adj* infirm•us -a -um; *(sexually)* steril•is -is -e
impound *tr* publicare; *(animals)* includĕre
impoverish *tr* in egestatem redigĕre
impoverished *adj* eg•ens -entis
impractical *adj* inutil•is -is -e
imprecate *tr* imprecari, exsecrari
imprecation *s* exsecrati•o -onis *f*
impregnable *adj* inexpugnabil•is -is -e
impregnate *tr* gravidam facĕre
impregnation *s* fecundati•o -onis *f*
impress *tr* imprimĕre; *(a person)* movēre; **to — s.th. on s.o.** alicui inculcare aliquid
impression *s* impressi•o -onis *f; (copy)* exempl•ar -aris *n;* **to make an — on** (com)movēre
impressive *adj* grav•is -is -e
impressively *adv* graviter
imprint *s* impressi•o -onis *f*
imprint *tr* imprimĕre; **to be —ed on the mind** in animum imprimi
imprison *tr* in vincula conjicĕre
imprisonment *s* custodi•a -ae *f*
improbable *adj* haud credibil•is -is -e
impromptu *adj* subit(ari)•us -a -um
impromptu *adv* ex tempore
improper *adj* indecor•us -a -um
improperly *adv* indecore
improve *tr* mel•iorem -iorem -ius facĕre; *(where a fault exists)* emendare; *(soil)* laetificare **‖** *intr* mel•ior -ior -ius fieri
improvement *s* emendati•o -onis *f; (progress made)* profect•us -ūs *m;* **to make —** proficĕre
improvident *adj* improvid•us -a -um
improvise *tr* ex tempore dicĕre *or* componĕre
imprudence *s* imprudenti•a -ae *f*
imprudent *adj* imprud•ens -entis
imprudently *adv* imprudenter
impugn *tr* inpugnare, in dubium vocare
impulse *s* impet•us -ūs *m* animi
impulsive *adj* temerari•us -a -um
impulsively *adv* impetu quodam animi
impunity *s* impunit•as -atis *f;* **with —** impune
impure *adj* impur•us -a -um
impurely *adv* impure
impurity *s* impurit•as -atis *f*
in *prep* in *(w. abl); (in the writings of)* apud *(w. acc); (of time) render by abl; (denoting rule, standard or manner)* in *(w. acc), e.g.,* **— the manner of slaves** servilem in modum; **— that** quod; **— the course of the night** de nocte; **— the course of the third watch** de tertia vigilia; **— the likeness of** ad similitudinem *(w. gen);* **— the month of September** (de) mense Septembri; **— the same manner** ad eundem modum, eodem modo
in *adv (motion)* intro; *(rest)* intra, intus
inability *s* impotenti•a -ae *f*
inaccessible *adj* inacess•us -a -um; **to be —** *(of a person)* rari aditūs esse
inaccuracy *s* indiligenti•a -ae *f*

inaccurate *adj* parum accurat•us -a -um
inaccurately *adv* parum accurate
inactive *adj* iner•s -tis
inactivity *s* inerti•a -ae *f*
inadequate *adj* im•par -paris
inadequately *adv* parum, haud satis
inadmissible *adj* illicit•us -a -um
inadvertent *adj* imprud•ens -entis
inadvertently *adv* imprudenter; *more frequently expressed by the adjective* imprud•ens -entis
inalienable *adj* quod alienari non potest
inane *adj* inan•is -is -e
inanimate *adj* inanim•us -a -um
inapplicable *adj* **to be —** non valēre
inappropriate *adj* haud apt•us -a -um
inappropriately *adv* parum apte
inarticulate *adj* indistinct•us -a -um
inartistic *adj* dur•us -a -um
inasmuch as *conj* quandoquidem
inattentive *adj* haud attent•us -a -um
inattentively *adv* neglegenter
inaudible *adj* **to be —** audiri non posse
inaugurate *tr* inaugurare
inauguration *s* inaugurati•o -onis *f*
inauspicious *adj* infaust•us -a -um
inauspiciously *adv* malo omine
inborn *adj* innat•us -a -um
incalculable *adj* inaestimabil•is -is -e; *(fig)* immens•us -a -um
incantation *s* incantament•um -i *n*
incapable *adj* incap•ax -acis; **to be — of** non posse *(w. inf)*
incapacitate *tr* debilitare
incarcerate *tr* in carcerem conjicĕre
incarnate *adj* incarnat•us -a -um
incarnation *s* incarnati•o -onis *f*
incautious *adj* incaut•us -a -um
incautiously *adv* incaute
incendiary *adj* incendiari•us -a -um
incense *s* tu•s -ris *n*
incense *tr* ture fumigare; *(to anger)* incendĕre
incentive *s* incitament•um -i *n*
incessant *adj* assidu•us -a -um
incessantly *adv* assidue
incest *s* incest•us -ūs *m*
incestuous *adj* incest•us -a -um
inch *s* unci•a -ae *f;* **— by —** unciatim
incident *s* cas•us -ūs *m*
incidental *adj* fortuit•us -a -um
incidentally *adv* casu, inter alias res
incision *s* incisur•a -ae *f*
incisive *adj* a•cer -cris -cre
incite *tr* incitare
incitement *s* incitament•um -i *n*
incivility *s* rusticit•as -atis *f*
inclemency *s* inclementi•a -ae *f; (of weather)* asperit•as -atis *f*
inclement *adj* asp•er -era -erum
inclination *s (act, propensity)* inclinati•o -onis *f; (slope)* proclivit•as -atis *f*
incline *s* acclivit•as -atis *f*
incline *tr & intr* inclinare
inclined *adj* propens•us -a -um; **I am — to believe** crediderim
include *tr (to enclose)* includĕre; *(to comprise)* comprehendĕre; **—ing me** me haud excepto; **—ing your brother** in his frater tuus
inclusive *adj expressed by* adnumerare: **from the 1st to the 10th —** a primo die ad decimum adnumeratum *(or* ipso decimo adnumerato)
incognito *adv* alienā indutā personā
incoherent *adj* perturbat•us -a -um; **to be —** non cohaerēre
incoherently *adv* **to speak —** male cohaerentia loqui
income *s* quaest•us -ūs *m*
incomparable *adj* incomparabil•is -is -e
incomparably *adv* unice
incompatibility *s* repugnanti•a -ae *f*
incompatible *adj* repugn•ans -antis
incompetence *s* insciti•a -ae *f*
incompetent *adj* inscit•us -a -um
incomplete *adj* imperfect•us -a -um
incomprehensible *adj* quod mente non comprehendi potest
inconceivable *adj* incredibil•is -is -e
inconclusive *adj* anc•eps -ipitis
incongruous *adj* male congru•ens -entis, inconveni•ens -entis
inconsiderable *adj* exigu•us -a -um
inconsiderate *adj* inconsiderat•us -a -um
inconsistency *s* discrepanti•a -ae *f*
inconsistent *adj* inconst•ans -antis; **to be — with** abhorrēre ab *(w. abl)*
inconsistently *adv* inconstanter
inconsolable *adj* inconsolabil•is -is -e
inconstancy *s* inconstanti•a -ae *f*
inconstant *adj* inconst•ans -antis
incontestible *adj* non contentend•us -a -um
incontinence *s* incontinenti•a -ae *f*
incontinent *adj* incontin•ens -entis
incontrovertible *adj* quod refutari non potest
inconvenience *s* incommod•um -i *n*
inconvenience *tr* incommodare
inconvenient *adj* incommod•us -a -um
inconveniently *adv* incommode
incorporate *tr* adjicĕre; *(to unite, esp. politically)* contribuĕre; *(to form into a corporation)* constituĕre
incorporeal *adj* incorporal•is -is -e
incorrect *adj* mendos•us -a -um
incorrectly *adv* perperam
incorrigible *adj* perdit•us -a -um
incorrigibly *adv* perdite
incorrupt *adj* incorrupt•us -a -um
incorruptibility *s* incorruptibilit•as -atis *f*
incorruptible *adj* incorruptibil•is -is -e; *(upright)* inte•ger -gra -grum
increase *s* increment•um -i *n; (act)* accreti•o -onis *f*
increase *tr* augēre, ampliare ‖ *intr* augeri,

crescĕre
incredible *adj* incredibil•is -is -e
incredibly *adv* incredibiliter
incredulity *s* incredulit•as -atis *f*
incredulous *adj* incredul•us -a -um
increment *s* increment•um -i *n*
incriminate *tr* criminari
incubate *tr* incubare
incubation *s* incubati•o -onis *f*
inculcate *tr* inculcare
inculcation *s* inculcati•o -onis *f*
incumbent *adj* **it is — on** oportet *(w. acc)*
incumbent *s* qui honorem gerit
incur *tr* subire; *(guilt)* admittĕre
incurable *adj* insanabil•is -is -e
incursion *s* incursi•o -onis *f*
indebted *adj* obaerat•us -a -um; *(obliged)* obnoxi•us -a -um; **to be — to s.o. for a sum of money** pecuniam alicui debēre
indecency *s* impudicit•as -atis *f*
indecent *adj* impudic•us -a -um
indecently *adv* impudice
indecision *s* haesitati•o -onis *f*
indecisive *adj* anc•eps -ipitis
indeclinable *adj* indeclinabil•is -is -e
indeed *adv* vere, profecto; *(concessive)* quidem; *(reply)* certe, vero; *(interrog)* itane?
indefatigable *adj* indefatigabil•is -is -e
indefensible *adj (an action)* non excusand•us -a -um; *(mil)* parum firm•us -a -um; **to be —** defendi non posse
indefinite *adj* incert•us -a -um; *(vague)* anc•eps -ipitis; *(gram)* infinit•us -a -um
indelible *adj* indelibil•is -is -e
indelicate *adj* putid•us -a -um
indemnify *tr* damnum restitutĕre *(w. dat)*
indemnity *s* indemnit•as -atis *f*
indent *tr* incisuris signare
indentation *s* incisur•a -ae *f*
indented *adj* incis•us -a -um; *(serrated)* serrat•us -a -um
independence *s* libert•as -atis *f*
independent *adj* lib•er -era -erum; *(one's own master)* sui pot•ens -entis; *(leg)* sui juris
independently *adv* libere, suo arbitrio
indescribable *adj* inenarrabil•is -is -e
indescribably *adv* inenarrabiliter
indestructible *adj* perenn•is -is -e, indelebil•is -is -e
indeterminate *adj* indefinit•us -a -um
index *s* ind•ex -icis *m*
Indian *adj* Indic•us -a -um
Indian *s* Ind•us -i *m*
indicate *tr* indicare, significare; **to — that** docēre *(w. acc & inf)*
indication *s* indic•ium -(i)i *n*
indicative *s (gram)* indicativus mod•us -i *m*
indict *tr* nomen *(w. gen)* deferre
indictment *s* nominis delati•o -onis *f;* **bill of —** libell•us -i *m*
indifference *s* aequus anim•us -i *m; (apathy)* lentitud•o -inis *f*
indifferent *adj (apathetic)* indiffer•ens -entis; *(mediocre)* mediocr•is -is -e; **to be — to s.th.** aliquid nil morari
indifferently *adv* indifferenter
indigenous *adj (home-grown)* vernacul•us -a -um; *(of people)* indigen•a -ae; **the — Latins** indigenae Latini
indigent *adj* eg•ens -entis
indigestible *adj* crud•us -a -um
indigestion *s* crudit•as -atis *f*
indignant *adj* indignabund•us -a -um; **— at** indign•ans -antis *(w. gen);* **to be —** indignari
indignantly *adv* indignanter
indignation *s* indignati•o -onis *f*
indignity *s* indignit•as -atis *f*
indirect *adj* indirect•us -a -um; **— discourse** obliqua orati•o -onis *f*
indirectly *adv* indirecte
indiscreet *adj* inconsult•us -a -um
indiscreetly *adv* inconsulte
indiscretion *s* imprudenti•a -ae *f;* **driven by youthful —** licentiā juvenali impuls•us -a -um
indiscriminate *adj* promiscu•us -a -um
indiscriminately *adv* sine discrimine
indispensable *adj* omnino necessari•us -a -um
indisposed *adj* **(to)** avers•us -a -um (ab + *abl); (sick)* aegrot•us -a -um
indisputable *adj* cert•us -a -um
indissoluble *adj* indissolubil•is -is -e
indistinct *adj* parum clar•us -a -um
indistinctly *adv* parum clare
individual *adj (of one only)* singular•is -is -e; *(of more than one)* singul•i -ae -a; *(particular)* quidam quaedam, quoddam; *(peculiar)* propri•us -a -um
individual *s* hom•o -inis *mf;* **—s** singul•i -ae -a; **to benefit the country or —s** civitatem aut singulis civibus prodesse
individually *adv* singulatim
individuality *s* proprium ingen•ium -(i)i *n*
indivisible *adj* indivisibil•is -is -e
indolence *s* inerti•a -ae *f*
indolent *adj* in•ers -ertis
indomitable *adj* indomit•us -a -um
indorse *tr* ratum facĕre
indubitable *adj* indubitabil•is -is -e
indubitably *adv* sine dubio
induce *tr* inducĕre, adducĕre
inducement *s* incitament•um -i *n*
indulge *tr* indulgēre *(w. dat)*
indulgent *adj* indulg•ens -entis
indulgently *adv* indulgenter
industrial *adj* ad artes quaestuosas pertin•ens -entis
industrialist *s* magis•ter -tri *m* officinarum
industrious *adj* industri•us -a -um
industriously *adv* industrie

industry *s (effort)* industri•a -ae *f; (com)* art•es -ium *fpl* quaestuosae
inebriated *adj* ebri•us -a -um
ineffable *adj* ineffabil•is -is -e
ineffective *adj* irrit•us -a -um; **to be —** effectu carēre
ineffectual *adj* ineffic•ax -acis
ineffectually *adv* frustra
inefficiency *s* segniti•a -ae *f*
inefficient *adj* segn•is -is -e
inelegant *adj* ineleg•ans -antis
ineligible *adj* non eligend•us -a -um
inept *adj* inept•us -a -um
ineptitude *s* inepti•ae -arum *fpl*
inequality *s* inaequalit•as -atis *f (social)* iniquit•as -atis *f*
inequitable *adj* iniqu•us -a -um
inert *adj* in•ers -ertis
inertia *s* inerti•a -ae *f*
inevitable *adj* inevitabil•is -is -e
inevitably *adv* necessario
inexact *adj* haud accurat•us -a -um; *(of persons)* indilig•ens -entis
inexcusable *adj* inexcusabil•is -is -e
inexhaustible *adj* inexhaust•us -a -um
inexorable *adj* inexorabil•is -is -e
inexperience *s* imperiti•a -ae *f*
inexperienced *adj* imperit•us -a -um
inexplicable *adj* inexplicabil•is -is -e
inexpressible *adj* inenarrabil•is -is -e
inextricable *adj* inextricabil•is -is -e
infallibility *s* erroris immunit•as -atis *f*
infallible *adj* qui errare non potest
infamous *adj* infam•is -is -e
infamously *adv* cum infamia
infancy *s* infanti•a -ae *f*
infant *s* inf•ans -antis *mf*
infanticide *s (deed)* infanticid•ium -(i)i *n; (person)* infanticid•a -ae *m*
infantile *adj* infantil•is -is -e
infantry *s* peditat•us -ūs *m*
infatuate *tr* infatuare; *(w. love)* urěre
infatuated *adj* mente capt•us -a -um
infatuation *s* dementi•a -ae *f*
infect *tr* inficěre; *(fig)* contaminare
infection *s* contagi•o -onis *f*
infectious *adj* contagios•us -a -um
infer *tr* colligěre, conjicěre
inference *s* conjectur•a -ae *f*
inferior *adj* deter•ior -ior -ius
infernal *adj* infern•us -a -um
infertile *adj* steril•is -is -e
infertility *s* sterilit•as -atis *f*
infest *tr* infestare
infidel *s* infidel•is -is *mf*
infidelity *s* infidelit•as -atis *f*
infiltrate *tr* se insinuare in *(w. acc)*
infinite *adj* infinit•us -a -um
infinitely *adv* infinite; *(coll)* infinito
infinitive *s* infinitiv•um -i *n*
infinity *s* infinit•as -atis *f*
infirm *adj* infirm•us -a -um
infirmary *s* valetudinar•ium -(i)i *n*
infirmity *s* infirmit•as -atis *f*
inflame *tr (lit & fig)* inflammare; *(fig)* incenděre
inflammable *adj* ad exardescendum facil•is -is -e
inflammation *s* inflammati•o -onis *f*
inflammatory *adj* turbulent•us -a -um
inflate *tr* inflare
inflated *adj* inflat•us -a -um
inflation *s* inflati•o -onis *f*
inflect *tr (gram)* declinare
inflection *s* declinati•o -onis *f*
inflexible *adj* inflexibil•is -is -e; *(fig)* obstinat•us -a -um
inflexibly *adv* obstinate
inflict *tr* infligěre, inferre; **to — a deadly blow** mortiferam plagam infligěre; **to — punishment on s.o.** aliquem supplicio afficěre; **to — wounds on** vulnera inferre *(w. dat)*
influence *s* grati•a -ae *f;* **to have — on** valēre apud *(w. acc);* **to have (great, more, very great) influence on** magnum (plus, plurimum) posse apud *(w. acc)*
influence *tr* movēre
influential *adj* auctoritate grav•is -is -e
influenza *s* catarrh•us -i *m*
influx *s* influxi•o -onis *f*
inform *tr* certiorem facěre, docēre; **having been —ed about this** his rebus cognitis ‖ *intr* **to — against** deferre de *(w. abl)*
informant *s* ind•ex -icis *m*
information *s* re•s -rum *fpl,* nunt•ius -(i)i *m;* **having received this —** his rebus cognitis
informer *s* delat•or -oris *m*
infraction *s* infracti•o -onis *f*
infrequency *s* rarit•as -atis *f*
infrequent *adj* rar•us -a -um
infrequently *adv* raro
infringe *tr* infringěre ‖ *intr* **to — upon** usurpare
infringement *s* immunuti•o -onis *f*
infuriate *tr* efferare
infuse *tr* infunděre; *(fig)* injicěre
infusion *s* infusi•o -onis *f*
ingenious *adj* ingenios•us -a -um, soll•ers -ertis
ingeniously *adv* sollerter
ingenuity *s* sollerti•a -ae *f*
ingenuous *adj* ingenu•us -a -um
ingest *tr* ingerěre
inglorious *adj* inglori•us -a -um
ingloriously *adv* sine gloriā
ingrained *adj* insit•us -a -um
ingratiate *tr* **to — oneself with** gratiam inire ab *(w. abl)*
ingratitude *s* ingratus anim•us -i *m*
ingredient *s (generally not expressed by a noun)* element•um -i *n;* **a composition, the —s of which** compositio quae habet;

the medication consists of the following —s medicamentum constat ex his
inhabit *tr* incolĕre
inhabitable *adj* habitabil•is -is -e
inhabitant *s* incol•a -ae *mf*
inhale *tr* haurire, ducĕre ‖ *intr* spiritum ducĕre
inharmonious *adj* disson•us -a -um
inherent *adj* inhaer•ens -entis; **to be — in** inhaerēre in *(w. abl)*, inesse in *(w. abl)*
inherit *tr* excipĕre
inheritance *s* heredit•as -atis *f;* **to come into an —** hereditatem adire
inhospitable *adj* inhospital•is -is -e
inhuman *adj* inhuman•us -a -um
inhumanly *adv* inhumane
inhumanity *s* inhumanit•as -atis *f*
inimical *adj* inimic•us -a -um
inimitable *adj* inimitabil•is -is -e
iniquitous *adj* improb•us -a -um
iniquity *s* improbit•as -atis *f*
initial *adj* prim•us -a -um
initial *s* prima nominis litter•a -ae *f*
initiate *tr* initiare
initiation *s* initiati•o -onis *f*
initiative *s* vis *f*
inject *tr* injicĕre, immittĕre
injection *s* injecti•o -onis *f*
injudicious *adj* inconsult•us -a -um
injudiciously *adv* inconsulte
injunction *s* mandat•um -i *n;* **to get an —** ad interdictum venire
injure *tr* nocēre *(w. dat)*, laedĕre
injurious *adj* noxi•us -a -um
injury *s* detriment•um -i *n;* **to do great —** magnum detrimentum adferre
injustice *s* injustiti•a -ae *f; (act of injustice)* injuri•a -ae *f*
ink *s* atrament•um -i *n*
inkling *s* obscura significati•o -onis *f;* **to have an —** suspicari
inland *adj* mediterrane•us -a -um
in-law *s* affin•is -is *mf*
inlay *tr* inserĕre; *(with mosaic)* tessellare
inlet *s* aestuar•ium -(i)i *n*
inmate *s* inquilin•us -i *m*
inmost *adj* intim•us -a -um
inn *s* deversor•ium -(i)i *n, (esp. of an inferior type)* caupon•a -ae *f*
innate *adj* innat•us -a -um
inner *adj* inter•ior -ior -ius
innermost *adj* intim•us -a -um
innkeeper *s* caup•o -onis *m; (female)* caupon•a -ae *f*
innocence *s* innocenti•a -ae *f*
innocent *adj* innoc•ens -entis
innocently *adv* innocenter
innocuous *adj* innocu•us -a -um
innocuously *adv* innocue
innovate *tr* novare
innovation *s* novit•as -atis *f*
innovative *adj* multa nov•ans -antis
innovator *s* qui multa novat
innumerable *adj* innumerabil•is -is -e
inoculate *tr* serum inserĕre *(w. dat)*
inoffensive *adj* innoxi•us -a -um
inopportune *adj* inopportun•us -a -um
inopportunely *adv* parum in tempore
inordinate *adj* immoderat•us -a -um
inordinately *adv* immoderate
inquest *s* inquisiti•o -onis *f; (leg)* quaesti•o -onis *f;* **an — was held on the cause of death** quaesitum est quae mortis causa fuisset
inquire *intr* **(into)** inquirĕre
inquiry *s* quaesti•o -onis *f*
inquisition *s* inquisiti•o -onis *f*
inquisitive *adj* curios•us -a -um
inquisitor *s* quaesit•or -oris *m*
inroad *s* incursi•o -onis *f;* **to make —s into territory** incursiones in fines facĕre
insane *adj* insan•us -a -um
insanely *adv* insane
insanity *s* insanit•as -atis *f*
insatiable *adj* insatiabil•is -is -e
inscribe *tr* inscribĕre
inscription *s* inscripti•o -onis *f*
inscrutable *adj* occult•us -a -um
insect *s* insect•um -i *n*
insecure *adj* haud tut•us -a -um
insecurity *s* **feeling of —** sollicitud•o -inis *f*
insensible *adj* insensil•is -is -e; *(fig)* dur•us -a -um
inseparable *adj* inseparabil•is -is -e
insert *tr* inserĕre, interponĕre; *(in writing)* ascribĕre
insertion *s* interpositi•o -onis *f*
inside *adj* inter•ior -ior -ius
inside *adv* intus
inside *prep* intro *(w. acc)*
inside *s* interior par•s -tis *f*
inside of *prep* intra *(w. acc)*
insidious *adj* insidios•us -a -um
insidiously *adv* insidiose
insight *s* cogniti•o -onis *f;* **to have a profound — into human character** mores hominum atque ingenia penitus perspecta habēre
insignia *spl* insign•ia -ium *npl*
insignificance *s* exiguit•as -atis *f*
insignificant *adj* exigu•us -a -um, nullius momenti
insincere *adj* insincer•us -a -um
insincerely *adv* haud sincere
insincerity *s* ingen•ium -(i)i *n* haud sincerum
insinuate *tr* insinuare; *(to hint)* operte significare
insinuation *s* significati•o -onis *f*
insipid *adj* insuls•us -a -um
insipidly *adv* insulse
insist *intr* instare; **to — on** urgēre
insistence *s* pertinaci•a -ae *f*
insolence *s* insolenti•a -ae *f*
insolent *adj* insol•ens -entis

insoluble *adj* insolubil•is -is -e; *(fig)* inexplicabil•is -is -e
insolvent *adj* decoct•us -a -um; **I am insolvent** solvendo non sum
inspect *tr* inspicĕre; *(mil)* recensēre
inspection *s* inspecti•o -onis *f; (mil)* recensi•o -onis *f*
inspector *s* curat•or -oris *m*
inspiration *s (divine)* afflat•us -ūs *m; (prophetic)* fur•or -oris *m; (idea)* noti•o -onis *f*
inspire *tr* inspirare; **divinely —ed** divino spiritu instinct•us -a -um; **to — s.o. with courage** animos alicui addĕre; **to — s.o. with fear** alicui formidinem injicĕre
instability *s* instabilit•as -atis *f*
install *tr (mechanically)* instruĕre; *(w. augural solemnity)* inaugurare
installation *s* inaugurati•o -onis *f; (mechanical)* constructi•o -onis *f; (mil)* castr•a -orum *npl* stativa
installment *s (com)* pensi•o -onis *f*
instance *s* exempl•um -i *n;* **at my —** me auctore; **for —** exempli gratiā; **for — when** ut enim cum; **in this —** in hac re
instance *tr* memorare
instant *adj* praes•ens -entis; **this —** statim
instantaneous *adj* praes•ens -entis
instantaneously *adv* continuo
instead *adv* potius, magis
instead of *prep* pro *(w. abl)*
instigate *tr* instigāre, concitare
instigation *s* instigati•o -onis *f;* **at your —** te auctore
instigator *s* instigat•or -oris *m*
instill *tr* instillare
instinct *s* natur•a -ae *f*
instinctive *adj* natural•is -is -e
instinctively *adv* naturā
institute *tr* instituĕre
institute *s* institut•um -i *n*
institution *s (act)* instituti•o -onis *f; (thing instituted)* institut•um -i *n*
instruct *tr (to teach)* instituĕre; *(to order)* mandare *(w. dat or* ut, ne)
instruction *s* instituti•o -onis *f,* doctrin•a -ae *f;* **—s** mandat•a -orum *npl;* **to give —s to** mandare *(w. dat)*
instructive *adj* ad docendum apt•us -a -um
instructor *s* doc•ens -entis *mf*
instrument *s* instrument•um -i *n; (mus)* organ•um -i *n; (leg)* syngraph•a -ae *f*
instrumental *s* util•is -is -e; **you were — in bringing s.th. to pass** tuā operā factum est; *(in negative sentences)* **you were instrumental in not**...per te stetit quominus
instrumentality *s* oper•a -ae *f*
insubordinate *adj (mutinous)* seditios•us -a -um; *(disobedient)* male par•ens -entis
insubordination *s (mutiny)* sediti•o -onis *f;* **to be guilty of —** per licentiam ducibus non parēre
insufferable *adj* intolerand•us -a -um
insufficiency *s* inop•ia -ae *f*
insufficient *adj* haud suffici•ens -entis
insufficiently *adv* haud satis
insular *adj* insulan•us -a -um
insulate *tr* segregare
insult *s* contumeli•a -ae *f*
insult *tr* contumeliā afficĕre
insulting *adj* contumelios•us -a -um
insultingly *adv* contumeliose
insuperable *adj* insuperabil•is -is -e
insurance *s* cauti•o -onis *f* indemnitatis
insurance company *s* eran•us -i *m*
insurance policy *s* cauti•o -onis *f* indemnitatis
insure *tr* praecavēre de damnis
insurgent *adj* rebell•is -is -e
insurgent *s* rebell•is -is *m*
insurmountable *adj* inexsuperabil•is -is -e
insurrection *s* rebelli•o -onis *f; (civil strife)* sediti•o -onis *f*
intact *adj* incolum•is -is -e
intangible *adj* intactil•is -is -e
integral *adj* necessari•us -a -um
integrity *s* integrit•as -atis *f*
intellect *s* intellect•us -ūs *m*
intellectual *adj* intelleg•ens -entis
intelligence *s* intellegenti•a -ae *f; (information)* nunti•us -(i)i *m*
intelligent *adj* intelleg•ens -entis
intelligently *adv* intellegenter
intelligible *adj* intelligibil•is -is -e
intelligibly *adv* intellegibiliter
intemperance *s* intemperanti•a -ae *f*
intemperately *adv* intemperanter
intend *tr* in ànimo habēre
intended *adj* destinat•us -a -um; *(of future spouse)* spons•us -a
intense *adj* a•cer -cris -cre; *(heat, cold)* magn•us -a -um; *(excessive)* nimi•us -a -um
intensively *adv* vehementer
intensify *tr* intendĕre
intensity *s* vehementi•a -ae *f,* vis *f*
intent *adj* intent•us -a -um; **to be — on** animum intendĕre in *(w. acc)*
intently *adv* intente
intention *s* consil•ium -(i)i *n; (meaning)* significati•o -onis *f*
intentionally *adv* de industriā
inter *tr* inhumare
intercede *intr (on behalf of)* deprecari (pro + *abl)*
intercept *tr* excipĕre
intercession *s* deprecati•o -onis *f; (of a tribune)* intercessi•o -onis *f*
intercessor *s* deprecat•or -oris *m*
interchange *s* permutati•o -onis *f*
interchange *tr* permutare
intercourse *s (sexual)* coït•us -ūs *m; (social)* consuetud•o -inis *f*
interdict *tr* interdicĕre *(w. acc of person*

and abl of thing; dat of person and acc of thing)
interdiction *s* interdicti•o -onis *f*
interest *s (attention)* stud•ium -(i)i *n; (advantage)* us•us -ūs *m; (fin)* faen•us -oris *n;* **it is in my —** meā interest
interest *tr (to affect the mind)* tenēre; *(to delight)* delectare; **children are —ed in games** liberi ludis tenentur
interested *adj* **— in** studios•us -a -um *(w. gen),* attent•us -a -um *(w. dat)*
interesting *adj* jucund•us -a -um
interfere *intr* se interponĕre *(w. dat); (to prevent s.th.)* intercedĕre; **the tribunes will not — with the praetor's making a motion** tribuni non praetori intercessuri sunt, quominus referat
interference *s* intercessi•o -onis *f*
interim *s* intervall•um -i *n;* **in the —** interim
interior *adj* inter•ior -ior -ius
interior *s* interior par•s -tis *f*
interjection *s* interjecti•o -onis *f*
interlinear *adj* interscript•us -a -um
interlude *s* embol•ium -(i)i *n*
intermarriage *s* connub•ium -(i)i *n*
intermarry *intr* matrimonio inter se conjungi
intermediary *s* internunti•us -(i)i *m*
intermediate *adj* medi•us -a -um
interment *s* sepultur•a -ae *f*
interminable *adj* infinit•us -a -um
intermission *s* intercaped•o -inis *f*
intermittent *adj* intermitt•ens -entis
intermittently *adv* interdum
internal *adj* intestin•us -a -um
internally *adv* intus, interne
international *adj* inter gentes
interpolate *tr* interpolare
interpolation *s* interpolati•o -onis *f*
interpret *tr* interpretari
interpretation *s* interpretati•o -onis *f*
interpreter *s* interpr•es -etis *mf*
interrogate *tr* interrogare
interrogation *s* interrogati•o -onis *f*
interrogative *adj* interrogativ•us -a -um
interrupt *tr* interrumpĕre; *(speech)* interpellĕre
interruption *s* interrupti•o -onis *f; (of a speaker)* interpellati•o -onis
intersect *tr* intersecare
intersection *s* intersecti•o -onis *f; (of roads)* quadriv•ium -(i)i *n*
intersperse *tr* inmiscēre
intertwine *tr* intertexĕre
interval *s* intervall•um -i *n*
intervene *intr (to be between)* interjacēre; *(to come between)* intercedĕre, intervenire
intervening *adj* medi•us -a -um
intervention *s* intervent•us -ūs *m*
interview *s* colloqu•ium -(i)i *n*
interview *tr* percontari
interweave *tr* intertexĕre
intestinal *adj* ad intestina pertin•ens -entis
intestine *adj* intestin•us -a -um
intestine *s* intestin•um -i *n;* **the small —** intestin•um -i *n* tenue
intimacy *s* consuetud•o -inis *f*
intimate *adj* familiar•is -is -e; *(stronger than preced.)* intim•us -a -um
intimately *adv* familiariter, intime
intimate *tr* indicare
intimation *s* indic•ium -(i)i *n*
intimidate *tr* absterrēre
intimidation *s* min•ae -arum *fpl*
into *prep* in *(w. acc)*
intolerable *adj* intolerabil•is -is -e
intolerably *adv* intoleranter
intolerance *s* intoleranti•a -ae *f*
intolerant *adj* intoler•ans -antis
intonation *s* accent•us -ūs *m*
intone *tr* cantare
intoxicate *tr* ebrium *(or* ebriam) reddĕre
intoxicated *adj* ebri•us -a -um
intoxication *s* ebriet•as -atis *f*
intractable *adj* intractabil•is -is -e
intrepid *adj* intrepid•us -a -um
intrepidly *adv* intrepide
intricate *adj* contort•us -a -um
intricately *adv* contorte
intrigue *s* artifici•a -orum *npl*
intrigue *tr* tenēre, capĕre
intriguing *adj* illecebros•us -a -um
intrinsic *adj* ver•us -a -um; **it has no — worth** res ipsa per se nullius pretii est
intrinsically *adv* vere
introduce *tr* inducĕre; *(a person)* tradĕre
introduction *s (preamble)* praefati•o -onis *f; (of a speech)* exord•ium -(i)i *n; (to a person)* introducti•o -onis *f*
instrospection *s* sui contemplati•o -onis *f*
introspective *adj* se ipsum inspici•ens -entis
introvert *s* hom•o -inis *m* umbraticus
intrude *intr* se interponĕre; **to — on** se imponĕre *(w. dat)*
intruder *s* intervent•or -oris *m; (into a home)* effract•or -oris *m*
intrusion *s* irrupti•o -onis *f*
intuition *s* intuit•us -ūs *m*
intuitive *adj* intuitiv•us -a -um
intuitively *adv* mentis propriā vi ac naturā
inundate *tr* inundare
inundation *s* inundati•o -onis *f*
invade *tr* invadĕre in *(w. acc)*
invader *s* invas•or -oris *m*
invalid *adj* irrit•us -a -um
invalid *s* aegrot•us -i *m,* aegrot•a -ae *f*
invalidate *tr* irrit•um -am -um facĕre
invaluable *adj* inaestimabil•is -is -e
invariable *adj* immutabil•is -is -e
invariably *adv* semper
invasion *s* incursi•o -onis *f*
invective *s* convic•ium -(i)i *n*

inveigh *intr* **to — against** invehi in *(w. acc)*, insectari
invent *tr* invenire; *(to contrive)* excogitare, fingĕre
inventive *adj* ingenios•us -a -um
invention *s (act)* inventi•o -onis *f; (thing invented)* invent•um -i *n*
inventor *s* invent•or -oris *m*, inventr•ix -icis *f*
inventory *s* bonorum ind•ex -icis *m*
inverse *adj* invers•us -a -um
inversely *adv* inverso ordine
inversion *s* inversi•o -onis *f*
invert *tr* invertĕre
invest *tr (money)* collocare; *(to besiege)* obsidēre
investigate *tr* investigare; *(leg)* quaerĕre, cognoscĕre
investigation *s* investigati•o -onis *f; (leg)* cogniti•o -onis *f*
investigator *s* investigat•or -oris *m; (leg)* quaesit•or -oris *m*
investment *s (of money)* collocati•o -onis *f; (money invested)* locata pecuni•a -ae *f; (mil)* obsessi•o -onis *f*
inveterate *adj* inveterat•us -a -um
invigorate *tr* corroborare
invigorating *adj* apt•us -a -um ad corpus firmandum
invincible *adj* insuperabil•is -is -e, invict•us -a - um
inviolable *adj* sacrosanct•us -a -um
inviolate *adj* inviolat•us -a -um
invisible *adj* invisibil•is -is -e
invitation *s* invitati•o -onis *f*
invite *tr* invitare; **to — to dinner** ad cenam vocare
inviting *adj* suav•is -is -e
invitingly *adv* suaviter
invocation *s* invocati•o -onis *f*
invoice *s* libell•us -i *m*
invoke *tr* invocare
involuntarily *adv* sine voluntate
involuntary *adj* haud voluntari•us -a -um; **— bodily action** naturalis acti•o -onis *f* corporis
involve *tr* involvĕre; *(to comprise)* continēre
involved *adj (intricate)* involut•us -a -um; *(occupied)* implicat•us -a -um; **to be — in debt** aere alieno laborare; **to be — in many errors** multis erroribus implicari; **to be — in war** illigari bello
invulnerable *adj* invulnerabil•is -is -e
inward *adj* inter•ior -ior -ius
inwardly *adv* intus, intrinsecus
inwards *adv* introrsus
Ionian *adj* Ionic•us -a -um
irascible *adj* iracund•us -a -um
Ireland *s* Hiberni•a -ae *f*
iris *s* ir•is -idis *f*
Irish *adj* Hibernic•us -a -um
irk *tr* incommodare; **I am —ed, it irks me** me taedet
irksome *adj* molest•us -a -um
iron *s* ferr•um -i *n*
iron *adj* ferre•us -a -um
ironical *adj* ironic•us -a -um
ironically *adv* per ironiam
irony *s* ironi•a -ae *f*
irradiate *tr* illustrare ‖ *intr* effulgēre
irrational *adj* irrational•is -is -e
irrationally *adv* absurde
irreconcilable *adj* implacabil•is -is -e; *(incompatible)* omnino inter se contrari•i -ae -a
irrecoverable *adj* irreparabil•is -is -e
irrefutable *adj* certissim•us -a -um
irregular *adj (having no regular form)* enorm•is -is -e; *(not uniform)* inaequal•is -is -e; *(fever)* incert•us -a -um; *(gram)* anomal•us -a -um; **— army** exercit•us -ūs *m* tumultuarius
irregularity *s* enormit•as -atis *f; (gram)* anomali•a -ae *f;* **to be guilty of some —** peccare aliquid
irrelevant *adj* alien•us -a -um; **it is —** nil ad rem pertinet
irreligious *adj* impi•us -a -um erga deos; *(actions)* irreligios•us -a -um
irremediable *adj* insanabil•is -is -e
irreparable *adj* irreparabil•is -is -e
irreproachable *adj* inte•ger -gra -grum
irresistible *adj* invict•us -a -um
irresolute *adj* incert•us -a -um (sententiae); *(permanent characteristic)* parum firm•us -a -um
irresolutely *adv* dubitanter
irresolution *s* dubitati•o -onis *f*, anim•us -i *m* parum firmus
irresponsibility *s* incuri•a -ae *f*
irresponsible *adj* incurios•us -a -um
irretrievable *adj* irreparabil•is -is -e
irreverence *s* impiet•as -atis *f*
irreverent *adj* irrever•ens -entis (deorum)
irrevocable *adj* irrevocabil•is -is -e
irrigate *tr* irrigare
irrigation *s* irrigati•o -onis *f*
irritability *s* iracundi•a -ae *f*
irritable *adj* iracund•us -a -um
irritate *tr* irritare; *(a wound)* inflammare
irritation *s* irritati•o -onis *f*
island *s* insul•a -ae *f*
islander *s* insulan•us -i *m*
islet *s* parva insul•a -ae *f*
isolate *tr* secernĕre
issue *s (result)* event•us -ūs *m; (question)* res, rei *f; (offspring)* prol•es -is *f; (of a book)* editi•o -onis *f; (of money)* emissi•o -onis *f*
issue *tr (to distribute)* distribuĕre; *(orders)* edĕre, promulgare; *(money)* erogare; *(book)* edĕre ‖ *intr* emanare, egredi; *(to turn out, result)* evenire
isthmus *s* isthm•us -i *m*
it *pron* id
itch *s* prurig•o -inis *f*

itch *intr* prurire; *(fig)* gestire
item *s* res, rei *f*
itinerant *adj* circumforane•us -a -um
itinerary *s* itinerar•ium -(i)i *n*
its *pron* ejus; **— own** su•us -a -um
itself *pron (refl)* se, sese; *(intensive)* ipsum
ivory *s* eb•ur -oris *n*
ivory *adj* eburne•us -a -um
ivy *s* heder•a -ae *f*

J

jab *s* puls•us -ūs *m*
jab *tr* fodicare
jabber *intr* blaterare
jabbering *s* garrulit•as -atis *f*
jackass *s* asin•us -i *m*
jacket *s* tunic•a -ae *f*
jack-of-all-trades *s* hom•o -inis *m* omnis Minervae
jackpot *s* **to hit the —** Venerem jacěre
jaded *adj* defess•us -a -um
jagged *adj* serrat•us -a -um; *(of rocks)* praerupt•us -a -um
jail *s* carc•er -eris *m*
jail *tr* in carcere includěre
jailbird *s* furcif•er -eri *m*
jailer *s* carcerar•ius -(i)i *m*
jam *s* baccarum conditur•a -ae *f;* **to be in a —** in angustiis versari
jam *tr* frequentare; *(to obsbruct)* obstruěre
jamb *s* post•is -is *m*
jangle *tr & intr* crepitare
janitor *s* janit•or -oris *m*
January *s* Januar•ius -(i)i *m or* mens•is -is *m* Januarius; **on the first of —** Kalendis Januariis
jar *s* oll•a -ae *f; (large, with 2 handles)* amphor•a -ae *f*
jar *tr (to shock)* offenděre; *(of sound)* strepěre **‖** *intr* discrepare
jargon *s* confusae voc•es -ium *fpl*
jarring *adj* disson•us -a -um
jaundice *s* morb•us -i *m* regius
jaundiced *adj* icterici•us -a -um; **to see things with — eyes** omnia in deteriorem partem interpretari
jaunt *s* excursi•o -onis *f;* **to take a —** excurrěre
jaunty *adj* veget•us -a -um
javelin *s* jacul•um -i *n;* **to hurl a —** jaculari
jaw *s* mal•ae -arum *fpl;* **—s** fauc•es -ium *fpl*
jawbone *s* maxill•a -ae *f*
jay *s* gracul•us -i *m*
jealous *adj* zelotyp•us -a -um
jealousy *s* zel•us -i *m*
jeer *s* irris•us -ūs *m*
jeer *tr* deridēre **‖** *intr* deridēre; **to —at** irridēre
jelly *s* cyl•on -i *n*
jellyfish *s* pulm•o -onis *m*
jeopardize *tr* periclitari
jeopardy *s* pericul•um -i *n*
jerk *s* mot•us -ūs *m* subitus; *(person)* vapp•a -ae *m*
jerk *tr (to push)* subito truděre; *(to pull)* subito revellěre
jerky *adj* salebros•us -a -um
jest *s* joc•us -i *m;* **in —** jocose
jest *intr* jocari
jester *s* joculat•or -oris *m; (buffoon)* scurr•a -ae *m*
jestingly *adv* per jocum
Jesus *s* Jes•us -u *(dat, abl, voc:* Jesu; *acc:* Jesum) *m*
jet *s* scatebr•a -ae *f*
jet-black *adj* nigerrim•us -a -um
jetty *s* mol•es -is *f*
Jew *s* Judae•us -i *m*
jewel *s* gemm•a -ae *f*
jeweler *s* gemmar•ius -(i)i *m*
jewelry *s* gemm•ae -arum *fpl*
Jewess *s* Judae•a -ae *f*
Jewish *adj* Judae•us -a -um
jilt *tr* repudiare
jingle *s* tinnit•us -ūs *m*
jingle *intr* tinnire
jitters *spl* scrupul•um -i *n;* **to give s.o. the —** scrupulum alicui injicěre
job *s* negot•ium -(i)i *n*
jobless *adj* quaestūs exper•s -tis
jockey *s* agas•o -onis *m*
jocular *adj* jocular•is -is -e
jog *intr* tolutim currěre
join *tr (to connect)* conjungěre, connectěre; *(to come into the company of)* se jungěre *(w. dat); (to join as a companion)* supervenire *(w. dat); (to go over to)* transire; **—ing hands** manibus nex•i -ae -a **‖** *intr* conjungi; **to — in** particeps esse *(w. gen);* **to — together** inter se conjungi
joint *adj* commun•is -is -e
joint *s (anat)* articul•us -i *m; (of a plant)* genicul•um -i *n,* nod•us -i *m; (of a structure)* compag•es -inis *f*
jointed *adj* geniculat•us -a -um
jointly *adv* unā, communiter
joist *s* tign•um -i *n*
joke *s* joc•us -i *m;* **as a —** per jocum; **to make a — of** jocum risumque facěre
joke *intr* jocari; **to be —ing** jocari
joker *s* joculat•or -oris *m*
joking *s* jocati•o -onis *f;* **all — aside** joco remoto
jokingly *adv* per jocum
jolly *adj* hilar•is -is -e
jolt *s* (im)puls•us -ūs *m*
jolt *tr* jactare; *(fig)* percellěre **‖** *intr* jactari
jolting *s* jactati•o -onis *f*
jostle *tr* pulsare
jot *s* hil•um -i *n;* **not a —** minime; **to care not a — for** non flocci facěre
journal *s* ephemer•is -idis *f*

journalist *s* script•or -oris *m* actorum
journey *s* it•er -ineris *n*
journey *intr* iter facĕre; **to — abroad** peregrinari
journeyman *s* opif•ex -icis *m*
Jove *s* Jupiter Jovis *m*
jovial *adj* hilar•is -is -e
jowl *s* bucc•a -ae *f*
joy *s* gaud•ium -(i)i *n*
joyful *adj* laet•us -a -um
joyfully *adv* laete
joyless *adj* illaetabil•is -is -e
jubilant *adj* laetitiā exsult•ans -antis
jubilation *s* exsultati•o -onis *f*
jubilee *s* ann•us -i *m* anniversarius
Judaic *adj* Judaïc•us -a -um
Judaism *s* Judaïsm•us -i *m*
judge *s* jud•ex -icis *m; (in criminal cases)* quaesit•or -oris *m*
judge *tr* judicare; *(to think)* existimare; *(to value)* aestimare; *(to decide between)* dijudicare
judgment *s* judic•ium -(i)i *n,* sententi•a -ae *f;* **in my —** sententiā meā; **to pronounce —** jus dicĕre; **to sit in — over** jus dicĕre inter *(w. acc)*
judgment seat *s* tribun•al -alis *n*
judicial *adj* judicial•is -is -e; **— proceedings** judici•a -orum *npl*
judicially *adv* jure
judicious *adj* sapi•ens -entis
judiciously *adv* sapienter
jug *s* urce•us -i *m*
juggle *intr* praestigias agĕre
juggler *s* praestigiat•or -oris *m*
juice *s* suc•us -i *m*
juicy *adj* sucos•us -a -um
July *s* Jul•ius -(i)i *or* mens•is -is *m* Julius; **on the first of —** Kalendis Juliis
jumble *s* congeri•es -ei *f*
jumble *tr* permiscēre
jump *s* salt•us -ūs *m*
jump *tr* transalire ‖ *intr* salire; **to —at** *(opportunity)* captare; **to — for joy** dissilire gaudimonio; **to — up** exsurrigĕre
junction *s* conjuncti•o -onis *f; (roads)* compit•um -i *n*
juncture *s* temp•us -oris *n;* **at this —** hic
June *s* Jun•ius -(i)i *m or* mens•is -is *m* Junius; **on the first of —** Kalendis Juniis
jungle *s* silv•ae -arum *fpl*
junior *adj* min•or -or -us natu
juniper *s* juniper•us -i *f*
junk *s* scrut•a -orum *npl*
jurisdiction *s* jurisdicti•o -onis *f*
jurisprudence *s* jurisprudenti•a -ae *f*
jurist *s* jurisconsult•us -i *m*
juror *s* jud•ex -icis *m*
jury *s* judic•es -um *mpl*
just *adj* just•us -a -um; *(fair)* aequ•us -a -um; *(deserved)* merit•us -a -um
just *adv (only)* modo; *(exactly)* prorsus; *(w. adv)* demum, denique; **— after** sub *(w. acc);* **— as** perinde ac, sic ut; **— before** sub *(w. acc);* **— now** modo; **— so** ita prorsus; **— then** tunc maxime; **— what?** quidnam?; **— who?** quisnam?
justice *s* justiti•a -ae *f; (just treatment)* jus juris *n; (person)* praet•or -oris *m*
justifiable *adj* excusat•us -a -um
justifiably *adv* jure
justification *s* excusati•o -onis *f*
justify *tr* excusare, expurgare
jut *intr* prominēre; **to — out** procurrĕre; **to — out into the sea** in aequor procurrĕre
juvenile *adj* juvenil•is -is -e; **— delinquent** adulesc•ens -entis *m* noxius
juvenile *s* adulesc•ens -entis *mf*
juxtaposition *s* propinquit•as -atis *f;* **to put in —** apponĕre

K

kale *s* cramb•e -es *f*
keel *s* carin•a -ae *f*
keel *intr* **to — over** collabi
keen *adj* a•cer -cris -cre
keenly *adv* acriter
keenness *s (of scent)* sagacit•as -atis *f; (of sight)* aci•es -ei *f; (of pain)* acerbit•as -atis *f; (enthusiasm)* stud•ium -(i)i *n*
keep *tr* tenēre; *(to preserve)* servare; *(to celebrate)* agĕre; *(to guard)* custodire; *(to obey)* observare; *(to support)* alĕre; *(animals)* alĕre, pascĕre; *(to store)* condĕre; **to — annoying** subinde molestare; **to — apart** distinēre; **to — at bay** sustinēre; **to — away** arcēre; **to — back** retinēre, cohibēre; *(to conceal)* celare; **to — back nothing** nihil reticēre; **to — back tears** lacrimas tenēre; **to — company** comitari; **to — down** reprimĕre; **to — from** prohibēre; **to — in** cohibēre; **to — in custody** asservare; **to — in line the wavering Senate** confirmare labantem ordinem; **to — in mind** in memoria habēre; **to — off** arcēre, defendĕre; **to — to oneself** secum habēre; **to — pace with** pariter ire cum *(w. abl);* **to — secret** celare; **to — together** continēre; **to — under control** compescĕre; **to — under lock and key** clavi servare; **to — up** sustinēre; **to — up one's courage** animo erecto esse; **to — up with** subsequi; **to — your eyes on** oculos intentare in *(w. acc)* ‖ *intr (to last)* durare; **to — away from** abstinēre ab *(w. abl)*
keep *s* custodi•a -ae *f*
keeper *s* cust•os -odis *m*
keeping *s* tutel•a -ae *f;* **in — with** pro *(w. abl)*
keepsake *s* monument•m -i *n*
keg *s* cad•us -i *m*

kennel *s* stabul•um -i *n* caninum
kerchief *s* sudar•ium -(i)i *n*
kernel *s* nucle•us -i *m; (fig)* medull•um -i *n*
kettle *s* leb•es -etis *f*
kettledrum *s* tympan•um -i *n* aeneum
key *s* clav•is -is *f; (pitch)* voculati•o -onis *f; (clue)* ans•a -ae *f*
keyhole *s* claustell•um -i *n*
kick *s* cal•x -cis *mf*
kick *tr* calce ferire; **to — the bucket** *(coll)* animam ebullire ‖ *intr* calcitrare
kid *s* haed•us -i *m; (boy)* parvul•us -i *m*
kid *tr & intr* ludificari
kidnap *tr* surripĕre
kidnapper *s* plagiar•ius -(i)i *m,* plagiari•a -ae *f*
kidnapping *s* plag•ium -(i)i *n*
kidney *s* ren renis *m*
kidney bean *s* phasel•us -i *m*
kill *s* nex necis *f; (prey)* praed•a -ae *f*
kill *tr* interficĕre; *(by cruel means)* necare; *(by wounds or blows)* caedĕre; **to — time** tempus perdĕre
killer *s* interfect•or -oris *m*
kiln *s* forn•ax -acis *f*
kin *s* cognat•i -orum *mpl;* **next of —** proxim•i -orum *mpl*
kind *adj* benign•us -a -um
kind *s* gen•us -eris *n;* **that — of war** ejus modi bell•um -i *n;* **what — of** qual•is -is -e, qui quae quod
kindhearted *adj* benign•us -a -um
kindle *tr* incendĕre, accendĕre
kindly *adj* human•us -a -um
kindly *adv* benigne
kindness *s* benignit•as -atis *f; (deed)* benefic•ium -(i)i *n;* **to bestow a — on s.o.** beneficium apud aliquem collocare; **to do (return) an act of —** beneficium dare (reddĕre)
kindred *adj* consanguine•us -a -um
kindred *s* consanguinit•as -atis *f; (relatives)* consanguine•i -orum *mpl,* consanguine•ae -arum *fpl*
king *s* re•x -gis *m*
kingdom *s* regn•um -i *n*
kingfisher *s* alced•o -inis *f*
kingly *adj* regi•us -a -um; *(worthy of a king)* regal•is -is -e
kinsman *s* necessar•ius -(i)i *m*
kinswoman *s* necessari•a -ae *f*
kiss *s* oscul•um -i *n*
kiss *tr* osculari
kissing *s* osculati•o -onis *f*
kit *s* apparat•us -ūs *m*
kitchen *s* culin•a -ae *f*
kite *s (bird)* milv•us -i *m*
kith and kin *spl* propinqu•i -orum et adfin•es -ium *mpl*
kitten *s* catul•us -i *m* felinus
knack *s* sollerti•a -ae *f*
knapsack *s* per•a -ae *f*
knave *s* scelest•us -i *m*
knead *tr* subigĕre
knee *s* gen•u -us *n;* **on bended —** duplicato poplite; **to fall at s.o.'s —s** *(in entreaty)* se ad genua alicujus projicĕre; **to fall on one's —s to** genua ponĕre *(w. dat of person so honored)*
kneecap *s* patell•a -ae *f*
knee-deep *adj* genibus tenus alt•us -a -um
kneel *intr* genibus niti; **to — down** ad genua procumbĕre
knell *s* campan•a -ae *f* funebris
knife *s* cul•ter -tri *m; (for surgery)* scalpr•um -i *n*
knight *s* equ•es -itis *m*
knighthood *s* equestris dignit•as -atis *f*
knightly *adj* eques•ter -tris -tre
knit *tr* texĕre; **to — the brow** frontem contrahĕre
knob *s* tub•er -eris *n; (on door)* bull•a -ae *f*
knock *s* puls•us -ūs *m*
knock *tr* **to — down** dejicĕre, sternĕre; *(fig) (at auction)* addicĕre; **to — in** impellĕre; **to — one's head against the wall** caput ad parietem offendĕre; **to — out** excutĕre; **to — out s.o.'s brains** cerebrum alicui excutĕre ‖ *intr* **to — about** *(to ramble)* vagari; **to — at** pulsare, percutĕre
knocking *s* pulsati•ō- onis *f*
knock-kneed *adj* var•us -a -um
knoll *s* tumul•us -i *m*
knot *s* nod•us -i *m; (of people)* turbul•a -ae *f;* **to tie a —** nodum facĕre; **to untie a —** nodum expedire
knot *tr* nodare
knotty *adj* nodos•us -a -um; *(fig)* spinos•us -a -um
know *tr* scire; *(a person)* novisse; **not to —** ignorare, nescire; **to — how to** scire *(w. inf)*
knowing *adj* callid•us -a -um
knowingly *adv* scienter
knowledge *s* scienti•a -ae *f; (of s.th.)* cogniti•o -onis *f;* **without the — of** clam *(w. abl);* **without your —** clam vobis
known *adj* not•us -a -um; **— to me by sight** familiar•is -is -e oculis meis; **to become —** enotescĕre; **to make —** divulgare
knuckle *s* digiti articul•us -i *m*
knuckle *intr* **to — under to** cedĕre *(w. dat)*
kowtow *intr* **(to)** adulari *(w. dat)*

L

label *s* pittac•ium -(i)i *n*
labor *s* lab•or -oris *m; (manual)* oper•a -ae *f; (work done)* op•us -eris *n;* **to be in —** laborare in utero; **woman in —** puerper•a -ae *f*

labor *intr* laborare, eniti; **to — under** laborare *(w. abl)*
laboratory *s* officin•a -ae *f*
labored *adj* affectat•us -a -um
laborer *s* operar•ius -(i)i *m*
labyrinth *s* labyrinth•us -i *m*
labyrinthine *adj* labyrinthic•us -a -um; *(fig)* inextricabil•is -is -e
lace *s* op•us -eris *n* reticulatum
lace *tr (to tie)* nectĕre; *(to tighten)* astringĕre
lacerate *tr* lacerare
laceration *s* lacerati•o -onis *f*
lack *s* inopi•a -ae *f*
lack *tr* carēre *(w. abl)*
lackey *s* pedisequ•us -i *m*
laconic *adj* brev•is -is -e
lad *s* pu•er -eri *m*
ladder *s* scal•ae -arum *fpl;* **one —** unae scalae
laden *adj* onust•us -a -um
ladle *s* ligul•a -ae *f,* trull•a -ae *f*
ladle *tr* ligulā fundĕre
lady *s* domin•a -ae *f*
lag *intr* cessare
lagoon *s* lacun•a -ae *f*
lair *s* cubil•e -is *n*
laity *spl* laïc•i -orum *mpl*
lake *s* lac•us -ūs *m*
lamb *s* agn•us -i *m,* agn•a -ae *f; (meat)* agnin•a -ae *f*
lame *adj* claud•us -a -um; **— in one leg** claud•us -a -um altero pede; **to be —** claudicare
lamely *adv (fig)* inconcinne
lameness *s* claudit•as -atis *f*
lament *s* lament•um -i *n*
lament *tr* lamentari **II** *intr* deplorare
lamentable *adj* lamentabil•is -is -e
lamentation *s* lamentati•o -onis *f*
lamp *s* lucern•a -ae *f*
lampoon *s* libell•us -i *m*
lance *s* lance•a -ae *f*
lance *tr* incidĕre
land *s* terr•a -ae *f; (soil)* sol•um -i *n; (as a possession)* a•ger -gri *m;* **public —** ager publicus *(or* agri publici); **on — and sea** terrā marique
land *tr* in terram exponĕre **II** *intr* egredi, appellĕre
land *adj (animals, route)* terren•us -a -um; *(animals, route, troops)* terrestr•is -is -e; *(battle)* pedes•ter -tris -tre
landing *s* egress•us -ūs *m*
landing place *s* appuls•us -ūs *m*
landlady *s* domin•a -ae *f*
landlord *s* (insulae) domin•us -i *m*
landmark *s* lap•is -idis *m*
landscape *s* regionis sit•us -ūs *m*
landslide *s* terrae laps•us -ūs *m*
land tax *s* vectig•al -alis *n*
lane *s* semit•a -ae *f*
language *s* lingu•a -ae *f; (diction)* orati•o -onis *f;* **abusive and insulting — against s.o.** maledice contumelioseque dict•a -orum *npl* in aliquem
languid *adj* languid•us -a -um
languish *intr* languēre
languishing *adj* languid•us -a -um
languor *s* langu•or -oris *m*
lanky *adj* prolix•us -a -um
lantern *s* la(n)tern•a -ae *f*
lap *s* sin•us -ūs *m; (fig)* grem•ium -(i)i *n*
lap *tr* lambĕre
lapse *s* laps•us -ūs *m; (error)* peccat•um -i *n;* **after a — of one year** interjecto anno
lapse *intr* labi; **to — into** recidĕre in *(w. acc)*
larceny *s* furt•um -i *n*
lard *s* ad•eps -ipis *mf*
large *adj* magn•us -a -um; **to a — extent** magnā ex parte
largely *adv* plerumque
largess *s* largiti•o -onis *f;* **to give a —** largiri
lark *s* alaud•a -ae *f*
larynx *s* gutt•ur -uris *n*
lascivious *adj* lasciv•us -a -um
lasciviously *adv* lascive
lash *s (blow)* verb•er -eris *n; (whip)* flagell•um -i *n*
lash *tr* verberare, flagellare; *(to censure severely)* castigare; *(to fasten)* annectĕre, alligare
lashing *s* verberati•o -onis *f*
lass *s* puell•a -ae *f*
lassitude *s* lassitud•o -inis *f*
last *adj* postrem•us -a -um, ultim•us -a -um; *(immediately preceding)* proxim•us -a -um; *(in line)* novissim•us -a -um; **at — demum; for the — time** postremo; **— but one** paenultim•us -a -um; **— night** proximā nocte; **the night before —** superiore nocte
last *intr* durare; **to — for some time** aliquod tempus habēre; **to — long** *(of a fever, etc.)* diu permanēre
lasting *adj* diuturn•us -a -um
lastly *adv* denique, postremo
latch *s* pessul•us -i *m*
latch *tr* oppessulare
late *adj* ser•us -a -um; *(loitering behind time)* tard•us -a -um; *(far advanced)* mult•us -a -um; *(recent in date)* rec•ens -entis; *(deceased)* demortu•us -a -um; *(of an emperor)* divus; **Homer was not —er than Lycurgus** Homerus non infra Lycurgum fuit; **it was — in the day** serum erat diei; **till — at night** ad multam noctem
late *adv* sero; **all too —** immo jam sero; **— at night** multā nocte; **— in life** seri anni; **too —** serius
lately *adv* modo, nuper, recens
latent *adj* occult•us -a -um
lateral *adj* lateral•is -is -e

Latin *adj* Latin•us -a -um ‖ *s* **to learn —** Latine discĕre; **to speak —** Latine loqui; **to teach —** Latine docēre; **to translate into —** Latine reddĕre; **to understand —** Latine scire
Latinity *s* Latinit•as -atis *f*
latitude *s* latitud•o -inis *f; (fig)* libert•as -atis *f*
latter *adj* poster•ior -ior -ius; **the —** hic
lattice *s* cancell•i -orum *mpl*
laudable *adj* laudabil•is -is -e
laudably *adv* laudabiliter
laudatory *adj* laudativ•us -a -um
laugh *s* ris•us -ūs *m*
laugh *intr* ridēre; **to — at** ridēre; *(to mock)* irridēre
laughable *adj* ridicul•us -a -um
laughingstock *s* ludibr•ium -(i)i *n*
laughter *s* ris•us -ūs *m; (loud, indecorous)* cachinnati•o -onis *f*
launch *tr* deducĕre; *(to hurl)* jaculari ‖ *intr* **to — out** proficisci
laundress *s* lotr•ix -icis *f*
laundry *s* lavator•ium -(i)i *n*
laureate *adj* laureat•us -a -um
laurel *adj* laure•us -a -um
laurel tree *s* laur•us -i *f*
lava *s* liquefacta mass•a -ae *f*
lavish *adj* prodig•us -a -um
lavish *tr* prodigĕre, profundĕre
lavishly *adv* prodige
law *s* lex legis *f; (right)* jus juris *n; (divine)* fas *n (indecl);* **to break the —** leges violare; **to introduce a —** legem ferre; **to pass a —** legem perferre
law-abiding *adj* bene morat•us -a -um
law court *s* judic•ium -(i)i *n; (building)* basilic•a -ae *f*
lawful *adj* legitim•us -a -um; **it is —** fas est
lawfully *adv* legitime
lawless *adj* exl•ex -egis
lawlessness *s* licenti•a -ae *f*
lawn *s* pratul•um -i *n*
lawsuit *s* caus•a -ae *f*
lawyer *s* jurisconsult•us -i *m*
lax *adj* lax•us -a -um
laxity *s* remissi•o -onis *f*
lay *tr (to put)* ponĕre; *(eggs)* parĕre; *(foundations)* jacĕre; *(hands)* injicĕre; **to — an ambush** insidiari; **to be laid up** cubare; **to — aside** ponĕre; *(cares, fear)* amovēre; **to — before** proponĕre; **to — claim to** arrogare, vindicare; **to — down** *(office)* resignare; *(rules)* statuĕre; **to — down arms** ab armis discedĕre; **to — hands on s.th.** aliquid invadĕre; **to — hold of** prehendĕre; **to — it on the line** *(coll)* directum loqui; **to — out** *(money)* expendĕre; *(plans)* designare; **to — siege to** obsidēre; **to — the blame on** culpam conferre in *(w. acc);* **to — up** condĕre; **to — waste** vastare
lay *s (mus)* cantilen•a -ae *f*
layer *s* lamin•a -ae *f; (stratum)* cor•ium -(i)i *n; (of a plant)* propag•o -inis *f*
lazily *adv* ignave, pigre
laziness *s* pigriti•a -ae *f*
lazy *adj* ignav•us -a -um
lead *s* plumb•um -i *n*
lead *adj* plumbe•us -a -um
lead *tr* ducĕre; *(life)* agĕre; **to — about** circumducĕre; **to — away** abducĕre; **to — off** divertĕre; **to — on** conducĕre ‖ *intr (of a road)* **to — to** ducĕre ad; **to — up to** tendĕre ad *(w. acc)*
leaden *adj* plumbe•us -a -um
leader *s* du•x -cis *m,* duct•or -oris *m*
leadership *s* duct•us -ūs *m*
leading *adj* princ•eps -cipis
leaf *s* fol•ium -(i)i *n; (of vine)* pampin•us -i *m; (of paper)* sched•a -ae *f; (of metal)* bracte•a -ae *f;* **to turn over a new —** ad bonam frugem se recipere
leafless *adj* fronde nudat•us -a -um
leafy *adj* frondos•us -a -um
league *s* foed•us -eris *n*
leak *s* rim•a -ae *f*
leak *intr* rimas agĕre, perfluĕre
leaky *adj* rimos•us -a -um
lean *adj* ma•cer -cra -crum
lean *tr* inclinare ‖ *intr* inclinare, niti; **—ing forward** inclinat•us -a -um; **to — against** se applicare *(w. dat);* **to — back** se inclinare; **to — on** inniti in *(w. abl)*
leap *s* salt•us -ūs *m*
leap *intr* salire; **to — for joy** exsultare
leap year *s* bisextilis ann•us -i *m*
learn *tr* discĕre; *(from elders)* accipĕre; **to — by heart** ediscĕre ‖ *intr* **to — about** cognoscĕre; *(to be informed about)* certior fieri de *(w. abl)*
learned *adj* doct•us -a -um
learnedly *adv* docte
learning *s* doctrin•a -ae *f,* eruditi•o -onis *f*
lease *s* conducti•o -onis *f; (act on part of proprietor)* locati•o -onis *f*
lease *tr* conducĕre; **to — out** locare
leash *s* lor•um -i *n,* cingul•um -i *n*
leash *tr* cingulo alligare
least *adj* minim•us -a -um
least *adv* minime; **at —** utique; *(emphasizing a particular word)* saltem
least *n* minim•um -ī *n;* **not in the —** ne minimum quidem
leather *s (tanned or untanned)* cor•ium -(i)i *n; (tanned)* alut•a -ae *f*
leather *adj* scorte•us -a -um
leathery *adj* lent•us -a -um
leave *tr* relinquĕre; *(to entrust)* mandare, tradĕre; *(legacy)* legare; **to — behind** relinquĕre; **to — out** omittĕre ‖ *intr (to depart)* discedĕre, abire; **to — off** desinĕre
leave *s* permissi•o -onis *f;* **— of absence** commeat•us -ūs *m;* **to ask —** veniam petĕre; **to obtain —** impetrare; **to take**

— of valēre jubēre; **with your —** pace tuā (vestrā)
leaven *s* ferment•um -i *n*
leaven *tr* fermentare
lecherous *adj* libidinos•us -a -um
lector *s* lect•or -oris *m*
lecture *s* lecti•o -onis *f*, acroas•is -is *f;* **to give a —** acroasin facĕre
lecture *tr (to reprove)* objurgare ‖ *intr* acroases facĕre, scholas habēre
lecturer *s* lect•or -oris *m*
ledge *s* projectur•a -ae *f; (of a cliff)* dors•um -i *n*
ledger *s* cod•ex -icis *m* (accepti et expensi)
leech *s* sanguisug•a -ae *f*
leer *intr* limis oculis spectare
leering *adj* lim•us -a -um
left *adj* laev•us -a -um, sinis•ter -tra -trum; **on the —** a sinistrā; **to the —** sinistrorsum, ad sinistram
left-handed *adj* laev•us -a -um
leftover *adj* reliqu•us -a -um
leftovers *spl* reliqui•ae -arum *fpl*
leg *s* cru•s -ris *n; (of table, etc.)* pes pedis *m*
legacy *s* legat•um -i *n*
legacy hunter *s* captat•or -oris *m*
legal *adj* legitim•us -a -um
legally *adv* legitime, lege
legalize *tr* sancire
legate *s* legat•us -i *m*
legation *s* legati•o -onis *f*
legend *s* fabul•a -ae *f; (inscription)* titul•us -i *m*
legendary *adj* commentici•us -a -um, fabulos•us -a -um
legging *s* ocre•a -ae *f*
legible *adj* legibil•is -is -e
legion *s* legi•o -onis *f*
legislate *intr* leges dare
legislation *s* leg•es -um *fpl,* legum dati•o -onis *f*
legislator *s* legum lat•or -oris *m*
legitimate *adj* legitim•us -a -um
legitimately *adv* legitime
leisure *s* ot•ium -(i)i *n;* **at —** otios•us -a -um
leisure *adj* otios•us -a -um, vacu•us -a -um; **— activity** op•us -eris *n* subsicivum
leisure time *s* temp•us -oris *n* vacuum
leisurely *adj* lent•us -a -um
lemon *s* pom•um -i *n* citreum
lemonade *s* aqu•a -ae *f* limonata
lend *tr* commodare; **to — money** pecuniam mutuam dare; *(at interest)* pecuniam faenerare; **to — one's ear to** aures praebēre *(w. dat)*
length *s* longitud•o -inis *f; (of time)* longinquit•as -atis *f;* **at —** tandem
lengthen *tr* producĕre, protrahĕre
lengthwise *adv* in longitudinem
lengthy *adj* long•us -a -um
leniency *s* lenit•as -atis *f*
lenient *adj* len•is -is -e
leniently *adv* leniter
lentil *s* len•s -tis *f*
leopard *s* leopard•us -i *m*
leper *s* lepros•us -i *m*
leprosy *s* lepr•ae -arum *fpl*
less *adj* min•or -or -us
less *adv* minus
lessee *s* conduct•or -oris *m*
lessen *tr* minuĕre ‖ *intr* decrescĕre
lesson *s* document•um -i *n; (a portion for reading)* lecti•o -onis *f;* **let him learn a — from me** habeat me ipsum sibi documento; **to give —s in** docēre; **to give —s in grammar** grammaticam docēre
lessor *s* locat•or -oris *m*
lest *conj* ne
let *tr (to allow)* sinĕre, permittĕre; *(to lease)* locare; **to — alone** omittĕre; **to — down** *(to disappoint)* deësse *(w. dat);* **to — fall** a manibus mittĕre; **to — fly** emittĕre; **to — go** (di)mittĕre; **to — in** admittĕre; **to — off** absolvĕre; **to — out** emittĕre; **to — pass** omittĕre; **to — slip an opportunity** occasionem amittĕre ‖ *intr* **to — up** residēre; **the rain is letting up** imber detumescit
lethargic *adj* lethargic•us -a -um
lethargy *s* letharg•us -i *m*
letter *s (of alphabet)* litter•a -ae *f; (epistle)* litter•ae -arum *fpl,* epistul•a -ae *f;* **by —** per litteras; **to the —** ad verbum
letter carrier *s* tabellar•ius -(i)i *m*
lettered *adj* litterat•us -a -um
lettering *s* titul•us -i *m*
lettuce *s* lactuc•a -ae *f*
level *adj* plan•us -a -um
level *s* planiti•es -ei *f; (tool)* libr•a -ae *f;* **to be on a — with** par esse *(w. dat)*
level *tr* (ad)aequare; *(to destroy)* diruĕre; **to — to the ground** solo aequare
lever *s* vect•is -is *m*
levity *s* levit•as -atis *f*
levy *s* delect•us -ūs *m*
levy *tr (troops)* conscribĕre; *(tax)* exigĕre
lewd *adj* incest•us -a -um
lewdly *adv* inceste
lewdness *s* impudiciti•a -ae *f*
liable *adj* obnoxi•us -a -um
liar *s* mend•ax -acis *mf*
libation *s* libati•o -onis *f;* **to pour a —** libare
libel *s* calumni•a -ae *f*
libel *tr* calumniari
libelous *adj* famos•us -a -um
liberal *adj* liberal•is -is -e; *(free)* lib•er -era -erum; **— arts** art•es -ium *fpl* liberales
liberality *s* liberalit•as -atis *f*
liberally *adv* liberaliter
liberate *tr* liberare; *(a slave)* manumittĕre
liberation *s* liberati•o -onis *f*

liberator *s* liberat•or -oris *m*
libertine *s* hom•o -inis *m* dissolutus
liberty *s* libert•as -atis *f;* **at —** lib•er -era -erum; **to be at —** licet *(w. dat of English subject);* **to take liberties with s.o.** liberius se in aliquem gerĕre
librarian *s* librar•ius -(i)i *m*
library *s* bibliothec•a -ae *f*
license *s (permission)* copi•a -ae *f,* potest•as -atis *f; (freedom)* licenti•a -ae *f*
license *tr* potestatem dare *(w. dat)*
licentious *adj* dissolut•us -a -um
licentiously *adv* dissolute
lick *tr* lambĕre; *(daintily)* ligurrire; **to — the plate** catillare; **to — out** elingĕre; **to — up** delingĕre
lictor *s* lict•or -oris *m*
lid *s* operiment•um -i *n*
lie *s* mendac•ium -(i)i *n;* **to give the — to** redarguĕre; **to tell a —** mentiri
lie *intr (to tell a lie or lies)* mentiri; *(to be lying down)* jacēre, cubare; *(to be situated)* sit•us -a -um esse; **to — down** jacēre; **to — in wait for** insidiari *(w. dat);* **to — on** *or* **upon** incubare *(w. dat);* **to — on one's back** resupinus jacēre; **to — on one's left (right) side** in latus sinistrum (dextrum) cubare; **to — on one's stomach** pronus jacēre
lieu *s* **in — of** loco *(w. gen)*
lieutenant *s* legat•us -i *m; (mil)* centuri•o -onis *m*
life *s* vit•a -ae *f; (age)* aet•as -atis *f; (fig)* alacrit•as -atis *f;* **to lose one's —** animam amittĕre; **spark of —** animul•a -ae *f;* **to lead the — of Riley** vitam Chiam gerĕre
life blood *s* suc•us -i *m* et sangu•is -inis *m*
life-giving *adj* alm•us -a -um
lifeless *adj* inanim•us -a -um; *(fig)* exsangu•is -is -e, frigid•us -a -um
lifelessly *adv* frigide
life style *s* vitae proposit•um -i *n*
lifetime *s* aet•as -atis *f*
lift *tr* tollĕre; **to — her hand to her face** manum ad faciem suam admovēre; **to — up** attollĕre
ligament *s* ligament•um -i *n*
ligature *s* ligatur•a -ae *f*
light *s* lu•x -cis *f,* lum•en -inis *n; (lamp)* lucern•a -ae *f;* **— and shade** *(in painting)* lum•en -inis *n* et umbr•ae -arum *fpl;* **to bring to —** in lucem proferre; **to throw — on** lumen adhibēre *(w. dat)*
light *adj (in weight)* lev•is -is -e; *(bright)* lucid•us -a -um; *(of colors)* candid•us -a -um; *(easy)* facil•is -is -e; *(nimble)* agil•is -is -e; *(wine)* tenu•is -is -e, len•is -is -e; *(food)* lev•is -is -e; **to grow —** lucescĕre
light *tr* accendĕre; *(to illuminate)* illuminare ‖ *intr* flammam concipĕre; **to — upon** offendĕre; **to — up** *(fig)* hilar•is -is -e fieri
lighten *tr (to illumintate)* illustrare; *(weight)* allevare, exonerare ‖ *intr (in the sky)* fulgurare
light-hearted *adj* hilar•is -is -e
lighthouse *s* phar•us -i *f*
lightness *s* levit•as -atis *f*
lightning *s* fulg•ur -uris *n; (in its destructive effects)* fulm•en -inis *n;* **struck by —** de caelo tact•us -a -um
like *adj* simil•is -is -e *(w. dat); (equal)* par *(w. dat),* aequ•us -a -um *(w. dat)*
like *prep* instar *(w. gen);* tamquam, ut
like *tr* amare; **he —s to paint** libentissime pingit; **I — this** hoc mihi placet; **I — to do this** me juvat hoc facĕre
likelihood *s* verisimilitud•o -inis *f*
likely *adj* verisimil•is -is -e, probabil•is -is -e; **it is most — that** proximum est ut
likely *adv* probabiliter
liken *tr* comparare
likeness *s* similitud•o -inis *f; (portrait)* effigi•es -ei *f*
likewise *adv* pariter, similiter, item
liking *s* am•or -oris *m; (fancy)* libid•o -inis *f;* **according to one's —** ex libidine
lilac *s* syring•a -ae *f* vulgaris
lily *s* lil•ium -(i)i *n*
lily of the valley *s* convallaria majal•is -is *f*
limb *s* art•us -ūs *m,* membr•um -i *n; (of tree)* ram•us -i *m*
limber *adj* flexil•is -is -e
lime *s* cal•x -cis *f*
limestone *s* cal•x -cis *f*
lime tree *s* tili•a -ae *f*
limit *s* fin•is -is *m,* mod•us -i *m;* **to set —s to** finire
limit *tr* finire, terminare; *(to restrict)* circumscribĕre
limitation *s* circumscripti•o -onis *f*
limited *adj* finit•us -a -um; *(time)* brev•is -is -e; *(resources)* exigu•us -a -um
limp *s* claudicati•o -onis *f*
limp *intr* claudicare
limp *adj* flaccid•us -a -um
limpid *adj* limpid•us -a -um
linden tree *s* tili•a -ae *f*
line *s (drawn)* line•a -ae *f; (row)* seri•es -ei *f; (lineage)* stirp•s -is *m,* gen•us -eris *n; (mil)* aci•es -ei *f; (of poetry)* vers•us -ūs *m; (cord)* fun•is -is *m;* **in a straight —** rectā lineā; **I will write a few —s in answer to your letter** pauca ad tuas litteras rescribam; **the front —** *(mil)* principi•a -orum *npl;* **to draw a —** lineam ducĕre; **to keep s.o. in —** imperare *(w. dat)*
line *tr (the streets)* saepire; **to — a garment with wool** vestem introrsum lanā obducĕre
lineage *s* gen•us -eris *n*
lineal *adj* linear•is -is -e
lineally *adv* rectā lineā
lineament *s* lineament•um -i *n*

linear *adj* linear•is -is -e
linen *s* linte•um -i *n,* lin•um -i *n*
linen *adj* linte•us -a -um; **— cloth** linteol•um -i *n*
linger *intr* morari, cunctari
lingering *adj* cunctabund•us -a -um
lingering *s* cunctati•o -onis *f*
linguist *s* linguarum perit•us -i *m*
linguistics *s* linguistic•a -ae *f*
liniment *s* linit•us -ūs *m*
link *s (of chain)* anul•us -i *m; (bond)* vincul•um -i *n*
link *tr* connectĕre, conjungĕre
linseed *s* lini sem•en -inis *n*
lint *s* linament•um -i *n*
lintel *s* lim•en -inis *n* superum
lion *s* le•o -onis *m*
lioness *s* leaen•a -ae *f*
lip *s* labr•um -i *n; (edge)* or•a -ae *f;* **to be on everyone's —s** in ore esse omni populo
liquefy *tr* liquefacĕre
liquid *adj* liquid•us -a -um
liquid *s* um•or -oris *m*
liquidate *tr* persolvĕre
liquor *s* temet•um -i *n*
lisp *s* balbutire
lisping *adj* blaes•us -a -um
list *s* numer•us -i *m; (naut)* inclinati•o -onis *f;* **— of charges** subscripti•o -onis *f*
list *tr* enumerare ‖ *intr (naut)* inclinare
listen *intr* auscultare; **to — to** auscultare *(w. dat);* **— to me!** ausculta mihi!
listless *adj* languid•us -a -um
listlessly *adv* languide
litany *s* litani•a -ae *f*
literal *adj* litteral•is -is -e
literally *adv* ad verbum
literary *adj (person)* litterat•us -a -um; **— pursuits** studi•a -orum *npl* litterarum; **— style** scribendi gen•us -eris *n*
literature *s* litter•ae -arum *fpl*
litigant *s* litig•ans -antis *mf*
litigate *intr* litigare
litigation *s* li•s -tis *f*
litter *s (vehicle)* lectic•a -ae *f; (of straw, etc.)* strament•um -i *n; (brood)* fet•us -ūs *m; (refuse)* reject•a -orum *npl*
litter *tr* spargĕre; **to — the streets** scruta viis spargĕre ‖ *intr* rejecta dispergĕre
little *adj* parv•us -a -um
little *adv* parum, paulum; **a —** paulum, pusillum; **— by —** paulatim
little *s* aliquantul•um -i *n*
little people *spl (coll)* popul•us -i *m* minutus
live *tr* **to — it up** ferias agĕre ‖ *intr* vivĕre, vitam agĕre; *(to reside)* habitare; **to — on** vesci *(w. abl);* **to — up to** aequiparare
live *adj* viv•us -a -um
livelihood *s* vict•us -ūs *m;* **to gain a —** victum quaeritare
lively *adj* veget•us -a -um
liver *s* jec•ur -oris *n*
livid *adj* livid•us -a -um; **to be —** livēre
living *adj* viv•us -a -um
living *s (livelihood)* vict•us -ūs *m*
lizard *s* lacert•a -ae *f*
load *s* on•us -eris *n*
load *tr* onerare
loaded *adj (rich)* saplut•us -a -um; *(drunk)* uvid•us -a -um
loaf *s* pan•is -is *m*
loaf *intr* cessare
loafer *s* cessat•or -oris *m,* cessatr•ix -icis *f*
loafing *s* cessati•ō -ōnis *f*
loam *s* lut•um -i *n*
loan *s* mutu•um -i *n*
loan *tr* faenerari
loathe *tr* fastidire
loathing *s* fastid•ium -(i)i *n*
loathsome *adj* tae•ter -tra -trum
lobby *s* vestibul•um -i *n*
lobe *s* lob•us -i *m*
lobster *s* astac•us -i *m*
local *adj* loci *(gen),* regionis *(gen)*
locality *s* loc•us -i *m*
lock *s (of door)* ser•a -ae *f; (of hair)* crin•is -is *m;* **—, stock, and barrel** cum porcis, cum fiscinā; **to be kept under — and key** esse sub clavi
lock *tr* obserare, oppessulare; **to — in** includĕre; **to — out** excludĕre; **to — up** concludĕre
locker *s* loculament•um -i *n*
locket *s* capsell•a -a *f*
locust *s* locust•a -ae *f*
lodge *tr* **to — a complaint against s.o.** nomen alicujus deferre ‖ *intr (with)* deversari (apud + *acc); (to stick)* inhaerēre
lodger *s* hosp•es -itis *m; (in a tenement)* insular•ius -(i)i *m*
lodging *s* hospit•ium -(i)i *n;* **to take up —** hospitium accipĕre
loft *s* tabulat•um -i *n*
lofty *adj* (ex)cels•us -a -um; *(fig)* sublim•is -is -e
log *s* stip•es -itis *m*
logic *s* dialectic•a -orum *npl*
logical *adj* logic•us -a -um; *(reasonable)* rational•is -is -e
logically *adv* ex ratione
loin *s* lumb•us -i *m*
loiter *intr* cessare
loiterer *s* cessat•or -oris *m*
loll *intr* recumbĕre
lone *adj* sol•us -a -um
loneliness *s* solitud•o -inis *f*
lonely *adj* solitari•us -a -um
lonesome *adj* solitari•us -a -um
long *adj* long•us -a -um; *(of time)* diuturn•us -a -um; *(lengthened; syllable)* product•us -a -um; **a — way off** longinqu•us -a -um; **for a — time** jam diu

long *adv* diu; **a little —er** paulo longius; **— how long?** quamdiu? **— after** multo post; **— ago** jamdudum, jampridem; **— before** multo ante; **too —** nimis diu
long *intr* avēre; **to — for** desiderare
longed-for *adj* expectat•us -a -um
longevity *s* longaevit•as -atis *f*
longing *s* desider•ium -(i)i *n*
longing *adj* avid•us -a -um
longingly *adv* avide
longitude *s* longitud•o -inis *f*
long-lasting *adj* diutin•us -a -um
long-lived *adj* viv•ax -acis
long-standing *adj* vetustissim•us -a -um
long-suffering *adj* pati•ens -entis
long-winded *adj* long•us -a -um
look *s (act of looking)* aspect•us -ūs *m; (facial expression)* vult•us -ūs *m; (appearance)* speci•es -ei *f;* **—s** *(general appearance)* habit•us -ūs *m*
look *intr* aspicĕre; *(to seem)* videri; **he —s stern** severitas inest in vultu ejus; **— !** aspice!; **to — about** circumspicĕre; **to — after** curare; **to — after oneself** sibi consulĕre; **to — around** respicĕre, circumspicĕre; **to — around for** prospicĕre; **to — at** intuēri, aspicĕre; *(to study)* considerare; **to — back** respicĕre; **to — down** despicĕre; **to — down upon** despicĕre *(w. acc);* **to — for** quaerĕre; **to — forward to** exspectare; **to — glad** laetitiam vultu aperte ferre; **to look into** *(lit & fig)* inspicĕre; *(to examine)* perscrutari; **to — into one's own mind** introspicĕre in mentem suam; **to — on** intueri, observare; **to — out** prospicĕre; **to — out for** quaerĕre; **to — out of the window** ex fenestra prospicĕre; **to — s.o. in the face** rectis oculis aliquem adspicĕre; **to — towards** spectare; **to — up** suspicĕre, oculos erigĕre; **to — up to** *(implying respect)* suspicĕre; **to — up to heaven** in caelum suspicĕre; **to — upon** habēre
looker-on *s* spectat•or -oris *m*
look-out *s (person)* speculat•or -oris *m;* **to keep a careful —** omnia circumspectare
loom *s* tel•a -ae *f*
loom *intr* in conspectum prodire
loop *s* sin•us -ūs *m*
loophole *s (fig)* effug•ium -(i)i *n*
loose *adj* lax•us -a -um; *(flowing, slack)* flux•us -a -um; *(not chaste)* dissolut•us -a -um; **— bowels** fusa alv•us -i *f*
loosely *adv* laxe; *(dissolutely)* dissolute
loosen *tr* solvĕre, laxare ‖ *intr* solvi
lop *tr* **to — off** praecidĕre; *(in pruning)* amputare
lop-sided *adj* inaequal•is -is -e
loquacious *adj* loqu•ax -acis
lord *s* domin•us -i *m*
Lord *s* Domin•us -i *m*
lord *intr* **to — it over** dominari in *(w. acc)*
lordly *adj* imperios•us -a -um
lordship *s* dominati•o -onis *f*
lore *s* doctrin•a -ae *f*
lose *tr* amittĕre, perdĕre; **to — one eye** altero oculo capi; **to — heart** deficĕre; **to — one's way** (ab)errare
loss *s (act)* amissi•o -onis *f;* damn•um -i *n; (mil, pol)* repuls•a -ae *f;* **to incur some —** aliquid damni contrahĕre; **to suffer a —** damnum *(or* jacturam) facĕre
lost *adj* perdit•us -a -um; **— in admiration** satur•us -a -um admiratione; **to be —** perire; **to get —** aberrare
lot *s* sor•s -tis *f; (destiny)* fat•um -i *n; (piece of land)* agell•us -i *m;* **a —** *(coll)* multum; **a — better** *(coll)* multo melior; **casting of —s** sortiti•o -onis *f;* **—s of people** mult•i -orum *mpl;* **to draw —s for** sortiri
lotion *s* liniment•um -i *n*
lottery *s* sortiti•o -onis *f*
loud *adj* magn•us -a -um ‖ *adv* magnā voce
lounge *s (room)* exedr•ium -(i)i *n; (couch)* lectul•us -i *m*
lounge *intr* otiari
louse *s* pedicul•us -i *m*
lousy *adj* pediculos•us -a -um; *(coll)* foed•us -a -um
lout *s* rustic•us -i *m*
loutish *adj* rustic•us -a -um
love *s* am•or -oris *m;* **to fall in — with** in amorem *(w. gen)* incidĕre
love *tr* amare, diligĕre
love affair *s* am•or -oris *m*
loveliness *s* venust•as -atis *f*
lovely *adj* venust•us -a -um
love potion *s* philtr•um -i *n*
lover *s* am•ans -antis *mf; (homosexual partner)* fra•ter -tris *m*
lovesick *adj* amore ae•ger -gra -grum
loving *adj* am•ans -antis
low *adj (close to the ground; in status)* humil•is -is -e; *(of price)* vil•is -is -e; *(of birth)* obscur•us -a -um; *(low-pitched)* grav•is -is -e; *(not loud)* summiss•us -a -um; *(depressed)* trist•is -is -e; *(vile)* turp•is -is -e; **at — tide** ubi aestus recessit
low *adv* humiliter; summissā voce
low *intr* mugire
lowborn *adj* degen•er -eris
lower *tr* demittĕre, deprimĕre; *(price)* imminuĕre
lower *adj* infer•ior -ior -ius; **of the — world** infer•us -a -um; **the — world** infer•i -orum *mpl*
lowermost *adj* infim•us -a -um
lowing *s* mugit•us -ūs *m*
lowlands *spl* campestr•ia -ium *npl*
lowly *adj* humil•is -is -e
loyal *adj* fidel•is -is -e, fid•us -a -um
loyally *adv* fideliter
loyalty *s* fidelit•as -atis *f*

lubricate *tr* unguĕre
lucid *adj* lucid•us -a -um; **if a madman has a — interval** si furiosus intermissionem habet
Lucifer *s* Lucif•er -eri *m*
luck *s* fortun•a -ae *f;* **bad —** fortun•a -ae *f,* infortun•ium -(i)i *n;* **good —** fortun•a -ae *f*
luckily *adv* feliciter
luckless *adj* infel•ix -icis
lucky *adj* fel•ix -icis; **— stiff** Fortunae fil•ius -(i)i *m*
lucrative *adj* lucrativ•us -a -um
lucre *s* lucr•um -i *n*
ludicrous *adj* ridicul•us -a -um
ludicrously *adv* ridicule
luggage *s* sarcin•ae -arum *fpl*
lukewarm *adj* tepid•us -a -um; *(fig)* segn•is -is -e, frigid•us -a -um
lukewarmly *adv* segniter
lull *s* qui•es -etis *f*
lull *tr* sopire; *(to calm, as a storm)* sedare; *(fig)* demulcēre
lullaby *s* lall•um -i *n*
lumber *s* materi•a -ae *f*
luminary *s* lum•en -inis *n*
luminous *adj* lucid•us -a -um; *(fig)* dilucid•us -a -um
lump *s* glaeb•a -ae *f,* mass•a -ae *f; (on the body)* tub•er -eris *n*
lump *tr* **to — together** coacervare
lumpy *adj* glaebos•us -a -um
lunacy *s* alienati•o -onis *f* mentis
lunar *adj* lunar•is -is -e
lunatic *s* insan•us -i *n*
lunch *s* prand•ium -(i)i *n;* **to have for —** in prandium habēre
lunch *intr* prandēre
luncheon *s* prand•ium -(i)i *n*
lung *s* pulm•o -onis *m*
lunge *s* ict•us -ūs *m*
lunge *intr* prosalire
lurch *s* propuls•us -ūs *m;* **to leave in a —** derelinquĕre
lurch *intr* titubare
lure *s* illecebr•a -ae *f,* esc•a -ae *f*
lure *tr* allicĕre; *(an animal)* inescare
lurk *intr* latēre
luscious *adj* praedulc•is -is -e
lush *adj* luxurios•us -a -um
lust *s* libid•o -inis *f; (for power, etc.)* cupidit•as -atis *f*
lust *intr* concupiscĕre
luster *s* splend•or -oris *m*
lustful *adj* libidinos•us -a -um
lustfully *adv* libidinose, lascive
lustily *adv* valide
lusty *adj* valid•us -a -um
luxuriance *s* luxuri•es -ei *f*
luxuriant *adj* luxurios•us -a -um
luxuriate *intr* luxuriare
luxurious *adj* sumptuos•us -a -um
luxuriously *adv* sumptuose
luxury *s* luxuri•a -ae *f*
lye *s* lixivi•a -ae *f*
lying *adj* mend•ax -acis
lying *s* mendacit•as -atis *f*
lymph *s* lymph•a -ae *f*
lynx *s* lyn•x -cis *mf*
lyre *s* lyr•a -ae *f*
lyric *adj* lyric•us -a -um
lyric *s* (lyricum) carm•en -inis *n*

M

macaroni *s* collyr•a -ae *f*
mace *s* virg•a -ae *f*
machination *s* dol•us -i *m*
machine *s* machin•a -ae *f*
machinery *s* machinament•um -i *n*
mackerel *s* scom•ber -bri *m*
mad *adj* furios•us -a -um; **to be —** furĕre
madam *s* domin•a -ae *f*
madden *tr* mentem alienare *(w. dat); (fig)* furiare
madly *adv* furiose; **to be — in love** insane amare
madman *s* hom•o -inis *m* furiosus
madness *s* fur•or -oris *m*
magazine *s (journal)* ephemer•is -idis *f; (storehouse)* horre•um -i *n*
maggot *s* verm•is -is *m*
magic *adj* magic•us -a -um
magic *s* magica ar•s -tis *f*
magically *adv* velut magicā quadam arte et vi
magician *s* mag•us -i *m*
magisterial *adj* ad magistratum pertin•ens -entis
magistracy *s* magistrat•us ūs *m*
magistrate *s* magistrat•us ūs *m*
magnanimity *s* magnanimit•as -atis *f*
magnanimous *adj* magnanim•us -a -um
magnet *s* magn•es -etis *m*
magnetic *adj* magnetic•us -a -um
magnetism *s* vis *f* magnetica
magnetize *tr* megneticā vi afficĕre
magnificence *s* magnificenti•a -ae *f*
magnificent *adj* magnific•us -a -um
magnificently *adv* magnifice
magnify *tr* amplificare
magnitude *s* magnitud•o -inis *f*
maid *s* ancill•a -ae *f*
maiden *s* virg•o -inis *f*
maidenhood *s* virginit•as -atis *f*
maidenly *adj* virginal•is -is -e
mail *s (letters)* epistol•ae -arum *fpl; (armor)* loric•a -ae *f*
mail *tr* dare
mailman *s* tabellar•ius -(i)i *m*
maim *tr* mutilare
maimed *adj* manc•us -a -um
main *adj* praecipu•us -a -um; **the — point** cap•ut -itis *n;* **in the —** magnā ex parte

main *s* pelag•us -i *m*
mainland *s* contin•ens -entis *f*
mainly *adv* praecipue
maintain *tr (to keep)* tenēre; *(to keep alive)* alěre; *(to defend)* sustinēre; *(to argue)* affirmare
maintenance *s (support)* sustentati•o -onis *f; (means of living)* vict•us -ūs *m*
majestic *adj* august•us -a -um; **how — was his address!** quanta fuit in oratione majestas!
majesty *s* majest•as -atis *f*
major *adj* ma•jor -jor -jus
major *s (mil)* tribun•us -i *m* militaris; *(in logic)* major praemiss•a -ae *f*
majority *s* major par•s -tis *f*
make *s* form•a -ae *f,* figur•a -ae *f*
make *tr* facěre; *(by molding, shaping)* fingěre; *(to render)* redděre; *(to appoint)* creare; *(to force)* cogěre; **to — amends for** corrigěre; **to — haste** festinare; **to — light of** parvi facěre; **to — money** pecuniam facěre; **to — much of** magni facěre; **to — over** transferre; **to — peace** pacem parěre; **to — public** publicare; **to — the bed** lectum sterněre; **to — up** *(story)* fingěre; **to — up with (s.o)** reverti in gratiam cum *(w. abl);* **to — use of** uti *(w. abl);* **to — way for** ceděre *(w. dat),* viam dare *(dat)* ‖ *intr* **to — away with** amovēre; **to — for** petěre
make-believe *adj* fict•us -a -um
maker *s* fabricat•or -oris *m*
make-up *s* compositi•o -onis *f; (disposition)* indol•es -is *f; (cosmetics)* fuc•us -i *m*
maladministration *s* mala administrati•o -onis *f*
malady *s* morb•us -i *m*
malcontent *adj* dissid•ens -entis
male *adj* masculin•us -a -um
male *s* ma•s -ris *m*
malefactor *s* hom•o -inis *m* maleficus
malevolence *s* malevolenti•a -ae *f*
malevolent *adj* malevol•us -a -um
malice *s* malevolenti•a -ae *f*
malicious *adj* malevol•us -a -um
maliciously *adv* malevolo animo
malign *tr* obtrectare
malignant *adj* malevol•us -a -um; *(med)* malign•us -a -um
malleable *adj* ductil•is -is -e
mallet *s* malle•us -i *m*
malpractice *s* delict•a -orum *npl*
maltreat *tr* vexare; *(w. blows, etc.)* mulcare
mama *s* mamm•a -ae *f*
man *s (human being)* hom•o -inis *m; (male)* vir viri *m*
man *tr (ships)* complēre; *(the walls)* praesidio firmare
manacle *s* manic•a -ae *f*
manacle *tr* manicas injicěre *(w. dat)*
manage *tr* curare; *(esp. on large scale)* administrare, gerěre
manageable *adj* tractabil•is -is -e
management *s* cur•a -ae *f,* administrati•o -onis *f*
manager *s* curat•or -oris *m; (steward)* procurat•or -oris *m; (of an estate)* villic•us -i *m*
mandate *s* mandat•um -i *n*
mane *s* jub•a -ae *f*
maneuver *s (mil)* decurs•us -ūs *m; (trick)* dol•us -i *m*
maneuver *intr (mil)* decurrěre; *(fig)* machinari, tractare
mange *s* scabi•es -ei *f*
manger *s* praesep•e -is *n*
mangle *tr* lacerare, dilaniare
mangy *adj* sca•ber -bra -brum
manhood *s* virilit•as -atis *f; (period of puberty)* pubert•as -atis *f*
mania *s* insani•a -ae *f*
maniac *s* furios•us -i *m*
manifest *adj* manifest•us -a -um
manifest *tr* manifestare, declarare
manifestation *s* patefacti•o -onis *f*
manifestly *adv* manifeste
manifesto *s* edict•um -i *n*
manifold *adj* vari•us -a -um
manipulate *intr* tractare
manipulation *s* tractati•o -onis *f*
mankind *s* gen•us -eris *n* humanum
manliness *s* virt•us -utis *f;* **to act with —** viriliter agěre
manly *adj* viril•is -is e
manner *s* mod•us -i *m; (custom)* consuetud•o -inis *f;* **after the — of** ritu *(w. gen),* more *(w. gen);* **bad —s** rusticit•as -atis *f;* **good —s** urbanit•as -atis *f*
mannerism *s* mala affectati•o -onis *f*
mannerly *adj* urban•us -a -um
mannikin *s* homuncul•us -i *m*
man-of-war *s* nav•is -is *f* longa
manor *s* praed•ium -(i)i *n*
man servant *s* serv•us -i *m*
mansion *s* dom•us ūs *f*
manslaughter *s* homicid•ium -(i)i *n*
mantel *s* plute•us -i *m* fornacis
mantle *s (women's outdoor wear)* pall•a -ae *f; (fig)* velament•um -i *n*
mantle *tr* tegěre, dissimulare
manual *adj* manual•is -is -e; **— labor** oper•a -ae *f* quae manibus exercetur
manual *s* enchiridi•on -onis *n*
manufacture *s* fabric•a -ae *f*
manufacture *tr* fabrefacěre
manufacturer *s* fabricat•or -oris *m*
manure *s* sterc•us -oris *n*
manure *tr* stercorare
manuscript *s* cod•ex -icis *m*
many *adj* mult•i -ae -a; **a good —** nonnull•i -ae -a; **as —...as** quot...tot; **how —** quot *(indecl);* **in — ways** multifariam; **so —** tot *(indecl)*
many-colored *adj* multicol•or -oris
map *s* tabul•a -ae *f* geographica

map *tr* **to — out** designare
maple *adj* acern•us -a -um
maple tree *s* ac•er -eris *n*
mar *tr* foedare; *(esp. fig)* deformare
marauder *s* praedat•or -oris *m*
marauding *s* praedati•o -onis *f*
marble *adj* marmore•us -a -um
marble *s* marm•or -oris *n*
March *s* Mart•ius -(i)i *m or* mens•is -is *m* Martius; **on the first of —** Kalendis Martiis
march *s* it•er -ineris *n*
march *tr* ducĕre ‖ *intr* iter facĕre, incedĕre; **to — on** signa proferre; **to — on a town** oppidum aggredi
mare *s* equ•a -ae *f*
margin *s* marg•o -inis *mf*
marginal *adj* margini ascript•us -a -um
marigold *s* calth•a -ae *f*
marine *adj* marin•us -a -um
marine *s* mil•es -itis *m* classicus
mariner *s* naut•a -ae *m*
maritime *adj* maritim•us -a -um
mark *s* not•a -ae *f; (sign, token)* indic•ium -(i)i *n; (brand)* stigm•a -atis *n; (target)* scop•us -i *m; (of wound)* cicatr•ix -icis *f; (characteristic) expressed with gen after verb* esse, *e.g.,* **it is the — of a small mind** pusilli animi est
mark *tr* notare; *(to observe)* animadvertĕre; *(with pencil, etc.)* designare; **to — out** metari
marker *s* ind•ex -icis *mf*
market *s* macell•um -i *n*
marketable *adj* venal•is -is -e
market day *s* nundin•ae -arum *fpl*
marketing *s* empti•o -onis *f*
marketplace *s* for•um -i *n*
market town *s* empor•ium -(i)i *n*
marmalade *s* quil•on -onis *n* ex aurantiis confectum
marquee *s* tabernacul•um -i *n*
marriage *s* matrimon•ium -(i)i *n;* **to give a daughter in —** filiam in matrimonio collocare
marriageable *adj (girl)* nubil•is -is -e
marriage alliance *s* affinit•as -atis *f*
marriage contract *s* pacti•o -onis *f* nuptialis
married *adj (of a woman)* nupta; *(of a man)* maritus; **to get —** matrimonio conjungi
marrow *s* medull•a -ae *f*
marry *tr (said of a man)* in matrimonium ducĕre, uxorem ducĕre; *(said of a woman)* nubĕre *(w. dat)*
marsh *s* pal•us -udis *f*
marshal *s* du•x -cis *m*
marshal *tr* disponĕre
marshy *adj* palus•ter -tris -tre
mart *s* empor•ium -(i)i *n*
martial *adj* bellicos•us -a -um
martyr *s* mart•yr -yris *mf*
martyrdom *s* martyr•ium -(i)i *n*
marvel *s* miracul•um -i *n*
marvel *intr* **to — at** mirari
marvelous *adj* mir•us -a -um
marvelously *adv* mire
masculine *adj* mascul•us -a -um; *(gram)* masculin•us -a -um
mash *s* mixtur•a -ae *f; (for cattle)* forag•o -inis *f*
mash *tr* commiscēre; *(to bruise)* contundĕre
mask *s* person•a -ae *f*
mask *tr (fig)* dissimulare
mason *s* lapidar•ius -(i)i *m*
masonry *s* op•us -eris *n* caementicium
mass *adj* tot•us -a -um; *(large-scale)* magnari•us -a -um
mass *s* mol•es -is *f; (large amount)* copi•a -ae *f; (of people)* turb•a -ae *f; (eccl)* miss•a -ae *f;* **the —es** vulg•us -i *n*
mass *tr* congerĕre, coacervare ‖ *intr* congeri, coacervari
massacre *s* trucidati•o -onis *f*
massacre *tr* trucidare
massage *s* iatraliptic•e -es *f*
massage *tr* fricare
masseur *s* iatralipt•es -ae *m*
massive *adj* solid•us -a -um
mast *s (of ship)* mal•us -i *m; (for cattle)* glan•s -dis *f*
master *s* domin•us -i *m; (teacher)* magis•ter -tri *m; (controller)* arbi•ter -tri *m;* **to be — of** potens esse *(w. gen),* compos esse *(w. gen);* **not be — of** impotens esse *(w. gen)*
master *tr* superare; *(to learn)* perdiscĕre; *(passion)* continēre
masterful *adj* pot•ens -entis, imperios•us -a -um
masterly *adj* perit•us -a -um
masterpiece *s* magnum op•us -eris *n*
mastery *s* dominati•o -onis *f;* **having — of** pot•ens -entis *(w. gen)*
masticate *tr* mandĕre
mastiff *s* Moloss•us -i *m*
mat *s* teg•es -etis *f*
match *s (marriage)* nupti•ae -arum *fpl; (contest)* certam•en -inis *n; (an equal)* par paris *mf;* **a — for** par *(w. dat);* **not a — for** impar *(w. dat)*
match *tr* adaequare ‖ *intr* quadrare
matchless *adj* incomparabil•is -is -e
match maker *s* nuptiarum conciliat•or -oris *m,* conciliatr•ix -icis *f*
mate *s* soc•ius -(i)i *m,* soci•a -ae *f; (spouse)* conju•(n)x -gis *mf*
mate *intr* coïre
material *adj* corpore•us -a -um; *(significant)* haud lev•is -is -e
material *s* materi•a -ae *f*
materially *adv* magnopere
maternal *adj* matern•us -a -um; **— aunt** materter•a -ae *f;* **— uncle** avuncul•us -i *m*

maternity *s* condici•o -onis *f* matris
mathematical *adj* mathematic•us -a -um
mathematician *s* mathematic•us -i *m*
mathematics *s* mathematic•a -ae *f*
matrimony *s* matrimon•ium -(i)i *n*
matrix *s* form•a -ae *f*
matron *s* matron•a -ae *f*
matronly *adj* matronal•is -is -e
matter *s (substance)* materi•a -ae *f; (affair)* res, rei *f; (med)* pus puris *n;* **no —** nihil interest; **what's the — with you?** quid tibi est?
matter *intr impers* refert; **it does not —** nihil interest, nihil refert; **it —s a lot** multum *or* magnopere refert; **what does that — to me (to you)?** quid refert meā (tuā)?
matting *s* teget•es -um *fpl*
mattress *s* culcit•a -ae *f*
mature *adj* matur•us -a -um
mature *intr* maturare
maturely *adv* mature
maturity *s* maturit•as -atis *f*
maul *tr* mulcare
mausoleum *s* mausole•um -i *n*
maw *s* ingluvi•es -ei *f*
mawkish *adj* putid•us -a -um
mawkishly *adv* putide
maxim *s* axiom•a -atis *n*
maximum *adj* quam maxim•us -a -um
May *s* Mai•us -i *m or* mens•is -is *m* Maius; **on the first of —** Kalendis Maiis
may *intr* posse; **I may go** *(denoting lawfulness, permission)* licet mihi ire; *(possibility, expressed by subj):* eam; **perhaps s.o. may say** fortasse quispiam dixerit
maybe *adv* forsitan, fortasse
mayor *s* praet•or -oris *m*
maze *s* labyrinth•us -i *m*
me *pron* **by —** a me; **to —** mihi; **with —** mecum
mead *s (drink)* muls•um -i *n*
meadow *s* prat•um -i *n*
meager *adj* exil•is -is -e; *(insufficient)* exigu•us -a -um
meagerly *adv* exiliter
meagerness *s* exilit•as -atis *f*
meal *s* cib•us -i *m; (flour)* farin•a -ae *f;* **to eat a —** cibum sumĕre
mean *adj (middle)* medi•us -a -um; *(low)* humil•is -is -e; *(cruel)* vil•is -is -e
mean *s* med•ium -(i)i *n*
mean *tr* significare; *(after s.th. has been mentioned)* dicĕre, *e.g.,* **of course, you — Plato** Platonem videlicet dicis; *(to intend)* velle, in animo habēre; **quid sibi vult pater?** what does my father mean?
meander *intr* sinuoso cursu labi
meaning *s* sens•us -ūs *m,* significati•o -onis *f*
meaningful *adj* signific•ans -antis
meanness *s (lowliness)* humilit•as -atis *f; (cruelty)* crudelit•as -atis *f*
means *spl (way, method)* rati•o -onis *f,* mod•us -i *m;* **by all —** maxime, omnino; **by fair —** recte; **by — of** *render by abl or* per *(w. acc);* **by no —** haudquaquam
meanwhile *adv* interea, interim
measles *spl* morbill•i -orum *mpl*
measurable *adj* mensurabil•is -is -e
measure *s* mensur•a -ae *f; (proper measure)* mod•us -i *m; (course of action)* rati•o -onis *f; (leg)* rogati•o -onis *f;* **beyond —** supra modum; **in some —** aliquā ex parte; **to take —s** consulĕre *(w. dat of that on behalf of which;* in + *acc of person against whom)*
measure *tr* metiri; **to — off** metari
measurement *s* mensur•a -ae *f*
meat *s* car•o -nis *f*
meat tray *s* carnar•ium -(i)i *n*
mechanic *s* opif•ex -icis *m*
mechanical *adj* mechanic•us -a -um
mechanically *adv* mechanicā quādam arte
mechanics *s* mechanica ar•s -tis *f*
mechanism *s* mechanati•o -onis *f*
medal *s* insign•e -is *n*
medallion *s* numism•a -atis *n* sollemne
meddle *intr* **(in)** se interponĕre (in + *acc)*
meddler *s* ardali•o -onis *m*
meddlesome *adj* curios•us -a -um
medial *adj* medi•us -a -um
median *adj* dimidi•us -a -um
median *s* mediocrit•as -atis *f*
mediate *tr* conciliare ‖ *intr* se interponĕre ad componendam litem; **to — between estranged friends** aversos amicos componĕre
mediation *s* intercessi•o -onis *f*
mediator *s* intercess•or -oris *m*
medical *adj* medic•us -a -um; **— practice** medicin•a -ae *f*
medicate *tr* medicare
medication *s* medicament•um -i *n*
medicinal *adj* medic•us -a -um
medicine *s (science)* medicin•a -ae *f; (remedy)* medicament•um -i *n;* **to practice —** medicinam exercēre
medieval *adj* medii aevi *(gen used as adj)*
mediocre *adj* mediocr•is -is -e
mediocrity *s* mediocrit•as -atis *f*
meditate *intr* cogitare
meditation *s* cogitati•o -onis *f*
meditative *adj* cogitabund•us -a -um
Mediterranean *s* mar•e -is *n* internum, mar•e -is *n* nostrum
medium *s (middle)* med•ium -(i)i *n; (expedient)* mod•us -i *m; (agency)* conciliat•or -oris *m*
medium *adj* mediocr•is -is -e
medley *s* farrag•o -inis *f*
meek *adj* mit•is -is -e; *(unassuming)* summiss•us -a -um
meekly *adv* summisse

meekness *s* anim•us -i *m* summissus
meet *adj* apt•us -a -um; **it is —** convenit
meet *tr* convenire, obviam ire *(w. dat); (danger, death, etc.)* obire ‖ *intr* convenire; **to — with** offendĕre
meet *s (contest)* certam•en -inis *n*
meeting *s (of two or many individuals)* congressi•o -onis *f; (assembly)* convent•us -ūs *m; (for consultation)* consil•ium -(i)i *n;* **to hold a —** conventum habēre, consilium habēre
melancholy *s* maestiti•a -ae *f*
melancholy *adj* maest•us -a -um
melee *s* tumult•us -ūs *m*
mellow *adj* matur•us -a -um; *(from drinking)* temulent•us -a -um
melodious *adj* canor•us -a -um
melodiously *adv* canore, modulate
melodramatic *adj* **to be —** paratragoedare
melody *s* mel•os -eos *n*
melt *tr* liquefacĕre; **to — down** conflare ‖ *intr* liquescĕre
melting *s* liquati•o -onis *f*
melting pot *s* fictil•e -is *n*
member *s* membr•um -i *n; (fig)* sodal•is -is *m*
membrane *s* membran•a -ae *f*
memento *s* monument•um -i *n*
memoirs *spl* commentari•i -orum *mpl*
memorable *adj* memorabil•is -is -e
memorandum *s* not•a -ae *f*
memorial *adj* monument•um -i *n*
memory *s* memori•a -ae *f;* **from —** ex memoriā, memoriter; **in — of** in memoriam *(w. gen);* **in the — of man** post hominum memoriam; **to commit to —** ediscĕre; **to have a good —** esse memoriā bonā
menace *s* min•ae -arum *fpl*
menace *tr* minari, minitari; *(of things)* imminēre *(w. dat)*
menacing *adj* min•ax -acis; *(only of persons)* minitabund•us -a -um
mend *tr* emendare; *(clothes)* sarcire ‖ *intr (to improve in health)* mel•ior -ior -ius fieri
mendicant *s* mendic•us -i *m,* mendic•a -ae *f*
menial *adj* servil•is -is -e
menial *s* serv•us -i *m,* serv•a -ae *f*
menses *spl* menstru•a -orum *npl*
mental *adj* mente concept•us -a -um
mentally *adv* mente, animo
mention *s* menti•o -onis *f;* **to make — of** mentionem facĕre *(w. gen)*
mention *tr* commemorare; *(by name)* nominare; **not to —** silentio praeterire; **not to — the others** ne de alteris referam
mercantile *adj* mercatori•us -a -um
mercenary *adj* mercenari•us -a -um
mercenary *s* mil•es -itis *m* mercenarius
merchandise *s* merc•es -ium *fpl*
merchant *s* mercat•or -oris *m; (in a market)* macellar•ius -(i)i *m*
merchant ship *s* nav•is -is *f* mercatoria
merciful *adj* misericor•s -dis
mercifully *adv* misericorditer
merciless *adj* immisericor•s -dis
mercilessly *adv* immisericorditer
mercurial *adj* a•cer -cris -cre
Mercury *s* Mercur•ius -(i)i *m*
mercury *s* argent•um -i *n* vivum
mercy *s* misericordi•a -ae *f*
mere *adj* mer•us -a -um
merely *adv* tantummodo, solum
meretricious *adj* meretrici•us -a -um
merge *tr* confundĕre ‖ *intr* confundi
meridian *s* meridianus circul•us -i *m*
merit *s* merit•um -i *n*
merit *tr* merēre, merēri
meritorious *adj* laudabil•is -is -e
mermaid *s* nymph•a -ae *f*
merrily *adv* festive, hilare
merry *adj* festiv•us -a -um, fest•us -a -um; **Merry Christmas** fausta festa Christi Nataliti•a -ae *f*
merrymaking *s* festivit•as -atis *f*
mesh *s (of net)* macul•a -ae *f*
mess *s (dirt)* squal•or -oris *m; (confusion)* rerum perturbati•o -onis *f*
message *s* nunt•ius -(i)i *m,* nunt•ium -(i)i *n*
messenger *s* nunt•ius -(i)i *m*
metal *adj* metallic•us -a -um
metal *s* metall•um -i *n*
metallurgy *s* metallurgi•a -ae *f*
metamorphosis *s* transfigurati•o -onis *f*
metaphor *s* translati•o -onis *f*
metaphorical *adj* translat•us -a -um
metaphorically *adv* per translationem
metaphysical *adj* metaphysic•us -a -um
metaphysics *s* metaphysic•a -ae *f; (as a title)* metaphysic•a -orum *npl*
meteor *s* fa•x -cis *f* caelestis
meteorology *s* meteorologi•a -ae *f*
mete out *tr* emetiri
meter *s* metr•um -i *n*
method *s* rati•o -onis *f*
methodical *adj (of things)* ratione et viā fact•us -a -um; *(of a person)* dilig•ens -entis
methodically *adv* ratione et viā
meticulous *adj* accurat•us -a -um
meticulously *adv* accurate
metonymy *s* metonymi•a -ae *f*
metrical *adj* metric•us -a -um
metropolis *s* cap•ut -itis *n*
mettle *s* anim•us -i *m*
miasma *s* halit•us -ūs *m*
microscope *s* microscop•ium -(i)i *n*
mid *adj* medi•us -a -um
midday *adj* meridian•us -a -um
midday *s* meridi•es -ei *f*
middle *adj* medi•us -a -um; **— age** aet•as -atis *f* media
middle *s* med•ium -(i)i *n;* **in the middle of the road** in mediā viā
midget *s* pumili•o -onis *mf*

midnight *s* media no•x -ctis *f;* **around —** mediā circiter nocte
midriff *s* diaphragm•a -atis *n*
midst *s* med•ium -(i)i *n;* **in the midst of** inter *(w. acc)*
midsummer *s* summa aest•as -atis *f*
midway *adv* medi•us -a -um; **he stood — between the lines** stabat medius inter acies
midwife *s* obstetr•ix -icis *f*
midwinter *s* brum•a -ae *f*
midwinter *adj* brumal•is -is -e
mien *s* habit•us -ūs *m; (facial expression)* vult•us -ūs *m*
might *s* vis *f;* **with all one's —** summā ope
might *intr render by imperfect subjunctive*
mightily *adv* valde
mighty *adj* validissim•us -a -um; **— Homer** ingens Homer•us -i *m*
migrate *intr* migrare
migration *s* peregrinati•o -onis *f*
migratory *adj* migr•ans -antis; **— birds** volucr•es -um *fpl* advenae
mild *adj* mit•is -is -e; *(esp. of weather)* clem•ens -entis; **to grow —** mitescěre
mildew *s* muc•or -oris *m*
mildewed *adj* **to become —** mucorem contrahěre
mildness *s* lenit•as -atis *f; (of weather)* clementi•a -ae *f*
mile *s* mille *n* passūs; **three —s** tria milia passuum
milestone *s* milliar•ium -i(i) *n*
militant *adj* milit•ans -antis
military *adj* militar•is -is -e; **— command** imper•ium -(i)i *n;* **— service** militi•a -ae *f*
military *s* militi•a -ae *f*
militia *s* militi•a -ae *f* domestica
milk *s* lac lactis *n*
milk *tr* mulgēre
milky *adj* lacte•us -a -um
Milky Way *s* Vi•a -ae *f* Lactea
mill *s* mol•a -ae *f*
millenium *s* mille ann•i -orum *mpl*
miller *s* pist•or -oris *m*
million *adj* decies centena milia *(w. gen)*
millionaire *s* hom•o -inis *m* praedives
millstone *s* mol•a -ae *f*
mime *s* mim•us -i *m*
mimic *s* imitat•or -oris *m*
mimic *tr* imitari
mimicry *s* imitati•o -onis *f*
mince *tr* conciděre; **not to — words** Latine loqui
mind *s* men•s -tis *f;* **to be in one's right —** compo•s -tis mentis suae esse; **to call to —** recordari; **to change one's —** mentem mutare; **to come to —** in mentem venire, *(coll)* in buccam venire; **to make up one's —** constituěre; **to show presence of —** schemas non loqui
mind *tr (to look after)* curare; *(to regard)* respicěre; *(to object to)* aegre ferre; **to — one's own business** suum negotium agěre
mindful *adj* mem•or -oris
mine *s* fodin•a -ae *f,* metall•um -i *n; (fig)* thesaur•us -i *m*
mine *tr* effoděre
mine *adj* me•us -a -um
miner *s* metallic•us -i *m*
mineral *s* metall•um -i *n*
mineral *adj* metallic•us -a -um
mineralogist *s* metallorum perit•us -i *m*
mineralogy *s* metallorum scienti•a -ae *f*
mingle *tr* commiscēre **‖** *intr* se immiscēre
miniature *s* minuta tabul•a -ae *f*
minimum *adj* quam minim•us -a -um
minimum *s* minim•um -i *n*
minion *s* clien•s -tis *mf*
minister *s* adminis•ter -tri *m*
minister *intr* ministrare
ministry *s* ministrati•o -onis *f*
minor *s* pupill•us -i *m,* pupill•a -ae *f*
minor *adj* min•or -or -us
minority *s* minor par•s -tis *f*
minstrel *s* fidic•en -enis *m*
mint *s (for making money)* monet•a -ae *f; (bot)* menth•a -ae *f*
mint *tr* cuděre
minute *s* temporis moment•um -i *n;* **to keep —s** acta diurna conficěre
minute *adj (small)* minut•us -a -um; *(exact)* accurat•us -a -um
minutely *adv* minute, subtiliter
miracle *s* miracul•um -i *n*
miraculous *adj* miraculos•us -a -um
miraculously *adv* miraculose
mirage *s* imag•o -inis *f* ficta
mire *s* lut•um -i *n*
mirror *s* specul•um -i *n*
mirth *s* hilarit•as -atis *f*
mirthful *adj* hilar•is -is -e
misadventure *s* infortun•ium -i(i) *n*
misapply *tr* abuti *(w. abl)*
misapprehend *tr* male intellegěre
misapprehension *s* falsa concepti•o -onis *f*
misbehave *intr* indecore se gerěre
misbehavior *s* morum pravit•as -atis *f*
miscalculate *intr* errare
miscalculation *s* err•or -oris *m*
miscarriage *s* abort•us -ūs *m; (fig)* malus success•us -ūs *m*
miscarry *intr* abortum facěre; *(fig)* male succeděre
miscellaneous *adj* miscellane•us -a -um
mischance *s* infortun•ium -(i)i *n*
mischief *s* malefic•ium -(i)i *n; (of children)* lascivi•a -ae *f;* **to refrain from doing any —** ab injuria et maleficio temperare
mischievous *adj* malefic•us -a -um; *(playful)* lasciv•us -a -um
misconceive *tr* male intellegěre

misconception *s* falsa opini•o -onis *f*
misconduct *s* delict•um -i *n;* **to be guilty of —** delictum in se admittĕre
misconstrue *tr* male interpretari
misdeed *s* delict•um -i *n*
misdemeanor *s* levius delict•um -i *n*
misdirect *tr* fallĕre
miser *s* avar•us -i *m*
miserable *adj* mis•er -era -erum
miserably *adv* misere
miserly *adj* avar•us -a -um
misery *s* miseri•a -ae *f*
misfortune *s* infortun•ium -(i)i *n*
misgiving *s* sollicitud•o -inis *f;* **to have —s about** diffidĕre *(w. dat)*
misgovern *tr* male administrare
misguide *tr* seducĕre
misguided *adj (fig)* dem•ens -entis
mishap *s* incommod•um -i *n*
misinform *tr* falsa docēre *(w. acc)*
misinterpret *tr* male interpretari
misinterpretation *s* prava interpretati•o -onis *f*
misjudge *tr* male judicare
mislay *tr* amittĕre
mislead *tr* seducĕre, decipĕre
mismanage *tr* male gerĕre
mismanagement *s* mala administrati•o -onis *f*
misnomer *s* falsum nom•en -inis *n*
misplace *tr* alieno loco ponĕre; **confidence in such persons is —ed** iis male creditur
misprint *s* errat•um -i *n* typographicum, mend•um -i *n*
misquote *tr* aliis verbis ponĕre
misquotation *s* falsa prolati•o -onis *f*
misrepresent *tr* detorquēre
misrepresentation *s* sinistra interpretati•o -onis *f*
misrule *s* prava administrati•o -onis *f*
miss *s* err•or -oris *m; (term of respect)* domin•a -ae *f*
miss *tr (to overlook)* omittĕre; *(one's aim)* non attingĕre; *(to feel the want of)* desiderare ‖ *intr (to fall short)* errare
misshapen *adj* deform•is -is -e
missile *s* missil•e -is *n*
missing *adj* abs•ens -entis; **to be —** deësse
mission *s (delegation, sending)* missi•o -onis *f; (goal)* fin•is -is *m*
misspell *tr* perperam scribĕre
misspend *tr* prodigĕre
misstate *tr* parum accurate memorare
misstatement *s* fals•um -i *n*
mist *s* nebul•a -ae *f*
mistake *s* err•or -oris *m; (written)* mend•um -i *n;* **to make a —** errare
mistake *tr* **to —** *(s.o. or s.th.)* **for** habēre pro *(w. abl)*
mistaken *adj* fals•us -a -um; **to be —** falli; **unless I am —** ni fallor
mistletoe *s* visc•um -i *n*
mistress *s* domin•a -ae *f,* her•a -ae *f; (paramour)* concubin•a -ae *f; (teacher)* magistr•a -ae *f*
mistrust *s* diffidenti•a -ae *f*
mistrust *tr* diffidĕre *(w. dat)*
mistrustful *adj* diffid•ens -entis
mistrustfully *adv* diffidenter
misty *adj* nebulos•us -a -um
misunderstand *tr* perperam intellegĕre
misunderstanding *s* falsa opini•o -onis *f; (among friends)* offensi•o -onis *f*
misuse *s* abus•us -ūs *m;* **that is a — of the term** id est verbum alieno loco adhibēre
misuse *tr* abuti *(w. abl); (to revile)* conviciari
mite *s (bit)* parvul•us -i *m; (coin)* sext•ans -antis *m*
miter *s* mitr•a -ae *f*
mitigate *tr* mitigare
mitigation *s* mitigati•o -onis *f*
mix *tr* miscēre; **to — in** admiscēre; **to — up** commiscēre; *(fig)* confundĕre
mixed *adj* promiscu•us -a -um
mixture *s* mixtur•a -ae *f*
moan *s* gemit•us -ūs *m*
moan *intr* gemĕre
moat *s* foss•a -ae *f*
mob *s* turb•a -ae *f,* vulg•us -i *n*
mob *tr* stipare
mobile *adj* mobil•is -is -e
mobility *s* mobilit•as -atis *f*
mock *tr* irridēre
mock *adj* mimic•us -a -um; **— death** mimica mor•s -tis *f;* **— sea battle show** naumachiae spectacul•um -i *n*
mockery *s* irrisi•o -onis *f*
mode *s* mod•us -i *m; (fashion)* us•us -ūs *m;* **— of life** vitae praeposit•um -i *n*
model *s* exempl•ar -aris *n;* **on the — of** ad simulacrum *(w. gen)*
model *tr* formare; *(e.g., a statue)* fingĕre; **to — oneself after** imitari
moderate *adj* moderat•us -a -um
moderate *tr* moderari, temperare
moderately *adv* moderate
moderation *s* moderati•o -onis *f*
moderator *s* praes•es -idis *mf*
modern *adj* rec•ens -entis
modest *adj (restricted)* modest•us -a -um; *(slight)* modic•us -a -um
modestly *adv* verecunde
modesty *s* modesti•a -ae *f*
modification *s* mutati•o -onis *f*
modify *tr* (im)mutare
modulate *tr* flectĕre
modulation *s* flexi•o -onis *f*
moist *adj* (h)umid•us -a -um
moisten *tr* (h)umectare
moisture *s* hum•or -oris *m*
molar *s* den•s -tis *m* genuinus
molasses *s* sacchari fae•x -cis *f*
mold *s* form•a -ae *f; (mustiness)* muc•or -oris *m*
mold *tr* formare, fingĕre ‖ *intr* mucescĕre

molder *intr* putrescĕre
moldiness *s* muc•or -oris *m*
moldy *adj* mucid•us -a -um
mole *s (animal)* talp•a -ae *f; (sea wall)* mol•es -is *f; (on skin)* naev•us -i *m*
molecule *s* particul•a -ae *f*
molehill *s* **to make mountains out of —s** e rivo flumina magna facĕre
molest *tr* vexare
molt *tr* plumas ponĕre
molten *adj* liquefact•us -a -um
moment *s* temporis moment•um -i *n;* **at any —** omnibus momentis; **at the very —** ipso tempore; **for a —** paulisper; **in a —** momento temporis
momentarily *adv* statim
momentary *adj* brev•is -is -e
momentous *adj* magni momenti *(gen, used adjectively)*
monarch *s* re•x -gis *m*
monarchical *adj* regi•us -a -um
monarchy *s* regn•um -i *n*
monastery *s* monaster•ium -(i)i *n*
monetary *adj* pecuniari•us -a -um
money *s* pecuni•a -ae *f*
moneychanger *s* numular•ius -(i)i *m*
moneylender *s* faenerat•or -oris *m*
mongrel *s* hybrid•a -ae *m*
monitor *m* admonit•or -oris *m*
monk *s* monach•us -i *m*
monkey *s* sim•ius -(i)i *m,* simi•a -ae *f*
monogram *s* monogramm•a -atis *n*
monologue *s* monologi•a -ae *f*
monopolize *tr* monopolium exercēre in *(w. acc)*
monopoly *s* monopol•ium -(i)i *n*
monosyllabic *adj* monosyllab•us -a -um
monosyllable *s* monosyllab•um -i *n*
monotonous *adj* semper idem (eadem, idem); *(sing-song)* canor•us-a -um
monotony *s* taed•ium -(i)i *n*
monster *s* monstr•um -i *n*
monstrosity *s* monstr•um -i *n*
monstrous *adj* monstros•us -a -um
monstrously *adv* monstrose
month *s* mens•is -is *m;* **on the first of the —** Kalendis
monthly *adj* menstru•us -a -um
monthly *adv* singulis mensibus
monument *s* monument•um -i *n*
monumental *adj (huge)* ing•ens -entis; *(important)* grav•is -is -e
mood *s* animi habit•us -i *m; (gram)* mod•us -i *m*
moodiness *s* morosit•as -atis *f*
moody *adj* moros•us -a -um
moon *s* lun•a -ae *f;* **the — is shining** luna nitescit
moonlight *s* lunae lum•en -inis *n;* **by —** per lunam
moonstruck *adj* lunatic•us -a -um
Moor *s* Maur•us -i *m*
moor *tr* religare, ancoris retinēre
moor *s* tesc•a -orum *npl*
mop *s* penicul•us -i *m*
mop *tr* detergēre
mope *intr* maerēre
moral *adj (relating to morals)* moral•is -is -e; *(morally proper)* honest•us -a -um
moral *s (of story)* document•um -i *n*
morale *s* anim•us -i *m; (of several)* anim•i -orum *mpl;* **— is low** animi deficiunt
morality *s* boni mor•es -um *mpl*
moralize *intr* de moribus disserĕre
morals *spl* mor•es -um *mpl*
morass *s* pal•us -udis *f*
morbid *adj* morbid•us -a -um
more *adj* plus *(w. gen); (pl)* plur•es -es -ia; *(denoting greater extent of space or time)* amplius: **for — than four hours** amplius quattuor horis; **— and —** magis magisque; **— or less** plus minus; **— than** plus quam; **— than enough** ultra quam satis; **no —** non diutius; **and what's —, he even comes into the senate** immo vero etiam in senatum venit
moreover *adv* praeterea
morning *s* mane *n (indecl),* temp•us -oris *n* matutinum; **early in the —** bene mane; **from — till evening** a mane usque ad vesperam; **good —!** salve!; **in the —** mane; **this —** hodie mane
morning *adj* matutin•us -a -um
morning star *s* Lucif•er -eri *m*
morose *adj* moros•us -a -um
morosely *adv* morose
moroseness *s* morosit•as -atis *f*
morsel *s* off•a -ae *f*
mortal *adj* mortal•is -is -e; *(deadly)* mortif•er -era -erum
mortal *s* mortal•is -is *mf*
mortality *s* mortalit•as -atis *f*
mortally *adv* mortifere; **to be — wounded** mortiferum vulnus accipĕre
mortar *s* mortar•ium -(i)i *n*
mortgage *s* hypothec•a -ae *f*
mortgage *tr* obligare
mortify *tr (to vex)* offendĕre
mosaic *s* tessellatum op•us -eris *n*
mosaic floor *s* tesselatum et sectile paviment•um -i *n*
mosquito *s* cul•ex -icis *m*
moss *s* musc•us -i *m*
mossy *adj* muscos•us -a -um
most *adj* plurim•us -a -um, plerusque, -aque, -umque; **for the — part** maximam partem; **— people** plerique
most *adv (w. verbs)* maxime; *(w. adjectives and adverbs, expressed by superl., or w. adjectives ending in* -ius, *expressed w.* maxime *w. positive);* **— enthusiastically** animosissime
mostly *adv* plerumque
moth *s* blatt•a -ae *f*
moth-eaten *adj* blattis peres•us -a -um
mother *s* ma•ter -tris *f*

motherhood *s* matris condici•o -onis *f*
mother-in-law *s* socr•us -ūs *f*
motherless *adj* matre orb•us -a -um
motherly *adj* matern•us -a -um
motion *s* moti•o -onis *f; (proposal of a bill)* rogati•o -onis *f;* **to make a —** ferre; **to set in —** ciēre
motionless *adj* immot•us -a -um
motive *s* caus•a -ae *f,* rati•o -onis *f*
motive *adj* mov•ens -entis
motley *adj* vari•us -a -um
mottled *adj* maculos•us -a -um
motto *s* sententi•a -ae *f*
mound *s (round)* tumul•us -i *m; (reaching lengthwise)* agg•er -eris *m*
mount *s* mon•s -tis *m*
mount *tr* conscendĕre ‖ *intr* ascendĕre
mountain *s* mon•s -tis *m*
mountaineer *s* montan•us -i *m*
mountainous *adj* montan•us -a -um
mountain top *s* culm•en -inis *n* summi montis
mounted *adj* inscens•us -a -um; *(on horse)* equistr•is -is -e
mourn *tr & intr* lugēre
mourner *s* plorat•or -oris *m*
mournful *adj* lugubr•is -is -e
mournfully *adv* maeste
mourning *s* luct•us -ūs *m; (dress)* vest•is -is *f* lugubris; **in —** pullat•us -a -um; **to go into —** vestitum mutare
mouse *s* mu•s -ris *m*
mousetrap *s* muscipul•um -i *n*
mouth *s* os, oris *n; (of beast)* fau•x -cis *f; (of river)* ost•ium -(i)i *n; (of bottle)* lur•a -ae *f*
mouthful *s* buccell•a -ae *f*
mouthpiece *s* interpr•es -etis *m*
movable *adj* mobil•is -is -e
movables *spl* mobil•ia -ium *npl*
move *tr* movēre; *(emotionally)* commovēre; *(to propose)* ferre ‖ *intr* movēri, se movēre; *(to change residence)* migrare; **to — on** progredi
movement *s* mot•us -ūs *m*
moving *adj* flebil•is -is -e
mow *tr* secare
mower *s* faenis•ex -icis *mf*
mowing *s* faenisic•ium -(i)i *n*
much *adj* mult•us -a -um; **as —...as** tantus...quantus; **how —** quant•us -a -um; **how — does this cost?** quanti hoc constat?; **— less** nedum; **so —** tant•us -a -um; **too —** nimi•us -a -um; **very —** plurim•us -a -um
much *adv* multum; *(w. comparatives)* multo; **very —** plurimum
muck *s* sterc•us -oris *n*
mucous *adj* mucos•us -a -um
mucus *s* muc•us -i *m*
mud *s* lut•um -i *n,* lim•us -i *m*
muddle *tr* turbare; *(fig)* perturbare
muddle *s* turb•a -ae *f*
muddy *adj* lutulent•us -a -um; *(troubled)* turbid•us -a -um
muffle *tr* involvĕre; **to — up** obvolvĕre
muffled *adj* surd•us -a -um
mug *s* pocul•um -i *n*
mug *tr* mulcare
mugger *s* percuss•or -oris *m*
muggy *adj* humid•us -a -um
mulberry *s* mor•um -i *n*
mulberry tree *s* mor•us -i *f*
mule *s* mul•us -i *m*
muleteer *s* muli•o -onis *m*
mulish *adj* obstinat•us -a -um
multifarious *adj* vari•us -a -um
multiplication *s* multiplicati•o -onis *f*
multiply *tr* multiplicare ‖ *intr* augēri
multitude *s* multitud•o -inis *f; (crowd)* turb•a -ae *f*
mumble *tr & intr* murmurare
munch *tr* manducare
mundane *adj* mundan•us -a -um
municipal *adj* municipal•is -is -e
municipality *s* municip•ium -(i)i *n*
munificence *s* munificenti•a -ae *f*
munificent *adj* munific•us -a -um
munificently *adv* munifice
munitions *spl* belli apparat•us -ūs *m*
mural *adj* mural•is -is -e
murder *s* caed•es -is *f,* nex, necis *f*
murder *tr* necare; **to — a song** lacerare canticum
murderer *s* homicid•a -ae *mf*
murderous *adj* cruent•us -a -um
murky *adj* caliginos•us -a -um
murmur *s* murm•ur -uris *n*
murmur *tr & intr* murmurare
murmuring *s* admurmurati•o -onis *f*
muscle *s* muscul•us -i *m*
muscular *adj* musculos•us -a -um
Muse *s* Mus•a -ae *f*
muse *intr* secum agitare
mushroom *s* bolet•us -i *m*
music *s* music•a -ae *f; (of instruments and voices)* cant•us ūs *m*
musical *adj (of persons)* music•us -a -um; *(of sound)* canor•us -a -um
musician *s* music•us -i *m,* music•a *f; (of stringed instrument)* fidic•en -inis *m; (of wind instruments)* tibic•en -inis *m*
must *s* must•um -i *n*
must *intr* **I — go** mihi eundum est, me oportet ire, debeo ire, necesse est (ut) eam
mustard *s* sinap•i -is *n*
muster *tr* lustrare; *(fig)* cogĕre; **to — up courage** animum sumĕre ‖ *intr* coïre
muster *s* copiarum lustrati•o -onis *f*
musty *adj* mucid•us -a -um
mutable *adj* mutabil•is -is -e
mute *adj* mut•us -a -um
mutilate *tr* mutilare, truncare
mutilated *adj* mutil•us -a -um
mutilation *s* mutilati•o -onis *f*
mutineer *s* seditios•us -i *m*

mutinous *adj* seditios•us -a -um
mutiny *s* sediti•o -onis *f*
mutiny *intr* seditionem facĕre
mutter *s* murmurati•o -onis *f*
mutter *tr & intr* mussare
mutton *s* ovillin•a -ae *f*
mutual *adj* mutu•us -a -um
mutually *adv* mutuo, inter se
muzzle *s* capistr•um -i *n*
muzzle *tr* capistrare
my *adj* me•us -a -um; **— own** propri•us -a -um
myriad *adj (innumerable)* sescent•i -ae -a
myrrh *s* myrrh•a -ae *f*
myrtle *s* myrt•us -i *f*
myself *pron (refl)* me; *(intensive)* ipse, egomet; **to —** mihi
mysterious *adj* arcan•us -a -um
mysteriously *adv* arcane
mystery *s* myster•ium -(i)i *n; (fig)* res, rei *f* occultissima
mystical *adj* mystic•us -a -um
mystically *adv* mystice
mystify *tr* confundĕre
myth *s* myth•os -i *m*
mythical *adj* fabulos•us -a -um
mythology *s* histori•a -ae *f* fabularum

N

nab *tr* prehendĕre
nadir *s* fund•us -i *m*
nag *s* caball•us -i *m*
nag *tr* objurgitare
naiad *s* naï•as -adis *f*
nail *s* clav•us -i *m; (of finger, of toe)* ungu•is -is *m*
nail *tr* clavīs (con)figĕre *(w. dat of that to which);* **to — to the cross** cruci figĕre
naive *adj* simpl•ex -icis
naively *adv* simpliciter
naked *adj* nud•us -a -um
nakedly *adv (fig)* aperte
name *s* nom•en -inis *n; (a significant designation)* appellati•o -onis *f; (good name, reputation)* fam•a -ae *f; (term)* vocabul•um -i *n;* **by —** nominatim; **her — is Fortunata** Fortunata appellatur *or* illi nomen est Fortunata *or* illi nomen est Fortunatae
name *tr (to call by a name; to mention by name)* nominare; *(to appoint)* dicĕre; **to be —ed after one's father** nominari a patre
nameless *adj* nominis exper•s -tis
namely *adv* scilicet
nap *s* brevis somn•us -i *n; (of cloth)* vill•us -i *m;* **to take a —** brevi somno uti
nape *s* **— of the neck** cerv•ix -icis *f*
napkin *s* mapp•a -ae *f*
narcotic *adj* somnific•us -a -um
narcotic *s* medicament•um -i *n* somnificum
nard *s* nard•um -i *n*
narrate *tr* narrare
narration *s* narrati•o -onis *f*
narrative *s* narrati•o *f*
narrator *s* narrat•or -oris *m*
narrow *adj* angust•us -a -um; *(fig)* arct•us -a -um
narrow *tr* coarctare ‖ *intr* coarctari
narrowly *adv* vix, aegre
narrow-minded *adj* animi angusti *or* parvi *(gen used adjectively)*
narrowness *s* angusti•ae -arum *fpl*
nasty *adj (foul)* foed•us -a -um; *(mean)* turp•is -is -e
natal *adj* natal•is -is -e
nation *s* gen•s -tis *f,* nati•o -onis *f; (organized political community)* popul•us -i *m*
national *adj (expr. by gen of* gens *or* natio *or* populus): **— customs** gentis mor•es -um *mpl;* **— assembly** concil•ium -(i)i *n* populi
nationality *s* civit•as -atis *f*
nationalize *tr* confiscare
native *adj* indigen•a -ae *mf;* **— land** patri•a -ae *f;* **— language** patrius serm•o -onis *m*
native *s* indigen•a -ae *mf*
nativity *s* ort•us -ūs *m*
natural *adj (history, law, daughter, death)* natural•is -is -e; *(not man-made)* nativ•us -a -um; *(innate; opp:* traditus) innat•us -a -um
natural disposition *s* indol•es -is *f*
naturalization *s* civitatis donati•o -onis *f*
naturalize *tr* civitate donare
naturally *adv* naturā, naturaliter; *(unaffectedly)* simpliciter; *(of its own accord)* sponte
natural science *s* physic•a -ae *f*
nature *s (of a specific thing)* natur•a -ae *f; (universal nature)* rerum natur•a -ae *f; (mostly of persons)* ingen•ium -(i)i *n;* **second —** altera natur•a -ae *f;* **beauties of —** amoenitat•es -um *fpl* locorum
naught *s* nihil; **to set at —** nihili facĕre
naughty *adj* improbul•us -a -um
nausea *s* nause•a -ae *f; (fig)* fastid•ium -(i)i *n*
nauseate *tr (fig)* fastidium movēre *(w. dat);* **to be —ed** fastidire
nautical *adj* nautic•us -a -um
naval *adj* naval•is -is -e
nave *s (archit)* nav•is -is *f*
navel *s* umbilic•us -i *m*
navigable *adj* navigabil•is -is -e
navigate *tr* gubernare ‖ *intr* navigare
navigation *s* navigati•o -onis *f; (as a field)* re•s -rum *fpl* nauticae
navigator *s* gubernat•or -oris *m*
navy *s* class•is -is *f*
nay *adv* non ita
near *prep* prope *(w. acc); (esp. to denote a*

battle site) ad *(w. acc)*, apud *(w. acc)*; *(in the vicinity, e.g., of a city)* apud *(w. acc)*
near *adj* propinqu•us -a -um; *(of relation)* proxim•us -a -um; **— at hand** in promptu, praesto
near *adv* prope, juxta
near *tr* appropinquare *(w. dat)*
nearly *adv* prope, fere, ferme
nearness *s* propinquit•as -atis *f*
nearsighted *adj* myop•s -is
neat *adj* mund•us -a -um; *(properly groomed)* compt•us -a -um; *(in good taste)* concinn•us -a -um
neatly *adv* munde; concinne
neatness *s* munditi•a -ae *f*
necessarily *adv* necessario
necessary *adj* necessari•us -a -um; **it is —** opus est; **consultation is —** consulto opus est
necessitate *tr* cogĕre
necessity *s* necessit•as -atis *f; (want)* egest•as -atis *f; (thing)* res necessaria *f;* **— is the mother of invention** ingeniosa est rerum egestas
neck *s (of body or bottle)* cerv•ix -icis *f (often pl. without change of meaning); (of animal)* coll•um -i *n*
necklace *s* monil•e -is *n*
necktie *s* collar•e -is *n*
nectar *s* nect•ar -aris *n*
need *s (necessity)* necessit•as -atis *f; (want)* inopi•a -ae *f;* **there is — of** opus est *(w. abl)*
need *tr* egēre *(w. abl)*, indigēre *(w. abl); (to require)* requirĕre
needle *s* ac•us -ūs *f*
needless *adj* minime necessari•us -a -um; **— to say** sine dubio
needlessly *adv* sine causā
needy *adj* egen•s -tis
nefarious *adj* nefari•us -a -um
negation *s* negati•o -onis *f*
negative *adj* negativ•us -a -um
negative *s* negati•o -onis *f;* **to answer in the —** negare
neglect *tr* neglegĕre
neglect *s* neglect•us -ūs *m*
neglectful *adj* neglegen•s -tis
negligible *adj* tenu•is -is -e
negotiable *adj* mercabil•is -is -e
negotiate *tr* agĕre de *(w. abl);* **to — a peace** de pacis condicionibus agĕre **||** *intr* negotiari
negotiation *s* transacti•o -onis *f;* **to settle disputes by —** controversias per colloquia componĕre
negotiator *s* conciliat•or -oris *m; (spokesman)* orat•or -oris *m*
Negro *s* Aethiop•s -is *m*
neigh *intr* hinnire
neigh *s* hinnit•us -ūs *m*
neighbor *s* vicin•us -i *m*
neighborhood *s* vicini•a -ae *f*
neighboring *adj* vicin•us -a -um
neighborly *adj* benign•us -a -um
neither *pron* neu•ter -tra -trum
neither *conj* nec, neque; **—...nor** neque...neque
neophyte *s* tir•o -onis *m*
nephew *s* fratris *(or* sororis) fil•ius -(i)i *m*
nepotism *s* nimius in necessarios fav•or -oris *m*
Nereid *s* Nere•is -idos *f*
nerve *s (fig)* audaci•a -ae *f*
nervous *adj* trepid•us -a -um
nervously *adv* trepide
nervousness *s* trepidati•o -onis *f*
nest *s* nid•us -i *m*
nest *intr* nidificare
nestle *intr* recubare
net *s* ret•e -is *n*
net *tr* irritire
netting *s* reticul•um -i *n*
nettle *s* urtic•a -ae *f*
nettle *tr* vexare
network *s* op•us -eris *n* reticulatum
neuter *adj (gram)* neu•ter -tra -trum
neutral *adj* medi•us -a -um
neutrality *s* nullam in partem propensi•o -onis *f*
neutralize *tr* aequare
never *adv* numquam
nevermore *adv* numquam posthac
nevertheless *adv* nihilominus
new *adj* nov•us -a -um
newly *adv* nuper, modo
newcomer *s* adven•a -ae *mf*
news *s (no single Latin counterpart exists) (message)* nunt•ium -(i)i *n,* nunt•ius -(i)i *m;* **any — ?** num quidnam novi?; **good —** boni nuntii *mpl;* **to bring good —** gaudium nuntiare; **— came** nuntiatum est; **when he heard this —** his auditis
newspaper *s* act•a -orum *npl* diurna
next *adj* proxim•us -a -um; *(of time)* insequen•s -tis; **— day** postridie
nibble *tr* arrodĕre; *(fig)* carpĕre **||** *intr* rodĕre
nice *adj (dainty)* delicat•us -a -um; *(cute)* bell•us -a -um; *(exact)* accurat•us -a -um; *(weather)* seren•us -a -um
nicely *adv (well)* bene; *(exactly)* subtiliter; *(prettily)* belle
nicety *s* subtilit•as -atis *f*
niche *s* aedicul•a -ae *f*
nick *s* incisur•a -ae *f;* **in the very — of time** in ipso articulo temporis
nick *tr* incidĕre
nickname *s* agnom•en -inis *n*
niece *s* fratris *(or* sororis) fili•a -ae *f*
niggardly *adj* parc•us -a -um
nigh *adj* propinqu•us -a -um
night *s* no•x -ctis *f;* **at —, by —** nocte, noctu; **good —!** bene valeas et quiescas!; **— after —** per singulas noctes; **to spend the —** pernoctare

nightcap *s (drink)* embasiocoet•as -ae *f*
nightfall *s* **at —** sub noctem
nightingale *s* luscini•a -ae *f*
nightly *adj* nocturn•us -a -um
nightly *adv* de nocte
nightmare *s* tumultuosum somn•ium -(i)i *n;* **to have —s** per somnium exterrēri
night watch *s* vigili•a -ae *f; (guard)* vig•il -ilis *m*
nimble *adj* agil•is -is -e
nine *adj* novem *(indecl);* **— times** noviens
nineteen *adj* undeviginti *(indecl)*
nineteenth *adj* undevicesim•us -a -um
ninetieth *adj* nonagesim•us -a -um
ninety *adj* nonaginta *(indecl)*
ninth *adj* non•us -a -um
nip *tr* vellicare; *(of frost)* urĕre; **— the thing in the bud!** principiis obsta!; **to — off** desecare
nippers *spl* for•ceps -cipitis *m*
nipple *s* papill•a -ae *f*
no *adj* null•us -a -um; **he has — more money** non plus pecuniae habet; **— more than three times** ter nec amplius; **there is — news** nihil novi est
no *adv* non; **— indeed** minime vero; **to say —** negare
nobility *s* nobilit•as -atis *f; (the nobles as a group)* nobil•es -ium *mpl*
noble *adj* nobil•is -is -e; *(morally)* honest•us -a -um
noble *s* hom•o -inis *m* nobilis
nobleman *s* vir• -i *m* nobilis
nobly *adv* praeclare
nobody *pron* nem•o -inis *m;* **some — or other** nescio qui terrae filius
nocturnal *adj* nocturn•us -a -um
nod *s* nut•us -ūs *m*
nod *intr* nutare; *(to doze)* dormitare; *(in assent)* annuĕre
noise *s* strepit•us -ūs *m; (high-pitched)* strid•or -oris *m; (crash)* frag•or -oris *m; (crackling, rattling)* crepit•us -ūs *m; (esp. of people talking loud)* convic•ium -(i)i *n;* **to make —** strepĕre, crepitare
noise *tr* **to — abroad** evulgare
noiseless *adj* tacit•us -a -um
noiselessly *adv* tacite
noisily *adv* cum strepitu
noisy *adj* clamos•us -a -um
nomad *s* nom•as -adis *mf*
nomadic *adj* vag•us -a -um
nominal *adj* nominal•is -is -e
nominally *adv* nomine, verbo
nominate *tr* nominare
nomination *s* nominati•o -onis *f*
nominative *adj* nominativ•us -a -um
nominee *s* hom•o -inis *m* destinatus
none *pron* nem•o -inis *m*
nonentity *s* nihil•um -i *n*
nones *spl* Non•ae -arum *fpl*
nonplus *tr (to puzzle)* ad incitas redigĕre
nonsense *s* nug•ae -arum *fpl;* **—!** nugas!; **to talk —** garrire
nonsensical *adj* inept•us -a -um
nook *s* angul•us -i *m*
noon *s* meridi•es -ei *m;* **at —** meridie; **before —** ante meridiem
noonday *adj* meridian•us -a -um
no one *pron* nem•o -inis *m*
noose *s* laque•us -i *m*
nor *conj* nec, neque
norm *s* norm•a -ae *f*
normal *adj* solit•us -a -um
normally *adv* plerumque
north *s* septentrion•es -um *mpl;* **to face —** in septentriones spectare
north *adj* septentrional•is -is -e; **— of** supra + *acc)*
northern *adj* septentrional•is -is -e
northern lights *spl* auror•a -ae *f* Borealis
north pole *s* arct•os -i *f*
northwards *adv* (ad) septentriones versus
north wind *s* aquil•o -onis *m*
nose *s (as a feature of the face)* nas•us -ūs *m; (as a function of smell)* nar•es -ium *mpl;* **having a large —** nasut•us -a -um; **to blow the —** emungĕre
nostril *s* nar•is -is *f*
not *adv* non; *(more emphatic)* haud; **— at all** nullo modo, haudquaquam; **— even** ne...quidem
notable *adj* notabil•is -is -e
notably *adv* insigniter
notary *s* scrib•a -ae *m*
notation *s* notati•o -onis *f*
notch *s* incisur•a -ae *f*
notch *tr* incidĕre
note *s (mark)* not•a -ae *f; (comment)* adnotati•o -onis *f; (mus)* son•us -i *m,* vo•x -cis *f; (com)* chirograph•um -i *n;* **a brief —** scriptur•a -ae *f* brevis
note *tr* notare; *(to notice)* animadvertĕre
notebook *s* libell•us -i *m,* pugillar•es -ium *mpl*
noted *adj* not•us -a -um
noteworthy *adj* notabil•is -is -e
nothing *pron* nihil, nil; **for —** *(free)* gratis, gratuito; *(in vain)* frustra; **good for —** nequam; **— but** nihil nisi; **to think — of** nihili facĕre
notice *s (act of noticing)* notati•o -onis *f; (announcement)* denuntiati•o -onis *f; (sign)* proscripti•o -onis *f,* titul•us -i *m;* **to escape —** latēre; **to escape the — of** fallĕre; **to give — of** denuntiare
notice *tr* animadvertĕre
noticeable *adj* insign•is -is -e
noticeably *adv* insigniter
notification *s* denuntiati•o -onis *f*
notify *tr* certiorem facĕre
notion *s* noti•o -onis *f*
notoriety *s* infami•a -ae *f*
notorious *adj* infam•is -is -e
notwithstanding *adv* nihilominus

notwithstanding *prep expr. by various participles, e.g.,* **notwithstanding the auspices** neglectis auspiciis
nought *pron* nihil; **to set at —** nihili facĕre
noun *s* nom•en -inis *n;* **proper and common —s** nomina propria et appellativa
nourish *tr* alĕre, nutrire
nourishment *s* aliment•um -i *n*
novel *adj* novici•us -a -um, inaudit•us -a -um
novel *s* histori•a -ae *f* commenticia
novelty *s* novit•as -atis *f*
November *s* Novem•ber -bris *m or* mens•is -is *m* November; **on the first of November** Kalendis Novembribus
novice *s* tir•o -onis *m*
now *adv* nunc; *(denoting urgency and emphasis)* jam; *(transitional, esp. in argumentation; never the first word in the sentence)* autem; **— and then** iterdum; **—…—** modo…modo
nowhere *adv* nusquam
noxious *adj* noxi•us -a -um
nozzle *s* ans•a -ae *f*
nude *adj* nud•us -a -um
nudge *tr* fodicare
nudity *s* nudati•o -onis *f*
nugget *s* mass•a -ae *f*
nuisance *s* molesti•a -ae *f;* **what a — it is!** quam molestum est
null *adj* **— and void** irrit•us -a -um; **to be — and void** cessare; **to render —** infringĕre
nullify *tr* irritum facĕre
numb *adj* torpid•us -a -um; **to become —** torpescĕre; **to be —** torpēre
number *s (gram & math)* numer•us -i *m;* **a — of** aliquot; **relying on their superior —s** multitudine freti; **to assemble in large —** frequentissimi convenire; **without —** innumerabil•is -is -e
number *tr* numerare; **a fleet —ing 1000 ships** classis mille numero navium; **to be —ed among** adnumerat•us -a -um *(w. dat)*
numberless *adj* innumer•us -a -um
numbness *s* torp•or -oris *m; (fig)* stup•or -oris *m*
numerical *adj* numeral•is -is -e
numerically *adv* numero
numerous *adj* cre•ber -bra -brum
numismatics *s* doctrin•a -ae *f* nummorum
nuptial *adj* nuptial•is -is -e
nuptials *spl* nupti•ae -arum *fpl*
nurse *s* nutr•ix -icis *f*
nurse *tr (a baby)* nutrire; *(the sick)* curare; *(fig)* fovēre
nursery *s (for children)* infantium diaet•a -ae *f; (for plants)* seminar•ium -(i)i *n*
nurture *tr* nutrire
nut *s* nu•x -cis *f;* **a hard — to crack** *(fig)* quaesti•o -onis *f* nodosa; **he is a —** *(pej)* nuga iste est
nutriment *s* nutriment•um -i *n*
nutrition *s* nutriti•o -onis *f*
nutritious *adj* alibil•is -is -e
nutshell *s* putam•en -inis *n;* **in a —** *(fig)* paucis verbis
nutty *adj* vecor•s -dis
nymph *s* nymph•a -ae *f*

O

oaf *s* stult•us -i *m*
oak *adj* querce•us -a -um
oak *s* querc•us -ūs *f; (esp. timber)* rob•ur -uris *n*
oar *s* rem•us -i *m;* **to pull the —s** remos ducĕre
oarsman *s* rem•ex -igis *m*
oath *s* jusurandum *(gen:* jurisjurandi) *n; (mil)* sacrament•um -i *n;* **false —** perjur•ium -(i)i *n;* **to take an —** jurare; *(mil)* sacramentum dicĕre
oats *spl* aven•a -ae *f*
obdurate *adj* obstinat•us -a -um
obdurately *adv* obstinate
obedience *s* obedienti•a -ae *f*
obedient *adj* obedien•s -tis
obediently *adv* obedienter
obeisance *s* **to make — to** adorare
obelisk *s* obelisc•us -i *m*
obese *adj* obes•us -a -um
obesity *s* obesit•as -atis *f*
obey *tr* parēre *(w. dat)*
obituary *s* Libitinae ind•ex -icis *m*
object *s* object•um -i *n,* res, rei *f; (aim)* proposit•um -i *n*
object *intr (to feel annoyance)* gravari; *(to make objections)* recusare; **to — to** aegre ferre; **I do not —, provided that**…non repugno dummodo…; **I do not — to your leaving** non recuso quominus abeas
objection *s* oppositi•o -onis *f;* **to raise many —s** multa in contrariam partem afferre
objectionable *adj* improbabil•is -is -e
objective *s* proposit•um -i *n*
obligation *s* offic•ium -(i)i *n;* **under —** noxi•us -a -um
obligatory *adj* necessari•us -a -um
oblige *tr (to force)* cogĕre; *(to put under obligation)* obligare; *(to do a favor for)* morigerari *(w. dat);* **to be —ed to** debēre *(w. inf); (to feel gratitude toward)* gratiam habēre *(w. dat)*
obliging *adj* officios•us -a -um
obligingly *adv* officiose
oblique *adj* obliqu•us -a -um
obliquely *adv* oblique
oblong *adj* oblong•us -a -um
obnoxious *adj* invis•us -a -um
obscene *adj* obscen•us -a -um

obscenely *adv* obscene
obscenity *s* obscenit•as -atis *f*
obscure *adj* obscur•us -a -um
obscure *tr* obscurare
obscurely *adv* obscure
obscurity *s* obscurit•as -atis *f; (of birth)* humilit•as -atis *f*
obsequies *spl* exsequi•ae -arum *fpl*
obsequious *adj* nimis obsequen•s -tis
obsequiousness *s* obsequ•ium -(i)i *n*
observable *adj* notabil•is -is -e
observance *s* observanti•a -ae *f; (rite)* rit•us -ūs *m*
observant *adj* attent•us -a -um; **— of** diligen•s -tis *(w. gen)*
observation *s* observati•o -onis *f; (remark)* notati•o -onis *f*
observe *tr (to watch, keep)* observare; *(to remark)* dicĕre
observer *s* spectat•or -oris *m*
obsess *tr* occupare
obsession *s* mentis prehensi•o -onis *f*
obsolescent *adj* **to be —** obsolescĕre
obsolete *adj* obsolet•us -a -um; **to become —** exsolescĕre
obstacle *s* impediment•um -i *n; (barrier)* ob•ex -icis *m*
obstinacy *s* obstinati•o -onis *f*
obstinate *adj* obstinat•us -a -um
obstinately *adv* obstinate
obstreperous *adj* tumultuos•us -a -um
obstruct *tr* obstare *(w. dat)*
obstruction *s* impediment•um -i *n*
obtain *tr* adipisci; *(by asking)* impetrare; **to — pardon** veniam impetrare
obtainable *adj* impetrabil•is -is -e
obtrusive *adj* molest•us -a -um
obtuse *adj* obtus•us -a -um
obviate *tr* praevertĕre
obvious *adj* apert•us -a -um; **it was — that** apparebat *(w. acc & inf)*
obviously *adv* aperte, manifesto
occasion *s* occasi•o -onis *f; (reason)* caus•a -ae *f; (time)* temp•us -oris *n;* **for the —** *(temporary)* ad tempus
occasion *tr* locum dare *(w. dat)*
occasional *adj* rar•us -a -um
occasionally *adv* interdum
occidental *adj* occidental•is -is -e
occult *adj* occult•us -a -um
occupant *s* possess•or -oris *m*
occupation *s* possessi•o -onis *f; (employment)* quaest•us -ūs *m*
occupy *tr* occupare; *(to possess)* possidēre; *(space)* complēre
occur *intr* accidĕre; *(to show up, appear)* nasci; *(to the mind)* in mentem venire; **it —ed to me** mihi in mentem venit; **to — at the right time** competĕre
occurrence *s* cas•us -ūs *m*
ocean *s* ocean•us -i *m*
oceanic *adj* oceanens•is -is -e
October *s* Octo•ber -bris *m or* mens•is -is *m* October; **on the first of —** Kalendis Octobribus
ocular *adj* ocular•is -is -e
oculist *s* ocularius medic•us -i *m*
odd *adj (of number)* im•par -paris; *(quaint)* insolit•us -a -um; *(remaining)* reliqu•us -a -um
oddity *s* rarit•as -atis *f; (thing)* mir•um -i *n*
oddly *adv* mirum in modum
odds *spl* **— and ends** quisquili•ae -arum *fpl;* **the — are against us** impares sumus; **to be at — with** disidēre ab *(w. abl);* **to lay — that not** pignore certare ne *(w. subj)*
odious *adj* odios•us -a -um
odium *s* invidi•a -ae *f*
odor *s* od•or -oris *m*
odorous *adj* odorat•us -a -um
Odyssey *s* Odysse•a -ae *f*
of *prep (possession) rendered by gen; (origin)* de *(w. abl),* ex *(w. abl); (concerning)* de *(w. abl); (denoting description or quality) expr. by gen or abl:* **a man — of highest talents** vir summi ingenii *(or* summo ingenio); **one — them** unús de illis *(or* ex illis); **statue of bronze** statua ex aere facta
off *adv* procul, longe; **far —** procul; **to be a long way —** longe abesse; **— with you!** aufer te modo!; **well —** bene nummerat•us -a -um
off *prep* de *(w. abl)*
offend *tr* offendĕre ‖ *intr* **to — against** violare
offender *s* re•us -i *m*
offense *s (fault)* offens•a -ae *f,* delict•um -i *n; (insult)* injuri•a -ae *f; (displeasure)* offensi•o -onis *f;* **to give — to** offendĕre
offensive *adj* injurios•us -a -um; *(odors, etc.)* odios•us -a -um, foed•us -a -um; *(language)* malign•us -a -um; *(aggressive)* bellum inferens; **to go on the —** bellum inferre
offer *tr* offerre, praebēre; **to — help to** opem ferre *(w. dat);* **to — violence to** vim afferre *(w. dat)*
offer *s* condici•o -onis *f*
offering *s* don•um -i *n*
offhand *adj* incurios•us -a -um
offhand *adv* confestim, illico
office *s (place of work)* officin•a -ae *f; (pol)* hon•or -oris *m; (duty)* offic•ium -(i)i *n;* **through the good —s of** per *(w. acc);* **to reach high —** ad honorem pervenire
officer *s* magistrat•us -ūs *m; (mil)* sagat•us -i *m; (police)* vig•il -ilis *m*
official *adj* public•us -a -um; **— residence** dom•us -ūs *f* publica
official *s* magistrat•us -ūs *m*
officiate *intr* officio *(or* munere) fungi; *(of a clergyman)* rem divinam facĕre
officious *adj* officios•us -a -um

officiously *adv* officiose
offing *s* **in the —** in promptu
offset *tr* compensare
offspring *s* prol•es -is *f*
often *adv* saepe; **very —** persaepe
ogre *s* larv•a -ae *f*
oh *interj* oh!, ohe!
oil *s* ole•um -i *n*
oil *tr* ung(u)ĕre
oil press *s* torcul•ar -aris *n*
oily *adj* oleos•us -a -um; *(like oil)* oleace•us -a -um; **to have an — taste** oleum sapĕre
ointment *s* unguent•um -i *n*
old *adj (aged)* sen•ex -is; *(out of use)* obsolet•us -a -um; *(worn)* trit•us -a -um; *(ancient)* antiqu•us -a -um; **good — days** prisca tempor•a -um *npl;* **of —** olim, quondam; **—er** ma•jor -jor -jus (natu); *(among old people)* sen•ior -ior -ius; **—est** maxim•us -a -um (natu); **to be no more than ten years —** non plus quam decem annos habēre; **to be ten years —** decem annos nat•us -a -um esse; **to grow —** senescĕre
old age *s* senect•us -utis *f*
old-fashioned *adj* prisc•us -a -um
old maid *s* an•us -us *f* innupta
old lady *s* an•us -ūs *f;* **little —** anicul•a -ae *f*
old man *s* sen•ex -is *m*
oligarchy *s* paucorum administrati•o -onis *f* civitatis; *(members of the oligarchy)* opimat•es -um *mpl*
olive *s* ole•a -ae *f,* oliv•a -ae *f*
olive oil *s* ole•um -i *n*
olive grove *s* olivet•um -i *n*
olive tree *s* oliv•a -ae *f*
Olympia *s* Olympi•a -ae *f*
Olympiad *s* Olympi•as -adis *f*
Olympic *adj* Olympic•us -a -um
omelet *s* lagan•um -i *n* de ovis confectum
omen *s* om•en -inis *n;* **to announce unfavorable —s** obnuntiare; **to get favorable —s** litare
ominous *adj* ominos•us -a -um
omission *s* praetermissi•o -onis *f*
omit *tr* (o)mittĕre
omnipotence *s* omnipotenti•a -ae *f*
omnipotent *adj* omnipoten•s -tis
omnivorous *adj* omnivor•us -a -um
on *prep (place)* in *(w. abl); (about, concerning)* de *(w. abl); (ranged with)* ab *(w. abl); (depending, hanging on)* de *(w. abl); (close to, e.g., a river)* juxta *(w. acc),* ad *(w. acc); (on the side of, in the direction of)* ab *(w. abl):* **— the east** ab oriente; **— the west** ab occidente
on *adv* porro; *(continually)* usque; **and so —** et cetera; **from then —** ex eo (tempore); **to drink — till daylight** potare usque ad primam lucem; **to go —** pergĕre; **to move—** procedĕre
once *adv (one time)* semel; *(formerly)* olim, quondam; **at —** statim, illico, continuo; **for —** demum; **—...twice...a third time** semel...iterum...tertio; **— and for all** semel (et) in perpetuum; **— more** iterum; **— or twice** semel iterumque; **— upon a time** olim
one *adj* un•us -a -um; **— day** *(in the past)* quodam die; *(in the future)* aliquando; **at — time** simul; **— ladder** unae scal•ae -arum *fpl;* **to have — and the same wish** idem velle
one *pron* un•us -a -um; *(a certain person)* quidam, quaedam, quoddam; **it is all —** perinde est; **— after another** ali•us -a -um ex alio; **— another** inter se, alius alium; **— by —** singulatim; **— or the other** alterut•er alterut•ra alterut•rum; **— or two** un•us -a -um et alt•er -era -erum *(w. pl verb);* **— would think that time stood still** putes stare tempus; **only —** unic•us -a -um
one-eyed *adj* lusc•us -a -um
onerous *adj* oneros•us -a -um
oneself *pron (refl)* se; **by —** per se; **to —** sibi; **with —** secum; *(intensive)* ips•e -a -um
one-sided *adj* inaequal•is -is -e
onion *s* caep•a -ae *f*
only *adj* sol•us -a -um, unic•us -a -um, un•us -a -um
only *adv* solum, tantum; **not —...but also** non solum...sed etiam
only-begotten *adj* unigenit•us -a -um
onset *s* impet•us -ūs *m*
onslaught *s* incurs•us -ūs *m*
onward *adv* porro; **—, soldiers!** porro, milites!
ooze *intr* manare
opaque *adj* opac•us -a -um
open *adj (not shut)* apert•us -a -um, paten•s -tis; *(evident)* manifest•us -a -um; *(sincere)* candid•us -a -um; *(public)* public•us -a -um; *(of a question, undecided)* inte•ger -gra -grum; **in the — (air)** sub divo; **to be — to** *(e.g, bribery, disease)* patēre *(w. dat);* **to lie —** patēre
open *tr* aperire; *(to uncover)* retegĕre; *(letter)* resignare; *(book)* evolvĕre; *(conversation)* exordiri; *(w. ceremony)* inaugurare; *(mouth)* diducĕre; *(door)* recludĕre; **to — up a hole** foramen laxare **‖** *intr* patescĕre, se pandĕre; *(gape)* dehiscĕre; *(of a wound)* recrudescĕre
open-handed *adj* larg•us -a -um
open-hearted *adj* ingenu•us -a -um
opening *s (act)* aperti•o -onis *f; (aperture)* foram•en -inis *n; (e.g., of a cave)* os, oris *n; (opportunity)* loc•us -i *m*
openly *adv* (pro)palam
open-minded *adj* docil•is -is -e
operate *tr* agĕre; *(to manage, e.g., a business)* exercēre **‖** *intr* operari; **to — on** *(surgically)* secare
operation *s (act of doing or working)*

effecti•o -onis *f; (surgical)* secti•o -onis *f; (business)* negot•ium -(i)i *n*
operative *adj* effica•x -cis
operator *s* opif•ex -icis *m*
opinion *s* opini•o -onis *f*, sententi•a -ae *f*; **good — of** aestimati•o -onis *f* de *(w. abl)*; **in my —** meā sententiā; **public —** fam•a -ae *f*; **to be of the —** opinari; **to hold the — that** opinionem habēre *(w. acc & inf)*
opium *s* op•ium -(i)i *n*
opponent *s* adversar•ius -(i)i *m; (pol)* competit•or -oris *m*
opportune *adj* opportun•us -a -um
opportunity *s* occasi•o -onis *f*; **as — offered** ex occasione; **— for revenge** occasio vindictae; **to give s.o. the — to** alicui potestatem dare *(w. gen of gerundive)*; **to take** *or* **get the —** occasionem nancisci
oppose *tr* adversari *(w. dat)*; *(w. words)* contra dicĕre *(w. dat)*; **to — the idea that** adversari ne *(w. subj)*
opposite *adj* advers•us -a -um
opposite *prep* contra *(w. acc)*
opposition *s* oppositi•o -onis *f; (obstacle)* impediment•um -i *n*; **— party** par•s -tis *f* diversa
oppress *tr* opprimĕre, gravare
oppression *s* injuri•a -ae *f*
oppressive *adj* praegrav•is -is -e; **to become —** ingravescĕre
oppressor *s* tyrann•us -i *m*
opprobrium *s* ignomini•a -ae *f*
optical *adj* opticus -a -um
optician *s* hom•o -inis *m* optices peritus
option *s* opti•o -onis *f*; **you have the — either to...or to** tibi optio datur utrum...an
or *conj* vel, aut, —ve; *(in questions)* an; **either...or** *(mutually exclusive)* aut...aut; *(optional)* vel...vel; **— else** alioquin; **— not** annnon; *(in indirect questions)* necne
oracle *s* oracul•um -i *n*
oracular *adj* fatidic•us -a -um
oral *adj* verbal•is -is -e, verbo tradit•us -a -um
orally *adv* voce, verbis
orange *s* mal•um -i *n* aureum
oration *s* orati•o -onis *f*; **to deliver an —** orationem habēre
orator *s* orat•or -oris *m*
oratorical *adj* oratori•us -a -um
oratory *s* oratoria ar•s -tis *f*
orb *s* orb•is -is *m*
orbit *tr* **to — the earth** orbem terrae circumagĕre
orbit *s (astr)* gyr•us -i *m*
orchard *s* pomar•ium -(i)i *n*
orchestra *s* symphoni•a -ae *f; (part of theater)* orchestr•a -ae *f*
orchid *s* orch•is -is *f*
ordain *tr* edicĕre; *(eccl)* ordinare
ordeal *s* discrim•en -inis *n*
order *s (class, arrangement, sequence)* ord•o -inis *m; (command)* juss•um -i *n; (mil)* imperat•um -i *n*; **to call to —** convocare; **in — to** ut *(w. subj)*; **in — not to** ne *(w. subj)*; **in short —** brevi; **out of —** ex usu; **out of the regular —** extra ordinem; **to arrange in —** ordinare; **to draw up an army in — of battle** aciem ordinare
order *tr (to command)* jubēre, imperare *(w. dat); (to arrange)* disponĕre, ordinare; *(to ask for)* postulare, poscĕre
orderly *adj* composit•us -i -um; *(well behaved)* modest•us -a -um
orderly *s* accens•us -ūs *m; (mil)* tessarari•us -(i)i *m*
ordinal *adj* ordinal•is -is -e
ordinance *s* edict•um -i *n*
ordinarily *adv* plerumque, fere
ordinary *adj* usitat•us -a -um, solit•us -a -um; *(everyday)* cotidian•us -a -um; *(traditional, not novel)* tralatici•us -a -um
ordnance *s* torment•a -orum *npl*
ore *s* ae•s -ris *n*
organ *s (anat)* par•s *f* corporis, visc•us -eris *n; (mus)* organ•um -i *n*; **the —s** viscer•a -um *npl*
organic *adj* pertinen•s -tis ad partem corporis
organism *s* compag•es -is *f*
organization *s* structur•a -ae *f; (society)* sodalit•as -atis *f*
orgy *s* comissati•o -onis *f*
Orient *s* orien•s -tis *m*
oriental *adj* Asiatic•us -a -um
origin *s* orig•o -inis *f; (birth)* gen•us -eris *n; (source)* fon•s -tis *m*
original *adj* primitiv•us -a -um; *(one's own)* propri•us -a -um; *(new)* inaudit•us -a -um
original *s* archetyp•um -i *n*, exempl•ar -aris *n; (writing)* autograph•um -i *n*
originality *s* propriet•as -atis *f* ingenii
originally *adv* initio, principio
originate *tr* instituĕre ‖ *intr* oriri
originator *s* auct•or -oris *m*
ornament *s* ornament•um -i *n*
ornamental *adj* decor•us -a -um
ornate *adj* ornat•us -a -um
ornately *adv* ornate
orphan *s* orb•us -i *m*, orb•a -ae *f*
orphaned *adj* orbat•us -a -um
orphanage *s* orphanotroph•ium -(i)i *n*
orthodox *adj* orthodox•us -a -um
orthography *s* orthographi•a -ae *f*
oscillate *intr* ultro citroque se inclinare; *(fig)* dubitare
oscillation *s* ultro citroque inclinati•o -onis *f; (fig)* dubitati•o -onis *f*
ostensible *adj* simulat•us -a -um
ostensibly *adv* per speciem
ostentation *s* ostentati•o -onis *f*
ostentatious *adj* specios•us -a -um

ostracism *s* relegati•o -onis *f; (Athenian custom)* testarum suffragi•a -orum *npl*
ostrich *s* struthiocamel•us -i *m*
other *adj (different)* ali•us -a -ud; *(remaining)* ceter•us -a -um; **every — day** tertio quoque die; **on the — hand** contra; **the —** alt•er -era -erum; **the — day** nuper; **to attend to — people's affairs** aliena curare
otherwise *adv* aliter; *(in the contrary supposition)* alioquin; **to think —** aliter sentire; **you didn't do it yet; — you would have told me** nondum id fecisti; alioquin mihi narasses
otter *s* lutr•a -ae *f*
ought *intr* **I —** debeo, oportet me
ounce *s* unci•a -ae *f*
our *adj* nos•ter -tra -trum; **— men** nostr•i -orum *mpl*
ours *pron* nos•ter -tra -trum
ourselves *pron refl* nos(met); **by —** per nos; **to —** nobis; *(intensive)* nosmet ips•i -ae
oust *tr* ejicĕre
out *adv (outside)* foris; *(motion)* foras; **— of** de *(w. abl)*, ex *(w. abl); (on account of)* ob *(w. acc)*; **— of doors** extra ostium, foris; **— of the way** devi•us -a -um; **to dine —** foris cenare; **to flee — of the temple** extra templum profugĕre
outbreak *s* erupti•o -onis *f; (disturbance)* sediti•o -onis *f*
outburst *s* erupti•o -onis *f;* **in an — of anger** impoten•s -tis irae
outcast *s* ex•sul -sulis *m*
outcome *s* event•us -ūs *m*
outcry *s* clam•or -oris *m; (noisy shouting)* convic•ium -(i)i *n*
outdo *tr* superare
outdoors *adv* foris; *(motion)* foras
outer *adj* exter•ior -ior -ius; **— space** intermundi•a -orum *npl*
outermost *adj* extrem•us -a -um
outfit *s* apparat•us -ūs *m; (costume)* habit•us -ūs *m*
outfit *tr* ornare
outflank *tr* circumire
outgrow *tr* excedĕre ex *(w. abl)*, staturā superare
outing *s* excursi•o -onis *f*
outlandish *adj* absurd•us -a -um
outlast *tr* diutius durare *(w. abl)*
outlaw *s* proscript•us -i *m*
outlaw *tr* aquā et igni interdicĕre *(w. dat)*, proscribĕre
outlay *s* impens•a -ae *f*
outlet *s* exit•us -ūs *m; (for water)* emissar•ium -(i)i *n*
outline *s* adumbrati•o -onis *f;* **to draw the — of a thing** primas modo lineas alicujus rei ducĕre
outline *tr* delineare, adumbrare
outlive *tr* supervivĕre *(w. dat)*
outlook *s* occasi•o -onis *f*, prospect•us -ūs *m*
outlying *adj* extern•us -a -um
outnumber *tr* multitudine superare
outpost *s* stati•o -onis *f*
outpouring *s* effusi•o -onis *f*
output *s* fruct•us -ūs *m*
outrage *s* injuri•a -ae *f*
outrage *tr* injuriā afficĕre
outrageous *adj* flagitios•us -a -um
outrageously *adv* flagitiose
outrank *tr* et aetate et dignitate antecedĕre *(w. dat)*
outright *adj* manifest•us -a -um
outright *adv* prorsus; *(at once)* statim
outrun *tr* cursu superare
outset *s* init•ium -(i)i *n*
outshine *tr* praelucĕre *(w. dat)*
outside *s* par•s -tis *f* exterior; *(appearance)* speci•es -ei *f;* **on the —** extrinsecus
outside *prep* extra *(acc)*
outside *adv* foris, extra; *(motion)* foras; **from —** extrinsecus
outside *adj* extern•us -a -um
outskirts *spl* suburb•ium -(i)i *n;* **just on the — of the province** fere ad extremum provinciae finem
outspoken *adj* liberius dic•ax -acis
outspread *adj* patul•us -a -um
outstanding *adj* praestan•s -tis; *(of debts)* residu•us -a -um
outstretched *adj* porrect•us -a -um
outstrip *tr* cursu superare
outward *adj* extern•us -a -um
outwardly *adv* extrinsecus
outweigh *tr* praeponderare; *(fig)* praevertĕre *(w. dat)*
outwit *tr* deludĕre, dolis vincĕre
oval *adj* ovat•us -a -um
oval *s* ovata form•a -ae *f*
ovation *s* plaus•us -ūs *m; (second-class triumph)* ovati•o -onis *f*
oven *s* furn•us -i *m*
over *prep (across)* super *(w. acc)*, trans *(w. acc); (w. verbs of motion, denoting space traversed)* per *(w. acc); (motion over)* super *(w. acc); (position above)* supra *(w. acc); (w. numbers)* plus quam; **— and above** super *(w. acc);* **the water was — a man's head** humanā magnitudine major erat fluminis altitudo
over *adv* supra; *(excess)* nimis; **all —** ubique; **— and above** insuper; **— and —** identidem
overall *adj* tot•us -a -um
overawe *tr* (de)terrēre
overbalance *tr* praeponderare
overbearing *adj* superb•us -a -um
overboard *adv* ex nave
overburden *tr* nimis onerare
overcast *adj* nubil•us -a -um
overcharge *tr* plus aequo exigĕre ab *(w. abl)*

overcoat *s* paenul•a -ae *f*
overdo *tr* exaggerare, in majus extollĕre; **to — it** se supra vires extendĕre
overdue *adj (money)* residu•us -a -um
overestimate *tr* majoris aestimare
overflow *s* inundati•o -onis *f*
overflow *tr* inundare ‖ *intr* abundare
overgrown *adj* obsit•us -a -um; *(too big)* praegrand•is -is -e
overhang *tr* impendēre *(w. dat)*
overhanging *adj* impenden•s -tis
overhasty *adj* praeproper•us -a -um
overhaul *tr* reficĕre; *(to pass)* consequi
overhead *adv* desuper
overhear *tr* auscultare
overjoyed *adj* **I am —!** *(coll)* immortaliter gaudeo!; **to be — at the sight of a son** ad conspectum filii laetitiā exsultare
overladen *adj* praegravat•us -a -um
overland *adj* per terram
overlay *tr* inducĕre, illinĕre
overload *tr* nimis onerare
overlook *tr (not to notice)* praetermittĕre; *(to pardon)* ignoscĕre *(w. dat)*; *(a view)* prospicĕre, spectare
overlord *s* domin•us -i *m*
overpower *tr* opprimĕre
overrate *tr* nimis magni aestimare; **to be an —ed man** famā minor esse
overreach *tr* circumvenire
overriding *adj* praecipu•us -a -um
overripe *adj* permatur•us -a -um
overrun *tr* occupare
overseas *adj* transmarin•us -a -um
oversee *tr* praeesse *(w. dat)*
overseer *s* curat•or -oris *m*
overshadow *tr* obumbrare; *(fig)* obscurare
overshoot *tr* excedĕre; **to — the mark** ex orbita ire; **don't — the mark** ne ultra quam est opus contendas
oversight *s (superintendence)* cur•a -ae *f*; *(carelessness)* incuri•a -ae *f*
oversleep *intr* diutius dormire
overspread *tr* obducĕre
overstate *tr* in majus extollĕre
overstep *tr* transgredi
overstock *tr* **to — a shop** tabernam super quam est opus rebus venalibus instruĕre
overt *adj* apert•us -a -um
overtime *adj* **— work** oper•a -ae *f* subsiciva
overtly *adv* palam
overtake *tr* consequi
overtax *tr (fig)* abuti *(w. abl)*
overthrow *s* eversi•o -onis *f*
overthrow *tr* evertĕre, dejicĕre
overture *s (proposal)* condici•o -onis *f*; *(mus)* exord•ium -(i)i *n*; **to make —s to** agĕre cum *(w. abl)*
overturn *tr* evertĕre; **—ed tables** eversae mens•ae -arum *fpl* ‖ *intr* everti
overwhelm *tr* obruĕre, opprimĕre
overwork *tr* immodico labore onerare; **to — oneself** plus aequo laborare

owe *tr* debēre
owing to *prep* propter *(w. acc)*
owl *s* bub•o -onis *m*
own *adj* propri•us -a -um; **one's —** su•us -a -um, propri•us -a -um
own *tr* tenēre, possidēre; *(to acknowledge)* confitēri
owner *s* domin•us -i *m*
ownership *s* domin•ium -(i)i *n*
ox *s* bo•s -vis *m*
oyster *s* ostre•a -ae *f*
oyster shell *s* ostreae test•a -ae *f*

P

pace *s (step)* pass•us -ūs *m*, grad•us -ūs *m*; *(measure of length; five Roman feet)* pass•us -ūs *m*; *(speed)* velocit•as -atis *f*; **to keep — with** pariter ire cum *(w. abl)*
pace *tr* **to — off** passibus emetiri ‖ *intr* gradi; **to — up and down** inambulare
pacific *adj* pacific•us -a -um
pacification *s* pacificati•o -onis *f*
pacify *tr* placare
pack *s (bundle)* sarcin•a -ae *f*; *(of animals, of people)* gre•x -gis *m*
pack *tr (items of luggage)* colligĕre; *(to fill completely)* frequentare, complēre; *(to compress)* stipare ‖ *intr* **to — up** vasa colligĕre
package *s* sarcin•a -ae *f*
packet *s* fascicul•us -i *m*
pack horse *s* equ•us -i *m* clitellarius
packsaddle *s* clitell•ae -arum *fpl*
pact *s* pact•um -i *n*; **to make a —** pacisci
pad *s* pulvill•us -i *m*
pad *tr* suffarcinare
padding *s* fartur•a -ae *f*
paddle *s* rem•us -i *m*
paddle *intr* remigare
paddock *s* saept•um -i *n*
pagan *adj* pagan•us -a -um
pagan *s* pagan•us -i *m*
paganism *s* paganit•as -atis *f*
page *s (of book)* pagin•a -ae *f*; *(boy)* pu•er -eri *m*; **at the top (bottom) of the —** ab summā (imā) paginā
page *tr* arcessĕre
pageant *s* pomp•a -ae *f*
pail *s* situl•a -ae *f*
pain *s* dol•or -oris *m*; *(fig)* ang•or -oris *m*; **— in the neck** *(coll)* molest•us -i *m*; **to be in —** dolēre; **to take —s** operam dare; **to take great —s to** in magno negotio habēre *(w. inf)*
pain *tr* dolore afficĕre ‖ *intr* dolēre
painful *adj* molest•us -a -um; *(bitter, distressful)* acerb•us -a -um; **to be extremely —** dolores magnos movēre
painfully *adv* magno cum dolore
painkiller *s* medicament•um -i *n* anodynum

painless *adj* doloris exper•s -tis
painstaking *adj* operos•us -a -um
paint *s* pigment•um -i *n*
paint *tr* pingĕre
paintbrush *s* penicill•us -i *m*
painter *s* pict•or -oris *m*
pair *s* par, paris *n; (of oxen)* jug•um -i *n*
pair *tr* conjungĕre ‖ *intr* coïre
palace *s* regi•a -ae *f,* aul•a -ae *f*
palatable *adj* sapid•us -a -um
palate *s* palat•um -i *n; (sense of taste)* gustat•us -ūs *m*
palatial *adj* regi•us -a -um
pale *adj* pallid•us -a -um; **to be —** pallēre; **to grow —** pallescĕre
pale *s* pal•us -i *m; (enclosure)* saept•um -i *n*
paleography *s* palaeographi•a -ae *f*
palette *s* pictoris tabul•a -ae *f*
palisade *s* vall•um -i *n*
pall *s* pall•ium -(i)i *n*
pall *tr* satiare ‖ *intr* vapescĕre
pallet *s* grabat•us -i *m*
palliative *s* leniment•um -i *n*
pallid *adj* pallid•us -a -um
pallor *s* pall•or -oris *m*
palm *s (of the hand; palm tree; palm branch, as token of victory)* palm•a -ae *f;* **to grease s.o.'s —** aliquem pecuniā corrumpĕre; **to win the —** palmam ferre
palmist *s* chiromant•is -idos *mf*
palm off *tr* **(on)** imponĕre *(w. dat)*
palpable *adj* tractabil•is -is -e; *(fig)* manifest•us -a -um
palpitate *tr* palpitare
palsied *adj* paralytic•us -a -um
palsy *s* paralys•is -is *f*
paltry *adj* vil•is -is -e
pamper *tr* indulgēre *(w. dat)*
pamphlet *s* libell•us -i *m*
pan *s* patin•a -ae *f; (for frying)* sartag•o -inis *f*
pan *intr* **to — out** *(coll)* evenire
panacea *s* panace•a -ae *f*
pancake *s* lagan•um -i *n*
pandemic *adj* evagat•us -a -um
pandemonium *s* tumult•us -ūs *m*
pander *intr* lenocinari; **to — to** indulgēre *(w. dat)*
panderer *s* len•o -onis *m*
pandering *s* lenocin•ium -(i)i *n*
panegyric *s* laudati•o -onis *f*
panel *s (of wall)* abac•us -i *m; (of ceiling)* lacun•ar -aris *n; (of door)* tympan•um -i *n; (of jury)* judic•es -um *mpl; (discussion group)* colleg•ium -(i)i *n*
paneled *adj* laqueat•us -a -um
pang *s* dol•or -oris *m*
panic *s* pav•or -oris *m*
panicky, panic-stricken *adj* pavid•us -a -um
panoply *s* arm•a -orum *npl*
panorama *s* prospect•us -ūs *m*
pant *intr* anhelare; **to — after** *(fig)* gestire
pantheism *s* pantheism•us -i *m*
pantheist *s* pantheist•a -ae *m*
Pantheon *s* Panthe•um -i *n*
panther *s* panther•a -ae *f*
panting *adj* anhel•us -a -um
panting *s* anhelit•us -ūs *m*
pantomime *s (play; actor)* mim•us -i *m; (actress)* mima -ae *f*
pantry *s* cell•a -ae *f* penaria
pap *s* papill•a -ae *f*
papa *s* tat•a -ae *m*
paper *s (stationery)* chart•a -ae *f; (newspaper)* act•a -orum *npl* diurna; **—s** script•a -orum *npl*
paper *adj* chartace•us -a -um
papyrus *s* papyr•us -i *f*
par *s* **to be on a — with** par esse *(w. dat)*
parable *s* parabol•e -es *f*
parade *s* pomp•a -ae *f; (mil)* decurs•us -ūs *m*
parade *tr* ostentare ‖ *intr (mil)* decurrĕre
paradise *s* paradis•us -i *m*
paradox *s* paradox•um -i *n*
paragon *s* specim•en -inis *n*
paragraph *s* cap•ut -itis *n*
parallel *adj* parallel•us -a -um; *(fig)* consimil•is -is -e
parallel *tr* exaequare
paralysis *s* paralys•is -is *f*
paralytic *adj* paralytic•us -a -um
paralyze *tr* enervare; *(fig)* percellĕre
paralyzed *adj* per omnia membra resolut•us -a -um
paramount *adj* suprem•us -a -um
paramour *s (male)* moech•us -i *m; (female)* meretr•ix -icis *f*
parapet *s* plute•us -i *m*
paraphernalia *s* apparat•us -ūs *m*
paraphrase *s* paraphras•is -is *f*
paraphrase *tr* laxius liberiusque interpretari
parasite *s* parasit•us -i *m*
parasol *s* umbell•a -ae *f*
parcel *s* fascicul•us -i *m; (plot of land)* agell•us -i *m*
parcel *tr* **to — out** dispertire
parch *tr* torrēre
parched *adj* torrid•us -a -um
parchment *s* membran•a -ae *f*
pardon *s* veni•a -ae *f;* **to obtain a —** veniam impetrare; **to grant a — to** *(leg)* absolvĕre
pardon *tr* ignoscĕre *(dat);* condonare *(w. acc of thing & dat of person); (leg)* absolvĕre; **after being —ed** post impetratam veniam
pardonable *adj* ignoscend•us -a -um
pare *tr (vegetables)* deglubĕre; *(the nails)* resecare
parent *s* paren•s -tis *mf*
parentage *s* gen•us -eris *n*
parental *adj* parental•is -is -e

parenthesis *s* interclusi•o -onis *f*
pariah *s* sentin•a -ae *f* reipublicae
parity *s* parit•as -atis *f*
park *s* hort•i -orum *mpl*
parlance *s* serm•o -onis *m*
parley *s* colloqu•ium -(i)i *n*
parley *intr* colloqui
parliament *s* parlament•um -i *n*
parlor *s* exedr•ium -(i)i *n*
parody *s* parodi•a -ae *f*
parole *s* fid•es -ei *f;* **on —** custodiae immun•is -is -e
parole *tr* fide interpositā demittĕre
paroxysm *s* access•us -ūs *m*
parricide *s (murder)* parricid•ium -(i)i *n; (murderer)* parricid•a -ae *mf*
parrot *s* psittac•us -i *m*
parry *tr* avertĕre
parse *tr* notare proprietatesque describĕre
parsimonious *adj* parc•us -a -um
parsimoniously *adv* parce
parsing *s* partium orationis flexi•o -onis *f*
parsley *s* selin•um -i *n*
part *s* par•s -tis *f; (role)* part•es -ium *fpl; (duty)* offic•ium -(i)i *n;* **for the most —** maximā ex parte; **in —** partim; **on the — of** ab *(w. abl);* **to act the — of** sustinēre partes *(w. gen);* **to take — in** interesse *(w. dat)*
part *tr* separare, dividĕre; **to — company** discedĕre **‖** *intr* discedĕre, abire; *(to go open)* dehiscĕre; **to — with** dimittĕre
partial *adj (unfair)* iniqu•us -a -um; *(incomplete)* manc•us -a -um, per partes
partiality *s* iniquit•as -atis *f*
partially *adv* aliquā ex parte
participant *s* parti•ceps -cipis *mf*
participate *intr* **to — in** interesse *(w. dat),* particeps esse *(w. gen)*
participation *s* participati•o -onis *f*
participle *s* particip•ium -(i)i *n*
particle *s* particul•a -ae *f*
particular *adj (special)* praecipu•us -a -um; *(fussy)* fastidios•us -a -um; **in —** potissimum
particularly *adv* praecipue, praesertim
particularize *tr* exsequi
particulars *spl* singul•a -orum *npl*
parting *s* discess•us -ūs *m*
partisan *s* faut•or -oris *m; (guerilla)* factiosus armig•er -eri *m*
partition *s* partiti•o -onis *f; (between rooms)* pari•es -etis *m; (compartment)* loculament•um -i *n*
partition *tr* dividĕre
partitive *adj (gram)* partitiv•us -a -um
partly *adv* partim, ex parte
partner *s* soc•ius -(i)i *m,* soci•a -ae *f,* partic•eps -ipis *mf; (in office)* colleg•a -ae *m; (in marriage)* con•ju(n)x -jugis *mf*
partnership *s* societ•as -atis *f;* **to dissolve a —** dissociari; **to form a —** societatem inire
partridge *s* perd•ix -icis *mf*
party *s (for entertainment)* conviv•ium -(i)i *n; (pol)* part•es -ium *fpl; (detachment)* man•us -ūs *f;* **opposite —** partes diversae; **to join a —** partes sequi
pass *s (defile)* angusti•ae -arum *fpl; (free ticket)* tesser•a -ae *f* gratuita; **things have come to such a — that** eo rerum ventum erat ut
pass *tr (to go by)* praeterire; *(exceed)* excedĕre; *(to approve)* probare; *(time)* degĕre; *(a law)* perferre; *(by the assembly)* jubēre; **he tried to — himself off for Philip** se Philippum ferebat; **pass me the vegetables!** porrige mihi holera!; **to — around** circumferre; **to — down** tradĕre; **to — sentence** jus dicĕre; **to — the test** approbari; **to — up** praetermittĕre **‖** *intr (of time)* transire; *(to walk by)* praeterire; *(to ride by)* praetervehi; **to come to —** fieri, evenire; **to let —** praetermittĕre; **to let an army — through the country** exercitum per fines transmittĕre; **to — away** *(to die)* perire; *(to come to an end)* transire; **to — by** *(e.g.,* **a park)** praeterire (hortos); *(in a carriage or ship)* praetervehi; **to — for** haberi; **to — on** *(to go forward)* pergĕre; *(to another subject)* transire; *(to die)* perire; **to — out** collabi, intermori; **to — over** *(e.g., of a storm)* transire; *(to make no mention of)* praeterire; **to — over the fact that** mittĕre quod *(w. subj);* **to — through** *(e.g.,* **a town)** transire; *(of an arrow, spear)* ire per *(w. acc);* **to — through enemy lines** per hostes vadĕre
passable *adj (of road)* pervi•us -a -um; *(tolerable)* tolerabil•is -is -e
passably *adv* tolerabiliter
passage *s (act)* transit•us -ūs *m; (by water)* trajecti•o -onis *f; (road)* it•er -ineris *n; (in a book)* loc•us -i *m (pl:* loc•i -orum); **to allow anyone a passage through the province** alicui transitum dare per provinciam
passenger *s* viat•or -oris *m; (in a carriage, aboard ship)* vect•or -oris *m*
passer-by *s* praeter•iens -euntis *mf*
passing *s* obit•us -ūs *m*
passion *s (strong desire of any kind, esp. lust)* cupidit•as -atis *f; (strong emotion)* animi permoti•o -onis *f; (lust)* libid•o -inis *f; (violent anger)* iracundi•a -ae *f;* **to fly into a —** exardescĕre iracundiā et stomacho
passionate *adj* arden•s -tis; *(given to bursts of anger)* iracund•us -a -um
passionately *adv* ardenter; iracunde
passive *adj* passiv•us -a -um
passively *adv* passive
passport *s* diplom•a -atis *n*
password *s* tesser•a -ae *f*
past *adj* praeterit•us -a -um; *(immediately*

preceding) proxim•us -a -um, super•ior -ior -ius
past *s* praeterit•um -i *n; (past tense)* praeteritum temp•us -oris *n*
past *prep* praeter *(w. acc)*
paste *s* farin•a -ae *f* chartaria
paste *tr* glutinare
pasteboard *s* chart•a -ae *f* crassa
pastime *s* oblectament•um -i *n;* **by way of —** oblectamenti causā
pastoral *adj (poetry)* bucolic•us -a -um; *(of shepherds)* pastoral•is -is -e
pastoral *s* bucolic•um -i *n*
pastry *s* crustul•a -orum *npl*
pasture *s* past•us -ūs *m*
pasture *tr* pascĕre ‖ *intr* pasci
pat *tr* permulcēre
patch *s* pann•us -i *m*
patch *tr* resarcire; **to — up** *(fig)* refovēre
patchwork *s* cent•o -onis *m*
patent *adj* manifest•us -a -um
patently *adv* manifesto
paternal *adj* patern•us -a -um; *(like a father)* patri•us -a -um
paternity *s* paternit•as -atis *f*
path *s* semit•a -ae *f*
pathetic *adj* flebil•is -is -e
pathless *adj* invi•us -a -um
pathos *s* vis *f* ad misericordiam movendam
pathway *s* semit•a -ae *f*
patience *s* patienti•a -ae *f*
patient *adj* patien•s -tis
patient *s* ae•ger -gri *m,* aegr•a -ae *f*
patiently *adv* aequo animo
patriarch *s* patriarch•a -ae *m*
patriarchal *adj* patriarchic•us -a -um
patrician *adj* patrici•us -a -um
patrician *s* patric•ius -(i)i *m*
patrimony *s* patrimon•ium -(i)i *n*
patriot *s* aman•s -tis *mf* patriae
patriotic *adj* aman•s -tis patriae
patriotism *s* am•or -oris *m* patriae
patrol *s* circuitor•es -um *mpl*
patrol *tr & intr* circumire
patron *s* patron•us -i *m*
patronage *s* patrocin•ium -(i)i *n*
patroness *s* patron•a -ae *f*
patronize *tr* favēre *(w. dat); (a shop)* frequentare
pattern *s* exempl•ar -aris *n*
paucity *s* paucit•as -atis *f*
paunch *s* ingluvi•es -ei *f*
pauper *s* egen•s -tis *mf*
pause *s* paus•a -ae *f; (break)* intercaped•o -inis *f; (mus)* intermissi•o -onis *f*
pause *intr* subsistĕre; *(to halt)* insistĕre; **to — in speaking** in dicendo subsistĕre
pave *tr* sternĕre; **to — the way to** *(fig)* viam facĕre ad *(w. acc)*
pavement *s* paviment•um -i *n*
pavilion *s* tentor•ium -(i)i *n*
paving stone *s* sax•um -i *n* quadratum
paw *s* pe•s -dis *m*
paw *tr* pedibus pulsare
pawn *s* pign•us -oris *n*
pawn *tr* pignerare
pawnbroker *s* pignernat•or -oris *m*
pay *s* merc•es -edis *f; (mil)* stipend•ium -(i)i *n*
pay *tr (money)* solvĕre; *(in full)* persolvĕre, pendĕre; *(a person)* pecuniam (mercedem) solvĕre *(dat); (mil)* stipendium numerare *(w. dat);* **to — back** restituĕre; *(to avenge)* vindicare; **to — in cash** numerare; **to — off a debt** nomen exsolvĕre, aes alienum persolvĕre; **to — out** numerare; **to — s.o. a compliment** laudare; **to — (s.o.) for** solvĕre *(w. acc of thing and dat of person);* **to — respects to** salutare; **to — the penalty** poenam dare, poenam luĕre ‖ *intr* **it —s** operae pretium est; **to — for** *(merchandise)* emĕre; *(a misdeed)* poenas dare ob *(w. acc)*
payable *adj* solvend•us -a -um
payday *s* di•es -ei *f* pecuniae
paymaster *s* dispensat•or -oris *m*
payment *s (act)* soluti•o -onis *f; (sum of money)* pensi•o -onis *f*
pea *s* pis•um -i *n*
peace *s* pa•x -cis *f;* **in a state of —** pacat•us -a -um; **to hold one's —** tacēre; **to live in —** pacem agitare
peaceably *adv* cum bona pace
peaceful *adj* tranquill•us -a -um
peacefully *adv* tranquille
peace-loving *adj* pacis aman•s -tis
peacemaker *s* pacificat•or -oris *m*
peace offering *s* placam•en -inis *n*
peacetime *s* ot•ium -(i)i *n*
peach *s* Persic•um -i *n*
peacock *s* pav•o -onis *mf*
peak *s* vert•ex -icis *m; (of a mountain)* cacum•en -inis *n*
peal *s (of thunder)* frag•or -oris *m; (of bells)* concent•us -ūs *m*
peal *intr* resonare
pear *s* pir•um -i *n*
pearl *s* margarit•a -ae *f*
pearly *adj* gemme•us -a -um
peasant *s* rustic•us -i *m*
peasantry *s* agrest•es -ium *mpl*
pebble *s* calcul•us -i *m*
peck *s* mod•ius -(i)i *m; (perfunctory kiss)* basiol•um -i *n*
peck *tr* vellicare
peculiar *adj* peculiar•is -is -e; *(belonging to one person or thing only)* propri•us -a -um; *(odd)* inusitat•us -a -um, absurd•us -a -um
peculiarity *s* propriet•as -atis *f*
pedagogue *s* paedagog•us -i *m*
pedant *s* scholastic•us -i *m*
pedantic *adj* umbratic•us -a -um
pedantry *s* morosit•as -atis *f*
peddle *tr* venditare

peddler *s* instit•or -oris *m;* **door-to-door —** qui merces suas ostiatim venditat
pedestal *s* bas•is -is *f*
pedestrian *adj* pedes•ter -tris -tre
pedestrian *s* ped•es -itis *m*
pedigree *s* stemm•a -atis *n*
pediment *s* fastig•ium -(i)i *n*
pedophile *s* pedicat•or -oris *m*
pee *intr* (aquam) facĕre
peel *s* cut•is -is *f*
peel *tr* resecare cutem *(w. gen)*
peep *s* conspect•us -ūs *m* fugax
peep *intr* furtim conspicĕre
peephole *s* conspicill•um -i *n*
peer *s* par paris *m*
peer *intr* **to — at** intuēri
peerless *adj* incomparabil•is -is -e
peevish *adj* stomachos•us -a -um
peevishly *adv* stomachose
peg *s* paxill•us -i *m*
pelican *s* pelican•us -i *m*
pellet *s* globul•us -i *m*
pelt *s* pell•is -is *f*
pelt *tr (to hurl)* conjicĕre; **to — s.o. with stones** aliquem lapidare
pen *s* calam•us -i *m; (enclosure)* saept•um -i *n; (for pigs)* suil•e -is *n; (for sheep)* ovil•e -is *n*
pen *tr* scribĕre; **to — in** includĕre
penal *adj* poenal•is -is -e
penalize *tr* mul(c)tare
penalty *s* mul(c)t•a -ae *f*
penance *s* satisfacti•o -onis *f*
pencil *s* graph•is -idis *f*
pencil box *s* graphiar•ium -(i)i *n*
pending *adj* suspens•us -a -um; *(leg)* sub judice
pending *prep* inter *(acc)*
pendulum *s* librament•um -i *n*
penetrate *tr* penetrare ad *(w. acc)* ‖ *intr* penetrare
penetrating *adj (cold)* acut•us -a -um *(keen-sighted)* perspic•ax -acis
penetration *s* aci•es -ei *f* mentis
peninsula *s* paeninsul•a -ae *f*
penitence *s* paenitenti•a -ae *f*
penitent *adj* paenit•ens -entis
penitentiary *s* ergastul•um -i *n*
penknife *s* cultell•us -i *m*
penmanship *s* man•us -ūs *f*
pennant *s* vexill•um -i *n*
penniless *adj* in•ops -opis
penny *s* quadr•ans -antis *m*
pension *s* annu•a -orum *npl*
pensive *adj* meditabund•us -a -um
penultimate *adj* paenultim•us -a -um
people *s* homin•es -um *mpl; (as political entity)* popul•us -i *m; (of a country)* gen•s -tis *f;* **common —** vulg•us -i *n;* **— say** dicunt; **— who say** qui dicunt
people *tr* frequentare
pep *s* alacrit•as -atis *f*
pep talk *s* conti•o -onis *f;* **to give a —** contionem habēre
pepper *s* pip•er -eris *n*
pepper *tr* pipere condire; *(w. blows)* verberare
peppermint *s* menth•a -ae *f*
perceive *tr* percipĕre
percent *s* per centum
percentage *s* porti•o -onis *f*
perceptible *adj* percipiend•us -a -um
perceptibly *adv* sensim
perch *s (for birds)* pertic•a -ae *f; (fish)* perc•a -ae *f*
perch *intr* insidēre
perchance *adv* forte
percolate *tr* percolare ‖ *intr* permanare
percussion *s* percuss•us -ūs *m*
percussion instrument *s* percussionale instrument•um -i *n* musicum
perdition *s* interit•us -ūs *m*
peremptory *adj* arrogan•s -tis
perennial *adj* perenn•is -is -e
perfect *adj* perfect•us -a -um; **to enjoy almost — health** inlaesā prope valetudine uti
perfect *s (gram)* (tempus) praeterit•um perfect•um -i *n*
perfect *tr* perficĕre
perfectly *adv* perfecte
perfidious *adj* perfid•us -a -um
perfidy *s* perfidi•a -ae *f*
perforate *tr* perforare
perforation *s* foram•en -inis *n*
perform *tr* perficĕre, peragĕre; *(duty)* fungi *(w. abl); (theat)* agĕre
performance *s* perfuncti•o -onis *f; (work)* op•us -eris *n; (of a play)* acti•o -onis *f; (play)* fabul•a -ae *f*
performer *s* act•or -oris *m; (theat)* histri•o -onis *f*
perfume *s* od•or -oris *m*
perfume *tr* odoribus imbuĕre
perfunctorily *adv* perfunctorie
perfunctory *adj* perfunctori•us -a -um
perhaps *adv* fortasse, forsitan
peril *s* pericul•um -i *n*
perilous *adj* periculos•us -a -um
perilously *adv* periculose
period *s (of time)* spat•ium -(i)i *n; (chronological)* temp•us -oris *n; (punctuation mark)* punct•um -i *n; (complete phrase or sentence)* period•us -i *m;* **— of life** aet•as -atis *f;* **over a long — of time** in diuturno spatio
periodic *adj* recurr•ens -entis
periodical *s* libell•us -i *m* diurnus
periodically *adv* temporibus statis
periphery *s* peripheri•a -ae *f*
periphrastic *adj* periphrastic•us -a -um
perish *intr* interire, perire
perishable *adj* quae cito corrumpuntur
peristyle *s* peristyl•ium -(i)i *n*
perjure *tr* **to — oneself** perjurare
perjured *adj* perjur•us -a -um

perjury *s* perjur•ium -(i)i *n;* **to commit —** perjurare
perk *intr* **to — up** reviviscĕre
permanence *s* stabilit•as -atis *f*
permanent *adj* perpetu•us -a -um
permanently *adv* perpetuo
permeable *adj* pervi•us -a -um
permeate *tr* permanare, permeare
permissible *adj* **it is — for me to** licet mihi ire *(or* licet eam)
permission *s* potest•as -atis *f;* **to grant — to** permittĕre *(w. dat);* **with your —** bonā tuā veniā
permit *tr* permittĕre *(w. dat)*
permutation *s* permutati•o -onis *f*
pernicious *adj* pernicios•us -a -um
perniciously *adv* perniciose
peroration *s* perorati•o -onis *f*
perpendicular *adj* perpendicular•is -is -e
perpendicular *s* line•a -ae *f* perpendicularis
perpetrate *tr* perficĕre
perpetrator *s* auct•or -oris *m*
perpetual *adj* perpetu•us -a -um
perpetually *adv* perpetuo
perpetuate *tr* perpetuare
perpetuity *s* perpetuit•as -atis *f*
perplex *tr* distrahĕre
perplexing *adj* perplex•us -a -um
perplexity *s* dubitati•o -onis *f*
persecute *tr* insectari
persecution *s* insectati•o -onis *f*
persecutor *s* insectat•or -oris *m*
perseverance *s* perseveranti•a -ae *f*
persevere *intr* perseverare, perstare
persevering *adj* persever•ans -antis
persist *intr* perseverare, perstare
persistence *s* perseveranti•a -ae *f*
persistent *adj* pertin•ax -acis
persistently *adv* pertinaciter
person *s* hom•o -inis *m,* person•a -ae *f;* *(gram)* persona *f;* **in —** ips•e -a
personage *s* person•a -ae *f*
personal *adj* privat•us -a -um; *(gram, leg)* personal•is -is -e; **— appearance** form•a -ae *f* et habit•us -ūs *m*
personality *s* indol•es -is *f*
personally *adv rendered by* ips•e -a
personification *s* prosopopei•a -ae *f*
personify *tr (inanimate objects)* vitam sensumque tribuĕre *(dat);* **to — evil** malum in personam suam constituĕre
personnel *s* soci•i -orum *mpl*
perspective *s (viewpoint)* conspect•us -ūs *m* animi; *(in drawing)* scaenographi•a -ae *f*
perspicacious *adj* perspic•ax -acis
perspicacity *s* perspicacit•as -atis *f*
perspiration *s (sweating)* sudati•o -onis *f;* *(sweat)* sud•or -oris *m*
perspire *intr* sudare
persuade *tr* persuadēre *(w. dat)*
persuasion *s* persuasi•o -onis *f*
persuasive *adj* suasori•us -a -um
persuasively *adv* persuabiliter
pert *adj* proc•ax -acis
pertain *intr* **(to)** pertinēre (ad *w. acc)*
pertinence *s* congruenti•a -ae *f*
pertinent *adj* apposit•us -a -um; **to be —** ad rem pertinēre
perturb *tr* perturbare
perturbation *s* perturbati•o -onis *f*
perusal *s* perlecti-o -onis *f*
peruse *tr* perlegĕre
pervade *tr* permanare per *(w. acc)*
perverse *adj* pervers•us -a -um
perversely *adv* perverse
perversion *s* perversit•as -atis *f*
perversity *s* perversit•as -atis *f*
pervert *s* hom•o -inis *m* perversus
pervert *tr* depravare; *(words)* detorquēre
pest *s* pest•is -is *f*
pester *tr* vexare
pestilence *s* pestilenti•a -ae *f*
pestle *s* pistill•um -i *n*
pet *s* delici•ae -arum *fpl;* **to have a dog as a —** canem in deliciis habēre
pet *tr* permulcēre
petal *s* floris fol•ium -(i)i *n*
petition *s* petiti•o -onis *f;* *(pol)* libell•us -i *m*
petition *tr* supplicare
petitioner *s* suppl•ex -icis *m*
petrify *tr* in lapidem convertĕre ‖ *intr* lapidescĕre
petticoat *s* inducul•a -ae *f*
pettiness *s* anim•us -i *m* angustus
petty *adj* minut•us et angust•us -a -um
petulance *s* petulanti•a -ae *f*
petulant *adj* petul•ans -antis
pew *s* subsell•ium -(i)i *n*
phantasy *s* phantasi•a -ae *f*
phantom *s* larv•a -ae *f*
pharmacy *s* tabern•a -ae *f* medicamentaria
phase *s* lunae faci•es -ei *f;* *(fig)* vic•es -ium *fpl*
pheasant *s* phasian•us -i *m,* phasian•a -ae *f*
phenomenal *adj* singular•is -is -e
phenomenon *s* res, rei *f;* *(s.th. remarkable)* miracul•um -i *n*
philanthropic *adj* human•us -a -um
philanthropy *s* humanit•as -atis *f*
philologist *s* philolog•us -i *m*
philology *s* philologi•a -ae *f*
philosopher *s* philosoph•us -i *m*
philosophical *adj* philosophic•us -a -um
philosophically *adv* philosophice; *(calmly)* aequo animo
philosophize *intr* philosophari
philosophy *s* philosophi•a -ae *f;* *(theory)* rati•o -onis *f*
phlegm *s* phlegm•a -atis *n*
phlegmatic *adj* lent•us -a -um
phone *s* telephon•um -i *n*
phone *tr* per telephonum loqui cum *(w. abl)*
phosphorus *s* phosphor•us -i *m*
phrase *s* locuti•o -onis *f*

phrase *tr* verbis exprimĕre
phraseology *s* loquendi rati•o -onis *f*
physical *adj (relating to nature)* physic•us -a -um; — **strength** corporis vir•es -ium *fpl*
physician *s* medic•us -i *m*
physicist *s* physic•us -i *m*
physics *s* physic•a -orum *npl*
physiognomy *s* physiognomi•a -ae *f*
physiological *adj* physiologic•us -a -um
physiologist *s* physiolog•us -i *m*
physiology *s* physiologi•a -ae *f*
physique *s* corporis habit•us -ūs *m*
pick *tr (to choose)* eligĕre; *(fruit)* carpĕre, legĕre; **to — a quarrel** jurgii causam inferre; **to — out** eligĕre; **to — pockets** manticulari; **to — the teeth** dentes perfodĕre; **to — up** tollĕre
pick *s (tool)* dolabr•a -ae *f; (the best)* flo•s -ris *m*
pickax *s* dolabr•a -ae *f*
picked *adj* elect•us -a -um
picket *s (mil)* stati•o -onis *f*
pickle *s (brine)* muri•a -ae *f; (vegetable)* oxycucum•er -eris *m*
pickled *adj* muria condit•us -a -um; *(drunk)* ebri•us -a -um; — **olives** oxycomin•a -orum *npl*
pickpocket *s* saccular•ius -(i)i *m*
picnic *s* conviv•ium -(i)i *n* sub divo
pictorial *adj* pictori•us -a -um
picture *s* pictur•a -ae *f*
picture gallery *s* pinacothec•a -ae *f*
picturesque *adj* amoen•us -a -um
pie *s* crust•um -i *n;* **apple —** mal•a -orum *npl* in crusto cocta
piece *s* par•s -tis *f; (of food)* frust•um -i *n; (broken off)* fragment•um -i *n; (drama)* fabul•a -ae *f; (very often not expressed by a separate word, e.g.,* **a — of cheese** case•us -i *m;* **a — of ground** agell•us -i *m;* **a — of meat** car•o -nis *f;* **a — of paper** chart•a -ae *f);* **to cut in —s** minute concidĕre; **to fall to —s** dilabi; **to tear to —s** dilaniare; *(e.g., paper)* conscindĕre
piece *tr* **to — together** fabricari
piecemeal *adv* frustatim, separatim
pier *s* mol•es -is *f*
pierce *tr* perforare; *(w. a sword)* perfodĕre; *(fig)* pungĕre
piercing *adj* acut•us -a -um
piety *s* piet•as -atis *f*
pig *s* porc•us -i *m*
pigeon *s* columb•a -ae *f*
pigheaded *adj* obstinat•us -a -um
pigment *s* pigment•um -i *n*
pigsty *s* suil•e -is *n*
pike *s* hast•a -ae *f; (fish)* lup•us -i *m*
pilaster *s* parastatic•a -ae *f*
pile *s* acerv•us -i *m; (nap of cloth)* vill•us -i *m; (for cremation)* rog•us -i *m*
pile *tr* **(on)** congerĕre *(w. dat);* **to — up** exstruĕre ‖ *intr* crescĕre
pilgrim *s* peregrinat•or -oris *m* religionis causā
pilgrimage *s* peregrinati•o -onis *f* religionis causā
pill *s* pilul•a -ae *f*
pillage *s* rapin•a -ae *f*
pillage *tr* diripĕre ‖ *intr* praedari
pillar *s* pil•a -ae *f*
pillow *s* cervic•al •alis *n*
pillowcase *s* cervicalis tegim•en -inis *n*
pilot *s* gubernat•or -oris *m*
pilot *tr* gubernare
pimp *s* len•o -onis *m*
pimp *tr & intr* lenocinari
pimple *s* pustul•a -ae *f*
pin *s* ac•us -ūs *f; (peg)* clav•us -i *m*
pin *tr* acu figĕre; **to — down** defigĕre; *(fig)* devincire
pin cushion *s* pulvill•us -i *m* acibus servandis
pincers *spl* forc•eps -ipis *mf*
pinch *tr* vellicare; *(of cold; of shoe)* (ad)urĕre
pinch *s (e.g., of salt)* mensur•a -ae *f* duorum *(or* trium) digitorum
pine *s* pin•us -i *f*
pine *intr* **to — away** tabescĕre; **to — for** desiderare
pineapple *s* nu•x -cis *f* pinea
pink *adj* punice•us -a -um; **to be in the — of health** optimā valetudine uti
pinnacle *s* fastig•ium -(i)i *n*
pint *s* sextar•ius -(i)i *m*
pioneer *s* praecurs•or -oris *m*
pious *adj* pi•us -a -um, prob•us -a -um; *(spotless)* sanct•us -a -um
piously *adv* pie, religiose, sancte
pipe *s* tub•us -i *m; (conduit)* canal•is -is *m; (mus)* fistul•a -ae *f*
pipe *tr & intr (mus)* fistulā canĕre
piper *s* fistulat•or -oris *m*
piquant *adj* a•cer -cris -cre; *(fig)* sals•us -a -um
pique *s* offensi•o -onis *f*
pique *tr* offendĕre
piracy *s* latrocin•ium -(i)i *n*
pirate *s* pirat•a -ae *m*
piratical *adj* piratic•us -a -um
pistachio *s* pistac•ium -(i)i *n*
pit *s* fove•a -ae *f; (quarry)* fodin•a -ae *f; (theat)* cave•a -ae *f*
pit *tr* **to — one against another** alium cum alio committĕre
pitch *s* pi•x -cis *f; (sound)* son•us -i *m; (degree)* grad•us -ūs *m; (slope)* fastig•ium -(i)i *n;* **to such a — of** eo *(w. gen)*
pitch *tr (to fling)* conjicĕre; *(camp)* ponĕre; *(tent)* tendĕre
pitcher *s* urce•us -i *m*
pitchfork *s* furc•a -ae *f*
piteous *adj* miserabil•is -is -e
piteously *adv* miserabiliter
pitfall *s* fove•a -ae *f*

pith *s* medull•a -ae *f*
pithy *adj* sententios•us -a -um
pitiable *adj* miserand•us -a -um
pitiful *adj* misericor•s -dis; *(pitiable)* miserand•us -a -um
pitifully *adv* misere
pitiless *adj* immisericor•s -dis
pitilessly *adv* immisericorditer
pittance *s* mercedul•a -ae *f*
pity *s* misericordi•a -ae *f*
pity *tr* misereri *(w. gen)*; **I — him** miseret me ejus
pivot *s* cnod•ax -acis *m; (fig)* card•o -inis *m*
placard *s* titul•us -i *m*
place *s* loc•us -i *m (pl:* loc•a -orum *npl)*; **in — of** in locum *(w. gen)*; **in the first —** primum; **in the last —** postremo; **in the same —** ibidem; **out of —** alien•us -a -um; **to take —** fieri
place *tr* ponĕre; *(pointing to the placing of an object in connection with other objects)* (col)locare
placid *adj* placid•us -a -um
placidly *adv* placide
plagiarism *s* furt•um -i *n* litterarium
plagiarist *s* fu•r -ris *m* litterarius
plagiarize *tr* furari
plague *s* pestilenti•a -ae *f; (fig)* pest•is -is *f*
plague *tr* vexare
plain *s* camp•us -i *m*
plain *adj (clear)* manifest•us -a -um; *(unadorned)* simpl•ex -icis; *(of one color)* unicol•or -oris; *(frank)* sincer•us -a -um; *(homely)* invenust•us -a -um
plainly *adv* plane; simpliciter
plaintiff *s* petit•or -oris *m*
plaintive *adj* flebil•is -is -e
plaintively *adv* flebiliter
plan *s* consil•ium -(i)i *n; (for a building)* form•a -ae *f*; **to form a —** consilium inire
plan *tr* destinare, in animo habēre; *(to scheme)* meditari ‖ *intr* **to — on** in animo habēre
plane *s (tool)* runcin•a -ae *f; (level surface)* planiti•es -ei *f*
plane *tr* runcinare
planet *s* planet•a -ae *f*
plank *s* ax•is -is *m*
plant *s* plant•a -ae *f*
plant *tr* serĕre; **his feet are —ed on** pedes stipantur in *(w. abl)*; **to — one's feet on the ground** pedes in terram deferre
plantation *s* plantar•ium -(i)i *n*
planter *s* sat•or -oris *m*
planting *s* sat•us -ūs *m*
plaster *s* tector•ium -(i)i *n*
plaster *tr* tectorium inducĕre *(w. dat)*
plasterer *s* tect•or -oris *m*
plaster of Paris *s* gyps•um -i *n*
plastic *adj* plastic•us -a -um
plastic *s* materi•a -ae *f* plastica
plate *s (dish)* patell•a -ae *f; (of metal)* lamin•a -ae *f; (dish of silver or gold)* argent•um -i *n*
plateau *s* aequ•um -i *n*
platform *s* suggest•us -ūs *m*
platitude *s* trita sententi•a -ae *f*
Platonic *adj* Platonic•us -a -um
platoon *s* manipul•us -i *m*
platter *s* lan•x -cis *f*
plaudits *spl* plaus•us -ūs *m*
plausible *adj* verisimil•is -is -e
play *s* lud•us -i *m; (theat)* fabul•a -ae *f*; **to be at —** ludĕre
play *tr* ludĕre; *(instrument)* canĕre *(w. abl)*; **to — ball** pilā ludĕre; **to — a trick on** ludificari; **to — Latin songs** Latine ludĕre; **to — the lead role** primas partes agĕre; **to — the role of a parasite** parasitum agĕre; **to — with** *(sexually)* ludĕre cum *(w. abl)*
player *s* lus•or -oris *m; (theat)* histri•o -onis *m; (on wind instrument)* tibic•en -inis *m; (on stringed instrument)* fidic•en -inis *m*
playful *adj* ludibund•us -a -um; *(frolicsome)* lasciv•us -a -um
playfully *adv* per ludum
playfulness *s* lascivi•a -ae *f*
playground *s* are•a -ae *f* lusoria
playmate *s* collus•or -oris *m*
plaything *s* ludibr•ium -(i)i *n*
playwright *s* fabularum script•or -oris *m*
plea *s* supplicati•o -onis *f; (one of the grounds for defense as stated in the praetor's edict)* excepti•o -onis *f*; **to enter a — against s.o.** exceptionem objicĕre alicui; **well-founded —** justa exceptio *f*
plead *tr (ignorance)* causari; **to — a case** causam agĕre ‖ *intr* **to — for** petĕre; **to — with s.o.** aliquem supplicare
pleasant *adj* amoen•us -a -um, jucund•us -a -um
pleasantly *adv* jucunde
pleasantry *s* jocosa dicacit•as -atis *f*
please *tr* placēre *(w. dat)*; **anyone you —** quilibet, quaelibet; **anything you —** quidlibet; **if you —** si placet; si videtur; **—!** sis (= si vis); amabo te *(coll)*; **— God!** Deo volente
pleasing *adj* grat•us -a -um
pleasurable *adj* jucund•us -a -um
pleasure *s* volupt•as -atis *f*; **it is my —** libet; **to derive — from** voluptatem capĕre de *(w. abl)*
plebeian *adj* plebei•us -a -um
plebeians *spl* pleb•s -is *f*
plebiscite *s* plebiscit•um -i *n*
pledge *s* pign•us -oris *n; (proof)* testimon•ium -(i)i *n*
pledge *tr* (op)pignerare, obligare; **to — one's word** fidem obligare
Pleiads *spl* Pleiad•es -um *fpl*
plenary *adj* plen•us -a -um

plenipotentiary *s* legat·us -i *m* praepotens
plentiful *adj* larg·us -a -um
plenty *s* copi·a -ae *f*
plethora *s* redundanti·a -ae *f*
pleurisy *s* pleurit·is -idis *f*
pliable *adj* tractabil·is -is -e
pliant *adj* lent·us -a -um
plight *s* discrim·en -inis *n;* **in a sorry —** male perdit·us -a -um
plod *intr* assidue laborare
plodder *s* sedulus hom·o -inis *m*
plodding *adj* sedul·us -a -um
plot *s (conspiracy)* conjurati·o -onis *f; (of ground)* agell·us -i *m; (of a play)* argument·um -i *n*
plot *intr* conjurare, moliri
plow *s* aratr·um -i *n*
plow *tr* arare; **to — under** inarare; **to — up** exarare
plowing *s* arati·o -onis *f*
plowman *s* arat·or -oris *m*
plowshare *s* vom·er -eris *m*
pluck *s* anim·us -i *m*
pluck *tr (flowers, fruit)* carpĕre; *(feathers)* vellĕre; **to — off** decerpĕre; **to — out** evellĕre; **to — up one's courage** animo esse
plug *s* obturament·um -i *n*
plug *tr* obturare
plum *s* prun·um -i *n*
plumage *s* plum·ae -arum *fpl*
plumber *s* plumbar·ius -(i)i *m*
plume *s* crist·a -ae *f*
plummet *s* perpendicul·um -i *n*
plummet *intr* praecipitare
plump *adj* pingu·is -is -e
plum tree *s* prun·us -i *f*
plunder *s (act)* rapin·a -ae *f; (booty)* praed·a -ae *f*
plunder *tr* praedari
plunderer *s* praedat·or -oris *m*
plundering *s* rapin·a -ae *f*
plundering *adj* praedatori·us -a -um
plunge *tr* mergĕre; *(sword, etc.)* condĕre ‖ *intr* se mergĕre; **to — into the midst of the enemy** inter mucrones hostium se immergĕre
pluperfect *s* plus quam perfectum temp·us -oris *n*
plural *adj* plural·is -is -e
plural *s* numer·us -i *m* multitudinis; **in the —** pluraliter
plurality *s* multitud·o -inis *f; (majority)* major par·s -tis *f*
plush *adj* laut·us -a -um
ply *tr* exercēre, urgēre
poach *tr (eggs)* frigĕre ‖ *intr* illicita venatione uti
poacher *s* venat·or -oris *m* illicitus
pocket *s* sin·us -ūs *m,* saccul·us -i *m*
pocket *tr* in sacculis condĕre
pocketbook *s (small book)* pugillar·ia -ium *npl; (purse)* marsup·ium -(i)i *n*
pockmark *s* cicatr·ix -icis *f*
pod *s* siliqu·a -ae *f*
poem *s* poëm·a -atis *n*
poet *s* poët·a -ae *m*
poetess *s* poëtri·a -ae *f*
poetic *adj* poëtic·us -a -um
poetically *adv* poëtice
poetics *s* ar·s -tis *f* poëtica
poetry *s (art)* poëtic·e -es *f; (poems)* poës·is -is *f,* carm·en -inis *n*
poignancy *s* acerbit·as -atis *f*
poignant *adj* acerb·us -a -um
point *s* punct·um -i *n; (pointed end)* acum·en -inis *n; (of sword, etc.)* mucr·o -onis *m; (point in dispute)* quaesti·o -onis *f; (in time)* articul·a -ae *f* temporis; **at this very —** hoc ipso in loco; **beside the —** ab re; **from this — on** posthac, hinc; **main —** cap·ut -itis *n;* **— of view** sententi·a -ae *f,* opini·o -onis *f;* to come to a — acui; **to be on the — of** in eo esse ut, *e.g., he was on the point of being arrested* in eo erat *(or* haud abfuit) ut comprehenderetur; **to such a — that** eo ut; **to the —** ad rem; **up to this —** hactenus
point *tr (to sharpen)* acuĕre; **to — out** monstrare, indicare; **to — the finger at** digitum intendĕre ad *(w. acc)* ‖ *intr* **to — at** digito monstrare
pointed *adj* acut·us -a -um; *(fig) (stinging)* aculeat·us -a -um
pointer *s* ind·ex -icis *mf*
pointless *adj* supervacu·us -a -um
poise *s* urbanit·as -atis *f*
poise *tr* librare
poison *s* venen·um -i *n*
poison *tr* venenare; *(fig)* vitiare
poisoning *s* venefic·ium -(i)i *n*
poke *tr (to jab)* fodicare, pungĕre; *(w. the elbow)* cubito pulsare; *(fire)* fodĕre; **to — fun at** eludĕre
poker *s* rutabul·um -i *n*
polar *adj* arctic·us -a -um
polarity *s* polarit·as -atis *f*
pole *s* ass·er -eris *m; (short pole)* asserul·us -i *m; (long pole)* longur·ius -(i)i *m; (of the earth)* pol·us -i *m;* **North (South) Pole** ax·is -is *m* septentrionalis (meridianus)
police *s* vigil·es -um *mpl*
policeman *s* vig·il -ilis *m*
policy *s* rati·o -onis *f; (document)* chirograph·um -i *n*
polish *s (shine)* nit·or -oris *m; (refined manners)* urbanit·as -atis *f*
polish *tr* polire; **to — up** expolire
polite *adj* urban·us -a -um
politely *adv* urbane
politeness *s* urbanit·as -atis *f*
politic *adj* pruden·s -tis
political *adj* civil·is -is -e; **from — motives** per ambitionem; **— supporter** suffragat·or -oris *m*

politician *s* vir viri *m* civilium rerum peritus
politics *s* respublica *(gen:* reipublicae) *f;* **to enter —** rempublicam inire; **to talk — at table** ad mensam res publicas crepare
poll *s* diribitorium -(i)i *n; (survey)* rogati•o -onis *f* sententiarum; **the —s** comiti•a -orum *npl*
polling booth *s* saept•um -i *n*
poll tax *s* capitum exacti•o -onis *f*
pollute *tr* polluĕre, contaminare
pollution *s* polluti•o -onis *f*
polygamy *s* polygami•a -ae *f*
polysyllabic *adj* polysyllab•us -a -um
polytheism *s* multorum deorum cult•us -ūs *m*
pomegranate *s* mal•um -i *n* Punicum
pommel *tr* pulsare, verberare
pomp *s* apparat•us -ūs *m*
pompous *adj* magnific•us -a -um
pompously *adv* magnifice
pond *s* stagn•um -i *n*
ponder *tr* animo volutare
ponderous *adj* ponderos•us -a -um
pontiff *s* pontif•ex -icis *m*
pontifical *adj* pontifical•is -is -e
pontificate *s* pontificat•us -ūs *m*
pontoon *s* pont•o -onis *m*
pony *s* mannul•us -i *m*
pool *s* lacun•a -ae *f*
pool *tr* conferre
poor *adj* paup•er -eris: *(soil)* ma•cer -cra -crum; *(pitiable)* mis•er -era -erum; *(meager)* exil•is -is -e
poorly *adv* parum, mediocriter
pop *s* crepit•us -ūs *m; (father)* pap•a -ae *m*
pop *intr* crepare; **to — out** exsilire
pope *s* pap•a -ae *m*
poplar *s* popul•us -i *f*
poppy, poppyseed *s* papav•er -eris *n*
populace *s* vulg•us -i *n*
popular *adj* popular•is -is -e; **— feeling** sens•us -ūs *m* populi
popularity *s* fav•or -oris *m,* grati•a-ae *f;* **to enjoy —** gratiam habēre
populate *tr* frequentare
population *s* multitud•o -inis *f*
populous *adj* frequ•ens -entis
porcelain *s* fictil•ia -ium *npl* elegantia
porch *s* pergul•a -ae *f*
porcupine *s* hystr•ix -icis *f*
pore *s* foram•en -inis *n*
pore *intr* **to — over** scrutari
pork *s* porcin•a -ae *f*
pork chop *s* off•a -ae *f* porcina
porpoise *s* porcul•us -i *m* marinus
porridge *s* pul•s -tis *f*
port *s* port•us -ūs *m*
portal *s* port•a -ae *f*
portend *tr* portendĕre
portent *s* portent•um -i *n*
portentous *adj* prodigios•us -a -um
porter *s* atriens•is is *m; (carrier)* bajul•us -i *m*
portfolio *s* scrin•ium -(i)i *n*
portico *s* portic•us -ūs *f*
portion *s* porti•o -onis *f*
portion *tr* partire; **to — out** dispertire
portly *adj* **to be —** opimo corporis habitu esse
portrait *s* imag•o -inis *f*
portray *tr* depingĕre, exprimĕre
pose *s* stat•us -ūs *m*
pose *intr* statum sumĕre
position *s* positi•o -onis *f; (of the body)* gest•us -ūs *m; (office)* hon•or -oris *m; (rank)* dignit•as -atis *f; (state)* conditi•o -onis *f*
positive *adj* cert•us -a -um; *(opp: negative)* affirmativ•us -a -um; *(gram)* positiv•us -a -um
positively *adv* certo, praecise
possess *tr* possidēre
possession *s* possessi•o -onis *f;* **in the — of** penes *(w. acc);* **to gain — of** potiri *(w. abl)*
possessive *adj* quaestuos•us -a -um; *(gram)* possessiv•us -a -um
possessor *s* possess•or -oris *m*
possibility *s* facult•as -atis *f*
possible *adj* **as quickly as —** quam celerrime; **it is —** fieri potest; **it is — for me to** possum *(w. inf)*
possibly *adv (perhaps)* fortasse; **as carefully as I — can** quam diligentissime possum; **I may — go to Sicily** fieri potest ut in Siciliam proficiscar
post *s (stake)* post•is -is *m; (station)* stati•o -onis *f; (in a race)* met•a -ae *f*
post *tr (a notice)* in publicum proponĕre; *(to station)* collocare: **to — a letter** litteras dare
postage *s* vectur•a -ae *f* litterarum
postdate *tr* diem seriorem scribĕre *(w. dat)*
poster *s* libell•us -i *m;* **to put up a —** libellum proponĕre
posterior *adj* poster•ior -ior -ius
posterity *s* posterit•as -atis *f; (descendants)* poster•i -orum *mpl*
posthaste *adv* quam celerrime
postumous *adj* postum•us -a -um
postman *s* tabellar•ius -(i)i *m*
postpone *tr* differre
postscript *s* adjecti•o -onis *f* litterarum
posture *s* stat•us -ūs *m*
pot *s (of clay)* oll•a -ae *f; (of bronze)* ahen•um -i *n; (chamber pot)* matell•a -ae *f;* **to go to —** pessum ire
pot-bellied *adj* ventrios•us -a -um
potato *s* solan•um -i *n* tuberosum
potentate *s* tyrann•us -i *m*
potential *adj* futur•us -a -um
potion *s* poti•o -onis *f*
potter *s* figul•us -i *m*

pottery *s* fictil•ia -ium *npl*
pouch *s* saccul•us -i *m*
poultry *s* av•es -ium *fpl* cohortales
pounce *intr* **to — on** insilire *(w. dat or* in + *acc)*
pound *s* libr•a -ae *f (w.* pondo *sometimes added);* **a half —** selibr•a -ae *f;* **a — and a half** sesquilibr•a -ae *f;* **a —** *(or* **per —**) in libras; **a quarter —** quadran•s -tis *f* pondo; **per —** in libras
pound *tr* contundĕre
pour *tr* fundĕre; **to — into** infundĕre *(*in + *acc);* **to — out** effundĕre; **to — water on his hands** aquam in ejus manūs infundĕre; **to — water on his head** caput illi aquā perfundĕre ‖ *intr* fundi, fluĕre; **to come —ing out** *(of people)* se effundĕre; **to — down** *(of rain)* ruĕre; **to — into** *(of people)* se infundĕre in *(w. acc)*
pouring *adj (rain)* effus•us -a -um
pout *intr* labellum extendĕre
poverty *s* paupert•as -atis *f; (inadequacy)* egest•as -atis *f*
poverty-stricken *adj* inop•s -is
powder *s* pulv•is -eris *m*
powder *tr* pulvere conspergĕre
power *s (strength)* vis *f; (control, dominium)* potest•as -atis *f; (excessive; nonconstitutional)* potenti•a -ae *f; (mil, pol)* imper•ium -(i)i *n;* **as far as is in our —** quantum in nobis est; **— of the mind** vir•es -ium *fpl* ingenii; **to have great —** multum posse
powerful *adj (physically)* valid•us -a -um; *(kings, etc.)* poten•s -tis
powerfully *adv* valde
powerless *adj* invalid•us -a -um; **to be —** nil valēre
practical *adj* util•is -is -e; *(sensible)* pruden•s -tis; *(philosophy)* effectiv•us -a -um
practically *adv* usu; *(almost)* fere
practice *s (actual employment or experience)* us•us -ūs *m; (rehearsal)* meditati•o -onis *f; (custom)* consuetud•o -inis *f;* **to have a large — as a doctor** medicus praecipuae celebritatis esse
practice *tr (medicine, patience)* exercēre; *(to rehearse)* meditari
practitioner *s* exercitat•or -oris *m; (medical)* medic•us -i *m*
pragmatic *adj* pragmatic•us -a -um
prairie *s* camp•us -i *m* latissime patens herbisque obsitus
praise *s* lau•s -dis *f*
praise *tr* laudare
praiseworthy *adj* laudabil•is -is -e
prance *intr* exsilire
prank *s* lud•us -i *m*
pray *intr* precari, orare; **to — for** petĕre, precari; **to — to** adorare; **to — to the gods for peace** deos pacem precari
prayer *s* pre•x -cis *f*
preach *tr & intr* praedicare
preacher *s* praedicat•or -oris *m*
preamble *s* exord•ium -(i)i *n*
precarious *adj* precari•us -a -um; **in a most — position** in summo discrimine
precariously *adv* precario
precaution *s* cauti•o -onis *f;* **to take —s** praecavēre
precede *tr* antecedĕre *(w. acc or dat)*
precedence *s* prior loc•us -i *m;* **to take — over** antecedĕre
precedent *s* exempl•um -i *n*
preceding *adj* pr•ior -ior -ius
precept *s* praecept•um -i *n*
preceptor *s* praecept•or -oris *m*
precinct *s* termin•i -orum *mpl; (pol)* regi•o -onis *f*
precious *adj* pretios•us -a -um; **— stone** gemm•a -ae *f*
precipice *s* praec•eps -ipitis *n;* **down a —** in praeceps; **over the —** per praecipitia
precipitate *tr* praecipitare
precipitious *adj* praec•eps -ipitis
precise *adj (exact)* exact•us -a -um; *(particular)* accurat•us -a -um
precisely *adv* subtiliter
precision *s* accurati•o -onis *f*
preclude *tr* praecludĕre
precocious *adj* praec•ox -ocis
preconceive *tr* praecipĕre; **—d idea** praejudic•ium -(i)i *n*
preconception *s* praejudicata opini•o -onis *f*
precursor *s* praenunt•ius -(i)i *m*
predatory *adj* praedatori•us -a -um
predecessor *s* decess•or -oris *m*
predestine *tr* praedestinare
predicament *s* discrim•en -inis *n*
predicate *tr* praedicare
predicate *s* praedicat•um -i *n*
predict *tr* praedicĕre
prediction *s* praedicti•o -onis *f*
predilection *s* **(for)** stud•ium -(i)i *n (w. gen)*
predispose *tr* inclinare
predisposed *adj* **(to)** obnoxi•us -a -um *(w. dat)*
predispostion *s* inclinati•o -onis *f*
predominant *adj* praevalen•s -tis
predominate *intr* praevalēre
preeminent *adj* praecipu•us -a -um
preempt *tr* praeoccupare
preexist *intr* antea exstare *or* esse
preface *s* praefati•o -onis *f*
prefatory *adj* **to make a few — remarks** pauca praefari
prefect *s* praefect•us -i *m*
prefecture *s* praefectur•a -ae *f*
prefer *tr* praeponĕre, praeferre; *(charges)* deferre; **to — to** *(would rather)* malle *(w. inf)*
preferable *adj* pot•ior -ior-ius, praestan-

t•ior -ior -ius; *(when more than two are compared)* potissim•us -a -um
preference *s* fav•or -oris *m;* **in — to** potius quam; **to give — to s.o. over** aliquem anteponĕre *(w. dat)*
prefix *s* praepositi•o -onis *f*
prefix *tr* **(to)** praeponĕre *(dat)*
pregnancy *s* gravidit•as -atis *f*
pregnant *adj* gravid•us -a -um; *(of language)* press•us -a -um
prejudge *tr* praejudicare
prejudice *s* praejudicata opini•o -onis *f*
prejudice *tr* **to be —d against** praejudicatam opinionem habēre in *(w. acc);* **to — the people against** studia hominum inclinare in *(w. acc)*
prejudicial *adj* noxi•us -a -um
preliminary *adj* pr•ior -ior -ius; **to make a few — remarks** pauca praefari
prelude *s (mus)* proœm•ium -(i)i *n; (fig)* praelusi•o -onis *f*
premature *adj* praematur•us -a -um
prematurely *adv* ante tempus
premeditate *tr* praemeditari
premier *s* princ•eps -ipitis *m*
premise *s (major)* propositi•o -onis *f; (minor)* assumpti•o -onis *f;* **—s** praed•ium -(i)i *n*
premium *s* praem•ium -(i)i *n;* **at a —** car•us -a -um
premonition *s* monit•um -i *n*
preoccupation *s* nescio qua de re sollicitati•o -onis *f*
preoccupied *adj* nescio qua de re sollicit•us -a -um
preoccupy *tr* distringĕre
preparation *s* praeparati•o -onis *f;* **to make careful —s** diligentem praeparationem adhibēre
prepare *tr* parare; *(a medicine)* componĕre; *(a speech, case)* meditari; **to — to** parare *(w. inf)*
preponderance *s* praestanti•a -ae *f*
preposition *s* praepositi•o -onis *f*
preposterous *adj* praeposter•us -a -um
preposterously *adv* praepostere
prerogative *s* ju•s -ris *n*
presage *tr* praesagire
prescribe *tr* mandare; *(a medicine)* praescribĕre
prescription *s (med)* compositi•o -onis *f;* **to write a —** medicinam praescribĕre
presence *s* praesenti•a -ae *f;* **in my —** me praesente; **in the — of** coram *(w. abl);* **— of mind** praesenti•a -ae *f* animi
present *adj* praesen•s -tis; **for the —** in praesens tempus; **to be —** adesse; *(of fever, infection)* inesse
present *s* don•um -i *n*
present *tr (to give)* donare; *(to introduce)* introducĕre; *(in court)* sistĕre; *(to bring forward)* praebēre, offerre; **an opportunity —s itself** occasio obvenit
presentation *s (of gifts)* donati•o -onis *f; (show)* spectacul•um -i *n; (introduction)* introducti•o -onis *f*
presentiment *s* praesag•ium -(i)i *n*
presently *adv* mox, statim
preservation *s* conservati•o -onis *f*
preserve *tr* conservare; *(fruit)* condire
preserver *s* conservat•or -oris *m*
preside *intr* **(over)** praesidēre *(w. dat)*
presidency *s* praefectur•a -ae *f; (term of office)* magister•ium -(i)i *n*
president *s* praes•es -idis *m*
press *s (for wine; for printing)* prel•um -i *n;* **hot off the —** modo ex prelo typographico; **to send to the —** prelo subjicĕre
press *tr* primĕre; *(fig)* urgēre; **to — down** deprimĕre; **to — together** comprimĕre ‖ *intr* **to — forward** anniti; **to — on** pergĕre
pressing *adj* urg•ens -entis
pressure *s* pressur•a -ae *f*
pressure *vt* urgēre
prestige *s* auctorit•as -atis *f*
presumably *adv* sane
presume *tr* sumĕre, conjicĕre; *(to take liberties)* sibi arrogare
presumption *s* praesumpti•o -onis *f*
presumptuous *adj* praesumptios•us -a -um
presuppose *tr* praesumĕre
pretend *tr* simulare, fingĕre; **to — to be shocked** fingĕre se inhorrescĕre
pretender *s* simulat•or -oris *m*
pretense *s* simulati•o -onis *f;* **under the — of** per speciem *(w. gen);* **without —** sine fuco
pretension *s (claim)* postulati•o -onis *f; (display)* ostentati•o -onis *f;* **to make —s to** affectare
preterite *s* temp•us -oris *n* praeteritum
preternatural *adj* praeter naturam
pretext *s* speci•es -ei *f;* **under the — of** (sub) specie *(w. gen)*
pretor *s* praet•or -oris *m*
pretorian *adj* praetorian•us -a -um
pretorship *s* praetur•a -ae *f*
prettily *adv* belle
pretty *adj* bell•us -a -um
pretty *adv* satis, admodum; **a — considerable quantity** aliquantul•um -i *n;* **— well** mediocriter
prevail *intr (to be prevalent)* esse, obtinēre; *(to win)* vincĕre; **to — upon** persuadēre *(w. dat)*
prevalent *adj* (per)vulgat•us -a -um; **to become —** increbrescĕre
prevaricate *intr* praevaricari
prevarication *s* praevaricati•o -onis *f*
prevaricator *s* praevaricat•or -oris *m*
prevent *tr* prohibēre; **to — s.th. from happening** prohibēre ne *(or* quominus) quid fiat
prevention *s* impediti•o -onis *f*

preventive *adj* **to adopt all — measures** omnia providēre et curare
previous *adj* super•ior -ior -ius
previously *adv* antehac
prey *s* praed•a -ae *f*
prey *intr* **to — on** praedari
price *s* pret•ium -(i)i *n;* **at a high —** magni; **at a low —** parvi; **to purchase at an enormous —** immenso pretio comparare
priceless *adj* inaestimabil•is -is -e
price tag *s* titul•us -i *m*
prick *tr* pungĕre; *(fig)* stimulare; **to — up the ears** aures arrigĕre
prickle *s* acule•us -i *m*
prickly *adj* spinos•us -a -um
pride *s* superbi•a -ae *f; (source of pride)* dec•us -oris *n*
pride *tr* **to — oneself on** jactare
priest *s* sacerd•os -otis *m; (of a particular god)* flam•en -inis *m*
priestess *s* sacerd•os -otis *f*
priesthood *s (office)* sacerdot•ium -(i)i *n*
priestly *adj* sacerdotal•is -is -e
prig *s* hom•o -inis *m* fastidiosus
prim *adj* (nimis) dilig•ens -entis
primarily *adv* praecipue
primary *adj* principal•is -is -e; *(chief)* praecipu•us -a -um
prime *s* flo•s -ris *m;* **to be in one's —** aetate florēre
prime *adj* prim•us -a -um, optim•us -a -um
primeval *adj* pristin•us -a -um
primitive *adj* primitiv•us -a -um
primordial *adj* primordi•us -a -um
primrose *s* primul•a -ae *f* vulgaris
prince *s* regis fil•ius -(i)i *m*
princely *adj* regi•us -a -um
princess *s* regis fili•a -ae *f*
principal *adj* principal•is -is -e, praecipu•us -a -um
principal *s (of a school)* rect•or -oris *m; (fin)* cap•ut -itis *n*
principality *s* principat•us -ūs *m*
principally *adv* praecipue
principle *s* princip•ium -(i)i *n; (rule of conduct)* praecept•um -i *n;* **a man of —** vi•r -ri *m* gravis et severus
print *s* not•a -ae *f* impressa; *(cloth)* pann•us -i *m* imaginibus impressus
print *tr* imprimĕre
printer *s* typograph•us -i *m*
printing *s* typographi•a -ae *f*
printing press *s* prel•um -i *n* typographicum
prior *adj* pr•ior -ior -ius
priority *s* primat•us -ūs *m*
prism *s* prism•a -atis *n*
prison *s* carc•er -eris *m;* **to throw into —** in carcerem conjicĕre
prisoner *s* captiv•us -i *m,* captiv•a -ae *f;* **(for debt)** nex•us -i *m*
pristine *adj* pristin•us -a -um
privacy *s* secret•um -i *n*
private *adj (secluded)* secret•us -a -um; *(person)* privat•us -a -um; *(tutor)* domestic•us -a -um; *(one's own)* propri•us -a -um; *(mil)* gregari•us -a -um
private *s* mil•es -itis *m* gregarius
privately *adv* clam, secreto; *(in a private capacity)* privatim
privation *s* egest•as -atis *f*
privilege *s* privileg•ium -(i)i *n*
privy *adj* privat•us -a -um; **— to** consci•us -a -um *(w. gen)*
prize *s (reward)* praem•ium -(i)i *n; (prey)* praed•a -ae *f*
prize *tr* magni aestimare
prize fighter *s* pug•il -ilis *m*
probability *s* veri similitud•o -inis *f*
probable *adj* veri simil•is -is -e
probably *adv* probabiliter
probation *s* probati•o -onis *f*
probe *s (med)* specill•um -i *n*
probe *tr* scrutari
problem *s* quaesti•o -onis *f,* aerumn•a -ae *f; (math)* problem•a -atis *n*
problematical *adj* anc•eps -ipitis
procedure *s* mod•us -i *m* operandi
proceed *intr* procedĕre; *(to go on)* pergĕre; **to — against** persequi; **to — from** oriri ex *(w. abl)*
proceedings *spl* act•a -orum *npl; (leg)* acti•o -onis *f*
proceeds *spl* redit•us -ūs *m*
process *s* rati•o -onis *f; (leg)* acti•o -onis *f*
proclaim *tr* pronuntiare
proclamation *s* pronunt•ium -(i)i *n*
proclivity *s* proclivit•as -atis *f*
proconsul *s* procons•ul -ulis *m*
proconsular *adj* proconsular•is -is -e
proconsulship *s* pronconsulat•us -ūs *m*
procrastinate *intr* procrastinare
procrastination *s* procrastinati•o -onis *f*
procreate *tr* procreare
procreation *s* procreati•o -onis *f*
proctor *s* procurat•or -oris *m*
procurable *adj* comparand•us -a -um
procure *tr* comparare
procurement *s* comparati•o -onis *f*
prodigal *adj* prodig•us -a -um
prodigality *s* dissipati•o -onis *f*
prodigious *adj* imman•is -is -e
prodigy *s* prodig•ium -(i)i *n; (fig)* miracul•um -i *n*
produce *s* fruct•us -ūs *m*
produce *tr (to bring forward)* producĕre, proferre; *(to bring into existence)* parĕre, gignĕre; *(to cause)* efficĕre, movēre; *(a play)* docēre; *(public games)* edĕre; *(crops)* ferre
product *s* op•us -eris *n*
production *s (act)* fabricati•o -onis *f*
productive *adj* efficien•s -tis; *(fertile)* fer•ax -acis
productivity *s* feracit•as -atis *f*
profanation *s* violati•o -onis *f*

profane *adj* profan•us -a -um
profanity *s* verb•a -orum *npl* profana
profess *tr* profiteri
professed *adj* manifest•us -a -um
profession *s* professi•o -onis *f*
professional *adj* ad professionem pertinen•s -tis; *(expert)* perit•us -a -um
professor *s* profess•or -oris *m*
proffer *tr* promittěre
proficiency *s* progress•us -ūs *m*
proficient (in) *adj* perit•us -a -um (*w. gen*)
profile *s* faci•es -ei *f* obliqua; *(portrait)* imag•o -inis *f* obliqua; *(description)* descripti•o -onis *f*
profit *s (financial)* lucr•um -i *n; (benefit)* emolument•um -i *n* bonum
profit *tr* prodesse *(w. dat)* ‖ *intr* **to — by** uti *(w. abl)*; **to — from** proficěre *(w. abl)*
profitable *adj* fructuos•us -a -um; *(fin)* quaestuos•us -a -um; **to be — for s.o.** prodesse alicui
profitably *adv* utiliter
profitless *adj* inutil•is -is -e
profligacy *s* nequiti•a -ae *f*
profligate *adj* nequam *(indecl)*
profligate *s* nep•os -otis *m*
profound *adj* alt•us -a -um; *(recondite)* abstrus•us -a -um
profoundly *adv* funditus
profundity *s* altitud•o -inis *f*
profuse *adj* profus•us -a -um
profusely *adv* profuse
profusion *s* profusi•o -onis *f*
progeny *s* progeni•es -ei *f*
prognosticate *tr* praedicěre
prognostication *s* praedicti•o -onis *f*
program *s* institut•um -i *n*, rati•o -onis *f; (booklet)* libell•us -i *m*
progress *s* progress•us -ūs *m;* **to make —** proficěre
progress *intr* progredi
progression *s* progress•us -ūs *m*
progressive *adj* profici•ens -entis
progressively *adv* gradatim
prohibit *tr* vetare
prohibition *s* interdicti•o -onis *f*
project *s* proposit•um -i *n*
project *tr* projicěre ‖ *intr* prominēre, exstare; *(of land)* excurrěre
projectile *s* missil•e -is *n*
projecting *adj* emin•ens -entis
projection *s* projectur•a -ae *f*
proletarian *adj* proletari•us -a -um
proletariat *s* pleb•s -is *f*
prolific *adj* fecund•us -a -um
prologue *s* prolog•us -i *m*
prolong *tr* producěre; *(term of office)* prorogare
prolongation *s* dilati•o -onis *f; (of term of office)* prorogati•o -onis *f*
promenade *s (walk)* ambulati•o -onis *f; (place)* ambulacr•um -i *n*
promenade *intr* spatiari
prominence *s* eminenti•a -ae *f*
prominent *adj* promin•ens -entis
promiscuous *adj* promiscu•us -a -um
promiscuously *adv* promiscue
promise *s* promiss•um -i *n;* **— of immunity** fid•es -ei *f* publica; **to break a —** fidem fallěre; **to keep a —** promissum tenēre; **to make a —** fidem dare; **to make many —s** multa promittěre
promise *tr* promittěre, polliceri; *(in marriage)* despondēre
promising *adj* bonā spe *(abl used adjectively)*; **less —** min•or -or -us opinione
promissory note *s* chirograph•um -i *n*
promontory *s* promontor•ium -(i)i *n*
promote *tr (in rank)* promovēre; *(a cause, etc.)* favēre *(w. dat)*; **to — to a higher rank** in ampliorem gradum promovēre
promoter *s* faut•or -oris *m*
promotion *s* amplior grad•us -ūs *m*
prompt *adj* prompt•us -a -um
prompt *tr* subjicěre, suggerěre; *(incite)* commovēre
promptly *adv* statim, extemplo
promulgate *tr* promulgare
promulgation *s* promulgati•o -onis *f*
prone *adj* **(to)** pron•us -a -um (ad *or* in + *acc)*
prong *s* den•s -tis *m*
pronominal *adj* pronominal•is -is -e
pronoun *s* pronom•en -inis *n*
pronounce *tr (to declare)* pronuntiare; *(a word, judicial sentence)* dicěre
pronunciation *s* pronuntiati•o -onis *f*
proof *s* document•um -i *n; (indication)* indic•ium -(i)i *n*
proof *adj* **— against** impervi•us -a -um *(w. dat)*
proofs *spl (from the press)* plagul•ae -arum *fpl;* **to correct —s** plagulas corrigěre
prop *s* fulcr•um -i *n*
prop *tr* fulcire; **to — oneself up on** se fulcire *(w. dat)*
propaganda *s* re•s -rum *fpl* ad animos hominum movendos
propagate *tr* propagare; *(information)* disseminare
propagation *s* propagati•o -onis *f;* disseminati•o -onis *f*
propel *tr* propellěre
propeller *s* propuls•or -oris *m*
propensity *s* propensi•o -onis *f*
proper *adj (becoming)* decor•us -a -um; *(suitable)* idone•us -a -um; **it is — for an orator to speak** decet oratorem loqui
properly *adv (in the strict sense)* proprie; *(fitly)* apte, commode
property *s* bon•a -orum *npl; (characteristic)* virt•us -utis *f*, propriet•as -atis *f;* **private —** res, rei *f* familiaris
prophecy *s* vaticinati•o -onis *f*
prophesy *tr* vaticinari

prophet *s* vat•es -is *mf; (Biblical)* prophet•a -ae *m*
prophetess *s* vat•es -is *f*
propitiate *tr* propitiare
propitiation *s* propitiati•o -onis *f*
propitious *adj* propiti•us -a -um
proportion *s* proporti•o -onis *f;* **in —** pro rata parte; **in — to** pro *(w. abl)*
proportionately *adv* pro portione
proposal *s* propositi•o -onis *f,* condici•o -onis *f;* **to accept a —** condicionem accipĕre; **to make a — that** condicionem ferre ut
propose *tr (esp. a law)* ferre; **to — a toast to** propinare *(w. dat)*
proposition *s (offer)* condici•o -onis *f; (logic)* propositi•o -onis *f*
propound *tr* proponĕre, exponĕre
proprietor *s* domin•us -i *m*
propriety *s* decor•um -i *n*
propulsion *s* propulsi•o -onis *f*
prosaic *adj* jejun•us -a -um
proscribe *tr* proscribĕre
proscription *s* proscripti•o -onis *f*
prose *s* pros•a -ae *f*
prosecute *tr (to carry out)* exsequi; *(leg)* litem intendĕre *(w. dat);* **to — offenses** delicta exsequi
prosecution *s* exsecuti•o -onis *f; (leg)* accusati•o -onis *f*
prosecutor *s* accusat•or -oris *m*
prospect *s* prospect•us -ūs *m; (hope)* spes, spei *f;* **his —s are good** is in bonā spe est
prospective *adj* futur•us -a -um
prosper *intr* vigēre
prosperity *s* re•s -rum *fpl* secundae
prosperous *adj* prosper•us -a -um
prosperously *adv* prospere
prostitute *s* meretr•ix -icis *f*
prostitute *tr* prostituĕre
prostrate *tr* sternĕre; **to — oneself at the feet of** se projicĕre ad pedes *(w. gen)*
prostrate *adj* prostrat•us -a -um; *(fig)* fract•us -a -um; **to fall —** se projicĕre
prostration *s (act)* prostrati•o -onis *f; (state)* anim•us -i *m* fractus
protect *tr* (pro)tegĕre
protection *s* praesid•ium -(i)i *n; (protecting power)* tutel•a -ae *f*
protective *adj* protegen•s -tis
protector *s* tut•or -oris *m*
protest *s* obtestati•o -onis *f*
protest *tr (to assert positively)* asseverare; *(to object to)* obtestari ‖ *intr* contra dicĕre; **to — against** contra dicĕre *(w. dat)*
prototype *s* exempl•ar -aris *n*
protract *tr* producĕre
protracted *adj* product•us -a -um
protrude *tr* protrudĕre ‖ *intr* prominēre, eminēre
protuberance *s* tub•er -eris *n; (small lump)* tubercul•um -i *n*

proud *adj* superb•us -a -um; **to be — of** superbire *(w. abl)*
proudly *adv* superbe
prove *tr* probare ‖ *intr (of persons)* se praebēre, se praestare; *(of a thing, event)* evadĕre, fieri, exire
proverb *s* proverb•ium -(i)i *n*
proverbial *adj* proverbial•is -is -e
provide *tr (to get ready)* parare; *(to furnish)* suppeditare; *(to equip)* ornare; **to — by law that** sancire ut ‖ *intr* **to — for** providēre *(w. dat); (of laws)* jubēre
provided *adj* instruct•us -a -um; **well —** refert•us -a -um
provided (that) *conj* dummodo *(w. subj)*
providence *s* providenti•a -ae *f*
provident *adj* provid•us -a -um
providential *adj* divin•us -a -um
providentially *adv* divinitus
provider *s* provis•or -oris *m*
province *s* provinci•a -ae *f*
provincial *adj* provincial•is -is -e; *(pej)* rustic•us -a -um
provision *s (stipulation)* condici•o -onis *f;* **—s** vict•us -ūs *m; (mil)* commeat•us -ūs *m;* **with the added —** exceptione adjectā
provisional *adj* temporari•us -a -um
provisionally *adv* ad tempus
proviso *s* condici•o -onis *f;* **with the — that** eā condicione ut
provocation *s* provocati•o -onis *f*
provoke *tr (to cause)* (com)movēre; *(to irritate)* irritare, movēre
provoking *adj* molest•us -a -um
prow *s* pror•a -ae *f*
prowess *s* vir•es -ium *fpl*
prowl *intr* vagari, grassari
prowler *s* praedat•or -oris *m*
proximity *s* propinquit•as -atis *f*
proxy *s* vicar•ius -(i)i *m*
prude *s* tetric•a -ae *f*
prudence *s* prudenti•a -ae *f*
prudent *adj* prud•ens -entis
prudently *adv* prudenter
prudish *adj* tetric•us -a -um
prune *s* prun•um -i *n* passum
prune *tr* (am)putare, resecare
pruning *s* putati•o -onis *f*
pruning shears *spl* fal•x -cis *f*
pry *intr* perscrutari; **to — into** investigare
prying *adj* curios•us -a -um
pseudonym *s* falsum nom•en -inis *n*
puberty *s* pubert•as -atis *f*
public *adj* public•us -a -um; *(known)* vulgat•us -a -um; **in a — capacity** publice; **— affairs** respublica *(gen:* reipublicae) *f*
public *s* public•um -i *n,* vulg•us -i *n;* **in —** propalam; *(outdoors)* foris; **to appear in —** prodire in publicum; **to open** *(e.g., a road)* **to the —** publicare
publican *s* publican•us -i *m*

publication *s* publicati•o -onis *f; (of a book)* editi•o -onis *f; (book)* li•ber -bri *m*
publicity *s* celebrit•as -atis *f*
publicly *adv* propalam
publish *tr* publicare, patefacĕre; *(book)* edĕre
publisher *s* edit•or -oris *m*
pucker *intr* **to — up the lips** osculari
puddle *s* lacun•a -ae *f*
puerile *adj* pueril•is -is -e
puff *s* flat•us -ūs *m*
puff *tr* inflare; **to be —ed up** tumēre ‖ *intr (to pant)* anhelare; **to — up** intumescĕre
puffy *adj* sufflat•us -a -um; *(swollen)* tum•ens -entis
pugilist *s* pug•il -ilis *m*
pugnacious *adj* pugn•ax -acis
pull *tr (to drag)* trahĕre, tractare; **to — apart** distrahĕre; **to — away** avellĕre; **to — down** detrahĕre; *(buildings)* demoliri, destruĕre; **to — out** extrahĕre; *(hair)* evellĕre; *(e.g., a weapon, tooth)* eximĕre; **to — out by the roots** exstirpare; *(weeds)* eruncare ‖ *intr* **to — at** vellicare; **to — through** pervincĕre; *(an illness)* convalescĕre
pull *s (act)* tract•us -ūs *m; (influence)* grati•a -ae *f*
pulley *s* trochle•a -ae *f*
pulmonary *adj* pulmone•us -a -um; *(disease)* pulmonari•us -a -um
pulp *s* pulp•a -ae *f*
pulpit *s (eccl)* cathedr•a -ae *f*
pulsate *intr* palpitare
pulse *s* puls•us -ūs (venarum) *m;* **to feel the —** venas temptare
pulverize *tr* pulverare, contundĕre
pumice *s* pum•ex -icis *m*
pump *s* antli•a -ae *f*
pump *tr* haurire; **to — out, — dry** exhaurire; **to — with questions** percontari
pumpkin *s* pep•o-onis *m*
pun *s* verborum lus•us -ūs *m*
punch *s (tool)* verucul•um -i *n; (blow)* pugn•us -i *m; (drink)* poti•o -onis *f* ex fructuum suco; **to give s.o. a —** pugnum alicui ducĕre
punch *tr* pugnum ducĕre *(w. dat);* **to — a hole in** pungĕre
punch-drunk *adj* stupefact•us -a -um
punching bag *s* coryc•us -i *m*
punctilious *adj* scrupulos•us -a -um
punctual *adj* **to be —** ad tempus venire
punctually *adv* ad tempus
punctuate *tr* interpungĕre
punctuation *s* interpuncti•o -onis *f*
punctuation mark *s* interpunct•um -i *n*
puncture *s* puncti•o -onis *f*
puncture *tr* pungĕre
pungent *adj* acut•us -a -um
Punic *adj* Punic•us -a -um
punish *tr* punire, animadvertĕre in *(w. acc),* supplicium sumĕre de *(w. abl);* **to — with loss of one half of one's property** multare dimidiā parte; **to — with loss of the priesthood and dowry** multare sacerdotio et uxoris dote
punishable *adj* puniend•us -a -um
punishment *s (act)* puniti•o -onis *f; (penalty)* poen•a -ae *f,* supplic•ium -(i)i *n;* **to inflict — on s.o.** aliquem poenā afficĕre; **without —** impune
puny *adj* pusill•us -a -um
pup *s* catul•us -i *m,* catell•a -ae *f;* **to have —s** catulos parĕre
pupil *s* discipul•us -i *m,* discipul•a -ae *f; (of the eye)* pupill•a -ae *f*
puppet *s* pup•a -ae *f*
puppy *s* catul•us -i *m,* catell•a -ae *f*
purchase *s (act)* empti•o -onis *f; (merchandise)* mer•x -cis *f*
purchase *tr* emĕre, comparare
purchase price *s* pret•ium -(i)i *n; (of grain)* annon•a -ae *f*
purchaser *s* empt•or -oris *m*
pure *adj* pur•us -a -um; *(unmixed)* mer•us -a -um; *(morally)* cast•us -a -um
purely *adv* pure; *(quite)* omnino; *(solely)* solum
purge *tr* purgare, mundare
purge *s* purgati•o -onis *f; (pol)* proscripti•o -onis *f*
purification *s* purificati•o -onis *f*
purify *tr* purificare; *(fig)* expiare
purity *s* purit•as -atis *f; (moral)* castit•as -atis *f*
purple *s* purpur•a -ae *f;* **dressed in —** purpurat•us -a -um
purple *adj* purpure•us -a -um
purport *s* sigificati•o -onis *f,* sententi•a -ae *f;* **a communication to the same —** tabell•ae -arum *fpl* in eandem fere sententiam
purport *tr* significare
purpose *s (aim, end)* proposit•um -i *n,* fin•is -is *m; (wish)* men•s -tis *f;* **on —** consulto; **to no —** frustra, nequaquam; **to what —** quorsum
purpose *tr* in animo habēre
purposely *adv* consulto, de industriā
purr *s* murm•ur -uris *n*
purr *intr* murmurare
purring *s* murmurati•o -onis *f*
purse *s* marsup•ium -(i)i *n*
purse *tr (to pucker up)* astringĕre
pursuance *s* exsecuti•o -onis *f;* **in — of** secundum *(w. acc),* ex *(w. abl)*
pursuant to *prep* secundum *(w. acc)*
pursue *tr (an enemy)* insequi; *(a course, plan)* insistĕre *(w. acc or dat);* **I will not — this subject further** quod non prosequar longius; **to — one's studies** studiis insistĕre; **to — an advantage** utilitatem sequi; **to — wealth and power** opes et potentiam consectari

pursuit *s* insectati•o -onis *f; (striving after)* consectati•o -onis *f; (eager desire for and aiming at; occupation)* stud•ium -(i)i *n*
pus *s* pu•s -ris *n*
push *tr* truděre, impellěre; **to — away** *or* **back** repellěre ‖ *intr* **to — on** contenděre, iter facěre
push *s* puls•us -ūs *m; (strong effort)* nis•us -ūs *m; (mil)* impet•us -ūs *m*
pushy *adj* aud•ax -acis, molest•us -a -um
put *tr* poněre, collocare; **to — an end to** finem facěre *(w. dat)*; **to — aside** poněre; **to — away** seponěre, abděre; *(in safety)* reconděre; **to — back** reponěre; **to — down** deponěre; *(to suppress)* supponěre, sedare; *(in writing)* scriběre; **to — his hand to his mouth** manum ad os apponěre; **to — in** inserěre; **to — in order** ordinare; **to — off** *(to postpone)* differre; **to — on** imponěre *(w. dat)*; *(to add)* adděre; *(clothes)* se induěre *(w. abl)*; *(a ring)* (anulum) digito aptare; *(a cap)* (pilleum) capiti suo imponěre; *(a sword)* cingěre latus (gladio); **to — on the table** poněre super mensam; **to — out** *(the hand)* proferre; *(to remove, e.g., from office)* submovēre; *(a fire)* exstinguěre; **to — out of one's mind** ex animo delēre; **to — out of the way** demovēre; *(to murder)* de medio tollěre; **to — together** componěre, conferre; **to — up** *(to erect)* statuěre; *(to raise, e.g., hands)* erigěre; **to — up for sale** venum dare; ‖ *intr* **to — in** *(of ships)* appellěre; **to — in to port** portum petěre; **to — out to sea** solvěre; **to — up with** tolerare
putrefy *intr* putrescěre
putrid *adj* putrid•us -a -um
putty *s* glut•en -inis *n* vitrariorum
puzzle *s* aenigm•a -atis *n*
puzzle *tr* confunděre
puzzled *adj* confus•us -a -um
puzzling *adj* perplex•us -a -um
pygmy *s* pygmae•us -i *m*
pylon *s* colum•en -inis *n*
pyramid *s* pyram•is -idis *f*
pyre *s* rog•us -i *m*
Pythagorean *adj* Pythagorae•us -a -um
Pythian *adj* Pythi•us -a -um

Q

quack *s (phoney)* circulat•or -oris *m; (bad physician)* pharmacopol•a -ae *m; (of a duck)* tetrissitat•us -ūs *m*
quack *intr* tetrissitare
quadrangle *s* are•a -ae *f*
quadruped *s* quadrup•es -edis *mf*
quadruple *tr* quadruplicare
quaestor *s* quaest•or -oris *m*
quaestorship *s* quaestur•a -ae *f;* **to hold the —** quaesturam gerěre
quaff *tr* ducěre, haurire
quagmire *s* pal•us -udis *f*
quail *s* coturn•ix -icis *f*
quaint *adj* insolit•us -a -um
quake *intr* treměre
qualification *s (endowment)* indol•es -is *f; (limitation)* excepti•o -onis *f*
qualified *adj (competent)* perit•us -a -um; *(limited)* modic•us -a -um; **— for** apt•us -a -um ad *(w. acc)*, habil•is -is -e ad *(w. acc)*
qualify *tr* aptum *or* idoneum redděre; *(to limit)* temperare
quality *s* qualit•as -atis *f; (excellence)* virt•us -utis *f*
qualm *s* fastid•ium -(i)i *n;* **— of conscience** scrupul•us -i *m*
quantity *s* numer•us -i *m,* quantit•as -atis *f;* **a large —** frequenti•a -ae *f*
quarrel *s* jurg•ium -(i)i *n*
quarrel *intr* jurgare, altercari
quarrelsome *adj* jurgios•us -a -um
quarry *s* lapicidin•ae -arum *fpl; (prey)* praed•a -ae *f*
quart *s* duo sextari•i -orum *mpl*
quarter *s (fourth part)* quarta par•s -tis *f,* quadran•s -tis *m; (side, direction)* par•s -tis *f; (district)* regi•o -onis *f;* **at close —s** comminus *(adv)*; **—s** *(dwelling)* tect•um -i *n; (temporary abode)* hospit•ium -(i)i *n;* **neither giving nor asking for —** sine missione
quarter *tr* in quattuor partes dividěre; *(to give lodgings to)* hospitium praebēre *(w. dat)*
quarterly *adj* trimestr•is -is -e
quarterly *adv* tertio quoque mense
quartermaster *s* castrorum praefect•us -i *m*
quash *tr (rebellion)* oppriměre; *(a law)* rescinděre
quatrain *s* tetrastich•on -i *n*
quavering *adj* tremul•us -a -um
queasy *adj* nauseabund•us -a -um; **to feel —** nauseare
queen *s* regin•a -ae *f*
queen bee *s* re•x -gis *m* apium
queer *adj* insolit•us -a -um; *(strange)* inept•us -a -um
quell *tr* sedare
quench *tr* exstinguěre; **to — a thirst** sitim sedare
querulous *adj* querul•us -a -um
query *s* quaesti•o -onis *f*
query *tr & intr* quaerěre
quest *s* inquisiti•o -onis *f;* **to be in — of** requirěre; **to go in — of** investigare
question *s* quaesti•o -onis *f,* interrogati•o -onis *f;* **I ask you this —** hoc te rogo; **there is no — that** non dubium est quin; **to ask a —** interrogare, quaerere; **to ask many —s** multa interrogare; **to answer**

a — ad rogatum respondēre; **to call into —** in dubium vocare; **to keep asking —s** rogitare; **without —** sine dubio
question *tr* interrogare, percontari; *(to doubt)* dubitare, in dubium vocare; *(to examine)* scrutari
questionable *adj* dubi•us -a -um
questioning *s* interrogati•o -onis *f*
questor *s* quaest•or -oris *m*
questorship *s* quaestur•a -ae *f;* **to hold the —** quaesturam gerĕre
quibble *s* capti•o -onis *f*
quibble *intr* cavillari
quibbler *s* cavillat•or -oris *m*
quibbling *s* cavillati•o -onis *f*
quick *adj* cel•er -eris -ere; *(agile)* agil•is -is -e; *(mentally)* astut•us -a -um; *(w. hands)* facil•is -is -e; *(w. wits)* argut•us -a -um
quicken *tr* accelerare
quickly *adv* cito
quickness *s* celerit•as -atis *f; (of mind)* acum•en -inis *n; (agility)* agilit•as -atis *f*
quicksand *s* syrt•is -is *f*
quicksilver *s* argent•um -i *n* vivum
quiet *adj* quiet•us -a -um; *(silent)* tacit•us -a -um; **to keep —** quiescĕre; *(to refrain from talking)* silēre
quiet *s* qui•es -etis *f; (leisure)* ot•ium -(i)i *n; (silence)* silent•ium -(i)i *n*
quiet *tr* tranquillare, sedare
quill *s* penn•a -ae *f*
quilt *s* culcit•a -ae *f*
quince *s* cydon•ium -(i)i *n*
quintessence *s* medull•a -ae *f*
quip *s* faceti•ae -arum *fpl*
quip *tr & intr* per jocum dicĕre
quirk *s* propr•ium -(i)i *n*
quit *tr (to leave)* relinquĕre; *(to stop)* cessare, desinĕre; **— laughing!** noli *(pl:* nolite) ridēre!
quite *adv* omnino, admodum; **not —** parum; *(not yet)* nondum
quiver *s* pharetr•a -ae *f;* **wearing a —** pharetrat•us -a -um
quiver *intr* tremĕre
quivering *s* trem•or -oris *m*
Quixotic *adj* ridicul•us -a -um
quoit *s* disc•us -i *m;* **to play —s** disco ludĕre
quota *s* rata par•s -tis *f*
quotation *s (act)* prolati•o -onis *f; (words quoted)* loc•us -i *m* allatus
quote *tr* ponĕre

R

rabbi *s* rabbi *indecl m*
rabbit *s* cunicul•us -i *m*
rabble *s* turb•a -ae *f*
rabid *adj* rabid•us -a -um
race *s (lineage)* gen•us -eris *n; (foot race)* certam•en -inis *n* cursūs; *(horse race)* curs•us -ūs *m* equorum; *(of chariots)* curricul•um -i *n*
race *intr* certare; *(running)* pedibus certare; *(on horseback)* cursu equestri certare
racecourse *s* stad•ium -(i)i *n*
racehorse *s* cel•es -etis *m*
racer *s* curs•or -oris *m*
racetrack *s* curricul•um -i *n*
rack *s (shelf)* plute•us -i *m; (for punishment)* equule•us -i *m;* **to put to the —** equuleo torquēre
rack *tr* **to be —ed with pain** dolore distineri; **to — one's brain about s.th.** aliquā re scrutandā fatigari
racket *s (noise)* strepit•us -ūs *m; (for tennis)* reticul•um -i *n*
racketeer *s* circulat•or -oris *m*
radiance *s* fulg•or -oris *m*
radiant *adj* fulgid•us -a -um
radiate *tr* emittĕre ‖ *intr* radiare
radiation *s* radiati•o -onis *f*
radical *adj* innat•us -a -um; *(thorough)* tot•us - a -um
radical *s* rerum novarum cupid•us -i *m*
radically *adv* penitus
radish *s* radicul•a -ae *f*
radius *s* rad•ius -(i)i *m*
raffle *s* ale•a -ae *f*
raffle *tr* **to — off** aleā vendĕre
raft *s* rat•is -is *f*
rafter *s* trab•s -is *f*
rag *s* pannicul•us -i *m*
rage *s* fur•or -oris *m*
rage *intr* furĕre, saevire
ragged *adj* pannos•us -a -um
ragman *s* centonar•ius -(i)i *m*
raid *s* incursi•o -onis *f*
raid *tr* praedari
raider *s* praedat•or -oris *m*
rail *s* longur•ius -(i)i *m*
rail *tr* **to — off** consaepire ‖ *intr* **to — at** insectari
railing *s (fence)* saepiment•um -i *n; (abuse)* convic•ium -(i)i *n*
railroad *s* ferrata vi•a -ae *f*
railroad car *s* viae ferratae curr•us -ūs *m*
railroad station *s* viae ferratae stati•o -onis *f*
raiment *s* vestit•us -ūs *m*
rain *s* pluvi•a -ae *f,* imb•er -ris *m*
rain *intr* pluĕre; **it is —ing** pluit
rainbow *s* pluvius arc•us -ūs *m*
rain cloud *s* imb•er -ris *m*
rainy *adj* pluvi•us -a -um
raise *tr* tollĕre; *(finger, ladder, eyes)* erigĕre; *(to build)* exstruĕre; *(money)* expedire; *(an army)* (con)scribĕre, comparare; *(siege)* solvĕre; *(children)* educare; *(to stir up)* excitare; *(to promote)* provehĕre; *(price)* augēre; *(crops)* colĕre; *(beard)* demittĕre; **to — the cur-**

tain aulaea preměre; **to — the head (eyes)** caput (oculos) attollěre
raisin *s* (uva) pass•a -ae *f*
rake *s* rastell•us -i *m; (person)* nep•os -otis *m*
rake *tr* raděre; **to — up** corraděre
rally *s* conti•o -onis *f*
rally *tr (mil)* in ordines revocare ‖ *intr* se colligěre; *(after a retreat)* se ex fuga colligěre; *(from sickness)* convalescěre
ram *s* ari•es -etis *m*
ram *tr* fistucare; *(to cram)* infercire
ramble *s* vagati•o -onis *f*
ramble *intr* vagari, errare; **to — on** *(in speech)* garrire
rambling *adj* erran•s -tis; *(fig)* vag•us -a -um
ramification *s* ramificati•o -onis *f*
ramp *s* agg•er -eris *m*
rampage *s* **to go on a —** ferocire
rampage *intr* furěre
rampant *adj* effrenat•us -a -um; *(widespread)* divulgat•us -a -um
rampart *s* vall•um -i *n*
ranch *s* latifund•ium -(i)i *n*
rancher *s* pecuar•ius -(i)i *m*
rancid *adj* rancid•us -a -um
rancor *s* iracundi•a -ae *f*
random *adj* fortuit•us -a -um; **at —** temere
range *s (row)* ord•o -inis *m; (of mountain)* jug•um -i *n; (reach)* jact•us -ūs *m; (extent)* fin•es -ium *mpl;* **to be in —** esse intra teli jactum; **to be out of —** extra teli jactum abesse; **the enemy were just within —** non longius hostes aberant quam quo telum adjici posset
range *tr* ordinare, disponěre ‖ *intr (to rove at large)* pervagari; *(to vary)* discrepare
rank *s* ord•o -inis *m,* grad•us -ūs *m; (high rank)* dignit•as -atis *f;* **in close —** *(mil)* firmis ordinibus; **the — and file** *(i.e., ordinary soldiers)* manipular•es -ium *mpl*
rank *tr* in numero habēre ‖ *intr* in numero haberi; **to — first** primum locum obtiněre
rank *adj* luxurios•us -a -um; *(extreme)* summ•us -a -um; *(of smell)* fo͡etid•us -a -um
rankle *intr (fig)* suppurare
ransack *tr* diripěre; *(to search thoroughly)* exquirěre
ransom *s (act)* redempti•o -onis *f; (money)* pret•ium -(i)i *n*
ransom *tr* rediměre
rant *intr* ampullari; **to — and rave** debacchari
rap *s (slap)* alap•a -ae *f; (blow)* ict•us -ūs *m; (at door)* pulsati•o -onis *f; (w. knuckles)* talitr•um -i *n;* **not to give a —** non flocci facěre
rap *tr (to criticize)* exagitare ‖ *intr* **to — at** pulsare
rapacious *adj* rap•ax -acis
rape *s* stupr•um -i *n* per vim
rape *tr* per vim stuprare
rapid *adj* rapid•us -a -um
rapidity *s* rapidit•as -atis *f*
rapidly *adv* rapide
rapine *s* rapin•a -ae *f*
rapist *s* constuprat•or -oris *m*
rapture *s* exsultati•o -onis *f;* **to be in —s of delight** gaudio efferi
rapturous *adj* exsult•ans -antis
rare *adj* rar•us -a -um; *(meat)* semicoct•us -a -um
rarefy *tr* rarefacěre
rarely *adv* raro
rarity *s* rarit•as -atis *f,* paucit•as -atis *f; (thing)* res, rei *f* rara
rascal *s* scelest•us -i *m*
rascally *adj* scelest•us -a -um
rash *adj* temerari•us -a -um
rash *s* erupti•o -onis *f* pustulae
rashly *adv* temere
rashness *s* temerit•as -atis *f*
raspberry *s* mor•um -i *n* Idaeum
raspberry bush *s* mor•a -ae *f* Idaea
rat *s* mu•s -ris *m; (person)* transfug•a -ae *m;* **like drowned —s** tamquam mures udi
rate *s* proporti•o -onis *f; (price)* pret•ium -(i)i *n; (scale)* norm•a -ae *f;* **at any —** utique; **— of exchange** collyb•us -i *m;* **— of interest** faen•us -oris *n*
rate *tr* aestimare, taxare; **to — s.o. highly** aliquem magni facěre
rather *adv* potius, prius; *(somewhat)* aliquantum, paulo, *or render by comparative of adjective or adverb*
ratification *s* sancti•o -onis *f*
ratify *tr* sancire, comprobare
rating *s* aestimati•o -onis *f*
ratio *s* proporti•o -onis *f*
ration *s (portion)* demens•um -i *n;* **—s** *(mil)* cibari•a -orum *npl*
ration *tr* demetiri
rational *adj* ratione praedit•us -a -um
rationalize *intr* ratiocinari
rationally *adv* ratione, sapienter
rattle *s* crepit•us -ūs *m; (toy)* crepitacul•um -i *n*
rattle *tr* crepitare *(w. abl)* ‖ *intr* crepare, crepitare; **to — on** garrire
raucous *adj* rauc•us -a -um
ravage *tr* vastare, populari
ravages *spl* vastati•o -onis *f*
rave *intr* furěre, saevire
ravel *tr* involvěre
raven *s* corv•us -i *m,* corn•ix -icis *f*
ravenous *adj* vor•ax -acis
ravenously *adv* voraciter
ravine *s* fauc•es -ium *fpl*
raving *adj* furios•us -a -um; **to be — mad** plane furěre
ravish *tr* stuprare
raw *adj* crud•us -a -um; *(weather)* asp•er -era -erum; *(jokes)* incondit•us -a -um
rawboned *adj* strigos•us -a -um

ray *s* rad•ius -(i)i *m*
raze *tr* solo aequare
razor *s* novacul•a -ae *f*
reach *s* *(grasp, capacity)* capt•us -ūs *m; (of weapon)* jact•us -ūs *m;* **out of my —** extra ictum meum
reach *tr (e.g., a high branch)* contingĕre, attingĕre; *(of space)* pertinēre ad *(w. acc),* extendi ad *(w. acc); (to come up to)* assequi; *(to arrive at)* pervenire ad *or* in *(w. acc); (to hand)* porrigĕre; *(to attain to, e.g., old age)* adipisci
react *intr* affici; **to — to** referre
reaction *s* affect•us -ūs *m*
reactionary *s* qui pristinum rerum statum revocare vult
read *tr & intr* legĕre; **to — aloud** recitare; **to — over** translegĕre; **to — through** perlegĕre; **to — well** commode legĕre
readable *adj* lectu facil•is -is -e
reader *s* lect•or -oris *m*
readily *adv (willingly)* libenter; *(easily)* facile
readiness *s* facilit•as -atis *f;* **in —** in promptu
ready *adj* **(for)** parat•us -a -um, prompt•us -a -um (ad + *acc)*
real *adj* ver•us -a -um
real estate *s* re•s -rum *fpl* soli *(opp:* re•s -rum *fpl* mobiles); **piece of —** praed•ium -(i)i *n*
real estate broker *s* praediat•or -oris *m*
realistic *adj* verisimil•is -is -e
reality *s* res, rei *f,* verit•as -atis *f;* **in —** re verā
realization *s (e.g., of plans)* effect•us -ūs *m; (of ideas)* comprehensi•o -onis *f*
realize *tr* sentire; *(to effect)* efficĕre, ad exitum perducĕre; **to — great profits from** magnas pecunias facĕre ex *(w. abl)*
really *adv* vero, profecto, re verā; *(surely)* sane, certe
realm *s* regn•um -i *n*
reap *tr* metĕre; *(fig)* percipĕre; **to — the reward for** fructum percipĕre ex *(w. abl)*
reaper *s* mess•or -oris *m*
reappear *intr* redire, revenire; *(from below)* resurgĕre
rear *tr* educare ‖ *intr (of horses)* arrectum se tollĕre
rear *s* terg•um -i *n; (mil)* novissimum agm•en -inis *n;* **on the —** a tergo; **to bring up the —** agmen cogĕre
rearing *s* educati•o -onis *f*
reascend *tr & intr* denuo ascendĕre
reason *s (faculty; reasonable ground)* rati•o -onis *f; (cause)* caus•a -ae *f; (moderation)* mod•us -i *m;* **for good —s** justis de causis; **for that —** ideo, idcirco; **for this —** hāc de causā, itaque, quamobrem; **for —s of poor health** valetudinis causā; **there is no — why** nihil causae est, cur; **to give a — why** adferre rationem, quamobrem; **what is the — why** quid est, cur; **with —** cum causā
reasonable *adj (fair)* aequ•us -a -um; *(moderate)* modic•us -a -um; *(judicious)* prud•ens -entis
reasonably *adv* ratione, juste; modice
reasoning *s* ratiocinati•o -onis *f; (discussing)* disceptati•o -onis *f*
reassemble *tr* recolligĕre, cogĕre
reassert *tr* iterare
reassure *tr* confirmare, redintegrare
rebate *s* deminuti•o -onis *f*
rebel *s* rebell•is -is *m*
rebel *intr* rebellare, desciscĕre
rebellion *s* rebelli•o -onis *f*
rebellious *adj* rebell•is -is -e; *(disobedient)* contum•ax -acis
rebirth *s* novus ort•us -ūs *m*
rebound *s* result•us -ūs *m*
rebound *intr* resultare, resilire
rebuff *s* repuls•a -ae *f*
rebuff *tr* repellĕre, rejicĕre
rebuild *tr* reficĕre
rebuke *s* reprehensi•o -onis *f*
rebuke *tr* reprehendĕre, vituperare
rebuttal *s* refutati•o -onis *f*
recall *s* revocati•o -onis *f*
recall *tr* revocare; **to — to mind** in memoriam redigĕre
recant *tr* recantare, retractare
recapitulate *tr* summatim colligĕre
recapitulation *s* repetiti•o -onis *f*
recapture *s* recuperati•o -onis *f*
recapture *tr* recuperare
recede *intr* recedĕre
receipt *s (act)* accepti•o -onis *f; (document)* apoch•a -ae *f;* **—s and expeditures** accept•a -orum *npl* et dat•a -orum *npl*
receive *tr* accipĕre
receiver *s* recept•or -oris *m*
recent *adj* rec•ens -entis
recently *adv* nuper
receptacle *s* receptacul•um -i *n*
reception *s (act)* accepti•o -onis *f; (social event)* hospit•ium -(i)i *n*
receptive *adj* docil•is -is -e; **to be — to treatment** recipĕre curationem
recess *s (place)* recess•us -ūs *m; (in a wall)* adyt•um *-n; (intermission)* intermissi•o -onis *f; (vacation)* feri•ae -arum *fpl; (leg)* justit•ium -(i)i *n*
recipe *s* praescript•um -i *n*
recipient *s* accept•or -oris *m*
reciprocal *adj* mutu•us -a -um
reciprocally *adv* mutuo, invicem
reciprocate *tr* reddĕre ‖ *intr* reciprocare
reciprocity *s* reciprocati•o -onis *f*
recital *s* recitati•o -onis *f*
recitation *s* recitati•o -onis *f*
reckless *adj* temerari•us -a -um
recklessly *adv* temere

reckon *tr* aestimare ‖ *intr* **to — on** confidĕre *(w. dat)*
reckoning *s* numerati•o -onis *f; (account to be given)* rati•o -onis *f;* **— of time** ratio *f* temporis
reclaim *tr* reposcĕre, repetĕre
recline *intr* recubare; *(at table)* accumbĕre, recumbĕre; *(said of several guests)* discumbĕre
recluse *s* solitarius hom•o -inis *m*
recognition *s* agniti•o -onis *f*
recognizance *s* vadimon•ium -(i)i *n*
recognize *tr* agnoscĕre; *(to acknowledge)* noscĕre; *(to admit)* accipĕre
recoil *intr* resilire; *(in horror)* **(from)** refugĕre (ab + *acc)*
recoil *s* recessi•o -onis *f*
recollect *tr* recordari
recollection *s* recordati•o -onis *f*
recommence *tr* redintegrare ‖ *intr* redire
recommend *tr* commendare
recommendation *s* commendati•o -onis *f;* **letter of —** litter•ae -arum *fpl* commendaticiae
recompense *s* remunerati•o -onis *f*
recompense *tr* remunerare; *(to indemnify)* compensare
reconcilable *adj* placabil•is -is -e; *(of things)* conveni•ens -entis
reconcile *tr* reconciliare, componĕre; **to be —ed** in gratiam restitui
reconciliation *s* reconciliati•o -onis *f*
reconnoiter *tr* perspeculari
reconquer *tr* revincĕre
reconsider *tr* retractare
reconstruct *tr* restituĕre, renovare
reconstruction *s* renovati•o -onis *f*
record *s* monument•um -i *n; (top performance)* palm•a -ae *f;* **—s** act•a -orum *npl,* annal•es -ium *mpl; (in bookkeeping)* tabul•ae -arum *fpl*
record *tr* referre (in tabulas)
recorder *s* procurat•or -oris *m* ab actis
recount *tr* enarrare
recoup *tr* recuperare
recourse *s* refug•ium -(i)i *n;* **to have — to** fugĕre ad; *(to resort to)* descendĕre ad
recover *tr* recuperare ‖ *intr (from an illness)* convalescĕre; *(to come to one's senses)* ad se redire
recoverable *adj* reparabil•is -is -e; *(of persons)* sanabil•is -is -e
recovery *s* recuperati•o -onis *f; (from illness)* recreati•o -onis *f*
recreate *tr* recreare
recreation *s* oblectati•o -onis *f*
recriminate *tr* invicem accusare
recrimination *s* mutua accusati•o -onis *f*
recruit *s* tir•o -onis *m*
recruit *tr (mil)* conscribĕre; *(one's strength)* reficĕre
recuiting *s* delect•us -ūs *m*
recruiting officer *s* conquisit•or -oris *m*
rectify *tr* corrigĕre, emendare
rectitude *s* probit•as -atis *f*
rector *s* rect•or -oris *m*
recumbent *adj* resupin•us -a -um
recur *intr* redire
recurrence *s* redit•us -ūs *m*
recurrent *adj* assidu•us -a -um
red *adj* ru•ber -bra -brum; *(ruddy)* rubicund•us -a -um; **to be —** rubēre; **to grow —** rubescĕre
redden *tr* rubefacĕre, rutilare ‖ *intr* rubescĕre; *(to blush)* erubescĕre
reddish *adj* subru•ber -bra -brum; *(hair)* subruf•us -a -um
redeem *tr* redimĕre
redeemer *s* liberat•or -oris *m; (eccl)* Redempt•or -oris *m*
redemption *s* redempti•o -onis *f*
redhead *s* ruf•us -i *m,* ruf•a -ae *f*
red-hot *adj* cand•ens -entis
redness *s* rub•or -oris *m*
redolent *adj* redol•ens -entis
redouble *tr* ingeminare
redoubt *s* propugnacul•um -i *n*
redound *intr* redundare
redress *s* satisfacti•o -onis *f;* **to demand —** res repetĕre
redress *tr* restituĕre
reduce *tr* minuĕre; *(to a condition)* redigĕre; *(mil)* expugnare
reduction *s* deminuti•o -onis *f; (mil)* expugnati•o -onis *f*
redundancy *s* redundanti•a -ae *f*
redundant *adj* supervacu•us -a -um
reed *s* harund•o -inis *f*
reef *s* scopul•us -i *m*
reek *intr* fumare; **to — of** olēre
reel *s* fus•us -i *m*
reel *intr (to stagger)* titubare
reestablish *tr* restituĕre
reestablishment *s* restituti•o -onis *f*
refer *tr* referre, remittĕre ‖ *intr* **to — to** attingĕre, alludĕre
referee *s* arbi•ter -tri *m*
reference *s* rati•o -onis *f; (place in a book)* loc•us -i *m; (as to character)* commendati•o -onis *f;* **in — to s.th.** ex relatione ad aliquid; **with — to our annals** ad nostrorum annalium rationem
refine *tr* expolire; *(metals)* excoquĕre; *(manners)* excolĕre
refinement *s (of liquids)* purgati•o -onis *f; (fig)* humanit•as -atis *f*
reflect *tr* repercutĕre ‖ *intr* **to — on** considerare, reputare
reflection *s* repercussi•o -onis *f; (thing reflected)* imag•o -inis *f; (thinking over)* considerati•o -onis *f;* **without —** inconsulte
reflective *adj* cogitabund•us -a -um
reflexive *adj* reciproc•us -a -um
reform *tr* reficĕre; *(to amend)* corrigĕre ‖ *intr* se corrigĕre

reform *s* correcti•o -onis *f*
reformation *s* correcti•o -onis *f*
Reformation *s* Reformati•o -onis *f*
reformer *s* correct•or -oris *m*
refract *tr* refringĕre
refraction *s* refracti•o -onis *f*
refractory *adj* contum•ax -acis
refrain *s* vers•us -ūs *m* intercularis
refrain *intr* **to — from** abstinēre ab *(w. abl)*; **I — from speaking** abstineo quin dicam; **he will not — from boasting** non temperabit quin jactet
refresh *tr* recreare, reficĕre; *(the memory)* redintegrare
refreshing *adj* jucund•us -a -um
refreshment *s (food)* cib•us -i *m; (drink)* pot•us -ūs *m*
refuge *s* refug•ium -(i)i *n;* **to take — with** confugĕre in *(w. acc)*
refugee *s* profug•us -i *m,* ex(s)•ul -ulis *mf*
refulgent *adj* fulgid•us -a -um
refund *tr* restituĕre
refund *s* pecuni•a -ae *f* restituta
refusal *s* recusati•o -onis *f*
refuse *tr* recusare, negare
refutation *s* refutati•o -onis *f*
refute *tr* refutare, redarguĕre
regain *tr* recuperare
regal *adj* regal•is -is -e
regally *adv* regaliter
regard *s* rati•o -onis *f; (concern)* cur•a -ae *f; (esteem)* grati•a -ae *f;* **give my —s to your brother!** fratrem tuum jube salvēre! **to have — for** rationem *(w. gen)* habēre; **to send best — to** salutem plurimam ascribĕre *(w. dat)*
regard *tr (to look at)* respicĕre, intueri; *(to concern)* spectare ad *(w. acc); (to esteem)* aestimare; *(to consider)* habēre; **to — his word as law** pro legibus habēre quae dicat
regarding *prep* de *(w. abl)*
regardless *adj* **— of** neglegen•s -tis *(w. acc);* **— of order of preference** omisso ordine
regency *s* interregn•um -i *n*
regenerate *tr* regenerare
regeneration *s* regenerati•o -onis *f*
regent *s* inter•rex -regis *m*
regicide *s (murderer)* regis occis•or -oris *m; (deed)* caed•es -is *f* regis
regime *s* administrati•o -onis *f*
regimen *s* vict•us -ūs *m*
region *s* regi•o -onis *f;* **in the — of** circa *(w. acc)*
register *s (list)* tabul•ae -arum *fpl*
register *tr* perscribĕre, in tabulas referre; *(emotions)* ostendĕre ‖ *intr* nomen dare
registrar *s* tabular•ius -(i)i *m*
registration *s* in tabulas relati•o -onis *f,* perscripti•o -onis *f*
registry *s* tabular•ium -(i)i *n*
regret *s* paenitenti•a -ae *f*
regret *tr* **I —** me paenitet *(w. gen)*
regretful *adj* paenit•ens -entis
regular *adj (common)* usitat•us -a -um; *(proper)* just•us -a -um; *(consistent)* const•ans -antis; *(arranged, coming in order)* ordinari•us -a -um
regularity *s (orderly arrangement)* ord•o -inis *m; (evenness, unbroken succession)* constanti•a -ae *f*
regularly *adv* ordine, constanter
regulate *tr* ordinare, disponĕre; *(to control)* moderari
regulation *s (act)* ordinati•o -onis *f; (rule)* praecept•um -i *n,* juss•um -i *n*
rehabilitate *tr* restituĕre
rehearsal *s* meditati•o -onis *f*
rehearse *tr* meditari
reign *s* regn•um -i *n*
reign *intr* regnare; **to — over** regnare in *(w. abl),* dominari *(w. dat)*
reimburse *tr* rependĕre
reimbursement *s* pecuniae restituti•o -onis *f*
rein *s* haben•a -ae *f;* **to give full — to** habenas immittĕre *(w. dat);* **to loosen the —s** frenos dare; **to tighten the —s** habenas adducĕre
reindeer *s* ren•o -onis *f*
reinforce *tr* firmare, supplēre
reinforcement *s* subsid•ium -(i)i *n;* **—s** *(mil)* supplement•um -i *n; (fresh troops)* novae copi•ae -arum *fpl*
reinstate *tr* restituĕre
reinstatement *s* restituti•o -onis *f*
reinvest *tr* iterum locare
reiterate *tr* iterare
reiteration *s* iterati•o -onis *f*
reject *tr* rejicĕre
rejection *s* rejecti•o -onis *f*
rejoice *intr* gaudēre
rejoin *tr* redire ad *(w. acc)* ‖ *intr* respondēre
rejoinder *s* respons•um -i *n*
rekindle *tr* resuscitare
relapse *s* **to have a —** recidĕre
relapse *intr* recidĕre
relate *tr* referre, narrare ‖ *intr* **to — to** pertinēre ad
related *adj* propinqu•us -a -um; *(by birth)* **(to)** cognat•us -a -um *(w. dat); (by marriage)* **(to)** affin•is -is -e *(w. dat)*
relation *s* narrati•o -onis *f; (reference)* rati•o -onis *f; (relative)* cognat•us -i *m,* cognat•a -ae *f; (relationship)* cognati•o -onis *f*
relationship *s (by blood)* consanguinit•as -atis *f,* cognati•o -onis *f; (by marriage; connection)* affinit•as -atis *f*
relative *adj* cum ceteris comparat•us -a -um; *(gram)* relativ•us -a -um; **— to** de *(w. abl)*
relative *s* cognat•us -i *m,* cognat•a -ae *f*
relatively *adv* comparate; **not absolutely but —** non simpliciter sed comparatione

relax *tr* remittĕre, relaxare ‖ *intr* se remittĕre
relaxation *s* relaxati•o -onis *f*
relaxing *adj* remissiv•us -a -um
release *s* liberati•o -onis *f*
release *tr* solvĕre; *(a prisoner)* liberare
relegate *tr* relegare
relent *intr* mitescĕre
relentless *adj* inexorabil•is -is -e
relentlessly *adv* sine missione
relevant *adj* **to be —** ad rem attinēre
reliable *adj* cert•us -a -um; *(person)* fid•us -a -um
reliance *s* fiduci•a -ae *f*
reliant *adj* **(on)** fret•us -a -um *(w. abl)*
relic *s* reliqui•ae -arum *fpl*
relief *s (alleviation)* levati•o -onis *f; (comfort)* lenim•en -inis *n; (help)* auxil•ium -(i)i *n; (in sculpture)* toreum•a -atis *n; (of sentries)* mutati•o -onis *f*
relieve *tr* levare, mitigare; *(to aid)* succurrĕre *(w. dat); (a guard)* succedĕre *(w. dat),* excipĕre; **to — oneself** vesicam exonerare; *(coll)* facĕre
religion *s* religi•o -onis *f;* **regard for —** religi•o -onis *f*
religious *adj* religios•us -a -um; **— ceremonies, — rites** religion•es -um *fpl*
relinquish *tr* relinquĕre; *(office)* se abdicare ab *(w. abl)*
relish *s (flavor)* sap•or -oris *m; (enthusiasm)* stud•ium -(i)i *n; (seasoning)* condiment•um -i *n*
relish *tr* gustare, non male appetĕre
reluctance *s* aversati•o -onis *f;* **with —** invite
reluctant *adj* invit•us -a -um
reluctantly *adv* invite
rely *intr* **to — on** confidĕre *(w. dat),* niti *(w. abl)*
remain *intr* manēre, permanēre; *(of things)* restare; *(to be left over)* superesse; **to — in that condition** subsistĕre in eo habitu
remainder *s* reliqu•um -i *n*
remaining *adj* reliqu•us -a -um
remains *spl* reliqui•ae -arum *fpl*
remark *tr* dicĕre
remark *s* dict•um -i *n*
remarkable *adj* notabil•is -is -e
remarkably *adv* mire, egregie
remedial *adj* remedial•is -is -e; *(med)* medicabil•is -is -e
remedy *s* **(for)** remed•ium -(i)i *n* (contra + *acc); (a healing drug)* medicament•um -i *n*
remedy *tr* corrigĕre; *(med)* mederi *(w. dat)*
remember *tr* meminisse *(w. gen),* recordari; **if I — right** si bene memini
remembrance *s* recordati•o -onis *f*
remind *tr* (ad)monēre
reminder *s* admoniti•o -onis *f*
reminisce *intr* meditari; **to — about** recordari
reminiscence *s* recordati•o -onis *f*
remiss *adj* negleg•ens -entis
remission *s* remissi•o -onis *f*
remit *tr* remittĕre
remittance *s* remissi•o -onis *f,* pecuni•a -ae *f*
remnant *s* reliqu•um -i *n;* **—s** reliqui•ae -arum *fpl*
remodel *intr* reformare, transfigurare
remonstrate *intr* **to — with** objurgare
remorse *s* paenitenti•a -ae *f*
remorseless *adj* immisericor•s -dis
remote *adj* remot•us -a -um
remotely *adv* procul
remoteness *s* longinquit•as -atis *f*
removable *adj* mobil•is -is -e
removal *s* amoti•o -onis *f; (of fear, pain)* depulsi•o -onis *f*
remove *tr* amovēre, tollĕre
remunerate *tr* remunerari
remuneration *s* remunerati•o -onis *f*
rend *tr* lacerare, scindĕre; *(to split)* findĕre
render *tr* reddĕre; *(to translate)* vertĕre; **to — thanks** gratias reddĕre
rendezvous *s* constitut•um -i *n*
renegade *s* transfug•a -ae *f*
renew *tr* renovare, redintegrare; **to — one's strength** recipere ex integro vires
renewal *s* renovati•o -onis *f*
renown *s* fam•a -ae *f*
renowned *adj* praeclar•us -a-um
rent *s* merc•es -edis *f; (tear)* scissur•a -ae *f;* **to pay the — for the room** mercedem cellae dare; **year's —** annua habitati•o -onis *f*
rent *tr (to let out)* locare; *(to hire)* conducĕre; **to — out** locare
renunciation *s* repudiati•o -onis *f*
reopen *tr* iterum aperire; **the discussion was —ed** res retractata est
reorganize *tr* ordinare, constituĕre
repair *tr* reparare, reficĕre; *(clothes)* resarcire
repair *s* refecti•o -onis *f;* **in bad —** ruinos•us -a -um
reparation *s* satisfacti•o -onis *f;* **to make —s** satisfacĕre
repartee *s* sal•es -ium *mpl*
repast *s* cib•us -i *m*
repay *tr* remunerari; *(money)* reponĕre, retribuĕre
repayment *s* remunerati•o -onis *f*
repeal *tr* abrogare, tollĕre
repeal *s* abrogati•o -onis *f*
repeat *tr* iterare, repetĕre; *(a ritual)* instaurare
repeatedly *adv* identidem
repel *tr* repellĕre; *(fig)* aspernari
repent *tr* **I —** me paenitet *(w. gen)* ‖ *intr* **I —** paenitet me
repentance *s* paenitenti•a -ae *f*
repentant *adj* paenit•ens -entis
repercussion *s* repercuss•us -ūs *m*

repetition *s* iterati•o -onis *f*
replace *tr* reponĕre
replant *tr* reserĕre
replenish *tr* replēre
replete *adj* replet•us -a -um
reply *s* respons•um -i *n*
reply *tr & intr* respondēre
report *s (rumor)* fam•a -ae *f; (official)* renuntiati•o -onis *f; (noise)* frag•or -oris *m;* **the — spread** fama percrebuit
report *tr* **(to)** referre, nuntiare, *(officially)* renuntiare *(w. dat)*
reporter *s* relat•or -oris
repose *s* qui•es -etis *f*
repose *intr* quiescĕre
repository *s* receptacul•um -i *n*
reprehend *tr* reprehendĕre
reprehensible *adj* vituperabil•is -is -e
represent *tr (to portray)* repraesentare; *(to stand in the place of another)* personam *(w. gen)* gerĕre; *(a character)* partes *(w. gen)* agĕre
representation *s (act)* repraesentati•o -onis *f; (likness)* imag•o -inis *f*
representative *s* vicar•ius -(i)i *m*
repress *tr* reprimĕre, cohibēre
repression *s* cohibiti•o -onis *f*
reprieve *s* supplicii dilati•o -onis *f;* **to grant a —** supplicium differre
reprimand *s* reprehensi•o -onis *f*
reprimand *tr* reprehendĕre
reprint *tr* denuo imprimĕre
reprisal *s* ulti•o -onis *f;* **to make —s** retaliare
reproach *s* exprobrati•o -onis *f; (disgrace)* opprobr•ium -(i)i *n*
reproach *tr* opprobrare, vituperare
reproachful *adj* objurgatori•us -a -um, contumelios•us -a -um
reprobate *s* perdit•us -i *m*
reproduce *tr* regenerare, propagare; **to — a play** iterum fabulam referre
reproduction *s* regenerati•o -onis *f; (likeness)* effigi•es -ei *f*
reproductive *adj* genital•is -is -e; **— organs** genital•ia -ium *npl*
reproof *s* objurgati•o -onis *f*
reprove *tr* objurgare
reptile *s* besti•a -ae *f* serpens
republic *s* respublica *(gen:* reipublicae) *f; (modern form)* civit•as -atis *f* popularis
republican *adj* optimatibus addict•us -a -um
repudiate *tr* repudiare
repudiation *s* repudiati•o -onis *f*
repugnance *s* aversati•o -onis *f*
repugnant *adj* avers•us -a -um
repulse *s* depulsi•o -onis *f; (political defeat)* repuls•a -ae *f*
repulse *tr* repellĕre
repulsive *adj* odios•us -a -um
reputable *adj* honest•us -a -um
reputation *s* fam•a -ae *f*
repute *s* fam•a -ae *f*
request *s* petiti•o -onis *f;* **to deny a —** negare roganti; **to grant a —** satisfacĕre petenti
request *tr* petĕre, rogare
require *tr* poscĕre, postulare; *(to need)* egēre *(w. gen); (to call for)* requirĕre, desiderare
requirement *s* necessar•ium -(i)i *n*
requisite *adj* necessari•us -a -um
requisition *s* postulati•o -onis *f*
requital *s* retributi•o -onis *f*
requite *tr* compensare, retribuĕre; *(for a favor)* remunerari
rescind *tr* rescindĕre
rescue *s* liberati•o -onis *f;* **to come to s.o.'s —** subvenire alicui
rescue *tr (to snatch away)* **(from)** eripĕre *(dat or* ab, de, ex + *abl); (to free)* liberare
research *s* investigati•o -onis *f*
resemblance *s* similitud•o -inis *f*
resemble *tr* simil•is -is -e esse *(w. gen, esp. of persons, or w. dat)*
resembling *adj* simil•is -is -e *(w. gen, esp. of persons, or w. dat)*
resent *tr* aegre ferre
resentful *adj* iracund•us -a -um
resentment *s* indignati•o -onis *f*
reservation *s* retenti•o -onis *f;* **mental —s** exception•es -um *fpl* animo conceptae
reserve *s (restraint)* pud•or -oris *m; (stock)* copi•a -ae *f; (mil)* subsid•ium -(i)i *n;* **—s** *(mil)* subsidiari•i -orum *mpl*
reserve *adj (mil)* subsidiari•us -a -um
reserve *tr* reservare
reserved *adj (of seat)* assignat•us -a -um; *(of disposition)* taciturn•us -a -um
reservoir *s* lac•us -ūs *m; (of an aqueduct)* castell•um -i *n*
reset *tr* reponĕre
reside *intr* habitare; **to — in** inhabitare
residence *s* sed•es -is *f*
resident *s* incol•a -ae *mf*
residue *s* residu•um -i *n*
resign *tr (an office)* se abdicare ab *(w. abl);* **to — oneself to** animum summittĕre *(w. dat)* **||** *intr* se abdicare
resignation *s* abdicati•o -onis *f; (fig)* aequus anim•us -i *m*
resigned *adj* summiss•us -a -um; **to be —** aequo animo esse; **to be — to** aequo animo ferre
resilience *s* molliti•a -ae *f*
resilient *adj* resili•ens -entis
resin *s* resin•a -ae *f*
resist *tr* resistĕre *(w. dat),* obstare *(w. dat),* repugnare *(w. dat)*
resistance *s* repugnanti•a -ae *f;* **to offer — to** obsistĕre *(w. dat)*
resolute *adj* const•ans -antis
resolutely *adv* constanter
resolution *s (determination)* constanti•a

-ae *f; (decision, decree)* decret•um -i *n; (of Senate)* consult•um -i *n*
resolve *s* constanti•a -ae *f*
resolve *tr* constituĕre; *(to reduce, convert)* resolvĕre, dissolvĕre
resonance *s* resonanti•a -ae *f*
resonant *adj* reson•us -a -um
resort *s* loc•us -i *m* celeber
resort *intr* **to — to** *(to frequent)* frequentare; *(to have recourse to)* confugĕre ad *(w acc.); (to lower oneself)* descendĕre ad *(w. acc.)*
resource *s* subsid•ium -(i)i *n;* **—s** op•es -ium *fpl*
respect *s (high esteem)* observanti•a -ae *f,* hon•or -oris *m; (regard)* respect•us -ūs *m; (religious awe)* religi•o -onis *f, e.g,* **respect for an oath** religio juris jurandi; **in every —** ex omni parte; **in other —s** ceterum; **in — to knowledge** scientiā; **to mention s.o. out of —** aliquem honoris causā nominare
respect *tr (to esteem highly)* observare; *(to esteem with fear)* vereri
respectability *s* honest•as -atis *f*
respectable *adj* honest•us -a -um
respectably *adv* honeste
respectful *adj* rever•ens -entis
respectfully *adv* reverenter
respecting *prep* de *(w. abl)*
respective *adj* propri•us -a -um
respectively *adv* proprie
respiration *s* respirati•o -onis *f*
respite *s* intermissi•o -onis *f*
resplendent *adj* splendid•us -a -um
respond *tr & intr* respondēre
respondent *s (leg)* re•us -i *m*
response *s* respons•um -i *n*
responsibility *s* cur•a -ae *f;* **it is my —** est mihi curae; **it is the — of a father to say this** patris est haec dicĕre; **sense of —** piet•as -atis *f*
responsible *adj* obnoxi•us -a -um; *(reliable)* fid•us -a -um; **to be — for** praestare *(w. acc);* **to hold anyone —** rationem reposcĕre ab aliquo
rest *s* qui•es -etis *f; (support)* fulcr•um -i *n; (remainder)* reliqu•um -i *n;* **the — of the men** ceter•i -orum *mpl*
rest *tr (to lean)* reclinare ‖ *intr* (re)-quiescĕre; *(to pause)* cessare; **to — on** inniti in *(w. abl),* niti *(w. abl);* **—ing on his elbow** reclinatus in cubitum
restitution *s* restituti•o -onis *f*
restive *adj* contum•ax -acis
restless *adj* inquiet•us -a -um
restlessly *adv* inquiete
restoration *s* restaurati•o -onis *f*
restore *tr* restituĕre, reddĕre; *(to rebuild)* restaurare, reficĕre; **to — to health** recurare; **to — to order** in integrum reducĕre
restrain *tr* coercēre; *(tears, laughter)* tenēre; *(emotions)* cohibēre
restraint *s* moderati•o -onis *f*
restrict *tr* restringĕre; *(to limit)* **(to)** definire *(w. dat)*
restriction *s* restricti•o -onis *f*
restrictive *adj (gram)* restringen•s -tis
result *s* exit•us -ūs *m,* event•us -ūs *m;* **without —** nequiquam
resume *tr* resumĕre
resumption *s* resumpti•o -onis *f*
resurrection *s* resurrecti•o -onis *f*
resuscitate *tr* resuscitare
retail *tr* divendĕre
retailer *s* caup•o -onis *m*
retail shop *s* caupon•a -ae *f*
retain *tr* retinēre
retainer *s (adherent)* assectat•or -oris *m; (fee)* arrab•o -onis *m*
retake *tr* recuperare
retaliate *intr* ulcisci
retaliation *s* ulti•o -onis *f*
retard *tr* retardare
retch *intr* sine vomitu nauseare
retention *s* retenti•o -onis *f*
retentive *adj* ten•ax -acis
reticence *s* taciturnit•as -atis *f*
reticent *adj* taciturn•us -a -um
retinue *s* comitat•us -ūs *m*
retire *intr* recedĕre; *(from work)* secedĕre; *(from office)* abire; *(for the night)* dormitum ire
retired *adj* emerit•us -a -um
retirement *s (act)* recess•us -ūs *m; (state)* ot•ium -(i)i *n*
retiring *adj* modest•us -a -um
retort *s* respons•um -i *n*
retort *tr* respondēre
retrace *tr* repetĕre
retract *tr (words)* retractare; *(a promise)* revocare
retraction *s* retractati•o -onis *f*
retreat *s (act; place)* recess•us -ūs *m; (mil)* recept•us -ūs *m;* **to sound the —** *(mil)* receptui canĕre
retreat *intr* recedĕre, se recipĕre
retrench *intr* sumptūs recidĕre
retrenchment *s* recisi•o -onis *f*
retribution *s* retributi•o -onis *f*
retrieve *tr* recuperare, recipĕre
retrievable *adj (loss)* pensabil•is -is -e
retrogression *s* retrogress•us -ūs *m*
retrospect *s* **in —** respicienti
retrospective *adj* respicien•s -tis
return *s (coming back)* redit•us -ūs *m; (gain)* quaest•us -ūs *m; (profit)* fruct•us -ūs *m*
return *tr (to give back)* reddĕre; *(to send back)* remittĕre; **to — a favor** gratiam referre ‖ *intr (to go back)* redire; *(to come back)* reverti
reunion *s* readunati•o -onis *f*
reunite *tr* iterum conjungĕre; *(to reconclie)* reconciliare ‖ *intr* reconciliari
reveal *tr* retegĕre, recludĕre; *(to unveil)* revelare

revel *s* comissati•o -onis *f*
revel *intr* comissari, debacchari
revelation *s* revelati•o -onis *f*
reveler *s* comissat•or -oris *m*
revelry *s* comissati•o -onis *f*
revenge *tr* ulcisci
revenge *s* ulti•o -onis *f*, vindict•a -ae *f;* **to seek —** ultionem petĕre; **to take — for s.th. small** vindictam parvae rei quaerĕre; **to take — on** se vindicare in *(w. acc)*
revengeful *adj* ulciscendi cupid•us -a -um
revenue *s* vectig•al -alis *n*
reverberate *intr* resonare
reverberation *s* resonanti•a -ae *f*
revere *tr* revereri, venerari
reverence *s* reverenti•a -ae *f;* **— due to the gods** deorum caerimoni•a -ae *f*
reverend *adj* reverend•us -a -um
reverent *adj* reveren•s -tis
reverential *adj* venerabund•us -a -um
reverently *adv* reverenter
reverie *s* meditati•o -onis *f*
reversal *s* reversi•o -onis *f*
reverse *s* contrar•ium -(i)i *n; (change)* conversi•o -onis *f; (defeat)* clad•es -is *f;* **to suffer a —** *(mil)* cladem accipĕre; *(pol)* repulsam ferre
reverse *tr* invertĕre, (com)mutare; *(decision)* rescindĕre, abrogare
revert *intr* reverti
review *s* recogniti•o -onis *f; (of a book)* censur•a -ae *f; (mil)* recensi•o -onis *f*
review *tr* recensēre
reviewer *s* cens•or -oris *m*
revile *tr* maledicĕre *(w. dat)*
revise *tr* corrigĕre; *(laws)* retractare
revision *s* emendati•o -onis *f; (literary);* recensi•o -onis *f*
revisit *tr* revisĕre, revisitare
revival *s* redanimati•o -onis *f; (fig)* renovati•o -onis *f*
revive *tr* resuscitare; *(to renew)* renovare; *(strength)* refovēre ‖ *intr* reviviscĕre
revocation *s* revocati•o -onis *f*
revoke *tr* revocare; *(a law)* rescindĕre, abrogare
revolt *s* rebelli•o -onis *f; (civil discord)* sediti•o -onis *f;* **to rise in — against s.o.** cooriri in aliquem
revolt *tr* offendĕre ‖ *intr* deficĕre
revolting *adj* tae•ter -tra -trum
revolution *s (e.g., of a wheel)* conversi•o -onis *f; (change)* commutati•o -onis *f; (of planets)* ambit•us -ūs *m; (pol)* res novae *fpl*
revolutionary *adj* seditios•us -a -um
revolutionary *s* hom•o -inis *m* rerum novarum cupidus
revolutionize *tr* novare
revolve *tr (in mind)* volutare ‖ *intr* revolvi
revulsion *s* revulsi•o -onis *f*
reward *s* praem•ium -(i)i *n*
reward *tr* praemio afficĕre
rewrite *tr* rescribĕre
rhapsody *s* rhapsodi•a -ae *f*
rhetoric *s* rhetoric•a -ae *f;* **to practice —** declamare
rhetorical *adj* rhetoric•us -a -um
rhetorician *s* rhet•or -oris *m*
rheumatism *s* dol•or -oris *m* artuum
rhinoceros *s* rhinocer•os -i *m*
rhubarb *s* rad•ix -cis *f* Pontica
rhyme *s* homoeoteleut•on -i *n*
rhythm *s* numer•us -i *m*
rhythmical *adj* numeros•us -a -um
rib *s* cost•a -ae *f*
ribbed *adj* costat•us -a -um
ribbon *s* taeni•a -ae *f; (as badge of honor)* inful•a -ae *f*
rice *s* oryz•a -ae *f*
rich *adj* div•es -itis; *(of soil)* opim•us -a -um; *(food)* pingu•is -is -e; *(costly)* laut•us -a -um
richly *adv* copiose, laute
riches *spl* diviti•ae -arum *fpl*
rickety *adj* instabil•is -is -e
rid *tr* liberare; **to get — of** dimittĕre
riddle *s* aenigm•a -atis *n*
ride *tr* **to — a horse** equo vehi ‖ *intr* equitare, equo vehi; **to — off** avehi
rider *s (on horse)* rect•or -oris *m; (in carriage)* vect•or -oris *m; (attached to documents)* adjecti•o -onis *f*
ridge *s* jug•um -i *n*, dors•um -i *n*
ridicule *s* ridicul•um -i *n*
ridicule *tr* irridēre
ridiculous *adj* ridicul•us -a -um
ridiculously *adv* ridicule
riding *s* equitati•o -onis *f; (in a carriage)* vectati•o -ōnis *f*
rife *adj* **(with)** frequ•ens -entis *(w. abl)*
riffraff *s* fae•x -cis *f* populi
rifle *tr* expilare
rifle *s* scoplet•um -i *n* striatum
rig *tr* adornare; *(ship)* ornare
rigging *s* fun•es -ium *mpl*
right *adj (correct)* rect•us -a -um; *(opp. of left)* dex•ter -tra -trum; *(just)* just•us -a -um; *(suitable)* idone•us -a -um, apt•us -a -um; *(true, reasonable)* ver•us -a -um; **on the — hand** dextrā; **to do the — thing** frugem facĕre
right *s (hand)* dextr•a -ae *f; (leg)* ju•s -ris *n; (what is permitted by God or conscience)* fas *n (indecl);* **by what —** quo jure; **on the — as you come in** dextrā introeunti; **the —** *(of knights and senators)* **to wear the gold ring** jus anuli
right *tr* emendare, corrigĕre; *(a fallen statue)* restituĕre; *(to avenge)* vindicare
righteous *adj* just•us -a -um
righteousness *s* justiti•a -ae *f*
rightful *adj* legitim•us -a -um
rightfully *adv* juste
right-hand *adj* dex•ter -tra -trum; **— man** dextell•a -ae *f*

rigid *adj* rigid•us -a -um
rigidity *s* rigidit•as -atis *f*
rigidly *adv* rigide
rigor *s* rig•or -oris *m*
rigorous *adj* dur•us -a -um
rill *s* rivul•us -i *m*
rim *s* or•a -ae *f,* marg•o -inis *f; (of a jar)* labr•um -i *n; (of a wheel)* canth•us -i *m*
rind *s* crust•a -ae *f*
ring *s* anul•us -i *m; (of people)* coron•a -ae *f; (for fighting)* aren•a -ae *f; (sound)* sonit•us -ūs *m; (of bells)* tinnit•us -ūs *m*
ring *tr* **to — a bell** tintinnabulum tractare ‖ *intr* tinnire, resonare; **to — with laughter** exsonare omni risu
ringing *s* tinnit•us -ūs *m*
ringleader *s* instigat•or -oris *m,* instigatr•ix -icis *f*
rinse *tr* colluĕre; **to — out** eluĕre
rinsing *s* colluvi•es -ei *f*
riot *s* tumult•us -ūs *m;* **to run —** luxuriari
riot *intr* tumultuari, seditionem movēre
rioter *s* seditios•us -i *m*
riotous *adj* seditios•us -a -um; **— living** luxuri•a -ae *f*
rip *tr* scindĕre; **to — apart** discindĕre; *(fig)* discerpĕre
ripe *adj* matur•us -a -um
ripen *tr* maturare ‖ *intr* maturescĕre
ripple *intr* trepidare
ripple *s* flucticul•us -i *m*
rise *intr* oriri; *(from a seat, from sleep; of the sun)* surgĕre; *(in a body)* consurgĕre; *(out of respect)* assurgĕre; *(of the voice)* crescĕre; **to — again** resurgĕre; **to — up against** adoriri
rise *s* ort•us -ūs *m; (to higher office)* ascens•us -ūs *m; (slope)* cliv•us -i *m;* **— in the ground** loc•us -i *m* editus; **to give — to** parĕre, gignĕre, excitare
riser *s* **early —** tempestiv•us -i *m*
rising *s* ort•us -ūs *m*
rising *adj* orien•s -tis; **gently — ground** loc•us -i *m* paulatim ab imo acclivis; **— star** *(fig)* adolescen•s -tis *m* summā spe et animi et ingenii praeditus
risk *s* pericul•um -i *n;* **to be at —** periclitari; **to run a —** periculum subire
risk *tr* in periculum vocare
rite *s* rit•us -ūs *m,* caeremoni•a -ae *f*
ritual *adj* ritual•is -is -e
ritual *s* rit•us -ūs *m*
rival *s* rival•is -is *mf; (pol)* competit•or -oris *m*
rival *adj* aemul•us -a -um
rival *tr* aemulari
rivalry *s* aemulati•o -onis *f; (among lovers)* rivalit•as -atis *f*
river *s* flum•en -inis *n,* amn•is -is *m*
rivet *s* clav•us -i *m*
rivet *tr (eyes, attention)* defigĕre
rivulet *s* rivul•us -i *m*
road *s* vi•a -ae *f; (route)* it•er -ineris *n;* **on the —** in itinere; **paved —** strat•a -ae *f;* **to build a —** viam munire
roadside *s* **by the —** secundum viam
roam *intr* errare, vagari
roar *s* fremit•us -ūs *m*
roar *intr* fremĕre, rugire
roast *adj* ass•us -a -um
roast *s* ass•um -i *n*
roast *tr* torrēre; *(esp. meat)* assare
rob *tr* rapĕre; **to — s.o. of** spoliare aliquem *(w. abl)* ‖ *intr* latrocinari
robber *s* latr•o -onis *f*
robbery *s* latrocin•ium -(i)i *n*
robe *s* vest•is -is *m; (of kings, augurs, knights)* trabe•a -ae *f; (of tragic actors)* pall•a -ae *f*
robe *tr* vestire
robin *s* rubecul•a -ae *f*
robust *adj* robust•us -a -um
rock *s* sax•um -i *n; (cliff)* rup•es -is *f;* **between a — and a hard place** inter sacrum saxumque
rock *tr* movēre; **to — the cradle** cunas agitare ‖ *intr* vibrare; **to — from side to side** in utramque partem toto corpore vacillare
rocket *s* missil•e -is *n*
rocky *adj* saxos•us -a -um
rod *s* virg•a -ae *f,* ferul•a -ae *f*
roe *s* capre•a -ae *f; (of fish)* ov•a -orum *npl*
roebuck *s* capreol•us -i *m*
rogue *s* furcif•er -eri *m*
roguish *adj* nequam *(indecl)*
role *s* part•es -ium *fpl;* **to take the lead —** primas partes suscipĕre
roll *tr* volvĕre; **to — back** revolvĕre; **to — over** evolvĕre; **to — over and over** pervolvĕre; **to — the dice** mittĕre talos; **to — together** *(to twist)* convolvĕre; **to — up** convolvĕre; *(from below)* subvolvĕre ‖ *intr* volvi
roll *s (book)* volum•en -inis *f; (of names)* catalog•us -i *m; (leg)* alb•um -i *n; (bun)* collyr•a -ae *f; (sweet roll)* pastill•us -i *m*
rollcall *s* catalogi recitat•o -onis *f*
roller *s* cylindr•us -i *m*
Roman *adj* Roman•us -a -um
Roman *s* Roman•us -i *m*
romance *s* fabul•a -ae *f* amatoria; *(affair)* amor•es -um *mpl*
romantic *adj* amatori•us -a -um
Romeo *s* agag•a -ae *m*
roof *s* tect•um -i *n;* **— of the mouth** palat•um -i *n*
roof *tr* contegĕre, integĕre
room *s (of house)* conclav•e -is *n; (small room)* cell•a -ae *f; (tiny room)* cellul•a -ae *f; (space)* loc•us -i *m,* spat•ium -(i)i *n*
room *intr* manēre
roomer *s* hosp•es -itis *m,* deversit•or -oris *m*
roominess *s* laxit•as -atis *f*
roommate *s* contubernal•is -is *mf*
roomy *adj* lax•us -a -um

roost *s* pertic•a -ae *f*
roost *intr* cubitare, insistĕre
rooster *s* gall•us -i *m* gallinaceus
root *s* rad•ix -icis *f; (fig)* fon•s -tis *m;* **to take —** coalescĕre
root *tr* **to become —ed** *(lit & fig)* radices agĕre; **to be —ed** inhaerēre; **to — out** eradicare ‖ *intr* **to — for** acclamare
rope *s* fun•is -is *m,* rest•is -is *f*
rosary *s* rosar•ium -(i)i *n*
rose *s* ros•a -ae *f*
rosebed *s* rosar•ium -(i)i *n*
rosebud *s* rosae cal•yx -ycis *m*
rosebush *s* frut•ex -icis *f* rosae
rose garden *s* roset•um -ī *n*
rosemary *s* ro•s -ris *m* marinus
rosin *s* resin•a -ae *f*
rostrum *s* rostr•a -orum *npl;* **to speak from the —** pro rostris loqui
rosy *adj* rose•us -a -um; *(fig)* festiv•us -a -um
rot *intr* putrescĕre, tabescĕre
rot *s* putred•o -inis *f,* tab•es -is *f*
rotate *intr* volvi
rotation *s* rotati•o -onis *f;* **in —** per *or* in orbem; **— of command** vicissitud•o -inis *f* imperitandi
rote *s* **by —** memoriter
rotten *adj* putrid•us -a -um
rotunda *s* thol•us -i *m*
rouge *s* fuc•us -i *m*
rough *adj* asp•er -era -erum; *(of character)* dur•us -a -um; *(weather)* inclem•ens -entis; *(shaggy)* hirsut•us -a -um; *(masonry)* impolit•us -a -um
rough-and-ready *adj* prompt•us -a -um
roughen *tr* asperare
roughly *adv* aspere, duriter; *(approximately)* fere
roughneck *s* rup•ex -icis *m*
roughness *s* asperit•as -atis *f; (brutality)* ferit•as -atis *f*
round *adj* rotund•us -a -um
round *s (in boxing)* congress•us -ūs *m;* **to give a — of applause** plausum dare; **— of beef** fem•ur -oris *n* bubulum transverse sectum; **—s of applause** plaus•us -ūs *m* multiplex; **to go the —s** *(of a policeman)* vigilias circumire; **to go the —s of** circumire *(w. acc)*
round *tr (a corner)* circumire; *(a cape)* superare; **to — off** concludĕre; **to — out** complĕre; **to — up** cogĕre
roundabout *adj* **in a — way** per ambages, circuitu; **— route** circuit•us -ūs *m;* **to tell a — story to** ambages narrare *(w. dat)*
rouse *tr* excitare; **a —ing harangue** incitata et vehemens conti•o -onis *f*
rout *s* fug•a -ae *f; (defeat)* clad•es -is *f; (rabble)* vulg•us -i *n;* **to put to —** in fugam convertĕre
rout *tr* fugare, fundĕre
route *s* it•er -ineris *n,* vi•a -ae *f*
routine *s* ord•o -inis *m;* **daily —** cotidianus ordo *m*
rove *intr* errare, vagari
rover *s* err•o -onis *m*
row *s* ord•o -inis *m,* seri•es -ei *f;* **in a row** continu•us -a -um; **for seven days in a —** per septem continuos dies; **— of seats** grad•us -ūs *m;* **— of trees** ordo arborum; **three days in a —** triennio continuo
row *tr* remis propellĕre ‖ *intr* remigare; **to — hard** remis contendĕre
rower *s* rem•ex -igis *m*
rowing *s* remig•ium -(i)i *n*
royal *adj* regi•us -a -um; *(worthy of a king)* regal•is -is -e; **— power** regn•um -i *n*
royally *adv* regie, regaliter
royalty *s* regn•um -i *n*
rub *tr* fricare; **to — away** detergēre; **to — down** defricare; **to — in** infricare
rub *s* fricat•us -ūs *m;* **and that's the —** hoc opus, hic labor est
rubbing *s* fricti•o -onis *f*
rubbish *s (lit & fig)* quisquili•ae -arum *fpl*
rubble *s* rud•us -eris *n*
rubric *s* rubric•a -ae *f*
ruby *s* carbuncul•us -i *m*
rudder *s* gubernacul•um -i *n*
ruddy *adj* rubicund•us -a -um
rude *adj* rud•is -is -e; *(impolite)* inurban•us -a -um, rustic•us -a -um
rudeness *s* inhumanit•as -atis *f*
rudiment *s* element•um -i *n*
rudimentary *adj* elementari•us -a -um
rue *tr* **I rue** me paenitet *(w. gen)*
rueful *adj* maest•us -a -um
ruffian *s* grassat•or -oris *m*
ruffle *s* limb•us -i *m*
rug *s* stragul•um -i *n*
rugged *adj* dur•us -a -um; *(terrain)* praerupt•us -a -um
ruin *s* exit•ium -(i)i *n;* **—s** rud•us -eris *n;* **to go to —** ruĕre, pessum ire, perire
ruin *tr* perdĕre, corrumpĕre; *(morally)* depravare
ruinous *adj* exitios•us -a -um
rule *s (instrument; regulation)* regul•a -ae *f; (government)* regim•en -inis *n;* **absolute —** dominati•o -onis *f*
rule *tr* regĕre, imperare ‖ *intr* regnare, dominari; **to — out** excludĕre; **to — over** imperare *(w. dat),* dominari in *(w. acc)*
ruler *s* rect•or -oris *m; (instrument)* regul•a -ae *f*
ruling *s* sententi•a -ae *f*
rum *s* sicer•a -ae *f*
rumble *s* murm•ur -uris *n*
rumble *intr* murmurare; **my stomach is —ing** sonat mihi circum stomachum
rumbling *s* murm•ur -uris *n*
ruminate *intr* ruminare
rummage *intr* **to — through** perscrutari

rummage sale *s* venditi•o -onis *f* scrutaria
rumor *s* rum•or -oris *m*
rump *s* clun•is -is *f*
rumple *s (in garment)* rug•a -ae *f*
rumple *tr* corrugare
run *tr (to manage)* exercēre; **to — a fever** febricitare; **to — down** *(to disparage)* detrectare; *(w. vehicle)* obterĕre; **to — her hand over my hair** ducĕre capillos meos lentā manu; **to — up** *(increase)* augēre; **to — up bills** aes alienum conflare ‖ *intr* currĕre; *(to flow)* fluĕre; **to — about** discurrĕre; **to — after** petĕre; **to — around** discurrĕre; **to — around the table** discurrĕre circa mensam; **to — away** aufugĕre; **to — aground** offendĕre; **to — down** decurrĕre; *(of water)* defluĕre; **to — for office** honorem petĕre; **to — foul of** impingĕre; **to — high** *(of a river, sea)* tumēre; **to — into** *(to meet)* occurrĕre *(w. dat)*, incidĕre in *(w. acc)*; **to — low** deficĕre; **to — off** aufugĕre; *(of water)* defluĕre; **to — on** percurrĕre, continuare; **to — out** excurrĕre; *(of time)* exire; *(of supplies)* deficĕre; **to — over** *(of fluids)* superfluĕre; *(details)* percurrĕre; **to — short** deficĕre; **to — through** *(to dissipate)* dissipare; **to — through a list of** exsequi; **to — together** concurrĕre; **to — up to s.o.** accurrĕre ad aliquem
run *s* curs•us -ūs *m;* **in the long —** in exitu; **on the —** cursim; **to have the —s** citā alvo laborare
runaway *s* transfug•a -ae *mf*
rundown *s* compend•ium -(i)i *n*
run-down *adj* defatigat•us -a -um; *(dilapidated)* ruinos•us -a -um
rung *s (of ladder)* grad•us -ūs *m*
run-in *s* altercati•o -onis *f*
runner *s* curs•or -oris *m*
running *s* curs•us -ūs *m;* **— for office** petiti•o -onis *f* honoris; **— of the government** administrati•o -onis *f* rei publicae
runny nose *s* distillation•es -um *fpl*
rupture *s (of relations)* discid•ium -(i)i *n; (med)* herni•a -ae *f*
rupture *tr* rumpĕre ‖ *intr* rumpi
rural *adj* rural•is -is -e
ruse *s* dol•us -i *m*
rush *s (plant)* junc•us -i *m; (charge)* impet•us -ūs *m; (of people)* **(on)** concurs•us -ūs *m* (ad + *acc.*)
rush *tr (to attack)* oppugnare; *(to do in a hurry)* festinare; *(to cause to hurry)* urgēre ‖ *intr* festinare, ruĕre; **to — away** avolare; **to — forth** se proripĕre; **to — in** irruĕre; **to — into** irruĕre in *(w. acc)*; **to — out** evolare, erumpĕre
russet *adj* russ•us -a -um
rust *s* rubig•o -inis *f; (of iron)* ferrug•o -inis *f*
rust *intr* rubiginem trahĕre
rustic *adj* rustic•us -a -um
rustic *s* rustic•us -i *m*
rustle *intr* crepitare
rustle *s* crepit•us -ūs *m*
rusty *adj* rubiginos•us -a -um; **to become —** rubigine obduci; *(fig)* desuescĕre
rut *s* orbit•a -ae *f*
ruthless *adj* immisericor•s -dis
ruthlessly *adv* immisericorditer
rye *s* secal•e -is *n*

S

Sabbath *s* sabbat•a -orum *npl;* **to keep the —** sabbatizare
saber *s* acinac•es -is *m*
sable *s* pell•is -is *f* zibellina
sabotage *s* vastati•o -onis *f* occulta
sabotage *tr* occulte evertĕre
saccharin *s* sacchar•on -i *n*
sack *s* sacc•us -i *m; (of leather)* cule•us -i *m; (mil)* direpti•o -onis *f*
sack *tr* in saccos condĕre; *(mil)* diripĕre
sackcloth *s* cilic•ium -(i)i *n;* **in — and ashes** sordidat•us -a -um
sacrament *s (eccl)* sacrament•um -i *n*
sacred *adj* sa•cer -cra -crum
sacrifice *s (act)* sacrific•ium -(i)i *n; (victim)* hosti•a -ae *f; (fig)* jactur•a -ae *f;* **to offer (perform) a —** sacrificium agĕre (facĕre), rem divinam facĕre
sacrifice *tr* sacrificare, immolare; **to — an eye for** oculum impendĕre pro *(w. abl)*; **to — one's life for another** vitam pro aliquo profundĕre
sacrilege *s* sacrileg•ium -(i)i *n*
sacrilegious *adj* sacrileg•us -a -um
sad *adj* trist•is -is -e, maest•us -a -um
sadden *tr* contristare
saddle *s* ephipp•ium -(i)i *n*
saddle *tr (fig)* imponĕre *(w. acc of thing and dat of person)*; **to — a horse** equum sternĕre
saddlebags *spl* clitell•ae -arum *fpl*
sadly *adv* maeste
safe *adj* tut•us -a -um; *(unharmed)* incolum•is -is -e; *(harmless)* innocu•us -a -um; *(sure)* cert•us -a -um **— and sound** salv•us -a -um
safe *s* arc•a -ae *f*
safe-conduct *s* **under —** publicā fide interpositā
safeguard *tr* tueri
safeguard *s* cauti•o -onis *f;* **there is but one — against these troubles** horum incommodorum cautio una est *(followed by* ut *or* ne)
safekeeping *s* **for —** in fidem
safely *adv* tute
safety *s* sal•us -utis *f;* **in —** tuto

safety pin *s* fibul•a -ae *f*
safety valve *s* spirament•um -i *n*
saffron *s* croc•us -i *m*
saffron *adj* croce•us -a -um
sagacious *adj* sag•ax -acis
sagacity *s* sagacit•as -atis *f*
sage *s (wise man)* vi•r -ri *m* sapi•ens -entis
sage *adj* sapi•ens -entis
sail *s* vel•um -i *n;* **to set —** vela dare
sail *intr* nave vehi, navigare; **to — down to** devehi ad *or* in *(w. acc);* **to — up to** subvehi ad *or* in *(w. acc)*
sailing *s* navigati•o -onis *f*
sailor *s* naut•a -ae *m*
saint *s* vi•r -ri *m* sanctus; femin•a -ae *f* sancta
saintly *adj* sanct•us -a -um
sake *s* **for heaven's — !** pro deum fidem! **for the — of** causā *or* gratiā *(w. gen);* **for the — of glory** gloriae causā *(or* gratiā)
salable *adj* vendibil•is -is -e
salacious *adj* sal•ax -acis
salad *s* acetari•a -orum *npl*
salamander *s* salamandr•a -ae *f*
salary *s* salar•ium -(i)i *n*
sale *s* venditi•o -onis *f;* **for —** venal•is -is -e; **to advertise a house for —** aedes venales inscribĕre; **to go up for —** venum ire; **to put up for —** venum dare, prostare
salesman *s* instit•or -oris *m*
saline *adj* sals•us -a -um
saliva *s* saliv•a -ae *f*
sallow *adj* pallid•us -a -um
sally *intr* eruptionem facĕre
sally *s* erupti•o -onis *f*
salmon *s* salm•o -onis *m*
saloon *s* caupon•a -ae *f*
salt *s* sa•l -lis *m*
salt *tr* salire, sale condire
salting *s* salsur•a -ae *f*
saltless *adj* insals•us -a -um
salt mine *s* salifodin•a -ae *f*
salt shaker *s* salin•um -i *n*
salty *adj* sals•us -a -um
salt water *s* aqu•a -ae *f* marina
salubrious *adj* salu•ber -bris -bre
salutary *adj* salutar•is -is -e
salutation *s* salutati•o -onis *f*
salute *s* sal•us -utis *f*
salute *tr* salutare
salvage *tr* eripĕre, servare
salvage *s* id quod e nave fracta servatur
salvation *s* sal•us -utis *f*
salve *s* unguent•um -i *n*
same *adj* idem, eadem, idem; **at the — time** simul, eodem tempore; **the very —** ipsissim•us -a -um
sameness *s* identit•as -atis *f*
sample *s* exempl•um -i *n*
sample *tr* libare
sanctify *tr* sanctificare
sanctimonious *adj* sanctitatem affect•ans -antis
sanction *s* auctorit•as -atis *f;* **with the — of the people** jussu populi; **without the — of the people** injussu populi
sanction *tr* ratum facĕre
sanctity *s* sanctit•as -atis *f*
sanctuary *s* sanctuar•ium -(i)i *n; (refuge)* asyl•um -i *n*
sand *s* (h)aren•a -ae *f*
sandal *s* sole•a -ae *f*
sandstone *s* tof•us -i *m*
sandy *adj* (h)arnenos•us -a -um
sandy-haired *adj* ruf•us -a -um
sane *adj* san•us -a -um
sanitary *adj* salubr•is -is -e
sanity *s* sanit•as -atis *f*
sap *s* suc•us -i *m*
sap *tr* haurire
sapling *s* surcul•us -i *m*
Sapphic *adj* Sapphic•us -a -um
sapphire *s* sapphir•us -i *f*
sarcasm *s* asperae faceti•ae -arum *fpl*
sarcastic *adj* acerb•us -a -um
sarcastically *adv* acerbe
sarcophagus *s* sarcophag•us -i *m*
sardine *s* sard•a -ae *f*
sardonic *adj* amar•us -a -um
sash *s* zon•a -ae *f*
Satan *s* Satan *m (indecl)*
Satanic *adj* Satanic•us -a -um
satchel *s* per•a -ae *f*
satellite *s* satell•es -itis *mf*
satiate *tr* satiare
satire *s* satur•a -ae *f*
satirical *adj* satiric•us -a -um; *(biting)* mord•ax -acis
satirist *s* script•or -oris *m* saturarum
satirize *tr* arripĕre, notare
satisfaction *s* volupt•as -atis *f; (of a creditor)* satisfacti•o -onis *f;* **to derive the greatest — from** incredibilem voluptatem capĕre ex *(w. abl);* **my house gives me great —** domus mea mihi valde placet
satisfactorily *adv* satis bene
satisfactory *adj* idone•us -a -um
satisfied *adj* content•us -a -um
satisfy *tr* satis facĕre *(w. dat); (thirst, hunger, expectation)* explēre; *(creditors)* satisfacĕre *(w. dat);* **to — your rage** satiare iracundiam tuam
saturate *tr* saturare
Saturday *s* di•es -ei *m* Saturni
Saturn *s* Saturn•us -i *m;* **feast of —** Saturnal•ia -ium *npl*
satyr *s* satyr•us -i *m*
sauce *s* condiment•um -i *n; (of meat)* liquam•en -inis *n*
saucepan *s* cacub•us -i *m*
saucer *s* patell•a -ae *f*
saucily *adv* petulanter
saucy *adj* petul•ans -antis

saunter *intr* vagari
sausage *s* farcim•en -inis *n*
savage *adj (wild, untamed)* fer•us -a -um; *(cruel)* saev•us -a -um
savagely *adv* atrociter
save *tr* **(from)** servare (ex + *abl)*; **to — up** reservare
save *prep* praeter *(w. acc)*
saving *s* conservati•o -onis *f*; **—s** pecul•ium -(i)i *n*
savior *s* servat•or -oris *m*
Savior *s* Salvat•or -oris *m*
savor *s* sap•or -oris *m*
savor *tr* sapĕre
savory *adj* sapid•us -a -um
saw *s (tool)* serr•a -ae *f*; *(saying)* proverb•ium -(i)i *n*
saw *tr* serrā secare **‖** *intr* serram ducĕre
sawdust *s* scob•is -is *f*
say *tr* dicĕre; **no sooner said than done** dictum (ac) factum; **that is to —** scilicet; **to — that...not** negare *(w. acc & inf)*
saying *s* dict•um -i *n*; **as the — goes** ut aiunt
scab *s* crust•a -ae *f*
scabbard *s* vagin•a -ae *f*
scaffold *s* machin•a -ae *f* aedificationis
scald *tr* urĕre
scale *s (for weighing)* trutin•a -ae *f*; *(of fish)* squam•a -ae *f*; *(gradation)* grad•us -ūs *m*; *(mus)* diagramm•a -atis *f*; **pair of —s** stater•a -ae *f*
scale *tr (fish)* desquamare; **to — a wall** murum per scalas ascendĕre
scallop *s (shellfish)* pect•en -inis *m*; *(curve)* sin•us -ūs *m*
scalp *s* pericran•ium -(i)i *n*
scaly *adj* squamos•us -a -um
scam *s* frau•s -dis *f*
scam artist *s* plan•us -i *m*
scamp *s* furcif•er -eri *m*
scamper *intr* cursare; **to — about** cursitare, discurrĕre; **to — away** aufugĕre
scan *tr* examinare; *(verse)* scandĕre
scandal *s* opprobr•ium -(i)i *n*; **to be a — to the community** opprobrio esse civitati
scandalize *tr* offendĕre
scandalous *adj* probros•us -a -um
scantily *adv* exigue
scanty *adj* exigu•us -a -um
scapegoat *s* piacul•um -i *n*
scar *s* cicatr•ix -icis *f*
scar *tr* cicatricibus foedare
scarce *adj* rar•us -a -um
scarcely *adv* vix; *(with effort)* aegre
scarcity *s* inopi•a -ae *f*
scare *tr* terrēre; **to — off** absterrēre
scarecrow *s* terricul•um -i *n*
scared *adj* territ•us -a -um
scarf *s* amictor•ium -(i)i *n*
scarlet *adj* coccin•us -a -um
scathing *adj* aculeat•us -a -um
scatter *tr* spargĕre, dispergĕre **‖** *intr* dilabi, diffugĕre
scavenger *s* colacar•ius -(i)i *m*
scene *s (vista)* prospect•us -ūs *m*; *(picture)* pictur•a -ae *f*; *(theat)* scaen•a -ae *f*; **behind the —s** post siparium; **Italy, the — of the civil war** Italia, arena belli civilis; **on the —** in re praesenti; **to make a —** convicium facĕre
scenery *s (theat)* scenae apparat•us -ūs *m*; *(of nature)* speci•es -ei *f* regionis
scent *s (sense)* odorat•us -ūs *m*; *(of dogs)* sagacit•as -atis *f*; *(fragrance)* od•or -oris *m*
scent *tr* odorari
scented *adj* odorat•us -a -um
scepter *s* sceptr•um -i *n*
sceptic *s* sceptic•us -i *m*
sceptical *adj* **to be —** dubitare
schedule *s* schedul•a -ae *f*
scheme *s* consil•ium -(i)i *n*; *(pej)* dol•us -i *m*
scheme *intr* moliri
scholar *s* philolog•us -i *m*
scholarly *adj* doct•us -a -um
scholarship *s* litter•ae -arum *fpl*; *(grant)* pecuni•ae -arum *fpl* quae scholari alendo praebentur
scholastic *adj* scholastic•us -a -um
scholiast *s* scholiast•es -ae *m*
school *s* lud•us -i *m*; *(an advanced school)* schol•a -ae *f*; **elementary —** lud•us -i *m* litterarius; *(group holding like opinions)* sect•a -ae *f*
schoolboy *s* discipul•us -i *m*
schoolgirl *s* discipul•a -ae *f*
schoolmaster *s* ludi magis•ter -tri *m*
schoolroom *s* schol•a -ae *f*
science *s* disciplin•a -ae *f*; **natural —** rati•o -onis *f* physica
scientific *adj* physic•us -a -um
scientifically *adv* ratione
scientist *s* physic•us -i *m*
scimitar *s* acinac•es -is *m*
scion *s* edit•us -i *m*
scissors *spl* forficul•ae -arum *fpl*
scoff *s* cavillati•o -onis *f*
scoff *intr* cavillari; **to — at** irridēre
scoffer *s* irris•or -oris *m*
scold *tr* objurgare
scolding *s* objurgati•o -onis *f*
scoop *s* trull•a -ae *f*
scoop *tr* **to — out** excavare
scoot *intr* provolare
scope *s (extent)* spat•ium -(i)i *n*; *(range)* aspect•us -ūs *m*
scorch *tr* adurĕre
score *s (total)* summ•a -ae *f*; *(twenty)* viginti *(indecl)*; *(reckoning)* rati•o -onis *f*; **to even the — with** *(fig)* ulcisci; **to keep —** rationem notare; **to know the —** scire quid agatur
score *tr* notare

scorn *s* contempti•o -onis *f*
scorn *tr* contemněre
scornful *adj* fastidios•us -a -um
scornfully *adv* contemptim
scorpion *s* scorpi•o -onis *m*
Scot *adj* Scotic•us -a -um
Scotchman *s* Scot•us -i *m*
Scotland *s* Scoti•a -ae *f*
scoundrel *s* furci•fer -feri *m*
scour *tr (to rub clean)* tergēre; *(to roam over)* pervagari
scourge *s* flagell•um -i *n; (fig)* pest•is -is *f*
scourge *tr* flagellare
scourging *s* flagellati•o -onis *f*
scout *s* explorat•or -oris *m*
scout *tr* explorare
scowl *intr* frontem contrahěre
scowlingly *adv* fronte contractā
scramble *intr* **to — for** diripěre; **to — up** scanděre
scrap *s (small piece)* frust•um -i *n; (junk)* metall•um -i *n* scrutarium
scrap *tr* rejicěre
scrape *s* difficult•as -atis *f; (quarrel)* rix•a -ae *f*
scrape *tr* raděre; **to — together** *(money, etc.)* corraděre
scraping *s* rasur•a -ae *f*
scratch *tr* raděre; *(the head)* scaběre; **to — up** *(e.g., the earth)* scalpěre
scratch *s* levis incisur•a -ae *f*
scrawl *s* mala scriptur•a -ae *f*
scrawl *tr & intr* male scriběre
scream *s* ululat•us -ūs *m,* clam•or -oris *m; (of child)* vagit•us -ūs *m*
scream *intr* ululare; *(of child)* vagire
screech *s* strid•or -oris *m*
screech *intr* stridēre
screen *s* umbracul•um -i *n*
screen *tr* tegěre
screw *s* cochle•a -ae *f*
screw *tr* torquēre; *(sl)* debattuěre
scribble *tr & intr* conscribillare
scribe *s* scrib•a -ae *m*
script *s* script•um -i *n; (hand)* man•us -ūs *f*
scroll *s* volum•en -inis *n*
scrub *tr* tergēre
scruple *s* scrupul•us -i *m*
scrupulous *adj* scrupulos•us -a -um
scrupulously *adv* diligenter
scrutinize *tr* scrutari
scrutiny *s* scrutati•o -onis *f*
scuffle *s* rix•a -ae *f*
scuffle *intr* rixari
sculptor *s* sculpt•or -oris *m*
sculpture *s (art)* sculptur•a -ae *f; (work)* sign•um -i *n* (marmoreum)
sculpture *tr* sculpěre
scum *s* spum•a -ae *f; (fig)* sentin•a -ae *f* reipublicae
scurrilous *adj* scurril•is -is -e
scurry *intr* volitare, properare
scuttle *tr* pertunděre ac depriměre
scythe *s* fal•x -cis *f*
sea *s* mar•e -is *n;* **by —** mari, nave
sea captain *s* navarch•us -i *m*
seacoast *s* or•a -ae *f* maritima
seafaring *adj* maritim•us -a -um
sea gull *s* lar•us -i *m*
seal *s* sigill•um -i *n; (animal)* phoc•a -ae *f*
seal *tr* signare; **to — up** obsignare
seam *s* sutur•a -ae *f*
seaman *s* naut•a -ae *m*
seamanship *s* nauticarum rerum us•us -ūs *m*
seamstress *s* sarcinatr•ix -icis *f*
sear *tr* adurěre
search *s* investigati•o -onis *f,* indagati•o -onis *f*
search *tr* investigare; *(to shake down a person)* excutěre ‖ *intr* quaerěre; **to — for** quaerěre; **to — out** exquirěre
seasick *adj* nauseabund•us -a -um; **to be —** nauseare
seasickness *s* nause•a -ae *f*
season *s* anni temp•us -oris *n; (proper time)* opportunit•as -atis *f,* tempus *n;* **in due —** (in) tempore; **in —** tempestiv•us -a -um
season *tr* condire; *(fig)* assuefacěre
seasonable *adj* temptestiv•us -a -um
seasoning *s* condiment•um -i *n*
seat *s* sed•es -is *f,* sell•a -ae *f; (fixed abode)* domicil•ium -(i)i *n;* **— of honor** *(in dining room)* loc•us -i *m* praetorius; **to take one's —** considěre
seat *tr* sede locare; **to — oneself** considěre
seaweed *s* alg•a -ac *f*
secede *intr* seceděre
secession *s* secessi•o -onis *f*
seclude *tr* secluděre
secluded *adj* secret•us -a -um
seclusion *s* solitud•o -inis *f*
second *adj* secund•us -a -um; **a — alt•er** -era -erum; **a — time** iterum; **in the — place** deinde; **ranking — to s.o.** alter ab aliquo; **— to Achilles** ab Achille secundus; **to play — fiddle** secundas partes agěre
second *s (handler)* adjut•or -oris *m; (of time)* moment•um -i *n* temporis
second *tr* adesse *(w. dat),* favēre *(w. dat);* **to — a motion** in sententiam alicujus dicěre
secondary *adj* secundari•us -a -um
secondhand *adj* trit•us -a -um
second-rate *adj* infer•ior -ior -ius
secrecy *s* secret•um -i *n; (keeping secret)* silent•ium -(i)i *n*
secret *adj* secret•us -a -um; **to keep —** celare
secret *s* secret•um -i *n;* **he makes no — of it** neque id occulte fert; **in —** clam; **keep this a —!** haec tu tecum habeto!

to keep a — commissum celare; to reveal a — commissum enuntiare
secretary *s* a manu serv•us -i *m*
secrete *tr (to hide)* abdĕre; *(med)* secernĕre
secretion *s* secreti•o -onis *f*
sect *s* sect•a -ae *f*
section *s* secti•o -onis *f*
sector *s* sect•or -oris *m*
secular *adj* profan•us -a -um
secure *adj* tut•us -a -um
secure *tr (to make safe)* munire; *(to obtain)* comparare; *(to fasten)* religare; **to — oneself against fraud** muniri contra fraudes
securely *adv* tuto
security *s* securit•as -atis *f; (pledge)* satisdati•o -onis *f,* pign•us -oris *n*
sedate *adj* sedat•us -a -um
sedate *tr* sedare
sedentary *adj* sedentari•us -a -um
sedge *s* ul•va -ae *f*
sediment *s* sediment•um -i *n*
sedition *s* sediti•o -onis *f*
seditious *adj* seditios•us -a -um
seduce *tr* corrumpĕre, stuprum inferre *(w. dat)*
seducer *s* corrupt•or -oris *m*
seduction *s* corruptel•a -ae *f*
seductive *adj* illecebros•us -a -um
see *tr* vidēre; *(to distinguish w. the eyes)* cernĕre; **to go to —** visĕre; **to — to it that** curare ut ‖ *intr* vidēre; **to — to s.o.'s safety** prospicĕre alicujus saluti
seed *s* sem•en -inis *n; (offspring)* progeni•es -ei *f; (in fruit)* acin•um -i *n*
seedling *s* surcul•us -i *m*
seed-time *s* sement•is -is *f*
seek *tr* quaerĕre, petĕre; *(to strive after)* consectari; **to — to** conari *(w. inf)*
seem *intr* videri
seeming *adj* specios•us -a -um
seemingly *adv* ut videtur, in speciem
seemly *adj* decor•us -a -um
seep *intr* manare
seer *s* vat•es -is *m*
seethe *intr* aestuare
segment *s* segment•um -i *n*
segregate *tr* segregare
segregation *s* separati•o -onis *f*
seismograph *s* apparat•us -ūs *m* ad terrae motum observandum
seize *tr* prehendĕre, arripĕre; *(mil)* occupare; *(fig)* afficĕre
seizure *s* comprehensi•o -onis *f; (med)* accessi•o -onis *f*
seldom *adv* raro; **very —** perraro
select *tr* seligĕre, eligĕre
selection *s (act)* selecti•o -onis *f; (things chosen)* elect•a -orum *npl*
self *pron* ips•e -a -um; **he was never again his old —** coloris sui numquam fuit
self-appointed *adj* sibi arrogan•s -tis
self-assurance *s* confidenti•a -ae *f*
self-centered *adj* sibi dedit•us -a -um
self-confidence *s* fiduci•a -ae *f*
self-confident *adj* sibi fiden•s -tis
self-conscious *adj* pudibund•us -a -um
self-control *s* continenti•a -ae *f*
self-denial *s* abstinenti•a -ae *f*
self-evident *adj* manifest•us -a -um
self-indulgent *adj* intemperan•s -tis
selfish *adj* avar•us -a -um
selfishness *s* avariti•a -ae *f*
self-made *adj* **he is a — man** de nihilo crevit
self-respect *s* pud•or -oris *m*
sell *tr* vendĕre; *(as a practice)* venditare; **to — for 3000 sesterces per pound** vendĕre ternis milibus nummum in libras ‖ *intr* venire, venum ire
seller *s* vendit•or -oris *m*
semblance *s* speci•es -ei *f,* umbr•a -ae *f;* **under the — of a just treaty** sub umbrā foederis aequi
semicircle *s* semicircul•us -i *m*
semicircular *adj* semicircul•us -a -um
Senate *s* senat•us -ūs *m; (building)* curi•a -ae *f;* **— session** senatus *m;* **a — session was held on that very day** senatus eo ipso die agebatur
senatorial *adj* senatori•us -a -um
send *tr* mittĕre; *(on public business)* legare; **to — away** dimittĕre; **to — back** remittĕre; **to — flying into s.o.'s face** immittĕre in alicujus faciem; **to — forward** praemittĕre; **to — into** intromittĕre in *(w. acc)* ‖ *intr* **to — for** arcessĕre
sender *s* script•or -oris *m;* qui mittit
senile *adj* senil•is -is -e
senior *adj* natu maj•or -or -us
seniority *s* aetatis praerogativ•a -ae *f*
seniors *spl* senior•es -um *mpl*
sensation *s* sens•us -ūs *m; (fig)* mir•um -i *n;* **a painful —** doloris sensus; **to make a —** conspici
sensational *adj* mirabil•is -is -e
sense *s (faculty; meaning)* sens•us -ūs *m; (understanding)* prudenti•a -ae *f; (meaning)* vis *f,* significati•o -onis *f*
sense *tr* sentire
senseless *adj* absurd•us -a -um; *(unconscious)* omni sensu caren•s -tis
sensible *adj* prud•ens -entis
sensibly *adv* prudenter
sensitive *adj* sensil•is -is -e; *(touchy)* moll•is -is -e
sensual *adj* voluptari•us -a -um; **— pleasure** corporis volupt•as -atis *f*
sensuality *s* libid•o -inis *f*
sentence *s (gram, leg)* sententi•a -ae *f; (decision of an arbiter)* arbitr•ium (i)i *n;* **to pass — on s.o.** arbitrium de aliquo agĕre; **to pronounce the —** sententiam dicĕre

sentence *tr* damnare, condemnare
sententious *adj* sententios•us -a -um
sentiment *s (opinion)* sententi•a -e *f,* opini•o -onis *f; (feeling)* sens•us -ūs *m*
sentimental *adj* moll•is -is -e
sentimentality *s* animi molliti•es -ei *f*
sentinel, sentry *s* cust•os -odis *m,* vig•il -is *m; (collectively)* stati•o -onis *f;* **to be on sentry duty** in statione esse
separable *adj* separabil•is -is -e
separate *tr* separare, disjungĕre ‖ *intr* separari, disjungi
separate *adj* separat•us -a -um
separately *adv* separatim
separation *s* separati•o -onis *f*
September *s* Septem•ber -bris *m or* mens•is -is *m* Septmber; **on the first of —** Kalendis Septembribus
sepulcher *s* sepulcr•um -i *n*
sepulchral *adj* sepulcral•is -is -e
sequel *s* postprincip•ium -(i)i *n*
sequence *s* ord•o -inis *m*
serenade *tr* occentare
serene *adj* seren•us -a -um
serenely *adv* serene
serenity *s* serenit•as -atis *f*
serf *s* serv•us -i *m*
serfdom *s* servit•ium -(i)i *n*
sergeant *s* opti•o -onis *m*
series *s* seri•es -ei *f*
serious *adj* seri•us -a -um, grav•is -is -e
seriously *adv* serio, graviter; **to take —** in serium convertĕre
seriousness *s* gravit•as -atis *f*
sermon *s* orati•o -onis *f* sacra
serpent *s* serp•ens -entis *m*
servant *s* famul•us -i *m,* famul•a -ae *f,* serv•us -i *m,* serv•a -ae *f*
serve *tr (to be a servant to)* servire *(w. dat); (food)* apponĕre; *(to be useful)* prodesse *(w. dat);* **to — a sentence** poenam subire ‖ *intr (mil)* (stipendia) merēre; *(to suffice)* sufficĕre; **the trunk — the elephant as a hand** proboscis elephanto pro manu est
service *s (favor)* offic•ium -(i)i *n; (mil)* militi•a -ae *f,* stipendi•a -orum *npl; (work)* minister•ium -(i)i *n;* **to be of — to** prodesse *(w. dat)*
serviceable *adj* util•is -is -e
servile *adj* servil•is -is -e
servitude *s* servit•us -utis *f*
sesame *s* sesam•um -i *n*
session *s* sessi•o -onis *f*
sesterce *s* sestert•ius -(i)i *m (used in smaller sums; large sums are expressed by the collective form* sestertium = mille sestertii, *usually with the distributive numeral, e.g.,* **hundred thousand sesterces** centena sestertia, *but also with the cardinal, as,* septem sestertia **seven hundred thousand sesterces)**
set *tr (to place)* ponĕre; *(to make to stand)* sistĕre, statuĕre; *(diamonds, etc.)* includĕre; *(a broken limb)* collocare; *(course)* dirigĕre; *(example)* praebēre; *(limit)* imponĕre; *(table)* instruĕre; *(plants)* serĕre; *(the clock)* constituĕre; **to — apart** seponĕre; **to — aside** ponĕre; *(to rescind)* rescindĕre; **to — a trap** insidias tendĕre; **to — bounds to** modum *(w. gen)* habēre; **to — down** deponĕre; *(in writing)* perscribĕre; **to — foot in** attingĕre; **to — forth** exponĕre, proponĕre; **to — free** liberare; **to — in motion** ciēre; **to — in order** componĕre; **to — off** *(to adorn)* adornare; **to — on fire** incendĕre; **to — one's hopes on** spem collocare in *(w. abl);* **to — s.o. over** aliquem praeficĕre *(w. dat);* **to — up** statuĕre ‖ *intr (of stars, sun)* occidĕre; **to — about waging wars** bella incipĕre; **to — in** *(to begin)* incipĕre; **to — out** proficisci
set *adj (fixed)* cert•us -a -um; *(prescribed, e.g., day, sacrifice)* stat•us -a -um; *(prepared)* parat•us -a -um; **in — terms** composite; **— speech** declamati•o -onis *f*
set *s (a set of two)* pa•r -ris *n; (gear, set of tools)* instrument•um -i *n; (number of persons customarily associated)* glob•us -i *m;* **a — of tools for one's trade** artis instrumentum *n*
setback *s* **to suffer a —** *(mil)* adversum casum experiri; *(pol)* repulsam ferre
setting *s (of sun)* occas•us -ūs *m; (situation)* res, rerum *fpl*
settle *tr* statuĕre; *(business)* transigĕre; *(colony)* deducĕre; *(people, e.g., on public lands)* constituĕre; *(argument)* componĕre; *(debt)* expedire; **to — accounts with** rationes putare cum *(w. abl)* ‖ *intr (to the bottom)* subsidēre; *(to alight, land)* **(on)** insidĕre *(w. dat); (to fix one's home)* **(in)** considĕre *or* insidĕre (in + *abl);* **we —ed among ourselves to** constituimus inter nos ut
settled *adj (sure, certain)* cert•us -a -um
settlement *s (of a colony)* deducti•o -onis *f; (the colony itself)* coloni•a -ae *f; (of an affair)* compositi•o -onis *f; (terms)* pact•um -i *n*
settler *s* colon•us -i *m*
seven *adj* septem *(indecl);* **— times** septies
sevenfold *adj* septempl•ex -icis
seventeen *adj* septendecim *(indecl)*
seventeenth *adj* septim•us decim•us -a -um
seventh *adj* septim•us -a -um
seventieth *adj* septuagesim•us -a -um
seventy *adj* septuaginta *(indecl)*
sever *tr* separare ‖ *intr* disjungi
several *adj* aliquot *(indecl)*
severally *adv* singulatim

severe *adj (rigorous, strict)* sever•us -a -um; *(wound, punishment)* grav•is -is -e; *(winter)* a•cer -cris -cre; *(cold, pain)* dur•us -a -um
severely *adv* severe, graviter
severity *s* severit•as -atis *f*, gravit•as -atis *f*
sew *tr* suĕre; **to — up** consuĕre
sewer *s* cloac•a -ae *f*
sewing *s* sutur•a -ae *f*
sex *s (gender)* sex•us -ūs *m; (intercourse)* Ven•us -eris *f*, coït•us -ūs *m;* **to have illicit — with** stuprum inferre *(w. dat)*
sextant *s* sext•ans -antis *m*
sexton *s* aeditu•us -i *m*
sexual *adj* sexual•is -is -e; **— desire** libid•o -inis *f;* **— intercourse** Ven•us -eris *f*, coït•us -ūs *m*
shabbily *adv* sordide
shabbiness *s* sord•es -ium *fpl*
shabby *adj* sordid•us -a -um; *(worn out, torn)* obsolet•us -a -um
shackle *tr* compedibus constringĕre
shackles *spl* vincul•a -orum *npl; (on the legs)* comped•es -ium *fpl*
shade *s* umbr•a -ae *f;* **—s** *(of the dead)* man•es -ium *mpl*
shade *tr* opacare, adumbrare
shadow *s* umbr•a -ae *f*
shadowy *adj* umbros•us -a -um; *(fig)* inan•is -is -e, exil•is -is -e
shady *adj* opac•us -a -um
shaft *s (arrow)* sagitt•a -ae *f; (of spear)* hastil•e -is *n; (of a mine)* pute•us -i *m*
shaggy *adj* villos•us -a -um
shake *tr* quatĕre, concutĕre; *(head)* nutare; **to — hands with** dextram jungĕre cum *(w. abl);* **to — off a bad reputation** infamiam discutĕre ‖ *intr* tremĕre; *(to totter)* vacillare; **her sides shook with laughter** ejus latera commoverunt risu; **to begin to —** intremescĕre
shaking *s* quassati•o -onis *f; (w. cold, fear)* trem•or -oris *m*
shaky *adj* instabil•is -is -e
shallow *adj (river, sea)* vados•us -a -um; *(trench)* humil•is -is -e; *(well)* brev•is -is -e; *(fig)* lev•is -is -e; **quite —** minime alt•us -a -um
shallows *spl* vad•a -orum *npl*
sham *s* dol•us -i *m*
sham *adj* simulat•us -a -um
shambles *spl* turb•a -ae *f*
shame *s* pud•or -oris *m; (disgrace)* dedec•us -oris *n;* **— on our Senate and morals!** pro senatu et moribus! **— on you!** sit pudor! **to have lost all sense of —** omnem pudorem exuisse; **to put s.o. to —** ruborem alicui incutĕre
shame *tr* rubrem incutĕre *(w. dat)*
shamefaced *adj* verecund•us -a -um
shameful *adj* probros•us -a -um
shamefully *adv* probrose, turpiter
shamless *adj* impud•ens -entis
shamelessly *adv* impudenter
shamrock *s* trifol•ium -(i)i *n*
shank *s* cru•s -ris *n*
shanty *s* tugur•ium -(i)i *n*
shape *s* form•a -ae *f*, figur•a -ae *f;* **to be in good (bad) —** boni (mali) habitūs esse
shape *tr* figurare, formare
shapeless *adj* inform•is -is -e
shapely *adj* formos•us -a -um; *(limbs)* ter•es -etis
shard *s* test•a -ae *f*
share *s* par•s -tis *f*, porti•o -onis *f*
share *tr* partire; *(to enjoy with, have in common with, others)* **(with)** communicare (cum + *abl)* ‖ *intr* **to — in** particeps esse *(w. gen)*
shark *s* p(r)istr•ix -icis *m*
sharp *adj* acut•us -a -um; *(mind)* ac•er -ris -re, sag•ax -acis; *(taste)* acerb•is -is -e
sharpen *tr* acuĕre
sharply *adv* acriter
shatter *tr* quassare, confringĕre; *(to knock apart)* discutĕre
shave *tr* radĕre; **to — off** deradĕre ‖ *intr* barbam radĕre
shaven *adj* adras•us -a -um
shavings *spl* rament•a -orum *npl*
shawl *s* amicul•um -i *n*
she *pron* ea, illa, haec
sheaf *s* fasc•is -is *m*
shear *tr* tondēre
shearing *s* tonsur•a -ae *f*
shears *spl* forfic•es -um *fpl*
sheath *s* vagin•a -ae *f*
sheathe *tr* in vaginam recondĕre
shed *tr (tears, blood, etc.)* fundĕre, effundĕre; *(feathers, leaves)* ponĕre; **to — light on a subject** lumen alicui rei adhibēre
shed *s* tugur•ium -(i)i *n; (mil)* vine•a -ae *f*
sheep *s* ov•is -is *f*
sheepfold *s* ovil•e -is *n*
sheepish *adj* pudibund•us -a -um
sheepishly *adv* pudenter
sheepskin *s* pell•is -is *f* ovilla
sheer *adj (pure, utter)* mer•us -a -um; *(steep)* praerupt•us -a -um
sheet *s* linte•um -i *n; (of paper)* sched•a -ae *f; (of metal)* lamin•a -ae *f;* **— of papyrus** *s* chart•a -ae *f*
shelf *s* plute•us -i *m*
shell *s* conch•a -ae *f; (of nuts)* putam•en -inis *n*
shellfish *s* conch•a -ae *f*
shelter *s* tegm•en -inis *n; (refuge)* refug•ium -(i)i *n; (lodgings)* hospit•ium -(i)i *n*
shelter *tr* tegĕre; *(refugees)* excipĕre
shepherd *s* past•or -oris *m*
shield *s (round)* parm•a-ae *f; (oblong)* scut•um -i *n*
shift *tr (to change)* mutare; *(transfer)*

transferre ‖ *intr* mutari; **to — for oneself** sibi providēre
shift *s (change)* mutati•o -onis *f*
shifty *adj* mobil•is -is -e
shin *s* tibi•a -ae *f*
shine *s* nit•or -oris *n*
shine *intr* lucēre; *(with a bright light)* fulgēre; *(to excel)* praestare; **to — forth** elucēre, enitēre; **to — on** affulgēre *(w. dat)*
shingle *s* tegul•a -ae *f*
shiny *adj* fulgid•us -a -um
ship *s* nav•is -is *f*
ship *tr* navi invehĕre; *(to send)* mittĕre
shipbuilder *s* naupeg•us -i *m*
ship owner *s* navicular•ius -(i)i *m*
shipwreck *s* naufrag•ium -(i)i *n;* **to suffer —** naufragium facĕre
shipwrecked *adj* naufract•us -a -um
shirk *tr* abhorrēre ab *(w. abl)*
shirt *s* subucul•a -ae *f*
shiver *intr* horrēre
shiver *s* horr•or -oris *m*
shoal *s (of fish)* exam•en -inis *n; (shallow)* vad•um -i *n*
shock *s* offensi•o -onis *f*
shock *tr* percutĕre; **to be —** inhorrescĕre
shocked *adj* attonit•us -a -um
shocking *adj* tae•ter -tra -trum
shoe *s* calce•us -i *m*
shoemaker *s* sut•or -oris *m*
shook up *adj* consternat•us -a -um, conterrit•us -a -um
shoot *tr (missile)* conjicĕre; *(person)* transfigĕre ‖ *intr* volare; **to — up** crescĕre
shoot *s* surcul•us -i *m*
shooting star *s* fae•x -cis *f* caelestis
shop *s* tabern•a -ae *f*
shop *intr* obsonare, mercari; **to — for** mercari; *(groceries)* obsonare
shopkeeper *s* tabernar•ius -(i)i *m*
shopper *s* obsonat•or -oris *m*
shopping *s* obsonat•us -ūs *m*
shore *s* lit•us -oris *n,* or•a -ae *f*
shore *tr* **to — up** fulcire
short *adj* brev•is -is -e; **in a — time** brevi; **in —** ad summam; **to run —** deficĕre
shortage *s* inopi•a -ae *f*
shortcoming *s* defect•us -ūs *m*
shortcut *s* compendari•a -ae *f*
shorten *tr* contrahĕre; *(to limit)* coarctare; *(a syllable)* corripĕre ‖ *intr* contrahi, minui
shorthand *s* not•ae -arum *fpl;* **to take down in —** notis excipĕre
short-lived *adj* brev•is -is -e
shortly *adv* brevi, mox
shortness *s* brevit•as -atis *f;* **— of breath** asthm•a -atis *n*
shortsighted *adj* my•ops -opis; *(fig)* improvid•us -a -um
short-winded *adj* anhel•us -a -um
shot *s* ict•us -ūs *m;* **long —** dubia ale•a -ae *f;* **within —** intra teli jactum
should *intr (ought)* debēre; **I — go** mihi eundum est; **if I — say no** si negem
shoulder *s* umer•us -i *m; (of animals)* arm•us -i *m*
shoulder *tr* suscipĕre
shoulder blade *s* scapul•a -ae *f*
shout *s* clam•or -oris *m; (of approval)* acclamati•o -onis *f*
shout *tr & intr* clamare, acclamare
shove *tr* trudĕre, pulsare; **to — the book under the bed** mittĕre librum subter lectum
shove *s* impulsi•o -onis *f*
shovel *s* rutr•um -i *n*
shovel *tr* rutro tollĕre; **to — out** rutro ejicĕre
show *tr* monstrare; *(to display)* exhibēre; *(to explain)* docēre; **to — off** ostendĕre ‖ *intr* manifest•us -a -um esse; **to — off** se jactare; **to — up** apparēre
show *s (appearance)* speci•es -ei *f; (display)* ostentati•o -onis *f; (pretense)* simulati•o -onis *f; (public entertainment)* spectacul•um -i *n;* **for —** ad speciem; **to put on a public —** spectaculum edĕre
shower *s (rain)* im•ber -bris *m; (of stones, darts)* vis *f,* multitud•o -inis *f; (for bathing)* balne•um -i *n* pensile; **to take a —** balneo pensili uti
shower *tr* fundĕre; **to — down arrows on** infundĕre sagittas *(w. dat)*
showy *adj* specios•us -a -um
shred *s* segment•um -i *n* panni; **not a — of evidence** nihil omnino testimonii; **to tear to —s** discindĕre
shrew *s* muli•er -eris *f* jurgiosa
shrewd *adj* callid•us -a -um
shrewdly *adv* callide
shrewdness *s* callidit•as -atis *f*
shriek *s* ululat•us -ūs *m*
shriek *intr* ululare, ejulare
shrill *adj* peracut•us -a -um
shrimp *s* can•cer -cri *m* pagurus; *(person)* homul•us -i *m*
shrine *s* delubr•um -i *n,* fan•um -i *n*
shrink *tr* contrahĕre ‖ *intr* contrahi; *(to withdraw)* refugĕre; **to — from** abhorrēre *or* refugĕre ab *(w. abl)*
shrivel *tr* corrugare ‖ *intr* corrugari
shriveled *adj* rugos•us -a -um
shroud *s* integument•um -i *n*
shroud *tr* involvĕre
shrub *s* frut•ex -icis *m*
shrubbery *s* frutect•um -i *n*
shrug *tr* **to — the shoulders** umeros allevare
shrug *s* umerorum allevati•o -onis *f*
shudder *intr* horrēre; **to — at the sight** horrēre visu

shudder *s* horr•or -oris *m*
shuffle *tr* miscēre ‖ *intr* claudicare
shun *tr* vitare, devitare
shut *tr* claudĕre; **to — in** includĕre; **to — off** occludĕre; **to — out** excludĕre; **to — up** concludĕre ‖ *intr* conticescĕre
shutter *s* foricul•a -ae *f*
shy *adj* timid•us -a -um
shy *intr (of horses)* consternari; **to — away from** abhorrēre ab *(w. abl)*
shyly *adv* timide
shyness *s* verecundi•a -ae *f*
sibyl *s* sibyll•a -ae *f*
sic *tr* **to — the dog on** instigare canem in *(w. acc)*
sick *adj (mentally or physically)* ae•ger -gra -grum; *(physically)* aegrot•us -a -um; **I am — and tired of** me taedet *(w. gen)*; **to be —** aegrotare
sicken *tr* fastidium movēre *(w. dat)* ‖ *intr* in morbum incidĕre
sickening *adj* tae•ter -tra -trum
sickle *s* fal•x -cis *f*
sickly *adj* morbos•us -a -um
sickness *s* morb•us -i *m*
side *s (of a body, hill, camp, ship, etc.)* lat•us -eris *n; (direction)* par•s -tis *f; (faction)* part•es -ium *fpl; (kinship)* gen•us -eris *n;* **at the — of** a latere *(w. gen);* **from all —s** undique; **having heard only one —, he condemned her** alterā tantum parte auditā condemnavit eam; **on all —s** undique; **on both —s** utrimque; **one — of the island** unum latus insulae; **on one —** unā ex parte; **on that —** illinc; **on the one —...on the other** hinc...illinc; **on their —** pro illa parte; **on the mother's —** materno genere; **on this —** hinc; **on this — of** cis *(w. acc),* citra *(w. acc);* **to be on the — of** stare ab *(w. abl),* sentire cum *(w. abl);* **to leave s.o.'s —** a latere alicujus discedĕre; **to lie on his —** in latus cubare; **to walk at s.o.'s —** tegĕre latus alicui
side *adj* lateral•is -is -e
side *intr* **to — with** partes sequi *(w. gen),* stare ab *(w. abl),* sentire cum *(w. abl)*
sideboard *s* abac•us -i *m*
sided *adj* **many-sided** multilater•us -a -um; **one-sided** unilter•us -a -um
sidelong *adj* obliqu•us -a -um
sideways *adv* in obliquum, oblique
siege *s* obsidi•o -onis *f;* **to lay — to** obsidēre
siesta *s* meridiati•o -onis *f;* **to take a —** meridiare
sieve *s* cribr•um -i *n; (little sieve)* cribell•um -i *n*
sift *tr* cribrare; *(fig)* scrutari
sigh *s* suspir•ium -(i)i *n*
sigh *intr* suspirare; **to — for** desiderare
sight *s (sense)* vis•us -ūs *m; (act of seeing)* aspect•us -ūs *m; (range)* conspect•us -ūs *m; (appearance)* speci•es -ei *f; (show)* spectacul•um -i *n;* **at first —** *(on the first appearance of a person or thing)* primā specie; *(looking at it subjectively)* primo aspectu; **to catch — of** conspicĕre; **to lose — of** e conspectu amittĕre
sight *tr* conspicari
sign *s* sign•um -i *n,* indic•ium -(i)i *n; (mark)* not•a -ae *f; (distinction)* insign•e -is *n; (omen)* portent•um -i *n*
sign *tr (document)* subscribĕre; *(to ratify by signature and seal)* signare; **to — one's name to a letter** nomen epistolae notare
signal *intr* signum dare; *(by a nod)* annuĕre
signal *s* sign•um -i *n; (mil)* classic•um -i *n*
signal *adj* insign•is -is -e
signature *s* nom•en -inis *n*
signer *s* signat•or -oris *m*
signet *s* sigill•um -i *n*
significance *s (meaning)* significati•o -onis *f; (importance)* moment•um -i *n*
significant *adj* signific•ans -antis, magni momenti
signify *tr* significare
silence *s* silent•ium -(i)i *n;* **—!** tace! *(pl:* tacite); **to call for —** silentium facĕre; **to pass over in —** silentio praeterire
silence *tr* comprimĕre; *(by argument)* refutare
silent *adj* tacit•us -a -um; **to become —** conticescĕre; **to be —** tacēre; **to keep s.th. —** aliquid tacēre; **to keep — about s.th.** de aliquo silēre
silently *adv* tacite
silk *s* seric•um -i *n*
silk *adj* seric•us -a -um
silkworm *s* bomb•yx -ycis *mf*
sill *s* lim•en -inis *n* inferum
silly *adj* stult•us -a -um
silver *s* argent•um -i *n*
silversmith *s* fa•ber -bri *m* argentarius
silvery *adj* argente•us -a -um; *(of hair)* can•us -a -um
similar *adj* simil•is -is -e
similarity *s* similitud•o -inis *f*
similarly *adv* similiter, pariter
simile *s* translat•um -i *n*
simmer *intr* lente fervēre
simple *adj* simpl•ex -icis; *(easy)* facil•is -is -e; *(weak-minded)* inept•us -a -um; *(frank)* sincer•us -a -um
simpleton *s* inept•us -i *m*
simplicity *s* simplicit•as -atis *f*
simplify *tr* facil•iorem -iorem -ius reddĕre
simply *adv (in a simple manner)* simpliciter; *(only)* tantummodo
simulate *tr* simulare
simulation *s* simulati•o -onis *f*
simultaneous *adj* eodem tempore

simultaneously *adv* simul, unā
sin *s* peccat•um -i *n*
sin *intr* peccare
since *prep* ex *(w. abl),* ab *(w. abl),* post *(w. acc);* **ever —** usque ab *(w. abl)*
since *adv* abhinc; **long —** jamdudum
since *conj (temporal)* ex quo tempore, postquam, cum; *(causal)* quod, quia, quoniam, cum
sincere *adj* sincer•us -a -um
sincerely *adv* sincere
sincerity *s* sincerit•as -atis *f*
sinew *s* nerv•us -i *m*
sinewy *adj* nervos•us -a -um
sinful *adj* prav•us -a -um
sing *tr & intr* canĕre, cantare
singe *tr* adurĕre, amburĕre
singer *s* cantat•or -oris *m,* cantatr•ix -icis *f*
singing *s* cant•us -ūs *m*
single *adj* sol•us -a -um, unic•us -a -um; *(unmarried)* caeleb•s -is; **in — combat** vir unus cum viro congrediendo; **not a — one** ne unus quidem
single *tr* **to — out** eligĕre
singly *adv* singulatim
singsong *s* cantic•um -i *n*
singsong *adj* canor•us -a -um
singular *adj (only one; outstanding; gram)* singular•is -is -e; **in the —** singulariter
singularly *adv* singulariter, unice
sinister *adj* malevol•us -a -um
sink *tr* submergĕre; *(as a hostile act)* deprimĕre; *(money)* collocare ‖ *intr (to settle at the bottom)* (de)sidĕre; *(of ships)* mergi; *(of morale)* cadĕre; **to — in the mud** limo se immergĕre
sink *s* fusor•ium -(i)i *n*
sinless *adj* peccati exper•s -tis
sinner *s* peccat•or -oris *m*
sinuous *adj* sinuos•us -a -um
sip *tr* sorbillare
siphon *s* siph•o -onis *m*
sir interj *(to a master)* ere! *(to an equal)* bone vir! *(to a superior)* vir clarissime!
sire *s* genit•or -oris *m*
siren *s* sir•en -enis *f; (alarm)* classic•um -i *n*
sister *s* sor•or -oris *f*
sisterhood *s* sororum societ•as -atis *f*
sister-in-law *s* glo•s -ris *f*
sisterly *adj* sorori•us -a -um
sit *intr* sedēre; **to — as judge** jus dicĕre; **to — beside** assidēre *(w. dat);* **to — down (on)** considĕre (super + *acc);* **to — on** insidēre *(w. dat);* **to — up** residĕre; *(to stay awake)* vigilare; **to — up all night** pervigilare
site *s* sit•us -ūs *m*
sitting room *s* sessor•ium -(i)i *n*
situated *adj* sit•us -a -um
situation *s* sit•us -ūs *m; (circumstances)* res, rei *f;* **that's the —** res sic se habet

six *adj* sex *(indecl);* **— times** sexies
sixfold *adj* sextupl•us -a -um
sixteen *adj* sedecim *(indecl)*
sixteenth *adj* sext•us decim•us -a -um
sixth *adj* sext•us -a -um
sixth *s* sexta par•s -tis *f*
sixtieth *adj* sexagesim•us -a -um
sixty *adj* sexaginta *(indecl)*
size *s* magnitud•o -inis *f;* **of huge —** ingen•s -tis
skein *s* glom•us -i *m*
skeleton *s* oss•a -ium *npl* corporis
sketch *s* adumbrati•o -onis *f*
sketch *tr* adumbrare, delineare; *(in words)* describĕre
skiff *s* scaph•a -ae *f*
skill *s* sollerti•a -ae *f; (derived from experience)* periti•a -ae *f*
skilled *adj* perit•us -a -um
skillful *adj* scit•us -a -um; *(w. hands)* habil•is -is -e
skillfully *adv* sollerter, scite
skillet *s* cucumell•a -ae *f*
skim *tr* despumare; *(fig)* percurrĕre
skin *s (of man)* cut•is -is *f; (of animals)* pell•is -is *f*
skin *tr* pellem detrahĕre *(w. dat)*
skinny *adj* macilent•us -a -um
skip *tr* praeterire ‖ *intr* subsultare; **to — over** transilire
skirmish *s* leve certam•en -inis *n*
skirmish *intr* levia proelia conserĕre
skirt *s* inducul•a -ae *f*
skirt *tr* tangĕre
skittish *adj* timid•us -a -um
skull *s* cran•ium -(i)i *n;* **fractured —** cap•ut -itis *n* fractum
sky *s* cael•um -i *n;* **under the open —** sub divo
sky-blue *adj* caerule•us -a -um
skylark *s* alaud•a -ae *f*
slab *s* tabul•a -ae *f*
slack *adj* lax•us -a -um
slacken *tr* remittĕre, laxare ‖ *intr* remitti, minui
slag *s* scori•a -ae *f*
slain *adj* occis•us -a -um
slake *tr* exstinguĕre
slander *s* calumni•a -ae *f*
slander *tr* calumniari
slanderer *s* obtrectat•or -oris *m*
slanderous *adj* calumnios•us -a -um
slang *s* vulgaria verb•a -orum *npl*
slant *tr* acclinare; *(fig)* detorquēre ‖ *intr* proclinari
slanted *adj* transvers•us -a -um
slanting *adj* obliqu•us -a -um
slap *s* alap•a -ae *f*
slap *tr* alapam dare *(w. dat);* **to — s.o. in the face** os alicujus palmā pulsare
slash *s (cut)* caesur•a -ae *f; (blow)* ict•us -ūs *m; (wound)* vuln•us -eris *n*
slash *tr* caedĕre

slaughter *s* trucidati•o -onis *f*
slaughter *tr* trucidare, mactare
slaughterhouse *s* carnar•ium -(i)i *n*
slave *s* serv•us -i *m*, serv•a -ae *f*
slave *intr* sudare
slave dealer *s* mang•o -onis *m*
slavery *s* servitud•o -inis *f*
slave trade *s* venalic•ium -(i)i *n*
slavish *adj* servil•is -is -e
slavishly *adv* serviliter
slay *tr* interficĕre
slayer *s* interfect•or -oris *m*
sledge *s* trahe•a -ae *f*
sleek *adj* nitid•us -a -um
sleep *s* somn•us -i *m*
sleep *tr* **to — off a hangover** crapulam edormire ‖ *intr* dormire
sleepless *adj* insomn•is -is -e,
sleepy *adj* somniculos•us -a -um
sleet *s* nivosa grand•o -inis *f*
sleeve *s* manic•a -ae *f*
slender *adj* gracil•is -is -e
slice *s* lamin•a -ae *f*
slice *tr* secare
slide *intr* labi
slight *adj* exigu•us -a -um; *(of small account)* lev•is -is -e
slight *s* neglegenti•a -ae *f*
slightly *adv* parum
slily *adv* astute, callide
slim *adj* gracil•is -is -e; **— hope** angusta spe•s -ei *f*
slime *s* lēv•c -is *n*
slimy *adj* lēv•is -is -e
sling *s* fund•a -ae *f; (med)* fasci•a -ae *f*
sling *tr* jaculari
slink *intr* **to — away** furtim se subducĕre
slip *s* laps•us -ūs *m; (of paper)* schedul•a *f; (error)* peccat•um -i *n; (in grafting)* surcul•us -i *m; (underdress)* subucul•a -ae *f;* **— of the tongue** lapsus -us *m* linguae; **— of the pen** mend•um -i *n;* **to give s.o. the —** aliquem fallĕre
slip *tr (to give furtively)* furtim dare ‖ *intr* labi; **to let —** amittĕre, praetermittĕre; **to — away** elabi; *(to leave furtively)* se subducĕre; **to — out of** elabi ex *(w. abl); (to escape from)* excidĕre ex *(w. abl)*
slipper *s* sole•a -ae *f;* **wearing —s** soleat•us -a -um
slippery *adj* lubric•us -a -um; *(deceitful)* subdol•us -a -um
slipshot *adj* neglig•ens -entis
slit *s* incisur•a -ae *f*
slit *tr* incidĕre
sliver *s* schidi•a -ae *f*
slobber *intr* **to — on** conspuĕre
slop *s* quisquili•ae -arum *fpl*
slope *s* cliv•us -i *m*
slope *intr* proclinari, vergĕre
sloping *adj* decliv•is -is -e; *(upwards)* accliv•is -is -e
sloppy *adj (roads)* lutulent•us -a -um; *(work)* neglig•ens -entis
slot *s* rim•a -ae *f*
sloth *s* pigriti•a -ae *f*
slothful *adj* pi•ger -gra -grum
slothfully *adv* pigre
slouch *intr* languide incedĕre; **to — down** *(in a chair)* parum erecte sedēre
slough *s (of snake)* exuvi•ae -arum *fpl*
slovenly *adj* incompt•us -a -um
slow *adj* tard•us -a -um
slowly *adv* tarde, lente
sluggish *adj* pi•ger -gra -grum
sluggishly *adv* pigre
sluice *s* cataract•a -ae *f*
slumber *s* sop•or -oris *m*
slumber *intr* dormitare
slur *s* macul•a -ae *f*
slur *tr* inquinare; **to — over** mussitare
slut *s* meretr•ix -icis *f*
sly *adj* astut•us -a -um; **on the —** clam
slyness *s* astuti•a -ae *f*
smack *s (flavor)* sap•or -oris *m; (blow)* alap•a -ae *f; (kiss)* bas•ium -(i)i *n*
smack *tr* ferire; *(to kiss)* basiare ‖ *intr* **to — of** sapĕre *(w. acc)*
small *adj* parv•us -a -um; *(comp:* min•or -or -us; *superl:* minim•us -a -um)
smart *adj (clever)* callid•us -a -um; *(elegant)* elegan•s -tis; *(impertinent)* insolen•s -tis; *(of pace)* vel•ox -ocis
smart *s* dol•or -oris *m*
smart *intr* dolēre
smartly *adv* callide; eleganter
smash *s* concussi•o -onis *f*
smash *tr (also* **— up)** confringĕre
smashup *s* collisi•o -onis *f*
smattering *s* cogniti•o -onis *f* manca
smear *tr* oblinĕre, illinĕre
smell *s (sense)* odorat•us -ūs *m; (odor)* od•or -oris *m;* **to have a keen sense of —** bene olēre
smell *tr* olfacĕre ‖ *intr* olēre; **to — bad** male olēre; **to — good** bene olēre, jucunde olēre; **to — like** *or* **of** olēre *(w. acc)*
smelly *adj* olid•us -a -um
smelt *tr* coquĕre, fundĕre
smile *s* subris•us -ūs *m;* **with a —** subrid•ens -entis
smile *intr* subridēre; **to — at** arridēre *(w. dat)*
smirk *s* molestus subris•us -ūs *m*
smirk *intr* moleste subridēre
smite *tr* ferire, percutĕre
smith *s* fab•er -bri *m*
smithy *s* officin•a -ae *f* ferraria
smock *s* tunic•a -ae *f*
smoke *s* fum•us -i *m;* **where there's — there's fire** flamm•a -ae *f* fumo est proxima
smoke *tr (meat)* infumare ‖ *intr* fumare
smoky *adj* fumos•us -a -um

smooth *adj* lēv•is -is -e; *(hairless)* gla•ber -bra -brum; *(polished)* ter•es -itis; *(calm)* placid•us -a -um; *(of talk)* bland•us -a -um
smoothly *adv* lēviter; blande
smooth *tr* lēvare; *(to file)* limare; **to — the path to** viam facĕre ad *(w. acc)*
smoothness *s* lev•or -oris *m*
smother *tr (flames, tears, anger)* opprimĕre; *(to choke)* suffocare
smudge *s* lab•es -is *f*, macul•a -ae *f; (smear)* litur•a -ae *f*
smudge *tr* inquinare, maculare
smug *adj* sui content•us -a -um
smuggle *tr* sine portorio exportare *or* importare
smut *s (soot)* fulig•o -inis *f; (foul language, writing)* obscenit•as -atis *f*
smutty *adj* fumos•us -a -um; *(obscene)* obscen•us -a -um
snack *s* merend•a -ae *f*
snack *intr* adedĕre
snail *s* cochle•a -ae *f; (without shell)* lim•ax -acis *f*
snake *s* angu•is -is *m; (large snake)* drac•o -onis *m*
snap *s* crepit•us -ūs *m*
snap *tr (to break off suddenly)* praefrangĕre; **to — the fingers** digitis concrepare; **to — up** corripĕre ‖ *intr (to break with a sharp noise)* dissilire; *(to make a sharp sound)* crepare; **to — at** *(w. teeth)* morsu petĕre; *(in speaking)* increpare
snare *s* laque•us -i *m;* **to lay —s for a rival** rivali laqueos disponĕre
snare *tr* illaquēre
snarl *intr* hirrire
snarl *s* hirrit•us -ūs *m*
snatch *tr* rapĕre, corripĕre; **to — away** eripĕre; **to — up** surripĕre
sneak *s* lucifug•a -ae *m*
sneak *intr* repĕre; **to — into** corripĕre in *(w. acc);* **to — out of** repĕre ex *(w. abl);* **to — up on** obrepĕre *(w. dat)*
sneer *s* rhonch•us -i *m*
sneer *intr* irridēre; **to — at** irridēre
sneeze *s* sternument•um -i *n*
sneeze *intr* sternuĕre
sniff *s* **to get a — of** olfacĕre
sniff *tr* naribus captare; *(cocaine)* naribus ducĕre ‖ *intr* odorari
snip *tr* **to — off** praecidĕre
snivel *s* muc•us -i *m*
snivel *intr* mucum resorbēre
snob *s* hom•o -inis *m* fastidiosus
snobbish *adj* fastidios•us -a -um
snore *s* rhonch•us -i *m*
snore *intr* stertĕre
snort *s* fremit•us -ūs *m*
snort *intr* fremĕre
snout *s* rostr•um -i *n*
snow *s* nix, nivis *f*
snow *tr* **to — in** nive obruĕre ‖ *v impers* ningĕre; **it is —ing** ningit
snowball *s* glebul•a -ae *f* nivis
snowbound *adj* nivibus obrut•us -a -um
snowdrift *s* niveus agg•er -eris *m*
snowfall *s* nivis cas•us -ūs *m*
snowflakes *spl* ningu•es -um *fpl*
snowstorm *s* ning•or -oris *m*
snow-white *adj* nive•us -a -um
snowy *adj* nival•is -is -e
snub *tr* neglegĕre
snub *s* repuls•a -ae *f*
snuff *tr* **to — out** exstinguĕre
snug *adj* commod•us -a -um
snugly *adv* commode
so *adv* sic, ita, *(before adjectives)* tam; **and — forth** et cetera; **— far** eatenus, adhuc; **— help me** mehercules; **— many** tot; **— much** tant•us -a -um; *(so greatly)* tantopere; **— often** totiens; **— slight a** *(e.g., fever)* tantul•us -a -um; **— so** sic tenuiter; **— that** ut; **— that not** ne; **— then** quapropter; **— what?** quid ergo?
so *pron* **— and —** ille et ille
soak *tr* madefacĕre; *(to soften while soaking)* macerare ‖ *intr* madēre
soap *s* sap•o -onis *m*
soar *intr* in sublime ferri; *(of birds)* subvolare
sob *s* singult•us -ūs *m*
sob *intr* singultare
sober *adj* sobri•us -a -um; *(fig)* moderat•us -a -um
soberly *adv* sobrie; moderate
sobriety *s* sobriet•as -atis *f*
sociable *adj* sociabil•is -is -e; *(pleasant in society)* facil•is -is -e
social *adj (companionable)* social•is -is -e; *(life)* commun•is -is -e; *(institutions, laws, customs, duties)* civil•is -is -e; **— call** offic•ium -(i)i *n*
society *s* societ•as -atis *f;* **high —** optimat•es -ium *mpl;* **secret —** sodalit•as -atis *f;* **— as a whole** omnes homin•es -um *mpl*
sock *s* pedal•e -is *n*
socket *s (anat)* cav•um -i *n*
sod *s* caesp•es -itis *m*
soda *s (in natural state)* nitr•um -i *n*
sofa *s* lectul•us -i *m*
soft *adj* moll•is -is -e; *(fruit)* mit•is -is -e; *(fig)* delicat•us -a -um
soften *tr* mollire; *(fig)* lenire ‖ *intr* mollescĕre; *(of fruit)* mitescĕre; *(fig)* mitescĕre
softhearted *adj* miseric•ors -ordis
softly *adv* molliter; *(noiselessly)* leniter; *(opp. of loudly)* summissā voce
soil *s* sol•um -i *n*, hum•us -i *f*
soil *tr* inquinare, spurcare
sojourn *s* commorati•o -onis *f*
sojourn *intr* commorari
solace *s* solat•ium -(i)i *n*

solace *tr* consolari
solar *adj* solar•is -is -e
solder *tr* ferruminare
soldier *s* mil•es -itis *m*
soldierly *adj* militar•is -is -e
soldiery *s* mil•es -itis *m*
sole *adj* sol•us -a -um, unic•us -a -um
sole *s (of shoe)* sol•um -i *n; (anat)* plant•a -ae *f; (fish)* sole•a -ae *f*
solely *adv* solum, tantummodo
solemn *adj* sollemn•is -is -e
solemnity *s* sollemnit•as -atis *f*
solemnly *adv* sollemniter; **to swear —** religiosissimis verbis jurare
solemnize *tr* celebrare
solicit *tr* flagitare; **to — sex from s.o.** aliquem stuprum rogare
solicitation *s* flagiti•o -onis *f*
solicitor *s* flagitat•or -oris *m; (leg)* jurisperit•us -i *m*
solicitous *adj* anxi•us -a -um
solicitude *s* sollicitud•o -inis *f*
solid *adj* solid•us -a -um; *(food)* plen•ior -ior -ius; *(real, true)* firm•us -a -um; **men of — character** homin•es -um *mpl* probati; **— gold** totum aur•um -i *n*
solidly *adv* solide, firme
soliloquize *intr* secum loqui
soliloquy *s* soliloqu•ium -(i)i *n*
solitary *adj* solitari•us -a -um
solitude *s* solitud•o -inis *f*
solstice *s* solstit•ium -(i)i *n*
soluble *adj* dissolubil•is -is -e
solution *s* dilut•um -i *n; (fig)* soluti•o -onis *f*, explicati•o -onis *f*
solve *tr* (dis)solvĕre
solvency *s* facult•as -atis *f* solvendi
some *adj* ali•qui -qua -quod; *(a certain)* quidam quaedam quoddam; *(several)* nonnull•i -ae -a; *(a few)* aliquot *(indecl)*; **— twenty days later** aliquos viginti dies post; **— war or other** aliquod bellum, nescio quod bellum; **to drink — wine** aliquid vini bibĕre
some *pron* aliqu•i -ae -a; *(several)* nonnull•i -ae -a; *(certain people)* quidam, quaedam, quaedam; **—...others** alii...alii
somebody *pron* aliquis; **— or other** nescio quis
someday *adv* olim, aliquando
somehow *adv* aliquā (viā); **— or other** nescio quomodo
someone *pron* aliquis; **— else** ali•us -a
something *pron* aliquid; **— else** aliud ultra; **— or other** nescio quid
sometime *adv* aliquando
sometimes *adv* interdum, nonnumquam; **—...—** modo...modo
somewhat *adv* aliquantum; *(w. comparatives)* aliquanto, paulo
somewhere *adv* alicubi; *(w. motion)* aliquo; **— else** alibi; *(w. motion)* alio
somnolence *s* somnolenti•a -ae *f*
somnolent *adj* somnolent•us -a -um
son *s* fil•ius -(i)i *m*
song *s* cant•us -ūs *m*
son-in-law *s* gen•er -eri *m*
sonorous *adj* sonor•us -a -um
soon *adv* mox, brevi (tempore); **as —as** simulatque; **as — as possible** quam primum
sooner *adv* prius; *(preference)* potius; **— or later** serius ocius
soot *s* fulig•o -inis *f*
soothe *tr* mulcēre, lenire
soothsayer *s* vat•es -is *m*
soothsaying *s* vaticinati•o -onis *f*
sooty *adj* fuliginos•us -a -um
sop *s* offul•a -ae *f*
sophism *s* sophism•a -atis *n*
sophist *s* sophist•es -ae *m*
sophisticated *adj* urban•us -a -um
sophistry *s* capti•o -onis *f*
soporific *adj* soporif•er -era -erum
sorcerer *s* mag•us -i *m*
sorceress *s* mag•a -ae *f*
sorcery *s* magae art•es -ium *fpl*
sordid *adj* sordid•us -a -um
sordidly *adv* sordide
sore *adj (aching)* dol•ens -entis; *(angry)* irat•us -a -um
sore *s* ulc•us -eris *n*
sorely *adv* vehementer
sorrow *s* dol•or -oris *m*
sorrow *intr* dolēre
sorrowful *adj* maest•us -a -um
sorrowfully *adv* maeste
sorry *adj* mis•er -era -erum; **I am — about** me paenitet *(w. gen)*; **I feel — for** me miseret *(w. gen)*
sort *s* gen•us -eris *n*; **that — of man** ejus generis *(or* modi) vi•r -ri *m*
sort *tr* digerĕre; *(ballots)* diribēre
sot *s* fatu•us -i *m; (drunkard)* potat•or -oris *m*
soul *s (principle of life)* anim•a -ae *f; (principle of intellection and sensation)* anim•us -i *m*; **not a —** nem•o -inis *m*; *(human being)* mortal•is -is *m*
sound *adj (healthy)* san•us -a -um; *(strong)* valid•us -a -um; *(e.g., apple)* inte•ger -gra -grum; *(true, genuine)* ver•us -a -um; *(sleep)* art•us -a -um; *(stomach)* firm•us -a -um; **to be of — mind** comp•os -otis mentis esse
sound *s* son•us -i *m; (noise)* strepit•us -ūs *m; (of trumpet)* clang•or -oris *m; (strait)* fret•um -i *n*; **loud —** frag•or -oris *m*
sound *tr* **to — the alarm** classicum canĕre; **to — the signal for battle** bellicum canĕre; **to — the retreat** receptui canĕre; **to — the trumpet** bucinam inflare ‖ *intr* sonare; *(to seem)* videri; **to — off** clamitare
soundly *adv (of beating)* egregie; *(of sleeping)* arte

soundness *s* sanit•as -atis *f; (firmness)* firmit•as -atis *f; (correctness)* integrit•as -atis *f*
soup *s* ju•s -ris *n;* **noodle —** jus collyricum
sour *adj* acid•us -a -um, acerb•us -a -um; *(fig)* amar•us -a -um, moros•us -a -um; **I have a — stomach** cibus mihi acescit; **to turn —** acescĕre
source *s* fon•s -tis *m*
souse *s (sl)* potat•or -oris *m*
soused *adj (sl)* uvid•us -a -um
south *s* meridi•es -ei *m;* **to face —** in meridiem spectare
south *adj* meridian•us -a -um; **— of** infra *(w. acc)*
southeast *adv* inter meridiem et solis ortum
southern *adj* austral•is -is -e, meridional•is -is -e
southward *adv* in meridiem
southwest *adv* inter solis occasum et meridiem
south wind *s* aus•ter -tri *m*
souvenir *s* monument•um -i *n*
sovereign *adj* suprem•us -a -um
sovereign *s* princ•eps -ipis *m*
sovereignty *s* principat•us -ūs *m*
sow *s* scrof•a -ae *f*
sow *tr* serĕre; *(a field)* conserĕre
sower *s* sat•or -oris *m*
space *s* spat•ium -(i)i *n; (of time)* intervall•um -i *n*
spacious *adj* ampl•us -a -um
spaciousness *s* amplitud•o -inis *f*
spade *s* pal•a -ae *f;* **to call a — a —** quamque rem suo nomine appellare
span *s (exent)* spat•ium -(i)i *n; (measure)* palm•us -i *m;* **brief — of life** exigua brevit•as -atis *f* vitae
spangle *s* bracte•a -ae *f*
Spaniard *s* Hispan•us -a -um
Spanish *adj (esp. people)* Hispan•us -a -um; *(esp. things)* Hispanic•us -a -um; *(esp. foreign things connected with Spain)* Hispaniens•is -is -e; **to speak —** Hispanice loqui
spank *tr* ferire palmā
spanking *s* **to get a —** vapulare
spar *s* tign•um -i *n*
spar *intr* dimicare; *(fig)* digladiari
spare *tr* parcĕre *(w. dat)*
spare time *s* tempor•a -rum *npl* subsiciva
sparing *adj* parc•us -a -um
sparingly *adv* parce
spark *s* scintill•a -ae *f; (fig)* ignicul•us -i *m*
sparkle *intr* scintillare
sparkling *adj* corusc•us -a -um
sparrow *s* pass•er -eris *m*
sparse *adj* rar•us -a -um
Spartan *adj* Laconic•us -a -um
spasm *s* distenti•o -onis *f* nervorum
spasmodically *adv* interdum
spatter *tr* aspergĕre; **—ed with rain and mud** imbre lutoque aspers•us -a -um
spatula *s* spath•a -ae *f*
spawn *s* ov•a -orum *npl*
spawn *intr* ova parĕre
speak *tr* loqui, dicĕre; **to — Latin** Latine loqui ‖ *intr* loqui; **to — of** dicĕre de *(w. abl);* **to — to** alloqui *(w. acc);* **to — with** colloqui *(w. abl)*
speaker *s* dic•ens -entis *mf; (speech maker)* orat•or -oris *m*
spear *s* hast•a -ae *f*
spear *tr* hastā transfigĕre
special *adj* praecipu•us -a -um
speciality *s* propriet•as -atis *f*
specially *adv* praecipue
species *s* speci•es -ei *f*
specific *adj* cert•us -a -um
specify *tr* subtiliter enumerare
specimen *s* exempl•um -i *n*
specious *adj* specios•us -a -um
speck *s* macul•a -ae *f*
speckled *adj* maculos•us -a -um
spectacle *s* spectacul•um -i *n*
spectator *s* spectat•or -oris *m*
specter *s* larv•a -ae *f*
spectral *adj* larval•is -is -e
spectrum *s* spectr•um -i *n*
speculate *intr* conjecturam facĕre; *(com)* foro uti
speculation *s (guess)* conjectur•a -ae *f; (com)* ale•a -ae *f*
speculative *adj* conjectural•is -is -e
speculator *s* contemplat•or -oris *m; (com)* dardanar•ius -(i)i *m*
speech *s (faculty of speech; address)* orati•o -onis *f;* **to make a —** verba facĕre, orationem habēre
speechless *adj* elingu•is -is -e; **he was struck —** mutus erat ilico
speed *s* celerit•as -atis *f*
speed *tr* **to — up** accelerare ‖ *intr* properare
speedily *adv* celeriter
speedy *adj* cit•us -a -um
spell *tr* scribĕre
spell *s* incantament•um -i *n*
spellbound *adj* fascinat•us -a -um
spelling *s* orthographi•a -ae *f*
spend *tr (money, time, effort)* impendĕre; *(time)* agĕre, consumĕre; *(w. the idea of waste)* terĕre; **to — effort, money (on)** operam, pecuniam impendĕre (in + *acc or w. dat)*
spendthrift *s* prodig•us -i *m*
spew *tr* vomĕre
sphere *s* sphaer•a -ae *f; (fig)* provinci•a -ae *f*
spherical *adj* sphaeric•us -a -um
sphinx *s* sphin•x -gis *f*
spice *s* condiment•um -i *n*
spice *tr* condire
spicy *adj* a•cer -cris -cre

spider *s* aren•a -ae *f*
spider web *s* arane•um -i *n*
spigot *s* epistom•ium -(i)i *n*
spike *s* clav•us -i *m* tabular•is
spill *tr* effunděre; **to — blood** sanguinem funděre
spin *tr* versare; *(thread)* nēre; **to — a top** turbinem versare; **to — a web** telam texěre **II** *intr* versari
spinach *s* spinace•a -ae *f* oleracea
spinal *adj* spinae *(gen)*
spine *s* spin•a -ae *f*
spinster *s* innupt•a -ae *f*
spiral *adj* spiral•is -is -e
spiral *s* spir•a -ae *f*
spirit *s* spirit•us -ūs *m;* anim•us -i *m; (temper, disposition)* ingen•ium -(i)i *n;* **full of —** animos•us -a -um; **—s of the dead** man•es -ium *fpl;* **to be in high —s** hilar•is -is -e esse; **to defend with such —** tam enixe defenděre
spirited *adj* animos•us -a -um
spiritless *adj* ignav•us -a -um
spiritual *adj* animi *(gen)*
spit *s* ver•u -us *n; (spittle)* sput•um -i *n*
spit *tr* spuěre; **to — out** exspuěre **II** *intr* spuěre; **to — in s.o.'s face** in faciem *(w. gen)* inspuěre
spite *tr* offenděre
spite *s* malevolenti•a -ae *f;* **for —** consulto; **in — of** *(no exact Latin equivalent, sometimes expressed by an abl. absolute, e.g.,* **in — of all the arguments of his opponent, he stuck to this guns** contemptis omnibus adversarii rationibus, in sententia sua perseveravit
spiteful *adj* malevol•us -a -um
splash *tr* aspergěre; **to — the face with warm water** faciem aquā tepidā fovēre
splash *s* sonit•us -ūs *m* undae; *(display)* ostentati•o -onis *f*
splendid *adj* splendid•us -a -um
splendidly *adv* splendide
splendor *s* splend•or -oris *m*
splint *s* ferul•a -ae *f*
splinter *s* assul•a -ae *f*; **bone —** fragment•um -i *n* ossis
splinter *tr* assulatim finděre
split *s* fissur•a -ae *f*
split *tr* finděre; **to — one's sides laughing** ilia sua risu dissolvěre **II** *intr* findi
spoil *tr (to make faulty)* vitiare; *(a child)* depravare; *(food)* corrumpěre **II** *intr (of food)* corrumpi
spoils *spl* spoli•a -orum *npl*
spoke *s* rad•ius -(i)i *m*
spokesman *s* interpr•es -etis *m*
spondee *s* sponde•us -i *m*
sponge *s* spongi•a -ae *f*
sponge *tr* **to — a meal** cenam captare
sponsor *s* spons•or -oris *m*
sponsor *tr* favēre *(w. dat);* **to — games** ludos eděre
spontaneity *s* alacrit•as -atis *f*
spontaneous *adj* automat•us -a -um
spontaneously *adv* sponte, ultro
spool *s* fus•us -i *m*
spoon *s* cochle•ar -aris *n*
spoonful *s* cochlearis mensur•a -ae *f*
sporadic *adj* rar•us -a -um
sporadically *adv* dispersim
sport *s* lud•us -i *m*
sport *tr* ostentare
sportive *adj* jocos•us -a -um
sportsman *s* venat•or -oris *m; (fig)* aequus lus•or -oris *m*
spot *s* macul•a -ae *f; (stain)* lab•es -is *f; (place)* loc•us -i *m;* **on the —** *(immediately)* ilico; *(in trouble)* in angustiis; **to the same —** eodem
spot *tr* conspicěre
spotless *adj* immaculat•us -a -um
spotted *adj* maculos•us -a -um
spouse *s* conju(n)•x -gis *mf*
spout *s (rain spout)* o•s -ris *n* canalis; *(of jug)* o•s -ris *n*
spout *tr* ejaculare; *(speeches)* declamare **II** *intr* emicare
sprain *tr* intorquēre; **to — an ankle** talum intorquēre
sprawl *intr* se funděre
spray *s* asperg•o -inis *f*
spray *tr* aspergěre
spread *tr* panděre; *(to make known)* divulgare; **to — a blanket on the floor** extenděre lodiculam in pavimento **II** *intr* patēre; *(of rumor)* percrebrescěre; *(of disease)* serpěre
spread *s (ranch)* latifund•ium -(i)i *n*
sprig *s* ramul•us -i *m*
sprightly *adj* veget•us -a -um
spring *s (season)* ve•r -ris *n; (leap)* salt•us -ūs *m; (of water)* scaturg•o -inis *f*, fon•s -tis *m*
spring *adj* vern•us -a -um
spring *tr* **to — a leak** rimas agěre **II** *intr (to come from)* oriri, enasci; *(of rivers, etc.)* exoriri; *(to leap)* salire; **to — down** desilire; **to suddenly — open** subito se panděre
springboard *s* petaur•us -i *m*
springtime *s* vernum temp•us -oris *n*
sprinkle *tr* spargěre; **to — s.th. on** inspergěre aliquid *(w. dat or super + acc)* **II** *intr* rorare
sprout *s* pull•us -i *m*
sprout *intr* pullulare
spruce *adj* laut•us -a -um
spruce *tr* **to — up** mundare **II** *intr* **to — up** se mundare
spur *s* calc•ar -aris *n; (fig)* incitament•um -i *n;* **on the — of the moment** de improviso
spur *tr (a horse)* calcaribus concitare; *(fig)* urgēre, stimulare

spurious *adj* spuri•us -a -um
spurn *tr* spernĕre
spurt *intr* emicare
sputter *intr* balbutire
spy *s* speculat•or -oris *m*
spy *intr* speculari
squabble *s* rix•a -ae *f*
squabble *intr* rixari
squad *s* manipul•us -i *m*
squadron *s (of cavalry)* turm•a -ae *f; (of ships)* class•is -is *f*
squalid *adj* squalid•us -a -um
squall *s* procell•a -ae *f*
squalor *s* squal•or -oris *m*
squander *tr* dissipare
squanderer *s* prodig•us -i *m*
square *adj* quadrat•us -a -um; *(fig)* honest•us -a -um; **— foot** quadratus pe•s pedis *m;* **— meal** largior cib•us -i *m*
square *s* quadrat•um -i *n; (tool)* norm•a -ae *f*
square *tr (math)* quadrare ‖ *intr* convenire, congruĕre; **to — off** pugnis minitari
squash *tr* conterĕre
squash *s* cucurbit•a -ae *f*
squat *intr* subsidĕre
squat *adj* parv•us atque obes•us -a -um
squeak *intr* stridēre
squeak *s* strid•or -oris *m*
squeamish *adj* fastidios•us -a -um; **to feel —** fastidire
squeeze *tr* comprimĕre; **to — out** exprimĕre
squint *intr* strabo esse
squint-eyed *adj* paet•us -a -um
squire *s* armig•er -eri *m*
squirrel *s* sciur•us -i *m*
squirt *tr* projicĕre ‖ *intr* emicare
stab *s* punct•a -ae *f*
stab *tr* fodĕre, perforare
stability *s* stabilit•as -atis *f*
stabilize *tr* stabilire, firmare
stable *adj* stabil•is -is -e
stable *s* stabul•um -i *n; (for horses)* equil•e -is *n; (for cows, oxen)* bubil•e -is *n; (of boxers, gladiators)* famili•a -ae *f*
stack *s* acerv•us -i *m,* stru•es -is *f*
stack *tr* coacervare
staff *s* scipi•o -onis *m; (of a magistrate)* contubern•ium -(i)i *n*
staff member, staff officer *s* contubernal•is -is *m*
stag *s* cerv•us -i *m*
stag party *s* conviv•ium -(i)i *n* sine feminis
stage *s (theat)* scaen•a -ae *f; (degree)* grad•us -ūs *m;* **during the early —s of** inter initia *(w. gen);* **— of life** par•s -tis *f* aetatis
stage play *s* lud•us -i *m* scaenicus
stagger *tr* obstupefacĕre ‖ *intr* titubare
stagnant *adj* stagn•ans -antis; *(fig)* in•ers -ertis
stagnate *intr* stagnare
stagnation *s* cessati•o -onis *f*
stain *s* lab•es -is *f,* macul•a -ae *f*
stain *tr* maculare; *(to dye)* tingĕre
stainless *adj* immaculat•us -a -um
stair *s* grad•us -ūs *m;* **—s** scal•ae -arum *fpl,* grad•ūs -uum *mpl;* **to climb the —** per gradūs ascendĕre
staircase *s* scal•ae -arum *fpl*
stake *s* pal•us -i *m; (wager)* deposit•um -i *n;* **to be at —** agi
stake *tr* deponĕre; **to burn at the —** ad palum igni interficĕre
stale *adj* vet•us -eris; *(bread)* secund•us -a -um, hestern•us -a -um
stalk *s (of plant)* caul•is -is *m; (of grain)* calam•us -i *m;* **— of asparagus** stirp•s -itis *m* asparagi
stalk *tr (game)* venari; *(a person)* insidiis persequi
stall *s* stabul•um -i *n; (small shop)* tabern•a -ae *f*
stall *tr* sistĕre ‖ *intr* consistĕre
stallion *s* admissar•ius -(i)i *m*
stamina *s* patienti•a -ae *f*
stammer *tr & intr* balbutire
stammering *adj* balb•us -a -um
stammering *s* balbuti•es -ei *f*
stamp *s (mark)* not•a -ae *f; (impression made)* impressi•o -onis *f;* **— of the foot** subplosi•o -onis *f* pedis; *(on a letter)* imag•o -inis *f*
stamp *tr* imprimĕre, notare; *(money)* cudĕre; *(feet)* supplodĕre
stance *s* stat•us -ūs *m;* **to take the — of a fighter** statum proeliantis componĕre
stand *s (board with three legs)* tripes mens•a -ae *f; (platform)* suggest•us -ūs *m; (halt)* mor•a -ae *f;* **to make a — against** restare adversus *(w. acc)*
stand *tr (to set upright)* statuĕre; *(to tolerate)* tolerare; **to — one's ground** perstare; **to — one's ground against** subsistĕre *(w. dat)* ‖ *intr* stare; **to keep —ing** perstare; **to — aloof** abstare; **to — at the door** adsistĕre ad fores; **to — by** adesse *(w. dat);* **to — by one's promises** promissis manēre; **to — by one's word** in fide stare; **to — close to** adsistĕre ad *(w. acc);* **to — fast** consistĕre; **to — for office** honorem petĕre; **to — in awe of** in metu habēre; **to — in the way of** obstare *(w. dat);* **to — in need of** indigēre *(w. abl);* **to — on end** *(of hair)* inhorrescĕre; **to — out** exstare, eminēre; **to — still** consistĕre; **to — up** surgĕre; **to — up for s.o.** alicui adesse; **to — up to anyone** coram alicui resistĕre
standard *adj* solit•us -a -um

standard *s* norm•a -ae *f,* mensur•a -ae *f; (mil)* vexill•um -i *n*
standard-bearer *s* vexillar•ius -(i)i *m*
standard of living *s* consuetud•o -inis *f* victūs
stand-in *s* vicar•ius -(i)i *m*
standing *s* stat•us -ūs *m;* **of long —** vet•us -eris
standing *adj* perpetu•us -a -um
standstill *s* **to be at a —** haerēre; **to come to a —** consistĕre
stanza *s* vers•us -ūs *m; (of four lines)* tetrastich•on -i *n*
staple *adj* necessari•us -a -um; *(chief)* praecipu•us -a -um; **—s** vict•us -ūs *m*
star *s* stell•a -ae *f,* sid•us -eris *n; (fig)* lum•en -inis *n*
star *intr (theat)* primas partes agĕre
starch *s* amyl•um -i *n*
starch *tr* amylare
stare *s* obtut•us -ūs *m*
stare *intr* stupēre; **to — at** intueri
stark *adj* rigid•us -a -um
stark *adv* omnino, penitus
starlight *s* siderum lum•en -inis *n*
starling *s* sturn•us -i *m*
starry *adj* sidere•us -a -um
start *s* init•ium -(i)i *n; (sudden movement)* salt•us -ūs *m; (of journey)* profecti•o -onis *f;* **to get a — on s.o.** occupare aliquem; **to get off to a bad —** initia male ponĕre; **to have a two-day — on s.o.** biduo antecessĕre aliquem
start *tr* incipĕre, instituĕre ‖ *intr* incipĕre, (ex)oridiri; *(to take fright)* resilire; **to — out** proficisci
starting gate *s* carcer•es -um *mpl*
startle *tr* territare
starvation *s* fam•es -is *f;* **to go on a — diet** abstin•ax -acis esse
starve *tr* fame interficĕre ‖ *intr* fame confici
state *s* stat•us -ūs *m; (pol)* civit•as -atis *f,* respublica *(gen:* reipublicae) *f;* **— of affairs** re•s -rum *fpl;* **to be in a better —** in meliore loco esse; **to be in a worse —** deteriore statu esse; **to restore s.th. to its former —** in pristinum statum aliquid restituĕre
state *tr* affirmare; *(of writers)* auctor esse; *(in writing)* scribĕre
statement *s* dict•um -i *n,* affirmati•o -onis *f; (of a witness in court)* testimon•ium -(i)i *n;* **to make a —** profiteri
statesman *s* vir *m* reipublicae administrandae peritus
statesmanship *s* ar•s -tis *f* reipublicae administrandae
station *s* stati•o -onis *f*
station *tr* locare, disponĕre

stationary *adj* stabil•is -is -e, immot•us -a -um
stationery *s* re•s -rum *fpl* scriptoriae
stationery store *s* tabern•a -ae *f* chartaria
statistics *spl* cens•us -ūs *m*
statue *s* statu•a -ae *f,* sign•um -i *n*
stature *s* statur•a -ae *f*
status quo *s* praesens stat•us -ūs *m*
statute *s* constitut•um -i *n*
staunch *adj* fid•us -a -um, firm•us -a -um
staunch *tr* **to — the flow of blood** sanguinem cohibēre
stave *tr* **to — off** arcēre
stay *tr* detinēre; *(to curb)* coercēre ‖ *intr* manēre, commorari; **to — at home** se continēre; **to — away from** abstinēre *(w. abl)*
stay *s (sojourn)* mansi•o -onis *f; (delay)* mor•a -ae *f; (prop)* fulcr•um -i *n;* **— of execution** prolati•o -onis *f* supplicii extremi
steadfast *adj* const•ans -antis
steadfastly *adv* constanter
steadily *adv* firme, constanter
steadiness *s* constanti•a -ae *f*
steady *adj* stabil•is -is -e, firm•us -a -um; *(fig)* const•ans -antis; **— weather** aequales tempestat•es -um *fpl*
steak *s* off•a -ae *f* bubula
steal *tr* furari ‖ *intr* furari; **to — away** se subducĕre
stealth *s* furt•um -i *n;* **by —** furtim
stealthily *adv* furtim
stealthy *adj* furtiv•us -a -um
steam *s* vap•or -oris *m,* fum•us -i *m*
steam *intr* vaporare, fumare
steam bath *s* sudator•ium -(i)i *n*
steam pipe *s* vaporar•ium -(i)i *n*
steed *s* equ•us -i *m* bellator
steel *s* chalyb•s -is *m*
steel *tr* **to — oneself against** obdurescĕre contra *(w. acc)*
steep *adj* ardu•us -a -um
steep *tr* madefacĕre; **—ed in crime** inquinat•us -a -um sceleribus
steeple *s* turr•is -is *f*
steepness *s* arduit•as -atis *f*
steer *s* juvenc•us -i *m*
steer *tr* gubernare, dirigĕre
steering *s* gubernati•o -onis *f*
stem *s* stirp•s -is *f; (of a ship)* pror•a -ae *f*
stem *tr* obsistĕre *(w. dat)*
stench *s* foet•or -oris *m*
step *s* pass•us -ūs *m,* grad•us -ūs *m; (measure)* rati•o -onis *f;* **flight of —s** scal•ae -arum *fpl;* **— by —** gradatim
step *intr* gradi
stepbrother *s (on father's side)* vitrici fil•ius -(i)i *m; (on mother's side)* novercae fil•ius -(i)i *m*

stepdaughter *s* privign•a -ae *f*
stepfather *s* vitric•us -i *m*
stepmother *s* noverc•a -ae *f*
stepson *s* privign•us -i *m*
sterile *adj* steril•is -is -e
sterility *s* sterilit•as -atis *f*
sterling *adj* ver•us -a -um
stern *adj* sever•us -a -um
sternly *adv* severe
sternness *s* severit•as -atis *f*
stew *s* carn•es -ium *fpl* cum condimentis elixae; **to be in a —** turbid•us -a -um animi esse
stew *tr* lento igne coquĕre
steward *s* procurat•or -oris *m; (of country estate)* villic•us -i *m*
stewardship *s* procurati•o -onis *f*
stick *s* fust•is -is *m; (cane)* bacul•um -i *n*
stick *tr* figĕre; **to — out a foot on s.o.** *(in order to trip)* pedem alicui opponĕre; **to —one's neck in the noose** cervices nodo condĕre ‖ *intr* haerēre, haesitare; **to — to the usual order** ordinem conservare; **to — to the truth** in veritate manēre; **to — out** eminĕre
sticky *adj* viscos•us -a -um
stiff *adj* rigid•us -a -um; *(formal)* frigid•us -a -um
stiffly *adv* rigide; frigide
stiffen *tr* rigid•um -am -um facĕre; *(w. starch)* amylare ‖ *intr* obdurescĕre
stifle *tr* suffocare; *(fig)* opprimĕre
stigma *s* stigm•a -atis *n,* not•a -ae *f*
stigmatize *tr* notare
still *adj* quiet•us -a -um
still *adv (adversative)* tamen; *(as yet)* adhuc, etiamnum; *(w. comparatives)* etiam, etiamnum
still *tr* pacare, sedare
stillborn *adj* abortiv•us -a -um
stillness *s (silence)* silent•ium -(i)i *n; (quiet)* qui•es -etis *f*
stilts *spl* grall•ae -arum *fpl*
stimulant *s* irritament•um -i *n*
stimulate *tr* stimulare
stimulus *s* stimul•us -i *m*
sting *s (on an insect)* acule•us -i *m; (bite)* ict•us -ūs *m; (of conscience)* ang•or -oris *m*
sting *tr (of a bee)* icĕre; *(fig)* mordēre ‖ *intr (to hurt)* dolēre
stinginess *s* sord•es -ium *fpl*
stingy *adj* sordid•us -a -um
stink *s* foet•or -oris *m*
stink *intr* foetēre; **to — of garlic** obolēre allium
stinky *adj* foetid•us -a -um
stint *s* **without — or measure** sine modo aut mensurā
stint *tr* coercēre
stipend *s* salar•ium -(i)i *n*
stipulate *tr* stipulari
stipulation *s* stipulati•o -onis *f;* **with the — that** eā condicione ut
stir *s* tumult•us -ūs *m*
stir *tr* excitare ‖ *intr* se movēre
stirring *adj* ad movendos animos apt•us -a -um
stitch *tr* suĕre
stitch *s* tract•us -ūs *m* acūs; **— in the side** subitus lateris dol•or -oris *m*
stock *s (supply)* copi•a -ae *f; (race)* gen•us -eris *n; (handle)* lign•um -i *n;* **to take — of** permetiri
stock *tr (to provide with)* instruĕre; *(to store)* condĕre; **to — a fishpond** piscinam frequentare
stockade *s* vall•um *n*
stocking *s* tibial•e -is *n*
Stoic *adj* Stoic•us -a -um
Stoic *s* Stoic•us -i *m*
stoical *adj* dur•us -a -um
Stoicism *s* Stoica disciplin•a -ae *f*
stole *s* amict•us -ūs *m*
stolen *adj* furtiv•us -a -um; **— goods** furt•a -orum *npl*
stomach *s* stomach•us -i *m;* **to have — trouble** a stomacho laborare
stomach *tr* tolerare
stone *s* lap•is -idis *m,* sax•um -i *n*
stone *tr* lapidare
stonecutter *s* lapicid•a -ae *m*
stone quarry *s* lapidicin•a -ae *f*
stony *adj (full of stones)* lapidos•us -a -um; *(fig)* dur•us -a -um
stool *s (bench)* scabell•um -i *n; (feces)* alv•us -i *f;* **when the — is not passed** ubi alvus non descendit
stoop *intr* proclinare; *(fig)* se summittĕre
stop *tr* sistĕre ‖ *intr* consistĕre; *(to cease)* desistĕre; **to — off at Rome** Romae subsistĕre
stop *s* mor•a -ae *f;* **to come to a —** consistĕre; **to put a — to** comprimĕre
stopgap *s* tibic•en -inis *m*
stoppage *s* obstructi•o -onis *f*
stopper *s* obturament•um -i *n*
store *s (supply)* copi•a -ae *f; (shop)* tabern•a -ae *f*
store *tr* condĕre, reponĕre
storehouse *s* promptuar•ium -(i)i *n; (for grain)* horre•um -i *n; (fig)* thesaur•us -i *m*
stork *s* ciconi•a -ae *f*
storm *s* tempest•as -atis *f*
storm *tr* expugnare ‖ *intr* desaevire; **to come —ing in** se infundĕre
stormy *adj* turbid•us -a -um; *(fig)* tumultuos•us -a -um
story *s* fabul•a -ae *f; (of a building)* tabulat•um -i *n*
storyteller *s* narrat•or -oris *m*
stout *adj* corpulent•us -a -um, plen•us

-a -um; *(brave)* fort•is -is -e; *(strong)* valid•us -a -um
stoutly *adv* fortiter
stove *s* foc•us -i *m*
stow *tr* conděre ‖ *intr* **to — away** in navi delitescěre
straddle *tr* cruribus varicatis insistěre super *(w. acc)*
straggle *intr* palari; **to — over the countryside** palari per agros
straggler *s* palat•us -i *m*
straggly *adj* **— beard** horrida barb•a -ae *f*
straight *adj* rect•us -a -um, direct•us -a -um; **— as a line** lineae modo rect•us -a -um
straight *adv* directo, rectā
straighten *tr* rect•um -am -um facěre; **to — out** corrigěre
straightforward *adj* apert•us -a -um
straightway *adv* statim
strain *tr* contenděre; *(muscle)* luxare; *(to filter)* percolare ‖ *intr* eniti
strain *s* contenti•o -onis *f; (effort)* lab•or -oris *m; (mus)* mod•us -i *m*
strained *adj (style)* arcessit•us -a -um
strainer *s* col•um -i *n*
strait *s* fret•um -i *n;* **to be in dire —s** in angustiis esse
strand *s (of hair)* flocc•us -i *m*
strand *tr* vadis illiděre
strange *adj* nov•us -a -um, insolit•us -a -um; *(foreign)* peregrin•us -a -um; **— to say** mirabile dictu
strangely *adv* mirum in modum
strangeness *s* novit•as -atis *f*
stranger *s* peregrin•us -i *m;* **a perfect —** omnino ignot•us -i *m*
strangle *tr* strangulare
strap *s* lor•um -i *n*
stratagem *s* stratagem•a -atis *n*
strategic *adj* bellic•us -a -um
strategy *s* consil•ium -(i)i *n*
straw *adj* stramentici•us -a -um
straw *s* strament•um -i *n; (a single stalk)* culm•us -i *m; (for drinking)* fistul•a -ae *f;* **cottages thatched with —** cas•ae -arum *fpl* stramento tectae
strawberry *s* frag•um -i *n*
strawberry-blond *adj* fulv•us -a -um
stray *intr* errare, aberrare
stray *adj* err•ans -antis
streak *s* line•a -ae *f; (of character)* ven•a -ae *f*
streak *tr* lineis distinguěre
stream *s* flum•en -inis *n;* **—s of sweat** riv•i -orum *mpl* sudoris
stream *intr* se effunděre
streamer *s* vexill•um -i *n*
street *s* vi•a -ae *f; (in city)* vic•us -i *m; (very narrow)* tram•es -itis *m*
street clothes *spl* forens•ia -ium *npl*
street walker *s* muli•er -eris *f* secutuleia

strength *s* vir•es -ium *fpl*
strengthen *tr* confirmare
strenuous *adj* strenu•us -a -um
strenuously *adv* strenue
stress *s (accent)* ict•us -ūs *m; (emphasis)* vis *f; (tension)* tensi•o -onis *f; (importance)* pond•us -eris *n;* **not to lay much — upon a matter** aliquid levi momento aestimare; **to lay — on trifles** adděre pondus nugis
stress *tr* expriměre
stretch *tr* tenděre; *(to tighten what is already stretched)* contenděre; *(in different directions)* distenděre; *(to elongate, e.g., the skin)* producěre; **to — or relax the muscles** nervos intenděre aut remittěre; **to — out the hand to** *(to help s.o.)* manum intenděre *(w. dat);* **to — the legs** crura in longitudinem extenděre ‖ *intr* extendi, distendi; *(geog)* tenděre *(of a person while yawning)* pandiculari; **to — out on the couch** se extenděre super torum
stretch *s* tract•us -ūs *m*
stretcher *s* lecticul•a -ae *f*
strew *tr* spargěre, sterněre
stricken *adj* afflict•us -a -um
strict *adj (severe)* sever•us -a -um; *(accurate)* dilig•ens -entis; **according to the — letter of the law** summo jure; **— meaning of the word** verbi sens•us -ūs *m* proprius; **— truth** verit•as -atis *f* ipsa
strictly *adv* severe; *(carefully)* diligenter; **— speaking** proprie
stricture *s* vituperati•o -onis *f*
stride *s* pass•us -ūs *m* grandis
stride *intr* proceděre passibus grandibus
strife *s* jurg•ium -(i)i *n*
strike *tr* ferire, percutěre, icěre; **I was struck by his boldness** miratus sum audaciam ejus; **struck blind** oculis capt•us -a -um; **struck by lightning** de caelo percuss•us -a -um; **to — a bargain, deal** pacisci; **to — fear into s.o.** incutere timorem in *(w. acc)* ‖ *intr (of workers)* opere faciendo cessare
strike *s* cessati•o -onis *f* operis; *(blow)* ict•us -ūs *m*
striking *adj* insign•is -is -e
strikingly *adv* mirum in modum
string *s* fil•um -i *n; (for bow)* nerv•us -i *m; (mus)* chord•a -ae *f; (fig)* seri•es -ei *f;* **— of pearls** line•a -ae *f* margaritarum
string *tr (a bow)* intenděre; **to — together** colligare
stringent *adj* sever•us -a -um
stringy *adj* fibrat•us -a -um
strip *tr* (de)nudare, spoliare; **to — off**

(clothes) exuĕre; *(e.g., a tribune of power)* privare; *(of rights)* nudare ‖ *intr* se exuĕre vestibus
strip *s (of cloth; of land)* lacini•a -ae *f; (of paper)* sched•a -ae *f*
stripe *s (streak)* lim•es -itis *m; (welt)* vib•ex -icis *m; (blow)* ict•us -ūs *m; (on toga)* clav•us -i *m*
stripped *adj (e.g., for flogging)* despoliat•us -a -um
strive *intr* **(after, for)** niti (ad *or* in + *acc)*
striving *s* contenti•o -onis *f*
stroke *s* ict•us -ūs *m,* plag•a -ae *f; (of oar)* puls•us -ūs *m;* **— of luck** lus•us -ūs *m* fortunae mirabilis; **— of the pen** pennae duct•us -ūs *m*
stroke *tr* (per)mulcēre
stroll *s* ambulati•o -onis *f;* **to take a —** spatiari
stroll *intr* spatiari
strong *adj (body, remedy)* valid•us -a -um; *(smell)* grav•is -is -e; *(powerful)* pot•ens -entis; *(feeling)* a•cer -cris -cre; *(language)* vehem•ens -entis
strongly *adv* valide, vehementer
stronghold *s* castell•um -i *n*
structure *s* structur•a -ae *f; (building)* aedific•ium -(i)i *n*
struggle *s* certam•en -inis *f,* pugn•a -ae *f; (fig)* luctati•o -onis *f*
struggle *intr* contendĕre, luctari
strum *tr* pulsare
strumpet *s* scort•um -i *n*
strut *s* incess•us -ūs *m* magnificus
strut *intr* magnifice incedĕre
stubble *s* stipul•a -ae *f*
stubborn *adj* obstinat•us -a -um
stubbornly *adv* obstinate
stubbornness *s* obstinati•o -onis *f*
stuck-up *adj* vultuos•us -a -um
stud *s* clav•us -i *m; (horse)* admissar•ius -(i)i *m*
student *s* discipul•us -i *m,* discipul•a -ae *f; (at university)* scholastic•us -i *m*
studied *adj* meditat•us -a -um
studious *adj* studios•us -a -um discendi
study *s* stud•ium -(i)i *n; (room)* tablin•um -i *n*
study *tr* studēre *(w. dat); (to scrutinize)* perscrutari ‖ *intr* studēre; *(at night)* lucubrare; **to — under a teacher of rhetoric** operam dare dicendi magistro
stuff *s* materi•a -ae *f*
stuff *tr* farcire; *(w. food)* saginare; **to — it down s.o.'s throat** saginare aliquem recusantem
stuffing *s (in cooking)* fart•um -i *n; (in pillow, uphostery)* toment•um -i *n*
stultify *tr* ad irritum redigĕre
stumble *intr* offendĕre; **to — upon** incidĕre in *(w. acc)*
stumbling block *s* offensi•o -onis *f*
stump *s* caud•ex -icis *m*
stun *tr* stupefacĕre; *(fig)* obstupefacĕre
stunted *adj* curt•us -a -um
stupefy *tr* obstupefacĕre
stupendous *adj* permir•us -a -um
stupid *adj* stupid•us -a -um
stupidity *s* stupidit•as -atis *f*
stupidly *adv* stupide
stupor *s* stup•or -oris *m*
sturdiness *s* firmit•as -atis *f*
sturdy *adj* firm•us -a -um
sturgeon *s* acipens•er -eris *m*
stutter *intr* balbutire
stutterer *s* balb•us -i *m*
stye *s* suil•e -is *n*
style *s (kind, manner)* gen•us -eris *n; (literary)* scribendi genus *n; (rhetorical)* dicendi genus *n; (architectural)* structurae genus *n; (of dress)* habit•us -ūs *m;* **in the new —** novo more
style *tr* vocare, nominare
stylish *adj* specios•us -a -um
suave *adj* suav•is -is -e
subdivide *tr* iterum dividĕre
subdivision *s* par•s -tis *f*
subdue *tr* subjicĕre
subject *adj* subject•us -a -um; **— to** subjectus *(w. dat); (disease)* obnoxi•us -a -um *(w. dat)*
subject *tr* subjicĕre, subigĕre
subject *s* subject•us -i *m,* civ•is -is *m; (topic)* res, rei *f,* argument•um -i *n; (gram)* subject•um -i *n*
subjection *s* servit•us -utis *f*
subjective *adj* propri•us -a -um
subjugate *tr* subigĕre
subjunctive *s* subjunctivus mod•us -i *m*
sublime *adj* sublim•is -is -e
sublimely *adv* excelse
submerge *tr* demergĕre, inundare ‖ *intr* se demergĕre
submission *s* obsequ•ium -(i)i *n*
submissive *adj* summiss•us -a -um
submissively *adv* summisse
submit *tr (e.g., a proposal)* referre ‖ *intr* se submittĕre; **to — to** obtemperare *(w. dat)*
subordinate *tr* subjicĕre, supponĕre
subordinate *adj* subject•us -a -um
suborn *tr* subornare
subscribe *intr* **to — to** *(to agree with)* assentiri *(w. dat); (a magazine)* nomine subscripto profiteri se empturum esse *(w. acc)*
subscriber *s* subscript•or -oris *m*
subscription *s* collati•o -onis *f*
subsequent *adj* sequ•ens -entis
subsequently *adv* deinde, postea
subservient *adj* obsequios•us -a -um
subside *intr (of panic, the sea, wind)* desidĕre; *(of passion)* defervescĕre

subsidiary *adj* subsidiari•us -a -um
subsidy *s* subsid•ium -(i)i *n*
subsist *intr* subsistĕre
subsistence *s* vict•us -ūs *m*
substance *s* substanti•a -ae *f; (wealth)* res, rei *f; (gist)* summ•a -ae *f*
substantial *adj* solid•us -a -um; *(real)* ver•us -a -um; *(rich)* opulent•us -a -um; *(important)* magn•us -a -um; *(meal)* plen•us -a -um
substantially *adv* magnā ex parte
substantiate *tr* confirmare
substantive *s* substantiv•um -i *n*
substitute *s* vicar•ius -(i)i *m;* **as a —** in vicem; **I will go as a — for you** ibo pro te
substitute *tr* **(for)** substituĕre (pro + *abl),* supponĕre (pro + *abl)*
substitution *s* substituti•o -onis *f*
subterfuge *s* perfug•ium -(i)i *n*
subterranean *adj* subterrane•us -a -um
subtle *adj* subtil•is -is -e
subtlety *s* subtilit•as -atis *f*
subtract *tr* deducĕre; **to — the interest paid from the capital** de capite deducĕre quod usuris pernumeratum est
subtraction *s* deducti•o -onis *f*
suburb *s* suburb•ium -(i)i *n*
suburban *adj* suburban•us -a -um
subversion *s* eversi•o -onis *f*
subversive *adj* seditios•us -a -um
subvert *tr* evertĕre
succeed *tr* succedĕre *(w. dat),* insequi ‖ *intr (of persons)* rem bene gerĕre; *(of activities)* prospere evenire
success *s* success•us -ūs *m*
successful *adj (of persons)* fel•ix -icis; *(of things)* prosp•er -era -erum
successfully *adv* prospere, fortunate
succession *s* successi•o -onis *f; (series)* seri•es -ei *f*
successive *adj* continu•us -a -um; **on five — nights** quinque continuis noctibus
successor *s* success•or -oris *m*
succinct *adj* press•us -a -um
succinctly *adv* presse
succor *s* subsid•ium -(i)i *n*
succor *tr* succurrĕre *(w. dat)*
succulence *s* suc•us -i *m*
succulent *adj* suculent•us -a -um
succumb *intr* succumbĕre
such *adj* tal•is -is -e; **—...as** tal•is...qualis
suck *tr* sugĕre; **to — dry** ebibĕre; **to — in** sorbēre; **to — up** exsorbēre
sucker *s (fool)* barcal•a -ae *mf; (bot)* surcul•us -i *m*
suckle *tr* alĕre, mammam dare *(w. dat)*
suction *s* suct•us -ūs *m*
suction cup *s* cucurbitul•a -ae *f*
sudden *adj* subit•us -a -um
suddenly *adv* subito

suds *spl* aqu•a -ae *f* sapone infecta
sue *tr* litem intendĕre *(dat)* ‖ *intr* petĕre
suffer *tr* pati, tolerare; **to — the punishment** poenam dare ‖ *intr* pati; **to — from** laborare *(w. abl);* **—ing from** oppress•us -a -um *(w. abl)*
sufferable *adj* tolerabil•is -is -e
suffering *s* dol•or -oris *m*
suffice *intr* sufficĕre, satis esse
sufficient *adj* satis *(w. gen)*
sufficiently *adv* satis
suffocate *tr* suffocare ‖ *intr* suffocari
suffocation *s* suffocati•o -onis *f*
sugar *s* sacchar•um -i *n*
sugar *tr* saccharo condire
sugar cane *s* arund•o -inis *f* sacchari
suggest *tr* suggerĕre
suggestion *s* suggesti•o -onis *f*
suicide *s* mor•s -tis *f* voluntaria; **to commit —** sibi mortem consciscĕre
suit *s* li•s -tis *f;* **— of clothes** synthes•is -is *f*
suit *tr* accommodare, convenire *(w. dat);* **not —** displicēre *(w. dat)*
suitable *adj* apt•us -a -um
suitcase *s* vidul•us -i *m*
suite *s (apartment)* diaet•a -ae *f; (retinue)* comitat•us -ūs *m*
suitor *s* proc•us -i *m*
sulfur *s* sulf•ur -uris *n*
sulk *intr* aegre ferre
sulky *adj* moros•us -a -um
sullen *adj* contum•ax -acis
sullenly *adv best expressed by the adjective*
sully *tr* inquinare
sultry *adj* aestuos•us -a -um
sum *s* summ•a -ae *f;* **for a large —** magni *or* magno; **for a small —** parvi *or* parvo; **— and substance of a letter** cap•ut -itis *n* litterarum; **— total** summ•a -ae *f* summarum
sum *tr* **to — up** computare; *(to summarize)* summatim describĕre
summarily *adv* summatim
summarize *tr* summatim describĕre
summary *s* summar•ium -(i)i *n*
summer *s* aest•as -atis *f*
summer *adj* aestiv•us -a -um
summit *s* culm•en -inis *n; (fig)* fastig•ium -(i)i *n*
summon *tr* arcessĕre; *(meeting)* convocare; **—ed as a witness** citat•us -a -um testis; **to — to an inquiry** vocare ad disquisitionem; **to — up courage** animum erigĕre
summons *s (leg)* vocati•o -onis *f*
sumptuary *adj* sumptuari•us -a -um
sumptuous *adj* sumptuos•us -a -um
sumptuously *adv* sumptuose
sun *s* sol, solis *m*
sun *tr* **to — oneself** apricari
sunbeam *s* rad•ius -(i)i *m* solis

sunburnt *adj* adust•us -a -um
Sunday *s* di•es -ei *m* solis; *(eccl)* Dominic•a -ae *f*
sunder *tr* separare
sundial *s* solar•ium -(i)i *n*
sundry *adj* divers•i -ae -a
sunflower *s* helianth•us -i *m*
sunken *adj* depress•us -a -um
sunlight *s* sol, solis *m*
sunny *adj* apric•us -a -um
sunrise *s* solis ort•us -ūs *m*
sunset *s* solis occas•us -ūs *m*
sunshine *s* sol, solis *m*
superabundant *adj* nimi•us -a -um
superabundantly *adv* satis superque
superb *adj* magnific•us -a -um
superbly *adv* magnifice
supercilious *adj* superb•us -a -um
superficial *adj (fig)* lĕv•is -is -e; — **wound** vuln•us -eris *n* quod in summa parte est
superfluity *s* redundanti•a -ae *f*
superfluous *adj* supervacane•us -a -um; **to be regarded as** — pro supervacuo haberi
superhuman *adj* divin•us -a -um; *(fig)* incredibil•is -is -e; — **form** form•a -ae *f* major humanā
superintend *tr* praeesse *(w. dat)*
superintendence *s* cur•a -ae *f*
superintendent *s* curat•or -oris *m; (of an apt.bldg)* procurat•or -oris *m* insulae
superior *adj* super•ior -ior -ius; **to be — in cavalry** plus valēre equitatu
superior *s* praeposit•us -i *m*, qui praeest
superiority *s* praestanti•a -ae *f*
superlative *adj* eximi•us -a -um; *(gram)* superlativ•us -a -um
supernatural *adj* divin•us -a -um; supra naturam
supersede *tr* succedĕre *(w. dat)*
superstition *s* superstiti•o -onis *f*
superstitious *adj* superstitios•us -a -um
supervise *tr* procurare
supervision *s* cur•a -ae *f*
supine *adj* supin•us -a -um
supine *s* supin•um -i *n*
supper *s* cen•a -ae *f;* **after** — cenat•us -a -um; **to eat** — cenare
supple *adj* flexibil•is -is -e
supplement *s* supplement•um -i *n*
supplement *tr* amplificare
suppliant *s* suppl•ex -icis *mf*
supplicate *tr* supplicare
supplication *s* supplicati•o -onis *f*
supplied *adj* **well — with** copios•us -a -um *(w. abl)*
supply *s* copi•a -ae *f;* **supplies** *(mil)* commeat•us -ūs *m*
supply *tr (to furnish)* praebēre, suppeditare; *(to fill up)* supplēre; **to be supplied with** suppeditare *(w. abl)*
support *s (prop)* fulcr•um -i *n; (help)* subsid•ium -(i)i *n; (maintenance)* aliment•um -i *n; (backing)* stud•ium -(i)i *n*
support *tr (to hold up)* fulcire, sustinēre; *(to maintain)* alĕre; *(children) (leg)* exhibēre; *(to help)* adjuvare
supportable *adj* tolerabil•is -is -e
supporter *s* faut•or -oris *m; (pol)* suffragat•or -oris *m*
suppose *tr & intr* opinari, putare
supposition *s* opini•o -onis *f*
suppress *tr* comprimĕre; *(for a time)* reprimĕre; *(information)* opprimĕre
suppression *s* suppressi•o -onis *f*
supremacy *s* dominat•us -ūs *m; (supreme power)* imper•ium -(i)i *n;* **to exercise** — dominari
supreme *adj* suprem•us -a -um, summ•us -a -um
supremely *adv* unice, maxime
sure *adj* cert•us -a -um; *(faithful)* fid•us -a -um; **I am** — mihi persuadeo
surely *adv* certe, profecto
surf *s* aest•us -ūs *m*
surface *s* superfici•es -ei *f;* — **of the sea** summum mar•e -is *n*
surfeit *s* satiet•as -atis *f*
surfeit *tr* saturare; *(fig)* satiare
surge *s* aest•us -ūs *m*
surge *intr* surgĕre, tumescĕre; **to — forward** proruĕre
surgeon *s* chirurg•us -i *m*
surgery *s* chirugi•a -ae *f*
surgical *adj* chirurgic•us -a -um
surly *adj* moros•us -a -um et difficil•is -is -e
surmise *s* conjectur•a -ae *f;* **to make —s** opinari
surmise *tr* conjicĕre
surmount *tr* superare
surmountable *adj* superabil•is -is -e
surname *s* cognom•en -inis *n*
surpass *tr* superare, excedĕre
surplus *s* residu•um -i *n*
surprise *s (feeling)* mirati•o -onis *f; (thing)* mir•um -i *n;* **to catch by** — deprehendĕre; **to feel** — mirari; **to the — of all, he says**...cunctis improvisis ait; **to take s.o. by** — excipĕre aliquem incaut•um -am
surprise *tr* admirationem movēre *(w. dat); (mil)* opprimĕre; **to be —d at** mirari, admirari
surprise attack *s* subita incursi•o -onis *f*
surprising *adj* mir•us -a -um
surprisingly *adv* mire, mirabiliter
surrender *s* traditi•o -onis *f; (leg)* cessi•o -onis *f; (mil)* dediti•o -onis *f*
surrender *tr* tradĕre, dedĕre ‖ *intr* se dedĕre, se tradĕre
surreptitious *adj* furtiv•us -a -um

surreptitiously *adv* furtim
surround *tr* circumdare
surroundings *spl* vicini•a -ae *f*
survey *s* inspecti•o -onis *f; (of land)* mensur•a -ae *f*
survey *tr* oculis lustrare; *(land)* permetiri
surveyor *s* agrimens•or -oris *m*
survival *s* sal•us -utis *f*
survive *tr* supervivĕre *(w. dat)* ‖ *intr* superst•es -itis esse
surviving *adj* superst•es -itis
survivor *s* superst•es -itis *mf*
susceptible *adj* moll•is -is -e; **— to** obnoxi•us -a -um *(w. dat)*
suspect *tr* suspicari, suspectare; **to be —ed of** in suspicionem venire quasi *(w. verb in subjunctive)*
suspend *tr* suspendĕre, differre; **to be —ed from office** summoveri administratione rei publicae
suspense *s* exspectati•o -onis *f;* **in —** suspens•us -a -um; **to end the —** exspectationem discutĕre
suspicion *s* suspici•o -onis *f;* **to come under —** in suspicionem venire; **to throw — on** suspicionem adjungĕre ad *(w. acc)*
suspicious *adj* suspic•ax -acis; *(suspected)* suspect•us -a -um
suspiciously *adv* suspiciose
sustain *tr* sustinēre; *(hardships, loss, injury, etc.)* ferre
sustenance *s* vict•us -ūs *m*
swab *s* penicul•us -i *m*
swab *tr* detergēre
swaddling clothes *spl* incunabul•a -orum *npl*
swagger *intr* se inferre
swallow *s (bird)* hirund•o -inis *f*
swallow *tr* vorare; *(liquids)* sorbēre; **to — up** devorare, absorbēre
swamp *s* pal•us -udis *f*
swamp *tr* demergĕre
swampy *adj* paludos•us -a -um
swan *s* cygn•us -i *m*
swank *adj* laut•us -a -um
swap *tr* permutare
swap *s* permutati•o -onis *f*
swarm *s* exam•en -inis *n*
swarm *intr (of bees)* examinare; *(of people)* congregari
swarthy *adj* fusc•us -a -um
swathe *s* fasci•a -ae *f*
sway *s* dici•o -onis *f,* imper•ium -(i)i *n;* **to hold —** regnare
sway *tr (to influence)* suadēre *(w. dat)* ‖ *intr* vacillare
swear *tr* jurare; **to — in** sacramento adigĕre ‖ *intr* jurare; **to — off** ejurare
sweat *s* sud•or -oris *m;* **to break a —** insudare
sweat *intr* sudare
sweep *tr* verrĕre; **to — out** everrĕre ‖ *intr* **to — by** *(to dash by)* praetervolare
sweet *adj* dulc•is -is -e; *(fig)* bland•us -a -um
sweeten *tr* dulcem facĕre; *(fig)* lenire
sweetheart *s* delici•ae -arum *fpl*
sweetly *adv* dulce; *(fig)* suaviter
sweetness *s* dulced•o -inis *f*
sweets *spl* cuppedi•a -orum *npl*
swell *s* aest•us -ūs *m*
swell *tr* tumefacĕre ‖ *intr* tumēre
swelling *s* tum•or -oris *m*
swelter *intr* aestu laborare
swerve *intr* aberrare
swift *adj* cel•er -eris -ere
swiftness *s* celerit•as -atis *f*
swim *intr* natare; **to — across** tranare; **the floor was swimming in wine** pavimentum natabat vino
swimmer *s* natat•or -oris *m*
swimming *s* natati•o -onis *f; (of the head)* vertig•o -inis *f*
swimming pool *s* piscin•a -ae *f*
swindle *s* frau•s -dis *f*
swindle *tr* fraudare
swindler *s* fraudat•or -oris *m*
swine *s* sus, suis *mf*
swineherd *s* suar•ius -(i)i *m*
swing *s* oscillati•o -onis *f*
swing *tr* librare ‖ *intr* oscillare
swipe *tr (to steal)* subducĕre
switch *s (stick)* virgul•a -ae *f; (change)* transit•us -ūs *m*
switch *tr* commutare ‖ *intr* transire; **to — from wine to water** transire a vino ad aquam; **to — over to the plebs** transire ad plebem
swollen *adj* tumid•us -a -um
swoon *intr* intermori
swoop *s* impet•us -ūs *m*
swoop *intr* **to — down on** involare in *(w. acc);* **to — upon** petĕre
sword *s* glad•ius -(i)i *m;* **with fire and —** ferro ignique
sycamore *s* sycamor•us -i *f*
sycophant *s* sychophant•a -ae *m*
syllable *s* syllab•a -ae *f*
syllogism *s* syllogism•us -i *m*
symbol *s* symbol•us -i *m*
symbolic *adj* **to be — of s.th.** signum esse alicujus
symbolically *adv* symbolice
symbolize *tr* repraesentare
symmetrical *adj* congru•ens -entis
symmetry *s* symmetri•a -ae *f*
sympathetic *adj* misericor•s -dis
sympathy *s* misericordi•a -ae *f*
symphony *s* symphoni•a -ae *f*
symptom *s* sign•um -i *n*
synagogue *s* synagog•a -ae *f*
syndicate *s* societ•as -atis *f*
synonym *s* verb•um -i *n* idem declarans

synoymous *adj* idem declaran•s -tis; **a Latin word — with the Greek** verb•um -i *n* Latinum quod idem Graeco valet
synopsis *s* synops•is -is *f*
syntax *s* syntax•is -is *f*
system *s* rati•o -onis *f*
systematic *adj* ordinat•us -a -um
systematically *adv* certā ratione
systematize *tr* in ordinem redigĕre

T

tab *s* pittac•ium -(i)i *n; (coll)* rati•o -onis *f* (debiti)
tab *tr* designare, notare
tabernacle *s* tabernacul•um -i *n*
table *s* mens•a -ae *f; (list)* ind•ex -icis *m,* tabul•a -ae *f; (of bronze)* ae•s -ris *n;* **at** — apud mensam; **to clear the** — mensam auferre; **— of contents: Earthquakes; Chasms, etc.** continenter in hoc libro: De Terrae Motibus; De Terrae Hiatibus, etc.; **to set the** — mensam ponĕre; **to wait on —s** ad mensas ministrare
tablecloth *s* mantil•e -is *n*
tableland *s* planiti•es -ei *f*
tablespoon *s* ligul•a -ae *f*
tablet *s* tabul•a -ae *f; (pill)* catapot•ium -(i)i *n*
tacit *adj* tacit•us -a -um
tacitly *adv* tacite
taciturn *adj* taciturn•us -a -um
tack *s* clavul•us -i *m*
tack *tr* **to — on** *(in sewing)* assuĕre; *(to add on)* subjicĕre ‖ *intr (of ships)* reciprocari
tackle *tr* obsistĕre *(w. dat); (to deal with)* tractare
tackle *s (gear)* apparat•us -ūs *m*
tact *s* urbanit•as -atis *f*
tactful *adj* urban•us -a -um
tactician *s* rei militaris perit•us -i *m*
tactics *spl* belli rati•o -onis *f; (methods)* rati•o -onis *f* rei gerendae
tadpole *s* ranuncul•us -i *m*
tag *s* appendicul•a -ae *f*
tail *s* caud•a -ae *f;* **to turn** — tergum vertĕre
tail *tr* insequi
tailor *s* vestit•or -oris *m*
taint *s* contagi•o -onis *f; (blemish)* vit•ium -(i)i *n*
taint *tr* inficĕre; *(fig)* corrumpĕre
take *tr (in nearly all senses of the English word)* capĕre; *(w. eagerness or haste)* arripĕre; *(what is offered)* accipĕre; *(to require)* requirĕre; *(to grasp, take hold of)* comprehendĕre; *(food, drink, poison)* sumĕre; *(to suppose)* opinari; *(to regard, consider)* accipĕre, habēre, ducĕre; **to — a bath** balneo uti; **to — a dislike to** capĕre odium *(w. gen);* **to — as a certainty** sumĕre pro certo; **to — aside** seducĕre; **to — a trip** iter facĕre; **to — a walk** spatiari; **to — away (from)** adimĕre *(w. dat),* auferre *(w. abl);* **to — back** recipĕre, repetĕre; **to — by the hand** manu prehendĕre; **to — captive** capĕre; **to — charge of** curare; **to — credit for** capĕre gratiam *(w. gen);* **to — down** *(words of a speaker)* excipĕre; *(posters, signs)* refigĕre; **to — flight** capĕre fugam; **to — for granted** praesumĕre; **to — from** adimĕre *(w. dat or abl);* **to — great pains to** in magno negotio habēre *(w. inf);* **to — hold of** *(to grasp)* (com)prehendĕre; *(of a disease)* capĕre; **to — in** *(as guest)* recipĕre; *(to deceive)* decipĕre, fallĕre; **to — in hand** suscipĕre; **to — into consideration** respicĕre; **to — its name from** nomen capĕre ex *(w. abl);* **to — leave of your senses** a te exire; **to — notice of** observare; **to — off** *(clothes, shoes, ring, locket)* detrahĕre; **to — part in** capessĕre partem *(w. gen);* **to — place** fieri; **to — pleasure in** capĕre laetitiam ex *(w. abl);* **to — out** *(to produce)* proferre; *(from storage)* promĕre; **to — out a loan** pecuniam mutuam sumĕre; **to — out of his pocket** de sinu proferre; **to — pity on** capĕre misericordiam *(w. gen);* **to — possession of** occupare; **to — the opportunity** capĕre occasionem; **to — the place of** occupare locum *(w. gen);* **to — to task** exprobrare; **to — up** *(a day)* consumĕre; *(a task)* suscipĕre; *(space)* occupare; *(to snatch up)* corripĕre; *(arms)* capĕre; **to — (it) upon oneself** sibi sumĕre, in se conferre; **to — vengeance on** vindicare ‖ *intr* **I'm —ing off** apoculo *(coll);* **it would — too long to** longum esset *(w. inf);* **to — after** similis esse *(w. gen, esp. of persons; w. dat, esp. of things);* **to — off** abire, proficisci; **to — off from** *(e.g., work)* absistĕre *(w. abl);* **to — over completely** plane tenēre
take *s* praed•a -ae *f; (earnings, profits)* captur•a -ae *f*
tale *s* fabul•a -ae *f; (short tale)* fabell•a -ae *f*
talent *s* talent•um -i *n; (fig)* ingen•ium -(i)i *n*
talented *adj* ingenios•us -a -um
talk *s* serm•o -onis *m;* **idle** — nug•ae

-arum *fpl;* **small —** sermuncul•us -i *m*

talk *intr* loqui; **to — tough** durae buccae esse; **to — with** colloqui cum *(w. abl)*

talkative *adj* loqu•ax -acis

talker *s (idle)* blater•o -onis *m*

tall *adj* alt•us -a -um, cels•us -a -um; *(person)* procer•us -a -um; **to be —** excelsā staturā esse

tallow *s* seb•um -i *n*

tally *s* tesser•a -a *f*

tally *intr* convenire

talon *s* ungu•is -is *m*

tambourine *s* tympan•um -i *n*

tame *adj* mansuet•us -a -um

tame *tr* mansuefacĕre, domare

tamely *adv* mansuete; *(fig)* ignave

tamer *s* domit•or -oris *m*

taming *s* domit•us -ūs *m*

tamper *intr* **to — with** *(e.g., the jury)* sollicitare; *(writings)* depravare

tan *tr (hides)* perficĕre; *(by sun)* adurĕre

tan *s* adustus col•or -oris *m;* **to get a —** colorare

tangible *adj* tractabil•is -is -e

tangle *s* implicati•o -onis *f*

tangle *tr* implicare **‖** *intr* **to — with** se implicare in *(w. abl)*

tank *s* lac•us -ūs *m*

tankard *s* canthar•us -i *m*

tanned *adj* adust•us -a -um

tantalize *tr* vexare

tantamount *adj* pa•r -ris

tap *s* levis ict•us -ūs *m*

tap *tr* leviter ferire; *(wine, etc.)* relinĕre

tape *s* taeni•a -ae *f*

taper *s* cere•us -i *m*

taper *tr* fastigare **‖** *intr* fastigari

tapestry *s* tapet•e -is *n*

taproom *s* tabern•a -ae *f*

tar *s* pix, picis *f*

tardily *adv* tarde, lente

tardiness *s* tardit•as -atis *f*

tardy *adj* tard•us -a -um

target *s* scop•us -i *m*

tariff *s* portor•ium -(i)i *n*

tarnish *tr* infuscare **‖** *intr* infuscari

tarry *intr* commorari

tart *adj* acerb•us -a -um

tart *s* scriblit•a -ae *f*

task *s* pens•um -i *n;* **to take to —** exprobrare

taste *s (sense)* gustat•us -ūs *m; (flavor)* sap•or -oris *m; (fig)* judic•ium -(i)i *n*

taste *tr* gustare **‖** *intr* sapĕre; **to — bad, good** male, bene sapĕre; **to — like** reddĕre saporem *(w. gen),* sapĕre

tasteful *adj* eleg•ans -antis; *(neat in arrangement)* concinn•us -a -um

tastefully *adv* eleganter

tasteless *adj* insipid•us -a -um; *(fig)* insuls•us -a -um

tastelessly *adv* insulse

tasty *adj* sapid•us -a -um

tattered *adj* pannos•us -a -um

tatters *spl* pann•i -orum *mpl*

taunt *s* convic•ium -(i)i *n*

taunt *tr* conviciari; **to — s.o. with his low birth** ignobilitatem alicui objicĕre

taut *adj* intent•us -a -um

tavern *s* caupon•a -ae *f*

tavern keeper *s* caup•o -onis *m*

tawdry *adj* vil•is -is -e

tax *s* vectig•al -alis *n;* **to pay a — on water** vectigal pro aqua pendĕre

tax *tr* vectigal imponĕre *(w. dat);* **to — oneself to the utmost** contendĕre omnes nervos

taxable *adj* vectigal•is -is -e

tax collector *s* exact•or -oris *m*

teach *tr* docēre, instituĕre

teachable *adj* docil•is -is -e

teacher *s* docen•s -tis *mf,* magist•er -ri *m,* magistr•a -ae *f; (of elementary school)* litterat•or -oris *m; (of secondary school)* grammatic•us -i *m*

teaching *s* doctrin•a -ae *f*

team *s* jugal•es -ium *mpl; (of animals)* protel•um -i *n*

tear *s* lacrim•a -ae *f; (a rent)* scissur•a -ae *f*

tear *tr* scindĕre; **to — apart** discindĕre; **to — down** revellĕre; *(a building)* diruĕre; **to — off** abscindĕre; **to — open** rescindĕre; **to — out** evellĕre; **to — to pieces** (di)laniare, discerpĕre; **to — up** *(trees, shrubs)* convellĕre; *(paper)* discindĕre **‖** *intr (to rush)* volare, ruĕre

tease *tr* vexare, ludĕre

teat *s* mamm•a -ae *f*

technical *adj* propri•us -a -um

technique *s* ar•s -tis *f*

technology *s* officinarum art•es -ium *fpl*

tedious *adj* lent•us -a -um; **it would be — to** longum est *(w. inf)*

tedium *s* taed•ium -(i)i *n*

teem *intr* scatēre, redundare

teethe *intr* dentire

teething *s* dentiti•o -onis *f*

tell *tr* narrare, referre; *(to show, indicate)* docēre; **— me the truth!** dic mihi verum! **to — s.o. to** *(w. inf)* imperare alicui ut *(w. subj)*

teller *s* numerat•or -oris *m*

temerity *s* temerit•as -atis *f*

temper *s* temperati•o -onis *f; (anger)* iracundi•a -ae *f*

temper *tr* temperare

temperament *s* indol•es -is

temperance *s* temperanti•a -ae *f*

temperate *adj* temperat•us -a -um

temperature *s* temperati•o -onis *f*

tempest *s* tempest•as -atis *f*
tempestuous *adj* procellos•us -a -um
temple *s* templ•um -i *n; (anat)* temp•us -oris *n*
temporal *adj* profan•us -a -um
temporarily *adv* ad tempus
temporary *adj* temporari•us -a -um; **— stadium** stadi•um -i *n* ad tempus exstructum
temporize *intr* tempori servire
tempt *tr* temptare; **to — fate** experiri casūs
temptation *s* tentati•o -onis *f*
ten *adj* decem *(indecl);* **— times** decies
tenable *adj* defensibil•is -is -e
tenacious *adj* ten•ax -acis
tenaciously *adv* tenaciter
tenacity *s* tenacit•as -atis *f*
tenancy *s* conducti•o -onis *f*
tenant *s* conduct•or -oris *m; (of an apartment)* insular•ius -(i)i *m*
tenant farmer *s* colon•us -i *m*
tend *tr* curare ‖ *intr (to be wont)* solēre; **I tend to believe** crediderim
tendency *s* inclinati•o -onis *f*
tender *adj* ten•er -eris -ere
tender *tr* deferre
tenderly *adv* tenere
tenderness *s (softness)* tenerit•as -atis *f; (affection)* indulgenti•a -ae *f*
tendon *s* nerv•us -i *m*
tendril *s (of vine)* pampin•us -i *m; (of plants)* clavicul•us -i *m*
tenement *s* conduct•um -i *n*
tenet *s* dogm•a -atis *n*
tenfold *adj* decempl•ex -icis
tennis *s* **to play —** pilā ludĕre
tennis court *s* sphaerister•ium -(i)i *n*
tenor *s (purport)* sens•us -ūs *m; (mus)* vo•x -cis *f* tertia
tense *adj* tent•us -a -um
tense *s (gram)* temp•us -oris *n*
tension *s* intenti•o -onis *f*
tent *s* tentor•ium -(i)i *n*
tentative *adj* tent•ans -antis
tenth *adj* decim•us -a -um
tenuous *adj* tenu•is -is -e
tenure *s (fixed period)* spat•ium -(i)i *n; (possession)* possessi•o -onis *f; (pol)* imperii temp•us -oris *n*
tepid *adj* tepid•us -a -um
term *s (word)* appellati•o -onis *f; (limit)* termin•us -i *m; (condition)* condici•o -onis *f; (length of time)* spat•ium -(i)i *n; (math)* termin•us -i *m*
terminal *adj* extrem•us -a -um
terminal *s* stati•o -onis *f* ultima
terminate *tr* terminare ‖ *intr* terminari; *(of words)* cadĕre
termination *s* terminati•o -onis *f*
terrace *s* agg•er -eris *m; (patio)* solar•ium -(i)i *n*
terrain *s* locorum sit•us -ūs *m*
terrestrial *adj* terrestr•is -is -e
terrible *adj* terribil•is -is -e
terribly *adv* horrendum in modum
terrific *adj* terrific•us -a -um; *(great)* festiv•us -a -um
terrify *tr* terrēre
territory *s* a•ger -gri *m,* territor•ium -(i)i *n*
terror *s* terr•or -oris *m*
terse *adj* press•us -a -um
tersely *adv* presse
test *s* probati•o -onis *f*
test *tr* probare, experiri
testament *s* testament•um -i *n*
testamentary *adj* testamentari•us -a -um
testator *s* testat•or -oris *m*
testicle *s* testicul•us -i *m*
testify *tr* testificari
testimonial *s* laudati•o -onis *f*
testimony *s* testimon•ium -(i)i *n*
testy *adj* stomachos•us -a -um
tether *s* retinacul•um -i *n*
tether *tr* religare
text *s* verb•a -orum *npl* scriptoris
textbook *s* enchirid•ion -(i)i *n*
textile *adj* textil•is -is -e
textile *s* textil•e -is *n*
texture *s* text•us -ūs *m*
than *adv* quam
thank *tr* **to — s.o. for** gratias alicui agĕre ob *(w. acc)*
thankful *adj* grat•us -a -um
thankfully *adv* grate
thankless *adj* ingrat•us -a -um
thanks *spl* grati•ae -arum *fpl;* **— to Caesar, I am free** beneficio Caesaris liber sum; **to give —** gratias agĕre
thanks *interj* gratias!
thanksgiving *s* gratulati•o -onis *f; (public act)* supplicati•o -onis *f*
that *adj* ill•e -a -ud; is, ea id; *(sometimes contemptuous)* ist•e -a -ud
that *pron demonstrative* ill•e -a -ud; is, ea, id; ist•e -a -ud; **that is, if Aquila will allow me** si tamen per Aquila licerit; **— is to say** videlicet; **— was the life!** illud erat vivĕre!
that *conj (purpose, result, command)* ut; *(after verbs of fearing)* ne
thatch *s* strament•um -i *n*
thatch *tr* stramento tegĕre
thaw *tr* (dis)solvĕre ‖ *intr* tabescĕre
the *article not expressed in Latin; however to express celebrity, use* ill•e -a -ud: **the Hercules of Xenophon** Hercules Xenophontius ille
the *adv* **—...—** quo...eo; **— less he pursued glory, — more it followed him** quo minus gloriam petebat eo magis eum sequebatur
theater *s* theatr•um -i *n*
theatrical *adj* theatral•is -is -e

thee *pron* te; **of —** de te; **to —** tibi; **with —** tecum
theft *s* furt•um -i *n*
their *adj* illorum, illarum, illorum; eorum, earum, eorum; **— own** su•us -a -um
them *pron* eos, eas, ea; ill•os -as -a; ist•os -ae -a; **to —** eis, illis, istis
theme *s* argument•um -i *n*
themselves *pron refl* se; **to —** sibi
themselves *pron intensive* ips•i -ae -a
then *adv (at that time)* tum, tunc; *(after that)* deinde; *(therefore)* igitur, ergo; **now and —** interdum; **— and there** e vestigio, ilico
thence *adv* inde, illinc
thenceforth *adv* dehinc
theologian *s* theolog•us -i *m*
theological *adj* theologic•us -a -um
theology *s* theologi•a -ae *f*
theoretical *adj* rational•is -is -e
theorizing *s* ratiocinati•o -onis *f*
theory *s* rati•o -onis *f;* **the — and practice of war** ratio et usus belli
there *adv* ibi; *(thither)* illuc; **— are** sunt; **— is** est
thereabouts *adv* circa, circiter, fere
thereafter *adv* deinde
thereby *adv* eā re, eo
therefore *adv* itaque, igitur, ergo
therefrom *adv* exinde, ex eo
thereupon *adv* subinde
thesis *s* thes•is -is *f*
they *pron* ei eae ea; illi illae illa; isti istae ista
thick *adj* crass•us -a -um; *(closely packed)* dens•us -a -um, spiss•us -a -um
thicken *tr* densare, spissare ‖ *intr* crassescĕre
thicket *s* frutect•um -i *n*
thickly *adv* dense
thickness *s* crassitud•o -inis *f*
thick-headed *adj* bard•us -a -um
thick-skinned *adj* callos•us -a -um
thief *s* fur, furis *m;* **an out and out —** tri•fur -furis *m*
thievery *s* furt•um -i *n*
thigh *s* fem•ur -oris *n;* **to slap the —** femur percutĕre
thin *adj* tenu•is -is -e, exil•is -is -e; *(lean)* ma•cer -cra -crum; **to become —** macrescĕre
thin *tr* attenuare; **to — out** rarefacĕre
thine *adj* tu•us -a -um
thing *s* res, rei *f*
think *tr* cogitare; *(to believe, imagine, etc.)* putare, credĕre; *(to surmise)* suspicari; **to — over** in mente agitare; ‖ *intr* cogitare, putare; **to — highly of** magni habēre; **to — ill of Crassus** male opinari de Crasso
thinker *s* philosph•us -i *m*
thinking *s* cogitati•o -onis *f*
thinness *s* tenuit•as -atis *f*
third *adj* terti•us -a -um
third *s* tertia par•s -tis *f*
thirdly *adv* tertio
thirst *s* sit•is -is *f*
thirst *intr* sitire; **to — for** sitire
thirstily *adv* sitienter
thirsty *adj* siti•ens -entis
thirteen *adj* tredecim *(indecl)*
thirteenth *adj* terti•us decim•us -a -um
thirtieth *adj* tricesim•us -a -um
thirty *adj* triginta *(indecl)*
this *adj* hic, haec, hoc
thistle *s* cardu•us -i *m*
thither *adv* illuc, eo
thong *s* lor•um -i *n*
thorn *s* spin•a -ae *f*
thorn bush *s* vepr•es -is *m*
thorny *adj* spinos•us -a -um; *(fig)* nodos•us -a -um
thorough *adj* perfect•us -a -um
thoroughly *adv* penitus
thoroughbred *adj* generos•us -a -um
thoroughfare *s* perv•ium -(i)i *n*
those *adj see* **that**
thou *pron* tu
though *conj* quamquam, quamvis
though *adv* tamen
thought *s (act, faculty)* cogitati•o -onis *f; (product of thinking)* cogitat•um -i *n*
thoughtful *adj (reflecting)* cogitabund•us -a -um; *(careful)* provid•us -a -um; *(kind)* human•us -a -um
thoughtless *adj* inconsult•us -a -um
thoughtlessly *adv* inconsulte, temere
thousand *adj* mille *(indecl);* **a — times** millies
thousandth *adj* millesim•us -a -um
thrash *tr* verberare
thrashing *s* verber•a -orum *npl*
thread *s* fil•um -i *n*
thread *tr* inserĕre
threadbare *adj* obsolet•us -a -um
threat *s (act)* minati•o -onis *f;* **—s** min•ae -arum *fpl*
threaten *tr* minari *(w. acc of thing and dat of person);* **to — s.o. with death** comminari necem alicui ‖ *intr* imminēre, impendĕre
three *adj* tres, tres, tria; **— times** ter
threefold *adj* tripl•ex -icis
three-legged *adj* trip•es -edis
thresh *tr* terĕre
thresher *s* tribul•um -i *n*
threshing *s* tritur•a -ae *f*
threshing floor *s* are•a -ae *f*
threshold *s* lim•en -inis *n*
thrice *adv* ter
thrift *s* parsimoni•a -ae *f*
thriftily *adv* frugaliter
thriftiness *s* frugalit•as -atis *f*

thrifty *adj* parc•us -a -um
thrill *s (delight)* delectati•o -onis *f*
thrill *tr* commovēre
thrilling *adj* mir•us -a -um
thrive *intr* vigēre, virēre
thriving *adj* veget•us -a -um
throat *s* fauc•es -ium *fpl*
throb *s* palpitati•o -onis *f*
throb *intr* palpitare; *(of a vein)* agitare
throes *spl* dol•or -oris *m*
throne *s* sol•ium -(i)i *n; (fig) (regal power)* regn•um -i *n;* **to restore to the —** restituĕre in regnum; **to succeed to the —** recipĕre regnum; *(of emperors)* recipĕre imperium
throng *s* frequenti•a -ae *f*
throng *intr* **to — around** stipare
throttle *tr* strangulare
through *prep* per *(w. acc); (on account of)* ob *(w. acc)*
through *adv render by compound verb with* trans- *or* per-, *e.g.,* **to read —** perlegĕre; **— and —** omnino
throughout *adv* prorsus
throughout *prep* per *(w. acc)*
throw *tr* jacĕre; *(freq)* jactare; *(to hurl)* conjicĕre; *(esp. missiles)* mittĕre; **to — an apple at s.o.** aliquem malo petĕre; **to — a stone at s.o.** impingĕre lapidem alicui; **to — at** conjicĕre ad, in *(w. acc);* **to — away** abjicĕre; **to — back** rejicĕre; **to — down** dejicĕre; **to — food to the dogs** cibum canibus objicĕre; **to — in the way of** objicĕre *(w. dat);* **to — into the fire** projicĕre in ignem; **to — off** *(a rider)* ejicĕre, excutĕre; *(clothes, bonds)* exuĕre; **to — oneself at the feet of s.o.** ad pedes alicujus se projicĕre; **to — oneself down** *(from a height)* se praecipitare; **to — open** patefacĕre; **to — out** ejicĕre; **to —** *(e.g., a cloak)* **over s.o.** injicĕre (pallium) alicui; **to — together** conjicĕre in unum
throw *s* jact•us -ūs *m*
thrush *s* turd•us -i *m*
thrust *s* impet•us -ūs *m,* ict•us -ūs *m*
thrust *tr* trudĕre, impellĕre; **to — back** retrudĕre; **to — off** detrudĕre; **to — out** extrudĕre; **to — together** contrudĕre
thumb *s* poll•ex -icis *m*
thump *s* percussi•o -onis *f*
thump *tr* tundĕre
thunder *s* tonitr•us -ūs *m*
thunder *intr* tonare
thunderstruck *adj* attonit•us -a -um
thus *adv* ita, sic; **and —** itaque
thwart *tr* obstare *(w. dat)*
thy *adj* tu•us -a -um
tiara *s* diadem•a -atis *n*
tick *s (insect)* ricin•us -i *m; (clicking)* lĕvis ict•us -ūs *m*
ticket *s* tesser•a -ae *f; (label)* pittac•ium -(i)i *n*
tickle *tr & intr* titillare
tickling *s* titillati•o -onis *f*
tickish *adj* periculos•us -a -um
tide *s* aest•us -ūs *m*
tidiness *s* munditi•a -ae *f*
tidings *spl* nunt•ius -(i)i *m;* **to bring — of joy** gaudium nuntiare
tie *s* vincul•um -i *n; (of blood, kinship)* necessitud•o -inis *f*
tie *tr* (al)ligare; *(in a knot)* nodare, nectĕre; **to — one's hair in a knot** colligĕre capillos in nodum; **to — up** alligare; *(a wound)* deligare
tier *s* ord•o -inis *m*
tiger *s* tigr•is -is *m*
tight *adj* strict•us -a -um, art•us -a -um; *(tense)* intent•us -a -um; **to get — on wine** se vino devincire; **in a — spot** in angustiis
tighten *tr* adstringĕre
tightly *adv* arte; **too — bandaged** nimis adstrict•us -a -um
tile *s* tegul•a -ae *f*
till *conj* dum, donec
till *prep* usque ad *(w. acc)*
till *tr* colĕre
tillage *s* agricultur•a -ae *f*
tiller *s (person)* agricol•a -ae *f; (helm)* gubernacul•um -i *n*
tilt *tr* proclinare
timber *s* materi•a -ae *f*
time *s* temp•us -oris *n; (age, period)* aet•as -atis *f; (leisure)* ot•ium -(i)i *n; (opportunity)* occasi•o -onis *f; (interval)* invervall•um -i *n; (of day)* hor•a -ae *f;* **after so long a —** tanto intervallo; **another —** alias; **around the — of the battle** sub tempus proelii; **at about the same —** sub idem tempus; **at that —** *(at that hour)* ad id temporis; *(in the past)* tum; **at the right —** ad tempus, tempestive; **at the same —** simul; **at the wrong —** intempestive; **for all future —** in posterum; **for a short —** brevi tempore, paulisper; **for a long —** diu; **for a —** parumper; **for some —** aliquamdiu; **for the first —** primum; **for the — being** in tempus; **from that — on** ex eo (tempore); **from — to —** interdum; **I have no —** non est mihi tempus; **in a short —** brevi; **in —** ad tempus, temperi; **it is high — to** tempus maxime est *(w. inf)*; **many —s** saepius; **on time** tempestive, ad horam; **there is no — to cry** non vacat flēre; **there is no — to lose** maturato opus est; **there was a — when** tempus erat quum; **to ask what — it is** horas quaerĕre; **to say what — it is** quotas horas nuntiare;

to see what — it is horas inspicĕre; **what — is it?** quota hora est? **you couldn't have come at a better —** non potuisti magis per tempus advenire
time *tr* clepsydrā metiri
timeliness *s* tempestivit•as -atis *f*
timely *adj* tempestiv•us -a -um
timepiece *s* horolog•ium -(i)i *n*
timid *adj* timid•us -a -um
timidity *s* timidit•as -atis *f*
timorous *adj* pavid•us -a -um
tin *s* stann•um -i *n*
tin *adj* stanne•us -a -um
tincture *s* col•or -oris *m*
tinder *s* fom•es -itis *m*
tingle *intr* formicare
tinkle *intr* tinnire
tinsel *s* bracteol•a -ae *f*
tint *tr* tingĕre
tip *s* ap•ex -icis *m; (of sword, horn)* mucr•o -onis *m; (hint)* indic•ium -(i)i *n; (money)* stip•s -is *f;* **on the — of the tongue** in labris primoribus; **— of the nose** imus nas•us -i *m*
tip *tr (to make pointy)* praefigĕre; **to — over** vergĕre
tipple *intr* potare
tippler *s* pot•or -oris *m*
tipsy *adj* ebriol•us -a -um
tiptoe *adv* in digitos erect•us -a -um
tire *tr* fatigare; **to — out** defatigare ‖ *intr* defatigari; **I — of** me taedet *(w. gen)*
tire *s* canth•us -i *m*
tired *adj* fess•us -a -um; **I am sick and — of** me pertaedet *(w. gen);* **— out** defess•us -a -um
tiresome *adj* molest•us -a -um
tissue *s* text•us -ūs *m*
tit *s* **to give s.o. — for tat** alicui par pari respondĕre
titanic *adj* ing•ens -entis
tithe *s* decum•a -ae *f*
titillate *tr* titillare
title *s* titul•us -i *m; (of a book)* inscripti•o -onis *f; (of a person)* appellati•o -onis *f; (claim)* ju•s -ris *n*
title *tr* inscribĕre
title page *s* ind•ex -icis *m*
titter *s* ris•us -ūs *m*
to *prep often rendered by the dative; (motion, except with names of towns, small islands)* ad *(w. acc),* in *(w. acc); (reaching to)* tenus *(always placed after the case) (w. gen);* **— and fro** huc illuc; **— my, your, his house** ad me, te, eum; **— the country** rus; **up —** usque ad *(w. acc)*
toad *s* buf•o -onis *m*
toady *s* adulat•or -oris *m*
toast *s (bread)* panis tosti offul•a -ae *f; (health)* propinati•o -onis *f;* **to drink a — to** propinare *(w. dat)*
toast *tr* torrēre; *(in drinking)* propinare *(w. dat)*
today *adv* hodie
today *s* hodiernus di•es -ei *m*
toe *s* digit•us -i *m;* **big —** poll•ex -icis *m*
toga *s* tog•a -ae *f*
together *adv* simul, unā
toil *s* lab•or -oris *m*
toil *intr* laborare
token *s* sign•um -i *n*
tolerable *adj* tolerabil•is -is -e
tolerably *adv* mediocriter
tolerance *s* patienti•a -ae *f*
tolerant *adj* toler•ans -antis
tolerate *tr* tolerare
toleration *s* tolerati•o -onis *f*
toll *s* vectig•al -alis *n; (at ports)* portor•ium -(i)i *n*
toll booth *s* tabern•a -ae *f* portorii
toll collector *s* exact•or -oris *m*
tomb *s* sepulcr•um -i *n*
tombstone *s* stel•a -ae *f*
tomorrow *adv* cras; **day after —** perendie; **— morning** cras mane
tomorrow *s* crastinus di•es -ei *m;* **the day after —** perendinus di•es -ei *m*
ton *s* **to have —s of money** nummorum nummos habēre
tone *s* son•us -i *m; (in painting)* col•or -oris *m*
tongs *spl* for•ceps -cipis *mf*
tongue *s* lingu•a -ae *f; (of shoe)* ligul•a -ae *f;* **to hold one's —** linguam continēre; **his name was on the tip of my —** versabatur mihi nomen in primoribus labris
tonsils *spl* tonsill•ae -arum *fpl*
too *adv* nimis, nimium; *(also)* quoque
tool *s* instrument•um -i *n; (dupe)* minis•ter -tri *m*
tooth *s* den•s -tis *m;* **— and nail** totis viribus
toothache *s* dentium dol•or -oris *m*
toothbrush *s* penicul•us -i *m* dentibus purgandis
toothed *adj* dentat•us -a -um
toothless *adj* edentul•us -a -um
toothpick *s* dentiscalp•ium -(i)i *n*
tooth powder *s* dentifric•ium -(i)i *n*
top *adj* summ•us -a -um
top *s* ap•ex -icis *m; (of tree)* cacum•en -inis *n; (of house)* fastig•ium -(i)i *n; (toy)* turb•o -inis *m;* **at the — of the page** ab summā paginā; **on —** supra; **on — of that** insuper; **— of the head** vert•ex -icis *m;* **— of the mountain** summus mon•s -tis *m*
top *tr* superare; **to — it off** in summo
top-heavy *adj* praegrav•is -is -e a superiore parte

topic *s* res, rei *f,* argument•um -i *n*
topmost *adj* summ•us -a -um
topography *s* regionis descripti•o -onis *f*
topple *tr* evertĕre ‖ *intr* titubare
topsy-turvy *adv* **to turn things —** omnia sursum deorsum versare
torch *s* fax, facis *f*
torchlight *s* **by —** ad lumina
torment *s* torment•um -i *n*
torment *tr* cruciare
tormentor *s* carnif•ex -icis *m*
torn *adj* sciss•us -a -um
torpid *adj* torp•ens -entis; **to be —** torpēre
torpor *s* torp•or -oris *m*
torrent *s* torr•ens -entis *m*
torrid *adj* torrid•us -a -um
tortoise, tortoise shell *s* testud•o -inis *f*
torture *s* torment•um -i *n (almost always used in the plural); (pain inflicted by way of punishment or cruelty)* cruciat•us -ūs *m;* **instruments of —** torment•a -orum *npl;* **to question under —** tormentis quaerĕre
torture *tr* torquēre, cruciare
torturer *s* tort•or -oris *m*
toss *s* jact•us -ūs *m*
toss *tr* jactare ‖ *intr* jactari
total *adj* tot•us -a -um, univers•us -a -um
total *s* summ•a -ae *f*
totally *adv* omnino, prorsus
totter *intr* titubare
touch *tr* tangĕre; *(to stir)* movēre; **to — deeply** commovēre ‖ *intr* inter se contingĕre; **to — on** attingĕre
touch *s* tact•us -ūs *m*
touch-and-go *adj* anc•eps -itis
touching *adj* flexanim•us -a -um
touchstone *s (fig)* obruss•a -ae *f*
touchy *adj* stomachos•us -a -um
tough *adj* dur•us -a -um; *(fig)* strenu•us -a -um
tour *s (rounds)* circuit•us -ūs *m; (abroad)* peregrinati•o -onis *f*
tourist *s* peregrinat•or -oris *m*
tournament *s* certam•en -inis *n*
tow *s* stupp•a -ae *f*
tow *tr* remulco trahĕre
toward *prep* versus *(w. acc),* ad *(w. acc); (of feelings)* erga *(w. acc),* in *(w. acc); (of time)* sub *(w. acc)*
towel *s* linte•um -i *n,* mantel•e -is *n*
tower *s* turr•is -is *f*
tower *intr* **to — over** imminēre *(w. dat)*
towering *adj* excels•us -a -um
towline *s* remulc•um -i *n*
town *s* oppid•um -i *n,* urb•s -is *f*
town hall *s* curi•a -ae *f*
townsman *s* oppidan•us -i *m*
toy *s* ludibr•ium -(i)i *n*
toy *intr* **to — with** ludĕre cum *(w. abl)*
trace *s* vestig•ium -(i)i *n; (for horses)* helc•ium -(i)i *n;* **no — of a wound** nulla suspici•o -onis *f* vulneris
trace *tr* indagare; *(to outline)* delinēre; **to — back** repetĕre
track *s* vestig•ium -(i)i *n; (path)* semit•a -ae *f,* call•es -is *m*
track *tr* indagare
trackless *adj* avi•us -a -um
tract *s (land; treatise)* tract•us -ūs *m*
trade *s* commerc•ium -(i)i *n; (profession)* artific•ium -(i)i *n;* **to carry on — in** commercium *(w. gen)* facĕre
trade *tr* commutare ‖ *intr* mercaturas facĕre, negotiari; **to — in weapons** commercari tela
trader *s* mercat•or -oris *m*
tradesman *s* opif•ex -icis *m*
tradition *s* traditi•o -onis *f,* mo•s -ris *m* majorum; **there is an old —** ab antiquis traditur
traditional *adj* a majoribus tradit•us -a -um
traffic *s* commerc•ium -(i)i *n; (on street)* transit•us -ūs *m*
tragedian *s (playwright)* tragoed•us -i *m; (actor)* tragicus act•or -oris *m*
tragedy *s* tragoedi•a -ae *f*
tragic *adj (lit & fig)* tragic•us -a -um
tragically *adv* tragice
trail *s* vestig•ium -(i)i *n; (path)* call•es -is *m*
trail *tr* investigare; *(to drag)* trahĕre
train *s (line)* seri•es -ei *f,* ord•o -inis *m; (of robe)* peniculament•um -i *n; (retinue)* comitat•us -ūs *m; (rail)* hamaxostich•os -i *m*
train *tr* instituĕre, exercēre; *(to habituate)* assuefacĕre ‖ *intr* se exercēre
trainer *s* exercit•or -oris *m; (of gladiators)* lanist•a -ae *m*
training *s* instituti•o -onis *f; (practice)* exercitati•o -onis *f*
trait *s* mos, moris *m*
traitor *s* prodit•or -oris *m*
traitorous *adj* perfid•us -a -um
tramp *s* vagabund•us -i *m; (of feet)* puls•us -ūs *m*
tramp *intr* gradi
trample *tr* proterĕre ‖ *intr* **to — on, upon** proterĕre
trance *s* stup•or -oris *m;* **in a —** in excessu mentis; **she fell into a —** cecidit super eam mentis excessus
tranquil *adj* tranquill•us -a -um
tranquility *s* tranquillit•as -atis *f*
tranquilize *tr* tranquillare
transact *tr* transigĕre, agĕre
transaction *s* negot•ium -(i)i *n*
transatlantic *adj* transatlantic•us -a -um
transcend *tr* superare, antecedĕre

transcendental *adj* sublim•is -is -e
transcribe *tr* transcribĕre
transcription *s* transcripti•o -onis *f*
transfer *s* translati•o -onis *f; (of property)* alienati•o -onis *f*
transfer *tr* transferre; *(property)* abalienare
transference *s* translati•o -onis *f*
transfigure *tr* transfigurare
transform *tr* vertĕre, commutare
transformation *s* commutati•o -onis *f*
transgress *tr* violare, perfringĕre
transgression *s* violati•o -onis *f; (deed)* delict•um -i *n*
transgressor *s* violat•or -oris *m*
transient *adj* transitori•us -a -um
transition *s* transit•us -ūs *m*
transitive *adj* transitiv•us -a -um
transitively *adv* transitive
transitory *adj* transitori•us -a -um
translate *tr* convertĕre; **to — into Latin** in sermonem Latinum convertĕre
translation *s* translat•a -orum *npl; generally expressed by the verb:* **to do a good deal of — from** multa convertĕre ex (Graeco, etc.) in patrium sermonem
translator *s* interpr•es -etis *m*
transmission *s* transmissi•o -onis *f*
transmit *tr* transmittĕre
transmutation *s* transmutati•o -onis *f*
transparent *adj* pellucid•us -a -um; *(fig)* perspicu•us -a -um
transpire *intr (to happen)* fieri
transplant *tr* transferre
transport *tr* transportare, transvehĕre
transport *s* vectur•a -ae *f; (ship)* nav•is -is *f* oneraria; *(rapture)* sublimit•as -atis *f*
transportation *s* vectur•a -ae *f*
transpose *tr* transponĕre
trap *s* laque•us -i *m,* pedic•a -ae *f; (fig)* insidi•ae -arum *fpl*
trap *tr* irretire; *(fig)* inlaqueare
trappings *spl* apparat•us -ūs *m; (of horse)* phaler•ae -arum *fpl*
trash *s* scrut•a -orum *npl; (fig)* nug•ae -arum *fpl*
trashy *adj (cheap)* vil•is -is -e; *(obscene)* obscen•us -a -um
travel *tr* **to — a road** viā ire ‖ *intr* iter facĕre; **to — abroad** peregrinari
traveler *s* viat•or -oris *m; (abroad)* peregrinat•or -oris *m*
traverse *tr* peragrare, lustrare
travesty *s* perversa imitati•o -onis *f*
tray *s* fercul•um -i *n*
treacherous *adj* perfid•us -a -um; **to be on — ground** in lubrico versari
treacherously *adv* perfide
treachery *s* perfidi•a -ae *f*
tread *tr* calcare ‖ *intr* incedĕre; **to — upon** insistĕre *(w. dat)*
tread *s* incess•us -ūs *m*
treason *s* perduelli•o -onis *f*
treasonable *adj* perfid•us -a -um
treasure *s* thesaur•us -i *m*
treasure *tr* fovēre, magni aestimare
treasurer *s* aerarii praefect•us -i *m*
treasury *s (of the state)* aerar•ium -(i)i *n; (of the emperor)* fisc•us -i *m*
treat *tr* uti *(w. abl),* tractare; *(patient)* curare; *(topic)* tractare; *(to entertain)* invitare; **to — gold like mud** habēre aurum pro luto
treatise *s* libell•us -i *m*
treatment *s* tractati•o -onis *f; (med)* curati•o -onis *f*
treaty *s* foed•us -eris *n;* **to make a —** foedus icĕre
treble *adj* tripl•ex -icis; *(of sound)* acut•us -a -um
treble *tr* triplicare
tree *s* arb•or -oris *f*
trellis *s* cancell•i -orum *mpl*
tremble *intr* tremĕre
trembling *adj* tremul•us -a -um
trembling *s* trepidati•o -onis *f*
tremendous *adj* imman•is -is -e
tremendously *adv* valde, vehementer
tremulous *adj* tremul•us -a -um
trench *s* foss•a -ae *f;* **to dig a —** fossam fodĕre
trespass *intr* in alienum fundum ingredi (sine domini permissu)
trespass *n* peccat•um -i *n*
tress *s* crin•is -is *m*
trestle *s* fulciment•um -i *n*
trial *s (attempt)* conat•us -ūs *m; (experiment)* experienti•a -ae *f; (test)* probati•o -onis *f; (suffering)* tribulati•o -onis *f; (leg)* judic•ium -(i)i *n*
trial lawyer *s* act•or -oris *m* causarum
triangle *s* triangul•um -i *n*
triangular *adj* triquetr•us -a -um
tribe *s* trib•us -ūs *f*
tribulation *s* tribulati•o -onis *f*
tribunal *s* tribun•al -alis *n;* **on the —** pro tribunali
tribune *s* tribun•us -i *m*
tribuneship *s* tribunat•us -ūs *m*
tributary *adj* vectigal•is -is -e
tributary *s* amn•is -is *m* in alium influens
tribute *s* tribut•um -i *n;* **to pay a — to s.o.** aliquem laudibus debitis efferre
trick *s* dol•us -i *m; (feat of skill)* stroph•a -ae *f;* **to do some —s** aliqua portenta facĕre
trick *tr* fallĕre
trickle *s* stillicid•ium -(i)i *n*
trickle *intr* stillare
trickster *s* veterat•or -oris *m*
tricky *adj* dolos•us -a-um; *(difficult)* nodos•us -a -um
trident *s* trid•ens -entis *m*

triennial *adj* trienn•is -is -e
trifle *s* res rei *f* parva; **—s** nug•ae -arum *fpl*
trifle *intr* nugari
trifling *adj* lĕv•is -is -e
trigonometry *s* trigonometri•a -ae *f*
trill *s* son•us -i *m* vibratus
trill *tr* vibrare
trim *adj* compt•us -a -um
trim *tr* adornare; *(to prune)* putare; *(the hair)* tondēre
trim *s* **to be in —** boni habitūs esse
trimmings *spl* ornat•us -ūs *m*
trinket *s* tric•ae -arum *fpl*
trio *s* trini•o -onis *f*
trip *s* it•er -ineris *n;* **to take a —** iter facĕre
trip *tr* pedem opponĕre *(w. dat); (fig)* fallĕre ‖ *intr* pedem offendĕre; *(fig)* errare, labi
tripartite *adj* tripartit•us -a -um
tripe *s* omas•um -i *n*
triple *adj* tripl•ex -icis
triple *tr* triplicare
tripod *s* trip•us -odis *m*
trireme *s* trirem•is -is *f*
trisyllabic *adj* trisyllab•us -a -um
trite *adj* trit•us -a -um
triumph *s (victory)* victori•a -ae *f; (entry of victorious general)* triumph•us -i *m;* **to hold a —** triumphum agĕre
triumph *intr* triumphare; **to — over** devincĕre; *(of a general)* triumphare de *(w. abl)*
triumphal *adj* triumphal•is -is -e
triumphant *adj (masc)* vict•or -oris; *(fem)* victr•ix -icis
trivial *adj* lev•is -is -e
triviality *s* nug•ae -arum *fpl*
troop *s* caterv•a -ae *f; (of cavalry)* turm•a -ae *f;* **—s** copi•ae -arum *fpl*
trooper *s (coll)* veteran•us -i *m*
trophy *s* tropae•um -i *n*
tropical *adj* tropic•us -a -um
tropics *spl* zon•a -ae *f* torrida
trot *intr* tolutim ire
trouble *s* lab•or -oris *m,* aerumn•a -ae *f;* **to have — with** *(e.g., the kidneys)* laborare *(w. abl)*
trouble *tr* vexare, angĕre
troubled *adj* confus•us -a -um; **— face** vult•us -ūs *m* exercitatus
troublesome *adj* molest•us -a -um; **to be —** urgēre
trough *s* alve•us -i *m*
trounce *tr (to punish)* castigare; *(to defeat decisively)* devincĕre
troupe *s* gre•x -gis *m*
trousers *spl* brac•ae -arum *fpl*
trout *s* truct•a -ae *f*
trowel *s* trull•a -ae *f*
truant *s* cessat•or -oris *m;* **to play —** solita ludi munera neglegĕre
truce *s* induti•ae -arum *fpl;* **during the —** per indutias; **to agree to a —** indutias cum hostibus pacisci; **to break off a —** indutias tollĕre
truck *s* carr•us -i *m*
trudge *intr* repĕre; **to — over many places** calcare plura loca
true *adj* ver•us -a -um; *(genuine)* german•us -a -um; *(faithful)* fid•us -a -um; *(exact)* rect•us -a -um
truffle *s* tub•er -eris *n* terrae
truism *s* ver•um -i *n* tritum
truly *adv* vere, profecto
trump *tr* **to — up** effingĕre
trumpet *s (mil)* tub•a -ae *f,* aes, aeris *n; (for civilian purposes)* buccin•a -ae *f;* **to rouse the men with the —** aere viros ciēre
trumpeter *s* tubic•en -inis *m;* buccinat•or -oris *m*
truncheon *s* fust•is -is *m*
trundle *intr* volvĕre
trunk *s (of tree)* trunc•us -i *m; (for luggage)* cist•a -ae *f; (of elephant)* probosc•is -is *f,* man•us -ūs *f*
trust *s* fiduci•a -ae *f,* fid•es -ei *f;* **to put — in** (con)fidĕre *(w. dat)*
trust *tr (persons or acts)* fidĕre *(w. dat); (esp. words spoken)* credĕre *(w. dat); (to entrust)* committĕre; **not — his eyes** fidem oculorum timēre ‖ *intr* **to — in** fidĕre *(w. dat)*
trustee *s* fiduciar•ius -(i)i *m*
trusteeship *s* tutel•a -ae *f*
trustful *adj* credul•us -a -um
trusting *adj* fid•ens -entis
trustingly *adv* fidenter
trustworthiness *s* fid•es -ei *f*
trustworthy *adj* fid•us -a -um; *(witness)* locupl•es -etis
trusty *adj* fid•us -a -um
truth *s (abstract)* verit•as -atis *f; (concrete)* ver•um -i *n;* **in —** vero; **this is the —** haec sunt vera; **to speak the —** verum dicĕre
truthful *adj* ver•ax -acis
truthfully *adv* veraciter
try *tr* tentare, temptare; *(to put to the test)* experiri; *(leg)* judicare; *(to hold a judicial inquiry)* cognoscĕre; **to — a case** causam cognoscĕre; **to — one's patience** patientiā abuti; **to — to obtain** affectare
trying *adj* incommod•us -a -um
tub *s* labr•um -i *n*
tube *s* tubul•us -i *m,* fistul•a -ae *f*
tuberculosis *s* tab•es -is *f*
tuck *tr* **to — up** succingĕre; **with tunic —ed up** succint•us -a -um
Tuesday *s* di•es -ei *m* Martis
tuft *s* flocc•us -i *m*
tug *s* tract•us -ūs *m; (ship)* nav•is -is *f* tractoria

tug *tr* trahĕre ‖ *intr* **to — at** vellicare
tugboat *s* nav•is -is *f* tractoria
tuition *s* minerv•al -alis *n*
tumble *intr* volvi
tumbler *s* pocul•um -i *n* vitreum
tumor *s* tum•or -oris *m*
tumult *s* tumult•us -ūs *m*
tumultuous *adj* tumultuos•us -a -um
tumultuously *adv* tumultuose
tune *s* cant•us -ūs *m;* **in —** conson•us -a -um; **out of —** abson•us -a -um; **to be out of —** discrepare
tuneful *adj* canor•us -a -um
tunic *s* tunic•a -ae *f;* **long-sleeved —** tunica *f* manicata; **small —** tunicul•a -ae *f;* **— reaching to the ankles** tunica *f* talaris; **wearing a tunic** tunicat•us -a -um
tunnel *s* cunicul•us -i *m*
turban *s* mitr•a -ae *f*
turbid *adj* turbid•us -a -um
turbulence *s* agitati•o -onis *f; (air)* flabr•a -orum *npl* violenta
turbulent *adj* turbulent•us -a -um
turf *s* caesp•es -itis *m*
turgid *adj* turgid•us -a -um
turkey *s* meleagris gallopav•o -onis *f;* **to talk —** *(coll)* Latine loqui
turmoil *s* perturbati•o -onis *f;* **mental —** animi commoti•o -onis *f*
turn *s (circuit)* circuit•us -ūs *m; (revolution)* conversi•o -onis *f; (change, course)* vicissitud•o -inis *f; (inclination of the mind)* inclinati•o -onis *f;* **a good —** benefic•ium -(i)i *n;* **in —** invicem; **out of —** extra ordinem; **take a — for the better, worse** melius, pejus ire; **to take —s in fighting** per vices dimicare; **— in the road** flex•us -ūs *m* viae
turn *tr* (con)vertĕre; *(to twist)* torquēre; *(to bend)* flectĕre; **to — around** circumagĕre, volvĕre; **to — aside** deflectĕre; **to — away** avertĕre; **to — back** convertĕre; **to — down** *(to refuse)* recusare, detrectare; **to — into** vertĕre in *(w. acc);* **to — over** *(to hand over)* tradĕre; *(property)* alienare; *(in the mind)* agitare; *(to upset)* evertĕre; **to — over the pages of a book** librum evolvĕre; **to —one's attention to** animadvertĕre; **to — out** ejicĕre; **to — up** *(w. hoe)* invertĕre; **to — up the nose** nares corrugare; **to — upside down** quod sursum est, deorsum facĕre ‖ *intr* verti, versari; **to — against** disciscĕre ab *(w. abl);* **to — around** converti; **to — aside** se declinare; **to — away** aversari; **to — back** reverti; **to — into** mutari in *(w. acc),* vertĕre in *(w. acc);* **to — out** evenire, evadĕre; **to — up** intervenire, adesse
turnip *s* rap•um -i *n*
turpitude *s* turpitud•o -inis *f*
turret *s* turricul•a -ae *f*
turtle *s* testud•o -inis *f*
tusk *s* den•s -tis *m*
tutelage *s* tutel•a -ae *f*
tutor *s* domesticus praecept•or -oris *m*
tweezers *spl* volsell•a -ae *f*
twelfth *adj* duodecim•us -a -um
twelve *adj* duodecim *(indecl);* **— times** duodecies
twentieth *adj* vicesim•us -a -um
twenty *adj* viginti *(indecl);* **— times** vicies
twice *adv* bis
twig *s* ramul•us -i *m*
twilight *s (evening)* crepuscul•um -i *n; (early dawn)* dilucul•um -i *n*
twin *adj* gemin•us -a -um
twin *s* gemin•us -i *m,* gemell•us -i *m*
twine *s* fil•um -i *n*
twine *tr* circumplicare ‖ *intr* **to — around** circumplecti *(w. acc)*
twinge *s* dol•or -oris *m;* **to suffer such —s of conscience that** ita conscientia mentem excitam vexat ut
twinkle *intr* micare
twinkling *s (of eye)* nict•us -ūs *m*
twirl *tr* versare, circumagĕre ‖ *intr* versari
twist *tr* torquēre ‖ *intr* se torquēre
twit *tr* exprobrare, objurgare
twitch *s* vellicati•o -onis *f*
twitch *tr* vellicare ‖ *intr* formicare
twitter *s* pipul•um -i *n*
twitter *intr* minurire
two *adj* duo, duae, duo; **— at a time** bin•i -ae -a; **— camps** bina castr•a -orum *npl;* **— times** bis
two-bit *adj (worthless)* sestertiari•us -a -um
two-edged *adj* anc•eps -ipitis; **— ax** bipenn•is -is *f*
two-faced *adj (pej)* bilingu•is -is -e
twofold *adj* dupl•ex -icis
two-footed *adj* bip•es -edis
two-headed *adj* bic•eps -ipitis
two hundred *adj* ducent•i -ae -a
two-pronged *adj* bid•ens -entis
twosome *s* par, paris *n*
two-time *tr* fraudare
two-timer *s* infidel•is is *mf*
two-way *adj* bivi•us -a -um
type *s* exempl•um -i *n; (class)* gen•us -eris *n; (print)* typ•i -orum *mpl;* **this — of speech** hujus generis orati•o -onis *f*
type *tr* exarare in machinam scriptoriam
typewriter *s* machin•a -ae *f* scriptoria
typhoon *s* turb•o -inis *f*
typical *adj* typic•us -a -um
typically *adv* per typum
typify *tr* imaginem *(w. gen)* fingĕre

typist *s* scrib•a -ae *mf*
tyrannical *adj* tyrannic•us -a -um
tyrannically *adv* tyrannice
tyrannicide *s (act)* tyrannicid•ium -(i)i *n; (person)* tyrannicid•a -ae *m*
tyrannt *s* tyrann•us -i *m*
tyro *s* tir•o -onis *m*

U

ubiquitous *adj* ubique praes•ens -entis
udder *s* ub•er -eris *n*
ugliness *s* deformit•as -atis *f*
ugly *adj* deform•is -is -e; **to make —** deformare
ulcer *s* ulc•us -eris *n*
ulcerate *intr* ulcerari
ulcerous *adj* ulceros•us -a -um
ulterior *adj (place)* ulter•ior -ior -ius; *(time)* poster•us -a -um; **— motive** rati•o -onis *f* recondita
ultimate *adj* ultim•us -a -um
ultimately *adv* ultimo
umbrage *s* **to take — at** aegre ferre
umbrella *s* umbell•a -ae *f*
umpire *s* arbi•ter -tri *m*
unabashed *adj* intrepid•us -a -um; *(pej)* impud•ens -entis
unabated *adj* continu•us -a -um
unable *adj* **(to)** nequi•ens -entis *(w. inf)*; **— to control his anger** impot•ens -entis irae; **— to keep up with the words of the speaker** male subsequ•ens -entis verba dicentis; **to be — to** non posse *or* nequire *(w. inf)*
unaccented *adj* accentu caren•s -tis
unacceptable *adj* **(to)** invis•us -a -um *(w. dat)*
unaccompanied *adj* incomitat•us -a -um
unaccomplished *adj* infect•us -a -um
unaccountable *adj* inenodabil•is -is -e
unaccountably *adv* praeter opinionem
unaccustomed *adj* insuet•us -a -um
unacquainted *adj* **— with** ignar•us -a -um *(w. gen)*, exper•s -tis *(w. gen)*
unadorned *adj* inornat•us -a -um
unadulterated *adj* mer•us -a -um
unaffected *adj* simpl•ex -icis
unafraid *adj* impavid•us -a -um
unaided *adj* non adjut•us -a -um
unalterable *adj* immutabil•is -is -e
unaltered *adj* immutat•us -a -um
unanimous *adj* unanim•us -a -um
unanimously *adv* consensu omnium
unanswerable *adj* irrefragabil•is -is -e
unappeased *adj* implacat•us -a -um
unapproachable *adj* inaccess•us -a -um
unarmed *adj* inerm•is -is -e
unasked *adj* injuss•us -a -um
unassailable *adj* inexpugnabil•is -is -e
unassuming *adj* modest•us -a -um
unattached *adj* vacu•us -a -um
unattainable *adj* ardu•us -a -um
unattended *adj (unaccompanied)* sine comitatu; *(not cared for)* neglect•us -a -um; **— by pain** privat•us -a -um dolore
unattractive *adj* invenust•us -a -um
unauthorized *adj* illicit•us -a -um
unavailing *adj* inutil•is -is -e
unavenged *adj* inult•us -a -um
unavoidable *adj* inevitabil•is -is -e
unaware *adj* insci•us -a -um
unbearable *adj* intolerabil•is -is -e
unbeaten *adj* invict•us -a -um
unbecoming *adj* indecor•us -a -um; **it is —** dedecet
unbefitting *adj* indecor•us -a -um
unbend *intr* animum remittĕre
unbending *adj* inflexibil•is -is -e
unbiased *adj* sine ira et studio
unbidden *adj* injuss•us -a -um
unbleached *adj* crud•us -a -um
unblemished *adj* intact•us -a -um
unblest *adj* infortunat•us -a -um
unborn *adj* nondum nat•us -a -um
unbridled *adj (lit & fig)* infren•is -is -e
unbroken *adj* irrupt•us -a -um; *(of horses)* indomit•us -a -um
unbuckle *tr* refibulare
unburden *tr* exonerare
unbutton *tr* diloricare
uncalled-for *adj* alien•us -a -um
uncanny *adj* mir•us -a -um
uncared-for *adj* neglect•us -a -um
unceasing *adj* assidu•us -a -um
unceasingly *adv* assidue, sine fine
uncertain *adj* incert•us -a -um; **to be —** haerēre, vacillare
uncertainty *s* dubitati•o -onis *f*
unchangeable *adj* immutabil•is -is -e
unchanged *adj* immutat•us -a -um
unchanging *adj* immutat•us -a -um
uncharitable *adj* immisericor•s -dis
unchaste *adj* parum cast•us -a -um
uncivil *adj* inurban•us -a -um
uncivilized *adj* incult•us -a -um
unclasp *tr* refibulare
uncle *s (father's brother)* patru•us -i *m; (mother's brother)* avuncul•us -i *m;* **great —** magnus patruus *(or* avunculus) *m*
unclean *adj* immund•us -a -um
uncomfortable *adj* incommod•us -a -um
uncommon *adj* rar•us -a -um; *(outstanding)* egregi•us -a -um
uncommonly *adv* praeter solitum
unconcerned *adj* incurios•us -a -um
unconditional *adj* sine exceptione
unconditionally *adv* nullā condicione
unconnected *adj* disjunct•us -a -um
unconquerable *adj* invict•us -a -um
unconscionable *adj* iniqu•us -a -um

unconcious *adj* omni sensu car•ens -entis; **— of** ignar•us -a -um *(w. gen)*, insci•us -a -um *(w. gen)*
unconstitutional *adj* illicit•us -a -um
uncontrollable *adj* impot•ens -entis
unconventional *adj* insolit•us -a -um
unconvinced *adj* **I am — that** non adductus sum ut credam *(w. acc & inf)*
unconvincing *adj* non verisimil•is -is -e
uncooked *adj* crud•us -a -um
uncorrupted *adj* incorrupt•us -a -um
uncouth *adj* inurban•us -a -um
uncover *tr* detegĕre
uncritical *adj* credul•us -a -um
uncultivated *adj* incult•us -a -um
uncut *adj (hair)* intons•us -a -um; *(wood)* incaedu•us -a -um
undamaged *adj* incolum•is -is -e
undaunted *adj* intrepid•us -a -um
undecided *adj* anc•eps -ipitis; **— whether...or** cunctat•us -a -um utrum...an
undefended *adj* indefens•us -a -um
undefiled *adj* incontaminat•us -a -um
undeniable *adj* haud dubi•us -a -um
under *adv* subter, infra
under *prep (position)* sub *(w. abl)*; *(motion)* sub, subter *(w. acc)*; *(less than)* infra *(w. acc)*; **— the pretense of** per simulationem *(w. gen)*
underage *adj* impub•es -is
underbid *tr* minoris faciendum conducĕre
underbrush *s* frutect•um -i *n*
undercurrent *s* torr•ens -entis *m* subterfluens; **— of feeling** intimus animi sens•us -ūs *m*
under-done *adj* semicrud•us -a -um
underestimate *tr* minoris aestimare
underfoot *adj* obvi•us -a -um
undergarment *s* subucul•a -ae *f*; *(worn chiefly by women)* suppar•um -i *n*
undergo *tr* subire; **to — change** se mutare; **to — punishment** poenam dare, poenam sufferre
underground *adj* subterrane•us -a -um
undergrowth *s* virgult•a -orum *npl*
underhanded *adj* clandestin•us -a -um
underhandedly *adv* clam, furtive
underline *tr* subnotare
underling *s* minis•ter -tri *m*
undermine *tr* subruĕre; *(fig)* labefactare
underneath *adv* infra, subter
underneath *prep (position)* infra *(w. acc)*, sub *(w. abl)*; *(motion)* sub *(w. acc)*
underpin *tr* fulcire
underpinnings *spl* fulciment•a -orum *npl*
underrate *tr* minoris aestimare
understand *tr* intellegĕre; *(a language or art)* scire; **to — Latin** Latine scire
understanding *adj* prud•ens -entis
understanding *s* intellect•us -ūs *m*; *(agreement)* consens•us -ūs *m*; *(condition)* condici•o -onis *f*
undertake *tr* adire ad *(w. acc)*, suscipĕre; *(to begin)* incipĕre
undertaker *s* libitinar•ius -(i)i *m*
undertaking *s* incept•um -i *n*
undervalue *tr* minoris aestimare
underworld *s* infer•i -orum *mpl*
undeserved *adj* immerit•us -a -um
undeservedly *adv* immerito
undeserving *adj* **(of)** indign•us -a -um *(w. abl)*
undiminished *adj* imminut•us -a -um
undiscernible *adj* impercept•us -a -um
undiscerning *adj* heb•es -etis
undisciplined *adj* immoderat•us -a -um; *(mil)* inexercitat•us -a -um
undisguised *adj* apert•us -a -um
undismayed *adj* interrit•us -a -um
undisputed *adj* cert•us -a -um; **since this is —** quum hoc constet
undistinguished *adj* ignobil•is -is -e
undisturbed *adj* imperturbat•us -a -um; **— peace** immota pa•x -cis *f*
undivided *adj* indivis•us -a -um
undo *tr (knot)* solvĕre; *(fig)* infectum reddĕre, irritum facĕre; *(to ruin)* perdĕre; **you have undone everything** omnia irrita fecisti
undone *adj (no completed)* infect•us -a -um; *(ruined)* perdit•us -a -um; **to be —** *(to be ruined)* perire
undoubted *adj* haud dubi•us -a -um
undoubtedly *adv* haud dubie
undress *tr* exuĕre **‖** *intr* se exuĕre
undue *adj (excessive)* nimi•us -a -um; *(unfair)* iniqu•us -a -um
undulate *intr* undare, fluctuare
undulating *adj* undulabund•us -a -um
undulation *s* undarum agitati•o -onis *f*
unduly *adv* nimis, plus aequo
undying *adj* aetern•us -a -um
unearth *tr* effodĕre; *(fig)* detegĕre
unearthly *adj* haud mortal•is -is -e
uneasily *adv* turbate; **to sleep —** male dormire
uneasiness *s* sollicitud•o -inis *f*
uneasy *adj* sollicit•us -a -um
uneducated *adj* indoct•us -a -um
unemployed *adj* otios•us -a -um; **to be —** cessare
unemployment *s* cessati•o -onis *f*
unencumbered *adj* expedit•us -a -um
unending *adj* infinit•us -a -um
unendurable *adj* intolerand•us -a -um
unenjoyable *adj* injucund•us -a -um
unenlightened *adj* inerudit•us -a -um
unenviable *adj* non invidend•us -a -um
unequal *adj* inaequal•is -is -e; **— to** im•par -paris *(w. dat)*

unequalled *adj* singular•is -is -e
unequally *adv* impariter
unerring *adj* cert•us -a -um
unerringly *adv* certe
uneven *adj* iniqu•us -a -um; *(rough)* asp•era -era -erum
unevenness *s* iniquit•as -atis *f*
unexpected *adj* inopinat•us -a -um; *(unforeseen)* improvis•us -a -um
unexpectedly *adv* de improviso
unexplored *adj* inexplorat•us -a -um
unfading *adj* semper rec•ens -entis
unfailing *adj (friend)* cert•us -a -um; *(waters)* perenn•is -is -e
unfair *adj* iniqu•us -a -um
unfairly *adv* inique
unfaithful *adj* infid•us -a -um
unfamiliar *adj* ignot•us -a -um
unfamiliarity *s* **(with)** imprudenti•a -ae *f (w. gen)*
unfashionable *adj* obsolet•us -a -um
unfasten *tr* resolvĕre, laxare
unfavorable *adj* iniqu•us -a -um; — **and favorable omens** omin•a -um *npl* tristia et laeta
unfavorably *adv* male, inique
unfed *adj* impast•us -a -um
unfeeling *adj* dur•us -a -um
unfetter *tr* vincula demĕre *(w. dat)*
unfinished *adj* imperfect•us -a -um; *(crude)* rud•is -is -e
unfit *adj* inept•us -a -um
unfold *tr* explicare; *(story)* enarrare ‖ *intr* patescĕre
unforeseen *adj* improvis•us -a -um
unforgiving *adj* inexorabil•is -is -e
unfortified *adj* immunit•us -a -um
unfortunate *adj* infel•ix -icis
unfortunately *adv* infeliciter
unfounded *adj* van•us -a -um
unfriendly *adj* parum amic•us -a -um
unfruitful *adj* infecund•us -a -um
unfurl *tr* pandĕre
unfurnished *adj* nud•us -a -um
ungainly *adj* inhabil•is -is -e
ungenerous *adj* illiberal•is -is -e
ungentlemanly *adj* inurban•us -a -um
ungird *tr* discingĕre
ungodly *adj* impi•us -a -um
ungovernable *adj* intractabil•is -is -e
ungraceful *adj* invenust•us -a -um
ungracious *adj* petul•ans -antis
ungrateful *adj* ingrat•us -a -um
ungratefully *adv* ingrate
ungrudging *adj* non invit•us -a -um
ungrudgingly *adv* sine invidia
unguarded *adj* incustodit•us -a -um; *(of words)* inconsult•us -a -um
unhandy *adj* inhabil•is -is -e
unhappily *adv* infeliciter
unhappiness *s* infelicit•as -atis *f*
unhappy *adj* infel•ix -icis
unharness *tr* disjungĕre
unhealthiness *s* mala valetud•o -inis *f; (of a place)* gravit•as -atis *f*
unhealthy *adj* infirm•us -a -um, morbos•us -a -um; *(place, season, wind)* grav•is -is -e
unheard-of *adj* inaudit•us -a -um
unheeded *adj* neglect•us -a -um
unheroic *adj* ignav•us -a -um
unhesitating *adj* prompt•us -a -um
unhindered *adj* expedit•us -a -um
unhinge *tr* de cardine detrahĕre; *(fig)* perturbare
unholy *adj* impi•us -a -um
unhoped-for *adj* insperat•us -a -um
unhurt *adj* incolum•is -is -e
unicorn *s* unicorn•us -i *m*
uniform *adj* aequabil•is -is -e
uniform *s* ornat•us -ūs *m; (mil)* ornat•us -ūs *m* militaris; **in —** subornat•us -a -um
uniformed *adj* subornat•us -a -um
uniformity *s* aequabilit•as -atis *f*
uniformly *adv* aequabiliter
unify *tr* conjungĕre
unilateral *adj* de uno latere tantummodo
unimaginative *adj* heb•es -etis
unimpaired *adj* inte•ger -gra -grum
unimpeachable *adj* probatissim•us -a -um
unimportant *adj* lĕv•is -is -e
uninformed *adj* indoct•us -a -um
uninhabitable *adj* inhabitabil•is -is -e
uninhabited *adj* desert•us -a -um
uninjured *adj* incolum•is -is -e
uninspired *adj* non inspirat•us -a -um
unintelligible *adj* obscur•us -a -um
uninteresting *adj* jejun•us -a -um
uninterrupted *adj* continu•us -a -um
uninviting *adj* injucund•us -a -um
union *s (act)* conjuncti•o -onis *f; (social)* societ•as -atis *f; (agreement)* consens•us -ūs *m; (marriage)* conjug•ium -(i)i *n*
unique *adj* unic•us -a -um
unison *s* concent•us -ūs *m;* **to sing in —** unā voce canĕre
unit *s* unit•as -atis *f,* mon•as -adis *f*
unite *tr* conjungĕre; *(to make into one)* unire ‖ *intr* coïre, coalescĕre
united *adj* consociat•us -a -um; **— opposition** *(pol)* conspirati•o -onis *f*
unity *s* unit•as -atis *f*
universal *adj* universal•is -is -e
universally *adv* universe
universe *s* universit•as -atis *f*
university *s* academi•a -ae *f*
unjust *adj* unjust•us -a -um
unjustly *adv* injuste
unjustifiable *adj* quod nihil excusationis habet
unkempt *adj* incompt•us -a -um

unkind *adj* inhuman•us -a -um
unkindly *adv* inhumane
unknowingly *adv* inscienter
unknown *adj* ignot•us -a -um; **— to his wife** clam uxorem
unlawful *adj* contra jus; *(w. reference to state law)* contra legem; **it is — to** nefas est *(w. inf)*
unlawfully *adv* contra legem
unleavened *adj* non fermentat•us -a -um
unless *conj* nisi
unlike *adj* dissimil•is -is -e; **it is not — going** non est dissimile atque ire
unlimited *adj* infinit•us -a -um
unload *tr* exonerare
unlock *tr* reserare; **with the door unlocked** reseratis foribus
unlooked-for *adj* inopinat•us -a -um
unluckily *adv* infeliciter
unlucky *adj* infel•ix -icis; *(omen)* infaut•us -a -um; **— day** di•es -ei *m* ater
unmanageable *adj* intractabil•is -is -e
unmanly *adj* moll•is -is -e
unmannerly *adj* male morat•us -a -um, inurban•us -a -um
unmarried *adj (man)* cael•ebs -ibis; *(woman)* innupta
unmask *tr* detegĕre
unmatched *adj* singular•is -is -e
unmerciful *adj* immisericor•s -dis
unmercifully *adv* immisericorditer
unmistakable *adj* evid•ens -entis
unmistakably *adv* sine dubio
unmoved *adj* immot•us -a -um
unnatural *adj (event)* monstruos•us -a -um; *(deed)* imman•is -is -e
unnaturally *adv* contra naturam
unnecessarily *adv* ex supervacuo
unnecessary *adj* haud necessari•us -a -um
unnerve *tr* debilitare
unnoticed *adj* praetermiss•us -a -um; **to go — by** latēre inter *(w. acc)*
unobjectionable *adj* culpā exper•s -tis
unoccupied *adj* vacu•us -a -um; *(land)* apert•us -a -um; **to be —** vacare
unofficial *adj* privat•us -a -um
unpack *tr* e cistis eximĕre
unpaid *adj (of money)* debit•us -a -um; *(of service)* gratuit•us -a -um
unpalatable *adj* insuav•is -is -e
unparalleled *adj* singular•is -is -e
unpardonable *adj* cui ignosci non potest
unpatriotic *adj* immem•or -oris patriae
unpleasant *adj* injucund•us -a -um
unpleasantly *adv* injucunde
unpolluted *adj* impollut•us -a -um; *(fig)* intact•us -a -um
unpopular *adj* invis•us -a -um
unpopularity *s* invidi•a -ae *f*
unpracticed *adj* inexpert•us -a -um
unprecedented *adj* inaudit•us -a -um
unprejudiced *adj* candid•us -a -um
unpremeditated *adj* inconsult•us -a -um, subit•us -a -um
unprepared *adj* imparat•us -a -um
unprincipled *adj* improb•us -a -um
unproductive *adj* infecund•us -a -um
unprofitable *adj* inutil•is -is -e
unprofitably *adv* nullis fructibus
unprotected *adj* indefens•us -a -um
unprovoked *adj* ultro
unpunished *adj* inpunit•us -a -um; **to allow a crime to go —** maleficium impune habēre
unqualified *adj* haud idone•us -a -um; *(complete)* consummat•us -a -um
unquenchable *adj* inexstinct•us -a -um
unquestionable *adj* certissim•us -a -um
unquestionably *adv* facile
unquestioning *adj* credul•us -a -um
unravel *tr* retexĕre; *(fig)* enodare
unreasonable *adj* absurd•us -a -um
unreasonably *adv* absurde
unrefined *adj* crud•us -a -um
unrelenting *adj* inplacabil•is -is -e
unremitting *adj* assidu•us -a -um
unrepentant *adj* impaenit•ens -entis
unrestrained *adj* effrenat•us -a -um
unrighteous *adj* injust•us -a -um
unripe *adj* immatur•us -a -um
unrivaled *adj* incomparabil•is -is -e
unroll *tr* evolvĕre
unruffled *adj* immot•us -a -um
unruliness *s* impotenti•a -ae *f*
unruly *adj* impot•ens -entis
unsafe *adj* intut•us -a -um
unsalted *adj* insals•us -a -um
unsatisfied *adj* inexplet•us -a -um
unsatisfactory *adj* non idone•us -a -um
unsavory *adj* insipid•us -a -um; *(disreputable)* foed•us -a -um
unscrew *tr* retorquēre
unseal *tr (letter)* resignare; *(a jar)* relinĕre
unseasonable *adj* intempestiv•us -a -um
unseemly *adj* indecor•us -a -um
unseen *adj* invis•us -a -um
unselfish *adj* suae utilitatis immem•or -oris
unselfishly *adv* liberaliter
unsettle *tr* sollicitare
unsettled *adj* incert•us -a -um; *(of mind)* sollicit•us -a -um
unshaken *adj* immot•us -a -um
unshaved *adj* irras•us -a -um
unsheathe *tr* destringĕre
unsightly *adj* turp•is -is -e
unskilful *adj* imperit•us -a -um
unskilfully *adv* imperite
unskilled *adj* imperit•us -a -um
unsophisticated *adj* simpl•ex -icis
unsound *adj* infirm•us -a -um; *(of mind)* insan•us -a -um; *(ill-founded)* van•us -a -um

unsparing *adj (merciless)* inclem•ens -entis; *(lavish)* larg•us -a -um
unsparingly *adv* inclementer; large
unspeakable *adj* ineffabil•is -is -e
unstable *adj* instabil•is -is -e; *(fig)* lĕv•is -is -e, inconst•ans -antis
unstained *adj* pur•us -a -um; *(honor)* intaminat•us -a -um
unsteadily *adv* inconstanter
unsteady *adj* inconst•ans -antis
unsuccessful *adj* infel•ix -icis
unsuccessfully *adv* infeliciter
unsuitable *adj* incommod•us -a -um
unsuited *adj* haud idone•us -a -um
unsullied *adj* intaminat•us -a -um
unsuspected *adj* non suspect•us -a -um
untamed *adj* indomit•us -a -um
untasted *adj* ingustat•us -a -um
untaught *adj* indoct•us -a -um
unteachable *adj* indocil•is -is -e
untenable *adj* infirm•us -a -um, quod defendi non potest
unthankful *adj* ingrat•us -a -um
untie *tr* solvĕre
until *conj* dum, donec, quoad
until *prep* usque ad *(w. acc)*, in *(w. acc)*; **to put off — tomorrow** differre in crastinum; **— late at night** in multam noctem; **— now** adhuc
untimely *adj* intempestiv•us -a -um; *(premature)* praematur•us -a -um
untiring *adj* assidu•us -a -um
untold *adj (numberless)* innumer•us -a -um; *(story)* immemorat•us -a -um
untouched *adj* intact•us -a -um; *(fig)* immot•us -a -um
untrained *adj* inexercitat•us -a -um
untried *adj* intemptat•us -a -um
untrodden *adj* non trit•us -a -um
untroubled *adj* tranquill•us -a -um
untrue *adj* fals•us -a -um; *(disloyal)* infid•us -a -um
untrustworthy *adj* infid•us -a -um
unusual *adj* inusitat•us -a -um
unusually *adv* praeter solitum
unutterable *adj* infand•us -a -um
unvarnished *adj (fig)* nud•us -a -um
unveil *tr* detegĕre; *(fig)* patefacĕre
unversed *adj* **— in** imperit•us -a -um *(w. gen)*
unwanted *adj* ingrat•us -a -um; *(superfluous)* supervacane•us -a -um
unwarranted *adj* iniqu•us -a -um
unwary *adj* incaut•us -a -um
unweaned *adj* lacticulos•us -a -um
unwearied *adj* indefess•us -a -um
unwelcome *adj* ingrat•us -a -um
unwieldy *adj* inhabil•is -is -e
unwilling *adj* invit•us -a -um
unwillingly *adv* invite
unwind *tr* revolvĕre; **they unwound their threads** retro sua fila revolverunt
unwise *adj* imprud•ens -entis
unwisely *adv* imprudenter
unworthily *adv* indigne
unworthiness *s* indignit•as -atis *f*
unworthy *adj* **(of)** indign•us -a -um *(w. abl)*
unwrap *tr* explicare, evolvĕre
unwritten *adj* non script•us -a -um
unyielding *adj* inflexibil•is -is -e
unyoke *tr* disjungĕre
up *adv* sursum; (**up** is often expressed in Latin by the prefix con-, com-cor-, ex-, sub- combined with the verb: **to eat —** comesse; **to finish —** conficĕre; **to snatch —** corripĕre; **to rise —** exsurgĕre; **to lift —** sublevare); **to charge — the hill** erigĕre aciem per adversum collem; **to go — the mountains** ire in adversos montes; **to rise — against us** exsurgĕre adversus *(or* in) nos; **— and down** sursum deorsum; **to run — and down** modo huc modo illuc cursare; **— to** tenus *(w. abl) (always placed after its case, e.g.,* **the water come up to the waist** umbilico tenus aqua erat); **—s and downs** modo sic, modo sic
upbraid *tr* castigare verbis
upbringing *s* educati•o -onis *f*
upheaval *s* eversi•o -onis *f*
uphill *adj* accliv•is -is -e; **to have an — struggle** clivo laborare
uphill *adv* adversus clivum, in collen
uphold *tr* servare, sustentare
upkeep *s* impens•a -ae *f*
uplift *tr* sublevare
upon *prep (position)* super *(w. abl)*, in *(w. abl)*; *(motion)* super *(w. acc)*, in *(w. abl)*; *(directly after)* ex *(w. abl)*, sub *(w. abl)*; *(converning)* de *(w. abl)*; **— my word** fidem do
upper *adj* super•ior -ior -ius; *(world, air)* super•us -a -um; **an — room** superius cenacul•um -i *n*; **the — classes** superiores *(or* ampliores) ordin•es -um *mpl*; **to get the — hand** superare, vincĕre
uppermost *adj* summ•us -a -um
upright *adj* erect•us -a -um; *(of character)* honest•us -a -um, inte•ger -gra -grum
uproar *s* tumult•us -ūs *m*; **to cause an —** tumultuari
uproot *tr* eradicare, erurĕre
upset *tr* evertĕre, subvertĕre; *(to worry)* perturbare
upset *adj* perculs•us -a -um
upside down *adv* **to turn —** sursum deorsum versare
upstairs *adv* sursum
upstart *s* novus hom•o -inis *m*; *(pej)* terrae fil•ius -(i)i *m*

upstream *adv* adverso flumine
up to *prep* usque ad *(w. acc),* tenus *(postpositive, w. abl or gen)*
upwards *adv* sursum; **— of** *(of number)* plus quam
urban *adj* urban•us -a -um
urge *tr* urgēre, impellěre; **to — on** stimulare, incitare; *(horses)* admittěre
urge *s* impuls•us -ūs *m*
urgency *s* necessit•as -atis *f*
urgent *adj* grav•is -is -e; **whose need was most —** quibus summa necessitudo erat; **to be —** instare
urgently *adv* vehementer
urn *s* urn•a -ae
us *pron* nos; **to —** nobis; **with —** nobiscum
usage *s* us•us -ūs *m*
use *s* us•us -ūs *m;* **no —!** frustra!; **in common —** usitat•us -a -um; **it is no —** nihil opus est; **to be of —** usui esse; **to be of no —** inutile esse, usum nullum habēre; **to come into —** invalescěre, in morem venire; **to make — of** uti *(w. abl)*
use *tr* uti *(w. abl); (to take advantage of)* abuti *(w. abl);* **to — s.th. for** aliquid adhibēre *(w. dat);* **to — up** consuměre, exhaurire ‖ *intr* **I used to** solebam *(w. inf)*
used *adj* usitat•us -a -um; *(second-hand)* trit•us -a -um; **— to** *(accustomed to)* assuet•us -a -um *(w. dat)*
useful *adj* util•is -is -e; **to be —** usui esse
usefully *adv* utiliter, commode
useless *adj* inutil•is -is -e
uselessly *adv* frustra
usual *adj* solit•us -a -um; **as —** ut solet; **more than —** plus solito
usually *adv* plerumque, fere
usurp *tr* invaděre *(w. acc or* in + *acc),* usurpare
usurpation *s* usurpati•o -onis *f*
usurper *s* usurpat•or -oris *m*
usury *s* immodica usur•a -ae *f*
utensils *spl* untensil•ia -ium *npl;* **household —s** instrument•um -i *n;* **kitchen —s** coquinatori•a -orum *npl*
utility *s* utilit•as -atis *f*
utilize *tr* uti *(w. abl),* adhibēre
utmost *adj* summ•us -a -um
utmost *n* **to do one's —** omnibus viribus contenděre
utter *adj* tot•us -a -um
utter *tr* emittěre; *(to reveal what is a secret)* proloqui
utterance *s* dict•um -i *n;* **to give — to one's feelings** exprimere dicendo sensa
utterly *adv* omnino, funditus
uttermost *adj* extrem•us -a -um
uvula *s* uvul•a -ae *f*

V

vacancy *s* vacuit•as -atis *f; (in hotel)* cubicul•um -i *n* vacans
vacant *adj* vacu•us -a -um; *(look, stare)* inan•is -is -e; **to be —** vacare
vacate *tr* vacuefacěre
vacation *s* feri•ae -arum *fpl*
vaccinate *tr* vaccinum inserěre in *(w. acc)*
vaccination *s* vaccinati•o -onis *f*
vaccine *s* vaccin•um -i *n*
vacillate *intr* vacillare
vacillating *adj* vacill•ans -antis
vacuum *s* inan•e -is *n*
vagabond *s* larifug•a -ae *m*
vagary *s* libid•o -inis *f*
vagina *s* natural•e -is *n*
vagrancy *s* vagati•o -onis *f*
vagrant *adj* vag•us -a -um
vagrant *s* err•o -onis *m*
vague *adj* vag•us -a -um; *(not fixed)* incert•us -a -um; *(ambiguous)* ambigu•us -a -um
vaguely *adv* incerte
vagueness *s* obscurit•as -atis *f*
vain *adj (empty)* van•us -a -um; *(proud)* superb•us -a -um; **in —** frustra
vainly *adv* frustra
vainglorious *adj* glorios•us -a -um
valedictorian *s* valedic•ens -entis *mf*
valedictory *s* orati•o -onis *f* valedicens
valentine *s* chartul•a -ae *f* amatoria
valet *s* cubicular•ius -(i)i *m*
valiant *adj* fort•is -is -e
valid *adj* firm•us -a -um
valley *s* vall•es -is *f*
valor *s* fortitud•o -inis *f*
valuable *adj* pretios•us -a -um
valuables *spl* res, rerum *fpl* pretiosae
valuation *s* aestimati•o -onis *f*
value *s* pret•ium -(i)i *n*
value *tr* aestimare; **to — highly** magni aestimare; **to — s.o. for his prowess** aliquem probare a viribus
valueless *adj* vil•is -is -e
valve *s* epistom•ium -(i)i *n*
vampire *s* vespertili•o -onis *m*
vandal *s* evers•or -oris *m*
vanguard *s (mil)* primum agm•en -inis *n*
vanish *intr* (e)vanescěre, diffugěre
vanity *s* vanit•as -atis *f*
vanquish *tr* profligare, devincěre
vantage *s* commod•um -i *n;* **— point** superior loc•us -i *m*
vapid *adj* vapid•us -a -um
vapor *s* vap•or -oris *m*
variable *adj* vari•ans -antis
variance *s* differenti•a -ae *f;* **at — with** dissid•ens -entis ab *(w. abl);*

to set the state at — serĕre civiles discordias
variation *s* variet•as -atis *f*
varicose vein *s* var•ix -icis *f*
variety *s* variet•as -atis *f*
various *adj* vari•i -ae -a; **in — ways** varie
variously *adv* varie
vary *tr* variare, mutare ‖ *intr* mutari
vase *s* vascul•um -i *n*
vast *adj* vast•us -a -um
vastly *adv* valde, maxime
vastness *s* immensit•as -atis *f*
vat *s* cup•a -ae *f*
vault *s* *(archit)* camer•a -ae *f; (leap)* salt•us -ūs *m; (for valuables)* thesaur•us -i *m*
vault *intr* salire
vaunt *tr* jactare ‖ *intr* se jactare
veal *s* vitulin•a -ae *f*
veer *intr* se vertĕre
vegetable *s* hol•us -eris *n*
vegetable *adj* holitari•us -a -um
vehemence *s* vehementi•a -ae *f*
vehement *adj* vehem•ens -entis; *(violent)* violent•us -a -um
vehemently *adv* vehementer
vehicle *s* vehicul•um -i *n*
veil *s* velam•en -inis *n; (bridal)* flamme•um -i *n; (fig)* integument•um -i *n*
veil *tr* velare
vein *s* ven•a -ae *f*
velocity *s* velocit•as -atis *f*
velvet *s* velvet•um -i *n*
vend *tr* vendĕre
veneer *s* ligni bracte•a -ae *f; (fig)* speci•es -ei *f*
venerable *adj* venerabil•is -is -e
venerate *tr* venerari
veneration *s* venerati•o -onis *f*
venereal *adj* venere•us -a -um
vengeance *s* ulti•o -onis *f;* **to take — on s.o.** se vindicare ab *(w. abl)*
venison *s* ferin•a -ae *f*
venom *s* venen•um -i *n*
venomous *adj* venenat•us -a -um
vent *s* spirament•um -i *n*
vent *tr* aperire; **to — one's wrath on** iram erumpĕre in *(w. acc)*
ventilate *tr* ventilare
ventriloquist *s* ventriloqu•us -i *m*
venture *s* facin•us -eris *n;* **to risk a —** periculum subire
venture *tr* periclitari; **to — all** dare summam rerum in aleam
venturesome *adj* aud•ax -acis
veractiy *s* veracit•as -atis *f*
veranda *s* subdial•e -is *n*
verb *s* verb•um -i *n*
verbal *adj* verbal•is -is -e
verbally *adv* verbo
verbatim *adv* ad verbum
verbose *adj* verbos•us -a -um
verdict *s* sententi•a -ae *f;* **to deliver the —** sententiam pronuntiare
verge *s* marg•o -inis *m;* **to be on the — of** non procul abesse ut *(w. subj)*
verification *s* affirmati•o -onis *f*
verify *tr* probare
vermilion *adj* minian•us -a -um
vermilion *s* min•ium -(i)i *n*
vermin *spl* bestiol•ae -arum *fpl*
vernacular *s* patrius serm•o -onis *m*
versatile *adj* versatil•is -is -e
verse *s* vers•us -ūs *m*
versed *adj* **(in)** versat•us et exercitat•us -a -um (in + *abl)*
versification *s* versificati•o -onis *f*
version *s* translati•o -onis *f;* **to give a literal — of** plane vertĕre
vertex *s* vert•ex -icis *m*
vertical *adj* rect•us -a -um; **a — line** perpendicul•um -i *n*
vertically *adv* ad perpendiculum
very *adj* ips•e -a -um; **on the — day on which** ipso die quo
very *adv* valde, admodum, maxime
vessel *s* vas, vasis *n; (ship)* navig•ium -(i)i *n*
vest *s* thor•ax -acis *m*
vestal virgin *s* virg•o -inis *f* vestalis
vestibule *s* vestibul•um -i *n*
vestige *s* vestig•ium -(i)i *n*
vestment *s* vestiment•um -i *n*
veteran *s* veteran•us -i *m*
veterinarian *s* veterinar•ius -(i)i *m*
veterinary *adj* veterinari•us -a -um
veto *s* intercessi•o -onis *f*
veto *tr* intercedĕre *(w. dat)*
vex *tr* vexare
vexation *s* vexati•o -onis *f*
via *prep* per *(w. acc)*
vial *s* phial•a -ae *f*
vibrate *intr* vibrare
vibration *s* vibrat•us -ūs *m*
vicar *s* vicar•ius -(i)i *m*
vicarious *adj* vicari•us -a -um
vice *s* *(shameful deed)* flagit•ium -(i)i *n; (flaw)* vit•ium -(i)i *n*
vice admiral *s* classis subpraefect•us -i *m*
vice chancellor *s* procancellar•ius -(i)i *m*
vice president *s* praesidis vicar•ius -(i)i *m*
viceroy *s* subregul•us -i *m*
vicinity *s* vicini•a -ae *f;* **in the — of** circum *(w. acc)*
vicious *adj* crudel•is -is -e
viciously *adv* crudeliter
vicissitude *s* vicissitud•o -inis *f*
victim *s* victim•a -ae *f;* **to fall — to** obire *(w. dat)*
victimize *tr (to swindle)* circumvenire; *(to assault, kill)* vim inferre *(w. dat)*
victor *s* vict•or -oris *m,* victr•ix -icis *f*

victorious *adj* vict•or -oris, *(of a female)* victr•ix -icis *(used appositively);* **to be —** vincĕre
victory *s* victori•a -ae *f;* **news of —** litter•ae -arum *fpl* victrices; **to win a —** victoriam consequi *or* adipisci; **to gain a — over s.o.** ab aliquo victoriam reportare
vie *intr* certare, contendĕre
view *s* aspect•us -ūs *m,* conspect•us -ūs *m; (from above)* despect•us -ūs *m; (opinion)* sententi•a -ae *f;* **almost in — of the city** paene in conspectu urbis; **in my —** meo judicio; **this is my point of —** hoc sic mihi videtur; **to enjoy a view of** conspectu *(w. gen)* uti; **to get a bird's eye — of the city** omnem urbem sub uno aspectu despicĕre
view *tr* visĕre
vigil *s* vigili•ae -arum *fpl; (lasting all night)* pervigil•ium -(i)i *n*
vigilance *s* vigilanti•a -ae *f*
vigilant *adj* vigil•ans -antis
vigilantly *adv* vigilanter
vigor *s* vig•or -oris *m*
vigorous *adj* ala•cer -cris -cre
vigorously *adv* alacriter
vile *adj* vil•is -is -e
vilify *tr* infamare
villa *s* vill•a -ae *f;* **my — at Formiae** meum Formian•um -i *n*
village *s* pag•us -i *m*
villager *s* pagan•us -i *m*
villain *s* scelest•us -i *m*
villany *s* improbit•as -atis *f*
vindicate *tr* vindicare; *(to justify)* probare; *(person)* defendĕre
vindication *s* vindicati•o -onis *f*
vindictive *adj* ultionis cupid•us -a -um
vine *s* vit•is -is *f*
vine arbor *s* pergul•a -ae *f*
vinegar *s* acet•um -i *n*
vinegar bottle *s* acetabul•um -i *n*
vineyard *s* vine•a -ae *f*
vintage *s* vindemi•a -ae *f*
violate *tr* violare
violation *s* violati•o -onis *f*
violator *s* violat•or -oris *m*
violence *s* violenti•a -ae *f*
violent *adj* violent•us -a -um
violently *adv* violenter
virgin *adj* virg•o -inis *f (used appositively);* **— forest** silv•a -ae *f* intacta
virgin *s* virg•o -inis *f*
virile *adj* viril•is -is -e
virility *s* virilit•as -atis *f*
virtually *adv* fere
virtue *s* virt•us -utis *f; (power)* vis *f;* **by — of** per *(w. acc),* ex *(w. abl)*
virtuous *adj* prob•us -a -um, virtute praedit•us -a -um
virtuously *adv* cum virtute, honeste
virulence *s* vis *f*
virulent *adj* virulent•us -a -um
viscera *spl* viscer•a -um *npl*
viscous *adj* viscos•us -a -um
visible *adj* visibil•is -is -e; *(striking, noticeable)* manifest•us -a -um
visibly *adv* manifeste
vision *s (sense)* vis•us -ūs *m; (apparition)* visi•o -onis *f*
visionary *s* somni•ans -antis *mf*
visit *s* salutati•o -onis *f*
visit *tr* visĕre, visitare
visitor *s* hosp•es -itis *m*
visor *s* buccul•a -ae *f*
vista *s* prospect•us -ūs *m*
visual *adj* oculorum *(gen)*
vital *adj* vital•is -is -e; *(essential)* necessari•us -a -um
vitally *adv* praecipue
vitality *s* vis *f* vitalis
vitiate *tr* vitiare, corrumpĕre
vituperate *tr* vituperare
vituperation *s* vituperati•o -onis *f*
vivacious *adj* viv•ax -acis
vivaciously *adv* vivaciter
vivid *adj* vivid•us -a -um
vividly *adv* vivide
vivify *tr* vivificare
vocabulary *s* verborum copi•a -ae *f; (list of words)* vocabulorum ind•ex -icis *m*
vocal *adj* vocal•is -is -c
vocation *s* vocati•o -onis *f*
vociferous *adj* clamos•us -a -um
vogue *s* mos, moris *m;* **to be in —** moris esse
voice *s* vox vocis *f*
void *adj* inan•is -is -e; **— of** vacu•us -a -um *(w. abl)*
void *s* inan•e -is *n*
volatile *adj* volatic•us -a -um
volcanic *adj* vulcani•us -a -um
volcano *s* mon•s -tis *m* flammas et vaporem eructans
volition *s* volupt•as -atis *f*
volley *s (fig)* tempest•as -atis *f*
volume *s (book)* volum•en -inis *n; (quantity)* copi•a -ae *f; (of voice)* magnitud•o -inis *f*
voluminous *adj* voluminos•us -a -um; **— writer** script•or -oris *m* per multa diffusus volumina
voluntarily *adv* suā voluntate, ultro
voluntary *adj* voluntari•us -a -um; *(unpaid)* gratuit•us -a -um
volunteer *s* voluntar•ius -(i)i *m; (mil)* mil•es -itis *m* voluntarius
volunteer *intr (mil)* sponte nomen dare; **to — to do s.th.** aliquid ultro facĕre
voluptuous *adj* voluptari•us -a -um
vomit *s* vomiti•o -onis *f*
vomit *tr* vomĕre
voracious *adj* vor•ax -acis

voraciously *adv* voraciter
vortex *s* vort•ex -icis *m*
vote *s* suffrag•ium -(i)i *n; (fig) (judgment)* sententi•a -ae *f;* **to cast a —** suffragium ferre
vote *intr* suffragium ferre; *(of a judge)* sententiam ferre; *(of a senator)* censēre; **to — for** suffragari *(w. dat)*
voter *s* suffragat•or -oris *m*
votive *adj* votiv•us -a -um
vouch *intr* **to — for** testificari, affirmare
voucher *s* testimon•ium -(i)i *n*
vouchsafe *tr* concedĕre
vow *s* vot•um -i *n*
vow *tr* vovēre ‖ *intr* spondēre
vowel *s* vocal•is -is *f*
voyage *s* navigati•o -onis *f*
voyage *intr* navigare
voyager *s* navigat•or -oris *m*
vulgar *adj* vulgar•is -is -e; *(low)* vil•is -is -e
vulgarity *s* obscenit•as -atis *f*
vulnerable *adj* qui (quae, quod) vulnerari potest; *(of a fortress)* expugnabil•is -is -e
vulture *s* vult•ur -uris *m*

W

wad *s* fascicul•us -i *m*
wade *intr* per vada ire; **to — across** vado transire
wag *tr (the tail)* movēre
wage *tr* **to — war** bellum gerĕre
wager *tr* deponĕre
wager *s* sponsi•o -onis *f*
wages *spl* merc•es -edis *f*
wagon *s* plaustr•um -i *n; (toy)* plostell•um -i *n*
wail *intr* plorare
wailing *s* plorat•us -ūs *m*
waist *s* media par•s -tis *f* corporis
wait *intr* exspectare, opperiri; *(not to depart)* manēre; **to — at tables** ministrare; **to — for** exspectare, opperiri; **to — on** servire *(w. dat)*
wait *s* mor•a -ae *f;* **to lie in — for** insidiari *(w. dat)*
waiter *s* minis•ter -tri *m*
waitress *s* ministr•a -ae *f*
waive *tr* remittĕre
wake *tr* excitare ‖ *intr* **to — up** expergisci
wake *s* tract•us -ūs *m* aquarum a tergo navis; **in the — of** post *(w. acc)*
wakeful *adj* vig•il -is
walk *s (act)* ambulati•o -onis *f; (place)* ambulacr•um -i *n,* xyst•us -i *m; (covered)* portic•us -ūs *f; (gait)* incess•us -ūs *m*
walk *intr* ambulare, incedĕre; **to — out on** *(coll)* deserĕre
wall *s (interior)* pari•es -etis *m; (exterior)* mur•us -i *m; (of town)* moen•ia -ium *npl,* mur•us -i *m*
wall *tr* **to — in** moenibus munire; **to — up** *(w. stones, bricks)* concludĕre (saxis, lateribus)
walled *adj* moenibus munit•us -a -um
wallet *s* per•a -ae *f*
wallop *tr (coll)* percolopare
wallow *intr* volutari
walnut *s* jugl•ans -andis *f*
walrus *s* odoben•us -i *m*
waltz *s* saltati•o -onis *f* in gyrum
waltz *intr* saltare in gyrum
wan *adj* pallid•us -a -um
wander *intr* errare, vagari; **to — about** pervagari; **to — over** pererrare
wanderer *s* err•o -onis *m*
wandering *s* errati•o -onis *f*
wane *intr* decrescĕre
want *s (scarcity)* penuri•a -ae *f; (opp: copia)* inopi•a -ae *f; (extreme want)* egest•as -atis *f;* **to be in —, suffer —** egēre
want *tr* velle; *(to lack)* egēre *(w. abl)*
wanting *adj (defective)* vitios•us -a -um; *(missing)* abs•ens -entis; **to be —** deficĕre, deesse
wanton *adj (lewd)* libidinos•us -a -um; *(unwarranted)* iniqu•us -a -um
war *s* bell•um -i *n;* **to declare — on** bellum indicĕre *(w. dat)*
war *intr* **(against)** bellare adversus *(w. acc)*
warble *intr* canĕre; *(to twitter)* fritinnire
war cry *s* ululat•us -ūs *m*
ward *s (minor)* pupill•us -i *m,* pupill•a -ae *f; (of a city)* regi•o -onis *f;* **— by —** regionatim
ward *tr* **to — off** arcēre, avertĕre
warden *s* carcerar•ius -(i)i *m*
wardrobe *s* vestiar•ium -(i)i *n; (clothes)* vestiment•a -orum *npl*
warehouse *s* horre•um -i *n*
wares *spl* merc•es -ium *fpl*
warfare *s* res, rei *f* bellica
war-horse *s* equ•us -i *m* bellator
warily *adv* caute
warlike *adj* bellig•er -era -erum
warm *adj* callid•us -a -um; *(just warm)* tepid•us -a -um; *(fig)* fervid•us -a -um; **to be —** calēre
warm *tr* calefacĕre, tepefacĕre; *(with animal heat)* fovēre; **to — up** *(food)* recoquĕre; *(by exercise)* exercēre
warm-hearted *adj* am•ans -antis
warmly *adv* ardenter; *(kindly)* benigne
warmth *s* cal•or -oris *m; (fig)* ferv•or -oris *m*
warm-up *s* exercitati•o -onis *f*

warn *tr* monēre
warning *s* monit•um -i *n; (lesson)* document•um -i *n*
warp *s* stam•en -inis *n*
warp *tr* torquēre ‖ *intr (of wood)* panděre
warped *adj* pand•us -a -um
warping *s* pandati•o -onis *f*
warrant *tr (to guarantee)* praestare; *(to justify, call for)* probare
warrant *s* mandat•um -i *n;* **— for arrest** praemandat•a -orum *npl*
warranty *s* satisdati•o -onis *f*
warrior *s* bellat•or -oris *m*
wart *s* verruc•a -ae *f*
wary *adj* caut•us -a -um
wash *tr* lavare; **to — away** abluěre; **to — out** eluěre ‖ *intr* lavari
wash *s* linte•a -orum *npl* lavanda; **to send to the —** ad lavandum dare
wash basin *s* aqual•is -is *m*
washing *s* lavati•o -onis *f*
wasp *s* vesp•a -ae *f*
waste *s* detriment•um -i *n; (of time, property)* jactur•a -ae *f*
waste *tr* effunděre; *(time)* absuměre, terěre ‖ *intr* **to — away** tabescěre
waste *adj* vast•us -a -um; **to lay —** vastare
wasteful *adj* prodig•us -a -um
wastefully *adv* prodige
wasteland *s* solitud•o -inis *f*
watch *s (guard)* vigili•a -ae *f; (sentry)* excubi•ae -arum *fpl;* **to keep —** excubare; **to keep — over** invigilare *(w. dat),* custodire
watch *tr (to observe)* observare, spectare; *(to guard)* custodire
watchful *adj* vigil•ans -antis
watchman *s* vig•il -ilis *m*
watchtower *s* specul•a -ae *f*
watchword *s* tesser•a -ae *f*
water *s* aqu•a -ae *f*
water *tr* irrigare; *(animals)* adaquare
waterboy *s* aquar•ius -(i)i *m*
waterfall *s* deject•us -ūs *m* aquae
waterfront *s* naval•ia -ium *npl*
watering place *s* aquar•ium -(i)i *n*
watermellon *s* cucurbit•a -ae *f* citrulla
watery *adj* aquos•us -a -um
wattle *s* crat•es -is *f*
wave *s* und•a -ae *f,* fluct•us -ūs *m*
wave *tr (hands, arms)* jactare; *(weapon, flag)* quassare ‖ *intr* undare
waver *intr* labare, nutare
wavering *adj* nut•ans -antis
wavy *adj* und•ans -antis; *(hair)* crisp•us -a -um
wax *s* cer•a -ae *f*
wax *adj* cere•us -a -um
wax *tr* incerare ‖ *intr* crescěre
way *adv (coll)* longe, multo
way *s* vi•a -ae *f; (route)* it•er -ineris *n; (manner)* mod•us -i *m; (plan, system, method)* rati•o -onis *f; (habit)* mo•s -ris *m;* **all the — from** usque ab *(w. abl);* **all the — to** usque ad *(w. acc);* **a long — off** longinqu•us -a -um; **by the —** *(incidentally)* obiter; **by — of** viā *(w. gen);* **get out of the —!** abi, apage!; **have it your —!** esto ut lubet!; **in every —** omnibus modis; **in no —** nullo modo; **in the —** obvi•us -a -um; **in this way** ad hunc modum; **to be a long — off** longe distare; **to be in the — of** obesse *(w. dat);* **to be out of the —** devi•us -a -um esse; **to get in the — of** intervenire *(w. dat);* **to get under —** ancoram solvěre; **to give —** *(of a structure)* labare; *(to yield)* conceděre; *(mil)* pedem referre; **to give — to** indulgēre *(w. dat);* **to have one's own —** res pro arbitrio gerěre; **to stand in the — of** obstare *(w. dat);* **— in** ingress•us -ūs *m;* **— out** exit•us -ūs *m*
wayfarer *s* viat•or -oris *m*
waylay *tr* insidiari *(w. dat)*
wayward *adj* inconst•ans -antis
we *pron* nos; **— ourselves** *(masc)* nosmet ipsi; *(fem)* nosmet ipsae
weak *adj (in body, mind, resources)* infirm•us -a -um; *(from defects)* debil•is -is -e; *(argument, light, constitution)* tenu•is -is -e; *(senses)* heb•es -etis; *(voice)* exil•is -is -e
weaken *tr* infirmare, debilitare ‖ *intr* hebescěre, labare
weakly *adv* infirme
weakness *s* infirmit•as -atis *f,* debilit•as -atis *f; (of mind)* imbecillit•as -atis *f; (flaw)* vit•ium -(i)i *n; (of arguments)* levit•as -atis *f*
wealth *s* diviti•ae -arum *fpl; (resources)* op•es -um *fpl; (store, plenty)* copi•a -ae *f*
wealthy *adj* div•es -itis
wean *tr* ab ubere depellěre; *(fig)* desuefacěre
weapon *s* tel•um -i *n*
wear *tr (clothes)* gerěre, gestare; **to — out** terěre, exeděre ‖ *intr* durare
wear *s* trit•us -ūs *m;* **— and tear** intertriment•um -i *n*
weariness *s* lassitud•o -inis *f*
wearisome *adj* operos•us -a -um
weary *adj* fess•us -a -um
weather *s* tempest•as -atis *f;* **— conditions** tempestatum habit•us -ūs *m;* **types of —** gener•a -rum *npl* tempestatum
weather *tr* **to — a storm** procellam durare
weatherbeaten *adj* tempestate afflict•us -a -um
weave *tr* texěre

web *s (spider's)* arane•um -i *n; (on a loom)* tel•a -ae *f*
wed *tr (a woman)* ducĕre; *(a man)* nubĕre *(w. dat)* ‖ *intr (of bride)* nubĕre; *(of groom)* uxorem ducĕre
wedding *s* nupti•ae -arum *fpl*
wedding *adj* nuptial•is -is -e; **to set the — day** diem nuptiis dicere; **— day** dies -ei *m* nuptiarum; **— present** nuptiale don•um -i *n*; **— reception** cen•a -ae *f* nuptialis
wedge *s* cune•us -i *m*
wedlock *s* matrimon•ium -(i)i *n*
weed *s* herb•a -ae *f* mala
weed *tr* eruncare
week *s* hebdom•as -adis *f*, septiman•a -ae *f*
weekday *s* di•es -ei *m* profestus
weekly *adj* hebdomadal•is -is -e
weekly *adv* septimo quoque die
weep *intr* flēre; **to — for** deplorare
weeping *s* flet•us -ūs *m*
weigh *tr* pendĕre; *(fig)* examinare; **to — down** degravare; *(fig)* opprimĕre; **to — out** expendĕre ‖ *intr* **to — much** magni ponderis esse
weight *s* pond•us -eris *n; (heaviness)* gravit•as -atis *f; (influence)* auctorit•as -atis *f; (importance)* moment•um -i *n*
weighty *adj* grav•is -is -e
welcome *s* salutati•o -onis *f*; **I gave him a warm —** eum amantissime excepi
welcome *adj* opportunissim•us -a -um
welcome *tr* benigne excipĕre
welcome *interj* salve!; *pl:* salvete!
weld *tr* (con)ferruminare
welfare *s* sal•us -utis *f; (charity)* carit•as -atis *f*
well *s* pute•us -i *m*
well *adj (healthy)* san•us -a -um, salv•us -a -um; **it is — to** convenit *(w. inf)*
well *adv* bene, recte; **he is — off** bene se habet; **I am doing —** mihi bene est; **very —** optime
well *interj* immo; *(all right)* licet; **— now** age ergo
well-being *s* sal•us -tis *f*
well-born *adj* generos•us -a -um
well-bred *adj* bene educat•us -a -um
well-deserved *adj* rite merit•us -a -um
well-done *adj* optime fact•us -a -um; **— done!** macte virtute esto!
well-known *adj* nobil•is -is -e
well-read *adj* litterat•us -a -um
well-spoken *adj* disert•us -a -um
well-supplied *adj* copiosissim•us -a -um
well-timed *adj* opportun•us -a -um
welter *s* congeri•es -ei *f*
werewolf *s* versipell•is -is *m*
west *s* occas•us -ūs *m* (solis); **toward the —** in occasum
western *adj* occidental•is -is -e
westward *adv* in occasum
west wind *s* Zephyr•us -i *m*
wet *adj* uvid•us -a -um; *(through and through)* madid•us -a -um; **to get —** madefieri
wet *tr* madefacĕre
wet-nurse *s* nutr•ix -icis *f*
whale *s* balaen•a -ae *f*
wharf *s* naval•e -is *n*
what *adj interrog* qui, quae quod; **— sort of** qual•is -is -e
what *pron interrog* quid, quidnam; **— is this all about?** quid enim?
whatever *pron* quicquid
whatever *adj interrog* quicumque, quaecumque, quodcumque
wheat *s* tritic•um -i *n*
wheedle *tr* blandiri; **to — out of s.o.** eblandiri ex aliquo
wheel *s* rot•a -ae *f*
wheelbarrow *s* pab•o -onis *m*
when *adv* quando
when *conj* cum, ubi, ut; **— first** cum primum; **— joking** inter jocos
whence *adv* unde
whenever *adv* quandocumque, sicubi
where *adv* quā, ubi; *(motion)* quo
whereas *conj* quandoquidem
whereby *adv* quā viā, quo
wherefore *adv* quare, quamobrem
wherein *adv* in quo, in quibus, ubi
whereof *adv* de quo, de quibus
whereupon *adv* quo facto; *(then)* deinde
wherever *conj* quacumque, ubicumque
wherewithall *s* **to have the — to** unde habēre *(w. inf)*
whet *tr* acuĕre; **to — the appetite** exacuĕre appetentiam
whether *conj (in single indir. ques.)* num, -ne, an; **—...or** *(in multiple indir. ques.)* utrum...an, -ne...an, *or...*an; *(in disjunctive conditions)* sive...sive, seu...seu; **—...or not** utrum...necne
whetstone *s* co•s -tis *f*
which *pron interrog* quis quid; *(of two)* ut•er -ra -rum ‖ *pron rel* qui, quae, quod
which *adj interrog* qui, quae, quod; *(of two)* u•ter -tra -trum ‖ *adj rel* qui, quae, quod
whichever *pron* quicumque, quaecumque, quodcumque; *(of two)* utercumque, utracumque, utrumcumque
whiff *s (slight smell)* od•or -oris *m* exiguus; **to get a — of** subolēre; **— of air** aur•a -ae *f*
while *s* temp•us -oris *n*, spat•ium -(i)i *n*; **after a —** paulo post; **a good — after** aliquanto post; **a long —** diu; **for a short —** paulisper; **for a —**

aliquamdiu; **in a little —** in brevi spatio; **once in a —** interdum
while *conj* dum, quoad, donec
while *tr* **to — away the time** tempus fallĕre
whim *s* arbitr•ium -i *n;* **according to their — and pleasure** ad eorum arbitrium et nutum
whimper *s* vagit•us -ūs *m*
whimper *intr* vagire
whimsical *adj* mobil•is -is -e
whine *intr* plorare
whinny *s* hinnit•us -ūs *m*
whinny *intr* hinnire
whip *s* flagell•um -i *n*
whip *tr* flagellare; **to — out** eripĕre
whippersnapper *s* frust•um -i *n* pueri
whipping *s* **to get a —** vapulare
whirl *tr* torquēre, rotare ‖ *intr* torqueri, rotari
whirl *s* turb•o -inis *m*
whirlpool *s* gurg•es -itis *m*
whirlwind *s* turb•o -inis *m*
whirr *intr* stridēre, increpare
whisk *tr (to brush lightly)* everrĕre; **to — away** eripĕre ‖ *intr* **to — about** *(to move about quickly)* circumvolitare
whiskbroom *s* scopul•a -ae *f*
whisker *s (of animal)* saet•a -ae *f;* **by a —** vix; **—s** barb•a -ae *f*
whiskey *s* aqu•a -ae *f* vitae
whisper *s* susurr•us -i *m*
whisper *tr & intr* susurrare
whistle *s (sound)* sibil•us -i *m; (pipe)* fistul•a -ae *f; (of wind)* strid•or -oris *m*
whistle *tr* **to — some tune** exsibilare nescio quid ‖ *intr* sibilare; *(of the wind)* stridēre
whit *s* **every — as good** omnino par; **not a — better** nihilo melius
white *adj* alb•us -a -um; *(brilliant)* candid•us -a -um; *(hair)* can•us -a -um; **to be —** albēre, albicare; **— bread** pan•is -is *m* candidus
white *s (the color; of an egg, of the eye)* alb•um -i *n*
whiten *tr* dealbare, candefacĕre ‖ *intr* albescĕre, canescĕre
whitewash *s* albar•ium -(i)i *n; (fig)* fuc•us -i *m*
whitewash *tr* dealbare; *(fig)* fucare
whither *adv* quo, quorsum
whithersoever *adv* quocumque
whitish *adj* subalb•us -a -um
whiz *intr* increpare
who *pron interrog* quis ‖ *pron rel* qui, quae
whoever *pron* quicumque, quaecumque
whole *adj* tot•us -a -um, cunct•us -a -um, univers•us -a -um
whole *s* tot•um -i *n;* **on the —** plerumque, ex toto
wholehearted *adj* sincer•us -a -um
wholesale *adj* magnari•us -a -um; **to carry on — business** magnariam mercaturam facĕre
wholesale *adv* acervatim
wholesaler *s* magnarius negotiat•or -oris *m*
wholesome *adj* salutar•is -is -e
wholly *adv* omnino, prorsus
whoop *s* ululat•us -ūs *m*
whoop *intr* ululatum tollĕre
whore *s* scort•um-i *n*
whorehouse *s* lupan•ar -aris *n*
whoremonger *s* scortat•or -oris *m*
whose *pron* cujus; *pl:* quorum, quarum, quorum
why *adv* cur, quamobrem, quare; **just —** cur tandem; **that's —**...quo fit ut; **— not** quidni
wick *s* fil•um -i *n*
wicked *adj* improb•us -a -um
wickedly *adv* improbe, sceleste
wickedness *s* improbit•as -atis *f*
wicker *adj* vimine•us -a -um
wide *adj* lat•us -a -um
widely *adv* late
widen *tr* dilatare ‖ *intr* dilatari
widow *s* vidu•a -ae *f*
widower *s* vidu•us -i *m*
width *s* latitud•o -inis *f;* **ten feet in —** decem pedes in latitudinem
wield *tr (weapon)* tractare, vibrare; **to — supreme power** plurimum pollēre
wife *s* ux•or -oris *f; (of a slave)* contubernal•is -is *f*
wifely *adj* uxori•us -a -um
wig *s* capillament•um -i *n*
wiggle *tr* torquēre ‖ *intr* se torquēre; *(of a woman)* crisare
wild *adj* fer•us -a -um; *(desolate)* vast•us -a -um; *(mad)* insan•us -a -um; *(of trees, plants)* silvestr•is -is -e; *(of land)* incult•us -a -um; *(of disposition)* fer•ox -ocis; **— beast** fer•a -ae *f*, fera besti•a -ae *f*
wild *s* **growing in the —** silvestr•is -is -e; **the —s** incult•a -orum *npl*
wilderness *s* vastit•as -atis *f*
wildly *adv* saeve, ferociter
wile *s* dol•us -i *m*
wilful *adj* consult•us -a -um
wilfully *adv* consulto
wiliness *s* callidit•as -atis *f*
will *s* volunt•as -atis *f*, anim•us -i *m; (intent)* proposit•um -i *n; (document)* testament•um -i *n; (of gods)* nut•us -ūs *m;* **at —** ad libidinem
will *tr (a legacy)* legare
willing *adj* lib•ens -entis; **to be —** velle
willingly *adv* libenter, libenti animo
willingness *s* volunt•as -atis *f*
wily *adj* va•fer -fra -frum
win *tr* adipisci, consequi; *(victory)* reportare, adipisci; **to — a bet** spon-

sione vincĕre; **to — a court case** judicio vincĕre; **to — friends** amicos acquirĕre; **to — highest honors** amplissimos honores consequi; **to — the hearts of the people** conciliare animos plebis; **to — over** conciliare ‖ *intr* vincĕre

wince *intr* **to — with sudden pain** prae dolore subito horrēre

winch *s* sucul•a -ae *f*

wind *s* vent•us -i *m;* **I got — of it long ago** jam pridem id mihi subolebat

wind *tr* circumvolvĕre; **the plant wound itself around the tree** herba arbori se circumvolvit; **to — up** *(a speech)* concludĕre; *(a clock)* intendĕre; **to — up one's affairs** res domesticas et familiares in ordinem redigĕre

winded *adj* anhel•ans -antis

windfall *s (fig)* lucr•um -i *n* insperatum

winding *adj* flexuos•us -a -um

winding sheet *s* tunic•a -ae *f* funebris

windmill *s* venti mol•a -ae *f*

window *s* fenestr•a -ae *f*

windowpane *s* specular•e -is *n,* fenestrae vitr•um -i *n*

windpipe *s* arteri•a -ae *f* aspera

windy *adj* ventos•us -a -um

wine *s* vin•um -i *n; (undiluted)* mer•um -i *n; (cheap wine)* vapp•a -ae *f;* **dry —** austerum vinum *n*

wined and dined *adj* prans•us et pot•us -a -um

wine cellar *s* cell•a -ae *f* vinaria

wing *s* al•a -ae *f; (mil)* corn•u -ūs *n*

winged *adj* alat•us -a -um

wink *intr* nictare, connivēre

winner *s* vict•or -oris *m*

winning *adj (fig)* amoen•us -a -um

winnings *spl* lucr•um -i *n*

winnow *tr* ventilare

winter *s* hiem•s -is *f;* **in the dead of —** mediā hieme; **to spend the —** hiemare

winter *intr* hiemare, hibernare

winter *adj* hibern•us -a -um, hiemal•is, -is -e; **— clothes** hiberna vestiment•a -orum *npl;* **— time** hiemale temp•us -oris *n*

winter quarters *spl* hibern•a -orum *npl*

wintry *adj* hiemal•is -is -e, brumal•is -is -e

wipe *tr* tergēre; *(lips)* abstergēre; **to be —ed out** *(of a debt)* deperire; **to — away** abstergēre; *(tears)* extergēre; **to — off** *or* **clean** detergēre; **to — out** *(writing)* delēre; **to — the nose** emungĕre

wire *s* fil•um -i *n* ferreum; *(of silver)* fil•um -i *n* argenteum

wisdom *s* sapienti•a -ae *f*

wise *adj* sapi•ens -entis, prud•ens -entis

wise *s (way)* mod•us -i *m;* **in no —** nequaquam

wisely *adv* sapienter, prudenter

wish *s (act of wishing)* optati•o -onis *f; (thing wished)* optat•um -i *n; (prayer)* vot•um -i *n;* **according to one's —es** de sententiā; **best —es to your brother** salutem plurimam fratri tuo

wish *tr* optare, velle, cupĕre ‖ *intr* **to — for** exoptare, expetĕre

wishing *s* optati•o -onis *f*

wisp *s (of hair, grass, etc.)* manipul•us -i *m*

wistful *adj* desiderii plen•us -a -um

wistfully *adv* oculis intentis

wit *s (intellect)* ingen•ium -(i)i *n; (humor)* faceti•ae -arum *fpl; (person)* hom•o -inis *m* facetus; **to be at one's —s' end** delirare; **to —** scilicet

witch *s* strig•a -ae *f,* mag•a -ae *f*

witchcraft *s* ar•s -tis *f* magica

with *prep* cum *(w. abl); (at the house of)* apud *(w. acc)*

withdraw *tr* seducĕre, avocare; *(words)* revocare ‖ *intr* recedĕre

wither *tr* torrēre ‖ *intr* marcēre

withered *adj* marcid•us -a -um

withhold *tr* retinēre

within *adv* intus, intra; *(on the inside)* intrinsecus; **— and without** intrinsecus et extrinsecus

within *prep (place, time, the law)* intra *(w. acc); (during a definite period)* inter *(w. acc);* **— a few days** paucis diebus

without *adv* extra, exterius; *(out of doors)* foris; **from —** extrinsecus

without *prep* sine *(w. abl),* absque *(w. abl);* **I could in no way enter — their seeing me** nullo modo introire poteram quin me viderent; **to be —** carēre *(w. abl)*

withstand *tr* resistĕre *(w. dat),* obsistĕre *(w. dat)*

witness *s* test•is -is *mf; (to a signature)* obsignat•or -oris *m;* **to bear —** testificari; **to call to —** testari

witness *tr* testificari; *(to see)* interesse *(w. dat),* spectare

witticism *s* dicter•ium -(i)i *n*

wittily *adv* facete, festive

witty *adj* facet•us -a -um

wizard *s* mag•us -i *m*

woe *s* luct•us -ūs *m;* **—s** mal•a -orum *npl*

woeful *adj* luctuos•us -a -um

woefully *adv* misere, flebiliter

wolf *s* lup•us -i *m,* lup•a -ae *f*

woman *s* muli•er -eris *f,* femin•a -ae *f*

womanhood *s* muliebris stat•us -ūs *m*

womanly *adj* muliebr•is -is -e

womb *s* uter•us -i *m*

wonder *s* admirati•o -onis *f; (astonishing object)* miracul•um -i *n;* **to excite —** mirationem facĕre; **seven —s of the world** septem miracula mundi
wonder *intr* mirari; **I — where things are heading** reputo quorsum illa tendant; **to — at** admirari
wonderful *adj* mirabil•is -is -e
wonderfully *adv* mirabiliter
wont *adj* **to be — to** solēre *(w. inf)*
woo *tr* petĕre
wood *s* lign•um -i *n;* **—s** silv•a -ae *f*
wooded *adj* silvos•us -a -um
wooden *adj* ligne•us -a -um
woodland *s* salt•us -ūs *m*
woodman *s* lignat•or -oris *m*
wood nymph *s* Dry•as -adis *f*
woodpecker *s* pic•us -i *m*
woody *adj (full of wood fibers)* lignos•us -a -um; *(covered with woods)* silvos•us -a -um, silvestr•is -is -e
wooer *s* proc•us -i *m*
wool *s* lan•a -ae *f;* **to spin —** lanas ducĕre
woolen *adj* lane•us -a -um
word *s (in context)* verb•um -i *n; (out of context)* vocabul•um -i *n; (spoken)* vox vocis *f,* dict•um -i *n; (promise)* fid•es -ei *f; (news)* nunt•ius -(i)i *m;* **in a —** ad summam; **to break one's —** fidem fallĕre; **to give one's —** fidem dare; **to keep one's —** fidem praestare; **— for —** ad verbum; **—s fail me** quid dicam non invenio
wordy *adj* verbos•us -a -um
work *s (labor, pains)* oper•a -ae *f; (act of working and thing completed)* op•us -eris *n; (labor, trouble)* lab•or -oris *m;* **good —s** recte et honeste fact•a -orum *npl;* **one day's work** una opera *f;* **to throw out of —** de negotio dejicĕre; **you had spent more — and labor** plus operae laborisque consumpseras
work *tr (to exercise)* exercēre; *(to till)* colĕre ‖ *intr* laborare, operari
workman *s (unskilled)* operar•ius -(i)i *m; (skilled)* opif•ex -icis *m; (day laborer)* oper•a -ae *f*
workmanship *s* op•us -eris *n*
workshop *s* officin•a -ae *f*
world *s (universe)* mund•us -i *m,* summ•a -ae *f* rerum; *(earth)* orb•is -is *m* terrarum; *(mankind)* homin•es -um *mpl;* **where in the —** ubi terrarum
worldly *adj* profan•us -a -um
worm *s* verm•is -is *m*
worm *tr* **to — one's way into** se insinuare in *(w. acc)*
worm-eaten, wormy *adj* vermiculos•us -a -um
worry *s* sollicitud•o -inis *f*
worry *tr* sollicitare; **don't — yourself to death** ne te crucia ‖ *intr* sollicitari
worse *adj* pe•jor -jor -jus, deter•ior -ius; **to get —** ingravescĕre; **to turn out for the —** in pejus evenire
worsen *intr* ingravescĕre
worship *s* cult•us -ūs *m,* venerati•o -onis *f*
worship *tr* colĕre, venerari
worshiper *s* cult•or -oris *m*
worst *adj* pessim•us -a -um, deterrim•us -a -um; **— of all** maxime alien•us -a -um
worst *tr* vincĕre
worth *s (value)* pret•ium -(i)i *n; (merit)* dignit•as -atis *f;* **man is of little — worth** hom•o -inis *m* parvi pretii est
worth *adj* dign•us -a -um *(w. abl);* **a slave — any price** serv•us -i *m* quantivis pretii; **he is — a lot of money** divitias maximas habet; **he is — nothing** nihil est; **how much are pigs — here?** quibus hic pretiis porci veneunt?; **it is — knowing** est operae pretium cognoscĕre; **this is — s.th. to me** hoc mihi in lucro est; **to be — a lot** multum valēre
worthless *adj* vil•is -is -e; *(of persons)* nequam *(indecl)*
worthwhile *adj* **to be —** operae pretium esse
worthy *adj* **(of)** dign•us -a -um *(w. abl)*
wound *s* vuln•us -eris *n*
wound *tr* vulnerare; *(fig)* offendĕre
wounded *adj* sauci•us -a -um
wrangling *s* discordi•a -ae *f*
wrap *tr* involvĕre; **to — the head in his toga** caput obvolvĕre togā; **to — up** complicare; *(against the cold)* involvĕre
wrap *s* amict•us -ūs *m*
wrapper *s* involucr•um -i *n*
wrath *s* ir•a -ae *f,* iracundi•a -ae *f*
wrathful *adj* iracund•us -a -um
wreak *tr* **to — havoc** stragem dare; **to — vengeance on** ulcisci
wreath *s* sert•um -i *n*
wreathe *tr (to twist)* torquēre; *(to adorn with wreathes)* nectĕre
wreck *s (of ship)* naufrag•ium -(i)i *n;* **he is a —** naufragus est
wreck *tr* frangĕre; *(fig)* delēre
wren *s* regul•us -i *m*
wrench *tr* detorquēre, luxare
wrest *s* extorquēre, eripĕre
wrestle *intr* luctari
wretch *s* mis•er -eri *m*
wretched *adj* mis•er -era -erum
wretchedly *adv* misere
wretchedness *s* miseri•a -ae *f*
wring *tr* contorquēre; **to — the neck** gulam frangĕre; **—ing his hands**

manibus inter se constrictis; **to — out a cloth** linteolum exprimĕre
wrinkle *s* rug•a -ae *f*
wrinkle *tr* corrugare; **to — the forehead** frontem contrahĕre
wrinkled *adj* rugos•us -a -um
wrist *s* primoris man•us -ūs *f*
writ *s* mandat•um -i *n*
write *tr* scribĕre; *(poetry, book)* componĕre; *(history)* perscribĕre
writer *s* script•or -oris *m*
writhe *intr* torqueri
writing *s (act)* scripti•o -onis *f; (result)* script•um -i *n*
wrong *s* nefas *n (indecl),* injuri•a -ae *f,* mal•um -i *n;* **to do —** peccare
wrong *adj (opp:* erectus) prav•us -a -um; *(incorrect, mistaken)* fals•us -a -um; *(unfair)* iniqu•us -a -um; *(unsuitable)* alien•us -a -um; *(faulty)* vitios•us -a -um; **if I have done anything —** si quid perperam feci; **to be —** errare; **what's — with you?** quid est tecum?
wrong *tr* injuriam inferre *(w. dat)*
wrongdoing *s* probr•um -i *n*
wrongly *adv* perperam, male
wrought *adj* confect•us -a -um
wry *adj* contort•us -a -um; *(of humor)* mord•ax -acis

Y

yacht *s* priva trirem•is -is -e *f; (smaller model)* cel•ox -ocis *f*
yank *tr (coll)* vellĕre
yard *s* are•a -ae *f* domūs; *(measure)* tres pedes *mpl*
yarn *s (of linen)* fil•um -i *n* lini; *(of wool)* fil•um -i *n* laneum; *(story)* fabul•a -ae *f*
yawn *s* oscitati•o -onis *f*
yawn *intr* oscitare, hiare; *(to gape open)* dehiscĕre
year *s* ann•us -i *m;* **at the beginning (end) of the —** ineunte (exeunte) anno; **a — from now** ad annum; **every —** quotannis; **five —s** quinquenn•ium -(i)i *n;* **four —s** quadrenn•ium -(i)i *n;* **for a —** in annum; **he is twenty —s old** viginti annos natus est; **in his later —s** tempore extremo; **it's ten —s since the law was passed** decem anni sunt quum lata lex est; **I wish you a happy new —** in annum laeta opto tibi; **last —** anno superiore; **next —** anno proximo; **three —s** trienn•ium -(i)i *n;* **twice a —** bis (in) anno; **two —s** bienn•ium -(i)i *n*
yearly *adj* annu•us -a -um
yearly *adv* quotannis
yearn *intr* **to — for** desiderare
yearning *s* desider•ium -(i)i *n*
yeast *s* ferment•um -i *n*
yell *s* ululat•us -ūs *m*
yell *intr* ululare; *(in pain)* ejulare
yellow *adj (hair, gold, sand, grainfields, honey)* flav•us -a -us; *(teeth)* lurid•us -a -um; *(hair, sand)* fulv•us -a -um
yellowish *adj* subflav•us -a -um
yelp *intr (like a dog)* gannire; **what's he —ing for?** quid ille gannit?
yes *adv* ita, sic, sane, oppido *(but the most frequent way in Latin to express a simple yes is to repeat the word on which the emphasis rests in the question):* **do you want me? Yes.** visne me? Te.; **has he sold her? Yes.** eam vendidit? Vendidit.
yes-man *s* assecl•a -ae *m*
yesterday *adv* heri; **the day before —** nudiustertius; **— evening** heri vesperi; **— morning** heri mane
yet *adv (contrast, after adversative clause)* tamen; *(time)* adhuc; *(w. comparatives)* etiam; **as —** adhuc; **not —** nondum
yew *s* tax•us -i *f*
yield *tr (to produce)* ferre, parĕre; *(to surrender)* concedĕre ‖ *intr* cedĕre; **to — to** cedĕre *(w. dat)*
yield *s* fruct•us -ūs *m; (profit)* quaest•us -ūs *m*
yoke *s* jug•um -i *n; (fig)* servit•us -utis *f*
yoke *tr* conjungĕre
yokel *s* rustic•us -i *m*
yolk *s* vitell•us -i *m*
yonder *adv* illic
yonder *adj* ill•e -a -ud
you *pron* tu; *(ye)* vos; **to —** tibi; vobis; **with —** tecum; vobiscum
young *adj (children)* parv•us -a -um; *(goat, vine)* novell•us -a -um; **— bride** nova nupt•a -ae *f;* **— lady** muliercul•a -ae *f;* **— man** juven•is -is *m,* adulescentul•us -i *m,* adulesc•ens -entis *m*
younger *adj* jun•ior -ior -ius, min•or -or -us (natu)
youngster *s* adulescentul•us -i *m*
your *adj* tu•us -a -um; *pl:* ves•ter -tra -trum
yourself *pron refl* te; **by —** per te; **to —** tibi; **with —** tecum ‖ *pron intensive* **you —** *(masc)* tu ipse; *(fem)* tu ipsa
yourselves *pron refl* vos; **to —** vobis; **with —** vobiscum ‖ *pron intensive* **you —** *(masc)* vos ipsi; *(fem)* vos ipsae
youth *s (age)* adulescenti•a -ae *f; (collectively)* juvent•us -utis *f; (young man)* juven•is -is *m,* adulesc•ens -entis *m*

youthful *adj* juvenil•is -is -e
youthfully *adv* juveniliter

Z

zeal *s* stud•ium -(i)i *n*
zealot *s* fanatic•us -i *m*
zealous *adj* studios•us -a -um
zealously *adv* studiose, enixe
zenith *s* vert•ex -icis *m*
zephyr *s* Zephyr•us -i *m*
zero *s* nihil *n (indecl)*
zest *s* sap•or -oris *m; (fig)* gustat•us -ūs *m;* **— for true praise** gustatus *m* verae laudis
zig-zag *adj* tortuos•us -a -um; **— streets** anfract•us -uum *mpl* viarum
zodiac *s* Zodiac•us -i *m*
zone *s* zon•a -ae *f*
zoo *s* vivar•ium -(i)i *n*
zoology *s* zoologi•a -ae *f*

Abbreviations

abbr .... abbreviation
abl .... ablative
acc .... accusative
adj .... adjective
adjl .... adjectival
adv .... adverb
advl .... adverbial
anat .... anatomy
archit .... architecture
astr .... astronomy
bot .... botany
c. .... circa, about
cf. .... confer, compare
cent. .... century
coll .... colloquial
com .... commerce
comp .... comparative
conj .... conjunction
d. .... died
dat .... dative
defect .... defective verb
dim. .... diminutive
E. .... East(ern)
eccl .... ecclesiastical
educ .... education
euphem .... euphemism
esp. .... especially
expr. .... expressed
f .... feminine noun
fem .... feminine
fig .... figurative
fin .... finance
fl .... floruit, flourished
fpl .... feminine plural noun
fut .... future
gen .... genitive
geog .... geography
geol .... geology
gram .... grammar
hum .... humorous
imperf ...... imperfect
impers ...... impersonal verb
impv .... imperative
indecl .... indeclinable
indef .... indefinite
indic .... indicative
inf .... infinitive
interj .... interjection
interrog ... interrogative
intr .... intransitive
leg .... legal
lit .... literal
loc .... locative
m .... masculine noun
masc .... masculine
math .... mathematics
med .... medicine
mf .... masculine or feminine noun
mil .... military
mpl .... masculine plural noun
mus .... music
n .... neuter noun
N. .... North(ern)
naut .... nautical
neg. .... negative
neut .... neuter
nom .... nominative
npl .... neuter plural noun
opp .... opposite of
p .... participle
pass .... passive
pej .... pejorative
perf .... perfect
phil .... philosophy
pl .... plural
poet .... poetry
pol .... politics
pp .... past participle
pref .... prefix
prep .... preposition
pres .... present
pron .... pronoun
pros .... prosody
prov .... proverb
refl .... reflexive
rel .... relative
relig .... religion
rhet .... rhetoric
s .... substantive
S. .... South(ern)
singl .... singular
sl .... slang
s.o. .... someone
s.th. .... something
subj .... subjunctive
suf .... suffix
superl .... superlative
theat .... theater
topog .... topography
tr .... transitive verb
usu. .... usually
vbl .... verbal
v defect .... defective verb
v impers ... impersonal verb
vulg .... vulgar
w. .... with
W. .... West(ern)